D0762982

The Heath Anthology
of American Literature

Volume B

Early Nineteenth Century: 1800–1865

The Heath Anthology of American Literature

Seventh Edition

Volume B

Early Nineteenth Century: 1800–1865

Paul Lauter
Trinity College
General Editor

John Alberti
Northern Kentucky University
Editor, Instructor's Guide

Mary Pat Brady
Cornell University

Kirk Curnutt
Troy University

Daniel Heath Justice
University of British Columbia

James Kyung-Jin Lee
University of California, Irvine

Richard Yarborough
University of California, Los Angeles
Associate General Editor

Wendy Martin
Claremont Graduate University

D. Quentin Miller
Suffolk University

Bethany Schneider
Bryn Mawr College

Ivy Schweitzer
Dartmouth College

Sandra A. Zagarell
Oberlin College

WADSWORTH
CENGAGE Learning·

Australia • Brazil • Japan • Korea • Mexico • Singapore • Spain • United Kingdom • United States

WADSWORTH
CENGAGE Learning·

The Heath Anthology of American Literature, Seventh Edition
Volume B, *Early Nineteenth Century: 1800–1865*

Edited by Paul Lauter, Richard Yarborough, John Alberti, Mary Pat Brady, Kirk Curnutt, James Kyung-Jin Lee, Wendy Martin, D. Quentin Miller, Bethany Schneider, Ivy Schweitzer, and Sandra A. Zagarell

Editor in Chief: Lyn Uhl
Publisher: Michael Rosenberg
Senior Development Editor: Leslie Taggart
Development Editor: Craig Leonard
Assistant Editor: Erin Bosco
Editorial Assistant: Rebecca Donahue
Media Editor: Janine Tangney
Marketing Brand Manager: Lydia LeStar
Content Project Manager: Rosemary Winfield
Art Director: Marissa Falco
Production Technology Analyst: Jeff Joubert
Manufacturing Planner: Betsy Donaghey
Rights Acquisition Specialist: Jessica Elias
Production Service: Tania Andrabi, Cenveo® Publisher Services
Text Designer: Shawn Girsberger
Cover Designer: Tani Hasegawa
Cover Image: Alfred Jacob Miller (American, 1810–1874), *Caravan en Route, 1858–1860*, watercolor on paper, The Walters Art Gallery, Baltimore, MD
Compositor: Cenveo Publisher Services

For product information and technology assistance, contact us at **Cengage Learning Customer & Sales Support, 1-800-354-9706**.

For permission to use material from this text or product, submit all requests online at **www.cengage.com/permissions**.
Further permissions questions can be emailed to **permissionrequest@cengage.com**.

Library of Congress Control Number: 2012954880

ISBN 13: 978-1-133-31023-5
ISBN 10: 1-133-31023-0

Wadsworth
20 Channel Center Street
Boston, MA 02210
USA

Cengage Learning is a leading provider of customized learning solutions with office locations around the globe, including Singapore, the United Kingdom, Australia, Mexico, Brazil and Japan. Locate your local office at **international.cengage.com/region**.

Cengage Learning products are represented in Canada by Nelson Education, Ltd.

For your course and learning solutions, visit **www.cengage.com**.
Purchase any of our products at your local college store or at our preferred online store **www.cengagebrain.com**.

Instructors: Please visit **login.cengage.com** and log in to access instructor-specific resources.

Printed in the United States of America
4 5 6 7 8 21 20 19

CONTENTS

■

IN FOCUS
Race and Slavery   2075

RACE, SLAVERY, AND THE INVENTION   2104
OF THE "SOUTH"

THE EMERGENCE OF AMERICAN POETIC VOICES   3146

WALT WHITMAN (1819–1892) 3218

PREFACE

The *Heath Anthology of American Literature* represents a remarkable success story. It is not the story of a book, a small board of editors, or even a few publishing houses. It is, rather, the story of the thousands of students and faculty who have in the last quarter century transformed the study of American literature.

LITERATURE AS AN INCLUSIVE CULTURAL FORM

When in 1978 we began the Reconstructing American Literature project (from which the anthology developed), the definition of what constituted American literature was very narrow in terms of the authors covered, the forms of writing included, and the ideas of literary study then dominant. Today's students would hardly recognize the anthologies or the syllabi that characterized the work of critics and teachers back in the 1950s or 1960s. That work would appear as odd today as 1900 baseball uniforms or perhaps Victorian hoop skirts—recognizable but remote from our society or culture.

The *Heath Anthology of American Literature* was part of a movement for cultural change. That movement took as its goal conceiving American literature as an inclusive cultural form, a form of creativity that spoke of and to the lives of all Americans and that spoke with many voices and in many different ways. It has always been our intent and practice to represent the writers who traditionally had constituted American literature. It was and remains our goal to be as inclusive as the limits of these five volumes permit.

A DIVERSE COMMUNITY OF SCHOLARS

Because societies and cultures change, our understanding of the meaning of *inclusive* likewise changes. As readers will see, today's seventh edition of the *Heath Anthology* differs in what we think are interesting and useful ways from the first edition of 1980 or even from the more recent sixth edition. We have updated a large number of headnotes as well as introductions. And we have made certain changes in the literary texts contained in the anthology. Many of these changes are specified below.

Most of the ideas for change originated with teachers and students who have used the anthology. The particular character of the *Heath Anthology* has always depended on the participation in the project of a wide community of scholars and teachers. Unlike other anthologies, the *Heath* includes introductory notes that have been written by scholars who specialize in a particular author. In their diverse yet consistent approaches, these headnotes illustrate for students how writing about literature is not limited to any single standard.

More important, perhaps, these contributing editors, together with readers, consultants, and users of the anthology, have provided guidance to our large and diverse editorial board as we determine the changes that will make the anthology most useful. We hope that a new generation of students and teachers will share with us their ideas about what works in the anthology and what does not, what texts and configurations might be changed, and what more we might provide so that they can make the best use of these books.

BROADENING THE "LITERARY"

What is the "best use"? The answers to that question will, of course, vary enormously depending on the students and teachers involved. One could teach a fairly traditional course using *The Heath Anthology of American Literature*, emphasizing only the writers historically considered significant. There are rich selections in these volumes of writers like Edwards, Franklin, Emerson, Hawthorne, Melville, Thoreau, Whitman, Dickinson, James, Twain, and modernists like Eliot, Fitzgerald, Hemingway, Pound, Stevens, Wharton, and the like. But we have from the beginning of this project striven to include many writers who would not have been part of such a traditional course, like Frederick Douglass, Lydia Maria Child, Frances Harper, Sarah Piatt, Charles W. Chesnutt, Mary Wilkins Freeman, Kate Chopin, José Martí, and Randolph Bourne, just to name a few from earlier times. One of the accomplishments that we are most proud of is the transformative impact of the *Heath Anthology* on the American literary canon. The inclusion of a number of important new (that is, underappreciated) authors in the *Heath* has played an important role in catalyzing a wider and deeper awareness of their significance.

Likewise, these books contain abundant selections of fiction, poetry, drama, and also nonfictional prose, polemical and historical essays, songs, chants, speeches, and the like. Another major goal of the *Heath Anthology* has been to broaden our understanding of what constitutes the "literary." On the one hand, we want to provide students with a large selection of well-known texts whose literary power and cultural relevance had been established by generations of critics and teachers—William Bradford's "Of Plymouth Plantation," Benjamin Franklin's *Autobiography,* poetry by Bradstreet and Dickinson, "Young Goodman Brown," "Self-Reliance," "Civil Disobedience," "Annabel Lee," "Daisy Miller," "The Open Boat," *The Awakening, The Waste Land,* "Hills Like White Elephants," "Sonny's Blues," "Howl."

At the same time, we wish to provide exemplary texts that, because of their forms or subjects, have seldom been taught and often little read. Thus, we include, for example, "sorrow songs" or spirituals, nineteenth-century folk songs and stories, *corridos* and blues lyrics, and poems written on the walls of Angel Island prison by Chinese detainees.

Likewise, we include nonfictional forms such as the spiritual autobiographies of Thomas Shepard and Elizabeth Ashbridge, sketches by Fanny Fern, polemical letters by Angelina and Sarah Grimké, columns by Finley Peter Dunne, José Martí's important "Our America," Randolph Bourne's "Trans-National America," Martin Luther King's "I Have a Dream," and chapters from Gloria Anzaldúa's *Borderlands/La Frontera*. The sixth edition extended this goal by incorporating journal entries from several members of the Lewis and Clark expedition, letters protesting Cherokee removal, "proletarian" folk songs, and graphic narratives by Art Spiegelman, Lynda Barry, and others.

The seventh edition widens the lens still further by including a broader span of written texts by Native American authors from all parts of the country, the work of many more Spanish-language writers of all centuries, including those from the period of the Mexican Revolution, Chinese American immigrants such as novelist and future actor H. T. Tsiang, and essays such as Carlos Bulosan's "The Freedom from Want" that dramatize both the allure and the pitfalls of nationalism. A section of Spoken Word poetry now concludes the anthology. It is our hope that teachers and students will be able to take advantage of what remains, by far, the most inclusive and varied anthology in the field.

LONG AND SHORT WORKS

The *Heath Anthology* has also from its beginning balanced longer complete works with shorter texts by the wide variety of authors included. Thus, this edition includes the full texts of Royall Tyler's "The Contrast," Susanna Rowson's play *Slaves in Algiers; or, A Struggle for Freedom*, Melville's "Benito Cereno" and "Billy Budd," Frederick Douglass's *Narrative*, Abraham Cahan's "The Imported Bridegroom," Kate Chopin's *The Awakening*, Nella Larsen's *Passing*, George C. Wolfe's *The Colored Museum*, and Arthur Miller's *A View From the Bridge*, among many other longer works.

HISTORICAL AND SOCIAL CONTEXTS

It has always been our view that literature, like any art form, must in part be studied in relation to the historical and social contexts from which it develops and to which it speaks. We have therefore systematically included in the volumes important historical texts ranging from the Declaration of Independence to decisive court decisions like those that enabled Indian "removal" or imposed and finally helped end racial segregation. These "In Focus" sections can be read for their own interest, since they are vivid documents in and of themselves. But they can also be read to provide contexts to the more traditionally literary texts that constitute the primary content of the anthology. With the *Heath Anthology*'s unusually wide selection, they provide instructors with broadened opportunities to help students perceive continuity and change in the literary and cultural history of what is now the United States.

Likewise, in this electronic age, we have the following electronic resources for both instructors and students:

- **Heath Anthology Premium Website for Volumes A, B, C, D, and E**. This robust Premium Website includes a wide variety of multimedia resources to help bring to life the works and time periods featured in the *Anthology*. The website can be navigated by volume and centers around thirty of the most commonly taught works for each volume.

Each is supported by reading comprehension quizzes, interactive media such as audio or video, Web links, and author biographies. In addition, the Premium Website features materials to help provide historical, social, and political context for these works, such as maps and images. A glossary of literary terms is also provided, in both list form and as interactive flashcards. A variety of eBooks are available as an optional add-on to the Premium Website, including *The Scarlet Letter* and *Adventures of Huckleberry Finn*. Access the Premium Website at www.cengagebrain.com.

• **The Heath Blog**. Available as a link from the Instructor Companion Site and from the Premium Website, the Heath Blog is dedicated to providing tools, information, and pedagogical approaches for instructors and students of American literature and culture. It provides virtual space for conversations about what choices we make when we anthologize texts, how these texts are presented and received in the classroom, and how they resonate with contemporary concerns. All users are encouraged to respond to the blog articles with their own commentary and suggestions. Instructors may access the Instructor Companion Site at www.login.cengage.com, and the Premium Website is available for students via www.cengagebrain.com.

• *Online Instructor's Manual*. The *Online Instructor's Manual*, edited by John Alberti, offers suggestions for approaching texts and authors, model assignments, and useful exam and discussion questions. This helpful resource is available on the Instructor Companion Site, which can be accessed at www.login.cengage.com.

• **Instructor Companion Site**. This password-protected website provides access to both the downloadable Online Instructor's Manual and the Heath Blog.

CHANGES IN THE SEVENTH EDITION

The seventh edition includes 176 new works across the five volumes.

WHAT IS NEW IN VOLUME A, BEGINNINGS TO 1800

Changes to Volume A, Beginnings to 1800, are relatively few but draw on the latest scholarship to update translations and headnotes as well as enrich our offerings from Native and Spanish America. As in the other volumes in the seventh edition, we have added a new "In Focus: Northern New York—Mohegan/Brotherton Tribes" section that highlights the region of Northern New York. Included in this section are writers pulled from other places in the sixth edition, such as Handsome Lake, Samson Occom, and Hendrick Aupaumut, complemented by a new excerpt from Joseph Johnson, son-in-law and close associate of Occom, capped by an introductory headnote that discusses the many interrelations among these figures across tribal affiliation and the larger cultural movements they shaped. We have added Corn Tassel to "Native American Political Texts and Oratory" to continue integrating Native American writing and oratory throughout Volume A.

The selections from Gaspar Perez de Villagrá have been expanded and newly translated and form the hub of a group of hemispheric Spanish American writers recounting the exploration and conquest of North and South America, including new entries by Juan de Oñate, Fray Alonso Gregorio de Escobedo on the conquest of Florida, and Felipe Guaman Poma de Ayala on the conquest of Peru. Excerpts from Gaspar de Villagrá and Fray Alonso Gregorio de Escobedo are reprinted in the original Spanish.

Later in the volume, we have included two new selections from the revolutionary literature of Spanish America—a popular broadside by José Álvarez de Toledo and one of the founding documents of Latin American history, Simón Bolívar's "Letter from Jamaica," which now concludes Volume A.

The selections from New Netherland writer Adriaen van der Donck have been updated with a new translation, and we have added the entirety of Susanna Rowson's popular play *Slaves in Algiers* in the place of excerpts from her novel *Charlotte Temple*.

In the critical sections, we have added significant excerpts from Bartolomé de las Casas on the plight of the Indians, Aníbal Quijano and Immanuel Wallerstein on "Americanity," Trish Loughran on eighteenth-century print culture, and a blog post on "Decolonial Aesthetics" that reinforces the salience of colonial literature and coloniality to the present postmodern moment.

WHAT IS NEW IN VOLUME B, EARLY NINETEENTH CENTURY: 1800–1865

Volume B, Early Nineteenth Century: 1800–1865, has a newly restructured section on Native American literature, with new selections that include excerpts from Black Hawk and Mary Jemison, which frame the opening section as an exploration of complex and often misunderstood Native identities. Other Native writers, like William Appess and Jane Johnston Schoolcraft, are interspersed throughout the volume, working against the notion that Native voices precede other voices. A new "In Focus" section dedicated to the Cherokee nation and the literature surrounding Cherokee removal has been added. This enables instructors to focus on a particular Native nation, gaining a nation-specific focus that helps students understand both the Cherokee context in specific, and the larger imperative to encounter Native writing as nationally specific.

The "Cultures of Spanish America" section has been restructured and greatly expanded, with new works in English and in Spanish (with translations provided) by Victoria Moreno, José María Heredia, José María Tornel, and Vicente Pérez Rosales.

Finally, a new section focusing on "The Caribbean in the Antebellum Imagination," with works by Martin Delany, Lucy Holcombe Pickens, and Miguel Tolón, has been added.

WHAT IS NEW IN VOLUME C, LATE NINETEENTH CENTURY: 1865–1910

Thoroughly reconceived, Volume C, Late Nineteenth Century: 1865–1910, reflects even more vividly the extraordinary writing that flourished as the United States became a modern, diverse nation with an international presence. The overarching concept of this volume is that the literature written between 1865 and 1910 was so plentiful and so diverse that no single set of organizational categories does it justice. We have therefore devised several complementary categories to showcase this variety in a comprehensible manner.

Now book-ending the volume are sections on significant literary trends—"Varieties of Postwar Realism: Prose and Poetry" and literature "On the Cusp of a New Century." Of the other four sections in Volume C, one centers on Siouxian peoples ("Nation within a Nation: Lakotas/Dakotas/Nakotas"); two are organized geographically ("Writing and Place" and "Redefining the South"); and another ("Outside/Inside U.S.A.: Expansion and Immigration") foregrounds the era's cultural and political ferment with writing by or about immigrants and literature created in response to the shifting borders of the nation and to its geopolitical expansion.

All of these sections contain new material in addition to the literature of past editions. Most notably, we now feature four authors new to the *Heath Anthology*—the "Hoosier poet" James Whitcomb Riley, the witty Vermont regionalist Rowland E. Robinson, the Southern plantation tradition writer Thomas Nelson Page, and the proto-modernist poet Sadakichi Hartmann.

There are many new selections by familiar authors, among them Henry James's "The Figure in the Carpet," a section of Zitkala-Sa's "Impressions of an Indian Childhood," Mary E. Wilkins Freeman's "Old Woman Magoun," and Charles W. Chesnutt's "The Doll." We also restored the Frank Norris section.

Still further, we introduce two exciting, little-known Latino narratives—"Memories of California"/"Recuerdos de California" by Carlos F. Galán and "The Tale of a Glove"/"Historia de un guante" by N. Bolet Peraza. These selections are presented in Spanish and in English translations produced for the *Heath Anthology* by contributing editor John Alba Cutler.

In addition, Volume C now offers new or substantially revised headnotes on a number of authors included in earlier editions—Henry James, Sarah Orne Jewett, Mary E. Wilkins Freeman, Frances E. W. Harper, Alice Dunbar-Nelson, and Jack London. Finally, we also present new and revised "In Focus" sections, complete with new and updated introductory essays.

WHAT IS NEW IN VOLUME D, MODERN PERIOD: 1910–1945

Volume D, Modern Period: 1910–1945, continues to demonstrate the diversity of the literary period known as modernism by introducing readers to the array of modernisms that constitute it—the hermetic experiments of Ezra Pound and T. S. Eliot, the more commercial expression of loss and uncertainty in popular efforts by F. Scott Fitzgerald and Edna St. Vincent Millay, the ethnically complex fusion of African American and dominant-culture aesthetics that typify the Harlem Renaissance, and the political activism of the proletarian movement of the 1930s and its internal debates over the social functions of art.

Volume D continues to expand notions of both modernity and modernism by widening the scope of literary experience. Included here for the first time is a section on the literature of the Mexican Revolution, featuring Industrial Workers of the World (IWW) organizer Ricardo Flores Magón's *cri de guerre* "Land and Liberty" and a newly translated excerpt from the Spanish version of Leonor Villegas de Magnon's "La Rebelde," among others. There are two stories from Maria Cristina Mena, and a poem and two novel excerpts of H. T. Tsiang, who captures the despair of New York Chinatown like no other 1930s' writer. The famous "rent party" chapter from Wallace Thurman's *Infants of the Spring* (1932) features thinly veiled portraits of leading Harlem Renaissance writers. Also included are Meridel LeSueur's story "Annunciation" and an excerpt from her posthumously published novel, *The Girl*; Jose Garcia Villa's "Footnote to Youth" (the most famous Filipino short story of the 1930s); and a selection of poetry that expands our notions of modernist experimentation. Mexican American folklorist Jovita Gonzalez's essay "Shades of the Tenth Muses" provides a hallucinatory meditation on canon inclusion.

WHAT IS NEW IN VOLUME E, CONTEMPORARY PERIOD: 1945 TO THE PRESENT

Volume E, Contemporary Period: 1945 to the Present, has been radically restructured to reflect ongoing changes in what is considered contemporary and to make it easier for instructors and students to locate major trends and developments in the contemporary period. We have organized this section by decades, basing their placement on the date of publication rather than by the birth date of authors.

Some of the period's prolific, established authors such as Tennessee Williams, Arthur Miller, Toni Cade Bambara, Ishmael Reed, Sherman Alexie, and John Updike are represented by different works from the ones we included in previous editions.

Although we have had to reduce or cut some selections by authors previously represented in this section in the interest of limiting the volume to a reasonable length, more striking is the list of writers we have added to this volume. New authors to the seventh edition include John Cheever, Mitsuye Yamada, Kurt Vonnegut, Ralph Molina, Luís Valdez, Richard Ford, George C. Wolfe, Ann Beattie, Percival Everett, Martin Espada, Demetria Martinez, T. C. Boyle, Stephen Dunn, Natasha Trethewey, Junot Díaz, Dave Eggers, Jane Trenka, ZZ Packer, Francisco Goldman, and Manuel Munoz.

We have also added substantial new "In Focus" sections of Ojibway writings from the contemporary period, and the volume concludes with a section of "Spoken Word Poetry," which showcases some important new voices and the genre that they have helped to develop but which connects a current trend to the oral traditions that form the origin of American literature in its earliest years.

ACKNOWLEDGMENTS

We want to extend our thanks to all of the contributing editors who devoted their time and scholarship to introductory notes, choices of texts, and teaching materials. For the current edition, they include the following:

Katherine Bassard, Virginia Commonwealth University

Paula Bernat Bennett (Emerita), Southern Illinois University

Renée Bergland, Simmons College

Leah Blatt Glasser, Mount Holyoke College

David Budbill, poet and independent scholar

Raul Bueno, Dartmouth College

Keith Byerman, Indiana State University

Floyd Cheung, Smith College

Jonathan Chua, Ateneo de Manila

Hillary Chute, Harvard University

Michael C. Cohen, University of California, Los Angeles

Raúl Coronado, University of Chicago

Denise Cruz, Indiana University

Suzanne del Gizzo, Chestnut Hill College

Jared Demick, University of Connecticut

Joseph Dewey, University of Pittsburgh, Johnstown

Lyn Di Lorio, The City College of New York

Amy Doherty Mohr, Amerika Institut, Ludwig Maximilians Universität, Munich

Jennifer Emery-Peck, Oberlin College

Armando García, University of Pittsburgh

Caroline Gebhard, Tuskegee University

June Howard, University of Michigan

Caren Irr, Brandeis University

Gene Jarrett, Boston University

Ann Keniston, University of Nevada, Reno

Ryan James Kernan, Rutgers University

Kathy Knapp, University of Connecticut

Sara Kosiba, Troy University

Rodrigo Lazo, University of California, Irvine

Katherine E. Ledford, Appalachian State University

Marissa López, University of California, Los Angeles

Crystal J. Lucky, Villanova University

Manuel Martin-Rodriguez, University of California, Merced

Lauren R. Maxwell, The Citadel

Keith Mitchell, University of Massachusetts, Lowell

Charles Molesworth, City University of New York, Queens

Paula Moya, Stanford University

Viet Nguyen, University of Southern California

Ben V. Olguin, University of Texas, San Antonio

Yolana Padilla, University of Pennsylvania

Josephine Park, University of Pennsylvania

Robert Dale Parker, University of Illinois, Urbana-Champaign

Soojin Pate, Minneapolis Community and Technical College

Elizabeth Petrino, Fairfield University

Peter Reed, University of Mississippi

Domino Renee Perez, University of Texas, Austin

Ana Patricia Rodriguez, University of Maryland, College Park

Ramón Saldívar, Stanford University

James Schiff, University of Cincinnati

Lavina Dhingra, Bates College

E. Thomson Shields, East Carolina University

Susan Shillinglaw, San Jose State University

Amjrit Singh, Ohio University

Scott Slovic, University of Nevada, Reno

James Smethurst, University of Massachusetts, Amherst

Mayumi Takada, Bryn Mawr College

Justine Tally, Universidad de la Laguna

Kara Thompson, College of William and Mary

Lisa Thompson, State University of New York, Albany

Darlene Unrue, University of Nevada, Las Vegas

Joanne van der Woude, Columbia University

Ariana Vigil, University of North Carolina, Chapel Hill

Jennifer Wallach, University of North Texas

Hilary Wyss, Auburn University

Yvonne Yarbro-Bejarano, Stanford University

Thanks to Oberlin College for funding student researchers and to Amanda Shubert and Hillary Smith for the incomparable work they have done in that capacity. We also want to thank student researchers Carson Thomas and Kyle Lewis from Dartmouth College and Brandy Underwood from the University of California, Los Angeles for excellent editorial help.

We especially want to thank those who reviewed this edition:

David Anderson, University of North Texas

Craig Barrette, Brescia University

Robert Bennett, Montana State University

Brett Bodily, North Lake College

Kathryn Brewer-Strayer, Stillman College

Delmar Brewington, Piedmont Technical College

Brad Campbell, California Polytechnic State University

Beth Capo, Illinois College

Charles Cuthbertson, Southern Utah University

Joshua Dickinson, Jefferson Community College

Sharynn Owens Etheridge-Logan, Claflin University

April Gentry, Savannah State University

Wendy Gray, J. Sargeant Reynolds Community College

Deirdre Hall, University of North Carolina, Greensboro

Amy Hankins, Ottawa University

Tena Helton, University of Illinois, Springfield

Tai Houser, Broward College

Melanie Jenkins, Snow College

Bruce Johnson, Providence College

David Jones, University of Wisconsin, Eau Claire

Thomas Long, University of Connecticut

Marit MacArthur, California State University, Bakersfield

Bridget Marshall, University of
 Massachusetts, Lowell
John Miller, Longwood University
Keith Mitchell, University of
 Massachusetts, Lowell
Emmanuel Ngwang, Claflin
 University
Miles Orvell, Temple University
Priscilla Perkins, Roosevelt
 University
Jane Rosecrans, J. Sargeant
 Reynolds Community College
Christopher Schroeder,
 Northeastern Illinois University
Claudia Slate, Florida Southern
 College
Jimmy Smith, Union College

Blythe Tellefsen, Fullerton College
Ruthe Thompson, Southwest
 Minnesota State University
Stephanie Tingley, Youngstown
 State University
Terri Tucker, Southwest Texas
 Junior College
Tondalaya VanLear, Dabney S.
 Lancaster Community College
Trent Watts, Missouri University of
 Science and Technology
Michelle Weisman, College of the
 Ozarks
Eric Wertheimer, Arizona State
 University
Julie Wilhelm, Lamar University

We would like to continue to thank the many scholars who contributed to this as well as to earlier editions of this work. Their names are listed in the *Online Instructor's Manual* that accompanies this anthology.

AN IMAGE GALLERY
EARLY NINETEENTH CENTURY:
1800–1865

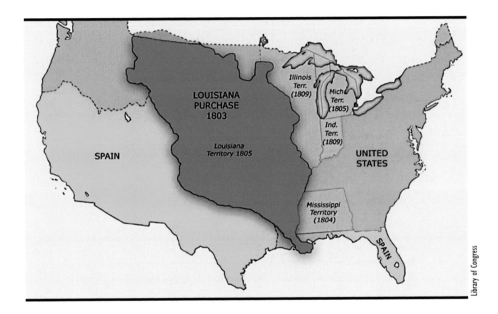

Library of Congress

■ **MAP SHOWING THE POLITICAL BOUNDARIES OF NORTH AMERICA IN THE ERA OF THE LOUISIANA PURCHASE (1803).** This map demonstrates the importance of Jefferson's purchase of the Louisiana Territory in 1803. Previously, other countries, especially France and Spain, controlled large pieces of land surrounding the growing United States. The opening of this new territory paved the way for Indian "removal" and the Trail of Tears, further European immigration throughout the nineteenth century, and the settlement of the West.

Camp Meeting of the Methodists in N. America

■ CAMP MEETING OF METHODISTS IN NORTH AMERICA

(c. 1819). This illustration displays the natural setting of camp meetings, which took place outside under temporary arbors or shelters, with rude benches for the congregation. In this picture, those gathered have put up tents for their families in the background. The nineteenth-century evangelical movement was part of the movement west, religion literally carved out of the wilderness. Camp meetings functioned as a time when congregants withdrew to a rural setting away from other responsibilities for a few days of preaching and social interaction with friends and neighbors. They were also a major instrument in the spread of religious fervor known as the Second Great Awakening.

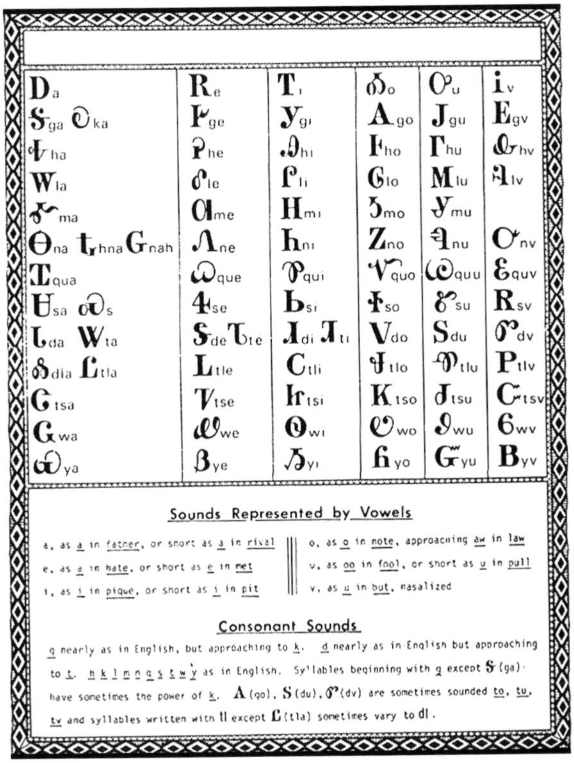

D a	R e	T i	ℬ o	O u	i v
S ga Ꭷ ka	Ᏺ ge	y gi	A go	J gu	E gv
Ꮼ ha	Ꭾ he	Ꭲ hi	Ꮻ ho	Γ hu	Ꮕ hv
W la	Ꭴ le	�p li	G lo	M lu	Ꮭ lv
Ꮼ ma	Ꭰ me	H mi	ℑ mo	y mu	
Ꮎ na Ꮏ hna G nah	Λ ne	Ꭿ ni	Z no	ꓴ nu	Ꮕ nv
Ꭲ qua	Ꮤ que	Ᏼ qui	Ꮴ quo	Ꮖ quu	Ꮕ quv
Ꮜ sa Ꮆ s	4 se	Ᏸ si	Ꮚ so	Ꮟ su	Rsv
Ꮇ da Ꮃ ta	Ꮝ de Ꮦ te	Ꭵ di Ꮧ ti	V do	Ꮪ du	ꓷ dv
Ꮧ dia Ꮭ tla	Ꮅ tle	Ꮳ tli	Ꮹ tlo	Ꮺ tlu	P tlv
Ꮳ tsa	� tse	Ir tsi	K tso	ꓮ tsu	C tsv
Ꮹ wa	Ꮺ we	O wi	Ꮼ wo	ꭹ wu	6 wv
Ꮽ ya	β ye	Ꭹ yi	Ꮀ yo	Ꮆ yu	B yv

Sounds Represented by Vowels

a, as _a_ in _father_, or short as _a_ in _rival_ ||| o, as _o_ in _note_, approaching _aw_ in _law_

e, as _a_ in _hate_, or short as _e_ in _met_ ||| v, as _oo_ in _fool_, or short as _u_ in _pull_

i, as _i_ in _pique_, or short as _i_ in _pit_ ||| v, as _u_ in _but_, nasalized

Consonant Sounds

g nearly as in English, but approaching to _k_.   d nearly as in English but approaching

to _t_.   _h k l m n q s t w y_ as in English. Syllables beginning with g except Ꮝ (ga)

have sometimes the power of _k_. A (go), S (du), Ꮝ (dv) are sometimes sounded _to_, _tu_,

_tv_ and syllables written with ll except Ꮭ (tla) sometimes vary to dl .

■ **CHEROKEE SYLLABARY.** The Cherokee syllabary was probably the most flexible of the many different forms of written communication known to have been used by Native Americans before the European alphabet was adopted. The Cherokee language consisted of combinations of about one hundred different syllables. Using the Bible, *McGuffey's Reader*, and Greek letters, Sequoyah created symbols for eighty-five of these syllables. The syllabary proved easy to use. Within months, many Cherokees learned to read and write using the new system. They exchanged letters and messages, transacted business, and read the Bible in Cherokee. The Cherokee also founded the *Cherokee Phoenix*, the first newspaper published in an American Indian language.

■ **THOMAS COLE, *THE LAST OF THE MOHICANS, CORA KNEELING AT THE FEET OF TAMENUND* (1827).** Thomas Cole's (1801–1848) painting was inspired by James Fenimore Cooper's novel *The Last of the Mohicans*, a hugely popular best seller that was published in 1826. Cole creates a lavish natural setting that dwarfs the tiny human drama of Cora begging for mercy in front of Tamenund, the chief of the Delaware.

$100 REWARD

WILL be given for the apprehension and delivery of my Servant Girl HARRIET. She is a light mulatto, 21 years of age, about 5 feet 4 inches high, of a thick and corpulent habit, having on her head a thick covering of black hair that curls naturally, but which can be easily combed straight. She speaks easily and fluently, and has an agreeable carriage and address. Being a good seamstress, she has been accustomed to dress well, has a variety of very fine clothes, made in the prevailing fashion, and will probably appear, if abroad, tricked out in gay and fashionable finery. As this girl absconded from the plantation of my son without any known cause or provocation, it is probable she designs to transport herself to the North.

The above reward, with all reasonable charges, will be given for apprehending her, or securing her in any prison or jail within the U. States.

All persons are hereby forewarned against harboring or entertaining her, or being in any way instrumental in her escape, under the most rigorous penalties of the law.

JAMES NORCOM.

Edenton, N. C. June 30

■ **RUNAWAY NOTICE FOR HARRIET JACOBS (1835).** Newspapers were full of notices like this one before American slaves were emancipated in 1863. The notice emphasizes the economic aspect of slavery and its financial rewards for the white owners. It also illustrates one of the uses to which slaveholders put literacy. Jacobs seized the tools of writing and publication to tell her story, which was very different from that produced by slaveholders.

■ **THOMAS COLE,** *VIEW FROM MOUNT HOLYOKE, NORTHAMPTON, MASSACHUSETTS, AFTER A THUNDER-STORM—THE OXBOW* **(c. 1836).** Thomas Cole's (1801–1848) image contrasts wilderness with domestication, the unresolved state of America in the nineteenth century. On the left, a violent storm moves in with uprooted trees in the foreground. On the right, Cole paints a scene of neat squares of farmland and a landscape cleared of trees. In *Hope Leslie*, Catherine Maria Sedgwick describes the scene of Cole's painting, visited by a party of Native Americans. The Native Americans compare themselves to the blasted trees, unearthed and displaced. In contrast, the European captive Everell Fletcher looks with longing at the smoke curling from the dwellings in the domesticated valley.

Eliza comes to tell Uncle Tom that he is sold, and that she is running away to save her child. Page 62.

■ **ILLUSTRATION BY HAMMATT BILLINGS FOR THE 1852 EDITION OF HARRIET BEECHER STOWE'S** *UNCLE TOM'S CABIN.* Eliza comes to tell Uncle Tom that she is sold and that she is running away to save her child (caption of illustration). Stowe's publisher, John Jewett, confident in the book's success, had six full-page illustrations drawn and engraved for the first printing. Hammatt Billings's (b. 1802) 1852 drawings were influential on later visualizations of the story.

■ **FREDERIC EDWIN CHURCH,** *NIAGARA* **(c. 1857).** Frederic Edwin Church's (1826–1900) painting was part of an effort by artists to invent an American style that took as its inspiration the vast scope and drama of the landscape of the United States. Across the nineteenth century, Niagara Falls symbolized both the continent's perceived wildness and its potential power to both Americans and a watching world.

■ *LINCOLN SHOWING SOJOURNER TRUTH THE BIBLE PRESENTED BY THE COLORED PEOPLE OF BALTIMORE, EXECUTIVE MANSION, WASHINGTON, D.C., OCT. 29, 1864.* This photograph of a painting displays President Abraham Lincoln's attentiveness to Sojourner Truth and the African Americans who are represented by the presentation of the Bible. Truth was illiterate and could not have read the Bible open before her. She is portrayed meekly sitting down, quietly dressed, with Lincoln standing, even though current accounts mention her imposing stature and loud voice. Her image and her roles as an abolitionist and early feminist have often been manipulated for various political purposes. The quiet image contrasts sharply with her famous impassioned speech, "Ar'n't I a Woman?"

■ **JOHN GAST,** *AMERICAN PROGRESS* **(c. 1872).** In this painting by John Gast (1772–1837), a goddess-like figure leads the pioneers west. Indians, buffalo, and a bear departing the image on the left are replaced by miners, a stagecoach, and a Conestoga wagon in the center. At the right, trains belch out smoke as they depart from cities. The female figure strings telegraph lines as she flies above the panorama holding a schoolbook, suggesting that education will be the key to the American achievement of Manifest Destiny.

■ **PORTRAIT OF EDGAR ALLAN POE, PROBABLY FROM A CIGAR BOX (c. 1900).** The photograph attests to Edgar Allan Poe's (1809–1849) continuing popularity, even at the turn of the century. The image of the writer on a cigar box is reminiscent of Benjamin Franklin's portrait on various souvenirs such as snuff-boxes during his time as minister of France. Both images show the writers as part of popular culture, not enshrined in a museum or between the pages of a book.

■ **CHEROKEE BASKETS.** Basket weaving lies at the center of Cherokee culture. Traditionally women are the basket weavers, and traditional materials were river reeds, cane, white oak, hickory bark, and honeysuckle, dyed with black walnut and blood root. Today the tradition of basket weaving continues among Cherokee artists, but the materials used have expanded to include contemporary, synthetic materials as well as traditional, natural fibers.

■ **COTTON GIN.** Eli Whitney's cotton "gin" (short for "engine") was invented in 1793 and patented in 1794. The machine separates cotton fibers from the seeds, a job that otherwise had to be done by hand. The invention reduced the amount of labor needed to process cotton, but it revolutionized cotton production in the United States and led to the expansion of slavery, as plantations could plant many more acres of the crop.

EARLY NINETEENTH CENTURY: 1800–1865

O n the morning of August 31, 1837, Waldo and Lidian Emerson stepped into their buggy outside their home in Concord, Massachusetts, and drove the twenty or so miles into Cambridge. The day was bright and warm, the summer's dust having been settled by an earlier rainstorm. It was a festive time at Harvard: the class of 1837, which included future writers Henry David Thoreau and Richard Henry Dana, Jr., had graduated the previous day, and this afternoon Emerson was to deliver the annual Phi Beta Kappa oration on what was already a somewhat hackneyed subject, "The American Scholar." Writers and commentators had often called for a distinctively American culture in the decades since political independence had been won. Indeed, William Ellery Channing, one of Harvard's better-known overseers and perhaps a member of Emerson's audience, had written about the subject at length seven years before. For Emerson the occasion did not call for yet another appeal to literary nationalism; indeed, only the beginning and end of his lecture dealt explicitly with American letters.

Still, almost fifty years later, Oliver Wendell Holmes would celebrate Emerson's speech as "our intellectual Declaration of Independence." James Russell Lowell, a Harvard junior when he attended the talk, would speak of it as "an event without any former parallel in our literary annals." In *My Study Windows* (1871), Lowell dramatized the event: "What crowded and breathless aisles, what windows clustering with eager heads, what enthusiasm of approval, what grim silence of foregone dissent!" But these were recollections highly colored by the subsequent influence of "The American Scholar" and the fame of Emerson's many other essays and lectures. At the time, many in the audience found Emerson's ideas "misty, dreamy, unintelligible," as an older listener put it; "not very good and very transcendental," as a younger doubter wrote in his diary. The speech did not instantly liberate American letters from "the courtly muses of Europe" nor free the young scholars hearing it from the "disgust which the principles on which business is managed inspire."

Nonetheless, "The American Scholar" serves usefully to signify a turning point in our culture, marking the beginning of what critics have named the "American Renaissance," a flourishing of literary art unprecedented in the brief history of the nation. More precisely, seen in retrospect, Emerson's talk came just as a remarkable cultural wave was gathering strength; it gave rhetorical form to that conjunction of publishing events, establishment of institutions, and development of personal networks that underlie such advances. Late in 1836, Henry Wadsworth Longfellow had returned from Europe to take up his literary professorship at Harvard; in that position, and as an anthologist and translator, he would introduce European literature to generations of American readers. As a reviewer and arbiter of literary taste, he would also significantly shape the reputations and careers of American writers, including most notably those of his fellow Bowdoin graduate, Nathaniel Hawthorne, whose first volume, *Twice-Told Tales*, came out in 1837. Oliver Wendell Holmes, too, had returned to Harvard in 1836 to complete his medical degree and to publish his first volume, *Poems*. In 1836, just as Texas declared itself independent of Mexico and adopted a proslavery constitution, Angelina Grimké had issued her *Appeal to the Christian Women of the South*, a tract that helped introduce the idea of civil disobedience into the intensifying debate over slavery and, with Grimké's precedent-setting lectures to sexually mixed audiences, extended women's participation in the political and literary life of the republic. The following year, John Greenleaf Whittier published his first volume, its politics explicit in its title, *Poems Written During the Progress of the Abolition Question*. Later in 1837, when Elijah P. Lovejoy was murdered and his antislavery newspaper, *The Observer*, destroyed by a mob in Alton, Illinois, the causes of abolition and a free press were even more closely linked and the political power of words tragically reaffirmed. Another year later, young Frederick Douglass would escape from slavery and within a few years add his to the voices demanding its abolition.

Some months before Emerson delivered "The American Scholar," Horace Mann became the chief officer of the Massachusetts board of education; from that position he would initiate a series of studies and reforms that widened the scope of literacy, regularized curricula, extended the reading public, and otherwise influenced the shape of education across the country for at least the remainder of the century. By the Civil War, the principle of free, publicly funded primary education had been established almost everywhere but in the South, and the rate of school attendance was increasing even more rapidly than the population. In 1836, Mary Lyon had founded the Mt. Holyoke Female Seminary (later Mt. Holyoke College), the first such institution for women in the country; in 1837, Oberlin became the first coeducational college—and the first to admit black students—and Emma Willard formed the Willard Association for the Mutual Improvement of Female Teachers. Two of the association's honorary vice presidents were the poet and novelist Lydia Sigourney and Sarah Josepha Hale, who in 1836 had become editor of the merged *Ladies Magazine* and *Godey's Lady's Book*. The merger produced the most influential women's magazine of its time; it shaped a range of ideas from women's rights to women's fashions and offered further opportunities for writers such as Emerson, Longfellow, Poe, and Stowe, as well as many lesser-known female authors, to write for a living. The year 1836 also marks Margaret Fuller's introduction to Emerson and the birth of the Transcendentalists' informal "club," whose members discussed and supported each other's ideas and later produced a journal, *The Dial* (1840–1844). In fact, Fuller met with the Emersons after Waldo's Phi Beta Kappa speech and returned with them to Concord. The next day she joined for the first time in the club's meeting—and feasting—at the Emersons' home, perhaps adding hers to others' praise for how his "noble discourse" emphasized the value of individual inspiration and an original relation to nature over the mass of unexamined tradition.

These historical details and many others one could list were not necessarily in the minds of Emerson or his listeners. It is only in looking back from a distance that one is struck by the conjunction of events to which "The American Scholar" seems to give point. In fact, many of Emerson's listeners were very likely more concerned with mundane problems. The year 1837 had not been a happy one from an economic or social point of view. It had begun with a collapse in Southern real estate and commodity prices, which had rapidly deepened into a widespread financial panic. By the time outgoing President Andrew Jackson gave his farewell address at the beginning of March, there had been riots in New York, and on May 10, banks in New York and Boston stopped redeeming their notes for silver or gold. Manufacturing was in decline, unemployment spreading, and the investments and savings of thousands upon thousands of persons disappearing into the mysterious operations of a market economy few even claimed to understand. Though Emerson's listeners were probably not yet fully aware of it, seven lean years were coming upon the United States, an economic depression as deep as that of the 1930s.

Emerson himself had noted the multiplying problems in his journal:

> Cold April; hard times; men breaking who ought not to break; banks bullied into the bolstering of desperate speculators; all the newspapers a chorus of owls. . . . Loud cracks in the social edifice.—Sixty thousand laborers, says rumor, to be presently thrown out of work, and these make a formidable mob to break open banks & rob the rich & brave the domestic government.

Yet it was not in Emerson's nature to turn gloomy at such prospects; besides, his comfortable situation in Concord sheltered him and his new family from the spreading distress. By the end of May he could write in his journal:

> Still hard times. Yet how can I lament, when I see the resources of this continent in which three months will anywhere yield a crop of wheat or potatoes. On the bosom of this vast plenty, the blight of trade & manufactures seems to me a momentary mischance.

Perhaps nothing in Emerson so endeared him to his fellow Americans as this supreme optimism. In the face of vast changes in how and where people lived, worked, played, obtained their clothing, practiced their religion, and exchanged their ideas, Emerson retained an almost unqualified serenity about the future. He was not naive: America in 1837 was not "the best of all possible worlds." But like many of his countrymen, he seldom doubted that it could be made better, ever more perfect, through the efforts of individuals—individual "men," he would have said—acting on their deepest convictions in the belief that "what is true for you in your private heart is true for all men" ("Self-Reliance").

Edgar Allan Poe, even more recently married, had just moved to New York in 1837 after losing his job with the *Southern Literary Messenger*. In difficult financial circumstances, he was completing his novella *The Narrative of Arthur Gordon Pym*, a book whose central voyage ends, like Herman Melville's later *Moby-Dick*, in disaster and ambiguity:

> And now we rushed into the embraces of the cataract, where a chasm threw itself open to receive us. But there arose in our pathway a shrouded human

figure, very far larger in its proportions than any dweller among men. And the hue of the skin of the figure was of the perfect whiteness of the snow.

Perhaps the mutability of Poe's world, the wild cycles of commerce, the uncertainty of employment, the very rush of urban life evoked fear as well as confidence. Human ingenuity, unaided, might not always penetrate the deepest natural barriers, nor even the closer mysteries of our own passion and will. What was "true for you in your private heart" might not, as Emerson hoped, be "true for all men," but might instead express the imps of an altogether singular perversity. At any rate, for Poe, peril and loss remained dominant features of experience; the pit yawned fathomless, obscure at the feet of his heroes; the women of his poems and tales, like "Ligeia" (a story of that time), died mysteriously out of reach. In one of the few poems he wrote in 1837, he anticipates the better-known refrain of "The Raven," "nevermore":

> How many scenes of what departed
>   bliss!
>   How many thoughts of what
>   entombéd hopes!
> How many visions of a maiden that is
>   No more—no more upon thy verdant
>   slopes!
> *No more!* alas, that magical sad sound
>   Transforming all! Thy charms shall
>   please *no more,*—
> Thy memory *no more!*

> > "Sonnet—To Zante"

However disparate, the views of Emerson and Poe by no means exhaust the range of responses to the vicissitudes of American society in the early nineteenth century. For a slave like Harriet Jacobs, change was neither a venture into possibility nor the threat of ruin; it would have been a blessing. But in 1837, her reality was confinement: hiding from her slavemaster, she was suffering through a second year in the tiny attic of her grandmother's shed:

> *The garret was only nine feet long and seven wide. The highest part was three feet high, and sloped down abruptly to the loose board floor. There was no admission for either light or air.... The air was stifling; the darkness total. A bed had been spread on the floor. I could sleep quite comfortably on one side; but the slope was so sudden that I could not turn on the other without hitting the roof. The rats and mice ran over my bed; but I was weary, and I slept such sleep as the wretched may, when a tempest has passed over them. Morning came. I knew it only by the noises I heard; for in my small den day and night were all the same. I suffered for air even more than for light. But I was not comfortless. I heard the voices of my children.*

> > Harriet Jacobs,
> > Incidents in the Life of a Slave Girl

   To say that the face of America was transformed in the first half of the nineteenth century is to tell much, and yet little. For how you experienced change—indeed, whether you did—and how you expressed those experiences depended critically on who you were—man or woman, slave or free, the owner of a mill or one of its "hands," a settler on the "virgin lands" of the West or an Indian defending on those lands the graves of your ancestors and the grounds of your hunt. Differing experiences, differing lives and cultures produced varieties of American literature. Thus, while it is important to perceive the world Emerson saw and articulated, it is equally important to perceive how dissimilar was Harriet Jacobs's world, how very different the aims, the opportunities, the audience, and even the *language* available for her writing. In short, as we think of the Emersons riding into Cambridge for Waldo's speech, we need to think simultaneously of Harriet Jacobs lying in that obscure crawl space. And as we note the relationships between Emerson and those who knew and were influenced by him, we need to perceive the very different relationships and influences shaping the writing of many other Americans physically and intellectually distant from Concord.

   Indeed, the culture of Concord, of New England, and of the United States was shaped more, perhaps, than has been acknowledged by influences from abroad. Thoreau, ensconced in his cabin on the shore of Walden Pond, has come to be seen as an iconic representation of New England provincialism: "It is not worth the while to go round the world to count the cats in Zanzibar." But even that wonderful sentence is set in a paragraph wherein Thoreau quotes from the Roman poet Claudian and evokes the explorers John Franklin, Mungo Park, Lewis and Clark, and Frobisher, if only to take issue with the impulse to explore abroad rather than within. If Concord was in certain ways parochial, it was also, like the text milieu Thoreau evokes, cosmopolitan, very much a part of an international flow of ideas. Longfellow and Holmes were not alone in traveling and studying abroad and, in ways small and large, bringing back to America the cultures of the Old World. The grand tour was established as an upper-class phenomenon, and a writer such as Catharine Maria Sedgwick uses grand-tour narratives to reflect on domestic conditions. Fuller spent the last years of her life living in Europe and writing back to America about the revolutionary events transpiring there. Many of Alcott's significant characters, like Fritz Bhaer in *Little Women*, come from overseas or live abroad, and they bring to the domestic scenes of her households a wisdom and perspective gained from foreign experience. Hawthorne, literally as well as figuratively, left the United States to reside in Europe.

   Melville claimed a whaling ship as his "Harvard" and was deeply engaged in the issues generated by American activity, missionary and commercial, in the Pacific and South America. Like another well-known New York writer, Washington Irving, many of his formative experiences took place outside the United States. Poe, of course, derived many of his settings from a European Gothic imaginary, perhaps gained from the years of his childhood spent in an English boarding school. In the real world, his reputation and his influence flourished first in France, where poets like Baudelaire found in him both inspiration and theoretical justification for their *symboliste* poetic practice. Such literary connections were, in fact, dwarfed by the cultural links maintained by many immigrants from Germany, Scandinavia, Scotland, and Ireland. Meantime, a city like New Orleans became, especially after the Mexican War, a peculiarly international venue—a major trading port, a destination for immigrants from Latin America and the Caribbean, and a place where the primary language was not English but French. In short, while Americans in the antebellum period struggled to establish a distinctively American culture, they did so in a world markedly altered by America's involvement in an international context of trade, movement, and ideas. The changes that were reshaping the country in which Emerson, Poe, Jacobs, and their contemporaries lived thus need to be understood in that wider global context. What, then, were those changes?

Publishing: Growth and Goals

When the century began, the nation consisted of sixteen states, mostly strung along the Atlantic coast; with the Gadsden Purchase in 1853, the United States more than tripled its size, achieving the continental dimensions it would retain for more than a century, until the admission of Alaska and Hawaii as states. In those fifty years, the country's population grew from 5.3 million to more than 23.1 million. Not only was that rate of increase extraordinary, but so was the rapidity with which those people moved on to ever new frontiers. As the nineteenth century began, most knowledgeable Americans believed it would take a hundred years or more for white people to settle in the western territories even then claimed by the United States, much less in the vast areas further west claimed by Spain and populated primarily by Indians; nevertheless, by 1850, California on the far Pacific coast had been sufficiently organized to be admitted as a state. At the same time, the urban population, especially in eastern cities, was climbing rapidly—mainly because of massive immigration from Ireland, Scandinavia, and elsewhere in western Europe.

This dramatic growth and spread of population offered new opportunities as well as presenting a variety of social problems. Urban expansion in particular generated a wide new audience for newspapers and magazines. The number of newspapers in the country increased during the first third of the century from about 200 to more than 1,200; in 1830, New York City alone had 47 newspapers printed in many languages (compared with perhaps a dozen today). These journals and a growing number of monthly and annual magazines served one of the most literate populations in the world. Similarly, debating societies and the lyceum movement, which combined the features of an entertainment and educational network, rapidly followed the spread of the white—and especially northern—population across the country. Founded by Josiah Holbrook in 1826, lyceums had sprung up in fifteen states by 1835; by 1860, there were more than 3,000 lyceums. People came to lyceum halls much as, a hundred years later, they would congregate at the movies. They heard lectures on the Oregon Trail and the South Seas, Napoleon and Black Elk, the new science of daguerreotyping and the pseudoscience of phrenology. They listened to debates on the burning issues of the time: who should be able to vote, chattel slavery versus wage slavery, the demon rum, whether married women could hold property, America's "manifest destiny" to extend its boundaries.

The American people having derived their origin from many other nations, and the Declaration of National Independence being entirely based on the great principle of human equality, these facts demonstrate at once our disconnected position as regards any other nation; that we have, in reality, but little connection with the past history of any of them, and still less with all antiquity, its glories, or its crimes. On the contrary, our national birth was the beginning of a new history, the formation and progress of an untried political system, which separates us from the past and connects us with the future only; and so far as regards the entire development of the natural rights of man, in moral, political, and national life, we may confidently assume that our country is destined to be the great nation of futurity. . . .

We have no interest in the scenes of antiquity, only as lessons of avoidance of nearly all their examples. The expansive future is our arena, and for our history. We are entering on its untrodden space, with the truths of God in our minds, beneficent objects in our hearts, and with a clear conscience unsullied by the past. We are the nation of human progress, and who will, what can, set limits to our onward march? Providence is with us, and no earthly power can. We point to the everlasting truth on the first page of our national declaration, and we proclaim to the millions of other lands, that "the gates of hell"—the powers of aristocracy and monarchy—"shall not prevail against it."

The far-reaching, the boundless future will be the era of American greatness. In its magnificent domain of space and time, the nation of many nations is destined to manifest to mankind the excellence of divine principles; to establish on earth the noblest temple ever dedicated to the worship of the Most High—the Sacred and the True. Its floor shall be a hemisphere—its roof the firmament of the star-studded heavens, and its congregation an Union of many republics, comprising hundreds of happy millions, calling, owning no man master, but governed by God's natural and moral law of equality, the law of brotherhood—of "peace and good will amongst men." . . .

For this blessed mission to the nations of the world, which are shut out from the life-giving light of truth, has America been chosen; and her high example shall smite unto death the tyranny of kings, hierarchs, and oligarchs, and carry the glad tidings of peace and good will where myriads now endure an existence scarcely more enviable than that of beasts of the field. Who, then, can doubt that our country is destined to be *the great nation* of futurity?

John L. O'Sullivan, "The Great Nation of Futurity,"
The United States Democratic Review, 1839

Such publishing and speaking outlets helped educate the majority of Americans who had had, up to that time, little formal schooling, and they probably fostered the national penchant for arguing issues large and small. They also, at one time or another, provided employment to almost every writer of this period. Bryant and Whitman ran newspapers; Fuller and Poe, Hawthorne and Higginson, Child, Whittier, Douglass and Ridge, among others, served as editors, often composing what they published. Emerson made much of his living as a star of the lyceum circuit; Phillips, Douglass, Angelina Grimké, Frances Harper, and others traveled as abolitionist "agents," lecturing in cities and towns across the North. Nor was such editing and lecturing literary hackwork or simply political lobbying. Most of the best stories of Hawthorne and Stoddard first appeared in literary annuals, gift books, or similar magazines; the criticism of Poe and Fuller appeared in newspapers and popular journals; and Emerson's essays were, for the most part, first developed as lectures.

Thinking perhaps of Hawthorne's complaints about how his career opportunities were blocked by the effusions of a "mob of scribbling women," commentators have argued that pre–Civil War America offered, at most, very limited opportunities for writers to live by their pens. There was no international copyright, the public generally preferred to buy cheaper pirated editions of popular British writers like Sir Walter Scott and Charles Dickens to homegrown products, and publishers paid American writers a pittance or were themselves paid by better-known authors like Washington Irving and James Fenimore Cooper to distribute their books. The conclusion drawn from these facts, along with the further contention that the popular audience wished to read work different from what "serious" writers—the Hawthornes and Melvilles—had to offer, is that pre–Civil War America provided an inhospitable climate for authors. But there were many overlapping audiences in the United States, and although an international copyright was not adopted until 1891, those audiences had long since found sustenance in and furnished support for many different groups of American writers.

It was in the early nineteenth century, in fact, that writing first became an available profession not only for white gentlemen but for others. *The Cherokee Phoenix*, established in Georgia in 1828, was the first newspaper published by an Indian tribe and the first published in a native language as well as in English. It was succeeded in the West, after the Cherokees were forced out of their homes, by *The Cherokee Advocate*, founded in 1844. George Copway, the well-known Ojibwa writer, published his newspaper, *Copway's American Indian*, in New York in 1851. *Freedom's Journal* was established in 1827, the first of some seventeen black-owned and -edited newspapers in the pre–Civil War period. Begun by John B. Russwurm, the nation's first black college graduate, and Samuel E. Cornish, who edited a number of other weeklies, the *Journal*, like its successor, *The Rights of All*, and the other black newspapers, was abolitionist in sentiment and in much of its content, including many of the sketches and poems it published. The spread of abolitionist societies—by 1850 there were almost 2,000 with more than 200,000 members—helped to provide further outlets for white and black writers like Child, Whittier, Douglass, Garnet, Harper, and Harriet Beecher Stowe; indeed, *Uncle Tom's Cabin* was initially serialized in the Washington-based *National Era*.

For white women in particular, writing opened new professional doors. A substantial portion of the novels published in the United States after 1820 were written by women—primarily for a female audience; indeed, most of the best sellers before the Civil War were the works of writers like Susan Warner (*The Wide, Wide World*, 1850, the first American work to sell more than a million copies), Maria Cummins (*The Lamplighter*, 1854), and E.D.E.N. Southworth (*The Hidden Hand*, 1859), not to speak of Stowe. In her autobiographical novel, *Ruth Hall* (1855), Fanny Fern (Sara Willis Parton) describes in often touching and satiric detail how, to keep her family together after her husband's death, she carved out a career as a writer against the advice, and often despite the opposition, of her litterateur brother, Nathaniel P. Willis. Many of these women, and others included in this anthology, turned to writing in similar circumstances in order to earn their living.

Writing books that sold required entertaining as well as edifying their readers. But a living or not, writing was also for most authors an opportunity to shape the outlook, to mold the consciousness of their audience. In the twentieth century, most of us have been taught that "art" is a form of discourse that lays no claims on our actions, that a poem should not "mean but be," and that "literature" and "propaganda" are as different as elephants and ivy. But in the early nineteenth century, there were few advocates of such "art for art's sake" theories in the United States. Thus Emerson writes that "it is not metres, but a metre-making argument that makes a poem—a thought so passionate and alive that like the spirit of a plant or animal it has an architecture of its own, and adorns nature with a new thing" ("The Poet"). And Thoreau says toward the beginning of *Walden:* "I do not propose to write an ode to dejection, but to brag as lustily as chanticleer in the morning, standing on his roost, if only to wake my neighbors up." Harriet Beecher Stowe is even more explicit in her "Concluding Remarks" to *Uncle Tom's Cabin*:

> Nothing of tragedy can be written, can be spoken, can be conceived, that equals the frightful reality of scenes daily and hourly acting on our shores, beneath the shadow of American law, and the shadow of the cross of Christ.
>
> And now, men and women of America, is this a thing to be trifled with, apologized for, and passed over in silence? . . . But, what can any individual do? Of that, every individual can judge. There is one thing that every individual can do,—they can see to it that they feel right. An atmosphere of sympathetic influence encircles every human being; and the man or woman who feels strongly, healthily and justly, on the great interests of humanity, is a constant benefactor to the human race. See, then, to your sympathies in this matter!

Even Hawthorne, whose *Twice-Told Tales* could hardly have seemed more distant from the daily pulse of American life, effectively drew certain morals about social change, the value of scientific progress, and the sanctity of the human heart.

While the writing of the early nineteenth century is often shaped by these desires to influence how readers understand the world, it is also formed by the conditions of that world, as well as by the character of the literary traditions available to American authors. We shall turn shortly to the swiftly changing, increasingly complex material and intellectual circumstances affecting the writers of the time. But it is also important to recognize that how writers write, and about what, is in some measure a product of how their predecessors have written. Hawthorne, for example, adopted the ideas of the prose "Romance," which he developed in the "Custom-House" introduction to *The Scarlet Letter* and in his prefaces to *The House of the Seven Gables* and *The Blithedale Romance*, from earlier essays in English and American periodicals. These essays maintained that the romance was an ideal form for depicting the past, providing the romancer maintained a degree of verisimilitude even while creating the atmospheric and often dreamlike effects characteristic of the genre. Like other writers of their generation, Hawthorne and Poe were also influenced by the "Gothic" fictions of English and Continental authors like Matthew Lewis and Mrs. Ann Radcliffe and their domestic counterparts such as the writings of Charles Brockden Brown. Such Gothic works as *The Monk* and *The Mysteries of Udolpho* featured remote castles, ghostly apparitions, mysterious villains, and imperiled maidens. Poe and Hawthorne, among others, adapted elements of such books, as well as material from the popular scientific and pseudoscientific literature concerned with phrenology, mesmerism, alchemy, and exploration of remote parts of the earth. By contrast, many female writers—for example, Caroline Kirkland and Alice Cary—were influenced by the realistic English village sketches of a writer like Mary Russell Mitford and the "love and money" focus of Jane Austen. Such literary traditions and the variety of popular forms in prose and verse existed side by side, but how writers chose to use them depended very much on their responses to the worlds of change they faced and, as they often hoped, were molding.

Religion and Common Culture

In few areas was change more profound than in the religious and ethical life of the nation. By the end of the Revolution, most of the dominant churches, whether New England Presbyterian and Congregationalist or Virginia Anglican, were in decline. The rationalist spirit of the Revolution undercut their credibility. Leaders like Ethan Allen and Thomas Paine wrote deistic attacks on the authority of the Bible and of the clergy, and Jefferson and Madison moved to disestablish state religions and to separate state from church. Besides, the war itself had scattered congregations, and the rapid westward expansion drew people even further from eastern church authority. Historians estimate that by the 1790s only one in twenty Americans was a church member.

Beginning late in the eighteenth century and continuing well into the nineteenth, a series of religious revivals, called the Second Great Awakening, swept the nation. Such periodic revivals continued with more or less intensity well into the twentieth century, but this early-nineteenth-century Awakening in many respects established the pattern of religious organization that characterized the United States until recently. It brought a large majority of Americans—perhaps as many as three in four by the 1830s—into some relationship with one or another of the evangelical Protestant churches. It confirmed that no one church would be dominant, much less established, in the United States—that, indeed, religion like business in America would thrive on a competition of denominations. Among these denominations, newer groups that sought to recruit

Dr. Finney's ... appearance in the pulpit on these memorable occasions is indelibly impressed on my mind. I can see him now, his great eyes rolling around the congregation and his arms flying about in the air like those of a windmill. One evening he described hell and the devil and the long procession of sinners being swept down the rapids, about to make the awful plunge into the burning depths of liquid fire below, and the rejoicing hosts in the inferno coming up to meet them with the shouts of the devils echoing through the vaulted arches. He suddenly halted, and, pointing his index finger at the supposed procession, he exclaimed:

"There, do you not see them!"

I was wrought up to such a pitch that I actually jumped up and gazed in the direction to which he pointed, while the picture glowed before my eyes and remained with me for months afterward. I cannot forbear saying that, although high respect is due to the intellectual, moral, and spiritual gifts of the venerable ex-president of Oberlin College, such preaching worked incalculable harm to the very souls he sought to save. Fear of the judgment seized my soul. Visions of the lost haunted my dreams. Mental anguish prostrated my health. Dethronement of my reason was apprehended by friends. But he was sincere, so peace to his ashes! Returning home, I often at night roused my father from his slumbers to pray for me, lest I should be cast into the bottomless pit before morning.

Elizabeth Cady Stanton, *Eighty Years and More*, 1897

ordinary people who farmed and labored, principally the Baptists and the Methodists, would emerge by the 1820s as the largest.

However fragmented, Protestantism came to provide a degree of common culture to much of the country. Most people were in some measure familiar with the Bible, with the language and meters of hymns, and many with Christian literary works like Bunyan's *Pilgrim's Progress*. Thus speakers and writers as diverse as Henry Highland Garnet and Emily Dickinson, Melville and Stowe could depend on their audience to recognize and respond to biblical and other religious allusions and quotations. Traditions of biblical citation and religious debate provided a basis for tracts like those of William Apess and David Walker. Religion, especially among Southern black slaves, also provided a context for the creation of great works of art, the "spirituals" or sorrow songs. For many of today's readers, unfamiliarity with these traditions of religious discourse may in part block access to works of the nineteenth century.

Nineteenth-century evangelical Protestantism also displayed a strong millennial component, closely connecting the coming of God's kingdom with the working out of the political future of the United States. The progress of democracy at home and abroad could be taken to demonstrate movement toward the millennium, and expansion of Protestant America into the territory of pagan Indians or Catholic French or Spaniards could be rationalized as fulfilling God's plan. Such pious justifications for, as well as criticisms of, American expansionism constituted a persistent note in many writings of the time.

To some extent, the Second Awakening, as well as subsequent revival campaigns, reflected a conscious organizing effort by clergymen and their supporters to win back ground lost in the Revolution. Large numbers of lay as well as institutionally trained preachers were ordained and sent to ride far-flung circuits. In the early nineteenth century, churches founded more than seventy denominational colleges, primarily to support their efforts, and all the denominations promoted great camp meetings at which thousands were urged to come forward, be "reborn," and find the "inner strength" needed to combat sin. In the years immediately following, as Elizabeth Cady Stanton reports, techniques for organizing revivals and for moving converts to respond—often with displays of uncontrolled emotion—repent, and be reborn were perfected by preachers like Charles Grandison Finney and Lyman Beecher, patriarch of the famous Beecher family. In other respects, however, the Awakenings reflected the search of Americans, especially on the frontier, for community and a source of order in a dangerous and often lawless society. The early nineteenth century saw the founding of many new denominations and sects, some of which, like the Mormons, tried to organize their converts into communities at once secular and religious. The periodic revivals also may have represented a desire to reinvest spiritual life with an emotional vitality missing from the well-humored, practical enlightenment prose of a Franklin.

That desire was also a significant component in the movement of Emerson and his Transcendentalist friends away from the bloodless Unitarianism of 1830s New England. In certain respects, Transcendentalism may be thought of as a secularized religion, an enthusiastic encounter with the "Over-Soul" entailing no outward display, an endless Sabbath kept, in Emily Dickinson's words,

> ... staying at Home—
> With a Bobolink for a Chorister—
> And an Orchard, for a Dome—
>
> #324

Deeply influenced by English Romantic writers like Coleridge and Wordsworth, and Continental thinkers like Kant and Swedenborg, the Transcendentalists, and those affected by them, opposed the reigning materialism and widespread conformity of American culture, trying instead to develop an "original relation to the universe." They believed that the commonplace, "the shop, the plough, and the ledger," could reveal the "form and order" of the mighty universe. As Whitman put it:

> I believe a leaf of grass is no less
>   perfect than the journey-work of
>   the stars,
> And the pismire is equally perfect, and
>   a grain of sand, and the egg of the
>   wren,
>
> "Song of Myself," #31

For their sources of value and inspiration, they looked not to the past, as embodied in scriptures or creeds, but to the present encounter with nature and their own inner light. Again to quote Whitman:

> There was never any more inception
> > than there is now,
> Nor any more youth or age than there
> > is now,
> And will never be any more perfection
> > than there is now,
> Nor any more heaven or hell than there
> > is now.

"Song of Myself," #3

Not everyone shared this Transcendentalist vision of being at home in a universe open to one's intuitions. Emily Dickinson wrote that

> … nature is a stranger yet;
> The ones that cite her most
> Have never passed her haunted house,
> Nor simplified her ghost.

#1400

And Melville, like Hawthorne and Poe, presented a far more ambiguous picture of the power of the natural world in his white whale. Indeed, in later essays such as "Circles," Emerson himself qualified his generally optimistic outlook, and as they increasingly engaged the political realities of slavery at home and revolution in Europe, writers like Thoreau and Fuller found a world less plastic and amenable to change.

In any case, whatever their longer-range impact, especially in literary circles, the Transcendentalists' immediate effect on their time was not extensive. The circulation of their journal, *The Dial*, never exceeded about 300, and most of the copies of Thoreau's first book were returned to him by the publisher. Emerson's Divinity School "Address" marked him among traditional clergymen as a heretic, Thoreau's neighbors viewed him as something of a crank, and Bronson Alcott's experiments with education were regarded as visionary failures. To the mainstream of evangelical Protestantism, they were intellectual bohemians, marginal if not altogether irrelevant.

This is not to say, however, that there was fundamental agreement among religious denominations. On the contrary, the divisions in American Protestantism reflected and helped widen growing sectional and political schisms. Take, for example, the question of what sorts of behavior being "born again" implied. For many churches, generally fundamentalist, and especially those in the South, salvation entailed struggling against sin, especially in oneself, in order that one might ensure redemption in a life to come. For others, however, being reborn in the spirit of Christ entailed working to eradicate sin from *this world*; to evangelical Christians, bringing in the kingdom of God depended on perfecting the character of human society. Such believers developed a social gospel, which engaged them in efforts to eradicate the sources of human misery: poverty, alcoholism,

More than fifty-seven years have elapsed since a band of patriots convened in this place to devise measures for the deliverance of this country from a foreign yoke. The cornerstone upon which they founded the temple of freedom was broadly this: "That all men are created equal; and they are endowed by their Creator with certain inalienable rights; that among these are life, LIBERTY, and the pursuit of happiness." At the sound of their trumpet call 3 million people rose up as from the sleep of death and rushed to the strife of blood, deeming it more glorious to die instantly as freemen than desirable to live one hour as slaves. They were few in number, poor in resources; but the honest conviction that TRUTH, JUSTICE, and RIGHT were on their side made them invincible.

We have met together for the achievement of an enterprise, without which that of our fathers is incomplete; and which, for its magnitude, solemnity, and probable results upon the destiny of the world as far transcends theirs as moral truth does physical force.

In purity of motive, in earnestness of zeal, in decision of purpose, in intrepidity of action, in steadfastness of faith, in sincerity of spirit, we would not be inferior to them.

Their principles led them to wage war against their oppressors and to spill human blood like water in order to be free. *Ours* forbid the doing of evil that good may come and lead us to reject, and to entreat the oppressed to reject the use of all carnal weapons for deliverance from bondage, relying solely upon those which are spiritual and mighty through God to the pulling down of strongholds.

"Declaration of the American Anti-Slavery Convention," 1834

war, discrimination against women, and above all slavery. These deep commitments to bring about fundamental change *in* the world invested the writing of activists such as William Lloyd Garrison, John Greenleaf Whittier, Henry Highland Garnet, and Lydia Maria Child with a moral fervor and a sense of righteousness; these commitments also helped carry them through poverty, obloquy, and even violent attacks on their persons. Garrison, for example, was at one point led down the streets of Boston with a rope around his neck by a mob of well-dressed "gentlemen." Such commitments also set these religious activists deeply at odds with their ostensibly Christian brethren, both North and South, especially over the issue of slavery.

To say this another way, Protestant Christianity provided certain common assumptions, a vocabulary, and a set of images and allusions to the majority of Americans in the early nineteenth century. But the uses to which these commonalities were put were extremely diverse. Religion was, in the hands of some, a powerful censor: It was used to condemn the Grimké sisters for speaking in public, Melville for criticizing missionary activities in the Pacific, Whitman for extolling sexuality. It was used to defend (as well as to condemn) slavery, as seen in Whittier's satire in "The Hunters of Men" and Douglass's attack in his

Narrative. Indeed, it was used to rationalize violent attacks on Irish Catholic immigrants.

For many blacks, however, the biblical stories of the Exodus, of Daniel, of Revelations provided images of consolation and hope. For a writer like Stowe, the primary problems of the nineteenth century were religious: how to sustain the moral seriousness of Puritanism without its terrorizing theology, a dilemma she dramatized in *The Minister's Wooing*. Hawthorne selectively used the language and some of the imagery of Puritanism, but worked out questions of "sin and sorrow" so central to earlier New England religious life in newer psychological rather than theological terms. For an activist like Elizabeth Cady Stanton, religion was often an inhibitor, if not a downright enemy, of change. Yet to many nineteenth-century reformers, religion provided both the motivation and the moral energy to sustain a struggle for temperance, peace, and most of all the abolition of slavery.

The Debates over Racism and Slavery

No issues during the middle decades of the nineteenth century so engaged the passions of Americans as those of slavery and race. Indeed, the period is marked by a series of political accords—the Missouri Compromise (1820), the Gag Rule (1836), the Compromise of 1850—designed to balance the interests of pro- and antislavery forces, and to postpone as long as possible the question of whether, in Lincoln's famous phrase, "a house divided against itself" could stand, whether the nation could "endure, permanently half *slave* and half *free*." The Founders had generally assumed that slavery would atrophy in the course of time and that slaveholders, constitutionally prevented from importing additional slaves, would ultimately turn to other, free sources of labor. But a number of factors—the invention of the cotton gin, which made practical the use of the kind of cotton grown in much of the South; the development of a device for pressing cotton into easily transported bales; and the vastly increased market for cotton resulting from the expansion of textile manufacturing in Great Britain and then in New England—actually increased the demand for slave labor early in the century. During the 1820s, while the living standards and hopes for the future of white American men were largely rising, those of black slaves were rapidly declining. Opportunities for slaves to become artisans or to hire out their time and perhaps earn freedom began to disappear. Laws against teaching slaves to read or write began to be harshly enforced, especially after the uprising led by Nat Turner in 1831 and the advent of militant abolitionism, as represented by David Walker and William Lloyd Garrison, among Northern blacks and whites. In many areas of the upper South, slave-breeding became a major source of income. In the lower South, on the cotton, sugar, and indigo plantations, working conditions became increasingly harsh as more and more labor was demanded from the larger corps of field hands.

Just as the character of slavery changed significantly over the half century preceding the Civil War, so the arguments for and against it altered. Initially, defenders of slavery—who were by no means confined to the South—argued that it was an institution as old as human history, dating back at least to biblical and classical Greek civilizations and sanctioned by biblical texts. Then and now,

The brain of the Negro, as I have stated, is, according to positive
measurements, smaller than the Caucasian by a full tenth; and this
deficiency exists particularly in the anterior portion of the brain,
which is known to be the seat of the higher faculties. History and
observation, both teach that in accordance with this defective organization, the Mongol, the Malay, the Indian and Negro, are now
and have been in all ages and all places, inferior to the Caucasian.

Look at the world as it now stands and say where is civilization to
be found except amongst the various branches of the Caucasian race?

Take Europe and start in the freezing climate of Russia, and
come down to the straights of Gibralter, and you find not a solitary
exception, not one that excites a doubt.

Take Asia in the same way, and the only approximation to civilization, is found in the mixt, or in some of the Mongol tribes. Take
China which is the nearest approximation—she has for centuries
had stability in her government, and many of the arts have been
carried to a high state of perfection, but take her religion, her laws,
her government, her literature, and how does the comparison
stand? The most you can say is, that the Chinese are an intermediate link between the Negro and Caucasian.

Take Africa next and the picture presented is truly deplorable—
with the exception of Egypt, and the Barbary States, which were in
their palmy days occupied by Caucasian colonies, and now by their
mixed descendants; and where I repeat, except here, will you find
from the Mediterranean to the Cape of Good Hope, a single record
or a single monument to show that civilization has ever existed?

Josiah C. Nott, *Two Lectures on The Natural History of the
Caucasian and Negro Races*, 1844

they said, it had helped civilize and Christianize a childlike if not barbaric people. It was a more humane system than the "wage slavery" of the North and of
Britain, which demanded that workers compete with one another to sell their
one "possession," their labor, for a "wage" and in hard times left them to fend
for themselves in conditions of unrelenting poverty. In any case, Southerners
insisted, the several States had the right to define for themselves their forms of
social organization without interference from a federal government. As the
debate intensified, more racist theories came into play; in their extreme form,
such arguments held that blacks (and other colored races) were less than
human, incapable of full development even in freedom, and thus by nature cut
out only to be drawers of water and hewers of wood.

Not all defenders of slavery were racists; nor were many abolitionists free of
racist ideas. In the earlier part of the century, many of those opposing slavery
believed that black people should be helped or more forcibly sent back to African

colonies. With the circulation of powerful tracts like David Walker's *Appeal* (1829), and with Garrison's founding of *The Liberator* (1831), the vogue of colonization began to fade. If blacks were men, argued the abolitionists, and they were, as the lives of Toussaint and of Douglass testified, then the ideas of the Declaration of Independence—that "all men are created equal"—applied to them as well as to whites. "Life, liberty and the pursuit of happiness" were therefore "inalienable rights" which could not be infringed by law or custom. The issue at the center of stories like Douglass's "The Heroic Slave" and Melville's "Benito Cereno" was that of the full humanity of black people.

Because blacks were human—if supposedly "inferior"—in the eyes of most Americans, they stood before God as souls equally to be redeemed. To religious abolitionists, chattel slavery—claiming property in another human being—was the most fundamental violation of God's laws. For writers like Child, Jacobs, and Stowe, that was most vividly illustrated by the way in which slavery undermined and finally destroyed black families. In Stowe's *Uncle Tom's Cabin*, the poles of the conflict are symbolized by Haley, the slavetrader, "a man alive to nothing but trade and profit," and Rachel Halliday, the Quaker matriarch, whose face and dress and domestic occupations "showed at once the community to which she belonged." Haley's commercial principles are responsible for tearing families apart, Halliday's religious home for reuniting them.

For some earlier writers, like Irving and Cooper, and others in the next generation like Hawthorne and, for a time, Emerson, the slavery issue was not central. But after the passage of the Fugitive Slave Act in 1850, which imposed on Northerners the legal obligation of helping slaveholders regain their "property," and with the Dred Scott decision (1857), which held that Negroes were not citizens of the United States and that slaveholding could not be excluded from any of the states or territories, it became increasingly difficult for any public figure to avoid the issue. Some politicians, like Lincoln, insisted that their objective was to maintain the Union, regardless of the disposition of slavery. But Garrison, among others, was willing to burn the Constitution, which had legalized slavery, as a "Covenant with Death and an Agreement with Hell."

It is often argued that such phrases illustrate the "extremism" of writers like Garrison, Child, Phillips, Higginson, or the Thoreau of "A Plea for Captain John Brown" and "Slavery in Massachusetts." With such intellectual radicals, along with activists like John Brown, on one side, and Southern firebrands like George Fitzhugh, on the other, the argument goes, the cause of "moderates" primarily committed to the preservation of the Union was a necessary but increasingly difficult one to maintain. Thoreau himself had little patience with that way of framing the issue. In "A Plea," he writes:

> Our foes are in our midst and all about us. There is hardly a house but is divided against itself, for our foe is the all but universal woodenness of both head and heart, the want of vitality in man, which is the effect of our vice; and hence are begotten fear, superstition, bigotry, persecution, and slavery of all kinds.

It is to such "woodenness" that he addressed his essays, to "wake his neighbors" from their moral slumbers. He saw John Brown's "treason" in this context:

"High treason, when it is resistance to tyranny here below, has its origin in, and is first committed by, the power that makes and forever recreates man." Thus he could go on to compare Brown with Jesus: "The same indignation that is said to have cleared the temple once will clear it again. The question is not about the weapon, but the spirit in which you use it." Moderation was thus not the issue for these writers: "Tell a man whose house is on fire," Garrison had written more than a quarter of a century before, "to give a moderate alarm; tell him to moderately rescue his wife from the hands of the ravisher...." Nor was nationalism, which deified the Union itself, an ultimate good: "I would remind my countrymen," Thoreau wrote in "Slavery in Massachusetts," "that they are to be men first, and Americans only at a late and convenient hour."

In the years leading to the Civil War, differing understandings of civic virtue and of a conclusive measure of morality were being bitterly contested—in the lyceums and the halls of Congress, on the printed page, in the streets, and finally on the battlefield. This long conflict of values produced endless oratory and a huge amount of writing. Good politics does not necessarily produce good writing, nor does even the most vile politics prevent the creation of interesting art, as some Nazi films demonstrate. In a collection of oratory, the speakers of the Old South like Henry Clay and John C. Calhoun would be more heavily represented. But for an anthology of primarily written texts, the compositions of the Old South fade into relative obscurity. One need only compare the shrill and sentimental efforts to answer *Uncle Tom's Cabin* with the original to see why. Earlier books in the tradition of the plantation novel such as George Tucker's *The Valley of Shenandoah* (1824), James Kirke Paulding's *Westward Ho!* (1832), or the better-known *Swallow-Barn* (1832) by John Pendleton Kennedy and *The Yemassee* (1835) by William Gilmore Simms, whatever their other virtues, consistently display glaring racial stereotypes and long-discredited apologies for the slave system. Furthermore, the literature defending slavery was, given the outcome of the war, essentially stillborn. Still, we have included some representative examples of these texts, however painful they may prove for many readers. They are a part of our literary heritage, whatever we think of them today, and it is our purpose to display as much of American culture as we can—not just what meets the standards of value and intellect on which most Americans have come to agree. Furthermore, there is much to learn, however abhorrent, from the arguments made to defend the South's "peculiar institution." While the institution was, indeed, distinctive, the justifications and rationalizations of it do not altogether differ from those made to support the perpetuation of racist habits and conventions in our time. As one commentator has put it, "By understanding how others have fashioned and maintained their systems of meaning, we shall be better equipped to evaluate, criticize, and perhaps even change our own." Moreover, racial stereotyping was hardly confined to the works of the Old South, nor, indeed, to proslavery writers. Nevertheless, we believe that the controversialist texts of Child, Douglass, Thoreau, and Higginson, among others, still live and have effects, in ways not true of books like George Fitzhugh's *Sociology for the South*—as the quoted passage suggests. As Thoreau put it, "Slavery and servility have produced no sweet-scented flower annually, to charm the senses of men, for they have no real life."

Most blacks in the United States remained slaves throughout the period. While slavery had deprived black people of their original African languages, it did not by any means succeed in extirpating all aspects of African culture—in music and dance, in folktales, in forms of extended family organization, for example. But Southern law forbade and Northern discrimination inhibited the teaching of reading and writing to blacks, and thus the production and consumption of traditional literary work was severely limited. It is all the more remarkable, therefore, that in this period two uniquely American art forms flourished among blacks. The spirituals were a singular blend of African and European music, of Hebrew and Christian religious images converted through slave experience into symbols of present torment and future hope. And the slave narratives were, along with white women's narratives of Indian captivity, the first distinctively American forms of prose composition.

Almost all African American writing of the period was produced by free blacks and by former slaves. George Moses Horton, who was a slave for much of his life, wrote verse—including love poetry for sale to undergraduates at Chapel Hill—in the thwarted hope that he might buy his freedom and emigrate. In important ways, literary production by free blacks before Emancipation was shaped by the conditions of its production and use. A number of writers, such as Frances Harper, James M. Whitfield, and James Madison Bell, wrote poetry that was designed more to be delivered from the platform than read silently in a book. Their poems were in a sense "scripts," which they declaimed in churches, at public meetings, or at other events usually connected with the antislavery cause. Thus Whitfield's long poem "America" begins almost as a parody of patriotic verse:

America, it is to thee,
Thou boasted land of liberty,—
It is to thee I raise my song,
Thou land of blood, and crime, and
    wrong.

Many other poems and stories published in black newspapers or in abolitionist journals were designed to demonstrate by their very existence the abilities of their authors, often quite young, and the virtues of supporting their further education. Thus when Ann Plato's volume of prose and poetry (1841) was published she may have been as young as fifteen, and Frances Harper's *Forest Leaves* (no copy of which seems to have survived) came out when she was barely twenty. Furthermore, the poets set out to demonstrate that they could utilize the forms and cadences of British verse, so their work is often quite as derivative as their white models.

In subject, in audience, and in intent, much of the writing by blacks in this period was thus closely tied to the movement for emancipation and to the efforts to develop and support black educational and religious institutions. Not surprisingly, therefore, the most widely used form was the slave narrative. The abolitionist and black presses published hundreds of these autobiographies, ranging in size from a few pages to whole volumes, like those of Gustavus Vassa, Frederick Douglass, James W. C. Pennington, Ellen and William Craft, and Harriet Jacobs. They describe firsthand the evils of slavery, and often of Northern racism as well, narrate what are often thrilling escapes, and sometimes discuss the problems a former slave has in learning to read, getting a job, and adapting to Northern ways. After the resounding success of *Uncle Tom's Cabin* in helping stir up antislavery sentiment, however, some black writers in the 1850s turned to fiction as an equally useful form. The decade saw the publication of the first four novels by black authors—William Wells Brown's *Clotel* (1853), Frank Webb's *The Garies and Their Friends* (1857), Martin Delany's *Blake* (1859), and Harriet Wilson's *Our Nig* (1859)—as well as Frederick Douglass's novella "The Heroic Slave" (1853) and Frances Harper's short story "The Two Offers" (1859).

Apart from such work, almost all of it published in the Northeast, there existed a well-developed tradition of French Creole writing, primarily in New Orleans. And, of course, there was an extremely vital oral tradition of songs and tales throughout the South and wherever in Northern communities black people gathered. Little of this oral material, which was after all the major expressive form among slaves, was collected until after the Civil War. Furthermore, slaves learned, as Douglass says, that "a still tongue makes a wise head," especially around whites. Thus, it is almost impossible to know precisely which stories were actually in circulation during slavery. What is clear, however, is that such oral traditions influenced post–Civil War black writers rather more than their earlier peers, for whose audience dialect and folk stories were too closely tied to the oppression and ignorance of slavery.

The Debate over Women's "Sphere"

Closely related to abolitionism, but strong in its own claims, was the movement for women's rights. Abolitionism, especially the Garrisonian branch, provided the feminist movement with a number of trained activists, such as Susan B. Anthony and Frances Ellen Watkins Harper; with an ideology that insisted on the fundamental equality of all human beings, regardless of accidents of birth like race and sex; and with an analysis that explained how institutions like the churches perpetuated inequality despite the good will of many members. Feminists also learned in abolitionist circles the tactics of agitation and education that helped shape their writing. And the first women's rights convention, in Seneca Falls, New York, in 1848, developed in an immediate way from a meeting of abolitionists.

But early-nineteenth-century attention to women's distinctive concerns was rooted in broad social and economic changes. As the production of many household goods moved out of the home around the turn of the century, white middle-class women, especially in the North, found themselves with more leisure and ultimately more education than their mothers or grandmothers had had. That enabled them to become a large audience, especially for fiction, and to participate in efforts for social betterment, such as temperance and prison reform. At the same time, their opportunities for meaningful work apart from child rearing and their ability to control their own property or even their own persons had probably narrowed since the Revolution. Moreover, while even the most debased of white men could vote, run for office, dispose of his own *and* his wife's property, and "chastise" both spouse and children, women were increasingly expected to devote themselves to a domestic "sphere," which for many—Stanton makes clear—was isolating, repetitive, and trivializing, narrowing minds and restricting horizons despite the pious assertions of its moral value. To be sure, the "bonds of womanhood" included intensely meaningful relationships among women, as Emily Dickinson's poems and letters dramatize and as Caroline Kirkland's comments about community suggest. Nevertheless, significant numbers of women trying to earn their living, to express themselves as people, or even to extend the range of their accomplishments found themselves hemmed in by custom and law.

The experience of slaves and of white working-class women differed significantly, of course. Most slave women would probably have welcomed the leisure and security of middle-class marriages, since they worked in the fields or in the household from "can see to can't see," just like the men. Notions of gallantry did not extend to them; nobody helped Sojourner Truth from a carriage, though she was a woman. Moreover, Harriet Jacobs makes us understand, what might have been an asset to a free white woman—physical beauty, for example—all too often became a danger, indeed a plague, for a slave. The dilemma of a writer like Jacobs, or of Child, was that middle-class propriety frowned on direct discussion of sex, yet the experience of rape and seduction was a fundamental part of the lives of black women. Moreover, because Southern law forbade teaching slaves to read, and Northern customs discouraged when it did not altogether bar black people from formal education, the primary audience for a writer like Jacobs was precisely white women of the middle class.

White women from Yankee farms constituted much of the original industrial workforce in New England mills and New York sweatshops. Writers like Fanny Fern, Herman Melville, and later Rebecca Harding Davis and Elizabeth Stuart Phelps brought aspects of these women's experiences to an audience largely unfamiliar with factories, much less with the lives of their "operatives." Some of the factory women themselves contributed poems and stories to volumes like *The Lowell Offering* and other gift books and annuals. In fact, in the early years of industrialism, paternalistic manufacturers in places like Lowell, Massachusetts, where the young women lived together in boardinghouses, offered morally proper cultural and religious events to their "girls." Factory work thus provided young women with opportunities to attend lyceums, to read, and otherwise to broaden their cultural horizons, as well as to accumulate modest nest eggs. With the panic of 1837, the subsequent depression, the worsening of working conditions, and the importation of large numbers of immigrant workers, such opportunities declined.

On the whole, however, more women attended school at least for a time and a significant few went on to college, while many bought and read the increasing variety of American books and magazines. Correspondingly, a greater number of women were able to take up teaching and writing as their professions. Many popular women writers, like Augusta Evans Wilson and Maria Cummins, did very well financially, and a few, like E.D.E.N. Southworth, became rich and famous. Sarah Josepha Hale, as editor of *Godey's Lady's Book*, emerged as a powerful arbiter of taste and morals. In New York in the 1850s, the homes of writers like Caroline Kirkland and Alice and Phoebe Cary were centers of female literary networks, as was, somewhat later, the Boston home of Annie Fields. At the same time, women's rights conventions, which had begun at Seneca Falls in 1848, spread across the North.

Yet the issue of what was "appropriate" to women remained conflicted in almost every area of social and cultural life. There were those like Catharine Beecher who believed in separate "spheres" for men and women and who, with sister Harriet, argued that a woman's duty—and her opportunity—was to sustain and to teach domestic female values as an alternative to the competitive marketplace principles increasingly governing the life of a man. Still, Beecher was a major proponent of and innovator in education for women, emphasizing that maintaining a household and teaching children required technical training equal to that of a physician or lawyer. Margaret Fuller and Elizabeth Cady Stanton, by contrast, argued that a woman should be able to participate in any activities of which she was capable, whether that meant running a business, voting, or interpreting the Bible. It thus followed, though nineteenth-century feminists did not always pursue this argument, that separate "spheres" were inherently unequal and the ideology that promoted such separation in fact operated to confine women to relative powerlessness, even within the home and church. Indeed, the early feminist movement, led by Stanton and Susan B. Anthony, more than most other reform movements of the time, saw itself in conflict with organized religion. Thus the major appeal in the Seneca Falls "Declaration of Sentiments" is not to Christian virtue but to the Enlightenment ideas and rationalist prose of the Declaration of Independence. Some traditionalists believed, and continued to argue well into the twentieth century, that the "excessive" thinking entailed in higher education would interfere with a woman's reproductive capacities and that, at best, women should learn domestic and cultural refinements like needlework and French. Others like Mary Lyon and Lucy Stone sought to break down the barriers that made female education separate from and unequal to that of males, even in the same institution. At Oberlin, which she attended, Stone insisted on taking the "full course," usually reserved for men, instead of the women's "literary" curriculum. Even women's clothing became an issue: Amelia Bloomer invented a costume, based on loose-fitting, Turkish-style pantaloons, designed to free women from the tight corsets and stays that restricted circulation and movement; but the "Bloomer" dress was too radical for its time.

It is to mothers and to teachers that the world is to look for the character which is to be enstamped on each succeeding generation, for it is to them that the great business of education is almost exclusively committed. And will it not appear by examination that neither mothers nor teachers have ever been properly educated for their profession? What is the *profession of a woman*? Is it not to form immortal minds, and to watch, to nurse, and to rear the bodily system, so fearfully and wonderfully made, and upon the order and regulation of which the health and well-being of the mind so greatly depends?

Catharine Beecher, *Suggestions Respecting Improvements in Education*, 1829

The writing of women, and of many men, reflected these crosscurrents. The end of *The Scarlet Letter* raises, at least in symbolic terms, the question of woman's role in the building of community in America; Hawthorne's later novel *The Blithedale Romance* brings into sharp contrast the dangerously "liberated" dark woman, Zenobia, with the fair and saving Priscilla. Many of the widely selling women's novels of the 1850s in effect promoted what were presumed to be female virtues of patience, submission to duty, obedience, and chastity; their plots rewarded young women displaying such values, though not so much by marriage as by the formation of a domestic community centered on them. Such patterns were not restricted to novels like Susan Warner's *The Wide, Wide World*; they provide structure to a book like Hawthorne's *The House of the Seven Gables* as well. Still, many women writers felt it necessary—since the very act of a woman writing was regarded with suspicion by many—to deprecate their literary productions as, in Caroline Kirkland's phrases, work "too slight to need a preface," "straggling and cloudy crayon-sketches," a "rude attempt." Some hid their identities behind pen names, often male.

In asking "How Should Women Write?" (1860) Mary E. Bryan lamented:

> *Men, after much demur and hesitation, have given women liberty to write; but they cannot yet consent to allow them full freedom. They may flutter out of the cage, but it must be with clipped wings; they may hop about the smooth-shaven lawn, but must, on no account, fly. With metaphysics they have nothing to do; it is too deep a sea for their lead to sound; nor must they grapple with those great social and moral problems with which every strong soul is now wrestling. They must not go beyond the surface of life, lest they should stir the impure sediment that lurks beneath.*
>
> *. . . Having prescribed these bounds to the female pen, men are the first to condemn her efforts as tame and commonplace, because they lack earnestness and strength.*

Bryan's complaint reflects the sense of restriction under which women writers of the period labored.

In fact, however, they often annulled such limitations. In *The Hidden Hand* (1859), E.D.E.N. Southworth created a female character, Capitola, who dons a boy's clothing in order to survive, fights a duel, rescues the passive heroine, and, like other adventurous female characters of the time, altogether defies the prescribed stereotypes for a proper woman. As early as the 1820s, women writers like Catharine Maria Sedgwick and Lydia Sigourney directed their attention to the public concerns of the new nation; later, Stowe, Jacobs, and Child consciously engaged the great human questions of the time, such as slavery and the growing disparities in wealth. Indeed, female writers of the period probably involved themselves more with daily concerns than did their male counterparts, who, like Emerson, often existed in a world of abstractions and fancy. Fern and Child, among others, tried to bring to their audience the problems of urban homelessness, the exploitation of women workers, and the experiences of prostitutes and female inmates; Fuller placed before her readers not only those issues but her immediate experiences of revolution and its causes in Europe. Moreover, many female fiction writers consciously worked in more realistic modes, largely eschewing the "romances" and allegories preferred by Hawthorne. They focused on everyday lives in Ohio or Maine, rather than on the remote settings and mad heroes of Poe or on Melville's larger-than-life confrontation of Captain Ahab and the white whale. In part, this realistic practice may have been imposed by the kinds of restrictions Bryan sketches; in part, it may have been a conscious choice, as Alice Cary suggests in concluding her second volume of stories, *Clovernook* (1853):

> In our country, though all men are not "created equal," such is the influence of the sentiment of liberty and political equality, that:
>> "All thoughts, all passions, all delights, Whatever stirs this
>> mortal frame,"
> may with as much probability be supposed to affect conduct and expectation in the log cabin as in the marble mansion; and to illustrate this truth, to dispel that erroneous belief of the necessary baseness of the "common people" which the great masters in literature have in all ages labored to create, is a purpose and an object in our nationality to which the finest and highest genius may wisely be devoted; but which may be effected in a degree by writings as unpretending as these reminiscences of what occurred in and about the little village where I from childhood watched the pulsations of surrounding hearts.

Just as many women writers of the period focused on subjects and adopted strategies somewhat different from those of men, so the forms in which women expressed themselves often differed. For example, writers like the Grimkés, Child, and Kirkland adapted the letter—a form between private and public expression—for important published work. One thinks also of Emily Dickinson's conception of her poems, which remained almost entirely "unpublished," at least to the general public, throughout her life:

> This is my letter to the World
> That never wrote to Me—

Cary's stories seem, like life or dreams, to shift focus as they proceed. Many of Stowe's later works employ a narrator whose relationship to the reader is posed as that of a domestic friend speaking the language of kitchen conversation. Jacobs, unlike male slave narrators, employs many of the conventions and the language of the domestic novel.

The point is *not* that such differences absolutely divided female from male writing. It was not the case that men wrote the "serious" books and women the "popular"; men composed as many potboilers as women, and probably more best sellers as the century went on. Nor was it true that women's fiction was inevitably "sentimental" or men's adventurous. Cooper, Child, and Sedgwick wrote adventure tales focused on the drama of Indian-white relations; what is striking, however, are the differences between their versions of those interactions. Cooper's is finally a vision of irreconcilably separate societies, the development of the white necessitating the destruction of the Indian. Sedgwick and Child explore social and sexual interactions—including those of white women with Indian men—as paths to a harmonious future. Still, for all their sympathy and protest, their ideas of that future continue to entail subordination of Indian aspirations to white dominance. A slave narrative like Harriet Jacobs's *Incidents* focuses directly on problems of family, sexuality, and relations between white and black women, matters seldom touched on in slave narratives by men. Nor is it that the work of women writers in this period is notably "better" than that of men, or vice versa. What we need to look at are the similarities and the differences in their work, where their subjects, their styles, and their audiences are alike and where they diverge. And we need to understand how those differences arose from the differing conditions of male and female life in the first half of the nineteenth century.

The Many Cultures of America

Needless to say, sexual differences constituted only one of the factors helping to create in the United States one of the world's most heterogeneous societies. Long before the advent of white settlers on the North American continent, the "Indian" populations were themselves extremely diverse in language, culture, and social organization. With the coming of a variety of Europeans, the importation of Africans as slaves, and, in the nineteenth century, the incorporation of large French- and Spanish-speaking areas into the United States and the arrival of Chinese workers and merchants, the pattern of racial and cultural diversity that has come to characterize twenty-first-century America was established, though the full mosaic of ethnicity would not be seen until much later.

Nevertheless, even before the onset of European colonization, and even more so once it had begun, the culture—indeed, the population—of the Americas presented a complex mosaic. The peoples inhabiting the Americas developed distinctive languages, religions, and social practices. In significant degree, too— certainly by the mid-nineteenth century—these differing peoples and cultures interacted and influenced one another. To an extent that scholars are only now beginning to recognize, *all* the cultures of the Americas (like those in other parts of the world) came to be the hybrid products of multiple interactions, borrowings, and border crossings. In this volume, we underline by our organizational format certain distinctions in cultural development based on differences in geography, ethnicity, and historical experience. We believe it is useful for an understanding of nineteenth-century literary development for readers to look at the somewhat separate cultural productions of Native America, Spanish America, New England, and the South. After all, while many northern whites looked to eastern cities like Boston and New York, or beyond to London, for cultural leadership, others in what is now the southwestern United States looked to Mexico and beyond to Madrid. And for many Native Americans, the "center" was altogether differently constituted and often a subject of intense controversy. As for Southerners, culture was a terrain of struggle played out along the centuries-old lines of conflict between Americans of European and of African extraction.

But it is important to remember that writers from one area or culture interacted in various ways with those differently situated, even across boundaries of place, language, and religion. The cultures and literatures of nineteenth-century America have to be seen not as separate, isolated enclaves but as changing, intermingling, growing organisms that—often to the grief of editors and teachers— simply will not altogether fit into any single organizational format.

Moreover, while every group of people possesses a culture that embodies norms, values, stories, hopes, and fears, these may not always take "literary" form. Consider, for example, the history of Asian people in America during the nineteenth century. Although the original inhabitants of North America very likely came from Asia, and Chinese were probably among the earliest modern explorers of the continent, Asians were among the latest and least welcomed immigrants to the United States. Trade between America and China, limited to the port of Guanzhou (Canton), had begun late in the eighteenth century; in the nineteenth, China was forced by European military powers to open additional ports. Initially, Chinese goods like tea, silk, and porcelain flowed outward, with little from the West being imported. But by 1807 Western missionaries had begun work in China, and after its military defeat by Great Britain in the two Opium Wars (1839–1842 and 1855–1860), China was compelled to import goods from England (and other Western nations, including the United States), particularly British opium. Additionally, China was forced to pay huge indemnities, to cede Hong Kong to England, and to make other humiliating concessions, such as granting extraterritoriality to Western citizens in China. The weakness of the Qing Dynasty, the burden of taxes levied to pay off indemnities, consequent civil rebellions (including the Taiping Revolution, 1851–1864), and massive floods and famine produced conditions encouraging emigration.

Like China, Japan in 1854 was forced by military might to open its ports to Western commerce. But unlike China, Japan readily began to import Western technology and experts, strengthening itself militarily and economically until it emerged by the end of the century as a world power. With international standing and internal stability, there was little drive for emigration, and it was thus not until early in the twentieth century that significant numbers of Japanese immigrated to the continental United States.

Despite internal conditions in China, few Chinese came to the United States before gold was discovered in California. Chum Ming, a merchant who arrived in San Francisco in 1847, was one of the first to join the gold rush and to strike it rich. He wrote the news about "Gold Mountain" home to Sam Yup (Three Districts) near Guanzhou. In 1848 three Chinese arrived in San Francisco; in 1849 there were 323. Their numbers increased gradually, peaking in 1854 at 13,100 and thereafter averaging 5,000 for the next twelve years. In all, about 35,000 Chinese, immigrants and sojourners, came to the United States during the 1850s, while about 2.5 million people immigrated from Europe. Yet for economic and racial reasons, resentment mounted against the Chinese, and one discriminatory law after another was passed, mostly in California. In 1849, a law forbade any people of color from testifying against whites, thus effectively denying blacks and Indians, as well as Chinese, legal recourse. In 1854, a foreign miner's tax law was passed; it was levied almost exclusively against Chinese miners for the next twenty years. As the Chinese moved into other work, such as agriculture, cigar making, and shoe manufacturing, other laws were passed prohibiting their employment in these industries and preventing them from buying land. Finally, the only labor that Chinese could undertake without objection was largely "women's work": laundry, cooking, and domestic service.

Shortages of labor in Hawaii and the Western states led to the importation of Chinese workers, the so-called "coolies." The first group of 180 Chinese men was brought to work on Hawaii's sugar plantations in 1852; their wages were three dollars a month. In 1868, pursuing a policy of divide and control, growers brought the first group of Japanese laborers to Hawaii, and in the early twentieth century Koreans and Filipinos. But it was in the construction of the transcontinental railroad that Chinese workers gained their greatest fame. They had helped build the California Central Railroad in 1858, but the Central Pacific, which had undertaken the challenging task of pushing the transcontinental line east from Sacramento through the Sierra Nevada and Rocky Mountains, would initially hire only whites. Failing to recruit a sufficient crew, Leland Stanford, president of the line, finally agreed to try out a group of 50 Chinese workers in 1865. They proved so industrious and efficient that fifty more were hired, and within two years 12,000 of the 13,500 workers on the railroad's payroll were Chinese. It was they who swung down from cliffs in straw baskets to set, and too often be blown up by, dynamite charges—thus coining the phrase "he didn't have a Chinaman's chance." It was they who lived and worked underground for months at a time during the bitter mountain winters, tunneling the roadbed east. Ironically, their very efficiency in bringing the transcontinental railroad to completion on May 10, 1869, may have helped stifle other Chinese immigration, for the agitation that culminated in passage of the Chinese Exclusion Act of 1882 began soon after the last rail spike was driven.

The vast majority of the Chinese who came to the United States during this period were men, often hoping to make enough money to provide themselves with a stake at home. Many of the laborers were from peasant origins, not literate in Chinese, much less in English, a language they did not speak among themselves. Largely excluded from the society of Westerners, reviled by them and proud of their own civilization, the Chinese immigrants retained a culture essentially Chinese in language as well as focus. Much of what they wrote, when they were able, was in the form of private letters back to families or brief Chinese poems about life in Gold Mountain.

A few Chinese were also able to study in eastern schools, mainly through the assistance of American missionaries. On April 12, 1847, Yung Wing arrived in New York City en route to Monson, Massachusetts, where he would enroll in the Monson Academy. He later graduated with Yale's class of 1854, the first Chinese to gain a degree from an American college. Yung Wing married an American woman and became a naturalized American citizen, though he frequently traveled between China and the United States, acting as a kind of bridge between his two countries. He purchased machinery in Fitchburg, Massachusetts, to establish an arms factory, which later became the famous Kiangnan Arsenal, near Shanghai. He also devised and directed the Chinese Educational Mission, a project that in the 1870s brought groups of Chinese boys to Hartford, Connecticut, to study at the expense of the Chinese government. The title of Yung Wing's graceful autobiography, *My Life in China and America* (1909), expresses something of the duality in his life.

The Rise of Industry

The immigration of Irish Catholics in the East and Chinese laborers in the West was met with mob violence, antiforeign political organization, and new legal constraints. Yet more deeply troubling to the young country in the long run were the related shifts of its economic base from agriculture to industry and its population from rural to urban. Jeffersonian democrats had envisioned a country made up primarily of small landholders ("franklins") and artisans—educated, independent farmers careful of their land, jealous of their political freedoms, and dependent only on their own hard work for success. In fact, however, early in the nineteenth century the smaller, self-sufficient, eastern-style family farm began a long decline as growers increasingly turned to producing cash crops like cotton, sugar, and wheat for national and international markets. In the South, as we have pointed out, that meant an even harsher slave system. In the West, it meant the creation of huge, widely separated farms, which offered an efficient way of organizing growing but sacrificed most of the virtues of community. And since the young nation's single greatest exploitable resource was land, those living on the largest "unclaimed" tracts, American Indians, were, by imposed treaties, callous chiseling, and continued violence, pushed off into ever more remote and barren stretches of the West.

The new mills of the Northeast brought their own social changes. At first they seemed to offer at least some opportunity to women from the declining Yankee farms, and they could certainly produce standardized products—clothing, boots, pots and pans—more cheaply than they could be produced even at home, much less by neighborhood artisans. But as competition increased, as the looms and spindles were speeded up, and as wages declined, especially after the panic of 1837, the limited attractiveness of factory work disappeared. Independent artisans, who sold their product for a price, who could take pride in the work their hands created, who worked at times and at rates of their own choosing, whose family income was supplemented by a garden plot and by fishing and hunting, disappeared. They were replaced by the factory "hand," who had little or nothing to sell but his or her labor and who worked the factory loom or wielded a pickaxe on the Erie Canal. The skills formerly learned and honed by craftspeople through apprentice systems began to be built into remarkably accurate machines, like those portrayed by Melville in "The Tartarus of Maids." They could be operated by relatively unskilled laborers, easily replaced in times of crisis by newcomers or even by cheaper child workers. These laborers were mostly immigrants from Ireland or Germany, who crowded into eastern and developing midwestern cities. They had none of the skills, the small landholdings, the community connections, or the bases for family self-sufficiency that had seen independent artisans and farmers through hard times and helped set them on the road to success. Thus there came into being—despite the misgivings even of some factory owners—a "permanent factory population." Differing in origins and religion, they were often at the edge of poverty, sometimes unemployed, and subject to the new industrial discipline of the time clock marking out fourteen-hour days, six days a week— "wage slaves," as Southern planters liked to call them.

Many writers of the time tried to bring their concern for those afflicted by the changes in American society to a public largely ignorant of or indifferent to them. As journalists, Margaret Fuller, Fanny Fern, and Lydia Maria Child wrote about the conditions of life and work for this new urban working class and the increasing disparities of income in the cities of the Northeast. Child's "Letters from New York" dealing with homeless families and the sharp contrasts of affluence and poverty can almost be read as accounts of urban America in parts of the twentieth century. In addition to Melville, Rebecca Harding Davis and Elizabeth Stuart Phelps focused stories on the lives of people who labored in the mills, and *The Quaker City; or, the Monks of Monk Hall* by George Lippard, a working-class reformer, became a best seller in 1845. Indeed, Melville's most famous book, *Moby-Dick*, can be read on one level as an industrial novel, deeply concerned with the processes by which raw materials are turned into commodities and with the complex interactions between those who work and those who increasingly determine their jobs. It deals with a variety of other themes, to be sure—men and nature, the existence of ultimate truths, the contest of fanaticism and liberalism—but Melville's intense concern with the processes of work suggests how deeply the changes wrought by the industrial revolution were affecting the consciousness of his contemporaries.

At the same time, the new accumulations of wealth, which permitted some Americans the leisure to read and learn, brought their own problems. While the belief persisted that every (white) American could make *his* fortune, the fact was that in the half century before the Civil War economic inequality increased rapidly—and noticeably. Preachers inveighed against Mammon, politicians denounced privilege, writers like Emerson deplored the "public and private avarice [which] make the air we breathe thick and fat," and Thoreau urged his readers to "simplify, simplify"; but the rich got richer, and the poor ... well, they could at least "go west." Americans whose grandparents had fought to overthrow the tyranny of king and nobles and "gentlemen" found themselves confronted with new forms of title based on wealth—as well as with new forms of poverty, which persisted from generation to generation of factory hands and farm laborers.

But the underlying issue was whether the technological and social changes that were producing these effects were themselves finally beneficial, whatever their short-term impact. No one could deny the enormity of these changes. Take, for example, the revolution in transportation. At the turn of the nineteenth century you traveled, if at all, along waterways cut over millions of years by natural forces, propelled—as human beings had always been propelled—by the current, by sail, or by oar and paddle. Or you followed narrow, rutted trails on foot or horseback, or perhaps in a lumbering Conestoga wagon that would all too often have to be pried out of deep mud sloughs. Writers like Cooper and Sedgwick, looking backward to earlier years, offer a sense of what such travel was like. A family moving from around Philadelphia to try their luck at farming in the northwest territories (Ohio or Indiana) could take many months—indeed, more than a year if they had to stop to construct their own fortified raft to float down the Ohio River—to reach their destination. Caroline Kirkland's *A New Home, Who'll Follow?* vividly pictures the hardships of travel to the West in the 1830s. In 1843 the caravan of wagons traversing the Oregon Trail from Independence, Missouri, to the Willamette Valley took more than five months; along the way, at least seven of the migrants were buried by the trailside. By 1857 our imaginary family could have made the trip from Philadelphia to St. Louis in a matter of *days* using the new "through line" organized by the Baltimore and Ohio Railroad; by then, of course, they would have had to move many hundreds of miles further to find land on which they could homestead. Just a dozen years later, passengers were making the railroad trip from Omaha to San Francisco in *four days*.

This revolution in transportation represents simply one aspect of the application of advanced industrial technologies. When in 1807 Robert Fulton first drove his steamboat *Clermont* up the Hudson River from New York to Albany in thirty hours, he was applying to transportation a new motive power already being put to industrial uses. The adaptation and development of such technology was, even from the perspective of our own day, amazingly rapid; together with the exploitation of bountiful natural resources, it constituted a major reason for the country's mighty growth. For example, in 1830 Peter Cooper set an old pumping engine on a flatcar to create the first locomotive made in the United States; though it could manage the phenomenal speed of 12 miles per hour, his engine lost its first race against a horse. By 1840 there were about as many miles of railroad track, some 3,328, as there were miles of canals—all built within the previous twenty-five years; by 1860 there were about 30,000 miles of rail. In certain respects, the locomotive became, as Walt Whitman called it, the "type of the modern." Not only had railroads—along with steam-driven boats—utterly changed travel and trade, but they stimulated ancillary industries like coal mining, lumbering, iron manufacture, and machine tool production, as well as cash-crop farming. The building of the railroads also became the basis of giant fortunes for their owners, entailed the importation of thousands of poor laborers, helped ensure the settlement by Euro-Americans of the vast territories between the Mississippi and the Rockies, and led to the final destruction of the Plains Indian ways of life.

Did all of this represent "progress" or "decline"? Whitman took the locomotive as an "emblem of motion and power—pulse of the continent," but his enthusiasm for the progress it represented was by no means universally shared. Emily Dickinson liked "to see it lap the Miles," a punctual though alarming steed. "But," asked Thoreau from Walden,

> if we stay at home and mind our business, who will want railroads? We do not ride on the railroad; it rides upon us. Did you ever think what those sleepers are that underlie the railroad? Each one is a man, an Irishman, or a Yankee man. The rails are laid on them, and they are covered with sand, and the cars run smoothly over them. They are sound sleepers, I assure you. And every few years a new lot is laid down and run over; so that, if some have the pleasure of riding on a rail, others have the misfortune to be ridden upon.

In his sketch "The Celestial Railroad," Hawthorne portrays a modern railroad trip in terms of Bunyan's *Pilgrim's Progress*—headed not in a celestial, but in an opposite direction.

As the railroad provided an appropriately powerful and ambiguous symbol for modernizing America, so the scientist, the Frankenstein responsible for releasing this enormous power, became an equivocal figure. In another mood, Whitman wrote:

> When I heard the learn'd astronomer,
> When the proofs, the figures, were
>   ranged in columns before me,

When I was shown the charts and
    diagrams, to add, divide, and
    measure them,
When I sitting heard the astronomer
    where he lectured with much
    applause in the lecture-room,
How soon unaccountable I became tired
    and sick,
Till rising and gliding out I wander'd
    off by myself,
In the mystical moist night-air, and from
    time to time,
Look'd up in perfect silence at the stars.

Hawthorne created, in works like "The Birthmark," "Rappaccini's Daughter," and *The House of the Seven Gables*, a series of "scientists" who risk violating the most secret recesses of nature or of the human heart. Indeed, Chillingworth in *The Scarlet Letter* is a character cut in their image. So, in many respects, is Melville's Captain Ahab. Such figures are far distant from the happy image of Benjamin Franklin flying his innocent kite into the gathering thunderclouds above Philadelphia. By the middle of the nineteenth century, the United States was no longer a nation of Franklins, and the society's power to understand and transform the world around it was an increasingly enigmatic heritage.

Individualism and/vs. Community

What, finally, is that national heritage? That was perhaps the most conflicted of all the questions that emerged in the early nineteenth century: "What is an American?" When that question was asked, as it frequently was in the early part of the nineteenth century, it usually meant "In what ways, if at all, do white American men differ from their British forebears?" Occasionally, a particularly perceptive commentator like Alexis de Tocqueville would write about the independent qualities of white American women. But even his *Democracy in America* (1835–1840) devotes only a single, though lengthy, chapter to "The Present and Probable Future Condition of the Three Races That Inhabit the Territory of the United States." Mexicans, like the Irish immigrants, were not of significance to his subject. Indeed, the United States Constitution essentially excluded Indians from its definition of American citizenship and counted black slaves only as three-fifths of a person.

Nevertheless, throughout the period, Indians, blacks, and ultimately Mexicans and the new immigrants, as well as white women, scrutinized the same issues being examined by white men. In part, these concerned the question of nationality: What did it mean to be resident in the American democracy? How did that separate one from the person living in the Old World, in France, perhaps, or in England, or even elsewhere in the New World, like Canada? In literary terms, what did it mean, writers like Emerson and Fuller asked, to write an "American" book, or to create an "American" literature? Was it merely a colonial branch of the British stock, or did it have qualities distinctively its own? Because even then the United States was an unusually heterogeneous country, such questions were also extended to how the meaning of "American" might differ for those, like Indians, who were at once part and *not* part of the democracy and for a black man like Frederick Douglass, whose experience of July 4, Independence Day, was distinct from that of whites.

In a larger sense, the basic issues concerned what it meant to be a "person," especially a person in this experimental social and political arrangement called "democracy." Gone, at least in theory, were the definitions of self once established by the hierarchy of king, nobles, and gentlemen. How, then, in this new, unformed world, did people define their "place" and consequently who they were or might become? In a country largely to be created, how could, how should men and women effect a relationship with their fellow human beings or with nature? "Self-Reliance" may strike today's reader as inevitable in free enterprise America, but the individualism that Emerson so eloquently promoted was of rather recent invention, and the image he paints of himself standing in a woodland clearing and becoming a "transparent eyeball" open to all the "currents of the Universal Being" *(Nature)* would have appalled his grandparents' generation in its pantheism and wild self-assertiveness.

American intellectuals in the early nineteenth century were deeply affected by the revolutionary impulses of Romanticism, with its emphasis on openness to nature and to feeling, its idea of grand individual selves set free—or at least capable of being set free—from the constraints of tradition and decorum, and its view of society as a set of illegitimate constraints on free development of the self. But while such Romantic currents ran deep in American culture, certain consuming realities also heavily shaped conceptions of an American self by determining the forms of self-definition in fact available to individuals. The frontier, for example, was on one side a synonym for individual opportunity, but on the other an ever-narrowing barbed-wire fence. Slave-masters were notorious for the extremes—of combativeness and hospitality, among other traits— they affected, but they were able to do so largely by constricting the world their slaves inhabited. This is by no means to suggest that the individual personalities of Indians or slaves were, as some once seemed to think, ground down into an undifferentiated mass. Rather, as one discovers in Harriet Jacobs's *Incidents* or in Douglass's *Narrative*, what some of us can take for granted in defining ourselves, those in fundamentally differing circumstances cannot. Even possession of one's body, much less one's land or traditions of language and culture, could not always be assumed. That Douglass remains uncertain, as the opening paragraphs of his book show, not only of the date of his birth but of the identity of his father may serve here as a symbol of such differences.

Still, the force of American society in the early nineteenth century was to atomize all groups. Walt Whitman best focuses the issue in the lines that came to open his book, *Leaves of Grass*:

> One's-self I sing, a simple separate
> person,
> Yet utter the word Democratic, the
> word En-masse.

"Inscriptions"

Does the word *yet* imply "still"—that is, that the poet must at once sing both the separate individual *and* the democratic mass? Or does it imply "but"—that is, a conflict between the writer as a separate "self" and the democratic "en masse"? In other words, is the relationship between individuals and society in a democracy harmonious and productive, or combative and draining? Do we say to our neighbors, "You are as good as I, so let us work together for our mutual betterment"? Or do we say, "I am as good as you, so get out of my way"?

Historians like David Brion Davis have rooted this tension in a change in the vision of the role of the United States from preserving the "virtuous republic" established by the Founders to ensuring above all "individual opportunity." In many ways, the key to the intellectual and social life of the United States during the first half of the nineteenth century is precisely this tension between the mission of a democratic community and the growing ideology of individual advancement. Obviously, many Americans saw no contradiction between these conceptions; indeed, for Benjamin Franklin, each entailed the other. Still, a certain discord emerges in writers concerned with the frontier, such as Cooper and Kirkland, in the conflicts between the need for community and the imperatives of individual self-assertion. One hears it as a ground tone in the struggle over slavery: will the United States become what its founding documents promise—a blessed nation "dedicated to the proposition that all men are created equal"; or will it continue to recognize the "right" of one person to hold another as property?

Individual and community—with what scale do we balance their claims? We are transfixed by the unique expressive forms devised by individual artists like

---

In order more effectually to promote the great purposes of human culture; to establish the external relations of life on a basis of wisdom and purity; to apply the principles of justice and love to our social organization in accordance with the laws of Divine Providence; to substitute a system of brotherly cooperation for one of selfish competition; to secure to our children and those who may be entrusted to our care the benefits of the highest physical, intellectual, and moral education, which, in the progress of knowledge, the resources at our command will permit; to institute an attractive, efficient, and productive system of industry; to prevent the exercise of worldly anxiety by the competent supply of our necessary wants; to diminish the desire of excessive accumulation by making the acquisition of individual property subservient to upright and disinterested uses; to guarantee to each other forever the means of physical support and of spiritual progress; and thus to impart a greater freedom, simplicity, truthfulness, refinement, and moral dignity to our mode of life; we, the undersigned, do unite in a voluntary association, and adopt and ordain the following articles of agreement....

"Constitution of the Brook-Farm Association," 1841

Dickinson, Whitman, and Melville. We are swayed, as indeed Americans in the nineteenth century were swayed, by the expression of individualist ideas in Emerson's electric language:

> Society everywhere is in conspiracy against the manhood of every one of its members. Society is a joint-stock company, in which the members agree, for the better securing of his bread to each shareholder, to surrender the liberty and culture of the eater. The virtue in most request is conformity. Self-reliance is its aversion.... Whoso would be a man, must be a nonconformist.... Nothing is at last sacred but the integrity of your own mind. Absolve you to yourself, and you shall have the suffrage of the world.

Self-Reliance

Yet even as Emerson wrote, some of his closest friends were trying to establish at Brook Farm one among dozens of experiments in communitarian living, which entailed holding the land as a joint-stock company and working it together. It is not that such communities were popular with most Americans. The Mormons, like other religious collectives, were violently driven from upstate New York, then from Illinois, and finally to the then wilds of Utah. Other secular communards were attacked, scorned, or satirized, as Hawthorne did for Brook Farm in his novel *The Blithedale Romance*. It is also possible that white hostility to the Cherokees of Georgia had to do not only with racism and greed for their land but also with the fact that, organized as a separate nation, they conducted their business communally, with great success.

Still, the efforts to establish communities based on shared values continued even in the face of hostility and the fundamental triumph of individualism. Although Hawthorne mocked the Utopianism of Brook Farm, the themes of sustaining human community and the torment of individual isolation persist in much of his fiction. Melville suggests, in his final novel, *The Confidence-Man*, that a form of Emersonian individualism can easily become the "me-first" ethic of the entrepreneur. In Alice Cary's Uncle Christopher, individualism has become gnarled and destructive to those subject to it. And Alexis de Tocqueville, one of the keenest observers of nineteenth-century America, suggests that individualism too easily emerges as a "selfishness" that finally will confine a person "entirely within the solitude of his own heart." Tocqueville's view echoes precisely the criticism Margaret Fuller made of the insularity and self-absorption of her friend Emerson. She apparently shared the suspicion of him the Italian leader Giuseppe Mazzini expressed in a letter: "I feel fearful that he leads or will lead men to too much contemplation.... We stand in need of one who will ... appeal to the collective influence and inspiring sources, more than to individual self-improvement."

Thus if individualism triumphed, it was not without a struggle, nor without its critics—nor, indeed, without alternatives being posed. Frederick Douglass writes of his fellow slaves on the plantation of Mr. Freeland:

> We were linked and interlinked with each other. I loved them with a love stronger than any thing I have experienced since. It is sometimes said that we slaves do not love and confide in each other. In answer to this assertion, I can say, I never loved any or confided in any people more than my fellow

Individualism is a novel expression, to which a novel idea has given birth. Our fathers were only acquainted with *égoïsme* (selfishness). Selfishness is a passionate and exaggerated love of self, which leads a man to connect everything with himself and to prefer himself to everything in the world. Individualism is a mature and calm feeling, which disposes each member of the community to sever himself from the mass of his fellows and to draw apart with his family and his friends, so that after he has thus formed a little circle of his own, he willingly leaves society at large to itself. Selfishness origi- nates in blind instinct; individualism proceeds from erroneous judgment more than from depraved feelings; it originates as much in deficiencies of mind as in perversity of heart.

Selfishness blights the germ of all virtue; individualism, at first, only saps the virtues of public life; but in the long run it attacks and destroys all others and is at length absorbed in downright self- ishness. Selfishness is a vice as old as the world, which does not belong to one form of society more than to another; individualism is of democratic origin, and it threatens to spread in the same ratio as the equality of condition. . . .

As social conditions become more equal, the number of persons increases who, although they are neither rich nor powerful enough to exercise any great influence over their fellows, have nevertheless acquired or retained sufficient education and fortune to satisfy their own wants. They owe nothing to any man, they expect noth- ing from any man; they acquire the habit of always considering themselves as standing alone, and they are apt to imagine that their whole destiny is in their own hands.

Thus not only does democracy make every man forget his ancestors, but it hides his descendants and separates his contempo- raries from him; it throws him back forever upon himself alone and threatens in the end to confine him entirely within the solitude of his own heart.

Alexis de Tocqueville, Democracy in America, Part II, 1840

slaves. . . . We never undertook to do any thing, of any importance, without a mutual consultation. We never moved separately. We were one; and as much so by our tempers and dispositions, as by the mutual hardships to which we were necessarily subjected by our condition as slaves.

Harriet Jacobs survives the rigors of nearly seven years hiding in an attic through the support of her family, which, much of the time, she can only hear. In *Uncle Tom's Cabin*, Stowe poses the Quaker community, led by its matriarch Rachel Halliday, as the center of values for her book. This idea of community was not simply her fiction; in *A New Home*, Caroline Kirkland writes of her fron- tier experience:

> *In this newly-formed world, the earlier settler has a feeling of hostess-ship toward the new comer. I speak only of women—men look upon each one, newly arrived, merely as an additional business-automaton—a somebody more with whom to try the race of enterprize, i.e., money-making.*

Even art might be created in and by a community; explaining the birth of a spiritual, an old former slave described a pre–Civil War religious meeting in these words:

> *I'd jump up dar and den and hollar and shout and sing and pat, and dey would all cotch de words and I'd sing it to some old shout song I'd heard 'em sing from Africa, and dey'd all take it up and keep at it, and keep a-addin' to it, and den it would be a spiritual.*

In a way Emerson might have appreciated, this all-but-anonymous woman and her congregation were creating an art that, as surely as Dickinson and Whitman, turned from the "courtly muses of Europe" toward a distinctively American form and substance.

NATIVE AMERICA

Differences in historical experience and cultural patterns are perhaps nowhere more clearly illustrated than with respect to American Indians during the first part of the nineteenth century. Native peoples continued to struggle for cultural and political sovereignty in New England and along the East Coast, but the young United States did not, for the most part, acknowledge the continued existence of East Coast nations. A great deal of Anglo U.S. writing in the early decades of the century was dedicated to perpetuating the idea that Native people were "vanished" from the eastern seaboard, and "doomed" to disappear from the interior of the continent as well. In this volume, we see Pequot minister and writer William Apess battling this project of erasure and forgetting.

For Native people living further to the west, the pressure from the expanding United States grew intense across the first decades of the century. Between the American Revolution and the Civil War, the United States expanded past the Alleghenies and far beyond, and Native nations in the Northwest Territory and then in the Southeast were pressed hard. The result was a period of extreme social discontinuity and sharply increasing violence. After the Mexican-American War, with the rapid Anglo settlement of California and the annexation of Texas, Native nations in the interior of the continent faced a U.S. frontier on three sides.

The dominant policy adopted by the U.S. government during the first part of this period was removal. President James Monroe expressed the common view in an 1817 letter to Andrew Jackson: "The hunter or savage state requires a greater extent of territory to sustain it, than is compatible with the progress and just claims of civilized life, and must yield to it." In fact, however, when nations like the Cherokees in Georgia adapted Euro-American agricultural models and organized themselves as a peaceful sovereign state, they were put under even more brutal pressure to leave. Under provisions of the Removal Act of 1830, tribes gave up their lands east of the Mississippi, willingly or otherwise, in exchange for lands in the West. Although the Supreme Court ruled in 1832 that the Indian nations were "distinct political communities" not subject to State jurisdiction, President Jackson refused to enforce that decision. Tricked and intimidated out of their lands, the southern Indians were forced to follow what became known as the Trail of Tears to the distant, and often barren, Oklahoma Territory. The Cherokee Removal, and the discourses of cultural and political sovereignty that grew out of that struggle, are examined closely in this volume.

By 1844, most Native nations east of the Mississippi had been removed to the West. President Jackson had applauded his policy of removal by claiming that it had "at length placed [Indians] beyond the reach of injury and oppression," in areas where the "paternal care of the General Government [would] watch over them and protect them." In fact, the tide of European American settlement rolled rapidly over the Mississippi, and within ten years the General Government had begun to embark on campaigns to concentrate Indians in ever-decreasing "reservations." The result was further decimation. Dispossessed of the lands that provided bases for their cultures, deprived of the means they had long used to sustain life and society, many nations found it impossible to reestablish the old tribal ways.

Literary production in English indicates directly the degree of acculturation of the nations and reflects the impact of removal and other assimilationist policies, such as Christian education. Most Indians who wrote in English belonged to nations that had been displaced in the East or had been forced to remove to western lands. Cut off from traditional homelands and lifestyles, they were forced to acculturate in order to survive. Thus, in the first half of the nineteenth century, most Indian literary activity occurred among the rapidly acculturating Cherokees in the South and the Six Nations and Ojibwas in New York and the Great Lakes regions. Publishing outlets for Indians were limited. Writers often published their own work by subscription, but because they were oddities, their works were sometimes printed by commercial presses or by national and religious newspapers and journals, as well as by the few Indian publishing outlets mentioned above.

Though most English works by Indians reflect the trends in popular writings by non-Indians, they have their own distinguishing characteristics. Much of the early poetry, by writers such as John Rollin Ridge and Jane Johnston Schoolcraft, derives largely from romantic and early Victorian models. But not all writers attempted to conform to the literary standards of the dominant society. Writers such as David Cusick, Nicholson Parker, and Nathaniel T. Strong sought to record the oral traditions and lore of their people. Others served as informants to the growing number of non-Indian writers who took an anthropological interest in tribal cultures and sought to preserve the rehearsed traditions, legends, and chants that remain popular among readers of American Indian literature today. Jane Johnston Schoolcraft, her mother, and brother, for instance, served as early informants for Jane's husband, Henry Rowe Schoolcraft, and Ely Parker was a major contributor to Lewis H. Morgan's work on the League of the Iroquois.

This new interest in Indian oral literatures reflected the convergence of several important themes in the development of a popular American national character. For one thing, a major current of American literary nationalism sought its source in aboriginal culture, which was appropriated by writers from Charles Brockden Brown to Henry Wadsworth Longfellow. In 1815, Walter Channing, writing in the first volume of the North American Review, soon to become a prestigious journal, argued that the only truly American literature was the "oral literature of the aborigines," whose common speech, he claimed, was "the very language of poetry." Second, expansion beyond the Trans-Appalachian and Trans-Mississippi frontiers, coupled with Jackson's removal policy, had precipitated armed conflict between the U.S. government and many Indian nations. Though the popular imagination later fixed on Custer and the Little Bighorn, the warfare of the 1840s and 1850s was far more widespread and destructive, in terms of the number of Indian casualties, than the post–Civil War battles. As would be the case after the Civil War, questions about the effectiveness and direction of Indian policy caused champions of the Indians to develop and publish evidence of the Indians' humanity and cultivation in the hope of affecting the public debate. Unfortunately, these sympathetic portrayals of Native cultures were linked with the popular but false notion that the Indians were a vanishing race. Neither the people themselves nor their cultures were vanishing. While some formally educated Indians became prominent as culture brokers through their English language publications, within tribal settings tradition-bearers maintained the cultural legacy represented by the oral poetry included in this volume. The advent of missions, English language education, vocational training, and acculturative measures altered but could not extinguish the native muse.

Despite the degree of acculturation that their works display, most Indian writers composing in English made some use of their native backgrounds, and they did not attempt to mask their sympathy for Indian causes. William Apess, for instance, wrote on behalf of the rights of New England's Native people. Elias Boudinot argued for conscious acculturation as a means of resisting removal. George Harkins chided the Americans for paying lip service to freedom while calling for Indian removal. And George Copway, while supporting Christianization of Indians, condemned the whiskey trade and urged establishment of an Indian territory controlled by Indians in the upper Midwest. These writers tried to focus on the realities of Indian life and to cut through the stereotypical images of savages, either noble or devilish, projected by popular Euro-American writers like Cooper and Longfellow. They were joined in these efforts by people like Child and Fuller, as well as Sedgwick and Osgood (see below), who rejected the common American views of Indian character and destiny. Fuller, indeed, wrote that "at some distant day, [the Indians] will no doubt be considered as having acted the Roman or Carthaginian part of heroic and patriotic self-defence."

Other Indian writers, however, fed the popular reading taste of the day. Biographical, autobiographical, and "told-to" works by Indians enjoyed a good deal of success. We must not ignore such works, such as the *Life of Black Hawk*, which is a translation by a Euro-American interlocutor of a series of interviews with the Sauk leader, who could neither write nor speak English. If we insist that the only Native works to be accepted into a canon of American literature are those written by Native hands, then we reify English reading and writing as the only possible American voice. Texts like the Speech of Chief Seattle—which cannot be proved to bear much relation to any words he might actually have spoken, but which was received as the most moving and "true" expression of Native grief for generations—or the *Life of Black Hawk* or *A Narrative of the Life of Mary Jemison* challenge us to recognize that the desire to read Native writing and incorporate it into an American symphony of literary expression is itself an effect of colonization. These difficult, interdicted, cross-ethnic, and sometimes even fraudulent texts seem, at first glance, to lose their "authenticity" in translation. But it is in translation that they carry an essential lesson, one that we lose if we are attentive only to the writing of Native people who could, and chose to, write in English. These texts show us how literacy was used in the struggle over Native land and help to remind us how wishful our reading practices often are.

■ RED JACKET (SENECA) ■
c. 1758–1830

Red Jacket, a Seneca, was a chief of the Wolf clan. His adult name in Seneca was Sagoyewatha, which means "Keeps Them Awake," an acknowledgment of his great skill as an orator. He loved to wear the many red coats he was given by British allies during the Revolutionary War, hence the name Red Jacket. In 1792 Red Jacket led a delegation to Philadelphia to meet the new American victors of the war and was given a "peace medal" by George Washington, a large silver oval depicting Washington and Red Cloud shaking hands. Two years later, on November 11, 1794, Red Jacket was one of fifty representatives of the Grand Council of the Six Nations of the Iroquois (Haudenosaunee) to sign the Treaty of Canandaigua, in which a great deal of land was lost.

In 1805 a Boston missionary society asked Red Jacket's permission to proselytize among the Seneca. Joseph Cram, their representative, said that "there is but one religion, and but one way to serve God, and if you do not embrace the right way, you cannot be happy hereafter." Red Jacket responded with a short speech that remains one of the most powerful critiques of imperialist monotheism ever made. When he was finished speaking, an enraged Cram refused to shake his hand and declared Seneca religion to be the work of the devil.

Red Jacket had many children, but none survived their father. He devoted his life to defending Seneca culture, religion, and land against encroachment. When he died, of cholera, he was buried in a mission cemetery in spite of his opposing beliefs; his remains were eventually removed to the Forest Lawn Cemetery in Buffalo.

Bethany Schneider
Bryn Mawr College

The Religion of the White Man and the Red

FRIEND AND BROTHER:—It was the will of the Great Spirit that we should meet together this day. He orders all things and has given us a fine day for our council. He has taken His garment from before the sun and caused it to shine with brightness upon us. Our eyes are opened that we see clearly; our ears are unstopped that we have been able to hear distinctly the words you have spoken. For all these favors we thank the Great Spirit, and Him only.

Brother, this council fire was kindled by you. It was at your request that we came together at this time. We have listened with attention to what you have said. You requested us to speak our minds freely. This gives us great joy; for we now consider that we stand upright before you and can speak what we think. All have heard your voice and all speak to you now as one man. Our minds are agreed.

Brother, you say you want an answer to your talk before you leave this place. It is right you should have one, as you are a great distance from home and we do not wish to detain you. But first we will look back a little and tell you what our fathers have told us and what we have heard from the white people.

Brother, listen to what we say. There was a time when our forefathers owned this great island. Their seats extended from the rising to the setting sun. The Great Spirit had made it for the use of Indians. He had created the buffalo, the deer, and other animals for food. He had made the bear and the beaver. Their skins served us for clothing. He had scattered them over the country and taught us how to take them. He had caused the earth to produce corn for bread. All this He had done for His red children because He loved them. If we had some disputes about our hunting-ground they were generally settled without the shedding of much blood.

But an evil day came upon us. Your forefathers crossed the great water and landed on this island. Their numbers were small. They found friends and not enemies. They told us they had fled from their own country for fear of wicked men and had come here to enjoy their religion. They asked for a small seat. We took pity on them, granted their request, and they sat down among us. We gave them corn and meat; they gave us poison in return.

The white people, brother, had now found our country. Tidings were carried back and more came among us. Yet we did not fear them. We took them to be friends. They called us brothers. We believed them and gave them a larger seat. At length their numbers had greatly increased. They wanted more land; they wanted our country. Our eyes were opened and our minds became uneasy. War took place. Indians were hired to fight against Indians, and many of our people were destroyed. They also brought strong liquor among us. It was strong and powerful, and has slain thousands.

Brother, our seats were once large and yours were small. You have now become a great people, and we have scarcely a place left to spread our blankets. You have got our country, but are not satisfied; you want to force your religion upon us.

Brother, continue to listen. You say that you are sent to instruct us how to worship the Great Spirit agreeably to His mind; and, if we do not take hold of the religion which you white people teach we shall be unhappy hereafter. You say that you are right and we are lost. How do we know this to be true? We understand that your religion is written in a Book. If it was intended for us, as well as you, why has not the Great Spirit given to us, and not only to us, but why did He not give to our forefathers the knowledge of that Book, with the means of understanding it rightly. We only know what you tell us about it. How shall we know when to believe, being so often deceived by the white people?

Brother, you say there is but one way to worship and serve the Great Spirit. If there is but one religion, why do you white people differ so much about it? Why not all agreed, as you can all read the Book?

Brother, we do not understand these things. We are told that your religion was given to your forefathers and has been handed down from father to son. We also have a religion which was given to our forefathers and has been handed down to us, their children. We worship in that way. It teaches us to be thankful for all the favors we receive, to love each other, and to be united. We never quarrel about religion.

Brother, the Great Spirit has made us all, but He has made a great difference between His white and His red children. He has given us different complexions and different customs. To you He has given the arts. To these He has not opened our eyes. We know these things to be true. Since He has made so great a difference between us in other things, why may we not conclude that He has given us a different religion according to our understanding? The Great Spirit does right. He knows what is best for His children; we are satisfied.

Brother, we do not wish to destroy your religion or take it from you. We only want to enjoy our own.

Brother, you say you have not come to get our land or our money, but to enlighten our minds. I will now tell you that I have been at your meetings and saw you collect money from the meeting. I can not tell what this money was intended for, but suppose that it was for your minister; and, if we should conform to your way of thinking, perhaps you may want some from us.

Brother, we are told that you have been preaching to the white people in this place. These people are our neighbors. We are acquainted with them. We will wait a little while and see what effect your preaching has upon them. If we find it does them good, makes them honest, and less disposed to cheat Indians, we will then consider again of what you have said.

Brother, you have now heard our answer to your talk, and this is all we have to say at present. As we are going to part, we will come and take you by the hand, and hope the Great Spirit will protect you on your journey and return you safe to your friends.

1805

■ **MARY JEMISON** ■
1743–1833

In 1737 William Penn's son, Thomas Penn, exploited a clause in his father's original 1686 treaty with the Lenape (Delaware). The infamous "walking purchase" cheated the Delaware of their best land and inaugurated a decades-long period of friction between Native people in Pennsylvania and the Anglo-Irish immigrants who pushed into and beyond the newly "purchased" land. Mary Jemison was born in 1743 aboard ship on the way to Philadelphia from Ireland. Her family settled near Gettysburg, Pennsylvania, in an area hotly contended between European settler colonists and Native people. In 1758, when she was a teenager, Jemison was captured, along with most of her family and some visitors, by a Shawnee and French raiding party. Everyone except Mary and one little boy, who was not related to her, was killed. After westward travel with her captors—which she described in vivid terms—Jemison was adopted by a Seneca family. She was ritually welcomed into the matrilineal culture as a sister, a replacement for a brother lost to warfare. Her Seneca family renamed her Deh-he-wä-mis, "a pretty girl, a handsome girl, or a pleasant, good thing."

For a few years Jemison lived with her new family, learning the language and rhythms of life. She then married a young Delaware man named Sheninjee, with whom she had a son. Concerned that white captives were being reclaimed after the end of the French and Indian Wars, Sheninjee and Jemison went on a long journey to the Genesee River in what is now New York. Sheninjee died of a fever, and Jemison stayed with his family until she married an older Seneca man named Hiokatoo, with whom she had six more children. The body of her narrative traces the ways in which white incursions transformed Seneca life. It shows Seneca culture shifting across decades of land loss, death, and growing alcoholism; we see the patterns of life shifting, the roles of men and women changing, and most of all the continued duplicity of white settlers through and after the American Revolution. Jemison narrates the ways in which her sons are caught up in those changes, but she looks hopefully to a different future for her grandchildren. By the narrative's end, Jemison is living on land to which she has gained legal title under U.S. definitions of property ownership, surrounded by white neighbors. After this narrative was published, Jemison sold her land and went to live on the Buffalo Creek Reservation, where she lived and died, at the age of 90, with the Seneca.

Jemison's narrative is a highly mediated text. In 1823 she spent three days telling the story of her life to a minister, James Everett Seaver. He transformed his notes into A Narrative of the Life of Mrs. Mary Jemison, which was published in 1824. It was, and for decades remained, a best seller, as popular as James Fenimore Cooper's novels. Jemison consequently became one of the most famous women of the American nineteenth century. Scholars have worked hard to discern how much of the text we can read as an accurate reflection of Jemison's experience. Although there are many obvious signs of Seaver's editorial hand, much of it is thought to bear at least a trace of the voice of Mary Jemison.

But is A Narrative of the Life of Mrs. Mary Jemison a Seneca text? It is the story of a white-skinned woman born on the Atlantic Ocean between Ireland and the British colonies in the Americas. It was narrated to a white-skinned man, the extent of whose editorial decisions regarding the story, its structure, its contents, and its sentiments will never be known. It is, looked at in one way, a text very removed from something like a "real" Seneca voice. But looked at another way, this narrative belongs firmly in the category of Seneca literature. Jemison was adopted, with full ritual pomp, into the Seneca Nation. Although she describes grief and ambivalence about her acculturation process, the Seneca family and nation that took her in saw her as Seneca, and she saw herself as Seneca, lived most of her life with a Seneca husband, defended Seneca rights, raised her children as Seneca, and ultimately chose to die Seneca, among Senecas. The complexities of the text we have and the impossibility of finding Jemison's "real" voice in it can be seen as expressions of the complexity of the relation between what we tend to think of as "Indian" and what we tend to think of as "white." If "race" was a firm demarcation of identity for white colonists, it was not for many Native people. This narrative is an exploration of that huge cultural difference. The Seneca women who adopted a teenaged Anglo-Irish girl to replace a lost son and brother, the teenager who went through the ritual process of becoming Seneca, and the Native people among whom she lived the rest of her life all considered Mary Jemison to be Native. As a best seller among white readers throughout the nineteenth century, the text is deeply imbricated in the history of white fantasies about Native people. Nevertheless we include it here among other, often equally complicated and compromised, examples of nineteenth-century Native American writing.

Bethany Schneider
Bryn Mawr College

from **A Narrative of the Life of Mrs. Mary Jemison**

Preface

That to biographical writings we are indebted for the greatest and best field in which to study mankind, or human nature, is a fact duly appreciated by a well-informed community. In them we can trace the effects of mental operations to their proper sources; and by comparing our own composition with that of those who have excelled in virtue, or with that of those who have been sunk in the lowest depths of folly and vice, we are enabled to select a plan of life that will at least afford self-satisfaction, and guide us through the world in paths of morality....

Few great men have passed from the stage of action, who have not left in the history of their lives indelible marks of ambition or folly, which produced insurmountable reverses, and rendered the whole a mere caricature, that can be examined only with disgust and regret. Such pictures, however, are profitable, for "by others' faults wise men correct their own."

The following is a piece of biography, that shows what changes may be effected in the animal and mental constitution of man; what trials may be surmounted; what cruelties perpetrated, and what pain endured, when stern necessity holds the reins, and drives the car of fate.

As books of this kind are sought and read with avidity, especially by children, and are well calculated to excite their attention, inform their understanding, and improve them in the art of reading, the greatest care has been observed to render the style easy, the language comprehensive, and the description natural. Prolixity has been studiously avoided. The line of distinction between virtue and vice has been rendered distinctly visible; and chastity of expression and sentiment have received due attention. Strict fidelity has been observed in the composition: consequently, no circumstance has been intentionally exaggerated by the paintings of fancy, nor by fine flashes of rhetoric: neither has the picture been rendered more dull than the original. Without the aid of fiction, what was received as matter of fact only has been recorded.

It will be observed that the subject of this narrative has arrived at least to the advanced age of eighty years; that she is destitute of education; and that her journey of life, throughout its texture, has been interwoven with troubles, which ordinarily are calculated to impair the faculties of the mind; and it will be remembered, that there are but few old people who can recollect with precision the circumstances of their lives (particularly those circumstances which transpired after middle age.) If, therefore, any error shall be discovered in the narration in respect to time, it will be overlooked by the kind reader, or charitably placed to the narrator's account, and not imputed to neglect, or to the want of attention in the compiler.

The appendix is principally taken from the words of Mrs. Jemison's statements. Those parts which were not derived from her, are deserving equal credit, having been obtained from authentic sources.

For the accommodation of the reader, the work has been divided into chapters, and a copious table of contents affixed. The introduction will facilitate the understanding of what follows; and as it contains matter that could not be inserted with propriety in any other place, will be read with interest and satisfaction.

Having finished my undertaking, the subsequent pages are cheerfully submitted to the perusal and approbation or animadversion of a candid, generous, and indulgent public. At the same time it is fondly hoped that the lessons of distress that are portrayed, may have a direct tendency to increase our love of liberty; to enlarge our views of the blessings that are derived from our liberal institutions; and to excite in our breasts sentiments of devotion and gratitude to the great Author and finisher of our happiness.

The Author.

Pembroke, March 1, 1824.

Introduction

The Peace of 1783, and the consequent cessation of Indian hostilities and barbarities, returned to their friends those prisoners, who had escaped the tomahawk, the gauntlet, and the savage fire, after their having spent many years in captivity, and restored harmony to society.

The stories of Indian cruelties which were common in the new settlements, and were calamitous realities previous to that propitious event; slumbered in the minds that had been constantly agitated by them, and were only roused occasionally, to become the fearful topic of the fireside.

It is presumed that at this time there are but few native Americans that have arrived to middle age, who cannot distinctly recollect of sitting in the chimney corner when children, all contracted with fear, and there listening to their parents or visitors, while they related stories of Indian conquests, and murders, that would make their flaxen hair nearly stand erect, and almost destroy the power of motion.

At the close of the Revolutionary war; all that part of the State of New-York that lies west of Utica was uninhabited by white people, and few indeed had ever passed beyond Fort Stanwix, except when engaged in war against the Indians, who were numerous, and occupied a number of large towns between the Mohawk river and lake Erie. Some time elapsed after this event, before the country about the lakes and on the Genesee river was visited, save by an occasional land speculator, or by defaulters who wished by retreating to what in those days was deemed almost the end of the earth, to escape the force of civil law.

At length, the richness and fertility of the soil excited emigration, and here and there a family settled down and commenced improvements in the country which had recently been the property of the aborigines. Those who settled near the Genesee river, soon became acquainted with "The White Woman," as Mrs. Jemison is called, whose history they anxiously sought, both as a matter of interest and curiosity. Frankness characterized her conduct, and without reserve she would readily gratify them by relating some of the most important periods of her life.

Although her bosom companion was an ancient Indian warrior, and notwithstanding her children and associates were all Indians; yet it was found that she possessed an uncommon share of hospitality, and that her friendship was well worth courting and preserving. Her house was the stranger's home; from her table the hungry were refreshed;—she made the naked as comfortable as her means would admit of; and in all her actions, discovered so much natural goodness of heart, that her admirers increased in proportion to the extension of her acquaintance, and she became celebrated as the friend of the distressed. She was the protectress of the homeless fugitive, and made welcome the weary wanderer. Many still live to commemorate her benevolence towards them, when prisoners during the war, and to ascribe their deliverance to the mediation of "The White Woman."

The settlements increased, and the whole country around her was inhabited by a rich and respectable people, principally from New-England, as much distinguished for their spirit of inquisitiveness as for their habits of industry and honesty, who had all heard from one source and another a part of her life in detached pieces, and had obtained an idea that the whole taken in connection would afford instruction and amusement.

Many gentlemen of respectability, felt anxious that her narrative might be laid before the public, with a view not only to perpetuate the remembrance of the atrocities of the savages in former times, but to preserve some historical facts which they supposed to be intimately connected with her life, and which otherwise must be lost.

Forty years had passed since the close of the Revolutionary war, and almost seventy years had seen Mrs. Jemison with the Indians, when Daniel W. Banister, Esq. at the instance of several gentlemen, and prompted by his own ambition to add something to the accumulating fund of useful knowledge, resolved, in the autumn of 1823, to embrace that time, while she was capable of recollecting and reciting the scenes through which she had passed, to collect from herself, and to publish to the world, an accurate account of her life.

I was employed to collect the materials, and prepare the work for the press; and accordingly went to the house of Mrs. Jennet Whaley in the town of Castile, Genesee co. N. Y. in company with the publisher, who procured the interesting subject of the following narrative, to come to that place (a distance of four miles) and there repeat the story of her eventful life. She came on foot in company with Mr. Thomas Clute, whom she considers her protector, and tarried almost three days, which time was busily occupied in taking a sketch of her narrative as she recited it.

Her appearance was well calculated to excite a great degree of sympathy in a stranger, who had been partially informed of her origin, when comparing her present situation with what it probably would have been, had she been permitted to have remained with her friends, and to have enjoyed the blessings of civilization.

In stature she is very short, and considerably under the middle size, and stands tolerably erect, with her head bent forward, apparently from her having for a long time been accustomed to carrying heavy burdens in a strap placed across her forehead. Her complexion is very white for a woman of her age, and although the wrinkles of fourscore years are deeply indented in her cheeks, yet the crimson of youth is distinctly visible. Her eyes are light blue, a little faded by age, and naturally brilliant and sparkling. Her sight is quite dim, though she is able to perform her necessary labor without the assistance of glasses. Her cheek bones are high, and rather prominent, and her front teeth, in the lower jaw, are sound and good. When she looks up and is engaged in conversation her countenance is very expressive; but from her long residence with the Indians, she has acquired the habit of peeping from under eye-brows as they do with the head inclined downwards. Formerly her hair was of a light chestnut brown—it is now quite grey, a little curled, of middling length and tied in a bunch behind. She informed me that she had never worn a cap nor a comb.

She speaks English plainly and distinctly, with a little of the Irish emphasis, and has the use of words so well as to render herself intelligible on any subject with which she is acquainted. Her recollection and memory exceeded my expectation. It cannot be reasonably supposed, that a person of her age has kept the events of seventy years in so complete a chain as to be able to assign to each its proper time and place; she, however, made her recital with as few obvious mistakes as might be found in that of a person of fifty.

She walks with a quick step without a staff, and I was informed by Mr. Clute, that she could yet cross a stream on a log or pole as steadily as any other person.

Her passions are easily excited. At a number of periods in her narration, tears trickled down her grief worn cheek, and at the same time a rising sigh would stop her utterance.

Industry is a virtue which she has uniformly practised from the day of her adoption to the present. She pounds her samp, cooks for herself, gathers and chops wood, feeds her cattle and poultry, and performs other laborious services. Last season she planted, tended and gathered corn—in short, she is always busy.

Her dress at the time I saw her, was made and worn after the Indian fashion, and consisted of a shirt, short gown, petticoat, stockings, moccasins, a blanket and a bonnet. The shirt was of cotton and made at the top, as I was informed, like a man's without collar or sleeves—was open before and extended down about midway of the hips.—The petticoat was a piece of broadcloth with the list at the top and bottom and the ends sewed together. This was tied on by a string that was passed over it and around the waist, in such a manner as to let the bottom of the petticoat down half way between the knee and ankle and leave one-fourth of a yard at the top to be turned down over the string—the bottom of the shirt coming a little below, and on the outside of the top of the fold so as to leave the list and two or three inches of the cloth uncovered. The stockings, were of blue broadcloth, tied, or pinned on, which reached from the knees, into the mouth of the moccasins.—Around her toes only she had some rags, and over these her buckskin moccasins. Her gown was of undressed flannel, colored brown. It was made in old yankee style, with long sleeves, covered the top of the hips, and was tied before in two places with strings of deer skin. Over all this, she wore an Indian blanket. On her head she wore a piece of old brown woollen cloth made somewhat like a sun bonnet.

Such was the dress that this woman was contented to wear, and habit had rendered it convenient and comfortable. She wore it not as a matter of necessity, but from choice, for it will be seen in the sequel, that her property is sufficient to enable her to dress in the best fashion, and to allow her every comfort of life.

Her house, in which she lives, is 20 by 28 feet; built of square timber, with a shingled roof, and a framed stoop. In the centre of the house is a chimney of stones and sticks, in which there are two fire places. She has a good framed barn, 26 by 36, well filled, and owns a fine stock of cattle and horses. Besides the buildings above mentioned, she owns a number of houses that are occupied by tenants, who work her flats upon shares.

Her dwelling is about one hundred rods north of the Great Slide, a curiosity that will be described in its proper place, on the west side of the Genesee river.

Mrs. Jemison appeared sensible of her ignorance of the manners of the white people, and for that reason, was not familiar, except with those with whom she was intimately acquainted. In fact she was (to appearance) so jealous of her rights, or that she should say something that would be injurious to herself or family, that if Mr. Clute had not been present, we should have been unable to have obtained her history. She, however, soon became free and unembarrassed in her conversation, and spoke with a degree of mildness, candor and simplicity, that is calculated to remove all doubts as to the veracity of the speaker. The vices of the Indians, she appeared disposed not to aggravate, and seemed to take pride in extoling their virtues. A kind of family pride inclined her to withhold whatever would blot the character of her descendants, and perhaps induced her to keep back many things that would have been interesting.

For the life of her last husband, we are indebted to her cousin, Mr. George Jemison, to whom she referred us for information on that subject generally. The thoughts of his deeds, probably chilled her old heart, and made her dread to rehearse them, and at the same time she well knew they were no secret, for she had frequently heard him relate the whole, not only to her cousin, but to others.

Before she left us she was very sociable, and she resumed her naturally pleasant countenance, enlivened with a smile.

Her neighbors speak of her as possessing one of the happiest tempers and dispositions, and give her the name of never having done a censurable act to their knowledge.

Her habits, are those of the Indians—she sleeps on skins without a bed-stead, sits upon the floor or on a bench, and holds her victuals on her lap, or in her hands.

Her ideas of religion, correspond in every respect with those of the great mass of the Senecas. She applauds virtue, and despises vice. She believes in a future state, in which the good will be happy, and the bad miserable; and that the acquisition of that happiness, depends primarily upon human voli-tion, and the consequent good deeds of the happy recipient of blessedness. The doctrines taught in the Christian religion, she is a stranger to.

Her daughters are said to be active and enterprizing women, and her grandsons, who arrived to manhood, are considered able, decent and re-spectable men in their tribe.

Having in this cursory manner, introduced the subject of the following pages, I proceed to the narration of a life that has been viewed with atten-tion, for a great number of years by a few, and which will be read by the public with the mixed sensations of pleasure and pain, and with interest, anxiety and satisfaction.

Chapter I

Nativity of her Parents.—Their removal to America.—Her Birth.—Parents settle in Pennsylvania.—Omen of her Captivity.

Although I may have frequently heard the history of my ancestry, my recol-lection is too imperfect to enable me to trace it further back than to my fa-ther and mother, whom I have often heard mention the families from whence they originated, as having possessed wealth and honorable stations under the government of the country in which they resided.

On the account of the great length of time that has elapsed since I was separated from my parents and friends, and having heard the story of their nativity only in the days of my childhood, I am not able to state positively, which of the two countries, Ireland or Scotland, was the land of my parents' birth and education. It, however, is my impression, that they were born and brought up in Ireland.

My Father's name was Thomas Jemison, and my mother's, before her marriage with him, was Jane Erwin. Their affection for each other was mutual, and of that happy kind which tends directly to sweeten the cup of life; to render connubial sorrows lighter; to assuage every discontentment; and to promote not only their own comfort, but that of all who come within the circle of their acquaintance. Of their happiness I recollect to have heard them speak; and the remembrance I yet retain of their mildness and perfect agreement in the government of their children, together with their mutual attention to our common education, manners, religious instruction and wants, renders it a fact in my mind, that they were ornaments to the married state, and examples of connubial love, worthy of imitation. After my remembrance, they were strict observers of religious duties; for it was the daily practice of my father, morning and evening, to attend, in his family, to the worship of God.

Resolved to leave the land of their nativity, they removed from their residence to a port in Ireland, where they lived but a short time before they set sail for this country, in the year 1742 or 3, on board the ship Mary William, bound to Philadelphia, in the state of Pennsylvania.

The intestine divisions, civil wars, and ecclesiastical rigidity and domination that prevailed in those days, were the causes of their leaving their mother country, to find a home in the American wilderness under the mild and temperate government of the descendants of William Penn; where, without fear, they might worship God, and perform their usual avocations.

In Europe my parents had two sons and one daughter, whose names were John, Thomas and Betsey; with whom, after having put their effects on board, they embarked, leaving a large connexion of relatives and friends, under all those painful sensations, which are only felt when kindred souls give the parting hand and last farewell to those to whom they are endeared by every friendly tie.

In the course of their voyage I was born, to be the sport of fortune and almost an outcast to civil society; to stem the current of adversity through a long chain of vicissitudes, unsupported by the advice of tender parents, or the hand of an affectionate friend; and even without the enjoyment, from others, of any of those tender sympathies that are adapted to the sweetening of society, except such as naturally flow from uncultivated minds, that have been calloused by ferocity.

Excepting my birth, nothing remarkable occurred to my parents on their passage, and they were safely landed at Philadelphia. My father being fond of rural life, and having been bred to agricultural pursuits, soon left the city, and removed his family to the then frontier settlements of Pennsylvania, to a tract of excellent land lying on Marsh creek. At that place he cleared a large farm, and for seven or eight years enjoyed the fruits of his industry.

Peace attended their labors; and they had nothing to alarm them, save the midnight howl of the prowling wolf, or the terrifying shriek of the ferocious panther, as they occasionally visited their improvements, to take a lamb or a calf to satisfy their hunger.

During this period my mother had two sons, between whose ages there was a difference of about three years: the oldest was named Matthew, and the other Robert.

Health presided on every countenance, and vigor and strength characterized every exertion. Our mansion was a little paradise. The morning of my childish, happy days, will ever stand fresh in my remembrance, notwithstanding the many severe trials through which I have passed, in arriving at my present situation, at so advanced an age. Even at this remote period, the recollection of my pleasant home at my father's, of my parents, of my brothers and sister, and of the manner in which I was deprived of them all at once, affects me so powerfully that I am almost overwhelmed with grief, that is seemingly insupportable. Frequently I dream of those happy days: but, alas! they are gone: they have left me to be carried through a long life, dependent for the little pleasures of nearly seventy years, upon the tender mercies of the Indians! In the spring of 1752, and through the succeeding seasons, the stories of Indian barbarities inflicted upon the whites in those days, frequently excited in my parents the most serious alarm for our safety.

The next year the storm gathered faster; many murders were committed; and many captives were exposed to meet death in its most frightful form, by having their bodies stuck full of pine splinters, which were immediately set on fire, while their tormentors, exulting in their distress, would rejoice at their agony!

In 1754, an army for the protection of the settlers, and to drive back the French and Indians, was raised from the militia of the colonial governments, and placed (secondarily) under the command of Col. George Washington. In that army I had an uncle, whose name was John Jemison, who was killed at the battle at the Great Meadows, or Fort Necessity. His wife had died some time before this, and left a young child, which my mother nursed in the most tender manner, till its mother's sister took it away, a few months after my uncle's death. The French and Indians, after the surrender of Fort Necessity by Col. Washington (which happened the same season, and soon after his victory over them at that place) grew more and more terrible. The death of the whites, and plundering and burning their property, was apparently their only object: But as yet we had not heard the death-yell, nor seen the smoke of a dwelling that had been lit by an Indian's hand.

The return of a new-year's day found us unmolested; and though we knew that the enemy was at no great distance from us, my father concluded that he would continue to occupy his land another season: expecting (probably from the great exertions which the government was then making) that as soon as the troops could commence their operations in the spring, the enemy would be conquered and compelled to agree to a treaty of peace.

In the preceding autumn my father either moved to another part of his farm, or to another neighborhood, a short distance from our former abode. I well recollect moving, and that the barn that was on the place we moved to was built of logs, though the house was a good one.

The winter of 1754–5 was as mild as a common fall season, and the spring presented a pleasant seed time, and indicated a plenteous harvest. My father, with the assistance of his oldest sons, repaired his farm as usual, and was daily preparing the soil for the reception or the seed. His cattle and sheep were numerous, and according to the best idea of wealth that I can now form, he was wealthy.

But alas! how transitory are all human affairs! how fleeting are riches! how brittle the invisible thread on which all earthly comforts are suspended! Peace in a moment can take health its rosy cheeks; and life will vanish like a vapor at the appearance of the sun! In one fatal day our prospects were all blasted; and death, by cruel hands, inflicted upon almost the whole of the family.

On a pleasant day in the spring of 1755, when my father was sowing flax-seed, and my brothers driving the teams, I was sent to a neighbor's house, a distance of perhaps a mile, to procure a horse and return with it the next morning. I went as I was directed. I was out of the house in the beginning of the evening, and saw a sheet wide spread approaching towards me, in which I was caught (as I have ever since believed) and deprived of my senses! The family soon found me on the ground, almost lifeless (as they said) took me in and made use of every remedy in their power for my recovery but without effect till day-break, when my senses returned, and I soon round myself in good health, so that I went home with the horse very early in the morning.

The appearance of that sheet, I have ever considered as a forerunner of the melancholy catastrophe that so soon afterwards happened to our family: and my being caught in it, I believe, was ominous of my preservation from death at the time we were captured.

Chapter II

Her Education.—Captivity.—Journey to Fort Pitt.—Mother's Farewell Address.—Murder of her Family.—Preparation of the Scalps.—Indian Precautions.—Arrival at Fort Pitt, &c.

My education had received as much attention from my parents, as their situation in a new country would admit of. I had been at school some, where I learned to read in a book that was about half as large as a Bible; and in the Bible I had read a little. I had also learned the Catechism, which I used frequently to repeat to my parents and every night, before I went to bed, I was obliged to stand up before my mother and repeat some words that I suppose was a prayer.

My reading, Catechism and prayers, I have long since forgotten; though for a number of the first years that I lived with the Indians, I repeated the prayers as often as I had an opportunity. After the revolutionary war, I remembered the names of some of the letters when I saw them but have never read a word since I was taken prisoner. It is but a few years since a Missionary kindly gave me a Bible, which I am very fond of hearing my neighbors read to me and should be pleased to learn to read it myself; but my sight has been for a number of years, so dim that I have not been able to distinguish one letter from another.

As I before observed, I got home with the horse very early in the morning, where I found a man that lived in our neighborhood and his sister-in-law who had three children, one son and two daughters I soon learned that they had come there to live a short time; but for what purpose I cannot say. The woman's husband, however was at that time in Washington's army, fighting for his country; and as her brother-in-law had a house she had lived with him in his absence. Their names I have forgotten.

Immediately after I got home, the man took the horse to go to his house after a bag of grain, and took his gun in his hand for the purpose of killing game, if he should chance to see any.—Our family as usual, was busily employed about their common business. Father was shaving an axe-helve at the side of the house; mother was making preparations for breakfast;—my two oldest brothers were at work near the barn; and the little ones, with myself, and the woman and her three children, were in the house.

Breakfast was not yet ready, when we were alarmed by the discharge of a number of guns, that seemed to be near. Mother and the women before mentioned, almost fainted at the report, and every one trembled with fear. On opening the door, the man and horse lay dead near the house, having just been shot by the Indians.

I was afterwards informed, that the Indians discovered him at his own house with his gun, and pursued him to father's, where they shot him as I have related. They first secured my father, and then rushed into the house, and without the least resistance made prisoners of my mother, Robert, Matthew, Betsey, the woman and her three children, and myself, and then commenced plundering.

My two brothers, Thomas and John, being at the barn, escaped and went to Virginia, where my grandfather Erwin then lived, as I was informed by a Mr. Fields, who was at my house about the close of the revolutionary war.

The party that took us consisted of six Indians and four Frenchmen, who immediately commenced plundering, as I just observed, and took what they considered most valuable; consisting principally of bread, meal and meat. Having taken as much provision as they could carry, they set out with their prisoners in great haste, for fear of detection, and soon entered the woods. On our march that day, an Indian went behind us with a whip, with which he frequently lashed the children to make them keep up. In this manner we travelled till dark without a mouthful of food or a drop of water; although we had not eaten since the night before. Whenever the little children cried for water, the Indians would make them drink urine or go thirsty. At night they encamped in the woods without fire and without shelter, where we were watched with the greatest vigilance. Extremely fatigued, and very hungry, we were compelled to lie upon the ground supperless and without a drop of water to satisfy the cravings of our appetites. As in the day time, so the little ones were made to drink urine in the night if they cried for water. Fatigue alone brought us a little sleep for the refreshment of our weary limbs; and at the dawn of day we were again started on our march in the same order that we had proceeded on the day before. About sunrise we were halted, and the Indians gave us a full breakfast of provision that they had brought from my father's house. Each of us being very hungry, partook of this bounty of the Indians, except father, who was so much overcome with his situation—so much exhausted by anxiety and grief, that silent despair seemed fastened upon his countenance, and he could not be prevailed upon to refresh his sinking nature by the use of a morsel of food. Our repast being finished, we again resumed our march, and before noon passed a small fort that I heard my father say was called Fort Canagojigge.

That was the only time that I heard him speak from the time we were taken till we were finally separated the following night.

Towards evening we arrived at the border of a dark and dismal swamp, which was covered with small hemlocks, or some other evergreen, and other bushes, into which we were conducted; and having gone a short distance we stopped to encamp for the night.

Here we had some bread and meat for supper: but the dreariness of our station, together with, the uncertainty under which we all labored as to our future destiny, almost deprived us of the sense of hunger, and destroyed our relish for food.

Mother, from the time we were taken had manifested a great degree of fortitude, and encouraged us to support our troubles without complaining; and by her conversation seemed to make the distance and time shorter, and the way more smooth. But father lost all his ambition in the beginning of our trouble, and continued apparently lost to every care—absorbed in melancholy. Here, as before, she insisted on the necessity of our eating; and we obeyed her, but it was done with heavy hearts.

As soon as I had finished my supper, an Indian took off my shoes and stockings and put a pair of moccasins on my feet, which my mother observed; and believing that they would spare my life, even if they should destroy the other captives, addressed me as near as I can remember in the following words:—

"My dear little Mary, I fear that the time has arrived when we must be parted forever. Your life, my child, I think will be spared; but we shall probably be tomahawked here in this lonesome place by the Indians. O! how can I part with you my darling? What will become of my sweet little Mary? Oh! how can I think of your being continued in captivity without a hope of your being rescued? O that death had snatched you from my embraces in your infancy; the pain of parting then would have been pleasing to what it now is; and I should have seen the end of your troubles!—Alas my dear my heart bleeds at the thoughts of what awaits you; but, if you leave us, remember my child your own name, and the name of your father and mother. Be careful and not forget your English tongue. If you shall have an opportunity to get away from the Indians, don't try to escape; for if you do they will find and destroy you. Don't forget my little daughter, the prayers that I have learned you—say them often; be a good child, and God will bless you. May God bless you my child, and make you comfortable and happy."

During this time, the Indians stripped the shoes and stockings from the little boy that belonged to the woman who was taken with us, and put moccasins on his feet, as they had done before on mine. I was crying. An Indian took the little boy and myself by the hand to lead us off from the company, when my mother exclaimed, "Don't cry Mary—don't cry my child. God will bless you! Farewell—farewell!"

The Indian led us some distance into the bushes, or woods, and there lay down with us to spend the night. The recollection of parting with my tender mother kept me awake, while the tears constantly flowed from my eyes. A number of times in the night the little boy begged of me earnestly to run away with him and get clear of the Indians; but remembering the advice I had so lately received, and knowing the dangers to which we should be exposed, in travelling without a path and without a guide, through a wilderness unknown to us, I told him that I would not go, and persuaded him to lie still till morning.

Early the next morning the Indians and Frenchmen that we had left the night before, came to us; but our friends were left behind. It is impossible for any one to form a correct idea of what my feelings were at the sight of those savages, whom I supposed had murdered my parents and brothers, sister, and friends, and left them in the swamp to be devoured by wild beasts! But what could I do? A poor little defenceless girl; without the power or means of escaping; without a home to go to, even if I could be liberated; without a knowledge of the direction or distance to my former place of residence; and without a living friend to whom to fly for protection, I felt a kind of horror, anxiety, and dread, that, to me, seemed insupportable. I durst not cry—I durst not complain; and to inquire of them the fate of my friends (even if I could have mustered resolution) was beyond my ability, as I could not speak their language, nor they understand mine. My only relief was in silent stifled sobs.

My suspicions as to the fate of my parents proved too true; for soon after I left them they were killed and scalped, together with Robert, Matthew, Betsey, and the woman and her two children, and mangled in the most shocking manner.

Having given the little boy and myself some bread and meat for breakfast, they led us on as fast as we could travel, and one of them went behind and with a long staff, picked up all the grass and weeds that we trailed down by going over them. By taking that precaution they avoided detection; for each weed was so nicely placed in its natural position that no one would have suspected that we had passed that way. It is the custom of Indians when scouting, or on private expeditions, to step carefully and where no impression of their feet can be left—shunning wet or muddy ground. They seldom take hold of a bush or limb, and never break one; and by observing those precautions and that of setting up the weeds and grass which they necessarily lop, they completely elude the sagacity of their pursuers, and escape that punishment which they are conscious they merit from the hand of justice.

After a hard day's march we encamped in a thicket, where the Indians made a shelter of boughs, and then built a good fire to warm and dry our benumbed limbs and clothing for it had rained some through the day. Here we were again fed as before. When the Indians had finished their supper they took from their baggage a number of scalps and went about preparing them for the market, or to keep without spoiling, by straining them over small hoops which they prepared for that purpose, and then drying and scraping them by the fire. Having put the scalps, yet wet and bloody, upon the hoops, and stretched them to their full extent, they held them to the fire till they were partly dried and then with their knives commenced scraping off the flesh; and in that way they continued to work, alternately drying and scraping them, till they were dry and clean. That being done they combed the hair in the neatest manner, and then painted it and the edges of the scalps yet on the hoops, red. Those scalps I knew at the time must have been taken from our family by the color of the hair. My mother's hair was red; and I could easily distinguish my father's and the children's from each other. That sight was most appalling; yet, I was obliged to endure it without complaining.

In the course of the night they made me to understand that they should not have killed the family if the whites had not pursued them.

Mr. Fields, whom I have before mentioned, informed me that at the time we were taken, he lived in the vicinity of my father; and that on hearing of our captivity, the whole neighborhood turned out in pursuit of the enemy, and to deliver us if possible: but that their efforts were unavailing. They however pursued us to the dark swamp, where they found my father, his family and companions, stripped and mangled in the most inhuman manner: That from thence the march of the cruel monsters could not be traced in any direction; and that they returned to their homes with the melancholy tidings of our misfortunes, supposing that we had all shared in the massacre.

The next morning we went on; the Indian going behind us and setting up the weeds as on the day before. At night we encamped on the ground in the open air, without a shelter or fire.

In the morning we again set out early, and travelled as on the two former days, though the weather was extremely uncomfortable, from the continual falling of rain and snow.

At night the snow fell fast, and the Indians built a shelter of boughs, and a fire, where we rested tolerably dry through that and the two succeeding nights.

When we stopped, and before the fire was kindled, I was so much fatigued from running, and so far benumbed by the wet and cold, that I expected that I must fail and die before I could get warm and comfortable. The fire, however, soon restored the circulation, and after I had taken my supper I felt so that I rested well through the night.

On account of the storm, we were two days at that place. On one of those days, a party consisting of six Indians who had been to the frontier settlements, came to where we were, and brought with them one prisoner, a young white man who was very tired and dejected. His name I have forgotten.

Misery certainly loves company. I was extremely glad to see him, though I knew from his appearance, that his situation was as deplorable as mine, and that he could afford me no kind of assistance. In the afternoon the Indians killed a deer, which they dressed, and then roasted it whole; which made them a full meal. We were each allowed a share of their venison, and some bread, so that we made a good meal also.

Having spent three nights and two days at that place, and the storm having ceased, early in the morning the whole company, consisting of twelve Indians, four Frenchmen, the young man, the little boy and myself, moved on at a moderate pace without an Indian behind us to deceive our pursuers.

In the afternoon we came in sight of Fort Pitt (as it is now called) where we were halted while the Indians performed some customs upon their prisoners which they deemed necessary. That fort was then occupied by the French and Indians, and was called Fort Du Quesne. It stood at the junction of the Monongahela, which is said to signify, in some of the Indian languages, the Falling-in-Banks,[1] and the Alleghany[2] rivers, where the Ohio river begins to take its name. The word O-hi-o, signifies bloody.

At the place where we halted, the Indians combed the hair of the young man, the boy and myself, and then painted our faces and hair red, in the finest Indian style. We were then conducted into the fort, where we received a little bread, and were then shut up and left to tarry alone through the night.

Chapter III

She is given to two Squaws.—Her Journey down the Ohio.—Passes a
Shawanee town where white men had just been burnt.—Arrives at the
Seneca town.—Her Reception.—She is adopted.—Ceremony of Adoption.
—Indian Custom.— Address.—She receives a new name.—Her
Employment.—Retains her own and learns the Seneca Language.—

---

[1]Navigator.
[2]The word Alleghenny, was derived from an ancient race of Indians called "Tallegnwe." The Delaware Indians, instead of saying

"Alleghenny," say "Allegawe," or "Allegawenink."

Western Tour—p. 455.

Situation of the Town, &c.—Indians go on a Hunting Tour to Sciota and
take her with them.—Returns.—She is taken to Fort Pitt, and then hurried
back by her Indian Sisters.—Her hopes of Liberty destroyed.—Second Tour
to Sciota.—Return to Wiishto, &c.—Arrival of Prisoners.—Priscilla
Ramsay.—Her Chain.— Mary marries a Delaware.—Her Affection for
him.—Birth and Death of her first Child.—Her Sickness and Recovery.—
Birth of Thomas Jemison.

The night was spent in gloomy forebodings. What the result of our captivity
would be, it was out of our power to determine or even imagine.—At times
we could almost realize the approach of our masters to butcher and scalp
us;—again we could nearly see the pile of wood kindled on which we were
to be roasted; and then we would imagine ourselves at liberty: alone and
defenceless in the forest, surrounded by wild beasts that were ready to
devour us. The anxiety of our minds drove sleep from our eyelids; and it
was with a dreadful hope and painful impatience that we waited for the
morning to determine our fate.

The morning at length arrived, and our masters came early and let us
out of the house, and gave the young man and boy to the French, who immediately took them away. Their fate I never learned; as I have not seen nor
heard of them since.

I was now left alone in the fort, deprived of my former companions, and
of every thing that was near or dear to me but life. But it was not long
before I was in some measure relieved by the appearance of two pleasant
looking squaws of the Seneca tribe, who came and examined me attentively
for a short time, and then went out. After a few minutes absence they
returned with my former masters who gave me to them to dispose of as
they pleased.

The Indians by whom I was taken were a party of Shawanees, if I
remember right, that lived, when at home, a long distance down the Ohio.

My former Indian masters, and the two squaws, were soon ready to
leave the fort, and accordingly embarked; the Indians in a large canoe, and
the two squaws and myself in a small one, and went down the Ohio.

When we set off, an Indian in the forward canoe took the scalps of my
former friends, strung them on a pole that he placed upon his shoulder, and
in that manner carried them, standing in the stern of the canoe, directly
before us as we sailed down the river, to the town where the two squaws
resided.

On our way we passed a Shawanee town, where I saw a number of
heads, arms, legs, and other fragments of the bodies of some white people
who had just been burnt. The parts that remained were hanging on a
pole which was supported at each end by a crotch stuck in the ground, and
were roasted or burnt black as a coal. The fire was yet burning; and the
whole appearances afforded a spectacle so shocking, that, even to this day,
my blood almost curdles in my veins when I think of them!

At night we arrived at a small Seneca Indian town, at the mouth of a small river, that was called by the Indians, in the Seneca language, She-nan-jee,[3] where the two Squaws to whom I belonged resided. There we landed, and the Indians went on; which was the last I ever saw of them.

Having made fast to the shore, the Squaws left me in the canoe while they went to their wigwam or house in the town, and returned with a suit of Indian clothing, all new, and very clean and nice. My clothes, though whole and good when I was taken, were now torn in pieces, so that I was almost naked. They first undressed me and threw my rags into the river; then washed me clean and dressed me in the new suit they had just brought, in complete Indian style; and then led me home and seated me in the center of their wigwam.

I had been in that situation but a few minutes, before all the Squaws in the town came in to see me. I was soon surrounded by them, and they immediately set up a most dismal howling, crying bitterly, and wringing their hands in all the agonies of grief for a deceased relative.

Their tears flowed freely, and they exhibited all the signs of real mourning. At the commencement of this scene, one of their number began, in a voice somewhat between speaking and singing, to recite some words to the following purport, and continued the recitation till the ceremony was ended; the company at the same time varying the appearance of their countenances, gestures and tone of voice, so as to correspond with the sentiments expressed by their leader:

"Oh our brother! Alas! He is dead—he has gone; he will never return! Friendless he died on the field of the slain, where his bones are yet lying unburied! Oh, who will not mourn his sad fate? No tears dropped around him; oh, no! No tears of his sisters were there! He fell in his prime, when his arm was most needed to keep us from danger! Alas! he has gone! and left us in sorrow, his loss to bewail: Oh where is his spirit? His spirit went naked, and hungry it wanders, and thirsty and wounded it groans to return! Oh helpless and wretched, our brother has gone! No blanket nor food to nourish and warm him; nor candles to light him, nor weapons of war:—Oh, none of those comforts had he! But well we remember his deeds!—The deer he could take on the chase! The panther shrunk back at the sight of his strength! His enemies fell at his feet! He was brave and courageous in war! As the fawn he was harmless: his friendship was ardent: his temper was gentle: his pity was great! Oh! our friend, our companion is dead! Our brother, our brother, alas! he is gone! But why do we grieve for his loss? In the strength of a warrior, undaunted he left us, to fight by the side of the Chiefs! His war-whoop was shrill! His rifle well aimed laid his enemies low: his tomahawk drank of their blood: and his knife flayed their scalps while

---

[3]That town, according to the geographical description given by Mrs. Jemison, must have stood at the mouth of Indian Cross creek, which is about 76 miles by water, below Pittsburgh; or at the mouth of Indian Short creek, 87 miles below Pittsburgh, where the town of Warren now stands: But at which of those places I am unable to determine.

Author.

yet covered with gore! And why do we mourn? Though he fell on the field of the slain, with glory he fell, and his spirit went up to the land of his fathers in war! Then why do we mourn? With transports of joy they received him, and fed him, and clothed him, and welcomed him there! Oh friends, he is happy; then dry up your tears! His spirit has seen our distress, and sent us a helper whom with pleasure we greet. Dickewamis has come: then let us receive her with joy! She is handsome and pleasant! Oh! she is our sister, and gladly we welcome her here. In the place of our brother she stands in our tribe. With care we will guard her from trouble; and may she be happy till her spirit shall leave us."

In the course of that ceremony, from mourning they became serene—joy sparkled in their countenances, and they seemed to rejoice over me as over a long lost child. I was made welcome amongst them as a sister to the two Squaws before mentioned, and was called Dickewamis; which being interpreted, signifies a pretty girl, a handsome girl, or a pleasant, good thing. That is the name by which I have ever since been called by the Indians.

I afterwards learned that the ceremony I at that time passed through, was that of adoption. The two squaws had lost a brother in Washington's war, sometime in the year before, and in consequence of his death went up to Fort Pitt, on the day on which I arrived there, in order to receive a prisoner or an enemy's scalp, to supply their loss.

It is a custom of the Indians, when one of their number is slain or taken prisoner in battle, to give to the nearest relative to the dead or absent, a prisoner, if they have chanced to take one, and if not, to give him the scalp of an enemy. On the return of the Indians from conquest, which is always announced by peculiar shoutings, demonstrations of joy, and the exhibition of some trophy of victory, the mourners come forward and make their claims. If they receive a prisoner, it is at their option either to satiate their vengeance by taking his life in the most cruel manner they can conceive of; or, to receive and adopt him into the family, in the place of him whom they have lost. All the prisoners that are taken in battle and carried to the encampment or town by the Indians, are given to the bereaved families, till their number is made good. And unless the mourners have but just received the news of their bereavement, and are under the operation of a paroxysm of grief, anger and revenge; or, unless the prisoner is very old, sickly, or homely, they generally save him, and treat him kindly. But if their mental wound is fresh, their loss so great that they deem it irreparable, or if their prisoner or prisoners do not meet their approbation, no torture, let it be ever so cruel, seems sufficient to make them satisfaction. It is family, and not national, sacrifices amongst the Indians, that has given them an indelible stamp as barbarians, and identified their character with the idea which is generally formed of unfeeling ferocity, and the most abandoned cruelty.

It was my happy lot to be accepted for adoption; and at the time of the ceremony I was received by the two squaws, to supply the place of their brother in the family; and I was ever considered and treated by them as a real sister, the same as though I had been born of their mother.

During my adoption, I sat motionless, nearly terrified to death at the appearance and actions of the company, expecting every moment to feel their vengeance, and suffer death on the spot. I was, however, happily disappointed, when at the close of the ceremony the company retired, and my sisters went about employing every means for my consolation and comfort.

Being now settled and provided with a home, I was employed in nursing the children, and doing light work about the house. Occasionally I was sent out with the Indian hunters, when they went but a short distance, to help them carry their game. My situation was easy; I had no particular hardships to endure. But still, the recollection of my parents, my brothers and sisters, my home, and my own captivity, destroyed my happiness, and made me constantly solitary, lonesome and gloomy.

My sisters would not allow me to speak English in their hearing; but remembering the charge that my dear mother gave me at the time I left her, whenever I chanced to be alone I made a business of repeating my prayer, catechism, or something I had learned in order that I might not forget my own language. By practising in that way I retained it till I came to Genesee flats, where I soon became acquainted with English people with whom I have been almost daily in the habit of conversing.

My sisters were diligent in teaching me their language; and to their great satisfaction I soon learned so that I could understand it readily, and speak it fluently. I was very fortunate in falling into their hands; for they were kind good natured women; peaceable and mild in their dispositions; temperate and decent in their habits, and very tender and gentle towards me. I have great reason to respect them, though they have been dead a great number of years.

The town where they lived was pleasantly situated on the Ohio, at the mouth of the Shenanjee: the land produced good corn; the woods furnished a plenty of game, and the waters abounded with fish. Another river emptied itself into the Ohio, directly opposite the mouth of the Shenanjee. We spent the summer at that place, where we planted, hoed, and harvested a large crop of corn, of an excellent quality.

About the time of corn harvest, Fort Pitt was taken from the French by the English.[4]

The corn being harvested, the Indians took it on horses and in canoes, and proceeded down the Ohio, occasionally stopping to hunt a few days, till we arrived at the mouth of Sciota river; where they established their winter quarters, and continued hunting till the ensuing spring, in the adjacent

---

[4]The above statement is apparently an error; and is to be attributed solely to the treachery of the old lady's memory; though she is confident that that event took place at the time above mentioned. It is certain that Fort Pitt was not evacuated by the French and given up to the English, till sometime in November 1758. It is possible, however, that an armistice was agreed upon and that for a time, between the spring of 1755 and 1758, both nations visited that post without fear of molestation. As the succeeding part of the narrative corresponds with the true historical chain of events, the public will overlook this circumstance, which appears unsupported by history.

Author.

wilderness. While at that place I went with the other children to assist the hunters to bring in their game. The forests on the Sciota were well stocked with elk, deer, and other large animals; and the marshes contained large numbers of beaver, muskrat, &c. which made excellent hunting for the Indians; who depended, for their meat, upon their success in taking elk and deer; and for ammunition and clothing, upon the beaver, muskrat, and other furs that they could take in addition to their peltry.

The season for hunting being passed, we all returned in the spring to the mouth of the river Shenanjee, to the houses and fields we had left in the fall before. There we again planted our corn, squashes, and beans, on the fields that we occupied the preceding summer.

About planting time, our Indians all went up to Fort Pitt, to make peace with the British, and took me with them.[5] We landed on the opposite side of the river from the fort, and encamped for the night. Early the next morning the Indians took me over to the fort to see the white people that were there. It was then that my heart bounded to be liberated from the Indians and to be restored to *my* friends and my country. The white people were surprized to see me with the Indians, enduring the hardships of a savage life, at so early an age, and with so delicate a constitution as I appeared to possess. They asked me my name; where and when I was taken—and appeared very much interested on my behalf. They were continuing their inquiries, when my sisters became alarmed, believing that I should be taken from them, hurried me into their canoe and recrossed the river—took their bread out of the fire and fled with me, without stopping, till they arrived at the river Shenanjee. So great was their fear of losing me, or of my being given up in the treaty, that they never once stopped rowing till they got home.

Shortly after we left the shore opposite the fort, as I was informed by one of my Indian brothers, the white people came over to take me back; but after considerable inquiry, and having made diligent search to find where I was hid, they returned with heavy hearts. Although I had then been with the Indians something over a year, and had become considerably habituated to their mode of living, and attached to my sisters, the sight of white people who could speak English inspired me with an unspeakable anxiety to go home with them, and share in the blessings of civilization. My sudden departure and escape from them, seemed like a second captivity, and for a long time I brooded the thoughts of my miserable situation with almost as much sorrow and dejection as I had done those of my first sufferings. Time, the destroyer of every affection, wore away my unpleasant feelings, and I became as contented as before.

We tended our cornfields through the summer; and after we had harvested the crop, we again went down the river to the hunting ground on the Sciota, where we spent the winter, as we had done the winter before.

---

[5]History is silent as to any treaty having been made between the English and French and Indians, at that time; though it is possible that a truce was agreed upon, and that the parties met for the purpose of concluding a treaty of peace.

Early in the spring we sailed up the Ohio river, to a place that the Indians called Wiishto,[6] where one river emptied into the Ohio on one side,
and another on the other. At that place the Indians built a town, and we
planted corn.

We lived three summers at Wiishto, and spent each winter on the
Sciota.

The first summer of our living at Wiishto, a party of Delaware Indians
came up the river, took up their residence, and lived in common with us.
They brought five white prisoners with them, who by their conversation,
made my situation much more agreeable, as they could all speak English. I
have forgotten the names of all of them except one, which was Priscilla
Ramsay. She was a very handsome, good natured girl, and was married soon
after she came to Wiishto to Capt. Little Billy's uncle, who went with her on
a visit to her friends in the states. Having tarried with them as long as she
wished to, she returned with her husband to Can-a-ah-tun, where he died.
She, after his death, married a white man by the name of Nettles, and now
lives with him (if she is living) on Grand River, Upper Canada.

Not long after the Delawares came to live with us, at Wiishto, my sisters
told me that I must go and live with one of them, whose name was She-nin-
jee. Not daring to cross them, or disobey their commands, with a great
degree of reluctance I went; and Sheninjee and I were married according to
Indian custom.

Sheninjee was a noble man; large in stature; elegant in his appearance;
generous in his conduct; courageous in war; a friend to peace, and a great
lover of justice. He supported a degree of dignity far above his rank, and
merited and received the confidence and friendship of all the tribes with
whom he was acquainted. Yet, Sheninjee was an Indian. The idea of spending my days with him, at first seemed perfectly irreconcilable to my feelings:
but his good nature, generosity, tenderness, and friendship towards me,
soon gained my affection; and, strange as it may seem, I loved him!—To me
he was ever kind in sickness, and always treated me with gentleness; in fact,
he was an agreeable husband, and a comfortable companion. We lived happily together till the time of our final separation, which happened two or
three years after our marriage, as I shall presently relate.

In the second summer of my living at Wiishto, I had a child at the time
that the kernels of corn first appeared on the cob. When I was taken sick,
Sheninjee was absent, and I was sent to a small shed, on the bank of the
river, which was made of boughs, where I was obliged to stay till my husband returned. My two sisters, who were my only companions, attended
me, and on the second day of my confinement my child was born; but it
lived only two days. It was a girl: and notwithstanding the shortness of the
time that I possessed it, it was a great grief to me to lose it.

[6]Wiishto I suppose was situated near the
mouth of Indian Guyundal, 327 miles below
Pittsburgh, and 73 above Big Sciota; or at
the mouth of Swan creek, 307 miles below
Pittsburgh.

After the birth of my child, I was very sick, but was not allowed to go into the house for two weeks; when, to my great joy, Sheninjee returned, and I was taken in and as comfortably provided for as our situation would admit of. My disease continued to increase for a number of days; and I became so far reduced that my recovery was despaired of by my friends, and I concluded that my troubles would soon be finished. At length, however, my complaint took a favorable turn, and by the time that the corn was ripe I was able to get about. I continued to gain my health, and in the fall was able to go to our winter quarters, on the Sciota, with the Indians.

From that time, nothing remarkable occurred to me till the fourth winter of my captivity, when I had a son born, while I was at Sciota: I had a quick recovery, and my child was healthy. To commemorate the name of my much lamented father, I called my son Thomas Jemison.

Chapter IV

She leaves Wiishto for Fort Pitt, in company with her Husband.—Her feelings on setting out.—Contrast between the labor of the white and Indian Women.—Deficiency of Arts amongst the Indians.—Their former Happiness.—Baneful effects of Civilization, and the introduction of ardent Spirits amongst them, &c.—Journey up the River.—Murder of three Traders by the Shawnees.—Her Husband stops at a Trading House.— Wantonness of the Shawnees.—Moves up the Sandusky.—Meets her Brother from Ge-nish-a-u.—Her Husband goes to Wiishto, and she sets out for Genishau in company with her Brothers.—They arrive at Sandusky.— Occurrences at that place.—Her Journey to Genishau, and Reception by her Mother and Friends.

In the spring, when Thomas was three or four moons [months] old, we returned from Sciota to Wiishto, and soon after set out to go to Fort Pitt, to dispose of our fur and skins, that we had taken in the winter, and procure some necessary articles for the use of our family.

I had then been with the Indians four summers and four winters, and had become so far accustomed to their mode of living, habits and dispositions, that my anxiety to get away, to be set at liberty, and leave them, had almost subsided. With them was my home; my family was there, and there I had many friends to whom I was warmly attached in consideration of the favors, affection and friendship with which they had uniformly treated me, from the time of my adoption. Our labor was not severe; and that of one year was exactly similar, in almost every respect, to that of the others, without that endless variety that is to be observed in the common labor of the white people. Notwithstanding the Indian women have all the fuel and bread to procure, and the cooking to perform, their task is probably not harder than that of white women, who have those articles provided for them; and their cares certainly are not half as numerous, nor as great. In the summer season, we planted, tended and harvested our corn, and generally had all our children with us; but had no master to oversee or drive us, so that we could work as leisurely as we pleased. We had no ploughs on the Ohio; but performed the whole process of planting and hoeing with a small tool that resembled, in some respects, a hoe with a very short handle.

Our cooking consisted in pounding our corn into samp or hommany, boiling the hommany, making now and then a cake and baking it in the ashes, and in boiling or roasting our venison. As our cooking and eating utensils consisted of a hommany block and pestle, a small kettle, a knife or two, and a few vessels of bark or wood, it required but little time to keep them in order for use.

Spinning, weaving, sewing, stocking knitting, and the like, are arts which have never been practised in the Indian tribes generally. After the revolutionary war, I learned to sew, so that I could make my own clothing after a poor fashion; but the other domestic arts I have been wholly ignorant of the application of, since my captivity. In the season of hunting, it was our business, in addition to our cooking, to bring home the game that was taken by the Indians, dress it, and carefully preserve, the eatable meat, and prepare or dress the skins. Our clothing was fastened together with strings of deer skin, and tied on with the same.

In that manner we lived, without any of those jealousies, quarrels, and revengeful battles between families and individuals, which have been common in the Indian tribes since the introduction of ardent spirits amongst them.

The use of ardent spirits amongst the Indians and the attempts which have been made to civilize and christianize them by the white people, has constantly made them worse and worse; increased their vices, and robbed them of many of their virtues; and will ultimately produce their extermination. I have seen, in a number of instances, the effects of education upon some of our Indians, who were taken when young, from their families, and placed at school before they had had an opportunity to contract many Indian habits, and there kept till they arrived to manhood, but I have never seen one of those but what was an Indian in every respect after he returned. Indians must and will be Indians, in spite of all the means that can be used for their cultivation in the sciences and arts.

One thing only marred my happiness, while I lived with them on the Ohio; and that was the recollection that I had once had tender parents and a home that I loved. Aside from that consideration, or, if I had been taken in infancy, I should have been contented in my situation. Notwithstanding all that has been said against the Indians, in consequence of their cruelties to their enemies—cruelties that I have witnessed, and had abundant proof of—it is a fact that they are naturally kind, tender and peaceable towards their friends, and strictly honest; and that those cruelties have been practised, only upon their enemies, according to their idea of justice.

At the time we left Wiishto, it was impossible for me to suppress a sigh of regret on parting with those who had truly been my friends—with those whom I had every reason to respect. On account of a part of our family living at Genishau, we thought it doubtful whether we should return directly from Pittsburgh, or go from thence on a visit to see them.

Our company consisted of my husband, my two Indian brothers, my little son and myself. We embarked in a canoe that was large enough to contain ourselves *and* our effects, and proceeded on our voyage up the river.

Nothing remarkable occurred to us on our way, till we arrived at the mouth of a creek which Sheninjee and my brothers said was the outlet of Sandusky lake; where, as they said, two or three English traders in fur and skins had kept a trading house but a short time before, though they were then absent. We had passed the trading house but a short distance, when we met three white men floating down the river, with the appearance of having been recently murdered by the Indians. We supposed them to be the bodies of the traders, whose store we had passed the same day. Sheninjee being alarmed for fear of being apprehended as one of the murderers, if he should go on, resolved to put about immediately, and we accordingly returned to where the traders had lived, and there landed.

At the trading house we found a party of Shawnee Indians, who had taken a young white man prisoner, and had just begun to torture him for the sole purpose of gratifying their curiosity in exulting at his distress. They at first made him stand up, while they slowly pared his ears and split them into strings; they then made a number of slight incisions in his face; and then bound him upon the ground, rolled him in the dirt, and rubbed it in his wounds: some of them at the same time whipping him with small rods! The poor fellow cried for mercy and yelled most piteously.

The sight of his distress seemed too much for me to endure: I begged of them to desist—I entreated them with tears to release him. At length they attended to my intercessions, and set him at liberty. He was shockingly disfigured, bled profusely, and appeared to be in great pain: but as soon as he was liberated he made off in haste, which was the last I saw of him.

We soon learned that the same party of Shawnees had, but a few hours before, massacred the three white traders whom we saw in the river, and had plundered their store. We, however, were not molested by them, and after a short stay at that place, moved up the creek about forty miles to a Shawnee town, which the Indians called Gaw-gush-shaw-ga (which being interpreted signifies a mask or a false face.) The creek that we went up was called Candusky.

It was now summer; and having tarried a few days at Gawgush-shawga, we moved on up the creek to a place that was called Yis-kah-wa-na (meaning in English open mouth.)

As I have before observed, the family to which I belonged was part of a tribe of Seneca Indians, who lived, at that time, at a place called Genishau, from the name of the tribe, that was situated on a river of the same name which is now called Genesee. The word Genishau signifies a shining, clear or open place. Those of us who lived on the Ohio, had frequently received invitations from those at Genishau, by one of my brothers, who usually went and returned every season, to come and live with them, and my two sisters had been gone almost two years.

While we were at Yiskahwana, my brother arrived there from Genishau, and insisted so strenuously upon our going home (as he called it) with him, that my two brothers concluded to go, and to take me with them.

By this time the summer was gone, and the time for harvesting corn had arrived. My brothers, for fear of the rainy season setting in early, thought it best to set out immediately that we might have good travelling. Sheninjee consented to have me go with my brothers; but concluded to go down the river himself with some fur and skins which he had on hand, spend the winter in hunting with his friends, and come to me in the spring following.

That was accordingly agreed upon, and he set out for Wiishto; and my three brothers and myself, with my little son on my back, at the same time set out for Genishau. We came on to Upper Sandusky, to an Indian town that we found deserted by its inhabitants, in consequence of their having recently murdered some English traders, who resided amongst them. That town was owned and had been occupied by Delaware Indians, who, when they left it, buried their provision in the earth, in order to preserve it from their enemies, or to have a supply for themselves if they should chance to return. My brothers understood the customs of the Indians when they were obliged to fly from their enemies; and suspecting that their corn at least must have been hid, made diligent search, and at length found a large quantity of it, together with beans, sugar and honey, so carefully buried that it was completely dry and as good as when they left it. As our stock of provision was scanty, we considered ourselves extremely fortunate in finding so seasonable a supply, with so little trouble. Having caught two or three horses, that we found there, and furnished ourselves with a good store of food, we travelled on till we came to the mouth of French Creek, where we hunted two days, and from thence came on to Conowongo Creek, where we were obliged to stay seven or ten days, in consequence of our horses having left us and straying into the woods. The horses, however, were found, and we again prepared to resume our journey. During our stay at that place the rain fell fast, and had raised the creek to such a height that it was seemingly impossible for us to cross it. A number of times we ventured in, but were compelled to return, barely escaping with our lives. At length we succeeded in swimming our horses and reached the opposite shore; though I but just escaped with my little boy from being drowned. From Sandusky the path that we travelled was crooked and obscure; but was tolerably well understood by my oldest brother, who had travelled it a number of times, when going to and returning from the Cherokee wars. The fall by this time was considerably advanced, and the rains, attended with cold winds, continued daily to increase the difficulties of travelling. From Conowongo we came to a place, called by the Indians Che-ua-shung-gau-tau, and from that to U-na-waum-gwa (which means an eddy, not strong,) where the early frosts had destroyed the corn so that the Indians were in danger of starving for the want of bread. Having rested ourselves two days at that place, we came on to Caneadea and stayed one day, and then continued our march till we arrived at Genishau. Genishau at that time was a large Seneca town, thickly inhabited, lying on Genesee river, opposite what is now called the Free Ferry, adjoining Fall-Brook, and about south west of the present village of Geneseo, the county seat for the county of Livingston, in the state of New-York.

Those only who have travelled on foot the distance of five or six hundred miles, through an almost pathless wilderness, can form an idea of the fatigue and sufferings that I endured on that journey. My clothing was thin and illy calculated to defend me from the continually drenching rains with which I was daily completely wet, and at night with nothing but my wet blanket to cover me, I had to sleep on the naked ground, and generally without a shelter, save such as nature had provided. In addition to all that, I had to carry my child, then about nine months old, every step of the journey on my back, or in my arms, and provide for his comfort and prevent his suffering, as far as my poverty of means would admit. Such was the fatigue that I sometimes felt, that I thought it impossible for me to go through, and I would almost abandon the idea of even trying to proceed. My brothers were attentive, and at length, as I have stated, we reached our place of destination, in good health, and without having experienced a day's sickness from the time we left Yiskahwana.

We were kindly received by my Indian mother and the other members of the family, who appeared to make me welcome; and my two sisters, whom I had not seen in two years, received me with every expression of love and friendship, and that they really felt what they expressed, I have never had the least reason to doubt. The warmth of their feelings, the kind reception which I met with, and the continued favors that I received at their hands, rivetted my affection for them so strongly that I am constrained to be believe that I loved them as I should have loved my own sister had she lived, and I had been brought up with her.

Chapter VI

Peace amongst the Indians.—Celebrations.—Worship. Exercises.—Business of the Tribes.—Former Happiness of the Indians in time of peace extolled.—Their Morals; Fidelity; Honesty; Chastity; Temperance. Indians called to German Flats.—Treaty with Americans.—They are sent for by the British Commissioners, and go to Oswego.—Promises made by those Commissioners.—Greatness of the King of England. Reward that was paid them for joining the British. They make a Treaty.—Bounty offered for Scalps. Return richly dressed and equipped.—In 1776 they kill a man at Cautega to provoke the Americans. Prisoners taken at Cherry Valley, brought to Beard's-Town; redeemed, &c.—Battle at Fort Stanwix.—Indians suffer a great loss.—Mourning at Beard's Town.—Mrs. Jemison's care of and services rendered to Butler and Brandt.

After the conclusion of the French war, our tribe had nothing to trouble it till the commencement of the Revolution. For twelve or fifteen years the use of the implements of war was not known, nor the war-whoop heard, save on days of festivity, when the achievements of former times were commemorated in a kind of mimic warfare, in which the chiefs and warriors displayed their prowess, and illustrated their former adroitness, by laying the ambuscade, surprizing their enemies, and performing many accurate manoeuvres with the tomahawk and scalping knife; thereby preserving and handing to their children, the theory of Indian warfare. During that period they also pertinaciously observed the religious rites of their progenitors, by attending with the most scrupulous exactness and a great degree of enthusiasm to the sacrifices, at particular times, to appease the anger of the evil deity, or to excite the commisseration and friendship of the Great Good Spirit, whom they adored with reverence, as the author, governor, supporter and disposer of every good thing of which they participated.

They also practised in various athletic games, such as running, wrestling, leaping, and playing bail, with a view that their bodies might be more supple, or rather that they might not become enervated, and that they might be enabled to make a proper selection of Chiefs for the councils of the nation and leaders for war.

While the Indians were thus engaged in their round of traditionary performances, with the addition of hunting, their women attended to agriculture, their families, and a few domestic concerns of small consequence, and attended with but little labor.

No people can live more happy than the Indians did in times of peace, before the introduction of spirituous liquors amongst them. Their lives were a continual round of pleasures. Their wants were few, and easily satisfied; and their cares were only for to-day; the bounds of their calculations for future comfort not extending to the incalculable uncertainties of tomorrow. If peace ever dwelt with men, it was in former times, in the recesses from war, amongst what are now termed barbarians. The moral character of the Indians was (if I may be allowed the expression) uncontaminated. Their fidelity was perfect, and became proverbial; they were strictly honest; they despised deception and falsehood; and chastity was held in high veneration, and a violation of it was considered sacrilege. They were temperate in their desires, moderate in their passions, and candid and honorable in the expression of their sentiments on every subject of importance.

Thus, at peace amongst themselves, and with the neighboring whites, though there were none at that time very near, our Indians lived quietly and peaceably at home, till a little before the breaking out of the revolutionary war, when they were sent for, together with the Chiefs and members of the Six Nations generally, by the people of the States, to go to the German Flats, and there hold a general council, in order that the people of the states might ascertain, in good season, who they should esteem and treat as enemies, and who as friends, in the great war which was then upon the point of breaking out between them and the King of England.

Our Indians obeyed the call, and the council was holden, at which the pipe of peace was smoked, and a treaty made, in which the Six Nations solemnly agreed that if a war should eventually break out, they would not take up arms on either side; but that they would observe a strict neutrality. With that the people of the states were satisfied, as they had not asked their assistance, nor did not wish it. The Indians returned to their homes well pleased that they could live on neutral ground, surrounded by the din of war, without being engaged in it.

About a year passed off, and we, as usual, were enjoying ourselves in the employments of peaceable times, when a messenger arrived from the British Commissioners, requesting all the Indians of our tribe to attend a general council which was soon to be held at Oswego. The council convened, and being opened, the British Commissioners informed the Chiefs that the object of calling a council of the Six Nations, was, to engage their assistance in subduing the rebels, the people of the states, who had risen up against the good King, their master, and were about to rob him of a great part of his possessions and wealth, and added that they would amply reward them for all their services.

The Chiefs then arose, and informed the Commissioners of the nature and extent of the treaty which they had entered into with the people of the states, the year before, and that they should not violate it by taking up the hatchet against them.

The Commissioners continued their entreaties without success, till they addressed their avarice, by telling our people that the people of the states were few in number, and easily subdued; and that on the account of their disobedience to the King, they justly merited all the punishment that it was possible for white men and Indians to inflict upon them; and added, that the King was rich and powerful, both in money and subjects. That his rum was as plenty as the water in lake Ontario: that his men were as numerous as the sands upon the lake shore:—and that the Indians, if they would assist in the war, and persevere in their friendship to the King, till it was closed, should never want for money or goods. Upon this the Chiefs concluded a treaty with the British Commissioners, in which they agreed to take up arms against the rebels, and continue in the service of his Majesty till they were subdued, in consideration of certain conditions which were stipulated in the treaty to be performed by the British government and its agents.

As soon as the treaty was finished, the Commissioners made a present to each Indian of a suit of clothes, a brass kettle, a gun and tomahawk, a scalping knife, a quantity of powder and lead, a piece of gold, and promised a bounty on every scalp that should be brought in. Thus richly clad and equipped, they returned home, after an absence of about two weeks, full of the fire of war, and anxious to encounter their enemies. Many of the kettles which the Indians received at that time are now in use on the Genesee Flats.

Hired to commit depredations upon the whites, who had given them no offence, they waited impatiently to commence their labor, till sometime in the spring of 1776, when a convenient opportunity offered for them to make an attack. At that time, a party of our Indians were at Cau-te-ga, who shot a man that was looking after his horse, for the sole purpose, as I was informed by my Indian brother, who was present, of commencing hostilities.

In May following, our Indians were in their first battle with the Americans; but at what place I am unable to determine. While they were absent at that time, my daughter Nancy was born.

The same year, at Cherry Valley, our Indians took a woman and her three daughters prisoners, and brought them on, leaving one at Canandaigua, one at Honeoy, one at Cattaraugus, and one (the woman) at Little Beard's Town, where I resided. The woman told me that she and her daughters might have escaped, but that they expected the British army only, and therefore made no effort. Her husband and sons got away. Sometime having elapsed, they were redeemed at Fort Niagara by Col. Butler, who clothed them well, and sent them home.

In the same expedition, Joseph Smith was taken prisoner at or near Cherry Valley, brought to Genesee, and detained till after the revolutionary war. He was then liberated, and the Indians made him a present, in company with Horatio Jones, of 6000 acres of land lying in the present town of Leicester, in the county of Livingston.

One of the girls just mentioned, was married to a British officer at Fort Niagara, by the name of Johnson, who at the time she was taken, took a gold ring from her finger, without any compliments or ceremonies. When he saw her at Niagara he recognized her features, restored the ring that he had so impolitely borrowed, and courted and married her.

Previous to the battle at Fort Stanwix, the British sent for the Indians to come and see them whip the rebels; and, at the same time stated that they did not wish to have them fight, but wanted to have them just sit down, smoke their pipes, and look on. Our Indians went, to a man; but contrary to their expectation, instead of smoking and looking on, they were obliged to fight for their lives, and at the end of the battle were completely beaten, with a great loss in killed and wounded. Our Indians alone had thirty-six killed, and a great number wounded. Our town exhibited a scene of real sorrow and distress, when our warriors returned and recounted their misfortunes, and stated the real loss they had sustained in the engagement. The mourning was excessive, and was expressed by the most doleful yells, shrieks, and howlings, and by inimitable gesticulations.

During the revolution, my house was the home of Col's Butler and Brandt, whenever they chanced to come into our neighborhood as they passed to and from Fort Niagara, which was the seat of their military operations. Many and many a night I have pounded samp for them from sun-set till sun-rise, and furnished them with necessary provision and clean clothing for their journey.

Chapter XVI

Conclusion.—Review of her Life.—Reflections on the loss of Liberty.—Care
she took to preserve her Health.—Indians' abstemiousness in Drinking,
after the French War.—Care of their Lives, &c.—General use of Spirits.—
Her natural Strength.—Purchase of her first Cow.—Means by which she
has been supplied with Food.—Suspicions of her having been a Witch.—Her
Constancy.—Number of Children.—Number Living.—Their Residence.—
Closing Reflection.

When I review my life, the privations that I have suffered, the hardships I
have endured, the vicissitudes I have passed, and the complete revolution
that I have experienced in my manner of living; when I consider my reduc-
tion from a civilized to a savage state, and the various steps by which that
process has been effected, and that my life has been prolonged, and my
health and reason spared, it seems a miracle that I am unable to account
for, and is a tragical medley that I hope will never be repeated.

The bare loss of liberty is but a mere trifle when compared with the circumstances that necessarily attend, and are inseparably connected with it. It
is the recollection of what we once were, of the friends, the home, and the
pleasures that we have left or lost; the anticipation of misery, the appearance of wretchedness, the anxiety for freedom, the hope of release, the
devising of means of escaping, and the vigilance with which we watch our
keepers, that constitute the nauseous dregs of the bitter cup of slavery. I am
sensible, however, that no one can pass from a state of freedom to that of
slavery, and in the last situation rest perfectly contented; but as every one
knows that great exertions of the mind tend directly to debilitate the body,
it will appear obvious that we ought, when confined, to exert all our faculties to promote our present comfort, and let future days provide their own
sacrifices. In regard to ourselves, just as we feel, we are.

For the preservation of my life to the present time I am indebted to an
excellent constitution, with which I have been blessed in as great a degree as
any other person. After I arrived to years of understanding, the care of my
own health was one of my principal studies; and by avoiding exposures to
wet and cold, by temperance in eating, abstaining from the use of spirits,
and shunning the excesses to which I was frequently exposed, I effected my
object beyond what I expected. I have never once been sick till within a year
or two, only as I have related.

Spirits and tobacco I have never used, and I have never once attended
an Indian frolic. When I was taken prisoner, and for sometime after that,
spirits was not known; and when it was first introduced, it was in small
quantities, and used only by the Indians; so that it was a long time before
the Indian women begun to even taste it.

After the French war, for a number of years, it was the practice of the
Indians of our tribe to send to Niagara and get two or three kegs of rum (in
all six or eight gallons,) and hold a frolic as long as it lasted. When the rum

was brought to the town, all the Indians collected, and before a drop was drank, gave all their knives, tomahawks, guns, and other instruments of war, to one Indian, whose business it was to bury them in a private place, keep them concealed, and remain perfectly sober till the frolic was ended. Having thus divested themselves, they commenced drinking, and continued their frolic till every drop was consumed. If any of them became quarrelsome, or got to fighting, those who were sober enough bound them upon the ground, where they were obliged to lie till they got sober, and then were unbound. When the fumes of the spirits had left the company, the sober Indian returned to each the instruments with which they had entrusted him, and all went home satisfied. A frolic of that kind was held but once a year, and that at the time the Indians quit their hunting, and come in with their deer-skins.

In those frolics the women never participated. Soon after the revolutionary war, however, spirits became common in our tribe, and has been used indiscriminately by both sexes; though there are not so frequent instances of intoxication amongst the squaws as amongst the Indians.

To the introduction and use of that baneful article, which has made such devastation in our tribes, and threatens the extinction of our people (the Indians,) I can with the greatest propriety impute the whole of my misfortune in losing my three sons. But as I have before observed, not even the love of life will restrain an Indian from sipping the poison that he knows will destroy him. The voice of nature, the rebukes of reason, the advice of parents, the expostulations of friends, and the numerous instances of sudden death, are all insufficient to reclaim an Indian, who has once experienced the exhilarating and inebriating effects of spirits, from seeking his grave in the bottom of his bottle!

My strength has been great for a woman of my size, otherwise I must long ago have died under the burdens which I was obliged to carry. I learned to carry loads on my back, in a strap placed across my forehead, soon after my captivity; and continue to carry in the same way. Upwards of thirty years ago, with the help of my young children, I backed all the boards that were used about my house from Allen's mill at the outlet of Silver Lake, a distance of five miles. I have planted, hoed, and harvested corn every season but one since I was taken prisoner. Even this present fall (1823) I have husked my corn and backed it into the house.

The first cow that I ever owned, I bought of a squaw sometime after the revolution. It had been stolen from the enemy. I had owned it but a few days when it fell into a hole, and almost died before we could get it out. After this, the squaw wanted to be recanted, but as I would not give up the cow, I gave her money enough to make, when added to the sum which I paid her at first, thirty-five dollars. Cows were plenty on the Ohio, when I lived there, and of good quality.

For provisions I have never suffered since I came upon the flats; nor have I ever been in debt to any other hands than my own for the plenty that I have shared.

My vices, that have been suspected, have been but few. It was believed for a long time, by some of our people, that I was a great witch; but they were unable to prove my guilt, and consequently I escaped the certain doom of those who are convicted of that crime, which, by Indians, is considered as heinous as murder. Some of my children had light brown hair, and tolerable fair skin, which used to make some say that I stole them; yet as I was ever conscious of my own constancy, I never thought that any one really believed that I was guilty of adultery.

I have been the mother of eight children; three of whom are now living, and I have at this time thirty-nine grand children, and fourteen great-grand children, all living in the neighborhood of Genesee River, and at Buffalo.

I live in my own house, and on my own land, with my youngest daughter, Polly, who is married to George Chongo, and has three children.

My daughter Nancy, who is married to Billy Green, lives about 80 rods south of my house, and has seven children.

My other daughter, Betsey, is married to John Green, has seven children, and resides 80 rods north of my house.

Thus situated in the midst of my children, I expect I shall soon leave the world, and make room for the rising generation. I feel the weight of years with which I am loaded, and am sensible of my daily failure in seeing, hearing and strength; but my only anxiety is for my family. If my family will live happily, and I can be exempted from trouble while I have to stay, I feel as though I could lay down in peace a life that has been checked in almost every hour, with troubles of a deeper dye, than are commonly experienced by mortals.

1824

■ **BLACK HAWK** ■
1767–1838

Black Hawk was a Sauk war leader. Born in Saukenuk on the Rock River (now Rock Island, Illinois) into a clan that did not provide the Sauks with "chiefs," or civil leaders, Black Hawk achieved his prominent status through leadership in war. As a young man, he led several war parties, mostly against the Osages; when his father died during one of these battles, Black Hawk inherited an important medicine bundle. A man who could muster a group of warriors and lead them successfully on a military excursion gained respect and power in the Sauk Nation.

In middle age, with his band of 200 Sauk warriors, Black Hawk sided with the British in the War of 1812. He disapproved of the Euro-American style of warfare, considering it was too wasteful of human life, and after battles in which the British lost at great cost, Black Hawk withdrew his warriors from the conflict and returned home—only to find that a warrior named Keokuk had become the military leader of the Sauk Nation. Black Hawk's disappointment and disapproval of Keokuk, whom he considered an opportunist, a coward, and too conciliatory to the United States and its expansionist greed, would last for the rest of his life. He returned to fight on the British side, and in 1816 he signed a peace treaty with the United States. Unbeknownst to him, this treaty reaffirmed the terms of an 1804 treaty that ceded all Sauk territory east of the Mississippi to the United States.

As a result, the Sauk Nation was forced to leave its land east of the Mississippi and cross to the west in 1828. Along with other Sauk leaders, Black Hawk contested the treaty. The original 1804 document had been signed by men not authorized to cede land and without the knowledge or agreement of the entire Sauk tribal council. Believing he had the military support of the British, Black Hawk led a group of 500 warriors and 1,000 older men, women, and children back across the Mississippi River in April 1832.

Black Hawk's band aimed to cross the land that had been Sauk territory and reach friendly Winnebago villages to which they had been invited. Some Foxes, Kickapoos, and Potowatomies joined them. Meanwhile, the militias of Michigan and Illinois were mobilized to hunt down Black Hawk's group. The military pursued them, and there were several skirmishes. On August 1, as the band was attempting to flee back across the Mississippi River to safety, the U.S. gunboat *Warrior* appeared and prevented them from crossing. Black Hawk attempted to surrender, waving a white flag, but his signal was either misunderstood or ignored, and there was a battle. At the end of the day, Black Hawk tried to convince his followers to flee to the north, but most of the nonwarriors chose to stay and build rafts to cross the river. The next day, caught between the gunboat and the pursuing militia and their Indian allies, most of the 400–500 remaining members of the band, largely women and children, were killed in a massacre that lasted eight hours. A total of five U.S. militiamen were killed.

President Andrew Jackson had Black Hawk incarcerated and then insisted that he and eight other leaders of the group be taken on a tour of the eastern United States to demonstrate U.S. power over the Native nations. In East Coast cities, however, the group was greeted by enormous crowds, many of whom considered the Black Hawk War to have been a debacle and a blot on the United States' honor. So great was Black Hawk's popularity that his crowds were larger than those that turned out to greet the president, who was also touring the East. On the return leg of the trip, the Native leaders continued to be a huge spectacle, but frontier Americans greeted them with violent distrust, and in Detroit the crowd burned them in effigy.

While in the East, Black Hawk decided he needed to communicate his story to the citizens of the United States. On his return, he narrated the story of his life to Antoine LeClaire, a government interpreter of French and Pottawatomi descent. Edited by a newspaper man, J. B. Patterson, the resulting book, published in 1833, was titled *Life of Ma-Ka-Tai-Me-She-Kia-Kiak or Black Hawk—Dictated by Himself*. It was an immediate best seller.

The autobiography is a fascinating document. Because of its multiple refractions through a translator and an editor, most readers' first response is to doubt the possibility of finding Black Hawk's "voice" in the text at all. At various points the text has been discounted, doubted, and critiqued for its obvious distance from "authenticity." Black Hawk neither wrote nor spoke English. How could this document be considered an autobiography at all? But as with the *Narrative of the Life of Mary Jemison*, also excerpted here, this text challenges us to encounter it as material evidence of the struggle itself. Reading between the lines is absolutely necessary, yet the lines themselves are testimony to the inherent violence of contact and the struggle for understanding, justice, and what scholars call "survivance"—the ongoing creative act of surviving in the face of unimaginable change.

Bethany Schneider
Bryn Mawr College

from Life of Black Hawk or ma-ne-se-no oke-maut wap-pi ma-quai

Indian Agency

Rock-Island, *October* 16, 1833

I do hereby certify, that Mà-ka-tai-me-she-kià-kiàk, or Black Hawk, did call upon me, on his return to his people in August last, and expressed a great desire to have a History of his Life written and published, in order, (as he said) "that the people of the United States, (among whom he had been travelling, and by whom he had been treated with great respect, friendship and hospitality,) might know the *causes* that had impelled him to act as he had done, and the *principles* by which he was governed." In accordance with his request, I acted as Interpreter; and was particularly cautious, to understand distinctly the narrative of Black Hawk throughout—and have examined the work carefully, since its completion—and have no hesitation in pronouncing it strictly correct, in all its particulars. Given under my hand, at the Sac and Fox Agency, the day and date above written.

Antoine Leclaire,
U. S. Interpreter for the Sacs and Foxes

Dedication

To Brigadier Gen'l. H. Atkinson

Sir,—The changes of fortune, and vicissitudes of war, made you my conqueror. When my last resources were exhausted, my warriors worn down with long and toilsome marches, we yielded, and I became your prisoner.

The story of my life is told in the following pages; it is intimately connected, and in some measure, identified with a part of the history of your own: I have, therefore, dedicated it to you.

The changes of many summers, have brought old age upon me,—and I cannot expect to survive many moons. Before I set out on my journey to the land of my fathers, I have determined to give my motives and reasons for my former hostilities to the whites, and to vindicate my character from misrepresentation. The kindness I received from you whilst a prisoner of war, assures me that you will vouch for the facts contained in my narrative, so far as they came under your observation.

I am now an obscure member of a nation, that formerly honored and respected my opinions. The path to glory is rough, and many gloomy hours obscure it. May the Great Spirit shed light on your's—and that you may never experience the humility that the power of the American government has reduced me to, is the wish of him, who, in his native forests, was once as proud and bold as yourself.

Black Hawk
10th Moon, 1833

Advertisement

It is presumed no apology will be required for presenting to the public, the life of a Hero who has lately taken such high rank among the distinguished individuals of America. In the following pages he will be seen in the characters of a Warrior, a Patriot and a State-prisoner—in every situation he is still the Chief of his Band, asserting their rights with dignity, firmness and courage. Several accounts of the late war having been published, in which he thinks justice is not done to himself or nation, he determined to make known to the world, the injuries his people have received from the whites—the causes which brought on the war on the part of his nation, and a general history of it throughout the campaign. In his opinion, this is the only method now left him to rescue his little Band—the remnant of those who fought bravely with him—from the effects of the statements that have already gone forth.

The facts which he states, respecting the Treaty of 1804, in virtue of the provisions of which the government claimed the country in dispute, and enforced its arguments with the sword, are worthy of attention. It purported to cede to the United States, all of the country, including the village and corn-fields of Black Hawk and his band, on the east side of the Mississippi. Four individuals of the tribe, who were on a visit to St. Louis to obtain the liberation of one of their people from prison, were prevailed upon, (says Black Hawk,) to make this important treaty, without the knowledge or authority of the tribes, or nation.

In treating with the Indians for their country, it has always been customary to assemble the whole nation; because, as has been truly suggested by the Secretary of War, the nature of the authority of the chiefs of the tribe is such, that it is not often that they dare make a treaty of much consequence,—and we might add, never, when involving so much magnitude as the one under consideration, without the presence of their young men. A rule so reasonable and just ought never to be violated—and the Indians might well question the right of the Government to dispossess them, when such violation was made the basis of its right.

The editor has written this work according to the dictation of Black Hawk, through the United States' Interpreter, at the Sac and Fox Agency of Rock Island. He does not, therefore, consider himself responsible for any of the facts, or views, contained in it—and leaves the old Chief and his story with the public, whilst he neither asks, nor expects any fame for his services as an amanuensis.

The Editor

Life of Black Hawk

I was born at the Sac Village, on Rock river, in the year 1767, and am now in my 67th year. My great grandfather, Na-nà-ma-kee, or Thunder, (according to the tradition given me by my father, Py-e-sa,) was born in the vicinity of Montreal, where the Great Spirit first placed the Sac Nation, and inspired him with a belief that, at the end of four years, he should see a *white man*, who would be to him a father. Consequently he blacked his face, and ate but once a day, (just as the sun was going down,) for three years, and continued dreaming throughout all this time whenever he slept—when the Great Spirit again appeared to him, and told him, that, at the end of one year more, he should meet his father,—and directed him to start seven days before its expiration, and take with him his two brothers *Nàmah*, or Sturgeon, and *Pau-ka-hum-ma-wa* or Sun Fish, and travel in a direction to the left of sun-rising. After pursuing this course five days, he sent out his two brothers to listen if they could hear a noise, and if so, to fasten some grass to the end of a pole, erect it, pointing in the direction of the sound, and then return to him.

Early next morning they returned, and reported that they had heard sounds which appeared near at hand, and that they had fulfilled his order. They all then started for the place where the pole had been erected; when, on reaching it, Na-nà-ma-kee left his party, and went alone to the place from whence the sounds proceeded, and found that the white man had arrived and pitched his tent. When he came in sight, his father came out to meet him. He took him by the hand, and welcomed him into his tent. He told him that he was the son of the King of France—that he had been dreaming for four years—that the Great Spirit had directed him to come here, where he should meet a nation of people who had never yet seen a white man—that they should be his children, and he should be their father—that he had communicated these things to the King, his father, who laughed at him, and called him a Ma-she-na—but he insisted on coming here to meet his children, where the Great Spirit had directed him. The King had told him that he would neither find land nor people—that this was an uninhabited region of lakes and mountains; but, finding that he would have no peace without it, fitted out a nà-pe-quâ, manned it, and gave it to him in charge, when he immediately loaded it, set sail, and had now landed on the very day that the Great Spirit had told him, in his dreams, he should meet his children. He had now met the man who should, in future, have charge of all the nation.

He then presented him with a medal, which he hung round his neck. Na-nà-ma-kee informed him of *his* dreaming,—and told him that his two brothers remained a little ways behind. His father gave him a shirt, blanket, and handkerchief, besides a variety of presents, and told him to go and bring his brothers. Having laid aside his buffalo robe, and dressed himself in his new dress, he started to meet his brethren. When they met, he explained to them his meeting with the white man, and exhibited to their view the presents that he had made him—took off his medal, and placed it upon Nàh-ma, his elder brother, and requested them both to go with him to his father. They proceeded thither,—were ushered into the tent, and, after some brief ceremony, his father opened his chest and took presents there-from for the new-comers. He discovered that Nà-nà-ma-kee had given his medal to Nàh-ma. He told him that he had done wrong—he should wear that medal himself, as he had others for his brethren: That which he had given him was a type of the rank he should hold in the nation: That his brothers could only rank as *civil* chiefs,—and their duties should consist of taking care of the village, and attending to its civil concerns—whilst his rank, from his superior knowledge, placed him over them all. If the nation gets into any difficulty with another, then his puc-co-hà-wà-ma, or sovereign decree, must be obeyed. If he declared war, he must lead them on to battle: That the Great Spirit had made him a great and brave general, and had sent him here to give him that medal, and make presents to him for his people.

His father remained four days—during which time he gave him guns, powder and lead, spears and lances, and showed him their use—so that in war he could chastise his enemies—and in peace they could kill buffalo, deer and other game, necessary for the comforts and luxuries of life. He then pre-sented the others with various kinds of cooking utensils, and learned them their uses—and having given them a large quantity of goods, as presents, and every other thing necessary for their comfort, he set sail for France, after promising to meet them again, at the same place after the twelfth moon.

The three newly-made chiefs returned to their village, and explained to Muk-a-tà-quet, their father, who was the principal chief of the nation, what had been said and done. The old chief had some *dogs* killed, and made a feast, preparatory to resigning his sceptre, to which all the nation were invited. Great anxiety prevailed among them, to know what the three brothers had seen and heard—when the old chief rose, and related to them the sayings and doings of his three sons; and concluded by observing, that "the Great Spirit had directed that these, his three children, should take the rank and power that had been his—and that he yielded these honors and duties willingly to them—because it was the wish of the Great Spirit, and he could never consent to make him angry!" He now presented the great medicine bag to Na-nà-ma-kee, and told him, "that he cheerfully resigned it to him—it is the soul of our nation—it has never yet been disgraced—and I will expect you to keep it unsullied!"

Some dissension arose among them, in consequence of so much power being given to Na-nà-ma-kee, he being so young a man. To quiet this, Na-nà-ma-kee, during a violent *thunderstorm*, told them that he had *caused* it! and that it was an exemplification of the *name* the Great Spirit had given him. During the storm, the *lightning* struck, and set fire to a tree, close by; (a sight they had never witnessed before.) He went to it, and brought away some of its burning branches, made a fire in the lodge, and seated his brothers thereby, opposite to each other; whilst he stood up, and addressed his people as follows:

"I am yet young—but the Great Spirit has called me to the rank I now hold among you. I have never sought to be anything more than my birth entitled me. I have not been ambitious—nor was it ever my wish, whilst my father lives, to have taken his place—nor have I now usurped his powers. The Great Spirit caused me to dream for four years—he told me where to go and meet the white man, who would be a kind father to us all. I obeyed his order. I went, and have seen our new father. You have all heard what was said and done. The Great Spirit directed him to come and meet me, and it is his order that places me at the head of my nation—the place which my father has willingly resigned.

"You have all witnessed the power which has been given to me by the Great Spirit, in making that fire—and all that I now ask is, that these, my two chiefs, may never let it go out: That they may preserve peace among you, and administer to the wants of the needy: And, should an enemy invade our country, I will then, but not until then, assume command, and go forth with my band of brave warriors, and endeavor to chastise them!"

At the conclusion of this speech, every voice cried out for Na-nà-ma-kee! All were satisfied, when they found that the *Great Spirit had done*, what they had suspected was the work of Na-nà-ma-kee, he being a very shrewd young man.

The next spring, according to promise, their French father returned, with his nà-pe-quâ richly laden with goods, which were distributed among them. He continued for a long time to keep up a regular trade with them—they giving him in exchange for his goods, furs and peltries.

After a long time the British overpowered the French, (the two nations being at war,) drove them away from Quebec, and took possession of it themselves. The different tribes of Indians around our nation, envying our people, united their forces against them, and succeeded, by their great strength, to drive them to Montreal, and from thence to Mackinac. Here our people first met our British father, who furnished them with goods. Their enemies still pursued them, and drove them to different places on the lake, until they made a village near Green Bay, on what is now called *Sac* river, having derived its name from this circumstance. Here they held a council with the Foxes, and a national treaty of friendship and alliance was concluded upon. The Foxes abandoned their village, and joined the Sacs. This arrangement being mutually obligatory upon both parties, as neither were sufficiently strong to meet their enemies with any hope of success, they soon became as one band or nation of people. They were driven, however, by the combined forces of their enemies, to the Ouisconsin. They remained here for some time, until a party of their young men, (who had descended Rock river to its mouth,) returned, and made a favorable report of the country. They all descended Rock river—drove the Kaskaskias from the country, and commenced the erection of their village, determined never to leave it.

At this village I was born, being a regular descendant of the first chief, Na-nà-ma-kee, or Thunder. Few, if any, events of note, transpired within my recollection, until about my fifteenth year. I was not allowed to paint, or wear feathers; but distinguished myself, at that early age, by wounding an enemy; consequently, I was placed in the ranks of the Braves!

Soon after this, a leading chief of the Muscow nation, came to our village for recruits to go to war against the Osages, our common enemy. I volunteered my services to go, as my father had joined him; and was proud to have an opportunity to prove to him that I was not an unworthy son, and that I had courage and bravery. It was not long before we met the enemy, when a battle immediately ensued. Standing by my father's side, I saw him kill his antagonist, and tear the scalp from his head. Fired with valor and ambition, I rushed furiously upon another, smote him to the earth with my tomahawk—run my lance through his body—took off his scalp, and returned in triumph to my father! He said nothing, but looked pleased. This was the first man I killed! The enemy's loss in this engagement having been great, they immediately retreated, which put an end to the war for the present. Our party then returned to our village, and danced over the scalps we had taken. This was the first time that I was permitted to join in a scalp-dance.

After a few moons had passed, (having acquired considerable fame as a *brave*,) I led a party of seven, and attacked *one hundred Osages*! I killed one man, and left him for my comrades to scalp, whilst I was taking an observation of the strength and preparations of the enemy; and finding that they were equally well armed with ourselves, I ordered a retreat, and came off without losing a man! This excursion gained for me great applause, and enabled me, before a great while, to raise a party of one hundred and eighty, to go against the Osages. We left our village in high spirits, and marched over a rugged country, until we reached that of the Osages, on the Missouri. We followed their trail until we arrived at their village, which we approached with great caution, expecting that they were all there; but found, to our sorrow, that they had deserted it! The party became dissatisfied, in consequence of this disappointment,—and all, with the exception of *five*, dispersed and returned home. I then placed myself at the head of this brave little band, and thanked the Great Spirit that *so many* remained—and took up the trail of our enemies, with a full determination never to return without some trophy of victory! We followed on for several days—killed one man and a boy, and then returned with their scalps.

In consequence of this mutiny in my camp, I was not again enabled to raise a sufficient party to go against the Osages, until about my nineteenth year. During this interim, they committed many outrages on our nation and people. I succeeded at length, in recruiting two hundred efficient warriors, and took up the line of march early in the morning. In a few days we were in the enemy's country, and had not travelled far before we met an equal force to contend with. A general battle immediately commenced, although my braves were considerably fatigued by forced marches. Each party fought desperately. The enemy seemed unwilling to yield the ground, and we were determined to conquer or die! A large number of the Osages were killed, and many wounded, before they commenced retreating. A band of warriors more brave, skilful, and efficient than mine, could not be found. In this engagement I killed five men and one squaw, and had the good fortune to take the scalps of all I struck, except one. The enemy's loss in this engagement was about one hundred men. Ours nineteen. We now returned to our village, well pleased with our success, and danced over the scalps which we had taken.

The Osages, in consequence of their great loss in this battle, became satisfied to remain on their own lands; and ceased, for a while, their depredations on our nation. Our attention, therefore, was directed towards an ancient enemy, who had decoyed and murdered some of our helpless women and children. I started, with my father, who took command of a small party, and proceeded against the enemy. We met near Merimack, and an action ensued; the Cherokees having greatly the advantage in numbers. Early in this engagement my father was wounded in the thigh—but had the pleasure of killing his antagonist before he fell. Seeing that he had fallen, I assumed command, and fought desperately, until the enemy commenced retreating before us. I returned to my father to administer to his necessities, but nothing could be done for him. The *medicine man* said the wound was *mortal!* from which he soon after *died!* In this battle I killed three men, and wounded several. The enemy's loss being twenty-eight, and ours seven.

I now fell heir to the great *medicine bag* of my forefathers, which had belonged to my father. I took it, buried our dead, and returned with my party, all sad and sorrowful, to our village, in consequence of the loss of my father. Owing to this misfortune, I blacked my face, fasted, and prayed to the Great Spirit for five years—during which time I remained in a civil capacity, hunting and fishing.

. . . . . .

Our village was situated on the north side of Rock river, at the foot of its rapids, and on the point of land between Rock river and the Mississippi. In its front, a prairie extended to the bank of the Mississippi; and in our rear, a continued bluff, gently ascending from the prairie. On the side of this bluff we had our corn-fields, extending about two miles up, running parallel with the Mississippi; where we joined those of the Foxes, whose village was on the bank of the Mississippi, opposite the lower end of Rock Island, and three miles distant from ours. We had about eight hundred acres in cultivation, including what we had on the islands of Rock river. The land around our village, uncultivated, was covered with blue-grass, which made excellent pasture for our horses. Several fine springs broke out of the bluff, near by, from which we were supplied with good water. The rapids of Rock river furnished us with an abundance of excellent fish, and the land, being good, never failed to produce good crops of corn, beans, pumpkins, and squashes. We always had plenty—our children never cried with hunger, nor our people were never in want. Here our village had stood for more than a hundred years, during all which time we were the undisputed possessors of the valley of the Mississippi, from the Ouisconsin to the Portage des Sioux, near the mouth of the Missouri, being about seven hundred miles in length.

At this time we had very little intercourse with the whites, except our traders. Our village was healthy, and there was no place in the country possessing such advantages, nor no hunting grounds better than those we had in possession. If another prophet had come to our village in those days, and told us what has since taken place, none of our people would have believed him! What! to be driven from our village and hunting grounds, and not even permitted to visit the graves of our forefathers, our relations, and friends?

This hardship is not known to the whites. With us it is a custom to visit the graves of our friends, and keep them in repair for many years. The mother will go alone to weep over the grave of her child! The brave, with pleasure, visits the grave of his father, after he has been successful in war, and re-paints the post that shows where he lies! There is no place like that where the bones of our forefathers lie, to go to when in grief. Here the Great Spirit will take pity on us!

But, how different is our situation now, from what it was in those days! Then were we as happy as the buffalo on the plains—but now, we are as miserable as the hungry, howling wolf in the prairie! But I am digressing from my story. Bitter reflection crowds upon my mind, and must find utterance.

When we returned to our village in the spring, from our wintering grounds, we would finish trading with our traders, who always followed us to our village. We purposely kept some of our fine furs for this trade; and, as there was great opposition among them, who should get these skins, we always got our goods cheap. After this trade was over, the traders would give us a few kegs of rum, which was generally promised in the fall, to encourage us to make a good hunt, and not go to war. They would then start with their furs and peltries for their homes.

Our old men would take a frolic, (at this time our young men never drank.) When this was ended, the next thing to be done was to bury our dead, (such as had died during the year.) This is a great *medicine feast*. The relations of those who have died, give all the goods they have purchased, as presents to their friends—thereby reducing themselves to poverty, to show the Great Spirit that they are humble, so that he will take pity on them. We would next open the caches, and take out corn and other provisions, which had been put up in the fall—and then commence repairing our lodges. As soon as this is accomplished, we repair the fences around our fields, and clean them off, ready for planting corn. This work is done by our women. The men, during this time, are feasting on dried venison, bear's meat, wild fowl, and corn, prepared in different ways; and recounting to each other what took place during the winter.

Our women plant the corn, and as soon as they get done, we make a feast, and dance the *crane* dance, in which they join us, dressed in their best, and decorated with feathers. At this feast our young braves select the young woman they wish to have for a wife. He then informs his mother, who calls on the mother of the girl, when the arrangement is made, and the time appointed for him to come. He goes to the lodge when all are asleep, (or pretend to be,) lights his matches, which have been provided for the purpose, and soon finds where his intended sleeps. He then awakens her, and holds the light to his face that she may know him—after which he places the light close to her. If she blows it out, the ceremony is ended, and he appears in the lodge the next morning, as one of the family. If she does not blow out the light, but leaves it to burn out, he retires from the lodge. The next day he places himself in full view of it, and plays his flute. The young women go out, one by one, to see who he is playing for. The tune changes, to let them know that he is not playing for them. When his intended makes her appearance at the door, he continues his *courting* tune, until she returns to the lodge. He then gives over playing, and makes another trial at night, which generally turns out favorable. During the first year they ascertain whether they can agree with each other, and can be happy—if not, they part, and each looks out again. If we were to live together and disagree, we should be as foolish as the whites! No indiscretion can banish a woman from her parental lodge—no difference how many children she may bring home, she is always welcome—the kettle is over the fire to feed them.

The crane dance often lasts two or three days. When this is over, we feast again, and have our *national* dance. The large square in the village is swept and prepared for the purpose. The chiefs and old warriors, take seats on mats, which have been spread at the upper end of the square—the drummers and singers come next, and the braves and women form the sides, leaving a large space in the middle. The drums beat, and the singers commence. A warrior enters the square, keeping time with the music. He shows the manner he started on a war party—how he approached the enemy—he strikes, and describes the way he killed him. All join in applause. He then leaves the square, and another enters and takes his place. Such of our young men as have not been out in war parties, and killed an enemy, stand back ashamed—not being able to enter the square. I remember that I was ashamed to look where our young women stood, before I could take my stand in the square as a warrior.

What pleasure it is to an old warrior, to see his son come forward and relate his exploits—it makes him feel young, and induces him to enter the square, and "fight his battles o'er again."

This national dance makes our warriors. When I was travelling last summer, on a steamboat, on a large river, going from New York to Albany, I was shown the place where the Americans dance their national dance [West Point]; where the old warriors recount to their young men, what they have done, to stimulate them to go and do likewise. This surprised me, as I did not think the whites understood our way of making braves.

When our national dance is over—our corn-fields hoed, and every weed dug up, and our corn about knee-high, all our young men would start in a direction towards sun-down, to hunt deer and buffalo—being prepared, also, to kill Sioux if any are found on our hunting grounds—a part of our old men and women to the lead mines to make lead—and the remainder of our people start to fish, and get mat stuff. Every one leaves the village, and remains about forty days. They then return: the hunting party bringing in dried buffalo and deer meat, and sometimes *Sioux scalps*, when they are found trespassing on our hunting grounds. At other times they are met by a party of Sioux too strong for them, and are driven in. If the Sioux have killed the Sacs last, they expect to be retaliated upon, and will fly before them, and vice versa. Each party knows that the other has a right to retaliate, which induces those who have killed last, to give way before their enemy—as neither wishes to strike, except to avenge the death of their relatives. All our wars are predicated by the relatives of those killed; or by aggressions upon our hunting grounds.

The party from the lead mines bring lead, and the others dried fish, and mats for our winter lodges. Presents are now made by each party; the first, giving to the others dried buffalo and deer, and they, in exchange, presenting them with lead, dried fish and mats. This is a happy season of the year—having plenty of provisions, such as beans, squashes, and other produce, with our dried meat and fish, we continue to make feasts and visit each other, until our corn is ripe. Some lodge in the village makes a feast daily, to the Great Spirit. I cannot explain this so that the white people would comprehend me, as we have no regular standard among us. Every one makes his feast as he thinks best, to please the Great Spirit, who has the care of all beings created. Others believe in two Spirits: one good and one bad, and make feasts for the Bad Spirit, *to keep him quiet*! If they can make peace with him, the Good Spirit will not hurt them! For my part, I am of the opinion, that so far as we have *reason*, we have a right to use it, in determining what is right or wrong; and should pursue that path which we believe to be right—believing, that "whatever is, is right." If the Great and Good Spirit wished us to believe and do as the whites, he could easily change our opinions, so that we would see, and think, and act as they do. We are *nothing* compared to His power, and we feel and know it. We have men among us, like the whites, who pretend to know the right path, but will not consent to show it without *pay*! I have no faith in their paths—but believe that every man must make his own path!

When our corn is getting ripe, our young people watch with anxiety for the signal to pull roasting-ears—as none dare touch them until the proper time. When the corn is fit to use, another great ceremony takes place, with feasting, and returning thanks to the Great Spirit for giving us corn.

I will here relate the manner in which corn first came. According to tradition, handed down to our people, a beautiful woman was seen to descend from the clouds, and alight upon the earth, by two of our ancestors, who had killed a deer, and were sitting by a fire, roasting a part of it to eat. They were astonished at seeing her, and concluded that she must be hungry, and had smelt the meat—and immediately went to her, taking with them a piece of the roasted venison. They presented it to her, and she ate—and told them to return to the spot where she was sitting, at the end of one year, and they would find a reward for their kindness and generosity. She then ascended to the clouds, and disappeared. The two men returned to their village, and explained to the nation what they had seen, done, and heard—but were laughed at by their people. When the period arrived, for them to visit this consecrated ground, where they were to find a reward for their attention to the beautiful woman of the clouds, they went with a large party, and found, where her right hand had rested on the ground, *corn* growing—and where the left hand had rested, *beans*, and immediately where she had been seated, *tobacco*.

The two first have, ever since, been cultivated by our people, as our principal provisions—and the last used for smoking. The white people have since found out the latter, and seem to relish it as much as we do—as they use it in different ways, viz. smoking, snuffing and eating!

We thank the Great Spirit for all the benefits he has conferred upon us. For myself, I never take a drink of water from a spring, without being mindful of his goodness.

We next have our great ball play—from three to five hundred on a side, play this game. We play for horses, guns, blankets, or any other kind of property we have. The successful party take the stakes, and all retire to our lodges in peace and friendship.

We next commence horse-racing, and continue our sport and feasting, until the corn is all secured. We then prepare to leave our village for our hunting grounds. The traders arrive, and give us credit for such articles as we want to clothe our families, and enable us to hunt. We first, however, hold a council with them, to ascertain the price they will give us for our skins, and what they will charge us for goods. We inform them where we intend hunting—and tell them where to build their houses. At this place, we deposit part of our corn, and leave our old people. The traders have always been kind to them, and relieved them when in want. They were always much respected by our people—and never since we have been a nation, has one of them been killed by our people.

We disperse, in small parties, to make our hunt, and as soon as it is over, we return to our traders' establishment, with our skins, and remain feasting, playing cards and other pastimes, until near the close of the winter. Our young men then start on the beaver hunt; others to hunt raccoons and muskrats—and the remainder of our people go to the sugar camps to make sugar. All leave our encampment, and appoint a place to meet on the Mississippi, so that we may return to our village together, in the spring. We always spent our time pleasantly at the sugar camp. It being the season for wild fowl, we lived well, and always had plenty, when the hunters came in, that we might make a feast for them. After this is over, we return to our village, accompanied, sometimes, by our traders. In this way, the year rolled round happily. But these are times that were!

I returned to my hunting ground, after an absence of one moon, and related what I had done. In a short time we came up to our village, and found that the whites had not left it—but that others had come, and that the greater part of our corn-fields had been enclosed. When we landed, the whites appeared displeased because we had come back. We repaired the lodges that had been left standing, and built others. Ke-o-kuck came to the village; but his object was to persuade others to follow him to the Ioway. He had accomplished nothing towards making arrangements for us to remain, or to exchange other lands for our village. There was no more friendship existing between us. I looked upon him as a coward, and no brave, to abandon his village to be occupied by strangers. What *right* had these people to our village, and our fields, which the Great Spirit had given us to live upon?

My reason teaches me that *land cannot be sold.* The Great Spirit gave it to his children to live upon, and cultivate, as far as is necessary for their subsistence; and so long as they occupy and cultivate it, they have the right to the soil—but if they voluntarily leave it, then any other people have a right to settle upon it. Nothing can be sold, but such things as can be carried away.

In consequence of the improvements of the intruders on our fields, we found considerable difficulty to get ground to plant a little corn. Some of the whites permitted us to plant small patches in the fields they had fenced, keeping all the best ground for themselves. Our women had great difficulty in climbing their fences, (being unaccustomed to the kind,) and were ill-treated if they left a rail down.

One of my old friends thought he was safe. His corn-field was on a small island of Rock river. He planted his corn; it came up well—but the white man saw it!—he wanted the island, and took his team over, ploughed up the corn, and replanted it for himself! The old man shed tears; not for himself, but the distress his family would be in if they raised no corn.

The white people brought whisky into our village, made our people drunk, and cheated them out of their horses, guns, and traps! This fraudulent system was carried to such an extent that I apprehended serious difficulties might take place, unless a stop was put to it. Consequently, I visited all the whites and begged them not to sell whisky to my people. One of them continued the practice openly. I took a party of my young men, went to his house, and took out his barrel and broke in the head and turned out the whisky. I did this for fear some of the whites might be killed by my people when drunk.

Our people were treated badly by the whites on many occasions. At one time, a white man beat one of our women cruelly, for pulling a few suckers of corn out of his field, to suck, when hungry! At another time, one of our young men was beat with clubs by two white men for opening a fence which crossed our road, to take his horse through. His shoulder blade was broken, and his body badly bruised, from which he soon after *died*!

Bad, and cruel, as our people were treated by the whites, not one of them was hurt or molested by any of my band. I hope this will prove that we are a peaceable people—having permitted ten men to take possession of our corn-fields; prevent us from planting corn; burn and destroy our lodges; ill-treat our women; and *beat to death* our men, without offering resistance to their barbarous cruelties. This is a lesson worthy for the white man to learn: to use forbearance when injured.

We acquainted our agent daily with our situation, and through him, the great chief at St. Louis—and hoped that something would be done for us. The whites were *complaining* at the same time that *we* were *intruding* upon *their rights!* THEY made themselves out the *injured* party, and *we* the *intruders!* and called loudly to the great war chief to protect *their* property.

How smooth must be the language of the whites, when they can make right look like wrong, and wrong like right.

During this summer, I happened at Rock Island, when a great chief arrived, whom I had known as the great chief of Illinois, [governor Cole] in company with another chief, who, I have been told, is a great writer [judge Jas. Hall.] I called upon them and begged to explain to them the grievances under which me and my people were laboring, hoping that they could do something for us. The great chief, however, did not seem disposed to council with me. He said he was no longer the great chief of Illinois—that his children had selected another father in his stead, and that he now only ranked as they did. I was surprised at this talk, as I had always heard that he was a good, brave, and great chief. But the white people never appear to be satisfied. When they get a good father, they hold councils, (at the suggestion of some bad, ambitious man, who wants the place himself,) and conclude, among themselves, that this man, or some other equally ambitious, would make a better father than they have, and nine times out of ten they don't get as good a one again.

I insisted on explaining to these two chiefs the true situation of my people. They gave their assent: I rose and made a speech, in which I explained to them the treaty made by Quash-qua-me, and three of our braves, according to the manner the trader and others had explained it to me. I then told them that Quash-qua-me and his party *denied*, positively, having ever sold my village; and that, as I had never known them to *lie*, I was determined to keep it in possession.

I told them that the white people had already entered our village, *burnt our lodges, destroyed our fences, ploughed up our corn, and beat our people*: that they had brought *whisky* into our country, *made our people drunk*, and taken from them their *horses*, *guns*, and *traps*; and that I had borne all this injury, without suffering any of my braves to raise a hand against the whites.

My object in holding this council, was to get the opinion of these two chiefs, as to the best course for me to pursue. I had appealed in vain, time after time, to our agent, who regularly represented our situation to the great chief at St. Louis, whose duty it was to call upon our Great Father to have justice done to us; but instead of this, we are told *that the white people want our country, and we must leave it to them!*

I did not think it possible that our Great Father wished us to leave our village, where we had lived so long, and where the bones of so many of our people had been laid. The great chief said that, as he was no longer a chief, he could do nothing for us; and felt sorry that it was not in his power to aid us—nor did he know how to advise us. Neither of them could do anything for us; but both evidently appeared very sorry. It would give me great pleasure, at all times, to take these two chiefs by the hand.

That fall I paid a visit to the agent, before we started to our hunting grounds, to hear if he had any good news for me. He had news! He said that

the land on which our village stood was now ordered to be sold to individuals; and that, when sold, *our right* to remain, by treaty, would be at an end,
and that if we returned next spring, we would be *forced* to remove!

We learned during the winter that *part* of the land where our village
stood had been sold to individuals, and that the *trader* at Rock Island had
bought the greater part that had been sold. The reason was now plain to
me, why *he* urged us to remove. His object, we thought, was to get our
lands. We held several councils that winter to determine what we should do,
and resolved, in one of them, to return to our village in the spring, as usual;
and concluded, that if we were removed by force, that the *trader*, agent, and
others, must be the cause; and that, if found guilty of having driven us from
our village, they should be *killed*! The trader stood foremost on this list. He
had purchased the land on which my lodge stood, and that of our *grave yard*
also! Ne-a-pope promised to kill him, the agent, interpreter, the great chief
at St. Louis, the war chief at fort Armstrong, Rock Island, and Ke-o-kuck—
these being the principal persons to blame for endeavoring to remove us.

Our women received bad accounts from the women that had been raising corn at the new village—the difficulty of breaking the new prairie with
hoes—and the small quantity of corn raised. We were nearly in the same situation with regard to the latter, it being the first time I ever knew our people to be in want of provision.

I prevailed upon some of Ke-o-kuck's band to return this spring to the
Rock river village. Ke-o-kuck would not return with us. I hoped that we
would get permission to go to Washington to settle our affairs with our
Great Father. I visited the agent at Rock Island. He was displeased because
we had returned to our village, and told me that we *must* remove to the west
of the Mississippi. I told him plainly that we *would not*! I visited the interpreter at his house, who advised me to do as the agent had directed me. I
then went to see the trader, and upbraided him for buying our lands. He
said that if he had not purchased them, some person else would, and that if
our Great Father would make an exchange with us, he would willingly give
up the land he had purchased to the government. This I thought was fair,
and began to think that he had not acted as badly as I had suspected. We
again repaired our lodges, and built others, as most of our village had been
burnt and destroyed. Our women selected small patches to plant corn,
(where the whites had not taken them within their fences,) and worked
hard to raise something for our children to subsist upon.

I was told that, according to the treaty, we had no *right* to remain upon
the lands *sold*, and that the government would *force* us to leave them. There
was but a small portion, however, that *had been sold*; the balance remaining
in the hands of the government, we claimed the right (if we had no other)
to "live and hunt upon, as long as it remained the property of the government," by a stipulation in the same treaty that required us to evacuate it *after* it had been sold. This was the land that we wished to inhabit, and
thought we had the best right to occupy.

I heard that there was a great chief on the Wabash, and sent a party to get his advice. They informed him that we had not sold our village. He assured them then, that if we had not sold the land on which our village stood, our Great Father would not take it from us.

I started early to Maiden to see the chief of my British Father, and told him my story. He gave the same reply that the chief on the Wabash had given; and in justice to him, I must say, that he never gave me any bad advice: but advised me to apply to our American Father, who, he said, would do us justice. I next called on the great chief at Detroit, and made the same statement to him that I had to the chief of our British Father. He gave the same reply. He said, if we had not sold our lands, and would remain peaceably on them, that we would not be disturbed. This assured me that I was right, and determined me to hold out, as I had promised my people.

I returned from Maiden late in the fall. My people were gone to their hunting ground, whither I followed. Here I learned that they had been badly treated all summer by the whites; and that a treaty had been held at Prairie du Chien. Ke-o-kuck and some of our people attended it, and found out that our Great Father had exchanged a small strip of the land that was ceded by Quàsh-quà-me and his party, with the Pottowatomies, for a portion of their land, near Chicago; and that the object of this treaty was to get it back again; and that the United States had agreed to give them *sixteen thousand dollars a year forever*, for this small strip of land—it being less than the twentieth part of that taken from our nation, for *one thousand dollars a year*! This bears evidence of something I cannot explain. This land, they say, belonged to the United States. What reason, then, could have induced them to exchange it with the Pottowatomies, if it was so valuable? Why not keep it? Or, if they found they had made a bad bargain with the Pottowatomies, why not take back their land at a fair proportion of what they gave our nation for it? If this small portion of the land that they took from us for *one thousand dollars* a year, be worth *sixteen thousand dollars a year forever*, to the Pottowatomies, then the whole tract of country taken from us ought to be worth, to our nation, *twenty times* as much as this small fraction.

Here I was again puzzled to find out how the white people reasoned; and began to doubt whether they had any standard of right and wrong!

Communication was kept up between myself and the Prophet. Runners were sent to the Arkansas, Red river and Texas—not on the subject of our lands, but a secret mission, which I am not, at present, permitted to explain.

It was related to me, that the chiefs and headmen of the Foxes had been invited to Prairie du Chien, to hold a council to settle the difficulties existing between them and the Sioux. That the chiefs and head men, amounting to *nine*, started for the place designated, taking with them one woman—and were met by the Menomonees and Sioux, near the Ouisconsin and all *killed*, except one man. Having understood that the whole matter was published shortly after it occurred, and is known to the white people, I will say no more about it.

I would here remark, that our pastimes and sports had been laid aside for the last two years. We were a divided people, forming two parties. Ke-o-kuck being at the head of one, willing to barter our rights merely for the good opinion of the whites; and cowardly enough to desert our village to them. I was at the head of the other party, and was determined to hold on to my village, although I had been *ordered* to leave it. But, I considered, as myself and band had no agency in selling our country—and that as provision had been made in the treaty, for us all to remain on it as long as it belonged to the United States, that we could not be *forced* away. I refused, therefore, to quit my village. It was here, that I was born—and here lie the bones of many friends and relations. For this spot I felt a sacred reverence, and never could consent to leave it, without being forced therefrom.

When I called to mind the scenes of my youth, and those of later days—and reflected that the theatre on which these were acted, had been so long the home of my fathers, who now slept on the hills around it, I could not bring my mind to consent to leave this country to the whites, for any earthly consideration.

The winter passed off in gloom. We made a bad hunt, for want of the guns, traps, &c. that the whites had taken from our people for whisky! The prospect before us was a bad one. I fasted, and called upon the Great Spirit to direct my steps to the right path. I was in great sorrow—because all the whites with whom I was acquainted, and had been on terms of friendship, advised me so contrary to my wishes, that I begun to doubt whether I had a *friend* among them.

Ke-o-kuck, who has a smooth tongue, and is a great speaker, was busy in persuading my band that I was wrong—and thereby making many of them dissatisfied with me. I had one consolation—for all the women were on my side, on account of their corn-fields.

On my arrival again at my village, with my band increased, I found it worse than before. I visited Rock Island. The agent again ordered me to quit my village. He said, that if we did not, troops would be sent to drive us off. He reasoned with me, and told me, it would be better for us to be with the rest of our people, so that we might avoid difficulty, and live in peace. The *interpreter* joined him, and gave me so many good reasons, that I almost wished I had not undertaken the difficult task that I had pledged myself to my brave band to perform. In this mood, I called upon the *trader*, who is fond of talking, and had long been my friend, but now amongst those advising me to give up my village. He received me very friendly, and went on to defend Ke-o-kuck in what he had done, and endeavored to show me that I was bringing distress on our women and children. He inquired, if some terms could not be made, that would be honorable to me, and satisfactory to my braves, for us to remove to the west side of the Mississippi? I replied, that if our Great Father could do us justice, and would make the proposition, I could then give up honorably. He asked me, "if the great chief at St. Louis would give us six thousand dollars, to purchase provisions and other articles, if I would give up peaceably, and remove to the west side of the Mississippi?" After thinking some time, I agreed that I could honorably give up, by being paid for it, according to our customs; but told him, that I could not make the proposal myself, even if I wished, because it would be dishonorable in me to do so. He said he would do it, by sending word to the great chief at St. Louis, that he could remove us peaceably, for the amount stated, to the west side of the Mississippi. A steam boat arrived at the island during my stay. After its departure, the *trader* told me that he had "requested a war chief, who was stationed at Galena, and was on board of the steam boat, to make the offer to the great chief at St. Louis, and that he would soon be back, and bring his answer." I did not let my people know what had taken place, for fear they would be displeased. I did not much like what had been done myself, and tried to banish it from my mind.

After a few days had passed, the war chief returned, and brought for answer, that "the great chief at St. Louis would give us *nothing*!—and said if we did not remove immediately, we should be *drove off*!"

I was not much displeased with the answer brought by the war chief, because I would rather have laid my bones with my forefathers, than remove for any consideration. Yet if a friendly offer had been made, as I expected, I would, for the sake of my women and children, have removed peaceably.

I now resolved to remain in my village, and make no resistance, if the military came, but submit to my fate! I impressed the importance of this course on all my band, and directed them, in case the military came, not to raise an arm against them.

About this time, our agent was put out of office—for what reason, I never could ascertain. I then thought, if it was for wanting to make us leave our village, it was right—because I was tired of hearing him talk about it. The interpreter, who had been equally as bad in trying to persuade us to leave our village, was retained in office—and the young man who took the place of our agent, told the same old story over, about removing us. I was then satisfied, that this could not have been the cause.

Our women had planted a few patches of com, which was growing finely, and promised a subsistence for our children—but the *white people again commenced ploughing it up*! I now determined to put a stop to it, by clearing our country of the *intruders*. I went to the principal men and told them, that they must and should leave our country—and gave them until the middle of the next day, to remove in. The worst left within the time appointed—but the one who remained, represented, that his family, (which was large,) would be in a starving condition, if he went and left his crop— and promised to behave well, if I would consent to let him remain until fall, in order to secure his crop. He spoke reasonably, and I consented.

We now resumed some of our games and pastimes—having been assured by the prophet that we would not be removed. But in a little while it was ascertained, that a great war chief, [Gen. Gaines,] with a large number of soldiers, was on his way to Rock river. I again called upon the prophet, who requested a little time to see into the matter. Early next morning he came to me, and said he had been *dreaming*! "That he saw nothing bad in this great war chief, [Gen. Gaines,] who was now near Rock river. That the *object* of his mission was to *frighten* us from our village, that the white people might get our land for *nothing*!" He assured us that this "great war chief dare not, and would not, hurt any of us. That the Americans were at peace with the British, and when they made peace, the British required, (which the Americans agreed to,) that they should never interrupt any nation of Indians that was at peace—and that all we had to do to retain our village, was to *refuse* any, and every offer that might be made by this war chief."

The war chief arrived, and convened a council, at the agency. Ke-o-kuck and Wà-pel-lo were sent for, and came with a number of their band. The council house was opened, and they were all admitted. Myself and band were then sent for to attend the council. When we arrived at the door, singing a *war song*, and armed with lances, spears, war clubs and bows and arrows, as if going to battle, I halted, and refused to enter—as I could see no necessity or propriety in having the room crowded with those who were already there. If the council was convened for us, why have others there in our room? The war chief having sent all out, except Ke-o-kuck, Wà-pel-lo, and a few of their chiefs and braves, we entered the council house, in this war-like appearance, being desirous to show the war chief that we were *not afraid*! He then rose and made a speech.

He said:

"The president is very sorry to be put to the trouble and expense of sending a large body of soldiers here, to remove you from the lands you have long since ceded to the United States. Your Great Father has already warned you repeatedly, through your agent, to leave the country; and he is very sorry to find that you have disobeyed his orders. Your Great Father wishes you well; and asks nothing from you but what is reasonable and right. I hope you will consult your own interest, and leave the country you are occupying, and go to the other side of the Mississippi."

I replied: "That *we* had never sold our country. *We* never received any annuities from our American father! and *we* are determined to hold on to our village!"

The war chief, apparently angry, rose and said:—"Who is *Black Hawk*? Who is *Black Hawk*?"

I responded: "I am a *Sac*! My forefather was a SAC! and all the nations call me a SAC!!"

The war chief said:

"I came here, neither to *beg* nor *hire* you to leave your village. My business is to remove you, peaceably if I can, but *forcibly* if I must! I will now give you two days to remove in—and if you do not cross the Mississippi within that time, I will adopt measures to *force* you away!"

I told him that I never could consent to leave my village, and was determined not to leave it!

The council broke up, and the war chief retired to the fort. I consulted the prophet again! He said "he had been dreaming, and that the Great Spirit had directed that a woman, the daughter of Mat-ta-tas, the old chief of the village, should take a stick in her hand and go before the war chief, and tell him that she is the daughter of Mat-ta-tas, and that he had always been the *white man's friend*! That he had fought their battles—been wounded in their service—and had always spoke well of them—and she had never heard him say that he had sold their village. The whites are numerous, and can take it from us if they choose, but she hoped they would not be so unfriendly. If they were, she had one favor to ask: she wished her people to be allowed to remain long enough to gather the provisions now growing in their fields: that she was a woman, and had worked hard to raise something to support her children! And, if we are driven from our village without being allowed to save our corn, many of our little children must perish with hunger!"

Accordingly, Mat-ta-tas' daughter was sent to the fort, accompanied by several of our young men. They were admitted. She went before the war chief, and told the story of the prophet! The war chief said that the president did not send him here to make treaties with the women, nor to hold council with them! That our young men must leave the fort, but she might remain if she wished!

All our plans were now defeated. We must cross the river, or return to our village and await the coming of the war chief with his soldiers....

We had been here but a little while, before we saw a steam boat (the "Warrior,") coming. I told my braves not to shoot, as I intended going on board, so that we might save our women and children. I knew the captain, [THROCKMORTON,] and was determined to give myself up to him. I then sent for my *white flag*. While the messenger was gone, I took a small piece of white cotton, and put it on a pole, and called to the captain of the boat, and told him to send his little canoe ashore, and let me come on board. The people on board asked whether we were Sacs or Winnebagoes. I told a Winnebago to tell them that we were Sacs, and wanted to give ourselves up! A Winnebago on the boat called out to us "*to run and hide, that the whites were going to shoot!*" About this time one of my braves had jumped into the river, bearing a white flag to the boat—when another sprang in after him and brought him to the shore. The firing then commenced from the boat, which was returned by my braves, and continued for some time. Very few of my people were hurt after the first fire, having succeeded in getting behind old logs and trees, which shielded them from the enemy's fire.

The Winnebago, on the steam boat must either have misunderstood what was told, or did not tell it to the captain correctly; because I am confident that he would not have fired upon us, if he had known my wishes. I have always considered him a good man, and too great a brave to fire upon an enemy when suing for quarters.

After the boat left us, I told my people to cross, if they could, and wished: that I intended going into the Chippewa country. Some commenced crossing, and such as had determined to follow them, remained—only three lodges going with me. Next morning, at daybreak, a young man overtook me, and said that all my party had determined to cross the Mississippi—that a number had already got over safe, and that he had heard the white army last night within a few miles of them. I now began to fear that the whites would come up with my people, and kill them, before they could get across. I had determined to go and join the Chippewas; but reflecting that by this I could only save myself, I concluded to return, and die with my people, if the Great Spirit would not give us another victory! During our stay in the thicket, a party of whites came close by us, but passed on without discovering us.

Early in the morning a party of whites, being in advance of the army, came upon our people, who were attempting to cross the Mississippi. They tried to give themselves-up—the whites paid no attention to their entreaties—but commenced *slaughtering* them! In a little while the whole army arrived. Our braves, but few in number, finding that the enemy paid no regard to age or sex, and seeing that they were murdering helpless women and little children, determined to *fight until they were killed*! As many women as could, commenced swimming the Mississippi, with their children on their backs. A number of them were drowned, and some shot, before they could reach the opposite shore.

One of my braves, who gave me this information, piled up some saddles before him, (when the fight commenced,) to shield himself from the enemy's fire, and killed three white men! But seeing that the whites were coming too close to him, he crawled to the bank of the river, without being perceived, and hid himself under it, until the enemy retired. He then came to me and told me what had been done. After hearing this sorrowful news, I started, with my little party, to the Winnebago village at Prairie La Cross. On my arrival there, I entered the lodge of one of the chiefs, and told him that I wished him to go with me to his father—that I intended to give myself up to the American war chief, and *die*, if the Great Spirit saw proper! He said he would go with me. I then took my *medicine bag*, and addressed the chief. I told him that it was "the soul of the Sac nation—that it never had been dishonored in any battle—take it, it is my life—dearer than life—and give it to the American chief!" He said he would keep it, and take care of it, and if I was suffered to live, he would send it to me.

During my stay at the village, the squaws made me a white dress of deer skin. I then started, with several Winnebagoes, and went to their agent, at Prairie du Chien, and gave myself up.

On my arrival there, I found to my sorrow, that a large body of Sioux had pursued, and killed, a number of our women and children, who had got safely across the Mississippi. The whites ought not to have permitted such conduct—and none but *cowards* would ever have been guilty of such cruelty—which has always been practiced on our nation by the Sioux.

The massacre, which terminated the war, lasted about two hours. Our loss in killed, was about sixty, besides a number that were drowned. The loss of the enemy could not be ascertained by my braves, exactly; but they think that they killed about *sixteen*, during the action.

I was now given up by the agent to the commanding officer at fort Crawford (the White Beaver having gone down the river.) We remained here a short time, and then started to Jefferson Barracks, in a steam boat, under the charge of a young war chief, [Lieut. Jefferson Davis] who treated us all with much kindness. He is a good and brave young chief, with whose conduct I was much pleased. On our way down, we called at Galena, and remained a short time. The people crowded to the boat to see us; but the war chief would not permit them to enter the apartment where we were—knowing, from what his own feelings would have been, if he had been placed in a similar situation, that we did not wish to have a gaping crowd around us.

We passed Rock Island, without stopping. The great war chief, [Gen. Scott,] who was then at fort Armstrong, came out in a small boat to see us; but the captain of the steam boat would not allow any body from the fort to come on board of his boat, in consequence of the cholera raging among the soldiers. I did think that the captain ought to have permitted the war chief to come on board to see me, because I could see no danger to be apprehended by it. The war chief looked well, and I have since heard, was constantly among his soldiers, who were sick and dying, administering to their wants, and had not caught the disease from them—and I thought it absurd to think that any of the people on the steam boat could be afraid of catching the disease from a *well* man. But these people have not got bravery like war chiefs, who never *fear* any thing!

On our way down, I surveyed the country that had cost us so much trouble, anxiety, and blood, and that now caused me to be a prisoner of war. I reflected upon the ingratitude of the whites, when I saw their fine houses, rich harvests, and every thing desirable around them; and recollected that all this land had been ours, for which me and my people had never received a dollar, and that the whites were not satisfied until they took our village and our grave-yards from us, and removed us across the Mississippi.

On our arrival at Jefferson Barracks, we met the great war chief, [White Beaver,] who had commanded the American army against my little band. I felt the humiliation of my situation; a little while before, I had been the leader of my braves, now I was a prisoner of war! but had surrendered myself. He received us kindly, and treated us well.

We were now confined to the barracks, and forced to wear the *ball and chain*! This was extremely mortifying, and altogether useless. Was the White Beaver afraid I would break out of his barracks, and run away? Or was he ordered to inflict this punishment upon me? If I had taken him prisoner on the field of battle, I would not have wounded his feelings so much, by such treatment—knowing that a brave war chief would prefer *death* to *dishonor*! But I do not blame the White Beaver for the course he pursued—it is the custom among white soldiers, and, I suppose, was a part of his duty.

The time dragged heavily and gloomy along throughout the winter, although the White Beaver done every thing in his power to render us comfortable. Having been accustomed, throughout a long life, to roam the forests o'er—to go and come at liberty-confinement, and under such circumstances, could not be less than torture!

We passed away the time making pipes, until spring, when we were visited by the agent, trader, and interpreter, from Rock Island, Ke-o-kuck, and several chiefs and braves of our nation, and my wife and daughter. I was rejoiced to see the two latter, and spent my time very agreeably with them and my people, as long as they remained.

The trader presented me with some dried venison, which had been killed and cured by some of my friends. This was a valuable present; and although he had given me many before, none ever pleased me so much. This was the first meat I had eaten for a long time, that reminded me of the former pleasures of my own wigwam, which had always been stored with plenty.

Ke-o-kuck and his chiefs, during their stay at the barracks, petitioned our Great Father, the President, to release us; and pledged themselves for our good conduct. I now began to hope that I would soon be restored to liberty, and the enjoyment of my family and friends; having heard that Ke-o-kuck stood high in the estimation of our Great Father, because he did not join me in the war. But I was soon disappointed in my hopes. An order came from our Great Father to the White Beaver, to send us on to Washington....

On our arrival at Washington, we called to see our Great Father, the President. He looks as if he had seen as many winters as I have, and seems to be a *great brave*! I had very little talk with him, as he appeared to be busy, and did not seem to be much disposed to talk. I think he is a good man; and although he talked but little, he treated us very well. His wigwam is well furnished with every thing good and pretty, and is very strongly built.

He said he wished to know the *cause* of my going to war against his white children. I thought he ought to have known this before; and, consequently, said but little to him about it—as I expected he knew as well as I could tell him.

He said he wanted us to go to fortress Monroe, and stay awhile with the war chief who commanded it. But, having been so long from my people, I told him that I would rather return to my nation—that Ke-o-kuck had come here once on a visit to see him, as we had done, and he had let him return again, as soon as he wished; and that I expected to be treated in the same way. He insisted, however, on our going to fortress Monroe; and as our interpreter could not understand enough of our language to interpret a speech, I concluded it was best to obey our Great Father, and say nothing contrary to his wishes.

During our stay at the city, we were called upon by many of the people, who treated us well, particularly the squaws! We visited the great *council house* of the Americans—the place where they keep their *big guns*—and all the public buildings, and then started to fortress Monroe. The war chief met us, on our arrival, and shook hands, and appeared glad to see me. He treated us with great friendship, and talked to me frequently. Previous to our leaving this fort, he gave us a feast, and made us some presents, which I intend to keep for his sake. He is a very good man, and a great *brave*! I was sorry to leave him, although I was going to return to my people, because he had treated me like a brother, during all the time I remained with him.

Having got a new guide, a war chief, [Maj. Garland,] we started for our own country, taking a circuitous route. Our Great Father being about to pay a visit to his children in the *big towns* towards sunrising, and being desirous that we should have an opportunity of seeing them, directed our guide to take us through.

On our arrival at Baltimore, we were much astonished to see so large a village; but the war chief told us we would soon see a *larger one*. This surprised us more. During our stay here, we visited all the public buildings and places of amusement—saw much to admire, and were well entertained by the people, who crowded to see us. Our Great Father was there at the same time, and seemed to be much liked by his white children, who flocked around him, (as they had done us,) to shake him by the hand. He did not remain long—having left the city before us.

We left Baltimore in a steam boat, and travelled in this way to the big village, where they make *medals* and *money*, [Philadelphia.] We again expressed surprise at finding this village so much larger than the one we had left; but the war chief again told us, that we would see another much larger than this. I had no idea that the white people had such large villages, and so many people. They were very kind to us—showed us all their great public works, their ships and steam boats. We visited the place where they make money, [the mint] and saw the men engaged at it. They presented each of us with a number of pieces of the *coin* as they fell from the mint, which are very handsome.

I witnessed a militia training in this city, in which were performed a number of singular military feats. The chiefs and men were well dressed, and exhibited quite a warlike appearance. I think our system of military parade far better than that of the whites—but, as I am now done going to war, I will not describe it, or say any thing more about war, or the preparations necessary for it.

We next started to New York, and on our arrival near the wharf, saw a large collection of people gathered at Castle-Garden. We had seen many wonderful sights in our way—large villages, the great *national road* over the mountains, the *railroads*, steam carriages, ships, steam boats and many other things; but we were now about to witness a sight more surprising than any of these. We were told that a man was going up into the air in a balloon! We watched with anxiety to see if it could be true; and to our utter astonishment, saw him ascend in the air until the eye could no longer perceive him. Our people were all surprised, and one of our young men asked the *prophet* if he was going up to see the Great Spirit?

After the ascension of the balloon, we landed, and got into a carriage, to go to the house that had been provided for our reception. We had proceeded but a short distance, before the street was so crowded that it was impossible for the carriage to pass. The war chief then directed the coachman to take another street, and stop at a different house from the one we had intended. On our arrival here, we were waited upon by a number of gentlemen, who seemed much pleased to see us. We were furnished with good rooms, good provisions, and every thing necessary for our comfort.

The chiefs of this *big village*, being desirous that all their people should have an opportunity to see us, fitted up their great *council house* for this purpose, where we saw an immense number of people; all of whom treated us with great friendship, and many with great generosity.

The chiefs were particular in showing us every thing that they thought would be pleasing or gratifying to us. We went with them to Castle-Garden to see the fire-works, which was quite an agreeable entertainment—but to the *whites* who witnessed it, less *magnificent* than the sight of one of our large *prairies* would be when on fire.

We visited all the public buildings and places of amusement, which to us were truly astonishing, yet very gratifying.

Every body treated us with friendship, and many with great liberality. The squaws presented us many handsome little presents, that are said to be valuable. They were very kind, very good, and very pretty—for *pale-faces!*

Among the men who treated us with marked friendship, by the presentation of many valuable, presents, I cannot omit to mention the name of my old friend CROOKS, of the American Fur Company. I have known him long, and have always found him to be a good chief—one who gives good advice, and treats our people right. I shall always be proud to recognize him as a friend, and glad to shake him by the hand.

Having seen all the wonders of this *big village*, and being anxious to return to our people, our guide started with us for our own country. On arriving at Albany, the people were so anxious to see us, that they crowded the streets and wharves, where the steam boat landed, so much, that it was almost impossible for us to pass to the hotel which had been provided for our reception.

We remained here but a short time, and then started for Detroit. I had spent many pleasant days at this place; and anticipated, on my arrival, to meet many of my old friends—but in this I was disappointed. What could be the cause of this? Are they all dead? Or what has become of them? I did not see our old father there, who had always given me good advice, and treated me with great friendship.

After leaving Detroit, it was but a few days before we landed at Prairie du Chien. The war chief at the fort treated us very kindly, as did the people generally. I called on the father of the Winnebagoes, [Gen. J. M. Street,] to whom I had surrendered myself after the battle of the Bad Axe, who received me very friendly. I told him that I had left my great *medicine bag* with his chiefs before I gave myself up; and now, that I was to enjoy my liberty again, I was anxious to get it, that I might hand it down to my nation unsullied.

He said it was safe; he had heard his chiefs speak of it, and would get it and send it to me. I hope he will not forget his promise, as the whites generally do—because I have always heard that he was a good man, and a good father—and made no promise that he did not fulfill.

Passing down the Mississippi, I discovered a large collection of people in the mining country, on the west side of the river, *and on the ground that we had given to our relation*, DUBUQUE, *a long time ago*. I was surprised at this, as I had understood from our Great Father, that the Mississippi was to be the dividing line between his red and white children, and that he did not wish *either* to *cross it*. I was much pleased with this talk, as I knew it would be much better for both parties. I have since found the country much settled by the whites further down, and near to our people, on the west side of the river. I am very much afraid, that in a few years, they will begin to drive and abuse our people, as they have formerly done. I may not live to *see* it, but I feel certain that the day is not distant. . . .

During my travels, my opinions were asked on different subjects—but for want of a good interpreter, were very seldom given. Presuming that they would be equally acceptable now, I have thought it a part of my duty, to lay the most important before the public.

The subject of colonizing the *negroes* was introduced, and my opinion asked, as to the best method of getting clear of these people. I was not pre-pared at the time, to answer—as I knew but little about their situation. I have since made many inquiries on the subject—and find that a number of states admit no slaves, whilst the balance hold these negroes as slaves, and are anxious, but do not know, how to get clear of them. I will now give my plan, which, when understood, I hope will be adopted.

Let the free states remove all the *male* negroes within their limits, to the slave states—then let our Great Father buy all the *female* negroes in the slave states, between the ages of twelve and twenty, and sell them to the people of the free states, for a term of years—say, those under fifteen until they are twenty-one—and those of, and over fifteen, for five years—and continue to buy all the females in the slave states, as soon as they arrive at the age of twelve, and take them to the free states, and dispose of them in the same way as the first—and it will not be long before the country is clear of the *black skins*, about which, I am told, they have been talking, for a long time; and for which they have expended a large amount of money.

I have no doubt but our Great Father would willingly do his part in accomplishing this object for his children—as he could not lose much by it, and would make them all happy. If the free states did not want them all for servants, we would take the balance in our nation, to help our women make corn!

I have not time now, nor is it necessary, to enter more into detail about my travels through the United States. The white people know all about them, and my people have started to their hunting grounds, and I am anx-ious to follow them.

Before I take leave of the public, I must contradict the story of some of *village criers*, who (I have been told,) accuse me of "having murdered women and children among the whites!" This assertion is *false*! I never did, nor have

I any knowledge that any of my nation ever killed a white woman or child. I make this statement of truth, to satisfy the white people among whom I have been travelling, (and by whom I have been treated with great kindness,) that, when they shook me by the hand so cordially, they did not shake the hand that had ever been raised against any but warriors.

It has always been our custom to receive all strangers that come to our village or camps, in time of peace, to share with them the best provisions we have, and give them all the assistance in our power. If on a journey, or lost, to put them on the right trail, and if in want of moccasins, to supply them. I feel grateful to the whites for the kind manner they treated me and my party, whilst travelling among them—and from my heart I assure them, that the white man will always be welcome in our village or camps, as a brother. The tomahawk is buried forever! We will forget what has passed—and may the watchword between the Americans and the Sacs and Foxes, ever be—*"Friendship!"*

I am now done. A few more moons, and I must follow my fathers to the shades! May the Great Spirit keep our people and the whites always at peace—is the sincere wish of

Black Hawk

1833

▪ Seattle (Duwamish) ▪
1786–1866

Seattle (or Seathl) was chief of the Duwamish and Suquamish tribes. Converted by Catholic missionaries in the 1830s, he was a powerful leader of Indian peoples in the Puget Sound area and supported peaceful coexistence with Anglo-American settlers. Shortly after the Washington Territory was organized in 1853, the new governor, Isaac Stevens, visited the tribes to discuss treaty arrangements. Seattle's speech was a formal response to that of Stevens. In 1887, Dr. Henry A. Smith, who attended the meeting, published the speech from what he claimed were his notes taken at the time. Smith professed to understand the Suquamish language, though later commentators have questioned his linguistic capabilities; in any case, Smith himself suggested that his rendition of whatever Seattle said was a pale shade of the original. Thus the authenticity of "Chief Seattle's speech" has been in question since it was first printed more than thirty years after the event.

The problem was further compounded a century later when other versions of a supposed speech by Seattle were fabricated, first by the poet William Arrowsmith during the 1960s and later by a script writer, Ted Perry, in the 1970s. Perry's version was widely circulated, primarily because it placed into Seattle's mouth sentiments popular in environmentalist circles. The speech has thus become a particularly vivid example of the problem of authenticity in dealing with many supposedly Indian texts, including famous ones like those of Black Hawk and Black Elk. Are these the words of Indian orators, or are they what white auditors wish to have heard, or thought they did hear, coming, often many years before, from an Indian speaker ... or, in fact, from a translator? There are no easy answers to such questions, and they have been extensively debated (on the Internet as well as in scholarly publications).

In the present instance, it is reasonably clear that Seattle delivered a speech on the stated occasion and he was a powerful orator and an imposing presence, and it is likely that some or much of what he said is contained in Smith's version. It is also true, perhaps ironically, that authentic or not, this speech has become a part of "Indian" culture, referred to, quoted, and used by Native American as well as white writers. This is not without reason, for the speech may profitably be compared with Lincoln's Gettysburg Address or his Second Inaugural—other, perhaps more familiar, reflections on the costs of history. Though the "vanishing Indian" was a common theme in the popular arts of the nineteenth century, as well as an expression of a politically expedient ideology, the speech penetrates to the genocidal guilt behind that image, a motivation well articulated in the twentieth century by D. H. Lawrence and William Faulkner.

In 1855 Seattle signed the Port Elliot Treaty, which confined his and other Washington tribes to a reservation. The city of Seattle is, of course, named after him, though he strongly objected to that appropriation of a part of himself and appears, thereafter, to have preferred not to use the name—though that story, too, may be a part of the complex legend that has been constructed about this man.

Andrew O. Wiget
New Mexico University

Paul Lauter
Trinity College

PRIMARY WORKS

Dr. Henry A. Smith, "Early Reminiscences," Seattle *Sunday Star*, October 29, 1887; W. C. Vanderwerth, *Indian Oratory*, 1971.

Speech of Chief Seattle

Yonder sky that has wept tears of compassion upon my people for centuries untold, and which to us appears changeless and eternal, may change. Today is fair. Tomorrow it may be overcast with clouds. My words are like the stars that never change. Whatever Seattle says the great chief at Washington can rely upon with as much certainty as he can upon the return of the sun or the seasons. The White Chief says that Big Chief at Washington sends us greetings of friendship and goodwill. This is kind of him for we know he has little need of our friendship in return. His people are many. They are like the grass that covers vast prairies. My people are few. They resemble the scattering trees of a storm-swept plain. The great—and I presume—good White Chief sends us word that he wishes to buy our lands but is willing to allow us enough to live comfortably. This indeed appears just, even generous, for the Red Man no longer has rights that he need respect, and the offer may be wise also, as we are no longer in need of an extensive country.

There was a time when our people covered the land as the waves of a wind-ruffled sea cover its shell paved floor, but that time long since passed away with the greatness of tribes that are now but a mournful memory. I will not dwell on, nor mourn over, our untimely decay, nor reproach my paleface brothers with hastening it as we too may have been somewhat to blame.

Youth is impulsive. When our young men grow angry at some real or imaginary wrong, and disfigure their faces with black paint, it denotes that their hearts are black, and that they are often cruel and relentless, and our old men and old women are unable to restrain them. Thus it has ever been. Thus it was when the white man first began to push our forefathers westward. But let us hope that the hostilities between us may never return. We would have everything to lose and nothing to gain. Revenge by young men is considered gain, even at the cost of their own lives, but old men who stay at home in times of war, and mothers who have sons to lose, know better.

Our good father at Washington—for I presume he is now our father as well as yours, since King George has moved his boundaries further north—our great and good father, I say, sends us word that if we do as he desires he will protect us. His brave warriors will be to us a bristling wall of strength, and his wonderful ships of war will fill our harbors so that our ancient enemies far to the northward—the Hydas and Tsimpsians—will cease to frighten our women, children, and old men. Then in reality will he be our father and we his children. But can that ever be? Your God is not our God! Your God loves your people and hates mine. He folds his strong protecting arms lovingly about the pale face and leads him by the hand as a father leads his infant son—but He has forsaken His red children—if they really are His. Our God, the Great Spirit, seems also to have forsaken us. Your God makes your people wax strong every day. Soon they will fill all the land. Our people are ebbing away like a rapidly receding tide that will never return. The white man's God cannot love our people or He would protect them. They seem to be orphans who can look nowhere for help. How then can we be brothers? How can your God become our God and renew our prosperity and awaken in us dreams of returning greatness. If we have a common heavenly father He must be partial—for He came to His paleface children. We never saw Him. He gave you laws but had no word for his red children whose teeming multitudes once filled this vast continent as stars fill the firmament. No; we are two distinct races with separate origins and separate destinies. There is little in common between us.

To us the ashes of our ancestors are sacred and their resting place is hallowed ground. You wander far from the graves of your ancestors and seemingly without regret. Your religion was written upon tables of stone by the iron finger of your God so that you could not forget. The Red Man could never comprehend nor remember it. Our religion is the traditions of our ancestors—the dreams of our old men, given them in the solemn hours of night by the Great Spirit; and the visions of our sachems, and is written in the hearts of our people.

Your dead cease to love you and the land of their nativity as soon as they pass the portals of the tomb and wander way beyond the stars. They are soon forgotten and never return. Our dead never forget the beautiful world that gave them being. They still love its verdant valleys, its murmuring rivers, its magnificent mountains, sequestered vales and verdant lined lakes and bays, and ever yearn in tender, fond affection over the lonely hearted living, and often return from the Happy Hunting Ground to visit, guide, console and comfort others.

Day and night cannot dwell together. The Red Man has ever fled the approach of the White Man, as the morning mist flees before the morning sun.

However, your proposition seems fair and I think that my people will accept it and will retire to the reservation you offer them. Then we will dwell in peace, for the words of the Great White Chief seem to be the words of nature speaking to my people out of dense darkness.

It matters little where we pass the remnant of our days. They will not be many. The Indians' night promises to be dark. Not a single star of hope hovers above his horizon. Sad-voiced winds moan in the distance. Grim fate seems to be on the Red Man's trail, and wherever he goes he will hear the approaching footsteps of his fell destroyer and prepare stolidly to meet his doom, as does the wounded doe that hears the approaching footsteps of the hunter.

A few more moons. A few more winters—and not one of the descendants of the mighty hosts that once moved over his broad land or lived in happy homes, protected by the Great Spirit, will remain to mourn over the graves of a people—once more powerful and hopeful than yours. But why should I mourn at the untimely fate of my people? Tribe follows tribe, and nation follows nation, like the waves of the sea. It is the order of nature, and regret is useless. Your time of decay may be distant, but it will surely come, for even the White Man whose God walked and talked with him as friend with friend, cannot be exempt from the common destiny. We may be brothers after all. We will see.

We will ponder your proposition and when we decide will let you know. But should we accept it, I here and now make this condition that we will not be denied the privilege without molestation of visiting at any time the tombs of our ancestors, friends and children. Every part of this soil is sacred in the estimation of my people. Every hillside, every valley, every plain and grove, has been hallowed by some sad or happy event in days long vanished. Even the rocks, which seem to be dumb and dead as they swelter in the sun along the silent shore, thrill with memories of stirring events connected with the lives of my people, and the very dust upon which you now stand responds more lovingly to their footsteps than to yours, because it is rich with the blood of our ancestors and our bare feet are conscious of the sympathetic touch. Our departed braves, fond mothers, glad, happy-hearted maidens, and even our little children who lived here and rejoiced here for a brief season, will love these somber solitudes and at eventide they greet shadowy returning spirits. And when the last Red Man shall have perished, and the memory of my tribe shall have become a myth among the White Men, these shores will swarm with the invisible dead of my tribe, and when your children's children think themselves alone in the field, the store, the shop, upon the highway, or in the silence of the pathless woods, they will not be alone. In all the earth there is no place dedicated to solitude. At night when the streets of your cities and villages are silent and you think them deserted, they will throng with the returning hosts that once filled them and still love this beautiful land. The White Man will never be alone.

Let him be just and deal kindly with my people, for the dead are not powerless. Dead, did I say? There is no death, only a change of worlds.

1855

▪ JOHN WANNUAUCON QUINNEY (MAHICAN) ▪
1797–1855

In his 1854 Fourth of July speech at Reidsville, New York, John Wannuaucon Quinney challenges his white audience to snap out of their nationalistic pieties about the sad but inevitable disappearance of Indians and pay attention to U.S. history as Native people would tell it. Quinney had spent his adult life fighting for the survival of the Stockbridge Indians through swindles and removals, from New York to Indiana to Wisconsin, over a period of forty years. A year before his death, near the birthplace that his tribe had been forced to abandon and in the historic territory of his people, he was exhausted but not too tired to set the record straight and to demand that his audience confront, on the national holiday, what exactly they might think the United States stood for.

The Stockbridges were a band of predominantly Mahican people who were converted to Christianity in the early eighteenth century. At first contact with Europeans, they lived in the Hudson River Valley, from Lake Champlain in the north to the Catskills in the south. The fur trade led to conflicts with other tribes and increasing numbers of European settlers. Gradually the Mahicans moved east into the Housatonic River Valley in western Massachusetts. In 1735, their leaders agreed to join a mission village, which was called Stockbridge. The village attracted other remnant groups from tribes in the region, although the Mahicans dominated.

By the 1760s, the Stockbridges were a minority in their own town, losing their land to whites who demanded payment in land for every kind of financial transaction. In 1783 they accepted the invitation of the Oneidas to settle on a parcel of their land in New York. But land speculators, often state and local officials, preyed on them, and the disarray motivated the Stockbridges to move again, this time to present-day Indiana, to land granted to them by the Miamis. The deal fell through, and the Stockbridges had to find yet another place to go.

As a boy, along with two others chosen by the tribe's leaders, Quinney was educated for several years at the U.S. government's expense. Although Quinney wrote that he felt himself "poorly qualified for public employment," he accepted the responsibility because his tribe needed him. Quinney's political career began in 1822, when he represented the Stockbridges at a treaty and secured payments to the Stockbridges for their land from the New York legislature. He was particularly proud, he wrote, that the act was "the first ever passed by the New York legislature, to give an Indian Tribe full value for their lands." It would be a rare instance of the Stockbridges, getting just treatment from government authorities.

Eventually, after a series of treaties in the 1830s, the Stockbridges moved again, this time to two townships on the east side of Lake Winnebago in Wisconsin. But Congress conferred citizenship on the Stockbridges in 1843 and allotted their lands to individuals, prefiguring its actions with regard to all Indian nations in the later nineteenth century. Again the tribe sent Quinney to Washington, to petition that recognition of tribal status be restored. "I can now return home gladly," Quinney wrote in his diary when the law restoring recognition was signed in August. "We Stockbridges are now Indians again." But in 1848, their land greatly reduced and with the influx of white settlers increasing, the Stockbridges sold their land at Lake Winnebago to the United States in exchange for land yet to be found west of the Mississippi and cash payments that amounted to a fraction of the land's value and the value of the improvements they had made.

The Stockbridges had not yet found a suitable place to which to remove when, in 1852, Quinney was elected Grand Sachem, and he made a highly unusual request for a Native person: he petitioned Congress for citizenship in the United States. He made the request not out of faith in the United States but rather because he did not want to have to leave his home one more time, and he wanted to secure legal standing for himself and financial security for his family. "I am growing old and poor by attending continually to the business of my people, who are poor and unable to give me adequate compensation," he wrote. "I am ... discouraged with that policy which keeps the tribe in continual mutations—I mean removals. I have not only witnessed its injurious effects upon the people, but have, to my sorrow, experienced it. I feel that I cannot go into the wilderness again and begin anew. I have long striven for a home, but, for my situation in the tribe I have been disappointed." Ironically, a year after Quinney's death, the Stockbridges settled on a parcel of land on the Menominee reservation, some eighty miles north of Lake Winnebago, where they remain today.

Quinney returned to New York one last time in 1854 to give his speech in a place that had been Mahican when Europeans arrived. In transmitting a copy of the speech to the Wisconsin Historical Society, the Reverend Cutting Marsh, missionary to the Stockbridges, observed that "unlike most speeches of the kind made by white men and put into Indians' mouths," the speech was unequivocally Quinney's. "I know that it is his style," Marsh wrote. "He was capable of making a speech, and no one in the nation was equally well acquainted with their traditions as he was."

Maureen Konkle
University of Missouri–Columbia

PRIMARY WORKS

"Speech of John W. Quinney" (1854) and "Memorial of John W. Quinney" (1852), *Collections of the State Historical Society of Wisconsin* 4 (1859); *Memorial of the Stockbridge Nation of Indians in Wisconsin*, 27th Congress, 2d Session, Senate Doc. No. 189, March 16, 1842.

Quinney's Speech

It may appear to those whom I have the honor to address, a singular taste, for me, an Indian, to take an interest in the triumphal days of a people, who occupy by conquest, or have usurped the possession of the territories of my fathers, and have laid and carefully preserved, a train of terrible miseries, to end when my race shall have ceased to exist. But thanks to the fortunate circumstances of my life, I have been taught in the schools, and been able to read your histories and accounts of Europeans, yourselves and the Red Man; which instruct me, that while your rejoicings today are commemorative of the free birth of this giant nation, they simply convey to my mind, the recollection of a transfer of the miserable weakness and dependance of my race from one great power to another.

My friends, I am getting old, and have witnessed, for many years, your increase in wealth and power, while the steady consuming decline of my tribe, admonishes me, that their extinction is inevitable—they know it themselves, and the reflection teaches them humility and resignation, directing their attention to the existence of those happy hunting-grounds which the Great Father has prepared for all his red children.

In this spirit, my friends (being invited to come here), as a Muh-he-connew, and now standing upon the soil which once was, and now ought to be, the property of this tribe, I have thought for once, and certainly the last time, I would shake you by the hand, and ask you to listen, for a little while, to what I have to say.

In the documentary papers of this state, and in the various histories of early events in the settlement of this part of the country by the whites, the many traditions of my tribe, which are as firmly believed as written annals by you, inform me that there are many errors. Without, however, intending to refer to, and correct those histories, I will give you what those traditions are.

About the year 1645, and when King Ben (the last of the hereditary chiefs of the Muh-he-con-new Nation) was in his prime, a Grand Council was convened of the Muh-he-con-new tribe, for the purpose of conveying from the old to the young men, a knowledge of the past. Councils, for this object especially, had ever, at stated periods, been held. Here, for the space of two moons, the stores of memory were dispensed; corrections and comparisons made, and the results committed to faithful breasts, to be transmitted again to succeeding posterity.

Many years after, another, and the last, Council of this kind was held; and the traditions reduced to writing, by two of our young men, who had been taught to read and write, in the school of the Rev. John Sargeant, of Stockbridge, Massachusetts.[1] They were obtained, in some way, by a white man, for publication, who soon after dying, all trace of them became lost. The traditions of the tribe, however, have mainly been preserved; of which I give you substantially, the following:

"A great people came from the North-West: crossed over the salt-waters, and after long and weary pilgrimages (planting many colonies on their track), took possession, and built their fires upon the Atlantic coast, extending from the Delaware on the south, to the Penobscot in the north. They became, in process of time, divided into different tribes and interests; all, however, speaking one common dialect. This great confederacy, comprising Delawares, Munsees, Mohegans, Narragansetts, Pequots, Penobscots, and many others (of whom a few are now scattered among the distant wilds of the West— others supporting a weak, tottering existence; while, by far, a larger remainder have passed that bourne, to which their brethren are tending), held its Council once a year, to deliberate on the general welfare. Patriarchal delegates from each tribe attended, assisted by priests and wise men, who communicated the will, and invoked the blessing, of the Great and Good Spirit. The policy and decisions of this Council were every where respected, and inviolably observed. Thus contentment smiled upon their existence, and they were happy. Their religion, communicated by priests and prophets, was simple and true. The manner of worship is imperfectly transmitted; but their reverence for a Great and Good Spirit—(whom they referred to by looking or pointing upwards), the observance of feasts and fasts, in each year; the offering of beasts in thanksgiving and for atonement, is clearly expressed. They believed the soul to be immortal;—in the existence of a happy land beyond the view, inhabited by those whose lives had been blameless: while for the wicked had been a region of misery reserved, covered with thorns and thistles, where comfort and pleasure were unknown. Time was divided into years and seasons; twelve moons for a year, and a number of years by so many winters."

The tribe, to which your speaker belongs, and of which there were many bands, occupied and possessed the country from the sea-shore, at Manhattan, to Lake Champlain. Having found an ebb and flow of the tide, they said: "This is Muh-he-con-new,"—"like our waters, which are never still." From this expression, and by this name, they were afterwards known, until their removal to Stockbridge, in the year 1730. Housatonic River Indians, Mohegan, Manhattas, were all names of bands in different localities, but bound together, as one family, by blood, marriage and descent.

[1] John Sargeant (1710–1749) graduated from Yale in 1729 and from 1731 to 1735 served as a tutor there. In 1735, at the behest of the Boston commissioners of the Society for the Propagation of the Gospel in New England, Sargeant went to the Housatonic River Indian settlements and established the mission town of Stockbridge.

At a remote period, before the advent of the Europeans, their wise men foretold the coming of a strange race, from the sunrise, as numerous as the leaves upon the trees, who would eventually crowd them from their fair possessions. But apprehension was mitigated by the knowledge and belief, at that time entertained, that their original home was not there, and after a period of years, they would return to the West, from whence they had come; and, moreover, said they, "all the red men are sprung from a common ancestor, made by the Great Spirit from red clay, who will unite their strength to avert a common calamity." This tradition is confirmed by the common belief, which prevails in our day with all the Indian tribes; for they recognize one another by their color, as brothers, and acknowledge one Great Creator.

Two hundred and fifty winters ago, this prophecy was verified, and the Muh-he-con-new, for the first time, beheld the "pale-face." Their number was small, but their canoes were big. In the select and exclusive circles of your rich men, of the present day, I should encounter the gaze of curiosity, but not such as overwhelmed the senses of the Aborigines, my ancestors. "Our visitors were white, and must be sick. They asked for rest and kindness, we gave them both. They were strangers, and we took them in—naked, and we clothed them."[2] The first impression of astonishment and pity, was succeeded by awe and admiration of superior art, intelligence and address. A passion for information and improvement possessed the Indian—a residence was freely offered—territory given—and covenants of friendship exchanged.

Your written accounts of events at this period are familiar to you, my friends. Your children read them every day in their school books; but they do not read—no mind at this time can conceive, and no pen record, the terrible story of recompense for kindness, which for two hundred years has been paid the simple, trusting, guileless Muh-he-con-new. I have seen much myself—have been connected with more, and, I tell you, I know all. The tradition of the wise men is figuratively true, "that our home, at last, will be found in the West;" for, another tradition informs us, that "far beyond the setting sun, upon the smiling, happy lands, we shall be gathered with our Fathers, and be at rest."

Promises and professions were freely given, and as ruthlessly—intentionally broken. To kindle your fires—to be of and with us, was sought as a privilege; and yet at that moment you were transmitting to your kings, beyond the water, intelligence of your possession, "by right of discovery," and demanding assistance to assert and maintain your hold.

Where are the twenty-five thousand in number, and the four thousand warriors, who constituted the power and population of the great Muh-he-con-new Nation in 1604? They have been victims to vice and disease, which the white man imported. The small-pox, measles, and "strong waters" have done the work of annihilation.

---

[2]"For I was an hungered, and ye gave me meat: I was thirsty, and ye gave me drink: I was a stranger, and ye took me in: Naked, and ye clothed me: I was sick, and ye visited me: I was in prison, and ye came unto me." Matthew 25:35–36. See also verses 37–40.

Divisions and feuds were insidiously promoted between the several bands. They were induced to thin each other's ranks without just cause; and subsequently were defeated and disorganized in detail.

It is curious, the history of my tribe, in its decline, during the last two centuries and a half. Nothing that deserved the name of purchase, was ever made. From various causes, they were induced to abandon their territory at intervals, and retire further to the inland. Deeds were given, indifferently to the Government, or to individuals, for which little or no consideration was paid. The Indian was informed, in many instances, that he was selling one parcel, while the conveyance described other, and much larger limits. Should a particular band, for purposes of hunting or fishing, desert, for a time, its usual place of residence, the land was said to be abandoned, and the Indian claim extinguished. To legalize and confirm titles thus acquired, laws and edicts were subsequently passed, and these laws were said then, and are now called, justice!! Oh! what a mockery!! to confound justice with law. Will you look steadily at the intrigues, bargains, corruption and log-rolling of your present Legislatures, and see any trace of the divinity of justice? And by what test shall be tried the acts of the old Colonial Courts and Councils?

Let it not surprise you, my friends, when I say, that the spot on which we stand, has never been purchased or rightly obtained; and that by justice, human and divine, it is the property now of the remnant of that great people from whom I am descended. They left it in the tortures of starvation, and to improve their miserable existence; but a cession was never made, and their title has never been extinguished.

The Indian is said to be the ward of the white man, and the negro his slave. Has it ever occurred to you, my friends, that while the slave is increasing, and increased by every appliance, the Indian is left to rot and die, before the humanities of this model *Republic!* You have your tears, and groans, and mobs, and riots, for individuals of the former, while your indifference of purpose, and vacillation of policy, is hurrying to extinction, whole communities of the latter.

What are the treaties of the general Government? How often, and when, has its plighted faith been kept? Indian occupation forever, is, next year, or by the next Commissioner, more wise than his predecessor, re-purchased. One removal follows another, and thus your sympathies and justice are evinced in speedily *fulfilling the terrible destinies of our race.*

My friends, your holy book, the Bible, teaches us, that individual offences are punished in an existence, when time shall be no more. And the annals of the earth are equally instructive, that national wrongs are avenged, and national crimes atoned for in this world, to which alone the conformations of existence adapt them.

These events are above our comprehension, and for wise purposes. For myself and for my tribe, I ask for justice—I believe it will sooner or later occur—and may the Great and Good Spirit enable me to die in hope.

Wannuaucon, *the Muh-he-con-new*

1854

▪ GEORGE COPWAY (KAH-GE-GA-GAH-BOWH; OJIBWE) ▪
1818–1869

Born in 1818 near the mouth of the Trent River in Upper Canada, Copway was raised as a traditional Ojibwe until 1827, when his parents converted to Christianity. In 1830 Copway became a Christian convert and later occasionally attended the Methodist Mission School at Rice Lake, Ontario. From 1834 to 1837, he helped Methodist missionaries spread the gospel among the Lake Superior Ojibwe. In 1838 he entered Ebenezer Manual Labor School at Jacksonville, Illinois, where for the next nineteen months he received his only formal education. After he left school, Copway traveled in the East before returning to Rice Lake, where he met and married Elizabeth Howell, a white woman. An educated and genteel woman, who wrote numerous articles in her own right and whose letters reveal a polished writing style, Elizabeth Copway may have assisted her husband in his writing.

Until 1842 the Copways served as missionaries to the Indian tribes of Wisconsin and Minnesota. The high point of George Copway's career in Canadian Indian affairs was his election in 1845 as vice president of the Grand Council of Methodist Ojibwes of Upper Canada. Later that year he was accused of embezzlement. After being imprisoned briefly in the summer of 1846, Copway was expelled from the Canadian Conference of the Wesleyan Methodist Church and left Canada for the United States. Befriended by American Methodists, Copway launched a new career as a lecturer and writer on Indian affairs. His first book was his autobiography, *The Life, History and Travels* (1847), later republished as *The Life, Letters and Speeches* (New York, 1850) and as *Recollections of a Forest Life* (London, 1850). Enthusiasm for this autobiography was so great that it was reprinted in seven editions in one year.

In 1847, when the *Life, History and Travels* was published, William Medill, Commissioner of Indian Affairs, began efforts to secure Ojibwe removal from ceded territory to central Minnesota. Despite the plea of a delegation of headmen to regain villages in Wisconsin and upper Michigan, President Zachary Taylor in 1850 authorized immediate and total removal of the Ojibwes from the land set aside for them in 1842. These removal efforts aroused Copway to lecture in the East, South, and Midwest on his plan for a separate Indian state, advocated in his pamphlet *Organization of a New Indian Territory, East of the Missouri River* (1850). His lectures in the East enabled him to meet the well-known scholars Henry Rowe Schoolcraft and Francis Parkman, as well as such famous writers as Longfellow, Irving, and Cooper, who provided moral and financial encouragement for his later publishing projects. Copway's second book was *The Traditional History and Characteristic Sketches of the Ojibway Nation* (London, 1850; Boston, 1851), later republished as *Indian Life and Indian History* (1858). In this first published, book-length history of the Ojibwe people, Copway is far more critical of whites than he was in his autobiography. Copway reached the zenith of his career in 1850, when he was selected to represent the Christian Indians at the Peace Congress held in Germany. He lectured in Great Britain and on the Continent before the congress, where he created a great stir by delivering a lengthy antiwar speech while garbed in his Ojibwe finery.

Returning from Europe in December 1850, Copway hurriedly stitched together *Running Sketches of Men and Places, in England, France, Germany, Belgium, and Scotland* (1851), one of the first travel books by an Indian. Between July and fall 1851, Copway established the short-lived journal *Copway's American Indian*. Gradually abandoned by his eastern intellectual friends because of his constant pleas for money and beset by financial difficulties, he had also endured the deaths of three of his four children between August 1849 and January 1850.

Copway's attempt to support his family by lecturing was unsuccessful because his novelty had worn off. Dropped by the eastern intellectuals, he was taken up by a nativist group who called themselves "native Americans." Members of this anti-immigrant, anti–Roman Catholic group later established the political party known as the Know-Nothings. Little is known of Copway's later life. In 1864 he recruited Canadian Indians to serve in the American Civil War, for which he received a bounty. He surfaced again in 1867, when he advertised himself in the *Detroit Free Press* as a healer. The following year, having abandoned his wife and daughter, Copway arrived alone at the Lac-des-deux Montagnes, a large Algonquian-Iroquois mission near Montreal. Describing himself as a pagan, Copway became a Catholic convert and was baptized "Joseph-Antoine" on 17 January 1869. Several days later he died.

Copway's autobiography incorporates traditions from earlier personal narratives and American Indian oral narratives. It is divided into four parts: an ethnographic account of Ojibwe culture; the conversions of his band, family, and himself; his role as mediator between Indians and whites; and a history of Ojibwe-white relations in the recent past. Copway's blending of myth, history, and personal experience created a structure that later American Indian autobiographies would follow.

In its nostalgia for the lost tribal past, Copway's autobiography bears a stronger relationship to the narratives published by African slaves in the late eighteenth century than to those by African American slaves in the nineteenth. In the ethnographic sections on Ojibwe life, Copway adopts an overwhelmingly romantic and nostalgic tone. Appealing to American affection for the Indian as a child of nature, he also portrays himself as an example of the Indian's adaptability to white civilization. The ethnographic sections are designed to persuade his audience of the value of tribal culture and the essential humanity of Indian people.

A. LaVonne Brown Ruoff
University of Illinois at Chicago

PRIMARY WORKS

The Life, History and Travels of Kah-ge-ga-gah-bowh (George Copway), a Young Indian Chief of the Ojebwa Nation, ... with a Sketch of the Present State of the Ojebwa Nation, in Regard to Christianity and Their Future Prospects, 1847; repub. as *The Life, Letters and Speeches of Kah-ge-ga-gah-bowh, or G. Copway ...*, 2nd ed. rev. 1850; and as *Recollections of a Forest Life; or, The Life and Travels of Kah-ge-ga-gah-bowh, or George Copway ...*, 1850; 2nd ed. 1851; *Organization of a New Indian Territory, East of the Missouri River: Arguments and Reasons Submitted to the Honorable the Members of the Senate and House of Representatives to the 31st Congress of the United States, by the Indian Chief Kah-ge-ga-gah-bouh [sic], or Geo. Copway*, 1850; *Running Sketches of Men and Places, in England, France, Germany, Belgium, and Scotland*, 1851; *The Traditional History and Characteristic Sketches of the Ojibway Nation, by G. Copway, or, Kah-ge-ga-gah-bowh, Chief of the*

Ojibway Nation, 1850; 1851; repub. as *Indian Life and Indian History, by an Indian Author, Embracing the Traditions of the North American Indian Tribes Regarding Themselves, Particularly of that Most Important of all Tribes, the Ojibways*, 1858; *Copway's American Indian* (July–October 1851); *Life, Letters, and Speeches*, 1997.

from **The Life of Kah-ge-ga-gah-bowh**

Chapter I

The Christian will no doubt feel for my poor people, when he hears the story of one brought from that unfortunate race called the Indians. The lover of humanity will be glad to see that once powerful race can be made to enjoy the blessings of life.

What was once impossible—or rather thought to be—is made possible through my experience. I have made many close observations of men, and things around me; but, I regret to say, that I do not think I have made as good use of my opportunities as I might have done. It will be seen that I know but little—yet O how precious *that little!*—I would rather lose my right hand than be deprived of it.

I loved the woods, and the chase. I had the nature for it, and gloried in nothing else. The mind for letters was in me, *but was asleep*, till the dawn of Christianity arose, and awoke the slumbers of the soul into energy and action.

You will see that I served the imaginary gods of my poor blind father. I was out early and late in quest of the favors of the *Mon-e-doos* (spirits,) who, it was said, were numerous—who filled the air! At early dawn I watched the rising of the *palace* of the Great Spirit—*the sun*—who, it was said, made the world!

Early as I can recollect, I was taught that it was the gift of the many spirits to be a good hunter and warrior; and much of my time I devoted in search of their favors. On the mountain top, or along the valley, or the water brook, I searched for some kind intimation from the spirits who made their residence in the noise of the waterfalls.

I dreaded to hear the voice of the angry spirit in the gathering clouds. I looked with anxiety to catch a glimpse of the wings of the Great Spirit, who shrouded himself in rolling white and dark clouds—who, with his wings, fanned the earth, and laid low the tall pines and hemlock in his course—who rode in whirlwinds and tornadoes, and plucked the trees from their woven roots—who chased other gods from his course—who drove the Bad Spirit from the surface of the earth, down to the dark caverns of the deep. Yet he was a kind spirit. My father taught me to call that spirit Ke-sha-mon-e-doo—*Benevolent spirit*[1]—for his ancestors taught him no other name to give

---

[1]"*Mone-doos* (spirits) . . . *Benevolent spirit*"—In Ojibwe world view, all elements are animate and contain potential hostility to men. However, they may be appeased through governing spirits. There are numerous eternal spirits of manitos who appear as spirit pro- tectors of plants, birds, beasts, elemental forces, and life circumstances. Evil manitos are the cannibalistic windigos and under- water creatures. (See Ruth Landes, *Ojibwa Religion and the Mide-wiwin*, 1968.)

to that spirit who made the earth, with all its variety and smiling beauty. His benevolence I saw in the running of the streams, for the animals to quench their thirst and the fishes to live; the fruit of the earth teemed wherever I looked. Every thing I saw smilingly said Ke-sha-mon-e-doo nin-ge-oo-she-ig—*the Benevolent spirit made me.*

Where is he? My father pointed to the sun. What is his will concerning me, and the rest of the Indian race? This was a question that I found no one could answer, until a beam from heaven shone on my pathway, which was very dark, when first I saw that there was a true heaven—not in the far-setting sun, where the Indian anticipated a rest, a home for his spirit—but in the bosom of the Highest.

I view my life like the mariner on the wide ocean, without a compass, in the dark night, as he watches the heavens for the north star, which his eye having discovered, he makes his way amidst surging seas, and tossed by angry billows into the very jaws of death, till he arrives safely anchored at port. I have been tossed with hope and fear in this life; no star-light shone on my way, until the men of God pointed me to a Star in the East, as it rose with all its splendor and glory. It was the Star of Bethlehem. I could now say in the language of the poet—

> *"Once on the raging seas I rode,*
> *The storm was loud, the night was dark;*
> *The ocean yawned, and rudely blowed*
> *The wind that tossed my foundering bark."*

Yes, I hope to sing some day in the realms of bliss—

> *"It was my guide, my light my all!*
> *It bade my dark foreboding cease;*
> *And through the storm and danger's thrall,*
> *It led me to the port of peace."*

I have not the happiness of being able to refer to written records in narrating the history of my forefathers; but I can reveal to the world what has long been laid up in my memory; so that when "I go the way of all the earth," the crooked and singular paths which I have made in the world, may not only be a warning to others, but may inspire them with a trust in God. And not only a warning and a trust, but also that the world may learn that there once lived such a man as Kah-ge-ga-gah-bowh, when they read his griefs and his joys.

My parents were of the Ojebwa nation, who lived on the lake back of Cobourg, on the shores of Lake Ontario Canada West. The lake was called Rice Lake,[2] where there was a quantity of wild rice, and much game of different kinds, before the whites cleared away the woods, where the deer and the bear then resorted.

---

[2]Located northeast of Toronto and south of Peterborough, Ontario.

My father and mother were taught the religion of their nation. My father became a medicine man in the early part of his life, and always had by him the implements of war, which generally distinguish our head men. He was a good hunter as any in the tribe. Very few brought more furs than he did in the spring. Every spring they returned from their hunting grounds. The Ojebwas each claimed, and claim to this day, hunting grounds, rivers, lakes, and whole districts of country. No one hunted on each other's ground. My father had the northern fork of the river Trent, above Bellmont lake.

My great-grandfather was the first who ventured to settle at Rice Lake, after the Ojebwa nation defeated the Hurons, who once inhabited all the lakes in Western Canada, and who had a large village just on the top of the hill of the Anderson farm, (which was afterwards occupied by the Ojebwas,) and which furnished a magnificent view of the lakes and surrounding country. He was of the *Crane tribe*, i.e. had a crane for totem—*coat of arms*—which now forms the totem of the villagers, excepting those who have since come amongst us from other villages by intermarriage, for there was a law that no one was to marry one of the same totem, for all considered each other as being related.[3] He must have been a daring adventurer—*a warrior*—for no one would have ventured to go and settle down on the land from which they had just driven the Hurons, whom the Ojebwas conquered and reduced, unless he was a great hero. It is said that he lived about the islands of Rice Lake, secreting himself from the enemy for several years, until some others came and joined him, when they formed a settlement on one of the islands. He must have been a great hunter, for this was one of the principal inducements that made him venture there, for there must have been abundance of game of every kind. The Ojebwas are called, here and all around, Massissuagays, because they came from Me-sey Sah-gieng, at the head of Lake Huron, as you go up to Sault St. Marie falls.

Here he lived in jeopardy—with his life in his hand—enduring the unpleasant idea that he lived in the land of bones—*amidst the gloom*, which shrouded the once happy and populous village of the Hurons; here their bones lay broad-cast around his wigwam; where, among these woods once

---

[3]"He was of the *Crane tribe*, ... as being related."

According to William Whipple Warren, each Ojibwe clan is identified with a symbol or totem taken from nature, usually an animal, bird, fish, or reptile. Among the Ojibwe, clan membership descends through the male line. An individual is considered a close blood relation to all other Indians of the same clan, regardless of the band to which they belong. Consequently, intermarriage among clan members was formerly strictly forbidden (*History of the Ojibway Nation*, 1885; 1974).

The original five clans were expanded: Warren lists 21 and Johnson, 27 (*Ojibway Heritage*, 1979). Of the original five clans, the most important bird clan was the Crane.

Warren notes that members of the Crane clan were numerous and that they resided mostly on the south shores of Lake Superior and toward the east in Canada. Warren translates the name for this clan, Bus-in-an-see, as "Echomaker," which alludes to the loud, clear, far-reaching cry of the crane. Johnston describes the crane as a symbol of leadership. Warren indicates that "members of this clan were noted for possessing naturally a loud, ringing voice, and are the acknowledged orators of the tribe; in former times, when different tribes met in councils, they acted as interpreter of the wishes of their tribe. They claim, with some apparent justice, the chieftainship over the other clans of the Ojibways."

rang the war cry of the Hurons, echoing along the valley of the river Trent, but whose sinewed arms now laid low, with their badges and arms of war, in one common grave, near the residence of Peter Anderson, Esq. Their graves, forming a hillock, are now all that remain of this once powerful nation. Their bones, gun barrels, tomahawks, war spears, large scalping knives, are yet to be found there. This must have taken place soon after the formation of the settlement in Quebec.

The *Crane tribe* became the sole proprietors of this part of the Ojebwa land; the descendants of this tribe will continue to wear the distinguishing sign; except in a few instances, the chiefs are of this tribe.

My grandfather lived here about this time, and held some friendly inter-course with the whites. My father here learned the manners, customs, and worship of the nation. He, and others, became acquainted with the early set-tlers, and have ever been friendly with the whites. And I know the day when he used to shake the hand of the white man, and, *very friendly*, the white man would say, *"take some whiskey."* When he saw any hungering for veni-son, he gave them to eat; and some, in return for his kindness, have repaid him after they became good and great farmers.

My mother was of the *Eagle tribe;*[4] she was a sensible woman; she was as good a hunter as any of the Indians; she could shoot the deer, and the ducks flying as well as they. Nature had done a great deal for her, for she was active; and she was much more cleanly than the majority of our women in those days. She lived to see the day when most of her children were given up to the Lord in Christian baptism; while she experienced a change of heart, and the fulness of God in man, for she lived daily in the enjoyment of God's favors. I will speak more of her at a proper time, respecting her life and happy death.

My father still lives; he is from sixty-five to seventy years old, and is one of the chiefs of Rice Lake Indian Village. He used to love fire-water before he was converted to God, but now lives in the enjoyment of religion, and he is happy without the devil's spittal—*whiskey.* If Christianity had not come, and the grace of God had not taken possession of his heart, his head would soon have been laid low beneath the fallen leaves of the forest, and I, left, in my youthful days, an orphan. But to God be all the praise for his timely deliverance.

The reader will see that I cannot boast of an exalted parentage, nor trace the past history to some renowned warrior in days of yore; but let the above suffice. My fathers were those who endured much; who first took possession of the conquered lands of the Hurons.

I was born in *nature's wide domain!* The trees were all that sheltered my infant limbs—the blue heavens all that covered me. I am one of Nature's children; I have always admired her; she shall be my glory; her features—her robes, and the wreath about her brow—the seasons—her stately oaks,

---

[4]According to Johnson, the Eagle clan was identified with foresight and courage. Warren indicates that this group was a branch of the Crane clan.

and the evergreen—her hair—ringlets over the earth, all contribute to my enduring love of her; and wherever I see her, emotions of pleasure roll in my breast, and swell and burst like waves on the shores of the ocean, in prayer and praise to Him who has placed me in her hand. It is thought great to be born in palaces, surrounded with wealth—but to be born in nature's wide domain is greater still!

I was born sometime in the fall of 1818, near the mouth of the river Trent, called in our language, Sah-ge-dah-we-ge-wah-noong, while my father and mother were attending the annual distribution of the presents from the government to the Indians. I was the third of our family; a brother and sister being older, both of whom died. My brother died without the knowledge of the Saviour, but my sister experienced the power of the loving grace of God. One brother, and two stepbrothers, are still alive.

I remember the tall trees, and the dark woods—the swamp just by, where the little wren sang so melodiously after the going down of the sun in the west—the current of the broad river Trent—the skipping of the fish, and the noise of the rapids a little above. It was here I first saw the light; a little fallen down shelter, made of evergreens, and a few dead embers, the remains of the last fire that shed its genial warmth around, were all that marked the spot. When I last visited it, nothing but fur poles stuck in the ground, and they were leaning on account of decay. Is this dear spot, made green by the tears of memory, any less enticing and hallowed than the palaces where princes are born? I would much more glory in this birth-place, with the broad canopy of heaven above me, and the giant arms of the forest trees for my shelter, than to be born in palaces of marble, studded with pillars of gold! Nature will be nature stil' while palaces shall decay and fall in ruins. Yes, Niagara will be Niagara a thousand years hence! the rainbow, a wreath over her brow, shall continue as long as the sun, and the flowing of the river! While the work of art, however impregnable, shall in atoms fall.

Our wigwam we always carried with us wherever we went. It was made in the following manner: Poles were cut about fifteen feet long; three with crotches at the end, which were stuck in the ground some distance apart, the upper ends meeting, and fastened with bark; and then other poles were cut in circular form and bound round the first, and then covered with plaited reeds, or sewed birch bark, leaving an opening on top for the smoke to escape. The skins of animals formed a covering for a gap, which answered for a door. The family all seated tailor-fashion on mats. In the fall and winter they were generally made more secure, for the purpose of keeping out the rain and cold. The covering of our wigwam was always carried by my mother, whenever we went through the woods. In the summer it was easier and pleasanter to move about from place to place, than in the winter. In the summer we had birch bark canoes, and with these we travelled very rapidly and easily. In the winter every thing was carried upon the back. I have known some Indians to carry a whole deer—not a small one, but a buck. If an Indian could lift up his pack off the ground by means of his arms, it was a good load, not too light nor too heavy. I once carried one hundred and ninety-six weight of flour, twelve pounds of shot, five pounds of coffee, and some sugar, about a quarter of a mile, without resting—the flour was in two bags. It felt very heavy. This was since I travelled with the missionaries, in going over one of the portages in the west.

Our summer houses were made like those in gardens among the whites, except that the skeleton is covered with bark.

The hunting grounds of the Indians were secured by right, a law and custom among themselves. No one was allowed to hunt on another's land, without invitation or permission. If any person was found trespassing on the ground of another, all his things were taken from him, except a handful of shot, powder sufficient to serve him in going *straight* home, a gun, a tomahawk, and a knife; all the fur, and other things, were taken from him. If he were found a second time trespassing, all his things were taken away from him, except food sufficient to subsist on while going home. And should he still come a third time to trespass on the same, or another man's hunting grounds, his nation, or tribe, are then informed of it, who take up his case. If still he disobey, he is banished from his tribe.

My father's hunting ground was at the head of Crow River, a branch of the River Trent, north of the Prince Edward District, Canada West. There are two branches to this river—one belongs to George Poudash, one of the principal chiefs of our nation; the other to my father; and the Crow River belongs to another chief by the name of John Crow. During the last war the Indians did not hunt or fish much for nearly six years, and at the end of that time there were large quantities of beaver, otter, minks, lynx, fishes, &c.

These hunting grounds abound with rivers and lakes; the face of the country is swampy and rocky; the deer and the bear abound in these woods; part of the surrendered territory is included in it. In the year 1818, 1,800,000 acres of it were surrendered to the British government. For how much, do you ask? For 62,960 per annum! What a *great sum* for British generosity!

Much of the back country still remains unsold, and I hope the scales will be removed from the eyes of my poor countrymen, that they may see the robberies perpetrated upon them, before they surrender another foot of territory.

From these lakes and rivers come the best furs that are caught in Western Canada. Buyers of fur get large quantities from here. They are then shipped to New York city, or to England. Whenever fruit is plenty, bears are also plenty, and there is much bear hunting. Before the whites came amongst us, the skins of these animals served for clothing; they are now sold from three to eight dollars apiece.

My father generally took one or two families with him when he went to hunt; all were to hunt, and place their gains into one common stock till spring, (for they were often out all winter,) when a division took place.

Chapter II

In the fall we gathered the wild rice, and in the winter we were in the interior. Some winters we suffered most severely, on account of the depth of snow, and the cold; our wigwams were often buried in snow. We not only suffered from the snow and the cold, but from hunger. Our party would be unable to hunt, and being far from the white settlements, we were often in want of food. I will narrate a circumstance of our sufferings, when I come to speak of the actual condition of our people, before Christianity was introduced among us, which, when I think of it, I cannot but bless God for his preserving kindness to us, in sparing us to hear his blessed word.

Soon after being Christianized, my father and another Indian, by the name of Big John, and myself, went out hunting; my father left his family near the mission station, living in the wigwam. While we were out on the hunting grounds, we found out that some Indians had gone before us on the route up the river, and every day we gained upon them: their tracks were fresh. The river and the lakes were frozen, and we had to walk on the ice. For some days together we did not fire a gun, for fear they would hear it and go from us, where we could not find them. At length we found them by the banks of the river, they were Nah-doo-ways or Mohawks, from Bay Quinty; they were seven of them, tall fellows. We shook hands with them: they received us kindly. My father had determined to take all they had, if we should overtake them. After they gave us a good dinner of boiled beaver, my father stepped across the fire and ripped open two packs of beaver furs, that were just by him. He said to them "We have only one custom among us, and that is well known to all; this river, and all that is in it are mine: I have come up the river behind you, and you appear to have killed all before you. This is mine, and this is mine," he said, as he touched with the handle of his tomahawk each of the packs of beaver, otter, and muskrat skins. I expected every moment to see my father knocked down with a tomahawk, but none dared touch him; he counted the skins and then threw them across the fire-place to us. After this was done, the same thing took place with the guns; only one was left them to use on their way home. He talked to them by signs, and bade them, as the sailors say, "weigh anchor and soon be under way;" they left, and we took possession of the temporary wigwam they had built. We never saw them afterwards on our hunting grounds, though some of them have been there since.

My father was ever kind and affectionate to me, particularly after the death of my brother, which was occasioned by the going off of a gun, the load passing through the arm, and so fractured it that it soon mortified and caused his death. He believed in persuasion; I know not that he ever used harsh means, but would talk to me for hours together. As soon as it was dark he would call me to his side and begin to talk, and tell me that the Great Spirit would bless me with a long life if I should love my friends, and particularly the aged. He would always take me with him when going any where near, and I learned his movements, for I watched him going through the woods. Often would he tell me that when I should be a man that I must do so, and so, and do as he did, while fording the rivers, shooting the deer, trapping the beaver, etc., etc. I always imitated him while I was a hunter.

My mother was also kind and affectionate; she seemed to be happy when she saw us enjoying ourselves by her; often she would not eat much for days together; she would leave all for us! She was an industrious woman; in the spring she made more sugar than any one else; she was never idle while the season for gathering wild rice lasted.

I was taught early to hunt the deer. It was a part of our father's duty to teach us how to handle the gun as well as the bow and arrow. I was early reminded to hunt for myself; a thirst to excel in hunting began to increase; no pains were spared, no fatigue was too great, and at all seasons I found something to stimulate me to exertion, that I might become a good hunter. For years I followed my father, observed how he approached the deer, the manner of getting it upon his shoulders to carry it home. The appearance of the sky, the sound of the distant water-falls in the morning, the appearance of the clouds and the winds, were to be noticed. The step, and the gesture, in travelling in search of the deer, were to be observed.

Many a lecture I received when the deer lay bleeding at the feet of my father; he would give me an account of the nobleness of the hunter's deeds, and said that I should never be in want whenever there was any game, and that many a poor aged man could be assisted by me. "If you reverence the aged, many will be glad to hear of your name," were the words of my father. "The poor man will say to his children, 'my children, let us go to him, for he is a great hunter, and is kind to the poor, he will not turn us away empty.' The Great Spirit, who has given the aged a long life, will bless you. You must never laugh at any suffering object, for you know not how soon you may be in the same condition: never kill any game needlessly." Such was his language when we were alone in the woods. Ah! they were lessons directed from heaven.

In the spring but a few deer were killed, because they were not in good order, the venison being poor, and the skin so thin, that it was no object to kill them. To hunt deer in the summer was my great delight, which I did in the following manner:—During the day I looked for their tracks, as they came on the shore of the lake or river during the night; they came there to feed. If they came on the bank of the river, I lighted pitch pine, and the current of the river took the canoe along the shore. My lantern was so constructed that the light could not fall on one spot, but sweep along the shore. The deer could see the light, but were not alarmed by it, and continued feeding on the weeds. In this way, I have approached so close that I could have reached them with my paddle. In this manner our forefathers shot them, not with a gun, as I did, but with the bow and arrow. Bows were made strong enough, so that the arrows might pierce through them.

Another mode of hunting on the lakes, preferred by some, is shooting without a light. Many were so expert, and possessed such an accuracy in hearing, that they could shoot successfully in the dark, with no other guide than the noise of the deer in the water; the position of the deer being well known, in this way, the darkest night. I will here relate an occurrence which took place in 1834. My father and I were hunting on the river Trent, in the night; after we had shot two deer, and while returning homewards, we heard the noise of a deer's footsteps. The night was dark as pitch. We approached the deer. I asked my father at what part of the animal I should aim. He replied, "at the head or neck." I poised my gun and fired; hearing no noise, I concluded that my game was sure. I lighted some pitch pine and walked towards the spot from which the noise had come. The deer lay dead and bleeding. On examination I found that I had shot it just below the ear. In the fall of the year, also, I was accustomed to hunt; the meat was very fine, and the skins, (from which our moccasons were made,) were much thicker at this season. Those that could track the deer on fallen leaves and shoot one each day, were considered first rate hunters. The fall is the best time to determine the skill of the huntsman.

Of all animals the bear is the most dangerous to hunt. I had heard so many stories about its cunning that I dreaded to meet one. One day a party of us were going out to hunt the bear, just below Crooke's rapids. After we had made a temporary place to stay for several days, we marched in file; after a while we halted, each took a different direction. My father said, "my son you had better loiter behind the rest. Do not go far, for you may lose yourself." We parted—I took my course, and the rest theirs. I trembled for fear I should see what I was hunting for! I went only where I least expected to see a bear, and every noise I heard in the woods, I thought must be one. As I stood on an old mossy log, there was such a crack on the side of the hill that my heart leaped within me. As I turned and looked, there was a large bear running towards me! I hid myself behind a tree; but on he came; I watched him; he came like a hogshead rolling down hill; there were no signs of stopping; when a few feet from me, I jumped aside, and cried *Yah!* (an exclamation of fear.) I fired my gun without taking sight; in turning suddenly to avoid me, he threw up the earth and leaves; for an instant I was led to believe that the bear was upon me. I dropped my gun and fell backwards, while the bear lay sprawling just by me. Having recovered, I took up my gun and went a few feet from where I fell, and loaded my gun in a hurry. I then sought for a long pole, and with it, I poked it on its side, to see if it was really dead. It did not move, it was dead; but even then I had not courage to go and touch it with my hands. When all was over, and I had told my father I had killed a bear, I felt as though my little leggings could hardly contain me. In examining it, I found the ball had gone through its heart.

Bear meat is like pork. It can be kept a long time when cured. For some weeks together this was the only kind of food we used to eat.

The oil of the bear is used for various purposes. One use is, to prevent the falling out of the hair. The apothecaries buy it from the Indians for about five dollars a gallon.

The skins of bears are what our forefathers wore, before the white people came amongst us, as blankets; but now *land-sharks*, called traders, buy them from the Indians for a mere trifle.

I loved to hunt the bear, the beaver, and the deer but now, the occupation has no charms for me. I will now take the goose quil, for my *bow*, and its point for my *arrow*. If perchance I may yet speak; when my poor aching head lies low in the grave; when the hand that wrote these recollections shall have crumbled into dust; then these pages will not have been written in vain.

> *"O! Land of rest for thee I sigh—*
> *When will the season come,*
> *When I shall lay my armor by,*
> *And dwell in peace at home."*

The beaver was hunted in the spring and fall. They were either trapped or shot. Among all the animals that live in the water, the beaver is of the kindest disposition, when tamed; it is a very cleanly animal; sits on its broad tail on the ground while feeding; feeds all night, and sleeps most of the day. The beaver skin was once worth from eight to ten dollars apiece, or four dollars per pound.

The otter, too, is much valued. The whites buy the skins, and make caps of them. They are mostly caught in traps. In the fall and spring they are always on the move.

The otter is a greedy animal; it can be tamed, but when hungry becomes cross, and often bites. If it be a half a mile off, it will scent any food preparing in the wigwam.

When about five years old, I commenced shooting birds, with a small bow and arrow. I have shot many a bird, but am no more a marksman. I used to feel proud when I used to carry home my own game. The first thing that any of the hunters shot, was cooked by the grand-father and grand-mother, and there was great rejoicing, to inspire the youthful hunter with fresh ardor. Day after day I searched for the grey squirrel, the woodpecker, the snipe, and the snow bird, for this was all my employment.

The gun was another instrument put into my hands, which I was taught to use both carefully and skilfully. Seldom do accidents occur from the use of fire arms among our people. I delighted in running after the deer, in order to head and shoot them. It was a well known fact that I ranked high among the hunters. I remember the first deer I ever shot, it was about one mile north of the village of Keene. The Indians, as has just been said, once had a custom, which is now done away, of making a great feast of the first deer that a young hunter caught: the young hunter, however, was not to partake of any of it, but wait upon the others. All the satisfaction he could realize, was to thump his heels on the ground, while he and others were singing the following hunter's song:

> *"Ah yah ba wah, ne gah me koo nah vah!*
> *Ah yah wa seeh, ne gah me koo nah nah."*[5]
>
> *The fattest of the bucks I'll take,*
> *The choicest of all animals I'll take*

---

[5]These lines are sung over and over again, for about half an hour.

In the days of our ignorance we used to dance around the fire. I shudder when I think of those days of our darkness. I thought the Spirit would be kind to me if I danced before the old men; and day after day, or night after night, I have been employed with others in this way. I thank God that those days will never return.

Chapter III

The Ojebwas, as well as many others, acknowledged that there was but one Great Spirit, who made the world; they gave him the name of good or benevolent; *kesha* is benevolent, *monedoo* is spirit; Ke-sha-mon-e-doo. They supposed he lived in the heavens; but the most of the time he was in the *Sun*. They said it was from him they received all that was good through life, and that he seldom needs the offering of his Red children, for he was seldom angry.

They also said he could hear all his children, and see them. He was the author of all things that they saw, and made the other spirits that were acknowledged by the Ojebwas. It was said that these other spirits took special care of the various departments of nature. The god of the *hunter* was one who presided over the animals; the god of *war* was one who controlled the destinies of men; the god of *medicine* was one who presided over the herbs of the earth. The fishes had theirs, and there was another over the moon and stars!

> "Millions of spiritual creatures walk the earth
> Unseen, both when we sleep and when we wake."

There was one unappeasable spirit, called Bad Spirit, Mah-je-mah-ne-doo. He, it was thought, lived under the earth; and to him was attributed all that was not good, bad luck, sickness, even death. To him they offered sacrifices more than to any other spirit, things most dear to them. There were three things that were generally offered to the Bad Spirit, viz a dog, whiskey and tobacco, a fit offering, with the exception of the poor dog. The poor dog was painted red on its paws, with a large stone and five plugs of tobacco tied about its neck; it was then sunk in the water; while the beating of the drum took place upon the shore, and words were chanted to the Bad Spirit.

The whiskey was thus offered to the Bad Spirit:—When the Indians were seated around the wigwam, or on the grass, and the person who deals out the whiskey had given all the Indians a dram, then the devil was to have his share; it was poured on the ground, and if it went down quickly, it was thought he accepted the offering.

Fire water was sometimes poured out near the head of the graves of the deceased, that their spirits might drink with their former friends. I have often seen them sit around the grave, and, as they drank, make mention of the name of their dead, and pour some whiskey on the ground.

Our religion consisted in observing certain ceremonies every spring. Most of the Ojebwas around us used to come and worship the Great Spirit with us at Rice Lake. At this festival a great many of the youth were initiated into the medical mysteries of the nation. We were taught the virtues of herbs, and the various kinds of minerals used in our medicine. I will here describe the Me-tae-we-gah-mig or Grand Medicine Lodge. It was a wigwam 150 feet long and 15 feet wide. The clan of medicine men and women alone were allowed to be inside, at each sitting, with their medicine badge, on each side of the wigwam. Then there were four old men who took the lead in singing, and beating the drum, as they stood near the centre. Before them were a company who were to take degrees. There were four grades in the institution; and, as I have thought, somewhat similar to the Masonic institution.

After the singing commenced, the whole company arose and danced, as they moved from one end of the wigwam to the other. As they go round, one-half of them cast their heads down upon their bosoms, as if affected by the medicine, which was kept in small skins, and which they pretended to thrust at each other; this was done to deceive the ignorant. These forms were continued several days. The party to be made medicine men and women, looked on in the mean time, to see what they would have to do themselves. Then they are taken to another place with our medicine men, and are taught the science of medicine. After receiving instructions, another day was allotted to give them instruction on morality. They were advised on various subjects. All were to keep silence, and endeavor to retain what they were taught. I will here give some of the sayings of our medicine men:

"If you are a good hunter, warrior, and a medicine man, when you die, you will have no difficulty in getting to the far west in the spirit land."

"Listen to the words of your parents, never be impatient, then the Great Spirit will give you a long life."

"Never pass by any indigent person without giving him something to eat. Owh wah-yah-bak-mek ke-gah-shah-wa-ne-mig—the spirit that sees you will bless you."

"If you see an orphan in want, help him; for you will be rewarded by his friends here, or thanked by his parents in the land of spirits."

"If you own a good hunting dog, give it to the first poor man who really needs it."

"When you kill a deer, or bear, never appropriate it to yourself alone, if others are in want; never withhold from them what the Great Spirit has blessed you with."

"When you eat, share with the poor children who are near you, for when you are old they will administer to your wants."

"Never use improper medicine to the injury of another, lest you yourself receive the same treatment."

"When an opportunity offers, call the aged together, and provide for them venison properly cooked, and give them a hearty welcome; then the gods that have favored them will be your friends."

These are a few specimens of the advice given by our fathers, and by adhering to their counsels the lives, peace, and happiness of the Indian race were secured; for then there was no whiskey among them. O! that accursed thing. O! why did the white man give it to my poor fathers? None but fiends in human shape could have introduced it among us.

I recollect the day when my people in Canada were both numerous and happy; and since then, to my sorrow, they have faded away like frost before the heat of the sun! Where are now that once numerous and happy people? The voice of but few is heard.

When I think of them, I feel pained to know that many have fallen a prey to its soul and body-destroying influence. I could adopt the language of the poet:

> *I will go to my tent and lie down in despair,*
> *I will paint me with black, and sever my hair,*
> *I will sit on the shore where the hurricane blows,*
> *And relate to the God of the tempest my woes;*
> *For my kindred are gone to the mounds of the dead,*
> *But they died not of hunger nor wasting decay,*
> *For the drink of the white man hath swept them away.*

The Ojebwa nation, that unconquered nation, has fallen a prey to the withering influence of intemperance. Their buoyant spirits could once mount the air as on the wings of a bird. Now they have no spirits. They are hedged in, bound, and maltreated, by both the American and British governments. They have no other hope, than that at some day they will be relieved from their privations and trials by death. The fire-water has rolled towards them like the waves of the sea. Alas! alas! my poor people! The tribe became dissipated, and consequently improvident, and often suffered intensely.

It was in visiting the interior that we always suffered most. I will here narrate a single circumstance which will convey a correct idea of the sufferings to which the Indians were often exposed. To collect furs of different kinds for the traders, we had to travel far into the woods and remain there the whole winter. Once we left Rice Lake in the fall, and ascended the river in canoes, above Bellmont Lake. There were five families about to hunt with my father, on his grounds. The winter began to set in, and the river having frozen over, we left the canoes, the dried venison, the beaver, and some flour and pork; and when we had gone farther north, say about sixty miles from the whites, for the purpose of hunting, the snow fell for five days in succession to such a depth that it was impossible to shoot or trap anything. Our provisions were exhausted, and we had no means to procure any more. Here we were. The snow about five feet deep; our wigwam buried; the branches of the trees falling around us, and cracking from the weight of the snow.

Our mother boiled birch bark for my sister and myself, that we might not starve. On the seventh day some of them were so weak that they could not raise themselves, and others could not stand alone. They could only crawl in and out of the wigwam. We parched beaver skins and old moccasons for food. On the ninth day none of the men were able to go abroad, except my father and uncle. On the tenth day, still being without food, those only who were able to walk about the wigwam were my father, my grand-mother, my sister, and myself. O how distressing to see the starving Indians lying about the wigwam with hungry and eager looks; the children would cry for something to eat. My poor mother would heave *bitter sighs of despair*, the tears falling from her cheeks profusely as she kissed us. Wood, though plenty, could not be obtained, on account of the feebleness of our limbs.

My father, at times, would draw near the fire, and rehearse some prayer to the gods. It appeared to him that there was no way of escape; the men, women and children dying; some of them were speechless. The wigwam was cold and dark, and covered with snow. On the eleventh day, just before daylight, my father fell into a sleep; he soon awoke and said to me, "My son, the Great Spirit is about to bless us; this night in my dream I saw a person coming from the east, walking on tops of the trees. He told me that we should obtain two beavers this morning about nine o'clock. Put on your moccasons and go along with me to the river, and we will hunt the beaver, perhaps for the last time." I saw that his countenance beamed with delight; he was full of confidence. I put on my moccasons and carried my snow shoes, staggering along behind him, about half a mile. Having made a fire near the river, where there was an air hole, through which the beaver had come up during the night, my father tied a gun to a stump, with the muzzle towards the air hole; he also tied a string to the trigger, and said "should you see the beaver rise, pull the string and you will kill it." I stood by the fire with the string in my hand. I soon heard a noise occasioned by the blow of his tomahawk; he had killed a beaver, and he brought it to me. As he laid it down, he said "then the Great Spirit will not let us die here;" adding, as before, "if you see the beaver rise, pull the string." He left me, I soon saw the nose of one; but I did not shoot. Presently another came up; I pulled the trigger, and off the gun went. I could not see for sometime for the smoke. My father ran towards me, took the two beavers and laid them side by side; then pointing to the sun, said, "Do you see the sun? The Great Spirit informed me that we should kill these two about this time this morning. We will yet see our relatives at Rice Lake; now let us go home and see if they are still alive." We hastened home, and arrived just in time to save them from death. Since which, we visited the same spot, the year after the missionaries came among us. My father, with feelings of gratitude, knelt down on the spot where we had nearly perished. Glory to God! But what have I done for him since? Comparatively nothing. We were just at death's door, when Christianity rescued us. I have heard of many, who have perished in this way, far in the woods. In my travels to the west, I have met many whose families had perished, and who had themselves merely escaped starvation. May God forgive me, for my ingratitude and indolence in his blessed cause!

I will here introduce a favorite war song of the Ojebwa nation. It was accompanied by dancing, and an occasional war-whoop. At the end of each stanza, a warrior rehearsed some former victories, which inspired them with ardor for war. Unchristianized Indians are often like greedy lions after their prey; yes, at times they are indeed cruel and blood thirsty. I have met with warriors, who, when they had killed their enemies, cut open their breasts, took our their hearts, and drank their blood; and all this was out of mere *revenge*. But to the *War Song*, which was first translated for Col McKinney, *"the Indian's friend,"* on the shore of Lake Superior.

> *"On that day when our heroes lay low—lay low—*
> *On that day when our heroes lay low,*
> *I fought by their side, and thought ere I died,*
> *Just vengeance to take on the foe—the foe—*
> *Just vengeance to take on the foe.*
>
> *"On that day when our chieftains lay dead—lay dead—*
> *On that day when our chieftains lay dead,*
> *I fought hand to hand, at the head of my band,*
> *And here, on my breast, have I bled—have I bled—*
> *And here, on my breast, have I bled.*
>
> *"Our chiefs shall return no more—no more—*
> *Our chiefs shall return no more—*
> *And their brothers in war who can't show scar for scar,*
> *Like women their fates shall deplore—shall deplore—*
> *Like women, their fates shall deplore.*
>
> *"Five winters in hunting we'll spend—we'll spend—*
> *Five winters in hunting we'll spend—*
> *Then our youths grown to men, to the war lead again,*
> *And our days like our fathers', we'll end—we'll end—*
> *And our days like our fathers', we'll end."*[6]

1850

■ JOHN ROLLIN RIDGE (CHEROKEE) ■
1827–1867

John Rollin Ridge was a member of the Treaty Party of Cherokees. His father and grandfather were among the founders of the party, so designated because of its support for the Treaty of New Echota (1835), which provided for removal of the

[6]"Col McKinney, 'the Indian's friend,' ... And our days like our fathers', we'll end." See Colonel Thomas L. McKenney's *Sketches of a Tour of the Lakes, of the Character and customs of the Chippeway Indians* ... , 1827. Copway and McKenney quote the war song of Wa-ba-jick, a great war chief of La Point, Lake Superior. The song was translated by his daughter, O-Shau-Guscoday-way-gua, wife of John Johnston (1762– 1828). Their daughter, Jane Johnston, married Henry Rowe Schoolcraft (see her translations of the Ojibwa stories "Mishosha, or the Magician and his Daughters" and "The Forsaken Brother").

Cherokees from the South to Indian Territory. Much of Ridge's writing on American Indians argues for the need of all Indians to become "civilized"—that is, to be assimilated into white society—in order to survive.

Born in Georgia in 1827, Ridge was no stranger to turmoil. During his childhood, the Cherokee Nation was under pressure from whites to vacate their traditional lands and move westward. The Cherokees protested, but despite their eloquent arguments, it eventually became clear to many tribesmen that the cause was lost. As a result, John Ridge (his father), Major Ridge, a nephew Elias Boudinot, and others signed the removal treaty, which resulted in the displacement of most of the Cherokees to Indian Territory.

Shortly after removal was completed in 1839, the two elder Ridges and Boudinot were assassinated on the same day in separate incidents by Ross Party Cherokees, who opposed removal. The assassins dragged John Ridge from his bed and, in full view of his wife and children, stabbed him repeatedly. The scene remained in John Rollin Ridge's mind all his life. Fearing for their lives, the family fled to Arkansas, where Ridge remained for ten years, except for a brief stint at Great Barrington Academy in Massachusetts. He received a classical education under Cephas Washburn in Arkansas and for a time studied law. In 1846 Ridge married and settled down to farm in the Indian Territory. As the result of an argument that grew out of factional divisions in the tribe, Ridge killed a member of the Ross Party and was forced to flee once more. He lived for a while in southern Missouri, where he agitated against the Ross faction and even announced plans for an armed invasion of the Cherokee Nation. In 1850, however, he joined a number of other Cherokees on their way to the California goldfields. He always planned to return to the Cherokee Nation and, on at least two different occasions, introduced schemes to establish an Indian newspaper in the area. Although he never returned to Indian Territory, he remained in contact with his family and members of the Treaty Party. He was obviously considered a member of the group since he was asked to lead the Cherokee Southern delegation in its treaty deliberations after the Civil War.

In California, Ridge edited several newspapers and was an outspoken opponent of the Republicans. A Douglas Democrat, he was heavily involved in California politics. He also continued his literary career in California. He had begun writing and publishing poetry in Indian Territory and Arkansas, and his writing earned him some degree of fame as a poet in California. In 1854 he published a volume of romance fiction, *Life and Adventures of Joaquin Murieta, the Celebrated California Bandit*, ostensibly a true story. Although the book was very popular and Ridge achieved some fame from it, it was not a financial success.

Ridge wrote and published poetry in Arkansas and California. Much of this poetry uses poetic conventions common in the works of English and American Romantic poets. The themes and structures in his work are often similar to those of earlier writers, especially in the pieces that deal with nature. Ridge's nature poems attempt to recreate the poet's personal experiences with the natural environment, which often have mystical or transcendental qualities. Imagination is nearly always the force that makes these experiences possible. His other poems are autobiographical and intensely personal, again following Romantic models. While in California, Ridge wrote occasional poems, many of which are testimonials to the nineteenth-century idea of progress and the doctrine of Manifest Destiny.

In both his poetry and his prose, John Rollin Ridge argued that the only chance for survival for the American Indian lay in assimilating into white society. Like many others in the nineteenth century, Ridge was convinced of the reality of Manifest Destiny. He believed that the march of European civilization and technological progress was inexorable and could not be ignored by Indian nations. Yet, like most assimilated Indians of his time, he argued that justice demanded that his less acculturated brothers be safeguarded from oppression while the gradual process of acculturation took place. That way they might be saved from extinction. In some measure, no doubt, the alienation projected by Ridge was part of the legacy of colonization and removal that had been the tragic fate of his people, the Cherokees.

James W. Parins
University of Arkansas at Little Rock

PRIMARY WORKS

Life and Adventures of Joaquin Murieta, the Celebrated California Bandit, 1854; *Poems*, 1868.

Oppression of Digger Indians[1]

The Daily Bee
Tuesday Evening, July 12, 1857

A gentleman residing in this city, who has but recently returned from a hunting trip in Humboldt county, informs us of certain outrages committed upon the Digger Indians of that region, which ought to be made public. He went up to a valley about thirty miles south of the mouth of Eel river, which empties into the Pacific, where, finding a plenty of elk, deer, and bear, he temporarily located. The region is filled at this season with American hunters. There is but one permanent white resident in the valley—a man who went there from Nevada county with a Digger squaw for his wife, and accompanied by the Indians of the rancheria from which he took her. He is living on a ranch, the limits of which have not yet been surveyed, and which is covered by a large number of cattle brought there and placed upon it, from time to time, by himself. The increase of his stock promises to be rapid; in fact, the man is already a wealthy individual, though occupying so isolated and semi-savage a condition. Losing some of his cattle recently, which our informant says he is certain were in some instances killed, and in others driven off, by the hunters, he attributed the depredations to the Indians belonging to that region, and requested the hunters to shoot down every Indian, (except those he brought with him from Nevada county,) that they should come across. Many of the hunters were more than ready to act upon the suggestion, for it gave them a

[1]This essay appeared in the Sacramento *Daily Bee* on July 12, 1857. It was reprinted in Farmer and Strickland's *A Trumpet of Our Own*, from which it is reprinted here.

still better chance for carrying on a traffic in which they had previously been engaged, to wit: kidnapping Digger children and selling them in different parts of the country. A great many Indians have thus been shot down in cold blood by these white savages, and the inhuman practice of kidnapping is now going on with the steadiness of a regular system.

It is a pity that these poor and imbecile people cannot better be protected than they are by the General Government. We do not think it is the fault of the Indian Superintendent or his agents, in every instance, that such outrages occur. Many of the tribes of Diggers straggle off from the main body of their people and hide themselves in the mountains in order to escape being put on the reservations, and by so doing place themselves completely in the power of the hundreds of lawless white men who pitch their camps from place to place through the mountains, and make their money partly by hunting, partly by stealing cattle and laying it to the Indians, and partly by the system of kidnapping above alluded to. This latter practice is common in various parts of the country.

There is no remedy for these impositions upon the unfortunate Diggers, but the one now at work, and that is the placing them, as fast as it can be done, upon the reservations for their reception. The fact that such flagrant impositions are committed should cause renewed energy and exertion in this regard by those whose business it is especially to attend to it. There is no plea for the poor Digger but that of humanity. He has none of the romance which gathers around the nobler savage of the western prairies— he cannot defend himself or his rights, and a prayer for mercy is his only argument against cruelty and oppression.

1857

The Stolen White Girl

The prairies are broad, and the woodlands are wide
And proud on his steed the wild half-breed may ride,
With the belt round his waist and the knife at his side.
And no white man may claim his beautiful bride.

Though he stole her away from the land of the whites,   5
Pursuit is in vain, for her bosom delights
In the love that she bears the dark-eyed, the proud,
Whose glance is like starlight beneath a night-cloud.

Far down in the depths of the forest they'll stray,
Where the shadows like night are lingering all day;   10
Where the flowers are springing up wild at their feet,
And the voices of birds in the branches are sweet.

Together they'll roam by the streamlets that run,
O'ershadowed at times then meeting the sun—
The streamlets that soften their varying tune,   15
As up the blue heavens calm wanders the moon!

The contrast between them is pleasing and rare;
Her sweet eye of blue, and her soft silken hair,
Her beautiful waist, and her bosom of white
That heaves to the touch with a sense of delight;   20

His form more majestic and darker his brow,
Where the sun has imparted its liveliest glow—
An eye that grows brighter with passion's true fire,
As he looks on his loved one with earnest desire.

Oh, never let Sorrow's cloud darken their fate,   25
The girl of the "pale face," her Indian mate!
But deep in the forest of shadows and flowers,
Let Happiness smile, as she wings their sweet hours.

                                                                 1868

A Scene Along the Rio de las Plumas

With solemn step I trace
A dark and dismal place,
Where moss with trailing ends,
From heavy boughs depends;
Where day resembles night,   5
And birds of sullen flight
Pierce darkness with their screams;
Where slow and sluggish streams
Crawl through the sleeping woods
And weirdful solitudes.   10
In dreamy languor bound,
Upon their slimy breast
The lolling lilies rest,
And from their depths profound
Strange things, with staring eyes   15
And uncouth limbs, arise—
A moment gaze with mute surprise
Then sink adown like lead,
And seek their oozy bed.
What looks a spirit there,   20
Snow-white upon the air,
And hov'ring over these

Deep pools and drooping trees,
As if some heavenly sprite
Had come from Day to Night,   25
Is but the crane that feeds
When hungered 'mong the reeds
Or sloughs, flag-margined, wades,
Meandering 'neath the shades
And makes his vulgar dish   30
Of creeping things and fish.

Yon ermined owl that flits
Through dusky leaves, or sits
In somber silence now
On yonder ivyed bough   35
And looks a druid priest—
No higher thoughts inspire
Than lowest wants require,
As how to make his feast,
When lurking mouse or bird   40
Hath from its convert stirred.
Those flaming eyes awake
In yonder thorny brake,
Which dilate as I pass,
Illumining the grass   45
And lighting darksome ground,
Are not from that profound,
Where cries of woe resound
And Dante's damned abound,[1]
Nor yet the wandering ghouls,—   50
The dread of dead men's souls,—
(Because their flesh he craves,
And digs it from their graves),
But orbs of sinuous snake
Who from the neighboring lake,   55
Or vapor-breeding bog,
His victim soon shall take—
Some luckless dozing frog.
Nor will thy lither shape,
Thou rodent sly escape,   60
If once thine eye hath caught
The fire within that head,
From venomed sources fed,
With fascination fraught.

[1]The reference is to Dante's *Inferno*, the first
part of his long poem *The Divine Comedy*.

I reach a dimmer nook,   65
And warily I look,
For where you night-shades grow
And baneful blossoms blow,
Beneath the toadstools, well
I know ill-creatures dwell—   70
Tarantula, whose bite
Would strongest heart affright;
The stinging centipede,
Whose hundred-footed speed,
And hundred arm-ed feet   75
Bring death and danger fleet,
That, with Briarean clasp[2]
The fated victim grasp,
And scorpion, single-stinged,
Fabled erst as winged,   80
And still reported wide,
If pressed, a suicide.
And here I see—but lo!
I can no further go,
For what's this hum I hear   85
Which fills the atmosphere,
And drums the tingling ear
Till, half distraught, I reel?
I heard, but no I feel!
Good sakes, what winged forms!   90
What singing, dizzying swarms!
Ten thousand needles flamed
Could not with them be named.

                                                  1868

---

[2]In Greek mythology, Briareus was a monster
of a hundred hands.

SPANISH AMERICAS

When the nineteenth century began, the United States stretched only one-third of the distance across the North American continent, its dreams of further westward expansion thwarted by the colonial empires of France and Spain. At that point, there were still doubts that the U.S. experiment in republican democracy would survive. The newly formed nation was just one very small part of a web of nations and empires struggling for control of the hemisphere's resources. The British had arrived belatedly in the Americas. Well before their arrival, Spaniards were leaving indelible cultural markings across what is now the United States as well as the rest of the hemisphere. This violent Spanish colonial era lasted nearly three hundred years, from the time Cabeza de Vaca began his monumental trek—on foot—across present Texas and northern Mexico in 1528 to the successful culmination of the Mexican independence movement in 1821. France retreated from the competition for dominance with the sale of its vast Louisiana Territory in 1803, and the United States then found itself abutting, along its southwestern flank, the tantalizing provinces of New Spain, a colony soon to undergo its own revolutionary upheaval and emerge as the sovereign nation of Mexico. While Anglo-Americans scorned *Mexicanos*, they nevertheless coveted their land and, over a thirty-year period—through settlement, purchase, deception, annexation, and the ultimate device of the Mexican War—systematically relieved Mexico of nearly half its territory: Texas, New Mexico, Arizona, California, Nevada, Utah, and much of Colorado. As it turned out, the U.S. victory was military and political but not cultural. From St. Augustine, Florida, on the Atlantic Coast, to New Orleans at the end of the Mississippi, to San Diego and points north on the Pacific, the legacy of Spain and Mexico is evident, from ranching and agricultural practices to the design and names of hundreds of towns and cities.

During this tumultuous period, marked by the Haitian Revolution on the one hand and the U.S. Civil War on the other, Cuban, Puerto Rican, Spanish, and Mexican intellectuals established newspapers, periodicals, and active communities of revolutionary foment in U.S., Spanish, and French cities including Philadelphia, New York, Tampa, and New Orleans. Their vast and impressive literary output has often been shielded from view, partly because of the monolingualism of many literary scholars and partly because the convulsive histories of slavery, abolition, and Native genocide have held such prominence in U.S. histories, both literary and otherwise. Owing to the efforts of many dedicated scholars, including Raymond Paredes and the collaborative work of the Hispanic Recovery Project, the literary wealth of this network and period have become better known and studied. During the first half of the nineteenth century, however, the work of these poets and novelists was far more prominent. William Cullen Bryant, for example, translated José Maria Heredia's poetry, and his translations circulated across the continents. One of the first historical novels

published in either the United States or Europe, *Xicotencatl*, inspired a generation of interest in Aztec history.

As Anglo-Americans entered what is now the southwestern United States,
the impact of their culture varied from one region to another. In Texas and
New Mexico, for example, Anglo-American influences transformed the standing
culture at a relatively moderate pace after 1821, when the Stephen Austin
settlement was established. Oral traditions continued to shape cultural practices. In California, the discovery of gold in 1848 precipitated a swarm of Anglo-
American fortune hunters and settlers who virtually swamped much of *californio*
culture. The 1836 annexation of Texas and the 1846–1848 war against Mexico
inspired a great deal of literary output as supporters and opponents weighed
the ethics and import of the war. The Treaty of Guadalupe Hidalgo, which ended
the Mexican War in 1848, granted U.S. citizenship to the 80,000 Mexicans
in the annexed territories and promised to support continued education in
Spanish as well as protect existing land and treaty rights. The move toward
annexation inspired many dreams of continuing U.S. expansion across the
Caribbean and Central America. It would take another war, this time against
Spain in 1898, before such dreams resulted in further territorial gains.

■ LA LLORONA ■

There was a woman, or so the story goes, who committed the most monstrous
of deeds and in doing so became a legend. In an act of revenge or desperation,
La Llorona (The Weeping Woman) is said to have murdered her offspring and
futilely searches for what can never be recovered—forgiveness and her children's lives. As punishment, her ghostly form wanders the shores of rivers, alley-
ways, or garbage dumps and can be heard wailing in the night, "Aye, mis hijos"
("Oh, my children!"). Those unlucky enough to cross paths with this threatening
figure tell of narrow escapes from a woman who steals living children as substitutes for her own dead ones and punishes men whom she blames for her fate.

For people of Mexican ancestry, La Llorona figures prominently in oral and
literary traditions on both sides of the U.S./Mexican border. Told as a ghost
story or a cautionary tale, a familiar version of the legend has La Llorona being
abandoned by her male lover for another woman. In an inconsolable rage, La
Llorona drags her children to the river and pushes them beneath the surface of
the water. Later horrified by her own actions, she dies grief-stricken. Although
the man in the story is often cited as the catalyst for La Llorona's suffering, his
bad behavior is rarely scrutinized; rather, the emphasis in the story is on La
Llorona's response to his actions. Variations of the story often substitute economic adversity or unspeakable violence from an external threat for the heterosexual romance, though the outcome is the same: La Llorona is doomed and
damned. Although familiar elements appear repeatedly in Llorona stories (a
woman, a heterosexual romance, infanticide, and a body of water), these

features are absent in many versions of the tale. The wide variation in these stories has led one folklorist to conclude that the only commonality among them is the name La Llorona itself. Further complicating her position in the cultural imaginary is the fact that she is alternately, and sometimes simultaneously, "a person, legend, ghost, goddess, metaphor, story, and/or symbol." However one chooses to view La Llorona, she has been a part of Mexican and Mexican American cultural tradition for nearly five hundred years.

According to Luis González Obregón in *Las Calles de Mexico* (1922), stories about La Llorona began to surface around 1550, during the early colonial period of Mexico immediately following the Spanish conquest (1519–1521). While a number of folklorists and scholars see La Llorona as representing an Old World allegory, one heavily influenced by Catholicism and brought to Mexico by Europeans, others hold a different view. For example, folklorist Thomas Janvier, as well as Chicana feminists Gloria Anzaldúa and Cherríe Moraga, see La Llorona and her story as a distinctly New World phenomenon. They see her as indigenous in origin, either representative of Native people in general or derived from females goddesses found in the Mexica-Aztec pantheon—specifically, Cihuacoatl ("Snake Woman"), who was said to wander through the city of Tenochtitlan, chalked in white and carrying a cradleboard that contained a knife strapped to her back, calling out for sacrifices; and Coatlicue ("Serpent Skirt"), mother of Huitzilopochtli, the god of war, who had the power to create and destroy, with whom the weeping woman shares similar characteristics. According to Tey Diana Rebolledo, La Llorona, like Coatlicue, "approximates in popular folklore all those ancient Nahuatl [Aztec] deities who had life-giving and -destroying abilities." La Llorona has since become an integral part of the Mexican ideological landscape, signifying, along with the Virgin de Guadalupe and La Malinche, one version of Mexican and Mexican American maternity.

Whereas Guadalupe and Malinche traditionally represent virtue and treachery, respectively, in this female triad, La Llorona signifies maternal failure. In her perceived moral transgressions and betrayal of the family as an institution, La Llorona is often conflated with La Malinche. As Rita Alcalá argues, the merging of these two figures is born from the fictionalized fate of Malinche's children with Cortés. She is said to have drowned their children rather than allow them to return to Spain with their father. There is no historical evidence to support this claim. Though both share a history of conflict with Old World, Spanish, Catholic patriarchy and are vilified, each retains distinct characteristics. Together, all three figure prominently in Mexican and Chicano cultural history.

In an effort to exercise interpretative control over these icons, Chicana feminists have performed critical interventions through their cultural considerations of La Virgen, La Malinche, and La Llorona. The poem which follows here provides just one example. Feminist analyses, such as Carmen Tafolla's poem "La Llorona, Crying Lady of the Creekbeds, 483 Years Old, and Aging," call attention to the way that men have put to use these figures, historically and politically, in the project of nation building. They also help to expose the subversive possibilities of figures like La Llorona, who weeps not only for her children or for herself but also for those who long to exercise authority over their own bodies and their own lives. A native of San Antonio, Texas, Carmen Tafolla (b. 1951) is an award-winning poet, short story writer, and author of children's books. Tafolla holds a Ph.D. in Bilingual and Foreign Language Education from the University of Texas (1982). Referencing a history that stretches back five hundred years, the poem substitutes the heterosexual romance for other oppressive forces, including politicians, environmental racism, and classism. In the contemporary world, La Llorona is the one who is threatened by loss and erasure.

Domino Renee Perez
University of Texas at Austin

Legend of La Llorona

As is generally known, Señor, many bad things are met with by night in the streets of the City; but this Wailing Woman, La Llorona, is the very worst of them all. She is worse by far than the *vaca de lumbre*[1]—that at midnight comes forth from the *potrero*[2] of San Pablo and goes galloping through the streets like a blazing whirlwind, breathing forth from her nostrils smoke and sparks and flames: because the Fiery Cow, Señor, while a dangerous animal to look at, really does no harm whatever and La Llorona is as harmful as she can be!

Seeing her walking quietly along the quiet street—at the times when she is not running, and shrieking for her lost children—she seems a respectable person, only odd looking because of her white petticoat and the white *reboso*[3] with which her head is covered, and anybody might speak to her. But whoever does speak to her, in that very same moment dies!

The beginning of her was so long ago that no one knows when was the beginning of her; nor does any one know anything about her at all. But it is known certainly that at the beginning of her, when she was a living woman, she committed bad sins. As soon as ever a child was born to her she would throw it into one of the canals which surround the City, and so would drown it; and she had a great many children, and this practice in regard to them she continued for a long time. At last her conscience began to prick her about what she did with her children; but whether it was that the priest spoke to her, or that some of the saints cautioned her in the matter, no one knows. But it is certain that because of her sinnings she began to go through the streets in the darkness weeping and wailing. And presently it was said that from night till morning there was a wailing woman in the streets; and to see her, being in terror of her, many people went forth at midnight; but none did see her, because she could be seen only when the street was deserted and she was alone.

Sometimes she would come to a sleeping watchman, and would waken him by asking: "What time is it?" And he would see a woman clad in white

[1]"fiery cow"
[2]"field"
[3]Alternate spelling of "rebozo," a triangular-shaped piece of cloth used as a functional accessory by women in Mexico. It can be used as a head-covering, shawl, or to carry infants and other items.

standing beside him with her *reboso* drawn over her face. And he would answer: "It is twelve hours of the night." And she would say: "At twelve hours
of this day I must be in Guadalajara!"—or it might be in San Luis Potosi, or
in some other far-distant city—and, so speaking, she would shriek bitterly:
"Where shall I find my children?"—and would vanish instantly and utterly
away. And the watchman would feel as though all his senses had gone from
him, and would become as a dead man. This happened many times to many
watchmen, who made report of it to their officers; but their officers would
not believe what they told. But it happened, on a night, that an officer of
the watch was passing by the lonely street beside the church of Santa Anita.
And there he met with a woman wearing a white *reboso* and a white petticoat; and to her he began to make love. He urged her, saying: "Throw off
your *reboso* that I may see your pretty face!" And suddenly she uncovered
her face—and what he beheld was a bare grinning skull set fast to the bare
bones of a skeleton! And while he looked at her, being in horror, there came
from her fleshless jaws an icy breath; and the iciness of it froze the very
heart's blood in him, and he fell to the earth heavily in a deathly swoon.
When his senses came back to him he was greatly troubled. In fear he
returned to the Diputacion,[4] and there told what had befallen him. And in a
little while his life forsook him and he died. What is most wonderful about
this Wailing Woman, Señor, is that she is seen in the same moment by different people in places widely apart: one seeing her hurrying across the
atrium of the Cathedral; another beside the *Arcos de San Cosme*; and yet
another near the *Salto del Agua*,[5] over by the prison of Belen. More than
that, in one single night she will be seen in Monterey and in Oaxaca and in
Acapulco—the whole width and length of the land apart—and whoever
speaks with her in those far cities, as here in Mexico, immediately dies in
fright. Also, she is seen at times in the country. Once some travellers coming
along a lonely road met with her, and asked: "Where go you on this lonely
road?" And for answer she cried: "Where shall I find my children?" and,
shrieking, disappeared. And one of the travellers went mad. Being come here
to the City they told what they had seen; and were told that this same Wailing Woman had maddened or killed many people here also. Because the
Wailing Woman is so generally known, Señor, and so greatly feared, few
people now stop her when they meet with her to speak with her—therefore
few now die of her, and that is fortunate. But her loud keen wailings, and
the sound of her running feet, are heard often; and especially in nights of
storm. I myself, Señor, have heard the running of her feet and her wailings;
but I never have seen her. God forbid that I ever shall!

1910

---

[4]Provincial or local government.   [5]Near Mexico City.

■   CARMEN TAFOLLA[1]   ■
                          B. 1951

La Llorona, Crying Lady of the Creekbeds, 483 Years Old, and Aging

(—when we were children, we were told how La Llorona had lost her children, how one could hear her cry at night, searching for their dead lives, wailing, flying hair, and wild eyes. Different versions and different reasons, each to tell us a moral, to warn us. Once, we found out what her phone number was and used to dial and listen to her cry, passing around the phone from one to the next.

Years later, we learned that the myth predated the arrival of the Spaniards. The crying lady, a *malinche*, had bemoaned the fate of her own children, a fate she had been accomplice to. We knew she would be forever with us, forever in our memories, crying for her dead children and for her children yet unborn that were to die.

But creekbeds got scarce in the barrio, and so, La Llorona had to get a phone installed so we could reach her, so we could hear her, so she could let us know the truth.)

La Llorona
they took away her children
    the welfare office came and stole away her children
    because she had no right, they said,
    to be a single parent, non-model American family

they took away her children
    (all unborn)
    because He was married and she was on the pill and
    He didn't care to fool with divorce and didn't care to
    have any bastard children and asked her
    not to have his.

they took away her children
    it was way-out-of-style to long for large families
    and staying home with one's babies and breast-feeding truth
    and love and all that rot, especially if you were a professional
    and should know better, and one was only allowed to have two
    anyway, and only if one let the day-care raise them.

[1]During the 1970s, poet Carmen Tafolla used
the pen name Victoria Moreno.

they took away her children
"how are you *PROTECTING* yourself?" they always asked,
as if one could be *attacked* by pregnancy at any minute
and torn to shreds like the most horrible distortion

they took away her children
because there was no time
to build them a world, no time
in the battlefront, soldiers always needed
and she had to struggle just
to stay alive

they took away her children
and made decrees about all children-to-be
(too soon) and slipped anti-fertility chemicals into
the water, to insure a society that was *clean* and
scheduled and *sterile*, like the clinics designed to—
(well, don't worry about preserving health, just make sure to
FIGHT DISEASE!)

they took away her children
And the Aztec Lady crying down the creekbeds
ran into a concrete wall and, puzzled blank,
stopped her wailing for her children
and just stared, realizing that
hope was gone.
While I took up the dirge
and, screaming down the streets at night,
carried on the insane truth, the pain
knowing that

they took away her children.

1977

VALENTÍN DE FORONDA
1751–1821

Valentín de Foronda has emerged as one of the most significant writers of the Spanish Enlightenment. He was one of the most liberal of the Spanish diplomats to the U.S., serving first as consul general and then as acting minister (1807–1809). He was a man of letters, who preferred to devote his energy to producing knowledge that could ameliorate Spain's worsening socio-economic conditions. He managed to combine his role as a royal diplomat with that of a travel writer, moving about Europe reading and imbibing from texts that were difficult—though not impossible—to acquire in Spain, and he became a professor at the prestigious *Seminario Patriótico* of the Royal Basque Economic Society of Friends of the Country in Vergara, Spain. He contributed regularly to Spanish periodicals, wrote widely on a variety of topics—penal reform, political economy, freedom of the press, public health, poverty and social reform programs, Locke's treatise on education, Cervantes' *Don Quixote*, Rousseau's *Social Contract*—and translated Condillac's *Logique*.

Foronda was one of the earliest Hispanic members of the American Philosophical Society and a close friend of Thomas Jefferson. Toward the end of 1803, he delivered a fascinating thought experiment to the American Philosophical Society in Philadelphia in which he contemplated ways that Spain might improve its economic standing among nations. Most telling, the paper was published in 1803, the year of the Louisiana Purchase, but dated 1800, the year that Spain secretly signed a treaty with France giving the Louisiana Territory to France (Spain would continue to rule the territory until 1803). The document is signed only with the initial F., but internal evidence makes it clear that Foronda is the author.[1]

The essay, in the form of a letter, is the earliest known published document to advocate for the separation of Spanish America from Spain in the name of improving the well-being of the *Spanish* nation. It is a convoluted essay, a fascinating allegory told in the guise of a dream. Foronda goes to great lengths to distance himself from the arguments presented, creating elaborate, confusing subterfuges—as well he should have. The Spanish Inquisition had clearly demonstrated that it had no qualms whatsoever in condemning previous Spanish political ministers for veering from political doctrine. Foronda later suffered bitterly at the hands of the Inquisition, was eventually imprisoned, and many of his writings were censored and left unpublished.

Raúl Coronado
University of Chicago

PRIMARY WORKS

Apuntes ligeros sobre los Estados Unidos de la América Septentrional, 1804; *Carta sobre el modo que tal vez convendría a las Cortes seguir en el examen de los objetos que conducen a su fin, y dictamen sobre ellos*, 1811; *Carta sobre lo que debe hacer un principe que tenga colonias a gran distancia*, 1803; *Cartas sobre la obra de Rousseau titulada: Contrato social en las que se vacía todo lo interesante de ella, y se suprime lo que puede herir la religion católica apostólica romana*, 1814; *Cartas sobre los asuntos más exquisitos de la economía-política, y sobre las leyes criminales*, 1789.

---

[1]The essay was written in Spanish, and the only Spanish members of the Society living in Philadelphia at the time were Casa Irujo and Foronda. Likewise, the narrator in the essay admits to having authored *Cartas económicas-políticas*, which Foronda had published in 1789. *Carta sobre lo que debe hacer un principe que tenga colonias a gran distancia* (Philadelphia: American Philosophical Society, 1803), 8, hereafter cited in text.

Letter concerning What a Prince Should Do with His Colonies Held at a Great Distance[1]

Editor's note: Being a lover of the Spanish language, I try to socialize with Spaniards. Recently the issue of their Colonies came up in a conversation I had with one of them. That is the reason I commented on the sheer happiness of his Nation that owned the Kingdoms of Mexico and Peru, but I realized that far from agreeing with my ideas, he rejected them. He finished by telling me: "I have a copy of a letter that a friend of mine wrote on the problem of the Colonies, to add to the ones he has written to an imaginary Prince, and I will share it with Your Grace if you wish." I immediately accepted his offer and read the letter, and believing that the ideas found in it are worthy of the attention of Spanish political-economists,[2] I have decided to publish it, being sure that political truths reveal themselves by having opinions fight amongst each other in public.

V.[3] . . . 1st of March, 1800

What vigils and bitterness, my dear friend, have not been caused by the politicians who have made plans and regulations regarding the behavior expected of Princes in their colonies, to make their agriculture, mines and trading prosper, and to keep their colonies restrained and safe from ambitious nations who would want to invade them! What contradictions and false principles have some superficial and cold dissertators not devoured to completely forget the foundational elements of political economy! How delighted have others not become with the wonderful realization of being able to treat the Colonies as sheep that must be kept by its owner, if only to shear its wool and suckle its milk! There are so many different opinions on this issue! But what will my opinion be about Your Grace's colonies? Shall I put my thoughts in press so that my ideas may be distilled into wisdom, and be able to draw my plan with its help? . . . No, my friend, I have no interest in exhausting myself, especially when I can ease the great burden of solving the question of the Colonies, by telling you of a dream I had the other night. Your Grace, listen to my nonsense.

I imagined that Your Grace was the ruler of a large country that had been found between the New World and Asia and that in all things was similar to our Americas, and that to complete your Principality you were missing a smaller neighboring Kingdom,[4] and a Military Base[5] that belonged to a trading Nation.

[1][Translated by Armando García and Raúl Coronado. Note: The editors' footnotes are bracketed. Footnotes from the original are translated but not bracketed.]

[2][Foronda writes during a period when political economy as a field of knowledge was flourishing. Although Adam Smith's *Wealth of Nations* was banned by the Inquisition in 1792, a translated abridged version of Smith's work was published in that same year by the Spanish ambassador to the United States, under whom Foronda had served. This essay is an indefatigable defense of Smith's theory.]

[3][The letter is dated during the period that Foronda was a professor in the Basque city of Vergara, Spain.]

[4]I didn't think to inquire about its name, but we shall call it "P."

[5]We shall call this Military Base "G" or however Your Grace may wish, since we must not pay much attention to dreams.

I immediately thought that Your Grace could acquire the bordering Kingdom by way of negotiation, and never by force, because even when I sleep I am driven by the ideas of justice and humanity that I have so proclaimed in all of my writings.

To carry out my ideas, I had offered my neighbor my entire much-dreamed-about southern island in exchange for his States. This proposition surprised him for a moment, but he soon accepted it gladly, and he thanked me after he had examined, weighed and compared what he was losing with what he was gaining in the barter. In an instant he saw that it was in his best interest: because of the immense territory he was acquiring; because of the greater number of vassals he would be adding; because of the climate; because of the richness and fruitfulness of the land; and because he could join the ranks of the first [world] Powers, and to find himself with the in-sipid and burdensome pleasure of having the European Cabinets seek his counsel, in case he found it in his heart to welcome this pathetic ambition; because he sought to shake off a kind of tutelage he suffers under the Empire of an arrogant Nation;[6] and because he wanted to be free of worry that one of Your Grace's successors could whimsically decide to conquer his States.

Before the exchange had taken place, I realized that the other Nations would not agree to it, but in an instant I solved this real predicament with the following idea: the bartering has been verified without being revealed, but let us assume that it has not yet been consummated and that every Power is arming itself to prevent it, (I asked myself) would this prevent its verification? And I told myself that no, it wouldn't, because the only thing that they could do would be to cover the Ocean Sea with Warships, in which case Your Grace would lock yours up in a Harbor and you would let those of the belligerent Powers pass through, at the expense of raising taxes on their people and letting lay idle a large portion of their factories they employed in Your Grace's Principality and in that of your neighbor's.

It is true, I told myself, that they would try and conquer some of the islands which Your Grace possesses, but the success of their attempts is questionable, it will always cost them much blood spilled, and they will not achieve anything else except what Your Grace should give them, since I also thought that you would have the generosity of gifting them some of your islands, especially to that Nation who could cede you the base that you needed to complete your ideas, and which is only a burden to it, especially when access to Your Grace's Harbors would be free of charge to all members of humanity who follow the charitable belief of treating every Nation as you would sisters.

Likewise, I thought that the resentful Powers would think about con-quering some of the new Empire's bases, but this did not cause me much

---

[6]We shall call this Nation "Y," but so that no one may try and lay claim to it, we will name it "P" or the two letters "G.B."

concern, since I reminded myself that it is an absurd plan to keep garrisons at such a great distance when these are surrounded by enemy nations led by an enlightened Government. But, assuming that their preservation would be possible, I would make sure that they would only be used to defend their commerce, but since they have none, because the new King of my imaginary island would not permit it, it would be madness to waste time, men and money only because of the simple whim of conquering lands.

As for the rest of Your Grace's possessions, you would sell them to trading companies and to Princes who, although they have more than enough near them, have the habit of owning territories thousands of miles from their home.

After I finished making note of my part and my sales, I asked myself what good would come from such a revolution,[7] and I became confused when I realized that the money produced for Your Grace from half of the island alone would pay all of your debts, that it would fill your Principality with roads, navigation and irrigation channels, it would pay for the construction of all of the bridges needed for the rivers and for the work required to prevent floods, it would turn into fertile lands all of the swamps who are only good enough to poison the air, and that it would cover your Principality with Hospitals, houses of mercy and pious shelters to relieve the misery of the public.[8]

Having barely begun to distribute the seed of true wealth on the objectives I have just put forth, I remembered about the tributes, and then happiness overwhelmed me when I realized that without having to pay interest rates, nor meet old and unpaid loans, that without knowing of the countless little offices that cost a lot of money and are necessary to keep track of the Crown's obligations, this Vampire sucker of pockets would soon grow weak. But it was when I considered that War, that monster and ravager of public tranquility, would be [out of place] like an exotic wild animal in Your Grace's Principality that my happy heart truly grew as big as a hot air balloon. This sweet idea made my entire body sweat tears of syrup, and to repeat that no more will we see in Your State those tragic scenes where men join together to kill each other, as if earthquakes, floods and famine were not sufficient enough to destroy humankind; a friend will no longer march over his friend's body, or a brother over his brother's body, all in search of death; nor will he exhale sorrowful breaths towards his country when he remembers a kind woman, young children, who are left without support, and perhaps his bedridden Parents who have no cure for their ailment except for what these children give them; no longer will we know of those fictitious earthquakes, who with the help of gunpowder can blow up a bastion and bury their defendants under a horrible pile of rocks and rubble; no longer will we see people be continuously torn from their homes, nor laborers from

---

[7][Note the understated reference to the French and Haitian revolutions.]

[8][A year prior to the date of this letter, Foronda had published in Spain an identical statement in a prospectus for a newspaper entitled *Humanidad*.]

their fields, to be transformed into Sailors, into soldiers; taxes will no longer be raised to feed ambitious projects that seek to conquer a Province, an island, a City: Your Majesty will soon have a new treasure by selling all of the Warships and other vessels of war, for these mobile bastions will be superfluous; You will no longer spend three-hundred thousand pesos constructing a Warship, nor will you need that large number of warehouses used to hold military supplies, and you will save the cost of maintaining an immensity of sailors, offices, officials and all of the other expenses that always come with a respectable squadron; you will save on all of the costs of maintaining military bases in the Colonies and a large Army on land, since only a small army will be necessary to defend a Principality like Your Grace's (which I am also assuming will be a Peninsula),[9] and your treasury will be increased by keeping to yourself the salaries of the Ambassadors, who will no longer be necessary (assuming you have rid yourself of all bellicose ideas); your Principality will be invulnerable, and you will not need to spy on the movements of ambitious Powers; because all of Europe's forces combined will be worthless if they attempt to conquer a country that is so well situated, such as Your Grace's, and so happy that it can adequately defend itself; and above all, Your Grace will no longer feel the pain of witnessing those formal conventions called treaties voided and torn at every moment, because even though the contracting parties testify to heaven in making their promises, they still violate these without shame, trampling over equality, good faith, and Reason, reason which should join to make these promises respectable.[10]

Far from diminishing, my joy continued to grow by the moment when I contemplated that once wars were done away with that the tributes decreased, the roads, canals and houses of mercy were built, trade guilds destroyed, agriculture and commerce enjoying a total liberty; exclusive privileges destroyed; Customs offices demolished; a good education system established; enlightenment spread across the land; a good legislative system

[9][Foronda at last drops all pretenses and makes clear that this "dream" is in reality a discussion regarding the Spanish Peninsula's American colonies.]

[10]Your Grace should not think that I speak of Spain. No, of course not; this glorious Nation has always distinguished itself through its good faith, and even in the time of the Romans it was known for this virtue, which it has not lost to this day. Your Grace should see what [Gabriel Bonnot de] Mably says in his work on public law, page 433, volume 2. It is remarkable. Spain has followed its contracts faithfully to this day, but this has not been the case with the other States. Probably not everyone has followed its example, especially that Nation of which I speak about, although not by name, who appropriates for itself the title of Philosopher, who has become intoxicated with the illusory, impracticable and unjust will to hold in its hands exclusively the world's commerce, that Nation who defends in open force and demands a 5 percent payment in exchange for the protection it gives to the clandestine commerce done by its Citizens in the Colonies belonging to its friends, closing its ears off to the voices of the treatises who prohibit such treachery; in a word, that Nation who has the intemperate imprudence of requesting that it be recognized as Lord of the seas. [Mably was a French diplomat and political philosopher whose works posthumously influenced the French Revolution, republican political thought, and communism. His complete works were published in French in 1794–1795.]

put in place; in one word, having sown all of the ideas that I have suggested to Your Grace in my epistolary correspondence, You would see that the barren lands would transform into fertile fields; that the resistant and ungrateful lands would bend to your efforts and the drive of industrialism; that the mountains would be covered in thick-topped trees; that the hills would be full of exquisite vineyards; that the meadows would be filled with enormous herds, that in the desserts thriving Cities would flourish, and that on your beaches would emerge safe ports that would revitalize both industry and agriculture.

In the middle of my pleasant excitement, I was accosted by all of those ideas that are read about in the Political-economic books regarding active and passive trade; the balance of commerce; of imports and exports; of the abundance of metals, and all of those ostentatious voices that speak up incessantly, without their logic having been examined, and in whose favor the most intricate of problems are resolved; but I soon regained peace when I remembered what I had written in my first Volume of the economical-political letters regarding such subjects, and with whose assistance it was easy for me to reconcile all of the difficulties being raised.[11]

Since I am a firm believer of that truth that one cannot be a buyer without being a seller, I, of course, noticed that Your Principality's commerce could not be passive [source of raw goods], since you would sell as much as you would buy: given that Your Grace does not accept a surplus of money from other Nations, but rather that they pay you with other merchandise, since gold is not meant to be eaten nor drunk and that its primary use comes from the ability to buy other merchandise with it, an unverifiable reality because of the supposition of achieving a profitable balance, in which case both gold and silver must be accumulated in a country, resources which in Your Grace's Principality will only be good for raising the prices of the goods because they are abundant, so that your vassals would do with three what now they can only do with one; therefore, so that Your Majesty should not have to worry about this, I have taken it upon myself to increase the pecuniary abundance, making sure that the balance, mercantile, monetary, metallic or however you wish to call it, would lean in your favor.[12]

I realized that commerce would be negatively affected or be altogether extinguished in this way, but I consoled myself by remembering the analysis made by a French author, who says that commerce is not but an equal exchange of one thing of value for another, and that only in this way can it

---

[11][Foronda attacks the dominant economic system in place during this period, which was mercantilism. Mercantilism measured wealth according to the amount of bullion that a nation possessed. Adam Smith revolutionized economic thinking by arguing that wealth should be measured by what a nation produced. Foronda also makes reference to his *Cartas económicas-políticas* (1789).]

[12]I realize that everything I have just suggested is nonsense for those who are not drenched in the ideas that I have written in the letters regarding the balance of commerce, and in those about silver and gold as only signs of wealth; hence, whoever is not able to decipher everything I am able to say in these few lines, and would like to, should turn to such letters. [A reference, again, to Foronda's *Cartas económicas-políticas*.]

be carried out between the proprietors of said valuables. And who are these proprietors? Those that own the fruits of the earth and industry, since those that call themselves merchants are nothing but dealers, the agents who actually only facilitate the trade and who are rewarded with a certain percentage, but these do not produce the materials they traffic. The Lawyer, the Clerk, the Notary are not the ones living the problems of their trade, but they are useful for the person whose problems they solve: we should say the same of the traffickers: in the market these are some instruments used by every consumer in need of carrying out his wishes. But the true merchant is the Laborer, the manufacturer, classes that far from being debilitated would acquire a new vigor when being taxed less, enjoying complete freedom and are assisted by good canals and roads.

These realizations consoled me, and at the same time they made me see just how wrong several Governments were in thinking that commerce should be given a voice, since in not thinking this thoroughly, they believed that to seek counsel from commerce meant asking the traffickers; to favor commerce meant granting privileges to the merchants; to enrich commerce meant increasing several times over the wealth of such and such business-men, even if it was at the expense of the other members of Society.

The thought that Your Grace would abandon vast lands did not discon-cert me much, since it is well known that happiness does not depend on one owning deserts, that a well cultivated square mile is alone worth more than thousands of uncultivated lands.

The lack of sugar, coffee, indigo, beets, and other sweet fruits from Asia and the Americas do not upset me, because I knew for sure that the wool, grains, wines, oils, silks, saffron, and the products from Your Grace's Princi-pality would bring in all of those goods in abundance. In sum, I saw that Your Grace would have a diamond mine in your fields and in your factories to make continuous exchanges with all of the Nations, and that your vassals would obtain as much as they would need without having to move from your peninsula.

"From the moment that this unexpected revolution takes place," I said in my dream, "Your Grace will be the most envied of Princes." It is true that they will no longer seek your alliance, since you will no longer have the troops with which to play at being Don Quixote and undo injustices, but only those with which to defend your home in case that some ambitious Prince attempts to disturb your peace. It is also true that you will no longer intervene in the management of Cabinets, nor have the proud and ill-fated pleasure of setting the [political] tone in Europe, but this shall be your greatest fortune, since you will also not take part in the carnage of human blood and will watch peacefully from your Estates those horrible squalls that devastate countries, and you will only think about governing a peaceful country, which must surely be the most glorious of crests for Princes.

With this, I awoke, and recalling everything that had passed through my imagination, I was glad to have dreamt about the happiness of mankind. What delight can equal the thought of diminishing the amount of evils that afflict our fellow man? ... I don't think that any can, and that is why I am overjoyed at having had a good night. What I wish for is that Your Grace would always have a good night, and that when your name is pronounced, your vassals would not think of shackles, dungeons, gallows, as when they hear the names of Tiberius and Caligula, but rather that within them are awakened those sweet ideas inseparable from the names of Antoninus and Titus. May God grant that my wishes come true, and that Your Grace live as many years as yours truly desires.

F.

1800

■ JOSÉ MARÍA HEREDIA ■
1803–1839

In 1822, at the end of most of the wars of independence in Spanish America, the greatly respected Cuban-Mexican poet José María Heredia wrote an allegorical, romantic poem while in exile in New York City capturing the sublimity of hurricanes. Translated into English by William Cullen Bryant in 1827 and republished across the Americas, the poem became extremely well known. Bryant's translation is not so much a literal one as an inspired one, but Bryant's engagement with Heredia's work (he also liberally translated and helped make famous another of Heredia's poems, "Niagara") showcases an important aspect of the inter-American movement of cultural products. As Kristen Silva Gruesz notes, "En una tempestad: Al huracán" was ultimately used long after its publication as an example of how the rich culture of Cuba should be liberated from Spanish rule. Others, however, sought to use the same poem to stir Cuban loyalties to the Spanish empire. That the poem inspired so many different interpretations indicates its crucial place in the battles waged across the nineteenth century for imaginative and physical control of "America."

Born in 1803 in Santiago de Cuba, by the time he was in his teens Heredia was already an active participant in revolutionary efforts to liberate Cuba from Spain. Barely escaping imprisonment and torture, he fled to Boston and then New York; he eventually settled in Mexico, where he participated in politics, continued to write, and lived until his death in 1839. Yet writing from New York in 1822, all he could do was watch as the hurricane of history unleashed its fury on the Antilles, on what remained of the Spanish empire in the Americas. Hurricanes have long served as a vivid political-aesthetic trope for Caribbean writers. In Heredia's poem, the tempest serves as an allegory for the antinomies of modernity, the epistemic shift involved in viewing the world not as a received order but as a produced order. Where once had existed seemingly permanent and immovable "clouds, hills, my dear forest," now only a "shadowy tempest" may be seen "bury[ing] everything." Unlike the spirit of modernity in Anglo-Protestant societies, where progress and history ostensibly went hand in hand and political teleologies abounded, no such thing emerges in the Hispanic world. Heredia's narrator must mourn the devastation of progress even while admiring its ability to shape the future. But the trope of progress and production brought with it the disenchantment of the world. No longer was it a world produced by God where one found everywhere the trace of God's finger. For now, Heredia and his kinsmen were left alone, without God, and with the hurricane.

Heredia's narrator faces the hurricane of history alone as it unfolds its machinations, reconstructing the world before his very eyes. The language of solitude invokes a yearning for companionship, someone with whom the narrator can seek comfort in witnessing the hurricane's devastation. Heredia writes for a reading public that does not yet exist. They had to set out to act in the world in order to produce their future.

Raúl Coronado
University of Chicago

PRIMARY WORKS

En una tempestad, 1853; *The Hurricane*, 1827.

En una tempestad: Oda al huracán (in Spanish)

Huracán, huracán, venir te siento,
y en tu soplo abrasado
respiro entusiasmado
del señor de los aires el aliento.

En las alas del viento suspendido   5
vedle rodar por el espacio inmenso,
silencioso, tremendo, irresistible
en su curso veloz. La tierra en calma
siniestra, misteriosa,
contempla con pavor su faz terrible.   10
¿Al toro no miráis? El suelo escarban
de insoportable ardor sus pies heridos,
la frente poderosa levantando,
y en la hinchada nariz fuego aspirando
llama la tempestad con sus bramidos.   15

¡Qué nubes! ¡qué furor! El sol temblando
vela en triste vapor su faz gloriosa,
y su disco nublado sólo vierte
luz fúnebre y sombría,
que no es noche ni día....   20
¡Pavoroso color, velo de muerte!
Los pajarillos tiemblan y se esconden
al acercarse el huracán bramando,

y en los lejanos montes retumbando
le oyen los bosques, y a su voz responden.   25

Llega ya ... ¿No lo veis? ¡Cuál desenvuelve
su manto aterrador y majestuoso! ...
¡Gigante de los aires, te saludo! ...
En fiera confusión el viento agita
las orlas de tu parda vestidura ...   30
¡Ved! ... en el horizonte
los brazos rapidísimos enarca,
y con ellos abarca
cuanto alcanzo a mirar de monte a monte!

¡Oscuridad universal! ... ¡Su soplo   35
levanta en torbellinos
el polvo de los campos agitados! ...
En las nubes retumba despeñado
el carro del Señor, y de sus ruedas
brota el rayo veloz, se precipita,   40
hiere y aterra al suelo,
y su lívida luz inunda el cielo.

¿Qué rumor? ¿Es la lluvia? ... Desatada
cae a torrentes, oscurece el mundo,
y todo es confusión, horror profundo.   45
Cielo, nubes, colinas, caro bosque,
¿Do estáis? ... Os busco en vano:
desaparecisteis ... La tormenta umbría
en los aires revuelve un océano
que todo lo sepulta ...   50
Al fin, mundo fatal, nos separamos:
el huracán y yo solos estamos.

¡Sublime tempestad! ¡Cómo en tu seno
de tu solemne inspiración henchido,
al mundo vil y miserable olvido,   55
y alzo la frente, de delicia lleno!
¿Dó está el alma cobarde
que teme tu rugir? ... Yo en ti me elevo
al trono del Señor: oigo en las nubes
el eco de su voz; siento a la tierra   60
escucharle y temblar. Ferviente lloro
desciende por mis pálidas mejillas,
y su alta majestad trémulo adoro.

September 1822

In a Tempest: An Ode to the Hurricane (in English)[1]

Hurricane, hurricane, I sense your arrival,
and in your gust of air am I enveloped,
that of the breath of the Lord of the heavens.

Hanging on the wings of the wind   5
see him tumbling through the immense outer space,
silent, tremendous, irresistible
in his swift path. The earth, with a
sinister, mysterious tranquility
contemplates with dread his devastating face.   10
Do you not see the bull? Its wounded feet
clawing at the earth with insufferable fervor:
raising its mighty forehead,
and inhaling flames through its flared nostrils,
it calls out to the tempest with its bellows.   15

What clouds! What fury! The trembling sun
veils its glorious face with gloomy haze,
and its clouded disc only pours out
a solemn and somber light
that is neither of day nor night . . .   20
Dreadful heat, veil of death!
The small birds tremble and hide
as the roaring hurricane comes near,
and in the distant mountains rumbling
the forests hear him, and to his voice they respond.   25

Here it comes . . . Do you not see it? How it unwraps
its terrifying and majestic mantle! . . .
Giant of the winds, I salute you! . . .
In wildly ferocious confusion the wind flutters
the hem of your brownish-gray garments . . .   30
Look! . . . On the horizon
his arms rapidly raise and arch,
and with them he envelops
everything I can see from mountaintop to mountaintop.

Universal darkness! . . . His squalls   35
lift in whirlwinds
the dust from the turbulent fields! . . .
In the clouds, the Lord's carriage

[1]Translated by Raúl Coronado and Armando
García.

rumbles headlong, and from its wheels
springs forth lightning, rushing out,   40
wounding and terrorizing the land,
and its livid light floods the sky.

What is that sound? Is it the rain? ... Unleashed
it falls in torrents, the world becomes dark,
and all is confusion, profound horror,   45
sky, clouds, hills, beloved forest,
where are you? ... I search for you in vain:
you've disappeared ... The dark storm
hurls an ocean in the winds
that then entombs everything ...   50
At long last, terrible world, we separate:
the hurricane and I remain alone.

Sublime tempest! In your bosom,
of swollen solemn inspiration,
I forget the vile and miserable world   55
and delightfully, I raise my head!
Where is the cowardly soul
who fears your roar? ... On you I raise myself
to the Lord's throne: in the clouds I hear
the echo of his voice; I sense the earth   60
shivering as it hears him. Fervent tears
descending down my pale cheeks,
and his high majesty I tremulously adore.

                                                                         1822

FÉLIX VARELA
1788–1853

Born into an elite family in Havana, Cuba, in 1788, Félix Varela straddles an important intellectual shift in Spanish America: the transformation from Scholasticism to an eclectic, modern, disenchanted worldview. His mother died when he was three, and at four he traveled with his grandfather, Colonel Bartolomé Morales, to what was then Spanish Saint Augustine, Florida. There he received an excellent education under the tutelage of Father Michel O'Reilly, who taught him Latin, grammar, and the violin. On his return to Havana in 1801, he enrolled at the San Carlos and San Ambrosio Royal and Conciliar Seminary, where he continued his education steeped in Catholic Scholasticism. He studied under the renowned scholar Father José Agustín Caballero, who taught him not only the required Aristotelian *Organon* (the foundation of Aristotelian logic) but also Francis Bacon's *Novum Organon* (in turn, one of the foundational texts of the modern scientific method). In 1805, Caballero was authorized to transform the traditional Scholastic curriculum; in doing so, he was part of a much larger intellectual shift throughout the Hispanic world. Although the new modern sciences and philosophy, with their doctrine of rationalism and skepticism, had long been studied by Hispanic Scholastics (in Spain and Spanish America alike), it was not until the eighteenth century that these new methods began to have a major impact on Scholastic thought. This development led to a vigorous debate among Hispanic Scholastics, described by one historian as "the last stand of the Schoolmen." The debate ultimately led in the late eighteenth century to the reconfiguration of the university curriculum, of which Caballero was a part. This syncretic philosophy, combining Scholasticism with modern philosophy, may have provided part of the impetus to think skeptically about the world and to imagine new social formations.

Varela continued to immerse himself in Scholastic political thought, long since marginalized within modern political philosophy, even while attempting to integrate it with the modern scientific and philosophical methods previously banned by Hispanic authorities. At nineteen, he continued his education at the University of Havana, where his intellectual abilities were rewarded on numerous occasions, and in 1811 he was named professor of philosophy at the University. He continued to reform Scholastic education, teaching Bacon, Descartes, and other modern philosophers; he was an incredibly popular lecturer and authored several volumes of eclectic philosophy. But situated within the revolutionary struggles throughout the Hispanic world of the 1810s, Varela's intellectual efforts must be seen as contributing to an epistemic transformation as well—one that began to see the world less as something received from God and more as something that was actively produced by humanity.

In 1822, Varela was given the opportunity to put his thoughts to the test. He was named to represent Cuba at the Spanish Cortes, the modern parliament established when Napoleon deposed the Spanish king in 1808. An active participant, Varela advocated for clerical reform, the abolition of slavery, and a political reconfiguration of Spanish America that would have addressed the revolutionaries' demands for sovereignty. But all was for naught. The king abolished the Cortes, as he had done on several occasions before, and signed a death warrant for Varela and many other liberal representatives. Varela barely escaped to the United States, as many previous liberal Hispanics had done. He arrived on December 17, 1823, and would live the rest of his life in the United States, first in Philadelphia, then in New York, and, finally, in St. Augustine, Florida, where he died in 1853.

Once in Philadelphia, Varela continued writing, published the newspaper *El Habanero* (which he continued to publish in New York), and authored what is recognized as the first Hispanic historical novel, *Jicoténcal* (Philadelphia, 1826). He was far from alone. Many other Spanish-American revolutionaries lived in Philadelphia, including José María Heredia and Vicente Rocafuerte among countless others, hoping to gain support from the United States and Anglo-Americans for the struggles of independence. His publications, along with most other Hispanophone publications from the U.S. East Coast, circulated throughout Spanish America. So powerful were these documents thought to be that the Spanish monarchy sought to have Varela and others assassinated.

Félix Varela had his novel *Jicoténcal* published anonymously in Philadelphia in 1826 (Luis Leal and Juan Cortina, however, have clearly established Varela as the author). In it, he dramatized the story of the Spanish defeat of Mesoamerica—but he revised the story by describing the Spaniards as tyrants and the "Americans" or Tlaxcalans as republicans. In doing so, he presents allegories of four related but competing political moralities. On the one hand, the novel rebukes both conservative Catholic thought, with its claim of divine right, and Machiavellianism, with its use of cynicism and deceit to gain power. On the other hand, it seeks to reconstitute a virtuous political morality by producing a hybrid of a reconfigured tradition of Catholic thought—with its emphasis on a complex structure of law that includes reason, natural law, and civil law—and republican political thought. The novel thus serves as a tightly written lesson that works at a variety of levels. It is an exercise in political philosophy that seeks to produce a modern, liberal Catholic world even while it seeks to offer what Doris Sommer famously described as a "foundational fiction" for Spanish-American republicanism. But it is this conundrum—of seeing the world as one that is actively produced by humans and one that must work to strive toward Christian perfection or justice—that is at the heart of the novel. Decades later, U.S. Latina/o authors such as María Amparo Ruiz de Burton continued to wrestle with how political morality should be reconfigured in a disenchanted world. Her 1885 novel, *The Squatter and the Don*, critiques the demise of republican political morality and its replacement by a solipsistic liberal capitalist morality.

Raúl Coronado
University of Chicago

PRIMARY WORKS

Jicoténcal, 1826; *El Habanero: papel político, científico, y literario*, 1824; *Letters to Elpidio*, 1989; *Xicoténcatl*, English translation, 1999.

from **Xicoténcatl**[1]

Xicoténcatl and Teutila bade their Mexican relatives good-bye and, accompanied by their Zocotlan friends and their families, went to Tlaxcala, where they were all received most effusively by the venerable elder Xicoténcatl. The family's patriarch set the wedding date for three days hence, a period of time that, even though long for the son in his ardor, had to be accepted out of consideration for the country's customs and Teutila's need for rest, so overwhelmed was she after so many stressful experiences.[2]

---

[1] The English translation modernized spelling and, in some cases, altered verb tenses, most notably from present to past tense.
[2] This excerpt opens with the marriage of the warrior hero Xicoténcatl the younger of the Tlaxcalan nation, and Teutila of the Zocotlán nation. Both were located south of the Aztec capital of Tenochtitlán, modern day Mexico City. The marriage sought to establish an alliance between the Tlaxcalans and Zoctlan nations against the Spaniards.

The day of the betrothal arrived, and the two lovers, seeming animated by the flush in their cheeks, appeared before the venerable elder who waited them to give them his blessing.

"May Heaven bless you, my children!" he said, shedding tears of joy and making those present shed them as well. "Go in peace to unite your innocent hearts and swear an oath of love and faithfulness that will last as long as you both live. This great act of the first alliance of man will raise you both to the great rank of parenthood, a rank of which your incomparable nobility has made you worthy because of your virtues. May the gods preserve you from failing to keep the sweet but sacred obligations to which you are going to commit yourselves, one toward the other, and both of you toward your children and toward society! Don't be halfhearted in your affection; don't let the torch of discord suffuse its fatal smoke over your peaceful home, and may your many offspring, educated like you both in virtue, make you as happy in your old age as your elderly father is now!

"Come into my arms, my children, and may Heaven bless, as I bless you with my heart and my soul. And you, my dear Xicoténcatl, do not let yourself be seduced by the sweet pleasures of your new state when your country calls you to come to its aid; this is every man's first duty in society, and yours grows today as you enlarge your place in society. Good-bye, my beloved children."

The bride and groom left the paternal home, decked in their wedding attire, the new groom dressed in a cloak and his beloved wearing a veil, both as white as snow. The father, relatives, and friends walked behind them in procession with a respectful bearing.

In such a manner, they walked toward the temple, where a priest asked them, employing the expressions required by law, if they loved each other and if they agreed mutually to become man and wife. Once an answer in the affirmative had been received, the priest took Teutila's veil in one hand and Xicoténcatl's cloak in the other and tied them together, one end to the other in God's name, in this way making manifest the sacred union of the two spouses.

Joined in this manner and accompanied by the same priest and the rest of the procession, they went toward their house, to the home where the domestic fires burned, and, after going around it seven times, everyone forming a respectful procession, the newly married couple sat down to receive the sacred warmth of their domestic fire, as a sign of the conjugal love that should inspire them for the rest of their lives. With the wedding ceremony thus concluded, all turned to the usual festivities and rejoicing in order to celebrate the marriage.

The innocent joy of this simple family did not last very long. Hernán Cortés[3] communicated to Magiscatzin[4] that he was preparing an important campaign whose glory he would share with his friends the Tlaxcalans, if they

[3]Hernán Cortés was a Spanish conquistador who used the tensions between the Aztecs, Tlaxcalans, Zocotlans, Cempoalans, among other Mesoamerican peoples to his advantage. In 1519, he conquered the Aztec civilization, but only with the military support of other Mesoamerican peoples.

[4]Magiscatzin is a corrupt Tlaxcalan senator and rival of Xicoténcatl the Elder and his son. He supported Cortés's efforts against the Aztecs.

joined him voluntarily, and that he would have the pleasure of seeing him at his home. The elder Xicoténcatl had learned via his friends the Cempoalans[5] that the newly arrived foreign troops were at war with Hernán Cortés and his troops, a fact that, together with the news that Teutile had sent him, impelled him to go before the Senate to strongly oppose Magiscatzin's proposal that Cortés be given an auxiliary army for his enterprise. The Tlaxcalans listened to the powerful reasoning of the prudent elder, and Magiscatzin's proposition was rejected.

When father and son were gathered together at home, after this session, the young Xicoténcatl said:

"The respect and deference that I have always had with regard to your advice have prevented me from speaking out before the Senate, but I don't understand what motivates you, in your prudence, to have been opposed to having a strong division of our republic observe that foreigner in his dangerous journey. Perhaps this is the best opportunity to force him to leave our country."

"When two wild beasts fight, it would be imprudent, my son, for the hunter not to wait for the end of the struggle, which must, without fail, be advantageous to him. As we can see, it seems that those people operate out of personal interest and that the principle of which they speak is only a pretext for their acts of piracy. Let those two great enemies fight each other: their bloody disagreements will end up destroying the prestige that they enjoy among the masses. And, believe me, these plagues that from time to time come to afflict humanity sooner or later yield to the inalterable constancy of patriotism.

"You have seen how, finally, the Senate has come to sense these truths and the intrigues fomented by Magiscatzin have been impotent. This, my son, is a triumph against our enemies; let us be satisfied for now and let us hope that Heaven will not permit it to be our last one. But after having thus tended to the interests of the nation, it is now necessary to look after our own. That captain is going to come to Tlaxcala; his brutal passion for Teutila can be kindled and thus involve all of us if he provokes our, jus resentment. It seems to me that the best thing will be for you to absent yourself with her and, as much as it is possible for us, avoid a calamity.

"As for me, Nature is taking me away from public concerns, and now that I see, with satisfaction, that the majority of the people's representatives are looking after their interests, I gladly leave the presidency of the Senate to Magiscatzin, designated by law to succeed me, since he has the greatest seniority among its members. I will not again return to that sanctuary of justice without a great cause to revive *my* weakness."

The new couple, obedient to their father's advice, withdrew to one of their landholdings, while Hernán Cortés was only passing through Tlaxcala, pretending not to have been offended by the republic's snub. Diego de Ordaz[6]

[5]A Mesoamerican nation inhabiting what is today Veracruz. They were the first to encounter Hernán Cortés.

[6]Spanish conquistador who attempts to seduce Teutila.

warmly embraced the elder Xicoténcatl and, with his customary frankness, branded as nonessential the precaution of having had his son leave the city. In his honesty he believed it impossible that an attempt against public morals could be made in such a scandalous way and by a man who had to maintain himself by force at the head of an expedition whose command he had usurped from the established authority. Since Hernán Cortés said not a word about either Teutila or her marriage, Xicoténcatl reined in his suspicion and, to put right his fault and to have the honest Spaniard embrace his friends, he had his children come once the foreigners had left for Cempoala. Poor wretch! Your simple honesty did not know well the art of European corruption.

A few days later Hernán Cortés returned from his expedition, his army having been increased by the soldiers who had come to fight against him and who exceeded his own in numbers. Upon entering Tlaxcala, he showed off his splendid new troops and the aggregates and supplies of war that he had acquired in his expedition. Placing himself at the head of his brilliant columns, he went directly to the house of Magiscatzin. The triumph that the patriots had obtained against that magistrate's faction, denying the auxiliary troops to Cortés, made the latter discover the weakness of his own troops, and thus confronting an imposing force, he sided with him, without reflection and openly, so as to become reinvigorated and enable himself to obtain victory against the good Tlaxcalans. Thus force presided in the councils of state. The weak gave in to his impulses, those who were evil and rebellious found support, and the good encountered defeat at the very moment when they had been the most hopeful.

Diego de Ordaz shared with his friends the sweet satisfaction that they were enjoying, and he opened his heart to them, placing his feelings in the open palm of the innocent and pure friendship of the only virtuous persons that he knew. Then he informed Xicoténcatl how Hernán Cortés had left the island of Cuba and how that new fleet and army had arrived to apprehend him and lead him back as a prisoner in order to be judged and punished for his crimes. But that he, shrewdly and serenely, had established peace talks with the leader who commanded them, entertaining him in this manner while he assured himself, with gifts and promises, of the loyalty of the soldiers that he had under his command in Mexico and while he managed to corrupt those of his adversary with the gold that he had wrenched away from Moctezuma in the midst of his fears.

Finally, he told them that fortune had favored Cortés so much that he managed to have the newly arrived troops rebel, and in this state he attacked them by night with one hand on his sword and the other in his pocket. The confusion served him marvelously in his enterprise, and from the outcome of one of the battles that he was able to lead against them, he found an excuse to treat the vanquished with the harshness and vigor that only he deserved. In this way, he got rid of some, placed others securely in prison, and increased his own army with the multitudes, blinded by the thirst for gold.

The infamous Magiscatzin, vaingloriously drunk because of the distinction accorded him by the man to whom he had sold himself, gave in unconditionally to the vilest dependency and, to complete his infamy, publicly forsook the religion of his ancestors to embrace that of his protector, who had power in his hands. This example produced some imitators, and the priest, Fray Bartolomé de Olmedo[7], who only saw in these events the effects of his zeal for the propagation of his beliefs, took charge of converting the elder Xicoténcatl.

Hernán Cortés encouraged him in his enterprise, suspecting the venerable senator to be weakened enough by the ravages of time to be open to scruples and fears about his fate after death, if they managed to make him waver in his beliefs. Thus, the kindly chaplain went to visit him and spoke to him in the following manner:

"My brother, since we are all children of the same God, we must all love our common father and our brothers, who are all men."

"You surprise me, stranger, with maxims that conform so much to those that exist in my heart, when your actions are so contrary to these same maxims. If we are all to love one another in such a brotherly manner, why do you come in the guise of our worst enemies?"

"We come to place you on the road to salvation; we come to make God known to you, the one and only true God. We come to teach you the only form of worship that He accepts, the one that He demands from us and the divine religion that alone can save you from eternal damnation."

"Let me disregard for now that your conduct contradicts that divine mission and those benevolent views. And you yourself cannot deny to me that it is impossible for God to make Himself known through crimes that our hearts condemn. I think you come in peace, and I do not wish to offend you by telling you what you touch and feel if you don't also practice it. I know there is a God; that is, a very powerful being who has provided the whole universe with such a great intelligence that each thing has a direct relationship with a great end with admirable precision. I feel it inside myself, in the most abstract things as well as in the most tangible ones. This is as far as my knowledge goes; but since you have more of it, as you say, make that God known to me, a God that I believe is very powerful and wise, but of whom I know no more than what His works make known to me."

"That same God, creator, maker, beginning and end of all things, infinitely good, wise, just, and powerful, has revealed to us His mysteries and the religion that we profess."

"I cannot conceive how the world could have been created, because I cannot conceive how something can be created out of nothing; my imagination rests when I suppose it to be as old as its arranger. Neither can I grasp the concept of infinite kindness, knowledge, justice, and power, because the

---

[7]A Spanish friar who accompanied Cortés, and helped in the conversion of Mesoamericans to Catholicism.

idea of something that is endless does not fit inside my comprehension. I walk around this room and I say: 'Since there is a space as large as this one, there can well be one that is larger; but no matter how far I take my imagination, I always find the limits.' I also place a weight on a scale, for example, a bit of corn; on the other I place a stone, and it makes the sack rise; therefore, the stone weighs more than the sack. But how much more does it weigh? This makes it impossible for me to find it out if I do not compare its weight with other objects. For this reason I say: 'The intelligence and power of the One who has ordered the world are undoubtedly very great, for they have been sufficient to produce such effects, but my knowledge cannot go beyond that point.' But since you are telling me that God has revealed His mysteries, teach me about them; tell me what they are."

The chaplain, then, seeing such clarity of thought in the elder Xicoténcatl, explained the articles of faith to him. The elder asked him for an explanation of the mysteries it contained, and, after being told that they are mysteries beyond the reach of our understanding, he replied in a lively manner:

"So God has revealed nothing. And you want to make me believe that this Being, who is so wise, has communicated to me certain things that are repugnant to my reason? What could He have had in mind to have behaved in such a manner?"

"That of proving your submission to his will, your recognition of your smallness and ignorance."

"And what need is there for the existence of some contradictory and absurd mysteries when I have my judgment, which is continually measuring my weakness, and a voice that speaks to me here, in my heart, and says to me that I must be recognized and be obedient to the Author of all good? My duties are very clear, and when my miserable nature attempts to make me stray from my path, I have an instinct inside me, something that reminds me of them and that you call reason. And do you want me to renounce that governing instinct in order to please God? Why would. He have given it to me, then? But in the end if, in your religion, everything is violence and blind submission, tell me where is the evidence upon which it is founded?"

"The many miracles that have taken place offer some of the proof that favors the doctrine that it teaches."

"What is a miracle?"

"It is a phenomenon that goes beyond all the laws of Nature, such as bringing a dead person back to life."

"Are you a minister of your God?"

"Yes, by his mercy, although I am an unworthy sinner."

"Well, then, perform a miracle: bring my wife back to life; she died twenty moons ago."

"I do not have that gift."

"Have you seen a miracle?"

"Yes, by the grace of God."

"Tell me about it."

At this point Fray Bartolomé found himself deeply embarrassed, because although he believed that many of the events that had occurred during the enterprise in which he found himself had been miraculous, he recognized the difficulty of proving that they were outside the laws of Nature. Xicoténcatl removed him from the midst of his embarrassment, saying to him:

"Look, stranger, a miracle is an impossible thing, and believing in it offends the wisdom and power of that same God that you refer to as wise and powerful. All that our intelligence is able to know in this world is ordered by immutable laws and with a relationship that is so intimate that, if any of them were to be infringed upon, it would go against the order of things. On the other hand, there is no need for those exceptions, because that Being which governs the world has known how to place inside us the knowledge that He has felt to be convenient, with no need to break these same laws."

The conversation spread too much into prophecies, tradition, and other evidence for the Christian religion; but Xicoténcatl insisted on listening only to the false light of his reason, so Fray Bartolomé was becoming desperate in his task; but, remembering the beginning of the conversation, he said to him:

"My obstinate elder: my divine religion prescribes certain moral rules which, if you follow them, assure of happiness in this world and take away any fears of the next. Here it is in short; love God above all things and your neighbor as yourself. Tell me now that the religion that expects that behavior from you is not divine."

"Undoubtedly, my friend, those rules come from God; they are inside me, and they have been given to me by the same one to whom I owe these hands, this tongue with which I speak to you, and the thoughts that it expresses to you. Yes, I feel, in the same way that I feel hunger and thirst, that it is necessary to be just and beneficent. And you feel this also, you who come from such distant regions, as do more than twenty nations that inhabit the country that I know. You are whiter than we are; you have a beard and other differences which, seemingly, make yon a man from a species other than ours; nevertheless, your morality is the same as mine. Thus, it comes from God.

"If you wish for me to worship this God with you, give me that white delicacy that you offer Him, because it matters not to me whether I offer him a bit of copal or anything else so long as I acknowledge Him. Look at domestic animals when they try to please us; each one does it its own way and we do not concern ourselves with *the* way they communicate with us but pay attention only to what they are showing us. Thus, the Creator of Nature will, undoubtedly, only attend to our intentions. And if He had wished for all of us to think in like manner about these mysteries, it would have been no harder for Him to have had us agree on morality.

"Now I am going to give you some advice. Preach the practice of these rules of your religion among your people; exhort them to fulfill those divine duties, and if perchance you manage to have them heed your voice, and we see in them some examples of virtue, some just, moderate men, lords over their passions, then throw away your weapons of war, considering them to be worthless, because we will all look at you as gods. There's more yet: we will also believe any number of mysteries you might propose to us, no matter how absurd they might be, because then the sacrifice of our natural light would be rewarded with the happiness of all humanity. But, friend, to preach such a doctrine with war, licentiousness, and the most scandalous vices! What a contradiction! My God, these events put to the test my belief in your wisdom!"

Fray Bartolomé had not come prepared for such an attack, and thus under the pretext that his duties called for him to go elsewhere, he left with no great wish to continue in the conversation with the elder Tlaxcalan. The holy zeal of his religion had so inflamed the good priest that he entirely forgot the charge made to him by Cortés: to insinuate how surprised both natives and foreigners had been to see that Teutila had missed going by to visit her friend doña Marina.

In this way Cortés was trying to attract her to the house of Magiscatzin, where, with more security than any place else, he could surrender himself to any extreme, a somewhat dangerous activity among his own people. With the same end in mind, he used political tact in communicating his complaint to Xicoténcatl when the latter went to visit him as general of the republic.

"Stranger," the brave Tlaxcalan answered him, "it seems to me you are addressing Xicoténcatl. He is incapable of duplicity and deceit, and he answers you without evasion that his wife will not debase herself by dealing with an unworthy woman who has prostituted herself. Tlaxcalans respect their wives' honor."

"You are insolent; be aware of my power and tremble before it."

"Never, never will Xicoténcatl be afraid of you. Nor should you think that Teutila has stopped seeing that wretch out of fear of your outrages. Teutila is today a Tlaxcalan."

Cortés, then, recognizing his growing disadvantage in the situation, changed his demeanor, barely holding back his rage:

"Ingrate!" he said to him; "you don't want to be my friend—well, you will be, by God! or—"

Several Spanish officers entered the room, interrupting this scene, and Xicoténcatl left for his house.

When Cortés was alone, he had Magiscatzin summoned.

"Friend," he said to him, "can I count on your advocacy?"

"Sir, do you doubt the faithfulness of your slave Magiscatzin? What can I do to enhance your glory? Tell me."

"Listen, friend. That insolent Xicoténcatl is the great enemy that you have to fear. Tlaxcala committed the imprudence of making him its general and this imprudence will weigh heavily on you. For your well-being and tranquillity, I should like to rein him in in such a way that his fiery character might feel the restraint and accept the fact that he has no recourse but to yield to force. With this end in mind, I kept that fool Teutila detained in my barracks, for after I discovered her affair with Xicoténcatl, she was useful to me in quieting her lover. Teutile asked for her and I, who am incapable of ignoring the call of justice, turned her over to him. But now that I see their marriage celebrated, and suspect that this unworthy Tlaxcalan has a pact with your enemies, I would wish to use that woman to hold back that fearsome man, who will lead all of you to ruin."

"Oh, my lord! No one would wish to cut down that insolent family's pride more than I do. I too am motivated by just resentment against the relatives of the infamous Teutila. But, Lord, how will the Senate look upon an outrage committed against a Tlaxcalan woman? Those imbeciles are so frightened when a woman is violated that they think the world is going to be turned upside down. I fear the outcome of the project; nevertheless, I am anxious that you in your wisdom find a way to put it into play. What a pleasure! The ridiculous anger of that decrepit old man and the desperation of that insolent young man would make for a most entertaining scene."

"Well, listen to me: tonight Captain Ordaz is invited to dine with them. I have my suspicions that this captain has been an accomplice in the Spaniards' betrayal of me, a betrayal which has turned out quite victoriously in Cempoala, and I will have him apprehended during the dinner. He is fierce and haughty; to arrest him I will send one of his enemies who is brave and entirely faithful to me. There will probably be a scandalous scene. Xicoténcatl, who owes his life to an act of brave daring by Ordaz, will attempt to defend him, and my envoy, following my instructions, will lead them all to prison. I will immediately place my troops on alert and appear in person before the Senate, where I expect you to support me so that this body will agree that they all be judged, according to the laws of our military discipline. As a result of the process, Xicoténcatl will be removed and placed in prison and I will take Teutila with me, ridding you in this way of such a terrible enemy and assuring myself against the claims of Teutila's relatives, for she will be judged by the authority of the republic."

The villainous senator applauded with the vilest demonstrations of adulation the infernal plot that he had just heard, and everything was agreed to on the spot. But fate had reserved the brave Tlaxcalan and his honest wife for scenes even more tragic, although no less vile.

The virtuous friends were gathered at the home of Xicoténcatl when people came to notify him of a slight disorder among workers in his lands; attentive to his domestic duties, he rushed to put in order what also belonged to his dear wife. At that moment, a patrol surrounded the house. The officer in charge entered without announcing himself; he found Ordaz alone with the venerable elder and the virtuous matron.

"You are under arrest," he said, "in the name of the king."

"I place myself under arrest," Ordaz answered him, without the least resistance.

The officer was left disconcerted, and all of the plans for the most infernal intrigue dissolved like the soap bubbles that children blow into the wind.

Hernán Cortés drooled in his anger. Magiscatzin was now aware of his weakness and all his enemies triumphant. His passions, thus aroused, broke free completely and the elimination of Xicoténcatl was decided without appeal or recourse. Diego de Ordaz was set free, after having indicted him, because of the uselessness and dangers that a prosecution could bring to bear.

Hernán Cortés determined to continue on to Mexico, from where he had received news that the natives had taken up arms against the Spaniards who had remained garrisoned in the barracks. With the same political considerations that marked past occasions, he refused to be accompanied by a large Tlaxcalan army, but he did choose a division from it led by those partial to him.

The journey was settled, but it had to be postponed because of an unexpected event. Doña Marina was afflicted by birth pains; her natural robustness was weakened as a result of the excesses to which she had vehemently devoted herself, and Nature, which never leaves these faults unpunished, was moved by mortal symptoms on an occasion during which temperance is quite easy to follow. Her religious education had been too superficial, and Death, surrounded by horrifying specters, appeared in her imagination.[8]

This "madwoman of the house," as she has been called by a Spanish saint, grew infinitely worried and terrified, and the cruelest feeling of remorse came to put her in a truly pitiful state. Amid these feelings of spiritual anguish, excited further by the violence of the pains, she called Fray Bartolomé de Olmedo and confessed to him all of her past conduct, hiding from him neither the daring scene with Ordaz, nor her guardianship of Teutila, nor her persecution by Hernán Cortés, nor the intrigues and political tales—absolutely nothing.

The good friar vainly lavished on her the health-giving consolation prescribed by his ministry: she saw Hell open under her feet; the endless torments took shape in her frenetic imagination, and, in this state, the only method that occurred to her to atone for her faults was that of making a public confession of them and to ask for forgiveness from all those persons mat she had offended.

For this purpose she wanted everyone to come to her room, and, without seeing anything other than the vengeance of a just God, she feared neither Hernán Cortés nor all of the earth's princes gathered together. What, *in* effect, are human considerations before the excited imagination of a woman?

"No, Father," she said to her confessor, "there is no remedy for me. I am a great sinner and the whole universe must know of my faults and see *my* remorse; let my suffering serve as example and lesson to those who, like me, abandon the path of virtue."

It is easy to understand the predicament of a chaplain who is suddenly faced with all the considerations created by such a scene, and all of this

---

[8]Doña Marina, also referred to as Malintzín and infamously as la Malinche, has long been seen as the mother of mestizos. She is a highly contested symbolic figure in Mexican and Chicana/o literary and cultural criticism.

without being allowed a moment of reflection by his penitent. Four or six strong pains and the screams from a baby that began to breathe air took Fray Bartolomé de Olmedo away from an embarrassment that was becoming already too large for his great prudence.

Amid great surprise, and not without the good friar's satisfaction, Hell, torment, scruples, faults, reparation, everything gave in as if miraculously, to maternal affection at the sight of the boy that had just been born. Violent in her passions, and lively and mischievous in her talents, this American could have been a woman worthy of appreciation without the corruption to which she devoted herself when she associated with the Spaniards. Nevertheless, tender maternal love spilled a sweet cover over her feelings, and, quite peacefully so as not to alarm her confessor, she asked him to have Diego de Ordaz come. When he had arrived, she spoke to him thus:

"Ordaz, I am a mother. I wish my past conduct did not make me unworthy of tins joy! Nevertheless, perhaps Nature will be stronger in me than corruption. I wish to ask you a favor: I am anxious to see Teutila. Her virtues make my seeing her extremely necessary; she will be a mother also, and the fruit of her womb will enjoy the purity of her soul. Have that angelic child come, for her presence will reanimate in me those sensations that Nature awakens in me. Do me that favor, Ordaz; not for me but for this innocent babe. See how beautiful he is!"

Diego de Ordaz was moved, and he promised that he would communicate the request to his friends and that he hoped Teutila would accede to her wish. Then Fray Bartolomé de Olmedo offered a moving prayer about the duties of mothers with their children; this he did with much peace and appropriateness.

Hernán Cortés was concerned with reinforcing Magiscatzin's support, and he was also in the process of preparing him for his plans against Xicoténcatl. The news concerning the Mexicans' uprising concerned him, but there was no way of leaving doña Marina behind, for he needed her very much. It was thus imperative that he await her recovery; meanwhile, he wasted no opportunity to enhance his support, encouraging some with promises and flattering others with presents.

The physiological changes that accompany weak, lactating mothers' showed themselves in doña Marina as a strong delirium as Xicoténcatl and his wife went to see her, persuaded by Diego de Ordaz's request and his convincing arguments mat the sick woman had had a change of heart. Doña Marina's sorrowful state moved the sensitive American, and she proposed to her husband that she stay to accompany her in her recovery. Xicoténcatl was too humane not to accede to the compassionate wish of his wife, and kind Teutila thus exposed herself to new insults, while she lavished tender care on the sick woman.

When Hernán Cortés finished his affairs and intrigues, he remembered, finally, that doña Marina was suffering greatly and went to her room. It is not easy to describe his great surprise when he saw Teutila at the sick woman's bedside, so preoccupied with her that she failed to notice that Cortés had entered.

"To what happy event do we owe the pleasure of a visit by the wife of Xicoténcatl?" he said to her.

"To a very unfortunate one—" answered Teutila, interrupting herself in order to take care of Marina, who tossed and turned violently in her bed.

Then Fray Bartolomé de Olmedo informed his general about the sufferer's good intentions, and of the good effect that her desire to see Teutila had had on the latter's sensitive heart and of the tender compassion with which she had remained behind to take care of her in her delirious condition.

1826

■ JOSÉ MARÍA TORNEL ■
1795–1853

José María Tornel was enraged when he heard, in May 1836, of the Texas revolt against Mexico and the United States' more than tacit support of the uprising. Texas had defeated Santa Anna's army in March 1836, effectively creating an independent Texan republic, but news of Mexico's loss did not trickle down to Mexico City until May. As Secretary of War for the Republic of Mexico and former ambassador to the United States, Tornel, along with many of his fellow Mexicans, had openly admired the ambitious republican project of the United States, but it was now with a great sense of betrayal that he turned to his pen and wrote one of the earliest and most penetrating critiques of U.S. imperialism. "For more than fifty years," he began, "that is, from the period of their political infancy, the prevailing thought in the United States of America has been ... the acquisition of the greater part of the territory that formerly belonged to Spain, particularly that which today belongs to the Mexican nation." This Mexican statesman and prolific writer was quite prophetic; eleven years later the United States would conquer Mexico and annex half of its territory.

In 1836, Tornel sensed that the Texas revolt was but a prelude to the United States' unchecked expansionism; a year and a half later, in November 1837, he published *Tejas y los Estados-Unidos de América en sus relaciones con la República Mexicana*, an elegantly written and carefully documented ninety-eight-page study in which he systematically analyzed the United States' path to empire. Tornel's astute observations comprise the substance of his argument, but his tract also gives voice to a subtext that reveals the political-ethical grounds on which he makes his critique. The United States may have represented a utopian vision of modernity—the establishment of democratic, republican government with peaceful presidential successions, the expansion of an industrializing economy, and the philosophical pronouncements of the rights of man—but this early observer of an increasingly imperialistic neighbor positions his critique in a modernity that was developing quite distinctly from that of the United States. His was a Mexican modernity that had only recently begun to struggle with the form of government it should take. It was a modernity whose tattered economy had not yet recovered from the wars of independence, one that was searching for a common ontological foundation upon which to plant the roots of a Mexican nation.

Tornel wrote at a crucial moment in history when the United States had not yet gone to war with Mexico—a war in which, for the first time, an independent nation in the American hemisphere would conquer another in order to annex its territory. His essay represents an embattled articulation and defense of a Mexican modernity-in-formation in the face of a looming U.S. imperialism. Tornel thus used writing and publishing much as his fellow postindependence Spanish Americans had done, as a means to help reconfigure political morality in the modern world. As such, his essay offers an opportunity to examine how an observer from outside the United States proleptically conceptualized the machinations of a modern imperial nation. In reading Tornel, one realizes that José Martí's warnings were almost belated.

Raúl Coronado
University of Chicago

PRIMARY WORKS

Tejas y los Estados-Unidos de América, en sus relaciones con la República Mexicana, 1837; *Breve reseña histórica de los acontecimientos mas notables de la nacion Mexicana, desde el año de 1821 hasta nuestros dias*, 1852.

Relations between Texas, the United States of America, and the Mexican Republic

For more than fifty years, that is, from the very period of their political infancy, the prevailing thought in the United States of America has been the acquisition of the greater part of the territory that formerly belonged to Spain, particularly that part which to-day belongs to the Mexican nation. Democrats and Federalists, all their political parties, whatever their old or new designations, have been in perfect accord upon one point, their desire to extend the limits of the republic to the north, to the south, and to the west, using for the purpose, all the means at their command, guided by cunning, deceit, and bad faith. It has been neither an Alexander nor a Napoleon, desirous of conquest in order to extend his dominions or add to his glory, who has inspired the proud Anglo-Saxon race in its desire, its frenzy to usurp and gain control of that which rightfully belongs to its neighbors; rather it has been the nation itself which, possessed of that roving spirit that moved the barbarous hordes of a former age in a far remote north, has swept away whatever has stood in the way of its aggrandizement.

Jefferson, the embodiment of the most exaggerated democratic principles, the philosopher who exercised the greatest influence upon the government and laws of his country, the statesman who stamped upon it its singular and national character, who voiced the aspirations of its thousands of settlers and adventurers, used to flatter his fellow-citizens with the future possession of the Isthmus of Panama, while promising the Colossus of the North to gain a foothold upon the banks of the Saint Laurence. The atheist of Monticello thoroughly understood the desires and ambitions of his countrymen. In order to win universal popularity, he used to encourage their ambitious dreams of expansion, founded on no other right than the ominous one of might. It will, therefore, be strange indeed to find a single American who does not revere Jefferson as a semi-god, because everyone considers him the prophet of his country's destiny, the man to whom Providence confided its secrets.

Other Americans who aspire to be called moderates, would content themselves with the extension of the boundary to the Pánuco, as claimed by some writer who stated that this formed the western limits of Florida. Still others who are accused of lacking spirit and of being timid in their aspirations would content themselves with the acquisition of the lands watered by the Rio Bravo del Norte. The treaty of limits of February 22nd, 1819, which gave to the United States title to a *contested territory*, had no other purpose than to pave the way for and bring closer the acquisition of the two Floridas, leaving for a better and more propitious occasion the deletion of the imaginary boundary line then traced. Although in 1832, after more than four years of delays, the same terms of that treaty were accepted by the Mexican republic, it was foreseen with all certainty that they would never be observed by the United States. Our continuous revolts made that country conceive the hope that we would neglect or abandon our national and sacred charge, while the ill-advised colonization laws and our still more imprudent and scandalous mismanagement of the public lands, so coveted and yet so freely and generously distributed and given away, clearly showed that we knew neither how to appreciate nor how to keep the precious heritage of the Spaniards. Unfortunately they were not mistaken in their assumption, for at every step we have displayed that candor, weakness, and inexperience so characteristic of infant nations. Too late have we come to know the restless and enterprising neighbor who set himself up as our mentor, holding up his institutions for us to copy them, institutions which transplanted to our soil could not but produce constant anarchy, and which, by draining our resources, perverting our character, and weakening our vigor, have left us powerless against the attacks and the invasions of this modern Rome. The example of an *ever increasing* prosperity was treacherously pointed out to us, and, attributing to the written law the influence of habit and custom, we adopted the first without the steadying influence of the second. Thus we have chosen to live in perpetual contradiction, in an anomalous state. How costly have been to us the gifts of these new Greeks!

As a native of America I cannot regret the triumph of the Revolution of 1776, nor can I condemn the vast experiment in social welfare that has been undertaken upon our continent. But that same Revolution which bore such happy results for the American people,—even though they may not be as extensive, as perfect, and as complete as its partisans would have us believe—brought many misfortunes to the human race when considered from other points of view. The greatest of these, the French Revolution, was the direct outcome of the American principles indiscreetly adopted with ardor by the young French soldiers who, by order of their sovereign, came to America in search of battlefields where the pride of England might be humbled. While the Anglo-American provinces were taking their place among the nations of the world, enjoying the advantages of English civilization, their prosperity multiplied and established now on a firmer basis by their independent existence, France was paying with the blood of her sons and the head of her king for the services which both rendered to democracy. But not only France, all Europe, the entire world, has suffered a profound shock which has shaken the stability of nations. It is undeniably true that the condition of man has been improved to a certain point, but it is doubtful whether this improvement is sufficient recompense for so many and such cruel sacrifices. If happiness were now secure beyond all doubt, France, the whole universe, would find consolation at the tomb of the millions of fallen victims. But the struggle between absolutism and liberalism still rages, and each has advanced its claim for domination and power. England may well say that she has secured ample and bloody vengeance for the help which her continental rival gave to her rebellious colonies.

To wish, to wait, and to act describe the distinctive character of the government and the people of the United States. No nation in the civilized world can equal them in their boundless ambition. The object of their heart's desire having been determined, they lie in wait for the propitious moment, assuming a disinterested and indifferent attitude in the meanwhile which is foreign to their true feelings, until circumstances favor their designs, when they ruthlessly trample everything in the way of their desire. This is a historical truth as clear as the light of day. Let us now turn to the facts.

The events of Madrid and Bayone in 1808, the subsequent uprising of the Spanish people against the hordes of Napoleon, the disordered state of the administration which naturally followed, the weakness of her revolutionary governments, barely able to maintain a precarious existence, all these circumstances united to favor the ambitious plans of the United States who now, ill-concealing their joy, threw off the hypocritical mask with which, for a time, they covered their true designs. The thinking men of the United States had clearly foreseen that their emancipation would be but the prelude to the emancipation of all the New World. They realized that sooner or later the important revelation that resistance to a remote and tyrannical power could be crowned with complete victory would not be disregarded by the Spanish colonies. Nor were they ignorant of the fact that their early independent existence, their progress in civilization, and the experience gained through their own administration would assure them a preeminent position of power and influence in determining the fate of the new nations when they became established. To cooperate in this great enterprise was to safe-guard their own existence by the most effective means. In spite of the advantageous position of the United States, of their growing maritime power, of the war-like disposition of their inhabitants, of the determination displayed in their struggles, of the abundant resources of their soil and the bright prospects of their industry, they could not aspire to a superior rank among the nations of the world, as long as they had to compete with the old and powerful countries of Europe. The setting changed, however, with the appearance of other independent nations in the New World. It was, therefore, to the essential interest of the United States to encourage by their example, their counsel, and their material help the insurrection of Spanish America. Here they saw the realization of their ulterior motives enhanced by the sympathy created for themselves and the inherent weakness of the ephemeral governments of the new nations. Egoism is an inseparable vice of the genius of the Anglo-Saxon race. If they proclaim or sustain the august rights of liberty and independence, it is not because of the noble sympathy felt for a just and sacred cause; rather it is out of regard for their interests, it is their own improvement which they seek with indefatigable zeal. The time that has elapsed since our fortunate emancipation, a time so rich in disappointments, has removed the band that inexperience placed over our eyes. Who is ignorant to-day of the real cause, the prime motive behind the decision taken by the United States in favor of the independence of the Spanish colonies? This general assertion does not preclude the existence of a few philosophers, in whose number I am glad to include the earnest John Quincy Adams, the Demosthenes of the west, Mr. Clay, the Cicero of New England, Mr. Webster; the ill-fated congressman from Louisiana, Livingston, and a few other sincere friends of the liberty of mankind, who worked for the independence of America out of pure, philanthropic, and disinterested motives. But it cannot be denied that the immense majority of the American people participated in our melancholic tragedies for the purpose of weakening the power of Spain and out of a desire to exercise a direct influence, inevitable as a result of the vigor of a people full of life and dynamic activity, upon the fate of poorly educated peoples who would in the end destroy themselves by their excesses and the horrors of continuous civil war. Nothing could withstand the popularity of the Anglo-American system of government. The influence of Spain seemed to end at the Pillars of Hercules. The newborn star of the nations that rose upon the ruins of a decrepit monarchy shined fitfully and with a reddish glow.

. . .

... Have not the ancient republics, including the ambitious Rome, been left far behind when compared with this tumultuous democracy that with its gigantic arms reaches out from the Atlantic to the Pacific and threatens to seize a whole continent? Sometimes she advances peacefully, drawn on by the lure of imaginary rights which pave the way for her diplomatic intrigues. At others, she does not disdain to use force or resort to conquest. Let us agree that the vicinity of a republic which intervenes in all the transactions of the Americas is very detrimental; that her school of politics stands as a new, complete, and unique phenomenon, exacting as its own whatever adds to its aggrandisement and to its strength, ignoring ancient and established rights and the tranquil and peaceful possession through centuries....

... We made a present of Texas to the Americans of the North, sometimes freely granting them our territory and sometimes giving it to Mexicans without resources or wealth for the ostensible purpose of colonizing it. With a few honorable exceptions the real object of the Mexicans in obtaining these grants was to sell at the lowest price and to the citizens of the United States the land thus acquired....

If it is written in the uncertain and obscure book of destiny that we are some day to lose the department of Texas, let the fact remain buried in the inscrutable designs of fate as evidence of the unexampled perfidy displayed by the colonists and settlers and as testimony of ill-requited Mexican generosity. Our generosity knew none of the bounds which prudence dictates. It has been seen how through unwisely granted contracts one-tenth of the population of the United States could have found its way to Texas if the empresarios had had at their command adequate facilities for its transportation. As a result of this difficulty, speculators have thrown open the door to all the adventurers that can transport themselves at their own cost. They have even encouraged the very scum of the United States, those who because of debt or crimes found themselves obliged to flee from the rigor of the law in search of a more secure refuge in an unsettled country which was nominally governed by a well-regulated and organized body politic. Personal interest, therefore, demanded a complete ignorance of the moral character and actions of those who made their way to *this new sociological garden*....
Texas was given to the colonists. The revenue of the public lands in the United States is one of the most valuable resources of the nation, the one that has been of greatest importance in funding their public debt. Well might we have followed their example to replenish our exhausted treasury by selling what we did not care to keep. But our blindness has been so great that we have given away lands that are a paradise. We have turned them over to our own enemies without exacting a penny or receiving anything else in exchange. We are forced to admit this truth by the facts that stare us squarely in the face. We are, today, reaping the fruit of our inadvertence.

. . .

With the astonishing increase of population in the United States as a result of the extraordinary immigration from Europe, the government began to feel that the permanence of the Indian tribes in the territories they formerly occupied was an embarrassment. Their permanence was guaranteed by sacred treaties and solemn agreements. Nowhere else on the face of the globe is the feeling of the white race stronger against those which, in its pride, it designates as colored. This was sufficient for the expulsion of the men of bronze, the redmen, and for the despoliation of their property.

This policy was all the more advisable because in the lands occupied by some of these tribes deposits of the fatal and coveted metal had been discovered. Furthermore, the Indians had cleared the woods, and the lands were now ready for cultivation. What was there to restrain Anglo-American greed? Nothing! Might was on their side, the miserable Indians had nothing but their weakness. . . . What I aim to point out clearly is that at the same time that the Indians were despoiled of their territory, it was planned to deprive the Mexican Republic of its own. All these tribes have been moved to territories along our frontier because, realizing its weak defence, it has been foreseen that the Indians will pass into our territory, freeing the United States of the redmen which they have always considered a burden. . . .

. . .

The bare outline we have just hastily sketched of the unscrupulous policy of the United States should serve as a warning to Mexicans, making them realize the dangers that threaten them. It is but natural to expect that when they come to a full realization of these acts of oppression and violence, their indignation will know how to average them. The imagination of the Anglo-Americans is stimulated by their own vanity, and in their dreams of grandeur, they look upon us as pigmies, objects deserving of their pity. They consider our possessions but a fair prize of their greed. While the attention of humanity has been held by other problems, while the world has turned its energy to their solution, they have exercised, through their might, a pernicious influence. . . .

. . . Mexico cannot give up her territory nor can it consent that a rival power should establish itself upon a strategic position in her rear, absorbing part of her provinces and menacing the others. . . . If Mexico should consent to such baseness, she would lose her position as a first-class nation among American powers and descend to an unworthy level that would force her to buy, through a series of continuous humiliations, a costly and precarious existence. The loss of Texas would reduce the value of our lands; real estate throughout the rest of the republic would be worth a fourth of its present value. . . . The loss of Texas will inevitably result in the loss of New Mexico and the Californias. Little by little our territory will be absorbed, until only an insignificant part is left to us. Our destiny will be similar to the sad lot of Poland. Our national existence, acquired at the cost of so much blood, recognized after so many difficulties, would end like those weak meteors which, from time to time, shine fitfully in the firmament and disappear. . . .

. . .

. . . If their diplomacy has been dictated by a preconceived plan,—and this cannot be doubted by those who have observed the skill with which the cabinet in Washington directs its affairs—it is obvious that their aim has been to acquire possession of the disputed territory by force if necessary. This will involve us in more serious difficulties than even those presented by the

Texas question itself. War with the United States, however, need not be feared, for our final salvation may depend upon it.

War is the greatest scourge that may afflict nations. It is a calamity that must be avoided if possible, whenever independent political existence and the inherent rights of sovereignty are not at stake. War among the nations of America is an attempt against their own happiness, and is contrary to those high aims which the New World should try to realize by maintaining peace, while the nations of Europe solve the serious problems confronting them. Therefore, the American nation that provokes the war will be responsible for an attempt against the political ideals of this continent as opposed to the system of government prevailing in Europe. Up to the present, we have given ample proof of our patience, and the judgment of the civilized world cannot help but absolve us of any charge of aggression against the United States. Consequently, the blame will fall upon them alone, and this will not be favorable to their designs. . . .

. . .

I have impartially analyzed the policy of the United States, supported by the facts I have presented, for the calm examination of the reader. More than once, I have applauded the progress of the institutions of that republic, prosperous because of its industry and its public spirit. I have never ceased to feel grateful for the many considerations extended to me by her inhabitants while attending to an important mission entrusted to me by my country before their government. I owe to my country, however, the fruit of my experience and of my observations, and it is because of this duty, as sweet as it is sacred, that I have been obliged to relate the events as they have occurred, expressing my fears and my hopes as I see them. The Mexican nation can never consent to the loss of a considerable part of her territory, without soiling her honor and being humiliated. She stands ready to buy peace at any cost, except that of her honor. . . .

1837

■ TALES FROM THE HISPANIC SOUTHWEST ■

In his pioneering *Cuentos Españoles de Colorado y de Nuevo México* (*Spanish Tales from Colorado and New Mexico*), 1977, Professor Juan B. Rael points out that the majority of the five hundred tales he collected between 1930 and 1940 "represent a part of the cultural heritage that the first settlers of this former Spanish frontier brought with them, a heritage which their descendants have faithfully preserved through more than three centuries." The *cuentos*, or folktales, that Rael and his predecessor and teacher Aurelio M. Espinosa collected represent a huge repository of oral narratives that are old world in type-origin, but often adapted to the southwestern geographic and social ecology in which they were performed. The stories Hispanics related included morality tales alongside tales of picaresque rogues, tales of enchantment filled with witches, ghosts, enchanted princesses and tales in which animals with the gift of speech and wisdom reminded humans of their filial and social responsibilities.

"La comadre Sebastiana" ("Doña Sebastiana") and "Los tres hermanos" ("The Three Brothers"), included here, represent *cuentos morales* (morality tales), the function of which is to instill a complex religio-social sensibility in young listeners. There are scores of tales like "Los tres hermanos" in which characters who fail to consider the needs of the thirsty and hungry, the unsheltered, or the old are justly served with moral ruin, death, and perhaps worst of all, eternal damnation. In "La comadre Sebastiana," death is personified, actually given full status as a character who functions to integrate the reality and certainty of death into everyday experience. Death is imaged not as the terrorizing grim reaper but as a familial figure, *una comadre* or godmother, who maintains filial ties with an individual over a lifetime. Notice also that the *cuento* contains within its orthodox Christian configuration a space in which the social injustices that Christianity has instituted over the centuries are exposed. For a poor man to openly chastise both Jesus and the Virgin Mary for failing to be equitable is a stunning class-conscious critique of Christian hypocrisy and the Church's complicity with the rich. In this particular story, the woodcutter is rewarded for his charity with the gift of healing. As a *curandero*, or folkhealer, he assumes a revered position in traditional Chicano society, a position he must not abuse for material gain. When he does, the results are grave.

If these stories appear somewhat stiff in this textual edition, it is because the intimate environment in which they were performed is lost in print. *Cuento* telling was a special event in which families, relatives, and friends gathered after a long day's work, ate together, drank a few beers perhaps while the children roasted piñon nuts, and then listened with rapt attention as an uncle, ranch hand, or grandmother told story after story in nuanced tones, with rich hand gestures, suspense-building pauses, and meaningful glances at the children. The storytelling session often ended late, with the children clamoring for one more *cuento* ("uno más, tio, no más uno"/"one more, uncle, just one more") while the adults pulled them away and made for home. There would be other days and more tales another time.

However much the oral storytelling tradition has declined in recent decades, it remains a crucial narrative superstructure for many contemporary Chicano writers. In fact, New Mexico's preeminent Chicano novelist Rudolfo A. Anaya's *Bless Me, Ultima and Heart of Aztlan*, as well as numerous short stories, resonate with the narrative apparatus that functions in the *cuento* tradition. One might say that the orally performed *cuento* has rather naturally imbricated itself upon the textual narratives that writers like Anaya are creating—"naturally" because Anaya was one of those children clamoring for one more *cuento*. The informality, the verbal intimacy, even the melodramatic delight one discovers in Anaya and other Chicano writers seem a continuation of the storytelling strategies of the *cuento* performance.

Genaro M. Padilla
University of California at Berkeley

PRIMARY WORK

José Griego y Maestas, *Cuentos: Tales from the Hispanic Southwest*, retold in English by Rudolfo A. Anaya, 1980.

La comadre Sebastiana (Doña Sebastiana)

Once there was a poor man who earned his living cutting wood in the common land of the land grant and selling it in the village. When he sold his wood his family ate well, when he couldn't sell it his family went hungry. He lived that way for a long time, but one day he was tempted by hunger and he decided to swipe one of his wife's setting hens.

He waited until everyone was asleep and then stole into the chicken coop, took a chicken and killed it. Then he stealthily made his way into the mountains where he planned to indulge himself. He made a big fire and put the chicken on a spit to roast. He was flavoring the chicken with a few spices and enjoying the drippings when he heard someone approach his camp.

God help me! he thought. Even here I can't be left alone to enjoy myself! Well, whoever it is, I'm not going to invite them to eat!

"How do you do, my friend," said the stranger as he approached the camp. The stranger's noble stature made the woodcutter cautious.

"*Buenas noches*," the woodcutter responded. "Who are you?"

"I am the Lord," the stranger answered. "Will you invite me to eat with you?"

The woodcutter looked at the small chicken and thought awhile. "No," he finally said, "I don't think I'll invite you to share my meal, and I'll tell you why. I think you neglect the poor. You give everything to the rich and so little to the poor. You don't treat us equally."

And so the woodcutter kept the chicken for himself, and the Lord went away saddened. The woodcutter was satisfied, but shortly he heard another person approaching.

"Good evening, my friend," said the woman as she drew near.

"*Buenas noches, señora*," the woodcutter replied. "And who might you be?"

"I am the Virgin Mary," the woman answered. "Will you share your food with me?"

The woodcutter scratched his beard, looked again at the small chicken and finally said, "No, I am not going to share my food with you, and I'll tell you why. I think your Son neglects the poor. Since you are the mother of God, you should intercede for us so He would make us all equal. Either we should all be rich, or we should all be poor. The way it is now, He makes some very rich and some very poor, and unfortunately I am one of the poor ones. For that reason I am not going to share my chicken with you."

So the Virgin Mary left, but it wasn't long before the woodcutter heard someone else approach. This time it was Doña Sebastiana, Death herself, who approached the woodcutter's fire.

"How goes it, friend?" Doña Sebastiana asked.

"*Buenas noches,*" the woodcutter answered, trembling at the sight of the old hag in front of him. "Who are you?" he asked.

"I am Death," Doña Sebastiana answered as she slowly got down from her cart. "Will you share your meal with me?"

"I never realized Death was so thin!" the woodcutter said as he looked at the skeleton in front of him. "Of course you are welcome to share my food, and I'll tell you why. You do things very well. You don't play favorites with the wealthy because of their money, nor the beautiful because of their beauty, nor do you play favorites with the ugly or the old or the young. No, you treat us all equally. Sit down and share my meal."

After they had finished eating the roasted chicken Doña Sebastiana was very pleased, so she told the woodcutter to ask for any favor he wished and it would be granted.

"*Señora,*" the woodcutter said in his most humble voice, "I can't ask for a favor. If you wish to grant me one, then grant me what you will."

"Very well," Death answered, "I am going to grant you the power to be a healer, a *curandero.* You shall be able to cure all kinds of sickness. However, I leave you with one commandment: When you are asked to cure a sick person and you go to that patient's bed and see me standing at the head of the bed, don't cure that person regardless of what his relatives will pay or promise you. I warn you, if I am there, don't cure that person! That person has no remedy but to die. He has been called by God.

"But if you see me at the patient's feet, then go ahead and cure him. Use water or earth or curing powders, and the patient will get well. But remember, if you see me at the head of the bed, don't dare to attempt a cure, no matter what you are promised!"

So the curandero practiced his craft for many years and he cured many people and became famous for his powers. But one day the richest man in the region became ill and offered the curandero a fortune for a cure, and so the healer broke the commandment of Doña Sebastiana.

When the curandero arrived at the rich man's home he saw Doña Sebastiana seated at the head of the bed where the sick man lay. The curandero immediately grabbed her and wrestled her back and forth until she was so dizzy that he was able to move her to the foot of the bed. In that way Death was overpowered, and the curandero then cured the rich man.

But when the curandero was returning home Death met him on the road and reminded him that he had broken the one commandment he had promised not to break when she had given him the power to cure sickness.

"I warned you *never* to cure a sick person if I was at the head of his bed," Doña Sebastiana said angrily. "Now you must come with me."

She took the curandero to a dark room and showed him two candles. One candle had burned low and was flickering as if ready to go out, the other was a tall candle burning brightly.

"You have made a grave mistake," Death told the curandero. "Once you were like the tall candle and the sick man was like the short candle. But now you are the small candle and the man you cured is the tall one."

At that moment the flame of the short candle went out, and the curandero's soul was added to Doña Sebastiana's cart as it slowly made its way into eternity.

1980

Los tres hermanos (The Three Brothers)

Once upon a time there lived an old couple who had three sons. When the eldest came of age, he asked his parents for permission to go where he could make his livelihood. His parents agreed and gave him their benediction and supplied him with provisions for his trip.

"May God bless you and keep you away from all evil," they said. "Be kind to old people and remember your parents."

So the young man set out on his journey. On the road he met a woman who asked him where he was going. He told her he was looking for work.

"You are a good son," she said. Then, as the day was very hot, she asked him for water, but he lied to her and told her he had no water.

"Very well," she said, "follow this road to the next city. There you will find a man who can help you. He is my son."

So he followed the road until he came to a simple but pleasing city. He knocked at the door where the woman had directed him and was received by the woman's son. The youth explained that he was looking for work.

"Very well," said the man, "in order to begin your work, go and catch that donkey and saddle him. I want you to deliver a letter to my mother. Take my dog with you. Wherever he stops you will know it is safe and you can rest there. But if he doesn't want to stop you should not stop there either."

So the boy mounted the donkey and started out. On the road he came upon a magnificent and dazzling city where there was every kind of entertainment. Everyone was singing and dancing or playing musical instruments. The youth wanted to stop awhile and join the wild entertainment of that tempting city, but the dog wouldn't stop there. They continued until they came to a river of blood. This strange sight filled the youth with dread and he would not cross the river. He returned and gave the letter back to the man.

"I didn't finish the errand," he explained. "I came upon a river of blood and I was afraid to cross it."

"Very well, I will pay you for your trouble anyway," the man answered. "What do you want as a reward for trying? A simple thanks which says, 'God repay your kindness,' or a bagful of money?"

"I'll take the money," replied the youth.

And as soon as he was paid he went straight to the beguiling city to indulge in its delights. He forgot all about his parents and never once thought of sharing his money with them.

In time the second son was eager to be on his own so he asked his parents for their blessing so that he might go out and make his way in life.

The old couple replied, "But what if what happened to your brother happens to you? He evidently had good luck, but he has forgotten us and never sent us a nickel."

He assured them he wouldn't forget them, so they blessed him and he went forth. He met the same gracious woman his brother had met on the road and, like his brother, he didn't share his water or food with her. Nevertheless she told him where he could find work. And so, like his brother before him, he arrived at the city and called at the door. The man came out, greeted him and offered him the same errand.

"Take the donkey and go deliver this letter," he said. "Take my small dog with you and wherever he stops you can rest, but if he doesn't stop you should not stop."

The second young man continued his journey, and like his brother before him he saw the city of many pleasures, and he too arrived at the river of blood, but wouldn't cross it. He returned to the house of the man and told him he had not delivered the letter because he had come to a river of blood which frightened him.

"Very well," the man replied, "now what do you want as your reward? A 'God repay your kindness' or a bagful of money?"

"The bagful of money," the second brother quickly replied, and from there he went immediately to the beautiful city where everyone sang, danced and played, and he forgot all about his parents.

Soon after, the youngest son asked for his parents' benediction so he could go out and look for work. But they cried and refused to allow him to go because they were afraid he might end up like his brothers. He pleaded with them until at last they gave him their blessing and their meager supply of bread and water for his journey.

The next day as he walked down the road he met the same woman, and she asked him where he was going. He told her he was looking for work in order to help his parents.

"In the city up the road you can work for my son," she said. Then she added, "I am hungry. Do you have bread or water?"

"Yes," he answered and he shared with her his loaf of bread and water. After eating he said to her, "Take what is left, *señora*."

"No," she replied, "I cannot. You have a long way to walk yet."

"But I am a man and my parents taught me to share what I have with those who are in need. You are a woman and need the food."

The woman thanked him, took the food and the water and disappeared. The boy had walked only a short distance when he felt his pack grow heavy. He checked it and to his surprise it was replenished with food and water. He was mystified at what had happened, and he wondered if the woman was a witch or a saint.

He continued until he came to the city where he found the house the woman had described. He knocked at the door and a man came out and asked him what he wanted.

"I am looking for work," the boy replied.

"Very well," the man said, "I have an errand for you to do: Deliver a letter to my mother. Go catch that donkey so you can begin your journey, and take my little dog with you. He is a good companion. Wherever he stops you can stop to rest, but if he doesn't stop then you must continue."

The boy followed the road until he arrived at the beautiful and gay city where everyone sang, played, danced and laughed. He was tempted to stop and look for his two lost brothers, but the little dog wouldn't stop so he went on. Soon he arrived at the river of blood and he stopped; for a few minutes he didn't know what to do, then he remembered his parents' blessing.

"With the blessing of my father and mother I can overcome every obstacle in my way," he said, and with the little dog at his side he waded into the river and crossed safely to the other side.

"If God grants me life and health I will ask my master the meaning of this," he said to himself.

He continued his journey and came next to a river of swords.

"Ay, this is truly a dangerous place!" he whispered as he saw the sharp swords which filled the river. "But I have the blessing of my parents and that will keep me safe from all danger."

He jumped into the river, and with the little dog and the donkey at his side, he crossed safely. Once on the other side he marveled at the strange meaning of the river of swords.

"If God grants me life and health," he said, "I am going to ask my master the meaning of this obstacle."

Next he came to a place in the road blocked by two huge mountains which appeared to be fighting each other. The earth shook with their groans and huge boulders fell everywhere. As he had safely passed the treacherous rivers, so now he followed the little dog with his donkey, and they worked their way through the narrow canyon and the falling rocks until they were safely on the other side.

Up ahead he came upon a flock of very fat sheep grazing on a plain so desolate there wasn't a blade of grass on it. Yet in the distance there was a very green meadow, so the boy got down from his donkey and tried to drive the flock towards the grass. But the fat sheep wouldn't move towards the meadow and stayed in the dry desert. While trying to drive the sheep he lost the dog and he became very worried. It was strange, he thought, but the dog had not helped him while he had tried to drive the sheep to better pasture.

Without his trusty dog he wouldn't know where to go, so he sat beneath a tree and said to himself, "I won't leave until my dog comes back."

Suddenly the little dog appeared and the boy was overjoyed to see him again. Together they continued their journey and it wasn't long before they came upon a flock of thin sheep grazing on grass so high it almost covered them.

"How can it be that the fat sheep are in a place so dry and desolate and these thin sheep are in such a beautiful meadow?" the boy wondered. "If God grants me life and health to return from this strange journey I will ask my master the meaning of this."

In the distance he caught sight of a marvelous city. He hoped it was the place where he was to deliver the letter so he hurried forward. He followed his little dog through the city until they came to the door of a certain house. The boy knocked at the door and a woman appeared. The boy thought she was the same woman he had met on the road and with whom he had shared his food, but he didn't say anything. He handed her the letter and she received it with a smile. Then she invited him in and fed him and gave him a place where he could rest. He felt happy and content that he had completed his errand, and he quickly fell asleep. He did not awaken until the woman called him softly.

"Wake up, my son, you have been asleep a long time."

"No, *señora*," he said when he opened his eyes, "I just now fell asleep."

"No, you have been asleep for a hundred years," she said.

The way she said it made him jump up and run to the mirror. He saw that he was older and bearded. He grew very sad.

"Let me go quickly, my parents may already be dead!"

"Don't worry about your parents," she consoled him. "They are just as you left them."

But he did not yet believe her, so she sent him back to his master's home. On the return journey he didn't encounter any of the previous obstacles; instead, the road was straight to his master's house. The master received him warmly and asked him if he had done his work. The boy replied that he had.

"Now," the master said, "what do you want as your reward, a 'God bless you for your kindness,' or a bagful of money?"

"God's blessing is more valuable than money," the boy answered.

"Then you may ask for a favor," the man nodded.

"Before I ask my favor I would like to ask you some questions," the boy said. "What was the first city I came to when I left here? It was very beautiful and everyone was singing, dancing and laughing wildly."

"That is hell," his master answered.

"Farther on I came to a river of blood. What river was that?"

"That is the river of blood which Jesus shed for all sinners."

"Later I came to a river of swords. What river was that?"

"Those are the swords which wounded our Lord."

"Later I came upon two mountains which seemed to do battle with each other. What did that mean?"

"Those are two angry *compadres* who fight with each other instead of living in peace."

"Then I met a flock of fat sheep on a desolate plain. What did that strange sight mean?"

"Those are the poor people of the world who know there is a God and believe in Him."

"Up ahead I met a flock of thin sheep, and they were grazing in a beautiful meadow. What does this mean?"

"Those are the rich of the world who don't think there is a God nor believe in Him."

"And the city where I delivered the letter, what city is that?"

"That is heaven."

"And the woman who was in the house, who is she?"

"That is my mother."

"And you, master, you must be—"

"I am Jesus, the one who suffered for all sinners. Have you heard that the soldiers opened my side with a sword when I was on the cross?"

"Yes, my parents have told me the story."

Then the Lord lifted His arm and showed the boy the wound, and the boy understood all of the strange events which had occurred during his journey. He then made this request:

"The only favor I have to ask is that you take my parents and me, together with my two brothers, to the city where I delivered the letter."

"You and your parents will go to heaven, but not your brothers."

"But why, Lord?" the boy asked.

"Because they were bad sons, and did not take care of their parents, they deserve to spend eternity in the fires of hell."

1980

El obispo (The New Bishop)

It had been many years since Archbishop Zubiría of Durango had crossed the Jornada del Muerto to visit his flock in the farthest part of his diocese in New Mexico. Thus people in a small and isolated village were very happy that his Excellency, the new bishop of Santa Fe, was coming to administer the sacrament of Confirmation to their children. A big feast was planned, and the local parish priest went about telling everyone to prepare for the visit of this very important church dignitary.

The people had never seen the bishop, so they were overjoyed to have the opportunity to meet him. The day the bishop arrived the priest took him to the sacristy where he could meet the people before he administered Confirmation to the children. But the people, in their excitement, forgot how to greet him.

The men came in first, but none remembered how to address the bishop, and in their awe of him they made many mistakes.

One bowed and said, "How do you do, your holiness San Joaquín."

Others greeted him by saying, "How do you do, most holy Saint Anthony."

And one woman was so flabbergasted she said, "How do you do, oh blessed Virgin Mary."

Finally one man entered and said, "How do you do, your Excellency."

When this man greeted him correctly the shocked bishop was pleased he had finally met someone who could speak good Castillian Spanish. He took the man aside and whispered confidently, "Isn't it a shame that these people are so backward and ignorant that they don't even know how to greet me?"

The man replied sarcastically, "Yes, my *paisanos* are a humble people. Who else would address Your Excellency as a saint or as the Virgin Mary, when it's plain to see you're neither a saint nor a virgin!"

1980

El indito de las cien vacas (The Indian and the Hundred Cows)

In a small pueblo there once lived an Indian who was so devoted to the church he never missed mass on Sunday. One Sunday, during his homily, the priest said:

"Have charity, my children. Give alms to the poor. If you expect God's help it is necessary that you also help the church. You know that when you make a donation to God, He returns it a hundredfold."

The Indian, who was listening carefully, decided to give a cow that he had to the priest. That afternoon he brought his cow to the church and told the priest, "Padre, I have brought you my cow so that God will give me a hundred cows."

"Yes, yes, my son," the priest answered. "Have faith in God and he will repay your gift." Then the priest took the cow and added it to his own herd.

The Indian returned home very satisfied and he began to build a large corral where he could keep his hundred cows when they arrived. When he finished his corral he sat down to wait for the cows. He waited some time and then thought, "Perhaps the cows don't come on their own, maybe I should go for them." So he set out to look for his promised hundred cows. Near the church he came upon a large herd which he drove home and locked securely in his corral.

Later that afternoon the two *vaqueros* who took care of the priest's herd rode to the Indian's home.

"Why do you have these cattle locked up?" they asked gruffly. "Have they done some damage?"

"No, they haven't done any damage," the Indian answered. "I have them locked up because they're mine. I gave the priest a cow and he promised me God would give me a hundred, and here they are!"

"These are the priest's cattle, not yours," the cowboys answered.

"No, these are mine because he promised me a hundred for one!" the Indian insisted.

The cowboys returned to tell the priest what had happened. When he heard the news the priest became very angry. He got on his mule and the three rode to the Indian's home. When they arrived at the corral the Indian was sitting by the gate, his bow and quiver of arrows ready.

"Why have you locked up my cattle in your corral!" the priest shouted. "Is this the way you show your gratitude?"

"But these are my cows," the Indian answered.

"And who gave them to you?"

"You did. You said at mass whoever gave one cow would get a hundred in return!"

"That's not what I meant, you thief!" the priest cried angrily. "You are a thief and you must turn my cattle loose." He got down from his mule to open the gate but stopped when he saw the Indian put an arrow to his bow.

"Padre, if you dare touch the lock I will stick this arrow into your heart. Then the devils in hell will give you a hundred more."

The priest backed away. He realized the Indian meant to make him keep the promise he had made in church, and there was nothing he could do. So he got on his mule and quietly rode home, reminding himself to be more careful with what he said in his sermons.

1980

■

Expansion and the War against Mexico

During the 1840s, while many nations were embroiled in social and revolutionary struggles over workers' rights, democracy, and fundamental questions of equality and freedom, the United States was also actively pursuing greater influence over the hemisphere and, in particular, power over adjacent territories held sovereign by many nations including those claimed by the Spanish, Cherokees, Hopis, Iroquois Confederacy, Russians, and Mexicans. These territorial ambitions were laced together with the economic and moral questions of a nation deeply ambivalent about its slaveholding future. By mid-decade, the United States had established a popular framework to narrate its desire for more land. "Manifest Destiny" lent the political and military struggles a religious valence, soothing moral qualms and justifying the violence and slaughter to follow.

The term, coined in 1845 by either John O'Sullivan or Jane McManus Storm Cazneau, attempted to hold at bay opposition to the annexation of Texas and the sure-to-follow war against Mexico, which was declared and waged over the next three years. So important was the concept of destiny to this effort that writer George Lippard proclaimed that the nation would establish an "empire of Freedom" as long as his countrymen obeyed the "mysterious Symbol of our destiny—THE UNSHEATHED SWORD OF WASHINGTON RESTING UPON THE MAP OF THE NEW WORLD."

If the war against Mexico (1846–1848) is little discussed today, it was certainly not absent from national view as the drumbeats for annexation and war began to sound in 1844, nor, two years later, when companies of volunteers were raised in each state. Writers and artists as well as political leaders and industrial scions argued vigorously throughout the conflict about whether the war was justified. Many said that the primary purpose of the war was to relieve the territorial pressure created by the Missouri Compromise. Opponents of the war argued that supporters of slavery wanted additional territory to create more slaveholding states. Any number of defenders of the war claimed as a benefit that the conflict would prove that an independent republic could wage war against another nation, thus creating a further toehold for democracy. The war would provide a new opportunity to test chivalry and heroism, so the popular opinion urged. Up until then, political theorists had argued that only monarchs and autocrats had sufficient power to compel their subjects to die for the national interest. Still others cynically observed that the war was inevitable given the growing population of the states and the increasing need for the resources demanded by a burgeoning industrial economy in the North. Such was the sense of Ralph Waldo Emerson who, according to Jaime Rodríguez, viewed the war as both inevitable and immoral. Meditating on the war, Emerson would note in one journal entry, "I found two poor English or Irishmen playing chequers on a little board where the spots were marked with ink, and the *men* were beans and coffee berries. They played on, game after game, one sure of beating, the other indignant at defeat, and I left them playing. Why not? & what difference? All the world is playing backgammon, some with beans and coffee, and some with Texas & Mexico, with states and nations."

Emerson's troubling inference signals racialization processes that were incorporating increasingly sophisticated technologies of differentiation and stratification as part of the process of expansion. Manifest Destiny, like the doctrines that had been used to justify slavery, tended to rationalize violence by proclaiming the animalistic nature of Mexicanos. Using images and metaphors that dated back to the early era of England's battles with Spain, writers, ministers, and politicians disparaged people of Mexican descent in sermons, songs, posters, and dime novels. This was a moment of U.S. territorial expansion but also of racial expansion. Whether for or against the war, writers tended to establish a vision of an "Anglo-Saxon race" that could be variously identified (via philosophy, dialect, clothing, and so forth) and held superior to everyone else in the world. Songs such as "Yankee Doodle" were repeatedly played by volunteers. Described by an army correspondent as eliciting an "honest cheer" from the "gallant fellows," the song, like the flag, accompanied volunteers from across the states. Returning volunteers were similarly greeted: bands played, businesses closed, fireworks displays colored the night skies, and the troops were showered with flowers and celebrated as invigorating the spirit of the Declaration of Independence while renewing "the fires of freedom."

Opponents of the war similarly gathered their metaphors together to lampoon these celebrants and critique the causes of the war. James Russell Lowell's *The Biglow Papers* (1848) is among the most famous of these critiques. The book is a complex hybrid of poetry and prose: Three letters by Birdofredum Sawin, a Yankee soldier, are fictionally rewritten into dialect poetry by the Yankee farmer, Hosea Biglow. These letters and poems are framed by fictional essays by Parson Homer Wilbur. Critical of both the war and slavery, *The Biglow Papers* nevertheless offer prowar speeches and celebrate a kind of romanticized Yankee Anglo-Saxon ethnicity through the use of dialect verse. Where the poems call out the war's hypocrisy and misguidedness, it is often in order to celebrate isolationism. Gavin Jones notes that "Biglow's dialect is largely presented as the natural voice of truth, pitched against the 'foreign tongue' of classical poetry and the standardized, school-mastered language that was spreading rapidly through mass education and popular journalism." Yet as Jones, Shelley Streeby, Rodríguez, and other scholars note, the use of dialect also aided the effort to give the nation a sense of "Anglo-Saxon" rootedness and to underscore a sense of superiority, as Lowell himself would note in a letter: "[I]t is the manifest destiny of the English race to occupy this whole continent and to display there that practical understanding in matters of government and colonization which no other race has given such proof of possessing since the romans."

Frederic Douglass was among the quickest to see the contradictions between celebrations of Anglo-Saxonism and the claims to freedom. Writing in the *North Star* in 1848, he noted how blatantly the rhetoric surrounding the war and Manifest Destiny depended on a form of white supremacist pride in "Anglo Saxon blood." This in turn, he argued, contradicted the claims that the war was waged to uphold freedom. Ironically perhaps, the agreement bringing the war to an end, the Treaty of Guadalupe Hidalgo, laid the foundation for a possible challenge to such supremacist thinking even as it sealed the expansion of U.S. territory at the expense of Mexico's. The treaty provides a legal guarantee of civil (including language) and land rights to those Mexicanos residing in the annexed lands. For the next 150 years, scholars and activists would question whether this guarantee had been honored or could be made to do so today.

Mary Pat Brady
Cornell University

▪ John L. O'Sullivan (1813–1895) or ▪
Jane McManus Storm Cazneau
(1807–1878)

Annexation[1]

It is time now for opposition to the Annexation of Texas to cease, all further agitation of the waters of bitterness and strife, at least in connexion with this question,—even though it may perhaps be required of us as a necessary condition of the freedom of our institutions, that we must live on for ever in a state of unpausing struggle and excitement upon some subject of party division or other. But, in regard to Texas, enough has now been given to party. It is time for the common duty of Patriotism to the Country to succeed;—or if this claim will not be recognized, it is at least time for common sense to acquiesce with decent grace in the inevitable and the irrevocable.

Texas is now ours. Already, before these words are written, her Convention has undoubtedly ratified the acceptance, by her Congress, of our proffered invitation into the Union; and made the requisite changes in her already republican form of constitution to adapt it to its future federal relations. Her star and her stripe may already be said to have taken their place in the glorious blazon of our common nationality; and the sweep of our eagle's wing already includes within its circuit the wide extent of her fair and fertile land. She is no longer to us a mere geographical space—a certain combination of coast, plain, mountain, valley, forest and stream. She is no longer to us a mere country on the map. She comes within the dear and sacred designation of Our Country; no longer a *"pays,"* she is a part of *"la patrie"*; and that which is at once a sentiment and a virtue, Patriotism, already begins to thrill for her too within the national heart. It is time then that all should cease to treat her as alien, and even adverse—cease to denounce and vilify all and everything connected with her accession—cease to thwart and oppose the remaining steps for its consummation; or where such efforts are felt to be unavailing, at least to embitter the hour of reception by all the most ungracious frowns of aversion and words of unwelcome. There has been enough of all this. It has had its fitting day during the period when, in common with every other possible question of practical policy that can arise, it unfortunately became one of the leading topics of party division, of presidential electioneering. But that period has passed, and with it let its prejudices and its passions, its discords and its denunciations, pass away too. The next session of Congress will see the representatives of the new young State in their places in both our halls of national legislation, side by side with

[1]From *United States Magazine and Democratic Review* (July 1845), Library of Congress.

those of the old Thirteen. Let their reception into "the family" be frank, kindly, and cheerful, as befits such an occasion, as comports not less with our own self-respect than patriotic duty towards them. Ill betide those foul birds that delight to file their own nest, and disgust the ear with perpetual discord of ill-omened croak.

Why, were other reasoning wanting, in favor of now elevating this question of the reception of Texas into the Union, out of the lower region of our past party dissensions, up to its proper level of a high and broad nationality, it surely is to be found, found abundantly, in the manner in which other nations have undertaken to intrude themselves into it, between us and the proper parties to the case, in a spirit of hostile interference against us, for the avowed object of thwarting our policy and hampering our power, limiting our greatness and checking the fulfilment of our manifest destiny to overspread the continent allotted by Providence for the free development of our yearly multiplying millions. . . .

. . . Nor is there any just foundation for the charge that Annexation is a great pro-slavery measure—calculated to increase and perpetuate that institution. Slavery had nothing to do with it. Opinions were and are greatly divided, both at the North and South, as to the influence to be exerted by it on Slavery and the Slave States. That it will tend to facilitate and hasten the disappearance of Slavery from all the northern tier of the present Slave States, cannot surely admit of serious question. The greater value in Texas of the slave labor now employed in those States, must soon produce the effect of draining off that labor southwardly, by the same unvarying law that bids water descend the slope that invites it. Every new Slave State in Texas will make at least one Free State from among those in which that institution now exists—to say nothing of those portions of Texas on which slavery cannot spring and grow—to say nothing of the far more rapid growth of new States in the free West and North-west, as these fine regions are overspread by the emigration fast flowing over them from Europe, as well as from the Northern and Eastern States of the Union as it exists. On the other hand, it is undeniably much gained for the cause of the eventual voluntary abolition of slavery, that it should have been thus drained off towards the only outlet which appeared to furnish much probability of the ultimate disappearance of the negro race from our borders. The Spanish-Indian-American populations of Mexico, Central America and South America, afford the only receptacle capable of absorbing that race whenever we shall be prepared to slough it off—to emancipate it from slavery, and (simultaneously necessary) to remove it from the midst of our own. Themselves already of mixed and confused blood, and free from the "prejudices" which among us so insuperably forbid the social amalgamation which can alone elevate the Negro race out of a virtually servile degradation, even though legally free, the regions occupied by those populations must strongly attract the black race in that direction; and as soon as the destined hour of emancipation shall arrive, will relieve the question of one of its worst difficulties, if not absolutely the greatest.

... Texas has been absorbed into the Union in the inevitable fulfilment of the general law which is rolling our population westward; the connexion of which with that ratio of growth in population which is destined within a hundred years to swell our numbers to the enormous population of *two hundred and fifty millions* (if not more), is too evident to leave us in doubt of the manifest design of Providence in regard to the occupation of this continent. It was disintegrated from Mexico in the natural course of events, by a process perfectly legitimate on its own part, blameless on ours; and in which all the censures due to wrong, perfidy and folly, rest on Mexico alone. And possessed as it was by a population which was in truth but a colonial detachment from our own, and which was still bound by myriad ties of the very heart-strings to its old relations, domestic and political, their incorporation into the Union was not only inevitable, but the most natural, right and proper thing in the world—and it is only astonishing that there should be any among ourselves to say it nay.

... California will, probably, next fall away from the loose adhesion which, in such a country as Mexico, holds a remote province in a slight equivocal kind of dependence on the metropolis. Imbecile and distracted, Mexico never can exert any real governmental authority over such a country. The impotence of the one and the distance of the other, must make the relation one of virtual independence; unless, by stunting the province of all natural growth, and forbidding that immigration which can alone develop its capabilities and fulfill the purposes of its creation, tyranny may retain a military dominion, which is no government in the legitimate sense of the term. In the case of California this is now impossible. The Anglo-Saxon foot is already on its borders. Already the advance guard of the irresistible army of Anglo-Saxon emigration has begun to pour down upon it, armed with the plough and the rifle, and marking its trail with schools and colleges, courts and representative halls, mills and meeting-houses. A population will soon be in actual occupation of California, over which it will be idle for Mexico to dream of dominion. They will necessarily become independent.... Whether they will then attach themselves to our Union or not, is not to be predicted with any certainty. Unless the projected railroad across the continent to the Pacific be carried into effect, perhaps they may not; though even in that case, the day is not distant when the Empires of the Atlantic and Pacific would again flow together into one, as soon as their inland border should approach each other. But that great work, colossal as appears the plan on its first suggestion, cannot remain long unbuilt. Its necessity for this very purpose of binding and holding together in its iron clasp our fast-settling Pacific region with that of the Mississippi valley—the natural facility of the route—the ease with which any amount of labor for the construction can be drawn in from the overcrowded populations of Europe, to be paid in the lands made valuable by the progress of the work itself—and its immense utility to the commerce of the world with the whole eastern coast of Asia, alone almost sufficient for the support of such a road—these considerations give assurance that the day cannot be distant which shall witness the conveyance of the representatives from Oregon and California to Washington within less time than a few years ago was devoted to a similar journey by those from Ohio; while the magnetic telegraph will enable the editors of the "San Francisco Union," the "Astoria Evening Post," or the "Nootka Morning News," to set up in type the first half of the President's Inaugural before the echoes of the latter half shall have died away beneath the lofty porch of the Capitol, as spoken from his lips.

Away, then, with all idle French talk of *balances of power* on the American Continent. There is no growth in Spanish America! Whatever progress of population there may be in the British Canadas, is only for their own early severance of their present colonial relation to the little island three thousand miles across the Atlantic; soon to be followed by Annexation, and destined to swell the still accumulating momentum of our progress. And whosoever may hold the balance, though they should cast into the opposite scale all the bayonets and cannon, not only of France and England, but of Europe entire, how would it kick the beam against the simple, solid weight of the two hundred and fifty, or three hundred millions—and American millions—destined to gather beneath the flutter of the stripes and stars, in the fast hastening year of the Lord 1945!

1845

■　　　　JAMES RUSSELL LOWELL　　　　■
1819–1891

from **The Biglow Papers**

Thrash away, you 'll *hev* to rattle
　　On them kittle drums o' yourn,—
'Taint a knowin' kind o' cattle
　　Thet is ketched with mouldy corn;
Put in stiff, you fifer feller,　　　　　　　　　5
　　Let folks see how spry you be,—
Guess you 'll toot till you are yeller
　　'Fore you git ahold o' me!

Thet air flag 's a leetle rotten,
　　Hope it aint your Sunday's best;—　　　　10
Fact! it takes a sight o' cotton
　　To stuff out a soger's chest:
Sence we farmers hev to pay fer 't,
　　Ef you must wear humps like these,

Sposin' you should try salt hay fer 't,   15
    It would du ez slick ez grease.

'T would n't suit them Southern fellers,
    They 're a dreffle graspin' set,
We must ollers blow the bellers
    Wen they want their irons het;   20
May be it 's all right ez preachin',
    But *my* narves it kind o' grates,
Wen I see the overreachin'
    O' them nigger-drivin' States.

Them thet rule us, them slave-traders,   25
    Haint they cut a thunderin' swarth
(Helped by Yankee renegaders),
    Thru the vartu o' the North!
We begin to think it 's nater
    To take sarse an' not be riled;—   30
Who 'd expect to see a tater
    All on eend at bein' biled?

Ez fer war, I call it murder,—
    There you hev it plain an' flat;
I don't want to go no furder   35
    Than my Testyment fer that;
God hez sed so plump an' fairly,
    It 's ez long ez it is broad,
An' you 've gut to git up airly
    Ef you want to take in God.   40

'Taint your eppyletts an' feathers
    Make the thing a grain more right;
Taint afollerin' your bell-wethers
    Will excuse ye in His sight;
Ef you take a sword an' dror it,   45
    An' go stick a feller thru,
Guv'ment aint to answer for it,
    God 'll send the bill to you.

Wut 's the use o' meetin-goin'
    Every Sabbath, wet or dry,   50
Ef it 's right to go amowin'
    Feller-men like oats an' rye?
I dunno but wut it's pooty
    Trainin' round in bobtail coats,—
But it 's curus Christian dooty   55
    This ere cuttin' folks's throats.

They may talk o' Freedom's airy
    Tell they 're pupple in the face,—
It 's a grand gret cemetary
    Fer the barthrights of our race;   60
They jest want this Californy
    So 's to lug new slave-states in
To abuse ye, an' to scorn ye,
    An' to plunder ye like sin.

Aint it cute to see a Yankee   65
    Take sech everlastin' pains
All to git the Devil's thankee,
    Helpin' on 'em weld their chains?
Wy, it 's jest ez clear ez figgers,
    Clear ez one an' one make two,   70
Chaps thet make black slaves o' niggers
    Want to make wite slaves o' you.

Tell ye jest the eend I've come to
    Arter cipherin' plaguy smart,
An' it makes a handy sum, tu,   75
    Any gump could larn by heart;
Laborin' man an' laborin' woman
    Hev one glory an' one shame,
Ev'y thin' thet 's done inhuman
    Injers all on 'em the same.   80

'Taint by turnin' out to hack folks
    You 're agoin' to git your right,
Nor by lookin' down on black folks
    Coz you 're put upon by wite;
Slavery aint o' nary colour,   85
    'Taint the hide thet makes it wus,
All it keers fer in a feller
    'S jest to make him fill its pus.

Want to tackle *me* in, du ye?
    I expect you 'll hev to wait;   90
Wen cold lead puts daylight thru ye
    You 'll begin to kal'late;
'Spose the crows wun't fall to pickin'
    All the carkiss from your bones,
Coz you helped to give a lickin'   95
    To them poor half-Spanish drones?

Jest go home an' ask our Nancy
    Wether I'd be sech a goose

Ez to jine ye,—guess you'd fancy
    The etarnal bung wuz loose!   100
She wants me fer home consumption,
    Let alone the hay 's to mow,—
Ef you 're arter folks o' gumption,
    You've a darned long row to hoe.

Take them editors thet 's crowin'   105
    Like a cockerel three months old,—
Don't ketch any on 'em goin',
    Though they *be* so blasted bold;
Aint they a prime set o' fellers?
    'Fore they think on 't they will sprout   110
(Like a peach thet's got the yellers),
    With the meanness bustin' out.

Wal, go 'long to help 'em stealin'
    Bigger pens to cram with slaves,
Help the men thet 's ollers dealin'   115
    Insults on your fathers' graves;
Help the strong to grind the feeble,
    Help the many agin the few,
Help the men thet call your people
    Witewashed slaves an' peddlin' crew!   120

Massachusetts, God forgive her,
    She's akneelin' with the rest,
She, thet ough' to ha' clung fer ever
    In her grand old eagle-nest;
She thet ough' to stand so fearless   125
    Wile the wracks are round her hurled,
Holdin' up a beacon peerless
    To the oppressed of all the world!

Haint they sold your coloured seamen?
    Haint they made your env'ys wiz?   130
Wut 'll make ye act like freemen?
    Wut 'll git your dander riz?
Come, I'll tell ye wut I 'm thinkin'
    Is our dooty in this fix,
They 'd ha' done 't ez quick ez winkin'   135
    In the days o' seventy-six.

Clang the bells in every steeple,
    Call all true men to disown
The tradoocers of our people,

The enslavers o' their own; 140
Let our dear old Bay State proudly
    Put the trumpet to her mouth,
Let her ring this messidge loudly
    In the ears of all the South:—

"I 'll return ye good fer evil 145
    Much ez we frail mortils can,
But I wun't go help the Devil
    Makin' man the cus o' man;
Call me coward, call me traiter,
    Jest ez suits your mean idees,— 150
Here I stand a tyrant-hater,
    An' the friend o' God an Peace!"

Ef I'd *my* way I hed ruther
    We should go to work an' part,—
They take one way, we take t'other,— 155
    Guess it would n't break my heart;
Men hed ough' to put asunder
    Them thet God has noways jined;
An' I should n't gretly wonder
    Ef there 's thousands o' my mind. 160

[The first recruiting sergeant on record I conceive to have been that individual who is mentioned in the Book of Job as *going to and fro in the earth, and walking up and down in it*. Bishop Latimer will have him to have been a bishop, but to me that other calling would appear more congenial. The sect of Cainites is not yet extinct, who esteemed the first-born of Adam to be the most worthy, not only because of that privilege of primogeniture, but inasmuch as he was able to overcome and slay his younger brother. That was a wise saying of the famous Marquis Pescara to the Papal Legate, that *it was impossible for men to serve Mars and Christ at the same time*. Yet in time past the profession of arms was judged to be κατ' τ'ξοχην[1] that of a gentleman, nor does this opinion want for strenuous upholders even in our day. Must we suppose, then, that the profession of Christianity was only intended for losels, or, at best, to afford an opening for plebeian ambition? Or shall we hold with that nicely metaphysical Pomeranian, Captain Vratz, who was Count Königsmark's chief instrument in the murder of Mr. Thynne, that the scheme of salvation has been arranged with an especial eye to the necessities of the upper classes, and that "God would consider *a gentleman*, and deal with him suitably to the condition and profession he had placed him in"? It may be said of us all, *Exemplo plus quam ratione vivimus.*[2]—H. W.]

1848

[1]Greek: Preeminently

[2]Latin: We live more by example than by reason.

■ FREDERICK DOUGLASS ■
1818–1895

The War with Mexico

North Star Editorial
January 21, 1848

From aught that appears in the present position and movements of the executive and cabinet—the proceedings of either branch of the national Congress,—the several State Legislatures, North and South—the spirit of the public press—the conduct of leading men, and the general views and feelings of the people of the United States at large, slight hope can rationally be predicated of a very speedy termination of the present disgraceful, cruel, and iniquitous war with our sister republic. Mexico seems a doomed victim to Anglo Saxon cupidity and love of dominion. The determination of our slaveholding President to prosecute the war, and the probability of his success in wringing from the people men and money to carry it on, is made evident, rather than doubtful, by the puny opposition arrayed against him. No politician of any considerable distinction or eminence, seems willing to hazard his popularity with his party, or stem the fierce current of executive influence, by an open and unqualified disapprobation of the war. None seem willing to take their stand for peace at all risks; and all seem willing that the war should be carried on, in some form or other. If any oppose the President's demands, it is not because they hate the war, but for want of information as to the aims and objects of the war. The boldest declaration on this point is that of Hon. John P. Hale, which is to the effect that he will not vote a single dollar to the President for carrying on the war, until he shall be fully informed of the purposes and objects of the war. Mr. Hale knows, as well as the President can inform him, for what the war is waged; and yet he accompanies his declaration with that prudent proviso. This shows how deep seated and strongly bulwarked is the evil against which we contend. The boldest dare not fully grapple with it.

Meanwhile, "the plot thickens"—the evil spreads. Large demands are made on the national treasury (to wit: the poor man's pockets). Eloquent and patriotic speeches are made in the Senate, House of Representatives and State Assemblies: Whig as well as Democratic governors stand stoutly up for the war: experienced and hoary-headed statesmen tax their declining strength and ingenuity in devising ways and means for advancing the infernal work. Recruiting sergeants and corporals perambulate the land in search of victims for the sword and food for powder. Wherever there is a sink of iniquity, or a den of pollution, these buzzards may be found in search of their filthy prey. They dive into the rum shop, and gambling house, and other sinks too infamous to name, with a swine-like avidity, in pursuit of degraded men to vindicate the insulted honor of our Christian country. Military chieftains and heroes multiply, and towering high above the level of common men, are glorified, if nor deified, by the people. The whole nation seems to "wonder after these (bloody) beasts." Grasping ambition, tyrannic usurpation, atrocious aggression, cruel and haughty pride, spread and pervade the land. The curse is upon us. The plague is abroad. No part of the country can claim entire exemption from its evils. They may be seen as well in the State of New York, as in South Carolina; on the Penobscot, as on the Sabine. The people appear to be completely in the hands of office seekers, demagogues, and political gamblers. Within the bewildering meshes of their political nets, they are worried, confused, and confounded, so that a general outcry is heard—"Vigorous prosecution of the war!"—"Mexico must be humbled!"—"Conquer a peace!"—"Indemnity!"—"War forced upon us!"—"National honor!"—"The whole of Mexico!"—"Our destiny!"—"This continent!"—"Anglo Saxon blood!"—"More territory!"—"Free institutions!"—"Our country!" till it seems indeed "that justice has fled to brutish beasts, and men have lost their reason." The taste of human blood and the smell of powder seem to have extinguished the senses, scared the conscience, and subverted the reason of the people to a degree that may well induce the gloomy apprehension that our nation has fully entered on her downward career, and yielded herself up to the revolting idea of battle and blood. "Fire and sword," are now the choice of our young republic. The loss of thousands of her own men, and the slaughter of tens of thousands of the sons and daughters of Mexico, have rather given edge than dullness to our appetite for fiery conflict and plunder. The civilization of the age, the voice of the world, the sacredness of human life, the tremendous expense, the dangers, hardships, and the deep disgrace which must forever attach to our inhuman course, seem to oppose no availing check to the mad spirit of proud ambition, blood, and carnage, let loose in the land.

We have no preference for parties, regarding this slaveholding crusade. The one is as bad as the other. The friends of peace have nothing to hope from either. The Democrats claim the credit of commencing, and the Whigs monopolize the glory of voting supplies and carrying on the war; branding the war as dishonorably commenced, yet boldly persisting in pressing it on. If we have any preference of two such parties, that preference inclines to the one whose practice, though wicked, most accords with its professions. We know where to find the so called Democrats. They are the accustomed panderers to slaveholders: nothing is either too mean, too dirty, or infamous for them, when commanded by the merciless man stealers of our country. No one expects any thing honorable or decent from that party, touching human rights. They annexed Texas under the plea of extending the area of freedom. They elected James K. Polk, the slaveholder, as the friend of freedom; and they have backed him up in his Presidential falsehoods. They have used their utmost endeavors to crush the right of speech, abridge the right of petition, and to perpetuate the enslavement of the colored people of this country. But we do not intend to go into any examination of panics just now. That we shall have frequent opportunities of doing hereafter. We wish merely to give our readers a general portrait of the present aspect of our country in regard to the Mexican war, its designs, and its results, as they have thus far transpired.

Of the settled determination to prosecute the war, there can be no doubt: Polk has avowed it; his organs have published it; his supporters have rallied round him; all their actions bend in that direction; and every effort is made to establish their purpose firmly in the hearts of the people, and to harden their hearts for the conflict. All danger must be defied; all suffering despised; all honor eschewed; all mercy dried up; and all the better promptings of the human soul blunted, silenced and repudiated, while all the furies of hell are invoked to guide our hired assassins,—our man-killing machines,—now in and out of Mexico, to the infernal consummation. Qualities of head and heart, principles and maxims, counsels and warnings, which once commanded respect, and secured a nation's reverence, must all now be scouted; sense of decency must be utterly drowned: age nor sex must exercise any humanizing effect upon our gallant soldiers, or restrain their satanic designs. The groans of slaughtered men, the screams of violated women, and the cries of orphan children, must bring no throb of pity from our national heart, but must rather serve as music to inspire our gallant troops to deeds of atrocious cruelty, lust, and blood. The work is thus laid out, commenced, and is to be continued. Where it will end is known only to the Great Ruler of the Universe; but where the responsibility rests, and upon whom retribution will fall, is sure and certain.

In watching the effects of the war spirit, prominent among them, will be seen, not only the subversion of the great principles of Christian morality, but the most horrid blasphemy.

While traveling from Rochester to Victor, a few days ago, we listened to a conversation between two persons of apparent gentility and intelligence, on the subject of the United States' war against Mexico. A wide difference of opinion appeared between them; the one contending for the rightfulness of the war, and the other against it. The main argument in favor of the war was the meanness and wickedness of the Mexican people; and, to cap the climax, he gave it as his solemn conviction, that the hand of the Lord was in the work! that the cup of Mexican iniquity was full; and that God was now making use of the Anglo Saxon race as a rod to chastise them! The effect of this religious outburst was to stun his opponent into silence: he seemed speechless; the ground was too high and holy for him; he did not dare reply to it; and thus the conversation ended. When men charge their sins upon God, argument is idle; rebuke alone is needful; and the poor man, lacking the moral courage to do this, sat silent.

Here, then, we have religion coupled with our murderous designs. We are, in the hands of the great God, a rod to chastise this rebellious people! What say our evangelical clergy to this blasphemy? That clergy seem as silent as the grave; and their silence is the greatest sanction of the crime.

They have seen the blood of the innocent poured out like water, and are dumb; they have seen the truth trampled in the dust—right sought by pursuing the wrong—peace sought by prosecuting the war—honor sought by dishonorable means,—and have not raised a whisper against it: they float down with the multitude in the filthy current of crime, and are hand in hand with the guilty. Had the pulpit been faithful, we might have been saved from this withering curse. We sometimes fear, that now our case as a nation is hopeless. May God grant otherwise! Our nation seems resolved to rush on in her wicked career, though the road be ditched with human blood, and paved with human skulls. Well, be it so. But, humble as we are, and unavailing as our voice may be, we wish to warn our fellow country-men, that they may follow the course which they have marked out for them-selves; no barrier may be sufficient to obstruct them; they may accomplish all they desire; Mexico may fall before them; she may be conquered and sub-dued; her government may be annihilated—her name among the great sisterhood of nations blotted out; her separate existence annihilated; her rights and powers usurped; her people put under the iron arm of a military despotism, and reduced to a condition little better than that endured by the Saxons when vanquished by their Norman invaders; but, so sure as there is a God of justice, we shall not go unpunished; the penalty is certain; we cannot escape; a terrible retribution awaits us. We beseech our country-men to leave off this horrid conflict, abandon their murderous plans, and forsake the way of blood. Peradventure our country may yet be saved. Let the press, the pulpit, the church, the people at large, unite at once; and let petitions flood the halls of Congress by the million, asking for the instant recall of our forces from Mexico. This may not save us, but it is our only hope.

1848

■   **U.S. CONGRESS AND UNITED MEXICAN**   ■
STATES

Treaty of Guadalupe Hidalgo

Treaty of Peace, Friendship, Limits, and Settlement between the United States of America and the United Mexican States Concluded at Guadalupe Hidalgo, February 2, 1848; Ratification Advised by Senate, with Amend-ments, March 10, 1848; Ratified by President, March 16, 1848; Ratifications Exchanged at Queretaro, May 30, 1848; Proclaimed, July 4, 1848.

In the Name of Almighty God

Article VIII

Mexicans now established in territories previously belonging to Mexico, and which remain for the future within the limits of the United States, as defined by the present treaty, shall be free to continue where they now reside, or to remove at any time to the Mexican Republic, retaining the property which they possess in the said territories, or disposing thereof, and removing the proceeds wherever they please, without their being subjected, on this account, to any contribution, tax, or charge whatever.

Those who shall prefer to remain in the said territories may either retain the title and rights of Mexican citizens, or acquire those of citizens of the United States. But they shall be under the obligation to make their election within one year from the date of the exchange of ratifications of this treaty; and those who shall remain in the said territories after the expiration of that year, without having declared their intention to retain the character of Mexicans, shall be considered to have elected to become citizens of the United States.

In the said territories, property of every kind, now belonging to Mexicans not established there, shall be inviolably respected. The present owners, the heirs of these, and all Mexicans who may hereafter acquire said property by contract, shall enjoy with respect to it guarantees equally ample as if the same belonged to citizens of the United States. . . .

Article XI

Considering that a great part of the territories, which, by the present treaty, are to be comprehended for the future within the limits of the United States, is now occupied by savage tribes, who will hereafter be under the exclusive control of the Government of the United States, and whose incursions within the territory of Mexico would be prejudicial in the extreme, it is solemnly agreed that all such incursions shall be forcibly restrained by the Government of the United States whensoever this may be necessary; and that when they cannot be prevented, they shall be punished by the said Government, and satisfaction for the same shall be exacted all in the same way, and with equal diligence and energy, as if the same incursions were meditated or committed within its own territory, against its own citizens.

It shall not be lawful, under any pretext whatever, for any inhabitant of the United States to purchase or acquire any Mexican, or any foreigner residing in Mexico, who may have been captured by Indians inhabiting the territory of either of the two republics; nor to purchase or acquire horses, mules, cattle, or property of any kind, stolen within Mexican territory by such Indians.

And in the event of any person or persons, captured within Mexican territory by Indians, being carried into the territory of the United States, the Government of the latter engages and binds itself, in the most solemn manner, so soon as it shall know of such captives being within its territory, and shall be able so to do, through the faithful exercise of its influence and power, to rescue them and return them to their country or deliver them to the agent or representative of the Mexican Government. The Mexican authorities will, as far as practicable, give to the Government of the United States notice of such captures; and its agents shall pay the expenses incurred in the maintenance and transmission of the rescued captives; who, in the mean time, shall be treated with the utmost hospitality by the American authorities at the place where they may be. But if the Government of the United States, before receiving such notice from Mexico, should obtain intelligence, through any other channel, of the existence of Mexican captives within its territory, it will proceed forthwith to effect their release and delivery to the Mexican agent, as above stipulated. . . .

Article XII

In consideration of the extension acquired by the boundaries of the United States, as defined in the fifth article of the present treaty, the Government of the United States engages to pay to that of the Mexican Republic the sum of fifteen millions of dollars. . . .

1848

Cuba in the Antebellum U.S. Imagination

THE CARIBBEAN ENCHANTED AND INSPIRED U.S. WRITERS AND LEGISLATORS FROM the first days of the republic, both as a potential region for expansion and as a site for imaginative revelry. "I candidly confess," wrote Thomas Jefferson, "that I have ever looked on Cuba as the most interesting addition which could ever be made to our system of states." Another island, Santo Domingo, prompted fear and promise because it contained Haiti, the first black-led republic in the hemisphere. The Caribbean–U.S. connection became even more pronounced in the two decades preceding the U.S. Civil War as the United States spread to the West and conquered new territories in Texas and Mexico. Would the United States also expand to the tropical islands east of Florida? Both in the North and in the South, business operatives and planters looked for new markets and resources to exploit. Puerto Rico and Cuba, which remained Spanish colonies for most of the century, maintained slave-based economies until 1873 and 1880, respectively. In addition, the area's geopolitical importance grew as the United States jockeyed with England and Spain for influence over the hemisphere. Cuba, which was often presented as the "key" to the Gulf of Mexico, was particularly attractive, and interest in it reached the highest level of government. Three U.S. presidents—James Polk, Franklin Pierce, and James Buchanan—were involved in efforts to purchase Cuba from Spain prior to the U.S. Civil War.

Men of military action known as "filibusters" launched a series of independent attacks to take over territories in the Caribbean and Central America. From the Dutch word for "freebooter," "filibuster" had multiple connotations and was sometimes used disparagingly to characterize the ventures as the work of soldiers of fortune and even pirates. The best known of the filibusters was William Walker, who seized control of Nicaragua, reinstituted slavery, and dreamed of a slave-based empire that would stretch from the U.S. South to Central America and into the Caribbean. In response to and in conjunction with such political and military events, writers published newspaper articles, novels, poems, travel pieces, and other forms focused on the Caribbean. Often these writings were connected to particular political projects such as abolition. In other cases, travel writing fed a national yearning to read about the region, which was sometimes portrayed as an enchanting tropical territory. Although some writers used media that facilitated political debate, such as the pamphlet, others turned to literary forms to engage with the region. A serialized novel, for example, took up the topic of revolution in the Caribbean, and poems used romantic tropes to express a yearning for acquisition of territories.

Because most of Latin America and Haiti had abolished slavery, Cuba remained one of the few territories that offered U.S. writers a window onto another slave-based economy in the Americas. The result was a growing appetite for travel literature about Cuba. Travel accounts included William Cullen Bryant's *Letters of a Traveler* (1850), Richard Henry Dana's *To Cuba and Back* (1859), and Julia Ward Howe's *A Trip to Cuba* (1860). Some of the most captivating sections of these books focus on descriptions of slavery on the island and racist depictions of Cubans, sometimes described as incapable of governing themselves. As such, Cuba became an important site for black abolitionists such as Frederick Douglass and Martin Delany.

Delany's serialized novel *Blake; or the Huts of America* (1859) offers a dream of black-led insurrection that stretches from the United States to Cuba. Delany (1812–1895) was a physician, editor, abolitionist, and black leader as well as a novelist. Because of its awkward presentation of political arguments, Eric Sundquist writes, "*Blake* has seldom been read with much attention to its remarkably potent message, its array of the language and song of early black American life, and its interesting formal devices." More radical in its view of potential responses to slavery than other texts circulating in the period, including *Uncle Tom's Cabin*, Delany's novel thematized the very possibility that inspired fear among some white readers, the potential for black insurrection. The leader of the revolution is Henry Blake, born Henrico Blacus in Cuba, who associates his project not only with figures such as Nat Turner and Denmark Vesey but also with leaders of the U.S. Revolution. The novel switches settings from the northeastern United States to the U.S. South and to the Caribbean, all the while emphasizing the participation of European empires in the conflicts taking place. The excerpt reprinted here depicts the plotting of a scheme to transport slaves to Cuba in violation of international treaties prohibiting the slave trade.

Like slavery, filibustering was a topic of discussion in newspapers and the halls of Congress and thus made its way into various novels and poems. In *The Free Flag of Cuba* (1851), Lucy Holcombe Pickens, known as the "queen of the Confederacy," offered a fictionalized account of Narciso López's filibustering expeditions to Cuba. Pickens (1832–1899) was well known in the South for her looks and her marriage to South Carolina's secessionist governor. The South was not as hostile to the filibustering schemes as the North, and writers like Pickens considered whether the Caribbean and the U.S. South might band together as a region. The historian Matthew Guterl has argued that Southern elites saw themselves as part of an "American Mediterranean," a ring of territories that stretched around the Gulf of Mexico and into the Caribbean and Central America. But there were complexities in how Southerners viewed their neighbors further south. In the selection from *The Free Flag of Cuba*, Pickens, although sympathetic to López, frames him as "dark" and portrays Cubans as influenced by the "passionate splendor of a southern clime" in contradistinction to the more sober attitudes of people from the United States.

Debates about the Caribbean in the United States were not monolingual, as exemplified by poems such "El filibustero" [The Filibuster] (1853), by Juan Clemente Zenea, and "En el segundo aniversario de *La Verdad*" [On the Second Anniversary of *La Verdad*] (1850), by Miguel Teurbe Tolón. These poems illustrate how writers not only responded to political issues, such as slavery and colonialism, but presented an exile vision that often gendered Cuba as a woman to be regained. Zenea (1832–1871), who began publishing poetry and articles in Havana newspapers, developed a Cuban strain of Romanticism. Involved in exile politics, Zenea published his work in several U.S.-based newspapers, including *El Filibustero*, which bore the same name as the selected poem. Zenea continued his involvement in Cuban politics while living in the United States and was ultimately killed by a firing squad after returning to the island during the Ten Years' War. Tolón (1820–1857) was one of the most prolific Cuban exiles publishing in New York and New Orleans during the 1850s. Among his books published in New York were *The Elementary Spanish Reader and Translator* (1853) and a poetry collection, *Leyendas cubanas* (1856). He worked as an editor at New York's *La Verdad* and wrote the poem to commemorate the newspaper's anniversary.

Rodrigo Lazo
University of California, Irvine

▪ MARTIN DELANY ▪
1812–1885

from **Blake; or the Huts of America**

Chapter 1. The Project

On one of those exciting occasions during a contest for the presidency of the United States, a number of gentlemen met in the city of Baltimore. They were few in number, and appeared little concerned about the affairs of the general government. Though men of intelligence, their time and attention appeared to be entirely absorbed in an adventure of self-interest. They met for the purpose of completing arrangements for refitting the old ship "Merchantman," which then lay in the harbor near Fell's Point. Colonel Stephen Franks, Major James Armsted, Captain Richard Paul and Captain George Royer composed those who represented the American side—Captain Juan Garcia and Captain Jose Castello, those of Cuban interest.

Here a conversation ensued upon what seemed a point of vital importance to the company; it related to the place best suited for the completion of their arrangements. The Americans insisted on Baltimore as affording the greatest facilities, and having done more for the encouragement and protection of the trade than any other known place, whilst the Cubans, on the other side, urged their objections on the ground that the continual increase of liberal principles in the various political parties, which were fast ushering into existence, made the objection beyond a controversy. Havana was contended for as a point best suited for adjusting their arrangements, and that too with many apparent reasons; but for some cause, the preference for Baltimore prevailed.

Subsequently to the adjustment of their affairs by the most complete arrangement for refitting the vessel, Colonel Franks took leave of the party for his home in the distant state of Mississippi.

Chapter 15. Interchange of Opinion

The landing of a steamer on her downward trip brought Judge Ballard and Major Armsted to Natchez. The Judge had come to examine the country, purchase a cotton farm, and complete the arrangements of an interest in the "Merchantman." Already the proprietor of a large estate in Cuba, he was desirous of possessing a Mississippi cotton place. Disappointed by the absence of his wife abroad, he was satisfied to know that her object was accomplished.

Major Armsted was a man of ripe intelligence, acquired by years of rigid experience and close observation, rather than literary culture, though his educational attainments as a business man were quite respectable. He for years had been the partner in business with Colonel Stephen Franks. In Baltimore, Washington City, Annapolis, Richmond, Norfolk, Charlestown, and Winchester, Virginia, a prison or receptacle for coffle gangs of slaves purchased and sold in the market, comprised their principal places of business in the slave growing states of the Union.

The Major was a great jester, full of humor, and fond of a good joke, ever ready to give and take such even from a slave. A great common sense man, by strict attention to men and things, and general observation, had become a philosopher among his fellows.

"Quite happy to meet you, Judge, in these parts!" greeted Franks. "Wonder you could find your way so far south, especially at such a period, these being election times!"

"Don't matter a bit, as he's not up for anything I believe just now, except for Negro trading! And in that he is quite a proselyte, and heretic to the teachings of his northern faith!" jocosely remarked Armsted.

"Don't mistake me, gentlemen, because it was the incident of my life to be born in a nonslaveholding state. I'm certain that I am not at all understood as I should be on this question!" earnestly replied the Judge.

"The North has given you a bad name, Judge, and it's difficult to separate yourself now from it, holding the position that you do, as one of her ablest jurists," said Armsted.

"Well, gentlemen!" seriously replied the Judge. "As regards my opinion of Negro slavery, the circumstances which brought me here, my large interest and responsibility in the slave-labor products of Cuba, should be, I think, sufficient evidence of my fidelity to Southern principles, to say nothing of my official records, which modesty should forbid my reference to."

"Certainly, certainly, Judge! The Colonel is at fault. He has lost sight of the fact that you it was who seized the first runaway Negro by the throat and held him by the compromise grasp until we Southern gentlemen sent for him and had him brought back!"

"Good, good, by hookie!" replied the Colonel, rubbing his hands together.

"I hope I'm understood, gentlemen!" seriously remarked the Judge.

"I think so, Judge, I think so!" replied Armsted, evidently designing a full commitment on the part of the Judge. "And if not, a little explanation will set us right."

"It is true that I have not before been engaged in the slave trade, because until recently I had conscientious scruples about the thing—and I suppose I'm allowed the right of conscience as well as other folks," smilingly said the Judge, "never having purchased but for peopling my own plantation. But a little sober reflection set me right on that point. It is plain that the right to buy implies the right to hold, also to sell; and if there be right in the one, there is in the other; the premise being right, the conclusion follows as a matter of course. I have therefore determined, not only to buy and hold, but buy and sell also. As I have heretofore been interested *for* the trade I will become interested *in* it."

"Capital, capital, by George! That's conclusive. Charles! A pitcher of cool water here; Judge, take another glass of brandy."

"Good, very good!" said Armsted. "So far, but there is such a thing as feeding out of two cribs—present company, you know, and so—ahem!—therefore we should like to hear the Judge's opinion of equality, what it means anyhow. I'm anxious to learn some of the doctrines of human rights, not knowing how soon I may be called upon to practice them, as I may yet marry some little Yankee girl, full of her Puritan notions. And I'm told an old bachelor 'can't come it' up that way, except he has a 'pocket full of rocks,' and can talk philanthropy like old Wilberforce."

"Here, gentlemen, I beg to make an episode, before replying to Major Armsted," suggested the Judge. "His jest concerning the Yankee girl reminds me—and I hope it may not be amiss in saying so—that my lady is the daughter of a clergyman, brought up amidst the sand of New England, and I think I'll not have to go from the present company to prove her a good slaveholder. So the Major may see that we northerners are not all alike."

"How about the Compromise measures, Judge? Stand up to the thing all through, and no flinching."

"My opinion, sir, is a matter of record, being the first judge before whom a case was tested, which resulted in favor of the South. And I go further than this; I hold as a just construction of the law, that not only has the slaveholder a right to reclaim his slave when and wherever found, but by its provision every free black in the country, North and South, are liable to enslavement by any white person. They are freemen by sufferance or slaves-at-large, whom any white person may claim at discretion. It was a just decision of the Supreme Court—though I was in advance of it by action—that persons of African descent have no rights that white men are bound to respect!"

"Judge Ballard, with this explanation, I am satisfied; indeed as a southern man I would say that you've conceded all that I could ask and more than we expected. But this is a legal disquisition; what is your private opinion respecting the justice of the measures?"

"I think them right, sir, according to our system of government."

"But how will you get away from your representative system, Judge? In this your blacks are either voters, or reckoned among the inhabitants."

"Very well, sir, they stand in the same relation as your Negroes. In some of the states they are permitted to vote, but can't be voted for, and this leaves them without any political rights at all. Suffrage, sir, is one thing, franchisement another; the one a mere privilege—a thing permitted—the other a right inherent, that which is inviolable—cannot be interfered with. And my good sir, enumeration is a national measure, for which we are not sectionally responsible."

"Well, Judge, I'm compelled to admit that you are a very good Southerner; upon the whole, you are severe upon the Negroes; you seem to allow them no chance."

"I like Negroes well enough in their place!"

"How can you reconcile yourself to the state of things in Cuba, where the blacks enter largely into the social system?"

"I don't like it at all, and never could become reconciled to the state of things there. I consider that colony as it now stands, a moral pestilence, a blighting curse, and it is useless to endeavor to disguise the fact; Cuba must cease to be a Spanish colony, and become American territory. Those mongrel Creoles are incapable of self-government, and should be compelled to submit to the United States."

"Well, Judge, admit the latter part of that, as I rather guess we are all of the same way of thinking—how do you manage to get on with society when you are there?"

"I cannot for a moment tolerate it! One of the hateful customs of the place is that you must exchange civilities with whomsoever solicits it, consequently, the most stupid and ugly Negro you meet in the street may ask for a 'light' from your cigar."

"I know it, and I invariably comply with the request. How do you act in such cases?"

"I invariably comply, but as invariably throw away my cigar! If this were all, it would not be so bad, but then the idea of meeting Negroes and mulattoes at the levees of the Captain General is intolerable! It will never do to permit this state of things so near our own shores."

"Why throw away the cigar, Judge? What objection could there be to it because a negro took a light from it?"

"Because they are certain to take hold of it with their black fingers!"

"Just as I've always heard, Judge Ballard. You Northerners are a great deal more fastidious about Negroes than we of the South, and you'll pardon me if I add, 'more nice than wise,' to use a homily. Did ever it occur to you that black fingers made that cigar, before it entered your white lips!—all tobacco preparations being worked by "Negro hands in Cuba—and very frequently in closing up the wrapper, they draw it through their lips to give it tenacity."

"The deuce! Is that a fact, Major!"

"Does that surprise you, Judge? I'm sure the victuals you eat is cooked by black hands, the bread kneaded and made by black hands, and the sugar and molasses you use, all pass through black hands, or rather the hands of Negroes pass through them; at least you could not refrain from thinking so, had you seen them as I have frequently, with arms full length immersed in molasses."

"Well, Major, truly there are some things we are obliged to swallow, and I suppose these are among them."

"Though a Judge, Your Honor, you perceive that there are some things you have not learned."

"True, Major, true; and I like the Negro well enough in his place, but there is a disposition peculiar to the race, to shove themselves into the notice of the whites."

"Not peculiar to them, Judge, but common to mankind. The black man desires association with the white because the latter is regarded his superior. In the South it is the poor white man with the wealthy, and in Europe the common with the gentlefolks. In the North you have not made these distinctions among the whites, which prevents you from noticing this trait among yourselves."

"Tell me, Major, as you seem so well to understand them, why a Negro swells so soon into importance?"

"Simply because he's just like you, Judge, and I! It is simply a manifestation of human nature in an humble position, the same as that developed in the breast of a conqueror. Our strictures are not just on this unfortunate race, as we condemn in them that which we approve in ourselves. Southerner as I am, I can joke with a slave just because he is a man; some of them indeed, fine warmhearted fellows, and intelligent, as was the Colonel's Henry."

"I can't swallow that, Major! Joking with a Negro is rather too large a dose for me!"

"Let me give you an idea of my feeling about these things: I have on my place two good-natured black fellows, full of pranks and jokes—Bob and Jef. Passing along one morning Jef was approaching me, when just as we met and I was about to give him the time of day, he made a sudden halt, placing himself in the attitude of a pugilist, "grasping the muscle of his left arm, looking me full in the eyes exclaimed, 'Maus Army, my arm aches for you!' when stepping aside he gave the path for me to pass by."

"Did you not rebuke him for the impudence?"

"I laid my hand upon his shoulders as we passed, and gave him a laugh instead. At another time, passing along in company, Bob was righting up a section of fence, when Jef came along. 'How is yeh, Jef?' saluted Bob, without a response. Supposing he had not seen me, I halloed out: 'How are you Jef!' but to this, he made no reply. A gentleman in company with me who enjoyed the joke, said: 'Why Jef, you appear to be above speaking to your old friends!' Throwing his head slightly down with a rocking motion in his walk, elongating his mouth after the manner of a sausage—which by the way needed no improvement in that direction—in a tone of importance still looking down he exclaimed, 'I totes a meat!' He had indeed, a fine gammon on his shoulder from which that evening, he doubtless intended a good supper with his wife, which made him feel important, just as Judge Ballard feels, when he receives the news that 'sugar is up,' and contemplates large profits from his crop of that season."

"I'll be plagued, Major, if your love of the ludicrous don't induce you to give the freest possible license to your Negroes! I wonder they respect you!"

"One thing, Judge, I have learned by my intercourse with men, that pleasantry is the life and soul of the social system; and good treatment begets more labor from the slave than bad. A smile from the master is better than cross looks, and one crack of a joke with him is worth a hundred cracks of the whip. Only confide in him, and let him be satisfied that you respect him as a man, he'll work himself to death to prove his worthiness."

"After all, Major, you still hold them as slaves, though you claim for them the common rights of other people!"

"Certainly! And I would just as readily hold a white as a black in slavery, were it the custom and policy of the country to do so. It is all a matter of self-interest with me; and though I am morally opposed to slavery, yet while the thing exists, I may as well profit by it, as others."

"Well, Major," concluded the Judge, "let us drop the subject, and I hope that the free interchange of opinion will prove no detriment to our future prospects and continued friendship."

"Not at all, sir, not at all!" concluded the Major with a smile.

1859

LUCY HOLCOMBE PICKENS
1832–1899

from The Free Flag of Cuba; or, The Martyrdom of Lopez

Chapter 2

In a spacious room, with brilliant lights and luxurious furniture, sat two men, in earnest conversation. They were very unlike, the American and Cuban General.[1] The face of the one was calm, almost stern, with clear searching eyes of patriotism's "true blue." The stiff military mustache gave

---

[1] John A. Quitman was a Mississippi governor and a U.S.-Mexico War hero whom Cuban filibusters tried to recruit for an expedition.   The Cuban General is Narciso López, who led the failed attack on Cuba.

the curved upper lip of his haughty mouth an expression still more determined. The voice was quick as a staccato strain in music, decided as one accustomed to command and be obeyed. As you looked on him you felt that he was a man, who with a knowledge of right would stand before a world's opposition as a strong marble pillar in a raging storm, never swerving, never yielding, unbending and defiant.

The other was dark, with the passionate splendor of a southern clime; his face, although open and generous, had an air of sturdy resolve and perseverance. His eyes flashed with patriotic enthusiasm as he paused in the statement he had been giving of that enterprise which now occupied his whole attention. He listened anxiously as the American replied—

"It seems, indeed, that the present juncture calls for your immediate action. But are you sure that the Creole forces on the island are organized and ready to co-operate with you on your landing?"

"Their organization is as far completed as the necessary secresy will permit. I do not fear to trust them. They would not sacrifice my gallant little army by any weak indecision.

"But, General, the Americans with whom I am associated, are most anxious to put themselves under your direction and control. Their confidence in your valor and skill will inspire them with a stronger hope and trust. Many of them have fought under you in other days, and will willingly obey your orders, and be entirely guided by your judgment. I have come then, once more, to offer you that position, whose acceptance will give Cuba powerful aid. It will give dignity to the expedition even in the eyes of the prejudiced; and, with its supporters, it will place its success beyond a doubt."

There was a hushed silence in the room. The Cuban's face was eager with intense interest, as if a nation's destiny depended on the answer. *Who can say!* The steadfast eyes of the American General looked earnestly forward as though they were searching into futurity. At length he said—

"General Lopez, you well know my sympathy with your hopes, my respect and hearty approval of your cause—a cause justifiable in the spirit, intent, and conscience of its supporters. I thank both of you and my own countrymen for this mark of trust, even while I decline the responsible position you offer me. I rely not less on your good faith and ability than on the courage and fidelity of your men. But I greatly doubt the expediency of the expedition at this present time. That the Cubans desire a change of government I do not deny. You have certainly strong proof to that effect. But are they now prepared to make a struggle in behalf of their liberty? To rise, that you may assist them to unfasten their yoke? Have you force enough to inspire them with confidence of success? For they will dread the fearful consequences of a failure; and they well know, in case of defeat, the garrote will be their fate. Then, again, should they flock unanimously around you without arms, they could render but little assistance. You should be strong enough, independent of their aid, to make your first battles decisive; for the men you take with you must necessarily do most of the fighting. The Creoles are not, as you know, a warlike people. Forbidden the use of arms, they are mostly ignorant of the ordinary management of a gun. Our own men, accustomed are they are from early boyhood to the free use of firearms, require the severest drilling and discipline. You should have, instead of five hundred, five thousand men, well trained and equipped; sufficient means to maintain the government which you establish until it is able to stand on its own strength. The military adage, 'discretion is the better part of valor,' is peculiarly applicable. In providing for a failure you avert it."

"Very true," answered Lopez; "but, General, I dare not wait longer. My men are impatient for action. They have been thwarted and delayed, until their hopes and trust are will nigh gone. Besides, it is not scheme of conquest. We do not go to *rouse* the natives to rebellion, but to *aid* them in driving from their land the dark oppressors who encumber its soil. I have the assurance of a people weary of their bondage, whose chains have long been festering on them; and who, from this attempt, can fear no consequences more grievous than the daily burden they have so long borne without resistance. I have this surety, beside their expressed promises and their actions already begun, that they will fly to the standard of freedom as soon as it is raised."

"I do not feel the confidence which you perhaps are right in placing *in* the firmness of the Creoles; therefore, in taking the direction of the Patriot forces, I should be acting contrary to my judgement and conviction of propriety. This I cannot do. It is not a love of inactive ease," continued the veteran soldier, "neither is it a regard for personal interest or safety that restrains me, but I cannot lead men where there is not a prospect of overcoming danger with hardy courage and skill. You land with five hundred men. Your first battle may be victorious, but your numbers, in all probability, much diminished, while those of the enemy will be hourly increased by the addition of fresh troops. Your band, Spartan though it be, can effect but little against the immense force that will be brought to bear upon it; for the whole strength of the Spanish army is, as you well know, concentrated on the island. Yet I would not discourage you. God grant your success may prove my fears groundless!"

"Your reasons," said the Cuban, thoughtfully, "may be just and true; but I am urged by convictions equally strong, though opposite, to proceed. If, in the singleness of my zeal, I am rash—if, in the greatness of my hopes, I am blind to the scruples of your superior judgement, it is, that I cannot put from me the reliance I have on the sturdy strength of my American allies, or the unshaken confidence I repose in the powerful support which will be given me by the natives of Cuba. If I fail, I shall have the honest knowledge, that I dared for good. This will, in a measure, compensate me for any misfortune to myself, which may follow my effort in behalf of my country's liberty. Yet hope is very strong in my breast. My aim is a high and glorious one—the elevation of a degraded people. The proclamation of the President is—"[2]

"A mere piece of coquetry with Spain," interrupted the American, with a lurking smile, "intended to open her friendly ear to any proposals which may

---

[2]In 1851, President Millard Fillmore issued a proclamation condemning filibustering expeditions and warning participants of possible penalties and even imprisonment.

hereafter be made relative to the purchase of Cuba, which Mr. Fillmore is doubtless anxious to secure for the glory of his administration. This severity is but seeming. Yet the proclamation is not only arbitrary, but most unwise. The President of the United States cannot, with propriety, by any act of his own, stop himself from claiming the right to protect the life of an American citizen under *all* circumstances; *he has no right to will away the lives of freemen.* If, through his mistaken policy, he deems them erring, they are still the sons of Washington, and their error is on the generous side of freedom. It is his duty, and should be his pride, to shield and protect American interest. It is not his province to wantonly assign away to a foreign power the lives and liberties of men by whose sufferance he holds his position of limited—*not absolute*—power. He is not their master, nor are they his slaves, to be thus delivered up at pleasure to the mercy of a despotic oppressor. The President is the servant of the sovereign people, not their arbiter. This assumption of absolute control—this taking on himself the right to withdraw a government's protection from her free-born sons, is unlawful and most derogatory to the patriotic dignity of the man who stands in that position once held by the 'immortal lover of the people.' It is an unnatural mother who forsakes her child, and permits him to be harshly dealt with by a stranger. A common sense of justice scorns the sophistry which admits that America can, with any show of consistency, condemn her children because they seek to extend the very principles which are the life-breath of her own existence—the very principles which she from their infancy instills into they minds, inculcates in their hearts, as the surest foundation of moral and political good. If, with this before her, she could bring herself to censure the advocacy of the fundamental doctrines of her own nationality—it should have been with the loving-kindness of a mother, and not with the violence of a despot. It was not *her* place to cast reproach and indignity upon them. These men are no cowards to be menaced with arms—no children to be frightened into a servile obedience! The proclamation was disgraceful! The President has laid down—given away his right to interfere in their behalf. It was wrong, sir—all wrong, injudicious, and uncalled for."—The general brought his hand down in the most empathic manner upon the table by which he sat.

"Its consequences," said General Lopez, "may indeed be deplorable, for if we are unfortunate, which God forbid, Spain will be emboldened to treat with the utmost rigor the Americans who fall into her hands."

"It is true, the President has evinced an unpardonable want of fore-thought—has given up his right to interfere in their behalf; yet I believe him to have the honest heart of a free man, and he will in case of emergency be true to his trust. He cannot with consistency stand between them and the tyrannic cruelty of Spain; but the consistency of an administration is a little thing to sacrifice for the preservation of American life and Republican honor. Spain will not dare to use harshness—save, sir, at the peril of her national existence."

There was silence for a moment. Lopez looked on the brave proud face before him, and said—

"General! I have much to thank you for the unfailing kindness which you have shown me as a man, the generous sympathy you have manifested in the cause which I represent. Your interest in behalf of my unhappy country is plainly without the stain of self, for what more can you ask of fortune or fame than that which you already possess! I daily feel the loss Cuba will sustain in your absence from this struggle. If you were but identified with the hopes of Cuba's friends! if you would be accept the commandancy, which I cannot, through regard for your scruples, urge upon you——

"Ah! sir, you have nothing to thank me for. I did but give you that hand whose fellowship shall never be withheld from those whom I conceive to be truly good, whatever censure may ensue. I am as honest in my good feeling for yourself, as in the deep abiding interest I cherish for the enslaved land whose just rights you are seeking to establish at such fearful hazard. This act, by which you risk your life for the honor and liberty of a people, I can but admire. An act which in its motive, its daring, and its intended results, is of the most chivalrous and patriotic character; and act whose performance is but the natural duty you owe to Cuba. It is a laudable undertaking, and I trust that you may remove the restraint and gloom of tyranny from that beautiful island, that you may live to see commerce, agriculture, and education, flourish even as in my own glorious country—the proudest nation the world ever saw. This, sir, would I know, compensate you for past misfortune, and all which you may yet incur. Then—bring your Creole forces to stand firm beside the American allies—put arms into the hands of the people who pine for freedom—lead them to battle against the enslavers—and God help you!"

The Cuban grasped the cordial hand of the bold, honest American hero. There were no further words between them, yet he felt that, whatever his fate, *Cuba would not be without a friend.*

1854

■   # JUAN CLEMENTE ZENEA   ■
1832–1871

from **El filibustero (in Spanish)**

La tierra en que yo he nacido
que sobre la mar se pierde,
parece por ser tan verde
Níobe de la juventud;
y es en esa misma tierra
dónde en apacible calma,

5

mece sus ramos la palma
anunciando esclavitud.
    Yo me alejé de su seno
probre mártir de las penas,   10
porque entre tantas cadenas
se enlutaba el corazón

      .   .   .

    Con fiebre de independencia
abandoné mis prisiones,
y en apartadas regiones
la libertad me acogió.   15
Mas el genio de mis dichas
se desnudó de sus galas,
y levantando las alas
en el éter se perdió.   20
    Quedé solo nuevamente
¡solo! ¡solo en este mundo!
y con un dolor profundo
compré un divino placer.
Dejé lejos mis amigos   25
y entre otras amadas glorias
dejé unas tristes memorias
en un alma de mujer.

      .   .   .

Compré el placer de ser libre
al borde de un precipicio,   30
ofreciendo en sacrificio
angustias del corazón.

      .   .   .

En vano el tirano evita
que torne al suelo nativo,
y decreta vengativo   35
alguna bárbara ley,
porque tengo por más honra
ser libre "Filibustero"
que ser "pirata negrero"
y torpe esclavo de un rey.   40

from El Filibustero (in English)[1]

    The land where I was born,
which loses itself at sea,

[1]Translated by Rodrigo Lazo.

is so green that it resembles
Niobe in her youth;
on that same stretch of land,
under winds pleasantly calm   5
sway the fronds of a palm
that shelters slavery.
       I departed from her shadow
in my sadness a poor martyr,
chains so numerous they   10
dressed my heart in mourning;

                    . . .

With the fever of independence
I abandoned my prisons
and in remote regions   15
liberty welcomed me.
But the spirit of my luck
removed all its attire
and raising its feathers
lost itself in the heavens.   20
       Alone I ended once again
alone! alone in this world!
and with sorrow profound
divine pleasure I purchased.
I left behind my friends   25
and among beloved glories
I left behind a woman
with the saddest memories.

                    . . .

The pleasure of freedom I purchased
at the edge of an abyss,   30
offering as a sacrifice
the heart's distress.

                    . . .

       The tyrant works in vain
To ban me from native soil,
Seeking retribution   35
Through barbaric decrees,
for I carry far more honor
being freedom's "Filibuster"
than the pirate of a slave ship
and a torpid slave to a king.   40

                                                                        1853

▪ MIGUEL TEURBE TOLÓN ▪
1820–1857

from **En el segundo aniversario de *La Verdad***

Dos veces ya del extranjero cielo
Cumplió su curso el sol: dos largos años
La luz he visto tras el pardo velo
De los climas del Norte, y nuestra Cuba
Aún no levanta la cerviz ufana   5
Con voz de Libertad que al cielo suba,
Ni el sol del Sibonei en la sabana
Las lanzas dora de legión cubana.

. . . .

Mas no, ¡por dios! que entre los rojos pliegues
Del sacro pabellón de Cuba libre,   10
Pronto será que a nuestra Patria llegues,
"Verdad," fanal del pueblo,
Y entre falanges bélicas cubanas,
Triunfante al fin tu alzado acento vibre
En alcázares, montes y sabanas,   15
Por la muerte y el baldón de las hispanas.

from **On the Second Anniversary of *La Verdad*[1]**

Twice now the sun has completed its
course through strange skies: two long years
The light have I seen through the grey veil
Of the North's weather, and our Cuba
Has yet to raise its proud profile   5
Lifting Liberty's voice to the skies,
Siboney's sunlight strong on the savannah
Has yet to shine on the lances of a Cuban legion.

. . . .

By God, may the red stripes
Of the sacred banner of Cuba free,   10
Soon at our motherland arrive,
"Verdad," beacon of the people,
Carried by bellicose phalanges of Cuba,
Triumphant in the end may your accent resound
In fortresses, fields, and savannahs,   15
Avenge the death and insult to Hispanic women.

1850

[1]Translated by Rodrigo Lazo.

■

Narratives from the Mexican and Early American Southwest

The narrative excerpts presented here depict the cultural and social conditions of what is now the American Southwest during the first half of the nineteenth century, when the region passed from Spanish to Mexican to American control. This sequence was probably inevitable. A weakening Spain could not be expected to hold restless colonial territories an ocean away. Mexico, as a newly independent state, was badly overmatched in its struggle against the United States with its surging spirit of Manifest Destiny. Not surprisingly, the spirit of resourcefulness and self-sufficiency so much valued along the U.S. frontier had its equivalent in the far-flung Spanish-Mexican territories from Texas to California. As the narratives reproduced here show, Mexicans and Americans frequently resented each other but had more in common than they liked to admit.

The first excerpt in this section is from the "Historical Narrative" of Pio Pico (1860–1894), a prominent *californio* whose life stretched through the three stages of political domination noted above. Although Pico lived nearly fifty years into the American era, like many of his brethren he never learned English and never mastered American culture, particularly its political and legal practices. A dominant figure in Spanish and Mexican California, Pico lost both his influence and his wealth and died a bitter, forgotten man—the old revolutionary a nearly perfect symbol of a vanquished tradition. Pico was not a literary man, and his narrative is a straightforward account of California life in the early nineteenth century before the *yanquis* arrived. He notes the cruelty of the Spanish mission system and its devastating impact on Native American cultures; Pico understood that such a system could not endure indefinitely. Far removed from the center of Spanish colonial authority in Mexico City, California was generally politically unstable and easy prey to political adventurers from within and outside the territory who were attracted to its ideal climate and vast natural resources. In this environment, Pico thrived and ascended to the governor's office twice.

Although of little literary interest, Pico's narrative does reveal a number of important historical facts that refute conventional American depictions of early California and other parts of the Mexican Southwest. Pico shows that both Spaniards and Mexicans had a lively interest in commerce and were certainly not oblivious to money-making possibilities. Also, Pico notes a pattern of active travel between California towns and settlements, contrary to the enervating isolation claimed by many American historians. Ultimately, what is most important about the Pico narrative is that it demonstrates once again that what is "history" very much depends on who is telling the story.

Another *californio* who told his story, with considerably more passion and bitterness, was Mariano Vallejo. H. H. Bancroft, author of the massive *History of California*, which appeared between 1884 and 1890, persuaded Vallejo (and Pico as well) to record his version of California events. Bancroft and his associates collected some 140 narratives by *californios*. Vallejo's *Recuerdos históricos y personales tocante a la alta California*, at nearly one thousand manuscript pages, is perhaps the most interesting and illuminating. An early supporter of American annexation, Vallejo lived to regret his original enthusiasm. Like Pico, Vallejo was no match for the *yanqui* entrepreneurs who swarmed into the region after the Gold Rush. Eventually, his vast land holdings were reduced to little more than his homestead in Sonoma. As his fortunes declined, Vallejo recalled Mexican California all the more fondly. As Genaro Padilla has noted, Vallejo's and Pico's memoirs represent a departure from the classic model of the American autobiography in which individual talent prospers in direct correlation with rising American prosperity and prominence. The Mexican dream of *californios* like Vallejo and Pico turned into an American nightmare, the consequence of *yanqui* bigotry, treachery, and avarice.

Americans began to arrive in California in significant numbers after 1830 and were inevitably fascinated by its limitless possibilities for profit. Prominent among these was Alfred Robinson (1807–1895), who in 1846 published his own account of the *californios*, *Life in California*. As a longtime resident of California, Robinson offered probably the most balanced American assessment of the region. His excerpt shows that the *californios*, while certainly lacking the benefits of modern medicine and other conveniences, nevertheless led rich lives culturally and socially and practiced their religious beliefs as devoutly as any New England Congregationalist. Robinson might lament the absence of the Protestant love of aggressive capitalism, but he saw in California a style of living attractive in many aspects.

Raymund Paredes
Commissioner of Higher Education, Texas

PRIMARY WORKS

Pio Pico, *Don Pio Pico's Historical Narrative*, trans. Arthur P. Botello, ed. Martin Cole and Henry Welcome, 1973; Mariano Vallejo, *Recuerdos históricos y personales tocante a la alta California*, 1975; Alfred Robinson, *Life in California during a Residence of Several Years in That Territory*, 1969.

▪   PIO PICO   ▪
1801–1894

from **Historical Narrative**

Dictated to Thomas Savage, Los Angeles, October 24, 1877[1]

The Early Years

I was born on the 5th of May 1801, at the San Gabriel Mission where my father, José María Pico, company corporal of the San Diego garrison,

---

[1] The text is derived from *Don Pio Pico's Historical Narrative*, trans. Arthur P. Botello, ed. Martin Cole and Henry Welcome (Glendale, CA: Arthur H. Clark, 1973).

commanded the cavalry. My father was a native of Fuerte, at that time in the province of Sinaloa. My mother's name was María Eustaquia Gutiérrez, a native of San Miguel de Horcasitas in Sonora.

My father had four brothers in California, namely: José Dolores, who was a sergeant of the Monterey Company; Patricio, whom I knew as a rancher at the Simí ranch; Javier and Miguel, soldiers at Santa Barbara.

My mother had here two half-brothers and four half-sisters, all born from the second marriage of my grandmother and bearing the surname of López, namely: Ignacio and José who were soldiers of the San Diego Company; Josefa, married to a Mexican named Véjar, a carpenter in San Diego; Juliana, married to Juan Osuna, a corporal of the San Diego Company— Osuna later on was majordomo of the San Diego Mission much before the secularization; María Antonia, married to a soldier from San Diego named Jóse María Aguilar, mason by trade and, after being licensed, practicing this at the missions of San Luis Rey and San Juan Capistrano; María Ignacia, married to Joaquín Carrillo, also a soldier of the San Diego Company. A daughter of this half-aunt of mine married Don Mariano Guadalupe Vallejo. Another daughter married his brother, Don Salvador, and still another married Capt. Romualdo Pacheco and were the parents of our ex-governor Pacheco.

I had two brothers, José Antonio and Andrés; seven sisters: Concepción, Tomasa, María, Isidora, Estéfana, Jacinta, and Feliciana, all of them married.

I was raised in San Diego. An old lady named Matilde Carrillo, wife of Joaquín Arce, sergeant of San Diego, taught me to read, and when I was about twelve years old, more or less, Don José Antonio Carrillo, who was my brother-in-law, having been the husband of two of my sisters, taught me to write.

Señor Carrillo had me draw lines on paper and then he would write from one margin to the other "Señor Don Félix María Callejas" so I could copy it. He never gave me other words and I do not know how many reams of paper I filled with those same words.

Señor Carrillo at that time had a kind of school at the presidio of San Diego attended by daughters of some friends and also some soldiers who had been named corporals. I knew three or four others who went there to learn to write.

I continued at my mother's side without leaving her except to attend to business.

The year 1812, the church of San Juan Capistrano fell down as the consequence of some strong earthquakes.

The year 1811, a conspiracy among the troops in San Diego was discovered. My father was a sergeant of the company and was accused of being involved in the movement. He was confined to quarters. Also taken prisoners and put in chains were four [sic] soldiers of the company of leatherjackets: Ramón Rubio, José María López, García, Canedo, and an artilleryman named Ignacio Zúñiga. Three of the soldiers died chained in the same quarters—of course, they had been imprisoned many years. Artilleryman Zúñiga was in chains until independence was achieved. The soldier García was set at liberty at the conclusion of the affair.

In the year 1813, there was an Indian insurrection at the San Gabriel Mission. The garrison companies were moved, part of the four companies going to San Gabriel. If my memory is correct, the troops from the north arrived commanded by Ensign Gabriel Moraga. Those from San Diego came commanded by my father who placed himself under the orders of officer Moraga. The rebellious Indians took part of a herd of sheep and other things to the mountains. They were pursued by the troops and quite a few of the things were recovered. Some of the Indians were brought back to the mission. Of these, some were taken to San Diego. Nearly all of the prisoners were whipped and those that lived remained in prison at San Diego until their deaths.

We were told by our father that at the battle in the mountains a handsome Indian (one of those taken to San Diego) fought heroically, wounding two of the soldiers. He was finally taken with great difficulty because he barricaded himself behind dead bodies. Four of his bows had been broken by shots but he continued the struggle. My father instructed the troops that he not be killed if he could be taken alive. And so it was done, but afterwards he was known as Bonaparte.

In 1815, my father came with the commandant's permission to await his retirement [papers] at San Gabriel.

The year 1818, when Bouchard's insurgent expedition came, the commandant called him to San Diego, placing in his [my father's] charge the force located on the esplanade of the fortification to defend it in case the enemy came to invade. He remained there until the insurgents left and there was no more danger.

Bouchard's insurgents disembarked first at Monterey, burning the presidio and plundering everything of value. They then disembarked in Refugio, plundering it. Then they were in Santa Barbara but did no harm there. From there they went to San Juan Capistrano and took everything they found in storage, including the church's silver ornaments. They then continued their voyage, passing San Diego without stopping at the port, and nothing more was heard of them.

During my father's absence in San Diego, I was left in charge of the guard at San Gabriel which was comprised of residents of Los Angeles.

The campaign having ended, my father again returned to San Gabriel commanding the guard comprised of fifteen soldiers. This was not customary as the missions' guards were usually made up of four soldiers and a corporal.

My father did not succeed in being retired as a veteran. He continued in active service until his death, which was in September of 1819.

After the death of my father all the family moved to San Diego. Nothing was left us—not even an inch of ground. My older brother, José Antonio, was already in service but the rest of my family, except for two sisters already married, stayed at my mother's side and I had to solicit help for her.

My sisters and my mother worked at find needlework. My sister, Tomasa, always finished before the rest because of her expertness.

I put up a small store where I sold liquors, provisions, chairs, and shoes. I always had a clerk in the store because I frequently went to Los Angeles and the missions and as far as the border of Baja California to sell goods and to bring back cattle and other goods in exchange.

One time I left San Diego with a load of sugar for the border of Baja California. Arriving at San Vicente, I lodged in the house of Lieutenant Commander Don Manuel Ruiz, brother of Francisco María. While there, I visited the *Padre Ministre* [Father Minister] of the San Vicente Mission, Fr. Antonio Menendez, and the padre invited me to play a game of cards. I accepted. We played and he won all the sugar. I did not know the game and I had no idea that the priest would win, but he did and I returned to my home with nothing. When I turned over the sugar to him, Father Menendez said to me: "See here, Pico, it has happened to you as it did to Christ when he came into the world." I asked, "What happened to Christ?" and he responded: "Christ came into the world to redeem sinners. He came for wool and left shorn. You came to sell your sugar and now leave penniless."

This same Father Menendez some years later was chaplain of the San Diego Company and parson of the town. Still later he was transferred to Los Angeles and thence to Monterey.

During the stay of the padre in San Diego, we again played and I won from him twelve mules which he had brought from Baja California. I then told him: "Father, I do not want to behave like a tyrant. I will return your saddled black mule" and that is what I did.

My mother never knew of my adventure in San Vicente with Father Menendez but my sister Tomasa did. She was my confidante and took care of my money.

Tomasa once loaned $30.00 to a soldier from Baja California. I came home and my sister asked me if I had seen the soldier. I answered that I knew the soldier had left for Baja. She told me that the soldier owed her $30.00 and I offered to go and catch up with him. I went immediately. I caught up with him at Rancho de la Nación, about eight leagues from San Diego, and he paid me the $30.00. After paying me he invited me to play. On the ranch was a corporal and four soldiers whose duty it was to watch after the interest of La Nación. The corporal liked me very much and urged me to play with the soldier. He carried quite a bit of money from Monterey and Los Angeles. I won all that he carried. The soldier had on a pair of corduroy pants trimmed with gold thread. I asked him if he had anything more with which to play and he answered that he had only his pants and, if I wished, he would wager them. I did not want to play for his pants but my friend, the corporal, persuaded me to do so. With the pants, he not only won back all my money but my sister's $30.00.

Afterwards, he continued playing with the corporal and the four soldiers and left them all bare. He did not even leave them the buttons on their uniforms. He won even their leather pants.

At that time I was about twenty-three years old and I had never been interested in things political. My mother was very strict with me and never allowed me to be away from home after 8 o'clock at night, and until I was twenty-five I observed this rule.

As a young child I was quite advanced in praying. I knew all Ripalda's catechism from beginning to end and when new people would arrive from Mexico, Don José Antonio Carrillo's mother would call me and I would recite all the catechism with my arms crossed. This brought me much praise. Also, at the San Diego Mission, Father Fernando Martínez—a man of little culture—had me assist at mass in Latin without me understanding one word of what he was saying. . . .

The year 1821, I left here for the town of San José Guadalupe in charge of a shipment of barrels of wine and *aguardiente* that Don José Antonio Carrillo was sending from Los Angeles as a gift to fathers Luis Martínez of San Luis Obispo, and Juan Cabot of San Miguel. After delivering the goods in San Miguel, I went on to Monterey with five barrels of aguardiente that I had of my own. I arrived at the Rancho Nacional and met my uncle, José Dolores Pico, who had it in his care. From the ranch I went to San José with my barrels. There I stayed in the company of Señor Ignacio Vallejo, brother of the general, arranging the sale of the aguardiente. He was about eighteen years old, more or less. I stayed in San José three or four months and, when my aguardiente was sold, I returned to San Diego.

The year 1826, if I remember right, I was a voting member of the Deputation [vocal de la Diputación] but it was not in session and the members [vocales] did not have a single privilege unless the chamber [la cámara] was in session.

In 1827 or 1828, I was named scribe or secretary to Captain Don Pablo de la Portilla, who was named attorney-general, to take down declarations from one Señor Bringas, a Mexican.

Señor Bringas was a merchant established in Los Angeles and it was said that the merchandise he sold belonged to Don José María Herrera, principal subcommissioner residing in Monterey, who was accused of misappropriation of public funds and of having purchased this merchandise with government money which had been given him in Mexico to pay the troops in California.

Captain Portilla and I arrived at Los Angeles and arranged a meeting with Señor Bringas at an office that had been established by the captain in the home of Don Antonio Rocha, situated where the city jail is now. Señor Bringas presented himself. The captain informed him of the object of his commission, at which Bringas answered that he respected and esteemed him very much as a private individual and as a friend, but as a captain of the Mexican Army he was nothing more to him than the sole of his shoe. This reply impressed me profoundly because we considered a captain a personage of high rank and distinction. Not only captains, but all officials and even sergeants and corporals and even the lowest of soldiers were treated with consideration.

I was even more surprised when I heard Bringas tell Portilla that the civilians [paisanos] were the sacred core of the nation, and that the military were nothing more than servants of the nation, which was constituted of the people and not of the military. Bringas declared he would not give his statement except in front of a person in civil authority, even though he were an Indian *alcalde* from the mission. But not before a military man, whatever his rank. Convinced, Señor Portilla decided to send a message to the commandant general and another to the commandant of San Diego Captain José María Estudillo, laying before them Bringas' reluctance.

I offered to take the communication to the commandant of San Diego and my offer was accepted. I arrived at San Diego and delivered the document and was told by Señor Estudillo that I should go to my home to rest until the next day, and that I should return to take the reply back to Los Angeles. By then I was beginning to feel the effects of Señor Bringas' words.

My mother and my family were all in need of my services in San Diego and made it plain to me that for this reason, they were opposed to my return to Los Angeles. I wanted to please my mother and at the same time show my sense of independence. I now considered myself a "sacred vessel"—words which sounded very good to my ears. I presented myself to Estudillo. He had the official letter ready in his hand and he asked me if I was prepared to depart as he handed me the letter. I told him that I was not able to return to Los Angeles as I was needed at home. Then Señor Estudillo issued orders to the sergeant that I should be taken to the jail. They imprisoned me in a cell with other prisoners though I had the luck not to be placed in irons. I was there all that day and that night and the next morning Estudillo ordered my release, and that I should be taken to the commandant's office. I went there and he asked me to excuse the manner in which I had been treated—that it had been a hot-headed action and that I should go and look after my mother. I retired to my home and stayed at my mother's side, but always it appeared to me, deep in my soul, that the citizens were the nation and that no military was superior to us.

1877

■ **MARIANO GUADALUPE VALLEJO** ■
1808–1890

from **Recuerdos históricos y personales tocante a la alta California**

[Vallejo, who had earlier favored American annexation, records the dismay and sense of betrayal he felt when a group of ragged "thieves" led by Captain John C. Frémont imprisoned him and other men during the Bear Flag insurrection (June 1846) that hastened the U.S.–Mexican War in California.]

All during the first week of the month of June various interviews took place between Captain Frémont and his compatriots. What passed between them is not public knowledge, but if the antecedents may be drawn from what followed, it is easy to presume that they were perfecting the plans they thought most appropriate for seizing Alta California and devising the means to come off victorious in their undertaking. That such may have been the object of their frequent meeting is proved by the fact that on the afternoon of June 11th Frémont and his men, without a previous declaration of war and under no other pretext than their own caprice or necessity, seized the three hundred horses (two hundred of which belonged to the Indians emancipated from San Rafael ex-mission, the interests of whom were managed by Timothy Murphy) which on the account and by the order of Commanding General Castro were grazing to the north of the Cosumnes River in charge of Lieutenant Francisco Arce and several soldiers.

This was the first hostile act that Captain Frémont committed against the property of the inhabitants of California, and although the enormity of his conduct is somewhat mitigated by the fact of his having allowed the cowboys to return to San José mounted upon the horses, the impartial historian should not for that reason fail to censure in severe terms a soldier who belies his glorious mission and becomes a leader of thieves. In spite of my desire to palliate as much as I can the conduct of the individuals who participated in the theft of the Indians' horses, I cannot but stigmatize them with the anathema which society fulminates against those who without legal right to do so appropriate the property of others.

After distributing the horses as they thought most advantageous to their plans, the gentlemen under Captain Frémont's command took the road leading through the Napa Hills to Sonoma and at dawn on the fourteenth of June they surrounded my house located on the *plaza* at Sonoma. At daybreak they raised the shout of alarm and when I heard it, I looked out of my bedroom window. To my great surprise, I made out groups of armed men scattered to the right and left of my residence. The recent arrivals were not in uniform, but were all armed and presented a fierce aspect. Some of them wore on their heads a visorless cap of coyote skin, some a low-crowned plush hat, [and] some a red cotton handkerchief. As for the balance of the clothing of the assaulters of my residence, I shall not attempt to describe it, for I acknowledge that I am incapable of doing the task justice. I suspected that the intruders had intentions harmful not to my [property] interests alone, but to my life and that of the members of my family. I realized that my situation was desperate. My wife advised me to try and flee by the rear door, but I told her that such a step was unworthy and that under no circumstances could I decide to desert my young family at such a critical time. I had my uniform brought, dressed quickly and then ordered the large vestibule door thrown open. The house was immediately filled with armed men. I went with them into the parlor of my residence. I asked them what the trouble was and who was heading the party, but had to repeat that question a second time, because almost all of those who were in the parlor replied at once, "Here we are all heads." When I again asked with whom I should take the matter up, they pointed out William B. Ide who was the eldest of all. I then addressed that gentleman and informed him that I wanted to know to what happy circumstance *I owed the visit of so many individuals.*

In reply he stated that both Captain Merritt and the other gentlemen who were in his company had decided not to continue living any longer under the Mexican government, whose representatives, Castro and Pío Pico, did not respect the rights of American citizens living in the *Departamento;* that Castro was every once in a while issuing proclamations treating them all as bandits and, in a desire to put a stop to all these insults, they had decided to declare California independent; that while he held none but sentiments of regard for me, he would be forced to take me prisoner along with all my family.

We were at this point when there appeared in the room *don* Salvador Vallejo, *don* Pepe de la Rosa, Jacob P. Leese, and *don* Victor Prudon, all friends of mine for whom an order of arrest was suggested until it was decided what should be my fate. I thought for a moment that through some sacrifice on my part I might get rid of so many and such little desired guests, but my hopes were frustrated by the unworthy action of the Canadian, Olivier Beaulieu, who, knowing from his own experiences that liquor is an incentive for all kinds of villainous acts, had gone to his house and procured there a barrel full of brandy, which he distributed among the companions of Merritt and Ide. Once under the influence of the liquor, they forgot the chief object of their mission and broke into shouts of "Get the loot, get the loot!"

Fortunately, these seditious cries emitted by Scott, Beaulieu, Sears and others attracted the attention of Doctor Semple who stepped very angrily to the door of the entrance vestibule and by means of a speech of much feeling, in which there were not a few threats, gave them to understand that he would kill the first man who by committing robbery would cast a blot upon the expedition he had helped organize to advance a political end and that, so long as he was alive, he would not allow it to be turned into a looting expedition....

Shortly after Lieutenant Misroon's arrival at Sonoma, he endeavored to enter into extra-official relations with William B. Ide and the companions of that impoverished commander, but his advances met with no response, because Ide and the others sheltered under the fateful "Bear Flag" did not leave the barracks, the entrance to which was protected by nine cannon of different calibers that they had taken away from me at dawn on June 14th and which they kept loaded to the muzzle. These were all in charge of their respective gunners (the artillerymen did not know their business, for they had been improvised) who never for a single instant relaxed their vigilance over the war materials of which they had been left in charge.

When Lieutenant Misroon had arranged everything as best he could, he left instructions for his subordinate and returned on board the frigate "Portsmouth," where it is to be presumed that he submitted to Captain Montgomery an account of all he had heard and witnessed at Sonoma.

Shortly after Doctor Semple had set out for the Sacramento, the *plaza* at Sonoma was taken in charge by William B. Ide, whom the rest of the force that had invaded my residence had agreed to obey. The number of those who along with William B. Ide remained in charge of the Sonoma garrison was at least fifty. I am aware that various historians have fixed the number at eighteen, but I absolutely know that they are in error. It only remains to determine whether the mistake has been accidental or intentional. I am of the opinion that it has been intentional, for it seems that a hidden but powerful hand has taken great pains to garble all the facts relative to the capture of the Sonoma *plaza* by the group of adventurers to whom history has given the name of "The Bear Flag Party." I, who was made the chief victim those *patriotic gentlemen* sacrificed upon the altar of their well-laid plans, have no interest whatsoever in bespattering them with mud, nor do I aspire to ennoble myself at the expense of their reputation. All I desire is that the impartial public may know what took place at Sonoma on fateful June 14th, 1846, and that it may, after learning all there is to know in regard to this scandalous violation of law that deprived of liberty those who for years had been making countless sacrifices to redeem from the hands of the barbarous heathen the territory known as the Sonoma Frontier, decide in favor of one or the other of the participants in the events I have just related. All I demand is that the decision arrived at may be upon a basis of fact.

On the fourth day that Mr. Ide was in command at the Sonoma *plaza* and when he saw that a great number of Americans and foreigners had hurried in to place themselves under his protection, being fearful lest the Californians would attack them on their *ranchos* should they continue to live scattered over the country, he issued a document in which he set forth the reasons that had impelled him to refuse to recognize the authority of the Mexican government. The original proclamation, which was very brief, merely stated that, since the lives of foreigners were in imminent danger, he had felt it his duty to declare Alta California independent and that, counting as he did upon the definite support and cooperation of the "fighting men" who had rallied around him, he aimed to do all he could to prevent the Californians or the Mexicans from recovering the military post and arms which the valor of his men had seized from them. This is approximately what "Captain" Ide read aloud before the flagpole in the Sonoma *plaza*. I am fully aware that the original proclamation was destroyed and that a few weeks later another was drawn up which, it was said, contained a list of the wrongs which the Mexican authorities had perpetrated against United States citizens.

After the reading of the Commander-in-chief's proclamation, they proceeded with great ceremony to hoist the flag by virtue of which those who had assaulted my home and who had by that time appropriated to themselves two hundred fifty muskets and nine cannon proposed to carry on their campaign.

This flag was nothing more nor less than a strip of white cotton stuff with a red edge and upon the white part, almost in the center, were written the words "California Republic." Also on the white part, almost in the center, there was painted a bear with lowered head. The bear was so badly painted, however, that it looked more like a pig than a bear. The material for the flag was furnished, according to some, by Mrs. Elliot; according to others by Mrs. Sears. I also heard it said that Mrs. Grigsby furnished it.

Those who helped to prepare, sew and paint the flag were the following young men: Alexander Todd, Thomas Cowie and Benjamin Duell. The latter was the one who suggested that a star be painted near the mouth of the bear. Of course, both the bear and the star were very badly drawn, but that should not be wondered at, if one takes into consideration the fact that they lacked brushes and suitable colors.

The running up of this queer flag caused much fear to the families of the Californians established in the neighborhood of Sonoma, Petaluma and San Rafael, for they realized that the instigators of the uprising that had disturbed the tranquility of the frontier had made up their minds to rule, come what might, and, as the rumor had been spread far and wide that Ide and his associates had raised the bear flag in order to enjoy complete liberty and not be obliged to render any account of their activities to any civilized governments, the ranchers, who would have remained unperturbed should the American flag have been run up in Sonoma and who would have considered it as the harbinger of a period of progress and enlightenment, seized their *machetes* and guns and fled to the woods, determined to await a propitious moment for getting rid of the disturbers of the peace. Strange to relate, the first victim that the ranchers sacrificed was the painter of the "Bear Flag," young Thomas Cowie who, along with P. Fowler, was on his way to Fitch's ranch to get one-eyed Moses Carson (brother of the famous explorer Colonel Kit Carson), who was employed as an overseer by Captain Henry Fitch, to give them a half barrel of powder he had locked up in one of the storage closets of his farmhouse. Fowler and Cowie were taken by surprise at the Yulupa Rancho by the party operating under the command of Captains Padilla and Ramón Carrillo, who at the request of the people had assumed direction of the hostilities it had been decided to undertake against "the Bears." Neither of the two extemporaneous commanders thought it right to take the lives of their young captives, upon whom there had been found letters that proved beyond any doubt that Moses Carson and certain others of the Americans employed at the Fitch Ranch were in accord with Ide, Merritt and others of those who had made up their minds to put an end to Mexican domination in California; so they decided to tie them up to a couple of trees while they deliberated as to what should be done with the captives, whose fate was to be decided at the meeting that night to which had been summoned all the ranchers who by their votes had shared in entrusting command of the Californian forces to those wealthy citizens, Padilla and Carrillo. I am of the opinion that the lives of Cowie and Fowler would have been spared, had it not been that a certain Bernardo García, better known under the name of "Three-fingered Jack," taken advantage of the darkness of the night, approached the trees to which the captives were tied and put an end to their existence with his well-sharpened dagger.

After committing the two murders I have just told about, Bernardo García entered the lonely hut in which Padilla, Carrillo and others had met and were discussing as to what disposition should be made of the prisoners. Without waiting for them to ask him any questions, he said to his compatriots, "I thought you here were going to decide to free the prisoners and, as that is not for the good of my country, I got ahead of you and took the lives of the Americans who were tied to the trees."

Those few words, spoken with the greatest of sang-froid by the wickedest man that California had produced up to that time, caused all who heard him to shudder. No one dared to object to what had been done, however, for they knew that such a step would have exposed them to falling under the knife of the dreaded Bernardo García, who for years past had been the terror of the Sonoma frontier.

Equally with the relatives of the unfortunate youths, Cowie and Fowler, I regretted their premature death, for, in spite of the fact that they belonged to a group of audacious men who had torn me from the bosom of my family and done as they pleased with my horses, saddles and arms, I did not consider that the simple fact that they were the bearers of a few letters made them deserving of the supreme penalty. Until that fatal June 21st, neither they nor their companions had shed any Mexican blood and it was not right for the Mexicans to begin a war *à outrance*, that could not help but bring very grievous consequences upon them and their families....

When we reached New Helvetia, the Canadian, Alexis, who was heading our escort, gave three knocks upon the main gate with his lance and it was immediately thrown open by Captain Sutter, who, feigning surprise at seeing us as prisoners, led us into his living quarters. He then promised to comply with the orders that Captain Frémont had delivered to him by the mouth of his lieutenant, Alexis, who had said in our presence, "Captain Frémont is turning these gentlemen over to you for you to keep as prisoners behind these walls and upon your own responsibility."

"All right," said Sutter, and without any further ceremony he turned to us and suggested that we accompany him to a large room situated on the second floor where the only furniture was a kind of rude benches. When we were all inside this room, Sutter locked the door and thought no more about us that night.

I leave my readers to imagine how we cursed at finding ourselves locked up in a narrow room and forced to sleep upon the floor, without a mattress and without a blanket, even without water with which to quench our burning thirst. There, seated upon a bench, I ran over in my mind all that I had witnessed since that fatal June 14th and I assure you I regretted very much not having accepted the offer of that brave captain of militia, *don* Cayetano Juárez, had ordered made to me through his brother, Vicente Juárez.

On June 14, 1846, Captain Juárez was at his Tulcay *hacienda*, when he learned that a group of adventurers had assaulted the Sonoma *plaza*. No sooner did he learn of it than, arming himself, he came to an understanding with Citizens Victorino Altamirano, Antonio Wilson, Vicente and Francisco

Juárez, Andrés Vaca, Pancho Cibrián and others. He went and took up a position in Portezuelo Pass, where he awaited the reply that was to be brought to him by a brother of his whom he had sent, disguised as a woman, to take up a position where I was to pass and ask me if I desired that he (Cayetano Juárez) should make an effort to snatch me from the hands of my guards. I do not recall what it was that caused me to refuse the generous offer of that devoted soldier who had made up his mind to risk his life to procure my freedom. I think that I was influenced above all by the thought I held as to the misfortunes that would inevitably overtake my family, if Captain Juárez and his friends had killed the comrades of those who had remained behind in Sonoma in possession of the *plaza* and war materials. My repentance came too late, for I was in the hands of a foresworn man, a foreigner who had received many favors from me and mine, [but] who had deliberately forgotten them all and, to cap the climax of [his] infamy, had consented to become my jailor, in order to curry favor with a lot of men who had nothing to their names but an extraordinary dose of boldness, who were not fighting under any recognized flag, and who apparently had no other object than robbery and looting.

After a sleepless night, I greeted the dawn of the new day with enthusiasm, for we were by then beginning to experience the urge of a voracious appetite. Our jailor, however, who had doubtless made up his mind to make us drain the last drop of gall which a perverse fate had meted out to us, sent us no food until eleven o'clock in the morning, at which time he came and opened the door to permit the entrance of an Indian carrying a jar filled with broth and pieces of meat. He did not send us a spoon, knives and forks, for Captain Sutter no doubt thought that since we had lost our liberty we had also ceased to retain our dignity. Such behavior on the part of a companion in arms (at that time Captain Sutter was still an official of the Mexican Government) could not help but inspire our disgust, for we all recognized the insult that he was inflicting upon us by taking advantage of the circumstances. There are times in life, however, when man should resign himself to suffering every kind of adversity. Doubtless, God had decreed that the month of June, 1846, should be the blackest month of my life.

Four days after our arrival at New Helvetia, Citizen Julio Carrillo appeared at that place. Furnished with a passport issued to him by Lieutenant Misroon, he had undertaken the journey to bring me news of my family. Inasmuch as my jailors did not have any great respect for officials of the United States, they paid no attention to the passport and locked *señor* Carrillo up in the same room in which I was enjoying Captain Sutter's hospitality, along with Victor Prudon, Jacob Leese and Salvador Vallejo. I regretted very much the imprisonment of that friend who, moved by a desire to put an end to my wife's worry, had undertaken the dangerous mission of entering the enemy's camp....

Some years ago (in 1868) when I was in Monterey, my friend, David Spence, showed me a book entitled "History of California," written by an author of recognized merit by the name of Franklin Tuthill, and called my attention to that part of the gentleman's narrative where he expresses the assurance that the guerrilla men whom Captain Frémont sent in pursuit of the Californian, Joaquín de la Torre, took nine field pieces from the latter. I could not help but be surprised when I read such a story, for I know for a fact that Captain de la Torre had only thirty cavalrymen under his command who as their only weapons carried a lance, carbine, saber and pistol. I think that Mr. Tuthill would have done better if, instead of inventing the capture of nine cannon, he had devoted a few lines to describing the vandal-like manner in which the "Bear" soldiers sacked the Olompalí Rancho and mal-treated the eighty year old Dámaso Rodríguez, alférez retired, whom they beat so badly as to cause his death in the presence of his daughters and granddaughters. Filled with dismay, they gathered into their arms the body of the venerable old man who had fallen as a victim of the thirst for blood that was the prime mover of the guerrilla men headed by Mr. Ford.

I should indeed like to draw a veil over such a black deed, but the inexo-rable impartiality that is the guiding light of the historian prevents me from passing over a fact that so helps to reveal the true character of the men who on June 14, 1846, assaulted the *plaza* at Sonoma at a time when its garrison was in the central part of the *Departamento* busy curbing raids by the barba-rous heathen. Let my readers not think that it is my desire to open up wounds that have healed over by now. I am very far from harboring any such thought, for ever since Alta California became a part of the great feder-ation of the United States of North [America], I have spared no effort to es-tablish upon a solid and enduring basis those sentiments of union and concord which are so indispensible for the progress and advancement of all those who dwell in my native land, and, so long as I live, I propose to use all the means at my command to see to it that both races cast a stigma upon the disagreeable events that took place on the Sonoma frontier in 1846. If before I pass on to render an account of my acts to the Supreme Creator, I succeed in being a witness to a reconciliation between victor and van-quished, conquerors and conquered, I shall die with the conviction of not having striven in vain.

In bringing this chapter to a close, I will remark that, if the men who hoisted the "Bear Flag" had raised the flag that Washington sanctified by his abnegation and patriotism, there would have been no war on the Sonoma frontier, for all our minds were prepared to give a brotherly embrace to the sons of the Great Republic, whose enterprising spirit had filled us with admiration. Ill-advisedly, however, as some say, or dominated by a desire to rule without let or hindrance, as others say, they placed them-selves under the shelter of a flag that pictured a bear, an animal that we took as the emblem of rapine and force. This mistake was the cause of all the trouble, for when the Californians saw parties of men running over their plains and forests under the "Bear Flag," they thought that they were deal-ing with robbers and took the steps they thought most effective for the pro-tection of their lives and property.

[An Account of the Gold Rush]

Gold in the mines! This cry, resounding throughout the length and breadth of California, created a veritable revolution, social and financial. The farmer left his plough in the furrow, the schoolmaster abandoned his books and blackboards, the sailor deserted his ship, the barber flung down his razor and the tailor his shears. Even the lover relinquished the hand of his sweetheart to clutch the pick and shovel and rush forth in search of the longed-for metal.

Some of the adventurers left Monterey mounted on fine horses. Speeding along the roads at twenty miles a day, they were not long in reaching their destination. Others, with an eye to the future, set out in oxcarts loaded with provisions; they spent more time on the road, but on reaching the goal of their desires found themselves in far better circumstances than those who had preceded them, since their carts served them as bedrooms, dining rooms, reception halls and kitchens. As rains fell frequently at the mines, it was not only a comfort but a necessity to have places in which to take refuge from the storms.

Shortly after the discovery of the gold diggings, San Diego, Los Angeles, Monterey, Branciforte [Santa Cruz] and San José lost the greater part of their population, for everyone who could dispose of his property left his home and took the road to the mines or "placers," as they called the spots where the coveted metal could be gathered by the handful.

The few wooden houses which existed in the country were torn apart and loaded into small coasting vessels and sent to Sacramento, whence the lumber went forward to the mines by oxcart. Picks, shovels, sheets of tinplate, nails, rubber boots and medicines ... sold at fabulous prices. But it must be remembered that as many of the miners were producing more than two hundred pesos in a day of twelve hours, they were not minded to resent the inflated prices which they were forced to pay for tools, medicines and food.

At this time, when the populous cities of the southern part of the state were deserted by their inhabitants, the frontier town of Sonoma, an essentially agricultural community, which up to that time had figured only as an outpost against the raids of the heathen savages, rose to the first rank among the cities of Alta California.[1]

All the caravans from Monterey and other parts of the state, and even those which arrived from the state of Sonora,[2] broke their journey at Sonoma, where they rested the wearied animals, repaired harness and wagons, shod their saddle horses and bought fresh provisions before resuming their march. On the other hand, the miners who had met with good fortune in the diggings came, for the most part, to Sonoma to dispose of their gold,

[1]Early in the Spanish colonial period, California was geographically sectioned, politically and imaginatively, into Baja or Lower, and Alta or Upper, provinces, with Monterey as the approximate dividing line. These designations remain in popular use today as Southern and Northern California.

[2]A state in northern Mexico that borders what is now California and Arizona.

to buy new clothing and to make other necessary preparations for their return to the mines.

In December, 1848, and during all of the year 1849, gold in dust or flakes was so abundant in Sonoma that it was difficult to obtain six dollars an ounce in exchange for coined money. This low rate was attributed in part to the large amount of gold brought in by the Indians....

At the diggings the food consisted of the flesh of wild animals, of ship biscuit or bread made by the miners, onions, potatoes, dried beans, salt pork, and from time to time, of salmon. This fish abounded in the Sacramento River, and at that time could be caught with astonishing ease. The fishermen loaded great carts with salmon and, traveling day and night, brought them still fresh to the mining camps, where they sold them for twenty *reales* [$2.50] a pound.

As a rule, a four-horse wagon carried to the mines a ton of salmon, which produced for its owner, when he had sold it to the miners, about $5,000.00. When it is taken into consideration that the round trip could be made in eight days, and sometimes in even shorter time, it can be seen that the earnings of the fishermen were on a level with those of the miners, without the exposure to the calamitous and unpleasant experiences peculiar to the life of the gold diggers.

When the rainy season drew near, the miners who had been fortunate came down from the diggings to spend the winter in Sacramento, which, by reason of its proximity to San Francisco, offered a thousand comforts which one would have sought in vain in the towns of the interior. There were undoubtedly many cases of miners, owners of rich placers, who feared to lose their claims if they abandoned them during the winter, and so remained in the diggings during the rainy season.

Some of these men lost their lives, buried under the snow, some were drowned in the rivers and some were devoured by wild beasts. Misfortunes of this sort were very frequent in the district behind Downieville, where in the winter the snow lies to a depth of eight, ten or twelve feet, and wild animals are abundant.

In the winter Sacramento was always crowded, since it was there that the gamblers assembled in droves to fleece the unwary. Gaming tables were set up everywhere; faro, monte, rouge et noire and lasquinet were the favorite games. The amounts waged on a single card were very great, and there were times when they reached five or six hundred ounces of gold.

To attract many persons to their gambling halls, the proprietors engaged musicians and singers to whom they paid high wages. I remember that one such family, composed of four persons, was paid a hundred dollars a day, in addition to lodging, meals, liquor and laundry. Anyone had the right to enter the houses of play and demand liquor and cigars without payment, since the astute proprietors knew that the fumes of tobacco and liquor were powerful auxiliaries in upsetting the judgment of those who came to risk their money. Of course, the bankers cheated continually and those who laid their money on the green cloth rarely won.

... Many Californians, drawn by the novelty of the spectacle (for gambling in public was not permitted under Mexican rule, although in private the common people played until they lost the clothes off their backs) and deluded into believing that they could easily enrich themselves by guessing the cards, lost in half an hour cattle and ranches that had been owned for half a century, perhaps, by their ancestors. Blinded by the passion for the game, they did not awaken to the truth of the situation until it was already too late to remedy.

Disputes frequently arose among those who played, and these disputes developed into blows, shootings or stabbings. The police never interfered until hostilities were concluded, and the judges, in fear of their lives, refrained from punishing the guilty if they belonged to the great society of Hounds.[3]

This society, at the beginning of 1849, ruled San Francisco and, by means of its ramifications, dominated all California. The Society of Hounds had been founded under the name of "Society for Mutual Aid" but it was in reality nothing but an organization of soulless wretches whose only object was pillage, robbery and banditry; naturally, human life had no value in the eyes of these malefactors.

The Californians living in San Francisco and its environs, and the Europeans of Latin race furnished most of the victims of the Hounds; but when the supply of "foreigners" began to run low, the Hounds were not above robbing their countrymen, the North Americans. ...

Malefactors who fell into the hands of the miners seldom escaped with their lives. As at that time there were no laws, everyone did justice for himself, either alone or with the aid of his friends and neighbors. It is well known that '48 and '49 were terrible times for bandits, as the industrious miners hanged them as fast as they caught them, without distinction of sex. A woman was hanged in Downieville, and in Placerville (alias Hangtown) also they hanged a young woman who had caused human blood to flow. ...

When gold was discovered, the flag of stars already waved over Alta California. No longer were we ruled by the Mexican laws, under whose shadow some had advanced while others fell back, but under which no one had perished of hunger, and only two individuals had been by law deprived of their lives, a very common event during the early years of the North American domination in California.

The language now spoken in our country, the laws which govern us, the faces which we encounter daily, are those of the masters of the land, and, of course, antagonistic to our interests and rights,[4] but what does that matter

---

[3]The Hounds were a group of thugs—many of them were former Australian penal convicts—who, ironically, were commissioned by the mayor of San Francisco to patrol the streets of the city. As Vallejo indicates, these Hounds actually swaggered through the streets intimidating and beating "foreigners." On July 14, 1849, they attacked a Chilean and Peruvian encampment, destroying personal property, robbing and terrifying people, raping women, and killing a few "greasers." After this outrage, the Law and Order party was formed to arrest and try them.

[4]Vallejo is referring to disputes over language use, land tenure and ownership, and a widespread feeling on the part of Mexican Californians that they had been politically disfranchised by the American newcomers after California became a state in 1849.

to the conqueror? He wishes his own well-being and not ours!—a thing that I consider only natural in individuals, but which I condemn in a government which has promised to respect and make respected our rights, and to treat us as its own sons. But what does it avail us to complain. The thing has happened and there is no remedy.

. . . I ask, what has the state government done for the Californians since the victory over Mexico? Have they kept the promises with which they deluded us? I do not ask for miracles; I am not and never have been exacting; I do not demand gold, a pleasing gift only to abject peoples. But I ask and I have a right to ask for an answer.

1875

▪ VICENTE PÉREZ ROSALES ▪
1807–1886

In 1848, Vicente Pérez Rosales, a Chilean politician, journalist, and entrepreneur, left home along with thousands of other Chileans to seek his fortunes in the golden hills of California. He documented his adventures in "Algo Sobre California," which appeared in the June 1850 issue of the Chilean journal *Revista de Santiago*, and in 1882 as part of his memoir *Recuerdos del Pasado*. Pérez Rosales paints a picture of the San Francisco Bay Area in the late 1840s as an international crossroads where race emerges as a product of global capital, as part of a colonizing, Anglo-American discourse that elides the complicated histories and social structures of Latin America.

San Francisco was only one of many world cities Pérez Rosales visited in a lifetime that covered a vast and transformative period of Chilean and world history. His memoir, a small fraction of his literary output, reflects a remarkably cosmopolitan worldview. "Algo Sobre California," reprinted in *Recuerdos*, is a light-hearted tale of his and his brothers' adventures as fortune hunters in nineteenth-century California. Despite the humorous tone, however, "Algo Sobre California" covers serious and frightening territory. He describes anarchy in the streets, a lynching, and increasing bodily violence against Chilean, Mexican, and other Latin American miners as competition for mining rights increases. The reader witnesses racial formation, seemingly as it happens. Pérez Rosales juxtaposes racial antagonisms in the Bay Area with haphazard, territorial maps, and race emerges as something very much like one of those cigarette-paper sketches of an imagined land: endlessly re-written, never the same, and subject to the whims of its creator.

Social organization through physical metaphors of blood existed before the discovery of gold at Sutter's Mill, of course; but in the wake of gold's discovery, such distinctions take on the modern cast of racial thinking as an Anglo-American majority used first national and then racial distinctions for political and financial gain. Latin Americans in particular were targeted because they tended to operate the most successful diggings (mining operations). Though they came from all corners of Latin America, including Peru, Chile, Argentina, Brazil, and Mexico, they were frequently understood by Anglo Americans as an undifferentiated mass of foreigners. This was particularly galling to Chilean miners who prided themselves on their independence, fighting spirit, political stability, and national successes, sentiments Pérez Rosales illustrates throughout his narrative, but particularly in his description of a solitary journey he makes from San Francisco to Monterey in search of milk. On the way he encounters Mexican Californians who, in addition to serving as moral leaders of Latin American mining communities, a position corroborated by historians of the period, prompt a meditation on how Chilean and Mexican mining skill was widely acknowledged.

"Algo Sobre California" depicts the effects of this mining success, as violence against non-Anglos, Latin Americans especially, at the mines increased in inverse proportion to the ease in extracting gold. Chileans, and all foreigners, quickly became scapegoats for mining failures, an animosity which soon developed into calls to exclude "foreign" miners, or to at least heavily tax them. Pérez Rosales narrates the increasing animosity and couples the nativist turn with the explicit racializing of Chileans. He writes of vigilante justice at the mines that migrated eventually to the cities, coming to a head in July 1849 when a group called the Hounds attacked Chilecito, or Little Chile, a tent encampment of Chileans in what is now San Francisco's Little Italy, or North Beach. According to Bancroft's *Popular Tribunals*, the Hounds were a makeshift police force composed of the "most unsavory elements" of a disbanded group of New York volunteers brought to California during the Mexican American War.

After the attack of the Hounds, public opinion swelled strongly in favor of tighter regulation. The California legislature approved the Foreign Miners Tax Law in 1850. The law stipulated that any non-citizen who wished to mine needed a license to do so, at a cost of $20 per month, an outrageous amount eventually lowered to the much more realistic tax of $3 per month. After repeated revisions and repeals, the law accomplished its clear purpose of controlling the non-Anglo, non-U.S. citizen population in the mines and establishing Anglo superiority in the state.

Notably, Pérez Rosales does not argue against the concepts of race or racial hierarchies, he simply describes Anglo animosity towards Chileans as misguided, and his narrative demonstrates how categories of race emerge in tandem with flows of global capital. Pérez Rosales manipulates the emerging, racial hierarchies in nineteenth-century California by exploiting the fact that race and nation can be made and remade as easily as an imagined map. In "Algo Sobre California," the transformation of space parallels the creation of race. Over the course of his narrative an imagined Latina/o other appears in the United States as U.S. hemispheric dominance increases, a dominance manifest in the laws and physical violence that eventually drive Pérez Rosales, his brothers, and thousands of other Latin Americans from the state.

Nativism may have created a de facto Latina/o collectivity in the Anglo American imagination, but many Latin American groups were resistant to such identification and homogenization of cultures and histories. That resistance grows, in part, from tensions between these different groups, but such resistance also emerged to combat the over-riding tendency to create a vision of the past that idealizes the Mexican presence in the southwest at the expense of other *latinidades* or Latin American communities. Pérez Rosales' remarkable memoir shows California's radical heterogeneity along with the desire to subsume that diversity into Anglo-dominant historical narratives.

Marissa López
University of California at Los Angeles

PRIMARY WORKS

Memoria sobre la colonización de Valdivia, 1852; *Memoria sobre emigración*, 1854; *Ensayo sobre Chile*, 1857; *Recuerdos del Pasado*, 1882.

from **Times Gone By**

The things I saw and heard at that time in California were so unusual, so beyond the natural order of human events, so extraordinary in the speed with which they followed one another, that only by having noted them down as they occurred and seeing them in my own hand later can I believe that all I am stating is not a dream.

We leaped resolutely to dry land—or rather mud, for the outgoing tide had left nothing between the point at which our ship became grounded in the slime and the base of the slope of solid earth on which the town began. To the right of our landing place stood a kind of plank fence enclosing some beeves. Perched on the boards sat a row of crows croaking their appreciation of the odor of blood.

Some of our friends had stressed the necessity for leaving the ship armed, and always in the company of at least one other person. This is in fact how we went, and how most of the tradesmen of the town also went, displaying not only their merchandise but a dagger at the waist or else a revolver, a weapon that was then becoming common. In order to hit upon Price's house we were obliged to cover the greater part of this most extravagant and singular town. The streets were wide arcs each of whose ends came down to the beach, arcs broken by other streets at right angles that came down to the water, in each case to piers that hindered rather than facilitated the unloading of vessels. Some of the buildings arrayed in lines at either side of the streets of this maze must have been worth $100,000. But there was no uniformity among them. By the side of a costly though rough and simple structure stood rows of tents covered with wretched awnings, board shacks and cabins, some already set up, others in the very active process of construction. The Parker House Hotel was leased for $175,000 a year. There were no sidewalks in the streets, nor anything resembling them, and the center was a slough of trampled mud whose solidest parts were formed by the thousands of broken bottles thrown from the buildings as emptied. The inhabitants, of heterogeneous nationality, numbering about fifteen hundred permanent residents and as many transients, might have been

thought to be celebrating a vast and noisy masquerade ball, such were their
exotic costumes, their language, and the very nature of their occupations.
Even the women we thought must be dressed as men, for, seek as one might
through that Babylon, one found never a skirt recognizable as such. The furs
of the Oregonian with his hectoring look, the Maule cap, the parasol-like
headgear of the Chinese, the enormous boots of the Russian that appeared
to swallow up their wearer, the Frenchman, the Englishman, the Italian in
sailor attire, the rustic whose coat was about to take its last farewell, the
gentleman with no coat at all; everything, in short, that might have been
found in some gigantic carnival was here to be found gathered together and
whirling in movement. At every step we were compelled to get out of the
way, plunging our legs into the mire to give passage to some former dandy
now arrayed in woolen shirt and rolled up pants and sweating under the
weight of some load he was carrying from the beach to the dwellings at four
dollars a burden. Or perhaps we had to avoid being picked up by a more fortunate porter who, the proud owner of a wheelbarrow, strode stiffly ahead
with perfect unconcern exciting the envy of those who lacked a comparable
tool. Quiet and ease were words without meaning in San Francisco. In the
midst of the tremendous din of hammering that went on all about, some
men were setting up tents, others were sawing boards; one man rolled a barrel, another struggled with a post or pounded loudly to fix it in the ground.
A tent was scarcely erected when business was in full swing, the goods displayed in the open: boots and flimsy clothing, Chanco cheeses, bundles of
jerked beef, piles of dried pears, shovels, picks, powder and liquors, objects
which, like toasted and untoasted flour, brought their weight in gold. Chilean brandy sold for seventy dollars a four-gallon jug, and the sweetened
soda water that they called champagne for eight to twelve dollars a bottle.
These prices were due not so much to the small supplies of commodities, as
to me necessity for economy of time, which no one wasted in haggling, even
though things might be cheaper a bit farther on. Gold dust was the commonest currency, and the best evidence of its abundance lay in the manner
in which it was handled in making a payment, little care being taken to
return to the leather bag the excess that fell into the scale.

We saw the splendid edifice of brick and mortar being built by
Mr. Howard, a poor sailor elevated to the rank of millionaire, and beyond,
on the square, another being finished as a luxurious restaurant by a second
sailor no less opulent than the other. After a slow and laborious but exciting
walk of a quarter of an hour, we reached a hotel of fine appearance that
belonged to a gringo who had been a soldier of fortune in the expeditionary
force in Mexico. At the door just then a servant, who was none other than a
young gentleman turned waiter, was beating an enormous metal pan called a
Chinese gong, belaboring it so that it deafened all who passed, inviting them
to dine. In the dining room we found Price and the effeminate young Chilean
J. L. C., who had started in business selling leather sheaths for daggers at two
dollars each. A long, narrow table filled the room, and around it could be
counted no less than thirty diners of extraordinary appearance, all devouring

with speed and appetite in order quickly to make room for the others who were impatiently awaiting an empty place. The American ate thrice daily in California in that period, but his food was limited to roast meat, fresh or preserved salmon, one or two bad dishes, molasses, tea, coffee and butter. He breakfasted at seven, dined at twelve, and supped at six. Prices were as follows: beefsteak, one dollar; coffee, seventy-five cents; bread and butter, fifty cents.

At the time of our arrival more or less poetic lies, fancies and suppositions held absolute sway in that promised land. No one knew the geography of any place, no one knew what distances must be traversed between one point and another, and much less whether they must be covered by land or by water; but all with one voice made statements about everything. The few who had returned from the placers either were little disposed to answer our questions, or intentionally turned them aside for reasons of their own. We were therefore under compulsion to listen to the reports of persons who might be more ignorant than ourselves. The phrases we heard everywhere were limited to such as these: "Don't go to the Sacramento, because there is little gold there; go to the Stanislaus as fast as you can." "Don't even think about going to the Stanislaus, but go to Sacramento; so-and-so got so many thousands there in one day." "The mineral is under water; so-and-so, who just came back yesterday, says he has stood with water up to his middle." "Water, nonsense!" another would say, "It's drier there in winter than in summer." But why go on? Fortunately it had occurred to a Mr. Prendergast to coin money without leaving San Francisco by improvising a geographical office of which he himself was the only member and collaborator. He found, I don't know where, an ancient map of the viceroyship of Mexico, giving inaccurate proportions to Alta California, and inundated the city with sketches which, though miserably drawn and reduced to the size of cigarette papers, reached the price of twenty-five dollars apiece.

Relations between Chileans and Americans were in no way cordial. And the decree of General Persifer Smith, sent up from Panama and voicing the decision that "every foreigner henceforth be deprived of the right to exploit mines in California," capped me list of injuries to the peaceful and defenseless Chileans. Business and authorities in alarm proposed that foreigners acquire citizenship in me Union, a status dispensed at the cheap rate of ten dollars. But such a safe-conduct was only partially useful in me place where it was issued, and elsewhere more an object of mockery than a protection. Shortly afterward the provisional government at San Jose declared mining open to foreigners on the sale payment by each of twenty dollars a month in advance. The receipt for this sum was to afford adequate authorization to work. But how many conflicts arose from this resolution between collectors and contributors!

The animus of the average American toward the natives of other countries, and particularly toward the Chileans, had increased as a result. A simple and conclusive argument was adduced: The Chileans were descendants of the Spaniards; the Spaniards had Moorish blood; ergo, the Chileans were Hottentots at the very least, or, to give them the utmost one possibly could, something very like the timid and humble Californians. The Americans had found it hard to swallow the Chileans' intrepidity. Compliant in their own country, Chileans cease to be so abroad, even in the face of a pistol aimed at their hearts, provided only they can lay hand on the knife hilt at their belts. The Chileans in turn detested the Americans, whom they constantly averred to be cowards; and this mutual detestation explains the bloody disasters and atrocities that we saw at every step in the land of gold and hope.

Soon a society of bandits was formed in San Francisco, known as the Hounds and composed of vagrants, gamblers and drunkards united by the fellowship of thieves and boasting the motto *Get what you want*. They were everywhere preceded by the loathing and fear inspired by their offensive presence; and wherever they pitched their camps followed terrorism, violence and outrage.

But they did not always *get what they wanted* on the little point of land to the right where, apart from the rest of the city, a kind of miniature Chile had been created. The evil Hounds therefore determined to administer a forceful drubbing; and since *time was money* in California, the conscienceless malefactors fell upon the defenseless Chileans of that district with clubs and pistols.

The disturbance and outcry raised by so brutal and unwarranted an assault can be imagined. When they had recovered from the shock, the Chileans began to shower stones on their attackers. One respectable Chilean gentleman, unable to escape by the door of his tent owing to the entrance of several Hounds about to seize him, laid low with a pistol shot the first to approach, ripped open the canvas with his knife, and was fortunately able to join the body of his friends uninjured. The ex-Mormon Brannan, owner of the unforgettable *Dysymy-nana,* was informed by some Chileans of the tragedy on the point. Boiling with indignation, he strode up to the roof of his house and shouted for the town to gather below. Briefly and energetically he asserted that it was high time to make an example of the perpetrators of these unheard-of outrages against the citizens of a friendly nation that daily exported to San Francisco not only the finest flour, but the best hands in the world at making bricks! He added a proposal that in order to give more complete satisfaction for the injury, all willing Chileans under the leadership of American citizens go at once to arrest the disturbers of the peace.

A general shout of approval from the point and the almost instantaneous presence of the posse put an end to a bit of savagery that might have brought the most disastrous consequences. Eighteen bandits forcibly removed from their lairs were imprisoned aboard the sloop *Warren* of the American squadron, and peace was reestablished.

Three days later, when I was making every effort to find means to return to my associates, I read to my terror in the San Francisco daily a report to the following alarming effect: "American blood shed by vile

Chileans In the goldfields! Citizens be on your guard!" Next day tile news had assumed dreadful proportions, and by nightfall it was rumored that not only had the Chileans been forcibly expelled from the San Joaquin, but the same band of criminals that had driven them away, still thirsting for vengeance and plunder, was headed for my compatriots on the tributaries of the American River.

Judge what must have been my situation when, as I nervously pondered what was left for me to do in this anxious plight, an acquaintance brought me a wild tale of indescribable atrocities just perpetrated against the Chileans at the Mill! I confess my weakness; neither the distance that lay between the Mill and San Francisco, a distance I knew so well, nor the obvious impossibility of sending news through the air, were sufficient to make me doubt what I heard. It was a question of my brothers. How could I do other than lose my power of reason? My brothers, my unfortunate brothers alone there, and I unable to share their misfortunes! Frantic, carrying only my weapons, and with no hope beyond that of avenging my family, I paid $200 for a boat to take me to Sacramento. And deaf to the counsels of prudence, daring to make no reflections, I cast myself into the hands of fate. Where was I going? What did I mean to do? I cannot say. I remember that anything seemed possible, anything easy, except to return to Chile without my brothers.

We rowed day and night without rest. We reached Sacramento. I jumped into the water without waiting to come up alongside the landing. And with anxiety in my heart I ran till I reached Gillespie's house. There, judge what must have been my surprise! God had not abandoned me! My brothers had arrived the day before in Sacramento, poor and stripped of all they possessed, but unharmed. They had been discussing with Gillespie how to join me as soon as possible in San Francisco. To arrive, to see them, to count them, and to faint with emotion, was all the work of an instant. One would have to have been in my situation to understand it!

As we lay together that evening under a modest shelter of *sarapes* and reported our mutual adventures, joy was not long in coming to reassure us that all that had happened was only a black and ridiculous nightmare. Indeed, we were well and sound, and by actual count not one of us was missing. What more could we ask? The Americans had not needed recourse to extreme violence to expel the unwanted Chileans from the Mill. To be sure, they had robbed them and taken from them all that they had, but this in California was of no great moment.

The rest of our associates had dispersed. That very night we sat in committee to decide what was now to be done. No one was in favor of a return to Chile; rather it was unanimously determined to reenter the struggle against adverse fortune, changing our plan of attack until finally victorious.

* * *

I obtained from my comrades permission to make a trip to Monterey, on the pretext of extending our sphere of action. I confess that my real purpose was to go and have my fill of milk in that town.

In order to reach Monterey I had to climb the coastal hills on foot, and use the same means of locomotion to cover the 95 miles that separated this city from San Francisco. But what was that to a veteran at corporal punishment, when in exchange he was to get a few days' respite from the exhausting masquerade in which he had been tripping the light fantastic since his arrival in California? Above all, what was that compared with the prospect of holding up to his dry lips whole pitchers of pure, white, foaming milk?

It seems a trifle, but let me recall that when in 1828 some Indians of the Osage tribe visited Paris, they began to grow faint with nostalgia in spite of being lodged in the palace of Charles X; they would have died, had not the odor of the whale oil that supplied the illumination made them exclaim, "Bring us barrels of that nectar! To our minds it's worth a lot more than the hangings they choke us with, and the accursed ragouts the European aborigines use to deceive their stomachs!" In the cool of a beautiful July morning I slung my rifle over my shoulder, girded myself with a slender belt stuffed with gold, stuck pistols through it, put on a dirty wool hat and *sarape,* and with head bowed set off through the hills and hummocks that separate San Francisco from the former capital of Alta California. I passed the first ridges along the coast in the company of some Sonorans who were returning to their homes disillusioned, and we entered a broad valley covered with grass and flowers. There was a great abundance of birds, and above all of squirrels. These nimble and charming little animals leaped out from under our feet as if by magic. Flocks of deer came up to us as the guanacos do at home, and stampeded away at our slightest movement, only to stop suddenly and come back again. The useful taller vegetation is as surprising in this valley as everywhere else in California. Oak, pine and ash occur in inexhaustible numbers. The region back of the coast near San Francisco is covered with a redwood very similar to our larches, and indeed, these trees yield nothing in size to our giant trees in the south. In my earlier wanderings I had occasion to contemplate in astonishment the marvelous group of conifers in the Mariposa gold area. I saw there specimens that measured from ninety to one hundred yards in height and from twenty-eight to thirty-one in circumference at the base; and what is more astounding, lateral branches with a diameter of three and a half yards, appearing forty-five yards up from the ground. These prodigies of vegetation, known to science as *Sequoia gigantea,* have so many names in California that the foreigner does not know which to apply. By some they are called *grizzly giants;* by others *redwoods;* the English call them *Wellingtons,* the Americans *Washingtons;* we, I suppose, should call them after San Martín.

We made camp in the shelter of a live oak. All night we were annoyed by the visits of greedy, malevolent coyotes. Fear of coyotes had driven away from California Senor Ortiz A., a prissy Argentine dandy, very well known in Santiago. He had attempted what everyone was doing, but on his venturing out on the road alone the coyotes pursued him without pause until they brought him howling back to civilization. These wretched beasts permitted us to have breakfast next morning only because almost under our noses they had despatched what was left of a stag we had killed for food.

In this as in my previous contacts with Mexicans from Sonora and with Spanish Californians, I wondered at the candor with which these poor people speak about the American invasion and dominion of their country. They believe that they themselves cannot expel those whom they still justly term the tyrants; but they also believe implicitly that the Chileans, if they had a mind to, could do so, in view of their determined resistance to the brutal oppression of the Americans. So they came in my company, apparently as secure from assault as if they were under the protection of a terrible Fierabras. And thus when the moment came for taking our leave, I am confident the Fierabras was no less frightened at being left alone than were they.

On the afternoon of the third day of my march, already half repentant of my foolish action, my spirits were revived by the sight of one of the towers of Monterey that rose up at no great distance. And with no small delight I exerted myself to arrive before dark.

The port of Monterey is one of the best on that coast; as a town Monterey, until then considered the capital of Alta California, was a good deal like our Casablanca in 1840, and its population was not over 1500 souls. On the other hand, the nature of the fields that surround it, and that of the region as a whole is, with Santa Cruz, among the best and most fertile that I found in California. The surroundings of this delicious spot were adorned by many homes set among beautiful groves of trees; and although the buildings kept the form of our heavy country houses of half a century ago, their wide porticos open to the public road revealed the hospitable character of the Spanish race.

Night was falling fast. And since neither my appearance nor the coarseness of my attire authorized me to ask for lodging anywhere within doors, I proposed to rest in the shelter of the portico of a house whose shut windows and half-closed door appeared to indicate that it was not at the moment occupied by its owners. As I approached, I noticed that the door was noisily pulled to. "Bad," I said to myself, "It's impossible they didn't see me. What does that slam mean?" Nevertheless, I stepped under the covered porch, gave three knocks in the Spanish style, and since there was no reply, remembered that I was still in California and banged heavily twice with the butt of my rifle. This time there was an immediate response.

"Who is it?" said an ancient female voice inside.

"*Deo gracias*, Señora," I replied. "It is a man of peace who asks only permission to spread his *sarape* for the night on the floor of this veranda."

Within I heard some quick movements, and a woman's voice saying, "But it isn't an American, it's a Spaniard!"

And after a late "Forever and ever" in response to my first greeting, the door was cautiously opened a bit and I saw a gentleman about forty-five years of age, simply and neatly dressed, who saluted me and asked me what

I wished. On hearing me speak, he exclaimed in delight, "God forgive you, my friend, for the fright you just gave us! When we saw you come, we thought you were one of the many barbarians who infest our roads and towns, since the peace gave us a change of masters. Come in, Sir, come in!"

His caution was justified. Only the California landowner knew to how many outrages he was exposed without appeal since the moment when what they called the invasion of northern barbarians had begun. Great was the pleasure aroused in that amiable and hospitable family, composed of the gentleman, his lovely wife and two sisters-in-law, who would have been pretty anywhere and to me looked angelic, on learning that not only were they addressing a civilized person, but a Chilean to boot. A Chilean veteran of the diggings was here a symbol of personal security, a bulwark against American oppression, and a brother to be received with outstretched hand.

Familiarity was not long in putting at ease the kind hosts and the new arrival, whom they plied with questions about Chile, about the Chileans in San Francisco, about his unhappy adventures, and his reasons for coming to Monterey. The ladies nearly burst with laughter when I avowed that my chief reason was the desire to have my fill of milk.

Don Juan de Alvarado, as the master of the house was called, took me by the hand and led me to his bedroom. He made me promise to rest in his home as long as I could. Then by dint of entreaties and even displeasure, he forced upon me a linen shirt and an overcoat, to avoid being constantly reminded by my appearance of the intruders whom he despised. Then he left me alone and, like Don Quixote changing clothes at the home of the Duke and Duchess, I washed myself thoroughly, trimmed my whiskers, and felt the incomparable sensation of cool, starched linen against a skin roughened by long contact with wool. That night I slept in a bed with sheets and pillow! And the following day I found waiting for me, near a beautiful arbor surrounded by gardens, two splendid cows who provided me with an endless supply of milk, handed to me, glass after glass, by the soft and willing hands of my host's kind sisters-in-law. If there is a seventh heaven as they say there is, I was in that heaven then. There is nothing like exhaustion to reveal what rest can be; and to know what ease could mean one had to have been an adventurer in California.

Through Don Juan I contracted with a *ranchero*, or California ranch owner, for the delivery of twelve milch cows and eight oxen in San Francisco. Then, because eight days of recreation seemed already too long to have taken, I announced my immediate departure to the family. Such entreaties were heard as only Latins can give to their guests. And when I heard that a party was to be given for me the next day I gladly yielded.

The guests were numerous. The fair sex of Monterey reminded me of the women of Chile, polished, attractive and eager to please. The men had many of the distinguishing gifts of our gay *elquinos*. When there is an earthquake, there is a dance to drive away fear; in case of a death outside the immediate family and friends, they call for another ball to erase the impression left on the mind by the funeral procession; and if there is reason to be merry, why much better the reason for still another dance!

The rooms were adorned in simple, but fresh and happy fashion. Delightful was the appearance of the halls and corridors adjoining the reception room; they were draped with green branches and flowers forming arches and borders, and illuminated with wax lights, an almost unheard-of luxury. In each corner of the exterior rooms there were fragrant baskets filled with boxes of cigars of various sizes, among which, artistically arranged, was a little spirit flame. I thought at first that this provision was for men alone. I was mistaken. In Monterey, ladies who do not use tobacco at least enjoy the smoke. And the fair guests, after a quadrille played on the piano by the sexton of the adjoining chapel, walked through the corridors two by two, helped themselves to cigars as they passed the baskets, and returned to the ballroom only after throwing away the stubs. Their mothers were privileged to smoke in the ballroom itself; this they did in a peculiar manner that caught my attention, carefully covering their mouths with their shawls on inhaling the smoke, and uncovering them when blowing it out.

The Chilean guest of honor was the general subject of conversation, and the farewells taken at about two in the morning were friendly and cordial.

In all my panoply of war I prepared next morning to leave. The whole family of my hospitable friend accompanied me to the portico outside, where to my surprise I found a fine mule with the richest Mexican saddle and trappings I had ever seen, made of velvet embroidered with gold, and having in front a beautiful eagle's head of pure silver. This was to lighten my journey. I could not refuse the urgings of Don Juan to accept this gift, this trifle as he called it; and after expressive farewells I rode off on my mule from that oasis in a desert of selfish indifference, going at a trot with my head full of hopes over the only road to San Francisco.

1850

THE CULTURES OF NEW ENGLAND

European settlement of the Americas had many starting points: Mexico, Florida, Nova Scotia, New Amsterdam, Virginia, Massachusetts Bay, among other places. Each region developed along rather different cultural avenues, influenced by language, religion, the class origins and educational backgrounds of settlers, relationships with the Native Americans, and other factors. New England was first settled by strongly religious women and men, many of them highly literate, with a penchant for arguing about beliefs and values. Perhaps as a result, New England developed a moralistic culture within which controversial writing in the form of sermons, editorials, and jeremiads, as well as poetry and fiction, held a high place. It is not surprising, therefore, that many of the works gathered in this section are deeply involved with conflict. They were not, by and large, solely exercises in imaginative display. Rather, they had designs on their readers' thoughts and ultimately on their actions. Today's readers have often been taught that such hortatory writing is inherently less valuable than what is called "belles lettres," writing that appears to make no claims on our actions. That is not a view of "literature" with which most nineteenth-century intellectuals, and certainly not those in New England, would have agreed. Regardless of how one evaluates persuasive literature, a great deal of nineteenth-century writing aimed to move readers to feel and to act.

That is as true of poems like Lydia H. H. Sigourney's "Indian Names" or John Greenleaf Whittier's "The Hunters of Men" as it is of Henry David Thoreau's "Resistance to Civil Government" (better known as "Civil Disobedience") or Margaret Fuller's "Woman in the Nineteenth Century." Each of these works, and most of the others included in this section, were designed to move readers, to open their eyes to features of a social landscape they had not sufficiently observed before, to alter their ways of thinking—or at least, as Thoreau put it in *Walden*, "to wake my neighbors up." The same might be said of other such quintessentially New England works as Harriet Beecher Stowe's *Uncle Tom's Cabin*, as well as the essays of writers like Thomas Wentworth Higginson, Wendell Phillips, and William Lloyd Garrison printed elsewhere in this volume.

Not all New England writers agreed with one another. On the contrary, many of these texts were designed to dispute or attack received wisdom or ideas the writers rejected. It is essential in reading these works to look through their surfaces to understand the positions against which their writers are implicitly arguing. Sigourney's "Indian Names," for example, is an attack on the ideology of the "vanishing Indian," a set of sentimental images and associations through which whites largely hid from themselves the fact that Indians were not "naturally" disappearing but were being pushed out or exterminated. Thoreau's "Civil Disobedience" is fundamentally a denunciation not just of slavery and of the Mexican War but of the ease with which many New Englanders accommodated themselves to these immoral policies. Emerson speaks against the low "principles on which business is managed" as well as against individuals who preach consistency and tradition—that is, against much of the economic and clerical leadership of his world.

Not all or even most writing in New England in the first half of the nineteenth century was polemical, however. In the first place, much of what ordinary people wrote and read took the form of letters, often to or from relatives now at a distance in the Ohio territory or elsewhere on the "frontier." Such letters, as Joan Hedrick has pointed out, were often read aloud to family and friends in New England parlors or in whatever circumstances frontier life afforded. Then, too, a good deal of poetry and fiction was printed and circulated in popular magazines, in gift books, and in annuals, a number of which were the products of Boston publishers. Hawthorne, for example, produced much of his fiction before *The Scarlet Letter* for such periodicals, and although his tales often had a moral point, they were on the whole not moralistic in the mode of polemical essays.

These letters, essays, and speeches were clearly not composed without art. Emerson, Fuller, and Thoreau crafted their essays with as much care as any poet or fiction writer. They often jotted down thoughts in journals, converted those jottings into more formal entries, and then transformed the entries into sections of their essays. They would have rejected the idea, developed later in the century, that polemical writing was one kind of creature, different from the creature called "art." Writers—nowhere more so than in New England—regarded the artful presentation of an argument as central not only to its success in capturing an audience but to the pleasure of the writer in writing. Indeed, it might well be argued that the early-nineteenth-century "flowering of New England," as Van Wyck Brooks named it, or the "American Renaissance" described by F. O. Matthiessen can be located as much in the nonfictional prose of the period as in its fiction or poetry. Indeed, in the nonfictional works contained in this section we find passages as evocative as those in any poetry or fiction.

■ LYDIA HOWARD HUNTLEY SIGOURNEY ■
1791–1865

When Lafayette, the French hero of the American Revolutionary War, visited the United States in the 1820s, a procession of schoolchildren with wreaths proclaiming "NOUS AIMONS LA FAYETTE" greeted him in the city of Hartford, Connecticut. The phrase was the refrain of a poem in his honor by Lydia Howard Huntley Sigourney. This event characterizes Sigourney's position as a writer. Her poetry, like her prose, was about public subjects—history, slavery, missionary work, as well as current events—or treated personal matters, especially loss and death, as experiences common to all. In contrast to Dickinson or

Emerson, she wrote for popular consumption; her work expressed a communal ethic based on compassionate Christianity and on conservative republicanism.

Sigourney was enormously popular. In 1848 the respected publishers Cary and Hart issued her selected poems in their series of works by American poets, the preceding volumes having been devoted to three highly regarded male writers—Bryant, Longfellow, and N. P. Willis. She was also enormously productive: at her death in 1865 she had published more than fifty books. Their range attests to the variety of forms in which antebellum writers could undertake to guide the public. She wrote communitarian narratives, educational volumes, advice manuals, travel literature, temperance pieces, meditative prose, and exemplary memoirs, as well as a vast and varied quantity of poetry.

Sigourney's personal history was testimony to women's possibilities for self-betterment in America. Born in Norwich, Connecticut, in 1791, she was the only child of a gardener-handyman and his wife. As a child she was the protégé of her father's employer, Mrs. Lathrop, and when Mrs. Lathrop died, her aristocratic family in Hartford assumed the position of patron to the talented girl. Lydia's commitments to education, writing, and charity were formed early. As a child she wrote poetry and essays and kept a journal. When her formal schooling ended, she was tutored in Latin and Hebrew and conducted classes for impoverished children, among them African Americans (usually deprived of formal education at that time). In 1811 she and a friend established a girls' school in Hartford. In 1814 a wealthy relation of Mrs. Lathrop established a school for her, gathering pupils from among members of his circle in Hartford. Here she pursued a progressive educational policy, dispensing with the ornamental aspects of girls' education like needlework and concentrating on comprehension and moral development. In 1815 pedagogical materials that Sigourney had written were published as *Moral Pieces in Prose and Verse*.

Despite her success, she gave up teaching upon her engagement to Charles Sigourney, a prominent Hartford widower whom she married in 1819; they had five children, only two of whom lived to adulthood. She continued to write, but her stern, conservative husband objected to public authorship, and the matter was long a source of conflict in their marriage. Her wish to publish prevailed, though she usually did so anonymously until her authorship of an advice book became publicly known in 1833. After that she published under her name, her output soaring: in her first two years of acknowledged authorship, she produced nine volumes along with many ephemeral pieces for newspapers and magazines. Charles Sigourney's deteriorating economic circumstances probably contributed to this rate and may have sharpened her entrepreneurial skills. She was adroit at negotiating contracts and obtaining remunerative terms for her work, taking advantage of the substantial royalties she received for *The Girl's Reading Book* (1838) and *The Boy's Reading Book* (1839), for instance, by arranging for their adoption in numerous schools.

However assertive Sigourney was, her activities always remained within the boundaries of feminine propriety of her era. Her work was not solely for personal gain; she supported her parents and family and devoted at least ten percent of her annual income to charity. Her writing itself conformed to the idea of ladyhood to which she paid homage in her portrait of Mrs. Lathrop in *Sketch of Connecticut* (1824): a conservative benevolence dedicated to the public good.

Written with great skill, it was accessible to the broad readership it sought to influence. Unlike Romantic poetry, her poems are not about the subjective ego of poetic persona, nor do they appeal to readers' subjective states. They use familiar language, often language associated with hymns and the Bible, to present events like the death of an infant or spouse as painful instances of humanity's common fate. They also encourage readers' compassion for others and urge them to draw religious conclusions from the contemplation of natural processes and historical events.

Her work asserts a notion of the American polity that embraces class hierarchy but stresses cross-class obligations and represents Americans as a diverse people. In *Sketch of Connecticut*, she grants voices to members of different groups in the community of Norwich—African Americans, Native Americans, the poor, members of various religions, as well as a "Yankee" farmer. In *Lucy Howard's Journal* (1858), she advances a vision of the American West as an interdependent, though stratified, community. Sigourney's beliefs also fueled her concern—quite unusual in her day—about white treatment of Native Americans. In her many works on Native Americans' history and circumstances, she treats whites' conduct as a violation of Christian principles. As Nina Baym has noted, she did not condemn settlers' appropriation of land, but she felt that they failed in Christian and republican virtues by not Christianizing Native Americans and granting them citizenship, and she tried to represent Native American perspectives.

Sigourney's professional conduct was sometimes questionable. She presented literary notables as friends when they were mere acquaintances, and she published papers intended to remain private, including, after his death, her son's personal journals. Nevertheless, she was always true to her sense of writing as public service. She distributed many copies of her books *gratis* and published at least one at her own expense so that she could give copies away. In her memoir, *Letters of Life*, she estimates that she responded to two thousand letters annually and lists some of the curious requests she received from complete strangers, including one for an ode to a dead canary. Numerous letters from readers attest to the consolation and sustenance her work provided her contemporaries. The low esteem in which public literature—and most female writers— have long been held has allowed twentieth-century commentators to repeat with contempt her antebellum sobriquet "the Sweet Singer of Hartford." Yet her great success and the seriousness with which she pursued her vocation make it worth our while to explore both the nature of her appeal and the potential, as well as the limits, of popular antebellum writing.

Sandra A. Zagarell
Oberlin College

PRIMARY WORKS

Traits of the Aborigines of America, 1822; *Sketch of Connecticut, Forty Years Since*, 1824; *Poems*, 1827; *Zinzendorff and Other Poems*, 1835; *Illustrated Poems*, 1848; *Past Meridian*, 1854; *Lucy Howard's Journal*, 1858; *Letters of Life*, 1866.

The Suttee[1]

She sat upon the pile by her dead lord,
And in her full, dark eye, and shining hair
Youth revell'd.—The glad murmur of the crowd
Applauding her consent to the dread doom,
And the hoarse chanting of infuriate priests   5
She heeded not, for her quick ear had caught
An infant's wail.—Feeble and low that moan,
Yet it was answer'd in her heaving heart,
For the Mimosa in its shrinking fold
From the rude pressure, is not half so true,   10
So tremulous, as is a mother's soul
Unto her wailing babe.—There was such wo
In her imploring aspect,—in her tones
Such thrilling agony, that even the hearts
Of the flame-kindlers soften'd, and they laid   15
The famish'd infant on her yearning breast.
There with his tear-wet cheek he lay and drew
Plentiful nourishment from that full fount
Of infant happiness,—and long he prest
With eager lip the chalice of his joy.—   20
And then his little hands he stretch'd to grasp
His mother's flower-wove tresses, and with smile
And gay caress embraced his bloated sire,—
As if kind Nature taught that innocent one
With fond delay to cheat the hour which seal'd   25
His hopeless orphanage.—But those were near
Who mock'd such dalliance, as that Spirit malign
Who twined his serpent length mid Eden's bowers
Frown'd on our parents' bliss.—The victim mark'd
Their harsh intent, and clasp'd the unconscious babe   30
With such convulsive force, that when they tore
His writhing form away, the very nerves
Whose deep-sown fibres rack the inmost soul
Uprooted seem'd.—
　　　　　　　　　With voice of high command   35
Tossing her arms, she bade them bring her son,—
And then in maniac rashness sought to leap
Among the astonish'd throng.—But the rough cord
Compress'd her slender limbs, and bound her fast
Down to her loathsome partner.—Quick the fire   40
In showers was hurl'd upon the reeking pile;—
But yet amid the wild, demoniac shout

---

[1]From *Poems by the Author of Moral Pieces in Prose and Verse* (1827). "Suttee" was an Indian (that is, from India) practice in which a widow was immolated along with her husband's corpse. Suttee was supposed to be voluntary.

Of priest and people, mid the thundering yell
Of the infernal gong,—was heard to rise
Thrice a dire death-shriek.—And the men who stood   45
Near the red pile and heard that fearful cry,
Call'd on their idol-gods, and stopp'd their ears,
And oft amid their nightly dream would start
As frighted Fancy echoed in her cell
That burning mother's scream.   50

                                                        1827

Death of an Infant[1]

Death found strange beauty on that polish'd brow,
And dash'd it out. There was a tint of rose
On cheek and lip. He touched the veins with ice,
And the rose faded.
               Forth from those blue eyes   5
There spake a wishful tenderness, a doubt
Whether to grieve or sleep, which innocence
Alone may wear. With ruthless haste he bound
The silken fringes of those curtaining lids
For ever.   10
          There had been a murmuring sound,
With which the babe would claim its mother's ear,
Charming her even to tears. The spoiler set
The seal of silence.
            But there beam'd a smile,   15
So fix'd, so holy, from that cherub brow,
Death gazed, and left it there. He dar'd not steal
The signet-ring of Heaven.

                                                        1827

To the First Slave Ship

First of that train which cursed the wave,
And from the rifled cabin bore,

[1]From *Select Poems*, sixth ed., revised and corrected, 1848. Sigourney's most widely anthologized poem. Sigourney notes, "This little poem has been inserted by mistake, in one of the American editions of the late Mrs. Hemans. Though this is accounted by the real author, as an honor, it is still proper to state, that it was originally composed at Hartford, in the winter of 1824, and comprised in a volume of poems, published in Boston, by S. G. Goodrich, Esq., in 1827. Should other testimony be necessary, it may be mentioned that a letter from Mrs. Hemans, to a friend in this country, pointing out some poems in that volume which pleased her, designated, among others, this "Death of an Infant."

Inheritor of wo,—*the slave*
To bless his palm-tree's shade no more,

Dire engine!—o'er the troubled main   5
Borne on in unresisted state,—
Know'st thou within thy dark domain
The secrets of thy prison'd freight?—

Hear'st thou *their* moans whom hope hath fled?—
Wild cries, in agonizing starts?—   10
Know'st thou thy humid sails are spread
With ceaseless sighs from broken hearts?—

The fetter'd chieftain's burning tear,—
The parted lover's mute despair,—
The childless mother's pang severe,—   15
The orphan's misery, are there.

Ah!—could'st thou from the scroll of fate
The annal read of future years,
Stripes,—tortures,—unrelenting hate,
And death-gasps drown'd in slavery's tears,   20

Down,—down,—beneath the cleaving main
Thou fain would'st plunge where monsters lie,
Rather than ope the gates of pain
For time and for Eternity.—

Oh Afric!—what has been thy crime?—   25
That thus like Eden's fratricide,
A mark is set upon thy clime,
And every brother shuns thy side.—

Yet are thy wrongs, thou long-distrest!—
Thy burdens, by the world unweigh'd,   30
Safe in that *Unforgetful Breast*
Where all the sins of earth are laid.—

Poor outcast slave!—Our guilty land
Should tremble while she drinks thy tears,
Or sees in vengeful silence stand,   35
The beacon of thy shorten'd years;—
Should shrink to hear her sons proclaim
The sacred truth that heaven is just,—
Shrink even at her Judge's name,—
"Jehovah,—Saviour of the opprest."   40

The Sun upon thy forehead frown'd,
But Man more cruel far than he,
Dark fetters on thy spirit bound:—
Look to the mansions of the free!

Look to that realm where chains unbind,—   45
Where the pale tyrant drops his rod,
And where the patient sufferers find
A friend,—a father in their God.

                                                            1827

The Indian's Welcome to the Pilgrim Fathers[1]

*"On Friday, March 16th, 1622, while the colonists were busied in their
usual labors, they were much surprised to see a savage walk boldly towards
them, and salute them with, 'much welcome, English, much welcome,
Englishmen.'"*

Above them spread a stranger sky
        Around, the sterile plain,
The rock-bound coast rose frowning nigh,
        Beyond,—the wrathful main:
Chill remnants of the wintry snow   5
        Still chok'd the encumber'd soil,
Yet forth these Pilgrim Fathers go,
        To mark their future toil.

'Mid yonder vale their corn must rise
        In Summer's ripening pride,   10
And there the church-spire woo the skies
        Its sister-school beside.
Perchance 'mid England's velvet green
        Some tender thought repos'd,—
Though nought upon their stoic mien.   15
        Such soft regret disclos'd.

When sudden from the forest wide
        A red-brow'd chieftain came,
With towering form, and haughty stride,
        And eye like kindling flame: 20
No wrath he breath'd, no conflict sought,
        To no dark ambush drew,
But simply to the Old World brought,
        The welcome of the New.

[1]From *Zinzendorff and Other Poems* (1835).

That welcome was a blast and ban　　　　　　　　　25
　　Upon thy race unborn.
Was there no seer, thou fated Man!
　　Thy lavish zeal to warn?
Thou in thy fearless faith didst hail
　　A weak, invading band,　　　　　　　　　　　30
But who shall heed thy children's wail,
　　Swept from their native land?

Thou gav'st the riches of thy streams,
　　The lordship o'er thy waves,
The region of thine infant dreams,　　　　　　　35
　　And of thy fathers' graves,
But who to yon proud mansions pil'd
　　With wealth of earth and sea,
Poor outcast from thy forest wild,
　　Say, who shall welcome thee?　　　　　　　40

　　　　　　　　　　　　　　　　　　　　　　1835

Indian Names[1]

"How can the red men be forgotten, while so many of our states and territories, bays, lakes and rivers, are indelibly stamped by names of their giving?"

Ye say they all have passed away,
　　That noble race and brave,
That their light canoes have vanished
　　From off the crested wave;
That 'mid the forests where they roamed　　　　5
　　There rings no hunter's shout;
But their name is on your waters,
　　Ye may not wash it out.

'Tis where Ontario's billow
　　Like Ocean's surge is curled,　　　　　　　10
Where strong Niagara's thunders wake
　　The echo of the world,
Where red Missouri bringeth
　　Rich tributes from the west,
And Rappahannock sweetly sleeps　　　　　　15
　　On green Virginia's breast.

[1]From *Poems* (1834). Sigourney published this poem in two versions. The poem that was published in 1834 contained the seven stanzas printed here, and another version that was first published in 1838 omitted the last two stanzas. We haven chosen to print the 1834 version in part because it is interesting to speculate about the differences between the versions, especially in light of the Trail of Tears of 1838 and 1839 and earlier forced removals of the Cherokees from Georgia.

Ye say their cone-like cabins,
　　That clustered o'er the vale,
Have fled away like withered leaves
　　Before the autumn gale:　　　　　　　　　20
But their memory liveth on your hills,
　　Their baptism on your shore,
Your everlasting rivers speak
　　Their dialect of yore.

Old Massachusetts wears it　　　　　　　　25
　　Within her lordly crown,
And broad Ohio bears it
　　Amid her young renown;
Connecticut hath wreathed it
　　Where her quiet foliage waves,　　　　　30
And bold Kentucky breathed it hoarse
　　Through all her ancient caves.

Wachuset hides its lingering voice
　　Within his rocky heart,
And Alleghany graves its tone　　　　　　　35
　　Throughout his lofty chart;
Monadnock on his forehead hoar
　　Doth seal the sacred trust,
Your mountains build their monument,
　　Though ye destroy their dust.　　　　　　40

Ye call these red-browed brethren
　　The insects of an hour,
Crushed like the noteless worm amid
　　The regions of their power;
Ye drive them from their father's lands,　　45
　　Ye break of faith the seal,
But can ye from the court of Heaven
　　Exclude their last appeal?

Ye see their unresisting tribes,
　　With toilsome step and slow,　　　　　　50
On through the trackless desert pass,
　　A caravan of woe;
Think ye the Eternal's ear is deaf?
　　His sleepless vision dim?
Think ye the soul's blood may not cry　　　55
　　From that far land to him?

1834

Niagara[1]

Flow on for ever, in thy glorious robe
Of terror and of beauty. Yea, flow on
Unfathom'd and resistless. God hath set
His rainbow on thy forehead, and the cloud
Mantled around thy feet. And he doth give   5
Thy voice of thunder power to speak of Him
Eternally—bidding the lip of man
Keep silence—and upon thine altar pour
Incense of awe-struck praise.
                                        Earth fears to lift   10
The insect-trump that tells her trifling joys
Or fleeting triumphs, mid the peal sublime
Of thy tremendous hymn. Proud Ocean shrinks
Back from thy brotherhood, and all his waves
Retire abash'd. For he hath need to sleep,   15
Sometimes, like a spent labourer, calling home
His boisterous billows, from their vexing play,
To a long dreary calm: but thy strong tide
Faints not, nor e'er with failing heart forgets
Its everlasting lesson, night nor day.   20
The morning stars, that hail'd creation's birth,
Heard thy hoarse anthem mixing with their song
Jehovah's name; and the dissolving fires,
That wait the mandate of the day of doom
To wreck the earth, shall find it deep inscribed   25
Upon thy rocky scroll.
                                        The lofty trees
That list thy teachings, scorn the lighter lore
Of the too fitful winds; while their young leaves
Gather fresh greenness from thy living spray,   30
Yet tremble at the baptism. Lo! yon birds,
How bold they venture near, dipping their wing
In all thy mist and foam. Perchance 'tis meet
For them to touch thy garment's hem, or stir
Thy diamond wreath, who sport upon the cloud   35
Unblamed, or warble at the gate of heaven
Without reproof. But, as for us, it seems
Scarce lawful with our erring lips to talk
Familiarly of thee. Methinks, to trace
Thine awful features with our pencil's point   40
Were but to press on Sinai.

[1]From *Illustrated Poems* (1849). Mrs. Sigourney's best-known nature poem.

<blockquote>

                Thou dost speak
Alone of God, who pour'd thee as a drop
From his right-hand,—bidding the soul that looks
Upon thy fearful majesty be still,   45
Be humbly wrapp'd in its own nothingness,
And lose itself in Him.

</blockquote>

                                           1849

To a Shred of Linen[1]

Would they swept cleaner!
                          Here's a littering shred
Of linen left behind—a vile reproach
To all good housewifery. Right glad am I
That no neat lady, train'd in ancient times   5
Of pudding-making, and of sampler-work,
And speckless sanctity of household care,
Hath happen'd here to spy thee. She, no doubt,
Keen looking through her spectacles, would say,
"This comes of reading books." Or some spruce beau,   10
Essenced and lily-handed, had he chanced
To scan thy slight superfices, 'twould be,
"This comes of writing poetry."—Well, well,
Come forth, offender!—hast thou aught to say?
Canst thou, by merry thought or quaint conceit,   15
Repay this risk that I have run for thee?
——Begin at alpha, and resolve thyself
Into thine elements. I see the stalk
And bright blue flower of flax, which erst o'erspread
That fertile land, where mighty Moses stretch'd   20
His rod miraculous. I see thy bloom
Tinging, too scantly, these New England vales.
But, lo! the sturdy farmer lifts his flail
To crush thy bones unpitying, and his wife,
With kerchief'd head and eye brimfull of dust,   25
Thy fibrous nerves with hatchel-tooth divides.
——I hear a voice of music—and behold!
The ruddy damsel singeth at her wheel,[2]
While by her side the rustic lover sits.
Perchance, his shrewd eye secretly doth count   30
The mass of skeins, which, hanging on the wall,
Increaseth day by day. Perchance his thought
(For men have deeper minds than women—sure!)

---

[1]From *Illustrated Poems* (1849).   [2]Spinning.

Is calculating what a thrifty wife
The maid will make; and how his dairy shelves   35
Shall groan beneath the weight of golden cheese,
Made by her dexterous hand, while many a keg
And pot of butter to the market borne,
May, transmigrated, on his back appear
In new thanksgiving coats.   40
               Fain would I ask,
Mine own New England, for thy once loved wheel,
By sofa and piano quite displaced.
Why dost thou banish from thy parlour hearth
That old Hygeian[3] harp, whose magic ruled   45
Dyspepsia, as the minstrel-shepherd's skill
Exorcised Saul's ennui? There was no need,
In those good times of callisthenics, sure;
And there was less of gadding, and far more
Of home-born, heart-felt comfort, rooted strong   50
In industry, and bearing such rare fruit
As wealth might never purchase.
                   But come back,
Thou shred of linen. I did let thee drop
In my harangue, as wiser ones have lost   55
The thread of their discourse. What was thy lot
When the rough battery of the loom had stretch'd
And knit thy sinews, and the chemist sun
Thy brown complexion bleach'd?
                   Methinks I scan   60
Some idiosyncrasy that marks thee out
A defunct pillow-case. Did the trim guest,
To the best chamber usher'd, e'er admire
The snowy whiteness of thy freshen'd youth,
Feeding thy vanity? or some sweet babe   65
Pour its pure dream of innocence on thee?
Say, hast thou listen'd to the sick one's moan,
When there was none to comfort?—or shrunk back
From the dire tossings of the proud man's brow?
Or gather'd from young beauty's restless sigh   70
A tale of untold love?
              Still close and mute!—
Wilt tell no secrets, ha?—Well then, go down,
With all thy churl-kept hoard of curious lore,
In majesty and mystery, go down   75
Into the paper-mill, and from its jaws,
Stainless and smooth, emerge. Happy shall be

---

[3]Hygeia was the Greek goddess of health.

The renovation, if on thy fair page
Wisdom and truth their hallow'd lineaments
Trace for posterity. So shall thine end   80
Be better than thy birth, and worthier bard
Thine apotheosis immortalize.

                                                          1849

The Indian Summer[1]

When was the red man's summer?
                    When the rose
Hung its first banner out? When the gray rock,
Or the brown heath, the radiant kalmia clothed?
Or when the loiterer by the reedy brooks   5
Started to see the proud lobelia glow
Like living flame? When through the forest gleam'd
The rhododendron? or the fragrant breath
Of the magnolia swept deliciously
O'er the half laden nerve?   10
                    No. When the groves
In fleeting colours wrote their own decay,
And leaves fell eddying on the sharpen'd blast
That sang their dirge; when o'er their rustling bed
The red deer sprang, or fled the shrill-voiced quail, 15
Heavy of wing and fearful; when, with heart
Foreboding or depress'd, the white man mark'd
The signs of coming winter: then began
The Indian's joyous season. Then the haze,
Soft and illusive as fairy dream,   20
Lapp'd all the landscape in its silvery fold.
The quiet rivers, that were wont to hide
'Neath shelving banks, beheld their course betray'd
By the white mist that o'er their foreheads crept,
While wrapp'd in morning dreams, the sea and sky   25
Slept 'neath one curtain, as if both were merged
In the same element. Slowly the sun,
And all reluctantly, the spell dissolved,
And then it took upon its parting wing
A rainbow glory.   30
                    Gorgeous was the time,
Yet brief as gorgeous. Beautiful to thee,
Our brother hunter, but to us replete
With musing thoughts in melancholy train.

[1]From *The Western Home* (1854).

Our joys, alas! too oft were wo to thee.   35
Yet ah, poor Indian! whom we fain would drive
Both from our hearts, and from thy father's lands,
The perfect year doth bear thee on its crown,
And when we would forget, repeat thy name.

                                                                 1854

Fallen Forests

Man's warfare on the trees is terrible.
He lifts his rude hut in the wilderness,
And, lo! the loftiest trunks, that age on age
Were nurtured to nobility, and bore
Their summer coronets so gloriously,   5
Fall with a thunder sound to rise no more.
He toucheth flame unto them, and they lie
A blackened wreck, their tracery and wealth
Of sky-fed emerald, madly spent, to feed
An arch of brilliance for a single night,   10
And scaring thence the wild deer, and the fox,
And the lithe squirrel from the nut-strewn home,
So long enjoyed.
He lifts his puny arm,
And every echo of the axe doth hew   15
The iron heart of centuries away.
He entereth boldly to the solemn groves
On whose green altar tops, since time was young
The wingéd birds have poured their incense stream
Of praise and love, within whose mighty nave   20
The wearied cattle from a thousand hills
Have found their shelter mid the heat of day;
Perchance in their mute worship pleasing Him
Who careth for the meanest He hath made.
I said, he entereth to the sacred groves   25
Where nature in her beauty bows to God,
And, lo! their temple arch is desecrate.
Sinks the sweet hymn, the ancient ritual fades,
And uptorn roots and prostrate columns mark
The invader's footsteps.   30
Silent years roll on,
His babes are men. His ant-heap dwelling grows
Too narrow—for his hand hath gotten wealth.
He builds a stately mansion, but it stands
Unblessed by trees. He smote them recklessly   35
When their green arms were found him, as a guard

Of tutelary deities, and feels
Their maledictions, now the burning noon
Maketh his spirit faint. With anxious care,
He casteth acorns in the earth, and woos   40
Sunbeam and rain; he planteth the young shoot,
And props it from the storm; but neither he,
Nor yet his children's children, shall behold
What he hath swept away.
Methinks, 'twere well   45
Not as a spoiler or a thief to prey
On Nature's bosom, that sweet, gentle nurse
Who loveth us, and spreads a sheltering couch
When our brief task is o'er. O'er that green mound
Affection's hand may set the willow tree,   50
Or train the cypress, and let none profane
Her pious care.
Oh, Father! grant us grace
In all life's toils, so, with a steadfast hand
Evil and good to poise, as not to pave   55
Our way with wrecks, nor leave our blackened name
A beacon to the way-worn mariner.

                                                   1854

■ WILLIAM APESS[1] (PEQUOT) ■
1798–?

William Apess was born in 1798 near Colrain, Massachusetts. His mother may have been Candace Apes, who was listed as a "Negro" woman owned as a slave by Captain Joseph Taylor of Colchester until he freed her in 1805 at age twenty-eight. The author's father, whose name was probably William A. Apes, was half white. His paternal grandmother was a full-blooded Pequot; Apess claimed she was descended from Metacomet (Wampanoag; c. 1639–1676, given the name King Philip by the English). After his parents separated when Apess was around three, he was reared by his maternal grandparents. Badly beaten by his alcoholic grandmother, Apess was subsequently bound out to whites at age four or five—a common practice for dealing with homeless children. Apess's

[1]Although Apess spelled his name as *Apes* in his early publications, he changed it to *Apess* in the second editon of *The Eulogy on King Philip* (1836) published in 1837 and in the second edition of *The Experience of Five* *Christian Indians* (1835). In legal documents of 1836 and 1837, his name also appears as *Apess*. His parents and other family members are alluded to as *Apes*. See Barry O'Connell, *On Our Own Ground*, xiv.

pranks and strong will resulted in his being transferred to a series of masters. During his service to his last master, Apess was converted to Methodism in March 1813, at age fifteen. Forbidden by his master to attend any more Methodist revivals, Apess ran away. He subsequently enlisted in the army during the War of 1812 and served during the 1814 invasions of Canada and defense of Plattsburgh, New York. In 1817 Apess returned to Connecticut, where he was reunited with Pequot relatives. He began serving as a lay preacher to mixed audiences although his preaching was opposed by both his father and the local Methodist circuit rider, who forbade him to preach. In 1821 Apess married Mary Wood, a woman "nearly the same color as himself" (*A Son of the Forest*, 98), and supported his wife and growing family with a variety of jobs. In 1829, after moving to Providence, Rhode Island, he was ordained as a minister by the Methodist Society.

Apess's *A Son of the Forest* (1829) is the first published autobiography written by an Indian. It appeared during the controversy over the Indian Removal Act (1830), which authorized the federal government to remove Indians from lands east of the Mississippi to Indian Territory and other areas deemed suitable. The autobiography is a testament both to the essential humanity of Indian people and to their potential for adapting to white concepts of civilization. *A Son of the Forest* follows the basic structure of the spiritual confession, popular at that time. Apess's account of his experiences is especially interesting because he was raised primarily by whites. He describes how he was terrified of his own people because whites filled him with stereotypical stories about Indian cruelty but never told him how cruelly they treated Indians.

Apess published a briefer life history in *The Experiences of Five Christian Indians of the Pequod Tribe* (1833). Probably written before *A Son of the Forest*, this account is more critical of whites than the autobiography; the first edition of this book contained the essay "An Indian's Looking-Glass for the White Man." This essay illustrates the themes present in Apess's work and the forceful style that made him a persuasive speaker. Apess contrasts whites' savage treatment of nonwhites with their professed Christianity—a frequent theme in nineteenth-century slave narratives and life histories of Indian converts. Here, as in *A Son of the Forest*, Apess blames whites for the alcoholism that has decimated Indian families. His criticism of Indian agents is another theme common in Indian life histories. Apess effectively focuses the essay on the equality of people of color with whites. This concept of equality of all people under God made Christianity very appealing to Indian converts and to slaves.

Apess's last two books grew out of his commitment to the fight for Indian rights. He describes the Mashpee struggle to retain self-government in *Indian Nullification of the Unconstitutional Laws of Massachusetts, Relative to the Marshpee [sic] Tribe* (1835), one of the most powerful pieces of Indian protest literature of the first half of the nineteenth century. A mixture of Indian, white, and black, the Mashpees were subjected to considerable white prejudice. Apess's contact with them and their fight for civil and political rights turned him into a dedicated social reformer. Apess organized a council to draw up grievances, moved his family to Mashpee, became a spokesman for the tribe, and publicized their case in the Boston press. By 1834 his efforts had gained success, as evidenced by the large audience that heard his Boston speech on the subject.

The same year William Lloyd Garrison, the abolitionist editor, took up the cause of the Mashpee in *The Liberator*. Apess's efforts helped the Mashpees regain their rights, one of the few such Indian victories in the 1830s. However, the nation's attention was increasingly drawn away from the plight of the American Indian to the debate over the abolition of slavery. To remind whites of what New England Indians had endured, Apess wrote his final work, the eloquent *Eulogy on King Philip* (1836). Originally delivered as a series of lectures at the Odeon in Boston, the *Eulogy on King Philip* is a study of white-Indian relations in seventeenth- and eighteenth-century New England. After this work was published, Apess disappeared from public view, and the details of his later life are unknown.

A. LaVonne Brown Ruoff
University of Illinois at Chicago

PRIMARY WORK

On Our Own Ground: The Complete Writings of William Apess, a Pequot, ed. Barry O'Connell, 1992.

An Indian's Looking-Glass for the White Man

Having a desire to place a few things before my fellow creatures who are travelling with me to the grave, and to that God who is the maker and preserver both of the white man and the Indian, whose abilities are the same, and who are to be judged by one God, who will show no favor to outward appearances, but will judge righteousness. Now I ask if degradation has not been heaped long enough upon the Indians? And if so, can there not be a compromise; is it right to hold and promote prejudices? If not, why not put them all away? I mean here amongst those who are civilized. It may be that many are ignorant of the situation of many of my brethren within the limits of New England. Let me for a few moments turn your attention to the reservations in the different states of New England, and, with but few exceptions, we shall find them as follows: The most mean, abject, miserable race of beings in the world—a complete place of prodigality and prostitution.

Let a gentleman and lady, of integrity and respectability visit these places, and they would be surprised; as they wandered from one hut to the other they would view with the females who are left alone, children half starved, and some almost as naked as they came into the world. And it is a fact that I have seen them as much so—while the females are left without protection, and are seduced by white men, and are finally left to be common prostitutes for them, and to be destroyed by that burning, fiery curse, that has swept millions, both of red and white men, into the grave with sorrow and disgrace—Rum. One reason why they are left so is, because their most sensible and active men are absent at sea. Another reason is, because they are made to believe they are minors and have not the abilities given them from God, to take care of themselves, without it is to see to a few little articles, such as baskets and brooms. Their land is in common stock, and they have nothing to make them enterprising.

Another reason is because those men who are Agents, many of them are unfaithful, and care not whether the Indians live or die; they are much imposed upon by their neighbors who have no principle. They would think it no crime to go upon Indian lands and cut and carry off their most valuable timber, or any thing else they chose; and I doubt not but they think it clear gain. Another reason is because they have no education to take care of themselves; if they had, I would risk them to take care of their property.

Now I will ask, if the Indians are not called the most ingenious people amongst us? And are they not said to be men of talents? And I would ask, could there be a more efficient way to distress and murder them by inches than the way they have taken? And there is no people in the world but who may be destroyed in the same way. Now if these people are what they are held up in our view to be, I would take the liberty to ask why they are not brought forward and pains taken to educate them? to give them all a common education, and those of the brightest and first-rate talents put forward and held up to office. Perhaps some unholy, unprincipled men would cry out, the skin was not good enough; but stop friends—I am not talking about the skin, but about principles. I would ask if there cannot be as good feelings and principles under a red skin as there can be under a white? And let me ask, is it not on the account of a bad principle, that we who are red children have had to suffer so much as we have? And let me ask, did not this bad principle proceed from the whites or their forefathers? And I would ask, is it worth while to nourish it any longer? If not, then let us have a change; although some men no doubt will spout their corrupt principles against it, that are in the halls of legislation and elsewhere. But I presume this kind of talk will seem surprising and horrible. I do not see why it should so long as they (the whites) say that they think as much of us as they do of themselves.

This I have heard repeatedly, from the most respectable gentlemen and ladies—and having heard so much precept, I should now wish to see the example. And I would ask who has a better right to look for these things than the naturalist himself—the candid man would say none.

I know that many say that they are willing, perhaps the majority of the people, that we should enjoy our rights and privileges as they do. If so, I would ask why are not we protected in our persons and property throughout the Union? Is it not because there reigns in the breast of many who are leaders, a most unrighteous, unbecoming and impure black principle, and as corrupt and unholy as it can be—while these very same unfeeling, self-esteemed characters pretend to take the skin as a pretext to keep us from our unalienable and lawful rights? I would ask you if you would like to be disfranchised from all your rights, merely because your skin is white, and for no other crime? I'll venture to say, these very characters who hold the skin to be such a barrier in the way, would be the first to cry out, injustice! awful injustice!

But, reader, I acknowledge that this is a confused world, and I am not seeking for office; but merely placing before you the black inconsistency that you place before me—which is ten times blacker than any skin that you will find in the Universe. And now let me exhort you to do away that principle, as it appears ten times worse in the sight of God and candid men, than skins of color—more disgraceful than all the skins that Jehovah ever made. If black or red skins, or any other skin of color is disgraceful to God, it appears that he has disgraced himself a great deal—for he has made fifteen colored people to one white, and placed them here upon this earth.

Now let me ask you, white man, if it is a disgrace for to eat, drink and sleep with the image of God, or sit, or walk and talk with them? Or have you the folly to think that the white man, being one in fifteen or sixteen, are the only beloved images of God? Assemble all nations together in your imagination, and then let the whites be seated amongst them, and then let us look for the whites, and I doubt not it would be hard finding them; for to the rest of the nations, they are still but a handful. Now suppose these skins were put together, and each skin had its national crimes written upon it—which skin do you think would have the greatest? I will ask one question more. Can you charge the Indians with robbing a nation almost of their whole Continent, and murdering their women and children, and then depriving the remainder of their lawful rights, that nature and God require them to have? And to cap the climax, rob another nation to till their grounds, and welter out their days under the lash with hunger and fatigue under the scorching rays of a burning sun? I should look at all the skins, and I know that when I cast my eye upon that white skin, and if I saw those crimes written upon it, I should enter my protest against it immediately, and cleave to that which is more honorable. And I can tell you that I am satisfied with the manner of my creation, fully—whether others are or not.

But we will strive to penetrate more fully into the conduct of those who profess to have pure principles, and who tell us to follow Jesus Christ and imitate him and have his Spirit. Let us see if they come any where near him and his ancient disciples. The first thing we are to look at, are his precepts, of which we will mention a few. "Thou shalt love the Lord thy God with all thy heart, with all thy soul, with all thy mind, and with all thy strength." The second is like unto it. "Thou shalt love thy neighbor as thyself." On these two precepts hang all the law and the prophets.—Matt. xxii. 37, 38, 39, 40. "By this shall all men know that they are my disciples, if ye have love one to another"—John xiii. 35. Our Lord left this special command with his followers, that they should love one another.

Again, John in his Epistles says, "He who loveth God, loveth his brother also"—iv. 21. "Let us not love in word but in deed"—iii. 18. "Let your love be without dissimulation. See that ye love one another with a pure heart fervently"—1. Peter, viii. 22. "If any man say, I love God, and hateth his brother, he is a liar"—John iv. 20. "Whosoever hateth his brother is a murderer, and no murderer hath eternal life abiding in him." The first thing that takes our attention, is the saying of Jesus, "Thou shalt love," &c. The first question I would ask my brethren in the ministry, as well as that of the membership, What is love, or its effects? Now if they who teach are not essentially affected with pure love, the love of God, how can they teach as they ought? Again, the holy teachers of old said, "Now if any man have not the spirit of Christ, he is none of his"—Rom. viii. 9. Now my brethren in the ministry, let me ask you a few sincere questions. Did you ever hear or read of Christ teaching his disciples that they ought to despise one because his skin was different from theirs? Jesus Christ being a Jew, and those of his Apostles certainly were not whites,—and did not he who completed the plan of salvation complete it for the whites as well as for the Jews, and others? And were not the whites the most degraded people on the earth at that time, and none were more so; for they sacrificed their children to dumb idols! And did not St. Paul labor more abundantly for building up a christian nation amongst you than any of the Apostles. And you know as well as I that you are not indebted to a principle beneath a white skin for your religious services, but to a colored one.

What then is the matter now; is not religion the same now under a colored skin as it ever was? If so I would ask why is not a man of color respected; you may say as many say, we have white men enough. But was this the spirit of Christ and his Apostles? If it had been, there would not have been one white preacher in the world—for Jesus Christ never would have imparted his grace or word to them, for he could forever have withheld it from them. But we find that Jesus Christ and his Apostles never looked at the outward appearances. Jesus in particular looked at the hearts, and his Apostles through him being discerners of the spirit, looked at their fruit without any regard to the skin, color or nation; as St. Paul himself speaks, "Where there is neither Greek nor Jew, circumcision nor uncircumcision, Barbarian nor Scythian, bond nor free—but Christ is all and in all."[1] If you can find a spirit like Jesus Christ and his Apostles prevailing now in any of the white congregations, I should like to know it. I ask, is it not the case that every body that is not white is treated with contempt and counted as barbarians? And I ask if the word of God justifies the white man in so doing? When the prophets prophesied, of whom did they speak? When they spoke of heathens, was it not the whites and others who were counted Gentiles? And I ask if all nations with the exception of the Jews were not counted heathens? and according to the writings of some, it could not mean the Indians, for they are counted Jews. And now I would ask, why is all this distinction made among these christian societies? I would ask what is all this ado about Missionary Societies, if it be not to christianize those who are not christians? And what is it for? To degrade them worse, to bring them into society where they must welter out their days in disgrace merely because their skin is of a different complexion. What folly it is to try to make the state of human society worse than it is. How astonished some may be at this—but let me ask, is it not so? Let me refer you to the churches only. And my brethren, is there any agreement? Do brethren and

[1]Colossians 3:11.

sisters love one another?—Do they not rather hate one another? Outward forms and ceremonies, the lusts of the flesh, the lusts of the eye and pride of life is of more value to many professors, than the love of God shed abroad in their hearts, or an attachment to his altar, to his ordinances or to his children. But you may ask who are the children of God? perhaps you may say none but white. If so, the word of the Lord is not true.

I will refer you to St. Peter's precepts—Acts 10. "God is no respecter of persons"—&c. Now if this is the case, my white brother, what better are you than God? And if no better, why do you profess his gospel and to have his spirit, act so contrary to it? Let me ask why the men of a different skin are so dispised, why are not they educated and placed in your pulpits? I ask if his services well performed are not as good as if a white man performed them? I ask if a marriage or a funeral ceremony, or the ordinance of the Lord's house would not be as acceptable in the sight of God as though he was white? And if so, why is it not to you? I ask again, why is it not as acceptable to have men to exercise their office in one place as well as in another? Perhaps you will say that if we admit you to all of these privileges you will want more. I expect that I can guess what that is—Why, say you, there would be intermarriages. How that would be I am not able to say— and if it should be, it would be nothing strange or new to me; for I can assure you that I know a great many that have intermarried, both of the whites and the Indians—and many are their sons and daughters—and people too of the first respectability. And I could point to some in the famous city of Boston and elsewhere. You may now look at the disgraceful act in the statute law passed by the Legislature of Massachusetts, and behold the fifty pound fine levied upon any Clergyman or Justice of the Peace that dare to encourage the laws of God and nature by a legitimate union in holy wedlock between the Indians and whites. I would ask how this looks to your law makers. I would ask if this corresponds with your sayings—that you think as much of the Indians as you do of the whites. I do not wonder that you blush many of you while you read; for many have broken the ill-fated laws made by man to hedge up the laws of God and nature. I would ask if they who have made the law have not broken it—but there is no other state in New England that has this law but Massachusetts; and I think as many of you do not, that you have done yourselves no credit.

But as I am not looking for a wife, having one of the finest cast, as you no doubt would understand while you read her experience and travail of soul in the way to heaven, you will see that it is not my object. And if I had none, I should not want any one to take my right from me and choose a wife for me; for I think that I or any of my brethren have a right to choose a wife for themselves as well as the whites—and as the whites have taken the liberty to choose my brethren, the Indians, hundreds and thousands of them as partners in life, I believe the Indians have as much right to choose their partners amongst the whites if they wish. I would ask you if you can see any thing inconsistent in your conduct and talk about the Indians? And if you do, I hope you will try to become more consistent. Now if the Lord

Jesus Christ, who is counted by all to be a Jew, and it is well known that the Jews are a colored people, especially those living in the East, where Christ was born—and if he should appear amongst us, would he not be shut out of doors by many, very quickly? and by those too, who profess religion?

By what you read, you may learn how deep your principles are. I should say they were skin deep. I should not wonder if some of the most selfish and ignorant would spout a charge of their principles now and then at me. But I would ask, how are you to love your neighbors as yourself? Is it to cheat them? is it to wrong them in any thing? Now to cheat them out of any of their rights is robbery. And I ask, can you deny that you are not robbing the Indians daily, and many others? But at last you may think I am what is called a hard and uncharitable man. But not so. I believe there are many who would not hesitate to advocate our cause; and those too who are men of fame and respectability—as well as ladies of honor and virtue. There is a Webster, an Everett, and a Wirt, and many others who are distinguished characters—besides an host of my fellow citizens, who advocate our cause daily. And how I congratulate such noble spirits—how they are to be prized and valued; for they are well calculated to promote the happiness of mankind. They well know that man was made for society, and not for hissing stocks and outcasts. And when such a principle as this lies within the hearts of men, how much it is like its God—and how it honors its Maker—and how it imitates the feelings of the good Samaritan, that had his wounds bound up, who had been among thieves and robbers.

Do not get tired, ye noble-hearted—only think how many poor Indians want their wounds done up daily; the Lord will reward you, and pray you stop not till this tree of distinction shall be levelled to the earth, and the mantle of prejudice torn from every American heart—then shall peace pervade the Union.

1833

from **Eulogy on King Philip**

I do not arise to spread before you the fame of a noted warrior, whose natural abilities shone like those of the great and mighty Philip of Greece, or of Alexander the Great, or like those of Washington—whose virtues and patriotism are engraven on the hearts of my audience. Neither do I approve of war as being the best method of bowing to the haughty tyrant, Man, and civilizing the world. No, far from me be such a thought. But it is to bring before you beings made by the God of Nature, and in whose hearts and heads he has planted sympathies that shall live forever in the memory of the world, whose brilliant talents shone in the display of natural things, so that the most cultivated, whose powers shown with equal luster, were not able to prepare mantles to cover the burning elements of an uncivilized world. What, then? Shall we cease to mention the mighty of the earth, the noble work of God?

Yet those purer virtues remain untold. Those noble traits that marked the wild man's course lie buried in the shades of night; and who shall stand? I appeal to the lovers of liberty. But those few remaining descendants who now remain as the monument of the cruelty of those who came to improve our race and correct our errors—and as the immortal Washington lives endeared and engraven on the hearts of every white in America, never to be forgotten in time—even such is the immortal Philip honored, as held in memory by the degraded but yet grateful descendants who appreciate his character; so will every patriot, especially in this enlightened age, respect the rude yet all-accomplished son of the forest, that died a martyr to his cause, though unsuccessful, yet as glorious as the *American* Revolution. Where, then, shall we place the hero of the wilderness?

Justice and humanity for the remaining few prompt me to vindicate the character of him who yet lives in their hearts and, if possible, melt the prejudice that exists in the hearts of those who are in the possession of his soil, and only by the right of conquest—is the aim of him who proudly tells you, the blood of a denominated savage runs in his veins. It is, however, true that there are many who are said to be honorable warriors, who, in the wisdom of their civilized legislation, think it no crime to wreak their vengeance upon whole nations and communities, until the fields are covered with blood and the rivers turned into purple fountains, while groans, like distant thunder, are heard from the wounded and the tens of thousands of the dying, leaving helpless families depending on their cares and sympathies for life; while a loud response is heard floating through the air from the ten thousand Indian children and orphans, who are left to mourn the honorable acts of a few—civilized men.

Now, if we have common sense and ability to allow the difference between the civilized and the uncivilized, we cannot but see that one mode of warfare is as just as the other; for while one is sanctioned by authority of the enlightened and cultivated men, the other is an agreement according to the pure laws of nature, growing out of natural consequences; for nature always has her defense for every beast of the field; even the reptiles of the earth and the fishes of the sea have their weapons of war. But though frail man was made for a nobler purpose—to live, to love, and adore his God, and do good to his brother—for this reason, and this alone, the God of heaven prepared ways and means to blast anger, man's destroyer, and cause the Prince of Peace to rule, that man might swell those blessed notes. My image is of God; I am not a beast.

But as all men are governed by animal passions who are void of the true principles of God, whether cultivated or uncultivated, we shall now lay before you the true character of Philip, in relation to those hostilities between himself and the whites; and in so doing, permit me to be plain and candid.

The first inquiry is: Who is Philip? He was the descendant of one of the most celebrated chiefs in the known world, for peace and universal benevolence toward all men;[1] for injuries upon injuries, and the most daring robberies and barbarous deeds of death that were ever committed by the

---

[1]Philip's father was the Pokanoket sachem Massasoit who, as the rest of the *Eulogy* makes clear, became the Pilgrims' crucial ally.

American Pilgrims, were with patience and resignation borne, in a manner that would do justice to any Christian nation or being in the world—especially when we realize that it was voluntary suffering on the part of the good old chief. His country extensive, his men numerous, so as the wilderness was enlivened by them, say, a thousand to one of the white men, and they also sick and feeble—where, then, shall we find one nation submitting so tamely to another, with such a host at their command? For injuries of much less magnitude have the people called Christians slain their brethren, till they could sing, like Samson: With a jawbone of an ass have we slain our thousands and laid them in heaps. It will be well for us to lay those deeds and depredations committed by whites upon Indians before the civilized world, and then they can judge for themselves.

It appears from history that, in 1614, "There came one Henry Harly unto me, bringing with him a native of the Island of Capawick [Chappaquiddick], a place at the south of Cape Cod, whose name was Epenuel. This man was taken upon the main by force, with some twenty-nine others," very probably good old Massasoit's men (see Harlow's Voyage, 1611), "by a ship, and carried to London, and from thence to be sold for slaves among the Spaniards; but the Indians being too shrewd, or, as they say, unapt for their use, they refused to traffic in Indians' blood and bones." This inhuman act of the whites caused the Indians to be jealous forever afterward, which the white man acknowledges upon the first pages of the history of his country. (See Drake's *History of the Indians*, 7.)

How inhuman it was in those wretches, to come into a country where nature shone in beauty, spreading her wings over the vast continent, sheltering beneath her shades those natural sons of an Almighty Being, that shone in grandeur and luster like the stars of the first magnitude in the heavenly world; whose virtues far surpassed their more enlightened foes, notwithstanding their pretended zeal for religion and virtue. How they could go to work to enslave a free people and call it religion is beyond the power of my imagination and outstrips the revelation of God's word. O thou pretended hypocritical Christian, whoever thou art, to say it was the design of God that we should murder and slay one another because we have the power. Power was not given us to abuse each other, but a mere power delegated to us by the King of heaven, a weapon of defense against error and evil; and when abused, it will turn to our destruction. Mark, then, the history of nations throughout the world.

But notwithstanding the transgression of this power to destroy the Indians at their first discovery, yet it does appear that the Indians had a wish to be friendly. When the Pilgrims came among them (Iyanough's men),[2] there appeared an old woman, breaking out in solemn lamentations, declaring one Captain Hunt had carried off three of her children, and they would never return here. The Pilgrims replied that they were bad and wicked men, but

[2]Iyanough of Cummaquid was one of the sachems who were counted as allies of the Plymouth colony until Miles Standish lashed out against a "conspiracy" of Massachusetts leaders in 1623, killing seven. From Salisbury, *Manitou and Providence*, 130–134.

they were going to do better and would never injure them at all. And, to pay the poor mother, gave her a few brass trinkets, to atone for her three sons and appease her present feelings, a woman nearly one hundred years of age. O white woman! What would you think if some foreign nation, unknown to you, should come and carry away from you three lovely children, whom you had dandled on the knee, and at some future time you should behold them and break forth in sorrow, with your heart broken, and merely ask, "Sirs, where are my little ones?" and some one should reply: "It was passion, great passion." What would you think of them? Should you not think they were beings made more like rocks than men? Yet these same men came to these Indians for support and acknowledge themselves that no people could be used better than they were; that their treatment would do honor to any nation; that their provisions were in abundance; that they gave them venison and sold them many hogsheads of corn to fill their stores, besides beans. This was in the year 1622. Had it not been for this humane act of the Indians, every white man would have been swept from the New England colonies. In their sickness, too, the Indians were as tender to them as to their own children; and for all this they were denounced as savages by those who had received all the acts of kindness they possibly could show them. After these social acts of the Indians toward those who were suffering, and those of their countrymen, who well knew the care their brethren had received by them—how were the Indians treated before that? Oh, hear! In the following manner, and their own words we presume, they will not deny.

December (O.S.)[3] 1620, the Pilgrims landed at Plymouth, and without asking liberty from anyone they possessed themselves of a portion of the country, and built themselves houses, and then made a treaty, and commanded them to accede to it. This, if now done, it would be called an insult and every white man would be called to go out and act the part of a patriot, to defend their country's rights; and if every intruder were butchered, it would be sung upon every hilltop in the Union that victory and patriotism was the order of the day....

But we will proceed to show another inhuman act. The whites robbed the Indian graves, and their corn, about the year 1632, which caused Chicataubut to be displeased, who was chief, and also a son to the woman that was dead.[4] And according to the Indian custom, it was a righteous act to be avenged of the dead. Accordingly, he called all his men together and addressed them thus: "When last the glorious light of the sky was underneath this globe, and birds grew silent, I began to settle, as is my custom, to take repose. Before my eyes were fast closed, methought I saw a vision, at which my spirit was much troubled. A spirit cried aloud, 'Behold, my son, whom I have cherished, see the paps that gave thee suck, the hands that clasped three warm, and fed thee oft. Can thou forget to take revenge of those wild people that have my monument defaced in a despiteful manner,

[3]Old Style. Dates were ten days earlier than they would be currently.

[4]A Massachusett who led a band of fifty to sixty followers.

disdaining our ancient antiquities and honorable customs? See, now, the sachem's grave lies, like unto the common people of ignoble race, defaced. Thy mother doth complain and implores thy aid against these thievish people, now come hither. If this be suffered, I shall not rest quiet within my everlasting habitation.' " War was the result. And where is there a people in the world that would see their friends robbed of their common property, their nearest and dearest friends; robbed, after their last respects to them? I appeal to you, who value your friends and affectionate mothers, if you would have robbed them of their fine marble, and your storehouses broken open, without calling those to account who did it. I trust not; and if another nation should come to these regions and begin to rob and plunder all that came in their way, would not the orators of the day be called to address the people and arouse them to war for such insults? And, for all this, would they not be called Christians and patriots? Yes, it would be rung from Georgia to Maine, from the ocean to the lakes, what fine men and Christians there were in the land. But when a few red children attempt to defend their rights, they are condemned as savages by those, if possible, who have indulged in wrongs more cruel than the Indians....

But we have more to present; and that is the violation of a treaty that the Pilgrims proposed for the Indians to subscribe to, and they the first to break it. The Pilgrims promised to deliver up every transgressor of the Indian treaty to them, to be punished according to their laws, and the Indians were to do likewise. Now it appears that an Indian had committed treason by conspiring against the king's life, which is punishable with death; and Massasoit makes demand for the transgressor, and the Pilgrims refuse to give him up, although by their oath of alliance they had promised to do so.[5] Their reasons were, he was beneficial to them. This shows how grateful they were to their former safeguard and ancient protector. Now, who would have blamed this venerable old chief if he had declared war at once and swept the whole colonies away? It was certainly in his power to do it, if he pleased; but no, he forbore and forgave the whites. But where is there a people, called civilized, that would do it? We presume, none; and we doubt not but the Pilgrims would have exerted all their powers to be avenged and to appease their ungodly passions. But it will be seen that this good old chief exercised more Christian forbearance than any of the governors of that age or since. It might well be said he was a pattern for the Christians themselves; but by the Pilgrims he is denounced, as being a savage.

It does not appear that Massasoit or his sons were respected because they were human beings but because they feared him; and we are led to believe that, if it had been in the power of the Pilgrims, they would have butchered them out and out, notwithstanding all the piety they professed.

---

[5]This passage refers to Squanto, who plotted against Massasoit but was protected by the Pilgrims, who needed his aid.

Only look for a few moments at the abuses the son of Massasoit received. Alexander being sent for with armed men, and while he and his men were breaking their fast in the morning, they were taken immediately away, by order of the governor, without the least provocation but merely through suspicion.[6] Alexander and his men saw them and might have prevented it but did not, saying the governor had no occasion to treat him in this manner; and the heartless wretch informed him that he would murder him upon the spot if he did not go with him, presenting a sword at his breast; and had it not been for one of his men he would have yielded himself up upon the spot. Alexander was a man of strong passion and of a firm mind; and this insulting treatment of him caused him to fall sick of a fever, so that he never recovered. Some of the Indians were suspicious that he was poisoned to death. He died in the year 1662. "After him," says that eminent divine, Dr. Mather,[7] "there rose up one Philip, of cursed memory." Perhaps if the Doctor was present, he would find that the memory of Philip was as far before his, in the view of sound, judicious men, as the sun is before the stars at noonday. But we might suppose that men like Dr. Mather, so well versed in Scripture, would have known his work better than to have spoken evil of anyone, or have cursed any of God's works. He ought to have known that God did not make his red children for him to curse; but if he wanted them cursed, he could have done it himself. But, on the contrary, his suffering Master commanded him to love his enemies and to pray for his persecutors, and to do unto others as he would that men should do unto him. Now, we wonder if the sons of the Pilgrims would like to have us, poor Indians, come out and curse the Doctor, and all their sons, as we have been by many of them. And suppose that, in some future day, our children should repay all these wrongs, would it not be doing as we, poor Indians, have been done to? But we sincerely hope there is more humanity in us than that....

The history of New England writers say that our tribes were large and respectable. How, then, could it be otherwise, but their safety rested in the hands of friendly Indians? In 1647, the Pilgrims speak of large and respectable tribes. But let us trace them for a few moments. How have they been destroyed? Is it by fair means? No. How then? By hypocritical proceedings, by being duped and flattered; flattered by informing the Indians that their God was a going to speak to them, and then place them before the cannon's mouth in a line, and then putting the match to it and kill thousands of them. We might suppose that meek Christians had better gods and weapons than cannon; weapons that were not carnal, but mighty through God, to the pulling down of strongholds. These are the weapons that modern Christians profess to have; and if the Pilgrims did not have them, they ought not to be honored as such. But let us again review their weapons to civilize the

---

[6]Alexander was the eldest son of Massasoit and Philip's brother. Apess's account captures what seems actually to have occurred.

[7]This is Increase Mather, Cotton Mather's father. Both wrote virulently against Indians, but it was Increase Mather who wrote most at length on King Philip's War.

nations of this soil. What were they? Rum and powder and ball, together with all the diseases, such as the smallpox and every other disease imaginable, and in this way sweep off thousands and tens of thousands. And then it has been said that these men who were free from these things, that they could not live among civilized people. We wonder how a virtuous people could live in a sink of diseases, a people who had never been used to them.

And who is to account for those destructions upon innocent families and helpless children? It was said by some of the New England writers that living babes were found at the breast of their dead mothers. What an awful sight! And to think, too, that these diseases were carried among them on purpose to destroy them. Let the children of the Pilgrims blush, while the son of the forest drops a tear and groans over the fate of his murdered and departed fathers. He would say to the sons of the Pilgrims (as Job said about his birthday), let the day be dark, the 22nd day of December 1622;[8] let it be forgotten in your celebration, in your speeches, and by the burying of the rock that your fathers first put their foot upon. For be it remembered, although the Gospel is said to be glad tidings to all people, yet we poor Indians never have found those who brought it as messengers of mercy, but contrawise. We say, therefore, let every man of color wrap himself in mourning, for the 22nd of December and the 4th of July are days of mourning and not of joy. (I would here say, there is an error in my book; it speaks of the 25th of December, but it should be the 22nd. See *Indian Nullification*.) Let them rather fast and pray to the great Spirit, the Indian's God, who deals out mercy to his red children, and not destruction.

O Christians, can you answer for those beings that have been destroyed by your hostilities, and beings too that lie endeared to God as yourselves, his Son being their Savior as well as yours, and alike to all men? And will you presume to say that you are executing the judgments of God by so doing, or as many really are approving the works of their fathers to be genuine, as it is certain that every time they celebrate the day of the Pilgrims they do? Although in words they deny it, yet in the works they approve of the iniquities of their fathers. And as the seed of iniquity and prejudice was sown in that day, so it still remains; and there is a deep-rooted popular opinion in the hearts of many that Indians were made, etc., on purpose for destruction, to be driven out by white Christians, and they to take their places; and that God had decreed it from all eternity. If such theologians would only study the works of nature more, they would understand the purposes of good better than they do: that the favor of the Almighty was good and holy, and all his nobler works were made to adorn his image, by being his grateful servants and admiring each other as angels, and not, as they say, to drive and devour each other....

But having laid a mass of history and exposition before you, the purpose of which is to show that Philip and all the Indians generally felt indignantly

---

[8]Apess, as he makes clear later in the speech, takes December 22 as the day the Pilgrims landed and stepped on Plymouth Rock. They in fact arrived in Massachusetts in December 1620.

toward whites, whereby they were more easily allied together by Philip, their king and emperor, we come to notice more particularly his history. As to His Majesty, King Philip, it was certain that his honor was put to the test, and it was certainly to be tried, even at the loss of his life and country. It is a matter of uncertainty about his age; but his birthplace was at Mount Hope, Rhode Island, where Massasoit, his father, lived till 1656, and died, as also his brother, Alexander, by the governor's ill-treating him (that is, Winthrop), which caused his death, as before mentioned, in 1662; after which, the kingdom fell into the hands of Philip, the greatest man that ever lived upon the American shores. Soon after his coming to the throne, it appears he began to be noticed, though, prior to this, it appears that he was not forward in the councils of war or peace. When he came into office it appears that he knew there was great responsibility resting upon himself and country, that it was likely to be ruined by those rude intruders around him, though he appears friendly and is willing to sell them lands for almost nothing....

But it appears that the Pilgrims could not be contented with what they had done, but they must send an Indian, and a traitor, to preach to Philip and his men, in order to convert him and his people to Christianity. The preacher's name was Sassamon. I would appeal to this audience: Is it not certain that the Plymouth people strove to pick a quarrel with Philip and his men? What could have been more insulting than to send a man to them who was false, and looked upon as such? For it is most certain that a traitor was above all others, the more to be detested than any other. And not only so, it was the laws of the Indians that such a man must die, that he had forfeited his life; and when he made his appearance among them, Philip would have killed him upon the spot if his council had not persuaded him not to. But it appears that in March 1674 one of Philip's men killed him and placed him beneath the ice in a certain pond near Plymouth, doubtless by the order of Philip. After this, search was made for him, and they found there a certain Indian, by the name of Patuckson; Tobias, also his son, were apprehended and tried. Tobias was one of Philip's counselors, as it appears from the records that the trial did not end here, that it was put over, and that two of the Indians entered into bonds for $400, for the appearance of Tobias at the June term, for which a mortgage of land was taken to that amount for his safe return. June having arrived, three instead of one are arraigned. There was no one but Tobias suspected at the previous court. Now two others are arraigned, tried, condemned, and executed (making three in all) in June the 8th, 1675, by hanging and shooting. It does not appear that any more than one was guilty, and it was said that he was known to acknowledge it; but the other two persisted in their innocence to the last.

This murder of the preacher brought on the war a year sooner than it was anticipated by Philip. But this so exasperated King Philip that from that day he studied to be revenged of the Pilgrims, judging that his white intruders had nothing to do in punishing his people for any crime and that it was in violation of treaties of ancient date. But when we look at this, how bold and how daring it was to Philip, as though they would bid defiance to him, and all his authority; we do not wonder at his exasperation. When the governor finds that His Majesty was displeased, he then sends messengers to him and wishes to know why he would make war upon him (as if he had done all right), and wished to enter into a new treaty with him. The king answered them thus: "Your governor is but a subject of King Charles of England; I shall not treat with a subject; I shall treat of peace only with a king, my brother; when he comes, I am ready."

This answer of Philip's to the messengers is worthy of note throughout the world. And never could a prince answer with more dignity in regard to his official authority than he did—disdaining the idea of placing himself upon a par of the minor subjects of a king; letting them know, at the same time, that he felt his independence more than they thought he did. And indeed it was time for him to wake up, for now the subjects of King Charles had taken one of his counselors and killed him, and he could no longer trust them. Until the execution of these three Indians, supposed to be the murderers of Sassamon, no hostility was committed by Philip or his warriors. About the time of their trial, he was said to be marching his men up and down the country in arms; but when it was known, he could no longer restrain his young men, who, upon the 24th of June [1675], provoked the people of Swansea by killing their cattle and other injuries, which was a signal to commence the war, and what they had desired, as a superstitious notion prevailed among the Indians that whoever fired the first gun of either party would be conquered, doubtless a notion they had received from the Pilgrims. It was upon a fast day, too, when the first gun was fired; and as the people were returning from church, they were fired upon by the Indians, when several of them were killed. It is not supposed that Philip directed this attack but was opposed to it. Though it is not doubted that he meant to be revenged upon his enemies; for during some time he had been cementing his countrymen together, as it appears that he had sent to all the disaffected tribes, who also had watched the movements of the comers from the New World and were as dissatisfied as Philip himself was with their proceedings.

> Now around the council fires they met,
> The young nobles for to greet;
> Their tales of woe and sorrows to relate,
> About the Pilgrims, their wretched foes.

> And while their fires were blazing high,
> Their king and Emperor to greet;
> His voice like lightning fires their hearts,
> To stand the test or die.

> See those Pilgrims from the world unknown,
> No love for Indians do know:
> Although our fathers fed them well
> With venison rich, of precious kinds.

No gratitude to Indians now is shown,
From people saved by them alone;
All gratitude that poor Indian do know,
Is, we are robbed of all our rights.

At this council it appears that Philip made the following speech to his chiefs, counselors, and warriors:

Brothers, you see this vast country before us, which the Great Spirit gave to our fathers and us; you see the buffalo and deer that now are our support. Brothers, you see these little ones, our wives and children, who are looking to us for food and raiment; and you now see the foe before you, that they have grown insolent and bold; that all our ancient customs are disregarded; the treaties made by our fathers and us are broken, and all of us insulted; our council fires disregarded, and all the ancient customs of our fathers; our brothers murdered before our eyes, and their spirits cry to us for revenge. Brothers, these people from the unknown world will cut down our groves, spoil our hunting and planting grounds, and drive us and our children from the graves of our fathers, and our council fires, and enslave our women and children.

This famous speech of Philip was calculated to arouse them to arms, to do the best they could in protecting and defending their rights. The blow had now been struck, the die was cast, and nothing but blood and carnage was before them. And we find Philip as active as the wind, as dexterous as a giant, firm as the pillows of heaven, and fierce as a lion, a powerful foe to contend with indeed, and as swift as an eagle, gathering together his forces to prepare them for the battle. And as it would swell our address too full to mention all the tribes in Philip's train of warriors, suffice it to say that from six to seven were with him at different times. When he begins the war, he goes forward and musters about 500 of his men and arms them complete, and about 900 of the other, making in all about fourteen hundred warriors when he commenced. It must be recollected that this war was legally declared by Philip, so that the colonies had a fair warning. It was no savage war of surprise, as some suppose, but one sorely provoked by the Pilgrims themselves. But when Philip and his men fought as they were accustomed to do and according to their mode of war, it was more than what could be expected. But we hear no particular acts of cruelty committed by Philip during the siege. But we find more manly nobility in him than we do in all the head Pilgrims put together, as we shall see during this quarrel between them. Philip's young men were eager to do exploits and to lead captive their haughty lords. It does appear that every Indian heart had been lighted up at the council fires, at Philip's speech, and that the forest was literally alive with this injured race. And now town after town fell before them. The Pilgrims with their forces were marching ever in one direction, while Philip and his forces were marching in another, burning all before them, until Middleborough, Taunton, and Dartmouth were laid in ruins and forsaken by its inhabitants.

The Pilgrims determined to break down Philip's power, if possible, with the Narragansetts: Thus they raised an army of 1,500 strong, to go against them and destroy them if possible. In this, Massachusetts, Plymouth, and Connecticut all join in severally, to crush Philip. Accordingly, in December, in 1675, the Pilgrims set forward to destroy them. Preceding their march, Philip had made all arrangements for the winter and had fortified himself beyond what was common for his countrymen to do, upon a small island near South Kingston, R.I. Here he intended to pass the winter with his warriors and their wives and children. About 500 Indian houses was erected of a superior kind, in which was deposited all their stores, tubs of corn, and other things, piled up to a great height, which rendered it bulletproof. It was supposed that 3,000 persons had taken up their residence in it. (I would remark that Indians took better care of themselves in those days than they have been able to since.) Accordingly, on the 19th day of December, after the Pilgrims had been out in the extreme cold for nearly one month, lodging in tents, and their provision being short, and the air full of snow, they had no other alternative than to attack Philip in the fort. Treachery, however, hastened his ruin; one of his men, by hope of reward from the deceptive Pilgrims, betrayed his country into their hands. The traitor's name was Peter. No white man was acquainted with the way, and it would have been almost impossible for them to have found it, much less to have captured it. There was but one point where it could have been entered or assailed with any success, and this was fortified much like a blockhouse, directly in front of the entrance, and also flankers to cover a crossfire—besides high palisades, an immense hedge of fallen trees of nearly a rod in thickness. Thus surrounded by trees and water, there was but one place that the Pilgrims could pass. Nevertheless, they made the attempt. Philip now had directed his men to fire, and every platoon of the Indians swept every white man from the path one after another, until six captains, with a great many of the men, had fallen. In the meantime, one Captain Moseley with some of his men had somehow or other gotten into the fort in another way and surprised them, by which the Pilgrims were enabled to capture the fort, at the same time setting fire to it and hewing down men, women, and children indiscriminately. Philip, however, was enabled to escape with many of his warriors. It is said at this battle eighty whites were killed and one hundred and fifty wounded, many of whom died of their wounds afterward, not being able to dress them till they had marched 18 miles, also leaving many of their dead in the fort. It is said that 700 of the Narragansetts perished, the greater part of them being women and children.

It appears that God did not prosper them much, after all. It is believed that the sufferings of the Pilgrims were without a parallel in history; and it is supposed that the horrors and burning elements of Moscow will bear but a faint resemblance of that scene. The thousands and ten thousands assembled there with their well-disciplined forces bear little comparison to that of modern Europe, when the inhabitants, science, manners, and customs are taken into consideration. We might as well admit the above fact and say the like was never known among any heathen nation in the world; for none but those worse than heathens would have suffered so much, for the sake of being revenged upon those of their enemies. Philip had repaired to his quarters to take care of his people and not to have them exposed. We should not have wondered quite so much if Philip had gone forward and acted thus. But when a people calling themselves Christians conduct in this manner, we think they are censurable, and no pity at all ought to be had for them.

It appears that one of the whites had married one of Philip's countrymen; and they, the Pilgrims, said he was a traitor, and therefore they said he must die. So they quartered him; and as history informs us, they said, he being a heathen, but a few tears were shed at his funeral. Here, then, because a man would not turn and fight against his own wife and family, or leave them, he was condemned as a heathen. We presume that no honest men will commend those ancient fathers for such absurd conduct. Soon after this, Philip and his men left that part of the country and retired farther back, near the Mohawks, where, in July 1676, some of his men were slain by the Mohawks. Notwithstanding this, he strove to get them to join him; and here it is said that Philip did not do that which was right, that he killed some of the Mohawks and laid it to the whites in order that he might get them to join him. If so, we cannot consistently believe he did right. But he was so exasperated that nothing but revenge would satisfy him. All this act was no worse than our political men do in our days, of their strife to wrong each other, who profess to be enlightened; and all for the sake of carrying their points. Heathenlike, either by the sword, calumny, or deception of every kind; and the late duels among the [so-] called high men of honor is sufficient to warrant any statements. But while we pursue our history in regard to Philip, we find that he made many successful attempts against the Pilgrims, in surprising and driving them from their posts, during the year 1676, in February and through till August, in which time many of the Christian Indians joined him. It is thought by many that all would have joined him, if they had been left to their choice, as it appears they did not like their white brethren very well. It appears that Philip treated his prisoners with a great deal more Christian-like spirit than the Pilgrims did; even Mrs. Rowlandson,[9] although speaking with bitterness sometimes of the Indians, yet in her journal she speaks not a word against him. Philip even hires her to work for him, and pays her for her work, and then invites her to dine with him and to smoke with him. And we have many testimonies that he was kind to his prisoners; and when the English wanted to redeem Philip's prisoners, they had the privilege.

Now, did Governor Winthrop or any of those ancient divines use any of his men so? No. Was it known that they received any of their female captives into their houses and fed them? No, it cannot be found upon history. Were not the females completely safe, and none of them were violated, as they acknowledge themselves? But was it so when the Indian women fell into the hands of the Pilgrims? No. Did the Indians get a chance to redeem

---

[9]Mary Rowlandson was captured, along with three of her children, by a group of Philip's allies in an attack that destroyed her home village of Lancaster, Massachusetts. She was ransomed after six months of living with Indian war parties. Her *Narrative* of her captivity, published in 1682, became almost instantly popular and inaugurated one of the most important genres in American literature.

their prisoners? No. But when they were taken they were either compelled to turn traitors and join their enemies or be butchered upon the spot. And this is the dishonest method that the famous Captain Church used in doing his great exploits; and in no other way could he ever gained one battle.[10] So, after all, Church only owes his exploits to the honesty of the Indians, who told the truth, and to his own deceptive heart in duping them. Here it is to be understood that the whites have always imposed upon the credulity of the Indians. It is with shame, I acknowledge, that I have to notice so much corruption of a people calling themselves Christians. If they were like my people, professing no purity at all, then their crimes would not appear to have such magnitude. But while they appear to be by profession more virtuous, their crimes still blacken. It makes them truly to appear to be like mountains filled with smoke, and thick darkness covering them all around.

But we have another dark and corrupt deed for the sons of Pilgrims to look at, and that is the fight and capture of Philip's son and wife and many of his warriors, in which Philip lost about 130 men killed and wounded; this was in August 1676. But the most horrid act was in taking Philip's son, about ten years of age, and selling him to be a slave away from his father and mother. While I am writing, I can hardly restrain my feelings, to think a people calling themselves Christians should conduct so scandalous, so outrageous, making themselves appear so despicable in the eyes of the Indians; and even now, in this audience, I doubt but there is men honorable enough to despise the conduct of those pretended Christians. And surely none but such as believe they did right will ever go and undertake to celebrate that day of their landing, the 22nd of December. Only look at it; then stop and pause: My fathers came here for liberty themselves, and then they must go and chain that mind, that image they professed to serve, not content to rob and cheat the poor ignorant Indians but must take one of the king's sons and make a slave of him. Gentlemen and ladies, I blush at these tales, if you do not, especially when they professed to be a free and humane people. Yes, they did; they took a part of my tribe and sold them to the Spaniards in Bermuda, and many others;[11] and then on the Sabbath day, these people would gather themselves together and say that God is no respecter of persons; while the divines would pour forth, "He says that he loves God and hates his brother is a liar, and the truth is not in him"—and at the same time they hating and selling their fellow men in bondage. And there is

---

[10] Benjamin Church was the most successful of the leaders of the forces of the United Colonies against Philip. His sympathy with the Indians, his close knowledge of them, and his careful wooing of groups who were either unfriendly to Philip or otherwise uncertain about the war enabled him, as Apess rightly argues, to succeed where most of the other English commanders failed—in part because of their disdain for the Indians and a refusal to consider their ways.

[11] At the end of the Pequot War of 1637 the English sold a number of Pequots, men, women, and children, into slavery in Bermuda as part of their determination to wipe out the culture so they would never again be at risk of being challenged by it. The Pequots on Bermuda, though long out of touch with their New England brethren, have maintained a somewhat distinctive cultural identity to the present.

no manner of doubt but that all my countrymen would have been enslaved if they had tamely submitted. But no sooner would they butcher every white man that come in their way, and even put an end to their own wives and children, and that was all that prevented them from being slaves; yes, *all*. It was not the good will of those holy Pilgrims that prevented. No. But I would speak, and I could wish it might be like the voice of thunder, that it might be heard afar off, even to the ends of the earth. He that will advocate slavery is worse than a beast, is a being devoid of shame, and has gathered around him the most corrupt and debasing principles in the world; and I care not whether he be a minister or member of any church in the world— no, not excepting the head men of the nation. And he that will not set his face against its corrupt principles is a coward and not worthy of being numbered among men and Christians—and conduct, too, that libels the laws of the country, and the word of God, that men profess to believe in.

After Philip had his wife and son taken, sorrow filled his heart, but notwithstanding, as determined as ever to be revenged, though [he] was pursued by the duped Indians and Church into a swamp, one of the men proposing to Philip that he had better make peace with the enemy, upon which he slew him upon the spot. And the Pilgrims, being also repulsed by Philip, were forced to retreat with the loss of one man in particular, whose name was Thomas Lucas, of Plymouth. We rather suspect that he was some related to Lucas and Hedge, who made their famous speeches against the poor Marshpees, in 1834, in the Legislature, in Boston, against freeing them from slavery that their fathers, the Pilgrims, had made of them for years.

Philip's forces had now become very small, so many having been duped away by the whites and killed that it was now easy surrounding him. Therefore, upon the 12th of August, Captain Church surrounded the swamp where Philip and his men had encamped, early in the morning, before they had risen, doubtless led on by an Indian who was either compelled or hired to turn traitor. Church had now placed his guard so that it was impossible for Philip to escape without being shot. It is doubtful, however, whether they would have taken him if he had not been surprised. Suffice it to say, however, this was the case. A sorrowful morning to the poor Indians, to lose such a valuable man. When coming out of the swamp, he was fired upon by an Indian and killed dead upon the spot.

I rejoice that it was even so, that the Pilgrims did not have the pleasure of tormenting him. The white man's gun, missing fire, lost the honor of killing the truly great man, Philip. The place where Philip fell was very muddy. Upon this news, the Pilgrims gave three cheers; then Church ordering his body to be pulled out of the mud, while one of those tenderhearted Christians exclaims, "What a dirty creature he looks like." And we have also Church's speech upon that subject, as follows: "For as much as he has caused many a Pilgrim to lie above ground unburied, to rot, not one of his bones shall be buried." With him fell five of his best and most trusty men, one the son of a chief, who fired the first gun in the war.

Captain Church now orders him to be cut up. Accordingly, he was quartered and hung up upon four trees, his head and one hand given to the Indian who shot him, to carry about to show, at which sight it so overjoyed the Pilgrims that they would give him money for it, and in this way obtained a considerable sum. After which his head was sent to Plymouth and exposed upon a gibbet for twenty years; and his hand to Boston, where it was exhibited in savage triumph; and his mangled body denied a resting place in the tomb, and thus adds the poet,

> Cold with the beast he slew, he sleeps,
> O'er him no filial spirit weeps.

I think that, as a matter of honor, that I can rejoice that no such evil conduct is recorded of the Indians, that they never hung up any of the white warriors who were head men. And we add the famous speech of Dr. Increase Mather; he says, during the bloody contest the pious fathers wrestled hard and long with their God, in prayer, that he would prosper their arms and deliver their enemies into their hands. And when upon stated days of prayer the Indians got the advantage, it was considered as a rebuke of divine providence (we suppose the Indian prayed best then), which stimulated them to more ardor. And on the contrary, when they prevailed they considered it as an immediate interposition in their favor. The Doctor closes thus: "Nor could they, the Pilgrims, cease crying to the Lord against Philip, until they had prayed the bullet through his heart." And in speaking of the slaughter of Philip's people at Narragansett, he says, "We have heard of two and twenty Indian captains slain, all of them, and brought down to hell in one day." Again, in speaking of a chief who had sneered at the Pilgrims' religion, and who had withal added a most hideous blasphemy, "Immediately upon which a bullet took him in the head, and dashed out his brains, sending his cursed soul in a moment among the devils and blasphemers in hell forever." It is true that this language is sickening and is as true as the sun is in the heavens that such language was made use of, and it was a common thing for all the Pilgrims to curse the Indians, according to the order of their priests. It is also wonderful how they prayed, that they should pray the bullet through the Indians' heart and their souls down into hell. If I had any faith in such prayers, I should begin to think that soon we should all be gone. However, if this is the way they pray, that is, bullets through people's hearts, I hope they will not pray for me; I should rather be excused. But to say the least, there is no excuse for their ignorance how to treat their enemies and pray for them. If the Doctor and his people had only turned to the 23rd of Luke, and the 34th verse,[12] and heard the words of their Master, whom they pretended to follow, they would see that their course did utterly condemn them; or the 7th of Acts, and the Goth verse,[13] and heard the language of the pious Stephen,

---

[12]"Then Jesus said, 'Father, forgive them; for they know not what they do.'"

[13]"Then he fell to his knees and cried out in a loud voice, 'Lord, do not hold this sin against them'; and when he said this, he fell asleep."

we think it vastly different from the Pilgrims; he prayed: "Lord, lay not this sin to their charge." No curses were heard from these pious martyrs.

I do not hesitate to say that through the prayers, preaching, and examples of those pretended pious has been the foundation of all the slavery and degradation in the American colonies toward colored people. Experience has taught me that this has been a most sorry and wretched doctrine to us poor ignorant Indians. I will mention two or three things to amuse you a little; that is, as I was passing through Connecticut, about 15 years ago, where they are so pious that they kill the cats for killing rats, and whip the beer barrels for working upon the Sabbath, that in a severe cold night, when the face of the earth was one glare of ice, dark and stormy, I called at a man's house to know if I could not stay with him, it being about nine miles to the house where I then lived, and knowing him to be rich man, and withal very pious, knowing if he had a mind he could do it comfortably, and withal we were both members of one church. My reception, however, was almost as cold as the weather, only he did not turn me out-of-doors; if he had, I know not but I should have frozen to death. My situation was a little better than being out, for he allowed a little wood but no bed, because I was an Indian. Another Christian asked me to dine with him and put my dinner behind the door; I thought this a queer compliment indeed.

About two years ago, I called at an inn in Lexington; and a gentleman present, not spying me to be an Indian, began to say they ought to be exterminated. I took it up in our defense, though not boisterous but coolly and when we came to retire, finding that I was an Indian, he was unwilling to sleep opposite my room for fear of being murdered before morning. We presume his conscience pled guilty. These things I mention to show that the doctrines of the Pilgrims has grown up with the people.

But not to forget Philip and his lady, and his prophecy: It is (that in 1671), when Philip went to Boston, his clothing was worth nearly one hundred dollars. It is said by some of the writers in those days that their money being so curiously wrought, that neither Jew nor devil could counterfeit it—high encomium upon Indian arts; and with it they used to adorn their sagamores in a curious manner. It was said that Philip's wife was neatly attired in the Indian style; some of the white females used to call her a proud woman because she would not bow down to them and was so particular in adorning herself. Perhaps, while these ladies were so careful to review the queen, they had forgot that she was truly one of the greatest women there was among them, although not quite so white. But while we censure others for their faults in spending so much time to view their fair and handsome features, whether colored or white, we would remind all the fair sex it is what they all love, that is, jewels and feathers. It was what the Indian women used to love, and still love—and customs, we presume, that the whites brought from their original savage fathers, 1,000 years ago. Every white that knows their own history knows there was not a whit of difference between them and the Indians of their days.

But who was Philip, that made all this display in the world, that put an enlightened nation to flight and won so many battles? It was a son of nature, with nature's talents alone. And who did he have to contend with? With all the combined arts of cultivated talents of the Old and New World. It was like putting one talent against a thousand. And yet Philip, with that, accomplished more than all of them. Yea, he outdid the well-disciplined forces of Greece, under the command of Philip, the Grecian emperor; for he never was enabled to lay such plans of allying the tribes of the earth together, as Philip of Mount Hope did. And even Napoleon patterned after him, in collecting his forces and surprising the enemy. Washington, too, pursued many of his plans in attacking the enemy and thereby enabled him to defeat his antagonists and conquer them. What, then, shall we say? Shall we not do right to say that Philip, with his one talent, outstrips them all with their ten thousand? No warrior, of any age, was ever known to pursue such plans as Philip did....

How deep, then, was the thought of Philip, when he could look from Maine to Georgia, and from the ocean to the lakes, and view with one look all his brethren withering before the more enlightened to come; and how true his prophecy, that the white people would not only cut down their groves but would enslave them. Had the inspiration of Isaiah been there, he could not have been more correct. Our groves and hunting grounds are gone, our dead are dug up, our council fires are put out, and a foundation was laid in the first Legislature to enslave our people, by taking from them all rights, which has been strictly adhered to ever since. Look at the disgraceful laws, disfranchising us as citizens. Look at the treaties made by Congress, all broken. Look at the deep-rooted plans laid, when a territory becomes a state, that after so many years the laws shall be extended over the Indians that live within their boundaries. Yea, every charter that has been given was given with the view of driving the Indians out of the states, or dooming them to become chained under desperate laws, that would make them drag out a miserable life as one chained to the galley; and this is the course that has been pursued for nearly two hundred years. A fire, a canker, created by the Pilgrims from across the Atlantic, to burn and destroy my poor unfortunate brethren, and it cannot be denied. What, then, shall we do? Shall we cease crying and say it is all wrong, or shall we bury the hatchet and those unjust laws and Plymouth Rock together and become friends? And will the sons of Pilgrims aid in putting out the fire and destroying the canker that will ruin all that their fathers left behind them to destroy? (By this we see how true Philip spoke.) If so, we hope we shall not hear it said from ministers and church members that we are so good no other people can live with us, as you know it is a common thing for them to say Indians cannot live among Christian people; no, even the president of the United States tells the Indians they cannot live among civilized people, and we want your lands and must have them and will have them. As if he had said to them, "We want your land for our use to speculate upon; it aids us in paying off our national debt and supporting us in Congress to drive you off.

"You see, my red children, that our fathers carried on this scheme of getting your lands for our use, and we have now become rich and powerful; and we have a right to do with you just as we please; we claim to be your fathers. And we think we shall do you a great favor, my dear sons and daughters, to drive you out, to get you away out of the reach of our civilized people, who are cheating you, for we have no law to reach them, we cannot protect you although you be our children. So it is no use, you need not cry, you must go, even if the lions devour you, for we promised the land you have to somebody else long ago, perhaps twenty or thirty years; and we did it without your consent, it is true.

But this has been the way our fathers first brought us up, and it is hard to depart from it; therefore, you shall have to protection from us." Now, while we sum up this subject, does it not appear that the cause of all wars from beginning to end was and is for the want to food usage? That the whites have always been the aggressors, and the wars, cruelties, and bloodshed is a job of their own seeking, and not the Indians? Did you ever know of Indians hurting those who was kind to them? No. We have a thousand witnesses to the contrary. Yea, every male and female declare it to be the fact. We often hear of the wars breaking out upon the frontiers, and it is because the same spirit reigns there that reigned here in New England; and wherever there are any Indians, that spirit still reigns; and at present, there is no law to stop it. What, then, is to be done? Let every friend of the Indians now seize the mantle of Liberty and throw it over those burning elements that has spread with such fearful rapidity, and at once extinguish them forever. It is true that now and then a feeble voice has been raised in our favor. Yes, we must speak of distinguished men, but they fall so far short in the minority that it is heard but at a small distance. We want trumpets that sound like thunder, and men to act as though they were going at war with those corrupt and degrading priciples that robs one of all rights, merely because he is ignorant and of a little different color. Let us have principles that will give everyone his due; and then shall wars cease, and the weary find rest. Give the Indian his rights, and you may be assured war will cease.

But by this time you have been enabled to see that Philip's prophecy has come to pass; therefore, as a man of natural abilities, I shall pronounce him the greatest man that was ever in America; and so it will stand, until he is proved to the contrary, to the everlasting disgrace of the Pilgrims' fathers.

Noo-chun kes-uk-qut-tiam-at-am unch koo-we-su-onk, kuk-ket-as-soo-tam-oonk pey-au-moo-utch, keet-te-nan-tam-oo-onk ne nai; ne-ya-ne ke-suk-qutkah oh-ke-it; aos-sa-ma-i-in-ne-an ko-ko-ke-stik-o-da-e nut-as-e-suk-ok-ke fu-tuk-qun-neg; kah ah-quo-an-tam-a-i-in-ne-an num-match-e-se-ong-an-on-ash, ne-match-ene-na-mun wonk neet-ah-quo-antam-au-o-un-non-og nish-noh pasuk noo-na-mortuk-quoh-who-nan, kah chaque sag-kom-pa-ginne-an en qutch-e-het-tu-ong-a-nit, qut poh-qud-wus-sin-ne-an watch match-i-tut.

Having now given historical facts, and an exposition in relation to ancient times, by which we have been enabled to discover the foundation which destroyed our common fathers in their struggle together; it was indeed nothing more than the spirit of avarice and usurpation of power that has brought people in all ages to hate and devour each other. And I cannot, for one moment, look back upon what is past and call it religion. No, it has not the least appearance like it. Do not then wonder, my dear friends, at my bold and unpolished statements, though I do not believe that truth wants any polishing whatever. And I can assure you that I have no design to tell an untruth, but facts alone. Oft have I been surprised at the conduct of those who pretend to be Christians, to see how they were affected toward those who were of a different cast, professing one faith. Yes, the spirit of degradation has always been exercised toward us poor and untaught people. If we cannot read, we can see and feel; and we find no excuse in the Bible for Christians conducting toward us as they do.

It is said that in the Christian's guide, God is merciful, and they that are his followers are like him. How much mercy do you think has been shown toward Indians, their wives, and their children? Not much, we think. No. And ye fathers, I will appeal to you that are white. Have you any regard for your wives and children, for those delicate sons and daughters? Would you like to see them slain and lain in heaps, and their bodies devoured by the vultures and wild beasts of prey, and their bones bleaching in the sun and air, till they molder away or were covered by the falling leaves of the forest, and not resist? No. Your hearts would break with grief, and with all the religion and knowledge you have, it would not impede your force to take vengeance upon your foe that had so cruelly conducted thus, although God has forbid you in so doing. For he has said, "Vengeance is mine, and I will repay." What, then, my dear affectionate friends, can you think of those who have been so often betrayed, routed, and stripped of all they possess, of all their kindred in the flesh? Can or do you think we have no feeling? The speech of Logan,[14] the white man's friend, is no doubt fresh in your memory, that he intended to live and die the friend of the white man; that he always fed them and gave them the best his cabin afforded; and he appealed to them if they had not been well used, to which they never denied. After which they murdered all of his family in cool blood, which roused his passions to be revenged upon the whites. This circumstance is but one in a thousand.

Upon the banks of Ohio, a party of two hundred white warriors, in 1757 or about that time, came across a settlement of Christian Indians and falsely accused them of being warriors, to which they denied, but all to no purpose; they were determined to massacre them all. They, the Indians,

---

[14]Logan's speech, made after having his home and family destroyed by the English in 1774, was often quoted in this period as follows: "I appeal to any white to say, if ever he entered Logan's cabin hungry, and he gave him not meat; if ever he came cold and naked, and he clothed him not. During the course of the last long bloody war, Logan remained idle in his cabin, an advocate for peace. Such was my love for the whites that my countrymen pointed as they passed and said, 'Logan is the friend of the white men.' I had even thought to have lived with you, but for the injuries of one man. Col. Cresap, the last spring, in cold blood, and unprovoked, murdered all the relations of Logan; not even sparing my women and children. There runs not a drop of my blood in the veins of any living creature. This called on me for revenge. I have sought it. I have killed many. I have fully glutted my vengeance. For my country, I rejoice at the beams of peace. But do not harbor a thought that mine is the joy of fear. Logan never felt fear. He will not turn on his heel to save his life. Who is there to mourn for Logan?— Not one!"

then asked liberty to prepare for the fatal hour. The white savages then gave them one hour, as the historian said. They then prayed together; and in tears and cries, upon their knees, begged pardon of each other, of all they had done, after which they informed the white savages that they were now ready. One white man then begun with a mallet and knocked them down and continued his work until he had killed fifteen, with his own hand; then, saying it ached, he gave his commission to another. And thus they continued till they had massacred nearly ninety men, women, and children, all these innocent of any crime. What sad tales are these for us to look upon the massacre of our dear fathers, mothers, brothers, and sisters; and if we speak, we are then called savages for complaining. Our affections for each other are the same as yours; we think as much of ourselves as you do of yourselves. When our children are sick, we do all we can for them; they lie buried deep in our affections; if they die, we remember it long and mourn in after years. Children also cleave to their parents; they look to them for aid; they do the best they know how to do for each other; and when strangers come among us, we use them as well as we know how; we feel honest in whatever we do; we have no desire to offend anyone. But when we are so deceived, it spoils all our confidence in our visitors. And although I can say that I have some dear, good friends among white people, yet I eye them with a jealous eye, for fear they will betray me. Having been deceived so much by them, how can I help it? Being brought up to look upon white people as being enemies and not friends, and by the whites treated as such, who can wonder? Yes, in vain have I looked for the Christian to take me by the hand and bid me welcome to his cabin, as my fathers did them, before we were born; and if they did, it was only to satisfy curiosity and not to look upon me as a man and a Christian. And so all of my people have been treated, whether Christians or not. I say, then, a different course must be pursued, and different laws must be enacted, and all men must operate under one general law. And while you ask yourselves, "What do they, the Indians, want?" you have only to look at the unjust laws made for them and say, "They want what I want," in order to make men of them, good and wholesome citizens. And this plan ought to be pursued by all missionaries or not pursued at all. That is not only to make Christians of us, but men, which plan as yet has never been pursued. And when it is, I will then throw my might upon the side of missions and do what I can to favor it. But this work must begin here first, in New England.

Having now closed, I would say that many thanks is due from me to you, though an unworthy speaker, for your kind attention; and I wish you to understand that we are thankful for every favor; and you and I have to rejoice that we have not to answer for our fathers' crimes; neither shall we do right to charge them one to another. We can only regret it, and flee from it; and from henceforth, let peace and righteousness be written upon our hearts and hands forever, is the wish of a poor Indian.

1836

RALPH WALDO EMERSON
1803–1882

Ralph Waldo Emerson is often positioned as the "father" of American literature. As a poet, preacher, orator, and essayist, he articulated the new nation's prospects and needs and became a weighty exemplum of the American artist. Throughout the nineteenth century, Emerson's portrait gazed down from schoolhouse and library walls, where he was enshrined as one of America's great poets. His daughter Ellen, accompanying her father on one of his frequent lecture tours, reported the fun of "seeing all the world burn incense to Father." His calls for a scholar and a poet who would exploit the untapped materials of the nation served as literary credos for subsequent generations of writers, from Rebecca Harding Davis, Walt Whitman, and Frederick Douglass to Hart Crane, Robert Frost, and A. R. Ammons. He was known for his critique of conventional values of property and ambition, yet his formulation of the self-reliant American was used to authorize the *laissez-faire* individualism of Horatio Alger and Andrew Carnegie. He was one of the first American writers to be recognized by the British and European literary establishments, read enthusiastically by Carlyle and Nietzsche. To Matthew Arnold, he is the "voice oracular" who challenges the "bitter knowledge" of his "monstrous, dead, unprofitable world." To Irving Howe, Emerson is the dominant spirit of his age, the proponent of "the American newness." In F. O. Matthiessen's formulation of the "American Renaissance," Emerson is the initiating force "on which Thoreau built, to which Whitman gave extension, and to which Hawthorne and Melville were indebted by being forced to react against its philosophical assumptions." To Whitman and, subsequently, to Alfred Kazin, Emerson is the "founder" of the "procession of American literature."

The eminence of his public position made Emerson's approval a valued commodity, as Whitman showed when he printed a congratulatory letter from Emerson with the second edition of *Leaves of Grass*. It also made him a formidable predecessor with whom younger writers had to contend. Writers as diverse as Thoreau, Louisa May Alcott, and Elizabeth Stuart Phelps describe their emergence onto the literary scene in relationship to Emerson, to his influence as a teacher or writer, a speaker or austere presence. Yet even such acknowledgments as Whitman's famous remark—"I was simmering, simmering, simmering, and Emerson brought me to a boil"—position Emerson primarily as a precursor, important for his influence on others rather than for his own work. As Joel Porte has argued, "Emerson's fate, somewhat like Shakespeare's, was that he came to be treated as an almost purely allegorical personage whose real character and work got submerged in his function as a touchstone of critical opinion." He becomes the founder of "Transcendentalism" or the spokesman for "Nature," the "optimist" who does not understand the world's evil or pain. He is thus removed from the march of time, idealized as a "primordial" figure whose vision isolates him from the political and social struggles of his age.

But Emerson was never simply a distant patriarchal figure sheltered from the material problems of his age. He constructed his "optative" exuberance despite the early deaths of his father, two of his brothers, his beloved young wife, and his first son, and despite his own serious bouts with lung disease and eye strain. He was a child of both privilege and penury, of family position and dependence. As he wrote early on in his journal: "It is my own humor to despise pedigree. I was educated to prize it." His father, the minister William Emerson, died when he was eight, and his mother, Ruth Haskins Emerson, supported the five children (three others died young) by taking in boarders and by periodically living with relatives in Concord. Emerson's education vacillated between Boston Latin school and private tutoring by his aunt Mary Moody Emerson. At Harvard, which he attended on scholarship, Emerson struggled with the academic curriculum and with his expected future as either a teacher or a minister. But he also conducted a more satisfying private education of reading and journal-writing that would prepare him to be a writer, an American scholar, and poet. Those aims had to wait, however, while Emerson helped support his family by teaching school. In 1825 he entered Harvard Divinity School, following nine generations of his family into the ministry. Yet six years after his ordination, he resigned the ministry, concerned that the "dogmatic theology" of "formal Christianity" looked only to past traditions and the words of the dead. "My business is with the living," he wrote in his journal. "I have sometimes thought that in order to be a good minister it was necessary to leave the ministry."

These years were full of personal tumult as well. In 1829 Emerson married Ellen Tucker, only to lose her sixteen months later to the tuberculosis that also threatened him. The pain of her death and his own sense of vulnerability may have hastened Emerson's decision to leave the ministry. With the substantial inheritance she left him, he had the means to make such a change, to travel on the continent, to buy books, and to write them. The inheritance, with the earnings he received from his lecture tours and his publications and with a lifetime of frugality and fiscal planning, made him financially secure. He supported an extended family, caring for his retarded brother for twenty years. In 1835 he married Lidian Jackson, and moved to Concord, where they had four children—Waldo, Ellen, Edith, and Edward Waldo, who later edited his father's works and journals. The death from scarlet fever of five-year-old Waldo was a blow to Emerson's faith in compensation. In his 1844 essay "Experience," he wrote from this loss, and from his urgent desire to regain the "practical power" that could persist despite personal and public griefs. "Life is not intellectual or critical, but sturdy," he argued. His subsequent career and personal life reflect a determined affirmation to be "an active soul." "I am *Defeated* all the time," he acknowledged, "yet to Victory I am born." Emerson continued his work into his seventies, relying on his daughter Ellen to help organize his last lectures and essays. He died in 1882, from pneumonia, and was buried in Concord, near Thoreau and Hawthorne.

Emerson's long career, and his financial and social security, allowed him to intervene decisively in the formation of American culture and letters. Although he generally resisted the call to public advocacy, he was sought after to support various social causes: he was urged to join the experimental commune of Brook Farm, prodded to take a leading role in the abolitionist movement and in the lobbying for women's rights. Emerson's efforts on behalf of his fellow writers were of material importance, addressing the social impediments to publication and reputation. Through financial support, personal connections, or editorial efforts, he made possible publication of work by Thoreau and Bronson Alcott, Margaret Fuller and Jones Very. He loaned Thoreau the property at Walden Pond for his celebrated retreat and raised money to support the impoverished Alcott family, despite his own belief that a philosopher should earn his keep. He oversaw American printings of Carlyle's books and wrote prefaces for translations of Persian poets and of Plutarch. With Margaret Fuller, he edited *The Dial*, a short-lived but influential periodical.

Emerson's initial fame came from his critique of the literary, religious, and educational establishments of his day. He was known as an experimenter who urged Americans to reject their deference to old modes and values, to continental traditions. His chiding lectures about Harvard's religious and literary training and his resignation from the clergy made him a spokesman for reformist positions, although it also aroused harsh criticism of him as a religious infidel, "a sort of mad dog," and a "dangerous man." At the first meeting of the Transcendental Club, Emerson decried the "tame" genius of the times that did not match the grandeur of "this Titanic continent," and he transformed Harvard's traditional Phi Beta Kappa oration on "The American Scholar" into a critique of the "meek young men" and "sluggard intellect of this continent" and a call for a new age when "we will walk on our own feet; we will work with our own hands; we will speak our own minds."

Emerson's work is characterized by a combination of homely metaphors and grandiose goals, by his insistence on the present and his expectations for the future. His outpouring of "private" writings reflects a practical economy of writing, in which journals serve as a "Savings Bank" for "deposit" of "earnings" to be reworked into lectures and essays. They demonstrate his incredible energy and discipline (he kept 182 journals and notebooks over his career, which he carefully reread, indexed, and cross-referenced for use in preparing his more "public" work); and they reflect an astounding ambition, evident in the titles of his college journals, "The Wide World" and "The Universe," and in such notebooks as "XO" ("Inexorable; Reality and Illusion").

Emerson's literary practices have always been provocative. A critic of his first book, *Nature*, was offended by language that is sometimes "coarse and blunt." He also protested that "the effort of perusal is often painful, the thoughts excited are frequently bewildering, and the results to which they lead us, uncertain and obscure. The reader feels as in a disturbed dream." Although modern readers are unlikely to be upset by Emerson's diction or references to sex and madness, he remains disturbing, seen as a "difficult" writer requiring vast annotation and philosophic glossing. Emerson was indeed an allusive writer, but his use of cultural materials provokes with a purpose. The context he constructs is adamantly untraditional, mixing quotations from classics and British poetry with Asian literature and Welsh bards. One metaphor will emerge from his interest in scientific or engineering experiments, another from local politics, and yet another from what his son Waldo said that morning. The problem in reading Emerson— as well as the pleasure—is in seeing how such eclecticism undermines conventions of authority and reference and challenges established modes of reading.

For himself, and for the American public, he advocated "creative reading as well as creative writing," rejecting traditional oppositions between thinking and acting, between the scholar and the worker, between the speculative and the practical. "Words are also actions," he wrote, "and actions are a kind of words." For despite the hopeful tone of much of the writing, Emerson's brand of self-reliance and his exuberant nationalism were an aspiration, to be achieved only through constant work, constant critique. Emerson's aim as a writer was less to originate a tradition than to produce active readers, who would then refashion themselves and their culture: "Let me remind the reader that I am only an experimenter. Do not set the least value on what I do, or the least discredit on what I do not, as if I pretended to settle anything as true or false. I unsettle all things. No facts are to me sacred; none are profane; I simply experiment, an endless seeker, with no Past at my back."

Jean Ferguson Carr
University of Pittsburgh

PRIMARY WORKS

Emerson's Complete Works, ed. J. E. Cabot, 12 vols., 1883–1893; *The Complete Works of Ralph Waldo Emerson*, ed. Edward W. Emerson, 12 vols., 1903–1904; *The Journals of Ralph Waldo Emerson*, ed. Edward W. Emerson and Waldo Emerson Forbes, 10 vols., 1909–1914; *Young Emerson Speaks* [sermons], ed. Arthur C. McGiffert, Jr., 1938; *The Letters of Ralph Waldo Emerson*, ed. Ralph L. Rusk, 1939; *The Early Lectures of R. W. Emerson*, ed. Stephen Whicher, Robert Spiller, and Wallace Williams, 3 vols., 1959–1971; *The Journals and Miscellaneous Notebooks of R. W. Emerson*, ed. William Gilman, Alfred R. Ferguson, Ralph H. Orth, et al., 16 vols., 1960–1986; *The Correspondence of Emerson and Carlyle*, ed. Joseph Slater, 1964; *The Collected Works of R. W. Emerson*, ed. Alfred R. Ferguson, Jean Ferguson Carr, and Douglas E. Wilson, 1971–; *Emerson in His Journals*, ed. Joel Porte, 1982; *The Poetry Notebooks of Ralph Waldo Emerson*, ed. Ralph H. Orth et al., 1986.

Nature

> *A subtle chain of countless rings*
> *The next unto the farthest brings;*
> *The eye reads omens where it goes,*
> *And speaks all languages the rose;*
> *And, striving to be man, the worm*
> *Mounts through all the spires of form.*[1]

Introduction

Our age is retrospective. It builds the sepulchres of the fathers. It writes biographies, histories, and criticism. The foregoing generations beheld God and nature face to face; we, through their eyes. Why should not we also enjoy an original relation to the universe? Why should not we have a poetry and philosophy of insight and not of tradition, and a religion by revelation to us, and not the history of theirs? Embosomed for a season in nature, whose floods of life stream

---

[1]The 1836 edition had as epigraph a quotation attributed to Plotinus: "Nature is but an image or imitation of wisdom, the last thing of the soul; nature being a thing which doth only do, but not know."

around and through us, and invite us by the powers they supply, to action proportioned to nature, why should we grope among the dry bones of the past, or put the living generation into masquerade out of its faded wardrobe? The sun shines to-day also. There is more wool and flax in the fields. There are new lands, new men, new thoughts. Let us demand our own works and laws and worship.

Undoubtedly we have no questions to ask which are unanswerable. We must trust the perfection of the creation so far, as to believe that whatever curiosity the order of things has awakened in our minds, the order of things can satisfy. Every man's condition is a solution in hieroglyphic to those inquiries he would put. He acts it as life, before he apprehends it as truth. In like manner, nature is already, in its forms and tendencies, describing its own design. Let us interrogate the great apparition, that shines so peacefully around us. Let us inquire, to what end is nature?

All science has one aim, namely, to find a theory of nature. We have theories of races and of functions, but scarcely yet a remote approach to an idea of creation. We are now so far from the road to truth, that religious teachers dispute and hate each other, and speculative men are esteemed unsound and frivolous. But to a sound judgment, the most abstract truth is the most practical. Whenever a true theory appears, it will be its own evidence. Its test is, that it will explain all phenomena. Now many are thought not only unexplained but inexplicable; as language, sleep, madness, dreams, beasts, sex.

Philosophically considered, the universe is composed of Nature and the Soul. Strictly speaking, therefore, all that is separate from us, all which Philosophy distinguishes as the NOT ME, that is, both nature and art, all other men and my own body, must be ranked under this name, NATURE. In enumerating the values of nature and casting up their sum, I shall use the word in both senses;—in its common and in its philosophical import. In inquiries so general as our present one, the inaccuracy is not material; no confusion of thought will occur. *Nature*, in the common sense, refers to essences unchanged by man; space, the air, the river, the leaf. *Art* is applied to the mixture of his will with the same things, as in a house, a canal, a statue, a picture. But his operations taken together are so insignificant, a little chipping, baking, patching, and washing, that in an impression so grand as that of the world on the human mind, they do not vary the result.

Chapter I

Nature

To go into solitude, a man needs to retire as much from his chamber as from society. I am not solitary whilst I read and write, though nobody is with me. But if a man would be alone, let him look at the stars. The rays that come from those heavenly worlds, will separate between him and what he touches. One might think the atmosphere was made transparent with this design, to give man, in the heavenly bodies, the perpetual presence of the sublime. Seen in the streets of cities, how great they are! If the stars should appear one night in a thousand years, how would men believe and adore; and preserve for many generations the remembrance of the city of

God which had been shown! But every night come out these envoys of beauty, and light the universe with their admonishing smile.

The stars awaken a certain reverence, because though always present, they are inaccessible; but all natural objects make a kindred impression, when the mind is open to their influence. Nature never wears a mean appearance. Neither does the wisest man extort her secret, and lose his curiosity by finding out all her perfection. Nature never became a toy to a wise spirit. The flowers, the animals, the mountains, reflected the wisdom of his best hour, as much as they had delighted the simplicity of his childhood.

When we speak of nature in this manner, we have a distinct but most poetical sense in the mind. We mean the integrity of impression made by manifold natural objects. It is this which distinguishes the stick of timber of the wood-cutter, from the tree of the poet. The charming landscape which I saw this morning, is indubitably made up of some twenty or thirty farms. Miller owns this field, Locke that, and Manning the woodland beyond. But none of them owns the landscape. There is a property in the horizon which no man has but he whose eye can integrate all the parts, that is, the poet. This is the best part of these men's farms, yet to this their warranty-deeds give no title.

To speak truly, few adult persons can see nature. Most persons do not see the sun. At least they have a very superficial seeing. The sun illuminates only the eye of the man, but shines into the eye and the heart of the child. The lover of nature is he whose inward and outward senses are still truly adjusted to each other; who has retained the spirit of infancy even into the era of manhood. His intercourse with heaven and earth becomes part of his daily food. In the presence of nature, a wild delight runs through the man, in spite of real sorrows. Nature says,—he is my creature, and maugre[1] all his impertinent griefs, he shall be glad with me. Not the sun or the summer alone, but every hour and season yields its tribute of delight; for every hour and change corresponds to and authorizes a different state of the mind, from breathless noon to grimmest midnight. Nature is a setting that fits equally well a comic or a mourning piece. In good health, the air is a cordial of incredible virtue. Crossing a bare common, in snow puddles, at twilight, under a clouded sky, without having in my thoughts any occurrence of special good fortune, I have enjoyed a perfect exhilaration. I am glad to the brink of fear. In the woods too, a man casts off his years, as the snake his slough, and at what period soever of life, is always a child. In the woods, is perpetual youth. Within these plantations of God, a decorum and sanctity reign, a perennial festival is dressed, and the guest sees not how he should tire of them in a thousand years. In the woods, we return to reason and faith. There I feel that nothing can befall me in life,—no disgrace, no calamity, (leaving me my eyes,) which nature cannot repair. Standing on the bare ground,—my head bathed by the blithe air, and uplifted into infinite space,—all mean egotism vanishes. I become a transparent eye-ball; I am nothing; I see all; the currents of the Universal Being circulate through me; I

[1]In spite of.

am part or particle of God. The name of the nearest friend sounds then foreign and accidental: to be brothers, to be acquaintances,—master or servant, is then a trifle and a disturbance. I am the lover of uncontained and immortal beauty. In the wilderness, I find something more dear and connate than in streets or villages. In the tranquil landscape, and especially in the distant line of the horizon, man beholds somewhat as beautiful as his own nature.

The greatest delight which the fields and woods minister, is the suggestion of an occult relation between man and the vegetable. I am not alone and unacknowledged. They nod to me, and I to them. The waving of the boughs in the storm, is new to me and old. It takes me by surprise, and yet is not unknown. Its effect is like that of a higher thought or a better emotion coming over me, when I deemed I was thinking justly or doing right.

Yet it is certain that the power to produce this delight, does not reside in nature, but in man, or in a harmony of both. It is necessary to use these pleasures with great temperance. For, nature is not always tricked[2] in holiday attire, but the same scene which yesterday breathed perfume and glittered as for the frolic of the nymphs, is overspread with melancholy today. Nature always wears the colors of the spirit. To a man laboring under calamity, the heat of his own fire hath sadness in it. Then, there is a kind of contempt of the landscape felt by him who has just lost by death a dear friend. The sky is less grand as it shuts down over less worth in the population.

Chapter II

Commodity

Whoever considers the final cause of the world, will discern a multitude of uses that enter as parts into that result. They all admit of being thrown into one of the following classes; Commodity; Beauty; Language; and Discipline.

Under the general name of Commodity, I rank all those advantages which our senses owe to nature. This, of course, is a benefit which is temporary and mediate, not ultimate, like its service to the soul. Yet although low, it is perfect in its kind, and is the only use of nature which all men apprehend. The misery of man appears like childish petulance, when we explore the steady and prodigal provision that has been made for his support and delight on this green ball which floats him through the heavens. What angels invented these splendid ornaments, these rich conveniences, this ocean of air above, this ocean of water beneath, this firmament of earth between? this zodiac of lights, this tent of dropping clouds, this striped coat of climates, this fourfold year? Beasts, fire, water, stones, and corn serve him. The field is at once his floor, his work-yard, his play-ground, his garden, and his bed.

> *"More servants wait on man*
> *Than he'll take notice of."*—[1]

---

[2]Dressed.

[1]From "Man" (1633) by the English poet George Herbert. The poem is also quoted in Chapter VIII, "Prospects."

Nature, in its ministry to man, is not only the material, but is also the process and the result. All the parts incessantly work into each other's hands for the profit of man. The wind sows the seed; the sun evaporates the sea; the wind blows the vapor to the field; the ice, on the other side of the planet, condenses rain on this; the rain feeds the plant; the plant feeds the animal; and thus the endless circulations of the divine charity nourish man.

The useful arts are reproductions or new combinations by the wit of man, of the same natural benefactors. He no longer waits for favoring gales, but by means of steam, he realizes the fable of Æolus's[2] bag, and carries the two and thirty winds in the boiler of his boat. To diminish friction, he paves the road with iron bars, and, mounting a coach with a ship-load of men, animals, and merchandise behind him, he darts through the country, from town to town, like an eagle or a swallow through the air. By the aggregate of these aids, how is the face of the world changed, from the era of Noah to that of Napoleon! The private poor man hath cities, ships, canals, bridges, built for him. He goes to the post-office, and the human race run on his errands; to the book-shop, and the human race read and write of all that happens, for him; to the court-house, and nations repair his wrongs. He sets his house upon the road, and the human race go forth every morning, and shovel out the snow, and cut a path for him.

But there is no need of specifying particulars in this class of uses. The catalogue is endless, and the examples so obvious, that I shall leave them to the reader's reflection, with the general remark, that this mercenary benefit is one which has respect to a farther good. A man is fed, not that he may be fed, but that he may work.

Chapter III

Beauty

A nobler want of man is served by nature, namely, the love of Beauty.

The ancient Greeks called the world κόσμος,[1] beauty. Such is the constitution of all things, or such the plastic power of the human eye, that the primary forms, as the sky, the mountain, the tree, the animal, give us a delight in and for themselves; a pleasure arising from outline, color, motion, and grouping. This seems partly owing to the eye itself. The eye is the best of artists. By the mutual action of its structure and of the laws of light, perspective is produced, which integrates every mass of objects, of what character soever, into a well colored and shaded globe, so that where the particular objects are mean and unaffecting, the landscape which they compose, is round and symmetrical. And as the eye is the best composer, so light is the first of painters. There is no object so foul that intense light will not make beautiful. And the stimulus it affords to the sense, and a sort of infinitude which it hath, like space and time, make all matter gay. Even the corpse

---

[2]The wind god. [1]Greek term suggesting order and harmony.

hath its own beauty. But besides this general grace diffused over nature, almost all the individual forms are agreeable to the eye, as is proved by our endless imitations of some of them, as the acorn, the grape, the pine-cone, the wheat-ear, the egg, the wings and forms of most birds, the lion's claw, the serpent, the butterfly, sea-shells, flames, clouds, buds, leaves, and the forms of many trees, as the palm.

For better consideration, we may distribute the aspects of Beauty in a threefold manner.

1. First, the simple perception of natural forms is a delight. The influence of the forms and actions in nature, is so needful to man, that, in its lowest functions, it seems to lie on the confines of commodity and beauty. To the body and mind which have been cramped by noxious work or company, nature is medicinal and restores their tone. The tradesman, the attorney comes out of the din and craft of the street, and sees the sky and the woods, and is a man again. In their eternal calm, he finds himself. The health of the eye seems to demand a horizon. We are never tired, so long as we can see far enough.

But in other hours, Nature satisfies by its loveliness, and without any mixture of corporeal benefit. I see the spectacle of morning from the hill-top over against my house, from day-break to sun-rise, with emotions which an angel might share. The long slender bars of cloud float like fishes in the sea of crimson light. From the earth, as a shore, I look out into that silent sea. I seem to partake its rapid transformations: the active enchantment reaches my dust, and I dilate and conspire with the morning wind. How does Nature deify us with a few and cheap elements! Give me health and a day, and I will make the pomp of emperors ridiculous. The dawn is my Assyria, the sun-set and moon-rise my Paphos,[2] and unimaginable realms of faerie; broad noon shall be my England of the senses and the understanding; the night shall be my Germany of mystic philosophy and dreams.

Not less excellent, except for our less susceptibility in the afternoon, was the charm, last evening, of a January sunset. The western clouds divided and subdivided themselves into pink flakes modulated with tints of unspeakable softness; and the air had so much life and sweetness, that it was a pain to come within doors. What was it that nature would say? Was there no meaning in the live repose of the valley behind the mill, and which Homer or Shakspeare could not re-form for me in words? The leafless trees become spires of flame in the sunset, with the blue east for their background, and the stars of the dead calices[3] of flowers, and every withered stem and stubble rimed with frost, contribute something to the mute music.

The inhabitants of cities suppose that the country landscape is pleasant only half the year. I please myself with the graces of the winter scenery, and believe that we are as much touched by it as by the genial influences of summer. To the attentive eye, each moment of the year has its own beauty, and in the same field, it beholds, every hour, a picture which was never seen before, and which shall never be seen again. The heavens change every

---

[2]"Assyria ... Paphos." Ancient civilizations.   [3]Calyxes, the outer coverings of flowers.

moment, and reflect their glory or gloom on the plains beneath. The state of the crop in the surrounding farms alters the expression of the earth from week to week. The succession of native plants in the pastures and roadsides, which makes the silent clock by which time tells the summer hours, will make even the divisions of the day sensible to a keen observer. The tribes of birds and insects, like the plants punctual to their time, follow each other, and the year has room for all. By water-courses, the variety is greater. In July, the blue pontederia or pickerel-weed blooms in large beds in the shallow parts of our pleasant river, and swarms with yellow butterflies in continual motion. Art cannot rival this pomp of purple and gold. Indeed the river is a perpetual gala, and boasts each month a new ornament.

But this beauty of Nature which is seen and felt as beauty, is the least part. The shows of day, the dewy morning, the rainbow, mountains, orchards in blossom, stars, moonlight, shadows in still water, and the like, if too eagerly hunted, become shows merely, and mock us with their unreality. Go out of the house to see the moon, and 't is mere tinsel; it will not please as when its light shines upon your necessary journey. The beauty that shimmers in the yellow afternoons of October, who ever could clutch it? Go forth to find it, and it is gone: 't is only a mirage as you look from the windows of diligence.

2. The presence of a higher, namely, of the spiritual element is essential to its perfection. The high and divine beauty which can be loved without effeminacy, is that which is found in combination with the human will. Beauty is the mark God sets upon virtue. Every natural action is graceful. Every heroic act is also decent, and causes the place and the bystanders to shine. We are taught by great actions that the universe is the property of every individual in it. Every rational creature has all nature for his dowry and estate. It is his, if he will. He may divest himself of it; he may creep into a corner, and abdicate his kingdom, as most men do, but he is entitled to the world by his constitution. In proportion to the energy of his thought and will, he takes up the world into himself. "All those things for which men plough, build, or sail, obey virtue," said Sallust. "The winds and waves," said Gibbon,[4] "are always on the side of the ablest navigators." So are the sun and moon and all the stars of heaven. When a noble act is done,—perchance in a scene of great natural beauty; when Leonidas[5] and his three hundred martyrs consume one day in dying, and the sun and moon come each and look at them once in the steep defile of Thermopylae; when Arnold Winkelried, in the high Alps, under the shadow of the avalanche, gathers in his side a sheaf of Austrian spears to break the line for his comrades; are not these heroes entitled to add the beauty of the scene to the beauty of the

[4]"Sallust ... Gibbon" Roman historian (86–34 B.C.) and British author of *Decline and Fall of the Roman Empire* (1788).

[5]Emerson gives several historical examples of "noble acts": Spartan King Leonidas who fought the Persians in 480 B.C., Swiss hero Winkelried who sacrificed himself in battle in 1386; Columbus; and two English politicians executed under Charles II.

deed? When the bark of Columbus nears the shore of America;—before it, the beach lined with savages, fleeing out of all their huts of cane; the sea behind; and the purple mountains of the Indian Archipelago around, can we separate the man from the living picture? Does not the New World clothe his form with her palm-groves and savannahs as fit drapery? Ever does natural beauty steal in like air, and envelope great actions. When Sir Harry Vane was dragged up the Tower-hill, sitting on a sled, to suffer death, as the champion of the English laws, one of the multitude cried out to him, "You never sate on so glorious a seat." Charles II., to intimidate the citizens of London, caused the patriot Lord Russel to be drawn in an open coach, through the principal streets of the city, on his way to the scaffold. "But," his biographer says, "the multitude imagined they saw liberty and virtue sitting by his side." In private places, among sordid objects, an act of truth or heroism seems at once to draw to itself the sky as its temple, the sun as its candle. Nature stretcheth out her arms to embrace man, only let his thoughts be of equal greatness. Willingly does she follow his steps with the rose and the violet, and bend her lines of grandeur and grace to the decoration of her darling child. Only let his thoughts be of equal scope, and the frame will suit the picture. A virtuous man is in unison with her works, and makes the central figure of the visible sphere. Homer, Pindar, Socrates, Phocion,[6] associate themselves fitly in our memory with the geography and climate of Greece. The visible heavens and earth sympathize with Jesus. And in common life, whosoever has seen a person of powerful character and happy genius, will have remarked how easily he took all things along with him,—the persons, the opinions, and the day, and nature became ancillary to a man.

3. There is still another aspect under which the beauty of the world may be viewed, namely, as it becomes an object of the intellect. Beside the relation of things to virtue, they have a relation to thought. The intellect searches out the absolute order of things as they stand in the mind of God, and without the colors of affection. The intellectual and the active powers seem to succeed each other, and the exclusive activity of the one, generates the exclusive activity of the other. There is something unfriendly in each to the other, but they are like the alternate periods of feeding and working in animals; each prepares and will be followed by the other. Therefore does beauty, which, in relation to actions, as we have seen, comes unsought, and comes because it is unsought, remain for the apprehension and pursuit of the intellect; and then again, in its turn, of the active power. Nothing divine dies. All good is eternally reproductive. The beauty of nature reforms itself in the mind, and not for barren contemplation, but for new creation.

All men are in some degree impressed by the face of the world; some men even to delight. This love of beauty is Taste. Others have the same love

---

[6]Greek poets (Homer and Pindar), philosopher (Socrates), and statesman (Phocion).

in such excess, that, not content with admiring, they seek to embody it in new forms. The creation of beauty is Art.

The production of a work of art throws a light upon the mystery of humanity. A work of art is an abstract or epitome of the world. It is the result or expression of nature, in miniature. For, although the works of nature are innumerable and all different, the result or the expression of them all is similar and single. Nature is a sea of forms radically alike and even unique. A leaf, a sun-beam, a landscape, the ocean, make an analogous impression on the mind. What is common to them all,—that perfectness and harmony, is beauty. The standard of beauty is the entire circuit of natural forms,—the totality of nature; which the Italians expressed by defining beauty "il piu nell' uno."[7] Nothing is quite beautiful alone: nothing but is beautiful in the whole. A single object is only so far beautiful as it suggests this universal grace. The poet, the painter, the sculptor, the musician, the architect, seek each to concentrate this radiance of the world on one point, and each in his several work to satisfy the love of beauty which stimulates him to produce. Thus is Art, a nature passed through the alembic[8] of man. Thus in art, does nature work through the will of a man filled with the beauty of her first works.

The world thus exists to the soul to satisfy the desire of beauty. This element I call an ultimate end. No reason can be asked or given why the soul seeks beauty. Beauty, in its largest and profoundest sense, is one expression for the universe. God is the all-fair. Truth, and goodness, and beauty, are but different faces of the same All. But beauty in nature is not ultimate. It is the herald of inward and eternal beauty, and is not alone a solid and satisfactory good. It must stand as a part, and not as yet the last or highest expression of the final cause of Nature.

Chapter IV
Language

Language is a third use which Nature subserves to man. Nature is the vehicle of thought, and in a simple, double, and threefold degree.

1. Words are signs of natural facts.
2. Particular natural facts are symbols of particular spiritual facts.
3. Nature is the symbol of spirit.

1. Words are signs of natural facts. The use of natural history is to give us aid in supernatural history: the use of the outer creation, to give us language for the beings and changes of the inward creation. Every word which is used to express a moral or intellectual fact, if traced to its root, is found to be borrowed from some material appearance. *Right* means *straight; wrong* means *twisted. Spirit* primarily means *wind; transgression*, the crossing of a *line; supercilious*, the *raising of the eyebrow.* We say the *heart* to express emotion, the *head* to denote thought; and *thought* and *emotion* are words borrowed from sensible things, and now appropriated to spiritual nature. Most

---

[7]"The many in one."   [8]Apparatus used for distilling or refining.

of the process by which this transformation is made, is hidden from us in the remote time when language was framed; but the same tendency may be daily observed in children. Children and savages use only nouns or names of things, which they convert into verbs, and apply to analogous mental acts.

2. But this origin of all words that convey a spiritual import,—so conspicuous a fact in the history of language,—is our least debt to nature. It is not words only that are emblematic; it is things which are emblematic. Every natural fact is a symbol of some spiritual fact. Every appearance in nature corresponds to some state of the mind, and that state of the mind can only be described by presenting that natural appearance as its picture. An enraged man is a lion, a cunning man is a fox, a firm man is a rock, a learned man is a torch. A lamb is innocence; a snake is subtle spite; flowers express to us the delicate affections. Light and darkness are our familiar expression for knowledge and ignorance; and heat for love. Visible distance behind and before us, is respectively our image of memory and hope.

Who looks upon a river in a meditative hour, and is not reminded of the flux of all things? Throw a stone into the stream, and the circles that propagate themselves are the beautiful type of all influence. Man is conscious of a universal soul within or behind his individual life, wherein, as in a firmament, the natures of Justice, Truth, Love, Freedom, arise and shine. This universal soul, he calls Reason: it is not mine, or thine, or his, but we are its; we are its property and men. And the blue sky in which the private earth is buried, the sky with its eternal calm, and full of everlasting orbs, is the type of Reason. That which, intellectually considered, we call Reason, considered in relation to nature, we call Spirit. Spirit is the Creator. Spirit hath life in itself. And man in all ages and countries, embodies it in his language, as the FATHER.

It is easily seen that there is nothing lucky or capricious in these analogies, but that they are constant, and pervade nature. These are not the dreams of a few poets, here and there, but man is an analogist, and studies relations in all objects. He is placed in the centre of beings, and a ray of relation passes from every other being to him. And neither can man be understood without these objects, nor these objects without man. All the facts in natural history taken by themselves, have no value, but are barren, like a single sex. But marry it to human history, and it is full of life. Whole Floras, all Linnaeus' and Buffon's[1] volumes, are dry catalogues of facts; but the most trivial of these facts, the habit of a plant, the organs, or work, or noise of an insect, applied to the illustration of a fact in intellectual philosophy, or, in any way associated to human nature, affects us in the most lively and agreeable manner. The seed of a plant,—to what affecting analogies in the nature of man, is that little fruit made use of, in all discourse, up to the voice of Paul, who calls the human corpse a seed,—"It is sown a natural body; it is raised a spiritual body."[2] The motion of the earth round its axis,

---

[1] Eighteenth-century Swedish botanist and French naturalist, who wrote famous plant classifications.

[2] I Cor. 15:44.

and round the sun, makes the day, and the year. These are certain amounts of brute light and heat. But is there no intent of an analogy between man's life and the seasons? And do the seasons gain no grandeur or pathos from that analogy? The instincts of the ant are very unimportant, considered as the ant's; but the moment a ray of relation is seen to extend from it to man, and the little drudge is seen to be a monitor, a little body with a mighty heart, then all its habits, even that said to be recently observed, that it never sleeps, become sublime.

Because of this radical correspondence between visible things and human thoughts, savages, who have only what is necessary, converse in figures. As we go back in history, language becomes more picturesque, until its infancy, when it is all poetry; or all spiritual facts are represented by natural symbols. The same symbols are found to make the original elements of all languages. It has moreover been observed, that the idioms of all languages approach each other in passages of the greatest eloquence and power. And as this is the first language, so is it the last. This immediate dependence of language upon nature, this conversion of an outward phenomenon into a type of somewhat in human life, never loses its power to affect us. It is this which gives that piquancy to the conversation of a strong-natured farmer or back-woodsman, which all men relish.

A man's power to connect his thought with its proper symbol, and so to utter it, depends on the simplicity of his character, that is, upon his love of truth, and his desire to communicate it without loss. The corruption of man is followed by the corruption of language. When simplicity of character and the sovereignty of ideas is broken up by the prevalence of secondary desires, the desire of riches, of pleasure, of power, and of praise,—and duplicity and falsehood take place of simplicity and truth, the power over nature as an interpreter of the will, is in a degree lost; new imagery ceases to be created, and old words are perverted to stand for things which are not; a paper currency is employed, when there is no bullion in the vaults. In due time, the fraud is manifest, and words lose all power to stimulate the understanding or the affections. Hundreds of writers may be found in every long-civilized nation, who for a short time believe, and make others believe, that they see and utter truths, who do not of themselves clothe one thought in its natural garment, but who feed unconsciously on the language created by the primary writers of the country, those, namely, who hold primarily on nature.

But wise men pierce this rotten diction and fasten words again to visible things; so that picturesque language is at once a commanding certificate that he who employs it, is a man in alliance with truth and God. The moment our discourse rises above the ground line of familiar facts, and is inflamed with passion or exalted by thought, it clothes itself in images. A man conversing in earnest, if he watch his intellectual processes, will find that a material image, more or less luminous, arises in his mind, cotemporaneous with every thought, which furnishes the vestment of the thought. Hence, good writing and brilliant discourse are perpetual allegories. This imagery is spontaneous. It is the blending of experience with the present action of the mind. It is proper creation. It is the working of the Original Cause through the instruments he has already made.

These facts may suggest the advantage which the country-life possesses for a powerful mind, over the artificial and curtailed life of cities. We know more from nature than we can at will communicate. Its light flows into the mind evermore, and we forget its presence. The poet, the orator, bred in the woods, whose senses have been nourished by their fair and appeasing changes, year after year, without design and without heed,—shall not lose their lesson altogether, in the roar of cities or the broil of politics. Long hereafter, amidst agitation and terror in national councils,—in the hour of revolution,—these solemn images shall reappear in their morning lustre, as fit symbols and words of the thoughts which the passing events shall awaken. At the call of a noble sentiment, again the woods wave, the pines murmur, the river rolls and shines, and the cattle low upon the mountains, as he saw and heard them in his infancy. And with these forms, the spells of persuasion, the keys of power are put into his hands.

3. We are thus assisted by natural objects in the expression of particular meanings. But how great a language to convey such pepper-corn informations! Did it need such noble races of creatures, this profusion of forms, this host of orbs in heaven, to furnish man with the dictionary and grammar of his municipal speech? Whilst we use this grand cipher to expedite the affairs of our pot and kettle, we feel that we have not yet put it to its use, neither are able. We are like travellers using the cinders of a volcano to roast their eggs. Whilst we see that it always stands ready to clothe what we would say, we cannot avoid the question, whether the characters are not significant of themselves. Have mountains, and waves, and skies, no significance but what we consciously give them, when we employ them as emblems of our thoughts? The world is emblematic. Parts of speech are metaphors, because the whole of nature is a metaphor of the human mind. The laws of moral nature answer to those of matter as face to face in a glass. "The visible world and the relation of its parts, is the dial plate of the invisible."[3] The axioms of physics translate the laws of ethics. Thus, "the whole is greater than its part;" "reaction is equal to action;" "the smallest weight may be made to lift the greatest, the difference of weight being compensated by time;" and many the like propositions, which have an ethical as well as physical sense. These propositions have a much more extensive and universal sense when applied to human life, than when confined to technical use.

In like manner, the memorable words of history, and the proverbs of nations, consist usually of a natural fact, selected as a picture or parable of a

---

[3]This essay uses many of the quotations Emerson copied into his journals. He rarely cites the source, although he does mark with double quotations when a passage is a "*bona fide* quotation from any person" rather than an imagined or rhetorical comment. In some cases he paraphrases or quotes from memory. Here he cites the eighteenth-century philosopher Swedenborg; other quotations are from Shakespeare's plays and sonnets, the English Quaker George Fox, Coleridge, Francis Bacon, the Bible, Goethe, Plato, and Milton. Emerson could expect most of his contemporary readers to recognize biblical passages, mythological allusions, and Shakespeare.

moral truth. Thus; A rolling stone gathers no moss; A bird in the hand is worth two in the bush; A cripple in the right way, will beat a racer in the wrong; Make hay while the sun shines; 'T is hard to carry a full cup even; Vinegar is the son of wine; The last ounce broke the camel's back; Long-lived trees make roots first;—and the like. In their primary sense these are trivial facts, but we repeat them for the value of their analogical import. What is true of proverbs, is true of all fables, parables, and allegories.

This relation between the mind and matter is not fancied by some poet, but stands in the will of God, and so is free to be known by all men. It appears to men, or it does not appear. When in fortunate hours we ponder this miracle, the wise man doubts, if, at all other times, he is not blind and deaf;

> ——"Can these things be,
> And overcome us like a summer's cloud,
> Without our special wonder?"[4]

for the universe becomes transparent, and the light of higher laws than its own, shines through it. It is the standing problem which has exercised the wonder and the study of every fine genius since the world began; from the era of the Egyptians and the Brahmins,[5] to that of Pythagoras, of Plato, of Bacon, of Leibnitz,[6] of Swedenborg. There sits the Sphinx at the road-side, and from age to age, as each prophet comes by, he tries his fortune at reading her riddle. There seems to be a necessity in spirit to manifest itself in material forms; and day and night, river and storm, beast and bird, acid and alkali, preëxist in necessary Ideas in the mind of God, and are what they are by virtue of preceding affections, in the world of spirit. A Fact is the end or last issue of spirit. The visible creation is the terminus or the circumference of the invisible world. "Material objects," said a French philosopher, "are necessarily kinds of *scoriae*[7] of the substantial thoughts of the Creator, which must always preserve an exact relation to their first origin; in other words, visible nature must have a spiritual and moral side."[8]

This doctrine is abstruse, and though the images of "garment," "scoriae," "mirror," &c., may stimulate the fancy, we must summon the aid of subtler and more vital expositors to make it plain. "Every scripture is to be interpreted by the same spirit which gave it forth,"—is the fundamental law of criticism. A life in harmony with nature, the love of truth and of virtue, will purge the eyes to understand her text. By degrees we may come to know the primitive sense of the permanent objects of nature, so that the world shall be to us an open book, and every form significant of its hidden life and final cause.

---

[4]*Macbeth*, III, iv, 110–112.
[5]Priests of seventh-century B.C. Indian religion.
[6]Seventeenth-century German mathematician and philosopher.

[7]Refuse from melting metals or ores.
[8]Quoted from Guillaume Oegger, *The True Messiah* (1829).

A new interest surprises us, whilst, under the view now suggested, we contemplate the fearful extent and multitude of objects; since "every object rightly seen, unlocks a new faculty of the soul." That which was unconscious truth, becomes, when interpreted and defined in an object, a part of the domain of knowledge,—a new weapon in the magazine of power.

Chapter V

Discipline

In view of the significance of nature, we arrive at once at a new fact, that nature is a discipline. This use of the world includes the preceding uses, as parts of itself.

Space, time, society, labor, climate, food, locomotion, the animals, the mechanical forces, give us sincerest lessons, day by day, whose meaning is unlimited. They educate both the Understanding and the Reason. Every property of matter is a school for the understanding,—its solidity or resistance, its inertia, its extension, its figure, its divisibility. The understanding adds, divides, combines, measures, and finds nutriment and room for its activity in this worthy scene. Meantime, Reason transfers all these lessons into its own world of thought, by perceiving the analogy that marries Matter and Mind.

1. Nature is a discipline of the understanding in intellectual truths. Our dealing with sensible objects is a constant exercise in the necessary lessons of difference, of likeness, of order, of being and seeming, of progressive arrangement; of ascent from particular to general; of combination to one end of manifold forces. Proportioned to the importance of the organ to be formed, is the extreme care with which its tuition is provided,—a care pretermitted in no single case. What tedious training, day after day, year after year, never ending, to form the common sense; what continual reproduction of annoyances, inconveniences, dilemmas; what rejoicing over us of little men; what disputing of prices, what reckonings of interest,—and all to form the Hand of the mind;—to instruct us that "good thoughts are no better than good dreams, unless they be executed!"

The same good office is performed by Property and its filial systems of debt and credit. Debt, grinding debt, whose iron face the widow, the orphan, and the sons of genius fear and hate;—debt, which consumes so much time, which so cripples and disheartens a great spirit with cares that seem so base, is a preceptor whose lessons cannot be forgone, and is needed most by those who suffer from it most. Moreover, property, which has been well compared to snow,—"if it fall level to-day, it will be blown into drifts to-morrow,"—is the surface action of internal machinery, like the index on the face of a clock. Whilst now it is the gymnastics of the understanding, it is hiving in the foresight of the spirit, experience in profounder laws.

The whole character and fortune of the individual are affected by the least inequalities in the culture of the understanding; for example, in the perception of differences. Therefore is Space, and therefore Time, that man may know that things are not huddled and lumped, but sundered and individual. A bell and a plough have each their use, and neither can do the office of the other. Water is good to drink, coal to burn, wool to wear; but wool cannot be drunk, nor water spun, nor coal eaten. The wise man shows his wisdom in separation, in gradation, and his scale of creatures and of merits is as wide as nature. The foolish have no range in their scale, but suppose every man is as every other man. What is not good they call the worst, and what is not hateful, they call the best.

In like manner, what good heed, nature forms in us! She pardons no mistakes. Her yea is yea, and her nay, nay.

The first steps in Agriculture, Astronomy, Zoölogy, (those first steps which the farmer, the hunter, and the sailor take,) teach that nature's dice are always loaded; that in her heaps and rubbish are concealed sure and useful results.

How calmly and genially the mind apprehends one after another the laws of physics! What noble emotions dilate the mortal as he enters into the counsels of the creation, and feels by knowledge the privilege to BE! His insight refines him. The beauty of nature shines in his own breast. Man is greater that he can see this, and the universe less, because Time and Space relations vanish as laws are known.

Here again we are impressed and even daunted by the immense Universe to be explored. "What we know, is a point to what we do not know."[1] Open any recent journal of science, and weigh the problems suggested concerning Light, Heat, Electricity, Magnetism, Physiology, Geology, and judge whether the interest of natural science is likely to be soon exhausted.

Passing by many particulars of the discipline of nature, we must not omit to specify two.

The exercise of the Will or the lesson of power is taught in every event. From the child's successive possession of his several senses up to the hour when he saith, "Thy will be done!"[2] he is learning the secret, that he can reduce under his will, not only particular events, but great classes, nay the whole series of events, and so conform all facts to his character. Nature is thoroughly mediate. It is made to serve. It receives the dominion of man as meekly as the ass on which the Saviour rode. It offers all its kingdoms to man as the raw material which he may mould into what is useful. Man is never weary of working it up. He forges the subtile and delicate air into wise and melodious words, and gives them wing as angels of persuasion and command. One after another, his victorious thought comes up with and reduces all things, until the world becomes, at last, only a realized will,—the double of the man.

2. Sensible objects conform to the premonitions of Reason and reflect the conscience. All things are moral; and in their boundless changes have an unceasing reference to spiritual nature. Therefore is nature glorious with

[1]Emerson's learned quotations often came from less elevated sources: he found this quote from Bishop Joseph Butler in a British novel *Tremaine* (1825) by Robert P. Ward.

[2]The Lord's Prayer, Matthew 6:10, 26:42.

form, color, and motion, that every globe in the remotest heaven; every chemical change from the rudest crystal up to the laws of life; every change of vegetation from the first principle of growth in the eye of a leaf, to the tropical forest and antediluvian coal-mine; every animal function from the sponge up to Hercules, shall hint or thunder to man the laws of right and wrong, and echo the Ten Commandments. Therefore is nature ever the ally of Religion: lends all her pomp and riches to the religious sentiment. Prophet and priest, David, Isaiah, Jesus, have drawn deeply from this source. This ethical character so penetrates the bone and marrow of nature, as to seem the end for which it was made. Whatever private purpose is answered by any member or part, this is its public and universal function, and is never omitted. Nothing in nature is exhausted in its first use. When a thing has served an end to the uttermost, it is wholly new for an ulterior service. In God, every end is converted into a new means. Thus the use of commodity, regarded by itself, is mean and squalid. But it is to the mind an education in the doctrine of Use, namely, that a thing is good only so far as it serves; that a conspiring of parts and efforts to the production of an end, is essential to any being. The first and gross manifestation of this truth, is our inevitable and hatred training in values and wants, in corn and meat.

It has already been illustrated, that every natural process is a version of a moral sentence. The moral law lies at the centre of nature and radiates to the circumference. It is the pith and marrow of every substance, every relation, and every process. All things with which we deal, preach to us. What is a farm but a mute gospel? The chaff and the wheat, weeds and plants, blight, rain, insects, sun,—it is a sacred emblem from the first furrow of spring to the last stack which the snow of winter overtakes in the fields. But the sailor, the shepherd, the miner, the merchant, in their several resorts, have each an experience precisely parallel, and leading to the same conclusion: because all organizations are radically alike. Nor can it be doubted that this moral sentiment which thus scents the air, grows in the grain, and impregnates the waters of the world, is caught by man and sinks into his soul. The moral influence of nature upon every individual is that amount of truth which it illustrates to him. Who can estimate this? Who can guess how much firmness the sea-beaten rock has taught the fisherman? how much tranquillity has been reflected to man from the azure sky, over whose unspotted deeps the winds forevermore drive flocks of stormy clouds, and leave no wrinkle or stain? how much industry and providence and affection we have caught from the pantomime of brutes? What a searching preacher of self-command is the varying phenomenon of Health!

Herein is especially apprehended the unity of Nature,—the unity in variety,—which meets us everywhere. All the endless variety of things make an identical impression. Xenophanes[3] complained in his old age, that, look where he would, all things hastened back to Unity. He was weary of seeing the same entity in the tedious variety of forms. The fable of Proteus[4] has a

---

[3]Sixth-century B.C. Greek philosopher.   [4]Greek god who could change his shape.

cordial truth. A leaf, a drop, a crystal, a moment of time is related to the whole, and partakes of the perfection of the whole. Each particle is a microcosm, and faithfully renders the likeness of the world.

Not only resemblances exist in things whose analogy is obvious, as when we detect the type of the human hand in the flipper of the fossil saurus,[5] but also in objects wherein there is great superficial unlikeness. Thus architecture is called "frozen music," by De Stael and Goethe. Vitruvius[6] thought an architect should be a musician. "A Gothic church," said Coleridge, "is a petrified religion." Michael Angelo maintained, that, to an architect, a knowledge of anatomy is essential. In Haydn's oratorios, the notes present to the imagination not only motions, as, of the snake, the stag, and the elephant, but colors also; as the green grass. The law of harmonic sounds reappears in the harmonic colors. The granite is differenced in its laws only by the more or less of heat, from the river that wears it away. The river, as it flows, resembles the air that flows over it; the air resembles the light which traverses it with more subtile currents; the light resembles the heat which rides with it through Space. Each creature is only a modification of the other; the likeness in them is more than the difference, and their radical law is one and the same. A rule of one art, or a law of one organization, holds true throughout nature. So intimate is this Unity, that, it is easily seen, it lies under the undermost garment of nature, and betrays its source in Universal Spirit. For, it pervades Thought also. Every universal truth which we express in words, implies or supposes every other truth. *Omne verum vero consonat.*[7] It is like a great circle on a sphere, comprising all possible circles; which, however, may be drawn, and comprise it, in like manner. Every such truth is the absolute Ens[8] seen from one side. But it has innumerable sides.

The central Unity is still more conspicuous in actions. Words are finite organs of the infinite mind. They cannot cover the dimensions of what is in truth. They break, chop, and impoverish it. An action is the perfection and publication of thought. A right action seems to fill the eye, and to be related to all nature. "The wise man, in doing one thing, does all; or, in the one thing he does rightly, he sees the likeness of all which is done rightly."

Words and actions are not the attributes of brute nature. They introduce us to the human form, of which all other organizations appear to be degradations. When this appears among so many that surround it, the spirit prefers it to all others. It says, 'From such as this, have I drawn joy and knowledge; in such as this have I found and beheld myself; I will speak to it; it can speak again; it can yield me thought already formed and alive.'[9] In fact, the eye,—the mind,—is always accompanied by these forms, male and female; and these are incomparably the richest informations of the power and order that lie at the heart of things. Unfortunately, every one of them

---

[5]Extinct reptile, lizard.
[6]French writer Madame de Stael (1766–1817), German philosopher-author Goethe (1749–1832), and Roman architect Vitruvius (1st cent. B.C.).
[7]Every truth is consonant with all other truth.
[8]Latin term for "abstract being."
[9]The single quotation marks indicate that this is an imagined or rhetorical quotation.

bears the marks as of some injury; is marred and superficially defective. Nevertheless, far different from the deaf and dumb nature around them, these all rest like fountain-pipes on the unfathomed sea of thought and virtue whereto they alone, of all organizations, are the entrances.

It were a pleasant inquiry to follow into detail their ministry to our education, but where would it stop? We are associated in adolescent and adult life with some friends, who, like skies and waters, are coextensive with our idea; who, answering each to a certain affection of the soul, satisfy our desire on that side; whom we lack power to put at such focal distance from us, that we can mend or even analyze them. We cannot choose but love them. When much intercourse with a friend has supplied us with a standard of excellence, and has increased our respect for the resources of God who thus sends a real person to outgo our ideal; when he has, moreover, become an object of thought, and, whilst his character retains all its unconscious effect, is converted in the mind into solid and sweet wisdom,—it is a sign to us that his office is closing, and he is commonly withdrawn from our sight in a short time.

Chapter VI

Idealism

Thus is the unspeakable but intelligible and practicable meaning of the world conveyed to man, the immortal pupil, in every object of sense. To this one end of Discipline, all parts of nature conspire.

A noble doubt perpetually suggests itself, whether this end be not the Final Cause of the Universe; and whether nature outwardly exists. It is a sufficient account of that Appearance we call the World, that God will teach a human mind, and so makes it the receiver of a certain number of congruent sensations, which we call sun and moon, man and woman, house and trade. In my utter impotence to test the authenticity of the report of my senses, to know whether the impressions they make on me correspond with outlying objects, what difference does it make, whether Orion is up there in heaven, or some god paints the image in the firmament of the soul? The relations of parts and the end of the whole remaining the same, what is the difference, whether land and sea interact, and worlds revolve and intermingle without number or end,—deep yawning under deep, and galaxy balancing galaxy, throughout absolute space,—or, whether, without relations of time and space, the same appearances are inscribed in the constant faith of man? Whether nature enjoy a substantial existence without, or is only in the apocalypse of the mind, it is alike useful and alike venerable to me. Be it what it may, it is ideal to me, so long as I cannot try the accuracy of my senses.

The frivolous make themselves merry with the Ideal theory, as if its consequences were burlesque; as if it affected the stability of nature. It surely does not. God never jests with us, and will not compromise the end of nature, by permitting any inconsequence in its procession. Any distrust of the permanence of laws, would paralyze the faculties of man. Their permanence is sacredly respected, and his faith therein is perfect. The wheels and springs of man are all set to the hypothesis of the permanence of nature. We are not built like a ship to be tossed, but like a house to stand. It is a natural consequence of this structure, that, so long as the active powers predominate over the reflective, we resist with indignation any hint that nature is more short-lived or mutable than spirit. The broker, the wheelwright, the carpenter, the toll-man, are much displeased at the intimation.

But whilst we acquiesce entirely in the permanence of natural laws, the question of the absolute existence of nature still remains open. It is the uniform effect of culture on the human mind, not to shake our faith in the stability of particular phenomena, as of heat, water, azote;[1] but to lead us to regard nature as a phenomenon, not a substance; to attribute necessary existence to spirit; to esteem nature as an accident and an effect.

To the senses and the unrenewed understanding, belongs a sort of instinctive belief in the absolute existence of nature. In their view, man and nature are indissolubly joined. Things are ultimates, and they never look beyond their sphere. The presence of Reason mars this faith. The first effort of thought tends to relax this despotism of the senses, which binds us to nature as if we were a part of it, and shows us nature aloof, and, as it were, afloat. Until this higher agency intervened, the animal eye sees, with wonderful accuracy, sharp outlines and colored surfaces. When the eye of Reason opens, to outline and surface are at once added, grace and expression. These proceed from imagination and affection, and abate somewhat of the angular distinctness of objects. If the Reason be stimulated to more earnest vision, outlines and surfaces become transparent, and are no longer seen; causes and spirits are seen through them. The best moments of life are these delicious awakenings of the higher powers, and the reverential withdrawing of nature before its God.

Let us proceed to indicate the effects of culture. 1. Our first institution in the Ideal philosophy is a hint from nature herself.

Nature is made to conspire with spirit to emancipate us. Certain mechanical changes, a small alteration in our local position apprizes us of a dualism. We are strangely affected by seeing the shore from a moving ship, from a balloon, or through the tints of an unusual sky. The least change in our point of view, gives the whole world a pictorial air. A man who seldom rides, needs only to get into a coach and traverse his own town, to turn the street into a puppet-show. The men, the women,—talking, running, bartering, fighting,—the earnest mechanic, the lounger, the beggar, the boys, the dogs, are unrealized at once, or, at least, wholly detached from all relation to the observer, and seen as apparent, not substantial beings. What new thoughts are suggested by seeing a face of country quite familiar, in the rapid movement of the rail-road car! Nay, the most wonted objects, (make a very slight change in the point of vision,) please us most.

---

[1]Nitrogen.

In a camera obscura,[2] the butcher's cart, and the figure of one of our own family amuse us. So a portrait of a well-known face gratifies us. Turn the eyes upside down, by looking at the landscape through your legs, and how agreeable is the picture, though you have seen it any time these twenty years!

In these cases, by mechanical means, is suggested the difference between the observer and the spectacle,—between man and nature. Hence arises a pleasure mixed with awe; I may say, a low degree of the sublime is felt from the fact, probably, that man is hereby apprized, that, whilst the world is a spectacle, something in himself is stable.

2. In a higher manner, the poet communicates the same pleasure. By a few strokes he delineates, as on air, the sun, the mountain, the camp, the city, the hero, the maiden, not different from what we know them, but only lifted from the ground and afloat before the eye. He unfixes the land and the sea, makes them revolve around the axis of his primary thought, and disposes them anew. Possessed himself by a heroic passion, he uses matter as symbols of it. The sensual man conforms thoughts to things; the poet conforms things to his thoughts. The one esteems nature as rooted and fast; the other, as fluid, and impresses his being thereon. To him, the refractory world is ductile and flexible; he invests dust and stones with humanity, and makes them the words of the Reason. The Imagination may be defined to be, the use which the Reason makes of the material world. Shakspeare possesses the power of subordinating nature for the purposes of expression, beyond all poets. His imperial muse tosses the creation like a bauble from hand to hand, and uses it to embody any caprice of thought that is uppermost in his mind. The remotest spaces of nature are visited, and the farthest sundered things are brought together, by a subtle spiritual connection. We are made aware that magnitude of material things is relative, and all objects shrink and expand to serve the passion of the poet. Thus, in his sonnets, the lays of birds, the scents and dyes of flowers, he finds to be the *shadow* of his beloved; time, which keeps her from him, is his *chest;* the suspicion she has awakened, is her *ornament;*

> *The ornament of beauty is Suspect,*
> *A crow which flies in heaven's sweetest air.*

His passion is not the fruit of chance; it swells, as he speaks, to a city, or a state.

> *No, it was builded far from accident;*
> *It suffers not in smiling pomp, nor falls*
> *Under the brow of thralling discontent;*
> *It fears not policy, that heretic,*
> *That works on leases of short numbered hours,*
> *But all alone stands hugely politic.*

[2]Nineteenth-century forerunner of the camera.

In the strength of his constancy, the Pyramids seem to him recent and transitory. The freshness of youth and love dazzles him with its resemblance to morning.

> *Take those lips away*
> *Which so sweetly were forsworn;*
> *And those eyes,—the break of day,*
> *Lights that do mislead the morn.*[3]

The wild beauty of this hyperbole, I may say, in passing, it would not be easy to match in literature.

This transfiguration which all material objects undergo through the passion of the poet,—this power which he exerts to dwarf the great, to magnify the small,—might be illustrated by a thousand examples from his Plays. I have before me the Tempest, and will cite only these few lines.

> ARIEL. *The strong based promontory*
> *Have I made shake, and by the spurs plucked up*
> *The pine and cedar.*

Prospero calls for music to soothe the frantic Alonzo, and his companions;

> *A solemn air, and the best comforter*
> *To an unsettled fancy, cure thy brains*
> *Now useless, boiled within thy skull.*

Again;

> *The charm dissolves apace,*
> *And, as the morning steals upon the night,*
> *Melting the darkness, so their rising senses*
> *Begin to chase the ignorant fumes that mantle*
> *Their clearer reason.*

> *Their understanding*
> *Begins to swell: and the approaching tide*
> *Will shortly fill the reasonable shores*
> *That now lie foul and muddy.*[4]

The perception of real affinities between events, (that is to say, of *ideal* affinities, for those only are real,) enables the poet thus to make free with the most imposing forms and phenomena of the world, and to assert the predominance of the soul.

3. Whilst thus the poet animates nature with his own thoughts, he differs from the philosopher only herein, that the one proposes Beauty as his main end; the other Truth. But the philosopher, not less than the poet, postpones the apparent order and relations of things to the empire of thought. "The problem of philosophy," according to Plato, "is, for all that

---

[3]Shakespeare, Sonnets 70, 124, and *Measure for Measure*, IV, i, 1–4.

[4]Shakespeare, *The Tempest*, V, i. The opening lines are spoken not by Ariel but by Prospero.

exists conditionally, to find a ground unconditioned and absolute." It proceeds on the faith that a law determines all phenomena, which being known, the phenomena can be predicted. That law, when in the mind, is an idea. Its beauty is infinite. The true philosopher and the true poet are one, and a beauty, which is truth, and a truth, which is beauty, is the aim of both. Is not the charm of one of Plato's or Aristotle's definitions, strictly like that of the Antigone of Sophocles? It is, in both cases, that a spiritual life has been imparted to nature; that the solid seeming block of matter has been pervaded and dissolved by a thought; that this feeble human being has penetrated the vast masses of nature with an informing soul, and recognized itself in their harmony, that is, seized their law. In physics, when this is attained, the memory disburthens itself of its cumbrous catalogues of particulars, and carries centuries of observation in a single formula.

Thus even in physics, the material is degraded before the spiritual. The astronomer, the geometer, rely on their irrefragable analysis, and disdain the results of observation. The sublime remark of Euler[5] on his law of arches, "This will be found contrary to all experience, yet is true;" had already transferred nature into the mind, and left matter like an outcast corpse.

4. Intellectual science has been observed to beget invariably a doubt of the existence of matter. Turgot[6] said, "He that has never doubted the existence of matter, may be assured he has no aptitude for metaphysical inquiries." It fastens the attention upon immortal necessary uncreated natures, that is, upon Ideas; and in their presence, we feel that the outward circumstance is a dream and a shade. Whilst we wait in this Olympus of gods, we think of nature as an appendix to the soul. We ascend into their region, and know that these are the thoughts of the Supreme Being. "These are they who were set up from everlasting, from the beginning, or ever the earth was. When he prepared the heavens, they were there; when he established the clouds above, when he strengthened the fountains of the deep. Then they were by him, as one brought up with him. Of them took he counsel."[7]

Their influence is proportionate. As objects of science, they are accessible to few men. Yet all men are capable of being raised by piety or by passion, into their region. And no man touches these divine natures, without becoming, in some degree, himself divine. Like a new soul, they renew the body. We become physically nimble and lightsome; we tread on air; life is no longer irksome, and we think it will never be so. No man fears age or misfortune or death, in their serene company, for he is transported out of the district of change. Whilst we behold unveiled the nature of Justice and Truth, we learn the difference between the absolute and the conditional or relative. We apprehend the absolute. As it were, for the first time, *we exist*.

---

[5]Eighteenth-century Swiss mathematician.
[6]Eighteenth-century French economist and statesman.

[7]Paraphrase of Proverbs 8:23–30.

We become immortal, for we learn that time and space are relations of matter; that, with a perception of truth, or a virtuous will, they have no affinity.

5. Finally, religion and ethics, which may be fitly called,—the practice of ideas, or the introduction of ideas into life,—have an analogous effect with all lower culture, in degrading nature and suggesting its dependence on spirit. Ethics and religion differ herein; that the one is the system of human duties commencing from man; the other, from God. Religion includes the personality of God; Ethics does not. They are one to our present design. They both put nature under foot. The first and last lesson of religion is, "The things that are seen, are temporal; the things that are unseen, are eternal."[8] It puts an affront upon nature. It does that for the unschooled, which philosophy does for Berkeley and Viasa.[9] The uniform language that may be heard in the churches of the most ignorant sects, is,—'Contemn the unsubstantial shows of the world; they are vanities, dreams, shadows, unrealities; seek the realities of religion.' The devotee flouts nature. Some theosophists have arrived at a certain hostility and indignation towards matter, as the Manichean[10] and Plotinus.[11] They distrusted in themselves any looking back to these flesh-pots of Egypt. Plotinus was ashamed of his body. In short, they might all say of matter, what Michael Angelo said of external beauty, "it is the frail and weary weed, in which God dresses the soul, which he has called into time."

It appears that motion, poetry, physical and intellectual science, and religion, all tend to affect our convictions of the reality of the external world. But I own there is something ungrateful in expanding too curiously the particulars of the general proposition, that all culture tends to imbue us with idealism. I have no hostility to nature, but a child's love to it. I expand and live in the warm day like corn and melons. Let us speak her fair. I do not wish to fling stones at my beautiful mother, nor soil my gentle nest. I only wish to indicate the true position of nature in regard to man, wherein to establish man, all right education tends; as the ground which to attain is the object of human life, that is, of man's connection with nature. Culture inverts the vulgar views of nature, and brings the mind to call that apparent, which it uses to call real, and that real, which it uses to call visionary. Children, it is true, believe in the external world. The belief that it appears only, is an afterthought, but with culture, this faith will as surely arise on the mind as did the first.

The advantage of the ideal theory over the popular faith, is this, that it presents the world in precisely that view which is most desirable to the mind. It is, in fact, the view which Reason, both speculative and practical, that is, philosophy and virtue, take. For, seen in the light of thought, the world always is phenomenal; and virtue subordinates it to the mind. Idealism sees the world in God. It beholds the whole circle of persons and things,

[8]II Cor. 4:18.
[9]Eighteenth-century idealist philosopher and British bishop, and the legendary author of the Sanscrit scriptures, the Vedas.
[10]A follower of the third-century Babylonian mystic Manes, who believes the world is divided between good and evil.
[11]Third-century Roman philosopher.

of actions and events, of country and religion, not as painfully accumulated, atom after atom, act after act, in an aged creeping Past, but as one vast picture, which God paints on the instant eternity, for the contemplation of the soul. Therefore the soul holds itself off from a too trivial and microscopic study of the universal tablet. It respects the end too much, to immerse itself in the means. It sees something more important in Christianity, than the scandals of ecclesiastical history, or the niceties of criticism; and, very incurious concerning persons or miracles, and not at all disturbed by chasms of historical evidence, it accepts from God the phenomenon, as it finds it, as the pure and awful form of religion in the world. It is not hot and passionate at the appearance of what it calls its own good or bad fortune, at the union or opposition of other persons. No man is its enemy. It accepts whatsoever befalls, as part of its lesson. It is a watcher more than a doer, and it is a doer, only that it may the better watch.

Chapter VII

Spirit

It is essential to a true theory of nature and of man, that it should contain somewhat progressive. Uses that are exhausted or that may be, and facts that end in the statement, cannot be all that is true of this brave lodging wherein man is harbored, and wherein all his faculties find appropriate and endless exercise. And all the uses of nature admit of being summed in one, which yields the activity of man an infinite scope. Through all its kingdoms, to the suburbs and outskirts of things, it is faithful to the cause whence it had its origin. It always speaks of Spirit. It suggests the absolute. It is a perpetual effect. It is a great shadow pointing always to the sun behind us.

The aspect of nature is devout. Like the figure of Jesus, she stands with bended head, and hands folded upon the breast. The happiest man is he who learns from nature the lesson of worship.

Of that ineffable essence which we call Spirit, he that thinks most, will say least. We can foresee God in the coarse, and, as it were, distant phenomena of matter; but when we try to define and describe himself, both language and thought desert us, and we are as helpless as fools and savages. That essence refuses to be recorded in propositions, but when man has worshipped him intellectually, the noblest ministry of nature is to stand as the apparition of God. It is the organ through which the universal spirit speaks to the individual, and strives to lead back the individual to it.

When we consider Spirit, we see that the views already presented do not include the whole circumference of man. We must add some related thoughts.

Three problems are put by nature to the mind; What is matter? Whence is it? and Whereto? The first of these questions only, the ideal theory answers. Idealism saith: matter is a phenomenon, not a substance. Idealism acquaints us with the total disparity between the evidence of our own being, and the evidence of the world's being. The one is perfect; the other, incapable of any assurance; the mind is a part of the nature of things; the world is a divine dream, from which we may presently awake to the glories and certainties of day. Idealism is a hypothesis to account for nature by other principles than those of carpentry and chemistry. Yet, if it only deny the existence of matter, it does not satisfy the demands of the spirit. It leaves God out of me. It leaves me in the splendid labyrinth of my perceptions, to wander without end. Then the heart resists it, because it balks the affections in denying substantive being to men and women. Nature is so pervaded with human life, that there is something of humanity in all, and in every particular. But this theory makes nature foreign to me, and does not account for that consanguinity which we acknowledge to it.

Let it stand, then, in the present state of our knowledge, merely as a useful introductory hypothesis, serving to apprize us of the eternal distinction between the soul and the world.

But when, following the invisible steps of thought, we come to inquire, Whence is matter? and Whereto? many truths arise to us out of the recesses of consciousness. We learn that the highest is present to the soul of man, that the dread universal essence, which is not wisdom, or love, or beauty, or power, but all in one, and each entirely, is that for which all things exist, and that by which they are; that spirit creates; that behind nature, throughout nature, spirit is present; one and not compound, it does not act upon us from without, that is, in space and time, but spiritually, or through ourselves: therefore, that spirit, that is, the Supreme Being, does not build up nature around us, but puts it forth through us, as the life of the tree puts forth new branches and leaves through the pores of the old. As a plant upon the earth, so a man rests upon the bosom of God; he is nourished by unfailing fountains, and draws, at his need, inexhaustible power. Who can set bounds to the possibilities of man? Once inhale the upper air, being admitted to behold the absolute natures of justice and truth, and we learn that man has access to the entire mind of the Creator, is himself the creator in the finite. This view, which admonishes me where the sources of wisdom and power lie, and points to virtue as to

> "The golden key
> Which opes the palace of eternity,"[1]

carries upon its face the highest certificate of truth, because it animates me to create my own world through the purification of my soul.

The world proceeds from the same spirit as the body of man. It is a remoter and inferior incarnation of God, a projection of God in the unconscious. But it differs from the body in one important respect. It is not, like that, now subjected to the human will. Its serene order is inviolable by us. It is, therefore, to us, the present expositor of the divine mind. It is a fixed point whereby we may measure our departure. As we degenerate, the contrast between us and our house is more evident We are as much strangers

---

[1]Milton, *Comus*, 13–14.

in nature, as we are aliens from God. We do not understand the notes of birds. The fox and the deer run away from us; the bear and tiger rend us. We do not know the uses of more than a few plants, as corn and the apple, the potato and the vine. Is not the landscape, every glimpse of which hath a grandeur, a face of him? Yet this may show us what discord is between man and nature, for you cannot freely admire a noble landscape, if laborers are digging in the field hard by. The poet finds something ridiculous in his delight, until he is out of the sight of men.

Chapter VIII

Prospects

In inquiries respecting the laws of the world and the frame of things, the highest reason is always the truest. That which seems faintly possible—it is so refined, is often faint and dim because it is deepest seated in the mind among the eternal verities. Empirical science is apt to cloud the sight, and, by the very knowledge of functions and processes, to bereave the student of the manly contemplation of the whole. The savant becomes unpoetic. But the best read naturalist who lends an entire and devout attention to truth, will see that there remains much to learn of his relation to the world, and that it is not to be learned by any addition or subtraction or other comparison of known quantities, but is arrived at by untaught sallies of the spirit, by a continual self-recovery, and by entire humility. He will perceive that there are far more excellent qualities in the student than preciseness and infallibility; that a guess is often more fruitful than an indisputable affirmation, and that a dream may let us deeper into the secret of nature than a hundred concerted experiments.

For, the problems to be solved are precisely those which the physiologist and the naturalist omit to state. It is not so pertinent to man to know all the individuals of the animal kingdom, as it is to know whence and whereto is this tyrannizing unity in his constitution, which evermore separates and classifies things, endeavoring to reduce the most diverse to one form. When I behold a rich landscape, it is less to my purpose to recite correctly the order and superposition of the strata, than to know why all thought of multitude is lost in a tranquil sense of unity. I cannot greatly honor minuteness in details, so long as there is no hint to explain the relation between things and thoughts; no ray upon the *metaphysics* of conchology, of botany, of the arts, to show the relation of the forms of flowers, shells, animals, architecture, to the mind, and build science upon ideas. In a cabinet of natural history, we become sensible of a certain occult recognition and sympathy in regard to the most unwieldy and eccentric forms of beast, fish, and insect. The American who has been confined, in his own country, to the sight of buildings designed after foreign models, is surprised on entering York Minster or St. Peter's at Rome, by the feeling that these structures are imitations also,—faint copies of an invisible archetype. Nor has science sufficient humanity, so long as the naturalist overlooks that wonderful congruity which subsists between man and the world; of which he is lord, not because he is the most subtile inhabitant, but because he is its head and heart, and finds something of himself in every great and small thing, in every mountain stratum, in every new law of color, fact of astronomy, or atmospheric influence which observation or analysis lay open. A perception of this mystery inspires the muse of George Herbert, the beautiful psalmist of the seventeenth century. The following lines are part of his little poem on Man.

> "Man is all symmetry,
> Full of proportions, one limb to another,
> And to all the world besides.
> Each part may call the farthest, brother;
> For head with foot hath private amity,
> And both with moons and tides.

> "Nothing hath got so far
> But man hath caught and kept it as his prey;
> His eyes dismount the highest star;
> He is in little all the sphere.
> Herbs gladly cure our flesh, because that they
> Find their acquaintance there.

> "For us, the winds do blow,
> The earth doth rest, heaven move, and fountains flow;
> Nothing we see, but means our good,
> As our delight, or as our treasure;
> The whole is either our cupboard of food,
> Or cabinet of pleasure.

> "The stars have us to bed:
> Night draws the curtain; which the sun withdraws.
> Music and light attend our head.
> All things unto our flesh are kind,
> In their descent and being; to our mind,
> In their ascent and cause.

> "More servants wait on man
> Than he'll take notice of. In every path,
> He treads down that which doth befriend him
> When sickness makes him pale and wan.
> Oh mighty love! Man is one world, and hath
> Another to attend him."

The perception of this class of truths makes the attraction which draws men to science, but the end is lost sight of in attention to the means. In view of this half-sight of science, we accept the sentence of Plato, that, "poetry comes nearer to vital truth than history." Every surmise and

vaticination of the mind is entitled to a certain respect, and we learn to prefer imperfect theories, and sentences, which contain glimpses of truth, to
digested systems which have no one valuable suggestion. A wise writer will
feel that the ends of study and composition are best answered by announcing undiscovered regions of thought, and so communicating, through hope,
new activity to the torpid spirit.

I shall therefore conclude this essay with some traditions of man and
nature, which a certain poet[1] sang to me; and which, as they have always
been in the world, and perhaps reappear to every bard, may be both history
and prophecy.

'The foundations of man are not in matter, but in spirit. But the element of spirit is eternity. To it, therefore, the longest series of events, the
oldest chronologies are young and recent. In the cycle of the universal man,
from whom the known individuals proceed, centuries are points, and all history is but the epoch of one degradation.

'We distrust and deny inwardly our sympathy with nature. We own and
disown our relation to it, by turns. We are, like Nebuchadnezzar,[2] dethroned,
bereft of reason, and eating grass like an ox. But who can set limits to the
remedial force of spirit?

'A man is a god in ruins. When men are innocent, life shall be longer,
and shall pass into the immortal, as gently as we awake from dreams. Now,
the world would be insane and rabid, if these disorganizations should last
for hundreds of years. It is kept in check by death and infancy. Infancy is
the perpetual Messiah, which comes into the arms of fallen men, and pleads
with them to return to paradise.

'Man is the dwarf of himself. Once he was permeated and dissolved by
spirit. He filled nature with his overflowing currents. Out from him sprang
the sun and moon; from man, the sun; from woman, the moon. The laws of
his mind, the periods of his actions externized themselves into day and
night, into the year and the seasons. But, having made for himself this huge
shell, his waters retired; he no longer fills the veins and veinlets; he is
shrunk to a drop. He sees, that the structure still fits him, but fits him
colossally. Say, rather, once it fitted him, now it corresponds to him from
far and on high. He adores timidly his own work. Now is man the follower
of the sun, and woman the follower of the moon. Yet sometimes he starts
in his slumber, and wonders at himself and his house, and muses strangely
at the resemblance betwixt him and it. He perceives that if his law is still
paramount, if still he have elemental power, if his word is sterling yet in nature, it is not conscious power, it is not inferior but superior to his will. It is
Instinct.' Thus my Orphic poet sang.

At present, man applies to nature but half his force. He works on the
world with his understanding alone. He lives in it, and masters it by a

---

[1]Emerson here "quotes" an imaginary poet.   [2]Cf. Daniel 4:25–33.
Most of these "orphic" passages are drawn
from his own journals.

penny-wisdom; and he that works most in it, is but a half-man, and whilst his arms are strong and his digestion good, his mind is imbruted, and he is a selfish savage. His relation to nature, his power over it, is through the understanding; as by manure; the economic use of fire, wind, water, and the mariner's needle; steam, coal, chemical agriculture; the repairs of the human body by the dentist and the surgeon. This is such a resumption of power, as if a banished king should buy his territories inch by inch, instead of vaulting at once into his throne. Meantime, in the thick darkness, there are not wanting gleams of a better light,—occasional examples of the action of man upon nature with his entire force,—with reason as well as understanding. Such examples are; the traditions of miracles in the earliest antiquity of all nations; the history of Jesus Christ; the achievements of a principle, as in religious and political revolutions, and in the abolition of the Slave-trade; the miracles of enthusiasm, as those reported of Swedenborg, Hohenlohe,[3] and the Shakers; many obscure and yet contested facts, now arranged under the name of Animal Magnetism;[4] prayer; eloquence; self-healing; and the wisdom of children. These are examples of Reason's momentary grasp of the sceptre; the exertions of a power which exists not in time or space, but an instantaneous in-streaming causing power. The difference between the actual and the ideal force of man is happily figured by the schoolmen, in saying, that the knowledge of man is an evening knowledge, *vespertina cognitio*, but that of God is a morning knowledge, *matutina cognitio*.

The problem of restoring to the world original and eternal beauty, is solved by the redemption of the soul. The ruin or the blank, that we see when we look at nature, is in our own eye. The axis of vision is not coincident with the axis of things, and so they appear not transparent but opake. The reason why the world lacks unity, and lies broken and in heaps, is, because man is disunited with himself. He cannot be a naturalist, until he satisfies all the demands of the spirit. Love is as much its demand, as perception. Indeed, neither can be perfect without the other. In the uttermost meaning of the words, thought is devout, and devotion is thought. Deep calls unto deep.[5] But in actual life, the marriage is not celebrated. There are innocent men who worship God after the tradition of their fathers, but their sense of duty has not yet extended to the use of all their faculties. And there are patient naturalists, but they freeze their subject under the wintry light of the understanding. Is not prayer also a study of truth,—a sally of the soul into the unfound infinite? No man ever prayed heartily, without learning something. But when a faithful thinker, resolute to detach every object from personal relations, and see it in the light of thought, shall, at the same time, kindle science with the fire of the holiest affections, then will God go forth anew into the creation.

[3]Nineteenth-century German bishop credited with miracle cures.
[4]Form of hypnotism or mesmerism, developed in 1775 by Friedrich Mesmer.
[5]Cf. Psalms 42:7.

It will not need, when the mind is prepared for study, to search for objects. The invariable mark of wisdom is to see the miraculous in the common. What is a day? What is a year? What is summer? What is woman? What is a child? What is sleep? To our blindness, these things seem unaffecting. We make fables to hide the baldness of the fact and conform it, as we say, to the higher law of the mind. But when the fact is seen under the light of an idea, the gaudy fable fades and shrivels. We behold the real higher law. To the wise, therefore, a fact is true poetry, and the most beautiful of fables. These wonders are brought to our own door. You also are a man. Man and woman, and their social life, poverty, labor, sleep, fear, fortune, are known to you. Learn that none of these things is superficial, but that each phenomenon has its roots in the faculties and affections of the mind. Whilst the abstract question occupies your intellect, nature brings it in the concrete to be solved by your hands. It were a wise inquiry for the closet, to compare, point by point, especially at remarkable crises in life, our daily history, with the rise and progress of ideas in the mind.

So shall we come to look at the world with new eyes. It shall answer the endless inquiry of the intellect,—What is truth? and of the affections,—What is good? by yielding itself passive to the educated Will. Then shall come to pass what my poet said; 'Nature is not fixed but fluid. Spirit alters, moulds, makes it. The immobility or bruteness of nature, is the absence of spirit; to pure spirit, it is fluid, it is volatile, it is obedient. Every spirit builds itself a house; and beyond its house a world; and beyond its world, a heaven. Know then, that the world exists for you. For you is the phenomenon perfect. What we are, that only can we see. All that Adam had, all that Caesar could, you have and can do. Adam called his house, heaven and earth; Caesar called his house, Rome; you perhaps call yours, a cobler's trade; a hundred acres of ploughed land; or a scholar's garret. Yet line for line and point for point, your dominion is as great as theirs, though without fine names. Build, therefore, your own world. As fast as you conform your life to the pure idea in your mind, that will unfold its great proportions. A correspondent revolution in things will attend the influx of the spirit. So fast will disagreeable appearances, swine, spiders, snakes, pests, madhouses, prisons, enemies, vanish; they are temporary and shall be no more seen. The sordor and filths of nature, the sun shall dry up, and the wind exhale. As when the summer comes from the south; the snow-banks melt, and the face of the earth becomes green before it, so shall the advancing spirit create its ornaments along its path, and carry with it the beauty it visits, and the song which enchants it; it shall draw beautiful faces, warm hearts, wise discourse, and heroic acts, around its way, until evil is no more seen. The kingdom of man over nature, which cometh not with observation,—a dominion such as now is beyond his dream of God,—he shall enter without more wonder than the blind man feels who is gradually restored to perfect sight.'

1836, 1849

The American Scholar[1]

An Oration delivered before the Phi Beta Kappa Society, at Cambridge, August 31, 1837

Mr. President and Gentlemen,

I greet you on the re-commencement of our literary year. Our anniversary is one of hope, and, perhaps, not enough of labor. We do not meet for games of strength or skill, for the recitation of histories, tragedies, and odes, like the ancient Greeks; for parliaments of love and poesy, like the Troubadours; nor for the advancement of science, like our cotemporaries in the British and European capitals. Thus far, our holiday has been simply a friendly sign of the survival of the love of letters amongst a people too busy to give to letters any more. As such, it is precious as the sign of an indestructible instinct. Perhaps the time is already come, when it ought to be, and will be, something else; when the sluggard intellect of this continent will look from under its iron lids, and fill the postponed expectation of the world with something better than the exertions of mechanical skill. Our day of dependence, our long apprenticeship to the learning of other lands, draws to a close. The millions, that around us are rushing into life, cannot always be fed on the sere remains of foreign harvests. Events, actions arise, that must be sung, that will sing themselves. Who can doubt, that poetry will revive and lead in a new age, as the star in the constellation Harp, which now flames in our zenith, astronomers announce, shall one day be the pole-star for a thousand years?

In this hope, I accept the topic which not only usage, but the nature of our association, seem to prescribe to this day,—the AMERICAN SCHOLAR. Year by year, we come up hither to read one more chapter of his biography. Let us inquire what light new days and events have thrown on his character, and his hopes.

It is one of those fables,[2] which, out of an unknown antiquity, convey an unlooked-for wisdom, that the gods, in the beginning, divided Man into men, that he might be more helpful to himself; just as the hand was divided into fingers, the better to answer its end.

The old fable covers a doctrine ever new and sublime; that there is One Man,—present to all particular men only partially, or through one faculty; and that you must take the whole society to find the whole man. Man is not a farmer, or a professor, or an engineer, but he is all. Man is priest, and scholar, and statesman, and producer, and soldier. In the *divided* or social state, these functions are parcelled out to individuals, each of whom aims to do his stint of the joint work, whilst each other performs his. The fable implies, that the individual, to possess himself, must sometimes return from

[1]The original title for the address and 1837 pamphlet was "An Oration Delivered before the Phi Beta Kappa Society, at Cambridge, August 31, 1937." The 1849 title is the assigned topic of the annual Phi Beta Kappa lectures.

[2]A version of this fable appears in Plato and in Plutarch.

his own labor to embrace all the other laborers. But unfortunately, this original unit, this fountain of power, has been so distributed to multitudes, has been so minutely subdivided and peddled out, that it is spilled into drops, and cannot be gathered. The state of society is one in which the members have suffered amputation from the trunk, and strut about so many walking monsters,—a good finger, a neck, a stomach, an elbow, but never a man.

Man is thus metamorphosed into a thing, into many things. The planter, who is Man sent out into the field to gather food, is seldom cheered by any idea of the true dignity of his ministry. He sees his bushel and his cart, and nothing beyond, and sinks into the farmer, instead of Man on the farm. The tradesman scarcely ever gives an ideal worth to his work, but is ridden by the routine of his craft, and the soul is subject to dollars. The priest becomes a form; the attorney, a statute-book; the mechanic, a machine; the sailor, a rope of a ship.

In this distribution of functions, the scholar is the delegated intellect. In the right state, he is, *Man Thinking*. In the degenerate state, when the victim of society, he tends to become a mere thinker, or, still worse, the parrot of other men's thinking.

In this view of him, as Man Thinking, the theory of his office is contained. Him nature solicits with all her placid, all her monitory pictures; him the past instructs; him the future invites. Is not, indeed, every man a student, and do not all things exist for the student's behoof? And, finally, is not the true scholar the only true master? But the old oracle[3] said, "All things have two handles: beware of the wrong one." In life, too often, the scholar errs with mankind and forfeits his privilege. Let us see him in his school, and consider him in reference to the main influences he receives.

I. The first in time and the first in importance of the influences upon the mind is that of nature. Every day, the sun; and, after sunset, night and her stars. Ever the winds blow; ever the grass grows. Every day, men and women, conversing, beholding and beholden. The scholar is he of all men whom this spectacle most engages. He must settle its value in his mind. What is nature to him? There is never a beginning, there is never an end, to the inexplicable continuity of this web of God, but always circular power returning into itself. Therein it resembles his own spirit, whose beginning, whose ending, he never can find,—so entire, so boundless. Far, too, as her splendors shine, system on system shooting like rays, upward, downward, without centre, without circumference,—in the mass and in the particle, nature hastens to render account of herself to the mind. Classification begins. To the young mind, every thing is individual, stands by itself. By and by, it finds how to join two things, and see in them one nature; then three, then three thousand; and so, tyrannized over by its own unifying instinct, it goes on tying things together, diminishing anomalies, discovering roots running under ground, whereby contrary and remote things cohere, and flower out

---

[3]The passage is from the Stoic philosopher Epictetus (1st–2nd cent. A.D.).

from one stem. It presently learns, that, since the dawn of history, there has been a constant accumulation and classifying of facts. But what is classification but the perceiving that these objects are not chaotic, and are not foreign, but have a law which is also a law of the human mind? The astronomer discovers that geometry, a pure abstraction of the human mind, is the measure of planetary motion. The chemist finds proportions and intelligible method throughout matter; and science is nothing but the finding of analogy, identity, in the most remote parts. The ambitious soul sits down before each refractory fact; one after another, reduces all strange constitutions, all new powers, to their class and their law, and goes on for ever to animate the last fibre of organization, the outskirts of nature, by insight.

Thus to him, to this school-boy under the bending dome of day, is suggested, that he and it proceed from one root; one is leaf and one is flower; relation, sympathy, stirring in every vein. And what is that Root? Is not that the soul of his soul?—A thought too bold,—a dream too wild. Yet when this spiritual light shall have revealed the law of more earthly natures,—when he has learned to worship the soul, and to see that the natural philosophy that now is, is only the first gropings of its gigantic hand, he shall look forward to an ever expanding knowledge as to a becoming creator. He shall see, that nature is the opposite of the soul, answering to it part for part. One is seal, and one is print. Its beauty is the beauty of his own mind. Its laws are the laws of his own mind. Nature then becomes to him the measure of his attainments. So much of nature as he is ignorant of, so much of his own mind does he not yet possess. And, in fine, the ancient precept, "Know thyself," and the modern precept, "Study nature," become at last one maxim.

II. The next great influence into the spirit of the scholar, is, the mind of the Past,—in whatever form, whether of literature, of art, of institutions, that mind is inscribed. Books are the best type of the influence of the past, and perhaps we shall get at the truth,—learn the amount of this influence more conveniently,—by considering their value alone.

The theory of books is noble. The scholar of the first age received into him the world around; brooded thereon; gave it the new arrangement of his own mind, and uttered it again. It came into him, life; it went out from him, truth. It came to him, short-lived actions; it went out from him, immortal thoughts. It came to him, business; it went from him, poetry. It was dead fact; now, it is quick thought. It can stand, and it can go. It now endures, it now flies, it now inspires. Precisely in proportion to the depth of mind from which it issued, so high does it soar, so long does it sing.

Or, I might say, it depends on how far the process had gone, of transmuting life into truth. In proportion to the completeness of the distillation, so will the purity and imperishableness of the product be. But none is quite perfect. As no air-pump can by any means make a perfect vacuum, so neither can any artist entirely exclude the conventional, the local, the perishable from his book, or write a book of pure thought, that shall be as efficient, in all respects, to a remote posterity, as to cotemporaries, or rather to the second age. Each age, it is found, must write its own books; or rather, each generation for the next succeeding. The books of an older period will not fit this.

Yet hence arises a grave mischief. The sacredness which attaches to the act of creation,—the act of thought,—is transferred to the record. The poet chanting, was felt to be a divine man: henceforth the chant is divine also. The writer was a just and wise spirit: henceforward it is settled, the book is perfect; as love of the hero corrupts into worship of his statue. Instantly, the book becomes noxious: the guide is a tyrant. The sluggish and perverted mind of the multitude, slow to open to the incursions of Reason, having once so opened, having once received this book, stands upon it, and makes an outcry, if it is disparaged. Colleges are built on it. Books are written on it by thinkers, not by Man Thinking; by men of talent, that is, who start wrong, who set out from accepted dogmas, not from their own sight of principles. Meek young men grow up in libraries, believing it their duty to accept the views, which Cicero, which Locke, which Bacon, have given, forgetful that Cicero, Locke, and Bacon[4] were only young men in libraries, when they wrote these books.

Hence, instead of Man Thinking, we have the bookworm. Hence, the book-learned class, who value books, as such; not as related to nature and the human constitution, but as making a sort of Third Estate[5] with the world and the soul. Hence, the restorers of readings, the emendators, the bibliomaniacs of all degrees.

Books are the best of things, well used; abused, among the worst. What is the right use? What is the one end, which all means go to effect? They are for nothing but to inspire. I had better never see a book, than to be warped by its attraction clean out of my own orbit, and made a satellite instead of a system. The one thing in the world, of value, is the active soul. This every man is entitled to; this every man contains within him, although, in almost all men, obstructed, and as yet unborn. The soul active sees absolute truth; and utters truth, or creates. In this action, it is genius; not the privilege of here and there a favorite, but the sound estate of every man. In its essence, it is progressive. The book, the college, the school of art, the institution of any kind, stop with some past utterance of genius. This is good, say they,— let us hold by this. They pin me down. They look backward and not forward. But genius looks forward: the eyes of man are set in his forehead, not in his hindhead: man hopes: genius creates. Whatever talents may be, if the man create not, the pure efflux of the Diety is not his;—cinders and smoke there may be, but not yet flame. There are creative manners, there are creative actions, and creative words; manners, actions, words, that is, indicative of

---

[4] Emerson lists "young men" who, as adults, altered Western intellectual practice: the Roman orator Cicero (106–43 B.C.), seventeenth-century British philosopher John Locke, and seventeenth-century essayist Francis Bacon.

[5] Term used in prerevolutionary France and in England to define the political class of commoners.

no custom or authority, but springing spontaneous from the mind's own sense of good and fair.

On the other part, instead of being its own seer, let it receive from another mind its truth, though it were in torrents of light, without periods of solitude, inquest, and self-recovery, and a fatal disservice is done. Genius is always sufficiently the enemy of genius by over influence. The literature of every nation bear me witness. The English dramatic poets have Shakspearized now for two hundred years.

Undoubtedly there is a right way of reading, so it be sternly subordinated. Man Thinking must not be subdued by his instruments. Books are for the scholar's idle times. When he can read God directly, the hour is too precious to be wasted in other men's transcripts of their readings. But when the intervals of darkness come, as come they must,—when the sun is hid, and the stars withdraw their shining,—we repair to the lamps which were kindled by their ray, to guide our steps to the East again, where the dawn is. We hear, that we may speak. The Arabian proverb says, "A fig tree, looking on a fig tree, becometh fruitful."

It is remarkable, the character of the pleasure we derive from the best books. They impress us with the conviction, that one nature wrote and the same reads. We read the verses of one of the great English poets, of Chaucer, of Marvell, of Dryden, with the most modern joy,—with a pleasure, I mean, which is in great part caused by the abstraction of all *time* from their verses. There is some awe mixed with the joy of our surprise, when this poet, who lived in some past world, two or three hundred years ago, says that which lies close to my own soul, that which I also had wellnigh thought and said. But for the evidence thence afforded to the philosophical doctrine of the identity of all minds, we should suppose some preëstablished harmony, some foresight of souls that were to be, and some preparation of stores for their future wants, like the fact observed in insects, who lay up food before death for the young grub they shall never see.

I would not be hurried by any love of system, by any exaggeration of instincts, to underrate the Book. We all know, that, as the human body can be nourished on any food, though it were boiled grass and the broth of shoes, so the human mind can be fed by any knowledge. And great and heroic men have existed, who had almost no other information than by the printed page. I only would say, that it needs a strong head to bear that diet. One must be an inventor to read well. As the proverb says, "He that would bring home the wealth of the Indies, must carry out the wealth of the Indies." There is then creative reading as well as creative writing. When the mind is braced by labor and invention, the page of whatever book we read becomes luminous with manifold allusion. Every sentence is doubly significant, and the sense of our author is as broad as the world. We then see, what is always true, that, as the seer's hour of vision is short and rare among heavy days and months, so is its record, perchance, the least part of his volume. The discerning will read, in his Plato or Shakspeare, only that least part,—only the authentic utterances of the oracle;—all the rest he rejects, were it never so many times Plato's and Shakspeare's.

Of course, there is a portion of reading quite indispensable to a wise man. History and exact science he must learn by laborious reading. Colleges, in like manner, have their indispensable office,—to teach elements. But they can only highly serve us, when they aim not to drill, but to create; when they gather from far every ray of various genius to their hospitable halls, and, by the concentrated fires, set the hearts of their youth on flame. Thought and knowledge are natures in which apparatus and pretension avail nothing. Gowns, and pecuniary foundations, though of towns of gold, can never countervail the least sentence or syllable of wit. Forget this, and our American colleges will recede in their public importance, whilst they grow richer every year.

III. There goes in the world a notion, that the scholar should be a recluse, a valetudinarian,—as unfit for any handiwork or public labor, as a penknife for an axe. The so-called 'practical men' sneer at speculative men, as if, because they speculate or *see*, they could do nothing. I have heard it said that the clergy,—who are always, more universally than any other class, the scholars of their day,—are addressed as women; that the rough, spontaneous conversation of men they do not hear, but only a mincing and diluted speech. They are often virtually disfranchised; and, indeed, there are advocates for their celibacy. As far as this is true of the studious classes, it is not just and wise. Action is with the scholar subordinate, but it is essential. Without it, he is not yet man. Without it, thought can never ripen into truth. Whilst the world hangs before the eye as a cloud of beauty, we cannot even see its beauty. Inaction is cowardice, but there can be no scholar without the heroic mind. The preamble of thought, the transition through which it passes from the unconscious to the conscious, is action. Only so much do I know, as I have lived. Instantly we know whose words are loaded with life, and whose not.

The world,—this shadow of the soul, or *other me*, lies wide around. Its attractions are the keys which unlock my thoughts and make me acquainted with myself. I run eagerly into this resounding tumult. I grasp the hands of those next me, and take my place in the ring to suffer and to work, taught by an instinct, that so shall the dumb abyss be vocal with speech. I pierce its order; I dissipate its fear; I dispose of it within the circuit of my expanding life. So much only of life as I know by experience, so much of the wilderness have I vanquished and planted, or so far have I extended my being, my dominion. I do not see how any man can afford, for the sake of his nerves and his nap, to spare any action in which he can partake. It is pearls and rubies to his discourse. Drudgery, calamity, exasperation, want, are instructors in eloquence and wisdom. The true scholar grudges every opportunity of action past by, as a loss of power.

It is the raw material out of which the intellect moulds her splendid products. A strange process too, this, by which experience is converted into thought, as a mulberry leaf is converted into satin. The manufacture goes forward at all hours.

The actions and events of our childhood and youth, are now matters of calmest observation. They lie like fair pictures in the air. Not so with our recent actions,—with the business which we now have in hand. On this we are quite unable to speculate. Our affections as yet circulate through it. We no more feel or know it, than we feel the feet, or the hand, or the brain of our body. The new deed is yet a part of life,—remains for a time immersed in our unconscious life. In some contemplative hour, it detaches itself from the life like a ripe fruit, to become a thought of the mind. Instantly, it is raised, transfigured; the corruptible has put on incorruption. Henceforth it is an object of beauty, however base its origin and neighborhood. Observe, too, the impossibility of antedating this act. In its grub state, it cannot fly, it cannot shine, it is a dull grub. But suddenly, without observation, the self-same thing unfurls beautiful wings, and is an angel of wisdom. So is there no fact, no event, in our private history, which shall not, sooner or later, lose its adhesive, inert form, and astonish us by soaring from our body into the empyrean. Cradle and infancy, school and playground, the fear of boys, and dogs, and ferules, the love of little maids and berries, and many another fact that once filled the whole sky, are gone already; friend and relative, profession and party, town and country, nation and world, must also soar and sing.

Of course, he who has put forth his total strength in fit actions, has the richest return of wisdom. I will not shut myself out of this globe of action, and transplant an oak into a flower-pot, there to hunger and pine; nor trust the revenue of some single faculty, and exhaust one vein of thought, much like those Savoyards,[6] who, getting their livelihood by carving shepherds, shepherdesses, and smoking Dutchmen, for all Europe, went out one day to the mountain to find stock, and discovered that they had whittled up the last of their pine-trees. Authors we have, in numbers, who have written out their vein, and who, moved by a commendable prudence, sail for Greece or Palestine, follow the trapper into the prairie, or ramble round Algiers, to replenish their merchantable stock.

If it were only for a vocabulary, the scholar would be covetous of action. Life is our dictionary. Years are well spent in country labors; in town,—in the insight into trades and manufactures; in frank intercourse with many men and women; in science; in art; to the one end of mastering in all their facts a language by which to illustrate and embody our perceptions. I learn immediately from any speaker how much he has already lived, through the poverty or the splendor of his speech. Life lies behind us as the quarry from whence we get tiles and copestones for the masonry of to-day. This is the way to learn grammar. Colleges and books only copy the language which the field and the work-yard made.

But the final value of action, like that of books, and better than books, is, that it is a resource. That great principle of Undulation in nature, that shows itself in the inspiring and expiring of the breath; in desire and satiety;

---

[6]Natives of Savoy, region in the French Alps.

in the ebb and flow of the sea; in day and night; in heat and cold; and as yet more deeply ingrained in every atom and every fluid, is known to us under the name of Polarity,—these "fits of easy transmission and reflection," as Newton called them, are the law of nature because they are the law of spirit.

The mind now thinks; now acts; and each fit reproduces the other. When the artist has exhausted his materials, when the fancy no longer paints, when thoughts are no longer apprehended, and books are a weariness,—he has always the resource *to live*. Character is higher than intellect. Thinking is the function. Living is the functionary. The stream retreats to its source. A great soul will be strong to live, as well as strong to think. Does he lack organ or medium to impart his truths? He can still fall back on this elemental force of living them. This is a total act. Thinking is a partial act. Let the grandeur of justice shine in his affairs. Let the beauty of affection cheer his lowly roof. Those 'far from fame,' who dwell and act with him, will feel the force of his constitution in the doings and passages of the day better than it can be measured by any public and designed display. Time shall teach him, that the scholar loses no hour which the man lives. Herein he unfolds the sacred germ of his instinct, screened from influence. What is lost in seemliness is gained in strength. Not out of those, on whom systems of education have exhausted their culture, comes the helpful giant to destroy the old or to build the new, but out of unhandselled[7] savage nature, out of terrible Druids and Berserkirs, come at last Alfred and Shakspeare.[8]

I hear therefore with joy whatever is beginning to be said of the dignity and necessity of labor to every citizen. There is virtue yet in the hoe and the spade, for learned as well as for unlearned hands. And labor is everywhere welcome; always we are invited to work; only be this limitation observed, that a man shall not for the sake of wider activity sacrifice any opinion to the popular judgments and modes of action.

I have now spoken of the education of the scholar by nature, by books, and by action. It remains to say somewhat of his duties.

They are such as become Man Thinking. They may all be comprised in self-trust. The office of the scholar is to cheer, to raise, and to guide men by showing them facts amidst appearances. He plies the slow, unhonored, and unpaid task of observation. Flamsteed and Herschel,[9] in their glazed observatories, may catalogue the stars with the praise of all men, and, the results being splendid and useful, honor is sure. But he, in his private observatory, cataloguing obscure and nebulous stars of the human mind, which as yet no man has thought of as such,—watching days and months, sometimes, for a few facts; correcting still his old records;—must relinquish display and immediate fame. In the long period of his preparation, he must betray often an ignorance and shiftlessness in popular arts, incurring the disdain of the

[7]Untamed, untouched by hand, inauspicious.

[8]Ancient Celtic priests and Norse warriors contrast with examples of British civilization, Shakespeare and Alfred, the ninth-century king who founded schools and instituted laws.

[9]Seventeenth- and eighteenth-century English astronomers.

able who shoulder him aside. Long he must stammer in his speech; often forego the living for the dead. Worse yet, he must accept,—how often! poverty and solitude. For the ease and pleasure of treading the old road, accepting the fashions, the education, the religion of society, he takes the cross of making his own, and, of course, the self-accusation, the faint heart, the frequent uncertainty and loss of time, which are the nettles and tangling vines in the way of the self-relying and self-directed; and the state of virtual hostility in which he seems to stand to society, and especially to educated society. For all this loss and scorn, what offset? He is to find consolation in exercising the highest functions of human nature. He is one, who raises himself from private considerations, and breathes and lives on public and illustrious thoughts. He is the world's eye. He is the world's heart. He is to resist the vulgar prosperity that retrogrades ever to barbarism, by preserving and communicating heroic sentiments, noble biographies, melodious verse, and the conclusions of history. Whatsoever oracles the human heart, in all emergencies, in all solemn hours, has uttered as its commentary on the world of actions,—these he shall receive and impart. And whatsoever new verdict Reason from her inviolable seat pronounces on the passing men and events of to-day,—this he shall hear and promulgate.

These being his functions, it becomes him to feel all confidence in himself, and to defer never to the popular cry. He and he only knows the world. The world of any moment is the merest appearance. Some great decorum, some fetish of a government, some ephemeral trade, or war, or man, is cried up by half mankind and cried down by the other half, as if all depended on this particular up or down. The odds are that the whole question is not worth the poorest thought which the scholar has lost in listening to the controversy. Let him not quit his belief that a popgun is a popgun, though the ancient and honorable of the earth affirm it to be the crack of doom. In silence, in steadiness, in severe abstraction, let him hold by himself; add observation to observation, patient of neglect, patient of reproach; and bide his own time,—happy enough, if he can satisfy himself alone, that this day he has seen something truly. Success treads on every right step. For the instinct is sure, that prompts him to tell his brother what he thinks. He then learns, that in going down into the secrets of his own mind, he has descended into the secrets of all minds. He learns that he who has mastered any law in his private thoughts, is master to that extent of all men whose language he speaks, and of all into whose language his own can be translated. The poet, in utter solitude remembering his spontaneous thoughts and recording them, is found to have recorded that, which men in crowded cities find true for them also. The orator distrusts at first the fitness of his frank confessions,—his want of knowledge of the persons he addresses,—until he finds that he is the complement of his hearers;—that they drink his words because he fulfills for them their own nature; the deeper he dives into his privatest, secretest presentiment, to his wonder he finds, this is the most acceptable, most public, and universally true. The people delight in it; the better part of every man feels, This is my music; this is myself.

In self-trust, all the virtues are comprehended. Free should the scholar be,—free and brave. Free even to the definition of freedom, "without any hindrance that does not arise out of his own constitution." Brave; for fear is a thing, which a scholar by his very function puts behind him. Fear always springs from ignorance. It is a shame to him if his tranquility, amid danger-ous times, arise from the presumption, that, like children and women, his is a protected class; or if he seek a temporary peace by the diversion of his thoughts from politics or vexed questions, hiding his head like an ostrich in the flowering bushes, peeping into microscopes, and turning rhymes, as a boy whistles to keep his courage up. So is the danger a danger still; so is the fear worse. Manlike let him turn and face it. Let him look into its eye and search its nature, inspect its origin,—see the whelping of this lion,—which lies no great way back; he will then find in himself a perfect comprehension of its nature and extent; he will have made his hands meet on the other side, and can henceforth defy it, and pass on superior. The world is his, who can see through its pretension. What deafness, what stone-blind custom, what overgrown error you behold, is there only by sufferance,—by your suf-ferance. See it to be a lie, and you have already dealt it its mortal blow.

Yes, we are the cowed,—we the trustless. It is a mischievous notion that we are come late into nature; that the world was finished a long time ago. As the world was plastic and fluid in the hands of God, so it is ever to so much of his attributes as we bring to it. To ignorance and sin, it is flint. They adapt themselves to it as they may; but in proportion as a man has any thing in him divine, the firmament flows before him and takes his signet and form. Not he is great who can alter matter, but he who can alter my state of mind. They are the kings of the world who give the color of their present thought to all nature and all art, and persuade men by the cheerful serenity of their car-rying the matter, that this thing which they do, is the apple which the ages have desired to pluck, now at last ripe, and inviting nations to the harvest. The great man makes the great thing. Wherever Macdonald sits, there is the head of the table. Linnæus makes botany the most alluring of studies, and wins it from the farmer and the herb-woman; Davy, chemistry; and Cuvier, fossils.[10] The day is always his, who works in it with serenity and great aims. The unstable estimates of men crowd to him whose mind is filled with a truth, as the heaped waves of the Atlantic follow the moon.

For this self-trust, the reason is deeper than can be fathomed,—darker than can be enlightened. I might not carry with me the feeling of my audi-ence in stating my own belief. But I have already shown the ground of my hope, in adverting to the doctrine that man is one. I believe man has been wronged; he has wronged himself. He has almost lost the light, that can lead him back to his prerogatives. Men are become of no account. Men in his-tory, men in the world of to-day are bugs, are spawn, and are called 'the

[10]Emerson extends the contemporary saying about a Scottish clan leader's authority to three influential scientists.

mass' and 'the herd.' In a century, in a millennium, one or two men; that is to say,—one or two approximations to the right state of every man. All the rest behold in the hero or the poet their own green and crude being,—ripened; yes, and are content to be less, so *that* may attain to its full stature. What a testimony,—full of grandeur, full of pity, is borne to the demands of his own nature, by the poor clansman, the poor partisan, who rejoices in the glory of his chief. The poor and the low find some amends to their immense moral capacity, for their acquiescence in a political and social inferiority. They are content to be brushed like flies from the path of a great person, so that justice shall be done by him to that common nature which it is the dearest desire of all to see enlarged and glorified. They sun themselves in the great man's light, and feel it to be their own element. They cast the dignity of man from their downtrod selves upon the shoulders of a hero, and will perish to add one drop of blood to make that great heart beat, those giant sinews combat and conquer. He lives for us, and we live in him.

Men such as they are, very naturally seek money or power; and power because it is as good as money,—the "spoils," so called, "of office." And why not? for they aspire to the highest, and this, in their sleep-walking, they dream is highest. Wake them, and they shall quit the false good, and leap to the true, and leave governments to clerks and desks. This revolution is to be wrought by the gradual domestication of the idea of Culture. The main enterprise of the world for splendor, for extent, is the upbuilding of a man. Here are the materials strown along the ground. The private life of one man shall be a more illustrious monarchy,—more formidable to its enemy, more sweet and serene in its influence to its friend, than any kingdom in history. For a man, rightly viewed, comprehendeth the particular natures of all men. Each philosopher, each bard, each actor, has only done for me, as by a delegate, what one day I can do for myself. The books which once we valued more than the apple of the eye, we have quite exhausted. What is that but saying, that we have come up with the point of view which the universal mind took through the eyes of one scribe; we have been that man, and have passed on. First, one; then, another; we drain all cisterns, and, waxing greater by all these supplies, we crave a better and more abundant food. The man has never lived that can feed us ever. The human mind cannot be enshrined in a person, who shall set a barrier on any one side to this unbounded, unboundable empire. It is one central fire, which, flaming now out of the lips of Etna, lightens the capes of Sicily; and, now out of the throat of Vesuvius, illuminates the towers and vineyards of Naples. It is one light which beams out of a thousand stars. It is one soul which animates all men.

But I have dwelt perhaps tediously upon this abstraction of the Scholar. I ought not to delay longer to add what I have to say, of nearer reference to the time and to this country.

Historically, there is thought to be a difference in the ideas which predominate over successive epochs, and there are data for marking the genius of the Classic, of the Romantic, and now of the Reflective or Philosophical age. With the views I have intimated of the oneness or the identity of the mind through all individuals, I do not much dwell on these differences. In fact, I believe each individual passes through all three. The boy is a Greek; the youth, romantic; the adult, reflective. I deny not, however, that a revolution in the leading idea may be distinctly enough traced.

Our age is bewailed as the age of Introversion. Must that needs be evil? We, it seems, are critical; we are embarrassed with second thoughts; we cannot enjoy any thing for hankering to know whereof the pleasure consists; we are lined with eyes; we see with our feet; the time is infected with Hamlet's unhappiness,—

> *"Sicklied o'er with the pale cast of thought."*[11]

Is it so bad then? Sight is the last thing to be pitied. Would we be blind? Do we fear lest we should outsee nature and God, and drink truth dry? I look upon the discontent of the literary class, as a mere announcement of the fact, that they find themselves not in the state of mind of their fathers, and regret the coming state as untried; as a boy dreads the water before he has learned that he can swim. If there is any period one would desire to be born in,—is it not the age of Revolution; when the old and the new stand side by side, and admit of being compared; when the energies of all men are searched by fear and by hope; when the historic glories of the old, can be compensated by the rich possibilities of the new era? This time, like all times, is a very good one, if we but know what to do with it.

I read with joy some of the auspicious signs of the coming days, as they glimmer already through poetry and art, through philosophy and science, through church and state.

One of these signs is the fact, that the same movement which effected the elevation of what was called the lowest class in the state, assumed in literature a very marked and as benign an aspect. Instead of the sublime and beautiful; the near, the low, the common, was explored and poetized. That, which had been negligently trodden under foot by those who were harnessing and provisioning themselves for long journeys into far countries, is suddenly found to be richer than all foreign parts. The literature of the poor, the feelings of the child, the philosophy of the street, the meaning of household life, are the topics of the time. It is a great stride. It is a sign,—is it not? of new vigor, when the extremities are made active, when currents of warm life run into the hands and the feet. I ask not for the great, the remote, the romantic; what is doing in Italy or Arabia; what is Greek art, or Provençal minstrelsy; I embrace the common, I explore and sit at the feet of the familiar, the low. Give me insight into to-day, and you may have the antique and future worlds. What would we really know the meaning of? The meal in the firkin;[12] the milk in the pan; the ballad in the street; the news of the boat; the glance of the eye; the form and the gait of the body;—show me the ultimate reason of these matters; show me the sublime presence of the highest spiritual cause lurking, as always it does lurk, in these suburbs

---

[11] *Hamlet,* III, i: 85.　　[12] Small wooden bowl.

and extremities of nature; let me see every trifle bristling with the polarity that ranges it instantly on an eternal law; and the shop, the plough, and the leger, referred to the like cause by which light undulates and poets sing;— and the world lies no longer a dull miscellany and lumber-room, but has form and order; there is no trifle; there is no puzzle; but one design unites and animates the farthest pinnacle and the lowest trench.

This idea has inspired the genius of Goldsmith, Burns, Cowper, and, in a newer time, of Goethe, Wordsworth, and Carlyle. This idea they have differently followed and with various success. In contrast with their writing, the style of Pope, of Johnson, of Gibbon, looks cold and pedantic. This writing is blood-warm. Man is surprised to find that things near are not less beautiful and wondrous than things remote. The near explains the far. The drop is a small ocean. A man is related to all nature. This perception of the worth of the vulgar is fruitful in discoveries. Goethe, in this very thing the most modern of the moderns, has shown us, as none ever did, the genius of the ancients.

There is one man of genius, who has done much for this philosophy of life, whose literary value has never yet been rightly estimated;—I mean Emanuel Swedenborg. The most imaginative of men, yet writing with the precision of a mathematician, he endeavored to engraft a purely philosophical Ethics on the popular Christianity of his time. Such an attempt, of course, must have difficulty, which no genius could surmount. But he saw and showed the connection between nature and the affections of the soul. He pierced the emblematic or spiritual character of the visible, audible, tangible world. Especially did his shade-loving muse hover over and interpret the lower parts of nature; he showed the mysterious bond that allies moral evil to the foul material forms, and has given in epical parables a theory of insanity, of beasts, of unclean and fearful things.

Another sign of our times, also marked by an analogous political movement, is, the new importance given to the single person. Every thing that tends to insulate the individual,—to surround him with barriers of natural respect, so that each man shall feel the world is his, and man shall treat with man as a sovereign state with a sovereign state;—tends to true union as well as greatness. "I learned," said the melancholy Pestalozzi,[13] "that no man in God's wide earth is either willing or able to help any other man." Help must come from the bosom alone. The scholar is that man who must take up into himself all the ability of the time, all the contributions of the past, all the hopes of the future. He must be an university of knowledges. If there be one lesson more than another, which should pierce his ear, it is, The world is nothing, the man is all; in yourself is the law of all nature, and you know not yet how a globule of sap ascends; in yourself slumbers the whole of Reason; it is for you to know all, it is for you to dare all. Mr. President and Gentlemen, this confidence in the unsearched might of man

---

[13]Swiss educator and theorist (1746–1827) who influenced Bronson Alcott.

belongs, by all motives, by all prophecy, by all preparation, to the American Scholar. We have listened too long to the courtly muses of Europe. The spirit of the American freeman is already suspected to be timid, imitative, tame. Public and private avarice make the air we breathe thick and fat. The scholar is decent, indolent, complaisant. See already the tragic consequence. The mind of this country, taught to aim at low objects, eats upon itself. There is no work for any but the decorous and the complaisant. Young men of the fairest promise, who begin life upon our shores, inflated by the mountain winds, shined upon by all the stars of God, find the earth below not in unison with these,—but are hindered from action by the disgust which the principles on which business is managed inspire, and turn drudges, or die of disgust,—some of them suicides. What is the remedy? They did not yet see, and thousands of young men as hopeful now crowding to the barriers for the career, do not yet see, that, if the single man plant himself indomitably on his instincts, and there abide, the huge world will come round to him. Patience,—patience;—with the shades of all the good and great for company; and for solace, the perspective of your own infinite life; and for work, the study and the communication of principles, the making those instincts prevalent, the conversion of the world. Is it not the chief disgrace in the world, not to be an unit;—not to be reckoned one character;—not to yield that peculiar fruit which each man was created to bear, but to be reckoned in the gross, in the hundred, or the thousand, of the party, the section, to which we belong; and our opinion predicted geographically, as the north, or the south? Not so, brothers and friends,—please God, ours shall not be so. We will walk on our own feet; we will work with our own hands; we will speak our own minds. The study of letters shall be no longer a name for pity, for doubt, and for sensual indulgence. The dread of man and the love of man shall be a wall of defence and a wreath of joy around all. A nation of men will for the first time exist, because each believes himself inspired by the Divine Soul which also inspires all men.

1837, 1849

Self-Reliance

"Ne te quæsiveris extra."[1]

"Man is his own star; and the soul that can
Render an honest and a perfect man,
Commands all light, all influence, all fate;
Nothing to him falls early or too late.
Our acts our angels are, or good or ill,
Our fatal shadows that walk by us still."

—EPILOGUE TO BEAUMONT AND FLETCHER'S *Honest Man's Fortune.*

---

[1]"Look to no one outside yourself," from Persius, *Satires* (1st cent. A.D.).

> Cast the bantling[2] on the rocks,
> Suckle him with the she-wolf's teat;
> Wintered with the hawk and fox,
> Power and speed be hands and feet.[3]

I read the other day some verses written by an eminent painter[4] which were original and not conventional. The soul always hears an admonition in such lines, let the subject be what it may. The sentiment they instil is of more value than any thought they may contain. To believe your own thought, to believe that what is true for you in your private heart, is true for all men,— that is genius. Speak your latent conviction and it shall be the universal sense; for the inmost in due time[5] becomes the outmost,—and our first thought is rendered back to us by the trumpets of the Last Judgment. Familiar as the voice of the mind is to each, the highest merit we ascribe to Moses, Plato, and Milton, is that they set at naught books and traditions, and spoke not what men but what they thought. A man should learn to detect and watch that gleam of light which flashes across his mind from within, more than the lustre of the firmament of bards and sages. Yet he dismisses without notice his thought, because it is his. In every work of genius we recognize our own rejected thoughts: they come back to us with a certain alienated majesty. Great works of art have no more affecting lesson for us than this. They teach us to abide by our spontaneous impression with good-humored inflexibility then most when the whole cry of voices is on the other side. Else, tomorrow a stranger will say with masterly good sense precisely what we have thought and felt all the time, and we shall be forced to take with shame our own opinion from another.

There is a time in every man's education when he arrives at the conviction that envy is ignorance; that imitation is suicide; that he must take himself for better, for worse, as his portion; that though the wide universe is full of good, no kernel of nourishing corn can come to him but through his toil bestowed on that plot of ground which is given to him to till. The power which resides in him is new in nature, and none but he knows what that is which he can do, nor does he know until he has tried. Not for nothing one face, one character, one fact makes much impression on him, and another none. This sculpture in the memory is not without preëstablished harmony. The eye was placed where one ray should fall, that it might testify of that particular ray. We but half express ourselves, and are ashamed of that divine idea which each of us represents. It may be safely trusted as proportionate and of good issues, so it be faithfully imparted, but God will not have his work made manifest by cowards. A man is relieved and gay when he has put his heart into his work and done his best; but what he has said or done otherwise, shall

---

[2]Young child.

[3]This verse is by Emerson.

[4]Probably refers to American painter Washington Allston (1779–1843).

[5]Emerson's replacement of the 1841 edition's more extreme "always" with "in due time" is

an example of how he moderated descriptors in his 1847 revision. He also altered such words as "ever," "all," "great," "most," and "whole."

give him no peace. It is a deliverance which does not deliver. In the attempt his genius deserts him; no muse befriends; no invention, no hope.

Trust thyself: every heart vibrates to that iron string. Accept the place the divine Providence has found for you; the society of your contemporaries, the connexion of events. Great men have always done so and confided themselves childlike to the genius of their age, betraying their perception that the absolutely trustworthy was seated at their heart, working through their hands, predominating in all their being. And we are now men, and must accept in the highest mind the same transcendent destiny; and not minors and invalids in a protected corner, not cowards fleeing before a revolution, but guides, redeemers, and benefactors, obeying the Almighty effort, and advancing on Chaos and the Dark.

What pretty oracles nature yields us on this text in the face and behavior of children, babes and even brutes. That divided and rebel mind, that distrust of a sentiment because our arithmetic has computed the strength and means opposed to our purpose, these have not. Their mind being whole, their eye is as yet unconquered, and when we look in their faces, we are disconcerted. Infancy conforms to nobody: all conform to it, so that one babe commonly makes four or five out of the adults who prattle and play to it. So God has armed youth and puberty and manhood no less with its own piquancy and charm, and made it enviable and gracious and its claims not to be put by, if it will stand by itself. Do not think the youth has no force because he cannot speak to you and me. Hark! in the next room his voice is sufficiently clear and emphatic.[6] It seems he knows how to speak to his contemporaries. Bashful or bold, then, he will know how to make us seniors very unnecessary.

The nonchalance of boys who are sure of a dinner, and would disdain as much as a lord to do or say aught to conciliate one, is the healthy attitude of human nature. A boy is in the parlour what the pit[7] is in the playhouse; independent, irresponsible, looking out from his corner on such people and facts as pass by, he tries and sentences them on their merits, in the swift summary way of boys, as good, bad, interesting, silly, eloquent, troublesome. He cumbers himself never about consequences, about interests: he gives an independent, genuine verdict. You must court him: he does not court you. But the man is, as it were, clapped into jail by his consciousness. As soon as he has once acted or spoken with eclat, he is a committed person, watched by the sympathy or the hatred of hundreds whose affections must now enter into his account. There is no Lethe[8] for this. Ah, that he could pass again into his neutrality! Who can thus avoid all pledges, and having

---

[6]Throughout the 1847 revision, Emerson altered the more colloquial and oral style of the 1841 first edition. Here he omits: "who spoke so clear and emphatic? Good Heaven! it is he! it is that very lump of bashfulness and phlegm which for weeks has done nothing but eat when you were by, that now rolls out these words like bellstrokes." Elsewhere,

he revises: sewing up your "guarded lips" with "packthread," "words as hard as cannon balls," what the "aged ladies" say, a "right fool's word," "rambling round creation as a moth round a lamp," "gadding abroad," and "as the eyes of a maid follow her mistress."

[7]Cheap seats in Elizabethan theater.

[8]Mythological river that induces forgetfulness.

observed, observe again from the same unaffected, unbiassed, unbribable, unaffrighted innocence, must always be formidable. He would utter opinions on all passing affairs, which being seen to be not private but necessary, would sink like darts into the ear of men, and put them in fear.

These are the voices which we hear in solitude, but they grow faint and inaudible as we enter into the world. Society everywhere is in conspiracy against the manhood of every one of its members. Society is a joint-stock company in which the members agree for the better securing of his bread to each shareholder, to surrender the liberty and culture of the eater. The virtue in most request is conformity. Self-reliance is its aversion. It loves not realities and creators, but names and customs.

Whoso would be a man must be a nonconformist. He who would gather immortal palms must not be hindered by the name of goodness, but must explore if it be goodness. Nothing is at last sacred but the integrity of your own mind. Absolve you to yourself, and you shall have the suffrage of the world. I remember an answer which when quite young I was prompted to make to a valued adviser who was wont to importune me with the dear old doctrines of the church. On my saying, What have I to do with the sacredness of traditions, if I live wholly from within? my friend suggested—"But these impulses may be from below, not from above." I replied, "They do not seem to me to be such; but if I am the Devil's child, I will live then from the Devil." No law can be sacred to me but that of my nature. Good and bad are but names very readily transferable to that or this; the only right is what is after my constitution, the only wrong what is against it. A man is to carry himself in the presence of all opposition as if every thing were titular and ephemeral but he. I am ashamed to think how easily we capitulate to badges and names, to large societies and dead institutions. Every decent and well-spoken individual affects and sways me more than is right. I ought to go upright and vital, and speak the rude truth in all ways. If malice and vanity wear the coat of philanthropy, shall that pass? If an angry bigot assumes this bountiful cause of Abolition, and comes to me with his last news from Barbadoes,[9] why should I not say to him, 'Go love thy infant; love thy wood-chopper: be good-natured and modest: have that grace; and never varnish your hard, uncharitable ambition with this incredible tenderness for black folk a thousand miles off. Thy love afar is spite at home.' Rough and grace-less would be such greeting, but truth is handsomer than the affectation of love. Your goodness must have some edge to it—else it is none. The doctrine of hatred must be preached as the counteraction of the doctrine of love when that pules and whines. I shun father and mother[10] and wife and brother, when my genius calls me. I would write on the lintels of the door-post,[11] *Whim.* I hope it is somewhat better than whim at last, but we cannot spend the day in explanation. Expect me not to show cause why I seek or

---

[9]Slavery was officially abolished in 1834 in the British West Indies.
[10]Cf. Matthew 10:37.

[11]Emerson refers to marking with blood the houses of believers so God would not "smite" them; cf. Deuteronomy 6:9 and Exodus 12:23.

why I exclude company. Then, again, do not tell me, as a good man did to-day, of my obligation to put all poor men in good situations. Are they *my* poor? I tell thee, thou foolish philanthropist, that I grudge the dollar, the dime, the cent I give to such men as do not belong to me and to whom I do not belong. There is a class of persons to whom by all spiritual affinity I am bought and sold; for them I will go to prison, if need be; but your miscella-neous popular charities; the education at college of fools; the building of meeting-houses to the vain end to which many now stand; alms to sots; and the thousandfold Relief Societies;—though I confess with shame I some-times succumb and give the dollar, it is a wicked dollar which by and by I shall have the manhood to withhold.

Virtues are in the popular estimate rather the exception than the rule. There is the man *and* his virtues. Men do what is called a good action, as some piece of courage or charity, much as they would pay a fine in expiation of daily non-appearance on parade. Their works are done as an apology or extenuation of their living in the world,—as invalids and the insane pay a high board. Their virtues are penances. I do not wish to expiate, but to live. My life is for itself and not for a spectacle. I much prefer that it should be of a lower strain, so it be genuine and equal, than that it should be glittering and unsteady. I wish it to be sound and sweet, and not to need diet and bleeding.[12] I ask primary evidence that you are a man, and refuse this appeal from the man to his actions. I know that for myself it makes no difference whether I do or forbear those actions which are reckoned excellent. I cannot consent to pay for a privilege where I have intrinsic right. Few and mean as my gifts may be, I actually am, and do not need for my own assurance or the assurance of my fellows any secondary testimony.

What I must do, is all that concerns me, not what the people think. This rule, equally arduous in actual and in intellectual life, may serve for the whole distinction between greatness and meanness. It is the harder, because you will always find those who think they know what is your duty better than you know it. It is easy in the world to live after the world's opinion; it is easy in solitude to live after our own; but the great man is he who in the midst of the crowd keeps with perfect sweetness the independence of solitude.

The objection to conforming to usages that have become dead to you, is, that it scatters your force. It loses your time and blurs the impression of your character. If you maintain a dead church, contribute to a dead Bible-So-ciety, vote with a great party either for the Government or against it, spread your table like base housekeepers,—under all these screens, I have difficulty to detect the precise man you are. And, of course, so much force is with-drawn from your proper life. But do your work,[13] and I shall know you. Do your work, and you shall reinforce yourself. A man must consider what a blindman's-buff is this game of conformity. If I know your sect, I anticipate

[12]Bloodletting.
[13]In various versions of this passage, Emerson recommended doing your "work," "office," and "thing."

your argument. I hear a preacher announce for his text and topic the expediency of one of the institutions of his church. Do I not know beforehand that not possibly can he say a new and spontaneous word? Do I not know that with all this ostentation of examining the grounds of the institution, he will do no such thing? Do I not know that he is pledged to himself not to look but at one side,—the permitted side, not as a man, but as a parish minister? He is a retained attorney, and these airs of the bench are the emptiest affectation. Well, most men have bound their eyes with one or another handkerchief, and attached themselves to some one of these communities of opinion. This conformity makes them not false in a few particulars, authors of a few lies, but false in all particulars. Their every truth is not quite true. Their two is not the real two, their four not the real four: so that every word they say chagrins us, and we know not where to begin to set them right. Meantime nature is not slow to equip us in the prison-uniform of the party to which we adhere. We come to wear one cut of face and figure, and acquire by degrees the gentlest asinine expression. There is a mortifying experience in particular which does not fail to wreak itself also in the general history; I mean "the foolish face of praise,"[14] the forced smile which we put on in company where we do not feel at ease in answer to conversation which does not interest us. The muscles, not spontaneously moved, but moved by a low usurping wilfulness, grow tight about the outline of the face with the most disagreeable sensation.

For nonconformity the world whips you with its displeasure. And therefore a man must know how to estimate a sour face. The bystanders look askance on him in the public street or in the friend's parlor. If this aversation had its origin in contempt and resistance like his own, he might well go home with a sad countenance; but the sour faces of the multitude, like their sweet faces, have no deep cause, but are put on and off as the wind blows, and a newspaper directs. Yet is the discontent of the multitude more formidable than that of the senate and the college. It is easy enough for a firm man who knows the world to brook the rage of the cultivated classes. Their rage is decorous and prudent, for they are timid as being very vulnerable themselves. But when to their feminine rage the indignation of the people is added, when the ignorant and the poor are aroused, when the unintelligent brute force that lies at the bottom of society is made to growl and mow,[15] it needs the habit of magnanimity and religion to treat it godlike as a trifle of no concernment.

The other terror that scares us from self-trust is our consistency; a reverence for our past act or word, because the eyes of others have no other data for computing our orbit than our past acts, and we are loath to disappoint them.

But why should you keep your head over your shoulder? Why drag about this corpse of your memory, lest you contradict somewhat you have stated in this or that public place? Suppose you should contradict yourself; what

---

[14]Pope, "Epistle to Dr. Arbuthnot" (1735).   [15]Grimace.

then? It seems to be a rule of wisdom never to rely on your memory alone, scarcely even in acts of pure memory, but to bring the past for judgment into the thousand-eyed present, and live ever in a new day. In your metaphysics you have denied personality to the Deity; yet when the devout motions of the soul come, yield to them heart and life, though they should clothe God with shape and color. Leave your theory as Joseph his coat in the hand of the harlot,[16] and flee.

A foolish consistency is the hobgoblin of little minds, adored by little statesmen and philosophers and divines. With consistency a great soul has simply nothing to do. He may as well concern himself with his shadow on the wall. Speak what you think now in hard words, and to-morrow speak what to-morrow thinks in hard words again, though it contradict every thing you said to-day.—'Ah, so you shall be sure to be misunderstood.'—Is it so bad then to be misunderstood? Pythagoras[17] was misunderstood, and Socrates, and Jesus, and Luther, and Copernicus, and Galileo, and Newton, and every pure and wise spirit that ever took flesh. To be great is to be misunderstood.

I suppose no man can violate his nature. All the sallies of his will are rounded in by the law of his being as the inequalities of Andes and Himmaleh are insignificant in the curve of the sphere. Nor does it matter how you gauge and try him. A character is like an acrostic or Alexandrian stanza;— read it forward, backward, or across, it still spells the same thing. In this pleasing contrite wood-life which God allows me, let me record day by day my honest thought without prospect or retrospect, and, I cannot doubt, it will be found symmetrical, though I mean it not, and see it not. My book should smell of pines and resound with the hum of insects. The swallow over my window should interweave that thread or straw he carries in his bill into my web also. We pass for what we are. Character teaches above our wills. Men imagine that they communicate their virtue or vice only by overt actions and do not see that virtue or vice emit a breath every moment.

There will be an agreement in whatever variety of actions, so they be each honest and natural in their hour. For of one will, the actions will be harmonious, however unlike they seem. These varieties are lost sight of at a little distance, at a little height of thought. One tendency unites them all. The voyage of the best ship is a zigzag line of a hundred tacks. See the line from a sufficient distance, and it straightens itself to the average tendency. Your genuine action will explain itself and will explain your other genuine actions. Your conformity explains nothing. Act singly, and what you have already done singly, will justify you now. Greatness appeals to the future. If I can be firm enough to-day to do right and scorn eyes, I must have done so much right before, as to defend me now. Be it how it will, do right now. Always scorn appearances, and you always may. The force of character is cumulative. All the foregone days of virtue work their health into this. What

---

[16]Joseph fled from the temptings of Potiphar's wife; cf. Genesis 39:12.

[17]Like the rest of the list, the sixth-century Greek philosopher and mathematician met resistance for his radical positions.

makes the majesty of the heroes of the senate and the field, which so fills the imagination? The consciousness of a train of great days and victories behind. They shed an united light on the advancing actor. He is attended as by a visible escort of angels. That is it which throws thunder into Chatham's voice, and dignity into Washington's port,[18] and America into Adams's eye.[19] Honor is venerable to us because it is no ephemeris. It is always ancient virtue. We worship it to-day, because it is not of to-day. We love it and pay it homage, because it is not a trap for our love and homage, but is self-dependent, self-derived, and therefore of an old immaculate pedigree, even if shown in a young person.

I hope in these days we have heard the last of conformity and consistency. Let the words be gazetted[20] and ridiculous henceforward. Instead of the gong for dinner, let us hear a whistle from the Spartan fife. Let us never bow and apologize more. A great man is coming to eat at my house. I do not wish to please him: I wish that he should wish to please me. I will stand here for humanity, and though I would make it kind, I would make it true. Let us affront and reprimand the smooth mediocrity and squalid contentment of the times, and hurl in the face of custom, and trade, and office, the fact which is the upshot of all history, that there is a great responsible Thinker and Actor working wherever a man works; that a true man belongs to no other time or place, but is the centre of things. Where he is, there is nature. He measures you, and all men, and all events. Ordinarily every body in society reminds us of somewhat else or of some other person. Character, reality, reminds you of nothing else; it takes place of the whole creation. The man must be so much that he must make all circumstances indifferent. Every true man is a cause, a country, and an age; requires infinite spaces and numbers and time fully to accomplish his design;—and posterity seem to follow his steps as a train of clients. A man Cæsar is born, and for ages after, we have a Roman Empire. Christ is born, and millions of minds so grow and cleave to his genius, that he is confounded with virtue and the possible of man. An institution is the lengthened shadow of one man; as, Monachism, of the Hermit Antony; the Reformation, of Luther; Quakerism, of Fox; Methodism, of Wesley; Abolition, of Clarkson. Scipio,[21] Milton called "the height of Rome;" and all history resolves itself very easily into the biography of a few stout and earnest persons.

Let a man then know his worth, and keep things under his feet. Let him not peep or steal, or skulk up and down with the air of a charity-boy, a bastard, or an interloper, in the world which exists for him. But the man in the street finding no worth in himself which corresponds to the force which built a tower or sculptured a marble god, feels poor when he looks on these. To him a palace, a statue, or a costly book have an alien and forbidding air,

---

[18]Demeanor, bearing.
[19]The list of politicians includes William Pitt (Earl of Chatham), George Washington, and one of the patriotic Adamses (Samuel, John, or John Quincy). In Emerson's journal, the thundering voice belonged to the American orator William Ellery Channing.
[20]Published in a newspaper.
[21]Roman general who conquered Carthage (201 B.C.).

much like a gay equipage, and seem to say like that, 'Who are you, sir?' Yet they all are his, suitors for his notice, petitioners to his faculties that they will come out and take possession. The picture waits for my verdict: it is not to command me, but I am to settle its claims to praise. That popular fable of the sot who was picked up dead drunk in the street, carried to the duke's house, washed and dressed and laid in the duke's bed, and, on his waking, treated with all obsequious ceremony like the duke, and assured that he had been insane, owes its popularity to the fact, that it symbolizes so well the state of man, who is in the world a sort of sot, but now and then wakes up, exercises his reason, and finds himself a true prince.

Our reading is mendicant and sycophantic. In history, our imagination plays us false. Kingdom and lordship, power and estate are a gaudier vocabulary than private John and Edward in a small house and common day's work: but the things of life are the same to both: the sum total of both is the same. Why all this deference to Alfred, and Scanderbeg, and Gustavus?[22] Suppose they were virtuous: did they wear out virtue? As great a stake depends on your private act to-day, as followed their public and renowned steps. When private men shall act with original views, the lustre will be transferred from the actions of kings to those of gentlemen.

The world has been instructed by its kings, who have so magnetized the eyes of nations. It has been taught by this colossal symbol the mutual reverence that is due from man to man. The joyful loyalty with which men have everywhere suffered the king, the noble, or the great proprietor to walk among them by a law of his own, make his own scale of men and things, and reverse theirs, pay for benefits not with money but with honor, and represent the Law in his person, was the hieroglyphic by which they obscurely signified their consciousness of their own right and comeliness, the right of every man.

The magnetism which all original action exerts is explained when we inquire the reason of self-trust. Who is the Trustee? What is the aboriginal Self on which a universal reliance may be grounded? What is the nature and power of that science-baffling star, without parallax,[23] without calculable elements, which shoots a ray of beauty even into trivial and impure actions, if the least mark of independence appear? The inquiry leads us to that source, at once the essence of genius, of virtue, and of life, which we call Spontaneity or Instinct. We denote this primary wisdom as Intuition, whilst all later teachings are tuitions. In that deep force, the last fact behind which analysis cannot go, all things find their common origin. For the sense of being which in calm hours rises, we know not how, in the soul, is not diverse from things, from space, from light, from time, from man, but one with them, and proceeds obviously from the same source whence their life and being also

---

[22]The list of national heroes includes Alfred the Great of England, Scanderbeg or Iskander Bey (the leader of a fifteenth-century Albanian rebellion against the Turks), and King Gustavus Adolphus of Sweden.

[23]Star whose distance from the Earth cannot be measured.

proceed. We first share the life by which things exist, and afterwards see them as appearances in nature, and forget that we have shared their cause. Here is the fountain of action and of thought. Here are the lungs of that inspiration which giveth man wisdom, and which cannot be denied without impiety and atheism. We lie in the lap of immense intelligence, which makes us receivers of its truth and organs of its activity. When we discern justice, when we discern truth, we do nothing of ourselves, but allow a passage to its beams. If we ask whence this comes, if we seek to pry into the soul that causes, all philosophy is at fault. Its presence or its absence is all we can affirm. Every man discriminates between the voluntary acts of his mind, and his involuntary perceptions, and knows that to his involuntary perceptions a perfect faith is due. He may err in the expression of them, but he knows that these things are so, like day and night, not to be disputed. My wilful actions and acquisitions are but roving;—the idlest reverie, the faintest native emotion, command my curiosity and respect. Thoughtless people contradict as readily the statement of perceptions as of opinions, or rather much more readily; for, they do not distinguish between perception and notion. They fancy that I choose to see this or that thing. But perception is not whimsical, but fatal. If I see a trait, my children will see it after me, and in course of time, all mankind,—although it may chance that no one has seen it before me. For my perception of it is as much a fact as the sun.

The relations of the soul to the divine spirit are so pure that it is profane to seek to interpose helps. It must be that when God speaketh, he should communicate not one thing, but all things; should fill the world with his voice; should scatter forth light, nature, time, souls, from the centre of the present thought; and new date and new create the whole. Whenever a mind is simple, and receives a divine wisdom, old things pass away,—means, teachers, texts, temples fall; it lives now and absorbs past and future into the present hour. All things are made sacred by relation to it,—one as much as another. All things are dissolved to their centre by their cause, and in the universal miracle petty and particular miracles disappear. If, therefore, a man claims to know and speak of God, and carries you backward to the phraseology of some old mouldered nation in another country, in another world, believe him not. Is the acorn better than the oak which is its fulness and completion? Is the parent better than the child into whom he has cast his ripened being? Whence then this worship of the past? The centuries are conspirators against the sanity and authority of the soul. Time and space are but physiological colors which the eye makes, but the soul is light; where it is, is day; where it was, is night; and history is an impertinence and an injury, if it be anything more than a cheerful apologue or parable of my being and becoming.

Man is timid and apologetic; he is no longer upright; he dares not say 'I think,' 'I am,' but quotes some saint or sage. He is ashamed before the blade of grass or the blowing rose. These roses under my window make no reference to former roses or to better ones; they are for what they are; they exist with God to-day. There is no time to them. There is simply the rose; it is perfect in every moment of its existence. Before a leaf-bud has burst, its whole life acts; in the full-blown flower, there is no more; in the leafless root, there is no less. Its nature is satisfied, and it satisfies nature, in all moments alike. But man postpones or remembers; he does not live in the present, but with reverted eye laments the past, or, heedless of the riches that surround him, stands on tiptoe to foresee the future. He cannot be happy and strong until he too lives with nature in the present, above time.

This should be plain enough. Yet see what strong intellects dare not yet hear God himself, unless he speak the phraseology of I know not what David, or Jeremiah, or Paul. We shall not always set so great a price on a few texts, on a few lives. We are like children who repeat by rote the senten-ces of grandames and tutors, and, as they grow older, of the men of talents and character they chance to see,—painfully recollecting the exact words they spoke; afterwards, when they come into the point of view which those had who uttered these sayings, they understand them, and are willing to let the words go; for, at any time, they can use words as good, when occasion comes. If we live truly, we shall see truly. It is as easy for the strong man to be strong, as it is for the weak to be weak. When we have new perception, we shall gladly disburden the memory of its hoarded treasures as old rub-bish. When a man lives with God, his voice shall be as sweet as the murmur of the brook and the rustle of the corn.

And now at last the highest truth on this subject remains unsaid; prob-ably, cannot be said; for all that we say is the far off remembering of the intuition. That thought, by what I can now nearest approach to say it, is this. When good is near you, when you have life in yourself, it is not by any known or accustomed way; you shall not discern the foot-prints of any other; you shall not see the face of man; you shall not hear any name;—the way, the thought, the good shall be wholly strange and new. It shall exclude example and experience. You take the way from man, not to man. All per-sons that ever existed are its forgotten ministers. Fear and hope are alike beneath it. There is somewhat low even in hope. In the hour of vision, there is nothing that can be called gratitude, nor properly joy. The soul raised over passion beholds identity and eternal causation, perceives the self-existence of Truth and Right, and calms itself with knowing that all things go well. Vast spaces of nature, the Atlantic Ocean, the South Sea,—long intervals of time, years, centuries,—are of no account. This which I think and feel underlay every former state of life and circumstances, as it does underlie my present, and what is called life, and what is called death.

Life only avails, not the having lived. Power ceases in the instant of repose; it resides in the moment of transition from a past to a new state, in the shooting of the gulf, in the darting to an aim. This one fact the world hates, that the soul *becomes*; for, that forever degrades the past, turns all riches to poverty, all reputation to a shame, confounds the saint with the rogue, shoves Jesus and Judas equally aside. Why then do we prate of self-reliance? Inasmuch as the soul is present, there will be power not confident but agent. To talk of reliance, is a poor external way of speaking. Speak rather of that which relies, because it works and is. Who has more obedience than I, masters me, though he should not raise his finger. Round him I must revolve by the gravitation of spirits. We fancy it rhetoric when we speak of eminent virtue. We do not yet see that virtue is Height, and that a man or a company of men plastic and permeable to principles, by the law of nature must over-power and ride all cities, nations, kings, rich men, poets, who are not.

This is the ultimate fact which we so quickly reach on this as on every topic, the resolution of all into the ever blessed ONE. Self-existence is the at-tribute of the Supreme Cause, and it constitutes the measure of good by the degree in which it enters into all lower forms. All things real are so by so much virtue as they contain. Commerce, husbandry, hunting, whaling, war, eloquence, personal weight, are somewhat, and engage my respect as exam-ples of its presence and impure action. I see the same law working in nature for conservation and growth. Power is in nature the essential measure of right. Nature suffers nothing to remain in her kingdoms which cannot help itself. The genesis and maturation of a planet, its poise and orbit, the bended tree recovering itself from the strong wind, the vital resources of ev-ery animal and vegetable, are demonstrations of the self-sufficing, and therefore self-relying soul.

Thus all concentrates; let us not rove; let us sit at home with the cause. Let us stun and astonish the intruding rabble of men and books and institu-tions by a simple declaration of the divine fact. Bid the invaders take the shoes from off their feet, for God is here within.[24] Let our simplicity judge them, and our docility to our own law demonstrate the poverty of nature and fortune beside our native riches.

But now we are a mob. Man does not stand in awe of man, nor is his ge-nius admonished to stay at home, to put itself in communication with the internal ocean, but it goes abroad to beg a cup of water of the urns of other men. We must go alone. I like the silent church before the service begins, better than any preaching. How far off, how cool, how chaste the persons look, begirt each one with a precinct or sanctuary. So let us always sit. Why should we assume the faults of our friend, or wife, or father, or child, because they sit around our hearth, or are said to have the same blood? All men have my blood, and I have all men's. Not for that will I adopt their pet-ulance or folly, even to the extent of being ashamed of it. But your isolation must not be mechanical, but spiritual, that is, must be elevation. At times the whole world seems to be in conspiracy to importune you with emphatic trifles. Friend, client, child, sickness, fear, want, charity, all knock at once at thy closet door and say,—'Come out unto us.' But keep thy state; come not into their confusion. The power men possess to annoy me, I give them by a weak curiosity. No man can come near me but through my act. "What we love that we have, but by desire we bereave ourselves of the love."[25]

[24]In Exodus 3:5, God warns Moses not to profane the holy ground of the burning bush.

[25]A paraphrase from the eighteenth-century German poet Schiller.

If we cannot at once rise to the sanctities of obedience and faith, let us at least resist our temptations; let us enter into the state of war, and wake Thor and Woden,[26] courage and constancy, in our Saxon breasts. This is to be done in our smooth times by speaking the truth. Check this lying hospitality and lying affection. Live no longer to the expectation of these deceived and deceiving people with whom we converse. Say to them, O father, O mother, O wife, O brother, O friend, I have lived with you after appearances hitherto. Henceforward I am the truth's. Be it known unto you that henceforward I obey no law less than the eternal law. I will have no covenants but proximities. I shall endeavor to nourish my parents, to support my family, to be the chaste husband of one wife,—but these relations I must fill after a new and unprecedented way. I appeal from your customs. I must be myself. I cannot break myself any longer for you, or you. If you can love me for what I am, we shall be the happier. If you cannot, I will still seek to deserve that you should. I will not hide my tastes or aversions. I will so trust that what is deep is holy, that I will do strongly before the sun and moon whatever inly rejoices me, and the heart appoints. If you are noble, I will love you; if you are not, I will not hurt you and myself by hypocritical attentions. If you are true, but not in the same truth with me, cleave to your companions; I will seek my own. I do this not selfishly, but humbly and truly. It is alike your interest and mine and all men's, however long we have dwelt in lies, to live in truth. Does this sound harsh to-day? You will soon love what is dictated by your nature as well as mine, and if we follow the truth, it will bring us out safe at last.—But so you may give these friends pain. Yes, but I cannot sell my liberty and my power, to save their sensibility. Besides, all persons have their moments of reason when they look out into the region of absolute truth; then will they justify me and do the same thing.

The populace think that your rejection of popular standards is a rejection of all standard, and mere antinomianism;[27] and the bold sensualist will use the name of philosophy to gild his crimes. But the law of consciousness abides. There are two confessionals, in one or the other of which we must be shriven. You may fulfil your round of duties by clearing yourself in the *direct*, or, in the *reflex* way. Consider whether you have satisfied your relations to father, mother, cousin, neighbor, town, cat, and dog; whether any of these can upbraid you. But I may also neglect this reflex standard, and absolve me to myself. I have my own stern claims and perfect circle. It denies the name of duty to many offices that are called duties. But if I can discharge its debts, it enables me to dispense with the popular code. If any one imagines that this law is lax, let him keep its commandment one day.

And truly it demands something godlike in him who has cast off the common motives of humanity, and has ventured to trust himself for a taskmaster. High be his heart, faithful his will, clear his sight, that he may in

[26]Norse gods of thunder and war.

[27]Belief that faith rather than moral law achieves salvation; by extension, an opposition to moral laws.

good earnest be doctrine, society, law to himself, that a simple purpose may be to him as strong as iron necessity is to others.

If any man consider the present aspects of what is called by distinction *society*, he will see the need of these ethics. The sinew and heart of man seem to be drawn out, and we are become timorous desponding whimperers. We are afraid of truth, afraid of fortune, afraid of death, and afraid of each other. Our age yields no great and perfect persons. We want men and women who shall renovate life and our social state, but we see that most natures are insolvent, cannot satisfy their own wants, have an ambition out of all proportion to their practical force, and do lean and beg day and night continually. Our housekeeping is mendicant, our arts, our occupations, our marriages, our religion we have not chosen, but society has chosen for us. We are parlor soldiers. We shun the rugged battle of fate, where strength is born.

If our young men miscarry in their first enterprizes, they lose all heart. If the young merchant fails, men say he is *ruined*. If the finest genius studies at one of our colleges, and is not installed in an office within one year afterwards in the cities or suburbs of Boston or New York, it seems to his friends and to himself that he is right in being disheartened and in complaining the rest of his life. A sturdy lad from New Hampshire or Vermont, who in turn tries all the professions, who *teams it, farms it, peddles*, keeps a school, preaches, edits a newspaper, goes to Congress, buys a township, and so forth, in successive years, and always, like a cat, falls on his feet, is worth a hundred of these city dolls. He walks abreast with his days, and feels no shame in not 'studying a profession,' for he does not postpone his life, but lives already. He has not one chance, but a hundred chances. Let a Stoic[28] open the resources of man, and tell men they are not leaning willows, but can and must detach themselves; that with the exercise of self-trust, new powers shall appear; that a man is the word made flesh, born to shed healing to the nations,[29] that he should be ashamed of our compassion, and that the moment he acts from himself, tossing the laws, the books, idolatries, and customs out of the window, we pity him no more but thank and revere him,—and that teacher shall restore the life of man to splendor, and make his name dear to all History.

It is easy to see that a greater self-reliance must work a revolution in all the offices and relations of men; in their religion; in their education; in their pursuits; their modes of living; their association; in their property; in their speculative views.

1. In what prayers do men allow themselves! That which they call a holy office, is not so much as brave and manly. Prayer looks abroad and asks for some foreign addition to come through some foreign virtue, and loses itself in endless mazes of natural and supernatural, and mediatorial and

---

[28]Ancient Greek philosophers who advocated impassivity, independence, and adherence to natural law.

[29]Cf. John 1:14 and Revelation 22:2.

miraculous. Prayer that craves a particular commodity,—any thing less than all good,—is vicious. Prayer is the contemplation of the facts of life from the highest point of view. It is the soliloquy of a beholding and jubilant soul. It is the spirit of God pronouncing his works good.[30] But prayer as a means to effect a private end, is meanness and theft. It supposes dualism and not unity in nature and consciousness. As soon as the man is at one with God, he will not beg. He will then see prayer in all action. The prayer of the farmer kneeling in his field to weed it, the prayer of the rower kneeling with the stroke of his oar, are true prayers heard throughout nature, though for cheap ends. Caratach, in Fletcher's Bonduca,[31] when admonished to inquire the mind of the god Audate, replies,—

> *"His hidden meaning lies in our endeavors,*
> *Our valors are our best gods."*

Another sort of false prayers are our regrets. Discontent is the want of self-reliance: it is infirmity of will. Regret calamities, if you can thereby help the sufferer; if not, attend your own work, and already the evil begins to be repaired. Our sympathy is just as base. We come to them who weep foolishly, and sit down and cry for company, instead of imparting to them truth and health in rough electric shocks; putting them once more in communication with their own reason. The secret of fortune is joy in our hands. Welcome evermore to gods and men is the self-helping man. For him all doors are flung wide: him all tongues greet, all honors crown, all eyes follow with desire. Our love goes out to him and embraces him, because he did not need it. We solicitously and apologetically caress and celebrate him, because he held on his way and scorned our disapprobation. The gods love him because men hated him. "To the persevering mortal," said Zoroaster,[32] "the blessed Immortals are swift."

As men's prayers are a disease of the will, so are their creeds a disease of the intellect. They say with those foolish Israelites, 'Let not God speak to us, lest we die. Speak thou, speak any man with us, and we will obey.'[33] Everywhere I am hindered of meeting God in my brother, because he has shut his own temple doors, and recites fables merely of his brother's, or his brother's brother's God. Every new mind is a new classification. If it prove a mind of uncommon activity and power, a Locke, a Lavoisier, a Hutton, a Bentham, a Fourier,[34] it imposes its classification on other men, and lo! a new system. In proportion to the depth of the thought, and so to the number of the objects it touches and brings within reach of the pupil, is his complacency. But chiefly is this apparent in creeds and churches, which are also classifications of some powerful mind acting on the elemental thought of Duty, and man's relation to the Highest. Such is Calvinism, Quakerism,

[30]God's pronouncement after creating the world; cf. Genesis 1:31.
[31]Jacobean drama by John Fletcher.
[32]Persian religious leader (6th cent. B.C.).
[33]Cf. Exodus 20:9.

[34]List of pioneers in natural and social sciences. Instead of Fourier, the advocate of communitarianism, the 1841 edition included the phrenologist Spurzheim.

Swedenborgianism. The pupil takes the same delight in subordinating every thing to the new terminology, as a girl who has just learned botany in seeing a new earth and new seasons thereby. It will happen for a time, that the pupil will find his intellectual power has grown by the study of his master's mind. But in all unbalanced minds, the classification is idolized, passes for the end, and not for a speedily exhaustible means, so that the walls of the system blend to their eye in the remote horizon with the walls of the universe; the luminaries of heaven seem to them hung on the arch their master built. They cannot imagine how you aliens have any right to see,—how you can see; 'It must be somehow that you stole the light from us.' They do not yet perceive, that light, unsystematic, indomitable, will break into any cabin, even into theirs. Let them chirp awhile and call it their own. If they are honest and do well, presently their neat new pinfold[35] will be too strait and low, will crack, will lean, will rot and vanish, and the immortal light, all young and joyful, million-orbed, million-colored, will beam over the universe as on the first morning.

2. It is for want of self-culture that the superstition of Travelling, whose idols are Italy, England, Egypt, retains its fascination for all educated Americans. They who made England, Italy, or Greece venerable in the imagination, did so by sticking fast where they were, like an axis of the earth. In manly hours, we feel that duty is our place. The soul is no traveller: the wise man stays at home, and when his necessities, his duties, on any occasion call him from his house, or into foreign lands, he is at home still, and shall make men sensible by the expression of his countenance, that he goes the missionary of wisdom and virtue, and visits cities and men like a sovereign, and not like an interloper or a valet.

I have no churlish objection to the circumnavigation of the globe, for the purposes of art, of study, and benevolence, so that the man is first domesticated, or does not go abroad with the hope of finding somewhat greater than he knows. He who travels to be amused, or to get somewhat which he does not carry, travels away from himself, and grows old even in youth among old things. In Thebes, in Palmyra, his will and mind have become old and dilapidated as they. He carries ruins to ruins.

Travelling is a fool's paradise. Our first journeys discover to us the indifference of places. At home I dream that at Naples, at Rome, I can be intoxicated with beauty, and lose my sadness. I pack my trunk, embrace my friends, embark on the sea, and at last wake up in Naples, and there beside me is the stern Fact, the sad self, unrelenting, identical, that I fled from. I seek the Vatican, and the palaces. I affect to be intoxicated with sights and suggestions, but I am not intoxicated. My giant goes with me wherever I go.

3. But the rage of travelling is a symptom of a deeper unsoundness affecting the whole intellectual action. The intellect is vagabond, and our system of education fosters restlessness. Our minds travel when our bodies are forced to stay at home. We imitate; and what is imitation but the

---

[35]Animal enclosure.

travelling of the mind? Our houses are built with foreign taste; our shelves are garnished with foreign ornaments; our opinions, our tastes, our faculties, lean, and follow the Past and the Distant. The soul created the arts wherever they have flourished. It was in his own mind that the artist sought his model. It was an application of his own thought to the thing to be done and the conditions to be observed. And why need we copy the Doric or the Gothic model? Beauty, convenience, grandeur of thought, and quaint expression are as near to us as to any, and if the American artist will study with hope and love the precise thing to be done by him, considering the climate, the soil, the length of the day, the wants of the people, the habit and form of the government, he will create a house in which all these will find themselves fitted, and taste and sentiment will be satisfied also.

Insist on yourself; never imitate. Your own gift you can present every moment with the cumulative force of a whole life's cultivation; but of the adopted talent of another, you have only an extemporaneous, half possession. That which each can do best, none but his Maker can teach him. No man yet knows what it is, nor can, till that person has exhibited it. Where is the master who could have taught Shakspeare? Where is the master who could have instructed Franklin, or Washington, or Bacon, or Newton? Every great man is a unique. The Scipionism of Scipio is precisely that part he could not borrow. Shakspeare will never be made by the study of Shakspeare. Do that which is assigned you, and you cannot hope too much or dare too much. There is at this moment for you an utterance brave and grand as that of the colossal chisel of Phidias,[36] or trowel of the Egyptians, or the pen of Moses, or Dante, but different from all these. Not possibly will the soul all rich, all eloquent, with thousand-cloven tongue, deign to repeat itself; but if you can hear what these patriarchs say, surely you can reply to them in the same pitch of voice: for the ear and the tongue are two organs of one nature. Abide in the simple and noble regions of thy life, obey thy heart, and thou shalt reproduce the Foreworld again.

4. As our Religion, our Education, our Art look abroad, so does our spirit of society. All men plume themselves on the improvement of society, and no man improves.

Society never advances. It recedes as fast on one side as it gains on the other. It undergoes continual changes: it is barbarous, it is civilized, it is christianized, it is rich, it is scientific; but this change is not amelioration. For every thing that is given, something is taken. Society acquires new arts and loses old instincts. What a contrast between the well-clad, reading, writing, thinking American, with a watch, a pencil, and a bill of exchange in his pocket, and the naked New Zealander, whose property is a club, a spear, a mat, and an undivided twentieth of a shed to sleep under. But compare the health of the two men, and you shall see that the white man has lost his aboriginal strength. If the traveller tell us truly, strike the savage with a broad axe, and

---

[36]Greek sculptor (5th cent. B.C.).

in a day or two the flesh shall unite and heal as if you struck the blow into soft pitch, and the same blow shall send the white to his grave.

The civilized man has built a coach, but has lost the use of his feet. He is supported on crutches, but lacks so much support of muscle. He has a fine Geneva watch, but he fails of the skill to tell the hour by the sun. A Greenwich nautical almanac he has, and so being sure of the information when he wants it, the man in the street does not know a star in the sky. The solstice he does not observe; the equinox he knows as little; and the whole bright calendar of the year is without a dial in his mind. His note-books impair his memory; his libraries overload his wit; the insurance office increases the number of accidents; and it may be a question whether machinery does not encumber; whether we have not lost by refinement some energy, by a christianity entrenched in establishments and forms, some vigor of wild virtue. For every stoic was a stoic; but in Christendom where is the Christian?

There is no more deviation in the moral standard than in the standard of height or bulk. No greater men are now than ever were. A singular equality may be observed between the great men of the first and of the last ages; nor can all the science, art, religion and philosophy of the nineteenth century avail to educate greater men than Plutarch's heroes, three or four and twenty centuries ago. Not in time is the race progressive. Phocion, Socrates, Anaxagoras, Diogenes,[37] are great men, but they leave no class. He who is really of their class will not be called by their name, but will be his own man, and, in his turn the founder of a sect. The arts and inventions of each period are only its costume, and do not invigorate men. The harm of the improved machinery may compensate its good. Hudson and Behring accomplished so much in their fishing-boats, as to astonish Parry and Franklin,[38] whose equipment exhausted the resources of science and art. Galileo, with an opera-glass, discovered a more splendid series of celestial phenomena than any one since. Columbus found the New World in an undecked boat. It is curious to see the periodical disuse and perishing of means and machinery which were introduced with loud laudation, a few years or centuries before. The great genius returns to essential man. We reckoned the improvements of the art of war among the triumphs of science, and yet Napoleon conquered Europe by the Bivouac,[39] which consisted of falling back on naked valor, and disencumbering it of all aids. The Emperor held it impossible to make a perfect army, says Las Cases,[40] "without abolishing our arms, magazines, commissaries, and carriages, until in imitation of the Roman custom, the soldier should receive his supply of corn, grind it in his hand-mill, and bake his bread himself."

---

[37]Statesmen and philosophers of classical Greece.

[38]Emerson contrasts sixteenth- and seventeenth-century navigators with nineteenth-century Arctic explorers.

[39]Emerson capitalizes what would then have been a technical term introduced during the Napoleonic wars, indicating a temporary encampment without tents.

[40]French historian and biographer of Napoleon (1766–1842).

Society is a wave. The wave moves onward, but the water of which it is composed, does not. The same particle does not rise from the valley to the ridge. Its unity is only phenomenal. The persons who make up a nation to-day, next year die, and their experience with them.

And so the reliance on Property, including the reliance on governments which protect it, is the want of self-reliance. Men have looked away from themselves and at things so long, that they have come to esteem the religious, learned, and civil institutions, as guards of property, and they deprecate assaults on these, because they feel them to be assaults on property. They measure their esteem of each other, by what each has, and not by what each is. But a cultivated man becomes ashamed of his property, out of new respect for his nature. Especially he hates what he has, if he see that it is accidental,—came to him by inheritance, or gift, or crime; then he feels that it is not having; it does not belong to him, has no root in him, and merely lies there, because no revolution or no robber takes it away. But that which a man is, does always by necessity acquire, and what the man acquires is living property, which does not wait the beck of rulers, or mobs, or revolutions, or fire, or storm, or bankruptcies, but perpetually renews itself wherever the man breathes. "Thy lot or portion of life," said the Caliph Ali,[41] "is seeking after thee; therefore be at rest from seeking after it." Our dependence on these foreign goods leads us to our slavish respect for numbers. The political parties meet in numerous conventions; the greater the concourse, and with each new uproar of announcement, The delegation from Essex! The Democrats from New Hampshire! The Whigs of Maine! the young patriot feels himself stronger than before by a new thousand of eyes and arms. In like manner the reformers summon conventions, and vote and resolve in multitude. Not so, O friends! will the God deign to enter and inhabit you, but by a method precisely the reverse. It is only as a man puts off all foreign support, and stands alone, that I see him to be strong and to prevail. He is weaker by every recruit to his banner. Is not a man better than a town? Ask nothing of men, and in the endless mutation, thou only firm column must presently appear the upholder of all that surrounds thee. He who knows that power is inborn, that he is weak because he has looked for good out of him and elsewhere, and so perceiving, throws himself unhesitatingly on his thought, instantly rights himself, stands in the erect position, commands his limbs, works miracles; just as a man who stands on his feet is stronger than a man who stands on his head.

So use all that is called Fortune. Most men gamble with her, and gain all, and lose all, as her wheel rolls. But do thou leave as unlawful these winnings, and deal with Cause and Effect, the chancellors of God. In the Will work and acquire, and thou hast chained the wheel of Chance, and shalt sit hereafter out of fear from her rotations. A political victory, a rise of rents,

---

[41]Emerson found this sentence by the seventh-century successor of Mohammed in Ockley's *History of the Saracens* (1718).

the recovery of your sick, or the return of your absent friend, or some other favorable event, raises your spirits, and you think good days are preparing for you. Do not believe it. Nothing can bring you peace but yourself. Nothing can bring you peace but the triumph of principles.

1841, 1847

The Poet

> *A moody child and wildly wise*
> *Pursued the game with joyful eyes,*
> *Which chose, like meteors, their way,*
> *And rived the dark with private ray:*
> *They overleapt the horizon's edge,*
> *Searched with Apollo's privilege;*
> *Through man, and woman, and sea, and star,*
> *Saw the dance of nature forward far;*
> *Through worlds, and races, and terms, and times,*
> *Saw musical order, and pairing rhymes.*
>
> *Olympian bards who sung*
> *Divine ideas below,*
> *Which always find us young,*
> *And always keep us so.*[1]

Those who are esteemed umpires of taste, are often persons who have acquired some knowledge of admired pictures or sculptures, and have an inclination for whatever is elegant; but if you inquire whether they are beautiful souls, and whether their own acts are like fair pictures, you learn that they are selfish and sensual. Their cultivation is local, as if you should rub a log of dry wood in one spot to produce fire, all the rest remaining cold. Their knowledge of the fine arts is some study of rules and particulars, or some limited judgment of color or form, which is exercised for amusement or for show. It is a proof of the shallowness of the doctrine of beauty, as it lies in the minds of our amateurs, that men seem to have lost the perception of the instant dependence of form upon soul. There is no doctrine of forms in our philosophy. We were put into our bodies, as fire is put into a pan, to be carried about; but there is no accurate adjustment between the spirit and the organ, much less is the latter the germination of the former. So in regard to other forms, the intellectual men do not believe in any essential dependence of the material world on thought and volition. Theologians think it a pretty air-castle to talk of the spiritual meaning of a ship or a cloud, of a city or a contract, but they prefer to come again to the solid ground of historical evidence; and even the poets are contented with a civil and conformed manner of living, and to write poems from the fancy, at a

[1]These two poetic mottoes are by Emerson. The first verse is taken from his unfinished masque, "A Discontented Poet," and the quatrain is from "Ode to Beauty."

safe distance from their own experience. But the highest minds of the world have never ceased to explore the double meaning, or, shall I say, the quadruple, or the centuple, or much more manifold meaning, of every sensuous fact: Orpheus,[2] Empedocles, Heraclitus,[3] Plato, Plutarch, Dante, Swedenborg, and the masters of sculpture, picture, and poetry. For we are not pans and barrows, nor even porters of the fire and torch-bearers, but children of the fire, made of it, and only the same divinity transmuted, and at two or three removes, when we know least about it. And this hidden truth, that the fountains whence all this river of Time, and its creatures, floweth, are intrinsically ideal and beautiful, draws us to the consideration of the nature and functions of the Poet, or the man of Beauty, to the means and materials he uses, and to the general aspect of the art in the present time.

The breadth of the problem is great, for the poet is representative. He stands among partial men for the complete man, and apprises us not of his wealth, but of the commonwealth. The young man reveres men of genius, because, to speak truly, they are more himself than he is. They receive of the soul as he also receives, but they more. Nature enhances her beauty to the eye of loving men, from their belief that the poet is beholding her shows at the same time. He is isolated among his contemporaries, by truth and by his art, but with this consolation in his pursuits, that they will draw all men sooner or later. For all men live by truth, and stand in need of expression. In love, in art, in avarice, in politics, in labor, in games, we study to utter our painful secret. The man is only half himself, the other half is his expression.

Notwithstanding this necessity to be published, adequate expression is rare. I know not how it is that we need an interpreter; but the great majority of men seem to be minors, who have not yet come into possession of their own, or mutes, who cannot report the conversation they have had with nature. There is no man who does not anticipate a supersensual utility in the sun, and stars, earth, and water. These stand and wait to render him a peculiar service.[4] But there is some obstruction, or some excess of phlegm in our constitution, which does not suffer them to yield the due effect. Too feeble fall the impressions of nature on us to make us artists. Every touch should thrill. Every man should be so much an artist, that he could report in conversation what had befallen him. Yet, in our experience, the rays or appulses have sufficient force to arrive at the senses, but not enough to reach the quick, and compel the reproduction of themselves in speech. The poet is the person in whom these powers are in balance, the man without impediment, who sees and handles that which others dream of, traverses the whole scale of experience, and is representative of man, in virtue of being the largest power to receive and to impart.

For the Universe has three children, born at one time, which reappear, under different names, in every system of thought, whether they be called

[2]The list includes the mythological poet Orpheus, whom Emerson and contemporaries treated as a historic figure.

[3]Empedocles and Heraclitus were fifth-century Greek philosophers.
[4]Cf. Milton, Sonnet XIX, line 14.

cause, operation, and effect; or, more poetically, Jove, Pluto, Neptune; or, theologically, the Father, the Spirit, and the Son; but which we will call here, the Knower, the Doer, and the Sayer. These stand respectively for the love of truth, for the love of good, and for the love of beauty. These three are equal. Each is that which he is essentially, so that he cannot be surmounted or analyzed, and each of these three has the power of the others latent in him, and his own patent.

The poet is the sayer, the namer, and represents beauty. He is a sovereign, and stands on the centre. For the world is not painted, or adorned, but is from the beginning beautiful; and God has not made some beautiful things, but Beauty is the creator of the universe. Therefore the poet is not any permissive potentate, but is emperor in his own right. Criticism is infested with a cant of materialism, which assumes that manual skill and activity is the first merit of all men, and disparages such as say and do not, overlooking the fact, that some men, namely, poets, are natural sayers, sent into the world to the end of expression, and confounds them with those whose province is action, but who quit it to imitate the sayers. But Homer's words are as costly and admirable to Homer, as Agamemnon's victories are to Agamemnon. The poet does not wait for the hero or the sage, but, as they act and think primarily, so he writes primarily what will and must be spoken, reckoning the others, though primaries also, yet, in respect to him, secondaries and servants; as sitters or models in the studio of a painter, or as assistants who bring building materials to an architect.

For poetry was all written before time was, and whenever we are so finely organized that we can penetrate into that region where the air is music, we hear those primal warblings, and attempt to write them down, but we lose ever and anon a word, or a verse, and substitute something of our own, and thus miswrite the poem. The men of more delicate ear write down these cadences more faithfully, and these transcripts, though imperfect, become the songs of the nations. For nature is as truly beautiful as it is good, or as it is reasonable, and must as much appear, as it must be done, or be known. Words and deeds are quite indifferent modes of the divine energy. Words are also actions, and actions are a kind of words.

The sign and credentials of the poet are, that he announces that which no man foretold. He is the true and only doctor;[5] he knows and tells; he is the only teller of news, for he was present and privy to the appearance which he describes. He is a beholder of ideas, and an utterer of the necessary and causal. For we do not speak now of men of poetical talents, or of industry and skill in metre, but of the true poet. I took part in a conversation the other day, concerning a recent writer of lyrics, a man of subtle mind, whose head appeared to be a music-box of delicate tunes and rhythms, and whose skill, and command of language, we could not sufficiently praise. But when the question arose, whether he was not only a lyrist, but a poet, we were obliged to confess that he is plainly a contemporary,

---

[5]Used in the earlier sense of "teacher."

not an eternal man. He does not stand out of our low limitations, like a Chimborazo under the line,[6] running up from the torrid base through all the climates of the globe, with belts of the herbage of every latitude on its high and mottled sides; but this genius is the landscape-garden of a modern house, adorned with fountains and statues, with well-bred men and women standing and sitting in the walks and terraces. We hear, through all the varied music, the ground-tone of conventional life. Our poets are men of talents who sing, and not the children of music. The argument is secondary, the finish of the verses is primary.

For it is not metres, but a metre-making argument, that makes a poem,—a thought so passionate and alive, that, like the spirit of a plant or an animal, it has an architecture of its own, and adorns nature with a new thing. The thought and the form are equal in the order of time, but in the order of genesis the thought is prior to the form. The poet has a new thought: he has a whole new experience to unfold; he will tell us how it was with him, and all men will be the richer in his fortune. For, the experience of each new age requires a new confession, and the world seems always waiting for its poet. I remember, when I was young, how much I was moved one morning by tidings that genius had appeared in a youth who sat near me at table. He had left his work, and gone rambling none knew whither, and had written hundreds of lines, but could not tell whether that which was in him was therein told: he could tell nothing but that all was changed,—man, beast, heaven, earth, and sea. How gladly we listened! how credulous! Society seemed to be compromised. We sat in the aurora of a sunrise which was to put out all the stars. Boston seemed to be at twice the distance it had the night before, or was much farther than that. Rome,— what was Rome? Plutarch and Shakspeare were in the yellow leaf,[7] and Homer no more should be heard of. It is much to know that poetry has been written this very day, under this very roof, by your side. What! that wonderful spirit has not expired! these stony moments are still sparkling and animated! I had fancied that the oracles were all silent,[8] and nature had spent her fires, and behold! all night, from every pore, these fine auroras have been streaming. Every one has some interest in the advent of the poet, and no one knows how much it may concern him. We know that the secret of the world is profound, but who or what shall be our interpreter, we know not. A mountain ramble, a new style of face, a new person, may put the key into our hands. Of course, the value of genius to us is in the veracity of its report. Talent may frolic and juggle; genius realizes and adds. Mankind, in good earnest, have arrived so far in understanding themselves and their work, that the foremost watchman on the peak announces his news. It is

---

[6]Ecuadorian mountain located below the equator.

[7]Cf. *Macbeth*, Act V, iii, 22–23: "I have lived long enough. My way of life is fallen into the sere, the yellow leaf."

[8]Cf. Milton, "On the Morning of Christ's Nativity," line 173: "The oracles are dumb."

the truest word ever spoken, and the phrase will be the fittest, most musical, and the unerring voice of the world for that time.

All that we call sacred history attests that the birth of a poet is the principal event in chronology. Man, never so often deceived, still watches for the arrival of a brother who can hold him steady to a truth, until he has made it his own. With what joy I begin to read a poem, which I confide in as an inspiration! And now my chains are to be broken; I shall mount above these clouds and opaque airs in which I live,—opaque, though they seem transparent,—and from the heaven of truth I shall see and comprehend my relations. That will reconcile me to life, and renovate nature, to see trifles animated by a tendency, and to know what I am doing. Life will no more be a noise; now I shall see men and women, and know the signs by which they may be discerned from fools and satans. This day shall be better than my birthday: then I became an animal: now I am invited into the science of the real. Such is the hope, but the fruition is postponed. Oftener it falls, that this winged man, who will carry me into the heaven, whirls me into mists, then leaps and frisks about with me as it were from cloud to cloud, still affirming that he is bound heavenward; and I, being myself a novice, am slow in perceiving that he does not know the way into the heavens, and is merely bent that I should admire his skill to rise, like a fowl or a flying fish, a little way from the ground or the water; but the all-piercing, all-feeding, and ocular air of heaven, that man shall never inhabit. I tumble down again soon into my old nooks, and lead the life of exaggerations as before, and have lost some faith[9] in the possibility of any guide who can lead me thither where I would be.

But leaving these victims of vanity, let us, with new hope, observe how nature, by worthier impulses, has ensured the poet's fidelity to his office of announcement and affirming, namely, by the beauty of things, which becomes a new, and higher beauty, when expressed. Nature offers all her creatures to him as a picture-language. Being used as a type, a second wonderful value appears in the object, far better than its old value, as the carpenter's stretched cord, if you hold your ear close enough, is musical in the breeze. "Things more excellent than every image," says Jamblichus,[10] "are expressed through images." Things admit of being used as symbols, because nature is a symbol, in the whole, and in every part. Every line we can draw in the sand, has expression; and there is no body without its spirit or genius. All form is an effect of character; all condition, of the quality of the life; all harmony, of health; (and, for this reason, a perception of beauty should be sympathetic, or proper only to the good). The beautiful rests on the foundations of the necessary. The soul makes the body, as the wise Spenser teaches:—

---

[9]In a correction copy of the 1844 edition, Emerson marked the change from "lost my faith."

[10]Fourth-century Neo-Platonic philosopher.

> *"So every spirit, as it is most pure,*
> *And hath in it the more of heavenly light,*
> *So it the fairer body doth procure*
> *To habit in, and it more fairly dight,*
> *With cheerful grace and amiable sight.*
> *For, of the soul, the body form doth take,*
> *For soul is form, and doth the body make."*[11]

Here we find ourselves, suddenly, not in a critical speculation, but in a holy place, and should go very warily and reverently. We stand before the secret of the world, there where Being passes into Appearance, and Unity into Variety.

The Universe is the externization of the soul. Wherever the life is, that bursts into appearance around it. Our science is sensual, and therefore superficial. The earth, and the heavenly bodies, physics, and chemistry, we sensually treat, as if they were self-existent; but these are the retinue of that Being we have. "The mighty heaven," said Proclus,[12] "exhibits, in its transfigurations, clear images of the splendor of intellectual perceptions; being moved in conjunction with the unapparent periods of intellectual natures." Therefore, science always goes abreast with the just elevation of the man, keeping step with religion and metaphysics; or, the state of science is an index of our self-knowledge. Since everything in nature answers to a moral power, if any phenomenon remains brute and dark, it is because the corresponding faculty in the observer is not yet active.

No wonder, then, if these waters be so deep, that we hover over them with a religious regard. The beauty of the fable proves the importance of the sense; to the poet, and to all others; or, if you please, every man is so far a poet as to be susceptible of these enchantments of nature: for all men have the thoughts whereof the universe is the celebration. I find that the fascination resides in the symbol. Who loves nature? Who does not? Is it only poets, and men of leisure and cultivation, who live with her? No; but also hunters, farmers, grooms, and butchers, though they express their affection in their choice of life, and not in their choice of words. The writer wonders what the coachman or the hunter values in riding, in horses, and dogs. It is not superficial qualities. When you talk with him, he holds these at as slight a rate as you. His worship is sympathetic; he has no definitions, but he is commanded in nature, by the living power which he feels to be there present. No imitation, or playing of these things, would content him; he loves the earnest of the north wind, of rain, of stone, and wood, and iron. A beauty not explicable, is dearer than a beauty which we can see to the end of. It is nature the symbol, nature certifying the supernatural, body overflowed by life, which he worships, with coarse, but sincere rites.

The inwardness, and mystery, of this attachment, drive men of every class to the use of emblems. The schools of poets, and philosophers, are not

---

[11]From Edmund Spenser's "An Hymn in Honour of Beauty" (1596).   [12]Fifth-century Greek Neo-Platonic philosopher.

more intoxicated with their symbols, than the populace with theirs. In our political parties, compute the power of badges and emblems. See the huge wooden ball[13] rolled by successive ardent crowds from Baltimore to Bunker hill! In the political processions, Lowell goes in a loom, and Lynn in a shoe, and Salem in a ship. Witness the cider-barrel, the log-cabin, the hickory-stick, the palmetto, and all the cognizances of party. See the power of national emblems. Some stars, lilies, leopards, a crescent, a lion, an eagle, or other figure, which came into credit God knows how, on an old rag of bunting, blowing in the wind, on a fort, at the ends of the earth, shall make the blood tingle under the rudest, or the most conventional exterior. The people fancy they hate poetry, and they are all poets and mystics!

Beyond this universality of the symbolic language, we are apprised of the divineness of this superior use of things, whereby the world is a temple, whose walls are covered with emblems, pictures, and commandments of the Diety, in this, that there is no fact in nature which does not carry the whole sense of nature; and the distinctions which we make in events, and in affairs, of low and high, honest and base, disappear when nature is used as a symbol. Thought makes everything fit for use. The vocabulary of an omniscient man would embrace words and images excluded from polite conversation. What would be base, or even obscene, to the obscene, becomes illustrious, spoken in a new connexion of thought. The piety of the Hebrew prophets purges their grossness. The circumcision is an example of the power of poetry to raise the low and offensive. Small and mean things serve as well as great symbols. The meaner the type by which a law is expressed, the more pungent it is, and the more lasting in the memories of men: just as we choose the smallest box, or case, in which any needful utensil can be carried. Bare lists of words are found suggestive, to an imaginative and excited mind; as it is related of Lord Chatham, that he was accustomed to read in Bailey's Dictionary,[14] when he was preparing to speak in Parliament. The poorest experience is rich enough for all the purposes of expressing thought. Why covet a knowledge of new facts? Day and night, house and garden, a few books, a few actions, serve us as well as would all trades and all spectacles. We are far from having exhausted the significance of the few symbols we use. We can come to use them yet with a terrible simplicity. It does not need that a poem should be long. Every word was once a poem. Every new relation is a new word. Also, we use defects and deformities to a sacred purpose, so expressing our sense that the evils of the world are such only to the evil eye. In the old mythology, mythologists observe, defects are ascribed to divine natures, as lameness to Vulcan, blindness to Cupid, and the like, to signify exuberances.

[13]The political slogan "Keep the ball rolling" was used by the Whigs in the 1840 presidential campaign. The passage goes on to list other political and manufacturing emblems.

[14]Renowned orator William Pitt, Earl of Chatham (1708–1778); widely used etymological dictionary (1721) by Nathan Bailey.

For, as it is dislocation and detachment from the life of God, that makes things ugly, the poet, who re-attaches things to nature and the Whole,— re-attaching even artificial things, and violations of nature, to nature, by a deeper insight,—disposes very easily of the most disagreeable facts. Readers of poetry see the factory-village, and the railway, and fancy that the poetry of the landscape is broken up by these; for these works of art are not yet consecrated in their reading; but the poet sees them fall within the great Order not less than the bee-hive, or the spider's geometrical web. Nature adopts them very fast into her vital circles, and the gliding train of cars she loves like her own. Besides, in a centred mind, it signifies nothing how many mechanical inventions you exhibit. Though you add millions, and never so surprising, the fact of mechanics has not gained a grain's weight. The spiritual fact remains unalterable, by many or by few particulars; as no mountain is of any appreciable height to break the curve of the sphere. A shrewd country-boy goes to the city for the first time, and the complacent citizen is not satisfied with his little wonder. It is not that he does not see all the fine houses, and know that he never saw such before, but he disposes of them as easily as the poet finds place for the railway. The chief value of the new fact, is to enhance the great and constant fact of Life, which can dwarf any and every circumstance, and to which the belt of wampum, and the commerce of America, are alike.

The world being thus put under the mind for verb and noun, the poet is he who can articulate it. For, though life is great, and fascinates, and absorbs,—and though all men are intelligent of the symbols through which it is named,—yet they cannot originally use them. We are symbols, and inhabit symbols; workmen, work, and tools, words and things, birth and death, all are emblems; but we sympathize with the symbols, and, being infatuated with the economical uses of things, we do not know that they are thoughts. The poet, by an ulterior intellectual perception, gives them a power which makes their old use forgotten, and puts eyes, and a tongue, into every dumb and inanimate object. He perceives the thought's independence of the symbol, the stability of the thought, the accidency and fugacity[15] of the symbol. As the eyes of Lynceus[16] were said to see through the earth, so the poet turns the world to glass, and shows us all things in their right series and procession. For, through that better perception, he stands one step nearer to things, and sees the flowing or metamorphosis; perceives that thought is multiform; that within the form of every creature is a force impelling it to ascend into a higher form; and, following with his eyes the life, uses the forms which express that life, and so his speech flows with the flowing of nature. All the facts of the animal economy,—sex, nutriment, gestation, birth, growth—are symbols of the passage of the world into the soul of man, to suffer there a change, and reappear a new and higher fact.

[15]Transitoriness, volatility.
[16]One of the Argonauts, noted for his eyesight; from Apollonius Rhodius, *The Argonautica* (3rd–2nd cent. B.C.).

He uses forms according to the life, and not according to the form. This is true science. The poet alone knows astronomy, chemistry, vegetation, and animation, for he does not stop at these facts, but employs them as signs. He knows why the plain, or meadow of space, was strown with these flowers we call suns, and moons, and stars; why the great deep is adorned with animals, with men, and gods; for, in every word he speaks he rides on them as the horses of thought.

By virtue of this science the poet is the Namer, or Language-maker, naming things sometimes after their appearance, sometimes after their essence, and giving to every one its own name and not another's, thereby rejoicing the intellect, which delights in detachment or boundary. The poets made all the words, and therefore language is the archives of history, and, if we must say it, a sort of tomb of the muses. For, though the origin of most of our words is forgotten, each word was at first a stroke of genius, and obtained currency, because for the moment it symbolized the world to the first speaker and to the hearer. The etymologist finds the deadest word to have been once a brilliant picture. Language is fossil poetry. As the limestone of the continent consists of infinite masses of the shells of animalcules, so language is made up of images, or tropes, which now, in their secondary use, have long ceased to remind us of their poetic origin. But the poet names the thing because he sees it, or comes one step nearer to it than any other. This expression, or naming, is not art, but a second nature, grown out of the first, as a leaf out of a tree. What we call nature, is a certain self-regulated motion, or change; and nature does all things by her own hands, and does not leave another to baptize her, but baptizes herself; and this through the metamorphosis again. I remember that a certain poet[17] described it to me thus:

Genius is the activity which repairs the decays of things, whether wholly or partly of a material and finite kind. Nature, through all her kingdoms, insures herself. Nobody cares for planting the poor fungus: so she shakes down from the gills of one agaric countless spores, any one of which, being preserved, transmits new billions of spores to-morrow or next day. The new agaric of this hour has a chance which the old one had not. This atom of seed is thrown into a new place, not subject to the accidents which destroyed its parent two rods off. She makes a man; and having brought him to ripe age, she will no longer run the risk of losing this wonder at a blow, but she detaches from him a new self, that the kind may be safe from accidents to which the individual is exposed. So when the soul of the poet has come to ripeness of thought, she detaches and sends away from it its poems or songs,—a fearless, sleepless, deathless progeny, which is not exposed to the accidents of the weary kingdom of time: a fearless, vivacious offspring, clad with wings (such was the virtue of the soul out of which they

[17]The framed passage is from Emerson's own journal.

came), which carry them fast and far, and infix them irrecoverably into the hearts of men. These wings are the beauty of the poet's soul. The songs, thus flying immortal from their mortal parent, are pursued by clamorous flights of censures, which swarm in far greater numbers, and threaten to devour them; but these last are not winged. At the end of a very short leap they fall plump down, and rot, having received from the souls out of which they came no beautiful wings. But the melodies of the poet ascend, and leap, and pierce into the deeps of infinite time.

So far the bard taught me, using his freer speech. But nature has a higher end, in the production of new individuals, than security, namely, *ascension*, or, the passage of the soul into higher forms. I knew, in my younger days, the sculptor who made the statue of the youth which stands in the public garden. He was, as I remember, unable to tell, directly, what made him happy, or unhappy, but by wonderful indirections he could tell. He rose one day, according to his habit, before the dawn, and saw the morning break, grand as the eternity out of which it came, and, for many days after, he strove to express this tranquillity, and, lo! his chisel had fashioned out of marble the form of a beautiful youth, Phosphor,[18] whose aspect is such, that, it is said, all persons who look on it become silent. The poet also resigns himself to his mood, and that thought which agitated him is expressed, but *alter idem*,[19] in a manner totally new. The expression is organic, or, the new type which things themselves take when liberated. As, in the sun, objects paint their images on the retina of the eye, so they, sharing the aspiration of the whole universe, tend to paint a far more delicate copy of their essence in his mind. Like the metamorphosis of things into higher organic forms, is their change into melodies. Over everything stands its dæmon, or soul, and, as the form of the thing is reflected by the eye, so the soul of the thing is reflected by a melody. The sea, the mountain-ridge, Niagara, and every flower-bed, pre-exist, or super-exist, in pre-cantations, which sail like odors in the air, and when any man goes by with an ear sufficiently fine, he overhears them, and endeavors to write down the notes, without diluting or depraving them. And herein is the legitimation of criticism, in the mind's faith, that the poems are a corrupt version of some text in nature, with which they ought to be made to tally. A rhyme in one of our sonnets should not be less pleasing than the iterated nodes of a sea-shell, or the resembling difference of a group of flowers. The pairing[20] of the birds is an idyl, not tedious as our idyls are; a tempest is a rough ode without falsehood or rant; a summer, with its harvest sown, reaped, and stored, is an epic song, subordinating how many admirably executed parts. Why should not the symmetry and truth that modulate these, glide into our spirits, and we participate the invention of nature?

---

[18]Greek god Lucifer, the morning star. In his journal, Emerson himself is the sculptor, cutting a statue of Hesperus, the evening star.

[19]Latin for "the same yet different."

[20]Mating.

This insight, which expresses itself by what is called Imagination, is a very high sort of seeing, which does not come by study, but by the intellect being where and what it sees, by sharing the path, or circuit of things through forms, and so making them translucid to others. The path of things is silent. Will they suffer a speaker to go with them? A spy they will not suffer; a lover, a poet, is the transcendency of their own nature,—him they will suffer. The condition of true naming, on the poet's part, is his resigning himself to the divine *aura* which breathes through forms, and accompanying that.

It is a secret which every intellectual man quickly learns, that, beyond the energy of his possessed and conscious intellect, he is capable of a new energy (as of an intellect doubled on itself), by abandonment to the nature of things; that, beside his privacy of power as an individual man, there is a great public power, on which he can draw, by unlocking, at all risks, his human doors, and suffering the ethereal tides to roll and circulate through him: then he is caught up into the life of the Universe, his speech is thunder, his thought is law, and his words are universally intelligible as the plants and animals. The poet knows that he speaks adequately, then only when he speaks somewhat wildly, or, "with the flower of the mind;"[21] not with the intellect, used as an organ, but with the intellect released from all service, and suffered to take its direction from its celestial life; or, as the ancients[22] were wont to express themselves, not with intellect alone, but with the intellect inebriated by nectar. As the traveller who has lost his way, throws his reins on his horse's neck, and trusts to the instinct of the animal to find his road, so must we do with the divine animal who carries us through this world. For if in any manner we can stimulate this instinct, new passages are opened for us into nature, the mind flows into and through things hardest and highest, and the metamorphosis is possible.

This is the reason why bards love wine, mead, narcotics, coffee, tea, opium, the fumes of sandal-wood and tobacco, or whatever other procurers of animal exhilaration. All men avail themselves of such means as they can, to add this extraordinary power to their normal powers; and to this end they prize conversation, music, pictures, sculpture, dancing, theatres, travelling, war, mobs, fires, gaming, politics, or love, or science, or animal intoxication, which are several coarser or finer *quasi*-mechanical substitutes for the true nectar, which is the ravishment of the intellect by coming nearer to the fact. These are auxiliaries to the centrifugal tendency of a man, to his passage out into free space, and they help him to escape the custody of that body in which he is pent up, and of that jail-yard of individual relations in which he is enclosed. Hence a great number of such as were professionally expressors of Beauty, as painters, poets, musicians, and actors, have been more than others wont to lead a life of pleasure and indulgence; all but the

[21]Translation of a Greek phrase from the "Chaldean Oracles," selections of which appeared in translation in *The Dial* in 1844.

[22]Emerson is paraphrasing Plotinus and Proclus.

few who received the true nectar; and, as it was a spurious mode of attaining freedom, as it was an emancipation not into the heavens, but into the freedom of baser places, they were punished for that advantage they won, by a dissipation and deterioration. But never can any advantage be taken of nature by a trick. The spirit of the world, the great calm presence of the creator, comes not forth to the sorceries of opium or of wine. The sublime vision comes to the pure and simple soul in a clean and chaste body. That is not an inspiration which we owe to narcotics, but some counterfeit excitement and fury. Milton says, that the lyric poet may drink wine and live generously, but the epic poet, he who shall sing of the gods, and their descent unto men, must drink water out of a wooden bowl.[23] For poetry is not 'Devil's wine,'[24] but God's wine. It is with this as it is with toys. We fill the hands and nurseries of our children with all manner of dolls, drums, and horses, withdrawing their eyes from the plain face and sufficing objects of nature, the sun, and moon, the animals, the water, and stones, which should be their toys. So the poet's habit of living should be set on a key so low, that the common influences should delight him. His cheerfulness should be the gift of the sunlight; the air should suffice for his inspiration, and he should be tipsy with water. That spirit which suffices quiet hearts, which seems to come forth to such from every dry knoll of sere grass, from every pine-stump, and half-imbedded stone, on which the dull March sun shines, comes forth to the poor and hungry, and such as are of simple taste. If thou fill thy brain with Boston and New York, with fashion and covetousness, and wilt stimulate thy jaded senses with wine and French coffee, thou shalt find no radiance of wisdom in the lonely waste of the pinewoods.

If the imagination intoxicates the poet, it is not inactive in other men. The metamorphosis excites in the beholder an emotion of joy. The use of symbols has a certain power of emancipation and exhilaration for all men. We seem to be touched by a wand, which makes us dance and run about happily, like children. We are like persons who come out of a cave or cellar into the open air. This is the effect on us of tropes, fables, oracles, and all poetic forms. Poets are thus liberating gods. Men have really got a new sense, and found within their world, another world, or nest of worlds; for, the metamorphosis once seen, we divine that it does not stop. I will not now consider how much this makes the charm of algebra and the mathematics, which also have their tropes, but it is felt in every definition; as, when Aristotle defines *space* to be an immovable vessel, in which things are contained;—or, when Plato defines a *line* to be a flowing point; or, *figure* to be a bound of solid; and many the like. What a joyful sense of freedom we have, when Vitruvius announces the old opinion of artists, that no architect can build any house well, who does not know something of anatomy. When Socrates, in Charmides, tells us that the soul is cured of its maladies by certain incantations, and that these incantations are beautiful reasons, from

---

[23]Paraphrase of Milton's "Elegia Sexta" (1629).

[24]Emerson attributed this definition to the Church Fathers.

which temperance is generated in souls; when Plato calls the world an animal; and Timæus affirms that the plants also are animals; or affirms a man
to be a heavenly tree, growing with his root, which is his head, upward; and,
as George Chapman, following him, writes,—

> "So in our tree of man, whose nervie root
> Springs in his top;"

when Orpheus speaks of hoariness as "that white flower which marks
extreme old age;" when Proclus calls the universe the statue of the intellect;
when Chaucer, in his praise of 'Gentilesse,' compares good blood in mean
condition to fire, which, though carried to the darkest house betwixt this
and the mount of Caucasus, will yet hold its natural office, and burn as
bright as if twenty thousand men did it behold; when John saw, in the apocalypse, the ruin of the world through evil, and the stars fall from heaven, as
the figtree casteth her untimely fruit; when Æsop reports the whole catalogue of common daily relations through the masquerade of birds and
beasts;—we take the cheerful hint of the immortality of our essence, and its
versatile habit and escapes, as when the gypsies say of themselves, "it is in
vain to hang them, they cannot die."[25]

The poets are thus liberating gods. The ancient British bards had for the
title of their order, "Those who are free throughout the world."[26] They are
free, and they make free. An imaginative book renders us much more service
at first, by stimulating us through its tropes, than afterward, when we arrive
at the precise sense of the author. I think nothing is of any value in books,
excepting the transcendental and extraordinary. If a man is inflamed and
carried away by his thought, to that degree that he forgets the authors and
the public, and heeds only this one dream, which holds him like an insanity,
let me read his paper, and you may have all the arguments and histories and
criticism. All the value which attaches to Pythagoras, Paracelsus, Cornelius
Agrippa, Cardan, Kepler, Swedenborg, Schelling, Oken,[27] or any other who
introduces questionable facts into his cosmogony, as angels, devils, magic,
astrology, palmistry, mesmerism, and so on, is the certificate we have of departure from routine, and that here is a new witness. That also is the best
success in conversation, the magic of liberty, which puts the world, like a
ball, in our hands. How cheap even the liberty then seems; how mean to
study, when an emotion communicates to the intellect the power to sap and
upheave nature: how great the perspective! nations, times, systems, enter
and disappear, like threads in tapestry of large figure and many colors;

[25]Emerson's catalogue of "poets" is hardly the usual literary tradition; it includes Greek philosophers, a Roman architect, a transla-tor of Homer, a mythological poet, as well as the authors of the Apocalypse, *The Can-terbury Tales*, and *Aesop's Fables*, and ends with a saying of the "gypsies" taken from George Borrow's *The Zincali* (1842).

[26]Emerson found this "motto" in a biography of the popular English poet Felicia Hemans, in which she discussed her interest in "Welsh Melodies."

[27]Catalogue of scientific and religious theoret-icians from ancient Greece to Emerson's own day.

dream delivers us to dream, and, while the drunkenness lasts, we will sell our bed, our philosophy, our religion, in our opulence.

There is good reason why we should prize this liberation. The fate of the poor shepherd, who, blinded and lost in the snowstorm, perishes in a drift within a few feet of his cottage door, is an emblem of the state of man. On the brink of the waters of life and truth, we are miserably dying. The inaccessibleness of every thought but that we are in, is wonderful. What if you come near to it,—you are as remote, when you are nearest, as when you are farthest. Every thought is also a prison; every heaven is also a prison. Therefore we love the poet, the inventor, who in any form, whether in an ode, or in an action, or in looks and behavior, has yielded us a new thought. He unlocks our chains, and admits us to a new scene.

This emancipation is dear to all men, and the power to impart it, as it must come from greater depth and scope of thought, is a measure of intellect. Therefore all books of the imagination endure, all which ascend to that truth, that the writer sees nature beneath him, and uses it as his exponent. Every verse or sentence, possessing this virtue, will take care of its own immortality. The religions of the world are the ejaculations of a few imaginative men.

But the quality of the imagination is to flow, and not to freeze. The poet did not stop at the color, or the form, but read their meaning; neither may he rest in this meaning, but he makes the same objects exponents of his new thought. Here is the difference betwixt the poet and the mystic, that the last nails a symbol to one sense, which was a true sense for a moment, but soon becomes old and false. For all symbols are fluxional; all language is vehicular and transitive, and is good, as ferries and horses are, for conveyance, not as farms and houses are, for homestead. Mysticism consists in the mistake of an accidental and individual symbol for an universal one. The morning-redness happens to be the favorite meteor to the eyes of Jacob Behmen,[28] and comes to stand to him for truth and faith; and he believes should stand for the same realities to every reader. But the first reader prefers as naturally the symbol of a mother and child, or a gardener and his bulb, or a jeweller polishing a gem. Either of these, or of a myriad more, are equally good to the person to whom they are significant. Only they must be held lightly, and be very willingly translated into the equivalent terms which others use. And the mystic must be steadily told,—All that you say is just as true without the tedious use of that symbol as with it. Let us have a little algebra, instead of this trite rhetoric,—universal signs, instead of these village symbols,—and we shall both be gainers. The history of hierarchies seems to show, that all religious error consisted in making the symbol too stark and solid, and, at last, nothing but an excess of the organ of language.

Swedenborg, of all men in the recent ages, stands eminently for the translator of nature into thought. I do not know the man in history to

---

[28](Jakob Böhme), German mystic (1575–1624).

whom things stood so uniformly for words. Before him the metamorphosis continually plays. Everything on which his eye rests, obeys the impulses of moral nature. The figs become grapes whilst he eats them. When some of his angels affirmed a truth, the laurel twig which they held blossomed in their hands. The noise which, at a distance, appeared like gnashing and thumping, on coming nearer was found to be the voice of disputants. The men, in one of his visions, seen in heavenly light, appeared like dragons, and seemed in darkness; but, to each other, they appeared as men, and, when the light from heaven shone into their cabin, they complained of the darkness, and were compelled to shut the window that they might see.

There was this perception in him, which makes the poet or seer an object of awe and terror, namely, that the same man, or society of men, may wear one aspect to themselves and their companions, and a different aspect to higher intelligences. Certain priests, whom he describes as conversing very learnedly together, appeared to the children, who were at some distance, like dead horses; and many the like misappearances. And instantly the mind inquires, whether these fishes under the bridge, yonder oxen in the pasture, those dogs in the yard, are immutably fishes, oxen, and dogs, or only so appear to me, and perchance to themselves appear upright men; and whether I appear as a man to all eyes. The Bramins and Pythagoras propounded the same question, and if any poet has witnessed the transformation, he doubtless found it in harmony with various experiences. We have all seen changes as considerable in wheat and caterpillars. He is the poet, and shall draw us with love and terror, who sees, through the flowing vest, the firm nature, and can declare it.

I look in vain for the poet whom I describe. We do not, with sufficient plainness, or sufficient profoundness, address ourselves to life, nor dare we chaunt[29] our own times and social circumstance. If we filled the day with bravery, we should not shrink from celebrating it. Time and nature yield us many gifts, but not yet the timely man, the new religion, the reconciler, whom all things await. Dante's praise is, that he dared to write his autobiography in colossal cipher, or into universality. We have yet had no genius in America, with tyrannous eye, which knew the value of our incomparable materials, and saw, in the barbarism and materialism of the times, another carnival of the same gods whose picture he so much admires in Homer; then in the middle age; then in Calvinism. Banks and tariffs, the newspaper and caucus, methodism and unitarianism, are flat and dull to dull people, but rest on the same foundations of wonder as the town of Troy, and the temple of Delphi, and are as swiftly passing away. Our logrolling, our stumps and their politics, our fisheries, our Negroes, and Indians, our boasts, and our repudiations,[30] the wrath of rogues, and the pusillanimity of honest men, the northern trade, the southern planting, the western clearing,

---

[29]Emerson's usual way of spelling "chant."
[30]William Gilman suggested this correction for the first edition's "boats," to contrast with

"repudiations," *i.e.*, refusals to acknowledge or pay debts.

Oregon, and Texas,[31] are yet unsung. Yet America is a poem in our eyes; its ample geography dazzles the imagination, and it will not wait long for metres. If I have not found that excellent combination of gifts in my countrymen which I seek, neither could I aid myself to fix the idea of the poet by reading now and then in Chalmers's[32] collection of five centuries of English poets. These are wits, more than poets, though there have been poets among them. But when we adhere to the ideal of the poet, we have our difficulties even with Milton and Homer. Milton is too literary, and Homer too literal and historical.

But I am not wise enough for a national criticism, and must use the old largeness a little longer, to discharge my errand from the muse to the poet concerning his art.

Art is the path of the creator to his work. The paths, or methods, are ideal and eternal, though few men ever see them, not the artist himself for years, or for a lifetime, unless he come into the conditions. The painter, the sculptor, the composer, the epic rhapsodist, the orator, all partake one desire, namely, to express themselves symmetrically and abundantly, not dwarfishly and fragmentarily. They found or put themselves in certain conditions, as, the painter and sculptor before some impressive human figures; the orator, into the assembly of the people; and the others, in such scenes as each has found exciting to his intellect; and each presently feels the new desire. He hears a voice, he sees a beckoning. Then he is apprised, with wonder, what herds of dæmons hem him in. He can no more rest; he says, with the old painter, "By God, it is in me, and must go forth of me." He pursues a beauty, half seen, which flies before him. The poet pours out verses in every solitude. Most of the things he says are conventional, no doubt; but by and by he says something which is original and beautiful. That charms him. He would say nothing else but such things. In our way of talking, we say, 'That is yours, this is mine;' but the poet knows well that it is not his; that it is as strange and beautiful to him as to you; he would fain hear the like eloquence at length. Once having tasted this immortal ichor,[33] he cannot have enough of it, and, as an admirable creative power exists in these intellections, it is of the last importance that these things get spoken. What a little of all we know is said! What drops of all the sea of our science are baled up! and by what accident it is that these are exposed, when so many secrets sleep in nature! Hence the necessity of speech and song; hence these throbs and heart-beatings in the orator, at the door of the assembly, to the end, namely, that thought may be ejaculated as Logos, or Word.

Doubt not, O poet, but persist. Say, 'It is in me, and shall out.' Stand there, baulked and dumb, stuttering and stammering, hissed and hooted, stand and strive, until, at last, rage draw out of thee that *dream*-power which every night shows thee is thine own; a power transcending all limit

---

[31]States involved in contemporary political disputes.

[32]Alexander Chalmers: *Works of the English Poets* (21 volumes; 1810).

[33]In Greek mythology, ethereal fluid that replaces the gods' blood.

and privacy, and by virtue of which a man is the conductor of the whole river of electricity. Nothing walks, or creeps, or grows, or exists, which must not in turn arise and walk before him as exponent of his meaning. Comes he to that power, his genius is no longer exhaustible. All the creatures, by pairs and by tribes, pour into his mind as into a Noah's ark, to come forth again to people a new world. This is like the stock of air for our respiration, or for the combustion of our fireplace, not a measure of gallons, but the entire atmosphere if wanted. And therefore the rich poets, as Homer, Chaucer, Shakspeare, and Raphael, have obviously no limits to their works, except the limits of their lifetime, and resemble a mirror carried through the street, ready to render an image of every created thing.

O poet! a new nobility is conferred in groves and pastures, and not in castles, or by the sword-blade, any longer. The conditions are hard, but equal. Thou shalt leave the world, and know the muse only. Thou shalt not know any longer the times, customs, graces, politics, or opinions of men, but shalt take all from the muse. For the time of towns is tolled from the world by funereal chimes, but in nature the universal hours are counted by succeeding tribes of animals and plants, and by growth of joy on joy. God wills also that thou abdicate a duplex and manifold life, and that thou be content that others speak for thee. Others shall be thy gentlemen, and shall represent all courtesy and worldly life for thee; others shall do the great and resounding actions also. Thou shalt lie close hid with nature, and canst not be afforded to the Capitol or the Exchange.[34] The world is full of renunciations and apprenticeships, and this is thine; thou must pass for a fool and a churl for a long season. This is the screen and sheath in which Pan has protected his well-beloved flower, and thou shalt be known only to thine own, and they shall console thee with tenderest love. And thou shalt not be able to rehearse the names of thy friends in thy verse, for an old shame before the holy ideal. And this is the reward: that the ideal shall be real to thee, and the impressions of the actual world shall fall like summer rain, copious, but not troublesome, to thy invulnerable essence. Thou shalt have the whole land for thy park and manor, the sea for thy bath and navigation, without tax and without envy; the woods and the rivers thou shalt own; and thou shalt possess that wherein others are only tenants and boarders. Thou true land-lord! sea-lord! air-lord! Wherever snow falls, or water flows, or birds fly, wherever day and night meet in twilight, wherever the blue heaven is hung by clouds, or sown with stars, wherever are forms with transparent boundaries, wherever are outlets into celestial space, wherever is danger, and awe, and love, there is Beauty, plenteous as rain, shed for thee, and though thou shouldst walk the world over, thou shalt not be able to find a condition inopportune or ignoble.

1844, 1847

---

[34]*I.e.*, to politics or banking.

Experience

The lords of life, the lords of life,—
I saw them pass,
In their own guise,
Like and unlike,
Portly and grim,
Use and Surprise,
Surface and Dream,
Succession swift, and spectral Wrong,
Temperament without a tongue,
And the inventor of the game
Omnipresent without name;—
Some to see, some to be guessed,
They marched from east to west:
Little man, least of all,
Among the legs of his guardians tall,
Walked about with puzzled look:—
Him by the hand dear nature took;
Dearest nature, strong and kind,
Whispered, 'Darling, never mind!
Tomorrow they will wear another face,
The founder thou! these are thy race!'[1]

Where do we find ourselves? In a series, of which we do not know the extremes, and believe that it has none. We wake and find ourselves on a stair: there are stairs below us, which we seem to have ascended; there are stairs above us, many a one, which go upward and out of sight. But the Genius which, according to the old belief, stands at the door by which we enter, and gives us the lethe[2] to drink, that we may tell no tales, mixed the cup too strongly, and we cannot shake off the lethargy now at noonday. Sleep lingers all our lifetime about our eyes, as night hovers all day in the boughs of the fir-tree. All things swim and glimmer. Our life is not so much threatened as our perception. Ghostlike we glide through nature, and should not know our place again. Did our birth fall in some fit of indigence and frugality in nature, that she was so sparing of her fire and so liberal of her earth, that it appears to us that we lack the affirmative principle, and though we have health and reason, yet we have no superfluity of spirit for new creation? We have enough to live and bring the year about, but not an ounce to impart or to invest. Ah that our Genius were a little more of a genius! We are like millers on the lower levels of a stream, when the factories above them have exhausted the water. We too fancy that the upper people must have raised their dams.

---

[1]The motto is by Emerson.
[2]In Greek mythology, drinking from the river
Lethe produces forgetfulness.

If any of us knew what we were doing, or where we are going, then when we think we best know! We do not know today whether we are busy or idle. In times when we thought ourselves indolent, we have afterwards discovered, that much was accomplished, and much was begun in us. All our days are so unprofitable while they pass, that 'tis wonderful where or when we ever got anything of this which we call wisdom, poetry, virtue. We never got it on any dated calendar day. Some heavenly days must have been intercalated somewhere, like those that Hermes won with dice of the Moon, that Osiris might be born.[3] It is said, all martyrdoms looked mean when they were suffered.[4] Every ship is a romantic object, except that we sail in. Embark, and the romance quits our vessel, and hangs on every other sail in the horizon. Our life looks trivial, and we shun to record it. Men seem to have learned of the horizon the art of perpetual retreating and reference. 'Yonder uplands are rich pasturage, and my neighbor has fertile meadow, but my field,' says the querulous farmer,[5] 'only holds the world together.' I quote another man's saying; unluckily, that other withdraws himself in the same way, and quotes me. 'Tis the trick of nature thus to degrade today; a good deal of buzz, and somewhere a result slipped magically in. Every roof is agreeable to the eye, until it is lifted; then we find tragedy and moaning women, and hard-eyed husbands, and deluges of lethe, and the men ask, 'What's the news?' as if the old were so bad. How many individuals can we count in society? how many actions? how many opinions? So much of our time is preparation, so much is routine, and so much retrospect, that the pith of each man's genius contracts itself to a very few hours. The history of literature—take the net result of Tiraboschi, Warton, or Schlegel,[6]—is a sum of very few ideas, and of very few original tales,—all the rest being variation of these. So in this great society wide lying around us, a critical analysis would find very few spontaneous actions. It is almost all custom and gross sense. There are even few opinions, and these seem organic in the speakers, and do not disturb the universal necessity.

What opium is instilled into all disaster! It shows formidable as we approach it, but there is at last no rough rasping friction, but the most slippery sliding surfaces: we fall soft on a thought: *Ate Dea* is gentle—

> "Over men's heads walking aloft,
> With tender feet treading so soft."[7]

People grieve and bemoan themselves, but it is not half so bad with them as they say. There are moods in which we court suffering, in the hope that here, at least, we shall find reality, sharp peaks and edges of truth. But it turns out to be scene-painting and counterfeit. The only thing grief has

---

[3]After the sun god had forbidden his wife to bear a child on any existing day, her lover Hermes won five extra days ("intercalated" or inserted) on which the Egyptian gods could be born. Cf. Plutarch's *Morals*.

[4]From Harriet Martineau's *Deerbrook: A Novel* (1839).

[5]The farmer's passages are from Emerson's journal.

[6]Authors of Italian, English, and German literary histories.

[7]Goddess of mischief and discord as described in Homer's *Iliad*, XIX, 92–93.

taught me, is to know how shallow it is. That, like all the rest, plays about the surface, and never introduces me into the reality, for contact with which, we would even pay the costly price of sons and lovers. Was it Bosco-vich[8] who found out that bodies never come in contact? Well, souls never touch their objects. An innavigable sea washes with silent waves between us and the things we aim at and converse with. Grief too will make us idealists. In the death of my son,[9] now more than two years ago, I seem to have lost a beautiful estate,—no more. I cannot get it nearer to me. If tomorrow I should be informed of the bankruptcy of my principal debtors, the loss of my property would be a great inconvenience to me, perhaps, for many years; but it would leave me as it found me,—neither better nor worse. So is it with this calamity: it does not touch me: something which I fancied was a part of me, which could not be torn away without tearing me, nor enlarged without enriching me, falls off from me, and leaves no scar. It was caducous. I grieve that grief can teach me nothing, nor carry me one step into real na-ture. The Indian[10] who was laid under a curse, that the wind should not blow on him, nor water flow to him, nor fire burn him, is a type of us all. The dearest events are summer-rain, and we the Para coats[11] that shed ev-ery drop. Nothing is left us now but death. We look to that with a grim sat-isfaction, saying, there at least is reality that will not dodge us.

I take this evanescence and lubricity of all objects, which lets them slip through our fingers then when we clutch hardest, to be the most unhand-some part of our condition. Nature does not like to be observed, and likes that we should be her fools and playmates. We may have the sphere for our cricket-ball, but not a berry for our philosophy. Direct strokes she never gave us power to make; all our blows glance, all our hits are accidents. Our relations to each other are oblique and casual.

Dream delivers us to dream, and there is no end to illusion. Life is a train of moods like a string of beads, and, as we pass through them, they prove to be many-colored lenses which paint the world their own hue, and each shows only what lies in its focus. From the mountain you see the mountain. We animate what we can, and we see only what we animate. Na-ture and books belong to the eyes that see them. It depends on the mood of the man, whether he shall see the sunset or the fine poem. There are always sunsets, and there is always genius; but only a few hours so serene that we can relish nature or criticism. The more or less depends on structure or tem-perament. Temperament is the iron wire on which the beads are strung. Of what use is fortune or talent to a cold and defective nature? Who cares what sensibility or discrimination a man has at some time shown, if he falls asleep in his chair? or if he laugh and giggle? or if he apologize? or is infected with egotism? or thinks of his dollar? or cannot pass by food? or

---

[8]Eighteenth-century Italian physicist.
[9]Emerson's first child Waldo died in 1842 at the age of five. His first wife Ellen had died in1831, and his brother Edward in 1834.

[10]From Robert Southey's "The Curse of Kehama" (1810).
[11]Rubber coats, introduced after the develop-ment of vulcanization in 1839.

has gotten a child in his boyhood? Of what use is genius, if the organ is too convex or too concave, and cannot find a focal distance within the actual horizon of human life? Of what use, if the brain is too cold or too hot, and the man does not care enough for results, to stimulate him to experiment, and hold him up in it? or if the web is too finely woven, too irritable by pleasure and pain, so that life stagnates from too much reception, without due outlet? Of what use to make heroic vows of amendment, if the same old lawbreaker is to keep them? What cheer can the religious sentiment yield, when that is suspected to be secretly dependent on the seasons of the year, and the state of the blood? I knew a witty physician who found the creed in the biliary duct, and used to affirm that if there was disease in the liver, the man became a Calvinist, and if that organ was sound, he became a Unitarian. Very mortifying is the reluctant experience that some unfriendly excess or imbecility neutralizes the promise of genius. We see young men who owe us a new world, so readily and lavishly they promise, but they never acquit the debt; they die young and dodge the account: or if they live, they lose themselves in the crowd.

Temperament also enters fully into the system of illusions, and shuts us in a prison of glass which we cannot see. There is an optical illusion about every person we meet. In truth, they are all creatures of given temperament, which will appear in a given character, whose boundaries they will never pass: but we look at them, they seem alive, and we presume there is impulse in them. In the moment, it seems impulse; in the year, in the lifetime, it turns out to be a certain uniform tune which the revolving barrel of the music-box must play. Men resist the conclusion in the morning, but adopt it as the evening wears on, that temper prevails over everything of time, place, and condition, and is inconsumable in the flames of religion. Some modifications the moral sentiment avails to impose, but the individual texture holds its dominion, if not to bias the moral judgments, yet to fix the measure of activity and of enjoyment.

I thus express the law as it is read from the platform of ordinary life, but must not leave it without noticing the capital exception. For temperament is a power which no man willingly hears any one praise but himself. On the platform of physics, we cannot resist the contracting influences of so-called science. Temperament puts all divinity to rout. I know the mental proclivity of physicians. I hear the chuckle of the phrenologists. Theoretic kidnappers and slave-drivers, they esteem each man the victim of another, who winds him round his finger by knowing the law of his being, and by such cheap signboards as the color of his beard, or the slope of his occiput, reads the inventory of his fortunes and character. The grossest ignorance does not disgust like this impudent knowingness. The physicians say, they are not materialists; but they are:—Spirit is matter reduced to an extreme thinness: O so thin!—But the definition of *spiritual* should be, *that which is its own evidence.* What notions do they attach to love! what to religion! One would not willingly pronounce these words in their hearing, and give them the occasion to profane them. I saw a gracious gentleman who adapts his conversation to the form of the head of the man he talks with! I had fancied that the value of life lay in its inscrutable possibilities; in the fact that I never know, in addressing myself to a new individual, what may befall me. I carry the keys of my castle in my hand, ready to throw them at the feet of my lord, whenever and in what disguise soever he shall appear. I know he is in the neighborhood, hidden among vagabonds. Shall I preclude my future, by taking a high seat, and kindly adapting my conversation to the shape of heads? When I come to that, the doctors shall buy me for a cent.—'But, sir, medical history; the report to the Institute; the proven facts!'—I distrust the facts and the inferences. Temperament is the veto or limitation-power in the constitution, very justly applied to restrain an opposite excess in the constitution, but absurdly offered as a bar to original equity. When virtue is in presence, all subordinate powers sleep. On its own level, or in view of nature, temperament is final. I see not, if one be once caught in this trap of so-called sciences, any escape for the man from the links of the chain of physical necessity. Given such an embryo, such a history must follow. On this platform, one lives in a sty of sensualism, and would soon come to suicide. But it is impossible that the creative power should exclude itself. Into every intelligence there is a door which is never closed, through which the creator passes. The intellect, seeker of absolute truth, or the heart, lover of absolute good, intervenes for our succor, and at one whisper of these high powers, we awake from ineffectual struggles with this nightmare. We hurl it into its own hell, and cannot again contract ourselves to so base a state.

The secret of the illusoriness is in the necessity of a succession of moods or objects. Gladly we would anchor, but the anchorage is quicksand. This onward trick of nature is too strong for us: *Pero si muove.*[12] When, at night, I look at the moon and stars, I seem stationary, and they to hurry. Our love of the real draws us to permanence, but health of body consists in circulation, and sanity of mind in variety or facility of association. We need change of objects. Dedication to one thought is quickly odious. We house with the insane, and must humor them; then conversation dies out. Once I took such delight in Montaigne, that I thought I should not need any other book; before that, in Shakspeare; then in Plutarch; then in Plotinus; at one time in Bacon; afterwards in Goethe; even in Bettine;[13] but now I turn the pages of either of them languidly, whilst I still cherish their genius. So with pictures; each will bear an emphasis of attention once, which it cannot retain, though we fain would continue to be pleased in that manner. How strongly I have felt of pictures, that when you have seen one well, you must take your leave of it; you shall never see it again. I have had good lessons from pictures, which I have since seen without emotion or remark. A deduction must be made from the opinion, which even the wise express of a new book or occurrence. Their opinion gives me tidings of their

[12]"Nevertheless it moves": a variant of Galileo's famous comment after the Church forced him to deny that the earth moves around the sun.

[13]German writer Elizabeth von Arnim (1785–1859), whose book on Goethe Emerson described in 1842 as "the most remarkable book ever written by a woman."

mood, and some vague guess at the new fact, but is nowise to be trusted as the lasting relation between that intellect and that thing. The child asks, 'Mamma, why don't I like the story as well as when you told it me yesterday?' Alas, child, it is even so with the oldest cherubim of knowledge. But will it answer thy question to say, Because thou wert born to a whole, and this story is a particular? The reason of the pain this discovery causes us (and we make it late in respect to works of art and intellect), is the plaint of tragedy which murmurs from it in regard to persons, to friendship and love.

That immobility and absence of elasticity which we find in the arts, we find with more pain in the artist. There is no power of expansion in men. Our friends early appear to us as representatives of certain ideas, which they never pass or exceed. They stand on the brink of the ocean of thought and power, but they never take the single step that would bring them there. A man is like a bit of Labrador spar,[14] which has no lustre as you turn it in your hand, until you come to a particular angle; then it shows deep and beautiful colors. There is no adaptation or universal applicability in men, but each has his special talent, and the mastery of successful men consists in adroitly keeping themselves where and when that turn shall be oftenest to be practised. We do what we must, and call it by the best names we can, and would fain have the praise of having intended the result which ensues. I cannot recall any form of man who is not superfluous sometimes. But is not this pitiful? Life is not worth the taking, to do tricks in.

Of course, it needs the whole society, to give the symmetry we seek. The parti-colored wheel must revolve very fast to appear white. Something is learned too by conversing with so much folly and defect. In fine, whoever loses, we are always of the gaining party. Divinity is behind our failures and follies also. The plays of children are nonsense, but very educative nonsense. So is it with the largest and solemnest things, with commerce, government, church, marriage, and so with the history of every man's bread, and the ways by which he is to come by it. Like a bird which alights nowhere, but hops perpetually from bough to bough, is the Power which abides in no man and in no woman, but for a moment speaks from this one, and for another moment from that one.

But what help from these fineries or pedantries? What help from thought? Life is not dialectics. We, I think, in these times, have had lessons enough of the futility of criticism. Our young people have thought and written much on labor and reform, and for all that they have written, neither the world nor themselves have got on a step. Intellectual tasting of life will not supersede muscular activity. If a man should consider the nicety of the passage of a piece of bread down his throat, he would starve. At Education-Farm,[15] the noblest theory of life sat on the noblest figures of young men and maidens, quite powerless and melancholy. It would not rake or pitch a ton of hay; it would not rub down a horse; and the men and maidens it left

[14]Crystalline rock.

[15]Probably referring to Brook Farm, a commune Emerson had been invited to join.

pale and hungry. A political orator wittily compared our party promises to western roads, which opened stately enough, with planted trees on either side, to tempt the traveller, but soon became narrow and narrower, and ended in a squirrel-track, and ran up a tree. So does culture with us; it ends in headache. Unspeakably sad and barren does life look to those, who a few months ago were dazzled with the splendor of the promise of the times. "There is now no longer any right course of action, nor any self-devotion left among the Iranis."[16] Objections and criticism we have had our fill of. There are objections to every course of life and action, and the practical wisdom infers an indifferency, from the omnipresence of objection. The whole frame of things preaches indifferency. Do not craze yourself with thinking, but go about your business anywhere. Life is not intellectual or critical, but sturdy. Its chief good is for well-mixed people who can enjoy what they find, without question. Nature hates peeping, and our mothers speak her very sense when they say, "Children, eat your victuals, and say no more of it." To fill the hour,—that is happiness; to fill the hour, and leave no crevice for a repentance or an approval. We live amid surfaces, and the true art of life is to skate well on them. Under the oldest mouldiest conventions, a man of native force prospers just as well as in the newest world, and that by skill of handling and treatment. He can take hold anywhere. Life itself is a mixture of power and form, and will not bear the least excess of either. To finish the moment, to find the journey's end in every step of the road, to live the greatest number of good hours, is wisdom. It is not the part of men, but of fanatics, or of mathematicians, if you will, to say, that, the shortness of life considered, it is not worth caring whether for so short a duration we were sprawling in want, or sitting high. Since our office is with moments, let us husband them. Five minutes of today are worth as much to me, as five minutes in the next millennium. Let us be poised, and wise, and our own, today. Let us treat the men and women well: treat them as if they were real: perhaps they are. Men live in their fancy, like drunkards whose hands are too soft and tremulous for successful labor. It is a tempest of fancies, and the only ballast I know, is a respect to the present hour. Without any shadow of doubt, amidst this vertigo of shows and politics, I settle myself ever the firmer in the creed, that we should not postpone and refer and wish, but do broad justice where we are, by whomsoever we deal with, accepting our actual companions and circumstances, however humble or odious, as the mystic officials to whom the universe has delegated its whole pleasure for us. If these are mean and malignant, their contentment, which is the last victory of justice, is a more satisfying echo to the heart, than the voice of poets and the casual sympathy of admirable persons. I think that however a thoughtful man may suffer from the defects and absurdities of his company, he cannot without affectation deny to any set of men and

[16]From *Desatir*, a collection of ancient Persian
prophetic works translated into English in
1818.

women, a sensibility to extraordinary merit. The coarse and frivolous have an instinct of superiority, if they have not a sympathy, and honor it in their blind capricious way with sincere homage.

The fine young people despise life, but in me, and in such as with me are free from dyspepsia, and to whom a day is a sound and solid good, it is a great excess of politeness to look scornful and to cry for company. I am grown by sympathy a little eager and sentimental, but leave me alone, and I should relish every hour and what it brought me, the potluck of the day, as heartily as the oldest gossip in the bar-room. I am thankful for small mercies. I compared notes with one of my friends who expects everything of the universe, and is disappointed when anything is less than the best, and I found that I begin at the other extreme, expecting nothing, and am always full of thanks for moderate goods. I accept the clangor and jangle of contrary tendencies. I find my account in sots and bores also. They give a reality to the circumjacent picture, which such a vanishing meteorous appearance can ill spare. In the morning I awake, and find the old world, wife, babes, and mother, Concord and Boston, the dear old spiritual world, and even the dear old devil not far off. If we will take the good we find, asking no questions, we shall have heaping measures. The great gifts are not got by analysis. Everything good is on the highway. The middle region of our being is the temperate zone. We may climb into the thin and cold realm of pure geometry and lifeless science, or sink into that of sensation. Between these extremes is the equator of life, of thought, of spirit, of poetry,—a narrow belt. Moreover, in popular experience, everything good is on the highway. A collector peeps into all the picture-shops of Europe, for a landscape of Poussin, a crayon-sketch of Salvator;[17] but the Transfiguration, the Last Judgment, the Communion of St. Jerome, and what are as transcendent as these, are on the walls of the Vatican, the Uffizi, or the Louvre,[18] where every footman may see them; to say nothing of nature's pictures in every street, of sunsets and sunrises every day, and the sculpture of the human body never absent. A collector recently bought at public auction, in London, for one hundred and fifty-seven guineas, an autograph of Shakspeare: but for nothing a schoolboy can read Hamlet, and can detect secrets of highest concernment yet unpublished therein. I think I will never read any but the commonest books,—the Bible, Homer, Dante, Shakspeare, and Milton. Then we are impatient of so public a life and planet, and run hither and thither for nooks and secrets. The imagination delights in the wood-craft of Indians, trappers, and bee-hunters. We fancy that we are strangers, and not so intimately domesticated in the planet as the wild man, and the wild beast and bird. But the exclusion reaches them also; reaches the climbing, flying, gliding, feathered and four-footed man. Fox and woodchuck, hawk and snipe, and bittern, when nearly seen, have no more root in the deep world

[17]Seventeenth-century French and Italian painters.

[18]Paintings by Raphael, Michelangelo, and Domenichino; museums of Rome, Florence, and Paris.

than man, and are just such superficial tenants of the globe. Then the new molecular philosophy shows astronomical interspaces betwixt atom and atom, shows that the world is all outside: it has no inside.

The mid-world is best. Nature, as we know her, is no saint. The lights of the church, the ascetics, Gentoos and corn-eaters,[19] she does not distinguish by any favor. She comes eating and drinking and sinning. Her darlings, the great, the strong, the beautiful, are not children of our law, do not come out of the Sunday School, nor weigh their food, nor punctually keep the commandments. If we will be strong with her strength, we must not harbor such disconsolate consciences, borrowed too from the consciences of other nations. We must set up the strong present tense against all the rumors of wrath, past or to come. So many things are unsettled which it is of the first importance to settle,—and, pending their settlement, we will do as we do. Whilst the debate goes forward on the equity of commerce, and will not be closed for a century or two, New and Old England may keep shop. Law of copyright and international copyright[20] is to be discussed, and, in the interim, we will sell our books for the most we can. Expediency of literature, reason of literature, lawfulness of writing down a thought, is questioned; much is to say on both sides, and, while the fight waxes hot, thou, dearest scholar, stick to thy foolish task, add a line every hour, and between whiles add a line. Right to hold land, right of property, is disputed, and the conventions convene, and before the vote is taken, dig away in your garden, and spend your earnings as a waif or godsend to all serene and beautiful purposes. Life itself is a bubble and a skepticism, and a sleep within a sleep.[21] Grant it, and as much more as they will,—but thou, God's darling! heed thy private dream: thou wilt not be missed in the scorning and skepticism: there are enough of them: stay there in thy closet, and toil, until the rest are agreed what to do about it. Thy sickness, they say, and thy puny habit, require that thou do this or avoid that, but know that thy life is a flitting state, a tent for a night, and do thou, sick or well, finish that stint. Thou art sick, but shalt not be worse, and the universe, which holds thee dear, shall be the better.

Human life is made up of the two elements, power and form, and the proportion must be invariably kept, if we would have it sweet and sound. Each of these elements in excess makes a mischief as hurtful as its defect. Everything runs to excess: every good quality is noxious, if unmixed, and, to carry the danger to the edge of ruin, nature causes each man's peculiarity to superabound. Here, among the farms, we adduce the scholars as examples of this treachery. They are nature's victims of expression. You who see the artist, the orator, the poet, too near, and find their life no more excellent than that of mechanics or farmers, and themselves victims of partiality, very hollow and

---

[19]Hindus and vegetarians; in the first edition Emerson paired Gentoos with Grahamites, the cultish followers of Sylvester Graham (1794–1851), a New England reformer and inventor of the graham cracker.

[20]The United States did not pass an international copyright law until 1891, after years of heated debates over unauthorized publications.

[21]Cf. *The Tempest*, IV, i, 156–158.

haggard, and pronounce them failures,—not heroes, but quacks,—conclude very reasonably, that these arts are not for man, but are disease. Yet nature will not bear you out. Irresistible nature made men such, and makes legions more of such, every day. You love the boy reading in a book, gazing at a drawing, or a cast: yet what are these millions who read and behold, but incipient writers and sculptors? Add a little more of that quality which now reads and sees, and they will seize the pen and chisel. And if one remembers how innocently he began to be an artist, he perceives that nature joined with his enemy. A man is a golden impossibility. The line he must walk is a hair's breadth. The wise through excess of wisdom is made a fool.

How easily, if fate would suffer it, we might keep forever these beautiful limits, and adjust ourselves, once for all, to the perfect calculation of the kingdom of known cause and effect. In the street and in the newspapers, life appears so plain a business, that manly resolution and adherence to the multiplication-table through all weathers, will insure success. But ah! presently comes a day—or is it only a half-hour, with its angel-whispering—which discomfits the conclusions of nations and of years! Tomorrow again, everything looks real and angular, the habitual standards are reinstated, common sense is as rare as genius,—is the basis of genius, and experience is hands and feet to every enterprise;—and yet, he who should do his business on this understanding, would be quickly bankrupt. Power keeps quite another road than the turnpikes of choice and will, namely, the subterranean and invisible tunnels and channels of life. It is ridiculous that we are diplomatists, and doctors, and considerate people: there are no dupes like these. Life is a series of surprises, and would not be worth taking or keeping, if it were not. God delights to isolate us every day, and hide from us the past and the future. We would look about us, but with grand politeness he draws down before us an impenetrable screen of purest sky, and another behind us of purest sky. 'You will not remember,' he seems to say, 'and you will not expect.' All good conversation, manners, and action, come from a spontaneity which forgets usages, and makes the moment great. Nature hates calculators; her methods are saltatory and impulsive. Man lives by pulses; our organic movements are such; and the chemical and ethereal agents are undulatory and alternate; and the mind goes antagonizing on, and never prospers but by fits. We thrive by casualties. Our chief experiences have been casual. The most attractive class of people are those who are powerful obliquely, and not by the direct stroke: men of genius, but not yet accredited: one gets the cheer of their light, without paying too great a tax. Theirs is the beauty of the bird, or the morning light, and not of art. In the thought of genius there is always a surprise; and the moral sentiment is well called "the newness," for it is never other; as new to the oldest intelligence as to the young child,—"the kingdom that cometh without observation."[22] In like manner, for practical success, there must not be too much design.

[22]Cf. Luke 17:20–21.

A man will not be observed in doing that which he can do best. There is a certain magic about his properest action, which stupefies your powers of observation, so that though it is done before you, you wist not of it. The art of life has a pudency, and will not be exposed. Every man is an impossibility, until he is born; every thing impossible, until we see a success. The ardors of piety agree at last with the coldest skepticism,—that nothing is of us or our works,—that all is of God. Nature will not spare us the smallest leaf of laurel. All writing comes by the grace of God, and all doing and having. I would gladly be moral, and keep due metes and bounds, which I dearly love, and allow the most to the will of man, but I have set my heart on honesty in this chapter, and I can see nothing at last, in success or failure, than more or less of vital force supplied from the Eternal. The results of life are uncalculated and uncalculable. The years teach much which the days never know. The persons who compose our company, converse, and come and go, and design and execute many things, and somewhat comes of it all, but an unlooked-for result. The individual is always mistaken. He designed many things, and drew in other persons as coadjutors, quarrelled with some or all, blundered much, and something is done; all are a little advanced, but the individual is always mistaken. It turns out somewhat new, and very unlike what he promised himself.

The ancients, struck with this irreducibleness of the elements of human life to calculation, exalted Chance into a divinity, but that is to stay too long at the spark,—which glitters truly at one point,—but the universe is warm with the latency of the same fire. The miracle of life which will not be expounded, but will remain a miracle, introduces a new element. In the growth of the embryo, Sir Everard Home,[23] I think, noticed that the evolution was not from one central point, but coactive from three or more points. Life has no memory. That which proceeds in succession might be remembered, but that which is coexistent, or ejaculated from a deeper cause, as yet far from being conscious, knows not its own tendency. So is it with us, now skeptical, or without unity, because immersed in forms and effects all seeming to be of equal yet hostile value, and now religious, whilst in the reception of spiritual law. Bear with these distractions, with this coetaneous[24] growth of the parts: they will one day be *members*, and obey one will. On that one will, on that secret cause, they nail our attention and hope. Life is hereby melted into an expectation or a religion. Underneath the inharmonious and trivial particulars, is a musical perfection, the Ideal journeying always with us, the heaven without rent or seam. Do but observe the mode of our illumination. When I converse with a profound mind, or if at any time being alone I have good thoughts, I do not at once arrive at satisfactions, as when, being thirsty, I drink water, or go to the fire, being cold: no! but I am at first apprised of my vicinity to a new and excellent region of life. By persisting to read or to

---

[23]Scottish surgeon and anatomist (1756–1832). [24]Simultaneous.

think, this region gives further sign of itself, as it were in flashes of light, in sudden discoveries of its profound beauty and repose, as if the clouds that covered it parted at intervals, and showed the approaching traveller the inland mountains, with the tranquil eternal meadows spread at their base, whereon flocks graze, and shepherds pipe and dance. But every insight from this realm of thought is felt as initial, and promises a sequel. I do not make it; I arrive there, and behold what was there already. I make! O no! I clap my hands in infantine joy and amazement, before the first opening to me of this august magnificence, old with the love and homage of innumerable ages, young with the life of life, the sunbright Mecca of the desert. And what a future it opens! I feel a new heart beating with the love of the new beauty. I am ready to die out of nature, and be born again into this new yet unapproachable America I have found in the West.

> "Since neither now nor yesterday began
> These thoughts, which have been ever, nor yet can
> A man be found who their first entrance knew."[25]

If I have described life as a flux of moods, I must now add, that there is that in us which changes not, and which ranks all sensations and states of mind. The consciousness in each man is a sliding scale, which identifies him now with the First Cause, and now with the flesh of his body; life above life, in infinite degrees. The sentiment from which it sprung determines the dignity of any deed, and the question ever is, not, what you have done or forborne, but, at whose command you have done or forborne it.

Fortune, Minerva,[26] Muse, Holy Ghost,—these are quaint names, too narrow to cover this unbounded substance. The baffled intellect must still kneel before this cause, which refuses to be named,—ineffable cause, which every fine genius has essayed to represent by some emphatic symbol, as, Thales by water, Anaximenes by air, Anaxagoras by (Noês) thought,[27] Zoroaster by fire, Jesus and the moderns by love: and the metaphor of each has become a national religion. The Chinese Mencius[28] has not been the least successful in his generalization. "I fully understand language," he said, "and nourish well my vast-flowing vigor."—"I beg to ask what you call vast-flowing vigor?" said his companion. "The explanation," replied Mencius, "is difficult. This vigor is supremely great, and in the highest degree unbending. Nourish it correctly, and do it no injury, and it will fill up the vacancy between heaven and earth. This vigor accords with and assists justice and reason, and leaves no hunger." In our more correct writing, we give to this generalization the name of Being, and therby confess that we have arrived as far as we can go. Suffice it for the joy of the universe, that we have not arrived at a wall, but at interminable oceans. Our life seems not present, so much as prospective; not for the affairs on which it is wasted, but as a hint

---

[25]Translation from Sophocles' *Antigone*, ll. 455–457.

[26]Roman goddess of wisdom.

[27]Thales ... Anaximenes ... Anaxagoras. Greek philosophers.

[28]Confucian philosopher Meng-Tse (3rd cent. B.C.).

of this vast-flowing vigor. Most of life seems to be mere advertisement of
faculty: information is given us not to sell ourselves cheap; that we are very
great. So, in particulars, our greatness is always in a tendency or direction,
not in an action. It is for us to believe in the rule, not in the exception. The
noble are thus known from the ignoble. So in accepting the leading of the
sentiments, it is not what we believe concerning the immortality of the soul,
or the like, but *the universal impulse to believe*, that is the material circumstance, and is the principal fact in the history of the globe. Shall we describe
this cause as that which works directly? The spirit is not helpless or needful
of mediate organs. It has plentiful powers and direct effects. I am explained
without explaining, I am felt without acting, and where I am not. Therefore
all just persons are satisfied with their own praise. They refuse to explain
themselves, and are content that new actions should do them that office.
They believe that we communicate without speech, and above speech, and
that no right action of ours is quite unaffecting to our friends, at whatever
distance; for the influence of action is not to be measured by miles. Why
should I fret myself, because a circumstance has occurred, which hinders my
presence where I was expected? If I am not at the meeting, my presence
where I am should be as useful to the commonwealth of friendship and wisdom, as would be my presence in that place. I exert the same quality of
power in all places. Thus journeys the mighty Ideal before us; it never was
known to fall into the rear. No man ever came to an experience which was
satiating, but his good is tidings of a better. Onward and onward! In liberated moments, we know that a new picture of life and duty is already possible; the elements already exist in many minds around you, of a doctrine of
life which shall transcend any written record we have. The new statement
will comprise the skepticisms, as well as the faiths of society, and out of
unbeliefs a creed shall be formed. For, skepticisms are not gratuitous or lawless, but are limitations of the affirmative statement, and the new philosophy must take them in, and make affirmations outside of them, just as
much as it must include the oldest beliefs.

It is very unhappy, but too late to be helped, the discovery we have
made, that we exist. That discovery is called the Fall of Man. Ever afterwards, we suspect our instruments. We have learned that we do not see
directly, but mediately, and that we have no means of correcting these colored and distorting lenses which we are, or of computing the amount of
their errors. Perhaps these subject-lenses have a creative power; perhaps
there are no objects. Once we lived in what we saw; now, the rapaciousness
of this new power, which threatens to absorb all things, engages us. Nature,
art, persons, letters, religions,—objects, successively tumble in, and God is
but one of its ideas. Nature and literature are subjective phenomena; every
evil and every good thing is a shadow which we cast. The street is full of
humiliations to the proud. As the fop contrived to dress his bailiffs in his
livery, and make them wait on his guests at table, so the chagrins which the
bad heart gives off as bubbles, at once take form as ladies and gentlemen in
the street, shopmen or bar-keepers in hotels, and threaten or insult

whatever is threatenable and insultable in us. 'Tis the same with our idolatries. People forget that it is the eye which makes the horizon, and the
rounding mind's eye which makes this or that man a type or representative
of humanity with the name of hero or saint. Jesus the "providential man,"
is a good man on whom many people are agreed that these optical laws shall
take effect. By love on one part, and by forbearance to press objection on
the other part, it is for a time settled, that we will look at him in the centre
of the horizion, and ascribe to him the properties that will attach to any
man so seen. But the longest love or aversion has a speedy term. The great
and crescive[29] self, rooted in absolute nature, supplants all relative existence, and ruins the kingdom of mortal friendship and love. Marriage (in
what is called the spiritual world) is impossible, because of the inequality
between every subject and every object. The subject is the receiver of God-
head, and at every comparison must feel his being enhanced by that cryptic
might. Though not in energy, yet by presence, this magazine[30] of substance
cannot be otherwise than felt: nor can any force of intellect attribute to the
object the proper deity which sleeps or wakes forever in every subject. Never
can love make consciousness and ascription equal in force. There will be the
same gulf between every me and thee, as between the original and the picture. The universe is the bride of the soul. All private sympathy is partial.
Two human beings are like globes, which can touch only in a point, and,
whilst they remain in contact, all other points of each of the spheres are
inert; their turn must also come, and the longer a particular union lasts, the
more energy of appetency the parts not in union acquire.[31]

Life will be imaged, but cannot be divided nor doubled. Any invasion of
its unity would be chaos. The soul is not twin-born, but the only begotten,
and though revealing itself as child in time, child in appearance, is of a fatal
and universal power, admitting no co-life. Every day, every act betrays the
ill-concealed deity. We believe in ourselves, as we do not believe in others.
We permit all things to ourselves, and that which we call sin in others, is
experiment for us. It is an instance of our faith in ourselves, that men never
speak of crime as lightly as they think: or, every man thinks a latitude safe
for himself, which is nowise to be indulged to another. The act looks very
differently on the inside, and on the outside; in its quality, and in its consequences. Murder in the murderer is no such ruinous thought as poets and
romancers will have it; it does not unsettle him, or fright him from his ordinary notice of trifles: it is an act quite easy to be contemplated, but in its
sequel, it turns out to be a horrible jangle and confounding of all relations.
Especially the crimes that spring from love, seem right and fair from the
actor's point of view, but, when acted, are found destructive of society. No
man at last believes that he can be lost, nor that the crime in him is as black
as in the felon. Because the intellect qualifies in our own case the moral

[29]Growing.
[30]Stored supply.
[31]Referring to contemporary physics experiments about static electricity. "Appetancy"
meant both physical propulsion toward
unity and sexual desire.

judgments. For there is no crime to the intellect. That is antinomian or hypernomian,[32] and judges law as well as fact. "It is worse than a crime, it is a blunder," said Napoleon, speaking the language of the intellect. To it, the world is a problem in mathematics or the science of quantity, and it leaves out praise and blame, and all weak emotions. All stealing is comparative. If you come to absolutes, pray who does not steal? Saints are sad, because they behold sin, (even when they speculate,) from the point of view of the conscience, and not of the intellect; a confusion of thought. Sin seen from the thought, is a diminution or *less:* seen from the conscience or will, it is pravity or *bad.* The intellect names it shade, absence of light, and no essence. The conscience must feel it as essence, essential evil. This it is not: it has an objective existence, but no subjective.

Thus inevitably does the universe wear our color, and every object fall successively into the subject itself. The subject exists, the subject enlarges; all things sooner or later fall into place. As I am, so I see; use what language we will, we can never say anything but what we are; Hermes,[33] Cadmus,[34] Columbus, Newton, Bonaparte, are the mind's ministers. Instead of feeling a poverty when we encounter a great man, let us treat the new comer like a travelling geologist, who passes through our estate, and shows us good slate, or limestone, or anthracite, in our brush pasture. The partial action of each strong mind in one direction, is a telescope for the objects on which it is pointed. But every other part of knowledge is to be pushed to the same extravagance, ere the soul attains her due sphericity. Do you see that kitten chasing so prettily her own tail? If you could look with her eyes, you might see her surrounded with hundreds of figures performing complex dramas, with tragic and comic issues, long conversations, many characters, many ups and downs of fate,—and meantime it is only puss and her tail. How long before our masquerade will end its noise of tambourines, laughter, and shouting, and we shall find it was a solitary performance?—A subject and an object,—it takes so much to make the galvanic circuit complete, but magnitude adds nothing. What imports it whether it is Kepler[35] and the sphere; Columbus and America; a reader and his book; or puss with her tail?

It is true that all the muses and love and religion hate these developments, and will find a way to punish the chemist, who publishes in the parlor the secrets of the laboratory. And we cannot say too little of our constitutional necessity of seeing things under private aspects, or saturated with our humors. And yet is the God the native of these bleak rocks. That need makes in morals the capital virtue of self-trust. We must hold hard to this poverty, however scandalous, and by more vigorous self-recoveries, after the sallies of action, possess our axis more firmly. The life of truth is cold, and so far mournful; but it is not the slave of tears, contributions, and perturbations. It does not attempt another's work, nor adopt another's

---

[32]Against or beyond the control of law.
[33]Greek god who invented the lyre.
[34]Legendary founder of Thebes, who taught the Greeks the alphabet.

[35]German astronomer (1571–1630), who discovered basic laws of planetary motion.

facts. It is a main lesson of wisdom to know your own from another's. I have learned that I cannot dispose of other people's facts; but I possess such a key to my own, as persuades me against all their denials, that they also have a key to theirs. A sympathetic person is placed in the dilemma of a swimmer among drowning men, who all catch at him, and if he give so much as a leg or a finger, they will drown him. They wish to be saved from the mischiefs of their vices, but not from their vices. Charity would be wasted on this poor waiting on the symptoms. A wise and hardy physician will say, *Come out of that*, as the first condition of advice.

In this our talking America, we are ruined by our good nature and listening on all sides. This compliance takes away the power of being greatly useful. A man should not be able to look other than directly and forthright. A preoccupied attention is the only answer to the importunate frivolity of other people: an attention, and to an aim which makes their wants frivolous. This is a divine answer, and leaves no appeal, and no hard thoughts. In Flaxman's[36] drawing of the Eumenides of Æschylus, Orestes supplicates Apollo, whilst the Furies sleep on the threshold. The face of the god expresses a shade of regret and compassion, but calm with the conviction of the irreconcilableness of the two spheres. He is born into other politics, into the eternal and beautiful. The man at his feet asks for his interest in turmoils of the earth, into which his nature cannot enter. And the Eumenides there lying express pictorially this disparity. The god is surcharged with his divine destiny.

Illusion, Temperament, Succession, Surface, Surprise, Reality, Subjectiveness,—these are threads on the loom of time, these are the lords of life. I dare not assume to give their order, but I name them as I find them in my way. I know better than to claim any completeness for my picture. I am a fragment, and this is a fragment of me. I can very confidently announce one or another law, which throws itself into relief and form, but I am too young yet by some ages to compile a code. I gossip for my hour concerning the eternal politics. I have seen many fair pictures not in vain. A wonderful time I have lived in. I am not the novice I was fourteen, nor yet seven years ago. Let who will ask, where is the fruit? I find a private fruit sufficient. This is a fruit,—that I should not ask for a rash effect from meditations, counsels, and the hiving of truths. I should feel it pitiful to demand a result on this town and county, an overt effect on the instant month and year. The effect is deep and secular as the cause. It works on periods in which mortal lifetime is lost. All I know is reception; I am and I have: but I do not get, and when I have fancied I had gotten anything, I found I did not. I worship with wonder the great Fortune. My reception has been so large, that I am not annoyed by receiving this or that superabundantly. I say to the Genius, if he will pardon the proverb, *In for a mill, in for a million*. When I receive a new gift, I do not macerate[37] my body to make the account square, for, if I should die, I could not make the account square. The benefit overran the

---

[36]British artist (1755–1826).   [37]Waste away from excessive fasting.

merit the first day, and has overran the merit ever since. The merit itself, so-called, I reckon part of the receiving.

Also, that hankering after an overt or practical effect seems to me an apostasy. In good earnest, I am willing to spare this most unnecessary deal of doing. Life wears to me a visionary face. Hardest, roughest action is visionary also. It is but a choice between soft and turbulent dreams. People disparage knowing and the intellectual life, and urge doing. I am very content with knowing, if only I could know. That is an august entertainment, and would suffice me a great while. To know a little, would be worth the expense of this world. I hear always the law of Adrastia,[38] "that every soul which had acquired any truth, should be safe from harm until another period."

I know that the world I converse with in the city and in the farms, is not the world I *think*. I observe that difference, and shall observe it. One day, I shall know the value and law of this discrepance. But I have not found that much was gained by manipular attempts to realize the world of thought. Many eager persons successively make an experiment in this way, and make themselves ridiculous. They acquire democratic manners, they foam at the mouth, they hate and deny. Worse, I observe, that, in the history of mankind, there is never a solitary example of success,—taking their own tests of success. I say this polemically, or in reply to the inquiry, why not realize your world? But far be from me the despair which prejudges the law by a paltry empiricism,—since there never was a right endeavor, but it succeeded. Patience and patience, we shall win at the last. We must be very suspicious of the deceptions of the element of time. It takes a good deal of time to eat or to sleep, or to earn a hundred dollars, and a very little time to entertain a hope and an insight which becomes the light of our life. We dress our garden, eat our dinners, discuss the household with our wives, and these things make no impression, are forgotten next week; but in the solitude to which every man is always returning, he has a sanity and revelations, which in his passage into new worlds he will carry with him. Never mind the ridicule, never mind the defeat: up again, old heart!—it seems to say,— there is victory yet for all justice; and the true romance which the world exists to realize, will be the transformation of genius into practical power.

1844, 1847

Concord Hymn[1]

Sung at the Completion of the Battle Monument, July 4, 1837

By the rude bridge that arched the flood,
    Their flag to April's breeze unfurled,

---

[38]Nemesis, Greek goddess of justice or destiny; cf. Plato's *Phaedrus*.
[1]Emerson's popular hymn was sung to the tune of Old Hundred at the dedication of the monument commemorating the Revolution-

ary War battles of April 19, 1775. First printed as a broadside and distributed at the 1837 ceremony, it was popularized in newspapers, memorized by schoolchildren, and carved on a memorial stone in Concord.

Here once the embattled farmers stood
    And fired the shot heard round the world.

The foe long since in silence slept;   5
    Alike the conqueror silent sleeps;
And Time the ruined bridge has swept
    Down the dark stream which seaward creeps.

On this green bank, by this soft stream,
    We set to-day a votive stone;   10
That memory may their deed redeem,
    When, like our sires, our sons are gone.

Spirit, that made those heroes dare
    To die, and leave their children free,
Bid Time and Nature gently spare   15
    The shaft we raise to them and thee.

                            1837

The Rhodora[1]

On Being Asked, Whence Is the Flower?

In May, when sea-winds pierced our solitudes,
I found the fresh Rhodora in the woods,
Spreading its leafless blooms in a damp nook,
To please the desert and the sluggish brook.
The purple petals, fallen in the pool,   5
Made the black water with their beauty gay;
Here might the red-bird come his plumes to cool,
And court the flower that cheapens his array.
Rhodora! if the sages ask thee why
This charm is wasted on the earth and sky,   10
Tell them, dear, that if eyes were made for seeing,
Then Beauty is its own excuse for being:
Why thou wert there, O rival of the rose!
I never thought to ask, I never knew:
But, in my simple ignorance, suppose   15
The self-same Power that brought me there brought you.

                            1839

[1]Written in 1834, the poem was first pub-
lished in James Freeman Clarke's *The West-* *ern Messenger* (Kentucky) in 1839. A rhodora
is a shrub that grows in New England.

The Snow-Storm[1]

Announced by all the trumpets of the sky,
Arrives the snow, and, driving o'er the fields,
Seems nowhere to alight: the whited air
Hides hills and woods, the river, and the heaven,
And veils the farm-house at the garden's end.   5
The sled and traveller stopped, the courier's feet
Delayed, all friends shut out, the housemates sit
Around the radiant fireplace, enclosed
In a tumultuous privacy of storm.

Come see the north wind's masonry.   10
Out of an unseen quarry evermore
Furnished with tile, the fierce artificer
Curves his white bastions with projected roof
Round every windward stake, or tree, or door.
Speeding, the myriad-handed, his wild work   15
So fanciful, so savage, nought cares he
For number or proportion. Mockingly,
On coop or kennel he hangs Parian[2] wreaths;
A swan-like form invests the hidden thorn;
Fills up the farmer's lane from wall to wall,   20
Maugre[3] the farmer's sighs; and, at the gate
A tapering turret overtops the work.
And when his hours are numbered, and the world
Is all his own, retiring, as he were not,
Leaves, when the sun appears, astonished Art   25
To mimic in slow structures, stone by stone,
Built in an age, the mad wind's night-work,
The frolic architecture of the snow.

1841

Compensation[1]

I

The wings of Time are black and white,
Pied[2] with morning and with night.
Mountain tall and ocean deep

---

[1]Written in 1833–1834, the poem first appeared in *The Dial* in 1841.
[2]White marble used by Greek sculptors.
[3]In spite of.

[1]Emerson added these verses in 1847 as mottoes to his essay "Compensation."
[2]Multicolored.

Trembling balance duly keep.
In changing moon and tidal wave   5
Glows the feud of Want and Have.
Gauge of more and less through space,
Electric star or pencil plays,
The lonely Earth amid the balls
That hurry through the eternal halls,   10
A makeweight flying to the void,
Supplemental asteroid,
Or compensatory spark,
Shoots across the neutral Dark.

II

Man's the elm, and Wealth the vine;   15
Stanch and strong the tendrils twine:
Though the frail ringlets thee deceive,
None from its stock that vine can reave.
Fear not, then, though child infirm,
There's no god dare wrong a worm;   20
Laurel crowns cleave to deserts,
And power to him who power exerts.
Hast not thy share? On winged feet,
Lo! it rushes thee to meet;
And all that Nature made thy own,   25
Floating in air or pent in stone,
Will rive the hills and swim the sea,
And, like thy shadow, follow thee.

                                                                          1841

Hamatreya[1]

Bulkeley, Hunt, Willard, Hosmer, Meriam, Flint[2]
Possessed the land which rendered to their toil
Hay, corn, roots, hemp, flax, apples, wool, and wood.
Each of these landlords walked amidst his farm,
Saying, "'T is mine, my children's, and my name's.   5
How sweet the west wind sounds in my own trees!
How graceful climb those shadows on my hill!

---

[1]First published in *Poems* (1847), and based on his reading the Hindu *Vishnu Purana*. In the Hindu source, the Earth chants a song to the god Maitreya (Hamatreya), "by listening to which ambition fades away like the snow before the sun."

[2]The first settlers of Concord, including Emerson's ancestor, Bulkeley.

I fancy these pure waters and the flags[3]
Know me, as does my dog: we sympathize;
And, I affirm, my actions smack of the soil.'   10

Where are these men? Asleep beneath their grounds:
And strangers, fond as they, their furrows plough.
Earth laughs in flowers, to see her boastful boys
Earth-proud, proud of the earth which is not theirs;
Who steer the plough, but cannot steer their feet   15
Clear of the grave.
They added ridge to valley, brook to pond,
And sighed for all that bounded their domain;
'This suits me for a pasture; that's my park;
We must have clay, lime, gravel, granite-ledge,   20
And misty lowland, where to go for peat.
The land is well,—lies fairly to the south.
'T is good, when you have crossed the sea and back,
To find the sitfast acres where you left them.'
Ah! the hot owner sees not Death, who adds   25
Him to his land, a lump of mould the more.
Hear what the Earth says:—
EARTH-SONG

'Mine and yours;
Mine, not yours.   30
Earth endures;
Stars abide—
Shine down in the old sea;
Old are the shores;
But where are old men?   35
I who have seen much,
Such have I never seen.

'The lawyer's deed
Ran sure,
In tail,[4]   40
To them, and to their heirs
Who shall succeed,
Without fail,
Forevermore.

'Here is the land,   45
Shaggy with wood,

---

[3]Wild irises.

[4]Variant of "entail," the legal system of restricting inheritance.

With its old valley,
Mound and flood.
But the heritors?—
Fled like the flood's foam.   50
The lawyer, and the laws,
And the kingdom,
Clean swept herefrom.

'They called me theirs,
Who so controlled me;   55
Yet every one
Wished to stay, and is gone.
How am I theirs,
If they cannot hold me,
But I hold them?'   60

When I heard the Earth-song,
I was no longer brave;
My avarice cooled
Like lust in the chill of the grave.

                                                              1847

Brahma[1]

If the red slayer think he slays,
　　Or if the slain think he is slain,
They know not well the subtle ways
　　I keep, and pass, and turn again.

Far or forgot to me is near;   5
　　Shadow and sunlight are the same;
The vanished gods to me appear;
　　And one to me are shame and fame.

They reckon ill who leave me out;
　　When me they fly, I am the wings;   10
I am the doubter and the doubt,
　　And I the hymn the Brahmin sings.

The strong gods pine for my abode,
　　And pine in vain the sacred Seven;[2]
But thou, meek lover of the good!   15
　　Find me, and turn thy back on heaven.

                                                              1857

[1]Derived from Emerson's reading in Hindu texts (*The Vishnu Purana, The Bhagavad-Gita,* and *The Upanishads*) and first published in *The Atlantic Monthly* (1857).
[2]The high saints of Hinduism.

Days[1]

Daughters of Time, the hypocritic Days,
Muffled and dumb, like barefoot dervishes,
And marching single in an endless file,
Bring diadems and fagots in their hands.
To each they offer gifts, after his will,   5
Bread, kingdoms, stars, and sky that holds them all.
I, in my pleached garden, watched the pomp,
Forgot my morning wishes, hastily
Took a few herbs and apples, and the Day
Turned and departed silent. I, too late,   10
Under her solemn fillet saw the scorn.

                                                                    1857

Terminus[1']

It is time to be old
To take in sail:—
The god of bounds,
Who sets to seas ashore,
Came to me in his fatal rounds,   5
And said: 'No more!
No farther shoot
Thy broad ambitious branches, and thy root.
Fancy departs: no more invent;
Contract thy firmament   10
To compass of a tent.
There's not enough for this and that,
Make thy option which of two;
Economize the failing river,
Not the less revere the Giver,   15
Leave the many and hold the few.
Timely wise accept the terms,
Soften the fall with wary foot;
A little while
Still plan and smile,   20
And,—fault of novel germs,—
Mature the unfallen fruit.
Curse, if thou wilt, thy sires,
Bad husbands of their fires,

---

[1]First published in *The Atlantic Monthly* (1857).

[1']First published in *The Atlantic Monthly* (1867). Terminus was the Roman god of boundaries.

Who, when they gave thee breath,   25
Failed to bequeath
The needful sinew stark as once,
The Baresark[2] marrow to thy bones,
But left a legacy of ebbing veins,
Inconstant heat and nerveless reins,   30
Amid the Muses, left thee deaf and dumb,
Amid the gladiators, halt and numb.'

As the bird trims her to the gale,
I trim myself to the storm of time,
I man the rudder, reef the sail,   35
Obey the voice at eve obeyed at prime:
'Lowly faithful, banish fear,
Right onward drive unharmed;
The port, well worth the cruise, is near,
And every wave is charmed.'   40

          1867

JOHN GREENLEAF WHITTIER
1807–1892

He is now remembered as an early local colorist, whose example and support blessed the careers of later regional artists (such as Sarah Orne Jewett, whom he championed and advised) and whose warm depictions of American rural life rise occasionally above the patterned sentimentality that makes so much nineteenth-century poetry inaccessible to twenty-first-century readers. His present reputation rests largely on a single poem—the nostalgic *Snowbound* (1866), in which the poet re-creates a scene of his childhood on the weatherbeaten, isolated Massachusetts farmstead where he was born; describing the family "snowbound" indoors together, the poet dwells with poignant affection on the firelit faces of beloved family members, now long dead, but then gathered in the midst of life around a winter fireside. Although he produced many volumes of poetry and prose and was widely published throughout his career, it was *Snowbound* that brought him national recognition as a poet and, after a lifetime of poverty, a comfortable income as a writer. But in his own time, and

[2]The berserkers were fierce and brave Norse warriors, who fought "bare of shirt," i.e., without armor.

his own estimation, John Greenleaf Whittier was an abolitionist first, and a poet second.

Whittier was born in 1807 to a devout, debt-ridden Quaker farm family, that was struggling to retain the homestead near Haverhill, Massachusetts, where the Whittiers had been farmers since 1648. It was a costly battle: heavy physical labor in childhood broke Whittier's constitution, and in later life he would be subject to chronic headaches and, on several occasions, severe physical breakdowns. His formal education was necessarily limited, and though as a Quaker he was encouraged to study and express himself, few books were allowed him beyond the Bible and the journals of the early Friends; however, when at fourteen he was exposed to the poetry of Robert Burns, he was inspired—for Burns, too, was poor and ill educated yet could use his rough dialect and rural environment as the medium and subject for poetic expression.

But the habits of mind and spirit that he developed in that Quaker homestead drew Whittier into a life dedicated to social reform. Though Quakers were no longer openly persecuted, their history and faith still set them on the margin of New England society and gave them a critical perspective on that society, as well as a tendency to look with compassion and under-standing on the outcast and the oppressed. Their belief in the Inner Light, by which God's grace may move in any human being regardless of outward condition, led them to honor all souls—including women, Native Americans, and blacks—as equally precious in God's sight, and therefore in man's: to treat a human being as property was an outrageous violation of both man and God. When in 1826 the young Whittier published his first poem, he met William Lloyd Garrison, the journal's editor—and they became comrades in the movement to end slavery in the United States.

Encouraged by Garrison to pursue his writing, Whittier threw off the cobbling trade for which he had been training and wrote—surviving by teaching school and editing an assortment of newspapers while his poetry and articles were being published in a number of publications. But with *Justice and Expediency* (1833), a significant abolitionist tract, he cast his lot—and his creative energies—with the then-outcast and abominated antislavery movement, a choice that exposed him to much abuse and, during the 1830s, physical danger: he and the British abolitionist George Thompson were attacked and stoned on a New Hampshire lecture tour in 1835, and on another occasion in 1838 he joined in secret a raid on his own offices in order to salvage his papers from the flames. He was elected as a delegate to the National Anti-Slavery Convention in Philadelphia, which in turn led to his election in 1835 to a term in the Massachusetts legislature; and while he poured out antislavery poetry for political journals, he was a tireless and skillful manipulator of politicians in the Whig party and later the antislavery Liberty party (which he helped found in 1839).

In 1836 he moved with his mother and sisters to Amesbury, Massachusetts, where he soon settled permanently; and from this rural hamlet he sent forth his tracts, articles, broadsides—and poems and fiction. In the 1850s, when abolition became more fashionable and the movement developed a larger following, Whittier's reputation improved considerably; with the publication of *Snowbound* in 1866 he achieved national reknown as a poet; and over the remaining two decades of his life his work enjoyed steadily increasing popularity.

Whittier is sometimes eulogized as an inadequately trained artist whose talents were martyred to mere topical journalism. His association with the abolition movement doomed for several decades any hopes he might have had for popular acceptance as a poet, but it also monopolized his creative energies throughout the 1830s and much of the '40s and '50s. Often-quoted lines from Whittier's meditative *Tent on the Beach* (1867) offer the self-portrait of "a dreamer born/Who, with a mission to fulfil,/Had left the Muses' haunts to turn/The crank of an opinion-mill,/Making his rustic reed of song/A weapon in the war with wrong." But perhaps more representative of his own self-perception is his remark that he placed a "higher value on my name as appended to the Anti-Slavery Declaration ... than on any title-page of any book." He threw himself into the emancipation movement with fierce commitment, for the fact of slavery simply enraged him; and as a devout Quaker, he believed that his verses should not be ends in themselves but *means* to the ends of spiritual understanding and practical piety—means by which good works in the world could be generated.

But it was also through his labors in the "opinion mill" that he found and developed his own simple, passionate poetic voice. In the poetry Whittier devoted to the struggle against slavery, the occasion demanded not just expression but *persuasion*;. To achieve his goal, the poet learned in some degree to discipline his language for effect; by lacing his verse with small inversions of language and eerily ironic impersonations, he hoped to stimulate thought and encourage the reader to examine his or her conscience. The poems here should be read not as imperfect precursors of some later and purer art, but *as topical poems*: they draw their power as much from Whittier's political theme as they do from his artistic techniques. In the abolition poems, strategies for compression and self-control are employed to express feelings of profound moral outrage—a combination that yields some of Whittier's most affecting and expressive poetry.

Elaine Sargent Apthorp
San Jose State University

PRIMARY WORKS

Complete Writings, 7 vols., 1904; *Whittier on Writers and Writing: The Uncollected Critical Writings of John Greenleaf Whitter*, ed. Edwin H. Cady and Harry Hayden Clark, 1950; *Legends of New England*, 1831, reprinted with intro. by John B. Pickard, 1965; *Letters of John Greenleaf Whitter*, ed. John B. Pickard, 3 vols., 1975.

The Hunters of Men[1]

Have ye heard of our hunting, o'er mountain and glen,
Through cane-brake[2] and forest,—the hunting of men?

---

[1] These lines were written when the orators of the American Colonization Society were demanding that the free blacks should be sent to Africa, and opposing Emancipation unless expatriation followed. See the report of the proceedings of the society at its annual meeting in 1834. [Whittier's note]
[2] A thicket of cane.

The lords of our land to this hunting have gone,
As the fox-hunter follows the sound of the horn;
Hark! the cheer and the hallo! the crack of the whip,   5
And the yell of the hound as he fastens his grip!
All blithe are our hunters, and noble their match,
Though hundreds are caught, there are millions to catch.
So speed to their hunting, o'er mountain and glen,
Through cane-brake and forest,—the hunting of men!   10

Gay luck to our hunters! how nobly they ride
In the glow of their zeal, and the strength of their pride!
The priest with his cassock flung back on the wind,
Just screening the politic[3] statesman behind;
The saint and the sinner, with cursing and prayer,   15
The drunk and the sober, ride merrily there.
And woman, kind woman, wife, widow, and maid,
For the good of the hunted, is lending her aid:
Her foot's in the stirrup, her hand on the rein,
How blithely she rides to the hunting of men!   20

Oh, goodly and grand is our hunting to see,
In this "land of the brave and this home of the free."
Priest, warrior, and statesman, from Georgia to Maine,
All mounting the saddle, all grasping the rein;
Right merrily hunting the black man, whose sin   25
Is the curl of his hair and the hue of his skin!
Woe, now, to the hunted who turns him at bay!
Will our hunters be turned from their purpose and prey?
Will their hearts fail within them? their nerves tremble, when
All roughly they ride to the hunting of men?   30

Ho! alms for our hunters! all weary and faint,
Wax the curse of the sinner and prayer of the saint.
The horn is wound faintly, the echoes are still,
Over cane-brake and river, and forest and hill.
Haste, alms for our hunters! the hunted once more   35
Have turned from their flight with their backs to the shore:
What right have they here in the home of the white,
Shadowed o'er by our banner of Freedom and Right?
Ho! alms for the hunters! or never again
Will they ride in their pomp to the hunting of men!   40

Alms, alms for our hunters! why will ye delay,
When their pride and their glory are melting away?

---

[3]Shrewd, artful, concerned with expediency.

The parson has turned; for, on charge of his own,
Who goeth a warfare, or hunting, alone?
The politic statesman looks back with a sigh,   45
There is doubt in his heart, there is fear in his eye.
Oh, haste, lest that doubting and fear shall prevail,
And the head of his steed take the place of the tail.
Oh, haste, ere he leave us! for who will ride then,
For pleasure or gain, to the hunting of men?   50

                                                        1835

The Farewell

of a Virginia Slave Mother to Her Daughters
Sold into Southern Bondage

Gone, gone,—sold and gone,
    To the rice-swamp dank and lone.
Where the slave-whip ceaseless swings,
Where the noisome insect stings,
Where the fever demon strews   5
Poison with the falling dews,
Where the sickly sunbeams glare
Through the hot and misty air;
        Gone, gone,—sold and gone,
        To the rice-swamp dank and lone,   10
        From Virginia's hills and waters;
        Woe is me, my stolen daughters!

        Gone, gone,—sold and gone,
        To the rice-swamp dank and lone.
There no mother's eye is near them,   15
There no mother's ear can hear them;
Never, when the torturing lash
Seams their back with many a gash,
Shall a mother's kindness bless them,
Or a mother's arms caress them.   20
        Gone, gone,—sold and gone,
        To the rice-swamp dank and lone,
        From Virginia's hills and waters;
        Woe is me, my stolen daughters!

        Gone, gone,—sold and gone,   25
        To the rice-swamp dank and lone.
Oh, when weary, sad and slow,
From the fields at night they go,

Faint with toil, and racked with pain,
To their cheerless homes again,   30
There no brother's voice shall greet them;
There no father's welcome meet them.
 Gone, gone,—sold and gone,
 To the rice-swamp dank and lone,
 From Virginia's hills and waters;   35
 Woe is me, my stolen daughters!

 Gone, gone,—sold and gone,
 To the rice-swamp dank and lone.
From the tree whose shadow lay
On their childhood's place of play;   40
From the cool spring where they drank;
Rock, and hill, and rivulet bank;
From the solemn house of prayer,
And the holy counsels there;
 Gone, gone,—sold and gone,   45
 To the rice-swamp dank and lone,
 From Virginia's hills and waters;
 Woe is me, my stolen daughters!

 Gone, gone,—sold and gone,
 To the rice-swamp dank and lone;   50
Toiling through the weary day,
And at night the spoiler's prey.[1]
Oh, that they had earlier died,
Sleeping calmly, side by side,
Where the tyrant's power is o'er,   55
And the fetter galls no more!
 Gone, gone,—sold and gone,
 To the rice-swamp dank and lone,
 From Virginia's hills and waters;
 Woe is me, my stolen daughters!   60

 Gone, gone,—sold and gone,
 To the rice-swamp dank and lone.
By the holy love He beareth;
By the bruised reed He spareth;
Oh, may He, to whom alone   65
All their cruel wrongs are known,
Still their hope and refuge prove,
With a more than mother's love.
 Gone, gone,—sold and gone,

[1]Victim of plunderer; vulnerable to violation.

To the rice-swamp dank and lone,   70
From Virginia's hills and waters;
Woe is me, my stolen daughters!

                                                                    1838

Massachusetts to Virginia[1]

The blast from Freedom's Northern hills, upon its Southern way,
Bears greeting to Virginia from Massachusetts Bay:
No word of haughty challenging, nor battle bugle's peal,
Nor steady tread of marching files, nor clang of horsemen's steel.

No trains of deep-mouthed cannon along our highways go;   5
Around our silent arsenals untrodden lies the snow;
And to the land-breeze of our ports, upon their errands far,
A thousand sails of commerce swell, but none are spread for war.

We hear thy threats, Virginia! thy stormy words and high,
Swell harshly on the Southern winds which melt along our sky;   10
Yet, not one brown, hard hand foregoes its honest labor here,
No hewer of our mountain oaks suspends his axe in fear.

Wild are the waves which lash the reefs along St. George's bank;
Cold on the shore of Labrador the fog lies white and dank;
Through storm, and wave, and blinding mist, stout are the hearts
     which man   15
The fishing-smacks of Marblehead, the sea-boats of Cape Ann.[2]

The cold north light and wintry sun glare on their icy forms,
Bent grimly o'er their straining lines or wrestling with the storms;
Free as the winds they drive before, rough as the waves they roam,
They laugh to scorn the slaver's threat against their rocky home. 20

What means the Old Dominion?[3] Hath she forgot the day
When o'er her conquered valleys swept the Briton's steel array?
How side by side, with sons of hers, the Massachusetts men
Encountered Tarleton's charge of fire, and stout Cornwallis, then?[4]

[1]Written on reading an account of the proceedings of the citizens of Norfolk, Va., in reference to George Latimer, the alleged fugitive slave, who was seized in Boston without warrant at the request of James B. Grey, of Norfolk, claiming to be his master. The case caused great excitement North and South, and led to the presentation of a petition to Congress, signed by more than fifty thousand citizens of Massachusetts, calling for such laws and proposed amendments to the Constitution as should relieve the Commonwealth from all further participation in the crime of oppression. George Latimer himself was finally given free papers for the sum of four hundred dollars. [Whittier's note]
[2]This and other place-names in this stanza refer to sections of the Massachusetts coastline, and to fishing grounds to the north.
[3]Virginia.
[4]British generals defeated in the War for Independence. Reference recalls Massachusetts' military aid to Virginia at critical moments in the War.

Forgets she how the Bay State,[5] in answer to the call   25
Of her old House of Burgesses, spoke out from Faneuil Hall?[6]
When, echoing back her Henry's cry, came pulsing on each breath
Of Northern winds, the thrilling sounds of "Liberty or Death!"[7]

What asks the Old Dominion? If now her sons have proved
False to their fathers' memory, false to the faith they loved;   30
If she can scoff at Freedom, and its great charter[8] spurn,
Must we of Massachusetts from truth and duty turn?

We hunt your bondmen, flying from Slavery's hateful hell;
Our voices, at your bidding, take up the blood-hound's yell;
We gather, at your summons, above our fathers' graves,   35
From Freedom's holy altar-horns[9] to tear your wretched slaves!

Thank God! not yet so vilely can Massachusetts bow;
The spirit of her early time is with her even now;
Dream not because her Pilgrim blood moves slow and calm and
      cool,
She thus can stoop her chainless neck, a sister's slave and tool!   40

All that a sister State should do, all that a free State may,
Heart, hand, and purse we proffer, as in our early day;
But that one dark loathsome burden ye must stagger with alone,
And reap the bitter harvest which ye yourselves have sown!

Hold, while ye may, your struggling slaves, and burden God's free
      air   45
With woman's shriek beneath the lash, and manhood's wild
      despair;
Cling closer to the "cleaving curse" that writes upon your plains
The blasting of Almighty wrath against a land of chains.

Still shame your gallant ancestry, the cavaliers of old,
By watching round the shambles[10] where human flesh is sold;   50
Gloat o'er the new-born child, and count his market value, when
The maddened mother's cry of woe shall pierce the slaver's den!

[5]Massachusetts.
[6]Refers to Virginia's colonial House of Burgesses and to the Boston meeting house where community leaders met during the Revolution.
[7]Virginia Revolutionary Patrick Henry, who in addressing the House of Burgesses exclaimed, "I know not what course others may take, but as for me, give me liberty or give me death!"

[8]Refers to the Declaration of Independence, drafted by Virginia's Thomas Jefferson, which asserted that "all men are created equal."
[9]Sanctuary.
[10]A slaughterhouse.

Lower than plummet soundeth,[11] sink the Virginia name;
Plant, if ye will, your fathers' graves with rankest weeds of shame;
Be, if ye will, the scandal of God's fair universe;   55
We wash our hands forever of your sin and shame and curse.

A voice from lips whereon the coal from Freedom's shrine hath
     been,
Thrilled, as but yesterday, the hearts of Berkshire's mountain
     men:[12]
The echoes of that solemn voice are sadly lingering still
In all our sunny valleys, on every wind-swept hill.   60

And when the prowling man-thief came hunting for his prey
Beneath the very shadow of Bunker's shaft of gray,[13]
How, through the free lips of the son, the father's warning spoke;
How, from its bonds of trade and sect, the Pilgrim city broke![14]

A hundred thousand right arms were lifted up on high,   65
A hundred thousand voices sent back their loud reply;
Through the thronged towns of Essex[15] the startling summons
     rang,
And up from bench and loom and wheel her young mechanics[16]
     sprang!

The voice of free, broad Middlesex,[17] of thousands as of one,
The shaft of Bunker calling to that of Lexington;   70
From Norfolk's ancient villages, from Plymouth's rocky bound
To where Nantucket feels the arms of ocean close her round;

From rich and rural Worcester, where through the calm repose
Of cultured vales and fringing woods the gentle Nashua flows,
To where Wachuset's wintry blasts the mountain larches stir,   75
Swelled up to Heaven the thrilling cry of "God save Latimer!"[18]

---

[11]Refers to a line in Shakespeare's *The Tempest* (Act III, sc. 3, 1.101).

[12]Refers to the farmers and trappers of the Berkshire mountains in western Massachusetts.

[13]Bunker Hill was the site of a famous battle of the Revolution, in which six hundred colonial soldiers held the hilltop successfully against the onslaught of a British force more than twice their number.

[14]Boston, which was founded by nonseparatist Puritan "pilgrims."

[15]Whittier's home county, where this poem was being read.

[16]Craft and trade workers; skilled laborers.

[17]Massachusetts county. In the verses that follow, a number of other Massachusetts counties, towns, and natural landmarks are named (Lexington, scene of the first battle of the Revolutionary War; Norfolk; Plymouth; Nantucket; Worcester; the river Nashua; Wachuset mountain; Barnstable; Bristol; Narragansett Bay; the Connecticut River, which flows past Hampden, Hampshire, and Holyoke Hill) to indicate the breadth of the Massachusetts protest against the seizure of Latimer.

[18]George Latimer. See Whittier's headnote.

And sandy Barnstable rose up, wet with the salt sea spray;
And Bristol sent her answering shout down Narragansett Bay!
Along the broad Connecticut old Hampden felt the thrill,
And the cheer of Hampshire's woodmen swept down from
    Holyoke Hill.   80

The voice of Massachusetts! Of her free sons and daughters,
Deep calling unto deep aloud, the sound of many waters!
Against the burden of that voice what tyrant power shall stand?
No fetters in the Bay State! No slave upon her land!

Look to it well, Virginians! In calmness we have borne,   85
In answer to our faith and trust, your insult and your scorn;
You've spurned our kindest counsels; you've hunted for our lives;
And shaken round our hearths and homes your manacles and
    gyves![19]

We wage no war, we lift no arm, we fling no torch within[20]
The fire-damps of the quaking mine beneath your soil of sin;[21]   90
We leave ye with your bondmen, to wrestle, while ye can,
With the strong upward tendencies and godlike soul of man!

But for us and for our children, the vow which we have given
For freedom and humanity is registered in heaven;
No slave-hunt in our borders,—no pirate on our strand!   95
No fetters in the Bay State,—no slave upon our land!

                                               1843

At Port Royal[1]

The tent-lights glimmer on the land,
    The ship-lights on the sea;
The night-wind smooths with drifting sand
    Our track on lone Tybee.
At last our grating keels outslide,   5
    Our good boats forward swing;

---

[19]Shackles.

[20]Explosive mixture formed by the release of methane gas into the air of underground mines.

[21]Whittier probably intended a double meaning here: soil as earth (above a mine), as well as moral stain.

[1]In November 1861, a Union force under Commodore Dupont and General Sherman captured Port Royal, and from this point as a basis of operations, the neighboring islands between Charleston and Savannah were taken possession of. The early occupation of this district, where the negro population was greatly in excess of the white, gave an opportunity which was at once seized upon, of practically emancipating the slaves and of beginning that work of civilization which was accepted as the grave responsibility of those who had labored for freedom. [Whittier's note]

And while we ride the land-locked tide,
    Our negroes row and sing.

For dear the bondman holds his gifts
    Of music and of song;   10
The gold that kindly Nature sifts
    Among his sands of wrong;

The power to make his toiling days
    And poor home-comforts please;
The quaint relief of mirth that plays   15
    With sorrow's minor keys.

Another glow than sunset's fire
    Has filled the west with light,
Where field and garner, barn and byre,[2]
    Are blazing through the night.   20

The land is wild with fear and hate,
    The rout runs mad and fast;
From hand to hand, from gate to gate
    The flaming brand is passed.

The lurid glow falls strong across   25
    Dark faces broad with smiles:
Not theirs the terror, hate, and loss
    That fire yon blazing piles.

With oar-strokes timing to their song,
    They weave in simple lays   30
The pathos of remembered wrong,
    The hope of better days,—

The triumph-note that Miriam sung,[3]
    The joy of uncaged birds:
Softening with Afric's mellow tongue   35
    Their broken Saxon words.[4]

SONG OF THE NEGRO BOATMEN

Oh, praise an' tanks! De Lord he come
    To set de people free;

---

[2]Garner is a granary, byre a cow barn.
[3]See Exodus 15:20–21.

[4]Colloquial for Old English, which was the language of the Angles and Saxons of the British Isles.

An' massa tink it day ob doom,[5]
    An' we ob jubilee.[6]
De Lord dat heap de Red Sea waves[7]   40
    He jus' as 'trong as den;
He say de word: we las' night slaves;
    To-day, de Lord's freemen.
        De yam will grow, de cotton blow,   45
            We'll hab de rice an' corn;
        Oh nebber you fear, if nebber you hear
            De driver[8] blow his horn!

Ole massa on he trabbels gone;
    He leaf de land behind: 50
De Lord's breff blow him furder on,
    Like corn-shuck[9] in de wind.
We own de hoe, we own de plough,
    We own de hands dat hold;

We sell de pig, we sell de cow,   55
    But nebber chile be sold.
        De yam will grow, de cotton blow,
            We'll hab de rice an' corn;
        Oh nebber you fear, if nebber you hear
            De driver blow his horn!   60

We pray de Lord: he gib us signs
    Dat some day we be free;
De norf-wind tell it to de pines,
    De wild-duck to de sea;
We tink it when de church-bell ring,   65
    We dream it in de dream;
De rice-bird mean it when he sing,
    De eagle when he scream.
        De yam will grow, de cotton blow,
            We'll hab de rice an' corn: 70
        Oh nebber you fear, if nebber you hear
            De driver blow his horn!

* * *

[5]Refers to the return of Christ on Judgment Day; for the unredeemed sinner, the moment of final damnation.

[6]Refers to the return of Christ on Judgment Day; for the saint and redeemed sinner, the moment of rejoicing and deliverance.

[7]To aid Moses and the Israelites as they fled from Egyptian persecution, Jehovah parted the waters of the Red Sea that they might pass across safely.

[8]Slave-driver.

[9]The outer husk of an ear of corn, usually stripped away and discarded.

We know de promise nebber fail,
    An' nebber lie de word;
So like de 'postles in de jail,[10]   75
    We waited for de Lord:
An' now he open ebery door,
    An' trow away de key;
He tink we lub him so before,
    We lub him better free.   80
De yam will grow, de cotton blow,
    He'll gib de rice an' corn;
Oh nebber you fear, if nebber you hear
    De driver blow his horn!

So sing our dusky gondoliers;[11]   85
    And with a secret pain,
And smiles that seem akin to tears,
    We hear the wild refrain.

We dare not share the negro's trust,
    Nor yet his hope deny;   90
We only know that God is just,
    And every wrong shall die.

Rude seems the song; each swarthy[12] face,
    Flame-lighted, ruder still:
We start to think that hapless[13] race   95
    Must shape our good or ill;

That laws of changeless justice bind
    Oppressor with oppressed;
And, close as sin and suffering joined,
    We march to Fate abreast.   100

Sing on, poor hearts! your chant shall be
    Our sign of blight or bloom,
The Vala-song[14] of Liberty,
    Or death-rune of our doom!

1862

---

[10]Paul and Silas, early leaders of the Christian church, who when imprisoned for their faith prayed in their cell continuously for release.
[11]Dark-skinned (African) boatmen, guiding long, narrow, flat-bottomed barges.

[12]Black.
[13]Unlucky.
[14]Perhaps health-song, as in "valedictory."

■   SARAH MARGARET FULLER   ■
                                  1810–1850

Margaret Fuller's father was disappointed when his first child was a girl. Still, when he was not away as a member of Congress or as Speaker of the Massachusetts House, he gave her the same education as any young man of their class might have received. At age fifteen, her daily schedule began at five in the morning, ended at eleven at night, and included reading literary and philosophical works in four languages, especially German, walking, singing, and playing the piano. The passages about "Miranda" in *Woman in the Nineteenth Century* reflect an idealized view of this upbringing, omitting the lifelong nightmares and headaches that may have been rooted in this imposing routine. When her family moved back to Cambridge in the early 1830s, Fuller met most of the people central to the Transcendentalist movement: Emerson, Thoreau, Bronson Alcott, and W. H. Channing, among others. She was already on her way to what Thomas Carlyle called a "predetermination to *eat* this big universe as her oyster or her egg," and she made an instant impression on those around her.

The death of her father in 1835 forced Fuller to take up school-teaching to support herself and her family. After a brief stint in Alcott's progressive Temple School in Boston, she accepted a post in Providence, Rhode Island, moving there in 1837. But Fuller saw teaching as a means, not an end, and she keenly felt her isolation from the intellectual circles in Boston, to which she returned in December 1838.

There she flourished. In May 1839, she published her translation of Eckermann's *Conversations with Goethe in the Last Years of His Life*, and in January 1840, she began a two-year period as editor of *The Dial*, the semi-official journal of the Transcendentalists. During this period, she supported herself by holding "Conversations" for women on topics such as poetry, ethics, Greek mythology, or the other subjects outlined in her letter to Sophia Ripley. Fuller believed that women had been educated solely for display and not to think. She saw herself as a catalyst for the women in her groups, and at her "Conversations" she attempted to guide and draw out the participants, to force them to realize the potential within themselves. Her "Conversations" between 1839 and 1844 were so popular—even though among the most expensive in Boston—that she was finally constrained to admit men. The "Conversations" anticipate the later organization of women's literary clubs and other efforts aimed at the self-development of women, who remained largely excluded from advanced educational institutions.

Between May and September 1843, Fuller and some friends toured the Midwest. On returning to Boston, Fuller set about writing up her account of the trip and in June 1844 published it as *Summer on the Lakes, in 1843*. The value of her book does not lie in its factual matter—Fuller's aim was to give her "poetic impression of the country at large." In her commentary, she sympathized with the plight of the Indians and their betrayal by the whites, worried about attempts to imitate Eastern standards of culture at the expense of losing what was unique to the West, and inserted many long passages of scenic description to convey her own sense of wonder at all the natural beauty she had seen.

Summer on the Lakes not only helped Fuller gain recognition as an author, it also brought her to the attention of Horace Greeley, who hired her as literary critic and general essayist for his New York *Tribune* and offered to publish her next book. Fuller revised and expanded her essay "The Great Lawsuit. Man *versus* Men. Woman *versus* Women" from the July 1843 *Dial* and moved to New York in December 1844 while still working on the book.

Woman in the Nineteenth Century, published in February 1845, is Fuller's best-known work—indeed, the only one of her works generally made available to students. In it she attacks the hypocrisy of man, a hypocrisy that allowed him to champion freedom for blacks while maintaining legislation to restrict the rights of woman; a hypocrisy that saw man complain about woman's physical and emotional unsuitability for positions of responsibility in public life, yet insist that she be a field hand, a nurse, and the one to raise and socialize children. She applied to "the woman question" ideas about self-development she shared with Emerson and adapted something of his hortatory style to her social purposes. "What woman needs," she wrote,

> is not as a woman to act or rule, but as a nature to grow, as an intellect to discern, as a soul to live freely, and unimpeded to unfold such powers as were given her when we left our common home.

Fuller's arguments for full equality of opportunity, for abolishing stereotyped gender roles—"there is no wholly masculine man," she wrote, "no purely feminine woman"—and for women themselves to represent their own best interests may sound strikingly apt to today's readers. In any case, the book remains the fullest statement of women's rights to come out of the Boston-centered literary renaissance of mid-nineteenth-century America.

Fuller wrote nearly 250 reviews and occasional essays for the *Tribune* in the intense year and a half she worked in New York. *Papers on Literature and Art* (1846) collected only a few of these, including her famous essay surveying American literature, much of which is reprinted in this volume. But as a reporter she was also able to visit and write about women's prisons; Hopper Home, a halfway house for female convicts; immigrant slums; and city hospitals. She focused her attention, as she had not before, on specific social issues of the day, including capital punishment, the abolitionist movement, the war on Mexico, and the treatment of madness.

In August 1846, Fuller sailed for England as one of the first American "foreign correspondents," male or female. She began with the expected literary tour of England, where the recently issued *Papers* won her a warm reception among British writers. She also met, and was deeply influenced by, social activists like the Italian patriot Giuseppe Mazzini and literary figures concerned with sexual liberation like the poet Adam Mickiewicz and the then-notorious French woman novelist George Sand. By the summer of 1847, she had taken up residence in Rome and soon became involved in the revolutionary movements that were to shake Italy and all of Europe. She was swept up in the republican uprising, her dispatches to the *Tribune* urged American support for the republican cause, and in the final siege of Rome she ran a military hospital. She also entered a relationship with Giovanni Ossoli, by whom she had a son, Angelo, in September 1848; they apparently married the following year. When the Roman Republic fell to French troops in July 1849, the Ossolis escaped to Rieti, where Angelo was almost starved by a wet nurse, and then to Florence, where many of their friends, including the poets Elizabeth and Robert Browning, appear to have been scandalized by their marriage and the fact that Giovanni was eleven years younger than Margaret. After a winter working on her history of the Roman Republic, Fuller set sail with Ossoli for America the following May. Their ship was caught in a storm, wrecked on a sandbar some fifty yards off Fire Island—almost within sight of New York City—and went down; only Angelo's body was ever found. Thoreau spent five days unsuccessfully combing the beach for their remains or for Fuller's missing manuscripts.

Although Fuller is famous today for *Woman in the Nineteenth Century*, she was best known by her contemporaries for her criticism, which attempted to establish well-defined standards; for her personality, which some friends experienced as "the presence of a rather mountainous ME"; and for her conversation, which some found much superior to her writing. Indeed, she seems both to have intrigued and threatened many of her contemporaries. Hawthorne called her a "great humbug" in his journal and may have mocked her in the character of Zenobia in his novel about Brook Farm, *The Blithedale Romance*. While her friend Emerson lamented that he had "lost in her my audience," he, W. H. Channing, and James Freeman Clarke attempted to smooth away the social and political radicalism of her last years, bowdlerizing her journals and rewriting her letters in their *Memoirs of Margaret Fuller Ossoli* (1852). In the hands of such ambivalent editors, Fuller came to be regarded as, at best, a seriocomic footnote in American literary history, her style—in the words of a prominent twentieth-century critic—that of a headstrong "galloping filly." The emergence of a renewed women's movement in the 1960s helped revive interest in Fuller's work. Recent scholarship has shown the continuing influence of her writing on nineteenth-century feminists, and contemporary criticism has begun to understand the tensions in her life and work, the successes and failures of her prose, as reflections of her original effort to imagine "the woman who shall vindicate their birthright for all women; who shall teach them what to claim, and how to use what they obtain."

Joel Myerson
University of South Carolina

PRIMARY WORKS

Summer on the Lakes, in 1843, 1844; *Woman in the Nineteenth Century*, 1845; *Papers on Literature and Art*, 1846; *At Home and Abroad*, ed. Arthur B. Fuller, 1856; *The Letters of Margaret Fuller*, ed. Robert N. Hudspeth, 6 vols. to date, 1983–1994; "*These Sad but Glorious Days*": *Dispatches from Europe, 1846–1850*, ed. Larry J. Reynolds and Susan Belasco Smith, 1991; *The Essential Margaret Fuller*, ed. Jeffrey Steele, 1992; *The Portable Margaret Fuller*, ed. Mary Kelley, 1994.

from **Woman in the Nineteenth Century**

"Frei durch Venunft, stark durch Gesetze,
Durch Sanftmuth gross, und reich durch Schätze,
Die lange Zeit dein Busen dir verschwieg."[1]

"I meant the day-star should not brighter rise,
Nor lend like influence from its lucent seat;
I meant she should be courteous, facile, sweet,
Free from that solemn vice of greatness, pride;
I meant each softest virtue there should meet,
Fit in that softer bosom to reside;
Only a (heavenward and instructed) soul
I purposed her, that should, with evea powers,
The rock, the spindle, and the shears control
Of destiny, and spin her own free hours."[2]

Preface

The following essay is a reproduction, modified and expanded, of an article published in "The Dial, Boston, July, 1843," under the title of "The Great Lawsuit. Man versus Men: Woman versus Women."

This article excited a good deal of sympathy, and still more interest. It is in compliance with wishes expressed from many quarters, that it is prepared for publication in its present form.

Objections having been made to the former title, as not sufficiently easy to be understood, the present has been substituted as expressive of the main purpose of the essay; though, by myself, the other is preferred, partly for the reason others do not like it,—that is, that it requires some thought to see what it means, and might thus prepare the reader to meet me on my own ground. Beside, it offers a larger scope, and is, in that way, more just to my desire. I meant, by that title, to intimate the fact that, while it is the destiny of Man, in the course of the Ages, to ascertain and fulfil the law of his being, so that his life shall be seen, as a whole, to be that of an angel or messenger, the action of prejudices and passions, which attend, in the day, the growth of the individual, is continually obstructing the holy work that is to make the earth a part of heaven. By Man I mean both man and woman: these are the two halves of one thought. I lay no especial stress on the welfare of either. I believe that the development of the one cannot be effected without that of the other. My highest wish is that this truth should be distinctly and rationally apprehended, and the conditions of life and freedom

[1]"Free through understanding, strong through principles,/Great through gentleness, and enriched by loved ones,/This long time your bosom has concealed you." (Source unidentified.)

[2]Ben Jonson (ca. 1573–1637), English essayist and dramatist, quoted from Epigram No. 76, "On Lucy, Countess of Bedford."

recognized as the same for the daughters and the sons of time; twin exponents of a divine thought.

I solicit a sincere and patient attention from those who open the following pages at all. I solicit of women that they will lay it to heart to ascertain what is for them the liberty of law. It is for this, and not for any, the largest, extension of partial privileges that I seek. I ask them, if interested by these suggestions, to search their own experience and intuitions for better, and fill up with fit materials and trenches that hedge them in. From men I ask a noble and earnest attention to any thing that can be offered on this great and still obscure subject, such as I have met from many with whom I stand in private relations.

And may truth, unpolluted by prejudice, vanity, or selfishness, be granted daily more and more, as the due inheritance, and only valuable conquest for us all!

November, 1844.

... It should be remarked that, as the principle of liberty is better understood, and more nobly interpreted, a broader protest is made in behalf of Woman. As men become aware that few men have had a fair chance, they are inclined to say that no women have had a fair chance. The French Revolution, that strangely disguised angel, bore witness in favor of Woman, but interpreted her claims no less ignorantly than those of Man. Its idea of happiness did not rise beyond outward enjoyment, unobstructed by the tyranny of others. The title it gave was "citoyen," "citoyenne," and it is not unimportant to Woman that even this species of equality was awarded her. Before, she could be condemned to perish on the scaffold for treason, not as a citizen, but as a subject. The right with which this title then invested a human being, was that of bloodshed and license. The Goddess of Liberty was impure. As we read the poem addressed to her not long since, by Beranger, we can scarcely refrain from tears as painful as the tears of blood that flowed when "such crimes were committed in her name."[3] Yes! Man, born to purify and animate the unintelligent and the cold, can, in his madness, degrade and pollute no less the fair and the chaste. Yet truth was prophesied in the ravings of that hideous fever, caused by long ignorance and abuse. Europe is conning a valued lesson from the blood-stained page. The same tendencies, farther unfolded, will bear good fruit in this country.

Yet, by men in this country, as by the Jews, when Moses was leading them to the promised land, every thing has been done that inherited depravity could do, to hinder the promise of Heaven from its fulfilment. The cross, here as elsewhere, has been planted only to be blasphemed by cruelty and fraud. The name of the Prince of Peace has been profaned by all kinds of injustice toward the Gentile whom he said he came to save. But I need not speak of what has been done towards the Red Man, the Black Man. Those deeds are the scoff of the world; and they have been accompanied by

---

[3]Pierre-Jean de Béranger (1780–1857), French lyric poet known for his "La Liberté." The quotation is attributed to Madame Roland (1754–1793), a French revolutionist.

such pious words that the gentlest would not dare to intercede with "Father, forgive them, for they know not what they do."

Here, as elsewhere, the gain of creation consists always in the growth of individual minds, which live and aspire, as flowers bloom and birds sing, in the midst of morasses; and in the continual development of that thought, the thought of human destiny, which is given to eternity adequately to express, and which ages of failure only seemingly impede. Only seemingly, and whatever seems to the contrary, this country is as surely destined to elucidate a great moral law, as Europe was to promote the mental culture of Man.

Though the national independence be blurred by the servility of individuals, though freedom and equality have been proclaimed only to leave room for a monstrous display of slave-dealing and slave-keeping; though the free American so often feels himself free, like the Roman, only to pamper his appetites and his indolence through the misery of his fellow beings; still it is not in vain that the verbal statement has been made, "All men are born free and equal." There it stands, a golden certainty wherewith to encourage the good, to shame the bad. The New World may be called clearly to perceive that it incurs the utmost penalty if it reject or oppress the sorrowful brother. And, if men are deaf, the angels hear. But men cannot be deaf. It is inevitable that an external freedom, an independence of the encroachments of other men, such as has been achieved for the nation, should be so also for every member of it. That which has once been clearly conceived in the intelligence cannot fail, sooner or later, to be acted out. It has become a law as irrevocable as that of the Medes in their ancient dominion;[4] men will privately sin against it, but the law, as expressed by a leading mind of the age,

> *"Tutti fatti a sembianza d'un Solo,*
> *Figli tutti d'un solo riscatto,*
> *In qual'ora, in qual parte del suolo*
> *Transcorriamo quest' aura vital,*
> *Siam fratelli, siam stretti ad un patto:*
> *Maladetto colui che lo infrange,*
> *Che s'innalza sul fiacco che piange*
> *Che contrista uno spirto immortal.*[5]

> *"All made in the likeness of the One,*
> * All children of one ransom,*
> *In whatever hour, in whatever part of the soil,*
> * We draw this vital air,*
> *We are brothers; we must be bound by one compact,*
> * Accursed he who infringes it,*
> *Who raises himself upon the weak who weep,*
> * Who saddens an immortal spirit."*

[4]The inhabitants of Medea (in what is now northwest Iran) who were conquered by the Persians under Cyrus the Great.

[5]Manzoni [Fuller's note]. Alessandro Manzoni (1785–1873), Italian romantic novelist, quoted from "Coro Dell' Atto Secondo," *Il Conte di Carmagnola,* canto 45.

This law cannot fail of universal recognition. Accursed be he who willingly saddens an immortal spirit—doomed to infamy in later, wiser ages, doomed in future stages of his own being to deadly penance, only short of death. Accursed be he who sins in ignorance, if that ignorance be caused by sloth.

We sicken no less at the pomp than the strife of words. We feel that never were lungs so puffed with the wind of declamation, on moral and religious subjects, as now. We are tempted to implore these "word-heroes," these word-Catos, word-Christs, to beware of cant[6] above all things; to remember that hypocrisy is the most hopeless as well as the meanest of crimes, and that those must surely be polluted by it, who do not reserve a part of their morality and religion for private use. Landor[7] says that he cannot have a great deal of mind who cannot afford to let the larger part of it lie fallow, and what is true of genius is not less so of virtue. The tongue is a valuable member, but should appropriate but a small part of the vital juices that are needful all over the body. We feel that the mind may "grow black and rancid in the smoke" even "of altars." We start up from the harangue to go into our closet and shut the door. There inquires the spirit, "Is this rhetoric the bloom of healthy blood or a false pigment artfully laid on?" And yet again we know where is so much smoke, must be some fire; with so much talk about virtue and freedom, must be mingled some desire for them; that it cannot be in vain that such have become the common topics of conversation among men, rather than schemes for tyranny and plunder, that the very newspapers see it best to proclaim themselves "Pilgrims," "Puritans," "Heralds of Holiness." The king that maintains so costly a retinue cannot be a mere boast, or Carabbas fiction.[8] We have waited here long in the dust; we are tired and hungry, but the triumphal procession must appear at last.

Of all its banners, none has been more steadily upheld, and under none have more valor and willingness for real sacrifices been shown, than that of the champions of the enslaved African. And this band it is, which, partly from a natural following out of principles, partly because many women have been prominent in that cause, makes, just now, the warmest appeal in behalf of Woman.

Though there has been a growing liberality on this subject, yet society at large is not so prepared for the demands of this party, but that they are and will be for some time, coldly regarded as the Jacobins[9] of their day.

"Is it not enough," cries the irritated trader, "that you have done all you could to break up the national union, and thus destroy the prosperity of our

---

[6]Dr. Johnson's one piece of advice should be written on every door: "Clear your mind of cant." But Byron, to whom it was so acceptable, in clearing away the noxious vine, shook down the building. Sterling's emendation is worthy of honor: "Realize your cant, not cast it off." [Fuller's note] Samuel Johnson (1709–1784), English lexicographer and essayist, quoted from James Boswell, *The Life of Samuel Johnson* (1791), dated May 15, 1873. John Sterling (1806–1844), English poet and dramatist.

[7]Walter Savage Landor (1775–1864), English essayist.

[8]Carabbas, a character in Perrault's *Le Chat Botté (Puss in Boots)*, whose name is synonymous with aristocratic pretension.

[9]Jacobins, the name given to a radical organization in the French Revolution and usually associated with the Reign of Terror under Robespierre.

country, but now you must be trying to break up family union, to take my wife away from the cradle and the kitchen hearth to vote at polls, and preach from a pulpit? Of course, if she does such things, she cannot attend to those of her own sphere. She is happy enough as she is. She has more leisure than I have, every means of improvement, every indulgence."

"Have you asked her whether she was satisfied with these *indulgences*?"

"No, but I know she is. She is too amiable to wish what would make me unhappy, and too judicious to wish to step beyond the sphere of her sex. I will never consent to have our peace disturbed by any such discussions."

"'Consent—you?' it is not consent from you that is in question, it is assent from your wife."

"Am not I the head of my house?"

"You are not the head of your wife. God has given her a mind of her own."

"I am the head and she the heart."

"God grant you play true to one another then. I suppose I am to be grateful that you did not say she was only the hand. If the head represses no natural pulse of the heart, there can be no question as to your giving your consent. Both will be of one accord, and there needs but to present any question to get a full and true answer. There is no need of precaution, of indulgence, or consent. But our doubt is whether the heart *does* consent with the head, or only obeys its decrees with a passiveness that precludes the exercise of its natural powers, or a repugnance that turns sweet qualities to bitter, or a doubt that lays waste the fair occasions of life. It is to ascertain the truth, that we propose some liberating measures."

Thus vaguely are these questions proposed and discussed at present. But their being proposed at all implies much thought and suggests more. Many women are considering within themselves, what they need that they have not, and what they can have, if they find they need it. Many men are considering whether women are capable of being and having more than they are and have, *and*, whether, if so, it will be best to consent to improvement in their condition.

This morning, I open the Boston "Daily Mail," and find in its "poet's corner," a translation of Schiller's "Dignity of Woman." In the advertisement of a book on America, I see in the table of contents this sequence, "Republican Institutions. American Slavery. American Ladies."

I open the *"Deutsche Schnellpost,"* published in New-York, and find at the head of a column, *Judenund Frauen-emancipation in Ungarn.* "Emancipation of Jews and Women in Hungary."

The past year has seen action in the Rhode-Island legislature, to secure married women rights over their own property, where men showed that a very little examination of the subject could teach them much; an article in the Democratic Review on the same subject more largely considered, written by a woman, impelled, it is said, by glaring wrong to a distinguished friend having shown the defects in the existing laws, and the state of opinion from which they spring; and an answer from the revered old man, J. Q. Adams, in some respects the Phocion of his time, to an address made him by some ladies.[10] To this last I shall again advert in another place.

These symptoms of the times have come under my view quite accidentally: one who seeks, may, each month or week, collect more.

The numerous party, whose opinions are already labelled and adjusted too much to their mind to admit of any new light, strive, by lectures on some model-woman of bride-like beauty and gentleness, by writing and lending little treatises, intended to mark out with precision the limits of Woman's sphere, and Woman's mission, to prevent other than the rightful shepherd from climbing the wall, or the flock from using any chance to go astray.

Without enrolling ourselves at once on either side, let us look upon the subject from the best point of view which to-day offers. No better, it is to be feared, than a high house-top. A high hill-top, or at least a cathedral spire, would be desirable.

It may well be an Anti-Slavery party that pleads for Woman, if we consider merely that she does not hold property on equal terms with men; so that, if a husband dies without making a will, the wife, instead of taking at once his place as head of the family, inherits only a part of his fortune, often brought him by herself, as if she were a child, or ward only, not an equal partner.

We will not speak of the innumerable instances in which profligate and idle men live upon the earnings of industrious wives; or if the wives leave them, and take with them the children, to perform the double duty of mother and father, follow from place to place, and threaten to rob them of the children, if deprived of the rights of a husband, as they call them, planting themselves in their poor lodgings, frightening them into paying tribute by taking from them the children, running into debt at the expense of these otherwise so overtasked helots. Such instances count up by scores within my own memory. I have seen the husband who had stained himself by a long course of low vice, till his wife was wearied from her heroic forgiveness, by finding that his treachery made it useless, and that if she would provide bread for herself and her children, she must be separate from his ill fame—I have known this man come to install himself in the chamber of a woman who loathed him and say she should never take food without his company. I have known these men steal their children whom they knew they had no means to maintain, take them into dissolute company, expose them to bodily danger, to frighten the poor woman, to whom, it seems, the fact that she alone had borne the pangs of their birth, and nourished their infancy, does not give an equal right to them. I do believe that this mode of kidnapping— and it is frequent enough in all classes of society—will be by the next age viewed as it is by Heaven now, and that the man who avails himself of the shelter of men's laws to steal from a mother her own children, or arrogate

[10]The article is "The Legal Wrongs of Women," *United States Magazine and Democratic Review*, 14 (May 1844): 477–483. John Quincy Adams (1767–1848), sixth president of the United States. Phocion (ca. 402–317 B.C.), leader of the aristocratic party in Athens.

any superior right in them, save that of superior virtue, will bear the stigma he deserves, in common with him who steals grown men from their mother land, their hopes, and their homes.

I said, we will not speak of this now, yet I *have* spoken, for the subject makes me feel too much. I could give instances that would startle the most vulgar and callous, but I will not, for the public opinion of their own sex is already against such men, and where cases of extreme tyranny are made known, there is private action in the wife's favor. But she ought not to need this, nor, I think, can she long. Men must soon see that, on their own ground, that Woman is the weaker party, she ought to have legal protection, which would make such oppression impossible. But I would not deal with "atrocious instances" except in the way of illustration, neither demand from men a partial redress in some one matter, but go to the root of the whole. If principles could be established, particulars would adjust themselves aright. Ascertain the true destiny of Woman, give her legitimate hopes, and a standard within herself; marriage and all other relations would by degrees be harmonized with these.

But to return to the historical progress of this matter. Knowing that there exists in the minds of men a tone of feeling towards women as towards slaves, such as is expressed in the common phrase, "Tell that to women and children," that the infinite soul can only work through them in already ascertained limits; that the gift of reason, Man's highest prerogative, is allotted to them in much lower degree; that they must be kept from mischief and melancholy by being constantly engaged in active labor, which is to be furnished and directed by those better able to think, &c. &c,—we need not multiply instances, for who can review the experience of last week without recalling words which imply, whether in jest or earnest, these views or views like these,—knowing this, can we wonder that many reformers think that measures are not likely to be taken in behalf of women, unless their wishes could be publicly represented by women?

"That can never be necessary," cry the other side. "All men are privately influenced by women; each has his wife, sister, or female friends, and is too much biased by these relations to fail of representing their interests, and, if this is not enough, let them propose and enforce their wishes with the pen. The beauty of home would be destroyed, the delicacy of the sex be violated, the dignity of halls of legislation degraded by an attempt to introduce them there. Such duties are inconsistent with those of a mother"; and then we have ludicrous pictures of ladies in hysterics at the polls, and senate chambers filled with cradles.

But if, in reply, we admit as truth that Woman seems destined by nature rather for the inner circle, we must add that the arrangements of civilized life have not been, as yet, such as to secure it to her. Her circle, if the duller, is not the quieter. If kept from "excitement," she is not from drudgery. Not only the Indian squaw carries the burdens of the camp, but the favorites of Louis XIV accompany him in his journeys, and the washerwoman stands at her tub and carries home her work at all seasons, and in all states of health.

Those who think the physical circumstances of Woman would make a part in the affairs of national government unsuitable, are by no means those who think it impossible for the negresses to endure field work, even during pregnancy, or the sempstresses to go through their killing labors.

As to the use of the pen, there was quite as much opposition to Woman's possessing herself of that help to free agency, as there is now to her seizing on the rostrum or the desk;[11] and she is likely to draw, from a permission to plead her cause that way, opposite inferences to what might be wished by those who now grant it.

As to the possibility of her filling with grace and dignity, any such position, we should think those who had seen the great actresses, and heard the Quaker preachers of modern times, would not doubt, that Woman can express publicly the fulness of thought and creation, without losing any of the peculiar beauty of her sex. What can pollute and tarnish is to act thus from any motive except that something needs to be said or done. Woman could take part in the processions, the songs, the dances of old religion; no one fancied their delicacy was impaired by appearing in public for such a cause.

As to her home, she is not likely to leave it more than she now does for balls, theatres, meetings for promoting missions, revival meetings, and others to which she flies, in hope of an animation for her existence, commensurate with what she sees enjoyed by men. Governors of ladies' fairs are no less engrossed by such a change, than the Governor of the state by his; presidents of Washingtonian societies[12] no less away from home than presidents of conventions. If men look straitly to it, they will find that, unless their lives are domestic, those of the women will not be. A house is no home unless it contain food and fire for the mind as well as for the body. The female Greek, of our day, is as much in the street as the male to cry, "What news?" We doubt not it was the same in Athens of old. The women, shut out from the market-place, made up for it at the religious festivals. For human beings are not so constituted that they can live without expansion. If they do not get it one way, they must another, or perish.

As to men's representing women fairly at present, while we hear from men who owe to their wives not only all that is comfortable or graceful, but all that is wise in the arrangement of their lives, the frequent remark, "You cannot reason with a woman,"—when from those of delicacy, nobleness, and poetic culture, falls the contemptuous phrase "women and children," and that in no light sally of the hour, but in works intended to give a permanent statement of the best experiences,—when not one man, in the million, shall I say? no, not in the hundred million, can rise above the belief that Woman was made *for man*,—when such traits as these are daily forced upon the attention, can we feel that Man will always do justice to the interests of Woman? Can we think that he takes a sufficiently discerning and religious

[11]That is, women were actively discouraged from speaking in public, especially to mixed audiences.

[12]Temperance societies named after George Washington, first president of the United States.

view of her office and destiny, *ever* to do her justice, except when prompted by sentiment,—accidentally or transiently, that is, for the sentiment will vary according to the relations in which he is placed. The lover, the poet, the artist, are likely to view her nobly. The father and the philosopher have some chance of liberality; the man of the world, the legislator for expediency, none.

Under these circumstances, without attaching importance, in themselves, to the changes demanded by the champions of Woman, we hail them as signs of the times. We would have every arbitrary barrier thrown down. We would have every path laid open to Woman as freely as to Man. Were this done and a slight temporary fermentation allowed to subside, we should see crystallizations more pure and of more various beauty. We believe the divine energy would pervade nature to a degree unknown in the history of former ages, and that no discordant collision, but a ravishing harmony of the spheres would ensue.

Yet, then and only then, will mankind be ripe for this, when inward and outward freedom for Woman as much as for Man shall be acknowledged as *a right*, not yielded as a concession. As the friend of the negro assumes that one man cannot by right, hold another in bondage, so should the friend of Woman assume that Man cannot, by right, lay even well-meant restrictions on Woman. If the negro be a soul, if the woman be a soul, apparelled in flesh, to one Master only are they accountable. There is but one law for souls, and if there is to be an interpreter of it, he must come not as man, or son of man, but as son of God.

Were thought and feeling once so far elevated that Man should esteem himself the brother and friend, but nowise the lord and tutor of Woman,— were he really bound with her in equal worship,—arrangements as to function and employment would be of no consequence. What Woman needs is not as a woman to act or rule, but as a nature to grow, as an intellect to discern, as a soul to live freely and unimpeded, to unfold such powers as were given her when we left our common home. If fewer talents were given her, yet if allowed the free and full employment of these, so that she may render back to the giver his own with usury, she will not complain; nay, I dare to say she will bless and rejoice in her earthly birth-place, her earthly lot. Let us consider what obstructions impede this good era, and what signs give reason to hope that it draws near.

I was talking on this subject with Miranda, a woman, who, if any in the world could, might speak without heat and bitterness of the position of her sex. Her father was a man who cherished no sentimental reverence for Woman, but a firm belief in the equality of the sexes. She was his eldest child, and came to him at an age when he needed a companion. From the time she could speak and go alone, he addressed her not as a plaything, but as a living mind. Among the few verses he ever wrote was a copy addressed to this child, when the first locks were cut from her head, and the reverence expressed on this occasion for that cherished head, he never belied. It was to him the temple of immortal intellect. He respected his child, however, too much to be an indulgent parent. He called on her for clear judgement, for courage, for honor and fidelity; in short, for such virtues as he knew. In so far as he possessed the keys to the wonders of this universe, he allowed free use of them to her, and by the incentive of a high expectation, he forbade, as far as possible, that she should let the privilege lie idle.

Thus this child was early led to feel herself a child of the spirit. She took her place easily, not only in the world of organized being, but in the world of mind. A dignified sense of self-dependence was given as all her portion, and she found it a sure anchor. Herself securely anchored, her relations with others were established with equal security. She was fortunate in a total absence of those charms which might have drawn to her bewildering flatteries, and in a strong electric nature, which repelled those who did not belong to her, and attracted those who did. With men and women her relations were noble,—affectionate without passion, intellectual without coldness. The world was free to her, and she lived freely in it. Outward adversity came, and inward conflict, but that faith and self-respect had early been awakened which must always lead at last, to an outward serenity and an inward peace.

Of Miranda I had always thought as an example, that the restraints upon the sex were insuperable only to those who think them so, or who noisily strive to break them. She had taken a course of her own, and no man stood in her way. Many of her acts had been unusual, but excited no uproar. Few helped, but none checked her; and the many men, who knew her mind and her life, showed to her confidence, as to a brother, gentleness as to a sister. And not only refined, but very coarse men approved and aided one in whom they saw resolution and clearness of design. Her mind was often the leading one, always effective.

When I talked with her upon these matters, and had said very much what I have written, she smilingly replied: "And yet we must admit that I have been fortunate, and this should not be. My good father's early trust gave the first bias, and the rest followed of course. It is true that I have had less outward aid, in after years, than most women; but that is of little consequence. Religion was early awakened in my soul,—a sense that what the soul is capable to ask it must attain, and that, though I might be aided and instructed by others, I must depend on myself as the only constant friend. This self-dependence, which was honored in me, is deprecated as a fault in most women. They are taught to learn their rule from without, not to unfold it from within.

"This is the fault to Man, who is still vain, and wishes to be more important to Woman than, by right, he should be."

"Men have not shown this disposition toward you," I said.

"No! because the position I early was enabled to take was one of self-reliance. And were all women as sure of their wants as I was, the result would be the same. But they are so overloaded with precepts by guardians, who think that nothing is so much to be dreaded for a woman as originality of thought or character, that their minds are impeded by doubts till they lose their chance of fair, free proportions. The difficulty is to get them to the point from which they shall naturally develope selfrespect, and learn self-help.

"Once I thought that men would help to forward this state of things more than I do now. I saw so many of them wretched in the connections they had formed in weakness and vanity. They seemed so glad to esteem women whenever they could.

"'The soft arms of affection' said one of the most discerning spirits, 'will not suffice for me, unless on them I see the steel bracelets of strength.'

"But early I perceived that men never, in any extreme of despair, wished to be women. On the contrary they were ever ready to taunt one another, at any sign of weakness, with,

"*'Art thou not like the women, who'*—

The passage ends various ways, according to the occasion and rhetoric of the speaker. When they admired any woman they were inclined to speak of her as 'above her sex.' Silently I observed this, and feared it argued a rooted scepticism, which for ages had been fastening on the heart, and which only an age of miracles could eradicate. Ever I have been treated with great sincerity; and I look upon it as a signal instance of this, that an intimate friend of the other sex said, in a fervent moment, that I 'deserved in some star to be a man.' He was much surprised when I disclosed my view of my position and hopes, when I declared my faith that the feminine side, the side of love, of beauty, of holiness, was now to have its full chance, and that, if either were better, it was better now to be a woman, for even the slightest achievement of good was furthering an especial work of our time. He smiled incredulously. 'She makes the best she can of it,' thought he. 'Let Jews believe the pride of Jewry, but I am of the better sort, and know better.'

"Another used as highest praise, in speaking of a character in literature, the words 'a manly woman.'

"So in the noble passage of Ben Jonson:

'I meant the day-star should not brighter ride,
  Nor shed like influence from its lucent seat;
I meant she should be courteous, facile, sweet,
  Free from that solemn vice of greatness, pride;
I meant each softest virtue there should meet,
  Fit in that softer bosom to abide,
Only a learned and a manly *soul*
  I purposed her, that should with even powers
The rock, the spindle, and the shears control
  Of destiny, and spin her own free hours.'"

"Methinks," said I, "you are too fastidious in objecting to this. Jonson, in using the word 'manly,' only meant to heighten the picture of this, the true, the intelligent fate, with one of the deeper colors."

"And yet," said she, "so invariable is the use of this word where a heroic quality is to be described, and I feel so sure that persistence and courage are the most womanly no less than the most manly qualities, that I would exchange these words for others of a larger sense at the risk of marring the fine tissue of the verse. Read, 'A heavenward and instructed soul,' and I should be satisfied. Let it not be said, wherever there is energy or creative genius, 'She has a masculine mind.'"

This by no means argues a willing want of generosity toward Woman. Man is as generous towards her as he knows how to be.

Wherever she has herself arisen in national or private history, and nobly shone forth in any form of excellence, men have received her, not only willingly, but with triumph. Their encomiums, indeed, are always, in some sense, mortifying; they show too much surprise. "Can this be you?" he cries to the transfigured Cinderella; "well, I should never have thought it, but I am very glad. We will tell every one that you have *surpassed your sex*.'"

In every-day life, the feelings of the many are stained with vanity. Each wishes to be lord in a little world, to be superior at least over one; and he does not feel strong enough to retain a life-long ascendency over a strong nature. Only a Theseus could conquer before he wed the Amazonian queen.[13] Hercules wished rather to rest with Dejanira, and received the poisoned robe as a fit guerdon. The tale should be interpreted to all those who seek repose with the weak.[14]

But not only is Man vain and fond of power, but the same want of development, which thus affects him morally, prevents his intellectually discerning the destiny of Woman. The boy wants no woman, but only a girl to play ball with him, and mark his pocket handkerchief.

Thus, in Schiller's Dignity of Woman,[15] beautiful as the poem is, there is no "grave and perfect man," but only a great boy to be softened and restrained by the influence of girls. Poets—the elder brothers of their race—have usually seen further; but what can you expect of every-day men, if Schiller was not more prophetic as to what women must be? Even with Richter,[16] one foremost thought about a wife was that she would "cook him something good." But as this is a delicate subject, and we are in constant danger of being accused of slighting what are called "the functions," let me say, in behalf of Miranda and myself, that we have high respect for those who "cook something good," who create and preserve fair order in houses, and prepare therein the shining raiment for worthy inmates, worthy guests.

[13]Theseus was a Greek hero; the Amazonian queen Hippolyte or Orethyia. Fuller seems to mean that it takes a man as strong as Theseus to wed a woman as strong as the Amazonian queen.

[14]The weak Dejanira, trying to win back the love of the wandering Greek demigod Hercules, gave him as a gift a shirt she had obtained from Nessus. She had been led to believe that the shirt was steeped in a love potion; instead, it contained a caustic poison which devoured Hercules' flesh.

[15]A poem by the German writer Friedrich von Schiller (1759–1805). It praises women for docility by way of contrast with "masculine" aspiration and passion.

[16]The German fiction writer Jean Paul Richter (1763–1825) generally drew sympathetic portraits of women, but in some of his work he puts forward many of the patriarchal assumptions about woman's "place."

Only these "functions" must not be a drudgery, or enforced necessity, but a part of life. Let Ulysses drive the beeves home, while Penelope there piles up the fragrant loaves; they are both well employed if these be done in thought and love, willingly. But Penelope is no more meant for a baker or weaver solely, than Ulysses for a cattle-herd.[17]

The sexes should not only correspond to and appreciate, but prophesy to one another. In individual instances this happens. Two persons love in one another the future good which they aid one another to unfold. This is imperfectly or rarely done in the general life. Man has gone but little way; now he is waiting to see whether Woman can keep step with him; but, instead of calling out, like a good brother, "You can do it, if you only think so," or impersonally, "Any one can do what he tries to do"; he often discourages with school-boy brag: "Girls can't do that; girls can't play ball." But let any one defy their taunts, break through and be brave and secure, they rend the air with shouts. . . .

A little while since, I was at one of the most fashionable places of public resort. I saw there many women, dressed without regard to the season or the demands of the place, in apery, or, as it looked, in mockery, of European fashions. I saw their eyes restlessly courting attention. I saw the way in which it was paid: the style of devotion, almost an open sneer, which it pleased those ladies to receive from men whose expression marked their own low position in the moral and intellectual world. Those women went to their pillows with their heads full of folly, their hearts of jealousy, or gratified vanity; those men, with the low opinion they already entertained of Woman confirmed. These were American *ladies;* that is, they were of that class who have wealth and leisure to make full use of the day, and confer benefits on others. They were of that class whom the possession of external advantages makes of pernicious example to many, if these advantages be misused.

Soon after, I met a circle of women, stamped by society as among the most degraded of their sex. "How," it was asked of them, "did you come here?" for, by the society that I saw in the former place, they were shut up in a prison. The causes were not difficult to trace: love of dress, love of flattery, love of excitement. They had not dresses like the other ladies, so they stole them; they could not pay for flattery by distinctions, and the dower of a worldly marriage, so they paid by the profanation of their persons. In excitement, more and more madly sought from day to day, they drowned the voice of conscience.

Now I ask you, my sisters, if the women at the fashionable house be not answerable for those women being in the prison?

As to position in the world of souls, we may suppose the women of the prison stood fairest, both because they had misused less light, and because

[17]Ulysses is the hero of Homer's epic, *The Od-yssey,* and Penelope is the faithful wife who awaits his return.

loneliness and sorrow had brought some of them to feel the need of better life, nearer truth and good. This was no merit in them, being an effect of circumstance, but it was hopeful. But you, my friends, (and some of you I have already met), consecrate yourselves without waiting for reproof, in free love and unbroken energy, to win and to diffuse a better life. Offer beauty, talents, riches, on the altar; thus shall ye keep spotless your own hearts, and be visibly or invisibly the angels to others.

I would urge upon those women who have not yet considered this subject, to do so. Do not forget the unfortunates who dare not cross your guarded way. If it do not suit you to act with those who have organized measures of reform, then hold not yourself excused from acting in private. Seek out these degraded women, give them tender sympathy, counsel, employment. Take the place of mothers, such as might have saved them originally.

If you can do little for those already under the ban of the world,—and the best considered efforts have often failed, from a want of strength in those unhappy ones to bear up against the sting of shame and the prejudices of the world, which makes them seek oblivion again in their old excitements,—you will at least leave a sense of love and justice in their hearts, that will prevent their becoming utterly embittered and corrupt. And you may learn the means of prevention for those yet uninjured. There will be found in a diffusion of mental culture, simple tastes, best taught by your example, a genuine self-respect, and above all, what the influence of Man tends to hide from Woman, the love and fear of a divine, in preference to a human tribunal.

But suppose you save many who would have lost their bodily innocence (for as to mental, the loss of that is incalculably more general,) through mere vanity and folly; there still remain many, the prey and spoil of the brute passions of Man; for the stories frequent in our newspapers outshame antiquity, and vie with the horrors of war.

As to this, it must be considered that, as the vanity and proneness to seduction of the imprisoned women represented a general degradation in their sex; so do these acts a still more general and worse in the male. Where so many are weak it is natural there should be many lost, where legislators admit that ten thousand prostitutes are a fair proportion to one city, and husbands tell their wives that it is folly to expect chastity from men, it is inevitable that there should be many monsters of vice. . . .

There are two aspects of Woman's nature, represented by the ancients as Muse and Minerva.[18] It is the former to which the writer in the Pathfinder looks.[19] It is the latter which Wordsworth has in mind, when he says,

> *"With a placid brow,*
> *Which woman ne'er should forfeit, keep thy vow."*[20]

---

[18]The Muses were goddesses of the arts, poetry, song, and the sciences; Fuller uses them to represent woman's artistic nature. Minerva, Roman goddess of wisdom and handicrafts, sometimes portrayed in armor, here represents intellectual strength.

[19]A New York newspaper writer had published two articles under the title "Femality."

[20]Slightly altered from *Liberty: Sequel to the Preceding* (1835) by the English poet William Wordsworth.

The especial genius of Woman I believe to be electrical in movement, intuitive in function, spiritual in tendency. She excels not so easily in classification, or recreation, as in an instinctive seizure of causes, and a simple breathing out of what she receives, that has the singleness of life, rather than the selecting and energizing of art.

More native is it to her to be the living model of the artist than to set apart from herself any one form in objective reality; more native to inspire and receive the poem, than to create it. In so far as soul is in her completely developed, all soul is the same; but in so far as it is modified in her as Woman, it flows, it breathes, it sings, rather than deposits soil, or finishes work; and that which is especially feminine flushes, in blossom, the face of earth, and pervades, like air and water, all this seeming solid globe, daily renewing and purifying its life. Such may be the especially feminine element spoken of as Femality. But it is no more the order of nature that it should be incarnated pure in any form, than that the masculine energy should exist unmingled with it in any form.

Male and female represent the two sides of the great radical dualism. But, in fact, they are perpetually passing into one another. Fluid hardens to solid, solid rushes to fluid. There is no wholly masculine man, no purely feminine woman.

History jeers at the attempts of physiologists to bind great original laws by the forms which flow from them. They make a rule; they say from observation what can and cannot be. In vain! Nature provides exceptions to every rule. She sends women to battle, and sets Hercules spinning; she enables women to bear immense burdens, cold, and frost; she enables the man, who feels maternal love, to nourish his infant like a mother. Of late she plays still gayer pranks. Not only she deprives organizations, but organs, of a necessary end. She enables people to read with the top of the head, and see with the pit of the stomach. Presently she will make a female Newton, and a male Syren.[21]

Man partakes of the feminine in the Apollo, Woman of the masculine as Minerva.

What I mean by the Muse is that unimpeded clearness of the intuitive powers, which a perfectly truthful adherence to every admonition of the higher instincts would bring to a finely organized human being. It may appear as prophecy or as poesy. It enabled Cassandra[22] to foresee the results of actions passing round her; the Seeress to behold the true character of the person through the mask of his customary life. (Sometimes she saw a feminine form behind the man, sometimes the reverse.) It enabled the daughter of Linnaeus to see the soul of the flower exhaling from the flower.[23] It gave

[21]Isaac Newton (1642–1727), the British mathematician. In Greek mythology, the Sirens were sea nymphs who lured mariners into shipwreck.

[22]Daughter of Priam, King of Troy, she was gifted with the power of prophecy, but also fated not to be believed by those around her.

[23]The daughter of Linnaeus states, that, while looking steadfastly at the red lily, she saw its spirit hovering above it, as a red flame. It is true, this, like many fair spirit-stories, may be explained away as an optical illusion, but its poetic beauty and meaning would, even then, make it valuable, as an illustration of the spiritual fact. [Fuller's note.] Karl Linnaeus, Swedish botanist (1707–1778) developed a system for classifying plants.

a man, but a poet-man, the power of which he thus speaks: "Often in my contemplation of nature, radiant intimations, and as it were sheaves of light, appear before me as to the facts of cosmogony, in which my mind has, perhaps, taken especial part." He wisely adds, "but it is necessary with earnestness to verify the knowledge we gain by these flashes of light." And none should forget this. Sight must be verified by light before it can deserve the honors of piety and genius. Yet sight comes first, and of this sight of the world of causes, this approximation to the region of primitive motions, women I hold to be especially capable. Even without equal freedom with the other sex, they have already shown themselves so; and should these faculties have free play, I believe they will open new, deeper and purer sources of joyous inspiration than have as yet refreshed the earth.

Let us be wise, and not impede the soul. Let her work as she will. Let us have one creative energy, one incessant revelation. Let it take what form it will, and let us not bind it by the past to man or woman, black or white. Jove sprang from Rhea, Pallas from Jove.[24] So let it be.

If it has been the tendency of these remarks to call Woman rather to the Minerva side,—if I, unlike the more generous writer, have spoken from society no less than the soul,—let it be pardoned! It is love that has caused this,—love for many incarcerated souls, that might be freed, could the idea of religious selfdependence be established in them, could the weakening habit of dependence on others be broken up.

Proclus[25] teaches that every life has, in its sphere, a totality or wholeness of the animating powers of the other spheres; having only, as its own characteristic, a predominance of some one power. Thus Jupiter comprises, within himself, the other twelve powers, which stand thus: The first triad is *demiurgic or fabricative*, that is, Jupiter, Neptune, Vulcan; the second, *defensive*, Vesta, Minerva, Mars; the third, *vivific*, Ceres, Juno, Diana; and the fourth, Mercury, Venus, Apollo, *elevating and harmonic*. In the sphere of Jupiter, energy is predominant—with Venus, beauty; but each comprehends and apprehends all the others.[26]

When the same community of life and consciousness of mind begin among men, humanity will have, positively and finally, subjugated its brute elements and Titanic childhood; criticism will have perished; arbitrary limits and ignorant censure be impossible; all will have entered upon the liberty of law, and the harmony of common growth.

Then Apollo will sing to his lyre what Vulcan forges on the anvil, and the Muse weave anew the tapestries of Minerva.

It is, therefore, only in the present crisis that the preference is given to Minerva. The power of continence must establish the legitimacy of freedom, the power of self-poise the perfection of motion.

---

[24]The chief Roman god, Jove or Jupiter, was born of Rhea. Pallas Athene sprang, fully armored, from his head.

[25]Greek philosopher (c. 410–485 B.C.).

[26]Fuller interprets Jupiter, the chief among Roman gods, as incorporating the qualities of all the other major Roman gods.

Every relation, every gradation of nature is incalculably precious, but only to the soul which is poised upon itself, and to whom no loss, no change, can bring dull discord, for it is in harmony with the central soul.

If any individual live too much in relations, so that he becomes a stranger to the resources of his own nature, he falls, after a while, into a distraction, or imbecility, from which he can only be cured by a time of isolation, which gives the renovating fountains time to rise up. With a society it is the same. Many minds, deprived of the traditionary or instinctive means of passing a cheerful existence, must find help in self-impulse, or perish. It is therefore that, while any elevation, in the view of union, is to be hailed with joy, we shall not decline celibacy as the great fact of the time. It is one from which no vow, no arrangement, can at present save a thinking mind. For now the rowers are pausing on their oars; they wait a change before they can pull together. All tends to illustrate the thought of a wise contemporary. Union is only possible to those who are units. To be fit for relations in time, souls, whether of Man or Woman, must be able to do without them in the spirit.

It is therefore that I would have Woman lay aside all thought, such as she habitually cherishes, of being taught and led by men. I would have her, like the Indian girl, dedicate herself to the Sun, the Sun of Truth, and go nowhere if his beams did not make clear the path. I would have her free from compromise, from complaisance, from helplessness, because I would have her good enough and strong enough to love one and all beings, from the fulness, not the poverty of being.

Men, as at present instructed, will not help this work, because they also are under the slavery of habit. I have seen with delight their poetic impulses. A sister is the fairest ideal, and how nobly Wordsworth, and even Byron, have written of a sister![27]

There is no sweeter sight than to see a father with his little daughter. Very vulgar men become refined to the eye when leading a little girl by the hand. At that moment, the right relation between the sexes seems established, and you feel as if the man would aid in the noblest purpose, if you ask him in behalf of his little daughter. Once, two fine figures stood before me, thus. The father of very intellectual aspect, his falcon eye softened by affection as he looked down on his fair child; she the image of himself, only more graceful and brilliant in expression. I was reminded of Southey's Kehama;[28] when, lo, the dream was rudely broken! They were talking of education, and he said,

"I shall not have Maria brought too forward. If she knows too much, she will never find a husband; superior women hardly ever can."

"Surely," said his wife, with a blush, "you wish Maria to be as good and wise as she can, whether it will help her to marriage or not."

[27]William Wordsworth paid poetic tribute to his sister Dorothy; Byron to Augusta Leigh, his half-sister.

[28]A narrative poem, *The Curse of Kehama* (1810) by British poet Robert Southey (1774–1843).

"No," he persisted, "I want her to have a sphere and a home, and some one to protect her when I am gone."

It was a trifling incident, but made a deep impression. I felt that the holiest relations fail to instruct the unprepared and perverted mind. If this man, indeed, could have looked at it on the other side, he was the last that would have been willing to have been taken himself for the home and protection he could give, but would have been much more likely to repeat the tale of Alcibiades with his phials.

But men do *not* look at both sides, and women must leave off asking them and being influenced by them, but retire within themselves, and explore the groundwork of life till they find their peculiar secret. Then, when they come forth again, renovated and baptized, they will know how to turn all dross to gold, and will be rich and free though they live in a hut, tranquil if in a crowd. Then their sweet singing shall not be from passionate impulse, but the lyrical overflow of a divine rapture, and a new music shall be evolved from this many-chorded world.

Grant her, then, for a while, the armor and the javelin.[29] Let her put from her the press of other minds, and meditate in virgin loneliness. The same idea shall reäppear in due time as Muse, or Ceres,[30] the all-kindly, patient Earth-Spirit. . . .

And now I have designated in outline, if not in fulness, the stream which is ever flowing from the heights of my thought.

In the earlier tract, I was told, I did not make my meaning sufficiently clear. In this I have consequently tried to illustrate it in various ways, and may have been guilty of much repetition. Yet, as I am anxious to leave no room for doubt, I shall venture to retrace, once more, the scope of my design in points, as was done in old-fashioned sermons.

Man is a being of two-fold relations, to nature beneath, and intelligences above him. The earth is his school, if not his birth-place; God his object; life and thought his means of interpreting nature, and aspiring to God.

Only a fraction of this purpose is accomplished in the life of any one man. Its entire accomplishment is to be hoped only from the sum of the lives of men, or Man considered as a whole.

As this whole has one soul and one body, any injury or obstruction to a part, or to the meanest member, affects the whole. Man can never be perfectly happy or virtuous, till all men are so.

To address Man wisely, you must not forget that his life is partly animal, subject to the same laws with Nature.

But you cannot address him wisely unless you consider him still more as soul and appreciate the conditions and destiny of soul.

The growth of Man is two-fold, masculine and feminine.

As far as these two methods can be distinguished they are so as
Energy and Harmony;

---

[29]The defense and weapon of Pallas Athene, the Greek goddess of wisdom.   [30]Roman goddess of agriculture, grain, and harvest.

Power and Beauty;

Intellect and Love;

or by some such rude classification; for we have not language primitive and pure enough to express such ideas with precision.

These two sides are supposed to be expressed in Man and Woman, that is, as the more and less, for the faculties have not been given pure to either, but only in preponderance. There are also exceptions in great number, such as men of far more beauty than power, and the reverse. But as a general rule, it seems to have been the intention to give a preponderance on the one side, that is called masculine, and on the other, one that is called feminine.

There cannot be a doubt that, if these two developments were in perfect harmony, they would correspond to and fulfil one another, like hemispheres, or the tenor and bass in music.

But there is no perfect harmony in human nature; and the two parts answer one another only now and then; or, if there be a persistent consonance, it can only be traced, at long intervals, instead of discoursing an obvious melody.

What is the cause of this?

Man, in the order of time, was developed first; as energy comes before harmony; power before beauty.

Woman was therefore under his care as an elder. He might have been her guardian and teacher.

But as human nature goes not straight forward, but by excessive action and then reaction in an undulated course, he misunderstood and abused his advantages, and became her temporal master instead of her spiritual sire.

On himself came the punishment. He educated Woman more as a servant than a daughter, and found himself a king without a queen.

The children of this unequal union showed unequal natures, and, more and more, men seemed sons of the hand-maid, rather than princess.

At last there were so many Ishmaelites that the rest grew frightened and indignant. They laid the blame on Hagar, and drove her forth into the wilderness.[31]

But there were none the fewer Ishmaelites for that.

At last men became a little wiser, and saw that the infant Moses was, in every case, saved by the pure instincts of Woman's breast.[32] For, as too much adversity is better for the moral nature than too much prosperity, Woman, in this respect, dwindled less than Man, though in other respects, still a child in leading strings.

So Man did her more and more justice, and grew more and more kind.

But yet, his habits and his will corrupted by the past—he did not clearly see that Woman was half himself, that her interests were identical with his,

---

[31]In Genesis, Hagar was Abraham's concubine, who bore him a son, Ishmael, when his wife, Sarah, proved barren. But after the birth of Sarah's son Isaac, the now-haughty Hagar was banished from Abraham's tents.

[32]A reference to the biblical story in which Pharaoh's daughter saves Moses.

and that, by the law of their common being, he could never reach his true proportions while she remained in any wise shorn of hers.

And so it has gone on to our day; both ideas developing, but more slowly than they would under a clearer recognition of truth and justice, which would have permitted the sexes their due influence on one another, and mutual improvement from more dignified relations.

Wherever there was pure love, the natural influences were, for the time, restored.

Wherever the poet or artist gave free course to his genius, he saw the truth, and expressed it in worthy forms, for these men especially share and need the feminine principle. The divine birds need to be brooded into life and song by mothers.

Wherever religion (I mean the thirst for truth and good, not the love of sect and dogma) had its course, the original design was apprehended in its simplicity, and the dove presaged sweetly from Dodona's oak.[33]

I have aimed to show that no age was left entirely without a witness of the equality of the sexes in function, duty and hope.

Also, that when there was unwillingness or ignorance, which prevented this being acted upon, women had not the less power for their want of light and noble freedom. But it was power which hurt alike them and those against whom they made use of the arms of the servile,—cunning, blandishment, and unreasonable emotion.

That now the time has come when a clearer vision and better action are possible—when Man and Woman may regard one another as brother and sister, the pillars of one porch, the priests of one worship.

I have believed and intimated that this hope would receive an ampler frution, than ever before, in our own land.

And it will do so if this land carry out the principles from which sprang our national life.

I believe that, at present, women are the best helpers of one another.

Let them think; let them act; till they know what they need.

We only ask of men to remove arbitrary barriers. Some would like to do more. But I believe it needs for Woman to show herself in her native dignity, to teach them how to aid her; their minds are so encumbered by tradition.

When Lord Edward Fitzgerald[34] travelled with the Indians, his manly heart obliged him at once to take the packs from the squaws and carry them. But we do not read that the red men followed his example, though they are ready enough to carry the pack of the white woman, because she seems to them a superior being.

Let Woman appear in the mild majesty of Ceres, and rudest churls will be willing to learn from her.

---

[33]The oak grove in Dodona, in ancient Greece, housed an oracle dedicated to Zeus.

[34]Lord Edward Fitzgerald (1763–1798), Irish politician who traveled down the Mississippi River.

You ask, what use will she make of liberty, when she has so long been sustained and restrained?

I answer; in the first place, this will not be suddenly given. I read yesterday a debate of this year on the subject of enlarging women's rights over property. It was a leaf from the class-book that is preparing for the needed instruction. The men learned visibly as they spoke. The champions of Woman saw the fallacy of arguments on the opposite side, and were startled by their own convictions. With their wives at home, and the readers of the paper, it was the same. And so the stream flows on; thought urging action, and action leading to the evolution of still better thought.

But, were this freedom to come suddenly, I have no fear of the consequences. Individuals might commit excesses, but there is not only in the sex a reverence for decorums and limits inherited and enhanced from generation to generation, which many years of other life could not efface, but a native love, in Woman as Woman, of proportion, of "the simple art of not too much,"—a Greek moderation, which would create immediately a restraining party, the natural legislators and instructors of the rest, and would gradually establish such rules as are needed to guard, without impeding, life.

The Graces would lead the choral dance, and teach the rest to regulate their steps to the measure of beauty.

But if you ask me what offices they may fill, I reply—any. I do not care what case you put; let them be sea-captains, if you will. I do not doubt there are women well fitted for such an office, and, if so, I should be glad to see them in it, as to welcome the maid of Saragossa, or the maid of Missolonghi, or the Suliote heroine, or Emily Plater.[35]

I think women need, especially at this juncture, a much greater range of occupation than they have, to rouse their latent powers. A party of travellers lately visited a lonely hut on a mountain. There they found an old woman that told them she and her husband had lived there forty years. "Why," they said, "did you choose so barren a spot?" She "did not know; *it was the man's notion.*"

And, during forty years, she had been content to act, without knowing why, upon "the man's notion." I would not have it so.

In families that I know, some little girls like to saw wood, others to use carpenters' tools. Where these tastes are indulged, cheerfulness and good humor are promoted. Where they are forbidden, because "such things are not proper for girls," they grow sullen and mischievous.

---

[35]Sargossa, a city in northern Spain and capital of the kingdom of Aragon. Missolonghi, a town in Greece at which the British poet Lord Byron died (1824) during the struggle for Greek independence from Turkey. Suliotes, people of Greece who were defeated by the Turks in 1822 but who nevertheless played an important role in the Greek war of liberation. Countess Emily Plater was involved in the Polish war for independence.

Fourier[36] had observed these wants of women, as no one can fail to do who watches the desires of little girls, or knows the ennui that haunts grown women, except where they make to themselves a serene little world by art of some kind. He, therefore, in proposing a great variety of employments, in manufactures or the care of plants and animals, allows for one third of women as likely to have a taste for masculine pursuits, one third of men for feminine.

Who does not observe the immediate glow and serenity that is diffused over the life of women, before restless or fretful, by engaging in gardening, building, or the lowest department of art. Here is something that is not routine, something that draws forth life toward the infinite.

I have no doubt, however, that a large proportion of women would give themselves to the same employments as now, because there are circumstances that must lead them. Mothers will delight to make the nest soft and warm. Nature would take care of that; no need to clip the wings of any bird that wants to soar and sing, or finds in itself the strength of pinion for a migratory flight unusual to its kind. The difference would be that *all* need not be constrained to employments for which *some* are unfit.

I have urged upon the sex self-subsistence in its two forms of self-reliance and self-impulse, because I believe them to be the needed means of the present juncture.

I have urged on Woman independence of Man, not that I do not think the sexes mutually needed by one another, but because in Woman this fact has led to an excessive devotion, which has cooled love, degraded marriage, and prevented either sex from being what it should be to itself or the other.

I wish Woman to live, *first* for God's sake. Then she will not make an imperfect man her god, and thus sink to idolatry. Then she will not take what is not fit for her from a sense of weakness and poverty. Then, if she finds what she needs in Man embodied, she will know how to love, and be worthy of being loved.

By being more a soul, she will not be less Woman, for nature is perfected through spirit.

Now there is no woman, only an overgrown child.

That her hand may be given with dignity, she must be able to stand alone. I wish to see men and women capable of such relations as are depicted by Landor[37] in his Pericles and Aspasia, where grace is the natural garb of strength, and the affections are calm, because deep. The softness is that of a firm tissue, as when

> *"The gods approve*
> *The depth, but not the tumult of the soul,*
> *A fervent, not ungovernable love."*

[36]Charles Fourier (1772–1837), a French socialist on whose model a number of utopian communities were set up in the United States and who influenced George Ripley, a major force in establishing the Brook Farm community at West Roxbury, Massachusetts.

[37]Walter Savage Landor (1775–1864), British author.

A profound thinker has said, "no married woman can represent the female world, for she belongs to her husband. The idea of Woman must be represented by a virgin."

But that is the very fault of marriage, and of the present relation between the sexes; that the woman *does* belong to the man, instead of forming a whole with him. Were it otherwise, there would be no such limitation to the thought.

Woman, self-centered, would never be absorbed by any relation; it would be only an experience to her as to man. It is a vulgar error that love, *a* love, to Woman is her whole existence; she also is born for Truth and Love in their universal energy. Would she but assume her inheritance, Mary would not be the only virgin mother. Not Manzoni alone would celebrate in his wife the virgin mind with the maternal wisdom and conjugal affections.[38] The soul is ever young, ever virgin.

And will not she soon appear?—the woman who shall vindicate their birthright for all women; who shall teach them what to claim, and how to use what they obtain? Shall not her name be for her era Victoria, for her country and life Virginia? Yet predictions are rash; she herself must teach us to give her the fitting name.

An idea not unknown to ancient times has of late been revived, that, in the metamorphoses of life, the soul assumes the form, first of Man, then of Woman, and takes the chances, and reaps the benefits of either lot. Why then, say some, lay such emphasis on the rights or needs of Woman? What she wins not as Woman, will come to her as Man.

That makes no difference. It is not Woman, but the law of right, the law of growth, that speaks in us, and demands the perfection of each being in its kind,—apple as apple, Woman as Woman. Without adopting your theory I know that I, a daughter, live through the life of Man; but what concerns me now is, that my life be a beautiful, powerful, in a word, a complete life in its kind. Had I but one more moment to live, I must wish the same.

Suppose, at the end of your cycle, your great world-year, all will be completed, whether I exert myself or not (and the supposition is *false.*— but suppose it true), am I to be indifferent about it? Not so! I must beat my own pulse true in the heart of the world; for *that* is virtue, excellence, health.

Thou, Lord of Day! didst leave us to-night so calmly glorious, not dismayed that cold winter is coming, not postponing thy beneficence to the fruitful summer! Thou didst smile on thy day's work when it was done, and adorn thy down-going as thy up-rising, for thou art loyal, and it is thy nature to give life, if thou canst, and shine at all events!

I stand in the sunny noon of life. Objects no longer glitter in the dews of morning, neither are yet softened by the shadows of evening. Every spot

---

[38]In the "Preface" to *Adelchi* (1822) a tragedy by Italian writer Alessandro Manzoni (1785–1873).

is seen, every chasm revealed. Climbing the dusty hill, some fair effigies that once stood for symbols of human destiny have been broken; those I still have with me, show defects in this broad light. Yet enough is left, even by experience, to point distinctly to the glories of that destiny; faint, but not to be mistaken streaks of the future day. I can say with the bard,

"Though many have suffered shipwreck, still beat noble hearts."[39]

Always the soul says to us all, Cherish your best hopes as a faith, and abide by them in action. Such shall be the effectual fervent means to their fulfilment;

> *For the Power to whom we bow*
> *Has given its pledge that, if not now,*
> *They of pure and stedfast mind,*
> *By faith exalted, truth refined,*
> *Shall hear all music loud and clear,*
> *Whose first notes they ventured here.*
> *Then fear not thou to wind the horn,*
> *Though elf and gnome thy courage scorn;*
> *Ask for the Castle's King and Queen;*
> *Though rabble rout may rush between,*
> *Beat thee senseless to the ground,*
> *In the dark beset thee round;*
> *Persist to ask and it will come,*
> *Seek not for rest in humbler home;*
> *So shalt thou see what few have seen,*
> *The palace home of King and Queen.*

1844

from **Things and Thoughts in Europe**

Foreign Correspondence of the Tribune

Dispatch 17

ROME, October 18, 1847[1]

In the Spring, when I came to Rome, the people were in the intoxication of joy at the first serious measures of reform taken by the Pope.[2] I saw with pleasure their childlike joy and trust: I saw with pleasure the Pope, who has not in his expression the signs of intellectual greatness so much as of

---

[39]From "Laodamia" by the British poet William Wordsworth (1770–1850).

[1]First published as "Things and Thoughts in Europe. No. XVII" in *New-York Daily Tribune*, November 27, 1847, p. 1:1–3.

[2]Fuller's initial enthusiasm for the role of the liberal Pope Pius IX in supporting reforms and the efforts to unite Italy were later reversed in response to his irresolution, his flight when a Roman Republic was declared, and his backing of a French invasion to restore him to the papal throne.

nobleness and tenderness of heart, of large and liberal sympathies. Heart had spoken to heart between the Prince and the People; it was beautiful to see the immediate good influence of human feeling, generous designs, on the part of a ruler: he had wished to be a father, and the Italians, with that readiness of genius that characterizes them, entered at once into the relation; they, the Roman people, stigmatized by prejudice as so crafty and ferocious, showed themselves children, eager to learn, quick to obey, happy to confide.

Still, doubts were always present whether all this joy was not premature. The task undertaken by the Pope seemed to present insuperable difficulties. It is never easy to put new wine into old bottles, and our age is one where all things tend to a great crisis, not merely to revolution but to radical reform. From the people themselves the help must come, and not from princes: in the new state of things there will be none but natural princes, great men. From the aspirations of the general heart, from the teachings of conscience in individuals, and not from an old ivy-covered church, long since undermined, corroded by Time and gnawed by vermin, the help must come. Rome, to resume her glory, must cease to be an ecclesiastical Capital; must renounce all this gorgeous mummery, whose poetry, whose picture charms no one more than myself, but whose meaning is all of the Past and finds no echo in the Future. Although I sympathized warmly with the warm love of the people, the adulation of leading writers, who were so willing to take all from the hand of the prince, of the Church, as a gift and a bounty instead of implying steadily that it was the right of the people, was very repulsive to me. The Moderate party, like all who, in a transition state, manage affairs with a constant eye to prudence, lacks dignity always in its expositions; it is disagreeable and depressing to read them.

Passing into Tuscany, I found the Liberty of the Press just established, and a superior preparation to make use of it. The '*Alba,*' the '*Patria,*' were begun, and have been continued with equal judgment and spirit. Their aim is to educate the youth, to educate the lower people; they see that this is to be done by promoting Thought fearlessly, yet urge temperance in action, while the time is yet so difficult, and many of its signs dubious. They aim at breaking down those barriers between the different States of Italy, relics of a barbarous state of polity, artificially kept up by the craft of her foes.[3] While anxious not to break down what is really native to the Italian character, defences and differences that give individual genius a chance to grow

[3]Fuller arrived in Italy during a period called the *Risorgimento*, or national revival. It expressed a generally nationalist and republican spirit, perhaps best articulated in the writings and speeches of Giuseppe Mazzini, who had been struggling in exile for some fifteen years to develop the movement for change. In political terms, the movement underway by 1847 sought to free Italy from foreign domination— especially that of the Austrian empire—to unify the many little separate and sometimes hostile Italian states, and to develop at least a constitutional, if not a republican, form of government. After a number of initial successes, which were linked to the revolutionary movements taking place all over Europe in 1848, the Italian cause was temporarily defeated, primarily through French intervention in 1849. It would take another decade for the goal of Italian unification to be accomplished under the leadership of Garibaldi and Cavour.

and the fruits of each region to ripen in their natural way, they aim at a harmony of spirit as to measures of education and for the affairs of business, without which Italy can never, as one nation, present a front strong enough to resist foreign robbery, and for want of which so much time and talent are wasted here, and internal development almost wholly checked.

There is in Tuscany a large corps of enlightened minds, well prepared to be the instructors, the elder brothers and guardians of the lower people, and whose hearts burn to fulfil that noble office. Hitherto it had been almost impossible to them, for the reasons I have named in speaking of Lombardy; but, during these last four months that the way has been opened by the Freedom of the Press and establishment of the National Guard—so valuable, first of all, as giving occasion for public meetings and free interchange of thought between the different classes, it is surprising how much light they have been able to diffuse already.

A Bolognese, to whom I observed, "How can you be so full of trust when all your hopes depend, not on the recognition of principles and wants throughout the people, but on the life of one mortal man?" replied, "Ah! but you don't consider that his life gives us a chance to effect that recognition. If Pius IX. be spared to us five years, it will be impossible for his successors ever to take a backward course. Our people is of a genius so vivacious; we are unhappy but not stupid, we Italians; we can learn as much in two months as other nations in twenty years." This seemed to me no brag when I returned to Tuscany and saw the great development and diffusion of thought that had taken place during my brief absence. The Grand Duke, a well-intentioned, though dull man, had dared to declare himself *"an* ITALIAN *Prince,"* and the heart of Tuscany had bounded with hope. It is now deeply as justly felt that *the* curse of Italy is foreign intrusion, that if she could dispense with foreign aid and be free from foreign aggression, she would find the elements of salvation within herself. All her efforts tend that way, to reestablish the natural position of things: may Heaven grant them success! For myself I believe they will attain it. I see more reason for hope, as I know more of the people. Their rash and baffled struggles have taught them prudence; they are wanted in the civilized world as a peculiar influence; their leaders are thinking men, their cause is righteous. I believe that Italy will revive to new life, and probably a greater, a more truly rich and glorious, than at either epoch of her former greatness.

During the period of my absence, the Austrians had entered Ferrara. It is well that they hazarded this step, for it showed them the difficulties in acting against a Prince of the Church who is at the same time a friend to the People. The position was new, and they were probably surprised at the result, surprised at the firmness of the Pope, surprised at the indignation, tempered by calm resolve, on the part of the Italians. Louis Philippe's mean apostacy has this time turned to the advantage of Freedom. He renounced the good understanding with England which it had been one of the leading features of his policy to maintain, in the hope of aggrandizing and enriching his family (not France; he did not care for France) he did not know that he was paving the way for Italian Freedom. England now is led to play a part a little nearer her pretensions as the Guardian of Progress than she often comes, and the ghost of Lafayette looks down, not unappeased, to see the "Constitutional King" decried by the subjects he has cheated and lulled so craftily. The King of Sardinia is a worthless man, in whom nobody puts any trust so far as regards his heart or honor, but the stress of things seems likely to keep him on the right side. The little sovereigns blustered at first, then ran away affrighted when they found there was really a spirit risen at last within the charmed circle, a spirit likely to defy, to transcend, the spells of haggard premiers and imbecile monarchs.

I arrived in Florence, unhappily, too late for the great fete of the 12th September, in honor of the grant of the National Guard.[4] But I wept at the mere recital of the events of that day, which, if it should lead to no important results, must still be hallowed for ever in the memory of Italy for the great and beautiful emotions that flooded the hearts of her children. The National Guard is hailed with no undue joy by Italians, as the earnest of Progress, the first step toward truly national institutions and a representation of the people. Gratitude had done its natural work in their hearts; it had made them better. Some days before were passed by reconciling all strifes, composing all differences between cities, districts, and individuals. They wished to drop all petty, all local differences, to wash away all stains, to bathe and prepare for a new great covenant of brotherly love, where each should act for the good of all. On that day they all embraced in sign of this—strangers, foes, all, exchanged the kiss of faith and love; they exchanged banners as a token that they would fight for, would animate, one another. All was done in that beautiful poetic manner peculiar to this artist people, but it was the spirit, so great and tender, that melts my heart to think of. It was the spirit of true religion—such, my Country; as welling freshly from some great hearts in thy early hours, won for thee all of value that thou canst call thy own, whose ground-work is the assertion, still sublime though thou hast not been true to it, that all men have equal rights, and that these are *birth*-rights, derived from God alone.

I rejoice to say that the Americans took their share in this occasion, and that Greenough[5]—one of the few Americans who, living in Italy, takes the pains to know whether it is alive or dead; who penetrates beyond the cheats of tradesmen and the cunning of a mob corrupted by centuries of slavery, to know the real mind, the vital blood, of Italy—took a leading part. I am sorry to say that a large portion of my countrymen here take the same slothful and prejudiced view as the English, and, after many years' sojourn, betray entire ignorance of Italian literature and Italian life beyond what is attainable in a month's passage through the thoroughfares. However, they did show, this time, a becoming spirit, and erected the American Eagle where its

---

[4]The establishment of such local popular militias was viewed as a significant step forward in asserting Italian pride and self-determination.

[5]Horatio Greenough (1805–1852), a well-known American sculptor.

cry ought to be heard from afar, where a Nation is striving for independent existence and a Government to represent the People. Crawford[6] here in Rome has had the just feeling to join the Guard, and it is a real sacrifice for an artist to spend time on the exercises; but it well becomes the sculptor of Orpheus,[7] of him who had such faith, such music of divine thought, that he made the stones move, turned the beasts from their accustomed haunts and shamed Hell itself into sympathy with the grief of love. I do not deny that such a spirit is wanted here in Italy; it is everywhere if anything great, anything permanent, is to be done. In reference to what I have said of many Americans in Italy, I will only add that they talk about the corrupt and degenerate state of Italy as they do about that of our slaves at home. They come ready trained to that mode of reasoning which affirms that, because men are degraded by bad institutions, they are not fit for better.

For the English, some of them, are full of generous, intelligent sympathy, as indeed what is more solidly, more wisely good than the right sort of Englishmen, but others are like a gentleman I traveled with the other day, a man of intelligence and refinement too as to the details of life and outside culture, who observed, "he did not see what the Italians wanted of a National Guard unless to wear these little caps." He was a man who had passed five years in Italy, but always covered with that non-conductor called by a witty French writer "the Britannic fluid."

Very sweet to my ear was the continual hymn in the streets of Florence, in honor of Pius IX. It is the Roman hymn, and none of the new ones written in Tuscany have been able to take its place.—The people thank the Grand Duke when he does them good, but they know well from whose mind that good originates, and all their love is for the Pope. Time presses, or I would fain describe in detail the troupe of laborers of the lowest class, marching home at night; keeping step as if they were in the National Guard, filling the air and cheering the melancholy moon, by the patriotic hymns sung, with the mellow tone and in the perfect time which belong to Italians. I would describe the extempore concerts in the streets, the rejoicings at the theatres, where the addresses of liberal souls to the people, through that best vehicle, the drama, may now be heard. But I am tired; what I have to write would fill volumes, and my letter must go. I will only add some words upon the happy augury I draw from the wise docility of the people. With what readiness they listened to wise counsel and the hopes of the Pope that they would give no advantage to his enemies at a time when they were so fevered by the knowledge that conspiracy was at work in their midst. That was a time of trial. On all these occasions of popular excitement their conduct is like music, in such order and with such union of the melody of feeling with discretion where to stop; but what is wonderful is that they acted in the same manner on that difficult occasion. The influence of the Pope

---

[6]Thomas Crawford (1813?–1857), American sculptor.

[7]In Greek mythology, a poet and musician whose playing of the lyre could calm savage beasts and make rocks move. His playing persuaded Pluto, king of the underworld, to return his wife, Euridice, to Orpheus.

here is without bounds; he can always calm the crowd at once. But in Tuscany where they have no such one idol, they listened in the same way on a very trying occasion. The first announcement of the regulation for the Tuscan National Guard terribly disappointed the people; they felt that the Grand Duke, after suffering them to demonstrate such trust and joy on this feast of the 12th, did not really trust, on his side; that he meant to limit them all he could; they felt baffled, cheated; hence young men in anger tore down at once the symbols of satisfaction and respect; but the leading men went among the people, begged them to be calm, and wait till a deputation had seen the Grand Duke. The people listened at once to men who, they were sure, had at heart their best good—waited; the Grand Duke became convinced, and all ended without disturbance. If the people continue to act thus, their hopes cannot be baffled. Certainly I, for one, do not think that the present road will suffice to lead Italy to her goal. But it *is* an onward, upward road, and the people learn as it advances. Where they can now seek and think fearless of prisons and bayonets, a healthy circulation of blood begins, and the heart frees itself from disease.

I earnestly hope some expression of sympathy from my country toward Italy. Take a good chance and do something; you have shown much good feeling toward the Old World in its physical difficulties—you ought to do so still more in its spiritual endeavor. This cause is OURS, above all others; we ought to show that we feel it to be so. At present there is no likelihood of war, but in case of it I trust the United States would not fail in some noble token of sympathy toward this country. The Soul of our Nation need not wait for its Government; these things are better done by the effort of individuals. I believe some in the United States will pay attention to these words of mine, will feel that I am not a person to be kindled by a childish, sentimental enthusiasm, but that I must be sure that I have seen something of Italy to speak as I do. I have been here only seven months, but my means of observation have been uncommon. I have been ardently desirous to judge fairly, and I had no prejudices to prevent; beside, I was not ignorant of the history and literature of Italy and had some common ground on which to stand with its inhabitants, and hear what they have to say. In many ways she is of kin to us; she is the country of Columbus, of Amerigo,[8] of Cabot.[9] It would please me much to see a cannon here bought by the contributions of Americans, at whose head should stand the name of Cabot, to be used by the Guard for salutes on festive occasions, if they should be so happy as to have no more serious need. In Tuscany they are casting one to be called the "Gioberti," from a writer who has given a great impulse to the present movement. I should like the gift of America to be called the AMERICA, the COLUMBO, or the WASHINGTON. Please think of this, some of my friends, who still care for

[8]Amerigo Vespucci (Americus Vespucius, 1451–1512), Italian navigator, whose name we still bear.

[9]John Cabot, originally Giovanni Caboto (1450–1498), Italian navigator in English service, who discovered for Europeans the North American continent in 1497.

the Eagle, the 4th July, and the old cries of Hope and Honor. See, if there are any objections that I do not think of, and do something if it is well and brotherly.[10] Ah! America, with all thy rich boons, thou hast a heavy account to render for the talent given; see in every way that thou be not found wanting.

Dispatch 18

[Undated][1]

This letter will reach the United States about the 1st of January; and it may not be impertinent to offer a few New-Year's reflections. Every new year, indeed, confirms the old thoughts, but also presents them under some new aspects.

The American in Europe, if a thinking mind, can only become more American. In some respects it is a great pleasure to be here. Although we have an independent political existence, our position toward Europe, as to Literature and the Arts, is still that of a colony, and one feels the same joy here that is experienced by the colonist in returning to the parent home. What was but picture to us becomes reality; remote allusions and derivations trouble no more: we see the pattern of the stuff, and understand the whole tapestry. There is a gradual clearing up on many points, and many baseless notions and crude fancies are dropped. Even the post-haste passage of the business American through the great cities, escorted by cheating couriers, and ignorant *valets de place*, unable to hold intercourse with the natives of the country, and passing all his leisure hours with his countrymen, who know no more than himself, clears his mind of some mistakes—lifts some mists from his horizon.

There are three species: first, the servile American—a being utterly shallow, thoughtless, worthless. He comes abroad to spend his money and indulge his tastes. His object in Europe is to have fashionable clothes, good foreign cookery, to know some titled persons, and furnish himself with coffee-house gossip, which he wins importance at home by retailing among those less traveled, and as uninformed as himself.

I look with unspeakable contempt on this class—a class which has all the thoughtlessness and partiality of the exclusive classes in Europe, without any of their refinement, or the chivalric feeling which still sparkles among them here and there. However, though these willing serfs in a free age do some little hurt, and cause some annoyance at present, it cannot last: our country is fated to a grand, independent existence, and as its laws develop, these parasites of a bygone period must wither and drop away.

[10]In fact, her letter appears to have helped stimulate the first mass meeting in the United States in support of the Italian revolution. Horace Greeley, editor of the *Tribune*, was among its sponsors.

[1]First published as "Things and Thoughts in Europe. No. XVIII" in *New-York Daily Tribune*, January 1, 1848, p. 1:1–3.

Then there is the conceited American, instinctively bristling and proud of—he knows not what—He does not see, not he, that the history of Humanity for many centuries is likely to have produced results it requires some training, some devotion, to appreciate and profit by. With his great clumsy hands only fitted to work on a steam-engine, he seizes the old Cremona violin, makes it shriek with anguish in his grasp, and then declares he thought it was all humbug before he came, and now he knows it; that there is not really any music in these old things; that the frogs in one of our swamps make much finer, for *they* are young and alive. To him the etiquettes of courts and camps, the ritual of the Church, seem simply silly— and no wonder, profoundly ignorant as he is of their origin and meaning. Just so the legends which are the subjects of pictures, the profound myths which are represented in the antique marbles, amaze and revolt him; as, indeed, such things need to be judged of by another standard from that of the Connecticut Blue-Laws. He criticises severely pictures, feeling quite sure that his natural senses are better means of judgment than the rules of connoisseurs—not feeling that to see such objects mental vision as well as fleshly eyes are needed, and that something is aimed at in Art beyond the imitation of the commonest forms of Nature.

This is Jonathan in the sprawling state, the booby truant, not yet aspiring enough to be a good school-boy. Yet in his folly there is meaning; add thought and culture to his independence, and he will be a man of might: he is not a creature without hope, like the thick-skinned dandy of the class first specified.

The Artistes form a class by themselves. Yet among them, though seeking special aims by special means may also be found the lineaments of these two classes, as well as of the third, of which I am to speak.

3d. The thinking American—a man who, recognizing the immense advantage of being born to a new world and on a virgin soil, yet does not wish one seed from the Past to be lost. He is anxious to gather and carry back with him all that will bear a new climate and new culture. Some will dwindle; others will attain a bloom and stature unknown before. He wishes to gather them clean, free from noxious insects. He wishes to give them a fair trial in his new world. And that he may know the conditions under which he may best place them in that new world, he does not neglect to study their history in this.

The history of our planet in some moments seems so painfully mean and little, such terrible bafflings and failures to compensate some brilliant successes—such a crashing of the mass of men beneath the feet of a few, and these, too, of the least worthy—such a small drop of honey to each cup of gall, and, in many cases, so mingled, that it is never one moment in life purely tasted,—above all, so little achieved for Humanity as a whole, such tides of war and pestilence intervening to blot out the traces of each triumph, that no wonder if the strongest soul sometimes pauses aghast! No wonder if the many indolently console themselves with gross joys and frivolous prizes. Yes! those men *are* worthy of admiration who can carry this cross faithfully through fifty years; it is a great while for all the agonies that beset a lover of good, a lover of men; it makes a soul worthy of a speedier ascent, a more productive ministry in the next sphere. Blessed are they who ever keep that portion of pure, generous love with which they began life! How blessed those who have deepened the fountains, and have enough to spare for the thirst of others! Some such there are; and, feeling that, with all the excuses for failure, still only the sight of those who triumph gives a meaning to life or makes its pangs endurable, we must arise and follow.

Eighteen hundred years of this Christian culture in these European Kingdoms, a great theme never lost sight of, a mighty idea, an adorable history to which the hearts of men invariably cling, yet are genuine results rare as grains of gold in the river's sandy bed! Where is the genuine Democracy to which the rights of all men are holy? where the child-like wisdom learning all through life more and more of the will of God? where the aversion to falsehood in all its myriad disguises of cant, vanity, covetousness, so clear to be read in all the history of Jesus of Nazareth? Modern Europe is the sequel to that history, and see this hollow England, with its monstrous wealth and cruel poverty, its conventional life and low, practical aims; see this poor France, so full of talent, so adroit, yet so shallow and glossy still, which could not escape from a false position with all its baptism of blood; see that lost Poland and this Italy bound down by treacherous hands in all the force of genius; see Russia with its brutal Czar and innumerable slaves; see Austria and its royalty that represents nothing, and its people who, as people, are and have nothing! If we consider the amount of truth that has really been spoken out in the world, and the love that has beat in private hearts—how Genius has decked each spring-time with such splendid flowers, conveying each one enough of instruction in its life of harmonious energy, and how continually, unquenchably the spark of faith has striven to burst into flame and light up the Universe—the public failure seems amazing, seems monstrous.

Still Europe toils and struggles with her idea, and, at this moment, all things bode and declare a new outbreak of the fire, to destroy old palaces of crime! May it fertilize also many vineyards!—Here at this moment a successor of St. Peter, after the lapse of near two thousand years, is called "Utopian" by a part of this Europe, because he strives to get some food to the mouths of the *leaner* of his flock. A wonderful state of things, and which leaves as the best argument against despair that men do not, *cannot* despair amid such dark experiences—and thou, my country! will thou not be more true? does no greater success await thee? All things have so conspired to teach, to aid! A new world, a new chance, with oceans to wall in the new thought against interference from the old!—Treasures of all kinds, gold, silver, corn, marble, to provide for every physical need! A noble, constant, star-like soul, an Italian, led the way to its shores, and, in the first days, the strong, the pure, those too brave, too sincere for the life of the Old World hastened to people them. A generous struggle then shook off what was foreign and gave the nation a glorious start for a worthy goal. Men rocked the cradle of its hopes, great, firm, disinterested men who saw, who wrote, as the basis of all that was to be done, a statement of the rights, the inborn rights of men, which, if fully interpreted and acted upon, leaves nothing to be desired.

Yet, oh Eagle, whose early flight showed this clear sight of the Sun, how often dost thou near the ground, how show the vulture in these later days! Thou wert to be the advance-guard of Humanity, the herald of all Progress; how often hast thou betrayed this high commission! Fain would the tongue in clear triumphant accents draw example from thy story, to encourage the hearts of those who almost faint and die beneath the old oppressions. But we must stammer and blush when we speak of many things. I take pride here that I may really say the Liberty of the Press works well, and that checks and balances naturally evolve from it which suffice to its government. I may say the minds of our people are alert, and that Talent has a free chance to rise. It is much. But dare I say that political ambition is not as darkly sullied as in other countries? Dare I say that men of most influence in political life are those who represent most virtue or even intellectual power? Is it easy to find names in that career of which I can speak with enthusiasm? Must I not confess in my country to a boundless lust of gain? Must I not confess to the weakest vanity, which bristles and blusters at each foolish taunt of the foreign press; and must I not admit that the men who make these undignified rejoinders seek and find popularity so? Must I not confess that there is as yet no antidote cordially adopted that will defend even that great, rich country against the evils that have grown out of the commercial system in the old world? Can I say our social laws are generally better, or show a nobler insight into the wants of man and woman? I do, indeed, say what I believe, that voluntary association for improvement in these particulars will be the grand means for my nation to grow and give a nobler harmony to the coming age. But it is only of a small minority that I can say they as yet seriously take to heart these things; that they earnestly meditate on what is wanted for their country,—for mankind,—for our cause is, indeed, the cause of all mankind at present. Could we succeed, really succeed, combine a deep religious love with practical development, the achievements of Genius with the happiness of the multitude, we might believe Man had now reached a commanding point in his ascent, and would stumble and faint no more. Then there is this horrible cancer of Slavery, and this wicked War, that has grown out of it.[2] How dare I speak of these things here? I listen to the same arguments against the emancipation of Italy, that are used against the emancipation of our blacks; the same arguments in favor of the spoliation of Poland as for the conquest of Mexico. I find the cause of tyranny and wrong everywhere the same—and lo! my Country the darkest offender, because with the least excuse, foresworn to

[2]Fuller refers to the Mexican War (1846–1848), which many Americans saw as a means to extend slavery territory.

the high calling with which she was called,—no champion of the rights of men, but a robber and a jailer; the scourge hid behind her banner; her eyes fixed, not on the stars, but on the possessions of other men.

How it pleases me here to think of the Abolitionists! I could never endure to be with them at home, they were so tedious, often so narrow, always so rabid and exaggerated in their tone.

But, after all, they had a high motive, something eternal in their desire and life; and, if it was not the only thing worth thinking of it was really something worth living and dying for to free a great nation from such a terrible blot, such a threatening plague. God strengthen them and make them wise to achieve their purpose!

I please myself, too, with remembering some ardent souls among the American youth who, I trust, will yet expand and help to give soul to the huge, over fed, too hastily grown-up body. May they be constant. "Were Man but constant he were perfect!" it has been said; and it is true that he who could be constant to those moments in which he has been truly human—not brutal, not mechanical—is on the sure path to his perfection and to effectual service of the Universe.

It is to the youth that Hope addresses itself, to those who yet burn with aspiration, who are not hardened in their sins. But I dare not expect too much of them. I am not very old, yet of those who, in life's morning, I saw touched by the light of a high hope, many have seceded. Some have become voluptuaries; some mere family men, who think it is quite life enough to win bread for half a dozen people and treat them decently; others are lost through indolence and vacillation. Yet some remain constant. "I have witnessed many a shipwreck, yet still beat noble hearts."

I have found many among the youth of England, of France—of Italy also— full of high desire, but will they have courage and purity to fight the battle through in the sacred, the immortal band? Of some of them I believe it and await the proof. If a few succeed amid the trial, we have not lived and loved in vain.

To these, the heart of my country, a Happy New Year! I do not know what I have written. I have merely yielded to my feelings in thinking of America; but something of true love must be in these lines—receive them kindly, my friends; it is, by itself, some merit for printed words to be sincere.

■ ## HENRY DAVID THOREAU ■
1817–1862

Henry Thoreau was the second son and third child of John Thoreau, whose father Jean had emigrated to America from the Isle of Jersey about the time of the American Revolution. The Thoreaus were of Huguenot stock, having been driven from France in the Protestant persecutions of the late seventeenth century, culminating in the revocation by Louis XIV of the Edict of Nantes in 1685. Thoreau's energetic mother, Cynthia Dunbar Thoreau, was of hardy Scotch lineage. Growing up in Concord, Massachusetts, home also to Nathaniel Hawthorne and Ralph Waldo Emerson, Thoreau attended Harvard College in nearby Cambridge from 1833 to 1837, graduating without conspicuous honors. The remainder of his life, except for visits to Canada, Maine, Minnesota, and nearby locales, he spent in his home community, whose flora and fauna he explored with a microscopic eye, recording his observations in a compendious journal which he faithfully kept from 1837 to 1860. Early interpreters of Thoreau understandably thought of him as a naturalist, because his observations of botanical phenomena were copious and he spent much of his time roaming the environs of Concord with spyglass, notebook, and pencil, recording the seasonal changes and life cycles of hundreds of plants.

But this interpretation of Thoreau is now universally adjudged to have been too narrow. The mistake lay in part in the failure to perceive Thoreau's immersion in the worldview of his Transcendentalist friend and neighbor, Ralph Waldo Emerson, who propounded in his seminal book, *Nature*, the doctrine that every physical fact is but the facade of a spiritual truth. Emerson counseled his generation to look *through* the transparency of nature to grasp the essential spirituality of the universe embosomed there; and Thoreau, of all Emerson's followers, acted on Emerson's teachings most consistently. His most dramatic act was his retirement for two years, two months, and two days in 1845, 1846, and 1847 to Walden Pond, where he built a hut and studied nature to discover what she had to teach of moral and spiritual truth, the record of which he narrated in one of the most influential books of the nineteenth century—*Walden*—a triumph of refined, condensed, figurative prose that provided the base for his present distinguished literary reputation.

Thoreau's Transcendental premises led him to take a negative view of the dominant values of pre–Civil War America. He wrote disparagingly of the destruction of the natural environment, of which human beings were an integral part; he deplored the implications of the rise of industrialism, with its emphasis on materialistic values; he condemned the institution of black slavery, which debased people to the level of property, and as a corollary, the government that fostered and perpetuated the institution. Astute readers will also discern in Thoreau an awareness of the philosophical systems of his day, particularly of Kant and Coleridge; the political and economic theories of the time; and even many scientific assumptions that were to flower in the twentieth century. In short, Thoreau was not only a writer of great skill but a man remarkably alert to the thinking of his age, who with remarkable prescience anticipated the crises in values of the centuries to follow him. He is a man of his time, it is true, but he is a man of our time also; and it is his perceptiveness of the human problems of all times that makes him such an engaging literary figure to the student today.

Though Thoreau considered his profession to be that of writer, he published only two books in his short lifetime of 44 years. The first, *A Week on the Concord and Merrimack Rivers* (1849) is the record of a two-week river excursion by rowboat taken by Thoreau and his brother, John, in the fall of 1839, condensed in the book to one week and embellished by Thoreau's reflections on a variety of subjects for the most part suggested to him by his wide reading in world litera-ture. For many readers, the book is a collection of remarkable essays that lack cohesion and relatedness. It is, however, the second book, *Walden* (1854), that has elevated Thoreau into the first rank of American authors and distinguished him throughout the world as an artist and philosopher of unique perceptiveness and vision. *Walden* breaks out of the structure of Emersonian Transcendental-ism current at the time (though influenced by it), lifting the perceptive reader to a rare and exhilarating self-knowledge, as Thoreau's romantic contemporary John Keats observed that poetry should do, "surprising by a fine excess." That is to say, by employing many of the devices of poetry—allusion, figures of speech, imagery—and through a disciplined process of refinement and constric-tion of his text that took portions of the book through seven versions, Thoreau achieved a work of such subtlety and suggestiveness that repeated readings do not exhaust its meanings or dim the brilliance of its insights. Though only a few chapters can be excerpted for inclusion in an anthology such as this, students of American literature should secure a copy of the complete *Walden*, perennially available in multiple inexpensive editions, and enjoy the coherence and unity of the book as a whole.

Next to *Walden*, Thoreau is best known for his essay "Resistance to Civil Government," often called "Civil Disobedience," which delineates his view in 1849 of the legitimate role of the private individual in a society whose govern-ment sanctions the immorality of black slavery. Published in a soon to be defunct journal, *Aesthetic Papers*, edited by Elizabeth Peabody, Thoreau's conten-tions that private morality is a privileged sanctuary that governments have no right to intrude upon, and that such intrusion by government should be pas-sively resisted by the individual, have elicited sympathetic responses in widely separated parts of the world, from Gandhi's India to Martin Luther King's American South. The immediate occasion that provoked the essay was Thoreau's incarceration in the Concord jail for one night for his refusal to pay his poll tax to a government that supported black slavery, a story that he narrates in his essay; but what chiefly interests the modern reader is Thoreau's perceptive defi-nition of the line of demarcation between individual prerogative and the power of the state. In other words, Thoreau universalizes his experience, seeking not so much to justify his own actions and motives as to illuminate the principles that provide the cutting edge that separates individual rights from state author-ity. Black slavery is to him a moral issue, and a government that condones it and even abets it has intruded into an area where governments, according to his principle, have no authority. Over against the American Constitution, which condones black slavery, Thoreau superimposes an eighteenth-century "higher law" resembling that of Jefferson in the Declaration of Independence, which accords supremacy to individual morality.

By 1859, Thoreau's passive resistance to governmental intrusion upon indi-vidual rights, so eloquently argued in 1849, had changed to a methodology of militancy. When John Brown made his abortive assault on the armory at Harpers Ferry, Thoreau applauded Brown's resort to arms, tacitly admitting, it would seem, that so entrenched an evil as Southern slavery was unresponsive to the passive resistance he had offered earlier as the appropriate weapon to use to confront state authority. Thoreau had met John Brown in Concord and had been impressed by his single-minded aversion to human slavery; and in "A Plea for Captain John Brown," delivered by Thoreau as a lecture on several occasions before Brown was executed by hanging on December 2, 1859, Thoreau elevates Brown to the level of mythical hero, a "man of principle" who defied personal danger in order to shock both North and South into a recognition of the moral obliquy that black slavery typified. Thoreau had written earlier of his horror of the institution of slavery, notably in "Slavery in Massachusetts" (1854), which excoriated the Fugitive Slave Law that permitted Southern sheriffs to pursue fleeing blacks across the boundaries of Northern states; but Thoreau's John Brown essays are perhaps the most polemic that he ever wrote, charged with outrage at the social institution that was soon to provoke the American Civil War. Ironically, Thoreau was not to live to see the day when the Emancipation Proclamation would extinguish the American government's approval of a practice he found so heinous.

He died in 1862 of tuberculosis, the scourge of his family, at the age of 44. Within four years, four books of his writings were in print, edited and published by his sister Sophia, his friend Ellery Channing, and Emerson. His remarkable journal was issued in 1906, adding to his growing fame. As he declined into death in the spring months of 1862, just as nature was renewing herself around him, he expressed no regrets for the life he had lived. To the deathbed question, "Have you made your peace with God?" he allegedly replied, "We never quarrelled." "Are you ready for the next world?" another acquaintance asked. Thoreau's response was: "One world at a time."

Wendell P. Glick
University of Minnesota

PRIMARY WORKS

A Week on the Concord and Merrimack Rivers, 1849; *Walden*, 1854. Posthumously published: *The Maine Woods*, 1864; *Cape Cod*, 1865; *Letters to Various Persons* (edited by Emerson), 1865; *A Yankee in Canada, with Anti-Slavery and Reform Papers*, 1866. *The Writings of Henry David Thoreau*, 1906, 20 vols., which includes the *Journal*, is currently being superseded by the Princeton Edition of *The Writings of Henry David Thoreau*, 1971–, which will also include the *Journal* in augmented form.

Resistance to Civil Government[1]

I heartily accept the motto,—"That government is best which governs least;"[2] and I should like to see it acted up to more rapidly and systematically. Carried out, it finally amounts to this, which also I believe,—"That government is best which governs not at all;" and when men are prepared for it, that will be the kind of government which they will have. Government

---

[1]This is the title Thoreau gave his essay when he published it in 1849. Diligent search has unearthed no evidence that the often used title, "Civil Disobedience," was Thoreau's, though "Civil Disobedience" was used as the title when the essay was republished in 1866.

[2]The motto Thoreau quotes would have been recognized by many of his readers as a quotation from the masthead of the journal *The Democratic Review*.

is at best but an expedient; but most governments are usually, and all governments are sometimes, inexpedient. The objections which have been brought against a standing army, and they are many and weighty, and deserve to prevail, may also at last be brought against a standing government. The standing army is only an arm of the standing government. The government itself, which is only the mode which the people have chosen to execute their will, is equally liable to be abused and perverted before the people can act through it. Witness the present Mexican war, the work of comparatively a few individuals using the standing government as their tool; for, in the outset, the people would not have consented to this measure.[3]

This American government,—what is it but a tradition, though a recent one, endeavoring to transmit itself unimpaired to posterity, but each instant losing some of its integrity? It has not the vitality and force of a single living man; for a single man can bend it to his will. It is a sort of wooden gun to the people themselves; and, if ever they should use it in earnest as a real one against each other, it will surely split. But it is not the less necessary for this; for the people must have some complicated machinery or other, and hear its din, to satisfy that idea of government which they have. Governments show thus how successfully men can be imposed on, even impose on themselves, for their own advantage. It is excellent, we must all allow; yet this government never of itself furthered any enterprise, but by the alacrity with which it got out of its way. *It* does not keep the country free. *It* does not settle the West. *It* does not educate. The character inherent in the American people has done all that has been accomplished; and it would have done somewhat more, if the government had not sometimes got in its way. For government is an expedient by which men would fain succeed in letting one another alone; and, as has been said, when it is most expedient, the governed are most let alone by it. Trade and commerce, if they were not made of India rubber, would never manage to bounce over the obstacles which legislators are continually putting in their way; and, if one were to judge these men wholly by the effects of their actions, and not partly by their intentions, they would deserve to be classed and punished with those mischievous persons who put obstructions on the railroads.

But, to speak practically and as a citizen, unlike those who call themselves no-government men, I ask for, not at once no government, but *at once* a better government. Let every man make known what kind of government would command his respect, and that will be one step toward obtaining it.

After all, the practical reason why, when the power is once in the hands of the people, a majority are permitted, and for a long period continue, to rule, is not because they are most likely to be in the right, not because this seems fairest to the minority, but because they are physically the strongest. But a government in which the majority rule in all cases cannot be based on

[3]There was much citizen protest over the United States' involvement in the Mexican War (1845–1848), in many respects similar to the protest over the war in Vietnam.

justice, even as far as men understand it. Can there not be a government in which majorities do not virtually decide right and wrong, but conscience?—in which majorities decide only those questions to which the rule of expediency is applicable? Must the citizen ever for a moment, or in the least degree, resign his conscience to the legislator? Why has every man a conscience, then? I think that we should be men first, and subjects afterward. It is not desirable to cultivate a respect for the law, so much as for the right. The only obligation which I have a right to assume, is to do at any time what I think right. It is truly enough said, that a corporation has no conscience; but a corporation of conscientious men is a corporation *with* a conscience. Law never made men a whit more just; and, by means of their respect for it, even the well-disposed are daily made the agents of injustice. A common and natural result of an undue respect for law is, that you may see a file of soldiers, colonel, captain, corporal, privates, powder-monkeys and all, marching in admirable order over hill and dale to the wars, against their wills, aye, against their common sense and consciences, which makes it very steep marching indeed, and produces a palpitation of the heart. They have no doubt that it is a damnable business in which they are concerned; they are all peaceably inclined. Now, what are they? Men at all? or small moveable forts and magazines, at the service of some unscrupulous man in power? Visit the Navy Yard, and behold a marine, such a man as an American government can make, or such as it can make a man with its black arts, a mere shadow and reminiscence of humanity, a man laid out alive and standing, and already, as one may say, buried under arms with funeral accompaniments, though it may be

> "Not a drum was heard, not a funeral note,
>   As his corse to the rampart we hurried;
> Not a soldier discharged his farewell shot
>   O'er the grave where our hero we buried."[4]

The mass of men serve the State thus, not as men mainly, but as machines, with their bodies. They are the standing army, and the militia, jailers, constables, *posse comitatus*, &c. In most cases there is no free exercise whatever of the judgment or of the moral sense; but they put themselves on a level with wood and earth and stones, and wooden men can perhaps be manufactured that will serve the purpose as well. Such command no more respect than men of straw, or a lump of dirt. They have the same sort of worth only as horses and dogs. Yet such as these even are commonly esteemed good citizens. Others, as most legislators, politicians, lawyers, ministers, and office-holders, serve the State chiefly with their heads; and, as they rarely make any moral distinctions, they are as likely to serve the devil, without intending it, as God. A very few, as heroes, patriots, martyrs, reformers in the great sense, and *men*, serve the State with their consciences also, and so necessarily resist it for the most part; and they are commonly

[4]The poem is by Charles Wolfe.

treated by it as enemies. A wise man will only be useful as a man, and will not submit to be "clay," and "stop a hole to keep the wind away,"[5] but leave that office to his dust at least:—

> *I am too high-born to be propertied,*
> *To be a secondary at control,*
> *Or useful serving-man and instrument*
> *To any sovereign state throughout the world."*[6]

He who gives himself entirely to his fellow-men appears to them useless and selfish; but he who gives himself partially to them is pronounced a benefactor and philanthropist.

How does it become a man to behave toward this American government today? I answer that he cannot without disgrace be associated with it. I cannot for an instant recognize that political organization as *my* government which is the *slave's* government also.

All men recognize the right of revolution; that is, the right to refuse allegiance to and to resist the government, when its tyranny or its inefficiency are great and unendurable. But almost all say that such is not the case now. But such was the case, they think, in the Revolution of '75. If one were to tell me that this was a bad government because it taxed certain foreign commodities brought to its ports, it is most probable that I should not make an ado about it, for I can do without them: all machines have their friction; and possibly this does enough good to counterbalance the evil. At any rate, it is a great evil to make a stir about it. But when the friction comes to have its machine, and oppression and robbery are organized, I say, let us not have such a machine any longer. In other words, when a sixth of the population of a nation which has undertaken to be the refuge of liberty are slaves, and a whole country is unjustly overrun and conquered by a foreign army, and subjected to military law, I think that it is not too soon for honest men to rebel and revolutionize. What makes this duty the more urgent is the fact, that the country so overrun is not our own, but ours is the invading army.

Paley, a common authority with many on moral questions, in his chapter on the "Duty of Submission to Civil Government,"[7] resolves all civil obligation into expediency; and he proceeds to say, "that so long as the interest of the whole society requires it, that is, so long as the established government cannot be resisted or changed without public inconveniency, it is the will of God that the established government be obeyed, and no longer." ... "This principle being admitted, the justice of every particular case of resistance is reduced to a computation of the quantity of the danger and grievance on the one side, and of the probability and expense of redressing it on the other." Of this, he says, every man shall judge for himself. But Paley

---

[5]Shakespeare, *Hamlet.*
[6]Shakespeare, *King John.*
[7]Paley, an English philosopher, taught that resistance to government which caused "public inconveniency" was an affront to God. The effect of such teaching, obviously, was to make resistance to the government in power very difficult, however corrupt such a government might be.

appears never to have contemplated those cases to which the rule of expediency does not apply, in which a people, as well as an individual, must do justice, cost what it may. If I have unjustly wrested a plank from a drowning man, I must restore it to him though I drown myself. This, according to Paley, would be inconvenient. But he that would save his life, in such a case, shall lose it. This people must cease to hold slaves, and to make war on Mexico, though it cost them their existence as a people.

In their practice, nations agree with Paley; but does any one think that Massachusetts does exactly what is right at the present crisis?

> *"A drab of state, a cloth-o'-silver slut,*
> *To have her train borne up, and her soul trail in the dirt."*[8]

Practically speaking, the opponents to a reform in Massachusetts are not a hundred thousand politicians at the South, but a hundred thousand merchants and farmers here, who are more interested in commerce and agriculture than they are in humanity, and are not prepared to do justice to the slave and to Mexico, *cost what it may*. I quarrel not with far-off foes, but with those who, near at home, co-operate with, and do the bidding of those far away, and without whom the latter would be harmless. We are accustomed to say, that the mass of men are unprepared; but improvement is slow, because the few are not materially wiser or better than the many. It is not so important that many should be as good as you, as that there be some absolute goodness somewhere; for that will leaven the whole lump. There are thousands who are *in opinion* opposed to slavery and to the war, who yet in effect do nothing to put an end to them; who, esteeming themselves children of Washington and Franklin, sit down with their hands in their pockets, and say that they know not what to do, and do nothing; who even postpone the question of freedom to the question of free-trade, and quietly read the prices-current along with the latest advices from Mexico, after dinner, and, it may be, fall asleep over them both. What is the price-current of an honest man and patriot to-day? They hesitate, and they regret, and sometimes they petition; but they do nothing in earnest and with effect. They will wait, well-disposed, for others to remedy the evil, that they may no longer have it to regret. At most, they give only a cheap vote, and a feeble countenance and God-speed, to the right, as it goes by them. There are nine hundred and ninety-nine patrons of virtue to one virtuous man; but it is easier to deal with the real possessor of a thing than with the temporary guardian of it.

All voting is a sort of gaming, like chequers or backgammon, with a slight moral tinge to it, a playing with right and wrong, with moral questions; and betting naturally accompanies it. The character of the voters is not staked. I cast my vote, perchance, as I think right; but I am not vitally concerned that that right should prevail. I am willing to leave it to the

[8]Cyril Tourneur, the playwright from whose
The Revenger's Tragedy (IV, iv) Thoreau is
quoting, was a contemporary of Shakespeare.

majority. Its obligation, therefore, never exceeds that of expediency. Even voting *for the right* is *doing* nothing for it. It is only expressing to men feebly your desire that it should prevail. A wise man will not leave the right to the mercy of chance, nor wish it to prevail through the power of the majority. There is but little virtue in the action of masses of men. When the majority shall at length vote for the abolition of slavery, it will be because they are indifferent to slavery, or because there is but little slavery left to be abolished by their vote. *They* will then be the only slaves. Only *his* vote can hasten the abolition of slavery who asserts his own freedom by his vote.

I hear of a convention to be held at Baltimore, or elsewhere, for the selection of a candidate for the Presidency, made up chiefly of editors, and men who are politicians by profession; but I think, what is it to any independent, intelligent, and respectable man what decision they may come to, shall we not have the advantage of his wisdom and honesty, nevertheless? Can we not count upon some independent votes? Are there not many individuals in the country who do not attend conventions? But no: I find that the respectable man, so called, has immediately drifted from his position, and despairs of his country, when his country has more reason to despair of him. He forthwith adopts one of the candidates thus selected as the only *available* one, thus proving that he is himself *available* for any purposes of the demagogue. His vote is of no more use than that of any unprincipled foreigner or hireling native, who may have been bought. Oh for a man who is a *man*, and, as my neighbor says, has a bone in his back which you cannot pass your hand through! Our statistics are at fault: the population has been returned too large. How many *men* are there to a square thousand miles in this country? Hardly one. Does not America offer any inducement for men to settle here? The American has dwindled into an Odd Fellow,—one who may be known by the development of his organ of gregariousness, and a manifest lack of intellect and cheerful self-reliance; whose first and chief concern, on coming into the world, is to see that the alms-houses are in good repair; and, before yet he has lawfully donned the virile garb, to collect a fund for the support of the widows and orphans that may be: who, in short, ventures to live only by the aid of the mutual insurance company, which has promised to bury him decently.

It is not a man's duty, as a matter of course, to devote himself to the eradication of any, even the most enormous wrong; he may still properly have other concerns to engage him; but it is his duty, at least, to wash his hands of it, and, if he gives it no thought longer, not to give it practically his support. If I devote myself to other pursuits and contemplations, I must first see, at least, that I do not pursue them sitting upon another man's shoulders. I must get off him first, that he may pursue his contemplations too. See what gross inconsistency is tolerated. I have heard some of my townsmen say, "I should like to have them order me out to help put down an insurrection of the slaves, or to march to Mexico,—see if I would go;" and yet these very men have each, directly by their allegiance, and so indirectly, at least, by their money, furnished a substitute. The soldier is applauded who refuses to serve in an unjust war by those who do not refuse to sustain the unjust government which makes the war; is applauded by those whose own act and authority he disregards and sets at nought; as if the State were penitent to that degree that it hired one to scourge it while it sinned, but not to that degree that it left off sinning for a moment. Thus, under the name of order and civil government, we are all made at last to pay homage to and support our own meanness. After the first blush of sin, comes its indifference and from immoral it becomes, as it were, *unmoral*, and not quite unnecessary to that life which we have made.

The broadest and most prevalent error requires the most disinterested virtue to sustain it. The slight reproach to which the virtue of patriotism is commonly liable, the noble are most likely to incur. Those who, while they disapprove of the character and measures of a government, yield to it their allegiance and support, are undoubtedly its most conscientious supporters, and so frequently the most serious obstacles to reform. Some are petitioning the State to dissolve the Union, to disregard the requisitions of the President. Why do they not dissolve it themselves,—the union between themselves and the State,—and refuse to pay their quota into its treasury? Do not they stand in the same relation to the State, that the State does to the Union? And have not the same reasons prevented the State from resisting the Union, which have prevented them from resisting the State?

How can a man be satisfied to entertain an opinion merely, and enjoy *it?* Is there any enjoyment in it, if his opinion is that he is aggrieved? If you are cheated out of a single dollar by your neighbor, you do not rest satisfied with knowing that you are cheated, or with saying that you are cheated, or even with petitioning him to pay you your due; but you take effectual steps at once to obtain the full amount, and see that you are never cheated again. Action from principle,—the perception and the performance of right,— changes things and relations; it is essentially revolutionary, and does not consist wholly with any thing which was. It not only divides states and churches, it divides families; aye, it divides the *individual*, separating the diabolical in him from the divine.

Unjust laws exist: shall we be content to obey them, or shall we endeavor to amend them, and obey them until we have succeeded, or shall we transgress them at once? Men generally, under such a government as this, think that they ought to wait until they have persuaded the majority to alter them. They think that, if they should resist, the remedy would be worse than the evil. But it is the fault of the government itself that the remedy *is* worse than the evil. *It* makes it worse. Why is it not more apt to anticipate and provide for reform? Why does it not cherish its wise minority? Why does it cry and resist before it is hurt? Why does it not encourage its citizens to be on the alert to point out its faults, and *do* better than it would have them? Why does it always crucify Christ, and excommunicate Copernicus and Luther, and pronounce Washington and Franklin rebels?

One would think, that a deliberate and practical denial of its authority was the only offence never contemplated by government; else, why has it not assigned its definite, its suitable and proportionate penalty? If a man who has no property refuses but once to earn nine shillings for the State, he is put in prison for a period unlimited by any law that I know, and determined only by the discretion of those who placed him there; but if he should steal ninety times nine shillings from the State, he is soon permitted to go at large again.

If the injustice is part of the necessary friction of the machine of government, let it go, let it go: perchance it will wear smooth,—certainly the machine will wear out. If the injustice has a spring, or a pulley, or a rope, or a crank, exclusively for itself, then perhaps you may consider whether the remedy will not be worse than the evil; but if it is of such a nature that it requires you to be the agent of injustice to another, then, I say, break the law. Let your life be a counter friction to stop the machine. What I have to do is to see, at any rate, that I do not lend myself to the wrong which I condemn.

As for adopting the ways which the State has provided for remedying the evil, I know not of such ways. They take too much time, and a man's life will be gone. I have other affairs to attend to. I came into this world, not chiefly to make this a good place to live in, but to live in it, be it good or bad. A man has not every thing to do, but something; and because he cannot do *every thing*, it is not necessary that he should do *something* wrong. It is not my business to be petitioning the governor or the legislature any more than it is theirs to petition me; and, if they should not hear my petition, what should I do then? But in this case the State has provided no way: its very Constitution is the evil. This may seem to be harsh and stubborn and unconciliatory; but it is to treat with the utmost kindness and consideration the only spirit that can appreciate or deserves it. So is all change for the better, like birth and death which convulse the body.

I do not hesitate to say, that those who call themselves abolitionists should at once effectually withdraw their support, both in person and property, from the government of Massachusetts, and not wait till they constitute a majority of one, before they suffer the right to prevail through them. I think that it is enough if they have God on their side, without waiting for that other one. Moreover, any man more right than his neighbors, constitutes a majority of one already.

I meet this American government, or its representative the State government, directly, and face to face, once a year, no more, in the person of its tax-gatherer; this is the only mode in which a man situated as I am necessarily meets it; and it then says distinctly, Recognize me; and the simplest, the most effectual, and, in the present posture of affairs, the indispensablest mode of treating with it on this head, of expressing your little satisfaction with and love for it, is to deny it then. My civil neighbor, the tax-gatherer, is the very man I have to deal with,—for it is, after all, with men and not with parchment that I quarrel,—and he has voluntarily chosen to be an agent of the government. How shall he ever know well what he is and does as an officer of the government, or as a man, until he is obliged to consider whether he shall treat me, his neighbor, for whom he has respect, as a neighbor and well-disposed man, or as a maniac and disturber of the peace, and see if he can get over this obstruction to his neighborliness without a ruder and more impetuous thought or speech corresponding with his action? I know this well, that if one thousand, if one hundred, if ten men whom I could name,—if ten *honest* men only,—aye, if *one* HONEST man, in this State of Massachusetts, *ceasing to hold slaves*, were actually to withdraw from this copartnership, and be locked up in the county jail therefor, it would be the abolition of slavery in America. For it matters not how small the beginning may seem to be: what is once well done is done for ever. But we love better to talk about it: that we say is our mission. Reform keeps many scores of newspapers in its service, but not one man. If my esteemed neighbor, the State's ambassador, who will devote his days to the settlement of the question of human rights in the Council Chamber, instead of being threatened with the prisons of Carolina, were to sit down the prisoner of Massachusetts, that State which is so anxious to foist the sin of slavery upon her sister,[9]—though at present she can discover only an act of inhospitality to be the ground of a quarrel with her,—the Legislature would not wholly waive the subject the following winter.

Under a government which imprisons any unjustly, the true place for a just man is also a prison. The proper place to-day, the only place which Massachusetts has provided for her freer and less desponding spirits, is in her prisons, to be put out and locked out of the State by her own act, as they have already put themselves out by their principles. It is there that the fugitive slave, and the Mexican prisoner on parole, and the Indian come to plead the wrongs of his race, should find them; on that separate, but more free and honorable ground, where the State places those who are not *with* her but *against* her,—the only house in a slave-state in which a free man can abide with honor. If any think that their influence would be lost there, and their voices no longer afflict the ear of the State, that they would not be as an enemy within its walls, they do not know by how much truth is stronger than error, nor how much more eloquently and effectively he can combat injustice who has experienced a little in his own person. Cast your whole vote, not a strip of paper merely, but your whole influence. A minority is powerless while it conforms to the majority; it is not even a minority then; but it is irresistible when it clogs by its whole weight. If the alternative is to keep all just men in prison, or give up war and slavery, the State will not hesitate which to choose. If a thousand men were not to pay their tax-bills this year, that would not be a violent and bloody measure, as it would be to pay them, and enable the State to commit violence and shed innocent blood. This is, in fact, the definition of a peaceable revolution, if any such is possible. If the tax-gatherer, or any other public officer, asks me, as one has done, "But what shall I do?" my answer is, "If you really wish to do any thing,

---

[9]Thoreau's "esteemed neighbor," Samuel Hoar, was expelled from South Carolina for defending black sailors from Massachusetts.

resign your office." When the subject has refused allegiance, and the officer has resigned his office, then the revolution is accomplished. But even suppose blood should flow. Is there not a sort of blood shed when the conscience is wounded? Through this wound a man's real manhood and immortality flow out, and he bleeds to an everlasting death. I see this blood flowing now.

I have contemplated the imprisonment of the offender, rather than the seizure of his goods,—though both will serve the same purpose,—because they who assert the purest right, and consequently are most dangerous to a corrupt State, commonly have not spent much time in accumulating property. To such the State renders comparatively small service, and a slight tax is wont to appear exorbitant, particularly if they are obliged to earn it by special labor with their hands. If there were one who lived wholly without the use of money, the State itself would hesitate to demand it of him. But the rich man—not to make any invidious comparison—is always sold to the institution which makes him rich. Absolutely speaking, the more money, the less virtue; for money comes between a man and his objects, and obtains them for him; and it was certainly no great virtue to obtain it. It puts to rest many questions which he would otherwise be taxed to answer; while the only new question which it puts is the hard but superfluous one, how to spend it. Thus his moral ground is taken from under his feet. The opportunities of living are diminished in proportion as what are called the "means" are increased. The best thing a man can do for his culture when he is rich is to endeavour to carry out those schemes which he entertained when he was poor. Christ answered the Herodians according to their condition. "Show me the tribute-money," said he;—and one took a penny out of his pocket;— If you use money which has the image of Caesar on it, and which he has made current and valuable, that is, *if you are men of the State*, and gladly enjoy the advantages of Caesar's government, then pay him back some of his own when he demands it; "Render therefore to Caesar that which is Caesar's, and to God those things which are God's,"—leaving them no wiser than before as to which was which; for they did not wish to know.

When I converse with the freest of my neighbors, I perceive that, whatever they may say about the magnitude and seriousness of the question, and their regard for the public tranquillity, the long and the short of the matter is, that they cannot spare the protection of the existing government, and they dread the consequences of disobedience to it to their property and families. For my own part, I should not like to think that I ever rely on the protection of the State. But, if I deny the authority of the State when it presents its tax-bill, it will soon take and waste all my property, and so harass me and my children without end. This is hard. This makes it impossible for a man to live honestly and at the same time comfortably in outward respects. It will not be worth the while to accumulate property; that would be sure to go again. You must hire or squat somewhere, and raise but a small crop, and eat that soon. You must live within yourself, and depend upon yourself, always tucked up and ready for a start, and not have many affairs. A man may grow rich in Turkey even, if he will be in all respects a good subject of the Turkish government. Confucius said,—"If a State is governed by the principles of reason, poverty and misery are subjects of shame; if a State is not governed by the principles of reason, riches and honors are the subjects of shame." No: until I want the protection of Massachusetts to be extended to me in some distant southern port, where my liberty is endangered, or until I am bent solely on building up an estate at home by peaceful enterprise, I can afford to refuse allegiance to Massachusetts, and her right to my property and life. It costs me less in every sense to incur the penalty of disobedience to the State, than it would to obey. I should feel as if I were worth less in that case.

Some years ago, the State met me in behalf of the church, and commanded me to pay a certain sum toward the support of a clergyman whose preaching my father attended, but never I myself. "Pay it," it said, "or be locked up in the jail." I declined to pay. But, unfortunately, another man saw fit to pay it. I did not see why the schoolmaster should be taxed to support the priest, and not the priest the schoolmaster; for I was not the State's schoolmaster, but I supported myself by voluntary subscription. I did not see why the lyceum[10] should not present its tax-bill, and have the State to back its demand, as well as the church. However, at the request of the selectmen, I condescended to make some such statement as this in writing:—"Know all men by these presents, that I, Henry Thoreau, do not wish to be regarded as a member of any incorporated society which I have not joined." This I gave to the town-clerk; and he has it. The State, having thus learned that I did not wish to be regarded as a member of that church, has never made a like demand on me since; though it said that it must adhere to its original presumption that time. If I had known how to name them, I should then have signed off in detail from all the societies which I never signed on to; but I did not know where to find a complete list.

I have paid no poll-tax for six years. I was put into a jail once on this account, for one night; and, as I stood considering the walls of solid stone, two or three feet thick, the door of wood and iron, a foot thick, and the iron grating which strained the light, I could not help being struck with the foolishness of that institution which treated me as if I were mere flesh and blood and bones, to be locked up. I wondered that it should have concluded at length that this was the best use it could put me to, and had never thought to avail itself of my services in some way. I saw that, if there was a wall of stone between me and my townsmen, there was a still more difficult one to climb or break through, before they could get to be as free as I was. I did not for a moment feel confined, and the walls seemed a great waste of stone and mortar. I felt as if I alone of all my townsmen had paid my tax. They plainly did not know how to treat me, but behaved like persons who are underbred. In every threat and in every compliment there was a blunder;

---

[10]Thoreau was active in the Concord Lyceum, a forum in which invited lecturers spoke on topics of interest to people in the community.

for they thought that my chief desire was to stand the other side of that stone wall. I could not but smile to see how industriously they locked the door on my meditations, which followed them out again without let or hinderance, and *they* were really all that was dangerous. As they could not reach me, they had resolved to punish my body; just as boys, if they cannot come at some person against whom they have a spite, will abuse his dog. I saw that the State was half-witted, that it was timid as a lone woman with her silver spoons, and that it did not know its friends from its foes, and I lost all my remaining respect for it, and pitied it.

Thus the State never intentionally confronts a man's sense, intellectual or moral, but only his body, his senses. It is not armed with superior wit or honesty, but with superior physical strength. I was not born to be forced. I will breathe after my own fashion. Let us see who is the strongest. What force has a multitude? They only can force me who obey a higher law than I. They force me to become like themselves. I do not hear of *men* being *forced* to live this way or that by masses of men. What sort of life were that to live? When I meet a government which says to me, "Your money or your life," why should I be in haste to give it my money? It may be in a great strait, and not know what to do: I cannot help that. It must help itself; do as I do. It is not worth the while to snivel about it. I am not responsible for the successful working of the machinery of society. I am not the son of the engineer. I perceive that, when an acorn and a chestnut fall side by side, the one does not remain inert to make way for the other, but both obey their own laws, and spring and grow and flourish as best they can, till one, perchance, overshadows and destroys the other. If a plant cannot live according to its nature, it dies; and so a man.

The night in prison was novel and interesting enough. The prisoners in their shirt-sleeves were enjoying a chat and the evening air in the door-way, when I entered. But the jailer said, "Come, boys, it is time to lock up;" and so they dispersed, and I heard the sound of their steps returning into the hollow apartments. My roommate was introduced to me by the jailer, as "a first-rate fellow and a clever man." When the door was locked, he showed me where to hang my hat, and how he managed matters there. The rooms were whitewashed once a month; and this one, at least, was the whitest, most simply furnished, and probably the neatest apartment in the town. He naturally wanted to know where I came from, and what brought me there; and, when I had told him, I asked him in turn how he came there, presuming him to be an honest man, of course; and, as the world goes, I believe he was. "Why," said he, "they accused me of burning a barn; but I never did it." As near as I could discover, he had probably gone to bed in a barn when drunk, and smoked his pipe there; and so a barn was burnt. He had the reputation of being a clever man, had been there some three months waiting for his trial to come on, and would have to wait as much longer; but he was quite domesticated and contented, since he got his board for nothing, and thought that he was well treated.

He occupied one window, and I the other; and I saw, that, if one stayed there long, his principal business would be to look out the window. I had soon read all the tracts that were left there, and examined where former prisoners had broken out, and where a grate had been sawed off, and heard the history of the various occupants of that room; for I found that even here there was a history and a gossip which never circulated beyond the walls of the jail. Probably this is the only house in the town where verses are composed, which are afterward printed in a circular form, but not published. I was shown quite a long list of verses which were composed by some young men who had been detected in an attempt to escape, who avenged themselves by singing them.

I pumped my fellow-prisoner as dry as I could, for fear I should never see him again; but at length he showed me which was my bed, and left me to blow out the lamp.

It was like travelling into a far country, such as I had never expected to behold, to lie there for one night. It seemed to me that I never had heard the town-clock strike before, nor the evening sounds of the village; for we slept with the windows open, which were inside the grating. It was to see my native village in the light of the middle ages, and our Concord was turned into a Rhine stream, and visions of knights and castles passed before me. They were the voices of old burghers that I heard in the streets. I was an involuntary spectator and auditor of whatever was done and said in the kitchen of the adjacent village-inn,—a wholly new and rare experience to me. It was a closer view of my native town. I was fairly inside of it. I never had seen its institutions before. This is one of its peculiar institutions; for it is a shire town. I began to comprehend what its inhabitants were about.

In the morning, our breakfasts were put through the hole in the door, in small oblong-square tin pans, made to fit, and holding a pint of chocolate, with brown bread, and an iron spoon. When they called for the vessels again, I was green enough to return what bread I had left; but my comrade seized it, and said that I should lay that up for lunch or dinner. Soon after, he was let out to work at haying in a neighboring field, whither he went every day, and would not be back till noon; so he bade me good-day, saying that he doubted if he should see me again.

When I came out of prison,—for some one interfered, and paid the tax,—I did not perceive that great changes had taken place on the common, such as he observed who went in a youth, and emerged a tottering and gray-headed man; and yet a change had to my eyes come over the scene,—the town, and State, and country,—greater than any that mere time could effect. I saw yet more distinctly the State in which I lived. I saw to what extent the people among whom I lived could be trusted as good neighbors and friends; that their friendship was for summer weather only; that they did not greatly purpose to do right; that they were a distinct race from me by their prejudices and superstitions, as the Chinamen and Malays are; that, in their sacrifices to humanity, they ran no risks, not even to their property; that, after all, they were not so noble but they treated the thief as he had treated them, and hoped, by a certain outward observance and a few prayers, and by walking in a particular straight though useless path from time to time, to save their souls. This may be to judge my neighbors harshly; for

I believe that most of them are not aware that they have such an institution as the jail in their village.

It was formerly the custom in our village, when a poor debtor came out of jail, for his acquaintances to salute him, looking through their fingers, which were crossed to represent the grating of a jail window, "How do ye do?" My neighbors did not thus salute me, but first looked at me, and then at one another, as if I had returned from a long journey. I was put into jail as I was going to the shoemaker's to get a shoe which was mended. When I was let out the next morning, I proceeded to finish my errand, and, having put on my mended shoe, joined a huckleberry party, who were impatient to put themselves under my conduct; and in half an hour,—for the horse was soon tackled,[11] was in the midst of a huckleberry field, on one of our highest hills, two miles off; and then the State was nowhere to be seen.

This is the whole history of "My Prisons."[12]

I have never declined paying the highway tax, because I am as desirous of being a good neighbor as I am of being a bad subject; and, as for supporting schools, I am doing my part to educate my fellow-countrymen now. It is for no particular item in the tax-bill that I refuse to pay it. I simply wish to refuse allegiance to the State, to withdraw and stand aloof from it effectually. I do not care to trace the course of my dollar, if I could, till it buys a man, or a musket to shoot one with,—the dollar is innocent,—but I am concerned to trace the effects of my allegiance. In fact, I quietly declare war with the State, after my fashion, though I will still make what use and get what advantage of her I can, as is usual in such cases.

If others pay the tax which is demanded of me,[13] from a sympathy with the State, they do but what they have already done in their own case, or rather they abet injustice to a greater extent than the State requires. If they pay the tax from a mistaken interest in the individual taxed, to save his property or prevent his going to jail, it is because they have not considered wisely how far they let their private feelings interfere with the public good.

This, then, is my position at present. But one cannot be too much on his guard in such a case, lest his action be biassed by obstinacy, or an undue regard for the opinions of men. Let him see that he does only what belongs to himself and to the hour.

I think sometimes, Why, this people mean well; they are only ignorant; they would do better if they knew how: why give your neighbors this pain to treat you as they are not inclined to? But I think, again, this is no reason why I should do as they do, or permit others to suffer much greater pain of a different kind. Again, I sometimes say to myself, When many millions of men, without heat, without ill-will, without personal feeling of any kind, demand of you a few shillings only, without the possibility, such is their constitution, of retracting or altering their present demand, and without

---

[11]*I.e.*, harnessed.

[12]"My Prisons" was the title of a book written by the Italian poet Silvio Pellico after he had spent years in prison.

[13]It is not known for certain who paid Thoreau's tax and thus secured his release from jail.

the possibility, on your side, of appeal to any other millions, why expose yourself to this overwhelming brute force? You do not resist cold and hunger, the winds and the waves, thus obstinately; you quietly submit to a thousand similar necessities. You do not put your head into the fire. But just in proportion as I regard this as not wholly a brute force, but partly a human force, and consider that I have relations to those millions as to so many millions of men, and not of mere brute or inanimate things, I see that appeal is possible, first and instantaneously, from them to the Maker of them, and, secondly, from them to themselves. But, if I put my head deliberately into the fire, there is no appeal to fire or to the Maker of fire, and I have only myself to blame. If I could convince myself that I have any right to be satisfied with men as they are, and to treat them accordingly, and not according, in some respects, to my requisitions and expectations of what they and I ought to be, then, like a good Mussulman[14] and fatalist, I should endeavor to be satisfied with things as they are, and say it is the will of God. And, above all, there is this difference between resisting this and a purely brute or natural force, that I can resist this with some effect; but I cannot expect, like Orpheus, to change the nature of the rocks and trees and beasts.[15]

I do not wish to quarrel with any man or nation. I do not wish to split hairs, to make fine distinctions, or set myself up as better than my neighbors. I seek rather, I may say, even an excuse for conforming to the laws of the land. I am but too ready to conform to them. Indeed I have reason to suspect myself on this head; and each year, as the tax-gatherer comes round, I find myself disposed to review the acts and position of the general and state governments, and the spirit of the people, to discover a pretext for conformity. I believe that the State will soon be able to take all my work of this sort out of my hands, and then I shall be no better a patriot than my fellow-countrymen. Seen from a lower point of view, the Constitution, with all its faults, is very good; the law and the courts are very respectable; even this State and this American government are, in many respects, very admirable and rare things, to be thankful for, such as a great many have described them; but seen from a point of view a little higher, they are what I have described them; seen from a higher still, and the highest, who shall say what they are, or that they are worth looking at or thinking of at all?

However, the government does not concern me much, and I shall bestow the fewest possible thoughts on it. It is not many moments that I live under a government, even in this world. If a man is thought-free, fancy-free, imagination-free, that which *is not* never for a long time appearing *to be* to him, unwise rulers or reformers cannot fatally interrupt him.

I know that most men think differently from myself; but those whose lives are by profession devoted to the study of these or kindred subjects, content me as little as any. Statesmen and legislators, standing so

---

[14]A Mussulman was a Mohammedan.
[15]Orpheus, according to Greek mythology, could play his lyre so beautifully that trees and rocks moved.

completely within the institution, never distinctly and nakedly behold it. They speak of moving society, but have no resting-place without it. They may be men of a certain experience and discrimination, and have no doubt invented ingenious and even useful systems, for which we sincerely thank them; but all their wit and usefulness lie within certain not very wide limits. They are wont to forget that the world is not governed by policy and expediency. Webster[16] never goes behind government, and so cannot speak with authority about it. His words are wisdom to those legislators who contemplate no essential reform in the existing government; but for thinkers, and those who legislate for all time, he never once glances at the subject. I know of those whose serene and wise speculations on this theme would soon reveal the limits of his mind's range and hospitality. Yet, compared with the cheap professions of most reformers, and the still cheaper wisdom and eloquence of politicians in general, his are almost the only sensible and valuable words, and we thank Heaven for him. Comparatively, he is always strong, original, and, above all, practical. Still his quality is not wisdom, but prudence. The lawyer's truth is not Truth, but consistency, or a consistent expediency. Truth is always in harmony with herself, and is not concerned chiefly to reveal the justice that may consist with wrong-doing. He well deserves to be called, as he has been called, the Defender of the Constitution. There are really no blows to be given by him but defensive ones. He is not a leader, but a follower. His leaders are the men of '87. "I have never made an effort," he says, "and never propose to make an effort; I have never countenanced an effort, and never mean to countenance an effort, to disturb the arrangement as originally made, by which the various States came into the Union." Still thinking of the sanction which the Constitution gives to slavery, he says, "Because it was a part of the original compact,—let it stand." Notwithstanding his special acuteness and ability, he is unable to take a fact out of its merely political relations, and behold it as it lies absolutely to be disposed of by the intellect,—what, for instance, it behoves a man to do here in America to-day with regard to slavery,—but ventures, or is driven, to make some such desperate answer as the following, while professing to speak absolutely, and as a private man,—from which what new and singular code of social duties might be inferred?—"The manner," says he, "in which the governments of those States where slavery exists are to regulate it, is for their own consideration, under their responsibility to their constituents, to the general laws of propriety, humanity, and justice, and to God. Associations formed elsewhere, springing from a feeling of humanity, or any other cause, have nothing whatever to do with it. They have never received any encouragement from me, and they never will."[17]

---

[16]Thoreau's objection to Daniel Webster, one of the most powerful senators in the 1840s, was that Webster considered the American Constitution, which condoned black slavery, to be the ultimate authority on moral issues. In the final paragraphs of this essay, Thoreau argues for a moral order transcending the Constitution.

[17]These extracts have been inserted since the Lecture was read. [Thoreau's note.]

They who know of no purer sources of truth, who have traced up its stream no higher, stand, and wisely stand, by the Bible and the Constitution, and drink at it there with reverence and humility; but they who behold where it comes trickling into this lake or that pool, gird up their loins once more, and continue their pilgrimage toward its fountain-head.

No man with a genius for legislation has appeared in America. They are rare in the history of the world. There are orators, politicians, and eloquent men, by the thousand; but the speaker has not yet opened his mouth to speak, who is capable of settling the much-vexed questions of the day. We love eloquence for its own sake, and not for any truth which it may utter, or any heroism it may inspire. Our legislators have not yet learned the comparative value of free-trade and of freedom, of union, and of rectitude, to a nation. They have no genius or talent for comparatively humble questions of taxation and finance, commerce and manufactures and agriculture. If we were left solely to the wordy wit of legislators in Congress for our guidance, uncorrected by the seasonable experience and the effectual complaints of the people, America would not long retain her rank among the nations. For eighteen hundred years, though perchance I have no right to say it, the New Testament has been written; yet where is the legislator who has wisdom and practical talent enough to avail himself of the light which it sheds on the science of legislation?

The authority of government, even such as I am willing to submit to,— for I will cheerfully obey those who know and can do better than I, and in many things even those who neither know nor can do so well,—is still an impure one: to be strictly just, it must have the sanction and consent of the governed. It can have no pure right over my person and property but what I concede to it. The progress from an absolute to a limited monarchy, from a limited monarchy to a democracy, is a progress toward a true respect for the individual. Is a democracy, such as we know it, the last improvement possible in government? Is it not possible to take a step further towards recognizing and organizing the rights of man? There will never be a really free and enlightened State, until the State comes to recognize the individual as a higher and independent power, from which all its own power and authority are derived, and treats him accordingly. I please myself with imagining a State at last which can afford to be just to all men, and to treat the individual with respect as a neighbor; which even would not think it inconsistent with its own repose, if a few were to live aloof from it, not meddling with it, nor embraced by it, who fulfilled all the duties of neighbors and fellow-men. A State which bore this kind of fruit, and suffered it to drop off as fast as it ripened, would prepare the way for a still more perfect and glorious State, which also I have imagined, but not yet anywhere seen.

1849

from **Walden**

Where I Lived, and What I Lived For

At a certain season of our life we are accustomed to consider every spot as the possible site of a house. I have thus surveyed the country on every side within a dozen miles of where I live. In imagination I have bought all the farms in succession, for all were to be bought, and I knew their price. I walked over each farmer's premises, tasted his wild apples, discoursed on husbandry with him, took his farm at his price, at any price, mortgaging it to him in my mind; even put a higher price on it,—took every thing but a deed of it,—took his word for his deed, for I dearly love to talk,—cultivated it, and him too to some extent, I trust, and withdrew when I had enjoyed it long enough, leaving him to carry it on. This experience entitled me to be regarded as a sort of real-estate broker by my friends. Wherever I sat, there I might live, and the landscape radiated from me accordingly. What is a house but a *sedes*, a seat?—better if a country seat. I discovered many a site for a house not likely to be soon improved, which some might have thought too far from the village, but to my eyes the village was too far from it. Well, there I might live, I said; and there I did live, for an hour, a summer and a winter life; saw how I could let the years run off, buffet the winter through, and see the spring come in. The future inhabitants of this region, wherever they may place their houses, may be sure that they have been anticipated. An afternoon sufficed to lay out the land into orchard woodlot and pasture, and to decide what fine oaks or pines should be left to stand before the door, and whence each blasted tree could be seen to the best advantage; and then I let it lie, fallow perchance, for a man is rich in proportion to the number of things which he can afford to let alone.

My imagination carried me so far that I even had the refusal of several farms,—the refusal was all I wanted,—but I never got my fingers burned by actual possession. The nearest that I came to actual possession was when I bought the Hollowell Place, and had begun to sort my seeds, and collected materials with which to make a wheelbarrow to carry it on or off with; but before the owner gave me a deed of it, his wife—every man has such a wife—changed her mind and wished to keep it, and he offered me ten dollars to release him. Now, to speak the truth, I had but ten cents in the world, and it surpassed my arithmetic to tell, if I was that man who had ten cents, or who had a farm, or ten dollars, or all together. However, I let him keep the ten dollars and the farm too, for I had carried it far enough; or rather, to be generous, I sold him the farm for just what I gave for it, and, as he was not a rich man, made him a present of ten dollars, and still had my ten cents, and seeds, and materials for a wheelbarrow left. I found thus that I had been a rich man without any damage to my poverty. But I retained the landscape, and I have since annually carried off what it yielded without a wheelbarrow. With respect to landscapes,—

"I am monarch of all I survey,
My right there is none to dispute."[1]

I have frequently seen a poet withdraw, having enjoyed the most valuable part of a farm, while the crusty farmer supposed that he had got a few wild apples only. Why, the owner does not know it for many years when a poet has put his farm in rhyme, the most admirable kind of invisible fence, has fairly impounded it, milked it, skimmed it, and got all the cream, and left the farmer only the skimmed milk.

The real attractions of the Hollowell farm, to me, were: its complete retirement, being about two miles from the village, half a mile from the nearest neighbor, and separated from the highway by a broad field; its bounding on the river, which the owner said protected it by its fogs from frosts in the spring, though that was nothing to me; the gray color and ruinous state of the house and barn, and the dilapidated fences, which put such an interval between me and the last occupant; the hollow and lichen-covered apple trees, gnawed by rabbits, showing what kind of neighbors I should have; but above all, the recollection I had of it from my earliest voyages up the river, when the house was concealed behind a dense grove of red maples, through which I heard the house-dog bark. I was in haste to buy it, before the proprietor finished getting out some rocks, cutting down the hollow apple trees, and grubbing up some young birches which had sprung up in the pasture, or, in short, had made any more of his improvements. To enjoy these advantages I was ready to carry it on; like Atlas,[2] to take the world on my shoulders,—I never heard what compensation he received for that,— and do all those things which had no other motive or excuse but that I might pay for it and be unmolested in my possession of it; for I knew all the while that it would yield the most abundant crop of the kind I wanted if I could only afford to let it alone. But it turned out as I have said.

All that I could say, then, with respect to farming on a large scale, (I have always cultivated a garden,) was, that I had had my seeds ready. Many think that seeds improve with age. I have no doubt that time discriminates between the good and the bad; and when at last I shall plant, I shall be less likely to be disappointed. But I would say to my fellows, once for all, As long as possible live free and uncommitted. It makes but little difference whether you are committed to a farm or the county jail.

Old Cato, whose "De Re Rusticâ" is my "Cultivator,"[3] says, and the only translation I have seen makes sheer nonsense of the passage, "When you think of getting a farm, turn it thus in your mind, not to buy greedily; nor spare your pains to look at it, and do not think it enough to go round it once. The oftener you go there the more it will please you, if it is good." I

---

[1] Thoreau was himself a surveyor; in italicizing *"survey"* in the quotation from William Cowper's *Verses Supposed to be Written by Alexander Selkirk* he is punning on Cowper's meaning. Puns are frequent in his writings.

[2] Atlas, according to Greek mythology, was compelled by Zeus to support the heavens on his shoulders as a punishment.

[3] A journal on farming being published at the time was called the *Cultivator*. Cato was a Roman writer on agriculture.

think I shall not buy greedily, but go round and round it as long as I live, and be buried in it first, that it may please me the more at last.

The present was my next experiment of this kind, which I purpose to describe more at length; for convenience, putting the experience of two years into one. As I have said, I do not propose to write an ode to dejection, but to brag as lustily as chanticleer in the morning, standing on his roost, if only to wake my neighbors up.

When first I took up my abode in the woods, that is, began to spend my nights as well as days there, which, by accident, was on Independence Day, or the fourth of July, 1845, my house was not finished for winter, but was merely a defence against the rain, without plastering or chimney, the walls being of rough weather-stained boards, with wide chinks, which made it cool at night. The upright white hewn studs and freshly planed door and window casings gave it a clean and airy look, especially in the morning, when its timbers were saturated with dew, so that I fancied that by noon some sweet gum would exude from them. To my imagination it retained throughout the day more or less of this auroral character, reminding me of a certain house on a mountain which I had visited the year before. This was an airy and unplastered cabin, fit to entertain a traveling god, and where a goddess might trail her garments. The winds which passed over my dwelling were such as sweep over the ridges of mountains, bearing the broken strains, or celestial parts only, of terrestrial music. The morning wind forever blows, the poem of creation is uninterrupted; but few are the ears that hear it. Olympus is but the outside of the earth every where.

The only house I had been the owner of before, if I except a boat, was a tent, which I used occasionally when making excursions in the summer, and this is still rolled up in my garret; but the boat, after passing from hand to hand, has gone down the stream of time. With this more substantial shelter about me, I had made some progress toward settling in the world. This frame, so slightly clad, was a sort of crystallization around me, and reacted on the builder. It was suggestive somewhat as a picture in outlines. I did not need to go out doors to take the air, for the atmosphere within had lost none of its freshness. It was not so much within doors as behind a door where I sat, even in the rainiest weather. The Harivansa[4] says, "An abode without birds is like a meat without seasoning." Such was not my abode, for I found myself suddenly neighbor to the birds; not by having imprisoned one, but having caged myself near them. I was not only nearer to some of those which commonly frequent the garden and the orchard, but to those wilder and more thrilling songsters of the forest which never, or rarely, serenade a villager,—the wood-thrush, the veery, the scarlet tanager, the field-sparrow, the whippoorwill, and many others.

I was seated by the shore of a small pond, about a mile and a half south of the village of Concord and somewhat higher than it, in the midst of an

[4]Thoreau read widely in Hindu literature. The Harivansa was a Hindu poem.

extensive wood between that town and Lincoln, and about two miles south of that our only field known to fame, Concord Battle Ground; but I was so low in the woods that the opposite shore, half a mile off, like the rest, covered with wood, was my most distant horizon. For the first week, whenever I looked out on the pond it impressed me like a tarn high up on the side of a mountain, its bottom far above the surface of other lakes, and, as the sun arose, I saw it throwing off its nightly clothing of mist, and here and there, by degrees, its soft ripples or its smooth reflecting surface was revealed, while the mists, like ghosts, were stealthily withdrawing in every direction into the woods, as at the breaking up of some nocturnal conventicle. The very dew seemed to hang upon the trees later into the day than usual, as on the sides of mountains.

This small lake was of most value as a neighbor in the intervals of a gentle rain storm in August, when, both air and water being perfectly still, but the sky overcast, mid-afternoon had all the serenity of evening, and the wood-thrush sang around, and was heard from shore to shore. A lake like this is never smoother than at such a time; and the clear portion of the air above it being shallow and darkened by clouds, the water, full of light and reflections, becomes a lower heaven itself so much the more important. From a hill top near by, where the wood had been recently cut off, there was a pleasing vista southward across the pond, through a wide indentation in the hills which form the shore there, where their opposite sides sloping toward each other suggested a stream flowing out in that direction through a wooded valley, but stream there was none. That way I looked between and over the near green hills to some distant and higher ones in the horizon, tinged with blue. Indeed, by standing on tiptoe I could catch a glimpse of some of the peaks of the still bluer and more distant mountain ranges in the north-west, those true-blue coins from heaven's own mint, and also of some portion of the village. But in other directions, even from this point, I could not see over or beyond the woods which surrounded me. It is well to have some water in your neighborhood, to give buoyancy to and float the earth. One value even of the smallest well is, that when you look into it you see that earth is not continent but insular. This is as important as that it keeps butter cool.[5] When I looked across the pond from this peak toward the Sudbury meadows, which in time of flood I distinguished elevated perhaps by a mirage in their seething valley, like a coin in a basin, all the earth beyond the pond appeared like a thin crust insulated and floated even by this small sheet of intervening water, and I was reminded that this on which I dwelt was but *dry land*.

Though the view from my door was still more contracted, I did not feel crowded or confined in the least. There was pasture enough for my imagination. The low shrub-oak plateau to which the opposite shore arose, stretched

---

[5]Thoreau is saying that the perspective that comes from studying Nature is more important than the narrow uses we put Nature to.

Butter was preserved in cool wells because there was no refrigeration.

away toward the prairies of the West and the steppes of Tartary, affording ample room for all the roving families of men. "There are none happy in the world but beings who enjoy freely a vast horizon,"—said Damodara, when his herds required new and larger pastures.[6]

Both place and time were changed, and I dwelt nearer to those parts of the universe and to those eras in history which had most attracted me. Where I lived was as far off as many a region viewed nightly by astronomers. We are wont to imagine rare and delectable places in some remote and more celestial corner of the system, behind the constellation of Cassiopeia's Chair, far from noise and disturbance. I discovered that my house actually had its site in such a withdrawn, but forever new and unprofaned, part of the universe. If it were worth the while to settle in those parts near to the Pleiades or the Hyades, to Aldebaran or Altair,[7] then I was really there, or at an equal remoteness from the life which I had left behind, dwindled and twinkling with as fine a ray to my nearest neighbor, and to be seen only in moonless nights by him. Such was that part of creation where I had squatted;—

> *"There was a shepherd that did live,*
> *And held his thoughts as high*
> *As were the mounts whereon his flocks*
> *Did hourly feed him by."*

What should we think of the shepherd's life if his flocks always wandered to higher pastures than his thoughts?

Every morning was a cheerful invitation to make my life of equal simplicity, and I may say innocence, with Nature herself. I have been as sincere a worshipper of Aurora as the Greeks.[8] I got up early and bathed in the pond; that was a religious exercise, and one of the best things which I did. They say that characters were engraven on the bathing tub of king Tching-thang to this effect: "Renew thyself completely each day; do it again, and again, and forever again." I can understand that. Morning brings back the heroic ages. I was as much affected by the faint hum of a mosquito making its invisible and unimaginable tour through my apartment at earliest dawn, when I was sitting with door and windows open, as I could be by any trumpet that ever sang of fame. It was Homer's requiem; itself an Iliad and Odyssey in the air, singing its own wrath and wanderings. There was something cosmical about it; a standing advertisement, till forbidden, of the everlasting vigor and fertility of the world. The morning, which is the most memorable season of the day, is the awakening hour. Then there is least somnolence in us; and for an hour, at least, some part of us awakes which slumbers all the rest of the day and night. Little is to be expected of that day, if it can be

---

[6]The steppes of Tartary are prairie-like areas of Russia. Damodara was Krishna, in Hindu mythology one of the deities of Hinduism.

[7]Thoreau is referring in this passage to stars and constellations of stars.

[8]Aurora was the goddess of the dawn in Roman mythology (Eos in Greek). Memnon was her son.

called a day, to which we are not awakened by our Genius, but by the mechanical nudgings of some servitor, are not awakened by our own newly-acquired force and aspirations from within, accompanied by the undulations of celestial music, instead of factory bells, and a fragrance filling the air—to a higher life than we fell asleep from; and thus the darkness bear its fruit, and prove itself to be good, no less than the light. That man who does not believe that each day contains an earlier, more sacred, and auroral hour than he has yet profaned, has despaired of life, and is pursuing a descending and darkening way. After a partial cessation of his sensuous life, the soul of man, or its organs rather, are reinvigorated each day, and his Genius tries again what noble life it can make. All memorable events, I should say, transpire in morning time and in a morning atmosphere. The Vedas say, "All intelligences awake with the morning." Poetry and art, and the fairest and most memorable of the actions of men, date from such an hour. All poets and heroes, like Memnon, are the children of Aurora, and emit their music at sunrise. To him whose elastic and vigorous thought keeps pace with the sun, the day is a perpetual morning. It matters not what the clocks say or the attitudes and labors of men. Morning is when I am awake and there is a dawn in me. Moral reform is the effort to throw off sleep. Why is it that men give so poor an account of their day if they have not been slumbering? They are not such poor calculators. If they had not been overcome with drowsiness they would have performed something. The millions are awake enough for physical labor; but only one in a million is awake enough for effective intellectual exertion, only one in a hundred millions to a poetic or divine life. To be awake is to be alive. I have never yet met a man who was quite awake. How could I have looked him in the face?

We must learn to reawaken and keep ourselves awake, not by mechanical aids, but by an infinite expectation of the dawn, which does not forsake us in our soundest sleep. I know of no more encouraging fact than the unquestionable ability of man to elevate his life by a conscious endeavor. It is something to be able to paint a particular picture, or to carve a statue, and so to make a few objects beautiful; but it is far more glorious to carve and paint the very atmosphere and medium through which we look, which morally we can do. To affect the quality of the day, that is the highest of arts. Every man is tasked to make his life, even in its details, worthy of the contemplation of his most elevated and critical hour. If we refused, or rather used up, such paltry information as we get, the oracles would distinctly inform us how this might be done.

I went to the woods because I wished to live deliberately, to front only the essential facts of life, and see if I could not learn what it had to teach, and not, when I came to die, discover that I had not lived. I did not wish to live what was not life, living is so dear; nor did I wish to practise resignation, unless it was quite necessary. I wanted to live deep and suck out all the marrow of life, to live so sturdily and Spartan-like as to put to rout all that was not life, to cut a broad swath and shave close, to drive life into a corner, and reduce it to its lowest terms, and, if it proved to be mean, why then to get the whole and genuine meanness of it, and publish its meanness to the world; or if it were sublime, to know it by experience, and be able to give a true account of it in my next excursion. For most men, it appears to me, are in a strange uncertainty about it, whether it is of the devil or of God, and have *somewhat hastily* concluded that it is the chief end of man here to "glorify God and enjoy him forever."

Still we live meanly, like ants; though the fable tells us that we were long ago changed into men; like pygmies we fight with cranes; it is error upon error, and clout upon clout, and our best virtue has for its occasion a superfluous and evitable wretchedness. Our life is frittered away by detail. An honest man has hardly need to count more than his ten fingers, or in extreme cases he may add his ten toes, and lump the rest. Simplicity, simplicity, simplicity! I say, let your affairs be as two or three, and not a hundred or a thousand; instead of a million count half a dozen, and keep your accounts on your thumb nail. In the midst of this chopping sea of civilized life, such are the clouds and storms and quicksands and thousand-and-one items to be allowed for, that a man has to live, if he would not founder and go to the bottom and not make his port at all, by dead reckoning, and he must be a great calculator indeed who succeeds. Simplify, simplify. Instead of three meals a day, if it be necessary eat but one; instead of a hundred dishes, five; and reduce other things in proportion. Our life is like a German Confederacy,[9] made up of petty states, with its boundary forever fluctuating, so that even a German cannot tell you how it is bounded at any moment. The nation itself, with all its so called internal improvements, which, by the way, are all external and superficial, is just such an unwieldy and overgrown establishment, cluttered with furniture and tripped up by its own traps, ruined by luxury and heedless expense, by want of calculation and a worthy aim, as the million households in the land; and the only cure for it as for them is in a rigid economy, a stern and more than Spartan simplicity of life and elevation of purpose. It lives too fast. Men think that it is essential that the *Nation* have commerce, and export ice, and talk through a telegraph, and ride thirty miles an hour, without a doubt, whether *they* do or not; but whether we should live like baboons or like men, is a little uncertain. If we do not get out sleepers,[10] and forge rails, and devote days and nights to the work, but go to tinkering upon our *lives* to improve *them*, who will build railroads? And if railroads are not built, how shall we get to heaven in season? But if we stay at home and mind our business, who will want railroads? We do not ride on the railroad; it rides upon us. Did you ever think what those sleepers are that underlie the railroad? Each one is a man, an Irish-man, or a Yankee man. The rails are laid on them, and they are covered with sand, and the cars run smoothly over them. They are sound sleepers, I assure you. And every few years a new lot is laid down and

[9]The German nation as we know it did not exist in Thoreau's time; what is now Germany consisted of many warring states that were not unified until 1871.

[10]Sleepers were railroad ties. Thoreau is punning.

run over; so that, if some have the pleasure of riding on a rail, others have the misfortune to be ridden upon. And when they run over a man that is walking in his sleep, a supernumerary sleeper in the wrong position, and wake him up, they suddenly stop the cars, and make a hue and cry about it, as if this were an exception. I am glad to know that it takes a gang of men for every five miles to keep the sleepers down and level in their beds as it is, for this is a sign that they may sometime get up again.

Why should we live with such hurry and waste of life? We are determined to be starved before we are hungry. Men say that a stitch in time saves nine, and so they take a thousand stitches to-day to save nine to-morrow. As for *work*, we haven't any of any consequence. We have the Saint Vitus' dance, and cannot possibly keep our heads still. If I should only give a few pulls at the parish bell-rope, as for a fire, that is, without setting the bell, there is hardly a man on his farm in the outskirts of Concord, notwithstanding that press of engagements which was his excuse so many times this morning, nor a boy, nor a woman, I might almost say, but would forsake all and follow that sound, not mainly to save property from the flames, but, if we will confess the truth, much more to see it burn, since burn it must, and we, be it known, did not set it on fire,—or to see it put out, and have a hand in it, if that is done as handsomely; yes, even if it were the parish church itself. Hardly a man takes a half hour's nap after dinner, but when he wakes he holds up his head and asks, "What's the news?" as if the rest of mankind had stood his sentinels. Some give directions to be waked every half hour, doubtless for no other purpose; and then, to pay for it, they tell what they have dreamed. After a night's sleep the news is as indispensable as the breakfast. "Pray tell me any thing new that has happened to a man any where on this globe",—and he reads it over his coffee and rolls, that a man has had his eyes gouged out this morning on the Wachito River; never dreaming the while that he lives in the dark unfathomed mammoth cave of this world, and has but the rudiment of an eye himself.[11]

For my part, I could easily do without the post-office. I think that there are very few important communications made through it. To speak critically, I never received more than one or two letters in my life—I wrote this some years ago—that were worth the postage. The penny-post is, commonly, an institution through which you seriously offer a man that penny for his thoughts which is so often safely offered in jest. And I am sure that I never read any memorable news in a newspaper. If we read of one man robbed, or murdered, or killed by accident, or one house burned, or one vessel wrecked, or one steamboat blown up, or one cow run over on the Western Railroad, or one mad dog killed, or one lot of grasshoppers in the winter,—we never need read of another. One is enough. If you are acquainted with the principle, what do you care for a myriad instances and applications? To a philosopher all *news*, as it is called, is gossip, and they who edit and read it are old

[11]Thoreau's reference is to Mammoth Cave in Kentucky, where the fish were blind.

women over their tea. Yet not a few are greedy after this gossip. There was such a rush, as I hear, the other day at one of the offices to learn the foreign news by the last arrival, that several large squares of plate glass belonging to the establishment were broken by the pressure,—news which I seriously think a ready wit might write a twelve-month or twelve years beforehand with sufficient accuracy. As for Spain, for instance, if you know how to throw in Don Carlos and the Infanta, and Don Pedro and Seville and Granada, from time to time in the right proportions,—they may have changed the names a little since I saw the papers,—and serve up a bull-fight when other entertainments fail, it will be true to the letter, and give us as good an idea of the exact state or ruin of things in Spain as the most succinct and lucid reports under this head in the newspapers: and as for England, almost the last significant scrap of news from that quarter was the revolution of 1649; and if you have learned the history of her crops for an average year, you never need attend to that thing again, unless your speculations are of a merely pecuniary character. If one may judge who rarely looks into the newspapers, nothing new does ever happen in foreign parts, a French revolution not excepted.

What news! how much more important to know what that is which was never old! "Kieou-pe-yu (great dignitary of the state of Wei) sent a man to Khoung-tseu to know his news. Khoung-tseu caused the messenger to be seated near him, and questioned him in these terms: What is your master doing? The messenger answered with respect: My master desires to diminish the number of his faults, but he cannot accomplish it. The messenger being gone, the philosopher remarked: What a worthy messenger! What a worthy messenger!" The preacher, instead of vexing the ears of drowsy farmers on their day of rest at the end of the week,—for Sunday is the fit conclusion of an ill-spent week, and not the fresh and brave beginning of a new one,—with this one other draggle-tail of a sermon, should shout with thundering voice,—"Pause! Avast! Why so seeming fast, but deadly slow?"

Shams and delusions are esteemed for soundest truths, while reality is fabulous. If men would steadily observe realities only, and not allow themselves to be deluded, life, to compare it with such things as we know, would be like a fairy tale and the Arabian Nights' Entertainments. If we respected only what is inevitable and has a right to be, music and poetry would resound along the streets. When we are unhurried and wise, we perceive that only great and worthy things have any permanent and absolute existence,—that petty fears and petty pleasures are but the shadow of the reality. This is always exhilarating and sublime. By closing the eyes and slumbering, and consenting to be deceived by shows, men establish and confirm their daily life of routine and habit every where, which still is built on purely illusory foundations. Children, who play life, discern its true law and relations more clearly than men, who fail to live it worthily, but who think that they are wiser by experience, that is, by failure. I have read in a Hindoo book, that "there was a king's son, who, being expelled in infancy from his native city, was brought up by a forester, and, growing up to maturity in that state, imagined himself to belong to the barbarous race with which he lived. One of his father's ministers having discovered him, revealed to him what he was, and the misconception of his character was removed, and he knew himself to be a prince. So soul," continues the Hindoo philosopher, "from the circumstances in which it is placed, mistakes its own character, until the truth is revealed to it by some holy teacher, and then it knows itself to be *Brahme.*"[12] I perceive that we inhabitants of New England live this mean life that we do because our vision does not penetrate the surface of things. We think that that *is* which *appears* to be. If a man should walk through this town and see only the reality, where, think you, would the "Mill-dam"[13] go to? If he should give us an account of the realities he beheld there, we should not recognize the place in his description. Look at a meeting-house, or a court-house, or a jail, or a shop, or a dwelling-house, and say what that thing really is before a true gaze, and they would all go to pieces in your account of them. Men esteem truth remote, in the outskirts of the system, behind the farthest star, before Adam and after the last man. In eternity there is indeed something true and sublime. But all these times and places and occasions are now and here. God himself culminates in the present moment, and will never be more divine in the lapse of all the ages. And we are enabled to apprehend at all what is sublime and noble only by the perpetual instilling and drenching of the reality which surrounds us. The universe constantly and obediently answers to our conceptions; whether we travel fast or slow, the track is laid for us. Let us spend our lives in conceiving then. The poet or the artist never yet had so fair and noble a design but some of his posterity at least could accomplish it.

Let us spend one day as deliberately as Nature, and not be thrown off the track by every nutshell and mosquito's wing that falls on the rails. Let us rise early and fast, or break fast, gently and without perturbation; let company come and let company go, let the bells ring and the children cry,— determined to make a day of it. Why should we knock under and go with the stream? Let us not be upset and overwhelmed in that terrible rapid and whirlpool called a dinner, situated in the meridian shallows. Weather this danger and you are safe, for the rest of the way is down hill. With unrelaxed nerves, with morning vigor, sail by it, looking another way, tied to the mast like Ulysses.[14] If the engine whistles, let it whistle till it is hoarse for its pains. If the bell rings, why should we run? We will consider what kind of music they are like. Let us settle ourselves, and work and wedge our feet downward through the mud and slush of opinion, and prejudice, and tradition, and delusion, and appearance, that alluvion which covers the globe, through Paris and London, through New York and Boston and Concord, through church and state, through poetry and philosophy and religion, till

[12]*I.e.*, Brahma, in Hindu mythology the creator.
[13]The Mill-dam was the central business section of Concord.
[14]Ulysses, returning from Troy in Homer's *Odyssey*, had ordered his men to tie him to the mast of his ship, so that he would be able to resist the seductive songs of the Sirens.

we come to a hard bottom and rocks in place, which we can call *reality*, and say, This is, and no mistake; and then begin, having a *point d'appui*,[15] below freshet and frost and fire, a place where you might found a wall or a state, or set a lamp-post safely, or perhaps a gauge, not a Nilometer, but a Realometer,[16] that future ages might know how deep a freshet of shams and appearances had gathered from time to time. If you stand right fronting and face to face to a fact, you will see the sun glimmer on both its surfaces, as if it were a cimeter,[17] and feel its sweet edge dividing you through the heart and marrow, and so you will happily conclude your mortal career. Be it life or death, we crave only reality. If we are really dying, let us hear the rattle in our throats and feel cold in the extremities; if we are alive, let us go about our business.

Time is but the stream I go a-fishing in. I drink at it; but while I drink I see the sandy bottom and detect how shallow it is. Its thin current slides away, but eternity remains. I would drink deeper; fish in the sky, whose bottom is pebbly with stars. I cannot count one. I know not the first letter of the alphabet. I have always been regretting that I was not as wise as the day I was born. The intellect is a cleaver; it discerns and rifts its way into the secret of things. I do not wish to be any more busy with my hands than is necessary. My head is hands and feet. I feel all my best faculties concentrated in it. My instinct tells me that my head is an organ for burrowing, as some creatures use their snout and fore-paws, and with it I would mine and burrow my way through these hills. I think that the richest vein is somewhere hereabouts; so by the divining rod and thin rising vapors I judge; and here I will begin to mine.

Higher Laws

As I came home through the woods with my string of fish, trailing my pole, it being now quite dark, I caught a glimpse of a woodchuck stealing across my path, and felt a strange thrill of savage delight, and was strongly tempted to seize and devour him raw; not that I was hungry then, except for that wildness which he represented. Once or twice, however, while I lived at the pond, I found myself ranging the woods, like a half-starved hound, with a strange abandonment, seeking some kind of venison which I might devour, and no morsel could have been too savage for me. The wildest scenes had become unaccountably familiar. I found in myself, and still find, an instinct toward a higher, or, as it is named, spiritual life, as do most men, and another toward a primitive rank and savage one, and I reverence them both.[18] I love the wild not less than the good. The wildness and

[15]A firm point of support.
[16]By "Nilometer" Thoreau means a gauge used by Egyptians at the head of the Nile to measure the water depth. Thoreau is punning between "Nil" (nothing) and "real" as in "reality."

[17]"Cimeter" is the obsolete form of "scimitar," a sharp, curved, single-edged sword. Compare below, the reference to "cleaver."
[18]In reverencing both the physical and spiritual in himself, Thoreau departs from the Christian tradition of disparaging the carnal desires of the body.

adventure that are in fishing still recommended it to me. I like sometimes to take rank hold on life and spend my day more as the animals do. Perhaps I have owed to this employment and to hunting, when quite young, my closest acquaintance with Nature. They early introduce us to and detain us in scenery with which otherwise, at that age, we should have little acquaintance. Fishermen, hunters, woodchoppers, and others, spending their lives in the fields and woods, in a peculiar sense a part of Nature themselves, are often in a more favorable mood for observing her, in the intervals of their pursuits, than philosophers or poets even, who approach her with expectation. She is not afraid to exhibit herself to them. The traveller on the prairie is naturally a hunter, on the head waters of the Missouri and Columbia a trapper, and at the Falls of St. Mary[19] a fisherman. He who is only a traveller learns things at second-hand and by the halves, and is poor authority. We are most interested when science reports what those men already know practically or instinctively, for that alone is a true *humanity*, or account of human experience.

They mistake who assert that the Yankee has few amusements, because he has not so many public holidays, and men and boys do not play so many games as they do in England, for here the more primitive but solitary amusements of hunting fishing and like have not yet given place to the former. Almost every New England boy among my contemporaries shouldered a fowling piece[20] between the ages of ten and fourteen; and his hunting and fishing grounds were not limited like the preserves of an English nobleman, but were more boundless even than those of a savage. No wonder, then, that he did not oftener stay to play on the common. But already a change is taking place, owing, not to an increased humanity, but to an increased scarcity of game, for perhaps the hunter is the greatest friend of the animals hunted, not excepting the Humane Society.

Moreover, when at the pond, I wished sometimes to add fish to my fare for variety. I have actually fished from the same kind of necessity that the first fishers did. Whatever humanity I might conjure up against it was all factitious, and concerned my philosophy more than my feelings. I speak of fishing only now, for I had long felt differently about fowling, and sold my gun before I went to the woods. Not that I am less humane than others, but I did not perceive that my feelings were much affected. I did not pity the fishes nor the worms. This was habit. As for fowling, during the last years that I carried a gun my excuse was that I was studying ornithology, and sought only new or rare birds. But I confess that I am now inclined to think that there is a finer way of studying ornithology than this. It requires so much closer attention to the habits of the birds, that, if for that reason only, I have been willing to omit the gun. Yet notwithstanding the objection on the score of humanity, I am compelled to doubt if equally valuable sports

---

[19]The Falls of St. Mary are probably those in British Columbia associated with salmon fishing, though Thoreau may have had in mind the St. Mary's River in Nova Scotia, also known for its fisheries.
[20]An archaic name for "gun."

are ever substituted for these; and when some of my friends have asked me anxiously about their boys, whether they should let them hunt, I have answered, yes,—remembering that it was one of the best parts of my education,—*make* them hunters, though sportsmen only at first, if possible, mighty hunters at last, so that they shall not find game large enough for them in this or any vegetable wilderness,—hunters as well as fishers of men.[21] Thus far I am of the opinion of Chaucer's nun, who

> *"yave not of the text a pulled hen*
> *That saith that hunters ben not holy men."*

There is a period in the history of the individual, as of the race, when the hunters are the "best men," as the Algonquins called them. We cannot but pity the boy who has never fired a gun; he is no more humane, while his education has been sadly neglected. This was my answer with respect to those youths who were bent on this pursuit, trusting that they would soon outgrow it. No humane being, past the thoughtless age of boyhood, will wantonly murder any creature, which holds its life by the same tenure that he does. The hare in its extremity cries like a child. I warn you, mothers, that my sympathies do not always make the usual phil-*anthropic* distinctions.[22]

Such is oftenest the young man's introduction to the forest, and the most original part of himself. He goes thither at first as a hunter and fisher, until at last, if he has the seeds of a better life in him, he distinguishes his proper objects, as a poet or naturalist it may be, and leaves the gun and fish-pole behind. The mass of men are still and always young in this respect. In some countries a hunting parson is no uncommon sight. Such a one might make a good shepherd's dog, but is far from being the Good Shepherd. I have been surprised to consider that the only obvious employment, except wood-chopping, ice-cutting, or the like business, which ever to my knowledge detained at Walden Pond for a whole half day any of my fellow-citizens, whether fathers or children of the town, with just one exception, was fishing. Commonly they did not think that they were lucky, or well paid for their time, unless they got a long string of fish, though they had the opportunity of seeing the pond all the while. They might go there a thousand times before the sediment of fishing would sink to the bottom and leave their purpose pure; but no doubt such a clarifying process would be going on all the while. The governor and his council faintly remember the pond, for they went a-fishing there when they were boys; but now they are too old and dignified to go a-fishing, and so they know it no more forever. Yet even they expect to go to heaven at last. If the legislature regards it, it is chiefly to regulate the number of hooks to be used there; but they know nothing about the hook of hooks with which to angle for the pond itself, impaling

---

[21]Christ, in calling Simon and Andrew from their fishing to follow him, told them: "I will make you to become fishers of men." Mark 1:17.

[22]As he does so often, Thoreau is playing with the etymology of words. He is saying that his love of animals is not limited to "love of man" only.

the legislature for a bait. Thus, even in civilized communities, the embryo man passes through the hunter stage of development.

I have found repeatedly, of late years, that I cannot fish without falling a little in self-respect. I have tried it again and again. I have skill at it, and, like many of my fellows, a certain instinct for it, which revives from time to time, but always when I have done I feel that it would have been better if I had not fished. I think that I do not mistake. It is a faint intimation, yet so are the first streaks of morning. There is unquestionably this instinct in me which belongs to the lower orders of creation; yet with every year I am less a fisherman, though without more humanity or even wisdom; at present I am no fisherman at all. But I see that if I were to live in a wilderness I should again be tempted to become a fisher and hunter in earnest. Beside, there is something essentially unclean about this diet and all flesh, and I began to see where housework commences, and whence the endeavor, which costs so much, to wear a tidy and respectable appearance each day, to keep the house sweet and free from all ill odors and sights. Having been my own butcher and scullion and cook, as well as the gentleman for whom the dishes were served up, I can speak from an unusually complete experience. The practical objection to animal food in my case was its uncleanness; and, besides, when I had caught and cleaned and cooked and eaten my fish, they seemed not to have fed me essentially. It was insignificant and unnecessary, and cost more than it came to. A little bread or a few potatoes would have done as well, with less trouble and filth. Like many of my contemporaries, I had rarely for many years used animal food, or tea, or coffee, &c.; not so much because of any ill effects which I had traced to them, as because they were not agreeable to my imagination. The repugnance to animal food is not the effect of experience, but is an instinct. It appeared more beautiful to live low and fare hard in many respects; and though I never did so, I went far enough to please my imagination. I believe that every man who has ever been earnest to preserve his higher or poetic faculties in the best condition has been particularly inclined to abstain from animal food, and from much food of any kind. It is a significant fact, stated by entomologists, I find it in Kirby and Spence, that "some insects in their perfect state, though furnished with organs of feeding, make no use of them;" and they lay it down as "a general rule, that almost all insects in this state eat much less than in that of larvae. The voracious caterpillar when transformed into a butterfly," ... "and the gluttonous maggot when become a fly," content themselves with a drop or two of honey or some other sweet liquid. The abdomen under the wings of the butterfly still represents the larva. This is the tid-bit which tempts his insectivorous fate. The gross feeder is a man in the larva state; and there are whole nations in that condition, nations without fancy or imagination, whose vast abdomens betray them.

It is hard to provide and cook so simple and clean a diet as will not offend the imagination; but this, I think, is to be fed when we feed the body; they should both sit down at the same table. Yet perhaps this may be done. The fruits eaten temperately need not make us ashamed of our appetites, nor interrupt the worthiest pursuits. But put an extra condiment into your dish, and it will poison you. It is not worth the while to live by rich cookery. Most men would feel shame if caught preparing with their own hands precisely such a dinner, whether of animal or vegetable food, as is every day prepared for them by others. Yet till this is otherwise we are not civilized, and, if gentlemen and ladies, are not true men and women. This certainly suggests what change is to be made. It may be vain to ask why the imagination will not be reconciled to flesh and fat. I am satisfied that it is not. Is it not a reproach that man is a carnivorous animal? True, he can and does live, in a great measure, by preying on other animals; but this is a miserable way,—as any one who will go to snaring rabbits, or slaughtering lambs, may learn,—and he will be regarded as a benefactor of his race who shall teach man to confine himself to a more innocent and wholesome diet. Whatever my own practice may be, I have no doubt that it is a part of the destiny of the human race, in its gradual improvement, to leave off eating animals, as surely as the savage tribes have left off eating each other when they came in contact with the more civilized.

If one listens to the faintest but constant suggestions of his genius,[23] which are certainly true, he sees not to what extremes, or even insanity, it may lead him; and yet that way, as he grows more resolute and faithful, his road lies. The faintest assured objection which one healthy man feels will at length prevail over the arguments and customs of mankind. No man ever followed his genius till it misled him. Though the result were bodily weakness, yet perhaps no one can say that the consequences were to be regretted, for these were a life in conformity to higher principles. If the day and the night are such that you greet them with joy, and life emits a fragrance like flowers and sweet-scented herbs, is more elastic, more starry, more immortal,—that is your success. All nature is your congratulation, and you have cause momentarily to bless yourself. The greatest gains and values are farthest from being appreciated. We easily come to doubt if they exist. We soon forget them. They are the highest reality. Perhaps the facts most astounding and most real are never communicated by man to man. The true harvest of my daily life is somewhat as intangible and indescribable as the tints of morning or evening. It is a little star-dust caught, a segment of the rainbow which I have clutched.

Yet, for my part, I was never unusually squeamish; I could sometimes eat a fried rat with a good relish, if it were necessary. I am glad to have drunk water so long, for the same reason that I prefer the natural sky to an opium-eater's heaven. I would fain keep sober always; and there are infinite degrees of drunkenness. I believe that water is the only drink for a wise man; wine is not so noble a liquor; and think of dashing the hopes of a morning with a cup of warm coffee, or of an evening with a dish of tea! Ah, how low I fall when I am tempted by them! Even music may be intoxicating.

---

[23]By "genius" Thoreau means an innate faculty in all people which, he believes, identi-fies the good, the true, the right, the beautiful. These are the "highest reality."

Such apparently slight causes destroyed Greece and Rome, and will destroy England and America. Of all ebriosity, who does not prefer to be intoxicated by the air he breathes? I have found it to be the most serious objection to coarse labors long continued, that they compelled me to eat and drink coarsely also. But to tell the truth, I find myself at present somewhat less particular in these respects. I carry less religion to the table, ask no blessing; not because I am wiser than I was, but, I am obliged to confess, because, however much it is to be regretted, with years I have grown more coarse and indifferent. Perhaps these questions are entertained only in youth, as most believe of poetry. My practice is "nowhere," my opinion is here. Nevertheless I am far from regarding myself as one of those privileged ones to whom the Ved refers when it says, that "he who has true faith in the Omnipresent Supreme Being may eat all that exists," that is, is not bound to inquire what is his food, or who prepares it; and even in their case it is to be observed, as a Hindoo commentator has remarked, that the Vedant limits this privilege to "the time of distress."

Who has not sometimes derived an inexpressible satisfaction from his food in which appetite had no share? I have been thrilled to think that I owed a mental perception to the commonly gross sense of taste, that I have been inspired through the palate, that some berries which I had eaten on a hill-side had fed my genius. "The soul not being mistress of herself," says Thseng-tseu, "one looks, and one does not see; one listens, and one does not hear; one eats, and one does not know the savor of food." He who distinguishes the true savor of his food can never be a glutton; he who does not cannot be otherwise. A puritan may go to his brown-bread crust with as gross an appetite as ever an alderman to his turtle. Not that food which entereth into the mouth defileth a man, but the appetite with which it is eaten. It is neither the quality nor the quantity, but the devotion to sensual savors; when that which is eaten is not a viand to sustain our animal, or inspire our spiritual life, but food for the worms that possess us. If the hunter has a taste for mud-turtles, musk-rats, and other such savage tid-bits, the fine lady indulges a taste for jelly made of a calf's foot, or for sardines from over the sea, and they are even. He goes to the mill-pond, she to her preserve-pot. The wonder is how they, how you and I, can live this slimy beastly life, eating and drinking.

Our whole life is startlingly moral. There is never an instant's truce between virtue and vice. Goodness is the only investment that never fails. In the music of the harp which trembles round the world it is the insisting on this which thrills us. The harp is the travelling patterer for the Universe's Insurance Company, recommending its laws, and our little goodness is all the assessment that we pay. Though the youth at last grows indifferent, the laws of the universe are not indifferent, but are forever on the side of the most sensitive. Listen to every zephyr for some reproof, for it is surely there, and he is unfortunate who does not hear it. We cannot touch a string or move a stop but the charming moral transfixes us. Many an irksome noise, go a long way off, is heard as music, a proud sweet satire on the meanness of our lives.

We are conscious of an animal in us, which awakens in proportion as our higher nature slumbers. It is reptile and sensual, and perhaps cannot be wholly expelled; like the worms which, even in life and health, occupy our bodies. Possibly we may withdraw from it, but never change its nature. I fear that it may enjoy a certain health of its own; that we may be well, yet not pure. The other day I picked up the lower jaw of a hog, with white and sound teeth and tusks, which suggested that there was an animal health and vigor distinct from the spiritual. This creature succeeded by other means than temperance and purity. "That in which men differ from brute beasts," says Mencius, "is a thing very inconsiderable; the common herd lose it very soon; superior men preserve it carefully." Who knows what sort of life would result if we had attained to purity? If I knew so wise a man as could teach me purity I would go to seek him forthwith. "A command over our passions, and over the external senses of the body, and good acts, are declared by the Ved to be indispensable in the mind's approximation to God." Yet the spirit can for the time pervade and control every member and function of the body, and transmute what in form is the grossest sensuality into purity and devotion. The generative energy, which, when we are loose, dissipates and makes us unclean, when we are continent invigorates and inspires us. Chastity is the flowering of man; and what are called Genius, Heroism, Holiness, and the like, are but various fruits which succeed it. Man flows at once to God when the channel of purity is open. By turns our purity inspires and our impurity casts us down. He is blessed who is assured that the animal is dying out in him day by day, and the divine being established. Perhaps there is none but has cause for shame on account of the inferior and brutish nature to which he is allied. I fear that we are such gods or demigods only as fauns and satyrs, the divine allied to beasts, the creatures of appetite, and that, to some extent, our very life is our disgrace.—

> *"How happy's he who hath due place assigned*
> *To his beasts and disaforested his mind!*
>
> *Can use his horse, goat, wolf, and ev'ry beast,*
> *And is not ass himself to all the rest!*
> *Else man not only is the herd of swine,*
> *But he's those devils too which did incline*
> *Them to a headlong rage, and made them worse."*[24]

All sensuality is one, though it takes many forms; all purity is one. It is the same whether a man eat, or drink, or cohabit, or sleep sensually. They are but one appetite, and we only need to see a person do any one of these

---

[24]The passage of poetry quoted from John Donne alludes to the biblical story of Christ's casting out the devils from afflicted persons and transferring them into a herd of swine, which then plunged headlong into the sea. Thoreau is warning against the danger of giving ourselves up completely to sensuality and failing to strive for "wisdom and purity."

things to know how great a sensualist he is. The impure can neither stand nor sit with purity. When the reptile is attacked at one mouth of his burrow, he shows himself at another. If you would be chaste, you must be temperate. What is chastity? How shall a man know if he is chaste? He shall not know it. We have heard of this virtue, but we know not what it is. We speak conformably to the rumor which we have heard. From exertion come wisdom and purity; from sloth ignorance and sensuality. In the student sensuality is a sluggish habit of mind. An unclean person is universally a slothful one, one who sits by a stove, whom the sun shines on prostrate, who reposes without being fatigued. If you would avoid uncleanness, and all the sins, work earnestly, though it be at cleaning a stable. Nature is hard to be overcome, but she must be overcome. What avails it that you are Christian, if you are not purer than the heathen, if you deny yourself no more, if you are not more religious? I know of many systems of religion esteemed heathenish whose precepts fill the reader with shame, and provoke him to new endeavors, though it be to the performance of rites merely.

I hesitate to say these things, but it is not because of the subject,—I care not how obscene my *words* are,—but because I cannot speak of them without betraying my impurity. We discourse freely without shame of one form of sensuality, and are silent about another. We are so degraded that we cannot speak simply of the necessary functions of human nature. In earlier ages, in some countries, every function was reverently spoken of and regulated by law. Nothing was too trivial for the Hindoo lawgiver, however offensive it may be to modern taste. He teaches how to eat, drink, cohabit, void excrement and urine, and the like, elevating what is mean, and does not falsely excuse himself by calling these things trifles.

Every man is the builder of a temple, called his body, to the god he worships, after a style purely his own, nor can he get off by hammering marble instead. We are all sculptors and painters, and our material is our own flesh and blood and bones. Any nobleness begins at once to refine a man's features, any meanness or sensuality to imbrute them.

John Farmer sat at his door one September evening, after a hard day's work, his mind still running on his labor more or less. Having bathed he sat down to recreate his intellectual man. It was a rather cool evening, and some of his neighbors were apprehending a frost. He had not attended to the train of his thoughts long when he heard some one playing on a flute, and that sound harmonized with his mood. Still he thought of his work; but the burden of his thought was, that though this kept running in his head, and he found himself planning and contriving it against his will, yet it concerned him very little. It was no more than the scurf of his skin, which was constantly shuffled off. But the notes of the flute came home to his ears out of a different sphere from that he worked in, and suggested work for certain faculties which slumbered in him. They gently did away with the street, and the village, and the state in which he lived. A voice said to him,—Why do you stay here and live this mean moiling life, when a glorious existence is

possible for you? Those same stars twinkle over other fields than these.—
But how to come out of this condition and actually migrate thither? All that
he could think of was to practise some new austerity, to let his mind
descend into his body and redeem it, and treat himself with ever increasing
respect.

Spring

The opening of large tracts by the ice-cutters commonly causes a pond to
break up earlier; for the water, agitated by the wind, even in cold weather,
wears away the surrounding ice. But such was not the effect on Walden that
year, for she had soon got a thick new garment to take the place of the old.
This pond never breaks up so soon as the others in this neighborhood, on
account both of its greater depth and its having no stream passing through
it to melt or wear away the ice. I never knew it to open in the course of a
winter, not excepting that of '52–3, which gave the ponds so severe a trial.
It commonly opens about the first of April, a week or ten days later than
Flint's Pond and Fair-Haven, beginning to melt on the north side and in the
shallower parts where it began to freeze. It indicates better than any water
hereabouts the absolute progress of the season, being least affected by transient changes of temperature. A severe cold of a few days' duration in March
may very much retard the opening of the former ponds, while the temperature of Walden increases almost uninterruptedly. A thermometer thrust into
the middle of Walden on the 6th of March, 1847, stood at 32°, or freezing
point; near the shore at 33°; in the middle of Flint's Pond, the same day, at
32½°; at a dozen rods from the shore, in shallow water, under ice a foot
thick, at 36°. This difference of three and a half degrees between the temperature of the deep water and the shallow in the latter pond, and the fact
that a great proportion of it is comparatively shallow, show why it should
break up so much sooner than Walden. The ice in the shallowest part was
at this time several inches thinner than in the middle. In mid-winter
the middle had been the warmest and the ice thinnest there. So, also, every
one who has waded about the shores of a pond in summer must have perceived how much warmer the water is close to the shore, where only three
or four inches deep, than a little distance out, and on the surface where
it is deep, than near the bottom. In spring the sun not only exerts an influence through the increased temperature of the air and earth, but its heat
passes through ice a foot or more thick, and is reflected from the bottom in
shallow water, and so also warms the water and melts the under side of the
ice, at the same time that it is melting it more directly above, making it
uneven, and causing the air bubbles which it contains to extend themselves
upward and downward until it is completely honey-combed, and at last disappears suddenly in a single spring rain. Ice has its grain as well as wood,
and when a cake begins to rot or "comb," that is, assume the appearance of
honey-comb, whatever may be its position, the air cells are at right angles
with what was the water surface. Where there is a rock or a log rising near

to the surface the ice over it is much thinner, and is frequently quite dissolved by this reflected heat; and I have been told that in the experiment at Cambridge to freeze water in a shallow wooden pond, though the cold air circulated underneath, and so had access to both sides, the reflection of the sun from the bottom more than counterbalanced this advantage. When a warm rain in the middle of the winter melts off the snow-ice from Walden, and leaves a hard dark or transparent ice on the middle, there will be a strip of rotten though thicker white ice, a rod or more wide, about the shores, created by this reflected heat. Also, as I have said, the bubbles themselves within the ice operate as burning glasses to melt the ice beneath.

The phenomena of the year take place every day in a pond on a small scale. Every morning, generally speaking, the shallow water is being warmed more rapidly than the deep, though it may not be made so warm after all, and every evening it is being cooled more rapidly until the morning. The day is an epitome of the year. The night is the winter, the morning and evening are the spring and fall, and the noon is the summer. The cracking and booming of the ice indicate a change of temperature. One pleasant morning after a cold night, February 24th, 1850, having gone to Flint's Pond to spend the day, I noticed with surprise, that when I struck the ice with the head of my axe, it resounded like a gong for many rods around, or as if I had struck on a tight drum-head. The pond began to boom about an hour after sunrise, when it felt the influence of the sun's rays slanted upon it from over the hills; it stretched itself and yawned like a waking man with a gradually increasing tumult, which was kept up three or four hours. It took a short siesta at noon, and boomed once more toward night, as the sun was withdrawing his influence. In the right stage of the weather a pond fires its evening gun with great regularity. But in the middle of the day, being full of cracks, and the air also being less elastic, it had completely lost its resonance, and probably fishes and muskrats could not then have been stunned by a blow on it. The fishermen say that the "thundering of the pond" scares the fishes and prevents their biting. The pond does not thunder every evening, and I cannot tell surely when to expect its thundering; but though I may perceive no difference in the weather, it does. Who would have suspected so large and cold and thick-skinned a thing to be so sensitive? Yet it has its law to which it thunders obedience when it should as surely as the buds expand in the spring. The earth is all alive and covered with papillae. The largest pond is as sensitive to atmospheric changes as the globule of mercury in its tube.

One attraction in coming to the woods to live was that I should have leisure and opportunity to see the spring come in. The ice in the pond at length begins to be honey-combed, and I can set my heel in it as I walk. Fogs and rains and warmer suns are gradually melting the snow; the days have grown sensibly longer; and I see how I shall get through the winter without adding to my wood-pile, for large fires are no longer necessary. I am on the alert for the first signs of spring, to hear the chance note of some arriving bird, or the striped squirrel's chirp, for his stores must be now nearly exhausted, or see the woodchuck venture out of his winter quarters. On the 13th of March, after I had heard the bluebird, song-sparrow, and red-wing, the ice was still nearly a foot thick. As the weather grew warmer, it was not sensibly worn away by the water, nor broken up and floated off as in rivers, but, though it was completely melted for half a rod in width about the shore, the middle was merely honey-combed and saturated with water, so that you could put your foot through it when six inches thick; but by the next day evening, perhaps, after a warm rain followed by fog, it would have wholly disappeared, all gone off with the fog, spirited away. One year I went across the middle only five days before it disappeared entirely. In 1845 Walden was first completely open on the 1st of April; in '46, the 25th of March; in '47, the 8th of April; in '51, the 28th of March; in '52, the 18th of April; in '53, the 23d of March; in '54, about the 7th of April.

Every incident connected with the breaking up of the rivers and ponds and the settling of the weather is particularly interesting to us who live in a climate of so great extremes. When the warmer days come, they who dwell near the river hear the ice crack at night with a startling whoop as loud as artillery, as if its icy fetters were rent from end to end, and within a few days see it rapidly going out. So the alligator comes out of the mud with quakings of the earth. One old man, who has been a close observer of Nature, and seems as thoroughly wise in regard to all her operations as if she had been put upon the stocks when he was a boy, and he had helped to lay her keel,—who has come to his growth, and can hardly acquire more of a natural lore if he should live to the age of Methuselah,[25]—told me, and I was surprised to hear him express wonder at any of Nature's operations, for I thought that there were no secrets between them, that one spring day he took his gun and boat, and thought that he would have a little sport with the ducks. There was ice still on the meadows, but it was all gone out of the river, and he dropped down without obstruction from Sudbury, where he lived, to Fair-Haven Pond, which he found, unexpectedly, covered for the most part with a firm field of ice. It was a warm day, and he was surprised to see so great a body of ice remaining. Not seeing any ducks, he hid his boat on the north or back side of an island in the pond, and then concealed himself in the bushes on the south side, to await them. The ice was melted for three or four rods from the shore, and there was a smooth and warm sheet of water, with a muddy bottom, such as the ducks love, within, and he thought it likely that some would be along pretty soon. After he had lain still there about an hour he heard a low and seemingly very distant sound, but singularly grand and impressive, unlike any thing he had ever heard, gradually swelling and increasing as if it would have a universal and memorable ending, a sullen rush and roar, which seemed to him all at once like the sound of a vast body of fowl coming in to settle there, and, seizing his gun, he started up in haste and excited; but he found, to his surprise, that

[25]According to Genesis 5:27, he lived 969 years.

the whole body of the ice had started while he lay there, and drifted in to the shore, and the sound he had heard was made by its edge grating on the shore,—at first gently nibbled and crumbled off, but at length heaving up and scattering its wrecks along the island to a considerable height before it came to a stand still.

At length the sun's rays have attained the right angle, and warm winds blow up mist and rain and melt the snow banks, and the sun dispersing the mist smiles on a checkered landscape of russet and white smoking with incense, through which the traveller picks his way from islet to islet, cheered by the music of a thousand tinkling rills and rivulets whose veins are filled with the blood of winter which they are bearing off.

Few phenomena gave me more delight than to observe the forms which thawing sand and clay assume in flowing down the sides of a deep cut on the railroad through which I passed on my way to the village, a phenomenon not very common on so large a scale, though the number of freshly exposed banks of the right material must have been greatly multiplied since railroads were invented. The material was sand of every degree of fineness and of various rich colors, commonly mixed with a little clay. When the frost comes out in the spring, and even in a thawing day in the winter, the sand begins to flow down the slopes like lava, sometimes bursting out through the snow and overflowing it where no sand was to be seen before. Innumerable little streams overlap and interlace one with another, exhibiting a sort of hybrid product, which obeys half way the law of currents, and half way that of vegetation. As it flows it takes the forms of sappy leaves or vines, making heaps of pulpy sprays a foot or more in depth, and resembling, as you look down on them, the laciniated lobed and imbricated thalluses of some lichens; or you are reminded of coral, of leopards' paws or birds' feet, of brains or lungs or bowels, and excrements of all kinds. It is a truly *grotesque* vegetation, whose forms and color we see imitated in bronze, a sort of architectural foliage more ancient and typical than acanthus, chiccory, ivy, vine, or any vegetable leaves; destined perhaps, under some circumstances, to become a puzzle to future geologists. The whole cut impressed me as if it were a cave with its stalactites laid open to the light. The various shades of the sand are singularly rich and agreeable, embracing the different iron colors, brown, gray, yellowish, and reddish. When the flowing mass reaches the drain at the foot of the bank it spreads out flatter into *strands*, the separate streams losing their semi-cylindrical form and gradually becoming more flat and broad, running together as they are more moist, till they form an almost flat *sand*, still variously and beautifully shaded, but in which you can trace the original forms of vegetation; till at length, in the water itself, they are converted into *banks*, like those formed off the mouths of rivers, and the forms of vegetation are lost in the ripple marks on the bottom.

The whole bank, which is from twenty to forty feet high, is sometimes overlaid with a mass of this kind of foliage, or sandy rupture, for a quarter of a mile on one or both sides, the produce of one spring day. What makes this sand foliage remarkable is its springing into existence thus suddenly.

When I see on the one side the inert bank,—for the sun acts on one side first,—and on the other this luxuriant foliage, the creation of an hour, I am affected as if in a peculiar sense I stood in the laboratory of the Artist who made the world and me,—had come to where he was still at work, sporting on this bank, and with excess of energy strewing his fresh designs about. I feel as if I were nearer to the vitals of the globe, for this sandy overflow is something such a foliaceous mass as the vitals of the animal body. You find thus in the very sands an anticipation of the vegetable leaf. No wonder that the earth expresses itself outwardly in leaves, it so labors with the idea inwardly. The atoms have already learned this law, and are pregnant by it. The overhanging leaf sees here its prototype. *Internally*, whether in the globe or animal body, it is a moist thick *lobe*, a word especially applicable to the liver and lungs and the *leaves* of fat, ($\lambda \epsilon i \beta \omega$, *labor, lapsus*, to flow or slip downward, a lapsing; $\lambda o \beta o \varsigma$, *globus*, lobe, globe; also lap, flap, and many other words,) *externally* a dry thin *leaf*, even as the *f* and *v* are a pressed and dried *b*. The radicals of lobe are *lb*, the soft mass of the *b* (single lobed, or B, double lobed,) with a liquid *l* behind it pressing it forward. In globe, *glb*, the guttural *g* adds to the meaning the capacity of the throat. The feathers and wings of birds are still drier and thinner leaves. Thus, also, you pass from the lumpish grub in the earth to the airy and fluttering butterfly. The very globe continually transcends and translates itself, and becomes winged in its orbit. Even ice begins with delicate crystal leaves, as if it had flowed into moulds which the fronds of water plants have impressed on the watery mirror. The whole tree itself is but one leaf, and rivers are still vaster leaves whose pulp is intervening earth, and towns and cities are the ova of insects in their axils.

When the sun withdraws the sand ceases to flow, but in the morning the streams will start once more and branch and branch again into a myriad of others. You here see perchance how blood vessels are formed. If you look closely you observe that first there pushes forward from the thawing mass a stream of softened sand with a drop-like point, like the ball of the finger, feeling its way slowly and blindly downward, until at last with more heat and moisture, as the sun gets higher, the most fluid portion, in its effort to obey the law to which the most inert also yields, separates from the latter and forms for itself a meandering channel or artery within that, in which is seen a little silvery stream glancing like lightning from one stage of pulpy leaves or branches to another, and ever and anon swallowed up in the sand. It is wonderful how rapidly yet perfectly the sand organizes itself as it flows, using the best material its mass affords to form the sharp edges of its channel. Such are the sources of rivers. In the silicious matter which the water deposits is perhaps the bony system, and in the still finer soil and organic matter the fleshy fibre or cellular tissue. What is man but a mass of thawing clay? The ball of the human finger is but a drop congealed. The fingers and toes flow to their extent from the thawing mass of the body. Who knows what the human body would expand and flow out to under a more genial heaven? Is not the hand a spreading *palm* leaf with its lobes and veins? The ear may be regarded, fancifully, as a lichen, *umbilicaria*, on the side of the head, with its lobe or drop. The lip (*labium* from *labor* (?)) laps or lapses from the sides of the cavernous mouth. The nose is a manifest congealed drop or stalactite. The chin is a still larger drop, the confluent dripping of the face. The cheeks are a slide from the brows into the valley of the face, opposed and diffused by the cheek bones. Each rounded lobe of the vegetable leaf, too, is a thick and now loitering drop, larger or smaller; the lobes are the fingers of the leaf; and as many lobes as it has, in so many directions it tends to flow, and more heat or other genial influences would have caused it to flow yet farther.

Thus it seemed that this one hillside illustrated the principle of all the operations of Nature. The Maker of this earth but patented a leaf. What Champollion will decipher this hieroglyphic for us,[26] that we may turn over a new leaf at last? This phenomenon is more exhilarating to me than the luxuriance and fertility of vineyards. True, it is somewhat excrementitious in its character, and there is no end to the heaps of liver lights and bowels, as if the globe were turned wrong side outward; but this suggests at least that Nature has some bowels, and there again is mother of humanity. This is the frost coming out of the ground; this is Spring. It precedes the green and flowery spring, as mythology precedes regular poetry. I know of nothing more purgative of winter fumes and indigestions. It convinces me that Earth is still in her swaddling clothes, and stretches forth baby fingers on every side. Fresh curls spring from the baldest brow. There is nothing inorganic. These foliaceous heaps lie along the bank like the slag of a furnace, showing that Nature is "in full blast" within. The earth is not a mere fragment of dead history, stratum upon stratum like the leaves of a book, to be studied by geologists and antiquaries chiefly, but living poetry like the leaves of a tree, which precede flowers and fruit,—not a fossil earth, but a living earth; compared with whose great central life all animal and vegetable life is merely parasitic. Its throes will heave our exuviae from their graves. You may melt your metals and cast them into the most beautiful moulds you can; they will never excite me like the forms which this molten earth flows out into. And not only it, but the institutions upon it, are plastic like clay in the hands of the potter.

Ere long, not only on these banks, but on every hill and plain and in every hollow, the frost comes out of the ground like a dormant quadruped from its burrow, and seeks the sea with music, or migrates to other climes in clouds. Thaw with his gentle persuasion is more powerful than Thor with his hammer.[27] The one melts, the other but breaks in pieces.

When the ground was partially bare of snow, and a few warm days had dried its surface somewhat, it was pleasant to compare the first tender signs of the infant year just peeping forth with stately beauty of the withered

---

[26]Jean François Champollion (1790–1832) deciphered the hieroglyphics on the Rosetta Stone, thus providing a key to ancient Egyptian culture.

[27]Norse god of Thunder.

vegetation which had withstood the winter,—life-everlasting, golden-rods, pinweeds, and graceful wild grasses, more obvious and interesting frequently than in summer even, as if their beauty was not ripe till then; even cotton-grass, cat-tails, mulleins, johnswort, hardhack, meadow-sweet, and other strong stemmed plants, those unexhausted granaries which entertain the earliest birds,—decent weeds, at least, which widowed Nature wears. I am particularly attracted by the arching and sheaf-like top of the wool-grass; it brings back the summer to our winter memories, and is among the forms which art loves to copy, and which, in the vegetable kingdom, have the same relation to types already in the mind of man that astronomy has. It is an antique style older than Greek or Egyptian. Many of the phenomena of Winter are suggestive of an inexpressible tenderness and fragile delicacy. We are accustomed to hear this king described as a rude and boisterous tyrant; but with the gentleness of a lover he adorns the tresses of Summer.

At the approach of spring the red-squirrels got under my house, two at a time, directly under my feet as I sat reading or writing, and kept up the queerest chuckling and chirruping and vocal pirouetting and gurgling sounds that ever were heard; and when I stamped they only chirruped the louder, as if past all fear and respect in their mad pranks, defying humanity to stop them. No you don't—chickaree—chickaree. They were wholly deaf to my arguments, or failed to perceive their force, and fell into a strain of invective that was irresistible.

The first sparrow of spring! The year beginning with younger hope than ever! The faint silvery warblings heard over the partially bare and moist fields from the blue-bird, the song-sparrow, and the red-wing, as if the last flakes of winter tinkled as they fell! What at such a time are histories, chronologies, traditions, and all written revelations? The brooks sing carols and glees to the spring. The marsh-hawk sailing low over the meadow is already seeking the first slimy life that awakes. The sinking sound of melting snow is heard in all dells, and the ice dissolves apace in the ponds. The grass flames up on the hillsides like a spring fire,—"et primitus oritur herba imbribus primoribus evocata,"[28]—as if the earth sent forth an inward heat to greet the returning sun; not yellow but green is the color of its flame;—the symbol of perpetual youth, the grass-blade, like a long green ribbon, streams from the sod into the summer, checked indeed by the frost, but anon pushing on again, lifting its spear of last year's hay with the fresh life below. It grows as steadily as the rill oozes out of the ground. It is almost identical with that, for in the growing days of June, when the rills are dry, the grass blades are their channels, and from year to year the herds drink at this perennial green stream, and the mower draws from it betimes their winter supply. So our human life but dies down to its root, and still puts forth its green blade to eternity.

---

[28]From the Latin poem *De Re Rustica* by Varro, c. 25 B.C.: "The grass starts to grow, summoned by the early rains."

Walden is melting apace. There is a canal two rods wide along the northerly and westerly sides, and wider still at the east end. A great field of ice has cracked off from the main body. I hear a song-sparrow singing from the bushes on the shore,—*olit, olit, olit,*—*chip, chip, chip, che char,*—*che wiss, wiss, wiss.* He too is helping to crack it. How handsome the great sweeping curves in the edge of the ice, answering somewhat to those of the shore, but more regular! It is unusually hard, owing to the recent severe but transient cold, and all watered or waved like a palace floor. But the wind slides eastward over its opaque surface in vain, till it reaches the living surface beyond. It is glorious to behold this ribbon of water sparkling in the sun, the bare face of the pond full of glee and youth, as if it spoke the joy of the fishes within it, and of the sands on its shore,—a silvery sheen as from the scales of a *leuciscus*, as it were all one active fish. Such is the contrast between winter and spring. Walden was dead and is alive again. But this spring it broke up more steadily, as I have said.

The change from storm and winter to serene and mild weather, from dark and sluggish hours to bright and elastic ones, is a memorable crisis which all things proclaim. It is seemingly instantaneous at last. Suddenly an influx of light filled my house, though the evening was at hand, and the clouds of winter still overhung it, and the eaves were dripping with sleety rain. I looked out the window, and lo! where yesterday was cold gray ice there lay the transparent pond already calm and full of hope as on a summer evening, reflecting a summer evening sky in its bosom, though none was visible overhead, as if it had intelligence with some remote horizon. I heard a robin in the distance, the first I had heard for many a thousand years, methought, whose note I shall not forget for many a thousand more,—the same sweet and powerful song of yore. O the evening robin, at the end of a New England summer day! If I could ever find the twig he sits upon! I mean *he;* I mean *the twig.* This at least is not the *Turdus migratorius.*[29] The pitch-pines and shrub-oaks about my house, which had so long drooped, suddenly resumed their several characters, looked brighter, greener, and more erect and alive, as if effectually cleansed and restored by the rain. I knew that it would not rain any more. You may tell by looking at any twig of the forest, ay, at your very wood-pile, whether its winter is past or not. As it grew darker, I was startled by the *honking* of geese flying low over the woods, like weary travellers getting in late from southern lakes, and indulging at last in unrestrained complaint and mutual consolation. Standing at my door, I could hear the rush of their wings; when, driving toward my house, they suddenly spied my light, and with hushed clamor wheeled and settled in the pond. So I came in, and shut the door, and passed my first spring night in the woods.

In the morning I watched the geese from the door through the mist, sailing in the middle of the pond, fifty rods off, so large and tumultuous that Walden appeared like an artificial pond for their amusement. But when

[29]The American robin.

I stood on the shore they at once rose up with a great flapping of wings at the signal of their commander, and when they had got into rank circled about over my head, twenty-nine of them, and then steered straight to Canada, with a regular *honk* from the leader at intervals, trusting to break their fast in muddier pools. A "plump"[30] of ducks rose at the same time and took the route to the north in the wake of their noisier cousins.

For a week I heard the circling groping clangor of some solitary goose in the foggy mornings, seeking its companion, and still peopling the woods with the sound of a larger life than they could sustain. In April the pigeons were seen again flying express in small flocks, and in due time I heard the martins twittering over my clearing, though it had not seemed that the township contained so many that it could afford me any, and I fancied that they were peculiarly of the ancient race that dwelt in hollow trees ere white men came. In almost all climes the tortoise and the frog are among the precursors and heralds of this season, and birds fly with song and glancing plumage, and plants spring and bloom, and winds blow, to correct this slight oscillation of the poles and preserve the equilibrium of Nature.

As every season seems best to us in its turn, so the coming in of spring is like the creation of Cosmos out of Chaos and the realization of the Golden Age.—

> *"Eurus ad Auroram, Nabathaeaque regna recessit,*
> *Persidaque, et radiis juga subdita matutinis."*[31]

> *"The East-Wind withdrew to Aurora and the Nabathaean kingdom,*
> *And the Persian, and the ridges placed under the morning rays.*

> *Man was born. Whether that Artificer of things,*
> *The origin of a better world, made him from the divine seed;*
> *Or the earth being recent and lately sundered from the high*
> *Ether, retained some seeds of cognate heaven."*

A single gentle rain makes the grass many shades greener. So our prospects brighten on the influx of better thoughts. We should be blessed if we lived in the present always, and took advantage of every accident that befell us, like the grass which confesses the influence of the slightest dew that falls on it; and did not spend our time in atoning for the neglect of past opportunities, which we call doing our duty. We loiter in winter while it is already spring. In a pleasant spring morning all men's sins are forgiven. Such a day is a truce to vice. While such a sun holds out to burn, the vilest sinner may return. Through our own recovered innocence we discern the innocence of our neighbors. You may have known your neighbor yesterday for a thief, a drunkard, or a sensualist, and merely pitied or despised him, and despaired of the world; but the sun shines bright and warm this first spring morning, re-creating the world, and you meet him at some serene work, and see how

---

[30]Flock.

[31]From Ovid, *Metamorphoses*, Book 1.

his exhausted and debauched veins expand with still joy and bless the new day, feel the spring influence with the innocence of infancy, and all his faults are forgotten. There is not only an atmosphere of good will about him, but even a savor of holiness groping for expression, blindly and ineffectually perhaps, like a new-born instinct, and for a short hour the south hill-side echoes to no vulgar jest. You see some innocent fair shoots preparing to burst from his gnarled rind and try another year's life, tender and fresh as the youngest plant. Even he has entered into the joy of his Lord. Why the jailer does not leave open his prison doors,—why the judge does not dismiss his case,—why the preacher does not dismiss his congregation! It is because they do not obey the hint which God gives them, nor accept the pardon which he freely offers to all.

"A return to goodness produced each day in the tranquil and beneficent breath of the morning, causes that in respect to the love of virtue and the hatred of vice, one approaches a little the primitive nature of man, as the sprouts of the forest which has been felled. In like manner the evil which one does in the interval of a day prevents the germs of virtues which began to spring up again from developing themselves and destroys them.

"After the germs of virtue have thus been prevented many times from developing themselves, then the beneficent breath of evening does not suffice to preserve them. As soon as the breath of evening does not suffice longer to preserve them, then the nature of man does not differ much from that of the brute. Men seeing the nature of this man like that of the brute, think that he has never possessed the innate faculty of reason. Are those the true and natural sentiments of man?"[32]

> "The Golden Age was first created, which without any avenger
> Spontaneously without law cherished fidelity and rectitude.
> Punishment and fear were not; nor were threatening words read
> On suspended brass; nor did the suppliant crowd fear
> The words of their judge; but were safe without an avenger.
> Not yet the pine felled on its mountains had descended
> To the liquid waves that it might see a foreign world,
> And mortals knew no shores but their own.
>
> There was eternal spring, and placid zephyrs with warm
> Blasts soothed the flowers born without seed."[33]

On the 29th of April, as I was fishing from the bank of the river near the Nine-Acre-Corner bridge, standing on the quaking grass and willow roots, where the muskrats lurk, I heard a singular rattling sound, somewhat like that of the sticks which boys play with their fingers, when, looking up, I observed a very slight and graceful hawk, like a night-hawk, alternately soaring like a ripple and tumbling a rod or two over and over, showing the

---

[32]From *The Book of Mencius.*   [33]From Ovid, *Metamorphoses,* Book 1.

underside of its wings, which gleamed like a satin ribbon in the sun, or like the pearly inside of a shell. This sight reminded me of falconry and what nobleness and poetry are associated with that sport. The Merlin it seemed to me it might be called: but I care not for its name. It was the most ethereal flight I had ever witnessed. It did not simply flutter like a butterfly, nor soar like the larger hawks, but it sported with proud reliance in the fields of air; mounting again and again with its strange chuckle, it repeated its free and beautiful fall, turning over and over like a kite, and then recovering from its lofty tumbling, as if it had never set its foot on *terra firma*. It appeared to have no companion in the universe,—sporting there alone,—and to need none but the morning and the ether with which it played. It was not lonely, but made all the earth lonely beneath it. Where was the parent which hatched it, its kindred, and its father in the heavens? The tenant of the air, it seemed related to the earth but by an egg hatched some time in the crevice of a crag;—or was its native nest made in the angle of a cloud, woven of the rainbow's trimmings and the sunset sky, and lined with some soft midsummer haze caught up from earth? Its eyry now some cliffy cloud.

Beside this I got a rare mess of golden and silver and bright cupreous fishes, which looked like a string of jewels. Ah! I have penetrated to those meadows on the morning of many a first spring day, jumping from hummock to hummock, from willow root to willow root, when the wild river valley and the woods were bathed in so pure and bright a light as would have waked the dead, if they had been slumbering in their graves, as some suppose. There needs no stronger proof of immortality. All things must live in such a light. O Death, where was thy sting? O Grave, where was thy victory, then?[34]

Our village life would stagnate if it were not for the unexplored forests and meadows which surround it. We need the tonic of wildness,—to wade sometimes in marshes where the bittern and the meadow-hen lurk, and hear the booming of the snipe; to smell the whispering sedge where only some wilder and more solitary fowl builds her nest, and the mink crawls with its belly close to the ground. At the same time that we are earnest to explore and learn all things, we require that all things be mysterious and unexplorable, that land and sea be infinitely wild, unsurveyed and unfathomed by us because unfathomable. We can never have enough of Nature. We must be refreshed by the sight of inexhaustible vigor, vast and Titanic features, the sea-coast with its wrecks, the wilderness with its living and its decaying trees, the thunder cloud, and the rain which lasts three weeks and produces freshets. We need to witness our own limits transgressed, and some life pasturing freely where we never wander. We are cheered when we observe the vulture feeding on the carrion which disgusts and disheartens us and deriving health and strength from the repast. There was a dead horse in the hollow by the path to my house, which compelled me sometimes to go out of my way, especially in the night when the air was heavy, but the assurance it

---

[34]I Corinthians 15:55.

gave me of the strong appetite and inviolable health of Nature was my compensation for this. I love to see that Nature is so rife with life that myriads can be afforded to be sacrificed and suffered to prey on one another; that tender organizations can be so serenely squashed out of existence like pulp,—tadpoles which herons gobble up, and tortoises and toads run over in the road; and that sometimes it has rained flesh and blood! With the liability to accident, we must see how little account is to be made of it. The impression made on a wise man is that of universal innocence. Poison is not poisonous after all, nor are any wounds fatal. Compassion is a very untenable ground. It must be expeditious. Its pleadings will not bear to be stereotyped.

Early in May, the oaks, hickories, maples, and other trees, just putting out amidst the pine woods around the pond, imparted a brightness like sunshine to the landscape, especially in cloudy days, as if the sun were breaking through mists and shining faintly on the hill-sides here and there. On the third or fourth of May I saw a loon in the pond, and during the first week of the month I heard the whippoorwill, the brown-thrasher, the veery, the wood-pewee, the chewink, and other birds. I had heard the wood-thrush long before. The phoebe had already come once more and looked in at my door and window, to see if my house was cavern-like enough for her, sustaining herself on humming wings with clinched talons, as if she held by the air, while she surveyed the premises. The sulphur-like pollen of the pitch-pine soon covered the pond and the stones and rotten wood along the shore, so that you could have collected a barrel-ful. This is the "sulphur showers" we hear of. Even in Calidas' drama of Sacontala, we read of "rills dyed yellow with the golden dust of the lotus."[35] And so the seasons went rolling on into summer, as one rambles into higher and higher grass.

Thus was my first year's life in the woods completed; and the second year was similar to it. I finally left Walden September 6th, 1847.

Conclusion

To the sick the doctors wisely recommend a change of air and scenery. Thank Heaven, here is not all the world. The buck-eye does not grow in New England, and the mocking-bird is rarely heard here. The wild-goose is more of a cosmopolite than we; he breaks his fast in Canada, takes a luncheon in the Ohio, and plumes himself for the night in a southern bayou. Even the bison, to some extent, keeps pace with the seasons, cropping the pastures of the Colorado only till a greener and sweeter grass awaits him by the Yellowstone. Yet we think that if rail-fences are pulled down, and stone-walls piled up on our farms, bounds are henceforth set to our lives and our fates decided. If you are chosen town-clerk, forsooth, you cannot go to Tierra del Fuego this summer: but you may go to the land of infernal fire nevertheless. The universe is wider than our views of it.

[35]A fifth-century Sanskrit drama by the Hindu
poet Kalidasa.

Yet we should oftener look over the tafferel of our craft, like curious passengers, and not make the voyage like stupid sailors picking oakum.[36] The other side of the globe is but the home of our correspondent. Our voyaging is only great-circle sailing, and the doctors prescribe for diseases of the skin merely. One hastens to Southern Africa to chase the giraffe; but surely that is not the game he would be after. How long, pray, would a man hunt giraffes if he could? Snipes and woodcocks also may afford rare sport; but I trust it would be nobler game to shoot one's self.—

> *"Direct your eye sight inward, and you'll find*
> *A thousand regions in your mind*
> *Yet undiscovered. Travel them, and be*
> *Expert in home-cosmography."*[37]

What does Africa,—what does the West stand for? Is not our own interior white on the chart? black though it may prove, like the coast, when discovered. Is it the source of the Nile, or the Niger, or the Mississippi, or a North-West Passage around this continent, that we would find? Are these the problems which most concern mankind? Is Franklin the only man who is lost, that his wife should be so earnest to find him? Does Mr. Grinnell know where he himself is?[38] Be rather the Mungo Park, the Lewis and Clarke and Frobisher, of your own streams and oceans; explore your own higher latitudes,—with shiploads of preserved meats to support you, if they be necessary; and pile the empty cans sky-high for a sign. Were preserved meats invented to preserve meat merely? Nay, be a Columbus to whole new continents and worlds within you, opening new channels, not of trade, but of thought. Every man is the lord of a realm beside which the earthly empire of the Czar is but a petty state, a hummock left by the ice. Yet some can be patriotic who have no *self*-respect, and sacrifice the greater to the less. They love the soil which makes their graves, but have no sympathy with the spirit which may still animate their clay. Patriotism is a maggot in their heads. What was the meaning of that South-Sea Exploring Expedition, with all its parade and expense, but an indirect recognition of the fact, that there are continents and seas in the moral world, to which every man is an isthmus or an inlet, yet unexplored by him, but that it is easier to sail many thousand miles through cold and storm and cannibals, in a government ship, with five hundred men and boys to assist one, than it is to explore the private sea, the Atlantic and Pacific Ocean of one's being alone.—

[36]Picking oakum meant, literally, twisting caulking material used to stuff cracks to prevent leakage of the boat. Sailors were assigned to do it when there were no important tasks to be done. In effect, picking oakum meant killing time.

[37]The poem quoted from William Habington reinforces Thoreau's insistence upon people's acknowledgment of the spiritual reality within them.

[38]Grinnell was a New York citizen who supported the search for the lost explorer Sir John Franklin. The other persons mentioned in this passage were all explorers.

> *"Erret, et extremos alter scrutetur Iberos.*
> *Plus habet hic vitae, plus habet ille viae."*
> Let them wander and scrutinize the outlandish Australians.
> I have more of God, they more of the road.[39]

It is not worth the while to go round the world to count the cats in Zanzibar. Yet do this even till you can do better, and you may perhaps find some "Symmes' Hole" by which to get at the inside at last.[40] England and France, Spain and Portugal, Gold Coast and Slave Coast, all front on this private sea; but no bark from them has ventured out of sight of land, though it is without doubt the direct way to India. If you would learn to speak all tongues and conform to the customs of all nations, if you would travel farther than all travellers, be naturalized in all climes, and cause the Sphinx to dash her head against a stone, even obey the precept of the old philosopher, and Explore thyself. Herein are demanded the eye and the nerve. Only the defeated and deserters go to the wars, cowards that run away and enlist. Start now on that farthest western way, which does not pause at the Mississippi or the Pacific, nor conduct toward a worn-out China or Japan, but leads on direct a tangent to this sphere, summer and winter, day and night, sun down, moon down, and at last earth down too.

It is said that Mirabeau took to highway robbery "to ascertain what degree of resolution was necessary in order to place one's self in formal opposition to the most sacred laws of society." He declared that "a soldier who fights in the ranks does not require half so much courage as a footpad,"—"that honor and religion have never stood in the way of a well-considered and a firm resolve." This was manly, as the world goes; and yet it was idle, if not desperate. A saner man would have found himself often enough "in formal opposition" to what are deemed "the most sacred laws of society," through obedience to yet more sacred laws, and so have tested his resolution without going out of his way. It is not for a man to put himself in such an attitude to society, but to maintain himself in whatever attitude he find himself through obedience to the laws of his being, which will never be one of opposition to a just government, if he should chance to meet with such.

I left the woods for as good a reason as I went there. Perhaps it seemed to me that I had several more lives to live, and could not spare any more time for that one. It is remarkable how easily and insensibly we fall into a particular route, and make a beaten track for ourselves. I had not lived there a week before my feet wore a path from my door to the pond-side; and though it is five or six years since I trod it, it is still quite distinct. It is true, I fear that others may have fallen into it, and so helped to keep it open. The surface of the earth is soft and impressible by the feet of men; and so with

---

[39]The quotation from the Roman poet Claudian (which alters "Spaniards" to "Australians") reiterates Thoreau's point in the "Conclusion" of *Walden* that it is more profitable to explore the treasures within ourselves than to explore the remote areas of the Earth.

[40]Symmes was an Englishman who argued that the Earth was hollow.

the paths which the mind travels. How worn and dusty, then, must be the highways of the world, how deep the ruts of tradition and conformity! I did not wish to take a cabin passage, but rather to go before the mast and on the deck of the world, for there I could best see the moonlight amid the mountains. I do not wish to go below now.

I learned this, at least, by my experiment;[41] that if one advances confidently in the direction of his dreams, and endeavors to live the life which he has imagined, he will meet with a success unexpected in common hours. He will put some things behind, will pass an invisible boundary; new, universal, and more liberal laws will begin to establish themselves around and within him; or the old laws be expanded, and interpreted in his favor in a more liberal sense, and he will live with the license of a higher order of beings. In proportion as he simplifies his life, the laws of the universe will appear less complex, and solitude will not be solitude, nor poverty poverty, nor weakness weakness. If you have built castles in the air, your work need not be lost; that is where they should be. Now put the foundations under them.

It is a ridiculous demand which England and America make, that you shall speak so that they can understand you. Neither men nor toad-stools grow so. As if that were important, and there were not enough to understand you without them. As if Nature could support but one order of understandings, could not sustain birds as well as quadrupeds, flying as well as creeping things, and *hush* and *who*, which Bright can understand, were the best English.[42] As if there were safety in stupidity alone. I fear chiefly lest my expression may not be *extra-vagant* enough, may not wander far enough beyond the narrow limits of my daily experience, so as to be adequate to the truth of which I have been convinced. *Extra vagance!* it depends on how you are yarded. The migrating buffalo, which seeks new pastures in another latitude, is not extravagant like the cow which kicks over the pail, leaps the cowyard fence, and runs after her calf, in milking time. I desire to speak somewhere *without* bounds; like a man in a waking moment, to men in their waking moments; for I am convinced that I cannot exaggerate enough even to lay the foundation of a true expression. Who that has heard a strain of music feared then lest he should speak extravagantly any more forever? In view of the future or possible, we should live quite laxly and undefined in front, our outlines dim and misty on that side; as our shadows reveal an insensible perspiration toward the sun. The volatile truth of our words should continually betray the inadequacy of the residual statement. Their truth is instantly *translated;* its literal monument alone remains. The words which express our faith and piety are not definite; yet they are significant and fragrant like frankincense to superior natures.

---

[41]His "experiment," *i.e.*, his attempt to discover what it meant to live well, in his two-year stay at Walden Pond.

[42]"Bright" was a common name for oxen, while *hush* and *who* were apparently terms used in driving them. Thoreau expresses his concern in this paragraph that language may be inadequate to express the magnitude of human potential.

Why level downward to our dullest perception always, and praise that as common sense? The commonest sense is the sense of men asleep, which they express by snoring. Sometimes we are inclined to class those who are once-and-a-half witted with the half-witted, because we appreciate only a third part of their wit. Some would find fault with the morning-red, if they ever got up early enough. "They pretend," as I hear, "that the verses of Kabir have four different senses; illusion, spirit, intellect, and the exoteric doctrine of the Vedas;" but in this part of the world it is considered a ground for complaint if a man's writings admit of more than one interpretation. While England endeavors to cure the potato-rot, will not any endeavor to cure the brain-rot, which prevails so much more widely and fatally?

I do not suppose that I have attained to obscurity, but I should be proud if no more fatal fault were found with my pages on this score than was found with the Walden ice. Southern customers objected to its blue color, which is the evidence of its purity, as if it were muddy, and preferred the Cambridge ice, which is white, but tastes of weeds. The purity men love is like the mists which envelop the earth, and not like the azure ether beyond.

Some are dinning in our ears that we Americans, and moderns generally, are intellectual dwarfs compared with the ancients, or even the Elizabethan men. But what is that to the purpose? A living dog is better than a dead lion. Shall a man go and hang himself because he belongs to the race of pygmies, and not be the biggest pygmy that he can? Let every one mind his own business, and endeavor to be what he was made.

Why should we be in such desperate haste to succeed, and in such desperate enterprises? If a man does not keep pace with his companions, perhaps it is because he hears a different drummer. Let him step to the music which he hears, however measured or far away. It is not important that he should mature as soon as an apple-tree or an oak. Shall he turn his spring into summer? If the condition of things which we were made for is not yet, what were any reality which we can substitute? We will not be shipwrecked on a vain reality. Shall we with pains erect a heaven of blue glass over ourselves, though when it is done we shall be sure to gaze still at the true ethereal heaven far above, as if the former were not?

There was an artist in the city of Kouroo who was disposed to strive after perfection. One day it came into his mind to make a staff. Having considered that in an imperfect work time is an ingredient, but into a perfect work time does not enter, he said to himself, It shall be perfect in all respects, though I should do nothing else in my life. He proceeded instantly to the forest for wood, being resolved that it should not be made of unsuitable material; and as he searched for and rejected stick after stick, his friends gradually deserted him, for they grew old in their works and died, but he grew not older by a moment. His singleness of purpose and resolution, and his elevated piety, endowed him, without his knowledge, with perennial youth. As he made no compromise with Time, Time kept out of his way, and only sighed at a distance because he could not overcome him. Before he had found a stock in all respects suitable the city of Kouroo was a hoary ruin, and he sat on one of its mounds to peel the stick. Before he had given it the proper shape the dynasty of the Candahars was at an end, and with the point of the stick he wrote the name of the last of that race in the sand, and then resumed his work. By the time he had smoothed and polished the staff Kalpa was no longer the pole-star; and ere he had put on the ferule and the head adorned with precious stones, Brahma had awoke and slumbered many times.[43] But why do I stay to mention these things? When the finishing stroke was put to his work, it suddenly expanded before the eyes of the astonished artist into the fairest of all the creations of Brahma. He had made a new system in making a staff, a world with full and fair proportions; in which, though the old cities and dynasties had passed away, fairer and more glorious ones had taken their places. And now he saw by the heap of shavings still fresh at his feet, that, for him and his work, the former lapse of time had been an illusion, and that no more time had elapsed than is required for a single scintillation from the brain of Brahma to fall on and inflame the tinder of a mortal brain. The material was pure, and his art was pure; how could the result be other than wonderful?

No face which we can give to a matter will stead us so well at last as the truth. This alone wears well. For the most part, we are not where we are, but in a false position. Through an infirmity of our natures, we suppose a case, and put ourselves into it, and hence are in two cases at the same time, and it is doubly difficult to get out. In sane moments we regard only the facts, the case that is. Say what you have to say, not what you ought. Any truth is better than make-believe. Tom Hyde, the tinker, standing on the gallows, was asked if he had any thing to say. "Tell the tailors," said he, "to remember to make a knot in their thread before they take the first stitch." His companion's prayer is forgotten.

However mean your life is, meet it and live it; do not shun it and call it hard names. It is not so bad as you are. It looks poorest when you are richest. The fault-finder will find faults even in paradise. Love your life, poor as it is. You may perhaps have some pleasant, thrilling, glorious hours, even in a poorhouse. The setting sun is reflected from the windows of the alms-house as brightly as from the rich man's abode; the snow melts before its door as early in the spring. I do not see but a quiet mind may live as contentedly there, and have as cheering thoughts, as in a palace. The town's poor seem to me often to live the most independent lives of any. May be they are simply great enough to receive without misgiving. Most think that they are above being supported by the town; but it oftener happens that they are not above supporting themselves by dishonest means, which should be more reputable. Cultivate poverty like a garden herb, like sage. Do not trouble yourself much to get new things, whether clothes or friends. Turn the old; return to them. Things do not change; we change. Sell your clothes and keep your thoughts. God will see that you do not want

---

[43]Kalpa ... Brahma: Thoreau's emphasis is upon the passage of aeons of time.

society. If I were confined to a corner of a garret all my days, like a spider, the world would be just as large to me while I had my thoughts about me. The philosopher said: "From an army of three divisions one can take away its general, and put it in disorder; from the man the most abject and vulgar one cannot take away his thought." Do not seek so anxiously to be developed, to subject yourself to many influences to be played on; it is all dissipation. Humility like darkness reveals the heavenly lights. The shadows of poverty and meanness gather around us, "and lo! creation widens to our view." We are often reminded that if there were bestowed on us the wealth of Croesus, our aims must still be the same, and our means essentially the same. Moreover, if you are restricted in your range by poverty, if you cannot buy books and newspapers, for instance, you are but confined to the most significant and vital experiences; you are compelled to deal with the material which yields the most sugar and the most starch. It is life near the bone where it is sweetest. You are defended from being a trifler. No man loses ever on a lower level by magnanimity on a higher. Superfluous wealth can buy superfluities only. Money is not required to buy one necessary of the soul.

I live in the angle of a leaden wall, into whose composition was poured a little alloy of bell metal. Often, in the repose of my mid-day, there reaches my ears a confused *tintinnabulum*[44] from without. It is the noise of my contemporaries. My neighbors tell me of their adventures with famous gentlemen and ladies, what notabilities they met at the dinner-table; but I am no more interested in such things than in the contents of the Daily Times. The interest and the conversation are about costume and manners chiefly; but a goose is a goose still, dress it as you will. They tell me of California and Texas, of England and the Indies, of the Hon. Mr.——of Georgia or of Massachusetts, all transient and fleeting phenomena, till I am ready to leap from their court-yard like the Mameluke bey.[45] I delight to come to my bearings,—not walk in procession with pomp and parade, in a conspicuous place, but to walk even with the Builder of the universe, if I may,—not to live in this restless, nervous, bustling, trivial Nineteenth Century, but stand or sit thoughtfully while it goes by. What are men celebrating? They are all on a committee of arrangements, and hourly expect a speech from somebody. God is only the president of the day, and Webster is his orator. I love to weigh, to settle, to gravitate toward that which most strongly and rightfully attracts me;—not hang by the beam of the scale and try to weigh less,—not suppose a case, but take the case that is; to travel the only path I can, and that on which no power can resist me. It affords me no satisfaction to commence to spring an arch before I have got a solid foundation. Let us not play at kittly-benders.[46] There is a solid bottom every where. We read that the traveller asked the boy if the swamp before him had a hard bottom. The boy replied that it had. But presently the traveller's horse sank in up to

[44]Din, racket.
[45]An Egyptian bey, or officer, who escaped capture by leaping from a wall onto his horse.

[46]A game of children that involved running over thin ice.

the girths, and he observed to the boy, "I thought you said that this bog had a hard bottom." "So it has," answered the latter, "but you have not got half way to it yet." So it is with the bogs and quicksands of society; but he is an old boy that knows it. Only what is thought said or done at a certain rare coincidence is good. I would not be one of those who will foolishly drive a nail into mere lath and plastering; such a deed would keep me awake nights. Give me a hammer, and let me feel for the furring.[47] Do not depend on the putty. Drive a nail home and clinch it so faithfully that you can wake up in the night and think of your work with satisfaction,—a work at which you would not be ashamed to invoke the Muse. So will help you God, and so only. Every nail driven should be as another rivet in the machine of the universe, you carrying on the work.

Rather than love, than money, than fame, give me truth. I sat at a table where were rich food and wine in abundance, and obsequious attendance, but sincerity and truth were not; and I went away hungry from the inhospitable board. The hospitality was as cold as the ices. I thought that there was no need of ice to freeze them. They talked to me of the age of the wine and the fame of the vintage; but I thought of an older, a newer, and purer wine, of a more glorious vintage, which they had not got, and could not buy. The style, the house and grounds and "entertainment" pass for nothing with me. I called on the king, but he made me wait in his hall, and conducted like a man incapacitated for hospitality. There was a man in my neighborhood who lived in a hollow tree. His manners were truly regal. I should have done better had I called on him.

How long shall we sit in our porticoes practising idle and musty virtues, which any work would make impertinent? As if one were to begin the day with long-suffering, and hire a man to hoe his potatoes; and in the afternoon go forth to practise Christian meekness and charity with goodness aforethought! Consider the China pride and stagnant self-complacency of mankind.[48] This generation reclines a little to congratulate itself on being the last of an illustrious line; and in Boston and London and Paris and Rome, thinking of its long descent, it speaks of its progress in art and science and literature with satisfaction. There are the Records of the Philosophical Societies, and the public Eulogies of *Great Men!* It is the good Adam contemplating his own virtue. "Yes, we have done great deeds, and sung divine songs, which shall never die,"—that is, as long as *we* can remember them. The learned societies and great men of Assyria,—where are they? What youthful philosophers and experimentalists we are! There is not one of my readers who has yet lived a whole human life. These may be but the spring months in the life of the race. If we have had the seven-years' itch, we have not seen the seventeen-year locust yet in Concord. We are acquainted with a mere pellicle of the globe on which we live. Most have not

---

[47]The solid structure of a wall in which a driven nail will hold firm, unlike a nail driven only into plaster.

[48]China and the East were in Thoreau's time largely cut off economically and culturally from the West.

delved six feet beneath the surface, nor leaped as many above it. We know not where we are. Beside, we are sound asleep nearly half our time. Yet we esteem ourselves wise, and have an established order on the surface. Truly, we are deep thinkers, we are ambitious spirits! As I stand over the insect crawling amid the pine needles on the forest floor, and endeavoring to conceal itself from my sight, and ask myself why it will cherish those humble thoughts, and hide its head from me who might perhaps be its benefactor, and impart to its race some cheering information, I am reminded of the greater Benefactor and Intelligence that stands over me the human insect.

There is an incessant influx of novelty into the world, and yet we tolerate incredible dulness. I need only suggest what kind of sermons are still listened to in the most enlightened countries. There are such words as joy and sorrow, but they are only the burden of a psalm, sung with a nasal twang, while we believe in the ordinary and mean. We think that we can change our clothes only. It is said that the British Empire is very large and respectable, and that the United States are a first-rate power. We do not believe that a tide rises and falls behind every man which can float the British Empire like a chip, if he should ever harbor it in his mind. Who knows what sort of seventeen-year locust will next come out of the ground? The government of the world I live in was not framed, like that of Britain, in after-dinner conversations over the wine.

The life in us is like the water in the river. It may rise this year higher than man has ever known it, and flood the parched uplands; even this may be the eventful year, which will drown out all our muskrats. It was not always dry land where we dwell. I see far inland the banks which the stream anciently washed, before science began to record its freshets. Every one has heard the story which has gone the rounds of New England, of a strong and beautiful bug which came out of the dry leaf of an old table of apple-tree wood, which had stood in a farmer's kitchen for sixty years, first in Connecticut, and afterward in Massachusetts,—from an egg deposited in the living tree many years earlier still, as appeared by counting the annual layers beyond it; which was heard gnawing out for several weeks, hatched perchance by the heat of an urn. Who does not feel his faith in a resurrection and immortality strengthened by hearing of this? Who knows what beautiful and winged life, whose egg has been buried for ages under many concentric layers of woodenness in the dead dry life of society, deposited at first in the alburnum of the green and living tree, which has been gradually converted into the semblance of its well-seasoned tomb,—heard perchance gnawing out now for years by the astonished family of man, as they sat round the festive board,—may unexpectedly come forth from amidst society's most trivial and handselled furniture, to enjoy its perfect summer life at last!

I do not say that John or Jonathan[49] will realize all this; but such is the character of that morrow which mere lapse of time can never make to

[49]John (John Bull) was a common nickname for an Englishman, Jonathan for an American.

dawn. The light which puts out our eyes is darkness to us. Only that day dawns to which we are awake. There is more day to dawn. The sun is but a morning star.

THE END

1854

A Plea for Captain John Brown[1]

I trust that you will pardon me for being here. I do not wish to force my thoughts upon you, but I feel forced myself. Little as I know of Captain Brown, I would fain do my part to correct the tone and the statements of the newspapers, and of my countrymen generally, respecting his character and actions. It costs us nothing to be just. We can at least express our sympathy with, and admiration of, him and his companions, and that is what I now propose to do.

First, as to his history.

I will endeavor to omit, as much as possible, what you have already read. I need not describe his person to you, for probably most of you have seen and will not soon forget him. I am told that his grandfather, John Brown, was an officer in the Revolution; that he himself was born in Connecticut about the beginning of this century, but early went with his father to Ohio. I heard him say that his father was a contractor who furnished beef to the army there, in the war of 1812; that he accompanied him to the camp, and assisted him in that employment, seeing a good deal of military life, more, perhaps, than if he had been a soldier, for he was often present at the councils of the officers. Especially, he learned by experience how armies are supplied and maintained in the field—a work which, he observed, requires at least as much experience and skill as to lead them in battle. He said that few persons had any conception of the cost, even the pecuniary cost, of firing a single bullet in war. He saw enough, at any rate, to disgust him with a military life, indeed to excite in him a great abhorrence of it; so much so, that though he was tempted by the offer of some petty office in the army, when he was about eighteen, he not only declined that, but he also refused to train when warned, and was fined for it. He then resolved that he would never have anything to do with war, unless it were a war for liberty.

[1]John Brown attacked the federal arsenal at Harpers Ferry on October 16, 1859, with twenty-two heavily armed men, hoping that the attack would incite the slaves in the South to revolt. He was wounded, was captured on October 18, was tried immediately, convicted, and hanged on December 2. Thoreau had met Brown earlier on two occasions when Brown was in Concord raising money to purchase arms to carry on attacks against proslavery settlers in Kansas. Delivered first as a lecture on October 30, 1859, in the Concord Town Hall, the "Plea" was published early in February 1860 in *Echoes of Harper's Ferry*, a collection of essays and poems on Brown edited by James Redpath.

Read to the citizens of Concord, Mass., Sunday Evening, October 30, 1859. Also as the fifth lecture of the Fraternity Course in Boston, November 1; and at Worcester, November 3. [Thoreau's note]

When the troubles in Kansas began, he sent several of his sons thither to strengthen the party of the Free State men, fitting them out with such weapons as he had; telling them that if the troubles should increase, and there should be need of him, he would follow to assist them with his hand and counsel. This, as you all know, he soon after did; and it was through his agency, far more than any other's that Kansas was made free.

For a part of his life he was a surveyor,[2] and at one time he was engaged in wool-growing, and he went to Europe as an agent about that business. There, as every where, he had his eyes about him, and made many original observations. He said, for instance, that he saw why the soil of England was so rich, and that of Germany (I think it was) so poor, and he thought of writing to some of the crowned heads about it. It was because in England the peasantry live on the soil which they cultivate, but in Germany they are gathered into villages, at night. It is a pity that he did not make a book of his observations.

I should say that he was an old-fashioned man in his respect for the Constitution, and his faith in the permanence of this Union. Slavery he deemed to be wholly opposed to these, and he was its determined foe.

He was by descent and birth a New England farmer, a man of great common sense, deliberate and practical as that class is, and tenfold more so. He was like the best of those who stood at Concord Bridge once, on Lexington Common, and on Bunker Hill, only he was firmer and higher principled than any that I have chanced to hear of as there. It was no abolition lecturer that converted him. Ethan Allen and Stark, with whom he may in some respects be compared, were rangers in a lower and less important field.[3] They could bravely face their country's foes, but he had the courage to face his country herself, when she was in the wrong. A Western writer says, to account for his escape from so many perils, that he was concealed under a "rural exterior;" as if, in that prairie land, a hero should, by good rights, wear a citizen's dress only.

He did not go to the college called Harvard, good old Alma Mater as she is. He was not fed on the pap that is there furnished. As he phrased it, "I know no more of grammar than one of your calves." But he went to the great university of the West, where he sedulously pursued the study of Liberty, for which he had early betrayed a fondness, and having taken many degrees, he finally commenced the public practice of Humanity in Kansas, as you all know. Such were *his humanities*, and not any study of grammar. He would have left a Greek accent slanting the wrong way, and righted up a falling man.

He was one of that class of whom we hear a great deal, but, for the most part, see nothing at all—the Puritans. It would be in vain to kill him. He

---

[2]Both Brown and Thoreau were surveyors.
[3]The early battles of the American Revolution mentioned by Thoreau were fought by hardy citizen-soldiers of New England who opposed British domination. Ethan Allen and John Stark distinguished themselves at the battles of Ticonderoga and Bunker Hill, respectively.

died lately in the time of Cromwell, but he reappeared here.[4] Why should he not? Some of the Puritan stock are said to have come over and settled in New England. They were a class that did something else than celebrate their forefathers' day, and eat parched corn in remembrance of that time. They were neither Democrats nor Republicans, but men of simple habits, straightforward, prayerful; not thinking much of rulers who did not fear God, not making many compromises, nor seeking after available candidates.

"In his camp," as one has recently written, and as I have myself heard him state, "he permitted no profanity; no man of loose morals was suffered to remain there, unless, indeed, as a prisoner of war. 'I would rather,' said he, 'have the small-pox, yellow fever, and cholera, all together in my camp, than a man without principle. ... It is a mistake, sir, that our people make, when they think that bullies are the best fighters, or that they are the fit men to oppose these Southerners. Give me men of good principles,—God-fearing men,—men who respect themselves, and with a dozen of them I will oppose any hundred such men as these Buford ruffians.'"[5] He said that if one offered himself to be a soldier under him, who was forward to tell what he could or would do, if he could only get sight of the enemy, he had but little confidence in him.

He was never able to find more than a score or so of recruits whom he would accept, and only about a dozen, among them his sons, in whom he had perfect faith. When he was here, some years ago, he showed to a few a little manuscript book,—his "orderly book" I think he called it,—containing the names of his company in Kansas, and the rules by which they bound themselves; and he stated that several of them had already sealed the contract with their blood. When some one remarked that, with the addition of a chaplain, it would have been a perfect Cromwellian troop, he observed that he would have been glad to add a chaplain to the list, if he could have found one who could fill that office worthily. It is easy enough to find one for the United States army. I believe that he had prayers in his camp morning and evening, nevertheless.

He was a man of Spartan habits, and at sixty was scrupulous about his diet at your table, excusing himself by saying that he must eat sparingly and fare hard, as became a soldier or one who was fitting himself for difficult enterprises, a life of exposure.

A man of rare common sense and directness of speech, as of action; a transcendentalist above all, a man of ideas and principles,—that was what distinguished him. Not yielding to a whim or transient impulse, but carrying out the purpose of a life. I noticed that he did not overstate any thing, but spoke within bounds. I remember, particularly, how, in his speech here, he

[4]Thoreau compares Brown to Oliver Cromwell, the stern, religious military leader who overthrew the English monarchy, executed Charles I, and ruled England from 1653 to 1658.
[5]Buford led proslavery men into what is now Kansas. Settlers from both North and South moved into this area in an attempt to form majorities that would bring Kansas into the Union as a state supporting their viewpoint on slavery. Tensions were very high.

referred to what his family had suffered in Kansas, without ever giving the least vent to his pent-up fire. It was a volcano with an ordinary chimney-flue. Also referring to the deeds of certain Border Ruffians, he said, rapidly paring away his speech, like an experienced soldier, keeping a reserve of force and meaning, "They had a perfect right to be hung." He was not in the least a rhetorician, was not talking to Buncombe[6] or his constituents any where, had no need to invent any thing, but to tell the simple truth, and communicate his own resolution; therefore he appeared incomparably strong, and eloquence in Congress and elsewhere seemed to me at a discount. It was like the speeches of Cromwell compared with those of an ordinary king.

As for his tact and prudence, I will merely say, that at a time when scarcely a man from the Free States was able to reach Kansas by any direct route, at least without having his arms taken from him, he, carrying what imperfect guns and other weapons he could collect, openly and slowly drove an ox-cart through Missouri, apparently in the capacity of a surveyor, with his surveying compass exposed in it, and so passed unsuspected, and had ample opportunity to learn the designs of the enemy. For some time after his arrival he still followed the same profession. When, for instance, he saw a knot of the ruffians on the prairie, discussing, of course, the single topic which then occupied their minds, he would, perhaps, take his compass and one of his sons, and proceed to run an imaginary line right through the very spot on which that conclave had assembled, and when he came up to them, he would naturally pause and have some talk with them, learning their news, and, at last, all their plans perfectly; and having thus completed his real survey, he would resume his imaginary one, and run on his line till he was out of sight.

When I expressed surprise that he could live in Kansas at all, with a price set upon his head, and so large a number, including the authorities, exasperated against him, he accounted for it by saying, "It is perfectly well understood that I will not be taken." Much of the time for some years he has had to skulk in swamps, suffering from poverty and from sickness, which was the consequence of exposure, befriended only by Indians and a few whites. But though it might be known that he was lurking in a particular swamp, his foes commonly did not care to go in after him. He could even come out into a town where there were more Border Ruffians[7] than Free State men, and transact some business, without delaying long, and yet not be molested; for said he, "No little handful of men were willing to undertake it, and a large body could not be got together in season."

As for his recent failure, we do not know the facts about it. It was evidently far from being a wild and desperate attempt. His enemy, Mr.

[6]A pompous speaker who says nothing.
[7]Proslavery partisans in Kansas.

Vallandigham,[8] is compelled to say, that "it was among the best planned and executed conspiracies that ever failed."

Not to mention his other successes, was it a failure, or did it show a want of good management, to deliver from bondage a dozen human beings, and walk off with them by broad daylight, for weeks if not months, at a leisurely pace, through one State after another, for half the length of the North, conspicuous to all parties, with a price set upon his head, going into a court room on his way and telling what he had done, thus convincing Missouri that it was not profitable to try to hold slaves in his neighborhood?—and this, not because the government menials were lenient, but because they were afraid of him.

Yet he did not attribute his success, foolishly, to "his star," or to any magic. He said, truly, that the reason why such greatly superior numbers quailed before him, was, as one of his prisoners confessed, because they *lacked a cause*—a kind of armor which he and his party never lacked. When the time came, few men were found willing to lay down their lives in defence of what they knew to be wrong; they did not like that this should be their last act in this world.

But to make haste to *his* last act, and its effects.

The newspapers seem to ignore, or perhaps are really ignorant of the fact, that there are at least as many as two or three individuals to a town throughout the North, who think much as the present speaker does about him and his enterprise. I do not hesitate to say that they are an important and growing party. We aspire to be something more than stupid and timid chattels, pretending to read history and our bibles, but desecrating every house and every day we breathe in. Perhaps anxious politicians may prove that only seventeen white men and five negroes were concerned in the late enterprise, but their very anxiety to prove this might suggest to themselves that all is not told. Why do they still dodge the truth? They are so anxious because of a dim consciousness of the fact, which they do not distinctly face, that at least a million of the free inhabitants of the United States would have rejoiced if it had succeeded. They at most only criticise the tactics. Though we wear no crape, the thought of that man's position and probable fate is spoiling many a man's day here at the North for other thinking. If any one who has seen him here can pursue successfully any other train of thought, I do not know what he is made of. If there is any such who gets his usual allowance of sleep, I will warrant him to fatten easily under any circumstances which do not touch his body or purse. I put a piece of paper and a pencil under my pillow, and when I could not sleep, I wrote in the dark.

On the whole, my respect for my fellow-men, except as one may outweigh a million, is not being increased these days. I have noticed the

---

[8]Vallandigham was an Ohio congressman who, along with Senator Mason of Virginia, interviewed Brown after his capture.

cold-blooded way in which newspaper writers and men generally speak of this event, as if an ordinary malefactor, though one of unusual "pluck,"—as the Governor of Virginia is reported to have said, using the language of the cock-pit, "the gamest man he ever saw,"—had been caught, and were about to be hung. He was not dreaming of his foes when the governor thought he looked so brave. It turns what sweetness I have to gall, to hear, or hear of, the remarks of some of my neighbors. When we heard at first that he was dead, one of my townsmen observed that "he died as the fool dieth;" which, pardon me, for an instant suggested a likeness in him dying to my neighbor living. Others, craven-hearted, said disparagingly, that "he threw his life away," because he resisted the government. Which way have they thrown *their* lives, pray?—Such as would praise a man for attacking singly an ordinary band of thieves or murderers. I hear another ask, Yankee-like, "What will he gain by it?" as if he expected to fill his pockets by this enterprise. Such a one has no idea of gain but in this worldly sense. If it does not lead to a "surprise" party, if he does not get a new pair of boots, or a vote of thanks, it must be a failure. "But he won't gain any thing by it." Well, no, I don't suppose he could get four-and-sixpence a day for being hung, take the year round; but then he stands a chance to save a considerable part of his soul—and *such* a soul!—when *you* do not. No doubt you can get more in your market for a quart of milk than for a quart of blood, but that is not the market that heroes carry their blood to.

Such do not know that like the seed is the fruit, and that, in the moral world, when good seed is planted, good fruit is inevitable, and does not depend on our watering and cultivating; that when you plant, or bury, a hero in his field, a crop of heroes is sure to spring up. This is a seed of such force and vitality, that it does not ask our leave to germinate.

The momentary charge at Balaclava,[9] in obedience to a blundering command, proving what a perfect machine the soldier is, has, properly enough, been celebrated by a poet laureate; but the steady, and for the most part successful charge of this man, for some years, against the legions of Slavery, in obedience to an infinitely higher command, is as much more memorable than that, as an intelligent and conscientious man is superior to a machine. Do you think that that will go unsung?

"Served him right"—"A dangerous man"—"He is undoubtedly insane." So they proceed to live their sane, and wise, and altogether admirable lives, reading their Plutarch a little, but chiefly pausing at that feat of Putnam,[10] who was let down into a wolf's den; and in this wise they nourish themselves for brave and patriotic deeds some time or other. The Tract Society could afford to print that story of Putnam. You might open the district

---

[9]The charge by outnumbered British cavalry in the Crimean War of 1854, celebrated as "The Charge of the Light Brigade" in a well-known poem by Tennyson.

[10]Israel Putnam, a hero of the American Revolution, allegedly crawled into a cave at night

and killed a savage wolf. Thoreau in this passage is ridiculing religious organizations and individuals who fail to take a stand—as Brown had done—against slavery.

schools with the reading of it, for there is nothing about Slavery or the Church in it; unless it occurs to the reader that some pastors are *wolves* in sheep's clothing. "The American Board of Commissioners for Foreign Missions" even, might dare to protest against *that* wolf. I have heard of boards, and of American boards, but it chances that I never heard of this particular lumber till lately. And yet I hear of Northern men, women, and children, by families, buying a "life membership" in such societies as these;—a life-membership in the grave! You can get buried cheaper than that.

Our foes are in our midst and all about us. There is hardly a house but is divided against itself, for our foe is the all but universal woodenness of both head and heart, the want of vitality in man, which is the effect of our vice; and hence are begotten fear, superstition, bigotry, persecution, and slavery of all kinds. We are mere figure-heads upon a hulk, with livers in the place of hearts. The curse is the worship of idols, which at length changes the worshipper into a stone image himself; and the New Englander is just as much an idolater as the Hindoo. This man was an exception, for he did not set up even a political graven image between him and his God.

A church that can never have done with excommunicating Christ while it exists! Away with your broad and flat churches, and your narrow and tall churches! Take a step forward, and invent a new style of out-houses. Invent a salt that will save you, and defend our nostrils.

The modern Christian is a man who has consented to say all the prayers in the liturgy, provided you will let him go straight to bed and sleep quietly afterward. All his prayers begin with "Now I lay me down to sleep," and he is forever looking forward to the time when he shall go to his "*long* rest." He has consented to perform certain old established charities, too, after a fashion, but he does not wish to hear of any new-fangled ones; he doesn't wish to have any supplementary articles added to the contract, to fit it to the present time. He shows the whites of his eyes on the Sabbath, and the blacks all the rest of the week. The evil is not merely a stagnation of blood, but a stagnation of spirit. Many, no doubt, are well disposed, but sluggish by constitution and by habit, and they cannot conceive of a man who is actuated by higher motives than they are. Accordingly they pronounce this man insane, for they know that *they* could never act as he does, as long as they are themselves.

We dream of foreign countries, of other times and races of men, placing them at a distance in history or space; but let some significant event like the present occur in our midst, and we discover, often, this distance and this strangeness between us and our nearest neighbors. *They* are our Austrias, and Chinas, and South Sea Islands. Our crowded society becomes well spaced all at once, clean and handsome to the eye, a city of magnificent distances. We discover why it was that we never got beyond compliments and surfaces with them before; we become aware of as many versts between us and them as there are between a wandering Tartar and a Chinese town. The thoughtful man becomes a hermit in the thorough-fares of the marketplace. Impassable seas suddenly find their level between us, or dumb steppes stretch themselves out there. It is the difference of constitution, of intelligence, and faith, and not streams and mountains, that make the true and impassable boundaries between individuals and between states. None but the like-minded can come plenipotentiary to our court.

I read all the newspapers I could get within a week after this event, and I do not remember in them a single expression of sympathy for these men. I have since seen one noble statement, in a Boston paper, not editorial. Some voluminous sheets decided not to print the full report of Brown's words to the exclusion of other matter. It was as if a publisher should reject the manuscript of the New Testament, and print Wilson's last speech.[11] The same journal which contained this pregnant news, was chiefly filled, in parallel columns, with the reports of the political conventions that were being held. But the descent to them was too steep. They should have been spared this contrast, been printed in an extra at least. To turn from the voices and deeds of earnest men to the *cackling* of political conventions! Office seekers and speech-makers, who do not so much as lay an honest egg, but wear their breasts bare upon an egg of chalk! Their great game is the game of straws, or rather that universal aboriginal game of the platter, at which the Indians cried *hub, bub!*[12] Exclude the reports of religious and political conventions, and publish the words of a living man.

But I object not so much to what they have omitted as to what they have inserted. Even the *Liberator*[13] called it "a misguided, wild, and apparently insane ... effort." As for the herd of newspapers and magazines, I do not chance to know an editor in the country who will deliberately print anything which he knows will ultimately and permanently reduce the number of his subscribers. They do not believe that it would be expedient. How then can they print truth? If we do not say pleasant things, they argue, nobody will attend to us. And so they do like some travelling auctioneers, who sing an obscene song in order to draw a crowd around them. Republican editors, obliged to get their sentences ready for the morning edition, and accustomed to look at every thing by the twilight of politics, express no admiration, nor true sorrow even, but call these men "deluded fanatics"—"mistaken men"—"insane," or "crazed." It suggests what a *sane* set of editors we are blessed with, *not* "mistaken men"; who know very well on which side their bread is buttered, at least.

A man does a brave and humane deed, and at once, on all sides, we hear people and parties declaring, "I didn't do it, nor countenance *him* to do it, in any conceivable way. It can't be fairly inferred from my past career." I, for one, am not interested to hear you define your position. I don't know that I ever was, or ever shall be. I think it is mere egotism, or impertinent at this time. Ye needn't take so much pains to wash your skirts of him. No intelligent man will ever be convinced that he was any creature of yours. He went

---

[11]Wilson was a senator from Massachusetts.
[12]*Hub, bub* was a name applied by New Englanders to a native Indian game played with bones.

[13]The *Liberator* was the best known and most radical of the abolitionist newspapers. William Lloyd Garrison was founder and editor.

and came, as he himself informs us, "under the auspices of John Brown and nobody else." The Republican party does not perceive how many his *failure* will make to vote more correctly than they would have them. They have counted the votes of Pennsylvania & Co., but they have not correctly counted Captain Brown's vote. He has taken the wind out of their sails, the little wind they had, and they may as well lie to and repair.

What though he did not belong to your clique! Though you may not approve of his method or his principles, recognize his magnanimity. Would you not like to claim kindredship with him in that, though in no other thing he is like, or likely, to you? Do you think that you would lose your reputation so? What you lost at the spile, you would gain at the bung.[14]

If they do not mean all this, then they do not speak the truth, and say what they mean. They are simply at their old tricks still.

"It was always conceded to him," *says one who calls him crazy,* "that he was a conscientious man, very modest in his demeanor, apparently inoffensive, until the subject of Slavery was introduced, when he would exhibit a feeling of indignation unparalleled."

The slave-ship is on her way, crowded with its dying victims; new cargoes are being added in mid ocean; a small crew of slaveholders, countenanced by a large body of passengers, is smothering four millions under the hatches, and yet the politician asserts that the only proper way by which deliverance is to be obtained, is by "the quiet diffusion of the sentiments of humanity," without any "outbreak." As if the sentiments of humanity were ever found unaccompanied by its deeds, and you could disperse them, all finished to order, the pure article, as easily as water with a watering-pot, and so lay the dust. What is that that I hear cast overboard? The bodies of the dead that have found deliverance. That is the way we are "diffusing" humanity, and its sentiments with it.

Prominent and influential editors, accustomed to deal with politicians, men of an infinitely lower grade, say, in their ignorance, that he acted "on the principle of revenge." They do not know the man. They must enlarge themselves to conceive of him. I have no doubt that the time will come when they will begin to see him as he was. They have got to conceive of a man of faith and of religious principle, and not a politician or an Indian; of a man who did not wait till he was personally interfered with, or thwarted in some harmless business, before he gave his life to the cause of the oppressed.

If Walker[15] may be considered the representative of the South, I wish I could say that Brown was the representative of the North. He was a superior man. He did not value his bodily life in comparison with ideal things. He did not recognize unjust human laws, but resisted them as he was bid. For once we are lifted out of the trivialness and dust of politics into the region of

---

[14]In other words, what you lose of the liquid at the top (vent) hole of a barrel, you gain at the spout (below) where the liquid is drawn.

[15]Robert Walker was governor of the Kansas Territory.

truth and manhood. No man in America has ever stood up so persistently and effectively for the dignity of human nature, knowing himself for a man, and the equal of any and all governments. In that sense he was the most American of us all. He needed no babbling lawyer, making false issues, to defend him. He was more than a match for all the judges that American-voters, or office-holders of whatever grade, can create. He could not have been tried by a jury of his peers, because his peers did not exist. When a man stands up serenely against the condemnation and vengeance of mankind, rising above them literally *by a whole body*,—even though he were of late the vilest murderer, who has settled that matter with himself,—the spectacle is a sublime one,—didn't ye know it, ye Liberators, ye Tribunes, ye Republicans?[16]—and we become criminal in comparison. Do yourselves the honor to recognize him. He needs none of your respect.

As for the Democratic journals, they are not human enough to affect me at all. I do not feel indignation at any thing they may say.

I am aware that I anticipate a little, that he was still, at the last accounts, alive in the hands of his foes; but that being the case, I have all along found myself thinking and speaking of him as physically dead.

I do not believe in erecting statues to those who still live in our hearts, whose bones have not yet crumbled in the earth around us, but I would rather see the statue of Captain Brown in the Massachusetts State-House yard, than that of any other man whom I know. I rejoice that I live in this age—that I am his contemporary.

What a contrast, when we turn to that political party which is so anxiously shuffling him and his plot out of its way,[17] and looking around for some available slaveholder, perhaps, to be its candidate, at least for one who will execute the Fugitive Slave Law, and all those other unjust laws which he took up arms to annul![18]

Insane! A father and six sons, and one son-in-law, and several more men besides,—as many at least as twelve disciples,—all struck with insanity at once; while the sane tyrant holds with a firmer gripe than ever his four millions of slaves, and a thousand sane editors, his abettors, are saving their country and their bacon! Just as insane were his efforts in Kansas. Ask the tyrant who is his most dangerous foe, the sane man or the insane. Do the thousands who know him best, who have rejoiced at his deeds in Kansas, and have afforded him material aid there, think him insane? Such a use of this word is a mere trope with most who persist in using it, and I have no doubt that many of the rest have already in silence retracted their words.

Read his admirable answers to Mason and others. How they are dwarfed and defeated by the contrast! On the one side, half brutish, half timid questioning; on the other, truth, clear as lightning, crashing into their obscene

---

[16]Liberators, Tribunes, Republicans: names of three New England newspapers.

[17]"That political party," *i.e.*, the newly organized Republican Party.

[18]The Fugitive Slave Law of 1850 required Northern states and their citizens to aid in capturing black slaves fleeing from their Southern masters.

temples. They are made to stand with Pilate, and Gessler, and the Inquisition.[19] How ineffectual their speech and action! and what a void their silence! They are but helpless tools in this great work. It was no human power that gathered them about this preacher.

What have Massachusetts and the North sent a few *sane* representatives to Congress for, of late years?—to declare with effect what kind of sentiments? All their speeches put together and boiled down,—and probably they themselves will confess it,—do not match for manly directness and force, and for simple truth, the few casual remarks of crazy John Brown, on the floor of the Harper's Ferry engine house;—that man whom you are about to hang, to send to the other world, though not to represent *you* there. No, he was not our representative in any sense. He was too fair a specimen of a man to represent the like of us. Who, then, *were* his constituents? If you read his words understandingly you will find out. In his case there is no idle eloquence, no made, nor maiden speech, no compliments to the oppressor. Truth is his inspirer, and earnestness the polisher of his sentences. He could afford to lose his Sharps' rifles, while he retained his faculty of speech, a Sharps' rifle of infinitely surer and longer range.

And the *New York Herald* reports the conversation "*verbatim*"! It does not know of what undying words it is made the vehicle.

I have no respect for the penetration of any man who can read the report of that conversation, and still call the principal in it insane. It has the ring of a saner sanity than an ordinary discipline and habits of life, than an ordinary organization, secure. Take any sentence of it—"Any questions that I can honorably answer, I will; not otherwise. So far as I am myself concerned, I have told every thing truthfully. I value my word, sir." The few who talk about his vindictive spirit, while they really admire his heroism, have no test by which to detect a noble man, no amalgam to combine with his pure gold. They mix their own dross with it.

It is a relief to turn from these slanders to the testimony of his more truthful, but frightened, jailers and hangmen. Governor Wise speaks far more justly and appreciatingly of him than any Northern editor, or politician, or public personage, that I chance to have heard from. I know that you can afford to hear him again on this subject. He says: "They are themselves mistaken who take him to be a madman. ... He is cool, collected, and indomitable, and it is but just to him to say, that he was humane to his prisoners. ... And he inspired me with great trust in his integrity as a man of truth. He is a fanatic, vain and garrulous," (I leave that part to Mr. Wise) "but firm, truthful, and intelligent. His men, too, who survive, are like him. ... Colonel Washington[20] says that he was the coolest and firmest man he ever saw in defying danger and death. With one son dead by his side, and another shot through, he felt the pulse of his dying son with one hand,

---

[19]Pontius Pilate, the Roman governor of Palestine, allowed Jesus to be crucified. Gessler, an Austrian tyrant, was killed by William Tell. The Inquisition of the Roman Catholic Church oppressed dissenters, executing many.

[20]Colonel Washington was a landowner near Harpers Ferry, kidnapped by Brown.

and held his rifle with the other, and commanded his men with the utmost composure, encouraging them to be firm, and to sell their lives as dear as they could. Of the three white prisoners, Brown, Stevens, and Coppoc,[21] it was hard to say which was most firm...."

Almost the first Northern men whom the slaveholder has learned to respect!

The testimony of Mr. Vallandigham, though less valuable, is of the same purport, that "it is vain to underrate either the man or his conspiracy. ... He is the farthest possible remove from the ordinary ruffian, fanatic, or madman."

"All is quiet at Harper's Ferry," say the journals. What is the character of that calm which follows when the law and the slaveholder prevail? I regard this event as a touchstone designed to bring out, with glaring distinctness, the character of this government. We needed to be thus assisted to see it by the light of history. It needed to see itself. When a government puts forth its strength on the side of injustice, as ours to maintain Slavery and kill the liberators of the slave, it reveals itself a merely brute force, or worse, a demoniacal force. It is the head of the Plug Uglies.[22] It is more manifest than ever that tyranny rules. I see this government to be effectually allied with France and Austria in oppressing mankind. There sits a tyrant holding fettered four millions of slaves; here comes their heroic liberator. This most hypocritical and diabolical government looks up from its seat on the gasping four millions, and inquires with an assumption of innocence, "What do you assault me for? Am I not an honest man? Cease agitation on this subject, or I will make a slave of you, too, or else hang you."

We talk about a *representative* government; but what a monster of a government is that where the noblest faculties of the mind, and the *whole* heart, are not *represented*. A semi-human tiger or ox, stalking over the earth, with its heart taken out and the top of its brain shot away. Heroes have fought well on their stumps when their legs were shot off, but I never heard of any good done by such a government as that.

The only government that I recognize,—and it matters not how few are at the head of it, or how small its army,—is that power that establishes justice in the land, never that which establishes injustice. What shall we think of a government to which all the truly brave and just men in the land are enemies, standing between it and those whom it oppresses? A government that pretends to be Christian and crucifies a million Christs every day!

Treason! Where does such treason take its rise? I cannot help thinking of you as you deserve, ye governments. Can you dry up the fountains of thought? High treason, when it is resistance to tyranny here below, has its origin in, and is first committed by the power that makes and forever

---

[21]Stevens and Coppoc were two of Brown's men. They were captured and later executed.

[22]*I.e.*, gangs of ruffians.

recreates man. When you have caught and hung all these human rebels, you have accomplished nothing but your own guilt, for you have not struck at the fountain head. You presume to contend with a foe against whom West Point cadets and rifled cannon *point* not. Can all the art of the cannon-founder tempt matter to turn against its maker? Is the form in which the founder thinks he casts it more essential than the constitution of it and of himself?

The United States have a coffle of four millions of slaves. They are determined to keep them in this condition; and Massachusetts is one of the confederated overseers to prevent their escape. Such are not all the inhabitants of Massachusetts, but such are they who rule and are obeyed here. It was Massachusetts, as well as Virginia, that put down this insurrection at Harper's Ferry. She sent the marines there, and she will have to pay the penalty of her sin.

Suppose that there is a society in this State that out of its own purse and magnanimity saves all the fugitive slaves that run to us, and protects our colored fellow-citizens, and leaves the other work to the Government, so-called. Is not that government fast losing its occupation, and becoming contemptible to mankind? If private men are obliged to perform the offices of government, to protect the weak and dispense justice, then the government becomes only a hired man, or clerk, to perform menial or indifferent services. Of course, that is but the shadow of a government whose existence necessitates a Vigilant Committee.[23] What should we think of the oriental Cadi even, behind whom worked in secret a Vigilant Committee? But such is the character of our Northern States generally; each has its Vigilant Committee. And, to a certain extent, these crazy governments recognize and accept this relation. They say, virtually, "We'll be glad to work for you on these terms, only don't make a noise about it." And thus the government, its salary being insured, withdraws into the back shop, taking the constitution with it, and bestows most of its labor on repairing that. When I hear it at work sometimes, as I go by, it reminds me, at best, of those farmers who in winter contrive to turn a penny by following the coopering business. And what kind of spirit is their barrel made to hold? They speculate in stocks, and bore holes in mountains, but they are not competent to lay out even a decent highway. The only *free* road, the Underground Railroad,[24] is owned and managed by the Vigilant Committee. *They* have tunnelled under the whole breadth of the land. Such a government is losing its power and respectability as surely as water runs out of a leaky vessel, and is held by one that can contain it.

I hear many condemn these men because they were so few. When were the good and the brave ever in a majority? Would you have had him wait till that time came?—till you and I came over to him? The very fact that he had

---

[23]*I.e.*, a citizen group assuming law enforcement responsibilities. Thoreau is thinking of the abolitionists.

[24]The Underground Railroad consisted of a loose chain of people dedicated to aiding runaway slaves trying to escape to Canada.

no rabble or troop of hirelings about him would alone distinguish him from ordinary heroes. His company was small indeed, because few could be found worthy to pass muster. Each one who there laid down his life for the poor and oppressed, was a picked man, called out of many thousands, if not millions; apparently a man of principle, of rare courage and devoted humanity, ready to sacrifice his life at any moment for the benefit of his fellow man. It may be doubted if there were as many more their equals in these respects in all the country—I speak of his followers only—for their leader, no doubt, scoured the land far and wide, seeking to swell his troop. These alone were ready to step between the oppressor and the oppressed. Surely, they were the very best men you could select to be hung. That was the greatest compliment which this country could pay them. They were ripe for her gallows. She has tried a long time, she has hung a good many, but never found the right one before.

When I think of him, and his six sons, and his son in law,—not to enumerate the others,—enlisted for this fight; proceeding coolly, reverently, humanely to work, for months if not years, sleeping and waking upon it, summering and wintering the thought, without expecting any reward but a good conscience, while almost all America stood ranked on the other side, I say again that it affects me as a sublime spectacle. If he had had any journal advocating *"his cause,"* any organ as the phrase is, monotonously and wearisomely playing the same old tune, and then passing round the hat, it would have been fatal to his efficiency. If he had acted in any way so as to be let alone by the government, he might have been suspected. It was the fact that the tyrant must give place to him, or he to the tyrant, that distinguished him from all the reformers of the day that I know.

It was his peculiar doctrine that a man has a perfect right to interfere by force with the slaveholder, in order to rescue the slave. I agree with him. They who are continually shocked by slavery have some right to be shocked by the violent death of the slaveholder, but no others. Such will be more shocked by his life than by his death. I shall not be forward to think him mistaken in his method who quickest succeeds to liberate the slave. I speak for the slave when I say, that I prefer the philanthropy of Captain Brown to that philanthropy which neither shoots me nor liberates me. At any rate, I do not think it is quite sane for one to spend his whole life in talking or writing about this matter, unless he is continuously inspired, and I have not done so. A man may have other affairs to attend to. I do not wish to kill nor to be killed, but I can foresee circumstances in which both these things would be by me unavoidable. We preserve the so-called "peace" of our community by deeds of petty violence every day. Look at the policeman's billy and hand cuffs! Look at the jail! Look at the gallows! Look at the chaplain of the regiment! We are hoping only to live safely on the outskirts of *this* provisional army. So we defend ourselves and our hen roosts, and maintain slavery. I know that the mass of my countrymen think that the only righteous use that can be made of Sharps' rifles and revolvers is to fight duels with them, when we are insulted by other nations, or to hunt Indians, or shoot fugitive slaves with them, or the like. I think that for once the Sharps' rifles and the revolvers were employed in a righteous cause. The tools were in the hands of one who could use them.

The same indignation that is said to have cleared the temple once will clear it again.[25] The question is not about the weapon, but the spirit in which you use it. No man has appeared in America as yet who loved his fellow man so well, and treated him so tenderly. He lived for him. He took up his life and he laid it down for him. What sort of violence is that which is encouraged, not by soldiers but by peaceable citizens, not so much by laymen as by ministers of the gospel, and not so much by the fighting sects as by the Quakers, and not so much by Quaker men as by Quaker women?

This event advertises me that there is such a fact as death—the possibility of a man's dying. It seems as if no man had ever died in America before, for in order to die you must first have lived. I don't believe in the hearses and palls and funerals that they have had. There was no death in the case, because there had been no life; they merely rotted or sloughed off, pretty much as they had rotted or sloughed along. No temple's vail was rent,[26] only a hole dug somewhere. Let the dead bury their dead. The best of them fairly ran down like a clock. Franklin—Washington—they were let off without dying; they were merely missing one day. I hear a good many pretend that they are going to die;—or that they have died for aught that I know. Nonsense! I'll defy them to do it. They haven't got life enough in them. They'll deliquesce like fungi, and keep a hundred eulogists mopping the spot where they left off. Only half a dozen or so have died since the world began. Do you think that you are going to die, sir? No! there's no hope of you. You haven't got your lesson yet. You've got to stay after school. We make a needless ado about capital punishment—taking lives, when there is no life to take. *Memento mori!*[27] We don't understand that sublime sentence which some worthy got sculptured on his gravestone once. We've interpreted it in a grovelling and snivelling sense; we've wholly forgotten how to die.

But be sure you do die, nevertheless. Do your work, and finish it. If you know how to begin, you will know when to end.

These men, in teaching us how to die, have at the same time taught us how to live. If this man's acts and words do not create a revival, it will be the severest possible satire on the acts and words that do. It is the best news that America has ever heard. It has already quickened the feeble pulse of the North, and infused more and more generous blood into her veins and heart, than any number of years of what is called commercial and political prosperity could. How many a man who was lately contemplating suicide has now something to live for!

---

[25]Christ, in anger, drove the money-changers from the temple in Jerusalem.

[26]According to the New Testament, when Christ died on the cross, the veil of the temple was torn.

[27]Remember that you must die.

One writer says that Brown's peculiar monomania made him to be "dreaded by the Missourians as a supernatural being." Sure enough, a hero in the midst of us cowards is always so dreaded. He is just that thing. He shows himself superior to nature. He has a spark of divinity in him.

> "Unless above himself he can
> Erect himself, how poor a thing is man!"

Newspaper editors argue also that it is a proof of his *insanity* that he thought he was appointed to do this work which he did—that he did not suspect himself for a moment! They talk as if it were impossible that a man could be "divinely appointed" in these days to do any work whatever; as if vows and religion were out of date as connected with any man's daily work,—as if the agent to abolish Slavery could only be somebody appointed by the President, or by some political party. They talk as if a man's death were a failure, and his continued life, be it of whatever character, were a success.

When I reflect to what a cause this man devoted himself, and how religiously, and then reflect to what cause his judges and all who condemn him so angrily and fluently devote themselves, I see that they are as far apart as the heavens and earth are asunder.

The amount of it is, our *"leading men"* are a harmless kind of folk, and they know *well enough* that *they* were not divinely appointed, but elected by the votes of their party.

Who is it whose safety requires that Captain Brown be hung? Is it indispensable to any Northern man? Is there no resource but to cast these men also to the Minotaur?[28] If you do not wish it say so distinctly. While these things are being done, beauty stands veiled and music is a screeching lie. Think of him—of his rare qualities! such a man as it takes ages to make, and ages to understand; no mock hero, nor the representative of any party. A man such as the sun may not rise upon again in this benighted land. To whose making went the costliest material, the finest adamant; sent to be the redeemer of those in captivity. And the only use to which you can put him is to hang him at the end of a rope! You who pretend to care for Christ crucified, consider what you are about to do to him who offered himself to be the savior of four millions of men.

Any man knows when he is justified, and all the wits in the world cannot enlighten him on that point. The murderer always knows that he is justly punished; but when a government takes the life of a man without the consent of his conscience, it is an audacious government, and is taking a step towards its own dissolution. Is it not possible that an individual may be right and a government wrong? Are laws to be enforced simply because they were made? or declared by any number of men to be good, if they are *not* good? Is there any necessity for a man's being a tool to perform a deed

---

[28]A monster in Greek mythology who devoured youths.

of which his better nature disapproves? Is it the intention of law-makers that *good* men shall be hung ever? Are judges to interpret the law according to the letter, and not the spirit? What right have *you* to enter into a compact with yourself that you *will* do thus or so, against the light within you? Is it for *you* to *make up* your mind—to form any resolution whatever—and not accept the convictions that are forced upon you, and which ever pass your understanding? I do not believe in lawyers, in that mode of attacking or defending a man, because you descend to meet the judge on his own ground, and, in cases of the highest importance, it is of no consequence whether a man breaks a human law or not. Let lawyers decide trivial cases. Business men may arrange that among themselves. If they were the interpreters of the everlasting laws which rightfully bind man, that would be another thing. A counterfeiting law-factory, standing half in a slave land and half in a free! What kind of laws for free men can you expect from that?

I am here to plead his cause with you. I plead not for his life, but for his character—his immortal life; and so it becomes your cause wholly, and is not his in the least. Some eighteen hundred years ago Christ was crucified; this morning, perchance, Captain Brown was hung. These are the two ends of a chain which is not without its links. He is not Old Brown any longer; he is an Angel of Light.

I see now that it was necessary that the bravest and humanest man in all the country should be hung. Perhaps he saw it himself. I *almost fear* that I may yet hear of his deliverance, doubting if a prolonged life, if *any* life, can do as much good as his death.

"Misguided"! "Garrulous"! "Insane"! "Vindictive"! So ye write in your easy chairs, and thus the wounded responds from the floor of the Armory, clear as a cloudless sky, true as the voice of nature is: "No man sent me here; it was my own prompting and that of my Maker. I acknowledge no master in human form."

And in what a sweet and noble strain he proceeds, addressing his captors, who stand over him: "I think, my friends, you are guilty of a great wrong against God and humanity, and it would be perfectly right for any one to interfere with you so far as to free those you wilfully and wickedly hold in bondage."

And referring to his movement: "It is, in my opinion, the greatest service a man can render to God."

"I pity the poor in bondage that have none to help them; that is why I am here; not to gratify any personal animosity, revenge, or vindictive spirit. It is my sympathy with the oppressed and the wronged, that are as good as you, and as precious in the sight of God."

You don't know your testament when you see it.

"I want you to understand that I respect the rights of the poorest and weakest of colored people, oppressed by the slave power, just as much as I do those of the most wealthy and powerful."

"I wish to say, furthermore, that you had better, all you people at the South, prepare yourselves for a settlement of that question, that must come up for settlement sooner than you are prepared for it. The sooner you are prepared the better. You may dispose of me very easily. I am nearly disposed of now; but this question is still to be settled—this negro question, I mean; the end of that is not yet."

I foresee the time when the painter will paint that scene, no longer going to Rome for a subject;[29] the poet will sing it; the historian record it; and, with the Landing of the Pilgrims and the Declaration of Independence, it will be the ornament of some future national gallery, when at least the present form of Slavery shall be no more here. We shall then be at liberty to weep for Captain Brown. Then, and not till then, we will take our revenge.

1860

Walking

I wish to speak a word for Nature, for absolute freedom and wildness, as contrasted with a freedom and culture merely civil,—to regard man as an inhabitant, or a part and parcel of Nature, rather than a member of society. I wish to make an extreme statement, if so I may make an emphatic one, for there are enough champions of civilization: the minister, and the school-committee, and every one of you will take care of that.

I have met with but one or two persons in the course of my life who understood the art of Walking, that is, of taking walks,—who had a genius, so to speak, for *sauntering*: which word is beautifully derived "from idle people who roved about the country, in the Middle Ages, and asked charity, under pretence of going *à la Sainte Terre*," to the Holy Land, till the children exclaimed, "There goes a *Sainte-Terrer*," a Saunterer,—a Holy-Lander. They who never go to the Holy Land in their walks, as they pretend, are indeed mere idlers and vagabonds; but they who do go there are saunterers in the good sense, such as I mean. Some, however, would derive the word from *sans terre*, without land or a home, which, therefore, in the good sense, will mean, having no particular home, but equally at home everywhere. For this is the secret of successful sauntering. He who sits still in a house all the time may be the greatest vagrant of all; but the saunterer, in the good sense, is no more vagrant than the meandering river, which is all the while sedulously seeking the shortest course to the sea. But I prefer the first, which, indeed, is the most probable derivation. For every walk is a sort of crusade, preached by some Peter the Hermit in us, to go forth and reconquer this Holy Land from the hands of the Infidels.[1]

It is true, we are but faint-hearted crusaders, even the walkers, nowadays, who undertake no perservering, never-ending enterprises. Our expeditions are but tours, and come round again at evening to the old hearth-side from which we set out. Half the walk is but retracing our steps. We should

---

[29]John Stewart Curry's famous mural of Brown with the flowing beard would seem to bear out Thoreau's prophecy.

[1]Peter the Hermit was a zealot who led an unsuccessful crusade to Jerusalem in 1096 to free the Holy Land from the "infidels."

go forth on the shortest walk, perchance, in the spirit of undying adventure, never to return,—prepared to send back our embalmed hearts only as relics to our desolate kingdoms. If you are ready to leave father and mother, and brother and sister, and wife and child and friends, and never see them again,[2]—if you have paid your debts, and made your will, and settled all your affairs, and are a free man, then you are ready for a walk.

To come down to my own experience, my companion and I, for I sometimes have a companion, take pleasure in fancying ourselves knights of a new, or rather an old, order,—not Equestrians or Chevaliers, not Ritters or Riders,[3] but Walkers, a still more ancient and honorable class, I trust. The chivalric and heroic spirit which once belonged to the Rider seems now to reside in, or perchance to have subsided into, the Walker,—not the Knight, but Walker Errant.[4] He is a sort of fourth estate,[5] outside of Church and State and People.

We have felt that we almost alone hereabouts practised this noble art; though, to tell the truth, at least, if their own assertions are to be received, most of my townsmen would fain walk sometimes, as I do, but they cannot. No wealth can buy the requisite leisure, freedom, and independence, which are the capital in this profession. It comes only by the grace of God. It requires a direct dispensation from Heaven to become a walker. You must be born into the family of the Walkers. *Ambulator nascitur, non fit.*[6] Some of my townsmen, it is true, can remember and have described to me some walks which they took ten years ago, in which they were so blessed as to lose themselves for half an hour in the woods; but I know very well that they have confined themselves to the highway ever since, whatever pretensions they may make to belong to this select class. No doubt they were elevated for a moment as by the reminiscence of a previous state of existence, when even they were foresters and outlaws.

> *"When he came to grene wode,*
> *In a mery mornynge,*
> *There he herde the notes small*
>
> *Of byrdes mery syngynge.*
> *"It is ferre gone, sayd Robyn,*[7]
> *That I was last here;*
> *Me lyste a lytell for to shote*
> *At the donne dere."*

---

[2]Christ so charged his disciples as a prerequisite to following Him.

[3]Thoreau may have been thinking of Karl Ritter, father of modern human geography. A Chevalier was a member of one of the orders of knighthood.

[4]Thoreau is punning on "Knight Errant," a knight who traveled in search of heroic exploits.

[5]The press.

[6]A walker is born, not made.

[7]Robyn (Robin Hood) was a legendary twelfth-century hero who lived in the forest and robbed the rich to give to the poor. He illegally hunted deer on the preserves of the nobility.

I think that I cannot preserve my health and spirits, unless I spend four hours a day at least—and it is commonly more than that—sauntering through the woods and over the hills and fields, absolutely free from all worldly engagements. You may safely say, A penny for your thoughts, or a thousand pounds. When sometimes I am reminded that the mechanics and shopkeepers stay in their shops not only all the forenoon, but all the afternoon too, sitting with crossed legs, so many of them,—as if the legs were made to sit upon, and not to stand or walk upon,—I think that they deserve some credit for not having all committed suicide long ago.

I, who cannot stay in my chamber for a single day without acquiring some rust, and when sometimes I have stolen forth for a walk at the eleventh hour of four o'clock in the afternoon, too late to redeem the day, when the shades of night were already beginning to be mingled with the daylight, have felt as if I had committed some sin to be atoned for,—I confess that I am astonished at the power of endurance, to say nothing of the moral insensibility, of my neighbors who confine themselves to shops and offices the whole day for weeks and months, ay, and years almost together. I know now what manner of stuff they are of,—sitting there now at three o'clock in the afternoon, as if it were three o'clock in the morning. Bonaparte[8] may talk of the three-o'clock-in-the-morning courage, but it is nothing to the courage which can sit down cheerfully at this hour in the afternoon over against one's self whom you have known all the morning, to starve out a garrison to whom you are bound by such strong ties of sympathy. I wonder that about this time, or say between four and five o'clock in the afternoon, too late for the morning papers and too early for the evening ones, there is not a general explosion heard up and down the street, scattering a legion of antiquated and housebred notions and whims to the four winds for an airing,—and so the evil cure itself.

How womankind, who are confined to the house still more than men, stand it I do not know; but I have ground to suspect that most of them do not *stand* it at all. When, early in a summer afternoon, we have been shaking the dust of the village from the skirts of our garments, making haste past those houses with purely Doric or Gothic fronts,[9] which have such an air of repose about them, my companion whispers that probably about these times their occupants are all gone to bed. Then it is that I appreciate the beauty and the glory of architecture, which itself never turns in, but forever stands out and erect, keeping watch over the slumberers.

No doubt temperament, and, above all, age, have a good deal to do with it. As a man grows older, his ability to sit still and follow in-door occupations increases. He grows vespertinal in his habits as the evening of life approaches, till at last he comes forth only just before sundown, and gets all the walk that he requires in half an hour.

[8]Napoleon.
[9]Doric: an early architectural form developed by the Greeks. Gothic: the dominant architectural mode of the Middle Ages.

But the walking of which I speak has nothing in it akin to taking exercise, as it is called, as the sick take medicine at stated hours,—as the swinging of dumbbells or chairs; but is itself the enterprise and adventure of the day. If you would get exercise, go in search of the springs of life. Think of a man's swinging dumbbells for his health, when those springs are bubbling up in far-off pastures unsought by him!

Moreover, you must walk like a camel, which is said to be the only beast which ruminates when walking.[10] When a traveller asked Wordsworth's servant to show him her master's study, she answered, "Here is his library, but his study is out of doors."

Living much out of doors, in the sun and wind, will no doubt produce a certain roughness of character,—will cause a thicker cuticle to grow over some of the finer qualities of our nature, as on the face and hands, or as severe manual labor robs the hands of some of their delicacy of touch. So staying in the house, on the other hand, may produce a softness and smoothness, not to say thinness of skin, accompanied by an increased sensibility to certain impressions. Perhaps we should be more susceptible to some influences important to our intellectual and moral growth, if the sun had shone and the wind blown on us a little less; and no doubt it is a nice matter to proportion rightly the thick and thin skin. But methinks that is a scurf that will fall off fast enough,—that the natural remedy is to be found in the proportion which the night bears to the day, the winter to the summer, thought to experience. There will be so much the more air and sunshine in our thoughts. The callous palms of the laborer are conversant with finer tissues of self-respect and heroism, whose touch thrills the heart, than the languid fingers of idleness. That is mere sentimentality that lies abed by day and thinks itself white, far from the tan and callus of experience.

When we walk, we naturally go to the fields and woods: what would become of us, if we walked only in a garden or a mall? Even some sects of philosophers have felt the necessity of importing the woods to themselves, since they did not go to the woods. "They planted groves and walks of Platanes," where they took *subdiales ambulationes*[11] in porticos open to the air. Of course it is of no use to direct our steps to the woods, if they do not carry us thither. I am alarmed when it happens that I have walked a mile into the woods bodily, without getting there in spirit. In my afternoon walk I would fain forget all my morning occupations and my obligations to society. But it sometimes happens that I cannot easily shake off the village. The thought of some work will run in my head, and I am not where my body is,—I am out of my senses. In my walks I would fain return to my senses. What business have I in the woods, if I am thinking of something out of the woods? I suspect myself, and cannot help a shudder, when I find myself so implicated even in what are called good works,—for this may sometimes happen.

---

[10]Thoreau is using "ruminates" as a pun; the principal meaning he has in mind is "contemplates."

[11]Walks in the open air.

My vicinity affords many good walks; and though for so many years I have walked almost every day, and sometimes for several days together, I have not yet exhausted them. An absolutely new prospect is a great happiness, and I can still get this any afternoon. Two or three hours' walking will carry me to as strange a country as I expect ever to see. A single farm-house which I had not seen before is sometimes as good as the dominions of the King of Dahomey.[12] There is in fact a sort of harmony discoverable between the capabilities of the landscape within a circle of ten miles' radius, or the limits of an afternoon walk, and the threescore years and ten of human life. It will never become quite familiar to you.

Nowadays almost all man's improvements, so called, as the building of houses, and the cutting down of the forest and of all large trees, simply deform the landscape, and make it more and more tame and cheap. A people who would begin by burning the fences and let the forest stand! I saw the fences half consumed, their ends lost in the middle of the prairie, and some worldly miser with a surveyor looking after his bounds, while heaven had taken place around him, and he did not see the angels going to and fro, but was looking for an old post-hole in the midst of paradise. I looked again, and saw him standing in the middle of a boggy, stygian fen, surrounded by devils, and he had found his bounds without a doubt, three little stones, where a stake had been driven, and looking nearer, I saw that the Prince of Darkness[13] was his surveyor.

I can easily walk ten, fifteen, twenty, any number of miles, commencing at my own door, without going by any house, without crossing a road except where the fox and the mink do: first along by the river, and then the brook, and then the meadow and the wood-side. There are square miles in my vicinity which have no inhabitant. From many a hill I can see civilization and the abodes of man afar. The farmers and their works are scarcely more obvious than woodchucks and their burrows. Man and his affairs, church and state and school, trade and commerce, and manufactures and agriculture, even politics, the most alarming of them all,—I am pleased to see how little space they occupy in the landscape. Politics is but a narrow field, and that still narrower highway yonder leads to it. I sometimes direct the traveller thither. If you would go to the political world, follow the great road,—follow that market-man, keep his dust in your eyes, and it will lead you straight to it; for it, too, has its place merely, and does not occupy all space. I pass from it as from a beanfield into the forest, and it is forgotten. In one half-hour I can walk off to some portion of the earth's surface where a man does not stand from one year's end to another, and there, consequently, politics are not, for they are but as the cigar-smoke of a man.

The village is the place to which the roads tend, a sort of expansion of the highway, as a lake of a river. It is the body of which roads are the arms

[12]Presumably King Gezo of the West African kingdom whose economy was based on the export of slaves. [13]Satan.

and legs,—a trivial or quadrivial place, the thoroughfare and ordinary of travellers. The word is from the Latin *villa*, which, together with *via*, a way, or more anciently *ved* and *vella*, Varro derives from *veho*, to carry, because the villa is the place to and from which things are carried. They who got their living by teaming were said *vellaturam facere*.[14] Hence, too, apparently, the Latin word *vilis* and our vile; also *villain*. This suggests what kind of degeneracy villagers are liable to. They are wayworn by the travel that goes by and over them, without travelling themselves.

Some do not walk at all; others walk in the highways; a few walk across lots. Roads are made for horses and men of business. I do not travel in them much, comparatively, because I am not in a hurry to get to any tavern or grocery or livery-stable or depot to which they lead. I am a good horse to travel, but not from choice a roadster. The landscape-painter uses the figures of men to mark a road. He would not make that use of my figure. I walk out into a Nature such as the old prophets and poets, Menu, Moses, Homer, Chaucer, walked in. You may name it America, but it is not America: neither Americus Vespucius,[15] nor Columbus, nor the rest were the discoverers of it. There is a truer account of it in mythology than in any history of America, so called, that I have seen.

However, there are a few old roads that may be trodden with profit, as if they led somewhere now that they are nearly discontinued. There is the Old Marlborough Road,[16] which does not go to Marlborough now, methinks, unless that is Marlborough where it carries me. I am the bolder to speak of it here, because I presume that there are one or two such roads in every town.

THE OLD MARLBOROUGH ROAD

> *Where they once dug for money,*
> *But never found any;*
> *Where sometimes Martial Miles*
> *Singly flies,*
> *And Elijah Wood,*
> *I fear for no good:*
> *No other man,*
> *Save Elisha Dugan,—*
> *O man of wild habits,*
> *Partridges and rabbits,*
> *Who hast no cares*
> *Only to set snares,*
> *Who liv'st all alone,*
> *Close to the bone,*
> *And where life is sweetest*
> *   Constantly eatest.*

[14]Literally, "to make a cart."
[15]The Italian navigator who gave America its name.

[16]A deserted road that once led from Concord to Marlborough.

When the spring stirs my blood
    With the instinct to travel,
    I can get enough gravel
On the Old Marlborough Road.
    Nobody repairs it,
    For nobody wears it;
    It is a living way,
    As the Christians say.
Not many there be
    Who enter therein,
Only the guests of the
    Irishman Quin.
What is it, what is it,
    But a direction out there,
And the bare possibility
    Of going somewhere?
        Great guide-boards of stone,
        But travellers none;
        Cenotaphs of the towns
        Named on their crowns.
        It is worth going to see
        Where you might be.
        What king
        Did the thing,
        I am still wondering;
        Set up how or when,
        By what selectmen,
        Gourgas or Lee,
        Clark or Darby?
        They're a great endeavor
        To be something forever;
        Blank tablets of stone,
        Where a traveller might groan,
        And in one sentence
        Grave all that is known;
        Which another might read,
        In his extreme need.
        I know one or two
        Lines that would do,
        Literature that might stand
        All over the land,
        Which a man could remember
        Till next December,
        And read again in the spring,
        After the thawing.
If with fancy unfurled
    You leave your abode,
You may go round the world

By the Old Marlborough Road.

At present, in this vicinity, the best part of the land is not private property; the landscape is not owned, and the walker enjoys comparative freedom. But possibly the day will come when it will be partitioned off into so-called pleasure-grounds, in which a few will take a narrow and exclusive pleasure only,—when fences shall be multiplied, and man-traps and other engines invented to confine men to the *public* road, and walking over the surface of God's earth shall be construed to mean trespassing on some gentleman's grounds. To enjoy a thing exclusively is commonly to exclude yourself from the true enjoyment of it. Let us improve our opportunities, then, before the evil days come.

What is it that makes it so hard sometimes to determine whither we will walk? I believe that there is a subtle magnetism in Nature, which, if we unconsciously yield to it, will direct us aright. It is not indifferent to us which way we walk. There is a right way; but we are very liable from heedlessness and stupidity to take the wrong one. We would fain take that walk, never yet taken by us through this actual world, which is perfectly symbolical of the path which we love to travel in the interior and ideal world; and sometimes, no doubt, we find it difficult to choose our direction, because it does not yet exist distinctly in our idea.

When I go out of the house for a walk, uncertain as yet whither I will bend my steps, and submit myself to my instinct to decide for me, I find, strange and whimsical as it may seem, that I finally and inevitably settle southwest, toward some particular wood or meadow or deserted pasture or hill in that direction. My needle[17] is slow to settle,—varies a few degrees, and does not always point due southwest, it is true, and it has good authority for this variation, but it always settles between west and south-southwest. The future lies that way to me, and the earth seems more unexhausted and richer on that side. The outline which would bound my walks would be, not a circle, but a parabola, or rather like one of those cometary orbits which have been thought to be non-returning curves, in this case opening westward, in which my house occupies the place of the sun. I turn round and round irresolute sometimes for a quarter of an hour, until I decide, for the thousandth time, that I will walk into the southwest or west. Eastward I go only by force; but westward I go free. Thither no business leads me. It is hard for me to believe that I shall find fair landscapes or sufficient wildness and freedom behind the eastern horizon. I am not excited by the prospect of a walk thither; but I believe that the forest which I see in the western horizon stretches uninterruptedly towards the setting sun, and that there are no towns nor cities in it of enough consequence to disturb me. Let me live where I will, on this side is the city, on that the wilderness, and ever I am leaving the city more and more, and withdrawing into the wilderness. I should not lay so much stress

[17]Thoreau means his inner "compass."

on this fact, if I did not believe that something like this is the prevailing tendency of my countrymen. I must walk toward Oregon, and not toward Europe. And that way the nation is moving, and I may say that mankind progress from east to west. Within a few years we have witnessed the phenomenon of a southeastward migration, in the settlement of Australia; but this affects us as a retrograde movement, and, judging from the moral and physical character of the first generation of Australians, has not yet proved a successful experiment. The eastern Tartars[18] think that there is nothing west beyond Thibet. "The world ends there," say they; "beyond there is nothing but a shoreless sea." It is unmitigated East where they live.

We go eastward to realize history and study the works of art and literature, retracing the steps of the race; we go westward as into the future, with a spirit of enterprise and adventure. The Atlantic is a Lethean stream,[19] in our passage over which we have had an opportunity to forget the Old World and its institutions. If we do not succeed this time, there is perhaps one more chance for the race left before it arrives on the banks of the Styx;[20] and that is in the Lethe of the Pacific, which is three times as wide.

I know not how significant it is, or how far it is an evidence of singularity, that an individual should thus consent in his pettiest walk with the general movement of the race; but I know that something akin to the migratory instinct in birds and quadrupeds,—which, in some instances, is known to have affected the squirrel tribe, impelling them to a general and mysterious movement, in which they were seen, say some, crossing the broadest rivers, each on its particular chip, with its tail raised for a sail, and bridging narrower streams with their dead,—that something like the *furor* which affects the domestic cattle in the spring,[21] and which is referred to a worm in their tails,—affects both nations and individuals, either perennially or from time to time. Not a flock of wild geese cackles over our town, but it to some extent unsettles the value of real estate here, and, if I were a broker, I should probably take that disturbance into account.

> *"Than longen folk to gon on pilgrimages,*
> *And palmeres for to seken strange strondes."*[22]

Every sunset which I witness inspires me with the desire to go to a West as distant and as fair as that into which the sun goes down. He appears to migrate westward daily, and tempt us to follow him. He is the Great Western Pioneer whom the nations follow. We dream all night of those mountain-ridges in the horizon, though they may be of vapor only, which were

---

[18]Nomads that once roamed over what is now Mongolia.

[19]In Greek mythology, the river Lethe flowed in Hades. Persons who drank the water forgot the past.

[20]The Styx, in Greek mythology, was a river in the world of the dead.

[21]The *"furor"* Thoreau is speaking of results from the itching in the hides of cattle when eggs laid there by cattle flies begin to hatch. The cattle are very restless during this period in the spring.

[22]The quotation is from Chaucer's *Canterbury Tales*, in which the characters narrate tales while pilgrimaging from London to Canterbury.

last gilded by his rays. The island of Atlantis,[23] and the islands and gardens of the Hesperides, a sort of terrestrial paradise, appear to have been the Great West of the ancients, enveloped in mystery and poetry. Who has not seen in imagination, when looking into the sunset sky, the gardens of the Hesperides, and the foundation of all those fables?

Columbus felt the westward tendency more strongly than any before. He obeyed it, and found a New World for Castile and Leon. The herd of men in those days scented fresh pastures, from afar.

> "And now the sun had stretched out all the hills,
> And now was dropped into the western bay;
> At last he rose, and twitched his mantle blue;
> To-morrow to fresh woods and pastures new."[24]

Where on the globe can there be found an area of equal extent with that occupied by the bulk of our States, so fertile and so rich and varied in its productions, and at the same time so habitable by the European, as this is? Michaux,[25] who knew but part of them, says that "the species of large trees are much more numerous in North America than in Europe; in the United States there are more than one hundred and forty species that exceed thirty feet in height; in France there are but thirty that attain this size." Later botanists more than confirm his observations. Humboldt came to America to realize his youthful dreams of a tropical vegetation, and he beheld it in its greatest perfection in the primitive forests of the Amazon, the most gigantic wilderness on the earth, which he has so eloquently described. The geographer Guyot, himself a European, goes farther,—farther than I am ready to follow him; yet not when he says,—"As the plant is made for the animal, as the vegetable world is made for the animal world, America is made for the man of the Old World. ... The man of the Old World sets out upon his way. Leaving the highlands of Asia, he descends from station to station towards Europe. Each of his steps is marked by a new civilization superior to the preceding, by a greater power of development. Arrived at the Atlantic, he pauses on the shore of this unknown ocean, the bounds of which he knows not, and turns upon his footprints for an instant." When he has exhausted the rich soil of Europe, and reinvigorated himself, "then recommences his adventurous career westward as in the earliest ages." So far Guyot.

From this western impulse coming in contact with the barrier of the Atlantic sprang the commerce and enterprise of modern times. The younger Michaux, in his "Travels West of the Alleghanies in 1802," says that the common inquiry in the newly settled West was, "'From what part of the world

---

[23]Atlantis was, according to the ancients, a lost sunken island, often sought for. The Hesperides was an imaginary garden that produced golden apples.

[24]Thoreau quotes the final four lines of Milton's pastoral elegy "Lycidas."

[25]André Michaux was a French botanist who traveled extensively in America; Alexander Humboldt was a German naturalist and traveler.

have you come?' As if these vast and fertile regions would naturally be the place of meeting and common country of all the inhabitants of the globe."

To use an obsolete Latin word, I might say, *Ex Oriente lux; ex Occidente* FRUX. From the East light; from the West fruit.

Sir Francis Head, an English traveller and a Governor-General of Canada, tells us that "in both the northern and southern hemispheres of the New World, Nature has not only outlined her works on a larger scale, but has painted the whole picture with brighter and more costly colors than she used in delineating and in beautifying the Old World. ... The heavens of America appear infinitely higher, the sky is bluer, the air is fresher, the cold is intenser, the moon looks larger, the stars are brighter, the thunder is louder, the lightning is vivider, the wind is stronger, the rain is heavier, the mountains are higher, the rivers longer, the forests bigger, the plains broader." This statement will do at least to set against Buffon's account of this part of the world and its productions.[26]

Linnaeus said long ago, "Nescio quæ facies *læta, glabra* plantis Americanis: I know not what there is of joyous and smooth in the aspect of American plants"; and I think that in this country there are no, or at most very few, *Africanæ bestiæ*, African beasts, as the Romans called them, and that in this respect also it is peculiarly fitted for the habitation of man. We are told that within three miles of the centre of the East-Indian city of Singapore, some of the inhabitants are annually carried off by tigers; but the traveller can lie down in the woods at night almost anywhere in North America without fear of wild beasts.

These are encouraging testimonies. If the moon looks larger here than in Europe, probably the sun looks larger also. If the heavens of America appear infinitely higher, and the stars brighter, I trust that these facts are symbolical of the height to which the philosophy and poetry and religion of her inhabitants may one day soar. At length, perchance, the immaterial heaven will appear as much higher to the American mind, and the intimations that star it as much brighter. For I believe that climate does thus react on man,—as there is something in the mountain-air that feeds the spirit and inspires. Will not man grow to greater perfection intellectually as well as physically under these influences? Or is it unimportant how many foggy days there are in his life? I trust that we shall be more imaginative, that our thoughts will be clearer, fresher, and more ethereal, as our sky,—our understanding more comprehensive and broader, like our plains,—our intellect generally on a grander scale, like our thunder and lightning, our rivers and mountains and forests,—and our hearts shall even correspond in breadth and depth and grandeur to our inland seas. Perchance there will appear to the traveller something, he knows not what, of *læta* and *glabra*, of joyous

[26]Buffon was an eighteenth-century French writer on natural history. Linnaeus was a well-known Swedish botanist.

and serene, in our very faces. Else to what end does the world go on, and why was America discovered?

To Americans I hardly need to say,—

> "Westward the star of empire takes its way."

As a true patriot, I should be ashamed to think that Adam in paradise was more favorably situated on the whole than the backwoodsman in this country.

Our sympathies in Massachusetts are not confined to New England; though we may be estranged from the South, we sympathize with the West. There is the home of the younger sons, as among the Scandinavians they took to the sea for their inheritance. It is too late to be studying Hebrew; it is more important to understand even the slang of to-day.

Some months ago I went to see a panorama of the Rhine. It was like a dream of the Middle Ages. I floated down its historic stream in something more than imagination, under bridges built by the Romans, and repaired by later heroes, past cities and castles whose very names were music to my ears, and each of which was the subject of a legend. There were Ehrenbreitstein and Rolandseck and Coblentz, which I knew only in history. They were ruins that interested me chiefly. There seemed to come up from its waters and its vine-clad hills and valleys a hushed music as of Crusaders departing for the Holy Land. I floated along under the spell of enchantment, as if I had been transported to an heroic age, and breathed an atmosphere of chivalry.

Soon after, I went to see a panorama of the Mississippi, and as I worked my way up the river in the light of today, and saw the steamboats wooding up, counted the rising cities, gazed on the fresh ruins of Nauvoo,[27] beheld the Indians moving west across the stream, and, as before I had looked up the Moselle, now looked up the Ohio and the Missouri, and heard the legends of Dubuque and of Wenona's Cliff,—still thinking more of the future than of the past or present,—I saw that this was a Rhine stream of a different kind; that the foundations of castles were yet to be laid, and the famous bridges were yet to be thrown over the river; and I felt that *this was the heroic age itself*, though we know it not, for the hero is commonly the simplest and obscurest of men.

The West of which I speak is but another name for the Wild; and what I have been preparing to say is, that in Wildness is the preservation of the world. Every tree sends its fibres forth in search of the Wild. The cities import it at any price. Men plough and sail for it. From the forest and wilderness come the tonics and barks which brace mankind. Our ancestors were savages. The story of Romulus and Remus being suckled by a wolf is not a meaningless fable.[28] The founders of every State which has risen to eminence have drawn their nourishment and vigor from a similar wild

---

[27] The Illinois city founded by the Mormons; it was attacked and destroyed by their opponents.

[28] Romulus and Remus, according to Roman legend, were twin sons of the god Mars. Discarded as infants, they were suckled by a she-wolf until found and raised by a shepherd.

source. It was because the children of the Empire were not suckled by the wolf that they were conquered and displaced by the children of the Northern forests who were.

I believe in the forest, and in the meadow, and in the night in which the corn grows. We require an infusion of hemlock-spruce or arbor-vitæ in our tea. There is a difference between eating and drinking for strength and from mere gluttony. The Hottentots eagerly devour the marrow of the koodoo and other antelopes raw, as a matter of course. Some of our Northern Indians eat raw the marrow of the Arctic reindeer, as well as various other parts, including the summits of the antlers, as long as they are soft. And herein, perchance, they have stolen a march on the cooks of Paris. They get what usually goes to feed the fire. This is probably better than stall-fed beef and slaughter-house pork to make a man of. Give me a wildness whose glance no civilization can endure,—as if we lived on the marrow of koodoos devoured raw.

There are some intervals which border the strain of the wood-thrush, to which I would migrate,—wild lands where no settler has squatted; to which, methinks, I am already acclimated.

The African hunter Cummings tells us that the skin of the eland, as well as that of most other antelopes just killed, emits the most delicious perfume of trees and grass. I would have every man so much like a wild antelope, so much a part and parcel of Nature, that his very person should thus sweetly advertise our senses of his presence, and remind us of those parts of Nature which he most haunts. I feel no disposition to be satirical, when the trapper's coat emits the odor of musquash even; it is a sweeter scent to me than that which commonly exhales from the merchant's or the scholar's garments. When I go into their wardrobes and handle their vestments, I am reminded of no grassy plains and flowery meads which they have frequented, but of dusty merchants' exchanges and libraries rather.

A tanned skin is something more than respectable, and perhaps olive is a fitter color than white for a man,—a denizen of the woods. "The pale white man!" I do not wonder that the African pitied him. Darwin the naturalist says, "A white man bathing by the side of a Tahitian was like a plant bleached by the gardener's art, compared with a fine, dark green one, growing vigorously in the open fields."

Ben Jonson exclaims,—

> *"How near to good is what is fair!"*

So I would say,—

> *"How near to good is what is wild!"*

Life consists with wildness. The most alive is the wildest. Not yet subdued to man, its presence refreshes him. One who pressed forward incessantly and never rested from his labors, who grew fast and made infinite demands on life, would always find himself in a new country or wilderness, and surrounded by the raw material of life. He would be climbing over the prostrate stems of primitive forest-trees.

Hope and the future for me are not in lawns and cultivated fields, not in towns and cities, but in the impervious and quaking swamps. When, formerly, I have analyzed my partiality for some farm which I had contemplated purchasing, I have frequently found that I was attracted solely by a few square rods of impermeable and unfathomable bog,—a natural sink in one corner of it. That was the jewel which dazzled me. I derive more of my subsistence from the swamps which surround my native town than from the cultivated gardens in the village. There are no richer parterres to my eyes than the dense beds of dwarf andromeda (*Cassandra calyculata*) which cover these tender places on the earth's surface. Botany cannot go farther than tell me the names of the shrubs which grow there,—the high-blueberry, panicled andromeda, lamb-kill, azalea, and rhodora,—all standing in the quaking sphagnum. I often think that I should like to have my house front on this mass of dull red bushes, omitting other flower plots and borders, transplanted spruce and trim box, even gravelled walks,—to have this fertile spot under my windows, not a few imported barrow-fulls of soil only to cover the sand which was thrown out in digging the cellar. Why not put my house, my parlor, behind this plot, instead of behind that meagre assemblage of curiosities, that poor apology for a Nature and Art, which I call my front-yard? It is an effort to clear up and make a decent appearance when the carpenter and mason have departed, though done as much for the passer-by as the dweller within. The most tasteful front-yard fence was never an agreeable object of study to me; the most elaborate ornaments, acorn-tops, or what not, soon wearied and disgusted me. Bring your sills up to the very edge of the swamp, then, (though it may not be the best place for a dry cellar,) so that there be no access on that side to citizens. Front-yards are not made to walk in, but, at most, through, and you could go in the back way.

Yes, though you may think me perverse, if it were proposed to me to dwell in the neighborhood of the most beautiful garden that ever human art contrived, or else of a dismal swamp, I should certainly decide for the swamp. How vain, then, have been all your labors, citizens, for me!

My spirits infallibly rise in proportion to the outward dreariness. Give me the ocean, the desert, or the wilderness! In the desert, pure air and solitude compensate for want of moisture and fertility. The traveller Burton says of it,—"Your *morale* improves; you become frank and cordial, hospitable and single-minded. ... In the desert, spirituous liquors excite only disgust. There is a keen enjoyment in a mere animal existence." They who have been travelling long on the steppes of Tartary say,—"On reëntering cultivated lands, the agitation, perplexity, and turmoil of civilization oppressed and suffocated us; the air seemed to fail us, and we felt every moment as if about to die of asphyxia." When I would recreate myself, I seek the darkest wood, the thickest and most interminable, and, to the citizen, most dismal swamp. I enter a swamp as a sacred place,—a *sanctum sanctorum*. There is the strength, the marrow of Nature. The wild-wood covers the virgin mould,—and the same soil is good for men and for trees. A man's health requires as many acres of meadow to his prospect as his farm does loads of muck. There are the strong meats on which he feeds. A town is saved, not more by the righteous men in it than by the woods and swamps that surround it. A township where one primitive forest waves above, while another primitive forest rots below,—such a town is fitted to raise not only corn and potatoes, but poets and philosophers for the coming ages. In such a soil grew Homer and Confucius and the rest, and out of such a wilderness comes the Reformer eating locusts and wild honey.[29]

To preserve wild animals implies generally the creation of a forest for them to dwell in or resort to. So is it with man. A hundred years ago they sold bark in our streets peeled from our own woods. In the very aspect of those primitive and rugged trees, there was, methinks, a tanning principle which hardened and consolidated the fibres of men's thoughts. Ah! already I shudder for these comparatively degenerate days of my native village, when you cannot collect a load of bark of good thickness,—and we no longer produce tar and turpentine.

The civilized nations—Greece, Rome, England—have been sustained by the primitive forests which anciently rotted where they stand. They survive as long as the soil is not exhausted. Alas for human culture! little is to be expected of a nation, when the vegetable mould is exhausted, and it is compelled to make manure of the bones of its fathers. There the poet sustains himself merely by his own superfluous fat, and the philosopher comes down on his marrow-bones.

It is said to be the task of the American "to work the virgin soil," and that "agriculture here already assumes proportions unknown everywhere else." I think that the farmer displaces the Indian even because he redeems the meadow, and so makes himself stronger and in some respects more natural. I was surveying for a man the other day a single straight line one hundred and thirty-two rods long, through a swamp, at whose entrance might have been written the words which Dante read over the entrance to the infernal regions,—"Leave all hope, ye that enter,"—that is, of ever getting out again; where at one time I saw my employer actually up to his neck and swimming for his life in his property, though it was still winter. He had another similar swamp which I could not survey at all, because it was completely under water, and nevertheless, with regard to a third swamp, which I did *survey* from a distance, he remarked to me, true to his instincts, that he would not part with it for any consideration, on account of the mud which it contained. And that man intends to put a girdling ditch round the whole in the course of forty months, and so redeem it by the magic of his spade. I refer to him only as the type of a class.

The weapons with which we have gained our most important victories, which should be handed down as heirlooms from father to son, are not the sword and the lance, but the bush-whack, the turf-cutter, the spade, and the

---

[29]In the New Testament, John the Baptist, who lived in the wilderness where he ate locusts and wild honey, announced the coming of Christ.

bog-hoe, rusted with the blood of many a meadow, and begrimed with the dust of many a hard-fought field. The very winds blew the Indian's cornfield into the meadow, and pointed out the way which he had not the skill to follow. He had no better implement with which to intrench himself in the land than a clamshell. But the farmer is armed with plough and spade.

In Literature it is only the wild that attracts us. Dulness is but another name for tameness. It is the uncivilized free and wild thinking in "Hamlet" and the "Iliad," in all the Scriptures and Mythologies, not learned in the schools, that delights us. As the wild duck is more swift and beautiful than the tame, so is the wild—the mallard—thought, which 'mid falling dews wings it way above the fens.[30] A truly good book is something as natural, and as unexpectedly and unaccountably fair and perfect, as a wild flower discovered on the prairies of the West or in the jungles of the East. Genius is a light which makes the darkness visible, like the lightning's flash, which perchance shatters the temple of knowledge itself,—and not a taper lighted at the hearth-stone of the race, which pales before the light of common day.

English literature, from the days of the minstrels to the Lake Poets,—Chaucer and Spenser and Milton, and even Shakespeare, included,—breathes no quite fresh and in this sense wild strain. It is an essentially tame and civilized literature, reflecting Greece and Rome. Her wilderness is a green-wood,—her wild man a Robin Hood. There is plenty of genial love of Nature, but not so much of Nature herself. Her chronicles inform us when her wild animals, but not when the wild man in her, became extinct.

The science of Humboldt is one thing, poetry is another thing. The poet to-day, notwithstanding all the discoveries of science, and the accumulated learning of mankind, enjoys no advantage over Homer.

Where is the literature which gives expression to Nature? He would be a poet who could impress the winds and streams into his service, to speak for him; who nailed words to their primitive senses, as farmers drive down stakes in the spring, which the frost has heaved; who derived his words as often as he used them,—transplanted them to his page with earth adhering to their roots; whose words were so true and fresh and natural that they would appear to expand like the buds at the approach of spring, though they lay half-smothered between two musty leaves in a library,—ay, to bloom and bear fruit there, after their kind, annually, for the faithful reader, in sympathy with surrounding Nature.

I do not know of any poetry to quote which adequately expresses this yearning for the Wild. Approached from this side, the best poetry is tame. I do not know where to find in any literature, ancient or modern, any account which contents me of that Nature with which even I am acquainted. You will perceive that I demand something which no Augustan nor Elizabethan age, which no *culture*, in short, can give. Mythology comes nearer to it than anything. How much more fertile a Nature, at least, has Grecian mythology its

---

[30]Thoreau is paraphrasing from Bryant's poem "To a Waterfowl."

root in than English literature! Mythology is the crop which the Old World bore before its soil was exhausted, before the fancy and imagination were affected with blight; and which it still bears, wherever its pristine vigor is unabated. All other literatures endure only as the elms which overshadow our houses; but this is like the great dragon-tree of the Western Isles, as old as mankind, and, whether that does or not, will endure as long; for the decay of other literatures makes the soil in which it thrives.

The West is preparing to add its fables to those of the East. The valleys of the Ganges, the Nile, and the Rhine, having yielded their crop, it remains to be seen what the valleys of the Amazon, the Plate, the Orinoco, the St. Lawrence, and the Mississippi will produce. Perchance, when, in the course of ages, American liberty has become a fiction of the past,—as it is to some extent a fiction of the present,—the poets of the world will be inspired by American mythology.

The wildest dreams of wild men, even, are not the less true, though they may not recommend themselves to the sense which is most common among Englishmen and Americans to-day. It is not every truth that recommends itself to the common sense. Nature has a place for the wild clematis as well as for the cabbage. Some expressions of truth are reminiscent,—others merely *sensible*, as the phrase is,—others prophetic. Some forms of disease, even, may prophesy forms of health. The geologist has discovered that the figures of serpents, griffins, flying dragons, and other fanciful embellishments of heraldry, have their prototypes in the forms of fossil species which were extinct before man was created, and hence "indicate a faint and shadowy knowledge of a previous state of organic existence." The Hindoos dreamed that the earth rested on an elephant, and the elephant on a tortoise, and the tortoise on a serpent; and though it may be an unimportant coincidence, it will not be out of place here to state, that a fossil tortoise has lately been discovered in Asia large enough to support an elephant. I confess that I am partial to these wild fancies, which transcend the order of time and development. They are the sublimest recreation of the intellect. The partridge loves peas, but not those that go with her into the pot.

In short, all good things are wild and free. There is something in a strain of music, whether produced by an instrument or by the human voice,—take the sound of a bugle in a summer night, for instance,—which by its wildness, to speak without satire, reminds me of the cries emitted by wild beasts in their native forests. It is so much of their wildness as I can understand. Give me for my friends and neighbors wild men, not tame ones. The wildness of the savage is but a faint symbol of the awful ferity with which good men and lovers meet.

I love even to see the domestic animals reassert their native rights,—any evidence that they have not wholly lost their original wild habits and vigor; as when my neighbor's cow breaks out of her pasture early in the spring and boldly swims the river, a cold, gray tide, twenty-five or thirty rods wide, swollen by the melted snow. It is the buffalo crossing the Mississippi. This exploit confers some dignity on the herd in my eyes,—already dignified. The seeds of instinct are preserved under the thick hides of cattle and horses, like seeds in the bowels of the earth, an indefinite period.

Any sportiveness in cattle is unexpected. I saw one day a herd of a dozen bullocks and cows running about and frisking in unwieldly sport, like huge rats, even like kittens. They shook their heads, raised their tails, and rushed up and down a hill, and I perceived by their horns, as well as by their activity, their relation to the deer tribe. But, alas! a sudden loud *Whoa!* would have damped their ardor at once, reduced them from venison to beef, and stiffened their sides and sinews like the locomotive. Who but the Evil One has cried, "Whoa!" to mankind? Indeed, the life of cattle, like that of many men, is but a sort of locomotiveness; they move a side at a time, and man, by his machinery, is meeting the horse and ox halfway. Whatever part the whip has touched is thenceforth palsied. Who would ever think of a *side* of any of the supple cat tribe, as we speak of a *side* of beef?

I rejoice that horses and steers have to be broken before they can be made the slaves of men, and that men themselves have some wild oats still left to sow before they become submissive members of society. Undoubtedly, all men are not equally fit subjects for civilization; and because the majority, like dogs and sheep, are tame by inherited disposition, this is no reason why the others should have their natures broken that they may be reduced to the same level. Men are in the main alike, but they were made several in order that they might be various. If a low use is to be served, one man will do nearly or quite as well as another; if a high one, individual excellence is to be regarded. Any man can stop a hole to keep the wind away,[31] but no other man could serve so rare a use as the author of this illustration did. Confucius says,—"The skins of the tiger and the leopard, when they are tanned, are as the skins of the dog and the sheep tanned." But it is not the part of a true culture to tame tigers, any more than it is to make sheep ferocious; and tanning their skins for shoes is not the best use to which they can be put.

When looking over a list of men's names in a foreign language, as of military officers, or of authors who have written on a particular subject, I am reminded once more that there is nothing in a name. The name Menschikoff, for instance, has nothing in it to my ears more human than a whisker, and it may belong to a rat. As the names of the Poles and Russians are to us, so are ours to them. It is as if they had been named by the child's rigmarole,—*I cry wiery ichery van, tittle-tol-tan.* I see in my mind a herd of wild creatures swarming over the earth, and to each the herdsman has affixed some barbarous sound in his own dialect. The names of men are of course as cheap and meaningless as *Bose* and *Tray*, the names of dogs.

Methinks it would be some advantage to philosophy, if men were named merely in the gross, as they are known. It would be necessary only to know

---

[31]Thoreau's phrase "stop a hole to keep the wind away" is from Hamlet (V, i, 236).

the genus, and perhaps the race or variety, to know the individual. We are not prepared to believe that every private soldier in a Roman army had a name of his own,—because we have not supposed that he had a character of his own. At present our only true names are nicknames. I knew a boy who, from his peculiar energy, was called "Buster" by his playmates, and this rightly supplanted his Christian name. Some travellers tell us that an Indian had no name given him at first, but earned it, and his name was his fame; and among some tribes he acquired a new name with every new exploit. It is pitiful when a man bears a name for convenience merely, who has earned neither name nor fame.

I will not allow mere names to make distinctions for me, but still see men in herds for all them. A familiar name cannot make a man less strange to me. It may be given to a savage who retains in secret his own wild title earned in the woods. We have a wild savage in us, and a savage name is perchance somewhere recorded as ours. I see that my neighbor, who bears the familiar epithet William, or Edwin, takes it off with his jacket. It does not adhere to him when asleep or in anger, or aroused by any passion or inspiration. I seem to hear pronounced by some of his kin at such a time his original wild name in some jaw-breaking or else melodious tongue.

Here is this vast, savage, howling mother of ours, Nature, lying all around, with such beauty, and such affection for her children, as the leopard; and yet we are so early weaned from her breast to society, to that culture which is exclusively an interaction of man on man,—a sort of breeding in and in, which produces at most a merely English nobility, a civilization destined to have a speedy limit.

In society, in the best institutions of men, it is easy to detect a certain precocity. When we should still be growing children, we are already little men. Give me a culture which imports much muck from the meadows, and deepens the soil,—not that which trusts to heating manures, and improved implements and modes of culture only!

Many a poor sore-eyed student that I have heard of would grow faster, both intellectually and physically, if, instead of sitting up so very late, he honestly slumbered a fool's allowance.

There may be an excess even of informing light. Niépce, a Frenchman, discovered "actinism," that power in the sun's rays which produces a chemical effect,—that granite rocks, and stone structures, and statues of metal, "are all alike destructively acted upon during the hours of sunshine, and, but for provisions of Nature no less wonderful, would soon perish under the delicate touch of the most subtile of the agencies of the universe." But he observed that "those bodies which underwent this change during the daylight possessed the power of restoring themselves to their original conditions during the hours of night, when this excitement was no longer influencing them." Hence it has been inferred that "the hours of darkness are as necessary to the inorganic creation as we know night and sleep are to the organic kingdom." Not even does the moon shine every night, but gives place to darkness.

I would not have every man nor every part of a man cultivated, any more than I would have every acre of earth cultivated: part will be tillage, but the greater part will be meadow and forest, not only serving an immediate use, but preparing a mould against a distant future, by the annual decay of the vegetation which it supports.

There are other letters for the child to learn than those which Cadmus invented.[32] The Spaniards have a good term to express this wild and dusky knowledge,—*Gramática parda*, tawny grammar,—a kind of mother-wit derived from that same leopard to which I have referred.

We have heard of a Society for the Diffusion of Useful Knowledge. It is said that knowledge is power; and the like. Methinks there is equal need of a Society for the Diffusion of Useful Ignorance, what we will call Beautiful Knowledge, a knowledge useful in a higher sense: for what is most of our boasted so-called knowledge but a conceit that we know something, which robs us of the advantage of our actual ignorance? What we call knowledge is often our positive ignorance; ignorance our negative knowledge. By long years of patient industry and reading of the newspapers—for what are the libraries of science but files of newspapers?—a man accumulates a myriad facts, lays them up in his memory, and then when in some spring of his life he saunters abroad into the Great Fields of thought, he, as it were, goes to grass like a horse, and leaves all his harness behind in the stable. I would say to the Society for the Diffusion of Useful Knowledge, sometimes,—Go to grass. You have eaten hay long enough. The spring has come with its green crop. The very cows are driven to their country pastures before the end of May; though I have heard of one unnatural farmer who kept his cow in the barn and fed her on hay all the year round. So, frequently, the Society for the Diffusion of Useful Knowledge treats its cattle.

A man's ignorance sometimes is not only useful, but beautiful,—while his knowledge, so called, is oftentimes worse than useless, besides being ugly. Which is the best man to deal with,—he who knows nothing about a subject, and, what is extremely rare, knows that he knows nothing, or he who really knows something about it, but thinks that he knows all?

My desire for knowledge is intermittent; but my desire to bathe my head in atmospheres unknown to my feet is perennial and constant. The highest that we can attain to is not Knowledge, but Sympathy with Intelligence. I do not know that this higher knowledge amounts to anything more definite than a novel and grand surprise on a sudden revelation of the insufficiency of all that we called Knowledge before,—a discovery that there are more things in heaven and earth than are dreamed of in our philosophy. It is the lighting up of the mist by the sun. Man cannot *know* in any higher sense than this, any more than he can look serenely, and with impunity in the face of the sun: 'Ὡς τὶ νοῶν, οὐκεῖνον νοήσειϛ,—"You will not perceive that, as perceiving a particular thing," say the Chaldean Oracles.[33]

---

[32]Cadmus was the character in Greek legend who sowed dragon's teeth from which sprang the ancestors of the nobility of Thebes.

[33]The empire of the Chaldeans flourished in what is now Iran about 600 B.C. Oracles were sayings of persons, usually priestesses in touch with the gods, that revealed hidden knowledge.

There is something servile in the habit of seeking after a law which we may obey. We may study the laws of matter at and for our convenience, but a successful life knows no law. It is an unfortunate discovery certainly, that of a law which binds us where we did not know before that we were bound. Live free, child of the mist,—and with respect to knowledge we are all children of the mist. The man who takes the liberty to live is superior to all the laws, by virtue of his relation to the lawmaker. "That is active duty," says the Vishnu Purana, "which is not for our bondage; that is knowledge which is for our liberation: all other duty is good only unto weariness; all other knowledge is only the cleverness of an artist."[34]

It is remarkable how few events or crises there are in our histories; how little exercised we have been in our minds; how few experiences we have had. I would fain be assured that I am growing apace and rankly, though my very growth disturb this dull equanimity,—though it be with struggle through long, dark, muggy nights or seasons of gloom. It would be well, if all our lives were a divine tragedy even, instead of this trivial comedy or farce. Dante, Bunyan, and others, appear to have been exercised in their minds more than we: they were subjected to a kind of culture such as our district schools and colleges do not contemplate. Even Mahomet, though many may scream at his name, had a good deal more to live for, ay, and to die for, than they have commonly.[35]

When, at rare intervals, some thought visits one, as perchance he is walking on a railroad, then indeed the cars go by without his hearing them. But soon, by some inexorable law, our life goes by and the cars return.

> "Gentle breeze, that wanderest unseen,
> And bendest the thistles round Loira of storms,
> Traveller of the windy glens,
> Why hast thou left my ear so soon?"

While almost all men feel an attraction drawing them to society, few are attracted strongly to Nature. In their relation to Nature men appear to me for the most part, notwithstanding their arts, lower than the animals. It is not often a beautiful relation, as in the case of the animals. How little appreciation of the beauty of the landscape there is among us! We have to be told that the Greeks called the world Κοσμος, Beauty, or Order, but we do not see clearly why they did so, and we esteem it at best only a curious philological fact.

For my part, I feel that with regard to Nature I live a sort of border life, on the confines of a world into which I make occasional and transient forays only, and my patriotism and allegiance to the State into whose territories I seem to retreat are those of a moss-trooper. Unto a life which I call natural

---

[34]The Vishnu Paranas elaborated the myths of Vishnu, one of the greatest gods of the Hindu religion.

[35]Dante was the Italian author of *The Divine Comedy*; John Bunyan was the English author of *Pilgrim's Progress*. Mahomet was the founder of the religion of Islam.

I would gladly follow even a will-o'-the-wisp through bogs and sloughs unima-ginable, but no moon nor fire-fly has shown me the causeway to it. Nature is a personality so vast and universal that we have never seen one of her features. The walker in the familiar fields which stretch around my native town some-times finds himself in another land than is described in their owners' deeds, as it were in some faraway field on the confines of the actual Concord, where her jurisdiction ceases, and the idea which the word Concord suggests ceases to be suggested. These farms which I have myself surveyed, those bounds which I have set up appear dimly still as through a mist; but they have no chemistry to fix them; they fade from the surface of the glass; and the picture which the painter painted stands out dimly from beneath. The world with which we are commonly acquainted leaves no trace, and it will have no anniversary.

I took a walk on Spaulding's Farm the other afternoon. I saw the setting sun lighting up the opposite side of a stately pine wood. Its golden rays straggled into the aisles of the wood as into some noble hall. I was impressed as if some ancient and altogether admirable and shining family had settled there in that part of the land called Concord, unknown to me,—to whom the sun was servant,—who had not gone into society in the village,—who had not been called on. I saw their park, their pleasure-ground, beyond through the wood, in Spaulding's cranberry-meadow. The pines furnished them with gables as they grew. Their house was not obvious to vision; the trees grew through it. I do not know whether I heard the sounds of a suppressed hilarity or not. They seemed to recline on the sunbeams. They have sons and daugh-ters. They are quite well. The farmer's cart-path, which leads directly through their hall, does not in the least put them out,—as the muddy bottom of a pool is sometimes seen through the reflected skies. They never heard of Spaulding, and do not know that he is their neighbor,—notwithstanding I heard him whistle as he drove his team through the house. Nothing can equal the serenity of their lives. Their coat of arms is simply a lichen. I saw it painted on the pines and oaks. Their attics were in the tops of the trees. They are of no politics. There was no noise of labor. I did not perceive that they were weaving or spinning. Yet I did detect, when the wind lulled and hearing was done away, the finest imaginable sweet musical hum,—as of a distant hive in May, which perchance was the sound of their thinking. They had no idle thoughts, and no one without could see their work, for their industry was not as in knots and excrescences embayed.

But I find it difficult to remember them. They fade irrevocably out of my mind even now while I speak and endeavor to recall them, and recollect myself. It is only after a long and serious effort to recollect my best thoughts that I become again aware of their cohabitancy. If it were not for such families as this, I think I should move out of Concord.

We are accustomed to say in New England that few and fewer pigeons visit us every year. Our forests furnish no mast for them. So, it would seem, few and fewer thoughts visit each growing man from year to year, for the grove in our minds is laid waste,—sold to feed unnecessary fires of ambition, or sent to mill, and there is scarcely a twig left for them to perch on. They no longer build nor breed with us. In some more genial season, perchance, a faint shadow flits across the landscape of the mind, cast by the *wings* of some thought in its vernal or autumnal migration, but, looking up, we are unable to detect the substance of the thought itself. Our winged thoughts are turned to poultry. They no longer soar, and they attain only to a Shanghai and Cochin-China grandeur.[36] Those *gra-a-ate thoughts*, those *gra-a-ate men* you hear of!

We hug the earth,—how rarely we mount! Methinks we might elevate ourselves a little more. We might climb a tree, at least. I found my account in climbing a tree once. It was a tall white pine, on the top of a hill; and though I got well pitched, I was well paid for it, for I discovered new mountains in the horizon which I had never seen before,—so much more of the earth and the heavens. I might have walked about the foot of the tree for threescore years and ten, and yet I certainly should never have seen them. But, above all, I discovered around me,—it was near the end of June,—on the ends of the topmost branches only, a few minute and delicate red cone-like blossoms, the fertile flower of the white pine looking heavenward. I carried straightway to the village the topmost spire, and showed it to stranger jurymen who walked the streets,—for it was court-week,—and to farmers and lumber-dealers and wood-choppers and hunters, and not one had ever seen the like before, but they wondered as at a star dropped down. Tell of ancient architects finishing their works on the tops of columns as perfectly as on the lower and more visible parts! Nature has from the first expanded the minute blossoms of the forest only toward the heavens, above men's heads and unobserved by them. We see only the flowers that are under our feet in the meadows. The pines have developed their delicate blossoms on the highest twigs of the wood every summer for ages, as well over the heads of Nature's red children as of her white ones; yet scarcely a farmer or hunter in the land has ever seen them.

Above all, we cannot afford not to live in the present. He is blessed over all mortals who loses no moment of the passing life in remembering the past. Unless our philosophy hears the cock crow in every barn-yard within our horizon, it is belated. That sound commonly reminds us that we are growing rusty and antique in our employments and habits of thought. His philosophy comes down to a more recent time than ours. There is something suggested by it that is a newer treatment,—the gospel according to this moment. He has not fallen astern; he has got up early, and kept up early, and to be where he is is to be in season, in the foremost rank of time. It is an expression of the health and soundness of Nature, a brag for all the world,—healthiness as of a spring burst forth, a new fountain of the Muses,[37] to celebrate this last instant of time. Where he lives no fugitive

---

[36]Shanghai and Cochin-China are breeds of heavy, domestic poultry.

[37]In Greek mythology, certain fountains in Greece were sacred to the nine Muses, patron goddesses of the arts.

slave laws are passed. Who has not betrayed his master many times since last he heard that note?

The merit of this bird's strain is in its freedom from all plaintiveness. The singer can easily move us to tears or to laughter, but where is he who can excite in us a pure morning joy? When, in doleful dumps, breaking the awful stillness of our wooden sidewalk on a Sunday, or, perchance, a watcher in the house of mourning, I hear a cockerel crow far or near, I think to myself, "There is one of us well, at any rate,"—and with a sudden gush return to my senses.

We had a remarkable sunset one day last November. I was walking in a meadow, the source of a small brook, when the sun at last, just before setting, after a cold gray day, reached a clear stratum in the horizon, and the softest, brightest morning sunlight fell on the dry grass and on the stems of the trees in the opposite horizon, and on the leaves of the shrub-oaks on the hill-side, while our shadows stretched long over the meadow eastward, as if we were the only motes in its beams. It was such a light as we could not have imagined a moment before, and the air also was so warm and serene that nothing was wanting to make a paradise of that meadow. When we reflected that this was not a solitary phenomenon, never to happen again, but that it would happen forever and ever an infinite number of evenings, and cheer and reassure the latest child that walked there, it was more glorious still.

The sun sets on some retired meadow, where no house is visible, with all the glory and splendor that it lavishes on cities, and, perchance, as it has never set before,—where there is but a solitary marsh-hawk to have his wings gilded by it, or only a musquash[38] looks out from his cabin, and there is some little black-veined brook in the midst of the marsh, just beginning to meander, winding slowly round a decaying stump. We walked in so pure and bright a light, gilding the withered grass and leaves, so softly and serenely bright, I thought I had never bathed in such a golden flood, without a ripple or a murmur to it. The west side of every wood and rising ground gleamed like the boundary of Elysium,[39] and the sun on our backs seemed like a gentle herdsman driving us home at evening.

So we saunter toward the Holy Land, till one day the sun shall shine more brightly than ever he has done, shall perchance shine into our minds and hearts, and light up our whole lives with a great awakening light, as warm and serene and golden as on a bank-side in autumn.

1862

Race and Slavery

DEBATES OVER RACE AND RACISM HAVE MARKED AMERICAN CULTURE ALMOST from the beginning of European exploration and settlement until this very day. In the antebellum period, these debates took particularly intense form. In large measure, that was a function not just of the existence of slavery but of its expansion. Despite the expectations of most of the Founders, including slave-holders, that the "peculiar institution" would likely atrophy or at least diminish in significance, in fact—for reasons discussed in the introduction to this volume—it became more economically, politically, and culturally significant in the years leading up to the Civil War. Slavery expanded geographically into new terri-tories in the West; indeed, the armed struggle in Kansas over whether it would be free or slave in certain respects presaged the Civil War itself, and the Mexican War was widely seen as an effort to expand the territory of slaveholding. In a sense, slavery expanded into the North as well, especially after the passage of the Fugitive Slave Act in 1850 and particularly with the Dred Scott decision, which held that slaveholding could not be barred from the "free" states. By the end of the 1850s, slavery could no longer be quarantined within the states of what, with the onset of the Civil War, would become the Confederacy.

In a different sense, slavery also expanded ideologically during the period. Earlier in the nineteenth century, even slaveholders like Jefferson questioned its legitimacy and the racist values underwriting its perpetuation. But as the eco-nomic stakes rose and the debate intensified (especially once the demand for immediate and unconditional abolition of slavery took root in the white community after 1831), defenders of slavery increasingly invoked a range of arguments—religious, ethnographic, practical, moral—to justify its continuing existence. This feature provides some representative examples of such argu-ments by Thomas Roderick Dew and Thornton Stringfellow.

The feature also contains examples of the variety of arguments mounted by those who opposed slavery. Abolitionists did not always agree with one another. They differed over fundamental matters such as the usefulness and morality of electoral politics, the legitimacy of violence, and the roles of women in the effort to end slavery. They also differed, as did many in the North as well as the South, in assessing the capabilities, indeed the humanity, of people of African heritage. Meanwhile, African Americans like David Walker, Henry Highland Garnet, Fred-erick Douglass, and Harriet Ann Jacobs—whose texts appear in the section im-mediately following this feature—ably demonstrated their own abilities as writers and speakers, challenging the moral values of those who would question their humanity or reduce them to bondage. Along with white allies, African Americans also implemented a system of aiding escaped slaves that came to be called the Underground Railroad, whose "tracks" led from below the Mason-Dixon line across Pennsylvania, Ohio, Indiana, and other Northern states to Canada and freedom. Here we provide one illustration of the operations of this "Railroad," but interested readers might wish to seek out the somewhat obscure but exciting accounts of its undertakings in postbellum volumes like those of Levi Coffin and William Still. Today's readers are fortunate in being able to access online texts not only by activists like Coffin and Still but also by a host of others who participated in the widespread debates over race, slavery, and abolition.

The change in the intensity of the contest over slavery is, in a sense, illustrated by the first and last documents in this In Focus feature. In his diary, John Quincy Adams relates an altogether civilized but disheartening encounter with John C. Calhoun, that quintessential spokesman for the interests of slaveholding. In his final statement to the court, John Brown upholds the values of the attack he led on the federal arsenal at Harpers Ferry. Between these historical "bookends," one can follow the calls and responses of the increasingly militant contest over race and slavery in the antebellum period.

Paul Lauter
Trinity College

■ JOHN QUINCY ADAMS ■
1767–1848

from **Memoirs of John Quincy Adams**[1]

After this meeting, I walked home with Calhoun, who said that ... in the Southern country ... domestic labor was confined to the blacks; and such was the prejudice that if he, who was the most popular man in his district, were to keep a white servant in his house, his character and reputation would be irretrievably ruined.

I said that this confounding of the ideas of servitude and labor was one of the bad effects of slavery; but he thought it attended with many excellent consequences. It did not apply to all kinds of labor—not, for example, to farming. He himself had often held the plough; so had his father. Manufacturing and mechanical labor was not degrading. It was only manual labor—the proper work of slaves. No white person could descend to that. And it was the best guarantee to equality among the whites. It produced an unvarying level among them. It not only did not excite but

[1]*Memoirs of John Quincy Adams, Comprising Portions of His Diary from 1795 to 1848*, vol. 5, Charles Francis Adams, ed., 1875, pp. 4–12.

did not even admit of inequalities, by which one white man could domineer over another.

I told Calhoun I could not see things in the same light. It is, in truth, all perverted sentiment—mistaking labor for slavery, and dominion for freedom. The discussion of this Missouri question has betrayed the secret of their souls. In the abstract they admit that slavery is an evil, they disclaim all participation in the introduction of it, and cast it all upon the shoulders of our old Grandam Britain. But when probed to the quick upon it, they show at the bottom of their souls pride and vainglory in their condition of masterdom. They fancy themselves more generous and noblehearted than the plain freemen who labor for subsistence. They look down upon the simplicity of a Yankee's manners, because he has no habits of overbearing like theirs and cannot treat Negroes like dogs.

It is among the evils of slavery that it taints the very sources of moral principle. It establishes false estimates of virtue and vice; for what can be more false and heartless than this doctrine which makes the first and holiest rights of humanity to depend upon the color of the skin? It perverts human reason, and reduces man endowed with logical powers to maintain that slavery is sanctioned by the Christian religion, that slaves are happy and contented in their condition, that between master and slave there are ties of mutual attachment and affection, that the virtues of the master are refined and exalted by the degradation of the slave; while at the same time they vent execrations upon the slave trade, curse Britain for having given them slaves, burn at the stake Negroes convicted of crimes for the terror of the example, and writhe in agonies of fear at the very mention of human rights as applicable to men of color. The impression produced upon my mind by the progress of this discussion is that the bargain between freedom and slavery contained in the Constitution of the United States is morally and politically vicious, inconsistent with the principles upon which alone our Revolution can be justified; cruel and oppressive, by riveting the chains of slavery, by pledging the faith of freedom to maintain and perpetuate the tyranny of the master; and grossly unequal and impolitic, by admitting that slaves are at once enemies to be kept in subjection, property to be secured or restored to their owners, and persons not to be represented themselves, but for whom their masters are privileged with nearly a double share of representation. The consequence has been that this slave representation has governed the Union.

Benjamin portioned above his brethren has ravined as a wolf. In the morning he has devoured the prey, and at night he has divided the spoil. It would be no difficult matter to prove, by reviewing the history of the Union under this Constitution, that almost everything which has contributed to the honor and welfare of the nation has been accomplished in spite of them or forced upon them, and that everything unpropitious and dishonorable, including the blunders and follies of their adversaries, may be traced to them.

I have favored this Missouri Compromise, believing it to be all that could be effected under the present Constitution, and from extreme unwillingness to put the Union at hazard. But perhaps it would have been a wiser as well as a bolder course to have persisted in the restriction upon Missouri, till it should have terminated in a convention of the states to revise and amend the Constitution. This would have produced a new Union of thirteen or fourteen States, unpolluted with slavery, with a great and glorious object to effect; namely, that of rallying to their standard the other states by the universal emancipation of their slaves. If the Union must be dissolved, slavery is precisely the question upon which it ought to break. For the present, however, this contest is laid asleep.

1820

▪ THOMAS RODERICK DEW ▪
1802–1846

An Argument Upholding Slavery

It is said slavery is wrong, in the abstract at least, and contrary to the spirit of Christianity. To this we answer ... that any question must be determined by its circumstances, and if, as really is the case, we cannot get rid of slavery without producing a greater injury to both the masters and slaves, there is no rule of conscience or revealed law of God which can condemn us.... If slavery had commenced even contrary to the laws of God and man, and the sin of its introduction rested upon our hands, and it was even carrying forward the nation by slow degrees to final ruin—yet if it were certain that an attempt to remove it would only hasten and heighten the final catastrophe ... then, we would not only not be found to attempt the extirpation, but we would stand guilty of a high offense in the sight of both God and man, if we should rashly make the effort. But the original sin of introduction rests not on our heads, and we shall soon see that all those dreadful calamities which the false prophets of our day are pointing to, will never in all probability occur.

With regard to the assertion that slavery is against the spirit of Christianity, we are ready to admit the general assertion, but deny most positively that there is anything in the Old or New Testament, which would go to show that slavery, when once introduced, ought at all events to be abrogated, or that the master commits any offense in holding slaves. The children of Israel themselves were slave holders, and were not condemned for it.... When we turn to the New Testament, we find not one single passage at all calculated to disturb the conscience of an honest slave holder. No one can read it without seeing and admiring that the meek and humble Saviour of the world in no instance meddled with the established institutions of mankind—he came to save a fallen world, and not to excite the black passions of men and array them in deadly hostility against each other. From no one did he turn away; his plan was offered alike to all—to the monarch and the subject, the rich and the poor—the master and the slave. He was born in the Roman world, a world in which the most galling slavery existed, a thousand times more cruel than the slavery in our own country—and yet he nowhere encourages insurrection—he nowhere fosters discontent—but exhorts always to implicit obedience and fidelity. What a rebuke does the practice of the Redeemer of mankind imply upon the conduct of some of his nominal disciples of the day, who seek to destroy the contentment of the slaves, to rouse their most deadly passions, to break up the deep foundations of society, and to lead on to a night of darkness and confusion! . . .

2dly. But it is further said that the moral effects of slavery are of the most deleterious and hurtful kind; and as Mr. Jefferson has given the sanction of his great name to this charge, we shall proceed to examine it with all that respectful deference to which every sentiment of so pure and philanthropic a heart is justly entitled.

"The whole commerce between master and slave," says he, "is a perpetual exercise of the most boisterous passions—the most unremitting despotism on the one part, and degrading submission on the other. Our children see this, and learn to imitate it, for man is an imitative animal—this quality is the germ of education in him. . . ." Now we boldly assert that the fact does not bear Mr. Jefferson out in his conclusions. He has supposed the master in a continual passion—in the constant exercise of the most odious tyranny, and the child, a creature of imitation, looking on and learning. But is not this master sometimes kind and indulgent to his slaves? Does he not mete out to them, for faithful service, the reward of his cordial approbation? Is it not his interest to do it? And when thus acting humanely, and speaking kindly, where is the child, the creature of imitation, that he does not look on and learn? We may rest assured, in this intercourse between a good master and his servant, more good than evil may be taught the child, the exalted principles of morality and religion may thereby be sometimes indelibly inculated upon his mind, and instead of being reared a selfish contracted being, with nought but self to look to—he acquires a more exalted benevolence, a greater generosity and elevation of soul, and embraces for the sphere of his generous actions a much wider field. Look to the slave holding population of our country, and you everywhere find them characterized by noble and elevated sentiment, by humane and virtuous feelings. We do not find among them that cold, contracted, calculating selfishness, which withers and repels everything around it, and lessens or destroys all the multiplied enjoyments of social intercourse. Go into our national councils, and ask for the most generous, the most disinterested, the most conscientious, and the least unjust and oppressive in their principles, and see whether the slave holder will be past by in the selection. . . .

Is it not a fact, known to every man in the South, that the most cruel masters are those who have been unaccustomed to slavery? It is well known that northern gentlemen who marry southern heiresses, are much severer masters than southern gentlemen. And yet, if Mr. Jefferson's reasoning were correct, they ought to be much milder: in fact, it follows from his reasoning, that the authority which the father is called on to exercise over his children, must be seriously detrimental; and yet we know that this is not the case; that on the contrary, there is nothing which so much humanizes and softens the heart, as this very authority; and there are none, even among those who have no children themselves, so disposed to pardon the follies and indiscretion of youth, as those who have seen most of them, and suffered greatest annoyance. There may be many cruel relentless masters, and there are unkind and cruel fathers too; but both the one and the other make all those around them shudder with horror. We are disposed to think that their example in society tends rather to strengthen than weaken the principle of benevolence and humanity.

Let us now look a moment to the slave, and contemplate his position. Mr. Jefferson has described him as hating, rather than loving his master, and as losing, too, all that "amor patriæ" which characterizes the true patriot. We assert again, that Mr. Jefferson is not borne out by the fact. We are well convinced that there is nothing but the mere relations of husband and wife, parent and child, brother and sister, which produce a closer tie, than the relation of master and servant. We have no hesitation in affirming that throughout the whole slave holding country, the slaves of a good master are his warmest, most constant, and most devoted friends; they have been accustomed to look up to him as their supporter, director and defender. Every one acquainted with southern slaves, knows that the slave rejoices in the elevation and prosperity of his master; and the heart of no one is more gladdened at the successful début of young master or miss on the great theater of the world, than that of either the young slave who has grown up with them, and shared in all their sports, and even partaken of all their delicacies—or the aged one who has looked on and watched them from birth to manhood, with the kindest and most affectionate solicitude, and has ever met from them, all the kind treatment and generous sympathies of feeling tender hearts. Judge Smith in his able speech on Foote's Resolutions in the Senate said, in an emergency he would rely upon his own slaves for his defense—he would put arms into their hands, and he had no doubt they would defend him faithfully. In the late Southampton insurrection, we know that many actually convened their slaves, and armed them for defense, although slaves were here the cause of the evil which was to be repelled. . . .

. . . A merrier being does not exist on the face of the globe than the negro slave of the United States. Even Captain Hall himself, with his thick "crust of prejudice," is obliged to allow that they are happy and contented, and the master much less cruel than is generally imagined. Why then, since the slave is happy, and happiness is the great object of all animated creation, should we endeavor to disturb his contentment by infusing into his mind a vain and indefinite desire for liberty—a something which he cannot comprehend, and which must inevitably dry up the very sources of his happiness. . . .

3dly. It has been contended that slavery is unfavorable to a republican spirit: but the whole history of the world proves that this is far from being the case. In the ancient republics of Greece and Rome, where the spirit of liberty glowed with most intensity, the slaves were more numerous than the freemen. . . . In modern times, too, liberty has always been more ardently desired by slave holding communities. . . . Burke says, "it is because freedom is to them not only an enjoyment, but a kind of rank and privilege." Another, and perhaps more efficient cause of this, is the perfect spirit of equality so prevalent among the whites of all the slave holding states. . . . The menial and low offices being all performed by the blacks, there is at once taken away the greatest cause of distinction and separation of the ranks of society. The man to the North will not shake hands familiarly with his servant, and converse, and laugh, and dine with him, no matter how honest and respectable he may be. But go to the South, and you will find that no white man feels such inferiority of rank as to be unworthy of association with those around him. Color alone is here the badge of distinction, the true mark of aristocracy, and all who are white are equal in spite of the variety of occupation. . . .

4thly. Insecurity of the whites, arising from plots, insurrections, &c., among the blacks. This is the evil, after all, let us say what we will, which really operates most powerfully upon the schemers and emancipating philanthropists of those sections where slaves constitute the principal property. Now, if we have shown, as we trust we have, that the scheme of deportation is utterly impracticable, and that emancipation, with permission to remain, will produce all these horrors in still greater degree, it follows that this evil of slavery, allowing it to exist in all its latitude, would be no argument of legislative action, and therefore we might well rest contented with this issue; but as we are anxious to exhibit this whole subject in its true bearings, and as we do believe that this evil has been most strangely and causelessly exaggerated, we have determined to examine it a moment, and point out its true extent. It seems to us that those who insist most upon it commit the enormous error of looking upon every slave in the whole slave-holding country as actuated by the most deadly enmity to the whites, and possessing all that reckless, fiendish temper, which would lead him to murder and assassinate the moment the opportunity occurs. This is far from being true; the slave, as we have already said, generally loves the master and his family; and few indeed there are, who can coldly plot the murder of men, women and children; and if they do, there are fewer still who can have the villainy to execute. We can sit down and imagine that all the negroes in the South have conspired to rise on a certain night, and murder all the whites in their respective families; we may suppose the secret to be kept, and that they have the physical power to exterminate; and yet, we say the whole is morally impossible. No insurrection of this kind can ever occur where the blacks are as much civilized as they are in the United States.... his whole education and course of life are at war with such fell deeds. Nothing, then, but the most subtle and poisonous principles, sedulously infused into his mind, can break his allegiance, and transform him into the midnight murderer. Any man who will attend to the history of the Southampton massacre, must at once see, that the cause of even the partial success of the insurrectionists, was the very circumstance that there was no extensive plot, and that Nat, a demented fanatic, was under the impression that heaven had enjoined him to liberate the blacks, and had made its manifestations by loud noises in the air, an eclipse, and by the greenness of the sun. It was these signs which determined him, and ignorance and superstition, together with implicit confidence in Nat, determined a few others, and thus the bloody work began.....

1832

ANGELA DAVIS
B. 1944

from Reflections on the Black Woman's Role in the Community of Slaves

If resistance was an organic ingredient of slave life, it had to be directly nurtured by the social organization which the slaves themselves improvised. The consciousness of their oppression, the conscious thrust towards its abolition could not have been sustained without impetus from the community they pulled together through the sheer force of their own strength. Of necessity, this community would revolve around the realm which was furthermost removed from the immediate arena of domination. It could only be located in and around the living quarters, the area where the basic needs of physical life were met.

In the area of production, the slaves—pressed into the mold of beasts of burden—were forcibly deprived of their humanity. (And a human being thoroughly dehumanized, has no desire for freedom.) But the community gravitating around the domestic quarters might possibly permit a retrieval of the man and the woman in their fundamental humanity. We can assume that in a very real material sense, it was only in domestic life—away from the eyes and whip of the overseer—that the slaves could attempt to assert the modicum of freedom they still retained. It was only there that they might be inspired to project techniques of expanding it further by leveling what few weapons they had against the slaveholding class whose unmitigated drive for profit was the source of their misery.

Via this path, we return to the African slave woman: in the living quarters, the major responsibilities "naturally" fell to her. It was the woman who was charged with keeping the "home" in order. This role was dictated by the male supremacist ideology of white society in America; it was also woven into the patriarchal traditions of Africa. As her biological destiny, the woman bore the fruits of procreation; as her social destiny, she cooked, sewed, washed, cleaned house, raised the children. Traditionally the labor of females, domestic work is supposed to complement and confirm their inferiority.

But with the black slave woman, there is a strange twist of affairs: in the infinite anguish of ministering to the needs of the men and children around her (who were not necessarily members of her immediate family), she was performing the *only* labor of the slave community which could not be directly and immediately claimed by the oppressor. There was no compensation for work in the fields; it served no useful purpose for the slaves. Domestic labor was the only meaningful labor for the slave community as a whole (discounting as negligible the exceptional situations where slaves received some pay for their work).

Precisely through performing the drudgery which has long been a central expression of the socially conditional inferiority of women, the black woman in chains could help to lay the foundation for some degree of autonomy, both for herself and her men. Even as she was suffering under her unique oppression as female, she was thrust by the force of circumstances into the center of the slave community. She was, therefore, essential to the *survival* of the community. Not all people have survived enslavement; hence her survival-oriented activities were themselves a form of resistance. Survival, moreover, was the prerequisite of all higher levels of struggle....

The black woman's consciousness of the oppression suffered by her people was honed in the bestial realities of daily experience. It would not be the stunted awareness of a woman confined to the home. She would be prepared to ascend to the same levels of resistance which were accessible to her men. Even as she performed her housework, the black woman's role in the slave community could not be identical to the historically evolved female role. Stripped of the palliative feminine veneer which might have encouraged a passive performance of domestic tasks, she was now uniquely capable of weaving into the warp and woof of domestic life a profound consciousness of resistance....

1971

■ LEVI COFFIN ■
1798–1877

from **Reminiscences of Levi Coffin, the Reputed President of the Underground Railroad**[1]

A Company of Twenty-eight Fugitives

The fugitives generally arrived in the night, and were secreted among the friendly colored people or hidden in the upper room of our house. They came alone or in companies, and in a few instances had a white guide to direct them.

One company of twenty-eight that crossed the Ohio River at Lawrenceburg, Indiana—twenty miles below Cincinnati—had for conductor a white man whom they had employed to assist them. The character of this man was full of contradictions. He was a Virginian by birth and spent much of his time in the South, yet he hated slavery. He was devoid of moral principle, but was a true friend to the poor slave.

Sometimes slaves would manage to accumulate a little money by working at making baskets at night or on the Sabbath, and when they had saved a few dollars they were very willing to give it all to some white man in whom they had confidence, if he would help them across the river and direct them how to reach the Underground Railroad.

Thus I have always contended that this road was a Southern institution, being conducted however on a different principle from what it was on this side Mason and Dixon's line. The company of twenty-eight slaves referred to, all lived in the same neighborhood in Kentucky, and had been planning for some time how they could make their escape from slavery. This white man—John Fairfield—had been in the neighborhood for some weeks buying poultry, etc., for market, and though among the whites he assumed to be very pro-slavery, the negroes soon found that he was their friend.

He was engaged by the slaves to help them across the Ohio River and conduct them to Cincinnati. They paid him some money which they had managed to accumulate. The amount was small, considering the risk the conductor assumed, but it was all they had. Several of the men had their wives with them, and one woman a little child with her, a few months old. John Fairfield conducted the party to the Ohio River opposite the mouth of the Big Miami, where he knew there were several skiffs tied to the bank, near a wood-yard. When I asked him afterward if he did not feel

<hr/>

[1] *Reminiscences of Levi Coffin, the Reputed President of the Underground Railroad: Being a Brief History of the Labors of a Lifetime in Behalf of the Slave, with the Stories of Numerous Fugitives, Who Gained Their Freedom through His Instrumentality, and Many Other Incidents* (Cincinnati: Robert Clark & Co., 1880).

compunctions of conscience for breaking these skiffs loose and using them, he replied: "No; slaves are stolen property, and it is no harm to steal boats or anything else that will help them gain their liberty." The entire party crowded into three large skiffs or yawls, and made their way slowly across the river. The boats were overloaded and sank so deep that the passage was made in much peril. The boat John Fairfield was in was leaky, and began to sink when a few rods from the Ohio bank, and he sprang out on the sand-bar, where the water was two or three feet deep, and tried to drag the boat to the shore. He sank to his waist in mud and quicksands, and had to be pulled out by some of the negroes. The entire party waded out through mud and water and reached the shore safely, though all were wet and several lost their shoes. They hastened along the bank toward Cincinnati, but it was now late in the night and daylight appeared before they reached the city. Their plight was a most pitiable one. They were cold, hungry and exhausted; those who had lost their shoes in the mud suffered from bruised and lacer-ated feet, while to add to their discomfort a drizzling rain fell during the lat-ter part of the night. They could not enter the city for their appearance would at once proclaim them to be fugitives. When they reached the out-skirts of the city, below Mill Creek, John Fairfield hid them as well as he could, in ravines that had been washed in the sides of the steep hills, and told them not to move until he returned. He then went directly to John Hatfield, a worthy colored man, a deacon in the Zion Baptist Church, and told his story. He had applied to Hatfield before and knew him to be a great friend to the fugitives—one who had often sheltered them under his roof and aided them in every way he could.

John Fairfield also knew me and knew that I was a friend to the slave. I had met him several times, and was acquainted with the plan of his opera-tions in the South, but I was opposed to the principles on which he worked. I will have occasion to refer to him at another time and will explain more fully his plans, and the reason why I opposed his operations in the South. When he arrived, wet and muddy, at John Hatfield's house, he was scarcely recognized. He soon made himself and his errand known, and Hatfield at once sent a messenger to me, requesting me to come to his house without delay, as there were fugitives in danger. I went at once and met several prominent colored men who had also been summoned. While dry clothes and a warm breakfast were furnished to John Fairfield, we anxiously dis-cussed the situation of the twenty-eight fugitives who were lying, hungry and shivering, in the hills in sight of the city.

Several plans were suggested, but none seemed practicable. At last I sug-gested that some one should go immediately to a certain German livery sta-ble in the city and hire two coaches, and that several colored men should go out in buggies and take the women and children from their hiding-places, then that the coaches and buggies should form a procession as if going to a funeral, and march solemnly along the road leading to Cumminsville, on the west side of Mill Creek. In the western part of Cumminsville was the Meth-odist Episcopal burying ground, where a certain lot of ground had been set apart for the use of the colored people. They should pass this and continue on the Colerain pike till they reached a right-hand road leading to College Hill. At the latter place they would find a few colored families, living in the outskirts of the village, and could take refuge among them. Jonathan Cable, a Presbyterian minister, who lived near Farmer's College, on the west side of the village, was a prominent abolitionist, and I knew that he would give prompt assistance to the fugitives.

I advised that one of the buggies should leave the procession at Cumminsville, after passing the burying-ground, and hasten to College Hill to apprise friend Cable of the coming of the fugitives, that he might make arrangements for their reception in suitable places. My suggestions and advice were agreed to, and acted upon as quickly as possible, John Hatfield agreeing to apprise friend Cable of the coming of the fugitives. We knew that we must act quickly and with discretion, for the fugitives were in a very unsafe position, and in great danger of being discovered and captured by the police, who were always on the alert for runaway slaves.

While the carriages and buggies were being procured, John Hatfield's wife and daughter, and other colored women of the neighborhood, busied themselves in preparing provisions to be sent to the fugitives. A large stone jug was filled with hot coffee, and this, together with a supply of bread and other provisions, was placed in a buggy and sent on ahead of the carriages, that the hungry fugitives might receive some nourishment before starting. The conductor of the party, accompanied by John Hatfield, went in the buggy, in order to apprise the fugitives of the arrangements that had been made, and have them in readiness to approach the road as soon as the carriages arrived. Several blankets were provided to wrap around the women and children, whom we knew must be chilled by their exposure to the rain and cold. The fugitives were very glad to get the supply of food, the hot coffee especially being a great treat to them, and felt much revived. About the time they finished their breakfast the carriages and buggies drove up and halted in the road, and the fugitives were quickly conducted to them and placed inside. The women in the tight carriages wrapped themselves in the blankets, and the woman who had a young babe muffled it closely to keep it warm, and to prevent its cries from being heard. The little thing seemed to be suffering much pain, having been exposed so long to the rain and cold.

All the arrangements were carried out, and the party reached College Hill in safety, and were kindly received and cared for. But, sad to relate, it was a funeral procession not only in appearance but in reality, for when they arrived at College Hill, and the mother unwrapped her sick child, she found to her surprise and grief that its stillness, which she supposed to be that of sleep, was that of death. All necessary preparations were made by the kind people of the village, and the child was decently and quietly interred the next day in the burying ground on the Hill.

When it was known by some of the prominent ladies of the village that a large company of fugitives were in the neighborhood, they met together to prepare some clothing for them. Jonathan Cable ascertained the number and size of the shoes needed, and the clothes required to fit the fugitives for traveling, and came down in his carriage to my house, knowing that the Anti-Slavery Sewing Society had their depository there. I went with him to purchase the shoes that were needed, and my wife selected all the clothing we had that was suitable for the occasion; the rest was furnished by the noble women of College Hill.

I requested friend Cable to keep the fugitives as secluded as possible until a way could be provided for safely forwarding them on their way to Canada. Friend Cable was a stockholder in the Underground Railroad, and we consulted together about the best route, finally deciding on the line by way of Hamilton, West Elkton, Eaton, Paris and Newport, Indiana. West Elkton, twenty-five or thirty miles from College Hill, was the first Under-ground Railroad depot. That line always had plenty of locomotives and cars in readiness. I agreed to send information to that point, and accordingly wrote to one of my particular friends at West Elkton, informing him that I had some valuable stock on hand which I wished to forward to Newport, and requested him to send three two-horse wagons—covered—to College Hill, where the stock was resting, in charge of Jonathan Cable. I said: "Please put straw in the wagons so that they may rest easy on the journey, for many of them have sore feet, having traveled hastily over rough ground. I wish you to get to College Hill to-morrow evening; come without fail."

The three wagons arrived promptly at the time mentioned, and a little after dark took in the party, together with another fugitive, who had arrived the night before, and whom we added to the company. They went through to West Elkton safely that night, and the next night reached Newport, Indi-ana. With little delay they were forwarded on from station to station through Indiana and Michigan to Detroit, having fresh teams and conduc-tors each night, and resting during the day. I had letters from different sta-tions, as they progressed, giving accounts of the arrival and departure of the train, and I also heard of their safe arrival on the Canada shore.

I often received intelligence of the arrival in Canada of fugitives whom I had helped on the way to liberty, and it was always very gratifying to me. I was well known on the different routes of the Underground Railroad, and people wrote to me of the success of my shipments.

1880

▪ THORNTON STRINGFELLOW ▪
1788–1869

from A Brief Examination of Scripture Testimony on the Institution of Slavery[1]

Locust Grove, Culpeper Co., Va., 1841

Brother Sands:

Circumstances exist among the inhabitants of these United States, which make it proper that the Scriptures should be carefully examined by Christians in reference to the institution of Slavery, which exists in several of the States, with the approbation of those who profess unlimited subjection to God's revealed will.

It is branded by one portion of people, who take their rules of moral rectitude from the Scriptures, as a great sin; nay, the greatest of sins that exist in the nation. And they hold the obligation to exterminate it, to be paramount to all others.

If slavery be thus sinful, it behooves all Christians who are involved in the sin, to repent in dust and ashes, and wash their hands of it, without consulting with flesh and blood. Sin in the sight of God is something which God in his Word makes known to be wrong, either by preceptive prohibition, by principles of moral fitness, or examples of inspired men, contained in the sacred volume. When these furnish no law to condemn human conduct, there is no transgression. Christians should produce a "thus saith the Lord," both for what they condemn as sinful, and for what they approve as lawful, in the sight of Heaven.

It is to be hoped, that on a question of such vital importance as this to the peace and safety of our common country, as well as to the welfare of the church, we shall be seen cleaving to the Bible, and taking all our decisions about this matter, from its inspired pages. With men from the North, I have observed for many years a palpable ignorance of the divine will, in reference to the institution of slavery. I have seen but a few, who made the Bible their study, that had obtained a knowledge of what it did reveal on this subject. Of late, their denunciation of slavery as a sin, is loud and long.

I propose, therefore, to examine the sacred volume briefly, and if I am not greatly mistaken, I shall be able to make it appear that the institution of slavery has received, in the first place,

1st. The sanction of the Almighty in the Patriarchal age.

2d. That it was incorporated into the only National Constitution which ever emanated from God.

---

[1] In an essay first published in the *Religious Herald* and republished by request, with remarks on a letter of Elder Galusha, of New York, to Dr. R. Fuller, of South Carolina, Locust Grove, Culpeper Co., Va. (1841).

3d. That its legality was recognized, and its relative duties regulated, by Jesus Christ in his kingdom; and

4th. That it is full of mercy.

Before I proceed further, it is necessary that the terms used to designate the thing, be defined. It is not a name, but a thing, that is denounced as sinful; because it is supposed to be contrary to, and prohibited by, the Scriptures.

Our translators have used the term servant, to designate a state in which persons were serving, leaving us to gather the relation, between the party served and the party rendering the service, from other terms. The term slave, signifies with us, a definite state, condition, or relation, which state, condition, or relation, is precisely that one which is denounced as sinful. This state, condition, or relation, is that in which one human being is held without his consent by another, as property; to be bought, sold, and transferred, together with the increase, as property, forever. Now, this precise thing, is denounced by a portion of the people of these United States as the greatest individual and national sin that is among us, and is thought to be so hateful in the sight of God, as to subject the nation to ruinous judgments, if it be not removed. Now, I propose to show, from the Scriptures, that this state, condition, or relation, did exist in the patriarchal age, and that the persons most extensively involved in the sin, if it be a sin, are the very persons who have been singled out by the Almighty as the objects of his special regard—whose character and conduct he has caused to be held up as models for future generations. Before we conclude slavery to be a thing hateful to God, and a great sin in his sight, it is proper that we should search the records he has given us with care, to see in what light he has looked upon it, and find the warrant, for concluding that we shall honor him by efforts to abolish it; which efforts, in their consequences, may involve the indiscriminate slaughter of the innocent and the guilty, the master and the servant. . . .

1841

LEON LITWACK

B. 1929

from North of Slavery: The Negro in the Free States, 1790–1860

Negroes did not share in the expansion of political democracy in the first half of the nineteenth century; indeed, such expansion frequently came at the expense of their rights and privileges. By 1840, some 93 per cent of the northern free Negro population lived in states which completely or practically excluded them from the right to vote. Only in Massachusetts, New Hampshire, Vermont, and Maine could Negroes vote on an equal basis with whites. In New York, they could vote if they first met certain property and residence requirements. In New Jersey, Pennsylvania, and Connecticut, they were completely disfranchised, after having once enjoyed the ballot.

In several states the adoption of white manhood suffrage led directly to the political disfranchisement of the Negro. Those who opposed an expanded electorate—for both whites and Negroes—warned that it would, among other things, grant the Negro political power. Adopt universal manhood suffrage, a Pennsylvania constitutional convention delegate declared in 1837, and "every negro in the State, worthy and worthless—degraded and debased, as nine tenths of them are, will rush to the polls in senseless and unmeaning triumph." Would this not constitute, he asked, "a highly *coloured* illustration of the beauty and perfectability of *universal suffrage*?" In New York, a Federalist opponent of universal manhood suffrage warned that "the whole host of Africans that now deluge our City (already too impertinent to be borne), would be placed upon an equal with the citizens." In the face of increasing demands for a liberalized suffrage, a Rhode Island legislative committee advised against extending the vote in 1829, citing as one of its reasons the addition of Negroes and Indians to the electorate. "We ought to recollect," the committee warned, "that all the evils which may result from the extension of suffrage will be evils beyond our reach. We shall entail them upon our latest posterity without remedy. Open this door, and the whole frame and character of our institutions are changed forever."[26] . . .

While statutes and customs circumscribed the Negro's political and judicial rights, extralegal codes—enforced by public opinion—relegated him to a position of social inferiority and divided northern society into "Brahmins and Pariahs."[87] In virtually every phase of existence, Negroes found themselves systematically separated from whites. They were either excluded from railway cars, omnibuses, stagecoaches, and steamboats or assigned to special "Jim Crow" sections; they sat, when permitted, in secluded and remote corners of theaters and lecture halls; they could not enter most hotels, restaurants, and resorts, except as servants; they prayed in "Negro pews" in the white churches, and if partaking of the sacrament of the Lord's Supper, they waited until the whites had been served the bread and wine. Moreover, they were often educated in segregated schools, punished in segregated prisons, nursed in segregated hospitals, and buried in segregated cemeteries. Thus,

[26]*Pennsylvania Constitutional Debates of 1837–38*, II, 541; New York Historical Society, *Collections, John Watts de Peyster Publication Fund Series* (80 vols.; New York, 1869–1954), XVIII, 306; *House Report*, 28 Cong., 1 sess., No. 546 (1844), p. 401.

[87]Edward S. Abdy, *Journal of a Residence and Tour in the United States*, Vol. 1 (London, 1835), 44; William Chambers, *Things as They Are in America* (London and Edinburch, 1854), pp. 354–58; Henry B. Fearson, *Sketches of America* (London, 1818), pp. 60–61, 168–69.

one observer concluded, racial prejudice "haunts its victim wherever he goes,—in the hospitals where humanity suffers,—in the churches where it kneels to God,—in the prisons where it expiates its offences,—in the graveyards where it sleeps the last sleep."[88]

To most northerners, segregation constituted not a departure from democratic principles, as certain foreign critics alleged, but simply the working out of natural laws, the inevitable consequence of the racial inferiority of the Negro. God and Nature had condemned the blacks to perpetual subordination. Within the context of ante bellum northern thought and "science," this was not an absurd or hypocritical position. Integration, it was believed, would result in a disastrous mixing of the races. "We were taught by our mothers," a New York congressman explained, "to avoid all communications with them" so that "the theorists and utopians never would be able to bring about an amalgamation."[89]

The education of northern youths—at home and in school—helped to perpetuate popular racial prejudices and stereotypes and to confirm the Negro in his caste position. In 1837, for example, a Boston Negro minister discussed the origins of racial attitudes in the younger generation. As children, whites were warned to behave or "the old nigger will carry you off," and they were reprimanded as being "worse than a little *nigger*." Later, parents encouraged their children to improve themselves, lest they "be poor or ignorant as a *nigger*" or "have no more credit than a *nigger*." Finally, teachers frequently punished their students by sending them to the "nigger-seat" or by threatening to put them in a Negro class. Such training, the Negro minister concluded, had been "most disastrous upon the mind of the community; having been instructed from youth to look upon a black man in no other light than a slave."[90] Under such circumstances, white adults could hardly be expected to afford Negroes equal political and social rights.

Northerners drew the Negro stereotype in the image of his political, economic, and social degradation and constantly reminded him of his inferiority. Newspapers and public places prominently displayed cartoons and posters depicting his alleged physical deformities and poking fun at his manners and customs. The minstrel shows, a popular form of entertainment in the ante bellum North, helped to fix a public impression of the clownish, childish, carefree, and irresponsible Negro and prompted one Negro newspaper to label these black-face imitators as "the filthy scum of white society,

[88]Gustave De Beaumont, *Marie, or Slavery in the United States* (tr. by Barbara Chapman, Stanford, 1958), pp. 66, 75–76; Andrew Bell, *Men and Things in America: Being the Experience of a Year's Residence in the United States* (London, 1838), pp. 179–81; [James Boardman], *America and the Americans* (London, 1833), p. 311; William Chambers, *American Slavery and Colour* (London, 1838), pp. 131–35; Francis J. Grund, *Aristocracy in America* (2 vols.; London, 1839), I, 177–78; [Thomas Hamilton], *Men and Manners in America* (2 vols.; London, 1834), I, 93–99; Charles Mackay, *Life and Liberty in America* (2 vols.; London, 1859), II, 41–42; Edward Sullivan, *Rambles and Scrambles in North and South America* (London, 1852), pp. 203–4.

[89]*Appendix to the Congressional Globe*, 30 Cong., 1 sess., p. 581.

[90]Hosea Easton, *A Treatise on the Intellectual Character, and Civil and Political Condition of the Colored People of the United States; and the Prejudice Exercised Towards Them* (Boston, 1837), pp. 40–41, 43.

who have stolen from us a complexion denied to them by nature, in which to make money, and pander to the corrupt taste of their fellow-citizens."[91] Nevertheless, the minstrel shows, newspapers, and magazines combined to produce a Negro stereotype that hardly induced northerners to accord this clownish race equal political and social rights. As late as 1860, a group of New York Negroes, in an appeal for equal suffrage, complained bitterly that every facet of northern opinion had been turned against them. "What American artist has not caricatured us?" they asked. "What wit has not laughed at us in our wretchedness? has not ridiculed and condemned us? Few, few, very few."[92]

In addition to persistent public reminders of their physical and mental inferiority, Negroes frequently complained that they had to endure "abusive epithets" and harassment when walking through white areas or shopping in white stores. In passing a group of white men, "ten chances to one" there would be a "sneer or snigger, with characteristic accompanying remarks." Children often tormented them in the streets and hurled insulting language and objects at them.[93] "There appears to be a fixed determination on the part of our oppressors in this country," a Negro wrote in 1849, "to destroy every vestige of self-respect, self-possession, and manly independence left in the colored people; and when all things else have failed, or may be inconvenient, a resort to brow-beating, bully-ragging, and ridicule is at once and at all times had."[94]

Anti-Negro sentiment did not confine itself to popular ridicule and petty harassment. It frequently took the forms of mob action and violence, especially in the large centers of Negro population. In 1829, Cincinnati mobs helped to convince more than half of the Negro inhabitants of that city that flight was preferable to violence and enforcement of the "Black Codes." Twelve years later, a mob descended on the Negro section and prompted its inhabitants to seek protection from city officials. Agreeing to disarm, Negro men found themselves placed in the city jail in order to avoid further violence. The mob then turned on their women and children. "Think, for one moment," the Cincinnati *Gazette* reported, "of a band calling themselves men, disarming, carrying away and securing in prison, the male negroes, promising security and protection to their women and children—and while they were confidently reposing in that security, returning with hellish shouts, to attack these helpless and unprotected persons!"[95]

Sporadic outbreaks, preludes to the disastrous Draft Riots of 1863, occurred in New York City, but violence flared even more frequently in

[91]*North Star*, October 27, 1848.
[92]Herbert Aptheker (ed.), *A Documentary History of the Negro People in the United States* (New York, 1951), p. 456.
[93]Easton, *A Treatise*, p. 41; *North Star*, March 30, 1849; Abdy, *Journal of a Residence and Tour*, III, 206–7; Mrs. Felton, *American Life: A Narrative of Two Years' City and Country Residence in the United States* (London, 1842), p. 58.
[94]*North Star*, March 30, 1849.
[95]*Tenth Annual Report of the Board of Managers of the Massachusetts Anti-Slavery Society* (Boston, 1842), pp. 99–102; J. Reuben Sheeler, "The Struggle of the Negro in Ohio for Freedom," *Journal of Negro History*, XXXI (1946), 213–14.

Philadelphia. Between 1832 and 1849, Philadelphia mobs set off five major anti-Negro riots. In July, 1834, a white mob stormed through the Negro section, clubbed and stoned its victims, destroyed homes, churches, and meeting halls, forced hundreds to flee the city, and left many others homeless. In assessing the causes of the riot, a citizens' committee cited the frequent hiring of Negroes during periods of depression and white unemployment and the tendency of Negroes to protect, and even forcibly rescue, their brethren when the latter were arrested as fugitive slaves. To prevent further violence, the committee called upon influential Negroes to impress upon their people "the necessity, as well as the propriety, of behaving themselves inoffensively and with civility at all times and upon all occasions; taking care, as they pass along the streets, or assemble together, not to be obtrusive."[96] …

1961

■ **U.S. CONGRESS** ■

from **Fugitive Slave Act of 1850**

§ 5. And be it further enacted, That it shall be the duty of all marshals and deputy marshals to obey and execute all warrants and precepts issued under the provisions of this act, when to them directed; and should any marshal or deputy marshal refuse to receive such warrant, or other process, when tendered, or to use all proper means diligently to execute the same, he shall, on conviction thereof, be fined in the sum of one thousand dollars, to the use of such claimant, on the motion of such claimant, by the Circuit or District Court for the district of such marshal; and after arrest of such fugitive, by such marshal or his deputy, or whilst at any time in his custody under the provisions of this act, should such fugitive escape, whether with or without the assent of such marshal or his deputy, such marshal shall be liable, on his official bond, to be prosecuted for the benefit of such claimant, for the full value of the service or labor of said fugitive in the State, Territory, or District whence he escaped: and the better to enable the said commissioners, when thus appointed, to execute their duties faithfully and efficiently, in conformity with the requirements of the Constitution of the United States and of this act, they are hereby authorized and empowered, within their counties respectively, to appoint, in writing under their hands, any one or more suitable persons, from time to time, to execute all such

[96]Turner, *Negro in Pennsylvania*, pp.160–65; Abdy, *Journal of a Residence and Tour*, III, 316–33; Joseph Sturge, *A Visit to the United States in 1841* (London, 1842), p. 46; Bell, *Men and Things in America*, pp. 178–79.

warrants and other process as may be issued by them in the lawful performance of their respective duties; with authority to such commissioners, or the
persons to be appointed by them, to execute process as aforesaid, to summon and call to their aid the bystanders, or posse comitatus of the proper
county, when necessary to ensure a faithful observance of the clause of the
Constitution referred to, in conformity with the provisions of this act; and
all good citizens are hereby commanded to aid and assist in the prompt and
efficient execution of this law, whenever their services may be required, as
aforesaid, for that purpose; and said warrants shall run, and be executed by
said officers, any where in the State within which they are issued.

§ 6. And be it further enacted, That when a person held to service or
labor in any State or Territory of the United States, has heretofore or shall
hereafter escape into another State or Territory of the United States, the
person or persons to whom such service or labor may be due, or his, her, or
their agent or attorney, duly authorized, by power of attorney, in writing,
acknowledged and certified under the seal of some legal officer or court of
the State or Territory in which the same may be executed, may pursue and
reclaim such fugitive person, either by procuring a warrant from some one
of the courts, judges, or commissioners aforesaid, of the proper circuit, district, or county, for the apprehension of such fugitive from service or labor,
or by seizing and arresting such fugitive, where the same can be done without process, and by taking, or causing such person to be taken, forthwith
before such court, judge, or commissioner, whose duty it shall be to hear
and determine the case of such claimant in a summary manner; and upon
satisfactory proof being made, by deposition or affidavit, in writing, to be
taken and certified by such court, judge, or commissioner, or by other satisfactory testimony, duly taken and certified by some court, magistrate, justice of the peace, or other legal officer authorized to administer an oath and
take depositions under the laws of the State or Territory from which such
person owing service or labor may have escaped, with a certificate of such
magistracy or other authority, as aforesaid, with the seal of the proper court
or officer thereto attached, which seal shall be sufficient to establish the
competency of the proof, and with proof, also by affidavit, of the identity of
the person whose service or labor is claimed to be due as aforesaid, that the
person so arrested does in fact owe service or labor to the person or persons
claiming him or her, in the State or Territory from which such fugitive may
have escaped as aforesaid, and that said person escaped, to make out and
deliver to such claimant, his or her agent or attorney, a certificate setting
forth the substantial facts as to the service or labor due from such fugitive
to the claimant, and of his or her escape from the State or Territory in
which he or she was arrested, with authority to such claimant, or his or her
agent or attorney, to use such reasonable force and restraint as may be necessary, under the circumstances of the case, to take and remove such fugitive person back to the State or Territory whence he or she may have
escaped as aforesaid. In no trial or hearing under this act shall the testimony of such alleged fugitive be admitted in evidence; and the certificates

in this and the first [fourth] section mentioned, shall be conclusive of the right of the person or persons in whose favor granted, to remove such fugitive to the State or Territory from which he escaped, and shall prevent all molestation of such person or persons by any process issued by any court, judge, magistrate, or other person whomsoever.

§ 7. And be it further enacted, That any person who shall knowingly and willingly obstruct, hinder, or prevent such claimant, his agent or attorney, or any person or persons lawfully assisting him, her, or them, from arresting such a fugitive from service or labor, either with or without process as aforesaid, or shall rescue, or attempt to rescue, such fugitive from service or labor, from the custody of such claimant, his or her agent or attorney, or other person or persons lawfully assisting as aforesaid, when so arrested, pursuant to the authority herein given and declared; or shall aid, abet, or assist such person so owing service or labor as aforesaid, directly or indirectly, to escape from such claimant, his agent or attorney, or other person or persons legally authorized as aforesaid; or shall harbor or conceal such fugitive, so as to prevent the discovery and arrest of such person, after notice or knowledge of the fact that such person was a fugitive from service or labor as aforesaid, shall, for either of said offences, be subject to a fine not exceeding one thousand dollars, and imprisonment not exceeding six months, by indictment and conviction before the District Court of the United States for the district in which such offence may have been committed, or before the proper court of criminal jurisdiction, if committed within any one of the organized Territories of the United States; and shall moreover forfeit and pay, by way of civil damages to the party injured by such illegal conduct, the sum of one thousand dollars for each fugitive so lost as aforesaid, to be recovered by action of debt, in any of the District or Territorial Courts aforesaid, within whose jurisdiction the said offence may have been committed....

§ 9. And be it further enacted, That, upon affidavit made by the claimant of such fugitive, his agent or attorney, after such certificate has been issued, that he has reason to apprehend that such fugitive will he rescued by force from his or their possession before he can be taken beyond the limits of the State in which the arrest is made, it shall be the duty of the officer making the arrest to retain such fugitive in his custody, and to remove him to the State whence he fled, and there to deliver him to said claimant, his agent, or attorney. And to this end, the officer aforesaid is hereby authorized and required to employ so many persons as he may deem necessary to overcome such force, and to retain them in his service so long as circumstances may require. The said officer and his assistants, while so employed, to receive the same compensation, and to be allowed the same expenses, as are now allowed by law for transportation of criminals, to be certified by the judge of the district within which the arrest is made, and paid out of the treasury of the United States.

Approved, September 18, 1850.

MARTIN R. DELANY 1812–1885 AND FREDERICK DOUGLASS 1818–1895

An Exchange

Pittsburgh, March 22, 1853

Frederick Douglass, Esq.:

Dear Sir:—

I notice in your paper of March 4 an article in which you speak of having paid a visit to Mrs. H. E. B. Stowe, for the purpose, as you say, of consulting her, "as to some method which should contribute successfully and permanently, in the improvement and elevation of the free people of color in the United States." Also, in the number of March 18th, in an article by a writer over the initials of "P. C. S.," in reference to the same subject, he concludes by saying, "I await with much interest the suggestions of Mrs. Stowe in this matter."

Now, I simply wish to say, that we have always fallen into great errors in efforts of this kind, going to others than the intelligent and experienced among ourselves; and in all due respect and deference to Mrs. Stowe, I beg leave to say, that she knows nothing about us, "the Free Colored people of the United States," neither does any other white person—and, consequently, can contrive no successful scheme for our elevation; it must be done by ourselves. I am aware, that I differ with many in thus expressing myself, but I cannot help it; though I stand alone, and offend my best friends, so help me God! in a matter of such moment and importance, I will express my opinion. Why, in God's name, don't the leaders among our people make suggestions, and consult the most competent among their own brethren concerning our elevation? This they do not do; and I have not known one, whose province it was to do so, to go ten miles for such a purpose. We shall never effect anything until this is done.

I accord with the suggestions of H. O. Wagoner for a National Council or Consultation of our people, provided intelligence, maturity and experience in matters among them, could be so gathered together; other than this, would be a mere mockery—like the Convention of 1848, a coming together of rivals, to test their success for the "biggest offices." As God lives, I will never, knowingly, lend my aid to any such work, while our brethren groan in vassalage and bondage, and I and mine under oppression and degradation, such as we now suffer.

I would not give the counsel of one dozen intelligent colored freeman of the right stamp, for that of all the white and unsuitable colored persons in the land. But something must be done, and that speedily.

The so called free states, by their acts, are now virtually saying to the South, "you shall not emancipate; your blacks must be slaves; and should they come North, there is no refuge for them." I shall not be surprised to see, at no distant day, a solemn Convention called by the whites in the North, to deliberate on the propriety of changing the whole policy to that of slave states. This will be the remedy to prevent dissolution; and it will come, mark that! anything on the part of the American people to save their Union. Mark me—the non-slaveholding states will become slave states.

Yours for God and Humanity,
M. R. Delany.
Rochester: April 1, 1853

That colored men would agree among themselves to do something for the efficient and permanent aid of themselves and their race, "is a consummation devoutly to be wished;" but until they do, it is neither wise nor graceful for them, or for any one of them to throw cold water upon plans and efforts made for that purpose by others. To scornfully reject all aid from our white friends, and to denounce them as unworthy of our confidence, looks high and mighty enough on paper; but unless the back ground is filled up with facts demonstrating our independence and self-sustaining power, of what use is such display of self-consequence? Brother DELANY has worked long and hard, he has written vigorously, and spoken eloquently to colored people—beseeching them, in the name of liberty, and all the dearest interests of humanity, to unite their energies, and to increase their activities in the work of their own elevation; yet where has his voice been heeded? and where is the practical result? Echo answers, where? Is not the field open? Why, then, should any man object to the efforts of Mrs. Stowe, or any one else, who is moved to do anything on our behalf? The assertion that Mrs. Stowe "knows nothing about us," shows that bro. DELANY knows nothing about Mrs. Stowe; for he certainly would not so violate his moral, or common sense if he did. When Brother DELANY will submit any plan for benefitting the colored people, or will candidly criticize any plan already submitted, he will be heard with pleasure. But we expect no plan from him. He has written a book—and we may say that it is, in many respects, an excellent book—on the condition, character and destiny of the colored people; but it leaves us just where it finds us, without chart or compass, and in more doubt and perplexity than before we read it.

Brother Delany is one of our strong men; and we are therefore all the more grieved, that at a moment when all our energies should be united in giving effect to the benevolent designs of our friends, his voice should be uplifted to strike a jarring note, or to awaken a feeling of distrust.

In respect to a national convention, we are for it—and will not only go "ten miles," but a thousand, if need be, to attend it. Away, therefore, with all unworthy flings on that score.

—F.D. [Frederick Douglass]

1853

■   CHIEF JUSTICE ROGER B. TANEY   ■
1777–1864

from **Dred Scott v. Sandford (1857)**

The question is simply this: Can a negro, whose ancestors were imported into this country, and sold as slaves, become a member of the political community formed and brought into existence by the Constitution of the United States, and as such become entitled to all the rights, and privileges, and immunities, guaranteed by that instrument to the citizen? One of which rights is the privilege of suing in a court of the United States in the cases specified in the Constitution. . . .

In discussing this question, we must not confound the rights of citizenship which a State may confer within its own limits, and the rights of citizenship as a member of the Union. It does not by any means follow, because he has all the rights and privileges of a citizen of a State, that he must be a citizen of the United States. . . .

It is very clear . . . that no State can, by any act or law of its own, passed since the adoption of the Constitution, introduce a new member into the political community created by the Constitution of the United States. It cannot make him a member of this community by making him a member of its own. And for the same reason it cannot introduce any person, or description of persons, who were not intended to be embraced in this new political family, which the Constitution brought into existence, but were intended to be excluded from it. . . .

It is true, every person, and every class and description of persons, who were at the time of the adoption of the Constitution recognized as citizens in the several States, became also citizens of this new political body; but none other; it was formed by them, and for them and their posterity, but for no one else. . . .

It becomes necessary, therefore, to determine who were citizens of the several States when the Constitution was adopted. . . .

In the opinion of the court, the legislation and histories of the times, and the language used in the Declaration of Independence, show that neither the class of persons who had been imported as slaves, nor their descendants, whether they had become free or not, were then acknowledged as a part of the people, nor intended to be included in the general words used in that memorable instrument.

It is difficult at this day to realize the state of public opinion in relation to that unfortunate race, which prevailed in the civilized and enlightened portions of the world at the time of the Declaration of Independence, and when the Constitution of the United States was framed and adopted. But the public history of every European nation displays it in a manner too plain to be mistaken.

They had for more than a century before been regarded as beings of an inferior order, and altogether unfit to associate with the white race, either in social or political relations; and so far inferior, that they had no rights which the white man was bound to respect; and that the negro might justly and lawfully be reduced to slavery for his benefit. He was bought and sold, and treated as an ordinary article of merchandise and traffic, whenever a profit could be made by it. This opinion was at that time fixed and universal in the civilized portion of the white race. It was regarded as an axiom in morals as well as in politics, which no one thought of disputing, or supposed to be open to dispute; and men in every grade and position in society daily and habitually acted upon it in their private pursuits, as well as in matters of public concern, without doubting for a moment the correctness of this opinion....

The language of the Declaration of Independence is equally conclusive....

... "We hold these truths to be self-evident: that all men are created equal; that they are endowed by their Creator with certain unalienable rights; that among them is life, liberty, and the pursuit of happiness; that to secure these rights, governments are instituted, deriving their just powers from the consent of the governed."

The general words above quoted would seem to embrace the whole human family, and if they were used in a similar instrument at this day would be so understood. But it is too clear for dispute, that the enslaved African race were not intended to be included, and formed no part of the people who framed and adopted this Declaration; for if the language, as understood in that day, would embrace them, the conduct of the distinguished men who framed the Declaration of Independence would have been utterly and flagrantly inconsistent with the principles they asserted; and instead of the sympathy of mankind, to which they so confidently appealed, they would have deserved and received universal rebuke and reprobation....

But there are two clauses in the Constitution which point directly and specifically to the negro race as a separate class of persons, and show clearly that they were not regarded as a portion of the people or citizens of the government then formed.

One of these clauses reserves to each of the thirteen States the right to import slaves until the year 1808, if it thinks proper.... And by the other provision the States pledge themselves to each other to maintain the right of property of the master, by delivering up to him any slave who may have escaped from his service, and be found within their respective territories.... And these two provisions show, conclusively, that neither the description of persons therein referred to, nor their descendants, were embraced in any of the other provisions of the Constitution; for certainly these two clauses were not intended to confer on them or their posterity the blessings of liberty, or any of the personal rights so carefully provided for the citizen....

The only two provisions which point to them and include them, treat them as property, and make it the duty of the government to protect it; no other power, in relation to this race, is to be found in the Constitution; and as it is a government of special, delegated, powers, no authority beyond these two provisions can be constitutionally exercised. The government of the United States had no right to interfere for any other purpose but that of protecting the rights of the owner, leaving it altogether with the several States to deal with this race, whether emancipated or not, as each State may think justice, humanity, and the interests and safety of society require. . . .

Now, as we have already said in an earlier part of this opinion, upon a different point, the right of property in a slave is distinctly and expressly affirmed in the Constitution. . . . This is done in plain words—too plain to be misunderstood. And no word can be found in the Constitution which gives Congress a greater power over slave property, or which entitles property of that kind to less protection than property of any other description. The only power conferred is the power coupled with the duty of guarding and protecting the owner in his rights.

Upon these considerations, it is the opinion of the court that the act of Congress which prohibited a citizen from holding and owning property of this kind in the territory of the United States north of the line therein mentioned, is not warranted by the Constitution, and is therefore void; and that neither Dred Scott himself, nor any of his family, were made free by being carried into this territory. . . .

1857

▪ **MORTIMER THOMSON** ▪
1831–1875

Great Auction Sales of Slaves at Savannah, Georgia

March 2nd and 3rd, 1859. Reported for *The Tribune*

The sale had been advertised largely for many weeks, though the name of Mr. Butler was not mentioned; and as the Negroes were known to be a choice lot and very desirable property, the attendance of buyers was large. The breaking up of an old family estate is so uncommon an occurrence that the affair was regarded with unusual interest throughout the South. For several days before the sale every hotel in Savannah was crowded with negro speculators from North and South Carolina, Virginia, Georgia, Alabama and Louisiana, who had been attracted hither by the prospects of making good bargains. Nothing was heard for days, in the bar-rooms and public rooms, but talk of the great sale, criticisms of business affairs of Mr. Butler, and speculations as to the probable prices the stock would bring. The office of Joseph Bryan, the negro broker who had the management of the sale, was thronged every day by eager inquirers in search of information, and by some who were anxious to buy, but were uncertain as to whether their securities would prove acceptable. Little parties were made up from the various hotels every day to visit the Race Course, distant some three miles from the city, to look over the chattels, discuss their points, and make memoranda for guidance on the day of sale. The buyers were generally of a rough breed, slangy, profane and bearish, being for the most part from the back river and swamp plantations, where the elegancies of polite life are not, perhaps, developed to their fullest extent. In fact, the humanities are sadly neglected by the petty tyrants of the rice fields that border the great Dismal Swamp, their knowledge of the luxuries of our best society comprehending only revolvers and kindred delicacies.

Your correspondent was present at an early date; but as he easily anticipated the touching welcome that would, at such a time, be officiously extended to a representative of *The Tribune*, and being a modest man withal, and not desiring to be the recipient of a public demonstration from the enthusiastic Southern population, who at times overdo their hospitality and their guests, he did not placard his mission and claim his honors. . . .

None of the Butler slaves have ever been sold before, but have been on these two plantations since they were born. Here have they lived their humble lives, and loved their simple loves; here were they born, and here have many of them had children born unto them; here had their parents lived before them, and are now resting in quiet graves on the old plantations that these unhappy ones are to see no more forever; here they left not only the well-known scenes dear to them from very babyhood by a thousand fond memories, and homes as much loved by them, perhaps, as brighter homes by men of brighter faces; but all the clinging ties that bound them to living hearts were torn asunder, for but one half of each of these two happy little communities was sent to the shambles, to be scattered to the four winds, and the other half was left behind. And who can tell how closely intertwined are the affections of a little band of four hundred persons living isolated from all the world beside, from birth to middle age? Do they not naturally become one great family, each man a brother unto each?

It is true they were sold "in families"; but let us see: a man and his wife were called a "family," their parents and kindred were not taken into account; the man and wife might be sold to the pine woods of North Carolina, their brothers and sisters be scattered through the cotton fields of Alabama and the rice swamps of Louisiana, while the parents might be left on the old plantation to wear out their weary lives in heavy grief, and lay their heads in far-off graves over which their children might never weep. And no account could be taken of loves that were as yet unconsummated by marriage; and how many aching hearts have been divorced by this summary proceeding, no man can ever know. And the separation is as utter, and is infinitely more hopeless, than that made by the Angel of Death, for then the loved ones are committed to the care of a merciful Deity; but in the other instance, to the tender mercies of a slave-driver. These dark-skinned unfortunates are perfectly unlettered, and could not communicate by writing even if they should know where to send their missives. And so to each other, and to the old familiar places of their youth, clung all their sympa-thies and affections, not less strong, perhaps, because they are so few. The blades of grass on all the Butler estates are outnumbered by the tears that are poured out in agony at the wreck that has been wrought in happy homes, and the crushing grief that has been laid on loving hearts.

But, then, what business have "niggers" with tears? Besides, didn't Pierce Butler give them a silver dollar apiece? which will in the sequel. And, sad as it is, it was all necessary, because a gentleman was not able to live on the beggarly pittance of half a million, and so must needs enter into specula-tions which turned out adversely.

How They Were Treated in Savannah

The Negroes were brought to Savannah in small lots, as many at a time as could be conveniently taken care of, the last of them reaching the city the Friday before the sale. They were consigned to the care of Mr. J. Bryan, Auc-tioneer and Negro Broker, who was to feed and keep them in condition until disposed of. Immediately on their arrival they were taken to the Race Course, and there quartered in the sheds erected for the accommodation of the horses and carriages of gentlemen attending the races. Into these sheds they were huddled pell-mell, without any more attention to their comfort than was necessary to prevent their becoming ill and unsalable. Each "fam-ily" had one or more boxes or bundles, in which were stowed such scanty articles of their clothing as were not brought into immediate requisition, and their tin dishes and gourds for their food and drink.

It is perhaps, a fit tribute to large-handed munificence to say that, when the negro man was sold, there was not extra charge for the negro man's clothes; they went with the man, and were not charged in the bill. Nor is this altogether a contemptible idea, for many of them had worldly wealth, in the shape of clothing and other valuables, to the extent of perhaps four or five dollars; and had all these been taken strictly into the account, the sum total of the sale would have been increased, possibly, a thousand dol-lars. In the North, we do not necessarily sell the harness with the horse; why, in the South, should the clothes go with the negro?

In these sheds were the chattels huddled together on the floor, there being no sign of bench or table. They eat and slept on the bare boards, their food being rice and beans, with occasionally a bit of bacon and corn bread. Their huge bundles were scattered over the floor, and thereon the slaves sat or reclined, when not restlessly moving about, or gathered into sorrowful groups, discussing the chances of their future fate. On the faces of all was an expression of heavy grief; some appeared to be resigned to the hard stroke of Fortune that had torn them from their homes, and were sadly try-ing to make the best of it; some sat brooding moodily over their sorrows, their chins resting on their hands, their eyes staring vacantly, and their bodies rocking to and fro, with a restless motion that was never stilled; few wept, the place was too public and the drivers too near, though some occasionally turned aside to give way to a few quiet tears....

1859

JOHN BROWN
1800–1859

from John Brown's Last Speech and Letters

I have, may it please the Court, a few words to say.

In the first place, I deny everything but what I have all along admitted, the design on my part to free the slaves. I intended certainly to have made a clean thing of that matter, as I did last winter, when I went into Missouri and there took slaves without the snapping of a gun on either side, moved them through the country, and finally left them in Canada. I designed to have done the same thing again, on a larger scale. That was all I intended. I never did intend murder, or treason, or the destruction of property, or to excite or incite slaves to rebellion, or to make insurrection.

I have another objection; and that is, it is unjust that I should suffer such a penalty. Had I interfered in the manner which I admit, and which I admit has been fairly proved (for I admire the truthfulness and candor of the greater portion of the witnesses who have testified in this case),—had I so interfered in behalf of the rich, the powerful, the intelligent, the so-called great, or in behalf of any of their friends,—either father, mother, brother, sister, wife, or children, or any of that class—and suffered and sacrificed what I have in this interference, it would have been all right; and every man in this court would have deemed it an act worthy of reward rather than punishment.

This court acknowledges, as I suppose, the validity of the law of God. I see a book kissed here which I suppose to be the Bible, or at least the New Testament. That teaches me that all things whatsoever I would that men should do to me, I should do even so to them. It teaches me, further, to "remember them that are in bonds, as bound with them." I endeavored to act up to that instruction. I say, I am yet too young to understand that God is any respecter of persons. I believe that to have interfered as I have done—as I have always freely admitted I have done—in behalf of His despised poor, was not wrong, but right. Now, if it is deemed necessary that I should forfeit my life for the furtherance of the ends of justice, and mingle my blood further with the blood of my children and with the blood of millions in this slave country whose rights are disregarded by wicked, cruel, and unjust enactments,—I submit; so let it be done!

1859

RACE, SLAVERY, AND THE INVENTION OF THE "SOUTH"

Much literature of the early nineteenth century was intended to influence readers' ideas about current issues and thus their actions in the world. This section presents a sample of such work focused on the most critical issues of the antebellum period. (See the general introduction to this volume for an overview of the texts contained in this section.)

Much of this writing takes essay or speech form, but some emerges as poetry or fiction, as in the case of John Greenleaf Whittier and Frances Ellen Watkins Harper. The Whittier poems included in the section on New England were primarily efforts to mobilize sentiment against slavery. And a poem like Harper's "Free Labor" is, among other things, implicitly an argument against purchasing slave-produced fabrics. But *essay* itself is a broadly inclusive term, covering work as varied as Fanny Fern's informal *Fern Leaves*, Thoreau's *Walden*, Nancy Prince's travel narrative, ceremonious addresses, and the religious controversy and public letters of the Grimké sisters. These works also illustrate the continuities with and changes from important forms of discourse developed in the seventeenth and eighteenth centuries. In fact, the forms of personal narrative and religious and political controversy did not disappear with the American Revolution; rather, they evolved in the ways illustrated by the works in this section.

Although this literature presents a mix of forms, it also offers a power of language too often obscured because those forms—essay, letter, and speech—have generally been placed at a discount relative to poetry or fiction. Nevertheless, we find phrases that have entered the common culture, like Sojourner Truth's question "Ain't I a woman?" And we find passages of prose as evocative as those in any fiction, like the conclusion of Thomas Wentworth Higginson's essay on Nat Turner's slave insurrection:

> While these things were going on, the enthusiasm for the Polish Revolution was rising to its height. The nation was ringing with a peal of joy, on hearing that at Frankfort the Poles had killed fourteen thousand Russians. The Southern Religious Telegraph *was publishing an impassioned address to Kosciuszko; standards were being consecrated for Poland in the larger cities; heroes like Skrzynecki, Czartoryski, Rozyski, Raminski, were choking the trump of Fame with their complicated patronymics. These are all forgotten now; and this poor negro, who did not even possess a name, beyond one abrupt monosyllable,—for even the name of Turner was the master's property,—still lives, a memory of terror, and a symbol of wild retribution.*

The issues these works address—racism, inequality between the sexes, nonviolence as a means for effecting change—remain alive today. We have organized the writing in this section on the basis of such issues, and on the ways they were being argued out in the antebellum period, so that readers can see how the issues are differently addressed by the writers and how they develop over time. For example, Thoreau's essay commonly called "Civil Disobedience" ("Resistance to Civil Government," 1849), printed in the New England section, is often thought of as the origin of the concept of nonviolent resistance to tyranny, but we see the idea posed more than a decade before in Angelina Grimké's "Appeal to the Christian Women of the South" (1836). In fact, the concept was deeply embedded in the evangelical Christianity of the time, especially in the work of reformers like William Lloyd Garrison and his followers. These debates, apart from their inherent interest, also affected the conceptions of character and conflict in many of the period's works of fiction, such as *The Scarlet Letter* and *Uncle Tom's Cabin*.

Although the issues provide our organizing principle, we have not included works simply because they are of historical interest. Rather, we feel that the essays, poems, sketches, and letters printed here continue to speak effectively to readers today.

Paul Lauter
Trinity College

DAVID WALKER
1785–1830

The sketchy details of David Walker's brief life blend inexorably into the history of the 1830s, when a somewhat diffuse antislavery sentiment largely taken up with the notion of "colonizing" blacks back to Africa was annealed into an increasingly militant and organized abolitionist movement. No single factor accounted for this change; Garrison's starting of *The Liberator* in 1831 was involved, as was the slave revolt led by Nat Turner later that year. But David Walker's *Appeal*,[1]—coming from within, addressed primarily to the black community, and unprecedented both in its militance and for its extended argument against colonization—was surely a critical ingredient in that process.

David Walker was born September 28, 1785, in Wilmington, North Carolina—a town that, more than a century later, would be the scene of the bloody race riot that forms the basis for Charles Chesnutt's novel *The Marrow of Tradition*. His mother was a free black woman and his father—who died some months before he was born—a slave; in accordance with the laws of the South's "peculiar institution," David followed the "condition of his mother." Of his youth we know virtually nothing: he traveled widely in the United States, somewhere acquired an education rare for a black person in that day, and developed

---

[1]The full title is *Walker's Appeal: in four articles, together with a preamble to the coloured citizens of the world, but in particular,* *and very expressly to those of the United States of America.*

an inveterate hatred of slavery and racism in all their manifestations. In Wilmington, he and his mother would have been required by a law passed the year of his birth to wear a patch of cloth with the legend "FREE" upon their left shoulders. They were forbidden to testify against whites in court, could not gather in meetings without suspicion that they were planning insurrection, and constantly lived in fear that, marked by their "FREE" patches, they would be kidnapped and sold off as slaves. No surprise, then, that in the 1820s, Walker moved north, settling in Boston, where he became a dealer in new and used clothing.

In the few remaining years of his life, Walker was one of the most active members of Boston's small community of free black people. He was assiduous in the Methodist church, sheltered fugitives, shared the little he earned with the poor, married a young woman named Eliza, and frequently spoke out in public against slavery. In 1827 he became an agent for the newly formed *Freedom's Journal*, which he distributed and wrote for. He issued his *Appeal* in 1829; by the next year, he was dead.

The cause of his death is unclear, though in his day such an early death was not unusual. Still, the suspicion lingered that he had been poisoned. Such speculation was fired by the intense responses to his *Appeal*. A price of $1,000 dead or $10,000 alive was put on his head in Georgia. The governor of Georgia wrote to the mayor of Boston demanding that he suppress circulation of the *Appeal*, and the mayor of Savannah requested Walker's arrest. Laws were passed across the South banning its distribution and reasserting the policy against teaching slaves to read or write. Even whites opposed to slavery, like Benjamin Lundy and William Lloyd Garrison, condemned the pamphlet as "injudicious" and inflammatory. Nevertheless, the tract continued to circulate—occasionally, it would seem, in the pockets of clothing that Walker sold to sailors shipping to Southern ports. Before Walker's death, it had gone into three editions, each more militant, and it continued to be reprinted and circulated for many years after.

Why was—is—the *Appeal* so thoroughly provocative? In the first place, it utterly breaks in language, tone, and strategy with the moderation that had largely characterized the antislavery movement. It rejects an approach emphasizing moral suasion or an appeal to the religious sentiments of whites. Indeed, it attacks the supposed Christianity and liberalism of white America, including founding fathers like Jefferson. It affirms the citizenship of black people in the Republic, scorning the central notion of the colonization societies that black Americans should remove themselves to Africa. And it calls upon blacks to unite—not a popular concept among assimilationists of his day—to take action and, in the extreme case, to kill or be killed if necessary to achieve liberation. A century before these ideas were widely diffused, it invokes pride in being black and hope in militancy, not servility; in a certain sense, it is the first expression of black nationalism to appear in print in the United States.

Walker's work should not be taken, however, as a diatribe against all whites. In the course of the four "Articles" that constitute the full text of the *Appeal*, he expresses gratitude toward those white Americans "who have volunteered their services for our redemption...."

Still, it is one of the ironies of our history that Patrick Henry's cry—"Give me liberty or give me death"—evokes intense sentiments of patriotism, whereas

David Walker's assertion—"Yea, would I meet death with avidity far! far!! in preference to such *servile submission*"—has evoked primarily fear.

Paul Lauter
Trinity College

PRIMARY WORKS

One Continual Cry: David Walker's Appeal to the Colored Citizens of the World, ed. Herbert Aptheker, 1965; *David Walker's Appeal, in Four Articles ...*, ed. Charles Wiltse, 1965; unedited reprint by Arno, 1969; *David Walker's Appeal to the Coloured Citizens of the World*, ed. Peter P. Hinks, 2000.

from **Appeal ... to the Coloured Citizens of the World (Third edition, 1829)**

Preamble

My dearly beloved Brethren and Fellow Citizens:

Having travelled over a considerable portion of these United States, and having, in the course of my travels taken the most accurate observations of things as they exist—the result of my observations has warranted the full and unshakened conviction, that we, (colored people of these United States) are the most degraded, wretched, and abject set of beings that ever lived since the world began, and I pray God, that none like us ever may live again until time shall be no more. They tell us of the Israelites in Egypt, the Helots[1] in Sparta, and of the Roman Slaves, which last, were made up from almost every nation under heaven, whose sufferings under those ancient and heathen nations were, in comparison with ours, under this enlightened and christian nation, no more than a cypher—or in other words, those heathen nations of antiquity, had but little more among them than the name and form of slavery, while wretchedness and endless miseries were reserved, apparently in a phial, to be poured out upon our fathers, ourselves and our children by christian Americans!

These positions, I shall endeavour, by the help of the Lord, to demonstrate in the course of this *appeal*, to the satisfaction of the most incredulous mind—and may God Almighty who is the father of our Lord Jesus Christ, open your hearts to understand and believe the truth.

The *causes*, my brethren, which produce our wretchedness and miseries, are so very numerous and aggravating, that I believe the pen only of a Josephus[2] or a Plutarch,[3] can well enumerate and explain them. Upon subjects, then, of such incomprehensible magnitude, so impenetrable, and so notorious,

[1] The lowest class among the Spartans. They were essentially serfs, tied to land held by upper-class Spartans, who rendered a portion of their production to their lords. They could not be sold and could be freed only by the state. They may have been the original inhabitants of the area.
[2] Jewish historian, A.D. 37–c. 100.
[3] Greek biographer and moralist, first century A.D.

I shall be obliged to omit a large class of, and content myself with giving you an exposition of a few of those, which do indeed rage to such an alarming pitch, that they cannot but be a perpetual source of terror and dismay to every reflecting mind.

I am fully aware, in making this appeal to my much afflicted and suffering brethren, that I shall not only be assailed by those whose greatest earthly desires are, to keep us in abject ignorance and wretchedness, and who are of the firm conviction that heaven has designed us and our children to be slaves and *beasts of burden* to them and their children.—I say, I do not only expect to be held up to the public as an ignorant, impudent and restless disturber of the public peace, by such avaricious creatures, as well as a mover of insubordination—and perhaps put in prison or to death, for giving a superficial exposition of our miseries, and exposing tyrants. But I am persuaded, that many of my brethren, particularly those who are ignorantly in league with slaveholders or tyrants, who acquire their daily bread by the blood and sweat of their more ignorant brethren—and not a few of those too, who are too ignorant to see an inch beyond their noses, will rise up and call me cursed—Yea, the jealous ones among us will perhaps use more abject subtlety by affirming that this work is not worth perusing; that we are well situated and there is no use in trying to better our condition, for we cannot. I will ask one question here.—Can our condition be any worse?—Can it be more mean and abject? If there are any changes, will they not be for the better, though they may appear for the worse at first? Can they get us any lower? Where can they get us? They are afraid to treat us worse, for they know well, the day they do it they are gone. But against all accusations which may or can be preferred against me, I appeal to heaven for my motive in writing—who knows that my object is, if possible, to awaken in the breasts of my afflicted, degraded and slumbering brethren, a spirit of enquiry and investigation respecting our miseries and wretchedness in this *Republican Land of Liberty!!!!!*

The sources from which our miseries are derived and on which I shall comment, I shall not combine in one, but shall put them under distinct heads and expose them in their turn; in doing which, keeping truth on my side, and not departing from the strictest rules of morality, I shall endeavor to penetrate, search out, and lay them open for your inspection. If you cannot or will not profit by them, I shall have done *my* duty to you, my country and my God.

And as the inhuman system of *slavery*, is the *source* from which most of our miseries proceed, I shall begin with that *curse to nations*, which has spread terror and devastation through so many nations of antiquity, and which is raging to such a pitch at the present day in Spain and in Portugal. It had one tug in England, in France, and in the United States of America; yet the inhabitants thereof, do not learn wisdom, and erase it entirely from their dwellings and from all with whom they have to do. The fact is, the labour of slaves comes so cheap to the avaricious usurpers, and is (as they think) of such great utility to the country where it exists, that those who are actuated by sordid avarice only, overlook the evils, which will as sure as the Lord lives, follow after the good. In fact, they are so happy to keep in ignorance and degradation, and to receive the homage and the labour of the slaves, they forget that God rules in the armies of heaven and among the inhabitants of the earth, having his ears continually open to the cries, tears and groans of his oppressed people; and being a just and holy Being will at one day appear fully in behalf of the oppressed, and arrest the progress of the avaricious oppressors; for although the destruction of the oppressors God may not effect by the oppressed, yet the Lord our God will bring other destructions upon them—for not unfrequently will he cause them to rise up one against another, to be split and divided, and to oppress each other, and sometimes to open hostilities with sword in hand....

All persons who are acquainted with history, and particularly the Bible, who are not blinded by the God of this world, and are not actuated solely by avarice—who are able to lay aside prejudice long enough to view candidly and impartially, things as they were, are, and probably will be, who are willing to admit that God made man to serve him *alone*, and that man should have no other Lord or Lords but himself—that God Almighty is the *sole proprietor* or *master* of the WHOLE human family, and will not on any consideration admit of a colleague, being unwilling to divide his glory with another.—And who can dispense with prejudice long enough to admit that we are men, notwithstanding our *improminent noses* and *woolly heads*, and believe that we feel for our fathers, mothers, wives and children as well as they do for theirs.—I say, all who are permitted to see and believe these things, can easily recognize the judgments of God among the Spaniards. Though others may lay the cause of the fierceness with which they cut each other's throats, to some other circumstances, yet they who believe that God is a God of justice, will believe that SLAVERY *is the principal cause*.

While the Spaniards are running about upon the field of battle cutting each other's throats, has not the Lord an afflicted and suffering people in the midst of them whose cries and groans in consequence of oppression are continually pouring into the ears of the God of justice? Would they not cease to cut each others throats if they could? But how can they? The very support which they draw from government to aid them in perpetrating such enormities, does it not arise in a great degree from the wretched victims of oppression among them? And yet they are calling for *Peace!—Peace!!* Will any peace be given unto them? Their destruction may indeed be procrastinated awhile, but can it continue long while they are oppressing the Lord's people? Has He not the hearts of all men in His hand? Will he suffer one part of his creatures to go on oppressing another like brutes always, with impunity? And yet those avaricious wretches are calling for *Peace!!!!* I declare it does appear to me, as though some nations think God is asleep, or that he made the Africans for nothing else but to dig their mines and work their farms, or they cannot believe history, sacred or profane. I ask every man who has a heart and is blessed with the privilege of believing—Is not God a God of justice to all his creatures? Do you say he is? Then if he gives peace and tranquility to tyrants, and permits them to keep our fathers, our mothers, ourselves and our children in eternal ignorance and wretchedness to support them and their families, would he be to us a God of *justice*? I ask O ye *christians!!!* who hold us and our children, in the most abject ignorance and degradation, that ever a people were afflicted with since the world began—I say, if God gives you peace and tranquility, and suffers you thus to go on afflicting us and our children, who have never given you the least provocation,—Would he be to us *a God of justice*? If you will allow that we are MEN, who feel for each other, does not the blood of our fathers and of us their children, cry aloud to the Lord of Sabaoth against you, for the cruelties and murders with which you have, and do continue to afflict us. But it is time for me to close my remarks on the suburbs, just to enter more fully into the interior of this system of cruelty and oppression.

Article I

Our Wretchedness in Consequence of Slavery

My beloved brethren: The Indians of North and of South America—the Greeks—the Irish subjected under the king of Great Britain—the Jews that ancient people of the Lord—the inhabitants of the islands of the sea—in fine, all the inhabitants of the earth, (except however, the sons of Africa) are called *men*, and of course are, and ought to be free. But we, (coloured people) and our children are *brutes!!* and of course are and ought to be SLAVES to the American people and their children forever! to dig their mines and work their farms; and thus go on enriching them, from one generation to another with our blood and our tears!!

I promised in a preceding page to demonstrate to the satisfaction of the most incredulous, that we, (colored people of these United States of America) are the *most wretched, degraded* and abject set of beings that ever *lived* since the world began, and that the white Americans having reduced us to the wretched state of *slavery*, treat us in that condition *more cruel* (they being an enlightened and christian people) than any heathen nation did any people whom it had reduced to our condition. These affirmations are so well confirmed in the minds of all unprejudiced men who have taken the trouble to read histories, that they need no elucidation from me. But to put them beyond all doubt, I refer you in the first place to the children of Jacob, or of Israel in Egypt, under Pharaoh and his people. Some of my brethren do not know who Pharaoh and the Egyptians were—I know it to be a fact that some of them take the Egyptians to have been a gang of *devils*, not knowing any better, and that they (Egyptians) having got possession of the Lord's people, treated them *nearly* as cruel as *christians Americans* do us, at the present day. For the information of such, I would only mention that the Egyptians, were Africans or colored people, such as we are—some of them yellow and others dark—a mixture of Ethiopians and the natives of Egypt—about the same as you see the colored people of the United States at the present day,—I say, I call your attention then, to the children of Jacob, while I point out particularly to you his son Joseph among the rest, in Egypt.

"And Pharaoh, said unto Joseph, thou shalt be over my house, and according unto thy word shall all my people be ruled; only in the throne will I be greater than thou."[4]

"And Pharaoh said unto Joseph, see, I have set thee over all the land of Egypt."[5]

"And Pharaoh said unto Joseph, I am Pharaoh, and without thee shall no man lift up his hand or foot in all the land of Egypt."[6]

Now I appeal to heaven and to earth, and particularly to the American people themselves who cease not to declare that our condition is not *hard*, and that we are comparatively satisfied to rest in wretchedness and misery, under them and their children. Not, indeed, to show me a colored President, a Governor, a Legislator, a Senator, a Mayor, or an Attorney at the Bar.—But to show me a man of color, who holds the low office of a Constable, or one who sits in a Juror Box, even on a case of one of his wretched brethren, throughout this great Republic!!—But let us pass Joseph the son of Israel a little further in review, as he existed with that heathen nation.

"And Pharaoh called Joseph's name Zaphnathpaaneah; and he gave him to wife Asenath the daughter of Potipherah priest of On. And Joseph went out over all the land of Egypt."[7]

Compare the above, with the American institutions. Do they not institute laws to prohibit us from marrying among the whites? I would wish, candidly, however, before the Lord, to be understood, that I would not give a *pinch of snuff* to be married to any white person I ever saw in all the days of my life. And I do say it, that the black man, or man of color, who will leave his own color (provided he can get one who is good for any thing) and marry a white woman, to be a double slave to her just because she is *white*, ought to be treated by her as he surely will be, viz; as a NIGER!!! It is not indeed what I care about intermarriages with the whites, which induced me to pass this subject in review; for the Lord knows, that there is a day coming when they will be glad enough to get into the company of the blacks, notwithstanding, we are, in this generation, levelled by them almost on a level with the brute creation; and some of us they treat even worse than they do the brutes that perish. I only made this extract to show how much lower we are held, and how much more cruel we are treated by the Americans, than were the children of Jacob, by the Egyptians. We will notice the sufferings of Israel some further, under *heathen Pharaoh*, compared with ours under the *enlightened christians of America.*

"And Pharaoh spake unto Joseph, saying, thy father and thy brethren are come unto thee:

The land of Egypt is before thee: in the best of the land make thy father and brethren to dwell; in the land of Goshen let them dwell; and if thou knowest any men of activity among them, then make them rulers over my cattle."[8]

[4]See Genesis, chap. xli, v. 40. [Walker's note]
[5]v. 41. [Walker's note]
[6]v. 44. [Walker's note]
[7]v. 45. [Walker's note]
[8]Genesis, chap. xlvii. v. 5, 6. [Walker's note]

I ask those people who treat us so *well*, Oh! I ask them, where is the most barren spot of land which they have given unto us? Israel had the most fertile land in all Egypt. Need I mention the very notorious fact, that I have known a poor man of color, who labored night and day, to acquire a little money, and having acquired it, he vested it in a small piece of land, and got him a house erected thereon, and having paid for the whole, he moved his family into it, where he was suffered to remain but nine months, when he was cheated out of his property by a white man, and driven out of door!—And is not this the case generally? Can a man of color buy a piece of land and keep it peaceably? Will not some white man try to get it from him even if it is in a *mud hole*? I need not comment any farther on a subject, which all, both black and white, will readily admit. But I must, really, observe that in this very city, when a man of color dies, if he owned any real estate it must generally fall into the hands of some white person. The wife and children of the deceased may weep and lament if they please, but the estate will be kept snug enough by its white posessors.

But to prove farther that the conditions of the Israelites was better under the Egyptians than ours is under the whites. I call upon the professing christians, I call upon the philanthropist, I call upon the very tyrant himself, to show me a page of history, either sacred or profane, on which a verse can be found, which maintains, that the Egyptians heaped the *insupportable insult* upon the children of Israel by telling them that they were not of the *human family*. Can the whites deny this charge? Have they not, after having reduced us to the deplorable condition of slaves under their feet, held us up as descending originally from the tribes of *Monkeys* or *Orang-Outangs*? O! my God! I appeal to every man of feeling—is not this insupportable? Is it not heaping the most gross insult upon our miseries, because they have got us under their feet and we cannot help ourselves? Oh! pity us we pray thee, Lord Jesus, Master.—Has Mr. Jefferson declared to the world, that we are inferior to the whites, both in the endowments of our bodies and of minds?[9] It is indeed surprising, that a man of such great learning, combined with such excellent natural parts, should speak so of a set of men in chains. I do not know what to compare it to, unless, like putting one wild deer in an iron cage, where it will be secured, and hold another by the side of the same, then let it go, and expect the one in the cage to run as fast as the one at liberty. So far, my brethren, were the Egyptians from heaping these insults upon their slaves, that Pharaoh's daughter took Moses, a son of Israel, for her own, as will appear by the following.

"And Pharaoh's daughter said unto her, [Moses' mother] take this child away, and nurse it for me and I will pay thee thy wages. And the woman took the child [Moses] and nursed it.

[9]The reference is to Jefferson's *Notes on the State of Virginia*, Query XIV, printed elsewhere in Volume A.

And the child grew, and she brought him unto Pharaoh's daughter and he became her son. And she called his name Moses: and she said because I drew him out of the water."[10]

In all probability, Moses would have become Prince Regent to the throne, and no doubt, in process of time but he would have been seated on the throne of Egypt. But he had rather suffer shame, with the people of God, than to enjoy pleasures with that wicked people for a season. O! that the colored people were long since of Moses' excellent disposition, instead of courting favor with, and telling news and lies to our *natural enemies*, against each other—aiding them to keep their hellish chains of slavery upon us. Would we not long before this time, have been respectable men, instead of such wretched victims of oppression as we are? Would they be able to drag our mothers, our fathers, our wives, our children and ourselves, around the world in chains and hand-cuffs as they do, to dig up gold and silver for them and theirs? This question, my brethren, I leave for you to digest; and may God Almighty force it home to your hearts. Remember that unless you are united, keeping your tongues within your teeth, you will be afraid to trust your secrets to each other, and thus perpetuate our miseries under the *christians!!!!!* [☞ ADDITION,—Remember, also to lay humble at the feet of our Lord and Master Jesus Christ, with prayers and fastings. Let our enemies go on with their butcheries, and at once fill up their cup. Never make an attempt to gain our freedom or *natural right*, from under our cruel oppressors and murderers, until you see your way clear;[11] when that hour arrives and you move, be not afraid or dismayed; for be you assured that Jesus Christ the king of heaven and of earth who is the God of justice and of armies, will surely go before you. And those enemies who have for hundreds of years stolen our *rights*, and kept us ignorant of Him and His divine worship, he will remove. Millions of whom, are this day, so ignorant and avaricious, that they cannot conceive how God can have an attribute of justice, and show mercy to us because it pleased Him to make us black—which color, Mr. Jefferson calls unfortunate!!!!!! As though we are not as thankful to our God for having made us as it pleased himself, as they (the whites) are for having made them white. They think because they hold us in their infernal chains of slavery that we wish to be white, or of their color—but they are dreadfully deceived—we wish to be just as it pleased our Creator to have made us, and no avaricious and unmerciful wretches, have any business to

---

[10]See Exodus, chap. ii. v. 9, 10. [Walker's note]

[11]Walker's note: "It is not to be understood here, that I mean for us to wait until God shall take us by the hair of our heads and drag us out of abject wretchedness and slavery, nor do I mean to convey the idea for us to wait until our enemies shall make preparations, and call us to seize those preparations, take it away from them, and put every thing before us to death, in order to gain our freedom which God has given us. For you must remember that we are men as well as they. God has been pleased to give us two eyes, two hands, two feet, and some sense in our heads as well as they. They have no more right to hold us in slavery than we have to hold them, we have just as much right, in the sight of God, to hold them and their children in slavery and wretchedness, as they have to hold us, and no more."

make slaves of or hold us in slavery. How would they like for us to make slaves of, or hold them in cruel slavery, and murder them as they do us? But is Mr. Jefferson's assertion true? viz. "that it is unfortunate for us that our Creator has been pleased to make us black." We will not take his say so, for the fact. The world will have an opportunity to see whether it is unfortunate for us, that our Creator *has made us* darker than the *whites*.

Fear not the number and education of our *enemies*, against whom we shall have to contend for our lawful right; guaranteed to us by our Maker; for why should we be afraid, when God is, and will continue (if we continue humble) to be on our side?

The man who would not fight under our Lord and Master Jesus Christ, in the glorious and heavenly cause of freedom and of God—to be delivered from the most wretched, abject and servile slavery, that ever a people was afflicted with since the foundation of the world, to the present day—ought to be kept with all of his children or family, in slavery, or in chains, to be butchered by his *cruel enemies*.

I saw a paragraph, a few years since, in a South Carolina paper, which, speaking of the barbarity of the Turks it said: "The Turks are the most "barbarous" people in the world—they treat the Greeks "more like *brutes* than human beings." And in the same paper was an advertisement, which said: "Eight well built Virginia and Maryland *Negro* "*fellows* and four *wenches* will positively be *sold* "for this day *to the highest bidder!*" And what astonished me still more was, to see in this same *humane* paper!! the cuts of three men, with clubs and budgets[12] on their backs, and an advertisement offering a considerable sum of money for their apprehension and delivery. I declare it is really so *funny* to hear the Southerners and Westerners of this country talk about *barbarity*, that it is positively, enough to make a man *smile*.

The sufferings of the Helots among the Spartans, were somewhat severe, it is true, but to say that theirs were as severe as ours among the Americans I do most strenuously deny—for instance, can any man show me an article on a page of ancient history which specifies, that, the Spartans chained, and hand-cuffed the Helots, and dragged them from their wives and children, children from their parents, mothers from their sucking babes, wives from their husbands, driving them from one end of the country to the other? Notice the Spartans were heathens, who lived long before our Divine Master made his appearance in the flesh. Can Christian Americans deny these barbarous cruelties? Have you not Americans, having subjected us under you, added to these miseries, by insulting us in telling us to our face, because we are helpless that we are not of the human family? I ask you, O! Americans, I ask you, in the name of the Lord, can you deny these charges? Some perhaps may deny, by saying, that they never thought or said that we were not men. But do not actions speak louder than words?—have they not made provisions for the Greeks and Irish? Nations who have never done the least thing for them, while *we* who have enriched their country

---

[12]A bag or sack.

with our blood and tears—have dug up gold and silver for them and their children, from generation to generation, and are in more miseries than any other people under heaven, are not seen, but by comparatively a handful of the American people? There are indeed, more ways to kill a dog besides choaking it to death with butter. Further. The Spartans or Lacedemonians, had some frivolous pretext for enslaving the Helots, for they (Helots) while being free inhabitants of Sparta, stirred up an intestine commotion, and were by the Spartans subdued, and made prisoners of war. Consequently they and their children were condemned to perpetual slavery.[13]

I have been for years troubling the pages of historians to find out what our fathers have done to the *white Christians of America*, to merit such condign punishment as they have inflicted on them, and do continue to inflict on us their children. But I must aver, that my researches have hitherto been to no effect. I have therefore come to the immovable conclusion, that they (Americans) have, and do continue to punish us for nothing else, but for enriching them and their country. For I cannot conceive of any thing else. Nor will I ever believe otherwise until the Lord shall convince me.

The world knows, that slavery as it existed among the Romans, (which was the primary cause of their destruction) was, comparatively speaking, no more than a *cypher*, when compared with ours under the Americans. Indeed, I should not have noticed the Roman slaves, had not the very learned and penetrating Mr. Jefferson said, "When a master was murdered, all his slaves in the same house or within hearing, were condemned to death."[14]—Here let me ask Mr. Jefferson, (but he is gone to answer at the bar of God, for the deeds done in his body while living,) I therefore ask the whole American people, had I not rather die, or be put to death than to be a slave to any tyrant, who takes not only my own, but my wife and children's lives by the inches? Yea, would I meet death with avidity far! far!! in preference to such *servile submission* to the murderous hands of tyrants. Mr. Jefferson's very severe remarks on us have been so extensively argued upon by men whose attainments in literature, I shall never be able to reach, that I would not have meddled with it, were it not to solicit each of my brethren, who has the spirit of a man, to buy a copy of Mr. Jefferson's "Notes on Virginia," and put it in the hand of his son. For let no one of us suppose that the refutations which have been written by our white friends are enough—they are *whites*—we are *blacks*. We, and the world wish to see the charges of Mr. Jefferson refuted by the blacks *themselves*, according to their chance: for we must remember that what the whites have written respecting this subject, is other men's labors and did not emanate from the blacks. I know well, that there are some talents and learning among the coloured people of this country, which we have not a chance to develope, in consequence of oppression; but our oppression ought not to hinder us from acquiring all we can.—For

---

[13]See Dr. Goldsmith's History of Greece— page 9. See also Plutarch's lives. The Helots subdued by Agis, king of Sparta. [Walker's note]

[14]See his Notes on Virginia, page 210. [Walker's note]

we will have a chance to develope them by and by. God will not suffer us, always to be oppressed. Our sufferings will come to an *end*, in spite of all the Americans this side of *eternity*. Then we will want all the learning and talents among ourselves, and perhaps more, to govern ourselves.—"Every dog must have its day," the American's is coming to an end.

But let us review Mr. Jefferson's remarks respecting us some further. Comparing our miserable fathers, with the learned philosophers of Greece, he says: "Yet notwithstanding these and other discouraging circumstances among the Romans, their slaves were often their rarest artists. They excelled too in science, insomuch as to be usually employed as tutors to their master's children; Epictetus, Terence and Phaedrus,[15] were slaves,—but they were of the race of whites. It is not their *condition* then, but *nature*, which has produced the distinction."[16] See this, my brethren!! Do you believe that this assertion is swallowed by millions of the whites? Do you know that Mr. Jefferson was one of as great characters as ever lived among the whites? See his writings for the world, and public labors for the United States of America. Do you believe that the assertions of such a man, will pass away into oblivion unobserved by this people and the world? If you do you are much mistaken—See how the American people treat us—have we souls in our bodies? are we men who have any spirits at all? I know that there are many *swell-bellied* fellows among us whose greatest object is to fill their stomachs. Such I do not mean—I am after those who know and feel, that we are MEN as well as other people; to them, I say, that unless we try to refute Mr. Jefferson's arguments respecting us, we will only establish them.

But the slaves among the Romans. Every body who has read history, knows, that as soon as a slave among the Romans obtained his freedom, he could rise to the greatest eminence in the State, and there was no law instituted to hinder a slave from buying his freedom. Have not the Americans instituted laws to hinder us from obtaining our freedom. Do any deny this charge? Read the laws of Virginia, North Carolina, &c. Further: have not the Americans instituted laws to prohibit a man of colour from obtaining and holding any office whatever, under the government of the United States of America? Now, Mr. Jefferson tells us that our condition is not so hard, as the slaves were under the Romans!!!!

It is time for me to bring this article to a close. But before I close it, I must observe to my brethren that at the close of the first Revolution in this country with Great Britain, there were but thirteen States in the Union, now there are twenty-four, most of which are slave-holding States, and the whites are dragging us around in chains and hand-cuffs to their new States and Territories to work their mines and farms, to enrich them and their children, and millions of them believing firmly that we being a little darker

---

[15]Respectively, a Greek Stoic philosopher held in Rome; Roman writer of comic drama; Roman writer of fables.

[16]See his Notes on Virginia, page 211. [Walker's note]

than they, were made by our creator to be an inheritance to them and their children forever—the same as a parcel of *brutes!!*

Are we MEN!!—I ask you, O my brethren! are we MEN? Did our creator make us to be slaves to dust and ashes like ourselves? Are they not dying worms as well as we? Have they not to make their appearance before the tribunal of heaven, to answer for the deeds done in the body, as well as we? Have we any other master but Jesus Christ alone? Is he not their master as well as ours?—What right then, have we to obey and call any other master, but Himself? How we could be so *submissive* to a gang of men, whom we cannot tell whether they are as *good* as ourselves or not, I never could conceive. However, this is shut up with the Lord and we cannot precisely tell—but I declare, we judge men by their works.

The whites have always been an unjust, jealous unmerciful, avaricious and blood thirsty set of beings, always seeking after power and authority.—We view them all over the confederacy of Greece, where they were first known to be any thing, (in consequence of education) we see them there, cutting each other's throats—trying to subject each other to wretchedness and misery, to effect which they used all kinds of deceitful, unfair and unmerciful means. We view them next in Rome, where the spirit of tyranny and deceit raged still higher.—We view them in Gaul, Spain and in Britain—in fine, we view them all over Europe, together with what were scattered about in Asia and Africa, as heathens, and we see them acting more like devils than accountable men. But some may ask, did not the blacks of Africa, and the mulattoes of Asia, go on in the same way as did the whites of Europe. I answer no—they never were half so avaricious, deceitful and unmerciful as the whites, according to their knowledge.

But we will leave the whites or Europeans as heathens and take a view of them as christians, in which capacity we see them as cruel, if not more so than ever. In fact, take them as a body, they are ten times more cruel avaricious and unmerciful than ever they were; for while they were heathens they were bad enough it is true, but it is positively a fact that they were not quite so audacious as to go and take vessel loads of men, women and children, and in cold blood and through devilishness, throw them into the sea, and murder them in all kinds of ways. While they were heathens, they were too ignorant for such barbarity. But being christians, enlightened and sensible, they are completely prepared for such hellish cruelties. Now suppose God were to give them more sense, what would they do. If it were possible would they not *dethrone* Jehovah and seat themselves upon his throne? I therefore, in the name and fear of the Lord God of heaven and of earth, divested of prejudice either on the side of my colour or that of the whites, advance my suspicion of them, whether they are *as good by nature* as we are or not. Their actions, since they were known as a people, have been the reverse, I do indeed suspect them, but this, as I before observed, is shut up with the Lord, we cannot exactly tell, it will be proved in succeeding generations.—The whites have had the essence of the gospel as it was preached by my master and his apostles—the Ethiopians have not, who are to have it in its meridian splendor—the Lord will give it to them to their satisfaction. I hope and pray my God, that they will make good use of it, that it may be well with them.[17]

1829

■   # WILLIAM LLOYD GARRISON   ■

1805–1879

Like Benjamin Franklin, William Lloyd Garrison came from a poor New England family, was apprenticed to a printer, thus developed his skills in editing and writing, and applied them to a revolutionary cause. Both also believed that human beings were capable of infinite improvement, and both devoted them-selves to their divergent ideas of doing good in a wide variety of arenas. There the similarities cease. Indeed, it would be difficult to find two men more unlike in temperament, habits of mind, and prose. Franklin—worldly, conscious of image, ever ready to compromise, to seize the main chance, to accept the politic bird in the hand; given a bit to fat and a bit to smugness; a man who brought others together with humor, hard work, a touch of irony. Garrison—provincial, indifferent to opinion, as uncompromising with friend as with foe, ever demanding the "last full measure of devotion"; spare, humorless in public, and self-righteous; a man who brought others together with the goad of his rhetoric and the heat of his passion. Franklin, whose final political act was to persuade the Constitutional delegates to accept the imperfect document they had created; Garrison, who came to denounce that document as a "covenant with Death and an agreement with Hell."

Garrison's father, an amiable sailing master somewhat given to drink, aban-doned the family in 1808, three years after the birth of William Lloyd in New-buryport, Massachusetts. Reduced to poverty, Garrison's mother sought employment as a nurse in Lynn, then in Baltimore. At age thirteen Garrison secured an apprenticeship in the office of the Newburyport *Herald*, where he

---

[17]Walker's note: "It is my solemn belief, that if ever the world becomes Christianized, (which must certainly take place before long) it will be through the means, under God of the *Blacks*, who are now held in wretchedness, and degradation, by the white *Christians* of the world, who before they learn to do justice to us before our Maker—and be reconciled to us, and recon-cile us to them, and by that means have clear consciences before God and man.— Send out Missionaries to convert the Hea-thens, many of whomafter they cease to worship gods, which neither see nor hear, become ten times more the children of Hell, then ever they were, why what is the rea-son? Why the reason is obvious, they must learn to do justice at home, before they go into distant lands, to display their charity, Christianity, and benevolence; when they learn to do justice, God will accept their offering, (no man may think that I am against Missionaries for I am not, my object is to see justice done at home, before we go to convert the Heathens.)"

learned printing and began to write anonymously for the paper. Concluding his apprenticeship in 1826, Garrison worked as a compositor and editor of newspapers committed to temperance and political causes. In 1828, however, he met Benjamin Lundy, editor of *The Genius of Universal Emancipation*, virtually the only national newspaper devoted solely to the somnolent antislavery cause. Garrison would, they agreed, become associate editor. By the time he took up that task, he had abandoned Lundy's position that slavery would be ended by gradually emancipating blacks and colonizing them in Africa. Instead, Garrison began to argue for immediate emancipation without colonization or compensation. He also denounced a Newburyport merchant for transporting slaves from Baltimore to New Orleans. Convicted of libel, Garrison was, in lieu of payment of a fine and costs, sent to jail for forty-nine days. Characteristically, he turned confinement into a platform for a stream of antislavery poems and letters affirming his right to free speech.

By January 1831, he had established himself in Boston, where, with Isaac Knapp, he began issuing the *Liberator*. Set in the few hours they could spare from their jobs, printed with borrowed type, issued from a dingy office that also served as their lodging, the paper had within a few years effected a sea change in antislavery sentiment. Garrison succeeded in confronting Americans with stark moral choices. Slavery, he argued, was a crime against God and man—*the* most heinous of crimes. Gradualism and colonization merely perpetuated that crime—indeed, compounded it by maintaining that whites and blacks could not live together in one harmonious society. Only immediate emancipation could eradicate that crime, restore the moral integrity of American society, and bring to fruition the promise of the Declaration of Independence. To this position Garrison held unswervingly, insistently, clamorously for more than thirty years. If friends held out political compromises for the sake of "ultimate" progress, he rejected them; if the Constitution was interpreted as sustaining slaveholding, he denounced it. And if others could not see the moral revolution entailed in immediate, unconditional emancipation, he would enlighten them.

He was effective. Quickened by his rhetoric and by his influence in organizing the American Anti-Slavery Society in 1833, Southern militants began defending slavery as a positive good and arguing for its extension into new territories. In turn, Northerners came to regard the South as aggressively pushing its peculiar institution throughout the democracy. In the North, the militance of Garrison and his supporters was often met with mob actions by proslavery forces, which helped mobilize moderates to defend at least the right of abolitionists to be heard. Garrison was, in short, a burr under the political saddle of antebellum America, which no amount of careful riding could dislodge—a "practical agitator," as John Jay Chapman later described him, keeping the issues to which he devoted himself at a boil.

These issues encompassed every significant reform proposed in his time: temperance, women's rights, pacifism. The American Anti-Slavery Society split in 1840, largely because the Garrisonians insisted that women could not on principle be excluded from full participation in the work of reform. Indeed, Garrison joined Elizabeth Cady Stanton and Lucretia Mott in the gallery at the World Anti-Slavery Congress in London because they had not been allowed to take their seats as delegates. He broke with Frederick Douglass over the latter's espousal of political action apart from appeals to conscience and Douglass's growing doubts about the practicality of Garrisonian nonresistance as a means for overcoming the slave power.

These were, for Garrison, not miscellaneous positions. Rather, they were rooted in the millennial beliefs of the Great Awakening that God's kingdom would be brought in by people actively committed to eradicating not just their own wrongdoings but sinfulness from the world. To be a Christian was, for Garrison, to carry out literally the injunctions of the Sermon on the Mount. In particular, he was committed to the principle of "non-resistance to evil by violence," for "he denied the right of any man whatsoever, or any body of men, forcibly to coerce another man in any way," to quote Leo Tolstoy, who was strongly influenced by him. Garrison, Tolstoy continues, "was the first to proclaim this principle as a rule for the organization of the life of men." For coercion, Garrison would substitute what he perceived as ultimately human: the rational and loving persuasion of one person by another. He saw in slavery, in male domination, in the practice of politics, instances of forcible coercion, and thus he opposed them, not so much because they were impractical or unlawful or cruel, but because they perpetuated inhuman relationships among people. The difficulties Garrison presents for today's readers may thus be less a matter of his alleged shrillness and fanaticism than our skepticism that nonviolence, whether articulated by Thoreau or practiced by Martin Luther King, Jr., is a ground upon which we can construct peaceful and free societies.

Garrison's "Preface" to Frederick Douglass's *Narrative* is printed with that work below.

Paul Lauter
Trinity College

PRIMARY WORKS

Selections from the Writings and Speeches of William Lloyd Garrison, 1852, reprinted 1968; Wendell Phillips Garrison and Francis Jackson Garrison, *William Lloyd Garrison: The Story of His Life*, 4 vols., 1885–1889; *Document of Upheaval*, ed. Truman Nelson, 1966; *William Lloyd Garrison*, ed. George M. Frederickson, 1968; *Letters of William Lloyd Garrison*, ed. Walter M. Merrill and Louis Ruchames, 6 vols. 1971–1981; *William Lloyd Garrison and the Fight Against Slavery: Selections from the Liberator*, ed. William E. Cain, 1995.

Editorial from the First Issue of *The Liberator*[1]

To the Public

In the month of August, I issued proposals for publishing "THE LIBERATOR" in Washington City; but the enterprise, though hailed in different sections of the country, was palsied by public indifference. Since that time, the removal of the *Genius of Universal Emancipation* to the Seat of Government

[1]From *William Lloyd Garrison, 1805–1879: The Story of His Life, Told by His Children* (New York: Century Co., 1885), Vol. 1, 224–226.

has rendered less imperious the establishment of a similar periodical in that quarter.

During my recent tour for the purpose of exciting the minds of the people by a series of discourses on the subject of slavery, every place that I visited gave fresh evidence of the fact, that a greater revolution in public sentiment was to be effected in the free States—*and particularly in New-England*—than at the South. I found contempt more bitter, opposition more active, detraction more relentless, prejudice more stubborn, and apathy more frozen, than among slave-owners themselves. Of course, there were individual exceptions to the contrary. This state of things afflicted, but did not dishearten me. I determined, at every hazard, to lift up the standard of emancipation in the eyes of the nation, *within sight of Bunker Hill and in the birthplace of liberty*. That standard is now unfurled; and long may it float, unhurt by the spoliations of time or the missiles of a desperate foe—yea, till every chain be broken, and every bondman set free! Let Southern oppressors tremble—let their secret abettors tremble—let their Northern apologists tremble—let all the enemies of the persecuted blacks tremble.

I deem the publication of my original Prospectus unnecessary, as it has obtained a wide circulation. The principles therein inculcated will be steadily pursued in this paper, excepting that I shall not array myself as the political partisan of any man. In defending the great cause of human rights, I wish to derive the assistance of all religions and of all parties.

Assenting to the "self-evident truth" maintained in the American Declaration of Independence, "that all men are created equal, and endowed by their Creator with certain inalienable rights—among which are life, liberty and the pursuit of happiness," I shall strenuously contend for the immediate enfranchisement of our slave population. In Park-Street Church, on the Fourth of July, 1829, in an address on slavery, I unreflectingly assented to the popular but pernicious doctrine of *gradual* abolition. I seize this opportunity to make a full and unequivocal recantation, and thus publicly to ask pardon of my God, of my country, and of my brethren the poor slaves, for having uttered a sentiment so full of timidity, injustice, and absurdity. A similar recantation, from my pen, was published in the *Genius of Universal Emancipation* at Baltimore, in September, 1829. My conscience is now satisfied.

I am aware that many object to the severity of my language; but is there not cause for severity? I *will be* as harsh as truth, and as uncompromising as justice. On this subject, I do not wish to think, or speak, or write, with moderation. No! no! Tell a man whose house is on fire to give a moderate alarm; tell him to moderately rescue his wife from the hands of the ravisher; tell the mother to gradually extricate her babe from the fire into which it has fallen;—but urge me not to use moderation in a cause like the present. I am in earnest—I will not equivocate—I will not excuse—I will not retreat a inch—AND I WILL BE HEARD. The apathy of the people is enough to mak statue leap from its pedestal, and to hasten the resurrection of the dea

It is pretended, that I am retarding the cause of emancipation coarseness of my invective and the precipitancy of my measures. *Th*

2122 ■ Early Nineteenth Century: 1800–1865

is not true. On this question my influence,—humble as it is,—is felt at this moment to a considerable extent, and shall be felt in coming years—not perniciously, but beneficially—not as a curse, but as a blessing; and posterity will bear testimony that I was right. I desire to thank God, that he enables me to disregard "the fear of man which bringeth a snare," and to speak his truth in its simplicity and power. And here I close with this fresh dedication:

> *"Oppression! I have seen thee, face to face,*
> *And met thy cruel eye and cloudy brow;*
> *But thy soul-withering glance I fear not now—*
> *For dread to prouder feelings doth give place*
> *Of deep abhorrence! Scorning the disgrace*
> *Of slavish knees that at thy footstool bow,*
> *I also kneel—but with far other vow*
> *Do hail thee and thy herd of hirelings base:—*
> *I swear, while life-blood warms my throbbing veins,*
> *Still to oppose and thwart, with heart and hand,*
> *Thy brutalising sway—till Afric's chains*
> *Are burst, and Freedom rules the rescued land,—*
> *Trampling Oppression and his iron rod:*
> *Such is the vow I take—SO HELP ME GOD"*[2]

William Lloyd Garrison.
Boston, January 1, 1831.

1831, 1885

Declaration of Sentiments of the American Anti-Slavery Convention, Done at Philadelphia, December 6th, A.D. 1833[1]

The Convention assembled in the city of Philadelphia, to organize a National Anti-Slavery Society, promptly seize the opportunity to promulgate the following Declaration of Sentiments, as cherished by them in relation to the enslavement of one-sixth portion of the American people.

More than fifty-seven years have elapsed, since a band of patriots convened in this place, to devise measures for the deliverance of this country from a foreign yoke. The corner-stone upon which they founded the Temple of Freedom was broadly this—"that all men are created equal; that they are endowed by their Creator with certain inalienable rights; that among these are life, LIBERTY, and the pursuit of happiness." At the sound of their trumpet-call, three millions of people rose up as from the sleep of death, and rushed to the strife of blood; deeming it more glorious to die instantly as freemen, than desirable to live one hour as slaves. They were few in

---

[2]The author of this sonnet was Thomas Pringle, the Scottish poet, 1789–1834, one of the founders of *Blackwood's Magazine* and Secretary of the London Society for the Abolition of Slavery throughout the British Dominions.

[1]*Selections from the Writings of W. L. Garrison* (Boston: R. F. Wallcut, 1852).

number—poor in resources; but the honest conviction that Truth, Justice and Right were on their side, made them invincible.

We have met together for the achievement of an enterprise, without which that of our fathers is incomplete; and which, for its magnitude, solemnity, and probable results upon the destiny of the world, as far transcends theirs as moral truth does physical force.

In purity of motive, in earnestness of zeal, in decision of purpose, in intrepidity of action, in steadfastness of faith, in sincerity of spirit, we would not be inferior to them.

Their principles led them to wage war against their oppressors, and to spill human blood like water, in order to be free.

Ours forbid the doing of evil that good may come, and lead us to reject, and to entreat the oppressed to reject, the use of all carnal weapons for deliverance from bondage; relying solely upon those which are spiritual, and mighty through God to the pulling down of strong holds.

Their measures were physical resistance—the marshalling in arms—the hostile array—the mortal encounter. Ours shall be such only as the opposition of moral purity to moral corruption—the destruction of error by the potency of truth—the overthrow of prejudice by the power of love—and the abolition of slavery by the spirit of repentance.

Their grievances, great as they were, were trifling in comparison with the wrongs and sufferings of those for whom we plead. Our fathers were never slaves—never bought and sold like cattle—never shut out from the light of knowledge and religion—never subjected to the lash of brutal taskmasters.

But those, for whose emancipation we are striving—constituting at the present time at least one-sixth part of our countrymen—are recognized by law, and treated by their fellow-beings, as marketable commodities, as goods and chattels, as brute beasts; are plundered daily of the fruits of their toil without redress; really enjoy no constitutional nor legal protection from licentious and murderous outrages upon their persons; and are ruthlessly torn asunder—the tender babe from the arms of its frantic mother—the heart-broken wife from her weeping husband—at the caprice or pleasure of irresponsible tyrants. For the crime of having a dark complexion, they suffer the pangs of hunger, the infliction of stripes, the ignominy of brutal servitude. They are kept in heathenish darkness by laws expressly enacted to make their instruction a criminal offence.

These are the prominent circumstances in the condition of more than two millions of our people, the proof of which may be found in thousands of indisputable facts, and in the laws of the slaveholding States.

Hence we maintain—that, in view of the civil and religious privileges of this nation, the guilt of its oppression is unequalled by any other on the face of the earth; and, therefore, that it is bound to repent instantly, to undo the heavy burdens, and to let the oppressed go free.

We further maintain—that no man has a right to enslave or imbrute his brother—to hold or acknowledge him, for one moment, as a piece of merchandise—to keep back his hire by fraud—or to brutalize his mind, by denying him the means of intellectual, social and moral improvement.

The right to enjoy liberty is inalienable. To invade it is to usurp the prerogative of Jehovah. Every man has a right to his own body—to the products of his own labor—to the protection of law—and to the common advantages of society. It is piracy to buy or steal a native African, and subject him to servitude. Surely, the sin is as great to enslave an American as an African.

Therefore we believe and affirm—that there is no difference, in principle, between the African slave trade and American slavery:

That every American citizen, who detains a human being in involuntary bondage as his property, is, according to Scripture, (Ex. xxi. 16,) a man-stealer:

That the slaves ought instantly to be set free, and brought under the protection of law:

That if they had lived from the time of Pharaoh down to the present period, and had been entailed through successive generations, their right to be free could never have been alienated, but their claims would have constantly risen in solemnity:

That all those laws which are now in force, admitting the right of slavery, are therefore, before God, utterly null and void; being an audacious usurpation of the Divine prerogative, a daring infringement on the law of nature, a base over-throw of the very foundations of the social compact, a complete extinction of all the relations, endearments and obligations of mankind, and a presumptuous transgression of all the holy commandments; and that therefore they ought instantly to be abrogated.

We further believe and affirm—that all persons of color, who possess the qualifications which are demanded of others, ought to be admitted forthwith to the enjoyment of the same privileges, and the exercise of the same prerogatives, as others; and that the paths of preferment, of wealth, and of intelligence, should be opened as widely to them as to persons of a white complexion.

We maintain that no compensation should be given to the planters emancipating their slaves:

Because it would be a surrender of the great fundamental principle, that man cannot hold property in man:

Because slavery is a crime, and therefore is not an article to be sold:

Because the holders of slaves are not the just proprietors of what they claim; freeing the slave is not depriving them of property, but restoring it to its rightful owner; it is not wronging the master, but righting the slave—restoring him to himself:

Because immediate and general emancipation would only destroy nominal, not real property; it would not amputate a limb or break a bone of the slaves, but by infusing motives into their breasts, would make them doubly valuable to the masters as free laborers; and

Because, if compensation is to be given at all, it should be given to the outraged and guiltless slaves, and not to those who have plundered and abused them.

We regard as delusive, cruel and dangerous, any scheme of expatriation which pretends to aid, either directly or indirectly, in the emancipation of the slaves, or to be a substitute for the immediate and total abolition of slavery.

We fully and unanimously recognise the sovereignty of each State, to legislate exclusively on the subject of the slavery which is tolerated within its limits; we concede that Congress, under the present national compact, has no right to interfere with any of the slave States, in relation to this momentous subject:

But we maintain that Congress has a right, and is solemnly bound, to suppress the domestic slave trade between the several States, and to abolish slavery in those portions of our territory which the Constitution has placed under its exclusive jurisdiction.

We also maintain that there are, at the present time, the highest obligations resting upon the people of the free States to remove slavery by moral and political action, as prescribed in the Constitution of the United States. They are now living under a pledge of their tremendous physical force, to fasten the galling fetters of tyranny upon the limbs of millions in the Southern States; they are liable to be called at any moment to suppress a general insurrection of the slaves; they authorize the slave owner to vote for three-fifths of his slaves as property, and thus enable him to perpetuate his oppression; they support a standing army at the South for its protection and they seize the slave, who has escaped into their territories, and send him back to be tortured by an enraged master or a brutal driver. This relation to slavery is criminal, and full of danger: IT MUST BE BROKEN UP.

These are our views and principles—these our designs and measures. With entire confidence in the overruling justice of God, we plant ourselves upon the Declaration of our Independence and the truths of Divine Revelation, as upon the Everlasting Rock.

We shall organize Anti-Slavery Societies, if possible, in every city, town and village in our land.

We shall send forth agents to lift up the voice of remonstrance, of warning, of entreaty, and of rebuke.

We shall circulate, unsparingly and extensively, anti-slavery tracts and periodicals.

We shall enlist the pulpit and the press in the cause of the suffering and the dumb.

We shalt aim at a purification of the churches from all participation in the guilt of slavery.

We shall encourage the labor of freemen rather than that of slaves, by giving a preference to their productions: and

We shall spare no exertions nor means to bring the whole nation to speedy repentance.

Our trust for victory is solely in God. We may be personally defeated, but our principles never. Truth, Justice, Reason, Humanity, must and will gloriously triumph. Already a host is coming up to the help of the Lord against the mighty, and the prospect before us is full of encouragement.

Submitting this Declaration to the candid examination of the people of this country, and of the friends of liberty throughout the world, we hereby affix our signatures to it; pledging ourselves that, under the guidance and by the help of Almighty God, we will do all that in us lies, consistently with this Declaration of our principles, to overthrow the most execrable system of slavery that has ever been witnessed upon earth; to deliver our land from its deadliest curse; to wipe out the foulest stain which rests upon our national escutcheon; and to secure to the colored population of the United States, all the rights and privileges which belong to them as men, and as Americans—come what may to our persons, our interests, or our reputation—whether we live to witness the triumph of Liberty, Justice and Humanity, or perish untimely as martyrs in this great, benevolent, and holy cause.

1833

LYDIA MARIA CHILD
1802–1880

Lydia Maria Child was one of America's first women of letters. For a half-century, she edited anthologies and annuals and wrote poetry, novels, short fiction, history, essays, and works for children. Among the Garrisonian abolitionists, Child was the most important writer, Garrison himself the most significant journalist, and Wendell Phillips the most influential speaker. The selections that follow focus on her antislavery publications.

Child became a popular author while young. In 1824, at age twenty-two, she published *Hobomok, A Tale of Early Times*, a novel based on the experiences of the Puritan settlers and their relationships with the Indians. The book presents the marriage of a young Puritan woman to an Indian man, Hobomok. Although their happy union ends after Mary's youthful white lover returns from overseas and her Indian husband nobly disappears into the forest, the novel offers a mythic view of interracial relations altogether different from that of Cooper. The book was sufficiently well received to enable Child to obtain library privileges at the all-male Boston Athenaeum and to write a second novel in 1825, *The Rebels, or Boston before the Revolution*. In the same year she opened a school for girls, and in the next year produced the first periodical for children in the United States, the *Juvenile Miscellany*, most of which she wrote. In 1828, she married David Child, an idealistic but profoundly impractical young man whose projects invariably ran the family into debt. In part to survive financially, Child began writing books of practical advice for women, such as *The Frugal Housewife* (1829) and *The Mother's Book* (1831). She then conceived a grand project, *The Ladies' Family Library*, designed to provide women with biographical models, information, and ideas about their history and lives. Of the four volumes completed by 1835, her *History of the Condition of Women, in Various Ages and Nations* was perhaps the most influential, both as a source for later writers like Angelina Grimké Weld and Sarah Grimké and in its broad view of women's accomplishments.

By 1833, Child had met William Lloyd Garrison and had committed herself to work for the immediate and unconditional emancipation of the slaves. Her first effort toward that end was *An Appeal in Favor of That Class of Americans Called Africans*. In her Preface, Child discusses the problem she faces as a woman writing about a public political issue in a society that restricts middle-class females to the "domestic sphere." Addressing an audience familiar with her fiction and her domestic how-to books (well within the accepted range of women's writing), she challenges them to read her inflammatory pamphlet. In doing so, Child does not adopt the "masculine" stance of a polemicist. Instead, using traditional patterns of female discourse, she presents herself as a supplicant. Despite this conciliatory stance, the literary establishment rejected both the *Appeal* and its author. Its publication in 1833 marked Child as a "radical," and "decent" people began to shun her works. The Athenaeum revoked her library privileges; subscribers canceled their subscriptions to the *Juvenile Miscellany*, which then failed; and the promise of her literary career disappeared. But the *Appeal* was a major force in persuading a generation of young New England intellectuals to support immediate emancipation, and for the rest of her long life, Child did much of her writing for that and other reform movements.

In 1841 Child left Northampton, Massachusetts, where she had been involved with David's attempt to grow sugar beets as a substitute for the cane sugar produced by slave labor in the South, and moved to New York City to edit the Garrisonian abolitionist newspaper *The National Anti-Slavery Standard*. In the *Standard*, Child published her informal "Letters from New York," which appeared weekly next to her editorials; she later edited and republished these columns in an effort to make some money.

In 1843 Child resigned from her position as editor of the *Standard*, wearied of the internal struggles that were splitting the abolitionist movement. In an effort to reestablish her literary career, she published two series of her *Letters from New York* (1843, 1845) and a collection of stories, *Fact and Fiction* (1846), and she began a huge work, *The Progress of Religious Ideas through Successive Ages* (1855). She also continued to write on behalf of Indians, publishing a story, "A Legend of the Falls of St. Anthony" (1846), and an *Appeal for the Indians* (1868). She persisted in her advocacy for blacks. Some 300,000 copies of her exchange of letters with Governor Wise and Mrs. Mason of Virginia, occasioned by John Brown's raid at Harpers Ferry, were circulated in 1860 and were important in preparing Northern consciousness for what would become a war against slavery. In 1865 she spent her own money to print and to circulate *The Freedmen's Book*, a collection of essays, biographical sketches, and poems by and about black people, which she compiled for the freedom schools in the postslavery South. It was designed, in the tradition of Child's commitment to "art for truth's sake," as a literacy text and to promote the ideas of voting rights for blacks and black pride. Many of her works, like her last novel, *A Romance of the Republic* (1867), focus on interracial marriages, which Child seems to offer as a symbol for her vision of a nation to be made one out of many. Since Emancipation, Child's dramas of racial and sexual power relationships under slavery have been adopted by later generations of American writers to figure power relationships in a racist, sexist society. Her mythic characters and plots appear and reappear in American letters, from Mark Twain's *Pudd'nhead Wilson* to William Faulkner's *Absalom! Absalom!*

Jean Fagan Yellin
Pace University

PRIMARY WORKS

Hobomok, A Tale of Early Times, 1824, republished as *Hobomok and Other Writings on Indians*, ed. Carolyn L. Karcher, 1986; *The Rebels, Boston before the Revolution*, 1825; *The Frugal Housewife*, 1829; *The Mother's Book*, 1831; *An Appeal in Favor of That Class of Americans Called Africans*, 1833, ed. Carolyn L. Karcher, 1996; *The History of the Condition of Women, in Various Ages and Nations*, vols. 4 and 5 of *Ladies' Family Library*, 1835; *Philothia: A Romance*, 1836; *Letters from New-York, First Series*, 1843, and *Letters from New-York, Second Series*, 1845, republished as *Letters from New York*, ed. Bruce Mills, 1999; *Fact and Fiction: A Collection of Stories*, 1846; *The Progress of Religious Ideas through Successive Ages*, 3 vols., 1855; *Correspondence between Lydia Maria Child and Gov. Wise and Mrs. Mason of Virginia*, 1860; *The Freedmen's Book*, 1865; *A Romance of the Republic*, 1867, ed. Dana D. Nelson, 1997; *An Appeal for the Indians*, 1868; *The Collected Correspondence of Lydia Maria Child, 1817–1880*, ed. Patricia G. Holland, Milton Meltzer, and Francine Krasno, 1980; *Lydia Maria Child: Selected Letters, 1817–1880*, ed. Milton Meltzer, Patricia G. Holland, and Francine Krasno, 1982; *A Lydia Maria Child Reader*, ed. Carolyn L. Karcher, 1997.

from Appeal in Favor of That Class of Americans Called Africans

Preface

READER, I beseech you not to throw down this volume as soon as you have glanced at the title. Read it, if your prejudices will allow, for the very truth's sake. If I have the most trifling claims upon your good will, for an hour's amusement to yourself, or benefit to your children, read it for *my* sake:— Read it, if it be merely to find fresh occasion to sneer at the vulgarity of the cause;—Read it, from sheer curiosity to see what a woman who had much better attend to her household concerns will say upon such a subject;—Read it, on any terms, and my purpose will be gained.

The subject I have chosen admits of no encomiums on my country; but as I generally make it an object to supply what is most needed, this circumstance is unimportant; the market is so glutted with flattery, that a little truth may be acceptable, were it only for its rarity.

I am fully aware of the unpopularity of the task I have undertaken; but though I *expect* ridicule and censure, it is not in my nature to *fear* them.

A few years hence, the opinion of the world will be a matter in which I have not even the most transient interest; but this book will be abroad on its mission of humanity, long after the hand that wrote it is mingling with the dust.

Should it be the means of advancing, even one single hour, the inevitable progress of truth and justice, I would not exchange the consciousness for all Rothschild's wealth,[1] or Sir Walter's fame.[2]

Chapter VIII. Prejudices against People of Color, and Our Duties in Relation to This Subject

While we bestow our earnest disapprobation on the system of slavery, let us not flatter ourselves that we are in reality any better than our brethren of the South. Thanks to our soil and climate, and the early exertions of the excellent Society of Friends, the *form* of slavery does not exist among us; but the very *spirit* of the hateful and mischievous thing is here in all its strength.... Our prejudice against colored people is even more inveterate than it is at the South. The planter is often attached to his negroes, and lavishes caresses and kind words upon them, as he would on a favorite hound: but our cold-hearted, ignoble prejudice admits of no exception—no intermission.... In order that my readers may not be ignorant of the extent of this tyrannical prejudice, I will as briefly as possible state the evidence, and leave them to judge of it, as their hearts and consciences may dictate.

In the first place, an unjust law exists in this Commonwealth, by which marriage between persons of different color is pronounced illegal.... The government ought not to be invested with power to control the affections, any more than the consciences of citizens. A man has at least as good a right to choose his wife, as he has to choose his religion....

There is among the colored people an increasing desire for information, and laudable ambition to be respectable in manners and appearance.... But in the public schools, colored children are subject to many discouragements and difficulties; and into the private schools they cannot gain admission....

In the theatre, it is not possible for respectable colored people to obtain a decent seat. They must either be excluded, or herd with the vicious.

A fierce excitement prevailed, not long since, because a colored man had bought a pew in one of our churches.... Even at the communion-table, the mockery of human pride is mingled with the worship of Jehovah....

Will any candid person tell me why respectable colored people should not be allowed to make use of public conveyances, open to all who are able and willing to pay for the privilege? Those who enter a vessel, or a stagecoach, cannot expect to select their companions. If they can afford to take a carriage or boat for themselves, then, and then only, they have a right to be exclusive....

The state of public feeling not only makes it difficult for the Africans to obtain information, but it prevents them from making profitable use of

[1] The wealth of the European financial house of Rothschild had, by Child's time, become legendary.

[2] Sir Walter Scott (1771–1832), prolific poet and novelist, was the most popular writer of the day.

what knowledge they have. A colored man, however intelligent, is not allowed to pursue any business more lucrative than that of a barber, a shoe-black, or a waiter. These, and all other employments, are truly respectable, whenever the duties connected with them are faithfully performed; but it is unjust that a man should, on account of his complexion, be prevented from performing more elevated uses in society. Every citizen ought to have a fair chance to try his fortune in any line of business, which he thinks he has ability to transact....

If it be disagreeable to allow colored people the same right and privileges as other citizens, we can do with our prejudice, what most of us often do with better feeling—we can conceal it.

Our almanacs and newspapers can fairly show both sides of the question; and if they lean to either party, let it not be the strongest. Our preachers can speak of slavery, as they do of other evils. Our poets can find in this subject abundant room for sentiment and pathos. Our orators (provided they do not want office) may venture an allusion to our *in-*"glorious institutions."

The union of individual influence produces a vast amount of moral force, which is not the less powerful because it is often unperceived. A mere change in the *direction* of our efforts, without any increased exertion, would in the course of a few years, produce an entire revolution of public feeling. This slow but sure way of doing good is almost the only means by which benevolence can effect its purpose....

By publishing this book I have put my mite into the treasury. The expectation of displeasing all classes has not been unaccompanied with pain. But it has been strongly impressed upon my mind that it was a duty to fulfil this task; and worldly considerations should never stifle the voice of conscience.

1833

from **Letters from New York**

14 [17][1]

[Weeks[2] have passed since I wrote you; not from want of inclination, but because the wrangling at Washington leaves no room for gentle thoughts and poetic fancies. I know not whether you long as earnestly as I do to have Congress stop its discord, and the birds begin their harmony.][3] I was always impatient for the spring-time, but never so much as now; [compelled as I

---

[1]Child revised her letters—in some cases only slightly and in other cases in significant ways—when she reprinted them in book form. We have mainly chosen to print the texts as she revised them. Each letter has two numbers: the first numeral is from the book and the second is from the *National Anti-Slavery Standard* newspaper, where it first was published. Here, letter 14 (in the book) was originally published as letter 17 in

the *National Anti-Slavery Standard* for February 12, 1842.

[2]Child deleted a number of sentences from the opening paragraph of this letter. These we have reinserted for their contemporary interest and placed within brackets to illustrate her revisions.

[3]Child is referring to the congressional debate over the "gag rule" to block consideration of antislavery petitions.

am to watch the vile game of venality and passion, which men dignify with the name of government. Patience yet a few months longer, and Congress will *disband;* I do not think it will ever *rise,* until slavery is abolished; unless, indeed, a portion of them "rise" in the *southern* sense of the phrase, to cut up facts with bowie-knives, and exterminate truth with rifle-balls.]

Patience yet a little longer! and I shall find delicate bells of trailing arbutus, fragrant as an infant's breath, hidden deep, under their coverlid of autumn leaves, like modest worth in this pretending world. My spirit is weary for rural rambles. It is sad walking in the city. The streets shut out the sky, even as commerce comes between the soul and heaven. The busy throng, passing and repassing, fetter freedom, while they offer no sympathy. The loneliness of the soul is deeper, and far more restless, than in the solitude of the mighty forest. Wherever are woods and fields I find a home; each tinted leaf and shining pebble is to me a friend; and wherever I spy a wild flower, I am ready to leap up, clap my hands, and exclaim, "Cockatoo! he know me very well!" as did the poor New Zealander, when he recognized a bird of his native clime, in the menageries of London.

But amid these magnificent masses of sparkling marble, hewn *in prison,* I am alone. For eight weary months, I have met in the crowded streets but two faces I had ever seen before. Of some, I would I could say that I should never see them again; but they haunt me in my sleep, and come between me and the morning. Beseeching looks, begging the comfort and the hope I have no power to give. Hungry eyes, that look as if they had pleaded long for sympathy, and at last gone mute in still despair. Through what woful, what frightful masks, does the human soul look forth, leering, peeping, and defying, in this thoroughfare of nations. Yet in each and all lie the capacities of an archangel; as the majestic oak lies enfolded in the acorn that we tread carelessly under foot, and which decays, perchance, for want of soil to root in.

The other day, I went forth for exercise merely, without other hope of enjoyment than a farewell to the setting sun, on the now deserted Battery, and a fresh kiss from the breezes of the sea, ere they passed through the polluted city, bearing healing on their wings. I had not gone far, when I met a little ragged urchin, about four years old, with a heap of newspapers, "more big as he could carry," under his little arm, and another clenched in his small, red fist. The sweet voice of childhood was prematurely cracked into shrillness, by screaming street cries, at the top of his lungs; and he looked blue, cold, and disconsolate. May the angels guard him! How I wanted to warm him in my heart. I stood, looking after him, as he went shivering along. Imagination followed him to the miserable cellar where he probably slept on dirty straw; I saw him flogged, after his day of cheerless toil, because he had failed to bring home pence enough for his parents' grog; I saw wicked ones come muttering and beckoning between his young soul and heaven; they tempted him to steal to avoid the dreaded beating. I saw him, years after, bewildered and frightened, in the police-office, surrounded by hard faces. Their law-jargon conveyed no meaning to his ear, awakened no slumbering moral sense, taught him no clear distinction between right and wrong; but from their cold, harsh tones, and heartless merriment, he drew the inference that they were enemies; and, as such, he hated them. At that moment, one tone like a mother's voice might have wholly changed his earthly destiny; one kind word of friendly counsel might have saved him—as if an angel standing in the genial sunlight, had thrown to him one end of a garland, and gently diminishing the distance between them, had drawn him safely out of the deep and tangled labyrinth, where all false echoes and winding paths conspired to make him lose his way.

But watchmen and constables were around him; and they have small fellowship with angels. The strong impulses that might have become overwhelming love for his race, are perverted to the bitterest hatred. He tries the universal resort of weakness against force; if they are too strong for *him*, he will be too cunning for *them*. *Their* cunning is roused to detect *his* cunning: and thus the gallows-game is played, with interludes of damnable merriment from police reports, whereat the heedless multitude laugh; while angels weep over the slow murder of a human soul.

When, O when, will men learn that society makes and cherishes the very crimes it so fiercely punishes, and *in* punishing reproduces?

> *The key of knowledge first ye take away,*
> *And then, because ye've robbed him, ye enslave;*
> *Ye shut out from him the sweet light of day,*
> *And then, because he's in the dark, ye pave*
> *The road, that leads him to his wished-for grave,*
> *With stones of stumbling: then, if he but tread*
> *Darkling and slow, ye call him "fool" and "knave";—*
> *Doom him to toil, and yet deny him bread:*
> *Chains round his limbs ye throw, and curses on his head.*

God grant the little shivering carrier-boy a brighter destiny than I have foreseen for him.

A little further on, I encountered two young boys fighting furiously for some coppers, that had been given them and had fallen on the pavement. They had matted black hair, large, lustrous eyes, and an olive complexion. They were evidently foreign children, from the sunny climes of Italy or Spain, and nature had made them subjects for an artist's dream. Near by on the cold stone steps, sat a ragged, emaciated woman, whom I conjectured, from the resemblance of her large, dark eyes, might be their mother; but she looked on their fight with languid indifference, as if seeing, she saw it not. I spoke to her, and she shook her head in a mournful way, that told me she did not understand my language. Poor, forlorn wanderer! would I could place thee and thy beautiful boys under shelter of sun-ripened vines, surrounded by the music of thy motherland! Pence I will give thee, though political economy reprove the deed. They can but appease the hunger of the body; they cannot soothe the hunger of thy heart; that I obey the kindly impulse may make the world none the better—perchance some iota the worse; yet I must needs follow it—I cannot otherwise.

I raised my eyes above the woman's weather-beaten head, and saw, behind the window of clear, plate glass, large vases of gold and silver, curiously wrought. They spoke significantly of the sad contrasts in this disordered world; and excited in my mind whole volumes, not of political, but of angelic economy. "Truly," said I, "if the Law of Love prevailed, vases of gold and silver might even more abound—but no homeless outcast would sit shivering beneath their glittering mockery. All would be richer, and no man the poorer. When will the world learn its best wisdom? When will the mighty discord come into heavenly harmony?" I looked at the huge stone structures of commercial wealth, and they gave an answer that chilled my heart. Weary of city walks, I would have turned homeward; but nature, ever true and harmonious, beckoned to me from the Battery,[4] and the glowing twilight gave me friendly welcome. It seemed as if the dancing Spring Hours had thrown their rosy mantles on old silvery winter in the lavishness of youthful love.

I opened my heart to the gladsome influence, and forgot that earth was not a mirror of the heavens. It was but for a moment; for there, under the leafless trees, lay two ragged little boys, asleep in each other's arms. I remembered having read in the police reports, the day before, that two little children, thus found, had been taken up as vagabonds. They told, with simple pathos, how both their mothers had been dead for months; how they had formed an intimate friendship, had begged together, ate together, hungered together, and together slept uncovered beneath the steel-cold stars.

The twilight seemed no longer warm; and brushing away a tear, I walked hastily homeward. As I turned into the street where God has provided me with a friendly shelter, something lay across my path. It was a woman, apparently dead; with garments all draggled in New-York gutters, blacker than waves of the infernal rivers. Those who gathered around, said she had fallen in intoxication, and was rendered senseless by the force of the blow. They carried her to the watch-house, and the doctor promised she should be well attended. But alas, for watch-house charities to a breaking heart! I could not bring myself to think otherwise than that hers *was* a breaking heart! Could she but give a full revelation of early emotions checked in their full and kindly flow, of affections repressed, of hopes blighted, and energies misemployed through ignorance, the heart would kindle and melt, as it does when genius stirs its deepest recesses.

It seemed as if the voice of human wo was destined to follow me through the whole of that unblest day. Late in the night I heard the sound of voices in the street, and raising the window, saw a poor, staggering woman in the hands of a watchman. My ear caught the words, "Thank you kindly, sir. I should *like* to go home." The sad and humble accents in which the simple phrase was uttered, the dreary image of the watch-house, which that poor wretch dreamed was her *home*, proved too much for my

---

[4]The southern tip of Manhattan Island, so named for a fort located there.

overloaded sympathies. I hid my face in the pillow, and wept; for "my heart was almost breaking with the misery of my kind."

I thought, then, that I would walk no more abroad, till the fields were green. But my mind and body grow alike impatient of being inclosed within four walls; both ask for the free breeze, and the wide, blue dome that over-arches and embraces *all*. Again I rambled forth, under the February sun, as mild and genial as the breath of June. Heart, mind, and frame grew glad and strong, as we wandered on, past the old Stuyvesant church, which a few years agone was surrounded by fields and Dutch farmhouses, but now stands in the midst of peopled streets;—and past the trim, new houses, with their green verandahs, in the airy suburbs. Following the railroad, which lay far beneath our feet, as we wound our way over the hills, we came to the burying-ground of the poor. Weeds and brambles grew along the sides, and the stubble of last year's grass waved over it, like dreary memories of the past; but the sun smiled on it, like God's love on the desolate soul. It was inexpressibly touching to see the frail memorials of affection, placed there by hearts crushed under the weight of poverty. In one place was a small rude cross of wood, with the initials J.S. cut with a penknife, and apparently filled with ink. In another a small hoop had been bent into the form of a heart, painted green, and nailed on a stick at the head of the grave. On one upright shingle was painted only "MUTTER"; the German word for MOTHER. On another was scrawled, as if with charcoal, *So ruhe wohl, du unser liebes kind.* (Rest well, our beloved child.) One recorded life's brief history thus: "H.G. born in Bavaria; died in New-York." Another short epitaph, in French, told that the sleeper came from the banks of the Seine.

The predominance of foreign epitaphs affected me deeply. Who could now tell with what high hopes those departed ones had left the heart-homes of Germany, the sunny hills of Spain, the laughing skies of Italy, or the wild beauty of Switzerland? Would not the friends they had left in their child-hood's home, weep scalding tears to find them in a pauper's grave, with their initials rudely carved on a fragile shingle? Some had not even these frail memorials. It seemed there was none to care whether they lived or died. A wide, deep trench was open; and there I could see piles of unpainted coffins heaped one upon the other, left uncovered with earth, till the yawn-ing cavity was filled with its hundred tenants.

Returning homeward, we passed a Catholic burying-ground. It belonged to the upper classes, and was filled with marble monuments, covered with long inscriptions. But none of them touched my heart like that rude shingle, with the simple word "Mutter" inscribed thereon. The gate was open, and hundreds of Irish, in their best Sunday clothes, were stepping reverently among the graves, and kissing the very sods. Tenderness for the dead is one of the loveliest features of their nation and their church.

The evening was closing in, as we returned, thoughtful but not gloomy. Bright lights shone through crimson, blue, and green, in the apothecaries' windows, and were reflected in prismatic beauty from the dirty pools in the street. It was like poetic thoughts in the minds of the poor and ignorant;

like the memory of pure aspirations in the vicious; like a rainbow of promise, that God's spirit never leaves even the most degraded soul. I smiled, as my spirit gratefully accepted this love-token from the outward; and I thanked our heavenly Father for a world beyond this.

1842

[33][1]

It is curious how a single note in the great hymn of Nature sometimes recalls the memories of years—opens whole galleries of soul-painting, stretching far off into the remote perspective of the past. Rambling on the Brooklyn side of the ferry the other evening, I heard the note of a Katy-did. Instantly it flashed upon my recollection, under what impressive circumstances I, for the first time in my life, heard the angular note of that handsome insect. Six years ago, George Thompson[2] accompanied us to New-York. It was August, a month which the persecuted abolitionists were wont to observe brought out a multitude of snakes and southerners....

The steamboat, which brought us to New-York, was filled with our masters.[3] We saw one after another pointing out George Thompson; and never has it been my fortune to witness such fierce manifestations of hatred written on the human countenance. Men, who a few moments before seemed like polished gentlemen, were suddenly transformed into demons.—They followed close behind us, as we walked the deck, with clenched fists, and uttering the most fearful imprecations. One man, from Georgia, drew a sword from his case, and swore he would kill whoever dares say a word against slavery. It was our intention to stop at Newport, to visit a relative; and I was glad that it so happened; for had we gone on, the boat would have arrived in New-York just at dusk; and I, for one, had no inclination to land at that hour, with such a set of ferocious characters, to whom our persons were well known, and whom we had observed in whispered consultation, ominous of mischief. We pursued our route the next day, without attracting attention; and fearing that George Thompson would bring ruin to the dwelling of any acquaintance we might wish to visit in the city, we crossed over to Brooklyn, to the house of a friend who had known and loved him in Europe. The katydids were then in full concert; and their name was legion. It was the first time I had ever heard them; and my mind was in that excited state, which made all sounds discordant....

Mr. Thompson seemed, as he did on all similar occasions, very little disturbed concerning his own danger; but our host was so obviously anxious, that it imparted a degree of uneasiness to us all. That night, I started at

---

[1]This letter was not included in the book of *Letters from New York*.

[2]George Thompson (1804–1878), a British abolitionist, toured the United States at Garrison's invitation from 1834 to 1835; he again visited America in 1850 and in 1864.

[3]This is an ironic reference to slaveholders, whom Child suggests were ruling over all Americans.

every sound, and when the harsh and unusual notes of that army of katy-dids met my ear, I was again and again deceived by the impression that they were the shouts of a mob in the distance. I shall never be able to get rid of the image this engraved; to my mind the katydids will forever speak of mobs. . . .

Our host was by no means quite reassured, even when Thompson and my husband[4] had both left. I was not of sufficient consequence to endanger anybody; but should I be recognized, it might naturally be reported that Thompson was in the same house. Resolving that no one should incur risk on my account, and being utterly without friends in New-York, I went to a hotel at Bath, and staid there alone. Never, before or since, have I experienced such utter desolation, as I did the few days I remained there. It seemed to me as if anti-slavery had cut me off from all the sympathies of my kind. As I sat there alone, I wrote the following lines, for George Thompson's magnificent album. They have been several times printed; but as my reminiscences are busy with him, I will repeat them:

> I've heard thee when thy powerful words
> Were like the cataract's roar—
> Or like the ocean's mighty waves
> Resounding on the shore
>
> But even in reproof of sin,
> Love brooded over all—
> As the mild rainbow's heavenly arch
> Rests on the waterfall.
>
> I've heard thee in the hour of prayer
> When dangers were around,
> Thy voice was like the royal harp,
> That breathed a charmed sound.
>
> The evil spirit felt its powers
> And howling turned away;
> And some, perchance, "who came to scoff
> Remained with thee to pray."
>
> I've seen thee, too, in playful mood,
> When words of magic spell
> Dropped from thy lips like fairy gems,
> That sparkled as they fell.
>
> Still great and good in every change!
> Magnificent and mild!

[4]David Lee Child (1794–1874) was, like Child, a staunch Garrisonian abolitionist.

As if a saraph's god-like power
Dwealt in a little child.

Among the various exciting recollections with which Thompson is associated, no one is as deeply on my mind as the 1st of August, 1835. It was the first anniversary of emancipation in the British West Indies; and the abolitionists of Boston proposed to hold a meeting in commemoration of that glorious event. The Tremont House[5] was swarming with southerners; and they swore that George Thompson should not be allowed to speak. The meeting was, however, held at Julian Hall. Few people were there, and I had a chance to observe them all. Near the stairs, was a line of men in fine broadcloth, whom I saw at once were slaveholders; the fact was plainly enough written in the clenched fist, the fiercely compressed lip, and the haughty carriage of the head. In front of them were a dozen or more stout truckmen, in shirtsleeves; there seemed to be an understanding between them; there were in fact "the glorious Union." . . .

> [Thompson, aware that there "were well-managed preparations for a savage mob," poured out "torrents of eloquence." The Southerners raged out of the hall, with the truckmen after them.]

When the meeting closed, the heart of every abolitionist beat with a quickened pulse, for Thompson's safety. From time to time, the fierce, impatient faces of the truckmen were seen above the staircase; their courage evidently reinforced by fresh supplies of rum, paid for by southern generosity. Abolitionists, who left the meeting, came back to tell that the stairway and entry were lined with desperate-looking fellows, brandishing clubs and cartwhips; and that a carriage, with the steps down, stood close to the door. I did not then know that a train was laid by our friends for Thompson's escape. All I could do, was to join the women, who formed a dense circle around him; a species of troops in much requisition at that period, and well known by the name of "Quaker militia". . . . Near the platform, where the speaker had stood, was a private door, leading, by a flight of back stairs, into a store-room, that opened into another street than the front entrance. The mob were either ignorant of this entrance, or forgetful; but our friends were neither. One of our number held the key; a second had engaged a carriage, with swift horses, and a colored driver; a third made a signal from a window, for the carriage to approach the store communicating with the back passage. Holding Thompson in friendly chat, the women, as it were quite accidentally, approached the private door. The circle opened—the door opened—a volley of oaths from the truckmen, and a deafening rush down the front stairs—but where was *he?*

---

[5]A Boston hotel.

For a few moments, we who remained in the hall could not answer. But presently, S.J. May[6] came to us, with a face like Carara marble, and breathed, rather than uttered, the welcome words, "Thank God! he's safe!"....

I never saw George Thompson again, after that hurried farewell at morning twilight, when "Judge Lynch" was lying in wait for him. He left the country a few months after.

1842

34 [50, 51][1]

You ask what are my opinions about "Women's Rights." I confess, a strong distaste to the subject, as it has been generally treated. On no other theme, probably, has there been uttered so much of false, mawkish sentiment, shallow philosophy, and sputtering, farthing-candle wit. If the style of its advocates has often been offensive to taste, and unacceptable to reason, assuredly that of its opponents has been still more so. College boys have amused themselves with writing dreams, in which they saw women in hotels, with their feet hoisted, and chairs tilted back, or growling and bickering at each other in legislative halls, or fighting at the polls, with eyes blackened by fisticuffs. But it never seems to have occurred to these facetious writers, that the proceedings which appear so ludicrous and improper in *women*, are also ridiculous and disgraceful in *men*. It were well that *men* should learn not to hoist their feet above their heads, and tilt their chairs backward, not to growl and snap in the halls of legislation, or give each other black eyes at the polls.

Maria Edgeworth[2] says, "We are disgusted when we see a woman's mind overwhelmed with a torrent of learning; that the tide of literature has passed over it should be betrayed only by its fertility." This is beautiful and true; but is it not likewise applicable to man? The truly great never seek to display themselves. If they carry their heads high above the crowd, it is only made manifest to others by accidental revelations of their extended vision. "Human duties and proprieties do not lie so very far apart," said Harriet Martineau; "if they did, there would be two gospels, and two teachers, one for man, and another for woman."[3]

It would seem, indeed, as if men were willing to give women the exclusive benefit of gospel-teaching. "*Women* should be gentle," say the advocates of subordination; but when Christ said, "Blessed are the meek," did he preach to women only? "*Girls* should be modest," is the language of common teaching, continually uttered in words and customs. Would it not be an

[6]Unitarian minister Samuel J. May (1794–1871), the uncle of writer Louisa May Alcott, was a founder of the American Antislavery Society.

[1]For this letter on "Women's Rights," Child amalgamated two original letters, number 50, dated February 16, 1843, and number 51, dated February 23, 1843.

[2]Maria Edgeworth (1767–1849) wrote fiction, most notably *Castle Rackrent* (1800) and *Ormond* (1817), as well as works for children and feminist essays.

[3]British by birth, Harriet Martineau (1802–1876) actively supported the abolitionist cause in books like *Society in America* (1837) and *The Hour and the Man* (1840), a biography of Toussaint L'Ouverture.

improvement for men, also, to be scrupulously pure in manners, conversation, and life? Books addressed to young married people abound with advice to the *wife*, to control her temper, and never to utter wearisome complaints, or vexatious words, when the husband comes home fretful or unreasonable, from his out-of-door conflicts with the world. Would not the advice be as excellent and appropriate, if the husband were advised to conquer *his* fretfulness, and forbear *his* complaints, in consideration of his wife's ill-health, fatiguing cares, and the thousand disheartening influences of domestic routine? In short, whatsoever can be named as loveliest, best, and most graceful in woman, would likewise be good and graceful in man. You will perhaps remind me of courage. If you use the word in its highest signification, I answer the woman, above others, has abundant need of it, in her pilgrimage; and the true woman wears it with a quiet grace. If you mean mere animal courage, *that* is not mentioned in the Sermon on the Mount,[4] among those qualities which enable us to inherit the earth, or become the children of God. That the feminine ideal approaches much nearer to the gospel standard, than the prevalent idea of manhood, is shown by the universal tendency to represent the Saviour and his most beloved disciple with mild, meek expression, and feminine beauty. None speak of the bravery, the might, or the intellect of Jesus; but the devil is always imagined as a being of acute intellect, political cunning, and the fiercest courage. These universal and instinctive tendencies of the human mind reveal much.

That the present position of women in society is the result of physical force, is obvious enough; whosoever doubts it, let her reflect why she is afraid to go out in the evening without the protection of a man. What constitutes the danger of aggression? Superior physical strength, uncontrolled by the moral sentiments. If physical strength were in complete subjection to moral influence, there would be no need of outward protection. That animal instinct and brute force now govern the world, is painfully apparent in the condition of women everywhere; from the Morduan Tartars,[5] whose ceremony of marriage consists in placing the bride on a mat, and consigning her to the bridegroom, with the words, "Here, wolf, take thy lamb,"—to the German remark, that "stiff ale, stinging tobacco, and a girl in her smart dress, are the best things." The same thing, softened by the refinements of civilization, peeps out in Stephen's remark, that "woman never looks so interesting, as when leaning on the arm of a soldier": and in Hazlitt's[6] complaint that "it is not easy to keep up a conversation with women in company. It is thought a piece of rudeness to differ from them; it is not quite fair to ask them a *reason* for what they say."[7]

[4]See Matthew 5–7.

[5]A people of Central Asia.

[6]William Hazlitt (1778–1830), a British essayist.

[7]Child omitted three paragraphs of her original letter here. Some omitted sentences suggest her political outlook: "*Every* subject, bearing any relation to the contending influences of moral attraction and physical force, is a *branch* of anti-slavery, or, more properly speaking, a branch *with* anti-slavery. All truths flow from One, and tend to one; and whosoever has a mind sufficiently comprehensive to follow out one great principle, reaches another in the process."

This sort of politeness to women is what men call gallantry; an odious word to every sensible woman, because she sees that it is merely the flimsy veil which foppery throws over sensuality, to conceal its grossness. So far is it from indicating sincere esteem and affection for women, that the profligacy of a nation may, in general, be fairly measured by its gallantry. This taking away *rights*, and *condescending* to grant *privileges*, is an old trick of the physical force principle; and with the immense majority, who only look on the surface of things, this mask effectually disguises an ugliness, which would otherwise be abhorred. The most inveterate slaveholders are probably those who take most pride in dressing their household servants handsomely, and who would be most ashamed to have the name of being *unnecessarily* cruel. And profligates, who form the lowest and most sensual estimate of women, are the very ones to treat them with an excess of outward deference.

There are few books, which I can read through, without feeling insulted as a woman; but this insult is almost universally conveyed through that which was intended for praise. Just imagine, for a moment, what impression it would make on men, if women authors should write about *their* "rosy lips," and "melting eyes," and "voluptuous forms," as they write about *us!* That women in general do not feel this kind of flattery to be an insult, I readily admit; for, in the first place, they do not perceive the gross chattel-principle, of which it is the utterance; moreover, they have, from long habit, become accustomed to consider themselves as household conveniences, or gilded toys. Hence, they consider it feminine and pretty to abjure all such use of their faculties, as would make them co-workers with man in the advancement of those great principles, on which the progress of society depends. "There is perhaps no *animal*," says Hannah More,[8] "so much indebted to subordination, for its good behaviour, as woman." Alas, for the animal age, in which such utterance could be tolerated by public sentiment! ...

I have said enough to show that I consider prevalent opinions and customs highly unfavourable to the moral and intellectual development of women: and I need not say, that, in proportion to their true culture, women will be more useful and happy, and domestic life more perfected. True culture, in them, as in men, consists in the full and free development of individual character, regulated by their *own* perceptions of what is true, and their *own* love of what is good.

This individual responsibility is rarely acknowledged, even by the most refined, as necessary to the spiritual progress of women. I once heard a very beautiful lecture from R. W. Emerson, on Being and Seeming.[9] In the course of many remarks, as true as they were graceful, he urged women to *be*,

---

[8]Hannah More (1745–1833) taught, wrote for the theater, took an active role in polite London society of the late eighteenth century, and then became an evangelical philanthropist.

[9]Emerson initially delivered the lecture on January 10 and March 15, 1838. It is included in *The Early Lectures of Ralph Waldo Emerson*, vol. 2.

rather than *seem*. He told them that all their laboured education of forms, strict observance of genteel etiquette, tasteful arrangement of the toilette, &c., all this *seeming* would not *gain hearts* like *being* truly what God made them; that earnest simplicity, the sincerity of nature, would kindle the eye, light up the countenance, and give an inexpressible charm to the plainest features.

The advice was excellent, but the motive, by which it was urged, brought a flush of indignation over my face. *Men* were exhorted to *be*, rather than to *seem*, that they might fulfil the sacred mission for which their souls were embodied; that they might, in God's freedom, grow up into the full stature of spiritual manhood; but *women* were urged to simplicity and truthfulness, that they might become more *pleasing*.

Are we not all immortal beings? Is not each one responsible for himself and herself? There is no measuring the mischief done by the prevailing tendency to teach women to be virtuous as a duty to *man*, rather than to *God*—for the sake of pleasing the creature, rather than the Creator. "*God* is thy law, *thou* mine," said Eve to Adam. May Milton be forgiven for sending that thought "out into everlasting time" in such a jewelled setting. What weakness, vanity, frivolity, infirmity of moral purpose, sinful flexibility of principle—in a word, what soul-stifling, has been the result of thus putting man in the place of God!

But while I see plainly that society is on a false foundation, and that prevailing views concerning women indicate the want of wisdom and purity, which they serve to perpetuate—still, I must acknowledge that much of the talk about Women's Rights offends both my reason and my taste. I am not of those who maintain there is no sex in souls; nor do I like the results deducible from that doctrine. Kinmont, in his admirable book, called the Natural History of Man,[10] speaking of the warlike courage of the ancient German women, and of their being respectfully consulted on important public affairs, says: "You ask me if I consider all this right, and deserving of approbation? or that women were here engaged in their appropriate tasks? I answer, yes; it is just *as* right that they should take this interest in the honour of their country, as the other sex. Of course, I do not think that women were *made* for war and battle; neither do I believe that *men* were. But since the fashion of the times had made it so, and settled it that war was a necessary element of greatness, and that no safety was to be procured without it, I argue that it shows a healthful state of feeling in other respects, that the feelings of both sexes were *equally* enlisted in the cause; that there was no *division* in the house, or the State; and that the serious pursuits and objects of the one were also the serious pursuits and objects of the other."

[10]*Twelve Lectures on the Natural History of Man, and the Rise and Progress of Philosophy* (1839) by Alexander Kinmont (1799–1838).

The nearer society approaches to divine order, the less separation will there be in the characters, duties, and pursuits of men and women. Women will not become less gentle and graceful, but men will become more so. Women will not neglect the care and education of their children, but men will find themselves ennobled and refined by sharing those duties with them; and will receive, in return, co-operation and sympathy in the discharge of various other duties, now deemed inappropriate to women. The more women become rational companions, partners in business and in thought, as well as in affection and amusement, the more highly will men appreciate *home*—that blessed word, which opens to the human heart the most perfect glimpse of Heaven, and helps to carry it thither, as on an angel's wings.

> "Domestic bliss,
> That can, the world eluding, be itself
> A world enjoyed; that wants no witnesses
> But its own sharers, and approving heaven;
> That, like a flower deep hid in rocky cleft,
> Smiles, though 'tis looking only at the sky."

Alas, for these days of Astor houses, and Tremonts, and Albions! where families exchange comfort for costliness, fireside retirement for flirtation and flaunting, and the simple, healthful, cozy meal, for gravies and gout, dainties and dyspepsia. There is no characteristic of my countrymen which I regret so deeply, as their slight degree of adhesiveness to home. Closely intertwined with this instinct, is the religion of a nation. The Home and the Church bear a near relation to each other. The French have no such word as home in their language, and I believe they are the least reverential and religious of all the Christian nations. A Frenchman had been in the habit of visiting a lady constantly for several years, and being alarmed at a report that she was sought in marriage, he was asked why he did not marry her himself. "*Marry* her!" exclaimed he; "Good heavens! *where should I spend my evenings?*" The idea of domestic happiness was altogether a foreign idea to his soul, like a word that conveyed no meaning. Religious sentiment in France leads the same roving life as the domestic affections; breakfasting at one restaurateur's and supping at another's. When some wag in Boston reported that Louis Philippe had sent over for Dr. Channing to manufacture a religion for the French people, the witty significance of the joke was generally appreciated.

There is a deep spiritual reason why all that relates to the domestic affections should ever be found in close proximity with religious faith. The age of chivalry was likewise one of unquestioning veneration, which led to the crusade for the holy sepulchre. The French Revolution, which tore down churches, and voted that there was no God, likewise annulled marriage; and the doctrine that there is no sex in souls has usually been urged by those of infidel tendencies. Carlyle says: "But what feeling it was in the ancient, devout, deep soul, which of marriage made a *sacrament*, this, of all things in the world, is what Diderot will think of for aeons without discovering; unless, perhaps, it were to increase the *vestry fees*."

The conviction that woman's present position in society is a false one, and therefore re-acts disastrously on the happiness and improvement of man, is pressing, by slow degrees, on the common consciousness, through all the obstacles of bigotry, sensuality, and selfishness. As man approaches to the truest life, he will perceive more and more that there is no separation or discord in their mutual duties. They will be one; but it will be as affection and thought are one; the treble and bass of the same harmonious tune.

1843

The Duty of Disobedience to the Fugitive Slave Act:
An Appeal to the Legislators of Massachusetts

One thousand five hundred years ago, Gregory, a Bishop in Asia Minor, preached a sermon in which he rebuked the sin of slaveholding. Indignantly he asked, "Who can be the possessor of human beings save God? Those men that you say belong to you, did not God create them free? Command the brute creation; that is well. Bend the beasts of the field beneath your yoke. But are your fellow-men to be bought and sold, like herds of cattle? Who can pay the value of a being created in the image of God? The whole world itself bears no proportion to the value of a soul, on which the Most High has set the seal his likeness. This world will perish, but the soul of man is immortal. Show me, then, your titles of possession. Tell me whence you derive this strange claim. Is not your own nature the same with that of those you call your slaves? Have they not the same origin with yourselves? Are they not born to the same immortal destinies?"

Thus spake a good old Bishop, in the early years of Christianity. Since then, thousands and thousands of noble souls have given their bodies to the gibbet and the stake, to help onward the slow progress of truth and freedom; a great unknown continent has been opened as a new, free starting point for the human race; printing has been invented, and the command, "Whatsoever ye would that men should do unto you, do ye even so unto them," has been sent abroad in all the languages of the earth. And here, in the noon-day light the nineteenth century, in a nation claiming to be the freest and most enlightened on the face of the globe, a portion the population of fifteen States have thus agreed among themselves: "Other men shall work for us, without wages while we smoke, and drink, and gamble, and race horses, and fight. We will have their wives and daughters for concubines, and sell their children in the market with horses and pigs. If they make any objection to this arrangement, we will break them into subjection with the cow-hide and the bucking-paddle. They shall not be permitted to read or write, because that would be likely to 'produce dissatisfaction in their minds.' If they attempt to run away from us, our blood-hounds shall tear the flesh from their bones, and any man who sees them may shoot them down like mad dogs. If they succeed in getting beyond our frontier, into States where it is the custom to pay men for their work, and to protect their wives and children from outrage, we will compel the people of those States to drive them back into the jaws of our blood-hounds."

And what do the people of the other eighteen States of that enlightened country answer to this monstrous demand? What says Massachusetts, with the free blood of the Puritans coursing in her veins, and with the sword uplifted in her right hand, to procure "peaceful repose under liberty"? Massachusetts answers: "O yes. We will be your blood-hounds, and pay our own expenses. Only prove to our satisfaction that the stranger who has taken refuge among us is one of the men you have agreed among yourselves to whip into working without wages, and we will hunt him back for you. Only prove to us that this woman, who has run away from your harem, was bought for a concubine, that you might get more drinking-money by the sale of the children she bears you, and our soldiers will hunt her back with alacrity."

Shame on my native State! Everlasting shame! Blot out the escutcheon of the brave old Commonwealth! Instead of the sword uplifted to protect liberty, let the slave-driver's whip be suspended over a blood-hound, and take for your motto, Obedience to tyrants is the highest law.

1850

■ ANGELINA GRIMKÉ ■
1805–1879

In the 1830s, Angelina and Sarah Grimké became major publicists on behalf of women's rights and antislavery. Earlier, they had shocked their prominent South Carolina slaveholding family by publicly aligning themselves with Garrisonian abolitionism. Because they lectured in public to "promiscuous" audiences of men and women, they placed themselves beyond the boundaries defining women's decent behavior in nineteenth-century America.

The slavery system had long distressed both women. After Sarah moved to Philadelphia and joined the Society of Friends, her younger sister followed. Then in 1835, reading that antislavery women had been mobbed in Boston, Angelina impulsively wrote to abolitionist William Lloyd Garrison and embraced the cause of the antislavery activists. When Garrison published her letter in his newspaper *The Liberator* (without her knowledge or her consent), even Sarah condemned her. Nonetheless, Angelina persisted in her radical behavior and politics. In *An Appeal to the Christian Women of the South* (1836), she argues the validity of her newfound public role and urges her Southern "sisters" to act to end chattel slavery and to break the laws, if necessary, to do so.

Angelina became an "agent" of the American Anti-Slavery Society, speaking to small groups of women in the New York City area. Sarah soon joined her on the platform, and increasingly, curious men came to listen. In the summer of 1837, both Grimké sisters lectured throughout New England for the antislavery movement. When the educator Catharine Beecher attacked them by arguing that women should restrict themselves to the domestic sphere, Angelina Grimké responded in ringing tones with *Letters to Catharine Beecher*, asserting the correctness of the abolitionist cause and arguing that women can act appropriately wherever and however men can—both in private and in public.

While her younger sister composed her vigorous reply to Beecher, Sarah Grimké was framing *Letters on the Equality of the Sexes, and the Condition of Woman*.[1] Sarah Grimké rooted her pioneering feminist arguments in her lifelong study of theology. Even the electric phrases that sometimes flash from her Latinate prose—such as the "root of bitterness" she identifies as "the mistaken notion of the inequality of the sexes"—are scriptural.

The public careers of the Grimké sisters ended in 1838, when Angelina married abolitionist Theodore Weld. The sisters' antislavery arguments, however, came to define abolitionism for many Americans, and their writings on women's rights became the grounding of later works by Margaret Fuller and the thinking of the women who established an American feminist movement at Seneca Falls in 1848. In addition, the presence of the Grimké sisters on the public platform inspired a new generation of women, like Abby Kelley Foster and Lucy Stone, to speak in public and to assert women's presence in public life.

Jean Fagan Yellin
Pace University

PRIMARY WORKS

"Letter to William Lloyd Garrison, 30 August, 1835," published in the *Liberator*, copied in other publications, and reprinted as a broadside; *Appeal to the Christian Women of the South*, 1836; *Appeal to the Women of the Nominally Free States*, 1837; *Letters to Catharine Beecher, in reply to an Essay on Slavery and Abolition, Addressed to A. E. Grimké*, revised edition, 1838; Sarah Grimké, *Letters on the Equality of the Sexes, and the Condition of Woman*, 1838, first published in a series in the *New England Spectator*, 1938; "Letter to the Women's Rights Convention, Syracuse, 1852," Women's Rights Tract No. 8, 1852.

from **Appeal to the Christian Women of the South**

Then Mordecai commanded to answer Esther, Think not within thyself that thou shalt escape in the king's house more than all the Jews. For if thou altogether holdest thy peace at this time, then shall there enlargement and deliverance arise to the Jews from another place: but thou and thy father's house shall be destroyed; and who knoweth whether thou art come to the kingdom for such a time as this. And Esther bade them return Mordecai this

---

[1] Excerpts from these *Letters* are reprinted in the section "Literature and the 'Woman Question.'"

> *answer:—and so will I go in unto the king, which is not according to law,*
> *and if I perish, I perish."*

—*Esther IV. 13–16.*

Respected Friends,

It is because I feel a deep and tender interest in your present and eternal welfare that I am willing thus publicly to address you. Some of you have loved me as a relative, and some have felt bound to me in Christian sympathy, and Gospel fellowship; and even when compelled by a strong sense of duty, to break those outward bonds of union which bound us together as members of the same community, and members of the same religious denomination, you were generous enough to give me credit, for sincerity as a Christian, though you believed I had been most strangely deceived. . . .

But there are other Christian women scattered over the Southern States, a very large number of whom have never seen me, and never heard my name, and who feel *no* interest whatever in *me*. But I feel an interest in *you*, as branches of the same vine from whose root I daily draw the principle of spiritual vitality—Yes! Sisters in Christ I feel an interest in *you*, and often has the secret prayer arisen on your behalf, Lord "open thou their eyes that they may see wondrous things out of thy Law"—It is then, because I *do feel* and *do pray* for you, that I thus address you upon a subject about which of all others, perhaps you would rather not hear any thing; but, "would to God ye could bear with me a little in my folly, and indeed bear with me, for I am jealous over you with godly jealousy." Be not afraid then to read my appeal; it is *not* written in the heat of passion or prejudice, but in that solemn calmness which is the result of conviction and duty. It is true, I am going to tell you unwelcome truths, but I mean to speak those *truths in love*, and remember Solomon says, "faithful are the *wounds* of a friend." I do not believe the time has yet come when *Christian women* "will not endure sound doctrine," even on the subject of Slavery, if it is spoken to them in tenderness and love, therefore I now address *you*. . . .

I have thus, I think, clearly proved to you seven propositions, viz.: First, that slavery is contrary to the declaration of our independence. Second, that it is contrary to the first charter of human rights given to Adam, and renewed to Noah. Third, that the fact of slavery having been the subject of prophecy, furnishes *no* excuse whatever to slavedealers. Fourth, that no such system existed under the patriarchal dispensation. Fifth, that *slavery never* existed under the Jewish dispensation; but so far otherwise, that every servant was placed under the *protection of law*, and care taken not only to prevent all *involuntary* servitude, but all *voluntary perpetual* bondage. Sixth, that slavery in America reduces a *man* to a *thing*, a "chattel personal," *robs him* of *all* his rights as a *human being*, fetters both his mind and body, and protects the *master* in the most unnatural and unreasonable power, whilst it *throws him out* of the protection of law. Seventh, that slavery is contrary to the example and precepts of our holy and merciful Redeemer, and of his apostles.

But perhaps you will be ready to query, why appeal to *women* on this subject? *We* do not make the laws which perpetuate slavery. *No* legislative power is vested in *us; we* can do nothing to overthrow the system, even if we wished to do so. To this I reply, I know you do not make the laws, but I also know that *you are the wives and mothers, the sisters and daughters of those who do*, and if you really suppose *you* can do nothing to overthrow slavery, you are greatly mistaken. You can do much in every way: four things I will name. 1st. You can read on this subject. 2d. You can pray over this subject. 3d. You can speak on this subject. 4th. You can *act* on this subject. I have not placed reading before praying because I regard it more important, but because, in order to pray aright, we must understand what we are praying for; it is only then we can "pray with the understanding and the spirit also."

1. Read then on the subject of slavery. Search the Scriptures daily, whether the things I have told you are true. Other books and papers might be a great help to you in this investigation, but they are not necessary, and it is hardly probable that your Committees of Vigilance[1] will allow you to have any other. The *Bible* then is the book I want you to read in the spirit of inquiry, and the spirit of prayer. Even the enemies of Abolitionists, acknowledge that their doctrines are drawn from it. In the great mob in Boston, last autumn, when the books and papers of the Anti-Slavery Society, were thrown out of the windows of their office, one individual laid hold of the Bible and was about tossing it out to the ground, when another reminded him that it was the Bible he had in his hand. *"O! 'tis all one,"* he replied, and out went the sacred volume, along with the rest. We thank him for the acknowledgment. Yes, *"it is all one,"* for our books and papers are mostly commentaries on the Bible, and the Declaration.[2] Read the *Bible* then, it contains the words of Jesus, and they are spirit and life. Judge for yourselves whether *he sanctioned* such a system of oppression and crime.

2. Pray over this subject. When you have entered into your closets, and shut to the doors, then pray to your father, who seeth in secret, that he would open your eyes to see whether slavery is *sinful*, and if it is, that he would enable you to bear a faithful, open and unshrinking testimony against it, and to do whatsoever your hands find to do, leaving the consequences entirely to him, who still says to us whenever we try to reason away duty from the fear of consequences, *"What is that to thee, follow thou me."* Pray also for that poor slave, that he may be kept patient and submissive under his hard lot, until God is pleased to open the door of freedom to him without violence or bloodshed. Pray too for the master that his heart may be softened. and he made willing to acknowledge, as Joseph's brethren[3] did, "Verily we are guilty concerning our brother," before he will be compelled to add in consequence of Divine judgment, "therefore is all this evil come upon

---

[1]Citizens' groups which, in the white South, attempted to buttress the institution of chattel slavery by preventing the publication or distribution of abolitionist writings and speeches; the black North later organized committees of vigilance to protect fugitive slaves from slave-catchers.

[2]Declaration of Independence.

[3]Genesis 42:21.

us." Pray also for all your brethren and sisters who are laboring in the righteous cause of Emancipation in the Northern States, England and the world. There is great encouragement for prayer in these words of our Lord. "Whatsoever ye shall ask the Father *in my name*, he *will give* it to you"—Pray then without ceasing, in the closet and the social circle.

3. Speak on this subject. It is through the tongue, the pen, and the press, that truth is principally propagated. Speak then to your relatives, your friends, your acquaintances on the subject of slavery; be not afraid if you are conscientiously convinced it is *sinful*, to say so openly, but calmly, and to let your sentiments be known. If you are served by the slaves of others, try to ameliorate their condition as much as possible; never aggravate their faults, and thus add fuel to the fire of anger already kindled, in a master and mistress's bosom; remember their extreme ignorance, and consider them as your Heavenly Father does the *less* culpable on this account, even when they do wrong things. Discountenance *all* cruelty to them, all starvation, all corporal chastisement; these may brutalize and *break* their spirits, but will never bend them to willing, cheerful obedience. If possible, see that they are comfortably and *seasonably* fed, whether in the house or the field; it is unreasonable and cruel to expect slaves to wait for their breakfast until eleven o'clock, when they rise at five or six. Do all you can, to induce their owners to clothe them well, and to allow them many little indulgences which would contribute to their comfort. Above all, try to persuade your husband, father, brothers and sons, that *slavery is a crime against God and man*, and that it is a great sin to keep *human beings* in such abject ignorance; to deny them the privilege of learning to read and write. The Catholics are universally condemned, for denying the Bible to the common people, but, *slaveholders must not* blame them, for *they* are doing the *very same thing*, and for the very same reason, neither of these systems can bear the light which bursts from the pages of that Holy Book. And lastly, endeavour to inculcate submission on the part of the slaves, but whilst doing this be faithful in pleading the cause of the oppressed.

> "Will you *behold unheeding,*
>   *Life's holiest feelings crushed,*
> *Where* woman's *heart is bleeding,*
>   *Shall* woman's *voice be hushed?*"[4]

4. Act on this subject. Some of you *own* slaves yourselves. If you believe slavery is *sinful*, set them at liberty, "undo the heavy burdens and let the oppressed go free." If they wish to remain with you, pay them wages, if not let them leave you. Should they remain teach them, and have them taught the common branches of an English education; they have minds and those minds, *ought to be improved.* So precious a talent as intellect, never was given to be wrapt in a napkin and buried in the earth. It is the *duty* of all, as far as

---

[4]Elizabeth Margaret Chandler, "Think of Our Country's Glory," *Poetical Works*, ed. Benjamin Lundy (Philadelphia: Howell, 1836), p. 64.

they can, to improve their own mental faculties, because we are commanded to love God with *all our minds*, as well as with all our hearts, and we commit a great sin, if we *forbid or prevent* that cultivation of the mind in others, which would enable them to perform this duty. Teach your servants then to read &c, and encourage them to believe it is their *duty* to learn, if it were only that they might read the Bible.

But some of you will say, we can neither free our slaves nor teach them to read, for the laws of our state forbid it. Be not surprised when I say such wicked laws *ought to be no barrier* in the way of your duty, and I appeal to the Bible to prove this position. What was the conduct of Shiphrah and Puah, when the king of Egypt issued his cruel mandate, with regard to the Hebrew children? "*They* feared *God*, and did *not* as the King of Egypt commanded them, but saved the men children alive." Did these *women* do right in disobeying that monarch? "*Therefore* (says the sacred text,) *God dealt well* with them, and made them houses" Ex. i. What was the conduct of Shadrach, Meshach, and Abednego, when Nebuchadnezzar set up a golden image in the plain of Dura, and commanded all people, nations, and languages, to fall down and worship it? "Be it known, unto thee, (said these faithful *Jews*) O king, that *we will not* serve thy gods, nor worship the image which thou hast set up." Did these men *do right in disobeying the law* of their sovereign? Let their miraculous deliverance from the burning fiery furnace, answer; Dan. iii. . . .

But some of you may say, if we do free our slaves, they will be taken up and sold, therefore there will be no use in doing it. Peter and John might just as well have said, we will not preach the gospel, for if we do, we shall be taken up and put in prison, therefore there will be no use in our preaching. *Consequences*, my friends, belong no more to *you*, than they did to these apostles. Duty is ours and events are God's. If you think slavery is sinful, all *you* have to do is to set your slaves at liberty, do all you can to protect them, and in humble faith and fervent prayer, commend them to your common Father. He can take care of them; but if for wise purposes he sees fit to allow them to be sold, this will afford you an opportunity of testifying openly, wherever you go, against the crime of *manstealing*. Such an act will be *clear robbery*, and if exposed, might, under the Divine direction, do the cause of Emancipation more good, than any thing that could happen, for, "He makes even the wrath of man to praise him, and the remainder of wrath he will restrain."[5]

I know that this doctrine of obeying *God*, rather than man, will be considered as dangerous, and heretical by many, but I am not afraid openly to avow it, because it is the doctrine of the Bible; but I would not be understood to advocate resistance to any law however oppressive, if, in obeying it, I was not obliged to commit *sin*. If for instance, there was a law, which

---

[5]"Surely the wrath of man shall praise thee:
The remainder of wrath shalt thou restrain."
Psalms 76:10.

imposed imprisonment or a fine upon me if I manumitted a slave, I would on no account resist that law, I would set the slave free, and then go to prison or pay the fine. If a law commands me to *sin I will break it;* if it calls me to *suffer*, I will let it take its course *unresistingly*. The doctrine of blind obedience and unqualified submission to *any human* power, whether civil or ecclesiastical, is the doctrine of despotism, and ought to have no place among Republicans and Christians.

But you will perhaps say, such a course of conduct would inevitably expose us to great suffering. Yes! my christian friends, I believe it would, but this will *not* excuse you or any one else for the neglect of *duty*. If Prophets and Apostles, Martyrs, and Reformers had not been willing to suffer for the truth's sake, where would the world have been now? If they had said, we cannot speak the truth, we cannot do what we believe is right, because the *laws of our country or public opinion are against us*, where would our holy religion have been now? . . .

But you may say we are *women*, how can *our* hearts endure persecution? And why not? Have not *women* stood up in all the dignity and strength of moral courage to be the leaders of the people, and to bear a faithful testimony for the truth whenever the providence of God has called them to do so? Are there no *women* in that noble army of martyrs who are now singing the song of Moses and the Lamb? Who led out the women of Israel from the house of bondage, striking the timbrel, and singing the song of deliverance on the banks of that sea whose waters stood up like walls of crystal to open a passage for their escape? It was a *woman;* Miriam, the prophetess, the sister of Moses and Aaron. Who went up with Barak to Kadesh to fight against Jabin, King of Canaan, into whose hand Israel had been sold because of their iniquities? It was a *woman!* Deborah the wife of Lapidoth, the judge, as well as the prophetess of that backsliding people; Judges iv, 9. Into whose hands was Sisera, the captain of Jabin's host delivered? Into the hand of a *woman*. Jael the wife of Heber! Judges vi, 21. Who dared to *speak the truth* concerning those judgments which were coming upon Judea, when Josiah, alarmed at finding that his people "had not kept the word of the Lord to do after all that was written in the book of the Law," sent to enquire of the Lord concerning these things? It was a *woman*. Huldah the prophetess, the wife of Shallum; 2, Chron. xxxiv, 22. Who was chosen to deliver the whole Jewish nation from that murderous decree of Persia's King, which wicked Haman had obtained by calumny and fraud? It was a *woman;* Esther the Queen; yes, weak and trembling *woman* was the instrument appointed by God, to reverse the bloody mandate of the eastern monarch, and save the *whole visible church* from destruction. What human voice first proclaimed to Mary that she should be the mother of our Lord? It was a *woman!* Elizabeth, the wife of Zacharias; Luke i, 42, 43. Who united with the good old Simeon in giving thanks publicly in the temple, when the child, Jesus, was presented there by his parents, "and spake of him to all them that looked for redemption in Jerusalem?" It was a *woman!* Anna the prophetess. Who first proclaimed Christ as the true Messiah in the streets of Samaria, once the capital of the ten tribes? It was a *woman!* Who ministered to the Son of God whilst on earth, a despised and persecuted Reformer, in the humble garb of a carpenter? They were *women!* Who followed the rejected King of Israel, as his fainting footsteps trod the road to Calvary? "A great company of people and of *women;*" and it is remarkable that to *them alone,* he turned and addressed the pathetic language, "Daughters of Jerusalem, weep not for me, but weep for yourselves and your children". . . .

To whom did he *first* appear after his resurrection? It was to a *woman!* Mary Magdalene; Mark xvi, 9. Who gathered with the apostles to wait at Jerusalem, in prayer and supplication, for "the promise of the Father;" the spiritual blessing of the Great High Priest of his Church, who had entered, *not* into the splendid temple of Solomon, there to offer the blood of bulls, and of goats, and the smoking censer upon the golden altar, but into Heaven itself, there to present his intercessions, after having "given himself for us, an offering and a sacrifice to God for a sweet smelling savor?" *Women* were among that holy company; Acts i, 14. And did *women* wait in vain? Did those who had ministered to his necessities, followed in his train, and wept at his crucifixion, wait in vain? No! No! Did the cloven tongues of fire descend upon the heads of *women* as well as men? Yes, my friends, "it sat upon *each one of them;*" Acts ii, 3. *Women* as well as men were to be living stones in the temple of grace, and therefore *their* heads were consecrated by the descent of the Holy Ghost as well as those of men. Were *women* recognized as fellow laborers in the gospel field? They were! Paul says in his epistle to the Philippians, "help those *women* who labored with me, in the gospel;" Phil. iv, 3. . . .

And what, I would ask in conclusion, have *women* done for the great and glorious cause of Emancipation? Who wrote that pamphlet which moved the heart of Wilberforce[6] to pray over the wrongs, and his tongue to plead the cause of the oppressed African? It was a *woman,* Elizabeth Heyrick.[7] Who labored assiduously to keep the sufferings of the slave continually before the British public? They were *women.* And how did they do it? By their needles, paint brushes and pens, by speaking the truth, and petitioning Parliament for the abolition of slavery. And what was the effect of their labors? Read it in the Emancipation bill of Great Britain. Read it, in the present state of her West India Colonies. Read it, in the impulse which has been given to the cause of freedom, in the United States of America. Have English women then done so much for the negro, and shall American women do nothing? Oh no! Already are there sixty female Anti-Slavery Societies in operation. These are doing just what the English women did, telling the story of the colored man's wrongs, praying for his deliverance, and presenting his kneeling image constantly before the public eye on bags and needle-books,

---

[6]The British abolitionist William Wilberforce (1759–1833), a member of Parliament, led the Committee to Abolish the Slave Trade.
[7]The English Quaker Elizabeth Heyrick first urged the doctrine of Immediate Emancipa-tion in an 1825 pamphlet; British abolitionists, who had previously argued for gradual emancipation, adopted her principles.

card-racks, pen-wipers, pin-cushions, &c. Even the children of the north are inscribing on their handy work, "May the points of our needles prick the slaveholder's conscience." Some of the reports of these Societies exhibit not only considerable talent, but a deep sense of religious duty, and a determination to persevere through evil as well as good report, until every scourge, and every shackle, is buried under the feet of the manumitted slave.

The Ladies' Anti-Slavery Society of Boston was called last fall, to a severe trial of their faith and constancy. They were mobbed by "the gentlemen of property and standing," in that city at their anniversary meeting, and their lives were jeoparded by an infuriated crowd; but their conduct on that occasion did credit to our sex, and affords a full assurance that they will *never* abandon the cause of the slave.... The Northern women may labor to produce a correct public opinion at the North, but if Southern women sit down in listless indifference and criminal idleness, public opinion cannot be rectified and purified at the South. It is manifest to every reflecting mind, that slavery must be abolished; the era in which we live, and the light which is overspreading the whole world on this subject, clearly show that the time cannot be distant when it will be done. Now there are only two ways in which it can be effected, by moral power or physical force, and it is for *you* to choose which of these you prefer. Slavery always has, and always will produce insurrections wherever it exists, because it is a violation of the natural order of things, and no human power can much longer perpetuate it....

Well may the poet exclaim in bitter sarcasm,

> *"The fustian flag that proudly waves*
> *In solemn mockery o'er a land of slaves."*[8]

Can you not, my friends, understand the signs of the times; do you not see the sword of retributive justice hanging over the South, or are you still slumbering at your posts?—Are there no Shiphrahs, no Puahs[9] among you, who will dare in Christian firmness and Christian meekness, to refuse to obey the *wicked laws* which require *woman to enslave, to degrade and to brutalize woman?* Are there no Miriams,[10] who would rejoice to lead out the captive daughters of the Southern States to liberty and light? Are there no Huldahs[11] there who will dare to *speak the truth* concerning the sins of the people and those judgments, which it requires no prophet's eye to see, must follow if repentance is not speedily sought? Is there no Esther[12] among you

---

[8]Thomas Moore (1779–1852), "To the Lord Viscount Forbes, Written from the City of Washington": "Where bastard Freedom waves/The fustian flag in mockery over slaves."

[9]Hebrew midwives who disobeyed Pharaoh's command to slay sons born to Hebrew women. Exodus 1:15–20.

[10]Sister of Moses, who led a dance celebrating the Lord's victory over the Egyptians. She is cited as an example of truly enthusiastic-worship of God. See Exodus 15:20–21.

[11]Speaks the Lord's prophecy of the destruction of the kingdom of Judah. 2 Chronicles 34:22–28.

[12]Intervened with her husband, the king of Persia, at considerable personal risk, to save Mordecai and all the Jews from the slaughter planned for them by Haman. See particularly Esther 4:16: "Then I will go to the King, though it is against the law; and if I perish, I perish."

who will plead for the poor devoted slave? Read the history of this Persian queen, it is full of instruction; she at first refused to plead for the Jews; but, hear the words of Mordecai, "Think not within thyself, that *thou* shalt escape in the king's house more than all the Jews, for *if thou altogether hold-est thy peace at this time*, then shall there enlargement and deliverance arise to the Jews from another place: but *thou and thy father's house shall be destroyed*." Listen, too, to her magnanimous reply to this powerful appeal; "*I will* go unto the king, which is *not* according to law, and if I perish, I perish." Yes! if there were but *one* Esther at the South, she *might* save her country from ruin; but let the Christian women there arise, as the Christian women of Great Britain did, in the majesty of moral power, and that salvation is certain. Let them embody themselves in societies, and send petitions up to their different legislatures, entreating their husbands, fathers, brothers and sons, to abolish the institution of slavery; no longer to subject *woman* to the scourge and the chain, to mental darkness and moral degradation; no longer to tear husbands from their wives, and children from their parents; no longer to make men, women, and children, work *without wages;* no longer to make their lives bitter in hard bondage; no longer to reduce *American citizens* to the abject condition of *slaves*, of "chattels personal;" no longer to barter the *image of God* in human shambles for corruptible things such as silver and gold.

The *women of the South can overthrow* this horrible system of oppression and cruelty, licentiousness and wrong. Such appeals to your legislatures would be irresistible, for there is something in the heart of man which *will bend under moral suasion*. There is a swift witness for truth in his bosom, which *will respond to truth* when it is uttered with calmness and dignity. If you could obtain but six signatures to such a petition in only one state, I would say, send up that petition, and be not in the least discouraged by the scoffs and jeers of the heartless, or the resolution of the house to lay it on the table. It will be a great thing if the subject can be introduced into your legislatures in any way, even by *women*, and *they* will be the most likely to introduce it there in the best possible manner, as a matter of *morals* and *religion*, not of expediency or politics. You may petition, too, the different ecclesiastical bodies of the slave states. Slavery must be attacked with the whole power of truth and the sword of the spirit. You must take it up on *Christian* ground, and fight against it with Christian weapons, whilst your feet are shod with the preparation of the gospel of peace. And *you are now* loudly called upon by the cries of the widow and the orphan, to arise and gird your-selves for this great moral conflict, with the whole armour of righteousness upon the right hand and on the left....

Sisters in Christ, I have done. As a Southerner, I have felt it was my duty to address you. I have endeavoured to set before you the exceeding sinful-ness of slavery, and to point you to the example of those noble women who have been raised up in the church to effect great revolutions, and to suffer for the truth's sake. I have appealed to your sympathies as women, to your sense of duty as *Christian women*. I have attempted to vindicate the

Abolitionists, to prove the entire safety of immediate Emancipation, and to plead the cause of the poor and oppressed. I have done—I have sowed the seeds of truth, but I well know, that even if an Apollos were to follow in my steps to water them, "*God only* can give the increase." To Him then who is able to prosper the work of his servant's hand, I commend this Appeal in fervent prayer, that as he "hath *chosen the weak things of the world*, to confound the things which are mighty," so He may cause His blessing, to descend and carry conviction to the hearts of many Lydias[13] through these speaking pages. Farewell—Count me not your "enemy because I have told you the truth," but believe me in unfeigned affection,

Your sympathizing Friend,
Angelina E. Grimké.
1836

■ HENRY HIGHLAND GARNET ■
1815–1882

Setting himself in direct opposition to Frederick Douglass, Henry Highland Garnet advocated for belligerent resistance to slavery, telling slaves to "Arise, arise! Strike for your lives and liberties." Unlike Garrisonian abolitionism that demanded immediate and nonviolent emancipation, Garnet called for the violent overthrow of the slave system, appealing to Christianity by calling slaves' submission "sinful" and by claiming that God would approve any measures slaves took to undo their bondage. Garnet, like David Walker before him, assured slaves and antislavery activists that God was on their side and cared only about the outcome of the struggle, not the methods of attack. While abolitionists initially rejected Garnet's position, his views became more acceptable during the 1850s as the violent removal of the slave system seemed inescapable as well as imminent.

Garnet was born a slave in 1815 on a Maryland plantation. His father, possibly the son of a Mandingo leader (as he told young Henry), engineered the family's escape to Wilmington, Delaware, in 1824 and then, with the aid of Quakers involved in the Underground Railroad, to New Hope, Pennsylvania. After settling in New York City in 1825, Garnet's father gave his family new names, including the new family name of Garnet (their original name was Trusty). In New York, Garnet attended the African Free School, joining soon-to-be luminaries such as Alexander Crummell (a leading black intellectual and advocate for black colonization), James McCune Smith (the first African American to receive a medical degree), and Ira Aldridge (a celebrated actor of international acclaim). After a few stints at sea in 1828 and 1829, Garnet continued his education at the Noyes Academy in Canaan, New Hampshire—before angry whites towed the schoolhouse away with oxen—and at the Oneida Institute in Whitesboro, New York, where he decided to become a Presbyterian minister. In 1843, the year of his ordination, Garnet attended the National Negro Convention in Buffalo. Although Garnet was by this time well known in abolitionist circles, the convention provided his first direct encounter with Frederick Douglass, and the meeting marked the beginning of a rivalry that persisted until the 1850s. Douglass, who embraced William Lloyd Garrison's approach to abolition as well as women's rights, believed that the use of violence was contrary to Christian teaching. In Garnet's view, abolition of slavery trumped any other cause, and in "An Address to the Slaves of the United States of America" he argued, like Douglass invoking Christian principles, that it was sinful *not* to use violence if the defeat of slavery demanded it. Though Douglass and Garnet were obviously opposed ideologically, Garnet's Buffalo speech fell only one vote short of publication by the convention, evidencing Garnet's powers of rhetorical suasion.

Garnet and Douglass disagreed not only on the issue of violence and emancipation, but also on black colonization and emigration. While Douglass vociferously opposed all attempts to remove African Americans from American soil (which was the general perception of most white-backed colonization projects), Garnet endorsed the establishment of a black nation for African Americans, and in 1858 founded the African Civilization Society, an organization dedicated to "the civilization and christianization of Africa, and of the descendants of African ancestors in any portion of the earth, wherever dispersed." Douglass opposed the principles of the African Civilization Society and, writing in his newspaper *The North Star*, argued that "No one idea has given rise to more oppression and persecution toward colored people of this country, than that which makes Africa, not America, their home. It is that wolfish idea that elbows us off the side walk, and denies us the rights of citizenship." Douglass did not attack Garnet's proselytizing leanings, but rather his insistence on creating an African homeland and his encouraging of business entrepreneurship there rather than in America where many African Americans were already established economically, socially, and culturally.

In the early 1850s, Garnet traveled to Germany and Britain to lecture, eventually moving to Jamaica for missionary work. He returned to the United States in 1855. By 1863, Garnet and Douglass were united in recruiting Negro troops for the Union Army. In February 1865, when Congress enacted the bill that became the Thirteenth Amendment, President Lincoln invited Garnet to deliver a sermon in the House of Representatives. He was the first African American to speak before that body. After serving as the president of Avery College in Pittsburgh and pastor of Shiloh Church in New York, Garnet, in declining health, petitioned for the position of minister to Liberia, a post he received in 1881. Garnet traveled to Liberia in December of 1881, but he died just six weeks later.

Garnet's voice may not have been as loud as Douglass's, but he embodied radical abolitionism, taking the principles of David Walker's *Appeal ... to the Coloured Citizens of the World* and quite literally giving them voice. Seen as possibly dangerous in the 1840s, by the outbreak of the Civil War, Garnet's principles and appeals for righteousness seemed essential and even prescient. Although black abolitionists such as Douglass have won the battle for historical memory, Garnet, along with contemporaries like Alexander Crummell, Martin Delaney, and Edward Wilmot Bylden, generated a global perspective on black oppression and attempted to pull the black diaspora into political cohesion.

Daniel Moos
Rhode Island College

PRIMARY WORKS

Herbert Aptheker, *A Documentary History of the Negro People in the United States*, 1971; Ernest Bormann, *Forerunners of Black Power*, 1971; Earl Ofari, *"Let Your Motto Be Resistance": The Life and Thought of Henry Highland Garnet*, 1972.

An Address to the Slaves of the United States of America, Buffalo, N.Y., 1843

Brethren and Fellow-Citizens:—Your brethren of the North, East, and West have been accustomed to meet together in National Conventions, to sympathize with each other, and to weep over your unhappy condition. In these meetings we have addressed all classes of the free, but we have never, until this time, sent a word of consolation and advice to you. We have been contented in sitting still and mourning over your sorrows, earnestly hoping that before this day your sacred liberties would have been restored. But, we have hoped in vain. Years have rolled on, and tens of thousands have been borne on streams of blood and tears, to the shores of eternity. While you have been oppressed, we have also been partakers with you; nor can we be free while you are enslaved. We, therefore, write to you as being bound with you.

Many of you are bound to us, not only by the ties of a common humanity, but we are connected by the more tender relations of parents, wives, husbands, children, brothers, and sisters, and friends. As such we most affectionately address you.

Slavery has fixed a deep gulf between you and us, and while it shuts out from you the relief and consolation which your friends would willingly render, it afflicts and persecutes you with a fierceness which we might not expect to see in the fiends of hell. But still the Almighty Father of mercies has left to us a glimmering ray of hope, which shines out like a lone star in a cloudy sky. Mankind are becoming wiser, and better—the oppressor's power is fading, and you, every day, are becoming better informed, and more numerous. Your grievances, brethren, are many. We shall not attempt, in this short address, to present to the world all the dark catalogue of this nation's sins, which have been committed upon an innocent people. Nor is it indeed necessary, for you feel them from day to day, and all the civilized world look upon them with amazement.

Two hundred and twenty-seven years ago, the first of our injured race were brought to the shores of America. They came not with glad spirits to select their homes in the New World. They came not with their own consent, to find an unmolested enjoyment of the blessings of this fruitful soil. The first dealings they had with men calling themselves Christians, exhibited to them the worst features of corrupt and sordid hearts: and convinced them that no cruelty is too great, no villainy and no robbery too abhorrent for even enlightened men to perform, when influenced by avarice and lust. Neither did they come flying upon the wings of Liberty, to a land of freedom. But they came with broken hearts, from their beloved native land, and were doomed to unrequited toil and deep degradation. Nor did the evil of their bondage end at their emancipation by death. Succeeding generations inherited their chains, and millions have come from eternity into time, and have returned again to the world of spirits, cursed and ruined by American slavery.

The propagators of the system, or their immediate ancestors, very soon discovered its growing evil, and its tremendous wickedness, and secret promises were made to destroy it. The gross inconsistency of a people holding slaves, who had themselves "ferried o'er the wave" for freedom's sake, was too apparent to be entirely overlooked. The voice of Freedom cried, "Emancipate your slaves." Humanity supplicated with tears for the deliverance of the children of Africa. Wisdom urged her solemn plea. The bleeding captive pleaded his innocence, and pointed to Christianity who stood weeping at the cross. Jehovah frowned upon the nefarious institution, and thunderbolts, red with vengeance, struggled to leap forth to blast the guilty wretches who maintained it. But all was vain. Slavery had stretched its dark wings of death over the land, the Church stood silently by—the priests prophesied falsely, and the people loved to have it so. Its throne is established, and now it reigns triumphant.

Nearly three millions of your fellow-citizens are prohibited by law and public opinion (which in this country is stronger than law) from reading the Book of Life. Your intellect has been destroyed as much as possible, and every ray of light they have attempted to shut out from your minds. The oppressors themselves have become involved in the ruin. They have become weak, sensual, and rapacious—they have cursed you—they have cursed themselves—they have cursed the earth which they have trod.

The colonists threw the blame upon England. They said that the mother country entailed the evil upon them, and that they would rid themselves of it if they could. The world thought they were sincere, and the philanthropic pitied them. But time soon tested their sincerity. In a few years the colonists grew strong, and severed themselves from the British Government. Their independence was declared, and they took their station among the sovereign powers of the earth. The declaration was a glorious document. Sages admired it, and the patriotic of every nation reverenced the God-like sentiments which it contained. When the power of Government returned to their hands, did they emancipate the slaves? No; they rather added new links to our chains. Were they ignorant of the principles of Liberty? Certainly they were not. The sentiments of their revolutionary orators fell in burning eloquence upon their hearts, and with one voice they cried, *Liberty or Death*.[1] Oh what a sentence was that! It ran from soul to soul like electric

---

[1]A reference to Patrick Henry's speech to the Virginia House of Burgesses: "I know not what course others may take, but as for me, give me liberty or give me death."

fire, and nerved the arm of thousands to fight in the holy cause of Freedom. Among the diversity of opinions that are entertained in regard to physical resistance, there are but a few found to gainsay that stern declaration. We are among those who do not.

Slavery! How much misery is comprehended in that single word. What mind is there that does not shrink from its direful effects? Unless the image of God be obliterated from the soul, all men cherish the love of Liberty. The nice discerning political economist does not regard the sacred right more than the untutored African who roams in the wilds of Congo. Nor has the one more right to the full enjoyment of his freedom than the other. In every man's mind the good seeds of liberty are planted, and he who brings his fellow down so low, as to make him contented with a condition of slavery, commits the highest crime against God and man. Brethren, your oppressors aim to do this. They endeavor to make you as much like brutes as possible. When they have blinded the eyes of your mind—when they have embittered the sweet waters of life—when they have shut out the light which shines from the word of God—then, and not till then, has American slavery done its perfect work.

To such Degradation it is sinful in the Extreme for you to make voluntary Submission. The divine commandments you are in duty bound to reverence and obey. If you do not obey them, you will surely meet with the displeasure of the Almighty. He requires you to love him supremely, and your neighbor as yourself—to keep the Sabbath day holy—to search the Scriptures—and bring up your children with respect for his laws, and to worship no other God but him. But slavery sets all these at nought, and hurls defiance in the face of Jehovah. The forlorn condition in which you are placed, does not destroy your moral obligation to God. You are not certain of heaven, because you suffer yourselves to remain in a state of slavery, where you cannot obey the commandments of the Sovereign of the universe. If the ignorance of slavery is a passport to heaven, then it is a blessing, and no curse, and you should rather desire its perpetuity than its abolition. God will not receive slavery, nor ignorance, nor any other state of mind, for love and obedience to him. Your condition does not absolve you from your moral obligation. The diabolical injustice by which your liberties are cloven down, *neither God, nor angels, or just men, command you to suffer for a single moment. Therefore it is your solemn and imperative duty to use every means, both moral, intellectual, and physical, that promises success.* If a band of heathen men should attempt to enslave a race of Christians, and to place their children under the influence of some false religion, surely, Heaven would frown upon the men who would not resist such aggression, even to death. If, on the other hand, a band of Christians should attempt to enslave a race of heathen men, and to entail slavery upon them, and to keep them in heathenism in the midst of Christianity, the God of heaven would smile upon every effort which the injured might make to disenthral themselves.

Brethren, it is as wrong for your lordly oppressors to keep you in slavery, as it was for the man thief to steal our ancestors from the coast of

Africa. You should therefore now use the same manner of resistance, as would have been just in our ancestors, when the bloody footprints of the first remorseless soul-thief was placed upon the shores of our fatherland. The humblest peasant is as free in the sight of God as the proudest monarch that ever swayed a sceptre. Liberty is a spirit sent out from God, and like its great Author, is no respecter of persons.

Brethren, the time has come when you must act for yourselves. It is an old and true saying that, "if hereditary bondmen would be free, they must themselves strike the blow." You can plead your own cause, and do the work of emancipation better than any others. The nations of the old world are moving in the great cause of universal freedom, and some of them at least will, ere long, do you justice. The combined powers of Europe have placed their broad seal of disapprobation upon the African slave-trade. But in the slave-holding parts of the United States, the trade is as brisk as ever. They buy and sell you as though you were brute beasts. The North has done much—her opinion of slavery in the abstract is known. But in regard to the South, we adopt the opinion of the *New York Evangelist*—"We have advanced so far, that the cause apparently waits for a more effectual door to be thrown open than has been yet." We are about to point you to that more effectual door. Look around you, and behold the bosoms of your loving wives heaving with untold agonies! Hear the cries of your poor children! Remember the stripes your fathers bore. Think of the torture and disgrace of your noble mothers. Think of your wretched sisters, loving virtue and purity, as they are driven into concubinage and are exposed to the unbridled lusts of incarnate devils. Think of the undying glory that hangs around the ancient name of Africa:—and forget not that you are native-born American citizens, and as such, you are justly entitled to all the rights that are granted to the freest. Think how many tears you have poured out upon the soil which you have cultivated with unrequited toil and enriched with your blood; and then go to your lordly enslavers and tell them plainly, that you *are determined to be free*. Appeal to their sense of justice, and tell them that they have no more right to oppress you, than you have to enslave them. Entreat them to remove the grievous burdens which they have imposed upon you, and to remunerate you for your labor. Promise them renewed diligence in the cultivation of the soil, if they will render to you an equivalent for your services. Point them to the increase of happiness and prosperity in the British West-Indies since the Act of Emancipation.[2] Tell them in language which they cannot misunderstand, of the exceeding sinfulness of slavery, and of a future judgment, and of the righteous retributions of an indignant God. Inform them that all you desire is *freedom*, and that nothing else will suffice. Do this, and for ever after cease to toil for the heartless tyrants, who give you no other reward but stripes and abuse. If they then

[2]The Act freeing the slaves in the British West Indies had been passed ten years before, in 1833.

commence the work of death, they, and not you, will be responsible for the consequences. You had far better all die—*die immediately*, than live slaves, and entail your wretchedness upon your posterity. If you would be free in this generation, here is your only hope. However much you and all of us may desire it, there is not much hope of redemption without the shedding of blood. If you must bleed, let it all come at once—rather *die freemen, than live to be the slaves*. It is impossible, like the children of Israel, to make a grand exodus from the land of bondage. The Pharaohs are on both sides of the blood-red waters! You cannot move *en masse*, to the dominions of the British Queen—nor can you pass through Florida and overrun Texas, and at last find peace in Mexico. The propagators of American slavery are spending their blood and treasure, that they may plant the black flag in the heart of Mexico and riot in the halls of the Montezumas. In the language of the Rev. Robert Hall, when addressing the volunteers of Bristol, who were rushing forth to repel the invasion of Napoleon, who threatened to lay waste the fair homes of England, "Religion is too much interested in your behalf, not to shed over you her most gracious influences."

You will not be compelled to spend much time in order to become inured to hardships. From the first moment that you breathed the air of heaven, you have been accustomed to nothing else but hardships. The heroes of the American Revolution were never put upon harder fare than a peck of corn and a few herrings per week. You have not become enervated by the luxuries of life. Your sternest energies have been beaten out upon the anvil of severe trial. Slavery has done this, to make you subservient to its own purposes; but it has done more than this, it has prepared you for any emergency. If you receive good treatment, it is what you could hardly expect; if you meet with pain, sorrow, and even death, these are the common lot of the slaves.

Fellow-men! patient sufferers! behold your dearest rights crushed to the earth! See your sons murdered, and your wives, mothers and sisters doomed to prostitution. In the name of the merciful God, and by all that life is worth, let it no longer be a debatable question, whether it is better to choose *Liberty* or *death*.

In 1822, Denmark Veazie, of South Carolina, formed a plan for the liberation of his fellow-men.[3] In the whole history of human efforts to overthrow slavery, a more complicated and tremendous plan was never formed. He was betrayed by the treachery of his own people, and died a martyr to freedom. Many a brave hero fell, but history, faithful to her high trust, will transcribe his name on the same monument with Moses, Hampden, Tell, Bruce and Wallace, Toussaint L'Ouverture, Lafayette and Washington. That tremendous movement shook the whole empire of slavery. The guilty soul-thieves were overwhelmed with fear. It is a matter of fact, that at that time, and in consequence of the threatened revolution, the slave States talked

---

[3]Denmark Vesey led the organization of a planned slave insurrection in Charleston, South Carolina, in 1822; it was betrayed before it was put into action.

strongly of emancipation. But they blew but one blast of the trumpet of freedom, and then laid it aside. As these men became quiet, the slaveholders ceased to talk about emancipation: and now behold your condition today! Angels sigh over it, and humanity has long since exhausted her tears in weeping on your account!

The patriotic Nathaniel Turner[4] followed Denmark Veazie. He was goaded to desperation by wrong and injustice. By despotism, his name has been recorded on the list of infamy, and future generations will remember him among the noble and brave.

Next arose the immortal Joseph Cinque, the hero of the *Amistad*.[5] He was a native African, and by the help of God he emancipated a whole shipload of his fellow-men on the high seas. And he now sings of liberty on the sunny hills of Africa and beneath his native palm-trees, where he hears the lion roar and feels himself as free as that king of the forest.

Next arose Madison Washington,[6] that bright star of freedom, and took his station in the constellation of true heroism. He was a slave on board the brig *Creole*, of Richmond, bound to New Orleans, that great slave mart, with a hundred and four others. Nineteen struck for liberty or death. But one life was taken, and the whole were emancipated, and the vessel was carried into Nassau, New Providence.

Noble men! Those who have fallen in freedom's conflict, their memories will be cherished by the true-hearted and the God-fearing in all future generations; those who are living, their names are surrounded by a halo of glory.

Brethren, arise, arise! Strike for your lives and liberties. Now is the day and the hour. Let every slave throughout the land do this, and the days of slavery are numbered. You cannot be more oppressed than you have been— you cannot suffer greater cruelties than you have already. *Rather die freemen than live to be slaves*. Remember that you are *four millions!*

It is in your power so to torment the God-cursed slaveholders, that they will be glad to let you go free. If the scale was turned, and black men were the masters and white men the slaves, every destructive agent and element would be employed to lay the oppressor low. Danger and death would hang over their heads day and night. Yes, the tyrants would meet with plagues more terrible than those of Pharaoh. But you are a patient people. You act as though you were made for the special use of these devils. You act as though your daughters were born to pamper the lusts of your masters and overseers. And worse than all, you tamely submit while your lords tear your wives from your embraces and defile them before your eyes. In the name of

[4]See the essay by Thomas Wentworth Higginson later in this section.
[5]The *Amistad* was a Spanish schooner that was seized, in the summer of 1839, by its "cargo" of fifty-four slaves, led by Joseph Cinque. By a ruse, the whites who had been spared to navigate the ship back to Africa steered it instead to Long Island, where the Africans were seized and charged with piracy. After an eighteen-month legal battle, the Supreme Court freed the Africans and they were able to return to Mendi, their homeland.
[6]See Frederick Douglass's story "The Heroic Slave."

God, we ask, are you men? Where is the blood of your fathers? Has it all run out of your veins? Awake, awake; millions of voices are calling you! Your dead fathers speak to you from their graves. Heaven, as with a voice of thunder, calls on you to arise from the dust.

AMERICAN ANTI-SLAVERY ALMANAC, FOR 1840, BEING BISSEXTILE OR LEAP-YEAR, AND THE 64TH OF AMERICAN INDEPENDENCE. CALCULATED FOR NEW YORK; ADAPTED TO THE NORTHERN AND MIDDLE STATES.

NORTHERN HOSPITALITY—NEW YORK NINE MONTHS' LAW.
The slave steps out of the slave-state, and his chains fall. A free state, with another chain, stands ready to re-enslave him.

Thus saith the Lord, Deliver him that is spoiled out of the hands of the oppressor.

NEW YORK:
PUBLISHED BY THE AMERICAN ANTI-SLAVERY SOCIETY, NO. 143 NASSAU STREET.

Let your motto be resistance! *resistance! resistance!* No oppressed people have ever secured their liberty without resistance. What kind of resistance you had better make, you must decide by the circumstances that surround you, and according to the suggestion of expediency. Brethren, adieu! Trust in the living God. Labor for the peace of the human race, and remember that you are *four millions.*

1848

FREDERICK DOUGLASS
1818–1895

Narrative of the Life of Frederick Douglass, an American Slave[1]

Preface [William Lloyd Garrison][2]

In the month of August, 1841, I attended an anti-slavery convention in Nantucket, at which it was my happiness to become acquainted with FREDERICK DOUGLASS, the writer of the following Narrative. He was a stranger to nearly every member of that body; but, having recently made his escape from the southern prisonhouse of bondage, and feeling his curiosity excited to ascertain the principles and measures of the abolitionists,—of whom he had heard a somewhat vague description while he was a slave,—he was induced to give his attendance, on the occasion alluded to, though at that time a resident in New Bedford.

Fortunate, most fortunate occurrence!—fortunate for the millions of his manacled brethren, yet panting for deliverance from their awful thraldom!—fortunate for the cause of negro emancipation, and of universal liberty!—fortunate for the land of his birth, which he has already done so much to save and bless!—fortunate for a large circle of friends and acquaintances, whose sympathy and affection he has strongly secured by the many sufferings he has endured, by his virtuous traits of character, by his ever-abiding remembrance of those who are in bonds, as being bound with them!—fortunate for the multitudes, in various parts of our republic, whose minds he has enlightened on the subject of slavery, and who have been melted to tears by his pathos, or roused to virtuous indignation by his stirring eloquence against the enslavers of men!—fortunate for himself, as it at

[1]First printed in May 1845 by the Anti-Slavery Office in Boston; their 1847 edition is the source of the present text. The words "Written by Himself" were included in the title.

[2]For information about Garrison, see the selection from his work elsewhere in this volume.

once brought him into the field of public usefulness, "gave the world assurance of a man," quickened the slumbering energies of his soul, and consecrated him to the great work of breaking the rod of the oppressor, and letting the oppressed go free!

I shall never forget his first speech at the convention—the extraordinary emotion it excited in my own mind—the powerful impression it created upon a crowded auditory, completely taken by surprise—the applause which followed from the beginning to the end of his felicitous remarks. I think I never hated slavery so intensely as at that moment; certainly, my perception of the enormous outrage which is inflicted by it, on the godlike nature of its victims, was rendered far more clear than ever. There stood one, in physical proportion and stature commanding and exact—in intellect richly endowed—in natural eloquence a prodigy—in soul manifestly "created but a little lower than the angels"[3]—yet a slave, ay, a fugitive slave,—trembling for his safety, hardly daring to believe that on the American soil, a single white person could be found who would befriend him at all hazards, for the love of God and humanity! Capable of high attainments as an intellectual and moral being—needing nothing but a comparatively small amount of cultivation to make him an ornament to society and a blessing to his race—by the law of the land, by the voice of the people, by the terms of the slave code, he was only a piece of property, a beast of burden, a chattel personal, nevertheless!

A beloved friend from New Bedford[4] prevailed on Mr. DOUGLASS to address the convention: He came forward to the platform with a hesitancy and embarrassment, necessarily the attendants of a sensitive mind in such a novel position. After apologizing for his ignorance, and reminding the audience that slavery was a poor school for the human intellect and heart, he proceeded to narrate some of the facts in his own history as a slave, and in the course of his speech gave utterance to many noble thoughts and thrilling reflections. As soon as he had taken his seat, filled with hope and admiration, I rose, and declared that PATRICK HENRY,[5] of revolutionary fame, never made a speech more eloquent in the cause of liberty, than the one we had just listened to from the lips of that hunted fugitive. So I believed at that time—such is my belief now. I reminded the audience of the peril which surrounded this self-emancipated young man at the North,—even in Massachusetts, on the soil of the Pilgrim Fathers, among the descendants of revolutionary sires; and I appealed to them, whether they would ever allow him to be carried back into slavery,—law or no law, constitution or no constitution. The response was unanimous and in thunder-tones—"NO!" "Will you succor and protect him as a brother-man—a resident of the old Bay

---

[3]Psalm 8:5.

[4]William C. Coffin, one of the town's leading abolitionists.

[5]Henry (1736–1799), the well-known statesman and orator, was perhaps best remembered for his March 23, 1775, speech to the Virginia House of Delegates, which included the following: "Is life so dear or peace so sweet as to be purchased at the price of chains and slavery? Forbid it, Almighty God! I know not what course others may take; but as for me, give me liberty, or give me death!"

State."[6] "YES!" shouted the whole mass, with an energy so startling, that the ruthless tyrants south of Mason and Dixon's line might almost have heard the mighty burst of feeling, and recognized it as the pledge of an invincible determination, on the part of those who gave it, never to betray him that wanders, but to hide the outcast, and firmly to abide the consequences.

It was at once deeply impressed upon my mind, that, if Mr. DOUGLASS could be persuaded to consecrate his time and talents to the promotion of the anti-slavery enterprise, a powerful impetus would be given to it, and a stunning blow at the same time inflicted on northern prejudice against a colored complexion. I therefore endeavored to instill hope and courage into his mind, in order that he might dare to engage in a vocation so anomalous and responsible for a person in his situation; and I was seconded in this effort by warm-hearted friends, especially by the late General Agent of the Massachusetts Anti-Slavery Society, Mr. JOHN A. COLLINS, whose judgment in this instance entirely coincided with my own. At first, he could give no encouragement; with unfeigned diffidence, he expressed his conviction that he was not adequate to the performance of so great a task; the path marked out was wholly an untrodden one; he was sincerely apprehensive that he should do more harm than good. After much deliberation, however, he consented to make a trial; and ever since that period, he has acted as a lecturing agent, under the auspices either of the American or the Massachusetts Anti-Slavery Society. In labors he has been most abundant; and his success in combating prejudice, in gaining proselytes, in agitating the public mind, has far surpassed the most sanguine expectations that were raised at the commencement of his brilliant career. He has borne himself with gentleness and meekness, yet with true manliness of character. As a public speaker, he excels in pathos, wit, comparison, imitation, strength of reasoning, and fluency of language. There is in him that union of head and heart, which is indispensable to an enlightenment of the heads and a winning of the hearts of others. May his strength continue to be equal to his day! May he continue to "grow in grace, and in the knowledge of God," that he may be increasingly serviceable in the cause of bleeding humanity, whether at home or abroad!

It is certainly a very remarkable fact, that one of the most efficient advocates of the slave population, now before the public, is a fugitive slave, in the person of FREDERICK DOUGLASS; and that the free colored population of the United States are as ably represented by one of their own number, in the person of CHARLES LENOX REMOND,[7] whose eloquent appeals have extorted the highest applause of multitudes on both sides of the Atlantic. Let the calumniators of the colored race despise themselves for their baseness and illiberality of spirit, and henceforth cease to talk of the natural

---

[6]Massachusetts.

[7]Remond (1810–1873), one of the first black abolitionist lecturers, had returned from Britain and Ireland in 1842 and spoken on a number of occasions with Douglass.

inferiority of those who require nothing but time and opportunity to attain to the highest point of human excellence.

It may, perhaps, be fairly questioned, whether any other portion of the population of the earth could have endured the privations, sufferings and horrors of slavery, without having become more degraded in the scale of humanity than the slaves of African descent. Nothing has been left undone to cripple their intellects, darken their minds, debase their moral nature, obliterate all traces of their relationship to mankind; and yet how wonderfully they have sustained the mighty load of a most frightful bondage, under which they have been groaning for centuries! To illustrate the effect of slavery on the white man,—to show that he has no powers of endurance, in such a condition, superior to those of his black brother,—DANIEL O'CONNELL,[8] the distinguished advocate of universal emancipation, and the mightiest champion of prostrate but not conquered Ireland, relates the following anecdote in a speech delivered by him in the Conciliation Hall, Dublin, before the Loyal National Repeal Association, March 31, 1845. "No matter," said Mr. O'CONNELL, "under what specious term it may disguise itself, slavery is still hideous. *It has a natural, an inevitable tendency to brutalize every noble faculty of man.* An American sailor, who was cast away on the shore of Africa, where he was kept in slavery for three years, was at the expiration of that period, found to be imbruted and stultified—he had lost all reasoning power; and having forgotten his native language, could only utter some savage gibberish between Arabic and English, which nobody could understand, and which even he himself found difficulty in pronouncing. So much for the humanizing influence of THE DOMESTIC INSTITUTION!" Admitting this to have been an extraordinary case of mental deterioration, it proves at least that the white slave can sink as low in the scale of humanity as the black one.

Mr. DOUGLASS has very properly chosen to write his own Narrative, in his own style, and according to the best of his ability, rather than to employ some one else. It is, therefore, entirely his own production; and, considering how long and dark was the career he had to run as a slave,—how few have been his opportunities to improve his mind since he broke his iron fetters,—it is, in my judgment, highly creditable to his head and heart. He who can peruse it without a tearful eye, a heaving breast, an afflicted spirit,—without being filled with an unutterable abhorrence of slavery and all its abettors, and animated with a determination to seek the the immediate overthrow of that execrable system,—without trembling for the fate of this country in the hands of a righteous God, who is ever on the side of the oppressed, and whose arm is not shortened that it cannot save,—must have a flinty heart, and be qualified to act the part of a trafficker "in slaves and the souls of men." I am confident that it is essentially true in all its statements; that nothing has been set down in malice, nothing exaggerated, nothing drawn from the imagination; that it comes short of the reality,

---

[8] Daniel O'Connell (1775–1847), Irish leader often called the "Liberator," was elected a member of Parliament but took his seat only after Catholic emancipation in 1829.

rather than overstates a single fact in regard to SLAVERY AS IT IS.[9] The experience of FREDERICK DOUGLASS, as a slave, was not a peculiar one; his lot was not especially a hard one; his case may be regarded as a very fair specimen of the treatment of slaves in Maryland, in which State it is conceded that they are better fed and less cruelly treated than in Georgia, Alabama, or Louisiana. Many have suffered incomparably more, while very few on the plantations have suffered less, than himself. Yet how deplorable was his situation! what terrible chastisements were inflicted upon his person! what still more shocking outrages were perpetrated upon his mind! with all his noble powers and sublime aspirations, how like a brute was he treated, even by those professing to have the same mind in them that was in Christ Jesus! to what dreadful liabilities was he continually subjected! how destitute of friendly counsel and aid, even in his greatest extremities! how heavy was the midnight of woe which shrouded in blackness the last ray of hope, and filled the future with terror and gloom! what longings after freedom took possession of his breast, and how his misery augmented, in proportion as he grew reflective and intelligent,—thus demonstrating that a happy slave is an extinct man! how he thought, reasoned, felt, under the lash of the driver, with the chains upon his limbs! what perils he encountered in his endeavors to escape from his horrible doom! and how signal have been his deliverance and preservation in the midst of a nation of pitiless enemies!

This Narrative contains many affecting incidents, many passages of great eloquence and power; but I think the most thrilling one of them all is the description DOUGLASS gives of his feelings, as he stood soliloquizing respecting his fate, and the chances of his one day being a freeman, on the banks of the Chesapeake Bay—viewing the receding vessels as they flew with their white wings before the breeze, and apostrophizing them as animated by the living spirit of freedom. Who can read that passage, and be insensible to its pathos and sublimity? Compressed into it is a whole Alexandrian library[10] of thought, feeling, and sentiment—all that can, all that need be urged, in the form of expostulation, entreaty, rebuke, against that crime of crimes,—making man the property of his fellow-man! O, how accursed is that system, which entombs the godlike mind of man, defaces the divine image, reduces those who by creation were crowned with glory and honor to a level with four-footed beasts, and exalts the dealer in human flesh above all that is called God! Why should its existence be prolonged one hour? Is it not evil, only evil, and that continually? What does its presence imply but the absence of all fear of God, all regard for man, on the part of the people of the United States? Heaven speed its eternal overthrow!

So profoundly ignorant of the nature of slavery are many persons, that they are stubbornly incredulous whenever they read or listen to any recital of the cruelties which are daily inflicted on its victims. They do not deny

---

[9]The title of a very important sourcebook and antislavery tract (1839) by Theodore Dwight Weld.

[10]The library at Alexandria, in Egypt, contained what may well have been the greatest collection in the ancient world.

that the slaves are held as property; but that terrible fact seems to convey to their minds no idea of injustice, exposure to outrage, or savage barbarity. Tell them of cruel scourgings, of mutilations and brandings, of scenes of pollution and blood, of the banishment of all light and knowledge, and they affect to be greatly indignant at such enormous exaggerations, such wholesale misstatements, such abominable libels on the character of the southern planters! As if all these direful outrages were not the natural results of slavery! As if it were less cruel to reduce a human being to the condition of a thing, than to give him a severe flagellation, or to deprive him of necessary food and clothing! As if whips, chains, thumb-screws, paddles, bloodhounds, overseers, drivers, patrols, were not all indispensable to keep the slaves down, and to give protection to their ruthless oppressors! As if, when the marriage institution is abolished, concubinage, adultery, and incest, must not necessarily abound; when all the rights of humanity are annihilated, any barrier remains to protect the victim from the fury of the spoiler; when absolute power is assumed over life and liberty, it will not be wielded with destructive sway! Skeptics of this character abound in society. In some few instances, their incredulity arises from a want of reflection; but, generally, it indicates a hatred of the light, a desire to shield slavery from the assaults of its foes, a contempt of the colored race, whether bond or free. Such will try to discredit the shocking tales of slaveholding cruelty which are recorded in this truthful Narrative; but they will labor in vain. Mr. DOUGLASS has frankly disclosed the place of his birth, the names of those who claimed ownership in his body and soul, and the names also of those who committed the crimes which he has alleged against them. His statements, therefore, may easily be disproved, if they are untrue.

In the course of his Narrative, he relates two instances of murderous cruelty,—in one of which a planter deliberately shot a slave belonging to a neighboring plantation, who had unintentionally gotten within his lordly domain in quest of fish; and in the other, an overseer blew out the brains of a slave who had fled to a stream of water to escape a bloody scourging. Mr. DOUGLASS states that in neither of these instances was any thing done by way of legal arrest or judicial investigation. The Baltimore American, of March 17, 1845, relates a similar case of atrocity, perpetrated with similar impunity—as follows:—"*Shooting a Slave.*—We learn, upon the authority of a letter from Charles county, Maryland, received by a gentleman of this city, that a young man, named Matthews, a nephew of General Matthews, and whose father, it is believed, holds an office at Washington, killed one of the slaves upon his father's farm by shooting him. The letter states that young Matthews had been left in charge of the farm; that he gave an order to the servant, which was disobeyed, when he proceeded to the house, *obtained a gun, and, returning, shot the servant.* He immediately, the letter continues, fled to his father's residence, where he still remains unmolested."—Let it never be forgotten, that no slaveholder or overseer can be convicted of any outrage perpetrated on the person of a slave, however diabolical it may be, on the testimony of colored witnesses, whether bond or free. By the slave code, they are adjudged to be as incompetent to testify against a white man, as though they were indeed a part of the brute creation. Hence, there is no legal protection in fact, whatever there may be in form, for the slave population; and any amount of cruelty may be inflicted on them with impunity. Is it possible for the human mind to conceive of a more horrible state of society?

The effect of a religious profession on the conduct of southern masters is vividly described in the following Narrative, and shown to be any thing but salutary. In the nature of the case, it must be in the highest degree pernicious. The testimony of Mr. DOUGLASS, on this point, is sustained by a cloud of witnesses, whose veracity is unimpeachable. "A slaveholder's profession of Christianity is a palpable imposture. He is a felon of the highest grade. He is a man-stealer. It is of no importance what you put in the other scale."

Reader! are you with the man-stealers in sympathy and purpose, or on the side of their down-trodden victims? If with the former, then are you the foe of God and man. If with the latter, what are you prepared to do and dare in their behalf? Be faithful, be vigilant, be untiring in your efforts to break every yoke, and let the oppressed go free. Come what may—cost what it may—inscribe on the banner which you unfurl to the breeze, as your religious and political motto—"NO COMPROMISE WITH SLAVERY! NO UNION WITH SLAVEHOLDERS!"

WM. LLOYD GARRISON

Boston, *May* 1, 1845.

Letter from Wendell Phillips, Esq.[11]

BOSTON, *April* 22, 1845.

My Dear Friend:

You remember the old fable of "The Man and the Lion," where the lion complained that he should not be so misrepresented "when the lions wrote history."

I am glad the time has come when the "lions write history." We have been left long enough to gather the character of slavery from the involuntary evidence of the masters. One might, indeed, rest sufficiently satisfied with what, it is evident, must be, in general, the results of such a relation, without seeking farther to find whether they have followed in every instance. Indeed, those who stare at the half-peck of corn a week, and love to count the lashes on the slave's back, are seldom the "stuff" out of which reformers and abolitionists are to be made. I remember that, in 1838, many were waiting for the results of the West India experiment,[12] before they could come into our ranks. Those "results" have come long ago; but, alas! few of that number have come with them, as converts. A man must be disposed to judge of emancipation by other tests than whether it has increased

[11]For information about Phillips, see the headnote to his work later in this section.
[12]Great Britain had abolished the African slave trade and then, as of August 1, 1834, had decreed an end to slavery in the British West Indies, thus inaugurating a period of significant change for the newly freed black population of the islands.

the produce of sugar,—and to hate slavery for other reasons than because it starves men and whips women,—before he is ready to lay the first stone of his anti-slavery life.

I was glad to learn, in your story, how early the most neglected of God's children waken to a sense of their rights, and of the injustice done them. Experience is a keen teacher; and long before you had mastered your A B C, or knew where the "white sails" of the Chesapeake were bound, you began, I see, to gauge the wretchedness of the slave, not by his hunger and want, not by his lashes and toil, but by the cruel and blighting death which gathers over his soul.

In connection with this, there is one circumstance which makes your recollections peculiarly valuable, and renders your early insight the more remarkable. You come from that part of the country where we are told slavery appears with its fairest features. Let us hear, then, what it is at its best estate—gaze on its bright side, if it has one; and then imagination may task her powers to add dark lines to the picture, as she travels southward to that (for the colored man) Valley of the Shadow of Death, where the Mississippi sweeps along.

Again, we have known you long, and can put the most entire confidence in your truth, candor, and sincerity. Every one who has heard you speak has felt, and, I am confident, every one who reads your book will feel, persuaded that you give them a fair specimen of the whole truth. No one-sided portrait,—no wholesale complaints,—but strict justice done, whenever individual kindliness has neutralized, for a moment, the deadly system with which it was strangely allied. You have been with us, too, some years, and can fairly compare the twilight of rights, which your race enjoy at the North, with that "noon of night" under which they labor south of Mason and Dixon's line. Tell us whether, after all, the half-free colored man of Massachusetts is worse off than the pampered slave of the rice swamps!

In reading your life, no one can say that we have unfairly picked out some rare specimens of cruelty. We know that the bitter drops, which even you have drained from the cup, are no incidental aggravations, no individual ills, but such as must mingle always and necessarily in the lot of every slave. They are the essential ingredients, not the occasional results, of the system.

After all, I shall read your book with trembling for you. Some years ago, when you were beginning to tell me your real name and birthplace, you may remember I stopped you, and preferred to remain ignorant of all. With the exception of a vague description, so I continued, till the other day, when you read me your memoirs. I hardly knew, at the time, whether to thank you or not for the sight of them, when I reflected that it was still dangerous, in Massachusetts, for honest men to tell their names! They say the fathers, in 1776, signed the Declaration of Independence with the halter about their necks. You, too, publish your declaration of freedom with danger compassing you around. In all the broad lands which the Constitution of the United States overshadows, there is no single spot,—however narrow or desolate,—where a fugitive slave can plant himself and say, "I am safe." The whole armory of Northern Law has no shield for you. I am free to say that, in your place, I should throw the MS. into the fire.

You, perhaps, may tell your story in safety, endeared as you are to so many warm hearts by rare gifts, and a still rare devotion of them to the service of others. But it will be owing only to your labors, and the fearless efforts of those who, trampling the laws and Constitution of the country under their feet, are determined that they will "hide the outcast," and that their hearths shall be, spite of the law, an asylum for the oppressed, if, some time or other, the humblest may stand in our streets, and bear witness in safety against the cruelties of which he has been the victim.

Yet it is sad to think, that these very throbbing hearts which welcome your story, and form your best safeguard in telling it, are all beating contrary to the "statute in such case made and provided." Go on, my dear friend, till you, and those who, like you, have been saved, so as by fire, from the dark prisonhouse, shall stereotype these free, illegal pulses into statutes; and New England, cutting loose from a blood-stained Union, shall glory in being the house of refuge for the oppressed;—till we no longer merely "*hide the outcast*," or make a merit of standing idly by while he is hunted in our midst; but, consecrating anew the soil of the Pilgrims as an asylum for the oppressed, proclaim our *welcome* to the slave so loudly, that the tones shall reach every hut in the Carolinas, and make the broken-hearted bondman leap up at the thought of old Massachusetts.

God speed the day!

Till then, and ever,
Yours truly,
WENDELL PHILLIPS

Chapter I

I was born in Tuckahoe, near Hillsborough, and about twelve miles from Easton, in Talbot county, Maryland. I have no accurate knowledge of my age, never having seen any authentic record containing it. By far the larger part of the slaves know as little of their ages as horses know of theirs, and it is the wish of most masters within my knowledge to keep their slaves thus ignorant. I do not remember to have ever met a slave who could tell of his birthday. They seldom come nearer to it than planting-time, harvest-time, cherry-time, spring-time, or fall-time. A want of information concerning my own was a source of unhappiness to me even during childhood. The white children could tell their ages. I could not tell why I ought to be deprived of the same privilege. I was not allowed to make any inquiries of my master concerning it. He deemed all such inquiries on the part of a slave improper and impertinent, and evidence of a restless spirit. The nearest estimate I can give makes me now between twenty-seven and twenty-eight years of age. I come to this, from hearing my master say, some time during 1835, I was about seventeen years old.

My mother was named Harriet Bailey. She was the daughter of Isaac and Betsey Bailey, both colored, and quite dark. My mother was of a darker complexion than either my grandmother or grandfather.

My father was a white man. He was admitted to be such by all I ever heard speak of my parentage. The opinion was also whispered that my master was my father; but of the correctness of this opinion, I know nothing; the means of knowing was withheld from me. My mother and I were separated when I was but an infant—before I knew her as my mother. It is a common custom, in the part of Maryland from which I ran away, to part children from their mothers at a very early age. Frequently, before the child has reached its twelfth month, its mother is taken from it, and hired out on some farm a considerable distance off, and the child is placed under the care of an old woman, too old for field labor. For what this separation is done, I do not know, unless it be to hinder the development of the child's affection toward its mother, and to blunt and destroy the natural affection of the mother for the child. This is the inevitable result.

I never saw my mother, to know her as such, more than four or five times in my life; and each of these times was very short in duration, and at night. She was hired by a Mr. Stewart, who lived about twelve miles from my home. She made her journeys to see me in the night, travelling the whole distance on foot, after the performance of her day's work. She was a field hand, and a whipping is the penalty of not being in the field at sunrise, unless a slave has special permission from his or her master to the contrary—a permission which they seldom get, and one that gives to him that gives it the proud name of being a kind master. I do not recollect of ever seeing my mother by the light of day. She was with me in the night. She would lie down with me, and get me to sleep, but long before I waked she was gone. Very little communication ever took place between us. Death soon ended what little we could have while she lived, and with it her hardships and suffering. She died when I was about seven years old, on one of my master's farms, near Lee's Mill. I was not allowed to be present during her illness, at her death, or burial. She was gone long before I knew anything about it. Never having enjoyed, to any considerable extent, her soothing presence, her tender and watchful care, I received the tidings of her death with much the same emotions I should have probably felt at the death of a stranger.

Called thus suddenly away, she left me without the slightest intimation of who my father was. The whisper that my master was my father, may or may not be true; and, true or false, it is of but little consequence to my purpose whilst the fact remains, in all its glaring odiousness, that slaveholders have ordained, and by law established, that the children of slave women shall in all cases follow the condition of their mothers; and this is done too obviously to administer to their own lusts, and make a gratification of their wicked desires profitable as well as pleasurable; for by this cunning arrangement, the slaveholder, in cases not a few, sustains to his slaves the double relation of master and father.

I know of such cases; and it is worthy of remark that such slaves invariably suffer greater hardships, and have more to contend with, than others. They are, in the first place, a constant offence to their mistress. She is ever disposed to find fault with them; they can seldom do any thing to please her; she is never better pleased than when she sees them under the lash, especially when she suspects her husband of showing to his mulatto children favors which he withholds from his black slaves. The master is frequently compelled to sell this class of his slaves, out of deference to the feelings of his white wife; and, cruel as the deed may strike any one to be, for a man to sell his own children to human flesh-mongers, it is often the dictate of humanity for him to do so; for, unless he does this, he must not only whip them himself, but must stand by and see one white son tie up his brother, of but few shades darker complexion than himself, and ply the gory lash to his naked back; and if he lisp one word of disapproval, it is set down to his parental partiality, and only makes a bad matter worse, both for himself and the slave whom he would protect and defend.

Every year brings with it multitudes of this class of slaves. It was doubtless in consequence of a knowledge of this fact, that one great statesman of the south predicted the downfall of slavery by the inevitable laws of population. Whether this prophecy is ever fulfilled or not, it is nevertheless plain that a very different-looking class of people are springing up at the south, and are now held in slavery, from those originally brought to this country from Africa; and if their increase will do no other good, it will do away the force of the argument, that God cursed Ham, and therefore American slavery is right.[13] If the lineal descendants of Ham are alone to be scripturally enslaved, it is certain that slavery at the south must soon become unscriptural; for thousands are ushered into the world, annually, who, like myself, owe their existence to white fathers, and those fathers most frequently their own masters.

I have had two masters. My first master's name was Anthony. I do not remember his first name. He was generally called Captain Anthony—a title which, I presume, he acquired by sailing a craft on the Chesapeake Bay. He was not considered a rich slaveholder. He owned two or three farms, and about thirty slaves. His farms and slaves were under the care of an overseer. The overseer's name was Plummer. Mr. Plummer was a miserable drunkard, a profane swearer, and a savage monster. He always went armed with a cowskin[14] and a heavy cudgel. I have known him to cut and slash the women's heads so horribly, that even master would be enraged at his cruelty, and would threaten to whip him if he did not mind himself. Master, however, was not a humane slaveholder. It required extraordinary barbarity on the part of an overseer to affect him. He was a cruel man, hardened by a long life of slaveholding. He would at times seem to take great pleasure in whipping a slave. I have often been awakened at the dawn of day by the most heartrending shrieks of an old aunt of mine, whom he used to tie up to a joist, and whip upon her naked back till she was literally covered with blood.

[13]In Genesis 9:20–27 Noah curses his son, Ham, consigning him to bondage to his brothers; the passage was cited as scriptural authority for slavery.

[14]A cowhide whip.

No words, no tears, no prayers, from his gory victim, seemed to move his iron heart from its bloody purpose. The louder she screamed, the harder he whipped; and where the blood ran fastest, there he whipped longest. He would whip her to make her scream, and whip her to make her hush; and not until overcome by fatigue, would he cease to swing the blood-clotted cowskin. I remember the first time I ever witnessed this horrible exhibition. I was quite a child, but I well remember it. I never shall forget it whilst I remember any thing. It was the first of a long series of such outrages, of which I was doomed to be a witness and a participant. It struck me with awful force. It was the bloodstained gate, the entrance to the hell of slavery, through which I was about to pass. It was a most terrible spectacle. I wish I could commit to paper the feelings with which I beheld it.

This occurrence took place very soon after I went to live with my old master, and under the following circumstances. Aunt Hester went out one night,— where or for what I do not know,—and happened to be absent when my master desired her presence. He had ordered her not to go out evenings, and warned her that she must never let him catch her in company with a young man, who was paying attention to her belonging to Colonel Lloyd. The young man's named was Ned Roberts, generally called Lloyd's Ned. Why master was so careful of her, may be safely left to conjecture. She was a woman of noble form, and of graceful proportions, having very few equals, and fewer superiors, in personal appearance, among the colored or white women of our neighborhood.

Aunt Hester had not only disobeyed his orders in going out, but had been found in company with Lloyd's Ned; which circumstance, I found, from what he said while whipping her, was the chief offence. Had he been a man of pure morals himself, he might have been thought interested in protecting the innocence of my aunt; but those who knew him will not suspect him of any such virtue. Before he commenced whipping Aunt Hester, he took her into the kitchen, and stripped her from neck to waist, leaving her neck, shoulders, and back, entirely naked. He then told her to cross her hands, calling her at the same time a d—d b—h. After crossing her hands, he tied them with a strong rope, and led her to a stool under a large hook in the joist, put in for the purpose. He made her get upon the stool, and tied her hands to the hook. She now stood fair for his infernal purpose. Her arms were stretched up at their full length, so that she stood upon the ends of her toes. He then said to her, "Now, you d—d b—h, I'll learn you how to disobey my orders!" and after rolling up his sleeves, he commenced to lay on the heavy cowskin, and soon the warm, red blood (amid heart-rending shrieks from her, and horrid oaths from him) came dripping to the floor. I was so terrified and horror-stricken at the sight, that I hid myself in a closet, and dared not venture out till long after the bloody transaction was over. I expected it would be my turn next. It was all new to me. I had never seen any thing like it before. I had always lived with my grandmother on the outskirts of the plantation, where she was put to raise the children of the younger women. I had therefore been, until now, out of the way of the bloody scenes that often occurred on the plantation.

Chapter II

My master's family consisted of two sons, Andrew and Richard; one daughter, Lucretia, and her husband, Captain Thomas Auld. They lived in one house, upon the home plantation of Colonel Edward Lloyd. My master was Colonel Lloyd's clerk and superintendent. He was what might be called the overseer of the overseers. I spent two years of childhood on this plantation in my old master's family. It was here that I witnessed the bloody transaction recorded in the first chapter; and as I received my first impressions of slavery on this plantation, I will give some description of it, and of slavery as it there existed. The plantation is about twelve miles north of Easton, in Talbot county, and is situated on the border of Miles River. The principal products raised upon it were tobacco, corn, and wheat. These were raised in great abundance; so that, with the products of this and the other farms belonging to him, he was able to keep in almost constant employment a large sloop, in carrying them to market at Baltimore. This sloop was named Sally Lloyd, in honor of one of the colonel's daughters. My master's son-in-law, Captain Auld, was master of the vessel; she was otherwise manned by the colonel's own slaves. Their names were Peter, Isaac, Rich, and Jake. These were esteemed very highly by the other slaves, and looked upon as the privileged ones of the plantation; for it was no small affair, in the eyes of the slaves, to be allowed to see Baltimore.

Colonel Lloyd kept from three to four hundred slaves on his home plantation, and owned a large number more on the neighboring farms belonging to him. The names of the farms nearest to the home plantation were Wye Town and New Design. "Wye Town" was under the overseership of a man named Noah Willis. New Design was under the overseership of a Mr. Townsend. The overseers of these, and all the rest of the farms, numbering over twenty, received advice and direction from the managers of the home plantation. This was the great business place. It was the seat of government for the whole twenty farms. All disputes among the overseers were settled here. If a slave was convicted of any high misdemeanor, became unmanageable, or evinced a determination to run away, he was brought immediately here, severely whipped, put on board the sloop, carried to Baltimore, and sold to Austin Woolfolk, or some other slave-trader, as a warning to the slaves remaining.

Here, too, the slaves of all the other farms received their monthly allowance of food, and their yearly clothing. The men and women slaves received, as their monthly allowance of food, eight pounds of pork, or its equivalent in fish, and one bushel of corn meal. Their yearly clothing consisted of two coarse linen shirts, one pair of linen trousers, like the shirts, one jacket, one pair of trousers for winter, made of coarse negro cloth, one pair of stockings, and one pair of shoes; the whole of which could not have cost more than seven dollars. The allowance of the slave children was given to their mothers, or the old women having the care of them. The children unable to work in the field had neither shoes, stockings, jackets, nor trousers, given to them; their clothing consisted of two coarse linen shirts per year. When these failed them, they went naked until the next allowance-day. Children from seven to ten years old, of both sexes, almost naked, might be seen at all seasons of the year.

There were no beds given the slaves, unless one coarse blanket be considered such, and none but the men and women had these. This, however, is not considered a very great privation. They find less difficulty from the want of beds, than from the want of time to sleep; for when their day's work in the field is done, the most of them having their washing, mending, and cooking to do, and having few or none of the ordinary facilities for doing either of these, very many of their sleeping hours are consumed in preparing for the field the coming day; and when this is done, old and young, male and female, married and single, drop down side by side, on one common bed,—the cold, damp floor,—each covering himself or herself with their miserable blankets; and here they sleep till they are summoned to the field by the driver's horn. At the sound of this, all must rise, and be off to the field. There must be no halting; every one must be at his or her post; and woe betides them who hear not this morning summons to the field; for if they are not awakened by the sense of hearing, they are by the sense of feeling: no age nor sex finds any favor. Mr. Severe, the overseer, used to stand by the door of the quarter, armed with a large hickory stick and heavy cowskin, ready to whip any one who was so unfortunate as not to hear, or, from any other cause, was prevented from being ready to start for the field at the sound of the horn.

Mr. Severe was rightly named: he was a cruel man. I have seen him whip a woman, causing the blood to run half an hour at the time; and this, too, in the midst of her crying children, pleading for their mother's release. He seemed to take pleasure in manifesting his fiendish barbarity. Added to his cruelty, he was a profane swearer. It was enough to chill the blood and stiffen the hair of an ordinary man to hear him talk. Scarce a sentence escaped him but that was commenced or concluded by some horrid oath. The field was the place to witness his cruelty and profanity. His presence made it both the field of blood and of blasphemy. From the rising till the going down of the sun, he was cursing, raving, cutting, and slashing among the slaves of the field, in the most frightful manner. His career was short. He died very soon after I went to Colonel Lloyd's; and he died as he lived, uttering, with his dying groans, bitter curses and horrid oaths. His death was regarded by the slaves as the result of a merciful providence.

Mr. Severe's place was filled by a Mr. Hopkins. He was a very different man. He was less cruel, less profane, and made less noise, than Mr. Severe. His course was characterized by no extraordinary demonstrations of cruelty. He whipped, but seemed to take no pleasure in it. He was called by the slaves a good overseer.

The home plantation of Colonel Lloyd wore the appearance of a country village. All the mechanical operations for all the farms were performed here. The shoemaking and mending, the black-smithing, cartwrighting, coopering, weaving, and grain-grinding, were all performed by the slaves on the home plantation. The whole place wore a business-like aspect very unlike the neighboring farms. The number of houses, too, conspired to give it advantage over the neighboring farms. It was called by the slaves the *Great House Farm*. Few privileges were esteemed higher, by the slaves of the out-farms, than that of being selected to do errands at the Great House Farm. It was associated in their minds with greatness. A representative could not be prouder of his election to a seat in the American Congress, than a slave on one of the out-farms would be of his election to do errands at the Great House Farm. They regarded it as evidence of great confidence reposed in them by their overseers; and it was on this account, as well as a constant desire to be out of the field from under the driver's lash, that they esteemed it a high privilege, one worth careful living for. He was called the smartest and most trusty fellow, who had this honor conferred upon him the most frequently. The competitors for this office sought as diligently to please their overseers, as the office-seekers in the political parties seek to please and deceive the people. The same traits of character might be seen in Colonel Lloyd's slaves, as are seen in the slaves of the political parties.

The slaves selected to go to the Great House Farm, for the monthly allowance for themselves and their fellow-slaves, were peculiarly enthusiastic. While on their way, they would make the dense old woods, for miles around, reverberate with their wild songs, revealing at once the highest joy and the deepest sadness. They would compose and sing as they went along, consulting neither time nor tune. The thought that came up, came out—if not in the word, in the sound;—and as frequently in the one as in the other. They would sometimes sing the most pathetic sentiment in the most rapturous tone, and the most rapturous sentiment in the most pathetic tone. Into all of their songs they would manage to weave something of the Great House Farm. Especially would they do this, when leaving home. They would then sing most exultingly the following words:—

> "I am going away to the Great House Farm!
> O, yea! O, yea! O!"

This they would sing, as a chorus, to words which to many would seem unmeaning jargon, but which, nevertheless, were full of meaning to themselves. I have sometimes thought that the mere hearing of those songs would do more to impress some minds with the horrible character of slavery, than the reading of whole volumes of philosophy on the subject could do.

I did not, when a slave, understand the deep meaning of those rude and apparently incoherent songs. I was myself within the circle; so that I neither saw nor heard as those without might see and hear. They told a tale of woe which was then altogether beyond my feeble comprehension; they were tones loud, long, and deep; they breathed the prayer and complaint of souls boiling over with the bitterest anguish. Every tone was a testimony against slavery, and a prayer to God for deliverance from chains. The hearing of those wild notes always depressed my spirit, and filled me with ineffable sadness. I have frequently found myself in tears while hearing them. The mere recurrence to those songs, even now, afflicts me; and while I am writing these lines, an expression of feeling has already found its way down my cheek. To those songs I trace my first glimmering conception of the dehumanizing character of slavery. I can never get rid of that conception. Those songs still follow me, to deepen my hatred of slavery, and quicken my sympathies for my brethren in bonds. If any one wishes to be impressed with the soul-killing effects of slavery, let him go to Colonel Lloyd's plantation, and, on allowance-day, place himself in the deep pine woods, and there let him, in silence analyze the sounds that shall pass through the chambers of his soul,—and if he is not thus impressed, it will only be because "there is no flesh in his obdurate heart."

I have often been utterly astonished, since I came to the north, to find persons who could speak of the singing, among slaves, as evidence of their contentment and happiness. It is impossible to conceive of a greater mistake. Slaves sing most when they are most unhappy. The songs of the slave represent the sorrows of his heart; and he is relieved by them, only as an aching heart is relieved by its tears. At least, such is my experience. I have often sung to drown my sorrow, but seldom to express my happiness. Crying for joy, and singing for joy, were alike uncommon to me while in the jaws of slavery. The singing of a man cast away upon a desolate island might be as appropriately considered as evidence of contentment and happiness, as the singing of a slave; the songs of the one and of the other are prompted by the same emotion.

Chapter III

Colonel Lloyd kept a large and finely cultivated garden, which afforded almost constant employment for four men, besides the chief gardener, (Mr. M'Durmond.) This garden was probably the greatest attraction of the place. During the summer months, people came from far and near—from Baltimore, Easton, and Annapolis—to see it. It abounded in fruits of almost every description, from the hardy apple of the north to the delicate orange of the south. This garden was not the least source of trouble on the plantation. Its excellent fruit was quite a temptation to the hungry swarms of boys, as well as the older slaves, belonging to the colonel, few of whom had the virtue or the vice to resist it. Scarcely a day passed, during the summer, but that some slave had to take the lash for stealing fruit. The colonel had to resort to all kinds of stratagems to keep his slaves out of the garden. The last and most successful one was that of tarring his fence all around, after which, if a slave was caught with any tar upon his person, it was deemed sufficient proof that he had either been into the garden, or had tried to get in. In either case, he was severely whipped by the chief gardener. This plan worked well; the slaves became as fearful of tar as of the lash. They seemed to realize the impossibility of touching *tar* without being defiled.

The colonel also kept a splendid riding equipage. His stable and carriage-house presented the appearance of some of our large city livery establishments. His horses were of the finest form and noblest blood. His carriage-house contained three splendid coaches, three or four gigs, besides dearborns and barouches of the most fashionable style.[15]

This establishment was under the care of two slaves—old Barney and young Barney—father and son. To attend to this establishment was their sole work. But it was by no means an easy employment; for in nothing was Colonel Lloyd more particular than in the management of his horses. The slightest inattention to these was unpardonable, and was visited upon those, under whose care they were placed, with the severest punishment; no excuse could shield them, if the colonel only suspected any want of attention to his horses—a supposition which he frequently indulged, and one which, of course, made the office of old and young Barney a very trying one. They never knew when they were safe from punishment. They were frequently whipped when least deserving, and escaped whipping when most deserving it. Every thing depended upon the looks of the horses, and the state of Colonel Lloyd's own mind when his horses were brought to him for use. If a horse did not move fast enough, or hold his head high enough, it was owing to some fault of his keepers. It was painful to stand near the stabledoor, and hear the various complaints against the keepers when a horse was taken out for use. "This horse has not had proper attention. He has not been sufficiently rubbed and curried, or he has not been properly fed; his food was too wet or too dry; he got it too soon or too late; he was too hot or too cold; he had too much hay, and not enough of grain; or he had too much grain, and not enough of hay; instead of old Barney's attending to the horse, he had very improperly left it to his son." To all these complaints, no matter how unjust, the slave must answer never a word. Colonel Lloyd could not brook any contradiction from a slave. When he spoke, a slave must stand, listen, and tremble; and such was literally the case. I have seen Colonel Lloyd make old Barney, a man between fifty and sixty years of age, uncover his bald head, kneel down upon the cold, damp ground, and receive upon his naked and toil-worn shoulders more than thirty lashes at the time. Colonel Lloyd had three sons—Edward, Murray, and Daniel,—and three sons-in-law, Mr. Winder, Mr. Nicholson, and Mr. Lowndes. All of these lived at the Great House Farm, and enjoyed the luxury of whipping the servants when they pleased, from old Barney down to William Wilkes, the coach-driver. I have seen Winder make one of the house-servants stand off from him a suitable distance to be touched with the end of his whip, and at every stroke raise great ridges upon his back.

To describe the wealth of Colonel Lloyd would be almost equal to describing the riches of Job.[16] He kept from ten to fifteen house-servants.

---

[15]Various kinds of horse-drawn carriages.
[16]Before being visited with misfortunes, the biblical Job was enormously wealthy.

He was said to own a thousand slaves, and I think this estimate quite within the truth. Colonel Lloyd owned so many that he did not know them when he saw them; nor did all the slaves of the out-farms know him. It is reported of him, that, while riding along the road one day, he met a colored man, and addressed him in the usual manner of speaking to colored people on the public highways of the south: "Well, boy, whom do you belong to?" "To Colonel Lloyd," replied the slave. "Well, does the colonel treat you well?" "No, sir," was the ready reply. "What, does he work you too hard?" "Yes, sir." "Well, don't he give you enough to eat?" "Yes, sir, he gives me enough, such as it is."

The colonel, after ascertaining where the slave belonged, rode on; the man also went on about his business, not dreaming that he had been conversing with his master. He thought, said, and heard nothing more of the matter, until two or three weeks afterwards. The poor man was then informed by his overseer that, for having found fault with his master, he was now to be sold to a Georgia trader. He was immediately chained and handcuffed; and thus, without a moment's warning, he was snatched away, and forever sundered, from his family and friends, by a hand more unrelenting than death. This is the penalty of telling the truth, of telling the simple truth, in answer to a series of plain questions.

It is partly in consequence of such facts, that slaves, when inquired of as to their condition and the character of their masters, almost universally say they are contented, and that their masters are kind. The slaveholders have been known to send in spies among their slaves, to ascertain their views and feelings in regard to their condition. The frequency of this has had the effect to establish among the slaves the maxim, that a still tongue makes a wise head. They suppress the truth rather than take the consequences of telling it, and in so doing prove themselves a part of the human family. If they have any thing to say of their masters, it is generally in their masters' favor, especially when speaking to an untried man. I have been frequently asked, when a slave, if I had a kind master, and do not remember ever to have given a negative answer; nor did I, in pursuing this course, consider myself as uttering what was absolutely false; for I always measured the kindness of my master by the standard of kindness set up among slaveholders around us. Moreover, slaves are like other people, and imbibe prejudices quite common to others. They think their own better than that of others. Many, under the influence of this prejudice, think their own masters are better than the masters of other slaves; and this, too, in some cases, when the very reverse is true. Indeed, it is not uncommon for slaves even to fall out and quarrel among themselves about the relative goodness of their masters, each contending for the superior goodness of his own over that of the others. At the very same time, they mutually execrate their masters when viewed separately. It was so on our plantation. When Colonel Lloyd's slaves met the slaves of Jacob Jepson, they seldom parted without a quarrel about their masters; Colonel Lloyd's slaves contending that he was the richest, and Mr. Jepson's slaves that he was the smartest, and most of a man. Colonel

Lloyd's slaves would boast his ability to buy and sell Jacob Jepson. Mr. Jepson's slaves would boast his ability to whip Colonel Lloyd. These quarrels would almost always end in a fight between the parties, and those that whipped were supposed to have gained the point at issue. They seemed to think that the greatness of their masters was transferable to themselves. It was considered as being bad enough to be a slave; but to be a poor man's slave was deemed a disgrace indeed!

Chapter IV

Mr. Hopkins remained but a short time in the office of overseer. Why his career was so short, I do not know, but suppose he lacked the necessary severity to suit Colonel Lloyd. Mr. Hopkins was succeeded by Mr. Austin Gore, a man possessing, in an eminent degree, all those traits of character indispensable to what is called a first-rate overseer. Mr. Gore had served Colonel Lloyd, in the capacity of overseer, upon one of the out-farms, and had shown himself worthy of the high station of overseer upon the home or Great House Farm.

Mr. Gore was proud, ambitious, and persevering. He was artful, cruel, and obdurate. He was just the man for such a place, and it was just the place for such a man. It afforded scope for the full exercise of all his powers, and he seemed to be perfectly at home in it. He was one of those who could torture the slightest look, word, or gesture, on the part of the slave, into impudence, and would treat it accordingly. There must be no answering back to him; no explanation was allowed a slave, showing himself to have been wrongfully accused. Mr. Gore acted fully up to the maxim laid down by slaveholders,—"It is better that a dozen slaves suffer under the lash, than that the overseer should be convicted, in the presence of the slaves, of having been at fault." No matter how innocent a slave might be—it availed him nothing, when accused by Mr. Gore of any misdemeanor. To be accused was to be convicted, and to be convicted was to be punished; the one always following the other with immutable certainty. To escape punishment was to escape accusation; and few slaves had the fortune to do either, under the overseership of Mr. Gore. He was just proud enough to demand the most debasing homage of the slave, and quite servile enough to crouch, himself, at the feet of the master. He was ambitious enough to be contented with nothing short of the highest rank of overseers, and persevering enough to reach the height of his ambition. He was cruel enough to inflict the severest punishment, artful enough to descend to the lowest trickery, and obdurate enough to be insensible to the voice of a reproving conscience. He was, of all the overseers, the most dreaded by the slaves. His presence was painful; his eye flashed confusion; and seldom was his sharp, shrill voice heard, without producing horror and trembling in their ranks.

Mr. Gore was a grave man, and, though a young man, he indulged in no jokes, said no funny words, seldom smiled. His words were in perfect keeping with his looks, and his looks were in perfect keeping with his words.

Overseers will sometimes indulge in a witty word, even with the slaves; not so with Mr. Gore. He spoke but to command, and commanded but to be obeyed; he dealt sparingly with his words, and bountifully with his whip, never using the former where the latter would answer as well. When he whipped, he seemed to do so from a sense of duty, and feared no consequences. He did nothing reluctantly, no matter how disagreeable; always at his post, never inconsistent. He never promised but to fulfil. He was, in a word, a man of the most inflexible firmness and stone-like coolness.

His savage barbarity was equalled only by the consummate coolness with which he committed the grossest and most savage deeds upon the slaves under his charge. Mr. Gore once undertook to whip one of Colonel Lloyd's slaves, by the name of Demby. He had given Demby but few stripes, when, to get rid of the scourging, he ran and plunged himself into a creek, and stood there at the depth of his shoulders, refusing to come out. Mr. Gore told him that he would give him three calls, and that, if he did not come out at the third call, he would shoot him. The first call was given. Demby made no response, but stood his ground. The second and third calls were given with the same result. Mr. Gore then, without consultation or deliberation with any one, not even giving Demby an additional call, raised his musket to his face, taking deadly aim at his standing victim, and in an instant poor Demby was no more. His mangled body sank out of sight, and blood and brains marked the water where he had stood.

A thrill of horror flashed through every soul upon the plantation, excepting Mr. Gore. He alone seemed cool and collected. He was asked by Colonel Lloyd and my old master, why he resorted to this extraordinary expedient. His reply was, (as well as I can remember,) that Demby had become unmanageable. He was setting a dangerous example to the other slaves,—one which, if suffered to pass without some such demonstration on his part, would finally lead to the total subversion of all rule and order upon the plantation. He argued that if one slave refused to be corrected, and escaped with his life, the other slaves would soon copy the example; the result of which would be, the freedom of the slaves, and the enslavement of the whites. Mr. Gore's defence was satisfactory. He was continued in his station as overseer upon the home plantation. His fame as an overseer went abroad. His horrid crime was not even submitted to judicial investigation. It was committed in the presence of slaves, and they of course could neither institute a suit, nor testify against him; and thus the guilty perpetrator of one of the bloodiest and most foul murders goes unwhipped of justice, and uncensured by the community in which he lives. Mr. Gore lived in St. Michael's, Talbot county, Maryland, when I left there; and if he is still alive, he very probably lives there now; and if so, he is now, as he was then, as highly esteemed and as much respected as though his guilty soul had not been stained with his brother's blood.

I speak advisedly when I say this,—that killing a slave, or any colored person, in Talbot county, Maryland, is not treated as a crime, either by the courts or the community. Mr. Thomas Lanman, of St Michael's, killed two slaves, one of whom he killed with a hatchet, by knocking his brains out. He used to boast of the commission of the awful and bloody deed. I have heard him do so laughingly, saying, among other things, that he was the only ben-efactor of his country in the company, and that when others would do as much as he had done, we should be relieved of "the d——d niggers."

The wife of Mr. Giles Hicks, living but a short distance from where I used to live, murdered my wife's cousin, a young girl between fifteen and sixteen years of age, mangling her person in the most horrible manner, breaking her nose and breastbone with a stick, so that the poor girl expired in a few hours afterward. She was immediately buried, but had not been in her untimely grave but a few hours before she was taken up and examined by the coroner, who decided that she had come to her death by severe beat-ing. The offence for which this girl was thus murdered was this:—She had been set that night to mind Mrs. Hicks's baby, and during the night she fell asleep, and the baby cried. She, having lost her rest for several night previ-ous, did not hear the crying. They were both in the room with Mrs. Hicks. Mrs. Hicks, finding the girl slow to move, jumped from her bed, seized an oak stick of wood by the fireplace, and with it broke the girl's nose and breastbone, and thus ended her life. I will not say that this most horrid murder produced no sensation in the community. It did produce sensation, but not enough to bring the murderess to punishment. There was a warrant issued for her arrest, but it was never served. Thus she escaped not only punishment, but even the pain of being arraigned before a court for her hor-rid crime.

Whilst I am detailing bloody deeds which took place during my stay on Colonel Lloyd's plantation, I will briefly narrate another, which occurred about the same time as the murder of Demby by Mr. Gore.

Colonel Lloyd's slaves were in the habit of spending a part of their nights and Sundays in fishing for oysters, and in this way made up the defi-ciency of their scanty allowance. An old man belonging to Colonel Lloyd, while thus engaged, happened to get beyond the limits of Colonel Lloyd's, and on the premises of Mr. Beal Bondly. At this trespass, Mr. Bondly took offence, and with his musket came down to the shore, and blew its deadly contents into the poor old man.

Mr. Bondly came over to see Colonel Lloyd the next day, whether to pay him for his property, or to justify himself in what he had done, I know not. At any rate, this whole fiendish transaction was soon hushed up. There was very little said about it at all, and nothing done. It was a common saying, even among little white boys, that it was worth a half-cent to kill a "nigger," and a half-cent to bury one.

Chapter V

As to my own treatment while I lived on Colonel Lloyd's plantation, it was very similar to that of the other slave children. I was not old enough to work in the field, and there being little else than field work to do, I had a great deal of leisure time. The most I had to do was to drive up the cows at evening, keep the fowls out of the garden, keep the front yard clean, and run of errands for my old master's daughter, Mrs. Lucretia Auld. The most of my leisure time I spent in helping Master Daniel Lloyd in finding his birds, after he had shot them. My connection with Master Daniel was of some advantage to me. He became quite attached to me, and was a sort of protector of me. He would not allow the older boys to impose upon me, and would divide his cakes with me.

I was seldom whipped by my old master, and suffered little from any thing else than hunger and cold. I suffered much from hunger, but much more from cold. In hottest summer and coldest winter, I was kept almost naked—no shoes, no stockings, no jacket, no trousers, nothing on but a coarse tow linen shirt, reaching only to my knees. I had no bed. I must have perished with cold, but that, the coldest nights, I used to steal a bag which was used for carrying corn to the mill. I would crawl into this bag, and there sleep on the cold, damp, clay floor, with my head in and feet out. My feet have been so cracked with the frost, that the pen with which I am writing might be laid in the gashes.

We were not regularly allowanced. Our food was coarse corn meal boiled. This was called *mush*. It was put into a large wooden tray or trough, and set down upon the ground. The children were then called, like so many pigs, and like so many pigs they would come and devour the mush; some with oyster-shells, others with pieces of shingle, some with naked hands, and none with spoons. He that ate fastest got most; he that was strongest secured the best place; and few left the trough satisfied.

I was probably between seven and eight years old when I left Colonel Lloyd's plantation. I left it with joy. I shall never forget the ecstasy with which I received the intelligence that my old master (Anthony) had determined to let me go to Baltimore, to live with Mr. Hugh Auld, brother to my old master's son-in-law, Captain Thomas Auld. I received this information about three days before my departure. They were three of the happiest days I ever enjoyed. I spent the most part of all these three days in the creek, washing off the plantation scurf, and preparing myself for my departure.

The pride of appearance which this would indicate was not my own. I spent the time in washing, not so much because I wished to, but because Mrs. Lucretia had told me I must get all the dead skin off my feet and knees before I could go to Baltimore; for the people in Baltimore were very cleanly, and would laugh at me if I looked dirty. Besides, she was going to give me a pair of trousers, which I should not put on unless I got all the dirt off me. The thought of owning a pair of trousers was great indeed! It was almost a sufficient motive, not only to make me take off what would be called by pigdrovers the mange, but the skin itself. I went at it in good earnest, working for the first time with the hope of reward.

The ties that ordinarily bind children to their homes were all suspended in my case. I found no severe trial in my departure. My home was charmless; it was not home to me; on parting from it, I could not feel that I was leaving any thing which I could have enjoyed by staying. My mother was dead, my grandmother lived far off, so that I seldom saw her. I had two sisters and one brother, that lived in the same house with me; but the early separation of us from our mother had well nigh blotted the fact of our relationship from our memories. I looked for home elsewhere, and was confident of finding none which I should relish less than the one which I was leaving. If, however, I found in my new home hardship, hunger, whipping, and nakedness, I had the consolation that I should not have escaped any one of them by staying. Having already had more than a taste of them in the house of my old master, and having endured them there, I very naturally inferred my ability to endure them elsewhere, and especially at Baltimore; for I had something of the feeling about Baltimore that is expressed in the proverb, that "being hanged in England is preferable to dying a natural death in Ireland." I had the strongest desire to see Baltimore. Cousin Tom, though not fluent in speech, had inspired me with that desire by his eloquent description of the place. I could never point out any thing at the Great House, no matter how beautiful or powerful, but that he had seen something at Baltimore far exceeding, both in beauty and strength, the object which I pointed out to him. Even the Great House itself, with all its pictures, was far inferior to many buildings in Baltimore. So strong was my desire, that I thought a gratification of it would fully compensate for whatever loss of comforts I should sustain by the exchange. I left without a regret, and with the highest hopes of future happiness.

We sailed out of Miles River for Baltimore on a Saturday morning. I remember only the day of the week, for at that time I had no knowledge of the days of the month, nor the months of the year. On setting sail, I walked aft, and gave to Colonel Lloyd's plantation what I hoped would be the last look. I then placed myself in the bows of the sloop, and there spent the remainder of the day in looking ahead, interesting myself in what was in the distance rather than in things near by or behind.

In the afternoon of that day, we reached Annapolis, the capital of the State. We stopped but a few moments, so that I had no time to go on shore. It was the first large town that I had ever seen, and though it would look small compared with some of our New England factory villages, I thought it a wonderful place for its size—more imposing even than the Great House Farm!

We arrived at Baltimore early on Sunday morning, landing at Smith's Wharf, not far from Bowley's Wharf. We had on board the sloop a large flock of sheep; and after aiding in driving them to the slaughterhouse of Mr. Curtis on Louden Slater's Hill, I was conducted by Rich, one of the hands belonging on board of the sloop to my new home in Alliciana Street, near Mr. Gardner's ship-yard, on Fells Point.

Mr. and Mrs. Auld were both at home, and met me at the door with their little son Thomas, to take care of whom I had been given. And here I saw what I had never seen before; it was a white face beaming with the most kindly emotions; it was the face of my new mistress, Sophia Auld. I wish

I could describe the rapture that flashed through my soul as I beheld it. It was a new and strange sight to me, brightening up my pathway with the light of happiness. Little Thomas was told, there was his Freddy,—and I was told to take care of little Thomas; and thus I entered upon the duties of my new home with the most cheering prospect ahead.

I looked upon my departure from Colonel Lloyd's plantation as one of the most interesting events of my life. It is possible, and even quite proba-ble, that but for the mere circumstance of being removed from that planta-tion to Baltimore, I should have to-day, instead of being here seated by my own table, in the enjoyment of freedom and the happiness of home, writing this Narrative, been confined in the galling chains of slavery. Going to live at Baltimore laid the foundation, and opened the gateway, to all my subse-quent prosperity. I have ever regarded it as the first plain manifestation of that kind providence which has ever since attended me, and marked my life with so many favors. I regarded the selection of myself as being somewhat remarkable. There were a number of slave children that might have been sent from the plantation to Baltimore. There were those younger, those older, and those of the same age. I was chosen from among them all, and was the first, last, and only choice.

I may be deemed superstitious, and even egotistical, in regarding this event as a special interposition of divine Providence in my favor. But I should be false to the earliest sentiments of my soul, if I suppressed the opinion. I prefer to be true to myself, even at the hazard of incurring the ridicule of others, rather than to be false, and incur my own abhorrence. From my earliest recollection, I date the entertainment of a deep conviction that slavery would not always be able to hold me within its foul embrace; and in the darkest hours of my career in slavery, this living word of faith and spirit of hope departed [not] from me, but remained like ministering angels to cheer me through the gloom. This good spirit was from God, and to him I offer thanksgiving and praise.

Chapter VI

My new mistress proved to be all she appeared when I first met her at the door,—a woman of the kindest heart and finest feelings. She had never had a slave under her control previously to myself, and prior to her marriage she had been dependent upon her own industry for a living. She was by trade a weaver; and by constant application to her business, she had been in a good degree preserved from the blighting and dehumanizing effects of slavery. I was utterly astonished at her goodness. I scarcely knew how to behave towards her. She was entirely unlike any other white woman I had ever seen. I could not approach her as I was accustomed to approach other white ladies. My early instruction was all out of place. The crouching servility, usu-ally so acceptable a quality in a slave, did not answer when manifested to-ward her. Her favor was not gained by it; she seemed to be disturbed by it. She did not deem it impudent or unmannerly for a slave to look her in the face. The meanest slave was put fully at ease in her presence, and none left without feeling better for having seen her. Her face was made of heavenly smiles, and her voice of tranquil music.

But, alas! this kind heart had but a short time to remain such. The fatal poison of irresponsible power was already in her hands, and soon commenced its infernal work. That cheerful eye, under the influence of slavery, soon became red with rage; that voice, made all of sweet accord, changed to one of harsh and horrid discord; and that angelic face gave place to that of a demon.

Very soon after I went to live with Mr. and Mrs. Auld, she kindly commenced to teach me the A, B, C. After I had learned this, she assisted me in learning to spell words of three or four letters. Just at this point of my progress, Mr. Auld found out what was going on, and at once forbade Mrs. Auld to instruct me further, telling her, among other things, that it was unlawful,[17] as well as unsafe, to teach a slave to read. To use his own words further, he said, "If you give a nigger an inch, he will take an ell. A nigger should know nothing but to obey his master—to do as he is told to do. Learning would *spoil* the best nigger in the world. Now," said he, "if you teach that nigger (speaking of myself) how to read, there would be no keeping him. It would forever unfit him to be a slave. He would at once become unmanageable, and of no value to his master. As to himself, it could do him no good, but a great deal of harm. It would make him discontented and unhappy." These words sank deep into my heart, stirred up sentiments within that lay slumbering, and called into existence an entirely new train of thought. It was a new and special revelation, explaining dark and mysterious things, with which my youthful understanding had struggled, but struggled in vain. I now understood what had been to me a most perplexing difficulty—to wit, the white man's power to enslave the black man. It was a grand achievement, and I prized it highly. From that moment, I understood the pathway from slavery to freedom. It was just what I wanted, and I got it at a time when I the least expected it. Whilst I was saddened by the thought of losing the aid of my kind mistress, I was gladdened by the invaluable instruction which, by the merest accident, I had gained from my master. Though conscious of the difficulty of learning without a teacher, I set out with high hope, and a fixed purpose, at whatever cost of trouble, to learn how to read. The very decided manner with which he spoke, and strove to impress his wife with the evil consequences of giving me instruction, served to convince me that he was deeply sensible of the truths he was uttering. It gave me the best assurance that I might rely with the utmost confidence on the results which, he said, would flow from teaching me to read. What he most dreaded, that I most desired. What he most loved, that I most hated. That which to him was a great evil, to be carefully shunned, was to me a great good, to be diligently sought; and the argument which he so warmly

[17]Most Southern states had statutes making the teaching of slaves to read or write illegal.

urged, against my learning to read, only served to inspire me with a desire and determination to learn. In learning to read, I owe almost as much to the bitter opposition of my master, as to the kindly aid of my mistress. I acknowledge the benefit of both.

I had resided but a short time in Baltimore before I observed a marked difference, in the treatment of slaves, from that which I had witnessed in the country. A city slave is almost a freeman, compared with a slave on the plantation. He is much better fed and clothed, and enjoys privileges altogether unknown to the slave on the plantation. There is a vestige of decency, a sense of shame, that does much to curb and check those outbreaks of atrocious cruelty so commonly enacted upon the plantation. He is a desperate slaveholder, who will shock the humanity of his non-slaveholding neighbors with the cries of his lacerated slave. Few are willing to incur the odium attaching to the reputation of being a cruel master; and above all things, they would not be known as not giving a slave enough to eat. Every city slaveholder is anxious to have it known of him, that he feeds his slaves well; and it is due to them to say, that most of them do give their slaves enough to eat. There are, however, some painful exceptions to this rule. Directly opposite to us, on Philpot Street, lived Mr. Thomas Hamilton. He owned two slaves. Their names were Henrietta and Mary. Henrietta was about twenty-two years of age, Mary was about fourteen; and of all the mangled and emaciated creatures I ever looked upon, these two were the most so. His heart must be harder than stone, that could look upon these unmoved. The head, neck, and shoulders of Mary were literally cut to pieces. I have frequently felt her head, and found it nearly covered with festering sores, caused by the lash of her cruel mistress. I do not know that her master ever whipped her, but I have been an eye-witness to the cruelty of Mrs. Hamilton. I used to be in Mr. Hamilton's house nearly every day. Mrs. Hamilton used to sit in a large chair in the middle of the room, with a heavy cowskin always by her side, and scarce an hour passed during the day but was marked by the blood of one of these slaves. The girls seldom passed her without her saying, "Move faster, you *black gip!*" at the same time giving them a blow with the cowskin over the head or shoulders, often drawing the blood. She would then say, "Take that, you *black gip!*"— continuing, "If you don't move faster, I'll move you!" Added to the cruel lashings to which these slaves were subjected, they were kept nearly half-starved. They seldom knew what it was to eat a full meal. I have seen Mary contending with the pigs for the offal thrown into the street. So much was Mary kicked and cut to pieces, that she was oftener called "*pecked*" than by her name.

Chapter VII

I lived in Master Hugh's family about seven years. During this time, I succeeded in learning to read and write. In accomplishing this, I was compelled to resort to various stratagems. I had no regular teacher. My mistress, who had kindly commenced to instruct me, had, in compliance with the advice and direction of her husband, not only ceased to instruct, but had set her face against my being instructed by any one else. It is due, however, to my mistress to say of her, that she did not adopt this course of treatment immediately. She at first lacked the depravity indispensable to shutting me up in mental darkness. It was at least necessary for her to have some training in the exercise of irresponsible power, to make her equal to the task of treating me as though I were a brute.

My mistress was, as I have said, a kind and tender-hearted woman; and in the simplicity of her soul she commenced, when I first went to live with her, to treat me as she supposed one human being ought to treat another. In entering upon the duties of a slaveholder, she did not seem to perceive that I sustained to her the relation of a mere chattel, and that for her to treat me as a human being was not only wrong, but dangerously so. Slavery proved as injurious to her as it did to me. When I went there, she was a pious, warm, and tender-hearted woman. There was no sorrow or suffering for which she had not a tear. She had bread for the hungry, clothes for the naked, and comfort for every mourner that came within her reach. Slavery soon proved its ability to divest her of these heavenly qualities. Under its influence, the tender heart became stone, and the lamblike disposition gave way to one of tigerlike fierceness. The first step in her downward course was in her ceasing to instruct me. She now commenced to practise her husband's precepts. She finally became even more violent in her opposition than her husband himself. She was not satisfied with simply doing as well as he had commanded; she seemed anxious to do better. Nothing seemed to make her more angry than to see me with a newspaper. She seemed to think that here lay the danger. I have had her rush at me with a face made all up of fury, and snatch from me a newspaper, in a manner that fully revealed her apprehension. She was an apt woman; and a little experience soon demonstrated, to her satisfaction, that education and slavery were incompatible with each other.

From this time I was most narrowly watched. If I was in a separate room any considerable length of time, I was sure to be suspected of having a book, and was at once called to give an account of myself. All this, however, was too late. The first step had been taken. Mistress, in teaching me the alphabet, had given me the *inch*, and no precaution could prevent me from taking the *ell*.

The plan which I adopted, and the one by which I was most successful, was that of making friends of all the little white boys whom I met in the street. As many of these as I could, I converted into teachers. With their kindly aid, obtained at different times and in different places, I finally succeeded in learning to read. When I was sent of errands, I always took my book with me, and by going one part of my errand quickly, I found time to get a lesson before my return. I used also to carry bread with me, enough of which was always in the house, and to which I was always welcome; for I was much better off in this regard than many of the poor white children in our neighborhood. This bread I used to bestow upon the hungry little urchins, who, in return, would give me that more valuable bread of knowledge. I am strongly tempted to give the names of two or three of those little boys, as a testimonial of the gratitude and affection I bear them; but prudence forbids;—not that it would injure me, but it might embarrass them; for it is almost an unpardonable offence to teach slaves to read in this Christian country. It is enough to say of the dear little fellows, that they lived on Philpot Street, very near Durgin and Bailey's ship-yard. I used to talk this matter of slavery over with them. I would sometimes say to them, I wished I could be as free as they would be when they got to be men. "You will be free as soon as you are twenty-one, *but I am a slave for life!* Have not I as good a right to be free as you have?" These words used to trouble them; they would express for me the liveliest sympathy, and console me with the hope that something would occur by which I might be free.

I was now about twelve years old, and the thought of being *a slave for life* began to bear heavily upon my heart. Just about this time, I got hold of a book entitled "The Columbian Orator."[18] Every opportunity I got, I used to read this book. Among much of other interesting matter, I found in it a dialogue between a master and his slave. The slave was represented as having run away from his master three times. The dialogue represented the conversation which took place between them, when the slave was retaken the third time. In this dialogue, the whole argument in behalf of slavery was brought forward by the master, all of which was disposed of by the slave. The slave was made to say some very smart as well as impressive things in reply to his master—things which had the desired though unexpected effect; for the conversation resulted in the voluntary emancipation of the slave on the part of the master.

In the same book, I met with one of Sheridan's[19] mighty speeches on and in behalf of Catholic emancipation. These were choice documents to me. I read them over and over again with unabated interest. They gave tongue to interesting thoughts of my own soul, which had frequently flashed through my mind, and died away for want of utterance. The moral which I gained from the dialogue was the power of truth over the conscience of even a slaveholder. What I got from Sheridan was a bold denunciation of slavery, and a powerful vindication of human rights. The reading of these documents enabled me to utter my thoughts, and to meet the arguments brought forward to sustain slavery; but while they relieved me of one difficulty, they brought on another even more painful than the one of which I was relieved. The more I read, the more I was led to abhor and detest my enslavers. I could regard them in no other light than a band of successful robbers, who had left their homes, and gone to Africa, and stolen us from

[18]An anthology of speeches, poems, dialogues, and plays which Douglass had obtained as a child.

[19]Richard Brinsley Sheridan (1751–1816), Irish-born playwright and satirist, became a member of the British Parliament and spoke out on behalf of Catholic emancipation.

our homes, and in a strange land reduced us to slavery. I loathed them as being the meanest as well as the most wicked of men. As I read and contemplated the subject, behold! that very discontentment which Master Hugh had predicted would follow my learning to read had already come, to torment and sting my soul to unutterable anguish. As I writhed under it, I would at times feel that learning to read had been a curse rather than a blessing. It had given me a view of my wretched condition, without the remedy. It opened my eyes to the horrible pit, but to no ladder upon which to get out. In moments of agony, I envied my fellow-slaves for their stupidity. I have often wished myself a beast. I preferred the condition of the meanest reptile to my own. Any thing, no matter what, to get rid of thinking! It was this everlasting thinking of my condition that tormented me. There was no getting rid of it. It was pressed upon me by every object within sight or hearing, animate or inanimate. The silver trump of freedom had roused my soul to eternal wakefulness. Freedom now appeared, to disappear no more forever. It was heard in every sound, and seen in every thing. It was ever present to torment me with a sense of my wretched condition. I saw nothing without seeing it, I heard nothing without hearing it, and felt nothing without feeling it. It looked from every star, it smiled in every calm, breathed in every wind, and moved in every storm.

I often found myself regretting my own existence, and wishing myself dead; and but for the hope of being free, I have no doubt but that I should have killed myself, or done something for which I should have been killed. While in this state of mind, I was eager to hear any one speak of slavery. I was a ready listener. Every little while, I could hear something about the abolitionists. It was some time before I found what the word meant. It was always used in such connections as to make it an interesting word to me. If a slave ran away and succeeded in getting clear, or if a slave killed his master, set fire to a barn, or did any thing very wrong in the mind of a slaveholder, it was spoken of as the fruit of *abolition*. Hearing the word in this connection very often, I set about learning what it meant. The dictionary afforded me little or no help. I found it was "the act of abolishing;" but then I did not know what was to be abolished. Here I was perplexed. I did not dare to ask any one about its meaning, for I was satisfied that it was something they wanted me to know very little about. After a patient waiting, I got one of our city papers, containing an account of the number of petitions from the north, praying for the abolition of slavery in the District of Columbia, and of the slave trade between the States. From this time I understood the words *abolition* and *abolitionist*, and always drew near when that word was spoken, expecting to hear something of importance to myself and fellow-slaves. The light broke in upon me by degrees. I went one day down on the wharf of Mr. Waters; and seeing two Irishmen unloading a scow of stone, I went, unasked, and helped them. When we had finished, one of them came to me and asked me if I were a slave. I told him I was. He asked, "Are ye a slave for life?" I told him that I was. The good Irishman seemed to be deeply affected by the statement. He said to the other that it was a pity so fine a little fellow as myself should be a slave for life. He said it was a shame to hold me. They both advised me to run away to the north; that I should find friends there, and that I should be free. I pretended not to be interested in what they said, and treated them as if I did not understand them; for I feared they might be treacherous. White men have been known to encourage slaves to escape, and then, to get the reward, catch them and return them to their masters. I was afraid that these seemingly good men might use me so; but I nevertheless remembered their advice, and from that time I resolved to run away. I looked forward to a time at which it would be safe for me to escape. I was too young to think of doing so immediately; besides, I wished to learn how to write, as I might have occasion to write my own pass. I consoled myself with the hope that I should one day find a good chance. Meanwhile, I would learn to write.

The idea as to how I might learn to write was suggested to me by being in Durgin and Bailey's ship-yard, and frequently seeing the ship carpenters, after hewing, and getting a piece of timber ready for use, write on the timber the name of that part of the ship for which it was intended. When a piece of timber was intended for the larboard side, it would be marked—"L." When a piece was for the starboard side, it would be marked thus—"S." A piece for the larboard side forward, would be marked thus—"L.F." When a piece was for starboard side forward, it would be marked thus—"S. F." For larboard aft, it would be marked thus—"L. A." For starboard aft, it would be marked thus—"S. A." I soon learned the names of these letters, and for what they were intended when placed upon a piece of timber in the ship-yard. I immediately commenced copying them, and in a short time was able to make the four letters named. After that, when I met with any boy who I knew could write, I would tell him I could write as well as he. The next word would be, "I don't believe you. Let me see you try it." I would then make the letters which I had been so fortunate as to learn, and ask him to beat that. In this way I got a good many lessons in writing, which it is quite possible I should never have gotten in any other way. During this time, my copy-book was the board fence, brick way, and pavement; my pen and ink was a lump of chalk. With these, I learned mainly how to write. I then commenced and continued copying the Italics in Webster's Spelling Book,[20] until I could make them all without looking on the book. By this time, my little Master Thomas had gone to school, and learned how to write, and had written over a number of copy-books. These had been brought home, and shown to some of our near neighbors, and then laid aside. My mistress used to go to class meeting at the Wilk Street meetinghouse every Monday afternoon, and leave me to take care of the house. When left thus, I used to spend the time in writing in the spaces left in Master Thomas's copy-book, copying what he had written. I continued to do this until I could write a hand very similar to

[20]A word-book (1782–1783) developed by lexicographer Noah Webster (1758–1843); it was used in virtually all American schools and sold perhaps as many as sixty million copies.

that of Master Thomas. Thus, after a long, tedious effort for years, I finally succeeded in learning how to write.

Chapter VIII

In a very short time after I went to live at Baltimore, my old master's youngest son Richard died; and in about three years and six months after his death, my old master, Captain Anthony, died, leaving only his son, Andrew, and daughter, Lucretia, to share his estate. He died while on a visit to see his daughter at Hillsborough. Cut off thus unexpectedly, he left no will as to the disposal of his property. It was therefore necessary to have a valuation of the property, that it might be equally divided between Mrs. Lucretia and Master Andrew. I was immediately sent for, to be valued with the other property. Here again my feelings rose up in detestation of slavery. I had now a new conception of my degraded condition. Prior to this, I had become, if not insensible to my lot, at least partly so. I left Baltimore with a young heart overborne with sadness, and a soul full of apprehension. I took passage with Captain Rowe, in the schooner Wild Cat, and, after a sail of about twenty-four hours, I found myself near the place of my birth. I had now been absent from it almost, if not quite, five years. I, however, remembered the place very well. I was only about five years old when I left it, to go and live with my old master on Colonel Lloyd's plantation; so that I was now between ten and eleven years old.

We were all ranked together at the valuation. Men and women, old and young, married and single, were ranked with horses, sheep and swine. There were horses and men, cattle and women, pigs and children, all holding the same rank in the scale of being, and were all subjected to the same narrow examination. Silvery-headed age and sprightly youth, maids and matrons, had to undergo the same indelicate inspection. At this moment, I saw more clearly than ever the brutalizing effects of slavery upon both slave and slaveholder.

After the valuation, then came the division. I have no language to express the high excitement and deep anxiety which were felt among us poor slaves during this time. Our fate for life was now to be decided. We had no more voice in that decision than the brutes among whom we were ranked. A single word from the white men was enough—against all our wishes, prayers, and entreaties—to sunder forever the dearest friends, dearest kindred, and strongest ties known to human beings. In addition to the pain of separation, there was the horrid dread of falling into the hands of Master Andrew. He was known to us all as being a most cruel wretch,—a common drunkard, who had, by his reckless mismanagement and profligate dissipation, already wasted a large portion of his father's property. We all felt that we might as well be sold at once to the Georgia traders, as to pass into his hands; for we knew that that would be our inevitable condition,—a condition held by us all in the utmost horror and dread.

I suffered more anxiety than most of my fellowslaves. I had known what it was to be kindly treated; they had known nothing of the kind. They had seen little or nothing of the world. They were in very deed men and women of sorrow, and acquainted with grief. Their backs had been made familiar with the bloody lash, so that they had become callous; mine was yet tender; for while at Baltimore I got few whippings, and few slaves could boast of a kinder master and mistress than myself; and the thought of passing out of their hands into those of Master Andrew—a man who, but a few days before, to give me a sample of his bloody disposition, took my little brother by the throat, threw him on the ground, and with the heel of his boot stamped upon his head till the blood gushed from his nose and ears—was well calculated to make me anxious as to my fate. After he had committed this savage outrage upon my brother, he turned to me, and said that was the way he meant to serve me one of these days,—meaning, I suppose, when I came into his possession.

Thanks to a kind Providence, I fell to the portion of Mrs. Lucretia, and was sent immediately back to Baltimore, to live again in the family of Master Hugh. Their joy at my return equalled their sorrow at my departure. It was a glad day to me. I had escaped a [fate] worse than lion's jaws. I was absent from Baltimore, for the purpose of valuation and division, just about one month, and it seemed to have been six.

Very soon after my return to Baltimore, my mistress, Lucretia, died, leaving her husband and one child, Amanda; and in a very short time after her death, Master Andrew died. Now all the property of my old master, slaves included, was in the hands of strangers,—strangers who had had nothing to do with accumulating it. Not a slave was left free. All remained slaves, from the youngest to the oldest. If any one thing in my experience, more than another, served to deepen my conviction of the infernal character of slavery, and to fill me with unutterable loathing of slaveholders, it was their base ingratitude to my poor old grandmother. She had served my old master faithfully from youth to old age. She had been the source of all his wealth; she had peopled his plantation with slaves; she had become a great grandmother in his service. She had rocked him in infancy, attended him in childhood, served him through life, and at his death wiped from his icy brow the cold death-sweat, and closed his eyes forever. She was nevertheless left a slave—a slave for life—a slave in the hands of strangers; and in their hands she saw her children, her grandchildren, and her great-grandchildren, divided, like so many sheep, without being gratified with the small privilege of a single word, as to their or her own destiny. And, to cap the climax of their base ingratitude and fiendish barbarity, my grandmother, who was now very old, having outlived my old master and all his children, having seen the beginning and end of all of them, and her present owners finding she was of but little value, her frame already racked with the pains of old age, and complete helplessness fast stealing over her once active limbs, they took her to the woods, built her a little hut, put up a little mud-chimney, and then made her welcome to the privilege of supporting herself there in perfect loneliness; thus virtually turning her out to die! If my poor old grandmother now lives, she lives to suffer in utter loneliness; she lives to remember and mourn over the loss of children, the loss of grandchildren, and the loss of great-grandchildren. They are, in the language of the slave's poet, Whittier,—

> *"Gone, gone, sold and gone*
> *To the rice swamp dank and lone,*
> *Where the slave-whip ceaseless swings,*
> *Where the noisome insect stings,*
> *Where the fever-demon strews*
> *Poison with the falling dews,*
> *Where the sickly sunbeams glare*
> *Through the hot and misty air:—*
>   *Gone, gone, sold and gone*
> *To the rice swamp dank and lone,*
> *From Virginia hills and waters—*
> *Woe is me, my stolen daughters!"*[21]

The hearth is desolate. The children, the unconscious children, who once sang and danced in her presence, are gone. She gropes her way, in the darkness of age, for a drink of water. Instead of the voices of her children, she hears by day the moans of the dove, and by night the screams of the hideous owl. All is gloom. The grave is at the door. And now, when weighed down by the pains and aches of old age, when the head inclines to the feet, when the beginning and ending of human existence meet, and helpless infancy and painful old age combine together—at this time, this most needful time, the time for the exercise of that tenderness and affection which children only can exercise toward a declining parent—my poor old grandmother, the devoted mother of twelve children, is left all alone, in yonder little hut, before a few dim embers. She stands—she sits—she staggers—she falls—she groans—she dies—and there are none of her children or grandchildren present, to wipe from her wrinkled brow the cold sweat of death, or to place beneath the sod her fallen remains. Will not a righteous God visit for these things?

In about two years after the death of Mrs. Lucretia, Master Thomas married his second wife. Her name was Rowena Hamilton. She was the eldest daughter of Mr. William Hamilton. Master now lived in St. Michael's. Not long after his marriage, a misunderstanding took place between himself and Master Hugh; and as a means of punishing his brother, he took me from him to live with himself at St. Michael's. Here I underwent another most painful separation. It, however, was not so severe as the one I dreaded at the division of property; for, during this interval, a great change had taken place in Master Hugh and his once kind and affectionate wife. The influence of brandy upon him, and of slavery upon her, had effected a disastrous change in the characters of both; so that, as far as they were

[21]From John Greenleaf Whittier's "The Farewell: Of a Virginia Slave Mother to Her Daughter Sold into Southern Bondage," the full text of which is printed earlier in this volume.

concerned, I thought I had little to lose by the change. But it was not to them that I was attached. It was to those little Baltimore boys that I felt the strongest attachment. I had received many good lessons from them, and was still receiving them, and the thought of leaving them was painful indeed. I was leaving, too, without the hope of ever being allowed to return. Master Thomas had said he would never let me return again. The barrier betwixt himself and brother he considered impassable.

I then had to regret that I did not at least make the attempt to carry out my resolution to run away; for the chances of success are tenfold greater from the city than from the country.

I sailed from Baltimore for St. Michael's in the sloop Amanda, Captain Edward Dodson. On my passage, I paid particular attention to the direction which the steamboats took to go to Philadelphia. I found, instead of going down, on reaching North Point they went up the bay, in a north-easterly direction. I deemed this knowledge of the utmost importance. My determination to run away was again revived. I resolved to wait only so long as the offering of a favorable opportunity. When that came, I was determined to be off.

Chapter IX

I have now reached a period of my life when I can give dates. I left Baltimore, and went to live with Master Thomas Auld, at St. Michael's, in March, 1832. It was now more than seven years since I lived with him in the family of my old master, on Colonel Lloyd's plantation. We of course were now almost entire strangers to each other. He was to me a new master, and I to him a new slave. I was ignorant of his temper and disposition; he was equally so of mine. A very short time, however, brought us into full acquaintance with each other. I was made acquainted with his wife not less than with himself. They were well matched, being equally mean and cruel. I was now, for the first time during a space of more than seven years, made to feel the painful gnawings of hunger—a something which I had not experienced before since I left Colonel Lloyd's plantation. It went hard enough with me then, when I could look back at no period at which I had enjoyed a sufficiency. It was tenfold harder after living in Master Hugh's family, where I had always had enough to eat, and of that which was good. I have said Master Thomas was a mean man. He was so. Not to give a slave enough to eat, is regarded as the most aggravated development of meanness even among slaveholders. The rule is, no matter how coarse the food, only let there be enough of it. This is the theory; and in the part of Maryland from which I came, it is the general practice,—though there are many exceptions. Master Thomas gave us enough of neither coarse nor fine food. There were four slaves of us in the kitchen—my sister Eliza, my aunt Priscilla, Henny, and myself; and we were allowed less than half of a bushel of cornmeal per week, and very little else, either in the shape of meat or vegetables. It was not enough for us to subsist upon. We were therefore reduced to the wretched necessity of living at the expense of our neighbors. This we did by begging and stealing, whichever came handy in the time of need, the one being considered as legitimate as the other. A great many times have we poor creatures been nearly perishing with hunger, when food in abundance lay mouldering in the safe and smoke-house,[22] and our pious mistress was aware of the fact; and yet that mistress and her husband would kneel every morning, and pray that God would bless them in basket and store!

Bad as all slaveholders are, we seldom meet one destitute of every element of character commanding respect. My master was one of this rare sort. I do not know of one single noble act ever performed by him. The leading trait in his character was meanness; and if there were any other element in his nature, it was made subject to this. He was mean; and, like most other mean men, he lacked the ability to conceal his meanness. Captain Auld was not born a slaveholder. He had been a poor man, master only of a Bay craft. He came into possession of all his slaves by marriage; and of all men, adopted slaveholders are the worst. He was cruel, but cowardly. He commanded without firmness. In the enforcement of his rules, he was at times rigid, and at times lax. At times, he spoke to his slaves with the firmness of Napoleon and the fury of a demon; at other times, he might well be mistaken for an inquirer who had lost his way. He did nothing of himself. He might have passed for a lion, but for his ears.[23] In all things noble which he attempted, his own meanness shone most conspicuous. His airs, words, and actions, were the airs, words, and actions of born slaveholders, and, being assumed, were awkward enough. He was not even a good imitator. He possessed all the disposition to deceive, but wanted the power. Having no resources within himself, he was compelled to be the copyist of many, and being such, he was forever the victim of inconsistency; and of consequence he was an object of contempt, and was held as such even by his slaves. The luxury of having slaves of his own to wait upon him was something new and unprepared for. He was a slaveholder without the ability to hold slaves. He found himself incapable of managing his slaves either by force, fear, or fraud. We seldom called him "master," we generally called him "Captain Auld," and were hardly disposed to title him at all. I doubt not that our conduct had much to do with making him appear awkward, and of consequence fretful. Our want of reverence for him must have perplexed him greatly. He wished to have us call him master, but lacked the firmness necessary to command us to do so. His wife used to insist upon our calling him so, but to no purpose. In August, 1832, my master attended a Methodist camp-meeting held in the Bay-side, Talbot county, and there experienced religion. I indulged a faint hope that his conversion would lead him to emancipate his slaves, and that, if he did not do this, it would at any rate, make him more kind and humane. I was disappointed in both these respects. It neither made him to be humane to his slaves, nor to emancipate them. If it had any

[22]Meat and fish were cured by smoking in the smokehouse and then stored there or in a meat safe.

[23]Which, like those of a jackass, showed him to be something other than what he claimed.

effect on his character, it made him more cruel and hateful in all his ways; for I believe him to have been a much worse man after his conversion than before. Prior to his conversion, he relied upon his own depravity to shield and sustain him in his savage barbarity; but after his conversion, he found religious sanction and support for his slaveholding cruelty. He made the greatest pretensions to piety. His house was the house of prayer. He prayed morning, noon, and night. He very soon distinguished himself among his brethren, and was soon made a class-leader and exhorter. His activity in revivals was great, and he proved himself an instrument in the hands of the church in converting many souls. His house was the preachers' home. They used to take great pleasure in coming there to put up; for while he starved us, he stuffed them. We have had three or four preachers there at a time. The names of those who used to come most frequently while I lived there, were Mr. Storks, Mr. Ewery, Mr. Humphry, and Mr. Hickey. I have also seen Mr. George Cookman at our house. We slaves loved Mr. Cookman. We believed him to be a good man. We thought him instrumental in getting Mr. Samuel Harrison, a very rich slaveholder, to emancipate his slaves; and by some means got the impression that he was laboring to effect the emancipation of all the slaves. When he was at our house, we were sure to be called in to prayers. When the others were there, we were sometimes called in and sometimes not. Mr. Cookman took more notice of us than either of the other ministers. He could not come among us without betraying his sympathy for us, and, stupid as we were, we had the sagacity to see it.

While I lived with my master in St. Michael's, there was a white young man, a Mr. Wilson, who proposed to keep a Sabbath school for the instruction of such slaves as might be disposed to learn to read the New Testament. We met but three times, when Mr. West and Mr. Fairbanks, both class-leaders, with many others, came upon with us with sticks and other missiles, drove us off, and forbade us to meet again. Thus ended our little Sabbath school in the pious town of St. Michael's.

I have said my master found religious sanction for his cruelty. As an example, I will state one of many facts going to prove the charge. I have seen him tie up a lame young woman, and whip her with a heavy cowskin upon her naked shoulders, causing the warm red blood to drip; and, in justification of the bloody deed, he would quote this passage of Scripture—"He that knoweth his master's will, and doeth it not, shall be beaten with many stripes."

Master would keep this lacerated young woman tied up in this horrid situation four or five hours at a time. I have known him to tie her up early in the morning, and whip her before breakfast; leave her, go to his store, return at dinner, and whip her again, cutting her in the places already made raw with his cruel lash. The secret of master's cruelty toward "Henny" is found in the fact of her being almost helpless. When quite a child, she fell into the fire, and burned herself horribly. Her hands were so burnt that she never got the use of them. She could do very little but bear heavy burdens. She was to master a bill of expense; and as he was a mean man, she was a constant offence to him. He seemed desirous of getting the poor girl out of existence. He gave her away once to his sister; but, being a poor gift, she was not disposed to keep her. Finally, my benevolent master, to use his own words, "set her adrift to take care of herself." Here was a recently-converted man, holding on upon the mother, and at the same time turning out her helpless child, to starve and die! Master Thomas was one of the many pious slaveholders who hold slaves for the very charitable purpose of taking care of them.

My master and myself had quite a number of differences. He found me unsuitable to his purpose. My city life, he said, had had a very pernicious effect upon me. It had almost ruined me for every good purpose, and fitted me for every thing which was bad. One of my greatest faults was that of letting his horse run away, and go down to his father-in-law's farm, which was about five miles from St. Michael's. I would then have to go after it. My reason for this kind of carelessness, or carefulness, was, that I could always get something to eat when I went there. Master William Hamilton, my master's father-in-law, always gave his slaves enough to eat. I never left there hungry, no matter how great the need of my speedy return. Master Thomas at length said he would stand it no longer. I had lived with him nine months, during which time he had given me a number of severe whippings, all to no good purpose. He resolved to put me out, as he said, to be broken; and, for this purpose, he let me for one year to a man named Edward Covey. Mr. Covey was a poor man, a farm-renter. He rented the place upon which he lived, as also the hands with which he tilled it. Mr. Covey had acquired a very high reputation for breaking young slaves, and this reputation was of immense value to him. It enabled him to get his farm tilled with much less expense to himself than he could have had it done without such a reputation. Some slaveholders thought it not much loss to allow Mr. Covey to have their slaves one year, for the sake of the training to which they were subjected, without any other compensation. He could hire young help with great ease, in consequence of this reputation. Added to the natural good qualities of Mr. Covey, he was a professor of religion—a pious soul—a member and a class-leader in the Methodist church. All of this added weight to his reputation as a "nigger-breaker." I was aware of all the facts, having been made acquainted with them by a young man who had lived there. I nevertheless made the change gladly; for I was sure of getting enough to eat, which is not the smallest consideration to a hungry man.

Chapter X

I left Master Thomas's house, and went to live with Mr. Covey, on the 1st of January, 1833. I was now, for the first time in my life, a field hand. In my new employment, I found myself even more awkward than a country boy appeared to be in a large city. I had been at my new home but one week before Mr. Covey gave me a very severe whipping, cutting my back, causing the blood to run, and raising ridges on my flesh as large as my little finger.

The details of this affair are as follows: Mr. Covey sent me, very early in the morning of one of our coldest days in the month of January, to the woods, to get a load of wood. He gave me a team of unbroken oxen. He told me which was the in-hand ox, and which the off-hand one. He then tied the end of a large rope around the horns of the in-hand ox, and gave me the other end of it, and told me, if the oxen started to run, that I must hold on upon the rope. I had never driven oxen before, and of course I was very awkward. I, however, succeeded in getting to the edge of the woods with little difficulty; but I had got a very few rods into the woods, when the oxen took fright, and started full tilt, carrying the cart against trees, and over stumps, in the most frightful manner. I expected every moment that my brains would be dashed out against the trees. After running thus for a considerable distance, they finally upset the cart, dashing it with great force against a tree, and threw themselves into a dense thicket. How I escaped death, I do not know. There I was, entirely alone, in a thick wood, in a place new to me. My cart was upset and shattered, my oxen were entangled among the young trees, and there was none to help me. After a long spell of effort, I succeeded in getting my cart righted, my oxen disentangled and again yoked to the cart. I now proceeded with my team to the place where I had, the day before, been chopping wood, and loaded my cart pretty heavily, thinking in this way to tame my oxen. I then proceeded on my way home. I had now consumed one half of the day. I got out of the woods safely, and now felt out of danger. I stopped my oxen to open the woods gate; and just as I did so, before I could get hold of my ox-rope, the oxen again started, rushed through the gate, catching it between the wheel and the body of the cart, tearing it to pieces, and coming within a few inches of crushing me against the gate-post. Thus twice, in one short day, I escaped death by the merest chance. On my return, I told Mr. Covey what had happened, and how it happened. He ordered me to return to the woods again immediately. I did so, and he followed on after me. Just as I got into the woods, he came up and told me to stop my cart, and that he would teach me how to trifle away my time, and break gates. He then went to a large gum-tree, and with his axe cut three large switches, and, after trimming them up neatly with his pocketknife, he ordered me to take off my clothes. I made him no answer, but stood with my clothes on. He repeated his order. I still made him no answer, nor did I move to strip myself. Upon this he rushed at me with the fierceness of a tiger, tore off my clothes, and lashed me till he had worn out his switches, cutting me so savagely as to leave the marks visible for a long time after. This whipping was the first of a number just like it, and for similar offences.

I lived with Mr. Covey one year. During the first six months, of that year, scarce a week passed without his whipping me. I was seldom free from a sore back. My awkwardness was almost always his excuse for whipping me. We were worked fully up to the point of endurance. Long before day we were up, our horses fed, and by the first approach of day we were off to the field with our hoes and ploughing teams. Mr. Covey gave us enough to eat, but scarce time to eat it. We were often less than five minutes taking our meals. We were often in the field from the first approach of day till its last lingering ray had left us; and at saving-fodder time, midnight often caught us in the field binding blades.[24]

Covey would be out with us. The way he used to stand it, was this. He would spend the most of his afternoons in bed. He would then come out fresh in the evening, ready to urge us on with his words, example, and frequently with the whip. Mr. Covey was one of the few slaveholders who could and did work with his hands. He was a hard-working man. He knew by himself just what a man or a boy could do. There was no deceiving him. His work went on in his absence almost as well as in his presence; and he had the faculty of making us feel that he was ever present with us. This he did by surprising us. He seldom approached the spot where we were at work openly, if he could do it secretly. He always aimed at taking us by surprise. Such was his cunning, that we used to call him, among ourselves, "the snake." When we were at work in the cornfield, he would sometimes crawl on his hands and knees to avoid detection, and all at once he would rise nearly in our midst, and scream out, "Ha, ha! Come, come! Dash on, dash on!" This being his mode of attack, it was never safe to stop a single minute. His comings were like a thief in the night. He appeared to us as being ever at hand. He was under every tree, behind every stump, in every bush, and at every window, on the plantation. He would sometimes mount his horse, as if bound to St. Michael's, a distance of seven miles, and in half an hour afterwards you would see him coiled up in the corner of the wood-fence, watching every motion of the slaves. He would, for this purpose, leave his horse tied up in the woods. Again, he would sometimes walk up to us, and give us orders as though he was upon the point of starting on a long journey, turn his back upon us, and make as though he was going to the house to get ready; and, before he would get half way thither, he would turn short and crawl into a fence-corner, or behind some tree, and there watch us till the going down of the sun.

Mr. Covey's *forte* consisted in his power to deceive. His life was devoted to planning and perpetrating the grossest deceptions. Every thing he possessed in the shape of learning or religion, he made conform to his disposition to deceive. He seemed to think himself equal to deceiving the Almighty. He would make a short prayer in the morning, and a long prayer at night; and, strange as it may seem, few men would at times appear more devotional than he. The exercises of his family devotions were always commenced with singing; and, as he was a very poor singer himself, the duty of raising the hymn generally came upon me. He would read his hymn, and nod at me to commence. I would at times do so; at others, I would not. My non-compliance would almost always produce much confusion. To show

---

[24]At harvest time, slaves might be in the fields until after midnight binding sheaves or "blades."

himself independent of me, he would start and stagger through with his hymn in the most discordant manner. In this state of mind, he prayed with more than ordinary spirit. Poor man! such was his disposition, and success at deceiving, I do verily believe that he sometimes deceived himself into the solemn belief, that he was a sincere worshipper of the most high God; and this, too, at a time when he may be said to have been guilty of compelling his woman slave to commit the sin of adultery. The facts in the case are these: Mr. Covey was a poor man; he was just commencing in life; he was only able to buy one slave; and, shocking as is the fact, he bought her, as he said, for a *breeder*. This woman was named Caroline. Mr. Covey bought her from Mr. Thomas Lowe, about six miles from St. Michael's. She was a large, able-bodied woman, about twenty years old. She had already given birth to one child, which proved her to be just what he wanted. After buying her, he hired a married man of Mr. Samuel Harrison, to live with him one year; and him he used to fasten up with her every night! The result was, that, at the end of the year, the miserable woman gave birth to twins. At this result Mr. Covey seemed to be highly pleased, both with the man and the wretched woman. Such was his joy, and that of his wife, that nothing they could do for Caroline during her confinement was too good, or too hard to be done. The children were regarded as being quite an addition to his wealth.

If at any one time of my life more than another, I was made to drink the bitterest dregs of slavery, that time was during the first six months of my stay with Mr. Covey. We were worked in all weathers. It was never too hot or too cold; it could never rain, blow, hail, or snow, too hard for us to work in the field. Work, work, work, was scarcely more the order of the day than of the night. The longest days were too short for him, and the shortest nights too long for him. I was somewhat unmanageable when I first went there, but a few months of this discipline tamed me. Mr. Covey succeeded in breaking me. I was broken in body, soul, and spirit. My natural elasticity was crushed, my intellect languished, the disposition to read departed, the cheerful spark that lingered about my eye died; the dark night of slavery closed in upon me, and behold a man transformed into a brute!

Sunday was my only leisure time. I spent this in a sort of beastlike stupor, between sleep and wake, under some large tree. At times I would rise up, a flash of energetic freedom would dart through my soul, accompanied with a faint beam of hope, that flickered for a moment, and then vanished. I sank down again, mourning over my wretched condition. I was sometimes prompted to take my life, and that of Covey, but was prevented by a combination of hope and fear. My sufferings on this plantation seem now like a dream rather than a stern reality.

Our house stood within a few rods of the Chesapeake Bay, whose broad bosom was ever white with sails from every quarter of the habitable globe. Those beautiful vessels, robed in purest white, so delightful to the eye of freemen, were to me so many shrouded ghosts, to terrify and torment me with thoughts of my wretched condition. I have often, in the deep stillness of a summer's Sabbath, stood all alone upon the lofty banks of that noble bay, and traced, with saddened heart and tearful eye, the countless number of sails moving off to the mighty ocean. The sight of these always affected me powerfully. My thoughts would compel utterance; and there, with no audience but the Almighty, I would pour out my soul's complaint, in my rude way, with an apostrophe to the moving multitude of ships:—

"You are loosed from your moorings, and are free; I am fast in my chains, and am a slave! You move merrily before the gentle gale, and I sadly before the bloody whip! You are freedom's swiftwinged angels, that fly round the world; I am confined in bands of iron! O that I were free! Oh, that I were on one of your gallant decks, and under your protecting wing! Alas! betwixt me and you, the turbid waters roll. Go on, go on. O that I could also go! Could I but swim! If I could fly! O, why was I born a man, of whom to make a brute! The glad ship is gone; she hides in the dim distance. I am left in the hottest hell of unending slavery. O God, save me! God, deliver me! Let me be free! Is there any God? Why am I a slave? I will run away. I will not stand it. Get caught, or get clear, I'll try it. I had as well die with ague as the fever. I have only one life to lose. I had as well be killed running as die standing. Only think of it; one hundred miles straight north, and I am free! Try it? Yes! God helping me, I will. It cannot be that I shall live and die a slave. I will take to the water. This very bay shall yet bear me into freedom. The steamboats steered in a north-east course from North Point. I will do the same; and when I get to the head of the bay, I will turn my canoe adrift, and walk straight through Delaware into Pennsylvania. When I get there, I shall not be required to have a pass; I can travel without being disturbed. Let but the first opportunity offer, and, come what will, I am off. Meanwhile, I will try to bear up under the yoke. I am not the only slave in the world. Why should I fret? I can bear as much as any of them. Besides, I am but a boy, and all boys are bound to some one. It may be that my misery in slavery will only increase my happiness when I get free. There is a better day coming."

Thus I used to think, and thus I used to speak to myself; goaded almost to madness at one moment, and at the next reconciling myself to my wretched lot.

I have already intimated that my condition was much worse, during the first six months of my stay at Mr. Covey's, than in the last six. The circumstances leading to the change in Mr. Covey's course toward me form an epoch in my humble history. You have seen how a man was made a slave; you shall see how a slave was made a man. On one of the hottest days of the month of August, 1833, Bill Smith, William Hughes, a slave named Eli, and myself, were engaged in fanning wheat.[25] Hughes was clearing the fanned wheat from before the fan. Eli was turning, Smith was feeding, and I was carrying wheat to the fan. The work was simple, requiring strength rather than intellect; yet, to one entirely unused to such work, it came very hard. About three o'clock of that day, I broke down; my strength failed me;

[25]Separating the wheat from the chaff.

I was seized with a violent aching of the head, attended with extreme dizziness; I trembled in every limb. Finding what was coming, I nerved myself up, feeling it would never do to stop work. I stood as long as I could stagger to the hopper with grain. When I could stand no longer, I fell, and felt as if held down by an immense weight. The fan of course stopped; every one had his own work to do; and no one could do the work of the other, and have his own go on at the same time.

Mr. Covey was at the house, about one hundred yards from the treading-yard where we were fanning. On hearing the fan stop, he left immediately, and came to the spot where we were. He hastily inquired what the matter was. Bill answered that I was sick, and there was no one to bring wheat to the fan. I had by this time crawled away under the side of the post and rail-fence by which the yard was enclosed, hoping to find relief by getting out of the sun. He then asked where I was. He was told by one of the hands. He came to the spot, and, after looking at me awhile, asked me what was the matter. I told him as well as I could, for I scarce had strength to speak. He then gave me a savage kick in the side, and told me to get up. I tried to do so, but fell back in the attempt. He gave me another kick, and again told me to rise. I again tried, and succeeded in gaining my feet; but, stooping to get the tub with which I was feeding the fan, I again staggered and fell. While down in this situation, Mr. Covey took up the hickory slat with which Hughes had been striking off the half-bushel measure, and with it gave me a heavy blow upon the head, making a large wound, and the blood ran freely; and with this again told me to get up. I made no effort to comply, having now made up my mind to let him do his worst. In a short time after receiving this blow, my head grew better. Mr. Covey had now left me to my fate. At this moment I resolved, for the first time, to go to my master, enter a complaint, and ask his protection. In order to do this, I must that afternoon walk seven miles; and this, under the circumstances, was truly a severe undertaking. I was exceedingly feeble; made so as much by the kicks and blows which I received, as by the severe fit of sickness to which I had been subjected. I, however, watched my chance, while Covey was looking in an opposite direction, and started for St. Michael's. I succeeded in getting a considerable distance on my way to the woods, when Covey discovered me, and called after me to come back, threatening what he would do if I did not come. I disregarded both his calls and his threats, and made my way to the woods as fast as my feeble state would allow; and thinking I might be overhauled by him if I kept the road, I walked through the woods, keeping far enough from the road to avoid detection, and near enough to prevent losing my way. I had not gone far before my little strength again failed me. I could go no farther. I fell down, and lay for a considerable time. The blood was yet oozing from the wound on my head. For a time I thought I should bleed to death; and think now that I should have done so, but that the blood so matted my hair as to stop the wound. After lying there about three quarters of an hour, I nerved myself up again, and started on my way, through bogs and briers, barefooted and bareheaded, tearing my feet sometimes at nearly every step; and after a journey of about seven miles, occupying some five hours to perform it, I arrived at master's store. I then presented an appearance enough to affect any but a heart of iron. From the crown of my head to my feet, I was covered with blood. My hair was all clotted with dust and blood; my shirt was stiff with blood. My legs and feet were torn in sundry places with briers and thorns, and were also covered with blood. I suppose I looked like a man who had escaped a den of wild beasts, and barely escaped them. In this state I appeared before my master, humbly entreating him to interpose his authority for my protection. I told him all the circumstances as well as I could, and it seemed, as I spoke, at times to affect him. He would then walk the floor, and seek to justify Covey by saying he expected I deserved it. He asked me what I wanted. I told him, to let me get a new home; that as sure as I lived with Mr. Covey again, I should live with but to die with him; that Covey would surely kill me; he was in a fair way for it. Master Thomas ridiculed the idea that there was any danger of Mr. Covey's killing me, and said that he knew Mr. Covey; that he was a good man, and that he could not think of taking me from him; that, should he do so, he would lose the whole year's wages; that I belonged to Mr. Covey for one year, and that I must go back to him, come what might; and that I must not trouble him with any more stories, or that he would himself *get hold of me*. After threatening me thus, he gave me a very large dose of salts, telling me that I might remain in St. Michael's that night, (it being quite late,) but that I must be off back to Mr. Covey's early in the morning; and that if I did not, he would *get hold of me*, which meant that he would whip me. I remained all night, and, according to his orders, I started off to Covey's in the morning, (Saturday morning), wearied in body and broken in spirit. I got no supper that night, or breakfast that morning. I reached Covey's about nine o'clock; and just as I was getting over the fence that divided Mrs. Kemp's fields from ours, out ran Covey with his cowskin, to give me another whipping. Before he could reach me, I succeeded in getting to the cornfield; and as the corn was very high, it afforded me the means of hiding. He seemed very angry, and searched for me a long time. My behavior was altogether unaccountable. He finally gave up the chase, thinking, I suppose, that I must come home for something to eat; he would give himself no further trouble in looking for me. I spent that day mostly in the woods, having the alternative before me,—to go home and be whipped to death, or stay in the woods and be starved to death. That night, I fell in with Sandy Jenkins, a slave with whom I was somewhat acquainted. Sandy had a free wife who lived about four miles from Mr. Covey's; and it being Saturday, he was on his way to see her. I told him my circumstances, and he very kindly invited me to go home with him. I went home with him, and talked this whole matter over, and got his advice as to what course it was best for me to pursue. I found Sandy an old adviser.[26] He told me, with great solemnity, I must go back to Covey; but that before I went, I must go with him into another part

---

[26]A wise man—perhaps a conjure man.

of the woods, where there was a certain *root*,[27] which, if I would take some of it with me, carrying it *always on my right side*, would render it impossible for Mr. Covey, or any other white man, to whip me. He said he had carried it for years; and since he had done so, he had never received a blow, and never expected to while he carried it. I at first rejected the idea, that the simple carrying of a root in my pocket would have any such effect as he had said, and was not disposed to take it; but Sandy impressed the necessity with much earnestness, telling me it could do no harm, if it did no good. To please him, I at length took the root, and, according to his direction, carried it upon my right side. This was Sunday morning. I immediately started for home; and upon entering the yard gate, out came Mr. Covey on his way to meeting. He spoke to me very kindly, bade me drive the pigs from a lot near by, and passed on towards the church. Now, this singular conduct of Mr. Covey really made me begin to think that there was something in the *root* which Sandy had given me; and had it been on any other day than Sunday, I could have attributed the conduct to no other cause than the influence of that root; and as it was, I was half inclined to think the *root* to be something more than I at first had taken it to be. All went well till Monday morning. On this morning, the virtue of the *root* was fully tested. Long before day-light, I was called to go and rub, curry, and feed, the horses. I obeyed, and was glad to obey. But whilst thus engaged, whilst in the act of throwing down some blades from the loft, Mr. Covey entered the stable with a long rope; and just as I was half out of the loft, he caught hold of my legs, and was about tying me. As soon as I found what he was up to, I gave a sudden spring, and as I did so, he holding to my legs, I was brought sprawling on the stable floor. Mr. Covey seemed now to think he had me, and could do what he pleased; but at this moment—from whence came the spirit I don't know—I resolved to fight; and, suiting my action to the resolution, I seized Covey hard by the throat; and as I did so, I rose. He held on to me, and I to him. My resistance was so entirely unexpected, that Covey seemed taken all aback. He trembled like a leaf. This gave me assurance, and I held him uneasy, causing the blood to run where I touched him with the ends of my fingers. Mr. Covey soon called out to Hughes for help. Hughes came, and, while Covey held me, attempted to tie my right hand. While he was in the act of doing so, I watched my chance, and gave him a heavy kick close under the ribs. This kick fairly sickened Hughes, so that he left me in the hands of Mr. Covey. This kick had the effect of not only weakening Hughes, but Covey also. When he saw Hughes bending over with pain, his courage quailed. He asked me if I meant to persist in my resistance. I told him I did, come what might; that he had used me like a brute for six months, and that I was determined to be used so no longer. With that, he strove to drag me to a stick that was lying just out of the stable door. He meant to knock me

---

[27]Perhaps a "High John the Conquer" root—
see the African American tales in Volume C,
and note 28, below.

down. But just as he was leaning over to get the stick, I seized him with both hands by his collar, and brought him by a sudden snatch to the ground. By this time, Bill came. Covey called upon him for assistance. Bill wanted to know what he could do. Covey said, "Take hold of him, take hold of him!" Bill said his master hired him out to work, and not to help to whip me; so he left Covey and myself to fight our own battle out. We were at it for nearly two hours. Covey at length let me go, puffing and blowing at a great rate, saying that if I had not resisted, he would not have whipped me half so much. The truth was, that he had not whipped me at all. I considered him as getting entirely the worst end of the bargain; for he had drawn no blood from me, but I had from him. The whole six months afterwards, that I spent with Mr. Covey, he never laid the weight of his finger upon me in anger. He would occasionally say, he didn't want to get hold of me again. "No," thought I, "you need not; for you will come off worse than you did before."

This battle with Mr. Covey was the turning-point in my career as a slave. It rekindled the few expiring embers of freedom, and revived within me a sense of my own manhood. It recalled the departed self-confidence, and inspired me again with a determination to be free. The gratification afforded by the triumph was a full compensation for whatever else might follow, even death itself. He only can understand the deep satisfaction which I experienced, who has himself repelled by force the bloody arm of slavery. I felt as I never felt before. It was a glorious resurrection, from the tomb of slavery, to the heaven of freedom. My long-crushed spirit rose, cowardice departed, bold defiance took its place; and I now resolved that, however long I might remain a slave in form, the day had passed forever when I could be a slave in fact. I did not hesitate to let it be known of me, that the white man who expected to succeed in whipping, must also succeed in killing me.

From this time I was never again what might be called fairly whipped, though I remained a slave four years afterwards. I had several fights, but was never whipped.

It was for a long time a matter of surprise to me why Mr. Covey did not immediately have me taken by the constable to the whipping-post, and there regularly whipped for the crime of raising my hand against a white man in defence of myself. And the only explanation I can now think of does not entirely satisfy me; but such as it is, I will give it. Mr. Covey enjoyed the most unbounded reputation for being a first-rate overseer and negro-breaker. It was of considerable importance to him. That reputation was at stake; and had he sent me—a boy about sixteen years old—to the public whipping-post, his reputation would have been lost; so, to save his reputation, he suffered me to go unpunished.

My term of actual service to Mr. Edward Covey ended on Christmas day, 1833. The days between Christmas and New Year's day are allowed as holidays; and, accordingly, we were not required to perform any labor, more than to feed and take care of the stock. This time we regarded as our own, by the grace of our masters; and we therefore used or abused it nearly as we pleased. Those of us who had families at a distance, were generally allowed to spend the whole six days in their society. This time, however, was spent in various ways. The staid, sober, thinking and industrious ones of our number would employ themselves in making corn-brooms, mats, horse-collars, and baskets; and another class of us would spend the time hunting opossums, hares, and coons. But by far the larger part engaged in such sports and merriments as playing ball, wrestling, running foot-races, fiddling, dancing, and drinking whisky; and this latter mode of spending the time was by far the most agreeable to the feelings of our master. A slave who would work during the holidays was considered by our masters as scarcely deserving them. He was regarded as one who rejected the favor of his master. It was deemed a disgrace not to get drunk at Christmas; and he was regarded as lazy indeed, who had not provided himself with the necessary means, during the year, to get whisky enough to last him through Christmas.

From what I know of the effect of these holidays upon the slave, I believe them to be among the most effective means in the hands of the slaveholder in keeping down the spirit of insurrection. Were the slaveholders at once to abandon this practice, I have not the slightest doubt it would lead to an immediate insurrection among the slaves. These holidays serve as conductors, or safety-valves, to carry off the rebellious spirit of enslaved humanity. But for these, the slave would be forced up to the wildest desperation; and woe betide the slaveholder, the day he ventures to remove or hinder the operation of those conductors! I warn him that, in such an event, a spirit will go forth in their midst, more to be dreaded than the most appalling earthquake.

The holidays are part and parcel of the gross fraud, wrong, and inhumanity of slavery. They are professedly a custom established by the benevolence of the slaveholders; but I undertake to say, it is the result of selfishness, and one of the grossest frauds committed upon the downtrodden slave. They do not give the slaves this time because they would not like to have their work during its continuance, but because they know it would be unsafe to deprive them of it. This will be seen by the fact, that the slaveholders like to have their slaves spend those days just in such a manner as to make them as glad of their ending as of their beginning. Their object seems to be, to disgust their slaves with freedom, by plunging them into the lowest depths of dissipation. For instance, the slaveholders not only like to see the slave drink of his own accord, but will adopt various plans to make him drunk. One plan is, to make bets on their slaves, as to who can drink the most whisky without getting drunk; and in this way they succeed in getting whole multitudes to drink to excess. Thus, when the slave asks for virtuous freedom, the cunning slaveholder, knowing his ignorance, cheats him with a dose of vicious dissipation, artfully labelled with the name of liberty. The most of us used to drink it down, and the result was just what might be supposed: many of us were led to think that there was little to choose between liberty and slavery. We felt, and very properly too, that we had almost as well be slaves to man as to rum. So, when the holidays ended, we staggered up from the filth of our wallowing, took a long breath, and marched to the field,—feeling, upon the whole, rather glad to go, from what our master had deceived us into a belief was freedom, back to the arms of slavery.

I have said that this mode of treatment is a part of the whole system of fraud and inhumanity of slavery. It is so. The mode here adopted to disgust the slave with freedom, by allowing him to see only the abuse of it, is carried out in other things. For instance, a slave loves molasses; he steals some. His master, in many cases, goes off to town, and buys a large quantity; he returns, takes his whip, and commands the slave to eat the molasses, until the poor fellow is made sick at the very mention of it. The same mode is sometimes adopted to make the slaves refrain from asking for more food than their regular allowance. A slave runs through his allowance, and applies for more. His master is enraged at him; but, not willing to send him off without food, gives him more than is necessary, and compels him to eat it within a given time. Then, if he complains that he cannot eat it, he is said to be satisfied neither full nor fasting, and is whipped for being hard to please! I have an abundance of such illustrations of the same principle, drawn from my own observation, but think the cases I have cited sufficient. The practice is a very common one.

On the first of January, 1834, I left Mr. Covey, and went to live with Mr. William Freeland, who lived about three miles from St. Michael's. I soon found Mr. Freeland a very different man from Mr. Covey. Though not rich, he was what would be called an educated southern gentleman. Mr. Covey, as I have shown, was a well-trained negro-breaker and slave-driver. The former (slaveholder though he was) seemed to possess some regard for honor, some reverence for justice, and some respect for humanity. The latter seemed totally insensible to all such sentiments. Mr. Freeland had many of the faults peculiar to slaveholders, such as being very passionate and fretful; but I must do him the justice to say, that he was exceedingly free from those degrading vices to which Mr. Covey was constantly addicted. The one was open and frank, and we always knew where to find him. The other was a most artful deceiver, and could be understood only by such as were skilful enough to detect his cunningly-devised frauds. Another advantage I gained in my new master was, he made no pretensions to, or profession of, religion; and this, in my opinion, was truly a great advantage. I assert most unhesitatingly, that the religion of the south is a mere covering for the most horrid crimes,—a justifier of the most appalling barbarity,—a sanctifier of the most hateful frauds,—and a dark shelter under, which the darkest, foulest, grossest, and most infernal deeds of slaveholders find the strongest protection. Were I to be again reduced to the chains of slavery, next to that enslavement, I should regard being the slave of a religious master the greatest calamity that could befall me. For of all slaveholders with whom I have ever met, religious slaveholders are the worst. I have ever found them the meanest and basest, the most cruel and cowardly, of all others. It was my unhappy lot not only to belong to a religious slaveholder, but to live in a community of such religionists. Very near Mr. Freeland lived the Rev. Daniel Weeden, and in the same neighborhood lived the Rev. Rigby Hopkins. These were members and ministers in the Reformed Methodist Church. Mr. Weeden owned, among others, a woman slave, whose name I have forgotten. This woman's back, for weeks, was kept literally raw, made so by the lash of this merciless, *religious* wretch. He used to hire hands. His maxim was, Behave well or behave ill, it is the duty of a master occasionally to whip a slave, to remind him of his master's authority. Such was his theory, and such his practice.

Mr. Hopkins was even worse than Mr. Weeden. His chief boast was his ability to manage slaves. The peculiar feature of his government was that of whipping slaves in advance of deserving it. He always managed to have one or more of his slaves to whip every Monday morning. He did this to alarm their fears, and strike terror into those who escaped. His plan was to whip for the smallest offences, to prevent the commission of large ones. Mr. Hopkins could always find some excuse for whipping a slave. It would astonish one, unaccustomed to a slave-holding life, to see with what wonderful ease a slave-holder can find things, of which to make occasion to whip a slave. A mere look, word, or motion,—a mistake, accident, or want of power,—are all matters for which a slave may be whipped at any time. Does a slave look dissatisfied? It is said, he has the devil in him, and it must be whipped out. Does he speak loudly when spoken to by his master? Then he is wanting in reverence, and should be whipped for it. Does he ever venture to vindicate his conduct, when censured for it? Then he is guilty of impudence,—one of the greatest crimes of which a slave can be guilty. Does he ever venture to suggest a different mode of doing things from that pointed out by his master? He is indeed presumptuous, and getting above himself; and nothing less than a flogging will do for him. Does he, while ploughing, break a plough,—or, while hoeing, break a hoe? It is owing to his carelessness, and for it a slave must always be whipped. Mr. Hopkins could always find something of this sort to justify the use of the lash, and he seldom failed to embrace such opportunities. There was not a man in the whole county, with whom the slaves who had the getting their own home, would not prefer to live, rather than with this Rev. Mr. Hopkins. And yet there was not a man any where round, who made higher professions of religion, or was more active in revivals,—more attentive to the class, love-feast, prayer and preaching meetings, or more devotional in his family,—that prayed earlier, later, louder, and longer,—than this same reverend slave-driver, Rigby Hopkins.

But to return to Mr. Freeland, and to my experience while in his employment. He, like Mr. Covey, gave us enough to eat; but, unlike Mr. Covey, he also gave us sufficient time to take our meals. He worked us hard, but always between sunrise and sunset. He required a good deal of work to be done, but gave us good tools with which to work. His farm was large, but he employed hands enough to work it, and with ease, compared with many of his neighbors. My treatment, while in his employment, was heavenly, compared with what I experienced at the hands of Mr. Edward Covey.

Mr. Freeland was himself the owner of but two slaves. Their names were Henry Harris and John Harris. The rest of his hands he hired. These consisted of myself, Sandy Jenkins,[28] and Handy Caldwell. Henry and John were quite intelligent, and in a very little while after I went there, I succeeded in creating in them a strong desire to learn how to read. This desire soon sprang up in the others also. They very soon mustered up some old spelling-books, and nothing would do but that I must keep a Sabbath school. I agreed to do so, and accordingly devoted my Sundays to teaching these my loved fellow-slaves how to read. Neither of them knew his letters when I went there. Some of the slaves of the neighboring farms found what was going on, and also availed themselves of this little opportunity to learn to read. It was understood, among all who came, that there must be as little display about it as possible. It was necessary to keep our religious masters at St. Michael's unacquainted with the fact, that, instead of spending the Sabbath in wrestling, boxing, and drinking whisky, we were trying to learn how to read the will of God; for they had much rather see us engaged in those degrading sports, than to see us behaving like intellectual, moral, and accountable beings. My blood boils as I think of the bloody manner in which Messrs. Wright Fairbanks and Garrison West, both class-leaders, in connection with many others, rushed in upon us with sticks and stones, and broke up our virtuous little Sabbath school, at St. Michael's—all calling themselves Christians! humble followers of the Lord Jesus Christ! But I am again digressing.

I held my Sabbath school at the house of a free colored man, whose name I deem it imprudent to mention; for should it be known, it might embarrass him greatly, though the crime of holding the school was committed ten years ago. I had at one time over forty scholars, and those of the right sort, ardently desiring to learn. They were of all ages, though mostly men and women. I look back to those Sundays with an amount of pleasure not to be expressed. They were great days to my soul. The work of instructing my dear fellow-slaves was the sweetest engagement with which I was ever blessed. We loved each other, and to leave them at the close of the Sabbath was a severe cross indeed. When I think that these precious souls are to-day shut up in the prison-house of slavery, my feelings overcome me, and I am almost ready to ask, "Does a righteous God govern the universe? and for what does he hold the thunders in his right hand, if not to smite the oppressor, and deliver the spoiled out of the hand of the spoiler?" These dear souls came not to Sabbath school because it was popular to do so, nor did I teach them because it was reputable to be thus engaged. Every moment they spent in that school, they were liable to be taken up, and given thirty-nine lashes. They came because they wished to learn. Their minds had been

---

[28]This is the same man who gave the roots to prevent my being whipped by Mr. Covey. He was a "clever soul." We used frequently to talk about the fight with Covey, and as often as we did so, he would claim my success as the result of the roots which he gave me. This superstition is very common among the more ignorant slaves. A slave seldom dies but that his death is attributed to trickery. [Douglass's note.]

starved by their cruel masters. They had been shut up in mental darkness. I taught them, because it was the delight of my soul to be doing something that looked like bettering the condition of my race. I kept up my school nearly the whole year I lived with Mr. Freeland; and, beside my Sabbath school, I devoted three evenings in the week, during the winter, to teaching the slaves at home. And I have the happiness to know, that several of those who came to Sabbath school learned how to read; and that one, at least, is now free through my agency.

The year passed off smoothly. It seemed only about half as long as the year which preceded it. I went through it without receiving a single blow. I will give Mr. Freeland the credit of being the best master I ever had, *till I became my own master.* For the ease with which I passed the year, I was, however, somewhat indebted to the society of my fellow-slaves. They were noble souls; they not only possessed loving hearts, but brave ones. We were linked and interlinked with each other. I loved them with a love stronger than any thing I have experienced since. It is sometimes said that we slaves do not love and confide in each other. In answer to this assertion, I can say, I never loved any or confided in any people more than my fellow-slaves, and especially those with whom I lived at Mr. Freeland's. I believe we would have died for each other. We never undertook to do any thing, of any importance, without a mutual consultation. We never moved separately. We were one; and as much so by our tempers and dispositions, as by the mutual hardships to which we were necessarily subjected by our condition as slaves.

At the close of the year 1834, Mr. Freeland again hired me of my master, for the year 1835. But, by this time, I began to want to live *upon free land* as well as *with Freeland;* and I was no longer content, therefore, to live with him or any other slaveholder. I began, with the commencement of the year, to prepare myself for a final struggle, which should decide my fate one way or the other. My tendency was upward. I was fast approaching manhood, and year after year had passed, and I was still a slave. These thoughts roused me—I must do something. I therefore resolved that 1835 should not pass without witnessing an attempt, on my part, to secure my liberty. But I was not willing to cherish this determination alone. My fellow-slaves were dear to me. I was anxious to have them participate with me in this, my life-giving determination. I therefore, though with great prudence, commenced early to ascertain their views and feelings in regard to their condition, and to imbue their minds with thoughts of freedom. I bent myself to devising ways and means for our escape, and meanwhile strove, on all fitting occasions, to impress them with the gross fraud and inhumanity of slavery. I went first to Henry, next to John, then to the others. I found, in them all, warm hearts and noble spirits. They were ready to hear, and ready to act when a feasible plan should be proposed. This was what I wanted. I talked to them of our want of manhood, if we submitted to our enslavement without at least one noble effort to be free. We met often, and consulted frequently, and told our hopes and fears, recounted the difficulties, real and imagined, which we should be called on to meet. At times we were almost disposed to give up and try to content ourselves with our wretched lot; at others, we were firm and unbending in our determination to go. Whenever we suggested any plan, there was shrinking—the odds were fearful. Our path was beset with the greatest obstacles; and if we succeeded in gaining the end of it, our right to be free was yet questionable—we were yet liable to be returned to bondage. We could see no spot, this side of the ocean, where we could be free. We knew nothing about Canada. Our knowledge of the north did not extend farther than New York; and to go there, and be forever harassed with the frightful liability of being returned to slavery— with the certainty of being treated tenfold worse than before—the thought was truly a horrible one, and one which it was not easy to overcome. The case sometimes stood thus: At every gate through which we were to pass, we saw a watchman—at every ferry a guard—on every bridge a sentinel— and in every wood a patrol. We were hemmed in upon every side. Here were the difficulties, real or imagined—the good to be sought, and the evil to be shunned. On the one hand, there stood slavery, a stern reality, glaring frightfully upon us,—its robes already crimsoned with the blood of millions, and even now feasting itself greedily upon our own flesh. On the other hand, away back in the dim distance, under the flickering light of the north star, behind some craggy hill or snow-covered mountain, stood a doubtful freedom—half frozen—beckoning us to come and share its hospitality. This in itself was sometimes enough to stagger us; but when we permitted our- selves to survey the road, we were frequently appalled. Upon either side we saw grim death, assuming the most horrid shapes. Now it was starvation, causing us to eat our own flesh;—now we were contending with the waves, and were drowned;—now we were overtaken, and torn to pieces by the fangs of the terrible bloodhound. We were stung by scorpions, chased by wild beasts, bitten by snakes, and finally, after having nearly reached the desired spot,—after swimming rivers, encountering wild beasts, sleeping in the woods, suffering hunger and nakedness,—we were overtaken by our pursuers, and in our resistance, we were shot dead upon the spot! I say, this picture sometimes appalled us, and made us

> "*rather bear those ills we had,*
> *Than fly to others, that we knew not of.*"[29]

In coming to a fixed determination to run away, we did more than Patrick Henry, when he resolved upon liberty or death. With us it was a doubtful liberty at most, and almost certain death if we failed. For my part, I should prefer death to hopeless bondage.

Sandy, one of our number, gave up the notion, but still encouraged us. Our company then consisted of Henry Harris, John Harris, Henry Bailey, Charles Roberts, and myself. Henry Bailey was my uncle, and belonged to my master. Charles married my aunt: he belonged to my master's father-in-law, Mr. William Hamilton.

[29]Shakespeare, *Hamlet*, III, i, 81–82.

The plan we finally concluded upon was, to get a large canoe belonging to Mr. Hamilton, and upon the Saturday night previous to Easter holidays, paddle directly up the Chesapeake Bay. On our arrival at the head of the bay, a distance of seventy or eighty miles from where we lived, it was our purpose to turn our canoe adrift, and follow the guidance of the north star till we got beyond the limits of Maryland. Our reason for taking the water route was, that we were less liable to be suspected as runaways; we hoped to be regarded as fishermen; whereas, if we should take the land route, we should be subjected to interruptions of almost every kind. Any one having a white face, and being so disposed, could stop us, and subject us to examination.

The week before our intended start, I wrote several protections, one for each of us. As well as I can remember they were in the following words, to wit:—

"This is to certify that I, the undersigned, have given the bearer, my servant, full liberty to go to Baltimore, and spend the Easter holidays. Written with mine own hand &c., 1835.

"William Hamilton,
"Near St. Michael's, in Talbot county, Maryland."

We were not going to Baltimore; but, in going up the bay, we went toward Baltimore, and these protections were only intended to protect us while on the bay.

As the time drew near for our departure, our anxiety became more and more intense. It was truly a matter of life and death with us. The strength of our determination was about to be fully tested. At this time, I was very active in explaining every difficulty, removing every doubt, dispelling every fear, and inspiring all with the firmness indispensable to success in our undertaking; assuring them that half was gained the instant we made the move; we had talked long enough; we were now ready to move; if not now, we never should be; and if we did not intend to move now, we had as well fold our arms, sit down, and acknowledge ourselves fit only to be slaves. This, none of us were prepared to acknowledge. Every man stood firm; and at our last meeting, we pledged ourselves afresh, in the most solemn manner, that at the time appointed, we would certainly start in pursuit of freedom. This was in the middle of the week, at the end of which we were to be off. We went, as usual, to our several fields of labor, but with bosoms highly agitated with thoughts of our truly hazardous undertaking. We tried to conceal our feelings as much as possible; and I think we succeeded very well.

After a painful waiting, the Saturday morning, whose night was to witness our departure, came. I hailed it with joy, bring what of sadness it might. Friday night was a sleepless one for me. I probably felt more anxious than the rest, because I was, by common consent, at the head of the whole affair. The responsibility of success or failure lay heavily upon me. The glory of the one, and the confusion of the other, were alike mine. The first two hours of that morning were such as I never experienced before, and hope never to again. Early in the morning, we went, as usual, to the field.

We were spreading manure; and all at once, while thus engaged, I was overwhelmed with an indescribable feeling, in the fulness of which I turned to Sandy, who was near by, and said, "We are betrayed!" "Well," said he, "that thought has this moment struck me." We said no more. I was never more certain of any thing.

The horn was blown as usual, and we went up from the field to the house for breakfast. I went for the form, more than for want of any thing to eat that morning. Just as I got to the house, in looking out at the lane gate, I saw four white men, with two colored men. The white men were on horseback, and the colored ones were walking behind, as if tied. I watched them a few moments till they got up to our lane gate. Here they halted, and tied the colored men to the gate-post. I was not yet certain as to what the matter was. In a few moments, in rode Mr. Hamilton, with a speed betokening great excitement. He came to the door, and inquired if Master William was in. He was told he was at the barn. Mr. Hamilton, without dismounting, rode up to the barn with extraordinary speed. In a few moments, he and Mr. Freeland returned to the house. By this time, the three constables rode up, and in great haste dismounted, tied their horses, and met Master William and Mr. Hamilton returning from the barn; and after talking awhile, they all walked up to the kitchen door. There was no one in the kitchen but myself and John. Henry and Sandy were up at the barn. Mr. Freeland put his head in at the door, and called me by name, saying, there were some gentlemen at the door who wished to see me. I stepped to the door, and inquired what they wanted. They at once seized me, and, without giving me any satisfaction, tied me—lashing my hands closely together. I insisted upon knowing what the matter was. They at length said, that they had learned I had been in a "scrape," and that I was to be examined before my master; and if their information proved false, I should not be hurt.

In a few moments, they succeeded in tying John. They then turned to Henry, who had by this time returned, and commanded him to cross his hands. "I won't!" said Henry, in a firm tone, indicating his readiness to meet the consequences of his refusal. "Won't you?" said Tom Graham, the constable. "No, I won't!" said Henry, in a still stronger tone. With this, two of the constables pulled out their shining pistols, and swore, by their Creator, that they would make him cross his hands or kill him. Each cocked his pistol, and, with fingers on the trigger, walked up to Henry, saying, at the same time, if he did not cross his hands, they would blow his damned heart out. "Shoot me, shoot me!" said Henry; "you can't kill me but once. Shoot, shoot,—and be damned! *I won't be tied!*" This he said in a tone of loud defiance; and at the same time, with a motion as quick as lightning, he with one single stroke dashed the pistols from the hand of each constable. As he did this, all hands fell upon him, and, after beating him some time, they finally overpowered him, and got him tied.

During the scuffle, I managed, I know not how, to get my pass out, and, without being discovered, put it into the fire. We were all now tied; and just as we were to leave for Easton jail, Betsy Freeland, mother of William

Freeland, came to the door with her hands full of biscuits, and divided them between Henry and John. She then delivered herself of a speech, to the following effect:—addressing herself to me, she said, "*You devil! You yellow devil!* it was you that put it into the heads of Henry and John to run away. But for you, you long-legged mulatto devil! Henry nor John would never have thought of such a thing." I made no reply, and was immediately hurried off towards St. Michael's. Just a moment previous to the scuffle with Henry, Mr. Hamilton suggested the propriety of making a search for the protections which he had understood Frederick had written for himself and the rest. But, just at the moment he was about carrying his proposal into effect, his aid was needed in helping to tie Henry; and the excitement attending the scuffle caused them either to forget, or to deem it unsafe, under the circumstances, to search. So we were not yet convicted of the intention to run away.

When we got about half way to St. Michael's, while the constables having us in charge were looking ahead, Henry inquired of me what he should do with his pass. I told him to eat it with his biscuit, and own nothing; and we passed the word around, "*Own nothing;*" and "*Own nothing!*" said we all. Our confidence in each other was unshaken. We were resolved to succeed or fail together, after the calamity had befallen us as much as before. We were now prepared for any thing. We were to be dragged that morning fifteen miles behind horses, and then to be placed in the Easton jail. When we reached St. Michael's, we underwent a sort of examination. We all denied that we ever intended to run away. We did this more to bring out the evidence against us, than from any hope of getting clear of being sold; for, as I have said, we were ready for that. The fact was, we cared but little where we went, so we went together. Our greatest concern was about separation. We dreaded that more than any thing this side of death. We found the evidence against us to be the testimony of one person; our master would not tell who it was; but we came to a unanimous decision among ourselves as to who their informant was.[30] We were sent off to the jail at Easton. When we got there, we were delivered up to the sheriff, Mr. Joseph Graham, and by him placed in jail. Henry, John, and myself, were placed in one room together— Charles, and Henry Bailey, in another. Their object in separating us was to hinder concert.

We had been in jail scarcely twenty minutes, when a swarm of slave traders, and agents for slave traders, flocked into jail to look at us, and to ascertain if we were for sale. Such a set of beings I never saw before! I felt myself surrounded by so many fiends from perdition. A band of pirates never looked more like their father, the devil. They laughed and grinned over us, saying, "Ah, my boys! we have got you, haven't we?" And after taunting us in various ways, they one by one went into an examination of

---

[30]In the 1892 version of his autobiography, *The Life and Times of Frederick Douglass,* Douglass explicitly names Sandy Jenkins as the suspect: "We suspected *one* person only. Several circumstances seemed to point Sandy out as our betrayer."

us, with intent to ascertain our value. They would impudently ask us if we would not like to have them for our masters. We would make them no answer, and leave them to find out as best they could. Then they would curse and swear at us, telling us that they could take the devil out of us in a very little while, if we were only in their hands.

While in jail, we found ourselves in much more comfortable quarters than we expected when we went there. We did not get much to eat, nor that which was very good; but we had a good clean room, from the windows of which we could see what was going on in the street, which was very much better than though we had been placed in one of the dark, damp cells. Upon the whole, we got along very well, so far as the jail and its keeper were concerned. Immediately after the holidays were over, contrary to all our expectations, Mr. Hamilton and Mr. Freeland came up to Easton, and took Charles, the two Henrys, and John, out of jail, and carried them home, leaving me alone. I regarded this separation as a final one. It caused me more pain than any thing else in the whole transaction. I was ready for any thing rather than separation. I supposed that they had consulted together, and had decided that, as I was the whole cause of the intention of the others to run away, it was hard to make the innocent suffer with the guilty; and that they had, therefore, concluded to take the others home, and sell me, as a warning to the others that remained. It is due to the noble Henry to say, he seemed almost as reluctant at leaving the prison as at leaving home to come to the prison. But we knew we should, in all probability, be separated, if we were sold; and since he was in their hands, he concluded to go peaceably home.

I was now left to my fate. I was all alone, and within the walls of a stone prison. But a few days before, and I was full of hope. I expected to have been safe in a land of freedom; but now I was covered with gloom, sunk down to the utmost despair. I thought the possibility of freedom was gone. I was kept in this way about one week, at the end of which, Captain Auld, my master, to my surprise and utter astonishment, came up, and took me out, with the intention of sending me, with a gentleman of his acquaintance, into Alabama. But, from some cause or other, he did not send me to Alabama, but concluded to send me back to Baltimore, to live again with his brother Hugh, and to learn a trade.

Thus, after an absence of three years and one month, I was once more permitted to return to my old home at Baltimore. My master sent me away, because there existed against me a very great prejudice in the community, and he feared I might be killed.

In a few weeks after I went to Baltimore, Master Hugh hired me to Mr. William Gardner, an extensive ship-builder, on Fell's Point. I was put there to learn how to calk. It, however, proved a very unfavorable place for the accomplishment of this object. Mr. Gardner was engaged that spring in building two large man-of-war brigs, professedly for the Mexican government. The vessels were to be launched in the July of that year, and in failure thereof, Mr. Gardner was to lose a considerable sum; so that when I entered, all was hurry. There was no time to learn any thing. Every man had to do that which he knew how to do. In entering the shipyard, my orders from Mr. Gardner were, to do whatever the carpenters commanded me to do. This was placing me at the beck and call of about seventy-five men. I was to regard all these as masters. Their word was to be my law. My situation was a most trying one. At times I needed a dozen pair of hands. I was called a dozen ways in the space of a single minute. Three or four voices would strike my ear at the same moment. It was—"Fred., come help me to cant this timber here."—"Fred., come carry this timber yonder."—"Fred., bring that roller here."—"Fred., go get a fresh can of water."—"Fred., come help saw off the end of this timber."—"Fred., go quick, and get the crowbar."— "Fred., hold on the end of this fall."[31]—"Fred., go to the blacksmith's shop, and get a new punch."—"Hurra, Fred.! run and bring me a cold chisel."—"I say, Fred., bear a hand, and get up a fire as quick as lightning under that steambox."—"Halloo, nigger! come, turn this grindstone."—"Come, come! move, move! and *bowse*[32] this timber forward."—"I say, darky, blast your eyes, why don't you heat up some pitch?"—"Halloo! halloo! halloo!" (Three voices at the same time.) "Come here!—Go there!—Hold on where you are! Damn you, if you move, I'll knock your brains out!"

This was my school for eight months; and I might have remained there longer, but for a most horrid fight I had with four of the white apprentices, in which my left eye was nearly knocked out and I was horribly mangled in other respects. The facts in the case were these: Until a very little while after I went there, white and black ship-carpenters worked side by side, and no one seemed to see any impropriety in it. All hands seemed to be very well satisfied. Many of the black carpenters were freemen. Things seemed to be going on very well. All at once, the white carpenters knocked off, and said they would not work with free colored workmen. Their reason for this, as alleged, was, that if free colored carpenters were encouraged, they would soon take the trade into their own hands, and poor white men would be thrown out of employment. They therefore felt called upon at once to put a stop to it. And, taking advantage of Mr. Gardner's necessities, they broke off, swearing they would work no longer, unless he would discharge his black carpenters. Now, though this did not extend to me in form, it did reach me in fact. My fellow-apprentices very soon began to feel it degrading to them to work with me. They began to put on airs, and talk about the "niggers" taking the country, saying we all ought to be killed; and, being encouraged by the journeymen, they commenced making my condition as hard as they could, by hectoring me around, and sometimes striking me. I, of course, kept the vow I made after the fight with Mr. Covey, and struck back again, regardless of consequences; and while I kept them from combining, I succeeded very well; for I could whip the whole of them, taking them separately. They, however, at length combined, and came upon me, armed with sticks, stones, and heavy handspikes. One came in front with a half

---

[31]The end of a tackle.　　[32]Haul.

brick. There was one at each side of me, and one behind me. While I was attending to those in front, and on either side, the one behind ran up with the handspike, and struck me a heavy blow upon the head. It stunned me. I fell, and with this they all ran upon me, and fell to beating me with their fists. I let them lay on for a while, gathering strength. In an instant, I gave a sudden surge, and rose to my hands and knees. Just as I did that, one of their number gave me, with his heavy boot, a powerful kick in the left eye. My eyeball seemed to have burst. When they saw my eye closed, and badly swollen, they left me. With this I seized the handspike, and for a time pursued them. But here the carpenters interfered, and I thought I might as well give it up. It was impossible to stand my hand against so many. All this took place in sight of not less than fifty white ship-carpenters, and not one interposed a friendly word; but some cried, "Kill the damned nigger! Kill him! kill him! He struck a white person." I found my only chance for life was in flight. I succeeded in getting away without an additional blow, and barely so, for to strike a white man is death by Lynch law,—and that was the law in Mr. Gardner's ship-yard; nor is there much of any other out of Mr. Gardner's ship-yard.

I went directly home, and told the story of my wrongs to Master Hugh; and I am happy to say of him, irreligious as he was, his conduct was heavenly, compared with that of his brother Thomas under similar circumstances. He listened attentively to my narration of the circumstances leading to the savage outrage, and gave many proofs of his strong indignation at it. The heart of my once overkind mistress was again melted into pity. My puffed-out eye and blood-covered face moved her to tears. She took a chair by me, washed the blood from my face, and, with a mother's tenderness, bound up my head, covering the wounded eye with a lean piece of fresh beef. It was almost compensation for my suffering to witness, once more, a manifestation of kindness from this, my once affectionate old mistress. Master Hugh was very much enraged. He gave expression to his feelings by pouring out curses upon the heads of those who did the deed. As soon as I got a little the better of my bruises, he took me with him to Esquire Watson's, on Bond Street, to see what could be done about the matter. Mr. Watson inquired who saw the assault committed. Master Hugh told him it was done in Mr. Gardner's ship-yard, at midday, where there were a large company of men at work. "As to that," he said, "the deed was done, and there was no question as to who did it." His answer was, he could do nothing in the case, unless some white man would come forward and testify. He could issue no warrant on my word. If I had been killed in the presence of a thousand colored people, their testimony combined would have been insufficient to have arrested one of the murderers. Master Hugh, for once, was compelled to say this state of things was too bad. Of course, it was impossible to get any white man to volunteer his testimony in my behalf, and against the white young men. Even those who may have sympathized with me were not prepared to do this. It required a degree of courage unknown to them to do so; for just at that time, the slightest manifestation of humanity toward a colored person was denounced as abolitionism, and that name subjected its bearer to frightful liabilities. The watchwords of the bloody-minded in that region, and in those days, were, "Damn the abolitionists!" and "Damn the niggers!" There was nothing done, and probably nothing would have been done if I had been killed. Such was, and such remains, the state of things in the Christian city of Baltimore.

Master Hugh, finding he could get no redress, refused to let me go back again to Mr. Gardner. He kept me himself, and his wife dressed my wound till I was again restored to health. He then took me into the ship-yard of which he was foreman, in the employment of Mr. Walter Price. There I was immediately set to calking, and very soon learned the art of using my mallet and irons. In the course of one year from the time I left Mr. Gardner's, I was able to command the highest wages given to the most experienced calkers. I was now of some importance to my master. I was bringing him from six to seven dollars per week. I sometimes brought him nine dollars per week: my wages were a dollar and a half a day. After learning how to calk, I sought my own employment, made my own contracts, and collected the money which I earned. My pathway became much more smooth than before; my condition was now much more comfortable. When I could get no calking to do, I did nothing. During these leisure times, those old notions about freedom would steal over me again. When in Mr. Gardner's employ-ment, I was kept in such a perpetual whirl of excitement, I could think of nothing, scarcely, but my life; and in thinking of my life, I almost forgot my liberty. I have observed this in my experience of slavery,—that whenever my condition was improved, instead of its increasing my contentment, it only increased my desire to be free, and set me to thinking of plans to gain my freedom. I have found that, to make a contented slave, it is necessary to make a thoughtless one. It is necessary to darken his moral and mental vision, and, as far as possible, to annihilate the power of reason. He must be able to detect no inconsistencies in slavery; he must be made to feel that slavery is right; and he can be brought to that only when he ceases to be a man.

I was now getting, as I have said, one dollar and fifty cents per day. I contracted for it; I earned it; it was paid to me; it was rightfully my own; yet, upon each returning Saturday night, I was compelled to deliver every cent of that money to Master Hugh. And why? Not because he earned it,—not because he had any hand in earning it,—not because I owed it to him,—nor because he possessed the slightest shadow of a right to it; but solely because he had the power to compel me to give it up. The right of the grim-visaged pirate upon the high seas is exactly the same.

Chapter XI

I now come to that part of my life during which I planned, and finally suc-ceeded in making, my escape from slavery. But before narrating any of the peculiar circumstances, I deem it proper to make known my intention not to state all the facts connected with the transaction. My reasons for pursuing this course may be understood from the following: First, were I to give a minute statement of all the facts, it is not only possible but quite probable, that others would thereby be involved in the most embarrassing difficulties. Secondly, such a statement would most undoubtedly induce greater vigilance on the part of slaveholders than has existed heretofore among them; which would, of course, be the means of guarding a door whereby some dear brother bondman might escape his galling chains. I deeply regret the necessity that impels me to suppress any thing of importance connected with my experience in slavery. It would afford me great pleasure indeed, as well as materially add to the interest of my narrative, were I at liberty to gratify a curiosity, which I know exists in the minds of many, by an accurate statement of all the facts pertaining to my most fortunate escape. But I must deprive myself of this pleasure, and the curious of the gratification which such a statement would afford. I would allow myself to suffer under the greatest imputations which evil-minded men might suggest, rather than exculpate myself, and thereby run the hazard of closing the slightest avenue by which a brother slave might clear himself of the chains and fetters of slavery.[33]

I have never approved of the very public manner in which some of our western friends have conducted what they call the *underground railroad*,[34] but which I think, by their open declarations, has been made most emphatically the *upperground railroad*. I honor those good men and women for their noble daring, and applaud them for willingly subjecting themselves to bloody persecution, by openly avowing their participation in the escape of slaves. I, however, can see very little good resulting from such a course, either to themselves or the slaves escaping; while, upon the other hand, I see and feel assured that those open declarations are a positive evil to the slaves remaining, who are seeking to escape. They do nothing towards enlightening the slave, whilst they do much towards enlightening the master. They stimulate him to greater watchfulness, and enhance his power to capture his slave. We owe something to the slave south of the line as well as to those north of it; and in aiding the latter on their way to freedom, we should be careful to do nothing which would be likely to hinder the former from escaping from slavery. I would keep the merciless slaveholder profoundly ignorant of the means of flight adopted by the slave. I would leave him to imagine himself surrounded by myriads of invisible tormentors, ever ready to snatch from his infernal grasp his trembling prey. Let him be left to feel his way in the dark; let darkness commensurate with his crime hover over him; and let him feel that at every step he takes, in pursuit of the flying

[33]In *The Life and Times of Frederick Douglass*, Douglass describes how he escaped: he borrowed the papers of a free black, an American sailor, boarded the Baltimore train dressed as a sailor, and proceeded to Philadelphia, then to New York.

[34]A system of safe houses, conveyors, and supporters that worked to help slaves escape.

bondman, he is running the frightful risk of having his hot brains dashed out by an invisible agency. Let us render the tyrant no aid; let us not hold the light by which he can trace the footprints of our flying brother. But enough of this. I will now proceed to the statement of those facts, connected with my escape, for which I am alone responsible, and for which no one can be made to suffer but myself.

In the early part of the year 1838, I became quite restless. I could see no reason why I should, at the end of each week, pour the reward of my toil into the purse of my master. When I carried to him my weekly wages, he would, after counting the money, look me in the face with a robber-like fierceness, and say, "Is this all?" He was satisfied with nothing less than the last cent. He would, however, when I made him six dollars, sometimes give me six cents, to encourage me. It had the opposite effect. I regarded it as a sort of admission of my right to the whole. The fact that he gave me any part of my wages was proof, to my mind, that he believed me entitled to the whole of them. I always felt worse for having received any thing; for I feared that the giving me a few cents would ease his conscience, and make him feel himself to be a pretty honorable sort of robber. My discontent grew upon me. I was ever on the look-out for means of escape; and, finding no direct means, I determined to try to hire my time, with a view of getting money with which to make my escape. In the spring of 1838, when Master Thomas came to Baltimore to purchase his spring goods, I got an opportunity, and applied to him to allow me to hire my time. He unhesitatingly refused my request, and told me this was another stratagem by which to escape. He told me I could go nowhere but that he could get me; and that, in the event of my running away, he should spare no pains in his efforts to catch me. He exhorted me to content myself, and be obedient. He told me, if I would be happy, I must lay out no plans for the future. He said, if I behaved myself properly, he would take care of me. Indeed, he advised me to complete thoughtlessness of the future, and taught me to depend solely upon him for happiness. He seemed to see fully the pressing necessity of setting aside my intellectual nature, in order to [insure] contentment in slavery. But in spite of him, and even in spite of myself, I continued to think, and to think about the injustice of my enslavement, and the means of escape.

About two months after this, I applied to Master Hugh for the privilege of hiring my time. He was not acquainted with the fact that I had applied to Master Thomas, and had been refused. He too, at first, seemed disposed to refuse; but, after some reflection, he granted me the privilege, and proposed the following terms: I was to be allowed all my time, make all contracts with those for whom I worked, and find my own employment; and, in return for this liberty, I was to pay him three dollars at the end of each week; find myself in calking tools, and in board and clothing. My board was two dollars and a half per week. This, with the wear and tear of clothing and calking tools, made my regular expenses about six dollars per week. This amount I was compelled to make up, or relinquish the privilege of hiring my time. Rain or shine, work or no work, at the end of each week the money must be forthcoming, or I must give up my privilege. This arrangement, it will be perceived, was decidedly in my master's favor. It relieved him of all need of looking after me. His money was sure. He received all the benefits of slave-holding without its evils; while I endured all the evils of a slave, and suffered all the care and anxiety of a freeman. I found it a hard bargain. But, hard as it was I thought it better than the old mode of getting along. It was a step towards freedom to be allowed to bear the responsibilities of a freeman, and I was determined to hold on upon it. I bent myself to the work of making money. I was ready to work at night as well as day, and by the most untiring perservance and industry, I made enough to meet my expenses, and lay up a little money every week. I went on thus from May till August. Master Hugh then refused to allow me to hire my time longer. The ground for his refusal was a failure on my part, one Saturday night, to pay him for my week's time. This failure was occasioned by my attending a camp meeting about ten miles from Baltimore. During the week, I had entered into an engagement with a number of young friends to start from Baltimore to the camp ground early Saturday evening; and being detained by my employer, I was unable to get down to Master Hugh's without disappointing the company. I knew that Master Hugh was in no special need of the money that night. I therefore decided to go to the camp meeting, and upon my return pay him the three dollars. I staid at the camp meeting one day longer than I intended when I left. But as soon as I returned, I called upon him to pay him what he considered his due. I found him very angry; he could scarce restrain his wrath. He said he had a great mind to give me a severe whipping. He wished to know how I dared go out of the city without asking his permission. I told him I hired my time, and while I paid him the price which he asked for it, I did not know that I was bound to ask him when and where I should go. This reply troubled him; and, after reflecting a few moments, he turned to me, and said I should hire my time no longer; that the next thing he should know of, I would be running away. Upon the same plea, he told me to bring my tools and clothing home forthwith. I did so; but instead of seeking work, as I had been accustomed to do previously to hiring my time, I spent the whole week without the performance of a single stroke of work. I did this in retaliation. Saturday night, he called upon me as usual for my week's wages. I told him I had no wages; I had done no work that week. Here we were upon the point of coming to blows. He raved, and swore his determination to get hold of me. I did not allow myself a single word; but was resolved, if he laid the weight of his hand upon me, it should be blow for blow. He did not strike me, but told me that he would find me in constant employment in future. I thought the matter over during the next day, Sunday, and finally resolved upon the third day of September, as the day upon which I would make a second attempt to secure my freedom. I now had three weeks during which to prepare for my journey. Early on Monday morning, before Master Hugh had time to make any engagement for me, I went out and got employment of Mr. Butler, at his ship-yard near the drawbridge, upon what is called the City Block, thus making it unnecessary for him to seek employment for me. At the end of the week, I brought him between eight and nine dollars. He seemed very well pleased, and asked why I did not do the same the week before. He little knew what my plans were. My object in working steadily was to remove any suspicion he might entertain of my intent to run away; and in this I succeeded admirably. I suppose he thought I was never better satisfied with my condition than at the very time during which I was planning my escape. The second week passed, and again I carried him my full wages; and so well pleased was he, that he gave me twenty-five cents, (quite a large sum for a slaveholder to give a slave), and bade me to make a good use of it. I told him I would.

Things went on without very smoothly indeed, but within there was trouble. It is impossible for me to describe my feelings as the time of my contemplated start drew near. I had a number of warm-hearted friends in Baltimore,—friends that I loved almost as I did my life,—and the thought of being separated from them forever was painful beyond expression. It is my opinion that thousands would escape from slavery, who now remain, but for the strong cords of affection that bind them to their friends. The thought of leaving my friends was decidedly the most painful thought with which I had to contend. The love of them was my tender point, and shook my decision more than all things else. Besides the pain of separation, the dread and apprehension of a failure exceeded what I had experienced at my first attempt. The appalling defeat I then sustained returned to torment me. I felt assured that, if I failed in this attempt, my case would be a hopeless one—it would seal my fate as a slave forever. I could not hope to get off with any thing less than the severest punishment, and being placed beyond the means of escape. It required no very vivid imagination to depict the most frightful scenes through which I should have to pass, in case I failed. The wretchedness of slavery, and the blessedness of freedom, were perpetually before me. It was life and death with me. But I remained firm, and, according to my resolution, on the third day of September, 1838, I left my chains, and succeeded in reaching New York without the slightest interruption of any kind. How I did so,—what means I adopted,—what direction I travelled, and by what mode of conveyance,—I must leave unexplained, for the reasons before mentioned.

I have been frequently asked how I felt when I found myself in a free State. I have never been able to answer the question with any satisfaction to myself. It was a moment of the highest excitement I ever experienced. I suppose I felt as one may imagine the unarmed mariner to feel when he is rescued by a friendly man-of-war from the pursuit of a pirate. In writing to a dear friend, immediately after my arrival at New York, I said I felt like one who had escaped a den of hungry lions. This state of mind, however, very soon subsided; and I was again seized by a feeling of great insecurity and loneliness. I was yet liable to be taken back, and subjected to all the tortures of slavery. This in itself was enough to damp the ardor of my enthusiasm. But the loneliness overcame me. There I was in the midst of thousands, and yet a perfect stranger; without home and without friends, in the midst of thousands of my own brethren—children of a common Father, and yet I dared not to unfold to any one of them my sad condition. I was afraid to speak to any one for fear of speaking to the wrong one, and thereby falling into the hands of money-loving kidnappers, whose business it was to lie in wait for the panting fugitive, as the ferocious beasts of the forest lie in wait for their prey. The motto which I adopted when I started from slavery was this—"Trust no man!" I saw in every white man an enemy, and in almost every colored man cause for distrust. It was a most painful situation; and, to understand it, one must needs experience it, or imagine himself in similar circumstances. Let him be a fugitive slave in a strange land—a land given up to be the hunting-ground for slaveholders—whose inhabitants are legalized kidnappers—where he is every moment subjected to the terrible liability of being seized upon by his fellowmen, as the hideous crocodile seizes upon his prey!—I say, let him place himself in my situation—without home or friends—without money or credit—wanting shelter, and no one to give it— wanting bread, and no money to buy it,—and at the same time let him feel that he is pursued by merciless men-hunters, and in total darkness as to what to do, where to go, or where to stay,—perfectly helpless both as to the means of defence and means of escape,—in the midst of plenty, yet suffer- ing the terrible gnawings of hunger,—in the midst of houses, yet having no home,—among fellow-men, yet feeling as if in the midst of wild beasts, whose greediness to swallow up the trembling and half-famished fugitive is only equalled by that with which the monsters of the deep swallow up the helpless fish upon which they subsist,—I say, let him be placed in this most trying situation,—the situation in which I was placed,—then, and not till then, will he fully appreciate the hardships of, and know how to sympathize with, the toil-worn and whip-scarred fugitive slave.

Thank Heaven, I remained but a short time in this distress situation. I was relieved from it by the humane hand of Mr. DAVID RUGGLES,[35] whose vigilance, kindness, and perseverance, I shall never forget. I am glad of an opportunity to express, as far as words can, the love and gratitude I bear him. Mr. Ruggles is now afflicted with blindness, and is himself in need of the same kind offices which he was once so forward in the performance of toward others. I had been in New York but a few days, when Mr. Ruggles sought me out, and very kindly took me to his boarding-house at the corner of Church and Lespenard Streets. Mr. Ruggles was then very deeply engaged in the memorable *Darg* case, as well as attending to a number of other fugi- tive slaves; devising ways and means for their successful escape; and, though watched and hemmed in on almost every side, he seemed to be more than a match for his enemies.

[35]David Ruggles (1810–1849), a black journal- ist, businessman, fund-raiser, and activist, became general secretary of the New York Committee of Vigilance in 1835. In that position he helped hundreds of runaways, including Douglass: he sheltered Douglass for two weeks, arranged for his marriage, and sent the newlywed couple on to New Bedford with a donation of five dollars and a letter of introduction.

Very soon after I went to Mr. Ruggles, he wished to know of me where I wanted to go; as he deemed it unsafe for me to remain in New York. I told him I was a calker, and should like to go where I could get work. I thought of going to Canada; but he decided against it, and in favor of my going to New Bedford, thinking I should be able to get work there at my trade. At this time, Anna,[36] my intended wife, came on; for I wrote to her immediately after my arrival at New York, (notwithstanding my homeless, houseless, and helpless condition,) informing her of my successful flight, and wishing her to come on forthwith. In a few days after her arrival, Mr. Ruggles called in the Rev. J.W.C. Pennington, who, in the presence of Mr. Ruggles, Mrs. Michaels, and two or three others, performed the marriage ceremony, and gave us a certificate, of which the following is an exact copy:—

> "This may certify, that I joined together in holy matrimony Frederick Johnson[37] and Anna Murray, as man and wife, in the presence of Mr. David Ruggles and Mrs. Michaels.

"James W.C. Pennington
"New York, Sept. 15, 1838."

Upon receiving this certificate, and a five-dollar bill from Mr. Ruggles, I shouldered one part of our baggage, and Anna took up the other, and we set out forthwith to take passage on board of the steamboat John W. Richmond for Newport, on our way to New Bedford. Mr. Ruggles gave me a letter to a Mr. Shaw in Newport, and told me, in case my money did not serve me to New Bedford, to stop in Newport and obtain further assistance; but upon our arrival at Newport, we were so anxious to get to a place of safety, that, notwithstanding we lacked the necessary money to pay our fare, we decided to take seats in the stage, and promise to pay when we got to New Bedford. We were encouraged to do this by two excellent gentlemen, residents of New Bedford, whose names I afterward ascertained to be Joseph Ricketson and William C. Taber. They seemed at once to understand our circumstances, and gave us such assurance of their friendliness as put us fully at ease in their presence. It was good indeed to meet with such friends, at such a time. Upon reaching New Bedford, we were directed to the house of Mr. Nathan Johnson, by whom we were kindly received, and hospitably provided for. Both Mr. and Mrs. Johnson took a deep and lively interest in our welfare. They proved themselves quite worthy of the name of abolitionists. When the stage-driver found us unable to pay our fare, he held on upon our baggage as security for the debt. I had but to mention the fact to Mr. Johnson, and he forthwith advanced the money.

We now began to feel a degree of safety, and to prepare ourselves for the duties and responsibilities of a life of freedom. On the morning after our arrival at New Bedford, while at the breakfast-table, the question arose

[36]She was free. [Douglass's note.]
[37]I had changed my name from Frederick Bailey to that of Johnson. [Douglass's note.]

as to what name I should be called by. The name given me by my mother was, "Frederick Augustus Washington Bailey." I, however, had dispensed with the two middle names long before I left Maryland so that I was generally known by the name of "Frederick Bailey." I started from Baltimore bearing the name of "Stanley." When I got to New York I again changed my name to "Frederick Johnson," and thought that would be the last change. But when I got to New Bedford, I found it necessary again to change my name. The reason of this necessity was, that there were so many Johnsons in New Bedford, it was already quite difficult to distinguish between them. I gave Mr. Johnson the privilege of choosing me a name, but told him he must not take from me the name of "Frederick." I must hold on to that, to preserve a sense of my identity. Mr. Johnson had just been reading the "Lady of the Lake," and at once suggested that my name be "Douglass."[38] From that time until now I have been called "Frederick Douglass"; and as I am more widely known by that name than by either of the others, I shall continue to use it as my own.

I was quite disappointed at the general appearance of things in New Bedford. The impression which I had received respecting the character and condition of the people of the north, I found to be singularly erroneous. I had very strangely supposed, while in slavery, that few of the comforts, and scarcely any of the luxuries, of life were enjoyed at the north, compared with what were enjoyed by the slaveholders of the south. I probably came to this conclusion from the fact that northern people owned no slaves. I supposed that they were about upon a level with the non-slaveholding population of the south. I knew *they* were exceedingly poor, and I had been accustomed to regard their poverty as the necessary consequence of their being non-slaveholders. I had somehow imbibed the opinion that, in the absence of slaves, there could be no wealth, and very little refinement. And upon coming to the north, I expected to meet with a rough, hard-handed, and uncultivated population, living in the most Spartanlike simplicity, knowing nothing of the ease, luxury, pomp, and grandeur of southern slaveholders. Such being my conjectures, any one acquainted with the appearance of New Bedford may very readily infer how palpably I must have seen my mistake.

In the afternoon of the day when I reached New Bedford, I visited the wharves, to take a view of the shipping. Here I found myself surrounded with the strongest proofs of wealth. Lying at the wharves, and riding in the stream, I saw many ships of the finest model, in the best order, and of the largest size. Upon the right and left, I was walled in by granite warehouses of the widest dimensions, stowed to their utmost capacity with the necessaries and comforts of life. Added to this, almost every body seemed to be at work, but noiselessly so, compared with what I had been accustomed to in Baltimore. There were no loud songs heard from those engaged in loading and unloading ships. I heard no deep oaths or horrid curses on the laborer.

---

[38]A central character in Sir Walter Scott's poem *Lady of the Lake.*

I saw no whipping of men; but all seemed to go smoothly on. Every man appeared to understand his work, and went at it with a sober, yet cheerful earnestness, which betokened the deep interest which he felt in what he was doing, as well as a sense of his own dignity as man. To me this looked exceedingly strange. From the wharves I strolled around and over the town, gazing with wonder and admiration at the splendid churches, beautiful dwellings, and finely-cultivated gardens; evincing an amount of wealth, comfort, taste, and refinement, such as I had never seen in any part of slaveholding Maryland.

Every thing looked clean, new, and beautiful. I saw few or no dilapidated houses, with poverty-stricken inmates; no half-naked children and barefooted women, such as I had been accustomed to see in Hillsborough, Easton, St. Michael's, and Baltimore. The people looked more able, stronger, healthier, and happier, than those of Maryland. I was for once made glad by a view of extreme wealth, without being saddened by seeing extreme poverty. But the most astonishing as well as the most interesting thing to me was the condition of the colored people, a great many of whom, like myself, had escaped thither as a refuge from the hunters of men. I found many, who had not been seven years out of their chains, living in finer houses, and evidently enjoying more of the comforts of life, than the average of slaveholders in Maryland. I will venture to assert, that my friend Mr. Nathan Johnson (of whom I can say with a grateful heart, "I was hungry, and he gave me meat; I was thirsty, and he gave me drink; I was a stranger, and he took me in"[39] lived in a neater house; dined at a better table; took, paid for, and read, more newspapers; better understood the moral, religious, and political character of the nation,—than nine tenths of the slaveholders in Talbot county Maryland. Yet Mr. Johnson was a working man. His hands were hardened by toil, and not his alone, but those also of Mrs. Johnson. I found the colored people much more spirited than I had supposed they would be. I found among them a determination to protect each other from the bloodthirsty kidnapper, at all hazards. Soon after my arrival, I was told a circumstance which illustrated their spirit. A colored man and a fugitive slave were on unfriendly terms. The former was heard to threaten the latter with informing his master of his whereabouts. Straightway a meeting was called among the colored people, under the stereotyped notice, "Business of importance!" The betrayer was invited to attend. The people came at the appointed hour, and organized the meeting by appointing a very religious old gentleman as president, who, I believe, made a prayer, after which he addressed the meeting as follows: *Friends, we have got him here, and I would recommend that you young men just take him outside the door, and kill him!*" With this, a number of them bolted at him; but they were intercepted by some more timid than themselves, and the betrayer escaped their vengeance, and has not been seen in New Bedford since. I believe there have been

---

[39] Matthew 25:35.

no more such threats, and should there be hereafter, I doubt not that death would be the consequence.

I found employment, the third day after my arrival, in stowing a sloop with a load of oil. It was new, dirty, and hard work for me; but I went at it with a glad heart and a willing hand. I was now my own master. It was a happy moment, the rapture of which can be understood only by those who have been slaves. It was the first work, the reward of which was to be entirely my own. There was no Master Hugh standing ready, the moment I earned the money, to rob me of it. I worked that day with a pleasure I had never before experienced. I was at work for myself and newly-married wife. It was to me the starting-point of a new existence. When I got through with that job, I went in pursuit of a job of calking; but such was the strength of prejudice against color, among the white calkers, that they refused to work with me, and of course I could get no employment.[40] Finding my trade of no immediate benefit, I threw off my calking habiliments, and prepared myself to do any kind of work I could get to do. Mr. Johnson kindly let me have his wood-horse and saw, and I very soon found myself, a plenty of work. There was no work too hard—none too dirty. I was ready to saw wood, shovel coal, carry wood, sweep the chimney, or roll oil casks,—all of which I did for nearly three years in New Bedford, before I became known to the anti-slavery world.

In about four months after I went to New Bedford, there came a young man to me, and inquired if I did not wish to take the "Liberator."[41] I told him I did; but, just having made my escape from slavery, I remarked that I was unable to pay for it then. I, however, finally became a subscriber to it. The paper came, and I read it from week to week with such feelings as it would be quite idle for me to attempt to describe. The paper became my meat and my drink. My soul was set all on fire. Its sympathy for my brethren in bonds—its scathing denunciations of slaveholders—its faithful exposures of slavery—and its powerful attacks upon the upholders of the institution—sent a thrill of joy through my soul, such as I had never felt before!

I had not long been a reader of the "Liberator," before I got a pretty correct idea of the principles, measures and spirit of the anti-slavery reform. I took right hold of the cause. I could do but little; but what I could, I did with a joyful heart, and never felt happier than when in an anti-slavery meeting. I seldom had much to say at the meetings, because what I wanted to say was said so much better by others. But, while attending an anti-slavery convention at Nantucket, on the 11th of August, 1841, I felt strongly moved to speak, and was at the same time much urged to do so by Mr. William C. Coffin, a gentleman who had heard me speak in the colored people's meeting at New Bedford. It was a severe cross, and I took it up reluctantly. The truth

---

[40]I am told that colored persons can now get employment at calking in New Bedford—a result of anti-slavery effort. [Douglass's note.]

[41]See headnote on William Lloyd Garrison, earlier in this section. As this episode indicates, many of the newspaper's readers were black.

was, I felt myself a slave, and the idea of speaking to white people weighed me down. I spoke but a few moments, when I felt a degree of freedom, and said what I desired with considerable ease. From that time until now, I have been engaged in pleading the cause of my brethren—with what success, and with what devotion, I leave those acquainted with my labors to decide.

Appendix

I find, since reading over the foregoing Narrative, that I have, in several instances, spoken in such a tone and manner, respecting religion, as may possibly lead those unacquainted with my religious views to suppose me an opponent of all religion. To remove the liability of such misapprehension, I deem it proper to append the following brief explanation. What I have said respecting and against religion, I mean strictly to apply to the *slaveholding religion* of this land, and with no possible reference to Christianity proper; for, between the Christianity of this land, and the Christianity of Christ, I recognize the widest possible difference—so wide, that to receive the one as good, pure, and holy, is of necessity to reject the other as bad, corrupt, and wicked. To be the friend of the one, is of necessity to be the enemy of the other. I love the pure, peaceable, and impartial Christianity of Christ: I therefore hate the corrupt, slaveholding, women-whipping, cradle-plundering, partial and hypocritical Christianity of this land. Indeed, I can see no reason, but the most deceitful one, for calling the religion of this land Christianity. I look upon it as the climax of all misnomers, the boldest of all frauds, and the grossest of all libels. Never was there a clearer case of "stealing the livery of the court of heaven to serve the devil in." I am filled with unutterable loathing when I contemplate the religious pomp and show, together with the horrible inconsistencies, which every where surrounded me. We have men-stealers for ministers, women-whippers for missionaries, and cradle-plunderers for church members. The man who wields the blood-clotted cowskin during the week fills the pulpit on Sunday, and claims to be a minister of the meek and lowly Jesus. The man who robs me of my earnings at the end of each week meets me as a class-leader on Sunday morning, to show me the way of life, and the path of salvation. He who sells my sister, for purposes of prostitution, stands forth as the pious advocate of purity. He who proclaims it a religious duty to read the Bible denies me the right of learning to read the name of the God who made me. He who is the religious advocate of marriage robs whole millions of its sacred influence, and leaves them to the ravages of wholesale pollution. The warm defender of the sacredness of the family relation is the same that scatters whole families,—sundering husbands and wives, parents and children, sisters and brothers,—leaving the hut vacant, and the hearth desolate. We see the thief preaching against theft, and the adulterer against adultery. We have men sold to build churches, women sold to support the gospel, and babes sold to purchase Bibles for the *poor heathen! all for the glory of God and the good of souls!* The slave auctioneer's bell and the church-going bell chime in with each other, and the bitter cries of the heart-broken slave are drowned in the religious shouts of his pious master. Revivals of religion and revivals in the slave-trade go hand in hand together. The slave prison and the church stand near each other. The clanking of fetters and the rattling of chains in the prison, and the pious psalm and solemn prayer in the church, may be heard at the same time. The dealers in the bodies and souls of men erect their stand in the presence of the pulpit, and they mutually help each other. The dealer gives his blood-stained gold to support the pulpit, and the pulpit, in return, covers his infernal business with the garb of Christianity. Here we have religion and robbery the allies of each other—devils dressed in angels' robes, and hell presenting the semblance of paradise.

> "Just God! and these are they,
>   Who minister at thine altar, God of right!
> Men who their hands, with prayer and blessing, lay
>   On Israel's ark of light.[42]
>
> "What! preach, and kidnap men?
>   Give thanks, and rob thy own afflicted poor?
> Talk of thy glorious liberty, and then
>   Bolt hard the captive's door?
>
> "What! servants of thy own
>   Merciful Son, who came to seek and save
> The homeless and the outcast, fettering down
>   The tasked and plundered slave!
>
> "Pilate and Herod friends[43]
>   Chief priests and rulers, as of old, combine!
> Just God and holy! is that church which lends
>   Strength to the spoiler thine?"[44]

The Christianity of America is a Christianity, of whose votaries it may be as truly said, as it was of the ancient scribes and Pharisees,[45] "They bind heavy burdens, and grievous to be borne, and lay them on men's shoulders, but they themselves will not move them with one of their fingers. All their works they do for to be seen of men.—They love the uppermost rooms at feasts, and the chief seats in the synagogues, ... and to be called of men, Rabbi, Rabbi.—But woe unto you, scribes and Pharisees, hypocrites! for ye shut up the kingdom of heaven against men; for ye neither go in yourselves,

---

[42]The ark of the covenant, which, in a synagogue, contains the Torah or holy scripture.
[43]Pontius Pilate, Roman official who condemned Jesus Christ; Herod Antipater, tetrarch of Galilee, presented the head of John the Baptist on a platter to his stepdaughter, Salome.
[44]From J. G. Whittier's poem "Clerical Oppressors."

[45]The scribes were Jewish scholars and biblical interpreters often historically at odds with those, like Jesus, asserting prophetic authority; the Pharisees were a school of ascetics who came to look at themselves as better than other men.

neither suffer ye them that are entering to go in. Ye devour widows' houses, and for a pretence make long prayers; therefore ye shall receive the greater damnation. Ye compass sea and land to make one proselyte, and when he is made, ye make him twofold more the child of hell than yourselves.—Woe unto you, scribes and Pharisees, hypocrites! for ye pay tithe of mint, and anise, and cumin, and have omitted the weightier matters of the law, judgment, mercy, and faith; these ought ye to have done, and not to leave the other undone. Ye blind guides! which strain at a gnat, and swallow a camel. Woe unto you, scribes and Pharisees, hypocrites! for ye make clean the outside of the cup and of the platter; but within, they are full of extortion and excess.—Woe unto you, scribes and Pharisees, hypocrites! for ye are like unto whited sepulchres, which indeed appear beautiful outward, but are within full of dead men's bones, and of all uncleanness. Even so ye also outwardly appear righteous unto men, but within ye are full of hypocrisy and iniquity."[46]

Dark and terrible as is this picture, I hold it to be strictly true of the overwhelming mass of professed Christians in America. They strain at a gnat, and swallow a camel. Could any thing be more true of our churches? They would be shocked at the proposition of fellowshipping, a *sheep*-stealer; and at the same time they hug to their communion a *man*-stealer, and brand me with being an infidel, if I find fault with them for it. They attend with Pharisaical strictness to the outward forms of religion, and at the same time neglect the weightier matters of the law, judgment, mercy, and faith. They are always ready to sacrifice, but seldom to show mercy. They are they who are represented as professing to love God whom they have not seen, whilst they hate their brother whom they have seen. They love the heathen on the other side of the globe. They can pray for him, pay money to have the Bible put into his hand, and missionaries to instruct him; while they despise and totally neglect the heathen at their own doors.

Such is, very briefly, my view of the religion of this land; and to avoid any misunderstanding, growing out of the use of general terms, I mean, by the religion of this land, that which is revealed in the words, deeds, and actions, of those bodies, north and south, calling themselves Christian churches, and yet in union with slaveholders. It is against religion, as presented by these bodies, that I have felt it my duty to testify.

I conclude these remarks by copying the following portrait of the religion of the south, (which is, by communion and fellowship, the religion of the north,) which I soberly affirm is "true to the life," and without caricature or the slightest exaggeration. It is said to have been drawn, several years before the present anti-slavery agitation began, by a northern Methodist preacher, who, while residing at the south, had an opportunity to see slaveholding morals, manners, and piety, with his own eyes. "Shall I not visit for these things? saith the Lord. Shall not my soul be avenged on such a nation as this?"[47]

[46]See Matthew 23.   [47]Jeremiah 5:9.

A PARODY[48]

"Come, saints and sinners, hear me tell
How pious priests whip Jack and Nell,
And women buy and children sell,
And preach all sinners down to hell,
    And sing of heavenly union.

"They'll bleat and baa, dona like goats,
Gorge down black sheep, and strain at motes,
Array their backs in fine black coats,
Then seize their negroes by their throats,
    And choke, for heavenly union.

"They'll church you if you sip a dram,
And damn you if you steal a lamb;
Yet rob old Tony, Doll, and Sam,
Of human rights, and bread and ham;
    Kidnapper's heavenly union.

"They'll loudly talk of Christ's reward,
And bind his image with a cord
And scold, and swing the lash abhorred,
And sell their brother in the Lord
    To handcuffed heavenly union.

"They'll read and sing a sacred song,
And make a prayer both loud and long,
And teach the right and do the wrong,
Hailing the brother, sister throng,
    With words of heavenly union.

"We wonder how such saints can sing,
Or praise the Lord upon the wing,
Who roar, and scold, and whip, and sting,
And to their slaves and mammon cling,
    In guilty conscience union.

"They'll raise tobacco, corn, and rye,
And drive, and thieve, and cheat, and lie,
And lay up treasures in the sky,
By making switch and cowskin fly,
    In hope of heavenly union.

[48]In the poem, Douglass is parodying "Heavenly Union," a hymn popular in Southern churches at the time.

"They'll crack old Tony on the skull,
And preach and roar like Bashan bull,[49]
Or braying ass, of mischief full,
Then seize old Jacob by the wool,
    And pull for heavenly union.

"A roaring, ranting, sleek man-thief,
Who lived on mutton, veal, and beef,
Yet never would afford relief
To needy, sable sons of grief,
    Was big with heavenly union.

"'Love not the world,' the preacher said,
And winked his eye, and shook his head;
He seized on Tom, and Dick, and Ned,
Cut short their meat, and clothes, and bread,
    Yet still loved heavenly union.

"Another preacher whining spoke
Of One whose heart for sinners broke:
He tied old Nanny to an oak,
And drew the blood at every stroke,
    And prayed for heavenly union.

"Two others oped their iron jaws,
And waved their children-stealing paws;
There sat their children in gewgaws;
By stinting negroes' backs and maws,
    They kept up heavenly union.

"All good from Jack another takes,
And entertains their flirts and rakes,
Who dress as sleek as glossy snakes,
And cram their mouths with sweetened cakes;
    And this goes down for union."

Sincerely and earnestly hoping that this little book may do something toward throwing light on the American slave system, and hastening the glad day of deliverance to the millions of my brethren in bonds—faithfully relying upon the power of truth, love, and justice, for success in my humble efforts—and solemnly pledging my self anew to the sacred cause,—I subscribe myself,

FREDERICK DOUGLASS
Lynn, Mass., April 28, 1845.

---

[49]In the Old Testament, proverbially powerful.

What to the Slave Is the Fourth of July?

An Address Delivered in Rochester, New York, on 5 July 1852[1]

Mr. President, Friends and Fellow Citizens: He who could address this audience without a quailing sensation, has stronger nerves than I have. I do not remember ever to have appeared as a speaker before any assembly more shrinkingly, nor with greater distrust of my ability, than I do this day. A feeling has crept over me, quite unfavorable to the exercise of my limited powers of speech. The task before me is one which requires much previous thought and study for its proper performance. I know that apologies of this sort are generally considered flat and unmeaning. I trust, however, that mine will not be so considered. Should I seem at ease, my appearance would much misrepresent me. The little experience I have had in addressing public meetings, in country school houses, avails me nothing on the present occasion.

The papers and placards say, that I am to deliver a 4th of July oration. This certainly sounds large, and out of the common way, for me. It is true that I have often had the privilege to speak in this beautiful Hall, and to address many who now honor me with their presence. But neither their familiar faces, nor the perfect gage I think I have of Corinthian Hall, seems to free me from embarrassment.

The fact is, ladies and gentlemen, the distance between this platform and the slave plantation, from which I escaped, is considerable—and the difficulties to be overcome in getting from the latter to the former, are by no means slight. That I am here to-day is, to me, a matter of astonishment as well as of gratitude. You will not, therefore, be surprised, if in what I have to say, I evince no elaborate preparation, nor grace my speech with any high sounding exordium. With little experience and with less learning, I have been able to throw my thoughts hastily and imperfectly together; and trusting to your patient and generous indulgence, I will proceed to lay them before you.

This, for the purpose of this celebration, is the 4th of July. It is the birthday of your National Independence, and of your political freedom. This, to you, is what the Passover was to the emancipated people of God. It carries your minds back to the day, and to the act of your great deliverance; and to the signs, and to the wonders, associated with that act, and that day. This celebration also marks the beginning of another year of your national life; and reminds you that the Republic of America is now 76 years old. I am glad, fellow-citizens, that your nation is so young. Seventy-six years, though a good old age for a man, is but a mere speck in the life of a nation. Three score years and ten is the allotted time for individual men; but nations number their years by thousands. According to this fact, you are, even now, only in the beginning of your national career, still lingering in the period of childhood. I repeat, I am glad this is so. There is hope in the thought, and hope

[1]The speech was delivered on July 5, 1852, at Corinthian Hall in Rochester, New York. The text is based on that of the pamphlet, published by Lee, Mann and Company, during the same year.

is much needed, under the dark clouds which lower above the horizon. The eye of the reformer is met with angry flashes, portending disastrous times; but his heart may well beat lighter at the thought that America is young, and that she is still in the impressible stage of her existence. May he not hope that high lessons of wisdom, of justice and of truth, will yet give direction to her destiny? Were the nation older, the patriot's heart might be sadder, and the reformer's brow heavier. Its future might be shrouded in gloom, and the hope of its prophets go out in sorrow. There is consolation in the thought that America is young. Great streams are not easily turned from channels, worn deep in the course of ages. They may sometimes rise in quiet and stately majesty, and inundate the land, refreshing and fertilizing the earth with their mysterious properties. They may also rise in wrath and fury, and bear away, on their angry waves, the accumulated wealth of years of toil and hardship. They, however, gradually flow back to the same old channel, and flow on as serenely as ever. But, while the river may not be turned aside, it may dry up, and leave nothing behind but the withered branch, and the unsightly rock, to howl in the abyss-sweeping wind, the sad tale of departed glory. As with rivers so with nations.

Fellow-citizens, I shall not presume to dwell at length on the associations that cluster about this day. The simple story of it is that, 76 years ago, the people of this country were British subjects. The style and title of your "sovereign people" in which you now glory was not then born. You were under the British Crown. Your fathers esteemed the English Government as the home government; and England as the fatherland. This home government, you know, although a considerable distance from your home, did, in the exercise of its parental prerogatives, impose upon its colonial children, such restraints, burdens and limitations, as, in its mature judgement, it deemed wise, right and proper.

But, your fathers, who had not adopted the fashionable idea of this day, of the infallibility of government, and the absolute character of its acts, presumed to differ from the home government in respect to the wisdom and the justice of some of those burdens and restraints. They went so far in their excitement as to pronounce the measures of government unjust, unreasonable, and oppressive, and altogether such as ought not to be quietly submitted to. I scarcely need say, fellow-citizens, that my opinion of those measures fully accords with that of your fathers. Such a declaration of agreement on my part would not be worth much to anybody. It would, certainly, prove nothing, as to what part I might have taken, had I lived during the great controversy of 1776. To say *now* that America was right, and England wrong, is exceedingly easy. Everybody can say it; the dastard, not less than the noble brave, can flippantly discant on the tyranny of England towards the American Colonies. It is fashionable to do so; but there was a time when to pronounce against England, and in favor of the cause of the colonies, tried men's souls.[2] They who did so were accounted in their day, plotters of

[2]Douglass is paraphrasing the First *Crisis* paper of Thomas Paine; see the earlier section of this volume.

mischief, agitators and rebels, dangerous men. To side with the right, against the wrong, with the weak against the strong, and with the oppressed against the oppressor! *here* lies the merit, and the one which, of all others, seems unfashionable in our day. The cause of liberty may be stabbed by the men who glory in the deeds of your fathers. But, to proceed.

Feeling themselves harshly and unjustly treated by the home government, your fathers, like men of honesty, and men of spirit, earnestly sought redress. They petitioned and remonstrated; they did so in a decorous, respectful, and loyal manner. Their conduct was wholly unexceptionable. This, however, did not answer the purpose. They saw themselves treated with sovereign indifference, coldness and scorn. Yet they persevered. They were not the men to look back.

As the sheet anchor takes a firmer hold, when the ship is tossed by the storm, so did the cause of your fathers grow stronger, as it breasted the chilling blasts of kingly displeasure. The greatest and best of British statesmen admitted its justice, and the loftiest eloquence of the British Senate came to its support. But, with that blindness which seems to be the unvarying characteristic of tyrants, since Pharoah and his hosts were drowned in the Red Sea, the British Government persisted in the exactions complained of.

The madness of this course, we believe, is admitted now, even by England; but we fear the lesson is wholly lost on our present rulers.

Oppression makes a wise man mad. Your fathers were wise men, and if they did not go mad, they became restive under this treatment. They felt themselves the victims of grievous wrongs, wholly incurable in their colonial capacity. With brave men there is always a remedy for oppression. Just here, the idea of a total separation of the colonies from the crown was born! It was a startling idea, much more so, than we, at this distance of time, regard it. The timid and the prudent (as has been intimated) of that day, were, of course, shocked and alarmed by it.

Such people lived then, had lived before, and will, probably, ever have a place on this planet; and their course, in respect to any great change, (no matter how great the good to be attained, or the wrong to be redressed by it), may be calculated with as much precision as can be the course of the stars. They hate all changes, but silver, gold and copper change! Of this sort of change they are always strongly in favor.

These people were called tories in the days of your fathers; and the appellation, probably, conveyed the same idea that is meant by a more modern, though a somewhat less euphonious term, which we often find in our papers, applied to some of our old politicians.[3]

Their opposition to the then dangerous thought was earnest and powerful; but, amid all their terror and affrighted vociferations against it, the alarming and revolutionary idea moved on, and the country with it.

[3]The term may be "hunker," used to refer to conservative Democrats of the time.

On the 2d of July, 1776, the old Continental Congress, to the dismay of the lovers of ease, and the worshippers of property, clothed that dreadful idea with all the authority of national sanction. They did so in the form of a resolution; and as we seldom hit upon resolutions, drawn up in our day, whose transparency is at all equal to this, it may refresh your minds and help my story if I read it.

> "Resolved, That these united colonies are, and of right, ought to be free and Independent States; that they are absolved from all allegiance to the British Crown; and that all political connection between them and the State of Great Britain is, and ought to be, dissolved."[4]

Citizens, your fathers made good that resolution. They succeeded; and to-day you reap the fruits of their success. The freedom gained is yours; and you, therefore, may properly celebrate this anniversary. The 4th of July is the first great fact in your nation's history—the very ring-bolt in the chain of your yet undeveloped destiny.

Pride and patriotism, not less than gratitude, prompt you to celebrate and to hold it in perpetual remembrance. I have said that the Declaration of Independence is the RING-BOLT to the chain of your nation's destiny; so, indeed, I regard it. The principles contained in that instrument are saving principles. Stand by those principles, be true to them on all occasions, in all places, against all foes, and at whatever cost.

From the round top of your ship of state, dark and threatening clouds may be seen. Heavy billows, like mountains in the distance, disclose to the leeward huge forms of flinty rocks! That *bolt* drawn, that *chain* broken, and all is lost. *Cling to this day—cling to it*, and to its principles, with the grasp of a storm-tossed mariner to a spar at midnight.

The coming into being of a nation, in any circumstances, is an interesting event. But, besides general considerations, there were peculiar circumstances which make the advent of this republic an event of special attractiveness.

The whole scene, as I look back to it, was simple, dignified and sublime.

The population of the country, at the time, stood at the insignificant number of three millions. The country was poor in the munitions of war. The population was weak and scattered, and the country a wilderness unsubdued. There were then no means of concert and combination, such as exist now. Neither steam nor lightning had then been reduced to order and discipline. From the Potomac to the Delaware was a journey of many days. Under these, and innumerable other disadvantages, your fathers declared for liberty and independence and triumphed.

Fellow Citizens, I am not wanting in respect for the fathers of this republic. The signers of the Declaration of Independence were brave men. They were great men too—great enough to give fame to a great age. It does

---

[4]Here, and elsewhere, Douglass quotes from or paraphrases the Declaration of Independence.

not often happen to a nation to raise, at one time, such a number of truly great men. The point from which I am compelled to view them is not, certainly, the most favorable; and yet I cannot contemplate their great deeds with less than admiration. They were statesmen, patriots and heroes, and for the good they did, and the principles they contended for, I will unite with you to honor their memory.

They loved their country better than their own private interests; and, though this is not the highest form of human excellence, all will concede that it is a rare virtue, and that when it is exhibited, it ought to command respect. He who will, intelligently, lay down his life for his country, is a man whom it is not in human nature to despise. Your fathers staked their lives, their fortunes, and their sacred honor, on the cause of their country. In their admiration of liberty, they lost sight of all other interests.

They were peace men; but they preferred revolution to peaceful submission to bondage. They were quiet men; but they did not shrink from agitating against oppression. They showed forbearance; but that they knew its limits. They believed in order; but not in the order of tyranny. With them, nothing was "*settled*" that was not right. With them, justice, liberty and humanity were "*final*"; not slavery and oppression. You may well cherish the memory of such men. They were great in their day and generation. Their solid manhood stands out the more as we contrast it with these degenerate times.

How circumspect, exact and proportionate were all their movements! How unlike the politicians of an hour! Their statesmanship looked beyond the passing moment, and stretched away in strength into the distant future. They seized upon eternal principles, and set a glorious example in their defence. Mark them!

Fully appreciating the hardship to be encountered, firmly believing in the right of their cause, honorably inviting the scrutiny of an on-looking world, reverently appealing to heaven to attest their sincerity, soundly comprehending the solemn responsibility they were about to assume, wisely measuring the terrible odds against them, your fathers, the fathers of this republic, did, most deliberately, under the inspiration of a glorious patriotism, and with a sublime faith in the great principles of justice and freedom, lay deep the corner-stone of the national superstructure, which has risen and still rises in grandeur around you.

Of this fundamental work, this day is the anniversary. Our eyes are met with demonstrations of joyous enthusiasm. Banners and pennants wave exultingly on the breeze. The din of business, too, is hushed. Even Mammon seems to have quitted his grasp on this day. The ear-piercing fife and the stirring drum unite their accents with the ascending peal of a thousand church bells. Prayers are made, hymns are sung, and sermons are preached in honor of this day; while the quick martial tramp of a great and multitudinous nation, echoed back by all the hills, valleys and mountains of a vast continent, bespeak the occasion one of thrilling and universal interest—a nation's jubilee.

Friends and citizens, I need not enter further into the causes which led to this anniversary. Many of you understand them better than I do. You could instruct me in regard to them. That is a branch of knowledge in which you feel, perhaps, a much deeper interest than your speaker. The causes which led to the separation of the colonies from the British crown have never lacked for a tongue. They have all been taught in your common schools, narrated at your firesides, unfolded from your pulpits, and thundered from your legislative halls, and are as familiar to you as household words. They form the staple of your national poetry and eloquence.

I remember, also, that, as a people, Americans are remarkably familiar with all facts which make in their own favor. This is esteemed by some as a national trait—perhaps a national weakness. It is a fact, that whatever makes for the wealth or for the reputation of Americans, and can be had *cheap!* will be found by Americans. I shall not be charged with slandering Americans, if I say I think the American side of any question may be safely left in American hands.

I leave, therefore, the great deeds of your fathers to other gentlemen whose claim to have been regularly descended will be less likely to be disputed than mine!

The Present

My business, if I have any here to-day, is with the present. The accepted time with God and his cause is the ever-living now.

> *"Trust no future, however pleasant,*
> *Let the dead past bury its dead;*
> *Act, act in the living present,*
> *Heart within, and God overhead."*[5]

We have to do with the past only as we can make it useful to the present and to the future. To all inspiring motives, to noble deeds which can be gained from the past, we are welcome. But now is the time, the important time. Your fathers have lived, died, and have done their work, and have done much of it well. You live and must die, and you must do your work. You have no right to enjoy a child's share in the labor of your fathers, unless your children are to be blest by your labors. You have no right to wear out and waste the hard-earned fame of your fathers to cover your indolence. Sydney Smith[6] tells us that men seldom eulogize the wisdom and virtues of their fathers, but to excuse some folly or wickedness of their own. This truth is not a doubtful one. There are illustrations of it near and remote, ancient and modern. It was fashionable, hundreds of years ago, for the children of Jacob to boast, we have "Abraham to our father," when they had

---

[5] From Henry Wadsworth Longfellow, "A Psalm of Life."

[6] Anglican essayist and minister (1771–1845), best known in the United States for questioning who, anywhere, "reads an American book."

long lost Abraham's faith and spirit.[7] That people contented themselves under the shadow of Abraham's great name, while they repudiated the deeds which made his name great. Need I remind you that a similar thing is being done all over this country to-day? Need I tell you that the Jews are not the only people who built the tombs of the prophets, and garnished the sepulchers of the righteous? Washington could not die till he had broken the chains of his slaves.[8] Yet his monument is built up by the price of human blood, and the traders in the bodies and souls of men, shout—"We have Washington to *our father*." Alas! that it should be so; yet so it is.

> "The evil that men do, lives after them,
> The good is oft' interred with their bones."[9]

Fellow-citizens, pardon me, allow me to ask, why am I called upon to speak here to-day? What have I, or those I represent, to do with your national independence? Are the great principles of political freedom and of natural justice, embodied in that Declaration of Independence, extended to us? and am I, therefore, called upon to bring our humble offering to the national altar, and to confess the benefits and express devout gratitude for the blessings resulting from your independence to us?

Would to God, both for your sakes and ours, that an affirmative answer could be truthfully returned to these questions! Then would my task be light, and my burden easy and delightful. For *who* is there so cold, that a nation's sympathy could not warm him? Who so obdurate and dead to the claims of gratitude, that would not thankfully acknowledge such priceless benefits? Who so stolid and selfish, that would not give his voice to swell the hallelujahs of a nation's jubilee, when the chains of servitude had been torn from his limbs? I am not that man. In a case like that, the dumb might eloquently speak, and the "lame man leap as an hart."

But, such is not the state of the case. I say it with a sad sense of the disparity between us. I am not included within the pale of this glorious anniversary! Your high independence only reveals the immeasurable distance between us. The blessings in which you, this day, rejoice, are not enjoyed in common. The rich inheritance of justice, liberty, prosperity and independence, bequeathed by your fathers, is shared by you, not by me. The sunlight that brought life and healing to you, has brought stripes and death to me. This Fourth [of] July is *yours*, not *mine*. *You* may rejoice, *I* must mourn. To drag a man in fetters into the grand illuminated temple of liberty, and call upon him to join you in joyous anthems, were inhuman mockery and sacrilegious irony. Do you mean, citizens, to mock me, by asking me to speak to-day? If so, there is a parallel to your conduct. And let me warn you that it is dangerous to copy the example of a nation whose crimes, towering up to heaven, were thrown down by the breath of the Almighty, burying that

---

[7]Luke 3:8.

[8]George Washington's will provided that, at his wife's death, the 300 and more slaves he owned should be freed.

[9]*Julius Caesar*, III, ii, 76.

nation in irrecoverable ruin! I can to-day take up the plaintive lament of a peeled and woe-smitten people!

"By the rivers of Babylon, there we sat down. Yea! we wept when we remembered Zion. We hanged our harps upon the willows in the midst thereof. For there, they that carried us away captive, required of us a song; and they who wasted us required of us mirth, saying, Sing us one of the songs of Zion. How can we sing the Lord's song in a strange land? If I forget thee, O Jerusalem, let my right hand forget her cunning. If I do not remember thee, let my tongue cleave to the roof of my mouth."[10]

Fellow-citizens; above your national, tumultous joy, I hear the mournful wail of millions! whose chains, heavy and grievous yesterday, are, to-day, rendered more intolerable by the jubilee shouts that reach them. If I do forget, if I do not faithfully remember those bleeding children of sorrow this day, "may my right hand forget her cunning, and may my tongue cleave to the roof of my mouth!" To forget them, to pass lightly over their wrongs, and to chime in with the popular theme, would be treason most scandalous and shocking, and would make me a reproach before God and the world. My subject, then fellow-citizens, is AMERICAN SLAVERY. I shall see, this day, and its popular characteristics, from the slave's point of view. Standing, there, identified with the American bondman, making his wrongs mine, I do not hesitate to declare, with all my soul, that the character and conduct of this nation never looked blacker to me than on this 4th of July! Whether we turn to the declarations of the past, or to the professions of the present, the conduct of the nation seems equally hideous and revolting. America is false to the past, false to the present, and solemnly binds herself to be false to the future. Standing with God and the crushed and bleeding slave on this occasion, I will, in the name of humanity which is outraged, in the name of liberty which is fettered, in the name of the constitution and the Bible, which are disregarded and trampled upon, dare to call in question and to denounce, with all the emphasis I can command, everything that serves to perpetuate slavery—the great sin and shame of America! "I will not equivocate; I will not excuse"[11]; I will use the severest language I can command; and yet not one word shall escape me that any man, whose judgement is not blinded by prejudice, or who is not at heart a slaveholder, shall not confess to be right and just.

But I fancy I hear some one of my audience say, it is just in this circumstance that you and your brother abolitionists fail to make a favorable impression on the public mind. Would you argue more, and denounce less, would you persuade more, and rebuke less, your cause would be much more likely to succeed. But, I submit, where all is plain there is nothing to be argued. What point in the anti-slavery creed would you have me argue? On what branch of the subject do the people of this country need light? Must I

---

[10]Psalm 137:1–6.

[11]Douglass is quoting William Lloyd Garrison's editorial from the first issue of the *Liberator*; the full text appears earlier in this section.

undertake to prove that the slave is a man? That point is conceded already. Nobody doubts it. The slaveholders themselves acknowledge it in the enactment of law, for their government. They acknowledge it when they punish disobedience on the part of the slave. There are seventy-two crimes in the State of Virginia, which, if committed by a black man, (no matter how ignorant he be), subject him to the punishment of death; while only two of the same crimes will subject a white man to the like punishment. What is this but the acknowledgement that the slave is a moral, intellectual and responsible being? The manhood of the slave is conceded. It is admitted in the fact that Southern statute books are covered with enactments forbidding, under severe fines and penalties, the teaching of the slave to read or to write. When you can point to any such laws, in reference to the beasts of the field, then I may consent to argue the manhood of the slave. When the dogs in your streets, when the fowls of the air, when the cattle on your hills, when the fish of the sea, and the reptiles that crawl, shall be unable to distinguish the slave from a brute, *then* will I argue with you that the slave is a man!

For the present, it is enough to affirm the equal manhood of the negro race. Is it not astonishing that, while we are ploughing, planting and reaping, using all kinds of mechanical tools, erecting houses, constructing bridges, building ships, working in metals of brass, iron, copper, silver and gold; that, while we are reading, writing and cyphering, acting as clerks, merchants and secretaries, having among us lawyers, doctors, ministers, poets, authors, editors, orators and teachers; that, while we are engaged in all manner of enterprises common to other man, digging gold in California, capturing the whale in the Pacific, feeding sheep and cattle on the hill-side, living, moving, acting, thinking, planning, living in families as husbands, wives and children, and, above all, confessing and worshipping the Christian's God, and looking hopefully for life and immortality beyond the grave, we are called upon to prove that we are men!

Would you have me argue that man is entitled to liberty? that he is the rightful owner of his own body? You have already declared it. Must I argue the wrongfulness of slavery? Is that a question for Republicans? Is it to be settled by the rules of logic and argumentation, as a matter beset with great difficulty, involving a doubtful application of the principle of justice, hard to be understood? How should I look to-day, in the presence of Americans, dividing, and subdividing a discourse, to show that men have a natural right to freedom? speaking of it relatively, and positively, negatively, and affirmatively. To do so, would be to make myself ridiculous, and to offer an insult to your understanding. There is not a man beneath the canopy of heaven, that does not know that slavery is wrong *for him.*

What, am I to argue that it is wrong to make men brutes, to rob them of their liberty, to work them without wages, to keep them ignorant of their relations to their fellow men, to beat them with sticks, to flay their flesh with the lash, to load their limbs with irons, to hunt them with dogs, to sell them at auction, to sunder their families, to knock out their teeth, to burn their flesh, to starve them into obedience and submission to their masters?

Must I argue that a system thus marked with blood, and stained with pollution, is *wrong*? No! I will not. I have better employments for my time and strength, than such arguments would imply.

What, then, remains to be argued? Is it that slavery is not divine; that God did not establish it; that our doctors of divinity are mistaken? There is blasphemy in the thought. That which is inhuman, cannot be divine! *Who* can reason on such a proposition? They that can, may; I cannot. The time for such argument is past.

At a time like this, scorching irony, not convincing argument, is needed. O! had I the ability, and could I reach the nation's ear, I would, to-day, pour out a fiery stream of biting ridicule, blasting reproach, withering sarcasm, and stern rebuke. For it is not light that is needed, but fire; it is not the gentle shower, but thunder. We need the storm, the whirlwind, and the earthquake. The feeling of the nation must be quickened; the conscience of the nation must be roused; the propriety of the nation must be startled; the hypocrisy of the nation must be exposed; and its crimes against God and man must be proclaimed and denounced.

What, to the American slave, is your 4th of July? I answer: a day that reveals to him, more than all other days in the year, the gross injustice and cruelty to which he is the constant victim. To him, your celebration is a sham; your boasted liberty, an unholy license; your national greatness, swelling vanity; your sounds of rejoicing are empty and heartless; your denunciations of tyrants, brass fronted impudence; your shouts of liberty and equality, hollow mockery; your prayers and hymns, your sermons and thanksgivings, with all your religious parade, and solemnity, are, to him, mere bombast, fraud, deception, impiety, and hypocrisy—a thin veil to cover up crimes which would disgrace a nation of savages. There is not a nation on the earth guilty of practices, more shocking and bloody, than are the people of these United States, at this very hour.

Go where you may, search where you will, roam through all the monarchies and despotisms of the old world, travel through South America, search out every abuse, and when you have found the last, lay your facts by the side of the everyday practices of this nation, and you will say with me, that, for revolting barbarity and shameless hypocrisy, America reigns without a rival.

The Internal Slave Trade

Take the American slave-trade, which, we are told by the papers, is especially prosperous just now. Ex-Senator Benton[12] tells us that the price of men was never higher than now. He mentions the fact to show that slavery is in no danger. This trade is one of the peculiarities of American institutions. It is carried on in all the large towns and cities in one-half of this confederacy; and millions are pocketed every year, by dealers in this horrid traffic. In

[12]Thomas Hart Benton (1782–1858), United
States Senator from Missouri, 1821–1851.

several states, this trade is a chief source of wealth. It is called (in contradistinction to the foreign slave-trade) *"the internal slave-trade."* It is, probably,
called so, too, in order to divert from it the horror with which the foreign
slave-trade is contemplated. That trade has long since been denounced by
this government, as piracy. It has been denounced with burning words, from
the high places of the nation, as an execrable traffic. To arrest it, to put an
end to it, this nation keeps a squadron, at immense cost, on the coast of
Africa. Everywhere, in this country, it is safe to speak of this foreign slave-
trade, as a most inhuman traffic, opposed alike to the laws of God and of
man. The duty to extirpate and destroy it, is admitted even by our DOCTORS
OF DIVINITY. In order to put an end to it, some of these last have consented
that their colored brethren (nominally free) should leave this country, and
establish themselves on the western coast of Africa! It is, however, a notable
fact that, while so much execration is poured out by Americans upon those
engaged in the foreign slave-trade, the men engaged in the slave-trade
between the states pass without condemnation, and their business is
deemed honorable.

Behold the practical operation of this internal slave-trade, the American
slave-trade, sustained by American politics and American religion. Here you
will see men and women reared like swine for the market. You know what is
a swine-drover? I will show you a man-drover. They inhabit all our Southern
States. They perambulate the country, and crowd the highways of the
nation, with droves of human stock. You will see one of these human flesh-
jobbers, armed with pistol, whip and bowie-knife, driving a company of a
hundred men, women, and children, from the Potomac to the slave market
at New Orleans. These wretched people are to be sold singly, or in lots, to
suit purchasers. They are food for the cotton-field, and the deadly sugar-
mill. Mark the sad procession, as it moves wearily along, and the inhuman
wretch who drives them. Hear his savage yells and his blood-chilling oaths,
as he hurries on his affrighted captives! There, see the old man, with locks
thinned and gray. Cast one glance, if you please, upon that young mother,
whose shoulders are bare to the scorching sun, her briny tears falling on the
brow of the babe in her arms. See, too, that girl of thirteen, weeping, *yes!*
weeping, as she thinks of the mother from whom she has been torn! The
drove moves tardily. Heat and sorrow have nearly consumed their strength;
suddenly you hear a quick snap, like the discharge of a rifle; the fetters
clank, and the chain rattles simultaneously; your ears are saluted with a
scream, that seems to have torn its way to the centre of your soul! The crack
you heard, was the sound of the slave-whip; the scream you heard, was from
the woman you saw with the babe. Her speed had faltered under the weight
of her child and her chains! that gash on her shoulder tells her to move on.
Follow this drove to New Orleans. Attend the auction; see men examined
like horses; see the forms of women rudely and brutally exposed to the
shocking gaze of American slave-buyers. See this drove sold and separated
forever; and never forget the deep, sad sobs that arose from that scattered
multitude. Tell me citizens, WHERE, under the sun, you can witness a

spectacle more fiendish and shocking. Yet this is but a glance at the American slave-trade, as it exists, at this moment, in the ruling part of the United States.

I was born amid such sights and scenes. To me the American slave-trade is a terrible reality. When a child, my soul was often pierced with a sense of its horrors. I lived on Philpot Street, Fell's Point, Baltimore, and have watched from the wharves, the slave ships in the Basin, anchored from the shore, with their cargoes of human flesh, waiting for favorable winds to waft them down the Chesapeake. There was, at that time, a grand slave mart kept at the head of Pratt Street, by Austin Woldfolk.[13] His agents were sent into every town and county in Maryland, announcing their arrival, through the papers, and on flaming "*hand-bills*," headed CASH FOR NEGROES. These men were generally well dressed men, and very captivating in their manners. Ever ready to drink, to treat, and to gamble. The fate of many a slave has depended upon the turn of a single card; and many a child has been snatched from the arms of its mother by bargains arranged in a state of brutal drunkenness.

The flesh-mongers gather up their victims by dozens, and drive them, chained, to the general depot at Baltimore. When a sufficient number have been collected here, a ship is chartered, for the purpose of conveying the forlorn crew to Mobile, or to New Orleans. From the slave prison to the ship, they are usually driven in the darkness of night; for since the anti-slavery agitation, a certain caution is observed.

In the deep still darkness of midnight, I have been often aroused by the dead heavy footsteps, and the piteous cries of the chained gangs that passed our door. The anguish of my boyish heart was intense; and I was often consoled, when speaking to my mistress in the morning, to hear her say that the custom was very wicked; that she hated to hear the rattle of the chains, and the heart-rending cries. I was glad to find one who sympathised with me in my horror.

Fellow-citizens, this murderous traffic is, to-day, in active operation in this boasted republic. In the solitude of my spirit, I see clouds of dust raised on the highways of the South; I see the bleeding footsteps; I hear the doleful wail of fettered humanity, on the way to the slave-markets, where the victims are to be sold like *horses*, *sheep*, and *swine*, knocked off to the highest bidder. There I see the tenderest ties ruthlessly broken, to gratify the lust, caprice and rapacity of the buyers and sellers of men. My soul sickens at the sight.

> "*Is this the land your Fathers loved,*
> *The freedom which they toiled to win?*
> *Is this the earth whereon they moved?*
> *Are these the graves they slumber in?*"[14]

---

[13]Actually Austin Woolfolk, a well-known slave trader in Baltimore, to whom Douglass refers in his 1845 *Narrative*.

[14]Douglass changes slightly the first four lines of John Greenleaf Whittier's "Stanzas for the Times."

But a still more inhuman, disgraceful, and scandalous state of things remains to be presented.

By an act of the American Congress, not yet two years old, slavery has been nationalized in its most horrible and revolting form. By that act, Mason & Dixon's line has been obliterated; New York has become as Virginia; and the power to hold, hunt, and sell men, women, and children as slaves remains no longer a mere state institution, but is now an institution of the whole United States. The power is co-extensive with the star-spangled banner and American Christianity. Where these go, may also go the merciless slave-hunter. Where these are, man is not sacred. He is a bird for the sportsman's gun. By that most foul and fiendish of all human decrees, the liberty and person of every man are put in peril. Your broad republican domain is hunting ground for *men. Not* for thieves and robbers, enemies of society, merely, but for men guilty of no crime. Your lawmakers have commanded all good citizens to engage in this hellish sport. Your President, your Secretary of State, your *lords, nobles,* and ecclesiastics, enforce, as a duty you owe to your free and glorious country, and to your God, that you do this accursed thing. Not fewer than forty Americans have, within the past two years, been hunted down and, without a moment's warning, hurried away in chains, and consigned to slavery and excruciating torture. Some of these have had wives and children, dependent on them for bread; but of this, no account was made. The right of the hunter to his prey stands superior to the right of marriage, and to *all* rights in this republic, the rights of God included! For black men there are neither law, justice, humanity, nor religion. The Fugitive Slave *Law* makes MERCY TO THEM, A CRIME; and bribes the judge who tries them. An American JUDGE GETS TEN DOLLARS FOR EVERY VICTIM HE CONSIGNS to slavery, and five, when he fails to do so. The oath of any two villains is sufficient, under this hell-black enactment, to send the most pious and exemplary black man into the remorseless jaws of slavery! His own testimony is nothing. He can bring no witnesses for himself. The minister of American justice is bound by the law to hear but *one* side; and *that* side, is the side of the oppressor. Let this damning fact be perpetually told. Let it be thundered around the world, that, in tyrant-killing, king-hating, people-loving, democratic, Christian America, the seats of justice are filled with judges, who hold their offices under an open and palpable *bribe,* and are bound, in deciding in the case of a man's liberty, *to hear only his accusers!*[15]

In glaring violation of justice, in shameless disregard of the forms of administering law, in cunning arrangement to entrap the defenceless, and in diabolical intent, this Fugitive Slave Law stands alone in the annals of tyrannical legislation. I doubt if there be another nation on the globe, having the brass and the baseness to put such a law on the statute-book. If any man in this assembly thinks differently from me in this matter, and feels

---

[15]The Fugitive Slave Act of 1850 did, in fact, provide that the testimony of the alleged fugitive would not "be admitted in evidence"; nor could the person call witnesses.

able to disprove my statements, I will gladly confront him at any suitable time and place he may select....

The Constitution

But it is answered in reply to all this, that precisely what I have now denounced is, in fact, guaranteed and sanctioned by the Constitution of the United States; that the right to hold and to hunt slaves is a part of that Constitution framed by the illustrious Fathers of this Republic.

Then, I dare to affirm, notwithstanding all I have said before, your fathers stooped, basely stooped

"To palter with us in a double sense:
And keep the word of promise to the ear,
But break it to the heart."[16]

And instead of being the honest men I have before declared them to be, they were the veriest imposters that ever practised on mankind. *This* is the inevitable conclusion, and from it there is no escape. But I differ from those who charge this baseness on the framers of the Constitution of the United States. *It is a slander upon their memory*, at least, so I believe. There is not time now to argue the constitutional question at length; nor have I the ability to discuss it as it ought to be discussed. The subject has been handled with masterly power by Lysander Spooner, Esq., by William Goodell, by Samuel E. Sewall, Esq., and last, though not least, by Gerritt Smith, Esq.[17] These gentlemen have, as I think, fully and clearly vindicated the Constitution from any design to support slavery for an hour.

Fellow-citizens! there is no matter in respect to which, the people of the North have allowed themselves to be so ruinously imposed upon, as that of the pro-slavery character of the Constitution. In *that* instrument I hold there is neither warrant, license, nor sanction of the hateful thing; but, interpreted as it *ought* to be interpreted, the Constitution is a GLORIOUS LIBERTY DOCUMENT. Read its preamble, consider its purposes. Is slavery among them? Is it at the gateway? or is it in the temple? It is neither. While I do not intend to argue this question on the present occasion, let me ask, if it be not somewhat singular that, if the Constitution were intended to be, by its framers and adopters, a slave-holding instrument, why neither *slavery*, *slaveholding*, nor *slave* can anywhere be found in it. What would be thought of an instrument, drawn up, *legally* drawn up, for the purpose of entitling the city of Rochester to a track of land, in which no mention of land was made? Now, there are certain rules of interpretation, for the proper understanding of all legal instruments. These rules are well established. They are plain, common-sense rules, such as you and I, and all of us, can understand

---

[16]*Macbeth* V, viii, 20–22.
[17]Lysander Spooner had published *The Unconstitutionality of Slavery* in 1845; William Goodell, *Views of American Constitutional Law, Its Bearing Upon American Slavery* (1844); Samuel E. Sewell, *Remarks on Slavery in the United States* (1827), was also active as an antislavery lawyer and politician in Massachusetts; Gerrit Smith wrote frequently on the subject.

and apply, without having passed years in the study of law. I scout the idea that the question of the constitutionality or unconstitutionality of slavery is not a question for the people. I hold that every American citizen has a right to form an opinion of the constitution, and to propagate that opinion, and to use all honorable means to make his opinion the prevailing one. Without this right, the liberty of an American citizen would be as insecure as that of a Frenchman. Ex-Vice-President Dallas[18] tells us that the constitution is an object to which no American mind can be too attentive, and no American heart too devoted. He further says, the constitution, in its words, is plain and intelligible, and is meant for the home-bred, unsophisticated under-standings of our fellow-citizens. Senator Berrien[19] tells us that the Constitu-tion is the fundamental law, that which controls all others. The charter of our liberties, which every citizen has a personal interest in understanding thoroughly. The testimony of Senator Breese, Lewis Cass,[20] and many others that might be named, who are everywhere esteemed as sound law-yers, so regard the constitution. I take it, therefore, that it is not presump-tion in a private citizen to form an opinion of that instrument.

Now, take the constitution according to its plain reading, and I defy the presentation of a single pro-slavery clause in it. On the other hand it will be found to contain principles and purposes, entirely hostile to the existence of slavery.

I have detained my audience entirely too long already. At some future period I will gladly avail myself of an opportunity to give this subject a full and fair discussion.

Allow me to say, in conclusion, notwithstanding the dark picture I have this day presented of the state of the nation, I do not despair of this coun-try. There are forces in operation, which must inevitably work the downfall of slavery. *"The arm of the Lord is not shortened,"*[21] and the doom of slavery is certain. I, therefore, leave off where I began, with *hope*. While drawing encouragement from the Declaration of Independence, the great principles it contains, and the genius of American Institutions, my spirit is also cheered by the obvious tendencies of the age. Nations do not now stand in the same relation to each other that they did ages ago. No nation can now shut itself up from the surrounding world, and trot round in the same old path of its fathers without interference. The time *was* when such could be done. Long established customs of hurtful character could formerly fence themselves in, and do their evil work with social impunity. Knowledge was then confined and enjoyed by the privileged few, and the multitude walked

---

[18]George Mifflin Dallas (1792–1864) had served as vice president (1845–1849) and was, at the time of this speech, an active candidate for the Democratic nomination for president and committed to enforce-ment of the Fugitive Slave Law.

[19]Georgia Senator John MacPherson Berrien (1781–1856), known as a constitutional law-yer and compromiser on the slavery issue.

[20]Sidney Breese and Lewis Cass were United States senators from Illinois and Michigan, respectively.

[21]Paraphrased from Isaiah 59:1.

on in mental darkness. But a change has now come over the affairs of mankind. Walled cities and empires have become unfashionable. The arm of commerce has borne away the gates of the strong city. Intelligence is penetrating the darkest corners of the globe. It makes its pathway over and under the sea, as well as on the earth. Wind, steam, and lightning are its chartered agents. Oceans no longer divide, but link nations together. From Boston to London is now a holiday excursion. Space is comparatively annihilated. Thoughts expressed on one side of the Atlantic are distinctly heard on the other.

The far off and almost fabulous Pacific rolls in grandeur at our feet. The Celestial Empire, the mystery of ages, is being solved. The fiat of the Almighty, "*Let there be Light,*" has not yet spent its force. No abuse, no outrage whether in taste, sport or avarice, can now hide itself from the all-pervading light. The iron shoe, and crippled foot of China must be seen, in contrast with nature. *Africa must rise and put on her yet unwoven garment.* "*Ethiopia shall stretch out her hand unto God.*"[22] In the fervent aspirations of William Lloyd Garrison, I say, and let every heart join in saying it:

> *God speed the year of jubilee*
> *The wide world o'er!*
> *When from their galling chains set free,*
> *Th' oppress'd shall vilely bend the knee,*
> *And wear the yoke of tyranny*
> *Like brutes no more.*
> *That year will come, and freedom's reign,*
> *To man his plundered rights again*
> *Restore.*
>
> *God speed the day when human blood*
> *Shall cease to flow!*
> *In every clime be understood,*
> *The claims of human brotherhood,*
> *And each return for evil, good,*
> *Not blow for blow;*
> *That day will come all feuds to end,*
> *And change into a faithful friend*
> *Each foe.*
>
> *God speed the hour, the glorious hour,*
> *When none on earth*
> *Shall exercise a lordly power,*
> *Nor in a tyrant's presence cower;*
> *But all to manhood's stature tower,*
> *By equal birth!*

[22]See Psalm 68:31: "Princes shall come out of Egypt; Ethiopia shall soon stretch out her hands unto God."

THAT HOUR WILL COME, to each, to all,
And from his prison-house, the thrall
    Go forth.

Until that year, day, hour, arrive,
With head, and heart, and hand I'll strive,
To break the rod, and rend the gyve,
The spoiler of his prey deprive—
    So witness Heaven!
And never from my chosen post,
Whate'er the peril or the cost,
    Be driven.[23]

1852

The Heroic Slave

PART I

Oh! child of grief, why weepest thou?
Why droops thy sad and mournful brow?
Why is thy look so like despair?
What deep, sad sorrow lingers there?

The State of Virginia is famous in American annals for the multitudinous array of her statesmen and heroes. She has been dignified by some the mother of statesmen. History has not been sparing in recording their names, or in blazoning their deeds. Her high position in this respect, has given her an enviable distinction among her sister States. With Virginia for his birth-place, even a man of ordinary parts, on account of the general partiality for her sons, easily rises to eminent stations. Men, not great enough to attract special attention in their native States, have, like a certain distinguished citizen in the State of New York, sighed and repined that they were not born in Virginia. Yet not all the great ones of the Old Dominion have, by the fact of their birth-place, escaped undeserved obscurity. By some strange neglect, *one* of the truest, manliest, and bravest of her children,— one who, in after years, will, I think, command the pen of genius to set his merits forth, holds now no higher place in the records of that grand old Commonwealth than is held by a horse or an ox. Let those account for it who can, but there stands the fact, that a man who loved liberty as well as did Patrick Henry,—who deserved it as much as Thomas Jefferson,—and who fought for it with a valor as high, an arm as strong, and against odds as great, as he who led all the armies of the American colonies through the

[23]William Lloyd Garrison, "The Triumph of Freedom."

great war for freedom and independence, lives now only in the chattel records of his native State.

Glimpses of this great character are all that can now be presented. He is brought to view only by a few transient incidents, and these afford but partial satisfaction. Like a guiding star on a stormy night, he is seen through the parted clouds and the howling tempests; or, like the gray peak of a menacing rock on a perilous coast, he is seen by the quivering flash of angry lightning, and he again disappears covered with mystery.

Curiously, earnestly, anxiously we peer into the dark, and wish even for the blinding flash, or the light of northern skies to reveal him. But alas! he is still enveloped in darkness, and we return from the pursuit like a wearied and disheartened mother, (after a tedious and unsuccessful search for a lost child,) who returns weighed down with disappointment and sorrow. Speaking of marks, traces, possibles, and probabilities, we come before our readers.

In the spring of 1835, on a Sabbath morning, within hearing of the solemn peals of the church bells at a distant village, a Northern traveller through the State of Virginia drew up his horse to drink at a sparkling brook, near the edge of a dark pine forest. While his weary and thirsty steed drew in the grateful water, the rider caught the sound of a human voice, apparently engaged in earnest conversation.

Following the direction of the sound, he descried, among the tall pines, the man whose voice had arrested his attention. "To whom can he be speaking?" thought the traveller. "He seems to be alone." The circumstance interested him much, and he became intensely curious to know what thoughts and feelings, or, it might be, high aspirations, guided those rich and mellow accents. Tieing his horse at a short distance from the brook, he stealthily drew near the solitary speaker; and, concealing himself by the side of a huge fallen tree, he distinctly heard the following soliloquy:—

"What, then, is life to me? it is aimless and worthless, and worse than worthless. Those birds, perched on yon swinging boughs, in friendly conclave, sounding forth their merry notes in seeming worship of the rising sun, though liable to the sportsman's fowling-piece, are still my superiors. They *live free*, though they may die slaves. They fly where they list by day, and retire in freedom at night. But what is freedom to me, or I to it? I am a *slave*,—born a slave, an abject slave,—even before I made part of this breathing world, the scourge was platted for my back; the fetters were forged for my limbs. How mean a thing am I. That accursed and crawling snake, that miserable reptile, that has just glided into its slimy home, is freer and better off than I. He escaped my blow, and is safe. But here am I, a man,—yes, a man!—with thoughts and wishes, with powers and faculties as far as angel's flight above that hated reptile,—yet he is my superior, and scorns to own me as his master, or to stop to take my blows. When he saw my uplifted arm, he darted beyond my reach, and turned to give me battle. I dare not do as much as that. I neither run nor fight, but do meanly stand, answering each heavy blow of a cruel master with doleful wails and piteous cries. I am galled with irons; but even these are more tolerable than the consciousness, the *galling* consciousness of cowardice and indecision. Can it be that I *dare* not run away? *Perish the thought, I dare* do any thing which may be done by another. When that young man struggled with the waves for life, and others stood back appalled in helpless horror, did I not plunge in, forgetful of life, to save his? The raging bull from whom all others fled, pale with fright, did I not keep at bay with a single pitchfork? Could a coward do that? *NO,—no,—*I wrong myself,—I am no coward. Liberty I will have, or die in the attempt to gain it. This working that others may live in idleness! This cringing submission to insolence and curses! This living under the constant dread and apprehension of being sold and transferred, like a mere brute, is *too* much for me. I will stand it no longer. What others have done, I will do. These trusty legs, or these sinewy arms shall place me among the free. Tom escaped; so can I. The North Star will not be less kind to me than to him. I will follow it. I will at least make the trial. I have nothing to lose. If I am caught, I shall only be a slave. If I am shot, I shall only lose a life which is a burden and a curse. If I get clear, (as something tells me I shall,) liberty, the inalienable birth-right of every man, precious and priceless, will be mine. My resolution is fixed. *I shall be free.*"

At these words the traveller raised his head cautiously and noiselessly, and caught, from his hiding-place, a full view of the unsuspecting speaker. Madison (for that was the name of our hero) was standing erect, a smile of satisfaction rippled upon his expressive countenance, like that which plays upon the face of one who has but just solved a difficult problem, or vanquished a malignant foe; for at that moment he was free, at least in spirit. The future gleamed brightly before him, and his fetters lay broken at his feet. His air was triumphant.

Madison was of manly form. Tall, symmetrical, round, and strong. In his movements he seemed to combine, with the strength of the lion, a lion's elasticity. His torn sleeves disclosed arms like polished iron. His face was "black, but comely." His eye, lit with emotion, kept guard under a brow as dark and as glossy as the raven's wing. His whole appearance betokened Herculean strength: yet there was nothing savage or forbidding in his aspect. A child might play in his arms, or dance on his shoulders. A giant's strength, but not a giant's heart was in him. His broad mouth and nose spoke only of good nature and kindness. But his voice, that unfailing index of the soul, though full and melodious, had that in it which could terrify as well as charm. He was just the man you would choose when hardships were to be endured, or danger to be encountered,—intelligent and brave. He had the head to conceive, and the hand to execute. In a word, he was one to be sought as a friend, but to be dreaded as an enemy.

As our traveller gazed upon him, he almost trembled at the thought of his dangerous intrusion. Still he could not quit the place. He had long desired to sound the mysterious depths of the thoughts and feelings of a slave. He was not, therefore, disposed to allow so providential an opportunity to pass unimproved. He resolved to hear more; so he listened again for those mellow and mournful accents which, he says made such an impression upon him as can never be erased. He did not have to wait long. There came another gush from the same full fountain; now bitter, and now sweet. Scathing denunciations of the cruelty and injustice of slavery; heart-touching narrations of his own personal suffering, intermingled with prayers to the God of the oppressed for help and deliverance, were followed by presentations of the dangers and difficulties of escape, and formed the burden of his eloquent utterances; but his high resolution clung to him,—for he ended each speech by an emphatic declaration of his purpose to be free. It seemed that the very repetition of this, imparted a glow to his countenance. The hope of freedom seemed to sweeten, for a season, the bitter cup of slavery, and to make it, for a time, tolerable; for when in the very whirlwind of anguish,— when his heart's cord seemed screwed up to snapping tension, hope sprung up and soothed his troubled spirit. Fitfully he would exclaim, "How can I leave her? Poor thing! what can she do when I am gone? Oh! oh! 'tis impossible that I can leave poor Susan!"

A brief pause intervened. Our traveller raised his head, and saw again the sorrow-smitten slave. His eye was fixed upon the ground. The strong man staggered under a heavy load. Recovering himself, he argued thus aloud: "All is uncertain here. To-morrow's sun may not rise before I am sold, and separated from her I love. What, then, could I do for her? I should be in more hopeless slavery, and she no nearer to liberty,—whereas if I were free,—my arms my own,—I might devise the means to rescue her."

This said, Madison cast around a searching glance, as if the thought of being overheard had flashed across his mind. He said no more, but, with measured steps, walked away, and was lost to the eye of our traveller amidst the wildering woods.

Long after Madison had left the ground, Mr. Listwell (our traveller) remained in motionless silence, meditating on the extraordinary revelations to which he had listened. He seemed fastened to the spot, and stood half hoping, half fearing the return of the sable preacher to his solitary temple. The speech of Madison rung through the chambers of his soul, and vibrated through his entire frame. "Here is indeed a man," thought he, "of rare endowments,—a child of God,—guilty of no crime but the color of his skin, hiding away from the face of humanity, and pouring out his thoughts and feelings, his hopes and resolutions to the lonely woods; to him those distant church bells have no grateful music. He shuns the church, the altar, and the great congregation of christian worshippers, and wanders away to the gloomy forest, to utter in the vacant air complaints and griefs, which the religion of his times and his country can neither console nor relieve. Goaded almost to madness by the sense of the injustice done him, he resorts, hither to give vent to his pent up feelings, and to debate with himself the feasibility of plans, plans of his own invention, for his own deliverance. From this hour I am an abolitionist. I have seen enough and heard enough, and I shall go to my home in Ohio resolved to atone for my past indifference to this ill-starred race, by making such exertions as I shall be able to do, for the speedy emancipation of every slave in the land."

PART II

"The gaudy, blabbling and remorseful day
 Is crept into the bosom of the sea;
And now loud-howling wolves arouse the jades
 That drag the tragic melancholy night;
Who with their drowsy, slow, and flagging wings
 Clip dead men's graves, and from their misty jaws
 Breathe foul contagions, darkness in the air."

—Shakespeare

Five years after the foregoing singular occurrence, in the winter of 1840, Mr. and Mrs. Listwell sat together by the fireside of their own happy home in the State of Ohio. The children were all gone to bed. A single lamp burnt brightly on the centre-table. All was still and comfortable within; but the night was cold and dark; a heavy wind sighed and moaned sorrowfully around the house and barn, occasionally bringing against the clattering windows a stray leaf from the large oak trees that embowered their dwelling. It was a night for strange noises and for strange fancies. A whole wilderness of thought might pass through one's mind during such an evening. The smouldering embers, partaking of the spirit of the restless night, became fruitful of varied and fantastic pictures, and revived many bygone scenes and old impressions. The happy pair seemed to sit in silent fascination, gazing on the fire. Suddenly this *reverie* was interrupted by a heavy growl. Ordinarily such an occurrence would have scarcely provoked a single word, or excited the least apprehension. But there are certain seasons when the slightest sound sends a jar through all the subtle chambers of the mind; and such a season was this. The happy pair started up, as if some sudden danger had come upon them. The growl was from their trusty watchdog.

"What can it mean? certainly no one can be out on such a night as this," said Mrs. Listwell.

"The wind has deceived the dog, my dear; he has mistaken the noise of falling branches, brought down by the wind, for that of the footsteps of persons coming to the house. I have several times to-night thought that I heard the sound of footsteps. I am sure, however, that it was but the wind. Friends would not be likely to come out at such an hour, or such a night; and thieves are too lazy and self-indulgent to expose themselves to this biting frost; but should there be anyone about, our brave old Monte, who is on the lookout, will not be slow in sounding the alarm."

Saying this they quietly left the window, whither they had gone to learn the cause of the menacing growl, and re-seated themselves by the fire, as if reluctant to leave the slowly expiring embers, although the hour was late. A few minutes only intervened after resuming their seats, when again their sober meditations were disturbed. Their faithful dog now growled and barked furiously, as if assailed by an advancing foe. Simultaneously the good couple arose, and stood in mute expectation. The contest without seemed fierce and violent. It was, however, soon over,—the barking ceased, for, with true canine instinct, Monte quickly discovered that a friend, not an enemy of the family, was coming to the house, and instead of rushing to repel the supposed intruder, he was now at the door, whimpering and dancing for the admission of himself and his newly made friend.

Mr. Listwell knew by this movement that all was well; he advanced and opened the door, and saw by the light that streamed out into the darkness, a tall man advancing slowly towards the house, with a stick in one hand, and a small bundle in the other. "It is a traveller," thought he, "who has missed his way, and is coming to inquire the road. I am glad we did not go to bed earlier,—I have felt all the evening as if somebody would be here tonight."

The man had now halted a short distance from the door, and looked prepared alike for flight or battle. "Come in, sir, don't be alarmed, you have probably lost your way."

Slightly hesitating, the traveller walked in; not, however, without regarding his host with a scrutinizing glance. "No, sir," said he "I have come to ask you a greater favor."

Instantly Mr. Listwell exclaimed, (as the recollection of the Virginia forest scene flashed upon him,) "Oh, sir, I know not your name, but I have seen your face, and heard your voice before. I am glad to see you. *I know all*. You are flying for your liberty,—be seated,—be seated,—banish all fear. You are safe under my roof."

This recognition, so unexpected, rather disconcerted and disquieted the noble fugitive. The timidity and suspicion of persons escaping from slavery are easily awakened, and often what is intended to dispel the one, and to allay the other, has precisely the opposite effect. It was so in this case. Quickly observing the unhappy impression made by his words and action, Mr. Listwell assumed a more quiet and inquiring aspect, and finally succeeded in removing the apprehensions which his very natural and generous salutation had aroused.

Thus assured, the stranger said, "Sir, you have rightly guessed, I am, indeed, a fugitive from slavery. My name is Madison,—Madison Washington my mother used to call me. I am on my way to Canada, where I learn that persons of my color are protected in all the rights of men; and my object in calling upon you was, to beg the privilege of resting my weary limbs for the night in your barn. It was my purpose to have continued my journey till morning; but the piercing cold, and the frowning darkness compelled me to seek shelter; and, seeing a light through the lattice of your window, I was encouraged to come here to beg the privilege named. You will do me a great favor by affording me shelter for the night."

"A resting-place, indeed, sir, you shall have; not, however, in my barn, but in the best room of my house. Consider yourself, if you please, under the roof of a friend; for such I am to you, and to all your deeply injured race." While this introductory conversation was going on, the kind lady had revived the fire, and was diligently preparing supper; for she, not less than her husband, felt for the sorrows of the oppressed and hunted ones of earth, and was always glad of an opportunity to do them a service. A bountiful repast was quickly prepared, and the hungry and toil-worn bondman was cordially invited to partake thereof. Gratefully he acknowledged the favor of his benevolent benefactress; but appeared scarcely to understand what such hospitality could mean. It was the first time in his life that he had met so humane and friendly a greeting at the hands of persons whose color was unlike his own; yet it was impossible for him to doubt the charitableness of his new friends, or the genuineness of the welcome so freely given; and he therefore, with many thanks, took his seat at the table with Mr. and Mrs. Listwell, who, desirous to make him feel at home, took a cup of tea themselves, while urging upon Madison the best that the house could afford.

Supper over, all doubts and apprehensions banished, the three drew around the blazing fire, and a conversation commenced which lasted till long after midnight.

"Now," said Madison to Mr. Listwell, "I was a little surprised and alarmed when I came in, by what you said; do tell me, sir, *why* you thought you had seen my face before, and by what you knew me to be a fugitive from slavery; for I am sure that I never was before in this neighborhood, and I certainly sought to conceal what I supposed to be the manner of a fugitive slave."

Mr. Listwell at once frankly disclosed the secret; describing the place where he first saw him; rehearsing the language which he (Madison) had used; referring to the effect which his manner and speech had made upon him; declaring the resolution he there formed to be an abolitionist; telling how often he had spoken of the circumstance, and the deep concern he had ever since felt to know what had become of him; and whether he had carried out the purpose to make his escape, as in the woods he declared he would do.

"Ever since that morning," said Mr. Listwell, "you have seldom been absent from my mind, and though now I did not dare to hope that I should ever see you again, I have often wished that such might be my fortune; for, from that hour, your face seemed to be daguerreotyped on my memory."

Madison looked quite astonished, and felt amazed at the narration to which he had listened. After recovering himself he said, "I well remember that morning, and the bitter anguish that wrung my heart; I will state the occasion of it. I had, on the previous Saturday, suffered a cruel lashing; had been tied tip to the limb of a tree, with my feet chained together, and a heavy iron bar placed between my ankles. Thus suspended, I received on my naked back forty stripes, and was kept in this distressing position three or four hours, and was then let down, only to have my torture increased; for my bleeding back, gashed by the cow-skin, was washed by the overseer with old brine, partly to augment my suffering, and partly, as he said, to prevent inflammation. My crime was that I had stayed longer at the mill, the day previous, than it was thought I ought to have done, which, I assured my master and the overseer, was no fault of mine; but no excuses were allowed. 'Hold your tongue, you impudent rascal,' met my every explanation.

Slave-holders are so imperious when their passions are excited, as to construe every word of the slave into insolence. I could do nothing but submit to the agonizing infliction. Smarting still from the wounds, as well as from the consciousness of being whipt for no cause, I took advantage of the absence of my master, who had gone to church, to spend the time in the woods, and brood over my wretched lot. Oh, sir, I remember it well, and can never forget it."

"But this was five years ago; where have you been since?"

"I will try to tell you," said Madison. "Just four weeks after that Sabbath morning, I gathered up the few rags of clothing I had, and started, as I supposed, for the North and for freedom. I must not stop to describe my feelings on taking this step. It seemed like taking a leap into the dark. The thought of leaving my poor wife and two little children caused me indescribable anguish; but consoling myself with the reflection that once free, I could, possibly, devise ways and means to gain their freedom also, I nerved myself up to make the attempt. I started, but ill-luck attended me; for after being out a whole week, strange to say, I still found myself on my master's grounds; the third night after being out, a season of clouds and rain set in, wholly preventing me from seeing the North Star, which I had trusted as my guide, not dreaming that clouds might intervene between us.

"This circumstance was fatal to my project, for in losing my star, I lost my way; so when I supposed I was far towards the North, and had almost gained my freedom, I discovered myself at the very point from which I had started. It was a severe trial, for I arrived at home in great destitution; my feet were sore, and in travelling in the dark, I had dashed my foot against a stump, and started a nail, and lamed myself. I was wet and cold; one week had exhausted all my stores; and when I landed on my master's plantation, with all my work to do over again,—hungry, tired, lame, and bewildered,—I almost cursed the day that I was born. In this extremity I approached the quarters. I did so stealthily, although in my desperation I hardly cared whether I was discovered or not. Peeping through the rents of the quarters, I saw my fellow-slaves seated by a warm fire, merrily passing away the time, as though their hearts knew no sorrow. Although I envied their seeming contentment, all wretched as I was, I despised the cowardly acquiescence in their own degradation which it implied, and felt a kind of pride and glory in my own desperate lot. I dared not enter the quarters,—for where there is seeming contentment with slavery, there is certain treachery to freedom. I proceeded towards the great house, in the hope of catching a glimpse of my poor wife, whom I knew might be trusted with my secrets even on the scaffold. Just as I reached the fence which divided the field from the garden, I saw a woman in the yard, who in the darkness I took to be my wife; but a nearer approach told me it was not she. I was about to speak; had I done so, I would not have been here this night; for an alarm would have been sounded, and the hunters been put on my track. Here were hunger, cold, thirst, disappointment, and chagrin, confronted only by the dim hope of liberty. I tremble to think of that dreadful hour. To face the deadly cannon's mouth in warm blood unterrified, is, I think, a small achievement, compared with a conflict like this with gaunt starvation. The gnawings of hunger conquers by degrees, till all that a man has he would give in exchange for a single crust of bread. Thank God, I was not quite reduced to this extremity.

"Happily for me, before the fatal moment of utter despair, my good wife made her appearance in the yard. It was she; I knew her step. All was well now. I was, however, afraid to speak lest I should frighten her. Yet speak I did; and, to my great joy, my voice was known. Our meeting can be more easily imagined than described. For a time hunger, thirst, weariness, and lameness were forgotten. But it was soon necessary for her to return to the house. She being a house-servant, her absence from the kitchen, if discovered, might have excited suspicion. Our parting was like tearing the flesh from my bones; yet it was the part of wisdom for her to go. She left me with the purpose of meeting me at midnight in the very forest where you last saw me. She knew the place well, as one of my melancholy resorts, and could easily find it, though the night was dark.

"I hastened away, therefore, and concealed myself, to await the arrival of my good angel. As I lay there among the leaves, I was strongly tempted to return again to the house of my master and give myself up; but remembering my solemn pledge on that memorable Sunday morning, I was able to linger out the two long hours between ten and midnight. I may well call them long hours. I have endured much hardship; I have encountered many perils; but the anxiety of those two hours, was the bitterest I ever experienced. True to her word, my wife came laden with provisions, and we sat down on the side of a log, at that dark and lonesome hour of the night. I cannot say we talked; our feelings were too great for that; yet we came to an understanding that I should make the woods my home, for if I gave myself up, I should be whipped and sold away; and if I started for the North, I should leave a wife doubly dear to me. We mutually determined, therefore, that I should remain in the vicinity. In the dismal swamps I lived, sir, five long years,—a cave for my home during the day. I wandered about at night with the wolf and the bear,— sustained by the promise that my good Susan would meet me in the pine woods at least once a week. This promise was redeemed, I assure you, to the letter, greatly to my relief. I had partly become contented with my mode of life, and had made up my mind to spend my days there; but the wilderness that sheltered me thus long took fire, and refused longer to be my hiding-place.

"I will not harrow up your feelings by portraying the terrific scene of this awful conflagration. There is nothing to which I can liken it. It was horribly and indescribably grand. The whole world seemed on fire, and it appeared to me that the day of judgment had come; that the burning bowels of the earth had burst forth, and that the end of all things was at hand. Bears and wolves, scorched from their mysterious hiding-places in the earth, and all the wild inhabitants of the untrodden forest, filled with a common dismay, ran forth, yelling, howling, bewildered amidst the smoke and flame. The very heavens seemed to rain down fire through the towering trees; it was by the merest chance that I escaped the devouring element.

Running before it, and stopping occasionally to take breath, I looked back to behold its frightful ravages, and to drink in its savage magnificence. It was awful, thrilling, solemn, beyond compare. When aided by the fitful wind, the merciless tempest of fire swept on, sparkling, creaking, cracking, curling, roaring, out-doing in its dreadful splendor a thousand thunder-storms at once. From tree to tree it leaped, swallowing them up in its lurid, baleful glare; and leaving them leafless, limbless, charred, and lifeless behind. The scene was overwhelming, stunning,—nothing was spared,— cattle, tame and wild, herds of swine and of deer, wild beasts of every name and kind,—huge night-birds, bats, and owls, that had retired to their homes in lofty tree-tops to rest, perished in that fiery storm. The long-winged buz-zard, and croaking raven mingled their dismal cries with those of the count-less myriads of small birds that rose up to the skies, and were lost to the sight in clouds of smoke and flame. Oh, I shudder when I think of it! Many a poor wandering fugitive, who, like myself, had sought among wild beasts the mercy denied by our fellow men, saw, in helpless consternation, his dwelling-place and city of refuge reduced to ashes forever. It was this grand conflagration that drove me hither; I ran alike from fire and from slavery."

After a slight pause, (for both speaker and hearers were deeply moved by the above recital,) Mr. Listwell, addressing Madison, said, "If it does not weary you too much, do tell us something of your journeyings since this dis-astrous burning,—we are deeply interested in everything which can throw light on the hardships of persons escaping from slavery; we could hear you talk all night; are there no incidents that you could relate of your travels hither? or are they such that you do not like to mention them."

"For the most part, sir, my course has been uninterrupted; and, consid-ering the circumstances, at times even pleasant. I have suffered little for want of food; but I need not tell you how I got it. Your moral code may dif-fer from mine, as your customs and usages are different. The fact is, sir, during my flight, I felt myself robbed by society of all my just rights; that I was in an enemy's land, who sought both my life and my liberty. They had transformed me into a brute; made merchandise of my body, and, for all the purposes of my flight, turned day into night,—and guided by my own neces-sities, and in contempt of their conventionalities, I did not scruple to take bread where I could get it."

"And just there you were right," said Mr. Listwell; "I once had doubts on this point myself, but a conversation with Gerrit Smith, (a man, by the way, that I wish you could see, for he is a devoted friend of your race, and I know he would receive you gladly,) put an end to all my doubts on this point. But do not let me interrupt you."

"I had but one narrow escape during my whole journey," said Madison.

"Do let us hear of it," said Mr. Listwell.

"Two weeks ago," continued Madison, "after travelling all night, I was overtaken by daybreak, in what seemed to me an almost interminable wood. I deemed it unsafe to go farther, and, as usual, I looked around for a suitable tree in which to spend the day. I liked one with a bushy top, and found one just to my mind. Up I climbed, and hiding myself as well I could, I, with this strap, (pulling one out of his old coat-pocket,) lashed myself to a bough, and flattered myself that I should get a *good night's* sleep that day; but in this I was soon disappointed. I had scarcely got fastened to my natural hammock, when I heard the voices of a number of persons, apparently approaching the part of the woods where I was. Upon my word, sir, I dreaded more these human voices than I should have done those of wild beasts. I was at a loss to know what to do. If I descended, I should probably be discovered by the men; and if they had dogs I should, doubtless, be '*treed*.' It was an anxious moment, but hardships and dangers have been the accompaniments of my life; and have, perhaps, imparted to me a certain hardness of character, which, to some extent, adapts me to them. In my present predicament, I decided to hold my place in the tree-top, and abide the consequences. But here I must disappoint you; for the men, who were all colored, halted at least a hundred yards from me, and began with their axes, in right good earnest, to attack the trees. The sound of their laughing axes was like the report of as many well-charged pistols. By and by there came down at least a dozen trees with a terrible crash. They leaped upon the fallen trees with an air of victory. I could see no dog with them, and felt myself comparatively safe, though I could not forget the possibility that some freak or fancy might bring the axe a little nearer my dwelling than comported with my safety.

"There was no sleep for me that day, and I wished for night. You may imagine that the thought of having the tree attacked under me was far from agreeable, and that it very easily kept me on the look-out. The day was not without diversion. The men at work seemed to be a gay set; and they would often make the woods resound with that uncontrolled laughter for which we, as a race, are remarkable. I held my place in the tree till sunset,—saw the men put on their jackets to be off. I observed that all left the ground except one, whom I saw sitting on the side of a stump, with his head bowed, and his eyes apparently fixed on the ground. I became interested in him. After sitting in the position to which I have alluded ten or fifteen minutes, he left the stump, walked directly towards the tree in which I was secreted, and halted almost under the same. He stood for a moment and looked around, deliberately and reverently took off his hat, by which I saw that I saw that he was a man in the evening of life, slightly bald and quite gray. After laying down his hat carefully, he knelt and prayed aloud, and such a prayer, the most fervent, earnest, and solemn, to which I think I ever listened. After reverently addressing the Almighty, as the all-wise, all-good, and the common Father of all mankind, he besought God for grace, for strength, to bear up under, and to endure, as a good soldier, all the hardships and trials which beset the journey of life, and to enable him to live in a manner which accorded with the gospel of Christ. His soul now broke out in humble supplication for deliverance from bondage. 'O thou,' said he, 'that hearest the raven's cry, take pity on poor me! O deliver me! O deliver me! in mercy, O God, deliver me from the chains and manifold hardships of slavery!

With thee, O Father, all things are possible. Thou canst stand and measure the earth. Thou hast beheld and drove asunder the nations,—all power is in thy hand,—thou didst say of old, "I have seen the affliction of my people, and am come to deliver them,"—Oh look down upon our afflictions, and have mercy upon us.' But I cannot repeat his prayer, nor can I give you an idea of its deep pathos. I had given but little attention to religion, and had but little faith in it; yet, as the old man prayed, I felt almost like coming down and kneel by his side, and mingle my broken complaint with his.

He had already gained my confidence; as how could it be otherwise? I knew enough of religion to know that the man who prays in secret is far more likely to be sincere than he who loves to pray standing in the street, or in the great congregation. When he arose from his knees, like another Zacheus, I came down from the tree. He seemed a little alarmed at first, but I told him my story, and the good man embraced me in his arms, and assured me of his sympathy.

"I was now about out of provisions, and thought I might safely ask him to help me replenish my store. He said he had no money; but if he had, he would freely give it me. I told him I had *one dollar*; it was all the money I had in the world. I gave it to him, and asked him to purchase some crackers and cheese, and to kindly bring me the balance; that I would remain in or near that place, and would come to him on his return; if he would whistle. He was gone only about an hour. Meanwhile, from some cause or other, I know not what, (but as you shall see very wisely,) I changed my place. On his return I started to meet him; but it seemed as if the shadow of approaching danger fell upon my spirit, and checked my progress. In a very few minutes, closely on the heels of the old man, I distinctly saw fourteen men, with something like guns in their hands."

"Oh! the old wretch!" exclaimed Mrs. Listwell "he had betrayed you, had betrayed you, had he?"

"I think not," said Madison, "I cannot believe that the old man was to blame. He probably went into a store, asked for the articles for which I sent, and presented the bill I gave him; and it is so unusual for slaves in the country to have money, that fact, doubtless, excited suspicion, and gave rise to inquiry. I can easily believe that the truthfulness of the old man's character compelled him to disclose the facts; and thus were these blood-thirsty men put on my track. Of course I did not present myself; but hugged my hiding-place securely. If discovered and attacked, I resolved to sell my life as dearly as possible.

"After searching about the woods silently for a time, the whole company gathered around the old man; one charged him with lying, and called him an old villain; said he was a thief; charged him with stealing money; said if he did not instantly tell where he got it, they would take the shirt from his old back, and give him thirty-nine lashes.

"'I did *not* steal the money,' said the old man, 'it was given me, as I told you at the store; and if the man who gave it me is not here, it is not my fault.'

"'Hush! you lying old rascal; we'll make you smart for it. You shall not leave this spot until you have told where you got that money.'

"They now took hold of him, and began to strip him; while others went to get sticks with which to beat him. I felt, at the moment, like rushing out in the midst of them; but considering that the old man would be whipped the more for having aided a fugitive slave, and that, perhaps, in the *melée* he might be killed outright, I disobeyed this impulse. They tied him to a tree, and began to whip him. My own flesh crept at every blow, and I seem to hear the old man's piteous cries even now. They laid thirty-nine lashes on his bare back, and were going to repeat that number, when one of the company besought his comrades to desist. 'You'll kill the d–d old scoundrel! You've already whipt a dollar's worth out of him, even if he stole it!' 'O yes,' said another, 'let him down. He'll never tell us another lie, I'll warrant ye!' With this, one of the company untied the old man, and bid him go about his business.

"The old man left, but the company remained as much as an hour, scouring the woods. Round and round they went, turning up the underbrush, and peering about like so many bloodhounds. Two or three times they came within six feet of where I lay. I tell you I held my stick with a firmer grasp than I did in coming up to your house tonight. I expected to level one of them at least. Fortunately, however, I eluded their pursuit, and they left me alone in the woods.

"My last dollar was now gone, and you may well suppose I felt the loss of it; but the thought of being once again free to pursue my journey, prevented that depression which a sense of destitution causes; so swinging my little bundle on my back, I caught a glimpse of the *Great Bear* (which ever points the way to my beloved star,) and I started again on my journey. What I lost in money I made up at a hen-roost that same night, upon which I fortunately came."

"But you did'nt [*sic*] eat your food raw? How did you cook it?" said Mrs. Listwell.

"O no, Madam," said Madison, turning to his little bundle:—"I had the means of cooking." Here he took out of his bundle an old-fashioned tinderbox, and taking up a piece of a file, which he brought with him, he struck it with a heavy flint, and brought out at least a dozen sparks at once. "I have had this old box," said he, "more than five years. It is the only property saved from the fire in the dismal swamp. It has done me good service. It has given me the means of broiling many a chicken!"

It seemed quite a relief to Mrs. Listwell to know that Madison had, at least, lived upon cooked food. Women have a perfect horror of eating uncooked food. By this time thoughts of what was best to be done about getting Madison to Canada, began to trouble Mr. Listwell; for the laws of Ohio were very stringent against anyone who should aid, or who were found aiding a slave to escape through that State. A citizen, for the simple act of taking a fugitive slave in his carriage, had just been stripped of all his property, and thrown penniless upon the world. Notwithstanding this,

Mr. Listwell was determined to see Madison safely on his way to Canada. "Give yourself no uneasiness," said he to Madison, "for if it cost my farm, I shall see you safely out of the States, and on your way to a land of liberty. Thank God that there *such* a land so near us! You will spend to-morrow with us, and to-morrow night I will take you in my carriage to the Lake. Once upon that, and you are safe."

"Thank you! thank you," said the fugitive; "I will commit myself to your care."

For the *first* time during *five* years, Madison enjoyed the luxury of resting his limbs on a comfortable bed, and inside a human habitation. Looking at the white sheets, he said to Mr. Listwell, "What, sir! you don't mean that I shall sleep in that bed?"

"Oh yes, oh yes."

After Mr. Listwell left the room, Madison said he really hesitated whether or not he should lie on the floor; for that was *far* more comfortable and inviting than any bed to which he had been used.

We pass over the thoughts and feelings, the hopes and fears, the plans and purposes, that revolved in the mind of Madison during the day that he was secreted at the house of Mr. Listwell. The reader will be content to know that nothing occurred to endanger his liberty, or to excite alarm. Many were the little attentions bestowed upon him in his quiet retreat and hiding-place. In the evening, Mr. Listwell, after treating Madison to a new suit of winter clothes, and replenishing his exhausted purse with five dollars, all in silver, brought out his two-horse wagon, well provided with buffaloes, and silently started off with him to Cleveland. They arrived there without interruption, a few minutes before sunrise the next morning. Fortunately the steamer Admiral lay at the wharf, and was to start for Canada at nine o'clock. Here the last anticipated danger was surmounted. It was feared that just at this point the hunters of men might be on the look-out, and, possibly, pounce upon their victim. Mr. Listwell saw the captain of the boat; cautiously sounded him on the matter of carrying liberty-loving passengers, before he introduced his precious charge. This done, Madison was conducted on board. With usual generosity this true subject of the emancipating queen welcomed Madison, and assured him that he should be safely landed in Canada, free of charge. Madison now felt himself no more a piece of merchandise, but a passenger, and, like any other passenger, going about his business, carrying with him what belonged to him, and nothing which rightfully belonged to anybody else.

Wrapped in his new winter suit, snug and comfortable, a pocket full of silver, safe from his pursuers, embarked for a free country, Madison gave every sign of sincere gratitude, and bade his kind benefactor farewell, with such a grip of the hand as bespoke a heart full of honest manliness, and a soul that knew how to appreciate kindness. It need scarcely be said that Mr. Listwell was deeply moved by the gratitude and friendship he had excited in a nature so noble as that of the fugitive. He went to his home that day with a joy and gratification which knew no bounds. He had done something "to deliver the spoiled out of the hands of the spoiler," he had given bread to the hungry, and clothes to the naked; he had befriended a man to whom the laws of his country forbade all friendship,—and in proportion to the odds against his righteous deed, was the delightful satisfaction that gladdened his heart. On reaching home, he exclaimed, "*He is safe,—he is safe,—he is safe,*"—and the cup of his joy was shared by his excellent lady. The following letter was received from Madison a few days after.

"WINDSOR, CANADA WEST, DEC. 16, 1840.

My dear Friend,—for such you truly are:—

Madison is out of the woods at last; I nestle in the mane of the British lion, protected by his mighty paw from the talons and the beak of the American eagle. I AM FREE, and breathe an atmosphere too pure for *slaves,* slave-hunters, or slave-holders. My heart is full. As many thanks to you, sir, and to your kind lady, as there are pebbles on the shores of Lake Erie; and may the blessing of God rest upon you both. You will never be forgotten by your profoundly grateful friend,

MADISON WASHINGTON."

PART III

—His head was with his heart,
And that was far away!

—*Childe Harold*

Just upon the edge of the great road from Petersburg, Virginia, to Richmond, and only about fifteen miles from the latter place, there stands a somewhat ancient and famous public tavern, quite notorious in its better days, as being the grand resort for most of the leading gamblers, horse-racers, cock-fighters, and slave-traders from all the country round about. This old rookery, the nucleus of all sorts of birds, mostly those of ill omen, has, like everything else peculiar to Virginia, lost much of its ancient consequence and splendor; yet it keeps up some appearance of gaiety and high life, and is still frequented, even by respectable travellers, who are unacquainted with its past history and present condition. Its fine old portico looks well at a distance, and gives the building an air of grandeur. A nearer view, however, does little to sustain this pretension. The house is large, and its style imposing, but time and dissipation, unfailing in their results, have made ineffaceable marks upon it, and it must, in the common course of events, soon be numbered with the things that were. The gloomy mantle of ruin is, already, outspread to envelop it, and its remains, even but now remind one of a human skull, after the flesh has mingled with the earth. Old hats and rags fill the places in the upper windows once occupied by large panes of glass, and the moulding boards along the roofing have dropped off from their places, leaving holes and crevices in the rented wall for bats and swallows to build their nests in. The platform of the portico, which fronts the highway is a rickety affair, its planks are loose, and in some places entirely gone, leaving effective mantraps in their stead for nocturnal ramblers. The wooden pillars, which once supported it, but which now hang as encumbrances, are all rotten, and tremble with the touch. A part of the stable, a fine old structure in its day, which has given comfortable shelter to hundreds of the noblest steeds of "the Old Dominion" at once, was blown down many years ago, and never has been, and probably never will be, rebuilt. The doors of the barn are in wretched condition; they will shut with a little human strength to help their worn out hinges, but not otherwise. The side of the great building seen from the road is much discolored in sundry places by slops poured from the upper windows, rendering it unsightly and offensive in other respects. Three or four great dogs, looking as dull and gloomy as the mansion itself, lie stretched out along the door-sills under the portico; and double the number of loafers, some of them completely rum-ripe, and others ripening, dispose themselves like so many sentinels about the front of the house. These latter understand the science of scraping acquaintance to perfection. They know every-body, and almost every-body knows them. Of course, as their title implies, they have no regular employment. They are (to use an expressive phrase) *hangers on*, or still better, they are what sailors would denominate *holders-on to the slack, in every-body's mess, and in nobody's watch*. They are, however, as good as the newspaper for the events of the day, and they sell their knowledge almost as cheap. Money they seldom have; yet they always have capital the most reliable. They make their way with a succeeding traveller by intelligence gained from a preceding one. All the great names of Virginia they know by heart, and have seen their owners often. The history of the house is folded in their lips, and they rattle off stories in connection with it, equal to the guides at Dryburgh Abbey. He must be a shrewd man, and well skilled in the art of evasion, who gets out of the hands of these fellows without being at the expense of a treat.

It was at this old tavern, while on a second visit to the State of Virginia in 1841, that Mr. Listwell, unacquainted with the fame of the place, turned aside, about sunset, to pass the night. Riding up to the house, he had scarcely dismounted, when one of the half dozen bar-room fraternity met and addressed him in a manner exceedingly bland and accommodating.

"Fine evening, sir."

"Very fine," said Mr. Listwell. "This is a tavern, I believe?"

"O yes, sir, yes; although you may think it looks a little the worse for wear, it was once as good a house as any in Virginy. I make no doubt if ye spend the night here, you'll think it a good house yet; for there aint a more accommodating man in the country than you'll find the landlord."

Listwell. "The most I want is a good bed for myself, and a full manger for my horse. If I get these, I shall be quite satisfied."

Loafer. "Well, I alloys like to hear a gentleman talk for his horse; and just becase the horse can't talk for itself. A man that don't care about his beast, and don't look arter it when he's travelling, aint much in my eye anyhow.

Now, sir I likes a horse, and I'll guarantee your horse will be taken good care on here. That old stable, for all you see it looks so shabby now, once sheltered the great Eclipse, when he run here agin *Batchelor* and *Jumping Jemmy.* Them was fast horses, but he beat 'em both."

Listwell. "Indeed."

Loafer. "Well, I rather reckon you've travelled a right smart distance to-day, from the look of your horse?"

Listwell. "Forty miles only."

Loafer. "Well! I'll be darned if that aint a pretty good *only.* Mister, that beast of yours is a singed cat, I warrant you. I never see'd a creature like that that was'nt good on the road. You've come about forty miles, then?"

Listwell. "Yes, yes, and a pretty good pace at that."

Loafer. "You're somewhat in a hurry, then, I make no doubt? I reckon I could guess if I would, what you're going to Richmond for? It would'nt be much of a guess either; for it's rumored hereabouts, that there's to be the greatest sale of niggers at Richmond to-morrow that has taken place there in a long time; and I'll be bound you're a going there to have a hand in it."

Listwell. "Why, you must think, then, that there's money to be made at that business?"

Loafer. "Well, 'pon my honor, sir, I never made any that way myself; but it stands to reason that it's a money making business; for almost all other business in Virginia is dropped to engage in this. One thing is sartain, I never see'd a nigger-buyer yet that had 'nt [*sic*] a plenty of money, and he was 'nt [*sic*] as free with it as water. I has known one on 'em to treat as high as twenty times in a night; and, ginerally speaking, they's men of edication, and knows all about the government. The fact is, sir, I alloys like to hear 'em talk, bekase I alloys can learn something from them."

Listwell. "What may I call your name, sir?"

Loafer. "Well, now, they calls me Wilkes. I'm known all around by the gentlemen that comes here. They all knows old Wilkes."

Listwell. "Well, Wilkes, you seem to be acquainted here, and I see you have a strong liking for a horse. Be so good as to speak a kind word for mine to the hostler to-night, and you'll not lose anything by it."

Loafer. "Well, sir, I see you don't say much, but you've got an insight into things. It's alloys wise to get the good will of them that's acquainted about a tavern; for a man don't know when he goes into a house what may happen, or how much he may need a friend." Here the loafer gave Mr. Listwell a significant grin, which expressed a sort of triumphant pleasure at having, as he supposed, by his tact succeeded in placing so fine appearing a gentleman under obligations to him. The pleasure, however, was mutual; for there was something so insinuating in the glance of this loquacious customer, that Mr. Listwell was very glad to get quit of him, and to do so more successfully, he ordered his supper to be brought to him in his private room, private to the eye, but not to the ear. This room was directly over the bar, and the plastering being off, nothing but pine boards and naked laths separated him from the disagreeable company below,—he could easily hear what was said in the bar-room, and was rather glad of the advantage it afforded, for, as you shall see, it furnished him important hints as to the manner and deportment he should assume during his stay at that tavern.

Mr. Listwell says he had got into his room but a few moments, when he heard the officious Wilkes below, in a tone of disappointment, exclaim, "Whar's that gentleman?" Wilkes was evidently expecting to meet with his friend at the bar-room, on his return, and had no doubt of his doing the handsome thing. "He has gone to his room," answered the landlord, "and has ordered his supper to be brought to him."

Here some one shouted out, "Who is he, Wilkes? Where's he going?"

"Well, now, I'll be hanged if I know; but I'm willing to make any man a bet of this old hat agin a five dollar bill, that that gent is as full of money as a dog is of fleas. He's going down to Richmond to buy niggers, I make no doubt. He's no fool, I warrant ye."

"Well, he acts d—d strange," said another, "anyhow. I likes to see a man, when he comes up to a tavern, to come straight into the bar-room, and show that he's a man among men. Nobody was going to bite him."

"Now, I don't blame him a bit for not corning in here. That man knows his business, and means to take care on his money," answered Wilkes.

"Wilkes, you're a fool. You only say that, becase you hope to get a few coppers out on him."

"You only measure my corn by your half-bushel, I won't say that you're only mad becase I got the chance of speaking to him first."

"O Wilkes! you're known here. You'll praise up any body that will give you a copper; besides, 'tis my opinion that that fellow who took his long slab-sides up stairs, for all the world just like a half-scared woman, afraid to look honest men in the face, is a *Northerner*, and as mean as dish-water."

"Now what will you bet of that," said Wilkes.

The speaker said, "I make no bets with you, 'kase you can get that fellow up stairs there to say anything."

"Well," said Wilkes, "I am willing to bet any man in the company that *that* gentleman is a *nigger-buyer*. He did'nt tell me so right down, but I reckon I knows enough about men to give a pretty clean guess as to what they are arter."

The dispute as to *who* Mr. Listwell was, what his business, where he was going, etc., was kept up with much animation for some time, and more than once threatened a serious disturbance of the peace. Wilkes had his friends as well as his opponents. After this sharp debate, the company amused themselves by drinking whiskey, and telling stories. The latter consisting of quarrels, fights, *rencontres*, and duels, in which distinguished persons of that neighborhood, and frequenters of that house, had been actors. Some of these stories were frightful enough, and were told, too, with a relish which bespoke the pleasure of the parties with the horrid scenes they portrayed. It would not be proper here to give the reader any idea of the vulgarity and dark profanity which rolled, as "a sweet morsel," under these corrupt tongues. A more brutal set of creatures, perhaps, never congregated.

Disgusted, and a little alarmed withal, Mr. Listwell, who was not accustomed to such entertainment, at length retired, but not to sleep. He was *too* much wrought upon by what he had heard to rest quietly, and what snatches of sleep he got, were interrupted by dreams which were anything than pleasant. At eleven o'clock, there seemed to be several hundreds of persons crowding into the house. A loud and confused clamour, cursing and cracking of whips, and the noise of chains startled him from his bed; for a moment he would have given the half of his farm in Ohio to have been at home. This uproar was kept up with undulating course, till near morning. There was loud laughing,—loud singing,—loud cursing,—and yet there seemed to be weeping and mourning in the midst of all. Mr. Listwell said he had heard enough during the forepart of the night to convince him that a buyer of men and women stood the best chance of being respected. And he, therefore, thought it best to say nothing which might undo the favorable opinion that had been formed of him in the barroom by at least one of the fraternity that swarmed about it. While he would not avow himself a purchaser of slaves, he deemed it not prudent to disavow it. He felt that he might, properly, refuse to cast such a pearl before parties which, to him, were worse than swine. To reveal himself, and to impart a knowledge of his real character and sentiments would, to say the least, be imparting intelligence with the certainty of seeing it and himself both abused, Mr. Listwell confesses, that this reasoning did not altogether satisfy his conscience, for, hating slavery as he did, and regarding it to be the immediate duty of every man to cry out against it, "without compromise and without concealment," it was hard for him to admit to himself the possibility of circumstances wherein a man might, properly, hold his tongue on the subject. Having as little of the spirit of a martyr as Erasmus, he concluded, like the latter, that it was wiser to trust the mercy of God for his soul, than the humanity of slave-traders for his body. Bodily fear, not conscientious scruples, prevailed.

In this spirit he rose early in the morning, manifesting no surprise at what he had heard during the night. His quondam friend was soon at his elbow, boring him with all sorts of questions. All, however, directed to find out his character, business, residence, purposes, and destination. With the most perfect appearance of good nature and carelessness, Mr. Listwell evaded these meddlesome inquiries, and turned conversation to general topics, leaving himself and all that specially pertained to him, out of discussion. Disengaging himself from their troublesome companionship, he made his way towards an old bowling-alley, which was connected with the house, and which, like all the rest, was in very bad repair.

On reaching the alley Mr. Listwell saw, for the first time in his life, a slave-gang on their way to market. A sad sight truly. Here were one hundred and thirty human beings,—children of a common Creator—guilty of no crime—men and women, with hearts, minds, and deathless spirits, chained and fettered, and bound for the market, in a christian country,—in a country boasting of its liberty, independence, and high civilization! Humanity converted into merchandise, and linked in iron bands, with no regard to decency or humanity! All sizes, ages, and sexes, mothers, fathers, daughters, brothers, sisters,—all huddled together, on their way to market to be sold and separated from home, and from each other forever. And all to fill the pockets of men too lazy to work for an honest living, and who gain their fortune by plundering the helpless, and trafficking in the souls and sinews of men. As he gazed upon this revolting and heart-rending scene, our informant said he almost doubted the existence of a God of justice! And he stood wondering that the earth did not open and swallow up such wickedness. In the midst of these reflections, and while running his eye up and down the fettered ranks, he met the glance of one whose face he thought he had seen before. To be resolved, he moved towards the spot. It was MADISON WASHINGTON! Here was a scene for the pencil! Had Mr. Listwell been confronted by one risen from the dead, he could not have been more appalled. He was completely stunned. A thunderbolt could not have struck him more dumb. He stood, for a few moments, as motionless as one petrified; collecting himself, he at length exclaimed, "*Madison! is that you?*"

The noble fugitive, but little less astonished than himself, answered cheerily, "O yes, sir, they've got me again."

Thoughtless of consequences for the moment, Mr. Listwell ran up to his old friend, placing his hands upon his shoulders, and looked him in the face! Speechless they stood gazing at each other as if to be doubly resolved that there was no mistake about the matter, till Madison motioned his friend away, intimating a fear lest the keepers should find him there, and suspect him of tampering with the slaves.

"They will soon be out to look after us. You can come when they go to breakfast, and I will tell you all."

Pleased with this arrangement, Mr. Listwell passed out of the alley; but only just in time to save himself, for, while near the door, he observed three men making their way to the alley. The thought occurred to him to await their arrival, as the best means of diverting the ever ready suspicions of the guilty.

While the scene between Mr. Listwell and his friend Madison was going on, the other slaves stood as mute spectators,—at a loss to know what all this could mean. As he left, he heard the man chained to Madison ask, "Who is that gentleman?"

"He is a friend of mine. I cannot tell you now. Suffice it to say he is a friend. You shall hear more of him before long, but mark me! whatever shall pass between that gentleman and me, in your hearing, I pray you will say nothing about it. We are all chained here together,—ours is a common lot; and that gentleman is not less *your* friend than *mine.*" At these words, all mysterious as they were, the unhappy company gave signs of satisfaction and hope. It seems that Madison, by that mesmeric power which is the invariable accompaniment of genius, had already won the confidence of the gang, and was a sort of general-in-chief among them.

By this time the keepers arrived. A horrid trio, well fitted for their demoniacal work. Their uncombed hair came down over foreheads "*villainously low*," and with eyes, mouths, and noses to match. "Hallo! hallo!" they growled out as they entered. "Are you all there!"

"All here," said Madison.

"Well, well, that's right! your journey will soon be over. You'll be in Richmond by eleven to-day, and then you'll have an easy time on it."

"I say, gal, what in the devil are you crying about?" said one of them. "I'll give you something to cry about, if you don't mind." This was said to a girl, apparently not more than twelve years old, who had been weeping bitterly. She had, probably, left behind her a loving mother, affectionate sisters, brothers, and friends, and her tears were but the natural expression of her sorrow, and the only solace. But the dealers in human flesh have *no* respect for such sorrow. They look upon it as a protest against their cruel injustice, and they are prompt to punish it.

This is a puzzle not easily solved. *How* came he here? what can I do for him? may I not even now be in some way compromised in this affair? were thoughts that troubled Mr. Listwell, and made him eager for the promised opportunity of speaking to Madison.

The bell now sounded for breakfast, and keepers and drivers, with pistols and bowie-knives gleaming from their belts, hurried in, as if to get the best places. Taking the chance now afforded, Mr. Listwell hastened back to the bowling-alley. Reaching Madison, he said, "Now *do* tell me all about the matter. Do you know me?"

"Oh, yes," said Madison, "I know you well, and shall never forget you nor that cold and dreary night you gave me shelter. I must be short," he continued, "for they'll soon be out again. This, then, is the story in brief. On reaching Canada, and getting over the excitement of making my escape, sir, my thoughts turned to my poor wife, who had well deserved my love by her virtuous fidelity and undying affection for me. I could not bear the thought of leaving her in the cruel jaws of slavery, without making an effort to rescue her. First, I tried to get money to buy her; but oh! the process was *too slow*. I despaired of accomplishing it. She was in all my thoughts by day, and my dreams by night. At times I could almost hear her voice, saying, 'O Madison! Madison! will you then leave me here? can you leave me here to die? No! no! you will come! you will come!' I was wretched. I lost my appetite. I could neither work, eat, nor sleep, till I resolved to hazard my own liberty, to gain that of my wife! But I must be short. Six weeks ago I reached my old master's place. I laid about the neighborhood nearly a week, watching my chance, and, finally, I ventured upon the desperate attempt to reach my poor wife's room by means of a ladder. I reached the window, but the noise in raising it frightened my wife, and she screamed and fainted. I took her in my arms, and was descending the ladder, when the dogs began to bark furiously, and before I could get to the woods the white folks were roused. The cool night air soon restored my wife, and she readily recognized me. We made the best of our way to the woods, but it was now *too* late,—the dogs were after us as though they would have torn us to pieces. It was all over with me now! My old master and his two sons ran out with loaded rifles, and before we were out of gunshot, our ears were assailed with *'Stop! stop! or be shot down.'* Nevertheless we ran on. Seeing that we gave no heed to their calls, they fired, and my poor wife fell by my side dead, while I received but a slight flesh wound. I now became desperate, and stood my ground, and awaited their attack over her dead body. They rushed upon me, with their rifles in hand. I parried their blows, and fought them 'till I was knocked down and overpowered."

"Oh! it was madness to have returned," said Mr. Listwell.

"Sir, I could not be free with the galling thought that my poor wife was still a slave. With her in slavery, my body, not my spirit, was free. I was taken to the house,—chained to a ring-bolt,—my wounds dressed. I was kept there three days. All the slaves, for miles around, were brought to see me. Many slaveholders came with their slaves, using me as proof of the completeness of their power, and of the impossibility of slaves getting away. I was taunted, jeered at, and berated by them, in a manner that pierced me to the soul. Thank God, I was able to smother my rage, and to bear it all with seeming composure. After my wounds were nearly healed, I was taken to a tree and stripped, and I received sixty lashes on my naked back. A few days after, I was sold to a slave-trader, and placed in this gang for the New Orleans market."

"Do you think your master would sell you to me?"

"O no, sir! I was sold on condition of my being taken South. Their motive is revenge."

"Then, then," said Mr. Listwell, "I fear I can do nothing for you. Put your trust in God, and bear your sad lot with the manly fortitude which becomes a man. I shall see you at Richmond, but don't recognize me." Saying this, Mr. Listwell handed Madison ten dollars; said a few words to the other slaves; received their hearty "God bless you," and made his way to the house.

Fearful of exciting suspicion by too long delay, our friend went to the breakfast table, with the air of one who half reproved the greediness of those who rushed in at the sound of the bell. A cup of coffee was all that he could manage. His feelings were too bitter and excited, and his heart was too full with the fate of poor Madison (whom he loved as well as admired) to relish his breakfast; and although he sat long after the company had left the table, he really did little more than change the position of his knife and fork. The strangeness of meeting again one whom he had met on two several occasions before, under extraordinary circumstances, was well calculated to suggest the idea that a supernatural power, a wakeful providence, or an inexorable fate, had linked their destiny together; and that no efforts of his could disentangle him from the mysterious web of circumstances which enfolded him.

On leaving the table, Mr. Listwell nerved himself up and walked firmly into the bar-room. He was at once greeted again by that talkative chatterbox, Mr. Wilkes.

"Them's a likely set of niggers in the alley there," said Wilkes.

"Yes, they're fine looking fellows, one of them I should like to purchase, and for him I would be willing to give a handsome sum."

Turning to one of his comrades, and with a grin of victory, Wilkes said, "Aha, Bill, did you hear that? I told you I know'd that gentleman wanted to buy niggers, and would bid as high as any purchaser in the market."

"Come, come," said Listwell, "don't be too loud in your praise, you are old enough to know that prices rise when purchasers are plenty."

"That's a fact," said Wilkes, "I see you knows the ropes—and there's not a man in old Virginy whom I'd rather help to make a good bargain than you, sir.

"Mr. Listwell here threw a dollar at Wilkes, (which the latter caught with a dexterous hand,) saying, "Take that for your kind good will." Wilkes held up the dollar to his right eye, with a grin of victory, and turned to the morose grumbler in the corner who had questioned the liberality of a man of whom he knew nothing.

Mr. Listwell now stood as well with the company as any other occupant of the bar-room. We pass over the hurry and bustle, the brutal vociferations of the slave-drivers in getting their unhappy gang in motion for Richmond; and we need not narrate every application of the lash to those who faltered in the journey. Mr. Listwell followed the train at a long distance, with a sad heart; and on reaching Richmond, left his horse at a hotel, and made his way to the wharf in the direction of which he saw the slave-coffle driven. He was just in time to see the whole company embark for New Orleans. The thought struck him that, while mixing with the multitude, he might do his friend Madison one last service, and he stept into a hardware store and purchased three strong *files*. These he took with him, and standing near the small boat, which lay in waiting to bear the company by parcels to the side of the brig that lay in the stream, he managed, as Madison passed him, to slip the files into his pocket, and at once darted back among the crowd. All the company now on board, the imperious voice of the captain sounded, and instantly a dozen hardy seamen were in the rigging, hurrying aloft to unfurl the broad canvas of our Baltimore built American Slaver. The sailors hung about the ropes, like so many black cats, now in the round-tops, now in the cross-trees, now on the yard-arms; all was bluster and activity. Soon the broad fore topsail, the royal and top gallant sail were spread to the breeze. Round went the heavy windlass, clank, clank went the fall-bit,—the anchors weighed, jibs, mainsails, and topsails hauled to the wind, and the long, low, black slaver, with her cargo of human flesh, careened and moved forward to the sea.

Mr. Listwell stood on the shore, and watched the slaver till the last speck of her upper sails faded from sight, and announced the limit of human vision. "Farewell! farewell! brave and true man! God grant that brighter skies may smile upon your future than have yet looked down upon your thorny pathway."

Saying this to himself, our friend lost no time in completing his business, and in making his way homewards, gladly shaking off from his feet the dust of Old Virginia.

PART IV

Oh, where's the slave so lowly
Condemn'd to chains unholy,
   Who could he burst
   His bonds at first
Would pine beneath them slowly?

—Moore

—Know ye not
Who would be free, *themselves* must strike the blow.

—Childe Harold

What a world of inconsistency, as well as of wickedness, is suggested by the smooth and gliding phrase, AMERICAN SLAVE TRADE; and how strange and perverse is that moral sentiment which loathes, execrates, and brands as piracy and as deserving of death the carrying away into captivity men, women, and children from the *African coast;* but which is neither shocked nor disturbed by a similar traffic, carried on with the same motives and purposes, and characterized by even *more* odious peculiarities on the coast of our MODEL REPUBLIC. We execrate and hang the wretch guilty of this crime on the coast of Guinea, while we respect and applaud the guilty participators in this murderous business on the enlightened shores of the Chesapeake. The inconsistency is so flagrant and glaring, that it would seem to cast a doubt on the doctrine of the innate moral sense of mankind.

Just two months after the sailing of the Virginia slave brig, which the reader has seen move off to sea so proudly with her human cargo for the New Orleans market, there chanced to meet, in the Marine Coffee-house at Richmond, a company of *ocean birds*, when the following conversation, which throws some light on the subsequent history, not only of Madison Washington, but of the hundred and thirty human beings with whom we last saw him chained.

"I say, shipmate, you had rather rough weather on your late passage to Orleans?" said Jack Williams, a regular old salt, tauntingly, to a trim, compact, manly looking person, who proved to be the first mate of the slave brig in question.

"Foul play, as well as foul weather," replied the firmly knit personage, evidently but little inclined to enter upon a subject which terminated so ingloriously to the captain and officers of the American slaver.

"Well, betwixt you and me," said Williams, that whole affair on board of the Creole was miserably and disgracefully managed. Those black rascals got the upper hand of ye altogether; and, in my opinion, the whole disaster was the result of ignorance of the real character of darkies in general. With half a dozen *resolute* white men, (I say it not boastingly,) I could have had the rascals in irons in ten minutes, not because I'm so strong, but I know how to manage 'em. With my back against the *caboose*, I could, myself, have flogged a dozen of them; and had I been on board, by every monster of the deep, every black devil of 'em all would have had his neck stretched from the yard-arm. Ye made a mistake in yer manner of fighting 'em. All that is needed in dealing with a set of rebellious *darkies*, is to show that yer not afraid of 'em. For my own part, I would not honor a dozen niggers by point-ing a gun at one on 'em,—a good stout whip, or a stiff rope's end, is better than all the guns at Old Point to quell a *nigger* insurrection. Why, sir, to take a gun to a *nigger* is the best way you can select to tell him you are afraid of him, and the best way of inviting his attack."

This speech made quite a sensation among the company, and a part of them indicated solicitude for the answer which might be made to it. Our first mate replied, "Mr. Williams, all that you've now said sounds very well *here* on shore, where, perhaps, you have studied negro character. I do not profess to understand the subject as well as yourself; but it strikes me, you apply the same rule in dissimilar cases. It is quite easy to talk of flogging niggers here on land, where you have the sympathy of the community, and the whole physical force of the government, State and national, at your command; and where, if a negro shall lift his hand against a white man, the white community, with one accord, are ready to unite in shooting him down. I say, in such circumstances, it's easy to talk of flogging negroes and of negro cowardice; but, sir, I deny that the negro is, naturally, a coward, or that your theory of managing slaves will stand the test of *salt* water. It may do very well for an overseer, a contemptible hireling, to take advantage of fears already in existence, and which his presence has no power to inspire; to swagger about whip in hand, and discourse on the timidity and cowardice of negroes; for they have a smooth sea and a fair wind. It is one thing to manage a company of slaves on a Virginia plantation, and quite another thing to quell an insurrection on the lonely billows of the Atlantic, where ev-ery breeze speaks of courage and liberty. For the negro to act cowardly on shore, may be to act wisely; and I've some doubts whether *you*, Mr. Williams, would find it very convenient were you a slave in Algiers, to raise your hand against the bayonets of a whole government."

"By George, shipmate," said Williams, "you're coming rather *too* near. Ei-ther I've fallen very low in your estimation, or your notions of negro courage have got up a button-hole too high. Now I more than ever wish I'd been on board of that luckless craft. I'd have given ye practical evidence of the truth of my theory. I don't doubt there's some difference in being at sea. But a nigger's a nigger, on sea or land; and is a coward, find him where you will; a drop of blood from one on 'em will skeer a hundred. A knock on the nose, or a kick on the shin, will tame the wildest 'darkey' you can fetch me. I say again, and will stand by it, I could, with half a dozen good men, put the whole nineteen on 'em in irons, and have carried them safe to New Orleans too. Mind, I don't blame you, but I do say, and every gentleman here will bear me out in it, that the fault was somewhere, or them niggers would never have got off as they have done. For my part I feel ashamed to have the idea go abroad, that a ship load of slaves can't be safely taken from

Richmond to New Orleans. I should like, merely to redeem the character of Virginia sailors, to take charge of a ship load on 'em to-morrow."

Williams went on in this strain, occasionally casting an imploring glance at the company for applause for his wit, and sympathy for his contempt of negro courage. He had, evidently, however, waked up the wrong passenger; for besides being in the right, his opponent carried that in his eye which marked him a man not to be trifled with.

"Well, Sir," said the sturdy mate, "you can select your own method for distinguishing yourself;—the path of ambition in this direction is quite open to you in Virginia, and I've no doubt that you will be highly appreciated and compensated for all your valiant achievements in that line; but for myself, while I do not profess to be a giant, I have resolved never to set my foot on the deck of a slave ship, either as officer, or common sailor again; I have got enough of it."

"Indeed! indeed!" exclaimed Williams, derisively.

"Yes, *indeed,*" echoed the mate; "but don't misunderstand me. It is not the high value that I set upon my life that makes me say what I have said; yet I'm resolved never to endanger my life again in a cause which my conscience does not approve. I dare say *here* what many men *feel,* but *dare not speak,* that this whole slave-trading business is a disgrace and scandal to Old Virginia."

"Hold! hold on! shipmate," said Williams, "I hardly thought you'd have shown your colors so soon,—I'll be hanged if you're not as good an abolitionist as Garrison himself."

The mate now rose from his chair, manifesting some excitement. "What do you mean, sir," said he, in a commanding tone. "*That man does not live who shall offer me an insult with impunity.*"

The effect of the words was marked; and the company clustered around. Williams, in an apologetic tone, said, "Shipmate! keep your temper. I meant no insult. We all know that Tom Grant is no coward, and what I said about your being an abolitionist was simply this: you *might* have put down them black mutineers and murderers, but your conscience held you back."

"In that, too," said Grant, "you were mistaken. I did all that any man with equal strength and presence of mind could have done. The fact is, Mr. Williams, you underrate the courage as well as the skill of these negroes, and further, you do not seem to have been correctly informed about the case in hand at all."

"All I know about it is," said Williams, "that on the ninth day after you left Richmond, a dozen or two of the niggers ye had on board, came on deck and took the ship from, you;—had her steered into a British port, where, by the by, every wooly head of them went ashore and was free. Now I take this to be a discreditable piece of business, and one demanding explanation."

"There are a great many discreditable things in the world," said Grant. "For a ship to go down under a calm sky is, upon the first flush of it, disgraceful either to sailors or caulkers. But when we learn, that by some mysterious disturbance in nature, the waters parted beneath, and swallowed the ship up, we lose our indignation and disgust in lamentation of the disaster, and in awe of the Power which controls the elements."

"Very true, very true," said Williams, "I should be very glad to have an explanation which would relieve the affair of its present discreditable features. I have desired to see you ever since you got home, and to learn from you a full statement of the facts in the case. To me the whole thing seems unaccountable. I cannot see how a dozen or two of ignorant negroes, not one of whom had ever been to sea before, and all of them were closely ironed between decks, should be able to get their fetters off, rush out of the hatchway in open daylight, kill two white men, the one the captain and the other their master, and then carry the ship into a British port, where every '*darkey*' of them was set free. There must have been great carelessness, or cowardice somewhere!"

The company which had listened in silence during most of this discussion, now became much excited. One said, I agree with Williams; and several said the thing looks black enough. After the temporary tumultuous exclamations had subsided,—

"I see," said Grant, "how you regard this case, and how difficult it will be for me to render our ship's company blameless in your eyes. Nevertheless, I will state the fact precisely as they came under my own observation. Mr. Williams speaks of 'ignorant negroes,' and, as a general rule, they are ignorant; but had he been on board the *Creole* as I was, he would have seen cause to admit that there are exceptions to this general rule. The leader of the mutiny in question was just as shrewd a fellow as ever I met in my life, and was as well fitted to lead in a dangerous enterprise as any one white man in ten thousand. The name of this man, strange to say, (ominous of greatness,) was MADISON WASHINGTON. In the short time he had been on board, he had secured the confidence of every officer. The negroes fairly worshipped him. His manner and bearing were such, that no one could suspect him of a murderous purpose. The only feeling with which we regarded him was, that he was a powerful, good-disposed negro. He seldom spake to anyone, and when he did speak, it was with the utmost propriety. His words were well chosen, and his pronunciation equal to that of any schoolmaster. It was a mystery to us *where* he got his knowledge of language; but as little was said to him, none of us knew the extent of his intelligence and ability till it was too late. It seems he brought three files with him on board, and must have gone to work upon his fetters the first night out; and he must have worked well at that; for on the day of the rising, he got the irons *off eighteen* besides himself.

"The attack began just about twilight in the evening. Apprehending a squall, I had commanded the second mate to order all hands on deck, to take in sail. A few minutes before this I had seen Madison's head above the hatchway, looking out upon the white-capped waves at the leeward. I think I never saw him look more good-natured. I stood just about midship, on the larboard side. The captain was pacing the quarter-deck on the starboard side, in company with Mr. Jameson, the owner of most of the slaves on board. Both were armed. I had just told the men to lay aloft, and was looking to see my orders obeyed, when I heard the discharge of a pistol on the starboard side; and turning suddenly around, the very deck seemed covered with fiends from the pit. The nineteen negroes were all on deck, with their broken fetters in their hands, rushing in all directions. I put my hand quickly in my pocket to draw out my jack-knife; but before I could draw it, I was knocked senseless to the deck. When I came to myself, (which I did in a few minutes, I suppose, for it was yet quite light,) there was not a white man on deck. The sailors were all aloft in the rigging, and dared not come down. Captain Clarke and Mr. Jameson lay stretched on the quarter-deck,—both dying,—while Madison himself stood at the helm unhurt.

"I was completely weakened by the loss of blood, and had not recovered from the stunning blow which felled me to the deck; but it was a little too much for me, even in my prostrate condition, to see our good brig commanded by a *black murderer*. So I called out to the men to come down and take the ship, or die in the attempt. Suiting the action to the word, I started aft. You murderous villain, said I, to the imp at the helm, and rushed upon him to deal him a blow, when he pushed me back with his strong, black arm, as though I had been a boy of twelve. I looked around for the men. They were still in the rigging. Not one had come down. I started towards Madison again. The rascal now told me to stand back. 'Sir,' said he, 'your life is in my hands. I could have killed you a dozen times over during this last half hour, and could kill you now. You call me a *black murderer*. I am not a murderer. God is my witness that LIBERTY, not *malice*, is the motive for this night's work. I have done no more to those dead men yonder, than they would have done to me in like circumstances. We have struck for our freedom, and if a true man's heart be in you, you will honor us for the deed. We have done that which you applaud your fathers for doing, and if we are murderers, so *were they*.'

"I felt little disposition to reply to this impudent speech. By heaven, it disarmed me. The fellow loomed up before me. I forgot his blackness in the dignity of his manner, and the eloquence of his speech. It seemed as if the souls of both the great dead (whose names he bore) had entered him. To the sailors in the rigging he said: 'Men! the battle is over,—your captain is dead. I have complete command of this vessel. All resistance to my authority will be in vain. My men have won their liberty, with no other weapons but their own BROKEN FETTERS. We are nineteen in number. We do not thirst for your blood, we demand only our rightful freedom. Do not flatter yourselves that I am ignorant of chart or compass. I know both. We are now only about sixty miles from Nassau. Come down, and do your duty. Land us in Nassau, and not a hair of your heads shall be hurt.'

"I shouted, *Stay where you are, men*,—when a sturdy black fellow ran at me with a handspike, and would have split my head open, but for the interference of Madison, who darted between me and the blow. 'I know what you are up to,' said the latter to me. 'You want to navigate this brig into a slave port, where you would have us all hanged; but you'll miss it; before this brig shall touch a slave-cursed shore while I am on board, I will myself put a match to the magazine, and blow her, and be blown with her, into a thousand fragments. Now I have saved your life twice within these last twenty minutes,—for, when you lay helpless on deck, my men were about to kill you. I held them in check. And if you now (seeing I am your friend and not your enemy) persist in your resistance to my authority, I give you fair warning YOU SHALL DIE.'

"Saying this to me, he cast a glance into the rigging where the terror-stricken sailors were clinging, like so many frightened monkeys, and commanded them to come down, in a tone from which there was no appeal; for four men stood by with muskets in hand, ready at the word of command to shoot them down.

"I now became satisfied that resistance was out of the question; that my best policy was to put the brig into Nassau, and secure the assistance of the American consul at that port. I felt sure that the authorities would enable us to secure the murderers, and bring them to trial.

"By this time the apprehended squall had burst upon us. The wind howled furiously,—the ocean was white with foam, which, on account of the darkness, we could see only by the quick flashes of lightning that darted occasionally from the angry sky. All was alarm and confusion. Hideous cries came up from the slave women. Above the roaring billows a succession of heavy thunder rolled along, swelling the terrific din. Owing to the great darkness, and a sudden shift of the wind, we found ourselves in the trough of the sea. When shipping a heavy sea over the starboard bow, the bodies of the captain and Mr. Jameson were washed overboard. For awhile we had dearer interests to look after than slave property. A more savage thunder-gust never swept the ocean. Our brig rolled and creaked as if every bolt would be started, and every thread of oakum would be pressed out of the seams. "To the pumps! to the pumps!" I cried, but not a sailor would quit his grasp. Fortunately this squall soon passed over, or we must have been food for sharks.

"During all the storm, Madison stood firmly at the helm,—his keen eye fixed upon the binnacle. He was not indifferent to the dreadful hurricane; yet he met it with the equanimity of an old sailor. He was silent but not agitated. The first words he uttered after the storm had slightly subsided, were characteristic of the man. 'Mr. mate, you cannot write the bloody laws of slavery on those restless billows. The ocean, if not the land, is free.' I confess, gentlemen, I felt myself in the presence of a superior man; one who, had he been a white man, I would have followed willingly and gladly in any honorable enterprise. Our difference of color was the only ground for difference of action. It was not that his principles were wrong in the abstract; for they are the principles of 1776. But I could not bring myself to recognize their application to one whom I deemed my inferior.

"But to my story. What happened now is soon told. Two hours after the frightful tempest had spent itself, we were plump at the wharf in Nassau. I sent two of our men immediately to our consul with a statement of facts, requesting his interference in our behalf. What he did, or whether he did anything, I don't know; but, by order of the authorities, a company of *black* soldiers came on board, for the purpose, as they said, of protecting the property. These impudent rascals, when I called on them to assist me in keeping the slaves on board, sheltered themselves adroitly under their instructions only to protect property,—and said they did not recognize *persons as property*. I told them that by the laws of Virginia and the laws of the United States, the slaves on board were as much property as the barrels of flour in the hold. At this the stupid blockheads showed their *ivory*, rolled up their white eyes in horror, as if the idea of putting men on a footing with merchandise were revolting to their humanity. When these instructions were understood among the negroes, it was impossible for us to keep them on board. They deliberately gathered up their baggage before our eyes, and, against our remonstrances, poured through the gangway,—formed themselves into a procession on the wharf,—bid farewell to all on board, and, uttering the wildest shouts of exultation, they marched, amidst the deafening cheers of a multitude of sympathizing spectators, under the triumphant leadership of their heroic chief and deliverer, MADISON WASHINGTON."

1853

NANCY GARDNER PRINCE
1799–c. 1859 (?)

Nancy Gardner Prince's accounts of her life and travels illustrate the significance of mobility for free blacks in the antebellum period and expand our sense of black women's agency and participation in the public sphere. *A Narrative of the Life and Travels of Mrs. Nancy Prince*, published in three editions (1850, 1853, and 1856), incorporates and develops her earlier pamphlet, *The West Indies: Being a Description of the Islands, Progress of Christianity, Education and Liberty Among the Colored Population Generally* (1841). These works contain fascinating linguistic strategies, survival tactics, and cross-cultural interventions into areas such as education, emancipation, religion, citizenship, philanthropy, and women's rights.

A Narrative of the Life and Travels of Mrs. Nancy Prince chronicles Prince's youth and upbringing, then describes her travels to and residence in Russia, where her husband Nero was a guard for the tsar and she ran her own successful garment-making business. Born in Newburyport, Massachusetts, in 1799, she was three months old when her father died. Her mother remarried twice, bearing many children and suffering from mental illness. Throughout her youth, Prince worked as a servant for some of the most prominent New England families, while also managing the care and placement of her siblings. Her writing style was influenced by her evangelical Christian beliefs and draws on scripture as well as on the genres of the travelogue, missionary report, and sentimental narrative. As a young woman, she rescued her sister Silvia from a brothel, and in an incident left out of her published accounts, at age forty-eight she led a rock-throwing retaliation against a slave catcher in the Smith Court houses in the Beacon Hill section Boston.

The longest and most politically charged sections of her narrative describe her itinerant travels to Jamaica, where, she wrote, "a field of usefulness seemed to spread out before me.... I hoped that I might aid, in some small degree, to raise up and encourage emancipated inhabitants, and teach the young children to read and work ... and put their trust in the Savior" (*Narrative*, 43–45). Widowed shortly after returning from Russia, Prince became involved in the Garrisonian abolitionist movement in Boston, but it was through mobility that she transcended the limited roles for free African Americans and women and found her voice. In the Jamaica sections, she blends traditional travel writing with moral suasion and exhortations most likely influenced by David Walker's *Appeal* or Maria Stewart's fiery speeches. Drawing on the example of the industriousness of the freed slaves she met, she argues for the value of black citizenship in the United States, warning her Northern black readers to beware of colonization schemes that urged them to relocate to the West Indies for a better life; she also chastises Northern white readers for hypocrisy. In the sections on Jamaica excerpted here, Prince describes dangerous journeys and illnesses, corrupt ships' captains, greedy missionaries, deceitful colonial administrators, and the stark reality of the lives of free blacks who had relocated to Jamaica. She illustrates the contingent nature of free blackness and its relationship to slavery, as Prince and other free blacks could have been beaten or enslaved when their ships docked in the Southern United States. She also displays ambivalence toward Africanized forms of religious and spiritual practices but admires the Maroons, descendents of fugitives who had escaped their Spanish and British slave owners.

In the final pages of her narrative, Prince describes the danger, bodily harm, and psychic pain inflicted on her in her travels between the United States and Jamaica. Because of the political instability on the island, she was unable to establish a manual labor school in Kingston as she had hoped. Back in Boston, she was "broken up in business, embarrassed and obliged to move, when not able to wait on myself" (85) and found refuge in her belief in God. By the time of the publication of the third edition of her narrative, Prince was physically disabled, and she is listed in the Boston directories as residing in various locations, most likely boardinghouses, until 1859.

Prince's writing deserves to be recognized and read alongside the fiction, slave narratives, spiritual autobiography, and travel writing of the period, with which it shares generic and thematic concerns. Nancy Prince should be acknowledged as a resistant truth teller and early American public intellectual from the North who expressed outrage and proposed revisions of many institutional practices and national policies. As an antebellum American voice from the African diaspora, she was an early practitioner of what today we call transnational, postcolonial gender studies, as she makes important claims based on examining and positioning herself in relation to different national, raced, and gendered policies.

Cheryl J. Fish
Manhattan Community College
City University of New York

PRIMARY WORKS

The West Indies: Being a Description of the Islands, Progress of Christianity, Education and Liberty Among the Colored Population Generally (Boston: Dow and Jackson, 1841); Nancy Prince, "To Mr. Garrison," Letter, *Liberator* (Boston), September 17, 1841; "To the Public," Letter, *Anti-Slavery Standard* (New York), May 25, 1843; *A Narrative of the Life and Travels of Mrs. Nancy Prince* (Boston: Published by the author, 1850); *A Narrative of the Life and Travels of Mrs. Nancy Prince, Written by Herself*, 1853, in *Collected Black Women's Narratives* (New York: Oxford University Press, 1988).

from A Narrative of the Life and Travels of Mrs. Nancy Prince

My mind, after the emancipation in the West Indies, was bent upon going to Jamaica. A field of usefulness seemed spread out before me. While I was thinking about it, the Rev. Mr. Ingraham, who had spent seven years there, arrived in the city. He lectured in the city at the Marlboro' Chapel, on the results arising from the emancipation at the British Islands. He knew much about them, he had a station at a mountain near Kingston, and was very desirous to have persons go there to labor. He wished some one to go with him to his station. He called on me with the Rev. Mr. William Collier, to persuade me to go. I told him it was my intention to go if I could make myself useful, but that I was sensible that I was very limited in education. He told me that the moral condition of the people was very bad, and needed labor aside from any thing else.

I left America, November 16th, 1840, in the ship Scion, Captain Mansfield, bound for Jamaica, freighted with ice and machinery for the silk factory. There were on board a number of handicraftsmen and other passengers. We sailed on Monday afternoon, from Charlestown, Massachusetts. It rained continually until Saturday. Sunday, the 23d, was a fine day. Mr. De Grass, a young colored clergyman, was invited to perform divine service, which he did with much propriety. He spoke of the dangers we had escaped and the importance of being prepared to meet our God, (he died of fever about three weeks after arriving at Jamaica,) some who were able to attend came on deck, and listened to him with respect, while others seemed to look on in derision; these spent the afternoon and evening in card-playing. About twelve at night a storm commenced; on Monday were in great peril; the storm continued until Friday, the 27th. On that day a sail was seen at some distance making towards us, the captain judging her to be a piratical vessel, ordered the women and children below, and the men to prepare for action. The pirates were not inclined to hazard an engagement; when they saw the deck filled with armed men they left us. Thus were we preserved from the storm and from the enemy. Sabbath, 29th, divine service,—our attention was directed to the goodness of God, in sparing us.

Monday, and we mortals are still alive. Tuesday, thus far the Lord had led us on. Wednesday, thus far his power prolongs our days. Thursday, December 3d, to-day made Turks Island. Friday, this day had a view of Hayti, its lofty mountains presented a sublime prospect. Saturday, we had a glance at Cuba. Sunday, December 6th, at six o'clock in the evening, dropped anchor at St. Ann Harbor, Jamaica. We blessed the Lord for his goodness in sparing us to see the place of our destination; and here I will mention my object in visiting Jamaica. I hoped that I might aid, in some small degree, to raise up and encourage the emancipated inhabitants, and teach the young children to read and work, to fear God, and put their trust in the Savior. Mr. Whitmarsh and his friend came on board and welcomed us. On Tuesday we went on shore to see the place and the people; my intention had been to go directly to Kingston, but the people urged me to stay with them, and I thought it my duty to comply, and wrote to Mr. Ingraham to that effect. I went first to see the minister, Mr. Abbott; I thought as he was out, I had better wait his return. The people promised to pay me for my services, or send me to Kingston. When Mr. Abbott returned he made me an offer, which I readily accepted. As I lodged in the house of one of the class-leaders I attended her class a few times, and when I learned the method, I stopped. She then commenced her authority and gave me to understand if I did not comply I should not have any pay from that society. I spoke to her of the necessity of being born of the spirit of God before we become members of the church of Christ, and told her I was sorry to see the people blinded in such a way.

She was very angry with me and soon accomplished her end by complaining of me to the minister; and I soon found I was to be dismissed, unless I would yield obedience to this class-leader. I told the minister that I did not come there to be guided by a poor foolish woman. He then told me that I had spoken something about the necessity of moral conduct in church members. I told him I had, and in my opinion, I was sorry to see it so much neglected. He replied, that he hoped I would not express myself so except to him; they have the gospel, he continued, and let them into the church. I do not approve of women societies; they destroy the world's convention; the American women have too many of them. I talked with him an hour. He paid me for the time I had been there. I continued with the same opinion, that something must be done for the elevation of the children, and it is for that I labor. I am sorry to say the meeting house is more like a play house than a place of worship. The pulpit stands about the middle of the building, behind me about six hundred children that belong to the society; there they are placed for Sabbath School, and there they remain until service is over, playing most of the time. The house is crowded with the aged and the young, the greater part of them barefooted. Some have on bonnets, but most of the women wear straw hats such as our countrymen wear.

I gave several Bibles away, not knowing that I was hurting the minister's sale, the people buy them of him at a great advance. I gave up my school at St. Ann, the 18th of March. I took the fever and was obliged to remain until the 7th of April. The people of St. Ann fulfilled their promise which they made to induce me to stop with them. On the 11th of April I arrived at Kingston, and was conducted to the Mico Institution, where Mr. Ingraham directed me to find him; he had lost his pulpit and his school, but Mr. Venning, the teacher kindly received me. I remained there longer than I expected; the next morning he kindly sent one of the young men with me to the packet for my baggage. I then called on the American Consul, he told me he was very glad to see me for such a purpose as I had in view visiting Jamaica, but he said it was folly for the Americans to come to the island to better their condition; he said they came to him every day praying him to send them home.

He likewise mentioned to me the great mortality among the emigrants. The same day I saw the Rev. J. S. Beadslee, one of our missionaries, who wished me to accompany him forty miles into the interior of the country.

On May the 18th, I attended the Baptist Missionary meeting, in Queen Street Chapel; the house was crowded. Several ministers spoke of the importance of sending the gospel to Africa; they complimented the congregation on their liberality the last year, having given one hundred pounds sterling; they hoped this year they would give five hundred pounds, as there were five thousand members at the present time. There was but one colored minister on the platform. It is generally the policy of these missionaries to have the sanction of colored ministers, to all their assessments and taxes. The colored people give more readily, and are less suspicious of imposition, if one from themselves recommends the measure; this the missionaries understand very well, and know how to take advantage of it. On the 22d and 23d of June, the colored Baptists held their missionary meeting, the number of ministers, colored and mulattoes, was 18, the colored magistrates were present. The resolutions that were offered were unanimously accepted, and every thing was done in love and harmony. After taking up a contribution, they concluded with song and prayer, and returned home saying jocosely, "they would turn macroon hunters."

Mack is the name of a small coin in circulation at Jamaica. I called, on my return, at the market, and counted the different stalls. For vegetables and poultry 196, all numbered and under cover; beside 70 on the ground; these are all attended by colored women. The market is conveniently arranged, as they can close the gates and leave all safe. There are nineteen stalls for fresh fish, eighteen for pork, thirty for beef, eighteen for turtle. These are all regular built markets, and are kept by colored men and women. These are all in one place. Others also may be found, as with us, all over the city. Thus it may be hoped they are not the stupid set of beings they have been called; here *surely we see industry;* they are enterprising and quick in their perceptions, determined to possess themselves, and to possess property besides, and quite able to take care of themselves. They wished to know why I was so inquisitive about them. I told them we had heard in America that you are lazy, and that emancipation has been of no benefit to you; I wish to inform myself of the truth respecting you, and give a true account on my return. Am I right? More than two hundred people were around me listening to what I said.

They thanked me heartily. I gave them some tracts, and told them if it so pleased God I would come back to them and bring them some more books, and try what could be done with some of the poor children to make them better. I then left them, and went to the East Market, where there are many of all nations. The Jews and Spanish looked at me very black. The colored people gathered around me. I gave them little books and tracts, and told them I hoped to see them again.

There are in this street upwards of a thousand young women and children, living in sin of every kind. From thence I went to the jail, where there were seventeen men, but no women. There were in the House of Correction three hundred culprits; they are taken from there, to work on plantations. I went to the Admiral's house, where the emigrants find a shelter until they can find employment, then they work and pay for their passage. Many leave their homes and come to Jamaica under the impression that they are to have their passage free, and on reaching the island are to be found, until they can provide for themselves.

How the mistake originated, I am not able to say, but on arriving here, strangers poor and unacclimated, find the debt for passage money hard and unexpected. It is remarkable that whether fresh from Africa, or from other islands, from the South or from New England, they all feel deceived on this point. I called on many Americans and found them poor and discontented,—rueing the day they left their country, where, notwithstanding many obstacles, their parents lived and died,—a country they helped to conquer with their toil and blood; now shall their children stray abroad and starve in foreign lands. . . .

Most of the people of Jamaica are emancipated slaves, many of them are old, worn out and degraded. Those who are able to work, have yet many obstacles to contend with, and very little to encourage them; every advantage is taken of their ignorance; the same spirit of cruelty is opposed to them that held them for centuries in bondage; even religious teaching is bartered for their hard earnings, while they are allowed but thirty-three cents a day, and are told if they will not work for that they shall not work at all; an extraordinary price is asked of them for every thing they may wish to purchase, even the Bibles are sold to them at a large advance on the first purchase. Where are their apologists, if they are found wanting in the strict morals that Christians ought to practice? Who kindly say, forgive them when they err. "Forgive them, this is the bitter fruit of slavery." Who has integrity sufficient to hold the balance when these poor people are to be weighed? Yet their present state is blissful, compared with slavery.

Many of the farmers bring their produce twenty or thirty miles. Some have horses or ponys, but most of them bring their burdens on their head. As I returned from St. Andrew's Mountain, where I had been sent for by a Mr. Rose, I was overtaken by a respectable looking man on horseback; we rode about ten miles in company. The story he told me of the wrongs he and his wife had endured while in slavery, are too horrible to narrate. My heart sickens when I think of it. He asked me many questions, such as where I came from? why I came to that Isle? where had I lived, &c. I told him I was sent for by one of the missionaries to help him in his school.

Indeed, said he, our color need the instruction. I asked him why the colored people did not hire for themselves? We would be very glad to, he replied, but our money is taken from us so fast we cannot. Sometimes they say we must all bring 1*l.*; to raise this, we have to sell at a loss or to borrow, so that we have nothing left for ourselves; the Macroon hunters take all—this is a nickname they give the missionaries and the class-leaders—a cutting sarcasm this!

Arrived at a tavern, about a mile from Kingston, I bade the man adieu, and stopped for my guide. The inn-keeper kindly invited me in; he asked me several questions, and I asked him as many. How do the people get along, and I, since the emancipation? The negroes, he replied, will have the island in spite of the d—. Do not you see how they live, and how much they can bear? We cannot do so. This man was an Englishman, with a large family of mulatto children. I returned with my mind fully made up what to do. Spent three weeks at the Mico establishment, and three with my colored friends from America. We thought something ought to be done for the poor girls that were destitute; they consulted with their friends, called a meeting, and formed a society of forty; each agreed to pay three dollars a year and collect, and provide a house, while I came back to America to raise the money for all needful articles for the school. Here I met Mr. Ingraham for the first time; he had come from the mountains, and his health had rapidly declined. Wishing to get his family home before the Lord took him away, he embarked for Baltimore in the Orb, and I sailed for Philadelphia, July 20th, 1841, twenty-one days from Jamaica, in good health. I found there, Fitz W. Sargent's family, from Gloucester, who I lived with when a little girl; they received me very kindly, and gave donations of books and money for that object.

I met the Anti Slavery Society at Mrs. Lucretia Motts, who took great interest in the cause. I visited among the friends, and spent my time very pleasantly. August 5th, I started for New York; arrived safely, and staid with an old friend; ascertained that Mr. Ingraham's family were at Newark, at Theodore Wells'. He died four days after his arrival. I was invited to Mrs. Ingraham's, (his cousin's widow) to spend a week. There I met with much encouragement to labor in the cause. Missionaries were coming and going, and all seemed to be interested in my object. Saturday evening I went to the bath room, where I left my neck ribbon: returning after it, I had the misfortune to fall through an open trap door, down fifteen feet, on hard coal. I had no light with me. I dislocated my left shoulder, and was generally very much bruised; my screams brought the girl to my assistance, and by the help of God she brought me out of the cellar; it was some time before a surgeon could be procured; at last Dr. Josselyn came to my relief, and set my shoulder. I was obliged to remain at Mrs. Ingraham's three weeks; as soon as I was able, I left there for Boston. I intended to have gone by the western boat, but by mistake got on board Captain Comstock's, and was exposed on deck all night in a damp east wind, and when I arrived at the landing I could not assist myself; a sailor, who saw and pitied my situation, kindly took care of me and my baggage, and, on my arrival in Boston, procured a carriage for me. If it had not been for his kindness, I know not how I should have got along.

As soon as I was able, I commenced my task of collecting funds for my Free Labor School in Jamaica. I collected in Boston and vicinity, in New York and Philadelphia, but not sufficient to make up the required sum, and I was obliged to take fifty dollars from my own purse, thinking that when I returned to Jamaica, they would refund the money to me. April 15th, embarked on board the brig Norma, of New York, for Jamaica. I arrived at Kingston May 6th, and found every thing different from what it was when I left; the people were in a state of agitation, several were hanged, and the insurrection was so great that it was found necessary to increase the army to quell it. Several had been hanged. On the very day I arrived a man was hanged for shooting a man as he passed through the street. Such was the state of things that it was not safe to be there.

A few young people met to celebrate their freedom on an open plain, where they hold their market; their former masters and mistresses, envious of their happiness, conspired against them, and thought to put them down by violence. This only served to increase their numbers; but the oppressors were powerful, and succeeded in accomplishing their revenge, although many of them were relations. There was a rule among the slave holders, to take care of the children they have by their slaves; they select them out and place them in asylums. Those who lived with their white fathers were allowed great power over their slave mothers and her slave children; my heart was often grieved to see their conduct to their poor old grand parents. Those over twenty-one were freed in 1834, all under twenty-one were to serve their masters till twenty-one. It is well known that at that time, the children, alike with others, received twenty-five dollars a head for their relatives. Were I to tell all my eyes have seen among that people, it would not be credited. It is well known that those that were freed, knowing their children were still in bondage, were not satisfied. In the year 1838, general freedom throughout the British Islands gave the death blow to the power of the master, and mothers received with joy their emancipated children; they no longer looked the picture of despair, fearing to see their mulatto son or daughter beating or abusing their younger brothers and sisters of a darker skin. On this occasion there was an outrage committed by those who were in power. What little the poor colored people had gathered during their four years of freedom, was destroyed by violence; their fences were broken down, and their horses and hogs taken from them. Most of the mulattoes and masters are educated, many of them are very poor, some are very rich; the property is left to the oldest daughter, she divides it with her brothers and sisters; since slavery ended many of them have married; those who are poor, and mean to live in sin, make for New Orleans and other slave States; many of the planters left the island when slavery was abolished. In June, 1841, a number of people arrived from Sierra Leone at Jamaica; these were Maroons who were banished from the island. They were some of the original natives who inhabited the mountains, and were determined to destroy the whites.

These Maroons would secret themselves in trees, and arrest the whites as they passed along; they would pretend to guide them, when they would beat and abuse them as the whites did their slaves; the English, finding themselves defeated in all their plans to subdue them, proposed to take them by craft. They made a feast in a large tavern in Kingston, and invited them to come. After they had eaten, they were invited on board three ships of war that were all ready to set sail for Sierra Leone; many of them were infants in their mother's arms, they were well taken care of by the English and instructed; they were removed about the year 1796—they are bright and intelligent; I saw and conversed with them; when they heard of the abolition of slavery, they sent a petition to Queen Victoria that they might return to Jamaica, which was granted. Several of them were very old when they returned; they were men and women when they left the island, they had not forgot the injuries they had received from the hands of man, nor the mercies of God to them, nor his judgments to their enemies. Their numbers were few, but their power was great; they say the island, of right, belongs to them. Had there been a vessel in readiness, I should have come back immediately, it seemed useless to attempt to establish a Manual Labor School, as the government was so unsettled that I could not be protected. Some of my former friends were gone as teachers to Africa, and some to other parts of the island. I called on the American Consul to consult with him, he said that although such a school was much wanted, yet every thing seemed so unsettled that I had no courage to proceed. I told him there was so much excitement that I wished to leave the island as soon as he could find me a passage, it seemed useless to spend my time there. As soon as it was known that I intended to return, a movement was made to induce me to remain. I was persuaded to try the experiment for three months, not thinking their motive was bad. Before I left the United States, I got all that was needed, within fifty dollars. The fifty dollars I got from my own purse, expecting they would pay me. It cost me ten dollars for freight, and twenty-five for passage money; these people that I had hoped to serve, were much taken up with all the things I had brought, they thought that I had money, and I was continually surrounded; the thought of color was no where exhibited, much notice was taken of me. I was invited to breakfast in one place, and to dine in another, &c. A society was organized, made up of men and women of authority. A constitution was drafted by my consent, by those who were appointed to meet at my rooms. Between the time of the adjournment they altered it to suit themselves. At the time appointed we came together with a spirit apparently becoming any body of Christians; most of them were members of Christian churches. The meeting was opened with reading the Scriptures and prayer. Then said the leader, since our dear sister had left her native land and her friends to come to us, we welcome her with our hearts and hands. She will dwell among us, and we will take care of her—Brethren think of it! after which he sat down, and the constitution was called for. The Preamble held out all the flattery that a fool could desire; after which they commenced the articles, supposing that they could do as they thought best. The fourth article unveiled their design. As we have designed to take care of our sister, *we the undersigned will take charge of all she has brought;* the vote was called, every person rose in a moment except myself: every eye was upon me; one asked me why I did not vote, I made no answer—they put the vote again and again, I remained seated. Well, said the President, we can do nothing without her vote; they remained some time silent, and then broke up the meeting. The next day the deacon called to see what the state of my mind was, and some of the women proposed that we should have another meeting. I told them no, I should do no more for them. As soon as they found they could not get the things in the way they intended, they started to plunder me; but I detected their design, and was on my guard. I disposed of the articles, and made ready to leave when an opportunity presented. A more skillful plan than this, Satan never designed, but the power of God was above it. It is not surprising that this people are full of deceit and lies, this is the fruits of slavery, it makes master and slaves knaves. It is the rule where slavery exists to swell the churches with numbers, and hold out such doctrines as, *obedience to tyrants*, is a duty to God. I went with a Baptist woman to the house of a minister of the Church of England, to have her grandchild christened before it died; she told me if she did not have it christened, it would rise up in judgment against her. This poor deluded creature was a class leader in the Baptist Church, and such is the condition of most of the people: they seemed blinded to every thing but money. They are great for trade, and are united in their determination for procuring property, of which they have amassed a vast amount. Notwithstanding I had made over various articles to one of the American missionaries, a Mr. J. S. O. Beadslee, of Clarendon Mountains, I also gave to others, where they were needed, which receipts and letters I have in my possession. Notwithstanding all this, they made another attempt to rob me, and as a passage could not be obtained for me to return home, I was obliged to go to the Mico establishment again for safety, such was the outrage. Houses were broken open and robbed every night. I came very near being shot: there was a certain place where we placed ourselves the first of the evening. A friend came to bring us some refreshments, I had just left the window when a gun was fired through it, by one that often sat with us; this was common in the time of slavery. Previous to vessels arriving, passages were engaged. I disposed of my articles and furniture at a very small profit. On the 1st of August, Capt. A. Miner arrived, and advertised for passengers. The American Consul procured me a passage, and on the 18th of August, myself and nine other passengers embarked for New York.

Before giving an account of the voyage from Jamaica, it may prove interesting to some readers, to have a brief description of the country. With her liberty secured to her, may she now rise in prosperity, morality, and religion, and become a happy people, whose God is the Lord. . . .

. . . After leaving Jamaica, the vessel was tacked to a south-west course. I asked the Captain what this meant. He said he must take the current as there was no wind. Without any ceremony, I told him it was not the case, and told the passengers that he had deceived us. There were two English men that were born on the island, that had never been on the water. Before the third day passed, they asked the Captain why they had not seen Hayti. He told them they passed when they were asleep. I told them it was not true, he was steering south south-west. The passengers in the steerage got alarmed, and every one was asking the Captain what this meant. The ninth day we made land. "By ____," said the Captain, "this is Key West; come, passengers, let us have a vote to run over the neck, and I will go ashore and bring aboard fruit and turtle." They all agreed but myself. He soon dropped anchor. The officers from the shore came on board and congratulated him on keeping his appointment, thus proving that my suspicions were well founded. The Captain went ashore with these men, and soon came back, called for the passengers, and asked for their vote for him to remain until the next day, saying that he could by this delay, make five or six hundred dollars, as there had been a vessel wrecked there lately. They all agreed but myself. The vessel was soon at the side of the wharf. In an hour there were twenty slaves at work to unload her; every inducement was made to persuade me to go ashore, or set my feet on the wharf. A law had just been passed there that every free colored person coming there, should be put in custody on their going ashore; there were five colored persons on board; none dared to go ashore, however uncomfortable we might be in the vessel, or however we might desire to refresh ourselves by a change of scene. We remained at Key West four days.

September 3d, we set sail for New York, at 3 o'clock in the afternoon. At 10 o'clock a gale took us, that continued thirty-six hours; my state-room was filled with water, and my baggage all upset; a woman, with her little boy, and myself, were seated on a trunk thirty-six hours with our feet pressed against a barrel to prevent falling; the water pouring over us at every breaker. Wednesday, the 9th, the sun shone out so that the Captain could take an observation. He found himself in great peril, near the coast of Texas. All hands were employed in pumping and bailing. On the eleventh, the New Orleans steamer came to our assistance; as we passed up the river, I was made to forget my own condition, as I looked with pity on the poor slaves, who were laboring and toiling, on either side, as far as could be seen with a glass. We soon reached the dock, and we were there on the old wreck a spectacle for observation; the whites went on shore and made themselves comfortable, while we poor blacks were obliged to remain on that broken, wet vessel. The people were very busy about me; one man asked me who I belonged to, and many other rude questions; he asked me where I was born; I told him Newburyport. "What were your parents' names?" I told him my father's name was Thomas Gardner; his countenance changed; said he, "I knew him well;" and he proved friendly to me. He appeared very kind, and offered to arrange my affairs so that I might return to New York through the States. I thought it best to decline his proposal, knowing my spirit would not suffer me to pass on, and see my fellow-creatures suffering without a rebuke. We remained four days on the wreck; the boxes that contained the sugar were taken out; the two bottom tiers were washed out clean. There were a great many people that came to see the vessel; they were astonished that she did not sink; they watched me very closely. I asked them what they wished. In the mean time, there came along a drove of colored people, fettered together in pairs by the wrist; some had weights, with long chains at their ankles, men and women, young and old. I asked them what that meant. They were all ready to answer. Said they, "these negroes have been impudent, and have stolen; some of them are free negroes from the northern ships;" "and what," I asked "are they there for?" "For being on shore, some of them at night." I asked them who made them Lord over God's inheritance. They told me I was very foolish; they should think I had suffered enough to think of myself. I looked pretty bad, it is true; I was seated on a box, but poorly dressed; the mate had taken my clothes to a washer-woman; why he took this care, he was afraid to send the cook or steward on shore, as they were colored people. I kept still; but the other woman seemed to be in perfect despair, running up and down the deck, wringing her hands and crying, at the thought of all her clothes being destroyed; then her mind dwelt upon other things, and she seemed as if she were deranged; she took their attention for a few minutes, as she was white. Soon the washer-woman came with my clothes; they spoke to her as if she had been a dog. I looked at them with as much astonishment as if I had never heard of such a thing. I asked them if they believe there was a God. "Of course we do," they replied. "Then why not obey him?" "We do." "You do not; permit me to say there is a God, and a just one, that will bring you all to account." "For what?" "For suffering these men that have just come in to be taken out of these vessels, and that awful sight I see in the streets." "O that is nothing; I should think you would be concerned about yourself." "I am sure," I replied, "the Lord will take care of me; you cannot harm me." "No; we do not wish to; we do not want you here." Every ship that comes in, the colored men are dragged to prison. I found it necessary to be stern with them; they were very rude; if I had not been so, I know not what would have been the consequences. They went off for that day; the next day some of them came again. "Good morning," said they; "we shall watch you like the d___ until you go away; you must not say any thing to these negroes whilst you are here." "Why, then, do you talk to me, if you do not want me to say any thing to you? If you will let me alone, I will you." "Let me see your protection," they replied, "they say it is under the Russian government." I pointed them to the 18th chapter of Revelations and 15th verse: "The merchants of these things which were made rich by her, shall stand afar off, for the fear of her torment, weeping and wailing. For strong is the Lord God who judgeth her." They made no answer, but asked the Captain how soon he should get away.

On the 17th, the Captain put eight of us on board the bark H. W. Tyler, for New York; we had about a mile to walk; the Captain was in honor bound to return us our passage money, which we had paid him at Jamaica; he came without it to see if we were there, and went away saying he would soon return with it; but we saw no more of him or our money! Our bark, and a vessel loaded with slaves, were towed down the river by the same steamer; we dropped anchor at the bottom of the bay, as a storm was rising. The 18th, on Sabbath, it rained all day. Capt. Tyler knocked at my door, wishing me to come out; it rained hard; the bulwark of the bark was so high I could not look over it; he placed something for me to stand on, that I might see the awful sight, which was the vessel of slaves laying at the side of our ship! the deck was full of young men, girls, and children, bound to Texas for sale! Monday, the 19th, Capt. Tyler demanded of us to pay him for our passage. I had but ten dollars, and was determined not to give it; he was very severe with all. I told him there were articles enough to pay him belonging to me. Those who had nothing, were obliged to go back in the steamer. Tuesday, the 20th, we set sail; the storm was not over. The 22nd the gale took us; we were dismasted, and to save sinking, sixty casks of molasses were stove in, and holes cut in the bulwarks to let it off. All the fowls, pigs, and fresh provisions were lost. We were carried seventy-five miles up the bay of Mexico. The Captain was determined not to pay the steamer for carrying him back to New Orleans, and made his way the best he could.

The 3d of October we arrived again at Key West. The Captain got the bark repaired, and took on board a number of turtles, and a plenty of brandy. Friday, the 7th, set sail for New York; the Captain asked me why I did not go ashore when there in the Comet; "had you," said he "they intended to beat you. John and Lucy Davenport, of Salem, laid down the first ten dollars towards a hundred for that person who should get you there." The Florida laws are about the same as those at New Orleans. He was very talkative: wished to know if I saw anything of the Creole's crew while at Jamaica. I told him they were all safe, a fine set of young men and women; one dear little girl, that was taken from her mother in Virginia, I should have taken with me, if I had had the money. He said his brother owned the Creole, and some of the slaves were his. "I never owned any; I have followed the sea all my life, and can tell you every port and town in your State."

October 19th, 1842, arrived at New York, and thankful was I to set my feet on land, almost famished for the want of food; we lost all of our provisions; nothing was left but sailors' beef, and that was tainted before it was salted. I went at once to those who professed to be friends, but found myself mistaken. I hardly knew what was best. I had put up at Mrs. Rawes'; she did all she could to raise the twenty-five dollars that I must pay before I could take my baggage from the vessel. This seemed hard to obtain; I traveled from one to another for three days; at last I called at the Second Advent office; Mr. Nath'l Southard left his business at once, and took me to Mr. Lewis Tappan, and others; he raised the money, and went with me to the ship after my baggage. It was three o'clock on Saturday afternoon when I called on Mr. Southard; the vessel and Captain belonged to Virginia, was all ready for sea, waiting for a wind; they had ransacked my things. I took from Jamaica forty dollars' worth of preserved fruits, part were lost when we were cast away in the Comet, and some they had stolen. At 8 o'clock on Saturday evening, I made out to have my things landed on the wharf; it was very dark, as it rained hard. My kind friend did not leave me until they were all safely lodged at my residence. I boarded there three weeks, thinking to come home; but it was thought best for me to wait, and see if Capt. Miner came or not, hoping that I might recover my loss through him. I took a room, and went to sewing, and found the people very kind.

February, 1843, the colored men that went back to New Orleans, for the want of passage money, arrived at New York, wearied out. All the white people remained there. I waited in New York until the last of July, when I started for Boston. August 1st, 1843, arrived, poor in health, and poor in purse, having sacrificed both, hoping to benefit my fellow creatures. I trust it was acceptable to God, who in his providence preserved me in perils by land, and perils by sea.

> "God moves in a mysterious way
> His wonders to perform;
> He plants his footsteps on the sea,
> And rides upon the storm.
>
> "Deep in unfathomable mines
> Of never failing skill,
> He treasures up his bright designs,
> And works his sovereign will."

1850

■ GEORGE FITZHUGH ■
1804–1881

George Fitzhugh lived out, before the Civil War, a decline of the sort that would be more typical of his class and race in the South after the war's end: the family's plantation in Virginia had to be sold in the 1820s, and his education came almost entirely by his own means. Yet Fitzhugh became a lawyer and, by the 1850s, began to publish what became a "steady stream" of defenses of the institution of slavery. Fitzhugh's thinking is notable in that it took the characteristic arguments for slavery to their logical extremes. If slavery was a positive good, if its effects were benevolent for the entire society, then—argued Fitzhugh—race should make no difference. Slavery was as good for whites as it was for blacks. "To justify her own social system," he wrote, "the South ... will have to justify the slavery principle ... as natural, normal, and necessitous.... In the absence of negro slavery there must be white slavery, else the white laboring class are remitted to slavery to capital, which is much more cruel and exacting than domestic slavery" (Faust, 277).

By 1856 Fitzhugh's work was well enough known to send him on a tour of the North to spread the word. Northerners were horrified at his "professed support for white as well as black slavery" (Faust, 273). Yet as the selection in this anthology shows, this argument does not deviate from so much as it extends the arguments for slavery that typified Southern thought. For slavery as a system was logically separable from race as a system.

Southerners rejected the "social contractual theories of Locke and the 'absurd' and 'dangerous' principles of the Declaration of Independence" (Faust, 273), believing instead that the healthy community depended on a particular sort of interdependence among its members. That interdependence, in turn, depended on very clear boundaries between social and economic entities: slave and master, for example, male and female, and—in many other apologists' thinking—black and white. Southern thought ascribed to each group a set of roles and responsibilities that it saw as natural and normal for that group's identity. The identities—seen to be equally natural and normal—established biological differences between sexes and races as well.

Contemporary interest in Fitzhugh and other less radical proslavery apologists comes in part from an awareness that these notions did not die with the Confederacy. The Agrarians, whose *I'll Take My Stand* is excerpted in the introduction to the modern period, picked up on their notions of interdependency and hierarchy, and in particular used these ideas—as had the proslavery apologists—to mount a critique of industrial capitalism. Thus the interest in proslavery writing today derives in part from what these arguments shared with other critiques, primarily Marxism, of the atomization of modern society. However "interested" their position, proslavery apologists saw, or said they saw, slavery to be a humane and economically feasible antidote to the dissociations of wage employment. In slavery, with its paternalistic "family black and white," even (they would say especially) a slave's needs were met by the system holistically, from birth to death, at work and away from it, in a community setting for which the factory could be no match. Of course, the fact of human ownership of other humans played a light part in these arguments; however, such ownership was justified by the Bible, according to the apologists, who pointed out their precedents in detail.

Fitzhugh, the most radical of the apologists, managed to eke out a living in various minor government positions—before the war in Washington at the attorney general's office, during it in the Confederacy in Richmond, and after it in the Freedmen's Bureau. In 1866 he left the Freedmen's Bureau to return to his war-devastated home in Port Royal, Virginia. His arguments against Reconstruction and emancipation began to take a virulently racist cast missing from his earlier separation of the issues. He sank into poverty and increasing silence, and died in 1881.

Anne G. Jones
Allegheny College

PRIMARY WORKS

Slavery Justified, 1851; *Sociology for the South*, 1854; "Southern Thought," *DeBow's Review* 23 (1857):338–50; "Southern Thought Again," *DeBow's Review* 23 (1857):449–62; *Cannibals All!*, 1957; *Ante-Bellum*, ed. Harvey Wish, 1960; *Slavery Defended*, ed. Eric McKitrick, 1963; *The Ideology of Slavery*, ed. Drew Gilpin Faust, 1981.

from **Sociology for the South**

It is clear the Athenian Democracy would not suit a Negro nation, nor will the government of mere law suffice for the individual Negro. He is but a grown-up child, and must be governed as a child, not as a lunatic or criminal. The master occupies towards him the place of parent or guardian. We shall not dwell on this view, for no one will differ with us who thinks as we do of the Negro's capacity, and we might argue till doomsday, in vain, with those who have a high opinion of the Negro's moral and intellectual capacity.

Second, the Negro is improvident; will not lay up in summer for the wants of winter; will not accumulate in youth for the exigencies of age. He would become an insufferable burden to society. Society has the right to prevent this, and can only do so by subjecting him to domestic slavery.

In the last place, the Negro race is inferior to the white race, and living in their midst, they would be far outstripped or outwitted in the chase of free competition. Gradual but certain extermination would be their fate. We presume the maddest abolitionist does not think the Negro's providence of habits and moneymaking capacity at all to compare to those of the whites. This defect of character would alone justify enslaving him, if he is to remain here. In Africa or the West Indies, he would become idolatrous, savage and cannibal, or be devoured by savages and cannibals. At the North he would freeze or starve.

We would remind those who deprecate . . . Negro slavery, that his slavery here relieves him from a far more cruel slavery in Africa, or from idolatry and cannibalism, and every brutal vice and crime that can disgrace humanity; and that it Christianizes, protects, supports, and civilizes him; that it governs him far better than free laborers at the North are governed.

1854

from **Southern Thought**

Twenty years ago the South had no thought—no opinions of her own. Then she stood behind all christendom, admitted her social structure, her habits, her economy, and her industrial pursuits to be wrong, deplored them as a necessity, and begged pardon for their existence. Now she is about to lead the thought and direct the practices of christendom; for christendom sees and admits that she has acted a silly and suicidal part in abolishing African slavery—the South a wise and prudent one in retaining it. France and England, who fairly represent the whole of so-called free society, are actively engaged in the slave-trade under more odious and cruel forms than were ever known before. They must justify their practices; and, to do so, must adopt and follow Southern thought. This, of itself, would put the South at the lead of modern civilization.

In the sneering ridicule of the false and fallacious philanthropy of Lord Brougham by the London Times, the leading paper of Western Europe, we see that they are breaking ground to condemn and repudiate the "rose-water philanthropy" of Clarkson, Wilbeforce, Howard, and Hannah More, that nursed scoundrels and savages at the expense of the honest, industrious, laboring whites.

The next inevitable step will be to approve and vindicate the conduct of Hercules, and Moses, and Joshua, and the discoverers and settlers of America, who have conquered, enslaved, and exterminated savages, just as fast as might be necessary to make room for free civilized whites. This is the only philosophy that can justify the subjugation of Algiers or the hundred southern conquests and annexations of England; and this philosophy is consistent with Southern thought and practices, but wholly at war with the maudlin sentimentality of Hannah More, Wilbeforce, and Lord Brougham. Southern thought alone can justify European practices, and Southern practices alone save Western Europe from universal famine; for cotton, sugar, rice, molasses, and other slave products are intolerably dear and intolerably scarce, and France and England must have slaves to increase their production, or starve. They have begun to follow in our wake, instead of our humbly imitating them. It is true they are still impertinent and presumptious, and loud in their abuse of our form of slavery, whilst they are busily adopting worse forms. But the veil of hypocrisy with which they would conceal their conduct is too transparent to avail them long. Besides, they can use no arguments to justify their conduct that will not equally justify ours. In any view of the subject Southern thought and Southern example must rule the world.

The South has acted wisely and prudently, acted according to the almost universal usage of civilized mankind, and the injunctions of the Bible, and she is about to gather her reward for so doing. She flourishes like the bay tree, whilst Europe starves, and she is as remarkable for her exemption from crime as her freedom from poverty. She is by far, very far, the most prosperous and happy country in the world. Her jealous and dependent rivals have begun to imitate her. They must soon openly approve her course in order to vindicate themselves.

But there is no narrow philosophy to justify slavery. No human or divine authority to vindicate mere negro slavery as an exceptional institution. All the authority is the other way. White slavery, not black, has been the normal element of civilized society. It is true that the authorities and the philosophy which approve white slavery, are still stronger authorities in favor of negro slavery, for the principle and the practices of mankind in the general have been to make inferior races and individuals slaves to their superiors. How fortunate for the South that she has this inferior race, which enables her to make the whites a privileged class, and to exempt them from all servile, menial, and debasing employments.

But we must force the reluctant admission from Western Europe that the emancipation of the white serfs or villians was a far more cruel failure, so far as those serfs were concerned, than West India emancipations.

In truth, the admission is made in fact, though not in form, in almost every review, newspaper, and work of fiction, that emanates from the press of Western Europe or our North. They concur in describing the emancipated whites as starving from year to year, and from generation to generation, whilst nobody pretends that the liberated negroes of the West Indies are starving. As for crime and ignorance, we suspect that the laboring liberated poor of Western Europe may well claim to rival, if not surpass, the negroes of Jamaica. But the liberated whites work harder and cheaper as freemen, or rather as slaves to capital, than they did as serfs; and, therefore, the rich who employ them think white emancipation a successful experiment, a glorious change for the better. Because, although it starves and brings to untimely graves some half million of the laboring poor annually, it nevertheless makes labor cheaper, and increases the profits of the rich.

We despise this flood of crocodile tears which England is shedding over the free negroes of the West Indies, whilst she has not one tear to shed on account of her laboring poor at home, who are ten times worse off than the free negroes.

In the absence of negro slavery there must be white slavery, else the white laboring class are remitted to slavery to capital, which is much more cruel and exacting than domestic slavery.

Southern thought must justify the slavery principle, justify slavery as natural, normal, and necessitous. He who justifies mere negro slavery, and condemns other forms of slavery, does not think at all—no, not in the least. To prove that such men do not think, we have only to recur to the fact that they always cite the usages of antiquity and the commands of the Bible to prove that negro slavery is right. Now if these usages and commands prove anything, they prove that all kinds of slavery are right.

By Southern thought, we mean a Southern philosophy, not excuses, apologies, and palliations.

The South has much work before her, for to justify her own social system, she will have to disprove and refute the whole social, ethical, political, and economical philosophy of the day. These philosophies have grown up in societies whose social relations are different from hers, and are intended to enforce and justify those relations. They all inculcate selfishness and competition as the great duties of man, and success in getting the better of our fellow beings in the war of the wits as the chiefest, if not the only merit. The opposite or protective philosophy, which takes care of the weak whilst it governs them, is the philosophy of the South.

The free trade or competitive philosophy is an admitted failure, and most of the literature of Europe is employed in exposing and condemning it. From the writings of the socialists, (and almost everybody is a socialist in Western Europe,) we can derive both facts and arguments quite sufficient to upset the whole moral philosophy of the day. From the Bible and Aristotle we can deduce (added to our own successful experiment) quite enough to build up a new philosophy on the ruins of the present false and vicious system.

The South is fulfilling her destiny and coming up to her work beautifully. She is multiplying her academies, her colleges, and her universities, and they are all well patronised and conducted by able professors. Several of these professors have written works defending slavery with great ability, on general and scientific principles. All of them are true to Southern institutions. From these schools thousands of educated and influential men annually proceed to every quarter of the South. They will mould and control thought and opinion, whether they settle down as private citizens or become editors, lawyers, divines, or politicians.

Female schools and colleges are also rapidly increasing in numbers, and this is an important gain, for it is the mother who first affects opinions, and it is difficult in after life to get rid even of erroneous principles which have been taught by the mother in the nursery. It is not safe, wise, or prudent, to commit the education of our daughters to Northern schools, nor to female teachers brought from the North.

Fashion is one of the most powerful engines in controlling opinion, and fashion will soon cease to be borrowed from the North. Southern watering places are full to overflowing, and few go to the North to be insulted by the helps in their hotels. These Southern watering places annually bring together intelligent and influential persons from the various States of the South, who form friendships, unite various sections in stronger bonds of amity, and confirm each other in the support of Southern institutions, by comparison and concurrence of opinion. People do not like to be out of the fashion in thought any more than in dress, and hence the prevalent anti-slavery doctrines at Northern watering places, must exercise a baleful and dangerous influence on Southerners who visit them.

The educational conventions held in various parts of the South exercise a similar influence to our watering places, but a far more important and potent one, for they are attended by the ablest men in the nation, whose every day business, duty, and occupation, is to form opinion, and to inaugurate a Southern thought. The importance of these conventions in cutting us off from imitative allegiance to the North and to Europe can hardly be overrated. Nay, they will do more; they will teach our revilers to respect, admire, and imitate us, by the unanswerable facts and arguments which they will adduce to justify our institutions.

Another fact for congratulation to the South is, that our people are beginning to write books—to build up a literature of our own. This is an essential prerequisite to the establishment of independence of thought amongst us. All Northern and European books teach abolition either directly or indirectly. The indirect method is more dangerous than the direct one. It consists in inculcating doctrines at war with slavery, without expressly assailing the institution. Now, all authors who write about law, religion, politics, ethics, social or political economy, if not pro-slavery men themselves, are continually inculcating doctrines accordant with their own social forms, and therefore at war with ours. Hence it follows, that all books in the whole range of moral science, if not written by Southern authors, within the last twenty or thirty years, inculcate abolition either directly or indirectly. If written before that time, even by Southern authors, they are likely to be as absurd and as dangerous as the Declaration of Independence, or the Virginia Bill of Rights.

It is all important that we should write our own books. It matters little who makes our shoes. Indeed, the South will commit a fatal blunder, if, in its haste to become nominally independent, it loses its present engines of power, and thereby ceases to be really independent. Cotton is king; and rice, sugar, Indian corn, wheat, and tobacco, are his chief ministers. It is our great agricultural surplus that gives us power, commands respect, and secures independence. The world is pinched now for agricultural products. The rebellion in India will increase the scarcity. Then, take away our surplus from the world's supply, and famine and nakedness would be the consequence. We should not jeopard this great lever of power in the haste to become, like Englishmen, shop-keepers, cobblers, and common carriers for the universe. Our present pursuits are more honorable, more lucrative, and more generative of power and independence than those we fondly aspire to. We cannot do double work. If we become a commercial and manufacturing people, we must cease to be an agricultural one, or at least we shall cease to have an agricultural surplus. We should become as feeble, as isolated and contemptible as Chinese or Japanese. Actual independence would be bartered off for formal independence, which no one would respect. An increase in our commerce and manufactures, so gradual as not to affect the amount of our agricultural surplus, would be desirable, provided that increase never extends so far as to make us a commercial and manufacturing people. That we can be all three is one of the most palpable absurdities ever conceived by the human brain. Foreigners cannot buy from us unless we buy an equivalent amount from them. If they should do so, our agricultural surplus would absorb the whole currency of the world in less than a century, and we should be oppressed with a plethora of money that would necessitate the carrying about a cart-load of silver to buy an ox.

We can afford to let foreigners be our cobblers, and carriers, and tradesmen for a while longer, but we cannot safely delay writing our own books for an hour.

In Congress, and in the courts of Europe, in the conflict of debate, and in the war of diplomacy, Southerners have always shown themselves the equals, generally the superiors, of the first intellects of the world. This is easily accounted for.

All true power, whether in speaking, writing, or fighting, proceeds quite as much from strength of will as from power of mind or body; and no men have half the strength of will that Southerners possess. We are accustomed to command from our cradle. To command becomes a want and a necessity of our nature, and this begets that noble strength of will that nerves the mind for intellectual conflict and intellectual exertion, just as it nerves the body for physical contest. We are sure to write well, because we shall write boldly, fearlessly, and energetically.

We have already made a start. A great many Southern books have been written within the last three or four years. They are almost all distinguished by that boldness of thought, and close and energetic logic, which characterizes the Southern mind. The North surpasses us in taste and imagination, equals us in learning, but is far behind us in logic. No doubt our greater intensity of will gives us this advantage, for in no intellectual effort is force of will so absolutely necessary as in moral reasoning. It is the most difficult intellectual exercise, and therefore the most perfect self-control and self-command are required to nerve to high effort in this direction.

Several of our distinguished professors are employed in preparing school books for academies and common schools, and text books for our colleges. It is all important to "teach the young idea how to shoot," and to give it, in early life, a Southern bent. We have been guilty of great remissness on this subject, but we shall speedily repair it, and soon no more school books from Europe or the North will be seen south of Mason's and Dixon's line. . . .

These conventions are composed of able, patriotic, and conservative men. Their proceeding, though firm, are calm, dignified, and moderate. They represent Southern feeling and opinion correctly, and excluding Russia, the South is the only conservative section of civilized christendom. The democracy of the North, it is true, are conservative, but there Black Republicanism is in the ascendant, and that is radical and revolutionary in the extreme. The Pope of Rome is a radical reformer. Louis Napoleon and Victoria are halfway socialists, and Henry the Fifth, the Bourbon heir to the French throne, is a thorough socialist. So desperate is the condition of the people throughout Western Europe, that no one in power dare tell them that there shall be no change, that all things shall remain as they are. The South is the only conservative section of christendom, because it is the only section satisfied with its own condition. Every where else, except in our North, the people are suffering intolerable ills, and ripe, at any moment, for revolution. There is no occasion for radicalism and revolutionary spirit at the North. Next to the South, it is the most prosperous, and should be the most contented country in the world. All of its discontent, and its political, moral, and religious heresies have grown out of abolition. Men who begin by assailing negro slavery find that all government begets slavery in some form, and hence all abolitionists are socialists, who propose to destroy all the institutions of society.

That slavery to capital, so intolerable in densely settled countries, where lands are monopolised by the few, can never be felt at the North, until our vast possessions in the West are peopled to the Pacific, and a refluent population begins to pour back upon the East. Then, like Western Europe, the North would have a laboring population slaves to capital, "slaves without masters." Famine would become perennial, and revolution the common order of the day, as in Western Europe. Nay, the condition of the laboring class of the North-east, would be far worse than in Europe, because there would be no checks to competition, no limitations to the despotism of capital over labor. The spirit of trade and commerce is universal, and it is as much the business of trade to devour the poor, as of the whales to swallow herrings. All its profits are derived from unjust exacting or "exploitation" of the common poor laboring class; for the professional and capitalist, and skilful laboring classes, manage to exact five times as much from the poor, as they pay to the tradesmen in way of profit. The poor produce everything and enjoy nothing. The people of the North are hugging to their breasts a silly delusion, in the belief that the poor can tax the rich, and thus prevent those evils that are starving and maddening the masses in Western Europe. You can't tax a rich man unless he be a slave-holder, because he produces nothing. You can't tax property, except in slave society, because it does not breed or produce anything itself. Labor pays all taxes, pays the rich man's income, educates his children, pays the professional man's fees, the merchant's profits, and pays all the taxes which support the Government; a property tax must take a part of the property proposed to be taxed, and such a tax never will be imposed; a property tax would soon divest all men of their property.

Gerrit Smith said most truly in Congress: "The poor pay all taxes, we (meaning the rich) are the mere conduits who pass them over to government." This was the noblest and the grandest truth that ever was uttered on the floor of legislative hall. It is this awful truth that is shaking free society to its base, and it will never recover from the shock. 'Tis now tottering to its fall. Property and not labor is taxed in slave society. 'Tis true the negro produces the wherewithal to pay the tax, but he loses nothing by it. Neither his food or his raiment are abridged. Both humanity and self-interest prevent the master from lowering his wages. The master pays the tax by abridging his own expenses. He has less of food and raiment, not the slave. The capitalist charges higher rents and profits to meet increased taxation, and lives as expensively as ever. The employer reduces the wages of his laborers for the same purpose, and dines and sups as luxuriously as ever.

Labor pays all taxes, but labor in slave society is property, and men will take care of their property. In free society, labor is not property, and there is nothing to shield the laborer from the grinding weight of taxation—all of which he pays, because he produces everything valuable.

We have made this digression to show that if the North ever becomes densely settled, there is no mode of escaping from the evils of free competition and from the taxing power or exploitation of skill and capital. In Europe, competition is not so fierce, the spirit of trade not so universal. They have still kings, nobles, and established churches, stripped, it is true of their fair proportions, reduced somewhat to the semblance of shadowy "phantasms;" yet, still, as the natural friends of the poor, interposing some check to the unfeeling exactions of the landholder, the tradesman, and the employer. In the palmy days of royalty, of feudal nobility, and of catholic rule, there were no poor in Europe. Every man had his house and his home, and both his brave and his pious protectors. The baron and the priest vied with each other in their care of the vassal. This was feudal slavery; and what is modern liberty? Why, quietly, slowly, almost insensibly, the poor have been turned over from the parental and protective rule of kings, barons, and churchmen, to the unfeeling despotism of capitalists, employers, usurers, and extortioners; and this was called emancipation!

Although, in the event of a dense population cooped up in the North, without means of escape, the evils which we have depicted, would occur more virulently there than in Europe; yet, it is not worth while to anticipate evils that may never happen. The North is now doing well. Her poor are not the slaves of capital, and never will be whilst there are vacant lands in the North. Population does not always increase. It has its ebbs and flows. Very large countries, such as America, are not likely to be overstocked with inhabitants. Secret causes at work will diminish population in some sections, whilst it is increasing in others. The situation of the North is natural, healthful, and progressive, but for the abolitionists and other agrarian isms. 'Tis treason in them to disturb society by the unnecessary agitation of questions as to contingent and future evils. But this is not their only treason. They propose, in their conventions, to dissolve the Union, not for any evils with which it afflicts them, but because the South hold slaves. Now, Black Republicans, who are under the rule of abolitionists, if not all abolitionists themselves, are radical and revolutionary in their doctrines, and dangerous to the Union; whilst Southern Commercial Conventions are composed entirely of men of the opposite character, of enlightened conservatives. . . .

Southern thought must be a distinct thought—not a half thought, but a whole thought. Domestic slavery must be vindicated in the abstract, and in the general, as a normal, natural, and, *in general*, necessitous element of civilized society, without regard to race or color.

This argument about races is an infidel procedure, and we had better give up the negroes than the Bible. It is a double assertion of the falsity of the Bible—first, as it maintains that mankind have not sprang from a common parentage; and, secondly, as it contends that it is morally wrong to enslave white men, who, the Bible informs us, were enslaved by the express command of God. But it is also utterly falsified by history. The little States of Greece, in their intestine wars, made slaves of their prisoners, and there was no complaint that they did not make good slaves; whilst the Macedonians, an inferior race, were proverbially unfit for slavery. The Georgians and Circassians, the most beautiful of the human family, make excellent slaves, whilst the Bedouin Arab and American Indian are as unfit for slavery as the Bengal tiger, or those tribes in Palestine whom God commanded Moses and Joshua to put to the sword without discrimination or mercy.

Again: to defend and justify mere negro slavery, and condemn other forms of slavery, is to give up expressly the whole cause of the South—for mulattoes, quadroons, and men with as white skins as any of us, may legally be, and in fact are, held in slavery in every State of the South. The abolitionists well know this, for almost the whole interest of Mrs. Stowe's Uncle Tom's Cabin, arises from the fact, that a man and woman, with fair complexion, are held as slaves.

We are all in the habit of maintaining that our slaves are far better off than the common laborers of Europe, and that those laborers were infinitely better situated as feudal serfs or slaves than as freemen, or rather as slaves to capital. Now, we stultify ourselves if we maintain it would be wrong to remit them back to domestic slavery, which we always argue is much milder and protective than that slavery to capital, to which emancipation has subjected them. They have been wronged and injured by emancipation, would we not restore them to slavery? Or are we, too, to become Socialists, and coop them up in Greely's Free-Love phalansteries? There are no other alternatives.

Again: every Southern man in defending slavery, habitually appeals to the almost universal usages of civilized man, and argues that slavery must be natural to man, and intended by Providence as the condition of the larger portion of the race, else it could not have been so universal. What a ridiculous and absurd figure does the defender of mere negro slavery cut, who uses this argument, when the abolitionist turns round on him and says— "why, you have just admitted that white slavery was wrong, and this universal usage which you speak of has been white, not black slavery. The latter is a very recent affair."

We must defend the principle of slavery as part of the constitution of man's nature. The defence of mere negro slavery, will, nay, has involved us in a thousand absurdities and contradictions. We must take high philosophical, biblical, and historical grounds, and soar beyond the little time and space around us to the earliest records of time, and the farthest verge of civilization. Let us quit the narrow boundaries of the rice, the sugar and the cotton field, and invite the abolitionists to accompany us in our flight to the tent of Abraham, to the fields of Judea, to the halls of David and of Solomon, to the palaces and the farms of Athens and of Rome, and to the castles of the grim Barons of medieval time. Let us point to their daily routine of domestic life. Then, not till then, may we triumphantly defend negro slavery. "You see slavery everywhere, and throughout all times: you see men subjected to it by express command or by permission of God, with skins as white and intellects as good as yours. Can it be wrong to enslave the poor negro, who needs a master more than any of these?" Less than this is inconsiderate assertion, not Southern thought; nay, not thought at all.

The temptation to confine the defence of slavery to mere negro slavery is very strong, for it is obvious that they require masters under all circumstances, whilst the whites need them only under peculiar circumstances, and those circumstances such as we can hardly realize the existence of in America. May the day never arrive when our lands shall be so closely monopolized, and our population become so dense, that the poor would find slavery a happy refuge from the oppression of capital.

In the South, there is another and a stronger reason for the feeling of indignation at the bare suggestion of white slavery—that is pride of caste. No man loves liberty and hates slavery so cordially as the Southerner. Liberty is with him a privilege, or distinction, belonging to all white men.

Slavery a badge of disgrace attached to an inferior race. Accustomed from childhood to connect the idea of slavery with the negro, and of liberty with the white man, it shocks his sensibilities barely to mention white slavery. 'Tis vain to talk to him of the usages of mankind, for his prejudices and pre-possessions were formed long before he heard of history, and they are too strong to be reasoned away.

This peculiarity of Southerners, and other slaveholders, is admirably described by Burke, who was the most philosophic and farseeing statesman of modern times. He says, "in Virginia and the Carolinas they have a vast multitude of slaves. Where this is the case in any part of the world, those who are free are by far the most proud and jealous of their freedom. Freedom is to them not only an enjoyment, but a kind of rank and privilege. Not seeing then that freedom, as in countries where it is a common blessing, and as broad and general as the air, may be united with much abject toil, with great misery, with all the exterior of servitude, liberty looks among them as something more noble and liberal. I do not mean to commend the superior morality of this sentiment, which has at least as much pride as virtue in it; but I cannot alter the nature of man. The fact is so; and those people of the Southern colonies are much more strongly, and with a more stubborn spirit attached to liberty, than those to the Northward. Such were all the ancient commonwealths; such were our Gothic ancestry; such, in our days, were the Poles; and such will be all masters of slaves who are not slaves themselves. In such a people, haughtiness of domination combines with the spirit of freedom, fortifies it, and renders it invisible."

1857

■ FRANCES ELLEN WATKINS HARPER ■
1825–1911

The long and remarkable career of Frances Ellen Watkins Harper ran from the middle of the nineteenth into the beginning of the twentieth century. Over her lifetime, she was directly involved in abolitionism, the Underground Railroad, the temperance movement, the labor for black education and economic self-determination, the antilynching movement, and the campaign for women's suffrage. Harper demonstrated in her life and work a fusion between her artistic and political lives. She refused to separate the two. Political issues suffused her literary creations; literary selections (especially poems that she wrote) laced her political speeches. Ardent activist, groundbreaking writer, and brilliant artist in the oral tradition, she stands as a model of integrated aesthetic and political commitment.

The only child of free parents, Frances Ellen Watkins was born in Baltimore, Maryland, a slaveholding state, where she witnessed slavery firsthand as she was growing up. Orphaned at three, she was adopted by an aunt and uncle, who ran a school for free blacks which she attended until the age of fourteen. At that time, she hired out as a domestic to a Baltimore family. Already a writer while still in her teens, she published a volume of poetry at sixteen, *Forest Leaves* (also cited as *Autumn Leaves*), no copies of which are known to exist.

She left the South in 1850, settling in a free state, Ohio, where she took a teaching job at Union Seminary near Columbus (relocated, this institution would become Wilberforce University). After a few years, she moved to Little York, Pennsylvania. When a law was passed in 1853 forbidding free blacks to enter Maryland without risking capture and sale, she became intensely involved in antislavery work. Vowing to fight slavery in whatever way she could, she immersed herself in the stories of runaway slaves arriving on the Underground Railroad and became a friend and colleague of William Still, later famous as the author of the monumental 1872 history *The Underground Railroad*.

Probably at this point, political passion and her calling as an artist truly began to fuse for Harper. With the delivery of her first antislavery speech in August 1854 in New Bedford, Massachusetts, "The Education and Elevation of the Colored Race," she inaugurated the long and brilliant public-speaking career that before the Civil War would carry her through Massachusetts, Pennsylvania, New York, New Jersey, Ohio, and Maine, where she was engaged by the state Anti-Slavery Society as a full-time lecturer. In 1860 in Cincinnati, she married a widower, Fenton Harper, who had two children, and settled with him on a farm she helped purchase outside Columbus. When he died four years later, she and their baby, Mary, moved to Philadelphia, where she resumed the teaching and anti-slavery work she had begun before her marriage.

Harper's brilliance as an artist in the oral tradition is testified to by contemporary descriptions. She spoke at length—up to two hours—without a written text (thereby leaving few verbatim records of her speeches). She is pictured by one audience member, Grace Greenwood (Sara J. Lippincott), quoted in William Still's book, as standing quietly beside her desk "with gestures few and fitting. Her manner is marked by dignity and composure. She is never assuming, never theatrical. . . . The woe of two hundred years sighed through her tones. Every glance of her sad eyes was a mournful remonstrance against injustice and wrong." Although she met with discrimination—she would later report that some listeners refused to believe she was a woman or that she was really black—Harper was hugely successful as an orator, at one point in 1854 giving at least thirty-three speeches in twenty-one different towns and cities in a six-week period.

Highly gifted as well in the written tradition, Harper was America's best-known and most popular black poet between Phillis Wheatley and Paul Laurence Dunbar. Publishing four volumes of poetry as an adult, she wrote about many topics, characteristically focusing on black characters and experiences, slavery, lynching, temperance, Christianity, or moral reform. As a poet, she worked in both the popular and high-culture traditions, often aiming in her work to stimulate in the reader a vivid emotional response, such as anger, pity, horror, exaltation, or compassion. She incorporated into her poetry African American oral subject matter and techniques and also used the conventions of sentimentalism—ultra regular rhyme and rhythm, elaborate and even artificial language, direct apostrophal exclamations—to bring black and poor people's experiences into the mainstream, which in terms of popular published poetry in the United States in the nineteenth century prized rather than avoided the indulgence of feeling. Her poems on slavery in this volume, for example, appeal directly and boldly to her readers' emotions of sympathy, outrage, shame, and patriotic pride.

As a fiction writer, Harper's position in American literary history is preeminent. Her 1859 short story "The Two Offers" is thought to be the first short story published by a black person in the United States. It appeared in the *Anglo-African Magazine*, a publication founded in 1859 by Thomas Hamilton and committed to printing the work only of black writers. Perhaps because of the freedom created by that policy, the story does not deal with racial issues; it focuses instead on the problems of drunkenness, wife abuse, and child neglect and the pressure on women to marry, even if the marriage in question is destructive. Grounded in the middle-class nineteenth-century feminine ideology that some historians have labeled the cult of "true womanhood," an ideology that praised the superior piety, domesticity, and moral rectitude of Christian womanhood, the story argues that dignity and happiness are available to the woman who remains single.

Following the Civil War, Harper did not diminish her commitment as a political activist, orator, poet, and fiction writer; she continued to be celebrated as the most popular and best-known black American poet of the nineteenth century and published her best-known long work, *Iola Leroy*, in 1892. Some of Harper's later works are included in the Volume C of this anthology. She died of heart disease in Philadelphia at the age of eighty-six and is buried there in Eden Cemetery.

Elizabeth Ammons
Tufts University

PRIMARY WORKS

Poems on Miscellaneous Subjects, 1854; "The Two Offers," 1859 (short story); *Sketches of Southern Life*, 1872 (poems); *Iola Leroy; or Shadows Uplifted*, 1892 (novel); *The Martyr of Alabama and Other Poems*, 1894; *Complete Poems of Frances E. W. Harper*, ed. Maryemma Graham, 1988; *A Brighter Day Coming: A Frances Ellen Watkins Harper Reader*, ed. Frances Smith Foster, 1990; *Minnie's Sacrifice, Sowing and Reaping, Trial and Triumph: Three Rediscovered Novels*, ed. Frances Smith Foster, 1994.

The Slave Mother

Heard you that shriek? It rose
   So wildly on the air,
It seemed as if a burden'd heart
   Was breaking in despair.

Saw you those hands so sadly clasped—   5
    The bowed and feeble head—
The shuddering of that fragile form—
    That look of grief and dread?

Saw you the sad, imploring eye?
    Its every glance was pain,   10
As if a storm of agony
    Were sweeping through the brain.

She is a mother, pale with fear,
    Her boy clings to her side,
And in her kirtle vainly tries   15
    His trembling form to hide.

He is not hers, although she bore
    For him a mother's pains;
He is not hers, although her blood
    Is coursing through his veins!   20

He is not hers, for cruel hands
    May rudely tear apart
The only wreath of household love
    That binds her breaking heart.

His love has been a joyous light   25
    That o'er her pathway smiled,
A fountain gushing ever new,
    Amid life's desert wild.

His lightest word has been a tone
    Of music round her heart,   30
Their lives a streamlet blent in one—
    Oh, Father! must they part?

They tear him from her circling arms,
    Her last and fond embrace.
Oh! never more may her sad eyes   35
    Gaze on his mournful face.

No marvel, then, these bitter shrieks
    Disturb the listening air:
She is a mother, and her heart
    Is breaking in despair.   40

1857

The Tennessee Hero

"He had heard his comrades plotting to obtain their liberty, and rather than betray them he received 750 lashes and died."

He stood before the savage throng,
    The base and coward crew;
A tameless light flashed from his eye,
    His heart beat firm and true.

He was the hero of his band,   5
    The noblest of them all;
Though fetters galled his weary limbs,
    His spirit spurned their thrall.

And towered, in its manly might,
    Above the murderous crew.   10
Oh! liberty had nerved his heart,
    And every pulse beat true.

"Now tell us," said the savage troop,
    "And life thy gain shall be!
Who are the men that plotting, say—   15
    'They must and will be free!'"

Oh, could you have seen the hero then,
    As his lofty soul arose,
And his dauntless eyes defiance flashed
    On his mean and craven foes!   20

"I know the men who would be free;
    They are the heroes of your land;
But death and torture I defy,
    Ere I betray that band.

And what! oh, what is life to me,   25
    Beneath your base control?
Nay! do your worst. Ye have no chains
    To bind my free-born soul."

They brought the hateful lash and scourge,
    With murder in each eye.   30
But a solemn vow was on his lips—
    He had resolved to die.

Yes, rather than betray his trust,
    He'd meet a death of pain;
'T was sweeter far to meet it thus   35
    Than wear a treason stain!

Like storms of wrath, of hate and pain,
    The blows rained thick and fast;
But the monarch soul kept true
    Till the gates of life were past.   40

And the martyr spirit fled
    To the throne of God on high,
And showed his gaping wounds
    Before the unslumbering eye.

                       1857

Free Labor

I wear an easy garment,
    O'er it no toiling slave
Wept tears of hopeless anguish,
    In his passage to the grave.

And from its ample folds   5
    Shall rise no cry to God,
Upon its warp and woof shall be
    No stain of tears and blood.

Oh, lightly shall it press my form,
    Unladened with a sigh,   10
I shall not 'mid its rustling hear,
    Some sad despairing cry.

This fabric is too light to bear
    The weight of bondsmen's tears,
I shall not in its texture trace   15
    The agony of years.

Too light to bear a smother'd sigh,
    From some lorn woman's heart,
Whose only wreath of household love
    Is rudely torn apart.   20

Then lightly shall it press my form,
    Unburden'd by a sigh;

And from its seams and folds shall rise,
  No voice to pierce the sky,

And witness at the throne of God,   25
  In language deep and strong,
That I have nerv'd Oppression's hand,
  For deeds of guilt and wrong.

                                                                    1857

The Colored People in America

Having been placed by a dominant race in circumstances over which we have
had no control, we have been the butt of ridicule and the mark of oppression.
Identified with a people over whom weary ages of degradation have passed,
whatever concerns them, as a race, concerns me. I have noticed among our
people a disposition to censure and upbraid each other, a disposition which
has its foundation rather, perhaps, in a want of common sympathy and consideration, than mutual hatred, or other unholy passions. Born to an inheritance of misery, nurtured in degradation, and cradled in oppression, with the
scorn of the white man upon their souls, his fetters upon their limbs, his
scourge upon their flesh, what can be expected from their offspring, but a
mournful reaction of that cursed system which spreads its baneful influence
over body and soul; which dwarfs the intellect, stunts its development,
debases the spirit, and degrades the soul? Place any nation in the same condition which has been our hapless lot, fetter their limbs and degrade their souls,
debase their sons and corrupt their daughters, and when the restless yearnings for liberty shall burn through heart and brain—when, tortured by wrong
and goaded by oppression, the hearts that would madden with misery, or
break in despair, resolve to break their thrall, and escape from bondage, then
let the bay of the bloodhound and the scent of the human tiger be upon their
track;—let them feel that, from the ceaseless murmur of the Atlantic to the
sullen roar of the Pacific, from the thunders of the rainbow-crowned Niagara
to the swollen waters of the Mexican gulf, they have no shelter for their
bleeding feet, or resting-place for their defenceless heads;—let them, when
nominally free, feel that they have only exchanged the iron yoke of oppression for the galling fetters of a vitiated public opinion;—let prejudice assign
them the lowest places and the humblest positions, and make them "hewers
of wood and drawers of water;"—let their income be so small that they must
from necessity bequeath to their children an inheritance of poverty and a limited education,—and tell me, reviler of our race! censurer of our people! if
there is a nation in whose veins runs the purest Caucasian blood, upon whom
the same causes would not produce the same effects; whose social condition,
intellectual and moral character, would present a more favorable aspect than
ours? But there is hope; yes, blessed be God! for our down-trodden and
despised race. Public and private schools accommodate our children; and in

my own southern home, I see women, whose lot is unremitted labor, saving a pittance from their scanty wages to defray the expense of learning to read. We have papers edited by colored editors, which we may consider it an honor to possess, and a credit to sustain. We have a church that is extending itself from east to west, from north to south, through poverty and reproach, persecution and pain. We have our faults, our want of union and concentration of purpose; but are there not extenuating circumstances around our darkest faults—palliating excuses for our most egregious errors? and shall we not hope, that the mental and moral aspect which we present is but the first step of a mighty advancement, the faintest corruscations of the day that will dawn with unclouded splendor upon our down-trodden and benighted race, and that ere long we may present to the admiring gaze of those who wish us well, a people to whom knowledge has given power, and righteousness exaltation?

1857

Speech: On the Twenty-Fourth Anniversary of the American Anti-Slavery Society

Could we trace the record of every human heart, the aspirations of every immortal soul, perhaps we would find no man so imbruted and degraded that we could not trace the word liberty either written in living characters upon the soul or hidden away in some nook or corner of the heart. The law of liberty is the law of God, and is antecedent to all human legislation. It existed in the mind of Deity when He hung the first world upon its orbit and gave it liberty to gather light from the central sun.

Some people say set the slaves free. Did you ever think, if the slaves were free, they would steal everything they could lay their hands on from now till the day of their death—that they would steal more than two thousand millions of dollars (applause)! Ask Maryland, with her tens of thousands of slaves, if she is not prepared for freedom, and hear her answer: "I help supply the coffle-gangs of the South." Ask Virginia, with her hundreds of thousands of slaves, if she is not weary with her merchandise of blood and anxious to shake the gory traffic from her hands, and hear her reply: "Though fertility has covered my soil, though a genial sky bends over my hills and vales, though I hold in my hand a wealth of waterpower, enough to turn the spindles to clothe the world, yet, with all these advantages, one of my chief staples has been the sons and daughters I send to the human market and human shambles" (applause). Ask the farther South, and all the cotton-growing States chime in, "We have need of fresh supplies to fill the ranks of those whose lives have gone out in unrequited toil on our distant plantations."

A hundred thousand new-born babes are annually added to the victims of slavery; twenty thousand lives are annually sacrificed on the plantations of the South. Such a sight should send a thrill of horror through the nerves of civilization and impel the heart of humanity to lofty alchemy by which this blood can be transformed into gold. Instead of listening to the cry of agony, they listen to the ring of dollars and stoop down to pick up the coin (applause).

But a few months since a man escaped from bondage and found a temporary shelter almost beneath the shadow of Bunker Hill. Had that man stood upon the deck of an Austrian ship, beneath the shadow of the house of the Hapsburgs, he would have found protection. Had he been wrecked upon an island or colony of Great Britain, the waves of the tempest-lashed ocean would have washed him deliverance. Had he landed upon the territory of vine-encircled France and a Frenchman had reduced him to a thing and brought him here beneath the protection of our institutions and our laws, for such a nefarious deed that Frenchman would have lost his citizenship in France. Beneath the feebler light which glimmers from the Koran, the Bey of Tunis would have granted him freedom in his own dominions. Beside the ancient pyramids of Egypt he would have found liberty, for the soil laved by the glorious Nile is now consecrated to freedom. But from Boston harbour, made memorable by the infusion of three-penny taxed tea, Boston in its proximity to the plains of Lexington and Concord, Boston almost beneath the shadow of Bunker Hill and almost in sight of Plymouth Rock, he is thrust back from liberty and manhood and reconverted into a chattel. You have heard that, down South, they keep bloodhounds to hunt slaves. Ye bloodhounds, go back to your kennels; when you fail to catch the flying fugitive, when his stealthy tread is heard in the place where the bones of the revolutionary sires repose, the ready North is base enough to do your shameful service (applause).

Slavery is mean, because it tramples on the feeble and weak. A man comes with his affidavits from the South and invites me before a commissioner; upon that evidence *ex parte* and alone he hitches me to the car of slavery and trails my womanhood in the dust. I stand at the threshold of the Supreme Court and ask for justice, simple justice. Upon my tortured heart is thrown the mocking words, "You are a negro; you have no rights which white men are bound to respect"[1] (loud and long-continued applause)! Had it been my lot to have lived beneath the Crescent instead of the Cross, had injustice and violence been heaped upon my head as a Mohammedan woman, as a member of a common faith, I might have demanded justice and been listened to by the Pasha, the Bey or the Vizier; but when I come here to ask for justice, men tell me, "We have no higher law than the Constitution" (applause).

[1] It was still true in 1857 that not even free blacks could assume any constitutional rights. An 1819 Virginia law restricted the mobility of free blacks and forbade them to "speak provocatively" to whites. An 1820 South Carolina law decreed that free Negroes on ships coming into state harbors be imprisoned until the ships departed. And although the Massachusetts State Constitution said that "all men, without distinction of color or race, are equal before the law," a Massachusetts Supreme Court ruling of 1849 upheld racial segregation in schools. Not until a new law was passed in 1855 did the school segregation end.

But I will not dwell on the dark side of the picture. God is on the side of freedom; and any cause that has God on its side, I care not how much it may be trampled upon, how much it may be trailed in the dust, is sure to triumph. The message of Jesus Christ is on the side of freedom, "I come to preach deliverance to the captives, the opening of the prison doors to them that are bound." The truest and noblest hearts in the land are on the side of freedom. They may be hissed at by slavery's minions, their names cast out as evil, their characters branded with fanaticism, but O,

> "To side with Truth is noble when we share her humble crust
> Ere the cause bring fame and profit and it's prosperous to be just."

May I not, in conclusion, ask every honest, noble heart, every seeker after truth and justice, if they will not also be on the side of freedom. Will you not resolve that you will abate neither heart nor hope till you hear the death-knoll of human bondage sounded, and over the black ocean of slavery shall be heard a song, more exulting than the song of Miriam when it floated o'er Egypt's dark sea,[2] the requiem of Egypt's ruined hosts and the anthem of the deliverance of Israel's captive people? (great applause)

(We have attempted to give a full report of Miss Watkins's speech.)

1857

The Two Offers

"What is the matter with you, Laura, this morning? I have been watching you this hour, and in that time you have commenced a half dozen letters and torn them all up. What matter of such grave moment is puzzling your dear little head, that you do not know how to decide?"

"Well, it is an important matter: I have two offers for marriage, and I do not know which to choose."

"I should accept neither, or to say the least, not at present."

"Why not?"

"Because I think a woman who is undecided between two offers, has not love enough for either to make a choice; and in that very hesitation, indecision, she has a reason to pause and seriously reflect, lest her marriage, instead of being an affinity of souls or a union of hearts, should only be a mere matter of bargain and sale, or an affair of convenience and selfish interest."

"But I consider them both very good offers, just such as many a girl would gladly receive. But to tell you the truth, I do not think that I regard either as a woman should the man she chooses for her husband. But then if I refuse, there is the risk of being an old maid, and that is not to be thought of."

---

[2]Miriam, the sister of Moses and Aaron and an important leader of the Jews, led her people in singing and dancing after they had safely crossed the Red Sea and escaped from bondage to the Egyptians (Exodus 15:20–21).

"Well, suppose there is, is that the most dreadful fate that can befall a woman? Is there not more intense wretchedness in an ill-assorted marriage—more utter loneliness in a loveless home, than in the lot of the old maid who accepts her earthly mission as a gift from God, and strives to walk the path of life with earnest and unfaltering steps?"

"Oh! what a little preacher you are. I really believe that you were cut out for an old maid; that when nature formed you, she put in a double portion of intellect to make up for a deficiency of love; and yet you are kind and affectionate. But I do not think that you know anything of the grand, over-mastering passion, or the deep necessity of woman's heart for loving."

"Do you think so?" resumed the first speaker; and bending over her work she quietly applied herself to the knitting that had lain neglected by her side, during this brief conversation; but as she did so, a shadow flitted over her pale and intellectual brow, a mist gathered in her eyes, and a slight quivering of the lips, revealed a depth of feeling to which her companion was a stranger.

But before I proceed with my story, let me give you a slight history of the speakers. They were cousins, who had met life under different auspices. Laura Lagrange, was the only daughter of rich and indulgent parents, who had spared no pains to make her an accomplished lady. Her cousin, Janette Alston, was the child of parents, rich only in goodness and affection. Her father had been unfortunate in business, and dying before he could retrieve his fortunes, left his business in an embarrassed state. His widow was unacquainted with his business affairs, and when the estate was settled, hungry creditors had brought their claims and the lawyers had received their fees, she found herself homeless and almost penniless, and she who had been sheltered in the warm clasp of loving arms, found them too powerless to shield her from the pitiless pelting storms of adversity. Year after year she struggled with poverty and wrestled with want, till her toil-worn hands became too feeble to hold the shattered chords of existence, and her tear-dimmed eyes grew heavy with the slumber of death. Her daughter had watched over her with untiring devotion, had closed her eyes in death, and gone out into the busy, restless world, missing a precious tone from the voices of earth, a beloved step from the paths of life. Too self reliant to depend on the charity of relations, she endeavored to support herself by her own exertions, and she had succeeded. Her path for a while was marked with struggle and trial, but instead of uselessly repining, she met them bravely, and her life became not a thing of ease and indulgence, but of conquest, victory, and accomplishments. At the time when this conversation took place, the deep trials of her life had passed away. The achievements of her genius had won her a position in the literary world, where she shone as one of its bright particular stars. And with her fame came a competence of worldly means, which gave her leisure for improvement, and the riper development of her rare talents. And she, that pale intellectual woman, whose genius gave life and vivacity to the social circle, and whose presence threw a halo of beauty and grace around the charmed atmosphere in which she moved, had at one period of her life, known the mystic and solemn strength of an all-absorbing love. Years faded into the misty past, had seen the kindling of her eye, the quick flushing of her cheek, and the wild throbbing of her heart, at tones of a voice long since hushed to the stillness of death. Deeply, wildly, passionately, she had loved. Her whole life seemed like the pouring out of rich, warm and gushing affections. This love quickened her talents, inspired her genius, and threw over her life a tender and spiritual earnestness. And then came a fearful shock, a mournful waking from that "dream of beauty and delight." A shadow fell around her path; it came between her and the object of her heart's worship; first a few cold words, estrangement, and then a painful separation; the old story of woman's pride—digging the sepulchre of her happiness, and then a new-made grave, and her path over it to the spirit world; and thus faded out from that young heart her bright, brief and saddened dream of life. Faint and spirit-broken, she turned from the scenes associated with the memory of the loved and lost. She tried to break the chain of sad associations that bound her to the mournful past; and so, pressing back the bitter sobs from her almost breaking heart, like the dying dolphin, whose beauty is born of its death anguish, her genius gathered strength from suffering and wonderous power and brilliancy from the agony she hid within the desolate chambers of her soul. Men hailed her as one of earth's strangely gifted children, and wreathed the garlands of fame for her brow, when it was throbbing with a wild and fearful unrest. They breathed her name with applause, when through the lonely halls of her stricken spirit, was an earnest cry for peace, a deep yearning for sympathy and heart-support.

But life, with its stern realities, met her; its solemn responsibilities confronted her, and turning, with an earnest and shattered spirit, to life's duties and trials, she found a calmness and strength that she had only imagined in her dreams of poetry and song. We will now pass over a period of ten years, and the cousins have met again. In that calm and lovely woman, in whose eyes is a depth of tenderness, tempering the flashes of her genius, whose looks and tones are full of sympathy and love, we recognize the once smitten and stricken Janette Alston. The bloom of her girlhood had given way to a higher type of spiritual beauty, as if some unseen hand had been polishing and refining the temple in which her lovely spirit found its habitation; and this had been the fact. Her inner life had grown beautiful, and it was this that was constantly developing the outer. Never, in the early flush of womanhood, when an absorbing love had lit up her eyes and glowed in her life, had she appeared so interesting as when, with a countenance which seemed overshadowed with a spiritual light, she bent over the death-bed of a young woman, just lingering at the shadowy gates of the unseen land.

"Has he come?" faintly but eagerly exclaimed the dying woman. "Oh! how I have longed for his coming, and even in death he forgets me."

"Oh, do not say so, dear Laura, some accident may have detained him," said Janette to her cousin; for on that bed, from whence she will never rise, lies the once-beautiful and light-hearted Laura Lagrange, the brightness of whose eyes has long since been dimmed with tears, and whose voice had become like a harp whose every chord is tuned to sadness—whose faintest thrill and loudest vibrations are but the variations of agony. A heavy hand was laid upon her once warm and bounding heart, and a voice came whispering through her soul, that she must die. But, to her, the tidings was a message of deliverance—a voice, hushing her wild sorrows to the calmness of resignation and hope. Life had grown so weary upon her head—the future looked so hopeless—she had no wish to tread again the track where thorns had pierced her feet, and clouds overcast her sky; and she hailed the coming of death's angel as the footsteps of a welcome friend. And yet, earth had one object so very dear to her weary heart. It was her absent and recreant husband; for, since that conversation, she had accepted one of her offers, and become a wife. But, before she married, she learned that great lesson of human experience and woman's life, to love the man who bowed at her shrine, a willing worshipper. He had a pleasing address, raven hair, flashing eyes, a voice of thrilling sweetness, and lips of persuasive eloquence; and being well versed in the ways of the world, he won his way to her heart, and she became his bride, and he was proud of his prize. Vain and superficial in his character, he looked upon marriage not as a divine sacrament for the soul's development and human progression, but as the title-deed that gave him possession of the woman he thought he loved. But alas for her, the laxity of his principles had rendered him unworthy of the deep and undying devotion of a purehearted woman; but, for awhile, he hid from her his true character, and she blindly loved him, and for a short period was happy in the consciousness of being beloved; though sometimes a vague unrest would fill her soul, when, overflowing with a sense of the good, the beautiful, and the true, she would turn to him, but find no response to the deep yearnings of her soul—no appreciation of life's highest realities—its solemn grandeur and significant importance. Their souls never met, and soon she found a void in her bosom, that his earth-born love could not fill. He did not satisfy the wants of her mental and moral nature—between him and her there was no affinity of minds, no intercommunion of souls.

Talk as you will of woman's deep capacity for loving, of the strength of her affectional nature. I do not deny it; but will the mere possession of any human love, fully satisfy all the demands of her whole being? You may paint her in poetry or fiction, as a frail vine, clinging to her brother man for support, and dying when deprived of it; and all this may sound well enough to please the imaginations of school-girls, or love-lorn maidens. But woman—the true woman—if you would render her happy, it needs more than the mere development of her affectional nature. Her conscience should be enlightened, her faith in the true and right established, and scope given to her Heaven-endowed and God-given faculties. The true aim of female education should be, not a development of one or two, but all the faculties of the human soul, because no perfect womanhood is developed by imperfect culture. Intense love is often akin to intense suffering, and to trust the whole wealth of a woman's nature on the frail bark of human love, may often be like trusting a cargo of gold and precious gems, to a bark that has never battled with the storm, or buffetted the waves. Is it any wonder, then, that so many life-barks go down, paving the ocean of time with precious hearts and wasted hopes? that so many float around us, shattered and dismasted wrecks? that so many are stranded on the shoals of existence, mournful beacons and solemn warnings for the thoughtless, to whom marriage is a careless and hasty rushing together of the affections? Alas that an institution so fraught with good for humanity should be so perverted, and that state of life, which should be filled with happiness, become so replete with misery. And this was the fate of Laura Lagrange. For a brief period after her marriage her life seemed like a bright and beautiful dream, full of hope and radiant with joy. And then there came a change—he found other attractions that lay beyond the pale of home influences. The gambling saloon had power to win him from her side, he had lived in an element of unhealthy and unhallowed excitements, and the society of a loving wife, the pleasures of a well-regulated home, were enjoyments too tame for one who had vitiated his tastes by the pleasures of sin. There were charmed houses of vice, built upon dead men's loves, where, amid a flow of song, laughter, wine, and careless mirth, he would spend hour after hour, forgetting the cheek that was paling through his neglect, heedless of the tear-dimmed eyes, peering anxiously into the darkness, waiting, or watching his return.

The influence of old associations was upon him. In early life, home had been to him a place of ceilings and walls, not a true home, built upon goodness, love and truth. It was a place where velvet carpets hushed his tread, where images of loveliness and beauty invoked into being by painter's art and sculptor's skill, pleased the eye and gratified the taste, where magnificence surrounded his way and costly clothing adorned his person; but it was not the place for the true culture and right development of his soul. His father had been too much engrossed in making money, and his mother in spending it, in striving to maintain a fashionable position in society, and shining in the eyes of the world, to give the proper direction to the character of their wayward and impulsive son. His mother put beautiful robes upon his body, but left ugly scars upon his soul; she pampered his appetite, but starved his spirit. Every mother should be a true artist, who knows how to weave into her child's life images of grace and beauty, the true poet capable of writing on the soul of childhood the harmony of love and truth, and teaching it how to produce the grandest of all poems—the poetry of a true and noble life. But in his home, a love for the good, the true and right, had been sacrificed at the shrine of frivolity and fashion. That parental authority which should have been preserved as a string of precious pearls, unbroken and unscattered, was simply the administration of chance. At one time obedience was enforced by authority, at another time by flattery and promises, and just as often it was not enforced [at] all. His early associations were formed as chance directed, and from his want of home-training, his character received a bias, his life a shade, which ran through every avenue of his existence, and darkened all his future hours. Oh, if we would trace the history of all the crimes that have o'ershadowed this sin-shrouded and sorrow-darkened world of ours, how many might be seen arising from the wrong home influences, or the weakening of the home ties. Home should always be the best school for the affections, the birth-place of high resolves, and the altar upon which lofty aspirations are kindled, from whence the soul may go forth strengthened, to act its part aright in the great drama of life, with conscience enlightened, affections cultivated, and reason and judgment dominant. But alas for the young wife. Her husband had not been blessed with such a home. When he entered the arena of life, the voices from home did not linger around his path as angels of guidance about his steps; they were not like so many messages to invite him to deeds of high and holy worth. The memory of no sainted mother arose between him and deeds of darkness; the earnest prayers of no father arrested him in his downward course: and before a year of his married life had waned, his young wife had learned to wait and mourn his frequent and uncalled-for absence. More than once had she seen him come home from his midnight haunts, the bright intelligence of his eye displaced by the drunkard's stare, and his manly gait changed to the inebriate's stagger; and she was beginning to know the bitter agony that is compressed in the mournful words, a drunkard's wife. And then there came a bright but brief episode in her experience; the angel of life gave to her existence a deeper meaning and loftier significance: she sheltered in the warm clasp of her loving arms, a dear babe, a precious child, whose love filled every chamber of her heart, and felt the fount of maternal love gushing so new within her soul. That child was hers. How overshadowing was the love with which she bent over its helplessness, how much it helped to fill the void and chasms in her soul. How many lonely hours were beguiled by its winsome ways, its answering smiles and fond caresses. How exquisite and solemn was the feeling that thrilled her heart when she clasped the tiny hands together and taught her dear child to call God "Our Father."

What a blessing was that child. The father paused in his headlong career, awed by the strange beauty and precocious intellect of his child; and the mother's life had a better expression through her ministrations of love. And then there came hours of bitter anguish, shading the sunlight of her home and hushing the music of her heart. The angel of death bent over the couch of her child and beaconed it away. Closer and closer the mother strained her child to her wildly heaving breast, and struggled with the heavy hand that lay upon its heart. Love and agony contended with death, and the language of the mother's heart was,

> Oh, Death, away! that innocent is mine;
> I cannot spare him from my arms
> To lay him, Death, in thine.

I am a mother, Death; I gave that darling birth
I could not bear his lifeless limbs
Should moulder in the earth.

But death was stronger than love and mightier than agony and won the child for the land of crystal founts and deathless flowers, and the poor, stricken mother sat down beneath the shadow of her mighty grief, feeling as if a great light had gone out from her soul, and that the sunshine had suddenly faded around her path. She turned in her deep anguish to the father of her child, the loved and cherished dead. For awhile his words were kind and tender, his heart seemed subdued, and his tenderness fell upon her worn and weary heart like rain on perishing flowers, or cooling waters to lips all parched with thirst and scorched with fever; but the change was evanescent, the influence of unhallowed associations and evil habits had vitiated and poisoned the springs of his existence. They had bound him in their meshes, and he lacked the moral strength to break his fetters, and stand erect in all the strength and dignity of a true manhood, making life's highest excellence his ideal, and striving to gain it.

And yet moments of deep contrition would sweep over him, when he would resolve to abandon the wine-cup forever, when he was ready to forswear the handling of another card, and he would try to break away from the associations that he felt were working his ruin; but when the hour of temptation came his strength was weakness, his earnest purposes were cobwebs, his well-meant resolutions ropes of sand, and thus passed year after year of the married life of Laura Lagrange. She tried to hide her agony from the public gaze, to smile when her heart was almost breaking. But year after year her voice grew fainter and sadder, her once light and bounding step grew slower and faltering. Year after year she wrestled with agony, and strove with despair, till the quick eyes of her brother read, in the paling of her cheek and the dimming eye, the secret anguish of her worn and weary spirit. On that wan, sad face, he saw the death-tokens, and he knew the dark wing of the mystic angel swept coldly around her path. "Laura," said her brother to her one day, "you are not well, and I think you need our mother's tender care and nursing. You are daily losing strength, and if you will go I will accompany you." At first, she hesitated, she shrank almost instinctively from presenting that pale sad face to the loved ones at home. That face was such a tell-tale; it told of heart-sickness, of hope deferred, and the mournful story of unrequited love. But then a deep yearning for home sympathy woke within her a passionate longing for love's kind words, for tenderness and heart-support, and she resolved to seek the home of her childhood, and lay her weary head upon her mother's bosom, to be folded again in her loving arms, to lay that poor, bruised and aching heart where it might beat and throb closely to the loved ones at home. A kind welcome awaited her. All that love and tenderness could devise was done to bring the bloom to her cheek and the light to her eye; but it was all in vain; hers was a disease that no medicine could cure, no earthly balm would heal. It was a slow wasting of the vital forces, the sickness of the soul. The unkindness and neglect of her husband, lay like a leaden weight upon her heart, and slowly oozed away its life-drops. And where was he that had won her love, and then cast it aside as a useless thing, who rifled her heart of its wealth and spread bitter ashes upon its broken altars? He was lingering away from her when the death-damps were gathering on her brow, when his name was trembling on her lips! lingering away! when she was watching his coming, though the death films were gathering before her eyes, and earthly things were fading from her vision. "I think I hear him now," said the dying woman, "surely that is his step;" but the sound died away in the distance. Again she started from an uneasy slumber, "that is his voice! I am so glad he has come." Tears gathered in the eyes of the sad watchers by that dying bed, for they knew that she was deceived. He had not returned. For her sake they wished his coming. Slowly the hours waned away, and then came the sad, soul-sickening thought that she was forgotten, forgotten in the last hour of human need, forgotten when the spirit, about to be dissolved, paused for the last time on the threshold of existence, a weary watcher at the gates of death. "He has forgotten me," again she faintly murmured, and the last tears she would ever shed on earth sprung to her mournful eyes, and clasping her hands together in silent anguish, a few broken sentences issued from her pale and quivering lips. They were prayers for strength and earnest pleading for him who had desolated her young life, by turning its sunshine to shadows, its smiles to tears. "He has forgotten me," she murmured again, "but I can bear it, the bitterness of death is passed, and soon I hope to exchange the shadows of death for the brightness of eternity, the rugged paths of life for the golden streets of glory, and the care and turmoils of earth for the peace and rest of heaven." Her voice grew fainter and fainter, they saw the shadows that never deceive flit over her pale and faded face, and knew that the death angel waited to soothe their weary one to rest, to calm the throbbing of her bosom and cool the fever of her brain. And amid the silent hush of their grief the freed spirit, refined through suffering, and brought into divine harmony through the spirit of the living Christ, passed over the dark waters of death as on a bridge of light, over whose radiant arches hovering angels bent. They parted the dark locks from her marble brow, closed the waxen lids over the once bright and laughing eye, and left her to the dreamless slumber of the grave. Her cousin turned from that death-bed a sadder and wiser woman. She resolved more earnestly than ever to make the world better by her example, gladden by her presence, and to kindle the fires of her genius on the altars of universal love and truth. She had a higher and better object in all her writings than the mere acquisition of gold, or acquirement of fame. She felt that she had a high and holy mission on the battle-field of existence, that life was not given her to be frittered away in nonsense, or wasted away in trifling pursuits. She would willingly espouse an unpopular cause but not an unrighteous one. In her the downtrodden slave found an earnest advocate; the flying fugitive remembered her kindness as he stepped cautiously through our Republic, to gain his freedom in a monarchial land, having broken the chains on which the rust of centuries had gathered. Little children learned to name her with affection, the poor called her blessed, as she broke her bread to the pale lips of hunger. Her life was like a beautiful story, only it was clothed with the dignity of reality and invested with the sublimity of truth. True, she was an old maid, no husband brightened her life with his love, or shaded it with his neglect. No children nestling lovingly in her arms called her mother. No one appended Mrs. to her name; she was indeed an old maid, not vainly striving to keep up an appearance of girlishness, when departed was written on her youth. Not vainly pining at her loneliness and isolation, the world was full of warm, loving hearts and her own beat in unison with them. Neither was she always sentimentally sighing for something to love, objects of affection were all around her, and the world was not so wealthy in love that it had no use for hers; in blessing others she made a life and benediction, and as old age descended peacefully and gently upon her, she had learned one of life's most precious lessons, that true happiness consists not so much in the fruition of our wishes as in the regulation of desires and the full development and right culture of our whole natures.

1859

▪ THOMAS WENTWORTH HIGGINSON ▪
1823–1911

Thomas Wentworth Higginson is remembered, when he is remembered at all, as Emily Dickinson's well-meaning but short-sighted "preceptor," who in coediting the first collection of her poetry smoothed away the vivid irregularity of her genius. By profession he was a Protestant clergyman; yet he organized and commanded the first regiment of black troops in the Civil War. By heritage he was a Boston Brahmin; yet in 1854 he led a vigilante assault to free a fugitive slave from a federal courthouse, in the course of which a marshal was shot to death. He was one of nineteenth-century America's best-known essayists and speakers; yet it was political activism on behalf of abolition, women's rights, and the demands of working people that gave joy to much of his life. His long career may seem to our later eyes filled with paradoxes if not outright contradictions, yet to Higginson, it was a life that, in looking back, he could describe as *Cheerful Yesterdays*.

Stephen and Louisa Storrow Higginson were descended from old Massachusetts and New Hampshire families. Wentworth, as he came to be called, was their tenth and last child, born December 22, 1823, in their home on "Professor's Row" in Cambridge, Massachusetts. The extensive Higginson library, the intellectual community of Cambridge, and later the broad education provided by

Harvard College, which Higginson entered in 1837 when he was thirteen, helped prepare him for life as an intellectual in what was then America's intellectual capital. He credited to his mother the development of the "leading motives" of his life: "the love of personal liberty, of religious freedom, and of the equality of the sexes." But like many of his friends, Higginson was deeply influenced by the Transcendentalism of Emerson, Theodore Parker, and Margaret Fuller. Whatever its specific doctrines, the movement seemed to sweep away the constraints of tradition and to offer to a new generation the opportunity for carrying out "numberless projects of social reform."

After graduating with the class of 1841, Higginson vacillated between the life of a poet and that of a preacher. He found little to interest him in Christian doctrine and was rather put off by church ritual. Still, the ministry did seem to provide opportunities for pursuing his passion for liberal reform, and especially the abolitionism to which he had become increasingly committed. "Preaching alone I should love," he wrote, "but I feel inwardly that something more will be sought of me—An aesthetic life—how beautiful—but the life of a Reformer, a People's Guide 'battling for the right'—glorious, but, oh how hard!" This question of a vocation—or even an appropriate subject—would haunt Higginson throughout his life and perhaps explains why, despite his many talents and vigorous style, he never emerged as one of the outstanding writers of the century.

In 1847 Higginson was chosen by the First Religious Society of Newburyport as its pastor; the essentially conservative parishioners came to regard him and his new bride, Mary Channing, "as if we were handsome spotted panthers, good to look at and roaring finely—something to be proud of, perhaps—but not to be approached incautiously, or too near." His ministry would last only a year—he later served six years at the decidedly unorthodox Free Church of Worcester—but Higginson quickly became involved with the concerns that would shape his life. He preached effectively against drink, and played an active role in the state Temperance Convention, as he later would in national temperance organizations. He opened an evening school for working people, and urged labor reforms, like the ten-hour day. He became active on behalf of women, in 1850 signing the call for the first national women's rights convention; later, after breaking with Elizabeth Cady Stanton and Susan B. Anthony over the issue of the Fifteenth Amendment, Higginson became a founder of the American Women's Suffrage Association and was for fourteen years coeditor of its periodical, *Women's Journal*.

But his primary commitment before the Civil War was to the abolition of slavery. While minister at Newburyport, he accepted John Greenleaf Whittier's nomination to run for Congress as the candidate of the antislavery Free Soil party—an action that essentially ended his first ministry. After the passage of the Fugitive Slave Act in 1850, he again ran for Congress, urging Newburyport voters to disobey the Act. In May 1854, he was one of the main planners and, as events transpired, a primary actor in an attack on the Boston Court House designed, unsuccessfully, to free the fugitive Anthony Burns from the slave power. Later, Higginson would travel and preach on behalf of the antislavery forces in "Bloody Kansas," and he would become one of the "Secret Six" who raised money and support for John Brown's raid. Late in the 1850s, he wrote a series of essays on black rebellions, which would not be published in the *Atlantic* until after the war had broken out; part of one of these, on Nat Turner, is printed here. But his major contribution to the work of Emancipation was to undertake the training and command of the First South Carolina Volunteers. Higginson's account of his command—and his education—is contained in *Army Life in a Black Regiment*, one of the most fascinating books to come out of the Civil War.

In the forty-six years he lived after the war, Higginson remained active in a variety of causes, though he devoted himself increasingly to the pen and the lectern. He wrote volumes of history for adults and children; biographies of Margaret Fuller, Longfellow, and Whittier; an unsuccessful novel, *Malbone* (1870); interesting regional sketches, *Oldport Days* (1869); one of the few sensible books on women by a man, *Common Sense About Women* (1881); and a flow of essays about writing and writers.

One of these, a "Letter to a Young Contributer" published in the *Atlantic* just as he was leaving to take up his army command, brought a flood of responses, among them an enigmatic note from a young woman named Emily Dickinson, who wrote asking "if my verse is alive." Thus began an irregular correspondence of twenty-five years, during which Dickinson played the role of pupil and Higginson that of "a preceptorship which," he wrote, "it is almost needless to say did not exist." His account of their only extended meeting is reprinted below; her letters to him are included with other works by Dickinson later in this volume. Higginson's advice to delay publication until she had "mastered" poetic orthodoxy has been cited as the cause of Dickinson's failure to print her poems during her lifetime—rather an insubstantial notion, given Dickinson's own ideas about publication and how she chose to share her poems. Undoubtedly, Higginson did not fully appreciate her work, he certainly took objectionable liberties in "regularizing" and titling her poems when he coedited the first volume of her verse after her death, and he shared many of the critical limits of his time—including a distaste for Whitman. But he did recognize in Dickinson a "wholly new and original poetic genius," and he played a significant role in bringing her into print.

History is nothing, if not ironic. Perhaps Higginson would have smiled to know that his long life had narrowed in literary history to a footnote in the tale of Emily Dickinson. And, perhaps, he would smile again to find his own work restored to a little of its independent value.

Paul Lauter
Trinity College

PRIMARY WORKS

The Writings of Thomas Wentworth Higginson, 7 vols, 1900; *Letters and Journals of Thomas Wentworth Higginson*, ed. Mary Thacher Higginson, 1921, 1969; *Black Rebellion*, ed. James M. McPherson, 1969; *Army Life in a Black Regiment*, ed. Howard N. Meyer, 1984 (also ed., with other writings, by R. D. Madison, 1997); *The Complete Civil War Journal and Selected Letters of Thomas Wentworth Higginson*, ed. Christopher Looby, 2000; *The Magnificent Activist: The Writings of Thomas Wentworth Higginson*, ed. Howard N. Meyer, 2000.

from **Nat Turner's Insurrection**

During the year 1831, up to the 23d of August, the Virginia newspapers seem to have been absorbed in the momentous problems which then occupied the minds of intelligent American citizens: What Gen. Jackson should do with the scolds, and what with the disreputables?[1] should South Carolina be allowed to nullify?[2] and would the wives of cabinet ministers call on Mrs. Eaton?[3] It is an unfailing opiate to turn over the drowsy files of the Richmond *Enquirer*, until the moment when those dry and dusty pages are suddenly kindled into flame by the torch of Nat Turner. Then the terror flared on increasing, until the remotest Southern States were found shuddering at nightly rumors of insurrection; until far-off European colonies—Antigua, Martinique, Caraccas, Tortola—recognized by some secret sympathy the same epidemic alarms; until the very boldest words of freedom were reported as uttered in the Virginia House of Delegates with unclosed doors; until an obscure young man named Garrison was indicted at common law in North Carolina, and had a price set upon his head by the Legislature of Georgia.[4]

Near the south-eastern border of Virginia, in Southampton County, there is a neighborhood known as "The Cross Keys." It lies fifteen miles from Jerusalem, the county-town, or "court-house," seventy miles from Norfolk, and about as far from Richmond. It is some ten or fifteen miles from Murfreesborough in North Carolina, and about twenty-five from the Great Dismal Swamp. Up to Sunday, the 21st of August, 1831, there was nothing to distinguish it from any other rural, lethargic, slipshod Virginia neighborhood, with the due allotment of mansion-houses and log huts, tobacco-fields and "old-fields," horses, dogs, negroes, "poor white folks," so called, and other white folks, poor without being called so. One of these last was Joseph Travis, who had recently married the widow of one Putnam Moore, and had unfortunately wedded to himself her negroes also.

In the woods on the plantation of Joseph Travis, upon the Sunday just named, six slaves met at noon for what is called in the Northern States a picnic, and in the Southern a barbecue. The bill of fare was to be simple: one brought a pig, and another some brandy, giving to the meeting an aspect so cheaply convivial that no one would have imagined it to be the final consummation of a conspiracy which had been for six months in preparation. In this plot four of the men had been already initiated,—Henry, Hark or Hercules, Nelson, and Sam. Two others were novices, Will and Jack by name. The party had remained together from twelve to three o'clock, when a seventh man joined them,—a short, stout, powerfully built person, of dark

---

[1] Political factions during Andrew Jackson's presidency.

[2] The doctrine that states had the right, within their territory, to nullify a federal law.

[3] Peggy O'Neale, originally a bar-maid, had married President Andrew Jackson's Secretary of War, John H. Eaton. Other members

of the cabinet, notably John C. Calhoun, and their wives tried to ostracize her socially, and the conflict carried over into political infighting within the administration.

[4] William Lloyd Garrison had, indeed, had a price set on his head after he began publishing *The Liberator*.

mulatto complexion, and strongly marked African features, but with a face full of expression and resolution. This was Nat Turner.

He was at this time nearly thirty-one years old, having been born on the 2d of October, 1800. He had belonged originally to Benjamin Turner,—from whom he took his last name, slaves having usually no patronymic;—had then been transferred to Putnam Moore, and then to his present owner. He had, by his own account, felt himself singled out from childhood for some great work; and he had some peculiar marks on his person, which, joined to his mental precocity, were enough to occasion, among his youthful companions, a superstitious faith in his gifts and destiny. He had some mechanical ingenuity also; experimentalized very early in making paper, gunpowder, pottery, and in other arts, which, in later life, he was found thoroughly to understand. His moral faculties appeared strong, so that white witnesses admitted that he had never been known to swear an oath, to drink a drop of spirits, or to commit a theft. And, in general, so marked were his early peculiarities that people said "he had too much sense to be raised; and, if he was, he would never be of any use as a slave." This impression of personal destiny grew with his growth: he fasted, prayed, preached, read the Bible, heard voices when he walked behind his plough, and communicated his revelations to the awe-struck slaves. They told him, in return, that, "If they had his sense, they would not serve any master in the world."

The biographies of slaves can hardly be individualized; they belong to the class. We know bare facts; it is only the general experience of human beings in like condition which can clothe them with life. The outlines are certain, the details are inferential. Thus, for instance, we know that Nat Turner's young wife was a slave; we know that she belonged to a different master from himself; we know little more than this, but this is much. For this is equivalent to saying, that, by day or by night, her husband had no more power to protect her than the man who lies bound upon a plundered vessel's deck has power to protect his wife on board the pirate schooner disappearing in the horizon. She may be well treated, she may be outraged; it is in the powerlessness that the agony lies. There is, indeed, one thing more which we do know of this young woman: the Virginia newspapers state that she was tortured under the lash, after her husband's execution, to make her produce his papers: this is all.

What his private experiences and special privileges or wrongs may have been, it is therefore now impossible to say. Travis was declared to be "more humane and fatherly to his slaves than any man in the county;" but it is astonishing how often this phenomenon occurs in the contemporary annals of slave insurrections. The chairman of the county court also stated, in pronouncing sentence, that Nat Turner had spoken of his master as "only too indulgent;" but this, for some reason, does not appear in his printed Confession, which only says, "He was a kind master, and placed the greatest confidence in me." It is very possible that it may have been so, but the printed accounts of Nat Turner's person look suspicious: he is described in Gov. Floyd's proclamation as having a scar on one of his temples, also one on the back of his neck, and a large knot on one of the bones of his right arm, produced by a blow; and although these were explained away in Virginia newspapers as having been produced by fights with his companions, yet such affrays are entirely foreign to the admitted habits of the man. It must therefore remain an open question, whether the scars and the knot were produced by black hands or by white.

Whatever Nat Turner's experiences of slavery might have been, it is certain that his plans were not suddenly adopted, but that he had brooded over them for years. To this day there are traditions among the Virginia slaves of the keen devices of "Prophet Nat." If he was caught with lime and lampblack in hand, conning over a half-finished county-map on the barn-door, he was always "planning what to do if he were blind;" or, "studying how to get to Mr. Francis's house." When he had called a meeting of slaves, and some poor whites came eavesdropping, the poor whites at once became the subjects for discussion: he incidentally mentioned that the masters had been heard threatening to drive them away; one slave had been ordered to shoot Mr. Jones's pigs, another to tear down Mr. Johnson's fences. The poor whites, Johnson and Jones, ran home to see to their homesteads, and were better friends than ever to Prophet Nat.

He never was a Baptist preacher, though such vocation has often been attributed to him. The impression arose from his having immersed himself, during one of his periods of special enthusiasm, together with a poor white man named Brantley. "About this time," he says in his Confession, "I told these things to a white man, on whom it had a wonderful effect; and he ceased from his wickedness, and was attacked immediately with a cutaneous eruption, and the blood oozed from the pores of his skin, and after praying and fasting nine days he was healed. And the Spirit appeared to me again, and said, as the Saviour had been baptized, so should we be also; and when the white people would not let us be baptized by the church, we went down into the water together, in the sight of many who reviled us, and were baptized by the Spirit. After this I rejoiced greatly, and gave thanks to God."

The religious hallucinations narrated in his Confession seem to have been as genuine as the average of such things, and are very well expressed. The account reads quite like Jacob Behmen. He saw white spirits and black spirits contending in the skies; the sun was darkened, the thunder rolled. "And the Holy Ghost was with me, and said, 'Behold me as I stand in the heavens!' And I looked, and saw the forms of men in different attitudes. And there were lights in the sky, to which the children of darkness gave other names than what they really were; for they were the lights of the Saviour's hands, stretched forth from east to west, even as they were extended on the cross on Calvary, for the redemption of sinners." He saw drops of blood on the corn: this was Christ's blood, shed for man. He saw on the leaves in the woods letters and numbers and figures of men,—the same symbols which he had seen in the skies. On May 12, 1828, the Holy Spirit appeared to him, and proclaimed that the yoke of Jesus must fall on him, and he must fight against the serpent when the sign appeared. Then came an eclipse of the sun in February, 1831: this was the sign; then he must arise and prepare himself, and slay his enemies with their own weapons; then also the seal was removed from his lips, and then he confided his plans to four associates.

When he came, therefore, to the barbecue on the appointed Sunday, and found not these four only, but two others, his first question to the intruders was, how they came thither. To this Will answered manfully, that his life was worth no more than the others, and "his liberty was as dear to him." This admitted him to confidence; and as Jack was known to be entirely under Hark's influence, the strangers were no bar to their discussion. Eleven hours they remained there, in anxious consultation: one can imagine those dusky faces, beneath the funereal woods, and amid the flickering of pine-knot torches, preparing that stern revenge whose shuddering echoes should ring through the land so long. Two things were at last decided: to begin their work that night; and to begin it with a massacre so swift and irresistible as to create in a few days more terror than many battles, and so spare the need of future bloodshed. "It was agreed that we should commence at home on that night, and, until we had armed and equipped ourselves and gained sufficient force, neither age nor sex was to be spared: which was invariably adhered to."

John Brown invaded Virginia with nineteen men, and with the avowed resolution to take no life but in self-defence. Nat Turner attacked Virginia from within, with six men, and with the determination to spare no life until his power was established. John Brown intended to pass rapidly through Virginia, and then retreat to the mountains.[5] Nat Turner intended to "conquer Southampton County as the white men did in the Revolution, and then retreat, if necessary, to the Dismal Swamp." Each plan was deliberately matured; each was in its way practicable; but each was defeated by a single false step, as will soon appear.

We must pass over the details of horror, as they occurred during the next twenty-four hours. Swift and stealthy as Indians, the black men passed from house to house,—not pausing, not hesitating, as their terrible work went on. In one thing they were humaner than Indians, or than white men fighting against Indians: there was no gratuitous outrage beyond the death-blow itself, no insult, no mutilation; but in every house they entered, that blow fell on man, woman, and child,—nothing that had a white skin was spared. From every house they took arms and ammunition, and from a few money. On every plantation they found recruits: those dusky slaves, so obsequious to their master the day before, so prompt to sing and dance before his Northern visitors, were all swift to transform themselves into fiends of retribution now; show them sword or musket, and they grasped it, though it were an heirloom from Washington himself. The troop increased from

[5]Higginson knew whereof he spoke; he had been among Brown's most intimate confidants prior to the raid on Harpers Ferry.

house to house,—first to fifteen, then to forty, then to sixty. Some were armed with muskets, some with axes, some with scythes, some came on their master's horses. As the numbers increased, they could be divided, and the awful work was carried on more rapidly still. The plan then was for an advanced guard of horsemen to approach each house at a gallop, and surround it till the others came up. Meanwhile, what agonies of terror must have taken place within, shared alike by innocent and by guilty! what memories of wrongs inflicted on those dusky creatures, by some,—what innocent participation, by others, in the penance! The outbreak lasted for but forty-eight hours; but, during that period, fifty-five whites were slain, without the loss of a single slave.

One fear was needless, which to many a husband and father must have intensified the last struggle. These negroes had been systematically brutalized from childhood; they had been allowed no legalized or permanent marriage; they had beheld around them an habitual licentiousness, such as can scarcely exist except under slavery; some of them had seen their wives and sisters habitually polluted by the husbands and the brothers of these fair white women who were now absolutely in their power. Yet I have looked through the Virginia newspapers of that time in vain for one charge of an indecent outrage on a woman against these triumphant and terrible slaves. Wherever they went, there went death, and that was all. It is reported by some of the contemporary newspapers, that a portion of this abstinence was the result of deliberate consultation among the insurrectionists; that some of them were resolved on taking the white women for wives, but were overruled by Nat Turner. If so, he is the only American slave-leader of whom we know certainly that he rose above the ordinary level of slave vengeance; and Mrs. Stowe's picture of Dred's[6] purposes is then precisely typical of his: "Whom the Lord saith unto us, 'Smite,' them will we smite. We will not torment them with the scourge and fire, nor defile their women as they have done with ours. But we will slay them utterly, and consume them from off the face of the earth."[7]

When the number of adherents had increased to fifty or sixty, Nat Turner judged it time to strike at the county-seat, Jerusalem. Thither a few white fugitives had already fled, and couriers might thence be despatched for aid to Richmond and Petersburg, unless promptly intercepted. Besides, he could there find arms, ammunition, and money; though they had already obtained, it is dubiously reported, from eight hundred to one thousand dollars. On the way it was necessary to pass the plantation of Mr. Parker, three miles from Jerusalem. Some of the men wished to stop here and enlist some of their friends. Nat Turner objected, as the delay might prove dangerous; he yielded at last, and it proved fatal.

---

[6]In *Dred*, a novel by Harriet Beecher Stowe.
[7]The passage contains Old Testament phrases but is not a precise quotation. It does illustrate Nat Turner's biblical style.

He remained at the gate with six or eight men; thirty or forty went to the house, half a mile distant. They remained too long, and he went alone to hasten them. During his absence a party of eighteen white men came up suddenly, dispersing the small guard left at the gate; and when the main body of slaves emerged from the house, they encountered, for the first time, their armed masters. The blacks halted; the whites advanced cautiously within a hundred yards, and fired a volley; on its being returned, they broke into disorder, and hurriedly retreated, leaving some wounded on the ground. The retreating whites were pursued, and were saved only by falling in with another band of fresh men from Jerusalem, with whose aid they turned upon the slaves, who in their turn fell into confusion. Turner, Hark, and about twenty men on horseback retreated in some order; the rest were scattered. The leader still planned to reach Jerusalem by a private way, thus evading pursuit; but at last decided to stop for the night, in the hope of enlisting additional recruits.

During the night the number increased again to forty, and they encamped on Major Ridley's plantation. An alarm took place during the darkness,—whether real or imaginary, does not appear,—and the men became scattered again. Proceeding to make fresh enlistments with the day-light, they were resisted at Dr. Blunt's house, where his slaves, under his orders, fired upon them; and this, with a later attack from a party of white men near Capt. Harris's, so broke up the whole force that they never re-united. The few who remained together agreed to separate for a few hours to see if any thing could be done to revive the insurrection, and meet again that evening at their original rendezvous. But they never reached it.

Gloomily came Nat Turner at nightfall into those gloomy woods where forty-eight hours before he had revealed the details of his terrible plot to his companions. At the outset all his plans had succeeded; every thing was as he predicted: the slaves had come readily at his call; the masters had proved perfectly defenceless. Had he not been persuaded to pause at Parker's plantation, he would have been master before now of the arms and ammunition at Jerusalem; and with these to aid, and the Dismal Swamp for a refuge, he might have sustained himself indefinitely against his pursuers.

Now the blood was shed, the risk was incurred, his friends were killed or captured, and all for what? Lasting memories of terror, to be sure, for his oppressors; but, on the other hand, hopeless failure for the insurrection, and certain death for him. What a watch he must have kept that night! To that excited imagination, which had always seen spirits in the sky and blood-drops on the corn and hieroglyphic marks on the dry leaves, how full the lonely forest must have been of signs and solemn warnings! Alone with the fox's bark, the rabbit's rustle, and the screech-owl's scream, the self-appointed prophet brooded over his despair. Once creeping to the edge of the wood, he saw men stealthily approach on horseback. He fancied them some of his companions; but before he dared to whisper their ominous names, "Hark" or "Dred,"—for the latter was the name, since famous, of one of his more recent recruits,—he saw them to be white men, and shrank back stealthily beneath his covert.

There he waited two days and two nights,—long enough to satisfy himself that no one would rejoin him, and that the insurrection had hopelessly failed. The determined, desperate spirits who had shared his plans were scattered forever, and longer delay would be destruction for him also. He found a spot which he judged safe, dug a hole under a pile of fence-rails in a field, and lay there for six weeks, only leaving it for a few moments at midnight to obtain water from a neighboring spring. Food he had previously provided, without discovery, from a house near by....

But the immediate danger was at an end, the short-lived insurrection was finished, and now the work of vengeance was to begin. In the frank phrase of a North-Carolina correspondent, "The massacre of the whites was over, and the white people had commenced the destruction of the negroes, which was continued after our men got there, from time to time, as they could fall in with them, all day yesterday." A postscript adds, that "passengers by the Fayetteville stage say, that, by the latest accounts, one hundred and twenty negroes had been killed,"—this being little more than one day's work....

Men were tortured to death, burned, maimed, and subjected to nameless atrocities. The overseers were called on to point out any slaves whom they distrusted, and if any tried to escape they were shot down. Nay, worse than this. "A party of horsemen started from Richmond with the intention of killing every colored person they saw in Southampton County. They stopped opposite the cabin of a free colored man, who was hoeing in his little field. They called out, 'Is this Southampton County?' He replied, 'Yes, sir, you have just crossed the line, by yonder tree.' They shot him dead, and rode on." This is from the narrative of the editor of the Richmond *Whig*, who was then on duty in the militia, and protested manfully against these outrages. "Some of these scenes," he adds, "are hardly inferior in barbarity to the atrocities of the insurgents."

These were the masters' stories. If even these conceded so much, it would be interesting to hear what the slaves had to report. I am indebted to my honored friend, Lydia Maria Child, for some vivid recollections of this terrible period, as noted down from the lips of an old colored woman, once well known in New York, Charity Bowery. "At the time of the old Prophet Nat," she said, "the colored folks was afraid to pray loud; for the whites threatened to punish 'em dreadfully, if the least noise was heard. The patrols was low drunken whites; and in Nat's time, if they heard any of the colored folks praying, or singing a hymn, they would fall upon 'em and abuse 'em, and sometimes kill 'em, afore master or missis could get to 'em. The brightest and best was killed in Nat's time. The whites always suspect such ones. They killed a great many at a place called Duplon. They killed Antonio, a slave of Mr. J. Stanley, whom they shot; then they pointed their guns at him, and told him to confess about the insurrection. He told 'em he didn't know any thing about any insurrection. They shot several balls through him, quartered him, and put his head on a pole at the fork of the road leading to the court." (This is no exaggeration, if the Virginia newspapers may be taken as evidence.) "It was there but a short time. He had no trial. They never do. In Nat's time, the patrols would tie up the free colored people, flog 'em, and try to make 'em lie against one another, and often killed them before anybody could interfere. Mr. James Cole, high sheriff, said, if any of the patrols came on his plantation, he would lose his life in defence of his people. One day he heard a patroller boasting how many niggers he had killed. Mr. Cole said, 'If you don't pack up, as quick as God Almighty will let you, and get out of this town, and never be seen in it again, I'll put you where dogs won't bark at you.' He went off, and wasn't seen in them parts again"[8]....

It is astonishing to discover, by laborious comparison of newspaper files, how vast was the immediate range of these insurrectionary alarms. Every Southern State seems to have borne its harvest of terror....

Meanwhile the cause of all this terror was made the object of desperate search. On Sept. 17 the governor offered a reward of five hundred dollars for his capture; and there were other rewards, swelling the amount to eleven hundred dollars,—but in vain. No one could track or trap him. On Sept. 30 a minute account of his capture appeared in the newspapers, but it was wholly false. On Oct. 7 there was another, and on Oct. 18 another; yet all without foundation. Worn out by confinement in his little cave, Nat Turner grew more adventurous, and began to move about stealthily by night, afraid to speak to any human being, but hoping to obtain some information that might aid his escape. Returning regularly to his retreat before daybreak, he might possibly have continued this mode of life until pursuit had ceased, had not a dog succeeded where men had failed. The creature accidentally smelt out the provisions hid in the cave, and finally led thither his masters, two negroes, one of whom was named Nelson. On discovering the formidable fugitive, they fled precipitately, when he hastened to retreat in an opposite direction. This was on Oct. 15; and from this moment the neighborhood was all alive with excitement, and five or six hundred men undertook the pursuit.

It shows a more than Indian adroitness in Nat Turner to have escaped capture any longer. The cave, the arms, the provisions, were found; and, lying among them, the notched stick of this miserable Robinson Crusoe,[9] marked with five weary weeks and six days. But the man was gone. For ten days more he concealed himself among the wheat-stacks on Mr. Francis's plantation, and during this time was reduced almost to despair. Once he decided to surrender himself, and walked by night within two miles of Jerusalem before his purpose failed him. Three times he tried to get out of that neighborhood, but in vain: travelling by day was of course out of the

[8]Higginson had solicited information on Nat Turner from Lydia Maria Child and is here quoting from her letter.

[9]The reference here is to the hero of Daniel Defoe's novel of that name, who was cast away on a barren island.

question, and by night he found it impossible to elude the patrol. Again and again, therefore, he returned to his hiding-place; and, during his whole two months' liberty, never went fives miles from the Cross Keys. On the 25th of October, he was at last discovered by Mr. Francis as he was emerging from a stack. A load of buckshot was instantly discharged at him, twelve of which passed through his hat as he fell to the ground. He escaped even then; but his pursuers were rapidly concentrating upon him, and it is perfectly astonishing that he could have eluded them for five days more.

On Sunday, Oct. 30, a man named Benjamin Phipps, going out for the first time on patrol duty, was passing at noon a clearing in the woods where a number of pine-trees had long since been felled. There was a motion among their boughs; he stopped to watch it; and through a gap in the branches he saw, emerging from a hole in the earth beneath, the face of Nat Turner. Aiming his gun instantly, Phipps called on him to surrender. The fugitive, exhausted with watching and privation, entangled in the branches, armed only with a sword, had nothing to do but to yield,—sagaciously reflecting, also, as he afterwards explained, that the woods were full of armed men, and that he had better trust fortune for some later chance of escape, instead of desperately attempting it then. He was correct in the first impression, since there were fifty armed scouts within a circuit of two miles. His insurrection ended where it began; for this spot was only a mile and a half from the house of Joseph Travis.

Torn, emaciated, ragged, "a mere scarecrow," still wearing the hat perforated with buckshot, with his arms bound to his sides, he was driven before the levelled gun to the nearest house, that of a Mr. Edwards. He was confined there that night; but the news had spread so rapidly that within an hour after his arrival a hundred persons had collected, and the excitement became so intense "that it was with difficulty he could be conveyed alive to Jerusalem." The enthusiasm spread instantly through Virginia; M. Trezvant, the Jerusalem postmaster, sent notices of it far and near; and Gov. Floyd himself wrote a letter to the Richmond *Enquirer* to give official announcement of the momentous capture.

When Nat Turner was asked by Mr. T.R. Gray, the counsel assigned him, whether, although defeated, he still believed in his own Providential mission, he answered, as simply as one who came thirty years after him, "Was not Christ crucified?" In the same spirit, when arraigned before the court, "he answered, 'Not guilty,' saying to his counsel that he did not feel so." But apparently no argument was made in his favor by his counsel, nor were any witnesses called,—he being convicted on the testimony of Levi Waller, and upon his own confession, which was put in by Mr. Gray, and acknowledged by the prisoner before the six justices composing the court, as being "full, free, and voluntary." He was therefore placed in the paradoxical position of conviction by his own confession, under a plea of "Not guilty." The arrest took place on the 30th of October, 1831, the confession on the 1st of November, the trial and conviction on the 5th, and the execution on the following Friday, the 11th of November, precisely at noon. He met his death with perfect composure, declined addressing the multitude assembled, and told the sheriff in a firm voice that he was ready. Another account says that he "betrayed no emotion, and even hurried the executioner in the performance of his duty." "Not a limb nor a muscle was observed to move. His body, after his death, was given over to the surgeons for dissection."

The confession of the captive was published under authority of Mr. Gray, in a pamphlet, at Baltimore. Fifty thousand copies of it are said to have been printed; and it was "embellished with an accurate likeness of the brigand, taken by Mr. John Crawley, portrait-painter, and lithographed by Endicott & Swett, at Baltimore." The newly established *Liberator* said of it, at the time, that it would "only serve to rouse up other leaders, and hasten other insurrections," and advised grand juries to indict Mr. Gray. I have never seen a copy of the original pamphlet; it is not easily to be found in any of our public libraries; and I have heard of but one as still existing, although the Confession itself has been repeatedly reprinted. Another small pamphlet, containing the main features of the outbreak, was published at New York during the same year, and this is in my possession. But the greater part of the facts which I have given were gleaned from the contemporary newspapers.

Who now shall go back thirty years, and read the heart of this extraordinary man, who, by the admission of his captors, "never was known to swear an oath, or drink a drop of spirits," who, on same authority, "for natural intelligence and quickness of apprehension was surpassed by few men," "with a mind capable of attaining any thing;" who knew no book but his Bible, and that by heart; who devoted himself soul and body to the cause of his race, without a trace of personal hope or fear; who laid his plans so shrewdly that they came at last with less warning than any earthquake on the doomed community around; and who, when that time arrived, took the life of man, woman, and child, without a throb of compunction, a word of exultation, or an act of superfluous outrage? Mrs. Stowe's "Dred" seems dim and melodramatic beside the actual Nat Turner, and De Quincey's "Avenger"[10] is his only parallel in imaginative literature. Mr. Gray, his counsel, rises into a sort of bewildered enthusiasm with the prisoner before him. "I shall not attempt to describe the effect of his narrative, as told and commented on by himself, in the condemned-hole of the prison. The calm, deliberate composure with which he spoke of his late deeds and intentions, the expression of his fiend-like face when excited by enthusiasm, still bearing the stains of the blood of helpless innocence about him, clothed with rags and covered with chains, yet daring to raise his manacled hands to heaven, with a spirit soaring above the attributes of man,—I looked on him, and the blood curdled in my veins."

---

[10]Central character in a highly romantic work by English author Thomas De Quincey.

But, the more remarkable the personal character of Nat Turner, the greater the amazement felt that he should not have appreciated the extreme felicity of his position as a slave. In all insurrections, the standing wonder seems to be that the slaves most trusted and best used should be most deeply involved. So in this case, as usual, men resorted to the most astonishing theories of the origin of the affair. One attributed it to Free-Masonry, and another to free whiskey,—liberty appearing dangerous, even in these forms. The poor whites charged it upon the free colored people, and urged their expulsion; forgetting that in North Carolina the plot was betrayed by one of this class, and that in Virginia there were but two engaged, both of whom had slave wives. The slaveholding clergymen traced it to want of knowledge of the Bible, forgetting that Nat Turner knew scarcely any thing else. On the other hand, "a distinguished citizen of Virginia" combined in one sweeping denunciation "Northern incendiaries, tracts, Sunday schools, religion, reading, and writing."

But whether the theories of its origin were wise or foolish, the insurrection made its mark; and the famous band of Virginia emancipationists, who all that winter made the House of Delegates ring with unavailing eloquence,—till the rise of slave-exportation to new cotton regions stopped their voices,—were but the unconscious mouthpieces of Nat Turner. In January, 1832, in reply to a member who had called the outbreak a "petty affair," the eloquent James McDowell thus described the impression it left behind:—

"Now, sir, I ask you, I ask gentlemen in conscience to say, was that a 'petty affair' which startled the feelings of your whole population; which threw a portion of it into alarm, a portion of it into panic; which wrung out from an affrighted people the thrilling cry, day after day, conveyed to your executive, *We are in peril of our lives; send us an army for defence*? Was that a 'petty affair' which drove families from their homes,—which assembled women and children in crowds, without shelter, at places of common refuge, in every condition of weakness and infirmity, under every suffering which want and terror could inflict, yet willing to endure all, willing to meet death from famine, death from climate, death from hardships, preferring any thing rather than the horrors of meeting it from a domestic assassin? Was that a 'petty affair' which erected a peaceful and confiding portion of the State into a military camp; which outlawed from pity the unfortunate beings whose brothers had offended; which barred every door, penetrated every bosom with fear or suspicion; which so banished every sense of security from every man's dwelling, that, let but a hoof or horn break upon the silence of the night, and an aching throb would be driven to the heart, the husband would look to his weapon, and the mother would shudder and weep upon her cradle? Was it the fear of Nat Turner, and his deluded, drunken handful of followers, which produced such effects? Was it this that induced distant counties, where the very name of Southampton was strange, to arm and equip for a struggle? No, sir: it was the suspicion eternally attached to the slave himself,—the suspicion that a Nat Turner might be in every family; that the same bloody deed might be acted over at any time and in any place; that the materials for it were spread through the land, and were always ready for a like explosion. Nothing but the force of this withering apprehension,—nothing but the paralyzing and deadening weight with which it falls upon and prostrates the heart of every man who has helpless dependants to protect,—nothing but this could have thrown a brave people into consternation, or could have made any portion of this powerful Commonwealth, for a single instant, to have quailed and trembled."

While these things were going on, the enthusiasm for the Polish Revolution was rising to its height. The nation was ringing with a peal of joy, on hearing that at Frankfort the Poles had killed fourteen thousand Russians. The *Southern Religious Telegraph* was publishing an impassioned address to Kosciuszko; standards were being consecrated for Poland in the larger cities; heroes like Skrzynecki, Czartoryski, Rozyski, Raminski, were choking the trump of Fame with their complicated patronymics. These are all forgotten now; and this poor negro, who did not even possess a name, beyond one abrupt monosyllable,—for even the name of Turner was the master's property,—still lives, a memory of terror, and a symbol of wild retribution.

1861

Letter to Mrs. Higginson on Emily Dickinson

I shan't sit up tonight to write you all about E.D. dearest but if you had read Mrs. Stoddard's[1] novels you could understand a house where each member runs his or her own selves. Yet I only saw her.

A large county lawyer's house, brown brick, with great trees & a garden—I sent up my card. A parlor dark & cool & stiffish, a few books & engravings & an open piano—Malbone & O D [Out Door] Papers[2] among other books.

A step like a pattering child's in entry & in glided a little plain woman with two smooth bands of reddish hair & a face a little like Belle Dove's; not plainer—with no good feature—in a very plain & exquisitely clean white pique & a blue net worsted shawl. She came to me with two day lilies which she put in a sort of childlike way into my hand & said "These are my introduction" in a soft frightened breathless childlike voice—& added under her breath Forgive me if I am frightened; I never see strangers & hardly know what I say—but she talked soon & thenceforward continuously—&

---

[1] The fiction of Elizabeth Drew Stoddard is represented later in this volume.

[2] The books are, respectively, a novel and a collection of essays by Higginson.

deferentially—sometimes stopping to ask me to talk instead of her—but readily recommencing. Manner between Angie Tilton & Mr. Alcott[3]—but thoroughly ingenuous & simple which they are not & saying many things which you would have thought foolish & I wise—& some things you wd. hv. liked. I add a few over the page.

This is a lovely place, at least the view Hills everywhere, hardly mountains. I saw Dr. Stearns the Pres't of College—but the janitor cd. not be found to show me into the building I may try again tomorrow. I called on Mrs. Banfield & saw her five children—She looks much like H.H. *when ill* & was very cordial & friendly. Goodnight darling I am very sleepy & do good to write you this much. Thine am I

I got here at 2 & leave at 9. E.D. dreamed all night of *you* (not me) & next day got my letter proposing to come here!! She only knew of you through a mention in my notice of Charlotte Hawes.[4]

"Women talk: men are silent: that is why I dread women."

"My father only reads on Sunday—he reads lonely & rigorous books."

"If I read a book [and] it makes my whole body so cold no fire ever can warm me I know that is poetry. If I feel physically as if the top of my head were taken off, I know that is poetry. These are the only way I know it. Is there any other way."

"How do most people live without any thoughts. There are many people in the world (you must have noticed them in the street) How do they live. How do they get strength to put on their clothes in the morning"

"When I lost the use of my Eyes it was a comfort to think there were so few real books that I could easily find some one to read me all of them"

"Truth is such a rare thing it is delightful to tell it."

"I find ecstasy in living—the mere sense of living is joy enough"

I asked if she never felt want of employment, never going off the place & never seeing any visitor "I never thought of conceiving that I could ever have the slightest approach to such a want in all future time" (& added) "I feel that I have not expressed myself strongly enough."

She makes all the bread for her father only likes hers & says "& people must have puddings" this very dreamily, as if they were comets—so she makes them. . . .

She said to me at parting "Gratitude is the only secret that cannot reveal itself". . . .

I saw Mr. Dickinson this morning a little—thin dry & speechless—I saw what her life has been. Dr. S[tearns] says her sister is proud of her. . . .

This picture of Mrs Browning's tomb is from E.D. "Timothy Titcomb" [Dr. Holland] gave it to her.

---

[3]Bronson Alcott, American Transcendentalist and educational reformer, known for his other-worldliness.

[4]Higginson had published a tribute to the memory of Charlotte Prince Hawes, a magazine writer, in the *Boston Radical* in 1867.

I think I will mail this here as I hv. found time to write so much. I miss you little woman & wish you were here but you'd hate travelling.

Ever

E D again

"Could you tell me what home is"

"I never had a mother. I suppose a mother is one to whom you hurry when you are troubled."

"I never knew how to tell time by the clock till I was 15. My father thought he had taught me but I did not understand & I was afraid to say I did not & afraid to ask any one else lest he should know."

Her father was not severe I should think but remote. He did not wish them to read anything but the Bible. One day her brother brought home Kavanagh[5] hid it under the piano cover & made signs to her & they read it: her father at last found it & was displeased. Perhaps it was before this that a student of his was amazed that they had never heard of Mrs. [Lydia Maria] Child[6] & used to bring them books & hide in a bush by the door. They were then little things in short dresses with their feet on the rungs of the chair. After the first book she thought in ecstasy "This then is a book! And there are more of them!"

"Is it oblivion or absorption when things pass from our minds?"

Major Hunt[7] interested her more than any man she ever saw. She remembered two things he said—that her great dog "understood gravitation" & when he said he should come again "in a year. If I say a shorter time it will be longer."

When I said I would come again *some time* she said "Say in a long time, that will be nearer. Some time is nothing."

After long disuse of her eyes she read Shakespeare & thought why is any other book needed.

I never was with any one who drained my nerve power so much. Without touching her, she drew from me. I am glad not to live near her. She often thought me *tired* & seemed very thoughtful of others.

[The postscript of a letter Higginson wrote his sisters (HCL) on Sunday, 21 August, adds:]

Of course I hv. enjoyed my trip very very much. In Amherst I had a nice aftn & evng with my singular poetic correspondent & the remarkable cabinets of the College.

1921

---

[5]A romance by Longfellow set in a small New England town.

[6]The work of Lydia Maria Child is represented earlier in this section.

[7]Edward Bissell Hunt, an army engineer killed during the Civil War, and husband of Helen Hunt Jackson, author of *Ramona*.

HARRIET ANN JACOBS
1813–1897

Harriet Ann Jacobs was born a slave in Edenton, North Carolina, in 1813. At six, after the death of her mother, Jacobs was taken into her mistress's home and taught to read and to sew. When she was eleven, she was willed to her mistress's little niece and sent to the nearby Norcom home to live. Her father died the following year. Aside from her younger brother, Jacobs's closest relative was her remarkable grandmother, Molly Horniblow, a freed woman who ran a bakery in her home. As Jacobs grew into adolescence, her master, Dr. James Norcom, subjected her to unrelenting sexual harassment. To prevent him from forcing her into concubinage, at sixteen Jacobs became involved in a sexual liaison with a white neighbor, Samuel Tredwell Sawyer. Their son Joseph was born c. 1829–1830, and their daughter Louisa Matilda in 1833.

Jacobs was determined to free her children. When she was twenty-one, she again refused to become Dr. Norcom's concubine and was punished by being sent out to a plantation. Then, learning that Dr. Norcom planned to take the children from her grandmother's care, she decided to run away to save them from becoming plantation slaves. Reasoning that Norcom would sell the children if she were gone, she hid with sympathetic black and white neighbors. As she had hoped, Norcom sold the children to their father, who permitted them to continue to stay with her grandmother. But Norcom's zealous efforts to find her, and her grandmother's fear that she would be caught and returned in chains—as an uncle had been—combined to keep her in Edenton. For almost seven years, Jacobs hid in a tiny attic crawlspace in her grandmother's house. She spent her days reading the Bible, sewing clothes for her children, and planning ways to free them all.

In 1842, Jacobs escaped north, was reunited with her daughter (who had been sent to Brooklyn), and found work in New York in the home of the littera-teur Nathaniel Parker Willis. She arranged for her son to be sent to her brother, John S. Jacobs, who had escaped from slavery and become an abolitionist lecturer. In 1849, Jacobs joined him in Rochester, New York, to run the local Anti-Slavery Reading Room. In Rochester, she became part of a circle of antislavery feminists. Amy Post, who had attended the 1848 Women's Rights Convention at Seneca Falls and played a major role in the follow-up Rochester meeting, became Jacobs's friend. Post urged Jacobs to write her life story as a weapon in the struggle against chattel slavery.

After passage of the 1850 Fugitive Slave Law, Jacobs returned to her job with the Willis family. In New York, the Norcoms repeatedly attempted to catch her, and in 1852 Mrs. Willis bought Jacobs's freedom. Although glad to be free, Jacobs had objected to being bought, and she wrote to Post, "I was robbed of my victory." Early the next year, she was struggling with the idea of writing her story: "since I have no fear of my name coming before those whom I have lived in dread of I cannot be happy without trying to be useful in some way." After an abortive effort to involve as an amanuensis Harriet Beecher Stowe, whose *Uncle*

Tom's Cabin had become a best seller, Jacobs began writing her own life story. She finished her book in 1858, but could not find a publisher. Then in 1861, a firm agreed to get it out if the well-known writer and editor Lydia Maria Child would supply a preface. Child agreed, but the publisher went bankrupt, and *Incidents* was finally printed privately early in 1861. The book was well reviewed in the African American press and in reform newspapers; an English edition appeared the following year.

Like other abolitionists, Jacobs eagerly involved herself in the effort to transform the developing Civil War into a war of emancipation. In 1862, she left New York to do relief work among the "contraband" (slaves who escaped to the Union army). Jacobs raised money for Southern blacks, using the celebrity she had won among reformers as the author of *Incidents*. For the next six years she served in Washington, D.C., Alexandria, Virginia, and Savannah, Georgia, as an "agent" of Philadelphia and New York Quakers. She wrote her 1867 letter to Ednah Dow Cheney, Secretary of the New England Freedman's Aid Society, while visiting Reconstruction Edenton. After 1868, Jacobs returned north. She spent her last years with her daughter in Cambridge, Massachusetts, and Washington, D.C.

In letters to Amy Post, Jacobs expressed the conflict she felt about revealing her life story. To write a book politicizing the sexual exploitation of female slaves, she would have to expose her own sexual history and reveal herself an unwed mother. Ultimately, she created an alter ego, Linda Brent, who narrates her history in the first person. In and through Brent's narrative of her experiences in slavery as a sexual object and as a mother, Harriet Jacobs moved her book beyond the limits of genteel nineteenth-century discourse.

Incidents is unique among slave narratives in its double thrust: it is at once the first-person tale of a heroic mother who rescues her children from slavery and the first-person confession of a "fallen woman." Distinctive discourses express these double themes. When writing as a triumphant slave mother, Jacobs's narrator recounts precise details and uses language directly; when confessing her sexual history, however, she presents herself as a repentant supplicant, omitting specifics and using the elevated vocabulary, elaborate sentence structures, and mannered prose associated with the popular fiction of the period. But this narrator does not present herself as the passive victim of the seduction novel. On the contrary, Linda Brent takes responsibility for her mistakes, as well as for her triumphs.

Telling the story of her struggle for freedom, Jacobs's narrator locates herself within a densely patterned social context. In contrast to male-authored slave narratives, which, like Frederick Douglass's *Narrative*, characteristically focused on a lone protagonist struggling against an unjust society, *Incidents* presents a protagonist enmeshed in family relationships who recounts her efforts to achieve freedom for herself and her children within the context of the struggle for freedom of an entire black community. In Linda Brent, Jacobs created a narrator with a voice that was new in African American literature, in women's literature, and in American literature.

Both the preface that Jacobs signed as Linda Brent and the introduction her editor Lydia Maria Child supplied make clear that *Incidents* was written for an audience of free white women and that its purpose was to involve these women in political action against the institution of chattel slavery and the ideology of white racism. On one level, *Incidents* is a literary expression of the struggle of black and white abolitionists against slavery and white racism, and the attempt of nineteenth-century black and white feminists to move women to act collectively in the public sphere. On another, it is one woman's effort "to give a true and just account of my own life in Slavery."

Jean Fagan Yellin
Pace University

PRIMARY WORKS

Incidents in the Life of a Slave Girl. Written By Herself, ed. L. Maria Child, 1861; republished as *The Deeper Wrong. Incidents in the Life of a Slave Girl*, 1862; the standard text was edited by Jean Fagan Yellin, 2000; Harriet A. Jacobs to Ednah Dow Cheney, Edenton [North Carolina] April 25th [1867], ALS, Sophia Smith Collection; included, along with several more of Jacobs's letters, in *We Are Your Sisters: Black Women in the Nineteenth Century*, ed. Dorothy Sterling, 1984, and in the Yellin edition, which also includes "A True Tale of Slavery," the narrative of her brother, John S. Jacobs.

from Incidents in the Life of a Slave Girl

Seven Years Concealed

I. Childhood

I was born a slave; but I never knew it till six years of happy childhood had passed away. My father[1] was a carpenter, and considered so intelligent and skilful in his trade, that, when buildings out of the common line were to be erected, he was sent for from long distances, to be head workman. On condition of paying his mistress two hundred dollars a year, and supporting himself, he was allowed to work at his trade, and manage his own affairs. His strongest wish was to purchase his children; but, though he several times offered his hard earnings for that purpose, he never succeeded. In complexion my parents were a light shade of brownish yellow, and were termed mulattoes. They lived together in a comfortable home; and, though we were all slaves, I was so fondly shielded that I never dreamed I was a piece of merchandise, trusted to them for safe keeping, and liable to be demanded of them at any moment. I had one brother, William, who was two years younger than myself—a bright, affectionate child. I had also a great treasure in my maternal grandmother, who was a remarkable woman in many respects. She was the daughter of a planter in South Carolina, who, at his death, left her mother and his three children free, with money to go to St. Augustine, where they had relatives. It was during the Revolutionary War; and they were captured on their passage, carried back, and sold to

---

[1] The family members referred to in this chapter include Jacobs's father, Daniel Jacobs (?–c. 1826), her brother John S. Jacobs (1815?–1875), and her grandmother, Molly Horniblow (c. 1771–1853).

different purchasers. Such was the story my grandmother used to tell me; but I do not remember all the particulars. She was a little girl when she was captured and sold to the keeper of a large hotel. I have often heard her tell how hard she fared during childhood. But as she grew older she evinced so much intelligence, and was so faithful, that her master and mistress could not help seeing it was for their interest to take care of such a valuable piece of property. She became an indispensable personage in the household, officiating in all capacities, from cook and wet nurse to seamstress. She was much praised for her cooking; and her nice crackers became so famous in the neighborhood that many people were desirous of obtaining them. In consequence of numerous requests of this kind, she asked permission of her mistress to bake crackers at night, after all the household work was done; and she obtained leave to do it, provided she would clothe herself and her children from the profits. Upon these terms, after working hard all day for her mistress, she began her midnight bakings, assisted by her two oldest children. The business proved profitable; and each year she laid by a little, which was saved for a fund to purchase her children. Her master died, and the property was divided among his heirs. The widow had her dower in the hotel, which she continued to keep open. My grandmother remained in her service as a slave; but her children were divided among her master's children. As she had five, Benjamin, the youngest one, was sold, in order that each heir might have an equal portion of dollars and cents. There was so little difference in our ages that he seemed more like my brother than my uncle. He was a bright, handsome lad, nearly white; for he inherited the complexion my grandmother had derived from Anglo-Saxon ancestors. Though only ten years old, seven hundred and twenty dollars were paid for him. His sale was a terrible blow to my grandmother; but she was naturally hopeful, and she went to work with renewed energy, trusting in time to be able to purchase some of her children. She had laid up three hundred dollars, which her mistress one day begged as a loan, promising to pay her soon. The reader probably knows that no promise or writing given to a slave is legally binding; for, according to Southern laws, a slave, *being* property, can *hold* no property. When my grandmother lent her hard earnings to her mistress, she trusted solely to her honor. The honor of a slaveholder to a slave!

To this good grandmother I was indebted for many comforts. My brother Willie and I often received portions of the crackers, cakes, and preserves, she made to sell; and after we ceased to be children we were indebted to her for many more important services.

Such were the unusually fortunate circumstances of my early childhood. When I was six years old, my mother died; and then, for the first time, I learned, by the talk around me, that I was a slave. My mother's mistress was the daughter of my grandmother's mistress. She was the foster sister of my mother; they were both nourished at my grandmother's breast. In fact, my mother had been weaned at three months old, that the babe of the mistress might obtain sufficient food. They played together as children; and, when they became women, my mother was a most faithful servant to her whiter foster sister. On her death-bed her mistress promised that her children should never suffer for any thing; and during her lifetime she kept her word. They all spoke kindly of my dead mother, who had been a slave merely in name, but in nature was noble and womanly. I grieved for her, and my young mind was troubled with the thought who would now take care of me and my little brother. I was told that my home was now to be with her mistress; and I found it a happy one. No toilsome or disagreeable duties were imposed upon me. My mistress was so kind to me that I was always glad to do her bidding, and proud to labor for her as much as my young years would permit. I would sit by her side for hours, sewing diligently, with a heart as free from care as that of any free-born white child. When she thought I was tired, she would send me out to run and jump; and away I bounded, to gather berries or flowers to decorate her room. Those were happy days—too happy to last. The slave child had no thought for the morrow; but there came that blight, which too surely waits on every human being born to be a chattel.

When I was nearly twelve years old, my kind mistress sickened and died. As I saw the cheek grow paler, and the eye more glassy, how earnestly I prayed in my heart that she might live! I loved her; for she had been almost like a mother to me. My prayers were not answered. She died, and they buried her in the little churchyard, where, day after day, my tears fell upon her grave.

I was sent to spend a week with my grandmother. I was now old enough to begin to think of the future; and again and again I asked myself what they would do with me. I felt sure I should never find another mistress so kind as the one who was gone. She had promised my dying mother that her children should never suffer for any thing; and when I remembered that, and recalled her many proofs of attachment to me, I could not help having some hopes that she had left me free. My friends were almost certain it would be so. They thought she would be sure to do it, on account of my mother's love and faithful service. But, alas! we all know that the memory of a faithful slave does not avail much to save her children from the auction block.

After a brief period of suspense, the will of my mistress was read, and we learned that she had bequeathed me to her sister's daughter, a child of five years old. So vanished our hopes. My mistress had taught me the precepts of God's Word: "Thou shalt love they neighbor as thyself." "Whatsoever ye would that men should do unto you, do ye even so unto them." But I was her slave, and I suppose she did not recognize me as her neighbor. I would give much to blot out from my memory that one great wrong. As a child, I loved my mistress; and, looking back on the happy days I spent with her, I try to think with less bitterness of this act of injustice. While I was with her, she taught me to read and spell; and for this privilege, which so rarely falls to the lot of a slave, I bless her memory.

She possessed but few slaves; and at her death those were all distributed among her relatives. Five of them were my grandmother's children, and had shared the same milk that nourished her mother's children. Notwithstanding my grandmother's long and faithful service to her owners, not one of her children escaped the auction block. These God-breathing machines are no more, in the sight of their masters, than the cotton they plant, or the horses they tend.

[Linda Brent was willed to her late mistress's little niece Emily Flint and sent to the Flint house to live.]

VI. The Jealous Mistress

I would ten thousand times rather that my children should be the half-starved paupers of Ireland than to be the most pampered among the slaves of America.[1] I would rather drudge out my life on a cotton plantation, till the grave opened to give me rest, than to live with an unprincipled master and a jealous mistress. The felon's home in a penitentiary is preferable. He may repent, and turn from the error of his ways, and so find peace; but it is not so with a favorite slave. She is not allowed to have any pride of character. It is deemed a crime in her to wish to be virtuous.

Mrs. Flint possessed the key to her husband's character before I was born. She might have used this knowledge to counsel and to screen the young and the innocent among her slaves; but for them she had no sympathy. They were the objects of her constant suspicion and malevolence. She watched her husband with unceasing vigilance; but he was well practised in means to evade it. What he could not find opportunity to say in words he manifested in signs. He invented more than were ever thought of in a deaf and dumb asylum. I let them pass, as if I did not understand what he meant; and many were the curses and threats bestowed on me for my stupidity. One day he caught me teaching myself to write. He frowned, as if he was not well pleased; but I suppose he came to the conclusion that such an accomplishment might help to advance his favorite scheme. Before long, notes were often slipped into my hand. I would return them, saying, "I can't read them, sir." "Can't you?" he replied; "then I must read them to you." He always finished the reading by asking, "Do you understand?" Sometimes he would complain of the heat of the tea room, and order his supper to be placed on a small table in the piazza. He would seat himself there with a well-satisfied smile, and tell me to stand by and brush away the flies. He would eat very slowly, pausing between the mouthfuls. These intervals were employed in describing the happiness I was so foolishly throwing away, and in threatening me with the penalty that finally awaited my stubborn disobedience. He boasted much of the forbearance he had exercised towards me, and reminded me that there was a limit to his patience. When I succeeded

[1]Abolitionists regularly compared the plight of the Irish starving in the potato famine with the plight of African Americans held in slavery.

in avoiding opportunities for him to talk to me at home, I was ordered to come to his office, to do some errand. When there, I was obliged to stand and listen to such language as he saw fit to address to me. Sometimes I so openly expressed my contempt for him that he would become violently enraged, and I wondered why he did not strike me. Circumstanced as he was, he probably thought it was better policy to be forbearing. But the state of things grew worse and worse daily. In desperation I told him that I must and would apply to my grandmother for protection. He threatened me with death, and worse than death, if I made any complaint to her. Strange to say, I did not despair. I was naturally of a buoyant disposition, and always I had a hope of somehow getting out of his clutches. Like many a poor, simple slave before me, I trusted that some threads of joy would yet be woven into my dark destiny.

I had entered my sixteenth year, and every day it became more apparent that my presence was intolerable to Mrs. Flint. Angry words frequently passed between her and her husband. He had never punished me himself, and he would not allow any body else to punish me. In that respect, she was never satisfied; but, in her angry moods, no terms were too vile for her to bestow upon me. Yet I, whom she detested so bitterly, had far more pity for her than he had, whose duty it was to make her life happy. I never wronged her, or wished to wrong her; and one word of kindness from her would have brought me to her feet.

After repeated quarrels between the doctor and his wife, he announced his intention to take his youngest daughter, then four years old, to sleep in his apartment. It was necessary that a servant should sleep in the same room, to be on hand if the child stirred. I was selected for that office, and informed for what purpose that arrangement had been made. By managing to keep within sight of people, as much as possible, during the day time, I had hitherto succeeded in eluding my master, though a razor was often held to my throat to force me to change this line of policy. At night I slept by the side of my great aunt, where I felt safe. He was too prudent to come into her room. She was an old woman, and had been in the family many years. Moreover, as a married man, and a professional man, he deemed it necessary to save appearances in some degree. But he resolved to remove the obstacle in the way of his scheme; and he thought he had planned it so that he should evade suspicion. He was well aware how much I prized my refuge by the side of my old aunt, and he determined to dispossess me of it. The first night the doctor had the little child in his room alone. The next morning, I was ordered to take my station as nurse the following night. A kind Providence interposed in my favor. During the day Mrs. Flint heard of this new arrangement, and a storm followed. I rejoiced to hear it rage.

After a while my mistress sent for me to come to her room. Her first question was, "Did you know you were to sleep in the doctor's room?"

"Yes, ma'am."

"Who told you?"

"My master."

"Will you answer truly all the questions I ask?"

"Yes, ma'am."

"Tell me, then, as you hope to be forgiven, are you innocent of what I have accused you?"

"I am."

She handed me a Bible, and said, "Lay your hand on your heart, kiss this holy book, and swear before God that you tell me the truth."

I took the oath she required, and I did it with a clear conscience.

"You have taken God's holy word to testify your innocence," said she. "If you have deceived me, beware! Now take this stool, sit down, look me directly in the face, and tell me all that has passed between your master and you."

I did as she ordered. As I went on with my account her color changed frequently, she wept, and sometimes groaned. She spoke in tones so sad, that I was touched by her grief. The tears came to my eyes; but I was soon convinced that her emotions arose from anger and wounded pride. She felt that her marriage vows were desecrated, her dignity insulted; but she had no compassion for the poor victim of her husband's perfidy. She pitied herself as a martyr; but she was incapable of feeling for the condition of shame and misery in which her unfortunate, helpless slave was placed.

Yet perhaps she had some touch of feeling for me; for when the conference was ended, she spoke kindly, and promised to protect me. I should have been much comforted by this assurance if I could have had confidence in it; but my experiences in slavery had filled me with distrust. She was not a very refined woman, and had not much control over her passions. I was an object of her jealousy, and, consequently, of her hatred; and I knew I could not expect kindness or confidence from her under the circumstances in which I was placed. I could not blame her. Slaveholders' wives feel as other women would under similar circumstances. The fire of her temper kindled from small sparks, and now the flame became so intense that the doctor was obliged to give up his intended arrangement.

I knew I had ignited the torch, and I expected to suffer for it afterwards; but I felt too thankful to my mistress for the timely aid she rendered me to care much about that. She now took me to sleep in a room adjoining her own. There I was an object of her especial care, though not of her especial comfort, for she spent many a sleepless night to watch over me. Sometimes I woke up, and found her bending over me. At other times she whispered in my ear, as though it was her husband who was speaking to me, and listened to hear what I would answer. If she startled me, on such occasions, she would glide stealthily away; and the next morning she would tell me I had been talking in my sleep, and ask who I was talking to. At last, I began to be fearful for my life. It had been often threatened; and you can imagine, better than I can describe, what an unpleasant sensation it must produce to wake up in the dead of night and find a jealous woman bending over you. Terrible as this experience was, I had fears that it would give place to one more terrible.

My mistress grew weary of her vigils; they did not prove satisfactory. She changed her tactics. She now tried the trick of accusing my master of crime, in my presence, and gave my name as the author of the accusation. To my utter astonishment, he replied, "I don't believe it: but if she did acknowledge it, you tortured her into exposing me." Tortured into exposing him! Truly, Satan had no difficulty in distinguishing the color of his soul! I understood his object in making this false representation. It was to show me that I gained nothing by seeking the protection of my mistress; that the power was still all in his own hands. I pitied Mrs. Flint. She was a second wife, many years the junior of her husband; and the hoary-headed miscreant was enough to try the patience of a wiser and better woman. She was completely foiled, and knew not how to proceed. She would gladly have had me flogged for my supposed false oath; but, as I have already stated, the doctor never allowed any one to whip me. The old sinner was politic. The application of the lash might have led to remarks that would have exposed him in the eyes of his children and grandchildren. How often did I rejoice that I lived in a town where all the inhabitants knew each other! If I had been on a remote plantation, or lost among the multitude of a crowded city, I should not be a living woman at this day.

The secrets of slavery are concealed like those of the Inquisition. My master was, to my knowledge, the father of eleven slaves. But did the mothers dare to tell who was the father of their children? Did the other slaves dare to allude to it, except in whispers among themselves? No, indeed! They knew too well the terrible consequences.

My grandmother could not avoid seeing things which excited her suspicions. She was uneasy about me, and tried various ways to buy me; but the neverchanging answer was always repeated: "Linda does not belong to *me*. She is my daughter's property, and I have no legal right to sell her." The conscientious man! He was too scrupulous to *sell* me; but he had no scruples whatever about committing a much greater wrong against the helpless young girl placed under his guardianship, as his daughter's property. Sometimes my persecutor would ask me whether I would like to be sold. I told him I would rather be sold to any body than to lead such a life as I did. On such occasions he would assume the air of a very injured individual, and reproach me for my ingratitude. "Did I not take you into the house, and make you the companion of my own children?" he would say. "Have I ever treated you like a negro? I have never allowed you to be punished, not even to please your mistress. And this is the recompense I get, you ungrateful girl!" I answered that he had reasons of his own for screening me from punishment, and that the course he pursued made my mistress hate me and persecute me. If I wept, he would say, "Poor child! Don't cry! don't cry! I will make peace for you with your mistress. Only let me arrange matters in my own way. Poor, foolish girl! you don't know what is for your own good. I would cherish you. I would make a lady of you. Now go, and think of all I have promised you."

I did think of it.

Reader, I draw no imaginary pictures of southern homes. I am telling you the plain truth. Yet when victims make their escape from this wild beast of Slavery, northerners consent to act the part of bloodhounds, and hunt the poor fugitive back into his den, "full of dead men's bones, and all uncleanness."[2] Nay, more, they are not only willing, but proud, to give their daughters in marriage to slaveholders. The poor girls have romantic notions of a sunny clime, and of the flowering vines that all the year round shade a happy home. To what disappointments are they destined! The young wife soon learns that the husband in whose hands she has placed her happiness pays no regard to his marriage vows. Children of every shade of complexion play with her own fair babies, and too well she knows that they are born unto him of his own household. Jealousy and hatred enter the flowery home, and it is ravaged of its loveliness.

Southern women often marry a man knowing that he is the father of many little slaves. They do not trouble themselves about it. They regard such children as property, as marketable as the pigs on the plantation; and it is seldom that they do not make them aware of this by passing them into the slavetrader's hands as soon as possible, and thus getting them out of their sight. I am glad to say there are some honorable exceptions.

I have myself known two southern wives who exhorted their husbands to free those slaves towards whom they stood in a "parental relation"; and their request was granted. These husbands blushed before the superior nobleness of their wives' natures. Though they had only counselled them to do that which it was their duty to do, it commanded their respect, and rendered their conduct more exemplary. Concealment was at an end, and confidence took the place of distrust.

Though this bad institution deadens the moral sense, even in white women, to a fearful extent, it is not altogether extinct. I have heard southern ladies say of Mr. Such a one, "He not only thinks it no disgrace to be the father of those little niggers, but he is not ashamed to call himself their master. I declare, such things ought not to be tolerated in any decent society!"

[Linda Brent was subjected to unrelenting sexual harassment by Dr. Flint. When she was in her early teens, she fell in love with a free black man, but Flint, who wanted her for himself, forbade her to marry.]

X. A Perilous Passage in the Slave Girl's Life

After my lover went away, Dr. Flint contrived a new plan. He seemed to have an idea that my fear of my mistress was his greatest obstacle. In the blandest tones, he told me that he was going to build a small house for me, in a secluded place, four miles away from the town. I shuddered; but I was constrained to listen, while he talked of his intention to give me a home of

[2]"Woe unto you, scribes and Pharisees, hypocrites! for ye are like unto whited sepulchres, which indeed appear beautiful outward, but are within full of dead men's bones, and of all uncleanness." Matthew 23:27.

my own, and to make a lady of me. Hitherto, I had escaped my dreaded fate, by being in the midst of people. My grandmother had already had high words with my master about me. She had told him pretty plainly what she thought of his character, and there was considerable gossip in the neighborhood about our affairs, to which the open-mouthed jealousy of Mrs. Flint contributed not a little. When my master said he was going to build a house for me, and that he could do it with little trouble and expense, I was in hopes something would happen to frustrate his scheme; but I soon heard that the house was actually begun. I vowed before my Maker that I would never enter it. I had rather toil on the plantation from dawn til dark; I had rather live and die in jail, than drag on, from day to day, through such a living death. I was determined that the master, whom I so hated and loathed, who had blighted the prospects of my youth, and made my life a desert, should not, after my long struggle with him, succeed at last in trampling his victim under his feet. I would do any thing, every thing, for the sake of defeating him. What *could* I do? I thought and thought, til I became desperate, and made a plunge into the abyss.

And now, reader, I come to a period in my unhappy life, which I would gladly forget if I could. The remembrance fills me with sorrow and shame. It pains me to tell you of it; but I have promised to tell you the truth, and I will do it honestly, let it cost me what it may. I will not try to screen myself behind the plea of compulsion from a master; for it was not so. Neither can I plead ignorance or thoughtlessness. For years, my master had done his utmost to pollute my mind with foul images, and to destroy the pure principles inculcated by my grandmother, and the good mistress of my childhood. The influences of slavery had had the same effect on me that they had on other young girls; they had made me prematurely knowing, concerning the evil ways of the world. I knew what I did, and I did it with deliberate calculation.

But, O, ye happy women, whose purity has been sheltered from childhood, who have been free to choose the objects of your affection, whose homes are protected by law, do not judge the poor desolate slave girl too severely! If slavery had been abolished, I, also, could have married the man of my choice; I could have had a home shielded by the laws; and I should have been spared the painful task of confessing what I am now about to relate; but all my prospects had been blighted by slavery. I wanted to keep myself pure; and, under the most adverse circumstances, I tried hard to preserve my self-respect; but I was struggling alone in the powerful grasp of the demon Slavery; and the monster proved too strong for me. I felt as if I was forsaken by God and man; as if all my efforts must be frustrated; and I became reckless in my despair.

I have told you that Dr. Flint's persecutions and his wife's jealousy had given rise to some gossip in the neighborhood. Among others, it chanced that a white unmarried gentleman had obtained some knowledge of the circumstances in which I was placed. He knew my grandmother, and often spoke to me in the street. He became interested for me, and asked questions about my master, which I answered in part. He expressed a great deal of sympathy, and a wish to aid me. He constantly sought opportunities to see me, and wrote to me frequently. I was a poor slave girl, only fifteen years old.

So much attention from a superior person was, of course, flattering; for human nature is the same in all. I also felt grateful for his sympathy, and encouraged by his kind words. It seemed to me a great thing to have such a friend. By degrees, a more tender feeling crept into my heart. He was an educated and eloquent gentleman; too eloquent, alas, for the poor slave girl who trusted in him. Of course I saw whither all this was tending. I knew the impassable gulf between us; but to be an object of interest to a man who is not married, and who is not her master, is agreeable to the pride and feelings of a slave, if her miserable situation has left her any pride or sentiment. It seems less degrading to give one's self, than to submit to compulsion. There is something akin to freedom in having a lover who has no control over you, except that which he gains by kindness and attachment. A master may treat you as rudely as he pleases, and you dare not speak; moreover, the wrong does not seem so great with an unmarried man, as with one who has a wife to be made unhappy. There may be sophistry in all this; but the condition of a slave confuses all principles of morality, and, in fact, renders the practice of them impossible.

When I found that my master had actually begun to build the lonely cottage, other feelings mixed with those I have described. Revenge, and calculations of interest, were added to flattered vanity and sincere gratitude for kindness. I knew nothing would enrage Dr. Flint so much as to know that I favored another; and it was something to triumph over my tyrant even in that small way. I thought he would revenge himself by selling me, and I was sure my friend, Mr. Sands, would buy me. He was a man of more generosity and feeling than my master, and I thought my freedom could be easily obtained from him. The crisis of my fate now came so near that I was desperate. I shuddered to think of being the mother of children that should be owned by my old tyrant. I knew that as soon as a new fancy took him, his victims were sold far off to get rid of them; especially if they had children. I had seen several women sold, with his babies at the breast. He never allowed his offspring by slaves to remain long in sight of himself and his wife. Of a man who was not my master I could ask to have my children well supported; and in this case, I felt confident I should obtain the boon. I also felt quite sure they they would be made free. With all these thoughts revolving in my mind, and seeing no other way of escaping the doom I so much dreaded, I made a headlong plunge. Pity me, and pardon me, O virtuous reader! You never knew what it is to be a slave; to be entirely unprotected by law or custom; to have the laws reduce you to the condition of a chattel, entirely subject to the will of another. You never exhausted your ingenuity in avoiding the snares, and eluding the power of a hated tyrant; you never shuddered at the sound of his footsteps, and trembled within hearing of his voice. I know I did wrong. No one can feel it more sensibly than I do.

The painful and humiliating memory will haunt me to my dying day. Still, in looking back, calmly, on the events of my life, I feel that the slave woman ought not to be judged by the same standard as others.

The months passed on. I had many unhappy hours. I secretly mourned over the sorrow I was bringing on my grandmother, who had so tried to shield me from harm. I knew that I was the greatest comfort of her old age, and that it was a source of pride to her that I had not degraded myself, like most of the slaves. I wanted to confess to her that I was no longer worthy of her love; but I could not utter the dreaded words.

As for Dr. Flint, I had a feeling of satisfaction and triumph in the thought of telling *him*. From time to time he told me of his intended arrangements, and I was silent. At last, he came and told me the cottage was completed, and ordered me to go to it. I told him I would never enter it. He said, "I have heard enough of such talk as that. You shall go, if you are carried by force; and you shall remain there."

I replied, "I will never go there. In a few months I shall be a mother."

He stood and looked at me in dumb amazement, and left the house without a word. I thought I should be happy in my triumph over him. But now that the truth was out, and my relatives would hear of it, I felt wretched. Humble as were their circumstances, they had pride in my good character. Now, how could I look them in the face? My self-respect was gone! I had resolved that I would be virtuous, though I was a slave. I had said, "Let the storm beat! I will brave it till I die." And now, how humiliated I felt!

I went to my grandmother. My lips moved to make confession, but the words stuck in my throat. I sat down in the shade of a tree at her door and began to sew. I think she saw something unusual was the matter with me. The mother of slaves is very watchful. She knows there is no security for her children. After they have entered their teens she lives in daily expectation of trouble. This leads to many questions. If the girl is of a sensitive nature, timidity keeps her from answering truthfully, and this well-meant course has a tendency to drive her from maternal counsels. Presently, in came my mistress, like a mad woman, and accused me concerning her husband. My grandmother, whose suspicions had been previously awakened, believed what she said. She exclaimed, "O Linda! has it come to this? I had rather see you dead than to see you as you are now. You are a disgrace to your dead mother." She tore from my fingers my mother's wedding ring and her silver thimble. "Go away!" she exclaimed, "and never come to my house, again." Her reproaches fell so hot and heavy, that they left me no chance to answer. Bitter tears, such as the eyes never shed but once, were my only answer. I rose from my seat, but fell back again, sobbing. She did not speak to me; but the tears were running down her furrowed cheeks, and they scorched me like fire. She had always been so kind to me! *So* kind! How I longed to throw myself at her feet, and tell her all the truth! But she had ordered me to go, and never to come there again. After a few minutes, I mustered strength, and started to obey her. With what feelings did I now close that little gate, which I used to open with such an eager hand in my childhood! It closed upon me with a sound I never heard before.

Where could I go? I was afraid to return to my master's. I walked on recklessly, not caring where I went, or what would become of me. When I had gone four or five miles, fatigue compelled me to stop. I sat down on the stump of an old tree. The stars were shining through the boughs above me. How they mocked me, with their bright, calm light! The hours passed by, and as I sat there alone a chilliness and deadly sickness came over me. I sank on the ground. My mind was full of horrid thoughts. I prayed to die; but the prayer was not answered. At last, with great-effort I roused myself, and walked some distance further, to the house of a woman who had been a friend of my mother. When I told her why I was there, she spoke soothingly to me; but I could not be comforted. I thought I could bear my shame if I could only be reconciled to my grandmother. I longed to open my heart to her. I thought if she could know the real state of the case, and all I had been bearing for years, she would perhaps judge me less harshly. My friend advised me to send for her. I did so; but days of agonizing suspense passed before she came. Had she utterly forsaken me? No. She came at last. I knelt before her, and told her the things that had poisoned my life; how long I had been persecuted; that I saw no way of escape; and in an hour of extremity I had become desperate. She listened in silence. I told her I would bear any thing and do any thing, if in time I had hopes of obtaining her forgiveness. I begged of her to pity me, for my dead mother's sake. And she did pity me. She did not say, "I forgive you"; but she looked at me lovingly, with her eyes full of tears. She laid her old hand gently on my head, and murmured, "Poor child! Poor child!"

[Mrs. Flint threw Linda Brent out of the house and her grandmother took her in. Brent's son Benjamin was born in her grandmother's house, as was her daughter Ellen. When Linda Brent was 21, Flint again tried to force her into concubinage. She objected and was sent out to the plantation.]

XVI. Scenes at the Plantation

Early the next morning I left my grandmother's with my youngest child. My boy was ill, and I left him behind. I had many sad thoughts as the old wagon jolted on. Hitherto, I had suffered alone; now, my little one was to be treated as a slave. As we drew near the great house, I thought of the time when I was formerly sent there out of revenge. I wondered for what purpose I was now sent. I could not tell. I resolved to obey orders so far as duty required; but within myself, I determined to make my stay as short as possible. Mr. Flint was waiting to receive us, and told me to follow him up stairs to receive orders for the day. My little Ellen was left below in the kitchen. It was a change for her, who had always been so carefully tended. My young master said she might amuse herself in the yard. This was kind of him, since the child was hateful to his sight. My task was to fit up the house for the reception of the bride. In the midst of sheets, tablecloths, towels, drapery, and carpeting, my head was as busy planning, as were my fingers with the needle. At noon I was allowed to go to Ellen. She had sobbed herself to sleep. I heard Mr. Flint say to a neighbor, "I've got her down here, and I'll soon take the town notions out of her head. My father is partly to blame for her nonsense. He ought to have broke her in long ago." The remark was made within my hearing, and it would have been quite as manly to have made it to my face. He *had* said things to my face which might, or might not, have surprised his neighbor if he had known of them. He was "a chip of the old block."

I resolved to give him no cause to accuse me of being too much of a lady, so far as work was concerned. I worked day and night, with wretchedness before me. When I lay down beside my child, I felt how much easier it would be to see her die than to see her master beat her about, as I daily saw him beat other little ones. The spirit of the mothers was so crushed by the lash, that they stood by, without courage to remonstrate. How much more must I suffer, before I should be "broke in" to that degree?

I wished to appear as contented as possible. Sometimes I had an opportunity to send a few lines home; and this brought up recollections that made it difficult, for a time, to seem calm and indifferent to my lot. Notwithstanding my efforts, I saw that Mr. Flint regarded me with a suspicious eye. Ellen broke down under the trials of her new life. Separated from me, with no one to look after her, she wandered about, and in a few days cried herself sick. One day, she sat under the window where I was at work, crying that weary cry which makes a mother's heart bleed. I was obliged to steel myself to bear it. After a while it ceased. I looked out, and she was gone. As it was near noon, I ventured to go down in search of her. The great house was raised two feet above the ground. I looked under it, and saw her about midway, fast asleep. I crept under and drew her out. As I held her in my arms, I thought how well it would be for her if she never waked up; and I uttered my thought aloud. I was startled to hear some one say, "Did you speak to me?" I looked up, and saw Mr. Flint standing beside me. He said nothing further, but turned, frowning, away. That night he sent Ellen a biscuit and a cup of sweetened milk. This generosity surprised me. I learned afterwards, that in the afternoon he had killed a large snake, which crept from under the house; and I supposed that incident had prompted his unusual kindness.

The next morning the old cart was loaded with shingles for town. I put Ellen into it, and sent her to her grandmother. Mr. Flint said I ought to have asked his permission. I told him the child was sick, and required attention which I had no time to give. He let it pass; for he was aware that I had accomplished much work in a little time.

I had been three weeks on the plantation, when I planned a visit home. It must be at night, after every body was in bed. I was six miles from town, and the road was very dreary. I was to go with a young man, who, I knew, often stole to town to see his mother. One night, when all was quiet, we started. Fear gave speed to our steps, and we were not long in performing the journey. I arrived at my grandmother's. Her bed room was on the first floor, and the window was open, the weather being warm. I spoke to her and she awoke. She let me in and closed the window, lest some late passer-by should see me. A light was brought, and the whole household gathered round me, some smiling and some crying. I went to look at my children, and thanked God for their happy sleep. The tears fell as I leaned over them. As I moved to leave, Benny stirred. I turned back, and whispered, "Mother is here." After digging at his eyes with his little fist, they opened, and he sat up in bed, looking at me curiously. Having satisfied himself that it was I, he exclaimed, "O mother! you ain't dead, are you? They didn't cut off your head at the plantation, did they?"

My time was up too soon, and my guide was waiting for me. I laid Benny back in his bed, and dried his tears by a promise to come again soon. Rapidly we retraced our steps back to the plantation. About half way we were met by a company of four patrols.[1] Luckily we heard their horse's hoofs before they came in sight, and we had time to hide behind a large tree. They passed, hallooing and shouting in a manner that indicated a recent carousal. How thankful we were that they had not their dogs with them! We hastened our footsteps, and when we arrived on the plantation we heard the sound of the hand-mill. The slaves were grinding their corn. We were safely in the house before the horn summoned them to their labor. I divided my little parcel of food with my guide, knowing that he had lost the chance of grinding his corn, and must toil all day in the field.

Mr. Flint often took an inspection of the house, to see that no one was idle. The entire management of the work was trusted to me, because he knew nothing about it; and rather than hire a superintendent he contented himself with my arrangements. He had often urged upon his father the necessity of having me at the plantation to take charge of his affairs, and make clothes for the slaves; but the old man knew him too well to consent to that arrangement.

When I had been working a month at the plantation, the great aunt of Mr. Flint came to make him a visit. This was the good old lady who paid fifty dollars for my grandmother, for the purpose of making her free, when she stood on the auction block. My grandmother loved this old lady, whom we all called Miss Fanny. She often came to take tea with us. On such occasions the table was spread with a snow-white cloth, and the china cups and silver spoons were taken from the old-fashioned buffet. There were hot muffins, tea rusks, and delicious sweetmeats. My grandmother kept two cows, and the fresh cream was Miss Fanny's delight. She invariably declared that it was the best in town. The old ladies had cosey times together. They would work and chat, and sometimes, while talking over old times, their spectacles would get dim with tears, and would have to be taken off and

[1]A system of patrols monitored the roads and periodically checked the slave quarters. Slaves leaving the plantation were required to have a pass signed by a master or overseer; if caught without such passes, they were summarily punished by the patrol.

wiped. When Miss Fanny bade us good by, her bag was filled with grand-mother's best cakes, and she was urged to come again soon.

There had been a time when Dr. Flint's wife came to take tea with us, and when her children were also sent to have a feast of "Aunt Marthy's" nice cooking. But after I became an object of her jealousy and spite, she was angry with grandmother for giving a shelter to me and my children. She would not even speak to her in the street. This wounded my grandmother's feelings, for she could not retain ill will against the woman whom she had nourished with her milk when a babe. The doctor's wife would gladly have prevented our intercourse with Miss Fanny if she could have done it, but fortunately she was not dependent on the bounty of the Flints. She had enough to be independent; and that is more than can ever be gained from charity, however lavish it may be.

Miss Fanny was endeared to me by many recollections, and I was rejoiced to see her at the plantation. The warmth of her large, loyal heart made the house seem pleasanter while she was in it. She staid a week, and I had many talks with her. She said her principal object in coming was to see how I was treated, and whether any thing could be done for me. She inquired whether she could help me in any way. I told her I believed not. She condoled with me in her own peculiar way; saying she wished that I and all my grandmother's family were at rest in our graves, for not until then should she feel any peace about us. The good old soul did not dream that I was planning to bestow peace upon her, with regard to myself and my chil-dren; not by death, but by securing our freedom.

Again and again I had traversed those dreary twelve miles, to and from the town; and all the way, I was meditating upon some means of escape for myself and my children. My friends had made every effort that ingenuity could devise to effect our purchase, but all their plans had proved abortive. Dr. Flint was suspicious, and determined not to loosen his grasp upon us. I could have made my escape alone; but it was more for my helpless children than for myself that I longed for freedom. Though the boon would have been precious to me, above all price, I would not have taken it at the expense of leaving them in slavery. Every trial I endured, every sacrifice I made for their sakes, drew them closer to my heart, and gave me fresh cour-age to beat back the dark waves that rolled and rolled over me in a seem-ingly endless night of storms.

The six weeks were nearly completed, when Mr. Flint's bride was expected to take possession of her new home. The arrangements were all completed, and Mr. Flint said I had done well. He expected to leave home on Saturday, and return with his bride the following Wednesday. After receiving various orders from him, I ventured to ask permission to spend Sunday in town. It was granted; for which favor I was thankful. It was the first I had ever asked of him, and I intended it should be the last. It needed more than one night to accomplish the project I had in view; but the whole of Sunday would give me an opportunity. I spent the Sabbath with my grandmother. A calmer, more beautiful day never came down out of heaven.

To me it was a day of conflicting emotions. Perhaps it was the last day I should ever spend under that dear, old sheltering roof! Perhaps these were the last talks I should ever have with the faithful old friend of my whole life! Perhaps it was the last time I and my children should be together! Well, better so, I thought, than that they should be slaves. I knew the doom that awaited my fair baby in slavery, and I determined to save her from it, or perish in the attempt. I went to make this vow at the graves of my poor parents, in the burying-ground of the slaves. "There the wicked cease from troubling, and there the weary be at rest. There the prisoners rest together; they hear not the voice of the oppressor; the servant is free from his master."[2] I knelt by the graves of my parents, and thanked God, as I had often done before, that they had not lived to witness my trials, or to mourn over my sins. I had received my mother's blessing when she died; and in many an hour of tribulation I had seemed to hear her voice, sometimes chiding me, sometimes whispering loving words into my wounded heart. I have shed many and bitter tears, to think that when I am gone from my children they cannot remember me with such entire satisfaction as I remembered my mother.

The graveyard was in the woods, and twilight was coming on. Nothing broke the death-like stillness except the occasional twitter of a bird. My spirit was over-awed by the solemnity of the scene. For more than ten years I had frequented this spot, but never had it seemed to me so sacred as now. A black stump, at the head of my mother's grave, was all that remained of a tree my father had planted. His grave was marked by a small wooden board, bearing his name, the letters of which were nearly obliterated. I knelt down and kissed them, and poured forth a prayer to God for guidance and support in the perilous step I was about to take. As I passed the wreck of the old meeting house, where, before Nat Turner's time, the slaves had been allowed to meet for worship, I seemed to hear my father's voice come from it, bidding me not to tarry till I reached freedom or the grave.[3] I rushed on with renovated hopes. My trust in God had been strengthened by that prayer among the graves.

My plan was to conceal myself at the house of a friend, and remain there a few weeks till the search was over. My hope was that the doctor would get discouraged, and, for fear of losing my value, and also of subsequently finding my children among the missing, he would consent to sell us; and I knew somebody would buy us. I had done all in my power to make my children comfortable during the time I expected to be separated from them. I was packing my things, when grandmother came into the room, and asked what I was doing. "I am putting my things in order," I replied. I tried to look and speak cheerfully; but her watchful eye detected something beneath the surface. She drew me towards her, and asked me to sit down. She looked

[2] Job 3:17–19.
[3] In 1831 in Southampton County, Virginia (about 40 miles upstream from Edenton), Nat Turner had led the bloodiest slave insur-

rection in American history. Subsequently, the white South retaliated by passing and enforcing repressive laws against slaves and free blacks.

earnestly at me, and said, "Linda, do you want to kill your old grandmother? Do you mean to leave your little, helpless children? I am old now, and cannot do for your babies as I once did for you."

I replied, that if I went away, perhaps their father would be able to secure their freedom.

"Ah, my child," said she, "don't trust too much to him. Stand by your own children, and suffer with them till death. Nobody respects a mother who forsakes her children; and if you leave them, you will never have a happy moment. If you go, you will make me miserable the short time I have to live. You would be taken and brought back, and your sufferings would be dreadful. Remember poor Benjamin. Do give it up, Linda. Try to bear a little longer. Things may turn out better than we expect."

My courage failed me, in view of the sorrow I should bring on that faithful, loving old heart. I promised that I would try longer, and that I would take nothing out of her house without her knowledge.

Whenever the children climbed on my knee, or laid their heads on my lap, she would say, "Poor little souls! what would you do without a mother? She don't love you as I do." And she would hug them to her own bosom, as if to reproach me for my want of affection; but she knew all the while that I loved them better than my life. I slept with her that night, and it was the last time. The memory of it haunted me for many a year.

On Monday I returned to the plantation, and busied myself with preparations for the important day. Wednesday came. It was a beautiful day, and the faces of the slaves were as bright as sunshine. The poor creatures were merry. They were expecting little presents from the bride, and hoping for better times under her administration. I had no such hopes for them. I knew that the young wives of slaveholders often thought their authority and importance would be best established and maintained by cruelty; and what I had heard of young Mrs. Flint gave me no reason to expect that her rule over them would be less severe than that of the master and overseer. Truly, the colored race are the most cheerful and forgiving people on the face of the earth. That their masters sleep in safety is owing to their superabundance of heart; and yet they look upon their sufferings with less pity than they would bestow on those of a horse or a dog.

I stood at the door with others to receive the bridegroom and bride. She was a handsome, delicate-looking girl, and her face flushed with emotion at sight of her new home. I thought it likely that visions of a happy future were rising before her. It made me sad; for I knew how soon clouds would come over her sunshine. She examined every part of the house, and told me she was delighted with the arrangements I had made. I was afraid old Mrs. Flint had tried to prejudice her against me, and I did my best to please her.

All passed off smoothly for me until dinner time arrived. I did not mind the embarrassment of waiting on a dinner party, for the first time in my life, half so much as I did the meeting with Dr. Flint and his wife, who would be among the guests. It was a mystery to me why Mrs. Flint had not made her appearance at the plantation during all the time I was putting the house in order. I had not met her, face to face, for five years, and I had no wish to see her now. She was a praying woman, and, doubtless, considered my present position a special answer to her prayers. Nothing could please her better than to see me humbled and trampled upon. I was just where she would have me—in the power of a hard, unprincipled master. She did not speak to me when she took her seat at table; but her satisfied, triumphant smile, when I handed her plate, was more eloquent than words. The old doctor was not so quiet in his demonstrations. He ordered me here and there, and spoke with peculiar emphasis when he said "your *mistress.*" I was drilled like a disgraced soldier. When all was over, and the last key turned, I sought my pillow, thankful that God had appointed a season of rest for the weary.

The next day my new mistress began her housekeeping. I was not exactly appointed maid of all work; but I was to do whatever I was told. Monday evening came. It was always a busy time. On that night the slaves received their weekly allowance of food. Three pounds of meat, a peck of corn, and perhaps a dozen herring were allowed to each man. Women received a pound and a half of meat, a peck of corn, and the same number of herring. Children over twelve years old had half the allowance of the women. The meat was cut and weighed by the foreman of the field hands, and piled on planks before the meat house. Then the second foreman went behind the building, and when the first foreman called out, "Who takes this piece of meat?" he answered by calling somebody's name. This method was resorted to as means of preventing partiality in distributing the meat. The young mistress came out to see how things were done on her plantation, and she soon gave a specimen of her character. Among those in waiting for their allowance was a very old slave, who had faithfully served the Flint family through three generations. When he hobbled up to get his bit of meat, the mistress said he was too old to have any allowance; that when niggers were too old to work, they ought to be fed on grass. Poor old man! He suffered much before he found rest in the grave.

My mistress and I got along very well together. At the end of a week, old Mrs. Flint made us another visit, and was closeted a long time with her daughter-in-law. I had my suspicions what was the subject of the conference. The old doctor's wife had been informed that I could leave the plantation on one condition, and she was very desirous to keep me there. If she had trusted me, as I deserved to be trusted by her, she would have had no fears of my accepting that condition. When she entered her carriage to return home, she said to young Mrs. Flint, "Don't neglect to send for them as quick as possible." My heart was on the watch all the time, and I at once concluded that she spoke of my children. The doctor came the next day, and as I entered the room to spread the tea table, I heard him say, "Don't wait any longer. Send for them to-morrow." I saw through the plan. They thought my children's being there would fetter me to the spot, and that it was a good place to break us all in to abject submission to our lot as slaves. After the doctor left, a gentleman called, who had always manifested friendly feelings towards my grandmother and her family. Mr. Flint carried him over the plantation to show him the results of labor performed by men and women who were unpaid, miserably clothed, and half famished. The cotton crop was all they thought of. It was duly admired, and the gentleman returned with specimens to show his friends. I was ordered to carry water to wash his hands. As I did so, he said, "Linda, how do you like your new home?" I told him I liked it as well as I expected. He replied, "They don't think you are contented, and to-morrow they are going to bring your children to be with you. I am sorry for you, Linda. I hope they will treat you kindly." I hurried from the room, unable to thank him. My suspicions were correct. My children were to be brought to the plantation to be "broke in."

To this day I feel grateful to the gentleman who gave me this timely information. It nerved me to immediate action.

[Linda Brent ran away. All avenues of escape from the town were put under surveillance, and for several weeks she was sheltered by black and white neighbors. When Dr. Flint persisted in his hunt for her, Linda Brent's friends secreted her in a nearby swamp while her uncle prepared a hiding place in her grandmother's house.]

XXI. The Loophole of Retreat[1]

A small shed had been added to my grandmother's house years ago. Some boards were laid across the joists at the top, and between these boards and the roof was a very small garret, never occupied by any thing but rats and mice. It was a pent roof, covered with nothing but shingles, according to the southern custom for such buildings. The garret was only nine feet long and seven wide. The highest part was three feet high, and sloped down abruptly to the loose board floor. There was no admission for either light or air. My uncle Philip, who was a carpenter, had very skilfully made a concealed trapdoor, which communicated with the storeroom. He had been doing this while I was waiting in the swamp. The storeroom opened upon a piazza. To this hole I was conveyed as soon as I entered the house. The air was stifling; the darkness total. A bed had been spread on the floor. I could sleep quite comfortably on one side; but the slope was so sudden that I could not turn on the other without hitting the roof. The rats and mice ran over my bed; but I was weary, and I slept such sleep as the wretched may, when a tempest has passed over them. Morning came. I knew it only by the noises I heard; for in my small den day and night were all the same. I suffered for air even more than for light. But I was not comfortless. I heard the voices of my children. There was joy and there was sadness in the sound. It made my tears flow. How I longed to speak to them! I was eager to look on their faces; but there was no hole, no crack, through which I could peep. This continued darkness was oppressive. It seemed horrible to sit or lie in a cramped

---

[1]A reference to William Cowper's "The Task," IV, 88–90:

'Tis pleasant, through the loopholes of retreat,/ To peep at such a world,—to see the stir/ Of the great Babel, and not feel the crowd.

position day after day, without one gleam of light. Yet I would have chosen this, rather than my lot as a slave, though white people considered it an easy one; and it was so compared with the fate of others. I was never cruelly overworked; I was never lacerated with the whip from head to foot; I was never so beaten and bruised that I could not turn from one side to the other; I never had my heel-strings cut to prevent my running away; I was never chained to a log and forced to drag it about, while I toiled in the fields from morning till night; I was never branded with hot iron, or torn by blood-hounds. On the contrary, I had always been kindly treated, and tenderly cared for, until I came into the hands of Dr. Flint. I had never wished for freedom till then. But though my life in slavery was comparatively devoid of hardships, God pity the woman who is compelled to lead such a life!

My food was passed up to me through the trap-door my uncle had contrived; and my grandmother, my uncle Phillip, and aunt Nancy would seize such opportunities as they could, to mount up there and chat with me at the opening. But of course this was not safe in the daytime. It must all be done in darkness. It was impossible for me to move in an erect position, but I crawled about my den for exercise. One day I hit my head against something, and found it was a gimlet. My uncle had left it sticking there when he made the trap-door. I was as rejoiced as Robinson Crusoe could have been at finding such a treasure. It put a lucky thought into my head. I said to myself, "Now I will have some light. Now I will see my children." I did not dare to begin my work during the daytime, for fear of attracting attention. But I groped round; and having found the side next the street, where I could frequently see my children, I stuck the gimlet in and waited for evening. I bored three rows of holes, one above another; then I bored out the interstices between. I thus succeeded in making one hole about an inch long and an inch broad. I sat by it till late into the night, to enjoy the little whiff of air that floated in. In the morning I watched for my children. The first person I saw in the street was Dr. Flint. I had a shuddering, superstitious feeling that it was a bad omen. Several familiar faces passed by. At last I heard the merry laugh of children, and presently two sweet little faces were looking up at me, as though they knew I was there, and were conscious of the joy they imparted. How I longed to *tell* them I was there!

My condition was now a little improved. But for weeks I was tormented by hundreds of little red insects, fine as a needle's point, that pierced through my skin, and produced an intolerable burning. The good grand-mother gave me herb teas and cooling medicines, and finally I got rid of them. The heat of my den was intense, for nothing but thin shingles protected me from the scorching summer's sun. But I had my consolations. Through my peeping-hole I could watch the children, and when they were near enough, I could hear their talk. Aunt Nancy brought me all the news she could hear at Dr. Flint's. From her I learned that the doctor had written to New York to a colored woman, who had been born and raised in our neighborhood, and had breathed his contaminating atmosphere. He offered her a reward if she could find out any thing about me. I know not what was the nature of her reply; but he soon after started for New York in haste, saying to his family that he had business of importance to transact. I peeped at him as he passed on his way to the steamboat. It was a satisfaction to have miles of land and water between us, even for a little while; and it was a still greater satisfaction to know that he believed me to be in the Free States. My little den seemed less dreary than it had done. He returned, as he did from his former journey to New York, without obtaining any satisfactory information. When he passed our house next morning, Benny was standing at the gate. He had heard them say that he had gone to find me, and he called out, "Dr. Flint, did you bring my mother home? I want to see her." The doctor stamped his foot at him in a rage, and exclaimed, "Get out of the way, you little damned rascal! If you don't, I'll cut off your head."

Benny ran terrified into the house, saying, "You can't put me in jail again. I don't belong to you now." It was well that the wind carried the words away from the doctor's ear. I told my grandmother of it, when we had our next conference at the trap-door; and begged of her not to allow the children to be impertinent to the irascible old man.

Autumn came, with a pleasant abatement of heat. My eyes had become accustomed to the dim light, and by holding my book or work in a certain position near the aperture I contrived to read and sew. That was a great relief to the tedious monotony of my life. But when winter came, the cold penetrated through the thin shingle roof, and I was dreadfully chilled. The winters there are not so long, or so severe, as in northern latitudes; but the houses are not built to shelter from cold, and my little den was peculiarly comfortless. The kind grandmother brought me bed-clothes and warm drinks. Often I was obliged to lie in bed all day to keep comfortable; but with all my precautions, my shoulders and feet were frostbitten. O, those long, gloomy days, with no object for my eye to rest upon, and no thoughts to occupy my mind, except the dreary past and the uncertain future! I was thankful when there came a day sufficiently mild for me to wrap myself up and sit at the loophole to watch the passers by. Southerners have the habit of stopping and talking in the streets, and I heard many conversations not intended to meet my ears. I heard slave-hunters planning how to catch some poor fugitive. Several times I heard allusions to Dr. Flint, myself, and the history of my children, who, perhaps, were playing near the gate. One would say, "I wouldn't move my little finger to catch her, as old Flint's property." Another would say, "I'll catch *any* nigger for the reward. A man ought to have what belongs to him, if he *is* a damned brute." The opinion was often expressed that I was in the Free States. Very rarely did any one suggest that I might be in the vicinity. Had the least suspicion rested on my grandmother's house, it would have been burned to the ground. But it was the last place they thought of. Yet there was no place, where slavery existed, that could have afforded me so good a place of concealment.

Dr. Flint and his family repeatedly tried to coax and bribe my children to tell something they had heard said about me. One day the doctor took them into a shop, and offered them some bright little silver pieces and gay handkerchiefs if they would tell where their mother was. Ellen shrank away from him, and would not speak; but Benny spoke up, and said, "Dr. Flint, I don't know where my mother is. I guess she's in New York; and when you go there again, I wish you'd ask her to come home, for I want to see her; but if you put her in jail, or tell her you'll cut her head off, I'll tell her to go right back."

> [After years in hiding, Linda Brent escaped to the North. She was reunited with her children, who had been bought by their white father, and found work in the Bruce household. The passage of the 1850 Fugitive Slave Law, however, made her and her children extremely vulnerable.]

XLI. Free at Last[1]

Mrs. Bruce, and every member of her family, were exceedingly kind to me. I was thankful for the blessings of my lot, yet I could not always wear a cheerful countenance. I was doing harm to no one; on the contrary, I was doing all the good I could in my small way; yet I could never go out to breathe God's free air without trepidation at my heart. This seemed hard; and I could not think it was a right state of things in any civilized country.

From time to time I received news from my good old grandmother. She could not write; but she employed others to write for her. The following is an extract from one of her last letters:—

> *"Dear Daughter: I cannot hope to see you again on earth; but I pray to God to unite us above, where pain will no more rack this feeble body of mine; where sorrow and parting from my children will be no more.[2] God has promised these things if we are faithful unto the end. My age and feeble health deprive me of going to church now; but God is with me here at home. Thank your brother for his kindness. Give much love to him, and tell him to remember the Creator in the days of his youth, and strive to meet me in the Father's kingdom.[3] Love to Ellen and Benjamin. Don't neglect him. Tell him for me, to be a good boy. Strive, my child, to train them for God's children. May he protect and provide for you, is the prayer of your loving old mother."*

These letters both cheered and saddened me. I was always glad to have tidings from the kind, faithful old friend of my unhappy youth; but her messages of love made my heart yearn to see her before she died, and I mourned over the fact that it was impossible. Some months after I returned from my flight to New England, I received a letter from her, in which she wrote, "Dr. Flint is dead. He has left a distressed family. Poor old man! I hope he made his peace with God."

---

[1]"Free at last, free at last,/ Thank God, almighty, I'm free at last." One version of a traditional spiritual.

[2]"And God shall wipe away all tears from their eyes; and there shall be no more death, neither sorrow, nor crying, neither shall there be any more pain; for the former things are passed away." Revelation 21:4.

[3]"Remember now thy Creator in the days of thy youth, while the evil days come not, nor the years draw nigh, when thou shalt say, I have no pleasure in them." Ecclesiastes 12:1.

I remembered how he had defrauded my grandmother of the hard earnings she had loaned; how he had tried to cheat her out of the freedom her mistress had promised her, and how he had persecuted her children; and I thought to myself that she was a better Christian than I was, if she could entirely forgive him. I cannot say, with truth, that the news of my old master's death softened my feelings towards him. There are wrongs which even the grave does not bury. The man was odious to me while he lived, and his memory is odious now.

His departure from this world did not diminish my danger. He had threatened my grandmother that his heirs should hold me in slavery after he was gone; that I never should be free so long as a child of his survived. As for Mrs. Flint, I had seen her in deeper afflictions than I supposed the loss of her husband would be, for she had buried several children; yet I never saw any signs of softening in her heart. The doctor had died in embarrassed circumstances, and had little to will to his heirs, except such property as he was unable to grasp. I was well aware what I had to expect from the family of Flints; and my fears were confirmed by a letter from the south, warning me to be on my guard, because Mrs. Flint openly declared that her daughter could not afford to lose so valuable a slave as I was.

I kept close watch of the newspapers for arrivals; but one Saturday night, being much occupied, I forgot to examine the Evening Express as usual. I went down into the parlor for it, early in the morning, and found the boy about to kindle a fire with it. I took it from him and examined the list of arrivals. Reader, if you have never been a slave, you cannot imagine the acute sensation of suffering at my heart, when I read the names of Mr. and Mrs. Dodge, at a hotel in Courtland Street. It was a third-rate hotel, and that circumstance convinced me of the truth of what I had heard, that they were short of funds and had need of my value, as *they* valued me; and that was by dollars and cents. I hastened with the paper to Mrs. Bruce. Her heart and hand were always open to every one in distress, and she always warmly sympathized with mine. It was impossible to tell how near the enemy was. He might have passed and repassed the house while we were sleeping. He might at that moment be waiting to pounce upon me if I ventured out of doors. I had never seen the husband of my young mistress, and therefore I could not distinguish him from any other stranger. A carriage was hastily ordered; and, closely veiled, I followed Mrs. Bruce, taking the baby again with me into exile. After various turnings and crossings, and returnings, the carriage stopped at the house of one of Mrs. Bruce's friends, where I was kindly received. Mrs. Bruce returned immediately, to instruct the domestics what to say if any one came to inquire for me.

It was lucky for me that the evening paper was not burned up before I had a chance to examine the list of arrivals. It was not long after Mrs. Bruce's return to her house, before several people came to inquire for me. One inquired for me, another asked for my daughter Ellen, and another said he had a letter from my grandmother, which he was requested to deliver in person.

They were told, "She *has* lived here, but she has left."

"How long ago?"

"I don't know, sir."

"Do you know where she went?"

"I do not, sir." And the door was closed.

This Mr. Dodge, who claimed me as his property, was originally a Yankee pedler in the south; then he became a merchant, and finally a slaveholder. He managed to get introduced into what was called the first society, and married Miss Emily Flint. A quarrel arose between him and her brother, and the brother cowhided him. This led to a family feud, and he proposed to remove to Virginia. Dr. Flint left him no property, and his own means had become circumscribed, while a wife and children depended upon him for support. Under these circumstances, it was very natural that he should make an effort to put me into his pocket.

I had a colored friend, a man from my native place, in whom I had the most implicit confidence. I sent for him, and told him that Mr. and Mrs. Dodge had arrived in New York. I proposed that he should call upon them to make inquiries about his friends at the south, with whom Dr. Flint's family were well acquainted. He thought there was no impropriety in his doing so, and he consented. He went to the hotel, and knocked at the door of Mr. Dodge's room, which was opened by the gentleman himself, who gruffly inquired, "What brought you here? How came you to know I was in the city?"

"Your arrival was published in the evening papers, sir; and I called to ask Mrs. Dodge about my friends at home. I didn't suppose it would give any offence."

"Where's that negro girl, that belongs to my wife?"

"What girl, sir?"

"You know well enough. I mean Linda, that ran away from Dr. Flint's plantation, some years ago. I dare say you've seen her, and know where she is."

"Yes, sir, I've seen her, and know where she is. She is out of your reach, sir."

"Tell me where she is, or bring her to me, and I will give her a chance to buy her freedom."

"I don't think it would be of any use, sir. I have heard her say she would go to the ends of the earth, rather than pay any man or woman for her freedom, because she thinks she has a right to it. Besides, she couldn't do it, if she would, for she has spent her earnings to educate her children."

This made Mr. Dodge very angry, and some high words passed between them. My friend was afraid to come where I was; but in the course of the day I received a note from him. I supposed they had not come from the south, in the winter, for a pleasure excursion; and now the nature of their business was very plain.

Mrs. Bruce came to me and entreated me to leave the city the next morning. She said her house was watched, and it was possible that some clew to me might be obtained. I refused to take her advice. She pleaded with an earnest tenderness, that ought to have moved me; but I was in a bitter, disheartened mood. I was weary of flying from pillar to post. I had been chased during half my life, and it seemed as if the chase was never to end. There I sat, in that great city, guiltless of crime, yet not daring to worship God in any of the churches. I heard the bells ringing for afternoon service, and, with contemptuous sarcasm, I said, "Will the preachers take for their text, 'Proclaim liberty to the captive, and the opening of prison doors to them that are bound'? or will they preach from the text. 'Do unto others as ye would they should do unto you'?"[4] Oppressed Poles and Hungarians could find a safe refuge in that city; John Mitchell was free to proclaim in the City Hall his desire for "a plantation well stocked with slaves;" but there I sat, an oppressed American, not daring to show my face.[5] God forgive the black and bitter thoughts I indulged on that Sabbath day! The Scripture says, "Oppression makes even a wise man mad"; and I was not wise.[6]

I had been told that Mr. Dodge said his wife had never signed away her right to my children, and if he could not get me, he would take them. This it was, more than any thing else, that roused such a tempest in my soul. Benjamin was with his uncle William in California, but my innocent young daughter had come to spend a vacation with me. I thought of what I had suffered in slavery at her age, and my heart was like a tiger's when a hunter tries to seize her young.

Dear Mrs. Bruce! I seem to see the expression of her face, as she turned away discouraged by my obstinate mood. Finding her expostulation unavailing, she sent Ellen to entreat me. When ten o'clock in the evening arrived and Ellen had not returned, this watchful and unwearied friend became anxious. She came to us in a carriage, bringing a well-filled trunk for my journey—trusting that by this time I would listen to reason. I yielded to her, as I ought to have done before.

The next day, baby and I set out in a heavy snow storm, bound for New England again. I received letters from the City of Iniquity, addressed to me under an assumed name. In a few days one came from Mrs. Bruce, informing me that my new master was still searching for me, and that she intended to put an end to this persecution by buying my freedom. I felt grateful for the kindness that prompted this offer, but the idea was not so pleasant to me as might have been expected. The more my mind had become enlightened, the more difficult it was for me to consider myself an

[4]"The spirit of the Lord God is upon me; because the Lord hath anointed one to preach good tidings unto the meek; he hath sent me to bind up the brokenhearted, to proclaim liberty to the captives, and the opening of the prison to them that are bound." Isaiah 61:1. "Therefore all things whatsoever ye would that men should do to you, do ye even so to them: for this is the law and the prophets." Matthew 7:12.

[5]In 1854 John Mitchell (1815–1875), Irish nationalist founder of the proslavery newspaper *The Citizen* of New York, wrote: "We, for our part, wish we had a good plantation, well-stocked with healthy negroes, in Alabama."

[6]"Surely oppression maketh a wise man mad; and a gift destroyeth the heart." Ecclesiastes 7:17.

article of property; and to pay money to those who had so grievously oppressed me seemed like taking from my sufferings the glory of triumph.[7] I wrote to Mrs. Bruce, thanking her, but saying that being sold from one owner to another seemed too much like slavery; that such a great obligation could not be easily cancelled; and that I preferred to go to my brother in California.

Without my knowledge, Mrs. Bruce employed a gentleman in New York to enter into negotiations with Mr. Dodge. He proposed to pay three hundred dollars down, if Mr. Dodge would sell me, and enter into obligations to relinquish all claim to me or my children forever after. He who called himself my master said he scorned so small an offer for such a valuable servant. The gentleman replied, "You can do as you choose, sir. If you reject this offer you will never get any thing; for the woman has friends who will convey her and her children out of the country."

Mr. Dodge concluded that "half a loaf was better than no bread," and he agreed to the proffered terms. By the next mail I received this brief letter from Mrs. Bruce: "I am rejoiced to tell you that the money for your freedom has been paid to Mr. Dodge. Come home to-morrow. I long to see you and my sweet babe."

My brain reeled as I read these lines. A gentleman near me said, "It's true; I have seen the bill of sale." "The bill of sale!" Those words struck me like a blow. So I was *sold* at last! A human being *sold* in the free city of New York! The bill of sale is on record, and future generations will learn from it that women were articles of traffic in New York, late in the nineteenth century of the Christian religion. It may hereafter prove a useful document to antiquaries, who are seeking to measure the progress of civilization in the United States. I well know the value of that bit of paper; but much as I love freedom, I do not like to look upon it. I am deeply grateful to the generous friend who procured it, but I despise the miscreant who demanded payment for what never rightfully belonged to him or his.

I had objected to having my freedom bought, yet I must confess that when it was done I felt as if a heavy load had been lifted from my weary shoulders. When I rode home in the cars I was no longer afraid to unveil my face and look at people as they passed. I should have been glad to have met Daniel Dodge himself; to have had him seen me and known me, that he might have mourned over the untoward circumstances which compelled him to sell me for three hundred dollars.

When I reached home, the arms of my benefactress were thrown round me, and our tears mingled. As soon as she could speak, she said, "O Linda, I'm *so* glad it's all over! You wrote to me as if you thought you were going to be transferred from one owner to another. But I did not buy you for your services. I should have done just the same, if you had been going to sail for

---

[7]"He hath stripped me of my glory, and taken
the crown from my head." Job 19:9.

California tomorrow. I should, at least, have the satisfaction of knowing that you left me a free woman."

My heart was exceedingly full. I remembered how my poor father had tried to buy me, when I was a small child, and how he had been disappointed. I hoped his spirit was rejoicing over me now. I remembered how my good old grandmother had laid up her earnings to purchase me in later years, and how often her plans had been frustrated. How that faithful, loving old heart would leap for joy, if she could look on me and my children now that we were free! My relatives had been foiled in all their efforts, but God had raised me up a friend among strangers, who had bestowed on me the precious, long-desired boon. Friend! It is a common word, often lightly used. Like other good and beautiful things, It may be tarnished by careless handling; but when I speak of Mrs. Bruce as my friend, the word is sacred.

My grandmother lived to rejoice in my freedom; but not long after, a letter came with a black seal. She had gone "where the wicked cease from troubling, and the weary are at rest."[8]

Time passed on, and a paper came to me from the south, containing an obituary notice of my uncle Phillip. It was the only case I ever knew of such an honor conferred upon a colored person. It was written by one of his friends, and contained these words: "Now that death has laid him low, they call him a good man and a useful citizen; but what are eulogies to the black man, when the world has faded from his vision? It does not require man's praise to obtain rest in God's kingdom." So they called a colored man a *citizen!* Strange words to be uttered in that region![9]

Reader, my story ends with freedom; not in the usual way, with marriage. I and my children are now free! We are as free from the power of slaveholders as are the white people of the north; and though that, according to my ideas, is not saying a great deal, it is a vast improvement in *my* condition. The dream of my life is not yet realized. I do not sit with my children in a home of my own. I still long for a hearthstone of my own, however humble. I wish it for my children's sake far more than for my own. But God so orders circumstances as to keep me with my friend Mrs. Bruce. Love, duty, gratitude, also bind me to her side. It is a privilege to serve her who pities my oppressed people, and who has bestowed the inestimable boon of freedom on me and my children.

It has been painful to me, in many ways, to recall the dreary years I passed in bondage. I would gladly forget them if I could. Yet the retrospection is not altogether without solace; for with those gloomy recollections come tender memories of my good old grandmother, like light, fleecy clouds floating over a dark and troubled sea.

1861

---

[8]Job 3:17.
[9]In 1844 the North Carolina Supreme Court had declared that "free persons of color in this State are not to be considered as citizens...." An older law, referred to by David Walker, required that free black people wear a patch on their clothing.

Harriet Jacobs to Ednah Dow Cheney

Edenton [North Carolina] April 25th [1867]

Dear Mrs Cheney[1]

I felt I would like to write you a line from my old home. I am sitting under the old roof twelve feet from the spot where I suffered all the crushing weight of slavery. thank God the bitter cup is drained of its last dreg.[2] there is no more need of hiding places to conceal slave Mothers. yet it was little to purchase the blessings of freedom. I could have worn this poor life out there to save my Children from the misery and degradation of Slavery.

I had long thought I had no attachment to my old home. as I often sit here and think of those I loved of their hard struggle in life—their unfaltering love and devotion toward myself and Children. I love to sit here and think of them. they have made the few sunny spots in that dark life sacred to me.

I cannot tell you how I feel in this place. the change is so great I can hardly take it all in I was born here, and amid all these new born blessings, the old dark cloud comes over me, and I find it hard to have faith in rebels.

the past winter was very severe for this region of Country it caused much suffering, and the freedmen with but few exceptions were cheated out of their crop of cotton. their contract masters shipped it for them, and when they ask for a settlement, they are answered I am daily expecting the returns. these men have gone to work cheerfully, planted another crop without the returns to live on until their present crop is made. many of the large plantations of the once wealthy Planter, is worked under the control of Colored Men. the Owners let their Plantations to the freedmen in prefference to the poor Whites. they believe the Negro determined to make money, and they will get the largest portion of it. last years experience I think will be a proffitable lesson many will learn to act for themselves. Negro suffrage is making a stir in this place. the rebels are striving to make these people feel they are their true friends, and they must not be led astray by the Yankees. the freedmen ask if Abraham Lincoln[3] led them astray, that his friends is their friends his enemies their enemies.

I have spent much of my time on the Plantations distributing seed and trying to teach the women to make Yankee gardens.[4] they plant everything

---

[1]Ednah Dow Little Hale Cheney (1824–1904), Boston philanthropist, writer, and abolitionist, served as Secretary of the New England Freedmen's Aid Society from 1867 until 1875. She evidently became acquainted with Jacobs in connection with Jacobs's relief work in Alexandria and Savannah. (*Notable American Women*.) The nonstandard usage in this letter exists in the original.

[2]"Awake, awake, stand up, O Jerusalem, which hast drunk at the hand of the Lord, the cup of his fury; thou has drunken the dregs of the cup of trembling, and wrung them out." Isaiah 51:17.

[3]Abraham Lincoln (1809–1865), sixteenth President of the United States and signer of the Emancipation Proclamation.

[4]Jacobs made a practice of this. Child noted, "I found eleven letters awaiting me.... One of them was from Mrs. Jacobs, asking for garden seeds for some freedmen in Georgia, where she is at present." (Child to [Lucy Osgood], April 1, 1866, Wayland [Massachusetts], L. M. Child Papers Microform 64/1715.)

to mature in the summer, like their corn and cotton fields. I have hunted up all the old people, done what I could for them. I love to work for these old people. many of them I have known from Childhood

there is one School in Edenton well attended.[5] on some of the Plantations there is from 15 to 25 Children that cannot attend School, the distance is so far. some of the freedmen are very anxious to establish Plantation schools, as soon as the more advanced Schools, can send out teachers. many of the freedmen are willing and will sustain their teachers. at present there is a great revival in the colored Churches. the Whites say the Niggers sung and prayed until they got their freedom, and they are not satisfied. now they are singing and praying for judgment. the white members of the Baptist Church invited the colored members to their Church, to help them sing and pray. I assure you they have done it with a will. I never saw such a state of excitement the Churches have been open night and day. these people have time to think of their souls, now they are not compelled to think for the Negro.

my love to Miss Daisy.[6] I send her some Jassmine blossoms tell her they bear the fragrance of freedom.

> Yours Truly
> H Jacobs
> 1867

■ MARY BOYKIN CHESNUT ■
1823–1886

Historians and literary critics alike have praised Mary Boykin Chesnut's "diary" for its vivid and sweeping narrative of Confederate life during the Civil War. As her editor C. Vann Woodward points out, the enduring value of Chesnut's autobiographical writing lies not so much in the information it contains but "in the life and reality with which it endows people and events and with which it evokes the chaos and complexity of a society at war." A politically astute, well-educated, and gregarious woman whose father and husband were Southern political figures, Mary Chesnut was in an ideal position to observe and record the intricacies of her society and her era. Born in Statesburg, South Carolina, she was the

---

[5]On October 23, 1866, it was ordered that the freedmen of the Town of Edenton be allowed to build a Schoolhouse in the Town Commons east of Oakum Street...." In 1868, "The Sewing Society of colored persons" was granted use of the Town Hall for a fair to raise money to pay for the schoolhouse lot. (Edenton, N.C., Town Minutes, 1865–1887, October 13, 1866, p. 19; July 2, 1868, p. 32. North Carolina State Archives.)

[6]Cheney's daughter Margaret Swan Cheney (b. 1855).

oldest daughter of Mary Boykin and Stephen Miller. Her father was, at various periods, a U.S. Congressman and Senator, governor, and state senator.

According to her biographer Elisabeth Muhlenfeld, young Mary Miller received an unusually solid education for a nineteenth-century Southern woman. She attended Madame Talvande's French School for Young Ladies in Charleston, where she excelled in a course of study that stressed foreign language, history, rhetoric, literature, and science, as well as traditional female "accomplishments." While in attendance at Madame Talvande's, she met James Chesnut Jr., whom she married when she was barely seventeen. From a wealthy Camden family, her husband, a Princeton graduate and lawyer, served in various political positions before the war, including a U.S. Senate seat which he gave up in 1860 when differences between the North and South became insurmountable. His connections with such figures as Jefferson Davis during the war years opened windows of opportunity for his wife's observations of and relationships with key figures in the national drama, as did her own enjoyment of friendships with a broad spectrum of the Confederacy's most prominent men and women. After the war, the Chesnuts' land and plantation near Camden were lost to debt, and after James's death in 1884, Mary was left with a struggling dairy farm and a strong desire to complete her memoirs. Always in danger from heart trouble, she died of an attack before seeing her work published.

Like many other Southern autobiographers writing about the Civil War, many of them women who struggled through the vicissitudes of a war on home territory, Chesnut created her "diary" out of a complexly rendered combination of an actual diary written during the war and her memories of the past. The 1984 publication of *The Private Mary Chesnut*, edited by Woodward and Muhlenfeld, makes the original and highly personal diary available for the first time. This actual diary, which she kept under lock and key, was not meant for publication; the autobiographical book known as her "diary" was actually written twenty years after the war, from 1881 to 1884. Woodward's 1981 edition, titled *Mary Chesnut's Civil War*, incorporates part of the original diary with the retrospective memoirs. Mary Chesnut's writing was first published in 1905 and later in 1949 in an edition by Ben Ames Williams with the title (not one of Chesnut's choosing) *A Diary from Dixie*. Unlike Williams's *Diary*, Woodward's edition provides a synthesis of the two forms of autobiography, the diary and the memoir, in a responsibly edited combination of what Chesnut actually wrote during the war and twenty years later. One of her stated purposes in her revision of the 1880s, Woodward discovered through her correspondence, was what she called "leaving myself out." To whatever extent she succeeded, Woodward attempts to right the balance by reinserting personal comments that the previous editions left unpublished. In the selections reprinted below from Woodward's edition, deleted passages have been indicated by brackets. *Mary Chesnut's Civil War* thus captures the sweep and chaos of a society at war, as did Williams's *A Diary from Dixie*, but the more recent edition also allows an intimate picture of the woman as writer of her own story of that society.

Chesnut describes herself as writing "like a spider, spinning [her] own entrails." This web of self, like Chesnut's sense of history, is complexly attached to and woven out of a keen awareness of the white woman's position in a patriarchal slave society. At a personal level, Chesnut, who was childless and married to the only son of a wealthy planter family, was painfully cognizant of the white woman's role as the bearer of legitimate heirs. Her attitude toward slavery and patriarchal ideology has been seen as radically feminist for the times, and it has become commonplace to point out that Chesnut saw miscegenation as the embodiment of the evil of slavery and of the double standard that allowed the white Southern male sexual freedom and marital infidelity while his wife and daughter were bound by the prohibitions of chastity. In her frequently quoted diatribes against this aspect of slavery, such as the one reproduced below, though, Chesnut seems so intent on pitying the white women whose husbands are involved in philanderings in the slave quarters that she has no sympathy left for the black women who become their victims. She views black women instead as symbols of sexuality, ironically with freedoms not allowed "respectable" white women. Moreover, she seems to blame black women for a sexual coercion only white men could instigate or force, thereby focusing her bitterness at the victims of slavery, not the victimizers.

Thus Chesnut, a member of the wealthy planter class, abhorred slavery and its sexual vices but, like many white women of her time and position, seemed to remain blind, or at least myopic, concerning the intersections of gender and race with the power structures of the system in which she lived much of her life. Yet despite her limited critique of the patriarchal underpinnings of slavery, Mary Boykin Chesnut's massive volume paints a valuable portrait, interior as well as exterior, of the Old South's physical and ideological struggle to survive, its ultimate failure to do so, and perhaps some of the reasons behind that failure.

Minrose C. Gwin
University of New Mexico

PRIMARY WORKS

Mary Chesnut's Civil War, ed. C. Vann Woodward, 1981; *The Private Mary Chesnut: The Unpublished Civil War Diaries*, ed. C. Vann Woodward and Elisabeth Muhlenfeld, 1984.

from **Mary Chesnut's Civil War**

March 18, 1861

... ⟨⟨I wonder if it be a sin to think slavery a curse to any land. Sumner said not one word of this hated institution which is not true. Men and women are punished when their masters and mistresses are brutes and not when they do wrong—and then we live surrounded by prostitutes. An abandoned woman is sent out of any decent house elsewhere. Who thinks any worse of a negro or mulatto woman for being a thing we can't name? God forgive us, but ours is a *monstrous* system and wrong and iniquity. Perhaps the rest of the world is as bad—this *only* I see. Like the patriarchs of old our men live all in one house with their wives and their concubines, and the mulattoes one sees in every family exactly resemble the white children—and every lady tells you who is the father of all the mulatto children in everybody's household, but those in her own she seems to think drop from the clouds, or pretends so to think. Good women we have, *but* they talk of all *nastiness*—tho' they never do wrong, they talk day and night of [*erasures illegible save for the words* "all unconsciousness"] my disgust sometimes is boiling over—but they are, I believe, in conduct the purest women God ever made. Thank God for my countrywomen—alas for the men! No worse than men everywhere, but the lower their mistresses, the more degraded they must be.

《My mother-in-law told me when I was first married not to send my female servants in the street on errands. They were then tempted, led astray—and then she said placidly, so they told *me* when I came here, and I was very particular, *but you see with what result.*

《Mr. Harris said it was so patriarchal. So it is—flocks and herds and slaves—and wife Leah does not suffice. Rachel must be *added*, if not *married*.[1] And all the time they seem to think themselves patterns—models of husbands and fathers.

《Mrs. Davis told me everybody described my husband's father as an odd character—"a millionaire who did nothing for his son whatever, left him to struggle with poverty, &c." I replied—"Mr. Chesnut Senior thinks himself the best of fathers—and his son thinks likewise. I have nothing to say—but it is true. He has no money but what he makes as a lawyer." And again I say, my countrywomen are as pure as angels, tho' surrounded by another race who are the social evil!&&

August 26, 1861

... Now, this assemblage of army women or Confederate matrons talked pretty freely today. Let us record....

"You people who have been everywhere, stationed all over the U.S.—states, frontiers—been to Europe and all that, tell us homebiding ones: are our men worse than the others? Does Mrs. Stowe know? You know?"

"No, Lady Mary Montagu did. After all, only men and women—everywhere.[2] But Mrs. Stowe's exceptional cases may be true. You can pick out horrors from any criminal court record or newspaper in any country."

"You see, irresponsible men, county magnates, city millionaires, princes, &c do pretty much as they please. They are above law and morals."

Russell once more, to whom London and Paris and India have been an everyday sight—and every night, too, streets and all—for him to go on in indignation because there are women on negro plantations who were not vestal virgins! Negro women are married and after marriage behave as well

---

[1] In Genesis 29–30, Jacob, unhappy with his wife Leah, also marries her sister Rachel. He has children by both women and by their handmaidens as well. M.B.C. apparently believed old Mr. Chesnut had children by a slave whom she calls "Rachel" (p. 72). She confesses no such suspicions of her husband.

[2] "This world consists of men, women, and Herveys." Lady Mary (Wortley) Montagu, *Letters* (1763), volume 1. Lady Montagu, the wife of an adviser to George I, chronicled the scandals of London society.

as other people. Marrying is the amusement of their life. They take life easily. So do their class everywhere. Bad men are hated here as elsewhere.

"I hate slavery. I hate a man who—You say there are no more fallen women on a plantation than in London, in proportion to numbers. What do you say to this? A magnate who runs a hideous black harem and its consequences under the same roof with his lovely white wife and his beautiful and accomplished daughters? He holds his head as high and poses as the model of all human virtues to these poor women whom God and the laws have given him. From the height of his awful majesty he scolds and thunders at them, as if he never did wrong in his life.

"Fancy such a man finding his daughter reading *Don Juan*.[3] 'You with that unmoral book!' And he orders her out of his sight.

"You see, Mrs. Stowe did not hit the sorest spot. She makes Legree[4] a bachelor. Remember George II and his like."[5]

"Oh, I knew half a Legree, a man said to be as cruel as Legree—but the other half of him did not correspond. He was a man of polished manners. And the best husband and father and member of the church in the world."

"Can that be so?"

"Yes, I know it. Exceptional case, that sort of thing, always."

"And I knew the dissolute half of Legree well. He was high and mighty. But the kindest creature to his slaves—and the unfortunate results of his bad ways were not sold, had not to jump over ice blocks. They were kept in full view and provided for handsomely in his will.

"His wife and daughters in the might of their purity and innocence are supposed never to dream of what is as plain before their eyes as the sunlight, and they play their parts of unsuspecting angels to the letter. They prefer to adore their father as model of all earthly goodness."

"Well, yes. If he is rich, he is the fountain from whence all blessings flow."

"The one I have in my eye—my half of Legree, the dissolute half—was so furious in his temper and thundered his wrath so at the poor women they were glad to let him do as he pleased in peace, if they could only escape his everlasting faultfinding and noisy bluster. Making everybody so uncomfortable."

"*Now*. Now, do you know any woman of this generation who would stand that sort of thing?"

"No, never—not for one moment. The make-believe angels were of the last century. We know—and we won't have it."

"Condition of women is improving, it seems. These are old-world stories."

"Women were brought up not to judge their fathers or their husbands. They took them as the Lord provided—and were thankful."

---

[3] Lord Byron, *Don Juan* (1824).
[4] Simon Legree of *Uncle Tom's Cabin*.
[5] The ten-year relationship of George II with Mrs. Henrietta Howard was an open secret, as were several more casual liaisons.

"If they should not go to heaven, after all—think of what lives most women lead."

"No heaven, no purgatory, no——, the other thing—never. I believe in future rewards and punishments."

"How about the wives of drunkards? I heard a woman say once to a friend of her husband, tell it as a cruel matter of fact, without bitterness, without comment: 'Oh, you have not seen him. He is changed. He has not gone to bed sober in thirty years.' She has had her purgatory—if not what Mrs.——calls 'the other thing'—here in this world. We all know what a drunken man is. To think, *for no crime* a person may be condemned to live with one thirty years."

"You wander from the question I asked. Are Southern men worse because of the slave system and the—facile black women?"

"Not a bit. They see too much of them. The barroom people don't drink. The confectionary people loathe candy. They are sick of the black sight of them."

"You think a nice man from the South is the nicest thing in the world."

"I know it. Put him by any other man and see!"

"And you say no saints and martyrs now—those good women who stand by bad husbands? Eh?"

"No use to mince matters—no use to pick words—everybody knows the life of a woman whose husband drinks."

"Some men have a hard time, too. I know women who are—well, the very devil and all his imps."

"And have you not seen girls cower and shrink away from a fierce brute of a father? Men are dreadful animals."

"Seems to me those of you who are hardest on men here are soft enough with them when they are present. Now, everybody knows I am 'the friend of man,' and I defend them behind their backs, as I take pleasure in their society—well—before their faces." . . .

October 13, 1861

Went to hear Tom Davis[6] preach. It was a political sermon. He ended it by commenting on a remark made by a celebrated person from Washington who said he was bored with politics all the week. And if he could not hear a little pure religion, undefiled, on Sunday, he would not go to church.

Nudged me: "That's you. You are always grumbling at political sermons." "But I am not the least celebrated." However, the whispered dispute was soon settled. Henry Clay was the man who hoped to eschew politics one day in seven.

Our parson cited Lord Nelson as a case of good prayer from a bad man. At the battle of Trafalgar he prayed fervently, and his prayer was answered.

---

[6]Thomas Frederick Davis, Jr., was associate pastor of the Grace Episcopal Church in Camden. His wife was M.B.C.'s first cousin.

And there he died, saying, "Thank God I die doing my duty." Again my whisper: "He prayed, too, for Lady Hamilton, and he left her a legacy to his country—ungrateful country would not accept the bequest."[7]

At Mulberry we went in the afternoon to the negro church on the plantation. Manning Brown,[8] Methodist minister, preached to a very large black congregation. Though glossy black, they were well dressed—some very stylishly gotten up. They were stout, comfortable-looking Christians. The house women in white aprons and white turbans were the nicest looking. How snow-white the turbans on their heads appeared. But the youthful sisters flaunted in pink and sky blue bonnets which tried their complexions. For *the family* they had a cushioned seat near the pulpit, neatly covered with calico.

Manning Brown preached hell fire—so hot I felt singed, if not parboiled, though I could not remember any of my many sins worthy of an eternity in torment. But if all the world's misery, sin, and suffering came from so small a sin as eating that apple, what mighty proportions mine take.

Jim Nelson, the driver—the stateliest darky I ever saw. He is tall and straight as a pine tree, with a fair face—not so very black, but full-blooded African. His forefathers must have been of royal blood over there.

This distinguished gentleman was asked to "lead in prayer." He became wildly excited. Though on his knees, facing us, with his eyes shut, he clapped his hands at the end of every sentence, and his voice rose to the pitch of a shrill shriek. Still, his voice was strangely clear and musical, occasionally in a plaintive minor key that went to your heart. Sometimes it rung out like a trumpet. I wept bitterly. It was all sound, however, and emotional pathos. There was literally nothing in what he said. The words had no meaning at all. It was the devotional passion of voice and manner which was so magnetic. The negroes sobbed and shouted and swayed backward and forward, some with aprons to their eyes, most clapping their hands and responding in shrill tones, "Yes, my God! Jesus!" "Aeih! Savior! Bless de Lord, amen—&c."

It was a little too exciting for me. I would very much have liked to shout, too. Jim Nelson, when he rose from his knees, trembled and shook as one in a palsy. And from his eye you could see the ecstasy had not left him yet. He could not stand at all—sunk back on his bench.

Now, all this leaves not a trace behind. Jim Nelson is a good man— honest and true. And so he continues. Those who stole before steal on, in spite of sobs and shouts on Sunday. Those who drink continue to drink when they can get it. Except that for any open, *detected* sin they are turned out of church. A Methodist parson is practical—no mealy-mouth creature. He requires them to keep the commandments. If they are not married and show they ought to be, out of the church they go. If married members are not true to their vows and it is made plain to him by their conduct, he has

[7]The night before his death at the battle of Trafalgar, Horatio Nelson added a codicil to his will, leaving his mistress Lady Emma Hamilton and their daughter Horatia "a legacy to my king and country" and asking that they be given a pension. The will was not made public, and no such grant was ever made.

[8]A nephew of Old Colonel Chesnut who lived in Sumter District.

them up before the church. They are devoted to their church membership. And it is a keen police court.

Suddenly, as I sat wondering what next, they broke out into one of those soul-stirring negro camp-meeting hymns. To me this is the saddest of all earthly music—weird and depressing beyond my powers to describe.

> *The wrestling of the world asketh a fall;*
> *Here is no home: here is a wildernesse.*
> *Forth Pilgrim! forth! Oh! beast out of thy stall!*
> *Look up on high—And thank thy God for all.*

—Chaucer

October 20, 1861

... Hume says, "Mighty governments are built up by a great deal of accident with a very little of human foresight and wisdom."[9]

We have seen the building of one lately with no end of Jefferson and a constant sprinkling of Calhoun, &c&c&c. Which is the wisdom—where the accident or foresight? Somebody said Jefferson and Calhoun were the stern lights and did not help us to see what is before us.

One thing Mrs. Browne and I discussed. There were in Richmond and in Montgomery the safe, sober, second thoughts of the cool, wise morning hours. There in that drawing room after dinner—how much more in the smoking congresses where women were not—came what we called ideas preserved in alcohol. The self-same wild schemes, mad talk, exaggerated statements, inflamed and irrational views—our might and the enemies' weakness, &c&c. If "in vino veritas," God help us. After all it was not, could not be, unadulterated truth—it was truth, alcoholized.

I care no more for alcoholized wisdom than I do for the chattering of blackbirds—[*remainder of page cut off*].

Hard on the poor innocent birds! They were made so. And the great statesmen and soldiers deliberately drink down their high inheritance of reason and with light hearts become mere gabbling geese. *Alcools*—

Hume, after his kind, talks of *accident*. Lamartine says, "Dieu est Dieu— ce que les hommes appellent *rencontre*, les anges l'appellent Providence."[10]

Thank God for pine knots. Gas and candles and oil are all disappearing in the Confederacy. Lamb thinks for social purposes candles so much better than the garish light of the sun.[11] The unsocial nights of our ancestors in

---

[9]David Hume, *History of England* (1754–62), volume 2, chapter 23.

[10]A paraphrase from *Geneviève*, part 116. "God is God—what people call meeting, the angels call Providence."

[11]Paraphrased from Charles Lamb, "Popular Fallacies, XV.—That We Should Lie Down with the Lamb," in *The Last Essays of Elia* (1833). The quotation at the end of this paragraph derives from the same essay, although M.B.C. does not reproduce Lamb's wording exactly.

their dark caves. They must have laid about and abused one another in the dark. No, they went to sleep. And women then were too much slaves to dream of curtain lectures—which is one form of lying about and abusing one another in the dark. "What repartees could have passed, when you had to feel around for a smile and had to handle your neighbor's cheek to see if he understood you?"

> Fool enough to attempt to advise.
>   Ah, gentle dames! It gars me greet,
> To think how many counsels sweet,
>   How many lengthened sage advices
> The husband from the wife despises.[12]

⟨⟨poor me—⟩⟩

January 16, 1865

My husband is at home once more—for how long, I do not know. And his aides fill the house, and a group of hopelessly wounded haunt the place. And the drilling and the marching goes on—and as far as I can see, for. bats. happily forgotten.

It rains a flood—freshet after freshet. The forces of nature are befriending us, for our enemies have to make their way through swamps.

A month ago my husband wrote me a letter which I promptly suppressed after showing it to Mrs. McCord. He warned us to make ready—for the end had come. Our resources were exhausted—and the means of resistance could not be found.

It was what we could not bring ourselves to believe. And now—he thinks, with the RR all blown up, the swamps impassable by freshets which have no time to subside, so constant is the rain. The negroes are utterly apathetic (would they be so, if they saw us triumphant!), and if we had but an army to seize the opportunity. No troops—that is the real trouble. Dr. Gibbes took it on himself to send a telegram. Some people are cool enough—and fools enough for anything.

"Does Jeff Davis so hate South Carolina that he means to abandon her to her fate?" I wonder if they showed Mr. Davis this.

The answer has come.

"No. Jeff Davis loves South Carolina—only Yankees hate her. He will do all he can to save her."

Hardee—he of Hardee's *Tactics*[13]—he has a head for tactics, but it is not large enough to plan a campaign. He can only fight well when under orders.

---

[12]Slightly misquoted from Robert Burns, "Tam o' Shanter" (1791).

[13]William Joseph Hardee was the author of a standard textbook, *Rifle and Light Infantry Tactics* (1853–1855).

We seem utterly without a head down here—utterly at sea. If some heavenborn genius would rush in and take command—

The pilot in calm weather lets any sea boy toy with his rudder—but when the winds howl and the waves rise, he seizes the helm himself.

And our pilot? Where is he?

"Napoleon had to go to St. Helena when he had exhausted his levies. No more soldiers until France could grow them."

"Suppose we try Stephen Elliott—everybody trusts him."

Today Mrs. McCord exchanged 16,000 dollars, Confederate bills, for gold—300 dollars. Sixteen thousand—for three hundred.

The bazaar will be a Belshazzar affair.[14] The handwriting is on the wall. Bad news everywhere.

Miss Garnett was in agony.

"I fear the very worst—before they find out, those stupid Yankees, that I am Irish."

The fears of old maids increase, apparently in proportion to their age and infirmities—and hideous ugliness.

Isabella fairly white and shining—resplendent in apparel—has gone down to Millwood.

She reproved the "weary heart" for dragging so in the road of life, or as she put it:

"What do you mean to do if your father dies—or anybody that you really care for dies? You leave yourself no margin for proper affliction— when the time comes."

January 17, 1865

Bazaar opens today.

Sherman marches always—all RR's smashed.

And if I laugh at any mortal thing, it is that I may not weep.

Generals as plenty as blackberries, none in command. Beauregard with his Shiloh green sickness again. Bad time for a general seized by *melancholia*.

And this refrain is beating in my brain—

> *March—March—Ettrick and Teviotdale—*
> *Why the de'il do ye not march all in order,*
> *March—March—Teviot and Clydesdale—*
> *All the blue bonnets are over the Border.*[15]

1981

[14]Daniel 5.
[15]The first lines, slightly misquoted, of a "ditty" sung to "the ancient air of 'Blue Bonnets over the Border,'" in Sir Walter Scott, *The Monastery: A Romance* (1820), volume 2, chapter 11.

▪ **WENDELL PHILLIPS** ▪
1811–1884

The eighth of nine children, Wendell Phillips was born in a Beacon Hill mansion into one of Boston's distinguished old families. The Reverend George Phillips, his ancestor, had arrived with John Winthrop on the *Arbella* in 1630, and the family fortune had been established before the Revolutionary War. His father John Phillips, a lawyer, had both inherited and married wealth, and he saw to it that Wendell received the education and cultural exposure appropriate to the son of a Boston Brahmin. He attended the Boston Latin School and went on to Harvard College and Harvard Law School. Handsome and athletic, Phillips was elected to the Porcellan, the Gentleman's Club, and the Hasty Pudding Club, certain signs of his aristocratic status. When he graduated from college in 1831 he had served as president of each of those elite organizations. Except for a report that he watched the English actress Fanny Kemble at the Tremont Theatre nineteen nights in a row, everything recorded of Phillips's early life was conservative and conventional; there were no hints of passion or political commitment. He took up the law with a classmate in Lowell, Massachusetts, in 1834, but returned to Boston the following year and rented an office from which he tried, and apparently failed, to establish a law practice.

Although his private income was such that he did not need to work, Wendell Phillips was at that juncture professionally adrift, in want of a vocation. Yet in November 1837, with the brother and sister-in-law of William Lloyd Garrison serving as best man and matron of honor, he married a member of the Female Anti-Slavery Society, Ann Greene, who he later said had "made an out and out abolitionist of me." The following month, at a meeting in Faneuil Hall organized by William Ellery Channing to protest the mob murder of the abolitionist Elijah Lovejoy in Alton, Illinois, Phillips spoke eloquently in opposition to the Massachusetts Attorney General, James T. Austin, who had defended the killing, and thus he began his career as a public orator against slavery.

In succeeding years, allied with Garrison, Phillips wrote and spoke locally, but in November 1854, he undertook the first of his "abolitionizing trips," following a speech-making circuit that took him to Utica, Rochester, Syracuse, Detroit, Cleveland, and Cincinnati. The circuit later widened to include Chicago, Madison, and Milwaukee. For the next twenty-five years, he made these journeys over and over, collecting fees of $250 for his appearances. In the early years, his speaker's fees, like much of his extensive private wealth, found their way into the hands of persons whose causes he espoused. In the waning years of his life, his personal fortune expended, Phillips was forced to continue his public speaking in order to support himself and his invalid wife.

It was the Lyceum lecture series that brought Phillips wide recognition as a speaker. Although he was principally known for his abolitionist speeches, his repertoire included such topics as "Water," "Geology," "Chartism," and a very famous historical piece called "The Lost Arts." Often, when Phillips was engaged to deliver one of these "improving" lectures to his audiences of middle-class

Northerners, on a succeeding evening he would speak without fee on abolition. Although the substance of his orations was set down in his "commonplace book," Phillips spoke from memory, without notes, and in a manner that dazzled his audiences. Thoreau called him "an eloquent speaker and a righteous man." A Southern newspaper, the Richmond *Enquirer*, called him an "infernal machine set to music." Frequently transcribed and reprinted, many of his speeches became set pieces reenacted in school recitations. In 1887, the black poet James Weldon Johnson heard his classmate "Shiny" recite "Toussaint L'Ouverture" as the centerpiece of his grammar school graduation exercises.

The special characteristic of Phillips's orations on black heroes was their insistence on qualitative racial equality. Unlike him, many of the abolitionists opposed slavery simply on the grounds of Christian charity. Thus, for example, some part of the sympathy engendered by Stowe's depiction of Eliza and George, the young couple in *Uncle Tom's Cabin*, had to do with the fact that they were mulatto, and therefore partly white. Many of Phillips's contemporaries held views like those of Louis Agassiz, the Harvard biologist, who came to the conclusion that the Negro race was separate from and inferior to the white race, but who was nevertheless opposed to the institution of slavery.

Two speeches in particular, "Crispus Attucks" and "Toussaint L'Ouverture," represent Wendell Phillips's uncompromising support of racial equality. These speeches were delivered literally hundreds of times. In Crispus Attucks, who fought and died in the Boston Massacre in 1770, Phillips finds his example of a black man who liberated colonials from British slavery. In Toussaint L'Ouverture, who led the revolution against the French in Haiti, Phillips does not come far short of making a case for black supremacy, for he sees in Toussaint a man whose vision rivals Edmund Burke's, a man greater than Cromwell, greater far than Napoleon, both a genius and a saint. The real purpose of Phillips's speech is, however, revealed by its date: 1863. A debate was raging about whether or not to enlist black men as Union soldiers; there were those who argued either that they would not fight or that they would fight like savages. Phillips offers Toussaint's military genius and his humanitarian conduct to exemplify the capabilities of black soldiers.

Allison Heisch
San Jose State University

PRIMARY WORKS

Speeches, Lectures, and Letters, 1863, 1968; *Speeches, Lectures, and Letters:* Second series, 1891, 1969; *Wendell Phillips on Civil Rights and Freedom*, ed. Louis Filler, 1982.

from **Toussaint L'Ouverture**

... He had been born a slave on a plantation in the north of the island, an unmixed Negro, his father stolen from Africa. If anything, therefore, that I say of him tonight moves your admiration, remember, the black race claims it all—we have no part nor lot in it. He was fifty years old at this time. An old Negro had taught him to read. His favorite books were Epictetus,

Raynal, military memoirs, Plutarch.[1] In the woods, he learned some of the qualities of herbs, and was village doctor. On the estate, the highest place he ever reached was that of coachman. At fifty, he joined the army as physician. Before he went, he placed his master and mistress on shipboard, freighted the vessel with a cargo of sugar and coffee, and sent them to Baltimore, and never afterward did he forget to send them, year by year, ample means of support. And I might add that, of all the leading Negro generals, each one saved the man under whose roof he was born, and protected the family. [Cheering.]

Let me add another thing. If I stood here tonight to tell the story of Napoleon, I should take it from the lips of Frenchmen, who find no language rich enough to paint the great captain of the nineteenth century. Were I here to tell you the story of Washington, I should take it from your hearts—you, who think no marble white enough on which to carve the name of the Father of His Country. [Applause.] I am about to tell you the story of a Negro who has left hardly one written line. I am to glean it from the reluctant testimony of Britons, Frenchmen, Spaniards—men who despised him as a Negro and a slave, and hated him because he had beaten them in many a battle. All the materials for his biography are from the lips of his enemies.

The second story told of him is this. About the time he reached the camp, the army had been subjected to two insults. First, their commissioners, summoned to meet the French Committee, were ignominiously and insultingly dismissed; and when, afterward, François, their general, was summoned to a second conference, and went to it on horseback, accompanied by two officers; a young lieutenant, who had known him as a slave, angered at seeing him in the uniform of an officer, raised his riding whip and struck him over the shoulders. If he had been the savage which the Negro is painted to us, he had only to breathe the insult to his twenty-five thousand soldiers, and they would have trodden out the Frenchmen in blood. But the indignant chief rode back in silence to his tent, and it was twenty-four hours before his troops heard of this insult to their general. Then the word went forth, "Death to every white man!" They had fifteen hundred prisoners. Ranged in front of the camp, they were about to be shot. Toussaint, who had a vein of religious fanaticism, like most great leaders—like Mohammed, like Napoleon, like Cromwell, like John Brown [cheers], he could preach as well as fight—mounting a hillock, and getting the ear of the crowd, exclaimed: "Brothers, this blood will not wipe out the insult to our chief; only the blood in yonder French camp can wipe it out. To shed that is courage; to shed this is cowardice and cruelty besides"; and he saved fifteen hundred lives. [Applause.]

[1] Greek, French, and Latin philosophers and historians. Epictetus was a first-century Greek stoic philosopher; Guillaume Raynal, an eighteenth-century historian who wrote on the Europeans in the West Indies; Plutarch, a first-century biographer and moral philosopher.

I cannot stop to give in detail every one of his efforts. This was in 1793. Leap with me over seven years; come to 1800; what has he achieved? He has driven the Spaniard back into his own cities, conquered him there, and put the French banner over every Spanish town; and for the first time, and almost the last, the island obeys one law. He has put the mulatto under his feet. He has attacked Maitland,[2] defeated him in pitched battles, and permitted him to retreat to Jamaica; and when the French army rose upon Laveaux, their general, and put him in chains, Toussaint defeated them, took Laveaux out of prison, and put him at the head of his own troops. The grateful French in return named him General in Chief. *"Cet homme fait l'ouverture partout,"* said one—"This man makes an opening everywhere,"— hence his soldiers named him L'Ouverture, *the opening.*

This was the work of seven years. Let us pause a moment, and find something to measure him by. You remember Macaulay[3] says, comparing Cromwell with Napoleon, that Cromwell showed the greater military genius, if we consider that he never saw an army till he was forty; while Napoleon was educated from a boy in the best military schools in Europe. Cromwell manufactured his own army; Napoleon at the age of twenty-seven was placed at the head of the best troops Europe ever saw. They were both successful; but, says Macaulay, with such disadvantages, the Englishman showed the greater genius. Whether you allow the inference or not, you will at least grant that it is a fair mode of measurement. Apply it to Toussaint. Cromwell never saw an army till he was forty; this man never saw a soldier till he was fifty. Cromwell manufactured his own army—out of what? Englishmen, the best blood in Europe. Out of the middle class of Englishmen, the best blood of the island. And with it he conquered what? Englishmen, their equals. This man manufactured his army out of what? Out of what you call the despicable race of Negroes, debased, demoralized by two hundred years of slavery, one hundred thousand of them imported into the island within four years, unable to speak a dialect intelligible even to each other. Yet out of this mixed, and, as you say, despicable mass, he forged a thunderbolt and hurled it at what? At the proudest blood in Europe, the Spaniard, and sent him home conquered [cheers]; at the most warlike blood in Europe, the French, and put them under his feet; at the pluckiest blood in Europe, the English, and they skulked home to Jamaica. [Applause.] Now if Cromwell was a general, at least this man was a soldier. I know it was a small territory; it was not as large as the continent; but it was as large as that Attica, which, with Athens for a capital, has filled the earth with its fame for two thousand years. We measure genius by quality, not by quantity.

Further—Cromwell was only a soldier; his fame stops there. Not one line in the statute book of Britain can be traced to Cromwell; not one step in the social life of England finds its motive power in his brain. The state he

[2]British general.
[3]Nineteenth-century British historian who wrote *History of England*.

founded went down with him to his grave. But this man no sooner put his hand on the helm of state than the ship steadied with an upright keel, and he began to evince a statesmanship as marvelous as his military genius. History says that the most statesmanlike act of Napoleon was his proclamation of 1802, at the Peace of Amiens, when, believing that the indelible loyalty of a native-born heart is always a sufficient basis on which to found an empire, he said: "Frenchmen, come home. I pardon the crimes of the last twelve years; I blot out its parties; I found my throne on the hearts of all Frenchmen,"—and twelve years of unclouded success showed how wisely he judged. That was in 1802. In 1800 this Negro made a proclamation; it runs thus: "Sons of St. Domingo, come home. We never meant to take your houses or your lands. The Negro only asked that liberty which God gave him. Your houses wait for you; your lands are ready; come and cultivate them"; and from Madrid and Paris, from Baltimore and New Orleans, the emigrant planters crowded home to enjoy their estates, under the pledged word that was never broken of a victorious slave. [Cheers.]

Again, Carlyle[4] has said, "The natural king is one who melts all wills into his own." At this moment he turned to his armies—poor, ill-clad, and half-starved—and said to them: Go back and work on these estates you have conquered; for an empire can be founded only on order and industry, and you can learn these virtues only there. And they went. The French admiral, who witnessed the scene, said that in a week his army melted back into peasants.

It was 1800. The world waited fifty years before, in 1846, Robert Peel[5] dared to venture, as a matter of practical statesmanship, the theory of free trade. Adam Smith[6] theorized, the French statesmen dreamed, but no man at the head of affairs had ever dared to risk it as a practical measure. Europe waited till 1846 before the most practical intellect in the world, the English, adopted the great economic formula of unfettered trade. But in 1800 this black, with the instinct of statesmanship, said to the committee who were drafting for him a Constitution: "Put at the head of the chapter of commerce that the ports of St. Domingo are open to the trade of the world." [Cheers.] With lofty indifference to race, superior to all envy or prejudice, Toussaint had formed this committee of eight white proprietors and one mulatto—not a soldier nor a Negro on the list, although Haitian history proves that, with the exception of Rigaud,[7] the rarest genius has always been shown by pure Negroes.

Again, it was 1800, at a time when England was poisoned on every page of her statute book with religious intolerance, when a man could not enter the House of Commons without taking an Episcopal communion, when every State in the Union, except Rhode Island, was full of the intensest

---

[4]Author of the monumental history *The French Revolution.*

[5]Tory Prime Minister of Britain (1788–1850) who repealed taxes to encourage free trade.

[6]Eighteenth-century Scot who wrote *The Wealth of Nations;* father of laissez-faire economics.

[7]Mulatto general who defeated the British in the southern part of Haiti.

religious bigotry. This man was a Negro. You say that is a superstitious blood. He was uneducated. You say that makes a man narrow-minded. He was a Catholic. Many say that is but another name for intolerance. And yet—Negro, Catholic, slave—he took his place by the side of Roger Williams, and said to his committee: "Make it the first line of my Constitution that I know no difference between religious beliefs." [Applause.]

Now, blue-eyed Saxon, proud of your race, go back with me to the commencement of the century, and select what statesman you please. Let him be either American or European; let him have a brain the result of six generations of culture; let him have the ripest training of university routine; let him add to it the better education of practical life; crown his temples with the silver of seventy years; and show me the man of Saxon lineage for whom his most sanguine admirer will wreathe a laurel rich as embittered foes have placed on the brow of this Negro—rare military skill, profound knowledge of human nature, content to blot out all party distinctions, and trust a state to the blood of its sons—anticipating Sir Robert Peel fifty years, and taking his station by the side of Roger Williams before any Englishman or American had won the right; and yet this is the record which the history of rival states makes up for this inspired black of St. Domingo. [Cheers.]

It was 1801. The Frenchmen who lingered on the island described its prosperity and order as almost incredible. You might trust a child with a bag of gold to go from Samana to Port-au-Prince without risk. Peace was in every household; the valleys laughed with fertility; culture climbed the mountains; the commerce of the world was represented in its harbors. At this time Europe concluded the Peace of Amiens, and Napoleon took his seat on the throne of France. He glanced his eyes across the Atlantic, and, with a single stroke of his pen, reduced Cayenne and Martinique back into chains. He then said to his Council, "What shall I do with St. Domingo?" The slaveholders said, "Give it to us." Napoleon turned to the Abbé Gregoire, "What is your opinion?" "I think those men would change their opinions, if they changed their skins." Colonel Vincent, who had been private secretary to Toussaint, wrote a letter to Napoleon, in which he said: "Sire, leave it alone; it is the happiest spot in your dominions; God raised this man to govern; races melt under his hand. He has saved you this island; for I know of my own knowledge that, when the Republic could not have lifted a finger to prevent it, George III offered him any title and any revenue if he would hold the island under the British crown. He refused, and saved it for France." Napoleon turned away from his Council, and is said to have remarked, "I have sixty thousand idle troops; I must find them something to do." He meant to say, "I am about to seize the crown; I dare not do it in the faces of sixty thousand republican soldiers: I must give them work at a distance to do." The gossip of Paris gives another reason for his expedition against St. Domingo. It is said that the satirists of Paris had christened Toussaint, the Black Napoleon; and Bonaparte hated his black shadow. Toussaint had unfortunately once addressed him a letter, "The first of the blacks to the first of the whites." He did not like the comparison. You would think it too slight a motive. But let me remind you of the present Napoleon, that when the epigrammatists of Paris christened his wasteful and tasteless expense at Versailles, *Soulouquerie*, from the name of Soulouque, the Black Emperor, he deigned to issue a specific order forbidding the use of the word. The Napoleon blood is very sensitive. So Napoleon resolved to crush Toussaint from one motive or another, from the prompting of ambition, or dislike of this resemblance, which was very close. If either imitated the other, it must have been the white, since the Negro preceded him several years. They were very much alike, and they were very French—French even in vanity, common to both. You remember Bonaparte's vainglorious words to his soldiers at the Pyramids: "Forty centuries look down upon us." In the same mood, Toussaint said to the French captain who urged him to go to France in his frigate, "Sir, your ship is not large enough to carry me." Napoleon, you know, could never bear the military uniform. He hated the restraint of his rank; he loved to put on the gray coat of the Little Corporal, and wander in the camp. Toussaint also never could bear a uniform. He wore a plain coat, and often the yellow Madras handkerchief of the slaves. A French lieutenant once called him a maggot in a yellow handkerchief. Toussaint took him prisoner next day, and sent him home to his mother. Like Napoleon, he could fast many days; could dictate to three secretaries at once; could wear out four or five horses. Like Napoleon, no man ever divined his purpose or penetrated his plan. He was only a Negro, and so, in him, they called it hypocrisy. In Bonaparte we style it diplomacy. For instance, three attempts made to assassinate him all failed, from not firing at the right spot. If they thought he was in the north in a carriage, he would be in the south on horseback; if they thought he was in the city in a house, he would be in the field in a tent. They once riddled his carriage with bullets; he was on horseback on the other side. The seven Frenchmen who did it were arrested. They expected to be shot. The next day was some saint's day; he ordered them to be placed before the high altar, and, when the priest reached the prayer for forgiveness, came down from his high seat, repeated it with him, and permitted them to go unpunished. [Cheers.] He had that wit common to all great commanders, which makes its way in a camp. His soldiers getting disheartened, he filled a large vase with powder, and, scattering six grains of rice in it, shook them up, and said: "See, there is the white, there is the black; what are you afraid of?" So when people came to him in great numbers for office, as it is reported they do sometimes even in Washington, he learned the first words of a Catholic prayer in Latin, and, repeating it, would say, "Do you understand that?" "No, sir." "What! want an office, and not know Latin? Go home and learn it!"

Then, again, like Napoleon—like genius always—he had confidence in his power to rule men. You remember when Bonaparte returned from Elba, and Louis XVIII sent an army against him, Bonaparte descended from his carriage, opened his coat, offering his breast to their muskets and saying, "Frenchmen, it is the Emperor!" and they ranged themselves behind him, *his* soldiers, shouting, *"Vive l'Empereur!"* That was in 1815. Twelve years before, Toussaint, finding that four of his regiments had deserted and gone to Leclerc,[8] drew his sword, flung it on the grass, went across the field to them, folded his arms, and said, "Children, can you point a bayonet at me?" The blacks fell on their knees, praying his pardon. His bitterest enemies watched him, and none of them charged him with love of money, sensuality, or cruel use of power. The only instance in which his sternest critic has charged him with severity is this. During a tumult, a few white proprietors who had returned, trusting his proclamation, were killed. His nephew, General Moise, was accused of indecision in quelling the riot. He assembled a court-martial, and, on its verdict, ordered his own nephew to be shot, sternly Roman in thus keeping his promise of protection to the whites. Above the lust of gold, pure in private life, generous in the use of his power, it was against such a man that Napoleon sent his army, giving to General Leclerc, the husband of his beautiful sister Pauline, thirty thousand of his best troops, with orders to reintroduce slavery. Among these soldiers came all of Toussaint's old mulatto rivals and foes.

Holland lent sixty ships. England promised by special message to be neutral; and you know neutrality means sneering at freedom and sending arms to tyrants. [Loud and long-continued applause.] England promised neutrality, and the black looked out on the whole civilized world marshaled against him. America, full of slaves, of course was hostile. Only the Yankee sold him poor muskets at a very high price. [Laughter.] Mounting his horse, and riding to the eastern end of the island, Samana, he looked out on a sight such as no native had ever seen before. Sixty ships of the line, crowded by the best soldiers of Europe, rounded the point. They were soldiers who had never yet met an equal, whose tread, like Caesar's, had shaken Europe— soldiers who had scaled the Pyramids, and planted the French banners on the walls of Rome. He looked a moment, counted the flotilla, let the reins fall on the neck of his horse, and, turning to Christophe, exclaimed: "All France is come to Haiti; they can only come to make us slaves; and we are lost!" He then recognized the only mistake of his life—his confidence in Bonaparte, which had led him to disband his army.

Returning to the hills, he issued the only proclamation which bears his name and breathes vengeance: "My children, France comes to make us slaves. God gave us liberty; France has no right to take it away. Burn the cities, destroy the harvests, tear up the roads with cannon, poison the wells, show the white man the hell he comes to make"; and he was obeyed. [Applause.] When the great William of Orange saw Louis XIV cover Holland with troops, he said, "Break down the dikes, give Holland back to ocean"; and Europe said, "Sublime!" When Alexander saw the armies of France descend upon Russia, he said, "Burn Moscow, starve back the invaders"; and

---

[8]Brother-in-law of Napoleon Bonaparte and head of the French expeditionary forces in Haiti.

Europe said, "Sublime!" This black saw all Europe marshaled to crush him, and gave to his people the same heroic example of defiance.

It is true, the scene grows bloodier as we proceed. But, remember, the white man fitly accompanied his infamous attempt to *reduce freemen to slavery* with every bloody and cruel device that bitter and shameless hate could invent. Aristocracy is always cruel. The black man met the attempt, as every such attempt should be met, with war to the hilt. In his first struggle to gain his freedom, he had been generous and merciful, saved lives and pardoned enemies, as the people in every age and clime have always done when rising against aristocrats. Now, to save his liberty, the Negro exhausted every means, seized every weapon, and turned back the hateful invaders with a vengeance as terrible as their own, though even now he refused to be cruel.

Leclerc sent word to Christophe that he was about to land at Cape City. Christophe said, "Toussaint is governor of the island. I will send to him for permission. If without it a French soldier sets foot on shore, I will burn the town, and fight over its ashes."

Leclerc landed. Christophe took two thousand *white* men, women, and children, and carried them to the mountains in safety, then with his own hands set fire to the splendid palace which French architects had just finished for him, and in forty hours the place was in ashes. The battle was fought in its streets, and the French driven back to their boats. [Cheers.] Wherever they went, they were met with fire and sword. Once, resisting an attack, the blacks, Frenchmen born, shouted the "Marseilles Hymn," and the French soldiers stood still; they could not fight the "Marseillaise." And it was not till their officers sabered them on that they advanced, and then they were beaten. Beaten in the field, the French then took to lies. They issued proclamations, saying, "We do not come to make you slaves; this man Toussaint tells you lies. Join us, and you shall have the rights you claim." They cheated every one of his officers, except Christophe and Dessalines, and his own brother Pierre, and finally these also deserted him, and he was left alone. He then sent word to Leclerc, "I will submit. I could continue the struggle for years—could prevent a single Frenchman from safely quitting your camp. But I hate bloodshed. I have fought only for the liberty of my race. Guarantee that, I will submit and come in." He took the oath to be a faithful citizen; and on the same crucifix Leclerc swore that he should be faithfully protected, and that the island should be free. As the French general glanced along the line of his splendidly equipped troops, and saw, opposite, Toussaint's ragged, ill-armed followers, he said to him, "L'Ouverture, had you continued the war, where could you have got arms?" "I would have taken yours" was the Spartan reply. [Cheers.] He went down to his house in peace; it was summer, Leclerc remembered that the fever months were coming, when his army would be in hospitals, and when one motion of that royal hand would sweep his troops into the sea. He was too dangerous to be left at large. So they summoned him to attend a council; and here is the only charge made against him—the only charge. They say he was fool enough to go. Grant it; what was the record? The white man lies shrewdly to cheat the Negro. Knight-errantry was truth. The foulest insult you can offer a man since the Crusades is, You lie. Of Toussaint, Hermona, the Spanish general, who knew him well, said, "He was the purest soul God ever put into a body." Of him history bears witness, "He never broke his word." Maitland was traveling in the depths of the woods to meet Toussaint, when he was met by a messenger, and told that he was betrayed. He went on, and met Toussaint, who showed him two letters—one from the French general, offering him any rank if he would put Maitland in his power, and the other his reply. It was, "Sir, I have promised the Englishman that he shall go back." [Cheers.] Let it stand, therefore, that the Negro, truthful as a knight of old, was cheated by his lying foe. Which race has reason to be proud of such a record?

But he was not cheated. He was under espionage. Suppose he had refused: the government would have doubted him, would have found some cause to arrest him. He probably reasoned thus: "If I go willingly, I shall be treated accordingly"; and he went. The moment he entered the room, the officers drew their swords, and told him he was prisoner; and one young lieutenant who was present says, "He was not at all surprised, but seemed very sad." They put him on shipboard, and weighed anchor for France. As the island faded from his sight, he turned to the captain, and said, "You think you have rooted up the tree of liberty, but I am only a branch; I have planted the tree so deep that all France can never root it up." [Cheers.] Arrived in Paris, he was flung into jail, and Napoleon sent his secretary, Caffarelli, to him, supposing he had buried large treasures. He listened a while, then replied, "Young man, it is true I have lost treasures, but they are not such as you come to seek." He was then sent to the Castle of St. Joux, to a dungeon twelve feet by twenty, built wholly of stone, with a narrow window, high up on the side, looking out on the snows of Switzerland. In winter, ice covers the floor; in summer, it is damp and wet. In this living tomb the child of the sunny tropic was left to die. From this dungeon he wrote two letters to Napoleon. One of them ran thus:

> *Sire, I am a French citizen. I never broke a law. By the grace of God, I have saved for you the best island of your realm. Sire, of your mercy grant me justice.*

Napoleon never answered the letters. The commandant allowed him five francs a day for food and fuel. Napoleon heard of it, and reduced the sum to three. The luxurious usurper, who complained that the English government was stingy because it allowed him only six thousand dollars a month, stooped from his throne to cut down a dollar to a half, and still Toussaint did not die quick enough.

This dungeon was a tomb. The story is told that, in Josephine's time, a young French marquis was placed there, and the girl to whom he was betrothed went to the Empress and prayed for his release. Said Josephine to her, "Have a model of it made, and bring it to me." Josephine placed it near Napoleon. He said, "Take it away—it is horrible!" She put it on his footstool, and he kicked it from him. She held it to him the third time, and said, "Sire, in this horrible dungeon you have put a man to die." "Take him out," said Napoleon, and the girl saved her lover. In this tomb Toussaint was buried, but he did not die fast enough. Finally, the commandant was told to go into Switzerland, to carry the keys of the dungeon with him, and to stay four days; when he returned, Toussaint was found starved to death. That imperial assassin was taken twelve years after to his prison at St. Helena, planned for a tomb, as he had planned that of Toussaint, and there he whined away his dying hours in pitiful complaints of curtains and titles, of dishes and rides. God grant that when some future Plutarch shall weigh the great men of our epoch, the whites against the blacks, he do not put that whining child at St. Helena into one scale, and into the other the Negro meeting death like a Roman, without a murmur, in the solitude of his icy dungeon!

From the moment he was betrayed, the Negroes began to doubt the French, and rushed to arms. Soon every Negro but Maurepas deserted the French. Leclerc summoned Maurepas to his side. He came, loyally bringing with him five hundred soldiers. Leclerc spiked his epaulettes to his shoulders, shot him, and flung him into the sea. He took his five hundred soldiers on shore, shot them on the edge of a pit, and tumbled them in. Desalines from the mountain saw it, and, selecting five hundred French officers from his prisons, hung them on separate trees in sight of Leclerc's camp; and born, as I was, not far from Bunker Hill, I have yet found no reason to think he did wrong. [Cheers.] They murdered Pierre Toussaint's wife at his own door, and after such treatment that it was mercy when they killed her. The maddened husband, who had but a year before saved the lives of twelve hundred white men, carried his next thousand prisoners and sacrificed them on her grave.

The French exhausted every form of torture. The Negroes were bound together and thrown into the sea; anyone who floated was shot, others sunk with cannon balls tied to their feet; some smothered with sulphur fumes, others strangled, scourged to death, gibbeted; sixteen of Toussaint's officers were chained to rocks in desert islands, others in marshes, and left to be devoured by poisonous reptiles and insects. Rochambeau sent to Cuba for bloodhounds. When they arrived, the young girls went down to the wharf, decked the hounds with ribbons and flowers, kissed their necks, and, seated in the amphitheater, the women clapped their hands to see a Negro thrown to these dogs, previously starved to rage. But the Negroes besieged this very city so closely that these same girls, in their misery, ate the very hounds they had welcomed.

Then flashed forth that defying courage and sublime endurance which show how alike all races are when tried in the same furnace. The Roman wife, whose husband faltered when Nero ordered him to kill himself, seized the dagger and, mortally wounding her own body, cried, "Poetus, it is not hard to die." The world records it with proud tears. Just in the same spirit, when a Negro colonel was ordered to execution and trembled, his wife seized his sword and, giving herself a death wound, said, "Husband, death is sweet when liberty is gone."

The war went on. Napoleon sent over thirty thousand more soldiers. But disaster still followed his efforts. What the sword did not devour, the fever ate up. Leclerc died. Pauline carried his body back to France. Napoleon met her at Bordeaux, saying, "Sister, I gave you an army—you bring me back ashes." Rochambeau—the Rochambeau of our history—left in command of eight thousand troops, sent word to Dessalines: "When I take you, I will not shoot you like a soldier, or hang you like a white man; I will whip you to death like a slave." Dessalines chased him from battlefield to battlefield, from fort to fort, and finally shut him up in Samana. Heating cannon balls to destroy his fleet, Dessalines learned that Rochambeau had begged of the British admiral to cover his troops with the English flag, and the generous Negro suffered the boaster to embark undisturbed.

Some doubt the courage of the Negro. Go to Haiti, and stand on those fifty thousand graves of the best soldiers France ever had, and ask them what they think of the Negro's sword. And if that does not satisfy you, go to France, to the splendid mausoleum of the Counts of Rochambeau, and to the eight thousand graves of Frenchmen who skulked home under the English flag, and ask them. And if that does not satisfy you, come home, and if it had been October 1859, you might have come by way of quaking Virginia, and asked her what she thought of Negro courage.

You may also remember this—that we Saxons were slaves about four hundred years, sold with the land, and our fathers never raised a finger to end that slavery. They waited till Christianity and civilization, till commerce and the discovery of America, melted away their chains. Spartacus in Italy led the slaves of Rome against the empress of the world. She murdered him, and crucified them. There never was a slave rebellion successful but once, and that was in St. Domingo. Every race has been, some time or other, in chains. But there never was a race that, weakened and degraded by such chattel slavery, unaided, tore off its own fetters, forged them into swords, and won its liberty on the battlefield, but one, and that was the black race of St. Domingo. God grant that the wise vigor of our government may avert that necessity from our land, may raise into peaceful liberty the four million committed to our care, and show under democratic institutions a statesmanship as farsighted as that of England, as brave as the Negro of Haiti!

So much for the courage of the Negro. Now look at his endurance. In 1805 he said to the white men, "This island is ours; not a white foot shall touch it." Side by side with him stood the South American republics, planted by the best blood of the countrymen of Lope de Vega and Cervantes. They topple over so often that you could no more daguerreotype their crumbling fragments than you could the waves of the ocean. And yet, at their side, the Negro has kept his island sacredly to himself. It is said that at first, with rare patriotism, the Haitian government ordered the destruction of all the sugar plantations remaining, and discouraged its culture, deeming that the temptation which lured the French back again to attempt their enslavement. Burn over New York tonight, fill up her canals, sink every ship, destroy her railroads, blot out every remnant of education from her sons, let her be ignorant and penniless, with nothing but her hands to begin the world again—how much could she do in sixty years? And Europe, too, would lend you money, but she will not lend Haiti a dollar. Haiti, from the ruins of her colonial dependence, is become a civilized state, the seventh nation in the catalogue of commerce with this country, inferior in morals and education to none of the West Indian isles. Foreign merchants trust her courts as willingly as they do our own. Thus far, she has foiled the ambition of Spain, the greed of England, and the malicious statesmanship of Calhoun. Toussaint made her what she is. In this work there was grouped around him a score of men, mostly of pure Negro blood, who ably seconded his efforts. They were able in war and skillful in civil affairs, but not, like him, remarkable for that rare mingling of high qualities which alone makes true greatness, and insures a man leadership among those otherwise almost his equals. Toussaint was indisputably their chief. Courage, purpose, endurance—these are the tests. He did plant a state so deep that all the world has not been able to root it up.

I would call him Napoleon, but Napoleon made his way to empire over broken oaths and through a sea of blood. This man never broke his word. "No Retaliation" was his great motto and the rule of his life; and the last words uttered to his son in France were these: "My boy, you will one day go back to St. Domingo; forget that France murdered your father." I would call him Cromwell, but Cromwell was only a soldier, and the state he founded went down with him into his grave. I would call him Washington, but the great Virginian held slaves. This man risked his empire rather than permit the slave trade in the humblest village of his dominions.

You think me a fanatic tonight, for you read history, not with your eyes, but with your prejudices. But fifty years hence, when Truth gets a hearing, the Muse of History will put Phocion for the Greek, and Brutus for the Roman, Hampden for England, Fayette for France, choose Washington as the bright, consummate flower of our earlier civilization, and John Brown the ripe fruit of our noonday [thunders of applause], then, dipping her pen in the sunlight, will write in the clear blue, above them all, the name of the soldier, the statesman, the martyr, Toussaint L'Ouverture. [Long-continued applause.]

1863

ABRAHAM LINCOLN
1809–1865

Tom Lincoln, born to poverty, almost illiterate, and raised to the mastery of a limited body of farming skills, struggled to squeeze, from a succession of small farms in Kentucky, Indiana, and Illinois, a livelihood for his family. But his son Abraham, burdened with the gift of an extraordinary intelligence, sensed nothing but weary futility in what seemed to him a treadmill of squatting and moving on; and though his formal schooling was as minimal as his father's, Abraham was inspired to educate himself by the few books that came his way and by the support of his sensitive and ambitious mother and stepmother. From these resources and from his own native sensitivity he gleaned that he ought to make his life, like the books he had cherished, a story with a meaningful end.

To say that he succeeded in this would be an understatement. At twenty-one he was on his own, working as a laborer, storekeeper, and postmaster in the small town of New Salem, Illinois—and teaching himself the law; by his mid-twenties he was not only a successful practicing lawyer but a member of the state legislature (in which he served four terms); at thirty-eight he was elected to Congress; at fifty-two he was elected president of the United States; and by the time of his death by assassination—only a few weeks after the inauguration of his second presidential term—he had made of himself so extraordinary a statesman that his end was all too painfully meaningful.

The ideals of the Republic that were celebrated in the histories he read as a child instilled in Lincoln the faith that, despite the poverty and squalor of his birth, he could determine his own destiny, and that the Constitution of his country guaranteed him the right to do so. Consequently, he both revered the Constitution and labored, in his legal and political career, to assure that the Constitution's guarantees extended as far in practice as they did in ideal. That these two concerns were incompatible—that the compromise with slavery which was written into the Constitution made the United States (as he was to describe it) "a house divided against itself," a union which could not honor the rights of its Southern states without making a mockery of its own Bill of Rights—occurred to him only gradually; for though he was vocal in his disapproval of slavery, throughout most of his political career he stood for free soil in the new territories but not for abolition. When he campaigned for the presidency in 1860, his platform emphasized not the problem of slavery, but the preservation of the Union, as his primary concern.

It seemed clear enough that the new president was not the avenging angel of liberty the abolitionists had waited for, but rather an adroit politician whose appearance of flexible moderation made him tolerable to many though satisfactory to few—not the man anyone really wanted, but the only man who could command a tentative majority among the now bitterly divided population. He was quick and resourceful in appeasing the conflicting interests of his constituents—as ready to paint himself a defender of segregation as of universal liberty, when doing either would persuade his audience to accept his vision of the Constitution.

Yet the hysterical dread and outrage with which his opponents—both North and South—viewed his candidacy, which caused them to brand him the "blackest" of the "black Republicans" and caused seven southern states to secede from the Union in response to his election in 1861, was not unfounded. Adherents of slavery had good reason to fear him, for in Lincoln the worldly pragmatism that made him a skillful manipulator of men was coupled with an extraordinary intellectual independence. He had demonstrated in Congress his willingness to jeopardize his own political future by taking an unpopular stand on principle, once the reins of power were in his hands; and the stand he had taken then indicated that as president he would be the enemy of slaveholders, despite his protestations of moderation. During his presidency, he was besieged as much by the defenders of slavery as by its enemies, but in 1862, at a critically unstable moment in the war, he cast the weight of his administration with immediate emancipation of the slaves in the Confederate states, against the wishes of what seemed an overwhelming majority of the people. In his efforts to preserve the Union, he was willing to appease, and reluctant to offend, the powerful adherents of slavery—a posture which dictated a number of half-measures and dubious compromises. But the Union he envisioned was one in which slavery—and all artificial perpetuation of inequality among men—should have no lasting place.

Lincoln's rhetorical posture shifted with the needs of the moment, much as his policies did; but like his policies, the language of Lincoln's presidential speeches has about it a ring of enlightened purposiveness which seems to reach beyond the merely strategic dimension of rhetoric. In early speeches, he employed the precise language and humorous illustrative fables appropriate to an attorney arguing a case in law, but in the later speeches—of which the selections offered here are the most famous examples—he turned steadily toward the rhetoric of the Bible, both in style and reference. This shift from the legal to the religious parallels Lincoln's shift from the legislative to the executive branches of government and from a posture of legislative compromise to one of military force; his biblical rhetoric, which had characterized the speeches of abolitionists for decades, appeals, as they did, to an authority that could not finally be found in the Constitution, but which might be counted on to unite a politically divided people under the banner of the Christianity they still shared.

The Address at the Dedication of the Gettysburg National Cemetery and the Second Inaugural Address are remarkable, however, not for their use of biblical cadence and reference but for the simplicity and clarity with which that rhetoric is fused with the self-educated lawyer's measured concern for justice in the affairs of men. Two addresses were given on November 19, 1863, at the dedication of the national cemetery at Gettysburg—the site, only three months before, of the bloodiest battle of the war—and *both* appealed to the Christian sentiments of the fifteen thousand Americans who gathered for the ceremonies; but it was Edward Everett's two-hour paean to the forces of armed righteousness that met the public standard for eloquence and piety. Lincoln's two-minute speech, over almost before the crowd could realize that the president was speaking, seemed a failure—for it was concise and simple, barren of the florid language that would demonstrate the speaker's passionate response to the occasion. The piece, however, like Lincoln himself, gained after a time the regard of a people who (as Lincoln once jested) could be fooled some of the time but not forever; and his little speech has gradually come to seem more eloquent than any less restrained or more complex statement could have been. The author seems to speak from a place above narrow rational self-interest yet below blind adherence to an extrarational authority, so that these pleas for unity and support become reassertions of faith in the rational humanist principles on which his precious, precarious Republic had been founded.

Elaine Sargent Apthorp
San Jose State University

PRIMARY WORKS

The Collected Works of Abraham Lincoln, ed. Roy Basler, 9 volumes, 1953–1955; *Supplement 1832–1865*, 1974.

Address at the Dedication
of the Gettysburg National Cemetery

Four score and seven years ago our fathers brought forth on this continent, a new nation, conceived in Liberty, and dedicated to the proposition that all men are created equal.

Now we are engaged in a great civil war; testing whether that nation, or any nation so conceived and so dedicated, can long endure. We are met on a great battlefield of that war. We have come to dedicate a portion of that field as a final resting-place for those who here gave their lives that that nation might live. It is altogether fitting and proper that we should do this.

But, in a larger sense, we cannot dedicate—we cannot consecrate—we cannot hallow—this ground. The brave men, living and dead, who struggled here have consecrated it, far above our poor power to add or detract. The world will little note, nor long remember, what we say here, but it can never forget what they did here. It is for us the living, rather, to be dedicated here to the unfinished work which they who fought here have thus far so nobly advanced. It is rather for us to be here dedicated to the great task remaining before us—that from these honored dead we take increased devotion to that cause for which they gave the last full measure of devotion; that we here highly resolve that these dead shall not have died in vain; that this nation, under God, shall have a new birth of freedom; and that government of the people, by the people, for the people, shall not perish from the earth.

1863

Second Inaugural Address

FELLOW-COUNTRYMEN:

At this second appearing to take the oath of the presidential office, there is less occasion for an extended address than there was at the first. Then a statement, somewhat in detail, of a course to be pursued, seemed fitting and proper. Now, at the expiration of four years, during which public declarations have been constantly called forth on every point and phase of the great contest which still absorbs the attention and engrosses the energies of the nation, little that is new could be presented. The progress of our arms,[1] upon which all else chiefly depends, is as well known to the public as to myself; and it is, I trust, reasonably satisfactory and encouraging to all. With high hope for the future, no prediction in regard to it is ventured.

On the occasion corresponding to this four years ago, all thoughts were anxiously directed to an impending civil war. All dreaded it—all sought to avert it. While the inaugural address was being delivered from this place, devoted altogether to saving the Union without war, insurgent agents were in the city seeking to destroy it without war—seeking to dissolve the Union, and divide effects, by negotiation. Both parties deprecated war; but one of them would make war rather than let the nation survive; and the other would accept war rather than let it perish. And the war came.

One-eighth of the whole population were colored slaves, not distributed generally over the Union, but localized in the Southern part of it. These slaves constituted a peculiar and powerful interest. All knew that this interest was, somehow, the cause of the war. To strengthen, perpetuate, and extend this interest was the object for which the insurgents would rend the Union, even by war; while the government claimed no right to do more than to restrict the territorial enlargement of it.

Neither party expected for the war the magnitude or the duration which it has already attained. Neither anticipated that the cause of the conflict might cease with, or even before, the conflict itself should cease.[2] Each looked for an easier triumph, and a result less fundamental and astounding. Both read the same Bible, and pray to the same God; and each invokes his aid against the other. It may seem strange that any men should dare to ask a just God's assistance in wringing their bread from the sweat of other men's faces; but let us judge not, that we be not judged.[3] The prayers of both could not be answered—that of neither has been answered fully.

The Almighty has his own purposes. "Woe unto the world because of offences! for it must needs be that offences come; but woe to that man by whom the offence cometh."[4] If we shall suppose that American slavery is

---

[1]The success of our armies. At the time of Lincoln's second inaugural, the Civil War was essentially over, the Union forces victorious.
[2]That the slaves would be freed before the war to decide their future was ended. Lin-

coln's Emancipation Proclamation went into effect on January 1, 1863.
[3]Reference to the Book of Matthew, 7:1.
[4]Reference to the Book of Matthew, 17:7.

one of those offences which, in the providence of God, must needs come, but which, having continued through His appointed time, He now wills to remove, and that He gives to both North and South this terrible war, as the woe due to those by whom the offence came, shall we discern therein any departure from those divine attributes which the believers in a Living God always ascribe to Him? Fondly do we hope—fervently do we pray—that this mighty scourge of war may speedily pass away. Yet, if God wills that it continue until all the wealth piled by the bondman's two hundred and fifty years of unrequited toil shall be sunk, and until every drop of blood drawn with the lash shall be paid by another drawn with the sword, as was said three thousand years ago, so still it must be said, "The judgments of the Lord are true and righteous altogether."[5]

With malice toward none; with charity for all; with firmness in the right, as God gives us to see the right, let us strive on to finish the work we are in; to bind up the nation's wounds; to care for him who shall have borne the battle, and for his widow, and his orphan—to do all which may achieve and cherish a just and lasting peace, among ourselves, and with all nations.

1865

---

[5]Reference to the Book of Psalms 9:9.

The Cherokee Nation and the Anglo Nation

THE TRADITIONAL HOMELANDS OF THE CHEROKEE NATION ARE IN WHAT IS NOW the southeastern United States, particularly the mountainous regions of Tennessee, Georgia, Kentucky, the Carolinas, Alabama, and the Virginias. There are some stories that point to a northern origin of the Cherokees, who in these accounts were driven southward by their Iroquois kin, or for a South American origin, in which the Cherokees originated on a now lost island and journeyed northward. Whatever the birthplace of the Nation, the Cherokees call the Southeast the crucible of Cherokee culture.

Part of the American impetus for the Revolution was Britain's decree that westward expansion by the colonies was forbidden; as Cherokee territory was in the territory forbidden by Britain, most Cherokee towns allied themselves with the English during the war and were brutally punished for that alliance, losing much of their land in its aftermath. One of the primary goals of American diplomacy was the dissolution of tribal title to lands in the East, a goal that could be accomplished in one of two ways: open warfare or assimilation into the American populace. With the fledgling United States still struggling to remain a solvent union, warfare was impractical, so starting with the Jefferson administration, assimilation became the primary method used to erase Cherokee title to their homelands. This policy took a two-pronged form: "civilization" and "Christianization." Traditional cultural practices and spiritual beliefs deemed "uncivilized" were discouraged and aggressively prosecuted by the U.S. government and its agents, who maintained strong control over access to resources such as food, clothing, trade goods, and livestock. Cherokees adapted quickly and successfully to these demands of "civilization," but most adaptations took place within a distinctly Cherokee worldview and context.

Before the European invasion, the Cherokees were associated in a loose confederation of individual towns connected by clan ties, cultural traditions, and language. Each town was governed by a council of clan elders, medicine people, and peace and war leaders (both male and female), who each held authority over different spheres of domestic and international relations. In the early nineteenth century, in response to increasing aggression by Euro-American settlers and the U.S. government's demands for Cherokee territory, the individual towns affiliated as a single political entity—the Cherokee Nation—that was deemed more efficient in facing the ever-encroaching threats against Cherokee lands and sovereignty. The governmental structure of the Cherokee Republic was in part modeled on the U.S. system of checks and balances; it included a representative council (Congress), a tribal judiciary (the Supreme Court), and a Principal Chief (President), in addition to a written Constitution. This restructuring, however, disenfranchised women—pushing into the background the strong influence women had long asserted in Cherokee politics—and also reflected some of the values of influential Cherokee mixed bloods who owned plantations and black slaves, thus excluding blacks and black Cherokees from voting or representation.

These changes were lauded by many non-Indians—especially in the more liberalized Northeast—as evidence that the Cherokees were the most "civilized" Indians; others, however, especially those citizens of Georgia who were particularly hungry for Cherokee lands, were outraged by what they saw as primitive and backward people presuming to claim white civilization for their own.

The Cherokee language was a prime example of both the power and threat posed by the Cherokee Nation. In 1821, Sequoya, a crippled silversmith and organic linguist, finished developing an eighty-five-symbol written alphabet for the Cherokee language—the syllabary—which spread quickly through the Nation and, within two years, made the Cherokees the most literate people in the world, with some estimates of more than 95 percent literacy in written Cherokee. This development, along with the later political restructuring and the creation of a bilingual newspaper, the *Cherokee Phoenix*, resulted in a socially informed, politically astute citizenry that was fully engaged with the issues of the time.

When gold was found in Cherokee territory in 1828, thousands of white settlers descended on the Nation, followed by strong harassment of the Nation by the state of Georgia, which claimed most of the land of the Cherokees as its own. This year also saw the election of Andrew Jackson, the Indian-hating advocate of white supremacy and Indian expulsion from the United States. In 1830, with Jackson's hearty support, Congress passed the notorious Indian Removal Act. "Removal" was a euphemism for what would today be considered ethnic cleansing, providing the legal justification for the forcible eviction and relocation of thousands of Indians from dozens of tribes in the East (and even the Far West) from resource-rich lands desired by Euro-Americans.

The leaders of the Cherokee Nation, most notably Principal Chief John Ross, fought removal through all available channels: appeals to Congress (supported by such figures as Daniel Webster and Davy Crockett), letters to newspapers throughout the country, and suits brought before the U.S. Supreme Court—*Cherokee Nation v. Georgia* (1831) and *Worcester v. Georgia* (1832), both of which would come to be foundational decisions for U.S. Indian policy. By 1835, however, the pressures of U.S. removal policy and coercive trade and commerce restrictions, Georgia's increasingly brutal and illegal attacks on the Nation, and U.S./Georgia-agitated intratribal conflict led a few hundred Cherokees (who would come to be known as the Treaty Party) to sign the Treaty of New Echota with the U.S. government, exchanging all Cherokee territory for land in the "Indian Territory" of what is now Oklahoma.

Despite the opposition of nearly 15,000 Cherokees, including the democratically elected leadership of the Nation, who had no voice in its illegal and unrepresentative creation, Congress ratified the treaty in 1836. Two years later, the Cherokees were driven from their homes and rounded up in filthy, disease-ridden concentration camps. Weeks later, U.S. troops and Georgia militiamen forced the Cherokees into a thousand-mile march that would come to be known as the Trail of Tears. From the beginning of the ordeal to the end, through a late blazing summer and an early bitter winter to resettlement and reconstruction, perhaps half of the Cherokee people perished. (About a thousand Cherokees managed to avoid capture; these escapees became the core of what is now the Eastern Band, the majority of Cherokees who remained in the homeland of the Nation.)

When the survivors arrived in their new home, a few thousand Cherokees were already living in Indian Territory, including the Old Settlers, who sought to avoid white expansion a few years before removal, and the Treaty Party, who avoided the agonies of the Trail of Tears through their betrayal. Three of the four leaders of the Treaty Party were assassinated within weeks of the newcomers' arrival, and the tribe became quickly torn between the minority loyal to Stand Watie, the surviving Treaty Party leader, and the majority loyal to John Ross, the Principal Chief of the combined Nation. The Old Settlers joined the Ross party, and all set to work on rebuilding the Nation, in spite of continued conflict with Watie's loyalists. This conflict ceased for a while following a treaty between the Ross and Watie parties in 1846.

The Nation rebuilt quickly and surpassed all expectations in its reconstruction. Male and female educational seminaries and a public school system were established, along with a new newspaper, a national capital, city improvements, homes, and farmsteads. Despite myriad problems that continued in the aftermath of removal, the Nation managed to establish itself strongly in its new home. Major challenges to sovereignty, cultural and political distinctiveness, and even survival would face the Cherokee Nation and its citizens in the decades to come—with the U.S. Civil War and the dissolution of Indian Territory tribal title in the lead-up to Oklahoma statehood among the most traumatic—but the Cherokees endured.

Today there are three federally recognized Cherokee governments in the United States: the Cherokee Nation, currently the second largest tribe in the United States with more than 300,000 citizens, centered in Tahlequah, Oklahoma; the Eastern Band of Cherokees of the Qualla Boundary in North Carolina; and the United Keetoowah Band of Cherokees in Oklahoma and Arkansas. Like the fabled phoenix that continues to serve as the symbol for the Nation's official newspaper, the Cherokee people have risen again and again from the ashes of catastrophe, each time to assert the continuing strength, commitment, and courage of the *Ani-yun-wiya*, the Real Human Beings.

Daniel Heath Justice
University of British Columbia

PRIMARY SOURCES

Russell Thornton, *The Cherokees: A Population History*, 1990; Theda Perdue and Michael D. Green, eds., *The Cherokee Removal: A Brief History with Documents*, 1993; Robert J. Conley, *The Cherokee Nation: A History*, 2005.

ANONYMOUS

Cherokee Vision of Elohi[1]

When we lived beyond the great waters there were twelve clans belonging to the Cherokee tribe.... back in the old country in which we lived[,] the country was subject to great floods. So in the course of time we held a council and decided to build a store reaching to heaven. The Cherokees said that when the [h]ouse was built and the floods came the tribe would just leave the earth and go to heaven.... we commenced to build the great structure and when it was towering into one of the highest heavens[,] the great powers destroyed the apex, cutting it down to about half of its height. But as the tribe was fully determined to build to heaven for safety[,] they were not discouraged but commenced to repair the damage done by the gods. Finally, they completed the lofty structure and considered themselves safe from the floods ... after it was completed[,] the gods destroyed the high part again.... Then the tribe held another council and concluded to move out of the floody [sic] country and hunt one more dry and suitable to their liking. So[,] they journeyed for many days and years and finally came to a country that had a good climate and [was] suitable for raising corn and other plenty upon which the tribe subsisted. Other red tribes or clans to the Cherokee tribe began to come also from the old country. The emigration continued for many years, never knowing that they crossed the great waters. In the course of time, the old pathway which had been traveled by the clans was cut by the submergence of a portion of the land into the deep sea. This path can be traced to this day by the broken boulders. This was no surprise to the clans as they were used to the workings of the floods.

Long years after they had settled in their new homes in the new country[,] they began to hunt for the clans of the Cherokee tribe; ... after a fruitless search for the others finally gave it up an[d] established a new system of seven sacred clans to the tribe. From that day to this[,] they have been searching for the five lost clans of the Cherokee.

CHEROKEE WOMEN

Petition, May 2, 1817

The Cherokee ladys now being present at the meeting of the chiefs and warriors in council have thought it their duty as mothers to address their beloved chiefs and warriors now assembled.

---

[1]This text is a nineteenth-century version of a much older oral history account, and was subsequently republished in the late twentieth century.

Our beloved children and head men of the Cherokee Nation, we address you warriors in council. We have raised all of you on the land which we now have, which God gave us to inhabit and raise provisions. We know that our country has once been extensive, but by repeated sales has become circumscribed to a small track, and [we] never have thought it our duty to interfere in the disposition of it till now. If a father or mother was to sell all their lands which they had to depend on, which their children had to raise their living on, which would be indeed bad & to be removed to another country. We do not wish to go to an unknown country [to] which we have understood some of our children wish to go over the Mississippi, but this act of our children would be like destroying your mothers.

Your mothers, your sisters ask and beg of you not to part with any more of our land. We say ours. You are our descendants; take pity on our request. But keep it for our growing children, for it was the good will of our creator to place us here, and you know our father, the great president,[1] will not allow his white children to take our country away. Only keep your hands off of paper talks for it is our own country. For [if] it was not, they would not ask you to put your hands to paper, for it would be impossible to remove us all. For as soon as one child is raised, we have others in our arms, for such is our situation & will consider our circumstance.

Therefore, children, don't part with any more of our lands but continue on it & enlarge your farms. Cultivate and raise corn & cotton and your mothers and sisters will make clothing for you which our father the president has recommended to us all. We don't charge any body for selling any lands, but we have heard such intentions of our children. But your talks become true at last; it was our desire to forwarn you all not to part with our lands.

Nancy Ward to her children: Warriors to take pity and listen to the talks of your sisters. Although I am very old yet cannot but pity the situation in which you will hear of their minds. I have great many grand children which [I] wish them to do well on our land.

Petition, June 30, 1818

Beloved Children,

We have called a meeting among ourselves to consult on the different points now before the council, relating to our national affairs. We have heard with painful feelings that the bounds of the land we now possess are to be drawn into very narrow limits. The land was given to us by the Great Spirit above as our common right, to raise our children upon, & to make support for our rising generations. We therefore humbly petition our beloved children, the head men & warriors, to hold out to the last in support of our common

---

[1] James Monroe.

rights, as the Cherokee nation have been the first settlers of this land; we therefore claim the right of the soil.

We well remember that our country was formerly very extensive, but by repeated sales it has become circumscribed to the very narrow limits we have at present. Our Father the President advised us to become farmers, to manufacture our own clothes, & to have our children instructed. To this advice we have attended in every thing as far as we were able. Now the thought of being compelled to remove the other side of the Mississippi is dreadful to us, because it appears to us that we, by this removal, shall be brought to a savage state again, for we have, by the endeavor of our Father the President, become too much enlightened to throw aside the privileges of a civilized life.

We therefore unanimously join in our meeting to hold our country in common as hitherto.

Some of our children have become Christians. We have missionary schools among us. We have hard the gospel in our nation. We have become civilized & enlightened, & are in hopes that in a few years our nation will be prepared for instruction in other branches of sciences & arts, which are both useful & necessary in civilized society.

There are some white men among us who have been raised in this country from their youth, are connected with us by marriage, & have considerable families, who are very active in encouraging the emigration of our nation. These ought to be our truest friends but prove our worst enemies. They seem to be only concerned how to increase their riches, but do not care what becomes of our Nation, nor even of their own wives and children.

Petition, October 17, 1821 [1831?]

To the Committee and Council,

We the females, residing in Salequoree and Pine Log, believing that the present difficulties and embarrassments under which this nation is placed demands a full expression of the mind of every individual, on the subject of emigrating to Arkansas, would take upon ourselves to address you. Although it is not common for our sex to take part in public measures, we nevertheless feel justified in expressing our sentiments on any subject where our interest is as much at stake as any other part of the community.

We believe the present plan of the General Government to effect our removal West of the Mississippi, and thus obtain our lands for the use of the State of Georgia, to be highly oppressive, cruel and unjust. And we sincerely hope there is no consideration which can induce our citizens to forsake the land of our fathers of which they have been in possession from time immemorial, and thus compel us, against our will, to undergo the toils and difficulties of removing with our helpless families hundreds of miles to unhealthy and unproductive country. We hope therefore the Committee and

Council will take into deep consideration our deplorable situation, and do everything in their power to avert such a state of things. And we trust by a prudent course their transactions with the General Government will enlist in our behalf the sympathies of the good people of the United States.

JOHN RIDGE (CHEROKEE)
c. 1802–1839

Letter to Albert Gallatin, February 27, 1826

The Cherokee Nation is bounded on the North by east Tennessee & North Carolina, east by Georgia, south by the Creek Nation & state of Alabama, & west by west Tennessee. The extreme length of the Nation must be upwards of 200 miles & extreme breadth about 150. At a rough conjecture, it has been supposed to contain about 10,000,000 of acres of land. It is divided into eight districts or Counties by a special act of the National Council, & their boundaries are distinctly designated and defined. A census of the Nation was taken last year (1825) by order of the Council to ascertain the amount of property and Taxable persons within the Nation. The correctness of this may be relied on, and the population proved to be 13,583 native citizens, 147 white men married in the Nation, 73 white women, and 1,277 African slaves, to which if we add 400 cherokees who took reservations in North Carolina & who are not included in the census & who have since merged again among us, the Cherokee Nation will contain 15,480 inhabitants.[1] There is a scanty instance of African mixture with the Cherokee blood, but that of the white may be as 1 to 4, occasioned by intermarriages which has been increasing in proportion to the march of civilization.[2] The above population is dispersed over the face of the Country on separate farms; villages, or a community, having a common enclosure to protect their hutches [cabins], have disappeared long since, & to my knowledge, there is but one of this character at Coosawattee, the inhabitants of which are

[1]The reservations to which Ridge refers were tracts of land (often 640 acres) within cessions that the United States deeded to individual Indians. The United States government originally intended to give private reservations to those Indians who wanted to become citizens and assimilate into Anglo-American society, but in practice officials often awarded these private reservations to prominent individuals as an inducement to sign cessions. The holders often sold this property, pocketed the money, and moved onto common land within the Cherokee Nation; unscrupulous whites defrauded others of their reservations, and they too moved into the Nation.

[2]The census of 1835 documents the racial composition of the Cherokee Nation. The census lists 12,776 Cherokees, or 77.7 percent, as "full bloods," that is, of only Cherokee ancestry.

gradually diminishing by emigration to the woods, where they prefer to clear the forest & govern their own individual plantations. In this view of their location, it really appears that they are farmers and herdsmen, which is their real character. It is true that there are distinctions now existing & increasingly so in the value of property possessed by individuals, but this only answers a good purpose, as a stimulus to those in the rear to equal their neighbors who have taken the lead. Their principal dependence for subsidence is on the production of their own farms. Indian corn is a staple production and is the most essential article of food in use. Wheat, rye & oats grow very well & some families have commenced to introduce them on their farms. Cotton is generally raised for domestic consumption and a few have grown it for market & have realized very good profits. I take pleasure to state, tho' cautiously, that there is not to my knowledge a solitary Cherokee to be found that depends upon the chase for subsistence and every head of a family has his house & farm. The hardest portion of manual labor is performed by the men, & the women occasionally lend a hand to the field, more by choice and necessity than any thing else. This is applicable to the poorer class, and I can do them the justice to say, they very contentedly perform the duties of the kitchen and that they are the most valuable portion of our Citizens. They sew, they weave, they spin, they cook our meals and act well the duties assigned them by Nature as mothers as far as they are able & improved. The African slaves are generally mostly held by Half breeds and full Indians of distinguished talents. In this class the principal value of property is retained and their farms are conducted in the same style with the southern white farmers of equal ability in point of property. Their houses are usually of hewed logs, with brick chimneys & shingled roofs, there are also a few excellent Brick houses & frames. Their furniture is better than the exterior appearance of their houses would incline a stranger to suppose. They have their regular meals as the whites, Servants to attend them in their repasts, and the tables are usually covered with a clean cloth & furnished with the usual plates, knives & forks &c.[3] Every family more or less possess hogs, Cattle & horses and a number have commenced to pay attention to the introduction of sheep, which are increasing very fast. The horse is in general use for purposes of riding, drawing the plough or wagon.

Domestic manufactures is still confined to women who were first prevailed to undertake it. These consist of white or striped homespun, coarse woolen Blankets & in many instances very valuable & comfortable, twilled & figured coverlets. Woolen & cotton Stockings are mostly manufactured for domestic use within the Nation. I can only say that these domestic cloths are preferred by us to those brought from the New England. Domestic plaids our people are most generally clothed with them, but calicoes, silks, cambricks, &c. Handkerchiefs & shawls &c. are introduced by Native merchants,

---

[3]Cherokees traditionally ate only when they were hungry, a practice many Anglo-Americans considered to be "savage."

who generally trade to Augusta in Georgia. The only trade carried on by the Cherokees with the adjoining States, is in hogs & horned Cattle. Skins formerly were sold in respectable quantities but that kind of trade is fast declining & getting less reputable. Cherokees on the Tennessee river have already commenced to trade in cotton & grow the article in large plantations and they have realized very handsome profit. All those who have it in their power, are making preparations to grow it for market & it will soon be the staple commodity of traffic for the Nation.

You will be able more fully to ascertain their state of improvement by giving the out lines of their Government. Having been honored with a seat in its National Councils, I have better acquaintance with this branch of your enquiry, than any other. All Indian Nations are either divided into tribes, distinguished by different names & these are subdivided into Towns.[4] In each of these tribes or Towns are of course some men, prominent for valor, humanity & wisdom. The Assemblage of such men forms their Council fire. They are a standing body, & indefinitely so in number of warriors. They possess within themselves Legislation, Judicial & Executive powers. The first law & most prominent law is against murder. This is to be revenged & by the tribe of the victim without trial, whilst the relatives of the offender are compelled to remain neuter by the law of the Nation. This kind of Government existed in our Nation. Their chiefs were numerous and their responsibility was a trifling. Lands then could be obtained of them at a price most convenient to the U. States as their commissioners with the assistance of their agent could always procure a majority for a Cession, & when this was done, all yielded to secure their shares for the trifling equivalent. At length the eyes of our Nation were opened to see their folly. Their existence was in danger & the Remedy was within themselves & this could only be affected in the amendment of their Government. Useless members were stricken off. A Treasurer was appointed & a National seat for their future Government was selected. In short, these Chiefs organized themselves into Standing body of Legislators who meet in October annually at New Town [New Echota], their seat of Government.

They are composed of two departments, the National Committee & the Representative Council. The former consist of 13 members including their President & have a Clerk to record their proceedings. They control & regulate their monied concerns: powers to inspect the Books of the Treasury, & acknowledge claims, power to Legislate & Negative the sets of the other Branch of the Legislative Council. The Representatives have also their Secretary, consist of 45 members including their Speaker. They have power to Legislate & Negative the proceedings of the Nat. committee fill their own vacancies & the vacancies in the Committee, to elect the two head chiefs, or their executive in conjunction with the National Committee. All laws of course are passed with the concurrences of these two departments & approved of by the head Chiefs. Their laws at present are written in the

[4]Ridge is using "tribe" as a synonym for "clan."

English Language and commence in the words, to wit. "Be it Resolved by the National Committee & Council" &c. and are signed by the speaker of the Representatives, the President of the Committee and when approved by the first head Chief & attested by the Clerks. These Branches of our Legislature are composed of men chosen from the eight districts heretofore mentioned in as satisfactory proportion as circumstances will allow. The Judiciary of our Nation is more perfect than the Legislature, having less obstacles to make it so than the latter. It is independent [and has the] Power to bring any Chief before it of any grade, to pass sentence & put it in execution. There is a Court of Justice in every district & its district Judge, who presides over two Districts. Every Court has a Jury and its district officers, Sheriff constables &c. to attend it. A plaintiff or defendant can object to any Jury to sit on his trial or suit & if reasonable, he is indulged by the laws of his Country. There is also a Supreme Court of the Nation held once annually at New Town when all appeals from the district Courts are finally decided. At this Court Costs are exacted, but the District Courts are not allowed the privilege. The Sheriffs, marshals and constable are allowed 8 percent for collecting Taxes and debts &c. We have as yet not prisons and Justice is quickly awarded. The thief as soon as convicted & sentence passed is tied to the first Tree & on the naked skin is impressed, his receipt, for release. We have not as yet many written laws, it being the policy of our Government to regulate itself to the capacity and state of improvement of our people. I will give you a sketch of a few of these laws.

1. Law to regulate our Citizens agreeable to the Intercourse laws of the U. States for the purpose of Securing peace on the frontiers.

2. A law prohibiting the introduction of Intoxicating liquors by the whites.

3. Regulating intermarriages with the whites, making it necessary for a white man to obtain license & be married by a Gospel minister or some authorized person.

4. Against Renting land & introducing white people without a special written permission of the Legislative Council. Penalty: Expulsion of the white people so introduced as intruders, a fine of $500 on the aggressor and one hundred stripes on the naked back.

5. Giving indefeasible title to Lands improved—houses &c.—to the Citizens with power to sell or transfer them among each other, but not to Citizens of the adjoining States.

6. Regulating Taxes and defining the duties of collectors.

7. Law, prohibiting the sale of any more Lands to the United States except it be done by the concurrences of the Nat. Committee & Council; Penalty: disgrace & death to the offender.

8. A law to protect the orphan & widow to the father's [and] husband's property after death.

9. Regulating the Salary of the two head Chiefs, District & circuit Judges, the pay of the members of the Legislative Council & their clerks during active service and officers of the Nation generally.

10. Regulating the Judicial Courts of the Nation, defining their Powers.

11. against stealing.

12. against murder.

13. Defining the power of the Chiefs and that only exercised in a body in their Legislative capacity at the times appointed by law, and in the recess to be on a level with private Citizens.

I am assured of the loyalty of our Citizens to their Government and their laws and are determined to secure these blessings to their descendants yet unborn as an inheritance.

Property belonging to the wife is not exclusively at the control & disposal of the husband, and in many respects she has exclusive & distinct control over her own, particularly among the less civilized & in fact in every class & grade of intelligence, the law is in favor of the females in this respect.[5] Rules & customs in the transfer of property are adopted & respected from the adjoining states in the absence of any law to regulate this branch of our trade. Property descends from parents, equally to the children; if none, to the next relatives &c. But if a will is made, it is respected to the fullest extent & every person, possessed of property, is entitled to dispose of his or her property in this way.

Superstition is the portion of all uncivilized Nations and Idolatry is only engendered in the Brain of rudeness. The Cherokees in their most savage state, never worshipped the work of their own hands—neither fire or water nor any one or portion of splendid fires that adorn heaven's Canopy above. They believed in a great first cause or Spirit of all Good & in a great being the author of all evil. These [were] at variance and at war with each other, but the good Spirit was supposed to be superior to the bad one. These immortal beings had on both sides numerous intelligent beings of analogous dispositions to their chieftains. They had a heaven, which consisted of a visible world to those who had undergone a change by death. This heaven was adorned with all the beauties which a savage imagination could conceive: An open forest, yet various, giving shade & fruit of every kind; Flowers of various hues & pleasant to the Smell; Game of all kinds in great abundance, enough of feasts & plenty of dances, & to crown the whole, the most beautiful women, prepared & adorned by the great Spirit, for every individual Indian that by wisdom, hospitality & Bravery was introduced to this happy & immortal region. The Bad place was the reverse of this & in the vicinity of the good place, where the wretched, compelled to live in hunger, hostility & darkness, could hear the rejoicings of the happy, without the possibility of reaching its shores.

[5]In 1826, the states followed English common law with respect to married women's property. Under this legal tradition, married women had no right to property, even property they had before they married. When a woman married, her husband gained title to everything she owned. In 1839, Mississippi became the first state to enact legislation to protect the property rights of married women. The Cherokee law that protected married women's property may have been a holdover from traditional practices in which women controlled houses and fields, but the Council probably enacted this law to prevent white men from marrying Cherokee women solely to gain control of their property, which the Nation regarded as commonly owned.

Witches or wizards were in existence and pretended to possess Supernatural powers & intercourse with the Devil or bad Spirit. They were supposed capable of transforming themselves into the beasts of the forest & fowls of the air & take their nocturnal excursions in pursuit of human victims, particularly those suffering from disease, & it was often necessary for their friends to employ witch shooters to protect the sick from such visitors. Such characters were the dread of the Country, & many a time have I trembled at the croaking of a frog, hooting of an owl or guttural hoarseness of a Raven by night in my younger days. After the people began to be a little more courageous, these witches had a bad time of it. They were often on suspicion butchered or tomahawked by the enraged parents, relatives or friends of the deceased, particularly if the sickness was of short duration. The severity of revenge fell most principally on the grey hairs of aged persons of both sexes. To stop this evil, it was necessary to pass a law considering all slaughters of this kind in the light of murder, which has effected the desired remedy. There [are] yet among us who pretend to possess powers of milder character, Such as making rain, allaying a storm or whirlwinds, playing with thunder & foretelling future events with many other trifling conjurations not worth mentioning, but they are generally living monuments of fun to the young and grave Ridicule for the those in maturer years. There [are] about 8 churches, where the gospel is preached on sabbath days with in the Nation. They are missionary stations supported by moravians, Presbyterians, Baptists and methodists and each of these churches have a goodly number of pious & exemplary members and others, not professors, attend to preaching with respectable deportment. I am not able to say the precise number of actual christians, but they are respectable in point of number & character. And many a drunken, idle & good for nothing Indian has been converted from error & have become useful Citizens: Portions of Scripture & sacred hymns are translated and I have frequently heard with astonishment a Cherokee, unacquainted with the English take his text & preach, read his hymn & sing it, Joined by his audience, and pray to his heavenly father with great propriety & devotion. The influence of Religion on the life of the Indians is powerful & lasting. I have an uncle, who was given to all the vices of savagism in drunkenness, fornication and roguery & he is now tho' poorer in this world's goods but rich in goodness & makes his living by hard labor & is in every respect an honest praying christian.

In respect to marriage, we have no law regulating it & polygamy is still allowed to Native Cherokees. Increase of morality among the men, the same among the women & a respect for their characters & matrimonial happiness is fast consuming this last vestige of our ignorance. We attempted to pass a law regulating marriage, but as nearly all the members of our Legislature, tho' convinced of the propriety, had been married under the old existing ceremony, [and] were afraid it would reflect dishonor on them, it failed. Time will effect the desired change in this system & it is worthy of mention, even now, that the most respectable portion of our females prefer, tho' not required by law to be united in marriage attended by the solemnities of the

Christian mode. Indians, tho' naturally highminded, are not addicted to as much revenge as they have been represented, and I can say this, much it is paid for them to endure an intended Insult but they are ready to forgive if they discover marks of repentance in the countenance of an enemy. In regard to Intemperance, we are still as a nation grossly degraded. We are however on the improve. Five years ago our best chiefs during their official labors would get drunk & continue so for two or three days. It is now not the case & any member who should thus depart from duty would now be expelled from the Council. Among the younger class, a large number are of fine habits, temperate & genteel in their deportment. The females aspire to gain the affection of such men & to the females we may always ascribe the honor of effecting the civilization of man. There are about 13 Schools established by missionaries in the Nation and may contain 250 students. They are entirely supported by the humane Societies in different parts of the U. States. The Nation has not as yet contributed to the support of these Schools. Besides this, some of our most respectable people have their children educated at the academies in the adjoining states. Two cherokee females have recently completed their Education, at the expense of their father, at a celebrated female Academy in Salem, North Carolina. They are highly accomplished & in point of appearance & deportment; they would pass for the genteel & wellbred ladies in any Country.

I know of some others who are preparing for an admission in the same institution. I suppose that there are one third of our Citizens, that can read & write in the English Language. George Guess a Cherokee who is unacquainted with the English has invented 86 characters, in which the cherokees read & write in their own Language and regularly correspond with their Arkansas friends. This mode of writing is most extensively adopted by our people particularly by those who are ignorant of the English Language. A National Academy of a high order is to be soon established by law at our seat of Government.[6] The edifice will be of Brick & will be supported by the Nation. It is also in contemplation to establish an English & Cherokee printing press & a paper edited in both languages at our seat of Government. In our last Session, $1500 was appropriated to purchase the press and regulations adopted to carry the object into effect.[7] We have also a Society organized called the "Moral & Literary Society of the Cherokee Nation." A library is attached to this Institution.

Provision has been made by our Delegation at this place, in a Treaty with John C. Calhoun, the Sec'y of War in 1819, to afford aid to education in our Nation, by Reserving twelve miles square of Land to be sold by the President & by him invested to draw interest & applied as he shall think

---

[6]The plan to establish a national academy materialized only after removal. In the 1850s the Cherokees opened the Cherokee Male Seminary and the Cherokee Female Seminary, publicly supported institutions of higher education.

[7]The Cherokee Nation began publication of a bilingual newspaper, the *Cherokee Phoenix*, in 1828 with Ridge's cousin, Elias Boudinot, as editor.

proper. This tract has not been sold as yet, owing as I have understood in the unfavorable condition of the market at this time.

Having given a view of the present of civilization of the Cherokee Nation, it may not be amiss to relate the time & manner when it was first introduced. About the year 1795 Missionaries were sent by the United Abraham Or Moravians to the Cherokees & established a Station called Spring place in the center of Nation.[8] At or about that time, Col. Silas Dinsmore was appointed by Genl. Washington as Agent of the Nation, who from the Indian Testimony itself labored indefatigably in Teaching the Cherokees the art of agriculture by distributing hoes & ploughs & giving to the women Spinning wheels, cards & Looms. It appears when this change of Hunter life to a civilized one was proposed by the Agent to the Chiefs in Council, that he was unanimously laughed at by the Council for attempting [to] introduce white peoples' habits among the Indians, who were created to pursue the chase. Not discouraged here, the Agent turned to Individuals & succeeded to gain some to pay their attention to his plan by way of experiment, which succeeded. An anecdote is related of a Chief who was heartily opposed to the Agent's view. He came to Col. Dinsmore & said, "I don't want you to recommend these things to my people. They may suit white people, but will do [nothing] for the Indians. I am now going to hunt & shall be gone six moons & when I return, I shall expect to hear nothing of your talks made in [my] absence to induce my people to take hold of your plan." But in his absence the Agent induced his wife & daughters to Spin & weave with so much assiduity as to make more cloth in value, than the Chief's Hunt of six months amounted to. He was astonished & came to the Agent with a smile, accusing him for making his wife & daughters better hunters than he & requested to be furnished a plough & went to work on his farm.

In the meantime, the Moravians opened their School for the Indians, cleared a farm, cultivated a garden & planted an orchard. The Venerable Rev. John Gambold & his amiable Lady were a standing monument of Industry, Goodness & friendship. As far as they had means, they converted the "Wilderness to blossom as the Rose." There the boys & girls were taught to read & write, & occasionally labor in the Garden & in the field. There they were first taught to sing & pray to their Creator, & here Gospel Worship was first Established. Never shall I forget father Gambold & mother Mrs. Gambold. By them the clouds of ignorance which surrounded me on all sides were dispersed. My heart received the rays of civilization & my intellect expanded & took a wider range. My superstition vanished & I began to reason correctly

"Curious to view the Kings of ancient days,"
"The mighty dead that live in endless praise".

---

[8]The Moravians actually established their mission in 1800.

I draw to a close. Solemn & gloomy is the thought that all the Indian nations who once occupied America are nearly Gone! Powerful in War & Sage in peace, the Chiefs now sleep with their heroic deeds silent, in the bosom of the Earth! It was not their destiny to become great. Their Council fires could not be united into one, as the Seat of a great empire. It was for strangers to effect this, and necessity now compels the last Remnants to look to it for protection. It is true we Govern ourselves, but yet we live in fear. We are urged by these strangers to make room for their settlements & go farther west. Our National existence is suspended on the faith & honor of the U. States, alone. Their convenience may cut this asunder, & with a little faint struggle we may cease to be. All Nations have had their rises & their falls. This has been the case with us. Within the orbit the U. States move the States & within these we move in a little circle, dependent on the great center. We may live in this way fifty years & then we shall by Natural causes merge in & mingle with the U. States. Cherokee blood, if not destroyed, will wind its courses in beings of fair complexions, who will read that their ancestors became civilized under the frowns of misfortunes & causes of their enemies.

1826

ELIAS BOUDINOT (CHEROKEE)
C. 1802–1839

An Address to the Whites[1]

To those who are unacquainted with the manners, habits, and improvements of the Aborigines of this country, the term *Indian* is pregnant with ideas the most repelling and degrading. But such impressions, originating as they frequently do, from infant prejudices, although they hold too true when applied to some, do great injustices to many of this race of beings.

Some there are, perhaps even in this enlightened assembly, who at the bare sight of an Indian, or at the mention of the name, would throw back their imaginations to ancient times, to the ravages of savage warfare, to the yells pronounced over the mangled bodies of women and children, thus creating an opinion, inapplicable and highly injurious to those for whose temporal interest and eternal welfare, I come to plead.

What is an Indian? Is he not formed of the same materials with yourself? For "of one blood God created all the nations that dwell on the face of the

---

[1]The speech was delivered in Philadelphia, where it was published by William F. Geddes in 1826 with the subtitle *Delivered in the* *First Presbyterian Church on the 26th of May, 1826.*

earth." Though it be true that he is ignorant, that he is a heathen, that he is a savage; yet he is no more than all others have been under similar circumstances. Eighteen centuries ago what were the inhabitants of Great Britain?

You here behold an *Indian*, my kindred are *Indians*, and my fathers sleeping in the wilderness grave—they too were *Indians*. But I am not as my fathers were—broader means and nobler influences have fallen upon me. Yet I was not born as thousands are, in a stately dome and amid the congratulations of the great, for on a little hill, in a lonely cabin, overspread by the forest oak, I first drew my breath; and in a language unknown to learned and polished nations, I learnt to lisp my fond mother's name. In after days, I have had greater advantages than most of my race; and I now stand before you delegated by my native country to seek her interest, to labour for her respectability, and by my public efforts to assist in raising her to an equal standing with other nations of the earth.

The time has arrived when speculations and conjectures as to the practicability of civilizing the Indians must forever cease. A period is fast approaching when the stale remark—"Do what you will, an Indian will still be an Indian," must be placed no more in speech. With whatever plausibility this popular objection may have heretofore been made, every candid mind must now be sensible that it can no longer be uttered, except by those who are uninformed with respect to us, who are strongly prejudiced against us, or who are filled with vindictive feelings towards us; for the present history of the Indians, particularly of that nation to which I belong, most incontrovertibly establishes the fallacy of this remark. I am aware of the difficulties which have ever existed to Indian civilization. I do not deny the almost insurmountable obstacles which we ourselves have thrown in the way of this improvement, nor do I say that difficulties no longer remain; but facts will permit me to declare that there are none which may not easily be overcome, by strong and continued exertions. It needs not abstract reasoning to prove this position. It needs not the display of language to prove to the minds of good men, that Indians are susceptible of attainments necessary to the formation of polished society. It needs not the power of argument on the nature of man, to silence forever the remark that "it is the purpose of the Almighty that the Indians should be exterminated." It needs only that the world should know what we have done in the few last years, to foresee what yet we may do with the assistance of our white brethren, and that of the common Parent of us all.

It is not necessary to present to you a detailed account of the various aboriginal tribes, who have been known to you only on the pages of history, and there but obscurely known. They have gone; and to revert back to their days, would be only to disturb their oblivious sleep; to darken these walls with deeds at which humanity must shudder; to place before your eyes the scenes of Muskingum Sahta-goo[2] and the plains of Mexico, to call up the

---

[2]Boudinot probably refers to the execution of ninety unarmed Indians on the Muskingum River in 1782.

crimes of the bloody Cortes and his infernal host;[3] and to describe the animosity and vengeance which have overthrown, and hurried into the shades of death those numerous tribes. But here let me say, that however guilty these unhappy nations may have been, yet many and unreasonable were the wrongs they suffered, many the hardships they endured, and many their wanderings through the trackless wilderness. Yes, "notwithstanding the obloquy with which the early historians of the colonies have overshadowed the character of the ignorant and unfortunate natives, some bright gleams will occasionally break through, that throw a melancholy lustre on their memories. Facts are occasionally to be met with in their rude annals, which, though recorded with all the colouring of prejudice and bigotry, yet speak for themselves, and will be dwelt upon with applause and sympathy when prejudice shall have passed away."

Nor is it my purpose to enter largely into the consideration of the remnants, of those who have fled with time and are no more—They stand as monuments of the Indian's fate. And should they ever become extinct, they must move off the earth, as did their fathers. My design is to offer a few disconnected facts relative to the present improved state, and to the ultimate prospects of that particular tribe called Cherokees to which I belong.

The Cherokee nation lies within the chartered limits of the states of Georgia, Tennessee, and Alabama. Its extent as defined by treaties is about 200 miles in length from East to West, and about 120 in breadth. This country which is supposed to contain about 10,000,000 of acres exhibits great varieties of surface, the most part being hilly and mountainous, affording soil of no value. The vallies, however, are well watered and afford excellent land, in many parts particularly on the large streams, that of the first quality. The climate is temperate and healthy, indeed I would not be guilty of exaggeration were I to say, that the advantages which this country possesses to render it salubrious, are many and superior. Those lofty and barren mountains, defying the labour and ingenuity of man, and supposed by some as placed there only to exhibit omnipotence, contribute to the healthiness and beauty of the surrounding plains, and give to us that free air and pure water which distinguish our country. Those advantages, calculated to make the inhabitants healthy, vigorous, and intelligent, cannot fail to cause this country to become interesting. And there can be no doubt that the Cherokee Nation, however obscure and trifling it may now appear, will finally become, if not under its present occupants, one of the Garden spots of America. And here, let me be indulged in the fond wish, that she may thus become under those who now possess her; and ever be fostered, regulated and protected by the generous government of the United States.

The population of the Cherokee Nation increased from the year 1810 to that of 1824, 2000 exclusive of those who emigrated in 1818 and 19 to the

---

[3]The Spanish conquest of Mexico under Hernando Cortés was ruthless and bloody.

west of the Mississippi—of those who reside on the Arkansas the number is supposed to be about 5000.[4]

The rise of these people in their movement towards civilization may be traced as far back as the relinquishment of their towns; when game became incompetent to their support, by reason of the surrounding white population. They then betook themselves to the woods, commenced the opening of small clearings, and the raising of stock; still however following the chase. Game has since become so scarce that little dependence for subsistence can be placed upon it. They have gradually and I could almost say universally forsaken their ancient employment. In fact, there is not a single family in the nation, that can be said to subsist on the slender support which the wilderness would afford. The love and the practice of hunting are not now carried to a higher degree, than among all frontier people whether white or red. It cannot be doubted, however, that there are many who have commenced a life of agricultural labour from mere necessity, and if they could, would gladly resume their former course of living. But these are individual feelings and ought to be passed over.

On the other hand it cannot be doubted that the nation is improving, rapidly improving in all those particulars which must finally constitute the inhabitants an industrious and intelligent people.

It is a matter of surprise to me, and must be to all those who are properly acquainted with the condition of the Aborigines of this country, that the Cherokees have advanced so far and so rapidly in civilization. But there are yet powerful obstacles, both within and without, to be surmounted in the march of improvement. The prejudices in regard to them in the general community are strong and lasting. The evil effects of their intercourse with their immediate white neighbours, who differ from them chiefly in name, are easily to be seen, and it is evident that from this intercourse proceed those demoralizing practices which in order to surmount, peculiar and unremitting efforts are necessary. In defiance, however, of these obstacles the Cherokees have improved and are still rapidly improving. To give you a further view of their condition, I will here repeat some of the articles of the two statistical tables taken at different periods.

In 1810 There were 19,500 cattle; 6,100 horses; 19,600 swine; 1,037 sheep; 467 looms; 1,600 spinning wheels; 30 waggons; 500 ploughs; 3 saw-mills; 13 grist-mills etc. At this time there are 22,000 cattle; 7,600 Horses; 46,000 swine; 2,500 sheep; 762 looms; 2,488 spinning wheels; 172 waggons; 2,943 ploughs; 10 saw-mills; 31 grist-mills; 62 Blacksmith-shops; 8 cotton machines; 18 schools; 18 ferries; and a number of public roads. In one district there were, last winter, upwards of 0000[5] volumes of good books; and 11 different periodical papers both religious and political, which were taken and read. On the public roads there are many decent Inns, and few houses

---

[4]In 1808–1809 the Eastern Cherokee numbered 12,395. In 1819 the total was 15,000, one third of whom were west of the Mississippi. And in 1825 there were 13,542 in the East.

[5]The number intended is unknown.

for convenience, etc., would disgrace any country. Most of the schools are under the care and tuition of christian missionaries, of different denominations, who have been of great service to the nation, by inculcating moral and religious principles into the minds of the rising generation. In many places the word of God is regularly preached and explained, both by missionaries and natives; and there are numbers who have publicly professed their belief and interest in the merits of the great Saviour of the world. It is worthy of remark, that in no ignorant country have the missionaries undergone less trouble and difficulty, in spreading a knowledge of the Bible, than in this. Here, they have been welcomed and encouraged by the proper authorities of the nation, their persons have been protected, and in very few instances have some individual vagabonds threatened violence to them. Indeed it may be said with truth, that among no heathen people has the faithful minister of God experienced greater success, greater reward for his labour, than in this. He is surrounded by attentive hearers, the words which flow from his lips are not spent in vain. The Cherokees have had no established religion of their own, and perhaps to this circumstance we may attribute, in part, the facilities with which missionaries have pursued their ends. They cannot be called idolators; for they never worshipped Images. They believed in a Supreme Being, the Creator of all, the God of the white, the red, and the black man. They also believed in the existence of an evil spirit who resided, as they thought, in the setting sun, the future place of all who in their life time had done iniquitously. Their prayers were addressed alone to the Supreme Being, and which if written would fill a large volume, and display much sincerity, beauty and sublimity. When the ancient customs of the Cherokees were in their full force, no warrior thought himself secure, unless he had addressed his guardian angel; no hunter could hope for success, unless before the rising sun he had asked the assistance of his God, and on his return at eve had offered his sacrifice to him.

There are three things of late occurance, which must certainly place the Cherokee Nation in a fair light, and act as a powerful argument in favor of Indian improvement.

First. The invention of letters.

Second. The translation of the New Testament into Cherokee.

And Third. The organization of a Government.

The Cherokee mode of writing lately invented by George Guest,[6] who could not read any language nor speak any other than his own, consists of eighty-six characters, principally syllabic, the combinations of which form all the words of the language. Their terms may be greatly simplified, yet they answer all the purposes of writing, and already many natives use them.

The translation of the New Testament, together with Guest's mode of writing, has swept away that barrier which has long existed, and opened a

[6]Also Gist or Guess, better known as Sequoyah (c. 1760–c. 1840), who gave his syllabary to the Cherokees in 1821.

spacious channel for the instruction of adult Cherokees. Persons of all ages and classes may now read the precepts of the Almighty in their own language. Before it is long, there will scarcely be an individual in the nation who can say, "I know not God neither understand I what thou sayest," for all shall know him from the greatest to the least. The aged warrior over whom has rolled three score and ten years of savage life, will grace the temple of God with his hoary head; and the little child yet on the breast of its pious mother shall learn to lisp its Maker's name.

The shrill sound of the Savage yell shall die away as the roaring of far distant thunder; and Heaven wrought music will gladden the affrighted wilderness. "The solitary places will be glad for them, and the desert shall rejoice and blossom as a rose." Already do we see the morning star, forerunner of approaching dawn, rising over the tops of those deep forests in which for ages have echoed the warrior's whoop. But has not God said it, and will he not do it? The Almighty decrees his purposes, and man cannot with all his ingenuity and device countervail them. They are more fixed in their course than the rolling sun—more durable than the everlasting mountains.

The Government, though defective in many respects, is well suited to the condition of the inhabitants. As they rise in information and refinement, changes in it must follow, until they arrive at that state of advancement, when I trust they will be admitted into all the privileges of the American family.

The Cherokee Nation is divided into eight districts, in each of which are established courts of justice, where all disputed cases are decided by a Jury, under the direction of a circuit Judge, who has jurisdiction over two districts. Sheriffs and other public officers are appointed to execute the decisions of the courts, collect debts, and arrest thieves and other criminals. Appeals may be taken to the Superior Court, held annually at the seat of Government. The Legislative authority is vested in a General Court, which consists of the National Committee and Council. The National Committee consists of thirteen members, who are generally men of sound sense and fine talents. The National Council consists of thirty-two members, beside the speaker, who act as the representatives of the people. Every bill passing these two bodies, becomes the law of the land. Clerks are appointed to do the writings, and record the proceedings of the Council. The executive power is vested in two principal chiefs, who hold their office during good behaviour, and sanction all the decisions of the legislative council. Many of the laws display some degree of civilization, and establish the respectability of the nation.

Polygamy is abolished. Female chastity and honor are protected by law. The Sabbath is respected by the Council during session. Mechanics are encouraged by law. The practice of putting aged persons to death for witchcraft is abolished and murder has now become a governmental crime.

From what I have said, you will form but a faint opinion of the true state and prospects of the Cherokees. You will, however, be convinced of three important truths.

First, that the means which have been employed for the christianization and civilization of this tribe, have been greatly blessed. Second, that the increase of these means will meet with final success. Third, that it has now become necessary, that efficient and more than ordinary means should be employed.

Sensible of this last point, and wishing to do something for themselves, the Cherokees have thought it advisable that there should be established, a Printing Press and a Seminary of respectable character; and for these purposes your aid and patronage are now solicited. They wish the types, as expressed in their resolution, to be composed of English letters and Cherokee characters. These characters have now become extensively used in the nation; their religious songs are written in them; there is an astonishing eagerness in people of all classes and ages to acquire a knowledge of them; and the New Testament has been translated into their language. All this impresses on them the immediate necessity of procuring types. The most informed and judicious of our nation, believe that such a press would go further to remove ignorance, and her offspring superstition and prejudice, than all other means. The adult part of the nation will probably grovel on in ignorance and die in ignorance, without any fair trial upon them, unless the proposed means are carried into effect. The simplicity of this method of writing, and the eagerness to obtain a knowledge of it, are evinced by the astonishing rapidity with which it is acquired, and by the numbers who do so. It is about two years since its introduction, and already there are a great many who can read it. In the neighbourhood in which I live, I do not recollect a male Cherokee, between the ages of fifteen and twenty five, who is ignorant of this mode of writing. But in connexion with those for Cherokee characters, it is necessary to have types for English letters. There are many who already speak and read the English language, and can appreciate the advantages which would result from the publication of their laws and transactions in a well conducted newspaper. Such a paper, comprising a summary of religious and political events, etc. on the one hand; and on the other, exhibiting the feelings, disposition, improvements, and prospects of the Indians; their traditions, their true character, as it once was and as it now is; the ways and means most likely to throw the mantle of civilization over all tribes; and such other matter as will tend to diffuse proper and correct impressions in regard to their condition—such a paper could not fail to create much interest in the American community, favourable to the aborigines, and to have a powerful influence on the advancement of the Indians themselves. How can the patriot or the philanthropist devise efficient means, without full and correct information as to the subjects of his labour. And I am inclined to think, after all that has been written in narratives, professedly to elucidate the leading traits of their character, that the public knows little of that character. To obtain a correct and complete knowledge of these people, there must exist a vehicle of Indian Intelligence, altogether different from those which have heretofore been employed. Will not a paper published in an Indian country, under proper and judicious regulations, have the desired effect? I do not say that Indians will produce learned and elaborate dissertations in explanation and vindication of their own character; but they may exhibit specimens of their intellectual efforts, of their eloquence, of their moral, civil and physical advancement, which will do quite as much to remove prejudice and to give profitable information.[7]

The Cherokees wish to establish their Seminary, upon a footing which will insure to it all the advantages, that belong to such institutions in the states. Need I spend one moment in arguments, in favour of such an institution; need I speak one word of the utility, of the necessity, of an institution of learning; need I do more than simply to ask the patronage of benevolent hearts, to obtain that patronage.[8]

When before did a nation of Indians step forward and ask for the means of civilization? The Cherokee authorities have adopted the measures already stated, with a sincere desire to make their nation an intelligent and a virtuous people, and with a full hope that those who have already pointed out to them the road of happiness, will now assist them to pursue it. With that assistance, what are the prospects of the Cherokees? Are they not indeed glorious, compared to that deep darkness in which the nobler qualities of their souls have slept. Yes, methinks I can view my native country, rising from the ashes of her degredation, wearing her purified and beautiful garments, and taking her seat with the nations of the earth. I can behold her sons bursting the fetters of ignorance and unshackling her from the vices of heathenism. She is at this instant, risen like the first morning sun, which grows brighter and brighter, until it reaches its fulness of glory.

She will become not a great, but a faithful ally of the United States. In times of peace she will plead the common liberties of America. In times of war her intrepid sons will sacrifice their lives in your defence. And because she will be useful to you in coming time, she asks you to assist her in her present struggles. She asks not for greatness; she seeks not wealth, she pleads only for assistance to become respectable as a nation, to enlighten and ennoble her sons, and to ornament her daughters with modesty and virtue. She pleads for this assistance, too, because on her destiny hangs that of many nations. If she completes her civilization—then may we hope that all our nations will—then, indeed, may true patriots be encouraged in their efforts to make this world of the West, one continuous abode of enlightened, free, and happy people.

But if the Cherokee Nation fail in her struggle, if she die away, then all hopes are blasted, and falls the fabric of Indian civilization. Their fathers were born in darkness, and have died in darkness; without your assistance so will their sons. You, see, however, where the probability rests. Is there a soul whose narrowness will not permit the exercise of charity on such an occasion? Where is he that can withhold his mite from an object so noble? Who can prefer a little of his silver and gold, to the welfare of nations of his

---

[7]The *Cherokee Phoenix*, a weekly, was established in 1828. Printed in both English and Sequoyan script, the paper was edited by Boudinot.

[8]Although the Cherokee Council appropriated money for seminaries (or high schools) for both boys and girls in 1846, they were not built until 1851.

fellow beings? Human wealth perishes with our clay, but that wealth gained in charity still remains on earth, to enrich our names, when we are gone, and will be remembered in Heaven, when the miser and his coffers have mouldered together in their kindred earth. The works of a generous mind sweeten the cup of affliction; they enlighten the dreary way to the cold tomb; they blunt the sting of death, and smooth his passage to the unknown world. When all the kingdoms of this earth shall die away and their beauty and power shall perish, his name shall live and shine as a twinkling star; those for whose benefit be done his deeds of charity shall call him blessed, and they shall add honor to his immortal head.

There are, with regard to the Cherokee and other tribes, two alternatives; they must either become civilized and happy, or sharing the fate of many kindred nations, become extinct. If the General Government continue its protection, and the American people assist them in their humble efforts, they will, they must rise. Yes, under such protection, and with such assistance, the Indian must rise like the Phoenix, after having wallowed for ages in ignorance and barbarity. But should this Government withdraw its care, and the American people their aid, then, to use the words of a writer, "they will go the way that so many tribes have gone before them; for the hordes that still linger about the shores of Huron, and the tributary streams of the Mississippi, will share the fate of those tribes that once lorded it along the proud banks of the Hudson; of that gigantic race that are said to have existed on the borders of the Susquehanna; of those various nations that flourished about the Potomac and the Rhappahannoc, and that peopled the forests of the vast valley of Shenandoah. They will vanish like a vapour from the face of the earth, their very history will be lost in forgetfulness, and places that now know them will know them no more."

There is, in Indian history, something very melancholy, and which seems to establish a mournful precedent for the future events of the few sons of the forest, now scattered over this vast continent. We have seen every where the poor aborigines melt away before the white population. I merely speak of the fact, without at all referring to the cause. We have seen, I say, one family after another, one tribe after another, nation after nation, pass away; until only a few solitary creatures are left to tell the sad story of extinction.

Shall this precedent be followed? I ask you, shall red men live, or shall they be swept from the earth? With you and this public at large, the decision chiefly rests. Must they perish? Must they all, like the unfortunate Creeks, (victims of the unchristian policy of certain persons,) go down in sorrow to their grave?[9]

They hang upon your mercy as to a garment. Will you push them from you, or will you save them? Let humanity answer.

1826

[9]The "unfortunate Creeks" were victims of the Creek War of 1813– 1814, also known as the Red Stick War. In this clash with American forces (and some Cherokees), Creek towns were burned, many Creek citizens were killed, and others took refuge in Florida.

CHEROKEE NATION

from **Constitution of the Cherokee Nation**

Formed by a Convention of Delegates from the Several Districts, at New Echota, July 1827

We, the representatives of the people of the Cherokee Nation, in Convention assembled, in order to establish justice, ensure tranquility, promote our common welfare, and secure to ourselves and our posterity the blessings of liberty; acknowledging with humility and gratitude the goodness of the sovereign Ruler of the Universe, in offering us an opportunity so favorable to the design, and imploring His aid and direction in its accomplishment, do ordain and establish this Constitution for the Government of the Cherokee Nation.

Article I

Sec. 2.... and the lands therein are, and shall remain, the common property of the Nation; but the improvements made thereon, and in the possession of the citizens of the Nation, are the exclusive and indefeasible property of the citizens respectively who made; or may rightfully be in possession of them; Provided, that the citizens of the Nation, possessing exclusive and indefeasible right to their respective improvements, as expressed in this article, shall possess no right nor power to dispose of their improvements in any manner whatsoever to the United States, individual states, nor individual citizens thereof; and that whenever any such citizen or citizens shall remove with their effects out of the limits of this Nation, and become citizens of any other Government, all their rights and privileges as citizens of this Nation shall cease; Provided, nevertheless, That the Legislature shall have power to re-admit by law to all the rights of citizenship, any such person or persons, who may at any time desire to return to the Nation on their memorializing the General Council for such readmission. Moreover, the Legislature shall have power to adopt such laws and regulations, as its wisdom may deem expedient and proper, to prevent the citizens from monopolizing improvements with the view to speculation.

Article II

Sec. 1. The power of this Government shall be divided into three distinct departments; the Legislative, the Executive, and Judicial.

Sec. 2. No person or persons belonging to one of these departments shall exercise any of the powers properly belonging to either of the others, except in the cases hereinafter expressly directed or permitted.

Article III

Sec. 4. No person shall be eligible to a seat in the General Council, but a free Cherokee male citizen, who shall have attained to the age of twenty-five years. The descendants of Cherokee men by all free women, except the African race, whose parents may have been living together as man and wife, according to the customs and laws of this Nation, shall be entitled to all the rights and privileges of this Nation, as well as the posterity of Cherokee women by all free men. No person who is of negro or mulatto parentage, either by the father or mother side, shall be eligible to hold any office of profit, honor or trust under this Government.

Sec. 6. In all elections by the people, the electors shall vote viva voce.

Sec. 15. The General Council shall have power to make all laws and regulations, which they shall deem necessary and proper for the good of the Nation, which shall not be contrary to this Constitution.

Sec. 18. No retrospective law, nor any law impairing the obligations of contracts shall be passed.

Article V

Sec. 14. In all criminal prosecutions, the accused shall have the right of being heard, of demanding the nature and cause of the accusation against him, of meeting the witnesses face to face, of having compulsory process for obtaining witnesses in his favor: and in prosecutions by indictment or information, a speedy public trial by an impartial jury of the vicinage; nor shall he be compelled to give evidence against himself.

Sec. 15. The people shall be secure in their persons, houses, papers and possessions, from unreasonable seizures and searches, and no warrant to search any place or to seize any person or things, shall be issued without describing them as nearly as may be, nor without good cause, supported by oath, or affirmation....

Article VI

Sec. 2. No person who denies the being of a God, or a future state of rewards and punishment, shall hold any office in the civil department of this Nation.

Sec. 3. The free exercise of religious worship, and serving God without distinction shall forever be allowed within this Nation; Provided, That this liberty of conscience shall not be so construed as to excuse acts of licentiousness, or justify practices inconsistent with the peace or safety of this Nation.

Sec. 8. No person shall for the same offence be twice put in jeopardy of life or limb, nor shall any person's property be taken or applied to public use without his consent; Provided, That nothing in this clause shall be so construed as to impair the right and power of the General Council to lay and collect taxes. All courts shall be open, and every person for an injury done him in his property, person or reputation, shall have remedy by due course of law.

Sec. 9. The right of trial by jury shall remain inviolate.

Sec. 10. Religion, morality and knowledge being necessary to good government, the preservation of liberty, and the happiness of mankind, schools and the means of education shall forever be encouraged in this Nation.

1827

GEORGIA STATE ASSEMBLY

Laws Extending Jurisdiction over the Cherokees, December 19, 1829, and December 22, 1830

An act to add the Territory lying within the chartered limits of Georgia, and now in the occupancy of the Cherokee Indians, to the counties of Carroll, DeKalb, Gwinnett, Hall and Habersham, and to extend the laws of this State over the same, and to annul all laws and ordinances made by the Cherokee nation of Indians, and to provide for the compensation of officers serving legal process in said Territory, and to regulate the testimony of Indians, and to repeal the ninth section of the act of eighteen hundred and twenty-eight, upon this subject....

Sec. 6. *And be it further enacted*, That all the laws both civil and criminal of this State be, and the same are hereby extended over said portions of territory respectively, and all persons whatever residing within the same, shall, after the first day of June next, be subject and liable to the operation of said laws, in the same manner as other citizens of this State or the citizens of said counties respectively, and all writs and processes whatever issued by the courts or officers of said courts, shall extend over, and operate on the portions of territory hereby added to the same respectively.

Sec. 7. *And be it further enacted*, That after the first day of June next, all laws, ordinances, orders and regulations of any kind whatever, made, passed, or enacted by the Cherokee Indians, either in general council or in any other way whatever, or by any authority whatever of said tribe, be, and the same are hereby declared to be null and void and of no effect, as if the same had never existed; and in all cases of indictment or civil suits, it shall not be lawful for the defendant to justify under any of said laws, ordinances, orders or regulations; nor shall the courts of this State permit the same to be given in evidence on the trial of any suit whatever....

Sec. 15. *And be it further enacted*, That no Indian or descendant of any Indian residing within the Creek or Cherokee nations of Indians, shall be deemed a competent witness in any court of this State to which a white person may be a party, except such white person resides within the said nation.

An act to prevent the exercise of assumed and arbitrary power, by all persons under pretext of authority from the Cherokee Indians, and their laws, and to prevent white persons from residing within that part of the chartered limits of Georgia, occupied by the Cherokee Indians, and to provide a guard for the protection of the gold mines, and to enforce the laws of the State within the aforesaid territory.

Be it enacted by the Senate and House of Representatives of the State of Georgia, in General Assembly met, and it is hereby enacted by the authority of the same, That after the first day of February, eighteen hundred and thirty-one, it shall not be lawful for any person, or persons, under colour or pretence, of authority from said Cherokee tribe, or as head men, chiefs, or warriors of said tribe, to cause or procure by any means the assembling of any council, or other pretended Legislative body of the said Indians, or others living among them, for the purpose of legislating, (or for any other purpose whatever.) ...

Sec. 4. *And be it further enacted by the authority aforesaid,* That after the time aforesaid, it shall not be lawful for any person or persons, as a ministerial officer, or in any other capacity, to execute any precept, command, or process, issued by any court or tribunal in the Cherokee tribe, on the persons or property of any of said tribe. ...

1829, 1830

■   ANDREW JACKSON   ■
1767–1845

On Indian Removal: The President's Message to Congress[1]

It gives me pleasure to announce to Congress that the benevolent policy of the Government, steadily pursued for nearly thirty years, in relation to the removal of the Indians beyond the white settlements is approaching to a happy consummation. Two important tribes have accepted the provision made for their removal at the last session of Congress, and it is believed that their example will induce the remaining tribes also to seek the same obvious advantages.

[1]Transcription courtesy of Civics Online, www.civics-online.org.

The consequences of a speedy removal will be important to the United States, to individual States, and to the Indians themselves. The pecuniary advantages which it promises to the Government are the least of its recommendations. It puts an end to all possible danger of collision between the authorities of the General and State Governments on account of the Indians. It will place a dense and civilized population in large tracts of country now occupied by a few savage hunters. By opening the whole territory between Tennessee on the north and Louisiana on the south to the settlement of the whites, it will incalculably strengthen the southwestern frontier and render the adjacent States strong enough to repel future invasions without remote aid. It will relieve the whole State of Mississippi and the western part of Alabama of Indian occupancy, and enable those States to advance rapidly in population, wealth, and power. It will separate the Indians from immediate contact with settlements of whites; free them from the power of the States; enable them to pursue happiness in their own way and under their own rude institutions; will retard the progress of decay, which is lessening their numbers, and perhaps cause them gradually, under the protection of the Government and through the influence of good counsels, to cast off their savage habits and become an interesting, civilized, and Christian community.

What good man would prefer a country covered with forests and ranged by a few thousand savages to our extensive Republic, studded with cities, towns, and prosperous farms embellished with all the improvements which art can devise or industry execute, occupied by more than 12,000,000 happy people, and filled with all the blessings of liberty, civilization and religion?

The present policy of the Government is but a continuation of the same progressive change by a milder process. The tribes which occupied the countries now constituting the Eastern States were annihilated or have melted away to make room for the whites. The waves of population and civilization are rolling to the westward, and we now propose to acquire the countries occupied by the red men of the South and West by a fair exchange, and, at the expense of the United States, to send them to land where their existence may be prolonged and perhaps made perpetual. Doubtless it will be painful to leave the graves of their fathers; but what do they more than our ancestors did or than our children are now doing? To better their condition in an unknown land our forefathers left all that was dear in earthly objects. Our children by thousands yearly leave the land of their birth to seek new homes in distant regions. Does Humanity weep at these painful separations from everything, animate and inanimate, with which the young heart has become entwined? Far from it. It is rather a source of joy that our country affords scope where our young population may range unconstrained in body or in mind, developing the power and facilities of man in their highest perfection. These remove hundreds and almost thousands of miles at their own expense, purchase the lands they occupy, and support themselves at their new homes from the moment of their arrival. Can it be cruel in this Government when, by events which it can not control, the Indian is made discontented in his ancient home to purchase his lands, to give him a new and extensive territory, to pay the expense of his removal, and support him a year in his new abode? How many thousands of our own people would gladly embrace the opportunity of removing to the West on such conditions! If the offers made to the Indians were extended to them, they would be hailed with gratitude and joy.

And is it supposed that the wandering savage has a stronger attachment to his home than the settled, civilized Christian? Is it more afflicting to him to leave the graves of his fathers than it is to our brothers and children? Rightly considered, the policy of the General Government toward the red man is not only liberal, but generous. He is unwilling to submit to the laws of the States and mingle with their population. To save him from this alternative, or perhaps utter annihilation, the General Government kindly offers him a new home, and proposes to pay the whole expense of his removal and settlement.

1830

■　　UNITED STATES CONGRESS　　■

from **Indian Removal Act, May 28, 1830**

Chapter CXLVIII

An Act to provide for an exchange of lands with the Indians residing in any of the states or territories, and for their removal west of the river Mississippi.

Be it enacted by the Senate and House of Representatives of the United States of America, in Congress assembled, That it shall and may be lawful for the President of the United States to cause so much of any territory belonging to the United States, west of the river Mississippi, not included in any state or organized territory, and to which the Indian title has been extinguished, as he may judge necessary, to be divided into a suitable number of districts, for the reception of such tribes or nations of Indians as may choose to exchange the lands where they now reside, and remove there; and to cause each of said districts to be so described by natural or artificial marks, as to be easily distinguished from every other.

Sec. 2 *And be it further enacted,* That it shall and may be lawful for the President to exchange any or all of such districts, so to be laid off and described, with any tribe or nation of Indians now residing within the limits of any of the states or territories, and with which the United States have existing treaties, for the whole or any part or portion of the territory claimed and occupied by such tribe or nation, within the bounds of any one or more of the states or territories, where the land claimed and occupied by the Indians, is owned by the United States, or the United States are bound to the state within which it lies to extinguish the Indian claim thereto.

Sec. 3 *And be it further enacted*, That in the making of any such exchange or exchanges, it shall and may be lawful for the President solemnly to assure the tribe or nation with which the exchange is made, that the United States will forever secure and guaranty to them, and their heirs or successors, the country so exchanged with them; and if they prefer it, that the United States will cause a patent or grant to be made and executed to them for the same: *Provided always*, That such lands shall revert to the United States, if the Indians become extinct, or abandon the same.

Sec. 4 *And be it further enacted*, That if, upon any of the lands now occupied by the Indians, and to be exchanged for, there should be such improvements as add value to the land claimed by any individual or individuals of such tribes or nations, it shall and may be lawful for the President to cause such value to be ascertained by appraisement or otherwise, and to cause such ascertained value to be paid to the person or persons rightfully claiming such improvements. And upon the payment of such valuation, the improvements so valued and paid for, shall pass to the United States, and possession shall not afterwards be permitted to any of the same tribe.

Sec. 5 *And be it further enacted*, That upon the making of any such exchange as is contemplated by this act, it shall and may be lawful for the President to cause such aid and assistance to be furnished to the emigrants as may be necessary and proper to enable them to remove to, and settle in, the country for which they may have exchanged; and also, to give them such aid and assistance as may be necessary for their support and subsistence for the first year after their removal.

Sec. 6 *And be it further enacted*, That it shall and may be lawful for the President to cause such tribe or nation to be protected, at their new residence, against all interruption or disturbance from any other tribe or nation of Indians, or from any other person or persons whatever.

Sec. 7 *And be it further enacted*, That it shall and may be lawful for the President to have the same superintendence and care over any tribe or nation in the country to which they may remove, as contemplated by this act, that he is now authorized to have over them at their present places of residence: *Provided*, That nothing in this act contained shall be construed as authorizing or directing the violation of any existing treaty between the United States and any of the Indian tribes.

Sec. 8 *And be it further enacted*, That for the purpose of giving effect to the provisions of this act, the sum of five hundred thousand dollars is hereby appropriated, to be paid out of any money in the treasury, not otherwise appropriated.

1830

■ CHIEF JUSTICE JOHN MARSHALL ■
1755–1835

from **Cherokee Nation v. Georgia (1831)**

Mr. Chief Justice Marshall delivered the opinion of the Court.

This bill is brought by the Cherokee nation, praying an injunction to restrain the state of Georgia from the execution of certain laws of that state, which, as is alleged, go directly to annihilate the Cherokees as a political society, and to seize, for the use of Georgia, the lands of the nation which have been assured to them by the United States in solemn treaties repeatedly made and still in force.

If courts were permitted to indulge their sympathies, a case better calculated to excite them can scarcely be imagined. A people once numerous, powerful, and truly independent, found by our ancestors in the quiet and uncontrolled possession of an ample domain, gradually sinking beneath our superior policy, our arts and our arms, have yielded their lands by successive treaties, each of which contains a solemn guarantee of the residue, until they retain no more of their formerly extensive territory than is deemed necessary to their comfortable subsistence. To preserve this remnant, the present application is made.

Before we can look into the merits of the case, a preliminary inquiry presents itself. Has this court jurisdiction of the cause?

... Do the Cherokees constitute a foreign state in the sense of the constitution?

The counsel have shown conclusively that they are not a state of the union, and have insisted that individually they are aliens, not owing allegiance to the United States. An aggregate of aliens composing a state must, they say, be a foreign state. Each individual being foreign, the whole must be foreign.

This argument is imposing, but we must examine it more closely before we yield to it. The condition of the Indians in relation to the United States is perhaps unlike that of any other two people in existence. In the general, nations not owing a common allegiance are foreign to each other. The term *foreign nation* is, with strict propriety, applicable by either to the other. But the relation of the Indians to the United States is marked by peculiar and cardinal distinctions which exist no where else. The Indian territory is admitted to compose a part of the United States. In all our maps, geographical treatises, histories, and laws, it is so considered. In all our intercourse with foreign nations, in our commercial regulations, in any attempt at intercourse between Indians and foreign nations, they are considered as within the jurisdictional limits of the United States, subject to many of those restraints which are imposed upon our own citizens. They acknowledge themselves in their treaties to be under the protection of the United States; they admit that the United States shall have the sole and exclusive right of regulating the trade with them, and managing all their affairs as they think proper; and the Cherokees in particular were allowed by the treaty of Hopewell, which preceded the constitution, 'to send a deputy of their choice, whenever they think fit, to congress.' Treaties were made with some tribes by the state of New York, under a then unsettled construction of the confederation, by which they ceded all their lands to that state, taking back a limited grant to themselves, in which they admit their dependence.

Though the Indians are acknowledged to have an unquestionable, and, heretofore, unquestioned right to the lands they occupy, until that right shall be extinguished by a voluntary cession to our government; yet it may well be doubted whether those tribes which reside within the acknowledged boundaries of the United States can, with strict accuracy, be denominated foreign nations. They may, more correctly, perhaps, be denominated domestic dependent nations. They occupy a territory to which we assert a title independent of their will, which must take effect in point of possession when their right of possession ceases. Meanwhile they are in a state of pupilage. Their relation to the United States resembles that of a ward to his guardian.

... The court has bestowed its best attention on this question, and, after mature deliberation, the majority is of opinion that an Indian tribe or nation within the United States is not a foreign state in the sense of the constitution, and cannot maintain an action in the courts of the United States.

... If it be true that the Cherokee nation have rights, this is not the tribunal in which those rights are to be asserted. If it be true that wrongs have been inflicted, and that still greater are to be apprehended, this is not the tribunal which can redress the past or prevent the future.

The motion for an injunction is denied.

1831

from **Worcester v. Georgia (1832)**

This cause, in every point of view in which it can be placed, is of the deepest interest.

The defendant is a State, a member of the Union, which has exercised the powers of government over a people who deny its jurisdiction, and are under the protection of the United States.

The plaintiff is a citizen of the State of Vermont, condemned to hard labor for four years in the penitentiary of Georgia under color of an act which he alleges to be repugnant to the Constitution, laws, and treaties of the United States.

The legislative power of a State, the controlling power of the Constitution and laws of the United States, the rights, if they have any, the political existence of a once numerous and powerful people, the personal liberty of a citizen, all are involved in the subject now to be considered....

It has been said at the bar that the acts of the Legislature of Georgia seize on the whole Cherokee country, parcel it out among the neighboring counties of the State, extend her code over the whole country, abolish its institutions and its laws, and annihilate its political existence.

If this be the general effect of the system, let us inquire into the effect of the particular statute and section on which the indictment is founded.

It enacts that "all white persons, residing within the limits of the Cherokee Nation on the 1st day of March next, or at any time thereafter, without a licence or permit from his excellency the governor … and who shall not have taken the oath hereinafter required, shall be guilty of a high misdemeanor, and upon conviction thereof, shall be punished by confinement to the penitentiary at hard labor for a term not less than four years." …

The extraterritorial power of every Legislature being limited in its action to its own citizens or subjects, the very passage of this act is an assertion of jurisdiction over the Cherokee Nation, and of the rights and powers consequent on jurisdiction.

The first step, then, in the inquiry which the Constitution and the laws impose on this court, is an examination of the rightfulness of this claim. …

From the commencement of our government Congress has passed acts to regulate trade and intercourse with the Indians; which treat them as nations, respect their rights, and manifest a firm purpose to afford that protection which treaties stipulate. All these acts, and especially that of 1802, which is still in force, manifestly consider the several Indian nations as distinct political communities, having territorial boundaries, within which their authority is exclusive, and having a right to all the lands within those boundaries, which is not only acknowledged, but guaranteed by the United States. …

The Cherokee Nation, then, is a distinct community, occupying its own territory, with boundaries accurately described, in which the laws of Georgia can have no force, and which the citizens of Georgia have no right to enter but with the assent of the Cherokees themselves or in conformity with treaties and with the acts of Congress. The whole intercourse between the United States and this nation is, by our Constitution and laws, vested in the government of the United States.

The act of the State of Georgia under which the plaintiff in error was prosecuted is consequently void, and the judgement a nullity. … The Acts of Georgia are repugnant to the Constitution, laws, and treaties of the United States.

They interfere forcibly with the relations established between the United States and the Cherokee Nation, the regulation of which according to the settled principles of our Constitution, are committed exclusively to the government of the Union. They are in direct hostility with treaties, repeated in a succession of years, which mark out the boundary that separates the Cherokee country from Georgia; guarantee to them all the land within their boundary; solemnly pledge the faith of the United States to restrain their citizens from trespassing on it; and recognize the pre-existing power of the nation to govern itself.

They are in equal hostility with the acts of Congress for regulating this intercourse, and giving effect to the treaties …

Judgement reversed.

1832

■ JOHN ROSS (CHEROKEE)
1790–1866

Letter to Lewis Cass

Brown's Hotel Washington City
February 14th 1833

Sir

In reviewing the principles upon which these views are predicated we have been impelled to look into those upon which the primitive and conventional rights of the Cherokee nation have been recognized and established by the solemn acts of this Government. And it is with deep regret and great diffidence we are constrained to say that in this scheme of Indian removal we can see more of expediency and policy to get rid of them than to perpetuate their race upon any fundamental principle. Were it possible for you to be placed, or to imagine yourself for a moment to be, in the peculiar situation in which we stand, with the existing treaties and laws and the subsequent acts of the Govt. all before your eyes, you cannot but feel and see as we do! It is impossible then for us to see that by a removal to the country west of the Mississippi all our difficulties would be terminated, and the prosperity of our people fixed upon a permanent basis. Would not a removal to the country west of the Mississippi, upon lands of the U.S. by the Indian tribes under the provisions of the act of Congress, denationalize their character as distinct communities? By what tenure would such tribes occupy the lands to be assigned to them? Is not the fee simple title vested in and will be retained by the U. States? What kind of a Govt. of their own, then, is designed for them to establish? And how is it possible for the U. States to afford them more adequate protection against your own citizens there, than where we are? These questions have never as yet been definitively settled down upon any fundamental law of Congress, that we know of, and we cannot avoid believing that the present system of policy towards the Indians, is founded upon contingencies growing out of the interests and desires of the States, without regarding the permanent prosperity & happiness of the Indians. We intend no reflection upon the Govt. in thus frankly communicating our views, but we deem it essential to a perfect understanding upon the subject. As to the climate, soil and extent of the country to which you have alluded, and the future prospects of the Cherokees who are living there— our people are correctly informed on those points from personal observations and otherwise. Withal they have no wish to remove there. What then would be the consequence of a whole nation of people driven by the force of necessity to leave their native land for a distant one, in a strange and inhospitable region and there to experience the sad effects of injured disappointments; to what source could they seek indemnity for their injuries? and what tribunal will there redress their wrongs? For in vain have our nation appealed to the protecting arm of the Genl. Govt. to fulfill treaty obligations, to shield our suffering people against illegal encroachments; and in vain will your supreme judicial tribunal have declared a verdict in favor of our nation against the exercise of usurped power, on the part of state authority. In the suggestions which we took the liberty to submit for the consideration of the President [Andrew Jackson], that some practicable arrangement might be entered into between the U.S. & Georgia to relieve our nation of its present embarrassments, we had entertained no doubt that with a corresponding desire on the part of the Genl. Govt. such an arrangement could be effected. And in that event that Georgia would not be permitted to subject our people to the obedience of her law, inasmuch as the Supreme Court of the U. States had already pronounced the exercise of her jurisdiction over our Territory & people to be unconstitutional & void. And we are at a loss to see the grounds you have taken in arriving to the opinion that "we would still be subject to the laws of Georgia." We cannot subscribe to the correctness of the idea, which has been so frequently recurred to by the advocates of Indian removal, that the evils which have befallen and swept away the numerous Tribes that once inhabited the old States are to be traced to the *mere circumstances* of their contiguity to a white population; but we humbly conceive that the true causes of their extinction are to be found in the catalogue of wrongs which have been heaped upon their ignorance, & credulity by the superior policies of the whiteman when dictated by avarice & cupidity. You appeal to our better feelings in regard to the situation of our people, and suggest that under existing circumstances, some sacrifices may well be encountered in removing from a contact with the white population, in order to escape the fate which has swept away so many Indian Tribes. Should the doctrine that Indian Tribes cannot exist contiguously to a white population prevail, and they be compelled to remove west of the States & Territories of this republic, what is to prevent a similar removal of them from there for the same reason. We can only plead, let equal justice be done between the red & the whiteman and so long as the faith of contracts is preserved inviolate there will be no just cause for complaints, much less for aggressions on the rights of the one or the other. And that so far as our, individually, sense of right, justice & honor will dictate to us a course to meet the wishes, the interest & the permanent prosperity & happiness of our nation, that no pecuniary sacrifices or human sufferings ever so great can or will deter us from encountering them.

Contrary to treaty stipulations and the intercourse act of 1802 there are numerous white families who have intruded upon the lands of our nation within the chartered limits of several of the adjoining States, & the repeated complaints made of the same to the agent [Hugh Montgomery], have not been regarded & the trespassers instead of being removed, have greatly increased in numbers and are daily multiplying. We are constrained to bring this grievous subject before the Department that the evil be corrected.

In addition to these, there are others who threaten to overrun and dispossess our nation of its Territory under the sanction of State authorities. Under the assumption of the right to exercise jurisdiction, it is known that Georgia has passed legislative acts to survey and draw a lottery for the occupation of our land; and which in part, have been carried into effect. And without the timely interposition of this government will doubtless rob us of our lands.

Can this be permitted or will the President extend the constitutional arm of the Govt. to save us from this impending calamity? His determination upon this delicate & important question, we most respectfully solicit. Also, if we are to understand from your communication that the propositions submitted thro' Mr. [Elisha W.] Chester, and which have been rejected by the Genl. Council of our nation, as containing the only basis upon which the government will relieve our nation of the injustice of state oppressions? On the subject of our annuities you reply "that none are withheld from us"—"that the Govt. has engaged to pay certain annuities to the Cherokees whether these are to be paid to persons representing the tribe or the individuals composing it, as the treaties do not provide, the govt. is at liberty to determine." The view you have taken of this subject, is at variance with the true intent & meaning of those treaties, as all the former practice of the govt. in relation thereto will show. The U. States of America thro' their Commissioners Plenipotentiary entered into certain treaties with the Chiefs, Headmen &c of the Cherokee nation who were duly authorized & empowered by said nation. And in consideration for sundry cessions of land, there are certain annuities stipulated in those treaties to be paid to the Cherokee nation. And the usual practice of the Govt. in paying those annuities has always been thro' the U States agent, to the authorities of the Cherokee nation, & by them disposed of as the legislative council thereof think fit to direct for the public welfare. Upon the complaints of certain discontented chiefs of the upper Cherokee towns to the Govt. Mr. [Thomas] Jefferson, the then President of the U States, on the 4th day of May, 1803 spoke to them in writing thus: "You *complain* that you do not receive your just proportion of the annuity we pay your *nation*, that the chiefs of the lower towns take for them more than their share. My children, this distribution is made *by the authorities of the Cherokee nation*, and according to *their* own rules, over which *we have no control*. We do our *duty* in delivering the annuity to the *Headmen of the nation, and we pretend to no authority over them, to no right of directing how they are to be distributed*." For the last thirteen years the Cherokee nation have had a treasurer and into whose hands the annuities have been paid by the agents of the U.S. and for the faithful performance of the duties assigned to this office, the treasurer has executed a bond, with ample security in the penal sum fifty thousand dollars. The annuities due our nation for the two last years the agent has refused to pay them over to the Treasurer as usual, notwithstanding the written request of the great mass of our people to do so. And upon his failing to induce the individuals of the nation to accept of this money agreeably to the direction of the Dept. these annuities have since been deposited in the U.S.

Branch Bank at Nashville to the credit of the Treasurer of the U. States; under these circumstances we felt justified in saying that our annuities are withheld from us. Since the unconstitutional proceedings of Georgia toward our nation, our public expenses have greatly increased and consequently debts have been incurred, for the payment of which the faith of our nation stands pledged. And we trust the President will see in this good reasons for directing the annuities to be paid over to us, as heretofore—for we can see no possible advantage, in the Govt. controuling the application of these annuities contrary to the interest and desire of our nation, where they constitute a debt from the U.S. to the Cherokee nation. No complaints have ever been made to the Govt. by our nation, against the dishonesty or misapplication of this annual stipend by our own constituted authorities. On the contrary they have required the agent to pay it over as usual. And without intending any reflection we feel justified in saying that the Cherokee people feel as much respect for and have as great confidence in the justice and integrity of their own public men as they can possibly entertain towards the public agents of this govt. in their nation. With great respect we have the honor to be Sir, yr. obt. Servts,

Jno Ross	Jno. F. Baldridge (X)
R. Taylor	Joseph Vann

1833

Letter to Andrew Jackson

Washington City Brown's Hotel
March 28th 1834

Honored Sir

We have received thro' the War Department a reply [March 13] to the communication which we had the honor to address you on the 12th inst. disclaiming on your part all right of interference with the question of our political condition and rights within the limits of those States which have extended their laws over our people. And the Hon. Secretary [Lewis Cass] has thought proper to glance over again the offers which have been made our Nation as an inducement to exchange our present residence for one west of the Mississippi, it is enough for us to repeat that our Nation have entirely disagreed in opinion with the Department in reference to the view taken of the liberality of those offers. The Hon. Secry. however has informed us that you have instructed him to say to us, that you are willing ["]to extend to us the most liberal terms and to make such an arrangement as will be just in itself and ought to be satisfactory to us, for the termination of our present embarrassments and for our removal west of the Mississippi." We have already assured you, with the utmost sincerity & truth that the great body of our people have refused and will never voluntarily consent to remove west of the Mississippi. And it is on this grave question rests the great difficulty. We cannot, and dare not lose sight of our political rights, which have been recognized and established by the laws and treaties of the United States—for it is on them solely that our security of protection hang. And from the peculiar circumstances of the painful grievances under which our people labour, we were induced to submit for your serious consideration the suggestion which we had the honor of laying before you. And now, after further reflection on this momentous question, we have determined once more to address you, and present the subject in another view for your further determination, and we would entreat you by every consideration of honor and truth to be assured, that in thus submitting this question, we are influenced solely by a desire to secure the permanent welfare and happiness of our people, who dearly love the land of their Fathers, and are devotedly attached to the Govt. of the United States. Feeble as the Cherokees are, and surrounded by a nation so powerful as the United States, we cannot but clearly see, that our existence and permanent welfare as a people, must depend upon that relation which will eventually lead to an amalgamation with the population of this great republic, and as the prospects of securing this object collectively in our present location in the character of a Territorial or State Government, seem to be seriously opposed, and is threatened by the states which are interested in their own aggrandizement; and as the Cherokees have refused and will never voluntarily consent to remove west of the Mississippi we are constrained in the most respectful manner to present the following questions for your decision.

Will you agree to enter into an arrangement on the basis of the Cherokees becoming prospectively citizens of the United States; provided the Nation will cede to the United States a portion of its Territory for the use of Georgia? And will you agree to have the laws and treaties executed and enforced for the effectual protection of the nation on the remainder of its Territory for a definite period? With the understanding that after that period, the Cherokees are to be subjected to the laws of the states within whose limits they may be and to take an individual standing as citizens thereof, the same as other free citizens of the United States—and to dispose of our surplus lands in such a manner as may be agreed upon. Such an arrangement as this, would put an end to all conflicting interests—and secure to the Cherokees time to prepare for the important change of their condition, and enable them by means of education to defend their individual rights as free citizens against any fraud or violence before the proper tribunals of the country. It is no more than reasonable and just, that ample time should be extended to the Cherokee people to prepare for so important a change of their political character, in their native land. No nation of people emerging from the natural state of man can ever prosper by an untimely amalgamation with a civilized and refined community. When we look on our own individual condition and review the circumstances which have placed us in the scale of civilized life above the condition of others of our fellow countrymen, we cannot but see that they and their children are all equally capable under similar circumstances to rise to the same degree of elevation.

It is therefore our imperious duty to endeavor to afford them all the advantages possible for their general improvement. Georgia and the other interested states, cannot rightfully oppose such an arrangement and there can be no doubt that they would readily acquiesce in it. The great cause of contention will have been removed, by making certain an object which under existing Treaties at this time to them, is uncertain. And finally, a peaceable and an honorable adjustment of all conflicting interests will have been accomplished.

Twenty years have now elapsed since we participated with you in the toils and dangers of war, and obtained a victory over the unfortunate and deluded red foe at Tehopekah, on the memorable 27th March 1814, that portentous day was shrouded by a cloud of darkness, besprinkled with the awful streaks of blood and death. It is in the hour of such times alone that the heart of man can be truly rested and correctly judged. We were then your friends—and the conduct of man is an index to his disposition. Now in these days of profound peace, why should the gallant soldiers who in time of war walked hand in hand thro' blood and carnage, be not still friends? We answer, that we are yet your friends. And we love our people, our country and the homes of the childhood of our departed sires. We have ever enjoyed the rights and liberties of freemen—and God forbid that we should ever live in vassalage to any power. And if we are too weak to live as freemen—it is easier for freemen to die, than live as slaves!!!

To afford our people full privilege & satisfaction, if the United States would furnish the necessary means, and our nation think it proper to appoint an exploring party for the purpose of examining all the countries beyond the Mississippi river, it may be done in addition to the arrangement which we have suggested. We have the honor to be, sir, very respectfully yr. obt. Hble. Servts.

Jno Ross	Hair Conrad (X)
R. Taylor	John Timson
Danl. McCoy	

1834

Letter to a Friend[1]

From John Ross of the Cherokee, Georgia
[Red Clay Council Ground, Cherokee Nation, September 28, 1836]

It is well known that for a number of years past we have been harassed by a series of vexations, which it is deemed unnecessary to recite in detail, but the evidence of which our delegation will be prepared to furnish. With a view to bringing our troubles to a close, a delegation was appointed on the

[1]John Ross, *Letter from John Ross, Principal Chief of the Cherokee Nation of Indians, in Answer to Inquires from a Friend Regarding the* Cherokee Affairs with the United States (Washington, DC, 1836), 22–24.

23rd of October, 1835, by the General Council of the nation, clothed with full powers to enter into arrangements with the Government of the United States, for the final adjustment of all our existing difficulties. The delegation failing to effect an arrangement with the United States commissioner, then in the nation, proceeded, agreeably to their instructions in that case, to Washington City, for the purpose of negotiating a treaty with the authorities of the United States.

After the departure of the Delegation, a contract was made by the Rev. John F. Schermerhorn, and certain individual Cherokees, purporting to be a "treaty, concluded at New Echota, in the State of Georgia, on the 29th day of December, 1835, by General William Carroll and John F. Schermerhorn, commissioners on the part of the United States, and the chiefs, headmen, and people of the Cherokee tribes of Indians." A spurious Delegation, in violation of a special injunction of the general council of the nation, proceeded to Washington City with this pretended treaty, and by false and fraudulent representations supplanted in the favor of the Government the legal and accredited Delegation of the Cherokee people, and obtained for this instrument, after making important alterations in its provisions, the recognition of the United States Government. And now it is presented to us as a treaty, ratified by the Senate, and approved by the President [Andrew Jackson], and our acquiescence in its requirements demanded, under the sanction of the displeasure of the United States, and the threat of summary compulsion, in case of refusal. It comes to us, not through our legitimate authorities, the known and usual medium of communication between the Government of the United States and our nation, but through the agency of a complication of powers, civil and military.

By the stipulations of this instrument, we are despoiled of our private possessions, the indefeasible property of individuals. We are stripped of every attribute of freedom and eligibility for legal self-defence. Our property may be plundered before our eyes; violence may be committed on our persons; even our lives may be taken away, and there is none to regard our complaints. We are denationalized; we are disfranchised. We are deprived of membership in the human family! We have neither land nor home, nor resting place that can be called our own. And this is effected by the provisions of a compact which assumes the venerated, the sacred appellation of treaty.

We are overwhelmed! Our hearts are sickened, our utterance is paralized, when we reflect on the condition in which we are placed, by the audacious practices of unprincipled men, who have managed their stratagems with so much dexterity as to impose on the Government of the United States, in the face of our earnest, solemn, and reiterated protestations.

The instrument in question is not the act of our Nation; we are not parties to its covenants; it has not received the sanction of our people. The makers of it sustain no office nor appointment in our Nation, under the designation of Chiefs, Head men, or any other title, by which they hold, or could acquire, authority to assume the reins of Government, and to make bargain and sale of our rights, our possessions, and our common country. And we are constrained solemnly to declare, that we cannot but contemplate the enforcement of the stipulations of this instrument on us, against our consent, as an act of injustice and oppression, which, we are well persuaded, can never knowingly be countenanced by the Government and people of the United States; nor can we believe it to be the design of these honorable and highminded individuals, who stand at the head of the Govt., to bind a whole Nation, by the acts of a few unauthorized individuals. And, therefore, we, the parties to be affected by the result, appeal with confidence to the justice, the magnanimity, the compassion, of your honorable bodies, against the enforcement, on us, of the provisions of a compact, in the formation of which we have had no agency.

In truth, our cause is your own; it is the cause of liberty and of justice; it is based upon your own principles, which we have learned from yourselves; for we have gloried to count your [George] Washington and your [Thomas] Jefferson our great teachers; we have read their communications to us with veneration; we have practised their precepts with success. And the result is manifest. The wildness of the forest has given place to comfortable dwellings and cultivated fields, stocked with the various domestic animals. Mental culture, industrious habits, and domestic enjoyments, have succeeded the rudeness of the savage state.

We have learned your religion also. We have read your Sacred books. Hundreds of our people have embraced their doctrines, practised the virtues they teach, cherished the hopes they awaken, and rejoiced in the consolations which they afford. To the spirit of your institutions, and your religion, which has been imbibed by our community, is mainly to be ascribed that patient endurance which has characterized the conduct of our people, under the laceration of their keenest woes. For assuredly, we are not ignorant of our condition; we are not insensible to our sufferings. We feel them! we groan under their pressure! And anticipation crowds our breasts with sorrows yet to come. We are, indeed, an afflicted people! Our spirits are subdued! Despair has well nigh seized upon our energies! But we speak to the representatives of a Christian country; the friends of justice; the patrons of the oppressed. And our hopes revive, and our prospects brighten, as we indulge the thought. On your sentence, our fate is suspended; prosperity or desolation depends on your word. To you, therefore, we look! Before your august assembly we present ourselves, in the attitude of deprecation, and of entreaty. On your kindness, on your humanity, on your compassion, on your benevolence, we rest our hopes. To you we address our reiterated prayers. Spare our people! Spare the wreck of our prosperity! Let not our deserted homes become the monuments of our desolation! But we forbear! We suppress the agonies which wring our hearts, when we look at our wives, our children, and our venerable sires! We restrain the forebodings of anguish and distress, of misery and devastation and death, which must be the attendants on the execution of this ruinous compact....

1836

Annual Message

[Tahlequah, Cherokee Nation]
October [28], 1840

Friends and Fellow Citizens

In meeting you after the lapse of more than a year from the term of our organization, once again as an united people, it affords me greater satisfaction than I can express, to have it in my power to congratulate you on the good spirit which seems to pervade our nation. Our thanks should be specially poured forth to the Great Source of Blessings for His fostering beneficence under circumstances of no common peril. There is no recorded instance within my memory, of an entire change in the position of so extensive a community, even when wrought with its own consent, which has not been made the pretext for frightful disorders, fomented by the restless & the disaffected. I think it due to our own people to remind them of the praise they merit, for having, although their position was altered, not voluntarily, but without their consent, and against their will, borne the necessity in a noble temper of philosophic endurance; and to encourage them to persevere in the same disposition, by picturing the gratitude they will gain from their posterity, for having, after only a few sad days of confusion, even while destitution, disease, and death in every appalling form raged around them, at once emerged from the tempestuous chaos into the calm sunshine of a settled government, to which neither suffering nor intrigue appear likely ever to render them untrue. When the clouds over us were the darkest, it afforded the true lovers of peace no ordinary consolation to be assured in communications from the Secretary of War [Joel Poinsett] at Washington City, and from the Indian Commissioner [T. Hartley Crawford], that it was the unalterable principle of the United States in dealing with all Indian nations, to respect the will of their majorities; and as such is the only principle ever to be tolerated among the Cherokees, we ought no longer to despair of satisfactorily adjusting our affairs with the Power by whom it is thus solemnly announced as her great law. I am the more encouraged in this impression when I observe, which I do with unfeigned delight, that some of those who lately differed most strenuously in opinion with their fellow countrymen, now array themselves on the side of the majority and are associated with you as representatives of the nation. The reconcilement of the minority to the constitution and laws cannot but destroy the misapprehensions growing out of the state of things prevailing while the few kept back from the many. If this spirit of unanimity is cherished, and continues thus hourly to extend, it will remove every cause of difficulty, and, under the express declarations of the Secretary himself, render our appeals for justice irresistible.

Had our true position in this respect been understood at Washington, I trust I should have been enabled to present you a less discouraging report from your delegation,[1] which has recently returned from that city. But, as it is, I am compelled to announce their entire failure to gain any of the objects of their mission. The memorial [February 28, 1840] presented by them to Congress is herewith enclosed, as well as their communication [April 20, 1840] to the Indian Committee to whom that Memorial was referred. These papers are accompanied by the official Reports[2] of the war Department and by a great number of letters illustrating the various points upon which they treat. The Report [not found] of the Indian Committee upon the whole matter, will be found in the same package. A letter [not found] of the Chairman [John Bell] will explain to you in part why there was no action upon the Resolutions following the report. It may not be irrelevant to add that the question of the pending Presidential election has too entirely absorbed the attention of every party in congress for the last few months, to leave the members leisure even for subjects of pressing local importance; those from a distance, and especially those which could not be entertained without calling for expenditures that are admitted at the present moment to be peculiarly inconvenient, were, of course, altogether evaded. The delegation, indeed, were assured from time to time that some of their business would soon be taken up; and, after the extremely protracted session of Congress was over they were still encouraged to remain; but the constitutional term for the Annual Council was already at hand; no certainty appeared that the decision would not continue to be delayed; and there was every probability that, whatever that decision might prove, it would involve a final reference to congress which could not be had before the approaching session. Under these circumstances, the delegation thought it their duty to return.

I abstain from remarking upon the postponement of the just dues to our nation, further than to add, that, the unanimity now prevailing among ourselves, and other circumstances, justify the expectation of a change of policy in the United States government, regarding our affairs. I will therefore hope that our country men will continue to be patient and to place every confidence in the honesty and honor the Government and People of the United States. Let us not afford an excuse for withholding our dues, by dissention among ourselves. Let us remain in the right and trust to Providence and an upright cause for the result. The points for adjustment at Washington are more numerous and important now than ever. The country taken from us east of the Mississippi still remains unpaid for; the tenure under which our present lands in the West are granted continues undefined, as do the relations which are to subsist between us and the United States. But these multifarious calls are too severely known to you to require that I should enumerate them here.

[1]Although the membership shifted from time to time, the delegation in its entirety included Ross, Joseph M. Lynch, Looney Price, Elijah Hicks, Edward Gunter, George Hicks, Archibald Campbell, John Looney, and William S. Coodey.

[2]These reports and letters are probably those found in Cong. Serial 366, House Doc. 188.

The utter disregard of all our claims at the American metropolis might have been more injurious than it proved, had it not been for the timely aid of friends, by whom your delegation were enabled to meet the expenses which were to have been defrayed with monies long overdue from the United States, that, when applied for under your requisition were withheld. Thus embarrassed, I claimed, under a protest, the proceeds of a partial valuation for improvements taken from me in our for country, and with these discharged the loan for the nation and paid all other demands against your delegates.

I must not forget while upon the subject of our negociations with the government of the United States, to call your attention to one topic which has too long escaped our notice—the education fund. From every side I hear appeals for the establishment of schools among ourselves, and am pressed to explain wherefore the large education fund held in trust for us by the United States is not put in action. To expect that the excellent persons who have so faithfully executed for so long a time the duties imposed on them by the Board of Missions, could meet the wants of a population spreading over so wide a surface and daily becoming more numerous and more extended would be indeed extravagant; nor can there by any reason whatever for overburthening them then our own provisions for the purpose of instruction are ample, though dormant. I recommend this matter to your attentive consideration.

It was my hope to have had it in my power to close the whole business of the emigration at the present Council, but I deeply lament that the course taken by the War Department in withholding a final settlement, renders it impracticable. When our account, formed upon the basis distinctly understood between General [Winfield] Scott and our Special Agents, was presented for payment, frivolous exceptions were taken against portions of it; and a balance due to the nation of five hundred & eighty one thousand, three hundred & forty six dollars, eighty eight & a half cents, was left unsettled; but, upon remonstrance to the President [Martin Van Buren] in person, the subject was reopened by the Department, and, when we left Washington, was in a train which leads me to expect that justice will yet be done.

There is one branch of this subject in which so many of our citizens are interested, that I must pause a moment to give it special notice. I allude to the stipulation for the hire of waggons.

The principle upon which the nation estimated our emigration expenses with General Scott, was to receive for them the same amount which the removal would have cost, had it been accomplished, not by us but by the United States. One of the items stipulated five dollars a day waggon lure, and two dollars a day for the forage of five horses to each waggon, making seven dollars in all; with an extra allowance at the same rates for returning, limited to forty days. After this basis was settled upon between our Special Agents and the United States the furnishing of the forage was included in our agreement with our own contractor. Hence the daily compensation of five dollars each was all that remained for waggon hire. At the same time it was found that our people, under their peculiarly distressful circumstances, required comforts for which no provision had been made. The appropriation assigned for the return journey not being needed for that purpose, because the waggons were not to return, was accordingly destined for the discharge of contingent expenses not otherwise provided for, such as extra physicians, and thousands of other calls so unavoidable amid the sickness and privations of the journey.

It will be remembered that I myself have made no charge for time nor services; but that I enrolled myself under a conductor of my own appointment, and moved, with my family, on the same terms with my fellow-countrymen; hence, I am only interested in common with them. Whenever the emigration account against the United States shall be closed, whatever surplus may remain after a discharge of the various claims due under it, will, of course, be paid over to the nation.

It would be incorrect to close this communication, without expressing my gratitude to the Almighty Source of All Health and Happiness, for having seen fit to render the diseases which have so sorely afflicted the new emigrants less fatal during the present year than they were throughout the one preceding. Though sickness has been unsparing, more have survived its ravages. I deeply lament that it has not been permitted to include in the number of those who have escaped, two of our most worthy citizens. I allude to Going-Snake, the late venerable Speaker of the Council, and to John Martin, the highly respected Chief-Justice of our Supreme Court.

I have already, in various parts of this communication, as I have uniformly done throughout my entire connection with public affairs, endeavoured to impress it upon you never to encourage any dispositions towards one another but those of kindness, and to be gentle and forbearing towards our white neighbours and the surrounding tribes of our red brethren, under whatever circumstances may arise. The more difficult our position, the more honor we shall merit in deporting ourselves with prudence. Whenever we are bound, under the faith of Treaties, to seek and deliver up aggressors against the whites, let it be done promptly; for it is only by scrupulously observing treaty obligations ourselves, that we can confirm our right to look for their observance towards us from others. In short, let justice, and peace, and friendship towards all, be perpetually our ruling motto. To your wisdom, as the chosen watchmen of our rights, I now submit all that I have said; conscious that in your hands the interests of our common country are safe. May your labours for the public good, merit the smile of Heaven!

1840

RALPH WALDO EMERSON
1803–1882

Letter to Martin Van Buren, President of the United States

Concord, Mass., April 23, 1838

... Sir, my communication respects the sinister rumors that fill this part of the country concerning the Cherokee people.... Even in our distant State some good rumor of their worth and civility has arrived. We have learned with joy their improvement in the social arts. We have read their newspapers. We have seen some of them in our schools and colleges. In common with the great body of the American people, we have witnessed with sympathy the painful labors of these red men to redeem their own race from the doom of eternal inferiority, and to borrow and domesticate in the tribe the arts and customs of the Caucasian race....

The newspapers now inform us that, in December, 1835, a treaty contracting for the exchange of all the Cherokee territory was pretended to be made by an agent on the part of the United States with some persons appearing on the part of the Cherokees; that the fact afterwards transpired that these deputies did by no means represent the will of the nation; and that, out of eighteen thousand souls composing the nation, fifteen thousand six hundred and sixty-eight have protested against the so-called treaty. It now appears that the government of the United States choose to hold the Cherokees to this sham treaty, and are proceeding to execute the same. Almost the entire Cherokee Nation stand up and say, "This is not our act. Behold us. Here are we. Do not mistake that handful of deserters for us ;" and the American President and the Cabinet, the Senate and the House of Representatives, neither hear these men nor see them, and are contracting to put this active nation into carts and boats, and to drag them over mountains and rivers to a wilderness at a vast distance beyond the Mississippi. And a paper purporting to be an army order fixes a month from this day as the hour for this doleful removal.

In the name of God, sir, we ask you if this be so. Do the newspapers rightly inform us? Men and women with pale and perplexed faces meet one another in the streets and churches here, and ask if this be so. We have inquired if this be a gross misrepresentation from the party opposed to the government and anxious to blacken it with the people. We have looked in the newspapers of different parties and find a horrid confirmation of the tale. We are slow to believe it. We hoped the Indians were misinformed, and that their remonstrance was pre-mature, and will turn out to be a need[l] act of terror.

The piety, the principle that is left in the United States, i[f] coarsest form, a regard to the speech of men,—forbid us t[o]

fact. Such a dereliction of all faith and virtue, such a denial of justice, and such deafness to screams for mercy were never heard of in times of peace and in the dealing of a nation with its own allies and wards, since the earth was made. Sir, does this government think that the people of the United States are become savage and mad? From their mind are the sentiments of love and a good nature wiped clean out? The soul of man, the justice, the mercy that is the heart's heart in all men, from Maine to Georgia, does abhor this business.

In speaking thus the sentiments of my neighbors and my own, perhaps I overstep the bounds of decorum. But would it not be a higher indecorum coldly to argue a matter like this? We only state the fact that a crime is projected that confounds our understandings by its magnitude, –a crime that really deprives us as well as the Cherokees of a country ? for how could we call the conspiracy that should crush these poor Indians our government, or the land that was cursed by their parting and dying imprecations our country, any more? You, sir, will bring down that renowned chair in which you sit into infamy if your seal is set to this instrument of perfidy; and the name of this nation, hitherto the sweet omen of religion and liberty, will stink to the world

... One circumstance lessens the reluctance with which I intrude at this time on your attention my conviction that the government ought to be admonished of a new historical fact, which the discussion of this question has disclosed, namely, that there exists in a great part of the Northern people a gloomy diffidence in the moral character of the government.

On the broaching of this question, a general expression of despondency, of disbelief that any good will accrue from a remonstrance on an act of fraud and robbery, appeared in those men to whom we naturally turn for aid and counsel. Will the American government steal? Will it lie? Will it kill?—We ask triumphantly. Our counsellors and old statesmen here say that ten years ago they would have staked their lives on the affirmation that the proposed Indian measures could not be executed; that the unanimous country would put them down. And now the steps of this crime follow each other so fast, at such fatally quick time, that the millions of virtuous citizens, whose agents the government are, have no place to interpose, and must shut their eyes until the last howl and wailing of these tormented villages and tribes shall afflict the ear of the world. . . .

With great respect, sir, I am your fellow citizen,

RALPH WALDO EMERSON.

1838

LITERATURE AND THE "WOMAN QUESTION"

The works in this section focus on the important ongoing issues of women's status and women's rights—ongoing both in the early nineteenth century and in our own time. The terms of debate have changed over time, and the arenas of conflict have likewise altered. A participant in the 1848 meeting at Seneca Falls, the first women's rights convention in the United States, would not have understood, much less used, 1960s terms like "women's liberation," and "consciousness raising," and "the problem that has no name," or today's "glass ceiling," "mommy track," and "having it all." Nor would she have openly discussed abortion, lesbianism, or, indeed, sexuality. In the mid-nineteenth century, the pertinent questions were whether women should be able to vote, keep control of their own property even when they were married, have access to a wider array of jobs, and cast off some of the stays and multiple skirts that encumbered them in twenty-five pounds of clothing—whether, ultimately, women had a "place" outside the home. Some, by no means all, of these nineteenth-century issues have been settled, at least in the United States, though whether satisfactorily or not may be a matter of controversy. But in critical ways, the questions remaining on the agenda were first placed there by writers like those represented in this section.

The works of this section remain interesting and often moving both because the issues they address remain alive a century and a half later and because of the creative passion with which the authors express their views. But these works are not uniformly serious and heavy. On the contrary, a speaker like Sojourner Truth and a writer like Fanny Fern brought vivid irony and satire to bear, especially on unconsidered expressions of male privilege. And Margaret Fuller (whose "Woman in the Nineteenth Century" appears in the section on New England) offers a rhetorical flair and deploys an arsenal of learning remarkable for any writer of her time. In short, these works demonstrate the same range of styles and forms evident in writings directed at other important nineteenth-century issues, like abolition or democracy.

These works should also be read in relation to the fiction by women and men in the "Development of Narrative" section that follows. A number of these—like Caroline Kirkland's *A New Home* and Herman Melville's "The Tartarus of Maids"—are similarly concerned with the situations of women at home and at work. Indeed, a complex relationship existed between the kinds of hortatory writing included here and various fictional ways of exploring issues of inequality, oppression, domesticity, and desire. The "woman question" was not solely and simply a subject of debate; rather, it provided an important impetus to a great deal of women's (and sometimes men's) creative expression in the period.

SARAH MOORE GRIMKÉ
1792–1873

See headnote to Angelina Grimké 1805–1879 (p. 634).

from Letters on the Equality of the Sexes, and the Condition of Woman

Letter VIII. The Condition of Women in the United States

Brookline, 1837

... I shall now proceed to make a few remarks on the condition of women in my own country.

During the early part of my life, my lot was cast among the butterflies of the *fashionable* world; and of this class of women, I am constrained to say, both from experience and observation, that their education is miserably deficient; that they are taught to regard marriage as the one thing needful, the only avenue to distinction; hence to attract the notice and win the attention of men, by their external charms, is the chief business of fashionable girls. They seldom think that men will be allured by intellectual acquirements, because they find, that where any mental superiority exists, a woman is generally shunned and regarded as stepping out of her "appropriate sphere," which, in their view, is to dress, to dance, to set out to the best possible advantage her person, to read the novels which inundate the press, and which do more to destroy her character as a rational creature, than any thing else. Fashionable women regard themselves, and are regarded by men, as pretty toys or as mere instruments of pleasure; and the vacuity of mind, the heartlessness, the frivolity which is the necessary result of this false and debasing estimate of women, can only be fully understood by those who have mingled in the folly and wickedness of fashionable life. . . .

There is another and much more numerous class in this country, who are withdrawn by education or circumstances from the circle of fashionable amusements, but who are brought up with the dangerous and absurd idea, that *marriage* is a kind of preferment; and that to be able to keep their husband's house, and render his situation comfortable, is the end of her being. Much that she does and says and thinks is done in reference to this situation; and to be married is too often held up to the view of girls as the sine qua non of human happiness and human existence. For this purpose more than for any other, I verily believe the majority of girls are trained. This is demonstrated by the imperfect education which is bestowed upon them, and the little pains taken to cultivate their minds, after they leave school, by the little time allowed them for reading, and by the idea being constantly inculcated, that although all household concerns should be attended to with scrupulous punctuality at particular seasons, the improvement of their intellectual capacities is only a secondary consideration, and may serve as an occupation to fill up the odds and ends of time. In most families, it is considered a matter of far more consequence to call a girl off from making a pie, or a pudding, than to interrupt her whilst engaged in her studies. This mode of training necessarily exalts, in their view, the animal above the intellectual and spiritual nature, and teaches women to regard themselves as a kind of machinery, necessary to keep the domestic engine in order, but of little value as the *intelligent* companions of men.

Let no one think, from these remarks, that I regard a knowledge of housewifery as beneath the acquisition of women. Far from it: I believe that a complete knowledge of household affairs is an indispensable requisite in a woman's education,—that by the mistress of a family, whether married or single, doing her duty thoroughly and *understandingly*, the happiness of the family is increased to an incalculable degree, as well as a vast amount of time and money saved. All I complain of is, that our education consists so almost exclusively in culinary and other manual operations. I do long to see the time, when it will no longer be necessary for women to expend so many precious hours in furnishing "a well spread table," but that their husbands will forego some of their accustomed indulgences in this way, and encourage their wives to devote some portion of their time to mental cultivation, even at the expense of having to dine sometimes on baked potatoes, or bread and butter. . . .

The influence of women over the minds and character of *children* of both sexes, is allowed to be far greater than that of men. This being the case by the very ordering of nature, women should be prepared by education for the performance of their sacred duties as mothers and as sisters. . . .

There is another way in which the general opinion, that women are inferior to men, is manifested, that bears with tremendous effect on the laboring class, and indeed on almost all who are obliged to earn a subsistence, whether it be by mental or physical exertion—I allude to the disproportionate value set on the time and labor of men and of women. A man who is engaged in teaching, can always, I believe, command a higher price for tuition than a woman—even when he teaches the same branches, and is not in any respect superior to the woman. This I know is the case in boarding and other schools with which I have been acquainted, and it is so in every occupation in which the sexes engage indiscriminately. As for example, in tailoring, a man has twice, or three times as much for making a waistcoat or pantaloons as a woman, although the work done by each may be equally good. In those employments which are peculiar to women, their time is estimated at only half the value of that of men. A woman who goes out to wash, works as hard in proportion as a wood sawyer, or a coal heaver, but she is not generally able to make more than half as much by a day's work. The low remuneration which women receive for their work, has claimed the attention of a few philanthropists, and I hope it will continue to do so until some remedy is applied for this enormous evil. . . . There is yet another and more disastrous consequence arising from this unscriptural notion—women being educated, from earliest childhood, to regard themselves as inferior creatures, have not that self-respect which conscious equality would engender, and hence when their virtue is assailed, they yield to temptation with facility, under the idea that it rather exalts than debases them, to be connected with a superior being.

There is another class of women in this country, to whom I cannot refer, without feelings of the deepest shame and sorrow. I allude to our female slaves. Our southern cities are whelmed beneath a tide of pollution; the virtue of female slaves is wholly at the mercy of irresponsible tyrants, and women are bought and sold in our slave markets, to gratify the brutal lust of those who bear the name of Christians. In our slave States, if amid all her degradation and ignorance, a woman desires to preserve her virtue unsullied, she is either bribed or whipped into compliance, or if she dares resist her seducer, her life by the laws of some of the slave States may be, and has actually been sacrificed to the fury of disappointed passion. Where such laws do not exist, the power which is necessarily vested in the master over his property, leaves the defenceless slave entirely at his mercy, and the sufferings of some females on this account, both physical and mental, are intense. Mr. Gholson,[1] in the House of Delegates of Virginia, in 1832, said, "He really had been under the impression that he owned his slaves. He had lately purchased four women and ten children, in whom he thought he had obtained a great bargain; for he supposed they were his own property, *as were his brood mares.*" But even if any laws existed in the United States, as in Athens formerly, for the protection of female slaves, they would be null and void, because the evidence of a colored person is not admitted against a white, in any of our Courts of Justice in the slave States. "In Athens, if a female slave had cause to complain of any want of respect to the laws of modesty, she could seek the protection of the temple, and demand a change of owners; and such appeals were never discountenanced, or neglected by the magistrate." In Christian America, the slave has no refuge from unbridled cruelty and lust.

S.A. Forrall, speaking of the state of morals at the South, says, "Negresses when young and likely, are often employed by the planter, or his friends, to administer to their sensual desires. This frequently is a matter of speculation, for if the offspring, a mulatto, be a handsome female, 800 or 1000 dollars may be obtained for her in the New Orleans market. It is an occurrence of no uncommon nature to see a Christian father sell his own daughter and the brother his own sister." ... I will add but one more from the numerous testimonies respecting the degradation of female slaves, and

---

[1]"It has always (perhaps erroneously) been considered by steady and old-fashioned people, that the owner of land had a reasonable right to its annual profits ... the owner of *brood mares*, to their product; and the owner of *female slaves, to their increase.*" Mr. Gohl-son's speech to the Virginia legislature, January 18, 1831, as reported in the Richmond *Whig* and quoted in *American Slavery As It Is* (1839; rpt. New York: Arno Press, 1969), p. 182.

the licentiousness of the South. It is from the Circular of the Kentucky Union, for the moral and religious improvement of the colored race. "To the female character among our black population, we cannot allude but with feelings of the bitterest shame. A similar condition of moral pollution and utter disregard of a pure and virtuous reputation, is to be found *only without the pale of Christendom*. That such a state of society should exist in a Christian nation, claiming to be the most enlightened upon earth, without calling forth any *particular attention* to its existence, though ever before our eyes and *in our* families, is a moral phenomenon at once unaccountable and disgraceful." Nor does the colored woman suffer alone: the moral purity of the white woman is deeply contaminated. In the daily habit of seeing the virtue of her enslaved sister sacrificed without hesitancy or remorse, she looks upon the crimes of seduction and illicit intercourse without horror, and although not personally involved in the guilt, she loses that value for innocence in her own, as well as the other sex, which is one of the strongest safeguards to virtue. She lives in habitual intercourse with men, whom she knows to be polluted by licentiousness, and often is she compelled to witness in her own domestic circle, those disgusting and heartsickening jealousies and strifes which disgraced and distracted the family of Abraham. In addition to all this, the female slaves suffer every species of degradation and cruelty, which the most wanton barbarity can inflict; they are indecently divested of their clothing, sometimes tied up and severely whipped, sometimes prostrated on the earth, while their naked bodies are torn by the scorpion lash.

> *"The whip on WOMAN's shrinking flesh!*
> *Our soil yet reddening with the stains*
> *Caught from her scourging warm and fresh."*[2]

Can any American woman look at these scenes of shocking licentiousness and cruelty, and fold her hands in apathy, and say, "I have nothing to do with slavery"? *She cannot and be guiltless*.

I cannot close this letter, without saying a few words on the benefits to be derived by men, as well as women, from the opinions I advocate relative to the equality of the sexes. Many women are now supported, in idleness and extravagance, by the industry of their husbands, fathers, or brothers, who are compelled to toil out their existence, at the counting house, or in the printing office, or some other laborious occupation, while the wife and daughters and sisters take no part in the support of the family, and appear to think that their sole business is to spend the hard bought earnings of their male friends. I deeply regret such a state of things, because I believe that if women felt their responsibility, for the support of themselves, or their families it would add strength and dignity to their characters, and teach them more true sympathy for their husbands, than is now generally manifested,—a sympathy which would be exhibited by actions as well as

[2]John Greenleaf Whittier, "Stanzas."

words. Our brethren may reject my doctrine, because it runs counter to common opinions, and because it wounds their pride; but I believe they would be "partakers of the benefit" resulting from the Equality of the Sexes, and would find that woman, as their equal, was unspeakably more valuable than woman as their inferior, both as a moral and an intellectual being.

Thine in the bonds of womanhood,

Sarah M. Grimké

1838

Letter XV. Man Equally Guilty with Woman in the Fall

Uxbridge, 10th Mo. 20th, 1837.

... To perform our duties, we must comprehend our rights and responsibilities; and it is because we do not understand, that we now fall so far short in the discharge of our obligations. Unaccustomed to think for ourselves, and to search the sacred volume, to see how far we are living up to the design of Jehovah in our creation, we have rested satisfied with the sphere marked out for us by man, never detecting the fallacy of that reasoning which forbids woman to exercise some of her noblest faculties, and stamps with the reproach of indelicacy those actions by which women were formerly dignified and exalted in the church.

I should not mention this subject again, if it were not to point out to my sisters what seems to me an irresistible conclusion from the literal interpretation of St. Paul, without reference to the context, and the peculiar circumstances and abuses which drew forth the expressions, "I suffer not a woman to teach"[1]— "Let your women keep silence in the church,"[2] i.e. congregation. It is manifest, that if the apostle meant what his words imply, when taken in the strictest sense, then women have no right to *teach* Sabbath or day schools, or to open their lips to sing in the assemblies of the people; yet young and delicate women are engaged in all these offices; they are expressly trained to exhibit themselves, and raise their voices to a high pitch in the choirs of our places of worship. I do not intend to sit in judgment on my sisters for doing these things; I only want them to see, that they are as really infringing a *supposed* divine command, by instructing their pupils in the Sabbath or day schools, and by singing in the congregation, as if they were engaged in preaching the unsearchable riches of Christ to a lost and perishing world. Why, then, are we permitted to break this injunction in some points, and so sedulously warned not to overstep the bounds set for us by our *brethren* in another? Simply, as I believe, because in the one case we subserve *their* views and *their* interests, and act *in subordination to them;* whilst in the other, we come in contact with their interests, and claim to be on an equality with them in the highest and most important trust ever committed to man, namely, the ministry of the word. It is manifest, that if women were permitted to be ministers of the gospel, as they unquestionably

---

[1] I Timothy 2:12.   [2] I Corinthians 14:34.

were in the primitive ages of the Christian church, it would interfere materially with the present organized system of spiritual power and ecclesiastical authority, which is now vested solely in the hands of men. It would either show that all the paraphernalia of theological seminaries, &c. &c. to prepare men to become evangelists, is wholly unnecessary, or it would create a necessity for similar institutions in order to prepare women for the same office; and this would be an encroachment on that learning, which our kind brethren have so ungenerously monopolized. I do not ask any one to believe my statements, or adopt my conclusions, because they are mine; but I do earnestly entreat my sisters to lay aside their prejudices, and examine these subjects *for themselves*, regardless of the "traditions of men," because they are intimately connected with their duty and their usefulness in the present important crisis.

All who know any thing of the present system of benevolent and religious operations, know that women are performing an important part in them, in *subserviency to men*, who guide our labors, and are often the recipients of those benefits of education we toil to confer, and which we rejoice they can enjoy, although it is their mandate which deprives us of the same advantages. Now, whether our brethren have defrauded us intentionally, or unintentionally, the wrong we suffer is equally the same. For years, they have been spurring us up to the performance of our duties. The immense usefulness and the vast influence of woman have been eulogized and called into exercise, and many a blessing has been lavished upon us, and many a prayer put up for us, because we have labored by day and by night to clothe and feed and educate young men, whilst our own bodies sometimes suffer for want of comfortable garments, and our minds are left in almost utter destitution of that improvement which we are toiling to bestow upon the brethren. . . .

If the sewing societies, the avails of whose industry are now expended in supporting and educating young men for the ministry, were to withdraw their contributions to these objects, and give them where they are *more needed*, to the advancement of their *own sex* in useful learning, the next generation might furnish sufficient proof, that in intelligence and ability to master the whole circle of sciences, woman is not inferior to man; and instead of a sensible woman being regarded as she now is, as a *lusses naturae*,[3] they would be quite as common as sensible men. I confess, considering the high claim men in this country make to great politeness and deference to women, it does seem a little extraordinary that we should be urged to work for the brethren. I should suppose it would be more in character with "the generous promptings of chivalry, and the poetry of romantic gallantry," for which Catharine E. Beecher gives them credit, for them to form societies to educate their sisters, seeing our inferior capacities require more cultivation to bring them into use, and qualify us to be helps meet for them. However, though I think this would be but a just return for all our past kindnesses in this way, I should be willing to balance our accounts, and

---

[3]Freak of nature.

begin a new course. Henceforth, let the benefit be reciprocated, or else let each sex provide for the education of their own poor, whose talents ought to be rescued from the oblivion of ignorance. Sure I am, the young men who are now benefitted by the handy work of their sisters, will not be less honorable if they occupy half their time in earning enough to pay for their own education, instead of depending on the industry of women, who not unfrequently deprive themselves of the means of purchasing valuable books which might enlarge their stock of useful knowledge, and perhaps prove a blessing to the family by furnishing them with instructive reading. If the minds of women were enlightened and improved, the domestic circle would be more frequently refreshed by intelligent conversation, a means of edification now deplorably neglected, for want of that cultivation which these intellectual advantages would confer. . . .

I have now, my dear sister, completed my series of letters. I am aware, they contain some new views; but I believe they are based on the immutable truths of the Bible. All I ask for them is, the candid and prayerful consideration of Christians. If they strike at some of our bosom sins, our deep-rooted prejudices, our long cherished opinions, let us not condemn them on that account, but investigate them fearlessly and prayerfully, and not shrink from the examination; because, if they are true, they place heavy responsibilities upon women. In throwing them before the public, I have been actuated solely by the belief, that if they are acted upon, they will exalt the character and enlarge the usefulness of my own sex, and contribute greatly to the happiness and virtue of the other. That there is a root of bitterness continually springing up in families and troubling the repose of both men and women, (must be manifest to even a superficial observer; and I believe) it is the mistaken notion of the inequality of the sexes.[4] As there is an assumption of superiority on the one part, which is not sanctioned by Jehovah, there is an incessant struggle on the other to rise to that degree of dignity, which God designed women to possess in common with men, and to maintain those rights and exercise those privileges which every woman's common sense, apart from the prejudices of education, tells her are inalienable; they are a part of her moral nature, and can only cease when her immortal mind is extinguished.

One word more. I feel that I am calling upon my sex to sacrifice what has been, what is still dear to their hearts, the adulation, the flattery, the attentions of trifling men. I am asking them to repel these insidious enemies whenever they approach them; to manifest by their conduct, that, although they value highly the society of pious and intelligent men, they have no taste for idle conversation, and for that silly preference which is manifested for their personal accommodation, often at the expense of great inconvenience to their male companions. As an illustration of what I mean, I will state a fact.

---

[4]"Looking diligently lest any man fail of the grace of God; lest any root of bitterness springing up trouble *you*, and thereby may be defiled." Hebrews 12:15.

I was traveling lately in a stage coach. A gentleman, who was also a passenger, was made sick by riding with his back to the horses. I offered to exchange seats, assuring him it did not affect me at all unpleasantly; but he was too polite to permit a lady to run the risk of being discommoded. I am sure he meant to be very civil, but I really thought it was a foolish piece of civility. This kind of attention encourages selfishness in woman, and is only accorded as a sort of quietus, in exchange for those *rights* of which we are deprived. Men and women are equally bound to cultivate a spirit of accommodation; but I exceedingly deprecate her being treated like a spoiled child, and sacrifices made to her selfishness and vanity. In lieu of these flattering but injurious attentions, yielded to her as an inferior, as a mark of benevolence and courtesy, I want my sex to claim nothing from their brethren but what their brethren may justly claim from them, in their intercourse as Christians. I am persuaded woman can do much in this way to elevate her own character. And that we may become duly sensible of the dignity of our nature, only a little lower than the angels, and bring forth fruit to the glory and honor of Emanuel's name, is the fervent prayer of

Thine in the bonds of womanhood,

Sarah M. Grimké

1838

ANGELINA GRIMKÉ
1805–1879

from Letters to Catharine Beecher

Letter XI

Brookline, Mass. 8th mo. 28th, 1837.

Dear Friend:

... I trust my sisters may always be permitted to *petition* for a redress of grievances. Why not? The right of petition is the only political right that women have: why not let them exercise it whenever they are aggrieved? Our fathers waged a bloody conflict with England, because *they* were taxed without being represented. This is just what unmarried women of property now are. *They* were not willing to be governed by laws which *they* had no voice in making; but this is the way in which women are governed in this Republic. If, then, *we* are taxed without being represented, and governed by laws *we* have no voice in framing, then, surely, we ought to be permitted at least to remonstrate against "every political measure that may tend to injure and oppress our sex in various parts of the nation, and under the various public measures that may hereafter be enforced."[1] Why not? Art thou afraid to trust the women of this country with discretionary power as to petitioning? Is there not sound principle and common sense enough among them, to regulate the exercise of this right? I believe they will always use it wisely. I am not afraid to trust my sisters—not I.

Thou sayest, "In this country, petitions to Congress, in reference to official duties of legislators, seem, IN ALL CASES, to fall entirely without the sphere of female duty. Men are the proper persons to make appeals to the rulers whom they appoint," &c. Here I entirely dissent from thee. The fact that women are denied the right of voting for members of Congress, is but a poor reason why they should also be deprived of the right of petition. If their numbers are counted to swell the number of Representatives in our State and National Legislatures, the *very least* that can be done is to give them the right of petition in all cases whatsoever; and without any abridgement. If not, they are mere slaves, known only through their masters....

Thy Friend,
A. E. Grimké
1837

Letter XII. Human Rights Not Founded on Sex

East Boylston, Mass. 10th mo. 2d, 1837.

Dear Friend:

... The investigation of the rights of the slave has led me to a better understanding of my own.... Human beings have *rights*, because they are *moral* beings: the rights of *all* men grow out of their moral nature; and as all men have the same moral nature, they have essentially the same rights.... Now if rights are founded in the nature of our moral being, then the *mere circumstance of sex* does not give to man higher rights and responsibilities, than to woman. To suppose that it does, would be to deny the self-evident truth, that the "physical constitution is the mere instrument of the moral nature." To suppose that it does, would be to break up utterly the relations, of the two natures, and to reverse their functions, exalting the animal nature into a monarch, and humbling the moral into a slave; making the former a proprietor, and the latter its property. When human beings are regarded as *moral* beings, *sex*, instead of being enthroned upon the summit, administering upon rights and responsibilities, sinks into insignificance and nothingness. My doctrine then is, that whatever it is morally right for man to do, it is morally right for woman to do. Our duties originate, not from difference of sex, but from the diversity of our relations in life, the various gifts and talents committed to our care, and the different eras in which we live.

---

[1]Here, and throughout these *Letters*, Grimké
is quoting from Beecher to refute her.

This regulation of duty by the mere circumstance of sex, rather than by the fundamental principle of moral being, has led to all that multifarious train of evils flowing out of the anti-christian doctrine of masculine and feminine virtues. By this doctrine, man has been converted into the warrior, and clothed with sternness, and those other kindred qualities, which in common estimation belong to his character as a *man;* whilst woman has been taught to lean upon an arm of flesh, to sit as a doll arrayed in "gold, and pearls, and costly array," to be admired for her personal charms, and caressed and humored like a spoiled child, or converted into a mere drudge to suit the convenience of her lord and master. Thus have all the diversified relations of life been filled with "confusion and every evil work." This principle has given to man a charter for the exercise of tyranny and selfishness, pride and arrogance, lust and brutal violence. It has robbed woman of essential rights, the right to think and speak and act on all great moral questions, just as men think and speak and act; the right to share their responsibilities, perils and toils; the right to fulfil the great end of her being, as a moral, intellectual and immortal creature, and of glorifying God in her body and her spirit which are His. Hitherto, instead of being a help meet to man, in the highest, noblest sense of the term, as a companion, a co-worker, an equal; she has been a mere appendage of his being, an instrument of his convenience and pleasure, the pretty toy with which he wiled away his leisure moments, or the pet animal whom he humored into playfulness and submission. Woman, instead of being regarded as the equal of man, has uniformly been looked down upon as his inferior, a mere gift to fill up the measure of his happiness. In "the poetry of romantic gallantry," it is true, she has been called "the last *best* gift of God to man";[1] but I believe I speak forth the words of truth and soberness when I affirm, that woman never was given to man. She was created, like him, in the image of God, and crowned with glory and honor; created only a little lower than the angels,[2]—not, as is almost universally assumed, a little lower than man; on her brow, as well as on his, was placed the "diadem of beauty," and in her hand the sceptre of universal dominion. Gen: i. 27, 28. "The last *best gift* of God to man!" Where is the scripture warrant for this "rhetorical flourish, this splendid absurdity"? Let us examine the account of her creation. "And the rib which the Lord God had taken from man, made he a woman, and brought her unto the man." Not as a gift—for Adam immediately recognized her *as a part of himself*— ("this is now bone of my bone, and flesh of my flesh")—a companion and equal, not one hair's breadth beneath him in the majesty and glory of her moral being; not placed under his authority as a *subject,* but by his side, on the same platform of human rights, under the government of God only. This idea of woman's being "the last best gift of God to man," however pretty it may sound to the ears of those who love to discourse upon

---

[1] John Milton, "Paradise Lost," Book V, line 19: "Heaven's last, best gift; my ever new delight."

[2] Psalms viii, 5.

"the poetry of romantic gallantry, and the generous promptings of chivalry," has nevertheless been the means of sinking her from an *end* into a mere *means*—of turning her into an *appendage* to man, instead of recognizing her as *a part of man*—of destroying her individuality, and rights, and responsibilities, and merging her moral being in that of man. Instead of *Jehovah* being *her* king, *her* lawgiver, and *her* judge, she has been taken out of the exalted scale of existence in which He placed her, and subjected to the despotic control of man....

I recognize no rights but *human* rights—I know nothing of men's rights and women's rights; for in Christ Jesus, there is neither male nor female. It is my solemn conviction, that, until this principle of equality is recognised and embodied in practice, the church can do nothing effectual for the permanent reformation of the world. Woman was the first transgressor, and the first victim of power. In all heathen nations, she has been the slave of man, and Christian nations have never acknowledged her rights.... Now, I believe it is woman's right to have a voice in all the laws and regulations by which she is to be *governed*, whether in Church or State; and that the present arrangements of society, on these points, are *a violation of human rights, a rank usurpation of power*, a violent seizure and confiscation of what is sacredly and inalienably hers—thus inflicting upon woman outrageous wrongs, working mischief incalculable in the social circle, and in its influence on the world producing only evil, and that continually. *If* Ecclesiastical and Civil governments are ordained of God, *then* I contend that woman has just as much right to sit in solemn counsel in Conventions, Conferences, Associations and General Assemblies, as man—just as much right to sit upon the throne of England, or in the Presidential chair of the United States....

1837

SOJOURNER TRUTH
c. 1797–1883

Everyone knows the name Sojourner Truth. Her life is a favorite topic within children's literature, sharing shelf space with colorful, large-type narratives about Frederick Douglass and Harriet Tubman. Yet despite calls for her establishment as a bowsprit of abolition, women's rights, and advocacy for the poor, Truth remains an enigma. Her life story is a complex and convoluted mix of slavery, reform movements, and evangelical Christianity. Truth has even been hailed as an early Freedom Rider. In 1865, she chased down—and stopped— Washington, D.C.'s recently integrated horse-drawn buses, yelling "I want to ride, I WANT TO RIDE!" Physically, Truth cut an imposing path. She was close to six feet tall, with a resounding voice, and, as reported by numerous presses, a commanding presence. In fact, in describing Truth, one of her listeners wrote that one might "as well attempt to report the seven apocalyptic thunders." Unafraid of controversy and unwilling to be bullied, Truth once bared her breast to an audience after proslavery hecklers contended that she was a man.

Sojourner Truth was born into slavery as Isabella Baumfree in Hurley, Ulster County, New York. She was the property of a wealthy Dutch master, Charles Ardinburgh. She lived with her parents, who worked a small property let to them by Ardinburgh, until she was nine. After Ardinburgh's death, Isabella, along with other members of her family, was sold. At this time, Isabella spoke only Dutch, a language that her next master did not speak. The miscommunications between Isabella and her new master led to numerous beatings. Eventually Isabella learned English, but she spoke with a Dutch inflection throughout her life. In 1810 Isabella was sold to John J. Dumont, who remained her master until 1826. She took her freedom by simply walking away from Dumont's property with her infant daughter, Sophia, in 1826 after Dumont broke his promise to free Isabella. (New York law emancipated adult slaves in 1827, but Dumont had promised Isabella freedom a year earlier.) Isabella suffered with Dumont, though not as much as she had with other masters. Still, she received beatings, occasional ill-treatment at the hands of his white hired help, and quite possibly sexual abuse by Dumont's wife, Sally. After leaving Dumont, Isabella worked for another Dutch family, the Van Wageners, before moving to New York City in 1828. But before leaving for New York, Isabella found herself in a legal tangle with Dumont, who had illegally sold her son, Peter, to a man who then sold him out of the state (it was illegal under New York state law to sell a slave where slavery would continue past 1827). Isabella sued for Peter's return in New York state court and won his return.

While in New York City, Isabella Van Wagener, as she now called herself (after her last employer), worked as a domestic and became involved in both the John Street Methodist Church and the Zion African Church. Prone toward evangelism and beliefs in direct communications with God as well as the primacy of scriptural narratives, Isabella soon followed the Prophet Mathias (Robert Mathews), a self-avowed holy man whose religious visions took form in the Burned Over District of New York during the Second Great Awakening. In 1843, about eight years after the dissolution of the somewhat notorious "Kingdom of Mathias," Isabella felt a call to leave New York City, so she changed her name to Sojourner Truth and became an itinerant preacher. She wandered across Long Island, eventually landing in Northampton, Massachusetts, via the Connecticut River Valley a few months later. In Northampton, Truth joined a utopian cooperative, the Northampton Association of Education and Industry, begun by William Lloyd Garrison's brother-in-law, George Benson, among others. It was here that Truth began her abolitionist career (though the cooperative was not solely abolitionist, but more generally utopian). Also in Northampton, Truth met Olive Gilbert, the amanuensis who would write her "autobiography," albeit in third person. Truth's *Narrative of Sojourner Truth* was published in 1850, and its sale became her primary means of subsistence. Just a year later, Truth attended the famous women's rights meeting in Akron, Ohio, where she gave what has come to be known as her "Ar'n't I a Woman?" speech. Soon thereafter Truth moved to Battle Creek, Michigan, where she lived until her death in 1883.

Up until 1851, Truth's life was driven primarily by her religious fervor, the foundation for all her later political work. But the period between her attendance at the Akron conference and her death just over thirty years later is what most people know of Truth's life. During this time, she was an outspoken abolitionist and became firmly attached to the women's rights movement. Harriet Beecher Stowe celebrated Truth in 1863 in her *Atlantic Monthly* essay "Sojourner Truth, the Libyan Sibyl," in which Stowe recounted their meeting in 1853. "The Libyan Sibyl" cemented Truth's image as plain, pious, frank, wise, and, quite mistakenly, dead. In the same year, Frances Dana Gage, the chair of the Akron conference, published her account of Truth at the meeting twelve years earlier. Gage included Truth's speech in Akron, rewriting her words and adding rhetorical flourishes like Truth's now familiar question, "Ar'n't I a woman?" In 1864 Truth went to Washington and met with Abraham Lincoln, remaining there to help newly freed slaves. She began advocating for jobs and land for freed slaves, possibly in the West, almost a decade before the Exodus to Kansas. Also during this period, Truth found herself caught in the schism within the women's rights movement as advocates such as Elizabeth Cady Stanton and Susan B. Anthony lobbied against the passage of the Fourteenth and Fifteenth Amendments unless women, black and white, were also granted the right to vote. Truth, among others, disagreed and supported black male suffrage.

The use of Truth both during her lifetime and since her death has been variable, though she became canonized within the women's rights movement with the inclusion of Gage's version of Truth's Akron speech in the 1881 *History of Woman Suffrage*. Few people have had direct access to Truth's words, for she was illiterate. Though her speeches appeared in the press, they were often heavily edited for effect and political expediency (note the differences between Truth's 1851 Akron speech as printed in the *Anti-Slavery Bugle* and Gage's version recollected twelve years later). As historian Nell Painter writes, "Depending on the reporter, Truth can appear as a northerner or a southerner, an insightful commentator or an ignoramus." Truth has been celebrated as an early black militant, even a black nationalist for her unaccounted belief in a black western state, a suffragette, and an advocate for the poor; rarely, though, has she been held up as a model Christian. Her *Narrative* was problematic for abolitionists as it had few points in common with celebrated antislavery texts such as the narratives of Frederick Douglass or Harriet Jacobs; her *Narrative* lacked the rhetorical familiarity of these other well-known plantation slave narratives. Some contemporary critics argue that Truth can too easily be read naively, her words easily and strategically cast within various political positions. Any contemporary reading of Truth, however, needs to engage, or at least account for, Truth's multifaceted politics as well as her religious identity; they are inseparable. Her evangelical Christianity informs her abolitionist and feminist positions as much as her experiences as a Northern slave. Likewise, her experiences as a slave gave rise to a complex reformism that developed at the intersection of social justice, feminism, and scripture.

Daniel Moos
Rhode Island College

PRIMARY WORKS

Olive Gilbert, *Narrative of Sojourner Truth* (1850), Frances W. Titus, ed., 1875, 1884; Susan Pollon Fitch and Roseann M. Mandziuk, *Sojourner Truth as Orator: With Song and Story*, 1997.

Reminiscences by Frances D. Gage of Sojourner Truth, for May 28–29, 1851

The leaders of the movement trembled on seeing a tall, gaunt black woman in a gray dress and white turban, surmounted with an uncouth sun-bonnet, march deliberately into the church, walk with the air of a queen up the aisle, and take her seat upon the pulpit steps. A buzz of disapprobation was heard all over the house, and there fell on the listening ear, "An abolition affair!" "Woman's rights and niggers!" "I told you so!" "Go it, darkey!"

I chanced on that occasion to wear my first laurels in public life as president of the meeting. At my request order was restored, and the business of the Convention went on. Morning, afternoon, and evening exercises came and went. Through all these sessions old Sojourner, quiet and reticent as the "Lybian Statue," sat crouched against the wall on the corner of the pulpit stairs, her sun-bonnet shading her eyes, her elbows on her knees, her chin resting upon her broad, hard palms. At intermission she was busy selling the "Life of Sojourner Truth," a narrative of her own strange and adventurous life. Again and again, timorous and trembling ones came to me and said, with earnestness, "Don't let her speak, Mrs. Gage, it will ruin us. Every newspaper in the land will have our cause mixed up with abolition and niggers, and we shall be utterly denounced." My only answer was, "We shall see when the time comes."

The second day the work waxed warm. Methodist, Baptist, Episcopal, Presbyterian, and Universalist ministers came in to hear and discuss the resolutions presented. One claimed superior rights and privileges for man, on the ground of "superior intellect"; another, because of the "manhood of Christ; if God had desired the equality of woman, He would have given some token of His will through the birth, life, and death of the Saviour." Another gave us a theological view of the "sin of our first mother."

There were very few women in those days who dared to "speak in meeting"; and the august teachers of the people were seemingly getting the better of us, while the boys in the galleries, and the sneerers among the pews, were hugely enjoying the discomfiture, as they supposed, of the "strongminded." Some of the tender-skinned friends were on the point of losing dignity, and the atmosphere betokened a storm. When, slowly from her seat in the corner rose Sojourner Truth, who, till now, had scarcely lifted her head. "Don't let her speak!" gasped half a dozen in my ear. She moved slowly and solemnly to the front, laid her old bonnet at her feet, and turned her great speaking eyes to me. There was a hissing sound of disapprobation above and below. I rose and announced "Sojourner Truth," and begged the audience to keep silence for a few moments.

The tumult subsided at once, and every eye was fixed on this almost Amazon form, which stood nearly six feet high, head erect, and eyes piercing the upper air like one in a dream. At her first word there was a profound hush. She spoke in deep tones, which, though not loud, reached every ear in the house, and away through the throng at the doors and windows.

"Wall, chilern, whar dar is so much racket dar must be somethin' out o' kilter. I tink dat 'twixt de niggers of de Souf and de womin at de Norf, all talkin' 'bout rights, de white men will be in a fix pretty soon. But what's all dis here talkin' 'bout?

"Dat man ober dar say dat womin needs to be helped into carriages, and lifted ober ditches, and to hab de best place everywhar. Nobody eber helps me into carriages, or ober mud-puddles, or gibs me any best place!" And raising herself to her full height, and her voice to a pitch like rolling thunder, she asked. "And a'n't I a woman? Look at me! Look at my arm! (and she bared her right arm to the shoulder, showing her tremendous muscular power). I have ploughed, and planted, and gathered into barns, and no man could head me! And a'n't I a woman? I could work as much and eat as much as a man—when I could get it—and bear de lash as well! And a'n't I a woman? I have borne thirteen chilern, and seen 'em mos' all sold off to slavery, and when I cried out with my mother's grief, none but Jesus heard me! And a'n't I a woman?

"Den dey talks 'bout dis ting in de head; what dis dey call it?" ("Intellect," whispered some one near.) "Dat's it, honey. What's dat got to do wid womin's rights or nigger's rights? If my cup won't hold but a pint, and yourn holds a quart, wouldn't ye be mean not to let me have my little half-measure full?" And she pointed her significant finger, and sent a keen glance at the minister who had made the argument. The cheering was long and loud.

"Den dat little man in black dar, he say women can't have as much rights as men, 'cause Christ wan't a woman! Whar did your Christ come from?" Rolling thunder couldn't have stilled that crowd, as did those deep, wonderful tones, as she stood there with outstretched arms and eyes of fire. Raising her voice still louder, she repeated, "Whar did your Christ come from? From God and a woman! Man had nothin' to do wid Him." Oh, what a rebuke that was to that little man.

Turning again to another objector, she took up the defense of Mother Eve. I can not follow her through it all. It was pointed, and witty, and solemn; eliciting at almost every sentence deafening applause; and she ended by asserting: "If de fust woman God ever made was strong enough to turn de world upside down all alone, dese women togedder (and she glanced her eye over the platform) ought to be able to turn it back, and get it right side up again! And now dey is asking to do it, de men better let 'em." Long-continued cheering greeted this. "'Bleeged to ye for hearin' on me, and now ole Sojourner han't got nothin' more to say."

Amid roars of applause, she returned to her corner, leaving more than one of us with streaming eyes, and hearts beating with gratitude. She had taken us up in her strong arms and carried us safely over the slough of difficulty turning the whole tide in our favor. I have never in my life seen anything like the magical influence that subdued the mobbish spirit of the day, and turned the sneers and jeers of an excited crowd into notes of respect and admiration. Hundreds rushed up to shake hands with her, and congratulate the glorious old mother, and bid her God-speed on her mission of "testifyin' agin concerning the wickedness of this 'ere people."

1881

Speech at the Akron, Ohio, Women's Rights Meeting

One of the most unique and interesting speeches of the Convention was made by Sojourner Truth, an emancipated slave. It is impossible to transfer it to paper, or convey any adequate idea of the effect it produced upon the audience. Those only can appreciate it who saw her powerful form, her whole-souled, earnest gesture, and listened to her strong and truthful tones. She came forward to the platform and addressing the President said with great simplicity: "May I say a few words?" Receiving an affirmative answer, she proceeded:

I wanted to say a few words about this matter. I am a woman's rights. I have as much muscle as any man, and can do as much work as any man. I have plowed and reaped and husked and chopped and mowed, and can any man do more than that? I have heard much about the sexes being equal. I can carry as much as any man, and can eat as much too, if I can get it. I am as strong as any man that is now. As for intellect, all I can say is, if woman have a pint and a man a quart—why can't she have her little pint full? You need not be afraid to give us our rights for fear we will take too much,—for we can't take more than our pint'll hold. The poor men seem to be all in confusion, and don't know what to do. Why children, if you have woman's rights, give it to her and you will feel better. You will have your own rights, and they won't be so much trouble. I can't read, but I can hear. I have heard the bible and learned that Eve caused man to sin. Well, if woman upset the world, do give her a chance to set it right side up again. The Lady has spoken about Jesus, how he never spurned woman from him, and she was right. When Lazarus died, Mary and Martha came to him with faith and love and besought him to raise their brother. And Jesus wept and Lazarus came forth. And how came Jesus into the world? Through God who created him and a woman who bore him. Man, where is your part? But the women are coming up blessed by God and a few of the men are coming up with them. But man is in a tight place, the poor slave is on him, woman is coming on him, he is surely between a hawk and a buzzard.

1851

Speech at New York City Convention

... Sojourner Truth, a tall colored woman, well known in anti-slavery circles, and called the Lybian Sybil, made her appearance on the platform. This was the signal for a fresh outburst from the mob; for at every session every man of them was promptly in his place, at twenty-five cents a head. And this was the one redeeming feature of this mob—it paid all expenses, and left a surplus in the treasury. Sojourner combined in herself, as an individual, the two most hated elements of humanity. She was black, and she was a woman, and all the insults that could be cast upon color and sex were together hurled at her; but there she stood, calm and dignified, a grand, wise woman, who could neither read nor write, and yet with deep insight could penetrate the very soul of the universe about her. As soon as the terrible turmoil was in a measure quelled

She said: Is it not good for me to come and draw forth a spirit, to see what kind of spirit people are of? I see that some of you have got the spirit of a goose, and some have got the spirit of a snake. I feel at home here. I come to you, citizens of New York, as I suppose you ought to be. I am a citizen of the State of New York; I was born in it, and I was a slave in the State of New York; and now I am a good citizen of this State. I was born here, and I can tell you I feel at home here. I've been lookin' round and watchin' things, and I know a little mite 'bout Woman's Rights, too. I come forth to speak 'bout Woman's Rights, and want to throw in my little mite, to keep the scales a-movin'. I know that it feels a kind o' hissin' and ticklin' like to see a colored woman get up and tell you about things, and Woman's Rights. We have all been thrown down so low that nobody thought we'd ever get up again; but we have been long enough trodden now; we will come up again, and now I am here.

I was a-thinkin', when I see women contendin' for their rights, I was a-thinkin' what a difference there is now, and what there was in old times. I have only a few minutes to speak; but in the old times the kings of the earth would hear a woman. There was a king in the Scriptures; and then it was the kings of the earth would kill a woman if she come into their presence; but Queen Esther[1] come forth, for she was oppressed, and felt there was a great wrong, and she said I will die or I will bring my complaint before the king. Should the king of the United States be greater, or more crueler, or more harder? But the king, he raised up his sceptre and said: "Thy request shall be granted unto thee—to the half of my kingdom will I grant it to thee!" Then he said he would hang Haman on the gallows he had made up high. But that is not what women come forward to contend. The women want their rights as Esther. She only wanted to explain her rights. And he was so liberal that he said, "the half of my kingdom shall be granted to thee," and he did not wait for her to ask, he was so liberal with her.

Now, women do not ask half of a kingdom, but their rights, and they don't get 'em. When she comes to demand 'em, don't you hear how sons hiss their mothers like snakes, because they ask for their rights; and can

[1]The Old Testament King Ahasuerus offered to fulfill any request made by his Jewish wife Esther, even if she asked for half of his kingdom. Esther asked for justice for her people. Prince Haman was slaughtering the Jews because he believed he had been insulted by the king's adviser, Mordecai. King Ahasuerus hanged Haman on the gallows Haman had built for Mordecai.

they ask for anything less? The king ordered Haman to be hung on the gallows which he prepared to hang others; but I do not want any man to be killed, but I am sorry to see them so short-minded. But we'll have our rights; see if we don't; and you can't stop us from them; see if you can. You may hiss as much as you like, but it is comin'. Women don't get half as much rights as they ought to; we want more, and we will have it. Jesus says: "What I say to one, I say to all—watch!" I'm a-watchin'. God says: "Honor your father and your mother." Sons and daughters ought to behave themselves before their mothers, but they do not. I can see them a-laughin', and pointin' at their mothers up here on the stage. They hiss when an aged woman comes forth. If they'd been brought up proper they'd have known better than hissing like snakes and geese. I'm 'round watchin' these things, and I wanted to come up and say these few things to you, and I'm glad of the hearin' you give me. I wanted to tell you a mite about Woman's Rights, and so I came out and said so. I am sittin' among you to watch; and every once and awhile I will come out and tell you what time of night it is.

1881

Address to the First Annual Meeting of the American Equal Rights Association

New York City, May 9, 1867

My friends, I am rejoiced that you are glad, but I don't know how you will feel when I get through. I come from another field—the country of the slave. They have got their liberty—so much good luck to have slavery partly destroyed; not entirely. I want it root and branch destroyed. Then we will all be free indeed. I feel that if I have to answer for the deeds done in my body just as much as a man, I have a right to have just as much as a man. There is a great stir about colored men getting their rights, but not a word about the colored women; and if colored men get their rights, and not colored women theirs, you see the colored men will be masters over the women, and it will be just as bad as it was before. So I am for keeping the thing going while things are stirring; because if we wait till it is still, it will take a great while to get it going again. White women are a great deal smarter, and know more than colored women, while colored women do not know scarcely anything. They go out washing, which is about as high as a colored woman gets, and their men go about idle, strutting up and down; and when the women come home, they ask for their money and take it all, and then scold because there is no food. I want you to consider on that, chil'n. I call you chil'n; you are somebody's chil'n, and I am old enough to be mother of all that is here. I want women to have their rights. In the courts women have no right, no voice; nobody speaks for them. I wish woman to have her voice there among the pettifoggers. If it is not a fit place for women, it is unfit for men to be there.

I am above eighty years old; it is about time for me to be going. I have been forty years a slave and forty years free, and would be here forty years more to have equal rights for all. I suppose I am kept here because something remains for me to do; I suppose I am yet to help to break the chain. I have done a great deal of work; as much as a man, but did not get so much pay. I used to work in the field and bind grain, keeping up with the cradler; but men doing no more, got twice as much pay; so with the German women. They work in the field and do as much work, but do not get the pay. We do as much, we eat as much, we want as much. I suppose I am about the only colored woman that goes about to speak for the rights of the colored women. I want to keep the thing stirring, now that the ice is cracked. What we want is a little money. You men know that you get as much again as women when you write, or for what you do. When we get our rights we shall not have to come to you for money, for then we shall have money enough in our own pockets; and may be you will ask us for money. But help us now until we get it. It is a good consolation to know that when we have got this battle once fought we shall not be coming to you any more. You have been having our rights so long, that you think, like a slaveholder, that you own us. I know that it is hard for one who has held the reins for so long to give up; it cuts like a knife. It will feel all the better when it closes up again. I have been in Washington about three years, seeing about these colored people. Now colored men have the right to vote. There ought to be equal rights now more than ever, since colored people have got their freedom. I am going to talk several times while I am here; so now I will do a little singing. I have not heard any singing since I came here.

Accordingly, suiting the action to the word, Sojourner sang, "We are going home." "There, children," said she, "in heaven we shall rest from all our labors; first do all we have to do here. There I am determined to go, not to stop short of that beautiful place, and I do not mean to stop till I get there, and meet you there, too."

1881

■ FANNY FERN (SARA WILLIS PARTON)[1] ■
1811–1872

Born in Portland, Maine, the daughter of Nathaniel and Hannah Parker Willis, Fern spent her early years in Boston, where her father established a religious newspaper and founded *Youth's Companion*. Fern learned journalism from him

---

[1]Although "Fanny Fern" was a pen name, Parton preferred it to her real name and used it even in her personal life, becoming "Fanny" to her family and friends.

but preferred her more broadminded mother, to whom she later attributed her literary talents. Fern was educated at the famous Beecher seminary; Catharine Beecher and her sister Harriet recalled her as a mischief-maker who neglected her studies but wrote witty essays.

Fern lived happily with her first husband, Charles Eldredge, a bank cashier whom she married in 1837. But when he died in 1846, soon after the deaths of her mother and the eldest of her three daughters, she was reduced to relative poverty with only grudging support from her father and in-laws. In 1849 she married Samuel Farrington, a Boston merchant; they quickly separated, and Fern later portrayed him as a "hypocrite" who tricks a reluctant widow into marriage and then deserts her.

Fern tried unsuccessfully to earn a living sewing and teaching and had to give up a daughter to her in-laws before she decided to make use of her background and write short sketches for Boston papers. She appealed to her brother, N. P. Willis, a successful poet and editor, for help in launching a literary career; apparently he pronounced her writing vulgar and advised making shirts instead. But Fern's sketches proved so popular that when she collected them in 1853, *Fern Leaves from Fanny's Portfolio* became an instant best seller. She continued the next year with a second series and a juvenile.

Fern's early sketches are heavily autobiographical: they treat the deaths of husbands or children, as in "A Thanksgiving Story." One prominent theme, which would become a Fern staple, is the difficult situation of the female writer; Fern's aspiring authors have trouble finding decent writing conditions, proper remuneration from editors, or fair treatment by critics.

Fern used material from her early sketches in *Ruth Hall* (1855), a novel about the struggles of a widow to gain financial security. Fern had thought herself protected by her pseudonym, but *Ruth Hall* caused a sensation when her identity was discovered—apparently hinted at by her publisher's ads—and Ruth's mean father, in-laws, and brother "Hyacinth" recognized as the author's own. While Nathaniel Hawthorne admired the novel, making Fern the one exception to his sweeping indictment of his female rivals as a "d—d mob of scribbling women," most critics attacked it for the same reason he praised it: the lack of "female delicacy" in satirizing one's relatives and allowing one's heroine to evolve from tearful victim to aggressive author and businesswoman. Fern was widely thought to have "demeaned herself" in creating "Ruthless Hall."

Neither disapproving critics nor the publication of *Life and Beauties of Fanny Fern* (1855), an anonymously authored book denouncing her, affected Fern's popularity with readers. She accepted the extravagant sum of $100 a week to write for the *New York Ledger*, reclaimed her daughter, and moved to New York. In 1856 she again broke with convention, marrying a man eleven years her junior (James Parton, the biographer) and publicly praising Walt Whitman's scandalous *Leaves of Grass*. She also published an inferior novel, *Rose Clark*, but thereafter restricted herself to the form she excelled at, the short, informal essay; from 1857 to her death in 1872 she published several collections of these from her *Ledger* columns.

Because her early work is best known (or because women writing in mid-nineteenth-century America have been lumped together), Fanny Fern has been mistakenly classified as a "sentimentalist." Fred Pattee in *The Feminine Fifties* calls her a "tearful moralizer," claiming she produced "goodygoody inanity." However, Fern's writing changed significantly after her initial success. The first three-quarters of *Fern Leaves* may be too lachrymose for modern taste, but the last quarter contains humorous and satirical pieces, and in the second series the proportion is exactly reversed. Fern was known to her contemporaries for her non-goody-goody wit and humor expressed in the "noisy, rattling" style—full of italics and exclamation points—that her brother deplored.

By 1859 and the publication of *Folly As It Flies*, Fern had developed a surer voice, still direct and fresh but more relaxed and unified. She also broadened her range of subject matter. Although her trademark continued to be women's and children's rights and everyday domestic topics like the annoying habits of husbands, Fern became more conscious of urban social and economic conditions. She began to express her empathy with working women, which had earlier revealed itself in pieces like "Soliloquy of a Housemaid," in greater detail, depicting poverty, prostitution, exploitation of workers, and prison life.

Barbara A. White
University of New Hampshire

PRIMARY WORK

Ruth Hall and Other Writings, Joyce W. Warren, ed., 1986.

Hints to Young Wives

Shouldn't I like to make a bon-fire of all the "Hints to Young Wives," "Married Woman's Friend," etc., and throw in the authors after them? I have a little neighbor who believes all they tell her is gospel truth, and lives up to it. The minute she sees her husband coming up the street, she makes for the door, as if she hadn't another minute to live, stands in the entry with her teeth chattering in her head till he gets all his coats and mufflers, and overshoes, and what-do-you-call'-ems off, then chases round (like a cat in a fit) after the boot-jack; warms his slippers and puts 'em on, and dislocates her wrist carving at the table for fear it will tire him.

Poor little innocent fool! she imagines that's the way to preserve his affection. Preserve a fiddlestick! The consequence is, he's sick of the sight of her; snubs her when she asks him a question, and after he has eaten her good dinners takes himself off as soon as possible, bearing in mind the old proverb "that too much of a good thing is good for nothing." Now the truth is just this, and I wish all the women on earth had but one ear in common, so that I could put this little bit of gospel into it:—Just so long as a man isn't quite as sure as if he knew for certain, whether nothing on earth could ever disturb your affection for him, he is your humble servant, but the very second he finds out (or thinks he does) that he has possession of every inch of your heart, and no neutral territory—he will turn on his heel and march off whistling "Yankee Doodle!"

Now it's no use to take your pocket handkerchief and go snivelling round the house with a pink nose and red eyes; not a bit of it! If you have made the interesting discovery that you were married for a sort of upper servant or housekeeper, just *fill that place and no other*, keep your temper, keep all his strings and buttons and straps on; and then keep him at a distance as a housekeeper should—"them's my sentiments!" I have seen one or two men in my life who could bear to be loved (as a woman with a soul knows how), without being spoiled by it, or converted into a tyrant—but they are rare birds, and should be caught, stuffed and handed over to Barnum! Now as the ministers say, "I'll close with an interesting little incident that came under my observation."

Mr. Fern came home one day when I had such a crucifying headache that I couldn't have told whether I was married or single, and threw an old coat into my lap to mend. Well, I tied a wet bandage over my forehead, "left all flying," and sat down to it—he might as well have asked me to make a *new* one; however I new lined the sleeves, mended the buttonholes, sewed on new buttons down the front, and all over the coat tails—when finally it occurred to me (I believe it was a suggestion of Satan), that the *pocket* might need mending; so I turned it inside out, and *what do you think I found?* A *love-letter from him to my dress-maker!!* I dropped the coat, I dropped the work-basket, I dropped the buttons, I dropped the baby (it was a *female*, and I thought it just as well to put her out of future misery) and then I hopped up into a chair front of the looking-glass, and remarked to the young woman I saw there, "F-a-n-n-y F-e-r-n! if you—are—ever—such—a—confounded fool again"—and I wasn't.

Olive Branch
Feb. 14, 1852

from **Fern Leaves, First Series**

Thanksgiving Story

"Mary!" said the younger of two little girls, as they nestled under a coarse coverlid, one cold night in December, "tell me about Thanksgiving-day before papa went to heaven. I'm cold and hungry, and I can't go to sleep;—I want something nice to think about."

"Hush!" said the elder child, "don't let dear mamma hear you; come nearer to me;"—and they laid their cheeks together.

"I fancy papa was rich. We lived in a very nice house. I know there were pretty pictures on the wall; and there were nice velvet chairs, and the carpet was thick and soft, like the green moss-patches in the wood;—and we had pretty gold-fish on the side-table, and Tony, my black nurse, used to feed them. And papa!—you can't remember papa, Letty,—he was tall and grand, like a prince, and when he smiled he made me think of angels. He brought me toys and sweetmeats, and carried me out to the stable, and set me on Romeo's live back, and laughed because I was afraid! And I used to watch to see him come up the street, and then run to the door to jump in his arms;—he was a dear, kind papa," said the child, in a faltering voice.

"Don't cry," said the little one; "please tell me some more."

"Well, Thanksgiving-day we were so happy; we sat around such a large table, with so many people,—aunts and uncles and cousins,—I can't think why they never come to see us now, Letty,—and Betty made such sweet pies, and we had a big—big turkey; and papa would have me sit next to him, and gave me the wishbone, and all the plums out of his pudding; and after dinner he would take me in his lap, and tell me 'Red Riding Hood,' and call me 'pet,' and 'bird,' and 'fairy.' O, Letty, I can't tell any more; I believe I'm going to cry."

"I'm very cold," said Letty. "Does papa know, up in heaven, that we are poor and hungry now?"

"Yes—no—I can't tell," answered Mary, wiping away her tears; unable to reconcile her ideas of heaven with such a thought. "Hush!—mamma will hear!"

Mamma had "heard." The coarse garment, upon which she had toiled since sunrise, dropped from her hands, and tears were forcing themselves, thick and fast, through her closed eyelids. The simple recital found but too sad an echo in that widowed heart.

1853

from **Fern Leaves, Second Series**

Soliloquy of a Housemaid

Oh, dear, dear! Wonder if my mistress *ever* thinks I am made of flesh and blood? Five times, within half an hour, I have trotted up stairs, to hand her things, that were only four feet from her rocking-chair. Then, there's her son, Mr. George,—it does seem to me, that a great able-bodied man like him, need n't call a poor tired woman up four pair of stairs to ask "what's the time of day?" Heigho!—its "*Sally* do this," and "*Sally* do that," till I wish I never had been baptized at all; and I might as well go farther back, while I am about it, and wish I had never been born.

Now, instead of ordering me round so like a dray horse, if they would only look up smiling-like, now and then; or ask me how my "rheumatiz" did; or say good morning, Sally; or show some sort of interest in a fellow-cretur, I could pluck up a bit of heart to work for them. A kind word would ease the wheels of my treadmill amazingly, and wouldn't cost *them* anything, either.

Look at my clothes, all at sixes and sevens. I can't get a minute to sew on a string or button, except at night; and then I'm so sleepy it is as much as ever I can find the way to bed; and what a bed it is, to be sure! Why, even the pigs are now and then allowed clean straw to sleep on; and as to bed-clothes, the less said about them the better; my old cloak serves for a blanket, and the sheets are as thin as a charity school soup. Well, well; one wouldn't think it, to see all the fine glittering things down in the drawing-room. Master's span of horses, and Miss Clara's diamond ear-rings, and mistresses rich dresses. I *try* to think it is all right, but it is no use.

To-morrow is Sunday—"day of *rest*," I believe they *call* it. H-u-m-p-h!—more cooking to be done—more company—more confusion than on any other day in the week. If I own a soul I have not heard how to take care of it for many a long day. Wonder if my master and mistress calculate to pay me for *that*, if I lose it? It is a *question* in my mind. Land of Goshen! I aint sure I've got a mind—there's the bell again!

1854

Critics

"Bilious wretches, who abuse you because you write better than they."

Slander and detraction! Even I, Fanny, know better than that. *I* never knew an editor to nib[1] his pen with a knife as sharp as his temper, and write a scathing criticism on a book, because the authoress had declined contributing to his paper. I never knew a man who had fitted himself to a promiscuous coat, cut out in merry mood by taper fingers, to seize his porcupine quill, under the agony of too tight a *self-inflicted* fit, to annihilate the offender. I never saw the bottled-up hatred of years, concentrated in a single venomous paragraph. I never heard of an unsuccessful masculine author, whose books were drugs in the literary market, speak with a sneer of successful literary feminity, and insinuate that it was by *accident*, not *genius*, that they hit the popular favor!

By the memory of "seventy-six," No! Do you suppose a *man's* opinions are in the market—to be bought and sold to the highest bidder? Do you suppose he would laud a vapid book, because the fashionable authoress once laved his toadying temples with the baptism of upper-tendom? or, do you suppose he'd lash a poor, but self-reliant wretch, who had presumed to climb to the topmost round of Fame's ladder, without *his* royal permission or assistance, and in despite of his repeated attempts to discourage her? No—no—bless your simple soul; a man never stoops to a meanness. There never was a criticism yet, born of envy, or malice, or repulsed love, or disappointed ambition. No—no. Thank the gods, *I* have a more exalted opinion of masculinity.

1854

Mrs. Adolphus Smith Sporting the "Blue Stocking"

Well, I think I'll finish that story for the editor of the "Dutchman." Let me see; where did I leave off? The setting sun was just gilding with his last ray—"Ma, I want some bread and molassees"—(yes, dear,) gilding with his last ray the church spire—"Wife, where's my Sunday pants?" (*Under the bed, dear,*) the church spire of Inverness, when a—"There's nothing under the bed, dear, but your lace cap"—(Perhaps they are in the coal hod in the closet,) when a horseman was seen approaching—"Ma'am, the *pertators* is

---

[1] To mend the point of a pen.

out; not one for dinner"—(Take some turnips,) approaching, covered with dust, and—"Wife! the baby has swallowed a button"—(*Reverse him*, dear—take him by the heels,) and waving in his hand a banner, on which was written—"Ma! I've torn my pantaloons"—liberty or death! The inhabitants rushed *en masse*—"Wife! WILL you leave off scribbling?" (Don't be disagreeable, Smith, I'm just getting inspired,) to the public square, where De Begnis, who had been secretly—"Butcher wants to see you, ma'am"—secretly informed of the traitors'—"Forgot *which* you said, ma'am, sausages or mutton chop"—movements, gave orders to fire; not less than twenty—My gracious! Smith, you have n't been *reversing* that child all this time; he's as black as your coat; and that boy of YOURS has torn up the first sheet of my manuscript. There! it's no use for a married woman to cultivate her intellect.—Smith, hand me those twins.

1854

Male Criticism on Ladies Books

"Courtship and marriage, servants and children, these are the great objects of a woman's thoughts, and they necessarily form the staple topics of their writings and their conversation. We have no right to expect anything else in a woman's book."

—*N.Y. Times*

Is it in feminine novels *only* that courtship, marriage, servants and children are the staple? Is not this true of all novels?—of Dickins, of Thackery, of Bulwer and a host of others? Is it peculiar to feminine pens, most astute and liberal of critics? Would a novel be a novel if it did not treat of courtship and marriage? and if it could be so recognized, would it find readers? When I see such a narrow, snarling criticism as the above, I always say to myself, the writer is some unhappy man, who has come up without the refining influence of mother, or sister, or reputable female friends; who has divided his migratory life between boarding-houses, restaurants, and the outskirts of editorial sanctums; and who knows as much about reviewing a woman's book, as I do about navigating a ship, or engineering an omnibus from the South Ferry, through Broadway, to Union Park. I think I see him writing that paragraph in a fit of spleen—of *male* spleen—in his small boarding-house upper chamber, by the cheerful light of a solitary candle, flickering alternately on cobwebbed walls, dusty wash-stand, begrimed bowl and pitcher, refuse cigar stumps, boot-jacks, old hats, buttonless coats, muddy trousers, and all the wretched accompaniments of solitary, selfish male existence, not to speak of his own puckered, unkissable face; perhaps, in addition, his boots hurt, his cravat-bow persists in slipping under his ear for want of a pin, and a wife to pin it (poor wretch!) or he has been refused by some pretty girl, as he deserved to be (narrow-minded old vinegar-cruet!) or snubbed by some lady authoress; or, more trying than all to the male constitution, has had a weak cup of coffee for that morning's breakfast.

But seriously—we have had quite enough of this shallow criticism (?) on lady-books. Whether the book which called forth the remark above quoted, was a good book or a bad one, I know not: I should be inclined to think the *former* from the dispraise of such a pen. Whether ladies can write novels or not, is a question I do not intend to discuss; but that some of them have no difficulty in finding either publishers or readers is a matter of history; and that gentlemen often write over feminine signatures would seem also to argue that feminine literature is, after all, in good odor with the reading public. Granted that lady-novels are not all that they should be—is such shallow, unfair, wholesale, sneering criticism (?) the way to reform them? Would it not be better and more manly to point out a better way kindly, justly, *and above all, respectfully?* or—what would be a much harder task for such critics—write a better book!

1857

A Law More Nice Than Just

Here I have been sitting twiddling the morning paper between my fingers this half hour, reflecting upon the following paragraph in it: "Emma Wilson was arrested yesterday for wearing man's apparel."[1] Now, why this should be an actionable offense is past my finding out, or where's the harm in it, I am as much at a loss to see. Think of the old maids (and weep) who have to stay at home evening after evening, when, if they provided themselves with a coat, pants and hat, they might go abroad, instead of sitting there with their noses flattened against the window-pane, looking vainly for "the Coming Man." Think of the married women who stay at home after their day's toil is done, waiting wearily for their thoughtless, truant husbands, when they might be taking the much needed independent walk in trousers, which custom forbids to petticoats. And this, I fancy, may be the secret of this famous law—who knows? It *wouldn't* be pleasant for some of them to be surprised by a touch on the shoulder from some dapper young fellow, whose familiar treble voice belied his corduroys. That's it, now. What a fool I was not to think of it—not to remember that men who make the laws, make them to meet all these little emergencies.

Everybody knows what an everlasting drizzle of rain we have had lately, but nobody but a woman, and a woman who lives on fresh air and out-door exercise, knows the thraldom of taking her daily walk through a three weeks' rain, with skirts to hold up, and umbrella to hold down, and puddles to skip over, and gutters to walk round, and all the time in a fright lest, in an unguarded moment, her calves should become visible to some one of those rainy-day philanthropists who are interested in the public study of female anatomy.

[1]Both custom and municipal law prohibited women from wearing breeches.

One evening, after a long rainy day of scribbling, when my nerves were in double-twisted knots, and I felt as if myriads of little ants were leisurely traveling over me, and all for want of the walk which is my daily salvation, I stood at the window, looking at the slanting, persistent rain, and took my resolve: "*I'll do it*," said I, audibly, planting my slipper upon the carpet. "Do what?" asked Mr. Fern, looking up from a big book. "Put on a suit of your clothes and take a tramp with you," was the answer. "You dare not," was the rejoinder; "you are a little coward, only saucy on paper." It was the work of a moment, with such a challenge, to fly up stairs and overhaul my philosopher's wardrobe. Of course we had fun. Tailors must be a stingy set, I remarked, to be so sparing of their cloth, as I struggled into a pair of their handiwork, undeterred by the vociferous laughter of the wretch who had solemnly vowed to "cherish me" through all my tribulations. "Upon my word, everything seems to be narrow where it ought to be broad, and the waist of this coat might be made for a hogshead; and, ugh! this shirt collar is cutting my ears off, and you have not a decent cravat in the whole lot, and your vests are frights, and what am I to do with my hair?" Still no reply from Mr. Fern, who lay on the floor, faintly ejaculating, between his fits of laughter, "Oh, my! by Jove!—oh! by Jupiter!"

Was that to hinder me? Of course not. Strings and pins, women's never-failing resort, soon brought broadcloth and kerseymere to terms. I parted my hair on one side, rolled it under, and then secured it with hairpins; chose the best fitting coat, and cap-ping the climax with one of those soft, cosy hats, looked in the glass, where I beheld the very fac-simile of a certain musical gentleman, whose photograph hangs this minute in Brady's entry.[2]

Well, Mr. Fern seized his hat, and out we went together. "Fanny," said he, "you must not take my arm; you are a fellow." "True," said I. "I forgot; and you must not help me over puddles, as you did just now, and do, for mercy's sake, stop laughing. There, there goes your hat—I mean *my* hat; confound the wind! and down comes my hair; lucky 'tis dark, isn't it?" But oh, the delicious freedom of that walk; after we were well started! No skirts to hold up, or to draggle their wet folds against my ankles; no stifling vail flapping in my face, and blinding my eyes; no umbrella to turn inside out, but instead, the cool rain driving slap into my face, and the resurrectionized blood coursing through my veins, and tingling in my cheeks. To be sure, Mr. Fern occasionally loitered behind, and leaned up against the side of a house to enjoy a little private "guffaw," and I could now and then hear a gasping "Oh, Fanny! Oh, my!" but none of these things moved me, and if I don't have a nicely-fitting suit of my own to wear rainy evenings, it is because— well, there *are* difficulties in the way. Who's the best tailor?

Now, if any male or female Miss Nancy who reads this feels shocked, let 'em! Any woman who likes, may stay at home during a three weeks' rain, till her skin looks like parchment, and her eyes like those of a dead fish, or she may go out and get a consumption dragging round wet petticoats; I won't—

[2]Fern's brother, Richard Storrs Willis.

I positively declare I won't. I shall begin *evenings* when *that* suit is made, and take private walking lessons with Mr. Fern, and they who choose may crook their backs at home for fashion, and then send for the doctor to straighten them; I prefer to patronize my shoe-maker and tailor. I've as good a right to preserve the healthy body God gave me, as if I were not a woman.

1858

Independence

"FOURTH OF JULY." Well—I don't feel patriotic. Perhaps I might if they would stop that deafening racket. Washington was very well, if he *couldn't* spell, and I'm glad we are all free; but as a woman—I shouldn't know it, didn't some orator tell me. Can I go out of an evening without a hat at my side? Can I go out with one on my head without danger of a station-house? Can I clap my hands at some public speaker when I am nearly bursting with delight? Can I signify the contrary when my hair stands on end with vexation? Can I stand up in the cars "like a gentleman" without being immediately invited "to sit down"? Can I get into an omnibus without having my sixpence taken from my hand and given to the driver? Can I cross Broadway without having a policeman tackled to my helpless elbow? Can I go to see anything *pleasant*, like an execution or a dissection? Can I drive that splendid "Lantern,"[1] distancing—like his owner—all competitors? Can I have the nomination for "Governor of Vermont," like our other contributor, John G. Saxe?[2] Can I be a Senator, that I may hurry up that millennial International Copyright Law?[3] Can I *even* be President? Bah—you know I can't. *"Free!"* Humph!

New York Ledger
July 30, 1859

The Working-Girls of New York

Nowhere more than in New York does the contest between squalor and splendor so sharply present itself. This is the first reflection of the observing stranger who walks its streets. Particularly is this noticeable with regard to its women. Jostling on the same pavement with the dainty fashionist is the care-worn working-girl. Looking at both these women, the question arises, which lives the more miserable life—she whom the world styles "fortunate," whose husband belongs to three clubs, and whose only meal with his family is an occasional breakfast, from year's end to year's end; who is as much a stranger to his own children as to the reader; whose young son of seventeen has already a detective on his track employed by his father to

---

[1] A horse belonging to Robert Bonner, Fern's editor.

[2] John Godfrey Saxe (1816–1887), a poet and frequent contributor to magazines, ran for governor of Vermont in 1859 and 1860.

[3] Fern supported an international copyright law to protect authors from having their works pirated in other countries.

ascertain where and how he spends his nights and his father's money; swift retribution for that father who finds food, raiment, shelter, equipages for his household; but love, sympathy, companionship—never? Or she—this other woman—with a heart quite as hungry and unappeased, who also faces day by day the same appalling question: *Is this all life has for me?*

A great book is yet unwritten about women. Michelet has aired his wax-doll theories regarding them.[1] The defender of "woman's rights" has given us her views. Authors and authoresses of little, and big repute, have expressed themselves on this subject, and none of them as yet have begun to grasp it: men—because they lack spirituality, rightly and justly to interpret women; women—because they dare not, or will not tell us that which most interests us to know. Who shall write this bold, frank, truthful book remains to be seen. Meanwhile woman's millennium is yet a great way off; and while it slowly progresses, conservatism and indifference gaze through their spectacles at the seething elements of to-day, and wonder "what ails all our women?"

Let me tell you what ails the working-girls. While yet your breakfast is progressing, and your toilet unmade, comes forth through Chatham Street and the Bowery, a long procession of them by twos and threes to their daily labor. Their breakfast, so called, has been hastily swallowed in a tenement house, where two of them share, in a small room, the same miserable bed. Of its quality you may better judge, when you know that each of these girls pays but three dollars a week for board, to the working man and his wife where they lodge.

The room they occupy is close and unventilated, with no accommodations for personal cleanliness, and so near to the little Flinegans that their Celtic night-cries are distinctly heard. They have risen unrefreshed, as a matter of course, and their ill-cooked breakfast does not mend the matter. They emerge from the doorway where their passage is obstructed by "nanny goats" and ragged children rooting together in the dirt, and pass out into the street. They shiver as the sharp wind of early morning strikes their temples. There is no look of youth on their faces; hard lines appear there. Their brows are knit; their eyes are sunken; their dress is flimsy, and foolish, and tawdry; always a hat, and feather or soiled artificial flower upon it; the hair dressed with an abortive attempt at style; a soiled petticoat; a greasy dress, a well-worn sacque or shawl, and a gilt breast-pin and earrings.

Now follow them to the large, black-looking building, where several hundred of them are manufacturing hoop-skirts. If you are a woman you have worn plenty; but you little thought what passed in the heads of these girls as their busy fingers glazed the wire, or prepared the spools for covering them, or secured the tapes which held them in their places. *You* could not stay five minutes in that room, where the noise of the machinery used is so

---

[1] Refers to misogynist writings of Jules Michelet (1798–1894), a French historian who preferred women to be docile and obedient.

deafening, that only by the motion of the lips could you comprehend a person speaking.

Five minutes! Why, these young creatures bear it, from seven in the morning till six in the evening; week after week, month after month, with only half an hour at midday to eat their dinner of a slice of bread and butter or an apple, which they usually eat in the building, some of them having come a long distance. As I said, the roar of machinery in that room is like the roar of Niagara. Observe them as you enter. Not one lifts her head. They might as well be machines, for any interest or curiosity they show, save always to know *what o'clock it is*. Pitiful! pitiful, you almost sob to yourself, as you look at these young girls. *Young?* Alas! it is only in years that they are young.

Folly As It Flies

1868

▪ ELIZABETH CADY STANTON ▪
1815–1902

Elizabeth Cady Stanton became one of the best known and most radical women's rights advocates of the nineteenth century. If Susan B. Anthony became the movement's most effective organizer, Stanton became its leading philosopher.

No one would have predicted Stanton's public role from the circumstances of her birth. She was born in Johnstown, New York, on November 12, 1815. Her father, Daniel Cady, was a judge, "a conservative of the conservatives," as Stanton later recalled. Her mother, Margaret, came from the landed Livingston family of eastern New York and remained, according to her daughter, "blue-blooded, socially as well as physically."

As a young girl, she was reminded often that sons would have been more welcome in her family than daughters. Of eleven children born to her parents, six died young, including all five of the Cady sons. When her eldest brother, Eleazer, died in 1826, Stanton tried desperately to comfort her father. All he would say was, "Oh, my daughter, I wish you were a boy!" Stanton learned early that such gender stereotyping was not personal but structural. In her father's law office, where she acted as assistant, she discovered that everywhere, men had legal, political, and economic dominance.

In the 1830s, Stanton saw a far different vision of the world when she visited her cousins, Gerrit and Ann Smith. The Smiths were committed antislavery activists, and there Stanton met her future husband, Henry Brewster Stanton, a tireless and enthusiastic abolitionist lecturer. Henry and Elizabeth were married, despite strong parental misgivings, in May 1840.

The Stantons spent their honeymoon in England, where they attended the World Anti-Slavery Convention. Among the delegates to the meeting, Lucretia Mott most attracted Stanton's attention. A Quaker minister from Philadelphia, founder of the Philadelphia Female Anti-Slavery Society, and mother of six, Mott epitomized for Stanton the freedom and independence for women that she had dreamed about but had never before seen.

The World Anti-Slavery Convention decided on the first day of its meeting not to seat female delegates. Angered by such discrimination, Stanton and Mott resolved to organize a convention, as soon as they returned home, solely to discuss women's rights.

For eight years, however, they postponed action. The Stantons were immersed in starting a new career and a new family, first in Johnstown and then in Boston, where Henry began work as a lawyer and politician. Not until the Stantons moved to Seneca Falls would Elizabeth and Lucretia carry out their plan. There in Seneca Falls, the Stantons would raise four more children, to make seven in all. There, too, Elizabeth would begin her active career as a women's rights reformer.

Perhaps three hundred people attended the Seneca Falls convention. One hundred of them (sixty-eight women and thirty-two men) signed the Declaration of Sentiments, asserting that "all men and women are created equal." While Stanton discussed her own reasons for organizing this meeting, she said very little about why so many other people, on such short notice, would attend such a radical gathering.

Local people were in fact inspired to support women's rights by their participation in three other reform movements. The first was the effort to pass a Married Women's Property Act. For twelve years, the right of married women to own property had been seriously discussed throughout New York State. Wealthy men supported it so that they could give land to their daughters. Yet such an act had unsettling implications. Public debate over the Married Women's Property Act was also a debate over the equality of women and men and, in fact, over the meaning of the Declaration of Independence itself. As republicans, Americans linked citizenship rights (including the right to vote) with economic independence. If married women could be economically self-sufficient, what would prevent them from demanding political independence as well? This debate over women's rights occurred simultaneously with efforts to give black males equal voting rights with white men in New York State. Both issues forced New Yorkers to consider the essential meaning of citizenship in their democratic republic.

Against this general background, two more reform efforts hit Seneca Falls and the neighboring village of Waterloo with particular intensity. In Waterloo, a large Quaker meeting split apart over issues relating to equality. One group formed the new Congregational Friends. Active in both abolitionism and women's rights, almost every family in this group would attend the Seneca Falls convention. In Seneca Falls at the same time, traditional political parties exploded under the impact of the new Free Soil party, whose goal was to eliminate slavery in the western territories. Free Soilers in Seneca Falls would also support the women's rights convention.

Because the Seneca Falls convention used the language of the Declaration of Independence, people reacted to its demands for women's equality more positively than Stanton remembered. Many Americans agreed with Horace Greeley, editor of the nation's most influential newspaper, the *New York Tribune*, when he admitted that "when a sincere republican is asked to say in sober earnest, what adequate reason he can give for refusing the demand of women to an equal participation with men in political rights, he must answer, None at all.... it is but the assertion of a natural right, and as such must be conceded."

The Seneca Falls convention raised issues that Americans would debate through the mid-twentieth century. It touched off a series of local and national conventions that led to the formation of national women's rights organizations, to women's active presence in public life, and finally, seventy-two years later, to the passage of the Nineteenth Amendment on August 26, 1920, giving women the right to vote. Americans remain ambivalent, however, about whether or not "all men and women are created equal."

Stanton herself never deviated from her uncompromising commitment to women's rights, which she called "the greatest revolution the world has ever known." In her last public act before her death in 1902, she wrote one letter to President Theodore Roosevelt and another, the day before she died, to his wife, Edith K. Roosevelt, asking them to support a constitutional amendment for women's right to vote.

Judith Wellman
State University of New York at Oswego

PRIMARY WORKS

Eighty Years & More: Reminiscences, 1815–1897, 1898, reprint 1971; *Elizabeth Cady Stanton as Revealed in Her Letters, Diary and Reminiscences,* Theodore Stanton and Harriot Stanton Blatch, eds., 2 vols., 1922; *The Selected Papers of Elizabeth Cady Stanton and Susan B. Anthony,* 1977; *Elizabeth Cady Stanton, Susan B. Anthony: Correspondence, Writings, Speeches,* Ellen Carol DuBois, ed., 1981.

from **Eighty Years and More: Reminiscences**

Up to this time life had glided by with comparative ease, but now the real struggle was upon me. My duties were too numerous and varied, and none sufficiently exhilarating or intellectual to bring into play my higher faculties. I suffered with mental hunger, which, like an empty stomach, is very depressing. I had books, but no stimulating companionship. To add to my general dissatisfaction at the change from Boston, I found that Seneca Falls was a malarial region, and in due time all the children were attacked with chills and fever which, under homeopathic treatment in those days, lasted three months. The servants were afflicted in the same way. Cleanliness, order, the love of the beautiful and artistic, all faded away in the struggle to accomplish what was absolutely necessary from hour to hour. Now I understood, as I never had before, how women could sit down and rest in the midst of general disorder. Housekeeping, under such conditions, was impossible, so I packed our clothes, locked up the house, and went to that harbor of safety, home, as I did ever after in stress of weather.

I now fully understood the practical difficulties most women had to contend with in the isolated household, and the impossibility of woman's best development if in contact, the chief part of her life, with servants and

children. Fourier's phalansterie community life and co-operative households[1] had a new significance for me. Emerson says, "A healthy discontent
is the first step to progress." The general discontent I felt with woman's
portion as wife, mother, housekeeper, physician, and spiritual guide, the
chaotic conditions into which everything fell without her constant supervision, and the wearied, anxious look of the majority of women impressed me
with a strong feeling that some active measures should be taken to remedy
the wrongs of society in general, and of women in particular. My experience
at the World's Anti-slavery Convention, all I had read of the legal status of
women, and the oppression I saw everywhere, together swept across my
soul, intensified now by many personal experiences. It seemed as if all the
elements had conspired to impel me to some onward step. I could not see
what to do or where to begin—my only thought was a public meeting for
protest and discussion.

In this tempest-tossed condition of mind I received an invitation to
spend the day with Lucretia Mott, at Richard Hunt's, in Waterloo. There I
met several members of different families of Friends, earnest, thoughtful
women. I poured out, that day, the torrent of my long-accumulating discontent, with such vehemence and indignation that I stirred myself, as well as
the rest of the party, to do and dare anything. My discontent, according to
Emerson, must have been healthy, for it moved us all to prompt action, and
we decided, then and there, to call a "Woman's Rights Convention." We
wrote the call that evening and published it in the *Seneca County Courier* the
next day, the 14th of July, 1848,[2] giving only five days' notice, as the convention was to be held on the 19th and 20th. The call was inserted without
signatures,—in fact it was a mere announcement of a meeting,—but the
chief movers and managers were Lucretia Mott, Mary Ann McClintock, Jane
Hunt, Martha C. Wright, and myself. The convention, which was held two
days in the Methodist Church,[3] was in every way a grand success. The house
was crowded at every session, the speaking good, and a religious earnestness
dignified all the proceedings.

These were the hasty initiative steps of "the most momentous reform
that had yet been launched on the world—the first organized protest
against the injustice which had brooded for ages over the character and destiny of one-half the race." No words could express our astonishment on
finding, a few days afterward, that what seemed to us so timely, so rational,
and so sacred, should be a subject for sarcasm and ridicule to the entire
press of the nation. With our Declaration of Rights and Resolutions for a
text, it seemed as if every man who could wield a pen prepared a homily on
"woman's sphere." All the journals from Maine to Texas seemed to strive

---

[1]Frenchman Charles Fourier developed a
scheme for organizing harmonious cooperative communities. Inspired by articles in the
New York Tribune, Americans established several of these in the 1840s, including one in
nearby Skaneateles, New York.

[2]This actually appeared first on July 11, 1848.
[3]The women's rights conventions actually met
in the Wesleyan Methodist Church.

with each other to see which could make our movement appear the most ridiculous. The anti-slavery papers stood by us manfully and so did Frederick Douglass,[4] both in the convention and in his paper, *The North Star*, but so pronounced was the popular voice against us, in the parlor, press, and pulpit, that most of the ladies who had attended the convention and signed the declaration, one by one, withdrew their names and influence and joined our persecutors. Our friends gave us the cold shoulder and felt themselves disgraced by the whole proceeding.

If I had had the slightest premonition of all that was to follow that convention, I fear I should not have had the courage to risk it, and I must confess that it was with fear and trembling that I consented to attend another, one month afterward, in Rochester. Fortunately, the first one seemed to have drawn all the fire, and of the second but little was said. But we had set the ball in motion, and now, in quick succession, conventions were held in Ohio, Indiana, Massachusetts, Pennsylvania, and in the City of New York, and have been kept up nearly every year since.

... The most noteworthy of the early conventions were those held in Massachusetts, in which such men as Garrison, Phillips, Channing, Parker, and Emerson took part.[5] It was one of these that first attracted the attention of Mrs. John Stuart Mill, and drew from her pen that able article on "The Enfranchisement of Woman," in the *Westminster Review* of October, 1852.[6] ...

Declaration of Sentiments

When, in the course of human events, it becomes necessary for one portion of the family of man to assume among the people of the earth a position different from that which they have hitherto occupied, but one to which the laws of nature and of nature's God entitle them, a decent respect to the opinions of mankind requires that they should declare the causes that impel them to such a course.

We hold these truths to be self-evident: that all men and women are created equal; that they are endowed by their Creator with certain inalienable rights; that among these are life, liberty, and the pursuit of happiness; that to secure these rights governments are instituted, deriving their just powers

[4]Escaped slave, abolitionist orator, and editor of *The North Star* in Rochester, New York, Douglass was the only known black person to attend the Seneca Falls meeting. He remained committed to women's rights throughout his life.

[5]William Lloyd Garrison, Wendell Phillips, William Henry Channing, and Theodore Parker were all nationally known radical abolitionists from the Boston area. Garrison edited *The Liberator*; Phillips was a brilliant antislavery orator; Channing and Parker were Unitarian ministers. Ralph Waldo Emerson of Concord, Massachusetts, was perhaps America's best-known essayist and philosopher.

[6]Mrs. John Stuart Mill: Harriet Taylor married John Stuart Mill in 1851, after a twenty-one year intimate friendship. Mill attributed much of his commitment to women's rights to Harriet's influence, including "all that is most striking and profound" in his influential *The Subjection of Women* (1869).

from the consent of the governed. Whenever any form of government becomes destructive of these ends, it is the right of those who suffer from it to refuse allegiance to it, and to insist upon the institution of a new government, laying its foundation on such principles, and organizing its powers in such form, as to them shall seem most likely to effect their safety and happiness. Prudence, indeed, will dictate that governments long established should not be changed for light and transient causes; and accordingly all experience hath shown that mankind are more disposed to suffer, while evils are sufferable, than to right themselves by abolishing the forms to which they were accustomed. But when a long train of abuses and usurpations, pursuing invariably the same object evinces a design to reduce them under absolute despotism, it is their duty to throw off such government, and to provide new guards for their future security. Such has been the patient sufferance of the women under this government, and such is now the necessity which constrains them to demand the equal station to which they are entitled.

The history of mankind is a history of repeated injuries and usurpations on the part of man toward woman, having in direct object the establishment of an absolute tyranny over her. To prove this, let facts be submitted to a candid world.

He has never permitted her to exercise her inalienable right to the elective franchise.

He has compelled her to submit to laws, in the formation of which she had no voice.

He has withheld from her rights which are given to the most ignorant and degraded men—both natives and foreigners.

Having deprived her of this first right of a citizen, the elective franchise, thereby leaving her without representation in the halls of legislation, he has oppressed her on all sides.

He has made her, if married, in the eye of the law, civilly dead.

He has taken from her all right in property, even to the wages she earns.

He has made her, morally, an irresponsible being, as she can commit many crimes with impunity, provided they be done in the presence of her husband. In the covenant of marriage, she is compelled to promise obedience to her husband, he becoming, to all intents and purposes, her master— the law giving him power to deprive her of her liberty, and to administer chastisement.

He has so framed the laws of divorce, as to what shall be the proper causes, and in case of separation, to whom the guardianship of the children shall be given, as to be wholly regardless of the happiness of women—the law, in all cases, going upon a false supposition of the supremacy of man, and giving all power into his hands.

After depriving her of all rights as a married woman, if single, and the owner of property, he has taxed her to support a government which recognizes her only when her property can be made profitable to it.

He has monopolized nearly all the profitable employments, and from those she is permitted to follow, she receives but a scanty remuneration.

He closes against her all the avenues to wealth and distinction which he considers most honorable to himself. As a teacher of theology, medicine, or law, she is not known.

He has denied her the facilities for obtaining a thorough education, all colleges being closed against her.

He allows her in Church, as well as State, but a subordinate position, claiming Apostolic authority for her exclusion from the ministry, and, with some exceptions, from any public participation in the affairs of the Church.

He has created a false public sentiment by giving to the world a different code of morals for men and women, by which moral delinquencies which exclude women from society, are not only tolerated, but deemed of little account in man.

He has usurped the prerogative of Jehovah himself, claiming it as his right to assign for her a sphere of action, when that belongs to her conscience and to her God.

He has endeavored, in every way that he could, to destroy her confidence in her own powers, to lessen her self-respect, and to make her willing to lead a dependent and abject life.

Now, in view of this entire disfranchisement of one-half the people of this country, their social and religious degradation—in view of the unjust laws above mentioned, and because women do feel themselves aggrieved, oppressed, and fraudulently deprived of their most sacred rights, we insist that they have immediate admission to all the rights and privileges which belong to them as citizens of the United States.

In entering upon the great work before us, we anticipate no small amount of misconception, misrepresentation, and ridicule; but we shall use every instrumentality within our power to effect our object. We shall employ agents, circulate tracts, petition the State and National legislatures, and endeavor to enlist the pulpit and the press in our behalf. We hope this Convention will be followed by a series of Conventions embracing every part of the country.

1898

THE DEVELOPMENT OF NARRATIVE

Every society, as it develops, produces a series of images and narratives that in some sense become the common property of its members. These "myths" and "legends" serve a variety of functions in the society: they can offer an explanation of its physical and cultural origins; justify its hierarchies and other public arrangements; explain its beliefs, its rituals, its standards of morality and value; and express its hopes as well as its fears. They present images of what the society regards as valued and deplored behavior, as in the stories of Miriam and of Cain and Abel in the Bible. They express what are often deep psychological and social conflicts, as in the story of Oedipus. They offer characters whom generations of readers can comfortably laugh at—as in "The Legend of Sleepy Hollow"—or can admire—as in "The Purloined Letter."

The origins of early tales, legends, and images are a matter of considerable speculation, but they probably emerge from an interaction of historical events, individual creations, and what the society comes to feel is of value. No doubt, too, whatever the initial form of a story, as it gets told and retold it is gradually developed, embellished, and altered over time, taking on the qualities of a legend, before it assumes a more or less definitive shape. Particularly in preliterate cultures (i.e., cultures in which writing has not been developed), even well-developed myths seem to change over time as the conditions of life change. Divergent, indeed conflicting, myths can coexist within a culture, at least for a while. Different groups within a society construct and pass on stories they prefer. Ultimately the stories of the dominant group in a society themselves may come to dominate, though alternate myths often continue to live a kind of "underground" existence, offering a form of resistance to cultural extinction, especially among oppressed minorities.

The creation of myths is not a phenomenon of the dim past. They continue to be produced by accident and by design in any living society. The Terminator is a contemporary example of a consciously created legendary character designed to express the unfulfilled desires of some American men. The strong, silent cowboy, familiar to us from the movies, was a similar invention of late-nineteenth-century male writers. The creators of such characters were, in effect, posing them as embodiments of what they saw as significant social values, and they are generally set against other figures who embody alternative values. Such was the case, for example, with Cooper's Leather-stocking, whose outlook on nature and human society contrasted sharply with that of the settlers. Whether over time such tales assume the proportions of true myths depends, in part, on how useful and significant they continue to be in the long-range cultural life of a society.

Myths, whatever their forms, are not expected to be "realistic"—that is, they do not depend for their impact on being "true to life" in any literal way. The Terminator version of combat is, of course, as removed from reality as are the tall tales of Paul Bunyan or Mike Fink's "Brags" (printed below). The legendary exploits of the lone cowboy belied the harsh, boring conditions of his actual existence. Certain features of Leather-stocking's character and experiences are rooted in historic figures like David Crockett and Daniel Boone, but legends take on a life of their own, increasingly distant from whatever historic roots they had. The appeal of such tales is not that they did or could happen but that they express desires or fears or values held by some number of people in a culture; others, who do not share such emotions, may find them remote or even silly, as indeed, many have found Leather-stocking and the Terminator and the lone cowhand.

The variety of stories gathered here represents some of the differing cultures that were coming in the early nineteenth century to constitute American literature. Their differences tell us not only about the ideas and styles of individual authors but about the values and outlooks of these heterogeneous groups. The Objibwe myths presented by Jane Johnston Schoolcraft (in the section "The Emergence of American Poetic Voices") and the tale about Mike Fink relate combat between larger-than-life figures; but the conflicts embody diverse worldviews and societies, and the stories served distinct functions in their cultures. Even when members of the same society, like Cooper and Sedgwick, write about the same subject—the relationships of Indians and whites—their views and images can be significantly distinct and, of course, quite at variance with those of the Indians themselves. It is important to be aware of such differences, their sources, and their significance.

The creation of myths, tales, and legends is not confined to preliterate societies. In fact, some of the most long-lasting and familiar figures of American literature are mythic characters that emerge in early-nineteenth-century fiction. Aside from Cooper's Leather-stocking, there are fictional people like Irving's Ichabod Crane, the repellant schoolmaster with the appetite of an anaconda, and his nemesis, Brom Bones, one of the first in a long line of American male adolescents whose calling in life seems to be the torment of pedagogues. There are the heartless scientists of Hawthorne and their daft counterparts in Poe. There are Stowe's icons, some of whose very names—Uncle Tom, Simon Legree—have come into the language as nouns.

But at what point, and in what ways, does the creation of tales and myths flower into a national literature? It has generally been argued, certainly since F. O. Matthiessen's 1941 book, *American Renaissance*, that that flowering took place in the 1840s and 1850s, with the emergence of Hawthorne, Melville, and perhaps Poe—presumed to be the "major" successors to Irving and Cooper. It was also generally assumed that almost everything else written at the time could be placed in the category of "popular" fiction, whose leading practitioner was Harriet Beecher Stowe. The problem with this account is not only that it dismisses Stowe and many other white women and black writers, but that it is inaccurate because it loses the richness of literary production in the period in the large shadows cast by the "major" figures. The strength of Hawthorne, Melville, and Poe as writers does not at all depend on obscuring their contemporaries. On the contrary, seeing them more fully in the context of the wide range of narratives produced in the decades before the Civil War offers a fresh view of their achievements and at the same time reestablishes the value of the other writers, many of them women, with whom they shared the artistic stage, especially in the 1850s.

In the twentieth century, Hawthorne and Melville were linked as writers and, in turn, contrasted with Harriet Beecher Stowe. The men were friends and read, appreciated, and wrote about each other's work. Unlike Stowe, neither man could really make a decent living by writing; each finally depended on political appointment to survive financially. It is usually argued, too, that Hawthorne's and Melville's concerns and fictional methods were similar: they composed romances about the darker side of human experience, about "sin and sorrow," creating striking symbols—like the scarlet letter, the minister's black veil, and the white whale Moby-Dick—to express the powerful ambiguity of their visions. There is much that is true in this account. Yet seen in the context of their times, the significant differences between Hawthorne and Melville come into focus as sharply as their similarities.

The history of their reputations illustrates the point. From the early 1840s, critics saw Hawthorne as America's "classic" writer of fiction, and he has retained that esteem for more than a century and a half, even though, as Jane Tompkins has pointed out, the measures of a "classic" have changed substantially. Melville, on the other hand, was regarded by his contemporaries as something of a failed teller of South Seas island tales, was largely forgotten from the beginning of the Civil War until the 1920s, and then was rapidly revived as the country's preeminent novelist.

In fact, if we view Hawthorne's longer fiction together with that being written by the "mob of scribbling women" he often deplored, their similarities are striking—as is their distance from Melville and Poe. Like Hawthorne, women writers, such as Stowe in *The Minister's Wooing* and Alice Cary or Elizabeth Drew Stoddard in stories like those in this section, focused on social and sexual interactions of people not unlike ourselves, living in relatively familiar contemporary or recognizable historical settings. They were concerned with matters like desire, jealousy, property, marriage, careers—"love and money," as Jane Austen put it. In short, they wrote fiction about society—some realistic, some touched with the imaginative moonlight of what Hawthorne termed the "romance."

To be sure, women like Cary and Caroline Kirkland, among others, were less drawn to elaborate symbols or allegory than Hawthorne. And they generally composed in a plainer, somewhat conversational style. They had learned a realistic approach to writing about everyday events from predecessors like the British writer of village sketches, Mary Russell Mitford, little known to American readers today. Kirkland and Cary helped extend the influence of this realistic strategy through the literary salons they convened at their New York homes in the 1850s. Indeed, realism became the dominant approach of many women writers, especially when their subject was domestic life.

Such "domestic" fiction reached a wide, predominantly female audience. The development of the power-driven rotary press in the 1840s enabled the circulation of hundreds of thousands of copies of successful novels in the next decade. Many, though by no means all, of these were written by women, for whom novel writing offered a whole new line of work. They knew their audience: women much like themselves often seeking through the reading of fiction to extend their experience beyond the shut doors of their middle-class homes. Many of these books offered an ideology that supported the virtues of domesticity and, within that, images of female steadfastness and strength. Some appear to today's reader as heavily sentimental, focused on the tearfully difficult story of a girl alone in *The Wide, Wide World*—to use the title of Susan Warner's best seller. Others, however, were presented with the humor of a Fanny Fern and the moral intensity represented by Stowe in *The Minister's Wooing*. Despite their popularity and the critical respect they received in the 1850s, women like Stowe, E.D.E.N. Southworth, Susan Warner, and Alice Cary suffered an even longer eclipse than did Melville; they were only rediscovered and reprinted in response to the concerns of the women's movement of the 1960s and 1970s.

By contrast with this more realistic tradition, the fiction of Melville and Poe was influenced by the extravagances of "Gothic" novels, with their remote settings, unlikely events, larger-than-life characters, and ambience of hallucination, danger, and fear. Their often mysterious worlds are inhabited largely by men, few of whom we would ordinarily encounter in everyday life—elements that may help to explain the limits of their popularity with a largely female readership of fiction in the 1850s. Their language is often as fanciful as their settings and characters. Particularly in his long fiction, Melville spreads a wide and colorful canvas before us, laced with many dark and ambiguous shadows. His political concerns with slavery and racism, or with the oppression of women, are akin to Stowe's, though rather at variance with the conservative views of his friend Hawthorne. To be sure, Melville's later work approaches political issues obliquely, unlike Stowe, who generally tackles them head-on.

Still other writers found models in the broad panorama of events and personages drawn in British eighteenth-century adventure novels like Henry Fielding's *Tom Jones*, in the contemporary works of Charles Dickens, or in American historical narratives of travel to exotic climes such as California, as in Richard Henry Dana's *Two Years Before the Mast*. In terms of scope, eventfulness of action, and variety of characters, Stowe's *Uncle Tom's Cabin* or, less successfully, Southworth's *The Hidden Hand*, reflects such influences. *Uncle Tom's Cabin*, shaped by both "domestic" and "adventure" traditions, was itself instrumental in stimulating black novelists, like William Wells Brown, as well as a host of attempted "answers" to Stowe's indictment of slavery. Black authors had long composed autobiographical slave narratives; only in the 1850s, however, did they begin to write fiction, like Brown's *Clotel* and Harper's "The Two Offers," and autobiographically based narratives like Harriet Wilson's *Our Nig*, perhaps because a market had emerged or perhaps because they appreciated the value of *Uncle Tom's Cabin* in the struggle against slavery and racism.

As we can see, then, in the decades before the Civil War, narratives developed along a number of lines and in a variety of forms. This section is designed to suggest something of that diversity, in its strengths and weaknesses, as well as to convey a rich picture of the period's fiction.

Paul Lauter
Trinity College

Humor of the Old Southwest

SOUTHWEST HUMOR THRIVES ON BORDERS. IT GREW ON A BORDER, THE OLD Southwest frontier that before the Civil War ran through what is now the Southeast and then was generally identified with Southern (rather than Western) attitudes. As writing, it crossed the border with orality, coming from storytelling and in turn shaping the telling of tales. (In fact, the selections included here are well worth reading aloud.) It straddles the line, too, between "popular" and "high" literature; it appeared in newspapers and almanacs, in popular theater, and then in Mark Twain and William Faulkner. It lives on the border of realism, presenting as sober reality material that may be wildly exaggerated or clearly fantastic. Although almost exclusively the domain of white men, Southwest humor crosses traditional boundaries of gender as well, if only in one direction: some of its later ringtailed roarers are women. And it crosses cultural boundaries; it represents both genteel and frontier values, and it can mock and subvert either or both. From its place on so many borders, this style of humor has maintained a vitality that continues to excite interest in contemporary readers.

The two voices in George Washington Harris's "Dedicatory" to his 1867 *Sut Lovingood* speak across several divides. Sut's hope to womanize with his writing opposes his friend's ideas about what is appropriate for a lady; Sut's language is as defiantly nonstandard as his friend's is aggressively conventional, and Sut's morality is as Machiavellian as his friend's is pious. Yet despite the attacks on "decent s'ciety," the piece seems clearly written for an audience of exactly such folk.

Sut Lovingood, who made his first book appearance in 1867, is the latecomer in this anthology's group of Southwest humorists. By then, this type of humor had already enjoyed its heyday, roughly the thirty years prior to the Civil War. One of the earliest practitioners, David Crockett (with the help of a ghostwriter) wrote the *Narrative* of his life as a campaign strategy when he was running for office in 1835. Most, if not all, of the rest of the Crockett writings come not from his pen but from numerous folk who wrote out of and thus contributed to the creation of the legendary Davy. The real David Crockett was born in Tennessee (though not on a mountaintop and metamorphosed into Davy, the legendary woodsman whose revival in the 1950s brought coontail hats and the popular "Ballad of Davy Crockett" into thousands of American homes. As a young man, David Crockett fought Indians under Andrew Jackson (whose policies he was later to oppose). He ran for and won a seat in the Tennessee state legislature in 1821; in 1827 he won a seat in Congress. By 1831 the legend-making had begun: James Kirke Paulding's *The Lion of the West* had as its leading character one Nimrod Wildfire, based on Crockett, and in 1833 Mathew St. Clair Clarke's *Life and Adventures of Colonel David Crockett of West Tennessee*, more famously reprinted as *Sketches and Eccentricities of Colonel David Crockett of West Tennessee*, was in print. After his heroic death at the Alamo in 1836, Crockett's fame spread through songs, poems, almanacs (known as Crockett Almanacs), plays, and silent movies. The year 1955 saw the Disney-inspired Crockett craze, and in 1986 his bicentennial was celebrated.

"Sunrise in His Pocket," taken from the posthumous *Crockett Almanacs* and clearly not attributable to David, shows the exuberant exaggeration typical of the tall-tale teller and hero Davy was made into. "A Pretty Predicament" and "Crockett's Daughters" simultaneously subvert cultural norms for women and perpetuate racial stereotyping.

The *Crockett Almanacs* contain stories about another legendary hero of the Old Southwest, Mike Fink. Although there is no evidence that Fink wrote down any stories himself, he apparently told them often and well. The earliest to claim to have heard and recorded Fink was Morgan Neville, whose *The Last of the Boatmen* appeared in 1829. Fink was a keelboatman on the Mississippi River. Before taking to the river, he had worked, like Crockett, as an Indian scout; when he left the river, it was to move west as a trapper, where he died in the wilderness. Fink's exploits led him to be called (or to call himself) "half-horse, half-alligator." Born around 1770 near Fort Pitt, Pennsylvania, Mike Fink had already earned a reputation for bravery and marksmanship when he took work poling keelboats, a sort of barge, down and up the Mississippi. On the river, his violence, his brutal jokes, his competitive spirit, and his love life earned him legendary status. In 1822 Fink left for the west as a trapper; he may have died in the manner described in our account from Joseph M. Field in the *St. Louis Reveille* (1844). "Mike Fink Trying to Scare Mrs. Crockett" provides an interesting counterpoint to "Fink's Brag," and comes from the *Crockett Almanacs*, as does the story about Mike's daughter Sal Fink, "The Mississippi Screamer."

The first examples of literary rather than folkloristic Southwest humor came from a Georgia lawyer, judge, politician, minister, and secessionist, Augustus Baldwin Longstreet. An energetic and restless man, Longstreet was born in Augusta, Georgia. A friend of John C. Calhoun, Longstreet followed him to Yale and then into the law, which he practiced back home in Georgia. There he began *Georgia Scenes*; he published his first story in a Milledgeville paper in 1832. By 1838 Longstreet had taken on another profession: Methodist minister. In 1839 he took the presidency of Emory College and after ten years moved to preside at Centenary College, followed by the University of Mississippi and the University of South Carolina. Longstreet's convictions and predilections remained typical for his class and region; he advocated secession and refused to attend an International Statistical Congress in London because of the presence of a black delegate.

The stories in *Georgia Scenes* are set in northeast Georgia, and Longstreet claimed that they represent "*real* incidents and characters" and "supply a chasm in history ... the [Southern] society of the first thirty years of the republic." Edgar Allan Poe reviewed it in the *Southern Literary Messenger* for March 1836, and the stories have since enjoyed considerable success. "The Horse Swap"

SUT LOVINGOOD.
YARNS SPUN
by a
"NAT'RAL BORN DURN'D FOOL.
WARPED AND WOVE FOR PUBLIC WEAR.
by
GEORGE W. HARRIS.
DEDICATORY.

───────

"Well, Sut, your stories are all ready for the printer; to whom do you wish to dedicate the work?"

"I don't keer much, George; haint hit a kine ove lickskillet bisness, enyhow—sorter like the waggin ove a dorg's tail, when he sees yu eatin ove sassengers? But yere goes: How wud Anner Dickinson du tu pack hit ontu?"

"Oh, Sut, that would never do. What! dedicate such nonsense as yours to a woman? How will this do?

DEDICATED TO
THE MEMORY OF
ELBRIDGE GERRY EASTMAN,
THE ABLE EDITOR, AND FINISHED GENTLEMAN, THE FRIEND, WHOSE KINDLY
VOICE FIRST INSPIRED MY TIMID PEN WITH HOPE.
GRATEFUL MEMORY
DROPS A TEAR AMONG THE FLOWERS, AS AFFECTION STREWS THEM
O'ER HIS GRAVE."

"Won't begin tu du, George. The idear ove enybody bein grateful, ur rememberin a dead friend now-a-days! Why, if that wer tu git out onto me, I'd never be able tu mix in decent s'ciety while I lived. Tare that up, George."

"Well, what do you say to this, Sut?

TO
WILLIAM CRUTCHFIELD, OF CHATTANOOGA,
MY FRIEND IN STORM AND SUNSHINE, BRAVE ENOUGH TO BE TRUE, AND TRUE
ENOUGH TO BE SINGULAR; ONE WHO SAYS WHAT HE THINKS,
AND VERY OFTEN THINKS WHAT HE SAYS."

"That won't du either, hoss. 'Tis mos' es bad tu be grateful tu the livin es the dead. I tell yu hit ain't smart. Ef ever yu is grateful *at all*, show hit tu them what yu *expeck will* du a favor, *never* tu the 'tarnil fool what *hes dun hit.* Never es yu expeck tu git tu heaven, *never pay fur a ded hoss.* An' more, every fice ur houn dorg what either him ur me has wallop'd fur thar nastiness, wud open ontu our trail—ontu him fur buyin me, an' ontu me fur bein bought. No, George, I'll do ontill Bill gets poor ur dus sum devilmint. I'll tell yu what I'll du, I'll jis' dedercate this yere perduction *tu the durndest fool* in the United States, an' Massachusets too, he or she. An then, by golly, I'll jis' watch hu claims hit."

"Very well, Sut; how shall I write it? how designate the proper one?"

"Jis' this way; hits the easiest dun thing in the world:

DEDERCATED
WIF THE SYMPERTHYS OVE THE ORTHUR,
TU THE MAN UR 'OMAN, HUEVER THEY BE,
WHAT *DON'T* READ THIS YERE BOOK.

Don't *that* kiver the case tu a dot? Hu knows but what I'se dedercatin hit tu mysef at las'. Well, I don't keer a durn, I kin stan hit, ef the rest ove em kin."

represents a situation that Faulkner would draw upon in "Spotted Horses" and *The Hamlet*. For Longstreet, it offers an opportunity to represent, and through the narration to comment upon, the conflict between frontier and genteel values, particularly as they concern the meaning of lying. Longstreet's use of a genteel narrator to frame the story is far more typical of the genre than Harris's later and more radical choice of a vernacular voice—Sut's—almost entirely free of framing.

George Washington Harris, like Longstreet both a talented and a restless man, was born in Pennsylvania but moved as a child to Tennessee, where he developed a fierce loyalty to the South. Like Longstreet, he argued for secession; he wrote opposing Lincoln, Yankees, and Republicans in various newspapers. Harris worked in metal, captained a steamboat, farmed, superintended a glassworks, worked as postmaster and alderman of Knoxville, Tennessee, worked for the railroad—and wrote. Sut stories began to appear in *Spirit of the Times* as early as 1843, though the volume of *Yarns* did not appear until 1867. Harris died in 1869 on a journey home from Lynchburg, Virginia, to arrange publication of his second book. *High Times and Hard Times* finally appeared 100 years after *Sut Lovingood*, in 1967. "Mrs. Yardley's Quilting Party" shows the character of Sut that led Faulkner to praise him in a *Paris Review* interview: "He had no illusions about himself, did the best he could; at certain times he was a coward and knew it and wasn't ashamed; he never blamed his misfortunes on anyone and never cursed God for them." Faulkner does not mention Sut's raucous, sometimes malicious brutality, but surely made use of it as well. The quilting story is of particular interest to feminists for several reasons: for the treatment of women, and for what it suggests—by means of Sut's profound desire to disrupt it—about the power of the quilting party.

Anne G. Jones
Allegheny College

PRIMARY WORKS

Mathew St. Claire Clarke [?], *Sketches and Eccentricities of Col. David Crockett, of West Tennessee*, 1833; Thomas Chilton, *A Narrative of the Life of David Crockett*, 1834, James A. Shackford and Stanley J. Folmsbee, eds., 1973; *Georgia Scenes*, 1835, Richard Harwell, ed., 1975; Anon., *The Crockett Almanacs*, 1835–1856; *Sut Lovingood. Yarns Spun by a "Nat'ral Born Durn'd Fool.["] Warped and Wove for Public Wear*, 1967; M. Thomas Inge, ed., [1868] 1988; J. Donald Wade, *Augustus Baldwin Longstreet*, 1924, M. Thomas Inge, ed., 1969; Constance M. Rourke, *Davy Crockett*, 1934; Richard M. Dorson, ed., *Davy Crockett, American Comic Legend*, 1939; Walter Blair and Franklin J. Meine, *Half Horse, Half Alligator: The Growth of the Mike Fink Legend*, 1956; James M. Shackford, *David Crockett, the Man and the Legend*, 1956; Ben H. McClary, ed., *The Lovingood Papers*, 1962–1965; Milton Rickels, *George Washington Harris*, 1965; M. Thomas Inge, ed., *High Times and Hard Times: Sketches and Tales by GWH*, 1967; Michael A. Lofaro, ed., *Davy Crockett: The Man, the Legend, the Legacy, 1786–1986*, 1985.

DAVY CROCKETT
1786–1836

from **The Crockett Almanacs**

Sunrise in His Pocket

One January morning it was so all screwen cold that the forest trees were stiff and they couldn't shake, and the very daybreak froze fast as it was trying to dawn. The tinder box in my cabin would no more ketch fire than a sunk raft at the bottom of the sea. Well, seein' daylight war so far behind time I thought creation war in a fair way for freezen fast: so, thinks I, I must strike a little fire from my fingers, light my pipe, an' travel out a few leagues, and see about it. Then I brought my knuckles together like two thunderclouds, but the sparks froze up afore I could begin to collect 'em, so out I walked, whistlin' "Fire in the mountains!" as I went along in three double quick time. Well, arter I had walked about twenty miles up the Peak O'Day and Daybreak Hill I soon discovered what war the matter. The airth had actually friz fast on her axes, and couldn't turn round; the sun had got jammed between two cakes o' ice under the wheels, an' thar he had been shinin' an' workin' to get loose till he friz fast in his cold sweat. C-r-e-a-t-i-o-n! thought I, this ar the toughest sort of suspension, an' it mustn't be endured. Somethin' must be done, or human creation is done for. It war then so anteluvian an' premature cold that my upper and lower teeth an' tongue war all collapsed together as tight as a friz oyster; but I took a fresh twenty-pound bear off my back that I'd picked up on my road, and beat the animal agin the ice till the hot ile began to walk out on him at all sides. I then took an' held him over the airth's axes an' squeezed him till I'd thawed 'em loose, poured about a ton on't over the sun's face, give the airth's cog-wheel one kick backward till I got the sun loose—whistled "Push along, keep movin'!" an' in about fifteen seconds the airth gave a grunt, an' began movin'. The sun walked up beautiful, salutin' me with sich a wind o' gratitude that it made me sneeze. I lit my pipe by the blaze o' his top-knot, shouldered my bear, an' walked home, introducin' people to the fresh daylight with a piece of sunrise in my pocket.

1835–1856

A Pretty Predicament

When I was a big boy, that had jist begun to go a galling, I got astray in the woods one arternoon; and being wandering about a good deel, and got pretty considerable soaked by a grist of rain, I sot down on to a stump, and begun to wring out my leggin's, and shake the drops off of my raccoon cap.

Whilst I was on the stump, I got kind of sleepy, and so laid my head back in the crotch of a young tree that growed behind me, and shot up my eyes. I had laid out of doors for many a night before, with a sky blanket over me—so I got to sleep pretty soon, and fell to snoring most beautiful. So somehow, or somehow else, I did not wake till near sundown; and I don't know when I should have waked, had it not been for somebody tugging at my hair. As soon as I felt this, though I wan't more than half awake, I begun to feel to see if my thum' nail was on, as that was all the ammunition I had about me. I lay still, to see what the feller would be at. The first idee I had was that a cussed Ingun was fixing to take off my scalp; so I thought I'd wait till I begun to feel the pint of his knife scraping against the skin, and then I should have full proof agin him, and could jerk out his copper-coloured liver with the law all on my side. At last I felt such a hard twitch, that I roared right out, but when I found my head was squeezed so tight in the crotch that I could not get it out, I felt like a gone sucker. I felt raal ridiculous, I can assure you; so I began to talk to the varmint, and told him to help me get my head out, like a man, and I would give him five dollars before I killed him.

At last my hair begun to come out by the roots, and then I was mad to be took advantage of in that way. I swore at the varmint, till the tree shed all its leaves, and the sky turned yaller. So, in a few minutes, I heerd a voice, and then a gall cum running up, and axed what was the matter. She soon saw what was to pay, and told me that the eagles were tearing out my hair to build nests with. I told her I had endured more than a dead possum could stand already, and that if she would drive off the eagles, I would make her a present of an iron comb.

"That I will," says she; "for I am a she steamboat, and have doubled up a crocodile in my day."

So she pulled up a small sapling by the roots, and went to work as if she hadn't another minnit to live. She knocked down two of the varmints, and screamed the rest out of sight. Then I told her the predicament I was in; and she said she would loosen the hold that the crotch had on my head. So she took and reached out her arm into a rattlesnake's hole, and pulled out three or four of them. She tied 'em awl together, and made a strong rope out of 'em. She tied one eend of the snakes to the top of one branch, and pulled as if she was trying to haul the multiplication table apart. The tightness about my head began to be different altogether, and I hauled out my cocoanut, though I left a piece of one of my ears behind.

As soon as I was clear, I could not tell which way to look for the sun, and I was afeared I should fall into the sky, for I did not know which way was up, and which way was down. Then I looked at the gal that had got me loose—she was a strapper: she was as tall as a sapling, and had an arm like a keel boat's tiller. So I looked at her like all wrath, and as she cum down from the tree, I says to her:

"I wish I may be utterly onswoggled if I don't know how to hate an Ingun or love a gal as well as any he this side of roaring river. I fell in love with three gals at once at a log rolling, and as for tea squalls my heart never shut pan for a minnit at a time; so if you will marry me, I will forgive the tree and the eagles for your sake."

Then she turned as white as an egg-shell, and I seed that her heart was busting, and I run up to her, like a squirrel to his hole, and gave her a buss that sounded louder than a musket. So her spunk was all gone, and she took my arm as tame as a pigeon, and we cut out for her father's house. She complained that I hung too heavy on her arm, for I was enermost used up after laying so long between the branches. So she took up a stone that would weigh about fifty pound, and put it in her pocket on the other side to balance agin my weight, and so she moved along as upright as a steamboat. She told me that her Sunday bonnet was a hornet's nest garnished with wolves' tails and eagles' feathers, and that she wore a bran new goun, made of a whole bear's-hide, the tail serving for a train. She said she could drink of the branch without a cup, could shoot a wild goose flying, and wade the Mississippi without wetting herself. She said she could not play on the piane, nor sing like a nightingale, but she could outscream a catamount and jump over her own shadow; she had good strong horse sense and new a woodchuck from a skunk. So I was pleased with her, and offered her all my plunder if she would let me split the difference and call her Mrs. Crockett.

She kinder said she must insult her father before she went so fur as to marry. So she took me into another room to introduce me to another beau that she had. He was setting on the edge of a grindstone at the back part of the room with his heels on the mantel-piece! He had the skullbone of a catamount for a snuff-box, and he was dressed like he had been used to seeing hard times. I got a side squint into one of his pockets, and saw it was full of eyes that had been gouged from people of my acquaintance. I knew my jig was up, for such a feller could outcourt me, and I thort the gal brot me in on proppus to have a fight. So I turned off, and threatened to call agin; and I cut through the bushes like a pint of whiskey among forty men.

1835–1856

Crockett's Daughters

I always had the praise o' raisin the tallest and fattest, and sassyest gals in all America. They can out-run, out-jump, out-fight, and out-scream any crittur in creation; and for scratchin', thar's not a hungry painter, or a patent horse-rake can hold a claw to 'em.

The oldest one growed so etarnally tall that her head had got nearly out o' sight, when she got into an all-thunderin' fight with a thunder storm that stunted her growth, and now I am afraid that she'll never reach her natural size. Still, it takes a hull winter's weavin' to make her walkin' and bed clothes; and when she goes to bed, she's so tarnal long, and sleeps so sound, that we can only waken her by degrees, and that's by chopping fire wood on her shins.

An' I guess I shall never forget how all horrificaciously flumexed a hull party of Indians war, the time they surprised and seized my middle darter,

Thebeann, when she war out gatherin' birch bark, to make a canoe. The var-mints knew as soon as they got hold of her that she war one of my breed, by her thunderbolt kickin', and they determined to cook half of her and eat the other half alive, out of revenge for the many lickin's I gin 'em. At last they concluded to tie her to a tree, and kindle a fire around her. But they couldn't come it, for while they war gone for wood, a lot of painters that war looking on at the cowardly work, war so gal-vanised an' pleased with the gal's true grit that they formed a guard around her, and wouldn't allow the red niggers to come within smellin' distance; they actually gnawed her loose, an' 'scorted her half way home.

But the youngest o' my darters takes arter me, and is of the regular earth-quake natur. Her body's flint rock, her soul's lightnin, her fist is a thunderbolt, and her teeth can out-cut any steam-mill saw in creation. She is a parfect infant prodigy, being only six years old; she has the biggest foot and widest mouth in all the west, and when she grins, she is splendifferous; she shows most beautiful intarnals, and can scare a flock o' wolves to total terrifications.

Well, one day, my sweet little infant was walking in the woods, and amus-ing herself by picking up walnuts, and cracking them with her front grind-stones, when suddenaciously she stumbled over an almitey great hungry he-barr. The critter seein' her fine red shoulders bare, sprung at her as if deter-mined to feast upon Crockett meat. He gin her a savaggerous hug, and was jist about biting a regular buss out on her cheek, when the child, resentin' her insulted vartue, gin him a kick with her south fist in his digestion that made him hug the arth instanterly. Jist as he war a-comin' to her a second time, the little gal grinned sich a double streak o' blue lightnin into his mouth that it cooked the critter to death as quick as think. She brought him home for dinner.

She'll be a thunderin' fine gal when she gets her nateral growth, if her stock o' Crockett lightnin don't burst her biler, and blow her up.

1835–1856

MIKE FINK
1770?–1823?

from **The Crockett Almanacs**

Mike Fink's Brag

I'm a Salt River roarer! I'm a ring-tailed squealer! I'm a reg'lar screamer from the ol' Massassip'! WHOOP! I'm the very infant that refused his milk before its eyes were open, and called out for a bottle of old Rye! I love the women an' I'm chockful o' fight! I'm half wild horse and half cock-eyed alligator and the rest o' me is crooked snags an' red-hot snappin' turtle. I can hit like fourth-proof lightnin' an' every lick I make in the woods lets in an acre o' sunshine. I can out-run, out-jump, out-shoot, out-brag, out-drink, an' out-fight, rough-an'-tumble, no holts barred, ary man on both sides the river from Pittsburgh to New Orleans an' back ag'in to St. Louiee. Come on, you flatters, you bargers, you milk-white mechanics, an' see how tough I am to chaw! I ain't had a fight for two days an' I'm spilein' for exercise. Cock-a-doodle-do!

1835–1856

Sal Fink, the Mississippi Screamer How She Cooked Injuns

I dar say you've all on you, if not more, frequently heerd this great she human crittur boasted of, an' pointed out as *"one o' the gals"*—but I tell you what, stranger, you have never really set your eyes on *"one of the gals,"* till you have seen Sal Fink, the Mississippi screamer, whose miniature pictur I here give, about as nat'ral as life, but not half as handsome—an' if thar ever was a gal that desarved to be christened *"one o' the gals,"* then this gal was that gal—and no mistake.

She fought a duel once with a thunderbolt, an' came off without a single, while at the fust fire she split the thunderbolt all to flinders, an' gave the pieces to Uncle Sam's artillerymen, to touch off their canon with. When a gal about six years old, she used to play see-saw on the Mississippi snags, and arter she war done she would snap 'em off, an' so cleared a large district of the river. She used to ride down the river on an alligator's back, standen upright, an' dancing *Yankee Doodle*, and could leave all the steamers behind. But the greatest feat she ever did, positively outdid anything that ever was did.

One day when she war out in the forest, making a collection o' wild cat skins for her family's winter beddin, she war captered in the most all-sneaken manner by about fifty Injuns, an' carried by 'em to Roast flesh Hollow, whar the blood drinkin wild varmits determined to skin her alive, sprinkle a leetle salt over her, an' devour her before her own eyes; so they took an' tied her to a tree, to keep till mornin' should bring the rest o' thar ring-nosed sarpints to enjoy the fun. Arter that, they lit a large fire in the Holler, turned the bottom o' thar feet towards the blaze, Injun fashion, and went to sleep to dream o' thar mornin's feast; well, after the critturs got into a somniferous snore, Sal got into an all-lightnin' of a temper, and burst all the ropes about her like an apron-string! She then found a pile o' ropes, too, and tied all the Injun's heels together all round the fire,—then fixin a cord to the shins of every two couple, she, with a suddenachous jerk, that made the intire woods tremble, pulled the intire lot o' sleepin' red-skins into that ar great fire, fast together, an' then sloped like a panther out of her pen, in the midst o' the tallest yellin, howlin, scramblin and singin', that war ever seen or heerd on, since the great burnin' o' Buffalo prairie!

1853

Augustus Baldwin Longstreet
1790–1870

The Horse Swap

During the session of the Superior Court, in the village of——, about three weeks ago, when a number of people were collected in the principal street of the village, I observed a young man riding up and down the street, as I supposed, in a violent passion. He galloped this way, then that, and then the other. Spurred his horse to one group of citizens, then to another. Then dashed off at half speed, as if fleeing from danger; and suddenly checking his horse, returned—first in a pace, then in a trot, and then in a canter. While he was performing these various evolutions, he cursed, swore, whooped, screamed, and tossed himself in every attitude which man could assume on horse back. In short, he *cavorted* most magnanimously, (a term which, in our tongue, expresses all that I have described, and a little more) and seemed to be setting all creation at defiance. As I like to see all that is passing, I determined to take a position a little nearer to him, and to ascertain if possible, what it was that affected him so sensibly. Accordingly I approached a crowd before which he had stopt for a moment, and examined it with the strictest scrutiny.—But I could see nothing in it, that seemed to have any thing to do with the cavorter. Every man appeared to be in a good humor, and all minding their own business. Not one so much as noticed the principal figure. Still he went on. After a semicolon pause, which my appearance seemed to produce, (for he eyed me closely as I approached) he fetched a whoop, and swore that "he could out-swap any live man, woman or child, that ever walked these hills, or that ever straddled horse flesh since the days of old daddy Adam." "Stranger," said he to me, "did you ever see the *Yellow Blossom* from Jasper?"

"No," said I, "but I have often heard of him."

"I'm the boy," continued he; "perhaps a *leetle*—jist a *leetle* of the best man, at a horse swap, that ever trod shoe-leather."

I began to feel my situation a little awkward, when I was relieved by a man somewhat advanced in years, who stept up and began to survey the "*Yellow Blossom's*" horse with much apparent interest. This drew the rider's attention, and he turned the conversation from me to the stranger.

"Well, my old coon," said he, "do you want to swap *hosses?*"

"Why, I don't know," replied the stranger; "I believe I've got a beast I'd trade with you for that one, if you like him."

"Well, fetch up your nag, my old cock; you're jist the lark I wanted to get hold of. I am perhaps a *leetle*, jist a *leetle*, of the best man at a horse swap, that ever stole *cracklins* out of his mammy's fat gourd. Where's your *hoss?*"

"I'll bring him presently; but I want to examine your horse a little."

"Oh! look at him," said the Blossom, alighting and hitting him a cut—
"look at him. He's the best piece of *hoss* flesh in the thirteen united universal worlds. There's no sort o' mistake in little Bullet. He can pick up miles
on his feet and fling 'em behind him as fast as the next man's *hoss*, I don't
care where he comes from.—And he can keep at it as long as the Sun can
shine without resting."

During this harangue, little Bullet looked as if he understood it all,
believed it, and was ready at any moment to verify it. He was a horse of
goodly countenance, rather expressive of vigilance than fire; though an
unnatural appearance of fierceness was thrown into it, by the loss of his
ears, which had been cropt pretty close to his head. Nature had done but little for Bullet's head and neck; but he managed, in a great measure, to hide
their defects, by bowing perpetually. He had obviously suffered severely for
corn; but if his ribs and hip bones had not disclosed the fact, *he* never would
have done it; for he was in all respects, as cheerful and happy, as if he commanded all the corn-cribs and fodder stacks in Georgia. His height was
about twelve hands; but as his shape partook somewhat of that of the Giraffe, his haunches stood much lower. They were short, straight, peaked and
concave. Bullet's tail, however, made amends for all his defects. All that the
artist could do to beautify it, had been done; and all that horse could do to
compliment the artist, Bullet did. His tail was nicked in superior style, and
exhibited the line of beauty in so many directions, that it could not fail to
hit the most fastidious taste in some of them. From the root it dropt into a
graceful festoon; then rose in a handsome curve; then resumed its first
direction; and then mounted suddenly upwards like a cypress knee to a perpendicular of about two and a half inches. The whole had a careless and
bewitching inclination to the right. Bullet obviously knew where his beauty
lay, and took all occasions to display it to the best advantage. If a stick
cracked, or if any one moved suddenly about him, or coughed, or hawked,
or spoke a little louder than common, up went Bullet's tail like lightning;
and if the *going up* did not please, the *coming down* must of necessity, for it
was as different from the other movement, as was its direction. The first,
was a bold and rapid flight upward; usually to an angle of forty-five
degrees. In this position he kept his interesting appendage, until he satisfied himself that nothing in particular was to be done; when he commenced dropping it by half inches, in second beats—then in triple time—
then faster and shorter, and faster and shorter still; until it finally died
away imperceptibly into its natural position. If I might compare sights to
sounds, I should say, its *settling*, was more like the note of a locust than
any thing else in nature.

Either from native sprightliness of disposition, from uncontrollable activity, or from an unconquerable habit of removing flies by the stamping of
the feet, Bullet never stood still; but always kept up a gentle fly-scaring
movement of his limbs, which was peculiarly interesting.

"I tell you, man," proceeded the Yellow Blossom, "he's the best live hoss
that ever trod the grit of Georgia. Bob Smart knows the hoss. Come here,

Bob, and mount this hoss and show Bullet's motions." Here, Bullet bristled up, and looked as if he had been hunting for Bob all day long, and had just found him. Bob sprang on his back. "Boo-oo-oo!" said Bob, with a fluttering noise of the lips; and away went Bullet, as if in a quarter race, with all his beauties spread in handsome style.

"Now fetch him back," said Blossom. Bullet turned and came in pretty much as he went out.

"Now trot him by." Bullet reduced his tail to "*customary*"—sidled to the right and left airily, and exhibited at least three varieties of trot, in the short space of fifty yards.

"Make him pace!" Bob commenced twitching the bridle and kicking at the same time. These inconsistent movements obviously (and most naturally) disconcerted Bullet; for it was impossible for him to learn, from them, whether he was to proceed or stand still. He started to trot—and was told that wouldn't do. He attempted a canter—and was checked again. He stopt—and was urged to go on. Bullet now rushed into the wide field of experiment, and struck out a gait of his own, that completely turned the tables upon his rider, and certainly deserved a patent. It seemed to have derived its elements from the jig, the minuet and the cotillon. If it was not a pace, it certainly had *pace* in it; and no man would venture to call it any thing else; so it passed off to the satisfaction of the owner.

"Walk him!" Bullet was now at home again; and he walked as if money was staked on him.

The stranger, whose name I afterwards learned was Peter Ketch, having examined Bullet to his heart's content, ordered his son Neddy to go and bring up Kit. Neddy soon appeared upon Kit; a well formed sorrel of the middle size, and in good order. His *tout ensemble* threw Bullet entirely in the shade; though a glance was sufficient to satisfy any one, that Bullet had the decided advantage of him in point of intellect.

"Why man," said Blossom, "do you bring such a hoss as that to trade for Bullet? Oh, I see you've no notion of trading."

"Ride him off, Neddy!" said Peter. Kit put off at a handsome lope.

"Trot him back!" Kit came in at a long, sweeping trot, and stopt suddenly at the crowd.

"Well," said Blossom, "let me look at him; may be he'll do to plough."

"Examine him!" said Peter, taking hold of the bridle close to the mouth; "He's nothing but a tacky. He an't as *pretty* a horse as Bullet, I know; but he'll do. Start 'em together for a hundred and fifty *mile;* and if Kit an't twenty mile ahead of him at the coming out, any man may take Kit for nothing. But he's a monstrous mean horse, gentlemen; any man may see that. He's the scariest horse, too, you ever saw. He won't do to hunt on, no how. Stranger, will you let Neddy have your rifle to shoot off him? Lay the rifle between his ears, Neddy, and shoot at the blaze in that stump. Tell me when his head is high enough."

Ned fired, and hit the blaze; and Kit did not move a hair's breadth.

"Neddy, take a couple of sticks and beat on that hogshead at Kit's tail."

Ned made a tremendous rattling; at which *Bullet* took fright, broke his bridle and dashed off in grand style; and would have stopt all farther negotiations, by going home in disgust, had not a traveller arrested him and brought him back; but Kit did not move.

"I tell you, gentlemen," continued Peter, "he's the scariest horse you ever saw. He an't as gentle as Bullet; but he won't do any harm if you watch him. Shall I put him in a cart, gig, or wagon for you, stranger? He'll cut the same capers there he does here. He's a monstrous mean horse."

During all this time, Blossom was examining him with the nicest scrutiny. Having examined his frame and limbs, he now looked at his eyes.

"He's got a curious look out of his eyes," said Blossom.

"Oh yes, sir," said Peter, "just as blind as a bat. Blind horses always have clear eyes. Make a motion at his eyes, if you please, sir."

Blossom did so, and Kit threw up his head rather as if something pricked him under the chin, than as if fearing a blow. Blossom repeated the experiment, and Kit jirked back in considerable astonishment.

"Stone blind, you see, gentlemen," proceeded Peter; "but he's just as good to travel of a dark night as if he had eyes."

"Blame my buttons," said Blossom, "if I like them eyes."

"No," said Peter, "nor I neither. I'd rather have 'em made of diamonds; but they'll do, if they don't show as much white as Bullet's."

"Well," said Blossom, "make a pass at me."

"No," said Peter; "you made the banter; now make your pass."

"Well, I'm never afraid to price my hosses. You must give me twenty-five dollars boot."

"Oh certainly; say fifty, and my saddle and bridle in. Here, Neddy, my son, take away daddy's horse."

"Well," said Blossom, "I've made my pass; now you make yours."

"I'm for short talk in a horse swap; and therefore always tell a gentleman, at once, what I mean to do. You must give me ten dollars."

Blossom swore absolutely, roundly and profanely, that he never would give boot.

"Well," said Peter, "I didn't care about trading; but you cut such high shines, that I thought I'd like to back you out; and I've done it. Gentlemen, you see I've brought him to a hack."

"Come, old man," said Blossom, "I've been joking with you. I begin to think you do want to trade; therefore, give me five dollars and take Bullet. I'd rather lose ten dollars, any time, than not make a trade; though I hate to fling away a good hoss."

"Well," said Peter, "I'll be as clever as you are. Just put the five dollars on Bullet's back and hand him over, it's a trade."

Blossom swore again, as roundly as before, that he would not give boot; and, said he, "Bullet wouldn't hold five dollars on his back, no how. But as I bantered you, if you say an even swap, here's at you."

"I told you," said Peter, "I'd be as clever as you; therefore, here goes two dollars more, just for trade sake. Give three dollars, and it's a bargain."

Blossom repeated his former assertion; and here the parties stood for a long time, and the by-standers (for many were now collected,) began to taunt both parties. After some time, however, it was pretty unanimously decided that the old man had backed Blossom out.

At length Blossom swore he "never would be backed out, for three dollars, after bantering a man;" and accordingly they closed the trade.

"Now," said Blossom, as he handed Peter the three dollars, "I'm a man, that when he makes a bad trade, makes the most of it until he can make a better. I'm for no rues and after-claps."

"That's just my way," said Peter; "I never goes to law to mend my bargains."

"Ah, you're the kind of boy I love to trade with. Here's your hoss, old man. Take the saddle and bridle off him, and I'll strip yours; but lift up the blanket easy from Bullet's back, for he's a mighty tenderbacked hoss."

The old man removed the saddle, but the blanket stuck fast. He attempted to raise it, and Bullet bowed himself, switched his tail, danced a little, and gave signs of biting.

"Don't hurt him, old man," said Blossom archly; "take it off easy. I am, perhaps, a leetle of the best man at a horse-swap that ever catched a coon."

Peter continued to pull at the blanket more and more roughly; and Bullet became more and more *cavortish:* in so much, that when the blanket came off, he had reached the *kicking* point in good earnest.

The removal of the blanket, disclosed a sore on Bullet's back-bone, that seemed to have defied all medical skill. It measured six full inches in length, and four in breadth; and had as many features as Bullet had motions. My heart sickened at the sight; and I felt that the brute who had been riding him in that situation, deserved the halter.

The prevailing feeling, however, was that of mirth. The laugh became loud and general, at the old man's expense; and rustic witticisms were liberally bestowed upon him and his late purchase. These, Blossom continued to provoke by various remarks. He asked the old man, "if he thought Bullet would let five dollars lie on his back." He declared most seriously, that he had owned that horse three months, and had never discovered before, that he had a sore back, "or he never should have thought of trading him," &c. &c.

The old man bore it all with the most philosophic composure. He evinced no astonishment at his late discovery, and made no replies. But his son, Neddy, had not disciplined his feelings quite so well. His eyes opened, wider and wider, from the first to the last pull of the blanket; and when the whole sore burst upon his view, astonishment and fright seemed to contend for the mastery of his countenance. As the blanket disappeared, he stuck his hands in his breeches pockets, heaved a deep sigh, and lapsed into a profound reverie; from which he was only roused by the cuts at his father. He bore them as long as he could; and when he could contain himself no longer, he began, with a certain wildness of expression, which gave a peculiar interest to what he uttered: "His back's mighty bad off; but dod drot my soul, if he's put it to daddy as bad as he thinks he has, for old Kit's both blind and *deef*, I'll be dod drot if he eint."

"The devil he is," said Blossom. "Yes, dod drot my soul if he *eint*. You walk him and see if he *eint*. His eyes don't look like it; but he *jist as live go agin* the house with you, or in a ditch, as any how. Now you go try him." The laugh was now turned on Blossom; and many rushed to test the fidelity of the little boy's report. A few experiments established its truth, beyond controversy.

"Neddy," said the old man, "you oughn't to try and make people discontented with their things." "Stranger, don't mind what the little boy says. If you can only get Kit rid of them little failings, you'll find him all sorts of a horse. You are a *leetle* the best man, at a horse swap, that ever I got hold of; but don't fool away Kit. Come, Neddy, my son, let's be moving; the stranger seems to be getting snappish."

1835

■ GEORGE WASHINGTON HARRIS ■
1814–1869

Mrs. Yardley's Quilting

"Thar's one durn'd nasty muddy job, an' I is jis' glad enuf tu take a ho'n ur two, on the straingth ove hit."

"What have you been doing, Sut?"

"Helpin tu salt ole Missis Yardley down."

"What do you mean by that?"

"Fixin her fur rotten cumfurtably, kiverin her up wif sile, tu keep the buzzards from cheatin the wurms."

"Oh, you have been helping to bury a woman."

"That's hit, by golly! Now why the devil can't I 'splain mysef like yu? I ladles out my words at random, like a calf kickin at yaller-jackids; yu jis' rolls em out tu the pint, like a feller a-layin bricks—every one fits. How is it that bricks fits so clost enyhow? Rocks won't ni du hit."

"Becaze they'se all ove a size," ventured a man with a wen over his eye.

"The devil yu say, hon'ey-head! haint reapin-mersheens ove a size? I'd like tu see two ove em fit clost. Yu wait ontil yu sprouts tuther ho'n, afore yu venters tu 'splain mix'd questions. George, did yu know ole Missis Yardley?"

"No."

"Well, she wer a curious 'oman in her way, an' she wore shiney specks. Now jis' listen: Whenever yu see a ole 'oman ahine a par ove *shiney* specks, yu keep yer eye skinn'd; they am dang'rus in the extreme. Thar is jis' no kno-win what they ken du. I hed one a-stradil ove me onst, fur kissin her gal. She went fur my har, an' she went fur my skin, ontil I tho't she ment tu kill me, an' wud a-dun hit, ef my hollerin hadent fotch ole Dave Jordan, a *bach-eler*, tu my aid. He, like a durn'd fool, cotch her by the laig, an' drug her back'ards ofen me. She jis' kivered him, an' I run, by golly! The nex time I seed him he wer bald headed, an' his face looked like he'd been a-fitin wildcats.

"Ole Missis Yardley wer a great noticer ove littil things, that nobody else ever seed. She'd say right in the middil ove sumbody's serious talk: 'Law sakes! thar goes that yaller slut ove a hen, a-flingin straws over her shoulder; she's arter settin now, an' haint laid but seven aigs. I'll disapint *her*, see ef I don't; I'll put a punkin in her ne's, an' a feather in her nose. An' bless my soul! jis' look at that cow wif the wilted ho'n, a-flingin up dirt an' a-smellin the place whar hit cum frum, wif the rale ginuine still-wurim twis' in her tail, too; what upon the face ove the yeath kin she be arter now, the ole fool? watch her, Sally. An' sakes alive, jis' look at that ole sow; she's a-gwine in a fas' trot, wif her empty bag a-floppin agin her sides. Thar, she hes stop't, an's a-listenin! massy on us! what a long yearnis grunt she gin; hit cum frum way back ove her kidneys. Thar she goes agin; she's arter no good, sich kerryin on means no good.'

"An' so she wud gabble, no odds who wer a-listenin. She looked like she mout been made at fust 'bout four foot long, an' the common thickness ove wimen when they's at tharsefs, an' then had her har tied tu a stump, a par ove steers hitched to her heels, an' then straiched out a-mos' two foot more—mos' ove the straichin cumin outen her laigs an' naik. Her stockins, a-hangin on the clothes-line tu dry, looked like a par ove sabre scabbards, an' her naik looked like a dry beef shank smoked, an' mout been ni ontu es tough. I never felt hit mysef, I didn't, I jis' jedges by looks. Her darter Sal wer bilt at fust 'bout the laingth ove her mam, but wer never straiched eny by a par ove steers an' she wer fat enuf tu kill; she wer taller lyin down than she wer a-standin up. Hit wer her who gin me the 'hump shoulder.' Jis' look at me; haint I'se got a tech ove the dromedary back thar bad? haint I humpy? Well, a-stoopin tu kiss that squatty lard-stan ove a gal is what dun hit tu me. She wer the fairest-lookin gal I ever seed. She allers wore thick woolin stockins 'bout six inches too long fur her laig; they rolled down over her garters, lookin like a par ove life-presarvers up thar. I tell yu she wer a tarin gal enyhow. Luved kissin, wrastlin, an' biled cabbige, an' hated tite clothes, hot weather, an' suckit-riders. B'leved strong in married folk's ways, cradles, an' the remishun ove sins, an' didn't b'leve in corsets, fleas, peaners, nur the fashun plates."

"What caused the death of Mrs. Yardley, Sut?"

"Nuffin, only her heart stop't beatin 'bout losin a nine dimunt quilt. True, she got a skeer'd hoss tu run over her, but she'd a-got over that ef a quilt hadn't been mix'd up in the catastrophy. Yu see quilts wer wun ove her speshul gifts; she run strong on the bed-kiver question. Irish chain, star ove

Texas, sun-flower, nine dimunt, saw teeth, checker board, an' shell quilts; blue, an' white, an' yaller an' black coverlids, an' callickercumfurts reigned triumphan' 'bout her hous'. They wer packed in drawers, layin in shelfs full, wer hung four dubbil on lines in the lof, packed in chists, piled on cheers, an' wer everywhar, even ontu the beds, an' wer changed every bed-makin. She told everybody she cud git tu listen tu hit that she ment tu give every durn'd one ove them tu Sal when she got married. Oh, lordy! what es fat a gal es Sal Yardley cud ever du wif half ove em, an' sleepin wif a husbun at that, is more nor I ever cud see through. Jis' think ove her onder twenty layer ove quilts in July, an' yu in thar too. Gewhillikins! George, look how I is sweatin' now, an' this is December. I'd 'bout es lief be shet up in a steam biler wif a three hundred pound bag ove lard, es tu make a bisiness ove sleepin wif that gal—'twould kill a glass-blower.

"Well, tu cum tu the serious part ove this conversashun, that is how the old quilt-mersheen an' coverlid-loom cum tu stop operashuns on this yeath. She hed narrated hit thru the neighborhood that nex Saterday she'd gin a quiltin—three quilts an' one cumfurt tu tie. 'Goblers, fiddils, gals, an' whisky,' wer the words she sent tu the men-folk, an' more tetchin ur wak-enin words never drap't ofen an 'oman's tongue. She sed tu the gals, 'Sweet toddy, huggin, dancin, an' huggers in 'bundunce.' Them words struck the gals rite in the pit ove the stumick, an' spread a ticklin sensashun bof ways, ontil they scratched thar heads wif one han, an' thar heels wif tuther.

"Everybody, he an' she, what wer baptized b'levers in the righteousnes ove quiltins wer thar, an' hit jis' so happen'd that everybody in them parts, frum fifteen summers tu fifty winters, wer unannamus b'levers. Strange, warn't hit? Hit wer the bigges' quiltin ever Missis Yardley hilt, an' she hed hilt hundreds; everybody wer thar, 'scept the constibil an' suckit-rider, two dam easily-spared pussons; the numbers ni ontu even too; jis' a few more boys nur gals; that made hit more exhitin, fur hit gin the gals a chance tu kick an' squeal a littil, wifout runnin eny risk ove not gittin kissed at all, an' hit gin reasonabil grouns fur a few scrimmages amung the he's. Now es kissin an' fitin am the pepper an' salt ove all soshul getherins, so hit wer more espish-ully wif this ove ours. Es I swung my eyes over the crowd, George, I thought quiltins, managed in a morril an' sensibil way, truly am good things—good fur free drinkin, good fur free eatin, good fur free huggin, good fur free dan-cin, good fur free fitin, an' goodest ove all fur poperlatin a country fas'.

"Thar am a fur-seein wisdom in quiltins, ef they hes proper trimmins: 'vittils, fiddils, an' sperrits in 'bundunce.' One holesum quiltin am wuf three old pray'r meetins on the poperlashun pint, purtickerly ef hits hilt in the dark ove the moon, an' runs intu the night a few hours, an' April ur May am the time chosen. The moon don't suit quiltins whar everybody is well ac-quainted an' already fur along in courtin. She dus help pow'ful tu begin a courtin match onder, but when hit draws ni ontu a head, nobody wants a moon but the ole mammys.

"The mornin cum, still, saft, sunshiney; cocks crowin, hens singin, birds chirpin, tuckeys gobblin—jis' the day tu sun quilts, kick, kiss, squeal, an' make love.

"All the plow-lines an' clothes-lines wer straiched tu every post an' tree. Quilts purvailed. Durn my gizzard ef two acres roun that ar house warn't jis' one solid quilt, all out a-sunnin, an' tu be seed. They dazzled the eyes, skeered the hosses, gin wimen the heart-burn, an' perdominated.

"To'ards sundown the he's begun tu drap in. Yearnis' needil-driven cummenced tu lose groun; threads broke ofen, thimbils got los', an' quilts needed anuther roll. Gigglin, winkin, whisperin, smoofin ove har, an' gals a-ticklin one anuther, wer a-gainin every inch ove groun what the needils los'. Did yu ever notis, George, at all soshul getherins, when the he's begin tu gather, that the young she's begin tu tickil one anuther an' the ole maids swell thar tails, roach up thar backs, an' sharpen thar nails ontu the bed-posts an' door jams, an' spit an' groan sorter like cats a-courtin? Dus hit mean *rale* rath, ur is hit a dare tu the he's, sorter kivered up wif the outside signs ove danger? I honestly b'leve that the young shes' ticklin means, 'Cum an' take this job ofen our hans.' But that swellin I jis' don't onderstan; dus yu? Hit looks skeery, an' I never tetch one ove em when they am in the swellin way. I may be mistaken'd 'bout the ticklin bisiness too; hit may be dun like a feller chaws poplar bark when he haint got eny terbacker, a-sorter better nur nun make-shif. I dus know one thing tu a certainty: that is, when the he's take hold the ticklin quits, an' ef yu gits one ove the ole maids out tu herself, then she subsides an' is the smoofes, sleekes, saft thing yu ever seed, an' dam ef yu can't hear her purr, jis' es plain!

"But then, George, gals an' ole maids haint the things tu fool time away on. Hits widders, by golly, what am the rale sensibil, steady-goin, never-skeerin, never-kickin, willin, sperrited, smoof pacers. They cum clost up tu the hoss-block, standin still wif thar purty silky years playin, an' the naik-veins a-throbbin, an' waits fur the word, which ove course yu gives, arter yu finds yer feet well in the stirrup, an' away they moves like a cradil on cushioned rockers, ur a spring buggy runnin in damp san'. A tetch ove the bridil, an' they knows yu wants em tu turn, an' they dus hit es willin es ef the idear wer thar own. I be dod rabbited ef a man can't 'propriate happiness by the skinful ef he is in contack wif sumbody's widder, an' is smart. Gin me a willin widder, the yeath over: what they don't know, haint worth larnin. They hes all been tu Jamakey an' larnt how sugar's made, an' knows how tu sweeten wif hit; an' by golly, they is always ready tu use hit. All yu hes tu du is tu find the spoon, an' then drink cumfort till yer blind. Nex tu good sperrits an' my laigs, I likes a twenty-five year ole widder, wif roun ankils, an' bright eyes, honestly an' squarly lookin intu yurn, an' sayin es plainly es a partrige sez 'Bob White,' 'Don't be afraid ove me; I hes been thar; yu know hit ef yu hes eny sense, an' thar's no use in eny humbug, ole feller—cum ahead!'

"Ef yu onderstans widder nater, they ken save yu a power ove troubil, onsartinty, an' time, an' ef yu is interprisin yu gits mons'rous well paid fur hit. The very soun ove thar littil shoe-heels speak full trainin, an' hes a knowin click as they tap the floor; an' the rustil ove thar dress sez, 'I dar you tu ax me.'

"When yu hes made up yer mind tu court one, jis' go at hit like hit wer a job ove rail-maulin. Ware yer workin close, use yer common, every-day moshuns an' words, an' abuv all, fling away yer cinamint ile vial an' burn all yer love songs. No use in tryin tu fool em, fur they sees plum thru yu, a durn'd sight plainer than they dus thru thar veils. No use in a pasted shut; she's been thar. No use in borrowin a cavortin fat hoss; she's been thar. No use in har-dye; she's been thar. No use in cloves, tu kill whisky breff; she's been thar. No use in buyin clost curtains fur yer bed, fur she has been thar. Widders am a speshul means, George, fur ripenin green men, killin off weak ones, an' makin 'ternally happy the soun ones.

"Well, es I sed afore, I flew the track an' got ontu the widders. The fellers begun tu ride up an' walk up, sorter slow, like they warn't in a hurry, the durn'd 'saitful raskils, hitchin thar critters tu enything they cud find. One red-comb'd, long-spurr'd, dominecker feller, frum town, in a red an' white grid-iron jackid an' patent leather gaiters, hitched his hoss, a wild, skeery, wall-eyed devil, inside the yard palins, tu a cherry tree lim'. Thinks I, that hoss hes a skeer intu him big enuf tu run intu town, an' perhaps beyant hif, ef I kin only tetch hit off; so I sot intu thinkin.

"One aind ove a long clothes-line, wif nine dimunt quilts ontu hit, wer tied tu the same cherry tree that the hoss wer. I tuck my knife and socked hit thru every quilt, 'bout the middil, an' jis' below the rope, an' tied them thar wif bark, so they cudent slip. Then I went tu the back aind, an' ontied hit frum the pos', knottin in a hoe-handil, by the middil, tu keep the quilts frum slippin off ef my bark strings failed, an' laid hit on the groun. Then I went tu the tuther aind: thar wer 'bout ten foot tu spar, a-lyin on the groun arter tyin tu the tree. I tuck hit atwix Wall-eye's hine laigs, an' tied hit fas' tu bof stirrups, an' then cut the cherry tree lim' betwix his bridil an' the tree, almos' off. Now, mine yu thar wer two ur three uther ropes full ove quilts atween me an' the hous', so I wer purty well hid frum thar. I jis' tore off a palin frum the fence, an' tuck hit in bof hans, an' arter raisin hit 'way up yander, I fotch hit down, es hard es I cud, flatsided to'ards the groun, an' hit acksidentally happen'd tu hit Wall-eye, 'bout nine inches ahead ove the root ove his tail. Hit landed so hard that hit made my hans tingle, an' then busted intu splinters. The first thing I did, wer tu feel ove mysef, on the same spot whar hit hed hit the hoss. I cudent help duin hit tu save my life, an' I swar I felt sum ove Wall-eye's sensashun, jis' es plain. The fust thing he did, wer tu tare down the lim' wif a twenty footjump, his head to'ards the hous'. Thinks I, now yu hev dun hit, yu durn'd wall-eyed fool! tarin down that lim' wer the beginin ove all the troubil, an' the hoss did hit hissef; my conshuns felt clar es a mountin spring, an' I wer in a frame ove mine tu obsarve things es they happen'd, an' they soon begun tu happen purty clost arter one anuther rite then, an' thar, an' tharabouts, clean ontu town, thru hit, an' still wer a-happenin, in the woods beyant thar ni ontu eleven mile frum ole man Yardley's gate, an' four beyant town.

"The fust line ove quilts he tried tu jump, but broke hit down; the nex one he ran onder; the rope cotch ontu the ho'n ove the saddil, broke at bof ainds, an' went along wif the hoss, the cherry tree lim' an' the fust line ove quilts, what I hed proverdensally tied fas' tu the rope. That's what I calls foresight, George. Right furnint the frunt door he cum in contack wif ole Missis Yardley herself, an' anuther ole 'oman; they wer a-holdin a nine dimunt quilt spread out, a-'zaminin hit, an' a-praisin hits purfeckshuns. The durn'd onmanerly, wall-eyed fool run plum over Missis Yardley, frum ahine, stompt one hine foot through the quilt, takin hit along, a-kickin ontil he made hits corners snap like a whip. The gals screamed, the men hollered wo! an' the ole 'oman wer toted intu the hous' limber es a wet string, an' every word she sed wer, 'Oh, my preshus nine dimunt quilt!'

"Wall-eye busted thru the palins, an' Dominicker sed 'im, made a mortal rush fur his bitts, wer too late fur them, but in good time fur the strings ove flyin quilts, got tangled amung em, an' the gridiron jackid patren wer los' tu my sight amung star an' Irish chain quilts; he went from that quiltin at the rate ove thuty miles tu the hour. Nuffin lef on the lot ove the hole consarn, but a nine biler hat, a par ove gloves, an' the jack ove hearts.

"What a onmanerly, suddin way ove leavin places sum folks hev got, enyhow.

"Thinks I, well, that fool hoss, tarin down that cherry tree lim', hes dun sum good, enyhow; hit hes put the ole 'oman outen the way fur the balance ove the quiltin, an' tuck Dominicker outen the way an' outen danger, fur that gridiron jackid wud a-bred a scab on his nose afore midnite; hit wer morrily boun tu du hit.

"Two months arterwards, I tracked the route that hoss tuck in his kalamatus skeer, by quilt rags, tufts ove cotton, bunches ove har, (human an' hoss,) an' scraps ove a gridiron jackid stickin ontu the bushes, an' plum at the aind ove hit, whar all signs gin out, I foun a piece ove watch chain an' a hosses head. The places what know'd Dominicker, know'd 'im no more.

"Well, arter they'd tuck the ole 'oman up stairs an' camfired her tu sleep, things begun tu work agin. The widders broke the ice, an' arter a littil gigilin, goblin, an' gabblin, the kissin begun. *Smack!*—'Thar, now,' a widder sed that. *Pop!*—'Oh, don't!' *Pfip!*—'Oh, yu quit!' *Plosh!*—'Go *way* yu awkerd critter, yu kissed me in the eye!' anuther widder sed that. *Bop!* 'Now yu ar satisfied, I recon, big mouf!' *Vip!*—'That haint fair!' *Spat!*—'Oh, lordy! May, cum pull Bill away; he's a-tanglin my har.' *Thut!*—'I jis' d-a-r-e you tu du that agin!' a widder sed that, too. Hit sounded all 'roun that room like poppin co'n in a hot skillet, an' wer pow'ful sujestif.

"Hit kep on ontil I be durn'd ef *my* bristils didn't begin tu rise, an' sumthin like a cold buckshot wud run down the marrow in my back-bone 'bout every ten secons, an' then run up agin, tolerabil hot. I kep a swallerin wif nuthin tu swaller, an' my face felt swell'd; an' yet I wer fear'd tu make a bulge. Thinks I, I'll ketch one out tu herself torreckly, an' then I guess we'll rastil. Purty soon Sal Yardley started fur the smoke 'ous, so I jis' gin my head I few short shakes, let down one ove my wings a-trailin, an' sirkiled roun her wif a side twis' in my naik, steppin sidewise, an' a-fetchin up my hinmos' foot wif a sorter jerkin slide at every step. Sez I, 'Too coo-took a-too.' She onderstood hit, an stopt, sorter spreadin her shoulders. An' jis' es I hed pouch'd out my mouf, an' wer a-reachin forrid wif hit, fur the article hitsef, sunthin interfared wif me, hit did. George, wer yu ever ontu yer hans an' knees, an' let a hell-tarin big, mad ram, wif a ten-yard run, but yu yearnis'ly, jis' onst, right squar ontu the pint ove yer back-bone?"

"No, you fool; why do you ask?"

"Kaze I wanted tu know ef yu cud hev a realizin' noshun ove my shock. Hits scarcely worth while tu try tu make yu onderstan the case by words only, onless yu hev been tetched in that way. Gr-eat golly! the fust thing I felt, I tuck hit tu be a back-ackshun yeathquake; an' the fust thing I seed wer my chaw'r terbacker a-flyin over Sal's head like a skeer'd bat. My mouf wer pouch'd out, ready fur the article hitsef, yu know, an' hit went outen the roun hole like the wad outen a pop-gun—thug! an' the fust thing I know'd, I wer a flyin over Sal's head too, an' a-gainin on the chaw'r terbacker fast. I wer straitened out strait, toes hinemos', middil fingernails foremos', an' the fust thing I hearn wer, 'Yu dam Shanghi!' Great Jerus-a-lam! I lit ontu my all fours jis' in time tu but the yard gate ofen hits hinges, an' skeer loose sum more hosses—kep on in a four-footed gallop, clean acrost the lane afore I cud straiten up, an' yere I cotch up wif my chaw'r terbacker, stickin flat agin a fence-rail. I hed got so good a start that I thot hit a pity tu spile hit, so I jis' jump'd the fence an' tuck thru the orchurd. I tell yu I dusted these yere close, fur I tho't hit wer arter me.

"Arter runnin a spell, I ventered tu feel roun back thar, fur sum signs ove what hed happened tu me. George, arter two pow'ful hardtugs, I pull'd out the vamp an' sole ove one ove ole man Yardley's big brogans, what he hed los' amung my coat-tails. Dre'ful! dre'ful! Arter I got hit away frum thar, my flesh went fas' asleep, frum abuv my kidneys tu my knees; about now, fur the fust time, the idear struck me, what hit wer that hed interfar'd wif me, an' los' me the kiss. Hit wer ole Yardley hed kicked me. I walked fur a month like I wer straddlin a thorn hedge. Sich a shock, at sich a time, an' on sich a place—jis' think ove hit! hit am tremenjus, haint hit? The place feels num, right now."

"Well, Sut, how did the quilting come out?"

"How the hell du yu 'speck me tu know? I warn't thar eny more."

1867

WASHINGTON IRVING
1783–1859

A merchant's son, born and raised in New York City, Washington Irving was writing satirical pieces for a local newspaper before he was twenty. It was not until he was thirty-seven, however, that he established himself as a professional author. The cheap importation and reproduction of English books made literature a precarious occupation in the United States at the beginning of the nineteenth century. Moreover, American commercial society tended to equate art with idleness. For years Irving halfheartedly pursued a career in law and business, while stealing as much time from work as possible for his writing. Only in 1818, with the bankruptcy of his brothers' importing firm, on which he depended financially, did he risk authorship for a living. Two years later, the remarkable popularity of *The Sketch Book* made him a marketable commodity in both England and America, and his future as the nation's first successful professional writer was guaranteed.

In his youth, while essentially an amateur in literature, he wrote an abundance of broad, often irreverent burlesque humor, parody, and satire primarily to amuse a local New York audience. The comic periodical *Salmagundi*, on which he collaborated with his brother William and James Kirke Paulding, and the facetious *History of New York*, ostensibly written by the eccentric and highly unreliable antiquarian Diedrich Knickerbocker, mocked literary conventions and simultaneously made fun of bourgeois manners, provincial high culture, American chauvinism, and republican politics—particularly Jefferson's.

From 1815 to 1832, Irving lived and traveled widely in England and on the European continent. Now much of his work shaped itself as a consciously American response to Old World culture. Seeking a large international audience, he became primarily a writer of short fiction and personalized sketches and essays. Burlesque satire gave way to a gentler, more subtle humor, and he developed the more ingratiating prose style for which he became famous. His persona Geoffrey Crayon, a shy, ironic, at times melancholy American bachelor writer traveling in Europe—a fictionalized version of Irving himself—gave a degree of thematic and tonal unity to his miscellanies, *The Sketch Book*, *Bracebridge Hall*, *Tales of a Traveller*, and *The Alhambra*. In addition, Crayon helped dramatize the author's ambivalent feelings toward both European aristocracy and American democracy.

Irving had grown up in a transitional America, a nation culturally unsure of itself and deeply divided as to how democratic it should become. He is often dismissed as a political reactionary, a would-be aristocrat in a democratic society. Such a view, however, overlooks complexities, if not contradictions, in his work. For him issues were seldom clear-cut, and he was prone to exploit his uncertainties. A mild (if not rampant) self-mockery is inherent in much of his satire and fiction.

By 1820 he had become a partial convert to Romanticism, catering to the vogue for tearful sentimentality (though he made fun of it too) and exhibiting

Romantic interests in landscape, folklore, and the past. Subsequently, as a historian and biographer, he was to focus on colorful drama, costumes, and pageantry. But though by temperament a dreamer, he lacked the High Romantic's faith in imagination. The undermining of common sense by illusion and the shattering of visions against an unyielding reality are persistent themes in his work, as in "Rip Van Winkle" and "The Legend of Sleepy Hollow." With these narratives (both from *The Sketch Book*), Irving is usually seen as having created the short story as a new genre, distinct from the moral or sentimental tale and tales of headlong action and Gothic mystery. Ironically, both stories, with their evocative American settings, were partly inspired by German folk motifs and composed in England.

His going to Spain in 1826 and being given access to a mass of largely unused materials relating to Christopher Columbus led to his biography of the explorer. The book was well received, and thereafter Irving wrote more history and biography than fiction. A national celebrity upon his return to America in 1832, he traveled west, gathering material for "A Tour on the Prairies" (in *The Crayon Miscellany*), which he followed shortly with *Astoria* and *Bonneville*, histories of Far Western fur-trading and exploring ventures. From 1842 to 1846, he served as American minister to Spain. In his final years, he continued to produce books and revised and published his complete works. He finished the five-volume *Life of Washington* shortly before his death.

William Hedges
Goucher College

PRIMARY WORKS

Salmagundi, 1807–1808; *A History of New York ... by Diedrich Knickerbocker*, 1809; *The Sketch Book of Geoffrey Crayon, Gent.*, 1819–1820; *Bracebridge Hall*, 1822; *Tales of a Traveller*, 1824; *The Life and Voyages of Christopher Columbus*, 1828; *The Alhambra*, 1832; *The Crayon Miscellany*, 1835; *Astoria*, 1836; *Adventures of Captain Bonneville*, 1837; *The Life of George Washington*, 1855–1859.

Rip Van Winkle

A Posthumous Writing of Diedrich Knickerbocker

> By Woden, God of Saxons,
> From whence comes Wensday, that is Wodensday.
> Truth is a thing that ever I will keep
> Unto thylke day in which I creep into
> My sepulchre—
>
> —CARTWRIGHT[1]

*The following Tale was found among the papers of the late Diedrich
Knickerbocker, an old gentleman of New York, who was very curious in the
Dutch history of the province, and the manners of the descendants from its*

---

[1]Lines from *The Ordinary*, by William Cartwright, English dramatist (1611–1643).

primitive settlers. His historical researches, however, did not lie so much among books as among men; for the former are lamentably scanty on his favorite topics; whereas he found the old burghers, and still more their wives, rich in that legendary lore so invaluable to true history. Whenever, therefore, he happened upon a genuine Dutch family, snugly shut up in its low-roofed farmhouse, under a spreading sycamore, he looked upon it as a little clasped volume of black-letter, and studied it with the zeal of a bookworm.

The result of all these researches was a history of the province during the reign of the Dutch governors, which he published some years since. There have been various opinions as to the literary character of his work, and, to tell the truth, it is not a whit better than it should be. Its chief merit is its scrupulous accuracy, which indeed was a little questioned on its first appearance, but has since been completely established; and it is now admitted into all historical collections as a book of unquestionable authority.

The old gentleman died shortly after the publication of his work; and now that he is dead and gone, it cannot do much harm to his memory to say that his time might have been much better employed in weightier labor. He, however, was apt to ride his hobby his own way; and though it did now and then kick up the dust a little in the eyes of his neighbors, and grieve the spirit of some friends, for whom he felt the truest deference and affection, yet his errors and follies are remembered "more in sorrow than in anger,"[2] and it begins to be suspected that he never intended to injure or offend. But however his memory may be appreciated by critics, it is still held dear by many folk whose good opinion is well worth having; particularly by certain biscuit-bakers, who have gone so far as to imprint his likeness on their New-Year cakes; and have thus given him a chance for immortality, almost equal to the being stamped on a Waterloo Medal, or a Queen Anne's Farthing.[3]

Whoever has made a voyage up the Hudson must remember the Kaatskill mountains. They are a dismembered branch of the great Appalachian family, and are seen away to the west of the river, swelling up to a noble height, and lording it over the surrounding country. Every change of season, every change of weather, indeed, every hour of the day, produces some change in the magical hues and shapes of these mountains, and they are regarded by all the good wives, far and near, as perfect barometers. When the weather is fair and settled, they are clothed in blue and purple, and print their bold outlines on the clear evening sky; but sometimes, when the rest of the landscape is cloudless, they will gather a hood of gray vapors about their summits, which, in the last rays of the setting sun, will glow and light up like a crown of glory.

At the foot of these fairy mountains, the voyager may have descried the light smoke curling up from a village, whose shingle-roofs gleam among the trees, just where the blue tints of the upland melt away into the fresh green of the nearer landscape. It is a little village, of great antiquity, having been

[2]*Hamlet*, I, ii.
[3]Waterloo Medals and Queen Anne's Farth-
ings were not scarce.

founded by some of the Dutch colonists in the early times of the province, just about the beginning of the government of the good Peter Stuyvesant, (may he rest in peace!) and there were some of the houses of the original settlers standing within a few years, built of small yellow bricks brought from Holland, having latticed windows and gable fronts, surmounted with weathercocks.

In that same village, and in one of these very houses (which, to tell the precise truth, was sadly time-worn and weather-beaten), there lived, many years since, while the country was yet a province of Great Britain, a simple, good-natured fellow, of the name of Rip Van Winkle. He was a descendant of the Van Winkles who figured so gallantly in the chivalrous days of Peter Stuyvesant, and accompanied him to the siege of Fort Christina. He inherited, however, but little of the martial character of his ancestors. I have observed that he was a simple, good-natured man; he was, moreover, a kind neighbor, and an obedient, hen-pecked husband. Indeed, to the latter circumstance might be owing that meekness of spirit which gained him such universal popularity; for those men are most apt to be obsequious and conciliating abroad, who are under the discipline of shrews at home. Their tempers, doubtless, are rendered pliant and malleable in the fiery furnace of domestic tribulation; and a curtain-lecture[4] is worth all the sermons in the world for teaching the virtues of patience and long-suffering. A termagant wife may, therefore, in some respects be considered a tolerable blessing; and if so, Rip Van Winkle was thrice blessed.

Certain it is, that he was a great favorite among all the good wives of the village, who, as usual with the amiable sex, took his part in all family squabbles; and never failed, whenever they talked those matters over in their evening gossipings, to lay all the blame on Dame Van Winkle. The children of the village, too, would shout with joy whenever he approached. He assisted at their sports, made their playthings, taught them to fly kites and shoot marbles, and told them long stories of ghosts, witches, and Indians. Whenever he went dodging about the village, he was surrounded by a troop of them, hanging on his skirts, clambering on his back, and playing a thousand tricks on him with impunity; and not a dog would bark at him throughout the neighborhood.

The great error in Rip's composition was an insuperable aversion to all kinds of profitable labor. It could not be from the want of assiduity or perseverance; for he would sit on a wet rock, with a rod as long and heavy as a Tartar's lance, and fish all day without a murmur, even though he should not be encouraged by a single nibble. He would carry a fowling-piece on his shoulder for hours together, trudging through woods and swamps, and up hill and down dale, to shoot a few squirrels or wild pigeons. He would never refuse to assist a neighbor even in the roughest toil, and was a foremost man at all country frolics for husking Indian corn, or building stone fences; the women of the village, too, used to employ him to run their errands, and to do such

[4]A wife scolding her husband in bed.

little odd jobs as their less obliging husbands would not do for them. In a word, Rip was ready to attend to anybody's business but his own; but as to doing family duty, and keeping his farm in order, he found it impossible.

In fact, he declared it was of no use to work on his farm; it was the most pestilent little piece of ground in the whole country; everything about it went wrong, and would go wrong, in spite of him. His fences were continually falling to pieces; his cow would either go astray, or get among the cabbages; weeds were sure to grow quicker in his fields than anywhere else; the rain always made a point of setting in just as he had some out-door work to do; so that though his patrimonial estate had dwindled away under his management, acre by acre, until there was little more left than a mere patch of Indian corn and potatoes, yet it was the worst conditioned farm in the neighborhood.

His children, too, were as ragged and wild as if they belonged to nobody. His son Rip, an urchin begotten in his own likeness, promised to inherit the habits, with the old clothes, of his father. He was generally seen trooping like a colt at his mother's heels, equipped in a pair of his father's cast-off galligaskins, which he had much ado to hold up with one hand, as a fine lady does her train in bad weather.

Rip Van Winkle, however, was one of those happy mortals, of foolish, well-oiled dispositions, who take the world easy, eat white bread or brown, whichever can be got with least thought or trouble, and would rather starve on a penny than work for a pound. If left to himself, he would have whistled life away in perfect contentment; but his wife kept continually dinning in his ears about his idleness, his carelessness, and the ruin he was bringing on his family. Morning, noon, and night, her tongue was incessantly going, and everything he said or did was sure to produce a torrent of household eloquence. Rip had but one way of replying to all lectures of the kind, and that, by frequent use, had grown into a habit. He shrugged his shoulders, shook his head, cast up his eyes, but said nothing. This, however, always provoked a fresh volley from his wife; so that he was fain to draw off his forces, and take to the outside of the house—the only side which, in truth, belongs to a hen-pecked husband.

Rip's sole domestic adherent was his dog Wolf, who was as much hen-pecked as his master; for Dame Van Winkle regarded them as companions in idleness, and even looked upon Wolf with an evil eye, as the cause of his master's going so often astray. True it is, in all points of spirit befitting an honorable dog, he was as courageous an animal as ever scoured the woods; but what courage can withstand the ever-during and all-besetting terrors of a woman's tongue? The moment Wolf entered the house his crest fell, his tail drooped to the ground, or curled between his legs, he sneaked about with a gallows air, casting many a sidelong glance at Dame Van Winkle, and at the least flourish of a broomstick or ladle he would fly to the door with yelping precipitation.

Times grew worse and worse with Rip Van Winkle as years of matrimony rolled on; a tart temper never mellows with age, and a sharp tongue is the only edged tool that grows keener with constant use. For a long while he used to console himself, when driven from home, by frequenting a kind of perpetual club of the sages, philosophers, and other idle personages of the village, which held its sessions on a bench before a small inn, designated by a rubicund portrait of His Majesty George the Third. Here they used to sit in the shade through a long, lazy summer's day, talking listlessly over village gossip, or telling endless sleepy stories about nothing. But it would have been worth any statesman's money to have heard the profound discussions that sometimes took place, when by chance an old newspaper fell into their hands from some passing traveller. How solemnly they would listen to the contents, as drawled out by Derrick Van Bummel, the schoolmaster, a dapper learned little man, who was not to be daunted by the most gigantic word in the dictionary; and how sagely they would deliberate upon public events some months after they had taken place.

The opinions of this junto were completely controlled by Nicholas Vedder, a patriarch of the village, and landlord of the inn, at the door of which he took his seat from morning till night, just moving sufficiently to avoid the sun and keep in the shade of a large tree; so that the neighbors could tell the hour by his movements as accurately as by a sun-dial. It is true he was rarely heard to speak, but smoked his pipe incessantly. His adherents, however (for every great man has his adherents), perfectly understood him, and knew how to gather his opinions. When anything that was read or related displeased him, he was observed to smoke his pipe vehemently, and to send forth short, frequent, and angry puffs; but when pleased, he would inhale the smoke slowly and tranquilly, and emit it in light and placid clouds; and sometimes, taking the pipe from his mouth, and letting the fragrant vapor curl about his nose, would gravely nod his head in token of perfect approbation.

From even this stronghold the unlucky Rip was at length routed by his termagant wife, who would suddenly break in upon the tranquillity of the assemblage and call the members all to naught; nor was that august personage, Nicholas Vedder himself, sacred from the daring tongue of this terrible virago, who charged him outright with encouraging her husband in habits of idleness.

Poor Rip was at last reduced almost to despair; and his only alternative, to escape from the labor of the farm and clamor of his wife, was to take gun in hand and stroll away into the woods. Here he would sometimes seat himself at the foot of a tree, and share the contents of his wallet with Wolf, with whom he sympathized as a fellow-sufferer in persecution. "Poor Wolf," he would say, "thy mistress leads thee a dog's life of it; but never mind, my lad, whilst I live thou shalt never want a friend to stand by thee!" Wolf would wag his tail, look wistfully in his master's face; and if dogs can feel pity, I verily believe he reciprocated the sentiment with all his heart.

In a long ramble of the kind on a fine autumnal day, Rip had unconsciously scrambled to one of the highest parts of the Kaatskill mountains. He was after his favorite sport of squirrel-shooting, and the still solitudes had echoed and re-echoed with the reports of his gun. Panting and fatigued, he threw himself, late in the afternoon, on a green knoll, covered with mountain herbage, that crowned the brow of a precipice. From an opening between the trees he could overlook all the lower country for many a mile of rich woodland. He saw at a distance the lordly Hudson, far, far below him, moving on its silent but majestic course, with the reflection of a purple cloud, or the sail of a lagging bark, here and there sleeping on its glassy bosom, and at last losing itself in the blue highlands.

On the other side he looked down into a deep mountain glen, wild, lonely, and shagged, the bottom filled with fragments from the impending cliffs, and scarcely lighted by the reflected rays of the setting sun. For some time Rip lay musing on this scene; evening was gradually advancing; the mountains began to throw their long blue shadows over the valleys; he saw that it would be dark long before he could reach the village, and he heaved a heavy sigh when he thought of encountering the terrors of Dame Van Winkle.

As he was about to descend, he heard a voice from a distance, hallooing, "Rip Van Winkle, Rip Van Winkle!" He looked round, but could see nothing but a crow winging its solitary flight across the mountain. He thought his fancy must have deceived him, and turned again to descend, when he heard the same cry ring through the still evening air: "Rip Van Winkle! Rip Van Winkle!"—at the same time Wolf bristled up his back, and giving a low growl, skulked to his master's side, looking fearfully down into the glen. Rip now felt a vague apprehension stealing over him; he looked anxiously in the same direction, and perceived a strange figure slowly toiling up the rocks, and bending under the weight of something he carried on his back. He was surprised to see any human being in this lonely and unfrequented place; but supposing it to be some one of the neighborhood in need of his assistance, he hastened down to yield it.

On nearer approach he was still more surprised at the singularity of the stranger's appearance. He was a short, square-built old fellow, with thick bushy hair, and a grizzled beard. His dress was of the antique Dutch fashion,—a cloth jerkin strapped round the waist—several pair of breeches, the outer one of ample volume, decorated with rows of buttons down the sides, and bunches at the knees. He bore on his shoulder a stout keg, that seemed full of liquor, and made signs for Rip to approach and assist him with the load. Though rather shy and distrustful of this new acquaintance, Rip complied with his usual alacrity; and mutually relieving one another, they clambered up a narrow gully, apparently the dry bed of a mountain torrent. As they ascended, Rip every now and then heard long, rolling peals, like distant thunder, that seemed to issue out of a deep ravine, or rather cleft, between lofty rocks, toward which their rugged path conducted. He paused for an instant, but supposing it to be the muttering of one of those transient thunder-showers which often take place in mountain heights, he proceeded. Passing through the ravine, they came to a hollow, like a small amphitheatre, surrounded by perpendicular precipices, over the brinks of which impending trees shot their branches, so that you only caught glimpses of the azure sky and the bright evening cloud. During the whole time Rip and his companion had labored on in silence; for though the former marvelled greatly what could be the object of carrying a keg of liquor up this wild mountain, yet there was something strange and incomprehensible about the unknown, that inspired awe and checked familiarity.

On entering the amphitheatre, new objects of wonder presented themselves. On a level spot in the centre was a company of odd-looking personages playing at ninepins. They were dressed in a quaint, outlandish fashion; some wore short doublets, others jerkins, with long knives in their belts, and most of them had enormous breeches, of similar style with that of the guide's. Their visages, too, were peculiar: one had a large beard, broad face, and small piggish eyes; the face of another seemed to consist entirely of nose, and was surmounted by a white sugar-loaf hat, set off with a little red cock's tail. They all had beards, of various shapes and colors. There was one who seemed to be the commander. He was a stout old gentleman, with a weather-beaten countenance; he wore a laced doublet, broad belt and hanger, high crowned hat and feather, red stockings, and high-heeled shoes, with roses in them. The whole group reminded Rip of the figures in an old Flemish painting, in the parlor of Dominie Van Shaick, the village parson, and which had been brought over from Holland at the time of the settlement.

What seemed particularly odd to Rip was, that, though these folks were evidently amusing themselves, yet they maintained the gravest faces, the most mysterious silence, and were, withal, the most melancholy party of pleasure he had ever witnessed. Nothing interrupted the stillness of the scene but the noise of the balls, which, whenever they were rolled, echoed along the mountains like rumbling peals of thunder.

As Rip and his companion approached them, they suddenly desisted from their play, and stared at him with such fixed, statue-like gaze, and such strange, uncouth, lack-lustre countenances, that his heart turned within him, and his knees smote together. His companion now emptied the contents of the keg into large flagons, and made signs to him to wait upon the company. He obeyed with fear and trembling; they quaffed the liquor in profound silence, and then returned to their game.

By degrees Rip's awe and apprehension subsided. He even ventured, when no eye was fixed upon him, to taste the beverage, which he found had much of the flavor of excellent Hollands. He was naturally a thirsty soul, and was soon tempted to repeat the draught. One taste provoked another; and he reiterated his visits to the flagon so often that at length his senses were overpowered, his eyes swam in his head, his head gradually declined, and he fell into a deep sleep.

On waking, he found himself on the green knoll whence he had first seen the old man of the glen. He rubbed his eyes—it was a bright sunny morning. The birds were hopping and twittering among the bushes, and the eagle was wheeling aloft, and breasting the pure mountain breeze. "Surely," thought Rip, "I have not slept here all night." He recalled the occurrences before he fell asleep. The strange man with a keg of liquor—the mountain ravine—the wild retreat among the rocks—the woe-begone party at ninepins—the flagon—"Oh! that flagon! that wicked flagon!" thought Rip,—"what excuse shall I make to Dame Van Winkle?"

He looked round for his gun, but in place of the clean, well-oiled fowling-piece, he found an old firelock lying by him, the barrel incrusted with rust, the lock falling off, and the stock worm-eaten. He now suspected that the grave roisters of the mountain had put a trick upon him, and, having dosed him with liquor, had robbed him of his gun. Wolf, too, had disappeared, but he might have strayed away after a squirrel or partridge. He whistled after him, and shouted his name, but all in vain; the echoes repeated his whistle and shout, but no dog was to be seen.

He determined to revisit the scene of the last evening's gambol, and if he met with any of the party, to demand his dog and gun. As he rose to walk, he found himself stiff in the joints, and wanting in his usual activity. "These mountain beds do not agree with me," thought Rip, "and if this frolic should lay me up with a fit of rheumatism, I shall have a blessed time with Dame Van Winkle." With some difficulty he got down into the glen: he found the gully up which he and his companion had ascended the preceding evening; but to his astonishment a mountain stream was now foaming down it, leaping from rock to rock, and filling the glen with babbling murmurs. He, however, made shift to scramble up its sides, working his toilsome way through thickets of birch, sassafras, and witch-hazel, and sometimes tripped up or entangled by the wild grape-vines that twisted their coils or tendrils from tree to tree, and spread a kind of network in his path.

At length he reached to where the ravine had opened through the cliffs to the amphitheatre; but no traces of such opening remained. The rocks presented a high, impenetrable wall, over which the torrent came tumbling in a sheet of feathery foam, and fell into a broad deep basin, black from the shadows of the surrounding forest. Here, then, poor Rip was brought to a stand. He again called and whistled after his dog; he was only answered by the cawing of a flock of idle crows, sporting high in air about a dry tree that overhung a sunny precipice; and who, secure in their elevation, seemed to look down and scoff at the poor man's perplexities. What was to be done? the morning was passing away, and Rip felt famished for want of his breakfast. He grieved to give up his dog and gun; he dreaded to meet his wife; but it would not do to starve among the mountains. He shook his head, shouldered the rusty firelock, and, with a heart full of trouble and anxiety, turned his steps homeward.

As he approached the village he met a number of people, but none whom he knew, which some what surprised him, for he had thought himself acquainted with every one in the country round. Their dress, too, was of a different fashion from that to which he was accustomed. They all stared at him with equal marks of surprise, and whenever they cast their eyes upon him, invariably stroked their chins. The constant recurrence of this gesture induced Rip, involuntarily, to do the same, when, to his astonishment, he found his beard had grown a foot long!

He had now entered the skirts of the village. A troop of strange children ran at his heels, hooting after him, and pointing at his gray beard. The dogs, too, not one of which he recognized for an old acquaintance, barked at him as he passed. The very village was altered; it was larger and more populous. There were rows of houses which he had never seen before, and those which had been his familiar haunts had disappeared. Strange names were over the doors—strange faces at the windows—everything was strange. His mind now misgave him; he began to doubt whether both he and the world around him were not bewitched. Surely this was his native village, which he had left but the day before. There stood the Kaatskill mountains—there ran the silver Hudson at a distance—there was every hill and dale precisely as it had always been. Rip was sorely perplexed. "That flagon last night," thought he, "has addled my poor head sadly!"

It was with some difficulty that he found the way to his own house, which he approached with silent awe, expecting every moment to hear the shrill voice of Dame Van Winkle. He found the house gone to decay—the roof fallen in, the windows shattered, and the doors off the hinges. A half-starved dog that looked like Wolf was skulking about it. Rip called him by name, but the cur snarled, showed his teeth, and passed on. This was an unkind cut indeed. "My very dog," sighed poor Rip, "has forgotten me!"

He entered the house, which, to tell the truth, Dame Van Winkle had always kept in neat order. It was empty, forlorn, and apparently abandoned. This desolateness overcame all his connubial fears—he called loudly for his wife and children—the lonely chambers rang for a moment with his voice, and then all again was silence.

He now hurried forth, and hastened to his old resort, the village inn—but it too was gone. A large rickety wooden building stood in its place, with great gaping windows, some of them broken and mended with old hats and petticoats, and over the door was painted, "The Union Hotel, by Jonathan Doolittle." Instead of the great tree that used to shelter the quiet little Dutch inn of yore, there now was reared a tall naked pole, with something on the top that looked like a red nightcap,[5] and from it was fluttering a flag, on which was a singular assemblage of stars and stripes;—all this was strange and incomprehensible. He recognized on the sign, however, the ruby face of King George, under which he had smoked so many a peaceful pipe; but even this was singularly metamorphosed. The red coat was changed for one of blue and buff, a sword was held in the hand instead of a sceptre, the head was decorated with a cocked hat, and underneath was painted in large characters, GENERAL WASHINGTON.

There was, as usual, a crowd of folk about the door, but none that Rip recollected. The very character of the people seemed changed. There was a busy, bustling, disputatious tone about it, instead of the accustomed phlegm and drowsy tranquility. He looked in vain for the sage Nicholas Vedder, with

---

[5]Liberty poles and liberty caps were symbols used in the American and French Revolutions.

his broad face, double chin, and fair long pipe, uttering clouds of tobacco-smoke instead of idle speeches; or Van Bummel, the schoolmaster, doling forth the contents of an ancient newspaper. In place of these, a lean, bilious-looking fellow, with his pockets full of hand-bills, was haranguing vehemently about rights of citizens—elections—members of congress—liberty—Bunker's Hill—heroes of seventy-six—and other words, which were a perfect Babylonish[6] jargon to the bewildered Van Winkle.

The appearance of Rip, with his long, grizzled beard, his rusty fowling-piece, his uncouth dress, and an army of women and children at his heels, soon attracted the attention of the tavern-politicians. They crowded round him, eyeing him from head to foot with great curiosity. The orator bustled up to him, and drawing him partly aside, inquired "On which side he voted?" Rip stared in vacant stupidity. Another short but busy little fellow pulled him by the arm, and, rising on tiptoe, inquired in his ear, "Whether he was Federal or Democrat?" Rip was equally at a loss to comprehend the question; when a knowing, self-important old gentleman, in a sharp cocked hat, made his way through the crowd, putting them to the right and left with his elbows as he passed, and planting himself before Van Winkle, with one arm akimbo, the other resting on his cane, his keen eyes and sharp hat penetrating, as it were, into his very soul, demanded, in an austere tone, "What brought him to the election with a gun on his shoulder, and a mob at his heels; and whether he meant to breed a riot in the village?"—"Alas! gentlemen," cried Rip, somewhat dismayed, "I am a poor quiet man, a native of the place, and a loyal subject of the King, God bless him!"

Here a general shout burst from the by-standers—"A tory! a tory! a spy! a refugee! hustle him! away with him!" It was with great difficulty that the self-important man in the cocked hat restored order; and, having assumed a tenfold austerity of brow, demanded again of the unknown culprit, what he came there for, and whom he was seeking? The poor man humbly assured him that he meant no harm, but merely came there in search of some of his neighbors, who used to keep about the tavern.

"Well—who are they?—name them."

Rip bethought himself a moment, and inquired, "Where's Nicholas Vedder?"

There was a silence for a little while, when an old man replied, in a thin piping voice, "Nicholas Vedder! why, he is dead and gone these eighteen years! There was a wooden tombstone in the churchyard that used to tell all about him, but that's rotten and gone too."

"Where's Brom Dutcher?"

"Oh, he went off to the army in the beginning of the war; some say he was killed at the storming of Stony Point—others say he was drowned in a squall at the foot of Antony's Nose. I don't know—he never came back again."

"Where's Van Bummel, the schoolmaster?"

"He went off to the wars too, was a great militia general, and is now in congress."

[6]Babel-like.

Rip's heart died away at hearing of these sad changes in his home and friends, and finding himself thus alone in the world. Every answer puzzled him too, by treating of such enormous lapses of time, and of matters which he could not understand: war—congress—Stony Point;—he had no courage to ask after any more friends, but cried out in despair, "Does nobody here know Rip Van Winkle?"

"Oh, Rip Van Winkle!" exclaimed two or three, "oh, to be sure! that's Rip Van Winkle yonder, leaning against the tree."

Rip looked, and beheld a precise counterpart of himself, as he went up the mountain; apparently as lazy, and certainly as ragged. The poor fellow was now completely confounded. He doubted his own identity, and whether he was himself or another man. In the midst of his bewilderment, the man in the cocked hat demanded who he was, and what was his name.

"God knows," exclaimed he, at his wit's end; "I'm not myself—I'm somebody else—that's me yonder—no—that's somebody else got into my shoes—I was myself last night, but I fell asleep on the mountain, and they've changed my gun, and everything's changed, and I'm changed, and I can't tell what's my name, or who I am!"

The by-standers began now to look at each other, nod, wink significantly, and tap their fingers against their foreheads. There was a whisper, also, about securing the gun, and keeping the old fellow from doing mischief, at the very suggestion of which the self-important man in the cocked hat retired with some precipitation. At this critical moment a fresh, comely woman pressed through the throng to get a peep at the gray-bearded man. She had a chubby child in her arms, which, frightened at his looks, began to cry. "Hush, Rip," cried she, "hush, you little fool; the old man won't hurt you." The name of the child, the air of the mother, the tone of her voice, all awakened a train of recollections in his mind. "What is your name, my good woman?" asked he.

"Judith Gardenier."

"And your father's name?"

"Ah, poor man, Rip Van Winkle was his name, but it's twenty years since he went away from home with his gun, and never has been heard of since,—his dog came home without him; but whether he shot himself, or was carried away by the Indians, nobody can tell. I was then but a little girl."

Rip had but one question more to ask; but he put it with a faltering voice:

"Where's your mother?"

Oh, she too had died but a short time since; she broke a bloodvessel in a fit of passion at a New-England pedler.

There was a drop of comfort, at least, in this intelligence. The honest man could contain himself no longer. He caught his daughter and her child in his arms. "I am your father!" cried he—"Young Rip Van Winkle once— old Rip Van Winkle now!—Does nobody know poor Rip Van Winkle?"

All stood amazed, until an old woman, tottering out from among the crowd, put her hand to her brow, and peering under it in his face for a moment, exclaimed, "Sure enough! it is Rip Van Winkle—it is himself! Welcome home again, old neighbor. Why, where have you been these twenty long years?"

Rip's story was soon told, for the whole twenty years had been to him but as one night. The neighbors stared when they heard it; some were seen to wink at each other, and put their tongues in their cheeks: and the self-important man in the cocked hat, who, when the alarm was over, had returned to the field, screwed down the corners of his mouth, and shook his head—upon which there was a general shaking of the head throughout the assemblage.

It was determined, however, to take the opinion of old Peter Vanderdonk, who was seen slowly advancing up the road. He was a descendant of the historian of that name, who wrote one of the earliest accounts of the province. Peter was the most ancient inhabitant of the village, and well versed in all the wonderful events and traditions of the neighborhood. He recollected Rip at once, and corroborated his story in the most satisfactory manner. He assured the company that it was a fact, handed down from his ancestor the historian, that the Kaatskill mountains had always been haunted by strange beings. That it was affirmed that the great Hendrick Hudson, the first discoverer of the river and country, kept a kind of vigil there every twenty years, with his crew of the Half-moon; being permitted in this way to revisit the scenes of his enterprise, and keep a guardian eye upon the river and the great city called by his name. That his father had once seen them in their old Dutch dresses playing at ninepins in a hollow of the mountain; and that he himself had heard, one summer afternoon, the sound of their balls, like distant peals of thunder.

To make a long story short, the company broke up and returned to the more important concerns of the election. Rip's daughter took him home to live with her; she had a snug, well-furnished house, and a stout, cheery farmer for a husband, whom Rip recollected for one of the urchins that used to climb upon his back. As to Rip's son and heir, who was the ditto of himself, seen leaning against the tree, he was employed to work on the farm; but evinced an hereditary disposition to attend to anything else but his business.

Rip now resumed his old walks and habits; he soon found many of his former cronies, though all rather the worse for the wear and tear of time; and preferred making friends among the rising generation, with whom he soon grew into great favor.

Having nothing to do at home, and being arrived at that happy age when a man can be idle with impunity, he took his place once more on the bench at the inn-door, and was reverenced as one of the patriarchs of the village, and a chronicle of the old times "before the war." It was some time before he could get into the regular track of gossip, or could be made to comprehend the strange events that had taken place during his torpor. How that there had been a revolutionary war,—that the country had thrown off the yoke of old England,—and that, instead of being a subject of his Majesty George the Third, he was now a free citizen of the United States. Rip, in fact, was no politician; the changes of states and empires made but little impression on him; but there was one species of despotism under which he had long groaned, and that was—petticoat government. Happily that was at an end; he had got his neck out of the yoke of matrimony, and could go in and out whenever he pleased, without dreading the tyranny of Dame Van Winkle. Whenever her name was mentioned, however, he shook his head, shrugged his shoulders, and cast up his eyes; which might pass either for an expression of resignation to his fate, or joy at his deliverance.

He used to tell his story to every stranger that arrived at Mr. Doolittle's hotel. He was observed, at first, to vary on some points every time he told it, which was, doubtless, owing to his having so recently awaked. It at last settled down precisely to the tale I have related, and not a man, woman, or child in the neighborhood but knew it by heart. Some always pretended to doubt the reality of it, and insisted that Rip had been out of his head, and that this was one point on which he always remained flighty. The old Dutch inhabitants, however, almost universally gave it full credit. Even to this day they never hear a thunder-storm of a summer afternoon about the Kaatskill, but they say Hendrick Hudson and his crew are at their game of ninepins; and it is a common wish of all hen-pecked husbands in the neighborhood, when life hangs heavy on their hands, that they might have a quieting draught out of Rip Van Winkle's flagon.

NOTE

The foregoing Tale, one would suspect, had been suggested to Mr. Knickerbocker by a little German superstition about the Emperor Frederick der Rothbart, and the Kypphäuser mountain:[7] the subjoined note, however, which he had appended to the tale, shows that it is an absolute fact, narrated with his usual fidelity.

"The story of Rip Van Winkle may seem incredible to many, but nevertheless I give it my full belief, for I know the vicinity of our old Dutch settlements to have been very subject to marvellous events and appearances. Indeed, I have heard many stranger stories than this, in the villages along the Hudson; all of which were too well authenticated to admit of a doubt. I have even talked with Rip Van Winkle myself, who, when last I saw him, was a very venerable old man, and so perfectly rational and consistent on every other point, that I think no conscientious person could refuse to take this into the bargain; nay, I have seen a certificate on the subject taken before a country justice and signed with a cross, in the justice's own handwriting. The story, therefore, is beyond the possibility of doubt.

—D.K."

POSTSCRIPT

The following are travelling notes from a memorandum-book of Mr. Knickerbocker.

The Kaatsberg, or Catskill Mountains, have always been a region full of fable. The Indians considered them the abode of spirits, who influenced the

---

[7]The legend was that Frederick I (1152–1190) lay asleep in a mountain cave awaiting Germany's rise to world eminence, at which time he would reemerge.

weather, spreading sunshine or clouds over the landscape, and sending good or bad hunting-seasons. They were ruled by an old squaw spirit, said to be their mother. She dwelt on the highest peak of the Catskills, and had charge of the doors of day and night to open and shut them at the proper hour. She hung up the new moons in the skies, and cut up the old ones into stars. In times of drought, if properly propitiated, she would spin light summer clouds out of cobwebs and morning dew, and send them off from the crest of the mountain, flake after flake, like flakes of carded cotton, to float in the air; until, dissolved by the heat of the sun, they would fall in gentle showers, causing the grass to spring, the fruits to ripen, and the corn to grow an inch an hour. If displeased, however, she would brew up clouds black as ink, sitting in the midst of them like a bottle-bellied spider in the midst of its web; and when these clouds broke, woe betide the valleys!

In old times, say the Indian traditions, there was a kind of Manitou or Spirit, who kept about the wildest recesses of the Catskill Mountains, and took a mischievous pleasure in wreaking all kinds of evils and vexations upon the red men. Sometimes he would assume the form of a bear, a panther, or a deer, lead the bewildered hunter a weary chase through tangled forests and among ragged rocks; and then spring off with a loud ho! ho! leaving him aghast on the brink of a beetling precipice or raging torrent.

The favorite abode of this Manitou is still shown. It is a great rock or cliff on the loneliest part of the mountains, and, from the flowering vines which clamber about it, and the wild flowers which abound in its neighborhood, is known by the name of the Garden Rock. Near the foot of it is a small lake, the haunt of the solitary bittern, with water-snakes basking in the sun on the leaves of the pond-lilies which lie on the surface. This place was held in great awe by the Indians, insomuch that the boldest hunter would not pursue his game within its precincts. Once upon a time, however, a hunter who had lost his way, penetrated to the Garden Rock, where he beheld a number of gourds placed in the crotches of trees. One of these he seized and made off with it, but in the hurry of his retreat he let it fall among the rocks, when a great stream gushed forth, which washed him away and swept him down precipices, where he was dashed to pieces, and the stream made its way to the Hudson, and continues to flow to the present day; being the identical stream known by the name of the Kaaters-kill.

1819/1820

The Legend of Sleepy Hollow

Found among the Papers of the Late Diedrich Knickerbocker

> A pleasing land of drowsy head it was,
>   Of dreams that wave before the half-shut eye;
> And of gay castles in the clouds that pass,
>   For ever flushing round a summer sky.

—CASTLE OF INDOLENCE[1]

---

[1]Poem (1748) by James Thomson, British poet.

In the bosom of one of those spacious coves which indent the eastern shore of the Hudson, at that broad expansion of the river denominated by the ancient Dutch navigators the Tappan Zee, and where they always prudently shortened sail, and implored the protection of St. Nicholas when they crossed, there lies a small market-town or rural port, which by some is called Greensburgh, but which is more generally and properly known by the name of Tarry Town. This name was given, we are told, in former days, by the good housewives of the adjacent country, from the inveterate propensity of their husbands to linger about the village tavern on market-days. Be that as it may, I do not vouch for the fact, but merely advert to it for the sake of being precise and authentic. Not far from this village, perhaps about two miles, there is a little valley, or rather lap of land, among high hills, which is one of the quietest places in the whole world. A small brook glides through it, with just murmur enough to lull one to repose; and the occasional whistle of a quail, or tapping of a woodpecker, is almost the only sound that ever breaks in upon the uniform tranquillity.

I recollect that, when a stripling, my first exploit in squirrel-shooting was in a grove of tall walnut-trees that shades one side of the valley. I had wandered into it at noon-time, when all nature is peculiarly quiet, and was startled by the roar of my own gun, as it broke the Sabbath stillness around, and was prolonged and reverberated by the angry echoes. If ever I should wish for a retreat, whither I might steal from the world and its distractions, and dream quietly away the remnant of a troubled life, I know of none more promising than this little valley.

From the listless repose of the place, and the peculiar character of its inhabitants, who are descendants from the original Dutch settlers, this sequestered glen has long been known by the name of SLEEPY HOLLOW, and its rustic lads are called the Sleepy Hollow Boys throughout all the neighboring country. A drowsy, dreamy influence seems to hang over the land, and to pervade the very atmosphere. Some say that the place was bewitched by a high German doctor, during the early days of the settlement; others, that an old Indian chief, the prophet or wizard of his tribe, held his pow-wows there before the country was discovered by Master Hendrick Hudson. Certain it is, the place still continues under the sway of some witching power, that holds a spell over the minds of the good people, causing them to walk in a continual reverie. They are given to all kinds of marvellous beliefs; are subject to trances and visions; and frequently see strange sights, and hear music and voices in the air. The whole neighborhood abounds with local tales, haunted spots, and twilight superstitions; stars shoot and meteors glare oftener across the valley than in any other part of the country, and the nightmare, with her whole ninefold,[2] seems to make it the favorite scene of her gambols.

The dominant spirit, however, that haunts this enchanted region, and seems to be commander-in-chief of all the powers of the air, is the

[2]See *King Lear*, III, iv.

apparition of a figure on horseback without a head. It is said by some to be the ghost of a Hessian trooper, whose head had been carried away by a cannonball, in some nameless battle during the Revolutionary War, and who is ever and anon seen by the country folk, hurrying along in the gloom of night, as if on the wings of the wind. His haunts are not confined to the valley, but extend at times to the adjacent roads, and especially to the vicinity of a church at no great distance. Indeed certain of the most authentic historians of those parts, who have been careful in collecting and collating the floating facts concerning this spectre, allege that the body of the trooper, having been buried in the churchyard, the ghost rides forth to the scene of battle in nightly quest of his head; and that the rushing speed with which he sometimes passes along the Hollow, like a midnight blast, is owing to his being belated, and in a hurry to get back to the church yard before daybreak.

Such is the general purport of this legendary superstition, which has furnished materials for many a wild story in that region of shadows; and the spectre is known, at all the country firesides, by the name of the Headless Horseman of Sleepy Hollow.

It is remarkable that the visionary propensity I have mentioned is not confined to the native inhabitants of the valley, but is unconsciously imbibed by every one who resides there for a time. However wide awake they may have been before they entered that sleepy region, they are sure, in a little time, to inhale the witching influence of the air, and begin to grow imaginative, to dream dreams, and see apparitions.

I mention this peaceful spot with all possible laud; for it is in such little retired Dutch valleys, found here and there embosomed in the great State of New York, that population, manners, and customs remain fixed; while the great torrent of migration and improvement, which is making such incessant changes in other parts of this restless country, sweeps by them unobserved. They are like those little nooks of still water which border a rapid stream; where we may see the straw and bubble riding quietly at anchor, or slowly revolving in their mimic harbor, undisturbed by the rush of the passing current. Though many years have elapsed since I trod the drowsy shades of Sleepy Hollow, yet I question whether I should not still find the same trees and the same families vegetating in its sheltered bosom.

In this by-place of nature, there abode, in a remote period of American history, that is to say, some thirty years since, a worthy wight of the name of Ichabod Crane; who sojourned, or, as he expressed it, "tarried," in Sleepy Hollow, for the purpose of instructing the children of the vicinity. He was a native of Connecticut, a State which supplies the Union with pioneers for the mind as well as for the forest, and sends forth yearly its legions of frontier woodsmen and country schoolmasters. The cognomen of Crane was not inapplicable to his person. He was tall, but exceedingly lank, with narrow shoulders, long arms and legs, hands that dangled a mile out of his sleeves, feet that might have served for shovels, and his whole frame most loosely hung together. His head was small, and flat at top, with huge ears, large green glassy eyes, and a long snipe nose, so that it looked like a weathercock perched upon his spindle neck, to tell which way the wind blew. To see him striding along the profile of a hill on a windy day, with his clothes bagging and fluttering about him, one might have mistaken him for the genius of famine descending upon the earth, or some scarecrow eloped from a cornfield.

His schoolhouse was a low building of one large room, rudely constructed of logs; the windows partly glazed, and partly patched with leaves of old copy-books. It was most ingeniously secured at vacant hours by a withe twisted in the handle of the door, and stakes set against the window-shutters; so that, though a thief might get in with perfect ease, he would find some embarrassment in getting out: an idea most probably borrowed by the architect, Yost Van Houten, from the mystery of an eel-pot. The schoolhouse stood in a rather lonely but pleasant situation, just at the foot of a woody hill, with a brook running close by, and a formidable birch-tree growing at one end of it. From hence the low murmur of his pupils' voices, conning over their lessons, might be heard in a drowsy summer's day, like the hum of a bee-hive; interrupted now and then by the authoritative voice of the master, in the tone of menace or command; or, peradventure, by the appalling sound of the birch, as he urged some tardy loiterer along the flowery path of knowledge. Truth to say, he was a conscientious man, and ever bore in mind the golden maxim, "Spare the rod and spoil the child."[3]—Ichabod Crane's scholars certainly were not spoiled.

I would not have it imagined, however, that he was one of those cruel potentates of the school, who joy in the smart of their subjects; on the contrary, he administered justice with discrimination rather than severity, taking the burden off the backs of the weak, and laying it on those of the strong. Your mere puny stripling, that winced at the least flourish of the rod, was passed by with indulgence; but the claims of justice were satisfied by inflicting a double portion on some little, tough, wrong-headed, broad-skirted Dutch urchin, who sulked and swelled and grew dogged and sullen beneath the birch. All this he called "doing his duty" by their parents; and he never inflicted a chastisement without following it by the assurance, so consolatory to the smarting urchin, that "he would remember it, and thank him for it the longest day he had to live."

When school-hours were over, he was even the companion and playmate of the larger boys; and on holiday afternoons would convoy some of the smaller ones home, who happened to have pretty sisters, or good house-wives for mothers, noted for the comforts of the cupboard. Indeed it behooved him to keep on good terms with his pupils. The revenue arising from his school was small, and would have been scarcely sufficient to furnish him with daily bread, for he was a huge feeder, and, though lank, had

[3]See *Hudibras* by Samuel Butler, English poet (1612–1680), bk. 2, canto 1; also Proverbs, 13:24.

the dilating powers of an anaconda; but to help out his maintenance, he was, according to country custom in those parts, boarded and lodged at the houses of the farmers, whose children he instructed. With these he lived successively a week at a time; thus going the rounds of the neighborhood, with all his worldly effects tied up in a cotten handkerchief.

That all this might not be too onerous on the purses of his rustic patrons, who are apt to consider the costs of schooling a grievous burden, and schoolmasters as mere drones, he had various ways of rendering himself both useful and agreeable. He assisted the farmers occasionally in the lighter labors of their farms; helped to make hay; mended the fences; took the horses to water; drove the cows from pasture; and cut wood for the winter fire. He laid aside, too, all the dominant dignity and absolute sway with which he lorded it in his little empire, the school, and became wonderfully gentle and ingratiating. He found favor in the eyes of the mothers, by petting the children, particularly the youngest; and like the lion bold, which whilom so magnanimously the lamb did hold,[4] he would sit with a child on one knee, and rock a cradle with his foot for whole hours together.

In addition to his other vocations, he was the singing-master of the neighborhood, and picked up many bright shillings by instructing the young folks in psalmody. It was a matter of no little vanity to him, on Sundays, to take his station in front of the church-gallery, with a band of chosen singers; where, in his own mind, he completely carried away the palm from the parson. Certain it is, his voice resounded far above all the rest of the congregation; and there are peculiar quavers still to be heard in that church, and which may even be heard half a mile off, quite to the opposite side of the mill-pond, on a still Sunday morning, which are said to be legitimately descended from the nose of Ichabod Crane. Thus, by divers little make-shifts in that ingenious way which is commonly denominated "by hook and by crook," the worthy pedagogue got on tolerably enough, and was thought, by all who understood nothing of the labor of headwork, to have a wonderfully easy life of it.

The schoolmaster is generally a man of some importance in the female circle of a rural neighborhood; being considered a kind of idle, gentleman-like personage, of vastly superior taste and accomplishments to the rough country swains, and, indeed, inferior in learning only to the parson. His appearance, therefore, is apt to occasion some little stir at the tea-table of a farm-house, and the addition of a supernumerary dish of cakes or sweet-meats, or, peradventure, the parade of a silver teapot. Our man of letters, therefore, was peculiarly happy in the smiles of all the country damsels. How he would figure among them in the churchyard, between services on Sundays! gathering grapes for them from the wild vines that overrun the surrounding trees; reciting for their amusement all the epitaphs on the tombstones; or sauntering, with a whole bevy of them, along the banks of

[4]Alludes to the seventeenth-century *New England Primer*, under the letter *L*.

the adjacent mill-pond; while the more bashful country bumpkins hung sheepishly back, envying his superior elegance and address.

From his half itinerant life, also, he was a kind of travelling gazette, carrying the whole budget of local gossip from house to house: so that his appearance was always greeted with satisfaction. He was, moreover, esteemed by the women as a man of great erudition, for he had read several books quite through, and was a perfect master of Cotton Mather's "History of New England Witchcraft,"[5] in which, by the way, he most firmly and potently believed.

He was, in fact, an odd mixture of small shrewdness and simple credulity. His appetite for the marvellous, and his powers of digesting it, were equally extraordinary; and both had been increased by his residence in this spellbound region. No tale was too gross or monstrous for his capacious swallow. It was often his delight, after his school was dismissed in the afternoon, to stretch himself on the rich bed of clover bordering the little brook that whimpered by his school-house, and there con over old Mather's direful tales, until the gathering dusk of the evening made the printed page a mere mist before his eyes. Then, as he wended his way, by swamp and stream, and awful woodland, to the farmhouse where he happened to be quartered, every sound of nature, at that witching hour, fluttered his excited imagination; the moan of the whippoorwill from the hill-side; the boding cry of the tree-toad, that harbinger of storm; the dreary hooting of the screech-owl, or the sudden rustling in the thicket of birds frightened from their roost. The fire-flies, too, which sparkled most vividly in the darkest places, now and then startled him, as one of uncommon brightness would stream across his path; and if, by chance, a huge blockhead of a beetle came winging his blundering flight against him, the poor varlet was ready to give up the ghost, with the idea that he was struck with a witch's token. His only resource on such occasions, either to drown thought or drive away evil spirits, was to sing psalm-tunes; and the good people of Sleepy Hollow, as they sat by their doors of an evening, were often filled with awe, at hearing his nasal melody, "in linked sweetness long drawn out,"[6] floating from the distant hill, or along the dusky road.

Another of his sources of fearful pleasure was, to pass long winter evenings with the old Dutch wives, as they sat spinning by the fire, with a row of apples roasting and spluttering along the hearth, and listen to their marvellous tales of ghosts and goblins, and haunted fields, and haunted brooks, and haunted bridges, and haunted houses, and particularly of the headless horseman, or Galloping Hessian of the Hollow, as they sometimes called him. He would delight them equally by his anecdotes of witchcraft, and of the direful omens and portentous sights and sounds in the air, which prevailed in the earlier times of Connecticut; and would frighten them wofully with speculations upon comets and shooting stars, and with the alarming

---

[5]An erroneous title, although Mather (1663–1728) did write extensively on witchcraft.   [6]Milton, *L'Allegro*, 1. 140.

fact that the world did absolutely turn round, and that they were half the time topsy-turvy!

But if there was a pleasure in all this, while snugly cuddling in the chimney-corner of a chamber that was all of a ruddy glow from the crackling wood-fire, and where, of course, no spectre dared to show his face, it was dearly purchased by the terrors of his subsequent walk homewards. What fearful shapes and shadows beset his path amidst the dim and ghastly glare of a snowy night!—With what wistful look did he eye every trembling ray of light streaming across the waste fields from some distant window!—How often was he appalled by some shrub covered with snow, which, like a sheeted spectre, beset his very path!—How often did he shrink with curdling awe at the sound of his own steps on the frosty crust beneath his feet; and dread to look over his shoulder, lest he should behold some uncouth being tramping close behind him!—and how often was he thrown into complete dismay by some rushing blast, howling among the trees, in the idea that it was the Galloping Hessian on one of his nightly scourings!

All these, however, were mere terrors of the night, phantoms of the mind that walk in darkness; and though he had seen many spectres in his time, and been more than once beset by Satan in divers shapes, in his lonely perambulations, yet daylight put an end to all these evils; and he would have passed a pleasant life of it, in despite of the devil and all his works, if his path had not been crossed by a being that causes more perplexity to mortal man than ghosts, goblins, and the whole race of witches put together, and that was—a woman.

Among the musical disciples who assembled, one evening in each week, to receive his instructions in psalmody, was Katrina Van Tassel, the daughter and only child of a substantial Dutch farmer. She was a blooming lass of fresh eighteen; plump as a partridge; ripe and melting and rosy-cheeked as one of her father's peaches, and universally famed, not merely for her beauty, but her vast expectations. She was withal a little of a coquette, as might be perceived even in her dress, which was a mixture of ancient and modern fashions, as most suited to set off her charms. She wore the ornaments of pure yellow gold, which her great-great-grandmother had brought over from Saardam; the tempting stomacher of the olden time; and withal a provokingly short petticoat, to display the prettiest foot and ankle in the country round.

Ichabod Crane had a soft and foolish heart towards the sex; and it is not to be wondered at that so tempting a morsel soon found favor in his eyes; more especially after he had visited her in her paternal mansion. Old Baltus Van Tassel was a perfect picture of a thriving, contented, liberal-hearted farmer. He seldom, it is true, sent either his eyes or his thoughts beyond the boundaries of his own farm; but within those everything was snug, happy, and well-conditioned. He was satisfied with his wealth, but not proud of it; and piqued himself upon the hearty abundance rather than the style in which he lived. His stronghold was situated on the banks of the Hudson, in one of those green, sheltered, fertile nooks in which the Dutch farmers are so fond of nestling. A great elm-tree spread its broad branches over it; at the foot of which bubbled up a spring of the softest and sweetest water, in a little well, formed of a barrel; and then stole sparkling away through the grass, to a neighboring brook that bubbled along among alders and dwarf willows. Hard by the farm-house was a vast barn, that might have served for a church; every window and crevice of which seemed bursting forth with the treasures of the farm; the flail was busily resounding within it from morning till night; swallows and martins skimmed twittering about the eaves; and rows of pigeons, some with one eye turned up, as if watching the weather, some with their heads under their wings, or buried in their bosoms, and others swelling, and cooing, and bowing about their dames, were enjoying the sunshine on the roof. Sleek unwieldly porkers were grunting in the repose and abundance of their pens; whence sallied forth, now and then, troops of sucking pigs, as if to snuff the air. A stately squadron of snowy geese were riding in an adjoining pond, convoying whole fleets of ducks; regiments of turkeys were gobbling through the farm-yard, and guinea fowls fretting about it, like ill-tempered housewives, with their peevish discontented cry. Before the barn-door strutted the gallant cock, that pattern of a husband, a warrior, and a fine gentleman, clapping his burnished wings, and crowing in the pride and gladness of his heart—sometimes tearing up the earth with his feet, and then generously calling his ever-hungry family of wives and children to enjoy the rich morsel which he had discovered.

The pedagogue's mouth watered, as he looked upon this sumptuous promise of luxurious winter fare. In his devouring mind's eye he pictured to himself every roasting-pig running about with a pudding in his belly, and an apple in his mouth; the pigeons were snugly put to bed in a comfortable pie, and tucked in with a coverlet of crust; the geese were swimming in their own gravy; and the ducks pairing cosily in dishes, like snug married couples, with a decent competency of onion-sauce. In the porkers he saw carved out the future sleek side of bacon, and juicy relishing ham; not a turkey but he beheld daintily trussed up, with its gizzard under its wing, and, peradventure, a necklace of savory sausages; and even bright chanticleer himself lay sprawling on his back, in a side-dish, with uplifted claws, as if craving that quarter which his chivalrous spirit disdained to ask while living.

As the enraptured Ichabod fancied all this, and as he rolled his great green eyes over the fat meadow-lands, the rich fields of wheat, of rye, of buckwheat, and Indian corn, and the orchard burdened with ruddy fruit, which surrounded the warm tenement of Van Tassel, his heart yearned after the damsel who was to inherit these domains, and his imagination expanded with the idea how they might be readily turned into cash, and the money invested in immense tracts of wild land, and shingle palaces in the wilderness. Nay, his busy fancy already realized his hopes, and presented to him the blooming Katrina, with a whole family of children, mounted on the top of a wagon loaded with household trumpery, with pots and kettles dangling beneath; and he beheld himself bestriding a pacing mare, with a colt at her heels, setting out for Kentucky, Tennessee, or the Lord knows where.

When he entered the house, the conquest of his heart was complete. It was one of those spacious farm-houses, with high-ridged, but lowly-sloping roofs, built in the style handed down from the first Dutch settlers; the low projecting eaves forming a piazza along the front, capable of being closed up in bad weather. Under this were hung flails, harness, various utensils of husbandry, and nets for fishing in the neighboring river. Benches were built along the sides for summer use; and a great spinning-wheel at one end, and a churn at the other, showed the various uses to which this important porch might be devoted. From this piazza the wondering Ichabod entered the hall, which formed the centre of the mansion and the place of usual residence. Here, rows of resplendent pewter, ranged on a long dresser, dazzled his eyes. In one corner stood a huge bag of wool ready to be spun; in another a quantity of linsey-woolsey just from the loom; ears of Indian corn, and strings of dried apples and peaches, hung in gay festoons along the walls, mingled with the gaud of red peppers; and a door left ajar gave him a peep into the best parlor, where the claw-footed chairs and dark mahogany tables shone like mirrors; and irons, with their accompanying shovel and tongs, glistened from their covert of asparagus tops; mock-oranges and conch-shells decorated the mantel-piece; strings of various colored birds' eggs were suspended above it; a great ostrich egg was hung from the centre of the room, and a corner-cupboard, knowingly left open, displayed immense treasures of old silver and well-mended china.

From the moment Ichabod laid his eyes upon these regions of delight, the peace of his mind was at an end, and his only study was how to gain the affections of the peerless daughter of Van Tassel. In this enterprise, however, he had more real difficulties than generally fell to the lot of a knight-errant of yore, who seldom had anything but giants, enchanters, fiery dragons, and such like easily conquered adversaries, to contend with; and had to make his way merely through gates of iron and brass, and walls of adamant, to the castle-keep, where the lady of his heart was confined; all which he achieved as easily as a man would carve his way to the centre of a Christmas pie; and then the lady gave him her hand as a matter of course. Ichabod, on the contrary, had to win his way to the heart of a country coquette, beset with a labyrinth of whims and caprices, which were forever presenting new difficulties and impediments; and he had to encounter a host of fearful adversaries of real flesh and blood, the numerous rustic admirers, who beset every portal to her heart; keeping a watchful and angry eye upon each other, but ready to fly out in the common cause against any new competitor.

Among these the most formidable was a burly, roaring, roistering blade, of the name of Abraham, or, according to the Dutch abbreviation, Brom Van Brunt, the hero of the country round, which rang with his feats of strength and hardihood. He was broad-shouldered, and double-jointed, with short curly black hair, and a bluff but not unpleasant countenance, having a mingled air of fun and arrogance. From his Herculean frame and great powers of limb, he had received the nickname of BROM BONES, by which he was universally known. He was famed for great knowledge and skill in horsemanship, being as dexterous on horseback as a Tartar. He was foremost at all races and cockfights; and, with the ascendency which bodily strength acquires in rustic life, was the umpire in all disputes, setting his hat on one side, and giving his decisions with an air and tone admitting of no gainsay or appeal. He was always ready for either a fight or a frolic; but had more mischief than ill-will in his composition; and, with all his overbearing roughness, there was a strong dash of waggish good-humor at bottom. He had three or four boon companions, who regarded him as their model, and at the head of whom he scoured the country, attending every scene of feud or merriment for miles round. In cold weather he was distinguished by a fur cap, surmounted with a flaunting fox's tail; and when the folks at a country gathering descried this well-known crest at a distance, whisking about among a squad of hard riders, they always stood by for a squall. Sometimes his crew would be heard dashing along past the farmhouses at midnight, with whoop and halloo, like a troop of Don Cossacks; and the old dames, startled out of their sleep, would listen for a moment till the hurry-scurry had clattered by, and then exclaim, "Ay, there goes Brom Bones and his gang!" The neighbors looked upon him with a mixture of awe, admiration, and good-will; and when any madcap prank, or rustic brawl, occurred in the vicinity, always shook their heads, and warranted Brom Bones was at the bottom of it.

This rantipole[7] hero had for some time singled out the blooming Katrina for the object of his uncouth gallantries; and though his amorous toyings were something like the gentle caresses and endearments of a bear, yet it was whispered that she did not altogether discourage his hopes. Certain it is, his advances were signals for rival candidates to retire, who felt no inclination to cross a lion in his amours; insomuch, that, when his horse was seen tied to Van Tassel's paling, on a Sunday night, a sure sign that his master was courting, or, as it is termed, "sparking," within, all other suitors passed by in despair, and carried the war into other quarters.

Such was the formidable rival with whom Ichabod Crane had to contend, and, considering all things, a stouter man than he would have shrunk from the competition, and a wiser man would have despaired. He had, however, a happy mixture of pliability and perseverance in his nature; he was in form and spirit like a supplejack—yielding, but tough; though he bent, he never broke; and though he bowed beneath the slightest pressure, yet, the moment it was away—jerk! he was as erect, and carried his head as high as ever.

To have taken the field openly against his rival would have been madness; for he was not a man to be thwarted in his amours, any more than that stormy lover, Achilles. Ichabod, therefore, made his advances in a quiet and gently insinuating manner. Under cover of his character of singingmaster, he had made frequent visits at the farm-house; not that he had

---

[7]Wild, reckless.

anything to apprehend from the meddlesome interference of parents, which is so often a stumbling-block in the path of lovers. Balt Van Tassel was an easy, indulgent soul; he loved his daughter better even than his pipe, and, like a reasonable man and an excellent father, let her have her way in everything. His notable little wife, too, had enough to do to attend to her housekeeping and manage her poultry; for, as she sagely observed, ducks and geese are foolish things, and must be looked after, but girls can take care of themselves. Thus while the busy dame bustled about the house, or plied her spinning-wheel at one end of the piazza, honest Balt would sit smoking his evening pipe at the other, watching the achievements of a little wooden warrior, who, armed with a sword in each hand, was most valiantly fighting the wind on the pinnacle of the barn. In the mean time, Ichabod would carry on his suit with the daughter by the side of the spring under the great elm, or sauntering along in the twilight,—that hour so favorable to the lover's eloquence.

I profess not to know how women's hearts are wooed and won. To me they have always been matters of riddle and admiration. Some seem to have but one vulnerable point, or door of access; while others have a thousand avenues, and may be captured in a thousand different ways. It is a great triumph of skill to gain the former, but a still greater proof of generalship to maintain possession of the latter, for the man must battle for his fortress at every door and window. He who wins a thousand common hearts is therefore entitled to some renown; but he who keeps undisputed sway over the heart of a coquette, is indeed a hero. Certain it is, this was not the case with the redoubtable Brom Bones; and from the moment Ichabod Crane made his advances, the interests of the former evidently declined; his horse was no longer seen tied at the palings on Sunday nights, and a deadly feud gradually arose between him and the preceptor of Sleepy Hollow.

Brom, who had a degree of rough chivalry in his nature, would fain have carried matters to open warfare, and have settled their pretensions to the lady according to the mode of those most concise and simple reasoners, the knights-errant of yore—by single combat; but Ichabod was too conscious of the superior might of his adversary to enter the lists against him: he had overheard a boast of Bones, that he would "double the schoolmaster up, and lay him on a shelf of his own school-house"; and he was too wary to give him an opportunity. There was something extremely provoking in this obstinately pacific system; it left Brom no alternative but to draw upon the funds of rustic waggery in his disposition, and to play off boorish practical jokes upon his rival. Ichabod became the object of whimsical persecution to Bones and his gang of rough riders. They harried his hitherto peaceful domains; smoked out his singing-school, by stopping up the chimney; broke into the school-house at night, in spite of its formidable fastenings of withe and window-stakes, and turned everything topsy-turvy: so that the poor schoolmaster began to think all the witches in the country held their meetings there. But what was still more annoying, Brom took opportunities of turning him into ridicule in presence of his mistress, and had a scoundrel dog whom he taught to whine in the most ludicrous manner, and introduced as a rival of Ichabod's to instruct her in psalmody.

In this way matters went on for some time, without producing any material effect on the relative situation of the contending powers. On a fine autumnal afternoon, Ichabod, in pensive mood, sat enthroned on the lofty stool whence he usually watched all the concerns of his little literary realm. In his hand he swayed a ferule, that sceptre of despotic power; the birch of justice reposed on three nails, behind the throne, a constant terror to evildoers; while on the desk before him might be seen sundry contraband articles and prohibited weapons, detected upon the persons of idle urchins; such as half-munched apples, popguns, whirligigs, fly-cages, and whole legions of rampant little paper game-cocks. Apparently there had been some appalling act of justice recently inflicted, for his scholars were all busily intent upon their books, or slyly whispering behind them with one eye kept upon the master; and a kind of buzzing stillness reigned throughout the school-room. It was suddenly interrupted by the appearance of a negro, in tow-cloth jacket and trousers, a round-crowned fragment of a hat, like the cap of Mercury, and mounted on the back of a ragged, wild, half-broken colt, which he managed with a rope by way of halter. He came clattering up to the school-door with an invitation to Ichabod to attend a merry-making or "quilting frolic," to be held that evening at Mynheer Van Tassel's; and having delivered his message with that air of importance, and effort at fine language, which a negro is apt to display on petty embassies of the kind, he dashed over the brook, and was seen scampering away up the Hollow, full of the importance and hurry of his mission.

All was now bustle and hubbub in the late quiet school-room. The scholars were hurried through their lessons, without stopping at trifles; those who were nimble skipped over half with impunity, and those who were tardy had a smart application now and then in the rear, to quicken their speed, or help them over a tall word. Books were flung aside without being put away on the shelves, inkstands were overturned, benches thrown down, and the whole school was turned loose an hour before the usual time, bursting forth like a legion of young imps, yelping and racketing about the green, in joy at their early emancipation.

The gallant Ichabod now spent at least an extra half-hour at his toilet, brushing and furbishing up his best and indeed only suit of rusty black, and arranging his looks by a bit of broken looking-glass, that hung up in the school-house. That he might make his appearance before his mistress in the true style of a cavalier, he borrowed a horse from the farmer with whom he was domiciliated, a choleric old Dutchman, of the name of Hans Van Ripper, and, thus gallantly mounted, issued forth, like a knight-errant in quest of adventures. But it is meet I should, in the true spirit of romantic story, give some account of the looks and equipments of my hero and his steed. The animal he bestrode was a broken-down plough-horse, that had outlived almost everything but his viciousness. He was gaunt and shagged, with a ewe neck and a head like a hammer; his rusty mane and tail were tangled and knotted with burrs; one eye had lost its pupil, and was glaring and spec-tral; but the other had the gleam of a genuine devil in it. Still he must have had fire and mettle in his day, if we may judge from the name he bore of Gunpowder. He had, in fact, been a favorite steed of his master's, the chol-eric Van Ripper, who was a furious rider, and had infused, very probably, some of his own spirit into the animal; for, old and broken-down as he looked, there was more of the lurking devil in him than in any young filly in the country.

Ichabod was a suitable figure for such a steed. He rode with short stir-rups, which brought his knees nearly up to the pommel of the saddle; his sharp elbows stuck out like grasshoppers'; he carried his whip perpendicu-larly in his hand, like a sceptre, and, as his horse jogged on, the motion of his arms was not unlike the flapping of a pair of wings. A small wool hat rested on the top of his nose, for so his scanty strip of forehead might be called; and the skirts of his black coat fluttered out almost to the horse's tail. Such was the appearance of Ichabod and his steed, as they shambled out of the gate of Hans Van Ripper, and it was altogether such an apparition as is seldom to be met with in broad daylight.

It was, as I have said, a fine autumnal day, the sky was clear and serene, and nature wore that rich and golden livery which we always associate with the idea of abundance. The forests had put on their sober brown and yellow, while some trees of the tenderer kind had been nipped by the frosts into brilliant dyes of orange, purple, and scarlet. Streaming files of wild ducks began to make their appearance high in the air; the bark of the squirrel might be heard from the groves of beech and hickory nuts, and the pensive whistle of the quail at intervals from the neighboring stubble-field.

The small birds were taking their farewell banquets. In the fulness of their revelry, they fluttered, chirping and frolicking, from bush to bush, and tree to tree, capricious from the very profusion and variety around them. There was the honest cockrobin, the favorite game of stripling sportsmen, with its loud querulous notes; and the twittering blackbirds flying in sable clouds; and the golden-winged woodpecker, with his crimson crest, his broad black gorget, and splendid plumage; and the cedar-bird, with its red-tipt wings and yellow-tipt tail, and its little monteiro cap of feathers; and the blue jay, that noisy coxcomb, in his gay light-blue coat and white under-clothes, screaming and chattering, nodding and bobbing and bowing, and pretending to be on good terms with every songster of the grove.

As Ichabod jogged slowly on his way, his eye, ever open to every symp-tom of culinary abundance, ranged with delight over the treasures of jolly autumn. On all sides he beheld vast store of apples; some hanging in oppres-sive opulence on the trees; some gathered into baskets and barrels for the market; others heaped up in rich piles for the cider-press. Farther on he beheld great fields of Indian corn, with its golden ears peeping from their leafy coverts, and holding out the promise of cakes and hasty-pudding; and the yellow pumpkins lying beneath them, turning up their fair round bellies to the sun, and giving ample prospects of the most luxurious of pies; and anon he passed the fragrant buckwheat fields, breathing the odor of the bee-hive, and as he beheld them, soft anticipations stole over his mind of dainty slapjacks, well buttered, and garnished with honey or treacle, by the delicate little dimpled hand of Katrina Van Tassel.

Thus feeding his mind with many sweet thoughts and "sugared suppositions," he journeyed along the sides of a range of hills which look out upon some of the goodliest scenes of the mighty Hudson. The sun gradually wheeled his broad disk down into the west. The wide bosom of the Tappan Zee lay motionless and glossy, excepting that here and there a gentle undulation waved and prolonged the blue shadow of the distant mountain. A few amber clouds floated in the sky, without a breath of air to move them. The horizon was of a fine golden tint, changing gradually into a pure apple-green, and from that into the deep blue of the mid-heaven. A slanting ray lingered on the woody crests of the precipices that overhung some parts of the river, giving greater depth to the dark-gray and purple of their rocky sides. A sloop was loitering in the distance, dropping slowly down with the tide, her sail hanging uselessly against the mast; and as the reflection of the sky gleamed along the still water, it seemed as if the vessel was suspended in the air.

It was toward evening that Ichabod arrived at the castle of the Heer Van Tassel, which he found thronged with the pride and flower of the adjacent country. Old farmers, a spare leathern-faced race, in homespun coats and breeches, blue stockings, huge shoes, and magnificent pewter buckles. Their brisk withered little dames, in close crimped caps, long-waisted shortgowns, homespun petticoats, with scissors and pincushions, and gay calico pockets hanging on the outside. Buxom lasses, almost as antiquated as their mothers, excepting where a straw hat, a fine ribbon, or perhaps a white frock, gave symptoms of city innovation. The sons, in short square-skirted coats with rows of stupendous brass buttons, and their hair generally queued in the fashion of the times, especially if they could procure an eel-skin for the purpose, it being esteemed, throughout the country, as a potent nourisher and strengthener of the hair.

Brom Bones, however, was the hero of the scene, having come to the gathering on his favorite steed, Daredevil, a creature, like himself, full of mettle and mischief, and which no one but himself could manage. He was, in fact, noted for preferring vicious animals, given to all kinds of tricks, which kept the rider in constant risk of his neck, for he held a tractable well-broken horse as unworthy of a lad of spirit.

Fain would I pause to dwell upon the world of charms that burst upon the enraptured gaze of my hero, as he entered the state parlor of Van Tassel's mansion. Not those of the bevy of buxom lasses, with their luxurious display of red and white; but the ample charms of a genuine Dutch country tea-table, in the sumptuous time of autumn. Such heaped-up platters of cakes of various and almost indescribable kinds, known only to experienced Dutch housewives! There was the doughty doughnut, the tenderer oly koek, and the crisp and crumbling cruller; sweet cakes and short cakes, ginger-cakes and honey-cakes, and the whole family of cakes. And then there were apple-pies and peach-pies and pumpkin-pies; besides slices of ham and smoked beef; and moreover delectable dishes of preserved plums, and peaches, and pears, and quinces; not to mention broiled shad and roasted chickens; together with bowls of milk and cream, all mingled higgledy-piggledy, pretty much as I have enumerated them, with the motherly tea-pot sending up its clouds of vapor from the midst—Heaven bless the mark! I want breath and time to discuss this banquet as it deserves, and am too eager to get on with my story. Happily, Ichabod Crane was not in so great a hurry as his historian, but did ample justice to every dainty.

He was a kind and thankful creature, whose heart dilated in proportion as his skin was filled with good cheer; and whose spirits rose with eating as some men's do with drink. He could not help, too, rolling his large eyes round him as he ate, and chuckling with the possibility that he might one day be lord of all this scene of almost unimaginable luxury and splendor. Then, he thought, how soon he'd turn his back upon the old school-house; snap his fingers in the face of Hans Van Ripper, and every other niggardly patron, and kick any itinerant pedagogue out-of-doors that should dare to call him comrade!

Old Baltus Van Tassel moved about among his guests with a face dilated with content and good-humor, round and jolly as the harvest-moon. His hospitable attentions were brief, but expressive, being confined to a shake of the hand, a slap on the shoulder, a loud laugh, and a pressing invitation to "fall to, and help themselves."

And now the sound of the music from the common room, or hall, sum-moned to the dance. The musician was an old gray-headed negro, who had been the itinerant orchestra of the neighborhood for more than half a cen-tury. His instrument was as old and battered as himself. The greater part of the time he scraped on two or three strings accompanying every movement of the bow with a motion of the head; bowing almost to the ground and stamping with his foot whenever a fresh couple were to start.

Ichabod prided himself upon his dancing as much as upon his vocal powers. Not a limb, not a fibre about him was idle; and to have seen his loosely hung frame in full motion, and clattering about the room, you would have thought Saint Vitus himself, that blessed patron of the dance, was fig-uring before you in person. He was the admiration of all the negroes; who, having gathered, of all ages and sizes, from the farm and the neighborhood, stood forming a pyramid of shining black faces at every door and window, gazing with delight at the scene, rolling their white eyeballs, and showing grinning rows of ivory from ear to ear. How could the flogger of urchins be otherwise than animated and joyous? the lady of his heart was his partner in the dance, and smiling graciously in reply to all his amorous oglings; while Brom Bones, sorely smitten with love and jealousy, sat brooding by himself in one corner.

When the dance was at an end, Ichabod was attracted to a knot of the sager folks, who, with old Van Tassel, sat smoking at one end of the piazza, gossiping over former times, and drawing out long stories about the war.

This neighborhood, at the time of which I am speaking, was one of those highly favored places which abound with chronicle and great men. The British and American line had run near it during the war; it had, therefore, been the scene of marauding, and infested with refugees, cow-boys,[8] and all kinds of border chivalry. Just sufficient time had elapsed to enable each story-teller to dress up his tale with a little becoming fiction, and, in the indistinctness of his recollection, to make himself the hero of every exploit.

There was the story of Doffue Martling, a large blue-bearded Dutchman, who had nearly taken a British frigate with an old iron nine-pounder from a mud breastwork, only that his gun burst at the sixth discharge. And there was an old gentleman who shall be nameless, being too rich a mynheer to be lightly mentioned, who, in the battle of Whiteplains, being an excellent master of defence, parried a musketball with a small sword, insomuch that he absolutely felt it whiz round the blade, and glance off at the hilt; in proof of which he was ready at any time to show the sword, with the hilt a little bent. There were several more that had been equally great in the field, not one of whom but was persuaded that he had a considerable hand in bringing the war to a happy termination.

But all these were nothing to the tales of ghosts and apparitions that succeeded. The neighborhood is rich in legendary treasures of the kind. Local tales and superstitions thrive best in these sheltered long-settled retreats; but are trampled underfoot by the shifting throng that forms the population of most of our country places. Besides, there is no encouragement for ghosts in most of our villages, for they have scarcely had time to finish their first nap, and turn themselves in their graves, before their surviving friends have travelled away from the neighborhood; so that when they turn out at night to walk their rounds, they have no acquaintance left to call upon. This is perhaps the reason why we so seldom hear of ghosts, except in our long-established Dutch communities.

The immediate cause, however, of the prevalence of supernatural stories in these parts was doubtless owing to the vicinity of Sleepy Hollow. There was a contagion in the very air that blew from that haunted region; it breathed forth an atmosphere of dreams and fancies infecting all the land. Several of the Sleepy Hollow people were present at Van Tassel's, and, as usual, were doling out their wild and wonderful legends. Many dismal tales were told about funeral trains, and mourning cries and wailings heard and seen about the great tree where the unfortunate Major André was taken,[9] and which stood in the neighborhood. Some mention was made also of the woman in white, that haunted the dark glen at Raven Rock, and was often heard to shriek on winter nights before a storm, having perished there in the snow. The chief part of the stories, however, turned upon the favorite spectre of Sleepy Hollow, the headless horseman, who had been heard

---

[8]Guerrilla troops, active in the region during the Revolution.

[9]British officer involved in Benedict Arnold's desertion, executed as a spy by the Americans.

several times of late, patrolling the country; and, it was said, tethered his horse nightly among the graves in the churchyard.

The sequestered situation of this church seems always to have made it a favorite haunt of troubled spirits. It stands on a knoll, surrounded by locust-trees and lofty elms, from among which its decent whitewashed walls shine modestly forth, like Christian purity beaming through the shades of retirement. A gentle slope descends from it to a silver sheet of water, bordered by high trees, between which, peeps may be caught at the blue hills of the Hudson. To look upon its grass-grown yard, where the sunbeams seem to sleep so quietly, one would think that there at least the dead might rest in peace. On one side of the church extends a wide woody dell, along which raves a large brook among broken rocks and trunks of fallen trees. Over a deep black part of the stream, not far from the church, was formerly thrown a wooden bridge; the road that led to it, and the bridge itself, were thickly shaded by overhanging trees, which cast a gloom about it, even in the daytime, but occasioned a fearful darkness at night. This was one of the favorite haunts of the headless horseman; and the place where he was most frequently encountered. The tale was told of old Brouwer, a most heretical disbeliever in ghosts, how he met the horseman returning from his foray into Sleepy Hollow, and was obliged to get up behind him; how they galloped over bush and brake, over hill and swamp, until they reached the bridge; when the horseman suddenly turned into a skeleton, threw old Brouwer into the brook, and sprang away over the tree-tops with a clap of thunder.

This story was immediately matched by a thrice marvellous adventure of Brom Bones, who made light of the galloping Hessian as an arrant jockey. He affirmed that, on returning one night from the neighboring village of Sing Sing, he had been overtaken by this midnight trooper; that he had offered to race with him for a bowl of punch, and should have won it too, for Daredevil beat the goblin horse all hollow, but, just as they came to the church-bridge, the Hessian bolted, and vanished in a flash of fire.

All these tales, told in that drowsy undertone with which men talk in the dark, the countenances of the listeners only now and then receiving a casual gleam from the glare of a pipe, sank deep in the mind of Ichabod. He repaid them in kind with large extracts from his invaluable author, Cotton Mather, and added many marvellous events that had taken place in his native State of Connecticut, and fearful sights which he had seen in his nightly walks about the Sleepy Hollow.

The revel now gradually broke up. The old farmers gathered together their families in their wagons, and were heard for some time rattling along the hollow roads, and over the distant hills. Some of the damsels mounted on pillions behind their favorite swains, and their light-hearted laughter, mingling with the clatter of hoofs, echoed along the silent woodlands, sounding fainter and fainter until they gradually died away—and the late scene of noise and frolic was all silent and deserted. Ichabod only lingered behind, according to the custom of country lovers, to have a *tête-à-tête* with the heiress, fully convinced that he was now on the high road to success.

What passed at this interview I will not pretend to say, for in fact I do not know. Something, however, I fear me, must have gone wrong, for he certainly sallied forth, after no very great interval, with an air quite desolate and chop-fallen.—Oh, these women! these women! Could that girl have been playing off any of her coquettish tricks?—Was her encouragement of the poor pedagogue all a mere sham to secure her conquest of his rival?—Heaven only knows, not I!—Let it suffice to say, Ichabod stole forth with the air of one who had been sacking a hen-roost, rather than a fair lady's heart. Without looking to the right or left to notice the scene of rural wealth on which he had so often gloated, he went straight to the stable, and with several hearty cuffs and kicks, roused his steed most uncourteously from the comfortable quarters in which he was soundly sleeping, dreaming of mountains of corn and oats, and whole valleys of timothy and clover.

It was the very witching time of night[10] that Ichabod, heavy hearted and crest-fallen, pursued his travel homewards, along the sides of the lofty hills which rise above Tarry Town, and which he had traversed so cheerily in the afternoon. The hour was as dismal as himself. Far below him, the Tappan Zee spread its dusky and indistinct waste of waters, with here and there the tall mast of a sloop riding quietly at anchor under the land. In the dead hush of midnight he could even hear the barking of the watch-dog from the opposite shore of the Hudson; but it was so vague and faint as only to give an idea of his distance from this faithful companion of man. Now and then, too, the long-drawn crowing of a cock, accidentally awakened, would sound far, far off, from some farm-house away among the hills—but it was like a dreaming sound in his ear. No signs of life occurred near him, but occasionally the melancholy chirp of a cricket, or perhaps the guttural twang of a bull-frog, from a neighboring marsh, as if sleeping uncomfortably, and turning suddenly in his bed.

All the stories of ghosts and goblins that he had heard in the afternoon, now came crowding upon his recollection. The night grew darker and darker; the stars seemed to sink deeper in the sky, and driving clouds occasionally hid them from his sight. He had never felt so lonely and dismal. He was, moreover, approaching the very place where many of the scenes of the ghost-stories had been laid. In the centre of the road stood an enormous tulip-tree, which towered like a giant above all the other trees of the neighborhood, and formed a kind of landmark. Its limbs were gnarled, and fantastic, large enough to form trunks for ordinary trees, twisting down almost to the earth, and rising again into the air. It was connected with the tragical story of the unfortunate André, who had been taken prisoner hard by; and was universally known by the name of Major André's tree. The common people regarded it with a mixture of respect and superstition, partly out of sympathy for the fate of its ill-starred namesake, and partly from the tales of strange sights and doleful lamentations told concerning it.

[10]*Hamlet*, III, ii.

As Ichabod approached this fearful tree, he began to whistle: he thought his whistle was answered,—it was but a blast sweeping sharply through the dry branches. As he approached a little nearer, he thought he saw something white, hanging in the midst of the tree,—he paused and ceased whistling; but on looking more narrowly, perceived that it was a place where the tree had been scathed by lightning, and the white wood laid bare. Suddenly he heard a groan,—his teeth chattered and his knees smote against the saddle: it was but the rubbing of one huge bough upon another, as they were swayed about by the breeze. He passed the tree in safety; but new perils lay before him.

About two hundred yards from the tree a small brook crossed the road, and ran into a marshy and thickly wooded glen, known by the name of Wiley's swamp. A few rough logs, laid side by side, served for a bridge over this stream. On that side of the road where the brook entered the wood, a group of oaks and chestnuts, matted thick with wild grape-vines, threw a cavernous gloom over it. To pass this bridge was the severest trial. It was at this identical spot that the unfortunate André was captured, and under the covert of those chestnuts and vines were the sturdy yeomen concealed who surprised him. This has ever since been considered a haunted stream, and fearful are the feelings of the school boy who has to pass it alone after dark.

As he approached the stream, his heart began to thump; he summoned up, however, all his resolution, gave his horse half a score of kicks in the ribs, and attempted to dash briskly across the bridge; but instead of starting forward, the perverse old animal made a lateral movement, and ran broadside against the fence. Ichabod, whose fears increased with the delay, jerked the reins on the other side, and kicked lustily with the contrary foot: it was all in vain; his steed started, it is true, but it was only to plunge to the opposite side of the road into a thicket of brambles and alder bushes. The schoolmaster now bestowed both whip and heel upon the starveling ribs of old Gunpowder, who dashed forward, snuffling and snorting, but came to a stand just by the bridge, with a suddenness that had nearly sent his rider sprawling over his head. Just at this moment a plashy tramp by the side of the bridge caught the sensitive ear of Ichabod. In the dark shadow of the grove, on the margin of the brook, he beheld something huge, misshapen, black, and towering. It stirred not, but seemed gathered up in the gloom, like some gigantic monster ready to spring upon the traveller.

The hair of the affrighted pedagogue rose upon his head with terror. What was to be done? To turn and fly was not too late; and besides, what chance was there of escaping ghost or goblin, if such it was, which could ride upon the wings of the wind? Summoning up, therefore, a show of courage, he demanded in stammering accents—"Who are you?" He received no reply. He repeated his demand in a still more agitated voice. Still there was no answer. Once more he cudgelled the sides of the inflexible Gunpowder, and, shutting his eyes, broke forth with involuntary fervor into a psalm-tune. Just then the shadowy object of alarm put itself in motion, and, with a scramble and a bound, stood at once in the middle of the road. Though the night was dark and dismal, yet the form of the unknown might now in some degree be ascertained. He appeared to be a horseman of large dimensions, and mounted on a black horse of powerful frame. He made no offer of molestation or sociability, but kept aloof on one side of the road, jogging along on the blind side of old Gunpowder, who had now got over his fright and waywardness.

Ichabod, who had no relish for this strange midnight companion, and bethought himself of the adventure of Brom Bones with the Galloping Hessian, now quickened his steed, in hopes of leaving him behind. The stranger, however, quickened his horse to an equal pace. Ichabod pulled up, and fell into a walk, thinking to lag behind,—the other did the same. His heart began to sink within him; he endeavored to resume his psalm-tune, but his parched tongue clove to the roof of his mouth, and he could not utter a stave. There was something in the moody and dogged silence of this pertinacious companion, that was mysterious and appalling. It was soon fearfully accounted for. On mounting a rising ground, which brought the figure of his fellow-traveller in relief against the sky, gigantic in height, and muffled in a cloak, Ichabod was horror-struck, on perceiving that he was headless!—but his horror was still more increased, on observing that the head, which should have rested on his shoulders, was carried before him on the pommel of the saddle: his terror rose to desperation; he rained a shower of kicks and blows upon Gunpowder, hoping, by a sudden movement, to give his companion the slip,—but the spectre started full jump with him. Away then they dashed, through thick and thin; stones flying, and sparks flashing at every bound. Ichabod's flimsy garments fluttered in the air, as he stretched his long lank body away over his horse's head, in the eagerness of his flight.

They had now reached the road which turns off to Sleepy Hollow; but Gunpowder, who seemed possessed with a demon, instead of keeping up it, made an opposite turn, and plunged headlong downhill to the left. This road leads through a sandy hollow, shaded by trees for about a quarter of a mile, where it crosses the bridge famous in goblin story, and just beyond swells the green knoll on which stands the whitewashed church.

As yet the panic of the steed had given his unskilful rider an apparent advantage in the chase; but just as he had got half-way through the hollow, the girths of the saddle gave way, and he felt it slipping from under him. He seized it by the pommel, and endeavored to hold it firm, but in vain; and had just time to save himself by clasping old Gunpowder round the neck, when the saddle fell to the earth, and he heard it trampled underfoot by his pursuer. For a moment the terror of Hans Van Ripper's wrath passed across his mind—for it was his Sunday saddle; but this was no time for petty fears; the goblin was hard on his haunches; and (unskilful rider that he was!) he had much ado to maintain his seat; sometimes slipping on one side, sometimes on another, and sometimes jolted on the high ridge of his horse's backbone, with a violence that he verily feared would cleave him asunder.

An opening in the trees now cheered him with the hopes that the church-bridge was at hand. The wavering reflection of a silver star in the bosom of the brook told him that he was not mistaken. He saw the walls of the church dimly glaring under the trees beyond. He recollected the place where Brom Bones's ghostly competitor had disappeared. "If I can but reach that bridge," thought Ichabod, "I am safe." Just then he heard the black steed panting and blowing close behind him; he even fancied that he felt his hot breath. Another convulsive kick in the ribs, and old Gunpowder sprang upon the bridge; he thundered over the resounding planks; he gained the opposite side; and now Ichabod cast a look behind to see if his pursuer should vanish, according to rule, in a flash of fire and brimstone. Just then he saw the goblin rising in his stirrups, and in the very act of hurling his head at him. Ichabod endeavored to dodge the horrible missile, but too late. It encountered his cranium with a tremendous crash,—he was tumbled headlong into the dust, and Gunpowder, the black steed, and the goblin rider, passed by like a whirlwind.

The next morning the old horse was found without his saddle, and with the bridle under his feet, soberly cropping the grass at his master's gate. Ichabod did not make his appearance at breakfast;—dinner-hour came, but no Ichabod. The boys assembled at the school-house, and strolled idly about the banks of the brook; but no schoolmaster. Hans Van Ripper now began to feel some uneasiness about the fate of poor Ichabod, and his saddle. An inquiry was set on foot, and after diligent investigation they came upon his traces. In one part of the road leading to the church was found the saddle trampled in the dirt; the tracks of horses' hoofs deeply dented in the road, and evidently at furious speed, were traced to the bridge, beyond which, on the bank of a broad part of the brook, where the water ran deep and black, was found the hat of the unfortunate Ichabod, and close beside it a shattered pumpkin.

The brook was searched, but the body of the schoolmaster was not to be discovered. Hans Van Ripper, as executor of his estate, examined the bundle which contained all his worldly effects. They consisted of two shirts and a half; two stocks for the neck; a pair or two of worsted stockings; an old pair of corduroy small-clothes; a rusty razor; a book of psalm-tunes, full of dogs' ears, and a broken pitchpipe. As to the books and furniture of the school-house, they belonged to the community, excepting Cotton Mather's "History of Witchcraft," a "New England Almanac," and a book of dreams and fortune-telling; in which last was a sheet of foolscap much scribbled and blotted in several fruitless attempts to make a copy of verses in honor of the heiress of Van Tassel. These magic books and the poetic scrawl were forthwith consigned to the flames by Hans Van Ripper; who from that time forward determined to send his children no more to school; observing, that he never knew any good come of this same reading and writing. Whatever money the school-master possessed, and he had received his quarter's pay but a day or two before, he must have had about his person at the time of his disappearance.

The mysterious event caused much speculation at the church on the following Sunday. Knots of gazers and gossips were collected in the church-yard, at the bridge, and at the spot where the hat and pumpkin had been found. The stories of Brouwer, of Bones, and a whole budget of others, were called to mind; and when they had diligently considered them all, and compared them with the symptoms of the present case, they shook their heads, and came to the conclusion that Ichabod had been carried off by the Galloping Hessian. As he was a bachelor, and in nobody's debt, nobody troubled his head any more about him. The school was removed to a different quarter of the Hollow, and another pedagogue reigned in his stead.

It is true, an old farmer, who had been down to New York on a visit several years after, and from whom this account of the ghostly adventure was received, brought home the intelligence that Ichabod Crane was still alive; that he had left the neighborhood, partly through fear of the goblin and Hans Van Ripper, and partly in mortification at having been suddenly dismissed by the heiress; that he had changed his quarters to a distant part of the country; had kept school and studied law at the same time, had been admitted to the bar, turned politician, electioneered, written for the newspapers, and finally had been made a justice of the Ten Pound Court. Brom Bones too, who shortly after his rival's disappearance conducted the blooming Katrina in triumph to the altar, was observed to look exceeding knowing whenever the story of Ichabod was related, and always burst into a hearty laugh at the mention of the pumpkin; which led some to suspect that he knew more about the matter than he chose to tell.

The old country wives, however, who are the best judges of these matters, maintain to this day that Ichabod was spirited away by supernatural means; and it is a favorite story often told about the neighborhood round the winter evening fire. The bridge became more than ever an object of superstitious awe, and that may be the reason why the road has been altered of late years, so as to approach the church by the border of the mill-pond. The schoolhouse, being deserted, soon fell to decay, and was reported to be haunted by the ghost of the unfortunate pedagogue; and the ploughboy, loitering homeward of a still summer evening, has often fancied his voice at a distance, chanting a melancholy psalm-tune among the tranquil solitudes of Sleepy Hollow.

POSTSCRIPT,

Found in the Handwriting of Mr. Knickerbocker

The preceding Tale is given, almost in the precise words in which I heard it related at a Corporation meeting of the ancient city of Manhattoes, at which were present many of its sagest and most illustrious burghers. The narrator was a pleasant, shabby, gentlemanly old fellow, in pepper-and-salt clothes, with a sadly humorous face; and one whom I strongly suspected of being poor,—he made such efforts to be entertaining. When his story was concluded, there was much laughter and approbation, particularly from two or three deputy aldermen, who had been asleep the greater part of the time. There was, however, one tall, dry-looking old gentleman, with beetling eyebrows, who maintained a grave and rather severe face throughout: now and then folding his arms, inclining his head, and looking down upon the floor, as if turning a doubt over in his mind. He was one of your wary men, who never laugh, but upon good grounds—when they have reason and the law on their side. When the mirth of the rest of the company had subsided and silence was restored, he leaned one arm on the elbow of his chair, and sticking the other akimbo, demanded, with a slight but exceedingly sage motion of the head, and contraction of the brow, what was the moral of the story, and what it went to prove?

The story-teller, who was just putting a glass of wine to his lips, as a refreshment after his toils, paused for a moment, looked at his inquirer with an air of infinite deference, and, lowering the glass slowly to the table, observed, that the story was intended most logically to prove:—

"That there is no situation in life but has its advantages and pleasures—provided we will but take a joke as we find it:

"That, therefore, he that runs races with goblin troopers is likely to have rough riding of it.

"Ergo, for a country schoolmaster to be refused the hand of a Dutch heiress, is a certain step to high preferment in the state."

The cautious old gentleman knit his brows tenfold closer after this explanation, being sorely puzzled by the ratiocination of the syllogism; while, methought, the one in pepper-and-salt eyed him with something of a triumphant leer. At length he observed, that all this was very well, but still he thought the story a little on the extravagant—there were one or two points on which he had his doubts.

"Faith, sir," replied the story-teller, "as to that matter, I don't believe one half of it myself."

D.K.

1819/1820

JAMES FENIMORE COOPER ■

1789–1851

James Fenimore Cooper was the first American novelist to gain international stature and the first to earn his living from royalties. A prodigious innovator, he has been credited with inventing sea fiction (Melville and Conrad expressed their indebtedness), the international novel, and distinctively American forms of the novel of manners and allegorical fiction. Cooper's thirty-two novels, spanning the period from 1820 to 1850, include works in all these genres. But, as Cooper himself knew, the novels for which he is best remembered are his five Leather-stocking tales. In these tales, Cooper explored the meanings of American frontier experience, creating the prototypical Western hero, Natty Bumppo (the Leather-stocking), whose wilderness adventures dramatize some of the central cultural tensions of antebellum America.

The writer was the son of one of the early republic's most ambitious land speculators and developers, William Cooper, founder of Cooperstown in central

New York State and later a U.S. congressman from that region. William Cooper, having struggled to surmount his lowly beginnings as a Philadelphia wheelwright, expected his sons to assume a place among America's Federalist gentry as lawyers, politicians, or gentleman farmers. Thus, James Fenimore Cooper seems an unlikely figure to have become a novelist. Indeed, he did not become one until he was thirty years old, after serving briefly in the merchant marine and the U.S. Navy and then living as a gentleman farmer in New York's Westchester County and in Cooperstown.

During this period, the vast real estate empire of William Cooper, who died in 1809, collapsed under the claims of creditors. By 1820, James Cooper (he added the Fenimore later) was the family's only surviving son and thus the primary bearer of its rapidly accumulating indebtedness. Although Cooper may not have become a writer in order to gain solvency (family legend has it that he wrote his first novel in response to a dare from his wife), his literary career, once undertaken, was driven by both creative passion and financial necessity.

That career began in 1820 with *Precaution*, an unsuccessful and imitative novel of manners set in England and published anonymously. But the following year, Cooper found his form and his audience with *The Spy*. In this best seller, set in the Hudson River highlands above New York City during the American Revolution, the novelist exploited the immense appeal of American history, characters, and settings during a time when the Revolutionary era and its leaders had become a subject for reverence and nostalgia.

While *The Spy* established Cooper's reputation as a novelist, his next work, *The Pioneers*, published in 1823, more directly reveals his family legacy and his concerns for American life. In this first of the Leather-stocking tales, Cooper depicted the frontier settlement of Cooperstown, situated at the foot of Lake Otsego and called Templeton in the novel, as he remembered it from his childhood. (Born in New Jersey in 1789, Cooper was brought to Cooperstown in the first year of his life.) At the center of the novel, which probes the issue of rightful land ownership and use, stands Judge Marmaduke Temple—clearly a representation of William Cooper, the patriarchal founder and developer of Cooperstown.

The novel is organized around the perspectives of the land's historical claimants: old Indian John (Chingachgook), the last survivor of Native American life in the region; the seventy-year-old woodsman Natty Bumppo, whose spiritual claims to a free wilderness life long predate the property claims of Judge Temple; Oliver Effingham (known as Edwards for much of the novel), a descendant of an aristocratic Tory family dispossessed by the Revolution, who believes that Temple usurped his family's rights; and the multiethnic group of settlers attempting to secure their own more limited forms of land tenure. Although Temple ultimately is exonerated from the charge of usurpation, Cooper's ambivalence toward the authority of the patriarch—the novel both shores up such authority and undercuts it—is an interesting and energizing aspect of this novel and of the Leather-stocking tales as a whole.

After his publication of *The Pioneers*, Cooper went on in the following year to repeat the success of *The Spy*. *The Pilot*, one of whose central characters is John Paul Jones, is regarded by many literary historians as the first authentic novel of the sea.

Shortly thereafter, in 1826, Cooper published the second of the Leather-stocking tales, *The Last of the Mohicans*, set during the French and Indian War when Natty Bumppo was in vigorous middle age. This novel is centrally concerned with the issue of Indian dispossession and with the conflict of cultures. The fast-paced action and elegiac portrayal of Native Americans made this work an enormous success with the reading public. Cooper's sympathetic and epic treatment of Native Americans in *The Last of the Mohicans* has been viewed in our time in two distinct ways: as a romantic strategy for dismissing Native Americans from national experience and as Cooper's authentic identification with and sympathy for Native American dispossession. These views, while opposing, are in fact not mutually exclusive and suggest the complexity of Cooper's literary legacy.

Soon after publication of *The Last of the Mohicans* in 1826, Cooper, now a national hero, left America for a European sojourn of seven years. In 1827 he published from Paris what he must have thought was the concluding volume in the Leather-stocking series, *The Prairie*. In this novel, Natty Bumppo has become a fully mythic figure leading the nation's westward movement.

When Cooper returned to America in 1833, resuming residence in Cooperstown, he was shocked by what he regarded as the excesses of Jacksonian democracy, and from this point forward until the end of his life he waged an insistent argument—in his writings and in lawsuits (mostly against newspaper editors he believed had libeled him)—with his country. During the 1830s, in fact, Cooper published little fiction. Then, surprisingly, in the early 1840s, he brought the Leather-stocking hero back to life in two novels, *The Pathfinder* (1840) and *The Deerslayer* (1841), and thereby revived his own languishing career. In their more classical depiction of the American wilderness, these novels reflect an altered sense of landscape that Cooper had derived from his European travels. *The Deerslayer*, set like *The Pioneers* at Lake Otsego but in a much earlier time (Natty here is a youth of twenty), renders a particularly serene and classical picture of the American forest prior to settlement.

Later in the 1840s, Cooper resumed his overt polemical attack on his enemies in a series of novels called the Littlepage Trilogy. In these works, he became the defender of landowners in the Hudson River Valley, taking their side against rebellious tenant farmers in the so-called anti-rent wars of this period. Cooper's late novel *The Crater* (1848), an allegory of the rise and fall of the United States, confirms the novelist's ever-deepening sense of historical doom. He ended his career with a bitter satire about American social life and legal practices called *The Ways of the Hour* (1850).

Through the course of his long career, Cooper explored in his fiction some of nineteenth-century America's most important issues, especially the role of elites in a democracy and the conflicting meanings of frontier experience. That experience was embodied and made mythic in Cooper's Leather-stocking hero, one of the most enduring and influential figures in American literature. Though many of Cooper's works are unread today, he was regarded throughout much of the nineteenth century as America's preeminent novelist, and in our own time his works are being vigorously reexamined as expressions of a troubled and ambivalent response to democratic culture.

H. Daniel Peck
Vassar College

PRIMARY WORKS

The Spy, 1821; *The Pioneers*, 1823; *The Pilot*, 1824; *The Last of the Mohicans*, 1826; *The Prairie*, 1827; *The Pathfinder*, 1840; *The Deerslayer*, 1841; in the State University of New York Press editions, edited by James F. Beard et al.; the Leather-stocking tales are reprinted in the following series: the Library of America, Oxford World's Classics, and Penguin Classics; *Letters and Journals*, James F. Beard, ed., 1960–1968.

from **The Pioneers, or the Sources of the Susquehanna: A Descriptive Tale**

[This selection from *The Pioneers*—three full continuous chapters showing the advance of spring in the frontier community of Templeton—renders the deep background of the novel's action. In chapter XXI, we find Judge Marmaduke Temple's daughter Elizabeth asking him to describe the moment, on Mount Vision, when he first looked down upon the future site of Templeton. After describing a period of deprivation (the "starving-time") in the early days of settlement (a story emphasizing Temple's role as village patriarch), the Judge complies. He renders his moment on the mountain as a visionary possession of a wilderness landscape. Implicitly pointing to Temple's erasure of earlier claimants, Oliver Effingham (Edwards) raises the issue of the Indians' rights (long ago "extinguished," Temple responds), and of Natty Bumppo's increasingly threatened rights to a life of wilderness freedom.

The ways in which that freedom, and the very environment that supports it, are being eroded by settlement are made vivid in the following two chapters. In chapter XXII the settlers bring down huge numbers of passenger pigeons by firing cannon shots into the flock, and in chapter XXIII they seine thousands of fish onto the shore where most are left to rot. Natty, scornful of the settlers' wastefulness, holds the Judge, and the process of settlement initiated by him, responsible for these actions. But Temple is himself a conservationist, sponsoring game laws and lamenting, as he does at the conclusion of chapter XXIII, "the wasteful extravagance of man." At issue here is the kind of law that best serves the future: the evolving and necessarily imperfect frontier law enforced by Judge Temple or the natural law represented by Natty.

These powerful chapters dramatizing environmental destruction reveal Cooper's prescience about such matters (the passenger pigeon, whose spectacular sky-covering migration was one of early America's most wondrous sights, would become extinct by the end of the nineteenth century) and suggest that, at times, his deeply engrained social conservatism could open out toward an enlightened spirit of conservation. His daughter Susan Fenimore Cooper would carry that spirit into her own book, *Rural Hours* (1850), a pioneering work of bioregional literature also set in the Lake Otsego watershed.]

Chapter XXI

"Speed! Malise, speed! such cause of haste
Thine active sinews never brac'd."

—SCOTT, *THE LADY OF THE LAKE*, III.xiii.3–4.

The roads of Otsego, if we except the principal highways, were, at the early day of our tale, but little better than woodpaths. The high trees that were growing on the very verge of the wheel-tracks, excluded the sun's rays, unless at meridian, and the slowness of the evaporation, united with the rich mould of vegetable decomposition, that covered the whole country, to the depth of several inches, occasioned but an indifferent foundation for the footing of travellers. Added to these were the inequalities of a natural surface, and the constant recurrence of enormous and slippery roots, that were laid bare by the removal of the light soil, together with stumps of trees, to make a passage not only difficult, but dangerous. Yet the riders, among these numerous obstructions, which were such as would terrify an unpractised eye, gave no demonstrations of uneasiness, as their horses toiled through the sloughs, or trotted with uncertain paces along the dark route. In many places, the marks on the trees were the only indications of a road, with, perhaps, an occasional remnant of a pine, that, by being cut close to the earth, so as to leave nothing visible but its base of roots, spreading for twenty feet in every direction, was apparently placed there as a beacon, to warn the traveller that it was the centre of a highway.

Into one of these roads the active Sheriff led the way, first striking out of the footpath, by which they had descended from the sugar-bush, across a little bridge, formed of round logs laid loosely on sleepers of pine, in which large openings, of a formidable width, were frequent. The nag of Richard, when it reached one of these gaps, laid its nose along the logs, and stepped across the difficult passage with the sagacity of a man; but the blooded filly which Miss Temple rode disdained so humble a move-ment. She made a step or two with an unusual caution, and then, on reaching the broadest opening, obedient to the curb and whip of her fear-less mistress, she bounded across the dangerous pass, with the activity of a squirrel.

"Gently, gently, my child," said Marmaduke, who was following in the manner of Richard—"this is not a country for equestrian feats. Much pru-dence is requisite, to journey through our rough paths with safety. Thou mayst practise thy skill in horsemanship on the plains of New-Jersey, with safety, but in the hills of Otsego, they must be suspended for a time."

"I may as well, then, relinquish my saddle at once, dear sir," returned his daughter; "for if it is to be laid aside until this wild country be improved, old age will overtake me, and put an end to what you term my equestrian feats."

"Say not so, my child," returned her father; "but if thou venturest again, as in crossing this bridge, old age will never overtake thee, but I shall be left to mourn thee, cut off in thy pride, my Elizabeth. If thou hadst seen this district of country, as I did, when it lay in the sleep of nature, and had witnessed its rapid changes, as it awoke to supply the wants of man, thou wouldst curb thy impatience for a little time, though thou shouldst not check thy steed."

"I recollect hearing you speak of your first visit to these woods, but the impression is faint, and blended with the confused images of childhood. Wild and unsettled as it may yet seem, it must have been a thousand times more dreary then. Will you repeat, dear sir, what you then thought of your enterprise, and what you felt?"

During this speech of Elizabeth, which was uttered with the fervour of affection, young Edwards rode more closely to the side of the Judge, and bent his dark eyes on his countenance, with an expression that seemed to read his thoughts.

"Thou wast then young, my child, but must remember when I left thee and thy mother, to take my first survey of these uninhabited mountains," said Marmaduke. "But thou dost not feel all the secret motives that can urge a man to endure privations in order to accumulate wealth. In my case they have not been trifling, and God has been pleased to smile on my efforts. If I have encountered pain, famine, and disease, in accomplishing the settlement of this rough territory, I have not the misery of failure to add to the grievances."

"Famine!" echoed Elizabeth; "I thought this was the land of abundance! had you famine to contend with?"

"Even so, my child," said her father. "Those who look around them now, and see the loads of produce that issue out of every wild path in these mountains, during the season of travelling, will hardly credit that no more than five years have elapsed, since the tenants of these woods were compelled to eat the scanty fruits of the forest to sustain life, and, with their unpractised skill, to hunt the beasts as food for their starving families."

"Ay!" cried Richard, who happened to overhear the last of this speech, between the notes of the wood-chopper's song, which he was endeavouring to breathe aloud; "that was the starving-time,[1] cousin Bess. I grew as lank as a weasel that fall, and my face was as pale as one of your fever-and-ague visages. Monsieur Le Quoi, there, fell away like a pumpkin in drying; nor do I think you have got fairly over it yet, Monsieur. Benjamin, I thought, bore it with a worse grace than any of the family, for he swore

---

[1]The author has no better apology for interrupting the interest of a work of fiction by these desultory dialogues, than that they have reference to facts. In reviewing his work, after so many years, he is compelled to confess it is injured by too many allusions to incidents that are not at all suited to satisfy the just expectations of the general reader. One of these events is slightly touched on, in the commencement of this chapter.

More than thirty years since, a very near and dear relative of the writer, an elder sister and a second mother, was killed by a fall from a horse, in a ride among the very mountains mentioned in this tale. Few of her sex and years were more extensively known, or more universally beloved, than the admirable woman who thus fell a victim to the chances of the wilderness. [1832]

it was harder to endure than a short allowance in the calm latitudes. Benjamin is a sad fellow to swear, if you starve him ever so little. I had half a mind to quit you then, 'duke, and to go into Pennsylvania to fatten; but, damn it, thinks I, we are sisters' children, and I will live or die with him, after all."

"I do not forget thy kindness," said Marmaduke, "nor that we are of one blood."

"But, my dear father," cried the wondering Elizabeth, "was there actual suffering? where were the beautiful and fertile vales of the Mohawk? could they not furnish food for your wants?"

"It was a season of scarcity; the necessities of life commanded a high price in Europe, and were greedily sought after by the speculators. The emigrants, from the east to the west, invariably passed along the valley of the Mohawk, and swept away the means of subsistence, like a swarm of locusts. Nor were the people on the Flats in a much better condition. They were in want themselves, but they spared the little excess of provisions, that nature did not absolutely require, with the justice of the German character. There was no grinding of the poor. The word speculator was then unknown to them. I have seen many a stout man, bending under the load of the bag of meal, which he was carrying from the mills of the Mohawk, through the rugged passes of these mountains, to feed his half-famished children, with a heart so light, as he approached his hut, that the thirty miles he had passed seemed nothing. Remember, my child, it was in our very infancy: we had neither mills, nor grain, nor roads, nor often clearings;——we had nothing of increase but the mouths that were to be fed; for, even at that inauspicious moment, the restless spirit of emigration was not idle; nay, the general scarcity, which extended to the east, tended to increase the number of adventurers."

"And how, dearest father, didst thou encounter this dreadful evil?" said Elizabeth, unconsciously adopting the dialect of her parent, in the warmth of her sympathy. "Upon thee must have fallen the responsibility, if not the suffering."

"It did, Elizabeth," returned the Judge, pausing for a single moment, as if musing on his former feelings. "I had hundreds at that dreadful time, daily looking up to me for bread. The sufferings of their families, and the gloomy prospect before them, had paralysed the enterprise and efforts of my settlers; hunger drove them to the woods for food, but despair sent them, at night, enfeebled and wan, to a sleepless pillow. It was not a moment for inaction. I purchased cargoes of wheat from the granaries of Pennsylvania; they were landed at Albany, and brought up the Mohawk in boats; from thence it was transported on pack-horses into the wilderness, and distributed amongst my people. Seines were made, and the lakes and rivers were dragged for fish. Something like a miracle was wrought in our favour, for enormous shoals of herrings were discovered to have wandered five hundred miles, through the windings of the impetuous Susquehanna, and the lake was alive with their numbers. These were at length caught, and dealt out to the people, with proper portions of salt; and from that moment, we again began to prosper."[2]

"Yes," cried Richard, "and I was the man who served out the fish and the salt. When the poor devils came to receive their rations, Benjamin, who was my deputy, was obliged to keep them off by stretching ropes around me, for they smelt so of garlic, from eating nothing but the wild onion, that the fumes put me out, often, in my measurement. You were a child then, Bess, and knew nothing of the matter, for great care was observed to keep both you and your mother from suffering. That year put me back, dreadfully, both in the breed of my hogs, and of my turkeys."

"No, Bess," cried the Judge, in a more cheerful tone, disregarding the interruption of his cousin, "he who hears of the settlement of a country, knows but little of the toil and suffering by which it is accomplished. Unimproved and wild as this district now seems to your eyes, what was it when I first entered the hills! I left my party, the morning of my arrival, near the farms of the Cherry Valley, and, following a deer-path, rode to the summit of the mountain, that I have since called Mount Vision; for the sight that there met my eyes seemed to me as the deceptions of a dream. The fire had run over the pinnacle, and, in a great measure, laid open the view. The leaves were fallen, and I mounted a tree, and sat for an hour looking on the silent wilderness. Not an opening was to be seen in the boundless forest, except where the lake lay, like a mirror of glass. The water was covered by myriads of the wild-fowl that migrate with the changes in the season; and, while in my situation on the branch of the beech, I saw a bear, with her cubs, descend to the shore to drink. I had met many deer, gliding through the woods, in my journey; but not the vestige of a man could I trace, during my progress, nor from my elevated observatory. No clearing, no hut, none of the winding roads that are now to be seen, were there; nothing but mountains rising behind mountains, and the valley, with its surface of branches, enlivened here and there with the faded foliage of some tree, that parted from its leaves with more than ordinary reluctance. Even the Susquehanna was then hid, by the height and density of the forest."

"And were you alone?" asked Elizabeth;——"passed you the night in that solitary state?"

"Not so, my child," returned her father. "After musing on the scene for an hour, with a mingled feeling of pleasure and desolation, I left my perch, and descended the mountain. My horse was left to browse on the twigs that grew within his reach, while I explored the shores of the lake, and the spot where Templeton stands. A pine of more than ordinary growth stood where my dwelling is now placed; a wind-row had been opened through the trees from thence to the lake, and my view was but little impeded. Under the branches of that tree I made my solitary dinner; I had just finished my repast as I saw a smoke curling from under the mountain, near the eastern bank of the lake. It was the only indication of the vicinity of man that I had

---

[2]All this was literally true. [1832]

then seen. After much toil, I made my way to the spot, and found a rough cabin of logs, built against the foot of a rock, and bearing the marks of a tenant, though I found no one within it.—"

"It was the hut of Leather-stocking," said Edwards, quickly.

"It was; though I, at first, supposed it to be a habitation of the Indians. But while I was lingering around the spot, Natty made his appearance, staggering under the carcass of a buck that he had slain. Our acquaintance commenced at that time; before, I had never heard that such a being tenanted the woods. He launched his bark canoe, and set me across the foot of the lake, to the place where I had fastened my horse, and pointed out a spot where he might get a scanty browsing until the morning; when I returned and passed the night in the cabin of the hunter."

Miss Temple was so much struck by the deep attention of young Edwards, during this speech, that she forgot to resume her interrogatories; but the youth himself continued the discourse, by asking—

"And how did the Leather-stocking discharge the duties of a host, sir?"

"Why, simply but kindly, until late in the evening, when he discovered my name and object, and the cordiality of his manner very sensibly diminished, or, I might better say, disappeared. He considered the introduction of the settlers as an innovation on his rights, I believe; for he expressed much dissatisfaction at the measure, though it was in his confused and ambiguous manner. I hardly understood his objections myself, but supposed they referred chiefly to an interruption of the hunting."

"Had you then purchased the estate, or were you examining it with an intent to buy?" asked Edwards, a little abruptly.

"It had been mine for several years. It was with a view to people the land that I visited the lake. Natty treated me hospitably, but coldly, I thought, after he learnt the nature of my journey. I slept on his own bear-skin, however, and in the morning joined my surveyors again."

"Said he nothing of the Indian rights, sir? The Leather-stocking is much given to impeach the justice of the tenure by which the whites hold the country."

"I remember that he spoke of them, but I did not clearly comprehend him, and may have forgotten what he said; for the Indian title was extinguished so far back as the close of the old war; and if it had not been at all, I hold under the patents of the Royal Governors, confirmed by an act of our own State Legislature, and no court in the country can affect my title."

"Doubtless, sir, your title is both legal and equitable," returned the youth, coldly, reining his horse back, and remaining silent till the subject was changed.

It was seldom Mr. Jones suffered any conversation to continue, for a great length of time, without his participation. It seems that he was of the party that Judge Temple had designated as his surveyors; and he embraced the opportunity of the pause that succeeded the retreat of young Edwards, to take up the discourse, and with it a narration of their further proceedings, after his own manner. As it wanted, however, the interest that had accompanied the description of the Judge, we must decline the task of committing his sentences to paper.

They soon reached the point where the promised view was to be seen. It was one of those picturesque and peculiar scenes, that belong to the Otsego, but which required the absence of the ice, and the softness of a summer's landscape, to be enjoyed in all its beauty. Marmaduke had early forewarned his daughter of the season, and of its effect on the prospect, and after casting a cursory glance at its capabilities, the party returned homeward, perfectly satisfied that its beauties would repay them for the toil of a second ride, at a more propitious season.

"The spring is the gloomy time of the American year," said the Judge; "and it is more peculiarly the case in these mountains. The winter seems to retreat to the fastnesses of the hills, as to the citadel of its dominion, and is only expelled, after a tedious siege, in which either party, at times, would seem to be gaining the victory."

"A very just and apposite figure, Judge Temple," observed the Sheriff; "and the garrison under the command of Jack Frost make formidable sorties—you understand what I mean by sorties, Monsieur; sallies, in English—and sometimes drive General Spring and his troops back again into the low countries."

"Yes, sair," returned the Frenchman, whose prominent eyes were watching the precarious footsteps of the beast he rode, as it picked its dangerous way among the roots of trees, holes, log-bridges, and sloughs, that formed the aggregate of the highway. "Je vous entend; de low countrie is freeze up for half de year."

The error of Mr. Le Quoi was not observed by the Sheriff; and the rest of the party were yielding to the influence of the changeful season, which was already teaching the equestrians that a continuance of its mildness was not to be expected for any length of time. Silence and thoughtfulness succeeded the gayety and conversation that had prevailed during the commencement of the ride, as clouds began to gather about the heavens, apparently collecting from every quarter, in quick motion, without the agency of a breath of air.

While riding over one of the cleared eminences that occurred in their route, the watchful eye of Judge Temple pointed out to his daughter the approach of a tempest. Flurries of snow already obscured the mountain that formed the northern boundary of the lake, and the genial sensation which had quickened the blood through their veins, was already succeeded by the deadening influence of an approaching *northwester*.

All of the party were now busily engaged in making the best of their way to the village, though the badness of the roads frequently compelled them to check the impatience of their horses, which often carried them over places that would not admit of any gait faster than a walk.

Richard continued in advance, followed by Mr. Le Quoi; next to whom rode Elizabeth, who seemed to have imbibed the distance which pervaded the manner of young Edwards, since the termination of the discourse between the latter and her father. Marmaduke followed his daughter, giving her frequent and tender warnings as to the management of her horse. It was, possibly, the evident dependence that Louisa Grant placed on his assistance, which induced the youth to continue by her side, as they pursued their way through a dreary and dark wood, where the rays of the sun could but rarely penetrate, and where even the daylight was obscured and rendered gloomy by the deep forests that surrounded them. No wind had yet reached the spot where the equestrians were in motion, but that dead stillness that often precedes a storm, contributed to render their situation more irksome than if they were already subjected to the fury of the tempest. Suddenly the voice of young Edwards was heard shouting, in those appalling tones that carry alarm to the very soul, and which curdle the blood of those that hear them—

"A tree! a tree! whip—spur for your lives! a tree! a tree!"

"A tree! a tree!" echoed Richard, giving his horse a blow, that caused the alarmed beast to jump nearly a rod, throwing the mud and water into the air, like a hurricane.

"Von tree! von tree!" shouted the Frenchman, bending his body on the neck of his charger, shutting his eyes, and playing on the ribs of his beast with his heels, at a rate that caused him to be conveyed, on the crupper of the Sheriff, with a marvellous speed.

Elizabeth checked her filly, and looked up, with an unconscious but alarmed air, at the very cause of their danger, while she listened to the crackling sounds that awoke the stillness of the forest; but, at the next instant, her bridle was seized by her father, who cried—

"God protect my child!" and she felt herself hurried onward, impelled by the vigour of his nervous arm.

Each one of the party bowed to his saddle-bows, as the tearing of branches was succeeded by a sound like the rushing of the winds, which was followed by a thundering report, and a shock that caused the very earth to tremble, as one of the noblest ruins of the forest fell directly across their path.

One glance was enough to assure Judge Temple that his daughter, and those in front of him, were safe, and he turned his eyes, in dreadful anxiety, to learn the fate of the others. Young Edwards was on the opposite side of the tree, his form thrown back in his saddle to its utmost distance, his left hand drawing up his bridle with its greatest force, while the right grasped that of Miss Grant, so as to draw the head of her horse under its body. Both the animals stood shaking in every joint with terror, and snorting fearfully. Louisa herself had relinquished her reins, and with her hands pressed on her face, sat bending forward in her saddle, in an attitude of despair mingled strangely with resignation.

"Are you safe?" cried the Judge, first breaking the awful silence of the moment.

"By God's blessing," returned the youth; "but if there had been branches to the tree we must have been lost—"

He was interrupted by the figure of Louisa, slowly yielding in her saddle; and but for his arm, she would have sunken to the earth. Terror, however, was the only injury that the clergyman's daughter had sustained, and, with the aid of Elizabeth, she was soon restored to her senses. After some little time was lost in recovering her strength, the young lady was replaced in her saddle, and, supported on either side, by Judge Temple and Mr. Edwards, she was enabled to follow the party in their slow progress.

"The sudden falling of the trees," said Marmaduke, "are the most dangerous accidents in the forest, for they are not to be foreseen, being impelled by no winds, nor any extraneous or visible cause, against which we can guard."

"The reason of their falling, Judge Temple, is very obvious," said the Sheriff. "The tree is old and decayed, and it is gradually weakened by the frosts, until a line drawn from the centre of gravity falls without its base, and then the tree comes of a certainty; and I should like to know, what greater compulsion there can be for any thing, than a mathematical certainty. I studied mathe——"

"Very true, Richard," interrupted Marmaduke; "thy reasoning is true, and, if my memory be not over treacherous, was furnished by myself, on a former occasion. But how is one to guard against the danger? canst thou go through the forests, measuring the bases, and calculating the centres of the oaks? answer me that, friend Jones, and I will say thou wilt do the country a service."

"Answer thee that, friend Temple!" returned Richard; "a well-educated man can answer thee any thing, sir. Do any trees fall in this manner, but such as are decayed? Take care not to approach the roots of a rotten tree, and you will be safe enough."

"That would be excluding us entirely from the forests," said Marmaduke. "But, happily, the winds usually force down most of these dangerous ruins, as their currents are admitted into the woods by the surrounding clearings, and such a fall as this has been is very rare."

Louisa, by this time, had recovered so much strength, as to allow the party to proceed at a quicker pace; but long before they were safely housed, they were overtaken by the storm; and when they dismounted at the door of the Mansion-house, the black plumes of Miss Temple's hat were drooping with the weight of a load of damp snow, and the coats of the gentlemen were powdered with the same material.

While Edwards was assisting Louisa from her horse, the warmhearted girl caught his hand with fervour, and whispered—

"Now, Mr. Edwards, both father and daughter owe their lives to you."

A driving, north-westerly storm succeeded; and before the sun was set, every vestige of spring had vanished; the lake, the mountains, the village, and the fields, being again hid under one dazzling coat of snow.

Chapter XXII

"Men, boys, and girls,
Desert th' unpeopled village; and wild crowds
Spread o'er the plain, by the sweet frenzy driven."

—SOMERVILLE, THE CHACE, II.197–99.

From this time to the close of April, the weather continued to be a succession of great and rapid changes. One day, the soft airs of spring seemed to be stealing along the valley, and, in unison with an invigorating sun, attempting, covertly, to rouse the dormant powers of the vegetable world; while on the next, the surly blasts from the north would sweep across the lake, and erase every impression left by their gentle adversaries. The snow, however, finally disappeared, and the green wheat fields were seen in every direction, spotted with the dark and charred stumps that had, the preceding season, supported some of the proudest trees of the forest. Ploughs were in motion, wherever those useful implements could be used, and the smokes of the sugar-camps were no longer seen issuing from the woods of maple. The lake had lost the beauty of a field of ice, but still a dark and gloomy covering concealed its waters, for the absence of currents left them yet hid under a porous crust, which, saturated with the fluid, barely retained enough strength to preserve the contiguity of its parts. Large flocks of wild geese were seen passing over the country, which hovered, for a time, around the hidden sheet of water, apparently searching for a resting-place; and then, on finding themselves excluded by the chill covering, would soar away to the north, filling the air with discordant screams, as if venting their complaints at the tardy operations of nature.

For a week, the dark covering of the Otsego was left to the undisturbed possession of two eagles, who alighted on the centre of its field, and sat eyeing their undisputed territory. During the presence of these monarchs of the air, the flocks of migrating birds avoided crossing the plain of ice, by turning into the hills, apparently seeking the protection of the forests, while the white and bald heads of the tenants of the lake were turned upward, with a look of contempt. But the time had come, when even these kings of birds were to be dispossessed. An opening had been gradually increasing, at the lower extremity of the lake, and around the dark spot where the current of the river prevented the formation of ice, during even the coldest weather; and the fresh southerly winds, that now breathed freely upon the valley, made an impression on the waters. Mimic waves begun to curl over the margin of the frozen field, which exhibited an outline of crystallizations, that slowly receded towards the north. At each step the power of the winds and the waves increased, until, after a struggle of a few hours, the turbulent little billows succeeded in setting the whole field in motion, when it was driven beyond the reach of the eye, with a rapidity, that was as magical as the change produced in the scene by this expulsion of the lingering remnant of winter. Just as the last sheet of agitated ice was disappearing in the distance, the eagles rose, and soared with a wide sweep above the clouds, while the waves tossed their little caps of snow into the air, as if rioting in their release from a thraldom of five months' duration.

The following morning Elizabeth was awakened by the exhilarating sounds of the martins, who were quarreling and chattering around the little boxes suspended above her windows, and the cries of Richard, who was calling, in tones animating as the signs of the season itself—

"Awake! awake! my fair lady! the gulls are hovering over the lake already, and the heavens are alive with pigeons. You may look an hour before you can find a hole, through which, to get a peep at the sun. Awake! awake! lazy ones! Benjamin is overhauling the ammunition, and we only wait for our breakfasts, and away for the mountains and pigeon-shooting."

There was no resisting this animated appeal, and in a few minutes Miss Temple and her friend descended to the parlour. The doors of the hall were thrown open, and the mild, balmy air of a clear spring morning was ventilating the apartment, where the vigilance of the ex-steward had been so long maintaining an artificial heat, with such unremitted diligence. The gentlemen were impatiently waiting for their morning's repast, each equipt in the garb of a sportsman. Mr. Jones made many visits to the southern door, and would cry—

"See, cousin Bess! see, 'duke! the pigeon-roosts of the south have broken up! They are growing more thick every instant. Here is a flock that the eye cannot see the end of. There is food enough in it to keep the army of Xerxes for a month, and feathers enough to make beds for the whole country. Xerxes, Mr. Edwards, was a Grecian king, who—no, he was a Turk, or a Persian, who wanted to conquer Greece, just the same as these rascals will overrun our wheat-fields, when they come back in the fall.—Away! away! Bess; I long to pepper them."

In this wish both Marmaduke and young Edwards seemed equally to participate, for the sight was exhilarating to a sportsman; and the ladies soon dismissed the party, after a hasty breakfast.

If the heavens were alive with pigeons, the whole village seemed equally in motion, with men, women, and children. Every species of fire-arms, from the French ducking-gun, with a barrel near six feet in length, to the common horseman's pistol, was to be seen in the hands of the men and boys; while bows and arrows, some made of the simple stick of a walnut sapling, and others in a rude imitation of the ancient cross-bows, were carried by many of the latter.

The houses, and the signs of life apparent in the village, drove the alarmed birds from the direct line of their flight, towards the mountains, along the sides and near the bases of which they were glancing in dense masses, equally wonderful by the rapidity of their motion, and their incredible numbers.

We have already said, that across the inclined plane which fell from the steep ascent of the mountain to the banks of the Susquehanna, ran the highway, on either side of which a clearing of many acres had been made, at a very early day. Over those clearings, and up the eastern mountain, and along the dangerous path that was cut into its side, the different individuals posted themselves, and in a few moments the attack commenced.

Amongst the sportsmen was the tall, gaunt form of Leather-stocking, walking over the field, with his rifle hanging on his arm, his dogs at his heels; the latter now scenting the dead or wounded birds, that were beginning to tumble from the flocks, and then crouching under the legs of their master, as if they participated in his feelings, at this wasteful and unsports-manlike execution.

The reports of the fire-arms became rapid, whole volleys rising from the plain, as flocks of more than ordinary numbers darted over the opening, shadowing the field, like a cloud; and then the light smoke of a single piece would issue from among the leafless bushes on the mountain, as death was hurled on the retreat of the affrighted birds, who were rising from a volley, in a vain effort to escape. Arrows, and missiles of every kind, were in the midst of the flocks; and so numerous were the birds, and so low did they take their flight, that even long poles, in the hands of those on the sides of the mountain, were used to strike them to the earth.

During all this time, Mr. Jones, who disdained the humble and ordinary means of destruction used by his companions, was busily occupied, aided by Benjamin, in making arrangements for an assault of a more than ordinarily fatal character. Among the relics of the old military excursions, that occasionally are discovered throughout the different districts of the western part of New-York, there had been found in Templeton, at its settlement, a small swivel, which would carry a ball of a pound weight. It was thought to have been deserted by a war-party of the whites, in one of their inroads into the Indian settlements, when, perhaps, convenience or their necessity induced them to leave such an encumbrance behind them in the woods. This miniature cannon had been released from the rust, and being mounted on little wheels, was now in a state for actual service. For several years, it was the sole organ for extraordinary rejoicings used in those mountains. On the mornings of the Fourths of July, it would be heard ringing among the hills, and even Captain Hollister, who was the highest authority in that part of the country on all such occasions, affirmed that, considering its dimensions, it was no despicable gun for a salute. It was somewhat the worse for the service it had performed, it is true, there being but a trifling difference in size between the touch-hole and the muzzle. Still, the grand conceptions of Richard had suggested the importance of such an instrument, in hurling death at his nimble enemies. The swivel was dragged by a horse into a part of the open space, that the Sheriff thought most eligible for planting a battery of the kind, and Mr. Pump proceeded to load it. Several handfuls of duck-shot were placed on top of the powder, and the Major-domo announced that his piece was ready for service.

The sight of such an implement collected all the idle spectators to the spot, who, being mostly boys, filled the air with cries of exultation and delight. The gun was pointed high, and Richard, holding a coal of fire in a pair of tongs, patiently took his seat on a stump, awaiting the appearance of a flock worthy of his notice.

So prodigious was the number of the birds, that the scattering fire of the guns, with the hurling of missiles, and the cries of the boys, had no other effect than to break off small flocks from the immense masses that continued to dart along the valley, as if the whole of the feathered tribe were pouring through that one pass. None pretended to collect the game, which lay scattered over the fields in such profusion, as to cover the very ground with the fluttering victims.

Leather-stocking was a silent, but uneasy spectator of all these proceedings, but was able to keep his sentiments to himself until he saw the introduction of the swivel into the sports.

"This comes of settling a country!" he said—"here have I known the pigeons to fly for forty long years, and, till you made your clearings, there was nobody to skear or to hurt them. I loved to see them come into the woods, for they were company to a body; hurting nothing; being, as it was, as harmless as a garter-snake. But now it gives me sore thoughts when I hear the frighty things whizzing through the air, for I know it's only a motion to bring out all the brats in the village. Well! the Lord won't see the waste of his creaters for nothing, and right will be done to the pigeons, as well as others, by-and-by.——There's Mr. Oliver, as bad as the rest of them, firing into the flocks as if he was shooting down nothing but Mingo warriors."

Among the sportsmen was Billy Kirby, who, armed with an old musket, was loading, and, without even looking into the air, was firing, and shouting as his victims fell even on his own person. He heard the speech of Natty, and took upon himself to reply—

"What! old Leather-stocking," he cried, "grumbling at the loss of a few pigeons! If you had to sow your wheat twice, and three times, as I have done, you wouldn't be so massyfully feeling'd to'ards the divils.—Hurrah, boys! scatter the feathers. This is better than shooting at a turkey's head and neck, old fellow."

"It's better for you, maybe, Billy Kirby," replied the indignant old hunter, "and all them that don't know how to put a ball down a rifle-barrel, or how to bring it up ag'in with a true aim; but it's wicked to be shooting into flocks in this wastey manner; and none do it, who know how to knock over a single bird. If a body has a craving for pigeon's flesh, why! it's made the same as all other creater's, for man's eating, but not to kill twenty and eat one. When I want such a thing, I go into the woods till I find one to my liking, and then I shoot him off the branches without touching a feather of another, though there might be a hundred on the same tree. You couldn't do such a thing, Billy Kirby—you couldn't do it if you tried."

"What's that, old corn-stalk! you sapless stub!" cried the wood-chopper. "You've grown wordy, since the affair of the turkey; but if you're for a single shot, here goes at that bird which comes on by himself."

The fire from the distant part of the field had driven a single pigeon below the flock to which it belonged, and, frightened with the constant reports of the muskets, it was approaching the spot where the disputants stood, darting first from one side, and then to the other, cutting the air with the swiftness of lightning, and making a noise with its wings, not unlike the rushing of a bullet. Unfortunately for the wood-chopper, notwithstanding his vaunt, he did not see this bird until it was too late to fire as it approached, and he pulled his trigger at the unlucky moment when it was darting immediately over his head. The bird continued its course with the usual velocity.

Natty lowered the rifle from his arm, when the challenge was made, and, waiting a moment, until the terrified victim had got in a line with his eye, and had dropped near the bank of the lake, he raised it again with uncommon rapidity, and fired. It might have been chance, or it might have been skill, that produced the result; it was probably a union of both; but the pigeon whirled over in the air, and fell into the lake, with a broken wing. At the sound of his rifle, both his dogs started from his feet, and in a few minutes the "slut" brought out the bird, still alive.

The wonderful exploit of Leather-stocking was noised through the field with great rapidity, and the sportsmen gathered in to learn the truth of the report.

"What," said young Edwards, "have you really killed a pigeon on the wing, Natty, with a single ball?"

"Haven't I killed loons before now, lad, that dive at the flash?" returned the hunter. "It's much better to kill only such as you want, without wasting your powder and lead, than to be firing into God's creaters in this wicked manner. But I come out for a bird, and you know the reason why I like small game, Mr. Oliver, and now I have got one I will go home, for I don't relish to see these wasty ways that you are all practysing, as if the least thing was not made for use, and not to destroy."

"Thou sayest well, Leather-stocking," cried Marmaduke, "and I begin to think it time to put an end to this work of destruction."

"Put an ind, Judge, to your clearings. An't the woods his work as well as the pigeons? Use, but don't waste. Wasn't the woods made for the beasts and birds to harbour in? and when man wanted their flesh, their skins, or their feathers, there's the place to seek them. But I'll go to the hut with my own game, for I wouldn't touch one of the harmless things that kiver the ground here, looking up with their eyes on me, as if they only wanted tongues to say their thoughts."

With this sentiment in his mouth, Leather-stocking threw his rifle over his arm, and, followed by his dogs, stepped across the clearing with great caution, taking care not to tread on one of the wounded birds in his path. He soon entered the bushes on the margin of the lake, and was hid from view.

Whatever impression the morality of Natty made on the Judge, it was utterly lost on Richard. He availed himself of the gathering of the sportsmen, to lay a plan for one "fell swoop" of destruction. The musketmen were drawn up in battle array, in a line extending on each side of his artillery, with orders to await the signal of firing from himself.

"Stand by, my lads," said Benjamin, who acted as an aide-de-camp, on this occasion, "stand by, my hearties, and when Squire Dickens heaves out the signal to begin the firing, d'ye see, you may open upon them in a broadside. Take care and fire low, boys, and you'll be sure to hull the flock."

"Fire low!" shouted Kirby—"hear the old fool! If we fire low, we may hit the stumps, but not ruffle a pigeon."

"How should you know, you lubber?" cried Benjamin, with a very unbecoming heat, for an officer on the eve of battle—"how should you know, you grampus? Havn't I sailed aboard of the Boadishy for five years? and wasn't it a standing order to fire low, and to hull your enemy? Keep silence at your guns, boys, and mind the order that is passed."

The loud laughs of the musketmen were silenced by the more authoritative voice of Richard, who called for attention and obedience to his signals.

Some millions of pigeons were supposed to have already passed, that morning, over the valley of Templeton; but nothing like the flock that was now approaching had been seen before. It extended from mountain to mountain in one solid blue mass, and the eye looked in vain over the southern hills to find its termination. The front of this living column was distinctly marked by a line, but very slightly indented, so regular and even was the flight. Even Marmaduke forgot the morality of Leather-stocking as it approached, and, in common with the rest, brought his musket to a poise.

"Fire!" cried the Sheriff, clapping a coal to the priming of the cannon. As half of Benjamin's charge escaped through the touch-hole, the whole volley of the musketry preceded the report of the swivel. On receiving this united discharge of small-arms, the front of the flock darted upward, while, at the same instant, myriads of those in the rear rushed with amazing rapidity into their places, so that when the column of white smoke gushed from the mouth of the little cannon, an accumulated mass of objects was gliding over its point of direction. The roar of the gun echoed along the mountains, and died away to the north, like distant thunder, while the whole flock of alarmed birds seemed, for a moment, thrown into one disorderly and agitated mass. The air was filled with their irregular flight, layer rising above layer, far above the tops of the highest pines, none daring to advance beyond the dangerous pass; when, suddenly, some of the leaders of the feathered tribe shot across the valley, taking their flight directly over the village, and hundreds of thousands in their rear followed the example, deserting the eastern side of the plain to their persecutors and the slain.

"Victory!" shouted Richard, "victory! we have driven the enemy from the field."

"Not so, Dickon," said Marmaduke; "the field is covered with them; and, like the Leather-stocking, I see nothing but eyes, in every direction, as the innocent sufferers turn their heads in terror. Full one half of those that have fallen are yet alive: and I think it is time to end the sport; if sport it be."

"Sport!" cried the Sheriff; "it is princely sport. There are some thousands of the blue-coated boys on the ground, so that every old woman in the village may have a pot-pie for the asking."

"Well, we have happily frightened the birds from this side of the valley," said Marmaduke, "and the carnage must of necessity end, for the present.— Boys, I will give thee sixpence a hundred for the pigeons' heads only; so go to work, and bring them into the village."

This expedient produced the desired effect, for every urchin on the ground went industriously to work to wring the necks of the wounded birds.

Judge Temple retired towards his dwelling with that kind of feeling, that many a man has experienced before him, who discovers, after the excitement of the moment has passed, that he has purchased pleasure at the price of misery to others. Horses were loaded with the dead; and, after this first burst of sporting, the shooting of pigeons became a business, with a few idlers, for the remainder of the season. Richard, however, boasted for many a year, of his shot with the "cricket;" and Benjamin gravely asserted, that he thought they killed nearly as many pigeons on that day, as there were Frenchmen destroyed on the memorable occasion of Rodney's victory.

Chapter XXIII

"Help, masters, help; here's a fish hangs in the net like a poor man's right in the law."

—*PERICLES*, II.i.116–17.

The advance of the season now became as rapid, as its first approach had been tedious and lingering. The days were uniformly mild, while the nights, though cool, were no longer chilled by frosts. The whip-poor-will was heard whistling his melancholy notes along the margin of the lake, and the ponds and meadows were sending forth the music of their thousand tenants. The leaf of the native poplar was seen quivering in the woods; the sides of the mountains began to lose their hue of brown, as the lively green of the different members of the forest blended their shades with the permanent colours of the pine and hemlock; and even the buds of the tardy oak were swelling with the promise of the coming summer. The gay and fluttering blue-bird, the social robin, and the industrious little wren, were all to be seen, enlivening the fields with their presence and their songs; while the soaring fish-hawk was already hovering over the waters of the Otsego, watching, with native voracity, for the appearance of his prey.

The tenants of the lake were far-famed for both their quantities and their quality, and the ice had hardly disappeared, before numberless little boats were launched from the shores, and the lines of the fishermen were dropped into the inmost recesses of its deepest caverns, tempting the unwary animals with every variety of bait, that the ingenuity or the art of man had invented. But the slow, though certain adventures with hook and line were ill-suited to the profusion and impatience of the settlers. More destructive means were resorted to; and, as the season had now arrived when the bass-fisheries were allowed by the provisions of the law, that Judge Temple had procured, the Sheriff declared his intention by availing himself of the first dark night, to enjoy the sport in person—

"And you shall be present, cousin Bess," he added, when he announced this design, "and Miss Grant, and Mr. Edwards; and I will show you what I call fishing—not nibble, nibble, nibble, as 'duke does, when he goes after the salmon-trout. There he will sit, for hours, in a broiling sun, or, perhaps, over a hole in the ice, in the coldest days in winter, under the lee of a few bushes, and not a fish will he catch, after all this mortification of the flesh.

No, no—give me a good seine, that's fifty or sixty fathoms in length, with a jolly parcel of boatmen to crack their jokes, the while, with Benjamin to steer, and let us haul them in by thousands; I call that fishing."

"Ah! Dickon," cried Marmaduke, "thou knowest but little of the pleasure there is in playing with the hook and line, or thou wouldst be more saving of the game. I have known thee to leave fragments enough behind thee, when thou hast headed a night-party on the lake, to feed a dozen famishing families."

"I shall not dispute the matter, Judge Temple: this night will I go; and I invite the company to attend, and then let them decide between us."

Richard was busy, during most of the afternoon, making his preparations for the important occasion. Just as the light of the setting sun had disappeared, and a new moon had begun to throw its shadows on the earth, the fishermen took their departure in a boat, for a point that was situated on the western shore of the lake, at the distance of rather more than half a mile from the village. The ground had become settled, and the walking was good and dry. Marmaduke, with his daughter, her friend, and young Edwards, continued on the high, grassy banks, at the outlet of the placid sheet of water, watching the dark object that was moving across the lake, until it entered the shade of the western hills, and was lost to the eye. The distance round by land, to the point of destination, was a mile, and he observed—

"It is time for us to be moving; the moon will be down ere we reach the point, and then the miraculous hauls of Dickon will commence."

The evening was warm, and, after the long and dreary winter from which they had just escaped, delightfully invigorating. Inspirited by the scene, and their anticipated amusement, the youthful companions of the Judge followed his steps, as he led them along the shores of the Otsego, and through the skirts of the village.

"See!" said young Edwards; "they are building their fire already; it glimmers for a moment, and dies again, like the light of a fire-fly."

"Now it blazes," cried Elizabeth; "you can perceive figures moving around the light. Oh! I would bet my jewels against the gold beads of Remarkable, that my impatient cousin Dickon had an agency in raising that bright flame;—and see; it fades again, like most of his brilliant schemes."

"Thou hast guessed the truth, Bess," said her father; "he has thrown an armful of brush on the pile, which has burnt out as soon as lighted. But it has enabled them to find a better fuel, for their fire begins to blaze with a more steady flame. It is the true fisherman's beacon now; observe how beautifully it throws its little circle of light on the water."

The appearance of the fire urged the pedestrians on, for even the ladies had become eager to witness the miraculous draught. By the time they reached the bank which rose above the low point, where the fishermen had landed, the moon had sunk behind the tops of the western pines, and, as most of the stars were obscured by clouds, there was but little other light than that which proceeded from the fire. At the suggestion of Marmaduke, his companions paused to listen to the conversation of those below them, and examine the party, for a moment, before they descended to the shore.

The whole group were seated around the fire, with the exception of Richard and Benjamin; the former of whom occupied the root of a decayed stump, that had been drawn to the spot as part of their fuel, and the latter was standing, with his arms a-kimbo, so near to the flame, that the smoke occasionally obscured his solemn visage, as it waved around the pile, in obedience to the night-airs, that swept gently over the water.

"Why, look you, Squire," said the Major-domo, "you may call a lake-fish that will weigh twenty or thirty pounds a serious matter; but to a man who has hauled in a shovel-nosed shirk, d'ye see, it's but a poor kind of fishing, after all."

"I don't know, Benjamin," returned the Sheriff; "a haul of one thousand Otsego bass, without counting pike, pickerel, perch, bull-pouts, salmon-trouts, and suckers, is no bad fishing, let me tell you. There may be sport in sticking a shark, but what is he good for after you have got him? Now any one of the fish that I have named is fit to set before a king."

"Well, Squire," returned Benjamin, "just listen to the philosophy of the thing. Would it stand to reason, that such fish should live and be catched in this here little pond of water, where it's hardly deep enough to drown a man, as you'll find in the wide ocean, where, as every body knows, that is, every body that has followed the seas, whales and grampuses are to be seen, that are as long as one of them pine trees on yonder mountain?"

"Softly, softly, Benjamin," said the Sheriff, as if he wished to save the credit of his favourite; "why some of the pines will measure two hundred feet, and even more."

"Two hundred or two thousand, it's all the same thing," cried Benjamin, with an air which manifested that he was not easily to be bullied out of his opinion, on a subject like the present—"Haven't I been there, and haven't I seen? I have said that you fall in with whales as long as one of them there pines; and what I have once said I'll stand to!"

During this dialogue, which was evidently but the close of a much longer discussion, the huge frame of Billy Kirby was seen extended on one side of the fire, where he was picking his teeth with splinters of the chips near him, and occasionally shaking his head, with distrust of Benjamin's assertions.

"I've a notion," said the wood-chopper, "that there's water in this lake to swim the biggest whale that ever was invented; and, as to the pines, I think I ought to know so'thing consarning them; I have chopped many a one that was sixty times the length of my helve, without counting the eye; and I b'lieve, Benny, that if the old pine that stands in the hollow of the Vision Mountain, just over the village,—you may see the tree itself by looking up, for the moon is on its top yet;—well, now I b'lieve, if that same tree was planted out in the deepest part of the lake, there would be water enough for the biggest ship that ever was built to float over it, without touching its upper branches, I do."

"Did'ee ever see a ship, Master Kirby?" roared the steward—"did'ee ever see a ship, man? or any craft bigger than a limescow, or a wood-boat, on this here small bit of fresh water?"

"Yes, I have," said the wood-chopper, stoutly; "I can say that I have, and tell no lie."

"Did'ee ever see a British ship, Master Kirby? an English line-of-battle ship, boy? Where away did'ee ever fall in with a regular-built vessel, with starn-post and cutwater, garboard streak and plank-shear, gangways and hatchways, and waterways, quarter-deck and forecastle, ay, and flush-deck?—tell me that, man, if you can; where away did'ee ever fall in with a full-rigged, regular-built, decked vessel?"

The whole company were a good deal astounded with this overwhelming question, and even Richard afterwards remarked, that it "was a thousand pities that Benjamin could not read, or he must have made a valuable officer to the British marine. It is no wonder that they overcome the French so easily on the water, when even the lowest sailor so well understood the different parts of a vessel." But Billy Kirby was a fearless wight, and had great jealousy of foreign dictation; he had arisen on his feet, and turned his back to the fire, during the voluble delivery of this interrogatory, and when the steward ended, contrary to all expectation, he gave the following spirited reply:—

"Where! why on the North River, and maybe on Champlain. There's sloops on the river, boy, that would give a hard time on't to the stoutest vessel King George owns. They carry masts of ninety feet in the clear, of good, solid pine, for I've been at the chopping of many a one in Varmount state. I wish I was captain in one of them, and you was in that Board-dish that you talk so much about, and we'd soon see what good Yankee stuff is made on, and whether a Varmounter's hide an't as thick as an Englishman's."

The echoes from the opposite hills, which were more than half a mile from the fishing point, sent back the discordant laugh that Benjamin gave forth at this challenge; and the woods that covered their sides, seemed, by the noise that issued from their shades, to be full of mocking demons.

"Let us descend to the shore," whispered Marmaduke, "or there will soon be ill blood between them. Benjamin is a fearless boaster, and Kirby, though good-natured, is a careless son of the forest, who thinks one American more than a match for six Englishmen. I marvel that Dickon is silent, where there is such a trial of skill in the superlative!"

The appearance of Judge Temple and the ladies produced, if not a pacification, at least a cessation of hostilities. Obedient to the directions of Mr. Jones, the fishermen prepared to launch their boat, which had been seen in the back-ground of the view, with the net carefully disposed on a little platform in its stern, ready for service. Richard gave vent to his reproaches at the tardiness of the pedestrians, when all the turbulent passions of the party were succeeded by a calm, as mild and as placid as that which prevailed over the beautiful sheet of water, that they were about to rifle of its best treasures.

The night had now become so dark as to render objects, without the reach of the light of the fire, not only indistinct, but, in most cases, invisible. For a little distance the water was discernible, glistening, as the glare from the fire danced over its surface, touching it, here and there, with red, quivering streaks; but at a hundred feet from the shore, there lay a boundary of impenetrable gloom. One or two stars were shining through the openings of the clouds, and the lights were seen in the village, glimmering faintly, as if at an immeasurable distance. At times, as the fire lowered, or as the horizon cleared, the outline of the mountain, on the other side of the lake, might be traced, by its undulations; but its shadow was cast, wide and dense, on the bosom of the water, rendering the darkness, in that direction, trebly deep.

Benjamin Pump was invariably the cockswain and net-caster of Richard's boat, unless the Sheriff saw fit to preside in person; and, on the present occasion, Billy Kirby, and a youth of about half his strength, were assigned to the oars. The remainder of the assistants were stationed at the drag ropes. The arrangements were speedily made, and Richard gave the signal to "shove off."

Elizabeth watched the motion of the batteau, as it pulled from the shore, letting loose its rope as it went, but it very soon disappeared in the darkness, when the ear was her only guide to its evolutions. There was great affectation of stillness, during all these manœuvres, in order, as Richard assured them, "not to frighten the bass, who were running into the shoal waters, and who would approach the light, if not disturbed by the sounds from the fishermen."

The hoarse voice of Benjamin was alone heard, issuing out of the gloom, as he uttered, in authoritative tones, "pull larboard oar," "pull starboard," "give way together, boys," and such other dictative mandates as were necessary for the right disposition of his seine. A long time was passed in this necessary part of the process, for Benjamin prided himself greatly on his skill in throwing the net, and, in fact, most of the success of the sport depended on its being done with judgment. At length a loud splash in the water, as he threw away the "staff," or "stretcher," with a hoarse call from the steward, of "clear," announced that the boat was returning; when Richard seized a brand from the fire, and ran to a point, as far above the centre of the fishing ground, as the one from which the batteau had started was below it.

"Stick her in dead for the Squire, boys," said the steward, "and we'll have a look at what grows in this here pond."

In place of the falling net, were now to be heard the quick strokes of the oars, and the noise of the rope, running out of the boat. Presently the batteau shot into the circle of light, and in an instant she was pulled to shore. Several eager hands were extended, to receive the line, and, both ropes being equally well manned, the fishermen commenced hauling in, with slow and steady drags, Richard standing in the centre, giving orders, first to one party and then to the other, to increase or slacken their efforts, as occasion required. The visiters were posted near him, and enjoyed a fair view of the whole operation, which was slowly advancing to an end.

Opinions, as to the result of their adventure, were now freely hazarded by all the men, some declaring that the net came in as light as a feather, and others affirming that it seemed to be full of logs. As the ropes were many hundred feet in length, these opposing sentiments were thought to be of little moment by the Sheriff, who would go first to one line and then to the other, giving each a small pull, in order to enable him to form an opinion for himself.

"Why, Benjamin," he cried, as he made his first effort in this way, "you did not throw the net clear. I can move it with my little finger. The rope slackens in my hand."

"Did you ever see a whale, Squire?" responded the steward: "I say that if that there net is foul, the devil is in the lake in the shape of a fish, for I cast it as fair as ever rigging was rove over the quarter-deck of a flag-ship."

But Richard discovered his mistake, when he saw Billy Kirby before him, standing with his feet in the water, at an angle of forty-five degrees, inclining shorewards, and expending his gigantic strength in sustaining himself in that posture. He ceased his remonstrances, and proceeded to the party at the other line.

"I see the 'staffs,'" shouted Mr. Jones;—"gather in, boys, and away with it; to shore with her—to shore with her."

At this cheerful sound, Elizabeth strained her eyes, and saw the ends of the two sticks on the seine, emerging from the darkness, while the men closed near to each other, and formed a deep bag of their net. The exertions of the fishermen sensibly increased, and the voice of Richard was heard, encouraging them to make their greatest efforts, at the present moment.

"Now's the time, my lads," he cried, "let us get the ends to land, and all we have will be our own—away with her!"

"Away with her it is," echoed Benjamin—"hurrah! ho-a-hoy, ho-a-hoy, ho-a!"

"In with her," shouted Kirby, exerting himself in a manner that left nothing for those in his rear to do, but to gather up the slack of the rope which passed through his hands.

"Staff, ho!" shouted the steward.

"Staff, ho!" echoed Kirby, from the other rope.

The men rushed to the water's edge, some seizing the upper rope, and some the lower, or lead-rope, and began to haul with great activity and zeal. A deep semicircular sweep, of the little balls that supported the seine in its perpendicular position, was plainly visible to the spectators, and, as it rapidly lessened in size, the bag of the net appeared, while an occasional flutter on the water, announced the uneasiness of the prisoners it contained.

"Haul in, my lads," shouted Richard—"I can see the dogs kicking to get free. Haul in, and here's a cast that will pay for the labour."

Fishes of various sorts were now to be seen, entangled in the meshes of the net, as it was passed through the hands of the labourers, and the water, at a little distance from the shore, was alive with the movements of the alarmed victims. Hundreds of white sides were glancing up to the surface of the water, and glistening in the fire-light, when, frightened at the uproar and the change, the fish would again dart to the bottom, in fruitless efforts for freedom.

"Hurrah!" shouted Richard; "one or two more heavy drags, boys, and we are safe."

"Cheerily, boys, cheerily!" cried Benjamin; "I see a salmon-trout that is big enough for a chowder."

"Away with you, you varmint!" said Billy Kirby, plucking a bull-pout from the meshes, and casting the animal back into the lake with contempt. "Pull, boys, pull; here's all kinds, and the Lord condemn me for a liar, if there an't a thousand bass!"

Inflamed beyond the bounds of discretion at the sight, and forgetful of the season, the wood-chopper rushed to his middle into the water, and begun to drive the reluctant animals before him from their native element.

"Pull heartily, boys," cried Marmaduke, yielding to the excitement of the moment, and laying his hands to the net, with no trifling addition to the force. Edwards had preceded him, for the sight of the immense piles of fish, that were slowly rolling over on the gravelly beach, had impelled him also to leave the ladies, and join the fishermen.

Great care was observed in bringing the net to land, and, after much toil, the whole shoal of victims was safely deposited in a hollow of the bank, where they were left to flutter away their brief existence, in the new and fatal element.

Even Elizabeth and Louisa were greatly excited and highly gratified, by seeing two thousand captives thus drawn from the bosom of the lake, and laid as prisoners at their feet. But when the feelings of the moment were passing away, Marmaduke took in his hands a bass, that might have weighed two pounds, and, after viewing it a moment, in melancholy musing, he turned to his daughter, and observed—

"This is a fearful expenditure of the choicest gifts of Providence. These fish, Bess, which thou seest lying in such piles before thee, and which, by to-morrow evening, will be rejected food on the meanest table in Templeton, are of a quality and flavour that, in other countries, would make them esteemed a luxury on the tables of princes or epicures. The world has no better fish than the bass of Otsego: it unites the richness of the shad[3] to the firmness of the salmon."

"But surely, dear sir," cried Elizabeth, "they must prove a great blessing to the country, and a powerful friend to the poor."

"The poor are always prodigal, my child, where there is plenty, and seldom think of a provision against the morrow. But if there can be any excuse for destroying animals in this manner, it is in taking the bass. During the winter, you know, they are entirely protected from our assaults by the ice, for they refuse the hook; and during the hot months, they are not seen. It is supposed they retreat to the deep and cool waters of the lake, at that season; and it is only in the spring and autumn, that, for a few days, they are to be found, around the points where they are within the reach of a seine.

[3]Of all the fish the writer has ever tasted, he thinks the one in question the best. [1832]

But, like all the other treasures of the wilderness, they already begin to disappear, before the wasteful extravagance of man."

"Disappear, 'duke! disappear!" exclaimed the Sheriff; "if you don't call this appearing, I know not what you will. Here are a good thousand of the shiners, some hundreds of suckers, and a powerful quantity of other fry. But this is always the way with you, Marmaduke; first it's the trees, then it's the deer, after that it's the maple sugar, and so on to the end of the chapter. One day, you talk of canals, through a country where there's a river or a lake every half-mile, just because the water won't run the way you wish it to go; and the next, you say something about mines of coal, though any man who has good eyes, like myself—I say with good eyes—can see more wood than would keep the city of London in fuel for fifty years;—wouldn't it, Benjamin?"

"Why, for that, Squire," said the steward, "Lon'on is no small place. If it was stretched an end, all the same as a town on one side of a river, it would cover some such matter as this here lake. Thof I dar'st to say, that the wood in sight might sarve them a good turn, seeing that the Lon'oners mainly burn coal."

"Now we are on the subject of coal, Judge Temple," interrupted the Sheriff, "I have a thing of much importance to communicate to you; but I will defer it until to-morrow. I know that you intend riding into the eastern part of the Patent, and I will accompany you, and conduct you to a spot, where some of your projects may be realized. We will say no more now, for there are listeners; but a secret has this evening been revealed to me, 'duke, that is of more consequence to your welfare, than all your estate united."

Marmaduke laughed at the important intelligence, to which in a variety of shapes he was accustomed, and the Sheriff, with an air of great dignity, as if pitying his want of faith, proceeded in the business more immediately before them. As the labour of drawing the net had been very great, he directed one party of his men to commence throwing the fish into piles, preparatory to the usual division, while another, under the superintendence of Benjamin, prepared the seine for a second haul.

1823

■ CATHARINE MARIA SEDGWICK ■
1789–1867

Catharine Maria Sedgwick came from an important Federalist family in western Massachusetts. Although Catharine always spoke with love and respect of her mother, Pamela Dwight Sedgwick suffered repeated periods of mental illness and does not seem to have been close to her daughter. Instead, Catharine admired her father, though he was often away for his political career, which culminated in his becoming Speaker of the House. In his absence, Catharine was surrounded by her many siblings. She was particularly attached to her four brothers. Even when they had all married and become lawyers like their father, they remained the central figures in her emotional life. Single herself, she passed part of every year in the family of one or the other of her brothers, and was a favorite aunt to many children. It was her brothers who encouraged her to write. Together they worked to sustain her often failing self-confidence and assisted her practically with contracts and reviews.

Sedgwick, who left the Calvinist church of her childhood to become a Unitarian, showed a consistent tolerance for members of minority groups. The hero of her first work, *A New-England Tale*, was a Quaker. A long section of *Redwood* concerns a Shaker community, and although Sedgwick analyzes the psychological pressures keeping members within the group, the religion is never condemned. Similarly, *Hope Leslie* shows a sympathetic understanding of Indians and Indian religious beliefs, based partly on her research into Mohawk customs. Unlike Cooper, whose *Last of the Mohicans* appeared the year before *Hope Leslie*, Sedgwick countenances marriage between an Indian man and a white woman: the heroine's sister, Faith Leslie, is carried into captivity as a child, marries an Indian, and refuses the opportunity to rejoin the Puritan community. Sedgwick may have been influenced here by the similar legend of Eunice Williams, a remote ancestor of hers.

Sedgwick was immediately recognized as one of the writers creating an indigenous American literature. *A New-England Tale* was subtitled "Sketches of New-England Character and Manners," and two of her later novels—*Hope Leslie*, set among the Puritans, and *The Linwoods, Or "Sixty Years Since in America,"* set during the Revolution—mingled historical events with romantic invention. Praised as a woman writer, she was nevertheless associated equally with Bryant, Irving, and Cooper. On his European tour, Cooper found he was assumed to be the author of *Redwood*.

Throughout her life, Sedgwick was ambivalent about her position as a single woman. She told a favorite niece that "so many I have loved have made shipwreck of happiness in marriage or have found it a dreary joyless condition." Nevertheless, her fiction always depicts marriage as a young girl's goal and reward. Even in her final novel, *Married or Single?*, which she wrote to assuage depression after the death of her last remaining brother, she reveals her conflict. Though she wrote the novel to "drive away the smile . . . at the name of 'old maid'," she concluded the book by marrying off the heroine.

The central figures in Sedgwick's novels are women, often noted for their independence. In *Redwood*, Aunt Debby, "a natural protector of the weak and oppressed," rescues a young girl held among the Shakers. Aunt Debby had decided to remain single after the Revolutionary War because she was "so imbued with the independent spirit of the times, that she would not then consent to the surrender of any of her rights." On two occasions, Hope Leslie follows her own conscience and frees Indian women from unjust imprisonment. Both Hope and her Indian double Magawisca question political authority that does not include them: Hope, unable as a woman to work through the political system, defies it, and Magawisca denies a Puritan jury's jurisdiction over her people.

Though sympathetic to women's rights and abolition, Sedgwick never took an active part in those reforms. Toward the end of her life, however, she became the first director of the Women's Prison Association. Her novels show a horror of prisons and a hatred of slavery. In *The Linwoods*, the heroine assists in releasing her brother from jail. She is aided by a free black family servant who tells the jailer she ties up, "remember, that you were strung up there by a 'd—n *nigger*'—a nigger *woman*!" In *Married or Single?*, one heroine undertakes to free her brother from the New York Tombs, and another assists a runaway slave. Sedgwick's fiction repeatedly emphasized the political and personal need for liberty and independence.

Barbara A. Bardes
Suzanne Gossett
Loyola University

PRIMARY WORKS

A New-England Tale, 1822; *Redwood*, 1824; *Hope Leslie*, 1827 (reprint, Feminist Press, 1987); *Clarence*, 1830; *The Linwoods*, 1835; *Married or Single?*, 1857; *The Power of Her Sympathy: The Autobiography and Journal*, 1993.

from Hope Leslie

[The first passage included here from *Hope Leslie* traces the consequences of an Indian attack on the Fletcher homestead outside Boston. Mr. Fletcher had emigrated to America in 1630 to join the Puritan settlements, but finding their community oppressive, he chose to build his home on the edge of the forest. During the attack, which occurs when Mr. Fletcher and his ward Hope Leslie are absent, the Pequod chief Mononotto reclaims his children, Magawisca and Oneco, and carries off Fletcher's eldest son, Everell, to avenge his own eldest son Samoset's murder by the English during a massacre of the Indians. Oneco takes with him his favorite, the child Faith Leslie. The scene, which recalls the story of Pocohontas, describes Magawisca's rescue of Everell Fletcher.]

from Volume 1, Chapter 7

It is not our purpose to describe, step by step, the progress of the Indian fugitives. Their sagacity in traversing their native forests, their skill in following and eluding an enemy, and all their politic devices, have been so well described in a recent popular work, that their usages have become familiar as household words, and nothing remains but to shelter defects of skill and knowledge under the veil of silence, since we hold it to be an immutable maxim, that a thing had better not be done than be ill done.

Suffice it to say, then, that the savages, after crossing the track of their pursuers, threaded the forest with as little apparent uncertainty as to their path as is now felt by travellers who pass through the same still romantic country in a stagecoach and on a broad turnpike. As they receded from the Connecticut the pine levels disappeared, the country was broken into hills, and rose into high mountains.

They traversed the precipitous sides of a river that, swollen by the vernal rains, wound its way among the hills, foaming and raging like an angry monarch. The river, as they traced its course, dwindled to a mountain rill, but still retaining its impetuous character, leaping and tumbling for miles through a descending defile, between high mountains, whose stillness, grandeur, and immobility contrasted with the noisy, reckless little stream as stern manhood with infancy. In one place, which the Indians called the throat of the mountain, they were obliged to betake themselves to the channel of the brook, there not being room on its margin for a footpath. The branches of the trees that grew from the rocky and precipitous declivities on each side met and interfaced, forming a sylvan canopy over the imprisoned stream. To Magawisca, whose imagination breathed a living spirit into all the objects of Nature, it seemed as if the spirits of the wood had stooped to listen to its sweet music.

After tracing this little sociable rill to its source, they again plunged into the silent forest, waded through marshy ravines, and mounted to the summits of steril hills, till at length, at the close of the third day, after having gradually descended for several miles, the hills on one side receded, and left a little interval of meadow, through which they wound into the lower valley of the Housatonic.

This continued and difficult march had been sustained by Everell with a spirit and fortitude that evidently won the favour of the savages, who always render homage to superiority over physical evil. There was something more than this common feeling in the joy with which Mononotto noted the boy's silent endurance, and even contempt of pain. One noble victim seemed to him better than a "human hecatomb." In proportion to his exultation in possessing an object worthy to avenge his son, was his fear that his victim would escape from him. During the march, Everell had twice, aided by Magawisca, nearly achieved his liberty. These detected conspiracies, though defeated, rendered the chief impatient to execute his vengeance, and he secretly resolved that it should not be delayed longer than the morrow....

They had entered the expanded vale by following the windings of the Housatonic around a hill, conical and easy of ascent, excepting on that side which overlooked the river, where, half way from the base to the summit, rose a perpendicular rock, bearing on its beetling front the age of centuries. On every other side the hill was garlanded with laurels, now in full and profuse bloom, here and there surmounted by an intervening pine, spruce, or hemlock, whose seared winter foliage was fringed with the bright, tender sprouts of spring. We believe there is a chord even in the heart of savage man that responds to the voice of Nature. Certain it is, the party paused, as it appeared, from a common instinct, at a little grassy nook, formed by the curve of the hill, to gaze on this singularly beautiful spot. Everell looked on the smoke that curled from the huts of the village, imbosomed in pine-trees on the adjacent plain. The scene to him breathed peace and happiness, and gushing thoughts of home filled his eyes with tears. Oneco plucked clusters of laurels, and decked his little favourite, and the old chief fixed his melancholy eye on a solitary pine, scathed and blasted by tempests, that, rooted in the ground where he stood, lifted its topmost branches to the bare rock, where they seemed, in their wild desolation, to brave the elemental fury that had stripped them of beauty and life.

The leafless tree was truly, as it appeared to the eye of Mononotto, a fit emblem of the chieftain of a ruined tribe. "See you, child," he said, addressing Magawisca, "those unearthed roots? the tree must fall: hear you the death-song that wails through those blasted branches?"

"Nay, father, listen not to the sad strain; it is but the spirit of the tree mourning over its decay; rather turn thine ear to the glad song of this bright stream, image of the good. She nourishes the aged trees, and cherishes the tender flowerets, and her song is ever of happiness till she reaches the great sea, image of our eternity."

"Speak not to me of happiness, Magawisca; it has vanished with the smoke of our homes. I tell ye, the spirits of our race are gathered about this blasted tree. Samoset points to that rock—that sacrifice-rock." His keen glance turned from the rock to Everell.

Magawisca understood its portentous meaning, and she clasped her hands in mute and agonizing supplication. He answered to the silent entreaty. "It is in vain; my purpose is fixed, and here it shall be accomplished. Why hast thou linked thy heart, foolish girl, to this English boy? I have sworn, kneeling on the ashes of our hut, that I would never spare a son of our enemy's race. The lights of heaven witnessed my vow, and think you that, now this boy is given into my hands to avenge thy brother, I will spare him? no, not to *thy* prayer, Magawisca. No; though thou lookest on me with thy mother's eye, and speakest with her voice, I will not break my vow."

Mononotto had indeed taken a final and fatal resolution; and prompted, as he fancied, by supernatural intimations, and perhaps dreading the relentings of his own heart, he determined on its immediate execution. He announced his decision to the Mohawks. A brief and animated consultation followed, during which they brandished their tomahawks, and cast wild and threatening glances at Everell, who at once comprehended the meaning of these menacing looks and gestures. He turned an appealing glance to Magawisca. She did not speak. "Am I to die now?" he asked; she turned, shuddering, from him....

Magawisca and her companions were conducted to a wigwam standing on that part of the plain on which they had first entered. It was completely enclosed on three sides by dwarf oaks. In front there was a little plantation of the edible luxuries of the savages. On entering the hut they perceived it had but one occupant, a sick, emaciated old woman, who was stretched on her mat, covered with skins. She raised her head as the strangers entered, and at the sight of Faith Leslie uttered a faint exclamation, deeming the fair creature a messenger from the spirit-land; but, being informed who they were and whence they came, she made every sign and expression of courtesy to them that her feeble strength permitted.

Her hut contained all that was essential to savage hospitality. A few brands were burning on a hearthstone in the middle of the apartment. The smoke that found egress passed out by a hole in the centre of the roof, over which a mat was skilfully adjusted, and turned to the windward side by a cord that hung within. The old woman, in her long pilgrimage, had accumulated stores of Indian riches: piles of sleeping-mats lay in one corner; nicely-dressed skins garnished the walls; baskets of all shapes and sizes, gayly decorated with rude images of birds and flowers, contained dried fruits, medicinal herbs, Indian corn, nuts, and game. A covered pail, made of folds of birch bark, was filled with a kind of beer—a decoction of various roots and aromatic shrubs. Neatly-turned wooden spoons and bowls, and culinary utensils of clay, supplied all the demands of the inartificial housewifery of savage life.

The travellers, directed by their old hostess, prepared their evening repast—a short and simple process to an Indian; and, having satisfied the cravings of hunger, they were all, with the exception of Magawisca and one of the Mohawks, in a very short time stretched on their mats and fast asleep.

Magawisca seated herself at the feet of the old woman, and had neither spoken nor moved since she entered the hut. She watched anxiously and impatiently the movements of the Indian, whose appointed duty it appeared to be to guard her. He placed a wooden bench against the mat which served for a door, and stuffing his pipe with tobacco from a pouch slung over his shoulder, and then filling a gourd with the liquor in the pail, and placing it beside him he quietly sat himself down to his night-watch.

The old woman became restless, and her loud and repeated groans at last withdrew Magawisca from her own miserable thoughts. She inquired if she could do aught to allay her pain; the sufferer pointed to a jar that stood on the embers, in which a medicinal preparation was simmering. She motioned to Magawisca to give her a spoonful of the liquor; she did so; and as she took it, "It is made," she said, "of all the plants on which the spirit of sleep has breathed"; and so it seemed to be, for she had scarcely swallowed it when she fell asleep.

Once or twice she waked and murmured something, and once Magawisca heard her say, "Hark to the wekolis![1] he is perched on the old oak by the sacrifice-rock, and his cry is neither musical nor merry: a bad sign in a bird."

But all signs and portents were alike to Magawisca; every sound rung a death-peal to her ear, and the hissing silence had in it the mystery and fearfulness of death. The night wore slowly and painfully away, as if, as in the fairy tale, the moments were counted by drops of heart's blood. But the most wearisome nights will end; the morning approached; the familiar notes of the birds of earliest dawn were heard, and the twilight peeped through the crevices of the hut, when a new sound fell on Magawisca's startled ear. It was the slow, measured tread of many feet. The poor girl now broke

---

[1]Whippoorwill.

silence, and vehemently entreated the Mohawk to let her pass the door, or at least to raise the mat.

He shook his head with a look of unconcern, as if it were the petulant demand of a child, when the old woman, awakened by the noise, cried out that she was dying; that she must have light and air; and the Mohawk started up, impulsively, to raise the mat. It was held between two poles that formed the doorposts; and, while he was disengaging it, Magawisca, as if inspired, and quick as thought, poured the liquor from the jar on the fire into the hollow of her hand, and dashed it into the gourd which the Mohawk had just replenished. The narcotic was boiling hot, but she did not cringe; she did not even feel it; and she could scarcely repress a cry of joy when the savage turned round and swallowed, at one draught, the contents of the cup.

Magawisca looked eagerly through the aperture, but, though the sound of the footsteps had approached nearer, she saw no one. She saw nothing but a gentle declivity that sloped to the plain, a few yards from the hut, and was covered with a grove of trees; beyond and peering above them were the hill and the sacrifice-rock; the morning star, its rays not yet dimmed in the light of day, shed a soft trembling beam on its summit. This beautiful star, alone in the heavens when all other lights were quenched, spoke to the superstitious, or, rather, the imaginative spirit of Magawisca. "Star of promise," she thought, "thou dost still linger with us when day is vanished, and now thou art there alone to proclaim the coming sun; thou dost send in upon my soul a ray of hope; and though it be but as the spider's slender pathway, it shall sustain my courage." She had scarcely formed this resolution when she needed all its efficacy, for the train whose footsteps she had heard appeared in full view.

First came her father, with the Housatonic chief; next, alone, and walking with a firm, undaunted step, was Everell, his arms folded over his breast, and his head a little inclined upward, so that Magawisca fancied she saw his full eye turned heavenward; after him walked all the men of the tribe, ranged according to their age, and the rank assigned to each by his own exploits.

They were neither painted nor ornamented according to the common usage at festivals and sacrifices, but everything had the air of hasty preparation. Magawisca gazed in speechless despair. The procession entered the wood, and for a few moments disappeared from her sight; again they were visible, mounting the acclivity of the hill by a winding, narrow footpath, shaded on either side by laurels. They now walked singly and slowly, but to Magawisca their progress seemed rapid as a falling avalanche. She felt that, if she were to remain pent in that prison-house, her heart would burst, and she sprang towards the doorway in the hope of clearing her passage; but the Mohawk caught her arm in his iron grasp, and putting her back, calmly retained his station. She threw herself on her knees to him; she entreated, she wept, but in vain: he looked on her with unmoved apathy. Already she saw the foremost of the party had reached the rock, and were forming a semicircle around it: again she appealed to her determined keeper, and again he denied her petition, but with a faltering tongue and a drooping eye.

Magawisca, in the urgency of a necessity that could brook no delay, had forgotten, or regarded as useless, the sleeping potion she had infused into the Mohawk's draught; she now saw the powerful agent was at work for her, and with that quickness of apprehension that made the operations of her mind as rapid as the impulses of instinct, she perceived that every emotion she excited but hindered the effect of the potion. Suddenly seeming to relinquish all purpose and hope of escape, she threw herself on a mat, and hid her face, burning with agonizing impatience, in her mantle. There we must leave her, and join that fearful company who were gathered together to witness what they believed to be the execution of exact and necessary justice.

Seated around their sacrifice-rock—their holy of holies—they listened to the sad story of the Pequod chief with dejected countenances and downcast eyes, save when an involuntary glance turned on Everell, who stood awaiting his fate, cruelly aggravated by every moment's delay, with a quiet dignity and calm resignation that would have become a hero or a saint. Surrounded by this dark cloud of savages, his fair countenance kindled by holy inspiration, he looked scarcely like a creature of earth.

There might have been among the spectators some who felt the silent appeal of the helpless, courageous boy; some whose hearts moved them to interpose to save the selected victim; but they were restrained by their interpretation of natural justice, as controlling to them as our artificial codes of laws to us.

Others, of a more cruel or more irritable disposition, when the Pequod described his wrongs and depicted his sufferings, brandished their tomahawks, and would have hurled them at the boy; but the chief said, "Nay, brothers, the work is mine; he dies by my hand—for my first-born—life for life; he dies by a single stroke, for thus was my boy cut off. The blood of sachems is in his veins. He has the skin, but not the soul of that mixed race, whose gratitude is like that vanishing mist," and he pointed to the vapour that was melting from the mountain tops into the transparent ether; "and their promises like this," and he snapped a dead branch from the pine beside which he stood, and broke it in fragments. "Boy as he is, he fought for his mother as the eagle fights for its young. I watched him in the mountain-path, when the blood gushed from his torn feet; not a word from his smooth lip betrayed his pain."

Mononotto embellished his victim with praises, as the ancients wreathed theirs with flowers. He brandished his hatchet over Everell's head, and cried exultingly, "See, he flinches not. Thus stood my boy when they flashed their sabres before his eyes and bade him betray his father. Brothers: My people have told me I bore a woman's heart towards the enemy. Ye shall see. I will pour out this English boy's blood to the last drop, and give his flesh and bones to the dogs and wolves."

He then motioned to Everell to prostrate himself on the rock, his face downward. In this position the boy would not see the descending stroke.

Even at this moment of dire vengeance the instincts of a merciful nature asserted their rights.

Everell sunk calmly on his knees, not to supplicate life, but to commend his soul to God. He clasped his hands together. He did not—he could not speak; his soul was

> "Rapt in still communion, that transcends
> The imperfect offices of prayer."

At this moment a sunbeam penetrated the trees that enclosed the area, and fell athwart his brow and hair, kindling it with an almost supernatural brightness. To the savages, this was a token that the victim was accepted, and they sent forth a shout that rent the air. Everell bent forward and pressed his forehead to the rock. The chief raised the deadly weapon, when Magawisca, springing from the precipitous side of the rock, screamed "Forbear!" and interposed her arm. It was too late. The blow was levelled—force and direction given; the stroke, aimed at Everell's neck, severed his defender's arm, and left him unharmed. The lopped, quivering member dropped over the precipice. Mononotto staggered and fell senseless, and all the savages, uttering horrible yells, rushed towards the fatal spot.

"Stand back!" cried Magawisca. "I have bought his life with my own. Fly, Everell—nay, speak not, but fly—thither—to the east!" she cried, more vehemently.

Everell's faculties were paralyzed by a rapid succession of violent emotions. He was conscious only of a feeling of mingled gratitude and admiration for his preserver. He stood motionless, gazing on her. "I die in vain, then," she cried, in an accent of such despair that he was roused. He threw his arms around her, and pressed her to his heart as he would a sister that had redeemed his life with her own, and then, tearing himself from her, he disappeared. No one offered to follow him. The voice of nature rose from every heart, and, responding to the justice of Magawisca's claim, bade him "God speed!" To all it seemed that his deliverance had been achieved by miraculous aid. All—the dullest and coldest—paid involuntary homage to the heroic girl, as if she were a superior being, guided and upheld by supernatural power....

from **Volume 2, Chapter 1**

[A number of years later, Hope, resisting both "the prejudices of the age" and conventional feminine behavior, secretly frees from prison the Indian woman Nelema, who has been condemned as a witch because she cured a case of snakebite with herbal medicine. Nelema promises to repay Hope by finding her long-lost sister, and months later Magawisca contacts Hope with news of the girl, who has been raised among the Pequods and married to Magawisca's brother Oneco. Meeting secretly at the cemetery where both their mothers are buried, Hope and Magawisca courageously plan a way for Hope to see her sister, although this action will violate colonial law.

Sedgwick uses this meeting as well as Nelema's medical success to underscore her respect for Indian culture and to emphasize the strength and solidarity of women.]

The stranger seemed equally interested in Miss Leslie's appearance; and, fixing her eye intently on her, "Pray try my moccasins, lady," she said, earnestly.

"Oh, certainly; I should of all things like to buy a pair of you," said Hope; and, advancing, she was taking them from her shoulder, over which they were slung, when she, ascertaining by a quick glance that the servant had disappeared, gently repressed Miss Leslie's hand, saying at the same time, "Tell me thy name, lady."

"My name! Hope Leslie. But who art thou?" Hope asked in return, in a voice rendered almost inarticulate by the thought that flashed into her mind.

The stranger cast down her eyes, and for half an instant hesitated; then looking apprehensively around, she said, in low, distinct accents, "Hope Leslie, I am Magawisca."

"Magawisca!" echoed Hope. "Oh, Everell!" and she sprang towards the parlour door to summon Everell.

"Silence! stay," cried Magawisca, with a vehement gesture, and at the same time turning to escape should Hope prosecute her intention.

Hope perceived this, and again approached her. "It cannot, then, be Magawisca," she said; and she trembled as she spoke with doubts, hopes, and fears.

Magawisca might have at once identified herself by opening her blanket and disclosing her person; but that she did not, no one will wonder who knows that a savage feels more even than ordinary sensibility at personal deformity. She took from her bosom a necklace of hair and gold entwined together. "Dost thou know this?" she asked. "Is it not like that thou wearest?"

Hope grasped it, pressed it to her lips, and answered by exclaiming passionately, "My sister! my sister!"

"Yes, it is a token from thy sister. Listen to me, Hope Leslie: my time is brief; I may not stay here another moment; but come to me this evening at nine o'clock, at the burial-place, a little beyond the clump of pines, and I will give thee tidings of thy sister: keep what I say in thine own bosom; tell no one thou hast seen me; come *alone*, and fear not." . . .

She arrived at the appointed rendezvous, and there saw Magawisca, and Magawisca alone, kneeling before an upright stake planted at one end of a grave. She appeared occupied in delineating a figure on the stake with a small implement she held in her hand, which she dipped in a shell placed on the ground beside her.

Hope paused with a mingled feeling of disappointment and awe; disappointment that her sister was not there, and awe inspired by the solemnity of the scene before her: the spirit-stirring figure of Magawisca, the duty she was performing, the flickering light, the monumental stones, and the dark shadows that swept over them as the breeze bowed the tall pines. She drew her mantle, that fluttered in the breeze, close around her, and almost suppressed her breath, that she might not disturb what she believed to be an act of filial devotion.

Magawisca was not unconscious of Miss Leslie's approach, but she deemed the office in which she was engaged too sacred to be interrupted. She accompanied the movement of her hand with a low chant in her native tongue; and so sweet and varied were the tones of her voice, that it seemed to Hope they might have been breathed by an invisible spirit.

When she had finished her work, she leaned her head for a moment against the stake, and then rose and turned to Miss Leslie; a moonbeam shot across her face; it was wet with tears, but she spoke in a tranquil voice. "You have come—and alone?" she said, casting a searching glance around her.

"I promised to come alone," replied Hope.

"Yes, and I trusted you; and I will trust you farther, for the good deed you did Nelema."

"Nelema, then, lived to reach you."

"She did; wasted, faint, and dying, she crawled into my father's wigwam. She had but scant time and short breath; with that she cursed your race, and blessed you, Hope Leslie; her day was ended; the hand of death pressed her throat, and even then she made me swear to perform her promise to you."

"And you will, Magawisca," cried Hope, impetuously, "you will give me back my sister?"

"Nay, that she never promised—that I cannot do. I cannot send back the bird that has mated, to its parent nest—the stream that has mingled with other waters, to its fountain."

"Oh, do not speak to me in these dark sayings," replied Hope, her smooth brow contracting with impatience and apprehension, and her hurried manner and convulsed countenance contrasting strongly with the calmness of Magawisca; "what is it you mean? Where is my sister?"

"She is safe—she is near to you—and you shall see her, Hope Leslie."

"But when—and where, Magawisca? Oh, if I could once clasp her in my arms, she never should leave me—she never should be torn from me again."

"Those arms," said Magawisca, with a faint smile, "could no more retain thy sister than a spider's web. The lily of the Maqua's valley will never again make the English garden sweet."

"Speak plainer to me," cried Hope, in a voice of entreaty that could not be resisted. "Is my sister—" she paused, for her quivering lips could not pronounce the words that rose to them.

Magawisca understood her, and replied. "Yes, Hope Leslie, thy sister is married to Oneco."

"God forbid!" exclaimed Hope, shuddering as if a knife had been plunged in her bosom. "My sister married to an Indian!"

"An Indian!" exclaimed Magawisca, recoiling with a look of proud contempt, that showed she reciprocated with full measure the scorn expressed for her race. "Yes, an Indian, in whose veins runs the blood of the strongest, the fleetest of the children of the forest, who never turned their backs on friends or enemies, and whose souls have returned to the Great Spirit stainless as they came from him. Think ye that your blood will be corrupted by mingling with this stream?"

Long before Magawisca ceased to pour out her indignation, Hope's first emotion had given place to a burst of tears; she wept aloud, and her broken utterance of "O, my sister! my sister! My dear mother!" emitted but imperfect glimpses of the ruined hopes, the bitter feelings that oppressed her.

There was a chord in Magawisca's heart that needed but the touch of tenderness to respond in harmony; her pride vanished, and her indignation gave place to sympathy. She said in a low, soothing voice, "Now do not weep thus; your sister is well with us. She is cherished as the bird cherishes her young. The cold winds may not blow on her, nor the fierce sun scorch her, nor a harsh sound ever be spoken to her; she is dear to Mononotto as if his own blood ran in her veins; and Oneco—Oneco worships and serves her as if all good spirits dwelt in her. Oh, she is indeed well with us."

"There lies my mother," cried Hope, without seeming to have heard Magawisca's consolations; "she lost her life in bringing her children to this wild world, to secure them in the fold of Christ. O, God! restore my sister to the Christian family."

"And here," said Magawisca, in a voice of deep pathos, "here is my mother's grave; think ye not that the Great Spirit looks down on these sacred spots, where the good and the peaceful rest, with an equal eye? think ye not their children are His children, whether they are gathered in yonder temple where your people worship, or bow to him beneath the green boughs of the forest?"

There was certainly something thrilling in Magawisca's faith, and she now succeeded in riveting Hope's attention. "Listen to me," she said; "your sister is of what you call the Christian family. I believe ye have many names in that family. She hath been signed with the cross by a holy father from France; she bows to the crucifix."

"Thank God!" exclaimed Hope, fervently, for she thought that any Christian faith was better than none.

"Perhaps ye are right," said Magawisca, as if she read Hope's heart; "there may be those that need other lights; but to me, the Great Spirit is visible in the life-creating sun. I perceive him in the gentle light of the moon that steals in through the forest boughs. I feel him here," she continued, pressing her hand on her breast, while her face glowed with the enthusiasm of devotion. "I feel him in these ever-living, ever-wakeful thoughts—but we waste time. You must see your sister."

"When—and where?" again demanded Hope.

"Before I answer you, you must promise me by this sign," and she pointed to the emblem of her tribe, an eagle, which she had rudely delineated on the post that served as a headstone to her mother's grave; "you must promise me by the bright host of Heaven, that the door of your lips shall be fast; that none shall know that you have seen me, or are to see me again."

"I promise," said Hope, with her characteristic precipitancy.

"Then, when five suns have risen and set, I will return with your sister. But hush!" she said; suddenly stopping, and turning a suspicious eye towards the thicket of evergreens.

"It was but the wind," said Hope, rightly interpreting Magawisca's quick glance, and the slight inclination of her head.

"You would not betray me!" said Magawisca, in a voice of mingled assurance and inquiry. "Oh, more than ever entered into thy young thoughts hangs upon my safety."

"But why any fear for your safety? why not come openly among us? I will get the word of our good governor that you shall come and go in peace. No one ever feared to trust his word."

"You know not what you ask."

"Indeed I do; but you, Magawisca, know not what you refuse; and why refuse? are you afraid of being treated like a recovered prisoner? Oh, no! every one will delight to honour you, for your very name is dear to all Mr. Fletcher's friends—most dear to Everell."

"Dear to Everell Fletcher! Does he remember me? Is there a place in his heart for an Indian?" she demanded, with a blended expression of pride and melancholy.

"Yes, yes, Magawisca, indeed is there," replied Hope, for now she thought she had touched the right key. "It was but this morning that he said he had a mind to take an Indian guide, and seek you out among the Maquas." Magawisca hid her face in the folds of her mantle, and Hope proceeded with increasing earnestness. "There is nothing in the wide world— there is nothing that Everell thinks so good and so noble as you. Of, if you could but have seen his joy, when, after your parting on that horrid rock, he first heard you was living! He has described you so often and so truly, that the moment I saw you and heard your voice, I said to myself, 'this is surely Everell's Magawisca.'"

"Say no more, Hope Leslie, say no more," exclaimed Magawisca, throwing back the envelope from her face, as if she were ashamed to shelter emotions she ought not to indulge. "I have promised my father, I have repeated the vow here on my mother's grave, and if I were to go back from it, those bright witnesses," she pointed to the heavens, "would break their silence. Do not speak to me again of Everell Fletcher."

"Oh yes, once again, Magawisca: if you will not listen to me; if you will but give me this brief, mysterious meeting with my poor sister, at least let Everell be with me; for his sake, for my sake, for your own sake, do not refuse me."

Magawisca looked on Hope's glowing face for a moment, and then shook her head with a melancholy smile. "They tell me," she said, "that no one can look on you and deny you aught; that you can make old men's hearts soft, and mould them at your will; but I have learned to deny even the cravings of my own heart; to pursue my purpose like the bird that keeps her wing stretched to the toilsome flight, though the sweetest note of her mate recalls her to the nest. But ah! I do but boast," she continued, casting her eyes to the ground. "I may not trust myself; that was a childish scream that escaped me when I saw Everell; had my father heard it, his cheek would have been pale with shame. No, Hope Leslie, I may not listen to thee. You must come alone to the meeting, or never meet your sister: will you come?"

Hope saw in the determined manner of Magawisca that there was no alternative but to accept the boon on her own terms, and she no longer withheld her compliance. . . .

Before they separated, Hope said, "You will allow me, Magawisca, to persuade my sister, if I can, to remain with me?"

"Oh yes, if you can; but do not hope to persuade her. She and my brother are as if one life-chord bound them together; and, besides, your sister cannot speak to you and understand you as I do. She was very young when she was taken where she has only heard the Indian tongue: some, you know, are like water, that retains no mark; and others like the flinty rock, that never loses a mark." Magawisca observed Hope's look of disappointment, and, in a voice of pity, added, "Your sister hath a face that speaketh plainly what the tongue should never speak—her own goodness."

When these two romantic females had concerted every measure they deemed essential to the certainty and privacy of their meeting, Magawisca bowed her head and kissed the border of Hope's shawl with the reverent delicacy of an Oriental salutation; she then took from beneath her mantle some fragrant herbs, and strewed them over her mother's grave, then prostrated herself in deep and silent devotion, feeling (as others have felt on earth thus consecrated) as if the clods she pressed were instinct with life. When this last act of filial love was done, she rose, muffled herself closely in her dark mantle, and departed.

Hope lingered for a moment. "Mysteriously," she said, as her eye followed the noble figure of Magawisca till it was lost in the surrounding darkness, "mysteriously have our destinies been interwoven. Our mothers brought from a far distance to rest together here—their children connected in indissoluble bonds!"

from **Volume 2, Chapter 8**

[Hope's meeting with her sister leads to the capture of Magawisca as well as that of Faith Leslie. At her trial for "brewing conspiracy amongst us among the Indian tribes," Magawisca is assisted by John Eliot, "the apostle of New England," whom Sedgwick identifies as the "first Protestant missionary to the Indians." As the passage begins, Magawisca is being slandered by Sir Philip Gardiner, a secret Catholic who has courted Hope unsuccessfully and attempts to take his revenge by harming her friend. In the dramatic climax of the scene, Magawisca denies the right of the Puritan magistrates to judge her or her people.]

He said "that, after conducting Miss Leslie to the governor's door, he had immediately returned to his own lodgings, and that, induced by the still raging storm to make his walk as short as possible, he took a cross-cut through the burial ground; that, on coming near the upper extremity of the enclosure, he fancied he heard a human voice mingling with the din of the storm; that he paused, and directly a flash of lightning discovered Magawisca kneeling on the bare wet earth, making those monstrous and violent contortions, which all who heard him well knew characterized the devil-worship of the powwows; he would not, he ought not repeat to Christian ears her invocations to the Evil One to aid her in the execution of her revenge on the English; nor would he more particularly describe her diabolical writhings and beatings of her person. His brethren might easily imagine his emotions at witnessing them by the sulphureous gleams of lightning, on which, doubtless, her prayers were sped."

Sir Philip had gained confidence as he proceeded in his testimony, for he perceived by the fearful and angry glances that were cast on the prisoner, that his tale was credited by many of his audience, and he hoped by all.

The notion that the Indians were the children of the devil was not confined to the vulgar; and the belief in a familiar intercourse with evil spirits, now rejected by all but the most ignorant and credulous, was then universally received.

All had, therefore, listened in respectful silence to Sir Philip's extraordinary testimony, and it was too evident that it had the effect to set the current of feeling and opinion against the prisoner. Her few friends looked despondent; but for herself, true to the spirit of her race, she manifested no surprise nor emotion of any kind.

The audience listened eagerly to the magistrate, who read from his note-book the particulars which had been received from the Indian informer, and which served to corroborate and illustrate Sir Philip's testimony. All the evidence being now before the court, the governor asked Magawisca "if she had aught to allege in her own defence."

"Speak humbly, maiden," whispered Mr. Eliot; "it will grace thy cause with thy judges."

"Say," said Everell, "that you are a stranger to our laws and usages, and demand some one to speak for you."

Magawisca bowed her head to both advisers, in token of acknowledgment of their interest, and then, raising her eyes to her judges, she said, "I am your prisoner, and ye may slay me, but I deny your right to judge me. My people have never passed under your yoke; not one of my race has ever acknowledged your authority."

"This excuse will not suffice thee," answered one of her judges; "thy pride is like the image of Nebuchadnezzar's dream—it standeth on feet of clay: thy race have been swift witnesses to that sure word of prophecy, 'Fear thou not, O Jacob, my servant, for I am with thee, and I will make a full end of the people whither I have driven thee'; thy people! truly, where are they?"

"My people! where are they?" she replied, raising her eyes to Heaven, and speaking in a voice that sounded like deep-toned music after the harsh tones addressed to her; "my people are gone to the isles of the sweet southwest—to those shores that the bark of an enemy can never touch: think ye I fear to follow them?"

There was a momentary silence throughout the assembly; all seemed, for an instant, to feel that no human power could touch the spirit of the captive. Sir Philip whispered to the magistrate who last spoke, "Is it not awful presumption for this woman thus publicly to glory in her heathen notions?"

The knight's prompting had the intended effect. "Has this Pequod woman," demanded the magistrate, "never been instructed in the principles of truth, that she dares thus to hold forth her heathenisms before us? Dost thou not know, woman," he continued, holding up a Bible, "that this book contains the only revelation of a future world—the only rule for the present life?"

"I know," she replied, "that it contains thy rule, and it may be needful for thy mixed race; but the Great Spirit hath written his laws on the hearts of his original children, and we need it not."

"She is of Satan's heritage, and our enemy—a proved conspirator against the peace of God's people, and I see not why she should not be cut off," said the same gentleman, addressing his brethren in office.

"The testimony," said another of the magistrates, in a low voice, in which reason and mildness mingled, and truly indicated the disposition of the speaker, "the testimony appeareth to me insufficient to give peace to our consciences in bringing her to extremity. She seems, after her own manner, to be guided by the truth. Let the governor put it to her whether she will confess the charges laid against her."

The governor accordingly appealed to the prisoner. "I neither confess nor deny aught," she said. "I stand here like a deer caught in a thicket, awaiting the arrow of the hunter." . . .

The governor replied, with a severe gravity, ominous to the knight, "That the circumstances he had alluded to certainly required explanation; if that should not prove satisfactory, they would demand a public investigation. In the mean time, he should suspend the trial of the prisoner, who, though the decision of her case might not wholly depend on the establishment of Sir Philip's testimony, was yet, at present, materially affected by it.

"He expressed a deep regret at the interruption that had occurred, as it must lead," he said, "to the suspension of the justice to be manifested, either in the acquittal or condemnation of the prisoner. Some of the magistrates being called away from town on the next morning, he found himself compelled to adjourn the sitting of the court till one month from the present date."

"Then," said Magawisca, for the first time speaking with a tone of impatience, "then, I pray you, send me to death now. Anything is better than wearing through another moon in my prison-house, thinking," she added, and cast down her eyelids, heavy with tears, "thinking of that old man—my father. I pray thee," she continued, bending low her head, "I pray thee now to set me free. Wait not for his testimony"—she pointed to Sir Philip: "as well may ye expect the green herb to spring up in your trodden streets, as the breath of truth to come from his false lips. Do you wait for him to prove that I am your enemy? Take my own word—I am your enemy; the sunbeam and the shadow cannot mingle. The white man cometh—the Indian vanisheth. Can we grasp in friendship the hand raised to strike us? Nay: and it matters not whether we fall by the tempest that lays the forest low, or are cut down alone by the stroke of the axe. I would have thanked you for life and liberty; for Mononotto's sake I would have thanked you; but if ye send me back to that dungeon—the grave of the living, feeling, thinking soul, where the sun never shineth, where the stars never rise nor set, where the free breath of Heaven never enters, where all is darkness without and within"—she pressed her hand on her breast—"ye will even now condemn me to death, but death more slow and terrible than your most suffering captive ever endured from Indian fires and knives." She paused; passed unresisted without the little railing that encompassed her, mounted the steps of the platform, and, advancing to the feet of the governor, threw back her mantle, and knelt before him. Her mutilated person, unveiled by this action, appealed to the senses of the spectators. Everell involuntarily closed his eyes, and uttered a cry of agony, lost, indeed, in the murmurs of the crowd. She spoke, and all again were as hushed as death. "Thou didst promise," she said, addressing herself to Governor Winthrop, "to my dying mother thou didst promise kindness to her children. In her name, I demand of thee death or liberty."

Everell sprang forward, and, clasping his hands, exclaimed, "In the name of God, liberty!"

The feeling was contagious, and every voice, save her judges, shouted "Liberty! liberty! Grant the prisoner liberty!" . . .

The governor bowed his assent. "Rise, Magawisca," he said, in a voice of gentle authority; "I may not grant thy prayer; but what I can do in remembrance of my solemn promise to thy dying mother, without leaving undone higher duty, I will do."

1827

CAROLINE KIRKLAND
1801–1864

Caroline Stansbury Kirkland, eldest of eleven children of Eliza Alexander and Samuel Stansbury, was born on January 11, 1801, in New York City, where she spent most of her childhood and adolescence in a family noted for its interest in literature and education. Kirkland's mother was herself a writer, and Kirkland later revised and published some of her mother's work in her own gift books. An aunt headed a series of distinguished schools, which Caroline attended and in which she later taught. In 1828 Caroline married William Kirkland, previously a teacher of classics at Hamilton College, and together they opened a girls' school in Geneva, New York. In 1835, however, they emigrated to Detroit, Michigan, for William, tired of teaching, had dreams of buying land and founding a "city" on the Michigan frontier. By 1837 they had acquired sufficient land and capital to move to the village of Pinckney, where they began the experience in frontier living recorded in *A New Home—Who'll Follow?* (1839).

After five years on the frontier, the Kirklands returned to New York City, where Caroline continued to pursue the writing career she had begun in Michigan. She had by this time published both *A New Home* and its sequel, *Forest Life* (1842), as well as essays and sketches in a variety of magazines. In 1846 William Kirkland died, and at forty-five Kirkland became the sole support of herself and her four children. To make a living, she managed and taught in several girls' schools and wrote. She collected many of her essays in the various gift books she edited; in contrast to many similar offerings, Kirkland's collections were deservedly popular for their intellectual and aesthetic superiority. In 1847 Kirkland became editor of the *Union Magazine of Literature and Art*. As an editor, Kirkland demonstrated a strong commitment to realism in the materials she accepted for publication and considerable critical skill in her reviews, including an enthusiastic response to Melville's early books. Moreover, Kirkland was seriously interested in women as writers. In her long review essay of Susan Warner's *The Wide, Wide World* (1851) and *Queechy* (1852) and Anna Warner's *Dollars and Cents* (1852), published in the *North American Review* in 1853, she provided, in addition to detailed analyses of the strengths and weaknesses of these books, a survey of the state of the art of the novel in America with particular reference to women writers. Kirkland herself was part of a social and professional friendship network of women writers, and her home frequently functioned as a literary salon. She died in New York City on April 6, 1864, and was buried in Greenwood Cemetery in Brooklyn.

A New Home—Who'll Follow?, published under the pseudonym Mary Clavers, describes the experience of a relatively well-educated middle-class white woman transported to the American frontier by virtue of her husband's ambition. As a follower, Kirkland takes advantage of the accident of her presence on the Michigan frontier to become a recorder of American social history. Defining herself against the romanticism of previous western chroniclers, Kirkland consciously asserts her commitment to realism. But what kind of a "story" can one tell if she has "never seen a cougar—nor been bitten by a rattlesnake?" In meeting the dual challenge posed by writing as a woman and a realist, Kirkland recognizes that she is doing something new in American literature. At the heart of her enterprise is the education of her readers to the significance of the American frontier. For Kirkland, the frontier is a true text, revealing a national character obsessed with issues of class and gender. The pressure exerted by the frontier toward "levelling downwards" derives its intensity from the fact that upward mobility is the prevailing motive for western emigration. Thus settlers who have come to Michigan to improve their class status wish no reminders of the class system they think they have left behind.

As a follower, Kirkland can view with some detachment those masculine impulses that have brought her to the frontier. While Mrs. Clavers as a woman struggles to establish a community with her neighbors, the desire to make money at the expense of one's neighbors dominates the male world that Mr. Clavers enters. The "factotum" who offers to build Montacute for Mr. Clavers clears out after having gotten rich on his money, and if Mrs. Jenkins does not effect the "thorough reformation" of Simeon, similar schemes will no doubt ensue from his presence in the "arena of public life." Kirkland's detachment from masculine "madness," however, does not blind her to the degree to which this madness shapes her life. Unable to save the fine oaks, she is granted only the symbolic power of naming the venture to be erected on their stumps. But her detachment does enable her to focus on the lives of women and to recognize that the experience of those who follow is not necessarily the experience of those who lead. Though the frontier may enlarge women's sphere to some degree, woman's world is still primarily the home. Kirkland devotes much of her text to describing the physical and material hardship of housekeeping in the wilderness. More seriously, she records the homelessness frequently experienced by women on the frontier. Since the westering impulse originates in the masculine agenda of upward mobility, men have little incentive to make homes; rather, they view their land as counters in the status game, and they are prepared to sell out and move on at the first good offer, leaving women to pay the hidden costs. *A New Home—Who'll Follow?* signals a realism in American fiction designed to counter not simply previous romanticism but equally that masculine "realism" which believes the whole story is told when the man's story is told. In the portrait of Eloise Fidler, which precedes Mark Twain's Emmeline Grangerford by almost fifty years, Kirkland insists on telling her own story about women and writing. Satirizing through Eloise conventional masculine stereotypes of the woman writer, Kirkland in *A New Home* provides her readers with an alternative persona and style, distinctively female but clearly not feminine.

Judith Fetterley
State University of New York at Albany

PRIMARY WORKS

A New Home—Who'll Follow?, 1939, 1990; *Forest Life*, 1842; *Western Clearings*, 1845; *The Evening Book*, 1852; *A Book for the Home Circle*, 1853.

from **A New Home—Who'll Follow?**

or, Glimpses of Western Life by Mrs. Mary Clavers, An Actual Settler.

Preface

I am glad to be told by those who live in the world, that it has lately become fashionable to read prefaces. I wish to say a few words, by way of introduction, to a work which may be deemed too slight to need a preface, but which will doubtless be acknowledged to require some recommendation.

I claim for these straggling and cloudy crayon sketches of life and manners in the remoter parts of Michigan the merit of general truth of outline. Beyond this I venture not to aspire. I felt somewhat tempted to set forth my little book as being entirely—what it is very nearly—a veritable history;

an unimpeachable transcript of reality; a rough picture, in detached parts, but pentagraphed from the life; a sort of "Emigrant's Guide";—considering with myself that these my adventurous journeyings and tarryings beyond the confines of civilization might fairly be held to confer the traveller's privilege. But conscience prevailed, and I must honestly confess, that there be glosses, and colorings, and lights, if not shadows, for which the author is alone accountable. Journals, published entire and unaltered, should be Parthian darts, sent abroad only when one's back is turned. To throw them in the teeth of one's every-day associates might diminish one's popularity rather inconveniently. I would desire the courteous reader to bear in mind, however, that whatever is quite unnatural, or absolutely incredible, in the few incidents which diversify the following pages, is to be received as literally true. It is only in the most common-place parts (if there be comparisons) that I have any leasing-making to answer for.

It will of course be observed that Miss Mitford's[1] charming sketches of village life must have suggested the form of my rude attempt. I dare not flatter myself that any one will be led to accuse me of further imitation of a deservedly popular writer. And with such brief salvo, I make my humble curtsey.

M.C.

Preface to the Fourth Edition

The improvements which have taken place in the social aspect of the great West since these unvarnished records were written, may lead some who observe the present to doubt the truthfulness of such delineations of the past; but much observation subsequent to the publication of this book, and much after reflection upon it, suggest to me nothing to be retracted or altered in the sketches, as an honest portraiture of rural life in a new country.

No peculiarity of custom or expression is here introduced which was not drawn directly from fact, and if the picture lack verity in any particular, it is not through exaggeration, but the opposite. Indeed, the immediate appropriation of the book in a dozen different parts of the country, before the authorship was known, is a sufficient voucher for its truth.

I am, therefore, much pleased to be able to present a New Edition; the fourth public favor has called for, with illustrations by a pencil which never fails to add grace to any subject, however homely.

C.M.K.

New York, November, 1849.

---

[1]Mary Russell Mitford, an early-nineteenth-century English writer of village stories and sketches.

Chapter I

Here are seen
No traces of man's pomp and pride; no silks
Rustle, nor jewels shine, nor envious eyes
Encounter.

Oh, there is not lost
One of earth's charms; upon her bosom yet
After the flight of untold centuries
The freshness of her far beginning lies.

—BRYANT[2]

Our friends in the "settlements" have expressed so much interest in such of our letters to them as happened to convey any account of the peculiar features of western life, and have asked so many questions, touching particulars which we had not thought worthy of mention that I have been for some time past contemplating the possibility of something like a detailed account of our experiences. And I have determined to give them to the world, in a form not very different from that in which they were originally recorded for our private delectation; nothing doubting, that a veracious history of actual occurrences, an unvarnished transcript of real characters, and an impartial record of every-day forms of speech (taken down in many cases from the lips of the speaker) will be pronounced "graphic" by at least a fair proportion of the journalists of the day.

It is true there are but meagre materials for anything that might be called a story. I have never seen a cougar—nor been bitten by a rattlesnake. The reader who has patience to go with me to the close of my desultory sketches, must expect nothing beyond a meandering recital of common-place occurrences—mere gossip about everyday people, little enhanced in value by any fancy or ingenuity of the writer; in short, a very ordinary pen-drawing; which, deriving no interest from coloring, can be valuable only for its truth.

A home on the outskirts of civilization—habits of society which allow the maid and her mistress to do the honors in complete equality, and to make the social tea visit in loving conjunction—such a distribution of the duties of life as compels all, without distinction, to rise with the sun or before him—to breakfast with the chickens—then,

"Count the slow clock, and dine exact at noon"—

to be ready for tea at four, and for bed at eight—may certainly be expected to furnish some curious particulars for the consideration of those whose daily course almost reverses this primitive arrangement—who "call night day and day night," and who are apt occasionally to forget, when speaking

[2]William Cullen Bryant, "A Forest Hymn."

of a particular class, that "those creatures" are partakers with themselves of a common nature.

I can only wish, like other modest chroniclers, my respected prototypes, that so fertile a theme had fallen into worthier hands. If Miss Mitford, who has given us such charming glimpses of Aberleigh, Hilton Cross, and the Loddon, had, by some happy chance, been translated to Michigan, what would she not have made of such materials as Tinkerville, Montacute, and the Turnip?

When my husband purchased two hundred acres of wild land on the banks of this to-be-celebrated stream, and drew with a piece of chalk on the bar-room table at Danforth's the plan of a village, I little thought I was destined to make myself famous by handing down to posterity a faithful record of the advancing fortunes of that favored spot.

"The madness of the people" in those days of golden dreams took more commonly the form of city-building; but there were a few who contented themselves with planning villages, on the banks of streams which certainly never could be expected to bear navies, but which might yet be turned to account in the more homely way of grinding or sawing—operations which must necessarily be performed somewhere, for the well-being of those very cities. It is of one of these humble attempts that it is my lot to speak, and I make my confession at the outset, warning any fashionable reader, who may have taken up my book, that I intend to be "decidedly low."

Whether the purchaser of *our* village would have been as moderate under all possible circumstances, I am not prepared to say, since, never having enjoyed a situation under government, his resources have not been unlimited; and for this reason any remark which may be hazarded in the course of these my lucubrations touching the more magnificent plans of wealthier aspirants, must be received with some grains of allowance. "Il est plus aisé d'être sage pour les autres, que de l'être pour soi-même."[3]

When I made my first visit to these remote and lonely regions, the scattered woods through which we rode for many miles were gay in their first gosling-green suit of half-opened leaves, and the forest odors which exhaled with the dews of morning and evening, were beyond measure delicious to one "long in populous cities pent." I desired much to be a little sentimental at the time, and feel tempted to indulge to some small extent even here—but I forbear; and shall adhere closely to matters more in keeping with my subject.

I think, to be precise, the time was the last, the very last of April, and I recollect well that even at that early season, by availing myself with sedulous application, of those times when I was fain to quit the vehicle through fear of the perilous mud-holes, or still more perilous half-bridged marshes, I picked upwards of twenty varieties of wild-flowers—some of them of rare and delicate beauty;—and sure I am, that if I had succeeded in inspiring my

---

[3]It is easier to be wise about others than about oneself.

companion with one spark of my own floral enthusiasm, our hundred miles of travel would have occupied a week's time.

The wild-flowers of Michigan deserve a poet of their own. Shelley[4] who sang so quaintly of "the pied wind-flowers and the tulip tall," would have found many a fanciful comparison and deep-drawn meaning for the thousand gems of the roadside. Charles Lamb[5] could have written charming volumes about the humblest among them. Bulwer[6] would find means to associate the common three-leaved white lily so closely with the Past, the Present, and the Future—the Wind, the Stars, and the Tripod of Delphos,[7] that all future botanists, and eke[8] all future philosophers, might fail to unravel the "linked sweetness." We must have a poet of our own.

Since I have casually alluded to a Michigan mud-hole, I may as well enter into a detailed memoir on the subject, for the benefit of future travellers, who, flying over the soil on railroads, may look slightingly back upon the achievements of their predecessors. In the "settlements," a mud-hole is considered as apt to occasion an unpleasant jolt—a breaking of the thread of one's reverie—or in extreme cases, a temporary stand-still, or even an overturn of the rash and unwary. Here, on approaching one of these characteristic features of the "West"—(how much does that expression mean to include? I have never been able to discover its limits)—the driver stops—alights—walks up to the dark gulf—and around it, if he can get around it. He then seeks a long pole and sounds it, measures it across to ascertain how its width compares with the length of his wagon—tries whether its sides are perpendicular, as is usually the case if the road is much used. If he find it not more than three feet deep, he remounts cheerily, encourages his team, and in they go, with a plunge and a shock, rather apt to damp the courage of the inexperienced. If the hole be narrow, the hinder wheels will be quite lifted off the ground by the depression of their precedents, and so remain until by unwearied chiruping and some judicious touches of "the string" the horses are induced to struggle as for their lives; and if the Fates are propitious they generally emerge on the opposite side, dragging the vehicle, or, at least, the forewheels, after them. When I first "penetrated the interior," (to use an indigenous phrase,) all I knew of the wilds was from Hoffman's Tour, or Captain Hall's "graphic" delineations. I had some floating idea of "driving a barouche-and-four any where through the oak-openings"—and seeing "the murdered Banquos[9] of the forest" haunting the scenes of their departed strength and beauty. But I confess these pictures, touched by the glowing pencil of fancy, gave me but incorrect notions of a real journey through Michigan.

---

[4]Percy Bysshe Shelley (1792–1822), English Romantic poet, wrote many poems about natural objects and phenomena.
[5]Charles Lamb (1775–1834), whose informal essays were widely read.
[6]Edward Bulwer-Lytton (1803–1873), an English writer, composed historical novels, among other works.

[7]Among the accoutrements of the oracle at Delphi.
[8]Archaic for "also."
[9]Whose ghost appears in Shakespeare's *Macbeth*.

Our vehicle was not perhaps very judiciously chosen—at least we have since thought so. It was a light, high-hung carriage—of the description commonly known as a buggy or shandrydan—names, of which I would be glad to learn the etymology. I seriously advise any of my friends, who are about flitting to Wisconsin or Oregon, to prefer a heavy lumber wagon, even for the use of the ladies of the family; very little aid or consolation being derived from making a "genteel" appearance in such cases.

At the first encounter of such a mud-hole as I have attempted to describe, we stopped in utter despair. My companion indeed would fain have persuaded me that the many wheel tracks which passed through the formidable gulf were proof positive that it might be forded. I insisted with all a woman's obstinacy that I could not and would not make the attempt, and alighted accordingly, and tried to find a path on one side or the other. But in vain, even putting out of the question my paper-soled shoes—sensible things for the woods. The ditch on each side was filled with water and quite too wide to jump over; and we were actually contemplating a return, when a man in an immense bear-skin cap and a suit of deer's hide, sprang from behind a stump just within the edge of the forest. He "poled" himself over the ditch in a moment, and stood beside us, rifle in hand, as wild and rough a specimen of humanity as one would wish to encounter in a strange and lonely road, just at the shadowy dusk of the evening. I did *not* scream, though I own I was prodigiously frightened. But our stranger said immediately, in a gentle tone and with a French accent, "Me watch deer—you want to cross?" On receiving an answer in the affirmative, he ran in search of a rail, which he threw over the terrific mud-hole—aided me to walk across by the help of his pole—showed my husband where to plunge—waited till he had gone safely through, and "slow circles dimpled o'er the quaking mud"— then took himself off by the way he came, declining any compensation with a most polite "rien! rien!" This instance of true and genuine and generous politeness I record for the benefit of all bearskin caps, leathern jerkins, and cowhide boots, which ladies from the eastward world may hereafter encounter in Michigan.

Our journey was marked by no incident more alarming than the one I have related, though one night passed in a wretched inn, deep in the "timbered land"—as all woods are called in Michigan—was not without its terrors, owing to the horrible drunkenness of the master of the house, whose wife and children were in constant fear of their lives from his insane fury. I can never forget the countenance of that desolate woman, sitting trembling, and with white compressed lips, in the midst of her children. The father raving all night, and coming through our sleeping apartment with the earliest ray of morning in search of more of the poison already boiling in his veins. The poor wife could not forbear telling me her story—her change of lot—from a well-stored and comfortable home in Connecticut to this wretched den in the wilderness—herself and children worn almost to shadows with the ague, and her husband such as I have described him. I may mention here, that not very long after, I heard of this man in prison in

Detroit, for stabbing a neighbor in a drunken brawl, and ere the year was out, he died of delirium tremens, leaving his family destitute. So much for turning our fields of golden grain into "fire water"—a branch of business in which Michigan is fast improving.

Our ride being a deliberate one, I felt, after the third day, a little wearied, and began to complain of the sameness of the oak openings, and to wish we were fairly at our journey's end. We were crossing a broad expanse of what seemed, at a little distance, a smooth shaven lawn of the most brilliant green, but which proved on trial little better than a quaking bog—embracing within its ridgy circumference all possible varieties of

> *"Muirs and mosses, slaps and styles"*—

I had just indulged in something like a yawn, and wished that I could see our hotel. At the word, my companion's face assumed rather a comical expression, and I was preparing to inquire somewhat testily what there was so laughable—I was getting tired and cross, reader—when down came our good horse to the very chin in a bog-hole, green as Erin on the top, but giving way on the touch, and seeming deep enough to have engulfed us entirely, if its width had been proportionate. Down came the horse—and this was not all—down came the driver; and I could not do less than follow, though at a little distance—our good steed kicking and floundering—covering us with hieroglyphics, which would be readily deciphered by any Wolverine we should meet, though perchance strange to the eyes of our friends at home. This mishap was soon amended. Tufts of long marsh grass served to assoilize our habiliments a little, and a clear stream which rippled through the marsh aided in removing the eclipse from our faces. We journeyed on cheerily, watching the splendid changes in the west, but keeping a bright look out for bog-holes.

Chapter XV

> *Honester men have stretch'd a rope, or the law has been sadly cheated. But this unhappy business of yours? Can nothing be done? Let me see the charge.*
>
> *He took the papers, and as he read them, his countenance grew hopelessly dark and disconsolate.*
>
> —ANTIQUARY

> *A strange fish! Were I in England now, and had but this fish painted, not a holiday fool there but would give me a piece of silver.*
>
> —SHAKSPEARE—TEMPEST

> *Sorrow chang'd to solace, and solace mixed with sorrow.*
>
> —THE PASSIONATE PILGRIM

Several lots had already been purchased in Montacute and some improvement marked each succeeding day. The mill had grown to its full stature, the dam was nearly completed; the tavern began to exhibit promise of its present ugliness, and all seemed prosperous as our best dreams, when certain rumours were set afloat touching the solvency of our disinterested friend Mr. Mazard. After two or three days' whispering, a tall black-browed man who "happened in" from Gullsborough, the place which had for some time been honoured as the residence of the Dousterswivel of Montacute, stated boldly that Mr. Mazard had absconded; or, in Western language "cleared." It seemed passing strange that he should run away from the large house which was going on under his auspices; the materials all on the ground and the work in full progress. Still more unaccountable did it appear to us that his workmen should go on so quietly, without so much as expressing any anxiety about their pay.

Mr. Clavers had just been telling me of these things, when the long genius above mentioned, presented himself at the door of the loggery. His *abord* was a singular mixture of coarseness, and an attempt at being civil; and he sat for some minutes looking round and asking various questions before he touched the mainspring of his visit.

At length, after some fumbling in his pocket, he produced a dingy sheet of paper, which he handed to Mr. Clavers.

"There; I want you to read that, and tell me what you think of it."

I did not look at the paper, but at my husband's face, which was black enough. He walked away with the tall man, "and I saw no more of them at that time."

Mr. Clavers did not return until late in the evening, and it was then I learned that Mr. Mazard had been getting large quantities of lumber and other materials on his account, and as his agent; and that the money which had been placed in the agent's hands, for the purchase of certain lands to be flowed by the mill-pond, had gone into government coffers in payment for sundry eighty acre lots, which were intended for his, Mr. Mazard's, private behoof and benefit. These items present but a sample of our amiable friends trifling mistakes. I will not fatigue the reader by dwelling on the subject. The results of all this were most unpleasant to us. Mr. Clavers found himself involved to a large amount; and his only remedy seemed to prosecute Mr. Mazard. A consultation with his lawyer, however, convinced him, that even by this most disagreeable mode, redress was out of the question, since he had through inadvertence rendered himself liable for whatever that gentleman chose to buy or engage in his name. All that could be done, was to get out of the affair with as little loss as possible, and to take warning against land sharks in future.

An immediate journey to Detroit became necessary, and I was once more left alone, and in no overflowing spirits. I sat,

> "Revolving in my *altered soul*
> The various turns of fate below,"

when a tall damsel, of perhaps twenty-eight or thirty came in to make a visit. She was tastefully attired in a blue gingham dress, with broad cuffs of black morocco, and a black cambric apron edged with orange worsted lace.

Her oily black locks were cut quite short round the ears, and confined close to her head by a black ribbon, from one side of which depended, almost in her eye, two very long tassels of black silk, intended to do duty as curls. Prunelle[10] slippers with high heels, and a cotton handkerchief tied under the chin, finished the costume, which I have been thus particular in describing, because I have observed so many that were nearly similar.

The lady greeted me in the usual style, with a familiar nod, and seated herself at once in a chair near the door.

"Well, how do like Michigan?"

This question received the most polite answer which my conscience afforded; and I asked the lady in my turn, if she was one of my neighbours?

"Why, massy, yes!" she replied; "do n't you know me? I tho't every body know'd me. Why, I'm the school ma'am, Simeon Jenkins' sister, Cleory Jenkins."

Thus introduced, I put all my civility in requisition to entertain my guest, but she seemed quite independent, finding amusement for herself, and asking questions on every possible theme.

"You're doing your own work now, a'n't ye?"

This might not be denied; and I asked if she did not know of a girl whom I might be likely to get.

"Well, I do n't know; I'm looking for a place where I can board and do chores myself. I have a good deal of time before school, and after I get back; and I did n't know but I might suite ye for a while."

I was pondering on this proffer, when the sallow damsel arose from her seat, took a short pipe from her bosom, (not "Pan's reedy pipe,"[11] reader) filled it with tobacco, which she carried in her "work-pocket," and reseating herself, began to smoke with the greatest gusto, turning ever and anon to spit at the hearth.

Incredible again? alas, would it were not true! I have since known a girl of seventeen, who was attending a neighbour's sick infant, smoke the live-long day, and take snuff besides; and I can vouch for it, that a large proportion of the married women in the interior of Michigan use tobacco in some form, usually that of the odious pipe.

I took the earliest decent opportunity to decline the offered help, telling the school-ma'am plainly, that an inmate who smoked would make the house uncomfortable to me.

"Why, law!" said she, laughing; "that's nothing but pride now: folks is often too proud to take comfort. For my part, I could n't do without my pipe to please nobody."

Mr. Simeon Jenkins, the brother of this independent young lady now made his appearance on some trifling errand; and his sister repeated to him what I had said.

---

[10]A smooth woolen or mixed fabric.
[11]A Greek god of forests, pastures, and wild life, famous for playing on the syrinx, or "Pan's pipes."

Mr. Jenkins took his inch of cigar from his mouth, and asked if I really disliked tobacco-smoke, seeming to think it scarcely possible.

"Do n't your old man smoke?" said he.

"No, indeed," said I, with more than my usual energy; "I should hope he never would."

"Well," said neighbour Jenkins, "I tell you what, I'm *boss* at home; and if my old woman was to stick up that fashion, I'd keep the house so blue she could n't see to snuff the candle."

His sister laughed long and loud at this sally, which was uttered rather angrily, and with an air of most manful bravery; and, Mr. Jenkins, picking up his end of cigar from the floor, walked off with an air evidently intended to be as expressive as the celebrated and oft-quoted nod of Lord Burleigh[12] in the Critic.

Chapter XVII

The house's form within was rude and strong,
*   Like an huge cave hewn out of rocky clift;*
From whose rough vault the ragged breaches hung:—

.   .   .

And over them Arachne high did lift
*   Her cunning web, and spread her subtle net,*
Enwrapped in foul smoke, and clouds more black than jet.

—SPENCER—*FAERY QUEENE*

It were good that men, in their innovations, would follow the example of
time itself, which, indeed, innovateth greatly, but quietly, and by degrees
scarce to be perceived.

—BACON

It was on one of our superlatively doleful ague days, when a cold drizzling rain had sent mildew into our unfortunate bones; and I lay in bed, burning with fever, while my stronger half sat by the fire, taking his chill with his great-coat, hat, and boots on, that Mr. Rivers came to introduce his young daughter-in-law. I shall never forget the utterly disconsolate air, which, in spite of the fair lady's politeness, would make itself visible in the pauses of our conversation. She *did* try not to cast a curious glance round the room. She fixed her eyes on the fire-place—but there were the clay-filled sticks, instead of a chimney-piece—the half-consumed wooden *crane*, which had, more than once, let our dinner fall—the Rocky-Mountain hearth, and the reflector, baking biscuits for tea—so she thought it hardly polite to appear to dwell too long there. She turned towards the window: there were the shelves, with our remaining crockery, a grotesque assortment! and, just

[12]A character in Richard Sheridan's *The Critic*
(1799) who has no lines, only a celebrated
nod.

beneath, the unnameable iron and tin affairs, that are reckoned among the indispensables, even of the half-civilized state. She tried the other side, but there was the ladder, the flour-barrel, and a host of other things—rather odd parlour furniture—and she cast her eyes on the floor, with its gaping cracks, wide enough to admit a massasauga from below, and its inequalities, which might trip any but a sylph. The poor thing looked absolutely confounded, and I exerted all the energy my fever had left me, to try to say something a little encouraging.

"Come to-morrow morning, Mrs. Rivers," said I, "and you shall see the aspect of things quite changed; and I shall be able to tell you a great deal in favour of this wild life."

She smiled faintly, and tried not to look miserable, but I saw plainly that she was sadly depressed, and I could not feel surprised that she should be so. Mr. Rivers spoke very kindly to her, and filled up all the pauses in our forced talk with such cheering observations as he could muster.

He had found lodgings, he said, in a farm-house, not far from us, and his son's house would, ere long, be completed, when we should be quite near neighbours.

I saw tears swelling in the poor girl's eyes, as she took leave, and I longed to be well for her sake. In this newly-formed world, the earlier settler has a feeling of hostess-ship toward the new comer. I speak only of women—men look upon each one, newly arrived, merely as an additional business-automaton—a somebody more with whom to try the race of enterprize, i.e., money-making.

The next day Mrs. Rivers came again, and this time her husband was with her. Then I saw at a glance why it was that life in the wilderness looked so peculiarly gloomy to her. Her husband's face shewed but too plainly the marks of early excess; and there was at intervals, in spite of an evident effort to play the agreeable, an appearance of absence, of indifference, which spoke volumes of domestic history. He made innumerable inquiries, touching the hunting and fishing facilities of the country around us, expressed himself enthusiastically fond of those sports, and said the country was a living death without them, regretting much that Mr. Clavers was not of the same mind.

Meanwhile, I had begun to take quite an interest in his little wife. I found that she was as fond of novels and poetry, as her husband was of field-sports. Some of her flights of sentiment went quite beyond my sobered-down views. But I saw we should get on admirably, and so we have done ever since. I did not mistake that pleasant smile, and that soft sweet voice. They are even now as attractive as ever. And I had a neighbour.

Chapter XXVII

Smelling so sweetly (all musk,) and so rushling, I warrant you, in silk and gold; and in such alligant terms.

—SHAKSPEARE—*MERRY WIVES OF WINDSOR*

Art thou not Romeo, and a Montague?

—SHAKSPEARE

> *My brain's in a fever, my pulses beat quick*
> *I shall die, or at least be exceedingly sick!*
> *Oh what do you think! after all my romancing*
> *My visions of glory, my sighing, my glancing—*

—MISS BIDDY FUDGE

An addition to our Montacute first circle had lately appeared in the person of Miss Eloise Fidler, an elder sister of Mrs. Rivers, who was to spend some months "in this peaceful retreat,"—to borrow one of her favourite expressions.

This young lady was not as handsome as she would fain have been, if I may judge by the cataracts of ash-coloured ringlets which shaded her cheeks, and the exceeding straitness of the stays which restrained her somewhat exuberant proportions. Her age was at a stand; but I could never discover exactly where, for this point proved an exception to the general communicativeness of her disposition. I guessed it at eight-and-twenty; but perhaps she would have judged this uncharitable, so I will not insist. Certain it is that it must have taken a good while to read as many novels and commit to memory as much poetry, as lined the head and exalted the sensibilities of our fair visitant.

Her dress was in the height of fashion, and all her accoutrements *point de vice*.[13] A gold pencil-case of the most delicate proportions was suspended by a kindred chain round a neck which might be called whity-brown; and a note-book of corresponding lady-like-ness was peeping from the pocket of her highly-useful apron of blue silk—ever ready to secure a passing thought or an elegant quotation. Her album—she was just the person to have an album—was resplendent in gold and satin, and the verses which meandered over its emblazoned pages were of the most unexceptionable quality, overlaid with flowers and gems—love and despair. To find any degree of appropriateness in these various offerings, one must allow the fortunate possessor of the purple volume, at least all the various perfections of an Admirable Crichton,[14] allayed in some small measure by the trifling faults of coldness, fickleness, and deceit; and to judge of Miss Fidler's friends by their handwriting, they must have been able to offer an edifying variety of bumps to the fingers of the phrenologist. But here is the very book itself at my elbow, waiting these three months, I blush to say, for a contribution which has yet to be pumped up from my unwilling brains; and I have a mind to steal a few specimens from its already loaded pages, for the benefit of the distressed, who may, like myself, be at their wits' end for something to put in just such a book.

[13]Perfectly correct.
[14]A sixteenth-century Scottish prodigy, well known for his beauty and accomplishments.

The first page, rich with embossed lilies, bears the invocation, written in a great black spattering hand, and wearing the air of a defiance. It runs thus:

> *If among the names of the stainless few*
> > *Thine own hath maintain'd a place,*
> *Come dip thy pen in the sable dew*
> > *And with it this volume grace.*
>
> *But oh! if thy soul e'er encouraged a thought*
> > *Which purity's self might blame,*
> *Close quickly the volume, and venture not*
> > *To sully its snows with thy name.*

Then we come to a wreath of flowers of gorgeous hues, within whose circle appears in a *miminee piminee*[15] hand, evidently a young lady's—

The Wreath of Sleep.

> *Oh let me twine this glowing wreath*
> > *Amid those rings of golden hair,*
> *'T will soothe thee with its odorous breath*
> > *To sweet forgetfulness of care.*
>
> *'T is form'd of every scented flower*
> > *That flings its fragrance o'er the night;*
> *And gifted with a fairy power*
> > *To fill thy dreams with forms of light.*
>
> *'T was braided by an angel boy*
> > *When fresh from Paradise he came*
> *To fill our earth-born hearts with joy—*
> > *Ah! need I tell the cherub's name?*

This contributor I have settled in my own mind to be a descendant of Anna Matilda, the high-priestess of the Della Cruscan order.[16] The next blazon[17] is an interesting view of a young lady, combing her hair. As she seems not to have been long out of bed, the lines which follow are rather appropriate, though I feel quite sure they come from the expert fingers of a merchant's clerk—from the finished elegance, and very sweeping tails of the chirography.[18]

---

[15]Absurdly nice.
[16]A school of affected English poets who had named themselves after the Accademia Della Crusa, established in the sixteenth century to purify the Italian language. Here, as else-
wherein this section, Kirkland is spoofing Miss Fidler's pretentions, partly by adopting her affected language.
[17]A description or ostentatious display.
[18]A fancy word for handwriting.

Morning.

Awake! arise! art thou slumbering still?
When the sun is above the mapled hill,
And the shadows are flitting fast away,
And the dews are diamond beneath his ray,
And every bird in our vine-roofed bower
Is waked into song by the joyous hour;
Come, banish sleep from thy gentle eyes,
Sister! sweet sister! awake! arise!

Yet I love to gaze on thy lids of pearl,
And to mark the wave of the single curl
That shades in its beauty thy brow of snow,
And the cheek that lies like a rose below;
And to list to the murmuring notes that fall
From thy lips, like music in fairy hall.
But it must not be—the sweet morning flies
Ere thou hast enjoyed it; awake! arise!

There is balm on the wings of this freshen'd air;
'T will make thine eye brighter, thy brow more fair,
And a deep, deep rose on thy cheek shall be
The meed of an early walk with me.
We will seek the shade by the green hill side,
Or follow the clear brook's whispering tide;
And brush the dew from the violet's eyes—
Sister! sweet sister! awake! arise!

This I transcribe for the good advice which it contains. And what have we here? It is tastefully headed by an engraving of Hero and Ursula in the "pleached bower,"[19] and Beatrice running "like a lap-wing"[20] in the background. It begins ominously.

To—.

Oh, look upon this pallid brow!
    Say, canst thou there discern one trace
Of that proud soul which oft ere now
    Thou'st sworn shed radiance o'er my face?
Chill'd is that soul—its darling themes,
    Thy manly honour, virtue, truth
Prove now to be but fleeting dreams,
    Like other lovely thoughts of youth.

---

[19]A Shakespearean phrase; a bower formed by intertwining boughs.

[20]A plover notable for its irregular flight and jumping behavior.

Meet, if thy coward spirit dare,
    This sunken eye; say, dost thou see
The rays thou saidst were sparkling there
    When first its gaze was turn'd on thee?
That eye's young light is quench'd forever;
    No change its radiance can repair:
Will Joy's keen touch relume it? Never!
    It gleams the watch-light of Despair.

I find myself growing hoarse by sympathy, and I shall venture only a single extract more, and this because Miss Fidler declares it, without exception, the sweetest thing she ever read. It is written with a crow-quill, and has other marks of femininity. Its vignette[21] is a little girl and boy playing at battle-door.[22]

Ballad.

The deadly strife was over, and across the field of fame,
With anguish in his haughty eye, the Moor Almanzor came;
He prick'd his fiery courser on among the scatter'd dead,
Till he came at last to what he sought, a sever'd human head.

It might have seem'd a maiden's, so pale it was, and fair;
But the lip and chin were shaded till they match'd the raven hair.
There lingered yet upon the brow a spirit bold and high,
And the stroke of death had scarcely closed the piercing eagle eye.

Almanzor grasp'd the flowing locks, and he staid not in his flight,
Till he reach'd a lonely castle's gate where stood a lady bright.
"Inez! behold thy paramour!" he loud and sternly cried,
And threw his ghastly burden down, close at the lady's side.

"I sought thy bower at even-tide, thou syren, false as fair!"
"And, would that I had rather died! I found yon stripling there.
"I turn'd me from the hated spot, but I swore by yon dread Heaven,
"To know no rest until my sword the traitor's life had riven."

The lady stood like stone until he turn'd to ride away,
And then she oped her marble lips, and wildly thus did say:
"Alas, alas! thou cruel Moor, what is it thou hast done!
"This was my brother Rodriguez, my father's only son."

And then before his frenzied eyes, like a crush'd lily bell,
Lifeless upon the bleeding head, the gentle Inez fell.
He drew his glittering ataghan—he sheath'd it in his side—
And for his Spanish ladye-love the Moor Almanzor died.

---

[21]A decorative design or picture.   [22]What we would today call badminton.

This is not a very novel incident, but young ladies like stories of love and murder, and Miss Fidler's tastes were peculiarly young-lady-like. She praised Ainsworth and James, but thought Bulwer's works "very immoral," though I never could discover that she had more than skimmed the story from any of them. Cooper she found "pretty;" Miss Sedgwick, "pretty well, only her characters are such common sort of people."[23]

Miss Fidler wrote her own poetry, so that she had ample employment for her time while with us in the woods. It was unfortunate that she could not walk out much on account of her shoes. She was obliged to make out with diluted inspiration. The nearest approach she usually made to the study of Nature, was to sit on the wood-pile, under a girdled tree, and there, with her gold pencil in hand, and her "eyne,[24] grey as glas," rolled upwards, poefy by the hour. Several people, and especially one marriageable lady of a certain age, felt afraid Miss Fidler was "kind o' crazy."

And, standing marvel of Montacute, no guest at morning or night ever found the fair Eloise ungloved. Think of it! In the very wilds to be always like a cat in nutshells, alone useless where all are so busy! I do not wonder our good neighbours thought the damsel a little touched. And then her shoes! "Saint Crispin Crispianus"[25] never had so self-sacrificing a votary. No shoemaker this side of New-York could make a sole papery enough; no tannery out of France could produce materials for this piece of exquisite feminine foppery. Eternal imprisonment within doors, except in the warmest and driest weather, was indeed somewhat of a price to pay, but it was ungrudged. The sofa and its footstool, finery and novels, *would* have made a delicious world for Miss Eloise Fidler, *if*—

But alas! "all this availeth me nothing," has been ever the song of poor human nature. The mention of that unfortunate name includes the only real, personal, pungent distress which had as yet shaded the lot of my interesting heroine. Fidler! In the mortification adhering to so unpoetical, so unromantic, so inelegant a surname—a name irredeemable even by the highly classical elegance of the Eloise, or as the fair lady herself pronounced it, "Elovees;" in this lay all her wo; and the grand study of her life had been to sink this hated cognomen in one more congenial to her taste. Perhaps this very anxiety had defeated itself; at any rate, here she was at—I did not mean to touch on the ungrateful guess again, but at least at mateable years; neither married, nor particularly likely to be married.

Mrs. Rivers was the object of absolute envy to the pining Eloise. "Anna had been so fortunate," she said; "Rivers was the sweetest name! and Harley was such an elegant fellow!"

We thought poor Anna had been any thing but fortunate. She might better have been Fidler or Fiddlestring all her life than to have taken the name of an indifferent and dissipated husband. But not so thought Miss Fidler. It was not

---

[23]William Harrison Ainsworth, English author of *Old Saint Paul's* and other novels. George P. R. James, English novelist and critic. Edward Bulwer-Lytton (see note 6). James Fenimore Cooper and Catharine Maria Sedg-wick, the American novelists, are represented in this volume.
[24]Archaic for eyes.
[25]The patron saint of shoemakers.

long after the arrival of the elegant Eloise, that the Montacute Lyceum[26] held its first meeting in Mr. Simeon Jenkins's shop, lighted by three candles, supported by candelabra of scooped potatoes; Mr. Jenkins himself sitting on the head of a barrel, as president. At first the debates of the institute were held with closed doors; but after the youthful or less practised speakers had tried their powers for a few evenings, the Lyceum was thrown open to the world every Tuesday evening, at six o'clock. The list of members was not very select as to age, character, or standing; and it soon included the entire gentility of the town, and some who scarce claimed rank elsewhere. The attendance of the ladies was particularly requested; and the whole fair sex of Montacute made a point of showing occasionally the interest they undoubtedly felt in the gallant knights who tilted in this field of honour.

But I must not be too diffuse—I was speaking of Miss Fidler. One evening—I hope that beginning prepares the reader for something highly interesting—one evening the question to be debated was the equally novel and striking one which regards the comparative mental capacity of the sexes; and as it was expected that some of the best speakers on both sides would be drawn out by the interesting nature of the subject, every body was anxious to attend.

Among the rest was Miss Fidler, much to the surprise of her sister and myself, who had hitherto been so unfashionable as to deny ourselves this gratification.

"What new whim possesses you, Eloise?" said Mrs. Rivers; "you who never go out in the day-time."

"Oh, just *per passy le tong*,"[27] said the young lady, who was a great French scholar; and go she would and did.

The debate was interesting to absolute breathlessness, both of speakers and hearers, and was gallantly decided in favour of the fair by a youthful member who occupied the barrel as president for the evening. He gave it as his decided opinion, that if the natural and social disadvantages under which woman laboured and must ever continue to labour, could be removed; if their education could be entirely different, and their position in society the reverse of what it is at present, they would be very nearly, if not quite, equal to the nobler sex, in all but strength of mind, in which very useful quality it was his opinion that man would still have the advantage, especially in those communities whose energies were developed by the aid of debating societies. . . .

Chapter XLIII

On ne doit pas juger du merite d'un homme par ses grandes qualités, mais par l'usage qu'il en sait faire.[28]

—ROCHEFOUCAULT

[26]Meetings for lectures, debates, and discussions, which provided important educational opportunities as well as entertainment to frontier communities. See Introduction.

[27]A very corrupt French for passing the time.
[28]One can't judge a man's merits by his major qualities, but by the way in which he knows how to use them.

Des mots longs d'une toise,
De grands mots qui tiendroient d'ici jusqu' à Pontoise[29]

—RACINE—*LES PLAIDEURS*

But what he chiefly valued himself on, was his knowledge of metaphysics, in
which, having once upon a time ventured too deeply, he came well nigh
being smothered in a slough of unintelligible learning.

—W. IRVING—KNICKERBOCKER

Mr. Simeon Jenkins entered at an early stage of his career upon the arena of public life, having been employed by his honoured mother to dispose of a basket full of hard-boiled eggs, on election day, before he was eight years old. He often dwells with much unction upon this his debût; and declares that even at that dawning period, he had cut his eye-teeth.

"There was n't a feller there," Mr. Jenkins often says, "that could find out which side I was on, for all they tried hard enough. They thought I was soft, but I let 'em know I was as much baked as any on 'em. 'Be you a dimo-crat?' says one. Buy some eggs and I'll tell ye, says I; and by the time he'd bought his eggs, I could tell well enough which side *he* belonged to, and I'd hand him out a ticket according, for I had blue ones in one end o' my basket, and white ones in the other, and when night come, and I got off the stump to go home, I had eighteen shillin' and four pence in my pocket."

From this auspicious commencement may be dated Mr. Jenkins' glowing desire to serve the public. Each successive election day saw him at his post. From eggs he advanced to pies, from pies to almanacs, whiskey, powder and shot, foot-balls, playing-cards, and at length, for ambition ever "did grow with what it fed on," he brought into the field a large turkey, which was tied to a post and stoned to death at twenty-five cents a throw. By this time the still youthful aspirant had become quite the man of the world; could smoke twenty four cigars per diem, if any body else would pay for them; play cards, in old Hurler's shop, from noon till daybreak, and rise winner; and all this with suitable trimmings of gin and hard words. But he never lost sight of the main chance. He had made up his mind to serve his country, and he was all this time convincing his fellow-citizens of the disinterested purity of his sentiments.

"Patriotism," he would say, "patriotism is the thing! any man that's too proud to serve his country aint fit to live. Some thinks so much o' them-selves, that if they can't have just what they think they're fit for, they wont take nothing; but for my part, *I* call myself an American citizen; and any office that's in the gift o' the people will suit *me*. I'm up to any thing. And as there aint no other man about here,—no suitable man, I mean—that's got a horse, why I'd be willing to be constable, if the people's a mind to, though it would be a dead loss to me in my business, to be sure; but I

[29]Words a fathom long, huge words that stretch from here to Pontoise.

could do any thing for my country. Hurra for patriotism! them's my sentiments."

It can scarcely be doubted that Mr. Jenkins became a very popular citizen, or that he usually played a conspicuous part at the polls. Offices began to fall to his share, and though they were generally such as brought more honour than profit, office is office, and Mr. Jenkins did not grumble. Things were going on admirably.

> *The spoils of office glitter in his eyes,*
> *He climbs, he pants, he grasps them—*

Or thought he was just going to grasp them, when, presto! he found himself in the minority; the wheel of fortune turned, and Mr. Jenkins and his party were left undermost. Here was a dilemma! His zeal in the public service was ardent as ever, but how could he get a chance to show it unless his party was in power? His resolution was soon taken. He called his friends together, mounted a stump, which had fortunately been left standing not far from the door of his shop, and then and there gave "reasons for my ratting" in terms sublime enough for any meridian.[30]

"My friends and feller-citizens," said this self-sacrificing patriot, "I find myself conglomerated in sich a way, that my feelin's suffers severely. I'm sitivated in a peculiar sitivation. O' one side, I see my dear friends, pussonal friends—friends, that's stuck to me like wax, through thick and thin, never shinnyin' off and on, but up to the scratch, and no mistake. O' t' other side I behold my country, my bleedin' country, the land that fetch'd me into this world o' trouble. Now, sence things be as they be, and can't be no otherways as I see, I feel kind o' screwed into an augerhold to know what to do. If I hunt over the history of the universal world from the creation of man to the present day, I see that men has always had difficulties; and that some has took one way to get shut of 'em, and some another. My candid and unrefragable opinion is, that rather than remain useless, buckled down to the shop, and indulging in selfishness, it is my solemn dooty to change my ticket. It is severe, my friends, but dooty is dooty. And now, if any man calls me a turn-coat," continued the orator, gently spitting in his hands, rubbing them together, and rolling his eyes round the assembly, "all I say is, let him say it so that I can hear him."

The last argument was irresistible, if even the others might have brooked discussion, for Mr. Jenkins stands six feet two in his stockings, when he wears any, and gesticulates with a pair of arms as long and muscular as Rob Roy's.[31] So, though the audience did not cheer him, they contented themselves with dropping off one by one, without calling in question the patriotism of the rising statesman.

The very next election saw Mr. Jenkins justice of the peace, and it was in this honourable capacity that I have made most of my acquaintance with him,

[30]Highest point.
[31]The title character in a novel by Sir Walter Scott.

though we began with threatenings of a storm. He called to take the acknowledgement of a deed, and I, anxious for my country's honour, for I too am
something of a patriot in my own way, took the liberty of pointing out to his
notice a trifling slip of the pen; videlicet,[32] "Justas of Piece," which manner of
writing those words I informed him had gone out of fashion.

He reddened, looked at me very sharp for a moment, and then said he
thanked me; but subjoined,

"Book-learning is a good thing enough where there aint too much of it.
For my part, I've seen a good many that know'd books that did n't know
much else. The proper cultivation and edication of the human intellect, has
been the comprehensive study of the human understanding from the original creation of the universal world to the present day, and there has been a
good many ways tried besides book-learning. Not but what that's very well
in its place."

And the justice took his leave with somewhat of a swelling air. But we
are excellent friends, notwithstanding this hard rub; and Mr. Jenkins
favours me now and then with half an hour's conversation, when he has
had leisure to read up for the occasion in an odd volume of the Cyclopedia,
which holds an honoured place in the corner of his shop. He ought, in fairness, to give me previous notice, that I might study the dictionary a little,
for the hard words with which he arms himself for these "keen encounters,"
often push me to the very limits of my English.

I ought to add, that Mr. Jenkins has long since left off gambling, drinking, and all other vices of that class, except smoking; in this point he pro-
fesses to be incorrigible. But as his wife, who is one of the nicest women in
the world, and manages him admirably, pretends to like the smell of
tobacco, and takes care never to look at him when he disfigures her well-
scoured floor, I am not without hopes of his thorough reformation.

1839

■ NATHANIEL HAWTHORNE ■
1804–1864

Since the publication of *The Scarlet Letter* in 1850, Nathaniel Hawthorne has
been recognized as one of America's most important writers, both a "romancer"
who probed inner mysteries and a "realist" who assessed the American character
and experience.

Born in Massachusetts on the Fourth of July 1804, he was the descendant
of Puritan worthies and the son of a ship's captain who died at sea in 1808.

---

[32]For example. Usually abbreviated as viz.

His mother then brought her son and two daughters to live with her own family, the Mannings. Books freed Hawthorne's imagination, but the Eden of his youth was the lakeside wilderness of Raymond, Maine, where from 1816 to 1819 he lived with his mother and sisters, "free as a bird." Summoned back to Salem to prepare for college, and working part-time in the Mannings stagecoach office, he complained, "No Man can be a Poet & a Book-Keeper at the same time." The problem would recur.

From 1821 to 1825, Hawthorne was a student at Bowdoin College, graduating in the middle of his class of thirty-eight. From the Scottish philosophers, he absorbed the concepts of faculty psychology that would recur in his fiction: belief in a unitary mind with separate but interacting powers (including perception, reason, memory, association of ideas, and imagination) regulated by the will during waking hours but not in dreams; and a conviction that fulfillment requires living throughout the entire range of our faculties and sensibilities. Three classmates would become lifelong friends—Bridge (who helped arrange publication of his first book), Longfellow (who reviewed it), and Pierce (who became president of the United States and appointed Hawthorne consul to Liverpool).

Even before college, Hawthorne had rejected the major careers open to graduates—the ministry, medicine, and law. He mistrusted institutionalized authority, including organized religion, though he would always provisionally believe in a beneficent deity. "What do you think of my becoming an Author, and relying for support upon my pen," he had asked his mother, musing how proud she would be "to see my works praised." Although that ambition was unrealistic in mercantile America—since most books were imported from England or pirated, and most magazine fiction was low-paid and published anonymously—the new graduate was determined to pursue it. In the tales he produced in the Mannings' "chamber under the eaves," he exaggerated his plight as a lonely writer-dreamer, though his problems were real enough. In 1828, at his own expense, he published a slender novel drawn from his college experience titled *Fanshawe*, but it is characteristic of his lifelong diffidence that he soon repudiated it and tried to destroy all copies. He linked some of his tales into collections, but for lack of a publisher, he burned some and submitted others to periodicals and gift books. Editors were eager for his stories, and one offered hackwork: in 1836, with the assistance of his sister Elizabeth, Hawthorne edited *The American Magazine of Useful and Entertaining Knowledge* and wrote a best-selling children's text, *Peter Parley's Universal History*.

In 1837, Hawthorne's "twelve lonely years" as "the obscurest man of letters in America" came to an end when *Twice-Told Tales* was published with his name on the cover. Longfellow, already well established as a man of letters, enthusiastically praised the author's poetic imagination, his style, and his use of New England materials, and other critics followed suit, though neither this collection nor the expanded 1842 version attracted a large audience. The volume included "The Minister's Black Veil," a historically grounded parable about the guilt we hide from one another and about the dangers of self-absorption (which anticipates *The Scarlet Letter*). But Hawthorne had not chosen to include two even more complex early stories, "My Kinsman, Major Molineux" or "Young Goodman Brown." For the castles of Gothic romance, Hawthorne substituted the

American wilderness and the wilderness of the mind. As in a dream, his fiction pushes beyond surface reality, conveying knowledge that resists complete understanding.

The year 1837 brought another milestone: Hawthorne met Sophia Peabody, a frail amateur artist, to whom he became secretly engaged the following year. He was still writing stories for the magazines; but in January 1839, to supplement his income, Hawthorne sought political appointment, and became Measurer in the Boston Custom House. Predictably complaining that his imagination was dulled by routine, he produced only a few tales and two collections of children's stories (*Grandfather's Chair* and *Famous Old People*), as well as entries in the notebooks he used as literary storehouses and long letters telling Sophia (his "Dove" and his "Wife") how love had wakened him to life.

He left the custom house in November 1840. The following April, he began what he would call "the most romantic episode of his own life—essentially a daydream and yet a fact": he joined the Utopian commune of Brook Farm. Although skeptical about the community's socialist ideals, he hoped their way of life would enable him to combine authorship and marriage. But the drudgery of farmwork made writing impossible, and he left after half a year. His third novel, *The Blithedale Romance*, would dramatize that venture.

Next came an idyll that would last more than three years: in July 1842, Hawthorne married Sophia and moved into the Old Manse in Concord. He contentedly gardened, ice-skated with Emerson, and rowed with Thoreau. He also wrote prolifically, producing twenty published works, among them two of his most challenging stories—"The Birth-Mark" and "Rappaccini's Daughter." Perhaps working out his own apprehensions as a new groom, Hawthorne presented obsessed and cold-hearted men who destroy the innocent women who love and trust them. He had no trouble selling what he wrote, but his pen did not provide enough support, especially after the birth of his daughter Una in 1844. Political appointment was again the recourse.

In April 1846, Hawthorne became Surveyor of the Salem Custom House and returned to his birthplace. That June, *Mosses from an Old Manse* was published and his son Julian was born. Predictably, Hawthorne's imagination was inhibited by routine duty, but he was earning a comfortable living when the victorious Whigs dismissed him in 1849, Hawthorne struggled for reinstatement on the grounds that as a surveyor and a man of letters, he was apolitical. Then, anguished by his mother's death and frustrated by his dismissal, he wrote *The Scarlet Letter*.

His first novel, his masterpiece, is an indictment of Puritan America, but also of his own society. Its introductory essay, "The Custom-House," purportedly a straightforward account of his experience as surveyor, attacks officials who connived in his dismissal while vindicating himself as an artist. Like his heroine Hester, Hawthorne emerges from confrontation with a self-righteous society as an individual of integrity, passion, and moral superiority. The introduction also defines his requisites for writing romance: "a neutral territory, somewhere between the real world and fairy-land, where the Actual and the Imaginary may meet, and each imbue itself with the nature of the other"; enlivened by the heart, fiction could then "flow out on the brightening page." The romance itself also expresses Hawthorne's "romantic" belief in subjective perception, showing how imagination participates in creating the world we inhabit. Thus in the central scaffold scene, Dimmesdale perceives a meteor as an immense scarlet letter that signifies his guilt.

Leaving Salem forever, Hawthorne moved his family to a small house in the Berkshires in the spring of 1850 and soon produced his second novel, *The House of the Seven Gables*, centering on a Salem family burdened by ancestral guilt. He also wrote most of his third novel, *The Blithedale Romance*, drawing on his Brook Farm experience; his third major collection of short fiction, *The Snow-Image*; and a collection of Greek myths retold for children, titled *A Wonder-Book*. This was also the period of his friendship with Herman Melville—an ideal reader, whose review of *Mosses from an Old Manse* praised Hawthorne's "power of blackness," and who would dedicate *Moby-Dick* to him with "admiration for his genius."

Hawthorne's third child, Rose, was born in Lenox in 1851, and a year later, he bought a house in Concord, the only one he ever owned. The following year, however, the family sailed for England: as a reward for writing Pierce's campaign biography, Hawthorne was appointed consul to Liverpool, serving from 1853 to 1857. As in his other political positions, Hawthorne worked conscientiously, but his imagination became stultified; except for his notebooks, he wrote almost nothing. Then from 1857 to 1859, he lived in Rome and Florence, where his immersion in art and acquaintance with artists generated the last romance he would complete—*The Marble Faun*.

Returning to Concord in 1860, Hawthorne struggled to complete three other romances; but his health was broken and he was distraught by the prospect and then the actuality of civil war. Though he believed slavery was evil and hoped for Union victory, he remained skeptical about what abolitionists (or any other reformers) could accomplish. Except for the eyewitness report "Chiefly About War Matters," he published only a series of sketches drawn from his English notebooks (collected as *Our Old Home*). He died on May 19, 1864. Soon afterward, Sophia augmented her slim income by editing his American notebooks for publication, and memoirs by Julian and Rose Hawthorne expanded the biographical record.

For more than a century, despite changes in perspective and methodology, the verdict on Hawthorne's stature has remained virtually constant. The critical consensus continues to be that Hawthorne was a shrewd and large-minded writer who read widely and pondered deeply about the human condition and American identity from Puritan times to his own. Though afflicted by self-doubt and constrained by a materialistic society that did not adequately reward serious artists, he created texts whose power, profundity, and artistry command our attention. He wrote about his own society and its antecedents, but it turns out that he also wrote about ours.

Rita K. Gollin
State University of New York College at Geneseo

PRIMARY WORKS

Twice-Told Tales, 1837; *Mosses from an Old Manse*, 1846; *The Scarlet Letter*, 1850; *The House of the Seven Gables*, 1851; *The Snow-Image and Other Tales*, 1851; *A Wonder-Book for Boys and Girls*, 1851; *The Blithedale Romance*, 1852; *Tanglewood Tales for Boys and Girls*, 1853; *The Marble Faun*, 1860; *The Centenary Edition of the Works of Nathaniel Hawthorne*, 23 vols., W. Charvat et al., eds., 1962–1997.

My Kinsman, Major Molineux[1]

After the kings of Great Britain had assumed the right of appointing the colonial governors, the measures of the latter seldom met with the ready and general approbation, which had been paid to those of their predecessors, under the original charters.[2] The people looked with most jealous scrutiny to the exercise of power, which did not emanate from themselves, and they usually rewarded the rulers with slender gratitude, for the compliances, by which, in softening their instructions from beyond the sea, they had incurred the reprehension of those who gave them. The annals of Massachusetts Bay will inform us, that of six governors, in the space of about forty years from the surrender of the old charter, under James II., two were imprisoned by a popular insurrection; a third, as Hutchinson[3] inclines to believe, was driven from the province by the whizzing of a musket ball; a fourth, in the opinion of the same historian, was hastened to his grave by continual bickerings with the House of Representatives; and the remaining two, as well as their successors, till the Revolution, were favored with few and brief intervals of peaceful sway. The inferior members of the court party,[4] in times of high political excitement, led scarcely a more desirable life. These remarks may serve as preface to the following adventures, which chanced upon a summer night, not far from a hundred years ago. The reader, in order to avoid a long and dry detail of colonial affairs, is requested to dispense with an account of the train of circumstances, that had caused much temporary inflammation of the popular mind.

It was near nine o'clock of a moonlight evening, when a boat crossed the ferry with a single passenger, who had obtained his conveyance, at that unusual hour, by the promise of an extra fare. While he stood on the landing-place, searching in either pocket for the means of fulfilling his agreement, the ferryman lifted a lantern, by the aid of which, and the newly risen moon, he took a very accurate survey of the stranger's figure. He was a youth of barely eighteen years, evidently countrybred, and now, as it should seem, upon his first visit to town. He was clad in a coarse grey coat, well worn, but in excellent repair; his under garments were durably constructed of leather, and sat tight to a pair of serviceable and well-shaped limbs; his stockings of blue yarn, were the incontrovertible handiwork of a mother or a sister; and on his head was a three-cornered hat, which in its better days had perhaps sheltered the graver brow of the lad's father. Under his left arm was a heavy cudgel, formed of an oak sapling, and retaining a part of the hardened root; and his equipment was completed by a wallet,[5] not so abundantly stocked as to incommode the vigorous shoulders on which

---

[1]First published in the *Token* (1832) but not collected until *The Snow-Image, and Other Tales* (1851).

[2]Charles II annulled the Massachusetts Charter in 1684; James II appointed the first royal governor in 1685.

[3]Thomas Hutchinson (1711–1780), the last royal governor, who wrote *The History of the Colony and Province of Massachusetts-Bay* (1764, 1767).

[4]Supporters of the royal government.

[5]Knapsack.

it hung. Brown, curly hair, well-shaped features, and bright, cheerful eyes, were nature's gifts, and worth all that art could have done for his adornment.

The youth, one of whose names was Robin, finally drew from his pocket the half of a little province-bill of five shillings, which, in the depreciation of that sort of currency, did but satisfy the ferryman's demand, with the surplus of a sexangular piece of parchment valued at three pence.[6] He then walked forward into the town, with as light a step, as if his day's journey had not already exceeded thirty miles, and with as eager an eye, as if he were entering London city, instead of the little metropolis of a New England colony. Before Robin had proceeded far, however, it occurred to him, that he knew not whither to direct his steps; so he paused, and looked up and down the narrow street, scrutinizing the small and mean wooden buildings, that were scattered on either side.

"This low hovel cannot be my kinsman's dwelling," thought he, "nor yonder old house, where the moonlight enters at the broken casement; and truly I see none hereabouts that might be worthy of him. It would have been wise to inquire my way of the ferryman, and doubtless he would have gone with me, and earned a shilling from the Major for his pains. But the next man I meet will do as well."

He resumed his walk, and was glad to perceive that the street now became wider, and the houses more respectable in their appearance. He soon discerned a figure moving on moderately in advance, and hastened his steps to overtake it. As Robin drew nigh, he saw that the passenger was a man in years, with a full periwig of grey hair, a wide-skirted coat of dark cloth, and silk stockings rolled about his knees. He carried a long and polished cane, which he struck down perpendicularly before him, at every step; and at regular intervals he uttered two successive hems, of a peculiarly solemn and sepulchral intonation. Having made these observations, Robin laid hold of the skirt of the old man's coat, just when the light from the open door and windows of a barber's shop, fell upon both their figures.

"Good evening to you, honored Sir," said he, making a low bow, and still retaining his hold of the skirt. "I pray you to tell me whereabouts is the dwelling of my kinsman, Major Molineux?"

The youth's question was uttered very loudly; and one of the barbers, whose razor was descending on a well-soaped chin, and another who was dressing a Ramillies[7] wig, left their occupations, and came to the door. The citizen, in the meantime, turned a long favored countenance upon Robin, and answered him in a tone of excessive anger and annoyance. His two sepulchral hems, however, broke into the very centre of his rebuke, with most singular effect, like a thought of the cold grave obtruding among wrathful passions.

---

[6]Colonial paper money.
[7]Elaborate wig with a braided tail named for a British victory in Ramillies, Belgium.

"Let go my garment, fellow! I tell you, I know not the man you speak of. What! I have authority, I have—hem, hem—authority; and if this be the respect you show your betters, your feet shall be brought acquainted with the stocks,[8] by daylight, tomorrow morning!"

Robin released the old man's skirt, and hastened away, pursued by an ill-mannered roar of laughter from the barber's shop. He was at first considerably surprised by the result of his question, but, being a shrewd youth, soon thought himself able to account for the mystery.

"This is some country representative," was his conclusion, "who has never seen the inside of my kinsman's door, and lacks the breeding to answer a stranger civilly. The man is old, or verily—I might be tempted to turn back and smite him on the nose. Ah, Robin, Robin! even the barber's boys laugh at you, for choosing such a guide! You will be wiser in time, friend Robin."

He now became entangled in a succession of crooked and narrow streets, which crossed each other, and meandered at no great distance from the water-side. The smell of tar was obvious to his nostrils, the masts of vessels pierced the moonlight above the tops of the buildings, and the numerous signs, which Robin paused to read, informed him that he was near the centré of business. But the streets were empty, the shops were closed, and lights were visible only in the second stories of a few dwelling-houses. At length, on the corner of a narrow lane, through which he was passing, he beheld the broad countenance of a British hero swinging before the door of an inn,[9] whence proceeded the voices of many guests. The casement of one of the lower windows was thrown back, and a very thin curtain permitted Robin to distinguish a party at supper, round a well-furnished table. The fragrance of the good cheer steamed forth into the outer air, and the youth could not fail to recollect, that the last remnant of his travelling stock of provision had yielded to his morning appetite, and that noon had found, and left him, dinnerless.

"Oh, that a parchment three-penny might give me a right to sit down at yonder table," said Robin, with a sigh. "But the Major will make me welcome to the best of his victuals; so I will even step boldly in, and inquire my way to his dwelling."

He entered the tavern, and was guided by the murmur of voices, and fumes of tobacco, to the public room. It was a long and low apartment, with oaken walls, grown dark in the continual smoke, and a floor, which was thickly sanded, but of no immaculate purity. A number of persons, the larger part of whom appeared to be mariners, or in some way connected with the sea, occupied the wooden benches, or leather-bottomed chairs, conversing on various matters, and occasionally lending their attention to some topic of general interest. Three or four little groups were draining as many bowls of punch, which the great West India trade had long since made a

---

[8]Wooden instrument of punishment with holes for confining ankles and sometimes wrists.

[9]On a signboard.

familiar drink in the colony. Others, who had the aspect of men who lived by regular and laborious handicraft, preferred the insulated bliss of an unshared potation, and became more taciturn under its influence. Nearly all, in short, evinced a predilection for the Good Creature[10] in some of its various shapes, for this is a vice, to which, as the Fast-day sermons of a hundred years ago will testify, we have a long hereditary claim. The only guests to whom Robin's sympathies inclined him, were two or three sheepish countrymen, who were using the inn somewhat after the fashion of a Turkish Caravansary; they had gotten themselves into the darkest corner of the room, and, heedless of the Nicotian atmosphere,[11] were supping on the bread of their own ovens, and the bacon cured in their own chimney-smoke. But though Robin felt a sort of brotherhood with these strangers, his eyes were attracted from them, to a person who stood near the door, holding whispered conversation with a group of ill-dressed associates. His features were separately striking almost to grotesqueness, and the whole face left a deep impression in the memory. The forehead bulged out into a double prominence, with a vale between; the nose came boldly forth in an irregular curve, and its bridge was of more than a finger's breadth; the eyebrows were deep and shaggy, and the eyes glowed beneath them like fire in a cave.

While Robin deliberated of whom to inquire respecting his kinsman's dwelling, he was accosted by the innkeeper, a little man in a stained white apron, who had come to pay his professional welcome to the stranger. Being in the second generation from a French Protestant, he seemed to have inherited the courtesy of his parent nation; but no variety of circumstance was ever known to change his voice from the one shrill note in which he now addressed Robin.

"From the country, I presume, Sir?" said he, with a profound bow. "Beg to congratulate you on your arrival, and trust you intend a long stay with us. Fine town here, Sir, beautiful buildings, and much that may interest a stranger. May I hope for the honor of your commands in respect to supper?"

"The man sees a family likeness! the rogue has guessed that I am related to the Major!" thought Robin, who had hitherto experienced little superfluous civility.

All eyes were now turned on the country lad, standing at the door, in his worn three-cornered hat, grey coat, leather breeches, and blue yarn stockings, leaning on an oaken cudgel, and bearing a wallet on his back.

Robin replied to the courteous innkeeper, with such an assumption of consequence, as befitted the Major's relative.

"My honest friend," he said, "I shall make it a point to patronize your house on some occasion, when—"here he could not help lowering his voice—"I may have more than a parchment three-pence in my pocket.

---

[10]"For every creature of God is good, and nothing to be refused, if it be received with thanksgiving" (1 Timothy 4:4).

[11]Filled with tobacco smoke (from Jean Nicot, who introduced tobacco into France in 1560, when he was an ambassador at Lisbon).

My present business," continued he, speaking with lofty confidence, "is merely to inquire the way to the dwelling of my kinsman, Major Molineux."

There was a sudden and general movement in the room, which Robin interpreted as expressing the eagerness of each individual to become his guide. But the innkeeper turned his eyes to a written paper on the wall, which he read, or seemed to read, with occasional recurrences to the young man's figure.

"What have we here?" said he, breaking his speech into little dry fragments. 'Left the house of the subscriber, bounden servant,[12] Hezekiah Mudge—had on, when he went away, grey coat, leather breeches, master's third best hat. One pound currency reward to whoever shall lodge him in any jail in the province.' Better trudge, boy, better trudge!"

Robin had begun to draw his hand towards the lighter end of the oak cudgel, but a strange hostility in every countenance, induced him to relinquish his purpose of breaking the courteous innkeeper's head. As he turned to leave the room, he encountered a sneering glance from the bold-featured personage whom he had before noticed; and no sooner was he beyond the door, than he heard a general laugh, in which the innkeeper's voice might be distinguished, like the dropping of small stones into a kettle.

"Now is it not strange," thought Robin, with his usual shrewdness, "is it not strange, that the confession of an empty pocket, should outweigh the name of my kinsman, Major Molineux? Oh, if I had one of these grinning rascals in the woods, where I and my oak sapling grew up together, I would teach him that my arm is heavy, though my purse be light!"

On turning the corner of the narrow lane, Robin found himself in a spacious street, with an unbroken line of lofty houses on each side, and a steepled building at the upper end, whence the ringing of a bell announced the hour of nine. The light of the moon, and the lamps from numerous shop windows, discovered people promenading on the pavement, and amongst them, Robin hoped to recognize his hitherto inscrutable relative. The result of his former inquiries made him unwilling to hazard another, in a scene of such publicity, and he determined to walk slowly and silently up the street, thrusting his face close to that of every elderly gentleman, in search of the Major's lineaments. In his progress, Robin encountered many gay and gallant figures. Embroidered garments, of showy colors, enormous periwigs, gold-laced hats, and silver hilted swords, glided past him and dazzled his optics. Travelled youths, imitators of the European fine gentlemen of the period, trod jauntily along, half-dancing to the fashionable tunes which they hummed, and making poor Robin ashamed of his quiet and natural gait. At length, after many pauses to examine the gorgeous display of goods in the shop windows, and after suffering some rebukes for the impertinence of his scrutiny into people's faces, the Major's kinsman found himself near the

[12]A person who contracts to exchange a period of servitude for transportation to the colonies.

steepled building, still unsuccessful in his search. As yet, however, he had seen only one side of the thronged street; so Robin crossed, and continued the same sort of inquisition down the opposite pavement, with stronger hopes than the philosopher seeking an honest man,[13] but with no better fortune. He had arrived about midway towards the lower end, from which his course began, when he overheard the approach of some one, who struck down a cane on the flag-stones at every step, uttering, at regular intervals, two sepulchral hems.

"Mercy on us!" quoth Robin, recognizing the sound.

Turning a corner, which chanced to be close at his right hand, he hastened to pursue his researches, in some other part of the town. His patience was now wearing low, and he seemed to feel more fatigue from his rambles since he crossed the ferry, than from his journey of several days on the other side. Hunger also pleaded loudly within him, and Robin began to balance the propriety of demanding, violently and with lifted cudgel, the necessary guidance from the first solitary passenger, whom he should meet. While a resolution to this effect was gaining strength, he entered a street of mean appearance, on either side of which, a row of ill-built houses was straggling towards the harbor. The moonlight fell upon no passenger along the whole extent, but in the third domicile which Robin passed, there was a half-opened door, and his keen glance detected a woman's garment within.

"My luck may be better here," said he to himself.

Accordingly, he approached the door, and beheld it shut closer as he did so; yet an open space remained, sufficing for the fair occupant to observe the stranger, without a corresponding display on her part. All that Robin could discern was a strip of scarlet petticoat, and the occasional sparkle of an eye, as if the moonbeams were trembling on some bright thing.

"Pretty mistress,"—for I may call her so with a good conscience, thought the shrewd youth, since I know nothing to the contrary—"my sweet pretty mistress, will you be kind enough to tell me whereabouts I must seek the dwelling of my kinsman, Major Molineux?"

Robin's voice was plaintive and winning, and the female, seeing nothing to be shunned in the handsome country youth, thrust open the door, and came forth into the moonlight. She was a dainty little figure, with a white neck, round arms, and a slender waist, at the extremity of which her scarlet petticoat jutted out over a hoop, as if she were standing in a balloon. Moreover, her face was oval and pretty, her hair dark beneath the little cap, and her bright eyes possessed a sly freedom, which triumphed over those of Robin.

"Major Molineux dwells here," said this fair woman.

Now her voice was the sweetest Robin had heard that night, the airy counterpart of a stream of melted silver; yet he could not help doubting whether that sweet voice spoke Gospel truth. He looked up and down the mean street,

---

[13]The fifth-century Greek Cynic philosopher Diogenes supposedly roamed the world seeking an honest man.

and then surveyed the house before which they stood. It was a small, dark edifice of two stories, the second of which projected over the lower floor; and the front apartment had the aspect of a shop for petty commodities.

"Now truly I am in luck," replied Robin, cunningly, "and so indeed is my kinsman, the Major, in having so pretty a housekeeper. But I prithee trouble him to step to the door; I will deliver him a message from his friends in the country, and then go back to my lodgings at the inn."

"Nay, the Major has been a-bed this hour or more," said the lady of the scarlet petticoat; "and it would be to little purpose to disturb him to-night, seeing his evening draught was of the strongest. But he is a kind-hearted man, and it would be as much as my life's worth, to let a kinsman of his turn away from the door. You are the good old gentleman's very picture, and I could swear that was his rainy-weather hat. Also, he has garments very much resembling those leather—But come in, I pray, for I bid you hearty welcome in his name."

So saying, the fair and hospitable dame took our hero by the hand; and though the touch was light, and the force was gentleness, and though Robin read in her eyes what he did not hear in her words, yet the slender waisted woman, in the scarlet petticoat, proved stronger than the athletic country youth. She had drawn his half-willing footsteps nearly to the threshold, when the opening of a door in the neighborhood, startled the Major's housekeeper, and, leaving the Major's kinsman, she vanished speedily into her own domicile. A heavy yawn preceded the appearance of a man, who, like the Moonshine of Pyramus and Thisbe, carried a lantern,[14] needlessly aiding his sister luminary in the heavens. As he walked sleepily up the street, he turned his broad, dull face on Robin, and displayed a long staff, spiked at the end.

"Home, vagabond, home!" said the watchman, in accents that seemed to fall asleep as soon as they were uttered. "Home, or we'll set you in the stocks by peep of day!"

"This is the second hint of the kind," thought Robin. "I wish they would end my difficulties, by setting me there to-night."

Nevertheless, the youth felt an instinctive antipathy towards the guardian of midnight order, which at first prevented him from asking his usual question. But just when the man was about to vanish behind the corner, Robin resolved not to lose the opportunity, and shouted lustily after him—

"I say, friend! will you guide me to the house of my kinsman, Major Molineux?"

The watchman made no reply, but turned the corner and was gone; yet Robin seemed to hear the sound of drowsy laughter stealing along the solitary street. At that moment, also, a pleasant titter saluted him from the open window above his head; he looked up, and caught the sparkle of a saucy eye; a round arm beckoned to him, and next he heard light footsteps

[14]In the blundering enactment of the story of Pyramus and Thisbe in Shakespeare's *Midsummer Night's Dream*, one character plays the role of Moonshine.

descending the staircase within. But Robin, being of the household of a New England clergyman, was a good youth, as well as a shrewd one; so he resisted temptation, and fled away.

He now roamed desperately, and at random, through the town, almost ready to believe that a spell was on him, like that, by which a wizard of his country, had once kept three pursuers wandering, a whole winter night, within twenty paces of the cottage which they sought. The streets lay before him, strange and desolate, and the lights were extinguished in almost every house. Twice, however, little parties of men, among whom Robin distinguished individuals in outlandish attire, came hurrying along, but though on both occasions they paused to address him, such intercourse did not at all enlighten his perplexity. They did but utter a few words in some language of which Robin knew nothing, and perceiving his inability to answer, bestowed a curse upon him in plain English, and hastened away. Finally, the lad determined to knock at the door of every mansion that might appear worthy to be occupied by his kinsman, trusting that perseverance would overcome the fatality which had hitherto thwarted him. Firm in this resolve, he was passing beneath the walls of a church, which formed the corner of two streets, when, as he turned into the shade of its steeple, he encountered a bulky stranger, muffled in a cloak. The man was proceeding with the speed of earnest business, but Robin planted himself full before him, holding the oak cudgel with both hands across his body, as a bar to further passage.

"Halt, honest man, and answer me a question," said he, very resolutely. "Tell me, this instant, whereabouts is the dwelling of my kinsman, Major Molineux?"

"Keep your tongue between your teeth, fool, and let me pass," said a deep, gruff voice, which Robin partly remembered. "Let me pass, I say, or I'll strike you to the earth!"

"No, no, neighbor!" cried Robin, flourishing his cudgel, and then thrusting its larger end close to the man's muffled face. "No, no, I'm not the fool you take me for, nor do you pass, till I have an answer to my question. Whereabouts is the dwelling of my kinsman, Major Molineux?"

The stranger, instead of attempting to force his passage, stept back into the moonlight, unmuffled his own face and stared full into that of Robin.

"Watch here an hour, and Major Molineux will pass by," said he.

Robin gazed with dismay and astonishment, on the unprecedented physiognomy of the speaker. The forehead with its double prominence, the broad-hooked nose, the shaggy eyebrows, and fiery eyes, were those which he had noticed at the inn, but the man's complexion had undergone a singular, or, more properly, a two-fold change. One side of the face blazed of an intense red, while the other was black as midnight, the division line being in the broad bridge of the nose; and a mouth, which seemed to extend from ear to ear, was black or red, in contrast to the color of the cheek. The effect was as if two individual devils, a fiend of fire and a fiend of darkness, had united themselves to form this infernal visage. The stranger grinned in

Robin's face, muffled his parti-colored features, and was out of sight in a moment.

"Strange things we travellers see!" ejaculated Robin.

He seated himself, however, upon the steps of the church-door, resolving to wait the appointed time for his kinsman's appearance. A few moments were consumed in philosophical speculations, upon the species of the *genus homo*, who had just left him, but having settled this point shrewdly, rationally, and satisfactorily, he was compelled to look elsewhere for amusement. And first he threw his eyes along the street; it was of more respectable appearance than most of those into which he had wandered, and the moon, "creating, like the imaginative power, a beautiful strangeness in familiar objects," gave something of romance to a scene, that might not have possessed it in the light of day. The irregular, and often quaint architecture of the houses, some of whose roofs were broken into numerous little peaks; while others ascended, steep and narrow, into a single point; and others again were square; the pure milk-white of some of their complexions, the aged darkness of others, and the thousand sparklings, reflected from bright substances in the plastered walls of many; these matters engaged Robin's attention for awhile, and then began to grow wearisome. Next he endeavored to define the forms of distant objects, starting away with almost ghostly indistinctness, just as his eye appeared to grasp them; and finally he took a minute survey of an edifice, which stood on the opposite side of the street, directly in front of the church-door, where he was stationed. It was a large square mansion, distinguished from its neighbors by a balcony, which rested on tall pillars, and by an elaborate Gothic window, communicating therewith.

"Perhaps this is the very house I have been seeking," thought Robin.

Then he strove to speed away the time, by listening to a murmur, which swept continually along the street, yet was scarcely audible, except to an unaccustomed ear like his; it was a low, dull, dreamy sound, compounded of many noises, each of which was at too great a distance to be separately heard. Robin marvelled at this snore of a sleeping town, and marvelled more, whenever its continuity was broken, by now and then a distant shout, apparently loud where it originated. But altogether it was a sleep-inspiring sound, and to shake off its drowsy influence, Robin arose, and climbed a window-frame, that he might view the interior of the church. There the moonbeams came trembling in, and fell down upon the deserted pews, and extended along the quiet aisles. A fainter, yet more awful radiance, was hovering round the pulpit, and one solitary ray had dared to rest upon the opened page of the great Bible. Had Nature, in that deep hour, become a worshipper in the house, which man had builded? Or was that heavenly light the visible sanctity of the place, visible because no earthly and impure feet were within the walls? The scene made Robin's heart shiver with a sensation of loneliness, stronger than he had ever felt in the remotest depths of his native woods; so he turned away, and sat down again before the door. There were graves around the church, and now an uneasy thought obtruded into Robin's breast. What if the object of his search, which had been so often and so strangely thwarted, were all the time mouldering in his shroud? What if his kinsman should glide through yonder gate, and nod and smile to him in passing dimly by?

"Oh, that any breathing thing were here with me!" said Robin.

Recalling his thoughts from this uncomfortable track, he sent them over forest, hill, and stream, and attempted to imagine how that evening of ambiguity and weariness, had been spent by his father's household. He pictured them assembled at the door, beneath the tree, the great old tree, which had been spared for its huge twisted trunk, and venerable shade, when a thousand leafy brethren fell. There, at the going down of the summer sun, it was his father's custom to perform domestic worship, that the neighbors might come and join with him like brothers of the family, and that the wayfaring man might pause to drink at that fountain, and keep his heart pure by freshening the memory of home. Robin distinguished the seat of every individual of the little audience; he saw the good man in the midst, holding the Scriptures in the golden light that shone from the western clouds; he beheld him close the book, and all rise up to pray. He heard the old thanksgivings for daily mercies, the old supplications for their continuance, to which he had so often listened in weariness, but which were now among his dear remembrances. He perceived the slight inequality of his father's voice when he came to speak of the Absent One; he noted how his mother turned her face to the broad and knotted trunk; how his elder brother scorned, because the beard was rough upon his upper lip, to permit his features to be moved; how his younger sister drew down a low hanging branch before her eyes; and how the little one of all, whose sports had hitherto broken the decorum of the scene, understood the prayer for her playmate, and burst into clamorous grief. Then he saw them go in at the door; and when Robin would have entered also, the latch tinkled into its place, and he was excluded from his home.

"Am I here, or there?" cried Robin, starting; for all at once, when his thoughts had become visible and audible in a dream, the long, wide, solitary street shone out before him.

He aroused himself, and endeavored to fix his attention steadily upon the large edifice which he had surveyed before. But still his mind kept vibrating between fancy and reality; by turns, the pillars of the balcony lengthened into the tall, bare stems of pines, dwindled down to human figures, settled again in their true shape and size, and then commenced a new succession of changes. For a single moment, when he deemed himself awake, he could have sworn that a visage, one which he seemed to remember, yet could not absolutely name as his kinsman's, was looking towards him from the Gothic window. A deeper sleep wrestled with, and nearly overcame him, but fled at the sound of footsteps along the opposite pavement. Robin rubbed his eyes, discerned a man passing at the foot of the balcony, and addressed him in a loud, peevish, and lamentable cry.

"Halloo, friend! must I wait here all night for my kinsman, Major Molineux?"

The sleeping echoes awoke, and answered the voice; and the passenger, barely able to discern a figure sitting in the oblique shade of the steeple, traversed the street to obtain a nearer view. He was himself a gentleman in his prime, of open, intelligent, cheerful, and altogether prepossessing countenance. Perceiving a country youth, apparently homeless and without friends, he accosted him in a tone of real kindness, which had become strange to Robin's ears.

"Well, my good lad, why are you sitting here?" inquired he. "Can I be of service to you in any way?"

"I am afraid not, Sir," replied Robin, despondingly; "yet I shall take it kindly, if you'll answer me a single question. I've been searching half the night for one Major Molineux; now, Sir, is there really such a person in these parts, or am I dreaming?"

"Major Molineux! The name is not altogether strange to me," said the gentleman, smiling. "Have you any objection to telling me the nature of your business with him?"

Then Robin briefly related that his father was a clergyman, settled on a small salary, at a long distance back in the country, and that he and Major Molineux were brothers' children. The Major, having inherited riches, and acquired civil and military rank, had visited his cousin in great pomp a year or two before; had manifested much interest in Robin and an elder brother, and, being childless himself, had thrown out hints respecting the future establishment of one of them in life. The elder brother was destined to succeed to the farm, which his father cultivated, in the interval of sacred duties; it was therefore determined that Robin should profit by his kinsman's generous intentions, especially as he had seemed to be rather the favorite, and was thought to possess other necessary endowments.

"For I have the name of being a shrewd youth," observed Robin, in this part of his story.

"I doubt not you deserve it," replied his new friend, good naturedly; "but pray proceed."

"Well, Sir, being nearly eighteen years old, and well-grown, as you see," continued Robin, raising himself to his full height, "I thought it high time to begin the world. So my mother and sister put me in handsome trim, and my father gave me half the remnant of his last year's salary, and five days ago I started for this place, to pay the Major a visit. But would you believe it, Sir? I crossed the ferry a little after dusk, and have yet found nobody that would show me the way to his dwelling; only an hour or two since, I was told to wait here, and Major Molineux would pass by."

"Can you describe the man who told you this?" inquired the gentleman.

"Oh, he was a very ill-favored fellow, Sir," replied Robin, "with two great bumps on his forehead, a hook nose, fiery eyes, and, what struck me as the strangest, his face was of two different colors. Do you happen to know such a man, Sir?"

"Not intimately," answered the stranger, "but I chanced to meet him a little time previous to your stopping me. I believe you may trust his word, and that the Major will very shortly pass through this street. In the mean time, as I have a singular curiosity to witness your meeting, I will sit down here upon the steps, and bear you company."

He seated himself accordingly, and soon engaged his companion in animated discourse. It was but of brief continuance, however, for a noise of shouting, which had long been remotely audible, drew so much nearer, that Robin inquired its cause.

"What may be the meaning of this uproar?" asked he. "Truly, if your town be always as noisy, I shall find little sleep, while I am an inhabitant."

"Why, indeed, friend Robin, there do appear to be three or four riotous fellows abroad to-night," replied the gentleman. "You must not expect all the stillness of your native woods, here in our streets. But the watch will shortly be at the heels of these lads, and—"

"Aye, and set them in the stocks by peep of day," interrupted Robin, recollecting his own encounter with the drowsy lantern-bearer. "But, dear Sir, if I may trust my ears, an army of watchmen would never make head against such a multitude of rioters. There were at least a thousand voices went to make up that one shout."

"May not one man have several voices, Robin, as well as two complexions?" said his friend.

"Perhaps a man may; but Heaven forbid that a woman should!" responded the shrewd youth, thinking of the seductive tones of the Major's housekeeper.

The sounds of a trumpet in some neighboring street now became so evident and continual, that Robin's curiosity was strongly excited. In addition to the shouts, he heard frequent bursts from many instruments of discord, and a wild and confused laughter filled up the intervals. Robin rose from the steps, and looked wistfully towards a point, whither several people seemed to be hastening.

"Surely some prodigious merrymaking is going on," exclaimed he. "I have laughed very little since I left home, Sir, and should be sorry to lose an opportunity. Shall we just step round the corner by that darkish house, and take our share of the fun?"

"Sit down again, sit down, good Robin," replied the gentleman, laying his hand on the skirt of the grey coat. "You forget that we must wait here for your kinsman; and there is reason to believe that he will pass by, in the course of a very few moments."

The near approach of the uproar had now disturbed the neighborhood; windows flew open on all sides; and many heads, in the attire of the pillow, and confused by sleep suddenly broken, were protruded to the gaze of whoever had leisure to observe them. Eager voices hailed each other from house to house, all demanding the explanation, which not a soul could give. Half-dressed men hurried towards the unknown commotion, stumbling as they went over the stone steps, that thrust themselves into the narrow foot-walk. The shouts, the laughter, and the tuneless bray, the antipodes of music, came onward with increasing din, till scattered individuals, and then denser bodies, began to appear round a corner, at the distance of a hundred yards.

"Will you recognize your kinsman, Robin, if he passes in this crowd?" inquired the gentleman.

"Indeed, I can't warrant it, Sir; but I'll take my stand here, and keep a bright look out," answered Robin, descending to the outer edge of the pavement.

A mighty stream of people now emptied into the street, and came rolling slowly towards the church. A single horseman wheeled the corner in the midst of them, and close behind him came a band of fearful wind-instruments, sending forth a fresher discord, now that no intervening buildings kept it from the ear. Then a redder light disturbed the moon-beams, and a dense multitude of torches shone along the street, concealing by their glare whatever object they illuminated. The single horseman, clad in a military dress, and bearing a drawn sword, rode onward as the leader, and, by his fierce and variegated countenance, appeared like war personified; the red of one cheek was an emblem of fire and sword; the blackness of the other betokened the mourning which attends them. In his train, were wild figures in the Indian dress, and many fantastic shapes without a model, giving the whole march a visionary air, as if a dream had broken forth from some feverish brain, and were sweeping visibly through the midnight streets. A mass of people, inactive, except as applauding spectators, hemmed the procession in, and several women ran along the sidewalks, piercing the confusion of heavier sounds, with their shrill voices of mirth or terror.

"The double-faced fellow has his eye upon me," muttered Robin, with an indefinite but uncomfortable idea, that he was himself to bear a part in the pageantry.

The leader turned himself in the saddle, and fixed his glance full upon the country youth, as the steed went slowly by. When Robin had freed his eyes from those fiery ones, the musicians were passing before him, and the torches were close at hand; but the unsteady brightness of the latter formed a veil which he could not penetrate. The rattling of wheels over the stones sometimes found its way to his ear, and confused traces of a human form appeared at intervals, and then melted into the vivid light. A moment more, and the leader thundered a command to halt; the trumpets vomited a horrid breath, and held their peace; the shouts and laughter of the people died away, and there remained only a universal hum, nearly allied to silence. Right before Robin's eyes was an uncovered cart. There the torches blazed the brightest, there the moon shone out like day, and there, in tar-and-feathery dignity, sate his kinsman, Major Molineux!

He was an elderly man, of large and majestic person, and strong, square features, betokening a steady soul; but steady as it was, his enemies had found the means to shake it. His face was pale as death, and far more ghastly; the broad forehead was contracted in his agony, so that his eye-brows formed one grizzled line; his eyes were red and wild, and the foam hung white upon his quivering lip. His whole frame was agitated by a quick, and continual tremor, which his pride strove to quell, even in those circumstances of overwhelming humiliation. But perhaps the bitterest pang of all was when his eyes met those of Robin; for he evidently knew him on the instant, as the youth stood witnessing the foul disgrace of a head that had grown grey in honor. They stared at each other in silence, and Robin's knees shook, and his hair bristled, with a mixture of pity and terror. Soon, however, a bewildering excitement began to seize upon his mind; the preceding adventures of the night, the unexpected appearance of the crowd, the torches, the confused din, and the hush that followed, the spectre of his kinsman reviled by that great multitude, all this, and more than all, a perception of tremendous ridicule in the whole scene, affected him with a sort of mental inebriety. At that moment a voice of sluggish merriment saluted Robin's ears; he turned instinctively, and just behind the corner of the church stood the lantern-bearer, rubbing his eyes, and drowsily enjoying the lad's amazement. Then he heard a peal of laughter like the ringing of silvery bells; a woman twitched his arm, a saucy eye met his, and he saw the lady of the scarlet petticoat. A sharp, dry cachinnation appealed to his memory, and, standing on tiptoe in the crowd, with his white apron over his head, he beheld the courteous little innkeeper. And lastly, there sailed over the heads of the multitude a great, broad laugh, broken in the midst by two sepulchral hems; thus—

"Haw, haw, haw—hem, hem—haw, haw, haw, haw."

The sound proceeded from the balcony of the opposite edifice, and thither Robin turned his eyes. In front of the Gothic window stood the old citizen, wrapped in a wide gown, his grey periwig exchanged for a nightcap, which was thrust back from his forehead, and his silk stockings hanging down about his legs. He supported himself on his polished cane in a fit of convulsive merriment, which manifested itself on his solemn old features, like a funny inscription on a tombstone. Then Robin seemed to hear the voices of the barbers; of the guests of the inn; and of all who had made sport of him that night. The contagion was spreading among the multitude, when, all at once, it seized upon Robin, and he sent forth a shout of laughter that echoed through the street; every man shook his sides, every man emptied his lungs, but Robin's shout was the loudest there. The cloud-spirits peeped from their silvery islands, as the congregated mirth went roaring up the sky! The Man in the Moon heard the far bellow; "Oho," quoth he, "the old Earth is frolicsome to-night!"

When there was a momentary calm in that tempestuous sea of sound, the leader gave the sign, the procession resumed its march. On they went, like fiends that throng in mockery round some dead potentate, mighty no more, but majestic still in his agony. On they went, in counterfeited pomp, in senseless uproar, in frenzied merriment, trampling all on an old man's heart. On swept the tumult, and left a silent street behind.

"Well, Robin, are you dreaming?" inquired the gentleman, laying his hand on the youth's shoulder.

Robin started, and withdrew his arm from the stone post, to which he had instinctively clung, while the living stream rolled by him. His cheek was somewhat pale, and his eye not quite so lively as in the earlier part of the evening.

"Will you be kind enough to show me the way to the ferry?" said he, after a moment's pause.

"You have then adopted a new subject of inquiry?" observed his companion, with a smile.

"Why, yes, Sir," replied Robin, rather dryly. "Thanks to you, and to my other friends, I have at last met my kinsman, and he will scarce desire to see my face again. I begin to grow weary of a town life, Sir. Will you show me the way to the ferry?"

"No, my good friend Robin, not to-night, at least," said the gentleman. "Some few days hence, if you continue to wish it, I will speed you on your journey. Or, if you prefer to remain with us, perhaps, as you are a shrewd youth, you may rise in the world, without the help of your kinsman, Major Molineux."

1832

Young Goodman Brown[1]

Young Goodman[2] Brown came forth, at sunset, into the street of Salem village, but put his head back, after crossing the threshold, to exchange a parting kiss with his young wife. And Faith, as the wife was aptly named, thrust her own pretty head into the street, letting the wind play with the pink ribbons of her cap, while she called to Goodman Brown.

"Dearest heart," whispered she, softly and rather sadly, when her lips were close to his ear, "pr'y thee, put off your journey until sunrise, and sleep in your own bed to-night. A lone woman is troubled with such dreams and such thoughts, that she's afeard of herself, sometimes. Pray, tarry with me this night, dear husband, of all nights in the year!"

"My love and my Faith," replied young Goodman Brown, "of all nights in the year, this one night must I tarry away from thee. My journey, as thou callest it, forth and back again, must needs be done 'twixt now and sunrise. What, my sweet, pretty wife, dost thou doubt me already, and we but three months married!"

"Then, God bless you!" said Faith, with the pink ribbons, "and may you find all well, when you come back."

"Amen!" cried Goodman Brown. "Say thy prayers, dear Faith, and go to bed at dusk, and no harm will come to thee."

So they parted; and the young man pursued his way, until, being about to turn the corner by the meeting-house, he looked back, and saw the head of Faith still peeping after him, with a melancholy air, in spite of her pink ribbons.

"Poor little Faith!" thought he, for his heart smote him. "What a wretch am I, to leave her on such an errand! She talks of dreams, too. Methought, as

---

[1]First published in 1835 in *The New England Magazine* and included in *Mosses from an Old Manse* (1846).

[2]A polite term of address for a man of humble status who was head of a household.

she spoke, there was trouble in her face, as if a dream had warned her what work is to be done to-night. But, no, no! 'twould kill her to think it. Well; she's a blessed angel on earth; and after this one night, I'll cling to her skirts and follow her to Heaven."

With this excellent resolve for the future, Goodman Brown felt himself justified in making more haste on his present evil purpose. He had taken a dreary road, darkened by all the gloomiest trees of the forest, which barely stood aside to let the narrow path creep through, and closed immediately behind. It was all as lonely as could be; and there is this peculiarity in such a solitude, that the traveller knows not who may be concealed by the innumerable trunks and the thick boughs overhead; so that, with lonely footsteps, he may yet be passing through an unseen multitude.

"There may be a devilish Indian behind every tree," said Goodman Brown, to himself; and he glanced fearfully behind him, as he added, "What if the devil himself should be at my very elbow!"

His head being turned back, he passed a crook of the road, and looking forward again, beheld the figure of a man, in grave and decent attire, seated at the foot of an old tree. He arose, at Goodman Brown's approach, and walked onward, side by side with him.

"You are late, Goodman Brown," said he. "The clock of the Old South was striking as I came through Boston; and that is full fifteen minutes agone."[3]

"Faith kept me back awhile," replied the young man, with a tremor in his voice, caused by the sudden appearance of his companion, though not wholly unexpected.

It was now deep dusk in the forest, and deepest in that part of it where these two were journeying. As nearly as could be discerned, the second traveller was about fifty years old, apparently in the same rank of life as Goodman Brown, and bearing a considerable resemblance to him, though perhaps more in expression than features. Still, they might have been taken for father and son. And yet, though the elder person was as simply clad as the younger, and as simple in manner too, he had an indescribable air of one who knew the world, and would not have felt abashed at the governor's dinner-table, or in King William's court,[4] were it possible that his affairs should call him thither. But the only thing about him, that could be fixed upon as remarkable, was his staff, which bore the likeness of a great black snake, so curiously wrought, that it might almost be seen to twist and wriggle itself, like a living serpent. This, of course, must have been an ocular deception, assisted by the uncertain light.

"Come, Goodman Brown!" cried his fellow-traveller, "this is a dull pace for the beginning of a journey. Take my staff, if you are so soon weary."

---

[3] The Old South Church in Boston; such speed suggests supernatural power.

[4] King William III and his wife Queen Mary II jointly ruled England from 1689 to 1702.

"Friend," said the other, exchanging his slow pace for a full stop, "having kept covenant by meeting thee here, it is my purpose now to return whence I came. I have scruples, touching the matter thou wot'st of."

"Sayest thou so?" replied he of the serpent, smiling apart. "Let us walk on, nevertheless, reasoning as we go, and if I convince thee not, thou shalt turn back. We are but a little way in the forest, yet."

"Too far, too far!" exclaimed the goodman, unconsciously resuming his walk. "My father never went into the woods on such an errand, nor his father before him. We have been a race of honest men and good Christians, since the days of the martyrs.[5] And shall I be the first of the name of Brown, that ever took this path, and kept—"

"Such company, thou wouldst say," observed the elder person, interpreting his pause. "Well said, Goodman Brown! I have been as well acquainted with your family as with ever a one among the Puritans; and that's no trifle to say. I helped your grandfather, the constable, when he lashed the Quaker woman so smartly through the streets of Salem. And it was I that brought your father a pitch-pine knot, kindled at my own hearth, to set fire to an Indian village, in King Philip's war.[6] They were my good friends, both; and many a pleasant walk have we had along this path, and returned merrily after midnight. I would fain be friends with you, for their sake."

"If it be as thou sayest," replied Goodman Brown, "I marvel they never spoke of these matters. Or, verily, I marvel not, seeing that the least rumor of the sort would have driven them from New-England. We are a people of prayer, and good works, to boot, and abide no such wickedness."

"Wickedness or not," said the traveller with the twisted staff, "I have a very general acquaintance here in New-England. The deacons of many a church have drunk the communion wine with me; the selectmen, of divers towns, make me their chairman; and a majority of the Great and General Court[7] are firm supporters of my interest. The governor and I, too—but these are state-secrets."

"Can this be so!" cried Goodman Brown, with a stare of amazement at his undisturbed companion. "Howbeit, I have nothing to do with the governor and council; they have their own ways, and are no rule for a simple husbandman,[8] like me. But, were I to go on with thee, how should I meet the eye of that good old man, our minister, at Salem village? Oh, his voice would make me tremble, both Sabbath-day and lecture-day!"[9]

Thus far, the elder traveller had listened with due gravity, but now burst into a fit of irrepressible mirth, shaking himself so violently, that his snakelike staff actually seemed to wriggle in sympathy.

[5]Allusion to the murder of English Protestants during the reign of the Catholic monarch Mary Tudor (1553–1558).
[6]Uprising of the Wampanoag Indians (1675–1676) led by the chief called by settlers "King Philip."

[7]Colonial legislature.
[8]Farmer or small landowner.
[9]Midweek sermon day.

"Ha! ha! ha!" shouted he, again and again; then composing himself, "Well, go on, Goodman Brown, go on; but pr'y thee, don't kill me with laughing!"

"Well, then, to end the matter at once," said Goodman Brown, considerably nettled, "there is my wife, Faith. It would break her dear little heart; and I'd rather break my own!"

"Nay, if that be the case," answered the other, "e'en go thy ways, Goodman Brown. I would not, for twenty old women like the one hobbling before us, that Faith should come to any harm."

As he spoke, he pointed his staff at a female figure on the path, in whom Goodman Brown recognized a very pious and exemplary dame, who had taught him his catechism, in youth, and was still his moral and spiritual adviser, jointly with the minister and Deacon Gookin.

"A marvel, truly, that Goody Cloyse[10] should be so far in the wilderness, at night-fall!" said he. "But, with your leave, friend, I shall take a cut through the woods, until we have left this Christian woman behind. Bring a stranger to you, she might ask whom I was consorting with, and whither I was going."

"Be it so," said his fellow-traveller. "Betake you to the woods, and let me keep the path."

Accordingly, the young man turned aside, but took care to watch his companion, who advanced softly along the road, until he had come within a staff's length of the old dame. She, meanwhile, was making the best of her way, with singular speed for so aged a woman, and mumbling some indistinct words, a prayer, doubtless, as she went. The traveller put forth his staff, and touched her withered neck with what seemed the serpent's tail.

"The devil!" screamed the pious old lady.

"Then Goody Cloyse knows her old friend?" observed the traveller, confronting her, and leaning on his writhing stick.

"Ah, forsooth, and is it your worship, indeed?" cried the good dame. "Yea, truly is it, and in the very image of my old gossip, Goodman Brown, the grandfather of the silly fellow that now is. But—would your worship believe it?—my broomstick hath strangely disappeared, stolen, as I suspect, by that unhanged witch, Goody Cory, and that, too, when I was all anointed with the juice of smallage and cinque-foil and wolf's-bane—"

"Mingled with fine wheat and the fat of a new-born babe," said the shape of old Goodman Brown.

"Ah, your worship knows the receipt," cried the old lady, cackling aloud. "So, as I was saying, being all ready for the meeting, and no horse to ride on, I made up my mind to foot it; for they tell me, there is a nice young

[10]Abbreviation of goodwife, a polite term for a married woman of humble status. Goody Cloyse, like Goody Cory and Martha Carrier, was sentenced to death at the Salem witchcraft trials of 1692. Hawthorne's chief sources of information include Cotton Mather's *Wonders of the Invisible World* and *Magnalia Christi Americana*, written soon after the trials ended.

man to be taken into communion to-night. But now your good worship will lend me your arm, and we shall be there in a twinkling."

"That can hardly be," answered her friend. "I may not spare you my arm, Goody Cloyse, but here is my staff, if you will."

So saying, he threw it down at her feet, where, perhaps, it assumed life, being one of the rods which its owner had formerly lent to the Egyptian Magi.[11] Of this fact, however, Goodman Brown could not take cognizance. He had cast up his eyes in astonishment, and looking down again, beheld neither Goody Cloyse nor the serpentine staff, but his fellow-traveller alone, who waited for him as calmly as if nothing had happened.

"That old woman taught me my catechism!" said the young man; and there was a world of meaning in this simple comment.

They continued to walk onward, while the elder traveller exhorted his companion to make good speed and persevere in the path, discoursing so aptly, that his arguments seemed rather to spring up in the bosom of his auditor, than to be suggested by himself. As they went, he plucked a branch of maple, to serve for a walking-stick, and began to strip it of the twigs and little boughs, which were wet with evening dew. The moment his fingers touched them, they became strangely withered and dried up, as with a week's sunshine. Thus the pair proceeded, at a good free pace, until suddenly, in a gloomy hollow of the road, Goodman Brown sat himself down on the stump of a tree, and refused to go any farther.

"Friend," said he, stubbornly, "my mind is made up. Not another step will I budge on this errand. What if a wretched old woman do choose to go to the devil, when I thought she was going to Heaven! Is that any reason why I should quit my dear Faith, and go after her?"

"You will think better of this, by-and-by," said his acquaintance, composedly. "Sit here and rest yourself awhile; and when you feel like moving again, there is my staff to help you along."

Without more words, he threw his companion the maple stick, and was as speedily out of sight, as if he had vanished into the deepening gloom. The young man sat a few moments, by the road-side, applauding himself greatly, and thinking with how clear a conscience he should meet the minister, in his morning-walk, nor shrink from the eye of good old Deacon Gookin. And what calm sleep would be his, that very night, which was to have been spent so wickedly, but purely and sweetly now, in the arms of Faith! Amidst these pleasant and praiseworthy meditations, Goodman Brown heard the tramp of horses along the road, and deemed it advisable to conceal himself within the verge of the forest, conscious of the guilty purpose that had brought him thither, though now so happily turned from it.

On came the hoof-tramps and the voices of the riders, two grave old voices, conversing soberly as they drew near. These mingled sounds appeared

[11]Duplicating Aaron's feat, Egyptian magicians turned rods into serpents, but his rod swallowed theirs (Exodus 7:11–12).

to pass along the road, within a few yards of the young man's hiding-place; but owing, doubtless, to the depth of the gloom, at that particular spot, neither the travellers nor their steeds were visible. Though their figures brushed the small boughs by the way-side, it could not be seen that they intercepted, even for a moment, the faint gleam from the strip of bright sky, athwart which they must have passed. Goodman Brown alternately crouched and stood on tip-toe, pulling aside the branches, and thrusting forth his head as far as he durst, without discerning so much as a shadow. It vexed him the more, because he could have sworn, were such a thing possible, that he recognized the voices of the minister and Deacon Gookin, jogging along quietly, as they were wont to do, when bound to some ordination or ecclesiastical council. While yet within hearing, one of the riders stopped to pluck a switch.

"Of the two, reverend Sir," said the voice like the deacon's, "I had rather miss an ordination-dinner than to-night's meeting. They tell me that some of our community are to be here from Falmouth[12] and beyond, and others from Connecticut and Rhode-Island; besides several of the Indian powows, who, after their fashion, know almost as much deviltry as the best of us. Moreover, there is a goodly young woman to be taken into communion."

"Mighty well, Deacon Gookin!" replied the solemn old tones of the minister. "Spur up, or we shall be late. Nothing can be done, you know, until I get on the ground."

The hoofs clattered again, and the voices, talking so strangely in the empty air, passed on through the forest, where no church had ever been gathered, nor solitary Christian prayed. Whither, then, could these holy men be journeying, so deep into the heathen wilderness? Young Goodman Brown caught hold of a tree, for support, being ready to sink down on the ground, faint and overburthened with the heavy sickness of his heart. He looked up to the sky, doubting whether there really was a Heaven above him. Yet, there was the blue arch, and the stars brightening in it.

"With Heaven above, and Faith below, I will yet stand firm against the devil!" cried Goodman Brown.

While he still gazed upward, into the deep arch of the firmament, and had lifted his hands to pray, a cloud, though no wind was stirring, hurried across the zenith, and hid the brightening stars. The blue sky was still visible, except directly overhead, where this black mass of cloud was sweeping swiftly northward. Aloft in the air, as if from the depths of the cloud, came a confused and doubtful sound of voices. Once, the listener fancied that he could distinguish the accents of town's-people of his own, men and women, both pious and ungodly, many of whom he had met at the communion-table, and had seen others rioting at the tavern. The next moment, so indistinct were the sounds, he doubted whether he had heard aught but the murmur of the old forest, whispering without a wind. Then came a stronger

[12]Cape Cod town about seventy miles from Salem.

swell of those familiar tones, heard daily in the sunshine, at Salem village, but never, until now, from a cloud of night. There was one voice, of a young woman, uttering lamentations, yet with an uncertain sorrow, and entreating for some favor, which, perhaps, it would grieve her to obtain. And all the unseen multitude, both saints and sinners, seemed to encourage her onward.

"Faith!" shouted Goodman Brown, in a voice of agony and desperation; and the echoes of the forest mocked him, crying—"Faith! Faith!" as if bewildered wretches were seeking her, all through the wilderness.

The cry of grief, rage, and terror, was yet piercing the night, when the unhappy husband held his breath for a response. There was a scream, drowned immediately in a louder murmur of voices, fading into far-off laughter, as the dark cloud swept away, leaving the clear and silent sky above Goodman Brown. But something fluttered lightly down through the air, and caught on the branch of a tree. The young man seized it, and beheld a pink ribbon.

"My Faith is gone!" cried he, after one stupefied moment. "There is no good on earth; and sin is but a name. Come, devil! for to thee is this world given."

And maddened with despair, so that he laughed loud and long, did Goodman Brown grasp his staff and set forth again, at such a rate, that he seemed to fly along the forest-path, rather than to walk or run. The road grew wilder and drearier, and more faintly traced, and vanished at length, leaving him in the heart of the dark wilderness, still rushing onward, with the instinct that guides mortal man to evil. The whole forest was peopled with frightful sounds; the creaking of the trees, the howling of wild beasts, and the yell of Indians; while, sometimes, the wind tolled like a distant church-bell, and sometimes gave a broad roar around the traveller, as if all Nature were laughing him to scorn. But he was himself the chief horror of the scene, and shrank not from its other horrors.

"Ha! ha! ha!" roared Goodman Brown, when the wind laughed at him. "Let us hear which will laugh loudest! Think not to frighten me with your deviltry! Come witch, come wizard, come Indian powow,[13] come devil himself! and here comes Goodman Brown. You may as well fear him as he fear you!"

In truth, all through the haunted forest, there could be nothing more frightful than the figure of Goodman Brown. On he flew, among the black pines, brandishing his staff with frenzied gestures, now giving vent to an inspiration of horrid blasphemy, and now shouting forth such laughter, as set all the echoes of the forest laughing like demons around him. The fiend in his own shape is less hideous, than when he rages in the breast of man. Thus sped the demoniac on his course, until, quivering among the trees, he saw a red light before him, as when the felled trunks and branches of a clearing have been set on fire, and throw up their lurid blaze against the

[13]Medicine man.

sky, at the hour of midnight. He paused, in a lull of the tempest that had driven him onward, and heard the swell of what seemed a hymn, rolling solemnly from a distance, with the weight of many voices. He knew the tune; it was a familiar one in the choir of the village meeting-house. The verse died heavily away, and was lengthened by a chorus, not of human voices, but of all the sounds of the benighted wilderness, pealing in awful harmony together. Goodman Brown cried out; and his cry was lost to his own ear, by its unison with the cry of the desert.

In the interval of silence, he stole forward, until the light glared full upon his eyes. At one extremity of an open space, hemmed in by the dark wall of the forest, arose a rock, bearing some rude, natural resemblance either to an altar or a pulpit, and surrounded by four blazing pines, their tops aflame, their stems untouched, like candles at an evening meeting. The mass of foliage, that had overgrown the summit of the rock, was all on fire, blazing high into the night, and fitfully illuminating the whole field. Each pendent twig and leafy festoon was in a blaze. As the red light arose and fell, a numerous congregation alternately shone forth, then disappeared in shadow, and again grew, as it were, out of the darkness, peopling the heart of the solitary woods at once.

"A grave and dark-clad company!" quoth Goodman Brown.

In truth, they were such. Among them, quivering to-and-fro, between gloom and splendor, appeared faces that would be seen, next day, at the council-board of the province, and others which, Sabbath after Sabbath, looked devoutly heavenward, and benignantly over the crowded pews, from the holiest pulpits in the land. Some affirm, that the lady of the governor was there. At least, there were high dames well known to her, and wives of honored husbands, and widows, a great multitude, and ancient maidens, all of excellent repute, and fair young girls, who trembled, lest their mothers should espy them. Either the sudden gleams of light, flashing over the obscure field, bedazzled Goodman Brown, or he recognized a score of the church-members of Salem village, famous for their especial sanctity. Good old Deacon Gookin had arrived, and waited at the skirts of that venerable saint, his revered pastor. But, irreverently consorting with these grave, reputable, and pious people, these elders of the church, these chaste dames and dewy virgins, there were men of dissolute lives and women of spotted fame, wretches given over to all mean and filthy vice, and suspected even of horrid crimes. It was strange to see, that the good shrank not from the wicked, nor were the sinners abashed by the saints. Scattered, also, among their pale-faced enemies, were the Indian priests, or powows, who had often scared their native forest with more hideous incantations than any known to English witchcraft.

"But, where is Faith?" thought Goodman Brown; and, as hope came into his heart, he trembled.

Another verse of the hymn arose, a slow and mournful strain, such as the pious love, but joined to words which expressed all that our nature can conceive of sin, and darkly hinted at far more. Unfathomable to mere mortals is the lore of fiends. Verse after verse was sung, and still the chorus of the desert swelled between, like the deepest tone of a mighty organ. And, with the final peal of that dreadful anthem, there came a sound, as if the roaring wind, the rushing streams, the howling beasts, and every other voice of the unconverted wilderness, were mingling and according with the voice of guilty man, in homage to the prince of all. The four blazing pines threw up a loftier flame, and obscurely discovered shapes and visages of horror on the smoke-wreaths, above the impious assembly. At the same moment, the fire on the rock shot redly forth, and formed a glowing arch above its base, where now appeared a figure. With reverence be it spoken, the figure bore no slight similitude, both in garb and manner, to some grave divine of the New-England churches.

"Bring forth the converts!" cried a voice, that echoed through the field and rolled into the forest.

At the word, Goodman Brown stept forth from the shadow of the trees, and approached the congregation, with whom he felt a loathful brother-hood, by the sympathy of all that was wicked in his heart. He could have well nigh sworn, that the shape of his own dead father beckoned him to advance, looking downward from a smoke-wreath, while a woman, with dim features of despair, threw out her hand to warn him back. Was it his mother? But he had no power to retreat one step, nor to resist, even in thought, when the minister and good old Deacon Gookin seized his arms, and led him to the blazing rock. Thither came also the slender form of a veiled female, led between Goody Cloyse, that pious teacher of the cate-chism, and Martha Carrier, who had received the devil's promise to be queen of hell. A rampant hag was she! And there stood the proselytes, beneath the canopy of fire.

"Welcome, my children," said the dark figure, "to the communion of your race! Ye have found, thus young, your nature and your destiny. My children, look behind you!"

They turned; and flashing forth, as it were, in a sheet of flame, the fiend-worshippers were seen; the smile of welcome gleamed darkly on every visage.

"There," resumed the sable form, "are all whom ye have reverenced from youth. Ye deemed them holier than yourselves, and shrank from your own sin, contrasting it with their lives of righteousness, and prayerful aspirations heavenward. Yet, here are they all, in my worshipping assembly! This night it shall be granted you to know their secret deeds; how hoary-bearded elders of the church have whispered wanton words to the young maids of their households; how many a woman, eager for widow's weeds, has given her husband a drink at bedtime, and let him sleep his last sleep in her bosom; how beardless youths have made haste to inherit their fathers' wealth; and how fair damsels—blush not, sweet ones!—have dug little graves in the gar-den, and bidden me, the sole guest, to an infant's funeral. By the sympathy of your human hearts for sin, ye shall scent out all the places—whether in church, bed-chamber, street, field, or forest—where crime has been committed, and shall exult to behold the whole earth one stain of guilt, one mighty blood-spot. Far more than this! It shall be yours to penetrate, in every bosom, the deep mystery of sin, the fountain of all wicked arts, and which inexhaustibly supplies more evil impulses than human power—than my power, at its utmost!—can make manifest in deeds. And now, my children, look upon each other."

They did so; and, by the blaze of the hell-kindled torches, the wretched man beheld his Faith, and the wife her husband, trembling before that unhallowed altar.

"Lo! there ye stand, my children," said the figure, in a deep and solemn tone, almost sad, with its despairing awfulness, as if his once angelic nature could yet mourn for our miserable race. "Depending upon one another's hearts, ye had still hoped, that virtue were not all a dream. Now are ye undeceived! Evil is the nature of mankind. Evil must be your only happiness. Welcome, again, my children, to the communion of your race!"

"Welcome!" repeated the fiend-worshippers, in one cry of despair and triumph.

And there they stood, the only pair, as it seemed, who were yet hesitating on the verge of wickedness, in this dark world. A basin was hollowed, naturally, in the rock. Did it contain water, reddened by the lurid light? or was it blood? or, perchance, a liquid flame? Herein did the Shape of Evil dip his hand, and prepare to lay the mark of baptism upon their foreheads, that they might be partakers of the mystery of sin, more conscious of the secret guilt of others, both in deed and thought, than they could now be of their own. The husband cast one look at his pale wife, and Faith at him. What polluted wretches would the next glance shew them to each other, shuddering alike at what they disclosed and what they saw!

"Faith! Faith!" cried the husband. "Look up to Heaven, and resist the Wicked One!"

Whether Faith obeyed, he knew not. Hardly had he spoken, when he found himself amid calm night and solitude, listening to a roar of the wind, which died heavily away through the forest. He staggered against the rock and felt it chill and damp, while a hanging twig, that had been all on fire, besprinkled his cheek with the coldest dew.

The next morning, young Goodman Brown came slowly into the street of Salem village, staring around him like a bewildered man. The good old minister was taking a walk along the grave-yard, to get an appetite for breakfast and meditate his sermon, and bestowed a blessing, as he passed, on Goodman Brown. He shrank from the venerable saint, as if to avoid an anathema. Old Deacon Gookin was at domestic worship, and the holy words of his prayer were heard through the open window. "What God doth the wizard pray to?" quoth Goodman Brown. Goody Cloyse, that excellent old Christian, stood in the early sunshine, at her own lattice, catechising a little girl, who had brought her a pint of morning's milk. Goodman Brown snatched away the child, as from the grasp of the fiend himself. Turning the corner by the meeting-house, he spied the head of Faith, with the pink ribbons, gazing anxiously forth, and bursting into such joy at sight of him, that she skipt along the street, and almost kissed her husband before the whole village. But, Goodman Brown looked sternly and sadly into her face, and passed on without a greeting.

Had Goodman Brown fallen asleep in the forest, and only dreamed a wild dream of a witch-meeting?

Be it so, if you will. But, alas! it was a dream of evil omen for young Goodman Brown. A stern, a sad, a darkly meditative, a distrustful, if not a desperate man, did he become, from the night of that fearful dream. On the Sabbath-day, when the congregation were singing a holy psalm, he could not listen, because an anthem of sin rushed loudly upon his ear, and drowned all the blessed strain. When the minister spoke from the pulpit, with power and fervid eloquence, and, with his hand on the open Bible, of the sacred truths of our religion, and of saint-like lives and triumphant deaths, and of future bliss or misery unutterable, then did Goodman Brown turn pale, dreading, lest the roof should thunder down upon the gray blasphemer and his hearers. Often, awakening suddenly at midnight, he shrank from the bosom of Faith, and at morning or eventide, when the family knelt down at prayer, he scowled, and muttered to himself, and gazed sternly at his wife, and turned away. And when he had lived long, and was borne to his grave, a hoary corpse, followed by Faith, an aged woman, and children and grand-children, a goodly procession, besides neighbors, not a few, they carved no hopeful verse upon his tomb-stone; for his dying hour was gloom.

1835

The Minister's Black Veil[1]

A Parable[2]

The sexton stood in the porch of Milford[3] meeting-house, pulling lustily at the bell-rope. The old people of the village came stooping along the street. Children, with bright faces, tript merrily beside their parents, or mimicked a graver gait, in the conscious dignity of their Sunday clothes. Spruce bachelors looked sidelong at the pretty maidens, and fancied that the Sabbath sunshine made them prettier than on week-days. When the throng had mostly streamed into the porch, the sexton began to toll the bell, keeping his eye on the Reverend Mr. Hooper's door. The first glimpse of the clergy-man's figure was the signal for the bell to cease its summons.

---

[1]First published in the *Token* (1836) and included in *Twice-Told Tales* (1837).

[2]Another clergyman in New England, Mr. Joseph Moody, of York, Maine, who died about eighty years since, made himself remarkable by the same eccentricity that is here related of the Reverend Mr. Hooper. In his case,

however, the symbol had a different import. In early life he had accidentally killed a beloved friend; and from that day till the hour of his own death, he hid his face from men [Hawthorne's note].

[3]A town southwest of Boston.

"But what has good Parson Hooper got upon his face?" cried the sexton in astonishment.

All within hearing immediately turned about, and beheld the semblance of Mr. Hooper, pacing slowly his meditative way towards the meeting-house. With one accord they started, expressing more wonder than if some strange minister were coming to dust the cushions of Mr. Hooper's pulpit.

"Are you sure it is our parson?" inquired Goodman Gray of the sexton.

"Of a certainty it is good Mr. Hooper," replied the sexton. "He was to have exchanged pulpits with Parson Shute of Westbury; but Parson Shute sent to excuse himself yesterday, being to preach a funeral sermon."

The cause of so much amazement may appear sufficiently slight. Mr. Hooper, a gentlemanly person of about thirty, though still a bachelor, was dressed with due clerical neatness, as if a careful wife had starched his band, and brushed the weekly dust from his Sunday's garb. There was but one thing remarkable in his appearance. Swathed about his forehead, and hanging down over his face, so low as to be shaken by his breath, Mr. Hooper had on a black veil. On a nearer view, it seemed to consist of two folds of crape, which entirely concealed his features, except the mouth and chin, but probably did not intercept his sight, farther than to give a darkened aspect to all living and inanimate things. With this gloomy shade before him, good Mr. Hooper walked onward, at a slow and quiet pace, stooping somewhat and looking on the ground, as is customary with abstracted men, yet nodding kindly to those of his parishioners who still waited on the meeting-house steps. But so wonder-struck were they, that his greeting hardly met with a return.

"I can't really feel as if good Mr. Hooper's face was behind that piece of crape," said the sexton.

"I don't like it," muttered an old woman, as she hobbled into the meeting-house. "He has changed himself into something awful, only by hiding his face."

"Our parson has gone mad!" cried Goodman Gray, following him across the threshold.

A rumor of some unaccountable phenomenon had preceded Mr. Hooper into the meeting-house, and set all the congregation astir. Few could refrain from twisting their heads towards the door; many stood upright, and turned directly about; while several little boys clambered upon the seats, and came down again with a terrible racket. There was a general bustle, a rustling of the women's gowns and shuffling of the men's feet, greatly at variance with that hushed repose which should attend the entrance of the minister. But Mr. Hooper appeared not to notice the perturbation of his people. He entered with an almost noiseless step, bent his head mildly to the pews on each side, and bowed as he passed his oldest parishioner, a white-haired great-grandsire, who occupied an arm-chair in the centre of the aisle. It was strange to observe, how slowly this venerable man became conscious of something singular in the appearance of his pastor. He seemed not fully to partake of the prevailing wonder, till Mr. Hooper had ascended the stairs, and showed himself in the pulpit, face to face with his congregation, except for the black veil. That mysterious emblem was never once withdrawn. It shook with his measured breath as he gave out the psalm; it threw its obscurity between him and the holy page, as he read the Scriptures; and while he prayed, the veil lay heavily on his uplifted countenance. Did he seek to hide it from the dread Being whom he was addressing?

Such was the effect of this simple piece of crape, that more than one woman of delicate nerves was forced to leave the meeting-house. Yet perhaps the palefaced congregation was almost as fearful a sight to the minister, as his black veil to them.

Mr. Hooper had the reputation of a good preacher, but not an energetic one: he strove to win his people heavenward, by mild persuasive influences, rather than to drive them thither, by the thunders of the Word. The sermon which he now delivered, was marked by the same characteristics of style and manner, as the general series of his pulpit oratory. But there was something, either in the sentiment of the discourse itself, or in the imagination of the auditors, which made it greatly the most powerful effort that they had ever heard from their pastor's lips. It was tinged, rather more darkly than usual, with the gentle gloom of Mr. Hooper's temperament. The subject had reference to secret sin, and those sad mysteries which we hide from our nearest and dearest, and would fain conceal from our own consciousness, even forgetting that the Omniscient can detect them. A subtle power was breathed into his words. Each member of the congregation, the most innocent girl, and the man of hardened breast, felt as if the preacher had crept upon them, behind his awful veil, and discovered their hoarded iniquity of deed or thought. Many spread their clasped hands on their bosoms. There was nothing terrible in what Mr. Hooper said; at least, no violence; and yet, with every tremor of his melancholy voice, the hearers quaked. An unsought pathos came hand in hand with awe. So sensible were the audience of some unwonted attribute in their minister, that they longed for a breath of wind to blow aside the veil, almost believing that a stranger's visage would be discovered, though the form, gesture, and voice were those of Mr. Hooper.

At the close of the services, the people hurried out with indecorous confusion, eager to communicate their pent-up amazement, and conscious of lighter spirits, the moment they lost sight of the black veil. Some gathered in little circles, huddled closely together, with their mouths all whispering in the centre; some went homeward alone, wrapt in silent meditation; some talked loudly, and profaned the Sabbath-day with ostentatious laughter. A few shook their sagacious heads, intimating that they could penetrate the mystery; while one or two affirmed that there was no mystery at all, but only that Mr. Hooper's eyes were so weakened by the midnight lamp, as to require a shade. After a brief interval, forth came good Mr. Hooper also, in the rear of his flock. Turning his veiled face from one group to another, he paid due reverence to the hoary heads, saluted the middle-aged with kind dignity, as their friend and spiritual guide, greeted the young with mingled authority and love, and laid his hands on the little children's heads to bless them. Such was always his custom on the Sabbath-day. Strange and bewildered looks repaid him for his courtesy. None, as on former occasions, aspired to the honor of walking by their pastor's side. Old Squire Saunders, doubtless by an accidental lapse of memory, neglected to invite Mr. Hooper to his table, where the good clergyman had been wont to bless the food, almost every Sunday since his settlement. He returned, therefore, to the parsonage, and, at the moment of closing the door, was observed to look back upon the people, all of whom had their eyes fixed upon the minister. A sad smile gleamed faintly from beneath the black veil, and flickered about his mouth, glimmering as he disappeared.

"How strange," said a lady, "that a simple black veil, such as any woman might wear on her bonnet, should become such a terrible thing on Mr. Hooper's face!"

"Something must surely be amiss with Mr. Hooper's intellects," observed her husband, the physician of the village. "But the strangest part of the affair is the effect of this vagary, even on a sober-minded man like myself. The black veil, though it covers only our pastor's face, throws its influence over his whole person, and makes him ghost-like from head to foot. Do you not feel it so?"

"Truly do I," replied the lady; "and I would not be alone with him for the world. I wonder he is not afraid to be alone with himself!"

"Men sometimes are so," said her husband.

The afternoon service was attended with similar circumstances. At its conclusion, the bell tolled for the funeral of a young lady. The relatives and friends were assembled in the house, and the more distant acquaintances stood about the door, speaking of the good qualities of the deceased, when their talk was interrupted by the appearance of Mr. Hooper, still covered with his black veil. It was now an appropriate emblem. The clergyman stepped into the room where the corpse was laid, and bent over the coffin, to take a last farewell of his deceased parishioner. As he stooped, the veil hung straight down from his forehead, so that, if her eye-lids had not been closed for ever, the dead maiden might have seen his face. Could Mr. Hooper be fearful of her glance, that he so hastily caught back the black veil? A person, who watched the interview between the dead and living, scrupled not to affirm, that, at the instant when the clergyman's features were disclosed, the corpse had slightly shuddered, rustling the shroud and muslin cap, though the countenance retained the composure of death. A superstitious old woman was the only witness of this prodigy. From the coffin, Mr. Hooper passed into the chamber of the mourners, and thence to the head of the staircase, to make the funeral prayer. It was a tender and heart-dissolving prayer, full of sorrow, yet so imbued with celestial hopes, that the music of a heavenly harp, swept by the fingers of the dead, seemed faintly to be heard among the saddest accents of the minister. The people trembled, though they but darkly understood him, when he prayed that they, and himself, and all of mortal race, might be ready, as he trusted this young maiden had been, for the dreadful hour that should snatch the veil from their faces. The bearers went heavily forth, and the mourners followed, saddening all the street, with the dead before them, and Mr. Hooper in his black veil behind.

"Why do you look back?" said one in the procession to his partner.

"I had a fancy," replied she, "that the minister and the maiden's spirit were walking hand in hand."

"And so had I, at the same moment," said the other.

That night, the handsomest couple in Milford village were to be joined in wedlock. Though reckoned a melancholy man, Mr. Hooper had a placid cheerfulness for such occasions, which often excited a sympathetic smile, where livelier merriment would have been thrown away. There was no quality of his disposition which made him more beloved than this. The company at the wedding awaited his arrival with impatience, trusting that the strange awe, which had gathered over him throughout the day, would now be dispelled. But such was not the result. When Mr. Hooper came, the first thing that their eyes rested on was the same horrible black veil, which had added deeper gloom to the funeral, and could portend nothing but evil to the wedding. Such was its immediate effect on the guests, that a cloud seemed to have rolled duskily from beneath the black crape, and dimmed the light of the candles. The bridal pair stood up before the minister. But the bride's cold fingers quivered in the tremulous hand of the bridegroom, and her deathlike paleness caused a whisper, that the maiden who had been buried a few hours before, was come from her grave to be married. If ever another wedding were so dismal, it was that famous one, where they tolled the wedding-knell.[4] After performing the ceremony, Mr. Hooper raised a glass of wine to his lips, wishing happiness to the new-married couple, in a strain of mild pleasantry that ought to have brightened the features of the guests, like a cheerful gleam from the hearth. At that instant, catching a glimpse of his figure in the looking-glass, the black veil involved his own spirit in the horror with which it overwhelmed all others. His frame shuddered—his lips grew white—he spilt the untasted wine upon the carpet—and rushed forth into the darkness. For the Earth, too, had on her Black Veil.

The next day, the whole village of Milford talked of little else than Parson Hooper's black veil. That, and the mystery concealed behind it, supplied a topic for discussion between acquaintances meeting in the street, and good women gossiping at their open windows. It was the first item of news that the tavern-keeper told to his guests. The children babbled of it on their way to school. One imitative little imp covered his face with an old black handkerchief, thereby so affrighting his playmates, that the panic seized himself, and he well nigh lost his wits by his own waggery.

It was remarkable, that, of all the busy-bodies and impertinent people in the parish, not one ventured to put the plain question to Mr. Hooper,

[4]Hawthorne's story "The Wedding Knell," also published in the 1836 *Token* and included in *Twice-Told Tales*.

wherefore he did this thing. Hitherto, whenever there appeared the slightest call for such interference, he had never lacked advisers, nor shown himself averse to be guided by their judgment. If he erred at all, it was by so painful a degree of self-distrust, that even the mildest censure would lead him to consider an indifferent action as a crime. Yet, though so well acquainted with this amiable weakness, no individual among his parishioners chose to make the black veil a subject of friendly remonstrance. There was a feeling of dread, neither plainly confessed nor carefully concealed, which caused each to shift the responsibility upon another, till at length it was found expedient to send a deputation of the church, in order to deal with Mr. Hooper about the mystery, before it should grow into a scandal. Never did an embassy so ill discharge its duties. The minister received them with friendly courtesy, but became silent, after they were seated, leaving to his visiters the whole burthen of introducing their important business. The topic, it might be supposed, was obvious enough. There was the black veil, swathed round Mr. Hooper's forehead, and concealing every feature above his placid mouth, on which, at times, they could perceive the glimmering of a melancholy smile. But that piece of crape, to their imagination, seemed to hang down before his heart, the symbol of a fearful secret between him and them. Were the veil but cast aside, they might speak freely of it, but not till then. Thus they sat a considerable time, speechless, confused, and shrinking uneasily from Mr. Hooper's eye, which they felt to be fixed upon them with an invisible glance. Finally, the deputies returned abashed to their constituents, pronouncing the matter too weighty to be handled, except by a council of the churches, if, indeed, it might not require a general synod.

But there was one person in the village, unappalled by the awe with which the black veil had impressed all beside herself. When the deputies returned without an explanation, or even venturing to demand one, she, with the calm energy of her character, determined to chase away the strange cloud that appeared to be settling round Mr. Hooper, every moment more darkly than before. As his plighted wife, it should be her privilege to know what the black veil concealed. At the minister's first visit, therefore, she entered upon the subject, with a direct simplicity, which made the task easier both for him and her. After he had seated himself, she fixed her eyes steadfastly upon the veil, but could discern nothing of the dreadful gloom that had so overawed the multitude: it was but a double fold of crape, hanging down from his forehead to his mouth, and slightly stirring with his breath.

"No," said she aloud, and smiling, "there is nothing terrible in this piece of crape, except that it hides a face which I am always glad to look upon. Come, good sir, let the sun shine from behind the cloud. First lay aside your black veil: then tell me why you put it on."

Mr. Hooper's smile glimmered faintly.

"There is an hour to come," said he, "when all of us shall cast aside our veils. Take it not amiss, beloved friend, if I wear this piece of crape till then."

"Your words are a mystery too," returned the young lady. "Take away the veil from them, at least."

"Elizabeth, I will," said he, "so far as my vow may suffer me. Know, then, this veil is a type and a symbol, and I am bound to wear it ever, both in light and darkness, in solitude and before the gaze of multitudes, and as with strangers, so with my familiar friends. No mortal eye will see it withdrawn. This dismal shade must separate me from the world: even you, Elizabeth, can never come behind it!"

"What grievous affliction hath befallen you," she earnestly inquired, "that you should thus darken your eyes for ever?"

"If it be a sign of mourning," replied Mr. Hooper, "I, perhaps, like most other mortals, have sorrows dark enough to be typified by a black veil."

"But what if the world will not believe that it is the type of an innocent sorrow?" urged Elizabeth. "Beloved and respected as you are, there may be whispers, that you hide your face under the consciousness of secret sin. For the sake of your holy office, do away this scandal!"

The color rose into her cheeks, as she intimated the nature of the rumors that were already abroad in the village. But Mr. Hooper's mildness did not forsake him. He even smiled again—that same sad smile, which always appeared like a faint glimmering of light, proceeding from the obscurity beneath the veil.

"If I hide my face for sorrow, there is cause enough," he merely replied; "and if I cover it for secret sin, what mortal might not do the same?"

And with this gentle, but unconquerable obstinacy, did he resist all her entreaties. At length Elizabeth sat silent. For a few moments she appeared lost in thought, considering, probably, what new methods might be tried, to withdraw her lover from so dark a fantasy, which, if it had no other meaning, was perhaps a symptom of mental disease. Though of a firmer character than his own, the tears rolled down her cheeks. But, in an instant, as it were, a new feeling took the place of sorrow: her eyes were fixed insensibly on the black veil, when, like a sudden twilight in the air, its terrors fell around her. She arose, and stood trembling before him.

"And do you feel it then at last?" said he mournfully.

She made no reply, but covered her eyes with her hand, and turned to leave the room. He rushed forward and caught her arm.

"Have patience with me, Elizabeth!" cried he passionately. "Do not desert me, though this veil must be between us here on earth. Be mine, and hereafter there shall be no veil over my face, no darkness between our souls! It is but a mortal veil—it is not for eternity! Oh! you know not how lonely I am, and how frightened to be alone behind my black veil. Do not leave me in this miserable obscurity for ever!"

"Lift the veil but once, and look me in the face," said she.

"Never! It cannot be!" replied Mr. Hooper.

"Then, farewell!" said Elizabeth.

She withdrew her arm from his grasp, and slowly departed, pausing at the door, to give one long, shuddering gaze, that seemed almost to penetrate the mystery of the black veil. But, even amid his grief, Mr. Hooper smiled to think that only a material emblem had separated him from happiness, though the horrors which it shadowed forth, must be drawn darkly between the fondest of lovers.

From that time no attempts were made to remove Mr. Hooper's black veil, or, by a direct appeal, to discover the secret which it was supposed to hide. By persons who claimed a superiority to popular prejudice, it was reckoned merely an eccentric whim, such as often mingles with the sober actions of men otherwise rational, and tinges them all with its own semblance of insanity. But with the multitude, good Mr. Hooper was irreparably a bugbear. He could not walk the streets with any peace of mind, so conscious was he that the gentle and timid would turn aside to avoid him, and that others would make it a point of hardihood to throw themselves in his way. The impertinence of the latter class compelled him to give up his customary walk, at sunset, to the burial ground; for when he leaned pensively over the gate, there would always be faces behind the grave-stones, peeping at his black veil. A fable went the rounds, that the stare of the dead people drove him thence. It grieved him, to the very depth of his kind heart, to observe how the children fled from his approach, breaking up their merriest sports, while his melancholy figure was yet afar off. Their instinctive dread caused him to feel, more strongly than aught else, that a preternatural horror was interwoven with the threads of the black crape. In truth, his own antipathy to the veil was known to be so great, that he never willingly passed before a mirror, nor stooped to drink at a still fountain, lest, in its peaceful bosom, he should be affrighted by himself. This was what gave plausibility to the whispers, that Mr. Hooper's conscience tortured him for some great crime, too horrible to be entirely concealed, or otherwise than so obscurely intimated. Thus, from beneath the black veil, there rolled a cloud into the sunshine, an ambiguity of sin or sorrow, which enveloped the poor minister, so that love or sympathy could never reach him. It was said, that ghost and fiend consorted with him there. With self-shudderings and outward terrors, he walked continually in its shadow, groping darkly within his own soul, or gazing through a medium that saddened the whole world. Even the lawless wind, it was believed, respected his dreadful secret, and never blew aside the veil. But still good Mr. Hooper sadly smiled, at the pale visages of the worldly throng as he passed by.

Among all its bad influences, the black veil had the one desirable effect, of making its wearer a very efficient clergyman. By the aid of his mysterious emblem—for there was no other apparent cause—he became a man of awful power, over souls that were in agony for sin. His converts always regarded him with a dread peculiar to themselves, affirming, though but figuratively, that, before he brought them to celestial light, they had been with him behind the black veil. Its gloom, indeed, enabled him to sympathize with all dark affections. Dying sinners cried aloud for Mr. Hooper, and would not yield their breath till he appeared; though ever, as he stooped to whisper consolation, they shuddered at the veiled face so near their own.

Such were the terrors of the black veil, even when Death had bared his visage! Strangers came long distances to attend service at his church, with the mere idle purpose of gazing at his figure, because it was forbidden them to behold his face. But many were made to quake ere they departed! Once, during Governor Belcher's administration, Mr. Hooper was appointed to preach the election sermon.[5] Covered with his black veil, he stood before the chief magistrate, the council, and the representatives, and wrought so deep an impression, that the legislative measures of that year, were characterized by all the gloom and piety of our earliest ancestral sway.

In this manner Mr. Hooper spent a long life, irreproachable in outward act, yet shrouded in dismal suspicions; kind and loving, though unloved, and dimly feared; a man apart from men, shunned in their health and joy, but ever summoned to their aid in mortal anguish. As years wore on, shedding their snows above his sable veil, he acquired a name throughout the New-England churches, and they called him Father Hooper. Nearly all his parishioners, who were of mature age when he was settled, had been borne away by many a funeral: he had one congregation in the church, and a more crowded one in the church-yard; and having wrought so late into the evening, and done his work so well, it was now good Father Hooper's turn to rest.

Several persons were visible by the shaded candlelight, in the death-chamber of the old clergyman. Natural connections he had none. But there was the decorously grave, though unmoved physician, seeking only to mitigate the last pangs of the patient whom he could not save. There were the deacons, and other eminently pious members of his church. There, also, was the Reverend Mr. Clark, of Westbury, a young and zealous divine, who had ridden in haste to pray by the bed-side of the expiring minister. There was the nurse, no hired handmaiden of death, but one whose calm affection had endured thus long, in secresy, in solitude, amid the chill of age, and would not perish, even at the dying hour. Who, but Elizabeth! And there lay the hoary head of good Father Hooper upon the death-pillow, with the black veil still swathed about his brow and reaching down over his face, so that each more difficult gasp of his faint breath caused it to stir. All through life that piece of crape had hung between him and the world: it had separated him from cheerful brotherhood and woman's love, and kept him in that saddest of all prisons, his own heart; and still it lay upon his face, as if to deepen the gloom of his darksome chamber, and shade him from the sunshine of eternity.

For some time previous, his mind had been confused, wavering doubtfully between the past and the present, and hovering forward, as it were, at intervals, into the indistinctness of the world to come. There had been feverish turns, which tossed him from side to side, and wore away what

[5]Jonathan Belcher (1682–1757) was governor of both Massachusetts and New Hampshire between 1730 and 1741, which sets Hawthorne's story during the period of religious fervor known as "The Great Awakening." The annual election sermon was delivered by an eminent minister to solemnize the inauguration of a newly elected governor.

little strength he had. But in his most convulsive struggles, and in the wildest vagaries of his intellect, when no other thought retained its sober influence, he still showed an awful solicitude lest the black veil should slip aside. Even if his bewildered soul could have forgotten, there was a faithful woman at his pillow, who, with averted eyes, would have covered that aged face, which she had last beheld in the comeliness of manhood. At length the death-stricken old man lay quietly in the torpor of mental and bodily exhaustion, with an imperceptible pulse, and breath that grew fainter and fainter, except when a long, deep, and irregular inspiration seemed to prelude the flight of his spirit.

The minister of Westbury approached the bedside.

"Venerable Father Hooper," said he, "the moment of your release is at hand. Are you ready for the lifting of the veil, that shuts in time from eternity?"

Father Hooper at first replied merely by a feeble motion of his head; then, apprehensive, perhaps, that his meaning might be doubtful, he exerted himself to speak.

"Yea," said he, in faint accents, "my soul hath a patient weariness until that veil be lifted."

"And is it fitting," resumed the Reverend Mr. Clark, "that a man so given to prayer, of such a blameless example, holy in deed and thought, so far as mortal judgment may pronounce; is it fitting that a father in the church should leave a shadow on his memory, that may seem to blacken a life so pure? I pray you, my venerable brother, let not this thing be! Suffer us to be gladdened by your triumphant aspect, as you go to your reward. Before the veil of eternity be lifted, let me cast aside this black veil from your face!"

And thus speaking, the Reverend Mr. Clark bent forward to reveal the mystery of so many years. But, exerting a sudden energy, that made all the beholders stand aghast, Father Hooper snatched both his hands from beneath the bed-clothes, and pressed them strongly on the black veil, resolute to struggle, if the minister of Westbury would contend with a dying man.

"Never!" cried the veiled clergyman. "On earth, never!"

"Dark old man!" exclaimed the affrighted minister, "with what horrible crime upon your soul are you now passing to the judgment?"

Father Hooper's breath heaved; it rattled in his throat; but, with a mighty effort, grasping forward with his hands, he caught hold of life, and held it back till he should speak. He even raised himself in bed; and there he sat, shivering with the arms of death around him, while the black veil hung down, awful, at that last moment, in the gathered terrors of a life-time. And yet the faint, sad smile, so often there, now seemed to glimmer from its obscurity, and linger on Father Hooper's lips.

"Why do you tremble at me alone?" cried he, turning his veiled face round the circle of pale spectators. "Tremble also at each other! Have men avoided me, and women shown no pity, and children screamed and fled, only for my black veil? What, but the mystery which it obscurely typifies, has made this piece of crape so awful? When the friend shows his inmost heart to his friend; the lover to his best-beloved; when man does not vainly shrink from the eye of his Creator, loathsomely treasuring up the secret of his sin; then deem me a monster, for the symbol beneath which I have lived, and die! I look around me, and, lo! on every visage a Black Veil!"

While his auditors shrank from one another, in mutual affright, Father Hooper fell back upon his pillow, a veiled corpse, with a faint smile lingering on the lips. Still veiled, they laid him in his coffin, and a veiled corpse they bore him to the grave. The grass of many years has sprung up and withered on that grave, the burial-stone is moss-grown, and good Mr. Hooper's face is dust; but awful is still the thought, that it mouldered beneath the Black Veil!

1836

The Birth-Mark[1]

In the latter part of the last century, there lived a man of science—an eminent proficient in every branch of natural philosophy—who, not long before our story opens, had made experience of a spiritual affinity, more attractive than any chemical one. He had left his laboratory to the care of an assistant, cleared his fine countenance from the furnace-smoke, washed the stain of acids from his fingers, and persuaded a beautiful woman to become his wife. In those days, when the comparatively recent discovery of electricity, and other kindred mysteries of nature, seemed to open paths into the region of miracle, it was not unusual for the love of science to rival the love of woman, in its depth and absorbing energy. The higher intellect, the imagination, the spirit, and even the heart, might all find their congenial aliment in pursuits which, as some of their ardent votaries believed, would ascend from one step of powerful intelligence to another, until the philosopher should lay his hand on the secret of creative force, and perhaps make new worlds for himself. We know not whether Aylmer possessed this degree of faith in man's ultimate control over nature. He had devoted himself, however, too unreservedly to scientific studies, ever to be weaned from them by any second passion. His love for his young wife might prove the stronger of the two; but it could only be by intertwining itself with his love of science, and uniting the strength of the latter to its own.

Such a union accordingly took place, and was attended with truly remarkable consequences, and a deeply impressive moral. One day, very soon after their marriage, Aylmer sat gazing at his wife, with a trouble in his countenance that grew stronger, until he spoke.

"Georgiana," said he, "has it never occurred to you that the mark upon your cheek might be removed?"

[1]First published in 1843 in the *Pioneer Magazine* and included in *Mosses from an Old Manse* (1846).

"No, indeed," said she, smiling; but perceiving the seriousness of his manner, she blushed deeply. "To tell you the truth, it has been so often called a charm, that I was simple enough to imagine it might be so."

"Ah, upon another face, perhaps it might," replied her husband. "But never on yours! No, dearest Georgiana, you came so nearly perfect from the hand of Nature, that this slightest possible defect—which we hesitate whether to term a defect or a beauty—shocks me, as being the visible mark of earthly imperfection."

"Shocks you, my husband!" cried Georgiana, deeply hurt; at first reddening with momentary anger, but then bursting into tears. "Then why did you take me from my mother's side? You cannot love what shocks you!"

To explain this conversation, it must be mentioned, that, in the centre of Georgiana's left cheek, there was a singular mark, deeply interwoven, as it were, with the texture and substance of her face. In the usual state of her complexion,—a healthy, though delicate bloom,—the mark wore a tint of deeper crimson, which imperfectly defined its shape amid the surrounding rosiness. When she blushed, it gradually became more indistinct, and finally vanished amid the triumphant rush of blood, that bathed the whole cheek with its brilliant glow. But, if any shifting emotion caused her to turn pale, there was the mark again, a crimson stain upon the snow, in what Aylmer sometimes deemed an almost fearful distinctness. Its shape bore not a little similarity to the human hand, though of the smallest pigmy size. Georgiana's lovers were wont to say, that some fairy, at her birth-hour, had laid her tiny hand upon the infant's cheek, and left this impress there, in token of the magic endowments that were to give her such sway over all hearts. Many a desperate swain would have risked life for the privilege of pressing his lips to the mysterious hand. It must not be concealed, however, that the impression wrought by this fairy sign-manual varied exceedingly, according to the difference of temperament in the beholders. Some fastidious persons—but they were exclusively of her own sex—affirmed that the Bloody Hand, as they chose to call it, quite destroyed the effect of Georgiana's beauty, and rendered her countenance even hideous. But it would be as reasonable to say, that one of those small blue stains, which sometimes occur in the purest statuary marble, would convert the Eve of Powers[2] to a monster. Masculine observers, if the birth-mark did not heighten their admiration, contented themselves with wishing it away, that the world might possess one living specimen of ideal loveliness, without the semblance of a flaw. After his marriage—for he thought little or nothing of the matter before—Aylmer discovered that this was the case with himself.

Had she been less beautiful—if Envy's self could have found aught else to sneer at—he might have felt his affection heightened by the prettiness of this mimic hand, now vaguely portrayed, now lost, now stealing forth again,

[2]America's most famous sculptor, Hiram Powers (1805–1873), working in Florence, produced his nude marble statue of *Eve Tempted* in 1842 and the even more famous *Greek Slave* in 1843. During Hawthorne's stay in Italy, he and Powers were good friends.

and glimmering to-and-fro with every pulse of emotion that throbbed within her heart. But, seeing her otherwise so perfect, he found this one defect grow more and more intolerable, with every moment of their united lives.[3] It was the fatal flaw of humanity, which Nature, in one shape or another, stamps ineffaceably on all her productions, either to imply that they are temporary and finite, or that their perfection must be wrought by toil and pain. The Crimson Hand expressed the ineludible gripe, in which mortality clutches the highest and purest of earthly mould, degrading them into kindred with the lowest, and even with the very brutes, like whom their visible frames return to dust. In this manner, selecting it as the symbol of his wife's liability to sin, sorrow, decay, and death, Aylmer's sombre imagination was not long in rendering the birth-mark a frightful object, causing him more trouble and horror than ever Georgiana's beauty, whether of soul or sense, had given him delight.

At all the seasons which should have been their happiest, he invariably, and without intending it—nay, in spite of a purpose to the contrary—reverted to this one disastrous topic. Trifling as it at first appeared, it so connected itself with innumerable trains of thought, and modes of feeling, that it became the central point of all. With the morning twilight, Aylmer opened his eyes upon his wife's face, and recognized the symbol of imperfection; and when they sat together at the evening hearth, his eyes wandered stealthily to her cheek, and beheld, flickering with the blaze of the wood fire, the spectral Hand that wrote mortality, where he would fain have worshipped. Georgiana soon learned to shudder at his gaze. It needed but a glance, with the peculiar expression that his face often wore, to change the roses of her cheek into a deathlike paleness, amid which the Crimson Hand was brought strongly out, like a bas-relief of ruby on the whitest marble.

Late, one night, when the lights were growing dim, so as hardly to betray the stain on the poor wife's cheek, she herself, for the first time, voluntarily took up the subject.

"Do you remember, my dear Aylmer," said she, with a feeble attempt at a smile—"have you any recollection of a dream, last night, about this odious Hand?"

"None!—none whatever!" replied Aylmer, starting; but then he added in a dry, cold tone, affected for the sake of concealing the real depth of his emotion:—"I might well dream of it; for before I fell asleep, it had taken a pretty firm hold of my fancy."

"And you did dream of it," continued Georgiana, hastily; for she dreaded lest a gush of tears should interrupt what she had to say—"A terrible dream! I wonder that you can forget it. Is it possible to forget this one expression?—'It is in her heart now—we must have it out!'—Reflect, my husband; for by all means I would have you recall that dream."

---

[3]Hawthorne's story evolves from ideas in his notebooks, e.g., the 1837 entry, "A person to be in the possession of something as perfect as mortal man has a right to demand; he tries to make it better, and ruins it entirely."

The mind is in a sad note, when Sleep, the all-involving, cannot confine her spectres within the dim region of her sway, but suffers them to break forth, affrighting this actual life with secrets that perchance belong to a deeper one. Aylmer now remembered his dream. He had fancied himself, with his servant Aminadab, attempting an operation for the removal of the birth-mark. But the deeper went the knife, the deeper sank the Hand, until at length its tiny grasp appeared to have caught hold of Georgiana's heart; whence, however, her husband was inexorably resolved to cut or wrench it away.

When the dream had shaped itself perfectly in his memory, Aylmer sat in his wife's presence with a guilty feeling. Truth often finds its way to the mind close-muffled in robes of sleep, and then speaks with uncompromising directness of matters in regard to which we practise an unconscious self-deception, during our waking moments. Until now, he had not been aware of the tyrannizing influence acquired by one idea over his mind, and of the lengths which he might find in his heart to go, for the sake of giving himself peace.

"Aylmer," resumed Georgiana, solemnly, "I know not what may be the cost to both of us, to rid me of this fatal birth-mark. Perhaps its removal may cause cureless deformity. Or, it may be, the stain goes as deep as life itself. Again, do we know that there is a possibility, on any terms, of unclasping the firm gripe of this little Hand, which was laid upon me before I came into the world?"

"Dearest Georgiana, I have spent much thought upon the subject," hastily interrupted Aylmer—"I am convinced of the perfect practicability of its removal."

"If there be the remotest possibility of it," continued Georgiana, "let the attempt be made, at whatever risk. Danger is nothing to me; for life—while this hateful mark makes me the object of your horror and disgust—life is a burthen which I would fling down with joy. Either remove this dreadful Hand, or take my wretched life! You have deep science! All the world bears witness of it. You have achieved great wonders! Cannot you remove this little, little mark, which I cover with the tips of two small fingers? Is this beyond your power, for the sake of your own peace, and to save your poor wife from madness?"

"Noblest—dearest—tenderest wife!" cried Aylmer, rapturously. "Doubt not my power. I have already given this matter the deepest thought—thought which might almost have enlightened me to create a being less perfect than yourself. Georgiana, you have led me deeper than ever into the heart of science. I feel myself fully competent to render this dear cheek as faultless as its fellow; and then, most beloved, what will be my triumph, when I shall have corrected what Nature left imperfect, in her fairest work! Even Pygmalion, when his sculptured woman assumed life, felt not greater ecstasy than mine will be."

"It is resolved, then," said Georgiana, faintly smiling,—"And, Aylmer, spare me not, though you should find the birth-mark take refuge in my heart at last."

Her husband tenderly kissed her cheek—her right cheek—not that which bore the impress of the Crimson Hand.

The next day, Aylmer apprized his wife of a plan that he had formed, whereby he might have opportunity for the intense thought and constant watchfulness, which the proposed operation would require; while Georgiana, likewise, would enjoy the perfect repose essential to its success. They were to seclude themselves in the extensive apartments occupied by Aylmer as a laboratory, and where, during his toilsome youth, he had made discoveries in the elemental powers of nature, that had roused the admiration of all the learned societies in Europe. Seated calmly in this laboratory, the pale philosopher had investigated the secrets of the highest cloud-region, and of the profoundest mines; he had satisfied himself of the causes that kindled and kept alive the fires of the volcano; and had explained the mystery of fountains, and how it is that they gush forth, some so bright and pure, and others with such rich medicinal virtues, from the dark bosom of the earth. Here, too, at an earlier period, he had studied the wonders of the human frame, and attempted to fathom the very process by which Nature assimilates all her precious influences from earth and air, and from the spiritual world, to create and foster Man, her masterpiece. The latter pursuit, however, Aylmer had long laid aside, in unwilling recognition of the truth, against which all seekers sooner or later stumble, that our great creative Mother, while she amuses us with apparently working in the broadest sunshine, is yet severely careful to keep her own secrets, and, in spite of her pretended openness, shows us nothing but results. She permits us indeed, to mar, but seldom to mend, and, like a jealous patentee, on no account to make. Now, however, Aylmer resumed these half-forgotten investigations; not, of course, with such hopes or wishes as first suggested them; but because they involved much physiological truth, and lay in the path of his proposed scheme for the treatment of Georgiana.

As he led her over the threshold of the laboratory, Georgiana was cold and tremulous. Aylmer looked cheerfully into her face, with intent to reassure her, but was so startled with the intense glow of the birth-mark upon the whiteness of her cheek, that he could not restrain a strong convulsive shudder. His wife fainted.

"Aminadab! Aminadab!" shouted Aylmer, stamping violently on the floor.

Forthwith, there issued from an inner apartment a man of low stature, but bulky frame, with shaggy hair hanging about his visage, which was grimed with the vapors of the furnace. This personage had been Aylmer's under-worker during his whole scientific career, and was admirably fitted for that office by his great mechanical readiness, and the skill with which, while incapable of comprehending a single principle, he executed all the practical details of his master's experiments. With his vast strength, his shaggy hair, his smoky aspect, and the indescribable earthiness that incrusted him, he seemed to represent man's physical nature; while Aylmer's slender figure, and pale, intellectual face, were no less apt a type of the spiritual element.

"Throw open the door of the boudoir, Aminadab," said Aylmer, "and burn a pastille."

"Yes, master," answered Aminadab, looking intently at the lifeless form of Georgiana; and then he muttered to himself:—"If she were my wife, I'd never part with that birth-mark."

When Georgiana recovered consciousness, she found herself breathing an atmosphere of penetrating fragrance, the gentle potency of which had recalled her from her deathlike faintness. The scene around her looked like enchantment. Aylmer had converted those smoky, dingy, sombre rooms, where he had spent his brightest years in recondite pursuits, into a series of beautiful apartments, not unfit to be the secluded abode of a lovely woman. The walls were hung with gorgeous curtains, which imparted the combination of grandeur and grace, that no other species of adornment can achieve; and as they fell from the ceiling to the floor, their rich and ponderous folds, concealing all angles and straight lines, appeared to shut in the scene from infinite space. For aught Georgiana knew, it might be a pavilion among the clouds. And Aylmer, excluding the sunshine, which would have interfered with his chemical processes, had supplied its place with perfumed lamps, emitting flames of various hue, but all uniting in a soft, empurpled radiance. He now knelt by his wife's side, watching her earnestly, but without alarm; for he was confident in his science, and felt that he could draw a magic circle round her, within which no evil might intrude.

"Where am I?—Ah, I remember!" said Georgiana, faintly; and she placed her hand over her cheek, to hide the terrible mark from her husband's eyes.

"Fear not, dearest!" exclaimed he. "Do not shrink from me! Believe me, Georgiana, I even rejoice in this single imperfection, since it will be such rapture to remove it."

"Oh, spare me!" sadly replied his wife—"Pray do not look at it again. I never can forget that convulsive shudder."

In order to soothe Georgiana, and, as it were, to release her mind from the burthen of actual things, Aylmer now put in practice some of the light and playful secrets, which science had taught him among its profounder lore. Airy figures, absolutely bodiless ideas, and forms of unsubstantial beauty, came and danced before her, imprinting their momentary footsteps on beams of light. Though she had some indistinct idea of the method of these optical phenomena, still the illusion was almost perfect enough to warrant the belief, that her husband possessed sway over the spiritual world. Then again, when she felt a wish to look forth from her seclusion, immediately, as if her thoughts were answered, the procession of external existence flitted across a screen. The scenery and the figures of actual life were perfectly represented, but with that bewitching, yet indescribable difference, which always makes a picture, an image, or a shadow, so much more attractive than the original. When wearied of this, Aylmer bade her cast her eyes upon a vessel, containing a quantity of earth. She did so, with little interest at first, but was soon startled, to perceive the germ of a plant, shooting upward from the soil. Then came the slender stalk—the leaves gradually unfolded themselves—and amid them was a perfect and lovely flower.

"It is magical!" cried Georgiana, "I dare not touch it."

"Nay, pluck it," answered Aylmer, "pluck it, and inhale its brief perfume while you may. The flower will wither in a few moments, and leave nothing save its brown seed-vessels—but thence may be perpetuated a race as ephemeral as itself."

But Georgiana had no sooner touched the flower than the whole plant suffered a blight, its leaves turning coal-black, as if by the agency of fire.

"There was too powerful a stimulus," said Aylmer thoughtfully.

To make up for this abortive experiment, he proposed to take her portrait by a scientific process of his own invention. It was to be effected by rays of light striking upon a polished plate of metal. Georgiana assented—but, on looking at the result, was affrighted to find the features of the portrait blurred and indefinable,[4] while the minute figure of a hand appeared where the cheek should have been. Aylmer snatched the metallic plate, and threw it into a jar of corrosive acid.

Soon, however, he forgot these mortifying failures. In the intervals of study and chemical experiment, he came to her, flushed and exhausted, but seemed invigorated by her presence, and spoke in glowing language of the resources of his art. He gave a history of the long dynasty of the Alchemists, who spent so many ages in quest of the universal solvent, by which the Golden Principle might be elicited from all things vile and base. Aylmer appeared to believe, that, by the plainest scientific logic, it was altogether within the limits of possibility to discover this long-sought medium; but, he added, a philosopher who should go deep enough to acquire the power, would attain too lofty a wisdom to stoop to the exercise of it. Not less singular were his opinions in regard to the Elixir Vitæ.[5] He more than intimated, that it was his option to concoct a liquid that should prolong life for years—perhaps interminably—but that it would produce a discord in nature, which all the world, and chiefly the quaffer of the immortal nostrum, would find cause to curse.

"Aylmer, are you in earnest?" asked Georgiana, looking at him with amazement and fear; "it is terrible to possess such power, or even to dream of possessing it!"

"Oh, do not tremble, my love!" said her husband, "I would not wrong either you or myself by working such inharmonious effects upon our lives. But I would have you consider how trifling, in comparison, is the skill requisite to remove this little Hand."

At the mention of the birth-mark, Georgiana, as usual, shrank, as if a red-hot iron had touched her cheek.

Again Aylmer applied himself to his labors. She could hear his voice in the distant furnace-room, giving directions to Aminadab, whose harsh,

---

[4]In a daguerreotype—the first practical photographic process, introduced in 1839—a sitter's reflected image was fixed onto a silvered and sensitized metal plate after about thirty seconds. Any movement produced a blurred image.

[5]The main project of alchemy was to transmute base metals into gold, but it also involved seeking a panacea (or cure for all illnesses) and an elixir (or liquid) that might prolong life indefinitely.

uncouth, misshapen tones were audible in response, more like the grunt or growl of a brute than human speech. After hours of absence, Aylmer reappeared, and proposed that she should now examine his cabinet of chemical products, and natural treasures of the earth. Among the former he showed her a small vial, in which, he remarked, was contained a gentle yet most powerful fragrance, capable of impregnating all the breezes that blow across a kingdom. They were of inestimable value, the contents of that little vial; and, as he said so, he threw some of the perfume into the air, and filled the room with piercing and invigorating delight.

"And what is this?" asked Georgiana, pointing to a small crystal globe, containing a gold-colored liquid. "It is so beautiful to the eye, that I could imagine it the Elixir of Life."

"In one sense it is," replied Aylmer, "or rather the Elixir of Immortality. It is the most precious poison that ever was concocted in this world. By its aid, I could apportion the lifetime of any mortal at whom you might point your finger. The strength of the dose would determine whether he were to linger out years, or drop dead in the midst of a breath. No king, on his guarded throne, could keep his life, if I, in my private station, should deem that the welfare of millions justified me in depriving him of it."

"Why do you keep such a terrific drug?" inquired Georgiana in horror.

"Do not mistrust me, dearest!" said her husband, smiling; "its virtuous potency is yet greater than its harmful one. But, see! here is a powerful cosmetic. With a few drops of this, in a vase of water, freckles may be washed away as easily as the hands are cleansed. A stronger infusion would take the blood out of the cheek, and leave the rosiest beauty a pale ghost."

"Is it with this lotion that you intend to bathe my cheek?" asked Georgiana anxiously.

"Oh, no!" hastily replied her husband—"this is merely superficial. Your case demands a remedy that shall go deeper."

In his interviews with Georgiana, Aylmer generally made minute inquiries as to her sensations, and whether the confinement of the rooms, and the temperature of the atmosphere, agreed with her. These questions had such a particular drift, that Georgiana began to conjecture that she was already subjected to certain physical influences, either breathed in with the fragrant air, or taken with her food. She fancied, likewise—but it might be altogether fancy—that there was a stirring up of her system,—a strange indefinite sensation creeping through her veins, and tingling, half painfully, half pleasurably, at her heart. Still, whenever she dared to look into the mirror, there she beheld herself, pale as a white rose, and with the crimson birth-mark stamped upon her cheek. Not even Aylmer now hated it so much as she.

To dispel the tedium of the hours which her husband found it necessary to devote to the processes of combination and analysis, Georgiana turned over the volumes of his scientific library. In many dark old tomes, she met with chapters full of romance and poetry. They were the works of the philosophers of the middle ages, such as Albertus Magnus, Cornelius Agrippa, Paracelsus, and the famous friar who created the prophetic

Brazen Head.[6] All these antique naturalists stood in advance of their centuries, yet were imbued with some of their credulity, and therefore were believed, and perhaps imagined themselves, to have acquired from the investigation of nature a power above nature, and from physics a sway over the spiritual world. Hardly less curious and imaginative were the early volumes of the Transactions of the Royal Society,[7] in which the members, knowing little of the limits of natural possibility, were continually recording wonders, or proposing methods whereby wonders might be wrought.

But, to Georgiana, the most engrossing volume was a large folio from her husband's own hand, in which he had recorded every experiment of his scientific career, with its original aim, the methods adopted for its development, and its final success or failure, with the circumstances to which either event was attributable. The book, in truth, was both the history and emblem of his ardent, ambitious, imaginative, yet practical and laborious, life. He handled physical details, as if there were nothing beyond them; yet spiritualized them all, and redeemed himself from materialism, by his strong and eager aspiration towards the infinite. In his grasp, the veriest clod of earth assumed a soul. Georgiana, as she read, reverenced Aylmer, and loved him more profoundly than ever, but with a less entire dependence on his judgment than heretofore. Much as he had accomplished, she could not but observe that his most splendid successes were almost invariably failures, if compared with the ideal at which he aimed. His brightest diamonds were the merest pebbles, and felt to be so by himself, in comparison with the inestimable gems which lay hidden beyond his reach. The volume, rich with achievements that had won renown for its author, was yet as melancholy a record as ever mortal hand had penned. It was the sad confession, and continual exemplification, of the short-comings of the composite man—the spirit burthened with clay and working in matter—and of the despair that assails the higher nature, at finding itself so miserably thwarted by the earthly part. Perhaps every man of genius, in whatever sphere, might recognize the image of his own experience in Aylmer's journal.

So deeply did these reflections affect Georgiana, that she laid her face upon the open volume, and burst into tears. In this situation she was found by her husband.

"It is dangerous to read in a sorcerer's books," said he, with a smile, though his countenance was uneasy and displeased. "Georgiana, there are pages in that volume, which I can scarcely glance over and keep my senses. Take heed lest it prove as detrimental to you!"

"It has made me worship you more than ever," said she.

"Ah! wait for this one success," rejoined he, "then worship me if you will. I shall deem myself hardly unworthy of it. But, come! I have sought you for the luxury of your voice. Sing to me, dearest!"

---

[6]Medieval and Renaissance philosophers and scientists whose experiments were associated with magic. The friar was Roger Bacon.

[7]The Royal Society, founded in London in 1662, was committed to scientific experiment.

So she poured out the liquid music of her voice to quench the thirst of his spirit. He then took his leave, with a boyish exuberance of gaiety, assuring her that her seclusion would endure but a little longer, and that the result was already certain. Scarcely had he departed, when Georgiana felt irresistibly impelled to follow him. She had forgotten to inform Aylmer of a symptom, which, for two or three hours past, had begun to excite her attention. It was a sensation in the fatal birth-mark, not painful, but which induced a restlessness throughout her system. Hastening after her husband, she intruded, for the first time, into the laboratory.

The first thing that struck her eye was the furnace, that hot and feverish worker, with the intense glow of its fire, which, by the quantities of soot clustered above it, seemed to have been burning for ages. There was a distilling apparatus in full operation. Around the room were retorts, tubes, cylinders, crucibles, and other apparatus of chemical research. An electrical machine stood ready for immediate use. The atmosphere felt oppressively close, and was tainted with gaseous odors, which had been tormented forth by the processes of science. The severe and homely simplicity of the apartment, with its naked walls and brick pavement, looked strange, accustomed as Georgiana had become to the fantastic elegance of her boudoir. But what chiefly, indeed almost solely, drew her attention, was the aspect of Aylmer himself.

He was pale as death, anxious, and absorbed, and hung over the furnace as if it depended upon his utmost watchfulness whether the liquid, which it was distilling, should be the draught of immortal happiness or misery. How different from the sanguine and joyous mien that he had assumed for Georgiana's encouragement!

"Carefully now, Aminadab! Carefully, thou human machine! Carefully, thou man of clay!" muttered Aylmer, more to himself than his assistant. "Now, if there be a thought too much or too little, it is all over!"

"Hoh! hoh!" mumbled Aminadab—"look, master, look!"

Aylmer raised his eyes hastily, and at first reddened, then grew paler than ever, on beholding Georgiana. He rushed towards her, and seized her arm with a gripe that left the print of his fingers upon it.

"Why do you come hither? Have you no trust in your husband?" cried he impetuously. "Would you throw the blight of that fatal birth-mark over my labors? It is not well done. Go, prying woman, go!"

"Nay, Aylmer," said Georgiana, with the firmness of which she possessed no stinted endowment, "it is not you that have a right to complain. You mistrust your wife! You have concealed the anxiety with which you watch the development of this experiment. Think not so unworthily of me, my husband! Tell me all the risk we run; and fear not that I shall shrink, for my share in it is far less than your own!"

"No, no, Georgiana!" said Aylmer impatiently, "it must not be."

"I submit," replied she calmly. "And, Aylmer, I shall quaff whatever draught you bring me; but it will be on the same principle that would induce me to take a dose of poison, if offered by your hand."

"My noble wife," said Aylmer, deeply moved, "I knew not the height and depth of your nature, until now. Nothing shall be concealed. Know, then, that this Crimson Hand, superficial as it seems, has clutched its grasp into your being, with a strength of which I had no previous conception. I have already administered agents powerful enough to do aught except to change your entire physical system. Only one thing remains to be tried. If that fail us, we are ruined!"

"Why did you hesitate to tell me this?" asked she.

"Because, Georgiana," said Aylmer, in a low voice, "there is danger!"

"Danger? There is but one danger—that this horrible stigma shall be left upon my cheek!" cried Georgiana. "Remove it! remove it!—whatever be the cost—or we shall both go mad!"

"Heaven knows, your words are too true," said Aylmer, sadly. "And now, dearest, return to your boudoir. In a little while, all will be tested."

He conducted her back, and took leave of her with a solemn tenderness, which spoke far more than his words how much was now at stake. After his departure, Georgiana became wrapt in musings. She considered the character of Aylmer, and did it completer justice than at any previous moment. Her heart exulted, while it trembled, at his honorable love, so pure and lofty that it would accept nothing less than perfection, nor miserably make itself contented with an earthlier nature than he had dreamed of. She felt how much more precious was such a sentiment, than that meaner kind which would have borne with the imperfection for her sake, and have been guilty of treason to holy love, by degrading its perfect idea to the level of the actual. And, with her whole spirit, she prayed, that, for a single moment, she might satisfy his highest and deepest conception. Longer than one moment, she well knew, it could not be; for his spirit was ever on the march—ever ascending—and each instant required something that was beyond the scope of the instant before.

The sound of her husband's footsteps aroused her. He bore a crystal goblet, containing a liquor colorless as water, but bright enough to be the draught of immortality. Aylmer was pale; but it seemed rather the consequence of a highly wrought state of mind, and tension of spirit, than of fear or doubt.

"The concoction of the draught has been perfect," said he, in answer to Georgiana's look. "Unless all my science have deceived me, it cannot fail."

"Save on your account, my dearest Aylmer," observed his wife, "I might wish to put off this birth-mark of mortality by relinquishing mortality itself, in preference to any other mode. Life is but a sad possession to those who have attained precisely the degree of moral advancement at which I stand. Were I weaker and blinder, it might be happiness. Were I stronger, it might be endured hopefully. But, being what I find myself, methinks I am of all mortals the most fit to die."

"You are fit for heaven without tasting death!" replied her husband. "But why do we speak of dying? The draught cannot fail. Behold its effect upon this plant!"

On the window-seat there stood a geranium, diseased with yellow blotches, which had overspread all its leaves. Aylmer poured a small quantity of the liquid upon the soil in which it grew. In a little time, when the roots of the plant had taken up the moisture, the unsightly blotches began to be extinguished in a living verdure.

"There needed no proof," said Georgiana, quietly. "Give me the goblet. I joyfully stake all upon your word."

"Drink, then, thou lofty creature!" exclaimed Aylmer, with fervid admiration. "There is no taint of imperfection on thy spirit. Thy sensible frame, too, shall soon be all perfect!"

She quaffed the liquid, and returned the goblet to his hand.

"It is grateful," said she, with a placid smile. "Methinks it is like water from a heavenly fountain; for it contains I know not what of unobtrusive fragrance and deliciousness. It allays a feverish thirst, that had parched me for many days. Now, dearest, let me sleep. My earthly senses are closing over my spirit, like the leaves round the heart of a rose, at sunset."

She spoke the last words with a gentle reluctance, as if it required almost more energy than she could command to pronounce the faint and lingering syllables. Scarcely had they loitered through her lips, ere she was lost in slumber. Aylmer sat by her side, watching her aspect with the emotions proper to a man, the whole value of whose existence was involved in the process now to be tested. Mingled with this mood, however, was the philosophic investigation, characteristic of the man of science. Not the minutest symptom escaped him. A heightened flush of the cheek—a slight irregularity of breath—a quiver of the eyelid—a hardly perceptible tremor through the frame—such were the details which, as the moments passed, he wrote down in his folio volume. Intense thought had set its stamp upon every previous page of that volume; but the thoughts of years were all concentrated upon the last.

While thus employed, he failed not to gaze often at the fatal Hand, and not without a shudder. Yet once, by a strange and unaccountable impulse, he pressed it with his lips. His spirit recoiled, however, in the very act, and Georgiana, out of the midst of her deep sleep, moved uneasily and murmured, as if in remonstrance. Again, Aylmer resumed his watch. Nor was it without avail. The Crimson Hand, which at first had been strongly visible upon the marble paleness of Georgiana's cheek now grew more faintly outlined. She remained not less pale than ever; but the birth-mark, with every breath that came and went, lost somewhat of its former distinctness. Its presence had been awful; its departure was more awful still. Watch the stain of the rainbow fading out of the sky; and you will know how that mysterious symbol passed away.

"By Heaven, it is well nigh gone!" said Aylmer to himself, in almost irrepressible ecstasy. "I can scarcely trace it now. Success! Success! And now it is like the faintest rose-color. The slightest flush of blood across her cheek would overcome it. But she is so pale!"

He drew aside the window-curtain, and suffered the light of natural day to fall into the room, and rest upon her cheek. At the same time, he heard a gross, hoarse chuckle, which he had long known as his servant Aminadab's expression of delight.

"Ah, clod! Ah, earthly mass!" cried Aylmer, laughing in a sort of frenzy. "You have served me well! Matter and Spirit—Earth and Heaven—have both done their part in this! Laugh, thing of senses! You have earned the right to laugh."

These exclamations broke Georgiana's sleep. She slowly unclosed her eyes, and gazed into the mirror, which her husband had arranged for that purpose. A faint smile flitted over her lips, when she recognized how barely perceptible was now that Crimson Hand, which had once blazed forth with such disastrous brilliancy as to scare away all their happiness. But then her eyes sought Aylmer's face, with a trouble and anxiety that he could by no means account for.

"My poor Aylmer!" murmured she.

"Poor? Nay, richest! Happiest! Most favored!" exclaimed he. "My peerless bride, it is successful! You are perfect!"

"My poor Aylmer!" she repeated, with a more than human tenderness. "You have aimed loftily!—you have done nobly! Do not repent, that, with so high and pure a feeling, you have rejected the best that earth could offer. Aylmer—dearest Aylmer—I am dying!"

Alas, it was too true! The fatal Hand had grappled with the mystery of life, and was the bond by which an angelic spirit kept itself in union with a mortal frame. As the last crimson tint of the birth-mark—that sole token of human imperfection—faded from her cheek, the parting breath of the now perfect woman passed into the atmosphere, and her soul, lingering a moment near her husband, took its heavenward flight. Then a hoarse, chuckling laugh was heard again! Thus ever does the gross Fatality of Earth exult in its invariable triumph over the immortal essence, which, in this dim sphere of half-development, demands the completeness of a higher state. Yet, had Aylmer reached a profounder wisdom, he need not thus have flung away the happiness, which would have woven his mortal life of the self-same texture with the celestial. The momentary circumstance was too strong for him; he failed to look beyond the shadowy scope of Time, and living once for all in Eternity, to find the perfect Future in the present.

1843

Rappaccini's Daughter[1]

From the Writings of Aubépine[2]

We do not remember to have seen any translated specimens of the productions of M. de l'Aubépine; a fact the less to be wondered at, as his very name is unknown to many of his own countrymen, as well as to the student of

---

[1] First published in 1844 in *The United States Magazine and Democratic Review* and included in *Mosses from an Old Manse* (1846).

[2] Hawthorne.

foreign literature. As a writer, he seems to occupy an unfortunate position between the Transcendentalists (who, under one name or another, have their share in all the current literature of the world), and the great body of pen-and-ink men who address the intellect and sympathies of the multitude. If not too refined, at all events too remote, too shadowy and unsubstantial in his modes of development, to suit the taste of the latter class, and yet too popular to satisfy the spiritual or metaphysical requisitions of the former, he must necessarily find himself without an audience; except here and there an individual, or possibly an isolated clique. His writings, to do them justice, are not altogether destitute of fancy and originality; they might have won him greater reputation but for an inveterate love of allegory, which is apt to invest his plots and characters with the aspect of scenery and people in the clouds, and to steal away the human warmth out of his conceptions. His fictions are sometimes historical, sometimes of the present day, and sometimes, so far as can be discovered, have little or no reference either to time or space. In any case, he generally contents himself with a very slight embroidery of outward manners,—the faintest possible counterfeit of real life,—and endeavors to create an interest by some less obvious peculiarity of the subject. Occasionally, a breath of nature, a rain-drop of pathos and tenderness, or a gleam of humor, will find its way into the midst of his fantastic imagery, and make us feel as if, after all, we were yet within the limits of our native earth. We will only add to this very cursory notice, that M. de l'Aubépine's productions, if the reader chance to take them in precisely the proper point of view, may amuse a leisure hour as well as those of a brighter man; if otherwise, they can hardly fail to look excessively like nonsense.

Our author is voluminous; he continues to write and publish with as much praiseworthy and indefatigable prolixity, as if his efforts were crowned with the brilliant success that so justly attends those of Eugene Sue.[3] His first appearance was by a collection of stories, in a long series of volumes, entitled "*Contes deux fois recontées*." The titles of some of his more recent works (we quote from memory) are as follows:—"*Le Voyage Céleste à Chemin de Fer*," 3 tom. 1838. "*Le nouveau Père Adam et la nouvelle Mère Eve*," 2 tom. 1839. "*Roderic; ou le Serpent à l'estomac*," 2 tom. 1840. "*Le Culte de Feu*," a folio volume of ponderous research into the religion and ritual of the old Persian Ghebers, published in 1841. "*La Soirée du Château en Espagne*," 1 tom. 8 vo. 1842; and "*L'Artiste du Beau; ou le Papillon Mécanique*," 5 tom. 4to. 1843. Our somewhat wearisome perusal of this startling catalogue of volumes has left behind it a certain personal affection and sympathy, though by no means admiration, for M. de l'Aubépine; and we would fain do the little in our power towards introducing him favorably to the American public. The ensuing tale is a translation of his "*Beatrice; ou la Belle Empoisonneuse*," recently published in "*La Revue Anti-Aristocratique*." This journal, edited by the Comte de Bearhaven, has, for some years past, led the defence

[3]A popular French novelist (1804–1857).

of liberal principles and popular rights, with a faithfulness and ability worthy of all praise.[4]

A young man, named Giovanni Guasconti, came, very long ago, from the more southern region of Italy, to pursue his studies at the University of Padua. Giovanni, who had but a scanty supply of gold ducats in his pocket, took lodgings in a high and gloomy chamber of an old edifice, which looked not unworthy to have been the palace of a Paduan noble, and which, in fact, exhibited over its entrance the armorial bearings of a family long since extinct. The young stranger, who was not unstudied in the great poem of his country, recollected that one of the ancestors of this family, and perhaps an occupant of this very mansion, had been pictured by Dante as a partaker of the immortal agonies of his Inferno. These reminiscences and associations, together with the tendency to heart-break natural to a young man for the first time out of his native sphere, caused Giovanni to sigh heavily, as he looked around the desolate and ill-furnished apartment.

"Holy Virgin, Signor," cried old dame Lisabetta, who, won by the youth's remarkable beauty of person, was kindly endeavoring to give the chamber a habitable air, "what a sigh was that to come out of a young man's heart! Do you find this old mansion gloomy? For the love of heaven, then, put your head out of the window, and you will see as bright sunshine as you have left in Naples."

Guasconti mechanically did as the old woman advised, but could not quite agree with her that the Paduan sunshine was as cheerful as that of southern Italy. Such as it was, however, it fell upon a garden beneath the window, and expended its fostering influences on a variety of plants, which seemed to have been cultivated with exceeding care.

"Does this garden belong to the house?" asked Giovanni.

"Heaven forbid, Signor!—unless it were fruitful of better pot-herbs than any that grow there now," answered old Lisabetta. "No; that garden is cultivated by the own hands of Signor Giacomo Rappaccini, the famous Doctor, who, I warrant him, has been heard of as far as Naples. It is said that he distils these plants into medicines that are as potent as a charm. Oftentimes you may see the Signor Doctor at work, and perchance the Signora his daughter, too, gathering the strange flowers that grow in the garden."

The old woman had now done what she could for the aspect of the chamber, and, commending the young man to the protection of the saints, took her departure.

Giovanni still found no better occupation than to look down into the garden beneath his window. From its appearance, he judged it to be one of those botanic gardens, which were of earlier date in Padua than elsewhere in Italy, or in the world. Or, not improbably, it might once have been the pleasure-place of an opulent family; for there was the ruin of a marble

---

[4]Hawthorne's mock review of himself gives French renderings of *Twice-Told Tales*, the titles of individual stories, and *The Demo-* *cratic Review* (edited by his friend John O'Sullivan).

fountain in the centre, sculptured with rare art, but so wofully shattered that it was impossible to trace the original design from the chaos of remaining fragments. The water, however, continued to gush and sparkle into the sunbeams as cheerfully as ever. A little gurgling sound ascended to the young man's window, and made him feel as if the fountain were an immortal spirit, that sung its song unceasingly, and without heeding the vicissitudes around it; while one century embodied it in marble, and another scattered the perishable garniture on the soil. All about the pool into which the water subsided, grew various plants, that seemed to require a plentiful supply of moisture for the nourishment of gigantic leaves, and, in some instances, flowers gorgeously magnificent. There was one shrub in particular, set in a marble vase in the midst of the pool, that bore a profusion of purple blossoms, each of which had the lustre and richness of a gem; and the whole together made a show so resplendent that it seemed enough to illuminate the garden, even had there been no sunshine. Every portion of the soil was peopled with plants and herbs, which, if less beautiful, still bore tokens of assiduous care; as if all had their individual virtues, known to the scientific mind that fostered them. Some were placed in urns, rich with old carving, and others in common garden-pots; some crept serpent-like along the ground, or climbed on high, using whatever means of ascent was offered them. One plant had wreathed itself round a statue of Vertumnus,[5] which was thus quite veiled and shrouded in a drapery of hanging foliage, so happily arranged that it might have served a sculptor for a study.

While Giovanni stood at the window, he heard a rustling behind a screen of leaves, and became aware that a person was at work in the garden. His figure soon emerged into view, and showed itself to be that of no common laborer, but a tall, emaciated, sallow, and sickly-looking man, dressed in a scholar's garb of black. He was beyond the middle term of life, with grey hair, a thin grey beard, and a face singularly marked with intellect and cultivation, but which could never, even in his more youthful days, have expressed much warmth of heart.

Nothing could exceed the intentness with which this scientific gardener examined every shrub which grew in his path; it seemed as if he was looking into their inmost nature, making observations in regard to their creative essence, and discovering why one leaf grew in this shape, and another in that, and wherefore such and such flowers differed among themselves in hue and perfume. Nevertheless, in spite of this deep intelligence on his part, there was no approach to intimacy between himself and these vegetable existences. On the contrary, he avoided their actual touch, or the direct inhaling of their odors, with a caution that impressed Giovanni most disagreeably; for the man's demeanor was that of one walking among malignant influences, such as savage beasts, or deadly snakes, or evil spirits,

[5]The Roman god of changing seasons and thus of flowers and fruits, married to Pomona. Hawthorne's garden imagery includes allusions not only to classical myth but to the Garden of Eden, the Song of Songs, the Romance of the Rose, Dante, Spenser, and the University of Padua's experimental botanical gardens (founded in 1545).

which, should he allow them one moment of license, would wreak upon him some terrible fatality. It was strangely frightful to the young man's imagination, to see this air of insecurity in a person cultivating a garden, that most simple and innocent of human toils, and which had been alike the joy and labor of the unfallen parents of the race. Was this garden, then, the Eden of the present world?—and this man, with such a perception of harm in what his own hands caused to grow, was he the Adam?

The distrustful gardener, while plucking away the dead leaves or pruning the too luxuriant growth of the shrubs, defended his hands with a pair of thick gloves. Nor were these his only armor. When, in his walk through the garden, he came to the magnificent plant that hung its purple gems beside the marble fountain, he placed a kind of mask over his mouth and nostrils, as if all this beauty did but conceal a deadlier malice. But finding his task still too dangerous, he drew back, removed the mask, and called loudly, but in the infirm voice of a person affected with inward disease:

"Beatrice!—Beatrice!"[6]

"Here am I, my father! What would you?" cried a rich and youthful voice from the window of the opposite house; a voice as rich as a tropical sunset, and which made Giovanni, though he knew not why, think of deep hues of purple or crimson, and of perfumes heavily delectable.—"Are you in the garden?"

"Yes, Beatrice," answered the gardener, "and I need your help."

Soon there emerged from under a sculptured portal the figure of a young girl, arrayed with as much richness of taste as the most splendid of the flowers, beautiful as the day, and with a bloom so deep and vivid that one shade more would have been too much. She looked redundant with life, health, and energy; all of which attributes were bound down and compressed, as it were, and girdled tensely, in their luxuriance, by her virgin zone.[7] Yet Giovanni's fancy must have grown morbid, while he looked down into the garden; for the impression which the fair stranger made upon him was as if here were another flower, the human sister of those vegetable ones, as beautiful as they—more beautiful than the richest of them—but still to be touched only with a glove, nor to be approached without a mask. As Beatrice came down the garden path, it was observable that she handled and inhaled the odor of several of the plants, which her father had most sedulously avoided.

"Here, Beatrice," said the latter,—"see how many needful offices require to be done to our chief treasure. Yet, shattered as I am, my life might pay the penalty of approaching it so closely as circumstances demand. Henceforth, I fear, this plant must be consigned to your sole charge."

"And gladly will I undertake it," cried again the rich tones of the young lady, as she bent towards the magnificent plant, and opened her arms as if

---

[6]The name, literally "she who makes happy," is also that of Dante's beloved Beatrice Portonari (1266–1290), immortalized in his *Divine Comedy*.

[7]Belt worn by a young unmarried woman.

to embrace it. "Yes, my sister, my splendor, it shall be Beatrice's task to nurse and serve thee; and thou shalt reward her with thy kisses and perfumed breath, which to her is as the breath of life!"

Then, with all the tenderness in her manner that was so strikingly expressed in her words, she busied herself with such attentions as the plant seemed to require; and Giovanni, at his lofty window, rubbed his eyes, and almost doubted whether it were a girl tending her favorite flower, or one sister performing the duties of affection to another. The scene soon terminated. Whether Doctor Rappaccini had finished his labors in the garden, or that his watchful eye had caught the stranger's face, he now took his daughter's arm and retired. Night was already closing in; oppressive exhalations seemed to proceed from the plants, and steal upward past the open window; and Giovanni, closing the lattice, went to his couch, and dreamed of a rich flower and beautiful girl. Flower and maiden were different and yet the same, and fraught with some strange peril in either shape.

But there is an influence in the light of morning that tends to rectify whatever errors of fancy, or even of judgment, we may have incurred during the sun's decline, or among the shadows of the night, or in the less wholesome glow of moonshine. Giovanni's first movement on starting from sleep, was to throw open the window, and gaze down into the garden which his dreams had made so fertile of mysteries. He was surprised, and a little ashamed, to find how real and matter-of-fact an affair it proved to be, in the first rays of the sun, which gilded the dew-drops that hung upon leaf and blossom, and, while giving a brighter beauty to each rare flower, brought everything within the limits of ordinary experience. The young man rejoiced, that, in the heart of the barren city, he had the privilege of overlooking this spot of lovely and luxuriant vegetation. It would serve, he said to himself, as a symbolic language, to keep him in communion with Nature. Neither the sickly and thought-worn Doctor Giacomo Rappaccini, it is true, nor his brilliant daughter, were now visible; so that Giovanni could not determine how much of the singularity which he attributed to both, was due to their own qualities, and how much to his wonder-working fancy. But he was inclined to take a most rational view of the whole matter.

In the course of the day, he paid his respects to Signor Pietro Baglioni, professor of medicine in the University, a physician of eminent repute, to whom Giovanni had brought a letter of introduction. The Professor was an elderly personage, apparently of genial nature, and habits that might almost be called jovial; he kept the young man to dinner, and made himself very agreeable by the freedom and liveliness of his conversation, especially when warmed by a flask or two of Tuscan wine. Giovanni, conceiving that men of science, inhabitants of the same city, must needs be on familiar terms with one another, took an opportunity to mention the name of Doctor Rappaccini. But the Professor did not respond with so much cordiality as he had anticipated.

"Ill would it become a teacher of the divine art of medicine," said Professor Pietro Baglioni, in answer to a question of Giovanni, "to withhold due and well-considered praise of a physician so eminently skilled as Rappaccini.

But, on the other hand, I should answer it but scantily to my conscience, were I to permit a worthy youth like yourself, Signor Giovanni, the son of an ancient friend, to imbibe erroneous ideas respecting a man who might hereafter chance to hold your life and death in his hands. The truth is, our worshipful Doctor Rappaccini has as much science as any member of the faculty—with perhaps one single exception—in Padua, or all Italy. But there are certain grave objections to his professional character."

"And what are they?" asked the young man.

"Has my friend Giovanni any disease of body or heart, that he is so inquisitive about physicians?" said the Professor, with a smile. "But as for Rappaccini, it is said of him—and I, who know the man well, can answer for its truth—that he cares infinitely more for science than for mankind. His patients are interesting to him only as subjects for some new experiment. He would sacrifice human life, his own among the rest, or whatever else was dearest to him, for the sake of adding so much as a grain of mustard-seed to the great heap of his accumulated knowledge."

"Methinks he is an awful man, indeed," remarked Guasconti, mentally recalling the cold and purely intellectual aspect of Rappaccini. "And yet, worshipful Professor, is it not a noble spirit? Are there many men capable of so spiritual a love of science?"

"God forbid," answered the Professor, somewhat testily—"at least, unless they take sounder views of the healing art than those adopted by Rappaccini. It is his theory, that all medicinal virtues are comprised within those substances which we term vegetable poisons. These he cultivates with his own hands, and is said even to have produced new varieties of poison, more horribly deleterious than Nature, without the assistance of this learned person, would ever have plagued the world withal. That the Signor Doctor does less mischief than might be expected, with such dangerous substances, is undeniable. Now and then, it must be owned, he has effected—or seemed to effect—a marvellous cure. But, to tell you my private mind, Signor Giovanni, he should receive little credit for such instances of success—they being probably the work of chance—but should be held strictly accountable for his failures, which may justly be considered his own work."

The youth might have taken Baglioni's opinions with many grains of allowance, had he known that there was a professional warfare of long continuance between him and Doctor Rappaccini, in which the latter was generally thought to have gained the advantage. If the reader be inclined to judge for himself, we refer him to certain black-letter tracts on both sides, preserved in the medical department of the University of Padua.

"I know not, most learned Professor," returned Giovanni, after musing on what had been said of Rappaccini's exclusive zeal for science—"I know not how dearly this physician may love his art; but surely there is one object more dear to him. He has a daughter."

"Aha!" cried the Professor with a laugh. "So now our friend Giovanni's secret is out. You have heard of this daughter, whom all the young men in Padua are wild about, though not half a dozen have ever had the good hap to see her face. I know little of the Signora Beatrice, save that Rappaccini is said to have instructed her deeply in his science, and that, young and beautiful as fame reports her, she is already qualified to fill a professor's chair. Perchance her father destines her for mine! Other absurd rumors there be, not worth talking about, or listening to. So now, Signor Giovanni, drink off your glass of Lacryma."[8]

Guasconti returned to his lodgings somewhat heated with the wine he had quaffed, and which caused his brain to swim with strange fantasies in reference to Doctor Rappaccini and the beautiful Beatrice. On his way, happening to pass by a florist's, he bought a fresh bouquet of flowers.

Ascending to his chamber, he seated himself near the window, but within the shadow thrown by the depth of the wall, so that he could look down into the garden with little risk of being discovered. All beneath his eye was a solitude. The strange plants were basking in the sunshine, and now and then nodding gently to one another, as if in acknowledgment of sympathy and kindred. In the midst, by the shattered fountain, grew the magnificent shrub, with its purple gems clustering all over it; they glowed in the air, and gleamed back again out of the depths of the pool, which thus seemed to overflow with colored radiance from the rich reflection that was steeped in it. At first, as we have said, the garden was a solitude. Soon, however,—as Giovanni had half-hoped, half-feared, would be the case,—a figure appeared beneath the antique sculptured portal, and came down between the rows of plants, inhaling their various perfumes, as if she were one of those beings of old classic fable, that lived upon sweet odors. On again beholding Beatrice, the young man was even startled to perceive how much her beauty exceeded his recollection of it; so brilliant, so vivid was its character, that she glowed amid the sunlight, and, as Giovanni whispered to himself, positively illuminated the more shadowy intervals of the garden path. Her face being now more revealed than on the former occasion, he was struck by its expression of simplicity and sweetness; qualities that had not entered into his idea of her character, and which made him ask anew, what manner of mortal she might be. Nor did he fail again to observe, or imagine, an analogy between the beautiful girl and the gorgeous shrub that hung its gem-like flowers over the fountain; a resemblance which Beatrice seemed to have indulged a fantastic humor in heightening, both by the arrangement of her dress and the selection of its hues.

Approaching the shrub, she threw open her arms, as with a passionate ardor, and drew its branches into an intimate embrace; so intimate, that her features were hidden in its leafy bosom, and her glistening ringlets all intermingled with the flowers.

"Give me thy breath, my sister," exclaimed Beatrice; "for I am faint with common air! And give me this flower of thine, which I separate with gentlest fingers from the stem, and place it close beside my heart."

[8]Lachryma Christi ("Tears of Christ"), a famous Italian white wine.

With these words, the beautiful daughter of Rappaccini plucked one of the richest blossoms of the shrub, and was about to fasten it in her bosom. But now, unless Giovanni's draughts of wine had bewildered his senses, a singular incident occurred. A small orange-colored reptile, of the lizard or chameleon species, chanced to be creeping along the path, just at the feet of Beatrice. It appeared to Giovanni—but, at the distance from which he gazed, he could scarcely have seen anything so minute—it appeared to him, however, that a drop or two of moisture from the broken stem of the flower descended upon the lizard's head. For an instant, the reptile contorted itself violently, and then lay motionless in the sunshine. Beatrice observed this remarkable phenomenon, and crossed herself, sadly, but without surprise; nor did she therefore hesitate to arrange the fatal flower in her bosom. There it blushed, and almost glimmered with the dazzling effect of a precious stone, adding to her dress and aspect the one appropriate charm, which nothing else in the world could have supplied. But Giovanni, out of the shadow of his window, bent forward and shrank back, and murmured and trembled.

"Am I awake? Have I my senses?" said he to himself. "What is this being?—beautiful, shall I call her?—or inexpressibly terrible?"

Beatrice now strayed carelessly through the garden, approaching closer beneath Giovanni's window, so that he was compelled to thrust his head quite out of its concealment in order to gratify the intense and painful curiosity which she excited. At this moment, there came a beautiful insect over the garden wall; it had perhaps wandered through the city and found no flowers nor verdure among those antique haunts of men, until the heavy perfumes of Doctor Rappaccini's shrubs had lured it from afar. Without alighting on the flowers, this winged brightness seemed to be attracted by Beatrice, and lingered in the air and fluttered about her head. Now, here it could not be but that Giovanni Guasconti's eyes deceived him. Be that as it might, he fancied that while Beatrice was gazing at the insect with childish delight, it grew faint and fell at her feet;—its bright wings shivered; it was dead—from no cause that he could discern, unless it were the atmosphere of her breath. Again Beatrice crossed herself and sighed heavily, as she bent over the dead insect.

An impulsive movement of Giovanni drew her eyes to the window. There she beheld the beautiful head of the young man—rather a Grecian than an Italian head, with fair, regular features, and a glistening of gold among his ringlets—gazing down upon her like a being that hovered in midair. Scarcely knowing what he did, Giovanni threw down the bouquet which he had hitherto held in his hand.

"Signora," said he, "there are pure and healthful flowers. Wear them for the sake of Giovanni Guasconti!"

"Thanks, Signor," replied Beatrice, with her rich voice, that came forth as it were like a gush of music; and with a mirthful expression half childish and half woman-like. "I accept your gift, and would fain recompense it with this precious purple flower; but if I toss it into the air, it will not reach you. So Signor Guasconti must even content himself with my thanks."

She lifted the bouquet from the ground, and then as if inwardly ashamed at having stepped aside from her maidenly reserve to respond to a stranger's greeting, passed swiftly homeward through the garden. But, few as the moments were, it seemed to Giovanni when she was on the point of vanishing beneath the sculptured portal, that his beautiful bouquet was already beginning to wither in her grasp. It was an idle thought; there could be no possibility of distinguishing a faded flower from a fresh one at so great a distance.

For many days after this incident, the young man avoided the window that looked into Doctor Rappaccini's garden, as if something ugly and monstrous would have blasted his eyesight, had he been betrayed into a glance. He felt conscious of having put himself, to a certain extent, within the influence of an unintelligible power, by the communication which he had opened with Beatrice. The wisest course would have been, if his heart were in any real danger, to quit his lodgings and Padua itself, at once; the next wiser, to have accustomed himself, as far as possible, to the familiar and day-light view of Beatrice; thus bringing her rigidly and systematically within the limits of ordinary experience. Least of all, while avoiding her sight, ought Giovanni to have remained so near this extraordinary being, that the proximity and possibility even of intercourse, should give a kind of substance and reality to the wild vagaries which his imagination ran riot continually in producing. Guasconti had not a deep heart—or at all events, its depths were not sounded now—but he had a quick fancy, and an ardent southern temperament, which rose every instant to a higher fever-pitch. Whether or no Beatrice possessed those terrible attributes—that fatal breath—the affinity with those so beautiful and deadly flowers—which were indicated by what Giovanni had witnessed, she had at least instilled a fierce and subtle poison into his system. It was not love, although her rich beauty was a madness to him; nor horror, even while he fancied her spirit to be imbued with the same baneful essence that seemed to pervade her physical frame; but a wild offspring of both love and horror that had each parent in it, and burned like one and shivered like the other. Giovanni knew not what to dread; still less did he know what to hope; yet hope and dread kept a continual warfare in his breast, alternately vanquishing one another and starting up afresh to renew the contest. Blessed are all simple emotions, be they dark or bright! It is the lurid intermixture of the two that produces the illuminating blaze of the infernal regions.

Sometimes he endeavored to assuage the fever of his spirit by a rapid walk through the streets of Padua, or beyond its gates; his footsteps kept time with the throbbings of his brain, so that the walk was apt to accelerate itself to a race. One day, he found himself arrested; his arm was seized by a portly personage who had turned back on recognizing the young man, and expended much breath in overtaking him.

"Signor Giovanni!—stay, my young friend!" cried he. "Have you forgotten me? That might well be the case, if I were as much altered as yourself."

It was Baglioni, whom Giovanni had avoided, ever since their first meeting, from a doubt that the Professor's sagacity would look too deeply into his secrets. Endeavoring to recover himself, he stared forth wildly from his inner world into the outer one, and spoke like a man in a dream:

"Yes; I am Giovanni Guasconti. You are Professor Pietro Baglioni. Now let me pass!"

"Not yet—not yet, Signor Giovanni Guasconti," said the Professor, smiling, but at the same time scrutinizing the youth with an earnest glance.— "What; did I grow up side by side with your father, and shall his son pass me like a stranger, in these old streets of Padua? Stand still, Signor Giovanni; for we must have a word or two, before we part."

"Speedily, then, most worshipful Professor, speedily!" said Giovanni, with feverish impatience. "Does not your worship see that I am in haste?"

Now, while he was speaking, there came a man in black along the street, stooping and moving feebly, like a person in inferior health. His face was all overspread with a most sickly and sallow hue, but yet so pervaded with an expression of piercing and active intellect, that an observer might easily have overlooked the merely physical attributes, and have seen only this wonderful energy. As he passed, this person exchanged a cold and distant salutation with Baglioni, but fixed his eyes upon Giovanni with an intentness that seemed to bring out whatever was within him worthy of notice. Nevertheless, there was a peculiar quietness in the look, as if taking merely a speculative, not a human, interest in the young man.

"It is Doctor Rappaccini!" whispered the Professor, when the stranger had passed.—"Has he ever seen your face before?"

"Not that I know," answered Giovanni, starting at the name.

"He *has* seen you!—he must have seen you!" said Baglioni, hastily. "For some purpose or other, this man of science is making a study of you. I know that look of his! It is the same that coldly illuminates his face, as he bends over a bird, a mouse, or a butterfly, which, in pursuance of some experiment, he has killed by the perfume of a flower;—a look as deep as nature itself, but without Nature's warmth of love. Signor Giovanni, I will stake my life upon it, you are the subject of one of Rappaccini's experiments!"

"Will you make a fool of me?" cried Giovanni, passionately. "*That*, Signor Professor, were an untoward experiment."

"Patience, patience!" replied the imperturbable Professor.—"I tell thee, my poor Giovanni, that Rappaccini has a scientific interest in thee. Thou hast fallen into fearful hands! And the Signora Beatrice? What part does she act in this mystery?"

But Guasconti, finding Baglioni's pertinacity intolerable, here broke away, and was gone before the Professor could again seize his arm. He looked after the young man intently, and shook his head.

"This must not be," said Baglioni to himself. "The youth is the son of my old friend, and shall not come to any harm from which the arcana of medical science can preserve him. Besides, it is too insufferable an impertinence in Rappaccini, thus to snatch the lad out of my own hands, as I may say, and make use of him for his infernal experiments. This daughter of his! It shall be looked to. Perchance, most learned Rappaccini, I may foil you where you little dream of it!"

Meanwhile, Giovanni had pursued a circuitous route, and at length found himself at the door of his lodgings. As he crossed the threshold, he was met by old Lisabetta, who smirked and smiled, and was evidently desirous to attract his attention; vainly, however, as the ebullition of his feelings had momentarily subsided into a cold and dull vacuity. He turned his eyes full upon the withered face that was puckering itself into a smile, but seemed to behold it not. The old dame, therefore, laid her grasp upon his cloak.

"Signor!—Signor!" whispered she, still with a smile over the whole breadth of her visage, so that it looked not unlike a grotesque carving in wood, darkened by centuries—"Listen, Signor! There is a private entrance into the garden!"

"What do you say?" exclaimed Giovanni, turning quickly about, as if an inanimate thing should start into feverish life.—"A private entrance into Doctor Rappaccini's garden!"

"Hush! hush!—not so loud!" whispered Lisabetta, putting her hand over his mouth. "Yes; into the worshipful Doctor's garden, where you may see all his fine shrubbery. Many a young man in Padua would give gold to be admitted among those flowers."

Giovanni put a piece of gold into her hand.

"Show me the way," said he.

A surmise, probably excited by his conversation with Baglioni, crossed his mind, that this interposition of old Lisabetta might perchance be connected with the intrigue, whatever were its nature, in which the Professor seemed to suppose that Doctor Rappaccini was involving him. But such a suspicion, though it disturbed Giovanni, was inadequate to restrain him. The instant that he was aware of the possibility of approaching Beatrice, it seemed an absolute necessity of his existence to do so. It mattered not whether she were angel or demon; he was irrevocably within her sphere, and must obey the law that whirled him onward, in ever lessening circles, towards a result which he did not attempt to foreshadow. And yet, strange to say, there came across him a sudden doubt, whether this intense interest on his part were not delusory—whether it were really of so deep and positive a nature as to justify him in now thrusting himself into an incalculable position—whether it were not merely the fantasy of a young man's brain, only slightly, or not at all, connected with his heart!

He paused—hesitated—turned half about—but again went on. His withered guide led him along several obscure passages, and finally undid a door, through which, as it was opened, there came the sight and sound of rustling leaves, with the broken sunshine glimmering among them. Giovanni stepped forth, and forcing himself through the entanglement of a shrub that wreathed its tendrils over the hidden entrance, he stood beneath his own window, in the open area of Doctor Rappaccini's garden.

How often is it the case, that, when impossibilities have come to pass, and dreams have condensed their misty substance into tangible realities, we find ourselves calm, and even coldly self-possessed, amid circumstances which it would have been a delirium of joy or agony to anticipate! Fate delights to thwart us thus. Passion will choose his own time to rush upon the scene, and lingers sluggishly behind, when an appropriate adjustment of events would seem to summon his appearance. So was it now with Giovanni. Day after day, his pulses had throbbed with feverish blood, at the improbable idea of an interview with Beatrice, and of standing with her, face to face, in this very garden, basking in the Oriental sunshine of her beauty, and snatching from her full gaze the mystery which he deemed the riddle of his own existence. But now there was a singular and untimely equanimity within his breast. He threw a glance around the garden to discover if Beatrice or her father were present, and perceiving that he was alone, began a critical observation of the plants.

The aspect of one and all of them dissatisfied him; their gorgeousness seemed fierce, passionate, and even unnatural. There was hardly an individual shrub which a wanderer, straying by himself through a forest, would not have been startled to find growing wild, as if an unearthly face had glared at him out of the thicket. Several, also, would have shocked a delicate instinct by an appearance of artificialness, indicating that there had been such commixture, and, as it were, adultery of various vegetable species, that the production was no longer of God's making, but the monstrous offspring of man's depraved fancy, glowing with only an evil mockery of beauty. They were probably the result of experiment, which, in one or two cases, had succeeded in mingling plants individually lovely into a compound possessing the questionable and ominous character that distinguished the whole growth of the garden. In fine, Giovanni recognized but two or three plants in the collection, and those of a kind that he well knew to be poisonous. While busy with these contemplations, he heard the rustling of a silken garment, and turning, beheld Beatrice emerging from beneath the sculptured portal.

Giovanni had not considered with himself what should be his deportment; whether he should apologize for his intrusion into the garden, or assume that he was there with the privity, at least, if not by the desire, of Doctor Rappaccini or his daughter. But Beatrice's manner placed him at his ease, though leaving him still in doubt by what agency he had gained admittance. She came lightly along the path, and met him near the broken fountain. There was surprise in her face, but brightened by a simple and kind expression of pleasure.

"You are a connoisseur in flowers, Signor," said Beatrice with a smile, alluding to the bouquet which he had flung her from the window. "It is no marvel, therefore, if the sight of my father's rare collection has tempted you to take a nearer view. If he were here, he could tell you many strange and interesting facts as to the nature and habits of these shrubs, for he has spent a life-time in such studies, and this garden is his world."

"And yourself, lady"—observed Giovanni—"if fame says true—you, likewise, are deeply skilled in the virtues indicated by these rich blossoms, and these spicy perfumes. Would you deign to be my instructress, I should prove an apter scholar than if taught by Signor Rappaccini himself."

"Are there such idle rumors?" asked Beatrice, with the music of a pleasant laugh. "Do people say that I am skilled in my father's science of plants? What a jest is there! No; though I have grown up among these flowers, I know no more of them than their hues and perfume; and sometimes, methinks I would fain rid myself of even that small knowledge. There are many flowers here, and those not the least brilliant, that shock and offend me, when they meet my eye. But, pray, Signor, do not believe these stories about my science. Believe nothing of me save what you see with your own eyes."

"And must I believe all that I have seen with my own eyes?" asked Giovanni pointedly, while the recollection of former scenes made him shrink. "No, Signora, you demand too little of me. Bid me believe nothing, save what comes from your own lips."

It would appear that Beatrice understood him. There came a deep flush to her cheek; but she looked full into Giovanni's eyes, and responded to his gaze of uneasy suspicion with a queen-like haughtiness.

"I do so bid you, Signor!" she replied. "Forget whatever you may have fancied in regard to me. If true to the outward senses, still it may be false in its essence. But the words of Beatrice Rappaccini's lips are true from the depths of the heart outward. Those you may believe!"

A fervor glowed in her whole aspect, and beamed upon Giovanni's consciousness like the light of truth itself. But while she spoke, there was a fragrance in the atmosphere around her, rich and delightful, though evanescent, yet which the young man, from an indefinable reluctance, scarcely dared to draw into his lungs. It might be the odor of the flowers. Could it be Beatrice's breath, which thus embalmed her words with a strange richness, as if by steeping them in her heart? A faintness passed like a shadow over Giovanni, and flitted away; he seemed to gaze through the beautiful girl's eyes into her transparent soul, and felt no more doubt or fear.

The tinge of passion that had colored Beatrice's manner vanished; she became gay, and appeared to derive a pure delight from her communion with the youth, not unlike what the maiden of a lonely island might have felt, conversing with a voyager from the civilized world. Evidently her experience of life had been confined within the limits of that garden. She talked now about matters as simple as the day-light or summer-clouds, and now asked questions in reference to the city, or Giovanni's distant home, his friends, his mother, and his sisters; questions indicating such seclusion, and such lack of familiarity with modes and forms, that Giovanni responded as if to an infant. Her spirit gushed out before him like a fresh rill, that was just catching its first glimpse of the sunlight, and wondering at the reflections of earth and sky which were flung into its bosom. There came thoughts, too, from a deep source, and fantasies of a gem-like brilliancy, as if diamonds and rubies sparkled upward among the bubbles of the fountain.

Ever and anon, there gleamed across the young man's mind a sense of wonder, that he should be walking side by side with the being who had so
wrought upon his imagination—whom he had idealized in such hues of
terror—in whom he had positively witnessed such manifestations of dreadful attributes—that he should be conversing with Beatrice like a brother,
and should find her so human and so maiden-like. But such reflections were
only momentary; the effect of her character was too real, not to make itself
familiar at once.

In this free intercourse, they had strayed through the garden, and now,
after many turns among its avenues, were come to the shattered fountain,
beside which grew the magnificent shrub with its treasury of glowing blossoms. A fragrance was diffused from it, which Giovanni recognized as identical with that which he had attributed to Beatrice's breath, but incomparably
more powerful. As her eyes fell upon it, Giovanni beheld her press her hand
to her bosom, as if her heart were throbbing suddenly and painfully.

"For the first time in my life," murmured she, addressing the shrub, "I
had forgotten thee!"

"I remember, Signora," said Giovanni, "that you once promised to
reward me with one of these living gems for the bouquet, which I had the
happy boldness to fling to your feet. Permit me now to pluck it as a memorial of this interview."

He made a step towards the shrub, with extended hand. But Beatrice
darted forward, uttering a shriek that went through his heart like a dagger.
She caught his hand, and drew it back with the whole force of her slender
figure. Giovanni felt her touch thrilling through his fibres.

"Touch it not!" exclaimed she, in a voice of agony. "Not for thy life! It is
fatal!"

Then, hiding her face, she fled from him, and vanished beneath the
sculptured portal. As Giovanni followed her with his eyes, he beheld the
emaciated figure and pale intelligence of Doctor Rappaccini, who had been
watching the scene, he knew not how long, within the shadow of the
entrance.

No sooner was Guasconti alone in his chamber, than the image of Beatrice came back to his passionate musings, invested with all the witchery
that had been gathering around it ever since his first glimpse of her, and
now likewise imbued with a tender warmth of girlish womanhood. She was
human: her nature was endowed with all gentle and feminine qualities; she
was worthiest to be worshipped; she was capable, surely, on her part, of the
height and heroism of love. Those tokens, which he had hitherto considered
as proofs of a frightful peculiarity in her physical and moral system, were
now either forgotten, or, by the subtle sophistry of passion, transmuted into
a golden crown of enchantment, rendering Beatrice the more admirable, by
so much as she was the more unique. Whatever had looked ugly, was now
beautiful; or, if incapable of such a change, it stole away and hid itself
among those shapeless half-ideas, which throng the dim region beyond the
daylight of our perfect consciousness. Thus did he spend the night, nor fell

asleep, until the dawn had begun to awake the slumbering flowers in Doctor Rappaccini's garden, whither Giovanni's dreams doubtless led him. Up rose the sun in his due season, and flinging his beams upon the young man's eyelids, awoke him to a sense of pain. When thoroughly aroused, he became sensible of a burning and tingling agony in his hand—in his right hand— the very hand which Beatrice had grasped in her own, when he was on the point of plucking one of the gem-like flowers. On the back of that hand there was now a purple print, like that of four small fingers, and the likeness of a slender thumb upon his wrist.

Oh, how stubbornly does love—or even that cunning semblance of love which flourishes in the imagination, but strikes no depth of root into the heart—how stubbornly does it hold its faith, until the moment come, when it is doomed to vanish into thin mist! Giovanni wrapt a handkerchief about his hand, and wondered what evil thing had stung him, and soon forgot his pain in a reverie of Beatrice.

After the first interview, a second was in the inevitable course of what we call fate. A third; a fourth; and a meeting with Beatrice in the garden was no longer an incident in Giovanni's daily life, but the whole space in which he might be said to live; for the anticipation and memory of that ecstatic hour made up the remainder. Nor was it otherwise with the daughter of Rappaccini. She watched for the youth's appearance, and flew to his side with confidence as unreserved as if they had been playmates from early infancy—as if they were such playmates still. If, by any unwonted chance, he failed to come at the appointed moment, she stood beneath the window, and sent up the rich sweetness of her tones to float around him in his chamber, and echo and reverberate throughout his heart—"Giovanni! Giovanni! Why tarriest thou? Come down!"—And down he hastened into that Eden of poisonous flowers.

But, with all this intimate familiarity, there was still a reserve in Beatrice's demeanor, so rigidly and invariably sustained, that the idea of infringing it scarcely occurred to his imagination. By all appreciable signs, they loved; they had looked love, with eyes that conveyed the holy secret from the depths of one soul into the depths of the other, as if it were too sacred to be whispered by the way; they had even spoken love, in those gushes of passion when their spirits darted forth in articulated breath, like tongues of long-hidden flame; and yet there had been no seal of lips, no clasp of hands, nor any slightest caress, such as love claims and hallows. He had never touched one of the gleaming ringlets of her hair; her garment—so marked was the physical barrier between them—had never been waved against him by a breeze. On the few occasions when Giovanni had seemed tempted to overstep the limit, Beatrice grew so sad, so stern, and withal wore such a look of desolate separation, shuddering at itself, that not a spoken word was requisite to repel him. At such times, he was startled at the horrible suspicions that rose, monster-like, out of the caverns of his heart, and stared him in the face; his love grew thin and faint as the morning-mist; his doubts alone had substance. But when Beatrice's face brightened again, after the momentary shadow, she was transformed at once from the mysterious, questionable being, whom he had watched with so much awe and horror; she was now the beautiful and unsophisticated girl, whom he felt that his spirit knew with a certainty beyond all other knowledge.

A considerable time had now passed since Giovanni's last meeting with Baglioni. One morning, however, he was disagreeably surprised by a visit from the Professor, whom he had scarcely thought of for whole weeks, and would willingly have forgotten still longer. Given up, as he had long been, to a pervading excitement, he could tolerate no companions, except upon condition of their perfect sympathy with his present state of feeling. Such sympathy was not to be expected from Professor Baglioni.

The visitor chatted carelessly, for a few moments, about the gossip of the city and the University, and then took up another topic.

"I have been reading an old classic author lately," said he, "and met with a story that strangely interested me. Possibly you may remember it. It is of an Indian prince, who sent a beautiful woman as a present to Alexander the Great.[9] She was as lovely as the dawn, and gorgeous as the sunset; but what especially distinguished her was a certain rich perfume in her breath—richer than a garden of Persian roses. Alexander, as was natural to a youthful conqueror, fell in love at first sight with this magnificent stranger. But a certain sage physician, happening to be present, discovered a terrible secret in regard to her."

"And what was that?" asked Giovanni, turning his eyes downward to avoid those of the Professor.

"That this lovely woman," continued Baglioni, with emphasis, "had been nourished with poisons from her birth upward, until her whole nature was so imbued with them, that she herself had become the deadliest poison in existence. Poison was her element of life. With that rich perfume of her breath, she blasted the very air. Her love would have been poison!—her embrace death! Is not this a marvelous tale?"

"A childish fable," answered Giovanni, nervously starting from his chair. "I marvel how your worship finds time to read such nonsense, among your graver studies."

"By the bye," said the Professor, looking uneasily about him, "what singular fragrance is this in your apartment? Is it the perfume of your gloves? It is faint, but delicious, and yet, after all, by no means agreeable. Were I to breathe it long, methinks it would make me ill. It is like the breath of a flower—but I see no flowers in the chamber."

"Nor are there any," replied Giovanni, who had turned pale as the Professor spoke; "nor, I think, is there any fragrance, except in your worship's imagination. Odors, being a sort of element combined of the sensual and the spiritual, are apt to deceive us in this manner. The recollection of a perfume—the bare idea of it—may easily be mistaken for a present reality."

[9]Reported by the English doctor and writer Sir Thomas Brown in *Vulgar Errors* (1646), which Hawthorne quotes in an 1839 notebook entry.

"Aye; but my sober imagination does not often play such tricks," said Baglioni; "and were I to fancy any kind of odor, it would be that of some vile apothecary drug, wherewith my fingers are likely enough to be imbued. Our worshipful friend Rappaccini, as I have heard, tinctures his medicaments with odors richer than those of Araby. Doubtless, likewise, the fair and learned Signora Beatrice would minister to her patients with draughts as sweet as a maiden's breath. But wo to him that sips them!"

Giovanni's face evinced many contending emotions. The tone in which the Professor alluded to the pure and lovely daughter of Rappaccini was a torture to his soul; and yet, the intimation of a view of her character, opposite to his own, gave instantaneous distinctness to a thousand dim suspicions, which now grinned at him like so many demons. But he strove hard to quell them, and to respond to Baglioni with a true lover's perfect faith.

"Signor Professor," said he, "you were my father's friend—perchance, too, it is your purpose to act a friendly part towards his son. I would fain feel nothing towards you, save respect and deference. But I pray you to observe, Signor, that there is one subject on which we must not speak. You know not the Signora Beatrice. You cannot, therefore, estimate the wrong— the blasphemy, I may even say—that is offered to her character by a light or injurious word."

"Giovanni!—my poor Giovanni!" answered the Professor, with a calm expression of pity, "I know this wretched girl far better than yourself. You shall hear the truth in respect to the poisoner Rappaccini, and his poisonous daughter. Yes; poisonous as she is beautiful! Listen; for even should you do violence to my grey hairs, it shall not silence me. That old fable of the Indian woman has become a truth, by the deep and deadly science of Rappaccini, and in the person of the lovely Beatrice!"

Giovanni groaned and hid his face.

"Her father," continued Baglioni, "was not restrained by natural affection from offering up his child, in this horrible manner, as the victim of his insane zeal for science. For—let us do him justice—he is as true a man of science as ever distilled his own heart in an alembic. What, then, will be your fate? Beyond a doubt, you are selected as the material of some new experiment. Perhaps the result is to be death—perhaps a fate more awful still! Rappaccini, with what he calls the interest of science before his eyes, will hesitate at nothing."

"It is a dream!" muttered Giovanni to himself, "surely it is a dream!"

"But," resumed the Professor, "be of good cheer, son of my friend! It is not yet too late for the rescue. Possibly, we may even succeed in bringing back this miserable child within the limits of ordinary nature, from which her father's madness has estranged her. Behold this little silver vase! It was wrought by the hands of the renowned Benvenuto Cellini,[10] and is well worthy to be a love-gift to the fairest dame in Italy. But its contents

---

[10]Italian sculptor and goldsmith, and author of a famous autobiography (1500–1571).

are invaluable. One little sip of this antidote would have rendered the most virulent poisons of the Borgias innocuous.[11] Doubt not that it will be as efficacious against those of Rappaccini. Bestow the vase, and the precious liquid within it, on your Beatrice, and hopefully await the result."

Baglioni laid a small, exquisitely wrought silver phial on the table, and withdrew, leaving what he had said to produce its effect upon the young man's mind.

"We will thwart Rappaccini yet!" thought he, chuckling to himself, as he descended the stairs. "But, let us confess the truth of him, he is a wonderful man!—a wonderful man indeed! A vile empiric, however, in his practice, and therefore not to be tolerated by those who respect the good old rules of the medical profession!"

Throughout Giovanni's whole acquaintance with Beatrice, he had occasionally, as we have said, been haunted by dark surmises as to her character. Yet, so thoroughly had she made herself felt by him as a simple, natural, most affectionate and guileless creature, that the image now held up by Professor Baglioni, looked as strange and incredible, as if it were not in accordance with his own original conception. True, there were ugly recollections connected with his first glimpses of the beautiful girl; he could not quite forget the bouquet that withered in her grasp, and the insect that perished amid the sunny air, by no ostensible agency, save the fragrance of her breath. These incidents, however, dissolving in the pure light of her character, had no longer the efficacy of facts, but were acknowledged as mistaken fantasies, by whatever testimony of the senses they might appear to be substantiated. There is something truer and more real, than what we can see with the eyes, and touch with the finger. On such better evidence, had Giovanni founded his confidence in Beatrice, though rather by the necessary force of her high attributes, than by any deep and generous faith, on his part. But, now, his spirit was incapable of sustaining itself at the height to which the early enthusiasm of passion had exalted it; he fell down, grovelling among earthly doubts, and defiled therewith the pure whiteness of Beatrice's image. Not that he gave her up; he did but distrust. He resolved to institute some decisive test that should satisfy him, once for all, whether there were those dreadful peculiarities in her physical nature, which could not be supposed to exist without some corresponding monstrosity of soul. His eyes, gazing down afar, might have deceived him as to the lizard, the insect, and the flowers. But if he could witness, at the distance of a few paces, the sudden blight of one fresh and healthful flower in Beatrice's hand, there would be room for no further question. With this idea, he hastened to the florist's, and purchased a bouquet that was still gemmed with the morning dew-drops.

[11]An influential Italian aristocratic family that was notorious for corruption and licentiousness during the Renaissance.

It was now the customary hour of his daily interview with Beatrice. Before descending into the garden, Giovanni failed not to look at his figure in the mirror; a vanity to be expected in a beautiful young man, yet, as displaying itself at that troubled and feverish moment, the token of a certain shallowness of feeling and insincerity of character. He did gaze, however, and said to himself, that his features had never before possessed so rich a grace, nor his eyes such vivacity, nor his cheeks so warm a hue of superabundant life.

"At least," thought he, "her poison has not yet insinuated itself into my system. I am no flower to perish in her grasp!"

With that thought, he turned his eyes on the bouquet, which he had never once laid aside from his hand. A thrill of indefinable horror shot through his frame, on perceiving that those dewy flowers were already beginning to droop; they wore the aspect of things that had been fresh and lovely, yesterday. Giovanni grew white as marble, and stood motionless before the mirror, staring at his own reflection there, as at the likeness of something frightful. He remembered Baglioni's remark about the fragrance that seemed to pervade the chamber. It must have been the poison in his breath! Then he shuddered—shuddered at himself! Recovering from his stupor, he began to watch, with curious eye, a spider that was busily at work, hanging its web from the antique cornice of the apartment, crossing and recrossing the artful system of interwoven lines, as vigorous and active a spider as ever dangled from an old ceiling. Giovanni bent towards the insect, and emitted a deep, long breath. The spider suddenly ceased its toil; the web vibrated with a tremor originating in the body of the small artisan. Again Giovanni sent forth a breath, deeper, longer, and imbued with a venomous feeling out of his heart; he knew not whether he were wicked or only desperate. The spider made a convulsive gripe with his limbs, and hung dead across the window.

"Accursed! Accursed!" muttered Giovanni, addressing himself. "Hast thou grown so poisonous, that this deadly insect perishes by thy breath?"

At that moment, a rich, sweet voice came floating up from the garden:—

"Giovanni! Giovanni! It is past the hour! Why tarriest thou! Come down!"

"Yes," muttered Giovanni again. "She is the only being whom my breath may not slay! Would that it might!"

He rushed down, and in an instant, was standing before the bright and loving eyes of Beatrice. A moment ago, his wrath and despair had been so fierce that he could have desired nothing so much as to wither her by a glance. But, with her actual presence, there came influences which had too real an existence to be at once shaken off; recollections of the delicate and benign power of her feminine nature, which had so often enveloped him in a religious calm; recollections of many a holy and passionate outgush of her heart, when the pure fountain had been unsealed from its depths, and made visible in its transparency to his mental eye; recollections which, had Giovanni known how to estimate them, would have assured him that all this ugly mystery was but an earthly illusion, and that, whatever mist of evil might seem to have gathered over her, the real Beatrice was a heavenly angel. Incapable as he was of such high faith, still her presence had not utterly lost its magic. Giovanni's rage was quelled into an aspect of sullen insensibility. Beatrice, with a quick spiritual sense, immediately felt that there was a gulf of blackness between them, which neither he nor she could pass. They walked on together, sad and silent, and came thus to the marble fountain, and to its pool of water on the ground, in the midst of which grew the shrub that bore gem-like blossoms. Giovanni was affrighted at the eager enjoyment—the appetite, as it were—with which he found himself inhaling the fragrance of the flowers.

"Beatrice," asked he abruptly, "whence came this shrub?"

"My father created it," answered she, with simplicity.

"Created it! created it!" repeated Giovanni. "What mean you, Beatrice?"

"He is a man fearfully acquainted with the secrets of nature," replied Beatrice; "and, at the hour when I first drew breath, this plant sprang from the soil, the offspring of his science, of his intellect, while I was but his earthly child. Approach it not!" continued she, observing with terror that Giovanni was drawing nearer to the shrub. "It has qualities that you little dream of. But I, dearest Giovanni,—I grew up and blossomed with the plant, and was nourished with its breath. It was my sister, and I loved it with a human affection: for—alas! hast thou not suspected it? there was an awful doom."

Here Giovanni frowned so darkly upon her that Beatrice paused and trembled. But her faith in his tenderness reassured her, and made her blush that she had doubted for an instant.

"There was an awful doom," she continued,—"the effect of my father's fatal love of science—which estranged me from all society of my kind. Until Heaven sent thee, dearest Giovanni, Oh! how lonely was thy poor Beatrice!"

"Was it a hard doom?" asked Giovanni, fixing his eyes upon her.

"Only of late have I known how hard it was," answered she tenderly. "Oh, yes; but my heart was torpid, and therefore quiet."

Giovanni's rage broke forth from his sullen gloom like a lightning-flash out of a dark cloud.

"Accursed one!" cried he, with venomous scorn and anger. "And finding thy solitude wearisome, thou hast severed me, likewise, from all the warmth of life, and enticed me into thy region of unspeakable horror!"

"Giovanni!" exclaimed Beatrice, turning her large bright eyes upon his face. The force of his words had not found its way into her mind; she was merely thunder-struck.

"Yes, poisonous thing!" repeated Giovanni, beside himself with passion. "Thou hast done it! Thou hast blasted me! Thou hast filled my veins with poison! Thou hast made me as hateful, as ugly, as loathsome and deadly a creature as thyself,—a world's wonder of hideous monstrosity! Now—if our breath be happily as fatal to ourselves as to all others—let us join our lips in one kiss of unutterable hatred, and so die!"

"What has befallen me?" murmured Beatrice, with a low moan out of her heart. "Holy Virgin pity me, a poor heart-broken child!"

"Thou! Dost thou pray?" cried Giovanni, still with the same fiendish scorn. "Thy very prayers, as they come from thy lips, taint the atmosphere with death. Yes, yes; let us pray! Let us to church, and dip our fingers in the holy water at the portal! They that come after us will perish as by a pestilence. Let us sign crosses in the air! It will be scattering curses abroad in the likeness of holy symbols!"

"Giovanni," said Beatrice calmly, for her grief was beyond passion, "why dost thou join thyself with me thus in those terrible words? I, it is true, am the horrible thing thou namest me. But thou!—what hast thou to do, save with one other shudder at my hideous misery, to go forth out of the garden and mingle with thy race, and forget that there ever crawled on earth such a monster as poor Beatrice?"

"Dost thou pretend ignorance?" asked Giovanni, scowling upon her. "Behold! This power have I gained from the pure daughter of Rappaccini!"

There was a swarm of summer-insects flitting through the air, in search of the food promised by the flower-odors of the fatal garden. They circled round Giovanni's head, and were evidently attracted towards him by the same influence which had drawn them, for an instant, within the sphere of several of the shrubs. He sent forth a breath among them, and smiled bitterly at Beatrice, as at least a score of the insects fell dead upon the ground.

"I see it! I see it!" shrieked Beatrice. "It is my father's fatal science! No, no, Giovanni; it was not I! Never, never! I dreamed only to love thee, and be with thee a little time, and so to let thee pass away, leaving but thine image in mine heart. For, Giovanni—believe it—though my body be nourished with poison, my spirit is God's creature, and craves love as its daily food. But my father!—he has united us in this fearful sympathy. Yes; spurn me!—tread upon me!—kill me! Oh, what is death, after such words as thine? But it was not I! Not for a world of bliss would I have done it!"

Giovanni's passion had exhausted itself in its outburst from his lips. There now came across him a sense, mournful, and not without tenderness, of the intimate and peculiar relationship between Beatrice and himself. They stood, as it were, in an utter solitude, which would be made none the less solitary by the densest throng of human life. Ought not, then, the desert of humanity around them to press this insulated pair closer together? If they should be cruel to one another, who was there to be kind to them? Besides, thought Giovanni, might there not still be a hope of his returning within the limits of ordinary nature, and leading Beatrice—the redeemed Beatrice—by the hand? Oh, weak, and selfish, and unworthy spirit, that could dream of an earthly union and earthly happiness as possible, after such deep love had been so bitterly wronged as was Beatrice's love by Giovanni's blighting words! No, no; there could be no such hope. She must pass heavily, with that broken heart, across the borders of Time—she must bathe her hurts in some fount of Paradise, and forget her grief in the light of immortality—and *there* be well!

But Giovanni did not know it.

"Dear Beatrice," said he, approaching her, while she shrank away, as always at his approach, but now with a different impulse—"dearest Beatrice, our fate is not yet so desperate. Behold! There is a medicine, potent, as a wise physician has assured me, and almost divine in its efficacy. It is composed of ingredients the most opposite to those by which thy awful father has brought this calamity upon thee and me. It is distilled of blessed herbs. Shall we not quaff it together, and thus be purified from evil?"

"Give it me!" said Beatrice, extending her hand to receive the little silver phial which Giovanni took from his bosom. She added, with a peculiar emphasis: "I will drink—but do thou await the result."

She put Baglioni's antidote to her lips; and, at the same moment, the figure of Rappaccini emerged from the portal, and came slowly towards the marble fountain. As he drew near, the pale man of science seemed to gaze with a triumphant expression at the beautiful youth and maiden, as might an artist who should spend his life in achieving a picture or a group of statuary, and finally be satisfied with his success. He paused—his bent form grew erect with conscious power, he spread out his hands over them, in the attitude of a father imploring a blessing upon his children. But those were the same hands that had thrown poison into the stream of their lives! Giovanni trembled. Beatrice shuddered nervously, and pressed her hand upon her heart.

"My daughter," said Rappaccini, "thou art no longer lonely in the world! Pluck one of those precious gems from thy sister shrub, and bid thy bridegroom wear it in his bosom. It will not harm him now! My science, and the sympathy between thee and him, have so wrought within his system, that he now stands apart from common men, as thou dost, daughter of my pride and triumph, from ordinary women. Pass on, then, through the world, most dear to one another, and dreadful to all besides!"

"My father," said Beatrice, feebly—and still, as she spoke, she kept her hand upon her heart—"wherefore didst thou inflict this miserable doom upon thy child?"

"Miserable!" exclaimed Rappaccini. "What mean you, foolish girl? Dost thou deem it misery to be endowed with marvellous gifts, against which no power nor strength could avail an enemy? Misery, to be able to quell the mightiest with a breath? Misery, to be as terrible as thou art beautiful? Wouldst thou, then, have preferred the condition of a weak woman, exposed to all evil, and capable of none?"

"I would fain have been loved, not feared," murmured Beatrice, sinking down upon the ground.—"But now it matters not; I am going, father, where the evil, which thou hast striven to mingle with my being, will pass away like a dream—like the fragrance of these poisonous flowers, which will no longer taint my breath among the flowers of Eden. Farewell, Giovanni! Thy words of hatred are like lead within my heart—but they, too, will fall away as I ascend. Oh, was there not, from the first, more poison in thy nature than in mine?"

To Beatrice—so radically had her earthly part been wrought upon by Rappaccini's skill—as poison had been life, so the powerful antidote was death.

And thus the poor victim of man's ingenuity and of thwarted nature, and of the fatality that attends all such efforts of perverted wisdom, perished there, at the feet of her father and Giovanni. Just at that moment, Professor Pietro Baglioni looked forth from the window, and called loudly, in a tone of triumph mixed with horror, to the thunder-stricken man of science:

"Rappaccini! Rappaccini! And is *this* the upshot of your experiment?"

1844

Mrs. Hutchinson[1]

The character of this female suggests a train of thought which will form as natural an introduction to her story as most of the prefaces to Gay's Fables[2] or the tales of Prior,[3] besides that the general soundness of the moral may excuse any want of present applicability. We will not look for a living resemblance of Mrs. Hutchinson, though the search might not be altogether fruitless.—But there are portentous indications, changes gradually taking place in the habits and feelings of the gentle sex, which seem to threaten our posterity with many of those public women, whereof one was a burthen too grievous for our fathers. The press, however, is now the medium through which feminine ambition chiefly manifests itself, and we will not anticipate the period, (trusting to be gone hence ere it arrive,) when fair orators shall be as numerous as the fair authors of our own day. The hastiest glance may show, how much of the texture and body of cisatlantic literature is the work of those slender fingers, from which only a light and fanciful embroidery has heretofore been required, that might sparkle upon the garment without enfeebling the web. Woman's intellect should never give the tone to that of man, and even her morality is not exactly the material for masculine virtue. A false liberality which mistakes the strong division lines of Nature for arbitrary distinctions, and a courtesy, which might polish criticism but should never soften it, have done their best to add a girlish feebleness to the tottering infancy of our literature. The evil is likely to be a growing one. As yet, the great body of American women are a domestic race; but when a continuance of ill-judged incitements shall have turned their hearts away from the fireside, there are obvious circumstances which will render female pens more numerous and more prolific than those of men, though but equally encouraged; and (limited of course by the scanty support of the public, but increasing indefinitely within those limits) the ink-stained Amazons will expel their rivals by actual pressure, and petticoats wave triumphant over all the field. But, allowing that such forebodings are slightly exaggerated, is it good for woman's self that the path of feverish hope, of tremulous success, of bitter and ignominious disappointment, should be left

---

[1]First published in the *Salem Gazette* (December 7, 1830).

[2]John Gay (1688–1732), English poet and playwright, author of *The Beggar's Opera*.

[3]Matthew Prior (1664–1721), English poet, essayist, and diplomat.

wide open to her? Is the prize worth her having if she win it? Fame does not increase the peculiar respect which men pay to female excellence, and there is a delicacy, (even in rude bosoms, where few would think to find it) that perceives, or fancies, a sort of impropriety in the display of woman's naked mind to the gaze of the world, with indications by which its inmost secrets may be searched out. In fine, criticism should examine with a stricter, instead of a more indulgent eye, the merits of females at its bar, because they are to justify themselves for an irregularity which men do not commit in appearing there; and woman, when she feels the impulse of genius like a command of Heaven within her, should be aware that she is relinquishing a part of the loveliness of her sex, and obey the inward voice with sorrowing reluctance, like the Arabian maid who bewailed the gift of Prophecy. Hinting thus imperfectly at sentiments which may be developed on a future occasion, we proceed to consider the celebrated subject of this sketch.

Mrs. Hutchinson was a woman of extraordinary talent and strong imagination, whom the latter quality, following the general direction taken by the enthusiasm of the times, prompted to stand forth as a reformer in religion. In her native country, she had shown symptoms of irregular and daring thought, but, chiefly by the influence of a favorite pastor, was restrained from open indiscretion. On the removal of this clergyman, becoming dissatisfied with the ministry under which she lived, she was drawn in by the great tide of Puritan emigration, and visited Massachusetts within a few years after its first settlement. But she bore trouble in her own bosom, and could find no peace in this chosen land.—She soon began to promulgate strange and dangerous opinions, tending, in the peculiar situation of the colony, and from the principles which were its basis and indispensable for its temporary support, to eat into its very existence. We shall endeavor to give a more practical idea of this part of her course.

It is a summer evening. The dusk has settled heavily upon the woods, the waves, and the Trimontane peninsula, increasing that dismal aspect of the embryo town which was said to have drawn tears of despondency from Mrs. Hutchinson, though she believed that her mission thither was divine. The houses, straw-thatched and lowly roofed, stand irregularly along streets that are yet roughened by the roots of the trees, as if the forest, departing at the approach of man, had left its reluctant foot prints behind. Most of the dwellings are lonely and silent; from a few we may hear the reading of some sacred text, or the quiet voice of prayer; but nearly all the sombre life of the scene is collected near the extremity of the village. A crowd of hooded women, and of men in steeple-hats and close cropt hair, are assembled at the door and open windows of a house newly built. An earnest expression glows in every face, and some press inward as if the bread of life were to be dealt forth, and they feared to lose their share, while others would fain hold them back, but enter with them since they may not be restrained. We also will go in, edging through the thronged doorway to an apartment which occupies the whole breadth of the house. At the upper end, behind a table on which are placed the Scriptures and two glimmering lamps, we see a woman, plainly attired as befits her ripened years; her hair, complexion, and eyes are dark, the latter somewhat dull and heavy, but kindling up with a gradual brightness. Let us look round upon the hearers. At her right hand, his countenance suiting well with the gloomy light which discovers it, stands Vane the youthful governor, preferred by a hasty judgment of the people over all the wise and hoary heads that had preceded him to New-England. In his mysterious eyes we may read a dark enthusiasm, akin to that of the woman whose cause he has espoused, combined with a shrewd worldly fore-sight, which tells him that her doctrines will be productive of change and tumult, the elements of his power and delight. On her left, yet slightly drawn back so as to evince a less decided support, is Cotton, no young and hot enthusiast, but a mild, grave man in the decline of life, deep in all the learning of the age, and sanctified in heart and made venerable in feature by the long exercise of his holy profession. He also is deceived by the strange fire now laid upon the altar, and he alone among his brethren is excepted in the denunciation of the new Apostle, as sealed and set apart by Heaven to the work of the ministry. Others of the priesthood stand full in front of the woman, striving to beat her down with brows of wrinkled iron, and whisper-ing sternly and significantly among themselves, as she unfolds her seditious doctrines and grows warm in their support. Foremost is Hugh Peters, full of holy wrath, and scarce containing himself from rushing forward to convict her of damnable heresies; there also is Ward, meditating a reply of empty puns, and quaint antitheses, and tinkling jests that puzzle us with nothing but a sound. The audience are variously affected, but none indifferent. On the foreheads of the aged, the mature, and strong-minded, you may gener-ally read steadfast disapprobation, though here and there is one, whose faith seems shaken in those whom he had trusted for years; the females, on the other hand, are shuddering and weeping, and at times they cast a deso-late look of fear around them; while the young men lean forward, fiery and impatient, fit instruments for whatever rash deed may be suggested. And what is the eloquence that gives rise to all these passions? The woman tells them, (and cites texts from the Holy Book to prove her words,) that they have put their trust in unregenerated and uncommissioned men, and have followed them into the wilderness for naught. Therefore their hearts are turning from those whom they had chosen to lead them to Heaven, and they feel like children who have been enticed far from home, and see the features of their guides change all at once, assuming a fiendish shape in some frightful solitude.

These proceedings of Mrs. Hutchinson could not long be endured by the provincial government. The present was a most remarkable case, in which religious freedom was wholly inconsistent with public safety, and where the principles of an illiberal age indicated the very course which must have been pursued by worldly policy and enlightened wisdom. Unity of faith was the star that had guided these people over the deep, and a diversity of sects would either have scattered them from the land to which they had as yet so few attachments, or perhaps have excited a diminutive civil war among those who had come so far to worship together. The opposition to what may be termed the established church had now lost its chief support, by the removal of Vane from office and his departure for England, and Mr. Cotton began to have that light in regard to his errors, which will sometimes break in upon the wisest and most pious men, when their opinions are unhappily discordant with those of the Powers that be. A Synod, the first in New England, was speedily assembled, and pronounced its condemnation of the obnoxious doctrines. Mrs. Hutchinson was next summoned before the supreme civil tribunal, at which, however, the most eminent of the clergy were present, and appear to have taken a very active part as witnesses and advisers. We shall here resume the more picturesque style of narration.

It is a place of humble aspect where the Elders of the people are met, sitting in judgment upon the disturber of Israel. The floor of the low and narrow hall is laid with planks hewn by the axe,—the beams of the roof still wear the rugged bark with which they grew up in the forest, and the hearth is formed of one broad unhammered stone, heaped with logs that roll their blaze and smoke up a chimney of wood and clay. A sleety shower beats fitfully against the windows, driven by the November blast, which comes howling onward from the northern desert, the boisterous and unwelcome herald of a New England winter. Rude benches are arranged across the apartment and along its sides, occupied by men whose piety and learning might have entitled them to seats in those high Councils of the ancient Church, whence opinions were sent forth to confirm or supersede the Gospel in the belief of the whole world and of posterity.—Here are collected all those blessed Fathers of the land, who rank in our veneration next to the Evangelists of Holy Writ, and here also are many, unpurified from the fiercest errors of the age and ready to propagate the religion of peace by violence. In the highest place sits Winthrop, a man by whom the innocent and the guilty might alike desire to be judged, the first confiding in his integrity and wisdom, the latter hoping in his mildness. Next is Endicott, who would stand with his drawn sword at the gate of Heaven, and resist to the death all pilgrims thither, except they travelled his own path. The infant eyes of one in this assembly beheld the faggots blazing round the martyrs, in bloody Mary's time; in later life he dwelt long at Leyden, with the first who went from England for conscience sake; and now, in his weary age, it matters little where he lies down to die. There are others whose hearts were smitten in the high meridian of ambitious hope, and whose dreams still tempt them with the pomp of the old world and the din of its crowded cities, gleaming and echoing over the deep. In the midst, and in the centre of all eyes, we see the Woman. She stands loftily before her judges, with a determined brow, and, unknown to herself, there is a flash of carnal pride half hidden in her eye, as she surveys the many learned and famous men whom her doctrines have put in fear. They question her, and her answers are ready and acute; she reasons with them shrewdly, and brings scripture in support of every argument; the deepest controversialists of that scholastic day find here a woman, whom all their trained and sharpened intellects are inadequate to foil. But by the excitement of the contest, her heart is made to rise and swell within her, and she bursts forth into eloquence. She tells them of the long unquietness which she had endured in England, perceiving the corruption of the church, and yearning for a purer and more perfect light, and how, in a day of solitary prayer, that light was given; she claims for herself the peculiar power of distinguishing between the chosen of man and the Sealed of Heaven, and affirms that her gifted eye can see the glory round the foreheads of the Saints, sojourning in their mortal state. She declares herself commissioned to separate the true shepherds from the false, and denounces present and future judgments on the land, if she be disturbed in her celestial errand. Thus the accusations are proved from her own mouth. Her judges hesitate, and some speak faintly in her defence; but, with a few dissenting voices, sentence is pronounced, bidding her go out from among them, and trouble the land no more.

Mrs. Hutchinson's adherents throughout the colony were now disarmed, and she proceeded to Rhode Island, an accustomed refuge for the exiles of Massachusetts, in all seasons of persecution. Her enemies believed that the anger of Heaven was following her, of which Governor Winthrop does not disdain to record a notable instance, very interesting in a scientific point of view, but fitter for his old and homely narrative than for modern repetition. In a little time, also, she lost her husband, who is mentioned in history only as attending her footsteps, and whom we may conclude to have been (like most husbands of celebrated women) a mere insignificant appendage of his mightier wife. She now grew uneasy among the Rhode-Island colonists, whose liberality towards her, at an era when liberality was not esteemed a christian virtue, probably arose from a comparative insolicitude on religious matters, more distasteful to Mrs. Hutchinson than even the uncompromising narrowness of the Puritans. Her final movement was to lead her family within the limits of the Dutch Jurisdiction, where, having felled the trees of a virgin soil, she became herself the virtual head, civil and ecclesiastical, of a little colony.

Perhaps here she found the repose, hitherto so vainly sought. Secluded from all whose faith she could not govern, surrounded by the dependents over whom she held an unlimited influence, agitated by none of the tumultuous billows which were left swelling behind her, we may suppose, that, in the stillness of Nature, her heart was stilled. But her impressive story was to have an awful close. Her last scene is as difficult to be portrayed as a shipwreck, where the shrieks of the victims die unheard along a desolate sea, and a shapeless mass of agony is all that can be brought home to the imagination. The savage foe was on the watch for blood. Sixteen persons assembled at the evening prayer; in the deep midnight, their cry rang through the forest; and daylight dawned upon the lifeless clay of all but one. It was a circumstance not to be unnoticed by our stern ancestors, in considering the fate of her who had so troubled their religion, that an infant daughter, the sole survivor amid the terrible destruction of her mother's household, was bred in a barbarous faith, and never learned the way to the Christian's Heaven. Yet we will hope, that there the mother and the child have met.

1830

from **Abraham Lincoln**[1]
(March–April 1862)

By and by there was a little stir on the staircase and in the passage-way, and in lounged a tall, loose-jointed figure, of an exaggerated Yankee port and demeanor, whom (as being about the homeliest man I ever saw, yet by no means repulsive or disagreeable) it was impossible not to recognize as Uncle Abe.

Unquestionably, Western man though he be, and Kentuckian by birth, President Lincoln is the essential representative of all Yankees, and the veritable specimen, physically, of what the world seems determined to regard as our characteristic qualities. It is the strangest and yet the fittest thing in the jumble of human vicissitudes, that he, out of so many millions, unlooked for, unselected by any intelligible process that could be based upon his genuine qualities, unknown to those who chose him, and unsuspected of what endowments may adapt him for his tremendous responsibility, should have found the way open for him to fling his lank personality into the chair of state,—where, I presume, it was his first impulse to throw his legs on the council-table, and tell the Cabinet Ministers a story. There is no describing his lengthy awkwardness, nor the uncouthness of his movement; and yet it seemed as if I had been in the habit of seeing him daily, and had shaken hands with him a thousand times in some village street; so true was he to the aspect of the pattern American, though with a certain extravagance which, possibly, I exaggerated still further by the delighted eagerness with which I took it in. If put to guess his calling and livelihood, I should have taken him for a country schoolmaster as soon as anything else. He was dressed in a rusty black frock-coat and pantaloons, unbrushed, and worn so faithfully that the suit had adapted itself to the curves and angularities of his figure, and had grown to be an outer skin of the man. He had shabby slippers on his feet. His hair was black, still unmixed with gray, stiff, somewhat bushy, and had apparently been acquainted with neither brush nor comb that morning, after the disarrangement of the pillow; and as to a nightcap, Uncle Abe probably knows nothing of such effeminacies. His complexion is dark and sallow, betokening, I fear, an insalubrious atmosphere around the White House; he has thick black eyebrows and an impending brow; his nose is large, and the lines about his mouth are very strongly defined.

The whole physiognomy is as coarse a one as you would meet anywhere in the length and breadth of the States; but, withal, it is redeemed, illuminated, softened, and brightened by a kindly though serious look out of his eyes, and an expression of homely sagacity, that seems weighted with rich results of village experience. A great deal of native sense; no bookish cultivation, no

---

[1]Three of the five paragraphs Hawthorne reluctantly agreed to omit from "Chiefly About War Matters" (published in the *Atlantic Monthly* in 1862) after his publisher, James T. Fields, thought the description of Lincoln's "uncouth aspect" would outrage readers. Nine years later, in his memoir of Hawthorne (prepared for the *Atlantic* in 1871 and then included in *Yesterdays with Authors*), Fields printed the censored paragraphs, granting that he might have been too squeamish.

refinement; honest at heart, and thoroughly so, and yet, in some sort, sly,—
at least, endowed with a sort of tact and wisdom that are akin to craft, and
would impel him, I think, to take an antagonist in flank, rather than to make
a bull-run at him right in front. But, on the whole, I liked this sallow, queer,
sagacious visage, with the homely human sympathies that warmed it; and, for
my small share in the matter, would as lief have Uncle Abe for a ruler as any
man whom it would have been practicable to put in his place....

1872

Letter to Henry Wadsworth Longfellow

Salem, June 4th, 1837

Dear Sir,

Not to burthen you with my correspondence, I have delayed a rejoinder to
your very kind and cordial letter, until now. It gratifies me to find that you
have occasionally felt an interest in my situation; but your quotation from
Jean Paul,[1] about the "lark's nest," makes me smile. You would have been
nearer the truth if you had pictured me as dwelling in an owl's nest; for
mine is about as dismal; and, like the owl I seldom venture abroad till after
dark. By some witchcraft or other—for I really cannot assign any reasonable
why and wherefore—I have been carried apart from the main current of life,
and find it impossible to get back again. Since we last met—which, I remember, was in Sawtell's[2] room, where you read a farewell poem to the relics of
the class—ever since that time, I have secluded myself from society; and yet I
never meant any such thing, nor dreamed what sort of life I was going to lead.
I have made a captive of myself and put me into a dungeon and now I cannot
find the key to let myself out—and if the door were open, I should be almost
afraid to come out. You tell me that you have met with troubles and changes. I
know not what they may have been; but I can assure you that trouble is the
next best thing to enjoyment, and that there is no fate in this work so horrible
as to have no share in either its joys or sorrows. For the last ten years, I have
not lived, but only dreamed about living. It may be true that there have been
some unsubstantial pleasures here in the shade, which I should have missed in
the sunshine, but you cannot conceive how utterly devoid of satisfaction all my
retrospects are. I have laid up no treasure of pleasant remembrances, against
old age; but there is some comfort in thinking that my future years can hardly
fail to be more varied, and therefore more tolerable, than the past.

You give me more credit than I deserve, in supposing that I have led
a studious life. I have, indeed, turned over a good many books, but in so

---

[1] Johann Paul Friedrich Richter (1763–1825),
well-known German Romantic novelist, called
Jean Paul.

[2] Cullen Sawtelle (1805–1887); like Longfellow, one of Hawthorne's classmates at Bowdoin College.

desultory a way that it cannot be called study, nor has it left me the fruits of study. As to my literary efforts, I do not think much of them—neither is it worth while to be ashamed of them. They would have been better, I trust, if written under more favorable circumstances. I have had no external excitement—no consciousness that the public would like what I wrote, nor much hope nor a very passionate desire that they should do so. Nevertheless, having nothing else to be ambitious of, I have felt considerably interested in literature; and if my writings had made any decided impression, I should probably have been stimulated to greater exertions; but there has been no warmth of approbation, so that I have always written with benumbed fingers. I have another great difficulty, in the lack of materials; for I have seen so little of the world, that I have nothing but thin air to concoct my stories of, and it is not easy to give a lifelike semblance to such shadowy stuff. Sometimes, through a peep-hole, I have caught a glimpse of the real world; and the two or three articles in which I have portrayed such glimpses, please me better than the others. I have now, or shall soon have, one sharp spur to exertion, which I lacked at an earlier period; for I see little prospect but that I must scribble for a living. But this troubles me much less than you would suppose. I can turn my pen to all sorts of drudgery, such as children's books, etc., and by and by, I shall get some editorship that will answer my purpose. Frank Pierce, who was with us at college, offered me his influence to obtain an office in the Exploring Expedition; but I believe that he was mistaken in supposing that a vacancy existed. If such a post were attainable, I should certainly accept it; for, though fixed so long to one spot, I have always had a desire to run around the world.

The copy of my Tales[3] was sent to Mr. Owen's, the bookseller's in Cambridge. I am glad to find that you had read and liked some of the stories. To be sure, you could not well help flattering me a little; but I value your praise too highly not to have faith in its sincerity. When I last heard from the publisher—which was not very recently—the book was doing pretty well. Six or seven hundred copies had been sold. I suppose, however, these awful times have now stopped the sale.

I intend in a week or two to come out of my owl's nest, and not return to it till late in the summer—employing the interval in making a tour somewhere in New England. You, who have the dust of distant countries on your "sandal-shoon," cannot imagine how much enjoyment I shall have in this little excursion. Whenever I get abroad, I feel just as young as I did, ten years ago. What a letter I am inflicting on you! I trust you will answer it.

Yours sincerely,

Nath. Hawthorne.

1837

---

[3] *Twice-Told Tales*, whose publication provided the occasion for Hawthorne's letter and ultimately for a laudatory review by Longfellow.

Letter to Sophia Peabody

Oak Hill, April 13th. 1841

Ownest love,

Here is thy poor husband in a polar Paradise! I know not how to interpret this aspect of Nature—whether it be of good or evil omen to our enterprise. But I reflect that the Plymouth pilgrims arrived in the midst of storm and stept ashore upon mountain snow-drifts; and nevertheless they prospered, and became a great people—and doubtless it will be the same with us. I laud my stars, however, that thou wilt not have thy first impressions of our future home from such a day as this. Thou wouldst shiver all thy life afterwards, and never realise that there could be bright skies, and green hills and meadows, and trees heavy with foliage, when now the whole scene is a great snow-bank, and the sky full of snow likewise. Through faith, I persist in believing that spring and summer will come in their due season; but the unregenerated man shivers within me, and suggests a doubt whether I may not have wandered within the precincts of the Arctic circle, and chosen my heritage among ever-lasting snows. Dearest, provide thyself with a good stock of furs; and if thou canst obtain the skin of a polar bear, thou wilt find it a very suitable summer dress for this region. Thou must not hope ever to walk abroad, except upon snow-shoes, nor to find any warmth, save in thy husband's heart.

Belovedest, I have not yet taken my first lesson in agriculture, as thou mayst well suppose—except that I went to see our cows foddered, yesterday afternoon. We have eight of our own; and the number is now increased by a transcendental heifer, belonging to Miss Margaret Fuller. She is very frac-tious, I believe, and apt to kick over the milk pail. Thou knowest best, whether in these traits of character, she resembles her mistress.[1] Thy hus-band intends to convert himself into a milk-maid, this evening; but I pray heaven that Mr. Ripley[2] may be moved to assign him the kindliest cow in the herd—otherwise he will perform his duty with fear and trembling:

Ownest wife, I like my brethren in affliction very well; and couldst thou see us sitting round our table, at meal-times, before the great kitchen-fire, thou wouldst call it a cheerful sight. Mrs. Parker is a most comfortable woman to behold; she looks as if her ample person were stuffed full of ten-derness—indeed, as if she were all one great, kind heart. Wert thou here, I should ask for nothing more—not even for sunshine and summer weather; for thou wouldst be both, to thy husband. And how is that cough of thine, my belovedest? Hast thou thought of me, in my perils and wanderings? I trust that thou dost muse upon me with hope and joy; not with repining. Think that I am gone before, to prepare a home for my Dove, and will return for her, all in good time.

---

[1]Fuller's work is represented earlier in this volume. Hawthorne's attitude toward her was, at best, ambivalent.

[2]The Reverend George Ripley (1802–1880), American reformer and journalist instrumen-tal in organizing Brook Farm.

Thy husband has the best chamber in the house, I believe; and though not quite so good as the apartment I have left, it will do very well. I have hung up thy two pictures; and they give me a glimpse of summer and of thee. The vase I intended to have brought in my arms, but could not very conveniently do it yesterday; so that it still remains at Mrs. Hillard's,[3] together with my carpet. I shall bring them [at] the next opportunity.

Now farewell, for the present, most beloved. I have been writing this in my chamber; but the fire is getting low, and the house is old and cold: so that the warmth of my whole person has retreated to my heart, which burns with love for thee. I must run down to the kitchen or parlor hearth, when thy image shall sit beside me—yea, be pressed to my breast. At bed-time, thou shalt have a few lines more. Now I think of it, dearest, wilt thou give Mrs. Ripley a copy of Grandfather's Chair and Liberty Tree;[4] she wants them for some boys here. I have several copies of Famous Old People.

April 14th, 10 A.M. Sweetest, I did not milk the cows last night, because Mr. Ripley was afraid to trust them to my hands, or me to their horns—I know not which. But this morning, I have done wonders. Before breakfast, I went out to the barn, and began to chop hay for the cattle; and with such "righteous vehemence" (as Mr. Ripley says) did I labor, that in the space of ten minutes, I broke the machine. Then I brought wood and replenished the fires; and finally sat down to breakfast and ate up a huge mound of buckwheat cakes. After breakfast, Mr. Ripley put a four-pronged instrument into my hands, which he gave me to understand was called a pitch-fork; and he and Mr. Farley[5] being armed with similar weapons, we all then commenced a gallant attack upon a heap of manure. This office being concluded, and thy husband having purified himself, he sits down to finish this letter to his most beloved wife. Dearest, I will never consent that thou come within half a mile of me, after such an encounter as that of this morning. Pray Heaven that his letter retain none of the fragrance with which the writer was imbued. As for thy husband himself, he is peculiarly partial to the odor; but that whimsical little nose of thine might chance to quarrel with it.

Belovedest, Miss Fuller's cow hooks the other cows, and has made herself ruler of the herd, and behaves in a very tyrannical manner. Sweetest, I know not when I shall see thee; but I trust it will not be longer than the end of next week. I love thee! I love thee! I wouldst thou wert with me; for then would my labor be joyful—and even now it is not sorrowful. Dearest, I shall make an excellent husbandman. I feel the original Adam reviving within me.

Miss Sophia A. Peabody,
13 West street,
Boston.

1841

---

[3]Susan Howe Hillard, a friend of the Peabodys and Hawthorne's Boston landlady.
[4]Books by Hawthorne.

[5]Another participant in the Brook Farm experiment.

Letter to H. W. Longfellow, Cambridge

[Salem] Custom House, June 5th. 1849

Dear Longfellow,

I meant to have written you before now about Kavanaugh,[1] but have had no quiet time, during my letter-writing hours; and now the freshness of my thoughts has exhaled away. It is a most precious and rare book—as fragrant as a bunch of flowers, and as simple as one flower. A true picture of life, moreover—as true as those reflections of the trees and banks that I used to see in the Concord, but refined to a higher degree than they; as if the reflection were itself reflected. Nobody but yourself would dare to write so quiet a book; nor could any other succeed in it. It is entirely original; a book by itself; a true work of genius, if ever there were one; and yet I should not wonder if many people (God confound them!) were to see no such matter in it. In fact, I doubt whether hardly anybody else has enjoyed it so much as I; although I have heard or seen none but favorable opinions.

I should like to have written a long notice of it, and would have done so for the Salem Advertiser; but, on the strength of my notice of Evangeline[2] and some half-dozen other books, I have been accused of a connection with the editorship of that paper, and of writing political articles—which I never did one single time in my whole life! I must confess, it stirs up a little of the devil within me, to find myself hunted by these political bloodhounds. If they succeed in getting me out of office, I will surely immolate one or two of them. Not that poor monster of a Conolly,[3] whom I desire only to bury in oblivion, far out of my own remembrance. Nor any of the common political brawlers, who work on their own level, and can conceive of no higher ground than what they occupy. But if there be among them (as there must be, if they succeed) some men who claim a higher position, and ought to know better, I may perhaps select a victim, and let fall one little drop of venom on his heart, that shall make him writhe before the grin of the multitude for a considerable time to come. This I will do, not as an act of individual vengeance, but in your behalf as well as mine, because he will have violated the sanctity of the priesthood to which we both, in our different degrees, belong. I do not claim to be a poet; and yet I cannot but feel that some of the sacredness of that character adheres to me, and ought to be respected in me, unless I step out of its immunities, or make it a plea for violating any of the rules of ordinary life. When other people concede me this privilege, I never think that I possess it; but when they disregard it, the consciousness makes itself felt. If they will pay no reverence to the imaginative power when it causes herbs of grace and sweet-scented flowers to spring up along their pathway, then they should be taught what it can do in the way of producing nettles, skunk-cabbage, deadly nightshade, wolf's bane,

---

[1] A romance by Longfellow.
[2] Another of Longfellow's well-known narrative poems.

[3] A local political figure.

dog-wood.[4] If they will not be grateful for its works of beauty and beneficence, then let them dread it as a pervasive and penetrating mischief, that
can reach them at their firesides and in their bedchambers, follow them to
far countries, and make their very graves refuse to hide them. I have often
thought that there must be a good deal of enjoyment in writing personal
satire; but, never having felt the slightest ill-will towards any human being,
I have hitherto been debarred from this peculiar source of pleasure. I almost
hope I shall be turned out, so as to have an opportunity of trying it. I cannot
help smiling in anticipation of the astonishment of some of these local magnates here, who suppose themselves quite out of the reach of any retribution on my part.

I have spent a good deal of time in Boston, within a few weeks; my two
children having been ill of the scarlet-fever there; and the little boy was in
quite an alarming way. I could not have submitted in the least, had it gone
ill with him; but God spared me that trial—and there was no real misfortunes, save such as that. Other troubles may irritate me superficially; nothing else can go near the heart.

I mean to come and dine with you, the next time you invite me; and
Hillard said he would come too. Do not let it be within a week, however; for
Bridge and his wife expect to be here in the course of that time.

Please to present my regards to Mrs. Longfellow, and believe me

ever your friend,
Nath Hawthorne.

1849

Letter to J. T. Fields, Boston

Salem, January 20th. 1850.

My dear Fields,[1]

I am truly glad that you like the introduction; for I was rather afraid that it
might appear absurd and impertinent to be talking about myself, when
nobody, that I know of, has requested any information on that subject.

As regards the size of the book, I have been thinking a good deal about
it. Considered merely as a matter of taste and beauty, the form of publication which you recommend seems to me much preferable to that of the
'Mosses.'[2] In the present case, however, I have some doubts of the expediency; because, if the book is made up entirely of 'The Scarlet Letter,' it will
be too sombre. I found it impossible to relieve the shadows of the story with

---

[4]Various poisonous or foul-sounding plants.
[1]James Thomas Fields (1817–1881), the junior partner in Boston's major publishing
firm, Ticknor and Fields, who published all
Hawthorne's books from this point on. By
encouraging Hawthorne to expand *The Scarlet Letter* for separate book publication

instead of inclusion in a collection of tales,
Fields helped launch Hawthorne's career as a
romancer. He was a shrewd literary pro-
moter but also Hawthorne's trusted friend.
[2]Hawthorne's collection of tales, *Mosses from
an Old Manse*.

so much light as I would gladly have thrown in. Keeping so close to its point as the tale does, and diversified no otherwise than by turning different sides of the same dark idea to the reader's eye, it will weary very many people, and disgust some. Is it safe, then, to stake the fate of the book entirely on this one chance? A hunter loads his gun with a bullet and several buck-shot; and, following his sagacious example, it was my purpose to conjoin the one long story with half a dozen shorter ones; so that, failing to kill the public outright with my biggest and heaviest lump of lead, I might have other chances with the smaller bits, individually and in the aggregate.

However, I am willing to leave these considerations to your judgment, and should not be sorry to have you decide for the separate publication.

In this latter event, it appears to me that the only proper title for the book would be 'The Scarlet Letter'; for 'The Custom House' is merely introductory—an entrance-hall to the magnificent edifice which I throw open to my guests. It would be funny, if, seeing the further passages so dark and dismal, they should all choose to stop there!

If 'The Scarlet Letter' is to be the title, would it not be well to print it on the title-page in red ink? I am not quite sure about the good taste of so doing; but it would certainly be piquant and appropriate—and, I think, attractive to the great gull whom we are endeavoring to circumvent.

Very truly Yours,
Nath[l]. Hawthorne

J.T. Fields, Esq.

1850

[An undated draft of the letter:]

As regards the book, I have been thinking and considering—I was rather afraid that it appears sagacious absurd and impertinent to have some doubts, of the introduction to the book, which you recommend. I have found it impossible to relieve the shadows of the story with so much light as I would gladly stake the fate of the book entirely on the public. However, I am willing to leave these considerations to your judgment, and should not be sorry to have you decide for the separate publication.

If the Judgment Letter is to be the title—print it on the title page in red ink. I think that the only proper title for the book would be the Scarlet Letter. I am quite sure about the taste of so doing. I think it is attractive and appropriate—

from **Letter to H. W. Longfellow, Cambridge**

Concord, Jan[y] 2[d] 1864.

Dear Longfellow . . .

. . . I have been much out of sorts of late, and do not well know what is the matter with me, but am inclined to draw the conclusion that I shall have little more to do with pen and ink. One more book I should like well enough to write, and have indeed begun it, but with no assurance of ever bringing it to an end. As is always the case, I have a notion that this last book would be my best; and full of wisdom about matters of life and death—and yet it will be no deadly disappointment if I am compelled to drop it. You can tell, far better than I, whether there is ever anything worth having a literary reputation, and whether the best achievements seem to have any substance after they grow cold.

Your friend,
Nath[1] Hawthorne.

1864

Preface to *The House of the Seven Gables*

When a writer calls his work a Romance, it need hardly be observed that he wishes to claim a certain latitude, both as to its fashion and material, which he would not have felt himself entitled to assume had he professed to be writing a Novel. The latter form of composition is presumed to aim at a very minute fidelity, not merely to the possible, but to the probable and ordinary course of man's experience. The former—while, as a work of art, it must rigidly subject itself to laws, and while it sins unpardonably so far as it may swerve aside from the truth of the human heart—has fairly a right to present that truth under circumstances, to a great extent, of the writer's own choosing or creation. If he think fit, also, he may so manage his atmospherical medium as to bring out or mellow the lights and deepen and enrich the shadows of the picture. He will be wise, no doubt, to make a very moderate use of the privileges here stated, and, especially, to mingle the Marvellous rather as a slight, delicate, and evanescent flavor, than as any portion of the actual substance of the dish offered to the public. He can hardly be said, however, to commit a literary crime even if he disregard this caution.

In the present work, the author has proposed to himself—but with what success, fortunately, it is not for him to judge—to keep undeviatingly within his immunities. The point of view in which this tale comes under the Romantic definition lies in the attempt to connect a bygone time with the very present that is flitting away from us. It is a legend prolonging itself, from an epoch now gray in the distance, down into our own broad daylight, and bringing along with it some of its legendary mist, which the reader, according to his pleasure, may either disregard, or allow it to float almost imperceptibly about the characters and events for the sake of a picturesque effect. The narrative, it may be, is woven of so humble a texture as to require this advantage, and, at the same time, to render it the more difficult of attainment.

Many writers lay very great stress upon some definite moral purpose, at which they profess to aim their works. Not to be deficient in this particular, the author has provided himself with a moral,—the truth, namely, that the wrong-doing of one generation lives into the successive ones, and, divesting itself of every temporary advantage, becomes a pure and uncontrollable mischief; and he would feel it a singular gratification if this romance might effectually convince mankind—or, indeed, any one man—of the folly of tumbling down an avalanche of ill-gotten gold, or real estate, on the heads of an unfortunate posterity, thereby to maim and crush them, until the accumulated mass shall be scattered abroad in its original atoms. In good faith, however, he is not sufficiently imaginative to flatter himself with the slightest hope of this kind. When romances do really teach anything, or produce any effective operation, it is usually through a far more subtle process than the ostensible one. The author has considered it hardly worth his while, therefore, relentlessly to impale the story with its moral as with an iron rod,—or, rather, as by sticking a pin through a butterfly,—thus at once depriving it of life, and causing it to stiffen in an ungainly and unnatural attitude. A high truth, indeed, fairly, finely, and skilfully wrought out, brightening at every step, and crowning the final development of a work of fiction, may add an artistic glory, but is never any truer, and seldom any more evident, at the last page than at the first.

The reader may perhaps choose to assign an actual locality to the imaginary events of this narrative. If permitted by the historical connection,—which, though slight, was essential to his plan,—the author would very willingly have avoided anything of this nature. Not to speak of other objections, it exposes the romance to an inflexible and exceedingly dangerous species of criticism, by bringing his fancy-pictures almost into positive contact with the realities of the moment. It has been no part of his object, however, to describe local manners, nor in any way to meddle with the characteristics of a community for whom he cherishes a proper respect and a natural regard. He trusts not to be considered as unpardonably offending by laying out a street that infringes upon nobody's private rights, and appropriating a lot of land which had no visible owner, and building a house of materials long in use for constructing castles in the air. The personages of the tale—though they give themselves out to be of ancient stability and considerable prominence—are really of the author's own making, or, at all events, of his own mixing; their virtues can shed no lustre, nor their defects redound, in the remotest degree, to the discredit of the venerable town of which they profess to be inhabitants. He would be glad, therefore, if—especially in the quarter to which he alludes—the book may be read strictly as a Romance, having a great deal more to do with the clouds overhead than with any portion of the actual soil of the County of Essex.

Lenox
January 27, 1851

EDGAR ALLAN POE
1809–1849

Edgar Allan Poe is one of the best-known American authors, but his literary legacy is complex and confusing. Poe pioneered many of the most enduring forms of American popular culture, including the detective story, science fiction, and the gothic or sensational tale; yet he also exerted a profound influence on Modernism through the enthusiasm of Charles Baudelaire and the French Symbolist poets. Poe's fiction celebrates both the hyper-rationality of his detective double, C. Auguste Dupin, and the inability of philosophy to account for the perverse. Poe maintained that authors should begin by considering their writing's effect on the reader, yet he was highly critical of sentimentality and didacticism, insisting that beauty, understood as the elevation of the soul, was the essence of true poetry.

Poe's life was as contradictory as his literary legacy. He suffered the early death of his parents, disinheritance by his foster father, poverty, anonymity, and a series of professional failures, but he also enjoyed some notable successes: a reputation as a discerning, if severe, literary critic; sudden celebrity after the publication of "The Raven"; notoriety for his involvement in a number of literary scandals; and the beginnings of a European reputation as a misunderstood American genius. Many myths about Poe's life have taken powerful hold on the popular imagination, partly due to Poe's exaggeration of his own life story, to his creation of memorable pathological narrators, which readers have confused with Poe himself, and to society's difficulty in coming to grips with the contradiction between Poe's aesthetic of writerly mastery and his apparent lack of control over his finances, his drinking, and his career. Critics have come to value Poe's writing both for his acute representations of extreme psychological states and for the ways in which his poetry and tales speak to the darker side of nineteenth-century American culture, probing the limits of scientific method, the affective dynamics of sentimentalism, the challenge posed by the urban masses to a sense of social and civic belonging, and the preoccupation with property, depersonalization, incarceration, purity, and defilement endemic to a democracy that practiced and accommodated slavery.

Born in Boston on January 19, 1809, Edgar Poe was the second child of Elizabeth and David Poe, itinerant actors who performed in theaters in Eastern Seaboard cities from Massachusetts to South Carolina. David Poe abandoned the family while Poe was still an infant. When his mother died in December 1811 while appearing at the Richmond Theater, Poe was taken in by a prosperous Virginia merchant and his wife, John and Frances Allan.

An exporter of tobacco and importer of a variety of merchandise, John Allan moved his family to England in 1815 to set up a branch of his firm in London. There, Poe attended boarding school until he was eleven, when Allan moved the family back to Richmond. Poe completed school in Richmond, entering the newly opened University of Virginia in 1826. He excelled at ancient and modern languages but incurred large gambling debts that Allan refused to pay.

Quarreling with his foster father over his irresponsibility and extravagance, Poe fled to Boston, arranged for the publication of his first volume of poetry— *Tamerlane and Other Poems* (1827)—and enlisted in the United States Army under the name Edgar A. Perry. Poe left the army and reconciled with Allan when his foster mother died in 1829, obtaining a nomination to West Point in part through Allan's influence. While waiting to take up his appointment, Poe published his second book, *Al Aaraaf, Tamerlane, and Minor Poems* (1829).

Poe resumed his studies at West Point but continued to quarrel with Allan, who refused to support him financially and whose remarriage in the fall of 1830 dashed Poe's hopes that he would become Allan's heir. Poe got himself dismissed from West Point by deliberately disobeying orders; then he set out for New York City, where he published *Poems* (1831) on the strength of a subscription list generated by his fellow cadets. Poe struggled in the following years to support himself by his writing, moving to Baltimore to live with his grandmother, his aunt, and his young cousin Virginia Clemm, and submitting stories for newspaper prize competitions. Early in 1835, he began to publish tales and book reviews in a newly established Richmond magazine, the *Southern Literary Messenger*. By the end of the year, Poe had been hired as an editor and regular contributor and had reconstituted a family in Richmond consisting of his aunt Mrs. Clemm and thirteen-year-old Virginia, whom he married in the spring of 1836.

While at the *Messenger*, Poe developed a national reputation as a "tomahawk" critic, one who mercilessly subjected authors to unrelenting criticism in the manner of the British quarterly reviews. However, the magazine's financial troubles and Poe's disagreements with its owner over editorial and personal matters, including Poe's drinking, forced his resignation from the *Messenger* in 1837. Not for the last time, Poe turned to literary hackwork to support himself. In 1838, the Harper Brothers published his serialized adventure novel *The Narrative of Arthur Gordon Pym*, but it sold poorly in the United States despite being enthusiastically reviewed and pirated in England. In 1839 Poe finally obtained steady work in Philadelphia as editor of *Burton's Gentleman's Magazine*, where he published "The Fall of the House of Usher" and a number of other tales and reviews. His first collection of fiction, *Tales of the Grotesque and Arabesque*, was published in Philadelphia later that year, but reviewers found the tales extravagant and mystical, and the book sold poorly. Fired from *Burton's* in 1840, Poe attempted to garner subscribers for a literary magazine of his own; but when this project proved unfeasible, he accepted a job as literary editor and reviewer for *Graham's Lady's and Gentleman's Magazine*, a monthly journal that published literature and criticism alongside sentimental illustrations and the latest fashions.

Poe published "The Man of the Crowd" and the first of his detective stories in *Graham's*, along with numerous other tales, poems, and reviews. In January 1842, Virginia Poe burst a blood vessel while singing, almost died, and never fully recovered her health. Poe's own ill health prompted his replacement at *Graham's*, and he spent the next two years publishing wherever he could, unsuccessfully angling for a government appointment and gaining a measure of celebrity by winning a Philadelphia newspaper contest with the cryptographic tale "The Gold Bug." After experimenting with the lecture circuit, Poe moved his family to

New York in 1844. There, failing to find better work, he wrote anonymous articles as a "mechanical paragraphist" for the *New York Mirror*.

Poe burst onto the New York literary scene rather suddenly in January 1845, when James Russell Lowell's favorable sketch of Poe's life and works was followed by the publication of "The Raven," a poem that was immediately copied, parodied, and anthologized. As the "Author of 'The Raven,'" Poe was introduced into fashionable New York literary society, attending the salon of Ann Lynch, carrying on a literary flirtation with the poet Frances Sargent Osgood, and sharpening his critical credentials by accusing Henry Wadsworth Longfellow of plagiarism. Poe's sudden celebrity and his reputation for critical independence endeared him to a group of literary nationalists who sponsored the publication of his *Tales* and *The Raven and Other Poems* in 1845. Poe gradually assumed editorship and part ownership of a weekly literary magazine, the *Broadway Journal*, using it as a vehicle for printing revised versions of tales and poems that had been scattered among a variety of periodicals. Just as Poe seemed to be gaining a measure of control over his career and literary corpus, however, his personal and professional life began to unravel. Out of perversity, anxiety, strategy, or some combination of the three, Poe gave a disastrous reading at the Boston Lyceum, presenting his early poem "Al Aaraaf" as if it were a new production. When the substitution was discovered, he claimed to have been drunk at the time and to have hoaxed the Bostonians by getting them to applaud for an inferior poem. Poe's war of words with the Bostonians increased his notoriety and his reputation for unreliability; meanwhile, the *Broadway Journal* collapsed under the weight of considerable debt. Poe continued to publish tales and criticism and to become embroiled in literary scandals, finally fleeing the city in the spring of 1846 for a cottage in Fordham, New York, hoping the change of pace would relieve him from pressure and improve Virginia's health. Destitute and ill, Poe and his wife appeared in the papers as charity cases, much to Poe's chagrin. Virginia's health declined, and she died early in 1847.

In the last years of his life, Poe wrote poems, tales, and criticism and lectured on poetry and poetic theory, devoting considerable energy to *Eureka* (1848), a book-length prose poem detailing his theory of the universe. Reviving his plan to found an elite literary magazine, Poe traveled to Richmond to seek Southern support in the summer of 1849. There he took the temperance pledge and became engaged to his boyhood sweetheart before returning north on literary business. Stopping in Baltimore, he apparently broke his pledge, became drunk and disoriented, and was found unconscious outside a polling station on Election Day. Taken to a hospital, Poe died days later of "congestion of the brain." Shortly after the funeral, his character was maligned in a pseudonymous obituary by Rufus Wilmot Griswold, the man Poe had named as his literary executor. Griswold's posthumous edition of Poe's *Works* (1850) sealed Poe's literary fame, but the volumes were prefaced both by laudatory sketches of Poe's life and work and by Griswold's melodramatic and damning "Memoir of the Author," giving lasting form to the split subject of Poe biography.

Meredith L. McGill
Rutgers University

PRIMARY WORKS

Tamerlane and Other Poems, 1827; *Al Aaraaf Tamerlane, and Minor Poems*, 1829; *Poems*, 1831; *The Narrative of Arthur Gordon Pym, of Nantucket*, 1838; *Tales of the Grotesque and Arabesque*, 1840; *Tales*, 1845; *The Raven and Other Poems*, 1845; *Eureka: A Prose Poem*, 1848; *Works*, 1850; *Collected Works of Edgar Allan Poe*, 3 vols., Thomas Ollive Mabbott, ed., 1969–1978; *Collected Writings of Edgar Allan Poe*, 5 vols., Burton R. Pollin, ed., 1981–1997; *Poetry and Tales*, Patrick F. Quinn, ed., 1984; *Essays and Reviews*, G. R. Thompson, ed., 1984.

Ligeia

And the will therein lieth, which dieth not. Who knoweth the mysteries of the will, with its vigor? For God is but a great will pervading all things by nature of its intentness. Man doth not yield himself to the angels, nor unto death utterly, save only through the weakness of his feeble will.

—JOSEPH GLANVILL[1]

I cannot, for my soul, remember how, when, or even precisely where, I first became acquainted with the lady Ligeia. Long years have since elapsed, and my memory is feeble through much suffering. Or, perhaps, I cannot *now* bring these points to mind, because, in truth, the character of my beloved, her rare learning, her singular yet placid cast of beauty, and the thrilling and enthralling eloquence of her low musical language, made their way into my heart by paces so steadily and stealthily progressive that they have been unnoticed and unknown. Yet I believe that I met her first and most frequently in some large, old, decaying city near the Rhine. Of her family— I have surely heard her speak. That it is of a remotely ancient date cannot be doubted. Ligeia! Ligeia! Buried in studies of a nature more than all else adapted to deaden impressions of the outward world, it is by that sweet word alone—by Ligeia—that I bring before mine eyes in fancy the image of her who is no more. And now, while I write, a recollection flashes upon me that I have *never known* the paternal name of her who was my friend and my betrothed, and who became the partner of my studies, and finally the wife of my bosom. Was it a playful charge on the part of my Ligeia? or was it a test of my strength of affection, that I should institute no inquiries upon this point? or was it rather a caprice of my own—a wildly romantic offering on the shrine of the most passionate devotion? I but indistinctly recall the fact itself—what wonder that I have utterly forgotten the circumstances which originated or attended it? And, indeed, if ever that spirit which is entitled *Romance*—if ever she, the wan and the misty-winged

[1]First published in the *(Baltimore) American Museum* in September 1838, "Ligeia" was included in *Tales of the Grotesque and Arabesque* (1840) and substantially revised and republished in 1845 in the *(New York) New World* and the *Broadway Journal*. One of Poe's revisions was to insert his poem "The Conqueror Worm" as one of Ligeia's compositions. Joseph Glanvill was a seventeenth-century religious philosopher, but this quotation has never been located and may have been invented for the occasion.

Ashtophet[2] of idolatrous Egypt, presided, as they tell, over marriages ill-omened, then most surely she presided over mine.

There is one dear topic, however, on which my memory fails me not. It is the *person* of Ligeia. In stature she was tall, somewhat slender, and, in her later days, even emaciated. I would in vain attempt to portray the majesty, the quiet ease, of her demeanor, or the incomprehensible lightness and elasticity of her footfall. She came and departed as a shadow. I was never made aware of her entrance into my closed study save by the dear music of her low sweet voice, as she placed her marble hand upon my shoulder. In beauty of face no maiden ever equalled her. It was the radiance of an opium-dream—an airy and spirit-lifting vision more wildly divine than the phantasies which hovered about the slumbering souls of the daughters of Delos.[3] Yet her features were not of that regular mould which we have been falsely taught to worship in the classical labors of the heathen. "There is no exquisite beauty," says Bacon, Lord Verulam, speaking truly of all the forms and *genera* of beauty, "without some *strangeness* in the proportion."[4] Yet, although I saw that the features of Ligeia were not of a classic regularity—although I perceived that her loveliness was indeed "exquisite," and felt that there was much of "strangeness" pervading it, yet I have tried in vain to detect the irregularity and to trace home my own perception of "the strange." I examined the contour of the lofty and pale forehead—it was faultless—how cold indeed that word when applied to a majesty so divine!—the skin rivalling the purest ivory, the commanding extent and repose, the gentle prominence of the regions above the temples; and then the raven-black, the glossy, the luxuriant and naturally-curling tresses, setting forth the full force of the Homeric epithet, "hyacinthine!" I looked at the delicate outlines of the nose—and nowhere but in the graceful medallions of the Hebrews had I beheld a similar perfection. There were the same luxurious smoothness of surface, the same scarcely perceptible tendency to the aquiline, the same harmoniously curved nostrils speaking the free spirit. I regarded the sweet mouth. Here was indeed the triumph of all things heavenly—the magnificent turn of the short upper lip—the soft, voluptuous slumber of the under—the dimples which sported, and the color which spoke—the teeth glancing back, with a brilliancy almost startling, every ray of the holy light which fell upon them in her serene and placid, yet most exultingly radiant of all smiles. I scrutinized the formation of the chin—and here, too, I found the gentleness of breadth, the softness and the majesty, the fullness and the spirituality, of the Greek—the contour which the god Apollo revealed but in a dream, to Cleomenes, the son of the Athenian.[5] And then I peered into the large eyes of Ligeia.

---

[2]A deity associated with Ashtoreth, love goddess of the early Phoenicians.

[3]A poetic term for Greece.

[4]Poe was fond of the Francis Bacon quotation and used it several times in his works. Bacon wrote: "There is no excellent beauty ...," which Poe transforms to "There is no exquisite beauty...."

[5]Cleomenes was the sculptor of *Venus de Medici*.

For eyes we have no models in the remotely antique. It might have been, too, that in these eyes of my beloved lay the secret to which Lord Verulam alludes. They were, I must believe, far larger than the ordinary eyes of our own race. They were even fuller than the fullest of the gazelle eyes of the tribe of the valley of Nourjahad.[6] Yet it was only at intervals—in moments of intense excitement—that this peculiarity became more than slightly noticeable in Ligeia. And at such moments was her beauty—in my heated fancy thus it appeared perhaps—the beauty of beings either above or apart from the earth—the beauty of the fabulous Houri of the Turk.[7] The hue of the orbs was the most brilliant of black, and, far over them, hung jetty lashes of great length. The brows, slightly irregular in outline, had the same tint. The "strangeness," however, which I found in the eyes, was of a nature distinct from the formation, or the color, or the brilliancy of the features, and must, after all, be referred to the *expression*. Ah, word of no meaning! behind whose vast latitude of mere sound we intrench our ignorance of so much of the spiritual. The expression of the eyes of Ligeia! How for long hours have I pondered upon it! How have I, through the whole of a midsummer night, struggled to fathom it! What was it—that something more profound than the well of Democritus[8]—which lay far within the pupils of my beloved? What *was* it? I was possessed with a passion to discover. Those eyes! those large, those shining, those divine orbs! they became to me twin stars of Leda,[9] and I to them devoutest of astrologers.

There is no point, among the many incomprehensible anomalies of the science of mind, more thrillingly exciting than the fact—never, I believe, noticed in the schools—that, in our endeavors to recall to memory something long forgotten, we often find ourselves *upon the very verge* of remembrance, without being able, in the end, to remember. And thus how frequently, in my intense scrutiny of Ligeia's eyes, have I felt approaching the full knowledge of their expression—felt it approaching—yet not quite be mine—and so at length entirely depart! And (strange, oh strangest mystery of all!) I found, in the commonest objects of the universe, a circle of analogies to that expression. I mean to say that, subsequently to the period when Ligeia's beauty passed into my spirit, there dwelling as in a shrine, I derived, from many existences in the material world, a sentiment such as I felt always aroused within me by her large and luminous orbs. Yet not the more could I define that sentiment, or analyze, or even steadily view it. I recognized it, let me repeat, sometimes in the commonest objects of the universe. It has flashed upon me in the survey of a rapidly-growing vine—in the contemplation of a moth, a butterfly, a chrysalis, a stream of running water.

---

[6]Poe's reference is to Frances Sheridan's *History of the Nourjahad*, an orientalist novel.
[7]The Houri are maidens in the Mohammedan paradise.
[8]The proverb "Of truth we know nothing, for truth is in the depths" has been attributed to Democritus, a Greek philosopher who lived in the fifth century B.C.

[9]Leda was a beautiful mortal whom Zeus found irresistible. After Zeus, in the form of a swan, raped her, she gave birth to Helen of Troy and to Castor and Pollux, whom Zeus transformed into the constellation Gemini.

I have felt it in the ocean; in the falling of a meteor. I have felt it in the glances of unusually aged people. And there are one or two stars in heaven— (one especially, a star of the sixth magnitude, double and changeable, to be found near the large star in Lyra)[10] in a telescopic scrutiny of which I have been made aware of the feeling. I have been filled with it by certain sounds from stringed instruments, and not unfrequently by passages from books. Among innumerable other instances, I well remember something in a volume of Joseph Glanvill, which (perhaps merely from its quaintness—who shall say?) never failed to inspire me with the sentiment;—"And the will therein lieth, which dieth not. Who knoweth the mysteries of the will, with its vigor? For God is but a great will pervading all things by nature of its intentness. Man doth not yield him to the angels, nor unto death utterly, save only through the weakness of his feeble will."

Length of years, and subsequent reflection, have enabled me to trace, indeed, some remote connection between this passage in the English moralist and a portion of the character of Ligeia. An *intensity* in thought, action, or speech, was possibly, in her, a result, or at least an index, of that gigantic volition which, during our long intercourse, failed to give other and more immediate evidence of its existence. Of all the women whom I have ever known, she, the outwardly calm, the ever-placid Ligeia, was the most violently a prey to the tumultuous vultures of stern passion. And of such passion I could form no estimate, save by the miraculous expansion of those eyes which at once so delighted and appalled me—by the almost magical melody, modulation, distinctness and placidity of her very low voice—and by the fierce energy (rendered doubly effective by contrast with her manner of utterance) of the wild words which she habitually uttered.

I have spoken of the learning of Ligeia: it was immense—such as I have never known in woman. In the classical tongues was she deeply proficient, and as far as my own acquaintance extended in regard to the modern dialects of Europe, I have never known her at fault. Indeed upon any theme of the most admired, because simply the most abstruse of the boasted erudition of the academy, have I *ever* found Ligeia at fault? How singularly—how thrillingly, this one point in the nature of my wife has forced itself, at this late period only, upon my attention! I said her knowledge was such as I have never known in woman—but where breathes the man who has traversed, and successfully, *all* the wide areas of moral, physical, and mathematical science? I saw not then what I now clearly perceive, that the acquisitions of Ligeia were gigantic, were astounding; yet I was sufficiently aware of her infinite supremacy to resign myself, with a childlike confidence, to her guidance through the chaotic world of metaphysical investigation at which I was most busily occupied during the earlier years of our marriage. With how vast a triumph—with how vivid a delight—with how much of all that is ethereal in hope—did I *feel*, as she bent over me in studies but little sought—but less

[10]Lyra is a constellation of stars that form a heavenly harp.

known—that delicious vista by slow degrees expanding before me, down whose long, gorgeous, and all untrodden path, I might at length pass onward to the goal of a wisdom too divinely precious not to be forbidden!

How poignant, then, must have been the grief with which, after some years, I beheld my well-grounded expectations take wings to themselves and fly away! Without Ligeia I was but as a child groping benighted. Her presence, her readings alone, rendered vividly luminous the many mysteries of the transcendentalism[11] in which we were immersed. Wanting the radiant lustre of her eyes, letters, lambent and golden, grew duller than Saturnian lead.[12] And now those eyes shone less and less frequently upon the pages over which I pored. Ligeia grew ill. The wild eyes blazed with a too—too glorious effulgence; the pale fingers became of the transparent waxen hue of the grave, and the blue veins upon the lofty forehead swelled and sank impetuously with the tides of the most gentle emotion. I saw that she must die—and I struggled desperately in spirit with the grim Azrael.[13] And the struggles of the passionate wife were, to my astonishment, even more energetic than my own. There had been much in her stern nature to impress me with the belief that, to her, death would have come without its terrors;—but not so. Words are impotent to convey any just idea of the fierceness of resistance with which she wrestled with the Shadow. I groaned in anguish at the pitiable spectacle. I would have soothed—I would have reasoned; but, in the intensity of her wild desire for life,—for life—*but* for life—solace and reason were alike the uttermost of folly. Yet not until the last instance, amid the most convulsive writhings of her fierce spirit, was shaken the external placidity of her demeanor. Her voice grew more gentle—grew more low—yet I would not wish to dwell upon the wild meaning of the quietly uttered words. My brain reeled as I hearkened entranced, to a melody more than mortal—to assumptions and aspirations which mortality had never before known.

That she loved me I should not have doubted; and I might have been easily aware that, in a bosom such as hers, love would have reigned no ordinary passion. But in death only, was I fully impressed with the strength of her affection. For long hours, detaining my hand, would she pour out before me the overflowing of a heart whose more than passionate devotion amounted to idolatry. How had I deserved to be so blessed by such confession?—how had I deserved to be so cursed with the removal of my beloved in the hour of her making them? But upon this subject I cannot bear to dilate. Let me say only, that in Ligeia's more than womanly abandonment to a love, alas! all unmerited, all unworthily bestowed, I at length recognized the principle of her longing with so wildly earnest a desire for the life which was now fleeing so rapidly away. It is this wild longing—it is

---

[11]Poe refers here not to the New England school of thought headed by Emerson but to spiritual realities above and beyond the physical world.

[12]A reference to alchemy, a medieval pseudo-science which contended that lead could be transformed into gold. Saturnine in alchemical terminology means leadlike.

[13]The Mohammedan angel of death.

this eager vehemence of desire for life—*but* for life—that I have no power to portray—no utterance capable of expressing.

At high noon of the night in which she departed, beckoning me, peremptorily, to her side, she bade me repeat certain verses composed by herself not many days before. I obeyed her.—They were these:

> Lo! 't is a gala night
>> Within the lonesome latter years!
> An angel throng, bewinged, bedight
>> In veils, and drowned in tears,
> Sit in a theatre, to see
>> A play of hopes and fears,   5
> While the orchestra breathes fitfully
>> The music of the spheres.
>
> Mimes, in the form of God on high,
>> Mutter and mumble low,
> And hither and thither fly—   10
>> Mere puppets they, who come and go
> At bidding of vast formless things
>> That shift the scenery to and fro,
> Flapping from out their Condor wings
>> Invisible Wo!   15
>
> That motley drama!—oh, be sure
>> It shall not be forgot!
> With its Phantom chased forever more,
>> By a crowd that seize it not,
> Through a circle that ever returneth in   20
>> To the self-same spot,
> And much of Madness and more of Sin
>> And Horror the soul of the plot.
> But see, amid the mimic rout,
>> A crawling shape intrude!   25
> A blood-red thing that writhes from out
>> The scenic solitude!
> It writhes!—it writhes!—with mortal pangs
>> The mimes become its food,
> And the seraphs sob at vermin fangs   30
>> In human gore imbued.
>
> Out—out are the lights—out all!
>> And over each quivering form,
> The curtain, a funeral pall,
>> Comes down with the rush of a storm,   35
> And the angels, all pallid and wan,

Uprising, unveiling, affirm
That the play is the tragedy, "Man,"
And its hero the Conqueror Worm.[14]   40

"O God!" half shrieked Ligeia, leaping to her feet and extending her arms aloft with a spasmodic movement, as I made an end of these lines— "O God! O Divine Father!—shall these things be undeviatingly so?—shall this Conqueror be not once conquered? Are we not part and parcel in Thee? Who—who knoweth the mysteries of the will with its vigor? Man doth not yield him to the angels, *nor unto death utterly*, save only through the weakness of his feeble will."

And now, as if exhausted with emotion, she suffered her white arms to fall, and returned solemnly to her bed of death. And as she breathed her last sighs, there came mingled with them a low murmur from her lips. I bent to them my ear and distinguished, again, the concluding words of the passage in Glanvill—"*Man doth not yield him to the angels, nor unto death utterly, save only through the weakness of his feeble will.*"

She died;—and I, crushed into the very dust with sorrow, could no longer endure the lonely desolation of my dwelling in the dim and decaying city by the Rhine. I had no lack of what the world calls wealth. Ligeia had brought me far more, very far more than ordinarily falls to the lot of mortals. After a few months, therefore, of weary and aimless wandering, I purchased, and put in some repair, an abbey, which I shall not name, in one of the wildest and least frequented portions of fair England. The gloomy and dreary grandeur of the building, the almost savage aspect of the domain, the many melancholy and time-honored memories connected with both, had much in unison with the feelings of utter abandonment which had driven me into that remote and unsocial region of the country. Yet although the external abbey, with its verdant decay hanging about it, suffered but little alteration, I gave way, with a child-like perversity, and perchance with a faint hope of alleviating my sorrows, to a display of more than regal magnificence within.—For such follies, even in childhood, I had imbibed a taste and now they came back to me as if in the dotage of grief. Alas, I feel how much even of incipient madness might have been discovered in the gorgeous and fantastic draperies, in the solemn carvings of Egypt, in the wild cornices and furniture, in the Bedlam patterns of the carpets of tufted gold! I had become a bounden slave in the trammels of opium, and my labors and my orders had taken a coloring from my dreams. But these absurdities I must not pause to detail. Let me speak only of that one chamber, ever accursed, whither in a moment of mental alienation, I led from the altar as my bride—as the successor of the unforgotten Ligeia—the fair-haired and blue-eyed Lady Rowena Trevanion, of Tremaine.

[14]This poem was first published in 1843 under the title "The Conqueror Worm" and incorporated into "Ligeia" in 1845.

There is no individual portion of the architecture and decoration of that bridal chamber which is not now visibly before me. Where were the souls of the haughty family of the bride, when, through thirst of gold, they permitted to pass the threshold of an apartment *so* bedecked, a maiden and a daughter so beloved? I have said that I minutely remember the details of the chamber—yet I am sadly forgetful on topics of deep moment—and here there was no system, no keeping, in the fantastic display, to take hold upon the memory. The room lay in a high turret of the castellated abbey, was pentagonal in shape, and of capacious size. Occupying the whole southern face of the pentagon was the sole window—an immense sheet of unbroken glass from Venice—a single pane, and tinted of a leaden hue, so that the rays of either the sun or moon, passing through it, fell with a ghastly lustre on the objects within. Over the upper portion of this huge window, extended the trellice-work of an aged vine, which clambered up the massy walls of the turret. The ceiling, of gloomy-looking oak, was excessively lofty, vaulted, and elaborately fretted with the wildest and most grotesque specimens of a semi-Gothic, semi-Druidical device. From out the most central recess of this melancholy vaulting, depended, by a single chain of gold with long links, a huge censer of the same metal, Saracenic in pattern, and with many perforations so contrived that there writhed in and out of them, as if endued with a serpent vitality, a continual succession of parti-colored fires.

Some few ottomans and golden candelabra, of Eastern figure, were in various stations about—and there was the couch, too—the bridal couch—of an Indian model, and low, and sculptured of solid ebony, with a pall-like canopy above. In each of the angles of the chamber stood on end a gigantic sarcophagus of black granite, from the tombs of the kings over against Luxor,[15] with their aged lids full of immemorial sculpture. But in the draping of the apartment lay, alas! the chief phantasy of all. The lofty walls, gigantic in height—even unproportionably so—were hung from summit to foot, in vast folds, with a heavy and massive-looking tapestry—tapestry of a material which was found alike as a carpet on the floor, as a covering for the ottomans and the ebony bed, as a canopy for the bed, and as the gorgeous volutes of the curtains which partially shaded the window. The material was the richest cloth of gold. It was spotted all over, at irregular intervals, with arabesque figures, about a foot in diameter, and wrought upon the cloth in patterns of the most jetty black. But these figures partook of the true character of the arabesque only when regarded from a single point of view. By a contrivance now common, and indeed traceable to a very remote period of antiquity, they were made changeable in aspect. To one entering the room, they bore the appearance of simple monstrosities; but upon a farther advance, this appearance gradually departed; and step by step, as the visiter moved his station in the chamber, he saw himself surrounded by an endless succession of the ghastly forms which belong to the superstition of the

[15]Site of famous ruins on the Nile River near ancient Thebes.

Norman, or arise in the guilty slumbers of the monk. The phantasmagoric effect was vastly heightened by the artificial introduction of a strong continual current of wind behind the draperies—giving a hideous and uneasy animation to the whole.

In halls such as these—in a bridal chamber such as this—I passed, with the Lady of Tremaine, the unhallowed hours of the first month of our marriage—passed them with but little disquietude. That my wife dreaded the fierce moodiness of my temper—that she shunned me and loved me but little—I could not help perceiving; but it gave me rather pleasure than otherwise. I loathed her with a hatred belonging more to demon than to man. My memory flew back, (oh, with what intensity of regret!) to Ligeia, the beloved, the august, the beautiful, the entombed. I revelled in recollections of her purity, of her wisdom, of her lofty, her ethereal nature, of her passionate, her idolatrous love. Now, then, did my spirit fully and freely burn with more than all the fires of her own. In the excitement of my opium dreams (for I was habitually fettered in the shackles of the drug) I would call aloud upon her name, during the silence of the night, or among the sheltered recesses of the glens by day, as if, through the wild eagerness, the solemn passion, the consuming ardor of my longing for the departed, I could restore her to the pathway she had abandoned—ah, *could* it be forever?—upon the earth.

About the commencement of the second month of the marriage, the Lady Rowena was attacked with sudden illness, from which her recovery was slow. The fever which consumed her rendered her nights uneasy; and in her perturbed state of half-slumber, she spoke of sounds, and of motions, in and about the chamber of the turret, which I concluded had no origin save in the distemper of her fancy, or perhaps in the phantasmagoric influences of the chamber itself. She became at length convalescent—finally well. Yet but a brief period elapsed, ere a second more violent disorder again threw her upon a bed of suffering; and from this attack her frame, at all times feeble, never altogether recovered. Her illnesses were, after this epoch, of alarming character, and of more alarming recurrence, defying alike the knowledge and the great exertions of her physicians. With the increase of the chronic disease which had thus, apparently, taken too sure hold upon her constitution to be eradicated by human means, I could not fail to observe a similar increase in the nervous irritation of her temperament, and in her excitability by trivial causes of fear. She spoke again, and now more frequently and pertinaciously, of the sounds—of the slight sounds—and of the unusual motions among the tapestries, to which she had formerly alluded.

One night, near the closing in of September, she pressed this distressing subject with more than usual emphasis upon my attention. She had just awakened from an unquiet slumber, and I had been watching, with feelings half of anxiety, half of vague terror, the workings of her emaciated countenance. I sat by the side of her ebony bed, upon one of the ottomans of India. She partly arose, and spoke, in an earnest low whisper, of sounds which she *then* heard, but which I could not hear—of motions which she *then* saw, but which I could not perceive. The wind was rushing hurriedly behind the tapestries, and I wished to show her (what, let me confess it, I could not *all* believe) that those almost inarticulate breathings, and those very gentle variations of the figures upon the wall, were but the natural effects of that customary rushing of the wind. But a deadly pallor, over-spreading her face, had proved to me that my exertions to reassure her would be fruitless. She appeared to be fainting, and no attendants were within call. I remembered where was deposited a decanter of light wine which had been ordered by her physicians, and hastened across the chamber to procure it. But, as I stepped beneath the light of the censer, two circum-stances of a startling nature attracted my attention. I had felt that some pal-pable although invisible object had passed lightly by my person; and I saw that there lay upon the golden carpet, in the very middle of the rich lustre thrown from the censer, a shadow—a faint, indefinite shadow of angelic aspect—such as might be fancied for the shadow of a shade. But I was wild with the excitement of an immoderate dose of opium, and heeded these things but little, nor spoke of them to Rowena. Having found the wine, I recrossed the chamber, and poured out a goblet-ful, which I held to the lips of the fainting lady. She had now partially recovered, however, and took the ves-sel herself, while I sank upon an ottoman near me, with my eyes fastened upon her person. It was then that I became distinctly aware of a gentle foot-fall upon the carpet, and near the couch; and in a second thereafter, as Row-ena was in the act of raising the wine to her lips, I saw, or may have dreamed that I saw, fall within the goblet, as if from some invisible spring in the atmosphere of the room, three or four large drops of a brilliant and ruby col-ored fluid. If this I saw—not so Rowena. She swallowed the wine unhesitat-ingly, and I forbore to speak to her of a circumstance which must, after all, I considered, have been but the suggestion of a vivid imagination, rendered morbidly active by the terror of the lady, by the opium, and by the hour.

Yet I cannot conceal it from my own perception that, immediately sub-sequent to the fall of the ruby-drops, a rapid change for the worse took place in the disorder of my wife; so that, on the third subsequent night, the hands of her menials prepared her for the tomb, and on the fourth, I sat alone, with her shrouded body, in that fantastic chamber which had received her as my bride.—Wild visions, opium-engendered, flitted, shadow-like, before me. I gazed with unquiet eye upon the sarcophagi in the angles of the room, upon the varying figures of the drapery, and upon the writhing of the parti-colored fires in the censer overhead. My eyes then fell, as I called to mind the circumstances of a former night, to the spot beneath the glare of the censer where I had seen the faint traces of the shadow. It was there, however, no longer; and breathing with greater freedom, I turned my glan-ces to the pallid and rigid figure upon the bed. Then rushed upon me a thou-sand memories of Ligeia—and then came back upon my heart, with the turbulent violence of a flood, the whole of that unutterable wo with which I had regarded *her* thus enshrouded. The night waned; and still, with a bosom full of bitter thoughts of the one only and supremely beloved, I remained gazing upon the body of Rowena.

It might have been midnight, or perhaps earlier, or later, for I had taken no note of time, when a sob, low, gentle, but very distinct, startled me from my revery.—I *felt* that it came from the bed of ebony—the bed of death. I listened in an agony of superstitious terror—but there was no repetition of the sound. I strained my vision to detect any motion in the corpse—but there was not the slightest perceptible. Yet I could not have been deceived. I *had* heard the noise, however faint, and my soul was awakened within me. I resolutely and perseveringly kept my attention riveted upon the body. Many minutes elapsed before any circumstance occurred tending to throw light upon the mystery. At length it became evident that a slight, a very feeble, and barely noticeable tinge of color had flushed up within the cheeks, and along the sunken small veins of the eyelids. Through a species of unutterable horror and awe, for which the language of mortality has no sufficiently energetic expression, I felt my heart cease to beat, my limbs grow rigid where I sat. Yet a sense of duty finally operated to restore my self-possession. I could no longer doubt that we had been precipitate in our preparations—that Rowena still lived. It was necessary that some immediate exertion be made; yet the turret was altogether apart from the portion of the abbey tenanted by the servants—there were none within call—I had no means of summoning them to my aid without leaving the room for many minutes—and this I could not venture to do. I therefore struggled alone in my endeavors to call back the spirit still hovering. In a short period it was certain, however, that a relapse had taken place; the color disappeared from both eyelid and cheek, leaving a wanness even more than that of marble; the lips became doubly shrivelled and pinched up in the ghastly expression of death; a repulsive clamminess and coldness overspread rapidly the surface of the body; and all the usual rigorous stiffness immediately supervened. I fell back with a shudder upon the couch from which I had been so startlingly aroused, and again gave myself up to passionate waking visions of Ligeia.

An hour thus elapsed when (could it be possible?) I was a second time aware of some vague sound issuing from the region of the bed. I listened—in extremity of horror. The sound came again—it was a sigh. Rushing to the corpse, I saw—distinctly saw—a tremor upon the lips. In a minute afterward they relaxed, disclosing a bright line of the pearly teeth. Amazement now struggled in my bosom with the profound awe which had hitherto reigned there alone. I felt that my vision grew dim, that my reason wandered; and it was only by a violent effort that I at length succeeded in nerving myself to the task which duty thus once more had pointed out. There was now a partial glow upon the forehead and upon the cheek and throat; a perceptible warmth pervaded the whole frame; there was even a slight pulsation at the heart. The lady *lived*; and with redoubled ardor I betook myself to the task of restoration. I chafed and bathed the temples and the hands, and used every exertion which experience, and no little medical reading, could suggest. But in vain. Suddenly, the color fled, the pulsation ceased, the lips resumed the expression of the dead, and, in an instant afterward, the whole body took upon itself the icy chilliness, the livid hue, the intense rigidity, the sunken outline, and all the loathsome peculiarities of that which has been, for many days, a tenant of the tomb.

And again I sunk into visions of Ligeia—and again, (what marvel that I shudder while I write?) *again* there reached my ears a low sob from the region of the ebony bed. But why shall I minutely detail the unspeakable horrors of that night? Why shall I pause to relate how, time after time, until near the period of the gray dawn, this hideous drama of revivification was repeated; how each terrific relapse was only into a sterner and apparently more irredeemable death; how each agony wore the aspect of a struggle with some invisible foe; and how each struggle was succeeded by I know not what of wild change in the personal appearance of the corpse? Let me hurry to a conclusion.

The greater part of the fearful night had worn away, and she who had been dead, once again stirred—and now more vigorously than hitherto, although arousing from a dissolution more appalling in its utter hopelessness than any. I had long ceased to struggle or to move, and remained sitting rigidly upon the ottoman, a helpless prey to a whirl of violent emotions, of which extreme awe was perhaps the least terrible, the least consuming. The corpse, I repeat, stirred, and now more vigorously than before. The hues of life flushed up with unwonted energy into the countenance—the limbs relaxed—and, save that the eyelids were yet pressed heavily together, and that the bandages and draperies of the grave still imparted their charnel character to the figure, I might have dreamed that Rowena had indeed shaken off, utterly, the fetters of Death. But if this idea was not, even then, altogether adopted, I could at least doubt no longer, when, arising from the bed, tottering, with feeble steps, with closed eyes, and with the manner of one bewildered in a dream, the thing that was enshrouded advanced boldly and palpably into the middle of the apartment.

I trembled not—I stirred not—for a crowd of unutterable fancies connected with the air, the stature, the demeanor of the figure, rushing hurriedly through my brain, had paralyzed—had chilled me into stone. I stirred not—but gazed upon the apparition. There was a mad disorder in my thoughts—a tumult unappeasable. Could it, indeed, be the *living* Rowena who confronted me? Could it indeed be Rowena *at all*—the fair-haired, the blue-eyed Lady Rowena Trevanion of Tremaine? Why, *why* should I doubt it? The bandage lay heavily about the mouth—but then might it not be the mouth of the breathing Lady of Tremaine? And the cheeks—there were the roses as in her noon of life—yes, these might indeed be the fair cheeks of the living Lady of Tremaine. And the chin, with its dimples, as in health, might it not be hers?—but *had she then grown taller since her malady?* What inexpressible madness seized me with that thought? One bound, and I had reached her feet! Shrinking from my touch, she let fall from her head, unloosened, the ghastly cerements which had confined it, and there streamed forth, into the rushing atmosphere of the chamber, huge masses of long and dishevelled hair; *it was blacker than the raven wings of the mid-night!* And now slowly opened *the eyes* of the figure which stood before me. "Here then, at least," I shrieked aloud, "can I never—can I never be mistaken—these are the full, and the black, and the wild eyes—of my lost love—of the lady—of the LADY LIGEIA."

1838, 1845

The Fall of the House of Usher

Son coeur est un luth suspendu;
Sitôt qu'on le touche il résonne.[1]

—DE BÉRANGER

During the whole of a dull, dark, and soundless day in the autumn of the year, when the clouds hung oppressively low in the heavens, I had been passing alone, on horseback, through a singularly dreary tract of country, and at length found myself, as the shades of the evening drew on, within view of the melancholy House of Usher. I know not how it was—but, with the first glimpse of the building, a sense of insufferable gloom pervaded my spirit. I say insufferable; for the feeling was unrelieved by any of that half-pleasurable, because poetic, sentiment, with which the mind usually receives even the sternest natural images of the desolate or terrible. I looked upon the scene before me—upon the mere house, and the simple landscape features of the domain—upon the bleak walls—upon the vacant eye-like windows—upon a few rank sedges—and upon a few white trunks of decayed trees—with an utter depression of soul which I can compare to no earthly sensation more properly than to the after-dream of the reveller upon opium—the bitter lapse into every-day life—the hideous dropping off of the veil. There was an iciness, a sinking, a sickening of the heart—an unredeemed dreariness of thought which no goading of the imagination could torture into aught of the sublime. What was it—I paused to think—what was it that so unnerved me in the contemplation of the House of Usher? It was a mystery all insoluble; nor could I grapple with the shadowy fancies that crowded upon me as I pondered. I was forced to fall back upon the unsatisfactory conclusion, that while, beyond doubt, there *are* combinations of very simple natural objects which have the power of thus affecting us, still the analysis of this power lies among considerations beyond our depth. It was possible, I reflected, that a mere different arrangement of the particulars of the scene, of the details of the picture, would be sufficient to modify, or perhaps to annihilate its capacity for sorrowful impression; and, acting upon this idea, I reined my horse to the precipitous brink of a black

---

[1]Originally published in *Burton's Gentleman's Magazine* in 1839, "The Fall of the House of Usher" was included in both *Tales of the Grotesque and Arabesque* (1840) and *Tales* (1845). The epigraph, from the French poet Pierre-Jean de Béranger, translates as "His heart is a lute suspended; when touched, it resounds."

and lurid tarn[2] that lay in unruffled lustre by the dwelling, and gazed down—but with a shudder even more thrilling than before—upon the remodelled and inverted images of the gray sedge, and the ghastly tree-stems, and the vacant and eye-like windows.

Nevertheless, in this mansion of gloom I now proposed to myself a sojourn of some weeks. Its proprietor, Roderick Usher, had been one of my boon companions in boyhood; but many years had elapsed since our last meeting. A letter, however, had lately reached me in a distant part of the country—a letter from him—which, in its wildly importunate nature, had admitted of no other than a personal reply. The MS. gave evidence of nervous agitation. The writer spoke of acute bodily illness—of a mental disorder which oppressed him—and of an earnest desire to see me, as his best, and indeed his only personal friend, with a view of attempting, by the cheerfulness of my society, some alleviation of his malady. It was the manner in which all this, and much more, was said—it was the apparent *heart* that went with his request—which allowed me no room for hesitation; and I accordingly obeyed forthwith what I still considered a very singular summons.

Although, as boys, we had been even intimate associates, yet I really knew little of my friend. His reserve had been always excessive and habitual. I was aware, however, that his very ancient family had been noted, time out of mind, for a peculiar sensibility of temperament, displaying itself, through long ages, in many works of exalted art, and manifested, of late, in repeated deeds of munificent yet unobtrusive charity, as well as in a passionate devotion to the intricacies, perhaps even more than to the orthodox and easily recognizable beauties, of musical science. I had learned, too, the very remarkable fact, that the stem of the Usher race, all time-honoured as it was, had put forth, at no period, any enduring branch; in other words, that the entire family lay in the direct line of descent, and had always, with very trifling and very temporary variation, so lain. It was this deficiency, I considered, while running over in thought the perfect keeping of the character of the premises with the accredited character of the people, and while speculating upon the possible influence which the one, in the long lapse of centuries, might have exercised upon the other—it was this deficiency, perhaps of collateral issue, and the consequent undeviating transmission, from sire to son, of the patrimony with the name, which had, at length, so identified the two as to merge the original title of the estate in the quaint and equivocal appellation of the "House of Usher"—an appellation which seemed to include, in the minds of the peasantry who used it, both the family and the family mansion.

I have said that the sole effect of my somewhat childish experiment—that of looking down within the tarn—had been to deepen the first singular impression. There can be no doubt that the consciousness of the rapid increase of my superstition—for why should I not so term it?—served

[2]A small mountain lake.

mainly to accelerate the increase itself. Such, I have long known, is the paradoxical law of all sentiments having terror as a basis. And it might have been for this reason only, that, when I again uplifted my eyes to the house itself, from its image in the pool, there grew in my mind a strange fancy—a fancy so ridiculous, indeed, that I but mention it to show the vivid force of the sensations which oppressed me. I had so worked upon my imagination as really to believe that about the whole mansion and domain there hung an atmosphere peculiar to themselves and their immediate vicinity—an atmosphere which had no affinity with the air of heaven, but which had reeked up from the decayed trees, and the gray wall, and the silent tarn—a pestilent and mystic vapour, dull, sluggish, faintly discernible, and leaden-hued.

Shaking off from my spirit what *must* have been a dream, I scanned more narrowly the real aspect of the building. Its principal feature seemed to be that of an excessive antiquity. The discoloration of ages had been great. Minute fungi overspread the whole exterior, hanging in a fine tangled web-work from the eaves. Yet all this was apart from an extraordinary dilapidation. No portion of the masonry had fallen; and there appeared to be a wild inconsistency between its still perfect adaptation of parts, and the crumbling condition of the individual stones. In this there was much that reminded me of the specious totality of old woodwork which has rotted for long years in some neglected vault, with no disturbance from the breath of the external air. Beyond this indication of extensive decay, however, the fabric gave little token of instability. Perhaps the eye of a scrutinizing observer might have discovered a barely perceptible fissure, which, extending from the roof of the building in front, made its way down the wall in a zigzag direction, until it became lost in the sullen waters of the tarn.

Noticing these things, I rode over a short causeway to the house. A servant in waiting took my horse, and I entered the Gothic archway of the hall. A valet, of stealthy step, thence conducted me, in silence, through many dark and intricate passages in my progress to the *studio* of his master. Much that I encountered on the way contributed, I know not how, to heighten the vague sentiments of which I have already spoken. While the objects around me—while the carvings of the ceilings, the sombre tapestries of the walls, the ebon blackness of the floors, and the phantasmagoric armorial trophies which rattled as I strode, were but matters to which, or to such as which, I had been accustomed from my infancy—while I hesitated not to acknowledge how familiar was all this—I still wondered to find how unfamiliar were the fancies which ordinary images were stirring up. On one of the staircases, I met the physician of the family. His countenance, I thought, wore a mingled expression of low cunning and perplexity. He accosted me with trepidation and passed on. The valet now threw open a door and ushered me into the presence of his master.

The room in which I found myself was very large and lofty. The windows were long, narrow, and pointed, and at so vast a distance from the black oaken floor as to be altogether inaccessible from within. Feeble gleams of encrimsoned light made their way through the trellissed panes, and served to render sufficiently distinct the more prominent objects around; the eye, however, struggled in vain to reach the remoter angles of the chamber, or the recesses of the vaulted and fretted ceiling. Dark draperies hung upon the walls. The general furniture was profuse, comfortless, antique, and tattered. Many books and musical instruments lay scattered about, but failed to give any vitality to the scene. I felt that I breathed an atmosphere of sorrow. An air of stern, deep, and irredeemable gloom hung over and pervaded all.

Upon my entrance, Usher arose from a sofa on which he had been lying at full length, and greeted me with a vivacious warmth which had much in it, I at first thought of an overdone cordiality—of the constrained effort of the *ennuyé*[3] man of the world. A glance, however, at his countenance convinced me of his perfect sincerity. We sat down; and for some moments, while he spoke not, I gazed upon him with a feeling half of pity, half of awe. Surely, man had never before so terribly altered, in so brief a period, as had Roderick Usher! It was with difficulty that I could bring myself to admit the identity of the wan being before me with the companion of my early boyhood. Yet the character of his face had been at all times remarkable. A cadaverousness of complexion; an eye large, liquid, and luminous beyond comparison; lips somewhat thin and very pallid, but of a surpassingly beautiful curve; a nose of a delicate Hebrew model, but with a breadth of nostril unusual in similar formations; a finely moulded chin, speaking, in its want of prominence, of a want of moral energy; hair of a more than web-like softness and tenuity; these features, with an inordinate expansion above the regions of the temple, made up altogether a countenance not easily to be forgotten. And now in the mere exaggeration of the prevailing character of these features, and of the expression they were wont to convey, lay so much of change that I doubted to whom I spoke. The now ghastly pallor of the skin, and the now miraculous lustre of the eye, above all things startled and even awed me. The silken hair, too, had been suffered to grow all unheeded, and as, in its wild gossamer texture, it floated rather than fell about the face, I could not, even with effort, connect its Arabesque[4] expression with any idea of simple humanity.

In the manner of my friend I was at once struck with an incoherence—an inconsistency; and I soon found this to arise from a series of feeble and futile struggles to overcome an habitual trepidancy—an excessive nervous agitation. For something of this nature I had indeed been prepared, no less by his letter, than by reminiscences of certain boyish traits, and by conclusions deducted from his peculiar physical conformation and temperament. His action was alternately vivacious and sullen. His voice varied rapidly from a tremulous indecision (when the animal spirits seemed utterly in abeyance) to that species of energetic concision—that abrupt, weighty, unhurried, and

[3]French for bored.
[4]Poe uses the word *Arabesque* to describe some of his fictional tales. Here it means unfamiliar, exotic.

hollow-sounding enunciation—that leaden, self-balanced, and perfectly modulated guttural utterance, which may be observed in the lost drunkard, or the irreclaimable eater of opium, during the periods of his most intense excitement.

It was thus that he spoke of the object of my visit, of his earnest desire to see me, and of the solace he expected me to afford him. He entered, at some length, into what he conceived to be the nature of his malady. It was, he said, a constitutional and a family evil, and one for which he despaired to find a remedy—a mere nervous affection, he immediately added, which would undoubtedly soon pass off. It displayed itself in a host of unnatural sensations. Some of these, as he detailed them, interested and bewildered me; although, perhaps, the terms and the general manner of their narration had their weight. He suffered much from a morbid acuteness of the senses; the most insipid food was alone endurable; he could wear only garments of certain texture; the odours of all flowers were oppressive; his eyes were tortured by even a faint light; and there were but peculiar sounds, and these from stringed instruments, which did not inspire him with horror.

To an anomalous species of terror I found him a bounden slave. "I shall perish," said he, "I *must* perish in this deplorable folly. Thus, thus, and not otherwise, shall I be lost. I dread the events of the future, not in themselves, but in their results. I shudder at the thought of any, even the most trivial, incident, which may operate upon this intolerable agitation of soul. I have, indeed, no abhorrence of danger, except in its absolute effect—in terror. In this unnerved—in this pitiable condition—I feel that the period will sooner or later arrive when I must abandon life and reason together, in some struggle with the grim phantasm, FEAR."

I learned, moreover, at intervals, and through broken and equivocal hints, another singular feature of his mental condition. He was enchained by certain superstitious impressions in regard to the dwelling which he tenanted, and whence, for many years, he had never ventured forth—in regard to an influence whose supposititious force was conveyed in terms too shadowy here to be re-stated—an influence which some peculiarities in the mere form and substance of his family mansion had, by dint of long sufferance, he said, obtained over his spirit—an effect which the *physique* of the gray wall and turrets, and of the dim tarn into which they all looked down, had, at length, brought about upon the *morale* of his existence.

He admitted, however, although with hesitation, that much of the peculiar gloom which thus afflicted him could be traced to a more natural and far more palpable origin—to the severe and long-continued illness—indeed to the evidently approaching dissolution—of a tenderly beloved sister, his sole companion for long years, his last and only relative on earth. "Her decease," he said, with a bitterness which I can never forget, "would leave him (him the hopeless and the frail) the last of the ancient race of the Ushers." While he spoke, the lady Madeline (for so was she called) passed slowly through a remote portion of the apartment, and, without having noticed my presence, disappeared. I regarded her with an utter astonishment not unmingled with dread—and yet I found it impossible to account for such feelings. A sensation of stupor oppressed me, as my eyes followed her retreating steps. When a door, at length, closed upon her, my glance sought instinctively and eagerly the countenance of the brother—but he had buried his face in his hands, and I could only perceive that a far more than ordinary wanness had overspread the emaciated fingers through which trickled many passionate tears.

The disease of the lady Madeline had long baffled the skill of her physicians. A settled apathy, a gradual wasting away of the person, and frequent although transient affections of a partially cataleptical character were the unusual diagnosis. Hitherto she had steadily borne up against the pressure of her malady, and had not betaken herself finally to bed; but on the closing in of the evening of my arrival at the house, she succumbed (as her brother told me at night with inexpressible agitation) to the prostrating power of the destroyer; and I learned that the glimpse I had obtained of her person would thus probably be the last I should obtain—that the lady, at least while living, would be seen by me no more.

For several days ensuing, her name was unmentioned by either Usher or myself: and during this period I was busied in earnest endeavours to alleviate the melancholy of my friend. We painted and read together, or I listened, as if in a dream, to the wild improvisations of his speaking guitar. And thus, as a closer and still closer intimacy admitted me more unreservedly into the recesses of his spirit, the more bitterly did I perceive the futility of all attempt at cheering a mind from which darkness, as if an inherent positive quality, poured forth upon all objects of the moral and physical universe in one unceasing radiation of gloom.

I shall ever bear about me a memory of the many solemn hours I thus spent alone with the master of the House of Usher. Yet I should fail in any attempt to convey an idea of the exact character of the studies, or of the occupations, in which he involved me, or led me the way. An excited and highly distempered ideality threw a sulphureous lustre over all. His long improvised dirges will ring forever in my ears. Among other things, I hold painfully in mind a certain singular perversion and amplification of the wild air of the last waltz of Von Weber.[5] From the paintings over which his elaborate fancy brooded, and which grew, touch by touch, into vagueness at which I shuddered the more thrillingly, because I shuddered knowing not why;—from these paintings (vivid as their images now are before me) I would in vain endeavour to educe more than a small portion which should lie within the compass of merely written words. By the utter simplicity, by the nakedness of his designs, he arrested and overawed attention. If ever mortal painted an idea, that mortal was Roderick Usher. For me at least—in the circumstances then surrounding me—there arose out of the pure abstractions which the hypochondriac contrived to throw upon

---

[5]A German composer who died in 1826. "Weber's Last Waltz," a popular piece of music, was believed to have been composed shortly before his death.

his canvas, an intensity of intolerable awe, no shadow of which I felt ever yet in the contemplation of the certainly glowing yet too concrete reveries of Fuseli.[6]

One of the phantasmagoric conceptions of my friend, partaking not so rigidly of the spirit of abstraction, may be shadowed forth, although feebly, in words. A small picture presented the interior of an immensely long and rectangular vault or tunnel, with low walls, smooth, white, and without interruption or device. Certain accessory points of the design served well to convey the idea that this excavation lay at an exceeding depth below the surface of the earth. No outlet was observed in any portion of its vast extent, and no torch or other artificial source of light was discernible; yet a flood of intense rays rolled throughout, and bathed the whole in a ghastly and inappropriate splendour.

I have just spoken of that morbid condition of the auditory nerve which rendered all music intolerable to the sufferer, with the exception of certain effects of stringed instruments. It was, perhaps, the narrow limits to which he thus confined himself upon the guitar, which gave birth, in great measure, to the fantastic character of his performances. But the fervid *facility* of his *impromptus* could not be so accounted for. They must have been, and were, in the notes, as well as in the words of his wild fantasias (for he not unfrequently accompanied himself with rhymed verbal improvisations), the result of that intense mental collectedness and concentration to which I have previously alluded as observable only in particular moments of the highest artificial excitement. The words of one of these rhapsodies I have easily remembered. I was, perhaps, the more forcibly impressed with it, as he gave it, because, in the under or mystic current of its meaning, I fancied that I perceived, and for the first time, a full consciousness on the part of Usher, of the tottering of his lofty reason upon her throne. The verses, which were entitled "The Haunted Palace," ran very nearly, if not accurately, thus:

I

In the greenest of our valleys,
    By good angels tenanted,
Once a fair and stately palace—
    Radiant palace—reared its head.
In the monarch Thought's dominion—
    It stood there!
Never seraph spread a pinion
    Over fabric half so fair.

---

[6]A Swiss-English painter who specialized in fantastic scenes with grotesque figures.

II

Banners yellow, glorious, golden,
    On its roof did float and flow;
(This—all this—was in the olden
    Time long ago)
And every gentle air that dallied,
    In that sweet day,
Along the ramparts plumed and pallid,
    A winged odour went away.

III

Wanderers in that happy valley
    Through two luminous windows saw
Spirits moving musically
    To a lute's well-tunèd law,
Round about a throne, where sitting
    (Porphyrogene!)[7]
In state his glory well befitting,
    The ruler of the realm was seen.

IV

And all with pearl and ruby glowing
    Was the fair palace door,
Through which came flowing, flowing, flowing
    And sparkling evermore,
A troop of Echoes whose sweet duty
    Was but to sing,
In voices of surpassing beauty,
    The wit and wisdom of their king.

V

But evil things, in robes of sorrow,
    Assailed the monarch's high estate;
(Ah, let us mourn, for never morrow
    Shall dawn upon him, desolate!)
And, round about his home, the glory
    That blushed and bloomed
Is but a dim-remembered story
    Of the old time entombed.

[7]A word Poe coined from Greek roots meaning
"born to the purple"—in other words, royal.

VI

And travellers now within that valley,
    Through the red-litten windows see
Vast forms that move fantastically
    To a discordant melody;
While, like a rapid ghastly river,
    Through the pale door,
A hideous throng rush out forever,
    And laugh—but smile no more.

I well remember that suggestions arising from this ballad, led us into a train of thought, wherein there became manifest an opinion of Usher's which I mention not so much on account of its novelty, (for other men have thought thus,) as on account of the pertinacity with which he maintained it. This opinion, in its general form, was that of the sentience of all vegetable things. But, in his disordered fancy, the idea had assumed a more daring character, and trespassed, under certain conditions, upon the kingdom of inorganization. I lack words to express the full extent, or the earnest *abandon* of his persuasion. The belief, however, was connected (as I have previously hinted) with the gray stones of the home of his forefathers. The conditions of the sentience had been here, he imagined, fulfilled in the method of collocation of these stones—in the order of their arrangement, as well as in that of the many *fungi* which overspread them, and of the decayed trees which stood around—above all, in the long undisturbed endurance of this arrangement, and in its reduplication in the still waters of the tarn. Its evidence—the evidence of the sentience—was to be seen, he said (and I here started as he spoke), in the gradual yet certain condensation of an atmosphere of their own about the waters and the walls. The result was discoverable, he added, in that silent yet importunate and terrible influence which for centuries had moulded the destinies of his family, and which made *him* what I now saw him—what he was. Such opinions need no comment, and I will make none.

Our books—the books which, for years, had formed no small portion of the mental existence of the invalid—were, as might be supposed, in strict keeping with his character of phantasm. We pored together over such works as the Ververt et Chartreuse of Gresset; the Belphegor of Machiavelli; the Heaven and Hell of Swedenborg; the Subterranean Voyage of Nicholas Klimm of Holberg; the Chiromancy of Robert Flud, of Jean D'Indaginé, and of De la Chambre; the Journey into the Blue Distance of Tieck; and the City of the Sun of Campanella. One favourite volume was a small octavo edition of the *Directorium Inquisitorum*, by the Dominican Eymeric de Gironne; and there were passages in Pomponius Mela, about the old African Satyrs and Œgipans, over which Usher would sit dreaming for hours. His chief delight, however, was found in the perusal of an exceedingly rare and curious book in quarto Gothic—the manual of a forgotten church—the *Vigiliœ Mortuorum secundum Chorum Ecclesiœ Maguntinœ*.[8]

I could not help thinking of the wild ritual of this work, and of its probable influence upon the hypochondriac, when, one evening, having informed me abruptly that the lady Madeline was no more, he stated his intention of preserving her corpse for a fortnight, (previously to its final interment,) in one of the numerous vaults within the main walls of the building. The worldly reason, however, assigned for this singular proceeding, was one which I did not feel at liberty to dispute. The brother had been led to his resolution (so he told me) by consideration of the unusual character of the malady of the deceased, of certain obtrusive and eager inquiries on the part of her medical men, and of the remote and exposed situation of the burial-ground of the family. I will not deny that when I called to mind the sinister countenance of the person whom I met upon the staircase, on the day of my arrival at the house, I had no desire to oppose what I regarded as at best but a harmless, and by no means an unnatural, precaution.[9]

At the request of Usher, I personally aided him in the arrangements for the temporary entombment. The body having been encoffined, we two alone bore it to its rest. The vault in which we placed it (and which had been so long unopened that our torches, half smothered in its oppressive atmosphere, gave us little opportunity for investigation) was small, damp, and entirely without means of admission for light; lying, at great depth, immediately beneath that portion of the building in which was my own sleeping apartment. It had been used, apparently, in remote feudal times, for the worst purposes of a donjon-keep, and, in later days, as a place of deposit for powder, or some other highly combustible substance, as a portion of its floor, and the whole interior of a long archway through which we reached it, were carefully sheathed with copper. The door, of massive iron, had been, also, similarly protected. Its immense weight caused an unusually sharp grating sound, as it moved upon its hinges.

Having deposited our mournful burden upon tressels within this region of horror, we partially turned aside the yet unscrewed lid of the coffin, and looked upon the face of the tenant. A striking similitude between the brother and sister now first arrested my attention; and Usher, divining, perhaps, my thoughts, murmured out some few words from which I learned that the deceased and himself had been twins, and that sympathies of a scarcely intelligible nature had always existed between them. Our glances, however, rested not long upon the dead—for we could not regard her unawed. The disease which had thus entombed the lady in the maturity of youth, had left, as usual in all maladies of a strictly cataleptical character, the mockery of a faint blush upon the bosom and the face, and that suspiciously lingering smile upon the lip which is so terrible in death. We

[8]All the books listed deal with pseudoscience, demonism, or persecution.

[9]Usher is afraid that Lady Madeline's body will be dug up for instructional use in some medical college—a practice all too common in Poe's day.

replaced and screwed down the lid, and, having secured the door of iron, made our way, with toil, into the scarcely less gloomy apartments of the upper portion of the house.

And now, some days of bitter grief having elapsed, an observable change came over the features of the mental disorder of my friend. His ordinary manner had vanished. His ordinary occupations were neglected or forgotten. He roamed from chamber to chamber with hurried, unequal, and objectless step. The pallor of his countenance had assumed, if possible, a more ghastly hue—but the luminousness of his eye had utterly gone out. The once occasional huskiness of his tone was heard no more; and a tremulous quaver, as if of extreme terror, habitually characterized his utterance. There were times, indeed, when I thought his unceasingly agitated mind was labouring with some oppressive secret, to divulge which he struggled for the necessary courage. At times, again, I was obliged to resolve all into the mere inexplicable vagaries of madness, for I beheld him gazing upon vacancy for long hours, in an attitude of the profoundest attention, as if listening to some imaginary sound. It was no wonder that his condition terrified—that it infected me. I felt creeping upon me, by slow yet certain degrees, the wild influences of his own fantastic yet impressive superstitions.

It was, especially, upon retiring to bed late in the night of the seventh or eighth day after the placing of the lady Madeline within the donjon, that I experienced the full power of such feelings. Sleep came not near my couch—while the hours waned and waned away. I struggled to reason off the nervousness which had dominion over me. I endeavoured to believe that much, if not all of what I felt, was due to the bewildering influence of the gloomy furniture of the room—of the dark and tattered draperies, which, tortured into motion by the breath of a rising tempest, swayed fitfully to and fro upon the walls, and rustled uneasily about the decorations of the bed. But my efforts were fruitless. An irrepressible tremour gradually pervaded my frame; and, at length, there sat upon my very heart an incubus of utterly causeless alarm. Shaking this off with a gasp and a struggle, I uplifted myself upon the pillows, and, peering earnestly within the intense darkness of the chamber, hearkened—I know not why, except that an instinctive spirit prompted me—to certain low and indefinite sounds which came, through the pauses of the storm, at long intervals, I knew not whence. Overpowered by an intense sentiment of horror, unaccountable yet unendurable, I threw on my clothes with haste, (for I felt that I should sleep no more during the night,) and endeavoured to arouse myself from the pitiable condition into which I had fallen, by pacing rapidly to and fro through the apartment.

I had taken but few turns in this manner, when a light step on an adjoining staircase arrested my attention. I presently recognised it as that of Usher. In an instant afterward he rapped, with a gentle touch, at my door, and entered, bearing a lamp. His countenance was, as usual, cadaverously wan—but, moreover, there was a species of mad hilarity in his eyes—an evidently restrained *hysteria* in his whole demeanour. His air appalled me—but anything was preferable to the solitude which I had so long endured, and I even welcomed his presence as a relief.

"And you have not seen it?" he said abruptly, after having stared about him for some moments in silence—"you have not then seen it?—but, stay! you shall." Thus speaking, and having carefully shaded his lamp, he hurried to one of the casements, and threw it freely open to the storm.

The impetuous fury of the entering gust nearly lifted us from our feet. It was, indeed, a tempestuous yet sternly beautiful night, and one wildly singular in its terror and its beauty. A whirlwind had apparently collected its force in our vicinity; for there were frequent and violent alterations in the direction of the wind; and the exceeding density of the clouds (which hung so low as to press upon the turrets of the house) did not prevent our perceiving the life-like velocity with which they flew careering from all points against each other, without passing away into the distance. I say that even their exceeding density did not prevent our perceiving this—yet we had no glimpse of the moon or stars—nor was there any flashing forth of the lightning. But the under surfaces of the huge masses of agitated vapour, as well as all terrestrial objects immediately around us, were glowing in the unnatural light of a faintly luminous and distinctly visible gaseous exhalation which hung about and enshrouded the mansion.

"You must not—you shall not behold this!" said I, shudderingly, to Usher, as I led him, with a gentlè violence, from the window to a seat. "These appearances, which bewilder you, are merely electrical phenomena not uncommon—or it may be that they have their ghastly origin in the rank miasma of the tarn. Let us close this casement;—the air is chilling and dangerous to your frame. Here is one of your favourite romances. I will read, and you shall listen;—and so we will pass away this terrible night together."

The antique volume which I had taken up was the "Mad Trist" of Sir Launcelot Canning;[10] but I had called it a favourite of Usher's more in sad jest than in earnest; for, in truth, there is little in its uncouth and unimaginative prolixity which could have had interest for the lofty and spiritual ideality of my friend. It was, however, the only book immediately at hand; and I indulged a vague hope that the excitement which now agitated the hypochondriac, might find relief (for the history of mental disorder is full of similar anomalies) even in the extremeness of the folly which I could read. Could I have judged, indeed, by the wild overstrained air of vivacity with which he hearkened, or apparently hearkened, to the words of the tale, I might well have congratulated myself upon the success of my design.

I had arrived at that well-known portion of the story where Ethelred, the hero of the Trist, having sought in vain for peaceable admission into the dwelling of the hermit, proceeds to make good an entrance by force. Here, it will be remembered, the words of the narrative run thus:

[10]Scholars have failed to find Canning's name among lists of real authors, although Poe used the reference on more than one occasion.

"And Ethelred, who was by nature of a doughty heart, and who was now mighty withal, on account of the powerfulness of the wine which he had drunken, waited no longer to hold parley with the hermit, who, in sooth, was of an obstinate and maliceful turn, but, feeling the rain upon his shoulders, and fearing the rising of the tempest, uplifted his mace outright, and, with blows, made quickly room in the plankings of the door for his gauntleted hand; and now pulling therewith sturdily, he so cracked, and ripped, and tore all asunder, that the noise of the dry and hollow-sounding wood alarmed and reverberated throughout the forest."

At the termination of this sentence I started and, for a moment, paused; for it appeared to me (although I at once concluded that my excited fancy had deceived me)—it appeared to me that, from some very remote portion of the mansion, there came, indistinctly, to my ears, what might have been, in its exact similarity of character, the echo (but a stifled and dull one certainly) of the very cracking and ripping sound which Sir Launcelot had so particularly described. It was, beyond doubt, the coincidence alone which had arrested my attention; for, amid the rattling of the sashes of the casements, and the ordinary commingled noises of the still increasing storm, the sound, in itself, had nothing, surely, which should have interested or disturbed me. I continued the story:

"But the good champion Ethelred, now entering within the door, was sore enraged and amazed to perceive no signal of the maliceful hermit; but, in the stead thereof, a dragon of a scaly and prodigious demeanour, and of a fiery tongue, which sate in guard before a palace of gold, with a floor of silver; and upon the wall there hung a shield of shining brass with this legend enwritten—

Who entereth herein, a conqueror hath bin;
Who slayeth the dragon, the shield he shall win.

And Ethelred uplifted his mace, and struck upon the head of the dragon, which fell before him, and gave up his pesty breath, with a shriek so horrid and harsh, and withal so piercing, that Ethelred had fain to close his ears with his hands against the dreadful noise of it, the like whereof was never before heard."

Here again I paused abruptly, and now with a feeling of wild amazement—for there could be no doubt whatever that, in this instance, I did actually hear (although from what direction it proceeded I found it impossible to say) a low and apparently distant, but harsh, protracted, and most unusual screaming or grating sound—the exact counterpart of what my fancy had already conjured up for the dragon's unnatural shriek as described by the romancer.

Oppressed, as I certainly was, upon the occurrence of the second and most extraordinary coincidence, by a thousand conflicting sensations, in which wonder and extreme terror were predominant, I still retained sufficient presence of mind to avoid exciting, by any observation, the sensitive nervousness of my companion. I was by no means certain that he had noticed the sounds in question; although, assuredly, a strange alteration had, during the last few minutes, taken place in his demeanour. From a position fronting my own, he had gradually brought round his chair, so as to sit with his face to the door of the chamber; and thus I could but partially perceive his features, although I saw that his lips trembled as if he were murmuring inaudibly. His head had dropped upon his breast—yet I knew that he was not asleep, from the wide and rigid opening of the eye as I caught a glance of it in profile. The motion of his body, too, was at variance with this idea—for he rocked from side to side with a gentle yet constant and uniform sway. Having rapidly taken notice of all this, I resumed the narrative of Sir Launcelot, which thus proceeded:

"And now, the champion, having escaped from the terrible fury of the dragon, bethinking himself of the brazen shield, and of the breaking up of the enchantment which was upon it, removed the carcass from out of the way before him, and approached valorously over the silver pavement of the castle to where the shield was upon the wall; which in sooth tarried not for his full coming, but fell down at his feet upon the silver floor, with a mighty great and terrible ringing sound."

No sooner had these syllables passed my lips, than—as if a shield of brass had indeed, at the moment, fallen heavily upon a floor of silver—I became aware of a distinct, hollow, metallic, and clangorous, yet apparently muffled reverberation. Completely unnerved, I leaped to my feet; but the measured rocking movement of Usher was undisturbed. I rushed to the chair in which he sat. His eyes were bent fixedly before him, and throughout his whole countenance there reigned a stony rigidity. But, as I placed my hand upon his shoulder, there came a strong shudder over his whole person; a sickly smile quivered about his lips; and I saw that he spoke in a low, hurried, and gibbering murmur, as if unconscious of my presence. Bending closely over him, I at length drank in the hideous import of his words.

"Not hear it?—yes, I hear it, and *have* heard it. Long—long—long—many minutes, many hours, many days, have I heard it—yet I dared not—oh, pity me, miserable wretch that I am!—I dared not—I *dared* not speak! *We have put her living in the tomb!* Said I not that my senses were acute? I *now* tell you that I heard her first feeble movements in the hollow coffin. I heard them—many, many days ago—yet I dared not—I *dared not speak!* And now—to-night—Ethelred—ha! ha!—the breaking of the hermit's door, and the death-cry of the dragon, and the clangour of the shield!—say, rather, the rending of her coffin, and the grating of the iron hinges of her prison, and her struggles within the coppered archway of the vault! Oh whither shall I fly? Will she not be here anon? Is she not hurrying to upbraid me for my haste? Have I not heard her footsteps on the stair? Do I not distinguish that heavy and horrible beating of her heart? MADMAN!"—here he sprang furiously to his feet, and shrieked out his syllables, as if in the effort he were giving up his soul—"MADMAN! I TELL YOU THAT SHE NOW STANDS WITHOUT THE DOOR!"

As if in the superhuman energy of his utterance there had been found the potency of a spell—the huge antique panels to which the speaker pointed threw slowly back, upon the instant, their ponderous and ebony jaws. It was the work of the rushing gust—but then without those doors there DID stand the lofty and enshrouded figure of the lady Madeline of Usher. There was blood upon her white robes, and the evidence of some bitter struggle upon every portion of her emaciated frame. For a moment she remained trembling and reeling to and fro upon the threshold, then, with a low moaning cry, fell heavily inward upon the person of her brother, and in her violent and now final death-agonies, bore him to the floor a corpse, and a victim to the terrors he had anticipated.

From that chamber, and from that mansion, I fled aghast. The storm was still abroad in all its wrath as I found myself crossing the old causeway. Suddenly there shot along the path a wild light, and I turned to see whence a gleam so unusual could have issued; for the vast house and its shadows were alone behind me. The radiance was that of the full, setting, and blood-red moon, which now shone vividly through that once barely discernible fissure, of which I have before spoken as extending from the roof of the building, in a zigzag direction, to the base. While I gazed, this fissure rapidly widened—there came a fierce breath of the whirlwind—the entire orb of the satellite burst at once upon my sight—my brain reeled as I saw the mighty walls rushing asunder—there was a long tumultuous shouting sound like the voice of a thousand waters—and the deep and dank tarn at my feet closed sullenly and silently over the fragments of the "HOUSE OF USHER."

1839, 1845

The Man of the Crowd

Ce grand malheur, de ne pouvoir être seul.[1]

—*LA BRUYÈRE*

It was well said of a certain German book that *"er lasst sich nicht lesen"*—it does not permit itself to be read. There are some secrets which do not permit themselves to be told. Men die nightly in their beds, wringing the hands of ghostly confessors, and looking them piteously in the eyes—die with despair of heart and convulsion of throat, on account of the hideousness of mysteries which will not *suffer themselves* to be revealed. Now and then, alas, the conscience of man takes up a burthen so heavy in horror that it can be thrown down only into the grave. And thus the essence of all crime is undivulged.

Not long ago, about the closing in of an evening in autumn, I sat at the large bow window of the D—— Coffee-House in London. For some months I had been ill in health, but was now convalescent, and, with returning

[1]First published in December 1840 in *The Casket* and *Burton's Gentleman's Magazine*, journals that would be merged to form *Graham's Magazine*, "The Man of the Crowd" was revised and published in Poe's 1845 collection, *Tales*. The epigraph, "That great evil, to be unable to be alone," is taken from Jean de La Bruyère's *Les Charactères* (1688).

strength, found myself in one of those happy moods which are so precisely the converse of *ennui*—moods of the keenest appetency, when the film from the mental vision departs—the αχλυς ος πριν επηεν[2]—and the intellect, electrified, surpasses as greatly its every-day condition, as does the vivid yet candid reason of Leibnitz, the mad and flimsy rhetoric of Gorgias.[3] Merely to breathe was enjoyment; and I derived positive pleasure even from many of the legitimate sources of pain. I felt a calm but inquisitive interest in every thing. With a cigar in my mouth and a newspaper in my lap, I had been amusing myself for the greater part of the afternoon, now in poring over advertisements, now in observing the promiscuous company in the room, and now in peering through the smoky panes into the street.

This latter is one of the principal thoroughfares of the city, and had been very much crowded during the whole day. But, as the darkness came on, the throng momently increased; and, by the time the lamps were well lighted, two dense and continuous tides of population were rushing past the door. At this particular period of the evening I had never before been in a similar situation, and the tumultuous sea of human heads filled me, therefore, with a delicious novelty of emotion. I gave up, at length, all care of things within the hotel, and became absorbed in contemplation of the scene without.

At first my observations took an abstract and generalizing turn. I looked at the passengers in masses, and thought of them in their aggregate relations. Soon, however, I descended to details, and regarded with minute interest the innumerable varieties of figure, dress, air, gait, visage, and expression of countenance.

By far the greater number of those who went by had a satisfied business-like demeanor, and seemed to be thinking only of making their way through the press. Their brows were knit, and their eyes rolled quickly; when pushed against by fellow-wayfarers they evinced no symptom of impatience, but adjusted their clothes and hurried on. Others, still a numerous class, were restless in their movements, had flushed faces, and talked and gesticulated to themselves, as if feeling in solitude on account of the very denseness of the company around. When impeded in their progress, these people suddenly ceased muttering, but redoubled their gesticulations, and awaited, with an absent and overdone smile upon the lips, the course of the persons impeding them. If jostled, they bowed profusely to the jostlers, and appeared overwhelmed with confusion.—There was nothing very distinctive about these two large classes beyond what I have noted. Their habiliments belonged to that order which is pointedly termed the decent. They were undoubtedly noblemen, merchants, attorneys, tradesmen, stock-jobbers—

[2]"The mist that previously was upon them," a phrase adapted from the *Iliad*, in which Athena removes the haze from the eyes of Diomedes to enable him to distinguish the gods in battle.

[3]Gorgias, a skeptical philosopher and rhetorician of the fourth century B.C., was known for his rhetorical excessiveness. Gottfried Wilhelm Leibnitz (1646–1716), a German philosopher and mathematician, was a pioneer of modern symbolic logic.

the Eupatrids[4] and the common-places of society—men of leisure and men actively engaged in affairs of their own—conducting business upon their own responsibility. They did not greatly excite my attention.

The tribe of clerks was an obvious one and here I discerned two remarkable divisions. There were the junior clerks of flash houses—young gentlemen with tight coats, bright boots, well-oiled hair, and supercilious lips. Setting aside a certain dapperness of carriage, which may be termed *deskism* for want of a better word, the manner of these persons seemed to me an exact facsimile of what had been the perfection of *bon ton*[5] about twelve or eighteen months before. They wore the cast-off graces of the gentry;—and this, I believe, involves the best definition of the class.

The division of the upper clerks of staunch firms, or of the "steady old fellows," it was not possible to mistake. These were known by their coats and pantaloons of black or brown, made to sit comfortably, with white cravats and waistcoats, broad solid-looking shoes, and thick hose or gaiters.— They had all slightly bald heads, from which the right ears, long used to pen-holding, had an odd habit of standing off on end. I observed that they always removed or settled their hats with both hands, and wore watches, with short gold chains of a substantial and ancient pattern. Theirs was the affectation of respectability;—if indeed there be an affectation so honorable.

There were many individuals of dashing appearance, whom I easily understood as belonging to the race of swell pickpockets, with which all great cities are infested. I watched these gentry with much inquisitiveness, and found it difficult to imagine how they should ever be mistaken for gentlemen by gentlemen themselves. Their voluminousness of wristband, with an air of excessive frankness, should betray them at once.

The gamblers, of whom I descried not a few, were still more easily recognisable. They wore every variety of dress, from that of the desperate thimble-rig bully,[6] with velvet waistcoat, fancy neckerchief, gilt chains, and filagreed buttons, to that of the scrupulously inornate clergyman, than which nothing could be less liable to suspicion. Still all were distinguished by a certain sodden swarthiness of complexion, a filmy dimness of eye, and pallor and compression of lip. There were two other traits, moreover, by which I could always detect them;—a guarded lowness of tone in conversation, and a more than ordinary extension of the thumb in a direction at right angles with the fingers.—Very often, in company with these sharpers, I observed an order of men somewhat different in habits, but still birds of a kindred feather. They may be defined as the gentlemen who live by their wits. They seem to prey upon the public in two battalions—that of the dandies and that of the military men. Of the first grade the leading features are long locks and smiles; of the second frogged coats and frowns.

[4]Members of the hereditary aristocracy in ancient Athens.

[5]Fashion.

[6]The shell game, a con artist's trick.

Descending in the scale of what is termed gentility, I found darker and deeper themes for speculation. I saw Jew pedlars, with hawk eyes flashing from countenances whose every other feature wore only an expression of abject humility; sturdy professional street beggars scowling upon mendicants of a better stamp, whom despair alone had driven forth into the night for charity; feeble and ghastly invalids, upon whom death had placed a sure hand, and who sidled and tottered through the mob, looking every one beseechingly in the face, as if in search of some chance consolation, some lost hope; modest young girls returning from long and late labor to a cheerless home, and shrinking more tearfully than indignantly from the glances of ruffians, whose direct contact, even, could not be avoided; women of the town of all kinds and of all ages—the unequivocal beauty in the prime of her womanhood, putting one in mind of the statue in Lucian, with the surface of Parian marble and the interior filled with filth[7]—the loathsome and utterly lost leper in rags—the wrinkled, bejewelled and paint-begrimed beldame, making a last effort at youth—the mere child of immature form, yet, from long association, an adept in the dreadful coquetries of her trade, and burning with a rabid ambition to be ranked the equal of her elders in vice; drunkards innumerable and indescribable—some in shreds and patches, reeling, inarticulate, with bruised visage and lack-lustre eyes—some in whole although filthy garments, with a slightly unsteady swagger, thick sensual lips, and hearty-looking rubicund faces—others clothed in materials which had once been good, and which even now were scrupulously well brushed—men who walked with a more than naturally firm and springy step, but whose countenances were fearfully pale, whose eyes hideously wild and red, and who clutched with quivering fingers, as they strode through the crowd, at every object which came within their reach; beside these, pie-men, porters, coal-heavers, sweeps; organ-grinders, monkey-exhibiters and ballad mongers, those who vended with those who sang; ragged artizans and exhausted laborers of every description, and all full of a noisy and inordinate vivacity which jarred discordantly upon the ear, and gave an aching sensation to the eye.

As the night deepened, so deepened to me the interest of the scene; for not only did the general character of the crowd materially alter (its gentler features retiring in the gradual withdrawal of the more orderly portion of the people, and its harsher ones coming out into bolder relief, as the late hour brought forth every species of infamy from its den,) but the rays of the gas-lamps, feeble at first in their struggle with the dying day, had now at length gained ascendancy, and threw over every thing a fitful and garish lustre. All was dark yet splendid—as that ebony to which has been likened the style of Tertullian.[8]

---

[7]Poe paraphrases the Greek satirist Lucian, who lived in the second century A.D. Parian marble is used in fine statuary.

[8]One of the fathers of the Roman Church in the third century A.D., Tertullian wrote theological treatises attacking heresy and worldliness.

The wild effects of the light enchained me to an examination of individual faces; and although the rapidity with which the world of light flitted before the window, prevented me from casting more than a glance upon each visage, still it seemed that, in my then peculiar mental state, I could frequently read, even in that brief interval of a glance, the history of long years.

With my brow to the glass, I was thus occupied in scrutinizing the mob, when suddenly there came into view a countenance (that of a decrepid old man, some sixty-five or seventy years of age,)—a countenance which at once arrested and absorbed my whole attention, on account of the absolute idiosyncracy of its expression. Any thing even remotely resembling that expression I had never seen before. I well remember that my first thought, upon beholding it, was that Retzch,[9] had he viewed it, would have greatly preferred it to his own pictural incarnations of the fiend. As I endeavored, during the brief minute of my original survey, to form some analysis of the meaning conveyed, there arose confusedly and paradoxically within my mind, the ideas of vast mental power, of caution, of penuriousness, of avarice, of coolness, of malice, of blood-thirstiness, of triumph, of merriment, of excessive terror, of intense—of supreme despair. I felt singularly aroused, startled, fascinated. "How wild a history," I said to myself, "is written within that bosom!" Then came a craving desire to keep the man in view—to know more of him. Hurriedly putting on an overcoat, and seizing my hat and cane, I made my way into the street, and pushed through the crowd in the direction which I had seen him take; for he had already disappeared. With some little difficulty I at length came within sight of him, approached, and followed him closely, yet cautiously, so as not to attract his attention.

I had now a good opportunity of examining his person. He was short in stature, very thin, and apparently very feeble. His clothes, generally, were filthy and ragged; but as he came, now and then, within the strong glare of a lamp, I perceived that his linen, although dirty, was of beautiful texture; and my vision deceived me, or, through a rent in a closely-buttoned and evidently second-handed *roquelaire*[10] which enveloped him, I caught a glimpse both of a diamond and of a dagger. These observations heightened my curiosity, and I resolved to follow the stranger whithersoever he should go.

It was now fully night-fall, and a thick humid fog hung over the city, soon ending in a settled and heavy rain. This change of weather had an odd effect upon the crowd, the whole of which was at once put into new commotion, and overshadowed by a world of umbrellas. The waver, the jostle, and the hum increased in a tenfold degree. For my own part I did not much regard the rain—the lurking of an old fever in my system rendering the moisture somewhat too dangerously pleasant. Tying a handkerchief about my mouth, I kept on. For half an hour the old man held his way with

[9]Friedrich August Mortiz Retzsch (1779–1857) was a German engraver best known for his illustrations of Goethe's *Faust*.

[10]A knee-length coat.

difficulty along the great thoroughfare; and I here walked close at his elbow through fear of losing sight of him. Never once turning his head to look back, he did not observe me. By and bye he passed into a cross street, which, although densely filled with people, was not quite so much thronged as the main one he had quitted. Here a change in his demeanor became evident. He walked more slowly and with less object than before—more hesitatingly. He crossed and re-crossed the way repeatedly without apparent aim; and the press was still so thick that, at every such movement, I was obliged to follow him closely. The street was a narrow and long one, and his course lay within it for nearly an hour, during which the passengers had gradually diminished to about that number which is ordinarily seen at noon in Broadway near the Park—so vast a difference is there between a London populace and that of the most frequented American city. A second turn brought us into a square, brilliantly lighted, and overflowing with life. The old manner of the stranger re-appeared. His chin fell upon his breast, while his eyes rolled wildly from under his knit brows, in every direction, upon those who hemmed him in. He urged his way steadily and perseveringly. I was surprised, however, to find, upon his having made the circuit of the square, that he turned and retraced his steps. Still more was I astonished to see him repeat the same walk several times—once nearly detecting me as he came round with a sudden movement.

In this exercise he spent another hour, at the end of which we met with far less interruption from passengers than at first. The rain fell fast; the air grew cool; and the people were retiring to their homes. With a gesture of impatience, the wanderer passed into a bye-street comparatively deserted. Down this, some quarter of a mile long, he rushed with an activity I could not have dreamed of seeing in one so aged, and which put me to much trouble in pursuit. A few minutes brought us to a large and busy bazaar, with the localities of which the stranger appeared well acquainted, and where his original demeanor again became apparent, as he forced his way to and fro, without aim, among the host of buyers and sellers.

During the hour and a half, or thereabouts, which we passed in this place, it required much caution on my part to keep him within reach without attracting his observation. Luckily I wore a pair of caoutchouc[11] overshoes, and could move about in perfect silence. At no moment did he see that I watched him. He entered shop after shop, priced nothing, spoke no word, and looked at all objects with a wild and vacant stare. I was now utterly amazed at his behaviour, and firmly resolved that we should not part until I had satisfied myself in some measure respecting him.

A loud-toned clock struck eleven, and the company were fast deserting the bazaar. A shop-keeper, in putting up a shutter, jostled the old man, and at the instant I saw a strong shudder come over his frame. He hurried into the street, looked anxiously around him for an instant, and then ran with incredible swiftness through many crooked and people-less lanes, until we

[11]Rubber.

emerged once more upon the great thoroughfare whence we had started—the street of the D—— Hotel. It no longer wore, however, the same aspect. It was still brilliant with gas; but the rain fell fiercely, and there were few persons to be seen. The stranger grew pale. He walked moodily some paces up the once populous avenue, then, with a heavy sigh, turned in the direction of the river, and, plunging through a great variety of devious ways, came out, at length, in view of one of the principal theatres. It was about being closed, and the audience were thronging from the doors. I saw the old man gasp as if for breath while he threw himself amid the crowd; but I thought that the intense agony of his countenance had, in some measure, abated. His head again fell upon his breast; he appeared as I had seen him at first. I observed that he now took the course in which had gone the greater number of the audience—but, upon the whole, I was at a loss to comprehend the waywardness of his actions.

As he proceeded, the company grew more scattered, and his old uneasiness and vacillation were resumed. For some time he followed closely a party of some ten or twelve roisterers; but from this number one by one dropped off, until three only remained together, in a narrow and gloomy lane little frequented. The stranger paused, and, for a moment, seemed lost in thought; then, with every mark of agitation, pursued rapidly a route which brought us to the verge of the city, amid regions very different from those we had hitherto traversed. It was the most noisome[12] quarter of London, where every thing wore the worst impress of the most deplorable poverty, and of the most desperate crime. By the dim light of an accidental lamp, tall, antique, worm-eaten, wooden tenements were seen tottering to their fall, in directions so many and capricious that scarce the semblance of a passage was discernible between them. The paving-stones lay at random, displaced from their beds by the rankly-growing grass. Horrible filth festered in the dammed-up gutters. The whole atmosphere teemed with desolation. Yet, as we proceeded, the sounds of human life revived by sure degrees, and at length large bands of the most abandoned of a London populace were seen reeling to and fro. The spirits of the old man again flickered up, as a lamp which is near its death-hour. Once more he strode onward with elastic tread. Suddenly a corner was turned, a blaze of light burst upon our sight, and we stood before one of the huge suburban temples of Intemperance—one of the palaces of the fiend, Gin.

It was now nearly day-break; but a number of wretched inebriates still pressed in and out of the flaunting entrance. With a half shriek of joy the old man forced a passage within, resumed at once his original bearing, and stalked backward and forward, without apparent object, among the throng. He had not been thus long occupied, however, before a rush to the doors gave token that the host was closing them for the night. It was something even more intense than despair that I then observed upon the countenance of the singular being whom I had watched so pertinaciously. Yet he did not

---

[12]Disgusting; foul and filthy.

hesitate in his career, but, with a mad energy, retraced his steps at once, to the heart of the mighty London. Long and swiftly he fled, while I followed him in the wildest amazement, resolute not to abandon a scrutiny in which I now felt an interest all-absorbing. The sun arose while we proceeded, and, when we had once again reached that most thronged mart of the populous town, the street of the D——Hotel, it presented an appearance of human bustle and activity scarcely inferior to what I had seen on the evening before. And here, long, amid the momently increasing confusion, did I persist in my pursuit of the stranger. But, as usual, he walked to and fro, and during the day did not pass from out the turmoil of that street. And, as the shades of the second evening came on, I grew wearied unto death, and, stopping fully in front of the wanderer, gazed at him steadfastly in the face. He noticed me not, but resumed his solemn walk, while I, ceasing to follow, remained absorbed in contemplation. "This old man," I said at length, "is the type and the genius of deep crime. He refuses to be alone. *He is the man of the crowd.* It will be in vain to follow; for I shall learn no more of him, nor of his deeds. The worst heart of the world is a grosser book than the 'Hortulus Animae,' and perhaps it is but one of the great mercies of God that '*er lasst sich nicht lesen.*'"

1840, 1845

The Tell-Tale Heart[1]

True!—nervous—very, very dreadfully nervous I had been and am; but why *will* you say that I am mad? The disease had sharpened my senses—not destroyed—not dulled them. Above all was the sense of hearing acute. I heard all things in the heaven and in the earth. I heard many things in hell. How, then, am I mad? Hearken! and observe how healthily—how calmly I can tell you the whole story.

It is impossible to say how first the idea entered my brain; but once conceived, it haunted me day and night. Object there was none. Passion there was none. I loved the old man. He had never wronged me. He had never given me insult. For his gold I had no desire. I think it was his eye! yes, it was this! He had the eye of a vulture—a pale blue eye, with a film over it. Whenever it fell upon me, my blood ran cold; and so by degrees—very gradually—I made up my mind to take the life of the old man, and thus rid myself of the eye forever.

Now this is the point. You fancy me mad. Madmen know nothing. But you should have seen *me*. You should have seen how wisely I proceeded—with what caution—with what foresight—with what dissimulation I went to work! I was never kinder to the old man than during the whole week before I killed him. And every night, about midnight, I turned the latch of

---

[1]The story was first published in *The Pioneer* for January 1843 and republished in *The Broadway Journal* in August 1845.

his door and opened it—oh so gently! And then, when I had made an opening sufficient for my head, I put in a dark lantern, all closed, closed, so that no light shone out, and then I thrust in my head. Oh, you would have laughed to see how cunningly I thrust it in! I moved it slowly—very, very slowly, so that I might not disturb the old man's sleep. It took me an hour to place my whole head within the opening so far that I could see him as he lay upon his bed. Ha!—would a madman have been so wise as this? And then, when my head was well in the room, I undid the lantern cautiously—oh, so cautiously—cautiously (for the hinges creaked)—I undid it just so much that a single thin ray fell upon the vulture eye. And this I did for seven long nights—every night just at midnight—but I found the eye always closed; and so it was impossible to do the work; for it was not the old man who vexed me, but his Evil Eye. And every morning, when the day broke, I went boldly into the chamber, and spoke courageously to him, calling him by name in a hearty tone, and inquiring how he had passed the night. So you see he would have been a very profound old man, indeed, to suspect that every night, just at twelve, I looked in upon him while he slept.

Upon the eighth night I was more than usually cautious in opening the door. A watch's minute hand moves more quickly than did mine. Never before that night, had I *felt* the extent of my own powers—of my sagacity. I could scarcely contain my feelings of triumph. To think that there I was, opening the door, little by little, and he not even to dream of my secret deeds or thoughts. I fairly chuckled at the idea; and perhaps he heard me; for he moved on the bed suddenly, as if startled. Now you may think that I drew back—but no. His room was as black as pitch with the thick darkness, (for the shutters were close fastened, through fear of robbers,) and so I knew that he could not see the opening of the door, and I kept pushing it on steadily, steadily.

I had my head in, and was about to open the lantern, when my thumb slipped upon the tin fastening, and the old man sprang up in bed, crying out—"Who's there?"

I kept quite still and said nothing. For a whole hour I did not move a muscle, and in the meantime I did not hear him lie down. He was still sitting up in the bed listening;—just as I have done, night after night, hearkening to the death watches in the wall.[2]

Presently I heard a slight groan, and I knew it was the groan of mortal terror. It was not a groan of pain or of grief—oh, no!—it was the low stifled sound that arises from the bottom of the soul when overcharged with awe. I knew the sound well. Many a night, just at midnight, when all the world slept, it has welled up from my own bosom, deepening, with its dreadful echo, the terrors that distracted me. I say I knew it well. I knew what the old man felt, and pitied him, although I chuckled at heart. I knew that he had been lying awake ever since the first slight noise, when he had turned

[2]The death watch was a beetle that was thought to make sounds predicting someone's death.

in the bed. His fears had been ever since growing upon him. He had been trying to fancy them causeless, but could not. He had been saying to himself—"It is nothing but the wind in the chimney—it is only a mouse crossing the floor," or "it is merely a cricket which has made a single chirp." Yes, he had been trying to comfort himself with these suppositions: but he had found all in vain. *All in vain;* because Death, in approaching him had stalked with his black shadow before him, and enveloped the victim. And it was the mournful influence of the unperceived shadow that caused him to feel—although he neither saw nor heard—to *feel* the presence of my head within the room.

When I had waited a long time, very patiently, without hearing him lie down, I resolved to open a little—a very, very little crevice in the lantern. So I opened it—you cannot imagine how stealthily, stealthily—until, at length a simple dim ray, like the thread of the spider, shot from out the crevice and fell full upon the vulture eye.

It was open—wide, wide open—and I grew furious as I gazed upon it. I saw it with perfect distinctness—all a dull blue, with a hideous veil over it that chilled the very marrow in my bones; but I could see nothing else of the old man's face or person: for I had directed the ray as if by instinct, precisely upon the damned spot.

And have I not told you that what you mistake for madness is but over acuteness of the senses?—now, I say, there came to my ears a low, dull, quick sound, such as a watch makes when enveloped in cotton. I knew *that* sound well, too. It was the beating of the old man's heart. It increased my fury, as the beating of a drum stimulates the soldier into courage.

But even yet I refrained and kept still. I scarcely breathed. I held the lantern motionless. I tried how steadily I could maintain the ray upon the eye. Meantime the hellish tattoo[3] of the heart increased. It grew quicker and quicker, and louder and louder every instant. The old man's terror *must* have been extreme! It grew louder, I say, louder every moment!—do you mark me well? I have told you that I am nervous: so I am. And now at the dead hour of the night, amid the dreadful silence of that old house, so strange a noise as this excited me to uncontrollable terror. Yet, for some minutes longer I refrained and stood still. But the beating grew louder, louder! I thought the heart must burst. And now a new anxiety seized me—the sound would be heard by a neighbour! The old man's hour had come! With a loud yell, I threw open the lantern and leaped into the room. He shrieked once—once only. In an instant I dragged him to the floor, and pulled the heavy bed[4] over him. I then smiled gaily, to find the deed so far done. But, for many minutes, the heart beat on with a muffled sound. This, however, did not vex me; it would not be heard through the wall. At length it ceased. The old man was dead. I removed the bed and examined the corpse. Yes, he was

---

[3]Drumbeat.
[4]Featherbed or heavy comforter, which in Poe's day sometimes served as a mattress.

stone, stone dead. I placed my hand upon the heart and held it there many minutes. There was no pulsation. He was stone dead. His eye would trouble me no more.

If still you think me mad, you will think so no longer when I describe the wise precautions I took for the concealment of the body. The night waned, and I worked hastily, but in silence. First of all I dismembered the corpse. I cut off the head and the arms and the legs.

I then took up three planks from the flooring of the chamber, and deposited all between the scantlings.[5] I then replaced the boards so cleverly, so cunningly, that no human eye—not even *his*—could have detected any thing wrong. There was nothing to wash out—no stain of any kind—no blood-spot whatever. I had been too wary for that. A tub had caught all—ha! ha!

When I had made an end of these labors, it was four o'clock—still dark as midnight. As the bell sounded the hour, there came a knocking at the street door. I went down to open it with a light heart,—for what had I *now* to fear? There entered three men, who introduced themselves, with perfect suavity, as officers of the police. A shriek had been heard by a neighbour during the night; suspicion of foul play had been aroused; information had been lodged at the police office, and they (the officers) had been deputed to search the premises.

I smiled,—for *what* had I to fear? I bade the gentlemen welcome. The shriek, I said, was my own in a dream. The old man, I mentioned, was absent in the country. I took my visitors all over the house. I bade them search—search *well*. I led them, at length, to *his* chamber. I showed them his treasures, secure, undisturbed. In the enthusiasm of my confidence, I brought chairs into the room, and desired them *here* to rest from their fatigues, while I myself, in the wild audacity of my perfect triumph, placed my own seat upon the very spot beneath which reposed the corpse of the victim.

The officers were satisfied. My *manner* had convinced them. I was singularly at ease. They sat, and while I answered cheerily, they chatted of familiar things. But, ere long, I felt myself getting pale and wished them gone. My head ached, and I fancied a ringing in my ears: but still they sat and still chatted. The ringing became more distinct:—it continued and became more distinct: I talked more freely to get rid of the feeling: but it continued and gained definiteness—until, at length, I found that the noise was *not* within my ears.

No doubt I now grew *very* pale;—but I talked more fluently, and with a heightened voice. Yet the sound increased—and what could I do? It was *a low, dull, quick sound—much such a sound as a watch makes when enveloped in cotton.* I gasped for breath—and yet the officers heard it not. I talked more quickly—more vehemently; but the noise steadily increased. I arose and argued about trifles, in a high key and with violent gesticulations; but the noise steadily increased. Why *would* they not be gone? I paced the floor to

---

[5]Floor beams.

and fro with heavy strides, as if excited to fury by the observations of the men—but the noise steadily increased. Oh God! what *could* I do? I foamed—I raved—I swore! I swung the chair upon which I had been sitting, and grated it upon the boards, but the noise arose over all and continually increased. It grew louder—louder—*louder!* And still the men chatted pleasantly, and smiled. Was it possible they heard not? Almighty God!—no, no! They heard!—they suspected!—they *knew!*—they were making a mockery of my horror!—this I thought, and this I think. But anything was better than this agony! Anything was more tolerable than this derision! I could bear those hypocritical smiles no longer! I felt that I must scream or die! and now—again!—hark! louder! louder! louder! *louder!*

"Villains!" I shrieked, "dissemble no more! I admit the deed!—tear up the planks! here, here!—it is the beating of his hideous heart!"

1843, 1845

The Purloined Letter

Nil sapientiae odiosius acumine nimio.

—SENECA[1]

At Paris, just after dark one gusty evening in the autumn of 18—, I was enjoying the twofold luxury of meditation and a meerschaum,[2] in company with my friend C. Auguste Dupin, in his little back library, or book-closet, *au troisième,*[3] *No. 33, Rue Dunôt, Faubourg St. Germain.* For one hour at least we had maintained a profound silence; while each, to any casual observer, might have seemed intently and exclusively occupied with the curling eddies of smoke that oppressed the atmosphere of the chamber. For myself, however, I was mentally discussing certain topics which had formed matter for conversation between us at an earlier period of the evening; I mean the affair of the Rue Morgue, and the mystery attending the murder of Marie Rogêt. I looked upon it, therefore, as something of a coincidence, when the door of our apartment was thrown open and admitted our old acquaintance, Monsieur G——, the Prefect of the Parisian police.

We gave him a hearty welcome; for there was nearly half as much of the entertaining as of the contemptible about the man, and we had not seen him for several years. We had been sitting in the dark, and Dupin now arose for the purpose of lighting a lamp, but sat down again, without doing so,

---

[1] The story was first printed in *The Gift* for December 1844 and included in Poe's *Tales* (1845). A great favorite among storytellers and critics, it inspired fictional imitations by Wilkie Collins and Arthur Conan Doyle, as well as entire volumes of critical commentary. The epigraph translates as "Nothing is more distasteful to good sense than too much cunning." The source of the saying is not Seneca but Francis Bacon.

[2] Meerschaum is a soft, white mineral used in making pipes, because the stone draws the moisture and tar away from the tobacco. A Meerschaum pipe, usually ornately carved, was prized from the mid-eighteenth-century onward as the best pipe for a cool, dry smoke.

[3] French for "on the third." Americans would say "on the fourth floor."

upon G.'s saying that he had called to consult us, or rather to ask the opinion of my friend, about some official business which had occasioned a great deal of trouble.

"If it is any point requiring reflection," observed Dupin, as he forbore to enkindle the wick, "we shall examine it to better purpose in the dark."

"That is another of your odd notions," said the Prefect, who had a fashion of calling every thing "odd" that was beyond his comprehension, and thus lived amid an absolute legion of "oddities."

"Very true," said Dupin, as he supplied his visiter with a pipe, and rolled towards him a comfortable chair.

"And what is the difficulty now?" I asked. "Nothing more in the assassination way, I hope?"

"Oh no; nothing of that nature. The fact is, the business is *very* simple indeed, and I make no doubt that we can manage it sufficiently well ourselves; but then I thought Dupin would like to hear the details of it, because it is so excessively *odd*."

"Simple and odd," said Dupin.

"Why, yes; and not exactly that, either. The fact is, we have all been a good deal puzzled because the affair *is* so simple, and yet baffles us altogether."

"Perhaps it is the very simplicity of the thing which puts you at fault," said my friend.

"What nonsense you *do* talk!" replied the Prefect, laughing heartily.

"Perhaps the mystery is a little *too* plain," said Dupin.

"Oh, good heavens! who ever heard of such an idea?"

"A little *too* self-evident."

"Ha! ha! ha!—ha! ha! ha!—ho! ho! ho!"—roared our visiter, profoundly amused, "oh, Dupin, you will be the death of me yet!"

"And what, after all, *is* the matter on hand?" I asked.

"Why, I will tell you," replied the Prefect, as he gave a long, steady, and contemplative puff, and settled himself in his chair. "I will tell you in a few words; but, before I begin, let me caution you that this is an affair demanding the greatest secrecy, and that I should most probably lose the position I now hold, were it known that I confided it to any one."

"Proceed," said I.

"Or not," said Dupin.

"Well, then; I have received personal information, from a very high quarter, that a certain document of the last importance, has been purloined from the royal apartments. The individual who purloined it is known; this beyond a doubt; he was seen to take it. It is known, also, that it still remains in his possession."

"How is this known?" asked Dupin.

"It is clearly inferred," replied the Prefect, "from the nature of the document, and from the nonappearance of certain results which would at once arise from its passing *out* of the robber's possession;—that is to say, from his employing it as he must design in the end to employ it."

"Be a little more explicit," I said.

"Well, I may venture so far as to say that the paper gives its holder a certain power in a certain quarter where such power is immensely valuable." The Prefect was fond of the cant of diplomacy.

"Still I do not quite understand," said Dupin.

"No? Well; the disclosure of the document to a third person, who shall be nameless, would bring in question the honor of a personage of most exalted station; and this fact gives the holder of the document an ascendancy over the illustrious personage whose honor and peace are so jeopardized."

"But this ascendancy," I interposed, "would depend upon the robber's knowledge of the loser's knowledge of the robber. Who would dare—"

"The thief," said G., "is the Minister D——,[4] who dares all things, those unbecoming as well as those becoming a man. The method of the theft was not less ingenious than bold. The document in question—a letter, to be frank—has been received by the personage robbed while alone in the royal *boudoir*. During its perusal she was suddenly interrupted by the entrance of the other exalted personage from whom especially it was her wish to conceal it. After a hurried and vain endeavor to thrust it in a drawer, she was forced to place it, open as it was, upon a table. The address, however, was uppermost, and, the contents thus unexposed, the letter escaped notice. At this juncture enters the Minister D——. His lynx eye immediately perceives the paper, recognises the handwriting of the address, observes the confusion of the personage addressed, and fathoms her secret. After some business transactions, hurried through in his ordinary manner, he produces a letter somewhat similar to the one in question, opens it, pretends to read it, and then places it in close juxtaposition to the other. Again he converses, for some fifteen minutes, upon the public affairs. At length, in taking leave, he takes also from the table the letter to which he had no claim. Its rightful owner saw, but, of course, dared not call attention to the act, in the presence of the third personage who stood at her elbow. The minister decamped; leaving his own letter—one of no importance—upon the table."

"Here, then," said Dupin to me, "you have precisely what you demand to make the ascendancy complete—the robber's knowledge of the loser's knowledge of the robber."

"Yes," replied the Prefect; "and the power thus attained has, for some months past, been wielded, for political purposes, to a very dangerous extent. The personage robbed is more thoroughly convinced, every day, of the necessity of reclaiming her letter. But this, of course, cannot be done openly. In fine, driven to despair, she has committed the matter to me."

"Than whom," said Dupin, amid a perfect whirlwind of smoke, "no more sagacious agent could, I suppose, be desired, or even imagined."

[4]A convention of nineteenth-century fiction writers was to give the initial letters rather than whole names of story characters. The implication was that the characters had real-life identities, which the author concealed to protect the innocent.

"You flatter me," replied the Prefect; "but it is possible that some such opinion may have been entertained."

"It is clear," said I, "as you observe, that the letter is still in possession of the minister; since it is this possession, and not any employment of the letter, which bestows the power. With the employment the power departs."

"True," said G.; "and upon this conviction I proceeded. My first care was to make thorough search of the minister's hotel; and here my chief embarrassment lay in the necessity of searching without his knowledge. Beyond all things, I have been warned of the danger which would result from giving him reason to suspect our design."

"But," said I, "you are quite *au fait*[5] in these investigations. The Parisian police have done this thing often before."

"O yes; and for this reason I did not despair. The habits of the minister gave me, too, a great advantage. He is frequently absent from home all night. His servants are by no means numerous. They sleep at a distance from their master's apartment, and, being chiefly Neapolitans, are readily made drunk. I have keys, as you know, with which I can open any chamber or cabinet in Paris. For three months a night has not passed, during the greater part of which I have not been engaged, personally, in ransacking the D—— Hôtel. My honor is interested, and, to mention a great secret, the reward is enormous. So I did not abandon the search until I had become fully satisfied that the thief is a more astute man than myself. I fancy that I have investigated every nook and corner of the premises in which it is possible that the paper can be concealed."

"But is it not possible," I suggested, "that although the letter may be in possession of the minister, as it unquestionably is, he may have concealed it elsewhere than upon his own premises?"

"This is barely possible," said Dupin. "The present peculiar condition of affairs at court, and especially of those intrigues in which D—— is known to be involved, would render the instant availability of the document—its susceptibility of being produced at a moment's notice—a point of nearly equal importance with its possession."

"Its susceptibility of being produced?" said I.

"That is to say, of being *destroyed*," said Dupin.

"True," I observed; "the paper is clearly then upon the premises. As for its being upon the person of the minister, we may consider that as out of the question."

"Entirely," said the Prefect. "He has been twice waylaid, as if by footpads,[6] and his person rigorously searched under my own inspection."

"You might have spared yourself this trouble," said Dupin. "D——, I presume, is not altogether a fool, and, if not, must have anticipated these waylayings, as a matter of course."

"Not *altogether* a fool," said G., "but then he's a poet, which I take to be only one remove from a fool."

[5]Well informed.   [6]Highwaymen.

"True," said Dupin, after a long and thoughtful whiff from his meer-schaum, "although I have been guilty of certain doggerel myself."

"Suppose you detail," said I, "the particulars of your search."

"Why the fact is, we took our time, and we searched *every where*. I have had long experience in these affairs. I took the entire building, room by room; devoting the nights of a whole week to each. We examined, first, the furniture of each apartment. We opened every possible drawer; and I presume you know that, to a properly trained police agent, such a thing as a *secret* drawer is impossible. Any man is a dolt who permits a 'secret' drawer to escape him in a search of this kind. The thing is *so* plain. There is a certain amount of bulk—of space—to be accounted for in every cabinet. Then we have accurate rules. The fiftieth part of a line could not escape us. After the cabinets we took the chairs. The cushions we probed with the fine long needles you have seen me employ. From the tables we removed the tops."

"Why so?"

"Sometimes the top of a table, or other similarly arranged piece of furniture, is removed by the person wishing to conceal an article; then the leg is excavated, the article deposited within the cavity, and the top replaced. The bottoms and tops of bed-posts are employed in the same way."

"But could not the cavity be detected by sounding?" I asked.

"By no means, if, when the article is deposited, a sufficient wadding of cotton be placed around it. Besides, in our case, we were obliged to proceed without noise."

"But you could not have removed—you could not have taken to pieces *all* articles of furniture in which it would have been possible to make a deposit in the manner you mention. A letter may be compressed into a thin spiral roll, not differing much in shape or bulk from a large knitting-needle, and in this form it might be inserted into the rung of a chair, for example. You did not take to pieces all the chairs?"

"Certainly not; but we did better—we examined the rungs of every chair in the hotel, and, indeed, the jointings of every description of furniture, by the aid of a most powerful microscope.[7] Had there been any traces of recent disturbance we should not have failed to detect it instantly. A single grain of gimlet-dust, for example, would have been as obvious as an apple. Any disorder in the glueing—any unusual gaping in the joints—would have sufficed to insure detection."

"I presume you looked to the mirrors, between the boards and the plates, and you probed the beds and the bed-clothes, as well as the curtains and carpets."

"That of course; and when we had absolutely completed every particle of the furniture in this way, then we examined the house itself. We divided its entire surface into compartments, which we numbered, so that none might be missed; then we scrutinized each individual square inch throughout the

[7]Old-fashioned term for a magnifying glass.

premises, including the two houses immediately adjoining, with the microscope, as before."

"The two houses adjoining!" I exclaimed; "you must have had a great deal of trouble."

"We had; but the reward offered is prodigious."

"You include the *grounds* about the houses?"

"All the grounds are paved with brick. They gave us comparatively little trouble. We examined the moss between the bricks, and found it undisturbed."

"You looked among D——'s papers, of course, and into the books of the library?"

"Certainly; we opened every package and parcel; we not only opened every book, but we turned over every leaf in each volume, not contenting ourselves with a mere shake, according to the fashion of some of our police officers. We also measured the thickness of every book-*cover*, with the most accurate admeasurement, and applied to each the most jealous scrutiny of the microscope. Had any of the bindings been recently meddled with, it would have been utterly impossible that the fact should have escaped observation. Some five or six volumes, just from the hands of the binder, we carefully probed, longitudinally, with the needles."

"You explored the floors beneath the carpets?"

"Beyond doubt. We removed every carpet, and examined the boards with the microscope."

"And the paper on the walls?"

"Yes."

"You looked into the cellars?"

"We did."

"Then," I said, "you have been making a miscalculation, and the letter is *not* upon the premises, as you suppose."

"I fear you are right there," said the Prefect. "And now, Dupin, what would you advise me to do?"

"To make a thorough re-search of the premises."

"That is absolutely needless," replied G——. "I am not more sure that I breathe than I am that the letter is not at the Hôtel."

"I have no better advice to give you," said Dupin. "You have, of course, an accurate description of the letter?"

"Oh, yes!"—And here the Prefect, producing a memorandum-book, proceeded to read aloud a minute account of the internal, and especially of the external appearance of the missing document. Soon after finishing the perusal of this description, he took his departure, more entirely depressed in spirits than I had ever known the good gentleman before.

In about a month afterwards he paid us another visit, and found us occupied very nearly as before. He took a pipe and a chair and entered into some ordinary conversation. At length I said,—

"Well, but G——, what of the purloined letter? I presume you have at last made up your mind that there is no such thing as overreaching the Minister?"

"Confound him, say I—yes; I made the reexamination, however, as Dupin suggested—but it was all labor lost, as I knew it would be."

"How much was the reward offered, did you say?" asked Dupin.

"Why, a very great deal—a *very* liberal reward—I don't like to say how much, precisely; but one thing I *will* say, that I wouldn't mind giving my individual check for fifty thousand francs to any one who could obtain me that letter. The fact is, it is becoming of more and more importance every day; and the reward has been lately doubled. If it were trebled, however, I could do no more than I have done."

"Why, yes," said Dupin, drawlingly, between the whiffs of his meerschaum, "I really—think, G——, you have not exerted yourself—to the utmost in this matter. You might—do a little more, I think, eh?"

"How?—in what way?"

"Why—puff, puff—you might—puff, puff—employ counsel in the matter, eh?—puff, puff, puff. Do you remember the story they tell of Abernethy?"

"No; hang Abernethy!"

"To be sure! hang him and welcome. But, once upon a time, a certain rich miser conceived the design of spunging upon this Abernethy for a medical opinion. Getting up, for this purpose, an ordinary conversation in a private company, he insinuated his case to the physician, as that of an imaginary individual.

"'We will suppose,' said the miser, 'that his symptoms are such and such; now, doctor, what would *you* have directed him to take?'

"'Take!' said Abernethy, 'why, take *advice*, to be sure.'"

"But," said the Prefect, a little discomposed, "I am *perfectly* willing to take advice, and to pay for it. I would *really* give fifty thousand francs to any one who would aid me in the matter."

"In that case," replied Dupin, opening a drawer, and producing a checkbook, "you may as well fill me up a check for the amount mentioned. When you have signed it, I will hand you the letter."

I was astounded. The Prefect appeared absolutely thunder-stricken. For some minutes he remained speechless and motionless, looking incredulously at my friend with open mouth, and eyes that seemed starting from their sockets; then, apparently recovering himself in some measure, he seized a pen, and after several pauses and vacant stares, finally filled up and signed a check for fifty thousand francs, and handed it across the table to Dupin. The latter examined it carefully and deposited it in his pocket-book; then, unlocking an *escritoire*,[8] took thence a letter and gave it to the Prefect. This functionary grasped it in a perfect agony of joy, opened it with a trembling hand, cast a rapid glance at its contents, and then, scrambling and struggling to the door, rushed at length unceremoniously from the room and from the house, without having uttered a syllable since Dupin had requested him to fill up the check.

---

[8]Writing desk.

When he had gone, my friend entered into some explanations.

"The Parisian police," he said, "are exceedingly able in their way. They are persevering, ingenious, cunning, and thoroughly versed in the knowledge which their duties seem chiefly to demand. Thus, when G—— detailed to us his mode of searching the premises at the Hôtel D——, I felt entire confidence in his having made a satisfactory investigation—so far as his labors extended."

"So far as his labors extended?" said I.

"Yes," said Dupin. "The measures adopted were not only the best of their kind, but carried out to absolute perfection. Had the letter been deposited within the range of their search, these fellows would, beyond a question, have found it."

I merely laughed—but he seemed quite serious in all that he said.

"The measures, then," he continued, "were good in their kind, and well executed; their defect lay in their being inapplicable to the case, and to the man. A certain set of highly ingenious resources are, with the Prefect, a sort of Procrustean bed,[9] to which he forcibly adapts his designs. But he perpetually errs by being too deep or too shallow, for the matter in hand; and many a schoolboy is a better reasoner than he. I knew one about eight years of age, whose success at guessing in the game of 'even and odd' attracted universal admiration. This game is simple, and is played with marbles. One player holds in his hand a number of these toys, and demands of another whether that number is even or odd. If the guess is right, the guesser wins one; if wrong, he loses one. The boy to whom I allude won all the marbles of the school. Of course he had some principle of guessing; and this lay in mere observation and admeasurement of the astuteness of his opponents. For example, an arrant simpleton is his opponent, and, holding up his closed hand, asks, 'are they even or odd?' Our schoolboy replies, 'odd,' and loses; but upon the second trial he wins, for he then says to himself, 'the simpleton had them even upon the first trial, and his amount of cunning is just sufficient to make him have them odd upon the second; I will therefore guess odd;'—he guesses odd, and wins. Now, with a simpleton a degree above the first, he would have reasoned thus: 'This fellow finds that in the first instance I guessed odd, and, in the second, he will propose to himself upon the first impulse, a simple variation from even to odd, as did the first simpleton; but then a second thought will suggest that this is too simple a variation, and finally he will decide upon putting it even as before. I will therefore guess even;'—he guesses even, and wins. Now this mode of reasoning in the schoolboy, whom his fellows termed 'lucky,'—what, in its last analysis, is it?"

"It is merely," I said, "an identification of the reasoner's intellect with that of his opponent."

---

[9]Procrustes (Greek mythology) took extreme measures to make his guests' body length fit his couch. He either stretched guests to size or lopped off overhanging limbs. The reference to Procrustes no longer evokes a gruesome image but is in common use among logicians.

"It is," said Dupin; "and, upon inquiring of the boy by what means he effected the *thorough* identification in which his success consisted, I received answer as follows: 'When I wish to find out how wise, or how stupid, or how good, or how wicked is any one, or what are his thoughts at the moment, I fashion the expression of my face, as accurately as possible, in accordance with the expression of his, and then wait to see what thoughts or sentiments arise in my mind or heart, as if to match or correspond with the expression.' This response of the schoolboy lies at the bottom of all the spurious profundity which has been attributed to Rochefoucauld, to La Bougive, to Machiavelli, and to Campanella."[10]

"And the identification," I said, "of the reasoner's intellect with that of his opponent, depends, if I understand you aright, upon the accuracy with which the opponent's intellect is admeasured."

"For its practical value it depends upon this," replied Dupin; "and the Prefect and his cohort fail so frequently, first, by default of this identification, and, secondly, by ill-admeasurement, or rather through non-admeasurement, of the intellect with which they are engaged. They consider only their *own* ideas of ingenuity; and, in searching for anything hidden, advert only to the modes in which *they* would have hidden it. They are right in this much—that their own ingenuity is a faithful representative of that of *the mass;* but when the cunning of the individual felon is diverse in character from their own, the felon foils them, of course. This always happens when it is above their own, and very usually when it is below. They have no variation of principle in their investigations; at best, when urged by some unusual emergency—by some extraordinary reward—they extend or exaggerate their old modes of *practice,* without touching their principles. What, for example, in this case of D——, has been done to vary the principle of action? What is all this boring, and probing, and sounding, and scrutinizing with the microscope, and dividing the surface of the building into registered square inches—what is it all but an exaggeration *of the application* of the one principle or set of principles of search, which are based upon the one set of notions regarding human ingenuity, to which the Prefect, in the long routine of his duty, has been accustomed? Do you not see he has taken it for granted that *all* men proceed to conceal a letter,—not exactly in a gimlet-hole bored in a chair-leg—but, at least, in *some* out-of-the-way hole or corner suggested by the same tenor of thought which would urge a man to secrete a letter in a gimlet-hole bored in a chair-leg? And do you not see also, that such *recherchés*[11] nooks for concealment are adapted only for ordinary occasions, and would be adopted only by ordinary intellects; for, in all cases of concealment, a disposal of the article concealed—a disposal of it in this *recherché* manner,—is, in the very first instance, presumable and presumed; and thus its discovery depends, not at all upon the acumen, but

---

[10] Rochefoucauld wrote *Reflexions,* a compendium of moral axioms; La Bougive remains unidentified; Machiavelli was an Italian courtier and author of a famous political handbook, *The Prince;* Campanella was a monk who wrote a controversial volume of philosophy.

[11] Obscure, esoteric.

altogether upon the mere care, patience, and determination of the seekers; and where the case is of importance—or, what amounts to the same thing in the politicial eyes, when the reward is of magnitude,—the qualities in question have *never* been known to fail. You will now understand what I meant in suggesting that, had the purloined letter been hidden any where within the limits of the Prefect's examination—in other words, had the principle of its concealment been comprehended within the principles of the Prefect—its discovery would have been a matter altogether beyond question. This functionary, however, has been thoroughly mystified; and the remote source of his defeat lies in the supposition that the Minister is a fool, because he has acquired renown as a poet. All fools are poets; this the Prefect *feels;* and he is merely guilty of a *non distributio medii*[12] in thence inferring that all poets are fools."

"But is this really the poet?" I asked. "There are two brothers, I know; and both have attained reputation in letters. The Minister I believe has written learnedly on the Differential Calculus. He is a mathematician, and no poet."

"You are mistaken; I know him well; he is both. As poet *and* mathematician, he would reason well; as mere mathematician, he could not have reasoned at all, and thus would have been at the mercy of the Prefect."

"You surprise me," I said, "by these opinions, which have been contradicted by the voice of the world. You do not mean to set at naught the well-digested idea of centuries. The mathematical reason has long been regarded as *the* reason *par excellence.*"

"'*Il y a à parier,*'" replied Dupin, quoting from Chamfort, "'*que toute idée publique, toute convention reçue, est une sottise, car elle a convenu au plus grand nombre.*'[13] The mathematicians, I grant you, have done their best to promulgate the popular error to which you allude, and which is none the less an error for its promulgation as truth. With an art worthy a better cause, for example, they have insinuated the term 'analysis' into application to algebra. The French are the originators of this particular deception; but if a term is of any importance—if words derive any value from applicability—then 'analysis' conveys 'algebra' about as much as, in Latin, '*ambitus*' implies 'ambition,' '*religio*' 'religion,' or '*homines honesti*,' a set of *honorable* men."[14]

"You have a quarrel on hand, I see," said I, "with some of the algebraists of Paris; but proceed."

"I dispute the availability, and thus the value, of that reason which is cultivated in any especial form other than the abstractly logical. I dispute, in

---

12Poe's Latin phrase translates as "the undistributed middle"—an error in deductive logic in which the conclusion is not justified by the premises.

13"The odds are that every accepted idea is nonsense, since each one has been accepted by the multitude."

14Dupin argues that modern terms have altered and restricted the field of signifi-

cance connoted by their Latin roots. *Ambitus* suggested moving around a periphery and circumlocution as well as canvassing for office; *religio* implied scrupulousness and a sense of obligation, not simply reverence for the divine; and *homines honesti* referred to men of distinction and noble birth, not necessarily honest men.

particular, the reason educed by mathematical study. The mathematics are the science of form and quantity; mathematical reasoning is merely logic applied to observation upon form and quantity. The great error lies in supposing that even the truths of what is called *pure* algebra, are abstract or general truths. And this error is so egregious that I am confounded at the universality with which it has been received. Mathematical axioms are *not* axioms of general truth. What is true of *relation*—of form and quantity—is often grossly false in regard to morals, for example. In this latter science it is very usually *untrue* that the aggregated parts are equal to the whole. In chemistry also the axiom fails. In the consideration of motive it fails; for two motives, each of a given value, have not, necessarily, a value when united, equal to the sum of their values apart. There are numerous other mathematical truths which are only truths within the limits of *relation*. But the mathematician argues, from his *finite truths*, through habit, as if they were of an absolutely general applicability—as the world indeed imagines them to be. Bryant, in his very learned 'Mythology,'[15] mentions an analogous source of error, when he says that 'although the Pagan fables are not believed, yet we forget ourselves continually, and make inferences from them as existing realities.' With the algebraists, however, who are Pagans themselves, the 'Pagan fables' *are* believed, and the inferences are made, not so much through lapse of memory, as through an unaccountable addling of the brains. In short, I never yet encountered the mere mathematician who could be trusted out of equal roots, or one who did not clandestinely hold it as a point of his faith that $x^2 + px$ was absolutely and unconditionally equal to q. Say to one of these gentlemen, by way of experiment, if you please, that you believe occasions may occur where $x^2 + px$ is *not* altogether equal to q, and, having made him understand what you mean, get out of his reach as speedily as convenient, for, beyond doubt, he will endeavor to knock you down.

"I mean to say," continued Dupin, while I merely laughed at his last observations, "that if the Minister had been no more than a mathematician, the Prefect would have been under no necessity of giving me this check. I knew him, however, as both mathematician and poet, and my measures were adapted to his capacity, with reference to the circumstances by which he was surrounded. I knew him as a courtier, too, and as a bold *intriguant*.[16] Such a man, I considered, could not fail to be aware of the ordinary policial modes of action. He could not have failed to anticipate—and events have proved that he did not fail to anticipate—the waylayings to which he was subjected. He must have foreseen, I reflected, the secret investigations of his premises. His frequent absences from home at night, which were hailed by the Prefect as certain aids to his success, I regarded only as *ruses*, to afford opportunity for thorough search to the police, and thus the sooner to

[15]Jacob Bryant compiled and interpreted ancient myths in his *A New System of Ancient Mythology* (1774–1776).

[16]Intriguer, opportunist.

impress them with the conviction to which G——, in fact, did finally arrive—the conviction that the letter was not upon the premises. I felt, also, that the whole train of thought, which I was at some pains in detailing to you just now, concerning the invariable principle of policial action in searches for articles concealed—I felt that this whole train of thought would necessarily pass through the mind of the Minister. It would imperatively lead him to despise all the ordinary *nooks* of concealment. *He* could not, I reflected, be so weak as not to see that the most intricate and remote recess of his hotel would be as open as his commonest closets to the eyes, to the probes, to the gimlets, and to the microscopes of the Prefect. I saw, in fine, that he would be driven, as a matter of course, to *simplicity*, if not deliberately induced to it as a matter of choice. You will remember, perhaps, how desperately the Prefect laughed when I suggested, upon our first interview, that it was just possible this mystery troubled him so much on account of its being so *very* self-evident."

"Yes," said I, "I remember his merriment well. I really thought he would have fallen into convulsions."

"The material world," continued Dupin, "abounds with very strict analogies to the immaterial; and thus some color of truth has been given to the rhetorical dogma, that metaphor, or simile, may be made to strengthen an argument, as well as to embellish a description. The principle of the *vis inertiae*,[17] for example, seems to be identical in physics and metaphysics. It is not more true in the former, that a large body is with more difficulty set in motion than a smaller one, and that its subsequent *momentum* is commensurate with this difficulty, than it is, in the latter, that intellects of the vaster capacity, while more forcible, more constant, and more eventful in their movements than those of inferior grade, are yet the less readily moved, and more embarrassed and full of hesitation in the first few steps of their progress. Again: have you ever noticed which of the street signs, over the shop doors, are the most attractive of attention?"

"I have never given the matter a thought," I said.

"There is a game of puzzles," he resumed, "which is played upon a map. One party playing requires another to find a given word—the name of town, river, state or empire—any word, in short, upon the motley and perplexed surface of the chart. A novice in the game generally seeks to embarrass his opponents by giving them the most minutely lettered names; but the adept selects such words as stretch, in large characters, from one end of the chart to the other. These, like the over-largely lettered signs and placards of the street, escape observation by dint of being excessively obvious; and here the physical oversight is precisely analogous with the moral inapprehension by which the intellect suffers to pass unnoticed those considerations which are too obtrusively and too palpably self-evident. But this is a point, it appears, somewhat above or beneath the understanding of the Prefect. He never once thought it probable, or possible, that the Minister had

---

[17]Power of inertia.

deposited the letter immediately beneath the nose of the whole world, by way of best preventing any portion of that world from perceiving it.

"But the more I reflected upon the daring, dashing, and discriminating ingenuity of D——; upon the fact that the document must always have been *at hand*, if he intended to use it to good purpose; and upon the decisive evidence, obtained by the Prefect, that it was not hidden within the limits of that dignitary's ordinary search—the more satisfied I became that, to conceal this letter, the Minister had resorted to the comprehensive and sagacious expedient of not attempting to conceal it at all.

"Full of these ideas, I prepared myself with a pair of green spectacles, and called one fine morning, quite by accident, at the Ministerial hotel. I found D—— at home, yawning, lounging, and dawdling, as usual, and pretending to be in the last extremity of *ennui*.[18] He is, perhaps, the most really energetic human being now alive—but that is only when nobody sees him.

"To be even with him, I complained of my weak eyes, and lamented the necessity of the spectacles, under cover of which I cautiously and thoroughly surveyed the apartment, while seemingly intent only upon the conversation of my host.

"I paid special attention to a large writing-table near which he sat, and upon which lay confusedly, some miscellaneous letters and other papers, with one or two musical instruments and a few books. Here, however, after a long and very deliberate scrutiny, I saw nothing to excite particular suspicion.

"At length my eyes, in going the circuit of the room, fell upon a trumpery fillagree card-rack of pasteboard, that hung dangling by a dirty blue ribbon, from a little brass knob just beneath the middle of the mantelpiece. In this rack, which had three or four compartments, were five or six visiting cards and a solitary letter. This last was much soiled and crumpled. It was torn nearly in two, across the middle—as if a design, in the first instance, to tear it entirely up as worthless, had been altered, or stayed, in the second. It had a large black seal, bearing the D—— cipher *very* conspicuously, and was addressed, in a diminutive female hand, to D——, the minister, himself. It was thrust carelessly, and even, as it seemed, contemptuously, into one of the upper divisions of the rack.

"No sooner had I glanced at this letter, than I concluded it to be that of which I was in search. To be sure, it was, to all appearance, radically different from the one of which the Prefect had read us so minute a description. Here the seal was large and black, with the D—— cipher; there it was small and red, with the ducal arms of the S—— family. Here, the address, to the Minister, was diminutive and feminine; there the superscription, to a certain royal personage, was markedly bold and decided; the size alone formed a point of correspondence. But, then, the *radicalness* of these differences, which was excessive; the dirt; the soiled and torn condition of the paper, so inconsistent with the *true* methodical habits of D——, and so suggestive of

[18]Boredom.

a design to delude the beholder into an idea of the worthlessness of the document; these things, together with the hyperobtrusive situation of this document, full in the view of every visitor, and thus exactly in accordance with the conclusions to which I had previously arrived; these things, I say, were strongly corroborative of suspicion, in one who came with the intention to suspect.

"I protracted my visit as long as possible, and, while I maintained a most animated discussion with the Minister, on a topic which I knew well had never failed to interest and excite him, I kept my attention really riveted upon the letter. In this examination, I committed to memory its external appearance and arrangement in the rack; and also fell, at length, upon a discovery which set at rest whatever trivial doubt I might have entertained. In scrutinizing the edges of the paper, I observed them to be more *chafed* than seemed necessary. They presented the *broken* appearance which is manifested when a stiff paper, having been once folded and pressed with a folder, is refolded in a reversed direction, in the same creases or edges which had formed the original fold. This discovery was sufficient. It was clear to me that the letter had been turned, as a glove, inside out, re-directed, and re-sealed. I bade the Minister good morning, and took my departure at once, leaving a gold snuff-box upon the table.

"The next morning I called for the snuff-box, when we resumed, quite eagerly, the conversation of the preceding day. While thus engaged, however, a loud report, as if of a pistol, was heard immediately beneath the windows of the hotel, and was succeeded by a series of fearful screams, and the shoutings of a mob. D—— rushed to a casement, threw it open, and looked out. In the meantime, I stepped to the card-rack, took the letter, put it in my pocket, and replaced it by a *fac-simile*, (so far as regards externals,) which I had carefully prepared at my lodgings; imitating the D—— cipher, very readily, by means of a seal formed of bread.

"The disturbance in the street had been occasioned by the frantic behavior of a man with a musket. He had fired it among a crowd of women and children. It proved, however, to have been without ball, and the fellow was suffered to go his way as a lunatic or a drunkard. When he had gone, D—— came from the window, whither I had followed him immediately upon securing the object in view. Soon afterwards I bade him farewell. The pretended lunatic was a man in my own pay."

"But what purpose had you," I asked, "in replacing the letter by a *fac-simile*? Would it not have been better, at the first visit, to have seized it openly, and departed?"

"D——," replied Dupin, "is a desperate man, and a man of nerve. His hotel, too, is not without attendants devoted to his interests. Had I made the wild attempt you suggest, I might never have left the Ministerial presence alive. The good people of Paris might have heard of me no more. But I had an object apart from these considerations. You know my political prepossessions. In this matter, I act as a partisan of the lady concerned. For eighteen months the Minister has had her in his power. She has now him in hers; since, being unaware that the letter is not in his possession, he will proceed with his exactions as if it was. Thus will he inevitably commit himself, at once, to his political destruction. His downfall, too, will not be more precipitate than awkward. It is all very well to talk about the *facilis descensus Averni;*[19] but in all kinds of climbing, as Catalani[20] said of singing, it is far more easy to get up than to come down. In the present instance I have no sympathy—at least no pity—for him who descends. He is that *monstrum horrendum,*[21] an unprincipled man of genius. I confess, however, that I should like very well to know the precise character of his thoughts, when, being defied by her whom the Prefect terms 'a certain personage,' he is reduced to opening the letter which I left for him in the card-rack."

"How? did you put any thing particular in it?"

"Why—it did not seem altogether right to leave the interior blank—that would have been insulting. D——, at Vienna once, did me an evil turn, which I told him, quite good-humoredly, that I should remember. So, as I knew he would feel some curiosity in regard to the identity of the person who had outwitted him, I thought it a pity not to give him a clue. He is well acquainted with my MS., and I just copied into the middle of the blank sheet the words—

> —— *Un dessein si funeste,*
> *S'il n'est digne d'Atrée, est digne de Thyeste.*[22]

They are to be found in Crébillon's 'Atrée.'"

1844, 1845

The Philosophy of Composition[1]

Charles Dickens, in a note now lying before me, alluding to an examination I once made of the mechanism of "Barnaby Rudge," says—"By the way, are you aware that Godwin wrote his 'Caleb Williams' backwards? He first involved his hero in a web of difficulties, forming the second volume, and then, for the first, cast about him for some mode of accounting for what had been done."

I cannot think this the *precise* mode of procedure on the part of Godwin—and indeed what he himself acknowledges,[2] is not altogether in accordance with Mr. Dickens' idea—but the author of "Caleb Williams" was

---

[19]"The easy descent to hell," from Virgil's *Aeneid.*

[20]A famous Italian opera singer.

[21]Horrible monster, another quote from Virgil.

[22]"A design so deadly, if not worthy of Atreus is worthy of Thyestes." The quote is from *Atrée et Thyeste* by the French playwright Crébillon. In this drama, Thyestes seduces his brother's wife, and in revenge Atreus kills the three sons of Thyestes and serves them up in a pie at a banquet honoring their father.

[1]Originally published in *Graham's Magazine* for April 1846.

[2]Poe wrote a critical commentary on Dickens's *Barnaby Rudge* in which he predicted the conclusion before the last installment appeared in print. Godwin prefaces his *Caleb Williams* with the observation that he "invented" the third volume of his tale first, then the second, etc.

too good an artist not to perceive the advantage derivable from at least a somewhat similar process. Nothing is more clear than that every plot, worth the name, must be elaborated to its *dénouement*[3] before anything be attempted with the pen. It is only with the *dénouement* constantly in view that we can give a plot its indispensable air of consequence, or causation, by making the incidents, and especially the tone at all points, tend to the development of the intention.

There is a radical error, I think, in the usual mode of constructing a story. Either history affords a thesis—or one is suggested by an incident of the day—or, at best, the author sets himself to work in the combination of striking events to form merely the basis of his narrative—designing, generally, to fill in with description, dialogue, or autorial comment, whatever crevices of fact, or action, may, from page to page, render themselves apparent.

I prefer commencing with the consideration of an *effect*. Keeping originality *always* in view—for he is false to himself who ventures to dispense with so obvious and so easily attainable a source of interest—I say to myself, in the first place, "Of the innumerable effects, or impressions, of which the heart, the intellect, or (more generally) the soul is susceptible, what one shall I, on the present occasion, select?" Having chosen a novel, first, and secondly a vivid effect, I consider whether it can be best wrought by incident or tone—whether by ordinary incidents and peculiar tone, or the converse, or by peculiarity both of incident and tone—afterward looking about me (or rather within) for such combinations of event, or tone, as shall best aid me in the construction of the effect.

I have often thought how interesting a magazine paper[4] might be written by any author who would—that is to say who could—detail, step by step, the processes by which any one of his compositions attained its ultimate point of completion. Why such a paper has never been given to the world, I am much at a loss to say—but, perhaps, the autorial vanity has had more to do with the omission than any one other cause. Most writers—poets in especial—prefer having it understood that they compose by a species of fine frenzy—an ecstatic intuition—and would positively shudder at letting the public take a peep behind the scenes, at the elaborate and vacillating crudities of thought—at the true purposes seized only at the last moment—at the innumerable glimpses of idea that arrived not at the maturity of full view—at the fully matured fancies discarded in despair as unmanageable—at the cautious selections and rejections—at the painful erasures and interpolations—in a word, at the wheels and pinions—the tackle for scene-shifting—the step-ladders and demon-traps—the cock's feathers, the red paint and the black patches, which, in ninety-nine cases out of the hundred, constitute the properties of the literary *histrio*.

I am aware, on the other hand, that the case is by no means common, in which an author is at all in condition to retrace the steps by which his

---

[3]Unravelling or final solution.   [4]That is, a magazine article.

conclusions have been attained. In general, suggestions, having arisen pell-mell, are pursued and forgotten in a similar manner.

For my own part, I have neither sympathy with the repugnance alluded to, nor, at any time the least difficulty in recalling to mind the progressive steps of any of my compositions; and, since the interest of an analysis, or reconstruction, such as I have considered a *desideratum*,[5] is quite independent of any real or fancied interest in the thing analyzed, it will not be regarded as a breach of decorum on my part to show the *modus operandi* by which some one of my own works was put together. I select "The Raven," as most generally known. It is my design to render it manifest that no one point in its composition is referrible either to accident or intuition—that the work proceeded, step by step, to its completion with the precision and rigid consequence of a mathematical problem.

Let us dismiss, as irrelevant to the poem, *per se*, the circumstance—or say the necessity—which, in the first place, gave rise to the intention of composing *a* poem that should suit at once the popular and the critical taste.

We commence, then, with this intention.

The initial consideration was that of extent. If any literary work is too long to be read at one sitting, we must be content to dispense with the immensely important effect derivable from unity of impression—for, if two sittings be required, the affairs of the world interfere, and every thing like totality is at once destroyed. But since, *ceteris paribus*,[6] no poet can afford to dispense with *any thing* that may advance his design, it but remains to be seen whether there is, in extent, any advantage to counterbalance the loss of unity which attends it. Here I say no, at once. What we term a long poem is, in fact, merely a succession of brief ones—that is to say, of brief poetical effects. It is needless to demonstrate that a poem is such, only inasmuch as it intensely excites, by elevating, the soul; and all intense excitements are, through a psychal necessity, brief. For this reason, at least one half of the "Paradise Lost" is essentially prose—a succession of poetical excitements interspersed, *inevitably*, with corresponding depressions—the whole being deprived, through the extremeness of its length, of the vastly important artistic element, totality, or unity, of effect.

It appears evident, then, that there is a distinct limit, as regards length, to all works of literary art—the limit of a single sitting—and that, although in certain classes of prose composition, such as "Robinson Crusoe," (demanding no unity,) this limit may be advantageously overpassed, it can never properly be overpassed in a poem. Within this limit, the extent of a poem may be made to bear mathematical relation to its merit—in other words, to the excitement or elevation—again in other words, to the degree of the true poetical effect which it is capable of inducing; for it is clear that the brevity must be in direct ratio of the intensity of the intended effect:—this, with one proviso—that a certain degree of duration is absolutely requisite for the production of any effect at all.

[5]Something needed.   [6]Other things being equal.

Holding in view these considerations, as well as that degree of excitement which I deemed not above the popular, while not below the critical, taste, I reached at once what I conceived the proper *length* for my intended poem—a length of about one hundred lines. It is, in fact, a hundred and eight.

My next thought concerned the choice of an impression, or effect, to be conveyed: and here I may as well observe that, throughout the construction, I kept steadily in view the design of rendering the work *universally* appreciable. I should be carried too far out of my immediate topic were I to demonstrate a point upon which I have repeatedly insisted, and which, with the poetical, stands not in the slightest need of demonstration—the point, I mean, that Beauty is the sole legitimate province of the poem. A few words, however, in elucidation of my real meaning, which some of my friends have evinced a disposition to misrepresent. That pleasure which is at once the most intense, the most elevating, and the most pure, is, I believe, found in the contemplation of the beautiful. When, indeed, men speak of Beauty, they mean, precisely, not a quality, as is supposed, but an effect—they refer, in short, just to that intense and pure elevation of *soul*—*not* of intellect, or of heart—upon which I have commented, and which is experienced in consequence of contemplating "the beautiful." Now I designate Beauty as the province of the poem, merely because it is an obvious rule of Art that effects should be made to spring from direct causes—that objects should be attained through means best adapted for their attainment—no one as yet having been weak enough to deny that the peculiar elevation alluded to is *most readily* attained in the poem. Now the object, Truth, or the satisfaction of the intellect, and the object Passion, or the excitement of the heart, are, although attainable, to a certain extent, in poetry, far more readily attainable in prose. Truth, in fact, demands a precision, and Passion a *homeliness* (the truly passionate will comprehend me) which are absolutely antagonistic to that Beauty which, I maintain, is the excitement, or pleasurable elevation, of the soul. It by no means follows from any thing here said, that passion, or even truth, may not be introduced, and even profitably introduced, into a poem—for they may serve in elucidation, or aid the general effect, as do discords in music, by contrast—but the true artist will always contrive, first, to tone them into proper subservience to the predominant aim, and, secondly, to enveil them, as far as possible, in that Beauty which is the atmosphere and the essence of the poem.

Regarding, then, Beauty as my province, my next question referred to the *tone* of its highest manifestation—and all experience has shown that this tone is one of *sadness*. Beauty of whatever kind, in its supreme development, invariably excites the sensitive soul to tears. Melancholy is thus the most legitimate of all the poetical tones.

The length, the province, and the tone, being thus determined, I betook myself to ordinary induction, with the view of obtaining some artistic piquancy which might serve me as a key-note in the construction of the poem—some pivot upon which the whole structure might turn. In carefully thinking over all the usual artistic effects—or more properly *points*, in the theatrical sense—I did not fail to perceive immediately that no one had been so universally employed as that of the *refrain*. The universality of its employment sufficed to assure me of its intrinsic value, and spared me the necessity of submitting it to analysis. I considered it, however, with regard to its susceptibility of improvement, and soon saw it to be in a primitive condition. As commonly used, the *refrain*, or burden, not only is limited to lyric verse, but depends for its impression upon the force of monotone—both in sound and thought. The pleasure is deduced solely from the sense of identity—of repetition. I resolved to diversify, and so heighten, the effect, by adhering, in general, to the monotone of sound, while I continually varied that of thought: that is to say, I determined to produce continuously novel effects, by the variation *of the application* of the *refrain*—the *refrain* itself remaining, for the most part, unvaried.

These points being settled, I next bethought me of the *nature* of my *refrain*. Since its application was to be repeatedly varied, it was clear that the *refrain* itself must be brief, for there would have been an insurmountable difficulty in frequent variations of application in any sentence of length. In proportion to the brevity of the sentence, would, of course, be the facility of the variation. This led me at once to a single word as the best *refrain*.

The question now arose as to the *character* of the word. Having made up my mind to a *refrain*, the division of the poem into stanzas was, of course, a corollary: the *refrain* forming the close of each stanza. That such a close, to have force, must be sonorous and susceptible of protracted emphasis, admitted no doubt: and these considerations inevitably led me to the long *o* as the most sonorous vowel, in connection with *r* as the most producible consonant.

The sound of the *refrain* being thus determined, it became necessary to select a word embodying this sound, and at the same time in the fullest possible keeping with that melancholy which I had predetermined as the tone of the poem. In such a search it would have been absolutely impossible to overlook the word "Nevermore." In fact, it was the very first which presented itself.

The next *desideratum* was a pretext for the continuous use of the one word "nevermore." In observing the difficulty which I at once found in inventing a sufficiently plausible reason for its continuous repetition, I did not fail to perceive that this difficulty arose solely from the pre-assumption that the word was to be so continuously or monotonously spoken by *a human* being—I did not fail to perceive, in short, that the difficulty lay in the reconciliation of this monotony with the exercise of reason on the part of the creature repeating the word. Here, then, immediately arose the idea of a *non*-reasoning creature capable of speech; and, very naturally, a parrot, in the first instance, suggested itself, but was superseded forthwith by a Raven, as equally capable of speech, and infinitely more in keeping with the intended *tone*.

I had now gone so far as the conception of a Raven—the bird of ill omen—monotonously repeating the one word, "Nevermore," at the conclusion of each stanza, in a poem of melancholy tone, and in length about one hundred lines. Now, never losing sight of the object *supremeness*, or perfection, at all points, I asked myself—"Of all melancholy topics, what, according to the *universal* understanding of mankind, is the *most* melancholy?" Death—was the obvious reply. "And when," I said, "is this most melancholy of topics most poetical?" From what I have already explained at some length, the answer, here also, is obvious—"When it most closely allies itself to *Beauty*: the death, then, of a beautiful woman is, unquestionably, the most poetical topic in the world—and equally is it beyond doubt that the lips best suited for such topic are those of a bereaved lover."

I had now to combine the two ideas, of a lover lamenting his deceased mistress and a Raven continuously repeating the word "Nevermore."—I had to combine these, bearing in mind my design of varying, at every turn, the *application* of the word repeated; but the only intelligible mode of such combination is that of imagining the Raven employing the word in answer to the queries of the lover. And here it was that I saw at once the opportunity afforded for the effect on which I had been depending—that is to say, the effect of the *variation of application*. I saw that I could make the first query propounded by the lover—the first query to which the Raven should reply "Nevermore"—that I could make this first query a commonplace one—the second less so—the third still less, and so on—until at length the lover, startled from his original *nonchalance* by the melancholy character of the word itself—by its frequent repetition—and by a consideration of the ominous reputation of the fowl that uttered it—is at length excited to superstition, and wildly propounds queries of a far different character— queries whose solution he has passionately at heart—propounds them half in superstition and half in that species of despair which delights in self-torture—propounds them not altogether because he believes in the prophetic or demoniac character of the bird (which, reason assures him, is merely repeating a lesson learned by rote) but because he experiences a phrenzied pleasure in so modeling his questions as to receive from the *expected* "Nevermore" the most delicious because the most intolerable of sorrow. Perceiving the opportunity thus afforded me—or, more strictly, thus forced upon me in the progress of the construction—I first established in mind the climax, or concluding query—that query to which "Nevermore" should be in the last place an answer—that in reply to which this word "Nevermore" should involve the utmost conceivable amount of sorrow and despair.

Here then the poem may be said to have its beginning—at the end, where all works of art should begin—for it was here, at this point of my preconsiderations, that I first put pen to paper in the composition of the stanza:

> "Prophet," said I, "thing of evil! prophet still if bird or devil!
> By that heaven that bends above us—by that God we both adore,

Tell this soul with sorrow laden, if within the distant Aidenn,
It shall clasp a sainted maiden whom the angels name Lenore—
Clasp a rare and radiant maiden whom the angels name Lenore."
Quoth the raven "Nevermore."

I composed this stanza, at this point, first that, by establishing the climax, I might the better vary and graduate, as regards seriousness and importance, the preceding queries of the lover—and, secondly, that I might definitely settle the rhythm, the metre, and the length and general arrangement of the stanza—as well as graduate the stanzas which were to precede, so that none of them might surpass this in rhythmical effect. Had I been able, in the subsequent composition, to construct more vigorous stanzas, I should, without scruple, have purposely enfeebled them, so as not to interfere with the climacteric effect.[7]

And here I may as well say a few words of the versification. My first object (as usual) was originality. The extent to which this has been neglected, in versification, is one of the most unaccountable things in the world. Admitting that there is little possibility of variety in mere *rhythm*, it is still clear that the possible varieties of metre and stanza are absolutely infinite—and yet, *for centuries, no man, in verse, has ever done, or ever seemed to think of doing, an original thing.* The fact is, that originality (unless in minds of very unusual force) is by no means a matter, as some suppose, of impulse or intuition. In general, to be found, it must be elaborately sought, and although a positive merit of the highest class, demands in its attainment less of invention than negation.

Of course, I pretend to no originality in either the rhythm or metre of the "Raven." The former is trochaic—the latter is octameter acatalectic, alternating with heptameter catalectic repeated in the *refrain* of the fifth verse, and terminating with tetrameter catalectic. Less pedantically—the feet employed throughout (trochees) consist of a long syllable followed by a short: the first line of the stanza consists of eight of these feet—the second of seven and a half (in effect two-thirds)—the third of eight—the fourth of seven and a half—the fifth the same—the sixth three and a half. Now, each of these lines, taken individually, has been employed before, and what originality the "Raven" has, is in their *combination into stanza; nothing* even remotely approaching this combination has ever been attempted.[8] The effect of this originality of combination is aided by other unusual, and some altogether novel effects, arising from an extension of the application of the principles of rhyme and alliteration.

The next point to be considered was the mode of bringing together the lover and the Raven—and the first branch of this consideration was the *locale.* For this the most natural suggestion might seem to be a forest, or the fields—but it has always appeared to me that a close *circumscription of space* is absolutely necessary to the effect of insulated incident:—it has the force of a frame

---

[7]Climactic.
[8]An exaggeration, as Poe well knew. He had recently read Elizabeth Barrett Browning's "Lady Geraldine's Courtship," which is quite close to "The Raven" in rhyme and meter.

to a picture. It has an indisputable moral power in keeping concentrated the attention, and, of course, must not be confounded with mere unity of place.

I determined, then, to place the lover in his chamber—in a chamber rendered sacred to him by memories of her who had frequented it. The room is represented as richly furnished—this in mere pursuance of the ideas I have already explained on the subject of Beauty, as the sole true poetical thesis.

The *locale* being thus determined, I had now to introduce the bird—and the thought of introducing him through the window, was inevitable. The idea of making the lover suppose, in the first instance, that the flapping of the wings of the bird against the shutter, is a "tapping" at the door, originated in a wish to increase, by prolonging, the reader's curiosity, and in a desire to admit the incidental effect arising from the lover's throwing open the door, finding all dark, and thence adopting the half-fancy that it was the spirit of his mistress that knocked.

I made the night tempestuous, first, to account for the Raven's seeking admission, and secondly, for the effect of contrast with the (physical) serenity within the chamber.

I made the bird alight on the bust of Pallas, also for the effect of contrast between the marble and the plumage—it being understood that the bust was absolutely *suggested* by the bird—the bust of *Pallas* being chosen, first, as most in keeping with the scholarship of the lover, and, secondly, for the sonorousness of the word, Pallas, itself.

About the middle of the poem, also, I have availed myself of the force of contrast, with a view of deepening the ultimate impression. For example, an air of the fantastic—approaching as nearly to the ludicrous as was admissible—is given to the Raven's entrance. He comes in "with many a flirt and flutter."

> *Not the* least obeisance made be—*not a moment stopped or stayed*
> *he,*
> But with mien of lord or lady, *perched above my chamber door.*

In the two stanzas which follow, the design is more obviously carried out:—

> *Then this ebony bird beguiling my sad fancy into smiling*
> *By the grave and stern decorum of the countenance it wore,*
> *"Though thy crest be shorn and shaven thou," I said, "art sure no*
> *craven,*
> *Ghastly grim and ancient Raven wandering from the nightly shore—*
> *Tell me what thy lordly name is on the Night's Plutonian shore?"*
> *Quoth the Raven "Nevermore."*

> *Much I marvelled this ungainly fowl to hear discourse so plainly*
> *Though its answer little meaning—little relevancy bore;*
> *For we cannot help agreeing that no living human being*
> *Ever yet was blessed with seeing bird above his chamber door—*
> *Bird or beast upon the sculptured bust above his chamber door,*
> *With such name as "Nevermore."*

The effect of the *dénouement* being thus provided for, I immediately drop the fantastic for a tone of the most profound seriousness:—this tone commencing in the stanza directly following the one last quoted, with the line,

> But the Raven, sitting lonely on that placid bust, spoke only, etc.

From this epoch the lover no longer jests—no longer sees any thing even of the fantastic in the Raven's demeanor. He speaks of him as a "grim, ungainly, ghastly, gaunt, and ominous bird of yore," and feels the "fiery eyes" burning into his "bosom's core." This revolution of thought, or fancy, on the lover's part, is intended to induce a similar one on the part of the reader—to bring the mind into a proper frame for the *dénouement*—which is now brought about as rapidly and as *directly* as possible.

With the *dénouement* proper—with the Raven's reply, "Nevermore," to the lover's final demand if he shall meet his mistress in another world—the poem, in its obvious phase, that of a simple narrative, may be said to have its completion. So far, every thing is within the limits of the accountable—of the real. A raven, having learned by rote the single word "Nevermore," and having escaped from the custody of its owner, is driven at midnight, through the violence of a storm, to seek admission at a window from which a light still gleams—the chamber-window of a student, occupied half in poring over a volume, half in dreaming of a beloved mistress deceased. The casement being thrown open at the fluttering of the bird's wings, the bird itself perches on the most convenient seat out of the immediate reach of the student, who, amused by the incident and the oddity of the visitor's demeanor, demands of it, in jest and without looking for a reply, its name. The raven addressed, answers with its customary word, "Nevermore"—a word which finds immediate echo in the melancholy heart of the student, who, giving utterance aloud to certain thoughts suggested by the occasion, is again startled by the fowl's repetition of "Nevermore." The student now guesses the state of the base, but is impelled, as I have before explained, by the human thirst for self-torture, and in part by superstition, to propound such queries to the bird as will bring him, the lover, the most of the luxury of sorrow, through the anticipated answer "Nevermore." With the indulgence, to the extreme, of this self-torture, the narration, in what I have termed its first or obvious phase, has a natural termination, and so far there has been no overstepping of the limits of the real.

But in subjects so handled, however skilfully, or with however vivid an array of incident, there is always a certain hardness or nakedness, which repels the artistical eye. Two things are invariably required—first, some amount of complexity, or more properly, adaptation; and, secondly, some amount of suggestiveness—some undercurrent, however indefinite, of meaning. It is this latter, in especial, which imparts to a work of art so much of that *richness* (to borrow from colloquy a forcible term) which we are too fond of confounding with *the ideal*. It is the *excess* of the suggested meaning—it is the rendering this the upper instead of the under current of the theme—which turns into prose (and that of the very flattest kind) the so called poetry of the so called transcendentalists.

Holding these opinions, I added the two concluding stanzas of the poem—their suggestiveness being thus made to pervade all the narrative which has preceded them. The under-current of meaning is rendered first apparent in the lines—

> *"Take thy beak from out my heart, and take thy form from off my*
> *   door!"*
> *   Quoth the Raven "Nevermore!"*

It will be observed that the words, "from out my heart," involve the first metaphorical expression in the poem. They, with the answer, "Nevermore," dispose the mind to seek a moral in all that has been previously narrated. The reader begins now to regard the Raven as emblematical—but it is not until the very last line of the very last stanza, that the intention of making him emblematical of *Mournful and Never-ending Remembrance* is permitted distinctly to be seen:

> *And the Raven, never flitting, still is sitting, still is sitting,*
> *On the pallid bust of Pallas, just above my chamber door;*
> *And his eyes have all the seeming of a demon's that is dreaming,*
> *And the lamplight o'er him streaming throws his shadow on the floor;*
> *And my soul from out that shadow that lies floating on the floor*
> *   Shall be lifted—nevermore.*

1846

from **The Poetic Principle**

In speaking of the Poetic Principle, I have no design to be either thorough or profound. While discussing, very much at random, the essentiality of what we call Poetry, my principal purpose will be to cite for consideration, some few of those minor English or American poems which best suit my own taste, or which, upon my own fancy, have left the most definite impression. By "minor poems" I mean, of course, poems of little length. And here, in the beginning, permit me to say a few words in regard to a somewhat peculiar principle, which, whether rightfully or wrongfully, has always had its influence in my own critical estimate of the poem. I hold that a long poem does not exist. I maintain that the phrase, "a long poem," is simply a flat contradiction in terms.

I need scarcely observe that a poem deserves its title only inasmuch as it excites, by elevating the soul. The value of the poem is in the ratio of this elevating excitement. But all excitements are, through a psychal necessity, transient. That degree of excitement which would entitle a poem to be so called at all, cannot be sustained throughout a composition of any great length. After the lapse of half an hour, at the very utmost, it flags—fails—a revulsion ensues—and then the poem is, in effect and in fact, no longer such.

There are, no doubt, many who have found difficulty in reconciling the critical dictum that the "Paradise Lost" is to be devoutly admired throughout, with the absolute impossibility of maintaining for it, during perusal, the amount of enthusiasm which that critical dictum would demand. This great work, in fact, is to be regarded as poetical, only when, losing sight of that vital requisite in all works of Art, Unity, we view it merely as a series of minor poems. If, to preserve its Unity—its totality of effect or impression—we read it (as would be necessary) at a single sitting, the result is but a constant alteration of excitement and depression. After a passage of what we feel to be true poetry, there follows, inevitably, a passage of platitude which no critical prejudgment can force us to admire; but if, upon completing the work, we read it again, omitting the first book—that is to say, commencing with the second— we shall be surprised at now finding that admirable which we before condemned—that damnable which we had previously so much admired. It follows from all this that the ultimate, aggregate, or absolute effect of even the best epic under the sun, is a nullity:—and this is precisely the fact.

In regard to the *Iliad*, we have, if not positive proof, at least very good reason for believing it intended as a series of lyrics; but, granting the epic intention, I can say only that the work is based in an imperfect sense of art. The modern epic is, of the supposititious ancient model, but an inconsiderate and blindfold imitation. But the day of these artistic anomalies is over. If, at any time, any very long poem were popular in reality, which I doubt, it is at least clear that no very long poem will ever be popular again. . . .

While the epic mania, while the idea that to merit in poetry prolixity is indispensable, has for some years past been gradually dying out of the public mind, by mere dint of its own absurdity, we find it succeeded by a heresy too palpably false to be long tolerated, but one which, in the brief period it has already endured, may be said to have accomplished more in the corruption of our Poetical Literature than all its other enemies combined. I allude to the heresies of The Didactic. It has been assumed, tacitly and avowedly, directly and indirectly, that the ultimate object of all Poetry is Truth. Every poem, it is said, should inculcate a moral, and by this moral is the poetical merit of the work to be adjudged. We Americans especially have patronized this happy idea, and we Bostonians very especially have developed it in full. We have taken it into our heads that to write a poem simply for the poem's sake, and to acknowledge such to have been our design, would be to confess ourselves radically wanting in the true poetic dignity and force:—but the simple fact is that would we but permit ourselves to look into our own souls we should immediately there discover that under the sun there neither exists nor can exist any work more thoroughly dignified, more supremely noble, than this very poem, this poem per se, this poem which is a poem and nothing more, this poem written solely for the poem's sake.

With as deep a reverence for the True as ever inspired the bosom of man, I would nevertheless limit, in some measure, its modes of inculcation. I would limit to enforce them. I would not enfeeble them by dissipation. The demands of Truth are severe. She has no sympathy with the myrtles. All that which is so indispensable in Song is precisely all that with which she has nothing whatever to do. It is but making her a flaunting paradox to wreathe her in gems and flowers. In enforcing a truth we need severity rather than efflorescence of language. We must be simple, precise, terse. We must be cool, calm, unimpassioned. In a word, we must be in that mood which, as nearly as possible, is the exact converse of the poetical. He must be blind indeed who does not perceive the radical and chasmal difference between the truthful and the poetical modes of inculcation. He must be theory-mad beyond redemption who, in spite of these differences, shall still persist in attempting to reconcile the obstinate oils and waters of Poetry and Truth.

1850

Sonnet—To Science[1]

Science! true daughter of Old Time thou art!
   Who alterest all things with thy peering eyes.
Why preyest thou thus upon the poet's heart,
   Vulture, whose wings are dull realities?
How should he love thee? or how deem thee wise,   5
   Who wouldst not leave him in his wandering
To seek for treasure in the jewelled skies,
   Albeit he soared with an undaunted wing?
Hast thou not dragged Diana from her car?
   And driven the Hamadryad[2] from the wood   10
To seek a shelter in some happier star?
   Hast thou not torn the Naiad[3] from her flood,
The Elfin from the green grass, and from me
The summer dream beneath the tamarind tree?[4]

1829, 1845

Romance[1']

Romance, who loves to nod and sing,
With drowsy head and folded wing,
Among the green leaves as they shake
Far down within some shadowy lake,

---

[1]First published as a preface to the long poem "Al Aaraaf" in the collection *Al Aaraaf, Tamerlane, and Minor Poems* (1829), this sonnet was frequently revised and republished, appearing in its final form in *The Raven and Other Poems* (1845).

[2]Diana was an ancient Roman goddess associated with nature and fertility; Hamadryads are tree nymphs.

[3]Naiads are Greek female spirits who dwell in freshwater streams, lakes, etc.

[4]Tree noted for fragrance, found in the East and West Indies.

[1']First appearing under the title "Preface" in *Al Aaraaf, Tamerlane, and Minor Poems* (1829), this poem was included in *Poems* (1831) and in *The Raven and Other Poems* (1845).

To me a painted paroquet[2]　　　　　　　　　　　　5
Hath been—a most familiar bird—
Taught me my alphabet to say—
To lisp my very earliest word
While in the wild wood I did lie,
A child—with a most knowing eye.　　　　　　　　10

Of late, eternal Condor[3] years
So shake the very Heaven on high
With tumult as they thunder by,
I have no time for idle cares
Through gazing on the unquiet sky.　　　　　　　　15
And when an hour with calmer wings
Its down upon my spirit flings—
That little time with lyre and rhyme
To while away—forbidden things!
My heart would feel to be a crime　　　　　　　　20
Unless it trembled with the strings.

　　　　　　　　　　　　　　　　　　　　　1829

To Helen[1]

Helen, thy beauty is to me
　　Like those Nicéan[2'] barks of yore,
That gently, o'er a perfumed sea,
　　The weary, way-worn wanderer[3'] bore
　　　To his own native shore.　　　　　　　　　5

On desperate seas long wont to roam,
　　Thy hyacinth hair,[4] thy classic face,
Thy Naiad[5] airs have brought me home
　　To the glory that was Greece,
　　　And the grandeur that was Rome.　　　　　10

[2]Wooden bird hung from a pole outside a church tower to be shot at by archers.

[3]The condor is a scavenger with voracious appetite and vigorous flight.

[1]First published in *Poems* (1831) but revised and polished to its present form over a period of twelve years. The title figure refers to Helen of Troy, considered the most beautiful woman of antiquity. This version of the poem appeared in the (*Philadelphia*) *Saturday Museum* in 1843 before being collected in *The Raven and Other Poems* (1845).

[2']Nicéan might refer to Nicea, an ancient city associated with Dionysus, Greek god of wine and frenzy; or to Nike, the Greek word for victory.

[3']The wanderer has been variously identified as Bacchus, Catullus, Menelaus, and Odysseus. The last two were travelers on missions of love.

[4]Hyacinthus was a beautiful Greek youth beloved of Apollo. At his death, Apollo created the flower that bears his name. The term is also applied to the hairstyle of certain Greek statues and coins.

[5]Naiads are nymphs associated with freshwater lakes and rivers.

Lo! in yon brilliant window-niche
   How statue-like I see thee stand,
The agate[6] lamp within thy hand!
   Ah, Psyche,[7] from the regions which
   Are Holy-Land![8]   15

                                  1831, 1843

Israfel[1]

In Heaven a spirit doth dwell
   "Whose heart-strings are a lute;"
None sing so wildly well
As the angel Israfel,[2]
And the giddy stars (so legends tell)   5
Ceasing their hymns, attend the spell
   Of his voice, all mute.

Tottering above
   In her highest noon,
   The enamoured moon   10
Blushes with love,
   While, to listen, the red levin[3]
   (With the rapid Pleiads, even,
   Which were seven,)[4]
   Pauses in Heaven.   15

And they say (the starry choir
   And the other listening things)
That Israfeli's fire
Is owing to that lyre[5]
   By which he sits and sings—   20
The trembling living wire
   Of those unusual strings.

[6]The term "agate" is derived from *fidus Achates*, a faithful friend of Aeneas in Virgil.
[7]Psyche was the Greek immortal who represented spirit.
[8]Since everyday usage would associate the term with Jerusalem, Holy Land in this line might refer to that city or to ancient Rome or Athens, the holy land of art and culture.
[1]And the angel Israfel, whose heart-strings are a lute, and who has the sweetest voice of all God's creatures.—KORAN [Poe's note]. This work was first published in *Poems* (1831), then revised and reprinted several times in the 1830s and 1840s. This text is taken from *The Raven and Other Poems* (1845).

[2]Poe derived the name and the concept from Thomas Moore's *Lalla Rookh*, a popular orientalist tale.
[3]Lightning.
[4]The constellation Pleiades, which is supposed to represent seven sisters who were pursued by Orion.
[5]Probably to accommodate his rhyme scheme, Poe changes the basic image from a lute to a lyre, both stringed instruments with different frames. A lute looks like a mandolin with a bent neck, while a lyre is a small harp, the frame of which might be considered heart-shaped.

But the skies that angel trod,
　　Where deep thoughts are a duty—
Where Love's a grown-up God—　　　　　　　　25
　　Where the Houri[6] glances are
Imbued with all the beauty
　　Which we worship in a star.

Therefore, thou art not wrong,
　　Israfeli, who despisest　　　　　　　　　30
An unimpassioned song;
To thee the laurels belong,
　　Best bard, because the wisest!
Merrily live, and long!

The ecstasies above　　　　　　　　　　　35
　　With thy burning measures suit—
Thy grief, thy joy, thy hate, thy love,
　　With the fervour of thy lute—
　　Well may the stars be mute!

Yes, Heaven is thine; but this　　　　　　40
　　Is a world of sweets and sours;
　　Our flowers are merely—flowers,
And the shadow of thy perfect bliss
　　Is the sunshine of ours.

If I could dwell　　　　　　　　　　　　45
Where Israfel
　　Hath dwelt, and he where I,
He might not sing so wildly well
　　A mortal melody,
While a bolder note than this might swell　50
　　From my lyre within the sky.

　　　　　　　　　　　　　　　　　　1831, 1845

The City in the Sea[1]

Lo! Death has reared himself a throne
In a strange city lying alone
Far down within the dim West,

---

[6]Islamic maidens who dwell in paradise.
[1]First published under the title "The Doomed City" in the 1831 *Poems*, this poem was fre-

quently revised and reprinted. This version is taken from *The Raven and Other Poems* (1845).

Where the good and the bad and the worst and the best
Have gone to their eternal rest.   5
There shrines and palaces and towers
(Time-eaten towers that tremble not!)
Resemble nothing that is ours.
Around, by lifting winds forgot,[2]
Resignedly beneath the sky   10
The melancholy waters lie.

No rays from the holy heaven come down
On the long night-time of that town;
But light from out the lurid sea
Streams up the turrets silently—   15
Gleams up the pinnacles far and free—
Up domes—up spires—up kingly halls—
Up fanes—up Babylon-like walls—[3]
Up shadowy long-forgotten bowers
Of sculptured ivy and stone flowers—   20
Up many and many a marvellous shrine
Whose wreathéd friezes intertwine
The viol, the violet, and the vine.
Resignedly beneath the sky
The melancholy waters lie.   25
So blend the turrets and shadows there
That all seem pendulous in air,
While from a proud tower in the town
Death looks gigantically down.

There open fanes[4] and gaping graves   30
Yawn level with the luminous waves
But not the riches there that lie
In each idol's diamond eye—
Not the gaily-jewelled dead
Tempt the waters from their bed;   35
For no ripples curl, alas!
Along that wilderness of glass—
No swellings tell that winds may be
Upon some far-off happier sea—
No heavings hint that winds have been   40
On seas less hideously serene.

---

[2] Contemporary descriptions of the Dead Sea claimed that the waters were "so heavy that the winds cannot ruffle their surface."

[3] They are Babylon-like because they are doomed to fall.

[4] Archaic for temple or church.

But lo, a stir is in the air!
The wave—there is a movement there!
As if the towers had thrust aside,
In slightly sinking, the dull tide— 45
As if their tops had feebly given
A void within the filmy Heaven.
The waves have now a redder glow—
The hours are breathing faint and low—
And when, amid no earthly moans, 50
Down, down that town shall settle hence,
Hell, rising from a thousand thrones,
Shall do it reverence.

1831, 1845

Bridal Ballad[1]

The ring is on my hand,
    And the wreath is on my brow;
Satins and jewels grand
Are all at my command,
    And I am happy now. 5

And my lord he loves me well;
    But, when first he breathed his vow,
I felt my bosom swell—
For the words rang as a knell,
And the voice seemed *his* who fell 10
In the battle down the dell,
    And who is happy now.

But he spoke to re-assure me,
    And he kissed my pallid brow,
While a reverie came o'er me, 15
And to the church-yard bore me,
And I sighed to him before me,
(Thinking him dead D'Elormie,)
    "Oh, I am happy now!"

And thus the words were spoken; 20
    And this the plighted vow;
And, though my faith be broken,
And, though my heart be broken,

[1]First published in the *Southern Literary Messenger* in January 1837, "Bridal Ballad" was revised and reprinted in *The Raven and Other Poems* in 1845.

Here is a ring, as token
    That I am happy now!—   25
Behold the golden token
    That *proves* me happy now!

Would God I could awaken!
    For I dream I know not how,
And my soul is sorely shaken   30
Lest an evil step be taken,—
Lest the dead who is forsaken
    May not be happy now.

                                                        1837, 1845

Sonnet—Silence[1]

There are some qualities—some incorporate things,
    That have a double life, which thus is made
A type of that twin entity which springs
    From matter and light, evinced in solid and shade.
There is a two-fold *Silence*—sea and shore—   5
    Body and soul. One dwells in lonely places,
    Newly with grass o'ergrown; some solemn graces,
Some human memories and tearful lore,
Render him terrorless: his name's "No More."
He is the corporate Silence: dread him not!   10
    No power hath he of evil in himself;
But should some urgent fate (untimely lot!)
    Bring thee to meet his shadow (nameless elf,
That haunteth the lone regions where hath trod
No foot of man,) commend thyself to God!   15

                                                        1840, 1845

Dream-Land[1']

By a route obscure and lonely,
Haunted by ill angels only,
Where an Eidolon,[2] named NIGHT,
On a black throne reigns upright,

[1]First published in the *Philadelphia Saturday Courier* for January 4, 1840. Reprinted several times in the 1840s and included in *The Raven and Other Poems* (1845).
[1']Originally published in *Graham's Magazine* for June 1844 and included in *The Raven*

and Other Poems (1845), this text is taken from Poe's final corrections to the poem in the *Richmond Examiner* (1849).
[2]A phantom.

I have reached these lands but newly   5
From an ultimate dim Thule—[3]
From a wild weird clime that lieth, sublime,
    Out of SPACE—out of TIME.
Bottomless vales and boundless floods,
And chasms, and caves and Titan[4] woods,   10
With forms that no man can discover
For the tears that drip all over;
Mountains toppling evermore
Into seas without a shore;
Seas that restlessly aspire,   15
Surging, unto skies of fire;
Lakes that endlessly outspread
Their lone waters—lone and dead,—
Their still waters—still and chilly
With the snows of the lolling lily.   20

By the lakes that thus outspread
Their lone waters, lone and dead,—
Their sad waters, sad and chilly
With the snows of the lolling lily,—
By the mountains—near the river   25
Murmuring lowly, murmuring ever,—
By the grey woods,—by the swamp
Where the toad and the newt encamp,—
By the dismal tarns and pools
    Where dwell the Ghouls,—   30
By each spot the most unholy—
In each nook most melancholy,—
There the traveller meets, aghast,
Sheeted Memories of the Past—
Shrouded forms that start and sigh   35
As they pass the wanderer by—
White-robed forms of friends long given,
In agony, to the Earth—and Heaven.

For the heart whose woes are legion
'T is a peaceful, soothing region—   40
For the spirit that walks in shadow
'T is—oh 't is an Eldorado![5]

---

[3]Thule was the Greek name for an island north of Britain and thus remote from the center of things. Vergil used the phrase "ultima Thule" in his *Georgics*; it has come to mean remote beyond literal geography, so far off as to be unrecorded on maps.

[4]Titans were Greek gods before the Olympians. They were enormous and forbidding deities.
[5]A mythical city of gold.

But the traveller, travelling through it,
May not—dare not openly view it;
Never its mysteries are exposed   45
To the weak human eye unclosed;
So wills its King, who hath forbid
The uplifting of the fringéd lid;
And thus the sad Soul that here passes
Beholds it but through darkened glasses.   50
By a route obscure and lonely,
Haunted by ill angels only,
Where an Eidolon, named NIGHT,
On a black throne reigns upright,
I have wandered home but newly   55
From this ultimate dim Thule.

                                              1844, 1849

The Raven[1]

Once upon a midnight dreary, while I pondered, weak and weary,
Over many a quaint and curious volume of forgotten lore—
While I nodded, nearly napping, suddenly there came a tapping,
As of some one gently rapping, rapping at my chamber door.
"'T is some visiter," I muttered, "tapping at my chamber door—   5
            Only this and nothing more."

Ah, distinctly I remember it was in the bleak December;
And each separate dying ember wrought its ghost upon the floor.
Eagerly I wished the morrow;—vainly I had sought to borrow
From my books surcease of sorrow—sorrow for the lost Lenore—   10
For the rare and radiant maiden whom the angels name Lenore—
            Nameless *here* for evermore.

And the silken, sad, uncertain rustling of each purple curtain
Thrilled me—filled me with fantastic terrors never felt before;
So that now, to still the beating of my heart, I stood repeating   15
"'T is some visiter entreating entrance at my chamber door—
Some late visiter entreating entrance at my chamber door;—
            This it is and nothing more."

[1]First published in 1845 in the *American Review;* thereafter published numerous times in the year of initial publication. Poe's best-known poem in the United States and famous the world over, it has been reprinted, imitated, and satirized more than any other poem by an American, with the possible exception of Eliot's *Waste Land*. This text is taken from Poe's final revisions to the poem in the *Richmond Examiner* (1849).

Presently my soul grew stronger; hesitating then no longer,
"Sir," said I, "or Madam, truly your forgiveness I implore;   20
But the fact is I was napping, and so gently you came rapping,
And so faintly you came tapping, tapping at my chamber door,
That I scarce was sure I heard you"—here I opened wide the
    door;—
                      Darkness there and nothing more.

Deep into that darkness peering, long I stood there wondering,   25
    fearing,
Doubting, dreaming dreams no mortal ever dared to dream before;
But the silence was unbroken, and the stillness gave no token,
And the only word there spoken was the whispered word,
    "Lenore!"
This I whispered, and an echo murmured back the word
    "Lenore!"
                      Merely this and nothing more.   30

Back into the chamber turning, all my soul within me burning,
Soon again I heard a tapping somewhat louder than before.
"Surely," said I, "surely that is something at my window lattice;
Let me see, then, what thereat is, and this mystery explore—
Let my heart be still a moment and this mystery explore;—   35
                  'T is the wind and nothing more!"

Open here I flung the shutter, when, with many a flirt and flutter
In there stepped a stately Raven of the saintly days of yore.
Not the least obeisance made he; not a minute stopped or stayed
    he;
But, with mien of lord or lady, perched above my chamber door—   40
Perched upon a bust of Pallas[2] just above my chamber door—
               Perched, and sat, and nothing more.

Then this ebony bird beguiling my sad fancy into smiling,
By the grave and stern decorum of the countenance it wore,
"Though thy crest be shorn and shaven, thou," I said, "art sure no   45
    craven,[3]
Ghastly grim and ancient Raven wandering from the Nightly shore—
Tell me what thy lordly name is on the Night's Plutonian shore!"[4]
           Quoth the Raven, "Nevermore."

Much I marvelled this ungainly fowl to hear discourse so plainly,
Though its answer little meaning—little relevancy bore;   50

[2]Pallas Athena was the Greek goddess of
wisdom.
[3]A cowardly knight sometimes had his head
shaved as a sign of his disgrace.

[4]Relating to Pluto; thus the lower world,
hellish.

For we cannot help agreeing that no living human being
Ever yet was blessed with seeing bird above his chamber door—
Bird or beast upon the sculptured bust above his chamber door,
                With such name as "Nevermore."

But the Raven, sitting lonely on the placid bust, spoke only   55
That one word, as if his soul in that one word he did outpour.
Nothing farther then he uttered—not a feather then he fluttered—
Till I scarcely more than muttered "Other friends have flown
    before—
On the morrow *he* will leave me, as my hopes have flown before."
                Then the bird said "Nevermore."   60

Startled at the stillness broken by reply so aptly spoken,
"Doubtless," said I, "what it utters is its only stock and store
Caught from some unhappy master whom unmerciful Disaster
Followed fast and followed faster till his songs one burden bore—
Till the dirges of his Hope that melancholy burden bore   65
              Of 'Never—nevermore.'"

But the Raven still beguiling all my fancy into smiling,
Straight I wheeled a cushioned seat in front of bird, and bust and
    door;
Then, upon the velvet sinking, I betook myself to linking
Fancy unto fancy, thinking what this ominous bird of yore—   70
What this grim, ungainly, ghastly, gaunt, and ominous bird of yore
              Meant in croaking "Nevermore."

This I sat engaged in guessing, but no syllable expressing
To the fowl whose fiery eyes now burned into my bosom's core;
This and more I sat divining, with my head at ease reclining   75
On the cushion's velvet lining that the lamp-light gloated o'er,
But whose velvet violet lining with the lamp-light gloating o'er,
            She shall press, ah, nevermore!

Then, methought, the air grew denser, perfumed from an unseen
    censer
Swung by Seraphim[5] whose foot-falls tinkled on the tufted floor.   80
"Wretch," I cried, "thy God hath lent thee—by these angels he
    hath sent thee
Respite—respite and nepenthe[6] from thy memories of Lenore;
Quaff, oh quaff this kind nepenthe and forget this lost Lenore!"
            Quoth the Raven "Nevermore."

[5]Angels.
[6]A legendary drink supposed to soothe the
bereaved.

"Prophet!" said I, "thing of evil! prophet still, if bird or devil!—   85
Whether Tempter sent, or whether tempest tossed thee here
    ashore,
Desolate yet all undaunted, on this desert land enchanted—
On this home by Horror haunted—tell me truly, I implore—
Is there—*is* there balm in Gilead?[7]—tell me—tell me, I implore!"
              Quoth the Raven "Nevermore."   90

"Prophet!" said I, "thing of evil!—prophet still, if bird or devil!
By that Heaven that bends above us—by that God we both adore—

Tell this soul with sorrow laden if, within the distant Aidenn,[8]
It shall clasp a sainted maiden whom the angels name Lenore—
Clasp a rare and radiant maiden whom the angels name Lenore."   95
              Quoth the Raven "Nevermore."

"Be that word our sign of parting, bird or fiend!" I shrieked,
    upstarting—
"Get thee back into the tempest and the Night's Plutonian shore!
Leave no black plume as a token of that lie thy soul hath spoken!
Leave my loneliness unbroken!—quit the bust above my door!   100
Take thy beak from out my heart, and take thy form from off my
    door!"
              Quoth the Raven "Nevermore."

And the Raven, never flitting, still is sitting, *still* is sitting
On the pallid bust of Pallas just above my chamber door;
And his eyes have all the seeming of a demon's that is dreaming,   105
And the lamp-light o'er him streaming throws his shadow on the
    floor;
And my soul from out that shadow that lies floating on the floor
            Shall be lifted—nevermore!

                            1845, 1849

Annabel Lee[1]

It was many and many a year ago,
    In a kingdom by the sea

---

[7]A complex reference, meaning: is there solace in the future? or (biblical) is there hope for me in heaven?
[8]Poe's spelling of Eden.
[1]The initial authorized publication was in *Sartain's Union Magazine* for January 1850, but in his last summer, Poe distributed copies to several friends, who assumed he intended them to publish the poem—or who rushed it into print when they heard of Poe's death in October. Thus some versions appeared late in 1849.

That a maiden there lived whom you may know
    By the name of ANNABEL LEE;
And this maiden she lived with no other thought   5
    Than to love and be loved by me.

I was a child and *she* was a child,
    In this kingdom by the sea,
But we loved with a love that was more than love—
    I and my ANNABEL LEE—   10
With a love that the winged seraphs of heaven
    Coveted her and me.

And this was the reason that, long ago,
    In this kingdom by the sea,
A wind blew out of a cloud, chilling   15
    My beautiful ANNABEL LEE;
So that her highborn kinsmen came
    And bore her away from me,
To shut her up in a sepulchre
    In this kingdom by the sea.   20

The angels, not half so happy in heaven,
    Went envying her and me—
Yes!—that was the reason (as all men know,
    In this kingdom by the sea)
That the wind came out of the cloud by night,   25
    Chilling and killing my ANNABEL LEE.

But our love it was stronger by far than the love
    Of those who were older than we—
    Of many far wiser than we—
And neither the angels in heaven above,   30
    Nor the demons down under the sea,
Can ever dissever my soul from the soul
    Of the beautiful ANNABEL LEE:

For the moon never beams, without bringing me dreams
    Of the beautiful ANNABEL LEE;   35
And the stars never rise, but I feel the bright eyes
    Of the beautiful ANNABEL LEE:
And so, all the night-tide, I lie down by the side
Of my darling—my darling—my life and my bride,
    In the sepulchre there by the sea—   40
    In her tomb by the sounding sea.

                                          1849, 1850

Samuel Brown [a parody]

by Phoebe Cary

It was many and many a year ago,
    In a dwelling down in town,
That a fellow there lived whom you may know,
    By the name of Samuel Brown;
And this fellow lived with no other thought
    Than to our house to come down.

I was a child, and he was a child,
    In that dwelling down in town,
But we loved with a love that was more than love,
    I and my Samuel Brown,
With a love that the ladies coveted
    Me and Samuel Brown.

And this was the reason that, long ago,
    To that dwelling down in town,
A girl came out of her carriage, courting
    My beautiful Samuel Brown;-
So that her high-bred kinsman came
    And bore away Samuel Brown,
And shut him up in a dwelling-house,
    In a street quite up in town.

The ladies not half so happy up there,
    Went envying me and Brown;
Yes! that was the reason, (as all men know,
    In this dwelling down in town),
That the girl came out of the carriage by night,
    Coquetting and getting my Samuel Brown.

But our love is more artful by far than the love
    Of those who are older than we,—
Of many far wiser than we,
    And neither the girls that are living above,
Nor the girls that are down in town,
    Can ever dissever my soul from the soul
Of the beautiful Samuel Brown.

For the morn never shines without bringing me lines
    From my beautiful Samuel Brown;
And the night's never dark, but I sit in the park

With my beautiful Samuel Brown.
And often by day, I walk down in Broadway,
    With my darling, my darling, my life and my stay
To our dwelling down in town,
    To our house in the street down town.

1854

from *The Poems of Alice and Phoebe Cary*, 1903

■ ## HARRIET BEECHER STOWE ■
1811–1896

Harriet Beecher Stowe is known primarily for *Uncle Tom's Cabin*, the best-selling novel that is credited with creating such extreme public outrage over slavery that it set the stage for the Civil War. The popularity and political significance of Stowe's work underscores her importance as an author who skillfully represented the complexities and contradictions of nineteenth-century America.

Harriet Beecher Stowe was born on June 14, 1811, one of eleven children fathered by Lyman Beecher, a prominent but domineering Calvinist minister. She was influenced by the lively intellectual environment of her large and distinguished family, but she chafed under the limits imposed on her because of her gender; her father is recorded as saying that he wished she were a boy so that she could achieve as much as her brothers. Like her older sister Catherine Beecher, a well-known women's educator, Stowe sought to find opportunities for self-expression within the confines of household duties and familial obligations. Although Stowe did not agree with her sister's argument that women's influence should be restricted to the domestic sphere, neither did she embrace the radical egalitarian ideas championed by feminists like Elizabeth Cady Stanton. Stowe's successful career as an author would draw her into the public arena, but she struggled throughout her life to reconcile her political prominence with her responsibilities as a wife and mother.

In 1832 the Beecher family moved to Cincinnati, Ohio, a city separated from the slave state of Kentucky by the Ohio River, an important symbol in *Uncle Tom's Cabin*. There Stowe witnessed the practice of slavery and began to accept the validity of the abolitionist movement. She taught at Catherine Beecher's school for young women, the Western Female Institute, as she had at Beecher's Hartford Woman's Seminary in Connecticut, and began writing short fiction and essays for magazines. In 1836 she married Calvin Stowe, a professor of theology, and entered fully into family life; she would bear seven children in fourteen years. When Calvin was appointed to Bowdoin College, the Stowe family moved to Maine. It was there that Harriet Beecher Stowe began to compose *Uncle Tom's Cabin*, the genesis of which can be traced directly to the Fugitive Slave

Act of 1850; Stowe expressed her outrage over this law, writing "the time is come when even a woman or a child who can speak a word for freedom and humanity is bound to speak." In addition to these political considerations, writing was for Stowe a means of supporting a growing family and gaining financial independence so that she would not be what she described as "a mere domestic slave."

Uncle Tom's Cabin (1852) recounts the tale of Uncle Tom, a Southern slave of surpassing piety and humility, whose mistreatment by the cruel slave owner Simon Legree is depicted as a battle between good and evil. Through the novel, Stowe sought to transform the abstract concept of slavery into sympathetic slave characters like Uncle Tom and Eliza and George Harris with whom a white and Christian reading audience could identify. Her detailed portrait of the horrors of slavery demanded an emotional response from readers, who were guided by Stowe's authorial interventions to recognize their complicity with the slavery system. The Southern response to *Uncle Tom's Cabin* was venomous and challenged Stowe's legitimacy as an authority on slavery; an entire body of "anti-Tom" literature painted a contrasting portrait of contented slaves. The response by African American abolitionists was divided; Frederick Douglass endorsed the novel in his antislavery newspaper, overlooking its flaws in favor of its power to assist the abolitionist movement. But Martin R. Delany condemned Stowe's use of racial stereotypes and her endorsement of the plan to send freed American slaves to the African colony of Liberia.

These criticisms did nothing to temper the public embrace of the book. The first edition sold out within a few days, and by the end of 1852 more than three hundred thousand copies had sold in the United States. (By comparison, works like Hawthorne's *The Scarlet Letter* (1850) and Melville's *Moby-Dick* (1851) can be considered financial and popular failures.) By the end of the century, *Uncle Tom's Cabin* had sold more than a million copies and become the definitive best seller of its time. The novel's popularity resulted in a cultural phenomenon; Americans purchased numerous souvenirs of beloved characters like Uncle Tom, Little Eva, and Topsy—a marketing practice that is very common today but that began with *Uncle Tom's Cabin*.

Stowe was shocked by both her unexpected fame and the public criticism that accompanied it. She was determined to prove to the dubious that her account of slavery was accurate, even publishing a book titled *The Key to Uncle Tom's Cabin* (1853), a compendium of source material for the novel. Stowe's account of how she composed *Uncle Tom's Cabin* sheds light on her political motives and religious inspiration, as well as her method of integrating historical documents and true life accounts into her fictional projects. Stowe also wrote a novel, *Dred* (1856), in which the main character is not a Christian martyr like Uncle Tom but rather a militant escaped slave similar to George Harris; in *Dred*, Stowe explores the possibility that only a violent revolution will bring an end to slavery.

Although Stowe remained an active voice in the abolitionist movement and in the race debates of the post–Civil War era—as is evident in her support of African American authors like Sojourner Truth—her literary work increasingly addressed topics closer to her own experience. Stowe's family eventually settled in Hartford, Connecticut, and she embarked on a series of novels dealing with New England life that prefigures the regional or "local color" literature of authors like Mark Twain and Bret Harte. The autobiographical nature of her later fiction can be seen in *The Minister's Wooing* (1859); Stowe modeled the tragic drowning death of James Marvyn on two similar deaths close to her, including that of her eldest son, Henry. In the novel, Stowe challenges the harsh Calvinist ideology of Jonathan Edwards (and implicitly her own father) and proposes instead a loving religious experience built upon women's community. Although she criticized religious patriarchy, Stowe described herself as being only "to some extent a woman's rights woman," and novels like *My Wife and I* (1871) emphasize the value of feminine decorum and domestic skills over equality with men—an argument Stowe ironically makes by adopting a male persona.

Stowe's immense popularity did not survive long after her death in 1896. Characterized by literary critics and scholars as a writer of mawkish sentimental novels for women and as a perpetuator of negative racial stereotypes, Stowe fell into disrepute in the early twentieth century. In the 1980s, however, critics began to reconsider Stowe's place in the canon, arguing that the best-selling status of *Uncle Tom's Cabin* is a testament to its significance within American literary history. Scholars have noted the influence that *Uncle Tom's Cabin* had on African American authors like Frances Watkins Harper and Harriet Jacobs, who had uneasy relationships with Stowe's account of slavery. More and more critics are arguing that it is worthwhile to examine Stowe's contribution to American literature beyond *Uncle Tom's Cabin*, including feminist scholars who identify Stowe as one of the founders of the genre of "domestic fiction" that depicts and sometimes undercuts the conventions of true womanhood. Stowe is today recognized as one of the most important voices of her time, and though contemporary readers may find her work dated, she captures the complex struggles over racial equality, women's rights, and competing religious traditions that characterized nineteenth-century America.

Desirée Henderson
University of Texas at Arlington

PRIMARY WORKS

Uncle Tom's Cabin, 1852; *The Key to Uncle Tom's Cabin*, 1853; *Dred*, 1856; *The Minister's Wooing*, 1859; *The Pearl of Orr's Island*, 1862; *Oldtown Folks*, 1869; *Lady Byron Vindicated*, 1870; *Pink and White Tyranny*, 1871; *Sam Lawson's Oldtown Fireside Stories*, 1872; *Poganuc People*, 1878; *The Writings of Harriet Beecher Stowe*, 1896; *Life and Letters of Harriet Beecher Stowe*, Annie Fields, ed., 1897; *An Oxford Harriet Beecher Stowe Reader*, Joan D. Hedrick, ed., 1999.

from **Uncle Tom's Cabin**

or Life Among the Lowly

I. In Which the Reader Is Introduced to a Man of Humanity

Late in the afternoon of a chilly day in February, two gentlemen were sitting alone over their wine, in a well-furnished dining parlor, in the town of P——, in Kentucky. There were no servants present, and the gentlemen, with chairs closely approaching, seemed to be discussing some subject with great earnestness.

For convenience sake, we have said, hitherto, two *gentlemen*. One of the parties, however, when critically examined, did not seem, strictly speaking, to come under the species. He was a short, thick-set man, with coarse, commonplace features, and that swaggering air of pretension which marks a low man who is trying to elbow his way upward in the world. He was much over-dressed, in a gaudy vest of many colors, a blue neckerchief, bedropped gayly with yellow spots, and arranged with a flaunting tie, quite in keeping with the general air of the man. His hands, large and coarse, were plentifully bedecked with rings; and he wore a heavy gold watch-chain, with a bundle of seals of portentous size, and a great variety of colors, attached to it,— which, in the ardor of conversation, he was in the habit of flourishing and jingling with evident satisfaction. His conversation was in free and easy defiance of Murray's Grammar, and was garnished at convenient intervals with various profane expressions, which not even the desire to be graphic in our account shall induce us to transcribe.

His companion, Mr. Shelby, had the appearance of a gentleman; and the arrangements of the house, and the general air of the housekeeping, indicated easy, and even opulent circumstances. As we before stated, the two were in the midst of an earnest conversation.

"That is the way I should arrange the matter," said Mr. Shelby.

"I can't make trade that way—I positively can't, Mr. Shelby," said the other, holding up a glass of wine between his eye and the light.

"Why, the fact is, Haley, Tom is an uncommon fellow; he is certainly worth that sum anywhere,—steady, honest, capable, manages my whole farm like a clock."

"You mean honest, as niggers go," said Haley, helping himself to a glass of brandy.

"No; I mean, really, Tom is a good, steady, sensible, pious fellow. He got religion at a camp-meeting, four years ago; and I believe he really *did* get it. I've trusted him, since then, with everything I have,—money, house, horses,—and let him come and go round the country; and I always found him true and square in everything."

"Some folks don't believe there is pious niggers, Shelby," said Haley, with a candid flourish of his hand, "but *I do*. I had a fellow, now, in this yer last lot I took to Orleans—'t was as good as a meetin, now, really; to hear that critter pray; and he was quite gentle and quiet like. He fetched me a good sum, too, for I bought him cheap of a man that was 'bliged to sell out; so I realized six hundred on him. Yes, I consider religion a valeyable thing in a nigger, when it's the genuine article, and no mistake."

"Well, Tom's got the real article, if ever a fellow had," rejoined the other. "Why, last fall, I let him go to Cincinnati alone, to do business for me, and bring home five hundred dollars. 'Tom,' says I to him, 'I trust you, because I think you're a Christian—I know you would n't cheat.' Tom comes back, sure enough; I knew he would. Some low fellows, they say, said to him—

'Tom, why don't you make tracks for Canada?' 'Ah, master trusted me, and I could n't,'—they told me about it. I am sorry to part with Tom, I must say. You ought to let him cover the whole balance of the debt; and you would, Haley, if you had any conscience."

"Well, I've got just as much conscience as any man in business can afford to keep,—just a little, you know, to swear by, as 't were," said the trader, jocularly; "and, then, I'm ready to do anything in reason to 'blige friends; but this yer, you see, is a leetle too hard on a fellow—a leetle too hard." The trader sighed contemplatively, and poured out some more brandy.

"Well, then, Haley, how will you trade?" said Mr. Shelby, after an uneasy interval of silence.

"Well, have n't you a boy or gal that you could throw in with Tom?"

"Hum!—none that I could well spare; to tell the truth, it's only hard necessity makes me willing to sell at all. I don't like parting with any of my hands, that's a fact."

Here the door opened, and a small quadroon boy, between four and five years of age, entered the room. There was something in his appearance remarkably beautiful and engaging. His black hair, fine as floss silk, hung in glossy curls about his round, dimpled face, while a pair of large dark eyes, full of fire and softness, looked out from beneath the rich, long lashes, as he peered curiously into the apartment. A gay robe of scarlet and yellow plaid, carefully made and neatly fitted, set off to advantage the dark and rich style of his beauty; and a certain comic air of assurance, blended with bashfulness, showed that he had been not unused to being petted and noticed by his master.

"Hulloa, Jim Crow!" said Mr. Shelby, whistling, and snapping a bunch of raisins towards him, "pick that up, now!"

The child scampered, with all his little strength, after the prize, while his master laughed.

"Come here, Jim Crow," said he. The child came up, and the master patted the curly head, and chucked him under the chin.

"Now, Jim, show this gentleman how you can dance and sing." The boy commenced one of those wild, grotesque songs common among the negroes, in a rich, clear voice, accompanying his singing with many comic evolutions of the hands, feet, and whole body, all in perfect time to the music.

"Bravo!" said Haley, throwing him a quarter of an orange.

"Now, Jim, walk like old Uncle Cudjoe, when he has the rheumatism," said his master.

Instantly the flexible limbs of the child assumed the appearance of deformity and distortion, as, with his back humped up, and his master's stick in his hand, he hobbled about the room, his childish face drawn into a doleful pucker, and spitting from right to left, in imitation of an old man.

Both gentlemen laughed uproariously.

"Now, Jim," said his master, "show us how old Elder Robbins leads the psalm." The boy drew his chubby face down to a formidable length, and commenced toning a psalm tune through his nose, with imperturbable gravity.

"Hurrah! bravo! what a young 'un!" said Haley; "that chap's a case, I'll promise. Tell you what," said he, suddenly clapping his hand on Mr. Shelby's shoulder, "fling in that chap, and I'll settle the business—I will. Come, now, if that ain't doing the thing up about the rightest!"

At this moment, the door was pushed gently open, and a young quadroon woman, apparently about twenty-five, entered the room.

There needed only a glance from the child to her, to identify her as its mother. There was the same rich, full, dark eye, with its long lashes; the same ripples of silky black hair. The brown of her complexion gave way on the cheek to a perceptible flush, which deepened as she saw the gaze of the strange man fixed upon her in bold and undisguised admiration. Her dress was of the neatest possible fit, and set off to advantage her finely moulded shape;—a delicately formed hand and a trim foot and ankle were items of appearance that did not escape the quick eye of the trader, well used to run up at a glance the points of a fine female article.

"Well, Eliza?" said her master, as she stopped and looked hesitatingly at him.

"I was looking for Harry, please, sir;" and the boy bounded toward her, showing his spoils, which he had gathered in the skirt of his robe.

"Well, take him away, then," said Mr. Shelby; and hastily she withdrew, carrying the child on her arm.

"By Jupiter," said the trader, turning to him in admiration, "there's an article, now! You might make your fortune on that ar gal in Orleans, any day. I've seen over a thousand, in my day, paid down for gals not a bit handsomer."

"I don't want to make my fortune on her," said Mr. Shelby, dryly; and, seeking to turn the conversation, he uncorked a bottle of fresh wine, and asked his companion's opinion of it.

"Capital, sir,—first chop!" said the trader; then turning, and slapping his hand familiarly on Shelby's shoulder, he added—

"Come, how will you trade about the gal?—what shall I say for her— what'll you take?"

"Mr. Haley, she is not to be sold," said Shelby. "My wife would not part with her for her weight in gold."

"Ay, ay! women always say such things, cause they ha'nt no sort of calculation. Just show 'em how many watches, feathers, and trinkets, one's weight in gold would buy, and that alters the case, *I* reckon."

"I tell you, Haley, this must not be spoken of; I say no, and I mean no," said Shelby, decidedly.

"Well, you'll let me have the boy, though," said the trader; "you must own I've come down pretty handsomely for him."

"What on earth can you want with the child?" said Shelby.

"Why, I've got a friend that's going into this yer branch of the business—wants to buy up handsome boys to raise for the market. Fancy articles entirely—sell for waiters, and so on, to rich 'uns, that can pay for handsome 'uns. It sets off one of yer great places—a real handsome boy to open door, wait, and tend. They fetch a good sum; and this little devil is such a comical, musical concern, he's just the article."

"I would rather not sell him," said Mr. Shelby, thoughtfully; "the fact is, sir, I'm a humane man, and I hate to take the boy from his mother, sir."

"O, you do?—La! yes—something of that ar natur. I understand, perfectly. It is mighty onpleasant getting on with women, sometimes. I al'ays hates these yer screachin', screamin' times. They are *mighty* onpleasant; but, as I manages business, I generally avoids 'em, sir. Now, what if you get the girl off for a day, or a week, or so; then the thing's done quietly,—all over before she comes home. Your wife might get her some ear-rings, or a new gown, or some such truck, to make up with her."

"I'm afraid not."

"Lor bless ye, yes! These critters an't like white folks, you know; they gets over things, only manage right. Now, they say," said Haley, assuming a candid and confidential air, "that this kind o' trade is hardening to the feelings; but I never found it so. Fact is, I never could do things up the way some fellers manage the business. I've seen 'em as would pull a woman's child out of her arms, and set him up to sell, and she screechin' like mad all the time;—very bad policy—damages the article—makes 'em quite unfit for service sometimes. I knew a real handsome gal once, in Orleans, as was entirely ruined by this sort o' handling. The fellow that was trading for her did n't want her baby; and she was one of your real high sort, when her blood was up. I tell you, she squeezed up her child in her arms, and talked, and went on real awful. It kinder makes my blood run cold to think on't; and when they carried off the child, and locked her up, she jest went ravin' mad, and died in a week. Clear waste, sir, of a thousand dollars, just for want of management,—there's where 't is. It's always best to do the humane thing, sir; that's been *my* experience." And the trader leaned back in his chair, and folded his arm, with an air of virtuous decision, apparently considering himself a second Wilberforce.[1]

The subject appeared to interest the gentleman deeply; for while Mr. Shelby was thoughtfully peeling an orange, Haley broke out afresh, with becoming diffidence, but as if actually driven by the force of truth to say a few words more.

"It don't look well, now, for a feller to be praisin' himself; but I say it jest because it's the truth. I believe I'm reckoned to bring in about the finest droves of niggers that is brought in,—at least, I've been told so; if I have once, I reckon I have a hundred times,—all in good case,—fat and likely, and I lose as few as any man in the business. And I lays it all to my management, sir; and humanity, sir, I may say, is the great pillar of *my* management."

Mr. Shelby did not know what to say, and so he said, "Indeed!"

[1]William Wilberforce (1759–1833)—English philanthropist and member of Parliament whose antislavery speeches and support of the "Divine Light" missionary movement influenced the New Light Evangelical Reform movement in the United States.

"Now, I've been laughed at for my notions, sir, and I've been talked to. They an't pop'lar, and they an't common; but I stuck to 'em, sir; I've stuck to 'em, and realized well on 'em; yes, sir, they have paid their passage, I may say," and the trader laughed at his joke.

There was something so piquant and original in these elucidations of humanity, that Mr. Shelby could not help laughing in company. Perhaps you laugh too, dear reader; but you know humanity comes out in a variety of strange forms now-a-days, and there is no end to the odd things that humane people will say and do.

Mr. Shelby's laugh encouraged the trader to proceed.

"It's strange, now, but I never could beat this into people's heads. Now, there was Tom Loker, my old partner, down in Natchez; he was a clever fellow, Tom was, only the very devil with niggers,—on principle 't was, you see, for a better hearted feller never broke bread; 't was his *system*, sir. I used to talk to Tom. 'Why, Tom,' I used to say, 'when your gals takes on and cry, what's the use o' crackin on 'em over the head, and knockin' on 'em round? It's ridiculous,' says I, 'and don't do no sort o' good. Why, I don't see no harm in their cryin',' says I; 'it's natur,' says I, 'and if natur can't blow off one way, it will another. Besides, Tom,' says I, 'it jest spiles your gals; they get sickly, and down in the mouth; and sometimes they gets ugly,—particular yellow gals do,—and it's the devil and all gettin' on 'em broke in. Now,' says I, 'why can't you kinder coax 'em up, and speak 'em fair? Depend on it, Tom, a little humanity, thrown in along, goes a heap further than all your jawin' and crackin'; and it pays better,' says I, 'depend on 't.' But Tom couldn't get the hang on 't; and he spiled so many for me, that I had to break off with him, though he was a good-hearted fellow, and as fair a business hand as is goin'."

"And do you find your ways of managing do the business better than Tom's?" said Mr. Shelby.

"Why, yes, sir, I may say so. You see, when I any ways can, I takes a leetle care about the onpleasant parts, like selling young uns and that,—get the gals out of the way—out of sight, out of mind, you know,—and when it's clean done, and can't be helped, they naturally gets used to it. 'Tan't, you know, as if it was white folks, that's brought up in the way of 'spectin' to keep their children and wives, and all that. Niggers, you know, that's fetched up properly, ha' n't no kind of 'spectations of no kind; so all these things comes easier."

"I'm afraid mine are not properly brought up, then," said Mr. Shelby.

"S'pose not; you Kentucky folks spile your niggers. You mean well by 'em, but 'tan't no real kindness, arter all. Now, a nigger, you see, what's got to be hacked and tumbled round the world, and sold to Tom, and Dick, and the Lord knows who, 'tan't no kindness to be givin' on him notions and expectations, and bringin' on him up too well, for the rough and tumble comes all the harder on him arter. Now, I venture to say, your niggers would be quite chop-fallen in a place where some of your plantation niggers would be singing and whooping like all possessed. Every man, you know, Mr. Shelby, naturally thinks well of his own ways, and I think I treat niggers just about as well as it's ever worth while to treat 'em."

"It's a happy thing to be satisfied," said Mr. Shelby, with a slight shrug, and some perceptible feelings of a disagreeable nature.

"Well," said Haley, after they had both silently picked their nuts for a season, "what do you say?"

"I'll think the matter over, and talk with my wife," said Mr. Shelby. "Meantime, Haley, if you want the matter carried on in the quiet way you speak of, you'd best not let your business in this neighborhood be known. It will get out among my boys, and it will not be a particularly quiet business getting away any of my fellows, if they know it, I'll promise you."

"O! certainly, by all means, mum! of course. But I'll tell you, I'm in a devil of a hurry, and shall want to know, as soon as possible, what I may depend on," said he, rising and putting on his overcoat.

"Well, call up this evening, between six and seven, and you shall have my answer," said Mr. Shelby, and the trader bowed himself out of the apartment.

"I'd like to have been able to kick the fellow down the steps," said he to himself, as he saw the door fairly closed, "with his impudent assurance; but he knows how much he has me at advantage. If anybody had ever said to me that I should sell Tom down south to one of those rascally traders, I should have said, 'Is thy servant a dog, that he should do this thing?' And now it must come, for aught I see. And Eliza's child, too! I know that I shall have some fuss with wife about that; and, for that matter, about Tom, too. So much for being in debt,—heigho! The fellow sees his advantage, and means to push it."

Perhaps the mildest form of the system of slavery is to be seen in the State of Kentucky. The general prevalence of agricultural pursuits of a quiet and gradual nature, not requiring those periodic seasons of hurry and pressure that are called for in the business of more southern districts, makes the task of the negro a more healthful and reasonable one; while the master, content with a more gradual style of acquisition, has not those temptations to hardheartedness which always overcome frail human nature when the prospect of sudden and rapid gain is weighed in the balance, with no heavier counterpoise than the interests of the helpless and unprotected.

Whoever visits some estates there, and witnesses the good-humored indulgence of some masters and mistresses, and the affectionate loyalty of some slaves, might be tempted to dream the oft-fabled poetic legend of a patriarchal institution, and all that; but over and above the scene there broods a portentous shadow—the shadow of *law*. So long as the law considers all these human beings, with beating hearts and living affections, only as so many *things* belonging to a master,—so long as the failure, or misfortune, or imprudence, or death of the kindest owner, may cause them any day to exchange a life of kind protection and indulgence for one of hopeless misery and toil,—so long it is impossible to make anything beautiful or desirable in the best regulated administration of slavery.

Mr. Shelby was a fair average kind of man, good-natured and kindly, and disposed to easy indulgence of those around him, and there had never been a lack of anything which might contribute to the physical comfort of the negroes on his estate. He had, however, speculated largely and quite loosely; had involved himself deeply, and his notes to a large amount had come into the hands of Haley; and this small piece of information is the key to the preceding conversation.

Now, it had so happened that, in approaching the door, Eliza had caught enough of the conversation to know that a trader was making offers to her master for somebody.

She would gladly have stopped at the door to listen, as she came out; but her mistress just then calling, she was obliged to hasten away.

Still she thought she heard the trader make an offer for her boy;—could she be mistaken? Her heart swelled and throbbed, and she involuntarily strained him so tight that the little fellow looked up into her face in astonishment.

"Eliza, girl, what ails you to-day?" said her mistress, when Eliza had upset the wash-pitcher, knocked down the workstand, and finally was abstractedly offering her mistress a long night-gown in place of the silk dress she had ordered her to bring from the wardrobe.

Eliza started. "O, missis!" she said, raising her eyes; then, bursting into tears, she sat down in a chair, and began sobbing.

"Why, Eliza, child! what ails you?" said her mistress.

"O! missis, missis," said Eliza, "there's been a trader talking with master in the parlor! I heard him."

"Well, silly child, suppose there has."

"O, missis, *do* you suppose mas'r would sell my Harry?" And the poor creature threw herself into a chair, and sobbed convulsively.

"Sell him! No, you foolish girl! You know your master never deals with those southern traders, and never means to sell any of his servants, as long as they behave well. Why, you silly child, who do you think would want to buy your Harry? Do you think all the world are set on him as you are, you goosie? Come, cheer up, and hook my dress. There now, put my back hair up in that pretty braid you learnt the other day, and don't go listening at doors any more."

"Well, but, missis, *you* never would give your consent—to—to—"

"Nonsense, child! to be sure, I should n't. What do you talk so for? I would as soon have one of my own children sold. But really, Eliza, you are getting altogether too proud of that little fellow. A man can't put his nose into the door, but you think he must be coming to buy him."

Reassured by her mistress' confident tone, Eliza proceeded nimbly and adroitly with her toilet, laughing at her own fears, as she proceeded.

Mrs. Shelby was a woman of a high class, both intellectually and morally. To that natural magnanimity and generosity of mind which one often marks as characteristic of the women of Kentucky, she added high moral and religious sensibility and principle, carried out with great energy and ability into practical results. Her husband, who made no professions to any particular religious character, nevertheless reverenced and respected the consistency of hers, and stood, perhaps, a little in awe of her opinion. Certain it was that he gave her unlimited scope in all her benevolent efforts for the comfort, instruction, and improvement of her servants, though he never took any decided part in them himself. In fact, if not exactly a believer in the doctrine of the efficiency of the extra good works of saints, he really seemed somehow or other to fancy that his wife had piety and benevolence enough for two—to indulge a shadowy expectation of getting into heaven through her superabundance of qualities to which he made no particular pretension.

The heaviest load on his mind, after his conversation with the trader, lay in the foreseen necessity of breaking to his wife the arrangement contemplated,—meeting the importunities and opposition which he knew he should have reason to encounter.

Mrs. Shelby, being entirely ignorant of her husband's embarrassments, and knowing only the general kindliness of his temper, had been quite sincere in the entire incredulity with which she had met Eliza's suspicions. In fact, she dismissed the matter from her mind, without a second thought; and being occupied in preparations for an evening visit, it passed out of her thoughts entirely.

VII. The Mother's Struggle

[Eliza has been married to George Harris, a slave at a neighboring plantation, who has recently escaped from slavery. When Eliza overhears Mr. Shelby tell his wife that he has sold both Uncle Tom and Eliza's son Harry to a slave trader, Eliza decides to flee, but not before she stops by Uncle Tom's cabin to warn him that he has been sold. Tom declines Eliza's suggestion that he escape with her. The next day, Mrs. Shelby and two of the other slaves on the plantation covertly obstruct the slave trader's attempts to go after Eliza, thus buying her time to escape.]

It is impossible to conceive of a human creature more wholly desolate and forlorn than Eliza, when she turned her footsteps from Uncle Tom's cabin.

Her husband's suffering and dangers, and the danger of her child, all blended in her mind, with a confused and stunning sense of the risk she was running, in leaving the only home she had ever known, and cutting loose from the protection of a friend whom she loved and revered. Then there was the parting from every familiar object,—the place where she had grown up, the trees under which she had played, the groves where she had walked many an evening in happier days, by the side of her young husband,—everything, as it lay in the clear, frosty starlight, seemed to speak reproachfully to her, and ask her whither could she go from a home like that?

But stronger than all was maternal love, wrought into a paroxysm of frenzy by the near approach of a fearful danger. Her boy was old enough to have walked by her side, and, in an indifferent case, she would only have led him by the hand; but now the bare thought of putting him out of her arms made her shudder, and she strained him to her bosom with a convulsive grasp, as she went rapidly forward.

The frosty ground creaked beneath her feet, and she trembled at the sound; every quaking leaf and fluttering shadow sent the blood backward to her heart, and quickened her footsteps. She wondered within herself at the strength that seemed to be come upon her; for she felt the weight of her boy as if it had been a feather, and every flutter of fear seemed to increase the supernatural power that bore her on, while from her pale lips burst forth, in frequent ejaculations, the prayer to a Friend above—"Lord, help! Lord, save me!"

If it were *your* Harry, mother, or your Willie, that were going to be torn from you by a brutal trader, to-morrow morning,—if you had seen the man, and heard that the papers were signed and delivered, and you had only from twelve o'clock till morning to make good your escape,—how fast could *you* walk? How many miles could you make in those few brief hours, with the darling at your bosom,—the little sleepy head on your shoulder,—the small, soft arms trustingly holding on to your neck?

For the child slept. At first, the novelty and alarm kept him waking; but his mother so hurriedly repressed every breath or sound, and so assured him that if he were only still she would certainly save him, that he clung quietly round her neck, only asking, as he found himself sinking to sleep,

"Mother, I don't need to keep awake, do I?"

"No, my darling; sleep, if you want to."

"But, mother, if I do get asleep, you won't let him get me?"

"No! so may God help me!" said his mother, with a paler cheek, and a brighter light in her large dark eyes.

"You're *sure*, an't you, mother?"

"Yes, *sure!*" said the mother, in a voice that startled herself; for it seemed to her to come from a spirit within, that was no part of her; and the boy dropped his little weary head on her shoulder, and was soon asleep. How the touch of those warm arms, the gentle breathings that came in her neck, seemed to add fire and spirit to her movements! It seemed to her as if strength poured into her in electric streams, from every gentle touch and movement of the sleeping, confiding child. Sublime is the dominion of the mind over the body, that, for a time, can make flesh and nerve impregnable, and string the sinews like steel, so that the weak become so mighty.

The boundaries of the farm, the grove, the wood-lot, passed by her dizzily, as she walked on; and still she went, leaving one familiar object after another, slacking not, pausing not, till reddening daylight found her many a long mile from all traces of any familiar objects upon the open highway.

She had often been, with her mistress, to visit some connections, in the little village of T——, not far from the Ohio river, and knew the road well. To go thither, to escape across the Ohio river, were the first hurried outlines of her plan of escape; beyond that, she could only hope in God.

When horses and vehicles began to move along the highway, with that alert perception peculiar to a state of excitement, and which seems to be a sort of inspiration, she became aware that her headlong pace and distracted air might bring on her remark and suspicion. She therefore put the boy on the ground, and, adjusting her dress and bonnet, she walked on at as rapid a pace as she thought consistent with the preservation of appearances. In her little bundle she had provided a store of cakes and apples, which she used as expedients for quickening the speed of the child, rolling the apple some yards before them, when the boy would run with all his might after it; and this ruse, often repeated, carried them over many a half-mile.

After a while, they came to a thick patch of woodland, through which murmured a clear brook. As the child complained of hunger and thirst, she climbed over the fence with him; and, sitting down behind a large rock which concealed them from the road, she gave him a breakfast out of her little package. The boy wondered and grieved that she could not eat; and when, putting his arms round her neck, he tried to wedge some of his cake into her mouth, it seemed to her that the rising in her throat would choke her.

"No, no, Harry darling! mother can't eat till you are safe! We must go on—on—till we come to the river!" And she hurried again into the road, and again constrained herself to walk regularly and composedly forward.

She was many miles past any neighborhood where she was personally known. If she should chance to meet any who knew her, she reflected that the well-known kindness of the family would be of itself a blind to suspicion, as making it an unlikely supposition that she could be a fugitive. As she was also so white as not to be known as of colored lineage, without a critical survey, and her child was white also, it was much easier for her to pass on unsuspected.

On this presumption, she stopped at noon at a neat farmhouse, to rest herself, and buy some dinner for her child and self; for, as the danger decreased with the distance, the supernatural tension of the nervous system lessened, and she found herself both weary and hungry.

The good woman, kindly and gossipping, seemed rather pleased than otherwise with having somebody come in to talk with; and accepted, without examination, Eliza's statement, that she "was going on a little piece, to spend a week with her friends,"—all which she hoped in her heart might prove strictly true.

An hour before sunset, she entered the village of T——, by the Ohio river, weary and foot-sore, but still strong in heart. Her first glance was at the river, which lay, like Jordan, between her and the Canaan of liberty on the other side.

It was now early spring, and the river was swollen and turbulent; great cakes of floating ice were swinging heavily to and fro in the turbid waters. Owing to the peculiar form of the shore on the Kentucky side, the land bending far out into the water, the ice had been lodged and detained in great quantities, and the narrow channel which swept round the bend was full of ice, piled one cake over another, thus forming a temporary barrier to the descending ice, which lodged, and formed a great, undulating raft, filling up the whole river, and extending almost to the Kentucky shore.

Eliza stood, for a moment, contemplating this unfavorable aspect of things, which she saw at once must prevent the usual ferry-boat from running, and then turned into a small public house on the bank, to make a few inquiries.

The hostess, who was busy in various fizzing and stewing operations over the fire, preparatory to the evening meal, stopped, with a fork in her hand, as Eliza's sweet and plaintive voice arrested her.

"What is it?" she said.

"Is n't there any ferry or boat, that takes people over to B——, now?" she said.

"No, indeed!" said the woman; "the boats has stopped running."

Eliza's look of dismay and disappointment struck the woman, and she said, inquiringly,

"May be you're wanting to get over?—anybody sick? Ye seem mighty anxious?"

"I've got a child that's very dangerous," said Eliza. "I never heard of it till last night, and I've walked quite a piece to-day, in hopes to get to the ferry."

"Well, now, that's onlucky," said the woman, whose motherly sympathies were much aroused; "I'm re'lly consarned for ye. Solomon!" she called, from the window, towards a small back building. A man, in leather apron and very dirty hands, appeared at the door.

"I say, Sol," said the woman, "is that ar man going to tote them bar'ls over to-night?"

"He said he should try, if 't was any way prudent," said the man.

"There's a man a piece down here, that's going over with some truck this evening, if he durs' to; he'll be in here to supper to-night, so you'd better set down and wait. That's a sweet little fellow," added the woman, offering him a cake.

But the child, wholly exhausted, cried with weariness.

"Poor fellow! he is n't used to walking, and I've hurried him on so," said Eliza.

"Well, take him into this room," said the woman, opening into a small bedroom, where stood a comfortable bed. Eliza laid the weary boy upon it, and held his hands in hers till he was fast asleep. For her there was no rest. As a fire in her bones, the thought of the pursuer urged her on; and she gazed with longing eyes on the sullen, surging waters that lay between her and liberty. . . .

In consequence of all the various delays, it was about three-quarters of an hour after Eliza had laid her child to sleep in the village tavern that the party came riding into the same place. Eliza was standing by the window, looking out in another direction, when Sam's quick eye caught a glimpse of her. Haley and Andy were two yards behind. At this crisis, Sam contrived to have his hat blown off, and uttered a loud and characteristic ejaculation, which startled her at once; she drew suddenly back; the whole train swept by the window, round to the front door.

A thousand lives seemed to be concentrated in that one moment to Eliza. Her room opened by a side door to the river. She caught her child, and sprang down the steps towards it. The trader caught a full glimpse of her, just as she was disappearing down the bank; and throwing himself from his horse, and calling loudly on Sam and Andy, he was after her like a hound after a deer. In that dizzy moment her feet to her scarce seemed to touch the ground, and a moment brought her to the water's edge. Right on behind they came; and, nerved with strength such as God gives only to the desperate, with one wild cry and flying leap, she vaulted sheer over the turbid current by the shore, on to the raft of ice beyond. It was a desperate leap—impossible to anything but madness and despair; and Haley, Sam, and Andy, instinctively cried out, and lifted up their hands, as she did it.

The huge green fragment of ice on which she alighted pitched and creaked as her weight came on it, but she staid there not a moment. With wild cries and desperate energy she leaped to another and still another cake;—stumbling—leaping—slipping—springing upwards again! Her shoes are gone—her stockings cut from her feet—while blood marked every step; but she saw nothing, felt nothing, till dimly, as in a dream, she saw the Ohio side, and a man helping her up the bank.

"Yer a brave gal, now, whoever ye ar!" said the man, with an oath.

Eliza recognized the voice and face of a man who owned a farm not far from her old home.

"O, Mr. Symmes!—save me—do save me—do hide me!" said Eliza.

"Why, what's this?" said the man. "Why, if 'tan't Shelby's gal!"

"My child!—this boy!—he'd sold him! There is his Mas'r," said she, pointing to the Kentucky shore. "O, Mr. Symmes, you've got a little boy!"

"So I have," said the man, as he roughly, but kindly, drew her up the steep bank. "Besides, you're a right brave gal. I like grit, wherever I see it."

When they had gained the top of the bank, the man paused.

"I'd be glad to do something for ye," said he; "but then there's nowhar I could take ye. The best I can do is to tell ye to go *thar*," said he, pointing to a large white house which stood by itself, off the main street of the village. "Go thar; they're kind folks. Thar's no kind o' danger but they'll help you,— they're up to all that sort o' thing."

"The Lord bless you!" said Eliza, earnestly.

"No 'casion, no 'casion in the world," said the man. "What I've done 's of no 'count."

"And, oh, surely, sir, you won't tell any one!"

"Go to thunder, gal! What do you take a feller for? In course not," said the man. "Come, now, go along like a likely, sensible gal, as you are. You've arnt your liberty, and you shall have it, for all me."

The woman folded her child to her bosom, and walked firmly and swiftly away. The man stood and looked after her.

"Shelby, now, mebbe won't think this yer the most neighborly thing in the world; but what's a feller to do? If he catches one of my gals in the same fix, he'swelcome to pay back. Somehow I never could see no kind o' critter a strivin' and pantin', and trying to clar theirselves, with the dogs arter 'em, and go agin 'em. Besides, I don't see no kind of 'casion for me to be hunter and catcher for other folks, neither."

So spoke this poor, heathenish Kentuckian, who had not been instructed in his constitutional relations, and consequently was betrayed into acting in a sort of Christianized manner, which, if he had been better situated and more enlightened, he would not have been left to do.

Haley had stood a perfectly amazed spectator of the scene, till Eliza had disappeared up the bank, when he turned a blank, inquiring look on Sam and Andy.

"That ar was a tolable fair stroke of business," said Sam.

"The gal's got seven devils in her, I believe!" said Haley. "How like a wildcat she jumped!"

"Wal, now," said Sam, scratching his head, "I hope Mas'r 'll 'scuse us tryin' dat ar road. Don't think I feel spry enough for dat ar, no way!" and Sam gave a hoarse chuckle.

"*You* laugh!" said the trader, with a growl.

"Lord bless you, Mas'r, I could n't help it, now," said Sam, giving way to the long pent-up delight of his soul. "She looked so curi's, a leapin' and springin'—ice a crackin'—and only to hear her,—plump! ker chunk! ker splash! Spring! Lord! how she goes it!" said Sam and Andy laughed till the tears rolled down their cheeks.

"I'll make ye laugh t' other side yer mouths!" said the trader, laying about their heads with his riding-whip.

Both ducked, and ran shouting up the bank, and were on their horses before he was up.

"Good-evening, Mas'r!" said Sam, with much gravity. "I berry much spect Missis be anxious 'bout Jerry. Mas'r Haley won't want us no longer. Missis would n't hear of our ridin' the critters over Lizy's bridge to-night;" and, with a facetious poke into Andy's ribs, he started off, followed by the latter, at full speed,—their shouts of laughter coming faintly on the wind.

XI. In Which Property Gets into an Improper State of Mind

It was late in a drizzly afternoon that a traveller alighted at the door of a small country hotel, in the village of N——, in Kentucky. In the bar-room he found assembled quite a miscellaneous company, whom stress of weather had driven to harbor, and the place presented the usual scenery of such reunions. Great, tall, raw-boned Kentuckians, attired in hunting-shirts, and trailing their loose joints over a vast extent of territory, with the easy lounge peculiar to the race,—rifles stacked away in the corner, shot-pouches, game-bags, hunting-dogs, and little negroes, all rolled together in the corners,—were the characteristic features in the picture. At each end of the fireplace sat a long-legged gentleman, with his chair tipped back, his hat on his head, and the heels of his muddy boots reposing sublimely on the mantelpiece,—a position, we will inform our readers, decidedly favorable to the turn of reflection incident to western taverns, where travellers exhibit a decided preference for this particular mode of elevating their understandings.

Mine host, who stood behind the bar, like most of his countrymen, was great of stature, good-natured, and loose-jointed, with an enormous shock of hair on his head, and a great tall hat on the top of that.

In fact, everybody in the room bore on his head this characteristic emblem of man's sovereignty; whether it were felt hat, palm-leaf, greasy beaver, or fine new chapeau, there it reposed with true republican independence. In truth, it appeared to be the characteristic mark of every individual. Some wore them tipped rakishly to one side—these were your men of humor, jolly, free-and-easy dogs; some had them jammed independently down over their noses—these were your hard characters, thorough men, who, when they wore their hats, *wanted* to wear them, and to wear them just as they had a mind to; there were those who had them set far over back—wide-awake men, who wanted a clear prospect; while careless men, who did not know, or care, how their hats sat, had them shaking about in all directions. The various hats, in fact, were quite a Shakspearean study.

Divers negroes, in very free-and-easy pantaloons, and with no redundancy in the shirt line, were scuttling about, hither and thither, without bringing to pass any very particular results, except expressing a generic willingness to turn over everything in creation generally for the benefit of Mas'r and his guests. Add to this picture a jolly, crackling, rollicking fire, going rejoicingly up a great wide chimney,—the outer door and every window being set wide open, and the calico window-curtain flopping and snapping in a good stiff breeze of damp raw air,—and you have an idea of the jollities of a Kentucky tavern.

Your Kentuckian of the present day is a good illustration of the doctrine of transmitted instincts and peculiarities. His fathers were mighty hunters,—men who lived in the woods, and slept under the free, open heavens, with the stars to hold their candles; and their descendant to this day always acts as if the house were his camp,—wears his hat at all hours, tumbles himself about, and puts his heels on the tops of chairs or mantel-pieces, just as his father rolled on the green sward, and put his upon trees and logs,—keeps all the windows and doors open, winter and summer, that he may get air enough for his great lungs,—calls everybody "stranger," with nonchalant bonhommie, and is altogether the frankest, easiest, most jovial creature living.

Into such an assembly of the free and easy our traveller entered. He was a short, thick-set man, carefully dressed, with a round, good-natured countenance, and something rather fussy and particular in his appearance. He was very careful of his valise and umbrella, bringing them in with his own hands, and resisting, pertinaciously, all offers from the various servants to relieve him of them. He looked round the bar-room with rather an anxious air, and, retreating with his valuables to the warmest corner, disposed them under his chair, sat down, and looked rather apprehensively up at the worthy whose heels illustrated the end of the mantel-piece, who was spitting from right to left, with a courage and energy rather alarming to gentlemen of weak nerves and particular habits.

"I say, stranger, how are ye?" said the aforesaid gentleman, firing an honorary salute of tobacco-juice in the direction of the new arrival.

"Well, I reckon," was the reply of the other, as he dodged, with some alarm, the threatening honor.

"Any news?" said the respondent, taking out a strip of tobacco and a large hunting-knife from his pocket.

"Not that I know of," said the man.

"Chaw?" said the first speaker, handing the old gentleman a bit of his tobacco, with a decidedly brotherly air.

"No, thank ye—it don't agree with me," said the little man, edging off.

"Don't, eh?" said the other, easily, and stowing away the morsel in his own mouth, in order to keep up the supply of tobacco-juice, for the general benefit of society.

The old gentleman uniformly gave a little start whenever his long-sided brother fired in his direction; and this being observed by his companion, he very good-naturedly turned his artillery to another quarter, and proceeded to storm one of the fire-irons with a degree of military talent fully sufficient to take a city.

"What's that?" said the old gentleman, observing some of the company formed in a group around a large handbill.

"Nigger advertised!" said one of the company, briefly.

Mr. Wilson, for that was the old gentleman's name, rose up, and, after carefully adjusting his valise and umbrella, proceeded deliberately to take out his spectacles and fix them on his nose; and, this operation being performed, read as follows:

> "Ran away from the subscriber, my mulatto boy, George. Said George six feet in height, a very light mulatto, brown curly hair; is very intelligent, speaks handsomely, can read and write; will probably try to pass for a white man; is deeply scarred on his back and shoulders; has been branded in his right hand with the letter H.
>
> "I will give four hundred dollars for him alive, and the same sum for satisfactory proof that he has been killed."

The old gentleman read this advertisement from end to end, in a low voice, as if he were studying it.

The long-legged veteran, who had been besieging the fire-iron, as before related, now took down his cumbrous length, and rearing aloft his tall form, walked up to the advertisement, and very deliberately spit a full discharge of tobacco-juice on it.

"There's my mind upon that!" said he, briefly, and sat down again.

"Why, now, stranger, what's that for?" said mine host.

"I'd do it all the same to the writer of that ar paper, if he was here," said the long man, coolly resuming his old employment of cutting tobacco. "Any man that owns a boy like that, and can't find any better way o' treating on him, *deserves* to lose him. Such papers as these is a shame to Kentucky; that's my mind right out, if anybody wants to know!"

"Well, now, that's a fact," said mine host, as he made an entry in his book.

"I've got a gang of boys, sir," said the long man, resuming his attack on the fire-irons, "and I jest tells 'em—'Boys,' says I,—'*run* now! dig! put! jest when ye want to! I never shall come to look after you!' That's the way I keep mine. Let 'em know they are free to run any time, and it jest breaks up their wanting to. More'n all, I've got free papers for 'em all recorded, in case I gets keeled up any o' these times, and they knows it; and I tell ye, stranger, there an't a fellow in our parts gets more out of his niggers than I do. Why, my boys have been to Cincinnati, with five hundred dollars' worth of colts, and brought me back the money, all straight, time and agin. It stands to reason they should. Treat 'em like dogs, and you'll have dogs' works and dogs' actions. Treat 'em like men, and you'll have men's works." And the honest drover, in his warmth, endorsed this moral sentiment by firing a perfect *feu de joie* at the fireplace.

"I think you're altogether right, friend," said Mr. Wilson; "and this boy described here *is* a fine fellow—no mistake about that. He worked for me some half-dozen years in my bagging factory, and he was my best hand, sir. He is an ingenious fellow, too: he invented a machine for the cleaning of hemp—a really valuable affair; it's gone into use in several factories. His master holds the patent of it."

"I'll warrant ye," said the drover, "holds it and makes money out of it, and then turns round and brands the boy in his right hand. If I had a fair chance, I'd mark him, I reckon, so that he'd carry it *one* while."

"These yer knowin' boys is allers aggravatin' and sarcy," said a coarse-looking fellow, from the other side of the room; "that's why they gets cut up and marked so. If they behaved themselves, they would n't."

"That is to say, the Lord made 'em men, and it's a hard squeeze getting 'em down into beasts," said the drover, dryly.

"Bright niggers is n't no kind of 'vantage to their masters," continued the other, well intrenched, in a coarse, unconscious obtuseness, from the contempt of his opponent; "what's the use o' talents and them things, if you can't get the use on 'em yourself? Why, all the use they make on 't is to get round you. I've had one or two of these fellers, and I jest sold 'em down river. I knew I'd got to lose 'em, first or last, if I did n't."

"Better send orders up to the Lord, to make you a set, and leave out their souls entirely," said the drover.

Here the conversation was interrupted by the approach of a small one-horse buggy to the inn. It had a genteel appearance, and a well-dressed, gen-tlemanly man sat on the seat, with a colored servant driving.

The whole party examined the new comer with the interest with which a set of loafers in a rainy day usually examine every new comer. He was very tall, with a dark, Spanish complexion, fine, expressive black eyes, and close-curling hair, also of a glossy blackness. His well-formed aquiline nose, straight thin lips, and the admirable contour of his finely-formed limbs, impressed the whole company instantly with the idea of something uncom-mon. He walked easily in among the company, and with a nod indicated to his waiter where to place his trunk, bowed to the company, and, with his hat in his hand, walked up leisurely to the bar, and gave in his name as Henry Butler, Oaklands, Shelby County. Turning, with an indifferent air, he sauntered up to the advertisement, and read it over.

"Jim," he said to his man, "seems to me we met a boy something like this, up at Bernan's, did n't we?"

"Yes, Mas'r," said Jim, "only I an't sure about the hand."

"Well, I did n't look, of course," said the stranger, with a careless yawn. Then, walking up to the landlord, he desired him to furnish him with a private apartment, as he had some writing to do immediately.

The landlord was all obsequious, and a relay of about seven negroes, old and young, male and female, little and big, were soon whizzing about, like a covey of partridges, bustling, hurrying, treading on each other's toes, and tumbling over each other, in their zeal to get Mas'r's room ready, while he seated himself easily on a chair in the middle of the room, and entered into conversation with the man who sat next to him.

The manufacturer, Mr. Wilson, from the time of the entrance of the stranger, had regarded him with an air of disturbed and uneasy curiosity. He seemed to himself to have met and been acquainted with him somewhere, but he could not recollect. Every few moments, when the man spoke, or moved, or smiled, he would start and fix his eyes on him, and then suddenly withdraw them, as the bright, dark eyes met his with such unconcerned coolness. At last, a sudden recollection seemed to flash upon him, for he stared at the stranger with such an air of blank amazement and alarm, that he walked up to him.

"Mr. Wilson, I think," said he, in a tone of recognition, and extending his hand. "I beg your pardon, I did n't recollect you before. I see you remember me,—Mr. Butler, of Oaklands, Shelby County."

"Ye—yes—yes, sir," said Mr. Wilson, like one speaking in a dream.

Just then a negro boy entered, and announced that Mas'r's room was ready.

"Jim, see to the trunks," said the gentleman, negligently; then addressing himself to Mr. Wilson, he added—"I should like to have a few moments' conversation with you on business, in my room, if you please."

Mr. Wilson followed him, as one who walks in his sleep; and they proceeded to a large upper chamber, where a new-made fire was crackling, and various servants flying about, putting finishing touches to the arrangements.

When all was done, and the servants departed, the young man deliberately locked the door, and putting the key in his pocket, faced about, and folding his arms on his bosom, looked Mr. Wilson full in the face.

"George!" said Mr. Wilson.

"Yes, George," said the young man.

"I could n't have thought it!"

"I am pretty well disguised, I fancy," said the young man, with a smile. "A little walnut bark has made my yellow skin a genteel brown, and I've dyed my hair black; so you see I don't answer to the advertisement at all."

"O, George! but this is a dangerous game you are playing. I could not have advised you to it."

"I can do it on my own responsibility," said George, with the same proud smile.

We remark, *en passant*, that George was, by his father's side, of white descent. His mother was one of those unfortunates of her race, marked out by personal beauty to be the slave of the passions of her possessor, and the mother of children who may never know a father. From one of the proudest families in Kentucky he had inherited a set of fine European features, and a high, indomitable spirit. From his mother he had received only a slight mulatto tinge, amply compensated by its accompanying rich, dark eye. A slight change in the tint of the skin and the color of his hair had metamorphosed him into the Spanish-looking fellow he then appeared; and as gracefulness of movement and gentlemanly manners had always been perfectly natural to him, he found no difficulty in playing the bold part he had adopted—that of a gentleman travelling with his domestic.

Mr. Wilson, a good-natured but extremely fidgety and cautious old gentleman, ambled up and down the room, appearing, as John Bunyan hath it, "much tumbled up and down in his mind," and divided between his wish to help George, and a certain confused notion of maintaining law and order: so, as he shambled about, he delivered himself as follows:

"Well, George, I s'pose you 're running away—leaving your lawful master, George—(I don't wonder at it)—at the same time, I'm sorry, George,—yes, decidedly—I think I must say that, George—it's my duty to tell you so."

"Why are you sorry, sir?" said George, calmly.

"Why, to see you, as it were, setting yourself in opposition to the laws of your country."

"*My* country!" said George, with a strong and bitter emphasis; "what country have I, but the grave,—and I wish to God that I was laid there!"

"Why, George, no—no—it won't do; this way of talking is wicked—unscriptural. George, you've got a hard master—in fact, he is—well he conducts himself reprehensibly—I can't pretend to defend him. But you know how the angel commanded Hagar to return to her mistress, and submit herself under her hand; and the apostle sent back Onesimus to his master."

"Don't quote Bible at me that way, Mr. Wilson," said George, with a flashing eye, "don't! for my wife is a Christian, and I mean to be, if ever I get to where I can; but to quote Bible to a fellow in my circumstances, is enough to make him give it up altogether. I appeal to God Almighty;—I'm willing to go with the case to Him, and ask Him if I do wrong to seek my freedom."

"These feelings are quite natural, George," said the good-natured man, blowing his nose. "Yes they're natural, but it is my duty not to encourage 'em in you. Yes, my boy, I'm sorry for you, now; it's a bad case—very bad; but the apostle says, 'Let every one abide in the condition in which he is called.' We must all submit to the indications of Providence, George,—don't you see?"

George stood with his head drawn back, his arms folded tightly over his broad breast, and a bitter smile curling his lips.

"I wonder, Mr. Wilson, if the Indians should come and take you a prisoner away from your wife and children, and want to keep you all your life hoeing corn for them, if you'd think it your duty to abide in the condition in which you were called. I rather think that you'd think the first stray horse you could find an indication of Providence—should n't you?"

The little old gentleman stared with both eyes at this illustration of the case; but, though not much of a reasoner, he had the sense in which some logicians on this particular subject do not excel,—that of saying nothing, where nothing could be said. So, as he stood carefully stroking his umbrella, and folding and patting down all the creases in it, he proceeded on with his exhortations in a general way.

"You see, George, you know, now, I always have stood your friend; and whatever I've said, I've said for your good. Now, here, it seems to me, you're running an awful risk. You can't hope to carry it out. If you're taken, it will be worse with you than ever; they'll only abuse you, and half kill you, and sell you down river."

"Mr. Wilson, I know all this," said George. "I *do* run a risk, but—" he threw open his overcoat, and showed two pistols and a bowie-knife. "There!" he said, "I'm ready for 'em! Down south I never *will* go. No! if it comes to that, I can earn myself at least six feet of free soil,—the first and last I shall ever own in Kentucky!"

"Why, George, this state of mind is awful; it's getting really desperate, George. I'm concerned. Going to break the laws of your country!"

"My country again! Mr. Wilson, *you* have a country; but what country have *I*, or any one like me, born of slave mothers? What laws are there for us? We don't make them,—we don't consent to them,—we have nothing to do with them; all they do for us is to crush us, and keep us down. Have n't I heard your Fourth-of-July speeches? Don't you tell us all, once a year, that governments derive their just power from the consent of the governed? Can't a fellow *think*, that hears such things? Can't he put this and that together, and see what it comes to?"

Mr. Wilson's mind was one of those that may not unaptly be represented by a bale of cotton,—downy, soft, benevolently fuzzy and confused. He really pitied George with all his heart, and had a sort of dim and cloudy perception of the style of feeling that agitated him; but he deemed it his duty to go on talking *good* to him, with infinite pertinacity.

"George, this is bad. I must tell you, you know, as a friend, you'd better not be meddling with such notions; they are bad, George, very bad, for boys in your condition,—very;" and Mr. Wilson sat down to a table, and began nervously chewing the handle of his umbrella.

"See here, now, Mr. Wilson," said George, coming up and sitting himself determinately down in front of him; "look at me, now. Don't I sit before you, every way, just as much a man as you are? Look at my face,—look at my hands,—look at my body," and the young man drew himself up proudly; "why am I *not* a man, as much as anybody? Well, Mr. Wilson, hear what I can tell you. I had a father—one of your Kentucky gentlemen—who did n't think enough of me to keep me from being sold with his dogs and horses, to satisfy the estate, when he died. I saw my mother put up at sheriff's sale, with her seven children. They were sold before her eyes, one by one, all to different masters; and I was the youngest. She came and kneeled down before old Mas'r, and begged him to buy her with me, that she might have at least one child with her; and he kicked her away with his heavy boot. I saw him do it; and the last that I heard was her moans and screams, when I was tied to his horse's neck, to be carried off to his place."

"Well, then?"

"My master traded with one of the men, and bought my oldest sister. She was a pious, good girl,—a member of the Baptist church,—and as handsome as my poor mother had been. She was well brought up, and had good manners. At first, I was glad she was bought, for I had one friend near me. I was soon sorry for it. Sir, I have stood at the door and heard her whipped, when it seemed as if every blow cut into my naked heart, and I could n't do anything to help her; and she was whipped, sir, for wanting to live a decent Christian life, such as your laws give no slave girl a right to live; and at last I saw her chained with a trader's gang, to be sent to market in Orleans,—sent there for nothing else but that,—and that's the last I know of her. Well, I grew up,—long years and years,—no father, no mother, no sister, not a living soul that cared for me more than a dog; nothing but whipping, scolding, starving. Why, sir, I've been so hungry that I have been glad to take the bones they threw to their dogs; and yet, when I was a little fellow, and laid awake whole nights and cried, it was n't the hunger, it was n't the whipping, I cried for. No, sir; it was for *my mother* and *my sisters*,—it was because I had n't a friend to love me on earth. I never knew what peace or comfort was. I never had a kind word spoken to me till I came to work in your factory. Mr. Wilson, you treated me well; you encouraged me to do well, and to learn to read and write, and to try to make something of myself; and God knows how grateful I am for it. Then, sir, I found my wife; you've seen her,—you know how beautiful she is. When I found she loved me, when I married her, I scarcely could believe I was alive, I was so happy; and, sir, she is as good as she is beautiful. But now what? Why, now comes my master, takes me right away from my work, and my friends, and all I like, and grinds me down into the very dirt! And why? Because, he says, I forgot who I was; he says, to teach me that I am only a nigger! After all, and last of all, he comes between me and my wife, and says I shall give her up, and live with another woman. And all this your laws give him power to do, in spite of God or man. Mr. Wilson, look at it! There is n't *one* of all these things, that have broken the hearts of my mother and my sister, and my wife and myself, but your laws allow, and give every man power to do, in Kentucky, and none can say to him nay! Do you call these the laws of *my* country? Sir, I have n't any country, any more than I have any father. But I'm going to have one. I don't want anything of *your* country, except to be let alone,—to go peaceably out of it; and when I get to Canada, where the laws will own me and protect me, *that* shall be my country, and its laws I will obey. But if any man tries to stop me, let him take care, for I am desperate. I'll fight for my liberty to the last breath I breathe. You say your fathers did it; if it was right for them, it is right for me!"

This speech, delivered partly while sitting at the table, and partly walking up and down the room,—delivered with tears, and flashing eyes, and despairing gestures,—was altogether too much for the good-natured old body to whom it was addressed, who had pulled out a great yellow silk pocket-handkerchief, and was mopping up his face with great energy.

"Blast 'em all!" he suddenly broke out. "Have n't I always said so—the infernal old cusses! I hope I an't swearing, now. Well! go ahead, George, go ahead; but be careful, my boy; don't shoot anybody, George, unless—well—you'd *better* not shoot, I reckon; at least, I would n't *hit* anybody, you know. Where is your wife, George?" he added, as he nervously rose, and began walking the room.

"Gone, sir, gone, with her child in her arms, the Lord only knows where;—gone after the north star; and when we ever meet, or whether we meet at all in this world, no creature can tell."

"Is it possible! astonishing! from such a kind family?"

"Kind families get in debt, and the laws of *our* country allow them to sell the child out of its mother's bosom to pay its master's debts," said George, bitterly.

"Well, well," said the honest old man, fumbling in his pocket. "I s'pose, perhaps, I an't following my judgment,—hang it, I *won't* follow my judgment!" he added, suddenly; "so here, George," and, taking out a roll of bills from his pocketbook, he offered them to George.

"No, my kind, good sir!" said George, "you've done a great deal for me, and this might get you into trouble. I have money enough, I hope, to take me as far as I need it."

"No; but you must, George. Money is a great help everywhere;—can't have too much, if you get it honestly. Take it,—*do* take it, *now*,—do, my boy!"

"On condition, sir, that I may repay it at some future time, I will," said George, taking up the money.

"And now, George, how long are you going to travel in this way?—not long or far, I hope. It's well carried on, but too bold. And this black fellow,—who is he?"

"A true fellow, who went to Canada more than a year ago. He heard, after he got there, that his master was so angry at him for going off that he had whipped his poor old mother; and he has come all the way back to comfort her, and get a chance to get her away."

"Has he got her?"

"Not yet; he has been hanging about the place, and found no chance yet. Meanwhile, he is going with me as far as Ohio, to put me among friends that helped him, and then he will come back after her."

"Dangerous, very dangerous!" said the old man.

George drew himself up, and smiled disdainfully.

The old gentleman eyed him from head to foot, with a sort of innocent wonder.

"George, something has brought you out wonderfully. You hold up your head, and speak and move like another man," said Mr. Wilson.

"Because I'm a *freeman!*" said George, proudly. "Yes, sir; I've said Mas'r for the last time to any man. *I'm free!*"

"Take care! You are not sure,—you may be taken."

"All men are free and equal *in the grave*, if it comes to that, Mr. Wilson," said George.

"I'm perfectly dumb-foundered with your boldness!" said Mr. Wilson,— "to come right here to the nearest tavern!"

"Mr. Wilson, it is *so* bold, and this tavern is so near, that they will never think of it; they will look for me on ahead, and you yourself would n't know me. Jim's master don't live in this county; he is n't known in these parts. Besides, he is given up; nobody is looking after him, and nobody will take me up from the advertisement, I think."

"But the mark in your hand?"

George drew off his glove, and showed a newly-healed scar in his hand.

"That is a parting proof of Mr. Harris' regard," he said, scornfully. "A fortnight ago, he took it into his head to give it to me, because he said he believed I should try to get away one of these days. Looks interesting, does n't it?" he said, drawing his glove on again.

"I declare, my very blood runs cold when I think of it,—your condition and your risks!" said Mr. Wilson.

"Mine has run cold a good many years, Mr. Wilson; at present, it's about up to the boiling point," said George.

"Well, my good sir," continued George, after a few moments' silence, "I saw you knew me; I thought I'd just have this talk with you, lest your sur-prised looks should bring me out. I leave early to-morrow morning, before day-light; by tomorrow night I hope to sleep safe in Ohio. I shall travel by daylight, stop at the best hotels, go to the dinner-tables with the lords of the land. So, good-by, sir; if you hear that I'm taken, you may know that I'm dead!"

George stood up like a rock, and put out his hand with the air of a prince. The friendly little old man shook it heartily, and after a little shower of caution, he took his umbrella, and fumbled his way out of the room.

George stood thoughtfully looking at the door, as the old man closed it. A thought seemed to flash across his mind. He hastily stepped to it, and opening it, said,

"Mr. Wilson, one word more."

The old gentleman entered again, and George, as before, locked the door, and then stood for a few moments looking on the floor, irresolutely. At last, raising his head with a sudden effort—

"Mr. Wilson, you have shown yourself a Christian in your treatment of me,—I want to ask one last deed of Christian kindness of you."

"Well, George."

"Well, sir,—what you said was true. I *am* running a dreadful risk. There is n't, on earth, a living soul to care if I die," he added, drawing his breath hard, and speaking with a great effort,—"I shall be kicked out and buried like a dog, and nobody'll think of it a day after,—*only my poor wife!* Poor soul! she'll mourn and grieve; and if you'd only contrive, Mr. Wilson, to send this little pin to her. She gave it to me for a Christmas present, poor child! Give it to her, and tell her I loved her to the last. Will you? *Will* you?" he added, earnestly.

"Yes, certainly—poor fellow!" said the old gentleman, taking the pin, with watery eyes, and a melancholy quiver in his voice.

"Tell her one thing," said George; "it's my last wish, if she *can* get to Canada, to go there. No matter how kind her mistress is,—no matter how much she loves her home; beg her not to go back,—for slavery always ends in misery. Tell her to bring up our boy a free man, and then he won't suffer as I have. Tell her this, Mr. Wilson, will you?"

"Yes, George, I'll tell her; but I trust you won't die; take heart,—you're a brave fellow. Trust in the Lord, George. I wish in my heart you were safe through, though,—that's what I do."

"*Is* there a God to trust in?" said George, in such a tone of utter despair as arrested the old gentleman's words. "O, I've seen things all my life that have made me feel that there can't be a God. You Christians don't know how these things look to us. There's a God for you, but is there any for us?"

"O, now, don't—don't, my boy!" said the old man, almost sobbing as he spoke; "don't feel so! There is—there is; clouds and darkness are around about him, but righteousness and judgment are the habitation of his throne. There's a *God*, George,—believe it; trust in Him, and I'm sure He'll help you. Everything will be set right,—if not in this life, in another."

The real piety and benevolence of the simple old man invested him with a temporary dignity and authority, as he spoke. George stopped his distracted walk up and down the room, stood thoughtfully a moment, and then said, quietly,

"Thank you for saying that, my good friend; I'll *think of that*."

XIII. The Quaker Settlement

A quiet scene now rises before us. A large, roomy, neatly-painted kitchen, its yellow floor glossy and smooth, and without a particle of dust; a neat, well-blacked cooking-stove; rows of shining tin, suggestive of unmentionable good things to the appetite; glossy green wood chairs, old and firm; a small flag-bottomed rocking-chair, with a patch-work cushion in it, neatly contrived out of small pieces of different colored woollen goods, and a larger sized one, motherly and old, whose wide arms breathed hospitable invitation, seconded by the solicitation of its feather cushions,—a real comfortable, persuasive old chair, and worth, in the way of honest, homely enjoyment, a dozen of your plush or brochetelle drawing-room gentry; and in the chair, gently swaying back and forward, her eyes bent on some fine sewing, sat our old friend Eliza. Yes, there she is, paler and thinner than in her Kentucky home, with a world of quiet sorrow lying under the shadow of her long eyelashes, and marking the outline of her gentle mouth! It was plain to see how old and firm the girlish heart was grown under the discipline of heavy sorrow; and when, anon, her large dark eye was raised to follow the gambols of her little Harry, who was sporting, like some tropical butterfly, hither and thither over the floor, she showed a depth of firmness and steady resolve that was never there in her earlier and happier days.

By her side sat a woman with a bright tin pan in her lap, into which she was carefully sorting some dried peaches. She might be fifty-five or sixty; but hers was one of those faces that time seems to touch only to brighten and adorn. The snowy lisse crape cap, made after the strait Quaker pattern,—the plain white muslin handkerchief, lying in placid folds across her bosom,—the drab shawl and dress,—showed at once the community to which she belonged. Her face was round and rosy, with a healthful downy softness, suggestive of a ripe peach. Her hair, partially silvered by age, was parted smoothly back from a high placid forehead, on which time had written no inscription, except peace on earth, good will to men, and beneath shone a large pair of clear, honest, loving brown eyes; you only needed to look straight into them, to feel that you saw to the bottom of a heart as good and true as ever throbbed in woman's bosom. So much has been said and sung of beautiful young girls, why don't somebody wake up to the beauty of old women? If any want to get up an inspiration under this head, we refer them to our good friend Rachel Halliday, just as she sits there in her little rocking-chair. It had a turn for quacking and squeaking,—that chair had,—either from having taken cold in early life, or from some asthmatic affection, or perhaps from nervous derangement; but, as she gently swung backward and forward, the chair kept up a kind of subdued "creechy crawchy," that would have been intolerable in any other chair. But old Simeon Halliday often declared it was as good as any music to him, and the children all avowed that they would n't miss of hearing mother's chair for anything in the world. For why? for twenty years or more, nothing but loving words, and gentle moralities, and motherly loving kindness, had come from that chair;—head-aches and heart-aches innumerable had been cured there,—difficulties spiritual and temporal solved there,—all by one good, loving woman, God bless her!

"And so thee still thinks of going to Canada, Eliza?" she said, as she was quietly looking over her peaches.

"Yes, ma'am," said Eliza, firmly. "I must go onward. I dare not stop."

"And what'll thee do, when thee gets there? Thee must think about that, my daughter."

"My daughter" came naturally from the lips of Rachel Halliday; for hers was just the face and form that made "mother" seem the most natural word in the world.

Eliza's hands trembled, and some tears fell on her fine work; but she answered, firmly,

"I shall do—anything I can find. I hope I can find something."

"Thee knows thee can stay here, as long as thee pleases," said Rachel.

"O, thank you," said Eliza, "but"—she pointed to Harry—"I can't sleep nights; I can't rest. Last night I dreamed I saw that man coming into the yard," she said, shuddering.

"Poor child!" said Rachel, wiping her eyes; "but thee must n't feel so. The Lord hath ordered it so that never hath a fugitive been stolen from our village. I trust thine will not be the first."

The door here opened, and a little short, round, pincushiony woman stood at the door, with a cheery, blooming face, like a ripe apple. She was dressed, like Rachel, in sober gray, with the muslin folded neatly across her round, plump little chest.

"Ruth Stedman," said Rachel, coming joyfully forward; "how is thee, Ruth?" she said, heartily taking both her hands.

"Nicely," said Ruth, taking off her little drab bonnet, and dusting it with her handkerchief, displaying, as she did so, a round little head, on which the Quaker cap sat with a sort of jaunty air, despite all the stroking and patting of the small fat hands, which were busily applied to arranging it. Certain stray locks of decidedly curly hair, too, had escaped here and there, and had to be coaxed and cajoled into their place again; and then the new comer, who might have been five-and-twenty, turned from the small looking-glass, before which she had been making these arrangements, and looked well pleased,—as most people who looked at her might have been,—for she was decidedly a wholesome, wholehearted, chirruping little woman, as ever gladdened man's heart withal.

"Ruth, this friend is Eliza Harris; and this is the little boy I told thee of."

"I am glad to see thee, Eliza,—very," said Ruth, shaking hands, as if Eliza were an old friend she had long been expecting; "and this is thy dear boy,—I brought a cake for him," she said, holding out a little heart to the boy, who came up, gazing through his curls, and accepted it shyly.

"Where's thy baby, Ruth?" said Rachel.

"O, he's coming; but thy Mary caught him as I came in, and ran off with him to the barn, to show him to the children."

At this moment, the door opened, and Mary, an honest, rosy-looking girl, with large brown eyes, like her mother's, came in with the baby.

"Ah! ha!" said Rachel, coming up, and taking the great, white, fat fellow in her arms; "how good he looks, and how he does grow!"

"To be sure, he does," said little bustling Ruth, as she took the child, and began taking off a little blue silk hood, and various layers and wrappers of outer garments; and having given a twitch here, and a pull there, and variously adjusted and arranged him, and kissed him heartily, she set him on the floor to collect his thoughts. Baby seemed quite used to this mode of proceeding, for he put his thumb in his mouth (as if it were quite a thing of course), and seemed soon absorbed in his own reflections, while the mother seated herself, and taking out a long stocking of mixed blue and white yarn, began to knit with briskness.

"Mary, thee 'd better fill the kettle, had n't thee?" gently suggested the mother.

Mary took the kettle to the well, and soon reäppearing, placed it over the stove, where it was soon purring and steaming, a sort of censer of hospitality and good cheer. The peaches, moreover, in obedience to a few gentle whispers from Rachel, were soon deposited, by the same hand, in a stewpan over the fire.

Rachel now took down a snowy moulding-board, and, tying on an apron, proceeded quietly to making up some biscuits, first saying to Mary,—"Mary, had n't thee better tell John to get a chicken ready?" and Mary disappeared accordingly.

"And how is Abigail Peters?" said Rachel, as she went on with her biscuits.

"O, she's better," said Ruth; "I was in, this morning; made the bed, tidied up the house. Leah Hills went in, this afternoon, and baked bread and pies enough to last some days; and I engaged to go back to get her up, this evening."

"I will go in to-morrow, and do any cleaning there may be, and look over the mending," said Rachel.

"Ah! that is well," said Ruth. "I've heard," she added, "that Hannah Stanwood is sick. John was up there, last night,—I must go there to-morrow."

"John can come in here to his meals, if thee needs to stay all day," suggested Rachel.

"Thank thee, Rachel; will see, to-morrow; but, here comes Simeon."

Simeon Halliday, a tall, straight, muscular man, in drab coat and pantaloons, and broad-brimmed hat, now entered.

"How is thee, Ruth?" he said, warmly, as he spread his broad open hand for her little fat palm; "and how is John?"

"O! John is well, and all the rest of our folks," said Ruth, cheerily.

"Any news, father?" said Rachel, as she was putting her biscuits into the oven.

"Peter Stebbins told me that they should be along to-night, with *friends*," said Simeon, significantly, as he was washing his hands at a neat sink, in a little back porch.

"Indeed!" said Rachel, looking thoughtfully, and glancing at Eliza.

"Did thee say thy name was Harris?" said Simeon to Eliza, as he reëntered.

Rachel glanced quickly at her husband, as Eliza tremulously answered "yes;" her fears, ever uppermost, suggesting that possibly there might be advertisements out for her.

"Mother!" said Simeon, standing in the porch, and calling Rachel out.

"What does thee want, father?" said Rachel, rubbing her floury hands, as she went into the porch.

"This child's husband is in the settlement, and will be here to-night," said Simeon.

"Now, thee does n't say that, father?" said Rachel, all her face radiant with joy.

"It's really true. Peter was down yesterday, with the wagon, to the other stand, and there he found an old woman and two men; and one said his name was George Harris; and, from what he told of his history, I am certain who he is. He is a bright, likely fellow, too."

"Shall we tell her now?" said Simeon.

"Let's tell Ruth," said Rachel. "Here, Ruth,—come here."

Ruth laid down her knitting-work, and was in the back porch in a moment.

"Ruth, what does thee think?" said Rachel. "Father says Eliza's husband is in the last company, and will be here to-night."

A burst of joy from the little Quakeress interrupted the speech. She gave such a bound from the floor, as she clapped her little hands, that two stray curls fell from under her Quaker cap, and lay brightly on her white neckerchief.

"Hush thee, dear!" said Rachel, gently; "hush, Ruth! Tell us, shall we tell her now?"

"Now! to be sure,—this very minute. Why, now, suppose 't was my John, how should I feel? Do tell her, right off."

"Thee uses thyself only to learn how to love thy neighbor, Ruth," said Simeon, looking, with a beaming face, on Ruth.

"To be sure. Is n't it what we are made for? If I did n't love John and the baby, I should not know how to feel for her. Come, now, do tell her,— do!" and she laid her hands persuasively on Rachel's arm. "Take her into thy bed-room, there, and let me fry the chicken while thee does it."

Rachel came out into the kitchen, where Eliza was sewing, and opening the door of a small bed-room, said, gently, "Come in here with me, my daughter; I have news to tell thee."

The blood flushed in Eliza's pale face; she rose, trembling with nervous anxiety, and looked towards her boy.

"No, no," said little Ruth, darting up, and seizing her hands. "Never thee fear; it's good news, Eliza,—go in, go in!" And she gently pushed her to the door, which closed after her; and then, turning round, she caught little Harry in her arms, and began kissing him.

"Thee'll see thy father, little one. Does thee know it? Thy father is coming," she said, over and over again, as the boy looked wonderingly at her.

Meanwhile, within the door, another scene was going on. Rachel Halliday drew Eliza toward her, and said, "The Lord hath had mercy on thee, daughter; thy husband hath escaped from the house of bondage."

The blood flushed to Eliza's cheek in a sudden glow, and went back to her heart with as sudden a rush. She sat down, pale and faint.

"Have courage, child," said Rachel, laying her hand on her head. "He is among friends, who will bring him here to-night."

"To-night!" Eliza repeated, "to-night!" The words lost all meaning to her; her head was dreamy and confused; all was mist for a moment.

When she awoke, she found herself snugly tucked up on the bed, with a blanket over her, and little Ruth rubbing her hands with camphor. She opened her eyes in a state of dreamy, delicious languor, such as one has who has long been bearing a heavy load, and now feels it gone, and would rest. The tension of the nerves, which had never ceased a moment since the first hour of her flight, had given way, and a strange feeling of security and rest came over her; and, as she lay, with her large, dark eyes open, she followed, as in a quiet dream, the motions of those about her. She saw the door open into the other room; saw the supper-table, with its snowy cloth; heard the dreamy murmur of the singing tea-kettle; saw Ruth tripping backward and forward, with plates of cake and saucers of preserves, and ever and anon stopping to put a cake into Harry's hand, or pat his head, or twine his long curls round her snowy fingers. She saw the ample, motherly form of Rachel, as she ever and anon came to the bed-side, and smoothed and arranged something about the bed-clothes, and gave a tuck here and there, by way of expressing her good-will; and was conscious of a kind of sunshine beaming down upon her from her large, clear, brown eyes. She saw Ruth's husband come in,—saw her fly up to him, and commence whispering very earnestly, ever and anon, with impressive gesture, pointing her little finger toward the room. She saw her, with the baby in her arms, sitting down to tea; she saw them all at table, and little Harry in a high chair, under the shadow of Rachel's ample wing; there were low murmurs of talk, gentle tinkling of tea-spoons, and musical clatter of cups and saucers, and all mingled in a delightful dream of rest; and Eliza slept, as she had not slept before, since the fearful midnight hour when she had taken her child and fled through the frosty star-light.

She dreamed of a beautiful country,—a land, it seemed to her, of rest,— green shores, pleasant islands, and beautifully glittering water; and there, in a house which kind voices told her was a home, she saw her boy playing, a free and happy child. She heard her husband's footsteps; she felt him coming nearer; his arms were around her, his tears falling on her face, and she awoke! It was no dream. The daylight had long faded; her child lay calmly sleeping by her side; a candle was burning dimly on the stand, and her husband was sobbing by her pillow.

The next morning was a cheerful one at the Quaker house. "Mother" was up betimes, and surrounded by busy girls and boys, whom we had scarce time to introduce to our readers yesterday, and who all moved obediently to Rachel's gentle "Thee had better," or more gentle "Had n't thee better?" in the work of getting breakfast; for a breakfast in the luxurious valleys of Indiana is a thing complicated and multiform, and, like picking up the rose-leaves and trimming the bushes in Paradise, asking other hands than those of the original mother. While, therefore, John ran to the spring for fresh water, and Simeon the second sifted meal for corn-cakes, and Mary ground coffee, Rachel moved gently and quietly about, making biscuits, cutting up chicken, and diffusing a sort of sunny radiance over the whole proceeding generally. If there was any danger of friction or collision from the ill-regulated zeal of so many young operators, her gentle "Come! come!" or "I would n't, now," was quite sufficient to allay the difficulty. Bards have written of the cestus of Venus, that turned the heads of all the world in successive generations. We had rather, for our part, have the cestus of Rachel Halliday, that kept heads from being turned, and made everything go on harmoniously. We think it is more suited to our modern days, decidedly.

While all other preparations were going on, Simeon the elder stood in his shirt-sleeves before a little looking-glass in the corner, engaged in the anti-patriarchal operation of shaving. Everything went on so sociably, so quietly, so harmoniously, in the great kitchen,—it seemed so pleasant to every one to do just what they were doing, there was such an atmosphere of mutual confidence and good fellowship everywhere,—even the knives and forks had a social clatter as they went on to the table; and the chicken and ham had a cheerful and joyous fizzle in the pan, as if they rather enjoyed being cooked than otherwise;—and when George and Eliza and little Harry came out, they met such a hearty, rejoicing welcome, no wonder it seemed to them like a dream.

At last, they were all seated at breakfast, while Mary stood at the stove, baking griddle-cakes, which, as they gained the true exact golden-brown tint of perfection, were transferred quite handily to the table.

Rachel never looked so truly and benignly happy as at the head of her table. There was so much motherliness and full-heartedness even in the way she passed a plate of cakes or poured a cup of coffee, that it seemed to put a spirit into the food and drink she offered.

It was the first time that ever George had sat down on equal terms at any white man's table; and he sat down, at first, with some constraint and awkwardness; but they all exhaled and went off like fog, in the genial morning rays of this simple, overflowing kindness.

This, indeed, was a home,—*home*,—a word that George had never yet known a meaning for; and a belief in God, and trust in his providence, began to encircle his heart, as, with a golden cloud of protection and confidence, dark, misanthropic, pining, atheistic doubts, and fierce despair, melted away before the light of a living Gospel, breathed in living faces, preached by a thousand unconscious acts of love and good will, which, like the cup of cold water given in the name of a disciple, shall never lose their reward.

"Father, what if thee should get found out again?" said Simeon second, as he buttered his cake.

"I should pay my fine," said Simeon, quietly.

"But what if they put thee in prison?"

"Could n't thee and mother manage the farm?" said Simeon, smiling.

"Mother can do almost everything," said the boy. "But is n't it a shame to make such laws?"

"Thee must n't speak evil of thy rulers, Simeon," said his father, gravely. "The Lord only gives us our worldly goods that we may do justice and mercy; if our rulers require a price of us for it, we must deliver it up."

"Well, I hate those old slaveholders!" said the boy, who felt as unchristian as became any modern reformer.

"I am surprised at thee, son," said Simeon; "thy mother never taught thee so. I would do even the same for the slaveholder as for the slave, if the Lord brought him to my door in affliction."

Simeon second blushed scarlet; but his mother only smiled, and said, "Simeon is my good boy; he will grow older, by and by, and then he will be like his father."

"I hope, my good sir, that you are not exposed to any difficulty on our account," said George, anxiously.

"Fear nothing, George, for therefore are we sent into the world. If we would not meet trouble for a good cause, we were not worthy of our name."

"But, for *me*," said George, "I could not bear it."

"Fear not, then, friend George; it is not for thee, but for God and man, we do it," said Simeon. "And now thou must lie by quietly this day, and to-night, at ten o'clock, Phineas Fletcher will carry thee onward to the next stand,—thee and the rest of thy company. The pursuers are hard after thee; we must not delay."

"If that is the case, why wait till evening?" said George.

"Thou art safe here by daylight, for every one in the settlement is a Friend, and all are watching. It has been found safer to travel by night."

XIV. Evangeline

[Uncle Tom is taken into custody by Haley, the slave trader. Young George Shelby, who has taught Uncle Tom to read and write, is devastated by the sale and vows to get Tom back someday. Haley and Tom board a boat for New Orleans, where Haley plans to sell Tom.]

> *"A young star! which shone*
> *O'er life—too sweet an image for such glass!*
> *A lovely being, scarcely formed or moulded;*
> *A rose with all its sweetest leaves yet folded."*

The Mississippi! How, as by an enchanted wand, have its scenes been changed, since Chateaubriand wrote his prose-poetic description of it, as a river of mighty, unbroken solitudes, rolling amid undreamed wonders of vegetable and animal existence.

But, as in an hour, this river of dreams and wild romance has emerged to a reality scarcely less visionary and splendid. What other river of the world bears on its bosom to the ocean the wealth and enterprise of such another country?—a country whose products embrace all between the tropics and the poles! Those turbid waters, hurrying, foaming, tearing along, an apt resemblance of that headlong tide of business which is poured along its wave by a race more vehement and energetic than any the old world ever saw. Ah! would that they did not also bear along a more fearful freight,— the tears of the oppressed, the sighs of the helpless, the bitter prayers of poor, ignorant hearts to an unknown God—unknown, unseen and silent, but who will yet "come out of his place to save all the poor of the earth!"

The slanting light of the setting sun quivers on the sea-like expanse of the river; the shivery canes, and the tall, dark cypress, hung with wreaths of dark, funereal moss, glow in the golden ray, as the heavily-laden steamboat marches onward.

Piled with cotton-bales, from many a plantation, up over deck and sides, till she seems in the distance a square, massive block of gray, she moves heavily onward to the nearing mart. We must look some time among its crowded decks before we shall find again our humble friend Tom. High on the upper deck, in a little nook among the everywhere predominant cotton-bales, at last we may find him.

Partly from confidence inspired by Mr. Shelby's representations, and partly from the remarkably inoffensive and quiet character of the man, Tom had insensibly won his way far into the confidence even of such as man as Haley.

At first he had watched him narrowly through the day, and never allowed him to sleep at night unfettered; but the uncomplaining patience and apparent contentment of Tom's manner led him gradually to discontinue these restraints, and for some time Tom had enjoyed a sort of parole of honor, being permitted to come and go freely where he pleased on the boat.

Ever quiet and obliging, and more than ready to lend a hand in every emergency which occurred among the workmen below, he had won the good opinion of all the hands, and spent many hours in helping them with as hearty a good will as ever he worked on a Kentucky farm.

When there seemed to be nothing for him to do, he would climb to a nook among the cotton-bales of the upper deck, and busy himself in studying over his Bible,—and it is there we see him now.

For a hundred or more miles above New Orleans, the river is higher than the surrounding country, and rolls its tremendous volume between massive levees twenty feet in height. The traveller from the deck of the steamer, as from some floating castle top, overlooks the whole country for miles and miles around. Tom, therefore, had spread out full before him, in plantation after plantation, a map of the life to which he was approaching.

He saw the distant slaves at their toil; he saw afar their villages of huts gleaming out in long rows on many a plantation, distant from the stately mansions and pleasure-grounds of the master;—and as the moving picture passed on, his poor, foolish heart would be turning backward to the Kentucky farm, with its old shadowy beeches,—to the master's house, with its wide, cool halls, and, near by, the little cabin, overgrown with the multiflora and bignonia. There he seemed to see familiar faces of comrades, who had grown up with him from infancy; he saw his busy wife, bustling in her preparations for his evening meals; he heard the merry laugh of his boys at their play, and the chirrup of the baby at his knee; and then, with a start, all faded, and he saw again the cane-brakes and cypresses and gliding plantations, and heard again the creaking and groaning of the machinery, all telling him too plainly that all that phase of life had gone by forever.

In such a case, you write to your wife, and send messages to your children; but Tom could not write,—the mail for him had no existence, and the gulf of separation was unbridged by even a friendly word or signal.

Is it strange, then, that some tears fall on the pages of his Bible, as he lays it on the cotton-bale, and, with patient finger, threading his slow way from word to word, traces out its promises? Having learned late in life, Tom was but a slow reader, and passed on laboriously from verse to verse. Fortunate for him was it that the book he was intent on was one which slow reading cannot injure,—nay, one whose words, like ingots of gold, seem often to need to be weighed separately, that the mind may take in their priceless value. Let us follow him a moment, as, pointing to each word, and pronouncing each half aloud, he reads,

"Let—not—your—heart—be—troubled. In—my—Father's—house— are—many—mansions. I—go—to—prepare—a—place—for—you."

Cicero, when he buried his darling and only daughter, had a heart as full of honest grief as poor Tom's,—perhaps no fuller, for both were only men;—but Cicero could pause over no such sublime words of hope, and look to no such future reünion; and if he *had* seen them, ten to one he would not have believed,—he must fill his head first with a thousand questions of authenticity of manuscript, and correctness of translation. But, to poor Tom, there it lay, just what he needed, so evidently true and divine that the possibility of a question never entered his simple head. It must be true; for, if not true, how could he live?

As for Tom's Bible, though it had no annotations and helps in margin from learned commentators, still it had been embellished with certain waymarks and guide-boards of Tom's own invention, and which helped him more than the most learned expositions could have done. It had been his custom to get the Bible read to him by his master's children, in particular by young Master George; and, as they read, he would designate, by bold, strong marks and dashes, with pen and ink, the passages which more particularly gratified his ear or affected his heart. His Bible was thus marked through, from one end to the other, with a variety of styles and designations; so he could in a moment seize upon his favorite passages, without the labor of spelling out what lay between them;—and while it lay there before him, every passage breathing of some old home scene, and recalling some past enjoyment, his Bible seemed to him all of this life that remained, as well as the promise of a future one.

Among the passengers on the boat was a young gentleman of fortune and family, resident in New Orleans, who bore the name of St. Clare. He had with him a daughter between five and six years of age, together with a lady who seemed to claim relationship to both, and to have the little one especially under her charge.

Tom had often caught glimpses of this little girl,—for she was one of those busy, tripping creatures, that can be no more contained in one place than a sunbeam or a summer breeze,—nor was she one that, once seen, could be easily forgotten.

Her form was the perfection of childish beauty, without its usual chubbiness and squareness of outline. There was about it an undulating and aërial grace, such as one might dream of for some mythic and allegorical being. Her face was remarkable less for its perfect beauty of feature than for a singular and dreamy earnestness of expression, which made the ideal start when they looked at her, and by which the dullest and most literal were impressed, without exactly knowing why. The shape of her head and the turn of her neck and bust was peculiarly noble, and the long golden-brown hair that floated like a cloud around it, the deep spiritual gravity of her violet blue eyes, shaded by heavy fringes of golden brown,—all marked her out from other children, and made every one turn and look after her, as she glided hither and thither on the boat. Nevertheless, the little one was not what you would have called either a grave child or a sad one. On the contrary, an airy and innocent playfulness seemed to flicker like the shadow of summer leaves over her childish face, and around her buoyant figure. She was always in motion, always with a half smile on her rosy mouth, flying hither and thither, with an undulating and cloud-like tread, singing to herself as she moved as in a happy dream. Her father and female guardian were incessantly busy in pursuit of her,—but, when caught, she melted from them again like a summer cloud; and as no word of chiding or reproof ever fell on her ear for whatever she chose to do, she pursued her own way all over the boat. Always dressed in white, she seemed to move like a shadow through all sorts of places, without contracting spot or stain; and there was not a corner or nook, above or below, where those fairy footsteps had not glided, and that visionary golden head, with its deep blue eyes, fleeted along.

The fireman, as he looked up from his sweaty toil, sometimes found those eyes looking wonderingly into the raging depths of the furnace, and fearfully and pityingly at him, as if she thought him in some dreadful danger. Anon the steersman at the wheel paused and smiled, as the picture-like head gleamed through the window of the round house, and in a moment was gone again. A thousand times a day rough voices blessed her, and smiles of unwonted softness stole over hard faces, as she passed; and when she tripped fearlessly over dangerous places, rough, sooty hands were stretched involuntarily out to save her, and smooth her path.

Tom, who had the soft, impressible nature of his kindly race, ever yearning toward the simple and childlike, watched the little creature with daily increasing interest. To him she seemed something almost divine; and whenever her golden head and deep blue eyes peered out upon him from behind some dusky cotton-bale, or looked down upon him over some ridge of packages, he half believed that he saw one of the angels stepped out of his New Testament.

Often and often she walked mournfully round the place where Haley's gang of men and women sat in their chains. She would glide in among them, and look at them with an air of perplexed and sorrowful earnestness; and sometimes she would lift their chains with her slender hands, and then sigh wofully, as she glided away. Several times she appeared suddenly among them, with her hands full of candy, nuts, and oranges, which she would distribute joyfully to them, and then be gone again.

Tom watched the little lady a great deal, before he ventured on any overtures towards acquaintanceship. He knew an abundance of simple acts to propitiate and invite the approaches of the little people, and he resolved to play his part right skilfully. He could cut cunning little baskets out of cherry-stones, could make grotesque faces on hickory-nuts, or odd-jumping figures out of elder-pith, and he was a very Pan in the manufacture of whistles of all sizes and sorts. His pockets were full of miscellaneous articles of attraction, which he had hoarded in days of old for his master's children, and which he now produced, with commendable prudence and economy, one by one, as overtures for acquaintance and friendship.

The little one was shy, for all her busy interest in everything going on, and it was not easy to tame her. For a while, she would perch like a canary-bird on some box or package near Tom, while busy in the little arts afore-named, and take from him, with a kind of grave bashfulness, the little articles he offered. But at last they got on quite confidential terms.

"What's little missy's name?" said Tom, at last, when he thought matters were ripe to push such an inquiry.

"Evangeline St. Clare," said the little one, "though papa and everybody else call me Eva. Now, what's your name?"

"My name 's Tom; the little chil'en used to call me Uncle Tom, way back thar in Kentuck."

"Then I mean to call you Uncle Tom, because, you see, I like you," said Eva. "So, Uncle Tom, where are you going?"

"I don't know, Miss Eva."

"Don't know?" said Eva.

"No. I am going to be sold to somebody. I don't know who."

"My papa can buy you," said Eva, quickly; "and if he buys you, you will have good times. I mean to ask him to, this very day."

"Thank you, my little lady," said Tom.

The boat here stopped at a small landing to take in wood, and Eva, hearing her father's voice, bounded nimbly away. Tom rose up, and went forward to offer his service in wooding, and soon was busy among the hands.

Eva and her father were standing together by the railings to see the boat start from the landing-place, the wheel had made two or three revolutions in the water, when, by some sudden movement, the little one suddenly lost her balance, and fell sheer over the side of the boat into the water. Her father, scarce knowing what he did, was plunging in after her, but was held back by some behind him, who saw that more efficient aid had followed his child.

Tom was standing just under her on the lower deck, as she fell. He saw her strike the water, and sink, and was after her in a moment. A broad-chested, strong-armed fellow, it was nothing for him to keep afloat in the water, till, in a moment or two, the child rose to the surface, and he caught her in his arms, and, swimming with her to the boat-side, handed her up, all dripping, to the grasp of hundreds of hands, which, as if they had all belonged to one man, were stretched eagerly out to receive her. A few moments more, and her father bore her, dripping and senseless, to the ladies' cabin, where, as is usual in cases of the kind, there ensued a very well-meaning and kind-hearted strife among the female occupants generally, as to who should do the most things to make a disturbance, and to hinder her recovery in every way possible.

It was a sultry, close day, the next day, as the steamer drew near to New Orleans. A general bustle of expectation and preparation was spread through the boat; in the cabin, one and another were gathering their things together, and arranging them, preparatory to going ashore. The steward and chambermaid, and all, were busily engaged in cleaning, furbishing, and arranging the splendid boat, preparatory to a grand entree.

On the lower deck sat our friend Tom, with his arms folded, and anxiously, from time to time, turning his eyes towards a group on the other side of the boat.

There stood the fair Evangeline, a little paler than the day before, but otherwise exhibiting no traces of the accident which had befallen her. A graceful, elegantly-formed young man stood by her, carelessly leaning one elbow on a bale of cotton, while a large pocket-book lay open before him. It was quite evident, at a glance, that the gentleman was Eva's father. There was the same noble cast of head, the same large blue eyes, the same golden-brown hair; yet the expression was wholly different. In the large, clear blue eyes, though in form and color exactly similar, there was wanting that misty, dreamy depth of expression; all was clear, bold, and bright, but with a light wholly of this world: the beautifully cut mouth had a proud and somewhat sarcastic expression, while an air of free-and-easy superiority sat not ungracefully in every turn and movement of his fine form. He was listening, with a good-humored, negligent air, half comic, half contemptuous, to Haley, who was very volubly expatiating on the quality of the article for which they were bargaining.

"All the moral and Christian virtues bound in black morocco, complete!" he said, when Haley had finished. "Well, now, my good fellow, what's the damage, as they say in Kentucky; in short, what's to be paid out for this business? How much are you going to cheat me, now? Out with it!"

"Wal," said Haley, "if I should say thirteen hundred dollars for that ar fellow, I should n't but just save myself; I should n't, now, re'ly."

"Poor fellow!" said the young man, fixing his keen, mocking blue eye on him; "but I suppose you'd let me have him for that, out of a particular regard for me."

"Well, the young lady here seems to be sot on him, and nat'lly enough."

"O! certainly, there's a call on your benevolence, my friend. Now, as a matter of Christian charity, how cheap could you afford to let him go, to oblige a young lady that's particular sot on him?"

"Wal, now, just think on't," said the trader; "just look at them limbs,—broad-chested, strong as a horse. Look at his head; them high forrads allays shows calculatin niggers, that'll do any kind o' thing. I've marked that ar. Now, a nigger of that ar heft and build is worth considerable, just, as you may say, for his body, supposin he's stupid; but come to put in his calculatin faculties, and them which I can show he has oncommon, why, of course, it makes him come higher. Why, that ar fellow managed his master's whole farm. He has a strornary talent for business."

"Bad, bad, very bad; knows altogether too much!" said the young man, with the same mocking smile playing about his mouth. "Never will do, in the world. Your smart fellows are always running off, stealing horses, and raising the devil generally. I think you'll have to take off a couple of hundred for his smartness."

"Wal, there might be something in that ar, if it warnt for his character; but I can show recommends from his master and others, to prove he is one of your real pious,—the most humble, prayin, pious crittur ye ever did see. Why, he's been called a preacher in them parts he came from."

"And I might use him for a family chaplain, possibly," added the young man, dryly. "That 's quite an idea. Religion is a remarkably scarce article at our house."

"You're joking, now."

"How do you know I am? Did n't you just warrant him for a preacher? Has he been examined by any synod or council? Come, hand over your papers."

If the trader had not been sure, by a certain good-humored twinkle in the large blue eye, that all this banter was sure, in the long run, to turn out a cash concern, he might have been somewhat out of patience; as it was, he laid down a greasy pocketbook on the cotton-bales, and began anxiously studying over certain papers in it, the young man standing by, the while, looking down on him with an air of careless, easy drollery.

"Papa, do buy him! it's no matter what you pay," whispered Eva, softly, getting up on a package, and putting her arm around her father's neck. "You have money enough, I know. I want him."

"What for, pussy? Are you going to use him for a rattlebox, or a rocking-horse, or what?"

"I want to make him happy."

"An original reason, certainly."

Here the trader handed up a certificate, signed by Mr. Shelby, which the young man took with the tips of his long fingers, and glanced over carelessly.

"A gentlemanly hand," he said, "and well spelt, too. Well, now, but I'm not sure, after all, about this religion," said he, the old wicked expression returning to his eye; "the country is almost ruined with pious white people: such pious politicians as we have just before elections,—such pious goings on in all departments of church and state, that a fellow does not know who'll cheat him next. I don't know, either, about religion's being up in the market, just now. I have not looked in the papers lately, to see how it sells. How many hundred dollars, now, do you put on for this religion?"

"You like to be a jokin, now," said the trader; "but, then, there 's *sense* under all that ar. I know there's differences in religion. Some kinds is mis'r-able: there's your meetin pious; there's your singin, roarin pious; them ar an't no account, in black or white;—but these rayly is; and I've seen it in niggers as often as any, your rail softly, quiet, stiddy, honest, pious, that the hull world could n't tempt 'em to do nothing that they thinks is wrong; and ye see in this letter what Tom's old master says about him."

"Now," said the young man, stooping gravely over his book of bills, "if you can assure me that I really can buy *this* kind of pious, and that it will be set down to my account in the book up above, as something belonging to me, I would n't care if I did go a little extra for it. How d'ye say?"

"Wal, raily, I can't do that," said the trader. "I'm a thinkin that every man 'll have to hang on his own hook, in them ar quarters."

"Rather hard on a fellow that pays extra on religion, and can't trade with it in the state where he wants it most, an't it, now?" said the young man, who had been making out a roll of bills while he was speaking. "There, count your money, old boy!" he added, as he handed the roll to the trader.

"All right," said Haley, his face beaming with delight; and pulling out an old inkhorn, he proceeded to fill out a bill of sale, which, in a few moments, he handed to the young man.

"I wonder, now, if I was divided up and inventoried," said the latter, as he ran over the paper, "how much I might bring. Say so much for the shape of my head, so much for a high forehead, so much for arms, and hands, and legs, and then so much for education, learning, talent, honesty, religion! Bless me! there would be small charge on that last, I'm thinking. But come, Eva," he said; and taking the hand of his daughter, he stepped across the boat, and carelessly putting the tip of his finger under Tom's chin, said, good-humoredly, "Look up, Tom, and see how you like your new master."

Tom looked up. It was not in nature to look into that gay, young, handsome face, without a feeling of pleasure; and Tom felt the tears start in his eyes as he said, heartily, "God bless you, Mas'r!"

"Well, I hope he will. What's your name? Tom? Quite as likely to do it for your asking as mine, from all accounts. Can you drive horses, Tom?"

"I've been allays used to horses," said Tom. "Mas'r Shelby raised heaps on 'em."

"Well, I think I shall put you in coachy, on condition that you won't be drunk more than once a week, unless in cases of emergency, Tom."

Tom looked surprised, and rather hurt, and said, "I never drink, Mas'r."

"I've heard that story before, Tom; but then we'll see. It will be a special accommodation to all concerned, if you don't. Never mind, my boy," he added, good-humoredly, seeing Tom still looked grave; "I don't doubt you mean to do well."

"I sartin do, Mas'r," said Tom.

"And you shall have good times," said Eva. "Papa is very good to everybody, only he always will laugh at them."

"Papa is much obliged to you for his recommendation," said St. Clare, laughing, as he turned on his heel and walked away.

XL. The Martyr

[Simon Legree is a cruel man who drinks heavily and treats his slaves brutally. One night, one of his slaves, Cassy, drugs him and escapes, taking with her another slave, Emmeline, and urging Tom to escape also. Tom refuses to go, and after Legree is unsuccessful in catching the two women, he decides to question Tom.]

... Tom heard the message with a forewarning heart; for he knew all the plan of the fugitives' escape, and the place of their present concealment;—he knew the deadly character of the man he had to deal with, and his despotic power. But he felt strong in God to meet death, rather than betray the helpless.

He sat his basket down by the row, and, looking up, said, "Into thy hands I commend my spirit! Thou hast redeemed me, oh Lord God of truth!" and then quietly yielded himself to the rough, brutal grasp with which Quimbo seized him.

"Ay, ay!" said the giant, as he dragged him along; "ye'll cotch it, now! I'll boun' Mas'r's back's up *high*! No sneaking out, now! Tell ye, ye'll get it, and no mistake! See how ye'll look, now, helpin' Mas'r's niggers to run away! See what ye'll get!"

The savage words none of them reached that ear!—a higher voice there was saying, "Fear not them that kill the body, and, after that, have no more that they can do." Nerve and bone of that poor man's body vibrated to those words, as if touched by the finger of God; and he felt the strength of a thousand souls in one. As he passed along, the trees and bushes, the huts of his servitude, the whole scene of his degradation, seemed to whirl by him as the landscape by the rushing car. His soul throbbed,—his home was in sight,—and the hour of release seemed at hand.

"Well, Tom!" said Legree, walking up, and seizing him grimly by the collar of his coat, and speaking through his teeth, in a paroxysm of determined rage, "do you know I've made up my mind to KILL you?"

"It's very likely, Mas'r," said Tom calmly.

"I *have*," said Legree, with grim, terrible calmness, "*done—just—that—thing*, Tom, unless you'll tell me what you know about these yer gals!"

Tom stood silent.

"D'ye hear?" said Legree, stamping, with a roar like that of an incensed lion. "Speak!"

"*I han't got nothing to tell, Mas'r*," said Tom, with a slow, firm, deliberate utterance.

"Do you dare to tell me, ye old black Christian, ye don't *know*?" said Legree.

Tom was silent.

"Speak!" thundered Legree, striking him furiously. "Do you know anything?"

"I know, Mas'r; but I can't tell anything. *I can die!*"

Legree drew in a long breath; and, suppressing his rage, took Tom by the arm, and, approaching his face almost to his, said, in a terrible voice, "Hark 'e, Tom!—ye think, 'cause I've let you off before, I don't mean what I say; but, this time, I've *made up my mind*, and counted the cost. You've always stood it out agin' me: now, I'll *conquer ye; or kill ye!*—one or t'other. I'll count every drop of blood there is in you, and take 'em, one by one, till ye give up!"

Tom looked up to his master, and answered, "Mas'r, if you was sick, or in trouble, or dying, and I could save ye, I'd *give* ye my heart's blood; and, if taking every drop of blood in this poor old body would save your precious soul, I'd give 'em freely, as the Lord gave his for me. O, Mas'r! don't bring this great sin on your soul! It will hurt you more than 't will me! Do the worst you can, my troubles'll be over soon; but, if ye don't repent, yours won't *never* end!"

Like a strange snatch of heavenly music, heard in the lull of a tempest, this burst of feeling made a moment's blank pause. Legree stood aghast, and look at Tom; and there was such a silence, that the tick of the old clock could be heard, measuring, with silent touch, the last moments of mercy and probation to that hardened heart.

It was but a moment. There was one hesitating pause,—one irresolute, relenting thrill,—and the spirit of evil came back, with seven-fold vehemence; and Legree, foaming with rage, smote his victim to the ground.

Scenes of blood and cruelty are shocking to our ear and heart. What man has nerve to do, man has not nerve to hear. What brother-man and brother-Christian must suffer, cannot be told us, even in our secret chamber, it so harrows up the soul! And yet, oh my country! these things are done under the shadow of thy laws! O, Christ! thy church sees them, almost in silence!

But, of old, there was One whose suffering changed an instrument of torture, degradation and shame, into a symbol of glory, honor, and immortal life; and, where His spirit is, neither degrading stripes, nor blood, nor insults, can make the Christian's last struggle less than glorious.

Was he alone, that long night, whose brave, loving spirit was bearing up, in that old shed, against buffeting and brutal stripes?

Nay! There stood by him ONE,—seen by him alone,—"like unto the Son of God."

The tempter stood by him, too,—blinded by furious, despotic will,—every moment pressing him to shun that agony by the betrayal of the innocent. But the brave, true heart was firm on the Eternal Rock. Like his Master, he knew that, if he saved others, himself he could not save; nor could utmost extremity wring from him words, save of prayer and holy trust.

"He's most gone, Mas'r," said Sambo, touched, in spite of himself, by the patience of his victim.

"Pay away, till he gives up! Give it to him!—give it to him!" shouted Legree. "I'll take every drop of blood he has, unless he confesses!"

Tom opened his eyes, and looked upon his master. "Ye poor miserable critter!" he said, "there an't no more ye can do! I forgive ye, with all my soul!" and he fainted entirely away.

"I b'lieve, my soul, he's done for, finally," said Legree, stepping forward, to look at him. "Yes, he is! Well, his mouth's shut up, at last,—that's one comfort!"

Yes, Legree; but who shall shut up that voice in thy soul? that soul, past repentance, past prayer, past hope, in whom the fire that never shall be quenched is already burning!

Yet Tom was not quite gone. His wondrous words and pious prayers had struck upon the hearts of the imbruted blacks, who had been the instruments of cruelty upon him; and, the instant Legree withdrew, they took him down, and, in their ignorance, sought to call him back to life,—as if *that* were any favor to him.

"Sartin, we 's been doin' a drefful wicked thing!" said Sambo; "hopes Mas'r 'll have to 'count for it, and not we."

They washed his wounds,—they provided a rude bed, of some refuse cotton, for him to lie down on; and one of them, stealing up to the house, begged a drink of brandy of Legree, pretending that he was tired, and wanted it for himself. He brought it back, and poured it down Tom's throat.

"O, Tom!" said Quimbo, "we's been awful wicked to ye!"

"I forgive ye, with all my heart!" said Tom, faintly.

"O, Tom! do tell us who is *Jesus*, anyhow?" said Sambo;—"Jesus, that's been a standin' by you so, all this night!—Who is he?"

The word roused the failing, fainting spirit. He poured forth a few energetic sentences of that wondrous One,—his life, his death, his everlasting presence, and power to save.

They wept,—both the two savage men.

"Why did n't I never hear this before?" said Sambo; "but I do believe!—I can't help it! Lord Jesus, have mercy on us!"

"Poor critters!" said Tom, "I'd be willing to bar' all I have, if it 'll only bring ye to Christ! O, Lord! give me these two more souls, I pray!"

That prayer was answered!

XLI. The Young Master

... Tom had been lying two days since the fatal night; not suffering, for every nerve of suffering was blunted and destroyed. He lay, for the most part, in a quiet stupor; for the laws of a powerful and well-knit frame would not at once release the imprisoned spirit. By stealth, there had been there, in the darkness of the night, poor desolated creatures, who stole from their scanty hours' rest, that they might repay to him some of those ministrations of love in which he had always been so abundant. Truly, those poor disciples had little to give,—only the cup of cold water; but it was given with full hearts.

Tears had fallen on that honest, insensible face,—tears of late repentance in the poor, ignorant heathen, whom his dying love and patience had awakened to repentance, and bitter prayers, breathed over him to a late-found Saviour, of whom they scarce knew more than the name, but whom the yearning ignorant heart of man never implores in vain.

Cassy, who had glided out of her place of concealment, and, by overhearing, learned the sacrifice that had been made for her and Emmeline, had been there, the night before, defying the danger of detection; and, moved by the few last words which the affectionate soul had yet strength to breathe, the long winter of despair, the ice of years, had given way, and the dark, despairing woman had wept and prayed.

When George entered the shed, he felt his head giddy and his heart sick.

"Is it possible,—is it possible?" said he, kneeling down by him. "Uncle Tom, my poor, poor old friend!"

Something in the voice penetrated to the ear of the dying. He moved his head gently, smiled, and said,

> "Jesus can make a dying-bed
> Feel soft as downy pillows are."

Tears which did honor to his manly heart fell from the young man's eyes, as he bent over his poor friend.

"O, dear Uncle Tom! do wake,—do speak once more! Look up! Here's Mas'r George,—your own little Mas'r George. Don't you know me?"

"Mas'r George!" said Tom, opening his eyes, and speaking in a feeble voice; "Mas'r George!" He looked bewildered.

Slowly the idea seemed to fill his soul; and the vacant eye became fixed and brightened, the whole face lighted up, the hard hands clasped, and tears ran down the cheeks.

"Bless the Lord! it is,—it is,—it's all I wanted! They have n't forgot me. It warms my soul; it does my old heart good! Now I shall die content! Bless the Lord, oh my soul!"

"You shan't die! you *must n't* die, nor think of it! I've come to buy you, and take you home," said George, with impetuous vehemence.

"O, Mas'r George, ye're too late. The Lord's bought me, and is going to take me home,—and I long to go. Heaven is better than Kintuck."

"O, don't die! It'll kill me!—it'll break my heart to think what you've suffered,—and lying in this old shed, here! Poor, poor fellow!"

"Don't call me poor fellow!" said Tom, solemnly. "I *have* been poor fellow; but that's all past and gone, now. I'm right in the door, going into glory! O, Mas'r George! *Heaven has come!* I've got the victory!—the Lord Jesus has given it to me! Glory be to His name!"

George was awe-struck at the force, the vehemence, the power, with which these broken sentences were uttered. He sat gazing in silence.

Tom grasped his hand, and continued,—"Ye must n't, now, tell Chloe, poor soul! how ye found me;—'t would be so drefful to her. Only tell her ye found me going into glory; and that I could n't stay for no one. And tell her the Lord's stood by me everywhere and al'ays, and made everything light and easy. And oh, the poor chil'en, and the baby!—my old heart's been most broke for 'em, time and agin! Tell 'em all to follow me—follow me! Give my love to Mas'r, and dear good Missis, and everybody in the place! Ye don't know! 'Pears like I loves 'em all! I loves every creatur', everywhar!—it's nothing *but* love! O, Mas'r George! what a thing 't is to be a Christian!"

At this moment, Legree sauntered up to the door of the shed, looked in, with a dogged air of affected carelessness, and turned away.

"The old satan!" said George, in his indignation. "It's a comfort to think the devil will pay *him* for this, some of these days!"

"O, don't!—oh, ye must n't!" said Tom, grasping his hand; "he's a poor mis'able critter! it's awful to think on 't! O, if he only could repent, the Lord would forgive him now; but I'm 'feared he never will!"

"I hope he won't!" said George; "I never want to see *him* in heaven!"

"Hush, Mas'r George!—it worries me! Don't feel so! He an't done me no real harm,—only opened the gate of the kingdom for me; that's all!"

At this moment, the sudden flush of strength which the joy of meeting his young master had infused into the dying man gave way. A sudden sinking fell upon him; he closed his eyes; and that mysterious and sublime change passed over his face, that told the approach of other worlds.

He began to draw his breath with long, deep inspirations; and his broad chest rose and fell, heavily. The expression of his face was that of a conqueror.

"Who,—who,—who shall separate us from the love of Christ?" he said, in a voice that contended with mortal weakness; and, with a smile, he fell asleep.

George sat fixed with solemn awe. It seemed to him that the place was holy; and, as he closed the lifeless eyes, and rose up from the dead, only one thought possessed him,—that expressed by his simple old friend,—"What a thing it is to be a Christian!"

He turned: Legree was standing, sullenly, behind him.

Something in that dying scene had checked the natural fierceness of youthful passion. The presence of the man was simply loathsome to George; and he felt only an impulse to get away from him, with as few words as possible.

Fixing his keen dark eyes on Legree, he simply said, pointing to the dead, "You have got all you ever can of him. What shall I pay you for the body? I will take it away, and bury it decently."

"I don't sell dead niggers," said Legree doggedly. "You are welcome to bury him where and when you like."

"Boys," said George, in an authoritative tone, to two or three negroes, who were looking at the body, "help me lift him up, and carry him to my wagon; and get me a spade."

One of them ran for a spade; the other two assisted George to carry the body to the wagon.

George neither spoke to nor looked at Legree, who did not countermand his orders, but stood, whistling, with an air of forced unconcern. He sulkily followed them to where the wagon stood at the door.

George spread his cloak in the wagon, and had the body carefully disposed of in it,—moving the seat, so as to give it room. Then he turned, fixed his eyes on Legree, and said, with forced composure,

"I have not, as yet, said to you what I think of this most atrocious affair;—this is not the time and place. But, sir, this innocent blood shall have justice. I will proclaim this murder. I will go to the very first magistrate, and expose you."

"Do!" said Legree, snapping his fingers, scornfully. "I'd like to see you doing it. Where you going to get witnesses?—how you going to prove it?— Come, now!"

George saw, at once, the force of this defiance. There was not a white person on the place; and, in all southern courts, the testimony of colored blood is nothing. He felt, at that moment, as if he could have rent the heavens with his heart's indignant cry for justice; but in vain.

"After all, what a fuss, for a dead nigger!" said Legree.

The word was as a spark to a powder magazine. Prudence was never a cardinal virtue of the Kentucky boy. George turned, and, with one indignant blow, knocked Legree flat upon his face; and, as he stood over him, blazing with wrath and defiance, he would have formed no bad personification of his great namesake triumphing over the dragon.

Some men, however, are decidedly bettered by being knocked down. If a man lays them fairly flat in the dust, they seem immediately to conceive a respect for him; and Legree was one of this sort. As he rose, therefore, and brushed the dust from his clothes, he eyed the slowly-retreating wagon with some evident consideration; nor did he open his mouth till it was out of sight.

Beyond the boundaries of the plantation, George had noticed a dry, sandy knoll, shaded by a few trees: there they made the grave.

"Shall we take off the cloak, Mas'r?" said the negroes, when the grave was ready.

"No, no,—bury it with him! It's all I can give you, now, poor Tom, and you shall have it."

They laid him in; and the men shovelled away, silently. They banked it up, and laid green turf over it.

"You may go, boys," said George, slipping a quarter into the hand of each. They lingered about, however.

"If young Mas'r would please buy us—" said one.

"We'd serve him so faithful!" said the other.

"Hard times here, Mas'r!" said the first. "Do, Mas'r, buy us, please!"

"I can't!—I can't!" said George, with difficulty, motioning them off; "it's impossible!"

The poor fellows looked dejected, and walked off in silence.

"Witness, eternal God!" said George, kneeling on the grave of his poor friend; "oh, witness, that, from this hour, I will do *what one man can* to drive out this curse of slavery from my land!"

There is no monument to mark the last resting-place of our friend. He needs none! His Lord knows where he lies, and will raise him up, immortal, to appear with him when he shall appear in his glory.

Pity him not! Such a life and death is not for pity! Not in the riches of omnipotence is the chief glory of God; but in self-denying, suffering love! And blessed are the men whom he calls to fellowship with him, bearing their cross after him with patience. Of such it is written, "Blessed are they that mourn, for they shall be comforted."

1852

from **The Minister's Wooing**

XXIII. Views of Divine Government

[*The Minister's Wooing* is a romance about young Mary Scudder, a devout New England girl who is wooed by three men: Calvinist preacher Samuel Hopkins, the profligate colonel Aaron Burr, and her true love James

Marvyn. But the conventional romance plot provides a backdrop for Stowe's critique of traditional Calvinist doctrine.

The following selection describes the spiritual dilemma at the heart of the novel. News of James Marvyn's death at sea has reached the Marvyns and the Scudders. Mrs. Marvyn is distraught not only because her son is dead, but also because he has died unregenerate, without assurance that he has been saved. Mrs. Marvyn is not comforted by the Calvinist doctrine that has been preached to her by the abstract, highly intellectualized Reverend Hopkins. This doctrine states that the test of regeneration, or salvation, is the willingness to be damned and to undergo tremendous personal trials and self-sacrifice. Those who die unregenerate, and according to Hopkins there are only a few elect, will suffer greatly, sinners in the hands of an angry Edwardsian God.

This key chapter reveals the limitations of Calvinist doctrine as applied to the lives of women, particularly mothers. In its place, Stowe offers an alternative theological possibility, a gospel based on the faith that Jesus Christ died for the sins of all humans and that he is a God of love and mercy. This modern, evangelical model of conversion is preached by Candace, a black servant who shares the name of an African queen, and is grounded in the emotional realities of women's lives and their love for their families. It is this gospel which is finally able to comfort and heal Mrs. Marvyn.]

We have said before, what we now repeat, that it is impossible to write a story of New England life and manners for superficial thought or shallow feeling. They who would fully understand the springs which moved the characters with whom we now associate must go down with us to the very depths.

Never was there a community where the roots of common life shot down so deeply, and were so intensely grappled around things sublime and eternal. The founders of it were a body of confessors and martyrs, who turned their backs on the whole glory of the visible, to found in the wilderness a republic of which the God of Heaven and Earth should be the sovereign power. For the first hundred years grew this community, shut out by a fathomless ocean from the existing world, and divided by an antagonism not less deep from all the reigning ideas of nominal Christendom.

In a community thus unworldly must have arisen a mode of thought, energetic, original, and sublime. The leaders of thought and feeling were the ministry, and we boldly assert that the spectacle of the early ministry of New England was one to which the world gives no parallel. Living an intense, earnest, practical life, mostly tilling the earth with their own hands, they yet carried on the most startling and original religious investigations with a simplicity that might have been deemed audacious, were it not so reverential. All old issues relating to government, religion, ritual, and forms of church organization having for them passed away, they went straight to the heart of things, and boldly confronted the problem of universal being. They had come out from the world as witnesses to the most solemn and sacred of human rights. They had accustomed themselves boldly to challenge and dispute all sham pretensions and idolatries of past ages,—to question the right of kings in the State, and of prelates in the Church; and now they turned the same bold inquiries towards the Eternal Throne, and threw down their glove in the lists as authorized defenders of every mystery in the Eternal Government. The task they proposed to themselves was that of reconciling the most tremendous facts of sin and evil, present and eternal, with those conceptions of Infinite Power and Benevolence which their own strong and generous natures enabled them so vividly to realize. In the intervals of planting and harvesting, they were busy with the toils of adjusting the laws of a universe. Solemnly simple, they made long journeys in their old one-horse chaises, to settle with each other some nice point of celestial jurisprudence, and to compare their maps of the Infinite. Their letters to each other form a literature altogether unique. Hopkins sends to Edwards[1] the younger his scheme of the universe, in which he starts with the proposition, that God is infinitely above all obligations of any kind to his creatures. Edwards replies with the brusque comment,—"This is wrong; God has no more right to injure a creature than a creature has to injure God;" and each probably about that time preached a sermon on his own views, which was discussed by every farmer, in intervals of plough and hoe, by every woman and girl, at loom, spinning-wheel, or wash-tub. New England was one vast sea, surging from depths to heights with thought and discussion on the most insoluble of mysteries. And it is to be added, that no man or woman accepted any theory or speculation simply *as* theory or speculation; all was profoundly real and vital,—a foundation on which actual life was based with intensest earnestness.

The views of human existence which resulted from this course of training were gloomy enough to oppress any heart which did not rise above them by triumphant faith or sink below them by brutish insensibility; for they included every moral problem of natural or revealed religion, divested of all those softening poetries and tender draperies which forms, ceremonies, and rituals had thrown around them in other parts and ages of Christendom. The human race, without exception, coming into existence "under God's wrath and curse," with a nature so fatally disordered, that, although perfect free agents, men were infallibly certain to do nothing to Divine acceptance until regenerated by the supernatural aid of God's Spirit,—this aid being given only to a certain decreed number of the human race, the rest, with enough free agency to make them responsible, but without this indispensable assistance exposed to the malignant assaults of evil spirits versed in every art of temptation, were sure to fall hopelessly into perdition. The standard of what constituted a true regeneration, as presented in such

---

[1]Jonathan Edwards (1703–1758) and Samuel Hopkins (1721–1803)—theologians who had a dramatic influence on New England religious life. Edwards was known for "fire and brimstone" sermons that combined Calvinism with Locke's empiricism. Hopkins's extended study on the New Divinity led him to the doctrine that only those who had experienced religious conversion were redeemed. He was also an outspoken critic of slavery.

treatises as Edwards on the Affections, and others of the times, made this change to be something so high, disinterested, and superhuman, so removed from all natural and common habits and feelings, that the most earnest and devoted, whose whole life had been a constant travail of endeavor, a tissue of almost unearthly disinterestedness, often lived and died with only a glimmering hope of its attainment.

According to any views then entertained of the evidences of a true regeneration, the number of the whole human race who could be supposed as yet to have received this grace was so small, that, as to any numerical valuation, it must have been expressed as an infinitesimal. Dr. Hopkins in many places distinctly recognizes the fact, that the greater part of the human race, up to his time, had been eternally lost,—and boldly assumes the ground, that this amount of sin and suffering, being the best and most necessary means of the greatest final amount of happiness, was not merely permitted, but distinctly chosen, decreed, and provided for, as essential in the schemes of Infinite Benevolence. He held that this decree not only *permitted* each individual act of sin, but also took measures to make it certain, though, by an exercise of infinite skill, it accomplished this result without violating human free agency.

The preaching of those times was animated by an unflinching consistency which never shrank from carrying an idea to its remotest logical verge. The sufferings of the lost were not kept from view, but proclaimed with a terrible power. Dr. Hopkins boldly asserts, that "all the use which God will have for them is to suffer; this is all the end they can answer; therefore all their faculties, and their whole capacities, will be employed and used for this end...... The body can by omnipotence be made capable of suffering the greatest imaginable pain, without producing dissolution, or abating the least degree of life or sensibility...... One way in which God will show his power in punishing the wicked will be in strengthening and upholding their bodies and souls in torments which otherwise would be intolerable."

The sermons preached by President Edwards on this subject are so terrific in their refined poetry of torture, that very few persons of quick sensibility could read them through without agony; and it is related, that, when, in those calm and tender tones which never rose to passionate enunciation, he read these discourses, the house was often filled with shrieks and wailings, and that a brother minister once laid hold of his skirts, exclaiming, in an involuntary agony, "Oh! Mr. Edwards! Mr. Edwards! is God not a God of mercy?"

Not that these men were indifferent or insensible to the dread words they spoke; their whole lives and deportment bore thrilling witness to their sincerity. Edwards set apart special days of fasting, in view of the dreadful doom of the lost, in which he was wont to walk the floor, weeping and wringing his hands. Hopkins fasted every Saturday. David Brainerd[2] gave up

---

[2]David Brainerd (1718–1747)—a missionary to the Indians whose pietistic life, recorded in his journal, inspired others to enter the field.

every refinement of civilized life to weep and pray at the feet of hardened savages, if by any means he might save *one*. All, by lives of eminent purity and earnestness, gave awful weight and sanction to their words.

If we add to this statement the fact, that it was always proposed to every inquiring soul, as an evidence of regeneration, that it should truly and heartily accept all the ways of God thus declared right and lovely, and from the heart submit to Him as the only just and good, it will be seen what materials of tremendous internal conflict and agitation were all the while working in every bosom. Almost all the histories of religious experience of those times relate paroxysms of opposition to God and fierce rebellion, expressed in language which appalls the very soul,—followed, at length, by mysterious elevations of faith and reactions of confiding love, the result of Divine interposition, which carried the soul far above the region of the intellect, into that of direct spiritual intuition.

President Edwards records that he was once in this state of enmity,— that the facts of the Divine administration seemed horrible to him,—and that this opposition was overcome by no course of reasoning, but by an *"inward and sweet sense,"* which came to him once when walking alone in the fields, and, looking up into the blue sky, he saw the blending of the Divine majesty with a calm, sweet, and almost infinite meekness.

The piety which grew up under such a system was, of necessity, energetic,—it was the uprousing of the whole energy of the human soul, pierced and wrenched and probed from her lowest depths to her topmost heights with every awful life-force possible to existence. He whose faith in God came clear through these terrible tests would be sure never to know greater ones. He might certainly challenge earth or heaven, things present or things to come, to swerve him from this grand allegiance.

But it is to be conceded, that these systems, so admirable in relation to the energy, earnestness, and acuteness of their authors, when received as absolute truth, and as a basis of actual life, had, on minds of a certain class, the effect of a slow poison, producing life-habits of morbid action very different from any which ever followed the simple reading of the Bible. They differ from the New Testament as the living embrace of a friend does from his lifeless body, mapped out under the knife of the anatomical demonstrator;— every nerve and muscle is there, but to a sensitive spirit there is the very chill of death in the analysis.

All systems that deal with the infinite are, besides, exposed to danger from small, unsuspected admixtures of human error, which become deadly when carried to such vast results. The smallest speck of earth's dust, in the focus of an infinite lens, appears magnified among the heavenly orbs as a frightful monster.

Thus it happened, that, while strong spirits walked, palm-crowned, with victorious hymns, along these sublime paths, feebler and more sensitive ones lay along the track, bleeding away in life-long despair. Fearful to them were the shadows that lay over the cradle and the grave. The mother clasped her babe to her bosom, and looked with shuddering to the awful coming trial of free agency, with its terrible responsibilities and risks; and, as she thought of the infinite chances against her beloved, almost wished it might die in infancy. But when the stroke of death came, and some young, thoughtless head was laid suddenly low, who can say what silent anguish of loving hearts sounded the dread depths of eternity with the awful question, *Where?*

In no other time or place of Christendom have so fearful issues been presented to the mind. Some church interposed its protecting shield; the Christian born and baptized child was supposed in some wise rescued from the curse of the fall, and related to the great redemption,—to be a member of Christ's family, and, if ever so sinful, still infolded in some vague sphere of hope and protection. Augustine solaced the dread anxieties of trembling love by prayers offered for the dead, in times when the Church above and on earth presented itself to the eye of the mourner as a great assembly with one accord lifting interceding hands for the parted soul.

But the clear logic and intense individualism of New England deepened the problems of the Augustinian faith, while they swept away all those softening provisions so earnestly clasped to the throbbing heart of that great poet of theology. No rite, no form, no paternal relation, no faith or prayer of church, earthly or heavenly, interposed the slightest shield between the trembling spirit and Eternal Justice. The individual entered eternity alone, as if he had no interceding relation in the universe.

This, then, was the awful dread which was constantly underlying life. This it was which caused the tolling bell in green hollows and lonely dells to be a sound which shook the soul and searched the heart with fearful questions. And this it was that was lying with mountain weight on the soul of the mother, too keenly agonized to feel that doubt in such a case was any less a torture than the most dreadful certainty.

Hers was a nature more reasoning than creative and poetic; and whatever she believed bound her mind in strictest chains to its logical results. She delighted in the regions of mathematical knowledge, and walked them as a native home, but the commerce with abstract certainties fitted her mind still more to be stiffened and enchained by glacial reasonings, in regions where spiritual intuitions are as necessary as wings to birds.

Mary was by nature of the class who never reason abstractly, whose intellections all begin in the heart which sends them colored with its warm life-tint to the brain. Her perceptions of the same subjects were as different from Mrs. Marvyn's as his who revels only in color from his who is busy with the dry details of mere outline. The one mind was arranged like a map, and the other like a picture. In all the system which had been explained to her, her mind selected points on which it seized with intense sympathy, which it dwelt upon and expanded till all else fell away. The sublimity of disinterested benevolence,—the harmony and order of a system tending in its final results to infinite happiness,—the goodness of God,—the love of a self-sacrificing Redeemer,—were all so many glorious pictures, which she revolved in her mind with small care for their logical relations.

Mrs. Marvyn had never, in all the course of their intimacy, opened her mouth to Mary on the subject of religion. It was not an uncommon incident of those times for persons of great elevation and purity of character to be familiarly known and spoken of as living under a cloud of religious gloom; and it was simply regarded as one more mysterious instance of the workings of that infinite decree which denied to them the special illumination of the Spirit.

When Mrs. Marvyn had drawn Mary with her into her room, she seemed like a person almost in frenzy. She shut and bolted the door, drew her to the foot of the bed, and, throwing her arms round her, rested her hot and throbbing forehead on her shoulder. She pressed her thin hand over her eyes, and then, suddenly drawing back, looked her in the face as one resolved to speak something long suppressed. Her soft brown eyes had a flash of despairing wildness in them, like that of a hunted animal turning in its death-struggle on its pursuer.

"Mary," she said, "I can't help it,—don't mind what I say, but I must speak or die! Mary, I cannot, will not, be resigned!—it is all hard, unjust, cruel!—to all eternity I will say so! To me there is no goodness, no justice, no mercy in anything! Life seems to me the most tremendous doom that can be inflicted on a helpless being! *What had we done*, that it should be sent upon us? Why were we made to love so, to hope so,—our hearts so full of feeling, and all the laws of Nature marching over us,—never stopping for our agony? Why, we can suffer so in this life that we had better never have been born!

"But, Mary, think what a moment life is! think of those awful ages of eternity! and then think of all God's power and knowledge used on the lost to make them suffer! think that all but the merest fragment of mankind have gone into this,—are in it now! The number of the elect is so small we can scarce count them for anything! Think what noble minds, what warm, generous hearts, what splendid natures are wrecked and thrown away by thousands and tens of thousands! How we love each other! how our hearts weave into each other! how more than glad we should be to die for each other! And all this ends—O God, how must it end?—Mary! it isn't *my* sorrow only! What right have I to mourn? Is *my* son any better than any other mother's son? Thousands of thousands, whose mothers loved them as I love mine, are gone there!—Oh, my wedding-day! Why did they rejoice? Brides should wear mourning,—the bells should toll for every wedding; every new family is built over this awful pit of despair, and only one in a thousand escapes!"

Pale, aghast, horror-stricken, Mary stood dumb, as one who in the dark and storm sees by the sudden glare of lightning a chasm yawning under foot. It was amazement and dimness of anguish;—the dreadful words struck on the very centre where her soul rested. She felt as if the point of a wedge were being driven between her life and her life's life,—between her and her God. She clasped her hands instinctively on her bosom, as if to hold there some cherished image, and said, in a piercing voice of supplication, "My God! *my* God! oh, where art Thou?"

Mrs. Marvyn walked up and down the room with a vivid spot of red in each cheek, and a baleful fire in her eyes, talking in rapid soliloquy, scarcely regarding her listener, absorbed in her own enkindled thoughts.

"Dr. Hopkins says that this is all best,—better than it would have been in any other possible way,—that God *chose* it because it was for a greater final good,—that He not only chose it, but took means to make it certain,—that He ordains every sin, and does all that is necessary to make it certain,—that He creates the vessels of wrath and fits them for destruction, and that He has an infinite knowledge by which He can do it without violating their free agency.— So much the worse! What a use of infinite knowledge! What if men should do so? What if a father should take means to make it certain that his poor little child should be an abandoned wretch, without violating his free agency? So much the worse, I say!—They say He does this so that He may show to all eternity, by their example, the evil nature of sin and its consequences! This is all that the greater part of the human race have been used for yet; and it is all right, because an overplus of infinite happiness is yet to be wrought out by it!—It is *not* right! No possible amount of good to ever so many can make it right to deprave ever so few;—happiness and misery cannot be measured so! I never can think it right,—never!—Yet they say our salvation depends on our loving God,—loving Him better than ourselves,—loving Him better than our dearest friends.—It is impossible!—it is contrary to the laws of my nature! I can never love God! I can never praise Him!—I am lost! lost! lost! And what is worse, I cannot redeem my friends! Oh, I *could* suffer forever,—how willingly!—if I could save *him!*—But oh, eternity, eternity! Frightful, unspeakable woe! No end!—no bottom!—no shore!—no hope!—O God! O God!"

Mrs. Marvyn's eyes grew wilder,—she walked the floor, wringing her hands,—and her words, mingled with shrieks and moans, became whirling and confused, as when in autumn a storm drives the leaves in dizzy mazes.

Mary was alarmed,—the ecstacy of despair was just verging on insanity. She rushed out and called Mr. Marvyn.

"Oh! come in! do! quick!—I'm afraid her mind is going!" she said.

"It is what I feared," he said, rising from where he sat reading his great Bible, with an air of heartbroken dejection. "Since she heard this news, she has not slept nor shed a tear. The Lord hath covered us with a cloud in the day of his fierce anger."

He came into the room, and tried to take his wife into his arms. She pushed him violently back, her eyes glistening with a fierce light. "Leave me alone!" she said,—"I am a lost spirit!"

These words were uttered in a shriek that went through Mary's heart like an arrow.

At this moment, Candace, who had been anxiously listening at the door for an hour past, suddenly burst into the room.

"Lor' bress ye, Squire Marvyn, we won't hab her goin' on dis yer way," she said. "Do talk *gospel* to her, can't ye?—ef you can't, I will."

"Come, ye poor little lamb," she said, walking straight up to Mrs. Marvyn, "come to old Candace!"—and with that she gathered the pale form to her bosom, and sat down and began rocking her, as if she had been a babe. "Honey, darlin', ye a'n't right,—dar's a dreful mistake somewhar," she said. "Why, de Lord a'n't like what ye tink,—He *loves* ye, honey! Why, jes' feel how *I* loves ye,—poor ole black Candace,—an' I a'n't better'n Him as made me! Who was it wore de crown o' thorns, lamb?—who was it sweat great drops o' blood?—who was it said, 'Father, forgive dem'? Say, honey!—wasn't it de Lord dat made ye?—Dar, dar, now ye'r' cryin'!—cry away, and ease yer poor little heart! He died for Mass'r Jim,—loved him and *died* for him,—jes' give up his sweet, precious body and soul for him on de cross! Laws, jes' *leave* him in Jesus's hands! Why, honey, dar's de very print o' de nails in his hands now!"

The flood-gates were rent; and healing sobs and tears shook the frail form, as a faded lily shakes under the soft rains of summer. All in the room wept together.

"Now, honey," said Candace, after a pause of some minutes, "I knows our Doctor's a mighty good man, an' larned,—an' in fair weather I ha'n't no 'bjection to yer hearin' all about dese yer great an' mighty tings he's got to say. But, honey, dey won't do for you now; sick folks mus'n't hab strong meat; an' times like dese, dar jest a'n't but one ting to come to, an' dat ar's *Jesus.* Jes' come right down to whar poor ole black Candace has to stay allers,—it's a good place, darlin'! *Look right at Jesus.* Tell ye, honey, ye can't live no other way now. Don't ye 'member how He looked on His mother, when she stood faintin' an' tremblin' under de cross, jes' like you? He knows all about mothers' hearts; He won't break yours. It was jes' 'cause He know'd we'd come into straits like dis yer, dat he went through all dese tings,—Him, de Lord o' Glory! Is dis Him you was a-talkin' about?—Him you can't love? Look at Him, an' see ef you can't. Look an' see what He is!—don't ask no questions, and don't go to no reasonin's,—jes' look at *Him,* hangin' dar, so sweet and patient, on de cross! All dey could do couldn't stop his lovin' 'em; he prayed for 'em wid all de breath he had. Dar's a God you can love, a'n't dar? Candace loves Him,—poor, ole, foolish, black, wicked Candace,—and she knows He loves her,"—and here Candace broke down into torrents of weeping.

They laid the mother, faint and weary, on her bed, and beneath the shadow of that suffering cross came down a healing sleep on those weary eyelids.

"Honey," said Candace, mysteriously, after she had drawn Mary out of the room, "don't ye go for to troublin' yer mind wid dis yer. I'm clar Mass'r James is one o' de 'lect; and I'm clar dar's consid'able more o' de 'lect dan people tink. Why, Jesus didn't die for nothin',—all dat love a'n't gwine to be wasted. De 'lect is more'n you or I knows, honey! Dar's de *Spirit,*—He'll give it to 'em; and ef Mass'r James *is* called an' took, depend upon it de Lord has got him ready,—course He has,—so don't ye go to layin' on your poor heart what no mortal creetur can live under; 'cause, as we's got to live in dis yer world, it's quite clar de Lord must ha' fixed it so we *can;* and ef tings was as some folks suppose, why, we *couldn't* live, and dar wouldn't be no sense in anyting dat goes on."

The sudden shock of these scenes was followed, in Mrs. Marvyn's case, by a low, lingering fever. Her room was darkened, and she lay on her bed, a pale, suffering form, with scarcely the ability to raise her hand. The shimmering twilight of the sick-room fell on white napkins, spread over stands, where constantly appeared new vials, big and little, as the physician made his daily visit, and prescribed now this drug and now that, for a wound that had struck through the soul.

Mary remained many days at the white house, because, to the invalid, no step, no voice, no hand was like hers. We see her there now, as she sits in the glimmering by the bed-curtains,—her head a little drooped, as droops a snowdrop over a grave;—one ray of light from a round hole in the closed shutters falls on her smooth-parted hair, her small hands are clasped on her knees, her mouth has lines of sad compression, and in her eyes are infinite questionings.

1859

Sojourner Truth, the Libyan Sibyl[1]

Many years ago, the few readers of radical abolitionist papers must often have seen the singular name of Sojourner Truth announced as a frequent speaker at anti-slavery meetings, and as traveling on a sort of self-appointed agency through the country. I had myself often remarked the name, but never met the individual. On one occasion, when our house was filled with company, several eminent clergymen being our guests, notice was brought up to me that Sojourner Truth was below and requested an interview. Knowing nothing of her but her singular name, I went down, prepared to make this interview short, as the pressure of many other engagements demanded.

When I went into the room, a tall, spare form arose to meet me. She was evidently a full-blooded African, and, though now aged and worn with many hardships, still gave the impression of a physical development which in early youth must have been as fine a specimen of the torrid zone as Cumberworth's celebrated statuette of the Negro Woman at the Fountain. Indeed, she so strongly reminded me of that figure, that, when I recall the events of her life, as she narrated them to me, I imagine her as a living, breathing impersonation of that work of art.

I do not recollect ever to have been conversant with any one who had more of that silent and subtle power which we call personal presence than this woman. In the modern spiritualistic phraseology, she would be described as having a strong sphere. Her tall form, as she rose up before me, is still vivid to my mind. She was dressed in some stout, grayish stuff, neat and clean, though dusty from travel. On her head she wore a bright Madras

---

[1]Sojourner Truth (1797?–1883)—evangelist, abolitionist, reformer, and women's rights activist—traveled and spoke out against social injustice from the time of her emancipation in 1826 until her death. See selections earlier in this volume.

handkerchief, arranged as a turban, after the manner of her race. She seemed perfectly self-possessed and at her ease,—in fact, there was almost an unconscious superiority, not unmixed with a solemn twinkle of humor, in the odd, composed manner in which she looked down on me. Her whole air had at times a gloomy sort of drollery which impressed one strangely.

"So this is *you?*" she said.

"Yes," I answered.

"Well, honey, de Lord bless ye! I jes' thought I'd like to come an' have a look at ye. You's heerd o' me, I reckon?" she added.

"Yes, I think I have. You go about lecturing, do you not?"

"Yes, honey, that's what I do. The Lord has made me a sign unto this nation, an' I go round a-testifyin', an' showin' on 'em their sins agin my people."

So saying, she took a seat, and, stooping over and crossing her arms on her knees, she looked down on the floor, and appeared to fall into a sort of reverie. Her great gloomy eyes and her dark face seemed to work with some undercurrent of feeling; she sighed deeply, and occasionally broke out,—

"O Lord ! O Lord! O the tears, an' the groans, an' the moans! O Lord!"

I should have said that she was accompanied by a little grandson of ten years,—the fattest, jolliest woolly-headed little specimen of Africa that one can imagine. He was grinning and showing his glistening white teeth in a state of perpetual merriment, and at this moment broke out into an audible giggle, which disturbed the reverie into which his relative was falling.

She looked at him with an indulgent sadness, and then at me.

"Laws, ma'am, *he* don't know nothin' about it,—*he* don't. Why, I've seen them poor critturs, beat an' 'bused an' hunted, brought in all torn,—ears hangin' all in rags, where the dogs been a-bitin' of 'em!"

This set off our little African Puck into another giggle, in which he seemed perfectly convulsed.

She surveyed him soberly, without the slightest irritation.

"Well, you may bless the Lord you *can* laugh; but I tell you, 'twa'n't no laughin' matter."

By this time I thought her manner so original that it might be worth while to call down my friends; and she seemed perfectly well pleased with the idea. An audience was what she wanted,—it mattered not whether high or low, learned or ignorant. She had things to say, and was ready to say them at all times, and to any one.

I called down Dr. Beecher, Professor Allen, and two or three other clergymen, who, together with my husband and family, made a roomful. No princess could have received a drawing-room with more composed dignity than Sojourner her audience. She stood among them, calm and erect, as one of her own native palm-trees waving alone in the desert. I presented one after another to her, and at last said,—

"Sojourner, this is Dr. Beecher. He is a very celebrated preacher."

"*Is* he?" she said, offering her hand in a condescending manner, and looking down on his white head. "Ye dear lamb, I'm glad to see ye! De Lord bless ye! I loves preachers. I'm a kind o' preacher myself."

"You are?" said Dr. Beecher. "Do you preach from the Bible?"

"No, honey, can't preach from de Bible,—can't read a letter."

"Why, Sojourner, what do you preach from, then?"

Her answer was given with a solemn power of voice, peculiar to herself, that hushed every one in the room.

"When I preaches, I has just one text to preach from, an' I always preaches from this one. *My* text is, 'WHEN I FOUND JESUS.'"

"Well, you couldn't have a better one," said one of the ministers.

She paid no attention to him, but stood and seemed swelling with her own thoughts, and then began this narration:—

"Well, now, I'll jest have to go back, an' tell ye all about it. Ye see, we was all brought over from Africa, father an' mother an' I, an' a lot more of us; an' we was sold up an' down, an' hither an' yon; an' I can 'member when I was a little thing, not bigger than this 'ere," pointing to her grandson, "how my old mammy would sit out o' doors in the evenin', an' look up at the stars an' groan. She'd groan an' groan, an' says I to her,—

"'Mammy, what makes you groan so?'

"An' she'd say,—

"'Matter enough, chile! I'm groanin' to think o' my poor children: they don't know where I be, an' I don't know where they be; they looks up at the stars, an' I looks up at the stars, but I can't tell where they be.

"'Now,' she said, 'chile, when you're grown up, you may be sold away from your mother an' all your ole friends, an' have great troubles come on ye; an' when you has these troubles come on ye, ye jes' go to God, an' He'll help ye.'

"An' says I to her,—

"'Who is God anyhow, mammy?'

"An' says she,—

"'Why, chile, you jes' look up *dar!* It's Him that made all *dem!*'

"Well, I didn't mind much 'bout God in them days. I grew up pretty lively an' strong, an' could row a boat, or ride a horse, or work round, an' do 'most anything.

"At last I got sold away to a real hard massa an' missis. Oh, I tell you, they *was* hard! 'Peared like I couldn't please 'em, nohow. An' then I thought o' what my old mammy told me about God; an' I thought I'd got into trouble, sure enough, an' I wanted to find God, an' I heerd some one tell a story about a man that met God on a threshin'-floor, an' I thought, 'Well an' good, I'll have a threshin'-floor, too.' So I went down in the lot, an' I threshed down a place real hard, an' I used to go down there every day an' pray an' cry with all my might, a-prayin' to the Lord to make my massa an' missis better, but it didn't seem to do no good; an' so says I, one day,—

"'O God, I been a-askin' ye, an' askin' ye, for all this long time, to make my massa an' missis better, an' you don't do it, an' what *can* be the reason? Why, maybe you *can't.* Well, I shouldn't wonder ef you couldn't. Well, now, I tell you, I'll make a bargain with you. Ef you'll help me to git away from my massa an' missis, I'll agree to be good; but ef you don't help me, I really don't think I can be. Now,' says I, 'I want to git away; but the trouble's jest here: ef I try to git away in the night, I can't see; an' ef I try to git away in the daytime, they'll see me, an' be after me.'

"Then the Lord said to me, 'Git up two or three hours afore daylight, an' start off.'

"An' says I, 'Thank 'ee, Lord! that's a good thought.'

"So up I got, about three o'clock in the mornin,' an' I started an' traveled pretty fast, till, when the sun rose, I was clear away from our place an' our folks, an' out o'sight. An' then I begun to think I didn't know nothin' where to go. So I kneeled down, and says I,—

"'Well, Lord, you've started me out, an' now please to show me where to go.'

"Then the Lord made a house appear to me, an' He said to me that I was to walk on till I saw that house, an' then go in an' ask the people to take me. An' I traveled all day, an' didn't come to the house till late at night; but when I saw it, sure enough, I went in, an' I told the folks that the Lord sent me; an' they was Quakers, an' real kind they was to me. They jes' took me in, an' did for me as kind as ef I'd been one of 'em; an' after they'd give me supper, they took me into a room where there was a great, tall, white bed; an' they told me to sleep there. Well, honey, I was kind o' skeered when they left me alone with that great white bed; 'cause I never had been in a bed in my life. It never came into my mind they could mean me to sleep in it. An' so I jes' camped down under it on the floor, an' then I slep' pretty well. In the mornin', when they came in, they asked me ef I hadn't been asleep; an' I said, 'Yes, I never slep' better.' An' they said, 'Why, you haven't been in the bed!' An' says I, 'Laws, you didn't think o' sech a thing as my sleepin' in dat ar *bed*, did you? I never heerd o' sech a thing in my life.'

"Well, ye see, honey, I stayed an' lived with 'em. An' now jes' look here: instead o' keepin' my promise an' bein' good, as I told the Lord I would, jest as soon as everything got a-goin' easy, *I forgot all about God.*

"Pretty well don't need no help; an' I gin up prayin'. I lived there two or three years, an' then the slaves in New York were all set free, an' ole massa came to our house to make a visit, an' he asked me ef I didn't want to go back an' see the folks on the ole place. An' I told him I did. So he said, ef I'd jes' git into the wagon with him, he'd carry me over. Well, jest as I was goin' out to git into the wagon, *I met God!* an' says I, 'O God, I didn't know as you was so great!' An' I turned right round an' come into the house, an' set down in my room; for 't was God all around me. I could feel it burnin', burnin', burnin' all around me, an' goin' through me; an' I saw I was so wicked, it seemed as ef it would burn me up. An' I said, 'Oh,somebody, somebody, stand between God an' me, for it burns me!' Then, honey, when I said so, I felt as it were somethin' like an *amberill* [umbrella] that came between me an' the light, an' I felt it was *somebody*,—somebody that stood between me an' God; an' it felt cool, like a shade; an' says I, 'Who's this that stands between me an' God? Is it old Cato?' He was a pious old preacher; but then I seemed to see Cato in the light, an' he was all polluted an' vile, like me; an' I said, 'Is it old Sally?' an' then I saw her, an' she seemed jes' so. An' then says I, *'Who* is this?' An' then, honey, for a while it was like the sun shinin' in a pail o' water, when it moves up an' down; for I begun to feel 't was some-body that loved me; an' I tried to know him. An' I said, 'I know you! I know you! I know you!'—an' then I said, 'I don't know you! I don't know you! I don't know you!' An' when I said, 'I know you, I know you,' the light came; an' when I said, 'I don't know you, I don't know you,' it went, jes' like the sun in a pail o' water. An' finally somethin' spoke out in me an' said, *'This is Jesus!'* an' I spoke out with all my might, an' says I, *'This is Jesus!* Glory be to God!' An' then the whole world grew bright, an' the trees they waved an' waved in glory, an' every little bit o' stone on the ground shone like glass; an' I shouted an' said, 'Praise, praise, praise to the Lord!' An' I begun to feel sech a love in my soul as I never felt before,—love to all creatures. An' then, all of a sudden, it stopped, an' I said, 'Dar's de white folks, that have abused you an' beat you an' abused your people,—think o' them!' But then there came another rush of love through my soul, an' I cried out loud, 'Lord, Lord, I can love *even de white folks!'*

"Honey, I jes' walked round an' round in a dream. Jesus loved me! I knowed it,—I felt it. Jesus was my Jesus. Jesus would love me always. I didn't dare tell nobody; 't was a great secret. Everything had been got away from me that I ever had; an' I thought that ef I let white folks know about this, maybe they'd get *Him* away,—so I said, 'I'll keep this close. I won't let any one know.'"

"But, Sojourner, had you never been told about Jesus Christ?"

"No, honey. I hadn't heerd no preachin',—been to no meetin'. Nobody hadn't told me. I'd kind o' heerd of Jesus, but thought he was like Gineral Lafayette, or some o' them. But one night there was a Methodist meetin' somewhere in our parts, an' I went; an' they got up an' begun for to tell der 'speriences; an' de fust one begun to speak. I started, 'cause he told about Jesus. 'Why,' says I to myself, 'dat man's found him, too!' An' another got up an' spoke, an' I said, 'He's found him, too!' An' finally I said, 'Why, they all know him!' I was so happy! An' then they sung this hymn" (here Sojourner sang, in a strange, cracked voice, but evidently with all her soul and might, mispronouncing the English, but seeming to derive as much elevation and comfort from bad English as from good):—

> *"There is a holy city,*
> *A world of light above,*
> *Above the stairs and regions,*[2]
> *Built by the God of love.*

> *"An everlasting temple,*
> *And saints arrayed in white*
> *There serve their great Redeemer*
> *And dwell with him in light.*

---

[2]Starry regions.

"The meanest child of glory
    Outshines the radiant sun;
But who can speak the splendor
    Of Jesus on his throne?

"Is this the man of sorrows
    Who stood at Pilate's bar,
Condemned by haughty Herod
    And by his men of war?

"He seems a mighty conqueror,
    Who spoiled the powers below,
And ransomed many captives
    From everlasting woe.

"The hosts of saints around him
    Proclaim his work of grace,
The patriarchs and prophets,
    And all the godly race,

"Who speak of fiery trials
    And tortures on their way;
They came from tribulation
    To everlasting day.

"And what shall be my journey,
    How long I'll stay below,
Or what shall be my trials,
    Are not for me to know.

"In every day of trouble
    I'll raise my thoughts on high,
I'll think of that bright temple
    And crowns above the sky."

I put in this whole hymn, because Sojourner, carried away with her own feeling, sang it from beginning to end with a triumphant energy that held the whole circle around her intently listening. She sang with the strong barbaric accent of the native African, and with those indescribable upward turns and those deep gutterals which give such a wild, peculiar power to the negro singing,—but, above all, with such an overwhelming energy of personal appropriation that the hymn seemed to be fused in the furnace of her feelings and come out recrystallized as a production of her own.

It is said that Rachel was wont to chant the Marseillaise in a manner that made her seem, for the time, the very spirit and impersonation of the gaunt, wild, hungry, avenging mob which rose against aristocratic oppression; and in like manner Sojourner, singing this hymn, seemed to impersonate the fervor of Ethiopia, savage, hunted of all nations, but burning after God in her tropic heart, and stretching her scarred hands towards the glory to be revealed.

"Well, den, ye see, after a while I thought I'd go back an' see de folks on de ole place. Well, you know, de law had passed dat de cullud folks was all free; an' my old missis, she had a daughter married about dis time who went to live in Alabama,—an' what did she do but give her my son, a boy about de age of dis yer, for her to take down to Alabama? When I got back to de ole place, they told me about it, an' I went right up to see ole missis, an' says I,—

"'Missis, have you been an' sent my son away down to Alabama?'

"'Yes, I have,' says she; 'he's gone to live with your young missis.'

"'Oh, missis,' says I, 'how could you do it?'

"'Poh!' says she 'what a fuss you make about a little nigger! Got more of 'em now than you know what to do with.'

"I tell you, I stretched up. I felt as tall as the world!

"'Missis,' says I, '*I'll have my son back agin!*'

"She laughed.

"'*You* will, you nigger? How you goin' to do it? You ha'n't got no money.'

"'No, missis, but *God* has, an' you'll see He'll help me!' An' I turned round, an' went out.

"Oh, but I *was* angry to have her speak to me so haughty an' so scornful, as ef my chile wasn't worth anything. I said to God, 'O Lord, render unto her double!' It was a dreadful prayer, an' I didn't know how true it would come.

"Well, I didn't rightly know which way to turn; but I went to the Lord, an' I said to Him, 'O Lord, ef I was as rich as you be, an' you was as poor as I be, I'd help you,—you *know* I would; and, oh, do help me!' An' I felt sure then that He would.

"Well, I talked with people, an' they said I must git the case before a grand jury. So I went into the town, when they was holdin' a court, to see ef I could find any grand jury. An' I stood round the court-house, an' when they was a-comin' out I walked right up to the grandest-lookin' one I could see, an' says I to him,—

"'Sir, be you a grand jury?'

"An' then he wanted to know why I asked, an' I told him all about it; an' he asked me all sorts of questions, an' finally he says to me,—

"'I think, ef you pay me ten dollars, that I'd agree to git your son for you.' An' says he, pointin' to a house over the way, 'You go long an' tell your story to the folks in that house, an' I guess they'll give you the money.'

"Well, I went, an' I told them, an' they gave me twenty dollars; an' then I thought to myself, 'Ef ten dollars will git him, twenty dollars will git him *sartin.*' So I carried it to the man all out, an' said,—

"'Take it all,—only be sure an' git him.'

"Well, finally they got the boy brought back; an' then they tried to frighten him, an' to make him say that I wasn't his mammy, an' that he didn't know me; but they couldn't make it out. They gave him to me, an' I took him an' carried him home; an' when I came to take off his clothes, there was his poor little back all covered with scars an' hard lumps, where they'd flogged him.

"Well, you see, honey, I told you how I prayed the Lord to render unto her double. Well, it came true; for I was up at ole missis' house not long after, an' I heerd 'em readin' a letter to her how her daughter's husband had murdered her,—how he'd thrown her down an' stamped the life out of her when he was in liquor; an' my ole missis, she giv' a screech an' fell flat on the floor. Then says I, 'O Lord, I didn't mean all that! You took me up too quick.'

"Well, I went in an' tended that poor critter all night. She was out of her mind,—a-cryin,' an' callin' for her daughter; an' I held her poor ole head on my arm, an' watched for her as ef she'd been my babby. An' I watched by her, an' took care on her all through her sickness after that, an' she died in my arms, poor thing!"

"Well, Sojourner, did you always go by this name?"

"No, 'deed! My name was Isabella; but when I left the house of bondage, I left everything behind. I wa'n't goin' to keep nothin' of Egypt on me, an' so I went to the Lord an' asked Him to give me a new name. And the Lord gave me Sojourner, because I was to travel up an' down the land, showin' the people their sins, an' bein' a sign unto them. Afterwards I told the Lord I wanted another name, 'cause everybody else had two names; and the Lord gave me Truth, because I was to declare the truth to the people.

"Ye see, some ladies have given me a white satin banner," she said, pulling out of her pocket and unfolding a white banner, printed with many texts, such as, "Proclaim liberty throughout all the land unto all the inhabitants thereof," and others of like nature. "Well," she said, "I journeys round to camp-meetin's, an' wherever folks is, an' I sets up my banner, an' then I sings, an' then folks always comes up round me, an' then I preaches to 'em. I tells 'em about Jesus, an' I tells 'em about the sins of this people. A great many always comes to hear me; an' they're right good to me, too, an' say they want to hear me agin."

We all thought it likely; and as the company left her, they shook hands with her, and thanked her for her very original sermon; and one of the ministers was overheard to say to another, "There's more of the gospel in that story than in most sermons."

Sojourner stayed several days with us, a welcome guest. Her conversation was so strong, simple, shrewd, and with such a droll flavoring of humor, that the Professor was wont to say of an evening, "Come, I am dull, can't you get Sojourner up here to talk a little?" She would come up into the parlor, and sit among pictures and ornaments, in her simple stuff gown, with her heavy traveling-shoes, the central object of attention both to parents and children, always ready to talk or to sing, and putting into the common flow of conversation the keen edge of some shrewd remark.

"Sojourner, what do you think of Women's Rights?"

"Well, honey, I's ben to der meetings, an' harked a good deal. Dey wanted me fur to speak. So I got up. Says I, 'Sisters, I ain't clear what you'd be after. Ef women want any rights more'n dey's got, why don't dey jes' *take 'em*, an' not be talkin' about it?' Some on 'em came round me, an' asked why

I didn't wear bloomers. An' I told 'em I had bloomers enough when I was in bondage. You see," she said, "dey used to weave what dey called niggercloth, an' each one of us got jes' sech a strip, an' had to wear it width-wise. Them that was short got along pretty well, but as for me"—She gave an indescribably droll glance at her long limbs and then at us, and added, "Tell *you*, I had enough of bloomers in them days."

Sojourner then proceeded to give her views of the relative capacity of the sexes, in her own way.

"S'pose a man's mind holds a quart, an' a woman's don't hold but a pint; ef her pint is *full*, it's as good as his quart."

Sojourner was fond of singing an extraordinary lyric, commencing,—

> *"I'm on my way to Canada,*
> > *That cold but happy land;*
> *The dire effects of slavery*
> *I can no longer stand.*

> *O righteous Father,*
> > *Do look down on me,*
> *And help me on to Canada,*
> > *Where colored folks are free!"*

The lyric ran on to state that, when the fugitive crosses the Canada line,

> *"The Queen comes down unto the shore,*
> > *With arms extended wide,*
> *To welcome the poor fugitive*
> *Safe on to Freedom's side."*

In the truth thus set forth she seemed to have the most simple faith.

But her chief delight was to talk of "glory," and to sing hymns whose burden was,—

> *"O glory, glory, glory,*
> *Won't you come along with me?"*

and when left to herself she would often hum these with great delight, nodding her head.

On one occasion I remember her sitting at a window singing, and fervently keeping time with her head, the little black Puck of a grandson meanwhile amusing himself with ornamenting her red-and-yellow turban with green dandelion curls, which shook and trembled with her emotions, causing him perfect convulsions of delight.

"Sojourner," said the Professor to her one day when he heard her singing, "you seem to be very sure about heaven."

"Well, I be," she answered triumphantly.

"What makes you so sure there is any heaven?"

"Well, 'cause I got such a hankerin' arter it in here," she said, giving a thump on her breast with her usual energy.

There was at the time an invalid in the house, and Sojourner, on learning it, felt a mission to go and comfort her. It was curious to see the tall, gaunt, dusky figure stalk up to the bed, with such an air of conscious authority, and take on herself the office of consoler with such a mixture of authority and tenderness. She talked as from above, and at the same time if a pillow needed changing, or any office to be rendered, she did it with a strength and handiness that inspired trust. One felt as if the dark, strange woman were quite able to take up the invalid in her bosom and bear her as a lamb, both physically and spiritually. There was both power and sweetness in that great warm soul and that vigorous frame.

At length Sojourner, true to her name, departed. She had her mission elsewhere. Where now she is, I know not; but she left deep memories behind her.

To these recollections of my own, I will add one more anecdote, related by Wendell Phillips. Speaking of the power of Rachel to move and bear down a whole audience by a few simple words, he said he never knew but one other human being that had that power, and that other was Sojourner Truth. He related a scene of which he was witness. It was at a crowded public meeting in Faneuil Hall, where Frederick Douglass was one of the chief speakers. Douglass had been describing the wrongs of the black race, and as he proceeded he grew more and more excited, and finally ended by saying that they had no hope of justice from the whites, no possible hope except in their own right arms. It must come to blood; they must fight for themselves, and redeem themselves, or it would never be done. Sojourner was sitting, tall and dark, on the very front seat, facing the platform; and in the hush of deep feeling, after Douglass sat down, she spoke out in her deep, peculiar voice, heard all over the house,—

"Frederick, *is God dead?*"

The effect was perfectly electrical, and thrilled through the whole house, changing as by a flash the whole feeling of the audience. Not another word she said or needed to say; it was enough....

1863

WILLIAM WELLS BROWN
1815–1884

William Wells Brown has been criticized as an early proponent of the assimilationist policies of Booker T. Washington and hailed as black America's first professional man of letters. Despite being an advocate of economic aspirations similar to those of Washington, Brown demonstrated through his outspoken antislavery activity the militance and political shrewdness of Washington's opponent, W.E.B. Du Bois. He published one of the first African American novels, drama, a travel book, and military histories of blacks in the American Revolution, the War of 1812, and the Civil War. Although his writing reflects the sentimental standards of popular midcentury taste, his allegiance to the slave narratives' trope of the flight to freedom, his "worrying" again and again with the figure of the person of mixed blood, his concern with the concept of identity—both in his most famous character, Clotel(le), and in his own life—mark him as the ancestor not only of later writers like Charles Chesnutt but of contemporary black artists.

One way of understanding Brown's contribution to African American tradition is to read his pioneering literary efforts and his work for abolition, temperance, and black education as responses to what was at once a personal and racial imperative. Throughout his life, he was devoted to improving the condition of his people and also, emblematically and materially, to creating a self and a world of possibility for a former slave who never forgot how that "peculiar institution" had operated to limit and dehumanize him. Once released, Brown's Protean energies could not be contained by one literary genre, any more than by one professional career.

William Wells Brown was born the child of a slaveholding father and a slave mother in Kentucky in 1815. His first master, a Dr. Young, for whom he worked as both a house servant and, later, a part-time assistant, hired him out to a Major Freeland when he was around fourteen or fifteen. Freeland treated him so cruelly that, at this early age, Brown made his first escape attempt but was captured with the help of bloodhounds. In 1832, hired out again to James Walker, a slave trader, Brown witnessed many slave auctions, memories of which he drew upon in his subsequent writing.

In 1833 Brown made another escape attempt, this time with his mother, but they were captured after eleven days. His mother was sold down to New Orleans, and he was sold to Samuel Willi, a merchant tailor in Saint Louis. Willi sold Brown to Enoch Price, a Saint Louis commission merchant and steamboat owner, facilitating the young slave's final "leap to freedom": on New Year's Day 1834, Brown escaped in Cincinnati, Ohio. Quickly moving to Cleveland, the nineteen-year-old became a steamboat worker and a barber in the off season. There, the same year, he met and married Elizabeth Schooner and, two years later, settled with his family in Buffalo, New York, a center of antislavery activity. In Buffalo, Brown began the political involvement that was to make him well known among activists in America and abroad. He welcomed antislavery agents into his home and made his house a station on the Underground Railroad. Another social cause attracted him: temperance. He organized one of the first temperance societies in western New York, aiming his efforts particularly at blacks. At the same time, recognizing his need to catch up educationally, he was studying English grammar, mathematics, history, and literature.

In 1847 he launched what was to prove an extraordinarily prolific writing career by publishing the *Narrative* of his own escape from slavery, an autobiography that was to go through at least eight editions at home and abroad. He followed this piece in 1848 with a compilation, *The Antislavery Harp*, of interest not only historically but also for its inclusion of "Jefferson's Daughter," based on the well-known rumor of the sale of Thomas Jefferson's mulatto daughter at a New Orleans slave auction, the apparent inspiration for Brown's subsequent novel.

In 1849 Brown went to Europe as a delegate from the American Peace Society to the Peace Congress in Paris. He moved to London, becoming a journalist on several newspapers, and there, in 1850, commissioned the painting of a series of scenes representative of American slavery.

Because of the passage of the Fugitive Slave Law in 1850, Brown stayed in England longer than he had originally intended. In 1852 he published *Three Years in Europe*, a travel book consisting primarily of letters the author had written to friends and newspapers in America. In 1853 the first version of *Clotel, or The President's Daughter*, was published in London. Brown's British friends purchased his freedom in 1854, and he returned home the same year. After visiting Canada, Brown published a historical study, *The Black Man, His Antecedants, His Genius, and His Achievements*, in 1862.

By 1864, he had begun practicing medicine and opened a doctor's office in Boston. A second historical work, but the first of its kind, *The Negro in the American Rebellion*, appeared in 1867. An 1871 trip to Kentucky on behalf of temperance and black education resulted in Brown's hair-breadth escape from the Ku Klux Klan. His last historical work, which includes a sketch of Frances Harper, *The Rising Son*, was published in 1873; his final book, *My Southern Home*, which appeared in 1880, contains an account of Brown's trip to the South in the winter of 1879–1880 and is notable for its generous inclusion of slave songs and black folk songs of the Reconstruction period. William Wells Brown died in Chelsea, a suburb of Boston, on November 6, 1884.

Brown's *Clotel* was until recently accepted as the first novel written by an American black; it is certainly among the earliest known attempts at a fictional representation of American life from a black viewpoint. First published in London in 1853, the novel, which fiercely attacks slavery, attracted no special attention. When Brown returned to America, perhaps hoping to reach a larger audience, he changed the names of the major characters and made a number of other revisions in the narrative. For example, in *Clotel* the light-skinned heroine's beloved is near-white in appearance, whereas in the revision he is quite dark; thus Brown raises the issue of color preference, a theme frequently encountered in later African American texts. The revised novel, with essentially the same story line, was published as "Miralda; or, the Beautiful Quadroon: A Romance of American Slavery, Founded on Fact," in sixteen front-page installments in the *Weekly Anglo-African* between December 1, 1860, and March 16, 1861. Brown later shortened the novel, no doubt to fit the format of works in the Campfire Series, published by abolitionist James Redpath primarily for sale at ten cents a copy to Union soldiers. With the names of the characters again changed, the third revision, *Clotelle: A Tale of the Southern States*, was brought out by Redpath in 1864 and, simultaneously, in New York by Dexter, Hamilton, and Company. The final version of the story, *Clotelle; or, The Colored Heroine—A Tale of the Southern States*, appeared in 1867; it contains four new chapters in which Brown brought the action up to date, carrying it forward to two years after the Civil War.

Arlene Elder
University of Cincinnati

PRIMARY WORKS

The Travels of William Wells Brown: The Narrative of William Wells Brown, a fugitive slave, and *The American Fugitive in Europe, sketches of places and people abroad,* 1847, 1852, Paul Jefferson, ed., 1991; *Clotel, or The President's Daughter,* 1853, 1969; *Clotelle, or The Colored Heroine,* 1857, 1969.

from **Clotelle; or, The Colored Heroine**

[At this sale, eighteen-year-old Isabella, who will become Clotelle's mother, and her mother and sister are to be sold. Isabella, "admitted by all who knew her to be the handsomest girl, colored or white" in Richmond, will be bought by Henry Linwood who has become attracted to her at one of the city's "negro balls," "usually made up of quadroon women, a few negro men, and any number of white gentlemen."]

Chapter II. The Negro Sale

As might have been expected, the day of sale brought an unusually large number together to compete for the property to be sold. Farmers, who make a business of raising slaves for the market, were there, and slave-traders, who make a business of buying human beings in the slave-raising States and taking them to the far South, were also in attendance. Men and women, too, who wished to purchase for their own use, had found their way to the slave sale.

In the midst of the throng was one who felt a deeper interest in the result of the sale than any other of the bystanders. This was young Linwood. True to his promise, he was there with a blank bank-check in his pocket, awaiting with impatience to enter the list as a bidder for the beautiful slave.

It was indeed a heart-rending scene to witness the lamentations of these slaves, all of whom had grown up together on the old homestead of Mr. Graves, and who had been treated with great kindness by that gentleman, during his life. Now they were to be separated, and form new relations and companions. Such is the precarious condition of the slave. Even when with a good master, there is no certainty of his happiness in the future.

The less valuable slaves were first placed upon the auction-block, one after another, and sold to the highest bidder. Husbands and wives were separated with a degree of indifference that is unknown in any other relation in life. Brothers and sisters were torn from each other, and mothers saw their children for the last time on earth.

It was late in the day, and when the greatest number of persons were thought to be present, when Agnes and her daughters were brought out to the place of sale. The mother was first put upon the auction-block, and sold to a noted negro trader named Jennings. Marion was next ordered to ascend the stand, which she did with a trembling step, and was sold for $1200.

All eyes were now turned on Isabella, as she was led forward by the auctioneer. The appearance of the handsome quadroon caused a deep sensation among the crowd. There she stood, with a skin as fair as most white women, her features as beautifully regular as any of her sex of pure Anglo-Saxon blood, her long black hair done up in the neatest manner, her form tall and graceful, and her whole appearance indicating one superior to her condition.

The auctioneer commenced by saying that Miss Isabella was fit to deck the drawing-room of the finest mansion in Virginia.

"How much, gentlemen, for this real Albino!—fit fancy-girl for any one! She enjoys good health, and has a sweet temper. How much do you say?"

"Five hundred dollars."

"Only five hundred for such a girl as this? Gentlemen, she is worth a deal more than that sum. You certainly do not know the value of the article you are bidding on. Here, gentlemen, I hold in my hand a paper certifying that she has a good moral character."

"Seven hundred."

"Ah, gentlemen, that is something like. This paper also states that she is very intelligent."

"Eight hundred."

"She was first sprinkled, then immersed, and is now warranted to be a devoted Christian, and perfectly trustworthy."

"Nine hundred dollars."

"Nine hundred and fifty."

"One thousand."

"Eleven hundred."

Here the bidding came to a dead stand. The auctioneer stopped, looked around, and began in a rough manner to relate some anecdote connected with the sale of slaves, which he said had come under his own observation.

At this juncture the scene was indeed a most striking one. The laughing, joking, swearing, smoking, spitting, and talking, kept up a continual hum and confusion among the crowd, while the slave-girl stood with tearful eyes, looking alternately at her mother and sister and toward the young man whom she hoped would become her purchaser.

"The chastity of this girl," now continued the auctioneer, "is pure. She has never been from under her mother's care. She is virtuous, and as gentle as a dove."

The bids here took a fresh start, and went on until $1800 was reached. The auctioneer once more resorted to his jokes, and concluded by assuring the company that Isabella was not only pious, but that she could make an excellent prayer.

"Nineteen hundred dollars."

"Two thousand."

This was the last bid, and the quadroon girl was struck off, and became the property of Henry Linwood.

This was a Virginia slave-auction, at which the bones, sinews, blood, and nerves of a young girl of eighteen were sold for $500; her moral character for $200; her superior intellect for $100; the benefits supposed to accrue from her having been sprinkled and immersed, together with a warranty of her devoted Christianity, for $300; her ability to make a good prayer for

$200; and her chastity for $700 more. This, too, in a city thronged with churches, whose tall spires look like so many signals pointing to heaven, but whose ministers preach that slavery is a God-ordained institution!

The slaves were speedily separated, and taken along by their respective masters. Jennings, the slave-speculator, who had purchased Agnes and her daughter Marion, with several of the other slaves, took them to the county prison, where he usually kept his human cattle after purchasing them, previous to starting for the New Orleans market.

Linwood had already provided a place for Isabella, to which she was taken. The most trying moment for her was when she took leave of her mother and sister. The "Good-by" of the slave is unlike that of any other class in the community. It is indeed a farewell forever. With tears streaming down their cheeks, they embraced and commended each other to God, who is no respector of persons, and before whom master and slave must one day appear.

Chapter X. The Quadroon's Home

[Isabella's sister, Marion, aged sixteen, is bought from her original owner by Adolphus Morton, a northerner, opposed to slavery, who marries her and moves to another part of the city, where Marion passes for white. Morton attempts to purchase Isabella's and Marion's mother, Agnes, but she has died of a fever.]

A few miles out of Richmond is a pleasant place, with here and there a beautiful cottage surrounded by trees so as scarcely to be seen. Among these was one far retired from the public roads, and almost hidden among the trees. This was the spot that Henry Linwood had selected for Isabella, the eldest daughter of Agnes. The young man hired the house, furnished it, and placed his mistress there, and for many months no one in his father's family knew where he spent his leisure hours.

When Henry was not with her, Isabella employed herself in looking after her little garden and the flowers that grew in front of her cottage. The passion-flower, peony, dahlia, laburnum, and other plants, so abundant in warm climates, under the tasteful hand of Isabella, lavished their beauty upon this retired spot, and miniature paradise.

Although Isabella had been assured by Henry that she should be free and that he would always consider her as his wife, she nevertheless felt that she ought to be married and acknowledged by him. But this was an impossibility under the State laws, even had the young man been disposed to do what was right in the matter. Related as he was, however, to one of the first families in Virginia, he would not have dared to marry a woman of so low an origin, even had the laws been favorable.

Here, in this secluded grove, unvisited by any other except her lover, Isabella lived for years. She had become the mother of a lovely daughter, which its father named Clotelle. The complexion of the child was still fairer than that of its mother. Indeed, she was not darker than other white children, and as she grew older she more and more resembled her father.

As time passed away, Henry became negligent of Isabella and his child, so much so, that days and even weeks passed without their seeing him, or knowing where he was. Becoming more acquainted with the world, and moving continually in the society of young women of his own station, the young man felt that Isabella was a burden to him, and having as some would say, "outgrown his love," he longed to free himself of the responsibility; yet every time he saw the child, he felt that he owed it his fatherly care.

Henry had now entered into political life, and been elected to a seat in the legislature of his native State; and in his intercourse with his friends had become acquainted with Gertrude Miller, the daughter of a wealthy gentleman living near Richmond. Both Henry and Gertrude were very good-looking, and a mutual attachment sprang up between them.

Instead of finding fault with the unfrequent visits of Henry, Isabella always met him with a smile, and tried to make both him and herself believe that business was the cause of his negligence. When he was with her, she devoted every moment of her time to him, and never failed to speak of the growth and increasing intelligence of Clotelle.

The child had grown so large as to be able to follow its father on his departure out to the road. But the impression made on Henry's feelings by the devoted woman and her child was momentary. His heart had grown hard, and his acts were guided by no fixed principle. Henry and Gertrude had been married nearly two years before Isabella knew anything of the event, and it was merely by accident that she became acquainted with the facts.

One beautiful afternoon, when Isabella and Clotelle were picking wild strawberries some two miles from their home, and near the road-side, they observed a one-horse chaise driving past. The mother turned her face from the carriage not wishing to be seen by strangers, little dreaming that the chaise contained Henry and his wife. The child, however, watched the chaise, and startled her mother by screaming out at the top of her voice, "Papa! papa!" and clapped her little hands for joy. The mother turned in haste to look at the strangers, and her eyes encountered those of Henry's pale and dejected countenance. Gertrude's eyes were on the child. The swiftness with which Henry drove by could not hide from his wife the striking resemblance of the child to himself. The young wife had heard the child exclaim "Papa! papa!" and she immediately saw by the quivering of his lips and the agitation depicted in his countenance, that all was not right.

"Who is that woman? and why did that child call you papa?" she inquired, with a trembling voice.

Henry was silent; he knew not what to say, and without another word passing between them, they drove home.

On reaching her room, Gertrude buried her face in her handkerchief and wept. She loved Henry, and when she had heard from the lips of her companions how their husbands had proved false, she felt that he was an exception, and fervently thanked God that she had been so blessed.

When Gertrude retired to her bed that night, the sad scene of the day followed her. The beauty of Isabella, with her flowing curls, and the look of the child, so much resembling the man whom she so dearly loved, could not be forgotten; and little Clotelle's exclamation of "Papa! papa!" rang in her ears during the whole night.

The return of Henry at twelve o'clock did not increase her happiness. Feeling his guilt, he had absented himself from the house since his return from the ride.

Chapter XI. To-Day a Mistress, To-Morrow a Slave

The night was dark, the rain descended in torrents from the black and over-hanging clouds, and the thunder, accompanied with vivid flashes of light-ning, resounded fearfully, as Henry Linwood stepped from his chaise and entered Isabella's cottage.

More than a fortnight had elapsed since the accidental meeting, and Isa-bella was in doubt as to who the lady was that Henry was with in the car-riage. Little, however, did she think that it was his wife. With a smile, Isabella met the young man as he entered her little dwelling. Clotelle had al-ready gone to bed, but her father's voice aroused her from her sleep, and she was soon sitting on his knee.

The pale and agitated countenance of Henry betrayed his uneasiness, but Isabella's mild and laughing allusion to the incident of their meeting him on the day of his pleasure-drive, and her saying, "I presume, dear Henry, that the lady was one of your relatives," led him to believe that she was still in ignorance of his marriage. She was, in fact, ignorant who the lady was who accompanied the man she loved on that eventful day. He, aware of this, now acted more like himself, and passed the thing off as a joke. At heart, however, Isabella felt uneasy, and this uneasiness would at times show itself to the young man. At last, and with a great effort, she said,—

"Now, dear Henry, if I am in the way of your future happiness, say so, and I will release you from any promises that you have made me. I know there is no law by which I can hold you, and if there was, I would not resort to it. You are as dear to me as ever, and my thoughts shall always be devoted to you. It would be a great sacrifice for me to give you up to another, but if it be your desire, as great as the sacrifice is, I will make it. Send me and your child into a Free State if we are in your way."

Again and again Linwood assured her that no woman possessed his love but her. Oh, what falsehood and deceit man can put on when dealing with woman's love!

The unabated storm kept Henry from returning home until after the clock had struck two, and as he drew near his residence he saw his wife standing at the window. Giving his horse in charge of the servant who was waiting, he entered the house, and found his wife in tears. Although he had never satisfied Gertrude as to who the quadroon woman and child were, he had kept her comparatively easy by his close attention to her, and by telling her that she was mistaken in regard to the child's calling him "papa." His absence that night, however, without any apparent cause, had again aroused the jealousy of Gertrude; but Henry told her that he had been caught in the rain while out, which prevented his sooner returning, and she, anxious to believe him, received the story as satisfactory.

Somewhat heated with brandy, and wearied with much loss of sleep, Linwood fell into a sound slumber as soon as he retired. Not so with Gertrude. That faithfulness which has ever distinguished her sex, and the anxiety with which she watched all his movements, kept the wife awake while the husband slept. His sleep, though apparently sound, was nevertheless uneasy. Again and again she heard him pronounce the name of Isabella, and more than once she heard him say, "I am not married; I will never marry while you live." Then he would speak the name of Clotelle and say, "My dear child, how I love you!"

After a sleepless night, Gertrude arose from her couch, resolved that she would reveal the whole matter to her mother. Mrs. Miller was a woman of little or no feeling, proud, peevish, and passionate, thus making everybody miserable that came near her; and when she disliked any one, her hatred knew no bounds. This Gertrude knew; and had she not considered it her duty, she would have kept the secret locked in her own heart.

During the day, Mrs. Linwood visited her mother and told her all that had happened. The mother scolded the daughter for not having informed her sooner, and immediately determined to find out who the woman and child were that Gertrude had met on the day of her ride. Three days were spent by Mrs. Miller in this endeavor, but without success.

Four weeks had elapsed, and the storm of the old lady's temper had somewhat subsided, when, one evening, as she was approaching her daughter's residence, she saw Henry walking in the direction of where the quadroon was supposed to reside. Being satisfied that the young man had not seen her, the old woman at once resolved to follow him. Linwood's boots squeaked so loudly that Mrs. Miller had no difficulty in following him without being herself observed.

After a walk of about two miles, the young man turned into a narrow and unfrequented road, and soon entered the cottage occupied by Isabella. It was a fine starlight night, and the moon was just rising when they got to their journey's end. As usual, Isabella met Henry with a smile, and expressed her fears regarding his health.

Hours passed, and still old Mrs. Miller remained near the house, determined to know who lived there. When she undertook to ferret out anything, she bent her whole energies to it. As Michael Angelo, who subjected all things to his pursuit and the idea he had formed of it, painted the crucifixion by the side of a writhing slave and would have broken up the true cross for pencils, so Mrs. Miller would have entered the sepulchre, if she could have done it, in search of an object she wished to find.

The full moon had risen, and was pouring its beams upon surrounding objects as Henry stepped from Isabella's door, and looking at his watch, said,—

"I must go, dear; it is now half-past ten."

Had little Clotelle been awake, she too would have been at the door. As Henry walked to the gate, Isabella followed with her left hand locked in his. Again he looked at his watch, and said,—

"I must go."

"It is more than a year since you staid all night," murmured Isabella, as he folded her convulsively in his arms, and pressed upon her beautiful lips a parting kiss.

He was nearly out of sight when, with bitter sobs, the quadroon retraced her steps to the door of the cottage. Clotelle had in the mean time awoke, and now inquired of her mother how long her father had been gone. At that instant, a knock was heard at the door, and supposing that it was Henry returning for something he had forgotten, as he frequently did, Isabella flew to let him in. To her amazement, however, a strange woman stood in the door.

"Who are you that comes here at this late hour?" demanded the half-frightened Isabella.

Without making any reply, Mrs. Miller pushed the quadroon aside, and entered the house.

"What do you want here?" again demanded Isabella.

"I am in search of you," thundered the maddened Mrs. Miller; but thinking that her object would be better served by seeming to be kind, she assumed a different tone of voice, and began talking in a pleasing manner.

In this way, she succeeded in finding out the connection existing between Linwood and Isabella, and after getting all she could out of the unsuspecting woman, she informed her that the man she so fondly loved had been married for more than two years. Seized with dizziness, the poor, heart-broken woman fainted and fell upon the floor. How long she remained there she could not tell; but when she returned to consciousness, the strange woman was gone, and her child was standing by her side. When she was so far recovered as to regain her feet, Isabella went to the door, and even into the yard, to see if the old woman was not somewhere about.

As she stood there, the full moon cast its bright rays over her whole person, giving her an angelic appearance and imparting to her flowing hair a still more golden hue. Suddenly another change came over her features, and her full red lips trembled as with suppressed emotion. The muscles around her faultless mouth became convulsed, she gasped for breath, and exclaiming, "Is it possible that man can be so false!" again fainted.

Clotelle stood and bathed her mother's temples with cold water until she once more revived.

Although the laws of Virginia forbid the education of slaves, Agnes had nevertheless employed an old free negro to teach her two daughters to read and write. After being separated from her mother and sister, Isabella turned her attention to the subject of Christianity, and received that consolation from the Bible which is never denied to the children of God. This was now her last hope, for her heart was torn with grief and filled with all the bitterness of disappointment.

The night passed away, but without sleep to poor Isabella. At the dawn of day, she tried to make herself believe that the whole of the past night was a dream, and determined to be satisfied with the explanation which Henry should give on his next visit.

Chapter XVIII. A Slave-Hunting Parson

It was a delightful evening after a cloudless day, with the setting sun reflecting his golden rays on the surrounding hills which were covered with a beautiful greensward, and the luxuriant verdure that forms the constant garb of the tropics, that the steamer Columbia ran into the dock at Natchez, and began unloading the cargo, taking in passengers and making ready to proceed on her voyage to New Orleans. The plank connecting the boat with the shore had scarcely been secured in its place, when a good-looking man about fifty years of age, with a white neck-tie, and a pair of gold-rimmed glasses on, was seen hurrying on board the vessel. Just at that moment could be seen a stout man with his face pitted with the small-pox, making his way up to the above-mentioned gentleman.

"How do you do, my dear sir? this is Mr. Wilson, I believe," said the short man, at the same time taking from his mouth a large chew of tobacco, and throwing it down on the ship's deck.

"You have the advantage of me, sir," replied the tall man.

"Why, don't you know me? My name is Jennings; I sold you a splendid negro woman some years ago."

"Yes, yes," answered the Natchez man. "I remember you now, for the woman died in a few months, and I never got the worth of my money out of her."

"I could not help that," returned the slave-trader; "she was as sound as a roach when I sold her to you."

"Oh, yes," replied the parson, "I know she was; but now I want a young girl, fit for house use,—one that will do to wait on a lady."

"I am your man," said Jennings, "just follow me," continued he, "and I will show you the fairest little critter you ever saw." And the two passed to the stern of the boat to where the trader had between fifty and sixty slaves, the greater portion being women.

"There," said Jennings, as a beautiful young woman shrunk back with modesty. "There, sir, is the very gal that was made for you. If she had been made to your order, she could not have suited you better."

"Indeed, sir, is not that young woman white?" inquired the parson.

"Oh, no, sir; she is no whiter than you see!"

"But is she a slave?" asked the preacher.

"Yes," said the trader, "I bought her in Richmond, and she comes from an excellent family. She was raised by Squire Miller, and her mistress was one of the most pious ladies in that city, I may say; she was the salt of the earth, as the ministers say."

"But she resembles in some respect Agnes, the woman I bought from you," said Mr. Wilson. As he said the name of Agnes, the young woman started as if she had been struck. Her pulse seemed to quicken, but her face alternately flushed and turned pale, and tears trembled upon her eyelids. It was a name she had heard her mother mention, and it brought to her memory those days,—those happy days, when she was so loved and caressed. This young woman was Clotelle, the granddaughter of Agnes. The preacher, on learning the fact, purchased her, and took her home, feeling that his daughter Georgiana would prize her very highly. Clotelle found in Georgiana more a sister than a mistress, who, unknown to her father, taught the slave-girl how to read, and did much toward improving and refining Clotelle's manners, for her own sake. Like her mother fond of flowers, the "Virginia Maid," as she was sometimes called, spent many of her leisure hours in the garden. Beside the flowers which sprang up from the fertility of soil unplanted and unattended, there was the heliotrope, sweet-pea, and cup-rose, transplanted from the island of Cuba. In her new home Clotelle found herself saluted on all sides by the fragrance of the magnolia. When she went with her young mistress to the Poplar Farm, as she sometimes did, nature's wild luxuriance greeted her, wherever she cast her eyes.

The rustling citron, lime, and orange, shady mango with its fruits of gold, and the palmetto's umbrageous beauty, all welcomed the child of sorrow. When at the farm, Huckelby, the overseer, kept his eye on Clotelle if within sight of her, for he knew she was a slave, and no doubt hoped that she might some day fall into his hands. But she shrank from his looks as she would have done from the charm of the rattlesnake. The negro-driver always tried to insinuate himself into the good opinion of Georgiana and the company that she brought. Knowing that Miss Wilson at heart hated slavery, he was ever trying to show that the slaves under his charge were happy and contented. One day, when Georgiana and some of her Connecticut friends were there, the overseer called all the slaves up to the "great house," and set some of the young ones to dancing. After awhile whiskey was brought in and a dram given to each slave, in return for which they were expected to give a toast, or sing a short piece of his own composition; when it came to Jack's turn he said,—

"The big bee flies high, the little bee makes the honey: the black folks make the cotton, and the white folks gets the money."

Of course, the overseer was not at all elated with the sentiment contained in Jack's toast. Mr. Wilson had lately purchased a young man to assist about the house and to act as coachman. This slave, whose name was Jerome, was of pure African origin, was perfectly black, very fine-looking, tall, slim, and erect as any one could possibly be. His features were not bad, lips thin, nose prominent, hands and feet small. His brilliant black eyes lighted up his whole countenance. His hair which was nearly straight, hung in curls upon his lofty brow. George Combe or Fowler would have selected his head for a model. He was brave and daring, strong in person, fiery in spirit, yet kind and true in his affections, earnest in his doctrines. Clotelle had been at the parson's but a few weeks when it was observed that a mutual feeling had grown up between her and Jerome. As time rolled on, they became more and more attached to each other. After satisfying herself that these two really loved, Georgiana advised their marriage. But Jerome contemplated his escape at some future day, and therefore feared that if married it might militate against it. He hoped, also, to be able to get Clotelle away too, and it was this hope that kept him from trying to escape by himself. Dante did not more love his Beatrice, Swift his Stella, Waller his Saccharissa, Goldsmith his Jessamy bride, or Burns his Mary, than did Jerome his Clotelle. Unknown to her father, Miss Wilson could permit these two slaves to enjoy more privileges than any of the other servants. The young mistress taught Clotelle, and the latter imparted her instructions to her lover, until both could read so as to be well understood. Jerome felt his superiority, and always declared that no master should ever flog him. Aware of his high spirit and determination, Clotelle was in constant fear lest some difficulty might arise between her lover and his master.

One day Mr. Wilson, being somewhat out of temper and irritated at what he was pleased to call Jerome's insolence, ordered him to follow him to the barn to be flogged. The young slave obeyed his master, but those who saw him at the moment felt that he would not submit to be whipped.

"No, sir," replied Jerome, as his master told him to take off his coat: "I will serve you, Master Wilson, I will labor for you day and night, if you demand it, but I will not be whipped."

This was too much for a white man to stand from a negro, and the preacher seized his slave by the throat, intending to choke him. But for once he found his match. Jerome knocked him down, and then escaped through the back-yard to the street, and from thence to the woods.

Recovering somewhat from the effect of his fall, the parson regained his feet and started in pursuit of the fugitive. Finding, however, that the slave was beyond his reach, he at once resolved to put the dogs on his track. Tabor, the negro-catcher, was sent for, and in less than an hour, eight or ten men, including the parson, were in the woods with hounds, trying the trails. These dogs will attack a negro at their master's bidding; and cling to him as the bulldog will cling to a beast. Many are the speculations as to whether the negro will be secured alive or dead, when these dogs once get on his track. Whenever there is to be a negro hunt, there is no lack of participants. Many go to enjoy the fun which it is said they derive from these scenes.

The company had been in the woods but a short time ere they got on the track of two fugitives, one of whom was Jerome. The slaves immediately bent their steps toward the swamp, with the hope that the dogs, when put upon their scent would be unable to follow them through the water.

The slaves then took a straight course for the Baton Rouge and Bayou Sara road, about four miles distant. Nearer and nearer the whimpering pack pressed on; their delusion begins to dispel. All at once the truth flashes upon the minds of the fugitives like a glare of light,—'tis Tabor with his dogs!

The scent becomes warmer and warmer, and what was at first an irregular cry now deepens into one ceaseless roar, as the relentless pack presses on after its human prey.

They at last reach the river, and in the negroes plunge, followed by the catch-dog. Jerome is caught and is once more in the hands of his master, while the other poor fellow finds a watery grave. They return, and the preacher sends his slave to jail.

1867

■ HERMAN MELVILLE ■
1819–1891

When Herman Melville was twelve years old, his merchant father died bankrupt. The tragedy plunged young Herman from the comfortable, patrician world of his Melvill and Gansevoort ancestors into the precarious, drudging world of the sailors, clerks, farm laborers, factory workers, paupers, and slaves who would subsequently people his fiction. Melville's unique perspective on his society derives from his experience of living at the intersection of these opposing worlds.

As the impoverished grandson of two well-connected Revolutionary War heroes—the Brahmin Thomas Melvill, veteran of the Boston Tea Party, and the slaveowning Dutch patroon Peter Gansevoort, defender of Fort Stanwix—Melville acquired a firsthand understanding of what it meant to be excluded from the Revolution's promised benefits. Forced to drop out of school, temporarily after his father's death in 1832, permanently after his elder brother Gansevoort likewise fell victim to bankruptcy in the Panic of 1837, Melville launched on a fruitless search for stable employment, sampling the range of low-paid jobs open to young men with few marketable skills. He worked as a clerk in a bank and in his brother's fur store, as a laborer on his uncle's farm, and as a district schoolteacher in rural Massachusetts and New York, where he boarded with the families of his pupils and found himself defrauded of his salary on his second stint. He studied surveying and engineering, in the vain hope of procuring employment with the Erie Canal's engineering department. Finally, having exhausted all other options, he went to sea as a common sailor, first on a four-month voyage to Liverpool aboard the merchant ship *St. Lawrence* in 1839, then on a three-year voyage to the South Seas aboard a series of whaling ships beginning with the *Acushnet* in 1841.

Ten years later, Melville wrote in *Moby-Dick*, "if, at my death, my executors, or more properly my creditors, find any precious MSS. in my desk, then here I prospectively ascribe all the honor and the glory to whaling; for a whale-ship was my Yale College and my Harvard." Indeed Melville's roving life as a sailor, which provided the material for his first six books, also schooled his imagination. Exposed to brutal working conditions alongside men of all races, Melville learned to identify with slaves and to draw analogies between different forms of oppression. Confronted in the Marquesas, Tahiti, and Hawaii with warships training their guns on naked islanders and "rapacious hordes of enlightened individuals" rushing to seize the "depopulated land" from natives reduced to starving "interloper[s]" in their own country, Melville came to view "the white civilized man as the most ferocious animal on the face of the earth." Above all, a sojourn among one of the peoples his society denigrated as "savages" taught Melville to question his deepest cultural assumptions.

In July 1842, eighteen months of "tyrannical" usage at sea drove Melville and a shipmate named Toby Greene to jump ship at Nukahiva in the Marquesas. Falling into the hands of the Typee tribe, Melville discovered that these reputed cannibals "deal more kindly with each other, and are more humane" than many self-professed Christians. Although Melville chose to escape after four weeks of "indulgent captivity," he would never again take for granted either the superiority of white Christian civilization or the benefit of imposing it on others. Instead he began reexamining his own society through the eyes of "savages."

The Australian whaler *Lucy Ann*, on which Melville left Nukahiva, proved worse than the *Acushnet*, and he ended up embroiled in a mutiny that landed him in a Tahitian jail. Together with another shipmate, John Troy, Melville once more escaped and spent several weeks roaming around Tahiti and nearby Eimeo before shipping aboard the whaler *Charles and Henry*. Discharged in Hawaii, he clerked in a store for two and a half months. Finally, in August 1843, he joined the crew of the homeward bound warship *United States* as an ordinary seaman, arriving in Boston the following October 1844.

It was while narrating his adventures to his family that Melville found the métier he had sought for so long. His first book, *Typee: A Peep at Polynesian Life* (1846), was an instant success, but Melville's American publishers insisted on expurgating his attacks on the missionary and imperialist despoilers of Polynesia. "Try to get a living by the Truth," he would later complain in a famous letter to his friend Nathaniel Hawthorne "—and go to the Soup Societies." Melville wrestled with this dilemma throughout his literary career. His next book, *Omoo* (1847), a fictionalized account of the mutiny aboard the *Lucy Ann* and his ensuing adventures in Tahiti, retracted the concessions he had made to the censors of *Typee* and exposed white depredations in the South Seas more unsparingly than ever. Thereafter, he started experimenting with increasingly elaborate strategies for subverting his readers' prejudices and conveying unwelcome truths.

In 1847 Melville married Elizabeth Shaw, daughter of the Massachusetts Supreme Court's influential chief justice, Lemuel Shaw. A family friend and surrogate father, Shaw also emerged in the controversial Roberts and Sims cases of 1849 and 1851 as a staunch defender of racial segregation and of the infamous Fugitive Slave Law. Family obligations thus added to the pressures impelling Melville toward indirection.

His experimental allegory *Mardi* (1849) combined metaphysical speculation, political satire, and antislavery protest. Melville's public, however, rebelled against his formal innovations, forcing him to return to realistic narrative in *Redburn* (1849) and *White-Jacket: or The World in a Man-of-War* (1850). Based respectively on Melville's voyage to Liverpool and his stint on the frigate *United States*, these two books foreshadowed Melville's brilliant critiques of capitalism, slavery, war, and imperialism in such mature works as "Bartleby," "The Paradise of Bachelors and The Tartarus of Maids," "Benito Cereno," and *Billy Budd*.

The new technique Melville developed of fusing fact and symbol reached fruition in his most powerful and original work, *Moby-Dick* (1851). Conferring epic dignity on a class of men hitherto barred from the purview of literature and elevating their despised occupation, the whale hunt, to mythic stature, *Moby-Dick*'s matchless achievement was to transform the implements, raw materials, and processes of a lucrative, gory industry, which subsisted on the plunder of nature, into rich symbols of the struggle to fulfill humanity's potential under conditions threatening apocalyptic destruction. The book's Shakespearean grandeur, philosophical depth, and daring mixture of genres and forms reflected Melville's omnivorous reading since entering literary circles. Its dedication to Hawthorne, whom he had met while writing *Moby-Dick*, also indicated a debt to the allegorist he had hailed in his review "Hawthorne and His Mosses" (1850) as an American Shakespeare.

Unlike Hawthorne, however, Melville violated his public's literary tastes and offended its religious and political sensibilities. Thus his ambitious epic did not win him the acclaim he hoped for, let alone the financial rewards he needed to support his growing family. In a desperate attempt to recapture the literary marketplace, Melville set out to produce a psychological romance of the type Hawthorne had popularized. Perversely, *Pierre; or, The Ambiguities* (1852) burlesqued the very form it sought to emulate. Featuring incest, satirizing Christianity, lampooning the literary establishment, and even caricaturing Melville's own family, it called down a storm of abuse and convinced many that Melville had gone mad.

With his reemergence as a contributor to two of the period's leading monthly magazines, *Harper's* and *Putnam's*, Melville entered on a new phase of his literary career. Serialized in *Putnam's*, "The Encantadas" (1854), ten bleak sketches of the Galapagos Islands, and *Israel Potter* (1854–1855), a novella that paid homage to the common soldiers who had fought in the American Revolution but never tasted its fruits, marked the transition between Melville's novels and his magazine fiction.

Meanwhile, Melville had begun perfecting a very different literary style, exemplified at its best by "Bartleby" (1853), "Benito Cereno" (1855), and "The Paradise of Bachelors and The Tartarus of Maids" (1855). In these stories, Melville depicted the victims of capitalism and slavery no longer through the eyes of a sympathetic sailor narrator, but through the eyes of an obtuse observer representing the class of "gentlemen" whose smug prosperity rested on the extorted labor of the workers they dehumanized—the class constituting Melville's public and closest associates in the social milieu he had rejoined. Mouthing their racist clichés, mimicking their social snobbery, echoing their pious platitudes, and exposing their sublime obliviousness to the suffering on which they fattened, Melville mercilessly anatomized the readers he had given up hope of converting. Yet he also jarred them out of their complacency through language that insistently provoked discomfort and through the warning vision he held up again and again of the apocalyptic doom overtaking their society.

That vision culminated in *The Confidence-Man: His Masquerade* (1857). An allegorical apocalypse set on April Fools' Day, it imaged nineteenth-century America as a soot-streaked steamer heading down the Mississippi toward the financial capital of slavery, New Orleans, which the passengers have mistaken for the New Jerusalem.

The Confidence-Man and the volume of his *Putnam's* stories that Melville collected in *The Piazza Tales* (1856) were his last published works of prose fiction. By 1856 he had reached a psychological nadir, which his family attributed to the strain of writing. Stepping into the breach, his father-in-law Judge Shaw financed a trip to Europe and the Middle East. On his return in 1857, Melville tried for three years to support his family by lecturing, but he underwent a drawn-out repeat of the demoralizing search for remunerative employment that had driven him to sea. This time the search led in 1866 to a job as a customs inspector, which he held for nineteen years. The decade of trauma took a heavy toll, reaching a new low point in 1867, when Melville's wife Elizabeth considered leaving him, fearing that he had gone insane, and their eldest son Malcolm committed suicide at age eighteen.

Melville's personal crisis converged with the national crisis of the Civil War, which elicited his volume of poetry *Battle-Pieces* (1866), an attempt to speak for all parties to the conflict. In the interstices of his customhouse work, Melville continued to write poetry. *Clarel: A Poem and Pilgrimage in the Holy Land*, articulating the era's religious and political disillusionment, appeared in 1876. Two privately published volumes followed: *John Marr and Other Sailors* (1888) and *Timoleon* (1891).

In 1886, a legacy finally made it possible for Melville to retire from the customhouse. The result was *Billy Budd*, found in manuscript on Melville's death in 1891. Dramatizing the sacrifice of humanity to the god of war, it presciently evoked a world dominated by the forces of militarism and imperialism masquerading as the guardians of peace. Melville dedicated it to his heroic mentor aboard the *United States*, Jack Chase, "a stickler for the Rights of Man, and the liberties of the world."

Melville's critical fortunes have fluctuated strikingly over the past century. Forgotten by the end of his life, he was rediscovered in the 1920s but only as the author of a single masterpiece, *Moby-Dick*. Not until the early 1960s did Melville's short fiction begin to be widely read, anthologized, taught, and interpreted. The critics who first canonized Melville nevertheless abstracted him from his historical context and overlooked his engagement with the political controversies of his era—an engagement that became apparent to a later generation of critics shaped by the political controversies of their own era. Today, critics familiar with the full range of American writing made available by this anthology are once again reexamining Melville's relationship with his culture. Regardless of critical fashion, some readers will always value Melville primarily for his artistry, others for his profound insights into the systems of oppression and violence that governed his world and persist in ours.

Carolyn L. Karcher
Temple University

PRIMARY WORKS

Narrative of a Four Months' Residence among the Natives of a Valley of the Marquesan Islands; Or a Peep at Polynesian Life (London: John Murray, 1846), expurgated and retitled *Typee: A Peep at Polynesian Life* (New York: Wiley & Putnam, 1846); *Moby-Dick; or, The Whale* (New York: Harper & Brothers, 1851); *The Piazza Tales* (New York: Dix and Edwards, 1856); *Billy Budd, Sailor (An Inside Narrative)*, Harrison Hayford and Merton M. Sealts, Jr., eds., (Chicago: University of Chicago Press, 1962); *The Writings of Herman Melville*, Harrison Hayford, Hershel Parker, and G. Thomas Tanselle, eds., (Northwestern University Press and Newberry Library, 1968–; standard edition, in progress, includes Melville's *Journals* and *Correspondence*; volumes containing *Battle-Pieces, Billy Budd*, and Melville's late poetry and prose remain to be published); *The Melville Log: A Documentary Life of Herman Melville*, Jay Leyda, ed., 2 vols., 1951, 1969.

Bartleby, the Scrivener

A Story of Wall-Street[1]

I am a rather elderly man. The nature of my avocations for the last thirty years has brought me into more than ordinary contact with what would seem an interesting and somewhat singular set of men, of whom as yet nothing that I know of has ever been written:—I mean the law-copyists or scriveners. I have known very many of them, professionally and privately, and if I pleased, could relate divers histories, at which good-natured gentlemen might smile, and sentimental souls might weep. But I waive the biographies of all other scriveners for a few passages in the life of Bartleby, who was a scrivener the strangest I ever saw or heard of. While of other law-copyists I might write the complete life, of Bartleby nothing of that sort can be done. I believe that no materials exist for a full and satisfactory biography of this man. It is an irreparable loss to literature. Bartleby was one of those beings of whom nothing is ascertainable, except from the original sources, and in his case those are very small. What my own astonished eyes saw of Bartleby, *that* is all I know of him, except, indeed, one vague report which will appear in the sequel.

Ere introducing the scrivener, as he first appeared to me, it is fit I make some mention of myself, my *employés*, my business, my chambers, and general surroundings; because some such description is indispensable to an adequate understanding of the chief character about to be presented.

Imprimis:[2] I am a man who, from his youth upwards, has been filled with a profound conviction that the easiest way of life is the best. Hence,

---

[1] "Bartleby" was the first short story Melville published (though according to Merton Sealts's chronology of Melville's short fiction, it was the fourth story he wrote). It was serialized in the November and December 1853 issues of *Putnam's Monthly Magazine* and later collected in *The Piazza Tales*, where the subtitle was omitted. The present text is from the standard Northwestern-Newberry edition of *The Piazza Tales and Other Prose Pieces, 1839–1860*.

[2] In the first place: used to introduce the first in a number of items, as in an inventory or will.

though I belong to a profession proverbially energetic and nervous, even to turbulence, at times, yet nothing of that sort have I ever suffered to invade my peace. I am one of those unambitious lawyers who never addresses a jury, or in any way draws down public applause; but in the cool tranquillity of a snug retreat, do a snug business among rich men's bonds and mortgages and title-deeds. All who know me, consider me an eminently *safe* man. The late John Jacob Astor,[3] a personage little given to poetic enthusiasm, had no hesitation in pronouncing my first grand point to be prudence; my next, method. I do not speak it in vanity, but simply record the fact, that I was not unemployed in my profession by the late John Jacob Astor; a name which, I admit, I love to repeat, for it hath a rounded and orbicular sound to it, and rings like unto bullion. I will freely add, that I was not insensible to the late John Jacob Astor's good opinion.

Some time prior to the period at which this little history begins, my avocations had been largely increased. The good old office, now extinct in the State of New-York, of a Master in Chancery,[4] had been conferred upon me. It was not a very arduous office, but very pleasantly remunerative. I seldom lose my temper; much more seldom indulge in dangerous indignation at wrongs and outrages; but I must be permitted to be rash here and declare, that I consider the sudden and violent abrogation of the office of Master in Chancery, by the new Constitution, as a——premature act; inasmuch as I had counted upon a life-lease of the profits, whereas I only received those of a few short years. But this is by the way.

My chambers were up stairs at No.—Wall-street. At one end they looked upon the white wall of the interior of a spacious sky-light shaft, penetrating the building from top to bottom. This view might have been considered rather tame than otherwise, deficient in what landscape painters call "life." But if so, the view from the other end of my chambers offered, at least, a contrast, if nothing more. In that direction my windows commanded an unobstructed view of a lofty brick wall, black by age and everlasting shade; which wall required no spy-glass to bring out its lurking beauties, but for the benefit of all near-sighted spectators, was pushed up to within ten feet of my window panes. Owing to the great height of the surrounding

---

[3]German-born American multimillionaire (1763–1848), who made his vast fortune in the fur trade and in real estate speculation. On his death, he willed $350,000 (out of an estate totaling more than $20 million) to the founding of the New York Public Library. Astor's will had elicited much public comment only five years before the publication of "Bartleby." Stephen Zelnick has described Astor as a hated symbol of monopoly power, political corruption, antidemocratic values, and a new style of capitalist wage slavery. Also relevant, as Mario D'Avanzo has pointed out, is Astor's patronage of literary men, among them Washington Irving, whom he commissioned to write *Astoria*, a history of Astor's fur-trading colony in Oregon.

[4]A lucrative sinecure that guaranteed the Master his fees, regardless of which party won a case. Irving Adler has pointed out that the Court of Chancery, or Equity, was originally established in England "to provide remedies based on natural rights," rather than on "strict adherence to the written law." Its abolition expedited property settlements, but also subordinated natural rights to property rights, a central theme in the story.

buildings, and my chambers being on the second floor, the interval between this wall and mine not a little resembled a huge square cistern.

At the period just preceding the advent of Bartleby, I had two persons as copyists in my employment, and a promising lad as an office-boy. First, Turkey; second, Nippers; third, Ginger Nut. These may seem names, the like of which are not usually found in the Directory. In truth they were nicknames, mutually conferred upon each other by my three clerks, and were deemed expressive of their respective persons or characters. Turkey was a short, pursy[5] Englishman of about my own age, that is, somewhere not far from sixty. In the morning, one might say, his face was of a fine florid hue, but after twelve o'clock, meridian—his dinner hour—it blazed like a grate full of Christmas coals; and continued blazing—but, as it were, with a gradual wane—till 6 o'clock, P.M. or thereabouts, after which I saw no more of the proprietor of the face, which gaining its meridian with the sun, seemed to set with it, to rise, culminate, and decline the following day, with the like regularity and undiminished glory. There are many singular coincidences I have known in the course of my life, not the least among which was the fact, that exactly when Turkey displayed his fullest beams from his red and radiant countenance, just then, too, at that critical moment, began the daily period when I considered his business capacities as seriously disturbed for the remainder of the twenty-four hours. Not that he was absolutely idle, or averse to business then; far from it. The difficulty was, he was apt to be altogether too energetic. There was a strange, inflamed, flurried, flighty recklessness of activity about him. He would be incautious in dipping his pen into his inkstand. All his blots upon my documents, were dropped there after twelve o'clock, meridian. Indeed, not only would he be reckless and sadly given to making blots in the afternoon, but some days he went further, and was rather noisy. At such times, too, his face flamed with augmented blazonry, as if cannel[6] coal had been heaped on anthracite. He made an unpleasant racket with his chair; spilled his sand-box; in mending his pens, impatiently split them all to pieces, and threw them on the floor in a sudden passion; stood up and leaned over his table, boxing his papers about in a most indecorous manner, very sad to behold in an elderly man like him. Nevertheless, as he was in many ways a most valuable person to me, and all the time before twelve o'clock, meridian, was the quickest, steadiest creature too, accomplishing a great deal of work in a style not easy to be matched— for these reasons, I was willing to overlook his eccentricities, though indeed, occasionally, I remonstrated with him. I did this very gently, however, because, though the civilest, nay, the blandest and most reverential of men in the morning, yet in the afternoon he was disposed, upon provocation, to be slightly rash with his tongue, in fact, insolent. Now, valuing his morning services as I did, and resolved not to lose them; yet, at the same time made

---

[5]Short-winded due to obesity.
[6]A bituminous coal, rich in volatile matter, which burns with a very bright flame.

uncomfortable by his inflamed ways after twelve o'clock; and being a man of peace, unwilling by my admonitions to call forth unseemly retorts from him; I took upon me, one Saturday noon (he was always worse on Saturdays), to hint to him, very kindly, that perhaps now that he was growing old, it might be well to abridge his labors; in short, he need not come to my chambers after twelve o'clock, but, dinner over, had best go home to his lodgings and rest himself till tea-time. But no; he insisted upon his afternoon devotions. His countenance became intolerably fervid, as he oratorically assured me—gesticulating with a long ruler at the other end of the room—that if his services in the morning were useful, how indispensable, then, in the afternoon?

"With submission, sir," said Turkey on this occasion, "I consider myself your right-hand man. In the morning I but marshal and deploy my columns; but in the afternoon I put myself at their head, and gallantly charge the foe, thus!"—and he made a violent thrust with the ruler.

"But the blots, Turkey," intimated I.

"True,—but, with submission, sir, behold these hairs! I am getting old. Surely, sir, a blot or two of a warm afternoon is not to be severely urged against gray hairs. Old age—even if it blot the page—is honorable. With submission, sir, we *both* are getting old."

This appeal to my fellow-feeling was hardly to be resisted. At all events, I saw that go he would not. So I made up my mind to let him stay, resolving, nevertheless, to see to it, that during the afternoon he had to do with my less important papers.

Nippers, the second on my list, was a whiskered, sallow, and, upon the whole, rather piratical-looking young man of about five and twenty. I always deemed him the victim of two evil powers—ambition and indigestion. The ambition was evinced by a certain impatience of the duties of a mere copyist, an unwarrantable usurpation of strictly professional affairs, such as the original drawing up of legal documents. The indigestion seemed betokened in an occasional nervous testiness and grinning irritability, causing the teeth to audibly grind together over mistakes committed in copying; unnecessary maledictions, hissed, rather than spoken, in the heat of business; and especially by a continual discontent with the height of the table where he worked. Though of a very ingenious mechanical turn, Nippers could never get this table to suit him. He put chips under it, blocks of various sorts, bits of pasteboard, and at last went so far as to attempt an exquisite adjustment by final pieces of folding blotting-paper. But no invention would answer. If, for the sake of easing his back, he brought the table lid at a sharp angle well up towards his chin, and wrote there like a man using the steep roof of a Dutch house for his desk:—then he declared that it stopped the circulation in his arms. If now he lowered the table to his waistbands, and stooped over it in writing, then there was a sore aching in his back. In short, the truth of the matter was, Nippers knew not what he wanted. Or, if he wanted any thing, it was to be rid of a scrivener's table altogether. Among the manifestations of his diseased ambition was a fondness he had for receiving visits from certain ambiguous-looking fellows in seedy coats, whom he called his clients. Indeed I was aware that not only was he, at times, considerable of a ward-politician, but he occasionally did a little business at the Justices' courts, and was not unknown on the steps of the Tombs.[7] I have good reason to believe, however, that one individual who called upon him at my chambers, and who, with a grand air, he insisted was his client, was no other than a dun,[8] and the alleged title-deed, a bill. But with all his failings, and the annoyances he caused me, Nippers, like his compatriot Turkey, was a very useful man to me; wrote a neat, swift hand; and, when he chose, was not deficient in a gentlemanly sort of deportment. Added to this, he always dressed in a gentlemanly sort of way; and so, incidentally, reflected credit upon my chambers. Whereas with respect to Turkey, I had much ado to keep him from being a reproach to me. His clothes were apt to look oily and smell of eating-houses. He wore his pantaloons very loose and baggy in summer. His coats were execrable; his hat not to be handled. But while the hat was a thing of indifference to me, inasmuch as his natural civility and deference, as a dependent Englishman, always led him to doff it the moment he entered the room, yet his coat was another matter. Concerning his coats, I reasoned with him; but with no effect. The truth was, I suppose, that a man with so small an income, could not afford to sport such a lustrous face and a lustrous coat at one and the same time. As Nippers once observed, Turkey's money went chiefly for red ink. One winter day I presented Turkey with a highly-respectable looking coat of my own, a padded gray coat, of a most comfortable warmth, and which buttoned straight up from the knee to the neck. I thought Turkey would appreciate the favor, and abate his rashness and obstreperousness of afternoons. But no. I verily believe that buttoning himself up in so downy and blanket-like a coat had a pernicious effect upon him; upon the same principle that too much oats are bad for horses. In fact, precisely as a rash, restive horse is said to feel his oats, so Turkey felt his coat. It made him insolent. He was a man whom prosperity harmed.

Though concerning the self-indulgent habits of Turkey I had my own private surmises, yet touching Nippers I was well persuaded that whatever might be his faults in other respects, he was, at least, a temperate young man. But indeed, nature herself seemed to have been his vintner, and at his birth charged him so thoroughly with an irritable, brandy-like disposition, that all subsequent potations were needless. When I consider how, amid the stillness of my chambers, Nippers would sometimes impatiently rise from his seat, and stooping over his table, spread his arms wide apart, seize the whole desk, and move it, and jerk it, with a grim, grinding motion on the floor, as if the table were a perverse voluntary agent, intent on thwarting

---

[7]In short, Nippers is acting as a lawyer for the poor, the most numerous class held in the Tombs, the New York prison built in 1839. The Tombs received its name from the Egyp- tian tomb architecture it imitated, a style known as Egyptian Revival.

[8]An importunate creditor or agent employed to collect debts.

and vexing him; I plainly perceive that for Nippers, brandy and water were altogether superfluous.

It was fortunate for me that, owing to its peculiar cause—indigestion—the irritability and consequent nervousness of Nippers, were mainly observable in the morning, while in the afternoon he was comparatively mild. So that Turkey's paroxysms only coming on about twelve o'clock, I never had to do with their eccentricities at one time. Their fits relieved each other like guards. When Nippers' was on, Turkey's was off; and *vice versa*. This was a good natural arrangement under the circumstances.

Ginger Nut, the third on my list, was a lad some twelve years old. His father was a carman,[9] ambitious of seeing his son on the bench instead of a cart, before he died. So he sent him to my office as student at law, errand boy, and cleaner and sweeper, at the rate of one dollar a week. He had a little desk to himself, but he did not use it much. Upon inspection, the drawer exhibited a great array of the shells of various sorts of nuts. Indeed, to this quick-witted youth the whole noble science of the law was contained in a nut-shell. Not the least among the employments of Ginger Nut, as well as one which he discharged with the most alacrity, was his duty as cake and apple purveyor for Turkey and Nippers. Copying law papers being proverbially a dry, husky sort of business, my two scriveners were fain to moisten their mouths very often with Spitzenbergs[10] to be had at the numerous stalls nigh the Custom House and Post Office. Also, they sent Ginger Nut very frequently for that peculiar cake—small, flat, round, and very spicy—after which he had been named by them. Of a cold morning when business was but dull, Turkey would gobble up scores of these cakes, as if they were mere wafers—indeed they sell them at the rate of six or eight for a penny—the scrape of his pen blending with the crunching of the crisp particles in his mouth. Of all the fiery afternoon blunders and flurried rashnesses of Turkey, was his once moistening a ginger-cake between his lips, and clapping it on to a mortgage for a seal. I came within an ace of dismissing him then. But he mollified me by making an oriental bow, and saying—"With submission, sir, it was generous of me to find you in stationery on my own account."

Now my original business—that of a conveyancer[11] and title hunter, and drawer-up of recondite documents of all sorts—was considerably increased by receiving the master's office. There was now great work for scriveners. Not only must I push the clerks already with me, but I must have additional help. In answer to my advertisement, a motionless young man one morning, stood upon my office threshold, the door being open, for it was summer. I can see that figure now—pallidly neat, pitiably respectable, incurably forlorn! It was Bartleby.

[9]Carter, teamster.
[10]A variety of apple.
[11]A lawyer who prepares documents for the conveyance (transfer) of property and who investigates titles to property.

After a few words touching his qualifications, I engaged him, glad to have among my corps of copyists a man of so singularly sedate an aspect, which I thought might operate beneficially upon the flighty temper of Turkey, and the fiery one of Nippers.

I should have stated before that ground glass folding-doors divided my premises into two parts, one of which was occupied by my scriveners, the other by myself. According to my humor I threw open these doors, or closed them. I resolved to assign Bartleby a corner by the folding-doors, but on my side of them, so as to have this quiet man within easy call, in case any trifling thing was to be done. I placed his desk close up to a small side-window in that part of the room, a window which originally had afforded a lateral view of certain grimy back-yards and bricks, but which, owing to subsequent erections, commanded at present no view at all, though it gave some light. Within three feet of the panes was a wall, and the light came down from far above, between two lofty buildings, as from a very small opening in a dome. Still further to a satisfactory arrangement, I procured a high green folding screen, which might entirely isolate Bartleby from my sight, though not remove him from my voice. And thus, in a manner, privacy and society were conjoined.

At first Bartleby did an extraordinary quantity of writing. As if long famishing for something to copy, he seemed to gorge himself on my documents. There was no pause for digestion. He ran a day and night line, copying by sun-light and by candle-light. I should have been quite delighted with his application, had he been cheerfully industrious. But he wrote on silently, palely, mechanically.

It is, of course, an indispensable part of a scrivener's business to verify the accuracy of his copy, word by word. Where there are two or more scriveners in an office, they assist each other in this examination, one reading from the copy, the other holding the original. It is a very dull, wearisome, and lethargic affair. I can readily imagine that to some sanguine temperaments it would be altogether intolerable. For example, I cannot credit that the mettlesome poet Byron would have contentedly sat down with Bartleby to examine a law document of, say five hundred pages, closely written in a crimpy hand.

Now and then, in the haste of business, it had been my habit to assist in comparing some brief document myself, calling Turkey or Nippers for this purpose. One object I had in placing Bartleby so handy to me behind the screen, was to avail myself of his services on such trivial occasions. It was on the third day, I think, of his being with me, and before any necessity had arisen for having his own writing examined, that, being much hurried to complete a small affair I had in hand, I abruptly called to Bartleby. In my haste and natural expectancy of instant compliance, I sat with my head bent over the original on my desk, and my right hand sideways, and somewhat nervously extended with the copy, so that immediately upon emerging from his retreat, Bartleby might snatch it and proceed to business without the least delay.

In this very attitude did I sit when I called to him, rapidly stating what it was I wanted him to do—namely, to examine a small paper with me. Imagine my surprise, nay, my consternation, when without moving from his privacy, Bartleby in a singularly mild, firm voice, replied, "I would prefer not to."

I sat awhile in perfect silence, rallying my stunned faculties. Immediately it occurred to me that my ears had deceived me, or Bartleby had entirely misunderstood my meaning. I repeated my request in the clearest tone I could assume. But in quite as clear a one came the previous reply, "I would prefer not to."

"Prefer not to," echoed I, rising in high excitement, and crossing the room with a stride. "What do you mean? Are you moon-struck? I want you to help me compare this sheet here—take it," and I thrust it towards him.

"I would prefer not to," said he.

I looked at him steadfastly. His face was leanly composed; his gray eye dimly calm. Not a wrinkle of agitation rippled him. Had there been the least uneasiness, anger, impatience or impertinence in his manner; in other words, had there been any thing ordinarily human about him, doubtless I should have violently dismissed him from the premises. But as it was, I should have as soon thought of turning my pale plaster-of-paris bust of Cicero out of doors. I stood gazing at him awhile, as he went on with his own writing, and then reseated myself at my desk. This is very strange, thought I. What had one best do? But my business hurried me. I concluded to forget the matter for the present, reserving it for my future leisure. So calling Nippers from the other room, the paper was speedily examined.

A few days after this, Bartleby concluded four lengthy documents, being quadruplicates of a week's testimony taken before me in my High Court of Chancery. It became necessary to examine them. It was an important suit, and great accuracy was imperative. Having all things arranged I called Turkey, Nippers and Ginger Nut from the next room, meaning to place the four copies in the hands of my four clerks, while I should read from the original. Accordingly, Turkey, Nippers and Ginger Nut had taken their seats in a row, each with his document in hand, when I called to Bartleby to join this interesting group.

"Bartleby! quick, I am waiting."

I heard a slow scrape of his chair legs on the uncarpeted floor, and soon he appeared standing at the entrance of his hermitage.

"What is wanted?" said he mildly.

"The copies, the copies," said I hurriedly. "We are going to examine them. There"—and I held towards him the fourth quadruplicate.

"I would prefer not to," he said, and gently disappeared behind the screen.

For a few moments I was turned into a pillar of salt,[12] standing at the head of my seated column of clerks. Recovering myself, I advanced towards the screen, and demanded the reason for such extraordinary conduct.

---

[12] In Genesis 19:26, God turns Lot's wife into a pillar of salt when she disobeys the command not to look back toward her home, the city of Sodom, destroyed for its wicked-ness. Ironically, here it is the narrator, and not the disobedient Bartleby, who has been turned into a pillar of salt.

"*Why* do you refuse?"

"I would prefer not to."

With any other man I should have flown outright into a dreadful passion, scorned all further words, and thrust him ignominiously from my presence. But there was something about Bartleby that not only strangely disarmed me, but in a wonderful manner touched and disconcerted me. I began to reason with him.

"These are your own copies we are about to examine. It is labor saving to you, because one examination will answer for your four papers. It is common usage. Every copyist is bound to help examine his copy. Is it not so? Will you not speak? Answer!"

"I prefer not to," he replied in a flute-like tone. It seemed to me that while I had been addressing him, he carefully revolved every statement that I made; fully comprehended the meaning; could not gainsay the irresistible conclusion; but, at the same time, some paramount consideration prevailed with him to reply as he did.

"You are decided, then, not to comply with my request—a request made according to common usage and common sense?"

He briefly gave me to understand that on that point my judgment was sound. Yes: his decision was irreversible.

It is not seldom the case that when a man is browbeaten in some unprecedented and violently unreasonable way, he begins to stagger in his own plainest faith. He begins, as it were, vaguely to surmise that, wonderful as it may be, all the justice and all the reason is on the other side. Accordingly, if any disinterested persons are present, he turns to them for some reinforcement for his own faltering mind.

"Turkey," said I, "what do you think of this? Am I not right?"

"With submission, sir," said Turkey, with his blandest tone, "I think that you are."

"Nippers," said I, "what do *you* think of it?"

"I think I should kick him out of the office."

(The reader of nice perceptions will here perceive that, it being morning, Turkey's answer is couched in polite and tranquil terms, but Nippers replies in ill-tempered ones. Or, to repeat a previous sentence, Nippers's ugly mood was on duty, and Turkey's off.)

"Ginger Nut," said I, willing to enlist the smallest suffrage in my behalf, "what do *you* think of it?"

"I think, sir, he's a little *luny*," replied Ginger Nut, with a grin.

"You hear what they say," said I, turning towards the screen, "come forth and do your duty."

But he vouchsafed no reply. I pondered a moment in sore perplexity. But once more business hurried me. I determined again to postpone the consideration of this dilemma to my future leisure. With a little trouble we made out to examine the papers without Bartleby, though at every page or two, Turkey deferentially dropped his opinion that this proceeding was quite out of the common; while Nippers, twitching in his chair with a dyspeptic nervousness, ground out between his set teeth occasional hissing maledictions against the stubborn oaf behind the screen. And for his (Nippers's) part, this was the first and the last time he would do another man's business without pay.

Meanwhile Bartleby sat in his hermitage, oblivious to every thing but his own peculiar business there.

Some days passed, the scrivener being employed upon another lengthy work. His late remarkable conduct led me to regard his ways narrowly. I observed that he never went to dinner; indeed that he never went any where. As yet I had never of my personal knowledge known him to be outside of my office. He was a perpetual sentry in the corner. At about eleven o'clock though, in the morning, I noticed that Ginger Nut would advance toward the opening in Bartleby's screen, as if silently beckoned thither by a gesture invisible to me where I sat. The boy would then leave the office jingling a few pence, and reappear with a handful of ginger-nuts which he delivered in the hermitage, receiving two of the cakes for his trouble.

He lives, then, on ginger-nuts, thought I; never eats a dinner, properly speaking; he must be a vegetarian then; but no; he never eats even vegetables, he eats nothing but ginger-nuts. My mind then ran on in reveries concerning the probable effects upon the human constitution of living entirely on ginger-nuts. Ginger-nuts are so called because they contain ginger as one of their peculiar constituents, and the final flavoring one. Now what was ginger? A hot, spicy thing. Was Bartleby hot and spicy? Not at all. Ginger, then, had no effect upon Bartleby. Probably he preferred it should have none.

Nothing so aggravates an earnest person as a passive resistance. If the individual so resisted be of a not inhumane temper, and the resisting one perfectly harmless in his passivity; then, in the better moods of the former, he will endeavor charitably to construe to his imagination what proves impossible to be solved by his judgment. Even so, for the most part, I regarded Bartleby and his ways. Poor fellow! thought I, he means no mischief; it is plain he intends no insolence; his aspect sufficiently evinces that his eccentricities are involuntary. He is useful to me. I can get along with him. If I turn him away, the chances are he will fall in with some less indulgent employer, and then he will be rudely treated, and perhaps driven forth miserably to starve. Yes. Here I can cheaply purchase a delicious self-approval. To befriend Bartleby; to humor him in his strange wilfulness, will cost me little or nothing, while I lay up in my soul what will eventually prove a sweet morsel for my conscience. But this mood was not invariable with me. The passiveness of Bartleby sometimes irritated me. I felt strangely goaded on to encounter him in new opposition, to elicit some angry spark from him answerable to my own. But indeed I might as well have essayed to strike fire with my knuckles against a bit of Windsor soap. But one afternoon the evil impulse in me mastered me, and the following little scene ensued:

"Bartleby," said I, "when those papers are all copied, I will compare them with you."

"I would prefer not to."

"How? Surely you do not mean to persist in that mulish vagary?"

No answer.

I threw open the folding-doors near by, and turning upon Turkey and Nippers, exclaimed:

"Bartleby a second time says, he won't examine his papers. What do you think of it, Turkey?"

It was afternoon, be it remembered. Turkey sat glowing like a brass boiler, his bald head steaming, his hands reeling among his blotted papers.

"Think of it?" roared Turkey; "I think I'll just step behind his screen, and black his eyes for him!"

So saying, Turkey rose to his feet and threw his arms into a pugilistic position. He was hurrying away to make good his promise, when I detained him, alarmed at the effect of incautiously rousing Turkey's combativeness after dinner.

"Sit down, Turkey," said I, "and hear what Nippers has to say. What do you think of it, Nippers? Would I not be justified in immediately dismissing Bartleby?"

"Excuse me, that is for you to decide, sir. I think his conduct quite unusual, and indeed unjust, as regards Turkey and myself. But it may only be a passing whim."

"Ah," exclaimed I, "you have strangely changed your mind then—you speak very gently of him now."

"All beer," cried Turkey; "gentleness is effects of beer—Nippers and I dined together to-day. You see how gentle I am, sir. Shall I go and black his eyes?"

"You refer to Bartleby, I suppose. No, not to-day, Turkey," I replied; "pray, put up your fists."

I closed the doors, and again advanced towards Bartleby. I felt additional incentives tempting me to my fate. I burned to be rebelled against again. I remembered that Bartleby never left the office.

"Bartleby," said I, "Ginger Nut is away; just step round to the Post Office, won't you? (it was but a three minutes walk,) and see if there is any thing for me."

"I would prefer not to."

"You will not?"

"I prefer not."

I staggered to my desk, and sat there in a deep study. My blind inveteracy returned. Was there any other thing in which I could procure myself to be ignominiously repulsed by this lean, penniless wight?—my hired clerk? What added thing is there, perfectly reasonable, that he will be sure to refuse to do?

"Bartleby!"

No answer.

"Bartleby," in a louder tone.

No answer.

"Bartleby," I roared.

Like a very ghost, agreeably to the laws of magical invocation, at the third summons, he appeared at the entrance of his hermitage.

"Go to the next room, and tell Nippers to come to me."

"I prefer not to," he respectfully and slowly said, and mildly disappeared.

"Very good, Bartleby," said I, in a quiet sort of serenely severe self-possessed tone, intimating the unalterable purpose of some terrible retribution very close at hand. At the moment I half intended something of the kind. But upon the whole, as it was drawing towards my dinner-hour, I thought it best to put on my hat and walk home for the day, suffering much from perplexity and distress of mind.

Shall I acknowledge it? The conclusion of this whole business was, that it soon became a fixed fact of my chambers, that a pale young scrivener, by the name of Bartleby, had a desk there; that he copied for me at the usual rate of four cents a folio (one hundred words); but he was permanently exempt from examining the work done by him, that duty being transferred to Turkey and Nippers, out of compliment doubtless to their superior acuteness; moreover, said Bartleby was never on any account to be dispatched on the most trivial errand of any sort; and that even if entreated to take upon him such a matter, it was generally understood that he would prefer not to—in other words, that he would refuse point-blank.

As days passed on, I became considerably reconciled to Bartleby. His steadiness, his freedom from all dissipation, his incessant industry (except when he chose to throw himself into a standing revery behind his screen), his great stillness, his unalterableness of demeanor under all circumstances, made him a valuable acquisition. One prime thing was this,—*he was always there;*—first in the morning, continually through the day, and the last at night. I had a singular confidence in his honesty. I felt my most precious papers perfectly safe in his hands. Sometimes to be sure I could not, for the very soul of me, avoid falling into sudden spasmodic passions with him. For it was exceeding difficult to bear in mind all the time those strange peculiarities, privileges, and unheard of exemptions, forming the tacit stipulations on Bartleby's part under which he remained in my office. Now and then, in the eagerness of dispatching pressing business, I would inadvertently summon Bartleby, in a short, rapid tone, to put his finger, say, on the incipient tie of a bit of red tape with which I was about compressing some papers. Of course, from behind the screen the usual answer, "I prefer not to," was sure to come; and then, how could a human creature with the common infirmities of our nature, refrain from bitterly exclaiming upon such perverseness—such unreasonableness. However, every added repulse of this sort which I received only tended to lessen the probability of my repeating the inadvertence.

Here it must be said, that according to the custom of most legal gentlemen occupying chambers in densely-populated law buildings, there were several keys to my door. One was kept by a woman residing in the attic, which person weekly scrubbed and daily swept and dusted my apartments. Another was kept by Turkey for convenience sake. The third I sometimes carried in my own pocket. The fourth I knew not who had.

Now, one Sunday morning I happened to go to Trinity Church, to hear a celebrated preacher, and finding myself rather early on the ground, I thought I would walk round to my chambers for a while. Luckily I had my key with me; but upon applying it to the lock, I found it resisted by something inserted from the inside. Quite surprised, I called out; when to my consternation a key was turned from within; and thrusting his lean visage at me, and holding the door ajar, the apparition of Bartleby appeared, in his shirt sleeves, and otherwise in a strangely tattered dishabille, saying quietly that he was sorry, but he was deeply engaged just then, and—preferred not admitting me at present. In a brief word or two, he moreover added, that perhaps I had better walk round the block two or three times, and by that time he would probably have concluded his affairs.

Now, the utterly unsurmised appearance of Bartleby, tenanting my law-chambers of a Sunday morning, with his cadaverously gentlemanly *nonchalance*, yet withal firm and self-possessed, had such a strange effect upon me, that incontinently I slunk away from my own door, and did as desired. But not without sundry twinges of impotent rebellion against the mild effrontery of this unaccountable scrivener. Indeed, it was his wonderful mildness chiefly, which not only disarmed me, but unmanned me, as it were. For I consider that one, for the time, is a sort of unmanned when he tranquilly permits his hired clerk to dictate to him, and order him away from his own premises. Furthermore, I was full of uneasiness as to what Bartleby could possibly be doing in my office in his shirt sleeves, and in an otherwise dismantled condition of a Sunday morning. Was any thing amiss going on? Nay, that was out of the question. It was not to be thought of for a moment that Bartleby was an immoral person. But what could he be doing there?— copying? Nay again, whatever might be his eccentricities, Bartleby was an eminently decorous person. He would be the last man to sit down to his desk in any state approaching to nudity. Besides, it was Sunday; and there was something about Bartleby that forbade the supposition that he would by any secular occupation violate the proprieties of the day.

Nevertheless, my mind was not pacified; and full of a restless curiosity, at last I returned to the door. Without hindrance I inserted my key, opened it, and entered. Bartleby was not to be seen. I looked round anxiously, peeped behind his screen; but it was very plain that he was gone. Upon more closely examining the place, I surmised that for an indefinite period Bartleby must have ate, dressed, and slept in my office, and that too without plate, mirror, or bed. The cushioned seat of a ricketty old sofa in one corner bore the faint impress of a lean, reclining form. Rolled away under his desk, I found a blanket; under the empty grate, a blacking box and brush; on a chair, a tin basin, with soap and a ragged towel; in a newspaper a few crumbs of ginger-nuts and a morsel of cheese. Yes, thought I, it is evident enough that Bartleby has been making his home here, keeping bachelor's hall all by himself. Immediately then the thought came sweeping across me, What miserable friendlessness and loneliness are here revealed! His poverty is great; but his solitude, how horrible! Think of it. Of a Sunday, Wall-street is deserted as Petra;[13] and every night of every day it is an emptiness. This building too, which of week-days hums with industry and life, at nightfall echoes with sheer vacancy, and all through Sunday is forlorn. And here Bartleby makes his home; sole spectator of a solitude which he has seen all populous—a sort of innocent and transformed Marius brooding among the ruins of Carthage![14]

For the first time in my life a feeling of overpowering stinging melancholy seized me. Before, I had never experienced aught but a not-unpleasing sadness. The bond of a common humanity now drew me irresistibly to gloom. A fraternal melancholy! For both I and Bartleby were sons of Adam. I remembered the bright silks and sparkling faces I had seen that day, in gala trim, swan-like sailing down the Mississippi of Broadway; and I contrasted them with the pallid copyist, and thought to myself, Ah, happiness courts the light, so we deem the world is gay; but misery hides aloof, so we deem that misery there is none. These sad fancyings—chimeras, doubtless, of a sick and silly brain—led on to other and more special thoughts, concerning the eccentricities of Bartleby. Presentiments of strange discoveries hovered round me. The scrivener's pale form appeared to me laid out, among uncaring strangers, in its shivering winding sheet.

Suddenly I was attracted by Bartleby's closed desk, the key in open sight left in the lock.

I mean no mischief, seek the gratification of no heartless curiosity, thought I; besides, the desk is mine, and its contents too, so I will make bold to look within. Every thing was methodically arranged, the papers smoothly placed. The pigeon holes were deep, and removing the files of documents, I groped into their recesses. Presently I felt something there, and dragged it out. It was an old bandanna handkerchief, heavy and knotted. I opened it, and saw it was a savings' bank.

I now recalled all the quiet mysteries which I had noted in the man. I remembered that he never spoke but to answer; that though at intervals he had considerable time to himself, yet I had never seen him reading—no, not even a newspaper; that for long periods he would stand looking out, at his pale window behind the screen, upon the dead brick wall; I was quite sure he never visited any refectory or eating house; while his pale face clearly indicated that he never drank beer like Turkey, or tea and coffee even, like other men; that he never went any where in particular that I could learn; never went out for a walk, unless indeed that was the case at present; that he had declined telling who he was, or whence he came, or whether he had

[13]Ancient fortress-city of the Edom desert, uninhabited for centuries and rediscovered in 1812.

[14]Gaius Marius (157–86 B.C.), plebeian general and consul of Rome, after victorious campaigns in Africa and Gaul, lost a power struggle in Rome to patricians and fled back to Africa. A popular democratic symbol.

any relatives in the world; that though so thin and pale, he never complained of ill health. And more than all, I remembered a certain unconscious air of pallid—how shall I call it?—of pallid haughtiness, say, or rather an austere reserve about him, which had positively awed me into my tame compliance with his eccentricities, when I had feared to ask him to do the slightest incidental thing for me, even though I might know, from his long-continued motionlessness, that behind his screen he must be standing in one of those dead-wall reveries of his.

Revolving all these things, and coupling them with the recently discovered fact that he made my office his constant abiding place and home, and not forgetful of his morbid moodiness; revolving all these things, a prudential feeling began to steal over me. My first emotions had been those of pure melancholy and sincerest pity; but just in proportion as the forlornness of Bartleby grew and grew to my imagination, did that same melancholy merge into fear, that pity into repulsion. So true it is, and so terrible too, that up to a certain point the thought or sight of misery enlists our best affections; but, in certain special cases, beyond that point it does not. They err who would assert that invariably this is owing to the inherent selfishness of the human heart. It rather proceeds from a certain hopelessness of remedying excessive and organic ill. To a sensitive being, pity is not seldom pain. And when at last it is perceived that such pity cannot lead to effectual succor, common sense bids the soul be rid of it. What I saw that morning persuaded me that the scrivener was the victim of innate and incurable disorder. I might give alms to his body; but his body did not pain him; it was his soul that suffered, and his soul I could not reach.

I did not accomplish the purpose of going to Trinity Church that morning. Somehow, the things I had seen disqualified me for the time from church-going. I walked homeward, thinking what I would do with Bartleby. Finally, I resolved upon this;—I would put certain calm questions to him the next morning, touching his history, &c., and if he declined to answer them openly and unreservedly (and I supposed he would prefer not), then to give him a twenty dollar bill over and above whatever I might owe him, and tell him his services were no longer required; but that if in any other way I could assist him, I would be happy to do so, especially if he desired to return to his native place, wherever that might be, I would willingly help to defray the expenses. Moreover, if, after reaching home, he found himself at any time in want of aid, a letter from him would be sure of a reply.

The next morning came.

"Bartleby," said I, gently calling to him behind his screen.

No reply.

"Bartleby," said I, in a still gentler tone, "come here; I am not going to ask you to do any thing you would prefer not to do—I simply wish to speak to you."

Upon this he noiselessly slid into view.

"Will you tell me, Bartleby, where you were born?"

"I would prefer not to."

"Will you tell me *any thing* about yourself?"

"I would prefer not to."

"But what reasonable objection can you have to speak to me? I feel friendly towards you."

He did not look at me while I spoke, but kept his glance fixed upon my bust of Cicero, which as I then sat, was directly behind me, some six inches above my head.

"What is your answer, Bartleby?" said I, after waiting a considerable time for a reply, during which his countenance remained immovable, only there was the faintest conceivable tremor of the white attenuated mouth.

"At present I prefer to give no answer," he said, and retired into his hermitage.

It was rather weak in me I confess, but his manner on this occasion nettled me. Not only did there seem to lurk in it a certain calm disdain, but his perverseness seemed ungrateful, considering the undeniable good usage and indulgence he had received from me.

Again I sat ruminating what I should do. Mortified as I was at his behavior, and resolved as I had been to dismiss him when I entered my office, nevertheless I strangely felt something superstitious knocking at my heart, and forbidding me to carry out my purpose, and denouncing me for a villain if I dared to breathe one bitter word against this forlornest of mankind. At last, familiarly drawing my chair behind his screen, I sat down and said: "Bartleby, never mind then about revealing your history; but let me entreat you, as a friend, to comply as far as may be with the usages of this office. Say now you will help to examine papers to-morrow or next day: in short, say now that in a day or two you will begin to be a little reasonable:—say so, Bartleby."

"At present I would prefer not to be a little reasonable," was his mildly cadaverous reply.

Just then the folding-doors opened, and Nippers approached. He seemed suffering from an unusually bad night's rest, induced by severer indigestion than common. He overheard those final words of Bartleby.

"*Prefer not*, eh?" gritted Nippers—"I'd *prefer* him, if I were you, sir," addressing me—"I'd *prefer* him; I'd give him preferences, the stubborn mule! What is it, sir, pray, that he *prefers* not to do now?"

Bartleby moved not a limb.

"Mr. Nippers," said I, "I'd prefer that you would withdraw for the present."

Somehow, of late I had got into the way of involuntarily using this word "prefer" upon all sorts of not exactly suitable occasions. And I trembled to think that my contact with the scrivener had already and seriously affected me in a mental way. And what further and deeper aberration might it not yet produce? This apprehension had not been without efficacy in determining me to summary measures.

As Nippers, looking very sour and sulky, was departing, Turkey blandly and deferentially approached.

"With submission, sir," said he, "yesterday I was thinking about Bartleby here, and I think that if he would but prefer to take a quart of good ale every day, it would do much towards mending him, and enabling him to assist in examining his papers."

"So you have got the word too," said I, slightly excited.

"With submission, what word, sir," asked Turkey, respectfully crowding himself into the contracted space behind the screen, and by so doing, making me jostle the scrivener. "What word, sir?"

"I would prefer to be left alone here," said Bartleby, as if offended at being mobbed in his privacy.

"*That's* the word, Turkey," said I—"*that's* it."

"Oh, *prefer?* oh yes—queer word. I never use it myself. But, sir, as I was saying, if he would but prefer—"

"Turkey," interrupted I, "you will please withdraw."

"Oh certainly, sir, if you prefer that I should."

As he opened the folding-doors to retire, Nippers at his desk caught a glimpse of me, and asked whether I would prefer to have a certain paper copied on blue paper or white. He did not in the least roguishly accent the word prefer. It was plain that it involuntarily rolled from his tongue. I thought to myself, surely I must get rid of a demented man, who already has in some degree turned the tongues, if not the heads of myself and clerks. But I thought it prudent not to break the dismission at once.

The next day I noticed that Bartleby did nothing but stand at his window in his dead-wall revery. Upon asking him why he did not write, he said that he had decided upon doing no more writing.

"Why, how now? what next?" exclaimed I, "do no more writing?"

"No more."

"And what is the reason?"

"Do you not see the reason for yourself," he indifferently replied.

I looked steadfastly at him, and perceived that his eyes looked dull and glazed. Instantly it occurred to me, that his unexampled diligence in copying by his dim window for the first few weeks of his stay with me might have temporarily impaired his vision.

I was touched. I said something in condolence with him. I hinted that of course he did wisely in abstaining from writing for a while; and urged him to embrace that opportunity of taking wholesome exercise in the open air. This, however, he did not do. A few days after this, my other clerks being absent, and being in a great hurry to dispatch certain letters by the mail, I thought that, having nothing else earthly to do, Bartleby would surely be less inflexible than usual, and carry these letters to the post-office. But he blankly declined. So, much to my inconvenience, I went myself.

Still added days went by. Whether Bartleby's eyes improved or not, I could not say. To all appearance, I thought they did. But when I asked him if they did, he vouchsafed no answer. At all events, he would do no copying. At last, in reply to my urgings, he informed me that he had permanently given up copying.

"What!" exclaimed I; "suppose your eyes should get entirely well—better than ever before—would you not copy then?"

"I have given up copying," he answered, and slid aside.

He remained as ever, a fixture in my chamber. Nay—if that were possible—he became still more of a fixture than before. What was to be done? He would do nothing in the office: why should he stay there? In plain fact, he had now become a millstone to me, not only useless as a necklace, but afflictive to bear. Yet I was sorry for him. I speak less than truth when I say that, on his own account, he occasioned me uneasiness. If he would but have named a single relative or friend, I would instantly have written, and urged their taking the poor fellow away to some convenient retreat. But he seemed alone, absolutely alone in the universe. A bit of wreck in the mid Atlantic. At length, necessities connected with my business tyrannized over all other considerations. Decently as I could, I told Bartleby that in six days' time he must unconditionally leave the office. I warned him to take measures, in the interval, for procuring some other abode. I offered to assist him in this endeavor, if he himself would but take the first step towards a removal. "And when you finally quit me, Bartleby," added I, "I shall see that you go not away entirely unprovided. Six days from this hour, remember."

At the expiration of that period, I peeped behind the screen, and lo! Bartleby was there.

I buttoned up my coat, balanced myself; advanced slowly towards him, touched his shoulder, and said, "The time has come; you must quit this place; I am sorry for you; here is money; but you must go."

"I would prefer not," he replied, with his back still towards me.

"You *must*."

He remained silent.

Now I had an unbounded confidence in this man's common honesty. He had frequently restored to me sixpences and shillings carelessly dropped upon the floor, for I am apt to be very reckless in such shirt-button affairs. The proceeding then which followed will not be deemed extraordinary.

"Bartleby," said I, "I owe you twelve dollars on account; here are thirty-two; the odd twenty are yours.—Will you take it?" and I handed the bills towards him.

But he made no motion.

"I will leave them here then," putting them under a weight on the table. Then taking my hat and cane and going to the door I tranquilly turned and added—"After you have removed your things from these offices, Bartleby, you will of course lock the door—since every one is now gone for the day but you—and if you please, slip your key underneath the mat, so that I may have it in the morning. I shall not see you again; so good-bye to you. If hereafter in your new place of abode I can be of any service to you, do not fail to advise me by letter. Good-bye, Bartleby, and fare you well."

But he answered not a word; like the last column of some ruined temple, he remained standing mute and solitary in the middle of the otherwise deserted room.

As I walked home in a pensive mood, my vanity got the better of my pity. I could not but highly plume myself on my masterly management in getting rid of Bartleby. Masterly I call it, and such it must appear to any dispassionate thinker. The beauty of my procedure seemed to consist in its perfect quietness. There was no vulgar bullying, no bravado of any sort, no choleric hectoring, and striding to and fro across the apartment, jerking out vehement commands for Bartleby to bundle himself off with his beggarly traps. Nothing of the kind. Without loudly bidding Bartleby depart—as an inferior genius might have done—I *assumed* the ground that depart he must; and upon that assumption built all I had to say. The more I thought over my procedure, the more I was charmed with it. Nevertheless, next morning, upon awakening, I had my doubts,—I had somehow slept off the fumes of vanity. One of the coolest and wisest hours a man has, is just after he awakes in the morning. My procedure seemed as sagacious as ever,—but only in theory. How it would prove in practice—there was the rub. It was truly a beautiful thought to have assumed Bartleby's departure; but, after all, that assumption was simply my own, and none of Bartleby's. The great point was, not whether I had assumed that he would quit me, but whether he would prefer so to do. He was more a man of preferences than assumptions.

After breakfast, I walked down town, arguing the probabilities *pro* and *con*. One moment I thought it would prove a miserable failure, and Bartleby would be found all alive at my office as usual; the next moment it seemed certain that I should find his chair empty. And so I kept veering about. At the corner of Broadway and Canal-street, I saw quite an excited group of people standing in earnest conversation.

"I'll take odds he doesn't," said a voice as I passed.

"Doesn't go?—done!" said I, "put up your money."

I was instinctively putting my hand in my pocket to produce my own, when I remembered that this was an election day.[15] The words I had overheard bore no reference to Bartleby, but to the success or non-success of some candidate for the mayoralty. In my intent frame of mind, I had, as it were, imagined that all Broadway shared in my excitement, and were debating the same question with me. I passed on, very thankful that the uproar of the street screened my momentary absent-mindedness.

As I had intended, I was earlier than usual at my office door. I stood listening for a moment. All was still. He must be gone. I tried the knob. The door was locked. Yes, my procedure had worked to a charm; he indeed must be vanished. Yet a certain melancholy mixed with this: I was almost sorry for my brilliant success. I was fumbling under the door mat for the key,

---

[15]A complicated pun suggesting that this may be Judgment Day for the narrator, whose "election," in the religious sense of being chosen for salvation, may depend on how he chooses to treat Bartleby. H. Bruce Franklin and Donald M. Fiene have interpreted the story in the light of Matthew 25:31–42, where Christ prophesies that he will return at the end of the world to consign his professed disciples to heaven or to hell, according to whether they have treated those in need as they would treat Christ himself. I have drawn on their articles in identifying other relevant biblical passages below.

which Bartleby was to have left there for me, when accidentally my knee knocked against a panel, producing a summoning sound, and in response a voice came to me from within—"Not yet; I am occupied."

It was Bartleby.

I was thunderstruck. For an instant I stood like the man who, pipe in mouth, was killed one cloudless afternoon long ago in Virginia, by summer lightning; at his own warm open window he was killed, and remained leaning out there upon the dreamy afternoon, till some one touched him, when he fell.

"Not gone!" I murmured at last. But again obeying that wondrous ascendancy which the inscrutable scrivener had over me, and from which ascendancy, for all my chafing, I could not completely escape, I slowly went down stairs and out into the street, and while walking round the block, considered what I should next do in this unheard-of perplexity. Turn the man out by an actual thrusting I could not; to drive him away by calling him hard names would not do; calling in the police was an unpleasant idea; and yet, permit him to enjoy his cadaverous triumph over me,—this too I could not think of. What was to be done? or, if nothing could be done, was there any thing further that I could *assume* in the matter? Yes, as before I had prospectively assumed that Bartleby would depart, so now I might retrospectivelyassume that departed he was. In the legitimate carrying out of this assumption, I might enter my office in a great hurry, and pretending not to see Bartleby at all, walk straight against him as if he were air. Such a proceeding would in a singular degree have the appearance of a home-thrust. It was hardly possible that Bartleby could withstand such an application of the doctrine of assumptions. But upon second thoughts the success of the plan seemed rather dubious. I resolved to argue the matter over with him again.

"Bartleby," said I, entering the office, with a quietly severe expression, "I am seriously displeased. I am pained, Bartleby. I had thought better of you. I had imagined you of such a gentlemanly organization, that in any delicate dilemma a slight hint would suffice—in short, an assumption. But it appears I am deceived. Why," I added, unaffectedly starting, "you have not even touched that money yet," pointing to it, just where I had left it the evening previous.

He answered nothing.

"Will you, or will you not, quit me?" I now demanded in a sudden passion, advancing close to him.

"I would prefer *not* to quit you," he replied, gently emphasizing the *not*.

"What earthly right have you to stay here? Do you pay any rent? Do you pay my taxes? Or is this property yours?"

He answered nothing.

"Are you ready to go on and write now? Are your eyes recovered? Could you copy a small paper for me this morning? or help examine a few lines? or step round to the post-office? In a word, will you do any thing at all, to give a coloring to your refusal to depart the premises?"

He silently retired into his hermitage.

I was now in such a state of nervous resentment that I thought it but prudent to check myself at present from further demonstrations. Bartleby and I were alone. I remembered the tragedy of the unfortunate Adams and the still more unfortunate Colt[16] in the solitary office of the latter; and how poor Colt, being dreadfully incensed by Adams, and imprudently permitting himself to get wildly excited, was at unawares hurried into his fatal act—an act which certainly no man could possibly deplore more than the actor himself. Often it had occurred to me in my ponderings upon the subject, that had that altercation taken place in the public street, or at a private residence, it would not have terminated as it did. It was the circumstance of being alone in a solitary office, up stairs, of a building entirely unhallowed by humanizing domestic associations—an uncarpeted office, doubtless, of a dusty, haggard sort of appearance;—this it must have been, which greatly helped to enhance the irritable desperation of the hapless Colt.

But when this old Adam of resentment rose in me and tempted me concerning Bartleby, I grappled him and threw him. How? Why, simply by recalling the divine injunction: "A new commandment give I unto you, that ye love one another."[17] Yes, this it was that saved me. Aside from higher considerations, charity often operates as a vastly wise and prudent principle—a great safeguard to its possessor. Men have committed murder for jealousy's sake, and anger's sake, and hatred's sake, and selfishness' sake, and spiritual pride's sake; but no man that ever I heard of, ever committed a diabolical murder for sweet charity's sake. Mere self-interest, then, if no better motive can be enlisted, should, especially with high-tempered men, prompt all beings to charity and philanthropy. At any rate, upon the occasion in question, I strove to drown my exasperated feelings towards the scrivener by benevolently construing his conduct. Poor fellow, poor fellow! thought I, he don't mean any thing; and besides, he has seen hard times, and ought to be indulged.

I endeavored also immediately to occupy myself, and at the same time to comfort my despondency. I tried to fancy that in the course of the morning, at such time as might prove agreeable to him, Bartleby, of his own free accord, would emerge from his hermitage, and take up some decided line of march in the direction of the door. But no. Half-past twelve o'clock came; Turkey began to glow in the face, overturn his inkstand, and become generally obstreperous; Nippers abated down into quietude and courtesy; Ginger Nut munched his noon apple; and Bartleby remained standing at his window in one of his profoundest dead-wall reveries. Will it be credited? Ought

[16]John C. Colt, brother of the Colt revolver's inventor, murdered the printer Samuel Adams with a hatchet when Adams called on him in his Broadway office to collect a debt. Adams's body was found salted and crated for shipment to New Orleans in September 1841, and Colt was convicted of murder and sentenced to hanging in November 1842. The irony, however, is that the narrator views the murderer, Colt, as more unfortunate than the murdered man, Adams, whom he blames for provoking the murder.

[17]John 13:34.

I to acknowledge it? That afternoon I left the office without saying one further word to him.

Some days now passed, during which, at leisure intervals I looked a little into "Edwards on the Will," and "Priestley on Necessity."[18] Under the circumstances, those books induced a salutary feeling. Gradually I slid into the persuasion that these troubles of mine touching the scrivener, had been all predestined from eternity, and Bartleby was billeted upon me for some mysterious purpose of an all-wise Providence, which it was not for a mere mortal like me to fathom. Yes, Bartleby, stay there behind your screen, thought I; I shall persecute you no more; you are harmless and noiseless as any of these old chairs; in short, I never feel so private as when I know you are here. At last I see it, I feel it; I penetrate to the predestinated purpose of my life. I am content. Others may have loftier parts to enact; but my mission in this world, Bartleby, is to furnish you with office-room for such period as you may see fit to remain.

I believe that this wise and blessed frame of mind would have continued with me, had it not been for the unsolicited and uncharitable remarks obtruded upon me by my professional friends who visited the rooms. But thus it often is, that the constant friction of illiberal minds wears out at last the best resolves of the more generous. Though to be sure, when I reflected upon it, it was not strange that people entering my office should be struck by the peculiar aspect of the unaccountable Bartleby, and so be tempted to throw out some sinister observations concerning him. Sometimes an attorney having business with me, and calling at my office, and finding no one but the scrivener there, would undertake to obtain some sort of precise information from him touching my whereabouts; but without heeding his idle talk, Bartleby would remain standing immovable in the middle of the room. So after contemplating him in that position for a time, the attorney would depart, no wiser than he came.

Also, when a Reference[19] was going on, and the room full of lawyers and witnesses and business was driving fast; some deeply occupied legal gentlemen present, seeing Bartleby wholly unemployed, would request him to run round to his (the legal gentleman's) office and fetch some papers for him. Thereupon, Bartleby would tranquilly decline, and yet remain idle as before. Then the lawyer would give a great stare, and turn to me. And what could I say? At last I was made aware that all through the circle of my professional acquaintance, a whisper of wonder was running round, having reference to the strange creature I kept at my office. This worried me very much. And as the idea came upon me of his possibly turning out a long-lived man, and keep occupying my

[18]Arguing respectively from the premises of Calvinist theology and of philosophical determinism, the Massachusetts minister Jonathan Edwards, in his *Freedom of the Will* (1754), and the British clergyman-scientist Joseph Priestley, in his *Doctrine of Philosophical Necessity Illustrated* (1777), both maintained that the will was not free and that all history had been preordained. Both also believed that the apocalyptic prophecies in the Bible were being fulfilled in their lifetime.

[19]The act of referring a disputed matter to a referee.

chambers, and denying my authority; and perplexing my visitors; and scandalizing my professional reputation; and casting a general gloom over the premises; keeping soul and body together to the last upon his savings (for doubtless he spent but half a dime a day), and in the end perhaps outlive me, and claim possession of my office by right of his perpetual occupancy: as all these dark anticipations crowded upon me more and more, and my friends continually intruded their relentless remarks upon the apparition in my room; a great change was wrought in me. I resolved to gather all my faculties together, and for ever rid me of this intolerable incubus.

Ere revolving any complicated project, however, adapted to this end, I first simply suggested to Bartleby the propriety of his permanent departure. In a calm and serious tone, I commended the idea to his careful and mature consideration. But having taken three days to meditate upon it, he apprised me that his original determination remained the same; in short, that he still preferred to abide with me.

What shall I do? I now said to myself, buttoning up my coat to the last button. What shall I do? what ought I to do? what does conscience say I *should* do with this man, or rather ghost? Rid myself of him, I must; go, he shall. But how? You will not thrust him, the poor, pale, passive mortal,—you will not thrust such a helpless creature out of your door? you will not dishonor yourself by such cruelty? No, I will not, I cannot do that. Rather would I let him live and die here, and then mason up his remains in the wall. What then will you do? For all your coaxing, he will not budge. Bribes he leaves under your own paper-weight on your table; in short, it is quite plain that he prefers to cling to you.

Then something severe, something unusual must be done. What! surely you will not have him collared by a constable, and commit his innocent pallor to the common jail? And upon what ground could you procure such a thing to be done?—a vagrant, is he? What! he a vagrant, a wanderer, who refuses to budge? It is because he will *not* be a vagrant, then, that you seek to count him *as* a vagrant. That is too absurd. No visible means of support: there I have him. Wrong again: for indubitably he *does* support himself, and that is the only unanswerable proof that any man can show of his possessing the means so to do. No more then. Since he will not quit me, I must quit him. I will change my offices; I will move elsewhere; and give him fair notice, that if I find him on my new premises I will then proceed against him as a common trespasser.

Acting accordingly, next day I thus addressed him: "I find these chambers too far from the City Hall; the air is unwholesome. In a word, I propose to remove my offices next week, and shall no longer require your services. I tell you this now, in order that you may seek another place."

He made no reply, and nothing more was said.

On the appointed day I engaged carts and men, proceeded to my chambers, and having but little furniture, every thing was removed in a few hours. Throughout, the scrivener remained standing behind the screen, which I directed to be removed the last thing. It was withdrawn; and being folded up like a huge folio, left him the motionless occupant of a naked room. I stood in the entry watching him a moment, while something from within me upbraided me.

I re-entered, with my hand in my pocket—and—and my heart in my mouth.

"Good-bye, Bartleby; I am going—good-bye, and God some way bless you; and take that," slipping something in his hand. But it dropped upon the floor, and then,—strange to say—I tore myself from him whom I had so longed to be rid of.

Established in my new quarters, for a day or two I kept the door locked, and started at every footfall in the passages. When I returned to my rooms after any little absence, I would pause at the threshold for an instant, and attentively listen, ere applying my key. But these fears were needless. Bartleby never came nigh me.

I thought all was going well, when a perturbed looking stranger visited me, inquiring whether I was the person who had recently occupied rooms at No.—Wall-street.

Full of forebodings, I replied that I was.

"Then sir," said the stranger, who proved a lawyer, "you are responsible for the man you left there. He refuses to do any copying; he refuses to do any thing; he says he prefers not to; and he refuses to quit the premises."

"I am very sorry, sir," said I, with assumed tranquillity, but an inward tremor, "but, really, the man you allude to is nothing to me[20]—he is no relation or apprentice of mine, that you should hold me responsible for him."

"In mercy's name, who is he?"

"I certainly cannot inform you. I know nothing about him. Formerly I employed him as a copyist; but he has done nothing for me now for some time past."

"I shall settle him then,—good morning, sir."

Several days passed, and I heard nothing more; and though I often felt a charitable prompting to call at the place and see poor Bartleby, yet a certain squeamishness of I know not what withheld me.

All is over with him, by this time, thought I at last, when through another week no further intelligence reached me. But coming to my room the day after, I found several persons waiting at my door in a high state of nervous excitement.

"That's the man—here he comes," cried the foremost one, whom I recognized as the lawyer who had previously called upon me alone.

"You must take him away, sir, at once," cried a portly person among them, advancing upon me, and whom I knew to be the landlord of No.—Wall-street. "These gentlemen, my tenants, cannot stand it any longer; Mr. B——" pointing to the lawyer, "has turned him out of his room, and he

[20]Cf. Peter's denial of Christ, Mark 14:68, 70–71: "But he denied, saying, I know not, neither understand I what thou sayest.... And he denied it again.... But he began to curse and to swear, saying, I know not this man of whom ye speak."

now persists in haunting the building generally, sitting upon the banisters of the stairs by day, and sleeping in the entry by night. Every body is concerned; clients are leaving the offices; some fears are entertained of a mob; something you must do, and that without delay."

Aghast at this torrent, I fell back before it, and would fain have locked myself in my new quarters. In vain I persisted that Bartleby was nothing to me—no more than to any one else. In vain:—I was the last person known to have any thing to do with him, and they held me to the terrible account. Fearful then of being exposed in the papers (as one person present obscurely threatened) I considered the matter, and at length said, that if the lawyer would give me a confidential interview with the scrivener, in his (the lawyer's) own room, I would that afternoon strive my best to rid them of the nuisance they complained of.

Going up stairs to my old haunt, there was Bartleby silently sitting upon the banister at the landing.

"What are you doing here, Bartleby?" said I.

"Sitting upon the banister," he mildly replied.

I motioned him into the lawyer's room, who then left us.

"Bartleby," said I, "are you aware that you are the cause of great tribulation to me, by persisting in occupying the entry after being dismissed from the office?"

No answer.

"Now one of two things must take place. Either you must do something, or something must be done to you. Now what sort of business would you like to engage in? Would you like to re-engage in copying for some one?"

"No; I would prefer not to make any change."

"Would you like a clerkship in a dry-goods store?"[21]

"There is too much confinement about that. No, I would not like a clerkship; but I am not particular."

"Too much confinement," I cried, "why you keep yourself confined all the time!"

"I would prefer not to take a clerkship," he rejoined, as if to settle that little item at once.

"How would a bar-tender's business suit you? There is no trying of the eyesight in that."

"I would not like it at all; though, as I said before, I am not particular."

His unwonted wordiness inspirited me. I returned to the charge.

"Well then, would you like to travel through the country collecting bills for the merchants? That would improve your health."

"No, I would prefer to be doing something else."

"How then would going as a companion to Europe, to entertain some young gentleman with your conversation,—how would that suit you?"

"Not at all. It does not strike me that there is any thing definite about that. I like to be stationary. But I am not particular."

[21]Melville had clerked in his brother's fur store, as well as in a dry-goods store in Honolulu.

"Stationary you shall be then," I cried, now losing all patience, and for the first time in all my exasperating connection with him fairly flying into a passion. "If you do not go away from these premises before night, I shall feel bound—indeed I *am* bound—to—to—to quit the premises myself!" I rather absurdly concluded, knowing not with what possible threat to try to frighten his immobility into compliance. Despairing of all further efforts, I was precipitately leaving him, when a final thought occurred to me—one which had not been wholly unindulged before.

"Bartleby," said I, in the kindest tone I could assume under such exciting circumstances, "will you go home with me now—not to my office, but my dwelling—and remain there till we can conclude upon some convenient arrangement for you at our leisure? Come, let us start now, right away."

"No: at present I would prefer not to make any change at all."

I answered nothing; but effectually dodging every one by the suddenness and rapidity of my flight, rushed from the building, ran up Wall-street towards Broadway, and jumping into the first omnibus was soon removed from pursuit. As soon as tranquillity returned I distinctly perceived that I had now done all that I possibly could, both in respect to the demands of the landlord and his tenants, and with regard to my own desire and sense of duty, to benefit Bartleby, and shield him from rude persecution. I now strove to be entirely care-free and quiescent; and my conscience justified me in the attempt; though indeed it was not so successful as I could have wished. So fearful was I of being again hunted out by the incensed landlord and his exasperated tenants, that, surrendering my business to Nippers, for a few days I drove about the upper part of the town and through the suburbs, in my rockaway; crossed over to Jersey City and Hoboken, and paid fugitive visits to Manhattanville and Astoria. In fact I almost lived in my rockaway[22] for the time.

When again I entered my office, lo, a note from the landlord lay upon the desk. I opened it with trembling hands. It informed me that the writer had sent to the police, and had Bartleby removed to the Tombs as a vagrant. Moreover, since I knew more about him than any one else, he wished me to appear at that place, and make a suitable statement of the facts. These tidings had a conflicting effect upon me. At first I was indignant; but at last almost approved. The landlord's energetic, summary disposition, had led him to adopt a procedure which I do not think I would have decided upon myself; and yet as a last resort, under such peculiar circumstances, it seemed the only plan.

As I afterwards learned, the poor scrivener, when told that he must be conducted to the Tombs, offered not the slightest obstacle, but in his pale unmoving way, silently acquiesced.

Some of the compassionate and curious bystanders joined the party; and headed by one of the constables arm in arm with Bartleby, the silent

---

[22]A light, low carriage with open sides and a
fixed top.

procession filed its way through all the noise, and heat, and joy of the roaring thoroughfares at noon.

The same day I received the note I went to the Tombs, or to speak more properly, the Halls of Justice.[23] Seeking the right officer, I stated the purpose of my call, and was informed that the individual I described was indeed within. I then assured the functionary that Bartleby was a perfectly honest man, and greatly to be compassionated, however unaccountably eccentric. I narrated all I knew, and closed by suggesting the idea of letting him remain in as indulgent confinement as possible till something less harsh might be done—though indeed I hardly knew what. At all events, if nothing else could be decided upon, the alms-house must receive him. I then begged to have an interview.

Being under no disgraceful charge, and quite serene and harmless in all his ways, they had permitted him freely to wander about the prison, and especially in the inclosed grass-platted yards thereof. And so I found him there, standing all alone in the quietest of the yards, his face towards a high wall, while all around, from the narrow slits of the jail windows, I thought I saw peering out upon him the eyes of murderers and thieves.[24]

"Bartleby!"

"I know you," he said, without looking round,—"and I want nothing to say to you."

"It was not I that brought you here, Bartleby," said I, keenly pained at his implied suspicion. "And to you, this should not be so vile a place. Nothing reproachful attaches to you by being here. And see, it is not so sad a place as one might think. Look, there is the sky, and here is the grass."

"I know where I am," he replied, but would say nothing more, and so I left him.

As I entered the corridor again, a broad meat-like man, in an apron, accosted me, and jerking his thumb over his shoulder said—"Is that your friend?"

"Yes."

"Does he want to starve? If he does, let him live on the prison fare, that's all."

"Who are you?" asked I, not knowing what to make of such an unofficially speaking person in such a place.

"I am the grub-man. Such gentlemen as have friends here, hire me to provide them with something good to eat."

"Is this so?" said I, turning to the turnkey.

He said it was.

"Well then," said I, slipping some silver into the grub-man's hands (for so they called him). "I want you to give particular attention to my

---

[23]Melville is playing on the irony that the Tombs, officially designated the Halls of Justice and House of Detention, fulfilled two incompatible functions.

[24]Cf. Mark 15:27–28: "And with him they crucify two thieves.... And the scripture was fulfilled, which saith, And he was numbered with the transgressors."

friend there; let him have the best dinner you can get. And you must be as polite to him as possible."

"Introduce me, will you?" said the grub-man, looking at me with an expression which seemed to say he was all impatience for an opportunity to give a specimen of his breeding.

Thinking it would prove of benefit to the scrivener, I acquiesced; and asking the grub-man his name, went up with him to Bartleby.

"Bartleby, this is Mr. Cutlets; you will find him very useful to you."

"Your sarvant, sir, your sarvant," said the grub-man, making a low salutation behind his apron. "Hope you find it pleasant here, sir; nice grounds—cool apartments, sir—hope you'll stay with us some time—try to make it agreeable. May Mrs. Cutlets and I have the pleasure of your company to dinner, sir, in Mrs. Cutlets' private room?"

"I prefer not to dine to-day," said Bartleby, turning away. "It would disagree with me; I am unused to dinners." So saying he slowly moved to the other side of the inclosure, and took up a position fronting the dead-wall.

"How's this?" said the grub-man, addressing me with a stare of astonishment. "He's odd, aint he?"

"I think he is a little deranged," said I, sadly.

"Deranged? deranged is it? Well now, upon my word, I thought that friend of yourn was a gentleman forger; they are always pale and genteel-like, them forgers. I can't help pity 'em—can't help it, sir. Did you know Monroe Edwards?"[25] he added touchingly, and paused. Then, laying his hand pityingly on my shoulder, sighed, "he died of consumption at Sing-Sing. So you weren't acquainted with Monroe?"

"No, I was never socially acquainted with any forgers. But I cannot stop longer. Look to my friend yonder. You will not lose by it. I will see you again."

Some few days after this, I again obtained admission to the Tombs, and went through the corridors in quest of Bartleby; but without finding him.

"I saw him coming from his cell not long ago," said a turnkey, "may be he's gone to loiter in the yards."

So I went in that direction.

"Are you looking for the silent man?" said another turnkey passing me. "Yonder he lies—sleeping in the yard there. 'Tis not twenty minutes since I saw him lie down."

The yard was entirely quiet. It was not accessible to the common prisoners. The surrounding walls, of amazing thickness, kept off all sounds behind them. The Egyptian character of the masonry weighed upon me with its gloom. But a soft imprisoned turf grew under foot. The heart of the eternal

[25]A financier convicted of using forged letters of credit to defraud two firms of $25,000 each. His trial in June 1842 caused as much of a sensation as that of Colt.

pyramids, it seemed, wherein, by some strange magic, through the clefts, grass-seed, dropped by birds, had sprung.

Strangely huddled at the base of the wall, his knees drawn up, and lying on his side, his head touching the cold stones, I saw the wasted Bartleby. But nothing stirred. I paused; then went close up to him; stooped over, and saw that his dim eyes were open; otherwise he seemed profoundly sleeping. Something prompted me to touch him. I felt his hand, when a tingling shiver ran up my arm and down my spine to my feet.

The round face of the grub-man peered upon me now. "His dinner is ready. Won't he dine to-day, either? Or does he live without dining?"

"Lives without dining," said I, and closed the eyes.

"Eh!—He's asleep, aint he?"

"With kings and counsellors,"[26] murmured I.

There would seem little need for proceeding further in this history. Imagination will readily supply the meagre recital of poor Bartleby's interment. But ere parting with the reader, let me say, that if this little narrative has sufficiently interested him, to awaken curiosity as to who Bartleby was, and what manner of life he led prior to the present narrator's making his acquaintance, I can only reply, that in such curiosity I fully share, but am wholly unable to gratify it. Yet here I hardly know whether I should divulge one little item of rumor, which came to my ear a few months after the scrivener's decease. Upon what basis it rested, I could never ascertain; and hence, how true it is I cannot now tell. But inasmuch as this vague report has not been without a certain strange suggestive interest to me, however sad, it may prove the same with some others; and so I will briefly mention it. The report was this: that Bartleby had been a subordinate clerk in the Dead Letter Office at Washington, from which he had been suddenly removed by a change in the administration. When I think over this rumor, hardly can I express the emotions which seize me. Dead letters! does it not sound like dead men? Conceive a man by nature and misfortune prone to a pallid hopelessness, can any business seem more fitted to heighten it than that of continually handling these dead letters, and assorting them for the flames? For by the cart-load they are annually burned. Sometimes from out the folded paper the pale clerk takes a ring:—the finger it was meant for, perhaps, moulders in the grave; a bank-note sent in swiftest charity:—he whom it would relieve, nor eats nor hungers any more; pardon for those who died despairing; hope for those who died unhoping; good tidings for those who died stifled by unrelieved calamities. On errands of life, these letters speed to death.

Ah Bartleby! Ah humanity!

1853

---

[26]Job 3:14. After being smitten by God with boils, Job curses the day he was born and says that had he died in the womb or in infancy, he would have been "at rest, With kings and counsellors of the earth, which built desolate places for themselves."

The Paradise of Bachelors and The Tartarus of Maids[1]

I. The Paradise of Bachelors

It lies not far from Temple-Bar.[2]

Going to it, by the usual way, is like stealing from a heated plain into some cool, deep glen, shady among harboring hills.

Sick with the din and soiled with the mud of Fleet Street—where the Benedick[3] tradesmen are hurrying by, with ledger-lines ruled along their brows, thinking upon rise of bread and fall of babies—you adroitly turn a mystic corner—not a street—glide down a dim, monastic way, flanked by dark, sedate, and solemn piles, and still wending on, give the whole care-worn world the slip, and, disentangled, stand beneath the quiet cloisters of the Paradise of Bachelors.

Sweet are the oases in Sahara; charming the isle-groves of August prairies; delectable pure faith amidst a thousand perfidies: but sweeter, still more charming, most delectable, the dreamy Paradise of Bachelors, found in the stony heart of stunning London.

In mild meditation pace the cloisters;[4] take your pleasure, sip your leisure, in the garden waterward; go linger in the ancient library; go worship in the sculptured chapel: but little have you seen, just nothing do you know,

---

[1]Published in the April 1855 issue of *Harper's New Monthly Magazine*, this is one of three paired sketches that Melville wrote in spring 1854. The others are "Poor Man's Pudding and Rich Man's Crumbs," which compares the rural poor of preindustrial America with the urban poor of industrial England and indicts the hollow charity of the rich in both countries; and "The Two Temples," which contrasts a wealthy New York church congregation with the working-class audience of a London theater gallery and finds true Christian charity only in the latter (the sketch was regretfully turned down by *Putnam's*, whose editors feared "offending the religious sensibilities of the public"). The present text is from the standard Northwestern-Newberry edition of *The Piazza Tales and Other Prose Pieces, 1839–1860*.
"The Paradise of Bachelors" is based on Melville's experiences of dining at Elm Court, Temple, and of visiting the Temple and being feted by Robert Francis Cooke at a dinner for nine guests on December 19, 20, and 21, 1849, while peddling the manuscript of *White-Jacket* in London. Melville's *Journal of a Visit to London and the Continent, 1849–1850* conveys a vivid sense of the contradictory position in which he found himself on revisiting England ten years after his first voyage to Liverpool: "*then* a sailor, *now* H.M. author of 'Peedee' 'Hullabaloo' & 'Pog-Dog.'" Punctuating it are frequent complaints of

homesickness for Elizabeth and "the Little One"; accounts of "dodging about town to get a cheap dinner," cheap lodgings, and second-class travel accommodations; and comments on the "stiffness, formality & coldness" of the English upper classes. The *Journal* also indicates that although Melville "had a glorious time" and enjoyed the "fine dinner" and "exceedingly agreeable company" of his hosts at the "Paradise of Batchelors" (as he had already dubbed the Temple), he also regarded his contacts with England's social elites as grist for his literary mill.
Likewise autobiographical in origin, the second half of the diptych, "The Tartarus of Maids," was inspired by Melville's trip to Carson's Mill in Dalton, Massachusetts, to get "a sleigh-load of paper" in late January 1851. Critics have speculated that Elizabeth Melville's frequent pregnancies and their painful complications may have helped suggest the sketch's sexual symbolism.
[2]Stone gateway designed by Christopher Wren (1632–1723), separating Fleet Street, a publishers' and booksellers' district, from its prolongation, the Strand.
[3]A newly married man, once a confirmed bachelor, from Benedick in Shakespeare's *Much Ado about Nothing*.
[4]London's four Inns of Court (comprising Inner Temple, Middle Temple, Lincoln's Inn, and Gray's Inn), occupied by lawyers and law students.

not the sweet kernel have you tasted, till you dine among the banded Bachelors, and see their convivial eyes and glasses sparkle. Not dine in bustling commons, during term-time, in the hall; but tranquilly, by private hint, at a private table; some fine Templar's hospitably invited guest.

Templar? That's a romantic name. Let me see. Brian de Bois Guilbert was a Templar,[5] I believe. Do we understand you to insinuate that those famous Templars still survive in modern London? May the ring of their armed heels be heard, and the rattle of their shields, as in mailed prayer the monk-knights kneel before the consecrated Host? Surely a monk-knight were a curious sight picking his way along the Strand, his gleaming corselet and snowy surcoat spattered by an omnibus. Long-bearded, too, according to his order's rule; his face fuzzy as a pard's;[6] how would the grim ghost look among the crop-haired, close-shaven citizens? We know indeed—sad history recounts it—that a moral blight tainted at last this sacred Brotherhood. Though no sworded foe might outskill them in the fence, yet the worm of luxury crawled beneath their guard, gnawing the core of knightly troth, nibbling the monastic vow, till at last the monk's austerity relaxed to wassailing, and the sworn knights-bachelors grew to be but hypocrites and rakes.

But for all this, quite unprepared were we to learn that Knights-Templars (if at all in being) were so entirely secularized as to be reduced from carving out immortal fame in glorious battling for the Holy Land, to the carving of roast-mutton at a dinner-board. Like Anacreon,[7] do these degenerate Templars now think it sweeter far to fall in banquet than in war? Or, indeed, how can there be any survival of that famous order? Templars in modern London! Templars in their red-cross mantles smoking cigars at the Divan![8] Templars crowded in a railway train, till, stacked with steel helmet, spear, and shield, the whole train looks like one elongated locomotive!

No. The genuine Templar is long since departed. Go view the wondrous tombs in the Temple Church;[9] see there the rigidly-haughty forms stretched out, with crossed arms upon their stilly hearts, in everlasting and undreaming rest. Like the years before the flood, the bold-Knights-Templars are no more. Nevertheless, the name remains, and the nominal society, and the ancient grounds, and some of the ancient edifices. But the iron heel is changed to a boot of patent-leather; the long two-handed sword to a one-handed

---

[5]The Knights-Templars were monks of a military religious order established in twelfth-century Jerusalem to protect pilgrims and the Holy Sepulchre during the Crusades. Charges of sexual laxity, including sodomy, led to the order's disbanding in 1312. According to Beryl Rowland, several books published in the 1840s, one of which Melville owned, had revived the debate over the truth of those charges. The most popular source of information on the Templars, however, was Sir Walter Scott's novel *Ivanhoe* (1819), in which the evil Templar Brian de Bois-Guilbert abducts and tries to rape the

Jewess Rebecca, and then has her tried for witchcraft when she resists.
[6]Leopard.
[7]Late sixth-century B.C. Greek poet whose lyrics celebrated wine and love. According to legend, he died by choking on a grape seed.
[8]Melville is punning on the two main definitions of Divan: Oriental council chamber and smoking room.
[9]The Round Church of the Knights-Templars (1185), modeled on the Church of the Holy Sepulchre in Jerusalem and dedicated to St. Mary.

quill; the monk-giver of gratuitous ghostly counsel now counsels for a fee; the defender of the sarcophagus (if in good practice with his weapon) now has more than one case to defend; the vowed opener and clearer of all high-ways leading to the Holy Sepulchre, now has it in particular charge to check, to clog, to hinder, and embarrass all the courts and avenues of Law; the knight-combatant of the Saracen, breasting spear-points at Acre, now fights law-points in Westminster Hall. The helmet is a wig. Struck by Time's enchanter's wand, the Templar is to-day a Lawyer.[10]

But, like many others tumbled from proud glory's height—like the apple, hard on the bough but mellow on the ground—the Templar's fall has but made him all the finer fellow.

I dare say those old warrior-priests were but gruff and grouty at the best; cased in Birmingham[11] hardware, how could their crimped arms give yours or mine a hearty shake? Their proud, ambitious, monkish souls clasped shut, like horn-book missals;[12] their very faces clapped in bomb-shells; what sort of genial men were these? But best of comrades, most affable of hosts, capital diner is the modern Templar. His wit and wine are both of sparkling brands.

The church and cloisters, courts and vaults, lanes and passages, banquet-halls, refectories, libraries, terraces, gardens, broad walks, domicils, and dessert-rooms, covering a very large space of ground, and all grouped in central neighborhood, and quite sequestered from the old city's surrounding din; and every thing about the place being kept in most bachelor-like partic-ularity, no part of London offers to a quiet wight so agreeable a refuge.

The Temple is, indeed, a city by itself. A city with all the best appurte-nances, as the above enumeration shows. A city with a park to it, and flower-beds, and a river-side—the Thames flowing by as openly, in one part, as by Eden's primal garden flowed the mild Euphrates. In what is now the Temple Garden the old Crusaders used to exercise their steeds and lances; the modern Templars now lounge on the benches beneath the trees, and, switching their patent-leather boots, in gay discourse exercise at repartee.

Long lines of stately portraits in the banquet-halls, show what great men of mark—famous nobles, judges, and Lord Chancellors—have in their time been Templars. But all Templars are not known to universal fame; though, if the having warm hearts and warmer welcomes, full minds and fuller cellars, and giving good advice and glorious dinners, spiced with rare divertisements of fun and fancy, merit immortal mention, set down, ye muses, the names of R.F.C.[13] and his imperial brother.

---

[10]Jerusalem's Holy Sepulchre, believed to be the Tomb of Jesus, and the Palestinian sea-port of Acre, the last Christian stronghold of the Crusades, were two of the most fa-mous sites in the struggle between Christi-ans and Saracens (Muslims) for control of the Holy Land. London's Westminster Hall was used as a law court in the nineteenth century.

[11]English industrial city.

[12]Missals: devotional books used during mass; horn-books: children's primers consisting of parchment sheets mounted on boards, with handles and a protective covering of trans-parent horn.

[13]Robert Francis Cooke, Melville's dinner host at Elm Court, Temple.

Though to be a Templar, in the one true sense, you must needs be a law-yer, or a student at the law, and be ceremoniously enrolled as member of the order, yet as many such, though Templars, do not reside within the Temple's precincts, though they may have their offices there, just so, on the other hand, there are many residents of the hoary old domicils who are not admitted Templars. If being, say, a lounging gentleman and bachelor, or a quiet, unmarried, literary man, charmed with the soft seclusion of the spot, you much desire to pitch your shady tent among the rest in this serene encampment, then you must make some special friend among the order, and procure him to rent, in his name but at your charge, whatever vacant chamber you may find to suit.

Thus, I suppose, did Dr. Johnson,[14] that nominal Benedick and widower but virtual bachelor, when for a space he resided here. So, too, did that undoubted bachelor and rare good soul, Charles Lamb.[15] And hundreds more, of sterling spirits, Brethren of the Order of Celibacy, from time to time have dined, and slept, and tabernacled here. Indeed, the place is all a honeycomb of offices and domicils. Like any cheese, it is quite perforated through and through in all directions with the snug cells of bachelors. Dear, delightful spot! Ah! when I bethink me of the sweet hours there passed, enjoying such genial hospitalities beneath those time-honored roofs, my heart only finds due utterance through poetry; and, with a sigh, I softly sing, "Carry me back to old Virginny!"[16]

Such then, at large, is the Paradise of Bachelors. And such I found it one pleasant afternoon in the smiling month of May, when, sallying from my hotel in Trafalgar Square, I went to keep my dinner-appointment with that fine Barrister, Bachelor, and Bencher,[17] R.F.C. (he *is* the first and second, and *should be* the third; I hereby nominate him), whose card I kept fast pinched between my gloved forefinger and thumb, and every now and then snatched still another look at the pleasant address inscribed beneath the name, "No.—, Elm Court, Temple."

At the core he was a right bluff, care-free, right comfortable, and most companionable Englishman. If on a first acquaintance he seemed reserved, quite icy in his air—patience; this Champagne will thaw. And if it never do, better frozen Champagne than liquid vinegar.

There were nine gentlemen, all bachelors, at the dinner. One was from "No.—, King's Bench Walk, Temple;" a second, third, and fourth, and fifth, from various courts or passages christened with some similarly rich resounding syllables. It was indeed a sort of Senate of the Bachelors, sent to this dinner from widely-scattered districts, to represent the general celibacy of the Temple. Nay it was, by representation, a Grand Parliament of the best

---

[14]Samuel Johnson (1709–1784), English writer and lexicographer, whose haunts in Fleet Street Melville visited.
[15]English essayist (1775–1834), whose works Melville had begun reading on the sea passage to London.

[16]A pun on the virgin (bachelor) state, as well as one of several allusions linking the ruling classes of England and America and the systems of oppression over which they preside.
[17]One of the senior members presiding over the Inns of Court; a judge.

Bachelors in universal London; several of those present being from distant quarters of the town, noted immemorial seats of lawyers and unmarried men—Lincoln's Inn, Furnival's Inn; and one gentleman, upon whom I looked with a sort of collateral awe, hailed from the spot where Lord Verulam[18] once abode a bachelor—Gray's Inn.

The apartment was well up toward heaven. I know not how many strange old stairs I climbed to get to it. But a good dinner, with famous company, should be well earned. No doubt our host had his dining-room so high with a view to secure the prior exercise necessary to the due relishing and digesting of it.

The furniture was wonderfully unpretending, old, and snug. No new shining mahogany, sticky with undried varnish; no uncomfortably luxurious ottomans, and sofas too fine to use, vexed you in this sedate apartment. It is a thing which every sensible American should learn from every sensible Englishman, that glare and glitter, gimcracks and gewgaws, are not indispensable to domestic solacement. The American Benedick snatches, downtown, a tough chop in a gilded show-box; the English bachelor leisurely dines at home on that incomparable South Down of his, off a plain deal board.[19]

The ceiling of the room was low. Who wants to dine under the dome of St. Peter's? High ceilings! If that is your demand, and the higher the better, and you be so very tall, then go dine out with the topping giraffe in the open air.

In good time the nine gentlemen sat down to nine covers, and soon were fairly under way.

If I remember right, ox-tail soup inaugurated the affair. Of a rich russet hue, its agreeable flavor dissipated my first confounding of its main ingredient with teamster's gads and the raw-hides of ushers.[20] (By way of interlude, we here drank a little claret.) Neptune's was the next tribute rendered—turbot[21] coming second; snow-white, flaky, and just gelatinous enough, not too turtleish in its unctuousness.

(At this point we refreshed ourselves with a glass of sherry.) After these light skirmishers had vanished, the heavy artillery of the feast marched in, led by that well-known English generalissimo, roast beef. For aids-de-camp we had a saddle of mutton, a fat turkey, a chicken-pie, and endless other savory things; while for avant-couriers[22] came nine silver flagons of humming ale. This heavy ordnance having departed on the track of the light skirmishers, a picked brigade of game-fowl encamped upon the board, their camp-fires lit by the ruddiest of decanters.

---

[18]Francis Bacon (1561–1626), English philosopher and statesman.
[19]Mutton from the Southdown breed of sheep, served on a wooden trencher.
[20]Both ushers (assistant schoolmasters) and teamsters use gads (goads) or rawhide whips, made from oxtails.

[21]Rich, gelatinous white fish.
[22]The advance guard of an army. Note the elaborate military imagery.

Tarts and puddings followed, with innumerable niceties; then cheese and crackers. (By way of ceremony, simply, only to keep up good old fashions, we here each drank a glass of good old port.)

The cloth was now removed; and like Blucher's[23] army coming in at the death on the field of Waterloo, in marched a fresh detachment of bottles, dusty with their hurried march.

All these manœuvrings of the forces were superintended by a surprising old field-marshal (I can not school myself to call him by the inglorious name of waiter), with snowy hair and napkin, and a head like Socrates. Amidst all the hilarity of the feast, intent on important business, he disdained to smile. Venerable man!

I have above endeavored to give some slight schedule of the general plan of operations. But any one knows that a good, genial dinner is a sort of pell-mell, indiscriminate affair, quite baffling to detail in all particulars. Thus, I spoke of taking a glass of claret, and a glass of sherry, and a glass of port, and a mug of ale—all at certain specific periods and times. But those were merely the state bumpers,[24] so to speak. Innumerable impromptu glasses were drained between the periods of those grand imposing ones.

The nine bachelors seemed to have the most tender concern for each other's health. All the time, in flowing wine, they most earnestly expressed their sincerest wishes for the entire well-being and lasting hygiene of the gentlemen on the right and on the left. I noticed that when one of these kind bachelors desired a little more wine (just for his stomach's sake, like Timothy),[25] he would not help himself to it unless some other bachelor would join him. It seemed held something indelicate, selfish, and unfraternal, to be seen taking a lonely, unparticipated glass. Meantime, as the wine ran apace, the spirits of the company grew more and more to perfect genialness and unconstraint. They related all sorts of pleasant stories. Choice experiences in their private lives were now brought out, like choice brands of Moselle or Rhenish, only kept for particular company. One told us how mellowly he lived when a student at Oxford; with various spicy anecdotes of most frank-hearted noble lords, his liberal companions. Another bachelor, a gray-headed man, with a sunny face, who, by his own account, embraced every opportunity of leisure to cross over into the Low Countries,[26] on sudden tours of inspection of the fine old Flemish architecture there—this learned, white-haired, sunny-faced old bachelor, excelled in his

[23]Gebhard Leberecht von Blucher (1742–1819), leader of the Prussian troops allied with the English against Napoleon at the Battle of Waterloo, 1815. The victory over Napoleon inaugurated the era of British imperial rule.

[24]Large drinking glasses, filled to the brim; here used in the sense of official toasts.

[25]I Timothy 5:23: "Drink no longer water, but use a little wine for thy stomach's sake and thine often infirmities."

[26]Hershel Parker suggests that Melville may intend a bawdy Shakespearean pun on the lower parts of the body.

descriptions of the elaborate splendors of those old guild-halls, town-halls, and stadthold-houses, to be seen in the land of the ancient Flemings. A third was a great frequenter of the British Museum, and knew all about scores of wonderful antiquities, of Oriental manuscripts, and costly books without a duplicate. A fourth had lately returned from a trip to Old Granada, and, of course, was full of Saracenic scenery. A fifth had a funny case in law to tell. A sixth was erudite in wines. A seventh had a strange characteristic anecdote of the private life of the Iron Duke,[27] never printed, and never before announced in any public or private company. An eighth had lately been amusing his evenings, now and then, with translating a comic poem of Pulci's.[28] He quoted for us the more amusing passages.

And so the evening slipped along, the hours told, not by a water-clock,[29] like King Alfred's, but a wine-chronometer. Meantime the table seemed a sort of Epsom Heath;[30] a regular ring, where the decanters galloped round. For fear one decanter should not with sufficient speed reach his destination, another was sent express after him to hurry him; and then a third to hurry the second; and so on with a fourth and fifth. And throughout all this nothing loud, nothing unmannerly, nothing turbulent. I am quite sure, from the scrupulous gravity and austerity of his air, that had Socrates, the field-marshal, perceived aught of indecorum in the company he served, he would have forthwith departed without giving warning. I afterward learned that, during the repast, an invalid bachelor in an adjoining chamber enjoyed his first sound refreshing slumber in three long, weary weeks.

It was the very perfection of quiet absorption of good living, good drinking, good feeling, and good talk. We were a band of brothers. Comfort—fraternal, household comfort, was the grand trait of the affair. Also, you could plainly see that these easy-hearted men had no wives or children to give an anxious thought. Almost all of them were travelers, too; for bachelors alone can travel freely, and without any twinges of their consciences touching desertion of the fire-side.

The thing called pain, the bugbear styled trouble—those two legends seemed preposterous to their bachelor imaginations. How could men of liberal sense, ripe scholarship in the world, and capacious philosophical and convivial understandings—how could they suffer themselves to be imposed upon by such monkish fables? Pain! Trouble! As well talk of Catholic miracles. No such thing.—Pass the sherry, Sir.—Pooh, pooh! Can't be!—The port, Sir, if you please. Nonsense; don't tell me so.—The decanter stops with you, Sir, I believe.

And so it went.

---

[27]The Duke of Wellington (1769–1852), leader of the English army that defeated Napoleon at Waterloo.

[28]Luigi Pulci (1432–1484), Florentine comic poet.

[29]Instrument designed to measure time by the fall or flow of a quantity of water.

[30]English racetrack.

Not long after the cloth was drawn our host glanced significantly upon Socrates, who, solemnly stepping to a stand, returned with an immense convolved horn, a regular Jericho horn,[31] mounted with polished silver, and otherwise chased and curiously enriched; not omitting two life-like goat's heads, with four more horns of solid silver, projecting from opposite sides of the mouth of the noble main horn.

Not having heard that our host was a performer on the bugle, I was surprised to see him lift this horn from the table, as if he were about to blow an inspiring blast. But I was relieved from this, and set quite right as touching the purposes of the horn, by his now inserting his thumb and forefinger into its mouth; whereupon a slight aroma was stirred up, and my nostrils were greeted with the smell of some choice Rappee. It was a mull of snuff.[32] It went the rounds. Capital idea this, thought I, of taking snuff about this juncture. This goodly fashion must be introduced among my countrymen at home, further ruminated I.

The remarkable decorum of the nine bachelors—a decorum not to be affected by any quantity of wine—a decorum unassailable by any degree of mirthfulness—this was again set in a forcible light to me, by now observing that, though they took snuff very freely, yet not a man so far violated the proprieties, or so far molested the invalid bachelor in the adjoining room as to indulge himself in a sneeze. The snuff was snuffed silently, as if it had been some fine innoxious powder brushed off the wings of butterflies.

But fine though they be, bachelors' dinners, like bachelors' lives, can not endure forever. The time came for breaking up. One by one the bachelors took their hats, and two by two, and arm-in-arm they descended, still conversing, to the flagging of the court; some going to their neighboring chambers to turn over the Decameron[33] ere retiring for the night; some to smoke a cigar, promenading in the garden on the cool river-side; some to make for the street, call a hack, and be driven snugly to their distant lodgings.

I was the last lingerer.

"Well," said my smiling host, "what do you think of the Temple here, and the sort of life we bachelors make out to live in it?"

---

[31]Joshua 6:1–21 tells the story of how God delivered the city of Jericho into the hands of the Israelites. Carrying the ark and blowing "seven trumpets of rams' horns," seven priests circled the city for seven days, and on the seventh day, when they made a "long blast with the ram's horn," the people lifted up a "great shout" and "the wall of the city [fell] down flat." In the aftermath, the Israelites "utterly destroyed all that was in the city, both man and woman, young and old, and ox, and sheep, and ass, with the edge of the sword." Hence the Jericho horn is an apocalyptic symbol.

[32]Rappee: a moist, pungent snuff made from dark, rank tobacco leaves. Mull: a snuff-box

(derived from mill; the verbs "to mull" and "to mill" both mean "to grind"). Beryl Rowland has pointed out the ancient sexual connotations of the mill, and the link between the mull in the first sketch and the paper mill in the second.

[33]A collection of bawdy tales by the Italian writer Giovanni Boccaccio (1313–1375). The title refers to the ten days that the ten narrators have spent telling stories, in order to while away their seclusion in a country villa during the plague in Florence. Both the fictional content and the historical context of the Decameron are highly relevant to Melville's sketch.

"Sir," said I, with a burst of admiring candor—"Sir, this is the very Paradise of Bachelors!"

II. The Tartarus of Maids

It lies not far from Woedolor Mountain in New England. Turning to the east, right out from among bright farms and sunny meadows, nodding in early June with odorous grasses, you enter ascendingly among bleak hills. These gradually close in upon a dusky pass, which, from the violent Gulf Stream of air unceasingly driving between its cloven walls of haggard rock, as well as from the tradition of a crazy spinster's hut having long ago stood somewhere hereabouts, is called the Mad Maid's Bellows'-pipe.[1]

Winding along at the bottom of the gorge is a dangerously narrow wheel-road, occupying the bed of a former torrent. Following this road to its highest point, you stand as within a Dantean gateway.[2] From the steepness of the walls here, their strangely ebon hue, and the sudden contraction of the gorge, this particular point is called the Black Notch. The ravine now expandingly descends into a great, purple, hopper-shaped hollow, far sunk among many Plutonian, shaggy-wooded mountains. By the country people this hollow is called the Devil's Dungeon. Sounds of torrents fall on all sides upon the ear. These rapid waters unite at last in one turbid brick-colored stream, boiling through a flume among enormous boulders. They call this strange-colored torrent Blood River. Gaining a dark precipice it wheels suddenly to the west, and makes one maniac spring of sixty feet into the arms of a stunted wood of gray-haired pines, between which it thence eddies on its further way down to the invisible lowlands.

Conspicuously crowning a rocky bluff high to one side, at the cataract's verge, is the ruin of an old saw-mill, built in those primitive times when vast pines and hemlocks superabounded throughout the neighboring region. The black-mossed bulk of those immense, rough-hewn, and spike-knotted logs, here and there tumbled all together, in long abandonment and decay, or left in solitary, perilous projection over the cataract's gloomy brink, impart to this rude wooden ruin not only much of the aspect of one of rough-quarried stone, but also a sort of feudal, Rhineland, and Thurmberg[3] look, derived from the pinnacled wildness of the neighboring scenery.

Not far from the bottom of the Dungeon stands a large white-washed building, relieved, like some great whited sepulchre,[4] against the sullen

---

[1]Note the elaborate parallels linking the second sketch to the first, and the equally elaborate sexual symbolism, both inaugurated here and developed throughout.

[2]The gateway to hell, described in *The Inferno* by the Italian poet Dante Alighieri (1265–1321) as bearing the inscription: "Through me you pass into the city of woe:/Through me you pass into eternal pain/ . . . /All hope abandon, ye who enter here." This is the infernal counterpart of the Temple Bar gateway by Wren.

[3]A fourteenth-century fortified castle whose ruins dominated the Rhine near Welmich, south of Koblenz.

[4]Cf. Matthew 23:27: "Woe unto you, scribes and Pharisees, hypocrites! for ye are like unto whited sepulchres, which indeed appear beautiful outward, but are within full of dead men's bones, and of all uncleanness."

background of mountain-side firs, and other hardy evergreens, inaccessibly rising in grim terraces for some two thousand feet.

The building is a paper-mill.

Having embarked on a large scale in the seedsman's business (so extensively and broadcast, indeed, that at length my seeds were distributed through all the Eastern and Northern States, and even fell into the far soil of Missouri and the Carolinas), the demand for paper at my place became so great, that the expenditure soon amounted to a most important item in the general account. It need hardly be hinted how paper comes into use with seedsmen, as envelopes. These are mostly made of yellowish paper, folded square; and when filled, are all but flat, and being stamped, and superscribed with the nature of the seeds contained, assume not a little the appearance of business-letters ready for the mail. Of these small envelopes I used an incredible quantity—several hundreds of thousands in a year. For a time I had purchased my paper from the wholesale dealers in a neighboring town. For economy's sake, and partly for the adventure of the trip, I now resolved to cross the mountains, some sixty miles, and order my future paper at the Devil's Dungeon paper-mill.

The sleighing being uncommonly fine toward the end of January, and promising to hold so for no small period, in spite of the bitter cold I started one gray Friday noon in my pung,[5] well fitted with buffalo and wolf robes; and, spending one night on the road, next noon came in sight of Woedolor Mountain.

The far summit fairly smoked with frost; white vapors curled up from its white-wooded top, as from a chimney. The intense congelation made the whole country look like one petrifaction. The steel shoes of my pung craunched and gritted over the vitreous, chippy snow, as if it had been broken glass. The forests here and there skirting the route, feeling the same all-stiffening influence, their inmost fibres penetrated with the cold, strangely groaned—not in the swaying branches merely, but likewise in the vertical trunk—as the fitful gusts remorselessly swept through them. Brittle with excessive frost, many colossal tough-grained maples, snapped in twain like pipe-stems, cumbered the unfeeling earth.

Flaked all over with frozen sweat, white as a milky ram, his nostrils at each breath sending forth two horn-shaped shoots of heated respiration, Black, my good horse, but six years old, started at a sudden turn, where, right across the track—not ten minutes fallen—an old distorted hemlock lay, darkly undulatory as an anaconda.[6]

Gaining the Bellows'-pipe, the violent blast, dead from behind, all but shoved my high-backed pung up-hill. The gust shrieked through the shivered pass, as if laden with lost spirits bound to the unhappy world. Ere gaining the summit, Black, my horse, as if exasperated by the cutting wind, slung

---

[5]One-horse sleigh used in New England.
[6]A large snake of the boa constrictor type. The runaway horse is a common symbol of uncontrolled sexuality. Note the verbal echoes of the passage describing the Jericho horn.

out with his strong hind legs, tore the light pung straight up-hill, and sweeping grazingly through the narrow notch, sped downward madly past the ruined saw-mill. Into the Devil's Dungeon horse and cataract rushed together.

With might and main, quitting my seat and robes, and standing backward, with one foot braced against the dash-board, I rasped and churned the bit, and stopped him just in time to avoid collision, at a turn, with the bleak nozzle of a rock, couchant like a lion in the way—a road-side rock.

At first I could not discover the paper-mill.

The whole hollow gleamed with the white, except, here and there, where a pinnacle of granite showed one wind-swept angle bare. The mountains stood pinned in shrouds—a pass of Alpine corpses. Where stands the mill? Suddenly a whirling, humming sound broke upon my ear. I looked, and there, like an arrested avalanche, lay the large whitewashed factory. It was subordinately surrounded by a cluster of other and smaller buildings, some of which, from their cheap, blank air, great length, gregarious windows, and comfortless expression, no doubt were boarding-houses of the operatives. A snow-white hamlet amidst the snows. Various rude, irregular squares and courts resulted from the somewhat picturesque clusterings of these buildings, owing to the broken, rocky nature of the ground, which forbade all method in their relative arrangement. Several narrow lanes and alleys, too, partly blocked with snow fallen from the roof, cut up the hamlet in all directions.

When, turning from the traveled highway, jingling with bells of numerous farmers—who, availing themselves of the fine sleighing, were dragging their wood to market—and frequently diversified with swift cutters dashing from inn to inn of the scattered villages—when, I say, turning from that bustling main-road, I by degrees wound into the Mad Maid's Bellows'-pipe, and saw the grim Black Notch beyond, then something latent, as well as something obvious in the time and scene, strangely brought back to my mind my first sight of dark and grimy Temple-Bar. And when Black, my horse, went darting through the Notch, perilously grazing its rocky wall, I remembered being in a runaway London omnibus, which in much the same sort of style, though by no means at an equal rate, dashed through the ancient arch of Wren. Though the two objects did by no means completely correspond, yet this partial inadequacy but served to tinge the similitude not less with the vividness than the disorder of a dream. So that, when upon reining up at the protruding rock I at last caught sight of the quaint groupings of the factory-buildings, and with the traveled highway and the Notch behind, found myself all alone, silently and privily stealing through deep-cloven passages into this sequestered spot, and saw the long, high-gabled main factory edifice, with a rude tower—for hoisting heavy boxes—at one end, standing among its crowded outbuildings and boarding-houses, as the Temple Church amidst the surrounding offices and dormitories, and when the marvelous retirement of this mysterious mountain nook fastened its whole spell upon me, then, what memory lacked, all tributary imagination furnished, and I said to myself, "This is the very counterpart of the Paradise of Bachelors, but snowed upon, and frost-painted to a sepulchre."

Dismounting, and warily picking my way down the dangerous declivity—horse and man both sliding now and then upon the icy ledges—at length I drove, or the blast drove me, into the largest square, before one side of the main edifice. Piercingly and shrilly the shotted blast blew by the corner; and redly and demoniacally boiled Blood River at one side. A long wood-pile, of many scores of cords, all glittering in mail of crusted ice, stood crosswise in the square. A row of horse-posts, their north sides plastered with adhesive snow, flanked the factory wall. The bleak frost packed and paved the square as with some ringing metal.

The inverted similitude recurred—"The sweet, tranquil Temple garden, with the Thames bordering its green beds," strangely meditated I.

But where are the gay bachelors?

Then, as I and my horse stood shivering in the wind-spray, a girl ran from a neighboring dormitory door, and throwing her thin apron over her bare head, made for the opposite building.

"One moment, my girl; is there no shed hereabouts which I may drive into?"

Pausing, she turned upon me a face pale with work, and blue with cold; an eye supernatural with unrelated misery.

"Nay," faltered I, "I mistook you. Go on; I want nothing."

Leading my horse close to the door from which she had come, I knocked. Another pale, blue girl appeared, shivering in the doorway as, to prevent the blast, she jealously held the door ajar.

"Nay, I mistake again. In God's name shut the door. But hold, is there no man about?"

That moment a dark-complexioned well-wrapped personage passed, making for the factory door, and spying him coming, the girl rapidly closed the other one.

"Is there no horse-shed here, Sir?"

"Yonder, to the wood-shed," he replied, and disappeared inside the factory.

With much ado I managed to wedge in horse and pung between the scattered piles of wood all sawn and split. Then, blanketing my horse, and piling my buffalo on the blanket's top, and tucking in its edges well around the breast-band and breeching, so that the wind might not strip him bare, I tied him fast, and ran lamely for the factory door, stiff with frost, and cumbered with my driver's dread-naught.[7]

Immediately I found myself standing in a spacious place, intolerably lighted by long rows of windows, focusing inward the snowy scene without.

At rows of blank-looking counters sat rows of blank-looking girls, with blank, white folders in their blank hands, all blankly folding blank paper.

In one corner stood some huge frame of ponderous iron, with a vertical thing like a piston periodically rising and falling upon a heavy wooden block.

---

[7]Warm garment of thick cloth.

Before it—its tame minister—stood a tall girl, feeding the iron animal with half-quires[8] of rose-hued note paper, which, at every downward dab of the piston-like machine, received in the corner the impress of a wreath of roses. I looked from the rosy paper to the pallid cheek, but said nothing.

Seated before a long apparatus, strung with long, slender strings like any harp, another girl was feeding it with foolscap sheets, which, so soon as they curiously traveled from her on the cords, were withdrawn at the opposite end of the machine by a second girl. They came to the first girl blank; they went to the second girl ruled.

I looked upon the first girl's brow, and saw it was young and fair; I looked upon the second girl's brow, and saw it was ruled and wrinkled. Then, as I still looked, the two—for some small variety to the monotony—changed places; and where had stood the young, fair brow, now stood the ruled and wrinkled one.

Perched high upon a narrow platform, and still higher upon a high stool crowning it, sat another figure serving some other iron animal; while below the platform sat her mate in some sort of reciprocal attendance.

Not a syllable was breathed. Nothing was heard but the low, steady, overruling hum of the iron animals. The human voice was banished from the spot. Machinery—that vaunted slave of humanity—here stood menially served by human beings, who served mutely and cringingly as the slave serves the Sultan. The girls did not so much seem accessory wheels to the general machinery as mere cogs to the wheels.[9]

All this scene around me was instantaneously taken in at one sweeping glance—even before I had proceeded to unwind the heavy fur tippet from around my neck. But as soon as this fell from me the dark-complexioned man, standing close by, raised a sudden cry, and seizing my arm, dragged me out into the open air, and without pausing for a word instantly caught up some congealed snow and began rubbing both my cheeks.

"Two white spots like the whites of your eyes," he said; "man, your cheeks are frozen."

"That may well be," muttered I; "'tis some wonder the frost of the Devil's Dungeon strikes in no deeper. Rub away."

Soon a horrible, tearing pain caught at my reviving cheeks. Two gaunt blood-hounds, one on each side, seemed mumbling them. I seemed Actæon.[10]

Presently, when all was over, I re-entered the factory, made known my business, concluded it satisfactorily, and then begged to be conducted throughout the place to view it.

---

[8]Twelve sheets of folded paper.

[9]Cf. the famous passage in *The Communist Manifesto* explaining how laborers under capitalism become "a commodity" and "an appendage of the machine": "Not only are they slaves of the bourgeois class and the bourgeois state; they are daily and hourly enslaved by the machine, by the supervisor, and above all, by the individual bourgeois manufacturer himself."

[10]Hunter in classical mythology who watched the goddess Artemis (Diana) bathing and was punished by being turned into a stag and torn apart by his own dogs. The roles of Artemis as patroness of childbirth, chastity, and unmarried women are particularly relevant to Melville's story.

"Cupid is the boy for that," said the dark-complexioned man. "Cupid!" and by this odd fancy-name calling a dimpled, red-cheeked, spirited-looking, forward little fellow, who was rather impudently, I thought, gliding about among the passive-looking girls—like a gold fish through hueless waves— yet doing nothing in particular that I could see, the man bade him lead the stranger through the edifice.

"Come first and see the water-wheel," said this lively lad, with the air of boyishly-brisk importance.

Quitting the folding-room, we crossed some damp, cold boards, and stood beneath a great wet shed, incessantly showering with foam, like the green barnacled bow of some East Indiaman[11] in a gale. Round and round here went the enormous revolutions of the dark colossal water-wheel, grim with its one immutable purpose.

"This sets our whole machinery a-going, Sir; in every part of all these buildings; where the girls work and all."

I looked, and saw that the turbid waters of Blood River had not changed their hue by coming under the use of man.

"You make only blank paper; no printing of any sort, I suppose? All blank paper, don't you?"

"Certainly; what else should a paper-factory make?"

The lad here looked at me as if suspicious of my common-sense.

"Oh, to be sure!" said I, confused and stammering; "it only struck me as so strange that red waters should turn out pale chee—paper, I mean."

He took me up a wet and rickety stair to a great light room, furnished with no visible thing but rude, manger-like receptacles running all round its sides; and up to these mangers, like so many mares haltered to the rack, stood rows of girls. Before each was vertically thrust up a long, glittering scythe, immovably fixed at bottom to the manger-edge. The curve of the scythe, and its having no snath[12] to it, made it look exactly like a sword. To and fro, across the sharp edge, the girls forever dragged long strips of rags, washed white, picked from baskets at one side; thus ripping asunder every seam, and converting the tatters almost into lint. The air swam with the fine, poisonous particles, which from all sides darted, subtilely, as motes in sun-beams, into the lungs.

"This is the rag-room," coughed the boy.

"You find it rather stifling here," coughed I, in answer; "but the girls don't cough."

"Oh, they are used to it."

---

[11]Large sailing ship used in trade with India. That trade played a crucial role in the Industrial Revolution, first by contributing to capital accumulation, then by providing raw materials and a market for the British textile industry. During the very years when British military forces were busy defeating Napoleon, British manufacturing interests were gaining the upper hand over mercantile interests and developing the colonial policy that systematically destroyed the Indian hand-loom industry and transformed India from a major exporter into an importer of cotton textiles.
[12]Handle.

"Where do you get such hosts of rags?" picking up a handful from a basket.

"Some from the country round about; some from far over sea—Leghorn[13] and London."

"'Tis not unlikely, then," murmured I, "that among these heaps of rags there may be some old shirts, gathered from the dormitories of the Paradise of Bachelors. But the buttons are all dropped off. Pray, my lad, do you ever find any bachelor's buttons hereabouts?"

"None grow in this part of the country. The Devil's Dungeon is no place for flowers."

"Oh! you mean the *flowers* so called—the Bachelor's Buttons?"

"And was not that what you asked about? Or did you mean the gold bosom-buttons of our boss, Old Bach,[14] as our whispering girls all call him?"

"The man, then, I saw below is a bachelor, is he?"

"Oh, yes, he's a Bach."

"The edges of those swords, they are turned outward from the girls, if I see right; but their rags and fingers fly so, I can not distinctly see."

"Turned outward."

Yes, murmured I to myself; I see it now; turned outward; and each erected sword is so borne, edge-outward, before each girl. If my reading fails me not, just so, of old, condemned state-prisoners went from the hall of judgment to their doom: an officer before, bearing a sword, its edge turned outward, in significance of their fatal sentence. So, through consumptive pallors of this blank, raggy life, go these white girls to death.

"Those scythes look very sharp," again turning toward the boy.

"Yes; they have to keep them so. Look!"

That moment two of the girls, dropping their rags, plied each a whetstone up and down the sword-blade. My unaccustomed blood curdled at the sharp shriek of the tormented steel.

Their own executioners; themselves whetting the very swords that slay them; meditated I.

"What makes those girls so sheet-white, my lad?"

"Why"—with a roguish twinkle, pure ignorant drollery, not knowing heartlessness—"I suppose the handling of such white bits of sheets all the time makes them so sheety."

"Let us leave the rag-room now, my lad."

More tragical and more inscrutably mysterious than any mystic sight, human or machine, throughout the factory, was the strange innocence of cruel-heartedness in this usage-hardened boy.

"And now," said he, cheerily, "I suppose you want to see our great machine, which cost us twelve thousand dollars only last autumn. That's the machine that makes the paper, too. This way, Sir."

---

[13]Livorno, third-ranking west coast port of Italy, after Genoa and Naples.   [14]As in bachelor.

Following him, I crossed a large, bespattered place, with two great round vats in it, full of a white, wet, woolly-looking stuff, not unlike the albuminous part of an egg, soft-boiled.

"There," said Cupid, tapping the vats carelessly, "these are the first beginnings of the paper; this white pulp you see. Look how it swims bubbling round and round, moved by the paddle here. From hence it pours from both vats into that one common channel yonder; and so goes, mixed up and leisurely, to the great machine. And now for that."

He led me into a room, stifling with a strange, blood-like, abdominal heat, as if here, true enough, were being finally developed the germinous particles lately seen.

Before me, rolled out like some long Eastern manuscript, lay stretched one continuous length of iron frame-work—multitudinous and mystical, with all sorts of rollers, wheels, and cylinders, in slowly-measured and unceasing motion.

"Here first comes the pulp now," said Cupid, pointing to the nighest end of the machine. "See; first it pours out and spreads itself upon this wide, sloping board; and then—look—slides, thin and quivering, beneath the first roller there. Follow on now, and see it as it slides from under that to the next cylinder. There; see how it has become just a very little less pulpy now. One step more, and it grows still more to some slight consistence. Still another cylinder, and it is so knitted—though as yet mere dragon-fly wing—that it forms an air-bridge here, like a suspended cobweb, between two more separated rollers; and flowing over the last one, and under again, and doubling about there out of sight for a minute among all those mixed cylinders you indistinctly see, it reappears here, looking now at last a little less like pulp and more like paper, but still quite delicate and defective yet awhile. But—a little further onward, Sir, if you please—here now, at this further point, it puts on something of a real look, as if it might turn out to be something you might possibly handle in the end. But it's not yet done, Sir. Good way to travel yet, and plenty more of cylinders must roll it."

"Bless my soul!" said I, amazed at the elongation, interminable convolutions, and deliberate slowness of the machine; "it must take a long time for the pulp to pass from end to end, and come out paper."

"Oh! not so long," smiled the precocious lad, with a superior and patronizing air; "only nine minutes. But look; you may try it for yourself. Have you a bit of paper? Ah! here's a bit on the floor. Now mark that with any word you please, and let me dab it on here, and we'll see how long before it comes out at the other end."

"Well, let me see," said I, taking out my pencil; "come, I'll mark it with your name."

Bidding me take out my watch, Cupid adroitly dropped the inscribed slip on an exposed part of the incipient mass.

Instantly my eye marked the second-hand on my dial-plate.

Slowly I followed the slip, inch by inch; sometimes pausing for full half a minute as it disappeared beneath inscrutable groups of the lower cylinders, but only gradually to emerge again; and so, on, and on, and on—inch by inch; now in open sight, sliding along like a freckle on the quivering sheet; and then again wholly vanished; and so, on, and on, and on—inch by inch; all the time the main sheet growing more and more to final firmness—when, suddenly, I saw a sort of paper-fall, not wholly unlike a water-fall; a scissory sound smote my ear, as of some cord being snapped; and down dropped an unfolded sheet of perfect foolscap,[15] with my "Cupid" half faded out of it, and still moist and warm.

My travels were at an end, for here was the end of the machine.

"Well, how long was it?" said Cupid.

"Nine minutes to a second," replied I, watch in hand.

"I told you so."

For a moment a curious emotion filled me, not wholly unlike that which one might experience at the fulfillment of some mysterious prophecy. But how absurd, thought I again; the thing is a mere machine, the essence of which is unvarying punctuality and precision.

Previously absorbed by the wheels and cylinders, my attention was now directed to a sad-looking woman standing by.

"That is rather an elderly person so silently tending the machine-end here. She would not seem wholly used to it either."

"Oh," knowingly whispered Cupid, through the din, "she only came last week. She was a nurse[16] formerly. But the business is poor in these parts, and she's left it. But look at the paper she is piling there."

"Ay, foolscap," handling the piles of moist, warm sheets, which continually were being delivered into the woman's waiting hands. "Don't you turn out any thing but foolscap at this machine?"

"Oh, sometimes, but not often, we turn out finer work—cream-laid and royal sheets, we call them. But foolscap being in chief demand, we turn out foolscap most."

It was very curious. Looking at that blank paper continually dropping, dropping, dropping, my mind ran on in wonderings of those strange uses to which those thousand sheets eventually would be put. All sorts of writings would be writ on those now vacant things—sermons, lawyers' briefs, physicians' prescriptions, love-letters, marriage certificates, bills of divorce, registers of births, death-warrants, and so on, without end. Then, recurring back to them as they here lay all blank, I could not but bethink me of that celebrated comparison of John Locke, who, in demonstration of his theory that man had no innate ideas, compared the human mind at birth to a sheet of blank paper; something destined to be scribbled on, but what sort of characters no soul might tell.[17]

---

[15]Cheap writing paper, typically 16 by 13 inches. Derived from the watermark of a dunce's cap formerly applied to such paper.

[16]In the original meaning of the word, a woman employed to suckle and otherwise care for an infant.

[17]John Locke, English philosopher (1632–1704). His *Essay Concerning Human Understanding* (1690) denied the existence of innate ideas and compared the mind of a newborn infant to a "tabula rasa," or blank page.

Pacing slowing to and fro along the involved machine, still humming with its play, I was struck as well by the inevitability as the evolvement-power in all its motions.

"Does that thin cobweb there," said I, pointing to the sheet in its more imperfect stage, "does that never tear or break? It is marvelous fragile, and yet this machine it passes through is so mighty."

"It never is known to tear a hair's point."

"Does it never stop—get clogged?"

"No. It *must* go. The machinery makes it go just *so;* just that very way, and at that very pace you there plainly *see* it go. The pulp can't help going."

Something of awe now stole over me, as I gazed upon this inflexible iron animal. Always, more or less, machinery of this ponderous, elaborate sort strikes, in some moods, strange dread into the human heart, as some living, panting Behemoth might. But what made the thing I saw so specially terrible to me was the metallic necessity, the unbudging fatality which governed it. Though, here and there, I could not follow the thin, gauzy vail of pulp in the course of its more mysterious or entirely invisible advance, yet it was indubitable that, at those points where it eluded me, it still marched on in unvarying docility to the autocratic cunning of the machine. A fascination fastened on me. I stood spell-bound and wandering in my soul. Before my eyes—there, passing in slow procession along the wheeling cylinders, I seemed to see, glued to the pallid incipience of the pulp, the yet more pallid faces of all the pallid girls I had eyed that heavy day. Slowly, mournfully, beseechingly, yet unresistingly, they gleamed along, their agony dimly outlined on the imperfect paper, like the print of the tormented face on the handkerchief of Saint Veronica.[18]

"Halloa! the heat of the room is too much for you," cried Cupid, staring at me.

"No—I am rather chill, if any thing."

"Come out, Sir—out—out," and, with the protecting air of a careful father, the precocious lad hurried me outside.

In a few moments, feeling revived a little, I went into the folding-room—the first room I had entered, and where the desk for transacting business stood, surrounded by the blank counters and blank girls engaged at them.

"Cupid here has led me a strange tour," said I to the dark-complexioned man before mentioned, whom I had ere this discovered not only to be an old bachelor, but also the principal proprietor. "Yours is a most wonderful factory. Your great machine is a miracle of inscrutable intricacy."

"Yes, all our visitors think it so. But we don't have many. We are in a very out-of-the-way corner here. Few inhabitants, too. Most of our girls come from far-off villages."

---

[18]According to legend, when Christ was carrying his cross on the way to Calvary, she wiped his face with her veil or handkerchief, which miraculously retained its imprint.

"The girls," echoed I, glancing round at their silent forms. "Why is it, Sir, that in most factories, female operatives, of whatever age, are indiscriminately called girls, never women?"

"Oh! as to that—why, I suppose, the fact of their being generally unmarried—that's the reason, I should think. But it never struck me before. For our factory here, we will not have married women; they are apt to be off-and-on too much. We want none but steady workers: twelve hours to the day, day after day, through the three hundred and sixty-five days, excepting Sundays, Thanksgiving, and Fast-days. That's our rule. And so, having no married women, what females we have are rightly enough called girls."

"Then these are all maids," said I, while some pained homage to their pale virginity made me involuntarily bow.

"All maids."

Again the strange emotion filled me.

"Your cheeks look whitish yet, Sir," said the man, gazing at me narrowly. "You must be careful going home. Do they pain you at all now? It's a bad sign, if they do."

"No doubt, Sir," answered I, "when once I have got out of the Devil's Dungeon, I shall feel them mending."

"Ah, yes; the winter air in valleys, or gorges, or any sunken place, is far colder and more bitter than elsewhere. You would hardly believe it now, but it is colder here than at the top of Woedolor Mountain."

"I dare say it is, Sir. But time presses me; I must depart."

With that, remuffling myself in dread-naught and tippet, thrusting my hands into my huge seal-skin mittens, I sallied out into the nipping air, and found poor Black, my horse, all cringing and doubled up with the cold.

Soon, wrapped in furs and meditations, I ascended from the Devil's Dungeon.

At the Black Notch I paused, and once more bethought me of Temple-Bar. Then, shooting through the pass, all alone with inscrutable nature, I exclaimed—Oh! Paradise of Bachelors! and oh! Tartarus of Maids!

1855

Benito Cereno[1]

In the year 1799, Captain Amasa Delano,[2] of Duxbury, in Massachusetts, commanding a large sealer[3] and general trader, lay at anchor, with a

---

[1]"Benito Cereno" was serialized in the October, November, and December 1855 issues of *Putnam's Monthly* and collected the following year in *The Piazza Tales*. The present text is from the standard Northwestern-Newberry edition of *The Piazza Tales and Other Prose Pieces, 1839–1860*.

[2]As Horace Scudder first noted, Melville based his plot primarily on Chapter 18 of Captain

Amasa Delano's *Narrative of Voyages and Travels, in the Northern and Southern Hemispheres* (1817), but altered and amplified his source in significant ways. Two of his many changes were to backdate the events from 1805 to 1799 and to rechristen the Spanish ship *Tryal* the *San Dominick*.

[3]Seal-hunting ship.

valuable cargo, in the harbor of St. Maria—a small, desert, uninhabited island toward the southern extremity of the long coast of Chili. There he had touched for water.

On the second day, not long after dawn, while lying in his berth, his mate came below, informing him that a strange sail was coming into the bay. Ships were then not so plenty in those waters as now. He rose, dressed, and went on deck.

The morning was one peculiar to that coast. Everything was mute and calm; everything gray. The sea, though undulated into long roods of swells, seemed fixed, and was sleeked at the surface like waved lead that has cooled and set in the smelter's mould. The sky seemed a gray surtout. Flights of troubled gray fowl, kith and kin with flights of troubled gray vapors among which they were mixed, skimmed low and fitfully over the waters, as swallows over meadows before storms. Shadows present, foreshadowing deeper shadows to come.

To Captain Delano's surprise, the stranger, viewed through the glass, showed no colors; though to do so upon entering a haven, however uninhabited in its shores, where but a single other ship might be lying, was the custom among peaceful seamen of all nations. Considering the lawlessness and loneliness of the spot, and the sort of stories, at that day, associated with those seas, Captain Delano's surprise might have deepened into some uneasiness had he not been a person of a singularly undistrustful good nature, not liable, except on extraordinary and repeated incentives, and hardly then, to indulge in personal alarms, any way involving the imputation of malign evil in man. Whether, in view of what humanity is capable, such a trait implies, along with a benevolent heart, more than ordinary quickness and accuracy of intellectual perception, may be left to the wise to determine.

But whatever misgivings might have obtruded on first seeing the stranger, would almost, in any seaman's mind, have been dissipated by observing that, the ship, in navigating into the harbor, was drawing too near the land, for her own safety's sake, owing to a sunken reef making out off her bow. This seemed to prove her a stranger, indeed, not only to the sealer, but the island; consequently, she could be no wonted freebooter on that ocean. With no small interest, Captain Delano continued to watch her—a proceeding not much facilitated by the vapors partly mantling the hull, through which the far matin[4] light from her cabin streamed equivocally enough; much like the sun—by this time hemisphered on the rim of the horizon, and apparently, in company with the strange ship, entering the harbor—which, wimpled[5] by the same low, creeping clouds, showed not unlike a Lima intriguante's one sinister eye peering across the Plaza from the Indian loop-hole of her dusk *saya-y-manta*.[6]

---

[4]Early morning.
[5]Veiled; covered as with a wimple, the head-dress worn by nuns to cover the head, neck, and sides of the face.

[6]Skirt and shawl combination; the shawl could be used to veil the face of a woman involved in an intrigue, or illicit love affair.

It might have been but a deception of the vapors, but, the longer the stranger was watched, the more singular appeared her maneuvers. Ere long it seemed hard to decide whether she meant to come in or no—what she wanted, or what she was about. The wind, which had breezed up a little during the night, was now extremely light and baffling, which the more increased the apparent uncertainty of her movements.

Surmising, at last, that it might be a ship in distress, Captain Delano ordered his whale-boat to be dropped, and, much to the wary opposition of his mate, prepared to board her, and, at the least, pilot her in. On the night previous, a fishing-party of the seamen had gone a long distance to some detached rocks out of sight from the sealer, and, an hour or two before daybreak, had returned, having met with no small success. Presuming that the stranger might have been long off soundings, the good captain put several baskets of the fish, for presents, into his boat, and so pulled away. From her continuing too near the sunken reef, deeming her in danger, calling to his men, he made all haste to apprise those on board of their situation. But, some time ere the boat came up, the wind, light though it was, having shifted, had headed the vessel off, as well as partly broken the vapors from about her.

Upon gaining a less remote view, the ship, when made signally visible on the verge of the leaden-hued swells, with the shreds of fog here and there raggedly furring her, appeared like a white-washed monastery after a thunder-storm, seen perched upon some dun cliff among the Pyrenees. But it was no purely fanciful resemblance which now, for a moment, almost led Captain Delano to think that nothing less than a ship-load of monks was before him. Peering over the bulwarks were what really seemed, in the hazy distance, throngs of dark cowls; while, fitfully revealed through the open port-holes, other dark moving figures were dimly descried, as of Black Friars[7] pacing the cloisters.

Upon a still nigher approach, this appearance was modified, and the true character of the vessel was plain—a Spanish merchantman of the first class; carrying negro slaves, amongst other valuable freight, from one colonial port to another. A very large, and, in its time, a very fine vessel, such as in those days were at intervals encountered along that main; sometimes superseded Acapulco treasure-ships, or retired frigates of the Spanish king's navy,

---

[7]Dominicans, an order of mendicant preaching monks, called Black Friars because of the black mantles they wore. The Spanish priest St. Dominic founded the order in 1215 to combat the Albigensian heresy, but in Spain the Dominicans' main targets were the Moors, the North African Muslims who had conquered Spain in the eighth century A.D., and the Jews. When the Spanish Inquisition was launched under Ferdinand and Isabella, the Dominicans were entrusted with its execution, which involved the denunciation, torture, and burning at the stake of heretics, the confiscation of their property, and the forced mass conversion or expulsion of Moors and Jews.

The Dominican missionary Bartolomé de las Casas also played a key role in the history of the Americas, proposing that slaves be imported from Africa to save the Indians from slavery and extinction.

which, like superannuated Italian palaces, still, under a decline of masters, preserved signs of former state.

As the whale-boat drew more and more nigh, the cause of the peculiar pipe-clayed[8] aspect of the stranger was seen in the slovenly neglect pervading her. The spars, ropes, and great part of the bulwarks, looked woolly, from long unacquaintance with the scraper, tar, and the brush. Her keel seemed laid, her ribs put together, and she launched, from Ezekiel's Valley of Dry Bones.[9]

In the present business in which she was engaged, the ship's general model and rig appeared to have undergone no material change from their original war-like and Froissart[10] pattern. However, no guns were seen.

The tops were large, and were railed about with what had once been octagonal net-work, all now in sad disrepair. These tops hung overhead like three ruinous aviaries, in one of which was seen perched, on a ratlin,[11] a white noddy, a strange fowl, so called from its lethargic, somnambulistic character, being frequently caught by hand at sea. Battered and mouldy, the castellated forecastle seemed some ancient turret, long ago taken by assault, and then left to decay. Toward the stern, two high-raised quarter galleries— the balustrades here and there covered with dry, tindery sea-moss—opening out from the unoccupied state-cabin, whose dead lights,[12] for all the mild weather, were hermetically closed and calked—these tenantless balconies hung over the sea as if it were the grand Venetian canal. But the principal relic of faded grandeur was the ample oval of the shield-like stern-piece, intricately carved with the arms of Castile and Leon,[13] medallioned about by groups of mythological or symbolical devices; uppermost and central of which was a dark satyr in a mask, holding his foot on the prostrate neck of a writhing figure, likewise masked.

Whether the ship had a figure-head, or only a plain beak, was not quite certain, owing to canvas wrapped about that part, either to protect it while undergoing a refurbishing, or else decently to hide its decay. Rudely painted or chalked, as in a sailor freak, along the forward side of a sort of pedestal below the canvas, was the sentence, *"Seguid vuestro jefe,"* (follow your leader); while upon the tarnished headboards, near by, appeared, in stately capitals, once gilt, the ship's name, "SAN DOMINICK," each letter streakingly

---

[8]Whitened, from the grayish white clay used for making tobacco pipes and for whitening leather.

[9]Ezekiel 37:1–14 tells of how God set the prophet down in the midst of a valley full of dry bones and instructed him to prophesy to them that God would restore them to life. Accordingly, the dry bones "lived, and stood up upon their feet, an exceeding great army." God then explains that "these bones are the whole house of Israel," whose "bones are dried" because their "hope is lost," but who are shortly to be resurrected and restored to the land of Israel.

[10]Jean Froissart (c. 1333–c. 1405), medieval historian of the wars between France and England; hence medieval, feudal, or pertaining to national conquest.

[11]Small transverse rope attached to the shrouds of a ship and forming the steps of a rope ladder.

[12]Metal covers or shutters fitted to portholes to keep out light and water.

[13]Ancient kingdoms of Spain, united after 1230. Their arms included a closed castle symbolizing Castile and a rampant lion symbolizing Leon (see the description of the Spanish flag later in the story).

corroded with tricklings of copper-spike rust; while, like mourning weeds, dark festoons of sea-grass slimily swept to and fro over the name, with every hearse-like roll of the hull.

As at last the boat was hooked from the bow along toward the gangway amidship, its keel, while yet some inches separated from the hull, harshly grated as on a sunken coral reef. It proved a huge bunch of conglobated barnacles adhering below the water to the side like a wen; a token of baffling airs and long calms passed somewhere in those seas.

Climbing the side, the visitor was at once surrounded by a clamorous throng of whites and blacks, but the latter outnumbering the former more than could have been expected, negro transportation-ship as the stranger in port was. But, in one language, and as with one voice, all poured out a common tale of suffering; in which the negresses, of whom there were not a few, exceeded the others in their dolorous vehemence. The scurvy, together with a fever, had swept off a great part of their number, more especially the Spaniards. Off Cape Horn, they had narrowly escaped shipwreck; then, for days together, they had lain tranced without wind; their provisions were low; their water next to none; their lips that moment were baked.

While Captain Delano was thus made the mark of all eager tongues, his one eager glance took in all the faces, with every other object about him.

Always upon first boarding a large and populous ship at sea, especially a foreign one, with a nondescript crew such as Lascars[14] or Manilla men, the impression varies in a peculiar way from that produced by first entering a strange house with strange inmates in a strange land. Both house and ship, the one by its walls and blinds, the other by its high bulwarks like ramparts, hoard from view their interiors till the last moment; but in the case of the ship there is this addition; that the living spectacle it contains, upon its sudden and complete disclosure, has, in contrast with the blank ocean which zones it, something of the effect of enchantment. The ship seems unreal; these strange costumes, gestures, and faces, but a shadowy tableau just emerged from the deep, which directly must receive back what it gave.

Perhaps it was some such influence as above is attempted to be described, which, in Captain Delano's mind, heightened whatever, upon a staid scrutiny, might have seemed unusual; especially the conspicuous figures of four elderly grizzled negroes, their heads like black, doddered[15] willow tops, who, in venerable contrast to the tumult below them, were couched sphynx-like, one on the starboard cat-head,[16] another on the larboard, and the remaining pair face to face on the opposite bulwarks above the main-chains. They each had bits of unstranded old junk in their hands,

[14]East Indian sailors.
[15]Deprived of branches through age or decay. The word "sphynx-like" hints at a riddle of life-and-death importance to be solved, as in the Greek legend of Oedipus, in which the sphinx of Thebes destroyed all passers-by who could not solve the riddle she posed. A mythological creature, the sphinx was of Egyptian origin—one of many allusions in the story to this ancient African civilization, which abolitionists pointed to as evidence that Africans were not mere savages.
[16]A projecting piece of timber or iron near the bow of a ship to which the anchor is hoisted and secured. One is on the starboard (right) side, another on the larboard (left).

and, with a sort of stoical self-content, were picking the junk into oakum,[17] a small heap of which lay by their sides. They accompanied the task with a continuous, low, monotonous chant; droning and druling away like so many gray-headed bag-pipers playing a funeral march.

The quarter-deck rose into an ample elevated poop, upon the forward verge of which, lifted, like the oakum-pickers, some eight feet above the general throng, sat along in a row, separated by regular spaces, the cross-legged figures of six other blacks; each with a rusty hatchet in his hand, which, with a bit of brick and a rag, he was engaged like a scullion in scouring; while between each two was a small stack of hatchets, their rusted edges turned forward awaiting a like operation. Though occasionally the four oakum-pickers would briefly address some person or persons in the crowd below, yet the six hatchet-polishers neither spoke to others, nor breathed a whisper among themselves, but sat intent upon their task, except at intervals, when, with the peculiar love in negroes of uniting industry with pastime, two and two they sideways clashed their hatchets together, like cymbals, with a barbarous din. All six, unlike the generality, had the raw aspect of unsophisticated Africans.

But that first comprehensive glance which took in those ten figures, with scores less conspicuous, rested but an instant upon them, as, impatient of the hubbub of voices, the visitor turned in quest of whomsoever it might be that commanded the ship.

But as if not unwilling to let nature make known her own case among his suffering charge, or else in despair of restraining it for the time, the Spanish captain, a gentlemanly, reserved-looking, and rather young man to a stranger's eye, dressed with singular richness, but bearing plain traces of recent sleepless cares and disquietudes, stood passively by, leaning against the main-mast, at one moment casting a dreary, spiritless look upon his excited people, at the next an unhappy glance toward his visitor. By his side stood a black of small stature, in whose rude face, as occasionally, like a shepherd's dog, he mutely turned it up into the Spaniard's, sorrow and affection were equally blended.

Struggling through the throng, the American advanced to the Spaniard, assuring him of his sympathies, and offering to render whatever assistance might be in his power. To which the Spaniard returned, for the present, but grave and ceremonious acknowledgments, his national formality dusked by the saturnine mood of ill health.

But losing no time in mere compliments, Captain Delano returning to the gangway, had his baskets of fish brought up; and as the wind still continued light, so that some hours at least must elapse ere the ship could be brought to the anchorage, he bade his men return to the sealer, and fetch back as much water as the whale-boat could carry, with whatever soft bread the steward might have, all the remaining pumpkins on board, with a box of sugar, and a dozen of his private bottles of cider.

---

[17]Pieces of worn hemp rope impregnated with tar and used in caulking seams.

Not many minutes after the boat's pushing off, to the vexation of all, the wind entirely died away, and the tide turning, began drifting back the ship helplessly seaward. But trusting this would not long last, Captain Delano sought with good hopes to cheer up the strangers, feeling no small satisfaction that, with persons in their condition he could—thanks to his frequent voyages along the Spanish main—converse with some freedom in their native tongue.

While left alone with them, he was not long in observing some things tending to heighten his first impressions; but surprise was lost in pity, both for the Spaniards and blacks, alike evidently reduced from scarcity of water and provisions; while long-continued suffering seemed to have brought out the less good-natured qualities of the negroes, besides, at the same time, impairing the Spaniard's authority over them. But, under the circumstances, precisely this condition of things was to have been anticipated. In armies, navies, cities, or families, in nature herself, nothing more relaxes good order than misery. Still, Captain Delano was not without the idea, that had Benito Cereno been a man of greater energy, misrule would hardly have come to the present pass. But the debility, constitutional or induced by the hardships, bodily and mental, of the Spanish captain, was too obvious to be overlooked. A prey to settled dejection, as if long mocked with hope he would not now indulge it, even when it had ceased to be a mock, the prospect of that day or evening at furthest, lying at anchor, with plenty of water for his people, and a brother captain to counsel and befriend, seemed in no perceptible degree to encourage him. His mind appeared unstrung, if not still more seriously affected. Shut up in these oaken walls, chained to one dull round of command, whose unconditionality cloyed him, like some hypochondriac abbot he moved slowly about, at times suddenly pausing, starting, or staring, biting his lip, biting his finger-nail, flushing, paling, twitching his beard, with other symptoms of an absent or moody mind. This distempered spirit was lodged, as before hinted, in as distempered a frame. He was rather tall, but seemed never to have been robust, and now with nervous suffering was almost worn to a skeleton. A tendency to some pulmonary complaint appeared to have been lately confirmed. His voice was like that of one with lungs half gone, hoarsely suppressed, a husky whisper. No wonder that, as in this state he tottered about, his private servant apprehensively followed him. Sometimes the negro gave his master his arm, or took his handkerchief out of his pocket for him; performing these and similar offices with that affectionate zeal which transmutes into something filial or fraternal acts in themselves but menial; and which has gained for the negro the repute of making the most pleasing body servant in the world; one, too, whom a master need be on no stiffly superior terms with, but may treat with familiar trust; less a servant than a devoted companion.

Marking the noisy indocility of the blacks in general, as well as what seemed the sullen inefficiency of the whites, it was not without humane satisfaction that Captain Delano witnessed the steady good conduct of Babo.

But the good conduct of Babo, hardly more than the ill-behavior of others, seemed to withdraw the half-lunatic Don Benito from his cloudy languor. Not that such precisely was the impression made by the Spaniard on the mind of his visitor. The Spaniard's individual unrest was, for the present, but noted as a conspicuous feature in the ship's general affliction. Still, Captain Delano was not a little concerned at what he could not help taking for the time to be Don Benito's unfriendly indifference towards himself. The Spaniard's manner, too, conveyed a sort of sour and gloomy disdain, which he seemed at no pains to disguise. But this the American in charity ascribed to the harassing effects of sickness, since, in former instances, he had noted that there are peculiar natures on whom prolonged physical suffering seems to cancel every social instinct of kindness; as if forced to black bread themselves, they deemed it but equity that each person coming nigh them should, indirectly, by some slight or affront, be made to partake of their fare.

But ere long Captain Delano bethought him that, indulgent as he was at the first, in judging the Spaniard, he might not, after all, have exercised charity enough. At bottom it was Don Benito's reserve which displeased him; but the same reserve was shown towards all but his faithful personal attendant. Even the formal reports which, according to sea-usage, were, at stated times, made to him by some petty underling, either a white, mulatto or black, he hardly had patience enough to listen to, without betraying contemptuous aversion. His manner upon such occasions was, in its degree, not unlike that which might be supposed to have been his imperial countryman's, Charles V., just previous to the anchoritish retirement of that monarch from the throne.[18]

This splenetic disrelish of his place was evinced in almost every function pertaining to it. Proud as he was moody, he condescended to no personal mandate. Whatever special orders were necessary, their delivery was delegated to his body-servant, who in turn transferred them to their ultimate destination, through runners, alert Spanish boys or slave boys, like pages or pilot-fish[19] within easy call continually hovering round Don Benito. So that to have beheld this undemonstrative invalid gliding about, apathetic and mute, no landsman could have dreamed that in him was lodged a dictatorship beyond which, while at sea, there was no earthly appeal.

Thus, the Spaniard, regarded in his reserve, seemed as the involuntary victim of mental disorder. But, in fact, his reserve might, in some degree, have proceeded from design. If so, then here was evinced the unhealthy climax of that icy though conscientious policy, more or less adopted by all commanders of large ships, which, except in signal emergencies, obliterates alike the manifestation of sway with every trace of sociality; transforming the man into a block, or rather into a loaded cannon, which, until there is call for thunder, has nothing to say.

---

[18]Charles V (1500–1558) succeeded Ferdinand and Isabella to the throne of Spain in 1517 and became Holy Roman Emperor two years later. He inaugurated the importation of African slaves to the American colonies in 1517. After involving Spain in a long series of territorial and religious wars, Charles V abdicated the throne and retired to a monastery in the last years of his life, disappointed in his hopes and broken in health.

[19]Smaller fish that often swim in the company of sharks, seeming to pilot them.

Viewing him in this light, it seemed but a natural token of the perverse habit induced by a long course of such hard self-restraint, that, notwithstanding the present condition of his ship, the Spaniard should still persist in a demeanor, which, however harmless, or, it may be, appropriate, in a well appointed vessel, such as the San Dominick might have been at the outset of the voyage, was anything but judicious now. But the Spaniard perhaps thought that it was with captains as with gods: reserve, under all events, must still be their cue. But more probably this appearance of slumbering dominion might have been but an attempted disguise to conscious imbecility—not deep policy, but shallow device. But be all this as it might, whether Don Benito's manner was designed or not, the more Captain Delano noted its pervading reserve, the less he felt uneasiness at any particular manifestation of that reserve towards himself.

Neither were his thoughts taken up by the captain alone. Wonted to the quiet orderliness of the sealer's comfortable family of a crew, the noisy confusion of the San Dominick's suffering host repeatedly challenged his eye. Some prominent breaches not only of discipline but of decency were observed. These Captain Delano could not but ascribe, in the main, to the absence of those subordinate deck-officers to whom, along with higher duties, is entrusted what may be styled the police department of a populous ship. True, the old oakum-pickers appeared at times to act the part of monitorial constables to their countrymen, the blacks; but though occasionally succeeding in allaying trifling outbreaks now and then between man and man, they could do little or nothing toward establishing general quiet. The San Dominick was in the condition of a transatlantic emigrant ship, among whose multitude of living freight are some individuals, doubtless, as little troublesome as crates and bales; but the friendly remonstrances of such with their ruder companions are of not so much avail as the unfriendly arm of the mate. What the San Dominick wanted was, what the emigrant ship has, stern superior officers.[20] But on these decks not so much as a fourth mate was to be seen.

The visitor's curiosity was roused to learn the particulars of those mishaps which had brought about such absenteeism, with its consequences; because, though deriving some inkling of the voyage from the wails which at the first moment had greeted him, yet of the details no clear understanding had been had. The best account would, doubtless, be given by the captain. Yet at first the visitor was loth to ask it, unwilling to provoke some distant rebuff. But plucking up courage, he at last accosted Don Benito, renewing the expression of his benevolent interest, adding, that did he (Captain Delano) but know the particulars of the ship's misfortunes, he would, perhaps, be better able in the end to relieve them. Would Don Benito favor him with the whole story?

[20]In *Redburn* Melville pleaded passionately for improving conditions aboard emigrant ships, on which the "friendless emigrants" were "stowed away like bales of cotton, and packed like slaves in a slave-ship" (Chaps. 47, 58).

Don Benito faltered; then, like some somnambulist suddenly interfered with, vacantly stared at his visitor, and ended by looking down on the deck. He maintained this posture so long, that Captain Delano, almost equally disconcerted, and involuntarily almost as rude, turned suddenly from him, walking forward to accost one of the Spanish seamen for the desired information. But he had hardly gone five paces, when with a sort of eagerness Don Benito invited him back, regretting his momentary absence of mind, and professing readiness to gratify him.

While most part of the story was being given, the two captains stood on the after part of the main-deck, a privileged spot, no one being near but the servant.

"It is now a hundred and ninety days," began the Spaniard, in his husky whisper, "that this ship, well officered and well manned, with several cabin passengers—some fifty Spaniards in all—sailed from Buenos Ayres bound to Lima, with a general cargo, hardware, Paraguay tea and the like—and," pointing forward, "that parcel of negroes, now not more than a hundred and fifty, as you see, but then numbering over three hundred souls. Off Cape Horn we had heavy gales. In one moment, by night, three of my best officers, with fifteen sailors, were lost, with the main-yard; the spar snapping under them in the slings, as they sought, with heavers,[21] to beat down the icy sail. To lighten the hull, the heavier sacks of mate[22] were thrown into the sea, with most of the water-pipes lashed on deck at the time. And this last necessity it was, combined with the prolonged detentions afterwards experienced, which eventually brought about our chief causes of suffering. When—"

Here there was a sudden fainting attack of his cough, brought on, no doubt, by his mental distress. His servant sustained him, and drawing a cordial from his pocket placed it to his lips. He a little revived. But unwilling to leave him unsupported while yet imperfectly restored, the black with one arm still encircled his master, at the same time keeping his eye fixed on his face, as if to watch for the first sign of complete restoration, or relapse, as the event might prove.

The Spaniard proceeded, but brokenly and obscurely, as one in a dream.

—"Oh, my God! rather than pass through what I have, with joy I would have hailed the most terrible gales; but—"

His cough returned and with increased violence; this subsiding, with reddened lips and closed eyes he fell heavily against his supporter.

"His mind wanders. He was thinking of the plague that followed the gales," plaintively sighed the servant; "my poor, poor master!" wringing one hand, and with the other wiping the mouth. "But be patient, Señor," again turning to Captain Delano, "these fits do not last long; master will soon be himself."

Don Benito reviving, went on; but as this portion of the story was very brokenly delivered, the substance only will here be set down.

---

[21]Bars used as levers.　　　　　　[22]Mate: Paraguay tea; water-pipes: water casks.

It appeared that after the ship had been many days tossed in storms off the Cape, the scurvy broke out, carrying off numbers of the whites and blacks. When at last they had worked round into the Pacific, their spars and sails were so damaged, and so inadequately handled by the surviving mariners, most of whom were become invalids, that, unable to lay her northerly course by the wind, which was powerful, the unmanageable ship for successive days and nights was blown northwestward, where the breeze suddenly deserted her, in unknown waters, to sultry calms. The absence of the water-pipes now proved as fatal to life as before their presence had menaced it. Induced, or at least aggravated, by the more than scanty allowance of water, a malignant fever followed the scurvy; with the excessive heat of the lengthened calm, making such short work of it as to sweep away, as by billows, whole families of the Africans, and a yet larger number, proportionably, of the Spaniards, including, by a luckless fatality, every remaining officer on board. Consequently, in the smart west winds eventually following the calm, the already rent sails having to be simply dropped, not furled, at need, had been gradually reduced to the beggar's rags they were now. To procure substitutes for his lost sailors, as well as supplies of water and sails, the captain at the earliest opportunity had made for Baldivia, the southermost civilized port of Chili and South America; but upon nearing the coast the thick weather had prevented him from so much as sighting that harbor. Since which period, almost without a crew, and almost without canvas and almost without water, and at intervals giving its added dead to the sea, the San Dominick had been battle-dored about by contrary winds, inveigled by currents, or grown weedy in calms. Like a man lost in woods, more than once she had doubled upon her own track.

"But throughout these calamities," huskily continued Don Benito, painfully turning in the half embrace of his servant, "I have to thank those negroes you see, who, though to your inexperienced eyes appearing unruly, have, indeed, conducted themselves with less of restlessness than even their owner could have thought possible under such circumstances."

Here he again fell faintly back. Again his mind wandered: but he rallied, and less obscurely proceeded.

"Yes, their owner was quite right in assuring me that no fetters would be needed with his blacks; so that while, as is wont in this transportation, those negroes have always remained upon deck—not thrust below, as in the Guinea-men[23]—they have, also, from the beginning, been freely permitted to range within given bounds at their pleasure."

Once more the faintness returned—his mind roved—but, recovering, he resumed:

"But it is Babo here to whom, under God, I owe not only my own preservation, but likewise to him, chiefly, the merit is due, of pacifying his more ignorant brethren, when at intervals tempted to murmurings."

---

[23]Ships engaged in the African slave trade, of which the Guinea coast in West Africa was a center. Like American slaveholders, Don Benito considers the slave trade between ports of his own region less inhumane than the trade between Africa and the Americas.

"Ah, master," sighed the black, bowing his face, "don't speak of me; Babo is nothing; what Babo has done was but duty."

"Faithful fellow!" cried Capt. Delano. "Don Benito, I envy you such a friend; slave I cannot call him."

As master and man stood before him, the black upholding the white, Captain Delano could not but bethink him of the beauty of that relationship which could present such a spectacle of fidelity on the one hand and confidence on the other. The scene was heightened by the contrast in dress, denoting their relative positions. The Spaniard wore a loose Chili jacket of dark velvet; white small clothes and stockings, with silver buckles at the knee and instep; a high-crowned sombrero, of fine grass; a slender sword, silver mounted, hung from a knot in his sash; the last being an almost invariable adjunct, more for utility than ornament, of a South American gentleman's dress to this hour. Excepting when his occasional nervous contortions brought about disarray, there was a certain precision in his attire, curiously at variance with the unsightly disorder around; especially in the belittered Ghetto, forward of the main-mast, wholly occupied by the blacks.

The servant wore nothing but wide trowsers, apparently, from their coarseness and patches, made out of some old topsail; they were clean, and confined at the waist by a bit of unstranded rope, which, with his composed, deprecatory air at times, made him look something like a begging friar of St. Francis.

However unsuitable for the time and place, at least in the blunt-thinking American's eyes, and however strangely surviving in the midst of all his afflictions, the toilette of Don Benito might not, in fashion at least, have gone beyond the style of the day among South Americans of his class. Though on the present voyage sailing from Buenos Ayres, he had avowed himself a native and resident of Chili, whose inhabitants had not so generally adopted the plain coat and once plebeian pantaloons; but, with a becoming modification, adhered to their provincial costume, picturesque as any in the world. Still, relatively to the pale history of the voyage, and his own pale face, there seemed something so incongruous in the Spaniard's apparel, as almost to suggest the image of an invalid courtier tottering about London streets in the time of the plague.

The portion of the narrative which, perhaps, most excited interest, as well as some surprise, considering the latitudes in question, was the long calms spoken of, and more particularly the ship's so long drifting about. Without communicating the opinion, of course, the American could not but impute at least part of the detentions both to clumsy seamanship and faulty navigation. Eying Don Benito's small, yellow hands, he easily inferred that the young captain had not got into command at the hawse-hole,[24] but the

---

[24]Metal-lined hole in the bow of a ship through which cables pass. Don Benito's hands show that he has never worked among common sailors and has won his captaincy through social influence, not experience.

cabin-window; and if so, why wonder at incompetence, in youth, sickness, and gentility united?

But drowning criticism in compassion, after a fresh repetition of his sympathies, Captain Delano having heard out his story, not only engaged, as in the first place, to see Don Benito and his people supplied in their immediate bodily needs, but, also, now further promised to assist him in procuring a large permanent supply of water, as well as some sails and rigging; and, though it would involve no small embarrassment to himself, yet he would spare three of his best seamen for temporary deck officers; so that without delay the ship might proceed to Conception, there fully to refit for Lima, her destined port.

Such generosity was not without its effect, even upon the invalid. His face lighted up; eager and hectic, he met the honest glance of his visitor. With gratitude he seemed overcome.

"This excitement is bad for master," whispered the servant, taking his arm, and with soothing words gently drawing him aside.

When Don Benito returned, the American was pained to observe that his hopefulness, like the sudden kindling in his cheek, was but febrile and transient.

Ere long, with a joyless mien, looking up towards the poop, the host invited his guest to accompany him there, for the benefit of what little breath of wind might be stirring.

As during the telling of the story, Captain Delano had once or twice started at the occasional cymballing of the hatchet-polishers, wondering why such an interruption should be allowed, especially in that part of the ship, and in the ears of an invalid; and moreover, as the hatchets had anything but an attractive look, and the handlers of them still less so, it was, therefore, to tell the truth, not without some lurking reluctance, or even shrinking, it may be, that Captain Delano, with apparent complaisance, acquiesced in his host's invitation. The more so, since with an untimely caprice of punctilio, rendered distressing by his cadaverous aspect, Don Benito, with Castilian bows, solemnly insisted upon his guest's preceding him up the ladder leading to the elevation; where, one on each side of the last step, sat for armorial supporters and sentries two of the ominous file. Gingerly enough stepped good Captain Delano between them, and in the instant of leaving them behind, like one running the gauntlet, he felt an apprehensive twitch in the calves of his legs.

But when, facing about, he saw the whole file, like so many organ-grinders, still stupidly intent on their work, unmindful of everything beside, he could not but smile at his late fidgeting panic.

Presently, while standing with his host, looking forward upon the decks below, he was struck by one of those instances of insubordination previously alluded to. Three black boys, with two Spanish boys, were sitting together on the hatches, scraping a rude wooden platter, in which some scanty mess had recently been cooked. Suddenly, one of the black boys, enraged at a word dropped by one of his white companions, seized a knife, and though called to forbear by one of the oakum-pickers, struck the lad over the head, inflicting a gash from which blood flowed.

In amazement, Captain Delano inquired what this meant. To which the pale Don Benito dully muttered, that it was merely the sport of the lad.

"Pretty serious sport, truly," rejoined Captain Delano. "Had such a thing happened on board the Bachelor's Delight, instant punishment would have followed."

At these words the Spaniard turned upon the American one of his sudden, staring, half-lunatic looks; then relapsing into his torpor, answered, "Doubtless, doubtless, Señor."

Is it, thought Captain Delano, that this hapless man is one of those paper captains I've known, who by policy wink at what by power they cannot put down? I know no sadder sight than a commander who has little of command but the name.

"I should think, Don Benito," he now said, glancing towards the oakum-picker who had sought to interfere with the boys, "that you would find it advantageous to keep all your blacks employed, especially the younger ones, no matter at what useless task, and no matter what happens to the ship. Why, even with my little band, I find such a course indispensable. I once kept a crew on my quarter-deck thrumming mats[25] for my cabin, when, for three days, I had given up my ship—mats, men, and all—for a speedy loss, owing to the violence of a gale, in which we could do nothing but helplessly drive before it."

"Doubtless, doubtless," muttered Don Benito.

"But," continued Captain Delano, again glancing upon the oakum-pickers and then at the hatchet-polishers, near by, "I see you keep some at least of your host employed."

"Yes," was again the vacant response.

"Those old men there, shaking their pows[26] from their pulpits," continued Captain Delano, pointing to the oakum-pickers, "seem to act the part of old dominies to the rest, little heeded as their admonitions are at times. Is this voluntary on their part, Don Benito, or have you appointed them shepherds to your flock of black sheep?"

"What posts they fill, I appointed them," rejoined the Spaniard, in an acrid tone, as if resenting some supposed satiric reflection.

"And these others, these Ashantee[27] conjurors here," continued Captain Delano, rather uneasily eying the brandished steel of the hatchet-polishers, where in spots it had been brought to a shine, "this seems a curious business they are at, Don Benito?"

---

[25]Inserting short pieces of rope yarn into a piece of canvas, thus making a rough surface or mat that can be wrapped about rigging to prevent chafing or to stop a leak.

[26]Heads. Dominies: pedagogues, schoolmasters, ministers.

[27]A West African people in what is now Ghana. They formed a powerful kingdom in the seventeenth and eighteenth centuries after acquiring a regular supply of firearms. In the nineteenth century they fiercely resisted British conquest, beginning in 1824.

"In the gales we met," answered the Spaniard, "what of our general cargo was not thrown overboard was much damaged by the brine. Since coming into calm weather, I have had several cases of knives and hatchets daily brought up for overhauling and cleaning."

"A prudent idea, Don Benito. You are part owner of ship and cargo, I presume; but not of the slaves, perhaps?"

"I am owner of all you see," impatiently returned Don Benito, "except the main company of blacks, who belonged to my late friend, Alexandro Aranda."

As he mentioned this name, his air was heart-broken; his knees shook: his servant supported him.

Thinking he divined the cause of such unusual emotion, to confirm his surmise, Captain Delano, after a pause, said, "And may I ask, Don Benito, whether—since awhile ago you spoke of some cabin passengers—the friend, whose loss so afflicts you at the outset of the voyage accompanied his blacks?"

"Yes."

"But died of the fever?"

"Died of the fever.—Oh, could I but——"

Again quivering, the Spaniard paused.

"Pardon me," said Captain Delano lowly, "but I think that, by a sympathetic experience, I conjecture, Don Benito, what it is that gives the keener edge to your grief. It was once my hard fortune to lose at sea a dear friend, my own brother, then supercargo.[28] Assured of the welfare of his spirit, its departure I could have borne like a man; but that honest eye, that honest hand—both of which had so often met mine—and that warm heart; all, all—like scraps to the dogs—to throw all to the sharks! It was then I vowed never to have for fellow-voyager a man I loved, unless, unbeknown to him, I had provided every requisite, in case of a fatality, for embalming his mortal part for interment on shore. Were your friend's remains now on board this ship, Don Benito, not thus strangely would the mention of his name affect you."

"On board this ship?" echoed the Spaniard. Then, with horrified gestures, as directed against some specter, he unconsciously fell into the ready arms of his attendant, who, with a silent appeal toward Captain Delano, seemed beseeching him not again to broach a theme so unspeakably distressing to his master.

This poor fellow now, thought the pained American, is the victim of that sad superstition which associates goblins with the deserted body of man, as ghosts with an abandoned house. How unlike are we made! What to me, in like case, would have been a solemn satisfaction, the bare suggestion, even, terrifies the Spaniard into this trance. Poor Alexandro Aranda! what would

[28]Officer on a merchant ship whose duty is to manage the commercial concerns of the voyage.

you say could you here see your friend—who, on former voyages, when you for months were left behind, has, I dare say, often longed, and longed, for one peep at you—now transported with terror at the least thought of having you anyway nigh him.

At this moment, with a dreary grave-yard toll, betokening a flaw,[29] the ship's forecastle bell, smote by one of the grizzled oakum-pickers, proclaimed ten o'clock through the leaden calm; when Captain Delano's attention was caught by the moving figure of a gigantic black, emerging from the general crowd below, and slowly advancing towards the elevated poop. An iron collar was about his neck, from which depended a chain, thrice wound round his body; the terminating links padlocked together at a broad band of iron, his girdle.

"How like a mute Atufal moves," murmured the servant.

The black mounted the steps of the poop, and, like a brave prisoner, brought up to receive sentence, stood in unquailing muteness before Don Benito, now recovered from his attack.

At the first glimpse of his approach, Don Benito had started, a resentful shadow swept over his face; and, as with the sudden memory of bootless rage, his white lips glued together.

This is some mulish mutineer, thought Captain Delano, surveying, not without a mixture of admiration, the colossal form of the negro.

"See, he waits your question, master," said the servant.

Thus reminded, Don Benito, nervously averting his glance, as if shunning, by anticipation, some rebellious response, in a disconcerted voice, thus spoke:—

"Atufal, will you ask my pardon now?"

The black was silent.

"Again, master," murmured the servant, with bitter upbraiding eying his countryman, "Again, master; he will bend to master yet."

"Answer," said Don Benito, still averting his glance, "say but the one word *pardon*, and your chains shall be off."

Upon this, the black, slowly raising both arms, let them lifelessly fall, his links clanking, his head bowed; as much as to say, "no, I am content."

"Go," said Don Benito, with inkept and unknown emotion.

Deliberately as he had come, the black obeyed.

"Excuse me, Don Benito," said Captain Delano, "but this scene surprises me; what means it, pray?"

"It means that that negro alone, of all the band, has given me peculiar cause of offense. I have put him in chains; I—"

[29]Probably an allusion to the Liberty Bell, famous for the irreparable flaw that had made it crack repeatedly. Many abolitionists interpreted the flaw as a symbol of America's failure to obey the biblical command inscribed on the bell, which enjoined the Israelites to free their slaves on the Jubilee: "Proclaim liberty throughout all the land unto all the inhabitants thereof" (Leviticus 25:10).

Here he paused; his hand to his head, as if there were a swimming there, or a sudden bewilderment of memory had come over him; but meeting his servant's kindly glance seemed reassured, and proceeded:—

"I could not scourge such a form. But I told him he must ask my pardon. As yet he has not. At my command, every two hours he stands before me."

"And how long has this been?"

"Some sixty days."

"And obedient in all else? And respectful?"

"Yes."

"Upon my conscience, then," exclaimed Captain Delano, impulsively, "he has a royal spirit in him, this fellow."

"He may have some right to it," bitterly returned Don Benito, "he says he was king in his own land."

"Yes," said the servant, entering a word, "those slits in Atufal's ears once held wedges of gold; but poor Babo here, in his own land, was only a poor slave; a black man's slave was Babo, who now is the white's."

Somewhat annoyed by these conversational familiarities, Captain Delano turned curiously upon the attendant, then glanced inquiringly at his master; but, as if long wonted to these little informalities, neither master nor man seemed to understand him.

"What, pray, was Atufal's offense, Don Benito?" asked Captain Delano; "if it was not something very serious, take a fool's advice, and, in view of his general docility, as well as in some natural respect for his spirit, remit him his penalty."

"No, no, master never will do that," here murmured the servant to himself, "proud Atufal must first ask master's pardon. The slave there carries the padlock, but master here carries the key."

His attention thus directed, Captain Delano now noticed for the first time that, suspended by a slender silken cord, from Don Benito's neck hung a key. At once, from the servant's muttered syllables divining the key's purpose, he smiled and said:—"So, Don Benito—padlock and key—significant symbols, truly."

Biting his lip, Don Benito faltered.

Though the remark of Captain Delano, a man of such native simplicity as to be incapable of satire or irony, had been dropped in playful allusion to the Spaniard's singularly evidenced lordship over the black; yet the hypochondriac seemed in some way to have taken it as a malicious reflection upon his confessed inability thus far to break down, at least, on a verbal summons, the entrenched will of the slave. Deploring this supposed misconception, yet despairing of correcting it, Captain Delano shifted the subject; but finding his companion more than ever withdrawn, as if still sourly digesting the lees of the presumed affront above-mentioned, by-and-by Captain Delano likewise became less talkative, oppressed, against his own will, by what seemed the secret vindictiveness of the morbidly sensitive Spaniard. But the good sailor himself, of a quite contrary disposition, refrained, on his part, alike from the appearance as from the feeling of resentment, and if silent, was only so from contagion.

Presently the Spaniard, assisted by his servant, somewhat discourteously crossed over from his guest; a procedure which, sensibly enough, might have been allowed to pass for idle caprice of ill-humor, had not master and man, lingering round the corner of the elevated skylight, began whispering together in low voices. This was unpleasing. And more: the moody air of the Spaniard, which at times had not been without a sort of valetudinarian[30] stateliness, now seemed anything but dignified; while the menial familiarity of the servant lost its original charm of simple-hearted attachment.

In his embarrassment, the visitor turned his face to the other side of the ship. By so doing, his glance accidentally fell on a young Spanish sailor, a coil of rope in his hand, just stepped from the deck to the first round of the mizzen-rigging. Perhaps the man would not have been particularly noticed, were it not that, during his ascent to one of the yards, he, with a sort of covert intentness, kept his eye fixed on Captain Delano, from whom, presently, it passed, as if by a natural sequence, to the two whisperers.

His own attention thus redirected to that quarter, Captain Delano gave a slight start. From something in Don Benito's manner just then, it seemed as if the visitor had, at least partly, been the subject of the withdrawn consultation going on—a conjecture as little agreeable to the guest as it was little flattering to the host.

The singular alternations of courtesy and ill-breeding in the Spanish captain were unaccountable, except on one of two suppositions—innocent lunacy, or wicked imposture.

But the first idea, though it might naturally have occurred to an indifferent observer, and, in some respect, had not hitherto been wholly a stranger to Captain Delano's mind, yet, now that, in an incipient way, he began to regard the stranger's conduct something in the light of an intentional affront, of course the idea of lunacy was virtually vacated. But if not a lunatic, what then? Under the circumstances, would a gentleman, nay, any honest boor, act the part now acted by his host? The man was an impostor. Some low-born adventurer, masquerading as an oceanic grandee; yet so ignorant of the first requisites of mere gentlemanhood as to be betrayed into the present remarkable indecorum. That strange ceremoniousness, too, at other times evinced, seemed not uncharacteristic of one playing a part above his real level. Benito Cereno—Don Benito Cereno—a sounding name. One, too, at that period, not unknown, in the surname, to supercargoes and sea captains trading along the Spanish Main, as belonging to one of the most enterprising and extensive mercantile families in all those provinces; several members of it having titles; a sort of Castilian Rothschild,[31] with a noble brother, or cousin, in every great trading town of South America. The alleged Don Benito was in early manhood, about twenty-nine or thirty. To assume a sort of roving cadetship in the maritime affairs of such a house,

[30]Sickly, infirm.
[31]Wealthy German Jewish banking family with noble relatives in many European countries.

what more likely scheme for a young knave of talent and spirit? But the Spaniard was a pale invalid. Never mind. For even to the degree of simulating mortal disease, the craft of some tricksters had been known to attain. To think that, under the aspect of infantile weakness, the most savage energies might be couched—those velvets of the Spaniard but the silky paw to his fangs.

From no train of thought did these fancies come; not from within, but from without; suddenly, too, and in one throng, like hoar frost; yet as soon to vanish as the mild sun of Captain Delano's good-nature regained its meridian.

Glancing over once more towards his host—whose side-face, revealed above the skylight, was now turned towards him—he was struck by the profile, whose clearness of cut was refined by the thinness incident to ill-health, as well as ennobled about the chin by the beard. Away with suspicion. He was a true off-shoot of a true hidalgo Cereno.

Relieved by these and other better thoughts, the visitor, lightly humming a tune, now began indifferently pacing the poop, so as not to betray to Don Benito that he had at all mistrusted incivility, much less duplicity; for such mistrust would yet be proved illusory, and by the event; though, for the present, the circumstance which had provoked that distrust remained unexplained. But when that little mystery should have been cleared up, Captain Delano thought he might extremely regret it, did he allow Don Benito to become aware that he had indulged in ungenerous surmises. In short, to the Spaniard's black-letter text, it was best, for awhile, to leave open margin.[32]

Presently, his pale face twitching and overcast, the Spaniard, still supported by his attendant, moved over towards his guest, when, with even more than his usual embarrassment, and a strange sort of intriguing intonation in his husky whisper, the following conversation began:—

"Señor, may I ask how long you have lain at this isle?"

"Oh, but a day or two, Don Benito."

"And from what port are you last?"

"Canton."

"And there, Señor, you exchanged your seal-skins for teas and silks, I think you said?"

"Yes. Silks, mostly."

"And the balance you took in specie, perhaps?"

Captain Delano, fidgeting a little, answered—

"Yes; some silver; not a very great deal, though."

"Ah—well. May I ask how many men have you, Señor?"

Captain Delano slightly started, but answered—

---

[32]Black-letter was an early typeface imitating medieval manuscript lettering and hence difficult to read. Delano has decided to leave this text without explanatory notes in the margin—that is, to reserve judgment.

"About five-and-twenty, all told."

"And at present, Señor, all on board, I suppose?"

"All on board, Don Benito," replied the Captain, now with satisfaction.

"And will be to-night, Señor?"

At this last question, following so many pertinacious ones, for the soul of him Captain Delano could not but look very earnestly at the questioner, who, instead of meeting the glance, with every token of craven discomposure dropped his eyes to the deck; presenting an unworthy contrast to his servant, who, just then, was kneeling at his feet, adjusting a loose shoe-buckle; his disengaged face meantime, with humble curiosity, turned openly up into his master's downcast one.

The Spaniard, still with a guilty shuffle, repeated his question:—

"And—and will be to-night, Señor?"

"Yes, for aught I know," returned Captain Delano,—"but nay," rallying himself into fearless truth, "some of them talked of going off on another fishing party about midnight."

"Your ships generally go—go more or less armed, I believe, Señor?"

"Oh, a six-pounder or two, in case of emergency," was the intrepidly indifferent reply, "with a small stock of muskets, sealing-spears, and cutlasses, you know."

As he thus responded, Captain Delano again glanced at Don Benito, but the latter's eyes were averted; while abruptly and awkwardly shifting the subject, he made some peevish allusion to the calm, and then, without apology, once more, with his attendant, withdrew to the opposite bulwarks, where the whispering was resumed.

At this moment, and ere Captain Delano could cast a cool thought upon what had just passed, the young Spanish sailor before mentioned was seen descending from the rigging. In act of stooping over to spring inboard to the deck, his voluminous, unconfined frock, or shirt, of coarse woollen, much spotted with tar, opened out far down the chest, revealing a soiled under garment of what seemed the finest linen, edged, about the neck, with a narrow blue ribbon, sadly faded and worn. At this moment the young sailor's eye was again fixed on the whisperers, and Captain Delano thought he observed a lurking significance in it, as if silent signs of some Freemason[33] sort had that instant been interchanged.

This once more impelled his own glance in the direction of Don Benito, and, as before, he could not but infer that himself formed the subject of the conference. He paused. The sound of the hatchet-polishing fell on his ears. He cast another swift side-look at the two. They had the air of conspirators. In connection with the late questionings and the incident of the young sailor, these things now begat such return of involuntary suspicion, that the

---

[33]A worldwide secret society of men united for fraternal purposes, whose members used coded signs as means of communicating. Organized churches viewed freemasons as heretical, irreligious, and dangerous. A strong Anti-Mason movement influenced American politics in the 1820s and 1830s.

singular guilelessness of the American could not endure it. Plucking up a gay and humorous expression, he crossed over to the two rapidly, saying:—"Ha, Don Benito, your black here seems high in your trust; a sort of privy-counselor, in fact."

Upon this, the servant looked up with a good-natured grin, but the master started as from a venomous bite. It was a moment or two before the Spaniard sufficiently recovered himself to reply; which he did, at last, with cold restraint:—"Yes, Señor, I have trust in Babo."

Here Babo, changing his previous grin of mere animal humor into an intelligent smile, not ungratefully eyed his master.

Finding that the Spaniard now stood silent and reserved, as if involuntarily, or purposely giving hint that his guest's proximity was inconvenient just then, Captain Delano, unwilling to appear uncivil even to incivility itself, made some trivial remark and moved off; again and again turning over in his mind the mysterious demeanor of Don Benito Cereno.

He had descended from the poop, and, wrapped in thought, was passing near a dark hatchway, leading down into the steerage, when, perceiving motion there, he looked to see what moved. The same instant there was a sparkle in the shadowy hatchway, and he saw one of the Spanish sailors prowling there hurriedly placing his hand in the bosom of his frock, as if hiding something. Before the man could have been certain who it was that was passing, he slunk below out of sight. But enough was seen of him to make it sure that he was the same young sailor before noticed in the rigging.

What was that which so sparkled? thought Captain Delano. It was no lamp—no match—no live coal. Could it have been a jewel? But how come sailors with jewels?—or with silk-trimmed under-shirts either? Has he been robbing the trunks of the dead cabin passengers? But if so, he would hardly wear one of the stolen articles on board ship here. Ah, ah—if now that was, indeed, a secret sign I saw passing between this suspicious fellow and his captain awhile since; if I could only be certain that in my uneasiness my senses did not deceive me, then——

Here, passing from one suspicious thing to another, his mind revolved the point of the strange questions put to him concerning his ship.

By a curious coincidence, as each point was recalled, the black wizards of Ashantee would strike up with their hatchets, as in ominous comment on the white stranger's thoughts. Pressed by such enigmas and portents, it would have been almost against nature, had not, even into the least distrustful heart, some ugly misgivings obtruded.

Observing the ship now helplessly fallen into a current, with enchanted sails, drifting with increased rapidity seaward; and noting that, from a lately intercepted projection of the land, the sealer was hidden, the stout mariner began to quake at thoughts which he barely durst confess to himself. Above all, he began to feel a ghostly dread of Don Benito. And yet when he roused himself, dilated his chest, felt himself strong on his legs, and coolly considered it—what did all these phantoms amount to?

Had the Spaniard any sinister scheme, it must have reference not so much to him (Captain Delano) as to his ship (the Bachelor's Delight).[34] Hence the present drifting away of the one ship from the other, instead of favoring any such possible scheme, was, for the time at least, opposed to it. Clearly any suspicion, combining such contradictions, must need be delusive. Beside, was it not absurd to think of a vessel in distress—a vessel by sickness almost dismanned of her crew—a vessel whose inmates were parched for water—was it not a thousand times absurd that such a craft should, at present, be of a piratical character; or her commander, either for himself or those under him, cherish any desire but for speedy relief and refreshment? But then, might not general distress, and thirst in particular, be affected? And might not that same undiminished Spanish crew, alleged to have perished off to a remnant, be at that very moment lurking in the hold? On heart-broken pretense of entreating a cup of cold water, fiends in human form had got into lonely dwellings, nor retired until a dark deed had been done. And among the Malay pirates, it was no unusual thing to lure ships after them into their treacherous harbors, or entice boarders from a declared enemy at sea, by the spectacle of thinly manned or vacant decks, beneath which prowled a hundred spears with yellow arms ready to upthrust them through the mats. Not that Captain Delano had entirely credited such things. He had heard of them—and now, as stories, they recurred. The present destination of the ship was the anchorage. There she would be near his own vessel. Upon gaining that vicinity, might not the San Dominick, like a slumbering volcano, suddenly let loose energies now hid?

He recalled the Spaniard's manner while telling his story. There was a gloomy hesitancy and subterfuge about it. It was just the manner of one making up his tale for evil purposes, as he goes. But if that story was not true, what was the truth? That the ship had unlawfully come into the Spaniard's possession? But in many of its details, especially in reference to the more calamitous parts, such as the fatalities among the seamen, the consequent prolonged beating about, the past sufferings from obstinate calms, and still continued suffering from thirst; in all these points, as well as others, Don Benito's story had been corroborated not only by the wailing ejaculations of the indiscriminate multitude, white and black, but likewise—what seemed impossible to be counterfeit—by the very expression and play of every human feature, which Captain Delano saw. If Don Benito's story was throughout an invention, then every soul on board, down to the youngest negress, was his

---

[34]The name of a famous pirate ship belonging to William Cowley and William Dampier, who captured it from Danish slavers off the coast of Sierra Leone, sold the slaves found on board, and sailed it to South America and the Pacific, where they raided Spanish ports and shipping. Note the references to piracy that immediately follow. Melville mentions the "Buccaneers" Cowley and Dampier in Sketches Fifth and Sixth of "The Encantadas." The name of the historical Delano's ship was the *Perseverance*. The substitution offers a fascinating glimpse into the workings of Melville's imagination, showing how the activities Delano reports in his narrative remind Melville of earlier narratives by the pirates and slave-traders who plied the same waters.

carefully drilled recruit in the plot: an incredible inference. And yet, if there was ground for mistrusting his veracity, that inference was a legitimate one.

But those questions of the Spaniard. There, indeed, one might pause. Did they not seem put with much the same object with which the burglar or assassin, by day-time, reconnoitres the walls of a house? But, with ill purposes, to solicit such information openly of the chief person endangered, and so, in effect, setting him on his guard; how unlikely a procedure was that? Absurd, then, to suppose that those questions had been prompted by evil designs. Thus, the same conduct, which, in this instance, had raised the alarm, served to dispel it. In short, scarce any suspicion or uneasiness, however apparently reasonable at the time, which was not now, with equal apparent reason, dismissed.

At last he began to laugh at his former forebodings; and laugh at the strange ship for, in its aspect someway siding with them, as it were; and laugh, too, at the odd-looking blacks, particularly those old scissors-grinders, the Ashantees; and those bed-ridden old knitting-women, the oakum-pickers; and almost at the dark Spaniard himself, the central hobgoblin of all.

For the rest, whatever in a serious way seemed enigmatical, was now good-naturedly explained away by the thought that, for the most part, the poor invalid scarcely knew what he was about; either sulking in black vapors, or putting idle questions without sense or object. Evidently, for the present, the man was not fit to be entrusted with the ship. On some benevolent plea withdrawing the command from him, Captain Delano would yet have to send her to Conception, in charge of his second mate, a worthy person and good navigator—a plan not more convenient for the San Dominick than for Don Benito; for, relieved from all anxiety, keeping wholly to his cabin, the sick man, under the good nursing of his servant, would probably, by the end of the passage, be in a measure restored to health, and with that he should also be restored to authority.

Such were the American's thoughts. They were tranquilizing. There was a difference between the idea of Don Benito's darkly pre-ordaining Captain Delano's fate, and Captain Delano's lightly arranging Don Benito's. Nevertheless, it was not without something of relief that the good seaman presently perceived his whale-boat in the distance. Its absence had been prolonged by unexpected detention at the sealer's side, as well as its returning trip lengthened by the continual recession of the goal.

The advancing speck was observed by the blacks. Their shouts attracted the attention of Don Benito, who, with a return of courtesy, approaching Captain Delano, expressed satisfaction at the coming of some supplies, slight and temporary as they must necessarily prove.

Captain Delano responded; but while doing so, his attention was drawn to something passing on the deck below: among the crowd climbing the landward bulwarks, anxiously watching the coming boat, two blacks, to all appearances accidentally incommoded by one of the sailors, flew out against him with horrible curses, which the sailor someway resenting, the two blacks dashed him to the deck and jumped upon him, despite the earnest cries of the oakum-pickers.

"Don Benito," said Captain Delano quickly, "do you see what is going on there? Look!"

But, seized by his cough, the Spaniard staggered, with both hands to his face, on the point of falling. Captain Delano would have supported him, but the servant was more alert, who, with one hand sustaining his master, with the other applied the cordial. Don Benito restored, the black withdrew his support, slipping aside a little, but dutifully remaining within call of a whisper. Such discretion was here evinced as quite wiped away, in the visitor's eyes, any blemish of impropriety which might have attached to the attendant, from the indecorous conferences before mentioned; showing, too, that if the servant were to blame, it might be more the master's fault than his own, since when left to himself he could conduct thus well.

His glance thus called away from the spectacle of disorder to the more pleasing one before him, Captain Delano could not avoid again congratulating his host upon possessing such a servant, who, though perhaps a little too forward now and then, must upon the whole be invaluable to one in the invalid's situation.

"Tell me, Don Benito," he added, with a smile—"I should like to have your man here myself—what will you take for him? Would fifty doubloons be any object?"

"Master wouldn't part with Babo for a thousand doubloons," murmured the black, overhearing the offer, and taking it in earnest, and, with the strange vanity of a faithful slave appreciated by his master, scorning to hear so paltry a valuation put upon him by a stranger. But Don Benito, apparently hardly yet completely restored, and again interrupted by his cough, made but some broken reply.

Soon his physical distress became so great, affecting his mind, too, apparently, that, as if to screen the sad spectacle, the servant gently conducted his master below.

Left to himself, the American, to while away the time till his boat should arrive, would have pleasantly accosted some one of the few Spanish seamen he saw; but recalling something that Don Benito had said touching their ill conduct, he refrained, as a ship-master indisposed to countenance cowardice or unfaithfulness in seamen.

While, with these thoughts, standing with eye directed forward towards that handful of sailors, suddenly he thought that one or two of them returned the glance and with a sort of meaning. He rubbed his eyes, and looked again; but again seemed to see the same thing. Under a new form, but more obscure than any previous one, the old suspicions recurred, but, in the absence of Don Benito, with less of panic than before. Despite the bad account given of the sailors, Captain Delano resolved forthwith to accost one of them. Descending the poop, he made his way through the blacks, his movement drawing a queer cry from the oakum-pickers, prompted by whom, the negroes, twitching each other aside, divided before him; but, as if curious to see what was the object of this deliberate visit to their Ghetto, closing in behind, in tolerable order, followed the white stranger up. His progress thus proclaimed as by mounted kings-at-arms, and escorted as by a Caffre[35] guard of honor, Captain Delano, assuming a good humored, off-handed air, continued to advance; now and then saying a blithe word to the negroes, and his eye curiously surveying the white faces, here and there sparsely mixed in with the blacks, like stray white pawns venturously involved in the ranks of the chess-men opposed.

While thinking which of them to select for his purpose, he chanced to observe a sailor seated on the deck engaged in tarring the strap of a large block, with a circle of blacks squatted round him inquisitively eying the process.

The mean employment of the man was in contrast with something superior in his figure. His hand, black with continually thrusting it into the tarpot held for him by a negro, seemed not naturally allied to his face, a face which would have been a very fine one but for its haggardness. Whether this haggardness had aught to do with criminality, could not be determined; since, as intense heat and cold, though unlike, produce like sensations, so innocence and guilt, when, through casual association with mental pain, stamping any visible impress, use one seal—a hacked one.

Not again that this reflection occurred to Captain Delano at the time, charitable man as he was. Rather another idea. Because observing so singular a haggardness combined with a dark eye, averted as in trouble and shame, and then again recalling Don Benito's confessed ill opinion of his crew, insensibly he was operated upon by certain general notions, which, while disconnecting pain and abashment from virtue, invariably link them with vice.

If, indeed, there be any wickedness on board this ship, thought Captain Delano, be sure that man there has fouled his hand in it, even as now he fouls it in the pitch. I don't like to accost him. I will speak to this other, this old Jack here on the windlass.

He advanced to an old Barcelona tar, in ragged red breeches and dirty night-cap, cheeks trenched and bronzed, whiskers dense as thorn hedges. Seated between two sleepy-looking Africans, this mariner, like his younger shipmate, was employed upon some rigging—splicing a cable—the sleepy-looking blacks performing the inferior function of holding the outer parts of the ropes for him.

Upon Captain Delano's approach, the man at once hung his head below its previous level; the one necessary for business. It appeared as if he desired

[35]Kaffir (derived from the Arabic word for infidel), a Bantu people in Southern Africa; often applied to Africans in general.

to be thought absorbed, with more than common fidelity, in his task. Being addressed, he glanced up, but with what seemed a furtive, diffident air, which sat strangely enough on his weather-beaten visage, much as if a grizzly bear, instead of growling and biting, should simper and cast sheep's eyes. He was asked several questions concerning the voyage, questions purposely referring to several particulars in Don Benito's narrative, not previously corroborated by those impulsive cries greeting the visitor on first coming on board. The questions were briefly answered, confirming all that remained to be confirmed of the story. The negroes about the windlass joined in with the old sailor, but, as they became talkative, he by degrees became mute, and at length quite glum, seemed morosely unwilling to answer more questions, and yet, all the while, this ursine air was somehow mixed with his sheepish one.

Despairing of getting into unembarrassed talk with such a centaur, Captain Delano, after glancing round for a more promising countenance, but seeing none, spoke pleasantly to the blacks to make way for him; and so, amid various grins and grimaces, returned to the poop, feeling a little strange at first, he could hardly tell why, but upon the whole with regained confidence in Benito Cereno.

How plainly, thought he, did that old whiskerando yonder betray a consciousness of ill-desert. No doubt, when he saw me coming, he dreaded lest I, apprised by his Captain of the crew's general misbehavior, came with sharp words for him, and so down with his head. And yet—and yet, now that I think of it, that very old fellow, if I err not, was one of those who seemed so earnestly eying me here awhile since. Ah, these currents spin one's head round almost as much as they do the ship. Ha, there now's a pleasant sort of sunny sight; quite sociable, too.

His attention had been drawn to a slumbering negress, partly disclosed through the lace-work of some rigging, lying, with youthful limbs carelessly disposed, under the lee of the bulwarks, like a doe in the shade of a woodland rock. Sprawling at her lapped breasts was her wide-awake fawn, stark naked, its black little body half lifted from the deck, crosswise with its dam's; its hands, like two paws, clambering upon her; its mouth and nose ineffectually rooting to get at the mark; and meantime giving a vexatious half-grunt, blending with the composed snore of the negress.

The uncommon vigor of the child at length roused the mother. She started up, at distance facing Captain Delano. But as if not at all concerned at the attitude in which she had been caught, delightedly she caught the child up, with maternal transports, covering it with kisses.

There's naked nature, now; pure tenderness and love, thought Captain Delano, well pleased.

This incident prompted him to remark the other negresses more particularly than before. He was gratified with their manners; like most uncivilized women, they seemed at once tender of heart and tough of constitution; equally ready to die for their infants or fight for them. Unsophisticated as leopardesses; loving as doves. Ah! thought Captain Delano, these perhaps are some of the very women whom Mungo Park[36] saw in Africa, and gave such a noble account of.

These natural sights somehow insensibly deepened his confidence and ease. At last he looked to see how his boat was getting on; but it was still pretty remote. He turned to see if Don Benito had returned; but he had not.

To change the scene, as well as to please himself with a leisurely observation of the coming boat, stepping over into the mizzen-chains he clambered his way into the starboard quarter-gallery; one of those abandoned Venetian-looking water-balconies previously mentioned; retreats cut off from the deck. As his foot pressed the half-damp, half-dry sea-mosses matting the place, and a chance phantom cats-paw—an islet of breeze, unheralded, unfollowed—as this ghostly cats-paw came fanning his cheek, as his glance fell upon the row of small, round dead-lights, all closed like coppered eyes of the coffined, and the state-cabin door, once connecting with the gallery, even as the dead-lights had once looked out upon it, but now calked fast like a sarcophagus lid, to a purple-black, tarred-over panel, threshold, and post; and he bethought him of the time, when that state-cabin and this state-balcony had heard the voices of the Spanish king's officers, and the forms of the Lima viceroy's daughters had perhaps leaned where he stood— as these and other images flitted through his mind, as the cats-paw through the calm, gradually he felt rising a dreamy inquietude, like that of one who alone on the prairie feels unrest from the repose of the noon.

He leaned against the carved balustrade, again looking off toward his boat; but found his eye falling upon the ribbon grass, trailing along the ship's water-line, straight as a border of green box; and parterres[37] of seaweed, broad ovals and crescents, floating nigh and far, with what seemed long formal alleys between, crossing the terraces of swells, and sweeping round as if leading to the grottoes below. And overhanging all was the balustrade by his arm, which, partly stained with pitch and partly embossed with moss, seemed the charred ruin of some summer-house in a grand garden long running to waste.

Trying to break one charm, he was but becharmed anew. Though upon the wide sea, he seemed in some far inland country; prisoner in some deserted château, left to stare at empty grounds, and peer out at vague roads, where never wagon or wayfarer passed.

But these enchantments were a little disenchanted as his eye fell on the corroded main-chains. Of an ancient style, massy and rusty in link, shackle and bolt, they seemed even more fit for the ship's present business than the one for which probably she had been built.

[36]Scottish explorer (1771–1806), whose *Travels in the Interior of Africa* (1799) was one of the nineteenth century's main sources of information on African culture. Melville is probably referring to Park's tribute in Chapter 20 to the "disinterested charity, and tender solicitude" he received from "many of these poor heathens," especially the women, of whom he wrote: "I do not recollect a single instance of hardheartedness towards me in the women. In all my wanderings and wretchedness, I found them uniformly kind and compassionate."

[37]Gardens having ornamental and diversified arrangements of flower beds separated by paths.

Presently he thought something moved nigh the chains. He rubbed his eyes, and looked hard. Groves of rigging were about the chains; and there, peering from behind a great stay, like an Indian from behind a hemlock, a Spanish sailor, a marlingspike in his hand, was seen, who made what seemed an imperfect gesture towards the balcony, but immediately, as if alarmed by some advancing step along the deck within, vanished into the recesses of the hempen forest, like a poacher.

What meant this? Something the man had sought to communicate, unbeknown to any one, even to his captain. Did the secret involve aught unfavorable to his captain? Were those previous misgivings of Captain Delano's about to be verified? Or, in his haunted mood at the moment, had some random, unintentional motion of the man, while busy with the stay, as if repairing it, been mistaken for a significant beckoning?

Not unbewildered, again he gazed off for his boat. But it was temporarily hidden by a rocky spur of the isle. As with some eagerness he bent forward, watching for the first shooting view of its beak, the balustrade gave way before him like charcoal. Had he not clutched an outreaching rope he would have fallen into the sea. The crash, though feeble, and the fall, though hollow, of the rotten fragments, must have been overheard. He glanced up. With sober curiosity peering down upon him was one of the old oakum-pickers, slipped from his perch to an outside boom; while below the old negro, and, invisible to him, reconnoitering from a port-hole like a fox from the mouth of its den, crouched the Spanish sailor again. From something suddenly suggested by the man's air, the mad idea now darted into Captain Delano's mind, that Don Benito's plea of indisposition, in withdrawing below, was but a pretense: that he was engaged there maturing some plot, of which the sailor, by some means gaining an inkling, had a mind to warn the stranger against; incited, it may be, by gratitude for a kind word on first boarding the ship. Was it from foreseeing some possible interference like this, that Don Benito had, beforehand, given such a bad character of his sailors, while praising the negroes; though, indeed, the former seemed as docile as the latter the contrary? The whites, too, by nature, were the shrewder race. A man with some evil design, would he not be likely to speak well of that stupidity which was blind to his depravity, and malign that intelligence from which it might not be hidden? Not unlikely, perhaps. But if the whites had dark secrets concerning Don Benito, could then Don Benito be any way in complicity with the blacks? But they were too stupid. Besides, who ever heard of a white so far a renegade as to apostatize from his very species almost, by leaguing in against it with negroes?[38] These difficulties recalled former ones. Lost in their mazes, Captain Delano, who had now regained the deck, was

[38]Delano considers it both unnatural (like the crossbreeding of species) and irreligious (like the renunciation of one's inherited religious faith) for whites to side with blacks. He is echoing the racist theory that the human races are distinct species. Melville probably encountered this theory through a review in *Putnam's* of Josiah C. Nott's and George R. Gliddon's *Types of Mankind* (1854). He satirized scientific racism in "The 'Gees" (1856).

uneasily advancing along it, when he observed a new face; an aged sailor seated cross-legged near the main hatchway. His skin was shrunk up with wrinkles like a pelican's empty pouch; his hair frosted; his countenance grave and composed. His hands were full of ropes, which he was working into a large knot. Some blacks were about him obligingly dipping the strands for him, here and there, as the exigencies of the operation demanded.

Captain Delano crossed over to him, and stood in silence surveying the knot; his mind, by a not uncongenial transition, passing from its own entanglements to those of the hemp. For intricacy such a knot he had never seen in an American ship, or indeed any other. The old man looked like an Egyptian priest, making gordian knots for the temple of Ammon.[39] The knot seemed a combination of double-bowline-knot, treble-crown-knot, backhanded-well-knot, knot-in-and-out-knot, and jamming-knot.

At last, puzzled to comprehend the meaning of such a knot, Captain Delano addressed the knotter:—

"What are you knotting there, my man?"

"The knot," was the brief reply, without looking up.

"So it seems; but what is it for?"

"For some one else to undo," muttered back the old man, plying his fingers harder than ever, the knot being now nearly completed.

While Captain Delano stood watching him, suddenly the old man threw the knot towards him, saying in broken English,—the first heard in the ship,—something to this effect—"Undo it, cut it, quick." It was said lowly, but with such condensation of rapidity, that the long, slow words in Spanish, which had preceded and followed, almost operated as covers to the brief English between.

For a moment, knot in hand, and knot in head, Captain Delano stood mute; while, without further heeding him, the old man was now intent upon other ropes. Presently there was a slight stir behind Captain Delano. Turning, he saw the chained negro, Atufal, standing quietly there. The next moment the old sailor rose, muttering, and, followed by his subordinate negroes, removed to the forward part of the ship, where in the crowd he disappeared.

An elderly negro, in a clout like an infant's, and with a pepper and salt head, and a kind of attorney air, now approached Captain Delano. In

---

[39]Melville is compressing two episodes in the career of Alexander the Great. In 333 B.C. Alexander entered the ancient Phrygian city of Gordium (near present-day Ankara, Turkey). According to prophecy, whoever untied the intricate knot that bound the chariot of Gordius, the city's founder, to a pole, would rule Asia. Alexander cut the Gordian knot with his sword and went on to defeat the Persian army. The following year, on capturing Egypt from the Persians, he consulted the oracle of the Egyptian god Amon on the prospects of his conquest schemes and was supposedly hailed as a son of Amon. Unlike Alexander, Delano cannot cut this Gordian knot; like Alexander, however, who was initially welcomed by the Egyptians as a liberator, he is merely stepping into the place of the previous ruler. Also relevant here is the status of Amon as an African deity, worshipped both by the Egyptians and the Black Cushites of Nubia, and especially revered for his impartiality by the poor and oppressed.

tolerable Spanish, and with a good-natured, knowing wink, he informed him that the old knotter was simple-witted, but harmless; often playing his old tricks. The negro concluded by begging the knot, for of course the stranger would not care to be troubled with it. Unconsciously, it was handed to him. With a sort of congé,[40] the negro received it, and turning his back, ferreted into it like a detective Custom House officer after smuggled laces. Soon, with some African word, equivalent to pshaw, he tossed the knot overboard.

All this is very queer now, thought Captain Delano, with a qualmish sort of emotion; but as one feeling incipient sea-sickness, he strove, by ignoring the symptoms, to get rid of the malady. Once more he looked off for his boat. To his delight, it was now again in view, leaving the rocky spur astern.

The sensation here experienced, after at first relieving his uneasiness, with unforeseen efficacy, soon began to remove it. The less distant sight of that well-known boat—showing it, not as before, half blended with the haze, but with outline defined, so that its individuality, like a man's, was manifest; that boat, Rover[41] by name, which, though now in strange seas, had often pressed the beach of Captain Delano's home, and, brought to its threshold for repairs, had familiarly lain there, as a Newfoundland dog; the sight of that household boat evoked a thousand trustful associations, which, contrasted with previous suspicions, filled him not only with lightsome confidence, but somehow with half humorous self-reproaches at his former lack of it.

"What, I, Amasa Delano—Jack of the Beach, as they called me when a lad—I, Amasa; the same that, duck-satchel in hand, used to paddle along the waterside to the school-house made from the old hulk;—I, little Jack of the Beach, that used to go berrying with cousin Nat and the rest; I to be murdered here at the ends of the earth, on board a haunted pirate-ship by a horrible Spaniard?—Too nonsensical to think of! Who would murder Amasa Delano? His conscience is clean. There is some one above. Fie, fie, Jack of the Beach! you are a child indeed; a child of the second childhood, old boy; you are beginning to dote and drule, I'm afraid."

Light of heart and foot, he stepped aft, and there was met by Don Benito's servant, who, with a pleasing expression, responsive to his own present feelings, informed him that his master had recovered from the effects of his coughing fit, and had just ordered him to go present his compliments to his good guest, Don Amasa, and say that he (Don Benito) would soon have the happiness to rejoin him.

There now, do you mark that? again thought Captain Delano, walking the poop. What a donkey I was. This kind gentleman who here sends me his kind compliments, he, but ten minutes ago, dark-lantern in hand, was

---

[40] Ceremonious bow.
[41] Michael Rogin has suggested that the name is an allusion to the pirate ship disguised as a slave-trading vessel that gives its name to James Fenimore Cooper's novel, *The Red Rover* (1827), reviewed by Melville in 1850.

dodging round some old grind-stone in the hold, sharpening a hatchet for me, I thought. Well, well; these long calms have a morbid effect on the mind, I've often heard, though I never believed it before. Ha! glancing towards the boat; there's Rover; good dog; a white bone in her mouth. A pretty big bone though, seems to me.—What? Yes, she has fallen afoul of the bubbling tide-rip there. It sets her the other way, too, for the time. Patience.

It was now about noon, though, from the grayness of everything, it seemed to be getting towards dusk.

The calm was confirmed. In the far distance, away from the influence of land, the leaden ocean seemed laid out and leaded up, its course finished, soul gone, defunct. But the current from landward, where the ship was, increased; silently sweeping her further and further towards the tranced waters beyond.

Still, from his knowledge of those latitudes, cherishing hopes of a breeze, and a fair and fresh one, at any moment, Captain Delano, despite present prospects, buoyantly counted upon bringing the San Dominick safely to anchor ere night. The distance swept over was nothing; since, with a good wind, ten minutes' sailing would retrace more than sixty minutes' drifting. Meantime, one moment turning to mark "Rover" fighting the tide-rip, and the next to see Don Benito approaching, he continued walking the poop.

Gradually he felt a vexation arising from the delay of his boat; this soon merged into uneasiness; and at last, his eye falling continually, as from a stage-box into the pit, upon the strange crowd before and below him, and by and by recognising there the face—now composed to indifference—of the Spanish sailor who had seemed to beckon from the main chains, something of his old trepidations returned.

Ah, thought he—gravely enough—this is like the ague: because it went off, it follows not that it won't come back.

Though ashamed of the relapse, he could not altogether subdue it; and so, exerting his good nature to the utmost, insensibly he came to a compromise.

Yes, this is a strange craft; a strange history, too, and strange folks on board. But—nothing more.

By way of keeping his mind out of mischief till the boat should arrive, he tried to occupy it with turning over and over, in a purely speculative sort of way, some lesser peculiarities of the captain and crew. Among others, four curious points recurred.

First, the affair of the Spanish lad assailed with a knife by the slave boy; an act winked at by Don Benito. Second, the tyranny in Don Benito's treatment of Atufal, the black; as if a child should lead a bull of the Nile by the ring in his nose. Third, the trampling of the sailor by the two negroes; a piece of insolence passed over without so much as a reprimand. Fourth, the cringing submission to their master of all the ship's underlings, mostly blacks; as if by the least inadvertence they feared to draw down his despotic displeasure.

Coupling these points, they seemed somewhat contradictory. But what then, thought Captain Delano, glancing towards his now nearing boat,— what then? Why, Don Benito is a very capricious commander. But he is not the first of the sort I have seen; though it's true he rather exceeds any other. But as a nation—continued he in his reveries—these Spaniards are all an odd set; the very word Spaniard has a curious, conspirator, Guy-Fawkish[42] twang to it. And yet, I dare say, Spaniards in the main are as good folks as any in Duxbury, Massachusetts. Ah good! At last "Rover" has come.

As, with its welcome freight, the boat touched the side, the oakum-pickers, with venerable gestures, sought to restrain the blacks, who, at the sight of three gurried[43] water-casks in its bottom, and a pile of wilted pumpkins in its bow, hung over the bulwarks in disorderly raptures.

Don Benito with his servant now appeared; his coming, perhaps, hastened by hearing the noise. Of him Captain Delano sought permission to serve out the water, so that all might share alike, and none injure themselves by unfair excess. But sensible, and, on Don Benito's account, kind as this offer was, it was received with what seemed impatience; as if aware that he lacked energy as a commander, Don Benito, with the true jealousy of weakness, resented as an affront any interference. So, at least, Captain Delano inferred.

In another moment the casks were being hoisted in, when some of the eager negroes accidentally jostled Captain Delano, where he stood by the gangway; so that, unmindful of Don Benito, yielding to the impulse of the moment, with good-natured authority he bade the blacks stand back; to enforce his words making use of a half-mirthful, half-menacing gesture. Instantly the blacks paused, just where they were, each negro and negress suspended in his or her posture, exactly as the word had found them—for a few seconds continuing so—while, as between the responsive posts of a telegraph, an unknown syllable ran from man to man among the perched oakum-pickers. While the visitor's attention was fixed by this scene, suddenly the hatchet-polishers half rose, and a rapid cry came from Don Benito.

Thinking that at the signal of the Spaniard he was about to be massacred, Captain Delano would have sprung for his boat, but paused, as the oakum-pickers, dropping down into the crowd with earnest exclamations, forced every white and every negro back, at the same moment, with gestures friendly and familiar, almost jocose, bidding him, in substance, not be a fool. Simultaneously the hatchet-polishers resumed their seats, quietly as so many tailors, and at once, as if nothing had happened, the work

---

[42]Guy Fawkes (1570–1606), Catholic conspirator, participated in the Gunpowder Plot, aimed at blowing up the Parliament building while King James I and his chief ministers were meeting inside on November 5, 1605. Fawkes's name became a byword for Catholic villainy, and the annual celebration of Guy Fawkes Day regularly fanned anti-Catholic sentiment.
[43]Slimy from whale and fish refuse.

of hoisting in the casks was resumed, whites and blacks singing at the tackle.

Captain Delano glanced towards Don Benito. As he saw his meager form in the act of recovering itself from reclining in the servant's arms, into which the agitated invalid had fallen, he could not but marvel at the panic by which himself had been surprised on the darting supposition that such a commander, who upon a legitimate occasion, so trivial, too, as it now appeared, could lose all self-command, was, with energetic iniquity, going to bring about his murder.

The casks being on deck, Captain Delano was handed a number of jars and cups by one of the steward's aids, who, in the name of his captain, entreated him to do as he had proposed: dole out the water. He complied, with republican impartiality as to this republican element, which always seeks one level, serving the oldest white no better than the youngest black; excepting, indeed, poor Don Benito, whose condition, if not rank, demanded an extra allowance. To him, in the first place, Captain Delano presented a fair pitcher of the fluid; but, thirsting as he was for it, the Spaniard quaffed not a drop until after several grave bows and salutes. A reciprocation of courtesies which the sight-loving Africans hailed with clapping of hands.

Two of the less wilted pumpkins being reserved for the cabin table, the residue were minced up on the spot for the general regalement. But the soft bread, sugar, and bottled cider, Captain Delano would have given the whites alone, and in chief Don Benito; but the latter objected; which disinterested-ness, on his part, not a little pleased the American; and so mouthfuls all around were given alike to whites and blacks; excepting one bottle of cider, which Babo insisted upon setting aside for his master.

Here it may be observed that as, on the first visit of the boat, the American had not permitted his men to board the ship, neither did he now; being unwilling to add to the confusion of the decks.

Not uninfluenced by the peculiar good humor at present prevailing, and for the time oblivious of any but benevolent thoughts, Captain Delano, who from recent indications counted upon a breeze within an hour or two at furthest, dispatched the boat back to the sealer with orders for all the hands that could be spared immediately to set about rafting casks to the watering-place and filling them. Likewise he bade word be carried to his chief officer, that if against present expectation the ship was not brought to anchor by sunset, he need be under no concern, for as there was to be a full moon that night, he (Captain Delano) would remain on board ready to play the pilot, come the wind soon or late.

As the two Captains stood together, observing the departing boat—the servant as it happened having just spied a spot on his master's velvet sleeve, and silently engaged rubbing it out—the American expressed his regrets that the San Dominick had no boats; none, at least, but the unseaworthy old hulk of the long-boat, which, warped as a camel's skeleton in the desert, and almost as bleached, lay pot-wise inverted amidships, one side a little tipped, furnishing a subterraneous sort of den for family groups of the blacks, mostly women and small children; who, squatting on old mats below, or perched above in the dark dome, on the elevated seats, were descried, some distance within, like a social circle of bats, sheltering in some friendly cave; at intervals, ebon flights of naked boys and girls, three or four years old, darting in and out of the den's mouth.

"Had you three or four boats now, Don Benito," said Captain Delano, "I think that, by tugging at the oars, your negroes here might help along matters some.—Did you sail from port without boats, Don Benito?"

"They were stove in the gales, Señor."

"That was bad. Many men, too, you lost then. Boats and men.—Those must have been hard gales, Don Benito."

"Past all speech," cringed the Spaniard.

"Tell me, Don Benito," continued his companion with increased interest, "tell me, were these gales immediately off the pitch of Cape Horn?"

"Cape Horn?—who spoke of Cape Horn?"

"Yourself did, when giving me an account of your voyage," answered Captain Delano with almost equal astonishment at this eating of his own words, even as he ever seemed eating his own heart, on the part of the Spaniard. "You yourself, Don Benito, spoke of Cape Horn," he emphatically repeated.

The Spaniard turned, in a sort of stooping posture, pausing an instant, as one about to make a plunging exchange of elements, as from air to water.

At this moment a messenger-boy, a white, hurried by, in the regular performance of his function carrying the last expired half hour forward to the forecastle, from the cabin time-piece, to have it struck at the ship's large bell.

"Master," said the servant, discontinuing his work on the coat sleeve, and addressing the rapt Spaniard with a sort of timid apprehensiveness, as one charged with a duty, the discharge of which, it was foreseen, would prove irksome to the very person who had imposed it, and for whose benefit it was intended, "master told me never mind where he was, or how engaged, always to remind him, to a minute, when shaving-time comes. Miguel has gone to strike the half-hour afternoon. It is *now*, master. Will master go into the cuddy?"

"Ah—yes," answered the Spaniard, starting, somewhat as from dreams into realities; then turning upon Captain Delano, he said that ere long he would resume the conversation.

"Then if master means to talk more to Don Amasa," said the servant, "why not let Don Amasa sit by master in the cuddy, and master can talk, and Don Amasa can listen, while Babo here lathers and strops."

"Yes," said Captain Delano, not unpleased with this sociable plan, "yes, Don Benito, unless you had rather not, I will go with you."

"Be it so, Señor."

As the three passed aft, the American could not but think it another strange instance of his host's capriciousness, this being shaved with such uncommon punctuality in the middle of the day. But he deemed it more than likely that the servant's anxious fidelity had something to do with the matter; inasmuch as the timely interruption served to rally his master from the mood which had evidently been coming upon him.

The place called the cuddy was a light deck-cabin formed by the poop, a sort of attic to the large cabin below. Part of it had formerly been the quarters of the officers; but since their death all the partitionings had been thrown down, and the whole interior converted into one spacious and airy marine hall; for absence of fine furniture and picturesque disarray, of odd appurtenances, somewhat answering to the wide, cluttered hall of some eccentric bachelor-squire in the country, who hangs his shooting-jacket and tobacco-pouch on deer antlers, and keeps his fishing-rod, tongs, and walking-stick in the same corner.

The similitude was heightened, if not originally suggested, by glimpses of the surrounding sea; since, in one aspect, the country and the ocean seem cousins-german.

The floor of the cuddy was matted. Overhead, four or five old muskets were stuck into horizontal holes along the beams. On one side was a claw-footed old table lashed to the deck; a thumbed missal on it, and over it a small, meager crucifix attached to the bulk-head. Under the table lay a dented cutlass or two, with a hacked harpoon, among some melancholy old rigging, like a heap of poor friar's girdles. There were also two long, sharp-ribbed settees of malacca cane, black with age, and uncomfortable to look at as inquisitors' racks,[44] with a large, misshapen armchair, which, furnished with a rude barber's crutch at the back, working with a screw, seemed some grotesque, middle-age engine of torment. A flag locker was in one corner, open, exposing various colored bunting, some rolled up, others half unrolled, still others tumbled. Opposite was a cumbrous washstand, of black mahogany, all of one block, with a pedestal, like a font, and over it a railed shelf, containing combs, brushes, and other implements of the toilet. A torn hammock of stained grass swung near; the sheets tossed, and the pillow wrinkled up like a brow, as if whoever slept here slept but illy, with alternate visitations of sad thoughts and bad dreams.

The further extremity of the cuddy, overhanging the ship's stern, was pierced with three openings, windows or port holes, according as men or cannon might peer, socially or unsocially, out of them. At present neither men nor cannon were seen, though huge ring-bolts and other rusty iron fixtures of the wood-work hinted of twenty-four-pounders.

Glancing towards the hammock as he entered, Captain Delano said, "You sleep here, Don Benito?"

"Yes, Señor, since we got into mild weather."

"This seems a sort of dormitory, sitting-room, sail-loft, chapel, armory, and private closet all together, Don Benito," added Captain Delano, looking round.

[44]As John Bernstein has pointed out, references to the Spanish Inquisition, which reached its height under Charles V, structure the story.

"Yes, Señor; events have not been favorable to much order in my arrangements."

Here the servant, napkin on arm, made a motion as if waiting his master's good pleasure. Don Benito signified his readiness, when, seating him in the malacca arm-chair, and for the guest's convenience drawing opposite it one of the settees, the servant commenced operations by throwing back his master's collar and loosening his cravat.

There is something in the negro which, in a peculiar way, fits him for avocations about one's person. Most negroes are natural valets and hairdressers; taking to the comb and brush congenially as to the castinets, and flourishing them apparently with almost equal satisfaction. There is, too, a smooth tact about them in this employment, with a marvelous, noiseless, gliding briskness, not ungraceful in its way, singularly pleasing to behold, and still more so to be the manipulated subject of. And above all is the great gift of good humor. Not the mere grin or laugh is here meant. Those were unsuitable. But a certain easy cheerfulness, harmonious in every glance and gesture; as though God had set the whole negro to some pleasant tune.

When to all this is added the docility arising from the unaspiring contentment of a limited mind, and that susceptibility of blind attachment sometimes inhering in indisputable inferiors, one readily perceives why those hypochondriacs, Johnson and Byron—it may be something like the hypochondriac, Benito Cereno—took to their hearts, almost to the exclusion of the entire white race, their serving men, the negroes, Barber and Fletcher.[45] But if there be that in the negro which exempts him from the inflicted sourness of the morbid or cynical mind, how, in his most prepossessing aspects, must he appear to a benevolent one? When at ease with respect to exterior things, Captain Delano's nature was not only benign, but familiarly and humorously so. At home, he had often taken rare satisfaction in sitting in his door, watching some free man of color at his work or play. If on a voyage he chanced to have a black sailor, invariably he was on chatty, and half-gamesome terms with him. In fact, like most men of a good, blithe heart, Captain Delano took to negroes, not philanthropically, but genially, just as other men to Newfoundland dogs.

Hitherto the circumstances in which he found the San Dominick had repressed the tendency. But in the cuddy, relieved from his former uneasiness, and, for various reasons, more sociably inclined than at any previous period of the day, and seeing the colored servant, napkin on arm, so debonair about his master, in a business so familiar as that of shaving, too, all his old weakness for negroes returned.

Among other things, he was amused with an odd instance of the African love of bright colors and fine shows, in the black's informally taking from

[45]Francis Barber, the faithful black servant of Samuel Johnson (1709–1784), is mentioned frequently in James Boswell's *Life of Samuel Johnson*, which comments on the warm relationship between the two men. William Fletcher was the white English valet of Lord Byron (1788–1824). Melville apparently confused him with the black servant of Byron's companion Edward Trelawny.

the flag-locker a great piece of bunting of all hues, and lavishly tucking it under his master's chin for an apron.

The mode of shaving among the Spaniards is a little different from what it is with other nations. They have a basin, specifically called a barber's basin, which on one side is scooped out, so as accurately to receive the chin, against which it is closely held in lathering; which is done, not with a brush, but with soap dipped in the water of the basin and rubbed on the face.

In the present instance salt-water was used for lack of better; and the parts lathered were only the upper lip, and low down under the throat, all the rest being cultivated beard.

The preliminaries being somewhat novel to Captain Delano, he sat curiously eying them, so that no conversation took place, nor for the present did Don Benito appear disposed to renew any.

Setting down his basin, the negro searched among the razors, as for the sharpest, and having found it, gave it an additional edge by expertly strapping it on the firm, smooth, oily skin of his open palm; he then made a gesture as if to begin, but midway stood suspended for an instant, one hand elevating the razor, the other professionally dabbling among the bubbling suds on the Spaniard's lank neck. Not unaffected by the close sight of the gleaming steel, Don Benito nervously shuddered; his usual ghastliness was heightened by the lather, which lather, again, was intensified in its hue by the contrasting sootiness of the negro's body. Altogether the scene was somewhat peculiar, at least to Captain Delano, nor, as he saw the two thus postured, could he resist the vagary, that in the black he saw a headsman, and in the white, a man at the block. But this was one of those antic conceits, appearing and vanishing in a breath, from which, perhaps, the best regulated mind is not always free.

Meantime the agitation of the Spaniard had a little loosened the bunting from around him, so that one broad fold swept curtain-like over the chair-arm to the floor, revealing, amid a profusion of armorial bars and ground-colors—black, blue, and yellow—a closed castle in a blood-red field diagonal with a lion rampant in a white.

"The castle and the lion," exclaimed Captain Delano—"why, Don Benito, this is the flag of Spain you use here. It's well it's only I, and not the King, that sees this," he added with a smile, "but"—turning towards the black,— "it's all one, I suppose, so the colors be gay;" which playful remark did not fail somewhat to tickle the negro.

"Now, master," he said, readjusting the flag, and pressing the head gently further back into the crotch of the chair; "now master," and the steel glanced nigh the throat.

Again Don Benito faintly shuddered.

"You must not shake so, master.—See, Don Amasa, master always shakes when I shave him. And yet master knows I never yet have drawn blood, though it's true, if master will shake so, I may some of these times. Now master," he continued. "And now, Don Amasa, please go on with your talk about the gale, and all that, master can hear, and between times master can answer."

"Ah yes, these gales," said Captain Delano; "but the more I think of your voyage, Don Benito, the more I wonder, not at the gales, terrible as they must have been, but at the disastrous interval following them. For here, by your account, have you been these two months and more getting from Cape Horn to St. Maria, a distance which I myself, with a good wind, have sailed in a few days. True, you had calms, and long ones, but to be becalmed for two months, that is, at least, unusual. Why, Don Benito, had almost any other gentleman told me such a story, I should have been half disposed to a little incredulity."

Here an involuntary expression came over the Spaniard, similar to that just before on the deck, and whether it was the start he gave, or a sudden gawky roll of the hull in the calm, or a momentary unsteadiness of the servant's hand; however it was, just then the razor drew blood, spots of which stained the creamy lather under the throat; immediately the black barber drew back his steel, and remaining in his professional attitude, back to Captain Delano, and face to Don Benito, held up the trickling razor, saying, with a sort of half humorous sorrow, "See, master,—you shook so—here's Babo's first blood."

No sword drawn before James the First of England, no assassination in that timid King's presence,[46] could have produced a more terrified aspect than was now presented by Don Benito.

Poor fellow, thought Captain Delano, so nervous he can't even bear the sight of barber's blood; and this unstrung, sick man, is it credible that I should have imagined he meant to spill all my blood, who can't endure the sight of one little drop of his own? Surely, Amasa Delano, you have been beside yourself this day. Tell it not when you get home, sappy Amasa. Well, well, he looks like a murderer, doesn't he? More like as if himself were to be done for. Well, well, this day's experience shall be a good lesson.

Meantime, while these things were running through the honest seaman's mind, the servant had taken the napkin from his arm, and to Don Benito had said—"But answer Don Amasa, please, master, while I wipe this ugly stuff off the razor, and strop it again."

As he said the words, his face was turned half round, so as to be alike visible to the Spaniard and the American, and seemed by its expression to hint, that he was desirous, by getting his master to go on with the conversation, considerably to withdraw his attention from the recent annoying accident. As if glad to snatch the offered relief, Don Benito resumed, rehearsing to Captain Delano, that not only were the calms of unusual duration, but the ship had fallen in with obstinate currents; and other things he added, some of which were but repetitions of former statements, to explain how it came to pass that the passage from Cape Horn to St. Maria had been so exceedingly long, now and then mingling with his words, incidental praises, less qualified than before, to the blacks, for their general good conduct.

[46]Proverbially timid, James I (1566–1625) was haunted by fears of assassination at Catholic hands, especially after the Gunpowder Plot of 1605.

These particulars were not given consecutively, the servant, at convenient times, using his razor, and so, between the intervals of shaving, the story and panegyric went on with more than usual huskiness.

To Captain Delano's imagination, now again not wholly at rest, there was something so hollow in the Spaniard's manner, with apparently some reciprocal hollowness in the servant's dusky comment of silence, that the idea flashed across him, that possibly master and man, for some unknown purpose, were acting out, both in word and deed, nay, to the very tremor of Don Benito's limbs, some juggling play before him. Neither did the suspicion of collusion lack apparent support, from the fact of those whispered conferences before mentioned. But then, what could be the object of enacting this play of the barber before him? At last, regarding the notion as a whimsy, insensibly suggested, perhaps, by the theatrical aspect of Don Benito in his harlequin ensign, Captain Delano speedily banished it.

The shaving over, the servant bestirred himself with a small bottle of scented waters, pouring a few drops on the head, and then diligently rubbing; the vehemence of the exercise causing the muscles of his face to twitch rather strangely.

His next operation was with comb, scissors and brush; going round and round, smoothing a curl here, clipping an unruly whisker-hair there, giving a graceful sweep to the temple-lock, with other impromptu touches evincing the hand of a master; while, like any resigned gentleman in barber's hands, Don Benito bore all, much less uneasily, at least, than he had done the razoring; indeed, he sat so pale and rigid now, that the negro seemed a Nubian[47] sculptor finishing off a white statue-head.

All being over at last, the standard of Spain removed, tumbled up, and tossed back into the flag-locker, the negro's warm breath blowing away any stray hair which might have lodged down his master's neck; collar and cravat readjusted; a speck of lint whisked off the velvet lapel; all this being done; backing off a little space, and pausing with an expression of subdued self-complacency, the servant for a moment surveyed his master, as, in toilet at least, the creature of his own tasteful hands.

Captain Delano playfully complimented him upon his achievement; at the same time congratulating Don Benito.

But neither sweet waters, nor shampooing, nor fidelity, nor sociality, delighted the Spaniard. Seeing him relapsing into forbidding gloom, and still remaining seated, Captain Delano, thinking that his presence was undesired just then, withdrew, on pretense of seeing whether, as he had prophecied, any signs of a breeze were visible.

Walking forward to the mainmast, he stood awhile thinking over the scene, and not without some undefined misgivings, when he heard a noise

[47]Nubia, an ancient black kingdom in what is now Sudan, was cited by abolitionists along with Egypt as evidence that Africans had a heritage of civilization, not savagery. A Nubian dynasty ruled Egypt in the eighth and seventh centuries B.C., as Egyptian dynasties had earlier ruled Nubia, and a high degree of crossfertilization enriched the two cultures.

near the cuddy, and turning, saw the negro, his hand to his cheek. Advancing, Captain Delano perceived that the cheek was bleeding. He was about to ask the cause, when the negro's wailing soliloquy enlightened him.

"Ah, when will master get better from his sickness; only the sour heart that sour sickness breeds made him serve Babo so; cutting Babo with the razor, because, only by accident, Babo had given master one little scratch; and for the first time in so many a day, too. Ah, ah, ah," holding his hand to his face.

Is it possible, thought Captain Delano; was it to wreak in private his Spanish spite against this poor friend of his, that Don Benito, by his sullen manner, impelled me to withdraw? Ah, this slavery breeds ugly passions in man.—Poor fellow!

He was about to speak in sympathy to the negro, but with a timid reluctance he now reëntered the cuddy.

Presently master and man came forth; Don Benito leaning on his servant as if nothing had happened.

But a sort of love-quarrel, after all, thought Captain Delano.

He accosted Don Benito, and they slowly walked together. They had gone but a few paces, when the steward—a tall, rajah-looking mulatto, orientally set off with a pagoda turban formed by three or four Madras handkerchiefs wound about his head, tier on tier—approaching with a salaam, announced lunch in the cabin.

On their way thither, the two Captains were preceded by the mulatto, who, turning round as he advanced, with continual smiles and bows, ushered them on, a display of elegance which quite completed the insignificance of the small bare-headed Babo, who, as if not unconscious of inferiority, eyed askance the graceful steward. But in part, Captain Delano imputed his jealous watchfulness to that peculiar feeling which the full-blooded African entertains for the adulterated one. As for the steward, his manner, if not bespeaking much dignity of self-respect, yet evidenced his extreme desire to please; which is doubly meritorious, as at once Christian and Chesterfieldian.[48]

Captain Delano observed with interest that while the complexion of the mulatto was hybrid, his physiognomy was European; classically so.

"Don Benito," whispered he, "I am glad to see this usher-of-the-golden-rod[49] of yours; the sight refutes an ugly remark once made to me by a Barbadoes planter; that when a mulatto has a regular European face, look out for him; he is a devil. But see, your steward here has features more regular than King George's of England; and yet there he nods, and bows, and smiles; a king, indeed—the king of kind hearts and polite fellows. What a pleasant voice he has, too!"

"He has, Señor."

[48]Philip Dormer Stanhope, fourth Earl of Chesterfield (1694–1773), was famous for the worldly advice on policy and manners that he conveyed in letters to his illegitimate son. Melville often contrasts Chesterfield's code of morality with Christ's.

[49]Melville is punning on the usher-of-the-black-rod who attended the English king. Ushers were officers at court whose duty was to walk before dignitaries of high rank, bearing a rod. In the ensuing discussion, Delano once again echoes racist theories.

"But, tell me, has he not, so far as you have known him, always proved a good, worthy fellow?" said Captain Delano, pausing, while with a final genuflexion the steward disappeared into the cabin; "come, for the reason just mentioned, I am curious to know."

"Francesco is a good man," a sort of sluggishly responded Don Benito, like a phlegmatic appreciator, who would neither find fault nor flatter.

"Ah, I thought so. For it were strange indeed, and not very creditable to us white-skins, if a little of our blood mixed with the African's, should, far from improving the latter's quality, have the sad effect of pouring vitriolic acid into black broth; improving the hue, perhaps, but not the wholesomeness."

"Doubtless, doubtless, Señor, but"—glancing at Babo—"not to speak of negroes, your planter's remark I have heard applied to the Spanish and Indian inter-mixtures in our provinces. But I know nothing about the matter," he listlessly added.

And here they entered the cabin.

The lunch was a frugal one. Some of Captain Delano's fresh fish and pumpkins, biscuit and salt beef, the reserved bottle of cider, and the San Dominick's last bottle of Canary.

As they entered, Francesco, with two or three colored aids, was hovering over the table giving the last adjustments. Upon perceiving their master they withdrew, Francesco making a smiling congé, and the Spaniard, without condescending to notice it, fastidiously remarking to his companion that he relished not superfluous attendance.

Without companions, host and guest sat down, like a childless married couple, at opposite ends of the table, Don Benito waving Captain Delano to his place, and,weak as he was, insisting upon that gentleman being seated before himself.

The negro placed a rug under Don Benito's feet, and a cushion behind his back, and then stood behind, not his master's chair, but Captain Delano's. At first, this a little surprised the latter. But it was soon evident that, in taking his position, the black was still true to his master; since by facing him he could the more readily anticipate his slightest want.

"This is an uncommonly intelligent fellow of yours, Don Benito," whispered Captain Delano across the table.

"You say true, Señor."

During the repast, the guest again reverted to parts of Don Benito's story, begging further particulars here and there. He inquired how it was that the scurvy and fever should have committed such wholesale havoc upon the whites, while destroying less than half of the blacks. As if this question reproduced the whole scene of plague before the Spaniard's eyes, miserably reminding him of his solitude in a cabin where before he had had so many friends and officers round him, his hand shook, his face became hueless, broken words escaped; but directly the sane memory of the past seemed replaced by insane terrors of the present. With starting eyes he stared before him at vacancy. For nothing was to be seen but the hand of his servant pushing the Canary over towards him. At length a few sips served

partially to restore him. He made random reference to the different constitution of races, enabling one to offer more resistance to certain maladies
than another. The thought was new to his companion.

Presently Captain Delano, intending to say something to his host concerning the pecuniary part of the business he had undertaken for him, especially—
since he was strictly accountable to his owners—with reference to the new suit
of sails, and other things of that sort; and naturally preferring to conduct such
affairs in private, was desirous that the servant should withdraw; imagining
that Don Benito for a few minutes could dispense with his attendance. He,
however, waited awhile; thinking that, as the conversation proceeded, Don
Benito, without being prompted, would perceive the propriety of the step.

But it was otherwise. At last catching his host's eye, Captain Delano,
with a slight backward gesture of his thumb, whispered, "Don Benito, pardon me, but there is an interference with the full expression of what I have
to say to you."

Upon this the Spaniard changed countenance; which was imputed to his
resenting the hint, as in some way a reflection upon his servant. After a
moment's pause, he assured his guest that the black's remaining with them
could be of no disservice; because since losing his officers he had made Babo
(whose original office, it now appeared, had been captain of the slaves) not
only his constant attendant and companion, but in all things his confidant.

After this, nothing more could be said; though, indeed, Captain Delano
could hardly avoid some little tinge of irritation upon being left ungratified
in so inconsiderable a wish, by one, too, for whom he intended such solid
services. But it is only his querulousness, thought he; and so filling his glass
he proceeded to business.

The price of the sails and other matters was fixed upon. But while this
was being done, the American observed that, though his original offer of assistance had been hailed with hectic animation, yet now when it was
reduced to a business transaction, indifference and apathy were betrayed.
Don Benito, in fact, appeared to submit to hearing the details more out of
regard to common propriety, than from any impression that weighty benefit
to himself and his voyage was involved.

Soon, this manner became still more reserved. The effort was vain to
seek to draw him into social talk. Gnawed by his splenetic mood, he sat
twitching his beard, while to little purpose the hand of his servant, mute as
that on the wall,[50] slowly pushed over the Canary.

---

[50]In Daniel 5, in the midst of a great feast given by King Belshazzar of Babylon, the "fingers of a man's hand" mysteriously appear and begin writing on the palace wall. Like Cereno, Belshazzar blanches and trembles in terror. The Hebrew prophet Daniel interprets the handwriting on the wall to mean that the days of Belshazzar's kingdom are numbered, that Belshazzar has been "weighed in the balances, and ... found wanting," and that his kingdom is to be divided and given to the Medes and the Persians.

Lunch being over, they sat down on the cushioned transom; the servant placing a pillow behind his master. The long continuance of the calm had now affected the atmosphere. Don Benito sighed heavily, as if for breath.

"Why not adjourn to the cuddy," said Captain Delano; "there is more air there." But the host sat silent and motionless.

Meantime his servant knelt before him, with a large fan of feathers. And Francesco coming in on tiptoes, handed the negro a little cup of aromatic waters, with which at intervals he chafed his master's brow; smoothing the hair along the temples as a nurse does a child's. He spoke no word. He only rested his eye on his master's, as if, amid all Don Benito's distress, a little to refresh his spirit by the silent sight of fidelity.

Presently the ship's bell sounded two o'clock; and through the cabin-windows a slight rippling of the sea was discerned; and from the desired direction.

"There," exclaimed Captain Delano, "I told you so, Don Benito, look!"

He had risen to his feet, speaking in a very animated tone, with a view the more to rouse his companion. But though the crimson curtain of the stern-window near him that moment fluttered against his pale cheek, Don Benito seemed to have even less welcome for the breeze than the calm.

Poor fellow, thought Captain Delano, bitter experience has taught him that one ripple does not make a wind, any more than one swallow a summer. But he is mistaken for once. I will get his ship in for him, and prove it.

Briefly alluding to his weak condition, he urged his host to remain quietly where he was, since he (Captain Delano) would with pleasure take upon himself the responsibility of making the best use of the wind.

Upon gaining the deck, Captain Delano started at the unexpected figure of Atufal, monumentally fixed at the threshold, like one of those sculptured porters of black marble guarding the porches of Egyptian tombs.

But this time the start was, perhaps, purely physical. Atufal's presence, singularly attesting docility even in sullenness, was contrasted with that of the hatchet-polishers, who in patience evinced their industry; while both spectacles showed, that lax as Don Benito's general authority might be, still, whenever he chose to exert it, no man so savage or colossal but must, more or less, bow.

Snatching a trumpet which hung from the bulwarks, with a free step Captain Delano advanced to the forward edge of the poop, issuing his orders in his best Spanish. The few sailors and many negroes, all equally pleased, obediently set about heading the ship towards the harbor.

While giving some directions about setting a lower stu'n'-sail, suddenly Captain Delano heard a voice faithfully repeating his orders. Turning, he saw Babo, now for the time acting, under the pilot, his original part of captain of the slaves. This assistance proved valuable. Tattered sails and warped yards were soon brought into some trim. And no brace or halyard was pulled but to the blithe songs of the inspirited negroes.

Good fellows, thought Captain Delano, a little training would make fine sailors of them. Why see, the very women pull and sing too. These must be some of those Ashantee negresses that make such capital soldiers, I've heard. But who's at the helm. I must have a good hand there.

He went to see.

The San Dominick steered with a cumbrous tiller, with large horizontal pullies attached. At each pully-end stood a subordinate black, and between them, at the tiller-head, the responsible post, a Spanish seaman, whose countenance evinced his due share in the general hopefulness and confidence at the coming of the breeze.

He proved the same man who had behaved with so shame-faced an air on the windlass.

"Ah,—it is you, my man," exclaimed Captain Delano—"well, no more sheep's-eyes now;—look straight forward and keep the ship so. Good hand, I trust? And want to get into the harbor, don't you?"

The man assented with an inward chuckle, grasping the tiller-head firmly. Upon this, unperceived by the American, the two blacks eyed the sailor intently.

Finding all right at the helm, the pilot went forward to the forecastle, to see how matters stood there.

The ship now had way enough to breast the current. With the approach of evening, the breeze would be sure to freshen.

Having done all that was needed for the present, Captain Delano, giving his last orders to the sailors, turned aft to report affairs to Don Benito in the cabin; perhaps additionally incited to rejoin him by the hope of snatching a moment's private chat while his servant was engaged upon deck.

From opposite sides, there were, beneath the poop, two approaches to the cabin; one further forward than the other, and consequently communicating with a longer passage. Marking the servant still above, Captain Delano, taking the nighest entrance—the one last named, and at whose porch Atufal still stood—hurried on his way, till, arrived at the cabin threshold, he paused an instant, a little to recover from his eagerness. Then, with the words of his intended business upon his lips, he entered. As he advanced toward the seated Spaniard, he heard another footstep, keeping time with his. From the opposite door, a salver in hand, the servant was likewise advancing.

"Confound the faithful fellow," thought Captain Delano; "what a vexatious coincidence."

Possibly, the vexation might have been something different, were it not for the brisk confidence inspired by the breeze. But even as it was, he felt a slight twinge, from a sudden indefinite association in his mind of Babo with Atufal.

"Don Benito," said he, "I give you joy; the breeze will hold, and will increase. By the way, your tall man and time-piece, Atufal, stands without. By your order, of course?"

Don Benito recoiled, as if at some bland satirical touch, delivered with such adroit garnish of apparent good-breeding as to present no handle for retort.

He is like one flayed alive, thought Captain Delano; where may one touch him without causing a shrink?

The servant moved before his master, adjusting a cushion; recalled to civility, the Spaniard stiffly replied: "you are right. The slave appears where you saw him, according to my command; which is, that if at the given hour I am below, he must take his stand and abide my coming."

"Ah now, pardon me, but that is treating the poor fellow like an ex-king indeed. Ah, Don Benito," smiling, "for all the license you permit in some things, I fear lest, at bottom, you are a bitter hard master."

Again Don Benito shrank; and this time, as the good sailor thought, from a genuine twinge of his conscience.

Again conversation became constrained. In vain Captain Delano called attention to the now perceptible motion of the keel gently cleaving the sea; with lack-lustre eye, Don Benito returned words few and reserved.

By-and-by, the wind having steadily risen, and still blowing right into the harbor, bore the San Dominick swiftly on. Rounding a point of land, the sealer at distance came into open view.

Meantime Captain Delano had again repaired to the deck, remaining there some time. Having at last altered the ship's course, so as to give the reef a wide berth, he returned for a few moments below.

I will cheer up my poor friend, this time, thought he.

"Better and better, Don Benito," he cried as he blithely reëntered; "there will soon be an end to your cares, at least for awhile. For when, after a long, sad voyage, you know, the anchor drops into the haven, all its vast weight seems lifted from the captain's heart. We are getting on famously, Don Benito. My ship is in sight. Look through this side-light here; there she is; all a-taunt-o! The Bachelor's Delight, my good friend. Ah, how this wind braces one up. Come, you must take a cup of coffee with me this evening. My old steward will give you as fine a cup as ever any sultan tasted. What say you, Don Benito, will you?"

At first, the Spaniard glanced feverishly up, casting a longing look towards the sealer, while with mute concern his servant gazed into his face. Suddenly the old ague of coldness returned, and dropping back to his cushions he was silent.

"You do not answer. Come, all day you have been my host; would you have hospitality all on one side?"

"I cannot go," was the response.

"What? it will not fatigue you. The ships will lie together as near as they can, without swinging foul. It will be little more than stepping from deck to deck; which is but as from room to room. Come, come, you must not refuse me."

"I cannot go," decisively and repulsively repeated Don Benito.

Renouncing all but the last appearance of courtesy, with a sort of cadaverous sullenness, and biting his thin nails to the quick, he glanced, almost glared, at his guest; as if impatient that a stranger's presence should interfere with the full indulgence of his morbid hour. Meantime the sound of the parted waters came more and more gurglingly and merrily in at the windows; as reproaching him for his dark spleen; as telling him that, sulk as he might, and go mad with it, nature cared not a jot; since, whose fault was it, pray?

But the foul mood was now at its depth, as the fair wind at its height.

There was something in the man so far beyond any mere unsociality or sourness previously evinced, that even the forbearing good-nature of his guest could no longer endure it. Wholly at a loss to account for such demeanor, and deeming sickness with eccentricity, however extreme, no adequate excuse, well satisfied, too, that nothing in his own conduct could justify it, Captain Delano's pride began to be roused. Himself became reserved. But all seemed one to the Spaniard. Quitting him, therefore, Captain Delano once more went to the deck.

The ship was now within less than two miles of the sealer. The whaleboat was seen darting over the interval.

To be brief, the two vessels, thanks to the pilot's skill, ere long in neighborly style lay anchored together.

Before returning to his own vessel, Captain Delano had intended communicating to Don Benito the smaller details of the proposed services to be rendered. But, as it was, unwilling anew to subject himself to rebuffs, he resolved, now that he had seen the San Dominick safely moored, immediately to quit her, without further allusion to hospitality or business. Indefinitely postponing his ulterior plans, he would regulate his future actions according to future circumstances. His boat was ready to receive him; but his host still tarried below. Well, thought Captain Delano, if he has little breeding, the more need to show mine. He descended to the cabin to bid a ceremonious, and, it may be, tacitly rebukeful adieu. But to his great satisfaction, Don Benito, as if he began to feel the weight of that treatment with which his slighted guest had, not indecorously, retaliated upon him, now supported by his servant, rose to his feet, and grasping Captain Delano's hand, stood tremulous; too much agitated to speak. But the good augury hence drawn was suddenly dashed, by his resuming all his previous reserve, with augmented gloom, as, with half-averted eyes, he silently reseated himself on his cushions. With a corresponding return of his own chilled feelings, Captain Delano bowed and withdrew.

He was hardly midway in the narrow corridor, dim as a tunnel, leading from the cabin to the stairs, when a sound, as of the tolling for execution in some jail-yard, fell on his ears. It was the echo of the ship's flawed bell, striking the hour, drearily reverberated in this subterranean vault. Instantly, by a fatality not to be withstood, his mind, responsive to the portent, swarmed with superstitious suspicions. He paused. In images far swifter than these sentences, the minutest details of all his former distrusts swept through him.

Hitherto, credulous good-nature had been too ready to furnish excuses for reasonable fears. Why was the Spaniard, so superfluously punctilious at times, now heedless of common propriety in not accompanying to the side his departing guest? Did indisposition forbid? Indisposition had not forbidden more irksome exertion that day. His last equivocal demeanor recurred. He had risen to his feet, grasped his guest's hand, motioned toward his hat; then, in an instant, all was eclipsed in sinister muteness and gloom. Did this imply one brief, repentent relenting at the final moment, from some iniquitous plot, followed by remorseless return to it? His last glance seemed to express a calamitous, yet acquiescent farewell to Captain Delano forever. Why decline the invitation to visit the sealer that evening? Or was the Spaniard less hardened than the Jew, who refrained not from supping at the board of him whom the same night he meant to betray?[51] What imported all those day-long enigmas and contradictions, except they were intended to mystify, preliminary to some stealthy blow? Atufal, the pretended rebel, but punctual shadow, that moment lurked by the threshold without. He seemed a sentry, and more. Who, by his own confession, had stationed him there? Was the negro now lying in wait?

The Spaniard behind—his creature before: to rush from darkness to light was the involuntary choice.

The next moment, with clenched jaw and hand, he passed Atufal, and stood unharmed in the light. As he saw his trim ship lying peacefully at her anchor, and almost within ordinary call; as he saw his household boat, with familiar faces in it, patiently rising and falling on the short waves by the San Dominick's side; and then, glancing about the decks where he stood, saw the oakum-pickers still gravely plying their fingers; and heard the low, buzzing whistle and industrious hum of the hatchet-polishers, still bestirring themselves over their endless occupation; and more than all, as he saw the benign aspect of nature, taking her innocent repose in the evening; the screened sun in the quiet camp of the west shining out like the mild light from Abraham's tent; as charmed eye and ear took in all these, with the chained figure of the black, clenched jaw and hand relaxed. Once again he smiled at the phantoms which had mocked him, and felt something like a tinge of remorse, that, by harboring them even for a moment, he should, by implication, have betrayed an almost atheist doubt of the ever-watchful Providence above.[52]

There was a few minutes' delay, while, in obedience to his orders, the boat was being hooked along to the gangway. During this interval, a sort of saddened satisfaction stole over Captain Delano, at thinking of the kindly offices he had that day discharged for a stranger. Ah, thought he, after good actions one's conscience is never ungrateful, however much so the benefited party may be.

Presently, his foot, in the first act of descent into the boat, pressed the first round of the side-ladder, his face presented inward upon the deck. In

[51]Judas, who sat with Jesus at the Last Supper before betraying him (Matthew 26:20–25).
[52]In contrast to Delano, who considers it atheistic to doubt that Providence benevo-

lently keeps the black man in chains, Melville in the prose Supplement to his volume of Civil War poetry, *Battle-Pieces*, calls slavery an "atheistical iniquity."

the same moment, he heard his name courteously sounded; and, to his pleased surprise, saw Don Benito advancing—an unwonted energy in his air, as if, at the last moment, intent upon making amends for his recent discourtesy. With instinctive good feeling, Captain Delano, withdrawing his foot, turned and reciprocally advanced. As he did so, the Spaniard's nervous eagerness increased, but his vital energy failed; so that, the better to support him, the servant, placing his master's hand on his naked shoulder, and gently holding it there, formed himself into a sort of crutch.

When the two captains met, the Spaniard again fervently took the hand of the American, at the same time casting an earnest glance into his eyes, but, as before, too much overcome to speak.

I have done him wrong, self-reproachfully thought Captain Delano; his apparent coldness has deceived me; in no instance has he meant to offend.

Meantime, as if fearful that the continuance of the scene might too much unstring his master, the servant seemed anxious to terminate it. And so, still presenting himself as a crutch, and walking between the two captains, he advanced with them towards the gangway; while still, as if full of kindly contrition, Don Benito would not let go the hand of Captain Delano, but retained it in his, across the black's body.

Soon they were standing by the side, looking over into the boat, whose crew turned up their curious eyes. Waiting a moment for the Spaniard to relinquish his hold, the now embarrassed Captain Delano lifted his foot, to overstep the threshold of the open gangway; but still Don Benito would not let go his hand. And yet, with an agitated tone, he said, "I can go no further; here I must bid you adieu. Adieu, my dear, dear Don Amasa. Go—go!" suddenly tearing his hand loose, "go, and God guard you better than me, my best friend."

Not unaffected, Captain Delano would now have lingered; but catching the meekly admonitory eye of the servant, with a hasty farewell he descended into his boat, followed by the continual adieus of Don Benito, standing rooted in the gangway.

Seating himself in the stern, Captain Delano, making a last salute, ordered the boat shoved off. The crew had their oars on end. The bowsman pushed the boat a sufficient distance for the oars to be lengthwise dropped. The instant that was done, Don Benito sprang over the bulwarks, falling at the feet of Captain Delano; at the same time, calling towards his ship, but in tones so frenzied, that none in the boat could understand him. But, as if not equally obtuse, three sailors, from three different and distant parts of the ship, splashed into the sea, swimming after their captain, as if intent upon his rescue.

The dismayed officer of the boat eagerly asked what this meant. To which, Captain Delano, turning a disdainful smile upon the unaccountable Spaniard, answered that, for his part, he neither knew nor cared; but it seemed as if Don Benito had taken it into his head to produce the impression among his people that the boat wanted to kidnap him. "Or else—give way for your lives," he wildly added, starting at a clattering hubbub in the ship, above which rang the tocsin[53] of the hatchet-polishers; and seizing Don Benito by the throat he added, "this plotting pirate means murder!" Here, in apparent verification of the words, the servant, a dagger in his hand, was seen on the rail overhead, poised, in the act of leaping, as if with desperate fidelity to befriend his master to the last; while, seemingly to aid the black, the three white sailors were trying to clamber into the hampered bow. Meantime, the whole host of negroes, as if inflamed at the sight of their jeopardized captain, impended in one sooty avalanche over the bulwarks.

All this, with what preceded, and what followed, occurred with such involutions of rapidity, that past, present, and future seemed one.

Seeing the negro coming, Captain Delano had flung the Spaniard aside, almost in the very act of clutching him, and, by the unconscious recoil, shifting his place, with arms thrown up, so promptly grappled the servant in his descent, that with dagger presented at Captain Delano's heart, the black seemed of purpose to have leaped there as to his mark. But the weapon was wrenched away, and the assailant dashed down into the bottom of the boat, which now, with disentangled oars, began to speed through the sea.

At this juncture, the left hand of Captain Delano, on one side, again clutched the half-reclined Don Benito, heedless that he was in a speechless faint, while his right foot, on the other side, ground the prostrate negro;[54] and his right arm pressed for added speed on the after oar, his eye bent forward, encouraging his men to their utmost.

But here, the officer of the boat, who had at last succeeded in beating off the towing sailors, and was now, with face turned aft, assisting the bowsman at his oar, suddenly called to Captain Delano, to see what the black was about; while a Portuguese oarsman shouted to him to give heed to what the Spaniard was saying.

Glancing down at his feet, Captain Delano saw the freed hand of the servant aiming with a second dagger—a small one, before concealed in his wool—with this he was snakishly writhing up from the boat's bottom, at the heart of his master, his countenance lividly vindictive, expressing the centred purpose of his soul; while the Spaniard, half-choked, was vainly shrinking away, with husky words, incoherent to all but the Portuguese.

That moment, across the long-benighted mind of Captain Delano, a flash of revelation swept, illuminating in unanticipated clearness his host's whole mysterious demeanor, with every enigmatic event of the day, as well as the entire past voyage of the San Dominick. He smote Babo's hand down, but his own heart smote him harder. With infinite pity he withdrew his hold from Don Benito. Not Captain Delano, but Don Benito, the black, in leaping into the boat, had intended to stab.

[53]Alarm bell.
[54]Compare with the description of the "symbolical devices" on the *San Dominick*'s "shield-like stern-piece."

Both the black's hands were held, as, glancing up towards the San Dominick, Captain Delano, now with the scales dropped from his eyes, saw the negroes, not in misrule, not in tumult, not as if frantically concerned for Don Benito, but with mask torn away, flourishing hatchets and knives, in ferocious piratical revolt. Like delirious black dervishes, the six Ashantees danced on the poop. Prevented by their foes from springing into the water, the Spanish boys were hurrying up to the topmost spars, while such of the few Spanish sailors, not already in the sea, less alert, were descried, helplessly mixed in, on deck, with the blacks.

Meantime Captain Delano hailed his own vessel, ordering the ports up and the guns run out. But by this time the cable of the San Dominick had been cut; and the fag-end, in lashing out, whipped away the canvas shroud about the beak, suddenly revealing, as the bleached hull swung round towards the open ocean, death for the figure-head, in a human skeleton; chalky comment on the chalked words below, *"Follow your leader."*

At the sight, Don Benito, covering his face, wailed out: "'Tis he, Aranda! my murdered, unburied friend!"

Upon reaching the sealer, calling for ropes, Captain Delano bound the negro, who made no resistance, and had him hoisted to the deck. He would then have assisted the now almost helpless Don Benito up the side; but Don Benito, wan as he was, refused to move, or be moved, until the negro should have been first put below out of view. When, presently assured that it was done, he no more shrank from the ascent.

The boat was immediately dispatched back to pick up the three swimming sailors. Meantime, the guns were in readiness, though, owing to the San Dominick having glided somewhat astern of the sealer, only the aftermost one could be brought to bear. With this, they fired six times; thinking to cripple the fugitive ship by bringing down her spars. But only a few inconsiderable ropes were shot away. Soon the ship was beyond the gun's range, steering broad out of the bay; the blacks thickly clustering round the bowsprit, one moment with taunting cries towards the whites, the next with upthrown gestures hailing the now dusky moors of ocean—cawing crows escaped from the hand of the fowler.

The first impulse was to slip the cables and give chase. But, upon second thoughts, to pursue with whale-boat and yawl seemed more promising.

Upon inquiring of Don Benito what fire arms they had on board the San Dominick, Captain Delano was answered that they had none that could be used; because, in the earlier stages of the mutiny, a cabin-passenger, since dead, had secretly put out of order the locks of what few muskets there were. But with all his remaining strength, Don Benito entreated the American not to give chase, either with ship or boat; for the negroes had already proved themselves such desperadoes, that, in case of a present assault, nothing but a total massacre of the whites could be looked for. But, regarding this warning as coming from one whose spirit had been crushed by misery, the American did not give up his design.

The boats were got ready and armed. Captain Delano ordered his men into them. He was going himself when Don Benito grasped his arm.

"What! have you saved my life, señor, and are you now going to throw away your own?"

The officers also, for reasons connected with their interests and those of the voyage, and a duty owing to the owners, strongly objected against their commander's going. Weighing their remonstrances a moment, Captain Delano felt bound to remain; appointing his chief mate—an athletic and resolute man, who had been a privateer's-man,[55] and, as his enemies whispered, a pirate—to head the party. The more to encourage the sailors, they were told, that the Spanish captain considered his ship as good as lost; that she and her cargo, including some gold and silver, were worth more than a thousand doubloons. Take her, and no small part should be theirs. The sailors replied with a shout.

The fugitives had now almost gained an offing. It was nearly night; but the moon was rising. After hard, prolonged pulling, the boats came up on the ship's quarters, at a suitable distance laying upon their oars to discharge their muskets. Having no bullets to return, the negroes sent their yells. But, upon the second volley, Indian-like, they hurtled their hatchets. One took off a sailor's fingers. Another struck the whale-boat's bow, cutting off the rope there, and remaining stuck in the gunwale like a woodman's axe. Snatching it, quivering from its lodgment, the mate hurled it back. The returned gauntlet now stuck in the ship's broken quarter-gallery, and so remained.

The negroes giving too hot a reception, the whites kept a more respectful distance. Hovering now just out of reach of the hurtling hatchets, they, with a view to the close encounter which must soon come, sought to decoy the blacks into entirely disarming themselves of their most murderous weapons in a hand-to-hand fight, by foolishly flinging them, as missiles, short of the mark, into the sea. But ere long perceiving the stratagem, the negroes desisted, though not before many of them had to replace their lost hatchets with handspikes; an exchange which, as counted upon, proved in the end favorable to the assailants.

Meantime, with a strong wind, the ship still clove the water; the boats alternately falling behind, and pulling up, to discharge fresh volleys.

The fire was mostly directed towards the stern, since there, chiefly, the negroes, at present, were clustering. But to kill or maim the negroes was not the object. To take them, with the ship, was the object. To do it, the ship must be boarded; which could not be done by boats while she was sailing so fast.

A thought now struck the mate. Observing the Spanish boys still aloft, high as they could get, he called to them to descend to the yards, and cut

---

[55]A privateer was a pirate commissioned by a government to prey on foreign shipping, like the British pirates who preyed on Spanish shipping in the sixteenth and seventeenth centuries. In *The Piazza Tales* version, Melville omitted the phrase "and, as his enemies whispered, a pirate," perhaps to eliminate the distinction between privateering and piracy. He added this detail to his source.

adrift the sails. It was done. About this time, owing to causes hereafter to be shown, two Spaniards, in the dress of sailors and conspicuously showing themselves, were killed; not by volleys, but by deliberate marksman's shots; while, as it afterwards appeared, by one of the general discharges, Atufal, the black, and the Spaniard at the helm likewise were killed. What now, with the loss of the sails, and loss of leaders, the ship became unmanageable to the negroes.

With creaking masts, she came heavily round to the wind; the prow slowly swinging, into view of the boats, its skeleton gleaming in the horizontal moonlight, and casting a gigantic ribbed shadow upon the water. One extended arm of the ghost seemed beckoning the whites to avenge it.

"Follow your leader!" cried the mate; and, one on each bow, the boats boarded. Sealing-spears and cutlasses crossed hatchets and hand-spikes. Huddled upon the long-boat amidships, the negresses raised a wailing chant, whose chorus was the clash of the steel.

For a time, the attack wavered; the negroes wedging themselves to beat it back; the half-repelled sailors, as yet unable to gain a footing, fighting as troopers in the saddle, one leg sideways flung over the bulwarks, and one without, plying their cutlasses like carters' whips. But in vain. They were almost overborne, when, rallying themselves into a squad as one man, with a huzza, they sprang inboard; where, entangled, they involuntarily separated again. For a few breaths' space, there was a vague, muffled, inner sound, as of submerged sword-fish rushing hither and thither through shoals of black-fish. Soon, in a reunited band, and joined by the Spanish seamen, the whites came to the surface, irresistibly driving the negroes toward the stern. But a barricade of casks and sacks, from side to side, had been thrown up by the mainmast. Here the negroes faced about, and though scorning peace or truce, yet fain would have had a respite. But, without pause, overleaping the barrier, the unflagging sailors again closed. Exhausted, the blacks now fought in despair. Their red tongues lolled, wolf-like, from their black mouths. But the pale sailors' teeth were set; not a word was spoken; and, in five minutes more, the ship was won.

Nearly a score of the negroes were killed. Exclusive of those by the balls, many were mangled; their wounds—mostly inflicted by the long-edged sealing-spears—resembling those shaven ones of the English at Preston Pans, made by the poled scythes of the Highlanders.[56] On the other side, none were killed, though several were wounded; some severely, including the mate. The surviving negroes were temporarily secured, and the ship, towed back into the harbor at midnight, once more lay anchored.

Omitting the incidents and arrangements ensuing, suffice it that, after two days spent in refitting, the two ships sailed in company for Conception,

[56]At the battle of Prestonpans in 1745, Scottish Highlanders under Charles Edward Stuart, armed mainly with scythes, axes, and swords, routed and butchered British forces.

in Chili, and thence for Lima, in Peru; where, before the vice-regal courts, the whole affair, from the beginning, underwent investigation.

Though, midway on the passage, the ill-fated Spaniard, relaxed from constraint, showed some signs of regaining health with free-will; yet, agreeably to his own foreboding, shortly before arriving at Lima, he relapsed, finally becoming so reduced as to be carried ashore in arms. Hearing of his story and plight, one of the many religious institutions of the City of Kings opened an hospitable refuge to him, where both physician and priest were his nurses, and a member of the order volunteered to be his one special guardian and consoler, by night and by day.

The following extracts, translated from one of the official Spanish documents, will it is hoped, shed light on the preceding narrative, as well as, in the first place, reveal the true port of departure and true history of the San Dominick's voyage, down to the time of her touching at the island of St. Maria.[57]

But, ere the extracts come, it may be well to preface them with a remark.

The document selected, from among many others, for partial translation, contains the deposition of Benito Cereno; the first taken in the case.

---

[57]Melville substantially rewrote the Deposition found in Delano's *Narrative*. One effect of his revisions is to emphasize the biased, self-serving point of view from which the "official" version of events is being presented by accentuating the ferocity of the slaves and whitewashing Don Benito, the author of the Deposition. At the same time, the many embellishments Melville introduces have the effect of highlighting the brilliance of Babo's plot and the subtlety of his mind. For example, Melville invents and credits to Babo the devices of the oakumpickers, the hatchet-polishers, and the chains worn by Atufal; the use of the Spanish flag as a bib and sanbenito; and the preparation of the skeleton substituted for the figurehead of Columbus.

As mentioned in note 2, Melville also changed the date of the events from 1805 to 1799. H. Bruce Franklin has pointed out that the revised date and name link the slave revolt on board the *San Dominick* with the most famous slave revolt in history, the Santo Domingo uprising of 1791–1804, led by Toussaint L'Ouverture, who began extending his rule over the entire island in 1799.

Also relevant to the story, as Sidney Kaplan has shown, are the revolts on board the Spanish slave-trading schooner *Amistad* in 1839 and the American domestic slavetrading brig *Creole* in 1841. The *Amistad* case in particular seems to have furnished Melville with additional details, as Jean

Fagan Yellin, Carolyn Karcher, and Eric J. Sundquist have shown. Led by a West African captive named Cinque or Singbe, the *Amistad*'s fifty-three recently kidnapped Africans mutinied near Cuba, killed the captain and two crew members, and demanded that their Spanish owner, a former sea captain, navigate them back to Africa, threatening him with death if he betrayed them. He adopted the ruse of shifting the vessel's course at night, sailing north instead of east. After a voyage of two months, during which supplies gave out, barnacles accumulated, the sails disintegrated, and two American ships tried to take the *Amistad* in tow, but were frightened off when the Africans tried to board, the *Amistad* finally landed on Long Island. The American brig of war *Washington*, whose officers hoped to claim the *Amistad*'s cargo as salvage, took the rebels into custody, and the Africans remained in jail for two years until the Supreme Court freed them in 1841. Charges of piracy were central to the trial. The press had repeatedly described the *Amistad* as a pirate ship when it was sighted off the East Coast, but the Africans' abolitionist defense team, headed by former President John Quincy Adams, succeeded in casting the onus of piracy on the ship's captain and owner by proving that the *Amistad* rebels had been illegally kidnapped from Africa in violation of international laws branding the slave trade as piracy.

Some disclosures therein were, at the time, held dubious for both learned and natural reasons. The tribunal inclined to the opinion that the deponent, not undisturbed in his mind by recent events, raved of some things which could never have happened. But subsequent depositions of the surviving sailors, bearing out the revelations of their captain in several of the strangest particulars, gave credence to the rest. So that the tribunal, in its final decision, rested its capital sentences upon statements which, had they lacked confirmation, it would have deemed it but duty to reject.

I, DON JOSE DE ABOS AND PADILLA, His Majesty's Notary for the Royal Revenue, and Register of this Province, and Notary Public of the Holy Crusade of this Bishopric, etc.

Do certify and declare, as much as is requisite in law, that, in the criminal cause commenced the twenty-fourth of the month of September, in the year seventeen hundred and ninety-nine, against the negroes of the ship San Dominick, the following declaration before me was made.

   Declaration of the first witness, DON BENITO CERENO.

The same day, and month, and year, His Honor, Doctor Juan Martinez de Rozas, Councilor of the Royal Audience of this Kingdom, and learned in the law of this Intendency, ordered the captain of the ship San Dominick, Don Benito Cereno, to appear; which he did in his litter, attended by the monk Infelez; of whom he received the oath, which he took by God, our Lord, and a sign of the Cross; under which he promised to tell the truth of whatever he should know and should be asked;—and being interrogated agreeably to the tenor of the act commencing the process, he said, that on the twentieth of May last, he set sail with his ship from the port of Valparaiso, bound to that of Callao; loaded with the produce of the country beside thirty cases of hardware and one hundred and sixty blacks, of both sexes, mostly belonging to Don Alexandro Aranda, gentleman, of the city of Mendoza; that the crew of the ship consisted of thirty-six men, beside the persons who went as passengers; that the negroes were in part as follows:

[Here, in the original, follows a list of some fifty names, descriptions, and ages, compiled from certain recovered documents of Aranda's, and also from recollections of the deponent, from which portions only are extracted.]

—One, from about eighteen to nineteen years, named José, and this was the man that waited upon his master, Don Alexandro, and who speaks well the Spanish, having served him four or five years; *** a mulatto, named Francesco, the cabin steward, of a good person and voice, having sung in the Valparaiso churches, native of the province of Buenos Ayres, aged about thirty-five years. *** A smart negro, named Dago, who had been for many years a grave-digger among the Spaniards, aged forty-six years. *** Four old negroes, born in Africa, from sixty to seventy, but sound, calkers by trade, whose names are as follows:—the first was named Mure, and he was killed (as was also his son named Diamelo); the second, Natu; the third, Yola, likewise killed; the fourth, Ghofan; and six full-grown negroes, aged from thirty to forty-five, all raw, and born among the Ashantees—Matiluqui, Yau, Lecbe, Mapenda, Yambaio, Akim; four of whom were killed; *** a powerful negro named Atufal, who, being supposed to have been a chief in Africa, his owners set great store by him. *** And a small negro of Senegal, but some years among the Spaniards, aged about thirty, which negro's name was Babo; *** that he does not remember the names of the others, but that still expecting the residue of Don Alexandro's papers will be found, will then take due account of them all, and remit to the court; *** and thirty-nine women and children of all ages.

[The catalogue over, the deposition goes on:]

*** That all the negroes slept upon deck, as is customary in this navigation, and none wore fetters, because the owner, his friend Aranda, told him that they were all tractable; *** that on the seventh day after leaving port, at three o'clock in the morning, all the Spaniards being asleep except the two officers on the watch, who were the boatswain, Juan Robles, and the carpenter, Juan Bautista Gayete, and the helmsman and his boy, the negroes revolted suddenly, wounded dangerously the boatswain and the carpenter, and successively killed eighteen men of those who were sleeping upon deck, some with hand-spikes and hatchets, and others by throwing them alive overboard, after tying them; that of the Spaniards upon deck, they left about seven, as he thinks, alive and tied, to manoeuvre the ship, and three or four more who hid themselves, remained also alive. Although in the act of revolt the negroes made themselves masters of the hatchway, six or seven wounded went through it to the cockpit, without any hindrance on their part; that during the act of revolt, the mate and another person, whose name he does not recollect, attempted to come up through the hatchway, but being quickly wounded, they were obliged to return to the cabin; that the deponent resolved at break of day to come up the companion-way, where the negro Babo was, being the ringleader, and Atufal, who assisted him, and having spoken to them, exhorted them to cease committing such atrocities, asking them, at the same time, what they wanted and intended to do, offering, himself, to obey their commands; that, notwithstanding this, they threw, in his presence, three men, alive and tied, overboard; that they told the deponent to come up, and that they would not kill him; which having done, the negro Babo asked him whether there were in those seas any negro countries where they might be carried, and he answered them, No; that the negro Babo afterwards told him to carry them to Senegal, or to the neighboring islands of St. Nicolas; and he answered, that this was impossible, on account of the great distance, the necessity involved of rounding Cape Horn, the bad condition of the vessel, the want of provisions, sails, and water; but that the negro Babo replied to him he must carry them in any way; that they would do and conform themselves to everything the deponent should require as to eating and drinking; that after a long conference, being absolutely compelled to please them, for they threatened him to kill all the whites if they were not, at all events, carried to Senegal, he told them that what was most wanting for the voyage was water; that they would go near the coast to take it, and thence they would proceed on their course; that the negro Babo agreed to it; and the deponent steered towards the intermediate ports, hoping to meet some Spanish or foreign vessel that would save them; that within ten or eleven days they saw the land, and continued their course by it in the vicinity of Nasca; that the deponent observed that the negroes were now restless and mutinous, because he did not effect the taking in of water, the negro Babo having required, with threats, that it should be done, without fail, the following day; he told him they saw plainly that the coast was steep, and the rivers designated in the maps were not to be found, with other reasons suitable to the circumstances; that the best way would be to go to the island of Santa Maria, where they might water and victual easily, it being a solitary island, as the foreigners did; that the deponent did not go to Pisco, that was near, nor make any other port of the coast, because the negro Babo had intimated to him several times, that he would kill all the whites the very moment he should perceive any city, town, or settlement of any kind on the shores to which they should be carried: that having determined to go to the island of Santa Maria, as the deponent had planned, for the purpose of trying whether, on the passage or near the island itself, they could find any vessel that should favor them, or whether he could escape from it in a boat to the neighboring coast of Arauco; to adopt the necessary means he immediately changed his course, steering for the island; that the negroes Babo and Atufal held daily conferences, in which they discussed what was necessary for their design of returning to Senegal, whether they were to kill all the Spaniards, and particularly the deponent; that eight days after parting from the coast of Nasca, the deponent being on the watch a little after day-break, and soon after the negroes had their meeting, the negro Babo came to the place where the deponent was, and told him that he had determined to kill his master, Don Alexandro Aranda, both because he and his companions could not otherwise be sure of their liberty, and that, to keep the seamen in subjection, he wanted to prepare a warning of what road they should be made to take did they or any of them oppose him; and that, by means of the death of Don Alexandro, that warning would best be given; but, that what this last meant, the deponent did not at the time comprehend, nor could not, further than that the death of Don Alexandro was intended; and moreover, the negro Babo proposed to the deponent to call the mate Raneds, who was sleeping in the cabin, before the thing was done, for fear, as the deponent understood it, that the mate, who was a good navigator, should be killed with Don Alexandro and the rest; that the deponent, who was the friend, from youth, of Don Alexandro, prayed and conjured, but all was useless; for the negro Babo answered him that the thing could not be prevented, and that all the Spaniards risked their death if they should attempt to frustrate his will in this matter, or any other; that, in this conflict, the deponent

called the mate, Raneds, who was forced to go apart, and immediately the
negro Babo commanded the Ashantee Matiluqui and the Ashantee Lecbe to
go and commit the murder; that those two went down with hatchets to the
berth of Don Alexandro; that, yet half alive and mangled, they dragged him
on deck; that they were going to throw him overboard in that state, but the
negro Babo stopped them bidding the murder be completed on the deck
before him, which was done, when, by his orders, the body was carried
below, forward; that nothing more was seen of it by the deponent for three
days; *** that Don Alonzo Sidonia, an old man, long resident at Valparaiso,
and lately appointed to a civil office in Peru, whither he had taken passage,
was at the time sleeping in the berth opposite Don Alexandro's; that, awakening at his cries, surprised by them, and at the sight of the negroes with
their bloody hatchets in their hands, he threw himself into the sea through
a window which was near him, and was drowned, without it being in the
power of the deponent to assist or take him up; *** that, a short time after
killing Aranda, they brought upon deck his german-cousin, of middle-age,
Don Francisco Masa, of Mendoza, and the young Don Joaquin, Marques de
Arambaolaza, then lately from Spain, with his Spanish servant Ponce, and
the three young clerks of Aranda, José Morairi, Lorenzo Bargas, and Hermenegildo Gandix, all of Cadiz; that Don Joaquin and Hermenegildo Gandix,
the negro Babo for purposes hereafter to appear, preserved alive; but Don
Francisco Masa, José Morairi, and Lorenzo Bargas, with Ponce the servant,
beside the boatswain, Juan Robles, the boatswain's mates, Manuel Viscaya
and Roderigo Hurta, and four of the sailors, the negro Babo ordered to be
thrown alive into the sea, although they made no resistance, nor begged for
anything else but mercy; that the boatswain, Juan Robles, who knew how to
swim, kept the longest above water, making acts of contrition, and, in the
last words he uttered, charged this deponent to cause mass to be said for
his soul to our Lady of Succor; *** that, during the three days which followed, the deponent, uncertain what fate had befallen the remains of Don
Alexandro, frequently asked the negro Babo where they were, and, if still on
board, whether they were to be preserved for interment ashore, entreating
him so to order it; that the negro Babo answered nothing till the fourth
day, when at sunrise, the deponent coming on deck, the negro Babo showed
him a skeleton, which had been substituted for the ship's proper figure-
head, the image of Christopher Colon, the discoverer of the New World; that
the negro Babo asked him whose skeleton that was, and whether, from its
whiteness, he should not think it a white's; that, upon his covering his face,
the negro Babo, coming close, said words to this effect: "Keep faith with the
blacks from here to Senegal, or you shall in spirit, as now in body, follow
your leader," pointing to the prow; *** that the same morning the negro
Babo took by succession each Spaniard forward, and asked him whose skeleton that was, and whether, from its whiteness, he should not think it a
white's; that each Spaniard covered his face; that then to each the negro
Babo repeated the words in the first place said to the deponent; *** that
they (the Spaniards), being then assembled aft, the negro Babo harangued

them, saying that he had now done all; that the deponent (as navigator for the negroes) might pursue his course, warning him and all of them that they should, soul and body, go the way of Don Alexandro if he saw them (the Spaniards) speak or plot anything against them (the negroes)—a threat which was repeated every day; that, before the events last mentioned, they had tied the cook to throw him overboard, for it is not known what thing they heard him speak, but finally the negro Babo spared his life, at the request of the deponent; that a few days after, the deponent, endeavoring not to omit any means to preserve the lives of the remaining whites, spoke to the negroes peace and tranquillity, and agreed to draw up a paper, signed by the deponent and the sailors who could write, as also by the negro Babo, for himself and all the blacks, in which the deponent obliged himself to carry them to Senegal, and they not to kill any more, and he formally to make over to them the ship, with the cargo, with which they were for that time satisfied and quieted. *** But the next day, the more surely to guard against the sailors' escape, the negro Babo commanded all the boats to be destroyed but the long-boat, which was unseaworthy, and another, a cutter in good condition, which, knowing it would yet be wanted for towing the water casks, he had it lowered down into the hold.

[*Various particulars of the prolonged and perplexed navigation ensuing here follow, with incidents of a calamitous calm, from which portion one passage is extracted, to wit:*]

—That on the fifth day of the calm, all on board suffering much from the heat, and want of water, and five having died in fits, and mad, the negroes became irritable, and for a chance gesture, which they deemed suspicious—though it was harmless—made by the mate, Raneds, to the deponent, in the act of handing a quadrant, they killed him; but that for this they afterwards were sorry, the mate being the only remaining navigator on board, except the deponent.

—That omitting other events, which daily happened, and which can only serve uselessly to recall past misfortunes and conflicts, after seventy-three days' navigation, reckoned from the time they sailed from Nasca, during which they navigated under a scanty allowance of water, and were afflicted with the calms before mentioned, they at last arrived at the island of Santa Maria, on the seventeenth of the month of August, at about six o'clock in the afternoon, at which hour they cast anchor very near the American ship, Bachelor's Delight, which lay in the same bay, commanded by the generous Captain Amasa Delano; but at six o'clock in the morning, they had already descried the port, and the negroes became uneasy, as soon as at distance they saw the ship, not having expected to see one there; that the negro Babo pacified them, assuring them that no fear need be had; that straightway he ordered the figure on the bow to be covered with canvas, as for repairs, and had the decks a little set in order; that for a time the negro Babo and the negro Atufal conferred; that the negro Atufal was for sailing away, but the negro Babo would not, and, by himself, cast about what to do; that at last he came to the deponent, proposing to him to say and do all that the deponent declares to have said and done to the American captain; ****** that the negro Babo warned him that if he varied in the least, or uttered any word, or gave any look that should give the least intimation of the past events or present state, he would instantly kill him, with all his companions, showing a dagger, which he carried hid, saying something which, as he understood it, meant that that dagger would be alert as his eye; that the negro Babo then announced the plan to all his companions, which pleased them; that he then, the better to disguise the truth, devised many expedients, in some of them uniting deceit and defense; that of this sort was the device of the six Ashantees before named, who were his bravoes;[58] that them he stationed on the break of the poop, as if to clean certain hatchets (in cases, which were part of the cargo), but in reality to use them, and distribute them at need, and at a given word he told them; that, among other devices, was the device of presenting Atufal, his right-hand man, as chained, though in a moment the chains could be dropped; that in every particular he informed the deponent what part he was expected to enact in every device, and what story he was to tell on every occasion, always threatening him with instant death if he varied in the least: that, conscious that many of the negroes would be turbulent, the negro Babo appointed the four aged negroes, who were calkers, to keep what domestic order they could on the decks; that again and again he harangued the Spaniards and his companions, informing them of his intent, and of his devices, and of the invented story that this deponent was to tell, charging them lest any of them varied from that story; that these arrangements were made and matured during the interval of two or three hours, between their first sighting the ship and the arrival on board of Captain Amasa Delano; that this happened about half-past seven o'clock in the morning, Captain Amasa Delano coming in his boat, and all gladly receiving him; that the deponent, as well as he could force himself, acting then the part of principal owner, and a free captain of the ship, told Captain Amasa Delano, when called upon, that he came from Buenos Ayres, bound to Lima, with three hundred negroes; that off Cape Horn, and in a subsequent fever, many negroes had died; that also, by similar casualties, all the sea officers and the greatest part of the crew had died.

[*And so the deposition goes on, circumstantially recounting the fictitious story dictated to the deponent by Babo, and through the deponent imposed upon Captain Delano; and also recounting the friendly offers of Captain Delano, with other things, but all of which is here omitted. After the fictitious, strange story, etc., the deposition proceeds:*]

—that the generous Captain Amasa Delano remained on board all the day, till he left the ship anchored at six o'clock in the evening, deponent speaking to him always of his pretended misfortunes, under the fore-mentioned principles, without having had it in his power to tell a single word, or give him the least

[58]Hired soldiers or assassins.

hint, that he might know the truth and state of things; because the negro Babo, performing the office of an officious servant with all the appearance of submission of the humble slave, did not leave the deponent one moment; that this was in order to observe the deponent's actions and words, for the negro Babo understands well the Spanish; and besides, there were thereabout some others who were constantly on the watch, and likewise understood the Spanish; *** that upon one occasion, while deponent was standing on the deck conversing with Amasa Delano, by a secret sign the negro Babo drew him (the deponent) aside, the act appearing as if originating with the deponent; that then, he being drawn aside, the negro Babo proposed to him to gain from Amasa Delano full particulars about his ship, and crew, and arms; that the deponent asked "For what?" that the negro Babo answered he might conceive; that, grieved at the prospect of what might overtake the generous Captain Amasa Delano, the deponent at first refused to ask the desired questions, and used every argument to induce the negro Babo to give up this new design; that the negro Babo showed the point of his dagger; that, after the information had been obtained, the negro Babo again drew him aside, telling him that that very night he (the deponent) would be captain of two ships, instead of one, for that, great part of the American's ship's crew being to be absent fishing, the six Ashantees, without any one else, would easily take it; that at this time he said other things to the same purpose; that no entreaties availed; that, before Amasa Delano's coming on board, no hint had been given touching the capture of the American ship: that to prevent this project the deponent was powerless; ***—that in some things his memory is confused, he cannot distinctly recall every event; ***—that as soon as they had cast anchor at six of the clock in the evening, as has before been stated, the American Captain took leave to return to his vessel; that upon a sudden impulse, which the deponent believes to have come from God and his angels, he, after the farewell had been said, followed the generous Captain Amasa Delano as far as the gunwale, where he stayed, under pretense of taking leave, until Amasa Delano should have been seated in his boat; that on shoving off, the deponent sprang from the gunwale into the boat, and fell into it, he knows not how, God guarding him; that—

[Here, in the original, follows the account of what further happened at the escape, and how the San Dominick was retaken, and of the passage to the coast; including in the recital many expressions of "eternal gratitude" to the "generous Captain Amasa Delano." The deposition then proceeds with recapitulatory remarks, and a partial renumeration of the negroes, making record of their individual part in the past events, with a view to furnishing, according to command of the court, the data whereon to found the criminal sentences to be pronounced. From this portion is the following:]

—That he believes that all the negroes, though not in the first place knowing to the design of revolt, when it was accomplished, approved it. *** That the negro, José, eighteen years old, and in the personal service of Don Alexandro, was the one who communicated the information to the negro

Babo, about the state of things in the cabin, before the revolt; that this is
known, because, in the preceding midnights, he used to come from his
berth, which was under his master's, in the cabin, to the deck where the
ringleader and his associates were, and had secret conversations with the
negro Babo, in which he was several times seen by the mate; that, one night,
the mate drove him away twice; ** that this same negro José, was the one
who, without being commanded to do so by the negro Babo, as Lecbe and
Matiluqui were, stabbed his master, Don Alexandro, after he had been
dragged half-lifeless to the deck; ** that the mulatto steward, Francesco, was
of the first band of revolters, that he was, in all things, the creature and tool
of the negro Babo; that, to make his court, he, just before a repast in the
cabin, proposed, to the negro Babo, poisoning a dish for the generous Captain Amasa Delano; this is known and believed, because the negroes have
said it; but that the negro Babo, having another design, forbade Francesco;
** that the Ashantee Lecbe was one of the worst of them; for that, on the
day the ship was retaken, he assisted in the defense of her, with a hatchet
in each hand, with one of which he wounded, in the breast, the chief mate
of Amasa Delano, in the first act of boarding; this all knew; that, in sight of
the deponent, Lecbe struck, with a hatchet, Don Francisco Masa when, by
the negro Babo's orders, he was carrying him to throw him overboard, alive;
beside participating in the murder, before mentioned, of Don Alexandro
Aranda, and others of the cabin-passengers; that, owing to the fury with
which the Ashantees fought in the engagement with the boats, but this
Lecbe and Yau survived; that Yau was bad as Lecbe; that Yau was the man
who, by Babo's command, willingly prepared the skeleton of Don Alexandro,
in a way the negroes afterwards told the deponent, but which he, so long as
reason is left him, can never divulge; that Yau and Lecbe were the two who,
in a calm by night, riveted the skeleton to the bow; this also the negroes
told him; that the negro Babo was he who traced the inscription below it;
that the negro Babo was the plotter from first to last; he ordered every murder, and was the helm and keel of the revolt; that Atufal was his lieutenant
in all; but Atufal, with his own hand, committed no murder; nor did the negro Babo; ** that Atufal was shot, being killed in the fight with the boats,
ere boarding; ** that the negresses, of age, were knowing to the revolt, and
testified themselves satisfied at the death of their master, Don Alexandro;
that, had the negroes not restrained them, they would have tortured to
death, instead of simply killing, the Spaniards slain by command of the negro Babo; that the negresses used their utmost influence to have the deponent made away with; that, in the various acts of murder, they sang songs
and danced—not gaily, but solemnly; and before the engagement with the
boats, as well as during the action, they sang melancholy songs to the
negroes, and that this melancholy tone was more inflaming than a different
one would have been, and was so intended; that all this is believed, because
the negroes have said it.—that of the thirty-six men of the crew exclusive of
the passengers, (all of whom are now dead), which the deponent had knowledge of, six only remained alive, with four cabin-boys and ship-boys, not

included with the crew; **—that the negroes broke an arm of one of the cabin-boys and gave him strokes with hatchets.

[Then follow various random disclosures referring to various periods of time. The following are extracted:]

—That during the presence of Captain Amasa Delano on board, some attempts were made by the sailors, and one by Hermenegildo Gandix, to convey hints to him of the true state of affairs; but that these attempts were ineffectual, owing to fear of incurring death, and furthermore owing to the devices which offered contradictions to the true state of affairs; as well as owing to the generosity and piety of Amasa Delano incapable of sounding such wickedness; *** that Luys Galgo, a sailor about sixty years of age, and formerly of the king's navy, was one of those who sought to convey tokens to Captain Amasa Delano; but his intent, though undiscovered, being suspected, he was, on a pretense, made to retire out of sight, and at last into the hold, and there was made away with. This the negroes have since said; *** that one of the ship-boys feeling, from Captain Amasa Delano's presence, some hopes of release, and not having enough prudence, dropped some chance-word respecting his expectations, which being overheard and understood by a slave-boy with whom he was eating at the time, the latter struck him on the head with a knife, inflicting a bad wound, but of which the boy is now healing; that likewise, not long before the ship was brought to anchor, one of the seamen, steering at the time, endangered himself by letting the blacks remark some expression in his countenance, arising from a cause similar to the above; but this sailor, by his heedful after conduct, escaped; *** that these statements are made to show the court that from the beginning to the end of the revolt, it was impossible for the deponent and his men to act otherwise than they did; ***—that the third clerk, Hermenegildo Gandix, who before had been forced to live among the seamen, wearing a seaman's habit, and in all respects appearing to be one for the time; he, Gandix, was killed by a musket-ball fired through a mistake from the American boats before boarding; having in his fright ran up the mizzen-rigging, calling to the boats—"don't board," lest upon their boarding the negroes should kill him; that this inducing the Americans to believe he some way favored the cause of the negroes, they fired two balls at him, so that he fell wounded from the rigging, and was drowned in the sea; ***—that the young Don Joaquin, Marques de Arambaolaza, like Hermenegildo Gandix, the third clerk, was degraded to the office and appearance of a common seaman; that upon one occasion when Don Joaquin shrank, the negro Babo commanded the Ashantee Lecbe to take tar and heat it, and pour it upon Don Joaquin's hands; ***—that Don Joaquin was killed owing to another mistake of the Americans, but one impossible to be avoided, as upon the approach of the boats, Don Joaquin, with a hatchet tied edge out and upright to his hand, was made by the negroes to appear on the bulwarks; whereupon, seen with arms in his hands and in a questionable attitude, he was shot for a renegade seaman; ***—that on the person of Don Joaquin was found secreted a jewel, which, by papers that were discovered, proved to have been meant for the shrine of our Lady of Mercy in Lima; a votive offering, beforehand prepared and guarded, to attest his gratitude, when he should have landed in Peru, his last destination, for the safe conclusion of his entire voyage from Spain; ***—that the jewel, with the other effects of the late Don Joaquin, is in the custody of the brethren of the Hospital de Sacerdotes, awaiting the disposition of the honorable court; ***—that, owing to the condition of the deponent, as well as the haste in which the boats departed for the attack, the Americans were not forewarned that there were, among the apparent crew, a passenger and one of the clerks disguised by the negro Babo; ***—that, beside the negroes killed in the action, some were killed after the capture and re-anchoring at night, when shackled to the ring-bolts on deck; that these deaths were committed by the sailors, ere they could be prevented. That so soon as informed of it, Captain Amasa Delano used all his authority, and, in particular with his own hand, struck down Martinez Gola, who, having found a razor in the pocket of an old jacket of his, which one of the shackled negroes had on, was aiming it at the negro's throat; that the noble Captain Amasa Delano also wrenched from the hand of Bartholomew Barlo, a dagger secreted at the time of the massacre of the whites, with which he was in the act of stabbing a shackled negro, who, the same day, with another negro, had thrown him down and jumped upon him; ***—that, for all the events, befalling through so long a time, during which the ship was in the hands of the negro Babo, he cannot here give account; but that, what he has said is the most substantial of what occurs to him at present, and is the truth under the oath which he has taken; which declaration he affirmed and ratified, after hearing it read to him.

He said that he is twenty-nine years of age, and broken in body and mind; that when finally dismissed by the court, he shall not return home to Chili; but betake himself to the monastery on Mount Agonia without; and signed with his honor, and crossed himself, and, for the time, departed as he came, in his litter, with the monk Infelez, to the Hospital de Sacerdotes.

BENITO CERENO.

DOCTOR ROZAS.

If the Deposition have served as the key to fit into the lock of the complications which precede it, then, as a vault whose door has been flung back, the San Dominick's hull lies open to-day.[59]

Hitherto the nature of this narrative, besides rendering the intricacies in the beginning unavoidable, has more or less required that many things, instead of being set down in the order of occurrence, should be retrospectively, or

---

[59]Note the parallel to the key worn by Don Benito, which fits the padlock holding Atufal in chains. We readers are now standing in Don Benito's and Delano's shoes, as Melville offers us a key and invites us to unlock the problem symbolizing slavery.

irregularly given; this last is the case with the following passages, which will conclude the account:

During the long, mild voyage to Lima, there was, as before hinted, a period during which the sufferer a little recovered his health, or, at least in some degree, his tranquillity. Ere the decided relapse which came, the two captains had many cordial conversations—their fraternal unreserve in singular contrast with former withdrawments.

Again and again, it was repeated, how hard it had been to enact the part forced on the Spaniard by Babo.

"Ah, my dear friend," Don Benito once said, "at those very times when you thought me so morose and ungrateful, nay, when, as you now admit, you half thought me plotting your murder, at those very times my heart was frozen; I could not look at you, thinking of what, both on board this ship and your own, hung, from other hands, over my kind benefactor. And as God lives, Don Amasa, I know not whether desire for my own safety alone could have nerved me to that leap into your boat, had it not been for the thought that, did you, unenlightened, return to your ship, you, my best friend, with all who might be with you, stolen upon, that night, in your hammocks, would never in this world have wakened again. Do but think how you walked this deck, how you sat in this cabin, every inch of ground mined into honey-combs under you. Had I dropped the least hint, made the least advance towards an understanding between us, death, explosive death—yours as mine—would have ended the scene."

"True, true," cried Captain Delano, starting, "you have saved my life, Don Benito, more than I yours; saved it, too, against my knowledge and will."

"Nay, my friend," rejoined the Spaniard, courteous even to the point of religion, "God charmed your life, but you saved mine. To think of some things you did—those smilings and chattings, rash pointings and gesturings. For less than these, they slew my mate, Raneds; but you had the Prince of Heaven's safe conduct through all ambuscades."

"Yes, all is owing to Providence, I know; but the temper of my mind that morning was more than commonly pleasant, while the sight of so much suffering, more apparent than real, added to my good nature, compassion, and charity, happily interweaving the three. Had it been otherwise, doubtless, as you hint, some of my interferences might have ended unhappily enough. Besides that, those feelings I spoke of enabled me to get the better of momentary distrust, at times when acuteness might have cost me my life, without saving another's. Only at the end did my suspicions get the better of me, and you know how wide of the mark they then proved."

"Wide, indeed," said Don Benito, sadly; "you were with me all day; stood with me, sat with me, talked with me, looked at me, ate with me, drank with me; and yet, your last act was to clutch for a monster, not only an innocent man, but the most pitiable of all men. To such degree may malign machinations and deceptions impose. So far may even the best man err, in judging the conduct of one with the recesses of whose condition he is not acquainted. But you were forced to it; and you were in time undeceived. Would that, in both respects, it was so ever, and with all men."

"You generalize, Don Benito; and mournfully enough. But the past is passed; why moralize upon it? Forget it. See, yon bright sun has forgotten it all, and the blue sea, and the blue sky; these have turned over new leaves."

"Because they have no memory," he dejectedly replied; "because they are not human."

"But these mild trades that now fan your cheek, do they not come with a human-like healing to you? Warm friends, steadfast friends are the trades."

"With their steadfastness they but waft me to my tomb, Señor," was the foreboding response.

"You are saved," cried Captain Delano, more and more astonished and pained; "you are saved; what has cast such a shadow upon you?"

"The negro."

There was silence, while the moody man sat, slowly and unconsciously gathering his mantle about him, as if it were a pall.

There was no more conversation that day.

But if the Spaniard's melancholy sometimes ended in muteness upon topics like the above, there were others upon which he never spoke at all; on which, indeed, all his old reserves were piled. Pass over the worst, and, only to elucidate, let an item or two of these be cited. The dress so precise and costly, worn by him on the day whose events have been narrated, had not willingly been put on. And that silver-mounted sword, apparent symbol of despotic command, was not, indeed, a sword, but the ghost of one. The scabbard, artificially stiffened, was empty.

As for the black—whose brain, not body, had schemed and led the revolt, with the plot—his slight frame, inadequate to that which it held, had at once yielded to the superior muscular strength of his captor, in the boat. Seeing all was over, he uttered no sound, and could not be forced to. His aspect seemed to say, since I cannot do deeds, I will not speak words. Put in irons in the hold, with the rest, he was carried to Lima. During the passage Don Benito did not visit him. Nor then, nor at any time after, would he look at him. Before the tribunal he refused. When pressed by the judges he fainted. On the testimony of the sailors alone rested the legal identity of Babo.

Some months after, dragged to the gibbet at the tail of a mule, the black met his voiceless end. The body was burned to ashes; but for many days, the head, that hive of subtlety, fixed on a pole in the Plaza, met, unabashed, the gaze of the whites; and across the Plaza looked towards St. Bartholomew's church, in whose vaults slept then, as now, the recovered bones of Aranda; and across the Rimac bridge looked towards the monastery, on Mount Agonia without; where, three months after being dismissed by the court, Benito Cereno, borne on the bier, did, indeed, follow his leader.

1855

Billy Budd, Sailor

(An inside narrative)[1]

Dedicated

to

JACK CHASE

Englishman

Wherever that great heart may now be

Here on Earth or harbored in Paradise

Captain of the Maintop

in the year 1843

in the U.S. Frigate

United States[2]

1

In the time before steamships, or then more frequently than now, a stroller along the docks of any considerable seaport would occasionally have his attention arrested by a group of bronzed mariners, man-of-war's men or merchant sailors in holiday attire, ashore on liberty. In certain instances they would flank, or like a bodyguard, quite surround, some superior figure of their own class, moving along with them like Aldebaran[3] among the lesser lights of his constellation. That signal object was the "Handsome Sailor" of the less prosaic time alike of the military and merchant navies. With no perceptible trace of the vainglorious about him, rather with the offhand unaffectedness of natural regality, he seemed to accept the spontaneous homage of his shipmates.

A somewhat remarkable instance recurs to me. In Liverpool, now half a century ago, I saw under the shadow of the great dingy street-wall of Prince's Dock (an obstruction long since removed) a common sailor so intensely black that he must needs have been a native African of the unadulterate blood of Ham—a symmetric figure much above the average height. The two ends of a gay silk handkerchief thrown loose about the neck danced upon the displayed ebony of his chest, in his ears were big hoops of gold, and a

---

[1]Melville probably began working on *Billy Budd* after his retirement from the New York Custom House in December 1885. He was still revising it when he died in 1891. The story was first published by Raymond Weaver in 1924. The present text follows the edition of Harrison Hayford and Merton M. Sealts, Jr., the most reliable transcription to date, and draws throughout on their indispensable notes. According to Hayford and Sealts, the story began as a prose headnote to a ballad about a sailor condemned to hanging for having fomented mutiny. In later stages of composition, Melville successively changed Billy from a mutineer into an innocent, introduced the character of Claggart, and developed Vere from a minor into a major character.

[2]In *White-Jacket*, echoed throughout *Billy Budd*, Melville describes his shipmate Jack Chase as a "stickler for the Rights of Man, and the liberties of the world," who deserts temporarily from the *Neversink* to "befriend, heart and soul, what he deemed the cause of the Right" in Peru's war against Bolivian domination (Chap. 5).

[3]The "eye" and brightest star in the constellation Taurus, the Bull.

Highland bonnet with a tartan band set off his shapely head. It was a hot noon in July; and his face, lustrous with perspiration, beamed with barbaric good humor. In jovial sallies right and left, his white teeth flashing into view, he rollicked along, the center of a company of his shipmates. These were made up of such an assortment of tribes and complexions as would have well fitted them to be marched up by Anacharsis Cloots[4] before the bar of the first French Assembly as Representatives of the Human Race. At each spontaneous tribute rendered by the wayfarers to this black pagod of a fellow—the tribute of a pause and stare, and less frequently an exclamation—the motley retinue showed that they took that sort of pride in the evoker of it which the Assyrian priests doubtless showed for their grand sculptured Bull when the faithful prostrated themselves.

To return. If in some cases a bit of a nautical Murat[5] in setting forth his person ashore, the Handsome Sailor of the period in question evinced nothing of the dandified Billy-be-Dam, an amusing character all but extinct now, but occasionally to be encountered, and in a form yet more amusing than the original, at the tiller of the boats on the tempestuous Erie Canal or, more likely, vaporing in the groggeries along the towpath.[6] Invariably a proficient in his perilous calling, he was also more or less of a mighty boxer or wrestler. It was strength and beauty. Tales of his prowess were recited. Ashore he was the champion; afloat the spokesman; on every suitable occasion always foremost. Close-reefing topsails in a gale, there he was, astride the weather yardarm-end, foot in the Flemish horse as stirrup, both hands tugging at the earing as at a bridle, in very much the attitude of young Alexander curbing the fiery Bucephalus.[7] A superb figure, tossed up as by the horns of Taurus against the thunderous sky, cheerily hallooing to the strenuous file along the spar.

The moral nature was seldom out of keeping with the physical make. Indeed, except as toned by the former, the comeliness and power, always attractive in masculine conjunction, hardly could have drawn the sort of honest homage the Handsome Sailor in some examples received from his less gifted associates.

Such a cynosure, at least in aspect, and something such too in nature, though with important variations made apparent as the story proceeds, was

[4]Described in Thomas Carlyle's *The French Revolution*, Part II, Book I, Chapter 10, the procession of the Human Species that the Prussian-born revolutionary Jean Baptiste du Val de Grâce, Baron de Cloots (1755–1794), led before the French Assembly in 1790 as "mute representatives of their tongue-tied, befettered, heavy-laden Nations" became one of Melville's favorite metaphors for the brotherhood of humankind's diverse races. He calls the crew of the *Pequod* in *Moby-Dick* an "Anacharsis Clootz deputation" and the passengers of the *Fidele* in *The Confidence-Man* an "Anacharsis Clootz

congress," and he echoes Carlyle's description of Cloots's procession in *Redburn* while hymning America as a multiracial nation (Chaps. 27, 2, and 33, respectively).
[5]Joachim Murat (1767?–1815), who owed his throne to Napoleon, was known as the "Dandy King" of Naples.
[6]A joke, since tempests do not occur on canals. Unlike the Handsome Sailor, the Billy-be-Dam is fit only to steer canal boats, or more likely, to boast in barrooms.
[7]Alexander the Great (356–323 B.C.) tamed the fiery warhorse Bucephalus, whose head resembled a bull's (hence his name).

welkin-eyed[8] Billy Budd—or Baby Budd, as more familiarly, under circumstances hereafter to be given, he at last came to be called—aged twenty-one, a foretopman of the British fleet toward the close of the last decade of the eighteenth century. It was not very long prior to the time of the narration that follows that he had entered the King's service, having been impressed on the Narrow Seas from a homeward-bound English merchantman into a seventy-four[9] outward bound, H.M.S. *Bellipotent;* which ship, as was not unusual in those hurried days, having been obliged to put to sea short of her proper complement of men. Plump upon Billy at first sight in the gangway the boarding officer, Lieutenant Ratcliffe, pounced, even before the merchantman's crew was formally mustered on the quarter-deck for his deliberate inspection. And him only he elected. For whether it was because the other men when ranged before him showed to ill advantage after Billy, or whether he had some scruples in view of the merchantman's being rather short-handed, however it might be, the officer contented himself with his first spontaneous choice. To the surprise of the ship's company, though much to the lieutenant's satisfaction, Billy made no demur. But, indeed, any demur would have been as idle as the protest of a goldfinch popped into a cage.

Noting this uncomplaining acquiescence, all but cheerful, one might say, the shipmaster turned a surprised glance of silent reproach at the sailor. The shipmaster[10] was one of those worthy mortals found in every vocation, even the humbler ones—the sort of person whom everybody agrees in calling "a respectable man." And—nor so strange to report as it may appear to be—though a ploughman of the troubled waters, lifelong contending with the intractable elements, there was nothing this honest soul at heart loved better than simple peace and quiet. For the rest, he was fifty or thereabouts, a little inclined to corpulence, a prepossessing face, unwhiskered, and of an agreeable color—a rather full face, humanely intelligent in expression. On a fair day with a fair wind and all going well, a certain musical chime in his voice seemed to be the veritable unobstructed outcome of the innermost man. He had much prudence, much conscientiousness, and there were occasions when these virtues were the cause of overmuch disquietude in him. On a passage, so long as his craft was in any proximity to land, no sleep for Captain Graveling. He took to heart those serious responsibilities not so heavily borne by some shipmasters.

Now while Billy Budd was down in the forecastle getting his kit together, the *Bellipotent's* lieutenant, burly and bluff, nowise disconcerted by

---

[8]Blue-eyed, like the welkin (sky).
[9]Seized from the crew of a merchant ship on the channels separating England from the Continent and Ireland and forced to serve on a seventy-four-gun warship. British impressment of American sailors had helped provoke the War of 1812. Melville discusses impressment in *White-Jacket,* where he explains that in navies the world over, the low pay and

brutal discipline, epitomized by the practice of flogging, deterred all but the most desperate men from enlisting voluntarily (Chap. 90). Melville at first called this seventy-four the *Indomitable,* which connotes bravery, but later changed the name to the *Bellipotent,* which suggests mere brute force (potency in war).
[10]Captain.

Captain Graveling's omitting to proffer the customary hospitalities on an occasion so unwelcome to him, an omission simply caused by preoccupation of thought, unceremoniously invited himself into the cabin, and also to a flask from the spirit locker, a receptacle which his experienced eye instantly discovered. In fact he was one of those sea dogs in whom all the hardship and peril of naval life in the great prolonged wars of his time never impaired the natural instinct for sensuous enjoyment. His duty he always faithfully did; but duty is sometimes a dry obligation, and he was for irrigating its aridity, whensoever possible, with a fertilizing decoction of strong waters. For the cabin's proprietor there was nothing left but to play the part of the enforced host with whatever grace and alacrity were practicable. As necessary adjuncts to the flask, he silently placed tumbler and water jug before the irrepressible guest. But excusing himself from partaking just then, he dismally watched the unembarrassed officer deliberately diluting his grog a little, then tossing it off in three swallows, pushing the empty tumbler away, yet not so far as to be beyond easy reach, at the same time settling himself in his seat and smacking his lips with high satisfaction, looking straight at the host.

These proceedings over, the master broke the silence; and there lurked a rueful reproach in the tone of his voice: "Lieutenant, you are going to take my best man from me, the jewel of 'em."

"Yes, I know," rejoined the other, immediately drawing back the tumbler preliminary to a replenishing. "Yes, I know. Sorry."

"Beg pardon, but you don't understand, Lieutenant. See here, now. Before I shipped that young fellow, my forecastle was a rat-pit of quarrels. It was black times, I tell you, aboard the *Rights* here. I was worried to that degree my pipe had no comfort for me. But Billy came; and it was like a Catholic priest striking peace in an Irish shindy.[11] Not that he preached to them or said or did anything in particular; but a virtue went out of him, sugaring the sour ones. They took to him like hornets to treacle; all but the buffer of the gang, the big shaggy chap with the fire-red whiskers. He indeed, out of envy, perhaps, of the newcomer, and thinking such a "sweet and pleasant fellow," as he mockingly designated him to the others, could hardly have the spirit of a gamecock, must needs bestir himself in trying to get up an ugly row with him. Billy forebore with him and reasoned with him in a pleasant way—he is something like myself, Lieutenant, to whom aught like a quarrel is hateful—but nothing served. So, in the second dogwatch one day, the Red Whiskers in presence of the others, under pretense of showing Billy just whence a sirloin steak was cut—for the fellow had once been a butcher—insultingly gave him a dig under the ribs. Quick as lightning Billy let fly his arm. I dare say he never meant to do quite as much as he did, but anyhow he gave the burly fool a terrible drubbing. It took about half a minute, I should think. And, lord bless you, the lubber was astonished at the celerity. And will you believe it, Lieutenant, the Red Whiskers now

[11]Brawl.

really loves Billy—loves him, or is the biggest hypocrite that ever I heard of. But they all love him. Some of 'em do his washing, darn his old trousers for him; the carpenter is at odd times making a pretty little chest of drawers for him. Anybody will do anything for Billy Budd; and it's the happy family here. But now, Lieutenant, if that young fellow goes—I know how it will be aboard the *Rights*. Not again very soon shall I, coming up from dinner, lean over the capstan smoking a quiet pipe—no, not very soon again, I think. Ay, Lieutenant, you are going to take away the jewel of 'em; you are going to take away my peacemaker!" And with that the good soul had really some ado in checking a rising sob.

"Well," said the lieutenant, who had listened with amused interest to all this and now was waxing merry with his tipple; "well, blessed are the peace-makers, especially the fighting peacemakers. And such are the seventy-four beauties some of which you see poking their noses out of the portholes of yonder warship lying to for me," pointing through the cabin window at the *Bellipotent*. "But courage! Don't look so downhearted, man. Why, I pledge you in advance the royal approbation. Rest assured that His Majesty will be delighted to know that in a time when his hardtack is not sought for by sailors with such avidity as should be, a time also when some shipmasters privily resent the borrowing from them a tar or two for the service; His Majesty, I say, will be delighted to learn that *one* shipmaster at least cheerfully surrenders to the King the flower of his flock, a sailor who with equal loyalty makes no dissent.—But where's my beauty? Ah," looking through the cabin's open door, "here he comes; and, by Jove, lugging along his chest—Apollo with his portmanteau!—My man," stepping out to him, "you can't take that big box aboard a warship. The boxes there are mostly shot boxes. Put your duds in a bag, lad. Boot and saddle for the cavalryman, bag and hammock for the man-of-war's man."

The transfer from chest to bag was made. And, after seeing his man into the cutter and then following him down, the lieutenant pushed off from the *Rights-of-Man*. That was the merchant ship's name, though by her master and crew abbreviated in sailor fashion into the *Rights*. The hardheaded Dundee owner was a staunch admirer of Thomas Paine, whose book in rejoinder to Burke's arraignment of the French Revolution had then been published for some time and had gone everywhere.[12] In christening his vessel after the title of Paine's volume the man of Dundee was something like his contemporary shipowner, Stephen Girard of Philadelphia, whose sympathies, alike with his native land and its liberal philosophers, he evinced by naming his ships after Voltaire, Diderot,[13] and so forth.

[12]Thomas Paine wrote *The Rights of Man* (1791–1792) as a rejoinder to Edmund Burke's *Reflections on the Revolution in France* (1790). As Hayford and Sealts point out, the opposing positions the two authors take on the issue of natural rights "lie behind the dialectic of *Billy Budd*."

[13]The French-born merchant, banker, and philanthropist Stephen Girard of Philadelphia (1750–1831) named his ships for various French *philosophes* whose ideas laid the groundwork for the Revolution, such as Voltaire (1694–1778) and Denis Diderot (1713–1784).

But now, when the boat swept under the merchantman's stern, and officer and oarsmen were noting—some bitterly and others with a grin—the name emblazoned there; just then it was that the new recruit jumped up from the bow where the coxswain[14] had directed him to sit, and waving hat to his silent shipmates sorrowfully looking over at him from the taffrail, bade the lads a genial good-bye. Then, making a salutation as to the ship herself, "And good-bye to you too, old *Rights-of-Man*."

"Down, sir!" roared the lieutenant, instantly assuming all the rigor of his rank, though with difficulty repressing a smile.

To be sure, Billy's action was a terrible breach of naval decorum. But in that decorum he had never been instructed; in consideration of which the lieutenant would hardly have been so energetic in reproof but for the concluding farewell to the ship. This he rather took as meant to convey a covert sally on the new recruit's part, a sly slur at impressment in general, and that of himself in especial. And yet, more likely, if satire it was in effect, it was hardly so by intention, for Billy, though happily endowed with the gaiety of high health, youth, and a free heart, was yet by no means of a satirical turn. The will to it and the sinister dexterity were alike wanting. To deal in double meanings and insinuations of any sort was quite foreign to his nature.

As to his enforced enlistment, that he seemed to take pretty much as he was wont to take any vicissitude of weather. Like the animals, though no philosopher, he was, without knowing it, practically a fatalist. And it may be that he rather liked this adventurous turn in his affairs, which promised an opening into novel scenes and martial excitements.

Aboard the *Bellipotent* our merchant sailor was forthwith rated as an able seaman and assigned to the starboard watch of the foretop.[15] He was soon at home in the service, not at all disliked for his unpretentious good looks and a sort of genial happy-go-lucky air. No merrier man in his mess: in marked contrast to certain other individuals included like himself among the impressed portion of the ship's company; for these when not actively employed were sometimes, and more particularly in the last dogwatch[16] when the drawing near of twilight induced revery, apt to fall into a saddish mood which in some partook of sullenness. But they were not so young as our foretopman, and no few of them must have known a hearth of some sort, others may have had wives and children left, too probably, in uncertain circumstances, and hardly any but must have had acknowledged kith and kin, while for Billy, as will shortly be seen, his entire family was practically invested in himself.

[14]Boat steersman.
[15]Melville himself served as a maintopman on the *United States*. Crews were traditionally divided into two "watches," on duty for alternate periods at opposite sides of the ship, starboard (right) and port (left).
[16]From 6 to 8 P.M.

2

Though our new-made foretopman was well received in the top and on the gun decks, hardly here was he that cynosure he had previously been among those minor ship's companies of the merchant marine, with which companies only had he hitherto consorted.

He was young; and despite his all but fully developed frame, in aspect looked even younger than he really was, owing to a lingering adolescent expression in the as yet smooth face all but feminine in purity of natural complexion but where, thanks to his seagoing, the lily was quite suppressed and the rose had some ado visibly to flush through the tan.

To one essentially such a novice in the complexities of factitious life, the abrupt transition from his former and simpler sphere to the ampler and more knowing world of a great warship; this might well have abashed him had there been any conceit or vanity in his composition. Among her miscellaneous multitude, the *Bellipotent* mustered several individuals who however inferior in grade were of no common natural stamp, sailors more signally susceptive of that air which continuous martial discipline and repeated presence in battle can in some degree impart even to the average man. As the Handsome Sailor, Billy Budd's position aboard the seventy-four was something analogous to that of a rustic beauty transplanted from the provinces and brought into competition with the highborn dames of the court. But this change of circumstances he scarce noted. As little did he observe that something about him provoked an ambiguous smile in one or two harder faces among the bluejackets. Nor less unaware was he of the peculiar favorable effect his person and demeanor had upon the more intelligent gentlemen of the quarter-deck. Nor could this well have been otherwise. Cast in a mold peculiar to the finest physical examples of those Englishmen in whom the Saxon strain would seem not at all to partake of any Norman or other admixture, he showed in face that humane look of reposeful good nature which the Greek sculptor in some instances gave to his heroic strong man, Hercules. But this again was subtly modified by another and pervasive quality. The ear, small and shapely, the arch of the foot, the curve in mouth and nostril, even the indurated hand dyed to the orange-tawny of the toucan's[17] bill, a hand telling alike of the halyards[18] and tar bucket; but, above all, something in the mobile expression, and every chance attitude and movement, something suggestive of a mother eminently favored by Love and the Graces; all this strangely indicated a lineage in direct contradiction to his lot. The mysteriousness here became less mysterious through a matter of fact elicited when Billy at the capstan was being formally mustered into the service. Asked by the officer, a small, brisk little gentleman as it chanced, among other questions, his place of birth, he replied, "Please, sir, I don't know."

"Don't know where you were born? Who was your father?"

---

[17]Tropical bird native to Brazil, with bright-colored plumage and a broad orange beak.

[18]Ropes for hoisting sails and spars.

"God knows, sir."

Struck by the straightforward simplicity of these replies, the officer next asked, "Do you know anything about your beginning?"

"No, sir. But I have heard that I was found in a pretty silk-lined basket hanging one morning from the knocker of a good man's door in Bristol."

"*Found*, say you? Well," throwing back his head and looking up and down the new recruit; "well, it turns out to have been a pretty good find. Hope they'll find some more like you, my man; the fleet sadly needs them."

Yes, Billy Budd was a foundling, a presumable by-blow,[19] and, evidently, no ignoble one. Noble descent was as evident in him as in a blood horse.

For the rest, with little or no sharpness of faculty or any trace of the wisdom of the serpent, nor yet quite a dove,[20] he possessed that kind and degree of intelligence going along with the unconventional rectitude of a sound human creature, one to whom not yet has been proffered the questionable apple of knowledge. He was illiterate; he could not read, but he could sing, and like the illiterate nightingale was sometimes the composer of his own song.

Of self-consciousness he seemed to have little or none, or about as much as we may reasonably impute to a dog of Saint Bernard's breed.

Habitually living with the elements and knowing little more of the land than as a beach, or, rather, that portion of the terraqueous globe providentially set apart for dance-houses, doxies, and tapsters,[21] in short what sailors call a "fiddler's green,"[22] his simple nature remained unsophisticated by those moral obliquities which are not in every case incompatible with that manufacturable thing known as respectability. But are sailors, frequenters of fiddlers' greens, without vices? No; but less often than with landsmen do their vices, so called, partake of crookedness of heart, seeming less to proceed from viciousness than exuberance of vitality after long constraint: frank manifestations in accordance with natural law. By his original constitution aided by the co-operating influences of his lot, Billy in many respects was little more than a sort of upright barbarian, much such perhaps as Adam presumably might have been ere the urbane Serpent wriggled himself into his company.

And here be it submitted that apparently going to corroborate the doctrine of man's Fall, a doctrine now popularly ignored, it is observable that where certain virtues pristine and unadulterate peculiarly characterize anybody in the external uniform of civilization, they will upon scrutiny seem not to be derived from custom or convention, but rather to be out of keeping with these, as if indeed exceptionally transmitted from a period prior to

[19]Bastard child.
[20]"Behold, I send you forth as sheep in the midst of wolves: be ye therefore wise as serpents, and harmless as doves," Christ instructs his disciples (Matthew 10:16).
[21]Whores and bartenders.

[22]Traditional sailor's paradise, with unlimited fiddling, dancing, and liquor.

Cain's city[23] and citified man. The character marked by such qualities has to an unvitiated taste an untampered-with flavor like that of berries, while the man thoroughly civilized, even in a fair specimen of the breed, has to the same moral palate a questionable smack as of a compounded wine. To any stray inheritor of these primitive qualities found, like Caspar Hauser,[24] wandering dazed in any Christian capital of our time, the good-natured poet's famous invocation, near two thousand years ago, of the good rustic out of his latitude in the Rome of the Caesars, still appropriately holds:

> Honest and poor, faithful in word and thought,
> What hath thee, Fabian, to the city brought?[25]

Though our Handsome Sailor had as much of masculine beauty as one can expect anywhere to see; nevertheless, like the beautiful woman in one of Hawthorne's minor tales,[26] there was just one thing amiss in him. No visible blemish indeed, as with the lady; no, but an occasional liability to a vocal defect. Though in the hour of elemental uproar or peril he was everything that a sailor should be, yet under sudden provocation of strong heart-feeling his voice, otherwise singularly musical, as if expressive of the harmony within, was apt to develop an organic hesitancy, in fact more or less of a stutter or even worse. In this particular Billy was a striking instance that the arch interferer, the envious marplot of Eden, still has more or less to do with every human consignment to this planet of Earth. In every case, one way or another he is sure to slip in his little card, as much as to remind us—I too have a hand here.

The avowal of such an imperfection in the Handsome Sailor should be evidence not alone that he is not presented as a conventional hero, but also that the story in which he is the main figure is no romance.

3

At the time of Billy Budd's arbitrary enlistment into the *Bellipotent* that ship was on her way to join the Mediterranean fleet. No long time elapsed before the junction was effected. As one of that fleet the seventy-four participated in its movements, though at times on account of her superior sailing qualities, in the absence of frigates, dispatched on separate duty as a scout and at times on less temporary service. But with all this the story has little concernment, restricted as it is to the inner life of one particular ship and the career of an individual sailor.

[23]In Genesis 4:8–17, after Cain kills his brother Abel, God tells him that henceforth the earth he tills will no longer yield fruit. "And Cain went out from the presence of the LORD ... and he builded a city."

[24]A mysterious foundling (1812?–1833) who turned up in Nuremberg in 1828, bewildered and incoherent, after having allegedly been confined in a dark space all his life. He was thought to be of noble blood and to exemplify the innocence of human beings in a state of nature.

[25]Martial, *Epigrams* I.iv.1–2.

[26]"The Birth-Mark," included earlier in this volume, whose heroine dies when her scientist husband tries to remove the blemish from her cheek symbolizing "the fatal flaw of humanity which Nature, in one shape or another, stamps ineffaceably on all her productions...."

It was the summer of 1797. In the April of that year had occurred the commotion at Spithead followed in May by a second and yet more serious outbreak in the fleet at the Nore.[27] The latter is known, and without exaggeration in the epithet, as "the Great Mutiny." It was indeed a demonstration more menacing to England than the contemporary manifestoes and conquering and proselyting armies of the French Directory.[28] To the British Empire the Nore Mutiny was what a strike in the fire brigade would be to London threatened by general arson. In a crisis when the kingdom might well have anticipated the famous signal that some years later published along the naval line of battle what it was that upon occasion England expected of Englishmen;[29] *that* was the time when at the mastheads of the three-deckers and seventy-fours moored in her own roadstead—a fleet the right arm of a Power then all but the sole free conservative one of the Old World—the bluejackets, to be numbered by thousands, ran up with huzzas the British colors with the union and cross wiped out; by that cancellation transmuting the flag of founded law and freedom defined, into the enemy's red meteor of unbridled and unbounded revolt. Reasonable discontent growing out of practical grievances in the fleet had been ignited into irrational combustion as by live cinders blown across the Channel from France in flames.

The event converted into irony for a time those spirited strains of Dibdin[30]—as a song-writer no mean auxiliary to the English government at that European conjuncture—strains celebrating, among other things, the patriotic devotion of the British tar: "And as for my life, 'tis the King's!"

Such an episode in the Island's grand naval story her naval historians naturally abridge, one of them (William James)[31] candidly acknowledging that fain would he pass it over did not "impartiality forbid fastidiousness." And yet his mention is less a narration than a reference, having to do hardly at all with details. Nor are these readily to be found in the libraries. Like some other events in every age befalling states everywhere, including America, the Great Mutiny was of such character that national pride along with views of policy would fain shade it off into the historical background. Such

[27]According to Hayford and Sealts, Melville noted the exact dates of the Spithead and Nore uprisings (April 15 and May 20, 1797, respectively) on two library call-slips attached to Leaf 364 of the *Billy Budd* manuscript. Spithead is a roadstead (protected anchorage) in the English Channel, between Portsmouth and the Isle of Wight, and the Nore is a sandbank at the mouth of the Thames.

[28]Five-member executive body that governed France from 1795 to 1799, after the Revolution.

[29]Nelson's famous signal to his fleet at the Battle of Trafalgar (1805): "England expects every man to do his duty!"

[30]Charles Dibdin (1745–1814), English dramatist and songwriter. In *White-Jacket* Melville wrote that Dibdin's songs—"which would lead one to think that man-of-war's-men are the most carefree, contented, virtuous, and patriotic of mankind—were composed at a time when the English Navy was principally manned by felons and paupers.... Still more, these songs are pervaded by ... a reckless acquiescence in fate, and an implicit, unquestioning, dog-like devotion to whoever may be lord and master. Dibdin was a man of genius; but no wonder Dibdin was a government pensioner at £200 per annum" (Chap. 90).

[31]British historian, whose *Naval History of Great Britain* (6 vols., 1860) Melville is quoting somewhat inaccurately.

events cannot be ignored, but there is a considerate way of historically treating them. If a well-constituted individual refrains from blazoning aught amiss or calamitous in his family, a nation in the like circumstance may without reproach be equally discreet.

Though after parleyings between government and the ringleaders, and concessions by the former as to some glaring abuses, the first uprising—that at Spithead—with difficulty was put down, or matters for the time pacified; yet at the Nore the unforeseen renewal of insurrection on a yet larger scale, and emphasized in the conferences that ensued by demands deemed by the authorities not only inadmissible but aggressively insolent, indicated—if the Red Flag did not sufficiently do so—what was the spirit animating the men. Final suppression, however, there was; but only made possible perhaps by the unswerving loyalty of the marine corps[32] and a voluntary resumption of loyalty among influential sections of the crews.

To some extent the Nore Mutiny may be regarded as analogous to the distempering irruption of contagious fever in a frame constitutionally sound, and which anon throws it off.

At all events, of these thousands of mutineers were some of the tars who not so very long afterwards—whether wholly prompted thereto by patriotism, or pugnacious instinct, or by both—helped to win a coronet for Nelson at the Nile, and the naval crown of crowns for him at Trafalgar. To the mutineers, those battles and especially Trafalgar were a plenary absolution and a grand one. For all that goes to make up scenic naval display and heroic magnificence in arms, those battles, especially Trafalgar, stand unmatched in human annals.[33]

4

In this matter of writing, resolve as one may to keep to the main road, some bypaths have an enticement not readily to be withstood. I am going to err into such a bypath. If the reader will keep me company I shall be glad. At the least, we can promise ourselves that pleasure which is wickedly said to be in sinning, for a literary sin the divergence will be.

Very likely it is no new remark that the inventions of our time have at last brought about a change in sea warfare in degree corresponding to the revolution in all warfare effected by the original introduction from China into Europe of gunpowder. The first European firearm, a clumsy contrivance, was, as is well known, scouted by no few of the knights as a base implement, good enough peradventure for weavers too craven to stand up crossing steel with steel in frank fight. But as ashore knightly valor, though shorn of its blazonry, did not cease with the knights, neither on the seas—

[32]Melville discusses the "antagonism between the marine and the sailor" in *White-Jacket* and notes that officers habitually play the two groups against each other (Chap. 89).

[33]Nelson won a baron's coronet for defeating the French fleet at the Battle of the Nile

(1798). The "naval crown of crowns" was his hero's death at the Battle of Trafalgar (1805), which gave Britain undisputed mastery of the seas.

though nowadays in encounters there a certain kind of displayed gallantry be fallen out of date as hardly applicable under changed circumstances—did the nobler qualities of such naval magnates as Don John of Austria, Doria, Van Tromp, Jean Bart, the long line of British admirals, and the American Decaturs of 1812 become obsolete with their wooden walls.[34]

Nevertheless, to anybody who can hold the Present at its worth without being inappreciative of the Past, it may be forgiven, if to such an one the solitary old hulk at Portsmouth, Nelson's *Victory*, seems to float there, not alone as the decaying monument of a fame incorruptible, but also as a poetic reproach, softened by its picturesqueness, to the *Monitors*[35] and yet mightier hulls of the European ironclads. And this not altogether because such craft are unsightly, unavoidably lacking the symmetry and grand lines of the old battleships, but equally for other reasons.

There are some, perhaps, who while not altogether inaccessible to that poetic reproach just alluded to, may yet on behalf of the new order be disposed to parry it; and this to the extent of iconoclasm, if need be. For example, prompted by the sight of the star inserted in the *Victory*'s quarter-deck designating the spot where the Great Sailor fell, these martial utilitarians may suggest considerations implying that Nelson's ornate publication of his person in battle was not only unnecessary, but not military, nay, savored of foolhardiness and vanity. They may add, too, that at Trafalgar it was in effect nothing less than a challenge to death; and death came; and that but for his bravado the victorious admiral might possibly have survived the battle, and so, instead of having his sagacious dying injunctions overruled by his immediate successor in command, he himself when the contest was decided might have brought his shattered fleet to anchor, a proceeding which might have averted the deplorable loss of life by shipwreck in the elemental tempest that followed the martial one.

Well, should we set aside the more than disputable point whether for various reasons it was possible to anchor the fleet, then plausibly enough the Benthamites[36] of war may urge the above. But the *might-have-been* is but boggy ground to build on. And, certainly, in foresight as to the larger issue of an encounter, and anxious preparations for it—buoying the deadly way and mapping it out, as at Copenhagen[37]—few commanders have been so painstakingly circumspect as this same reckless declarer of his person in fight.

[34]Don John of Austria (1547–1578) commanded the fleet of the Holy League that defeated the Turks at Lepanto in 1571; Andrea Doria (1468?–1560) freed Genoa from the Turks; Maarten Tromp (1597–1653) commanded Dutch fleets against Spain, Portugal, and Britain; Jean Bart (1651?–1702), a French privateer, fought against the Dutch; Stephen Decatur (1779–1820) led American naval forces against the Tripoli pirates in 1803–1804 and against the British in 1812.

[35]See Melville's poem "A Utilitarian View of the Monitor's Fight," reprinted in the present anthology.

[36]Disciples of Jeremy Bentham (1748–1832), English philosopher who originated the concept of utilitarianism, or usefulness, as a guide to action.

[37]Prior to the Battle of Copenhagen (1801), the Danes had removed the buoys marking the intricate channel leading to the port, but Nelson took soundings and replaced the buoys, thus literally preparing the way to victory.

Personal prudence, even when dictated by quite other than selfish considerations, surely is no special virtue in a military man; while an excessive love of glory, impassioning a less burning impulse, the honest sense of duty, is the first. If the name *Wellington* is not so much of a trumpet to the blood as the simpler name *Nelson*, the reason for this may perhaps be inferred from the above. Alfred in his funeral ode on the victor of Waterloo ventures not to call him the greatest soldier of all time, though in the same ode he invokes Nelson as "the greatest sailor since our world began."[38]

At Trafalgar Nelson on the brink of opening the fight sat down and wrote his last brief will and testament. If under the presentiment of the most magnificent of all victories to be crowned by his own glorious death, a sort of priestly motive led him to dress his person in the jewelled vouchers of his own shining deeds; if thus to have adorned himself for the altar and the sacrifice were indeed vainglory, then affectation and fustian is each more heroic line in the great epics and dramas, since in such lines the poet but embodies in verse those exaltations of sentiment that a nature like Nelson, the opportunity being given, vitalizes into acts.

5

Yes, the outbreak at the Nore was put down. But not every grievance was redressed. If the contractors, for example, were no longer permitted to ply some practices peculiar to their tribe everywhere, such as providing shoddy cloth, rations not sound, or false in the measure; not the less impressment, for one thing, went on. By custom sanctioned for centuries, and judicially maintained by a Lord Chancellor as late as Mansfield,[39] that mode of manning the fleet, a mode now fallen into a sort of abeyance but never formally renounced, it was not practicable to give up in those years. Its abrogation would have crippled the indispensable fleet, one wholly under canvas, no steam power, its innumerable sails and thousands of cannon, everything in short, worked by muscle alone; a fleet the more insatiate in demand for men, because then multiplying its ships of all grades against contingencies present and to come of the convulsed Continent.

Discontent foreran the Two Mutinies, and more or less it lurkingly survived them. Hence it was not unreasonable to apprehend some return of trouble sporadic or general. One instance of such apprehensions: In the same year with this story, Nelson, then Rear Admiral Sir Horatio, being with the fleet off the Spanish coast, was directed by the admiral in command to shift his pennant from the *Captain* to the *Theseus;* and for this reason: that the latter ship having newly arrived on the station from home, where it had taken part in the Great Mutiny, danger was apprehended from the temper of the men; and it was thought that an officer like Nelson was the one, not

---

[38]Alfred, Lord Tennyson (1809–1892), in his *Ode on the Death of the Duke of Wellington*, from which Melville is quoting, pays tribute to the general who defeated Napoleon at Waterloo in 1815, but praises Nelson even more warmly.

[39]William Murray, Earl of Mansfield (1705–1793), became Lord Chief Justice of Britain in 1756.

indeed to terrorize the crew into base subjection, but to win them, by force of his mere presence and heroic personality, back to an allegiance if not as enthusiastic as his own yet as true.

So it was that for a time, on more than one quarter-deck, anxiety did exist. At sea, precautionary vigilance was strained against relapse. At short notice an engagement might come on. When it did, the lieutenants assigned to batteries felt it incumbent on them, in some instances, to stand with drawn swords behind the men working the guns.

6

But on board the seventy-four in which Billy now swung his hammock, very little in the manner of the men and nothing obvious in the demeanor of the officers would have suggested to an ordinary observer that the Great Mutiny was a recent event. In their general bearing and conduct the commissioned officers of a warship naturally take their tone from the commander, that is if he have that ascendancy of character that ought to be his.

Captain the Honorable Edward Fairfax Vere, to give his full title, was a bachelor of forty or thereabouts, a sailor of distinction even in a time prolific of renowned seamen. Though allied to the higher nobility, his advancement had not been altogether owing to influences connected with that circumstance. He had seen much service, been in various engagements, always acquitting himself as an officer mindful of the welfare of his men, but never tolerating an infraction of discipline; thoroughly versed in the science of his profession, and intrepid to the verge of temerity, though never injudiciously so. For his gallantry in the West Indian waters as flag lieutenant under Rodney in that admiral's crowning victory over De Grasse,[40] he was made a post captain.

Ashore, in the garb of a civilian, scarce anyone would have taken him for a sailor, more especially that he never garnished unprofessional talk with nautical terms, and grave in his bearing, evinced little appreciation of mere humor. It was not out of keeping with these traits that on a passage when nothing demanded his paramount action, he was the most undemonstrative of men. Any landsman observing this gentleman not conspicuous by his stature and wearing no pronounced insignia, emerging from his cabin to the open deck, and noting the silent deference of the officers retiring to leeward, might have taken him for the King's guest, a civilian aboard the King's ship, some highly honorable discreet envoy on his way to an important post. But in fact this unobtrusiveness of demeanor may have proceeded from a certain unaffected modesty of manhood sometimes accompanying a resolute

[40]The British admiral George Brydges, Baron Rodney (1719–1792), defeated the French admiral François de Grasse (1723–1788) off the West Indian island of Dominica in 1782. As Stanton Garner points out, De Grasse had just helped the Americans to defeat the British by keeping the English fleet in the Chesapeake from aiding Cornwallis at Yorktown in 1781. Charles Anderson suggests that Melville may be basing his account of Vere's career on that of Sir William George Fairfax, a hero of the Rodney–de Grasse engagement.

nature, a modesty evinced at all times not calling for pronounced action, which shown in any rank of life suggests a virtue aristocratic in kind. As with some others engaged in various departments of the world's more heroic activities, Captain Vere though practical enough upon occasion would at times betray a certain dreaminess of mood. Standing alone on the weather side of the quarter-deck, one hand holding by the rigging, he would absently gaze off at the blank sea. At the presentation to him then of some minor matter interrupting the current of his thoughts, he would show more or less irascibility; but instantly he would control it.

In the navy he was popularly known by the appellation "Starry Vere." How such a designation happened to fall upon one who whatever his sterling qualities was without any brilliant ones, was in this wise: A favorite kinsman, Lord Denton, a freehearted fellow, had been the first to meet and congratulate him upon his return to England from his West Indian cruise; and but the day previous turning over a copy of Andrew Marvell's poems had lighted, not for the first time, however, upon the lines entitled "Appleton House," the name of one of the seats of their common ancestor, a hero in the German wars of the seventeenth century, in which poem occur the lines:

> This 'tis to have been from the first
> In a domestic heaven nursed,
> Under the discipline severe
> Of Fairfax and the starry Vere.[41]

And so, upon embracing his cousin fresh from Rodney's great victory wherein he had played so gallant a part, brimming over with just family pride in the sailor of their house, he exuberantly exclaimed, "Give ye joy, Ed; give ye joy, my starry Vere!" This got currency, and the novel prefix serving in familiar parlance readily to distinguish the *Bellipotent*'s captain from another Vere his senior, a distant relative, an officer of like rank in the navy, it remained permanently attached to the surname.

7

In view of the part that the commander of the *Bellipotent* plays in scenes shortly to follow, it may be well to fill out that sketch of him outlined in the previous chapter.

Aside from his qualities as a sea officer Captain Vere was an exceptional character. Unlike no few of England's renowned sailors, long and arduous service with signal devotion to it had not resulted in absorbing and *salting* the entire man. He had a marked leaning toward everything intellectual. He loved books, never going to sea without a newly replenished library, compact but of the best. The isolated leisure, in some cases so wearisome, falling at intervals to commanders even during a war cruise, never

[41]English poet (1621–1678) whose "Upon Appleton House, to my Lord Fairfax" also refers to the Fairfax estate of Denton, from which Melville draws his "Lord Denton."

was tedious to Captain Vere. With nothing of that literary taste which less heeds the thing conveyed than the vehicle, his bias was toward those books to which every serious mind of superior order occupying any active post of authority in the world naturally inclines: books treating of actual men and events no matter of what era—history, biography, and unconventional writers like Montaigne, who, free from cant and convention, honestly and in the spirit of common sense philosophize upon realities. In this line of reading he found confirmation of his own more reserved thoughts—confirmation which he had vainly sought in social converse, so that as touching most fundamental topics, there had got to be established in him some positive convictions which he forefelt would abide in him essentially unmodified so long as his intelligent part remained unimpaired. In view of the troubled period in which his lot was cast, this was well for him. His settled convictions were as a dike against those invading waters of novel opinion social, political, and otherwise, which carried away as in a torrent no few minds in those days, minds by nature not inferior to his own. While other members of that aristocracy to which by birth he belonged were incensed at the innovators mainly because their theories were inimical to the privileged classes, Captain Vere disinterestedly opposed them not alone because they seemed to him insusceptible of embodiment in lasting institutions, but at war with the peace of the world and the true welfare of mankind.

With minds less stored than his and less earnest, some officers of his rank, with whom at times he would necessarily consort, found him lacking in the companionable quality, a dry and bookish gentleman, as they deemed. Upon any chance withdrawal from their company one would be apt to say to another something like this: "Vere is a noble fellow, Starry Vere. 'Spite the gazettes,[42] Sir Horatio" (meaning him who became Lord Nelson) "is at bottom scarce a better seaman or fighter. But between you and me now, don't you think there is a queer streak of the pedantic running through him? Yes, like the King's yarn in a coil of navy rope?"

Some apparent ground there was for this sort of confidential criticism; since not only did the captain's discourse never fall into the jocosely familiar, but in illustrating of any point touching the stirring personages and events of the time he would be as apt to cite some historic character or incident of antiquity as he would be to cite from the moderns. He seemed unmindful of the circumstance that to his bluff company such remote allusions, however pertinent they might really be, were altogether alien to men whose reading was mainly confined to the journals. But considerateness in such matters is not easy to natures constituted like Captain Vere's. Their honesty prescribes to them directness, sometimes far-reaching like that of a migratory fowl that in its flight never heeds when it crosses a frontier.

---

[42]Whatever the newspapers say.

8

The lieutenants and other commissioned gentlemen forming Captain Vere's staff it is not necessary here to particularize, nor needs it to make any mention of any of the warrant officers. But among the petty officers was one who, having much to do with the story, may as well be forthwith introduced. His portrait I essay, but shall never hit it. This was John Claggart, the master-at-arms.[43] But that sea title may to landsmen seem somewhat equivocal. Originally, doubtless, that petty officer's function was the instruction of the men in the use of arms, sword or cutlass. But very long ago, owing to the advance in gunnery making hand-to-hand encounters less frequent and giving to niter and sulphur the pre-eminence over steel, that function ceased; the master-at-arms of a great warship becoming a sort of chief of police charged among other matters with the duty of preserving order on the populous lower gun decks.

Claggart was a man about five-and-thirty, somewhat spare and tall, yet of no ill figure upon the whole. His hand was too small and shapely to have been accustomed to hard toil. The face was a notable one, the features all except the chin cleanly cut as those on a Greek medallion; yet the chin, beardless as Tecumseh's,[44] had something of strange protuberant broadness in its make that recalled the prints of the Reverend Dr. Titus Oates, the historic deponent with the clerical drawl in the time of Charles II and the fraud of the alleged Popish Plot.[45] It served Claggart in his office that his eye could cast a tutoring glance. His brow was of the sort phrenologically associated with more than average intellect; silken jet curls partly clustering over it, making a foil to the pallor below, a pallor tinged with a faint shade of amber akin to the hue of time-tinted marbles of old. This complexion, singularly contrasting with the red or deeply bronzed visages of the sailors, and in part the result of his official seclusion from the sunlight, though it was not exactly displeasing, nevertheless seemed to hint of something defective or abnormal in the constitution and blood. But his general aspect and manner were so suggestive of an education and career incongruous with his naval function that when not actively engaged in it he looked like a man of high quality, social and moral, who for reasons of his own was keeping incog. Nothing was known of his former life. It might be that he was an Englishman; and yet there lurked a bit of accent in his speech suggesting that possibly he was not such by birth, but through naturalization in early childhood. Among certain grizzled sea gossips of the gun decks and forecastle went a rumor perdue that the master-at-arms was a *chevalier*[46] who had

---

[43]In *White-Jacket* Melville described the master-at-arms as an officer "whom all sailors hate ... a universal informer and hunter-up of delinquents" (Chap. 6). The *Neversink's* master-at-arms Bland is an early version of Claggart.

[44]Shawnee chief (1768?–1813) who tried to unite Indian tribes from Florida to the head of the Missouri against whites and sided with the British in the War of 1812.

[45]In 1678 Titus Oates (1649–1705) fabricated evidence of an alleged Catholic plot to massacre English Protestants, burn London, and assassinate King Charles II. His unfounded accusations sent many people to their deaths before Oates's perjury was exposed in 1685.

[46]Swindler, sharper.

volunteered into the King's navy by way of compounding for some mysterious swindle whereof he had been arraigned at the King's Bench.[47] The fact that nobody could substantiate this report was, of course, nothing against its secret currency. Such a rumor once started on the gun decks in reference to almost anyone below the rank of a commissioned officer would, during the period assigned to this narrative, have seemed not altogether wanting in credibility to the tarry old wiseacres of a man-of-war crew. And indeed a man of Claggart's accomplishments, without prior nautical experience entering the navy at mature life, as he did, and necessarily allotted at the start to the lowest grade in it; a man too who never made allusion to his previous life ashore; these were circumstances which in the dearth of exact knowledge as to his true antecedents opened to the invidious a vague field for unfavorable surmise.

But the sailors' dogwatch gossip concerning him derived a vague plausibility from the fact that now for some period the British navy could so little afford to be squeamish in the matter of keeping up the muster rolls, that not only were press gangs[48] notoriously abroad both afloat and ashore, but there was little or no secret about another matter, namely, that the London police were at liberty to capture any able-bodied suspect, any questionable fellow at large, and summarily ship him to the dockyard or fleet. Furthermore, even among voluntary enlistments there were instances where the motive thereto partook neither of patriotic impulse nor yet of a random desire to experience a bit of sea life and martial adventure. Insolvent debtors of minor grade, together with the promiscuous lame ducks of morality, found in the navy a convenient and secure refuge, secure because, once enlisted aboard a King's ship, they were as much in sanctuary as the transgressor of the Middle Ages harboring himself under the shadow of the altar. Such sanctioned irregularities, which for obvious reasons the government would hardly think to parade at the time and which consequently, and as affecting the least influential class of mankind, have all but dropped into oblivion, lend color to something for the truth whereof I do not vouch, and hence have some scruple in stating; something I remember having seen in print though the book I cannot recall; but the same thing was personally communicated to me now more than forty years ago by an old pensioner in a cocked hat with whom I had a most interesting talk on the terrace at Greenwich, a Baltimore Negro, a Trafalgar man.[49] It was to this effect: In the case of a warship short of hands whose speedy sailing was imperative, the deficient quota, in lack of any other way of making it good, would be eked out by drafts culled direct from the jails. For reasons previously suggested it would not perhaps be easy at the present day directly to prove or

---

[47]Court of law.

[48]Impressment gangs serving to draft or kidnap men for the navy.

[49]Veteran of Trafalgar. An entry for November 21, 1849, in Melville's *Journal of a Visit to London and the Continent* contains the following telegraphic notes of an excursion to Greenwich Hospital near London: "The negro.... Pensioners in palaces! ... Walked in Greenwich Park ... talk with an old pensioner there."

disprove the allegation. But allowed as a verity, how significant would it be of England's straits at the time confronted by those wars which like a flight of harpies rose shrieking from the din and dust of the fallen Bastille.[50] That era appears measurably clear to us who look back at it, and but read of it. But to the grandfathers of us graybeards, the more thoughtful of them, the genius of it presented an aspect like that of Camoëns' Spirit of the Cape,[51] an eclipsing menace mysterious and prodigious. Not America was exempt from apprehension. At the height of Napoleon's unexampled conquests, there were Americans who had fought at Bunker Hill who looked forward to the possibility that the Atlantic might prove no barrier against the ultimate schemes of this French portentous upstart from the revolutionary chaos who seemed in act of fulfilling judgment prefigured in the Apocalypse.[52]

But the less credence was to be given to the gun-deck talk touching Claggart, seeing that no man holding his office in a man-of-war can ever hope to be popular with the crew. Besides, in derogatory comments upon anyone against whom they have a grudge, or for any reason or no reason mislike, sailors are much like landsmen: they are apt to exaggerate or romance it.

About as much was really known to the *Bellipotent*'s tars of the master-at-arms' career before entering the service as an astronomer knows about a comet's travels prior to its first observable appearance in the sky. The verdict of the sea quidnuncs[53] has been cited only by way of showing what sort of moral impression the man made upon rude uncultivated natures whose conceptions of human wickedness were necessarily of the narrowest, limited to ideas of vulgar rascality—a thief among the swinging hammocks during a night watch, or the man-brokers and land-sharks[54] of the seaports.

It was no gossip, however, but fact that though, as before hinted, Claggart upon his entrance into the navy was, as a novice, assigned to the least honorable section[55] of a man-of-war's crew, embracing the drudgery, he did not long remain there. The superior capacity he immediately evinced, his constitutional sobriety, an ingratiating deference to superiors, together with a peculiar ferreting genius manifested on a singular occasion; all this, capped by a certain austere patriotism, abruptly advanced him to the position of master-at-arms.

[50]Infamous prison stormed by the citizens of Paris on July 14, 1789, at the outbreak of the French Revolution. The Harpies were fierce, filthy monsters with the faces of women and the bodies and claws of vultures who served as ministers of divine vengeance and punished criminals.

[51]In *The Lusiads*, an epic on Vasco Da Gama's voyage to India by the Portuguese poet Luis de Camoëns (1524–1580), the Spirit embodies the natural forces that threaten to destroy Da Gama and his crew at the Cape of Good Hope. Melville acquired his love of Camoëns from his friend Jack Chase.

[52]Contemporary Christians who applied the prophecies in the book of Revelation to their own time often identified Napoleon with one of the blasphemous beasts given power to rule over all nations and to make war on the saints. They also equated the defeat of Napoleonic France with the fall of Babylon (Revelation 13–14).

[53]Literally "what now?" Hence busybodies, gossips.

[54]Man-brokers, or crimps, made money by impressing or shanghaiing sailors. Land-sharks swindled sailors ashore.

[55]The waisters, who, as Melville explains in *White-Jacket*, attended to "the drainage and sewerage below hatches" (Chap. 3).

Of this maritime chief of police the ship's corporals, so called, were the immediate subordinates, and compliant ones; and this, as is to be noted in some business departments ashore, almost to a degree inconsistent with entire moral volition. His place put various converging wires of underground influence under the chief's control, capable when astutely worked through his understrappers of operating to the mysterious discomfort, if nothing worse, of any of the sea commonalty.

9

Life in the foretop well agreed with Billy Budd. There, when not actually engaged on the yards yet higher aloft, the topmen, who as such had been picked out for youth and activity, constituted an aerial club lounging at ease against the smaller stun'sails rolled up into cushions, spinning yarns like the lazy gods, and frequently amused with what was going on in the busy world of the decks below. No wonder then that a young fellow of Billy's disposition was well content in such society. Giving no cause of offense to anybody, he was always alert at a call. So in the merchant service it had been with him. But now such a punctiliousness in duty was shown that his topmates would sometimes good-naturedly laugh at him for it. This heightened alacrity had its cause, namely, the impression made upon him by the first formal gang-way-punishment he had ever witnessed, which befell the day following his impressment. It had been incurred by a little fellow, young, a novice after-guardsman absent from his assigned post when the ship was being put about;[56] a dereliction resulting in a rather serious hitch to that maneuver, one demanding instantaneous promptitude in letting go and making fast. When Billy saw the culprit's naked back under the scourge, gridironed with red welts and worse, when he marked the dire expression in the liberated man's face as with his woolen shirt flung over him by the executioner he rushed forward from the spot to bury himself in the crowd, Billy was horrified. He resolved that never through remissness would he make himself liable to such a visitation or do or omit aught that might merit even verbal reproof. What then was his surprise and concern when ultimately he found himself getting into petty trouble occasionally about such matters as the stowage of his bag or something amiss in his hammock, matters under the police oversight of the ship's corporals of the lower decks, and which brought down on him a vague threat from one of them.

So heedful in all things as he was, how could this be? He could not understand it, and it more than vexed him. When he spoke to his young topmates about it they were either lightly incredulous or found something comical in his unconcealed anxiety. "Is it your bag, Billy?" said one. "Well,

---

[56]Melville's persona White-Jacket narrowly escapes a flogging for the same offense and is saved by the intervention of Jack Chase and the corporal of marines. According to *White-Jacket*, novices often found their way into the After-Guard, which demanded "little seamanship" (Chaps. 3, 67).

sew yourself up in it, bully boy, and then you'll be sure to know if anybody meddles with it."

Now there was a veteran aboard who because his years began to disqualify him for more active work had been recently assigned duty as mainmastman in his watch, looking to the gear belayed at the rail roundabout that great spar near the deck. At off-times the foretopman had picked up some acquaintance with him, and now in his trouble it occurred to him that he might be the sort of person to go to for wise counsel. He was an old Dansker[57] long anglicized in the service, of few words, many wrinkles, and some honorable scars. His wizened face, time-tinted and weather-stained to the complexion of an antique parchment, was here and there peppered blue by the chance explosion of a gun cartridge in action.

He was an *Agamemnon* man, some two years prior to the time of this story having served under Nelson when still captain in that ship immortal in naval memory, which dismantled and in part broken up to her bare ribs is seen a grand skeleton in Haden's etching.[58] As one of a boarding party from the *Agamemnon* he had received a cut slantwise along one temple and cheek leaving a long pale scar like a streak of dawn's light falling athwart the dark visage. It was on account of that scar and the affair in which it was known that he had received it, as well as from his blue-peppered complexion, that the Dansker went among the *Bellipotent*'s crew by the name of "Board-Her-in-the-Smoke."

Now the first time that his small weasel eyes happened to light on Billy Budd, a certain grim internal merriment set all his ancient wrinkles into antic play. Was it that his eccentric unsentimental old sapience, primitive in its kind, saw or thought it saw something which in contrast with the warship's environment looked oddly incongruous in the Handsome Sailor? But after slyly studying him at intervals, the old Merlin's[59] equivocal merriment was modified; for now when the twain would meet, it would start in his face a quizzing sort of look, but it would be but momentary and sometimes replaced by an expression of speculative query as to what might eventually befall a nature like that, dropped into a world not without some mantraps and against whose subtleties simple courage lacking experience and address, and without any touch of defensive ugliness, is of little avail; and where such innocence as man is capable of does yet in a moral emergency not always sharpen the faculties or enlighten the will.

However it was, the Dansker in his ascetic way rather took to Billy. Nor was this only because of a certain philosophic interest in such a character. There was another cause. While the old man's eccentricities, sometimes bordering on the ursine, repelled the juniors, Billy, undeterred thereby, revering him as a salt hero, would make advances, never passing the old *Agamemnon*

---

[57]Dane.

[58]"The Breaking Up of the *Agamemnon*," famous etching by Sir Francis Seymour Haden (1818–1910).

[59]The magician in the legends of King Arthur; hence a sage.

man without a salutation marked by that respect which is seldom lost on
the aged, however crabbed at times or whatever their station in life.

There was a vein of dry humor, or what not, in the mastman; and,
whether in freak of patriarchal irony touching Billy's youth and athletic
frame, or for some other and more recondite reason, from the first in
addressing him he always substituted *Baby* for Billy, the Dansker in fact
being the originator of the name by which the foretopman eventually
became known aboard ship.

Well then, in his mysterious little difficulty going in quest of the wrinkled one, Billy found him off duty in a dogwatch ruminating by himself,
seated on a shot box of the upper gun deck, now and then surveying with a
somewhat cynical regard certain of the more swaggering promenaders there.
Billy recounted his trouble, again wondering how it all happened. The salt
seer attentively listened, accompanying the foretopman's recital with queer
twitchings of his wrinkles and problematical little sparkles of his small ferret
eyes. Making an end of his story, the foretopman asked, "And now,
Dansker, do tell me what you think of it."

The old man, shoving up the front of his tarpaulin and deliberately rubbing the long slant scar at the point where it entered the thin hair, laconi-
cally said, "Baby Budd, *Jemmy Legs*" (meaning the master-at-arms) "is down
on you."

"*Jemmy Legs!*" ejaculated Billy, his welkin eyes expanding. "What for?
Why, he calls me 'the sweet and pleasant young fellow,' they tell me."

"Does he so?" grinned the grizzled one; then said, "Ay, Baby lad, a sweet
voice has Jemmy Legs."

"No, not always. But to me he has. I seldom pass him but there comes a
pleasant word."

"And that's because he's down upon you, Baby Budd."

Such reiteration, along with the manner of it, incomprehensible to a
novice, disturbed Billy almost as much as the mystery for which he had
sought explanation. Something less unpleasingly oracular he tried to extract;
but the old sea Chiron, thinking perhaps that for the nonce he had sufficiently instructed his young Achilles,[60] pursed his lips, gathered all his wrinkles together, and would commit himself to nothing further.

Years, and those experiences which befall certain shrewder men subordinated lifelong to the will of superiors, all this had developed in the Dansker
the pithy guarded cynicism that was his leading characteristic.

10

The next day an incident served to confirm Billy Budd in his incredulity as
to the Dansker's strange summing up of the case submitted. The ship at
noon, going large before the wind, was rolling on her course, and he below
at dinner and engaged in some sportful talk with the members of his mess,

[60]In Greek myth, the wise centaur Chiron tutored the warrior Achilles.

chanced in a sudden lurch to spill the entire contents of his soup pan upon the new-scrubbed deck. Claggart, the master-at-arms, official rattan[61] in hand, happened to be passing along the battery in a bay of which the mess was lodged, and the greasy liquid streamed just across his path. Stepping over it, he was proceeding on his way without comment, since the matter was nothing to take notice of under the circumstances, when he happened to observe who it was that had done the spilling. His countenance changed. Pausing, he was about to ejaculate something hasty at the sailor, but checked himself, and pointing down to the streaming soup, playfully tapped him from behind with his rattan, saying in a low musical voice peculiar to him at times, "Handsomely done, my lad! And handsome is as handsome did it, too!" And with that passed on. Not noted by Billy as not coming within his view was the involuntary smile, or rather grimace, that accompanied Claggart's equivocal words. Aridly it drew down the thin corners of his shapely mouth. But everybody taking his remark as meant for humorous, and at which therefore as coming from a superior they were bound to laugh "with counterfeited glee,"[62] acted accordingly; and Billy, tickled, it may be, by the allusion to his being the Handsome Sailor, merrily joined in; then addressing his messmates exclaimed, "There now, who says that Jemmy Legs is down on me!"

"And who said he was, Beauty?" demanded one Donald with some surprise. Whereat the foretopman looked a little foolish, recalling that it was only one person, Board-Her-in-the-Smoke, who had suggested what to him was the smoky idea that this master-at-arms was in any peculiar way hostile to him. Meantime that functionary, resuming his path, must have momentarily worn some expression less guarded than that of the bitter smile, usurping the face from the heart—some distorting expression perhaps, for a drummer-boy heedlessly frolicking along from the opposite direction and chancing to come into light collision with his person was strangely disconcerted by his aspect. Nor was the impression lessened when the official, impetuously giving him a sharp cut with the rattan, vehemently exclaimed, "Look where you go!"

11

What was the matter with the master-at-arms? And, be the matter what it might, how could it have direct relation to Billy Budd, with whom prior to the affair of the spilled soup he had never come into any special contact official or otherwise? What indeed could the trouble have to do with one so little inclined to give offense as the merchant-ship's "peacemaker," even him who in Claggart's own phrase was "the sweet and pleasant young fellow"? Yes, why should Jemmy Legs, to borrow the Dansker's expression, be "down" on the Handsome Sailor? But, at heart and not for nothing, as the

[61]Cane.
[62]Like the schoolboys in Oliver Goldsmith's "The Deserted Village" (1770), who laugh "with counterfeited glee" at their harsh schoolmaster's jokes.

late chance encounter may indicate to the discerning, down on him, secretly down on him, he assuredly was.

Now to invent something touching the more private career of Claggart, something involving Billy Budd, of which something the latter should be wholly ignorant, some romantic incident implying that Claggart's knowledge of the young blue-jacket began at some period anterior to catching sight of him on board the seventy-four—all this, not so difficult to do, might avail in a way more or less interesting to account for whatever of enigma may appear to lurk in the case. But in fact there was nothing of the sort. And yet the cause necessarily to be assumed as the sole one assignable is in its very realism as much charged with that prime element of Radcliffian romance, the mysterious, as any that the ingenuity of the author of *The Mysteries of Udolpho* could devise.[63] For what can more partake of the mysterious than an antipathy spontaneous and profound such as is evoked in certain exceptional mortals by the mere aspect of some other mortal, however harmless he may be, if not called forth by this very harmlessness itself?

Now there can exist no irritating juxtaposition of dissimilar personalities comparable to that which is possible aboard a great warship fully manned and at sea. There, every day among all ranks, almost every man comes into more or less of contact with almost every other man. Wholly there to avoid even the sight of an aggravating object one must needs give it Jonah's toss[64] or jump overboard himself. Imagine how all this might eventually operate on some peculiar human creature the direct reverse of a saint!

But for the adequate comprehending of Claggart by a normal nature these hints are insufficient. To pass from a normal nature to him one must cross "the deadly space between." And this is best done by indirection.

Long ago an honest scholar, my senior, said to me in reference to one who like himself is now no more, a man so unimpeachably respectable that against him nothing was ever openly said though among the few something was whispered, "Yes, X——is a nut not to be cracked by the tap of a lady's fan. You are aware that I am the adherent of no organized religion, much less of any philosophy built into a system. Well, for all that, I think that to try and get into X——, enter his labyrinth and get out again, without a clue derived from some source other that what is known as 'knowledge of the world'—that were hardly possible, at least for me."

---

[63]Ann Radcliffe (1764–1823), popular British author of Gothic novels, best known for *The Mysteries of Udolpho* (1794), in which all mysteries are ultimately explained away. In *The Confidence-Man* Melville disparages the "sallies of ingenuity" displayed by "certain psychological novelists" who "challenge astonishment at the tangled web of some character, and then raise admiration still greater at their satisfactory unraveling of it;

in this way throwing open, sometimes to the understanding even of school misses, the last complications of that spirit which is affirmed by its Creator to be fearfully and wonderfully made" (Chap. 14).
[64]When Jonah's disobedience provoked God to raise a storm at sea that endangered the ship, the sailors "took up Jonah, and cast him forth into the sea" (Jonah 1:15).

"Why," said I, "X——, however singular a study to some, is yet human, and knowledge of the world assuredly implies the knowledge of human nature, and in most of its varieties."

"Yes, but a superficial knowledge of it, serving ordinary purposes. But for anything deeper, I am not certain whether to know the world and to know human nature be not two distinct branches of knowledge, which while they may coexist in the same heart, yet either may exist with little or nothing of the other. Nay, in an average man of the world, his constant rubbing with it blunts that finer spiritual insight indispensable to the understanding of the essential in certain exceptional characters, whether evil ones or good. In a matter of some importance I have seen a girl wind an old lawyer about her little finger. Nor was it the dotage of senile love. Nothing of the sort. But he knew law better than he knew the girl's heart. Coke and Blackstone[65] hardly shed so much light into obscure spiritual places as the Hebrew prophets. And who were they? Mostly recluses."

At the time, my inexperience was such that I did not quite see the drift of all this. It may be that I see it now. And, indeed, if that lexicon which is based on Holy Writ were any longer popular, one might with less difficulty define and denominate certain phenomenal men. As it is, one must turn to some authority not liable to the charge of being tinctured with the biblical element.

In a list of definitions included in the authentic translation of Plato, a list attributed to him, occurs this: "Natural Depravity: a depravity according to nature,"[66] a definition which, though savoring of Calvinism, by no means involves Calvin's dogma as to total mankind. Evidently its intent makes it applicable but to individuals. Not many are the examples of this depravity which the gallows and jail supply. At any rate, for notable instances, since these have no vulgar alloy of the brute in them, but invariably are dominated by intellectuality, one must go elsewhere. Civilization, especially if of the austerer sort, is auspicious to it. It folds itself in the mantle of respectability. It has its certain negative virtues serving as silent auxiliaries. It never allows wine to get within its guard. It is not going too far to say that it is without vices or small sins. There is a phenomenal pride in it that excludes them. It is never mercenary or avaricious. In short, the depravity here meant partakes nothing of the sordid or sensual. It is serious, but free from acerbity. Though no flatterer of mankind it never speaks ill of it.

But the thing which in eminent instances signalizes so exceptional a nature is this: Though the man's even temper and discreet bearing would seem to intimate a mind peculiarly subject to the law of reason, not the less in heart he would seem to riot in complete exemption from that law, having apparently little to do with reason further than to employ it as an

[65]Sir Edward Coke (1552–1634) and Sir William Blackstone (1723–1780), who laid the foundations of British jurisprudence.
[66]According to Hayford and Sealts, Melville found this definition in the Bohn edition of Plato's works, Vol. 6 (1854). He distinguishes it from the Calvinist doctrine of total depravity, which applies not merely to individuals but to the entire human race.

ambidexter implement for effecting the irrational. That is to say: Toward the accomplishment of an aim which in wantonness of atrocity would seem to partake of the insane, he will direct a cool judgment sagacious and sound. These men are madmen, and of the most dangerous sort, for their lunacy is not continuous, but occasional, evoked by some special object; it is protectively secretive, which is as much as to say it is self-contained, so that when, moreover, most active it is to the average mind not distinguishable from sanity, and for the reason above suggested: that whatever its aims may be— and the aim is never declared—the method and the outward proceeding are always perfectly rational.

Now something such an one was Claggart, in whom was the mania of an evil nature, not engendered by vicious training or corrupting books or licentious living, but born with him and innate, in short "a depravity according to nature."

Dark sayings are these, some will say. But why? Is it because they somewhat savor of Holy Writ in its phrase "mystery of iniquity"?[67] If they do, such savor was far enough from being intended, for little will it commend these pages to many a reader of today.

The point of the present story turning on the hidden nature of the master-at-arms has necessitated this chapter. With an added hint or two in connection with the incident at the mess, the resumed narrative must be left to vindicate, as it may, its own credibility.

12

That Claggart's figure was not amiss, and his face, save the chin, well molded, has already been said. Of these favorable points he seemed not insensible, for he was not only neat but careful in his dress. But the form of Billy Budd was heroic; and if his face was without the intellectual look of the pallid Claggart's, not the less was it lit, like his, from within, though from a different source. The bonfire in his heart made luminous the rose-tan in his cheek.

In view of the marked contrast between the persons of the twain, it is more than probable that when the master-at-arms in the scene last given applied to the sailor the proverb "Handsome is as handsome does," he there let escape an ironic inkling, not caught by the young sailors who heard it, as to what it was that had first moved him against Billy, namely, his significant personal beauty.

Now envy and antipathy, passions irreconcilable in reason, nevertheless in fact may spring conjoined like Chang and Eng[68] in one birth. Is Envy then such a monster? Well, though many an arraigned mortal has in hopes of mitigated penalty pleaded guilty to horrible actions, did ever anybody

---

[67]II Thessalonians 2:7 warns believers against the "man of sin," or Antichrist, temporarily allowed by God to deceive the world: "For the mystery of iniquity doth already work."

[68]The original Siamese twins (1811–1874), exhibited as freaks in P. T. Barnum's American Museum.

seriously confess to envy? Something there is in it universally felt to be more shameful than even felonious crime. And not only does everybody disown it, but the better sort are inclined to incredulity when it is in earnest imputed to an intelligent man. But since its lodgment is in the heart not the brain, no degree of intellect supplies a guarantee against it. But Claggart's was no vulgar form of the passion. Nor, as directed toward Billy Budd, did it partake of that streak of apprehensive jealousy that marred Saul's visage perturbedly brooding on the comely young David.[69] Claggart's envy struck deeper. If askance he eyed the good looks, cheery health, and frank enjoyment of young life in Billy Budd, it was because these went along with a nature that, as Claggart magnetically felt, had in its simplicity never willed malice or experienced the reactionary bite of that serpent. To him, the spirit lodged within Billy, and looking out from his welkin eyes as from windows, that ineffability it was which made the dimple in his dyed cheek, suppled his joints, and dancing in his yellow curls made him pre-eminently the Handsome Sailor. One person excepted, the master-at-arms was perhaps the only man in the ship intellectually capable of adequately appreciating the moral phenomenon presented in Billy Budd. And the insight but intensified his passion, which assuming various secret forms within him, at times assumed that of cynic disdain, disdain of innocence—to be nothing more than innocent! Yet in an aesthetic way he saw the charm of it, the courageous free-and-easy temper of it, and fain would have shared it, but he despaired of it.

With no power to annul the elemental evil in him, though readily enough he could hide it; apprehending the good, but powerless to be it; a nature like Claggart's, surcharged with energy as such natures almost invariably are, what recourse is left to it but to recoil upon itself and, like the scorpion for which the Creator alone is responsible, act out to the end the part allotted it.

13

Passion, and passion in its profoundest, is not a thing demanding a palatial stage whereon to play its part. Down among the groundlings, among the beggars and rakers of the garbage, profound passion is enacted. And the circumstances that provoke it, however trivial or mean, are no measure of its power. In the present instance the stage is a scrubbed gun deck, and one of the external provocations a man-of-war's man's spilled soup.

Now when the master-at-arms noticed whence came that greasy fluid streaming before his feet, he must have taken it—to some extent wilfully, perhaps—not for the mere accident it assuredly was, but for the sly escape of a spontaneous feeling on Billy's part more or less answering to the antipathy on his own. In effect a foolish demonstration, he must have thought, and very harmless, like the futile kick of a heifer, which yet were the heifer a shod stallion would not be so harmless. Even so was it that into the gall of Claggart's envy he infused the vitriol of his contempt. But the incident confirmed to him certain telltale reports purveyed to his ear by "Squeak," one of his more cunning corporals, a grizzled little man, so nicknamed by the sailors on account of his squeaky voice and sharp visage ferreting about the dark corners of the lower decks after interlopers, satirically suggesting to them the idea of a rat in a cellar.

From his chief's employing him as an implicit tool in laying little traps for the worriment of the foretopman—for it was from the master-at-arms that the petty persecutions heretofore adverted to had proceeded—the corporal, having naturally enough concluded that his master could have no love for the sailor, made it his business, faithful understrapper that he was, to foment the ill blood by perverting to his chief certain innocent frolics of the good-natured foretopman, besides inventing for his mouth sundry contumelious epithets he claimed to have overheard him let fall. The master-at-arms never suspected the veracity of these reports, more especially as to the epithets, for he well knew how secretly unpopular may become a master-at-arms, at least a master-at-arms of those days, zealous in his function, and how the bluejackets shoot at him in private their raillery and wit; the nickname by which he goes among them (Jemmy Legs) implying under the form of merriment their cherished disrespect and dislike. But in view of the greediness of hate for pabulum[70] it hardly needed a purveyor to feed Claggart's passion.

An uncommon prudence is habitual with the subtler depravity, for it has everything to hide. And in case of an injury but suspected, its secretiveness voluntarily cuts it off from enlightenment or disillusion; and, not unreluctantly, action is taken upon surmise as upon certainty. And the retaliation is apt to be in monstrous disproportion to the supposed offense; for when in anybody was revenge in its exactions aught else but an inordinate usurer? But how with Claggart's conscience? For though consciences are unlike as foreheads, every intelligence, not excluding the scriptural devils who "believe and tremble,"[71] has one. But Claggart's conscience being but the lawyer to his will, made ogres of trifles, probably arguing that the motive imputed to Billy in spilling the soup just when he did, together with the epithets alleged, these, if nothing more, made a strong case against him; nay, justified animosity into a sort of retributive righteousness. The Pharisee is the Guy Fawkes[72] prowling in the hid chambers underlying some natures like Claggart's. And they can really form no conception of an unreciprocated malice. Probably the master-at-arms' clandestine persecution of Billy was started to try the temper

---

[70]Nourishment.

[71]James 2:19: "Thou believest that there is one God; ... the devils also believe, and tremble."

[72]In Matthew 22 and 23, the Pharisees try to entrap Jesus, who denounces them as hypocrites for splitting hairs over the letter of the law while neglecting "the weightier matters of the law, judgment, mercy, and faith." The Catholic conspirator Guy Fawkes, a participant in the Gunpowder Plot of 1605, was caught in the cellar of the Parliament building, which he was trying to blow up.

of the man; but it had not developed any quality in him that enmity could make official use of or even pervert into plausible self-justification; so that the occurrence at the mess, petty if it were, was a welcome one to that peculiar conscience assigned to be the private mentor of Claggart; and, for the rest, not improbably it put him upon new experiments.

14

Not many days after the last incident narrated, something befell Billy Budd that more graveled[73] him than aught that had previously occurred.

It was a warm night for the latitude; and the foretopman, whose watch at the time was properly below, was dozing on the uppermost deck whither he had ascended from his hot hammock, one of hundreds suspended so closely wedged together over a lower gun deck that there was little or no swing to them. He lay as in the shadow of a hillside, stretched under the lee[74] of the booms, a piled ridge of spare spars amidships between foremast and mainmast among which the ship's largest boat, the launch, was stowed. Alongside of three other slumberers from below, he lay near that end of the booms which approaches the foremast; his station aloft on duty as a foretopman being just over the deck-station of the forecastlemen, entitling him according to usage to make himself more or less at home in that neighborhood.

Presently he was stirred into semiconsciousness by somebody, who must have previously sounded the sleep of the others, touching his shoulder, and then, as the foretopman raised his head, breathing into his ear in a quick whisper, "Slip into the lee forechains, Billy; there is something in the wind. Don't speak. Quick, I will meet you there," and disappearing.

Now Billy, like sundry other essentially good-natured ones, had some of the weaknesses inseparable from essential good nature; and among these was a reluctance, almost an incapacity of plumply saying *no* to an abrupt proposition not obviously absurd on the face of it, nor obviously unfriendly, nor iniquitous. And being of warm blood, he had not the phlegm tacitly to negative any proposition by unresponsive inaction. Like his sense of fear, his apprehension as to aught outside of the honest and natural was seldom very quick. Besides, upon the present occasion, the drowse from his sleep still hung upon him.

However it was, he mechanically rose and, sleepily wondering what could be in the wind, betook himself to the designated place, a narrow platform, one of six, outside of the high bulwarks and screened by the great deadeyes and multiple columned lanyards of the shrouds and backstays;[75] and, in a great warship of that time, of dimensions commensurate to the hull's magnitude; a tarry balcony in short, overhanging the sea, and so secluded that one mariner of the *Bellipotent*, a Nonconformist old tar of a serious turn, made it even in daytime his private oratory.[76]

[73]Perplexed, bothered.
[74]Shelter (from the wind).
[75]Deadeyes are flat, round wooden blocks with holes for lanyards, short ropes that fasten the shrouds. Shrouds and backstays are sets of ropes extending sideways and back from the masts, to give them support.
[76]Place of prayer.

In this retired nook the stranger soon joined Billy Budd. There was no moon as yet; a haze obscured the starlight. He could not distinctly see the stranger's face. Yet from something in the outline and carriage, Billy took him, and correctly, for one of the afterguard.

"Hist! Billy," said the man, in the same quick cautionary whisper as before. "You were impressed, weren't you? Well, so was I"; and he paused, as to mark the effect. But Billy, not knowing exactly what to make of this, said nothing. Then the other: "We are not the only impressed ones, Billy. There's a gang of us.—Couldn't you—help—at a pinch?"

"What do you mean?" demanded Billy, here thoroughly shaking off his drowse.

"Hist, hist!" the hurried whisper now growing husky. "See here," and the man held up two small objects faintly twinkling in the night-light; "see, they are yours, Billy, if you'll only——"

But Billy broke in, and in his resentful eagerness to deliver himself his vocal infirmity somewhat intruded. "D—d—damme, I don't know what you are d—d—driving at, or what you mean, but you had better g—g—go where you belong!" For the moment the fellow, as confounded, did not stir; and Billy, springing to his feet, said, "If you d—don't start, I'll t—t—toss you back over the r—rail!" There was no mistaking this, and the mysterious emissary decamped, disappearing in the direction of the mainmast in the shadow of the booms.

"Hallo, what's the matter?" here came growling from a forecastleman awakened from his deck-doze by Billy's raised voice. And as the foretopman reappeared and was recognized by him: "Ah, Beauty, is it you? Well, something must have been the matter, for you st—st—stuttered."

"Oh," rejoined Billy, now mastering the impediment, "I found an afterguardsman in our part of the ship here, and I bid him be off where he belongs."

"And is that all you did about it, Foretopman?" gruffly demanded another, an irascible old fellow of brick-colored visage and hair who was known to his associate forecastlemen as "Red Pepper." "Such sneaks I should like to marry to the gunner's daughter!"—by that expression meaning that he would like to subject them to disciplinary castigation over a gun.

However, Billy's rendering of the matter satisfactorily accounted to these inquirers for the brief commotion, since of all the sections of a ship's company the forecastlemen, veterans for the most part and bigoted in their sea prejudices, are the most jealous in resenting territorial encroachments, especially on the part of any of the afterguard, of whom they have but a sorry opinion— chiefly landsmen, never going aloft except to reef or furl the mainsail, and in no wise competent to handle a marlinspike or turn in a deadeye, say.

15

This incident sorely puzzled Billy Budd. It was an entirely new experience, the first time in his life that he had ever been personally approached in underhand intriguing fashion. Prior to this encounter he had known nothing of the afterguardsman, the two men being stationed wide apart, one forward and aloft during his watch, the other on deck and aft.

What could it mean? And could they really be guineas, those two glittering objects the interloper had held up to his (Billy's) eyes? Where could the fellow get guineas? Why, even spare buttons are not so plentiful at sea. The more he turned the matter over, the more he was nonplussed, and made uneasy and discomfited. In his disgustful recoil from an overture which, though he but ill comprehended, he instinctively knew must involve evil of some sort, Billy Budd was like a young horse fresh from the pasture suddenly inhaling a vile whiff from some chemical factory, and by repeated snortings trying to get it out of his nostrils and lungs. This frame of mind barred all desire of holding further parley with the fellow, even were it but for the purpose of gaining some enlightenment as to his design in approaching him. And yet he was not without natural curiosity to see how such a visitor in the dark would look in broad day.

He espied him the following afternoon in his first dogwatch below, one of the smokers on that forward part of the upper gun deck allotted to the pipe. He recognized him by his general cut and build more than by his round freckled face and glassy eyes of pale blue, veiled with lashes all but white. And yet Billy was a bit uncertain whether indeed it were he—yonder chap about his own age chatting and laughing in freehearted way, leaning against a gun; a genial young fellow enough to look at, and something of a rattle-brain, to all appearance. Rather chubby too for a sailor, even an afterguardsman. In short, the last man in the world, one would think, to be overburdened with thoughts, especially those perilous thoughts that must needs belong to a conspirator in any serious project, or even to the underling of such a conspirator.

Although Billy was not aware of it, the fellow, with a sidelong watchful glance, had perceived Billy first, and then noting that Billy was looking at him, thereupon nodded a familiar sort of friendly recognition as to an old acquaintance, without interrupting the talk he was engaged in with the group of smokers. A day or two afterwards, chancing in the evening promenade on a gun deck to pass Billy, he offered a flying word of good-fellowship, as it were, which by its unexpectedness, and equivocalness under the circumstances, so embarrassed Billy that he knew not how to respond to it, and let it go unnoticed.

Billy was now left more at a loss than before. The ineffectual speculations into which he was led were so disturbingly alien to him that he did his best to smother them. It never entered his mind that here was a matter which, from its extreme questionableness, it was his duty as a loyal blue-jacket to report in the proper quarter. And, probably, had such a step been suggested to him, he would have been deterred from taking it by the thought, one of novice magnanimity, that it would savor overmuch of the dirty work of a telltale. He kept the thing to himself. Yet upon one occasion he could not forbear a little disburdening himself to the old Dansker, tempted thereto perhaps by the influence of a balmy night when the ship lay becalmed; the twain, silent for the most part, sitting together on deck, their heads propped against the bulwarks. But it was only a partial and anonymous account that Billy gave, the unfounded scruples above referred to preventing full disclosure to anybody. Upon hearing Billy's version, the sage Dansker seemed to divine more than he was told; and after a little meditation, during which his wrinkles were pursed as into a point, quite effacing for the time that quizzing expression his face sometimes wore: "Didn't I say so, Baby Budd?"

"Say what?" demanded Billy.

"Why, *Jemmy Legs* is *down* on you."

"And what," rejoined Billy in amazement, "has *Jemmy Legs* to do with that cracked afterguardsman?"

"Ho, it was an afterguardsman, then. A cat's-paw, a cat's-paw!"[77] And with that exclamation, whether it had reference to a light puff of air just then coming over the calm sea, or a subtler relation to the afterguardsman, there is no telling, the old Merlin gave a twisting wrench with his black teeth at his plug of tobacco, vouchsafing no reply to Billy's impetuous question, though now repeated, for it was his wont to relapse into grim silence when interrogated in skeptical sort as to any of his sententious oracles, not always very clear ones, rather partaking of that obscurity which invests most Delphic[78] deliverances from any quarter.

Long experience had very likely brought this old man to that bitter prudence which never interferes in aught and never gives advice.

16

Yes, despite the Dansker's pithy insistence as to the master-at-arms being at the bottom of these strange experiences of Billy on board the *Bellipotent*, the young sailor was ready to ascribe them to almost anybody but the man who, to use Billy's own expression, "always had a pleasant word for him." This is to be wondered at. Yet not so much to be wondered at. In certain matters, some sailors even in mature life remain unsophisticated enough. But a young seafarer of the disposition of our athletic foretopman is much of a child-man. And yet a child's utter innocence is but its blank ignorance, and the innocence more or less wanes as intelligence waxes. But in Billy Budd intelligence, such as it was, had advanced while yet his simplemindedness remained for the most part unaffected. Experience is a teacher indeed; yet did Billy's years make his experience small. Besides, he had none of that intuitive knowledge of the bad which in natures not good or incompletely so foreruns experience, and therefore may pertain, as in some instances it too clearly does pertain, even to youth.

[77]Hayford and Sealts point out that Melville is punning on the double meaning of the word as a light puff of air that barely ruffles the surface of the water, and as a "good-looking seaman employed to entice volunteers."

[78]The oracle of Delphi issued ambiguous and obscure prophecies.

And what could Billy know of man except of man as a mere sailor? And the old-fashioned sailor, the veritable man before the mast, the sailor from boyhood up, he, though indeed of the same species as a landsman, is in some respects singularly distinct from him. The sailor is frankness, the landsman is finesse. Life is not a game with the sailor, demanding the long head—no intricate game of chess where few moves are made in straightforwardness and ends are attained by indirection, an oblique, tedious, barren game hardly worth that poor candle burnt out in playing it.

Yes, as a class, sailors are in character a juvenile race. Even their deviations are marked by juvenility, this more especially holding true with the sailors of Billy's time. Then too, certain things which apply to all sailors do more pointedly operate here and there upon the junior one. Every sailor, too, is accustomed to obey orders without debating them; his life afloat is externally ruled for him; he is not brought into that promiscuous commerce with mankind where unobstructed free agency on equal terms—equal superficially, at least—soon teaches one that unless upon occasion he exercise a distrust keen in proportion to the fairness of the appearance, some foul turn may be served him. A ruled undemonstrative distrustfulness is so habitual, not with businessmen so much as with men who know their kind in less shallow relations than business, namely, certain men of the world, that they come at last to employ it all but unconsciously; and some of them would very likely feel real surprise at being charged with it as one of their general characteristics.

17

But after the little matter at the mess Billy Budd no more found himself in strange trouble at times about his hammock or his clothes bag or what not. As to that smile that occasionally sunned him, and the pleasant passing word, these were, if not more frequent, yet if anything more pronounced than before.

But for all that, there were certain other demonstrations now. When Claggart's unobserved glance happened to light on belted Billy rolling along the upper gun deck in the leisure of the second dogwatch, exchanging passing broadsides of fun with other young promenaders in the crowd, that glance would follow the cheerful sea Hyperion[79] with a settled meditative and melancholy expression, his eyes strangely suffused with incipient feverish tears. Then would Claggart look like the man of sorrows. Yes, and sometimes the melancholy expression would have in it a touch of soft yearning, as if Claggart could even have loved Billy but for fate and ban. But this was an evanescence, and quickly repented of, as it were, by an immitigable look, pinching and shriveling the visage into the momentary semblance of a wrinkled walnut. But sometimes catching sight in advance of the foretopman

[79]A Titan and sun god, later identified with
Apollo, and similarly depicted as an epitome
of youthful, manly beauty.

coming in his direction, he would, upon their nearing, step aside a little to let him pass, dwelling upon Billy for the moment with the glittering dental satire of a Guise.[80] But upon any abrupt unforeseen encounter a red light would flash forth from his eye like a spark from an anvil in a dusk smithy. That quick, fierce light was a strange one, darted from orbs which in repose were of a color nearest approaching a deeper violet, the softest of shades.

Though some of these caprices of the pit could not but be observed by their object, yet were they beyond the construing of such a nature. And the thews of Billy were hardly compatible with that sort of sensitive spiritual organization which in some cases instinctively conveys to ignorant innocence an admonition of the proximity of the malign. He thought the master-at-arms acted in a manner rather queer at times. That was all. But the occasional frank air and pleasant word went for what they purported to be, the young sailor never having heard as yet of the "too fair-spoken man."

Had the foretopman been conscious of having done or said anything to provoke the ill will of the official, it would have been different with him, and his sight might have been purged if not sharpened. As it was, innocence was his blinder.

So was it with him in yet another matter. Two minor officers, the armorer and captain of the hold, with whom he had never exchanged a word, his position in the ship not bringing him into contact with them, these men now for the first began to cast upon Billy, when they chanced to encounter him, that peculiar glance which evidences that the man from whom it comes has been some way tampered with, and to the prejudice of him upon whom the glance lights. Never did it occur to Billy as a thing to be noted or a thing suspicious, though he well knew the fact, that the armorer and captain of the hold, with the ship's yeoman, apothecary, and others of that grade, were by naval usage messmates of the master-at-arms, men with ears convenient to his confidential tongue.

But the general popularity that came from our Handsome Sailor's manly forwardness upon occasion and irresistible good nature, indicating no mental superiority tending to excite an invidious feeling, this good will on the part of most of his shipmates made him the less to concern himself about such mute aspects toward him as those whereto allusion has just been made, aspects he could not so fathom as to infer their whole import.

As to the afterguardsman, though Billy for reasons already given necessarily saw little of him, yet when the two did happen to meet, invariably came the fellow's offhand cheerful recognition, sometimes accompanied by a passing pleasant word or two. Whatever that equivocal young person's original design may really have been, or the design of which he might have been the deputy, certain it was from his manner upon these occasions that he had wholly dropped it.

[80]French ducal family notorious for anti-Protestant intrigues. Henri de Guise (1550–1588) helped mastermind the massacre of the Huguenots on St. Bartholomew's Day, 1572. "Glittering dental satire" is Melville's version of "one may smile, and smile, and be a villain" (*Hamlet* I.v.108).

It was as if his precocity of crookedness (and every vulgar villain is pre-cocious) had for once deceived him, and the man he had sought to entrap as a simpleton had through his very simplicity ignominiously baffled him.

But shrewd ones may opine that it was hardly possible for Billy to refrain from going up to the afterguardsman and bluntly demanding to know his purpose in the initial interview so abruptly closed in the fore-chains. Shrewd ones may also think it but natural in Billy to set about sounding some of the other impressed men of the ship in order to discover what basis, if any, there was for the emissary's obscure suggestions as to plotting disaffection aboard. Yes, shrewd ones may so think. But something more, or rather something else than mere shrewdness is perhaps needful for the due understanding of such a character as Billy Budd's.

As to Claggart, the monomania in the man—if that indeed it were—as involuntarily disclosed by starts in the manifestations detailed, yet in gen-eral covered over by his self-contained and rational demeanor; this, like a subterranean fire, was eating its way deeper and deeper in him. Something decisive must come of it.

18

After the mysterious interview in the forechains, the one so abruptly ended there by Billy, nothing especially germane to the story occurred until the events now about to be narrated.

Elsewhere it has been said that in the lack of frigates (of course better sailers than line-of-battle ships) in the English squadron up the Straits at that period, the *Bellipotent* 74 was occasionally employed not only as an available substitute for a scout, but at times on detached service of more im-portant kind. This was not alone because of her sailing qualities, not com-mon in a ship of her rate, but quite as much, probably, that the character of her commander, it was thought, specially adapted him for any duty where under unforeseen difficulties a prompt initiative might have to be taken in some matter demanding knowledge and ability in addition to those qualities implied in good seamanship. It was on an expedition of the latter sort, a somewhat distant one, and when the *Bellipotent* was almost at her furthest remove from the fleet, that in the latter part of an afternoon watch she unexpectedly came in sight of a ship of the enemy. It proved to be a frigate. The latter, perceiving through the glass that the weight of men and metal would be heavily against her, invoking her light heels crowded sail to get away. After a chase urged almost against hope and lasting until about the middle of the first dogwatch, she signally succeeded in effecting her escape.

Not long after the pursuit had been given up, and ere the excitement incident thereto had altogether waned away, the master-at-arms, ascending from his cavernous sphere, made his appearance cap in hand by the main-mast respectfully waiting the notice of Captain Vere, then solitary walking the weather side of the quarter-deck, doubtless somewhat chafed at the fail-ure of the pursuit. The spot where Claggart stood was the place allotted to men of lesser grades seeking some more particular interview either with the officer of the deck or the captain himself. But from the latter it was not often that a sailor or petty officer of those days would seek a hearing; only some exceptional cause would, according to established custom, have warranted that.

Presently, just as the commander, absorbed in his reflections, was on the point of turning aft in his promenade, he became sensible of Claggart's presence, and saw the doffed cap held in deferential expectancy. Here be it said that Captain Vere's personal knowledge of this petty officer had only begun at the time of the ship's last sailing from home, Claggart then for the first, in transfer from a ship detained for repairs, supplying on board the *Bellipotent* the place of a previous master-at-arms disabled and ashore.

No sooner did the commander observe who it was that now deferentially stood awaiting his notice than a peculiar expression came over him. It was not unlike that which uncontrollably will flit across the countenance of one at unawares encountering a person who, though known to him indeed, has hardly been long enough known for thorough knowledge, but something in whose aspect nevertheless now for the first provokes a vaguely repellent distaste. But coming to a stand and resuming much of his wonted official manner, save that a sort of impatience lurked in the intonation of the opening word, he said "Well? What is it, Master-at-arms?"

With the air of a subordinate grieved at the necessity of being a messenger of ill tidings, and while conscientiously determined to be frank yet equally resolved upon shunning overstatement, Claggart at this invitation, or rather summons to disburden, spoke up. What he said, conveyed in the language of no uneducated man, was to the effect following, if not altogether in these words, namely, that during the chase and preparations for the possible encounter he had seen enough to convince him that at least one sailor aboard was a dangerous character in a ship mustering some who not only had taken a guilty part in the late serious troubles, but others also who, like the man in question, had entered His Majesty's service under another form than enlistment.

At this point Captain Vere with some impatience interrupted him: "Be direct, man; say *impressed men.*"

Claggart made a gesture of subservience, and proceeded. Quite lately he (Claggart) had begun to suspect that on the gun decks some sort of movement prompted by the sailor in question was covertly going on, but he had not thought himself warranted in reporting the suspicion so long as it remained indistinct. But from what he had that afternoon observed in the man referred to, the suspicion of something clandestine going on had advanced to a point less removed from certainty. He deeply felt, he added, the serious responsibility assumed in making a report involving such possible consequences to the individual mainly concerned, besides tending to augment those natural anxieties which every naval commander must feel in view of extraordinary outbreaks so recent as those which, he sorrowfully said it, it needed not to name.

Now at the first broaching of the matter Captain Vere, taken by surprise, could not wholly dissemble his disquietude. But as Claggart went on, the former's aspect changed into restiveness under something in the testifier's manner in giving his testimony. However, he refrained from interrupting him. And Claggart, continuing, concluded with this: "God forbid, your honor, that the *Bellipotent*'s should be the experience of the ———"

"Never mind that!" here peremptorily broke in the superior, his face altering with anger, instinctively divining the ship that the other was about to name, one in which the Nore Mutiny had assumed a singularly tragical character that for a time jeopardized the life of its commander. Under the circumstances he was indignant at the purposed allusion. When the commissioned officers themselves were on all occasions very heedful how they referred to the recent events in the fleet, for a petty officer unnecessarily to allude to them in the presence of his captain, this struck him as a most immodest presumption. Besides, to his quick sense of self-respect it even looked under the circumstances something like an attempt to alarm him. Nor at first was he without some surprise that one who so far as he had hitherto come under his notice had shown considerable tact in his function should in this particular evince such lack of it.

But these thoughts and kindred dubious ones flitting across his mind were suddenly replaced by an intuitional surmise which, though as yet obscure in form, served practically to affect his reception of the ill tidings. Certain it is that, long versed in everything pertaining to the complicated gun-deck life, which like every other form of life has its secret mines and dubious side, the side popularly disclaimed, Captain Vere did not permit himself to be unduly disturbed by the general tenor of his subordinate's report.

Furthermore, if in view of recent events prompt action should be taken at the first palpable sign of recurring insubordination, for all that, not judicious would it be, he thought, to keep the idea of lingering disaffection alive by undue forwardness in crediting an informer, even if his own subordinate and charged among other things with police surveillance of the crew. This feeling would not perhaps have so prevailed with him were it not that upon a prior occasion the patriotic zeal officially evinced by Claggart had somewhat irritated him as appearing rather supersensible and strained. Furthermore, something even in the official's self-possessed and somewhat ostentatious manner in making his specifications strangely reminded him of a bandsman, a perjurous witness in a capital case before a court-martial ashore of which when a lieutenant he (Captain Vere) had been a member.

Now the peremptory check given to Claggart in the matter of the arrested allusion was quickly followed up by this: "You say that there is at least one dangerous man aboard. Name him."

"William Budd, a foretopman, your honor."

"William Budd!" repeated Captain Vere with unfeigned astonishment. "And mean you the man that Lieutenant Ratcliffe took from the merchantman not very long ago, the young fellow who seems to be so popular with the men—Billy, the Handsome Sailor, as they call him?"

"The same, your honor; but for all his youth and good looks, a deep one. Not for nothing does he insinuate himself into the good will of his shipmates, since at the least they will at a pinch say—all hands will—a good word for him, and at all hazards. Did Lieutenant Ratcliffe happen to tell your honor of that adroit fling of Budd's, jumping up in the cutter's bow under the merchantman's stern when he was being taken off? It is even masked by that sort of good-humored air that at heart he resents his impressment. You have but noted his fair cheek. A mantrap may be under the ruddy-tipped daisies."

Now the Handsome Sailor as a signal figure among the crew had naturally enough attracted the captain's attention from the first. Though in general not very demonstrative to his officers, he had congratulated Lieutenant Ratcliffe upon his good fortune in lighting on such a fine specimen of the *genus homo,* who in the nude might have posed for a statue of young Adam before the Fall. As to Billy's adieu to the ship *Rights-of-Man,* which the boarding lieutenant had indeed reported to him, but, in a deferential way, more as a good story than aught else, Captain Vere, though mistakenly understanding it as a satiric sally, had but thought so much the better of the impressed man for it; as a military sailor, admiring the spirit that could take an arbitrary enlistment so merrily and sensibly. The foretopman's conduct, too, so far as it had fallen under the captain's notice, had confirmed the first happy augury, while the new recruit's qualities as a "sailor-man" seemed to be such that he had thought of recommending him to the executive officer for promotion to a place that would more frequently bring him under his own observation, namely, the captaincy of the mizzentop, replacing there in the starboard watch a man not so young whom partly for that reason he deemed less fitted for the post. Be it parenthesized here that since the mizzentopmen have not to handle such breadths of heavy canvas as the lower sails on the mainmast and foremast, a young man if of the right stuff not only seems best adapted to duty there, but in fact is generally selected for the captaincy of that top, and the company under him are light hands and often but striplings. In sum, Captain Vere had from the beginning deemed Billy Budd to be what in the naval parlance of the time was called a "King's bargain": that is to say, for His Britannic Majesty's navy a capital investment at small outlay or none at all.

After a brief pause, during which the reminiscences above mentioned passed vividly through his mind and he weighed the import of Claggart's last suggestion conveyed in the phrase "mantrap under the daisies," and the more he weighed it the less reliance he felt in the informer's good faith, suddenly he turned upon him and in a low voice demanded: "Do you come to me, Master-at-arms, with so foggy a tale? As to Budd, cite me an act or spoken word of his confirmatory of what you in general charge against him. Stay," drawing nearer to him; "heed what you speak. Just now, and in a case like this, there is a yardarm-end[81] for the false witness."

---

[81]Used for hangings. Hayford and Sealts compare the scene to the one in which Shakespeare's Othello insists on "ocular proof" in response to Iago's accusations against Desdemona (III.iii).

"Ah, your honor!" sighed Claggart, mildly shaking his shapely head as in sad deprecation of such unmerited severity of tone. Then, bridling—erecting himself as in virtuous self-assertion—he circumstantially alleged certain words and acts which collectively, if credited, led to presumptions mortally inculpating Budd. And for some of these averments, he added, substantiating proof was not far.

With gray eyes impatient and distrustful essaying to fathom to the bottom Claggart's calm violet ones, Captain Vere again heard him out; then for the moment stood ruminating. The mood he evinced, Claggart—himself for the time liberated from the other's scrutiny—steadily regarded with a look difficult to render: a look curious of the operation of his tactics, a look such as might have been that of the spokesman of the envious children of Jacob deceptively imposing upon the troubled patriarch the blood-dyed coat of young Joseph.[82]

Though something exceptional in the moral quality of Captain Vere made him, in earnest encounter with a fellow man, a veritable touchstone of that man's essential nature, yet now as to Claggart and what was really going on in him his feeling partook less of intuitional conviction than of strong suspicion clogged by strange dubieties. The perplexity he evinced proceeded less from aught touching the man informed against—as Claggart doubtless opined—than from considerations how best to act in regard to the informer. At first, indeed, he was naturally for summoning that substantiation of his allegations which Claggart said was at hand. But such a proceeding would result in the matter at once getting abroad, which in the present stage of it, he thought, might undesirably affect the ship's company. If Claggart was a false witness—that closed the affair. And therefore, before trying the accusation, he would first practically test the accuser; and he thought this could be done in a quiet, undemonstrative way.

The measure he determined upon involved a shifting of the scene, a transfer to a place less exposed to observation than the broad quarter-deck. For although the few gun-room officers there at the time had, in due observance of naval etiquette, withdrawn to leeward the moment Captain Vere had begun his promenade on the deck's weather side; and though during the colloquy with Claggart they of course ventured not to diminish the distance; and though throughout the interview Captain Vere's voice was far from high, and Claggart's silvery and low; and the wind in the cordage and the wash of the sea helped the more to put them beyond earshot; nevertheless, the interview's continuance already had attracted observation from some topmen aloft and other sailors in the waist or further forward.

Having determined upon his measures, Captain Vere forthwith took action. Abruptly turning to Claggart, he asked, "Master-at-arms, is it now Budd's watch aloft?"

---

[82]After selling Joseph into slavery, his jealous brothers dipped his coat in blood to convince their father Jacob that Joseph had been killed by a wild beast (Genesis 37:31–33).

"No, your honor."

Whereupon, "Mr. Wilkes!" summoning the nearest midshipman. "Tell Albert to come to me." Albert was the captain's hammock-boy, a sort of sea valet in whose discretion and fidelity his master had much confidence. The lad appeared.

"You know Budd, the foretopman?"

"I do, sir."

"Go find him. It is his watch off. Manage to tell him out of earshot that he is wanted aft. Contrive it that he speaks to nobody. Keep him in talk yourself. And not till you get well aft here, not till then let him know that the place where he is wanted is my cabin. You understand. Go.—Master-at-arms, show yourself on the decks below, and when you think it time for Albert to be coming with his man, stand by quietly to follow the sailor in."

19

Now when the foretopman found himself in the cabin, closeted there, as it were, with the captain and Claggart, he was surprised enough. But it was a surprise unaccompanied by apprehension or distrust. To an immature nature essentially honest and humane, forewarning intimations of subtler danger from one's kind come tardily if at all. The only thing that took shape in the young sailor's mind was this: Yes, the captain, I have always thought, looks kindly upon me. Wonder if he's going to make me his coxswain. I should like that. And may be now he is going to ask the master-at-arms about me.

"Shut the door there, sentry," said the commander; "stand without, and let nobody come in.—Now, Master-at-arms, tell this man to his face what you told of him to me," and stood prepared to scrutinize the mutually con-fronting visages.

With the measured step and calm collected air of an asylum physician approaching in the public hall some patient beginning to show indications of a coming paroxysm, Claggart deliberately advanced within short range of Billy and, mesmerically looking him in the eye, briefly recapitulated the accusation.

Not at first did Billy take it in. When he did, the rose-tan of his cheek looked struck as by white leprosy. He stood like one impaled and gagged. Meanwhile the accuser's eyes, removing not as yet from the blue dilated ones, underwent a phenomenal change, their wonted rich violet color blur-ring into a muddy purple. Those lights of human intelligence, losing human expression, were gelidly protruding like the alien eyes of certain uncata-logued creatures of the deep. The first mesmeristic glance was one of ser-pent fascination; the last was as the paralyzing lurch of the torpedo fish.[83]

"Speak, man!" said Captain Vere to the transfixed one, struck by his as-pect even more than by Claggart's. "Speak! Defend yourself!" Which appeal caused but a strange dumb gesturing and gurgling in Billy; amazement at

[83]Also known as the electric ray, a flat fish
with a tapering tail that paralyzes its victims
with electricity.

such an accusation so suddenly sprung on inexperienced nonage;[84] this, and, it may be, horror of the accuser's eyes, serving to bring out his lurking defect and in this instance for the time intensifying it into a convulsed tongue-tie; while the intent head and entire form straining forward in an agony of ineffectual eagerness to obey the injunction to speak and defend himself, gave an expression to the face like that of a condemned vestal priestess in the moment of being buried alive, and in the first struggle against suffocation.[85]

Though at the time Captain Vere was quite ignorant of Billy's liability to vocal impediment, he now immediately divined it, since vividly Billy's aspect recalled to him that of a bright young schoolmate of his whom he had once seen struck by much the same startling impotence in the act of eagerly rising in the class to be foremost in response to a testing question put to it by the master. Going close up to the young sailor, and laying a soothing hand on his shoulder, he said, "There is no hurry, my boy. Take your time, take your time." Contrary to the effect intended, these words so fatherly in tone, doubtless touching Billy's heart to the quick, prompted yet more violent efforts at utterance—efforts soon ending for the time in confirming the paralysis, and bringing to his face an expression which was as a crucifixion to behold. The next instant, quick as the flame from a discharged cannon at night, his right arm shot out, and Claggart dropped to the deck. Whether intentionally or but owing to the young athlete's superior height, the blow had taken effect full upon the forehead, so shapely and intellectual-looking a feature in the master-at-arms; so that the body fell over lengthwise, like a heavy plank tilted from erectness. A gasp or two, and he lay motionless.

"Fated boy," breathed Captain Vere in tone so low as to be almost a whisper, "what have you done! But here, help me."

The twain raised the felled one from the loins up into a sitting position. The spare form flexibly acquiesced, but inertly. It was like handling a dead snake. They lowered it back. Regaining erectness, Captain Vere with one hand covering his face stood to all appearance as impassive as the object at his feet. Was he absorbed in taking in all the bearings of the event and what was best not only now at once to be done, but also in the sequel? Slowly he uncovered his face; and the effect was as if the moon emerging from eclipse should reappear with quite another aspect than that which had gone into hiding. The father in him, manifested towards Billy thus far in the scene, was replaced by the military disciplinarian. In his official tone he bade the foretopman retire to a stateroom aft (pointing it out), and there remain till thence summoned. This order Billy in silence mechanically obeyed. Then going to the cabin door where it opened on the quarter-deck, Captain Vere said to the sentry without, "Tell somebody to send Albert here." When the lad appeared, his master so contrived it that he should not catch sight of

---

[84]Youth.
[85]The vestal virgins, priestesses of the Roman goddess Vesta, were buried alive for violating their vows of chastity.

the prone one. "Albert," he said to him, "tell the surgeon I wish to see him. You need not come back till called."

When the surgeon entered—a self-poised character of that grave sense and experience that hardly anything could take him aback—Captain Vere advanced to meet him, thus unconsciously intercepting his view of Claggart, and, interrupting the other's wonted ceremonious salutation, said, "Nay. Tell me how it is with yonder man," directing his attention to the prostrate one.

The surgeon looked, and for all his self-command somewhat started at the abrupt revelation. On Claggart's always pallid complexion, thick black blood was now oozing from nostril and ear. To the gazer's professional eye it was unmistakably no living man that he saw.

"Is it so, then?" said Captain Vere, intently watching him. "I thought it. But verify it." Whereupon the customary tests confirmed the surgeon's first glance, who now, looking up in unfeigned concern, cast a look of intense inquisitiveness upon his superior. But Captain Vere, with one hand to his brow, was standing motionless. Suddenly, catching the surgeon's arm convulsively, he exclaimed, pointing down to the body, "It is the divine judgment on Ananias![86] Look!"

Disturbed by the excited manner he had never before observed in the *Bellipotent*'s captain, and as yet wholly ignorant of the affair, the prudent surgeon nevertheless held his peace, only again looking an earnest interrogatory as to what it was that had resulted in such a tragedy.

But Captain Vere was now again motionless, standing absorbed in thought. Again starting, he vehemently exclaimed, "Struck dead by an angel of God! Yet the angel must hang!"

At these passionate interjections, mere incoherences to the listener as yet unapprised of the antecedents, the surgeon was profoundly discomposed. But now, as recollecting himself, Captain Vere in less passionate tone briefly related the circumstances leading up to the event. "But come; we must dispatch," he added. "Help me to remove him" (meaning the body) "to yonder compartment," designating one opposite that where the foretopman remained immured. Anew disturbed by a request that, as implying a desire for secrecy, seemed unaccountably strange to him, there was nothing for the subordinate to do but comply.

"Go now," said Captain Vere with something of his wonted manner. "Go now. I presently shall call a drumhead court.[87] Tell the lieutenants what has happened, and tell Mr. Mordant" (meaning the captain of marines), "and charge them to keep the matter to themselves."

---

[86]In Acts 5:3–5, the Apostle Peter tells the false Christian Ananias, "thou hast not lied unto men, but unto God," whereupon Ananias falls dead.

[87]A court-martial held on the spot to try offenses committed during military operations (from the upturned drum used as a table).

20

Full of disquietude and misgiving, the surgeon left the cabin. Was Captain Vere suddenly affected in his mind, or was it but a transient excitement, brought about by so strange and extraordinary a tragedy? As to the drumhead court, it struck the surgeon as impolitic, if nothing more. The thing to do, he thought, was to place Billy Budd in confinement, and in a way dictated by usage, and postpone further action in so extraordinary a case to such time as they should rejoin the squadron, and then refer it to the admiral. He recalled the unwonted agitation of Captain Vere and his excited exclamations, so at variance with his normal manner. Was he unhinged?

But assuming that he is, it is not so susceptible of proof. What then can the surgeon do? No more trying situation is conceivable than that of an officer subordinate under a captain whom he suspects to be not mad, indeed, but yet not quite unaffected in his intellects. To argue his order to him would be insolence. To resist him would be mutiny.

In obedience to Captain Vere, he communicated what had happened to the lieutenants and captain of marines, saying nothing as to the captain's state. They fully shared his own surprise and concern. Like him too, they seemed to think that such a matter should be referred to the admiral.

21

Who in the rainbow can draw the line where the violet tint ends and the orange tint begins? Distinctly we see the difference of the colors, but where exactly does the one first blendingly enter into the other? So with sanity and insanity. In pronounced cases there is no question about them. But in some supposed cases, in various degrees supposedly less pronounced, to draw the exact line of demarcation few will undertake, though for a fee becoming considerate some professional experts will. There is nothing namable but that some men will, or undertake to, do it for pay.

Whether Captain Vere, as the surgeon professionally and privately surmised, was really the sudden victim of any degree of aberration, every one must determine for himself by such light as this narrative may afford.

That the unhappy event which has been narrated could not have happened at a worse juncture was but too true. For it was close on the heel of the suppressed insurrections, an aftertime very critical to naval authority, demanding from every English sea commander two qualities not readily interfusable—prudence and rigor. Moreover, there was something crucial in the case.

In the jugglery of circumstances preceding and attending the event on board the *Bellipotent*, and in the light of that martial code whereby it was formally to be judged, innocence and guilt personified in Claggart and Budd in effect changed places. In a legal view the apparent victim of the tragedy was he who had sought to victimize a man blameless; and the indisputable deed of the latter, navally regarded, constituted the most heinous of military crimes. Yet more. The essential right and wrong involved in the matter, the clearer that might be, so much the worse for the responsibility of a loyal sea commander, inasmuch as he was not authorized to determine the matter on that primitive basis.

Small wonder then that the *Bellipotent*'s captain, though in general a man of rapid decision, felt that circumspectness not less than promptitude was necessary. Until he could decide upon his course, and in each detail; and not only so, but until the concluding measure was upon the point of being enacted, he deemed it advisable, in view of all the circumstances, to guard as much as possible against publicity. Here he may or may not have erred. Certain it is, however, that subsequently in the confidential talk of more than one or two gun rooms and cabins he was not a little criticized by some officers, a fact imputed by his friends and vehemently by his cousin Jack Denton to professional jealousy of Starry Vere. Some imaginative ground for invidious comment there was. The maintenance of secrecy in the matter, the confining all knowledge of it for a time to the place where the homicide occurred, the quarter-deck cabin; in these particulars lurked some resemblance to the policy adopted in those tragedies of the palace which have occurred more than once in the capital founded by Peter the Barbarian.[88]

The case indeed was such that fain would the *Bellipotent*'s captain have deferred taking any action whatever respecting it further than to keep the foretopman a close prisoner till the ship rejoined the squadron and then submitting the matter to the judgment of his admiral.

But a true military officer is in one particular like a true monk. Not with more of self-abnegation will the latter keep his vows of monastic obedience than the former his vows of allegiance to martial duty.

Feeling that unless quick action was taken on it, the deed of the foretopman, so soon as it should be known on the gun decks, would tend to awaken any slumbering embers of the Nore among the crew, a sense of the urgency of the case overruled in Captain Vere every other consideration. But though a conscientious disciplinarian, he was no lover of authority for mere authority's sake. Very far was he from embracing opportunities for monopolizing to himself the perils of moral responsibility, none at least that could properly be referred to an official superior or shared with him by his official equals or even subordinates. So thinking, he was glad it would not be at variance with usage to turn the matter over to a summary court of his own officers, reserving to himself, as the one on whom the ultimate accountability would rest, the right of maintaining a supervision of it, or formally or informally interposing at need. Accordingly a drumhead court was summarily convened, he electing the individuals composing it: the first lieutenant, the captain of marines, and the sailing master.[89]

---

[88]Russian Czar Peter the Great (1672–1725).

[89]In *White-Jacket* Melville notes that officers habitually played marines against sailors, but the corporal of marines is also one of the two men who speak up for White-Jacket when he is arraigned at the mast to be flogged (Chaps. 67, 89). As Hayford and Sealts point out, the inclusion of these two officers in a drumhead court is "doubly a deviation 'from general custom.'" In fact British naval statutes provided that a captain refer court-martial cases to his Chief Commander, or admiral (as Vere's subordinate officers think he should have done). Critics are divided, however, as to whether Melville was familiar with those statutes.

In associating an officer of marines with the sea lieutenant and the sailing master in a case having to do with a sailor, the commander perhaps deviated from general custom. He was prompted thereto by the circumstance that he took that soldier to be a judicious person, thoughtful, and not altogether incapable of grappling with a difficult case unprecedented in his prior experience. Yet even as to him he was not without some latent misgiving, for withal he was an extremely good-natured man, an enjoyer of his dinner, a sound sleeper, and inclined to obesity—a man who though he would always maintain his manhood in battle might not prove altogether reliable in a moral dilemma involving aught of the tragic. As to the first lieutenant and the sailing master, Captain Vere could not but be aware that though honest natures, of approved gallantry upon occasion, their intelligence was mostly confined to the matter of active seamanship and the fighting demands of their profession.

The court was held in the same cabin where the unfortunate affair had taken place. This cabin, the commander's, embraced the entire area under the poop deck. Aft, and on either side, was a small stateroom, the one now temporarily a jail and the other a dead-house, and a yet smaller compartment, leaving a space between expanding forward into a goodly oblong of length coinciding with the ship's beam. A skylight of moderate dimension was overhead, and at each end of the oblong space were two sashed porthole windows easily convertible back into embrasures for short carronades.[90]

All being quickly in readiness, Billy Budd was arraigned, Captain Vere necessarily appearing as the sole witness in the case, and as such temporarily sinking his rank, though singularly maintaining it in a matter apparently trivial, namely, that he testified from the ship's weather side,[91] with that object having caused the court to sit on the lee side. Concisely he narrated all that had led up to the catastrophe, omitting nothing in Claggart's accusation and deposing as to the manner in which the prisoner had received it. At this testimony the three officers glanced with no little surprise at Billy Budd, the last man they would have suspected either of the mutinous design alleged by Claggart or the undeniable deed he himself had done. The first lieutenant, taking judicial primacy and turning toward the prisoner, said, "Captain Vere has spoken. Is it or is it not as Captain Vere says?"

In response came syllables not so much impeded in the utterance as might have been anticipated. They were these: "Captain Vere tells the truth. It is just as Captain Vere says, but it is not as the master-at-arms said. I have eaten the King's bread and I am true to the King."

"I believe you, my man," said the witness, his voice indicating a suppressed emotion not otherwise betrayed.

"God will bless you for that, your honor!" not without stammering said Billy, and all but broke down. But immediately he was recalled to self-

[90]Openings for light iron cannons.
[91]The side from which the wind is blowing, hence the higher side, raising Vere above the level of the court.

control by another question, to which with the same emotional difficulty of utterance he said, "No, there was no malice between us. I never bore malice against the master-at-arms. I am sorry that he is dead. I did not mean to kill him. Could I have used my tongue I would not have struck him. But he foully lied to my face and in presence of my captain, and I had to say something, and I could only say it with a blow, God help me!"

In the impulsive aboveboard manner of the frank one the court saw confirmed all that was implied in words that just previously had perplexed them, coming as they did from the testifier to the tragedy and promptly following Billy's impassioned disclaimer of mutinous intent—Captain Vere's words, "I believe you, my man."

Next it was asked of him whether he knew of or suspected aught savoring of incipient trouble (meaning mutiny, though the explicit term was avoided) going on in any section of the ship's company.

The reply lingered. This was naturally imputed by the court to the same vocal embarrassment which had retarded or obstructed previous answers. But in main it was otherwise here, the question immediately recalling to Billy's mind the interview with the afterguardsman in the forechains. But an innate repugnance to playing a part at all approaching that of an informer against one's own shipmates—the same erring sense of uninstructed honor which had stood in the way of his reporting the matter at the time, though as a loyal man-of-war's man it was incumbent on him, and failure so to do, if charged against him and proven, would have subjected him to the heaviest of penalties; this, with the blind feeling now his that nothing really was being hatched, prevailed with him. When the answer came it was a negative.

"One question more," said the officer of marines, now first speaking and with a troubled earnestness. "You tell us that what the master-at-arms said against you was a lie. Now why should he have so lied, so maliciously lied, since you declare there was no malice between you?"

At that question, unintentionally touching on a spiritual sphere wholly obscure to Billy's thoughts, he was nonplussed, evincing a confusion indeed that some observers, such as can readily be imagined, would have construed into involuntary evidence of hidden guilt. Nevertheless, he strove some way to answer, but all at once relinquished the vain endeavor, at the same time turning an appealing glance towards Captain Vere as deeming him his best helper and friend. Captain Vere, who had been seated for a time, rose to his feet, addressing the interrogator. "The question you put to him comes naturally enough. But how can he rightly answer it?—or anybody else, unless indeed it be he who lies within there," designating the compartment where lay the corpse. "But the prone one there will not rise to our summons. In effect, though, as it seems to me, the point you make is hardly material. Quite aside from any conceivable motive actuating the master-at-arms, and irrespective of the provocation to the blow, a martial court must needs in the present case confine its attention to the blow's consequence, which consequence justly is to be deemed not otherwise than as the striker's deed."

This utterance, the full significance of which it was not at all likely that Billy took in, nevertheless caused him to turn a wistful interrogative look toward the speaker, a look in its dumb expressiveness not unlike that which a dog of generous breed might turn upon his master, seeking in his face some elucidation of a previous gesture ambiguous to the canine intelligence.[92] Nor was the same utterance without marked effect upon the three officers, more especially the soldier. Couched in it seemed to them a meaning unanticipated, involving a prejudgment on the speaker's part. It served to augment a mental disturbance previously evident enough.

The soldier once more spoke, in a tone of suggestive dubiety addressing at once his associates and Captain Vere: "Nobody is present—none of the ship's company, I mean—who might shed lateral light, if any is to be had, upon what remains mysterious in this matter."

"That is thoughtfully put," said Captain Vere; "I see your drift. Ay, there is a mystery; but, to use a scriptural phrase, it is a 'mystery of iniquity,' a matter for psychologic theologians to discuss. But what has a military court to do with it? Not to add that for us any possible investigation of it is cut off by the lasting tongue-tie of—him—in yonder," again designating the mortuary stateroom. "The prisoner's deed—with that alone we have to do."

To this, and particularly the closing reiteration, the marine soldier, knowing not how aptly to reply, sadly abstained from saying aught. The first lieutenant, who at the outset had not unnaturally assumed primacy in the court, now overrulingly instructed by a glance from Captain Vere, a glance more effective than words, resumed that primacy. Turning to the prisoner, "Budd," he said, and scarce in equable tones, "Budd, if you have aught further to say for yourself, say it now."

Upon this the young sailor turned another quick glance toward Captain Vere; then, as taking a hint from that aspect, a hint confirming his own instinct that silence was now best, replied to the lieutenant, "I have said all, sir."

The marine—the same who had been the sentinel without the cabin door at the time that the foretopman, followed by the master-at-arms, entered it—he, standing by the sailor throughout these judicial proceedings, was now directed to take him back to the after compartment originally assigned to the prisoner and his custodian. As the twain disappeared from view, the three officers, as partially liberated from some inward constraint associated with Billy's mere presence, simultaneously stirred in their seats. They exchanged looks of troubled indecision, yet feeling that decide they

[92]In *White-Jacket* Melville objects to the "implicit, unquestioning, dog-like devotion to whoever may be lord and master" that Dibdin's songs inculcate in sailors (Chapter 90).

must and without long delay. For Captain Vere, he for the time stood—
unconsciously with his back toward them, apparently in one of his absent
fits—gazing out from a sashed porthole to windward upon the monotonous
blank of the twilight sea. But the court's silence continuing, broken only at
moments by brief consultations, in low earnest tones, this served to arouse
him and energize him. Turning, he to-and-fro paced the cabin athwart; in
the returning ascent to windward climbing the slant deck in the ship's lee
roll, without knowing it symbolizing thus in his action a mind resolute to
surmount difficulties even if against primitive instincts strong as the wind
and the sea. Presently he came to a stand before the three. After scanning
their faces he stood less as mustering his thoughts for expression than as
one inly deliberating how best to put them to well-meaning men not intellectually mature, men with whom it was necessary to demonstrate certain
principles that were axioms to himself. Similar impatience as to talking is
perhaps one reason that deters some minds from addressing any popular
assemblies.

When speak he did, something, both in the substance of what he said
and his manner of saying it, showed the influence of unshared studies modi-
fying and tempering the practical training of an active career. This, along
with his phraseology, now and then was suggestive of the grounds whereon
rested that imputation of a certain pedantry socially alleged against him by
certain naval men of wholly practical cast, captains who nevertheless would
frankly concede that His Majesty's navy mustered no more efficient officer
of their grade than Starry Vere.

What he said was to this effect: "Hitherto I have been but the witness,
little more; and I should hardly think now to take another tone, that of your
coadjutor for the time, did I not perceive in you—at the crisis too—a troubled hesitancy, proceeding, I doubt not, from the clash of military duty with
moral scruple—scruple vitalized by compassion. For the compassion, how
can I otherwise than share it? But, mindful of paramount obligations, I
strive against scruples that may tend to enervate decision. Not, gentlemen,
that I hide from myself that the case is an exceptional one. Speculatively
regarded, it well might be referred to a jury of casuists.[93] But for us here,
acting not as casuists or moralists, it is a case practical, and under martial
law practically to be dealt with.

"But your scruples: do they move as in a dusk? Challenge them. Make
them advance and declare themselves. Come now; do they import something
like this: If, mindless of palliating circumstances, we are bound to regard the
death of the master-at-arms as the prisoner's deed, then does that deed constitute a capital crime whereof the penalty is a mortal one. But in natural
justice is nothing but the prisoner's overt act to be considered? How can we
adjudge to summary and shameful death a fellow creature innocent before

---

[93]Those who seek to resolve difficult cases of conscience through close reading of scrip- tural rules or legal statutes (usually with connotations of twisting rules to suit their purposes).

God, and whom we feel to be so?—Does that state it aright? You sign sad assent. Well, I too feel that, the full force of that. It is Nature. But do these buttons that we wear attest that our allegiance is to Nature? No, to the King.[94] Though the ocean, which is inviolate Nature primeval, though this be the element where we move and have our being as sailors, yet as the King's officers lies our duty in a sphere correspondingly natural? So little is that true, that in receiving our commissions we in the most important regards ceased to be natural free agents. When war is declared are we the commissioned fighters previously consulted? We fight at command. If our judgments approve the war, that is but coincidence. So in other particulars. So now. For suppose condemnation to follow these present proceedings. Would it be so much we ourselves that would condemn as it would be martial law operating through us? For that law and the rigor of it, we are not responsible. Our vowed responsibility is in this: That however pitilessly that law may operate in any instances, we nevertheless adhere to it and administer it.

"But the exceptional in the matter moves the hearts within you. Even so too is mine moved. But let not warm hearts betray heads that should be cool. Ashore in a criminal case, will an upright judge allow himself off the bench to be waylaid by some tender kinswoman of the accused seeking to touch him with her tearful plea? Well, the heart here, sometimes the feminine in man, is as that piteous woman, and hard though it be, she must here be ruled out."

He paused, earnestly studying them for a moment; then resumed.

"But something in your aspect seems to urge that it is not solely the heart that moves in you, but also the conscience, the private conscience. But tell me whether or not, occupying the position we do, private conscience should not yield to that imperial one formulated in the code under which alone we officially proceed?"

Here the three men moved in their seats, less convinced than agitated by the course of an argument troubling but the more the spontaneous conflict within.

Perceiving which, the speaker paused for a moment; then abruptly changing his tone, went on.

---

[94]George III (1738–1820), against whom the American colonies had just successfully revolted. As Stanton Garner has pointed out, George III, whose mental instability was an open secret, was frequently caricatured in the press as "The Button-Maker" (an allusion to his hobby of making buttons on a lathe). See Thomas Wright's *England Under the House of Hanover . . . Illustrated from the Caricatures and Satires of the Day*, 2 vols. (London: Bentley, 1848), Chapter 9, for examples. One such caricature pictures the king "as he shews his buttons to two noblemen in attendance," saying, "I cannot attend to your remonstrance! Do not you see that I have been employed in business of much more consequence?" Wright also mentions a political satire that accuses the king of indulging his taste for making buttons while neglecting the needs of his subjects, and particularly of the sailors in his navy. Even more relevant are a pair of caricatures mocking the prostitution of Justice. In one, a partially blindfolded secretary of state insists: "Somebody must be hanged for this, right or wrong, to quiet the mob and save our credit." In the other, Britannia is depicted being hanged from the gallows.

"To steady us a bit, let us recur to the facts.—In wartime at sea a man-of-war's man strikes his superior in grade, and the blow kills. Apart from its effect the blow itself is, according to the Articles of War, a capital crime. Furthermore—"

"Ay, sir," emotionally broke in the officer of marines, "in one sense it was. But surely Budd purposed neither mutiny nor homicide."

"Surely not, my good man. And before a court less arbitrary and more merciful than a martial one, that plea would largely extenuate. At the Last Assizes[95] it shall acquit. But how here? We proceed under the law of the Mutiny Act. In feature no child can resemble his father more than that Act resembles in spirit the thing from which it derives—War. In His Majesty's service—in this ship, indeed—there are Englishmen forced to fight for the King against their will. Against their conscience, for aught we know. Though as their fellow creatures some of us may appreciate their position, yet as navy officers what reck we of it? Still less recks the enemy. Our impressed men he would fain cut down in the same swath with our volunteers. As regards the enemy's naval conscripts, some of whom may even share our own abhorrence of the regicidal French Directory, it is the same on our side. War looks but to the frontage, the appearance. And the Mutiny Act, War's child, takes after the father. Budd's intent or non-intent is nothing to the purpose.

"But while, put to it by those anxieties in you which I cannot but respect, I only repeat myself—while thus strangely we prolong proceedings that should be summary—the enemy may be sighted and an engagement result. We must do; and one of two things must we do—condemn or let go."

"Can we not convict and yet mitigate the penalty?" asked the sailing master, here speaking, and falteringly, for the first.

"Gentlemen, were that clearly lawful for us under the circumstances, consider the consequences of such clemency. The people" (meaning the ship's company) "have native sense; most of them are familiar with our naval usage and tradition; and how would they take it? Even could you explain to them—which our official position forbids—they, long molded by arbitrary discipline, have not that kind of intelligent responsiveness that might qualify them to comprehend and discriminate. No, to the people the foretopman's deed, however it be worded in the announcement, will be plain homicide committed in a flagrant act of mutiny. What penalty for that should follow, they know. But it does not follow. *Why?* they will ruminate. You know what sailors are. Will they not revert to the recent outbreak at the Nore? Ay. They know the well-founded alarm—the panic it struck throughout England. Your clement sentence they would account pusillanimous. They would think that we flinch, that we are afraid of them—afraid of practicing a lawful rigor singularly demanded at this juncture, lest it should provoke new troubles. What shame to us such a conjecture on their part, and how deadly to discipline. You see then, whither,

[95]The Last Judgment.

prompted by duty and the law, I steadfastly drive. But I beseech you, my friends, do not take me amiss. I feel as you do for this unfortunate boy. But did he know our hearts, I take him to be of that generous nature that he would feel even for us on whom in this military necessity so heavy a compulsion is laid."

With that, crossing the deck he resumed his place by the sashed port-hole, tacitly leaving the three to come to a decision. On the cabin's opposite side the troubled court sat silent. Loyal lieges, plain and practical, though at bottom they dissented from some points Captain Vere had put to them, they were without the faculty, hardly had the inclination, to gainsay one whom they felt to be an earnest man, one too not less their superior in mind than in naval rank. But it is not improbable that even such of his words as were not without influence over them, less came home to them than his closing appeal to their instinct as sea officers: in the forethought he threw out as to the practical consequences to discipline, considering the unconfirmed tone of the fleet at the time, should a man-of-war's man's violent killing at sea of a superior in grade be allowed to pass for aught else than a capital crime demanding prompt infliction of the penalty.

Not unlikely they were brought to something more or less akin to that harassed frame of mind which in the year 1842 actuated the commander of the U.S. brig-of-war *Somers* to resolve, under the so-called Articles of War, Articles modeled upon the English Mutiny Act, to resolve upon the execution at sea of a midshipman and two sailors as mutineers designing the seizure of the brig.[96] Which resolution was carried out though in a time of peace and within not many days' sail of home. An act vindicated by a naval court of inquiry subsequently convened ashore. History, and here cited without comment. True, the circumstances on board the *Somers* were different from those on board the *Bellipotent*. But the urgency felt, well-warranted or otherwise, was much the same.

Says a writer whom few know, "Forty years after a battle it is easy for a noncombatant to reason about how it ought to have been fought. It is another thing personally and under fire to have to direct the fighting while involved in the obscuring smoke of it. Much so with respect to other emergencies involving considerations both practical and moral, and when it is imperative promptly to act. The greater the fog the more it imperils the steamer, and speed is put on though at the hazard of running somebody down.[97] Little ween the snug card players in the cabin of the responsibilities of the sleepless man on the bridge."

[96]*White-Jacket* cites the *Somers* case to illustrate the arbitrary tyranny under which sailors lived and the harshness of the naval code embodied in the Articles of War (Chap. 72). Melville's cousin Guert Gansevoort, first lieutenant of the *Somers*, was implicated in the decision to hang the three alleged mutineers.

[97]Stanton Garner points out that in *Redburn* (Chap. 20), Melville describes the opposite practice of shortening sail to reduce speed in a fog, and that the practices of reducing speed and sounding warnings in a fog were "codified into international law" in 1889, while Melville was writing *Billy Budd*.

In brief, Billy Budd was formally convicted and sentenced to be hung at the yardarm in the early morning watch, it being now night. Otherwise, as is customary in such cases, the sentence would forthwith have been carried out. In wartime on the field or in the fleet, a mortal punishment decreed by a drumhead court—on the field sometimes decreed by but a nod from the general—follows without delay on the heel of conviction, without appeal.

22

It was Captain Vere himself who of his own motion communicated the finding of the court to the prisoner, for that purpose going to the compartment where he was in custody and bidding the marine there to withdraw for the time.

Beyond the communication of the sentence, what took place at this interview was never known. But in view of the character of the twain briefly closeted in that stateroom, each radically sharing in the rarer qualities of our nature—so rare indeed as to be all but incredible to average minds however much cultivated—some conjectures may be ventured.

It would have been in consonance with the spirit of Captain Vere should he on this occasion have concealed nothing from the condemned one— should he indeed have frankly disclosed to him the part he himself had played in bringing about the decision, at the same time revealing his actuating motives. On Billy's side it is not improbable that such a confession would have been received in much the same spirit that prompted it. Not without a sort of joy, indeed, he might have appreciated the brave opinion of him implied in his captain's making such a confidant of him. Nor, as to the sentence itself, could he have been insensible that it was imparted to him as to one not afraid to die. Even more may have been. Captain Vere in end may have developed the passion sometimes latent under an exterior stoical or indifferent. He was old enough to have been Billy's father. The austere devotee of military duty, letting himself melt back into what remains primeval in our formalized humanity, may in end have caught Billy to his heart, even as Abraham may have caught young Isaac on the brink of resolutely offering him up in obedience to the exacting behest.[98] But there is no telling the sacrament, seldom if in any case revealed to the gadding world, wherever under circumstances at all akin to those here attempted to be set forth two of great Nature's nobler order embrace. There is privacy at the time, inviolable to the survivor; and holy oblivion, the sequel to each diviner magnanimity, providentially covers all at last.

The first to encounter Captain Vere in act of leaving the compartment was the senior lieutenant. The face he beheld, for the moment one expressive of the agony of the strong, was to that officer, though a man

---

[98]In Genesis 22:1–13, God tries Abraham's faith by commanding him to sacrifice his only son Isaac, but as Abraham is standing over Isaac with upraised knife, an angel intervenes with the words: "Lay not thine hand upon the lad ... for now I know that thou fearest God, seeing thou has not withheld thy son. ..."

of fifty, a startling revelation. That the condemned one suffered less than
he who mainly had effected the condemnation was apparently indicated
by the former's exclamation in the scene soon perforce to be touched
upon.

23

Of a series of incidents within a brief term rapidly following each other, the
adequate narration may take up a term less brief, especially if explanation
or comment here and there seem requisite to the better understanding of
such incidents. Between the entrance into the cabin of him who never left it
alive, and him who when he did leave it left it as one condemned to die;
between this and the closeted interview just given, less than an hour and a
half had elapsed. It was an interval long enough, however, to awaken speculations among no few of the ship's company as to what it was that could be
detaining in the cabin the master-at-arms and the sailor; for a rumor that
both of them had been seen to enter it and neither of them had been seen
to emerge, this rumor had got abroad upon the gun decks and in the tops,
the people of a great warship being in one respect like villagers, taking microscopic note of every outward movement or non-movement going on.
When therefore, in weather not at all tempestuous, all hands were called in
the second dogwatch, a summons under such circumstances not usual in
those hours, the crew were not wholly unprepared for some announcement
extraordinary, one having connection too with the continued absence of the
two men from their wonted haunts.

There was a moderate sea at the time; and the moon, newly risen and
near to being at its full, silvered the white spar deck wherever not blotted
by the clear-cut shadows horizontally thrown of fixtures and moving men.
On either side the quarter-deck the marine guard under arms was drawn up;
and Captain Vere, standing in his place surrounded by all the wardroom
officers, addressed his men. In so doing, his manner showed neither more
nor less than that properly pertaining to his supreme position aboard his
own ship. In clear terms and concise he told them what had taken place in
the cabin: that the master-at-arms was dead, that he who had killed him
had been already tried by a summary court and condemned to death, and
that the execution would take place in the early morning watch. The word
mutiny was not named in what he said. He refrained too from making the
occasion an opportunity for any preachment as to the maintenance of discipline, thinking perhaps that under existing circumstances in the navy the
consequence of violating discipline should be made to speak for itself.

Their captain's announcement was listened to by the throng of standing
sailors in a dumbness like that of a seated congregation of believers in hell
listening to the clergyman's announcement of his Calvinistic text.

At the close, however, a confused murmur went up. It began to wax. All
but instantly, then, at a sign, it was pierced and suppressed by shrill whistles
of the boatswain and his mates. The word was given to about ship.

To be prepared for burial Claggart's body was delivered to certain petty officers of his mess. And here, not to clog the sequel with lateral matters, it may be added that at a suitable hour, the master-at-arms was committed to the sea with every funeral honor properly belonging to his naval grade.

In this proceeding as in every public one growing out of the tragedy strict adherence to usage was observed. Nor in any point could it have been at all deviated from, either with respect to Claggart or Billy Budd, without begetting undesirable speculations in the ship's company, sailors, and more particularly men-of-war's men, being of all men the greatest sticklers for usage. For similar cause, all communication between Captain Vere and the condemned one ended with the closeted interview already given, the latter being now surrendered to the ordinary routine preliminary to the end. His transfer under guard from the captain's quarters was effected without unusual precautions—at least no visible ones. If possible, not to let the men so much as surmise that their officers anticipate aught amiss from them is the tacit rule in a military ship. And the more that some sort of trouble should really be apprehended, the more do the officers keep that apprehension to themselves, though not the less unostentatious vigilance may be augmented. In the present instance, the sentry placed over the prisoner had strict orders to let no one have communication with him but the chaplain. And certain unobtrusive measures were taken absolutely to insure this point.

24

In a seventy-four of the old order the deck known as the upper gun deck was the one covered over by the spar deck, which last, though not without its armament, was for the most part exposed to the weather. In general it was at all hours free from hammocks; those of the crew swinging on the lower gun deck and berth deck, the latter being not only a dormitory but also the place for the stowing of the sailors' bags, and on both sides lined with the large chests or movable pantries of the many messes of the men.

On the starboard side of the *Bellipotent*'s upper gun deck, behold Billy Budd under sentry lying prone in irons in one of the bays formed by the regular spacing of the guns comprising the batteries on either side. All these pieces were of the heavier caliber of that period. Mounted on lumbering wooden carriages, they were hampered with cumbersome harness of breeching and strong side-tackles for running them out. Guns and carriages, together with the long rammers and shorter linstocks[99] lodged in loops overhead—all these, as customary, were painted black; and the heavy hempen breechings, tarred to the same tint, wore the like livery of the undertakers. In contrast with the funereal hue of these surroundings, the prone sailor's exterior apparel, white jumper and white duck trousers, each more or less soiled, dimly glimmered in the obscure light of the bay like a

---

[99]Sticks with pointed feet and forked tips, used to hold lighted matches when firing cannons.

patch of discolored snow in early April lingering at some upland cave's black mouth. In effect he is already in his shroud, or the garments that shall serve him in lieu of one. Over him but scarce illuminating him, two battle lanterns swing from two massive beams of the deck above. Fed with the oil supplied by the war contractors (whose gains, honest or otherwise, are in every land an anticipated portion of the harvest of death), with flickering splashes of dirty yellow light they pollute the pale moonshine all but ineffectually struggling in obstructed flecks through the open ports from which the tampioned[100] cannon protrude. Other lanterns at intervals serve but to bring out somewhat the obscurer bays which, like small confessionals or side-chapels in a cathedral, branch from the long dim-vistaed broad aisle between the two batteries of that covered tier.

Such was the deck where now lay the Handsome Sailor. Through the rose-tan of his complexion no pallor could have shown. It would have taken days of sequestration from the winds and the sun to have brought about the effacement of that. But the skeleton in the cheekbone at the point of its angle was just beginning delicately to be defined under the warm-tinted skin. In fervid hearts self-contained, some brief experiences devour our human tissue as secret fire in a ship's hold consumes cotton in the bale.

But now lying between the two guns, as nipped in the vice of fate, Billy's agony, mainly proceeding from a generous young heart's virgin experience of the diabolical incarnate and effective in some men—the tension of that agony was over now. It survived not the something healing in the closeted interview with Captain Vere. Without movement, he lay as in a trance, that adolescent expression previously noted as his taking on something akin to the look of a slumbering child in the cradle when the warm hearth-glow of the still chamber at night plays on the dimples that at whiles mysteriously form in the cheek, silently coming and going there. For now and then in the gyved[101] one's trance a serene happy light born of some wandering reminiscence or dream would diffuse itself over his face, and then wane away only anew to return.

The chaplain, coming to see him and finding him thus, and perceiving no sign that he was conscious of his presence, attentively regarded him for a space, then slipping aside, withdrew for the time, peradventure feeling that even he, the minister of Christ though receiving his stipend from Mars, had no consolation to proffer which could result in a peace transcending that which he beheld. But in the small hours he came again. And the prisoner, now awake to his surroundings, noticed his approach, and civilly, all but cheerfully, welcomed him. But it was to little purpose that in the interview following, the good man sought to bring Billy Budd to some godly understanding that he must die, and at dawn. True, Billy himself freely referred to his death as a thing close at hand; but it was something in the way that children will refer to death in general, who yet among their other sports will play a funeral with hearse and mourners.

---

[100]Plugged, muzzled. [101]Fettered, shackled.

Not that like children Billy was incapable of conceiving what death really is. No, but he was wholly without irrational fear of it, a fear more prevalent in highly civilized communities than those so-called barbarous ones which in all respects stand nearer to unadulterate Nature. And, as elsewhere said, a barbarian Billy radically was—as much so, for all the costume, as his countrymen the British captives, living trophies, made to march in the Roman triumph of Germanicus.[102] Quite as much so as those later barbarians, young men probably, and picked specimens among the earlier British converts to Christianity, at least nominally such, taken to Rome (as today converts from lesser isles of the sea may be taken to London), of whom the Pope of that time, admiring the strangeness of their personal beauty so unlike the Italian stamp, their clear ruddy complexion and curled flaxen locks, exclaimed, "Angles" (meaning *English*, the modern derivative), "Angles, do you call them? And is it because they look so like angels?"[103] Had it been later in time, one would think that the Pope had in mind Fra Angelico's seraphs, some of whom, plucking apples in gardens of the Hesperides,[104] have the faint rosebud complexion of the more beautiful English girls.

If in vain the good chaplain sought to impress the young barbarian with ideas of death akin to those conveyed in the skull, dial, and crossbones on old tombstones, equally futile to all appearance were his efforts to bring home to him the thought of salvation and a Savior. Billy listened, but less out of awe or reverence, perhaps, than from a certain natural politeness, doubtless at bottom regarding all that in much the same way that most mariners of his class take any discourse abstract or out of the common tone of the workaday world. And this sailor way of taking clerical discourse is not wholly unlike the way in which the primer of Christianity, full of transcendent miracles, was received long ago on tropic isles by any superior *savage*, so called—a Tahitian, say, of Captain Cook's[105] time or shortly after that time. Out of natural courtesy he received, but did not appropriate. It was like a gift placed in the palm of an outreached hand upon which the fingers do not close.

But the *Bellipotent*'s chaplain was a discreet man possessing the good sense of a good heart. So he insisted not in his vocation here. At the instance of Captain Vere, a lieutenant had apprised him of pretty much

---

[102]Germanicus Caesar (15 B.C.–A.D. 19), fought German tribes and received a hero's triumph in Rome in A.D. 17, described in the *Annals* of Tacitus, 2.41. The captives displayed were German, not British, however. Melville may be thinking of a later passage in the *Annals*, 12.33–37, describing the capture of the British hero Caractacus, displayed in Rome with his family in A.D. 50.

[103]Pope Gregory the Great (540?–604). This episode occurred before Gregory became Pope, however, and the Angles were not converts, but slaves being exposed for sale in the market.

[104]The Florentine painter Fra Angelico (1387–1455) was famous for his angels (hence his name). In Greek mythology, the Hesperides were daughters of Atlas in whose garden grew a tree with golden apples, guarded by a dragon.

[105]James Cook (1728–1779), English navigator, who first visited Tahiti in 1769. Melville discusses the attitude of the Tahitians toward Christian missionaries in *Omoo*, Chap. 45.

everything as to Billy; and since he felt that innocence was even a better thing than religion wherewith to go to Judgment, he reluctantly withdrew; but in his emotion not without first performing an act strange enough in an Englishman, and under the circumstances yet more so in any regular priest. Stooping over, he kissed on the fair cheek his fellow man,[106] a felon in martial law, one whom though on the confines of death he felt he could never convert to a dogma; nor for all that did he fear for his future.

Marvel not that having been made acquainted with the young sailor's essential innocence the worthy man lifted not a finger to avert the doom of such a martyr to martial discipline. So to do would not only have been as idle as invoking the desert, but would also have been an audacious transgression of the bounds of his function, one as exactly prescribed to him by military law as that of the boatswain or any other naval officer. Bluntly put, a chaplain is the minister of the Prince of Peace serving in the host of the God of War—Mars. As such, he is as incongruous as a musket would be on the altar at Christmas. Why, then, is he there? Because he indirectly subserves the purpose attested by the cannon; because too he lends the sanction of the religion of the meek to that which practically is the abrogation of everything but brute Force.

25

The night so luminous on the spar deck, but otherwise on the cavernous ones below, levels so like the tiered galleries in a coal mine—the luminous night passed away. But like the prophet in the chariot disappearing in heaven and dropping his mantle to Elisha,[107] the withdrawing night transferred its pale robe to the breaking day. A meek, shy light appeared in the East, where stretched a diaphanous fleece of white furrowed vapor. That light slowly waxed. Suddenly *eight bells* was struck aft, responded to by one louder metallic stroke from forward. It was four o'clock in the morning. Instantly the silver whistles were heard summoning all hands to witness punishment. Up through the great hatchways rimmed with racks of heavy shot the watch below came pouring, overspreading with the watch already on deck the space between the mainmast and foremast including that occupied by the capacious launch and the black booms tiered on either side of it, boat and booms making a summit of observation for the powder-boys and younger tars. A different group comprising one watch of topmen leaned over the rail of that sea balcony, no small one in a seventy-four, looking down on the crowd below. Man or boy, none spake but in whisper, and few spake at all. Captain Vere—as before, the central figure among the assembled commissioned officers—stood nigh the break of the poop deck facing forward. Just below him on the quarter-deck the marines in full

[106]Perhaps an allusion to the kiss with which Judas betrays Christ (Matthew 26:47–49).

[107]In II Kings 2:9–15, as the prophet Elijah is being carried to heaven in a chariot of fire, he drops his mantle to his disciple Elisha.

equipment were drawn up much as at the scene of the promulgated sentence.

At sea in the old time, the execution by halter of a military sailor was generally from the foreyard. In the present instance, for special reasons the mainyard was assigned. Under an arm of that yard the prisoner was presently brought up, the chaplain attending him. It was noted at the time, and remarked upon afterwards, that in this final scene the good man evinced little or nothing of the perfunctory. Brief speech indeed he had with the condemned one, but the genuine Gospel was less on his tongue than in his aspect and manner towards him. The final preparations personal to the latter being speedily brought to an end by two boatswain's mates, the consummation impended. Billy stood facing aft. At the penultimate moment, his words, his only ones, words wholly unobstructed in the utterance, were these: "God bless Captain Vere!" Syllables so unanticipated coming from one with the ignominious hemp about his neck—a conventional felon's benediction directed aft towards the quarters of honor; syllables too delivered in the clear melody of a singing bird on the point of launching from the twig— had a phenomenal effect, not unenhanced by the rare personal beauty of the young sailor, spiritualized now through late experiences so poignantly profound.

Without volition, as it were, as if indeed the ship's populace were but the vehicles of some vocal current electric, with one voice from alow and aloft came a resonant sympathetic echo: "God bless Captain Vere!" And yet at that instant Billy alone must have been in their hearts, even as in their eyes.

At the pronounced words and the spontaneous echo that voluminously rebounded them, Captain Vere, either through stoic self-control or a sort of momentary paralysis induced by emotional shock, stood erectly rigid as a musket in the ship-armorer's rack.

The hull, deliberately recovering from the periodic roll to leeward, was just regaining an even keel when the last signal, a preconcerted dumb one, was given. At the same moment it chanced that the vapory fleece hanging low in the East was shot through with a soft glory as of the fleece of the Lamb of God seen in mystical vision,[108] and simultaneously therewith, watched by the wedged mass of upturned faces, Billy ascended; and, ascending, took the full rose of the dawn.

In the pinioned figure arrived at the yard-end, to the wonder of all no motion was apparent, none save that created by the slow roll of the hull in moderate weather, so majestic in a great ship ponderously cannoned.

26

When some days afterwards, in reference to the singularity just mentioned, the purser,[109] a rather ruddy, rotund person more accurate as an

---

[108]In Revelation 1:10–16, St. John describes his vision of "one like unto the Son of man," whose "head and his hairs were white like wool," and whose "eyes were as a flame of fire."
[109]Paymaster.

accountant than profound as a philosopher, said at mess to the surgeon, "What testimony to the force lodged in will power," the latter, saturnine, spare, and tall, one in whom a discreet causticity went along with a manner less genial than polite, replied, "Your pardon, Mr. Purser. In a hanging scientifically conducted—and under special orders I myself directed how Budd's was to be effected—any movement following the completed suspension and originating in the body suspended, such movement indicates mechanical spasm in the muscular system. Hence the absence of that is no more attributable to will power, as you call it, than to horsepower—begging your pardon."

"But this muscular spasm you speak of, is not that in a degree more or less invariable in these cases?"

"Assuredly so, Mr. Purser."

"How then, my good sir, do you account for its absence in this instance?"

"Mr. Purser, it is clear that your sense of the singularity in this matter equals not mine. You account for it by what you call will power—a term not yet included in the lexicon of science. For me, I do not, with my present knowledge, pretend to account for it at all. Even should we assume the hypothesis that at the first touch of the halyards the action of Budd's heart, intensified by extraordinary emotion at its climax, abruptly stopped—much like a watch when in carelessly winding it up you strain at the finish, thus snapping the chain—even under that hypothesis how account for the phenomenon that followed?"

"You admit, then, that the absence of spasmodic movement was phenomenal."

"It was phenomenal, Mr. Purser, in the sense that it was an appearance the cause of which is not immediately to be assigned."

"But tell me, my dear sir," pertinaciously continued the other, "was the man's death effected by the halter, or was it a species of euthanasia?"[110]

"*Euthanasia*, Mr. Purser, is something like your *will power*: I doubt its authenticity as a scientific term—begging your pardon again. It is at once imaginative and metaphysical—in short, Greek.—But," abruptly changing his tone, "there is a case in the sick bay that I do not care to leave to my assistants. Beg your pardon, but excuse me." And rising from the mess he formally withdrew.

27

The silence at the moment of execution and for a moment or two continuing thereafter, a silence but emphasized by the regular wash of the sea against the hull or the flutter of a sail caused by the helmsman's eyes being

---

[110]Critics have suggested that Melville may be using the word either in the Greek sense of "patriotic self-sacrifice" or in the sense he found in Schopenhauer: "an easy death, not ushered in by disease, and free from all pain and struggle."

tempted astray, this emphasized silence was gradually disturbed by a sound not easily to be verbally rendered. Whoever has heard the freshet-wave of a torrent suddenly swelled by pouring showers in tropical mountains, showers not shared by the plain; whoever has heard the first muffled murmur of its sloping advance through precipitous woods may form some conception of the sound now heard. The seeming remoteness of its source was because of its murmurous indistinctness, since it came from close by, even from the men massed on the ship's open deck. Being inarticulate, it was dubious in significance further than it seemed to indicate some capricious revulsion of thought or feeling such as mobs ashore are liable to, in the present instance possibly implying a sullen revocation on the men's part of their involuntary echoing of Billy's benediction. But ere the murmur had time to wax into clamor it was met by a strategic command, the more telling that it came with abrupt unexpectedness: "Pipe down the starboard watch, Boatswain, and see that they go."

Shrill as the shriek of the sea hawk, the silver whistles of the boatswain and his mates pierced that ominous low sound, dissipating it; and yielding to the mechanism of discipline the throng was thinned by one-half. For the remainder, most of them were set to temporary employments connected with trimming the yards and so forth, business readily to be got up to serve occasion by any officer of the deck.

Now each proceeding that follows a mortal sentence pronounced at sea by a drumhead court is characterized by promptitude not perceptibly merging into hurry, though bordering that. The hammock, the one which had been Billy's bed when alive, having already been ballasted with shot and otherwise prepared to serve for his canvas coffin, the last offices of the sea undertakers, the sailmaker's mates, were now speedily completed. When everything was in readiness a second call for all hands, made necessary by the strategic movement before mentioned, was sounded, now to witness burial.

The details of this closing formality it needs not to give. But when the tilted plank let slide its freight into the sea, a second strange human murmur was heard, blended now with another inarticulate sound proceeding from certain larger seafowl who, their attention having been attracted by the peculiar commotion in the water resulting from the heavy sloped dive of the shotted hammock into the sea, flew screaming to the spot. So near the hull did they come, that the stridor or bony creak of their gaunt double-jointed pinions was audible. As the ship under light airs passed on, leaving the burial spot astern, they still kept circling it low down with the moving shadow of their outstretched wings and the croaked requiem of their cries.

Upon sailors as superstitious as those of the age preceding ours, men-of-war's men too who had just beheld the prodigy of repose in the form suspended in air, and now foundering in the deeps; to such mariners the action of the seafowl, though dictated by mere animal greed for prey, was big with no prosaic significance. An uncertain movement began among them, in which some encroachment was made. It was tolerated but for a moment. For suddenly the drum beat to quarters, which familiar sound happening at least twice every day, had upon the present occasion a signal peremptoriness in it. True martial discipline long continued superinduces in average man a sort of impulse whose operation at the official word of command much resembles in its promptitude the effect of an instinct.

The drumbeat dissolved the multitude, distributing most of them along the batteries of the two covered gun decks. There, as wonted, the guns' crews stood by their respective cannon erect and silent. In due course the first officer, sword under arm and standing in his place on the quarter-deck, formally received the successive reports of the sworded lieutenants commanding the sections of batteries below; the last of which reports being made, the summed report he delivered with the customary salute to the commander. All this occupied time, which in the present case was the object in beating to quarters at an hour prior to the customary one. That such variance from usage was authorized by an officer like Captain Vere, a martinet as some deemed him, was evidence of the necessity for unusual action implied in what he deemed to be temporarily the mood of his men. "With mankind," he would say, "forms, measured forms, are everything; and that is the import couched in the story of Orpheus[111] with his lyre spellbinding the wild denizens of the wood." And this he once applied to the disruption of forms going on across the Channel and the consequences thereof.

At this unwonted muster at quarters, all proceeded as at the regular hour. The band on the quarter-deck played a sacred air, after which the chaplain went through the customary morning service. That done, the drum beat the retreat; and toned by music and religious rites subserving the discipline and purposes of war, the men in their wonted orderly manner dispersed to the places allotted them when not at the guns.

And now it was full day. The fleece of low-hanging vapor had vanished, licked up by the sun that late had so glorified it. And the circumambient air in the clearness of its serenity was like smooth white marble in the polished block not yet removed from the marble-dealer's yard.

28

The symmetry of form attainable in pure fiction cannot so readily be achieved in a narration essentially having less to do with fable than with fact. Truth uncompromisingly told will always have its ragged edges; hence the conclusion of such a narration is apt to be less finished than an architectural finial.[112]

---

[111]In Greek mythology, the music of Orpheus, son of Apollo and the Muse Calliope, had the power to charm wild beasts, overcome destructive forces of nature, and even sway the relentless gods of the underworld.

[112]An ornament terminating or capping an architectural monument. Many critics have noted the contrast between this view of art and the "measured forms" Vere prefers.

How it fared with the Handsome Sailor during the year of the Great Mutiny has been faithfully given. But though properly the story ends with his life, something in way of sequel will not be amiss. Three brief chapters will suffice.

In the general rechristening under the Directory of the craft originally forming the navy of the French monarchy, the *St. Louis* line-of-battle ship was named the *Athée* (the *Atheist*). Such a name, like some other substituted ones in the Revolutionary fleet, while proclaiming the infidel audacity of the ruling power, was yet, though not so intended to be, the aptest name, if one consider it, ever given to a warship; far more so indeed than the *Devastation*, the *Erebus* (the *Hell*), and similar names bestowed upon fighting ships.

On the return passage to the English fleet from the detached cruise during which occurred the events already recorded, the *Bellipotent* fell in with the *Athée*. An engagement ensued, during which Captain Vere, in the act of putting his ship alongside the enemy with a view of throwing his boarders across her bulwarks, was hit by a musket ball from a porthole of the enemy's main cabin. More than disabled, he dropped to the deck and was carried below to the same cockpit where some of his men already lay. The senior lieutenant took command. Under him the enemy was finally captured, and though much crippled was by rare good fortune successfully taken into Gibraltar, an English port not very distant from the scene of the fight. There, Captain Vere with the rest of the wounded was put ashore. He lingered for some days, but the end came. Unhappily he was cut off too early for the Nile and Trafalgar. The spirit that 'spite its philosophic austerity may yet have indulged in the most secret of all passions, ambition, never attained to the fulness of fame.

Not long before death, while lying under the influence of that magical drug which, soothing the physical frame, mysteriously operates on the subtler element in man, he was heard to murmur words inexplicable to his attendant: "Billy Budd, Billy Budd." That these were not the accents of remorse would seem clear from what the attendant said to the *Bellipotent*'s senior officer of marines, who, as the most reluctant to condemn of the members of the drumhead court, too well knew, though here he kept the knowledge to himself, who Billy Budd was.

29

Some few weeks after the execution, among other matters under the head of "News from the Mediterranean," there appeared in a naval chronicle of the time, an authorized weekly publication, an account of the affair. It was doubtless for the most part written in good faith, though the medium, partly rumor, through which the facts must have reached the writer served to deflect and in part falsify them. The account was as follows:

"On the tenth of the last month a deplorable occurrence took place on board H.M.S. *Bellipotent*. John Claggart, the ship's master-at-arms, discovering that some sort of plot was incipient among an inferior section of the ship's company, and that the ringleader was one William Budd; he, Claggart, in the act of arraigning the man before the captain, was vindictively stabbed to the heart by the suddenly drawn sheath knife of Budd.

"The deed and the implement employed sufficiently suggest that though mustered into the service under an English name the assassin was no Englishman, but one of those aliens adopting English cognomens whom the present extraordinary necessities of the service have caused to be admitted into it in considerable numbers.

"The enormity of the crime and the extreme depravity of the criminal appear the greater in view of the character of the victim, a middle-aged man respectable and discreet, belonging to that minor official grade, the petty officers, upon whom, as none know better than the commissioned gentlemen, the efficiency of His Majesty's navy so largely depends. His function was a responsible one, at once onerous and thankless; and his fidelity in it the greater because of his strong patriotic impulse. In this instance as in so many other instances in these days, the character of this unfortunate man signally refutes, if refutation were needed, that peevish saying attributed to the late Dr. Johnson, that patriotism is the last refuge of a scoundrel.[113]

"The criminal paid the penalty of his crime. The promptitude of the punishment has proved salutary. Nothing amiss is now apprehended aboard H.M.S. *Bellipotent*."

The above, appearing in a publication now long ago superannuated and forgotten, is all that hitherto has stood in human record to attest what manner of men respectively were John Claggart and Billy Budd.

30

Everything is for a term venerated in navies. Any tangible object associated with some striking incident of the service is converted into a monument. The spar from which the foretopman was suspended was for some few years kept trace of by the bluejackets. Their knowledges followed it from ship to dockyard and again from dockyard to ship, still pursuing it even when at last reduced to a mere dockyard boom. To them a chip of it was as a piece of the Cross. Ignorant though they were of the secret facts of the tragedy, and not thinking but that the penalty was somehow unavoidably inflicted from the naval point of view, for all that, they instinctively felt that Billy was a sort of man as incapable of mutiny as of wilful murder. They recalled the fresh young image of the Handsome Sailor, that face never deformed by a sneer or subtler vile freak of the heart within. This impression of him was doubtless deepened by the fact that he was gone, and in a measure mysteriously gone. On the gun decks of the *Bellipotent* the general estimate of his nature and its unconscious simplicity eventually found rude utterance from another foretopman, one of his own watch, gifted, as some sailors are, with an artless *poetic* temperament. The tarry hand made some lines which, after

---

[113]As Hayford and Sealts note, James Boswell's *Life of Samuel Johnson* (1791) records this phrase under the date April 7, 1775, and explains that it refers to "pretended patriotism" used as "a cloak for self-interest."

circulating among the shipboard crews for a while, finally got rudely printed at Portsmouth as a ballad. The title given to it was the sailor's.

Billy in the Darbies[114]

Good of the chaplain to enter Lone Bay
And down on his marrowbones here and pray
For the likes just o' me, Billy Budd.—But, look:
Through the port comes the moonshine astray!
It tips the guard's cutlass and silvers this nook;
But 'twill die in the dawning of Billy's last day.
A jewel-block[115] they'll make of me tomorrow,
Pendant pearl from the yardarm-end
Like the eardrop I gave to Bristol Molly—
O, 'tis me, not the sentence they'll suspend.
Ay, ay, all is up; and I must up too,
Early in the morning, aloft from alow.
On an empty stomach now never it would do.
They'll give me a nibble—bit o' biscuit ere I go.
Sure, a messmate will reach me the last parting cup;
But, turning heads away from the hoist and the belay,[116]
Heaven knows who will have the running of me up!
No pipe to those halyards.[117]—But aren't it all sham?
A blur's in my eyes; it is dreaming that I am.
A hatchet to my hawser?[118] All adrift to go?
The drum roll to grog, and Billy never know?
But Donald he has promised to stand by the plank;
So I'll shake a friendly hand ere I sink.
But—no! It is dead then I'll be, come to think.
I remember Taff the Welshman when he sank.
And his cheek it was like the budding pink.

[114]Handcuffs.

[115]A block at the yardarm end through which the halyard of the studding-sail passes. Hayford and Sealts explain that the poet is punning on Billy's reputation as the "jewel" of the crew.

[116]Apparatus that will be used to hoist and secure Billy's body.

[117]Melville's comments in *White-Jacket* on the sailor's recourse to "the bottle to seek relief from the intolerable ennui" of man-of-war life perhaps shed light on this obscure line: "His ordinary government allowance of spirits … is not enough … he craves a more vigorous *nip at the cable*, a more sturdy *swig at the halyards*; and if opium were to be had, many would steep themselves a thousand fathoms down in the densest fumes of that oblivious drug" (Chap. 43). Melville may be punning on several slang and nautical meanings of pipe: the opium pipe; the large measure of wine containing two hogsheads (a meaning reflected in the expression "piped up," signifying drunk); and the boatswain's whistle that pipes the men to duty. The second meaning would fit the references to the "last parting cup" and the "drum roll to grog." Milton Stern suggests that Melville is using the word pipe in the sense of "pipe dream" (also derived from the opium pipe) and offers the interpretation: "The halyard from which he'll hang is very real and not his mere dream of it."

[118]Rope for towing a ship or securing it at a dock.

But me they'll lash in hammock, drop me deep.
Fathoms down, fathoms down, how I'll dream fast asleep.
I feel it stealing now. Sentry, are you there?
Just ease these darbies at the wrist,
And roll me over fair!
I am sleepy, and the oozy weeds about me twist.

1924

Hawthorne and His Mosses

By a Virginian Spending July in Vermont[1]

A papered chamber in a fine old farm-house—a mile from any other dwelling, and dipped to the eaves in foliage—surrounded by mountains, old woods, and Indian ponds,—this, surely, is the place to write of Hawthorne. Some charm is in this northern air, for love and duty seem both impelling to the task. A man of a deep and noble nature has seized me in this seclusion. His wild, witch voice rings through me; or, in softer cadences, I seem to hear it in the songs of the hill-side birds, that sing in the larch trees at my window.

Would that all excellent books were foundlings, without father or mother, that so it might be, we could glorify them, without including their ostensible authors. Nor would any true man take exception to this;—least of all, he who writes,—"When the Artist rises high enough to achieve the Beautiful, the symbol by which he makes it perceptible to mortal senses becomes of little value in his eyes, while his spirit possesses itself in the enjoyment of the reality."[2]

But more than this. I know not what would be the right name to put on the title-page of an excellent book, but this I feel, that the names of all fine authors are fictitious ones, far more so than that of Junius,[3]—simply

---

[1] The most substantial of five book reviews Melville published in the *Literary World*, edited by his friend Evert A. Duyckinck, this essay appeared in the issues of August 17 and 24, 1850. The present text is from the standard Northwestern-Newberry edition of *The Piazza Tales and Other Prose Pieces, 1839–1860* and draws on the editors' textual and historical notes. In it Merton M. Sealts, Jr., has restored a number of passages from the manuscript that were deleted or diluted by Duyckinck in the original published text to avoid offending contemporary authors. According to Sealts, the manuscript indicates that Melville's "Virginian" persona was an afterthought, to conceal his identity. Scholars disagree on whether Melville began the essay before meeting Hawthorne at an August 5 "literary outing" in the Berkshires or wrote the entire essay after the encounter. Through his praise of Hawthorne and Shakespeare as explorers of "blackness" and "masters of the great Art of Telling the Truth," Melville indirectly comments on his own aims and strategies as a writer covertly conveying dangerous truths to an unsympathetic public. A bold expression of literary nationalism, "Hawthorne and His Mosses" invites comparison with Emerson's "The American Scholar" and Whitman's 1855 Preface to *Leaves of Grass* and "Democratic Vistas."

[2] The concluding words of Hawthorne's "The Artist of the Beautiful," slightly modified by Melville.

[3] Unidentified pseudonymous author of the *Letters of Junius* (London, 1770; Philadelphia, 1791), which went through many editions and exerted a strong influence on American polemicists of the Revolutionary era as well as on the debates over ratification of the federal Constitution. "Junius" was best known for defending liberty of the press as the guardian of "all the civil, political, and religious rights of an Englishman."

standing, as they do, for the mystical, ever-eluding Spirit of all Beauty, which ubiquitously possesses men of genius. Purely imaginative as this fancy may appear, it nevertheless seems to receive some warranty from the fact, that on a personal interview no great author has ever come up to the idea of his reader. But that dust of which our bodies are composed, how can it fitly express the nobler intelligences among us? With reverence be it spoken, that not even in the case of one deemed more than man, not even in our Saviour, did his visible frame betoken anything of the augustness of the nature within. Else, how could those Jewish eyewitnesses fail to see heaven in his glance.

It is curious, how a man may travel along a country road, and yet miss the grandest, or sweetest of prospects, by reason of an intervening hedge, so like all other hedges, as in no way to hint of the wide landscape beyond. So has it been with me concerning the enchanting landscape in the soul of this Hawthorne, this most excellent Man of Mosses. His "Old Manse" has been written now four years, but I never read it till a day or two since. I had seen it in the book-stores—heard of it often—even had it recommended to me by a tasteful friend, as a rare, quiet book, perhaps too deserving of popularity to be popular. But there are so many books called "excellent", and so much unpopular merit, that amid the thick stir of other things, the hint of my tasteful friend was disregarded; and for four years the Mosses on the old Manse never refreshed me with their perennial green. It may be, however, that all this while, the book, like wine, was only improving in flavor and body. At any rate, it so chanced that this long procrastination eventuated in a happy result. At breakfast the other day, a mountain girl, a cousin of mine,[4] who for the last two weeks has every morning helped me to strawberries and raspberries,—which, like the roses and pearls in the fairy-tale, seemed to fall into the saucer from those strawberry-beds her cheeks,—this delightful creature, this charming Cherry says to me—"I see you spend your mornings in the hay-mow; and yesterday I found there 'Dwight's Travels in New England'.[5] Now I have something far better than that,—something more congenial to our summer on these hills. Take these raspberries, and then I will give you some moss."—"Moss!" said I.—"Yes, and you must take it to the barn with you, and good-bye to 'Dwight'".

With that she left me, and soon returned with a volume, verdantly bound, and garnished with a curious frontispiece in green,—nothing less, than a fragment of real moss cunningly pressed to a fly-leaf.—"Why this," said I spilling my raspberries, "this is the 'Mosses from an Old Manse'". "Yes" said cousin Cherry "yes, it is that flowery Hawthorne."—"Hawthorne and Mosses" said I "no more: it is morning: it is July in the country: and I am off for the barn".

---

[4]Melville's notation in his copy of *Mosses from an Old Manse* (1846) in fact indicates that he received the book from his Aunt Mary, widow of his Uncle Thomas Melvill, in Pittsfield, on July 18, 1850.

[5]Timothy Dwight's *Travels in New-England and New-York* (1821–1822).

Stretched on that new mown clover, the hill-side breeze blowing over me through the wide barn door, and soothed by the hum of the bees in the meadows around, how magically stole over me this Mossy Man! and how amply, how bountifully, did he redeem that delicious promise to his guests in the Old Manse, of whom it is written—"Others could give them pleasure, or amusement, or instruction—these could be picked up anywhere—but it was for me to give them rest. Rest, in a life of trouble! What better could be done for weary and world-worn spirits? what better could be done for any-body, who came within our magic circle, than to throw the spell of a magic spirit over him?"—So all that day, half-buried in the new clover, I watched this Hawthorne's "Assyrian dawn, and Paphian sunset and moonrise, from the summit of our Eastern Hill."[6]

The soft ravishments of the man spun me round about in a web of dreams, and when the book was closed, when the spell was over, this wizard "dismissed me with but misty reminiscences, as if I had been dreaming of him".

What a mild moonlight of contemplative humor bathes that Old Manse!— the rich and rare distilment of a spicy and slowly-oozing heart. No rollicking rudeness, no gross fun fed on fat dinners, and bred in the lees of wine,—but a humor so spiritually gentle, so high, so deep, and yet so richly relishable, that it were hardly inappropriate in an angel. It is the very religion of mirth; for nothing so human but it may be advanced to that. The orchard of the Old Manse seems the visible type of the fine mind that has described it. Those twisted, and contorted old trees, "that stretch out their crooked branches, and take such hold of the imagination, that we remember them as humorists, and odd-fellows." And then, as surrounded by these gro-tesque forms, and hushed in the noon-day repose of this Hawthorne's spell, how aptly might the still fall of his ruddy thoughts into your soul be symbol-ized by "the thump of a great apple, in the stillest afternoon, falling without a breath of wind, from the mere necessity of perfect ripeness"! For no less ripe than ruddy are the apples of the thoughts and fancies in this sweet Man of Mosses.

"Buds and Bird-voices"—What a delicious thing is that!—"Will the world ever be so decayed, that Spring may not renew its greenness?"—And the "Fire-Worship". Was ever the hearth so glorified into an altar before? The mere title of that piece is better than any common work in fifty folio volumes. How exquisite is this:—"Nor did it lessen the charm of his soft, fa-miliar courtesy and helpfulness, that the mighty spirit, were opportunity offered him, would run riot through the peaceful house, wrap its inmates in his terrible embrace, and leave nothing of them save their whitened bones. This possibility of mad destruction only made his domestic kindness the more beautiful and touching. It was so sweet of him, being endowed with

[6]Adapted from "The Old Manse," the prefa-tory sketch of *Mosses from an Old Manse*. The story titles and quotations that follow are all from *Mosses*, but Melville frequently introdu-ces slight alterations, a typical nineteenth-century practice.

such power, to dwell, day after day, and one long, lonesome night after another, on the dusky hearth, only now and then betraying his wild nature, by thrusting his red tongue out of the chimney-top! True, he had done much mischief in the world, and was pretty certain to do more, but his warm heart atoned for all. He was kindly to the race of man."

But he has still other apples, not quite so ruddy, though full as ripe;—apples, that have been left to wither on the tree, after the pleasant autumn gathering is past. The sketch of "The Old Apple Dealer" is conceived in the subtlest spirit of sadness; he whose "subdued and nerveless boyhood prefigured his abortive prime, which, likewise, contained within itself the prophecy and image of his lean and torpid age". Such touches as are in this piece can not proceed from any common heart. They argue such a depth of tenderness, such a boundless sympathy with all forms of being, such an omnipresent love, that we must needs say, that this Hawthorne is here almost alone in his generation,—at least, in the artistic manifestation of these things. Still more. Such touches as these,—and many, very many similar ones, all through his chapters—furnish clews, whereby we enter a little way into the intricate, profound heart where they originated. And we see, that suffering, some time or other and in some shape or other,—this only can enable any man to depict it in others. All over him, Hawthorne's melancholy rests like an Indian Summer, which though bathing a whole country in one softness, still reveals the distinctive hue of every towering hill, and each far-winding vale.

But it is the least part of genius that attracts admiration. Where Hawthorne is known, he seems to be deemed a pleasant writer, with a pleasant style,—a sequestered, harmless man, from whom any deep and weighty thing would hardly be anticipated:—a man who means no meanings. But there is no man, in whom humor and love, like mountain peaks, soar to such a rapt height, as to receive the irradiations of the upper skies;—there is no man in whom humor and love are developed in that high form called genius; no such man can exist without also possessing, as the indispensable complement of these, a great, deep intellect, which drops down into the universe like a plummet. Or, love and humor are only the eyes, through which such an intellect views this world. The great beauty in such a mind is but the product of its strength. What, to all readers, can be more charming than the piece entitled "Monsieur du Miroir"; and to a reader at all capable of fully fathoming it, what, at the same time, can possess more mystical depth of meaning?—Yes, there he sits, and looks at me,—this "shape of mystery", this "identical Monsieur du Miroir".—"Methinks I should tremble now, were his wizard power of gliding through all impediments in search of me, to place him suddenly before my eyes".

How profound, nay appalling, is the moral evolved by the "Earth's Holocaust"; where—beginning with the hollow follies and affectations of the world,—all vanities and empty theories and forms, are, one after another, and by an admirably graduated, growing comprehensiveness, thrown into the allegorical fire, till, at length, nothing is left but the all-engendering heart of man; which remaining still unconsumed, the great conflagration is nought.

Of a piece with this, is the "Intelligence Office", a wondrous symbolizing of the secret workings in men's souls. There are other sketches, still more charged with ponderous import.

"The Christmas Banquet", and "The Bosom Serpent" would be fine subjects for a curious and elaborate analysis, touching the conjectural parts of the mind that produced them. For spite of all the Indian-summer sunlight on the hither side of Hawthorne's soul, the other side—like the dark half of the physical sphere—is shrouded in a blackness, ten times black. But this darkness but gives more effect to the ever-moving dawn, that forever advances through it, and circumnavigates his world. Whether Hawthorne has simply availed himself of this mystical blackness as a means to the wondrous effects he makes it to produce in his lights and shades; or whether there really lurks in him, perhaps unknown to himself, a touch of Puritanic gloom,—this, I cannot altogether tell. Certain it is, however, that this great power of blackness in him derives its force from its appeals to that Calvinistic sense of Innate Depravity and Original Sin, from whose visitations, in some shape or other, no deeply thinking mind is always and wholly free. For, in certain moods, no man can weigh this world, without throwing in something, somehow like Original Sin, to strike the uneven balance. At all events, perhaps no writer has ever wielded this terrific thought with greater terror than this same harmless Hawthorne. Still more: this black conceit pervades him, through and through. You may be witched by his sunlight,—transported by the bright gildings in the skies he builds over you;—but there is the blackness of darkness beyond; and even his bright gildings but fringe, and play upon the edges of thunder-clouds.—In one word, the world is mistaken in this Nathaniel Hawthorne. He himself must often have smiled at its absurd misconception of him. He is immeasurably deeper than the plummet of the mere critic. For it is not the brain that can test such a man; it is only the heart. You cannot come to know greatness by inspecting it; there is no glimpse to be caught of it, except by intuition; you need not ring it, you but touch it, and you find it is gold.

Now it is that blackness in Hawthorne, of which I have spoken, that so fixes and fascinates me. It may be, nevertheless, that it is too largely developed in him. Perhaps he does not give us a ray of his light for every shade of his dark. But however this may be, this blackness it is that furnishes the infinite obscure of his back-ground,—that back-ground, against which Shakespeare plays his grandest conceits, the things that have made for Shakespeare his loftiest, but most circumscribed renown, as the profoundest of thinkers. For by philosophers Shakespeare is not adored as the great man of tragedy and comedy.—"Off with his head! so much for Buckingham!"[7]

<hr/>

[7] One of many lines interpolated into Shakespeare's *Richard III* (IV. iv) by the British actor and dramatist Colley Cibber (1671–1757), whose popular revision of the play dominated the American stage until the late nineteenth century.

this sort of rant, interlined by another hand, brings down the house,—those mistaken souls, who dream of Shakespeare as a mere man of Richard-the-Third humps, and Macbeth daggers. But it is those deep far-away things in him; those occasional flashings-forth of the intuitive Truth in him; those short, quick probings at the very axis of reality;—these are the things that make Shakespeare, Shakespeare. Through the mouths of the dark characters of Hamlet, Timon, Lear, and Iago, he craftily says, or sometimes insinuates the things, which we feel to be so terrifically true, that it were all but madness for any good man, in his own proper character, to utter, or even hint of them. Tormented into desperation, Lear the frantic King tears off the mask, and speaks the sane madness of vital truth. But, as I before said, it is the least part of genius that attracts admiration. And so, much of the blind, unbridled admiration that has been heaped upon Shakespeare, has been lavished upon the least part of him. And few of his endless commentators and critics seem to have remembered, or even perceived, that the immediate products of a great mind are not so great, as that undeveloped, (and sometimes undevelopable) yet dimly-discernable greatness, to which these immediate products are but the infallible indices. In Shakespeare's tomb lies infinitely more than Shakspeare ever wrote. And if I magnify Shakespeare, it is not so much for what he did do, as for what he did not do, or refrained from doing. For in this world of lies, Truth is forced to fly like a scared white doe in the woodlands; and only by cunning glimpses will she reveal herself, as in Shakespeare and other masters of the great Art of Telling the Truth,—even though it be covertly, and by snatches.

But if this view of the all-popular Shakespeare be seldom taken by his readers, and if very few who extol him, have ever read him deeply, or, perhaps, only have seen him on the tricky stage, (which alone made, and is still making him his mere mob renown)—if few men have time, or patience, or palate, for the spiritual truth as it is in that great genius;—it is, then, no matter of surprise that in a contemporaneous age, Nathaniel Hawthorne is a man, as yet, almost utterly mistaken among men. Here and there, in some quiet arm-chair in the noisy town, or some deep nook among the noiseless mountains, he may be appreciated for something of what he is. But unlike Shakespeare, who was forced to the contrary course by circumstances, Hawthorne (either from simple disinclination, or else from inaptitude) refrains from all the popularizing noise and show of broad farce, and blood-besmeared tragedy; content with the still, rich utterances of a great intellect in repose, and which sends few thoughts into circulation, except they be arterialized at his large warm lungs, and expanded in his honest heart.

Nor need you fix upon that blackness in him, if it suit you not. Nor, indeed, will all readers discern it, for it is, mostly, insinuated to those who may best understand it, and account for it; it is not obtruded upon every one alike.

Some may start to read of Shakespeare and Hawthorne on the same page. They may say, that if an illustration were needed, a lesser light might have sufficed to elucidate this Hawthorne, this small man of yesterday. But I am not, willingly, one of those, who, as touching Shakespeare at least, exemplify the maxim of Rochefoucault,[8] that "we exalt the reputation of some, in order to depress that of others";—who, to teach all noble-souled aspirants that there is no hope for them, pronounce Shakespeare absolutely unapproachable. But Shakespeare has been approached. There are minds that have gone as far as Shakespeare into the universe. And hardly a mortal man, who, at some time or other, has not felt as great thoughts in him as any you will find in Hamlet. We must not inferentially malign mankind for the sake of any one man, whoever he may be. This is too cheap a purchase of contentment for conscious mediocrity to make. Besides, this absolute and unconditional adoration of Shakespeare has grown to be a part of our Anglo Saxon superstitions. The Thirty Nine articles[9] are now Forty. Intolerance has come to exist in this matter. You must believe in Shakespeare's unapproachability, or quit the country. But what sort of a belief is this for an American, a man who is bound to carry republican progressiveness into Literature, as well as into Life? Believe me, my friends, that Shakespeares are this day being born on the banks of the Ohio. And the day will come, when you shall say who reads a book by an Englishman that is a modern?[10] The great mistake seems to be, that even with those Americans who look forward to the coming of a great literary genius among us, they somehow fancy he will come in the costume of Queen Elizabeth's day,—be a writer of dramas founded upon old English history, or the tales of Boccaccio.[11] Whereas, great geniuses are parts of the times; they themselves are the times; and possess a correspondent coloring. It is of a piece with the Jews, who while their Shiloh[12] was meekly walking in their streets, were still praying for his magnificent coming; looking for him in a chariot, who was already among them on an ass. Nor must we forget, that, in his own life-time, Shakespeare was not Shakespeare, but only Master William Shakespeare of the shrewd, thriving, business firm of Condell, Shakespeare & Co., proprietors of the Globe Theatre in London; and by a courtly author, of the name of Greene, was hooted at, as an "upstart crow" beautified "with other birds' feathers".[13] For, mark it well, imitation is often the first charge brought against real originality. Why this is so, there is not space to set forth here. You must have plenty of sea-room to tell the Truth in; especially, when it seems to have an aspect of newness, as America did in 1492, though it was then just as old, and perhaps older than Asia, only those

[8]François de la Rochefoucauld (1613–1680), French writer of moral maxims. The exact source for Melville's wording has not been identified.

[9]Tenets of the Anglican creed, metaphorically referring to the ironic worship of things English by a people whose ancestors threw off the yoke of the Anglican church and the British king.

[10]Melville is reversing the famous insult by the British critic Sydney Smith (1771–1845): "In the four quarters of the globe, who reads an American book?" (*Edinburgh Review*, 1820).

[11]Giovanni Boccaccio (1313–1375), Italian author of the *Decameron*.

[12]The name of the city and the sanctuary where the Ark of the Covenant was first kept after the entry into Canaan (Joshua 18:1) and the site of the early Israelites' great yearly sacrifice; hence used by Melville as a synonym for Messiah.

[13]An altered quotation from Robert Greene's *A Groatsworth of Wit* (1592). In both the manuscript and the original published text, Melville misattributed the quotation to Greene's publisher, Henry Chettle, but the Northwestern-Newberry editors have emended his error.

sagacious philosophers, the common sailors, had never seen it before; swearing it was all water and moonshine there.

Now, I do not say that Nathaniel of Salem is a greater than William of Avon, or as great. But the difference between the two men is by no means immeasurable. Not a very great deal more, and Nathaniel were verily William.

This, too, I mean, that if Shakespeare has not been equalled, he is sure to be surpassed, and surpassed by an American born now or yet to be born. For it will never do for us who in most other things out-do as well as out-brag the world, it will not do for us to fold our hands and say, In the highest department advance there is none. Nor will it at all do to say, that the world is getting grey and grizzled now, and has lost that fresh charm which she wore of old, and by virtue of which the great poets of past times made themselves what we esteem them to be. Not so. The world is as young today, as when it was created; and this Vermont morning dew is as wet to my feet, as Eden's dew to Adam's. Nor has Nature been all over ransacked by our progenitors, so that no new charms and mysteries remain for this latter generation to find. Far from it. The trillionth part has not yet been said; and all that has been said, but multiplies the avenues to what remains to be said. It is not so much paucity, as superabundance of material that seems to incapacitate modern authors.

Let America then prize and cherish her writers; yea, let her glorify them. They are not so many in number, as to exhaust her good-will. And while she has good kith and kin of her own, to take to her bosom, let her not lavish her embraces upon the household of an alien. For believe it or not England, after all, is, in many things, an alien to us. China has more bowels of real love for us than she. But even were there no Hawthorne, no Emerson, no Whittier, no Irving, no Bryant, no Dana, no Cooper, no Willis (not the author of the "Dashes", but the author of the "Belfry Pigeon")[14]—were there none of these, and others of like calibre among us, nevertheless, let America first praise mediocrity even, in her own children, before she praises (for everywhere, merit demands acknowledgment from every one) the best excellence in the children of any other land. Let her own authors, I say, have the priority of appreciation. I was much pleased with a hot-headed Carolina cousin of mine, who once said,—"If there were no other American to stand by, in Literature,—why, then, I would stand by Pop Emmons and his 'Fredoniad,'[15] and till a better epic came along, swear it was not very far behind the Iliad." Take away the words, and in spirit he was sound.

[14]In the original published text, Duyckinck deleted these names and substituted: "But even were there no strong literary individualities among us, as there are some dozens at least...." Richard Henry Dana, Jr. (1815–1882) was the author of *Two Years Before the Mast* (1840), which Melville hailed as a model for his own sea fiction. Nathaniel Parker Willis (1806–1867) was a dandified author and editor (and the employer of the escaped slave Harriet Jacobs, whose *Incidents in the Life of a Slave Girl* is reprinted earlier in this volume). Melville is referring to Willis's volume of short fiction, *Dashes at Life with a Free Pencil* (1845), and to his poem "The Belfry Pigeon" (1831). Willis, Irving, and Bryant were late additions to Melville's list.

[15]Identified by the Northwestern-Newberry editors as "the jocular nickname for Richard Emmons, author of the blatantly nationalistic and bathetic four-volume epic on the War of 1812, *The Fredondiad*" (1827).

Not that American genius needs patronage in order to expand. For that explosive sort of stuff will expand though screwed up in a vice, and burst it, though it were triple steel. It is for the nation's sake, and not for her authors' sake, that I would have America be heedful of the increasing greatness among her writers. For how great the shame, if other nations should be before her, in crowning her heroes of the pen. But this is almost the case now. American authors have received more just and discriminating praise (however loftily and ridiculously given, in certain cases) even from some Englishmen, than from their own countrymen. There are hardly five critics in America; and several of them are asleep. As for patronage, it is the American author who now patronizes his country, and not his country him. And if at times some among them appeal to the people for more recognition, it is not always with selfish motives, but patriotic ones.

It is true, that but few of them as yet have evinced that decided originality which merits great praise. But that graceful writer, who perhaps of all Americans has received the most plaudits from his own country for his productions,—that very popular and amiable writer, however good, and self-reliant in many things, perhaps owes his chief reputation to the self-acknowledged imitation of a foreign model, and to the studied avoidance of all topics but smooth ones.[16] But it is better to fail in originality, than to succeed in imitation. He who has never failed somewhere, that man can not be great. Failure is the true test of greatness. And if it be said, that continual success is a proof that a man wisely knows his powers,—it is only to be added, that, in that case, he knows them to be small. Let us believe it, then, once for all, that there is no hope for us in these smooth pleasing writers that know their powers. Without malice, but to speak the plain fact, they but furnish an appendix to Goldsmith, and other English authors. And we want no American Goldsmiths; nay, we want no American Miltons. It were the vilest thing you could say of a true American author, that he were an American Tompkins.[17] Call him an American, and have done; for you can not say a nobler thing of him.—But it is not meant that all American writers should studiously cleave to nationality in their writings; only this, no American writer should write like an Englishman, or a Frenchman; let him write like a man, for then he will be sure to write like an American. Let us away with this Bostonian leaven of literary flunkeyism towards England. If either must play the flunkey in this thing, let England do it, not us. And the time is not far off when circumstances may force her to it. While we are rapidly preparing for that political supremacy among the nations, which prophetically awaits us at the close of the present century; in a literary point of view,

---

[16]Washington Irving. Melville may be alluding either to the German sources of "Rip Van Winkle" and "The Legend of Sleepy Hollow" or to Irving's imitation of the British writer Oliver Goldsmith (1728–1774). See his reference later in this paragraph to Irving's reputation as the "American Goldsmith."

[17]Tompkins has not been identified, but some annotators have suggested that the name was commonly associated with liveried servants ("flunkeys")—hence Melville's references below to "literary flunkeyism" and "play[ing] the flunkey."

we are deplorably unprepared for it; and we seem studious to remain so. Hitherto, reasons might have existed why this should be; but no good reason exists now. And all that is requisite to amendment in this matter, is simply this: that, while freely acknowledging all excellence, everywhere, we should refrain from unduly lauding foreign writers and, at the same time, duly recognize the meritorious writers that are our own;—those writers, who breathe that unshackled, democratic spirit of Christianity in all things, which now takes the practical lead in this world, though at the same time led by ourselves—us Americans. Let us boldly contemn all imitation, though it comes to us graceful and fragrant as the morning; and foster all originality, though, at first, it be crabbed and ugly as our own pine knots. And if any of our authors fail, or seem to fail, then, in the words of my enthusiastic Carolina cousin, let us clap him on the shoulder, and back him against all Europe for his second round. The truth is, that in our point of view, this matter of a national literature has come to such a pass with us, that in some sense we must turn bullies, else the day is lost, or superiority so far beyond us, that we can hardly say it will ever be ours.

And now, my countrymen, as an excellent author, of your own flesh and blood,—an unimitating, and, perhaps, in his way, an inimitable man—whom better can I commend to you, in the first place, than Nathaniel Hawthorne. He is one of the new, and far better generation of your writers. The smell of your beeches and hemlocks is upon him; your own broad praries are in his soul; and if you travel away inland into his deep and noble nature, you will hear the far roar of his Niagara. Give not over to future generations the glad duty of acknowledging him for what he is. Take that joy to your self, in your own generation; and so shall he feel those grateful impulses in him, that may possibly prompt him to the full flower of some still greater achievement in your eyes. And by confessing him, you thereby confess others; you embrace the whole brotherhood. For genius, all over the world, stands hand in hand, and one shock of recognition runs the whole circle round.

In treating of Hawthorne, or rather of Hawthorne in his writings (for I never saw the man; and in the chances of a quiet plantation life, remote from his haunts, perhaps never shall) in treating of his works, I say, I have thus far omitted all mention of his "Twice Told Tales", and "Scarlet Letter". Both are excellent; but full of such manifold, strange and diffusive beauties, that time would all but fail me, to point the half of them out. But there are things in those two books, which, had they been written in England a century ago, Nathaniel Hawthorne had utterly displaced many of the bright names we now revere on authority. But I am content to leave Hawthorne to himself, and to the infallible finding of posterity; and however great may be the praise I have bestowed upon him, I feel, that in so doing, I have more served and honored myself, than him. For, at bottom, great excellence is praise enough to itself; but the feeling of a sincere and appreciative love and admiration towards it, this is relieved by utterance; and warm, honest praise ever leaves a pleasant flavor in the mouth; and it is an honorable thing to confess to what is honorable in others.

But I cannot leave my subject yet. No man can read a fine author, and relish him to his very bones, while he reads, without subsequently fancying to himself some ideal image of the man and his mind. And if you rightly look for it, you will almost always find that the author himself has somewhere furnished you with his own picture.—For poets (whether in prose or verse), being painters of Nature, are like their brethren of the pencil, the true portrait-painters, who, in the multitude of likenesses to be sketched, do not invariably omit their own; and in all high instances, they paint them without any vanity, though, at times, with a lurking something, that would take several pages to properly define.

I submit it, then, to those best acquainted with the man personally, whether the following is not Nathaniel Hawthorne;—and to himself, whether something involved in it does not express the temper of his mind,—that lasting temper of all true, candid men—a seeker, not a finder yet:—

> "A man now entered, in neglected attire, with the aspect of a thinker, but somewhat too rough-hewn and brawny for a scholar. His face was full of sturdy vigor, with some finer and keener attribute beneath; though harsh at first, it was tempered with the glow of a large, warm heart, which had force enough to heat his powerful intellect through and through. He advanced to the Intelligencer, and looked at him with a glance of such stern sincerity, that perhaps few secrets were beyond its scope.
> "'I seek for Truth', said he."[18]

Twenty four hours have elapsed since writing the foregoing. I have just returned from the hay mow, charged more and more with love and admiration of Hawthorne. For I have just been gleaning through the Mosses, picking up many things here and there that had previously escaped me. And I found that but to glean after this man, is better than to be in at the harvest of others. To be frank (though, perhaps, rather foolish) notwithstanding what I wrote yesterday of these Mosses, I had not then culled them all; but had, nevertheless, been sufficiently sensible of the subtle essence, in them, as to write as I did. To what infinite height of loving wonder and admiration I may yet be borne, when by repeatedly banquetting on these Mosses, I shall have thoroughly incorporated their whole stuff into my being,—that, I can not tell. But already I feel that this Hawthorne has dropped germinous seeds into my soul. He expands and deepens down, the more I contemplate him; and further, and further, shoots his strong New-England roots into the hot soil of my Southern soul.

By careful reference to the "Table of Contents", I now find, that I have gone through all the sketches; but that when I yesterday wrote, I had not at all read two particular pieces, to which I now desire to call special attention,—"A Select Party", and "Young Goodman Brown". Here, be it said to all

[18]Quoted from Hawthorne's "The Intelligence Office" in Mosses.

those whom this poor fugitive scrawl of mine may tempt to the perusal of the "Mosses," that they must on no account suffer themselves to be trifled with, disappointed, or deceived by the triviality of many of the titles to these Sketches. For in more than one instance, the title utterly belies the piece. It is as if rustic demijohns containing the very best and costliest of Falernian and Tokay, were labelled "Cider", "Perry," and "Elderberry wine".[19] The truth seems to be, that like many other geniuses, this Man of Mosses takes great delight in hoodwinking the world,—at least, with respect to himself. Personally, I doubt not, that he rather prefers to be generally esteemed but a so-so sort of author; being willing to reserve the thorough and acute appreciation of what he is, to that party most qualified to judge— that is, to himself. Besides, at the bottom of their natures, men like Hawthorne, in many things, deem the plaudits of the public such strong presumptive evidence of mediocrity in the object of them, that it would in some degree render them doubtful of their own powers, did they hear much and vociferous braying concerning them in the public pastures. True, I have been braying myself (if you please to be witty enough, to have it so) but then I claim to be the first that has so brayed in this particular matter; and therefore, while pleading guilty to the charge still claim all the merit due to originality.

But with whatever motive, playful or profound, Nathaniel Hawthorne has chosen to entitle his pieces in the manner he has, it is certain, that some of them are directly calculated to deceive—egregiously deceive, the superficial skimmer of pages. To be downright and candid once more, let me cheerfully say, that two of these titles did dolefully dupe no less an eagle-eyed reader than myself; and that, too, after I had been impressed with a sense of the great depth and breadth of this American man. "Who in the name of thunder" (as the country-people say in this neighborhood) "who in the name of thunder", would anticipate any marvel in a piece entitled "Young Goodman Brown"? You would of course suppose that it was a simple little tale, intended as a supplement to "Goody Two Shoes". Whereas, it is deep as Dante; nor can you finish it, without addressing the author in his own words—"It is yours to penetrate, in every bosom, the deep mystery of sin". And with Young Goodman, too, in allegorical pursuit of his Puritan wife, you cry out in your anguish,—

> "'Faith!' shouted Goodman Brown, in a voice of agony and desperation; and the echoes of the forest mocked him, crying—'Faith! Faith!' as if bewildered wretches were seeking her all through the wilderness."

Now this same piece, entitled "Young Goodman Brown", is one of the two that I had not all read yesterday; and I allude to it now, because it is, in itself, such a strong positive illustration of that blackness in Hawthorne, which I had assumed from the mere occasional shadows of it, as revealed in

---

[19]Falernian and Tokay were famous wines from Italy and Hungary, while apple cider, perry (pear cider), and elderberry wine were common home-fermented drinks.

several of the other sketches. But had I previously perused "Young Goodman Brown", I should have been at no pains to draw the conclusion, which I came to, at a time, when I was ignorant that the book contained one such direct and unqualified manifestation of it.

The other piece of the two referred to, is entitled "A Select Party", which, in my first simplicity upon originally taking hold of the book, I fancied must treat of some pumpkin-pie party in Old Salem, or some chowder party on Cape Cod. Whereas, by all the gods of Peedee![20] it is the sweetest and sublimest thing that has been written since Spencer wrote. Nay, there is nothing in Spencer that surpasses it, perhaps, nothing that equals it. And the test is this: read any canto in "The Faery Queen", and then read "A Select Party", and decide which pleases you the most,—that is, if you are qualified to judge. Do not be frightened at this; for when Spencer was alive, he was thought of very much as Hawthorne is now,—was generally accounted just such a "gentle" harmless man. It may be, that to common eyes, the sublimity of Hawthorne seems lost in his sweetness,—as perhaps in this same "Select Party" of his; for whom, he has builded so august a dome of sunset clouds, and served them on richer plate, than Belshazzar's when he banquetted his lords in Babylon.[21]

But my chief business now, is to point out a particular page in this piece, having reference to an honored guest, who under the name of "The Master Genius" but in the guise of "a young man of poor attire, with no insignia of rank or acknowledged eminence", is introduced to the Man of Fancy, who is the giver of the feast. Now the page having reference to this "Master Genius", so happily expresses much of what I yesterday wrote, touching the coming of the literary Shiloh of America, that I cannot but be charmed by the coincidence; especially, when it shows such a parity of ideas, at least in this one point, between a man like Hawthorne and a man like me.

And here, let me throw out another conceit of mine touching this American Shiloh, or "Master Genius", as Hawthorne calls him. May it not be, that this commanding mind has not been, is not, and never will be, individually developed in any one man? And would it, indeed, appear so unreasonable to suppose, that this great fullness and overflowing may be, or may be destined to be, shared by a plurality of men of genius? Surely, to take the very greatest example on record, Shakespeare cannot be regarded as in himself the concretion of all the genius of his time; nor as so immeasurably beyond Marlow, Webster, Ford, Beaumont, Jonson,[22] that those great men can be said to share none of his power? For one, I conceive that there were dramatists in Elizabeth's day, between whom and Shakespeare the distance was by no means great. Let anyone, hitherto little acquainted with those neglected

---

[20]River in the Carolinas (in keeping with Melville's Southern persona).

[21]Daniel 5:1 tells of how the Babylonian king Belshazzar "made a great feast to a thousand of his lords, and drank wine before the thousand."

[22]Christopher Marlowe (1564–1593), John Webster (c. 1580–c. 1625), John Ford (c. 1586–c. 1640), Francis Beaumont (c. 1584–1616), and Ben Jonson (1572–1637) were dramatists contemporary with Shakespeare.

old authors, for the first time read them thoroughly, or even read Charles Lamb's Specimens[23] of them, and he will be amazed at the wondrous ability of those Anaks[24] of men, and shocked at this renewed example of the fact, that Fortune has more to do with fame than merit,—though, without merit, lasting fame there can be none.

Nevertheless, it would argue too illy of my country were this maxim to hold good concerning Nathaniel Hawthorne, a man, who already, in some few minds, has shed "such a light, as never illuminates the earth, save when a great heart burns as the household fire of a grand intellect."

The words are his,—in the "Select Party"; and they are a magnificent setting to a coincident sentiment of my own, but ramblingly expressed yesterday, in reference to himself. Gainsay it who will, as I now write, I am Posterity speaking by proxy—and after times will make it more than good, when I declare—that the American, who up to the present day, has evinced, in Literature, the largest brain with the largest heart, that man is Nathaniel Hawthorne. Moreover, that whatever Nathaniel Hawthorne may hereafter write, "The Mosses from an Old Manse" will be ultimately accounted his masterpiece. For there is a sure, though a secret sign in some works which prove the culmination of the powers (only the developable ones, however) that produced them. But I am by no means desirous of the glory of a prophet. I pray Heaven that Hawthorne may *yet* prove me an impostor in this prediction. Especially, as I somehow cling to the strange fancy, that, in all men, hiddenly reside certain wondrous, occult properties—as in some plants and minerals—which by some happy but very rare accident (as bronze was discovered by the melting of the iron and brass in the burning of Corinth) may chance to be called forth here on earth; not entirely waiting for their better discovery in the more congenial, blessed atmosphere of heaven.

Once more—for it is hard to be finite upon an infinite subject, and all subjects are infinite. By some people, this entire scrawl of mine may be esteemed altogether unnecessary, inasmuch, "as years ago" (they may say) "we found out the rich and rare stuff in this Hawthorne, whom you now parade forth, as if only *yourself* were the discoverer of this Portuguese diamond in our Literature".—But even granting all this; and adding to it, the assumption that the books of Hawthorne have sold by the five-thousand,— what does that signify?—They should be sold by the hundred-thousand; and read by the million; and admired by every one who is capable of admiration.

1850

---

[23]The English essayist Charles Lamb (1775–1834) helped promote a revival of Elizabethan literature through his *Specimens of English Dramatic Poets, Who Lived about the Time of Shakespeare* (1808), which featured selections from most of the writers mentioned above.

[24]A race of reputedly unconquerable giants destroyed by Joshua. See Numbers 13:33 and Joshua 11:21.

from **Battle-Pieces and Aspects of the War**

The Portent[1] (1859)

Hanging from the beam,
    Slowly swaying (such the law),
Gaunt the shadow on your green,
    Shenandoah!
The cut is on the crown   5
(Lo, John Brown),
And the stabs shall heal no more.

Hidden in the cap
    Is the anguish none can draw;
So your future veils its face,   10
    Shenandoah!
But the streaming beard is shown
(Weird John Brown),
The meteor of the war.

                            1866

A Utilitarian View of the Monitor's Fight[1']

Plain be the phrase, yet apt the verse,
    More ponderous than nimble;
For since grimed War here laid aside
His Orient pomp, 'twould ill befit
    Overmuch to ply   5
    The rhyme's barbaric cymbal.
Hail to victory without the gaud
    Of glory; zeal that needs no fans
Of banners; plain mechanic power
Plied cogently in War now placed—   10
    Where War belongs—
    Among the trades and artisans.

---

[1]"The Portent" is the opening poem in *Battle-Pieces and Aspects of the War* (1866), the source of the present text. Set in italics in the original, it commemorates the hanging of John Brown after his unsuccessful raid on the Federal arsenal at Harpers Ferry, Virginia, in October 1859 and portrays Brown as a portent of the ensuing Civil War. The imagery suggests both an Old Testament prophet and a Christlike martyr—analogies common among antislavery sympathizers. Compare the poem with Thoreau's "A Plea for Captain John Brown" and the hanging of Brown with that of Billy Budd.

[1']Adopting a verse style in keeping with the new technology of warfare, the poem commemorates the battle of the first American ironclad battleships, the Union *Monitor* and the Confederate *Merrimack*, on May 9, 1862, at Hampton Roads, Virginia.

Yet this was battle, and intense—
    Beyond the strife of fleets heroic;
Deadlier, closer, calm 'mid storm;   15
No passion; all went on by crank,
       Pivot, and screw,

       And calculations of caloric.
Needless to dwell; the story's known.
    The ringing of those plates on plates   20
Still ringeth round the world—
The clangor of that blacksmiths' fray.
       The anvil-din
Resounds this message from the Fates:

War shall yet be, and to the end;   25
    But war-paint shows the streaks of weather;
War yet shall be, but warriors
Are now but operatives;[2] War's made
       Less grand than Peace,
And a singe runs through lace and feather.   30

                            1866

from **John Marr and Other Sailors**

The Maldive Shark

About the shark, phlegmatical one,
Pale sot of the Maldive sea,
The sleek little pilot-fish, azure and slim,
How alert in attendance be.
From his saw-pit of mouth, from his charnel of maw   5
They have nothing to harm to dread,
But liquidly glide on his ghastly flank
Or before in Gorgonian head;
Or lurk in the port of serrated teeth
In white triple tiers of glittering gates,   10
And there find a haven when peril's abroad,
An asylum in jaws of the Fates!
They are friends; and friendly they guide him to prey,
Yet never partake of the treat—
Eyes and brains to the dotard lethargic and dull,   15
Pale ravener of horrible meat.

                            1888

---

[2]Factory workers.

The Berg (A Dream)

I saw a ship of material build
(Her standards[1] set, her brave apparel on)
Directed as by madness mere
Against a solid iceberg steer,
Nor budge it, though the infatuate ship went down.   5
The impact made huge ice-cubes fall
Sullen in tons that crashed the deck;
But that one avalanche was all—
No other movement save the foundering wreck.

Along the spurs of ridges pale,   10
Not any slenderest shaft and frail,
A prism over glass-green gorges lone,
Toppled; nor lace of traceries fine,
Nor pendant drops in grot[2] or mine
Were jarred, when the stunned ship went down.   15
Nor sole the gulls in cloud that wheeled
Circling one snow-flanked peak afar,
But nearer fowl the floes that skimmed
And crystal beaches, felt no jar.
No thrill transmitted stirred the lock   20
Of jack-straw needle-ice at base;
Towers undermined by waves—the block
Atilt impending—kept their place.
Seals, dozing sleek on sliddery[3] ledges
Slipt never, when by loftier edges   25
Through the inertia overthrown,
The impetuous ship in bafflement went down.

Hard Berg (methought), so cold, so vast,
With mortal damps[4] self-overcast;
Exhaling still thy dankish breath—   30
Adrift dissolving, bound for death;
Though lumpish thou, a lumbering one—
A lumbering lubbard[5] loitering slow,
Impingers rue thee and go down,
Sounding thy precipice below,   35

---

[1]Flags.
[2]Grotto, cave.
[3]Slippery.

[4]Fog around the iceberg.
[5]Awkward, unseaworthy.

Nor stir the slimy slug that sprawls
Along thy dead indifference of walls.

1888

from **Timoleon**[1]

Monody

To have known him, to have loved him
    After loneness long;
And then to be estranged in life,
    And neither in the wrong;
And now for death to set his seal—   5
    Ease me, a little ease, my song!

By wintry hills his hermit-mound
    The sheeted snow-drifts drape,
And houseless there the snow-bird flits
    Beneath the fir-trees' crape: 10
Glazed now with ice the cloistral vine
    That hid the shyest grape.

1891

Art

In placid hours well-pleased we dream
Of many a brave unbodied scheme.
But form to lend, pulsed life create,
What unlike things must meet and mate:
A flame to melt—a wind to freeze;   5
Sad patience—joyous energies;
Humility—yet pride and scorn;
Instinct and study; love and hate;
Audacity—reverence. These must mate,
And fuse with Jacob's mystic heart,   10
To wrestle with the angel[1']—Art.

1891

---

[1]Melville had this volume of poems privately published in 1891. He seems to have composed "Monody" in response to Hawthorne's death in May 1864. A reclusive character named Vine, whom most critics identify as a portrait of Hawthorne, appears in *Clarel* (1876).

[1']In Genesis 32:24–29, Jacob wrestles all night long with an angel. The struggle ends with the angel's blessing Jacob and renaming him Israel.

JULIA WARD HOWE
1819–1910

Julia Ward Howe was a nineteenth-century one-hit wonder. This is certainly the best description of her place in the popular imagination today, but it was also somewhat true during her own lifetime. She was a prolific writer whose publishing career extended from 1836 to 1910, but nearly every time she entered a public room from 1862 until her death in 1911, a band would strike up, the audience would rise, and the group would begin to sing in unison: "Mine eyes have seen the glory of the coming of the Lord." Her most famous lyric, "The Battle Hymn of the Republic," cemented the bonds of sentimental nationalism in the United States both during and after the Civil War. Today, elementary school children parody the song, but it is also still a powerful nationalist anthem. On September 14, 2001, George W. Bush joined two thousand people in the National Cathedral in Washington, D.C., in singing Howe's famous words at the national day of prayer and remembrance.

It is surprising, to say the least, that Julia Ward Howe was also the author of a secret novel about a hermaphrodite that eschewed nationalism completely. In fact, Howe's career shows great reluctance to stay within any ideological boundaries, national or otherwise. She was a bold thinker whose works present a startling array of sometimes contradictory and often challenging ideas. Questions of sex and gender were often central to her work. In an 1874 essay defending women's education, Howe remarked, "The philosophy of sex is thus far little understood in America, or anywhere else" (*Sex and Education* 24). At that time—the 1870s—many others were also giving serious thought to philosophies of sex. Physicians and scientists were struggling to find the biological determinants of "true sex," while many artists were beginning to explore sexual identity. In the last years of the nineteenth century, terms like *homosexual, sexual invert*, and *Uranian* were coined.

But Howe's fascination with these questions had started much earlier. She wrote her hermaphrodite novel in the 1840s, a time when few others were putting their thoughts about sex, sexuality, or sexual sensibilities onto paper. Most scholars believe that, before the 1870s, sexual desire and personal identity were not linked to each other. *The Hermaphrodite* supports this belief to some extent, since the main character, Laurence, does not express desires. But the novel offers a thorough exploration of the tangled relations between sex, gender, and identity in the years before the Civil War. Until recently, few readers realized that Howe made such a sustained effort to think through philosophies of sex, since her most significant work, the hermaphrodite manuscript, was kept private. Her daughters saved most of the pages of the unfinished novel (though the first page is definitely missing), and they were preserved in a box in the Harvard University library. The box contained two long sections of the story and a third jumbled collection of fragments. In the first section, Laurence, the main character, explains his/her father's decision to raise him/her as male in spite of anomalous physiology and then recounts his/her schooling and three episodes—an almost conventional romance with a woman (Emma), a period of penitence in a chapel, and a passionate friendship with a man, Ronald. In the second section, Laurence travels to Rome and lives as a woman in a household of independent women. The other fragments include a fable about Eva and Rafael, thwarted lovers who achieve a miraculous spiritual union. Laurence does not achieve a similarly miraculous end. The manuscript is unfinished, and at its close, Laurence is unconscious, an object of study for scientists and philosophers who puzzle over his/her body. When asked whether Laurence is a man or a woman, the physician responds that "he is rather both than neither."

The Hermaphrodite was published in 2004, more than a hundred and fifty years after Howe had stopped working on it. With its publication, readers were offered a surprising chance to consider an early-nineteenth-century American woman's thinking about sex. Other books about androgynous figures had been published in France, and Julia Ward Howe had probably read them, but her manuscript was unlike anything published in America. The works published by her contemporaries (and by Howe herself) gave few hints at the possibility of gender confusion. One of the most surprising things about The Hermaphrodite is that it presents sex itself as mysterious. The mysteries are fascinating, but they are also painful and at times even deadly.

Julia Ward was born into a wealthy New York City family in 1819. Her mother had a literary turn of mind but died at age twenty-seven giving birth to her seventh child. Julia was five years old. Her father was one of the founders of the New York Stock Exchange. A strict Calvinist, he spent his money on private schooling for his sons and daughters, going so far as to buy Thomas Coles's huge Voyage of Life paintings to give his children's home a religious atmosphere. But in spite of their sheltered upbringing, Julia's three brothers were a little wild, and she and her sisters longed to be equally independent. Her brother Sam married Emily Astor, heir to an even larger fortune than the Wards', and became a well-known socialite who enlarged his younger sister's social circle by befriending the poet Henry Wadsworth Longfellow and the abolitionist politician Charles Sumner. He was a passionate collector of European literature who was celebrated for inventing a signature cocktail, the Sam Ward, a whole, peeled lemon suspended in an icy glass of chartreuse.

When she was seventeen, Julia Ward published her first essay, a review of Lamartine's Jocelyn, a French novel plotted around mistaken sexual identity. By her early twenties, she had established a reputation for her literary abilities in spite of her father's and uncle's disapproval. Hoping to escape the confines of her childhood home, she married the dashing war hero Samuel Gridley Howe, who was the physician-director of the Perkins Institution, a school for the blind. He turned out to be even less supportive of her literary ambitions than her father's family had been. From 1843, when they married, until her husband's death in 1876, the two were locked in a passionate struggle, and Julia's writing was often at the heart of it. In spite of this opposition, she wrote constantly, both in private diaries and manuscripts and for publication. Her first book of poems, Passion Flowers, was published in 1854 to wide acclaim, but it caused a great deal of family strife after her husband's friends pointed out to him that poems such as "Mind versus Mill-Stream" and "The Heart's Astronomy" could be read as discussions of their marriage and family. Julia Ward Howe made no secret of the painful conflicts that grew out of her passionate desires to think and to write. But in spite of them, she managed to publish four books of poetry, produce a play, publish two travel books, edit a collection of essays defending women's education, and write a biography of Margaret Fuller, along with numerous philosophical and biographical essays. She gave a final twist to her marital struggles by publishing a biography of her husband after his death, and in 1898, she published her own *Reminiscences*.

Howe had quite a bit to remember. In addition to her successes as a writer, she had been acquainted with many of the leading intellectual and cultural figures of her day, including the transcendentalist Margaret Fuller, the Unitarian preacher Theodore Parker, the radical abolitionist John Brown, the astronomer Maria Mitchell, and the suffragist Lucy Stone. She had traveled extensively, not only to England and Italy but also to Cuba and Greece. She had visited Civil War battlefields, become famous for her war song, and then used her fame to argue for women's political, economic, and educational rights. To cap it all off, she had established Mother's Day, a pacifist holiday based on her belief that women must get political rights in order to prevent the violence of war.

Howe's life was full of contradictions. At one time she was author of a martial hymn that worked as a stirring call to arms, and at another she was the leader of a peace movement. She puzzled about American philosophies of sex and wrote many pages exploring gender confusion, but she also defined herself as a "woman's woman," though she was never completely certain of what that meant. Her arguments with her husband were passionately public, but she published a hagiographic memoir of their marriage. Always, the contradictions seemed to swirl around questions about women—their place, their appropriate work, their talents, and more specifically, her talents. Howe's incandescent intelligence made the men in her life very uneasy, and at times it caused her great pain as well. But although Howe's personal contradictions make her a fascinating figure, her writing has much broader significance. From her private writings, particularly the unfinished *Hermaphrodite*, we can glean great insights into women's philosophies—and confusions—about sex in the early nineteenth century.

Renée Bergland
Simmons University

PRIMARY WORKS

Passion Flowers, 1854; *Words for the Hour*, 1857; *Trip to Cuba*, 1860; *Later Lyrics*, 1866; *From the Oak to the Olive: A Plain Record of a Pleasant Journey*, 1868; *World's Peace Congress*, 1870; *Sex and Education: A Reply to Dr. E. H. Clarke's "Sex in Education*," 1874; *Memoir of Dr. Samuel Gridley Howe*, 1876; *Margaret Fuller (Marchesa Ossoli)*, 1883; *Is Polite Society Polite? and Other Essays*, 1895; *Reminiscences, 1819–1899*, 1899; *From Sunset Ridge*, 1899; *At Sunset*, 1910; *Leonora, or the World's Own*, in *Representative American Plays*, Arthur Hobson Quinn, ed., 1917; *The Walk with God*, Laura E. Richards, ed., 1919; *Hippolytus*, in *Monte Cristo and Other Plays*, J. B. Russak, ed., 1945; *The Hermaphrodite*, Gary Williams, ed., 2004.

from **The Hermaphrodite**[1]

[In this section of the manuscript, the pages are numbered beginning with 2 and concluding with 163. The fragment does not include a first page and is missing pages 118–132.]

... ration on the part of my parents, it was resolved to invest me with the dignity and insignia of manhood, which would at least permit me to choose my own terms in associating with the world, and secure to me an independence of position most desirable for one who could never hope to become the half of another. I was baptized therefore by a masculine name, destined to a masculine profession, and sent to a boarding school for boys, that I might become robust and manly, and haply learn to seem that which I could never be.

At school, and afterward at college, my career was more prosperous than could have been anticipated. I learned quickly, was sensitive to reproof, and ambitious of approbation. I became a favorite with my tutors, and ranked among the first in my class. Even my rough comrades learned to play more gently with me than with each other—in my intercourse with them, I instinctively appealed to their generosity, rather than defy their force. "Laurence is tired, poor fellow, do not hurt him, he is not so strong as we—" thus they spoke of me, and the most hardy among them agreed to protect and defend one superior to themselves in grace and agility, but greatly their inferior in force. I was distinguishable from them chiefly by a stronger impulse of physical modesty, a greater sensitiveness to kindness, or its reverse, more quickness and less endurance, a more vivid imagination, and a feebler power of reasoning. But a child has, properly speaking, no sex, and my time of trial came not until childhood has passed—then only did I learn all that I was, and was not, and this fearful lesson has occupied my whole life.

I saw my parents only at long intervals during the years I passed at school. They were cold and reserved towards me, and seemed always to feel a certain relief at the termination of my short and infrequent vacations. I learned at last to dread rather than desire the arrival of those periods so golden in the lives of most children, and was scarcely sorry to learn that my visits at home were to cease with the beginning of my academic career. The college for which I was destined was remote from my father's residence, and on entering it, I saw him for the last time in several years. He came, on this occasion, to announce to me the birth of a younger and only brother, the death of my mother, and his own intention of being absent from the country for the space of a year or more. He seemed to me more cold and repulsive than ever, and I was surprised to find that he had taken pains to inform himself of the minutest details bearing any relation to my character

---

[1]From Julia Ward Howe, *The Hermaphrodite: Legacies of Nineteenth-Century American Women* Writers, ed. Gary Williams (Lincoln: University of Nebraska Press, 2004).

and conduct. His approbation and his counsel were briefly summed up in these words: "Laurence, you have studied well; continue to apply yourself, and to avoid all unnecessary intimacies."

"Yes, Sir."

"Embrace your father, Laurence," cried my old preceptor, who was present at this laconic parting.

"It is quite unnecessary," said the frigid Paternus.

"I am deuced glad of it," rejoined I, with a long breath.

My father fixed his eyes on mine with an expression of some astonishment—he read in my face an indifference and pride which might have seemed the reflection of his own. He coldly bade farewell, and left me—young as I was, I had at least determined that he should never know the pain he had given me.

At this period of my life, I know not how an impartial judge would have decided the doubtful question of my being—my powers of intellect had shot beyond those of my compeers, while yet my form threatened to take a strongly feminine development. My complexion was singularly delicate, and my hair, though continually cropped, would retain its silky softness, and fell in many curls around my neck and brow. At long intervals, my usually robust health was interrupted by fits of indisposition, each of which seemed a sort of crisis, a struggle between death and life. Strange to say, nature had endowed me with rare beauty. I grew tall and slender, my limbs were finely moulded, and my head might have been cited as a perfect model of classic grace. This beauty, under other circumstances, might have been a blessing; as it was, it proved the curse and torment of my life. In vain would I have shrunk into obscurity—I could nowhere show myself without being observed and pointed out of all. Women often gave me proofs of a stronger interest than any inspired by mere benevolence, while the eyes of men so scrutinized me that I was fain to hide myself from them with a perturbation for which I could scarce account to myself. I was anxious to propitiate the good will of all, but any intimacy beyond that of ordinary friendship was incomprehensible to me. For man or woman, as such, I felt an entire indifference—when I wished to trifle, I preferred the latter, when I wished to reason gravely, I chose the former. I sought sympathy from women, advice from men, but love from neither. Like all other young creatures, I was gladly in the company of the gay and of the gentle, but I could not be in it long without learning that a human soul, simply as such, and not invested with the capacity of either entire possession or entire surrender, has but a lame and unsatisfactory part to play in this world.

In the village that surrounded us, my college companions had many female friends, among whom I gradually became known. These pretty moths consumed no small portion of our learned leisure, and our holidays were entirely consecrated to their service. On these occasions, we often arranged parties of pleasure to various caves, ruins, and woods in the romantic neighbourhood, in which every youth was cavalier to some fair maiden, and the time was improved by most of them for the establishment of relations of a more or less intimate nature. Of these, some were passionate, some senti-mental, some transitory, some of life long duration, but all partaking of a feeling which was to me utterly incomprehensible. I enjoyed as keenly as any one a gallop on the greensward, or a ramble in the woods—our feasts and frolics, our songs and dances were all delightsome to me then in vivid reality, as now in softened remembrance—my eye was gratified by the grace and loveliness of the young girls, and my heart expanded in the sunshine of their gentle, happy nature, but they were to me even as the flowers, their sisters, and as the birds, their cousins, and as the distant clouds of heaven, and as all things else that were changeful and beautiful like unto them.

It was sufficiently easy for me to vie with my fellow-students in render-ing every courtesy to these fair creatures. Like all the rest, I led their gentle feet over rocks and mountain paths, or bent my knee that they might spring from it into the saddle—I twined chaplets for their festivals, and verses for their songs, but no passionate thought or wish was interwoven with either. The enthusiasm expressed in my verses was vague and abstract in its charac-ter, and though of warmer blood and more generous nature than most of my fellows, I yet in comparison with them seemed cold and statute-like. The innocence and purity of the young girls did not however lead them to sus-pect any peculiarity of kind in me. They found me ever gay, affable, and gracefully bold—they often turned from the amorous gabble of a stupid lover, to seek amusement from me, and I can still recall the rage of a senti-mental youth whose disdainful sweetheart, wearied, angry, or alarmed at the suit he was pressing, broke from him, and took refuge beside me, saying: I shall go to Laurence, for he never makes love.

Chapter 2nd

The relations which I have described lasted through a series of quiet, pleas-ant years, devoted otherwise to study, and marked by a gentle growth in the powers of thought and of action. Happy and golden do those days now look to me, though at the time, I was conscious of little more than a vague bien être, sometimes interrupted by deepest melancholy, and a hope of some thing far brighter and better, which methought time must soon bring me, but for which I am waiting still. Thus it is that we begin life in the expecta-tion of positive enjoyment, and look impatiently for the day which shall see us very great, very rich, or very happy. It is reserved for the positive evils of life to teach us that the negative happiness of early youth has in it more of actual delight than any thing else that awaits us; and that, from the toils and responsibilities of active life, and from the satiety of luxurious indul-gence, we are fain to turn back, and remember with longing the days in which we were neither oppressed with business, nor worn out with anxiety nor by ennuyé by the absence of either.

Yet the struggle from childhood to comparative maturity had had for me its secret agonies, its hours of depression and desolation—of these, I do not speak—I have never revealed them—I have never willingly laid upon another the lightest portion of the burthen which it was given to me to bear through life. Thus far, at least, God has ever been my friend, he has ever given me courage to support it.

It was in the last year of my Academic course that my quiet and harmless life met with a strange interruption. At this time, a handsome and sprightly widow, some twenty eight years of age, had added herself to the little circle of our neighbourhood. She came from a gay metropolis, where her life had been embellished by station and wealth, and, as some said, by a little gallantry. She appeared as something new and rare to all of us, a revelation of some thing as yet unseen and unimagined by us, and I fear me that maidenhood, with all its tender blushes, seemed to us quite tame and crude in comparison with the ever varying powers and beauties of the all accomplished, fully developed woman. The prettiest of our girls had perhaps the advantage of her in freshness and fragility of form and feature, but on the other hand, her beauty was heightened by her wit, displayed by her toilette, and rendered irresistible by an abandon which was not levity, a tact which was not worldliness, and a self-possession which was not impudence. As one may well imagine, the young ladies envied and imitated her, the young men vied with each other in their adoration of her, and I, occupying a middle ground, admired her at a respectful distance, giving her no reason to complain of either presumption or neglect on my part. But Emma von P. was not to be treated in this way. She was accustomed to see herself the queen of every circle in which she moved. The homage of the least was as necessary to her as that of the greatest, and while one heart remained unconquered by her charms, her triumph was incomplete.

One by one, rather in a body, the youths of our division had surrendered themselves at discretion. For her were the flowers, for her the verses and the serenades—it was who should ride beside her, who should drive or walk with her, who should go furthest and labour hardest for her pleasure. For such is the generous ambition of youth, it is who shall give most, and its day dream is to deserve the affection of one beloved by devotion and true service. Men of a riper age are better calculators—it is their business to receive as much, and give as little as possible, and the vision with which they delight themselves is one of fond, beautiful women, driven to distraction by their indifference, and vying with each other in their endeavors to win the worthless love of one who loves himself.

But let me do justice to the heroine-worship of our young gentlemen. I have seen the fools quarrel for the possession of a glove, or a faded flower from her hand, as they scramble for gold and precious stones at the largesse of some Eastern despot—bets were made upon her ribands, and duels were fought for her smiles. Nevertheless, as all human beings are said to esteem lightly that which is lightly got and as women especially are piqued by the indifference of a man and rejoice more in the subjugation of one rebel than in the loyal devotion of ninety and nine faithful ones that need no subjugation, so Emma von P. turned from the crowd of her admirers to look upon the unapproachable Laurence, whose greatest merit may have been that he seemed to trouble himself very little about her.

"Why does *he* never bring me any flowers?" said she, one evening, when her appearance in the ball room had been hailed by a perfect ovation of wreaths and banquets. A magnificent Camelia from my boutonnière was the only possible reply—it was honoured by a place in the bosom of the fair one, in which, however, I had no desire of succeeding it.

They were comparing several lyrics addressed to her on her birthday—she turned carelessly to me.

"I suppose that you have not the gift of writing verses."

"None worthy of being offered to Madame von P."

"He slanders himself," cried my fellow students: "Laurence is the best poet of his class—if he tries for the University prize, his poem is sure to receive it."

"There are other prizes worth striving for," said Emma von P. demurely looking down, and lancing to me a glance fuller of meaning than a thrown gauntlet. I hastily improvised some verses, and wrote them in pencil, the crown of my hat serving me for a desk. She received them triumphantly but having read them, her countenance expressed a certain disappointment.

"They are beautiful, but cold," said she.

"They are at least sincere, I say only that which I feel, and feel only the little that I know."

"Then you have still every thing to learn," said Emma, and bit her lip.

The challenge was now fairly given. I must either quarrel with Emma, or make love to her. The latter would be by far the most agreeable alternative to her, and the most advantageous to me. The incipient attacks were hazarded on the one side, and met on the other, with a skill & caution truly military—I cannot say that the same circumspection characterized all that followed. There is something of coquetry in all human beings, and mine could not but experience a certain elation when Emma repulsed for my sake a crowd of suitors, and when I marked that, in the admiring world of which she constituted the centre, she was seized with sudden blindness, and had no eye, no ear for any but me. My place was henceforth ever at her side in the salon, or in the green-wood. I was her chosen knight, and never have I been promoted to more gentle service. Many were the tête à tête wanderings arranged by herself, in which the charms of all that is loveliest in Nature, and in woman were combined by her, to give the fair picture the fairest surroundings, to place her image in the innermost shrine of my heart and to gather around every association of poetry and beauty. Long were our interviews, endlessly varied, our conversations. Unlike most women, she possessed the twofold gift of being graceful alike in speech and in silence—her voice was full of music, her words full of power, but when she listened, her features all spoke; and you read the eloquent answer in her eye long before you heard it from her lips, as lightning travels more swiftly than thunder. Gradually the charm of our intercourse deepened, the tone of coquetry grew into that of deepest feeling, and the eyes that had once flashed such proud defiance at me now sought mine with an expression by turns enthusiastic, tearful, even agonized. When we met, and when we parted, her hand lingering in mine, each finger seemed to interrogate each of mine, asking why its pressure was so slight, and so easily relaxed. Often, at the termination of a moonlight walk, or of a long session à quatres yeux in her little boudoir, she would fix her eyes on mine, as if in earnest interrogation and entreaty—not reading there the response she wished, she would turn abruptly from me, or push me from her, and close the door upon me with a nervous energy bordering on irritation.

The epoch of our last collegiate examination had arrived—we were all occupied in preparing for the exercises. Among various prizes had been announced one, to be adjudged to the author of the best poem, and this *concurrence* was to be crowned by the most imposing ceremony of the week of trial. For this, the last day had been chosen, a numerous company would be invited. The rival poems were to be read aloud, each by its author, and the successful candidate should receive the prize from the hand of Emma. The last clause in the prospectus of arrangements gave the keenest edge to the eagerness of the young competitors. They had all envied me the preference shown me by their new divinity, they were all determined to snatch from me, if possible, the crown made doubly precious by her hand. There was great agony of preparation throughout the college, and a sighing and groaning as of parturient mountains preparing to bring forth mice. During the last month of the term, all spoke in rhyme, thought in verse, ate and drank in strict measure. Those who had neither been born poets nor bred orators hoped in a few weeks to possess the attributes of both, not knowing that it needs a whole lifetime to acquire an art, of which the germ has not been given with life itself. They had each chosen themes suited to their various tastes and studies. I had written my poem without labour, almost without any fixed design—it was but a piece of my every day thought, more neatly fashioned than the crude jottings down which often recorded my soul's life, and which always spoke of states of feeling, not of events. I had only followed the guidance of the voices which, in those days, came to me at morn, at noon, and with the holy eventide, bringing me as from another world, thoughts and images of thoughts, which could only utter themselves in song.

"Here we are, all talking, consulting, and disputing about our poems," cried the students one day, "and no one has heard a syllable from Laurence, in any way explanatory of his intentions. Confess now, Laurence, that you have not yet thought of a subject."

"Not much in truth."

"Ah! For the first time, you will be behindhand. Know, gracilis puer, graceless boy, that moonlight rambles and metaphysical discussions with pretty women will not help you to the Muse."

"And tears will bedew the nose of the sweet old preceptor when, at the critical moment he shall thus interrogate you: 'Laurentsi, ubi est carmen tuum?'"

"Yet the poem has somehow written itself," said I.

"Has it so, and already? Then it is probably something brief and personal—to memory, hope, despair, or your mistress's eyelash."

"To the blessed wig of our chancellor?"

"Or to his ox, the Latin professor, or his ass, the Greek professor, or to his man-servant the chemist, or to his maid-servant, the old woman who presides over our theological studies and gives us, hebdomadally, a foretaste of damnation?"

"To nothing and nobody," cried I, stunned by their noise.

"Ah then, to one who is not a thing nor a body, but a heavenly essence, radiance, and effulgence—to the witching Emma?"

"I do not jest about Madame von P." said I, with some coldness, and turning to depart.

"Is he not shy, this Laurence?" said they, as I left them.

Chapter 3rd

On the evening that preceded the last day of trial, Wilhelm, a student who might have been my friend, had he not been Emma's lover, came to my room.

"Laurence," said he, "you have passed, thus far, a better examination than any of us. Are you not satisfied with your success? Do you still intend to present your poem for the prize tomorrow?"

I replied in the affirmative. He continued: "I implore you to listen to me. You are sure to receive the prize, and from Emma's hand. But for you, this happiness would be mine, but for you, I should still be as once I was, her favored one."

"As once you were?" repeated I, with contemptuous disbelief.

"Yes, but let me say all that I have to say. You do not love this woman, you have never loved her, you are but playing with her, and here stands one who would peril his life to obtain the boon which to me were blessedness, which to you will be but a trifling and transient gratification."

"What is the end and aim of this discourse?"

"It is briefly this—name your price, and sell me your poem."

"I am no Judas, to sell my soul for thirty pieces of silver."

"It shall be no mean price, my patrimony is large, ask whatever you will."

"If I should sell it thrice over, I could not make it yours," said I, with some haughtiness. "Children will claim their own parents."

"Then thus do I commit your first born to the flames," and before I could spring forward to prevent it, the excited youth had held my manu-script, which lay upon the table, in the blaze of the lamp—he waved it, flaming, around his head until nearly consumed, and then threw it from the window with a yell of triumph.

I stood and smiled upon him. "I will give you your revenge, if you wish it," said he.

"À demain," said I, courteously waving my hand, "I am in no hurry about it."

He looked at me in embarrassment and surprise, and was glad to seek the door.

That very evening and late into the night, I sat and talked with Emma von P. Our conversation had wandered hither and thither, as freely as our thoughts, but these, though widely discursive, ran ever in parallels. She had sung her sweetest, looked her beautifullest, and her discourse had been, as it ever was, full of point and of meaning. We had entered into a playful battle, tilting with golden lances, and pelting each other with rose leaves. At length, we became silent, she from very weariness, while I grew absorbed in painful forebodings. The conviction had forced itself more and more upon my mind that beneath Emma's jests there lurked a deep & dreadful earnest. I had begun to experience a malaise, an anxiety in her presence, for I felt the hidden strength of her nature, and I knew that it would soon be turned against her own happiness, and my peace. It was well, methought, that the hour of our separation was so near at hand.

"We have been very merry, and yet I am so sad!" sighed my companion from her corner of the causense.

"Your ladyship has then a fearful habit of deception, for I have observed that whenever you have been gayest, you turn to me with the smile yet on your lips to tell me that you are so sad!"

"Sadness and mirth are ever as near to each other as life and death," answered she musingly, "and there is always something of the one in the other."

Another pause: "What am I like?" said Emma to me.

"You are like a beautiful flower on an iron stem. The flower will fade, the iron will kill, so that you are mortal in yourself, and mortal to others."

"Thanks for a very bad compliment—shall I tell you what you are like?"

"Most certainly."—"You are like this marble against which I lean my head, whose pulses throb so that there seems to be a pulse in the cold stone itself—thus a heart that is near you may think to feel the presence of one in you, but it is all marble, only marble."

After a moment's silence, she continued: "How old are you, Laurence?"

"Nigh upon twenty one."

"Nearly twenty one? quite a man then, and still a trifler." Exquisitely touching was the tone in which this gentle reproach was uttered. I durst not betray the emotion it caused me, and my reply was cold and almost rude. "You have always invited me to trifle," I said, "and I thought that it was altogether to your taste, but since you have had enough of it, good night."

Oh, Emma! this should have been our last good night. As I left the house, she called me back. I heard her steps as she ran to overtake me, but I hastened mine, and did not look back. She returned and closed the door abruptly, but I heard a sob, as I passed near her window, on my way home.

* * *

On the afternoon of the day following, we were marshalled in the chapel of the college, for the reading of the prize poems. As we entered, we found the area filled by the members of the junior classes, the faculty of the college, our young friends of the neighbourhood, and some distinguished guests from the castle. At the upper end was the rostrum from which, by turns, we were to make our appeal to the favour of the audience—upon either side of this was a raised seat, on one of which was seated the chancellor of the University, and on the other, as upon a throne, our fair queen of love and beauty, Emma von P. to whom men forgave the pangs she sent to their hearts, for the delight she gave their eyes. It is so great a pleasure to see a woman finely trained and developed in person and in character. Your crude ore is cumbrous to carry, and difficult of estimation, but though Emma bore the guinea stamp of high breeding, she was yet of virgin gold, for a' that.

The compositions were really of a more respectable order than I had anticipated. There was unavoidably some pedantry displayed in the choice of subjects, and the young authors were obviously more familiar with their humanities than with humanity. It is true that we had a disquisition on the sufferings of Dido, and an ode commemorative of the constancy of Penelope, but I have often seen both of these heroines much more unkindly treated. There were several other productions, of which the theme alone could be called classic. A revolutionary poem followed, flaming and captious, at which the venerable Chancellor and other wigs there present winced somewhat. Then came a theological argument in blank verse, dogmatical, ambitious, and exceeding tedious to the young girls, delivered by a youth of pale complexion, red nose, and very indifferent digestion. After these exhibitions, Wilhelm really appeared to the greatest advantage, as he recited with a feeling voice a graceful lyric upon the ever old and ever new subject of love, into the closing lines of which was wrought an unmistakeable tribute to the charms of Emma. Universal applause followed his performance. He looked at Emma and at me, and seemed surprised to see a smile on my lips, and none on hers.

"I am the last, at least," said Wilhelm, with an air of satisfaction.

"You forget that the best and worst is yet to come, here is Laurence—"

Wilhelm hastily replied: "Laurence has no poem."

Emma overheard him, and changed colour, while she stole at me an anxious and inquiring glance.

"How know you that, Wilhelm?" said I—the countenance of my rival was instantly darkened. As my name was called, I ascended the platform, stated to the audience that my manuscript had accidentally been destroyed and requested permission to repeat memoratà, instead of reading my poem. This was granted me, as a matter of course. Then, with a voice of silvery sweetness, and in a measure peculiarly my own, I sang the sufferings of a soul exiled from heaven, and sent into this world invested with the semblance, but not the attributes of humanity. I told of its solitary wanderings on earth, how it could nothing make, nothing possess—how its abstract orphanhood could establish no relationship, and extort no sympathy from the souls of men, veiled in a flesh of whose wants and powers it knew nothing. The alternative was then offered to it of becoming utterly mortal, or of returning to its ghostland, and I closed with some thrilling numbers descriptive of the noble scorn with which the pure spirit refused to bear the unworthy burthen of the flesh, once contemplated and understood, and the fee and fearless courage with which it spread its wings, and flew back to the bosom of its God. My audience was deeply and attentively silent, and when my voice ceased, one long-drawn breath betrayed the interest with which I had been heard.

The committee appointed to decide upon the adjudication of the prize did not include (Deo sit gratias) the faculty of the college. It was composed of several gentlemen of the neighbourhood, among whom was the well accomplished Baron L———, who was present with several foreigners, his friends, and guests. The committee retired into an anteroom, whence they shortly returned, having been quite unanimous in their decision. The Baron, as foreman of the Jury, addressed the chancellor, and informed him that they had agreed, without one dissenting voice, to adjudge the prize to M. Laurence de ———. The Chancellor at first replied by a well bred stare and the whole Council of Pedagogues unhesitatingly expressed their disapproval.

"The poem of M. Laurence bears no marks of historical research," murmured the expounder of Sallust.

"In a theological point of view, it is an entire fallacy," growled the Doctor Divinitatis.

"There is nothing in it which would lead one to suppose that the author had been thoroughly grounded by me in trigonometry, integral calculus, conic sections, et alia," remarked the man of cubes and decahedrons.

"It is at least highly, beautifully poetical," rejoined the Baron, in his courtliest manner, "and as we came hither to listen to poems, and to decide upon their merits as such, you must allow me in the name of my friends of the Committee, to announce to the company the name of M. Laurence as the recipient of the prize, and to offer him our warmest thanks and congratulations upon his public desert of it."

A loud burst of applause confirmed the sanction of the whole assembly upon his decision. Some reply on my part seemed necessary, but I could only say to the Baron: "I have as yet small pretensions to knowledge of any kind. Thanks to you, who have recognized in me the presence of the poetic power."

"Turning from him, I knelt at Emma's feet to receive the prize—it was a crown woven of velvet oak leaves with golden acorns. I felt the tremulousness of the hand that placed it on my head, I saw by the tearful smile with which she greeted me, that her heart was moved at once to joy and grief. She was proud and happy in my triumph, but that another should have dedicated his services to her, while the poem of her chosen one bore no trace of her, this grieved her deeply. Yet she was alike incapable of feeling or of showing a petty vexation, and when she spoke to her [sic], her voice and her words were deeply sympathetic.

"Oh, Laurence, your flight is lofty, and the heaven you dwell in is beautiful, but why do you take no one with you?

"Could you not follow me then, Emma?"

"Did you expect it?"—"Yes—at least I hoped it. I have often wished to talk with you of the relations of pure spirit."

"Laurence, I hope that you are not one of those unsexed souls."

"Have you never been one?" said I.

"Never," she replied, "since I have learned what it is to be a woman."

These words made a strong impression upon me—"what is it to be a woman?" I asked of myself: "It is obviously a matter of which I have small conception."

As I looked from Emma's countenance, I saw that Wilhelm stood near, and glared on us with angry eyes. I went up to him, and offered him my hand.

"Come, Wilhelm, you cannot be angry that I have taken my revenge—I am at least glad that it is one which involves no injury to you"—"Why do you look so savagely upon me?" I continued. "I have entirely forgiven your foolish freak of last night."

"I shall never forgive you," muttered Wilhelm between his teeth.

I was ordered to wear my wreath through the evening. Music now sounded in the hall, and couples stood up to dance. I gave my arm to Emma, and led her to the head of the Quadrille. Her momentary sadness had passed away, and as she began to tread her graceful measure, she turned upon me a look of love and delight so radiant, that it sent a strange thrill to the very core of my frozen heart, and again I asked of myself: "what is it to be a woman?"

As we stood together in an interval of repose, I could not avoid overhearing the conversation of two strangers who occupied a place behind me, and of whom one spoke with a strongly marked Southern accent.

"What a beautiful antique head is this of the young Laureate's," remarked one, "so delicately chiselled, so finely set, one might say an Antinoüs, a Mercury, almost an Apollo."

"None of these," replied the Italian. "His beauty is of a more vague and undecided character—it is a face and form of strange contradictions—the eye and brow command, while the mouth persuades."

"The motions and gestures too are peculiar."

"Do you not see a striking resemblance to the lovely hermaphrodite in the villa Borghese?"

I heard no more—a mist came before my eyes, and a deadly faintness over my heart. With a hurried apology, I resigned Emma to the eager Wilhelm, and staggered to the open air—some minutes passed before I could recover strength to regain my room.

Chapter 4th

Once alone, in my own room, I could breathe more freely, but my whole being had received a shock, an impetus that hurried it to some deed, some resolution, I knew not what. A sort of galvanic agony had taken possession of my body, and forces foreign to itself were playing wildly with it. My vestments seemed to gird in my swelling heart, and I tore them off, half resolved to wear them no more. I was incapable of thought or of reason, but my brain was in a state of the highest spontaneous action, and a thousand horrible images of disgrace, despair, and utter confusion crowded each other in and out of my mind, like figures in a fever dream. Every thing around me seemed instinct with life—the very walls had eyes to spy out my secret, and tongues to betray it. I hurried hither and thither to escape the scrutiny of mocking spectres, who, all unseen, were yet present to me, and with hideous laughter followed me every where. At length, in very desperation, I threw myself, half undressed, on my bed, and drawing its covering around me, attempted to close my eyes, and compelled myself to lie still. Gradually, the confusion of my thoughts became greater, but less painful—the sounds of music and laughter became fainter in my ears, and soon ceased altogether. I know not how long it was before a light footstep at my bedside, told me that I must have been asleep.

A light footstep? oh how light! a gliding form, a gentle but fervent voice. Could it be? I rubbed my eyes, I was fully awake, and Emma, in all her brilliant beauty, stood before me.

"You were ill, dearest Laurence, and I could not rest until I had seen you—you are to leave tomorrow, and I could not live without one kind farewell from you. Oh Laurence, Laurence, do not look at me thus—you know well, you have long known what I am here to tell you."

I raised my head from the pillow and looked into her eyes. That look must have expressed the horror I felt, for it seemed to destroy the momentary courage which had given firmness to her step, and clearness to her voice. She sank upon her knees beside me, she buried her face in the curtain that hung near us, and was silent for a moment—then, raising it again, she clasped my knees, and spoke with a rapid, unequal, faltering intonation, as if she feared that her strength would desert her before she could speak out her meaning. "Listen to me Laurence," she said: "two deaths were before me. If I sought you not, I died of longing, if I came to you, I died of shame. The first I have long endured, it is slowly feeding upon my life—if the second fate must be mine, be merciful, and kill me quick." In stony silence, I sat and listened—she continued: "I do not ask you to marry me, Laurence, I am still young, rich, and perhaps handsome, but I do not pretend to be worthy of you—had I such a hope, I should scarce be at your feet, but look you, I am here alone, in your room, in your power, at dead of night—you cannot misinterpret this, it must convince you that I love you better than life, better than honour, better than my own soul and God. Give me but this one night, but this one hour—do you ask where I shall be tomorrow? I can die tomorrow—I shall have been happy."

I roused myself at length from my stupor—"Emma," said I, laying on hers a hand so cold that she started. "Emma, as you value your soul's peace, fly—fly from me, and think of me only as you think of the dead."

"Never!" cried Emma: "you may smite me, you may kill me, but I will die here at your feet—my last look shall be on you—my last prayer shall bless you."

I pointed to the time piece on the mantel, and said: "Emma, this is madness—to yield to it would be fatal to both of us. One of us must leave this room for the night, I give you five minutes to decide which it shall be."

She sprang to her feet, and stood before me, a beautiful impersonation of scorn and fury. Lightnings flashed from her eyes—a curse rose to her lips and died there—those lips were made for blessings only—tears and convulsive sobs burst forth instead, and brokenly these words: "you cannot cannot—cannot!"

"Listen to me, dearest Emma," I said, and drew her to a seat beside me—"listen to me—can you bear to hear the truth? will you hate me for telling it to you?"

"Tell it gently," she replied, with averted eyes. I continued: "Emma, your love is too beautiful, too glorious a thing to be thrown away upon one who can never make you his. There lies between us a deep, mysterious gulf, seek not to fathom it—with me, your human destiny would be hopelessly imperfect—were I to wed you, I should indeed deserve your curse." She was silent, and I proceeded: "there are between human beings relations independent of sex, relations of pure spirit, of heavenly sympathy of immaterial and undying affinities—such are the only relations that can exist between us, dearest Emma."

While I spoke, her eyes were suddenly turned upon mine with a look of almost superhuman intelligence. A new and dreadful suspicion seemed to dawn upon her mind. When I had ceased, she came slowly up to me, and uncovering my arm, held it up to the light—it was round and smooth as her own. With the same deliberation, she surveyed me from head to foot, the disordered habiliments revealing to her every outline of the equivocal form before her. She saw the bearded lip and earnest brow, but she saw also the falling shoulders, slender neck, and rounded bosom—then with a look like that of the Medusa, and a hoarse utterance, she murmured: "monster!"

"I am as God made me, Emma."

A shriek, fearful to hear, and thrice fearful to give, followed by another, and another, and a maniac lay foaming and writhing on the floor at my feet.

Over the memory of that night, I would gladly draw the thickest veil of oblivion. Like Job, I could pray that its name might be blotted out from the fair annals of the year, that no evening star might smile upon its birth, and no morning star weep for its departure, that its dews might bring no blessing, and its shades no rest. Methought it was a night on which God had slept, and permitted the power of evil to possess even the fairest of his creatures, for her own destruction. Yet it was not so—behind the worst that had happened there lurked an unfathomable *worse* from which the barriers of heavenly love and watchfulness had separated us. Emma was doomed, marked for her grave, but it would be a spotless one, and we were both guiltless of any crime against ourselves and God.

But for the moment, I was incapable of consolation. The curse of my nature had fallen upon another more heavily than upon myself—the shattered being before me was at once a monument of my past, and an earnest of my future: and kneeling over her, I almost prayed God to smite me with her madness. She heard me not, saw me not—a wild and frenzied smile distorted her features, and her lips were parted in incoherent ravings, of which

I could only distinguish these words: "like the hermaphrodite in the Villa Borghese," followed by a hideous laugh, after which she relapsed into broken and unintelligible mutterings. Almost as wild as herself, I struggled in vain to summon counsel for the exigency of the moment. The only idea that clearly presented itself to me was the necessity of restoring Emma at once, and unseen to the retirement of her own walls—there was but one way of effecting this—scarce knowing what I did, I raised her in my arms, and carried her down the staircase, and in the direction of her dwelling. My strength, though doubled by the energy of desperation, was scarcely adequate to so great and long continued an effort; and as I staggered, nearly fainting, under the burthen, it was almost a relief to hear the approaching footsteps of a man. This feeling vanished, however, when I recognized the voice of Wilhelm who, in no very happy or friendly mood, was wandering about the precincts of the college.

"Whom have we here?" he cried, at the unusual sight of a man bearing an inanimate form in his arms.

"You had better not interrupt me," I said, endeavouring to pass him, but he had recognized my voice, and planted himself in my way. A straggling moonbeam broke at that moment through the thick shade of the avenue, and fell upon the changed and convulsed countenance of Emma. Alas! He had seen her, she was in his power.

"Laurent, in the name of God, what means this?"

"Wilhelm, if you are a man, help me to bear Emma to her own house— she is ill, she is delirious, and every thing depends upon her being immediately at home, and under proper care."

Wilhelm spoke not, but placed his arm with mine around the form of Emma—together, and in silence, we carried her to the home that she would leave no more. We summoned her domestics, and ordered them to seek the promptest medical aid. We laid her on the couch unconscious of the presence [of] others. I knelt beside her, I clasped her hand, my eyes silently implored from hers one look of recognition and of blessing, but in vain. I was aroused by Wilhelm, who laid his hand upon my shoulder and pointed to the door. The surgeon had arrived, our presence in that chamber of despair was worse than unnecessary, and Wilhelm was impatient to demand of me an explanation of my mysterious conduct and position.

When we were alone, and out of sight and of hearing, Wilhelm, who had forced me to walk at a pace as rapid and nervous as his own, drew his arm from mine, and abruptly said: "Now Laurent, you must account for this either to me, or to the world."

"I am ready," I said, and drew my rapier.

"That will not suffice," he replied: "There are some things known to me which the shedding of your blood or of mine will scarcely elucidate—how came Emma in your room tonight?"

"How dare you assume that she was there?"

"Liar!"—"Slanderer!" Such words are not often exchanged with impunity. "I will die in defence of Emma's honour," cried I. "You shall die to avenge it," shouted Wilhelm. Another moment, and we closed in mortal combat.

Wilhelm fought with the ferocity of a tiger, almost it seemed to me, with the strength of one. At first, I was quite overwhelmed by the fury of his attack, yet scarcely daunted by it for I felt that his very rashness and violence must, in the end, defeat themselves. I cannot say whether it was by greater coolness, quickness of eye, or agility of body that the struggle was decided in my favour—this only I remember, that Wilhelm lay before me, prostrate and disarmed while with the point of my weapon at his throat, I held him at my mercy. At this moment, I paused. The steel that had let out our blood had perchance let out with it some of our madness, but, be that as it may, I could not slay the man now that I held him, defenceless in my grasp. I looked earnestly in his face, it was not the face of a coward. Even in the presence of death, his cheek blanched not, his look quailed not, and in his desperate danger, he even strove to taunt me.

"Don't be afraid to kill me," said he, with a bitter laugh: "It is safest, dead men tell no tales."

I threw away my sword: "I am not afraid to let you live," was my only answer. Wilhelm arose, and stood in silent surprize.

"Ask any thing of me but thanks," he said at length. "You have made the boon of life too worthless to me that I should thank you for it."

"I have nothing to ask of you for myself, but Wilhelm, as I have spared you, so I pray you to spare one whose reputation is in your power, even as your life has been in mine."

"Curses on her! She has trifled with me, scorned me, ruined herself. Is there any earthly reason why I should spare her?"

"Because you have loved her, because she is dying, most of all, because she is innocent."

"Prove to me her innocence, and I swear to respect it," replied Wilhelm.

I was silent. I saw clearly that the fates demanded an expiatory sacrifice, but the victim appointed was neither Wilhelm nor Emma. It was my own pride, almost my own life that I was called upon to immolate in behalf of one who had not hesitated to give up every thing for me. I must myself endure that fearful crucifixion. I must tear off that innermost sacred veil that shielded from scorn and pity the secret of my fate, and wrap it around Emma's defenceless honour. I was silent, but only for a moment. Oh Truth! Oh Emma! thank God, in that hour of trial, I loved you better than myself.

"Prove it—" repeated Wilhelm, in a defiant tone.

"I will do so," I replied, "but let me first tell you that the secret I am about to impart is not entrusted to you as a mark of confidence, you have deserved nothing of the kind from me. It is my desire to do justice to Emma alone that induces me to inform you of a fact, which, but for her unhappy position, would concern none but myself. Tell me now, Wilhelm, have I fought like a man?"

"Certainly."

"Have I treated you like a man?"

"I must say that you have."

"Have I, in all my college life maintained the integrity, the courage, the honour of a man?"

"Truly, I think so."

"Wilhelm, in all save these, I am none."

I did not repent me of my words, once spoken, but I felt that time, that eternity could never wring from me a confession more agonizing.

I turned me to depart, but I had not gone far, before Wilhelm came up to me, and laid his hand on my arm. He looked earnestly in my face, with an expression of doubt and wonder.

"You are no woman," said he, after a deliberate survey of my face and person.

"No," I replied, with a horrible sort of calmness: "I am no man, no woman, nothing. Let me go," and I pushed him from me, but he again seized me by both hands, and I saw in the cold moonlight that tears stood in his eyes.

"Laurence," he cried: "the sacrifice you have just made is heroic, and however lightly you may esteem me, I fully appreciate it—you have spared me, you have shielded Emma, and you cannot know that you have not ruined yourself. Hear me then while I swear, by the bloody agony of Christ, that the words you have spoken are, to all save me, as though they had never been uttered."

Wilhelm spoke in a tone of the deepest feeling, and as he did so, raised his right hand to heaven, so that his promise had all the solemnity of an oath.

"The vow is now registered in heaven," continued he, "and now tell me, what can I do to evince my gratitude for your forbearance, my appreciation of your noble conduct?"

I pointed, as nearly as I could, in the direction of Emma's dwelling—Wilhelm well understood the signal. "Remember her, and forget me," I said.

We parted sadly, but in perfect kindness.

Cold as duty, and stern as fate, the moon looked down upon me—and I was alone.

Home! I might indeed have been wise enough to know that no such place existed for me. What hearth, what heart would welcome me as its cherished guest? The only breast that had ever harboured my love had been as fearfully punished for its fondness as though it had opened its doors to a fiend, in the form of an angel.

Dim and vague indeed were my impressions of the scenes and companions of my childhood; cold and repulsive my remembrance of those who had borne to me the relation but scarcely the love of parents. The mother that bore me was dead to me long, long before the day that bade me mourn her death. And my father? It was with reluctance that I gave him even the name. In many years I had once seen him, or heard from him otherwise than through the medium of my tutor. He had indeed written to order that I should return to him immediately upon the close of the term, and had enclosed a sum of money amply sufficient for my expenses, but his letter was perfectly innocent of any hypocrisy of affection, and on reading it, I could not but acknowledge that he at least was entirely candid and constant in his indifference to his child. His parental tenderness, if any thing in his horny heart deserved the name, was doubtless monopolized by my younger brother, in whose person, but for my rights of primogeniture, would have been combined the succession of two princely estates.

Still, in my slowly weaned heart there dwelt the vision of a place where I had played in happy freedom, before I had borne the burthen of life, and learned how doubly heavy it was destined to be for me. There came to me images of trees that I had climbed, of waters that had held me in their sunny embrace, of grassy meadows on which I had laid me down to watch the gorgeous glory of sunset or the quiet beauty of a starry night. There lingered yet in my ear the echo of merry voices, and I thought that the laughing playmates who had so often caressed and tormented me still formed a rosy garland, of which I was the only blighted flower. The horrible event too which was still too fresh in my mind to be a memory, how did it chase me to some ark of safety, some spot sacred to kindest affections, to some heart whose sympathy should be spontaneous, whose love should be the involuntary tribute of nature. It was then with feelings of a mingled nature that I sought my father's house, yet in them hope predominated, and the very desperation of my condition, the sore need of my heart inspired me with a certain confidence in the ready succour and compassion of those nearest to me.

Once arrived, it needed little observation to dispel these consoling illusions. Cold and brief was my father's greeting, icy cold seemed the family circle that had been gathered to receive me. If the dinner that followed was not cold, it was at least utterly chilling and ungenial in its effects. The wine warmed no one, the food nourished no one—there were long pauses which nobody dared to interrupt, and brief remarks to which no one cared to reply. Paternus seemed to be the Evil Genius, the master magician of the feast, and one could have dreamed that the other figures around the table had been so many automata, animated only by his will. When he ate, the company ate, their very knives and forks keeping time with his. When he spoke, they listened and replied—when his voice ceased, they subsided into sympathetic silence. The dessert having been got through with, my health having been formally proposed and mechanically drunk, I wondered whether he would leave them rooted in their places until the next day, at the same hour; but he gave the signal of command, and they rose in concert, and marched like well drilled soldiers back to the drawing room.

I found my sisters changed past all remembrance, the world, matrimony and maternity having had full sway over them. The elder of them had married money, the younger had married love. Money was of course stupid and tedious, Love was a pretty man, but had probably seen his best days. Lady Money was cold and haughty, and iced me with a glittering smile. Lady Love was shy and timid, yet she glanced kindly at me when Paternus was not looking. Their children were not introduced at dessert, kept away doubtless in the fear lest they might catch their death of cold of their grandfather.

After having endured for an hour or two this purgatorial entertainment, it was a relief to hear a bounding step in the entry, and to see on the opening of the door, the glowing countenance of a beautiful boy. This was my brother, Philip, whom I had never before seen. The grim visage of Paternus relaxed into a smile at his approach, and patting him on the head, bade him go and shake hands with his brother. The boy glanced around the room, and having singled me out from the company, ran up to me, threw his arms about my neck and gave me, after his childish fashion, the heartiest welcome. Having hugged me to the extent of his ability, he drew back and took a survey of my person. It seemed on the whole not to displease him.

"Is your name Laurence?" he asked. I nodded affirmatively.

"I thought so; my name is Philip, but they call me Phil. I have been wanting a brother for a long time, but I am afraid you are too old to play with me."

"No indeed, I can shew you many fine games."

"Then you will be very kind—pray tell me what you have brought in that big trunk."

"We will go and see, Phil," and by a sort of joint diplomacy of the child's and of mine was effected a speedy escape from the forbidding presence in which, as no one seemed to be wanted, it was scarcely possible that any one should be missed.

"Somehow I have never much to say before papa," observed Phil confidentially, when we were once out of sight and of hearing. "He doesn't talk much himself and it seems to me that he does not like to have other people talk."

"Is he in one of his best moods tonight?" I carelessly inquired.

"Verbs have moods," said master Phil, proud to show his newly acquired grammatical knowledge. "Father is a common noun."

"Thank heaven, an uncommon one. Is he as pleasant as usual tonight?"

"I don't think that he ever is pleasant."

"Well, is he in a good humour, or in a bad one?"

"Why, brother Laurence, there is little difference in him when he is in a good humour and when he is not that I never can tell how it is." Truly, a satisfactory answer.

But we were not to be so easily let off from the family penance. Phil was soon deep in the mysteries of my dressing case and busied himself in opening every box drawer and inquiring its use. I was gazing with a mournful pleasure upon his fair face, and as I drew him to me, and looked in his eyes, I said to myself: Thou art indeed my own brother, my eyes and heart tell me so; but are we, can we be the children of that domestic iceberg?

At this moment a summons came to us from the drawing room, where coffee and cards awaited us. Excusing myself from the latter, I entered into conversations with a young man, the chaplain of the family, and Phil's tutor.

He seemed to me an amiable and genial person, and was anxious to be informed of my course of life and of study at the University. Thankful to pursue any subject which should lead me away from the unpleasant realities by which I was surrounded, I answered very fully all his questions, related anecdote after anecdote, and became so entirely emancipated from the yoke of the present that I was quite surprised at the end of the evening to find a knot of listeners gathered around us, and had been equally unconscious of the fact that Paternus, ensconced behind his evening gazette, had not lost a word of our conversation.

Welcome indeed was the nod of the master that released us all from further attendance upon us [sic] and dismissed us like a band of culprits, silent and ashamed, to the shelter of our bed chambers. I said to myself as I bade him good night: "I am glad that I do not love him—if habits of early intercourse had rendered him dear to me, I should feel a pang at every cold word and look of his."

I had been glad to leave the formal salon, but in the solitude of my own room, what fearful visions awaited me! The frantic ghost of Emma rose before me. I heard again the footstep that had roused me from my last dream of peace to my first real sorrow. I saw again the pleading look, the gesture of indignation, the tears of despair—again I heard, oh! I heard it all night long, the shriek of the agony which had rent asunder the moral veil of that most beautiful temple. Now, with glowing countenance, with eyes suffused, she told me of her love; now, rising in the might of her beauty, she spurned me from her foot like a crushed worm—now, her white arms sought to wind themselves about me, and now the lightning of her angry eye withered my very soul within me. And then I saw the strength of love, of courage, of anger, all give way beneath the weight of hopeless anguish, saw her totter, faint and fall, and the abyss of madness closed over her. Was it sleeping, was it waking? alas! It was one wild dream of wretchedness, a dream of many nights and days, and yet no dream.

Chapter [5]

The morrow brought a decisive interview with my father, and one that completely emancipated me from every filial relation towards him. Of him and of his words I wish to speak as briefly as possible, for many years and many thoughts have quite obliterated the painful impression then made upon me. Looking back from the varied experience, the wide range of thought through which life has led me, and viewing all things in the light of God's love, it seems to me a matter of infinitely small consequence that one who called himself my father was once cruel and unjust to me. He did not injure me, he had not the power to do so, but the evil intention in a father's heart—ah! it made an orphan of me at once and forever.

My father commenced the conversation by asking me if I had any preference in the choice of a profession. I told him that I had not thought of adopting one. He spoke of the church, of his influence among its dignitaries,

of the livings within his gift. I looked at him in astonishment—what inducement did the priesthood offer to me, the heir of a noble estate? I briefly
replied that I abhorred the clergy and would never willingly enter their
ranks. My father adroitly turned the current of his remarks upon the subject
of my college life, and questioned me concerning my standing in my class.
In reply, I presented to him the medals I had received, accompanied by various written commendations of my scholarship and good conduct from my
college instructors.

"I am satisfied that you have, on the whole, done much better than
might have been expected."

"I have done my duty, sir, I hope that you did not expect anything less
of me."

Paternus looked at me for a moment and then fixed his eyes upon the
credentials I had shown him.

"You seem to have been a favourite with your tutors," he remarked.

"They have never complained of me."

"You have had a duel; what was the occasion of it?"

"I fought to defend the honour of a lady from an unjust imputation."

"Let me advise you to trouble yourself as little as need be about women,
for the future."

"Your advice is quite needless, sir, I have never given myself any
unnecessary trouble about them."

My father did not relish the sharpness and decision with which I spoke,
and we entered into an altercation—not at all calculated to establish a good
understanding between us. Paternus, nettled by some profession of independence on my part, threw off at length his diplomatic *équivoque* and
appeared in his true colours.

"You stand there, and dictate terms to me, presuming yourself the heir
to my fortunes and estates. You know not, young sir, that I have power to
disinherit you, *if the inclination should not be wanting*."

"You the power?"—"Yes, the power to strip you of name, fortune, and
position, and to hold up your assumed manhood to the scorn of society."

"That is a point susceptible of some discussion. I shall take legal and
medical advice upon the subject; but supposing that you possess the power,
have you also the right?"

"You give me the right when you refuse me the respect due to a father."

"That can only be given in return for the kindness—the humanity due
to a son."

My father's coup d'état had failed. He had hoped to astonish and over-
whelm me, but he had not found me unarmed. I was better informed upon
the subject than he imagined. I knew that difficulties, that impossibilities
[lay] between him and the accomplishment of his wishes. He could not, he
would not dare attempt to prove my incapacity to inherit his estate. There
was danger and disgrace in the endeavour, and its result would be defeat. I
told him so, I defied him, and in the bitterness of my heart, I laughed him
to scorn.

Feeling the weakness of his position he endeavoured to fortify it by various statements. He told me that my mother had borne him many daughters in succession. His estate was entailed upon the heir male. At the epoch of my birth he was attacked by sudden and dangerous illness, and death appeared to him doubly formidable from the thought that his cherished lands and title must pass from his own family to that of a distant relative. At this critical moment, my birth had been a welcome event.

"You were born imperfect," related Paternus. "It was difficult to determine your sex with precision, it was in fact impossible. No time was to be lost however, and the exigency of the case decided for us. Under the circumstances we deemed it most expedient to bestow on you the name and rights of a man."

"It was expedient only because it was right," said I, "but having once decided thus, what has induced you to contemplate a change of purpose?"

"The desire to assure the integrity of the succession," replied Paternus, after some hesitation. "You can never transmit it to a lawful heir, but having once been permitted to represent it, you may see fit to abuse the trust confided to you, and bestow upon the son of another the heritage of your brother Philip."

These words fully roused my indignation: "Can you then suppose me so vile?" I cried. Paternus smiled grimly.

"We must be prepared for such things—it is easy to know men better than they know themselves."

I was cruelly angered, I was cruelly wounded—my father had confounded me, not by his threats, not by his arguments, but by the display of his wickedness. Encouraged by my silence, he went on to propose a compromise.

"Were you, instead of Philip, a younger son, your yearly income would be (he named a sum fully equal to my wishes). The enjoyment of such an income, I shall be happy to secure to you, and will add to it the sum of ten thousand pounds from my private fortune, in consideration of a formal relinquishment on your part of the expectations in which you have been brought up."

Before I could reply, my father left the room. I sat and mused in silence. The pang of those harsh words once over, my resolution was quickly taken. The succession so much dearer to my father's heart than his own child appeared to me a worthless bauble. Richly endowed and ancient as it was, it was in my eyes irrevocably degraded in his person. I had no ambition to represent him. The income he offered me was my right—it was shame enough that I should have to thank him for life, for aught else, I would never thank him. My reflections were interrupted by the reappearance of my father, who now returned, holding a paper in his hand.

"Here is the deed of the property I offer you," said he. "My terms are handsome, you will do well to accept them."

"From you, Sir, I will accept nothing. Let my brother Philip be summoned, and if he thinks fit, let the deed be made out in his name."

"Philip is a child!"—"Thank God, yes—he has the purity and the wisdom of a child."

Philip was sent for, and soon bounded into the room. There was a whole revelation in his manner as he eyed Paternus askance and nestled close at my side.

"Philip," said I, "your father wishes to have no son but you, and I am not going to be his son any longer."

The child looked at us both in wonder. I went on: "If you had been born before me, you would have been many times richer than I, you would have been called by a title, and the castle would have been your home; but now, as I happened to be born first, all these things are mine."

"I'm glad of it," cried Phil. "I'm very glad of it. I don't want anything except my pony, and Grandfather's sword, and the little lodge down by the lake."

"If I should die, there would be an end of my rights; you would be the rich and titled man, and there would be no one to stand in your way. Would you not be glad?"

"Brother Laurence, don't talk so!"

"Now Phil, I cannot die, but I am going away, and you will never see me here again. Your father wants to give all these fine things to you—I am willing. I leave them all to you, Phil, may you live long to enjoy them."

As the child looked upon my face, his beautiful countenance became pale as marble, and his dark eye grew eloquent with sadness, still, he spoke no word.

"Your father does not love me, and he has taught me not to love him. He wishes to give me money, to pay me for going away, for not being his son any more. I have told him that I would not take any thing from his hand. I will receive it from you, if you are willing to give me something to live upon."

Paternus, black with rage, beckoned Philip to him, and bade him write his name in several places upon the deed. Pale and speechless, the child obeyed, and scarce understanding wherefore, brought the paper to me. A bag of gold stood on the table, Paternus pointed to it, and Phil lifted it with all his strength, and laid it at my feet. My father now produced the deed of renunciation, which was signed and duly witnessed.

"Dear Philip, go and tell the servant to carry my luggage to the inn; I will follow on foot."

The child had, thus far, obeyed in passive silence, but as he listened to these words, his face flushed painfully and tears gathered in his eyes. I repeated the order, but instead of leaving me, he sprang into my arms, and hung weeping and sobbing upon my neck.

"Laurence, dear Laurence, don't leave me here! Take me with you!"

The child's heart already pined for sympathy and affection—in all his ignorance of life, and of human nature, he knew that the father who preferred him above me and who had despoiled me of every right in his heart and fortune, to lavish all upon his more favoured child, was yet an unlovely and unloving being.

"Laurence, don't be afraid to stay here—papa shall love you, if he does not, I will not love him."

At this threat, so likely to be fulfilled, Paternus and I exchanged a look of dreadful intelligence. I felt that for the sake of Philip's future peace, the scene must end. I held the boy near to me, and spoke a few quiet words to him. I was cold and immoveable as marble, and the child was somehow awed into tranquillity and obedience. Sadly and reluctantly he kissed me, and slowly went to do my bidding. I had a few words to say to Paternus, and walking nearer to him, I looked him full in the face.

"Now Sir, understand me. I do not give up the succession because I love my brother. He is very dear to me, but I know that he will be none the happier for the rank and wealth I resign to him—these I lay down because I despise them, and still more because I scorn to derive them from you. I will not even thank you for a name. As you disown me, I disown you, but your feeling may change, may soften with time, not so mine. God shield my brother from all harm—God preserve him long to life and its best happiness. But should any evil overtake him, should he die childless, and your old age be desolate, and your succession vacant, then never send for Laurence, then raise up an heir from the stones beneath your feet, for you will never find one in me—I swear—"

"Stop, stop, maniac!" cried Paternus arresting my words.

I left him without any other farewell than this. I hurried down the stairs, and out of the house. On the lawn I was met by the young tutor, who seized my arm, and attempted some expostulation. I broke from him. "Watch over Philip," I cried. "He has gained an inheritance, and lost a brother."

And farewell, and farewell, and farewell forever.

Chapter [6]

I had wished to travel by night as well as by day, partly to beguile the long hours of painful wakefulness, partly because my way led me through the scenes of my former peaceful life, and of the tragedy which so abruptly ended it. I dreaded to look upon those familiar spots in the daylight, and desired to avoid all encounters with my late associates. The weary day had sighed itself to rest, the twilight had deepened into the gloom of night before we reached the village. Post horses were ordered and instantly attached, but not quickly enough to satisfy my feverish impatience, and it was a relief to me when the postilion sprang into his saddle, cracked his whip, and gave his beasts the word of command. On past the Manor and its grounds—on, past the venerable college, and the shade of its rigid avenues—there was no light in the window of my old room, it needed none to make it painfully visible to me. I leaned back and closed my eyes to shut out the sight of things once lovely, but now harrowing to my soul. It was in vain—within my carriage, within my brain presided an attendant spirit that traced for me every landmark of my mournful way, and compelled me to measure with thought and remembrance, each step of my painful progress. Imagination grew worse than sight, the darkness of the carriage was frightful, its atmosphere oppressive to me—gasping for breath, I again leaned forward to the window that the real presence of objects might put to flight their monstrous phantoms.

Where was I? what was this? had I forgotten that pretty, fantastic mansion with its lovely shades and shrubberies? That window, who had stood beside me there? that threshold, how had I last crossed it? On, on, good postilion we dare not think, dare not look, dare not stop to ask of any one the dénouement of that tale of horrour! Ah! such secrets soon make themselves known. The oracles of evil wait not to be inquired of and propitiated—they are glad and in haste to scream their dreadful tidings in our ears. On, on, let us not pause to listen lest the wail of death and the sound of endless malediction make themselves heard to us. Oh, on, I say!

"But I cannot, good Sir—a funeral procession bars the road." Do you not hear the De Profundis? do you not see a form arrayed in white, borne on its flower crowned bier to its bridal bed? On, on! no—stop, stay—undo the door—let me out! let me fall prostrate in the way! let the icy car of death pass over me too, and offer up an expiatory victim to the manes of the unwittingly betrayed, of the irrevocably lost. Here is a solemnity in which I have a part to play, here is the only matter in which I shall have any interest for many years to come. Let me down, let me down, and thank God if He will give me tears!

An hour later, and the dirge is hushed. The mourners have gone their way to sleep and to forget—the saddest of them shall arise tomorrow, glad that the dead is buried out of their sight, glad that the mystic being they love and dread has no longer any claim upon them, any fellowship with them. Can you blame them? God himself—is not a God of the dead.

Did I say that she was buried? not yet, thank God, not yet. She lies before the high altar—its consecrated torches lend a gentle, life giving light to her dead beauty. She lies here alone with God, and the faithful priest who watched her remains, who will ask no reward to pray for her sweet spirit. Yield thy place to me, holy man—thou cannot pray for her as I can, thou art not bound to her as I am. Dost thou ask where I shall be tomorrow? I may be mad tomorrow.

A desperate man knelt at Emma's feet, as Emma had knelt at his—tears, groans and prayers he offered up at that holy shrine—when these were exhausted, he was mute and listened to voices heard never before. It is long but blessed, a night that we pass with the dead we love, and the dawn that succeeds it may usher in a better day than that which follows upon a bridal feast. No lover in the arms of his mistress ever received consolation so divine as that which came to me from the lips of that silent one, that night. Promises of divine guidance, of angelic companionship, assurances of immortal blessedness, and encouragements to a life of earnest striving and hope—all these were poured upon me as from a full urn, from the heart that had so loved me. Does any one doubt whether the souls of the dead have power to bless us? Let me tell such an one, solemnly and truly, that in my best hours, when the passionate music and the angry discords of life have been hushed and silent enough for the soul to hear other sounds than those of earth, then the holy dead, the living dead have walked with me, have spoken with me, and my heart and life have borne the record of their heavenly messages.

Let me say moreover that to these our periods of reception are appointed corresponding periods of reproduction. The sacred fire shall not merely afford us light and heat—it is like the genial warmth of Nature, quickening, fruitful, life-giving. The abstract truth revealed to us in our hour of agonizing prayer, of rapt meditation, grows into strength and courage in our day of trial and of action, and heavenly wisdom, the soul of our soul, becomes mortal and visible in heroic conflict in holy words and deeds, in patient labour, in calm endurance.

Thus did I pass the night. When the grey light of dawn warned me to recommence my journey, I arose and went on my way with gladness. I had laid down at Emma's feet the burthen of my humanity. I had taken up the heavier but more precious one of immortality. Upon her bosom I laid my poet's wreath—upon her lips I imprisoned the first, last kiss that woman and woman's love ever wrung from mine....

1840s

Mind versus Mill-Stream

A Miller wanted a mill-stream,
    A mild, efficient brook
To help him to his living, in
    Some snug and shady nook.

But our Miller had a brilliant taste,   5
    A love of flash and spray,
And so, the stream that charmed him most
    Was that of brightest play.

It wore a quiet look, at times,   10
    And steady seemed, and still,
But when its quicker depths were stirred,
    Wow! but it wrought its will.

And men had tried to bridle it   15
    By artifice, and force,
But madness from its rising grew,
    And all along its course.

'Twas on a sultry summer's day,
 The Miller chanced to stop   20
Where it invited to 'look in
 And take a friendly drop.'

Coiffed with long wreaths of crimson weed,   25
 Veiled by a passing cloud,
It looked a novice of the woods
 That dares not speak aloud.

Said he: 'I never met a stream   30
 More beautiful and bland,
'Twill gain my bread, and bless it too,
 So here my mill shall stand.'

And ere the summer's glow had passed,   35
 Or crimson flowers did fade,
The Miller measured out his ground,
 And his foundation laid.

The Miller toiled with might and main,   40
 Builded with thought and care;
And when the Spring broke up the ice
 The water-wheel stood there.

Like a frolic maiden come from school,   45
 The stream looked out, anew;
And the happy Miller bowing, said,
 'Now turn my mill-wheel, do!'

'Your mill-wheel?' cried the naughty Nymph, 50
 'That would, indeed, be fine!
You have your business, I suppose,
 Learn too that I have mine.'

'What better business can you have,   55
 Than turn this wheel for me?'
Leaping and laughing, the wild thing cried,
 'Follow, and you may see.'

The Miller trudged with measured pace,   60
 As Reason follows Rhyme,
And saw his mill-stream run to waste,
 In the very teeth of time.

'Fore heaven!' he swore, 'since thou'rt perverse,   65
 I've hit upon a plan;
A dam shall stay thine outward course,
 And then, break out who can.'

So he built a dam of wood and stone,   70
 Not sparing in the cost,
'For,' thought our friend, 'this water-power
 'Must not be lightly lost.'

'What? Will you force me?' said the sprite;   75
 'You shall not find it gain;'
So, with a flash, a dash, a crush,
 She made her way amain.

Then, freeing all her pent-up soul,   80
 She rushed, in frantic race
And fragments of the Miller's work
 Threw in the Miller's face.

The good man built his dam again,   85
 More stoutly than before;
He flung no challenge to the foe,
 But an oath he inly swore:

'Thou seest resistance is in vain,   90
 So yield with better grace.'
And the water sluices turned the stream
 To its appointed place.

'Aha! I've conquered now!' quoth he,   95
 For the water-fury bold
Was still an instant, ere she rose
 In wrath and power fourfold.

With roar and rush, and massive sweep   100
 She cleared the shameful bound,
And flung to utterness of waste
 The Miller, and his mound.

Moral.

If you would marry happily   105
 On the shady side of life,
Choose out some quietly-disposed
 And placid tempered wife,

To share the length of sober days,   110
    And dimly slumberous nights,
But well beware those fitful souls
    Fate wings for wilder flights!

For men will woo the tempest,   115
    And wed it, to their cost,
Then swear they took it for summer dew,
    And ah! their peace is lost!

                            1854

The Heart's Astronomy

This evening, as the twilight fell,
My younger children watched for me;
Like cherubs in the window framed,
I saw the smiling group of three.

While round and round the house I trudged,   5
Intent to walk a weary mile,
Oft as I passed within their range,
The little things would beck and smile.

They watched me, as Astronomers
Whose business lies in heaven afar,   10
Await, beside the slanting glass,
The re-appearance of a star.

Not so, not so, my pretty ones,
Seek stars in yonder cloudless sky;
But mark no steadfast path for me,   15
A comet dire and strange am I.

Now to the inmost spheres of light
Lifted, my wondering soul dilates,
Now dropped in endless depth of night,
My hope God's slow recall awaits.   20

Among the shining I have shone,
Among the blessing, have been blest,
Then wearying years have held me bound
Where darkness deadness gives, not rest.

Between extremes distraught and rent,   25
I question not the way I go;

Who made me, gave it me, I deem,
Thus to aspire, to languish so.

But Comets too have holy laws,
Their fiery sinews to restrain,   30
And from their outmost wanderings
Are drawn to heaven's dear heart again.

And ye, beloved ones, when ye know
What wild, erratic natures are,
Pray that the laws of heavenly force   35
Would hold and guide the Mother star.

                                                                       1854

The Battle Hymn of the Republic[1]

Mine eyes have seen the glory of the coming of the Lord;
He is trampling out the vintage where the grapes of wrath are
    stored;
He hath loosed the fateful lightning of His terrible swift sword;
    His truth is marching on.
      Chorus:
      Glory, glory, hallelujah,   5
      Glory, glory, hallelujah,
      Glory, glory, hallelujah,
        His truth is marching on.

I have seen Him in the watch-fires of a hundred circling camps;
They have builded Him an altar in the evening dews and damps;   10
I can read His righteous sentence by the dim and flaring lamps;
    His day is marching on.

I have read a fiery gospel writ in burnished rows of steel:
"As ye deal with My contemners, so with you My grace shall deal;
Let the Hero, born of woman, crush the serpent with His heel,   15
    Since God is marching on."

[1]In her *Reminiscences* (1899), Julia Ward Howe recounts how she came to write "The Battle Hymn of the Republic." She had visited an army camp near Washington in the company of her minister, a Mr. Clarke. Returning with a band of soldiers, they had joined in singing "John Brown's Body." Clarke asked why she did not "write some good words for that stirring tune," but she felt as yet uninspired, though she wished to do so. That night, as she later wrote, "as I lay waiting for the dawn, the long lines of the desired poem began to twine themselves in my mind." She quickly arose, lest she "fall asleep and forget them ... and scrawled the verses almost without looking at the paper." The poem was published in *The Atlantic Monthly* of February 1862, from which this text is taken.

The poem represents a striking instance of the adaptation by a self-conscious poet of the music and rhythms of an already popular, if simpler, song.

He has sounded forth the trumpet that shall never call retreat;
He is sifting out the hearts of men before His judgment seat:
Oh! be swift, my soul, to answer Him! be jubilant, my feet!
    Our God is marching on.   20

In the beauty of the lilies Christ was born across the sea,
With a glory in His bosom that transfigures you and me:
As He died to make men holy, let us die to make men free,
    While God is marching on.

1862

ALICE CARY
1820–1871

Alice Cary was born on a farm in Hamilton County, Ohio, eight miles north of Cincinnati. The village nearest this farm was called Mt. Healthy, and it is this village with its surrounding farms and houses that became the Clovernook memorialized in her short fiction. Her father, Robert Cary, had an American ancestry that could be traced to the Plymouth Colony in 1630. Her mother, Elizabeth Jessup Cary, was of Irish descent and, according to Alice Cary, "a woman of superior intellect and of a good, well-ordered life. In my memory she stands apart from all others, wiser and purer, doing more and loving better than any other woman" (*Ladies' Repository*, August 1855). Cary's fiction, however, does not support this vision of a loving mother; it records instead a motherless universe in which parents provide neither physical affection nor emotional support for their children and are often overtly hostile to them.

While she was growing up, Cary chose as her particular companion Rhoda, a sister two years older than herself, and, according to Cary, the most gifted member of the family. On the way to and from school, Rhoda would tell stories; "when we saw the house in sight, we would often sit down under a tree, that she might have more time to finish the story" (Mary Clemmer Ames, *A Memorial of Alice and Phoebe Cary, with Some of Their Later Poems*, 17). Cary never fully recovered from the death in 1833 of this sister who not only taught her the art and fascination of storytelling but also encouraged her first attempts at poetry.

Though both Cary parents were literate, apparently formal education for their children mattered little to them. In an early letter to Rufus Griswold, Cary described her formal education as "limited to the meagre and infrequent advantages of an obscure district school." Whether from lack of money or lack of interest, the Cary household contained few books. As Universalists, however, the Carys subscribed to the *Trumpet*, a Boston Universalist periodical, whose poet's corner, according to Phoebe Cary (1824–1871), Alice's younger sister, lifelong companion, and fellow writer, served as Cary's major model and source of inspiration.

Evidently, Alice Cary began writing poetry at an early age. In 1838 Cincinnati's Universalist paper, the *Sentinel*, printed "The Child of Sorrow," and for roughly a decade thereafter Cary continued to publish in local newspapers and periodicals. In 1847, however, she began to write fiction for the *National Era* (1847–1860), an abolitionist paper whose editor, Gamaliel Bailey, had recently moved from Cincinnati to Washington, D.C. The *Era*, best known perhaps for its serialization of *Uncle Tom's Cabin*, brought Cary a national audience; it also brought her the attention of John Greenleaf Whittier, notable for his support of nineteenth-century American women writers. In 1848 Rufus W. Griswold, editor of two anthologies of American poetry and prose, wrote to Alice and Phoebe Cary requesting material for inclusion in his latest project, *The Female Poets of America*. As a result of Griswold's often vexed but often amicable relations with Edgar Allan Poe, Poe wrote a review of this anthology for the *Southern Literary Messenger* (February 1849), in which he singled out the work of Alice Cary, declaring her "Pictures of Memory" to be *"decidedly the noblest poem in the collection."* In 1849 Griswold arranged for the publication of *Poems of Alice and Phoebe Cary*.

By 1850 Alice Cary was well on her way to becoming a writer with a national reputation. In the summer of that year, she made her first trip east, visiting New York, Boston, and Amesbury, Massachusetts, where Whittier lived. Shortly thereafter, Cary determined to make New York her home. In November 1850, she left Ohio; in the spring of 1851, Phoebe joined her in New York. Cary eventually purchased a house on East Twentieth Street, where she lived until her death. Here she set up a household that became famous for its Sunday evening receptions. Cary herself was the financial and executive center of this household, managing both its external and internal affairs. Though the events of her life tell a story of achievement against the odds of being poor, female, uneducated, and unsupported, Cary evidently paid a high price for her success. Her biographer presents her as working to live and living to work, finding pleasure only in labor and permanently destroying her health by refusing to rest. Alice Cary died on February 12, 1871, at her home in New York, and was buried two days later in Brooklyn's Greenwood cemetery.

Cary thought of herself primarily as a poet, and it was as a poet that she achieved her popular success. During her lifetime, she published four volumes of poetry, two collections of poetry and prose for children, and three novels. Cary deserves a place in American literary history, however, not for her poetry or her novels, but for her short fiction. There she was able to use her art to explore her consciousness. In so doing, Cary worked against the grain of a culture that labeled such privileging of the self in women as negatively egocentric or even pathologically narcissistic. This consciousness, located in the narrative "I" of her sketches, experiences human life primarily as a mystery, a fragment of some larger and essentially unknowable whole. For Cary, consciousness determined form. The sketch permitted her to accept and express the fragmentary nature of reality in fiction as she perceived it in life. Cary's interest lies not in plot but in character; action for her is rarely complete or completed. The strength of Cary's fiction lies in her insistence on specificity and her resistance to closure; her gift is recollections and sketches, by definition partial, personal, and incomplete, of one particular neighborhood in the West.

Cary shares with her female contemporaries a commitment to realism. With her male contemporaries she shares an understanding of fiction as psychic exploration and dream work. "Uncle Christopher's" demonstrates Cary's dual interest in realism and romance. It combines detailed descriptions of the contents of Uncle Christopher's attic with the portrait of seven women, exactly alike, knitting the same stocking in the same way at the same time. Indeed, the story contains much that we tend to associate with fairy tale and myth and might be taken for a bad dream, were it not from start to finish so chillingly realistic. Recording a world in which children don't matter and in which the death of a child transforms no one, Cary's fiction offers a harsh antidote to those child-centered works so popular with other nineteenth-century American writers.

Judith Fetterley
State University of New York at Albany

PRIMARY WORKS

Clovernook; or, Recollections of Our Neighborhood in the West, 1852; *Clovernook, Second Series*, 1853; *Pictures of Country Life*, 1859.

from **Clovernook, or Recollections of Our Neighborhood in the West, First Series**

Preface

The pastoral life of our country has not been a favorite subject of illustration by painters, poets, or writers of romance. Perhaps it has been regarded as wanting in the elements of beauty; perhaps it has been thought too passionless and even; or it may have been deemed too immediate and familiar. I have had little opportunity for its observation in the eastern and northern states, and in the south there is no such life, and in the far west where pioneers are still busy with feeling the opposing trees, it is not yet time for the reed's music; but in the interior of my native state, which was a wilderness when first my father went to it, and is now crowned with a dense and prosperous population, there is surely as much in the simple manners, and the little histories every day revealed, to interest us in humanity, as there can be in those old empires where the press of tyrannous laws and the deadening influence of hereditary acquiescence necessarily destroy the best life of society.

Without a thought of making a book, I began to recall some shadows and sunbeams that fell about me as I came up to womanhood, incidents for the most part of so little apparent moment or significance that they who live in what is called the world would scarcely have marked them had they been detained with me while they were passing, and before I was aware, the record of my memories grew to all I now have printed.

Looking over the proof sheets, as from day to day they have come from my publisher, the thought has frequently been suggested that such experiences as I have endeavored to describe will fail to interest the inhabitants of cities, where, however much they may be of pity there is surely little of sympathy for the poor and humble, and perhaps still less of faith in their capacity for those finer feelings which are too often deemed the blossoms of a high and fashionable culture. The masters of literature who at any time have attempted the exhibition of rural life, have, with few exceptions, known scarcely anything of it from participation, and however brilliant may have been their pictures, therefore, they have seldom been true. Perhaps in their extravagance has been their greatest charm. For myself, I confess I have no invention, and I am altogether too poor an artist to dream of any success which may not be won by the simplest fidelity. I believe that for these sketches I may challenge of competent witnesses at least this testimony, that the circumstances have a natural and probable air which should induce their reception as honest relations unless there is conclusive evidence against them. Having this merit, they may perhaps interest if they do not instruct readers who have regarded the farming class as essentially different and inferior, and entitled only to that peculiar praise they are accustomed to receive in the resolutions of political conventions.

1852

from **Clovernook, or Recollections of Our Neighborhood in the West, Second Series**

Uncle Christopher's

I

The night was intensely cold, but not dismal, for all the hills and meadows, all the steep roofs of the farm-houses, and the black roofs of the barns, were white as snow could make them. The haystacks looked like high, smooth heaps of snow, and the fences, in their zigzag course across the fields, seemed made of snow too, and half the trees had their limbs encrusted with the pure white.

Through the middle of the road, and between banks out of which it seemed to have been cut, ran a path, hard and blue and icy, and so narrow that only two horses could move in it abreast; and almost all the while I could hear the merry music of bells, or the clear and joyous voices of sleigh riders, exultant in the frosty and sparkling air.

With his head pushed under the curtain of the window next the road, so that his face touched the glass, stood my father, watching with as much interest, the things without, as I the pictures in the fire. His hands were thrust deep in his pockets; both his vest and coat hung loosely open; and so for a half hour he had stood, dividing my musings with joyous exclamations as the gay riders went by, singly, or in companies. Now it was a sled running over with children that he told me of; now an old man and woman wrapt in a coverlid and driving one poor horse; and now a bright sleigh with fine horses, jingling bells, and a troop of merry young folks. Then again he called out, "There goes a spider-legged thing that I wouldn't ride in," and this remark I knew referred to one of those contrivances which are gotten up on the spur of a moment, and generally after the snow begins to fall, consisting of two limber saplings on which a seat is fixed, and which serve for runners, fills, and all.

It was not often we had such a deep snow as this, and it carried the thoughts of my father away back to his boyhood, for he had lived among the mountains then, and been used to the hardy winters which keep their empire nearly half the year. Turning from the window, he remarked, at length, "This is a nice time to go to Uncle Christopher's, or some where."

"Yes," I said, "it would be a nice time;" but I did not think so, all the while, for the snow and I were never good friends. I knew, however, that my father would like above all things to visit Uncle Christopher, and that, better still, though he did not like to own it, he would enjoy the sleighing.

"I want to see Uncle Christopher directly," he continued, "about getting some spring wheat to sow."

"It is very cold," I said, "isn't it?" I really couldn't help the question.

"Just comfortably so," he answered, moving back from the fire.

Two or three times I tried to say, "Suppose we go," but the words were difficult, and not till he had said, "Nobody ever wants to go with me to Uncle Christopher's, nor anywhere," did I respond, heartily, "Oh, yes, father, I want to go."

In a minute afterwards, I heard him giving directions about the sleigh and horses.

"I am afraid, sir, you'll find it pretty cold," replied Billy, as he rose to obey.

"I don't care about going myself," continued my father apologetically, "but my daughter has taken a fancy to a ride, and so I must oblige her."

A few minutes, and a pair of handsome, well-kept horses were champing the bit, and pawing the snow at the door, while shawls, mittens, &c., were warmed at the fire. It was hard to see the bright coals smothered under the ashes, and the chairs set away; but I forced a smile to my lips, and as my father said "Ready?" I answered "Ready," and the door closed on the genial atmosphere—the horses stepped forward and backward, flung their heads up and down, curved their necks to the tightening rein, and we were off. The fates be praised, it is not to do again. All the shawls and muffs in Christendom could not avail against such a night—so still, clear, and intensely cold. The very stars seemed sharpened against the ice, and the white moonbeams slanted earthward, and pierced our faces like thorns—I think they had substance that night, and were stiff; and the thickest veil, doubled twice or thrice, was less than gossamer, and yet the wind did not blow, even so much as to stir one flake of snow from the bent boughs.

At first we talked with some attempts at mirth, but sobered presently and said little, as we glided almost noiselessly along the hard and smooth road. We had gone, perhaps, five miles to the northward, when we turned from the paved and level way into a narrow lane, or neighborhood road, as it was called, seeming to me hilly and winding and wild, for I had never been there before. The track was not so well worn, but my father pronounced it better than that we had left, and among the stumps and logs, and between hills and over hills, now through thick woods, and now through openings, we went crushing along. We passed a few cabins and old-fashioned houses, but not many, and the distances between them grew greater and greater, and there were many fields and many dark patches of woods between the lights. Every successive habitation I hoped would terminate our journey— our pleasure, I should have said—yet still we went on, and on.

"Is it much farther?" I asked, at length.

"Oh, no—only four or five miles," replied my father; and he added, "Why, are you getting cold?"

"Not much," I said, putting my hand to my face to ascertain that it was not frozen.

At last we turned into a lane, narrower, darker, and more lonesome still—edged with woods on either side, and leading up and up and up farther than I could see. No path had been previously broken, and the horses sunk knee deep at every step, their harness tightening as they strained forward, and their steamy breath drifting back, and freezing stiff my veil. At the summit the way was interrupted by a cross fence, and a gate was to be opened—a heavy thing, painted red, and fastened with a chain. It had been well secured, for after half an hour's attempts to open it, we found ourselves defied.

"I guess we'll have to leave the horses and walk to the house," said my father; "it's only a little step."

I felt terrible misgivings; the gate opened into an orchard; I could see no house, and the deep snow lay all unbroken; but there was no help; I must go forward as best I could, or remain and freeze. It was difficult to choose, but I decided to go on. In some places the snow was blown aside, and we walked a few steps on ground almost bare, but in the end high drifts met us, through which we could scarcely press our way. In a little while we began to descend, and soon, abruptly, in a nook sheltered by trees, and higher hills, I saw a curious combination of houses—brick, wood, and stone—and a great gray barn, looking desolate enough in the moonlight, though about it stood half a dozen of inferior size. But another and a more cheerful indication of humanity attracted me. On the brink of the hill stood two persons with a small hand-sled between them, which they seemed to have just drawn up; in the imperfect light, they appeared to be mere youths, the youngest not more than ten or twelve years of age. Their laughter rang on the cold air, and our approach, instead of checking, seemed to increase their mirth.

"Laugh, Mark, laugh," said the taller of the two, as we drew near, "so they will see our path—they're going right through the deep snow."

But instead, the little fellow stepped manfully forward, and directed us into the track broken by their sleds.

At the foot of the hill we came upon the medley of buildings, so incongruous that they might have been blown together by chance. Light appeared in the windows of that portion which was built of stone, but we heard no sound, and the snow about the door had not been disturbed since its fall. "And this," said I, "is where Uncle Christopher Wright lives?"

A black dog, with yellow spots under his eyes, stood suddenly before us, and growled so forbiddingly that we drew back.

"He will not bite," said the little boy; for the merry makers had landed on their sled at the foot of the hill, and followed us to the door; and in a moment the larger youth dashed past us, seized the dog by the fore paws, and dragged him violently aside, snarling and whimpering all the time. "Haven't you got no more sense," he exclaimed, "than to bark so at a gentleman and ladies?"

II

In answer to our quick rap, the door opened at once, and the circle about the great blazing log fire was broken by a general rising. The group consisted of eight persons—one man and seven women; the women so closely resembling each other, that one could not tell them apart; not even the mother from the daughters—for she appeared as young as the oldest of them—except by her cap and spectacles. All the seven were very slender, very straight, and very tall; all had dark complexions, black eyes, low foreheads, straight noses, and projecting teeth; and all were dressed precisely alike, in gowns of brown flannel, and coarse leather boots, with blue woollen stockings, and small capes, of red and yellow calico. The six daughters were all marriageable; at least the youngest of them was. They had staid, almost severe, expressions of countenances, and scarcely spoke during the evening. By one corner of the great fireplace they huddled together, each busy with knitting, and all occupied with long blue stockings, advanced in nearly similar degrees toward completion. Now and then they said "Yes, ma'm," or "No ma'm," when I spoke to them, but never or very rarely any thing more. As I said, Mrs. Wright differed from her daughters in appearance, only in that she wore a cap and spectacles; but she was neither silent nor ill at ease as they were; on the contrary, she industriously filled up all the little spaces unoccupied by her good man in the conversation; she set off his excellencies, as a frame does a picture; and before we were even seated, she expressed her delight that we had come when "Christopher" was at home, as, owing to his *gift*, he was much abroad.

Uncle Christopher was a tall muscular man of sixty or thereabouts, dressed in what might be termed stylish homespun coat, trowsers and waistcoat, of snuff-colored cloth. His cravat was of red-and-white-checked gingham, but it was quite hidden under his long grizzly beard, which he wore in full, this peculiarity being a part of his religion. His hair was of the same color, combed straight from his forehead, and turned over in one even curl on the back of the neck. Heavy gray eyebrows met over a hooked nose, and deep in his head twinkled two little blue eyes, which seemed to say, "I am delighted with myself, and, of course, you are with me." Between his knees he held a stout hickory stick, on which, occasionally, when he had settled something beyond the shadow of doubt, he rested his chin for a moment, and enjoyed the triumph. He rose on our entrance, for he had been seated beside a small table, where he monopolized a good portion of the light, and all the warmth, and having shaken hands with my father and welcomed him in a long and pompous speech, during which the good wife bowed her head, and listened as to an oracle, he greeted me in the same way, saying, "This, I suppose, is the virgin who abideth still in the house with you. She is not given, I hope, to gadding overmuch, nor to vain and foolish decorations of her person with ear-rings and finger-rings, and crisping-pins: for such are unprofitable, yea, abominable. My daughter, consider it well, and look upon it, and receive instruction." I was about replying, I don't know what, when he checked me by saying, "Much speech in a woman is as the crackling of thorns under a pot. Open rebuke," he continued, "is better than secret love." Then pointing with his cane in the direction of the six girls, he said, "Rise, maidens, and salute your kinswoman;" and as they stood up, pointing to each with his stick, he called their names, beginning with Abagail, eldest of the daughters of Rachael Wright and Christopher Wright, and ending with Lucinda, youngest born of Rachael Wright and Christopher Wright. Each, as she was referred to, made a quick ungraceful curtsy, and resumed her seat and her knitting.

A half hour afterward, seeing that we remained silent, the father said, by way of a gracious permission of conversation, I suppose, "A little talk of flax and wool, and of household diligence, would not ill become the daughters of our house." Upon hearing this, Lucinda, who, her mother remarked, had the "liveliest turn" of any of the girls, asked me if I liked to knit; to which I answered, "Yes," and added, "Is it a favorite occupation with you?" she replied, "Yes ma'm," and after a long silence, inquired how many cows we milked, and at the end of another pause, whether we had colored our flannel brown or blue; if we had gathered many hickory nuts; if our apples were keeping well, etc.

The room in which we sat was large, with a low ceiling, and bare floor, and so open about the windows and doors, that the slightest movement of the air without would keep the candle flame in motion, and chill those who were not sitting nearest the fire, which blazed and crackled and roared in the chimney. Uncle Christopher, as my father had always called him (though he was uncle so many degrees removed that I never exactly knew the relationship), laid aside the old volume from which he had been reading, removed the two pairs of spectacles he had previously worn, and hung them, by leather strings connecting their bows, on a nail in the stone jamb by which he sat, and talked, and talked; and talked, and I soon discovered by his conversation, aided by the occasional explanatory whispers of his wife, that he was one of those infatuated men who fancy themselves "called" to be teachers of religion, though he had neither talents, education, nor anything else to warrant such a notion, except a faculty for joining pompous and half scriptural phrases, from January to December.

That inward purity must be manifested by a public washing of the feet, that it was a sin to shave the beard, and an abomination for a man to be hired to preach, were his doctrines, I believe, and much time and some money he spent in their vindication. From neighborhood to neighborhood he traveled, now entering a blacksmith's shop and delivering a homily, now debating with the boys in the cornfield, and now obtruding into some church, where peaceable worshippers were assembled, with intimations that they had "broken teeth, and feet out of joint," that they were "like cold and snow in the time of harvest, yea, worse, even as pot-sheds covered with silver dross." And such exhortations he often concluded by quoting the passage: "Though thou shouldst bray a fool in a mortar among wheat, with a postle, yet will not his foolishness depart from him."

More than half an hour elapsed before the youths whose sliding down the hill had been interrupted by us, entered the house. Their hands and faces were red and stiffened with the cold, yet they kept shyly away from the fire, and no one noticed or made room for them. Both interested me at once, and partly, perhaps, that they seemed to interest nobody else. The taller was not so young as I at first imagined; he was ungraceful, shambling, awkward, and possessed one of those clean, pinky complexions which look so youthful; his hair was yellow, his eyes small and blue, with an unquiet expression, and his hands and feet inordinately large; and when he spoke, it was to the boy who sat on a low stool beside him, in a whisper, which he evidently meant to be inaudible to others, but which was, nevertheless, quite distinct to me. He seemed to exercise a kind of brotherly care over the boy, but he did not speak, nor move, nor look up, nor look down, nor turn aside, nor sit still, without an air of the most wretched embarrassment. I should not have written "sit still," for he changed his position continually, and each time his face grew crimson, and, to cover his confusion, as it were, he drew from his pocket a large silk handkerchief, rubbed his lips, and replaced it, at the same time moving and screwing and twisting the toe of his boot in every direction.

I felt glad of his attention to the boy, for he seemed silent and thoughtful beyond his years; perhaps he was lonesome, I thought; certainly he was not happy, for he leaned his chin on his hand, which was cracked and bleeding, and now and then when his companion ceased to speak, the tears gathered to his eyes; but he seemed willing to be pleased, and brushed the tears off his face and smiled, when the young man laid his great hand on his head, and, shaking it roughly, said, "Mark, Mark, Marky!"

"I can't help thinking about the money," said the boy, at last, "and how many new things it would have bought: just think of it, Andrew!"

"How Towser did bark at them people, didn't he, Mark?" said Andrew, not heeding what had been said to him.

"All new things!" murmured the boy, sorrowfully, glancing at his patched trowsers and ragged shoes.

"In three days it will be New-Year's; and then, Mark, won't we have fun!" and Andrew rubbed his huge hands together, in glee, at the prospect.

"It won't be no fun as I know of," replied the boy.

"May be the girls will bake some cakes," said Andrew, turning red, and looking sideways at the young women.

Mark laughed, and, looking up, he recognized the interested look with which I regarded him, and from that moment we were friends.

At the sound of laughter, Uncle Christopher struck his cane on the floor, and looking sternly toward the offenders, said, "A whip for the horse, a bridle for the ass, and a rod for the fool's back!" leaving to them the application, which they made, I suppose, for they became silent—the younger dropping his chin in his hands again, and the elder twisting the toe of his boot, and using his handkerchief very freely.

I thought we should never go home, for I soon tired of Uncle Christopher's conversation, and of Aunt Rachael's continual allusions to his "gift;" he was evidently regarded by her as not only the man of the house, but also as the man of all the world. The six young women had knitted their six blue stockings from the heel to the toe, and had begun precisely at the same time to taper them off, with six little white balls of yarn.

The clock struck eleven, and I ventured, timidly, to suggest my wish to return home. Mark, who sat drowsily in his chair, looked at me beseechingly, and when Aunt Rachael said, "Tut, tut! you are not going home to-night!" he laughed again, despite the late admonition. All the six young women also said, "You can stay just as well as not;" and I felt as if I were to be imprisoned, and began urging the impossibility of doing so, when Uncle Christopher put an end to remonstrance by exclaiming, "It is better to dwell in the corner of the housetop, than with a brawling woman, and in a wide house." It was soon determined that I should remain, not only for the night, but till the weather grew warmer; and I can feel now something of the pang I experienced when I heard the horses snorting on their homeward way, after the door had closed upon me.

"I am glad you didn't get to go!" whispered Mark, close to me, favored by a slight confusion induced by the climbing of the six young ladies upon six chairs, to hang over six lines, attached to the rafters, the six stockings.

There was no variableness in the order of things at Uncle Christopher's, but all went regularly forward without even a casual observation, and to see one day, was to see the entire experience in the family.

"He has a great gift in prayer," said Aunt Rachael, pulling my sleeve, as the hour for worship arrived.

I did not then, nor can I to this day, agree with her. I would not treat such matters with levity, and will not repeat the formula which this "gifted man" went over morning and evening, but he did not fail on each occasion to make known to the All-Wise the condition in which matters stood, and to assure him, that he himself was doing a great deal for their better management in the future. It was not so much a prayer as an announcement of the latest intelligence, even to "the visit of his kinswoman who was still detained by the severity of the elements."

It was through the exercise of his wonderful gift, that I first learned the histories of Andrew and Mark; that the former was a relation from the interior of Indiana, who, for feeding and milking Uncle Christopher's cows morning and evening, and the general oversight of affairs, when the great man was abroad, enjoyed the privilege of attending the district school in the neighborhood; and that the latter was the "son of his son," a "wicked and troublesome boy, for the present subjected to the chastening influences of a righteous discipline."

As a mere matter of form, Uncle Christopher always said, I will do so or so, "Providence permitting;" but he felt competent to do anything and everything on his own account, to "the drawing out of the Leviathan with an hook, or his tongue with a cord—to the putting a hook into his nose, or the boring his jaw through with a thorn."

"I believe it's getting colder," said Andrew, as he opened the door of the stairway, darkly winding over the great oven, to a low chamber; and, chuckling, he disappeared. He was pleased, as a child would be, with the novelty of a visitor, and perhaps half believed it was colder, because he hoped it was so. Mark gave me a smile as he sidled past his grandfather, and disappeared within the smoky avenue. We had scarcely spoken together, but somehow he had recognized the kindly disposition I felt toward him.

As I lay awake, among bags of meal and flour, boxes of hickory nuts and apples, with heaps of seed, wheat, oats, and barley, that filled the chamber into which I had been shown—cold, despite the twenty coverlids heaped over me—I kept thinking of little Mark, and wondering what was the story of the money he had referred to. I could not reconcile myself to the assumption of Uncle Christopher that he was a wicked boy; and, falling asleep at last, I dreamed the hard old man was beating him with his walking-stick, because the child was not big enough to fill his own snuff-colored coat and trowsers. And certainly this would have been little more absurd than his real effort to change the boy into a man.

There was yet no sign of daylight, when the stir of the family awoke me, and, knowing they would think very badly of me should I further indulge my disposition for sleep, I began to feel in the darkness for the various articles of my dress. At length, half awake, I made my way through and over the obstructions in the chamber, to the room below, which the blazing logs filled with light. The table was spread, and in the genial warmth sat Uncle Christopher, doing nothing. He turned his blue eyes upon me as I entered, and said, "Let a bear robbed of her whelps meet a man, rather than she who crieth, A little more sleep, and a little more slumber."

"Did he say anything to you?" asked Aunt Rachael, as I entered the kitchen in search of a wash-bowl. "It must have been just to the purpose," she continued; "Christopher always says something to the purpose."

There was no bowl, no accommodations, for one's toilet: Uncle Christopher did not approve of useless expenditures. I was advised to make an application of snow to my hands and face, and while I was doing so, I saw a light moving about the stables, and heard Andrew say, in a chuckling, pleased tone, "B'lieve it's colder, Mark—she can't go home to-day; and if she is only here till New-Years, maybe they will kill the big turkey." I felt, while melting on my cheeks the snow, that it was no warmer, and, perhaps, a little flattered with the evident liking of the young man and the boy, I resolved to make the best of my detention. I could see nothing to do, for seven women were already moving about by the light of a single tallow candle; the pork was frying, and the coffee boiling; the bread and butter were on the table, and there was nothing more, apparently, to be accomplished. I dared not sit down, however, and so remained in the comfortless kitchen, as some atonement for my involuntary idleness. At length the tin-horn was sounded, and shortly after Andrew and Mark came in, and breakfast was announced; in other words, Aunt Rachael placed her hand on her good man's chair, and said, "Come."

To the coarse fare before us we all helped ourselves in silence, except of the bread, and that was placed under the management of Uncle Christopher, and with the same knife he used in eating, slices were cut as they were required. The little courage I summoned while alone in the snow—thinking I might make myself useful, and do something to occupy my time, and oblige the family—flagged and failed during that comfortless meal. My poor attempts at cheerfulness fell like moonbeams on ice, except, indeed, that Andrew and Mark looked grateful.

Several times, before we left the table, I noticed the cry of a kitten, seeming to come from the kitchen, and that when Uncle Christopher turned his ear in that direction, Mark looked at Andrew, who rubbed his lips more earnestly than I had seen him before.

When the breakfast, at last, was ended, the old man proceeded to search out the harmless offender, with the instincts of some animal hungry for blood. I knew its doom, when it was discovered, clinging so tightly to the old hat, in which Mark had hidden it, dry and warm, by the kitchen fire; it had been better left in the cold snow, for I saw that the sharp little eyes which looked on it grew hard as stone.

"Mark," said Uncle Christopher, "into your hands I deliver this unclean beast: there is an old well digged by my father, and which lieth easterly a rod or more from the great barn—uncover the mouth thereof, and when you have borne the creature thither, cast it down!"

Mark looked as if he were suffering torture, and when, with the victim, he had reached the door, he turned, as if constrained by pity, and said, "Can't it stay in the barn?"

"No," answered Uncle Christopher, bringing down his great stick on the floor; "but you can stay in the barn, till you learn better than to gainsay my judgment." Rising, he pointed in the direction of the well, and followed, as I inferred, to see that his order was executed, deigning to offer neither reason nor explanation.

Andrew looked wistfully after, but dared not follow, and, taking from the mantle-shelf Walker's Dictionary, he began to study a column of definitions, in a whisper sufficiently loud for every one in the house to hear.

I inquired if that were one of his studies at school; but so painful was the embarrassment occasioned by the question, though he simply answered, "B'lieve it is," that I repented, and perhaps the more, as it failed of its purpose of inducing a somewhat lower whisper, in his mechanical repetitions of the words, which he resumed with the same annoying distinctness.

With the first appearance of daylight the single candle was snuffed out, and it now stood filling the room with smoke from its long limber wick, while the seven women removed the dishes, and I changed from place to place that I might seem to have some employment; and Andrew, his head and face heated in the blaze from the fireplace, studied the Dictionary. In half an hour Uncle Christopher returned, with stern satisfaction depicted in his face: the kitten was in the well, and Mark was in the barn; I felt that, and was miserable.

I asked for something to do, as the old man, resuming his seat, and, folding his hands over his staff, began a homily on the beauty of industry, and was given some patch-work; "There are fifty blocks in the quilt," said Aunt Rachael, "and each of them contains three hundred pieces."

I wrought diligently all the day, though I failed to see the use or beauty of the work on which I was engaged.

At last Andrew, putting his Dictionary in his pocket, saying, "I b'lieve I have my lesson by heart," and, a piece of bread and butter in the top of his hat, tucked the ends of his green woolen trowsers in his cowhide boots, and, without a word of kindness or encouragement, left the house for the school.

By this time the seven women had untwisted seven skeins of blue yarn, which they wound into seven blue balls, and each at the same time began the knitting of seven blue stockings.

That was a very long day to me, and as the hours went by I grew restless, and then wretched. Was little Mark all this time in the cold barn? Scratching the frost from the window pane, I looked in the direction from which I expected him to come, but he was nowhere to be seen.

The quick clicking of the knitting-needles grew hateful, the shut mouths and narrow foreheads of the seven women grew hateful, and hatefulest of all grew the small blue shining eyes of Uncle Christopher, as they bent on the yellow worm-eaten page of the old book he read. He was warm and comfortable, and had forgotten the existence of the little boy he had driven out into the cold.

I put down my work at last, and cold as it was, ventured out. There were narrow paths leading to the many barns and cribs, and entering one after another, I called to Mark, but in vain. Calves started up, and, placing their fore feet in the troughs from which they usually fed, looked at me, half in wonder and half in fear; the horses—and there seemed to be dozens of them—stamped, and whinnied, and, thrusting their noses through their mangers, pressed them into a thousand wrinkles, snuffing the air instead of expected oats. It was so intensely cold I began to fear the boy was dead, and turned over bundles of hay and straw, half expecting to find his stiffened corpse beneath them, but I did not, and was about leaving the green walls of hay that rose smoothly on each side of me, the great dusty beams and black cobwebs swaying here and there in the wind, when a thought struck me: the well—he might have fallen in! Having gone "a rod or more, easterly from the barn," directed by great footprints and little footprints, I discovered the place, and to my joy, the boy also. There was no curb about the well, and, with his hands resting on a decayed strip of plank that lay across its mouth, the boy was kneeling beside it, and looking in. He had not heard my approach, and, stooping, I drew him carefully back, showed him how the plank was decayed, and warned him against such fearful hazards.

"But," he said, half laughing, and half crying, "just see!" and he pulled me toward the well. The opening was small and dark, and seemed very deep, and as I looked more intently my vision gradually penetrated to the bottom; I could see the still pool there, and a little above it, crouching on a loose stone or other projection of the wall, the kitten, turning her shining eyes upward now and then, and mewing piteously.

"Do you think she will get any of it?" said Mark, the tears coming into his eyes; "and if she does, how long will she live there?" The kind-hearted child had been dropping down bits of bread for the prisoner.

He was afraid to go to the house, but when I told him Uncle Christopher might scold me if he scolded any one, and that I would tell him so, he was prevailed upon to accompany me. The hard man was evidently ashamed when he saw the child hiding behind my skirts for fear, and at first said nothing. But directly Mark began to cry—there was such an aching and stinging in his fingers and toes, he could not help it.

"Boo, hoo, hoo!" said the old man, making three times as much noise as the boy—"what's the matter now?"

"I suppose his hands and feet are frozen," said I, as though I knew it, and would maintain it in spite of him, and I confess I felt a secret satisfaction in showing him his cruelty.

"Oh, I guess not," Aunt Rachael said, quickly, alarmed for my cool assertion as well as for the child: "only a leetle frosted, I reckon. Whereabouts does it hurt you, my son?" she continued, stooping over him with a human sympathy and fondness I had not previously seen in any of the family.

"Frosted a leetle—that's all, Christopher," she said, by way of soothing her lord's compunction, and, at the same time, taking in her hands the feet of the boy, which he flung about for pain, crying bitterly. "Hush, little honey," she said, kissing him, and afraid the good man would be vexed at the crying; and as she sat there holding his feet, and tenderly soothing him, I at first could not believe she was the same dark and sedate matron who had been knitting the blue stocking.

"Woman, fret not thy gizzard!" said Christopher, slapping his book on the table, and hanging his spectacles on the jamb. The transient beauty all dropt away, the old expression of obsequious servility was back, and she resumed her seat and her knitting.

"There, let me doctor you," he continued, drawing the child's stocking off. The feet were covered with blisters, and presented the appearance of having been scalded. "Why, boy alive," said he, as he saw the blisters, "these are nothing—they will make you grow." He was forgetting his old pomposity, and, as if aware of it, resumed, "Thou hast been chastised according to thy deserts—go forth in the face of the wind, even the north wind, and, as the ox treadeth the mortar, tread thou the snow."

"You see, Markey," interposed Mrs. Wright, whose heart was really kind,—"you see your feet are a leetle frosted, and that will make them well."

The little fellow wiped his tears with his hand, which was cracked and bleeding from the cold; and, between laughing and crying, ran manfully out into the snow.

It was almost night, and the red clouds about the sunset began to cast their shadows along the hills. The seven women went into the kitchen for the preparation of dinner, (we ate but two meals in the day) and I went to the window to watch Mark as he trod the snow "even as an ox treadeth the mortar." There he was, running hither and thither, and up and down, but, to my surprise, not alone. Andrew, who had returned from school, and found his little friend in such a sorry plight, had, for the sake of giving him courage, bared his own feet, and was chasing after him in generously well-feigned enjoyment. Towser, too, had come forth from his kennel of straw, and a gay frolic they made of it, all together.

I need not describe the dinner—it differed only from the breakfast, in that it had potatoes added to the bread and pork.

I remember never days so long, before nor since; and that night, as the women resumed their knitting, and Uncle Christopher his old book, I could hardly keep from crying like a child, I was so lonesome and homesick. The wind roared in the neighboring woods, the frozen branches rattled against the stone wall, and sometimes the blaze was blown quite out of the fire-place. I could not see to make my patch-work, for Uncle Christopher monop-olized the one candle, and no one questioned his right to do so; and, at last, conscious of the displeasure that would follow me, I put by the patches, and joined Mark and Andrew, who were shelling corn in the kitchen. They were not permitted to burn a candle, but the great fire-place was full of blazing logs, and, on seeing me, their faces kindled into smiles, which helped to light the room, I thought. The floor was covered with red and white cobs, and there were sacks of ripe corn, and tubs of shelled corn, about the floor, and, taking a stool, I joined them at their work. At first, Andrew was so much confused, and rubbed his mouth so much with his handkerchief, that he shelled but little; gradually, however, he overcame his diffidence, and seemed to enjoy the privilege of conversation, which he did not often have, poor fellow. Little Mark made slow progress; his tender hands shrank from contact with the rough ears, and when I took his place, and asked him where he lived, and how old he was, his heart was quite won, and he found delight in communicating to me his little joys and sorrows. He was not pretty, certainly—his eyes were gray and large, his hair red, his expression surly, his voice querulous, and his manner unamiable, except, indeed, when talking with Andrew or myself.

I have been mistaken, I thought; he is really amiable and sweet-tempered; and, as I observed him very closely, his more habitual expression came to his face, and he said, abruptly, "I don't like grandfather!" "Why?" I said, smoothing back his hair, for I liked him better for saying so. "Because," he replied, "he don't like me;" and, in a moment, he continued, while his eyes moistened, "nobody likes me—everybody says I'm bad and ugly." "Oh, Mark!" exclaimed Andrew, "I like you, but I know somebody I don't like— somebody that wears spectaclesses, and a long beard—I don't say it's Uncle Christopher, and I don't say it ain't." Mark laughed, partly at the peculiar manner in which Andrew expressed himself; and when I told him I liked him too, and didn't think him either bad or ugly, he pulled at the hem of my apron as he remarked, that he should like to live with Andrew and me, always.

I answered that I would very gladly take him with me when I went home, and his face shone with pleasure, as he told me he had never yet ridden in a sleigh. But the pleasure lasted only a moment, and, with an altered and pained expression, he said, "I can't go—these things are all I have got," and he pointed to his homely and ill-conditioned clothes.

"Never mind, I will mend them," I said; and, wiping his eyes, he told me that once he had enough money to buy ever so many clothes, that he earned it by doing errands, sawing wood, and other services, for the man who lived next door to his father in the city, and that one Saturday night, when he had done something that pleased his employer, he paid him all he owed, and a little more, for being a good boy. "As I was running home," said he, "I met two boys that I knew; so I stopped to show them how much money I had, and when they told me to put it on the pavement in three little heaps, so we could see how much it made, I did so, and they, each one of them, seized a heap and ran away, and that," said Mark, "is just the truth."

"And what did you do then?" I asked.

"I told father," he answered, "and he said I was a simpleton, and it was good enough for me—that he would send me out here, and grandfather would straighten me."

"Never mind, Markey," said Andrew, "it will be New-Year's, day after tomorrow."

And so, sitting in the light of the cob-fire, and guessing what they would get in their stockings, I left them for the night.

I did not dampen their expectations of a good time, but I saw little cause to believe any pleasant dreams of their's would be realized, as I had seen no indications of preparation for the holidays, even to the degree of a plumb cake, or mince-pie. But I was certain of one thing—whatever Mark was, they would not make him any better. As he said, nobody loved him, nobody spoke to him, from morning till night, unless to correct or order him, in some way; and so, perhaps, he sometimes did things he ought not to do, merely to amuse his idleness. In all ways he was expected to have the wisdom of a man—to rise as early, and sit up as late, endure the heat and cold as well, and perform nearly as much labor. So, to say the truth, he was, for the most part, sulky and sullen, and did reluctantly that which he had to do, and no more, except, indeed, at the suggestion of Andrew, or while I was at the house, because it was at my request, and then work seemed only play to him.

The following morning was precisely like the morning that preceded it; the family rose before the daylight, and moved about by the tallow candle, and prepared breakfast, while Uncle Christopher sat in the great arm-chair, and Mark and Andrew fed the cattle by the light of a lantern.

"To-morrow will be New-Year's," said Mark, when breakfast was concluded, and Andrew took down the old Dictionary. No one noticed him, and he presently repeated it.

"Well, and what of it?" replied the old man, giving him a severe look.

"Nothing of it, as I know of," said the boy; "only I thought, maybe we would have something nice."

"Something nice!" echoed the grandfather; "don't we have something nice every day?"

"Well, but I want to do something," urged Mark, sure that he wished to have the dull routine broken in some way.

"Boys will be boys," said Aunt Rachael, in her most conciliatory tone, and addressing nobody in particular; and presently she asked Mark what had become of the potatoes he gleaned. He replied that they were in a barrel in the cellar.

"Eaten up by the rats," added Uncle Christopher.

"No, sir," said Mark, "they are as good as ever—may I sell them?"

"It's a great wonder you didn't let the rats eat them; but, I suppose, it's from no oversight of yours," Uncle Christopher said.

"Yes, sir, I covered them," replied the boy; "and now, may I sell them?— you said I might."

"Sell them—yes, you may sell them," replied the grandfather, in a mocking tone; "why don't you run along and sell them?"

Of course, the boy did not feel that he could sell his little crop, nor did the grandfather intend to grant any such permission.

"Uncle Christopher," said Andrew, looking up from his Dictionary, "do them ere potatoes belong to you, or do they belong to Markey?"

The old man did not reply directly, but said something about busy bodies and meddlers, which caused Andrew to study very earnestly, while Mark withdrew to the kitchen and cried, alone. Toward noon, however, his grandfather asked him if he could ride the old sorrel horse to the blacksmith's, three miles away, and get new shoes set on him, "because," said he, "if you can, you can carry a bag of the potatoes, and sell them."

Mark forgot how cold it was, forgot his ragged trowsers, forgot everything, except that the next day was New-Year's, and that he should have some money; and, mounting the old horse, with a bag of potatoes for a saddle, he was soon facing the north wind. He had no warm cap to turn against his ears, and no mittens for his hands, but he had something pleasant to think about, and so did not feel the cold so much.

When Andrew came from school, and found that Mark was gone to sell his potatoes, he was greatly pleased, and went out early to feed the cattle, first carrying the bundles of oats over the hill to the sheep—a portion of the work belonging to Mark; and he also made a blazing fire, and watched his coming at the window; but no one else seemed to think of him—the supper was served and removed, and not even the tea was kept by the fire for him. It was long after dark when he came, cold and hungry—but nobody made room at the hearth, and nobody inquired the result of his speculation, or what he had seen or heard during the day.

"You will find bread and butter in the cupboard," said Aunt Rachael, after a while, and that was all.

But he had received a dollar for the potatoes; that was fortune enough for one day, and he was careless and thoughtless of their indifference.

There was not light for my patch-work, and Aunt Rachael gave me instead a fine linen sheet to hem. "Isn't it fine and pretty?" said Mark, coming close to me before he went to bed; "I wish I could have it over me."

"Thoughtless child," said the grandfather, "you will have it over you soon enough, and nothing else about you, but your coffin-boards." And, with this benediction, he was dismissed for the night.

I awoke in the morning early, and heard the laughter of Andrew and Mark— it was New-Year's—and, in defiance of the gloomy prospect, they were merry; but when I descended the grandson looked grave—he had found nothing in his stockings.

"Put your feet in them," said Uncle Christopher, "and that will be something."

Fresh snow had fallen in the night, and the weather was milder than it had been, but within the house, the day began as usual.

"Grandfather," said Mark, "shall we not have the fat turkey-hen for dinner, today? I could run her down in the snow so easy!"

"So could I run you down in the snow, if I tried," he responded, with a surly quickness.

"New-Year's day," said Aunt Rachael, "is no better than any other, that I know of; and if you get very hungry, you can eat good bread and milk."

So, as in other mornings, Andrew whispered over the Dictionary, the old man sat in the corner, and the seven women began to knit.

Toward the noon, the happy thought came into the mind of Uncle Christopher: there would be wine-bibbers and mirthmakers at the village, three miles away—he would ride thither, and discourse to them of righteousness, temperance, and judgment to come. Mark was directed to bring his horse to the door, and, having combed his long beard with great care, and slipped over his head a knitted woollen cap, he departed on his errand, but not without having taken from little Mark the dollar he had received for his potatoes. "It may save a soul," he said, "and shall a wayward boy have his will, and a soul be lost?"

The child, however, was not likely in this way to be infused with religious feeling, whatever Uncle Christopher might think of the subject, and it was easy to see that a sense of the injustice he suffered had induced a change in his heart that no good angel would have joy to see. I tried to appease his anger, but he recounted, with the exactest particularity, all the history of the wrong he had suffered, and would not believe there was the slightest justification possible for robbing him of what was his own, instead of making him, as his grandfather should have done, a handsome present. About the middle of the afternoon Andrew came home from school, having been dismissed at so early an hour because it was a holiday, and to prepare for a spelling match to be held at the school-house in the evening. The chores were done long before sundown, and Andrew was in high spirits, partly in anticipation of the night's triumphs, and partly at the prospect of bringing some happiness to the heart of Mark, with whom he several times read over the lesson, impressing on his memory with all the skill he had the harder words which might come to him. Andrew went early, having in charge the school-house fire, and Mark did not accompany him, but I supposed he would follow presently, and so was not uneasy about him.

As the twilight darkened, Uncle Christopher came in, and, recounting his pious labors, with a conceited cant that was now become disgusting to me, he inquired for Mark, that the "brand" might hear and rejoice at the good accomplished with the money thus applied for the regeneration of the gentiles; but Mark was not to be found, and Aunt Rachael meekly hinted that from what she had overheard, she suspected he had gone with Andrew to the spelling match.

"Gone to the spelling match—and without asking me!" said the good man; "the rod has been spared too long." And taking from his pocket his knife, he opened it with deliberate satisfaction, and left the house.

I thought of the words of Mark, "I don't like my grandfather;" and I felt that he was not to blame. All the long evening the lithe sapling lay over the mantel, while Uncle Christopher knitted his brows, and the seven women knitted their seven stockings. I could not use my needle, nor think of what was being done about me; all the family practised their monotonous tasks in gloomy silence; the wind shrieked in the trees, whose branches were flung violently sometimes against the windows; Towser came scratching and whining at the door, without attracting the notice of any one; and Uncle Christopher sat in his easy-chair, in the most comfortable corner, seeming almost as if he were in an ecstasy with intense self-satisfaction, or, once in a while, looking joyously grim and stern as his eye rested on the instrument of torture he had prepared for poor Mark, for whose protection I found myself praying silently, as I half dreamed that he was in the hands of a pitiless monster.

The old clock struck eleven, from a distant part of the house, and we all counted the strokes, it was so still; the sheet I had finished lay on the settee beneath the window, where the rosevine creaked, and the mice peered out of the gnawed holes, and the rats ran through the mouldy cellar. There was a stamping at the door, in the moist snow; I listened, but could hear no voices; the door opened, and Andrew came in alone.

"Where is Mark?" asked the stern voice of the disciplinarian.

"I don't know," replied Andrew; "isn't he here?"

"No," said Aunt Rachael, throwing down her knitting, "nor hasn't been these many hours. Mercy on us, where can he be?"

"Fallen asleep somewhere about the house, likely," replied the old man; and taking up the candle, he began the search.

"And he hasn't been with you, Andrew?" asked Aunt Rachael again, in the faint hope that he would contradict his previous assertion.

"No ma'm, as true as I live and breathe," he replied, with childish simplicity and earnestness.

"Mercy on us!" she exclaimed again.

We could hear doors opening and shutting, and floors creaking in distant parts of the house; but nothing more.

"It's very strange," said the old man. "Don't be afraid, girls;" but he was evidently alarmed, and his hand shook as he lighted the lantern, saying, "he must be in the barn!"

Aunt Rachael would go, and I would go, too—I could not stay away. Andrew climbed along the scaffolds, stooping and reaching the lantern before him, and now and then we called to know if he had found him, as if he would not tell it when he did. So all the places we could think of had been searched, and we had began to call and listen, and call again.

"Hark," said Andrew, "I heard something."

We were all so still that it seemed as if we might hear the falling of flakes of snow.

"Only the howl of a dog," said Uncle Christopher.

"It's Towser's," suggested Andrew, fearfully; and with an anxious look he lowered the lantern to see what indications were in the way. Going toward the well were seen small footprints, and there were none returning. Even Uncle Christopher was evidently disturbed. Seeing the light, the dog began to yelp and whine, looking earnestly at us, and then suddenly down in the well, and when we came to the place every one felt a sinking of the heart, and no one dared to speak. The plank, on which I had seen him resting, was broken, and a part of it had fallen in. Towser whined, and his eyes shone as if he were in agony for words, and trying to throw all his intelligence into each piteous look he gave us.

"Get a rope, and lower the light," said one of the sisters; but the loose stones of the well were already rattling to the touch of Andrew, who, planting hands and feet on either side, was rapidly but cautiously descending. In a moment he was out of sight, but still we heard him, and soon there was a pause, then the sound of a hand, plashing the water, then a groan, sounding hollow and awful through the damp, dark opening, and a dragging, soughing movement, as if something were drawn up from the water. Presently we heard hands and feet once more against the sides of the well, and then, shining through the blackness into the light, two fiery eyes, and quickly after, as the bent head and shoulders of Andrew came nearer the surface, the kitten leaped from them, and dashed blindly past the old man, who was kneeling and looking down, pale with remorseful fear. Approaching the top, Andrew said, "I've got him!" and the grandfather reached down and lifted the lifeless form of the boy into his arms, where he had never reposed before. He was laid on the settee, by the window; the fine white sheet that I had hemmed, was placed over him; the stern and hard master walked backward and forward in the room, softened and contrite, though silent, except when occasional irrepressible groans disclosed the terrible action of his conscience; and Towser, who had been Mark's dearest playmate, nearly all the while kept his face, from without, against the window pane.

"Oh, if it were yesterday!" murmured Uncle Christopher, when the morning came; "Andrew," he said, and his voice faltered, as the young man took from the mantel the long, limber rod, and measured the shrouded form from the head to the feet, "get the coffin as good as you can—I don't care what it costs—get the best."

The Dictionary was not opened that day; Andrew was digging through the snow, on a lonesome hill-side, pausing now and then to wipe his eyes on his sleeve. Upright on the grave's edge, his only companion, sat the black dog.

Poor little Mark!—we dressed him very carefully, more prettily, too, than he had ever been in his life, and as he lay on the white pillow, all who saw him said, "How beautiful he is!" The day after the funeral, I saw Andrew, previously to his setting out for school, cutting from the sweet-brier such of the limbs as were reddest with berries, and he placed them over the heaped earth, as the best offering he could bring to beautify the last home of his companion. In the afternoon I went home, and have never seen him since, but, ignorant and graceless as he was, he had a heart full of sympathy and love, and Mark had owed to him the happiest hours of his life.

Perhaps, meditating of the injustice he himself was suffering, the unhappy boy, whose terrible death had brought sadness and perhaps repentance to the house of Uncle Christopher, had thought of the victim consigned by the same harsh master to the well, and determined, before starting for the schoolhouse, to go out and drop some food for it over the decayed plank on which I had seen him resting, and by its breaking had been precipitated down its uneven sides to the bottom, and so killed. But whether the result was by such accident, or by voluntary violence, his story is equally instructive to those straight and ungenial natures which see no beauty in childhood, and would drive before its time all childishness from life.

Conclusion

All things are beautiful in their time. Even Death, whom the poets have for ages made hideous, painting him as a skeleton reaper, cutting down tender flowers and ripe grain, and binding them into bundles for his dark garner, heedless of tears and prayers, is sometimes clothed with the wings and the mercy of an angel. It was one of the most beautiful conceptions of Blake, displayed in those illustrations of the Night Thoughts which forever should cause his name to be associated with the poet's, that his countenance who is called the Last Enemy was all sweetness and pitying gentleness; and how many, who have trembled with terror at his approach, have found the dearest rest in his embraces, as a frightened child has forgotten fear in wildest joy on discovering that some frightful being was only its mother, masqued for playing. Through this still messenger "He giveth his beloved sleep." How pleasant to the old and the worn to resign all their burdens in his hands, to lay by the staff, and lie down under canopies of flowers, assured that even through the night of the grave the morning will break! Thrice pleasant to the old, assured of having fought the good fight, and who feel, beneath the touch of Death, their white locks brightening with immortal crowns. They have done their work, and only Death can lead them up to hear from the master, "Well done, good and faithful servant." To the little child who has never sinned, he comes like a light slumber, and the temper, through the long bright ages, has no power. Only through the narrow and dark path of the grave could the tender feet have escaped the thorns—only to the bed which is low and cold may the delirium of passion and the torture of pain never come; so to the child the foe is the kindest of friends—dearest of friends!

One of the loveliest pictures that ever rises before me—I see it as I write—is that of a fair creature whose life was early rounded by that sleep which had in it the "rapture of repose" nothing could disturb forever. She had lain for days moaning and complaining, and we who loved her most could not help her, though she bent on us her mournfully beseeching eyes never so tenderly or imploringly. But when the writhing of anguish was gone, death gave to her cheek her beauty, and to her lips the old smile, and she was at rest. She had been lovely in her life and now she was transformed into an angel of the beautiful light, the fair soft light of the good and changeless world.

And for the wicked, looking over ruins they have made of life's beauty, friends they have changed to foes, love they have warped to hatred, one agonized moment of repentance has stretched itself up to the infinite mercy, and through radiance streaming from the cross, has sounded the soul-awakening and inspiring sentence, "Thy sins are forgiven!" What divine beauty covers the darkness that is before and around him! how blest to go with the friend who has come for him down into the grave, away from reproachful eyes—away from haughty and reviling words—away from the gentle rebuking of the injured, hardest of all to bear, and from the murmuring and complaining of a troubled conscience!

Whatever is dreariest in nature or saddest in life may in its time be bright and joyous—winter itself, with its naked boughs and bitter winds, and masses of clouds and snow. Poverty, too, with whom none of us voluntarily mate ourselves, has given birth to the sweetest humanities; its toils and privations have linked hand with hand, joined shoulder to shoulder, knit heart to heart; the armies of the poor are those who fight with the most indomitable courage, and like dust before the tempest are driven the obstacles that oppose their march; is it not the strength of their sinews that shapes the rough iron into axe and sickle? and does not the wheat-field stand smiling behind them and the hearth-light reach out from the cabin to greet their coming at night? Poverty is the pioneer about whose glowing forges and crashing forests burns and rings half the poetry that has filled the world. Many are the pleasant garlands that would be thrown aside if affluence were universal, and many the gentle oxen going from their plowing that would herd in wild droves but for men's necessities. The burdens of the poor are heavy indeed, and their tasks hard, but it has always seemed to me that in their modest homes and solitary by-paths is a pathos and tenderness in love, a bravery in adversity, a humility in prosperity, very rarely found in those conditions where character is less severely tried, and the virtues, if they make a fairer show, grow less strong than in the tempest, and the summer heat, and the winter cold.

It has been objected by some critics to the former series of these sketches of Western rural life, that they are of too sombre a tone; that a melancholy haze, an unnatural twilight, hangs too continually over every scene; but I think it is not so; if my recollections of "Clovernook" fail to suggest as much happiness as fall to the common lot, my observation has been unfortunate. I have not attempted any descriptions of the gay world; others—nearly all indeed of those writers of my sex who have essayed to amuse or instruct society—have apparently been familiar only with wealth and splendor, and such joys or sorrows as come gracefully to mingle with the refinements of luxury and art; but my days have been passed with the humbler classes, whose manners and experiences I have endeavored to exhibit in their customary lights and shadows, and in limiting myself to that domain to which I was born, it has never been in my thoughts to paint it as less lovely or more exposed to tearful influences than it is. If among those whose attention may be arrested by these unambitious delineations of scenes in "our neighborhood," there be any who have climbed through each gradation of fortune or consideration up to the stateliest distinctions, let them judge whether the "simple annals of the poor" are apt to be more bright, and the sum of enjoyment is greater in even those elevations, to attain to which is so often the most fondly cherished hope of youth and maturity.

In our country, though all men are not "created equal," such is the influence of the sentiment of liberty and political equality, that

> "All thoughts, all passions, all delights,
> Whatever stirs this mortal frame,"

may with as much probability be supposed to affect conduct and expectation in the log cabin as in the marble mansion; and to illustrate this truth, to dispel that erroneous belief of the necessary baseness of the "common people" which the great masters in literature have in all ages labored to create, is a purpose and an object in our nationality to which the finest and highest genius may wisely be devoted; but which may be effected in a degree by writings as unpretending as these reminiscences of what occurred in and about the little village where I from childhood watched the pulsations of surrounding hearts.

1853

ELIZABETH STODDARD
1823–1902

Elizabeth Stoddard's writings present women strongly moved by passion, struggling for self-realization, and rejecting conventional piety with its emphasis on female self-sacrifice. Writing in an era that endorsed "the cult of true womanhood," Stoddard failed to find an audience, not only because of her unconventional characterization of women, but also because of her cryptic narrative strategies. Nevertheless, during her lifetime, Stoddard managed to publish three novels, approximately seventy-five newspaper columns, forty or so poems, and more than eighty prose works.

Stoddard was born and raised in Mattapoisett, Massachusetts, a fishing village on the northwest shore of Buzzard's Bay. The bleak, seacoast landscape of Stoddard's youth, a landscape that seemingly gave rise to intense, fixated, and often bizarre passions, provided the setting and the characters found in her best work, including all three of her novels. Almost pathologically close to her family, particularly to her brother Wilson Barstow, Stoddard left Mattapoisett only briefly until her marriage, attending Wheaton Female Seminary for one term in 1837 and again in 1840–1841. She traveled in New England and to New York City, where in 1851 she met Richard Stoddard, an aspiring poet.

During an era that emphasized feminine domesticity, Stoddard struggled to find her own identity both as a woman and as a writer. In letters written to a friend in the early 1850s, she expresses her sense of being different from other women, sexually passionate, intellectual, and indomitably self-possessed, seeing marriage as a battle for mastery rather than a peaceful state, and estimating future motherhood as a distraction from her true purposes. Not surprisingly, the heroines of Stoddard's fiction display these attributes rather than those glorified in the ideology of true womanhood.

Married in 1852, Elizabeth and Richard lived in New York City, always on the edge of poverty. Elizabeth bore three children, only one of whom lived to adulthood. The couple sporadically held a salon for aspiring artists, actors, and writers, members of what literary historians have called "the genteel circle." Richard encouraged Elizabeth's writing and recognized her originality and her genius, but most of the other writers in their circle called her "The Pythoness" and wrote that she was mentally and morally diseased.

During the 1850s, Stoddard began publishing poetry, sketches, and short fiction. Most important among these apprentice efforts was a bimonthly column that she wrote between 1854 and 1858 for the *Daily Alta California*, San Francisco's oldest daily newspaper. With great wit, Stoddard's "letters" regularly reported on the New York cultural scene, the newest books, fashions, scandals, opera stars, and painters. These columns reveal Stoddard's iconoclasm about the received pieties of the day—manifest destiny, established religion, the confinement of women to the domestic sphere. In particular, Stoddard's columns mocked the values of the sentimental novel with its "eternal preachment about self-denial"; she asks, "Is goodness, then, incompatible with the enjoyment of the senses?" Stoddard looked to the Brontës rather than to American women writers as models for her own literary efforts.

Stoddard wrote all three of her novels during the 1860s. Although her work questions many of the cherished assumptions of the sentimental tradition, she uses the structure of the sentimental novel to mock its domestic feminism and to demonstrate that the romantic quest for total empowerment is inevitably defeated by the institutions of society. In her first novel, *The Morgesons* (1862), the heroine, Cassandra Morgeson, evolves into a mature, passionate woman who has accepted her essential isolation in a world in which social institutions are decaying, nature is indifferent, and the existence of God problematical. Lawrence Buell and Sandra Zagarell, in their excellent critical introduction to *The Morgesons and Other Writings*, aptly compare Stoddard's conception of Cassandra with Margaret Fuller's feminist insistence on self-realization.

Stoddard's other two novels, *Two Men* (1865) and *Temple House* (1867), present the New England family as the locus of power struggles, incestuous impulses, hatred, and guilt, rather than as a domestic sanctuary. When Thomas Wentworth Higginson first visited Emily Dickinson's household in Amherst, he wrote his wife that he was reminded of the families in Stoddard's novels. Indeed, Stoddard's New England, as the critic Mary Moss noted, is "A country of hereditary taints, of families divided against themselves, of violence, of excess."

During the 1860s, Stoddard also published the best of her short prose, often set in the New England of her childhood, utilizing popular stereotypes and plot conventions to question the values associated with those stereotypes. Her last major achievement was her collection of children's tales called *Lolly Dinks' Doings* (1874), a perplexing mixture of the whimsical and the bizarre. Increasingly, however, the poverty of her life with Richard forced her to become a hack writer; she became a bitter, often tiresome woman, who doubted her own gifts and alienated many of the couple's friends.

Despite the failure of Stoddard's three novels to sell, they impressed critics, including Nathaniel Hawthorne, William Dean Howells, and E. C. Stedman. The novels were reprinted twice in her lifetime, in 1888–1889 and in 1901, but again failed to capture the interest of the public, although the critical reception was favorable. Stoddard was long forgotten after her death in 1902, but the maverick qualities that put off so many of her contemporaries have contributed to the upsurge of interest in her today.

Sybil Weir
San Jose State University

Sandra A. Zagarell
Oberlin College

PRIMARY WORKS

The Morgesons, 1862; *Two Men*, 1865; *Temple House*, 1867; *Lolly Dinks' Doings*, 1874; *Poems*, 1895; *The Morgesons & Other Writings, Published and Unpublished, by Elizabeth Stoddard*, Lawrence Buell and Sandra A. Zagarell, eds., 1984.

Lemorne *versus* Huell[1]

The two months I spent at Newport[2] with Aunt Eliza Huell, who had been ordered to the sea-side for the benefit of her health, were the months that created all that is dramatic in my destiny. My aunt was troublesome, for she was not only out of health, but in a lawsuit. She wrote to me, for we lived apart, asking me to accompany her—not because she was fond of me, or wished to give me pleasure, but because I was useful in various ways. Mother insisted upon my accepting her invitation, not because she loved her late husband's sister, but because she thought it wise to cotton to her in every particular, for Aunt Eliza was rich, and we—two lone women—were poor.

I gave my music-pupils a longer and earlier vacation than usual, took a week to arrange my wardrobe—for I made my own dresses—and then started for New York, with the five dollars which Aunt Eliza had sent for my fare thither. I arrived at her house in Bond Street at 7 a.m., and found her man James in conversation with the milkman. He informed me that Miss Huell was very bad, and that the housekeeper was still in bed. I supposed that Aunt Eliza was in bed also, but I had hardly entered the house when I heard her bell ring as she only could ring it—with an impatient jerk.

"She wants hot milk," said James, "and the man has just come."

I laid my bonnet down, and went to the kitchen. Saluting the cook, who was an old acquaintance, and who told me that the "divil" had been in the range that morning, I took a pan, into which I poured some milk, and held it over the gaslight till it was hot; then I carried it up to Aunt Eliza.

"Here is your milk, Aunt Eliza. You have sent for me to help you, and I begin with the earliest opportunity."

"I looked for you an hour ago. Ring the bell."

I rang it.

"Your mother is well, I suppose. She would have sent you, though, had she been sick in bed."

"She has done so. She thinks better of my coming than I do."

The housekeeper, Mrs. Roll, came in, and Aunt Eliza politely requested her to have breakfast for her niece as soon as possible.

"I do not go down of mornings yet," said Aunt Eliza, "but Mrs. Roll presides. See that the coffee is good, Roll."

"It is good generally, Miss Huell."

"You see that Margaret brought me my milk."

---

[1]The text is that which originally appeared in *Harper's* 26 (1863).

[2]Newport, Rhode Island, was an extremely fashionable seaport resort during the nineteenth century.

"Ahem!" said Mrs. Roll, marching out.

At the beginning of each visit to Aunt Eliza I was in the habit of dwelling on the contrast between her way of living and ours. We lived from "hand to mouth." Every thing about her wore a hereditary air; for she lived in my grandfather's house, and it was the same as in his day. If I was at home when these contrasts occurred to me I should have felt angry; as it was, I felt them as in a dream—the china, the silver, the old furniture, and the excellent fare soothed me.

In the middle of the day Aunt Eliza came down stairs, and after she had received a visit from her doctor, decided to go to Newport on Saturday. It was Wednesday; and I could, if I chose, make any addition to my wardrobe. I had none to make, I informed her. What were my dresses?—had I a black silk? she asked. I had no black silk, and thought one would be unnecessary for hot weather.

"Who ever heard of a girl of twenty-four having no black silk! You have slimsy muslins, I dare say?"

"Yes."

"And you like them?"

"For present wear."

That afternoon she sent Mrs. Roll out, who returned with a splendid heavy silk for me, which Aunt Eliza said should be made before Saturday, and it was. I went to a fashionable dress-maker of her recommending, and on Friday it came home, beautifully made and trimmed with real lace.

"Even the Pushers could find no fault with this," said Aunt Eliza, turning over the sleeves and smoothing the lace. Somehow she smuggled into the house a white straw-bonnet, with white roses; also a handsome mantilla. She held the bonnet before me with a nod, and deposited it again in the box, which made a part of the luggage for Newport.

On Sunday morning we arrived in Newport, and went to a quiet hotel in the town. James was with us, but Mrs. Roll was left in Bond Street, in charge of the household. Monday was spent in an endeavor to make an arrangement regarding the hire of a coach and coachman. Several livery-stable keepers were in attendance, but nothing was settled, till I suggested that Aunt Eliza should send for her own carriage. James was sent back the next day, and returned on Thursday with coach, horses, and William her coachman. That matter being finished, and the trunks being unpacked, she decided to take her first bath in the sea, expecting me to support her through the trying ordeal of the surf. As we were returning from the beach we met a carriage containing a number of persons with a family resemblance.

When Aunt Eliza saw them she angrily exclaimed, "Am I to see those Uxbridges every day?"

Of the Uxbridges this much I knew—that the two brothers Uxbridge were the lawyers of her opponents in the lawsuit which had existed three or four years. I had never felt any interest in it, though I knew that it was concerning a tract of ground in the city which had belonged to my grandfather,

and which had, since his day, become very valuable. Litigation was a habit of
the Huell family. So the sight of the Uxbridge family did not agitate me as it
did Aunt Eliza.

"The sly, methodical dogs! but I shall beat Lemorne yet!"

"How will you amuse yourself then, aunt?"

"I'll adopt some boys to inherit what I shall save from his clutches."

The bath fatigued her so she remained in her room for the rest of the
day; but she kept me busy with a hundred trifles. I wrote for her, computed
interest, studied out bills of fare, till four o'clock came, and with it a fog.
Nevertheless I must ride on the Avenue, and the carriage was ordered.

"Wear your silk, Margaret; it will just about last your visit through—the
fog will use it up."

"I am glad of it," I answered.

"You will ride every day. Wear the bonnet I bought for you also."

"Certainly; but won't that go quicker in the fog than the dress?"

"Maybe; but wear it."

I rode every day afterward, from four to six, in the black silk, the mantilla, and the white straw. When Aunt Eliza went she was so on the alert for
the Uxbridge family carriage that she could have had little enjoyment of the
ride. Rocks never were a passion with her, she said, nor promontories,
chasms, or sand. She came to Newport to be washed with salt-water; when
she had washed up to the doctor's prescription she should leave, as ignorant
of the peculiar pleasures of Newport as when she arrived. She had no fancy
for its conglomerate societies, its literary cottages, its parvenue suits of
rooms, its saloon habits, and its bathing herds.

I considered the rides a part of the contract of what was expected in my
two months' performance. I did not dream that I was enjoying them, any
more than I supposed myself to be enjoying a sea-bath while pulling Aunt
Eliza to and fro in the surf. Nothing in the life around me stirred me, nothing in nature attracted me. I liked the fog; somehow it seemed to emanate
from me instead of rolling up from the ocean, and to represent me. Whether
I went alone or not, the coachman was ordered to drive a certain round; after that I could extend the ride in whatever direction I pleased, but I always
said, "Any where, William." One afternoon, which happened to be a bright
one, I was riding on the road which led to the glen, when I heard the
screaming of a flock of geese which were waddling across the path in front
of the horses. I started, for I was asleep probably, and, looking forward, saw
the Uxbridge carriage, filled with ladies and children, coming toward me;
and by it rode a gentleman on horseback. His horse was rearing among the
hissing geese, but neither horse nor geese appeared to engage him; his eyes
were fixed upon me. The horse swerved so near that its long mane almost
brushed against me. By an irresistible impulse I laid my ungloved hand upon
it, but did not look at the rider. Carriage and horseman passed on, and William resumed his pace. A vague idea took possession of me that I had seen
the horseman before on my various drives. I had a vision of a man galloping
on a black horse out of the fog, and into it again. I was very sure, however,

that I had never seen him on so pleasant a day as this! William did not bring his horses to time; it was after six when I went into Aunt Eliza's parlor, and found her impatient for her tea and toast. She was crosser than the occasion warranted; but I understood it when she gave me the outlines of a letter she desired me to write to her lawyer in New York. Something had turned up, he had written her; the Uxbridges believed that they had ferreted out what would go against her. I told her that I had met the Uxbridge carriage.

"One of them is in New York; how else could they be giving me trouble just now?"

"There was a gentleman on horseback beside the carriage."

"Did he look mean and cunning?"

"He did not wear his legal beaver up, I think; but he rode a fine horse and sat it well."

"A lawyer on horseback should, like the beggar of the adage, ride to the devil."

"Your business now is the 'Lemorne?'"

"You know it is."

"I did not know but that you had found something besides to litigate."

"It must have been Edward Uxbridge that you saw. He is the brain of the firm."

"You expect Mr. Van Horn?"

"Oh, he must come; I can not be writing letters."

We had been in Newport two weeks when Mr. Van Horn, Aunt Eliza's lawyer, came. He said that he would see Mr. Edward Uxbridge. Between them they might delay a term, which he thought would be best. "Would Miss Huell ever be ready for a compromise?" he jestingly asked.

"Are you suspicious?" she inquired.

"No; but the Uxbridge chaps are clever."

He dined with us; and at four o'clock Aunt Eliza graciously asked him to take a seat in the carriage with me, making some excuse for not going herself.

"Hullo!" said Mr. Van Horn when we had reached the country road; "there's Uxbridge now." And he waved his hand to him.

It was indeed the black horse and the same rider that I had met. He reined up beside us, and shook hands with Mr. Van Horn.

"We are required to answer this new complaint?" said Mr. Van Horn.

Mr. Uxbridge nodded.

"And after that the judgment?"

Mr. Uxbridge laughed.

"I wish that certain gore of land had been sunk instead of being mapped in 1835."

"The surveyor did his business well enough, I am sure."

They talked together in a low voice for a few minutes, and then Mr. Van Horn leaned back in his seat again. "Allow me," he said, "to introduce you, Uxbridge, to Miss Margaret Huell, Miss Huell's niece. Huell *vs.* Brown, you know," he added, in an explanatory tone; for I was Huell *vs.* Brown's daughter.

"Oh!" said Mr. Uxbridge bowing, and looking at me gravely. I looked at him also; he was a pale, stern-looking man, and forty years old certainly. I derived the impression at once that he had a domineering disposition, perhaps from the way in which he controlled his horse.

"Nice beast that," said Mr. Van Horn.

"Yes," he answered, laying his hand on its mane, so that the action brought immediately to my mind the recollection that I had done so too. I would not meet his eye again, however.

"How long shall you remain, Uxbridge?"

"I don't know. You are not interested in the lawsuit, Miss Huell?" he said, putting on his hat.

"Not in the least; nothing of mine is involved."

"We'll gain it for your portion yet, Miss Margaret," said Mr. Van Horn, nodding to Mr. Uxbridge, and bidding William drive on. He returned the next day, and we settled into the routine of hotel life. A few mornings after, she sent me to a matinée, which was given by some of the Opera people, who were in Newport strengthening the larynx with applications of brine. When the concert was half over, and the audience were making the usual hum and stir, I saw Mr. Uxbridge against a pillar, with his hands incased in pearl-colored gloves, and holding a shiny hat. He turned half away when he caught my eye, and then darted toward me.

"You have not been much more interested in the music than you are in the lawsuit," he said, seating himself beside me.

"The *tutoyer*[3] of the Italian voice is agreeable, however."

"It makes one dreamy."

"A child."

"Yes, a child; not a man nor a woman."

"I teach music. I can not dream over 'one, two, three.'"

"*You*—a music teacher!"

"For six years."

I was aware that he looked at me from head to foot, and I picked at the lace of my invariable black silk; but what did it matter whether I owned that I was a genteel pauper, representing my aunt's position for two months, or not?

"Where?"

"In Waterbury."

"Waterbury differs from Newport."

"I suppose so."

"You suppose!"

A young gentleman sauntered by us, and Mr. Uxbridge called to him to look up the Misses Uxbridge, his nieces, on the other side of the hall.

[3]*Tutoyer* means "to speak familiarly to" (to use the French *tu* form). Here its use also registers the singer's tone of voice.

"Paterfamilias Uxbridge has left his brood in my charge," he said. "I try to do my duty," and he held out a twisted pearl-colored glove, which he pulled off while talking. What white nervous fingers he had! I thought they might pinch like steel.

"You suppose," he repeated.

"I do not look at Newport."

"Have you observed Waterbury?"

"I observe what is in my sphere."

"Oh!"

He was silent then. The second part of the concert began; but I could not compose myself to appreciation. Either the music or I grew chaotic. So many tumultuous sounds I heard—of hope, doubt, inquiry, melancholy, and desire; or did I feel the emotions which these words express? Or was there magnetism stealing into me from the quiet man beside me? He left me with a bow before the concert was over, and I saw him making his way out of the hall when it was finished.

I had been sent in the carriage, of course; but several carriages were in advance of it before the walk, and I waited there for William to drive up. When he did so, I saw by the oscillatory motion of his head, though his arms and whiphand were perfectly correct, that he was inebriated. It was his first occasion of meeting fellow-coachmen in full dress, and the occasion had proved too much for him. My hand, however, was on the coach door, when I heard Mr. Uxbridge say, at my elbow.

"It is not safe for you."

"Oh, Sir, it is in the programme that I ride home from the concert." And I prepared to step in.

"I shall sit on the box, then."

"But your nieces?"

"They are walking home, squired by a younger knight."

Aunt Eliza would say, I thought, "Needs must when a lawyer drives"; and I concluded to allow him to have his way, telling him that he was taking a great deal of trouble. He thought it would be less if he were allowed to sit inside; both ways were unsafe.

Nothing happened. William drove well from habit; but James was obliged to assist him to dismount. Mr. Uxbridge waited a moment at the door, and so there was quite a little sensation, which spread its ripples till Aunt Eliza was reached. She sent for William, whose only excuse was "dampness."

"Uxbridge knew my carriage, of course," she said, with a complacent voice.

"He knew me," I replied.

"You do not look like the Huells."

"I look precisely like the young woman to whom he was introduced by Mr. Van Horn."

"Oh ho!"

"He thought it unsafe for me to come alone under William's charge."

"Ah ha!"

No more was said on the subject of his coming home with me. Aunt Eliza had several fits of musing in the course of the evening while I read aloud to her, which had no connection with the subject of the book. As I put it down she said that it would be well for me to go to church the next day. I acquiesced, but remarked that my piety would not require the carriage, and that I preferred to walk. Besides, it would be well for William and James to attend divine service. She could not spare James, and thought William had better clean the harness, by way of penance.

The morning proved to be warm and sunny. I donned a muslin dress of home manufacture and my own bonnet, and started for church. I had walked but a few paces when the consciousness of being *free* and *alone* struck me. I halted, looked about me, and concluded that I would not go to church, but walk into the fields. I had no knowledge of the whereabouts of the fields; but I walked straight forward, and after a while came upon some barren fields, cropping with coarse rocks, along which ran a narrow road. I turned into it, and soon saw beyond the rough coast the blue ring of the ocean—vast, silent, and splendid in the sunshine. I found a seat on the ruins of an old stone-wall, among some tangled bushes and briers. There being no Aunt Eliza to pull through the surf, and no animated bathers near, I discovered the beauty of the sea, and that I loved it.

Presently I heard the steps of a horse, and, to my astonishment, Mr. Uxbridge rode past. I was glad he did not know me. I watched him as he rode slowly down the road, deep in thought. He let drop the bridle, and the horse stopped, as if accustomed to the circumstance, and pawed the ground gently, or yawed his neck for pastime. Mr. Uxbridge folded his arms and raised his head to look seaward. It seemed to me as if he were about to address the jury. I had dropped so entirely from my observance of the landscape that I jumped when he resumed the bridle and turned his horse to come back. I slipped from my seat to look among the bushes, determined that he should not recognize me; but my attempt was a failure—he did not ride by the second time.

"Miss Huell!" And he jumped from his saddle, slipping his arm through the bridle.

"I am a runaway. What do you think of the Fugitive Slave Bill?"[4]

"I approve of returning property to its owners."

"The sea must have been God's temple first, instead of the groves."[5]

"I believe the Saurians were an Orthodox tribe."

"Did you stop yonder to ponder the sea?"

"I was pondering 'Lemorne vs. Huell.'"

---

[4]Reference to the Fugitive Slave Law, whose mandate that slaves who had escaped to the North must be returned to their owners was honored by conservative Northerners like Uxbridge.

[5]Adaptation of the first line of William Cullen Bryant's "A Forest Hymn" (1825).

He looked at me earnestly, and then gave a tug at the bridle, for his steed was inclined to make a crude repast from the bushes.

"How was it that I did not detect you at once?" he continued.

"My apparel is Waterbury apparel."

"Ah!"

We walked up the road slowly till we came to the end of it; then I stopped for him to understand that I thought it time for him to leave me. He sprang into the saddle.

"Give us good-by!" he said, bringing his horse close to me.

"We are not on equal terms; I feel too humble afoot to salute you."

"Put your foot on the stirrup then."

A leaf stuck in the horse's forelock, and I pulled it off and waved it in token of farewell. A powerful light shot into his eyes when he saw my hand close on the leaf.

"May I come and see you?" he asked, abruptly. "I will."

"I shall say neither 'No' nor 'Yes.'"

He rode on at a quick pace, and I walked homeward forgetting the sense of liberty I had started with, and proceeded straightway to Aunt Eliza.

"I have not been to church, aunt, but to walk beyond the town; it was not so nominated in the bond, but I went. The taste of freedom was so pleasant that I warn you there is danger of my 'striking.' When will you have done with Newport?"

"I am pleased with Newport now," she answered, with a curious intonation. "I like it."

"I do also."

Her keen eyes sparkled.

"Did you ever like anything when you were with me before?"

"Never. I will tell you why I like it: because I have met, and shall probably meet, Mr. Uxbridge. I saw him to-day. He asked permission to visit me."

"Let him come."

"He will come."

But we did not see him either at the hotel or when we went abroad. Aunt Eliza rode with me each afternoon, and each morning we went to the beach. She engaged me every moment when at home, and I faithfully performed all my tasks. I clapped to the door on self-investigation—locked it against any analysis or reasoning upon any circumstance connected with Mr. Uxbridge. The only piece of treachery to my code that I was guilty of was the putting of the leaf which I brought home on Sunday between the leaves of that poem whose motto is,

"*Mariana in the moated grange.*"[6]

---

[6]"Mariana" (1830), by Alfred, Lord Tennyson. The motto is from Shakespeare's *Measure for Measure*, III, i.

On Saturday morning, nearly a week after I saw him on my walk, Aunt Eliza proposed that we should go to Turo Street on a shopping excursion; she wanted a cap, and various articles besides. As we went into a large shop I saw Mr. Uxbridge at a counter buying gloves; her quick eye caught sight of him, and she edged away, saying she would look at some goods on the other side; I might wait where I was. As he turned to go out he saw me and stopped.

"I have been in New York since I saw you," he said. "Mr. Lemorne sent for me."

"There is my aunt," I said.

He shrugged his shoulders.

"I shall not go away soon again," he remarked. "I missed Newport greatly."

I made some foolish reply, and kept my eyes on Aunt Eliza, who dawdled unaccountably. He appeared amused, and after a little talk went away.

Aunt Eliza's purchase was a rose-colored moire antique, which she said was to be made for me; for Mrs. Bliss, one of our hotel acquaintances, had offered to chaperon me to the great ball which would come off in a few days, and she had accepted the offer for me.

"There will be no chance for you to take a walk instead," she finished with.

"I can not dance, you know."

"But you will be *there*."

I was sent to a dress-maker of Mrs. Bliss's recommending; but I ordered the dress to be made after my own design, long plain sleeves, and high plain corsage, and requested that it should not be sent home till the evening of the ball. Before it came off Mr. Uxbridge called, and was graciously received by Aunt Eliza, who could be gracious to all except her relatives. I could not but perceive, however, that they watched each other in spite of their lively conversation. To me he was deferential, but went over the ground of our acquaintance as if it had been the most natural thing in the world. But for my life-long habit of never calling in question the behavior of those I came in contact with, and of never expecting any thing different from that I received, I might have wondered over his visit. Every person's individuality was sacred to me, from the fact, perhaps, that my own individuality had never been respected by any person with whom I had any relation—not even by my own mother.

After Mr. Uxbridge went, I asked Aunt Eliza if she thought he looked mean and cunning? She laughed, and replied that she was bound to think that Mr. Lemorne's lawyer could not look otherwise.

When, on the night of the ball, I presented myself in the rose-colored moire antique for her inspection, she raised her eyebrows, but said nothing about it.

"I need not be careful of it, I suppose, aunt?"

"Spill as much wine and ice-cream on it as you like."

In the dressing room Mrs. Bliss surveyed me.

"I think I like this mass of rose-color," she said. "Your hair comes out in contrast so brilliantly. Why, you have not a single ornament on!"

"It is so easy to dress without."

This was all the conversation we had together during the evening, except when she introduced some acquaintance to fulfill her matronizing duties. As I was no dancer I was left alone most of the time, and amused myself by gliding from window to window along the wall, that it might not be observed that I was a fixed flower. Still I suffered the annoyance of being stared at by wandering squads of young gentlemen, the "curled darlings" of the ballroom. I borrowed Mrs. Bliss's fan in one of her visits for a protection. With that, and the embrasure of a remote window where I finally stationed myself, I hoped to escape further notice. The music of the celebrated band which played between the dances recalled the chorus of spirits which charmed Faust:

> "And the fluttering
> Ribbons of drapery
> Cover the plains,
> Cover the bowers,
> Where lovers,
> Deep in thought,
> Give themselves for life."[7]

The voice of Mrs. Bliss broke its spell.

"I bring an old friend, Miss Huell, and he tells me an acquaintance of yours."

It was Mr. Uxbridge.

"I had no thought of meeting you, Miss Huell."

And he coolly took the seat beside me in the window, leaving to Mrs. Bliss the alternative of standing or of going away; she chose the latter.

"I saw you as soon as I came in," he said, "gliding from window to window, like a vessel hugging the shore in a storm."

"With colors at half-mast; I have no dancing partner."

"How many have observed you?"

"Several young gentlemen."

"Moths."

"Oh no, butterflies."

"They must keep away now."

"Are you Rhadamanthus?"

"And Charon, too. I would have you row in the same boat with me."

"Now you are fishing."

"Won't you compliment me. Did I ever look better?"

[7]Johann Wolfgang von Goethe, *Faust*, Part I (1808), II, l. 1463–69. Gretchen, Faust's beloved and victim, is also called Margaret. *Faust* and "Lemorne vs. Huell" both feature illicit or illegal pacts and the theme of enchantment.

His evening costume *was* becoming, but he looked pale, and weary, and disturbed. But if we were engaged for a tournament, as his behavior indicated, I must do my best at telling. So I told him that he never looked better, and asked him how I looked. He would look at me presently, he said, and decide. Mrs. Bliss skimmed by us with nods and smiles; as she vanished our eyes followed her, and we talked vaguely on various matters, sounding ourselves and each other. When a furious redowa set in which cut our conversation into rhythm he pushed up the window and said, "Look out."

I turned my face to him to do so, and saw the moon at the full, riding through the strip of sky which our vision commanded. From the moon our eyes fell on each other. After a moment's silence, during which I returned his steadfast gaze, for I could not help it, he said:

"If we understand the impression we make upon each other, what must be said?"

I made no reply, but fanned myself, neither looking at the moon, nor upon the redowa, nor upon any thing.

He took the fan from me.

"Speak of yourself," he said.

"Speak you."

"I am what I seem, a man within your sphere. By all the accidents of position and circumstance suited to it. Have you not learned it?"

"I am not what I seem. I never wore so splendid a dress as this till tonight, and shall not again."

He gave the fan such a twirl that its slender sticks snapped, and it dropped like the broken wing of a bird.

"Mr. Uxbridge, that fan belongs to Mrs. Bliss."

He threw it out of the window.

"You have courage, fidelity, and patience—this character with a passionate soul. I am sure that you have such a soul?"

"I do not know."

"I have fallen in love with you. It happened on the very day when I passed you on the way to the Glen. I never got away from the remembrance of seeing your hand on the mane of my horse."

He waited for me to speak, but I could not; the balance of my mind was gone. Why should this have happened to me—a slave? As it had happened, why did I not feel exultant in the sense of power which the chance for freedom with him should give?

"What is it, Margaret? your face is as sad as death."

"How do you call me 'Margaret?'"

"As I would call my wife—Margaret."

He rose and stood before me to screen my face from observation. I supposed so, and endeavored to stifle my agitation.

"You are better," he said, presently. "Come go with me and get some refreshment." And he beckoned to Mrs. Bliss, who was down the hall with an unwieldly gentleman.

"Will you go to supper now?" she asked.

"We are only waiting for you," Mr. Uxbridge answered, offering me his arm.

When we emerged into the blaze and glitter of the supper-room I sought refuge in the shadow of Mrs. Bliss's companion, for it seemed to me that I had lost my own.

"Drink this Champagne," said Mr. Uxbridge. "Pay no attention to the Colonel on your left; he won't expect it."

"Neither must you."

"Drink."

The Champagne did not prevent me from reflecting on the fact that he had not yet asked whether I loved him.

The spirit chorus again floated through my mind:

> *"Where lovers,*
> *Deep in thought,*
> *Give themselves for life."*

I was not allowed to give myself—I was *taken*.

"No heel-taps," he whispered, "to the bottom quaff."

"Take me home, will you?"

"Mrs. Bliss is not ready."

"Tell her that I must go."

He went behind her chair and whispered something, and she nodded to me to go without her.

When her carriage came up, I think he gave the coachman an order to drive home in a round-about way, for we were a long time reaching it. I kept my face to the window, and he made no effort to divert my attention. When we came to a street whose thick rows of trees shut out the moonlight my eager soul longed to leap out into the dark and demand of him his heart, soul, life, for me.

I struck him lightly on the shoulder; he seized my hand.

"Oh, I know you, Margaret; you are mine!"

"We are at the hotel."

He sent the carriage back, and said that he would leave me at my aunt's door. He wished that he could see her then. Was it magic that made her open the door before I reached it?

"Have you come on legal business?" she asked him.

"You have divined what I come for."

"Step in, step in; it's very late. I should have been in bed but for neuralgia. Did Mr. Uxbridge come home with you, Margaret?"

"Yes, in Mrs. Bliss's carriage; I wished to come before she was ready to leave."

"Well, Mr. Uxbridge is old enough for your protector, certainly."

"I *am* forty, ma'am."

"Do you want Margaret?"

"I do."

"You know exactly how much is involved in your client's suit?"

"Exactly."

"You also know that his claim is an unjust one."

"Do I?"

"I shall not be poor if I lose; if I gain, Margaret will be rich."

"'Margaret will be rich,'" he repeated, absently.

"What! have you changed your mind respecting the orphans, aunt?"

"She has, and is—nothing," she went on, not heeding my remark. "Her father married below his station; when he died his wife fell back to her place—for he spent his fortune—and there she and Margaret must remain, unless Lemorne is defeated."

"Aunt, for your succinct biography of my position many thanks."

"Sixty thousand dollars," she continued. "Van Horn tells me that, as yet, the firm of Uxbridge Brothers have only an income—no capital."

"It is true," he answered, musingly.

The clock on the mantle struck two.

"A thousand dollars for every year of my life," she said. "You and I, Uxbridge, know the value and beauty of money."

"Yes, there is beauty in money, and"—looking at me—"beauty without it."

"The striking of the clock," I soliloquized, "proves that this scene is not a phantasm."

"Margaret is fatigued," he said, rising. "May I come to-morrow?"

"It is my part only," replied Aunt Eliza, "to see that she is, or is not, Cinderella."

"If you have ever thought of me, aunt, as an individual, you must have seen that I am not averse to ashes."

He held my hand a moment, and then kissed me with a kiss of appropriation.

"He is in love with you," she said, after he had gone. "I think I know him. He has found beauty ignorant of itself; he will teach you to develop it."

The next morning Mr. Uxbridge had an interview with Aunt Eliza before he saw me.

When we were alone I asked him how her eccentricities affected him; he could not but consider her violent, prejudiced, warped, and whimsical. I told him that I had been taught to accept all that she did on this basis. Would this explain to him my silence in regard to her?

"Can you endure to live with her in Bond Street for the present, or would you rather return to Waterbury?"

"She desires my company while she is in Newport only. I have never been with her so long before."

"I understand her. Law is a game, in her estimation, in which cheating can as easily be carried on as at cards."

"Her soul is in this case."

"Her soul is not too large for it. Will you ride this afternoon?"

I promised, of course. From that time till he left Newport we saw each other every day, and though I found little opportunity to express my own peculiar feelings, he comprehended many of my wishes, and all my tastes. I grew fond of him hourly. Had I not reason? Never was friend so considerate, never was lover more devoted.

When he had been gone a few days, Aunt Eliza declared that she was ready to depart from Newport. The rose-colored days were ended! In two days we were on the Sound, coach, horses, servants, and ourselves.

It was the 1st of September when we arrived in Bond Street. A week from that date Samuel Uxbridge, the senior partner of Uxbridge Brothers, went to Europe with his family, and I went to Waterbury, accompanied by Mr. Uxbridge. He consulted mother in regard to our marriage, and appointed it in November. In October Aunt Eliza sent for me to come back to Bond Street and spend a week. She had some fine marking to do, she wrote. While there I noticed a restlessness in her which I had never before observed, and conferred with Mrs. Roll on the matter. "She do be awake nights a deal, and that's the reason," Mrs. Roll said. Her manner was the same in other respects. She said she would not give me any thing for my wedding outfit, but she paid my fare from Waterbury and back.

She could not spare me to go out, she told Mr. Uxbridge, and in consequence I saw little of him while there.

In November we were married. Aunt Eliza was not at the wedding, which was a quiet one. Mr. Uxbridge desired me to remain in Waterbury till spring. He would not decide about taking a house in New York till then; by that time his brother might return, and if possible we would go to Europe for a few months. I acquiesced in all his plans. Indeed I was not consulted; but I was happy—happy in him, and happy in every thing.

The winter passed in waiting for him to come to Waterbury every Saturday; and in the enjoyment of the two days he passed with me. In March Aunt Eliza wrote me that Lemorne was beaten! Van Horn had taken up the whole contents of his snuff-box in her house the evening before in amazement at the turn things had taken.

That night I dreamed of the scene in the hotel at Newport. I heard Aunt Eliza saying, "If I gain, Margaret will be rich." And I heard also the clock strike two. As it struck I said, *"My husband is a scoundrel,"* and woke with a start.

1863

REBECCA HARDING DAVIS
1831–1910

When "Life in the Iron-Mills" appeared in the *Atlantic Monthly* in 1861, it was immediately recognized as a pioneering achievement, a story that captured a new subject for American literature—the grim lives of the industrial workers in the nation's mills and factories. Herman Melville's "The Tartarus of Maids" (1855) had previously but more briefly penetrated into the dark interiors of the industrial structures that were transfiguring the American landscape. Harding's story was the first extended treatment, a harsh portrayal of backbreaking labor and emotional and spiritual starvation. In its depiction of the lives of the workers, from their diet of cold, rancid potatoes to the crimes they were driven to commit, it introduced new elements of both realism and naturalism into American fiction.

"Life in the Iron-Mills" was the first published work of its thirty-year-old author, Rebecca Harding, resident of the industrial town of Wheeling, Virginia (now West Virginia). It brought her fame; the acquaintance of many eminent New England authors; a valued, lifelong friendship with Annie Fields, wife of James T. Fields, editor of the *Atlantic*; and further publication in that prestigious magazine, including the novel *Margret Howth* (1862). Ten years later, however, she had lost her literary position, and although she continued to write and publish prolifically, she was not to produce a literary work equal in imaginative power to her first. Well before her death in 1910, "Life in the Iron-Mills" had been forgotten, and for more than half a century thereafter, although mentioned in literary histories, it went largely unread until it was republished in 1972.

In her afterword to the 1972 edition, Tillie Olsen, the contemporary writer responsible for its rediscovery, attributed what she called "trespass vision" to Rebecca Harding, to underscore the unlikely nature of her achievement in writing about a way of life so different from her own. Born and raised in a well-to-do middle-class family, Harding led the relatively protected and circumscribed existence of one of her sex and class. Educated in her early years by her mother at home, she attended Washington Female Seminary in Pennsylvania, from which she graduated in 1848 at the age of seventeen. Thereafter she remained inside the family, helping, as the eldest daughter, with household chores and the education of the younger children; reading; and also registering and absorbing the life of Wheeling's cotton mills and iron-processing factories. A triumphal trip to Boston following publication of "Iron-Mills" introduced her to the world of professional authorship and to Nathaniel Hawthorne, whose work she had read and admired and whose influence can be seen in the supernatural and symbolic aspects of her "korl woman"—the statue that her main character, the furnace-tender Hugh Wolfe, a talented and self-taught sculptor, creates from the waste product, or korl, of steel-refining processes.

The story's publication also led to a correspondence between Harding and Philadelphia journalist L. Clarke Davis, whom she married in 1863. Moving to Philadelphia, the author entered into the complex responsibilities of nineteenth-century wifehood and motherhood: assuming the primary care of the three children born to the marriage (one of whom, Richard Harding Davis, would become a famous journalist with a reputation eclipsing her own); supervising the household in her husband's frequent absences; and serving, when he was at home, as hostess to his many friends. Although she continued to write and to publish, the family's often pressing financial needs led her to produce stories and serialized novels, including mysteries, gothics, and thrillers, for the popular magazines of the time, such as *Peterson's* and *Lippincott's*, which paid better than the *Atlantic*, and to write for the *New York Tribune* and a children's magazine, *Youth's Companion*, as well. In much of her work, including her final critical success, *Silhouettes of American Life* (1892), she continued to explore the issue of unused or wasted capacities, first treated in "Iron-Mills" in the story of Hugh Wolfe's unsatisfied artistic hunger. Again and again she probed the anguished conflict, for her female characters, of marriage and professional work—the seemingly exclusive longings for both family and artistic fulfillment—never arriving at a satisfactory resolution. Sometimes she celebrated the pleasures of domestic life; often she expressed ambivalence about the intellectually or artistically ambitious woman.

Throughout her career, Rebecca Harding Davis continued to introduce and explore new subject matter in accordance with her announced literary purpose, "to dig into this commonplace, this vulgar American life, and see what is in it." *Waiting for the Verdict* (1868) dealt with the educational, political, and economic needs of the newly emancipated slaves and the ways in which racial injustice frustrated the development of their talents. *John Andross* (1874) was one of the earliest novels to treat political corruption in the nation's government. *Earthen Pitchers*, serialized in *Scribner's Monthly* in 1873 and 1874, explored the reality of women earning their living professionally. In other works, she chose as heroines women who are unbeautiful by conventional standards and women who are unabashedly physical—significant departures from prevalent literary fashion and breakthroughs into a new realism in the depiction of women.

Until recently, even Davis's advocates accepted the assumption that the quality of her writing, as well as her literary reputation, declined after the publication of *Margret Howth* in 1862. One reason for misunderstanding Davis's later work is the mistaken belief that she wrote an antifeminist book, *Pro Aris et Focis*, in 1870.

Thanks to a new generation of Davis scholars, a different picture of her career is beginning to emerge. Regardless of the compromises she may have made in her life and her art, Rebecca Harding Davis left an impressive literary legacy. As Tillie Olsen has said, her "pioneering firsts in subject matter are unequaled. She extended the realm of fiction."

Judith Roman-Royer
Indiana University East

Elaine Hedges
Late of Towson State University

PRIMARY WORKS

Bits of Gossip, 1904; *Life in the Iron-Mills and Other Stories*, ed. with a biographical interpretation by Tillie Olsen, 1985; *Margret Howth: A Story of To-day*, Jean Fagan Yellin, ed., 1990; *A Rebecca Harding Davis Reader*, Jean Pfaelzer, ed., 1995; *Waiting for the Verdict*, Donald Dingledine, ed., 1996.

Life in the Iron-Mills[1]

"Is this the end?
O Life, as futile, then, as frail!
What hope of answer or redress?"[2]

A cloudy day: do you know what that is in a town of iron-works?[3] The sky sank down before dawn, muddy, flat, immovable. The air is thick, clammy with the breath of crowded human beings. It stifles me. I open the window, and, looking out, can scarcely see through the rain the grocer's shop opposite, where a crowd of drunken Irishmen are puffing Lynchburg tobacco[4] in their pipes. I can detect the scent through all the foul smells ranging loose in the air.

The idiosyncrasy of this town is smoke. It rolls sullenly in slow folds from the great chimneys of the iron-foundries, and settles down in black, slimy pools on the muddy streets. Smoke on the wharves, smoke on the dingy boats, on the yellow river,—clinging in a coating of greasy soot to the house-front, the two faded poplars, the faces of the passers-by. The long train of mules, dragging masses of pig-iron[5] through the narrow street, have a foul vapor hanging to their reeking sides. Here, inside, is a little broken figure of an angel pointing upward from the mantel-shelf; but even its wings are covered with smoke, clotted and black. Smoke everywhere! A dirty canary chirps desolately in a cage beside me. Its dream of green fields and sunshine is a very old dream,—almost worn out, I think.

From the back-window I can see a narrow brick-yard sloping down to the river-side, strewed with rain-butts and tubs. The river, dull and tawny-colored, *(la belle rivière!)*[6] drags itself sluggishly along, tired of the heavy weight of boats and coal-barges. What wonder? When I was a child, I used to fancy a look of weary, dumb appeal upon the face of the negro-like river slavishly bearing its burden day after day. Something of the same idle notion comes to me to-day, when from the street-window I look on the slow stream of human life creeping past, night and morning, to the great mills. Masses of men, with dull, besotted faces bent to the ground, sharpened here and there by pain or cunning; skin and muscle and flesh begrimed with smoke and ashes; stooping all night over boiling caldrons of metal, laired by day in dens of drunkenness and infamy; breathing from infancy to death an air saturated with fog and grease and soot, vileness for soul and body. What do you make of a case like that, amateur psychologist? You call it an altogether serious thing to be alive: to these men it is a drunken jest, a joke,—horrible to angels perhaps, to them commonplace enough. My fancy about

---

[1]The text is that of the *Atlantic Monthly* 7 (April 1861), pp. 430–51.
[2]The epigraph is a loose quotation of lines from sections XII and LVI of Alfred, Lord Tennyson's "In Memoriam A.H.H."
[3]The town is not named, but its characteristics match those of Harding's hometown, Wheeling, Virginia (now West Virginia).

[4]Cheap tobacco.
[5]Blocks of crude iron that will be refined into steel or wrought iron or remelted and cast into molds.
[6]The beautiful river"—used ironically.

the river was an idle one: it is no type of such a life. What if it be stagnant and slimy here? It knows that beyond there waits for it odorous sunlight,—quaint old gardens, dusky with soft, green foliage of apple-trees, and flushing crimson with roses,—air, and fields, and mountains. The future of the Welsh puddler[7] passing just now is not so pleasant. To be stowed away, after his grimy work is done, in a hole in the muddy graveyard, and after that,——not air, nor green fields, nor curious roses.

Can you see how foggy the day is? As I stand here, idly tapping the window-pane, and looking out through the rain at the dirty back-yard and the coal-boats below, fragments of an old story float up before me,—a story of this old house into which I happened to come today. You may think it a tiresome story enough, as foggy as the day, sharpened by no sudden flashes of pain or pleasure.—I know: only the outline of a dull life, that long since, with thousands of dull lives like its own, was vainly lived and lost: thousands of them,—massed, vile, slimy lives, like those of the torpid lizards in yonder stagnant water-butt.—Lost? There is a curious point for you to settle, my friend, who study psychology in a lazy, *dilettante*[8] way. Stop a moment. I am going to be honest. This is what I want you to do. I want you to hide your disgust, take no heed to your clean clothes, and come right down with me,—here, into the thickest of the fog and mud and foul effluvia. I want you to hear this story. There is a secret down here, in this nightmare fog, that has lain dumb for centuries: I want to make it a real thing to you. You, Egoist, or Pantheist, or Arminian,[9] busy in making straight paths for your feet on the hills, do not see it clearly,—this terrible question which men here have gone mad and died trying to answer. I dare not put this secret into words. I told you it was dumb. These men, going by with drunken faces and brains full of unawakened power, do not ask it of Society or of God. Their lives ask it; their deaths ask it. There is no reply. I will tell you plainly that I have a great hope; and I bring it to you to be tested. It is this: that this terrible dumb question is its own reply; that it is not the sentence of death we think it, but, from the very extremity of its darkness, the most solemn prophecy which the world has known of the Hope to come. I dare make my meaning no clearer, but will only tell my story. It will, perhaps, seem to you as foul and dark as this thick vapor about us, and as pregnant with death; but if your eyes are free as mine are to look deeper, no perfume-tinted dawn will be so fair with promise of the day that shall surely come.

My story is very simple,—only what I remember of the life of one of these men,—a furnace-tender in one of Kirby & John's rolling-mills,—Hugh Wolfe. You know the mills? They took the great order for the Lower Virginia

---

[7]The person who converts pig-iron into wrought iron by heating it and stirring in oxidizing substances.

[8]A person who pursues art or knowledge superficially.

[9]Person devoted to self-interest, person who believes in the unity of God and nature (similar to a Transcendentalist), and person who rejects predestination, respectively. Davis's point is that intellectuals who follow such philosophies do not understand the elemental nature of religious questions for persons like the immigrant ironworkers.

The "terrible question" may simply be: "Can I be saved?"

railroads there last winter; run usually with about a thousand men. I cannot tell why I choose the half-forgotten story of this Wolfe more than that of myriads of these furnace-hands. Perhaps because there is a secret underlying sympathy between that story and this day with its impure fog and thwarted sunshine,—or perhaps simply for the reason that this house is the one where the Wolfes lived. There were the father and son,—both hands, as I said, in one of Kirby & John's mills for making railroad-iron,—and Deborah, their cousin, a picker[10] in some of the cotton-mills. The house was rented then to half a dozen families. The Wolfes had two of the cellar-rooms. The old man, like many of the puddlers and feeders[11] of the mills, was Welsh,—had spent half of his life in the Cornish tin-mines. You may pick the Welsh emigrants, Cornish miners, out of the throng passing the windows, any day. They are a trifle more filthy; their muscles are not so brawny; they stoop more. When they are drunk, they neither yell, nor shout, nor stagger, but skulk along like beaten hounds. A pure, unmixed blood, I fancy: shows itself in the slight angular bodies and sharply-cut facial lines. It is nearly thirty years since the Wolfes lived here. Their lives were like those of their class: incessant labor, sleeping in kennel-like rooms, eating rank pork and molasses, drinking—God and the distillers only know what; with an occasional night in jail, to atone for some drunken excess. Is that all of their lives?—of the portion given to them and these their duplicates swarming the streets to-day?—nothing beneath?—all? So many a political reformer will tell you,—and many a private reformer, too, who has gone among them with a heart tender with Christ's charity, and come out outraged, hardened.

One rainy night, about eleven o'clock, a crowd of half-clothed women stopped outside of the cellar-door. They were going home from the cotton-mill.

"Good-night, Deb," said one, a mulatto, steadying herself against the gas-post. She needed the post to steady her. So did more than one of them.

"Dah's a ball to Miss Potts' to-night. Ye'd best come."

"Inteet, Deb, if hur 'll come, hur 'll hef fun," said a shrill Welsh voice in the crowd.

Two or three dirty hands were thrust out to catch the gown of the woman, who was groping for the latch of the door.

"No."

"No? Where's Kit Small, then?"

"Begorra![12] on the spools. Alleys behint, though we helped her, we dud. An wid ye! Let Deb alone! It's ondacent frettin' a quite body. Be the powers, an' we'll have a night of it! there 'll be lashin's o' drink,—the Vargent[13] be blessed and praised for't!"

---

[10]Person who operates a "picking machine," which pulls apart and separates cotton fibers.

[11]Person who feeds melted iron into the casting forms in which it will harden.

[12]Muted form of "By God."

[13]The Virgin Mary.

They went on, the mulatto inclining for a moment to show fight, and drag the woman Wolfe off with them; but, being pacified, she staggered away.

Deborah groped her way into the cellar, and, after considerable stumbling, kindled a match, and lighted a tallow dip, that sent a yellow glimmer over the room. It was low, damp,—the earthen floor covered with a green, slimy moss,—a fetid air smothering the breath. Old Wolfe lay asleep on a heap of straw, wrapped in a torn horse-blanket. He was a pale, meek little man, with a white face and red rabbit-eyes. The woman Deborah was like him; only her face was even more ghastly, her lips bluer, her eyes more watery. She wore a faded cotton gown and a slouching bonnet. When she walked, one could see that she was deformed, almost a hunchback. She trod softly, so as not to waken him, and went through into the room beyond. There she found by the half-extinguished fire an iron saucepan filled with cold boiled potatoes, which she put upon a broken chair with a pint-cup of ale. Placing the old candlestick beside this dainty repast, she untied her bonnet, which hung limp and wet over her face, and prepared to eat her supper. It was the first food that had touched her lips since morning. There was enough of it, however: there is not always. She was hungry,—one could see that easily enough,—and not drunk, as most of her companions would have been found at this hour. She did not drink, this woman,—her face told that, too,—nothing stronger than ale. Perhaps the weak, flaccid wretch had some stimulant in her pale life to keep her up,—some love or hope, it might be, or urgent need. When that stimulant was gone, she would take to whiskey. Man cannot live by work alone. While she was skinning the potatoes, and munching them, a noise behind her made her stop.

"Janey!" she called, lifting the candle and peering into the darkness. "Janey, are you there?"

A heap of ragged coats was heaved up, and the face of a young girl emerged, staring sleepily at the woman.

"Deborah," she said, at last, "I'm here the night."

"Yes, child. Hur 's welcome," she said, quietly eating on.

The girl's face was haggard and sickly; her eyes were heavy with sleep and hunger; real Milesian[14] eyes they were, dark, delicate blue, glooming out from black shadows with a pitiful fright.

"I was alone," she said, timidly.

"Where 's the father?" asked Deborah, holding out a potato, which the girl greedily seized.

"He's beyant,—wid Haley,—in the stone house." (Did you ever hear the word *jail* from an Irish mouth?) "I came here. Hugh told me never to stay me-lone."

"Hugh?"

---

[14]The ancestors of the Irish, the early Celts, are thought to have come from Miletus on the Aegean Sea. The genetic traits of the Celts included fair hair and blue eyes. Davis, like most people of her era, made many fine distinctions among people on the basis of racial and genetic inheritance.

"Yes."

A vexed frown crossed her face. The girl saw it, and added quickly,—

"I have not seen Hugh the day, Deb. The old man says his watch lasts till the mornin'."

The woman sprang up, and hastily began to arrange some bread and flitch[15] in a tin pail, and to pour her own measure of ale into a bottle. Tying on her bonnet, she blew out the candle.

"Lay ye down, Janey dear," she said, gently, covering her with the old rags. "Hur can eat the potatoes, if hur 's hungry."

"Where are ye goin', Deb? The rain 's sharp."

"To the mill, with Hugh's supper."

"Let him bide till th' morn. Sit ye down."

"No, no,"—sharply pushing her off. "The boy 'll starve."

She hurried from the cellar, while the child wearily coiled herself up for sleep. The rain was falling heavily, as the woman, pail in hand, emerged from the mouth of the alley, and turned down the narrow street, that stretched out, long and black, miles before her. Here and there a flicker of gas lighted an uncertain space of muddy footwalk and gutter; the long rows of houses, except an occasional lagerbier shop, were closed; now and then she met a band of mill-hands skulking to or from their work.

Not many even of the inhabitants of a manufacturing town know the vast machinery of system by which the bodies of workmen are governed, that goes on unceasingly from year to year. The hands of each mill are divided into watches that relieve each other as regularly as the sentinels of an army. By night and day the work goes on, the unsleeping engines groan and shriek, the fiery pools of metal boil and surge. Only for a day in the week, in half-courtesy to public censure, the fires are partially veiled; but as soon as the clock strikes midnight, the great furnaces break forth with renewed fury, the clamor begins with fresh, breathless vigor, the engines sob and shriek like "gods in pain."

As Deborah hurried down through the heavy rain, the noise of these thousand engines sounded through the sleep and shadow of the city like far-off thunder. The mill to which she was going lay on the river, a mile below the city-limits. It was far, and she was weak, aching from standing twelve hours at the spools. Yet it was her almost nightly walk to take this man his supper, though at every square she sat down to rest, and she knew she should receive small word of thanks.

Perhaps, if she had possessed an artist's eye, the picturesque oddity of the scene might have made her step stagger less, and the path seem shorter; but to her the mills were only "summat deilish[16] to look at by night."

The road leading to the mills had been quarried from the solid rock, which rose abrupt and bare on one side of the cinder-covered road, while the river, sluggish and black, crept past on the other. The mills for rolling iron[17]

---

[15]A poor grade of salt pork.
[16]"Somewhat devilish."
[17]Flattening iron for purposes such as railroad rails.

are simply immense tent-like roofs, covering acres of ground, open on every side. Beneath these roofs Deborah looked in on a city of fires, that burned hot and fiercely in the night. Fire in every horrible form: pits of flame waving in the wind; liquid metal-flames writhing in tortuous streams through the sand; wide caldrons filled with boiling fire, over which bent ghastly wretches stirring the strange brewing; and through all, crowds of half-clad men, looking like revengeful ghosts in the red light, hurried, throwing masses of glittering fire. It was like a street in Hell. Even Deborah muttered, as she crept through, "'T looks like t' Devil's place!" It did,—in more ways than one.

She found the man she was looking for, at last, heaping coal on a furnace. He had not time to eat his supper; so she went behind the furnace, and waited. Only a few men were with him, and they noticed her only by a "Hyur comes t' hunchback, Wolfe."

Deborah was stupid with sleep; her back pained her sharply; and her teeth chattered with cold, with the rain that soaked her clothes and dripped from her at every step. She stood, however, patiently holding the pail, and waiting.

"Hout, woman! ye look like a drowned cat. Come near to the fire,"—said one of the men, approaching to scrape away the ashes.

She shook her head. Wolfe had forgotten her. He turned, hearing the man, and came closer.

"I did no' think; gi' me my supper, woman."

She watched him eat with a painful eagerness. With a woman's quick instinct, she saw that he was not hungry,—was eating to please her. Her pale, watery eyes began to gather a strange light.

"Is't good, Hugh? T' ale was a bit sour, I feared."

"No, good enough." He hesitated a moment. "Ye're tired, poor lass! Bide here till I go. Lay down there on that heap of ash, and go to sleep."

He threw her an old coat for a pillow, and turned to his work. The heap was the refuse of the burnt iron, and was not a hard bed; the half-smothered warmth, too, penetrated her limbs, dulling their pain and cold shiver.

Miserable enough she looked, lying there on the ashes like a limp, dirty rag,—yet not an unfitting figure to crown the scene of hopeless discomfort and veiled crime: more fitting, if one looked deeper into the heart of things,—at her thwarted woman's form, her colorless life, her waking stupor that smothered pain and hunger,—even more fit to be a type of her class. Deeper yet if one could look, was there nothing worth reading in this wet, faded thing, half-covered with ashes? no story of a soul filled with groping passionate love, heroic unselfishness, fierce jealousy? of years of weary trying to please the one human being whom she loved, to gain one look of real heart-kindness from him? If anything like this were hidden beneath the pale, bleared eyes, and dull, washed-out-looking face, no one had ever taken the trouble to read its faint signs: not the half-clothed furnace-tender, Wolfe, certainly. Yet he was kind to her: it was his nature to be kind, even to the very rats that swarmed in the cellar: kind to her in just the same way. She knew that. And it might be that very knowledge had given to her face its apathy and vacancy more than her low, torpid life. One sees that dead, vacant look steal sometimes over the rarest, finest of women's faces,—in the very midst, it may be, of their warmest summer's day; and then one can guess at the secret of intolerable solitude that lies hid beneath the delicate laces and brilliant smile. There was no warmth, no brilliancy, no summer for this woman; so the stupor and vacancy had time to gnaw into her face perpetually. She was young, too, though no one guessed it; so the gnawing was the fiercer.

She lay quiet in the dark corner, listening, through the monotonous din and uncertain glare of the works, to the dull plash of the rain in the far distance,—shrinking back whenever the man Wolfe happened to look towards her. She knew, in spite of all his kindness, that there was that in her face and form which made him loathe the sight of her. She felt by instinct, although she could not comprehend it, the finer nature of the man, which made him among his fellow-workmen something unique, set apart. She knew, that, down under all the vileness and coarseness of his life, there was a groping passion for whatever was beautiful and pure,—that his soul sickened with disgust at her deformity, even when his words were kindest. Through this dull consciousness, which never left her, came, like a sting, the recollection of the dark blue eyes and lithe figure of the little Irish girl she had left in the cellar. The recollection struck through even her stupid intellect with a vivid glow of beauty and of grace. Little Janey, timid, helpless, clinging to Hugh as her only friend: that was the sharp thought, the bitter thought, that drove into the glazed eyes a fierce light of pain. You laugh at it? Are pain and jealousy less savage realities down here in this place I am taking you to than in your own house or your own heart,—your heart, which they clutch at sometimes? The note is the same, I fancy, be the octave high or low.

If you could go into this mill where Deborah lay, and drag out from the hearts of these men the terrible tragedy of their lives, taking it as a symptom of the disease of their class, no ghost Horror would terrify you more. A reality of soul-starvation, of living death, that meets you every day under the besotted faces on the street,—I can paint nothing of this, only give you the outside outlines of a night, a crisis in the life of one man: whatever muddy depth of soul-history lies beneath you can read according to the eyes God has given you.

Wolfe, while Deborah watched him as a spaniel its master, bent over the furnace with his iron pole, unconscious of her scrutiny, only stopping to receive orders. Physically, Nature had promised the man but little. He had already lost the strength and instinct vigor of a man, his muscles were thin, his nerves weak, his face (a meek, woman's face) haggard, yellow with consumption. In the mill he was known as one of the girl-men: "Molly Wolfe" was his *sobriquet*.[18] He was never seen in the cockpit,[19] did not own a terrier, drank but seldom; when he did, desperately. He fought sometimes, but was always thrashed, pommelled to a jelly. The man was game enough, when

[18]Nickname.   [19]A pit for cockfights.

his blood was up: but he was no favorite in the mill; he had the taint of school-learning on him,—not to a dangerous extent, only a quarter or so in the free-school in fact, but enough to ruin him as a good hand in a fight.

For other reasons, too, he was not popular. Not one of themselves, they felt that, though outwardly as filthy and ash-covered; silent, with foreign thoughts and longings breaking out through his quietness in innumerable curious ways: this one, for instance. In the neighboring furnace-buildings lay great heaps of the refuse from the ore after the pig-metal is run. *Korl* we call it here: a light, porous substance, of a delicate, waxen, flesh-colored tinge. Out of the blocks of this korl, Wolfe, in his off-hours from the furnace, had a habit of chipping and moulding figures,—hideous, fantastic enough, but sometimes strangely beautiful: even the mill-men saw that, while they jeered at him. It was a curious fancy in the man, almost a passion. The few hours for rest he spent hewing and hacking with his blunt knife, never speaking, until his watch came again,—working at one figure for months, and, when it was finished, breaking it to pieces perhaps, in a fit of disappointment. A morbid, gloomy man, untaught, unled, left to feed his soul in grossness and crime, and hard, grinding labor.

I want you to come down and look at this Wolfe, standing there among the lowest of his kind, and see him just as he is, that you may judge him justly when you hear the story of this night. I want you to look back, as he does every day, at his birth in vice, his starved infancy; to remember the heavy years he has groped through as boy and man,—the slow, heavy years of constant, hot work. So long ago he began, that he thinks sometimes he has worked there for ages. There is no hope that it will ever end. Think that God put into this man's soul a fierce thirst for beauty,—to know it, to create it; to *be*—something, he knows not what,—other than he is. There are moments when a passing cloud, the sun glinting on the purple thistles, a kindly smile, a child's face, will rouse him to a passion of pain,—when his nature starts up with a mad cry of rage against God, man, whoever it is that has forced this vile, slimy life upon him. With all this groping, this mad desire, a great blind intellect stumbling through wrong, a loving poet's heart, the man was by habit only a coarse, vulgar laborer, familiar with sights and words you would blush to name. Be just: when I tell you about this night, see him as he is. Be just,—not like man's law, which seizes on one isolated fact, but like God's judging angel, whose clear, sad eye saw all the countless cankering days of this man's life, all the countless nights, when, sick with starving, his soul fainted in him, before it judged him for this night, the saddest of all.

I called this night the crisis of his life. If it was, it stole on him unawares. These great turning-days of life cast no shadow before, slip by unconsciously. Only a trifle, a little turn of the rudder, and the ship goes to heaven or hell.

Wolfe, while Deborah watched him, dug into the furnace of melting iron with his pole, dully thinking only how many rails the lump would yield. It was late,—nearly Sunday morning; another hour, and the heavy work would be done,—only the furnaces to replenish and cover for the next day. The workmen were growing more noisy, shouting, as they had to do, to be heard over the deep clamor of the mills. Suddenly they grew less boisterous,—at the far end, entirely silent. Something unusual had happened. After a moment, the silence came nearer; the men stopped their jeers and drunken choruses. Deborah, stupidly lifting up her head, saw the cause of the quiet. A group of five or six men were slowly approaching, stopping to examine each furnace as they came. Visitors often came to see the mills after night: except by growing less noisy, the men took no notice of them. The furnace where Wolfe worked was near the bounds of the works; they halted there hot and tired: a walk over one of these great foundries is no trifling task. The woman, drawing out of sight, turned over to sleep. Wolfe, seeing them stop, suddenly roused from his indifferent stupor, and watched them keenly. He knew some of them: the overseer, Clarke,—a son of Kirby, one of the mill-owners,—and a Doctor May, one of the town-physicians. The other two were strangers. Wolfe came closer. He seized eagerly every chance that brought him into contact with this mysterious class that shone down on him perpetually with the glamour of another order of being. What made the difference between them? That was the mystery of his life. He had a vague notion that perhaps to-night he could find it out. One of the strangers sat down on a pile of bricks, and beckoned young Kirby to his side.

"This *is* hot, with a vengeance. A match, please?"—lighting his cigar. "But the walk is worth the trouble. If it were not that you must have heard it so often, Kirby, I would tell you that your works look like Dante's Inferno."[20]

Kirby laughed.

"Yes. Yonder is Farinata himself in the burning tomb,"—pointing to some figure in the shimmering shadows.

"Judging from some of the faces of your men," said the other, "they bid fair to try the reality of Dante's vision, some day."

Young Kirby looked curiously around, as if seeing the faces of his hands for the first time.

"They're bad enough, that's true. A desperate set, I fancy. Eh, Clarke?"

The overseer did not hear him. He was talking of net profits just then,—giving, in fact, a schedule of the annual business of the firm to a sharp peering little Yankee, who jotted down notes on a paper laid on the crown of his hat: a reporter for one of the city-papers, getting up a series of reviews of the leading manufactories. The other gentlemen had accompanied them merely for amusement. They were silent until the notes were finished, drying their feet at the furnaces, and sheltering their faces from the intolerable heat. At last the overseer concluded with—

"I believe that is a pretty fair estimate, Captain."

---

[20]Poem describing Dante Alighieri's imaginary journey into Hell. According to Dante, Farinata degli Uberti (below) is being punished for heresy by being submerged in a burning tomb. The references to Dante emphasize the gulf between the visitors and the workers.

"Here, some of you men!" said Kirby, "bring up those boards. We may as well sit down, gentlemen, until the rain is over. It cannot last much longer at this rate."

"Pig-metal,"—mumbled the reporter,—"um!—coal facilities,—um!—hands employed, twelve hundred,—bitumen,—um!—all right, I believe, Mr. Clarke;—sinking-fund,—what did you say was your sinking-fund?"

"Twelve hundred hands?" said the stranger, the young man who had first spoken. "Do you control their votes, Kirby?"

"Control? No." The young man smiled complacently. "But my father brought seven hundred votes to the polls for his candidate last November. No force-work, you understand,—only a speech or two, a hint to form themselves into a society, and a bit of red and blue bunting to make them a flag. The Invincible Roughs,—I believe that is their name. I forget the motto: 'Our country's hope,' I think."

There was a laugh. The young man talking to Kirby sat with an amused light in his cool gray eye, surveying critically the half-clothed figures of the puddlers, and the slow swing of their brawny muscles. He was a stranger in the city,—spending a couple of months in the borders of a Slave State,[21] to study the institutions of the South,—a brother-in-law of Kirby's,—Mitchell. He was an amateur gymnast,—hence his anatomical eye; a patron, in a *blasé* way, of the prize-ring; a man who sucked the essence out of a science or philosophy in an indifferent, gentlemanly way; who took Kant, Novalis, Humboldt,[22] for what they were worth in his own scales; accepting all, despising nothing, in heaven, earth, or hell, but one-idead men; with a temper yielding and brilliant as summer water, until his Self was touched, when it was ice, though brilliant still. Such men are not rare in the States.

As he knocked the ashes from his cigar, Wolfe caught with a quick pleasure the contour of the white hand, the blood-glow of a red ring he wore. His voice, too, and that of Kirby's touched him like music,—low, even, with chording cadences. About this man Mitchell hung the impalpable atmosphere belonging to the thorough-bred gentlemen. Wolfe, scraping away the ashes beside him, was conscious of it, did obeisance to it with his artist sense, unconscious that he did so.

The rain did not cease. Clarke and the reporter left the mills; the others, comfortably seated near the furnace, lingered, smoking and talking in a desultory way. Greek would not have been more unintelligible to the furnace-tenders, whose presence they soon forgot entirely. Kirby drew out a newspaper from his pocket and read aloud some article, which they discussed eagerly. At every sentence, Wolfe listened more and more like a dumb,

---

[21]In 1861, Wheeling was in a slave state although it was north of the Mason-Dixon line and west of the Appalachian mountains. Most of the residents of this area had abolitionist sympathies (as did Davis), so it was a poor place to study the "institutions of the South."

[22]Eighteenth-century German philosopher, poet, and naturalist, respectively. The implication is that Mitchell is sophisticated but lacks human understanding.

hopeless animal, with a duller, more stolid look creeping over his face, glancing now and then at Mitchell, marking acutely every smallest sign of refinement, then back to himself, seeing as in a mirror his filthy body, his more stained soul.

Never! He had no words for such a thought, but he knew now, in all the sharpness of the bitter certainty, that between them there was a great gulf never to be passed. Never!

The bell of the mills rang for midnight. Sunday morning had dawned. Whatever hidden message lay in the tolling bells floated past these men unknown. Yet it was there. Veiled in the solemn music ushering the risen Saviour was a key-note to solve the darkest secrets of a world gone wrong,—even this social riddle which the brain of the grimy puddler grappled with madly to-night.

The men began to withdraw the metal from the caldrons. The mills were deserted on Sundays, except by the hands who fed the fires, and those who had no lodgings and slept usually on the ash-heaps. The three strangers sat still during the next hour, watching the men cover the furnaces, laughing now and then at some jest of Kirby's.

"Do you know," said Mitchell, "I like this view of the works better than when the glare was fiercest? These heavy shadows and the amphitheatre of smothered fires are ghostly, unreal. One could fancy these red smouldering lights to be the half-shut eyes of wild beasts, and the spectral figures their victims in the den."

Kirby laughed. "You are fanciful. Come, let us get out of the den. The spectral figures, as you call them, are a little too real for me to fancy a close proximity in the darkness,—unarmed, too."

The others rose, buttoning their overcoats, and lighting cigars.

"Raining, still," said Doctor May, "and hard. Where did we leave the coach, Mitchell?"

"At the other side of the works.—Kirby, what's that?"

Mitchell started back, half-frightened, as, suddenly turning a corner, the white figure of a woman faced him in the darkness,—a woman, white, of giant proportions, crouching on the ground, her arms flung out in some wild gesture of warning.

"Stop! Make that fire burn there!" cried Kirby, stopping short.

The flame burst out, flashing the gaunt figure into bold relief.

Mitchell drew a long breath.

"I thought it was alive," he said, going up curiously.

The others followed.

"Not marble, eh?" asked Kirby, touching it.

One of the lower overseers stopped.

"Korl, Sir."

"Who did it?"

"Can't say. Some of the hands; chipped it out in off-hours."

"Chipped to some purpose, I should say. What a flesh-tint the stuff has! Do you see, Mitchell?"

"I see."

He had stepped aside where the light fell boldest on the figure, looking at it in silence. There was not one line of beauty or grace in it: a nude woman's form, muscular, grown coarse with labor, the powerful limbs instinct with some one poignant longing. One idea: there it was in the tense, rigid muscles, the clutching hands, the wild, eager face, like that of a starving wolf's. Kirby and Doctor May walked around it, critical, curious. Mitchell stood aloof, silent. The figure touched him strangely.

"Not badly done," said Doctor May. "Where did the fellow learn that sweep of the muscles in the arm and hand? Look at them! They are groping,—do you see?—clutching: the peculiar action of a man dying of thirst."

"They have ample facilities for studying anatomy," sneered Kirby, glancing at the half-naked figures.

"Look," continued the Doctor, "at this bony wrist, and the strained sinews of the instep! A working-woman,—the very type of her class."

"God forbid!" muttered Mitchell.

"Why?" demanded May. "What does the fellow intend by the figure? I cannot catch the meaning."

"Ask him," said the other, dryly. "There he stands,"—pointing to Wolfe, who stood with a group of men, leaning on his ash-rake.

The Doctor beckoned him with the affable smile which kind-hearted men put on, when talking to these people.

"Mr. Mitchell has picked you out as the man who did this,—I'm sure I don't know why. But what did you mean by it?"

"She be hungry."

Wolfe's eyes answered Mitchell, not the Doctor.

"Oh-h! But what a mistake you have made, my fine fellow! You have given no sign of starvation to the body. It is strong,—terribly strong. It has the mad, half-despairing gesture of drowning."

Wolfe stammered, glanced appealingly at Mitchell, who saw the soul of the thing, he knew. But the cool, probing eyes were turned on himself now,—mocking, cruel, relentless.

"Not hungry for meat," the furnace-tender said at last.

"What then? Whiskey?" jeered Kirby, with a coarse laugh.

Wolfe was silent a moment, thinking.

"I dunno," he said, with a bewildered look. "It mebbe. Summat to make her live, I think,—like you. Whiskey ull do it, in a way."

The young man laughed again. Mitchell flashed a look of disgust somewhere,—not at Wolfe.

"May," he broke out impatiently, "are you blind? Look at that woman's face! It asks questions of God, and says, 'I have a right to know.' Good God, how hungry it is!"

They looked a moment; then May turned to the mill-owner:—

"Have you many such hands as this? What are you going to do with them? Keep them at puddling iron?"

Kirby shrugged his shoulders. Mitchell's look had irritated him.

"*Ce n'est pas mon affaire.*[23] I have no fancy for nursing infant geniuses. I suppose there are some stray gleams of mind and soul among these wretches. The Lord will take care of his own; or else they can work out their own salvation. I have heard you call our American system a ladder which any man can scale. Do you doubt it? Or perhaps you want to banish all social ladders, and put us all on a flat table-land,—eh, May?"

The Doctor looked vexed, puzzled. Some terrible problem lay hid in this woman's face, and troubled these men. Kirby waited for an answer, and, receiving none, went on, warming with his subject.

"I tell you, there's something wrong that no talk of '*Liberté*' or '*Egalité*'[24] will do away. If I had the making of men, these men who do the lowest part of the world's work should be machines,—nothing more,—hands. It would be kindness. God help them! What are taste, reason, to creatures who must live such lives as that?" He pointed to Deborah, sleeping on the ash-heap. "So many nerves to sting them to pain. What if God had put your brain, with all its agony of touch, into your fingers, and bid you work and strike with that?"

"You think you could govern the world better?" laughed the Doctor.

"I do not think at all."

"That is true philosophy. Drift with the stream, because you cannot dive deep enough to find bottom, eh?"

"Exactly," rejoined Kirby. "I do not think. I wash my hands of all social problems,—slavery, caste, white or black. My duty to my operatives has a narrow limit,—the pay-hour on Saturday night. Outside of that, if they cut korl, or cut each other's throats, (the more popular amusement of the two,) I am not responsible."

The Doctor sighed,—a good honest sigh, from the depths of his stomach.

"God help us! Who is responsible?"

"Not I, I tell you," said Kirby, testily. "What has the man who pays them money to do with their souls' concerns, more than the grocer or butcher who takes it?"

"And yet," said Mitchell's cynical voice, "look at her! How hungry she is!"

Kirby tapped his boot with his cane. No one spoke. Only the dumb face of the rough image looking into their faces with the awful question, "What shall we do to be saved?" Only Wolfe's face, with its heavy weight of brain, its weak, uncertain mouth, its desperate eyes, out of which looked the soul of his class,—only Wolfe's face turned towards Kirby's. Mitchell laughed,—a cool, musical laugh.

---

[23]"It is not my affair." Here and elsewhere, Kirby echoes the Roman governor Pontius Pilate before the crucifixion of Jesus.

[24]"Liberty" and "Equality" were rallying cries of the French Revolution.

"Money has spoken!" he said, seating himself lightly on a stone with the air of an amused spectator at a play. "Are you answered?"—turning to Wolfe his clear, magnetic face.

Bright and deep and cold as Arctic air, the soul of the man lay tranquil beneath. He looked at the furnace-tender as he had looked at a rare mosaic in the morning; only the man was the more amusing study of the two.

"Are you answered? Why, May, look at him! *'De profundis clamavi.'*[25] Or, to quote in English, 'Hungry and thirsty, his soul faints in him.' And so Money sends back its answer into the depths through you, Kirby! Very clear the answer, too!—I think I remember reading the same words some-where:—washing your hands in Eau de Cologne, and saying, 'I am innocent of the blood of this man. See ye to it!'"

Kirby flushed angrily.

"You quote Scripture freely."

"Do I not quote correctly? I think I remember another line, which may amend my meaning: 'Inasmuch as ye did it unto one of the least of these, ye did it unto me.' Deist?[26] Bless you, man, I was raised on the milk of the Word. Now, Doctor, the pocket of the world having uttered its voice, what has the heart to say? You are a philanthropist, in a small way,—*n'est ce pas?*[27] Here, boy, this gentleman can show you how to cut korl better,—or your destiny. Go on, May!"

"I think a mocking devil possesses you to-night," rejoined the Doctor, seriously.

He went to Wolfe and put his hand kindly on his arm. Something of a vague idea possessed the Doctor's brain that much good was to be done here by a friendly word or two: a latent genius to be warmed into life by a waited-for sunbeam. Here it was: he had brought it. So he went on compla-cently:—

"Do you know, boy, you have it in you to be a great sculptor, a great man?—do you understand?" (talking down to the capacity of his hearer: it is a way people have with children, and men like Wolfe)—"to live a better, stronger life than I, or Mr. Kirby here? A man may make himself anything he chooses. God has given you stronger powers than many men,—me, for instance."

May stopped, heated, glowing with his own magnanimity. And it was magnanimous. The puddler had drunk in every word, looking through the Doctor's flurry, and generous heat, and self-approval, into his will, with those slow, absorbing eyes of his.

"Make yourself what you will. It is your right."

"I know," quietly. "Will you help me?"

Mitchell laughed again. The Doctor turned now, in a passion,—

---

[25]Latin words for Psalm 130:1, usually trans-lated as "Out of the depths I have cried unto thee."

[26]Person who believes God created the world but does not interfere in human affairs.
[27]"Aren't you?"

"You know, Mitchell, I have not the means. You know, if I had, it is in my heart to take this boy and educate him for"—

"The glory of God, and the glory of John May."

May did not speak for a moment; then, controlled, he said,—

"Why should one be raised, when myriads are left?—I have not the money, boy," to Wolfe, shortly.

"Money?" He said it over slowly, as one repeats the guessed answer to a riddle, doubtfully. "That is it? Money?"

"Yes, money,—that is it," said Mitchell, rising, and drawing his furred coat about him. "You've found the cure for all the world's diseases.—Come, May, find your good-humor, and come home. This damp wind chills my very bones. Come and preach your Saint-Simonian[28] doctrines to-morrow to Kirby's hands. Let them have a clear idea of the rights of the soul, and I'll venture next week they'll strike for higher wages. That will be the end of it."

"Will you send the coach-driver to this side of the mills?" asked Kirby, turning to Wolfe.

He spoke kindly: it was his habit to do so. Deborah, seeing the puddler go, crept after him. The three men waited outside. Doctor May walked up and down, chafed. Suddenly he stopped.

"Go back, Mitchell! You say the pocket and the heart of the world speak without meaning to these people. What has its head to say? Taste, culture, refinement? Go!"

Mitchell was leaning against a brick wall. He turned his head indolently, and looked into the mills. There hung about the place a thick, unclean odor. The slightest motion of his hand marked that he perceived it, and his insufferable disgust. That was all. May said nothing, only quickened his angry tramp.

"Besides," added Mitchell, giving a corollary to his answer, "it would be of no use. I am not one of them."

"You do not mean"—said May, facing him.

"Yes, I mean just that. Reform is born of need, not pity. No vital movement of the people's has worked down, for good or evil; fermented, instead, carried up the heaving, cloggy mass. Think back through history, and you will know it. What will this lowest deep—thieves, Magdalens, negroes—do with the light filtered through ponderous Church creeds, Baconian theories, Goethe schemes? Some day, out of their bitter need will be thrown up their own light-bringer,—their Jean Paul, their Cromwell, their Messiah."[29]

"Bah!" was the Doctor's inward criticism. However, in practice, he adopted the theory; for, when, night and morning, afterwards, he prayed

[28]Socialist.

[29]The first series of phrases is intended to designate overly intellectual religious and social philosophies, such as those of English essayist Francis Bacon (1561–1624) or German writer Johann Wolfgang von Goethe (1749–1832), as useless to people so unfortunate. The second series of phrases sug- gests that the people need a leader who will emerge from among themselves: German novelist Jean Paul Richter (1763–1825), military and religious protector of England Oliver Cromwell (1599–1658), or a spiritual Saviour such as the Messiah. Mitchell is espousing an essentially socialist position (not Davis's position).

that power might be given these degraded souls to rise, he glowed at heart, recognizing an accomplished duty.

Wolfe and the woman had stood in the shadow of the works as the coach drove off. The Doctor had held out his hand in a frank, generous way, telling him to "take care of himself, and to remember it was his right to rise." Mitchell had simply touched his hat, as to an equal, with a quiet look of thorough recognition. Kirby had thrown Deborah some money, which she found, and clutched eagerly enough. They were gone now, all of them. The man sat down on the cinder-road, looking up into the murky sky.

"'T be late, Hugh. Wunnot hur come?"

He shook his head doggedly, and the woman crouched out of his sight against the wall. Do you remember rare moments when a sudden light flashed over yourself, your world, God? when you stood on a mountain-peak, seeing your life as it might have been, as it is? one quick instant, when custom lost its force and everyday usage? when your friend, wife, brother, stood in a new light? your soul was bared, and the grave,—a fore-taste of the nakedness of the Judgment Day? So it came before him, his life, that night. The slow tides of pain he had borne gathered themselves up and surged against his soul. His squalid daily life, the brutal coarseness eating into his brain, as the ashes into his skin: before, these things had been a dull aching into his consciousness; to-night, they were reality. He gripped the filthy red shirt that clung, stiff with soot, about him, and tore it savagely from his arm. The flesh beneath was muddy with grease and ashes,—and the heart beneath that! And the soul? God knows.

Then flashed before his vivid poetic sense the man who had left him,— the pure face, the delicate, sinewy limbs, in harmony with all he knew of beauty or truth. In his cloudy fancy he had pictured a Something like this. He had found it in this Mitchell, even when he idly scoffed at his pain: a Man all-knowing, all-seeing, crowned by Nature, reigning,—the keen glance of his eye falling like a sceptre on other men. And yet his instinct taught him that he too—He! He looked at himself with sudden loathing, sick, wrung his hands with a cry, and then was silent. With all the phantoms of his heated, ignorant fancy, Wolfe had not been vague in his ambitions. They were practical, slowly built up before him out of his knowledge of what he could do. Through years he had day by day made this hope a real thing to himself,—a clear, projected figure of himself, as he might become.

Able to speak, to know what was best, to raise these men and women working at his side up with him: sometimes he forgot this defined hope in the frantic anguish to escape,—only to escape,—out of the wet, the pain, the ashes, somewhere, anywhere,—only for one moment of free air on a hill-side, to lie down and let his sick soul throb itself out in the sunshine. But to-night he panted for life. The savage strength of his nature was roused; his cry was fierce to God for justice.

"Look at me!" he said to Deborah, with a low, bitter laugh, striking his puny chest savagely. "What am I worth, Deb? Is it my fault that I am no better? My fault? My fault?"

He stopped, stung with a sudden remorse, seeing her hunchback shape writhing with sobs. For Deborah was crying thankless tears, according to the fashion of women.

"God forgi' me, woman! Things go harder wi' you nor me. It's a worse share."

He got up and helped her to rise; and they went doggedly down the muddy street, side by side.

"It's all wrong," he muttered, slowly,—"all wrong! I dunnot understan'. But it'll end some day."

"Come home, Hugh!" she said, coaxingly; for he had stopped, looking around bewildered.

"Home,—and back to the mill!" He went on saying this over to himself, as if he would mutter down every pain in this dull despair.

She followed him through the fog, her blue lips chattering with cold. They reached the cellar at last. Old Wolfe had been drinking since she went out, and had crept nearer the door. The girl Janey slept heavily in the corner. He went up to her, touching softly the worn white arm with his fingers. Some bitterer thought stung him, as he stood there. He wiped the drops from his forehead, and went into the room beyond, livid, trembling. A hope, trifling, perhaps, but very dear, had died just then out of the poor puddler's life, as he looked at the sleeping, innocent girl,—some plan for the future, in which she had borne a part. He gave it up that moment, then and forever. Only a trifle, perhaps, to us: his face grew a shade paler,—that was all. But, somehow, the man's soul, as God and the angels looked down on it, never was the same afterwards.

Deborah followed him into the inner room. She carried a candle, which she placed on the floor, closing the door after her. She had seen the look on his face, as he turned away: her own grew deadly. Yet, as she came up to him, her eyes glowed. He was seated on an old chest, quiet, holding his face in his hands.

"Hugh!" she said, softly.

He did not speak.

"Hugh, did hur hear what the man said,—him with the clear voice? Did hur hear? Money, money,—that it wud do all?"

He pushed her away,—gently, but he was worn out; her rasping tone fretted him.

"Hugh!"

The candle flared a pale yellow light over the cobwebbed brick walls, and the woman standing there. He looked at her. She was young, in deadly earnest; her faded eyes, and wet, ragged figure caught from their frantic eagerness a power akin to beauty.

"Hugh, it is true! Money ull do it! Oh, Hugh, boy, listen till me! He said it true! It is money!"

"I know. Go back! I do not want you here."

"Hugh, it is t' last time. I'll never worrit hur again."

There were tears in her voice now, but she choked them back.

"Hear till me only to-night! If one of t' witch people wud come, them we heard of t' home, and gif hur all hur wants, what then? Say, Hugh!"

"What do you mean?"

"I mean money."

Her whisper shrilled through his brain.

"If one of t' witch dwarfs wud come from t' lane moors to-night, and gif hur money, to go out,—*out*, I say,—out, lad, where t' sun shines, and t' heath grows, and t' ladies walk in silken gownds, and God stays all t' time,—where t' man lives that talked to us to-night,—Hugh knows,—Hugh could walk there like a king!"

He thought the woman mad, tried to check her, but she went on, fierce in her eager haste.

"If *I* were t' witch dwarf, if I had t' money, wud hur thank me? Wud hur take me out o' this place wid hur and Janey? I wud not come into the gran' house hur wud build, to vex hur wid t' hunch,—only at night when t' shadows were dark, stand far off to see hur."

Mad? Yes! Are many of us mad in this way?

"Poor Deb! poor Deb!" he said, soothingly.

"It is here," she said, suddenly jerking into his hand a small roll. "I took it! I did it! Me, me!—not hur! I shall be hanged, I shall be burnt in hell, if anybody knows I took it! Out of his pocket, as he leaned against t' bricks. Hur knows?"

She thrust it into his hand, and then, her errand done, began to gather chips together to make a fire, choking down hysteric sobs.

"Has it come to this?"

That was all he said. The Welsh Wolfe blood was honest. The roll was a small green pocket-book containing one or two gold pieces, and a check for an incredible amount, as it seemed to the poor puddler. He laid it down, hiding his face again in his hands.

"Hugh, don't be angry wud me! It's only poor Deb,—hur knows?"

He took the long skinny fingers kindly in his.

"Angry? God help me, no! Let me sleep. I am tired."

He threw himself heavily down on the wooden bench, stunned with pain and weariness. She brought some old rags to cover him.

It was late on Sunday evening before he awoke. I tell God's truth, when I say he had then no thought of keeping this money. Deborah had hid it in his pocket. He found it there. She watched him eagerly, as he took it out.

"I must gif it to him," he said, reading her face.

"Hur knows," she said with a bitter sigh of disappointment. "But it is hur right to keep it."

His right! The word struck him. Doctor May had used the same. He washed himself, and went out to find this man Mitchell. His right! Why did this chance word cling to him so obstinately? Do you hear the fierce devils whisper in his ear, as he went slowly down the darkening street?

The evening came on, slow and calm. He seated himself at the end of an alley leading into one of the larger streets. His brain was clear to-night, keen, intent, mastering. It would not start back, cowardly, from any hellish temptation, but meet it face to face. Therefore the great temptation of his life came to him veiled by no sophistry,[30] but bold, defiant, owning its own vile name, trusting to one bold blow for victory.

He did not deceive himself. Theft! That was it. At first the word sickened him; then he grappled with it. Sitting there on a broken cart-wheel, the fading day, the noisy groups, the church-bells' tolling passed before him like a panorama, while the sharp struggle went on within. This money! He took it out, and looked at it. If he gave it back, what then? He was going to be cool about it.

People going by to church saw only a sickly mill-boy watching them quietly at the alley's mouth. They did not know that he was mad, or they would not have gone by so quietly: mad with hunger; stretching out his hands to the world, that had given so much to them, for leave to live the life God meant him to live. His soul within him was smothering to death; he wanted so much, thought so much, and *knew*—nothing. There was nothing of which he was certain, except the mill and things there. Of God and heaven he had heard so little, that they were to him what fairy-land is to a child: something real, but not here; very far off. His brain, greedy, dwarfed, full of thwarted energy and unused powers, questioned these men and women going by, coldly, bitterly, that night. Was it not his right to live as they,—a pure life, a good, true-hearted life, full of beauty and kind words? He only wanted to know how to use the strength within him. His heart warmed, as he thought of it. He suffered himself to think of it longer. If he took the money?

Then he saw himself as he might be, strong, helpful, kindly. The night crept on, as this one image slowly evolved itself from the crowd of other thoughts and stood triumphant. He looked at it. As he might be! What wonder, if it blinded him to delirium,—the madness that underlies all revolution, all progress, and all fall?

You laugh at the shallow temptation? You see the error underlying its argument so clearly,—that to him a true life was one of full development rather than self-restraint? that he was deaf to the higher tone in a cry of voluntary suffering for truth's sake than in the fullest flow of spontaneous harmony? I do not plead his cause. I only want to show you the mote in my brother's eye: then you can see clearly to take it out.

The money,—there it lay on his knee, a little blotted slip of paper, nothing in itself; used to raise him out of the pit; something straight from God's hand. A thief! Well, what was it to be a thief? He met the question at last, face to face, wiping the clammy drops of sweat from his forehead. God made this money—the fresh air, too—for his children's use. He never made the difference between poor and rich. The Something who looked down on him that moment through the cool gray sky had a kindly face, he knew,—loved his children alike. Oh, he knew that!

---

[30]Argument or rationalization that sounds reasonable but is false.

There were times when the soft floods of color in the crimson and purple flames, or the clear depth of amber in the water below the bridge, had somehow given him a glimpse of another world than this,—of an infinite depth of beauty and of quiet somewhere,—somewhere,—a depth of quiet and rest and love. Looking up now, it became strangely real. The sun had sunk quite below the hills, but his last rays struck upward, touching the zenith. The fog had risen, and the town and river were steeped in its thick, gray damp; but overhead, the sun-touched smoke-clouds opened like a cleft ocean,—shifting, rolling seas of crimson mist, waves of billowy silver veined with blood-scarlet, inner depths unfathomable of glancing light. Wolfe's artist-eye grew drunk with color. The gates of that other world! Fading, flashing before him now! What, in that world of Beauty, Content, and Right, were the petty laws, the mine and thine, of mill-owners and mill-hands?

A consciousness of power stirred within him. He stood up. A man,—he thought, stretching out his hands,—free to work, to live, to love! Free! His right! He folded the scrap of paper in his hand. As his nervous fingers took it in, limp and blotted, so his soul took in the mean temptation, lapped it in fancied rights, in dreams of improved existences, drifting and endless as the cloud-seas of color. Clutching it, as if the tightness of his hold would strengthen his sense of possession, he went aimlessly down the street. It was his watch at the mill. He need not go, need never go again, thank God!—shaking off the thought with unspeakable loathing.

Shall I go over the history of the hours of that night? how the man wandered from one to another of his old haunts, with a half-consciousness of bidding them farewell,—lanes and alleys and backyards where the mill-hands lodged,—noting, with a new eagerness, the filth and drunkenness, the pig-pens, the ash-heaps covered with potato-skins, the bloated, pimpled women at the doors,—with a new disgust, a new sense of sudden triumph, and, under all, a new, vague dread, unknown before, smothered down, kept under, but still there? It left him but once during the night, when, for the second time in his life, he entered a church. It was a sombre Gothic pile, where the stained light lost itself in far-retreating arches; built to meet the requirements and sympathies of a far other class than Wolfe's. Yet it touched, moved him uncontrollably. The distances, the shadows, the still, marble figures, the mass of silent kneeling worshippers, the mysterious music, thrilled, lifted his soul with a wonderful pain. Wolfe forgot himself, forgot the new life he was going to live, the mean terror gnawing underneath. The voice of the speaker strengthened the charm; it was clear, feeling, full, strong. An old man, who had lived much, suffered much; whose brain was keenly alive, dominant; whose heart was summer-warm with charity. He taught it to-night. He held up Humanity in its grand total; showed the great world-cancer to his people. Who could show it better? He was a Christian reformer; he had studied the age thoroughly; his outlook at man had been free, world-wide, over all time. His faith stood sublime upon the Rock of Ages; his fiery zeal guided vast schemes by which the gospel was to be preached to all nations. How did he preach it to-night? In burning, light-laden words he painted the incarnate Life, Love, the universal Man: words that became reality in the lives of these people,—that lived again in beautiful words and actions, trifling, but heroic. Sin, as he defied it, was a real foe to them; their trials, temptations, were his. His words passed far over the furnace-tender's grasp, toned to suit another class of culture; they sounded in his ears a very pleasant song in an unknown tongue. He meant to cure this world-cancer with a steady eye that had never glared with hunger, and a hand that neither poverty nor strychnine-whiskey[31] had taught to shake. In this morbid, distorted heart of the Welsh puddler he had failed.

Wolfe rose at last, and turned from the church down the street. He looked up: the night had come on foggy, damp; the golden mists had vanished, and the sky lay dull and ash-colored. He wandered again aimlessly down the street, idly wondering what had become of the cloud-sea of crimson and scarlet. The trial-day of this man's life was over, and he had lost the victory. What followed was mere drifting circumstance,—a quicker walking over the path,—that was all. Do you want to hear the end of it? You wish me to make a tragic story out of it? Why, in the police-reports of the morning paper you can find a dozen such tragedies: hints of ship-wrecks unlike any that ever befell on the high seas; hints that here a power was lost to heaven,—that there a soul went down where no tide can ebb or flow. Commonplace enough the hints are,—jocose sometimes, done up in rhyme.

Doctor May, a month after the night I have told you of, was reading to his wife at breakfast from this fourth column of the morning-paper; an unusual thing,—these police-reports not being, in general, choice reading for ladies; but it was only one item he read.

"Oh, my dear! You remember that man I told you of, that we saw at Kirby's mill?—that was arrested for robbing Mitchell? Here he is; just listen:—'Circuit Court. Judge Day. Hugh Wolfe, operative in Kirby & John's Loudon Mills. Charge, grand larceny. Sentence, nineteen years hard labor in penitentiary.'—Scoundrel! Serves him right! After all our kindness that night! Picking Mitchell's pocket at the very time!"

His wife said something about the ingratitude of that kind of people, and then they began to talk of something else.

Nineteen years! How easy that was to read! What a simple word for Judge Day to utter! Nineteen years! Half a lifetime!

Hugh Wolfe sat on the window-ledge of his cell, looking out. His ankles were ironed. Not usual in such cases; but he had made two desperate efforts to escape. "Well," as Haley, the jailer, said, "small blame to him! Nineteen years' imprisonment was not a pleasant thing to look forward to." Haley was very good-natured about it, though Wolfe had fought him savagely.

"When he was first caught," the jailer said afterwards, in telling the story, "before the trial, the fellow was cut down at once,—laid there on that pallet like a dead man, with his hands over his eyes. Never saw a man

---

[31]Cheap, impure whiskey that can cause death.

so cut down in my life. Time of the trial, too, came the queerest dodge of any customer I ever had. Would choose no lawyer. Judge gave him one, of course. Gibson it was. He tried to prove the fellow crazy; but it wouldn't go. Thing was plain as day-light: money found on him. 'T was a hard sentence,—all the law allows; but it was for 'xample's sake. These mill-hands are gettin' onbearable. When the sentence was read, he just looked up, and said the money was his by rights, and that all the world had gone wrong. That night, after the trial, a gentleman came to see him here, name of Mitchell,—him as he stole from. Talked to him for an hour. Thought he came for curiosity, like. After he was gone, thought Wolfe was remarkable quiet, and went into his cell. Found him very low; bed all bloody. Doctor said he had been bleeding at the lungs. He was as weak as a cat; yet, if ye'll b'lieve me, he tried to get a-past me and get out. I just carried him like a baby, and threw him on the pallet. Three days after, he tried it again: that time reached the wall. Lord help you! he fought like a tiger,—giv' some terrible blows. Fightin' for life, you see; for he can't live long, shut up in the stone crib down yonder. Got a death-cough now. 'T took two of us to bring him down that day; so I just put the irons on his feet. There he sits, in there. Goin' to-morrow, with a batch more of 'em. That woman, hunchback, tried with him,—you remember?—she's only got three years. 'Complice. But *she's* a woman, you know. He's been quiet ever since I put on irons: giv' up, I suppose. Looks white, sick-lookin'. It acts different on 'em, bein' sentenced. Most of 'em gets reckless, devilish-like. Some prays awful, and sings them vile songs of the mills, all in a breath. That woman, now, she's desper't'. Been beggin' to see Hugh, as she calls him, for three days. I'm a-goin' to let her in. She don't go with him. Here she is in this next cell. I'm a-goin' now to let her in."

He let her in. Wolfe did not see her. She crept into a corner of the cell, and stood watching him. He was scratching the iron bars of the window with a piece of tin which he had picked up, with an idle, uncertain, vacant stare, just as a child or idiot would do.

"Tryin' to get out, old boy?" laughed Haley. "Them irons will need a crow-bar beside your tin, before you can open 'em."

Wolfe laughed, too, in a senseless way.

"I think I'll get out," he said.

"I believe his brain's touched," said Haley, when he came out.

The puddler scraped away with the tin for half an hour. Still Deborah did not speak. At last she ventured nearer, and touched his arm.

"Blood?" she said, looking at some spots on his coat with a shudder.

He looked up at her. "Why, Deb!" he said, smiling,—such a bright, boyish smile, that it went to poor Deborah's heart directly, and she sobbed and cried out loud.

"Oh, Hugh, lad! Hugh! dunnot look at me, when it wur my fault! To think I brought hur to it! And I loved hur so! Oh, lad, I dud!"

The confession, even in this wretch, came with the woman's blush through the sharp cry.

He did not seem to hear her,—scraping away diligently at the bars with the bit of tin.

Was he going mad? She peered closely into his face. Something she saw there made her draw suddenly back,—something which Haley had not seen, that lay beneath the pinched, vacant look it had caught since the trial, or the curious gray shadow that rested on it. That gray shadow,—yes, she knew what that meant. She had often seen it creeping over women's faces for months, who died at last of slow hunger or consumption. That meant death, distant, lingering: but this—Whatever it was the woman saw, or thought she saw, used as she was to crime and misery, seemed to make her sick with a new horror. Forgetting her fear of him, she caught his shoulders, and looked keenly, steadily, into his eyes.

"Hugh!" she cried, in a desperate whisper,—"oh, boy, not that! for God's sake, not *that!*"

The vacant laugh went off his face, and he answered her in a muttered word or two that drove her away. Yet the words were kindly enough. Sitting there on his pallet, she cried silently a hopeless sort of tears, but did not speak again. The man looked up furtively at her now and then. Whatever his own trouble was, her distress vexed him with a momentary sting.

It was market-day. The narrow window of the jail looked down directly on the carts and wagons drawn up in a long line, where they had unloaded. He could see, too, and hear distinctly the clink of money as it changed hands, the busy crowd of whites and blacks shoving, pushing one another, and the chaffering[32] and swearing at the stalls. Somehow, the sound, more than anything else had done, wakened him up,—made the whole real to him. He was done with the world and the business of it. He let the tin fall, and looked out, pressing his face close to the rusty bars. How they crowded and pushed! And he,—he should never walk that pavement again! There came Neff Sanders, one of the feeders at the mill, with a basket on his arm. Sure enough, Neff was married the other week. He whistled, hoping he would look up; but he did not. He wondered if Neff remembered he was there,—if any of the boys thought of him up there, and thought that he never was to go down that old cinder-road again. Never again! He had not quite understood it before; but now he did. Not for days or years, but never!—that was it.

How clear the light fell on that stall in front of the market! and how like a picture it was, the dark-green heaps of corn, and the crimson beets, and golden melons! There was another with game: how the light flickered on that pheasant's breast, with the purplish blood dripping over the brown feathers! He could see the red shining of the drops, it was so near. In one minute he could be down there. It was just a step. So easy, as it seemed, so natural to go! Yet it could never be—not in all the thousands of years to come—that he should put his foot on that street again! He thought of himself with a sorrowful pity, as of some one else. There was a dog down in the

[32]Bargaining, haggling over price.

market, walking after his master with such a stately, grave look!—only a dog, yet he could go backwards and forwards just as be pleased: he had good luck! Why, the very vilest cur, yelping there in the gutter, had not lived his life, had been free to act out whatever thought God had put into his brain; while he—No, he would not think of that! He tried to put the thought away, and to listen to a dispute between a countryman and a woman about some meat; but it would come back. He, what had he done to bear this?

Then came the sudden picture of what might have been, and now. He knew what it was to be in the penitentiary,—how it went with men there. He knew how in these long years he should slowly die, but not until soul and body had become corrupt and rotten,—how, when he came out, if he lived to come, even the lowest of the mill-hands would jeer him,—how his hands would be weak, and his brain senseless and stupid. He believed he was almost that now. He put his hand to his head with a puzzled, weary look. It ached, his head, with thinking. He tried to quiet himself. It was only right, perhaps; he had done wrong. But was there right or wrong for such as he? What was right? And who had ever taught him? He thrust the whole matter away. A dark, cold quiet crept through his brain. It was all wrong; but let it be! It was nothing to him more than the others. Let it be!

The door grated, as Haley opened it.

"Come, my woman! Must lock up for t' night. Come, stir yerself!"

She went up and took Hugh's hand.

"Good-night, Deb," he said, carelessly.

She had not hoped he would say more; but the tired pain on her mouth just then was bitterer than death. She took his passive hand and kissed it.

"Hur'll never see Deb again!" she ventured, her lips growing colder and more bloodless.

What did she say that for? Did he not know it? Yet he would not be impatient with poor old Deb. She had trouble of her own, as well as he.

"No, never again," he said, trying to be cheerful.

She stood just a moment, looking at him. Do you laugh at her, standing there, with her hunchback, her rags, her bleared, withered face, and the great despised love tugging at her heart?

"Come, you!" called Haley, impatiently.

She did not move.

"Hugh!" she whispered.

It was to be her last word. What was it?

"Hugh, boy, not THAT!"

He did not answer. She wrung her hands, trying to be silent, looking in his face in an agony of entreaty. He smiled again, kindly.

"It is best, Deb. I cannot bear to be hurted any more."

"Hur knows," she said, humbly.

"Tell my father good-bye; and—and kiss little Janey."

She nodded, saying nothing, looked in his face again, and went out of the door. As she went, she staggered.

"Drinkin' to-day?" broke out Haley, pushing her before him. "Where the Devil did you get it? Here, in with ye!" and he shoved her into her cell, next to Wolfe's, and shut the door.

Along the wall of her cell there was a crack low down by the floor, through which she could see the light from Wolfe's. She had discovered it days before. She hurried in now, and, kneeling down by it, listened, hoping to hear some sound. Nothing but the rasping of the tin on the bars. He was at his old amusement again. Something in the noise jarred on her ear, for she shivered as she heard it. Hugh rasped away at the bars. A dull old bit of tin, not fit to cut korl with.

He looked out of the window again. People were leaving the market now. A tall mulatto girl, following her mistress, her basket on her head, crossed the street just below, and looked up. She was laughing; but, when she caught sight of the haggard face peering out through the bars, suddenly grew grave, and hurried by. A free, firm step, a clear-cut olive face, with a scarlet turban tied on one side, dark, shining eyes, and on the head the basket poised, filled with fruit and flowers, under which the scarlet turban and bright eyes looked out half-shadowed. The picture caught his eye. It was good to see a face like that. He would try to-morrow, and cut one like it. *Tomorrow!* He threw down the tin, trembling, and covered his face with his hands. When he looked up again, the daylight was gone.

Deborah, crouching near by on the other side of the wall, heard no noise. He sat on the side of the low pallet, thinking. Whatever was the mystery which the woman had seen on his face, it came out now slowly, in the dark there, and became fixed,—a something never seen on his face before. The evening was darkening fast. The market had been over for an hour; the rumbling of the carts over the pavement grew more infrequent: he listened to each, as it passed, because he thought it was to be for the last time. For the same reason, it was, I suppose, that he strained his eyes to catch a glimpse of each passer-by, wondering who they were, what kind of homes they were going to, if they had children,—listening eagerly to every chance word in the street, as if—(God be merciful to the man! what strange fancy was this?)—as if he never should hear human voices again.

It was quite dark at last. The street was a lonely one. The last passenger, he thought, was gone. No,—there was a quick step: Joe Hill, lighting the lamps. Joe was a good old chap; never passed a fellow without some joke or other. He remembered once seeing the place where he lived with his wife. "Granny Hill" the boys called her. Bedridden she was; but so kind as Joe was to her! kept the room so clean!—and the old woman, when he was there, was laughing at "some of t' lad's foolishness." The step was far down the street; but he could see him place the ladder, run up, and light the gas. A longing seized him to be spoken to once more.

"Joe!" he called, out of the grating. "Good-bye, Joe!"

The old man stopped a moment, listening uncertainly; then hurried on. The prisoner thrust his hand out of the window, and called again, louder;

but Joe was too far down the street. It was a little thing; but it hurt him,—this disappointment.

"Good-bye, Joe!" he called, sorrowfully enough.

"Be quiet!" said one of the jailers, passing the door, striking on it with his club.

Oh, that was the last, was it?

There was an inexpressible bitterness on his face, as he lay down on the bed, taking the bit of tin, which he had rasped to a tolerable degree of sharpness, in his hand,—to play with, it may be. He bared his arms, looking intently at their corded veins and sinews. Deborah, listening in the next cell, heard a slight clicking sound, often repeated. She shut her lips tightly, that she might not scream; the cold drops of sweat broke over her, in her dumb agony.

"Hur knows best," she muttered at last, fiercely clutching the boards where she lay.

If she could have seen Wolfe, there was nothing about him to frighten her. He lay quite still, his arms outstretched, looking at the pearly stream of moonlight coming into the window. I think in that one hour that came then he lived back over all the years that had gone before. I think that all the low, vile life, all his wrongs, all his starved hopes, came then, and stung him with a farewell poison that made him sick unto death. (He made neither moan nor cry, only turned his worn face now and then to the pure light, that seemed so far off, as one that said, "How long, O Lord? how long?")

The hour was over at last. The moon, passing over her nightly path, slowly came nearer, and threw the light across his bed on his feet. He watched it steadily, as it crept up, inch by inch, slowly. It seemed to him to carry with it a great silence. He had been so hot and tired there always in the mills! The years had been so fierce and cruel! There was coming now quiet and coolness and sleep. His tense limbs relaxed, and settled in a calm languor. The blood ran fainter and slow from his heart. (He did not think now with a savage anger of what might be and was not; he was conscious only of deep stillness creeping over him.) At first he saw a sea of faces: the mill-men,—women he had known, drunken and bloated,—Janeys timid and pitiful,—poor old Debs: then they floated together like a mist, and faded away, leaving only the clear, pearly moonlight.

Whether, as the pure light crept up the stretched-out figure, it brought with it calm and peace, who shall say? His dumb soul was alone with God in judgment. A Voice may have spoken for it from far-off Calvary, "Father, forgive them, for they know not what they do!" Who dare say? Fainter and fainter the heart rose and fell, slower and slower, the moon floated from behind a cloud, until, when at last its full tide of white splendor swept over the cell, it seemed to wrap and fold into a deeper stillness the dead figure that never should move again. Silence deeper than the Night! Nothing that moved, save the black, nauseous stream of blood dripping slowly from the pallet to the floor!

There was outcry and crowd enough in the cell the next day. The coroner and his jury, the local editors, Kirby himself, and boys with their hands thrust knowingly into their pockets and heads on one side, jammed into the corners. Coming and going all day. Only one woman. She came late, and outstayed them all. A Quaker, or Friend, as they call themselves. I think this woman was known by that name in heaven. A homely body, coarsely dressed in gray and white. Deborah (for Haley had let her in) took notice of her. She watched them all—sitting on the end of the pallet, holding his head in her arms—with the ferocity of a watch-dog, if any of them touched the body. There was no meekness, no sorrow, in her face; the stuff out of which murderers are made, instead. All the time Haley and the woman were laying straight the limbs and cleaning the cell, Deborah sat still, keenly watching the Quaker's face. Of all the crowd there that day, this woman alone had not spoken to her,—only once or twice had put some cordial to her lips. After they all were gone, the woman, in the same still, gentle way, brought a vase of wood-leaves and berries, and placed it by the pallet, then opened the narrow window. The fresh air blew in, and swept the woody fragrance over the dead face. Deborah looked up with a quick wonder.

"Did hur know my boy wud like it? Did hur know Hugh?"

"I know Hugh now."

The white fingers passed in a slow, pitiful way over the dead, worn face. There was a heavy shadow in the quiet eyes.

"Did hur know where they'll bury Hugh?" said Deborah in a shrill tone, catching her arm.

This had been the question hanging on her lips all day.

"In t' town-yard? Under t' mud and ash? T' lad 'll smother, woman! He wur born on t' lane[33] moor, where t' air is frick[34] and strong. Take hur out, for God's sake, take hur out where t' air blows!"

The Quaker hesitated, but only for a moment. She put her strong arm around Deborah and led her to the window.

"Thee sees the hills, friend, over the river? Thee sees how the light lies warm there, and the winds of God blow all the day? I live there,—where the blue smoke is, by the trees. Look at me." She turned Deborah's face to her own, clear and earnest. "Thee will believe me? I will take Hugh and bury him there to-morrow."

Deborah did not doubt her. As the evening wore on, she leaned against the iron bars, looking at the hills that rose far off, through the thick sodden clouds, like a bright, unattainable calm. As she looked, a shadow of their solemn repose fell on her face: its fierce discontent faded into a pitiful, humble quiet. Slow, solemn tears gathered in her eyes: the poor weak eyes turned so hopelessly to the place where Hugh was to rest, the grave heights looking higher and brighter and more solemn than ever before. The Quaker watched her keenly. She came to her at last, and touched her arm.

---

[33] A Scottish variant of lone; hence, the lonely moor. [34] Fresh.

"When thee comes back," she said, in a low, sorrowful tone, like one who speaks from a strong heart deeply moved with remorse or pity, "thee shall begin thy life again,—there on the hills. I came too late; but not for thee,—by God's help, it may be."

Not too late. Three years after, the Quaker began her work. I end my story here. At evening-time it was light. There is no need to tire you with the long years of sunshine, and fresh air, and slow, patient Christ-love, needed to make healthy and hopeful this impure body and soul. There is a homely pine house, on one of these hills, whose windows overlook broad, wooded slopes and clover-crimsoned meadows,—niched into the very place where the light is warmest, the air freest. It is the Friends' meeting-house. Once a week they sit there, in their grave, earnest way, waiting for the Spirit of Love to speak, opening their simple hearts to receive His words. There is a woman, old, deformed, who takes a humble place among them: waiting like them: in her gray dress, her worn face, pure and meek, turned now and then to the sky. A woman much loved by these silent, restful people; more silent than they, more humble, more loving. Waiting: with her eyes turned to hills higher and purer than these on which she lives,—dim and far off now, but to be reached some day. There may be in her heart some latent hope to meet there the love denied her here,—that she shall find him whom she lost, and that then she will not be all-unworthy. Who blames her? Something is lost in the passage of every soul from one eternity to the other,— something pure and beautiful, which might have been and was not: a hope, a talent, a love, over which the soul mourns, like Esau deprived of his birthright. What blame to the meek Quaker, if she took her lost hope to make the hills of heaven more fair?

Nothing remains to tell that the poor Welsh puddler once lived, but this figure of the mill-woman cut in korl. I have it here in a corner of my library. I keep it hid behind a curtain,—it is such a rough, ungainly thing. Yet there are about it touches, grand sweeps of outline, that show a master's hand. Sometimes,—to-night, for instance,—the curtain is accidentally drawn back, and I see a bare arm stretched out imploringly in the darkness, and an eager, wolfish face watching mine: a wan, woful face, through which the spirit of the dead korl-cutter looks out, with its thwarted life, its mighty hunger, its unfinished work. Its pale, vague lips seem to tremble with a terrible question. "Is this the End?" they say,—"nothing beyond?—no more?" Why, you tell me you have seen that look in the eyes of dumb brutes,—horses dying under the lash. I know.

The deep of the night is passing while I write. The gas-light wakens from the shadows here and there the objects which lie scattered through the room: only faintly, though; for they belong to the open sunlight. As I glance at them, they each recall some task or pleasure of the coming day. A half-moulded child's head; Aphrodite;[35] a bough of forest-leaves; music; work; homely fragments, in which lie the secrets of all eternal truth and beauty.

[35]Greek goddess of love.

Prophetic all! Only this dumb, woful face seems to belong to and end with the night. I turn to look at it. Has the power of its desperate need commanded the darkness away? While the room is yet steeped in heavy shadow, a cool, gray light suddenly touches its head like a blessing hand, and its groping arm points through the broken cloud to the far East, where, in the flickering, nebulous crimson, God has set the promise of the Dawn.

1861

THE EMERGENCE OF AMERICAN
POETIC VOICES

There was a time not so very long ago when virtually every student who went through the American educational system would have read, or at least heard, lines like these:

> Listen, my children, and you shall hear
> Of the midnight ride of Paul Revere,
> On the eighteenth of April, in Seventy-five;
> Hardly a man is now alive
> Who remembers that famous day or year

If students remembered nothing else about this poem—apart from the innumerable parodies that drifted around most junior high schools—they were likely to recollect its famous warning signals against the British: "One, if by land, and two, if by sea."

They would almost certainly have read, as well, lines like the following:

> By the shore of Gitche Gumee,
> By the shining Big-Sea-Water,
> At the doorway of his wigwam,
> In the pleasant Summer morning,
> Hiawatha stood and waited.
> All the air was full of freshness,
> All the earth was bright and joyous,
> And before him, through the sunshine,
> Westward toward the neighboring forest
> Passed in golden swarms the Ahmo,
> Passed the bees, the honey-makers,
> Burning, singing in the sunshine.

Or they might have been taught to recite with patriotic fervor the whole of this poem:

> Ay, tear her tattered ensign down!
>   Long has it waved on high,
> And many an eye has danced to see
>   That banner in the sky;
> Beneath it rung the battle shout,
>   And burst the cannon's roar;—
> The meteor of the ocean air
>   Shall sweep the clouds no more!

Her deck, once red with heroes' blood
   Where knelt the vanquished foe,
When winds were hurrying o'er the flood
   And waves were white below,
No more shall feel the victor's tread,
   Or know the conquered knee;—
The harpies of the shore shall pluck
   The eagle of the sea!

O better that her shattered hulk
   Should sink beneath the wave;
Her thunders shook the mighty deep
   And there should be her grave;
Nail to the mast her holy flag,
   Set every thread-bare sail,
And give her to the god of storms,—
   The lightning and the gale!

The first two selections, as today's readers may or may not know, were written by Henry Wadsworth Longfellow; they are from "Paul Revere's Ride" (*Tales of a Wayside Inn*, 1860) and "The Song of Hiawatha" (1855). The full poem is Oliver Wendell Holmes's "Old Ironsides," which he wrote in 1830 in a successful effort to prevent the frigate *Constitution* from being dismantled.

For the better part of a century, such verse constituted the poetic mainstream of American literature. The "Schoolroom Poets" who wrote it, Cambridge gentlemen and Harvard professors like Longfellow, Holmes, and James Russell Lowell, embodied what many saw as the ideal of an American man of letters. The metrical regularity and linguistic simplicity of such verse recommended it for classroom recitation and study. Its unconflicted, ingenuous views of American history and of nature, its sentimental portraits of noble Indians and magnanimous Puritans, its elevated and highminded tone—all these appealed to generations of readers wishing to sustain an idealized view of the past.

To be sure, "Schoolroom" poetry did not constitute the full range of American verse in the first half of the nineteenth century. As this section demonstrates, a variety of distinctive folk traditions emerged in the early years of this republic. Black slaves in the South created from African and western European sources an altogether new genre, the "sorrow songs" or spirituals, as well as secular work songs to pace, and in a measure to complain against, their heavy labors. In many other areas, people used the work, conflicts, and loves attendant on building a new society to create what are generally described as "folk" songs and poems.

Among the more formal poets, William Cullen Bryant was the first American to successfully adapt the innovations in style and subject of British Romantics like Wordsworth, Keats, and Shelley and to win the reputation of poet on both sides of the Atlantic. In these respects, he set a pattern not only for the "Schoolroom" poets but for others, including Emerson, who found in nature both inspiration and symbol. Read perhaps as widely as Bryant and Longfellow in her day, but not since, Lydia Sigourney's work illustrates another dimension of nineteenth-century poetry, what has been demeaned—and therefore often misunderstood—as "sentimental." The popular reception—and large sales—of the work of these poets suggests a public function to their work unfamiliar to most twentieth-century readers of poetry.

Of the contemporaries of Emerson and Longfellow, however, it was Poe (represented earlier in this volume) whose work most influenced other poets—not so much in the United States, though works like "The Raven" and "The Bells" won wide attention and also lent themselves to the popular forms of oral recitation, but in France, where, through the responsive passion of writers like Baudelaire and Rimbaud, Poe's reputation flourished and his approach to invoking the mysterious states of mind was developed.

In the United States, as the nineteenth century drew to a close, as the men and women who wrote the best-known poetry died (Holmes, the last, in 1894), and as the first volumes of Emily Dickinson's poems began to be published, conceptions of poetic excellence were undergoing rapid change. Within a quarter century, and certainly into our own day, very different kinds of poetry came to be seen as the major achievements of American writers in the nineteenth century. Thinking about why helps us understand the changes from nineteenth-century ideas and tastes to those of our own day. Compare these lines, for example:

> Each heart has its haunted chamber,
>> Where the silent moonlight falls!
> On the floor are mysterious footsteps,
>> There are whispers along the walls!
>
> And mine at times is haunted
>> By phantoms of the Past,
> As motionless as shadows,
>> By the silent moonlight cast. . . .

Longfellow, from "The Haunted Chamber"

And now consider these:

> One need not be a Chamber—to be Haunted—
> One need not be a House—
> The Brain has Corridors—surpassing
> Material Place—
>
> Far safer, of a Midnight Meeting
> External Ghost
> Than its interior Confronting—
> That Cooler Host. . . .

Emily Dickinson, poem #670

In certain respects, the very regularity of Longfellow's lines works against the mood he is trying to create, and the abstractness and generality of his language make it far less startling or memorable than Dickinson's internal ghost. The jaggedness, the tension, the unusual concreteness of Dickinson's lines also came to appeal to twentieth-century sensibility far more; they came to be seen, in fact, as embodying many of the spasmodic, discordant qualities of contemporary life, even though the poem was written around 1863.

Or consider a further comparison. Here is the octave of a sonnet by Longfellow:

> The sea awoke at midnight from its sleep,
> And round the pebbly beaches far and wide
> I heard the first wave of the rising tide
> Rush onward with uninterrupted sweep;
> A voice out of the silence of the deep,
> A sound mysteriously multiplied
> As of a cataract from the mountain's side,
> Or roar of winds upon a wooded steep.

> "The Sound of the Sea"

And here is the opening of a poem from Walt Whitman's "Sea-Drift":

> Out of the cradle endlessly rocking,
> Out of the mocking-bird's throat, the musical shuttle,
> Out of the Ninth-month midnight,
> Over the sterile sands and the fields beyond, where the child leaving his
> bed wander'd alone, bareheaded, barefoot,
> Down from the shower'd halo,
> Up from the mystic play of shadows twining and twisting as if they were
> alive,
> Out from the patches of briers and blackberries,
> From the memories of the bird that chanted to me,
> From your memories sad brother, from the fitful risings and fallings I
> heard,
> From under that yellow half-moon late-risen and swollen as
> if with tears,
> From those beginning notes of yearning and love there in the mist,
> From the thousand responses of my heart never to cease....

> "Out of the cradle endlessly rocking"

The point of this comparison is not to demean Longfellow; on the contrary, we have included him in this anthology because some of his poetry continues to live and to move us. Besides, precisely because he was by far this country's most popular and respected poet, not only in the United States but also in Europe, reading him tells us a great deal about the sensibility of mid-nineteenth-century America.

By contrast, Whitman's "barbaric yawp" initially shocked many of his contemporaries. But his effort to create something new under the sun, a distinctively American poetic style, drawing from platform rhetoric, Quaker terminology, and youthful romantic yearnings, has come to appear a more vital voice in American literary history. The shift in valuation from Longfellow to Whitman can be used to mark the changes in critical standards from a century ago to our own day.

If we can perceive why most of their contemporaries much preferred Longfellow to Whitman, we can understand a great deal about the taste, the style, and the concerns of American poets during the first part of the nineteenth century.

Paul Lauter
Trinity College

■   # SONGS AND BALLADS   ■

Songs do not really exist on the printed page. Indeed, certain kinds of songs, notably those like spirituals given expression in congregational singing, do not exist even through music printed with their texts. They live only in the process of their fresh creation each time they are sung. Thus, printing the texts of some representative songs being sung in the first part of the nineteenth century in a sense falsifies them, as well as the cultural history of the time. Yet, it would be equally false to omit them, for the United States had a vigorous popular culture—or, more accurately, cultures—in which songs constituted a major element.

Determining which songs to include in such a selection is equally problematic. Although the composition of some songs can be dated with reasonable accuracy, many have been sung for decades before they are noted by collectors. Furthermore, new versions are always appearing: an old tune may be resurrected with fresh lyrics; simpler texts can be set to differing melodies. To some degree, therefore, placing certain of these songs in this particular time frame is arbitrary—some may well have been around since the previous century, and the printed versions may reflect late nineteenth- or even twentieth-century variations. In addition, no selection can fully reflect the range of the American people's cultures, even of the early nineteenth century. Here we have included a somewhat larger selection of African American songs of the time, in part because they represent the most characteristically "American," as distinct from imported, compositions and in part because of the enormous influence African American folk styles have had in the development of American culture generally.

Most of the songs in this section were not sung by performers observed and listened to by a silent audience. Singing was among the more vital activities people did together. In certain respects, as Bernice Reagon has put it, "the song is only a vehicle to get to the singing." It is the *singing*—in church, in the fields, at a quilting bee or a party, around a campfire or a piano—that unifies, inspires, moves people to hope and to act. The singing defines the nature of the gathering, predominantly for those engaged in it. Some of these verses were sung in meetings, for worship or for politics; some, like "John Brown's Body," were chanted by soldiers marching to battle; some were set out to pace or perhaps to ease work. One needs to imagine the circumstances in which they were created and re-created to gain a real sense of most of these songs.

Like other kinds of poetry, these songs convey a broad range of human emotions—affection, aspiration, complaint—but they are often more explicit about the roles they play in the lives of the people who sing them. Some songs were designed to support political parties, others, like "Paper of Pins," to give form to courting rituals. Some served multiple purposes: a spiritual like "Steal Away" could in some situations express the desire of slaves for a salvation beyond the oppression of daily life; in other circumstances, the song could serve as a signal for some to prepare to "steal away" literally on the Underground Railway. Often the songs voiced the common experiences and beliefs of particular groups of people—black slaves, Irish immigrants, forty-niners—as well as embodying images, rhythms, and harmonies characteristic of their cultures. In that sense, songs functioned to preserve and sustain important elements of group culture against the homogenizing tendencies of the developing nation.

Groups did borrow language and music from each other, but many songs bear the distinctive marks of particular historical cultures. Most African American congregational songs, for example, display a call-and-response pattern, in which the song leader sets out a line or phrase and the group responds by repeating or working variations on it. In one of the more famous examples, the leader cries out "Swing low, sweet chariot," and the congregation responds "Comin' for to carry me home"; or again, "When Israel was in Egypt land," and the response, "Let my people go." But the pattern of call-and-response is not limited to such fully structured lines; in fact, the essence of such African American congregational music depends on many individuals' extemporaneously singing out words or phrases—like "hallelujah" or "yes, Lord"—or even appropriate new lines. Many Anglo-American songs are marked by refrains whose "nonsense" syllables—e.g., "hoodle dang fol di dye yo, hoodle dang fol di day" in "Sweet Betsy from Pike"—vary according to the area of the country or the original nationality of the singers. In general, the language of these songs reflects the language of the people who sang them, just as the music significantly emerged from the European or African origins of the singers.

Most of the texts printed below are those of "folk songs," though a few are the compositions of specific writers. That is, the authors of most are unknown, the language of the songs colloquial, their images drawn from the common stock available to everyone in the group. They are designed to be *sung*, and thus their words may differ from versions a reader might know. The texts of such songs often changed, in fact, sometimes by accident as a song was re-created by people who might not have remembered all of the version they had once heard. Sometimes, however, songs were consciously changed to reflect new circumstances or to broaden their appeal. "Bury Me Not on the Lone Prairie" began as a sailor's lament about burial at sea. Songs like "Sweet Betsy from Pike" and "Pat Works on the Railway" probably had dozens of verses added or subtracted at one or another time. "The Battle Hymn of the Republic" was composed by Julia Ward Howe after she sang "John Brown's Body" with a troop of Union soldiers and her minister asked her to set new words to that "stirring tune." In still other cases, as with the version of "Go Down, Moses" included here, a song originally sung in dialect was later redone in more "standard" English when it began to be presented to a white audience. In the singing, then, the precise texts are less important than the process of reshaping the language to fit the inclinations of the singers.

In this respect, these texts represent snapshots of songs, freezing them into uncharacteristically stationary, historical forms. In fact, as readers will know, many of these songs have reemerged over the years as their sentiments or their phrases have come to echo the needs of new times and new singers.

Paul Lauter
Trinity College

Songs of the Slaves[1]

Lay Dis Body Down

I know moon-rise, I know star-rise
    I lay dis body down.
I walk in de moonlight, I walk in de starlight,
    To lay dis body down.
I walk in de graveyard, I walk troo de graveyard,   5
    To lay dis body down.
I lie in de grave an' stretch out my arms,
    I lay dis body down.
I go to de jedgment in de evenin' of de day
    When I lay dis body down,   10
An' my soul an' your soul will meet in de day
    When I lay dis body down.

Nobody Knows the Trouble I've Had

Nobody knows de trouble I've had [or, I've seen],
    Nobody knows but Jesus
Nobody knows de trouble I've had
    Glory hallelu.

One morning I was a-walking down,   5
    O yes, Lord!
I saw some berries a-hanging down,
    O yes, Lord!
    (Refrain)

[1]The texts of the following "spirituals" or "sorrow songs" are derived primarily from William Francis Allen, Charles Pickard Ware, and Lucy McKim Garrison, *Slave Songs of the United States*, 1867 (reprinted New York: Peter Smith, 1951), and James Weldon Johnson and J. Rosamond Johnson, *The Books of* *American Negro Spirituals*, 1925, 1926 (reprinted New York: Da Capo Press, 1977). Other sources, like Thomas Wentworth Higginson's *Army Life in a Black Regiment*, have also been consulted. The spellings are those of the volume from which the text is taken.

I pick de berry and I suck de juice, 10
    O yes, Lord!
Just as sweet as the honey in de comb,
    O yes, Lord!
    (Refrain)
Sometimes I'm up, sometimes I'm down, 15
Sometimes I'm almost on de groun'.
    (Refrain)
What make ole Satan hate me so?
Cause he got me once and he let me go.
    (Refrain) 20

Roll, Jordan, Roll

My brudder [sister, or a name] sittin' on de tree of life,
    An' he yearde when Jordan roll;
        Roll, Jordan, Roll, Jordan, Roll, Jordan, roll!
        O march de angel march, O march de angel march;
        O my soul arise in Heaven, Lord, 5
        For to year when Jordan roll.
Little chil'en, learn to fear de Lord,
    And let your days be long;
        Roll, Jordan, &c.
O, let no false nor spiteful word, 10
    Be found upon your tongue;
        Roll, Jordan, &c.

Michael Row the Boat Ashore

1. Michael row the boat ashore, Hallelujah! (repeat)
2. Michael boat a gospel boat, Hallelujah!
3. I wonder where my mudder deh [there].
4. See my mudder on de rock gwine home.
5. On de rock gwine home in Jesus' name.
6. Michael boat a music boat.
7. Gabriel blow de trumpet horn.
8. O you mind your boastin' talk.
9. Boastin' talk will sink your soul.
10. Brudder, lend a helpin' hand.
11. Sister, help for trim dat boat.
12. Jordan stream is wide and deep.
13. Jesus stand on t' oder side.
14. I wonder if my maussa der.
15. My fader gone to unknown land.
16. O de Lord he plant his garden deh.
17. He raise de fruit for you to eat.

18. He dat eat shall neber die.
19. When de riber overflow.
20. O poor sinner, how you land?
21. Riber run and darkness comin'.
22. Sinner row to save your soul.

Steal Away to Jesus

Steal away, steal away, steal away to Jesus!
Steal away, steal away home, I ain't got long to stay here.
Steal away, steal away, steal away to Jesus!
Steal away, steal away home, I ain't got long to stay here.
My Lord, He calls me, He calls me by the thunder,   5
The trumpet sounds within-a my soul, I ain't got long to stay here.
Steal away, steal away, steal away to Jesus!
Steal away, steal away home, I ain't got long to stay here.
Steal away, steal away, steal away to Jesus!
Steal away, steal away home, I ain't got long to stay here.   10
Green trees a-bending, po' sinner stand a-tembling,
The trumpet sounds within-a my soul.
I ain't got long to stay here, Oh, Lord, I ain't got long to stay here.

Many Thousand Go[1]

1. No more peck o' corn for me,
   No more, no more;
   No more peck o' corn for me,
   Many thousand go.
2. No more driver's lash for me.
3. No more pint o' salt for me.
4. No more hundred lash for me.
5. No more mistress' call for me.

Go Down, Moses

When Israel was in Egypt's land,
    Let my people go;
Oppressed so hard they could not stand,
    Let my people go.

[1]A song "to which the Rebellion had actually given rise. This was composed by nobody knows whom—though it was the most recent doubtless of all these 'spirituals,'—and had been sung in secret to avoid detection. It is certainly plaintive enough. The peck of corn and pint of salt were slavery's rations."—Thomas Wentworth Higginson. Lt. Col. Trowbridge learned that it was first sung when Beauregard took the slaves of the islands to build fortifications at Hilton Head and Bay Point. [Note of Allen, Ware, and Garrison]

Chorus:
> Go down, Moses, way down in Egypt's land;　　　　5
> Tell old Pharoah, to let my people go.

Thus saith the Lord, bold Moses said,
　Let my people go;
If not I'll smite your first born dead,
　Let my people go.　　　　　　　　　　10

No more shall they in bondage toil,
　Let my people go;
Let them come out with Egypt's spoil,
　Let my people go.

O 'twas a dark and dismal night,　　　　15
　Let my people go;
When Moses led the Israelites,
　Let my people go.

The Lord told Moses what to do,
　Let my people go;　　　　　　　　　　20
To lead the children of Israel through,
　Let my people go.

O come along, Moses, you won't get lost,
　Let my people go;
Stretch our your rod and come across,　　25
　Let my people go.

As Israel stood by the water side,
　Let my people go;
At the command of God it did divide,
　Let my people go.　　　　　　　　　　30

And when they reached the other side,
　Let my people go;
They sang a song of triumph o'er,
　Let my people go.

You won't get lost in the wilderness,　　35
　Let my people go;
With a lighted candle in your breast,
　Let my people go.

O let us all from bondage flee,
　Let my people go;　　　　　　　　　　40

And let us all in Christ be free,
    Let my people go.

We need not always weep and moan,
    Let my people go;
And wear these slavery chains forlorn,   45
    Let my people go.

What a beautiful morning that will be,
    Let my people go;
When time breaks up in eternity,
Let my people go.   50

Didn't My Lord Deliver Daniel

    Didn't my Lord deliver Daniel, deliver Daniel, deliver Daniel,
    Didn't my Lord deliver Daniel,
    An' why not every man.
He delivered Daniel from de lion's den,
Jonah from de belly of de whale,   5
An' de Hebrew chillun from de fiery furnace,
An' why not every man.
    Didn't my Lord deliver Daniel, deliver Daniel, deliver Daniel,
    Didn't my Lord deliver Daniel,
    An' why not every man.   10
De moon run down in a purple stream,
De sun forbear to shine,
An' every star disappear,
King Jesus shall-a be mine.
    (Refrain)   15
De win' blows eas' an' de win' blows wes',
It blows like de judgament day,
An' every po' soul dat never did pray
'll be glad to pray dat day.
    (Refrain)   20
I set my foot on de Gospel ship,
An de ship begin to sail,
It landed me over on Canaan's shore,
An' I'll never come back no mo'.
    (Refrain)   25

Songs of White Communities

John Brown's Body

John Brown's body lies a-moldering in the grave,
John Brown's body lies a-moldering in the grave,
John Brown's body lies a-moldering in the grave,
    But his soul goes marching on.

Chorus:
Glory, glory, hallelujah!   5
Glory, glory, hallelujah!
Glory, glory, hallelujah!
His soul goes marching on!

John Brown died that the slaves might be free,
John Brown died that the slaves might be free,   10
John Brown died that the slaves might be free,
    But his soul goes marching on.

He's gone to be a soldier in the army of the Lord,
He's gone to be a soldier in the army of the Lord,
He's gone to be a soldier in the army of the Lord,   15
    And his soul is marching on.

The stars of heaven are looking kindly down,
The stars of heaven are looking kindly down,
The stars of heaven are looking kindly down,
    On the grave of old John Brown.   20

Pat Works on the Railway

In eighteen hundred and forty-one
I put my corduroy breeches on.
I put my corduroy breeches on
To work upon the railway.
    Chorus:
    Fill-i-me-oo-ree-i-ree-ay (three times)   5
    To work upon the railway.

In eighteen hundred and forty-two
I left the Old World for the New.
Bad cess to the luck that brought me through
To work upon the railway.   10

In eighteen hundred and forty-three
'Twas then that I met sweet Biddy McGee.
An elegant wife she's been to me
While working on the railway.

In eighteen hundred and forty-four   15
I traveled the land from shore to shore,
I traveled the land from shore to shore
To work upon the railway.

In eighteen hundred and forty-five
I found myself more dead than alive.   20
I found myself more dead than alive
From working on the railway.

It's "Pat do this" and "Pat do that,"
Without a stocking or cravat,
Nothing but an old straw hat   25
While I worked upon the railway.

In eighteen hundred and forty-seven
Sweet Biddy McGee she went to heaven;
If she left one child she left eleven,
To work upon the railway.   30

Sweet Betsy from Pike[1]

Oh don't you remember sweet Betsy from Pike,
Who crossed the big mountains with her lover Ike,
With two yoke of oxen, a big yellow dog,
A tall Shanghai rooster, and one spotted hog?

   Chorus:
Singing dang fol dee dido,   5
   Singing dang fol dee day.

One evening quite early they camped on the Platte.
'Twas near by the road on a green shady flat,
Where Betsy, sore-footed, lay down to repose—
With wonder Ike gazed on that Pike County rose.   10

---

[1]To illustrate how traditional songs emerge in many variants, consider an alternative opening verse and chorus of "Sweet Betsy":
Did you ever hear of Sweet Betsy from Pike,
Who crossed the wide prairies with her lover Ike,
With two yoke of oxen and one spotted hog,
A tall Shanghai rooster and one yaller dog.

Saying "Good-bye Pike county, farewell for a while,
We'll come back again when we panned out our pile."
Other versions of the chorus take their character from groups supposed to have sung the song; an Irish-like chorus reads "Sing too ra li oo ra li oo ra li aye."

The Shanghai ran off, and their cattle all died;
That morning the last piece of bacon was fried;
Poor Ike was discouraged and Betsy got mad,
The dog drooped his tail and looked wondrously sad.

They stopped at Salt Lake to inquire of the way,   15
Where Brigham declared that sweet Betsy should stay;
But Betsy got frightened and ran like a deer,
While Brigham stood pawing the ground like a steer.

They soon reached the desert where Betsy gave out,
And down in the sand she lay rolling about;   20
While Ike, half distracted, looked on with surprise,
Saying, "Betsy, get up, you'll get sand in your eyes."

Sweet Betsy got up in a great deal of pain,
Declared she'd go back to Pike County again;
But Ike gave a sigh, and they fondly embraced,   25
And they traveled along with his arm round her waist.

The Injuns came down in a wild yelling horde,
And Betsy was scared they would scalp her adored;
Behind the front wagon wheel Betsy did crawl,
And there fought the Injuns with musket and ball.   30

They suddenly stopped on a very high hill,
With wonder looked down upon old Placerville;
Ike sighed when he said, and he cast his eyes down,
"Sweet Betsy, my darling, we've got to Hangtown."

Long Ike and sweet Betsy attended a dance;   35
Ike wore a pair of his Pike County pants;
Sweet Betsy was dressed up in ribbons and rings;
Says Ike, "You're an angel, but where are your wings?"

[Following are additional or alternative verses to "Sweet Betsy." Some
portray Betsy in rather a stronger light.]

'Twas out on the prairie one bright starry night,
They broke out the whiskey and Betsy got tight,
She sang and she howled and she danced o'er the plain,
And showed her bare legs to the whole wagon train.

The terrible desert was burning and bare,   5
And Isaac he shrank from the death lurkin' there,
"Dear old Pike County, I'll come back to you."
Says Betsy, "You'll go by yourself if you do."

They swam wild rivers and climbed the tall peaks,
And camped on the prairies for weeks upon weeks,   10
Starvation and cholera, hard work and slaughter,
They reached Californy, spite of hell and high water.

A miner said, "Betsy, will you dance with me?"
"I will, you old hoss, if you don't make too free.
But don't dance me hard, do you want to know why?   15
Doggone ye, I'm chock full of strong alkali.

Long Ike and sweet Betsy got married, of course,
But Ike, getting jealous, obtained a divorce,
While Betsy, well satisfied, said with a shout,
"Goodbye, you big lummox, I'm glad you backed out!"   20

Bury Me Not on the Lone Prairie[1]

"O bury me not on the lone prairie."
    These words came low and mournfully,
From the pallid lips of a youth who lay
    On his dying bed at the close of day.

He had wasted and pined till o'er his brow   5
    Death's shades were slowly gathering now.
He thought of home and loved ones nigh,
    As the cowboys gathered to see him die.

"O bury me not on the lone prairie,
    Where the coyotes howl and the wind blows free.   10
In a narrow grave just six by three—
    O bury me not on the lone prairie."

"It matters not, I've oft been told,
    Where the body lies when the heart grows cold.
Yet grant, o grant, this wish to me,   15
    O bury me not on the lone prairie."

"I've always wished to be laid when I died
    In a little churchyard on the green hillside.
By my father's grave there let me be,
    O bury me not on the lone prairie."   20

[1]This song probably originated as one among a number of ballads of the 1840s concerned with burial *at sea*. It appears to have migrated in some fashion to the Western range, where it became the most popular of early cowboy songs.

"I wish to lie where a mother's prayer
 And a sister's tear will mingle there.
Where friends can come and weep o'er me.
 O bury me not on the lone prairie."

"For there's another whose tears will shed   25
 For the one who lies in a prairie bed.
It breaks my heart to think of her now,
 She has curled these locks; she has kissed this brow"

"O bury me not ..." And his voice failed there.
 But they took no heed to his dying prayer.   30
In a narrow grave, just six by three,
 They buried him there on the lone prairie.

And the cowboys now as they roam the plain,
 For they marked the spot where his bones were lain,
Fling a handful of roses o'er his grave   35
 With a prayer to God, his soul to save.

Shenandoah[1]

Oh, Shenandoah, I long to hear you—
Away, you rolling river;
Oh, Shenandoah, I long to hear you—
Away, I'm bound away
'Cross the wide Missouri.   5

Oh, Shenandoah, I love your daughter—
Away, you rolling river;
I'll take her 'cross that rolling water—
Away, I'm bound away
'Cross the wide Missouri.   10

This white man loves your Indian maiden—
Away, you rolling river;
In my canoe with notions laden—
Away, I'm bound away
'Cross the wide Missouri.   15

[1]This song of a white trader who fell in love with the daughter of an Indian chieftain appears to have originated in the Missouri River valley in the early nineteenth century. Later, reversing the course of "Bury Me Not," it migrated east to the ocean, where in a slightly different version it emerged as a capstan chantey.

Farewell, goodbye, I shall not grieve you—
Away, you rolling river;
Oh, Shenandoah, I'll not deceive you—
Away, I'm bound away
'Cross the wide Missouri.   20

The ship sails free, a gale is blowing—
Away, you rolling river;
The braces taut, the sheets aflowing—
Away, I'm bound away
'Cross the wide Missouri.   25

Clementine[1]

In a cavern, in a canyon, excavating for a mine,
Lived a miner, forty-niner, and his daughter Clementine.
    Oh my darlin', oh my darlin', oh my darlin' Clementine,
    You are lost and gone forever, dreadful sorry Clementine.

Light she was and like a fairy, And her   5
    shoes were number nine;
Herring boxes without topses, Sandals
    were for Clementine.
(Chorus)

Drove she ducklings to the water, Every
    morning just at nine,   10
Hit her foot against a splinter, Fell into
    the foaming brine.
(Chorus)

Ruby lips above the water, Blowing
    bubbles soft and fine,
Alas for me, I was no swimmer, So I   15
    lost my Clementine.
(Chorus)

In a churchyard near the canyon,
    Where the myrtle doth entwine,
There grow roses and other posies,
    Fertilized by Clementine.   20
(Chorus)

[1]Both this and the following song, "Acres of
Clams," were popular among the gold miners
of California, the forty-niners.

In my dreams she oft doth haunt me,
    With her garments soaked in brine;
Though in life I used to hug her, Now
    she's dead I draw the line.
(Chorus)

Then the miner, forty-niner, Soon   25
    began to peak and pine;
Thought he 'oughter jin'e his daughter,
    Now he's with his Clementine.
(Chorus)

Cindy[1]

You ought to see my Cindy,
    She lives way down south;
She's so sweet the honey bees
    Swarm around her mouth.

Chorus:
    Get-a-long home, Cindy, Cindy,   5
    Get-a-long home, Cindy, Cindy,
    Get-a-long home, Cindy, Cindy,
        I'll marry you some day.

The first time I saw Cindy,
    She was standing in the door,   10
Her shoes and stockings in her hand,
    Her feet all over the floor.

She took me to her parlor,
    She cooled me with her fan;
She said I was the prettiest thing   15
    In the shape of mortal man.

She kissed me and she hugged me,
    She called me sugar plum;
She throwed her arms around me,
    I thought my time had come.   20

Oh, Cindy is a pretty girl,
    Cindy is a peach;

---

[1]"Cindy" is but one of a large group of ditties called "Play-Party Songs." They were generally sung and danced to without instrumental accompaniment, since many people viewed fiddle-playing as the work of the Devil. Verses were often improvised about local people and events as the song went along.

She throwed her arms around my neck,
    And hung on like a leech.

And if I was a sugar tree   25
    Standing in the town,
Every time my Cindy passed
    I'd shake some sugar down.

And if I had a needle and thread
    Fine as I could sew,   30
I'd sew that girl to my coat tails
    And down the road I'd go.

Come Home, Father

by Henry Clay Work[1]

Father, dear father, come home with me now!
The clock in the steeple strikes one.
You said you were coming right home from the shop,
As soon as your day's work was done.
Our fire has gone out, our house is all dark,   5
And mother's been watching since tea,
With poor brother Benny so sick in her arms,
And no one to help her but me.
Come home! come home! come home!
Please, father, dear father, come home.   10

    Chorus:
    Hear the sweet voice of the child
    Which the night winds repeat as they roam!
    Oh, who could resist this most plaintive of prayers?
    "Please, father, dear father, come home!
    Come home! come home! come home!   15
    Please, father, dear father, come home."

Father, dear father, come home with me now!
The clock in the steeple strikes two.
The night has grown colder and Benny is worse,
But he has been calling for you.   20
Indeed he is worse, Ma says he will die,
Perhaps before morning shall dawn;

---

[1]Work, an active abolitionist and temperance supporter, composed this song in 1864. For many years it was sung in what was probably the most popular temperance drama, "Ten Nights in a Barroom."

And this is the message she sent me to bring:
"Come quickly, or he will be gone."
Come home! come home! come home!   25
Please, father, dear father, come home.

Father, dear father, come home with me now!
The clock in the steeple strikes three.
The house is so lonely, the hours are so long,
For poor weeping mother and me.   30
Yes, we are alone, poor Benny is dead,
And gone with the angels of light;
And these were the very last words that he said:
"I want to kiss Papa good night."
Come home! come home! come home!   35
Please, father, dear father, come home.

Life Is a Toil

One day as I wandered, I heard a complaining,
  And saw an old woman, the picture of gloom;
She gazed at the mud on her doorstep ('twas raining),
  And this was her song as she wielded her broom:
  Chorus:
"Oh, life is a toil and love is a trouble,   5
  And beauty will fade and riches will flee;
Oh, pleasures they dwindle and prices they double,
  And nothing is as I would wish it to be.

"It's sweeping at six and it's dusting at seven,
  It's victuals at eight and it's dishes at nine;   10
It's potting and panning from ten to eleven—
  We scarce break our fast till we plan how to dine.

"There's too much of worriment goes in a bonnet,
  There's too much of ironing goes in a shirt;
There's nothing that pays for the time you waste on it,   15
  There's nothing that lasts us but trouble and dirt.

"In March it is mud, it is snow in December,
  The mid-summer breezes are loaded with dust;
In fall the leaves litter; in rainy September
  The wallpaper rots and the candlesticks rust.   20

"Last night in my dreams I was stationed forever
  On a far little isle in the midst of the sea;

My one chance for life was a ceaseless endeavor
   To sweep off the waves ere they swept over me.

"Alas, 'twas no dream, for ahead I behold it;   25
   I know I am helpless my fate to avert."
She put down her broom and her apron she folded,
   Then lay down and died, and was buried in dirt.

WILLIAM CULLEN BRYANT
1794–1878

Born in Cummington, Massachusetts, William Cullen Bryant was the son of a country doctor who served several terms in the Massachusetts state legislature and was both a stern Calvinist and a strict disciplinarian. Dr. Bryant's library, which contained at least seven hundred books, provided Bryant with a formidable basis for his copious early reading, which apparently began when he was sixteen months old. At thirteen Bryant was sent to live with an uncle so that he might begin to study Latin and Greek, and he learned so rapidly that at sixteen he entered Williams College as a sophomore. Despite his wish to continue working toward a classical education, Bryant was compelled by family financial circumstances to leave college during his first year, and he reluctantly turned to the law, reading for the bar in Worthington and entering practice in Plainfield, Massachusetts, at the age of twenty-one.

Bryant's precocity was evident also in his early poetry. At thirteen he wrote an anti-Jeffersonian poem called "The Embargo" after the manner of the seventeenth- and eighteenth-century satires of Dryden and Pope. Even though the political sentiments of the poem probably owed more to his father's opinions than to any political views young Cullen might claim, the poem so impressed Dr. Bryant that he had it printed in the *Hampshire Gazette*. Other early compositions that in their subject matter and manner prefigure the later poetry included a pair of odes in praise of the Connecticut River and patriotic stanzas called "The Genius of Columbia." In these, Bryant's style was influenced by his reading of English poets of the preceding generation, such as Thomas Gray, William Cowper, Henry Kirke White, Robert Southey, and Robert Blair. Their subjects, which tended to be pastoral and philosophical, helped to form Bryant's conception of what a poem should be: grave, somber, dignified, meditative, and above all, regular.

His most famous poem, "Thanatopsis," was composed when he was eighteen. His father, having discovered it, recopied the poem and submitted it to *The North American Review*, where it was published in September 1817. Although "Thanatopsis" means a "meditation on death," the poem is also a meditation on nature, and in its implicit pantheism the poem looks at once backward to

William Wordsworth's *Lyrical Ballads* (1798, 1800) and forward to the Transcendentalists. Of "Thanatopsis," Richard Henry Dana remarked that "no one on this side of the Atlantic is capable of writing such verses." Steeped as he was in English poetry, Bryant was able to manufacture American verses altogether as satisfactory as those produced abroad. Although poems such as "The Yellow Violet" and "To a Fringed Gentian" could as easily refer to English settings as American, the nationality of the author gave them a domestic stamp, and in poems such as "The Prairies" and "To Cole, the Painter, Departing for Europe," Bryant attempted to capture the spirit and landscape of the New World.

In 1821, the year of his marriage to Frances Fairchild, Bryant published a small book titled simply *Poems*. The connection established with Richard Henry Dana and Willard Philips at the *North American Review* had led to an invitation from the Phi Beta Kappa Society of Harvard College to present a "poetical address" at the 1821 commencement, and his poem for that occasion, "The Ages," together with seven others, was published in a forty-four-page pamphlet that was warmly reviewed by the *North American Review* and promptly reprinted in a British anthology of American poetry. Bryant's literary career was now launched.

Moving to New York in 1825, Bryant happily abandoned his job as justice of the peace in Berkshire County to become an editor of *The New York Review and Athenaeum*, but when the publication folded in 1827, he renewed his license to practice law in New York. His return to the legal profession was brief, however, as he was offered a job as assistant editor of the New York *Evening Post* and in 1829 became its editor-in-chief, a position he held until his death in 1878 at the age of eighty-four. During his years at the *Post*, he published a dozen volumes of his poetry to great acclaim. Although his poetic production fell off in his middle years, new collections of his poetry continued to be published and republished, and he achieved the sort of fame ordinarily reserved for traditional public figures, such as actors and politicians. Seemingly indefatigable, later in his life he undertook translations of both *The Iliad* and *The Odyssey*.

As editor of the *Evening Post*, he was first in the vanguard of the Free Soil movement and later a founder of the Republican party. Although relatively little of his published poetry even hints at the existence of politics, his editorials in the *Post* were influential in shaping public opinion, and he was a staunch supporter of Abraham Lincoln in 1860. Yet, even when he wrote on subjects that had some currency, Bryant was careful to keep his distance. In his poem "Civil War" (1861), for example, he drew on Horace's Epode VII and was ultimately ambiguous about the war, except to deplore its fraternal bloodshed. Thus, Bryant's phenomenal career existed in two carefully separated spheres: the political journalist and the philosophical poet were never confounded. He was lionized chiefly for his poetry, and his extraordinary popularity owed greatly to his ability to select subjects with which no one could disagree and then to cast them in forms recognizable and understandable to all.

Allison Heisch
San Jose State University

PRIMARY WORK

The Poetical Works of William Cullen Bryant, Henry C. Sturges, ed., 1903. AMS 1969, 1972.

Thanatopsis[1]

To him who in the love of Nature holds
Communion with her visible forms, she speaks
A various language; for his gayer hours
She has a voice of gladness, and a smile
And eloquence of beauty, and she glides   5
Into his darker musings, with a mild
And healing sympathy, that steals away
Their sharpness, ere he is aware. When thoughts
Of the last bitter hour come like a blight
Over thy spirit, and sad images   10
Of the stern agony, and shroud, and pall.
And breathless darkness, and the narrow house,
Make thee to shudder, and grow sick at heart;—
Go forth, under the open sky, and list
To Nature's teachings, while from all around—   15
Earth and her waters, and the depths of air—
Comes a still voice.—
Yet a few days, and thee
The all-beholding sun shall see no more
In all his course; nor yet in the cold ground,
Where thy pale form was laid, with many tears,   20
Nor in the embrace of ocean, shall exist
Thy image. Earth, that nourished thee, shall claim
Thy growth, to be resolved to earth again,
And, lost each human trace, surrendering up
Thine individual being, shalt thou go   25
To mix for ever with the elements,
To be a brother to the insensible rock
And to the sluggish clod, which the rude swain
Turns with his share,[2] and treads upon. The oak
Shall send his roots abroad, and pierce thy mould.   30

    Yet not to thine eternal resting-place
Shalt thou retire alone, nor couldst thou wish
Couch more magnificent. Thou shalt lie down
With patriarchs of the infant world—with kings,
The powerful of the earth—the wise, the good,   35
Fair forms, and hoary seers of ages past,
All in one mighty sepulchre. The hills
Rock-ribbed and ancient as the sun,—the vales

---

[1] Greek for meditation on death.   [2] Plowshare.

Stretching in pensive quietness between;
The venerable woods—rivers that move   40
In majesty, and the complaining brooks
That make the meadows green; and, poured round all,
Old Ocean's gray and melancholy waste,—
Are but the solemn decorations all
Of the great tomb of man. The golden sun,   45
The planets, all the infinite host of heaven,
Are shining on the sad abodes of death,
Through the still lapse of ages. All that tread
The globe are but a handful to the tribes
That slumber in its bosom.—Take the wings   50
Of morning, pierce the Barcan wilderness,[3]
Or lose thyself in the continuous woods
Where rolls the Oregon, and hears no sound,
Save his own dashings—yet the dead are there:
And millions in those solitudes, since first   55
The flight of years began, have laid them down
In their last sleep—the dead reign there alone.
So shalt thou rest, and what if thou withdraw
In silence from the living, and no friend
Take note of thy departure? All that breathe   60
Will share thy destiny. The gay will laugh
When thou art gone, the solemn brood of care
Plod on, and each one as before will chase
His favorite phantom; yet all these shall leave
Their mirth and their employments, and shall come   65
And make their bed with thee. As the long train
Of ages glides away, the sons of men,
The youth in life's fresh spring, and he who goes
In the full strength of years, matron and maid,
The speechless babe and the gray-headed man—   70
Shall one by one be gathered to thy side,
By those, who in their turn shall follow them.
        So live, that when thy summons comes to join
The innumerable caravan, which moves
To that mysterious realm, where each shall take   75
His chamber in the silent halls of death,
Thou go not like the quarry-slave at night,
Scourged to his dungeon, but, sustained and soothed
By an unfaltering trust, approach thy grave,
Like one who wraps the drapery of his couch   80
About him, and lies down to pleasant dreams.

                                                          1817

[3]A desert area of Libya.

To a Waterfowl

Whither, midst falling dew,
    While glow the heavens with the last steps of day,
Far, through their rosy depths, dost thou pursue
    Thy solitary way?

    Vainly the fowler's eye   5
Might mark thy distant flight to do thee wrong,
As, darkly painted on the crimson sky,
    Thy figure floats along.

    Seek'st thou the plashy brink
Of weedy lake, or marge of river wide,   10
Or where the rocking billows rise and sink
    On the chafed ocean-side?

    There is a Power whose care
Teaches thy way along that pathless coast—
The desert and illimitable air—   15
    Lone wandering, but not lost.

    All day thy wings have fanned,
At that far height, the cold, thin atmosphere,
Yet stoop not, weary, to the welcome land,
    Though the dark night is near.   20

    And soon that toil shall end;
Soon shalt thou find a summer home, and rest,
And scream among thy fellows; reeds shall bend,
    Soon, o'er thy sheltered nest.

    Thou'rt gone, the abyss of heaven   25
Hath swallowed up thy form; yet, on my heart
Deeply has sunk the lesson thou hast given,
    And shall not soon depart.

    He who, from zone to zone,
Guides through the boundless sky thy certain flight, 30
In the long way that I must tread alone,
    Will lead my steps aright.

                                 1815

To Cole, the Painter, Departing for Europe[1]

Thine eyes shall see the light of distant skies;
    Yet, COLE! thy heart shall bear to Europe's strand
    A living image of our own bright land,
Such as upon thy glorious canvas lies;
Lone lakes—savannas where the bison roves—   5
    Rocks rich with summer garlands—solemn streams—
    Skies, where the desert eagle wheels and screams—
Spring bloom and autumn blaze of boundless groves.
Fair scenes shall greet thee where thou goest—fair,
    But different—everywhere the trace of men,   10
    Paths, homes, graves, ruins, from the lowest glen
To where life shrinks from the fierce Alpine air.
    Gaze on them, till the tears shall dim thy sight,
    But keep that earlier, wilder image bright.

                                                      1829

To the Fringed Gentian

Thou blossom bright with autumn dew,
And colored with the heaven's own blue,
That openest when the quiet light
Succeeds the keen and frosty night.

Thou comest not when violets lean   5
O'er wandering brooks and springs unseen,
Or columbines, in purple dressed,
Nod o'er the ground-bird's hidden nest.

Thou waitest late and com'st alone,
When woods are bare and birds are flown,   10
And frosts and shortening days portend
The aged year is near his end.

Then doth thy sweet and quiet eye
Look through its fringes to the sky,
Blue—blue—as if that sky let fall   15
A flower from its cerulean wall.

I would that thus, when I shall see
The hour of death draw near to me,

[1]Thomas Cole, one of the Hudson River School of painters who, like his friend Bryant, was interested in presenting and preserving the beauties of the American landscape.

Hope, blossoming within my heart,
May look to heaven as I depart.   20

                                                                  1829

The Prairies

These are the gardens of the Desert, these
The unshorn fields, boundless and beautiful,
For which the speech of England has no name—[1]
The Prairies. I behold them for the first,
And my heart swells, while the dilated sight   5
Takes in the encircling vastness. Lo! they stretch,
In airy undulations, far away,
As if the ocean, in his gentlest swell,
Stood still, with all his rounded billows fixed,
And motionless forever.—Motionless?—   10
No—they are all unchained again. The clouds
Sweep over with their shadows, and, beneath,
The surface rolls and fluctuates to the eye;
Dark hollows seem to glide along and chase
The sunny ridges. Breezes of the South!   15
Who toss the golden and the flame-like flowers,
And pass the prairie-hawk that, poised on high,
Flaps his broad wings, yet moves not—ye have played
Among the palms of Mexico and vines
Of Texas, and have crisped the limpid brooks   20
That from the fountains of Sonora[2] glide
Into the calm Pacific—have ye fanned
A nobler or a lovelier scene than this?
Man hath no power in all this glorious work:
The hand that built the firmament hath heaved   25
And smoothed these verdant swells, and sown their slopes
With herbage, planted them with island groves,
And hedged them round with forests. Fitting floor
For this magnificent temple of the sky—
With flowers whose glory and whose multitude   30
Rival the constellations! The great heavens
Seem to stoop down upon the scene in love,—
A nearer vault, and of a tendered blue,
Than that which bends above our eastern hills.

          As o'er the verdant waste I guide my steed,   35
Among the high rank grass that sweeps his sides

[1]The term "prairie" is derived from the   [2]A state in northern Mexico.
French for meadow.

The hollow beating of his footstep seems
A sacrilegious sound. I think of those
Upon whose rest he tramples. Are they here—
The dead of other days?—and did the dust   40
Of these fair solitudes once stir with life
And burn with passion? Let the mighty mounds
That overlook the rivers, or that rise
In the dim forest crowded with old oaks,
Answer. A race, that long has passed away,   45
Built them;[3]—a disciplined and populous race
Heaped, with long toil, the earth, while yet the Greek
Was hewing the Pentelicus[4] to forms
Of symmetry, and rearing on its rock
The glittering Parthenon. These ample fields   50
Nourished their harvests, here their herds were fed,
When haply by their stalls the bison lowed,
And bowed his maned shoulder to the yoke.
All day this desert murmured with their toils,
Till twilight blushed, and lovers walked, and wooed   55
In a forgotten language, and old tunes,
From instruments of unremembered form,
Gave the soft winds a voice. The red man came—
The roaming hunter tribes, warlike and fierce,
And the mound-builders vanished from the earth.   60
The solitude of centuries untold
Has settled where they dwelt. The prairie-wolf
Hunts in their meadows, and his fresh-dug den
Yawns by my path. The gopher mines the ground
Where stood their swarming cities. All is gone;   65
All—save the piles of earth that hold their bones,
The platforms where they worshipped unknown gods,
The barriers which they builded from the soil
To keep the foe at bay—till o'er the walls
The wild beleaguerers broke, and, one by one,   70
The strongholds of the plain were forced, and heaped
With corpses. The brown vultures of the wood
Flocked to those vast uncovered sepulchres,
And sat unscared and silent at their feast.
Haply some solitary fugitive,   75
Lurking in marsh and forest, till the sense
Of desolation and of fear became
Bitterer than death, yielded himself to die.

[3]Such mounds, common to much of the Midwest, were erected for ceremonial or burial purposes. Bryant ascribes them to a race predating the Indians of the area.

[4]The mountain from which the Greeks quarried marble for structures like the Parthenon, the temple of the goddess Athena.

Man's better nature triumphed then. Kind words
Welcomed and soothed him; the rude conquerors   80
Seated the captive with their chiefs; he chose
A bride among their maidens, and at length
Seemed to forget—yet ne'er forgot—the wife
Of his first love, and her sweet little ones,
Butchered, amid their shrieks, with all his race.   85

   Thus change the forms of being. Thus arise
Races of living things, glorious in strength,
And perish, as the quickening breath of God
Fills them, or is withdrawn. The red man, too,
Has left the blooming wilds he ranged so long,   90
And, nearer to the Rocky Mountains, sought
A wilder hunting-ground. The beaver builds
No longer by these streams, but far away,
On waters whose blue surface ne'er gave back
The white man's face—among Missouri's springs,   95
And pools whose issues swell the Oregon—
He rears his little Venice. In these plains
The bison feeds no more. Twice twenty leagues
Beyond remotest smoke of hunter's camp,
Roams the majestic brute, in herds that shake   100
The earth with thundering steps—yet here I meet
His ancient footprints stamped beside the pool.

   Still this great solitude is quick with life.
Myriads of insects, gaudy as the flowers
They flutter over, gentle quadrupeds,   105
And birds, that scarce have learned the fear of man,
Are here, and sliding reptiles of the ground,
Startlingly beautiful. The graceful deer
Bounds to the wood at my approach. The bee,
A more adventurous colonist than man,   110
With whom he came across the eastern deep,
Fills the savannas with his murmurings,
And hides his sweets, as in the golden age,
Within the hollow oak. I listen long
To his domestic hum, and think I hear   115
The sound of that advancing multitude
Which soon shall fill these deserts. From the ground
Comes up the laugh of children, the soft voice
Of maidens, and the sweet and solemn hymn
Of Sabbath worshippers. The low of herds   120
Blends with the rustling of the heavy grain
Over the dark brown furrows. All at once

A fresher wind sweeps by, and breaks my dream,
And I am in the wilderness alone.

1832

Abraham Lincoln

Oh, slow to smite and swift to spare,
 Gentle and merciful and just!
Who, in the fear of God, didst bear
 The sword of power, a nation's trust!

In sorrow by thy bier we stand, 5
 Amid the awe that hushes all,
And speak the anguish of a land
 That shook with horror at thy fall.

Thy task is done; the bond are free:
 We bear thee to an honored grave, 10
Whose proudest monument shall be
 The broken fetters of the slave.

Pure was thy life; its bloody close
 Hath placed thee with the sons of light,
Among the noble host of those 15
 Who perished in the cause of Right.

1865

■ JANE JOHNSTON SCHOOLCRAFT (OJIBWE) ■
1800–1841

Jane Johnston Schoolcraft, the first known American Native literary writer,
wrote poetry and short fiction and translated songs from Ojibwe into English.
The daughter of an Ojibwe mother and an Irish father, she lived her daily life
speaking both Ojibwe and English. Her Ojibwe name was Bamewawagezhika-
quay, Woman of the Sound the Stars Make Rushing through the Sky. She was
born in 1800 in Sault Ste. Marie, in the upper peninsula of what is now Michigan, where two of her homes still stand, both listed on the National Register of
Historic Places. Schoolcraft's mother, Ozhaguscodaywayquay, grew up in what is
now northern Wisconsin and was the daughter of Waubojeeg, a famous war

chief and leader in civil life who was known for his eloquence in story and song. Schoolcraft's father, John Johnston, was an Irish fur trader.

The Sault was a center of Great Lakes Ojibwe culture. There were a few French-speaking whites, but the only English speakers were her father, her siblings, and the occasional British fur trader passing through. John Johnston was a book lover. Despite the high cost of books, and despite living in an area that to white people lay at the farthest reach of the frontier, he collected a huge library. He raised his children with a superb education in English and European literature, history, and theology, as Ozhaguscodaywayquay, who did not speak English, immersed the children in the traditions of Ojibwe song and storytelling.

Occasionally, young Jane traveled away from the Sault. In the fall of 1809, her father took her to Ireland and then to England. Returning home in the spring of 1810 along the St. Lawrence River, she felt a surge of emotion when she saw pine trees, which she had missed in Europe. Years later, as an adult, she recalled that feeling in "To the Pine Tree," which she wrote in Ojibwe and translated into English, varying the patterns of poetic repetition to suit the differences between the two languages. During the War of 1812, John fought with the British. For some reason, he brought Jane with him to Mackinac Island in 1814, when British forces, including John, repelled an American attack.

In 1820 a small American military force arrived at Sault Ste. Marie. The Americans pressed Ojibwe leaders to sign a treaty granting land for a fort. The Ojibwe leaders, still loyal to Great Britain, were reluctant to give up their lands and tempted to drive the Americans out, but Ozhaguscodaywayquay took the diplomatic initiative, calling the leaders together and convincing them to sign to avoid war. Although she may have prevented war, the treaty marked the beginning of a new American ascendancy that would change Jane Johnston's world.

In 1822 the Americans returned with a large force and a federal Indian agent, Henry Rowe Schoolcraft. The Johnstons, famous for their hospitality, took Henry in. He devoted himself to the study of Ojibwe language and culture, and in 1823 Jane and Henry married. Depending heavily on Jane and her family, Henry became one of the founding figures of American cultural anthropology. He gathered together the first large-scale collection of written-down and translated Native American stories, which he published in 1837 under the title *Algic Researches*. Though Henry minimized his acknowledgment of specific Native collaborators, the surviving manuscripts show that Jane wrote some of the stories. She probably varied in how much she gave traditional stories the stamp of her own personality and style, much as oral storytellers blend their own styles with other styles they have heard before. Henry Wadsworth Longfellow based *The Song of Hiawatha* (1855), the most famous American poem of the nineteenth century, on Henry's work and often on stories written by Jane, but until the recent publication of her work, her role has barely been recognized.

In marrying Henry, Jane Schoolcraft married into American federal and colonialist authority, yet she also held firmly to Ojibwe language and culture. In an early version of "The Contrast," written after Henry's arrival and before their marriage, she writes about the contrast between her happy childhood and the fearful emotions of falling in love. In a later version, included here, she contrasts her happy childhood to her mixed feelings about the onset of American colonialism, with the troops raising their flag each morning at the federal fort just outside her window. In a sense, the topic of both versions is the same, for Henry was both the object of her love and the official representative of the federal government.

Schoolcraft's earliest dated poem comes from 1815. After her two-year-old son, William Henry, died suddenly in 1827, she wrote at least five poems in his memory, including "To My Ever Beloved and Lamented Son William Henry." Though she usually wrote in English, she returned to writing in Ojibwe for poems about a small island in Lake Superior ("Lines Written at Castle Island") and about the pain of leaving her children at a boarding school. The boarding school poem carries special meaning for Native American history, because well into the twentieth century Native children were often forcibly taken from their families and sent to boarding schools where they were forbidden to speak their language and were often beaten and abused. Jane Schoolcraft did not leave an English translation of the boarding school poem, but Henry wrote what he called a "loose translation" in rhyme and meter, several times longer than the Ojibwe original or the new translation provided here. The two English versions of the boarding school poem provide an historical perspective on differences in aesthetic taste and poetic style between Schoolcraft's time and our own. Whereas readers today often look on rhyme and meter with distaste, in Schoolcraft's time readers expected rhyme and meter and would have looked with perplexity at the understated, more literal translation, which sounds more like a work of modern poetry.

In 1833 Jane Schoolcraft and her family moved to Mackinac Island, and in 1841, when Henry lost his position as Indian agent, they moved to New York City. Jane Schoolcraft died in 1842. Unrecognized in her lifetime except by friends and family, her now newly available writings offer a window onto a highly literate Native world that invites us to reenvision the cultural memory of early America.

Robert Dale Parker
University of Illinois at Urbana-Champaign

PRIMARY WORKS

The Sound the Stars Make Rushing through the Sky: The Writings of Jane Johnston Schoolcraft, Robert Dale Parker, ed., 2007; Mrs. (Anna Brownell) Jameson, *Winter Studies and Summer Rambles in Canada*, 3 vols. (London: Saunders and Otley, 1838).

SECONDARY WORKS

Robert Dale Parker, "Introduction: The World and Writings of Jane Johnston Schoolcraft." *The Sound the Stars Make Rushing through the Sky: The Writings of Jane Johnston Schoolcraft*, Robert Dale Parker, ed., 2007.

To the Pine Tree

on first seeing it
on returning from Europe

Shing wauk! Shing wauk! nin ge ik id,
Waish kee wau bum ug, shing wauk

Tuh quish in aun nau aub, ain dak nuk i yaun.
Shing wauk, shing wauk No sa
Shi e gwuh ke do dis au naun   5
Kau gega way zhau wus co zid.

Mes ah nah, shi egwuh tah gwish en aung
Sin da mik ke aum baun
Kag ait suh, ne meen wain dum
Me nah wau, wau bun dah maun   10
Gi yut wi au, wau bun dah maun een
Shing wauk, shing wauk nosa
Shi e gwuh ke do dis au naun.

Ka ween ga go, kau wau bun duh e yun
Tib isht co, izz henau gooz ze no an   15
Shing wauk wah zhau wush co zid
Ween Ait ah kwanaudj e we we
Kau ge gay wa zhau soush ko zid

Translation

The pine! the pine! I eager cried,
The pine, my father! see it stand,
As first that cherished tree I spied,
Returning to my native land.
The pine! the pine! oh lovely scene!   5
The pine, that is forever green.

Ah beauteous tree! ah happy sight!
That greets me on my native strand
And hails me, with a friend's delight,
To my own dear bright mother land   10
Oh 'tis to me a heart-sweet scene,
The pine—the pine! that's ever green.

Not all the trees of England bright,
Not Erin's lawns of green and light
Are half so sweet to memory's eye,   15
As this dear type of northern sky
Oh 'tis to me a heart-sweet scene,
The pine—the pine! that ever green.

unknown

Lines Written at Castle Island, Lake Superior[1]

Here in my native inland sea
From pain and sickness would I flee
And from its shores and island bright
Gather a store of sweet delight.
Lone island of the saltless sea!   5
How wide, how sweet, how fresh and free
How all transporting—is the view
Of rocks and skies and waters blue
Uniting, as a song's sweet strains
To tell, here nature only reigns.   10
Ah, nature! here forever sway
Far from the haunts of men away
For here, there are no sordid fears,
No crimes, no misery, no tears
No pride of wealth; the heart to fill,   15
No laws to treat my people ill.[2]

                                                     1838

Invocation

To my Maternal Grand-father on hearing his descent from Chippewa
ancestors misrepresented[1]

Rise bravest chief! of the mark of the noble deer,[2]
  With eagle glance,
  Resume thy lance,
And wield again thy warlike spear!
  The foes of thy line,   5
  With coward design,
Have dared with black envy to garble the truth,
And stain with a falsehood thy valorous youth.

They say when a child, thou wert ta'en from the Sioux,[3]
  And with impotent aim,   10
  To lessen thy fame

[1]A translation, by Jane Schoolcraft and/or her
husband Henry Schoolcraft, of a poem in
Ojibwe by Jane Schoolcraft. The Ojibwe version has not survived. Castle Island was
Schoolcraft's name for a small volcanic island
in Lake Superior near the present Marquette,
Michigan (not the same island called Castle
Island today). Schoolcraft traveled out onto
Lake Superior in the summer of 1838, hoping that the trip would aid her failing health.
[2]Referring partly to treaties between Native
nations and the United States government.

[1]The terms *Chippewa*, *Ojibwe*, and *Anishinaabe*
all refer to the same American Indian people
and language.
[2]The totem, or clan, of Schoolcraft's grandfather, Waubojeeg, was the reindeer.
[3]Waubojeeg had two Sioux half-brothers, but
the Sioux and the Ojibwe were traditional
enemies, especially as white settlers pressed
westward and left Ojibwe and Sioux people
to compete for shrinking territory.

Thy warlike lineage basely abuse;
 For they know that our band,
 Tread a far distant land,
And thou noble chieftain art nerveless and dead,   15
Thy bow all unstrung, and thy proud spirit fled.

Can the sports of thy youth, or thy deeds ever fade?
 Or those e'er forget,
 Who are mortal men yet,
The scenes where so bravely thou'st lifted the blade,   20
 Who have fought by thy side,
 And remember thy pride,
When rushing to battle, with valour and ire,
Thou saw'st the fell foes of thy nation expire?

Can the warrior forget how sublimely you rose?   25
 Like a star in the west,
 When the sun's sunk to rest,
That shines in bright splendour to dazzle our foes?
 Thy arm and thy yell,
 Once the tale could repel   30
Which slander invented, and minions detail,
And still shall thy actions refute the false tale.

Rest thou, noblest chief! in thy dark house of clay,
 Thy deeds and thy name,
 Thy child's child shall proclaim,   35
And make the dark forests resound with the lay;
 Though thy spirit has fled,
 To the hills of the dead,
Yet thy name shall be held in my heart's warmest core,
And cherish'd till valour and love be no more.   40

             1823

By an *Ojibwa Female* Pen: Invitation to Sisters to a Walk in the Garden, after a Shower

Come, sisters come! the shower's past,
The garden walks are drying fast,
The Sun's bright beams are seen again,
And nought[1] within, can now detain.
The rain drops tremble on the leaves,   5
Or drip expiring, from the eaves;

---

[1]Naught.

But soon the cool and balmy air,
Shall dry the gems that sparkle there,
With whisp'ring breath shake ev'ry spray,
And scatter every cloud away.   10

Thus sisters! shall the breeze of hope,
Through sorrow's clouds a vista ope;
Thus, shall affliction's surly blast,
By faith's bright calm be still'd at last;
Thus, pain and care,—the tear and sigh,   15
Be chased from every dewy eye;
And life's mix'd scene itself, but cease,
To show us realms of light and peace.

1826

The Contrast

With pen in hand, I shall contrast,
The present moments with the past
And mark difference, not by grains,
But weighed by feelings, joys and pains.
Calm, tranquil—far from fashion's gaze,   5
Passed all my earliest, happy days
Sweetly flew the golden hours,
In St. Mary's woodland bowers[1]
Or my father's simple hall,
Oped to whomsoe'er might call   10
Pains or cares we seldom knew
All the hours so peaceful flew
Concerts sweet we oft enjoyed,
Books our leisure time employed
Friends on every side appeared   15
From whose minds no ill I feared
If by chance, one gave me pain
The wish to wound me not again
Quick expressed in accents kind
Cast a joy throughout my mind   20
That, to have been a moment pained,
Seemed like bliss but just attained.
Whene'er in fault, to be reproved,

---

[1]Schoolcraft grew up along the St. Mary's River, which divides Sault Ste. Marie in the United States from Sault Ste. Marie in Canada.

With gratitude my heart was moved,
So mild and gentle were their words   25
It seemed as soft as song of birds
For well I knew, that each behest,
Was warmed by love—convincing test.

Thus passed the morning of my days,
My only wish, to gain the praise   30
Of friends I loved, and neighbours kind,
And keep a calm and heavenly mind.
My efforts, kindly were received,
Nor grieved, nor was myself aggrieved.
But ah! how changed is every scene,   35
Our little hamlet, and the green,
The long rich green, where warriors played,
And often, breezy elm-wood shade.
How changed, since full of strife and fear,
The world hath sent its votaries here.   40
The tree cut down—the cot removed,
The cot the simple Indian loved,
The busy strife of young and old
To gain one sordid bit of gold
By trade's o'er done plethoric moil,   45
And lawsuits, meetings, courts and toil.

Adieu, to days of homebred ease,
When many a rural care could please,
We trim our sail anew, to steer
By shoals we never knew were here,   50
And with the star flag, raised on high
Discover a new dominion nigh,
And half in joy, half in fear,
Welcome the proud Republic here.

                                                           1823

To My Ever Beloved and Lamented Son William Henry

Who was it, nestled on my breast,
"And on my cheek sweet kisses prest"[1]

---

[1]This line directly quotes line 3 of the once famous "My Mother" by Ann Taylor (1782–1866). In Taylor's poem, a child addresses its mother and the refrain is "My mother." In Schoolcraft's poem, by contrast, a mother addresses her child and the refrain is "My Willy."

And in whose smile I felt so blest?
> Sweet Willy.

Who hail'd my form as home I stept,   5
And in my arms so eager leapt,
And to my bosom joyous crept?
> My Willy.

Who was it, wiped my tearful eye,
And kiss'd away the coming sigh,   10
And smiling bid me say "good boy"?
> Sweet Willy.

Who was it, looked divinely fair,
Whilst lisping sweet the evening pray'r,
Guileless and free from earthly care?   15
> My Willy.

Where is that voice attuned to love,
That bid me say "my darling dove"?
But oh! that soul has flown above,
> Sweet Willy.   20

Whither has fled the rose's hue?
The lilly's whiteness blending grew,
Upon thy cheek—so fair to view.
> My Willy.

Oft have I gaz'd with rapt delight,   25
Upon those eyes that sparkled bright,
Emitting beams of joy and light!
> Sweet Willy.

Oft have I kiss'd that forehead high,
Like polished marble to the eye,   30
And blessing, breathed an anxious sigh.
> For Willy.

My son! thy coral lips are pale,
Can I believe the heart-sick tale,
That I, thy loss must ever wail?   35
> My Willy.

The clouds in darkness seemed to low'r,
The storm has past with awful pow'r,
And nipt my tender, beauteous flow'r!
> Sweet Willy.   40

But soon my spirit will be free,
And I, my lovely Son shall see,
For God, I know, did this decree!
> My Willy.

1827

On Leaving My Children John and Jane at School, in the Atlantic States, and Preparing to Return to the Interior[1]

Nyau nin de nain dum
May kow e yaun in
Ain dah nuk ki yaun
Waus sa wa kom eg
Ain dah nuk ki yaun   5

Ne dau nis ainse e
Ne gwis is ainse e
Ishe nau gun ug wau
Waus sa wa kom eg

She gwau go sha ween   10
Ba sho waud e we
Nin zhe ka we yea
Ishe ez hau jau yaun
Ain dah nuk ke yaun

Ain dah nuk ke yaun   15
Nin zhe ke we yea
Ishe ke way aun e
Nyau ne gush kain dum

1839

Free Translation[2]

Ah! when thought reverts to my country so dear,
My heart fills with pleasure, and throbs with a fear:
My country, my country, my own native land,
So lovely in aspect, in features so grand,
Far, far in the West. What are cities to me,   5
Oh! land of my mother, compared unto thee?

Fair land of the lakes! thou are blest to my sight,
With thy beaming bright waters, and landscapes of light;
The breeze and the murmur, the dash and the roar,
That summer and autumn cast over the shore,   10
They spring to my thoughts, like the lullaby tongue,
That soothed me to slumber when youthful and young.

[1]Henry Schoolcraft decided to leave his and Jane Schoolcraft's daughter Janee (age eleven) and son Johnston (age nine) at boarding schools, where he thought they would get a better education. Jane Schoolcraft objected, but she deferred to Henry's judgment.
[2]This free translation is by Henry Rowe Schoolcraft.

One feeling more strongly still binds me to thee,
There roved my forefathers, in liberty free—
There shook they the war lance, and sported the plume,   15
Ere Europe had cast o'er this country a gloom;
Nor thought they that kingdoms more happy could be,
White lords of a land so resplendent and free.

Yet it is not alone that my country is fair,
And my home and my friends are inviting me there;   20
While they beckon me onward, my heart is still here,
With my sweet lovely daughter, and bonny boy dear:
And oh! what's the joy that a home can impart,
Removed from the dear ones who cling to my heart.

It is learning that calls them; but tell me, can schools   25
Repay for my love, or give nature new rules?
They may teach them the lore of the wit and the sage,
To be grave in their youth, and be gay in their age;
But ah! my poor heart, what are schools to thy view,
While severed from children thou lovest so true!   30

I return to my country, I haste on my way,
For duty commands me, and duty must sway;
Yet I leave the bright land where my little ones dwell,
With a sober regret, and a bitter farewell;
For there I must leave the dear jewels I love,   35
The dearest of gifts from my Master above.

New York, March 18th, 1839.

New Translation[3]

As I am thinking
When I find you
My land
Far in the west
My land   5

My little daughter
My little son
I leave them behind
Far away land

[3]This 2005 translation is by Dennis Jones,
Heidi Stark, and James Vukelich.

[emphatically] But soon 10
It is close however
To my home I shall return
That is the way that I am, my being
My land

My land 15
To my home I shall return
I begin to make my way home
Ahh but I am sad

2005

Moowis, the Indian Coquette[1]

There was a village full of Indians, and a noted belle or *muh muh daw go qua* was living there. A noted beau or *muh muh daw go, nin nie* was there also. He and another young man went to court this young woman, and laid down beside her, when she scratched the face of the handsome beau. He went home and would not rise till the family prepared to depart, and he would not then arise. They then left him, as he felt ashamed to be seen even by his own relations. It was winter, and the young man, his rival, who was his cousin, tried all he could to persuade him to go with the family, for it was now winter, but to no purpose, till the whole village had decamped and had gone away. He then rose and gathered all the bits of clothing, and ornaments of beads and other things, that had been left. He then made a coat and leggins of the same, nicely trimmed with the beads, and the suit was fine and complete. After making a pair of moccasins, nicely trimmed, he also made a bow and arrows. He then collected the dirt of the village, and filled the garments he had made, so as to appear as a man, and put the bow and arrows in its hands, and it came to life. He then desired the dirt image to follow him to the camp of those who had left him, who thinking him dead by this time, were surprized to see him. One of the neighbors took in the dirt-man and entertained him. The belle saw them come and immediately fell in love with him. The family that took him in made a large fire to warm him, as it was winter. The image said to one of the children, "sit between me and the fire, it is too hot," and the child did so, but all smelt the dirt. Some said, "some one has trod on, and brought in dirt." The master of the family said to the child sitting in front of the guest, "get away from before our guest, you keep the heat from him." The boy answered saying, "he told me to sit between him and the fire." In the meantime, the belle wished the stranger would visit her. The image went to his master, and they went out to

---

[1]Reprinted from *The Sound the Stars Make Rushing through the Sky: The Writings of Jane Johnston Schoolcraft.* The source is a handwritten, unpublished magazine edited by Henry Schoolcraft in 1826 and 1827 and called *The Muzzeniegun or Literary Voyager* (*Muzzeniegun* is Ojibwe for "book" or "magazine"). The manuscript is in Henry Schoolcraft's papers in the Library of Congress. In Ojibwe, *moowis* is a derogatory and offensive term referring to filth or excrement.

different lodges, the image going as directed to the belle[']s. Towards morning, the image said to the young woman (as he had succeeded) "I must now go away," but she said, "I will go with you." He said "it is too far." She answered, "it is not so far but that I can go with you." He first went to the lodge where he was entertained, and then to his master, and told him of all that had happened, and that he was going off with her. The young man thought it a pity she had treated him so, and how sadly she would be punished. They went off, she following behind. He left her a great way behind, but she continued to follow him. When the sun rose high, she found one of his mittens and picked it up, but to her astonishment, found it full of dirt. She, however took it up and wiped it, and going on further, she found the other mitten in the same condition. She thought, "fie!! why does he do so," thinking he dirtied in them. She kept finding different articles of his dress, on the way all day, in the same condition. He kept ahead of her till towards evening, when the snow was like water, having melted by the heat of the day. No signs of her husband appearing, after having collected all the cloth[e]s that held him together, she began to cry, not knowing where to go, as their track was lost, on account of the snow's melting. She kept crying *Moowis* has led me astray, and she kept singing and crying Moowis nin ge won e win ig, ne won e win ig.[2]

1827

Mishösha, or the Magician and His Daughters: A Chippewa Tale or Legend[1]

In an early age of the world, when there were fewer inhabitants in the earth than there now are, there lived an Indian, who had a wife and two children, in a remote situation. Buried in the solitude of the forest, it was not often that he saw any one, out of the circle of his own family. Such a situation seemed favorable for his pursuits; and his life passed on in uninterrupted happiness, till he discovered a wanton disposition in his wife.

This woman secretly cherished a passion for a young man whom she accidentally met in the woods, and she lost no opportunity of courting his approaches. She even planned the death of her husband, who, she justly concluded, would put her to death, should he discover her infidelity. But this design was frustrated by the alertness of the husband, who having

[2]You have led me astray—you are leading me astray. Drawing on a version of "Moowis" that Henry Schoolcraft revised and included in *Algic Researches*, Henry Wadsworth Longfellow retells the story in his famous poem *Evangeline* (1847).

[1]Reprinted from *The Sound the Stars Make Rushing through the Sky: The Writings of Jane Johnston Schoolcraft*. The source for the first half of the story is a handwritten, unpublished magazine edited by Henry Schoolcraft in 1826 and 1827 and called *The Muzzenie-* gun or *Literary Voyager* (*Muzzeniegun* is Ojibwe for "book" or "magazine"). The second half probably appeared in a lost issue of the same magazine. The manuscript in *The Literary Voyager* (as it was usually called) is followed here because Jane Schoolcraft probably approved that copy of the story. The second half comes from a copy made by Jane Schoolcraft's brother William. Both manuscripts are in Henry Schoolcraft's papers in the Library of Congress.

cause to suspect her, determined to watch narrowly, to ascertain the truth, before he should come to a determination how to act. He followed her silently one day, at a distance, and hid himself behind a tree. He soon beheld a tall, handsome man approach his wife, and lead her away.

He was now convinced of her crime, and thought of killing her, the moment she returned. In the meantime he went home, and pondered on his situation. At last he came to the determination of leaving her forever, thinking that her own conscience would, in the end, punish her sufficiently; and relying on her maternal feelings, to take care of the two boys, whom he determined to leave behind.

When the wife returned, she was disappointed in not finding her husband, having concerted a plan to dispatch him. When she saw that day after day passed, and he did not return, she at last guessed the true cause of his absence. She then returned to her paramour, leaving the two helpless boys behind, telling them that she was going a short distance, and would return; but determined never to see them more.

The children thus abandoned, soon made way with the food that was left in the lodge, and were compelled to quit it, in search of more. The eldest boy possessed much intrepidity, as well as great tenderness for his little brother, frequently carrying him when he became weary, and gathering all the wild fruit he saw. Thus they went deeper into the forest, soon losing all traces of their former habitation, till they were completely lost in the labyrinths of the wilderness.

The elder boy fortunately had a knife, with which he made a bow and arrows, and was thus enabled to kill a few birds for himself and brother. In this way they lived some time, still pressing on, they knew not whither. At last they saw an opening through the woods, and were shortly after delighted to find themselves on the borders of a broad lake. Here the elder boy busied himself in picking the seed pods of the wild rose. In the meanwhile the younger, amused himself by shooting some arrows into the sand, one of which, happened to fall into the lake. The elder brother, not willing to lose his time in making another, waded into the water to reach it. Just as he was about to grasp the arrow, a canoe passed by him with the rapidity of lightning. An old man, sitting in the centre, seized the affrighted youth, and placed him in the canoe. In vain the boy addressed him. "My grandfather" (a term of respect for old people) "pray take my little brother also. Alone, I cannot go with you; he will starve if I leave him." The old magician (for such was his real character) laughed at him. Then giving his canoe a slap, and commanding it to go, it glided through the water with inconceivable swiftness. In a few minutes they reached the habitation of Mishosha, standing on an island in the centre of the lake. Here he lived, with his two daughters, the terror of all the surrounding country.

Leading the young man up to the lodge "Here my eldest daughter," said he, "I have brought a young man who shall become your husband." The youth saw surprize depicted in the countenance of the daughter, but she made no reply, seeming thereby to acquiesce in the commands of her father. In the evening he overheard the daughters in conversation. "There again":

said the elder daughter, "our father has brought another victim, under the pretence of giving me a husband. When will his enmity to the human race cease; or when shall we be spared witnessing such scenes of vice and wickedness, as we are daily compelled to behold."

When the old magician was asleep, the youth told the elder daughter, how he had been carried off, and compelled to leave his helpless brother on the shore. She told him to get up and take her father's canoe, and using the charm he had observed, it would carry him quickly to his brother. That he could carry him food, prepare a lodge for him, and return by morning. He did in every thing as he had been directed, and after providing for the subsistence of his brother, told him that in a short time he should come for him. Then returning to the enchanted island, resumed his place in the lodge before the magician awoke. Once during the night Mishosha awoke, and not seeing his son in law, asked his eldest daughter what had become of him. She replied that he had merely stepped out, and would be back soon. This satisfied him. In the morning, finding the young man in the lodge, his suspicions were completely lulled. "I see, my daughter, you have told me the truth."

As soon as the sun rose, Mishosha thus addressed the young man. "Come, my son, I have a mind to gather gulls eggs. I am acquainted with an island where there are great quantities; and I wish your aid in gathering them." The young man, saw no reasonable excuse, and getting into the canoe, the magician gave it a slap, and bidding it go, in an instant they were at the island. They found the shore covered with gulls eggs, and the island surrounded with birds of this kind. "Go, my son," said the old man, "and gather them, while I remain in the canoe." But the young man was no sooner ashore than Mishosha pushed his canoe a little from land and exclaimed: "Listen ye gulls: you have long expected something from me. I now give you an offering. Fly down, and devour him." Then striking his canoe, left the young man to his fate.

The birds immediately came in clouds around their victim, darkening all the air with their numbers. But the youth, seizing the first that came near him, and drawing his knife, cut off its head, and immediately skinning the bird, hung the feathers as a trophy on his breast. "Thus," he exclaimed, "will I treat every one of you who approaches me. Forbear, therefore, and listen to my words. It is not for you to eat human food. You have been given by the Great Spirit as food for man. Neither is it in the power of that old magician to do you any good. Take me on your beaks and carry me to his lodge, and you shall see that I am not ungrateful."

The gulls obeyed, collecting in a cloud for him to rest upon, and quickly flew to the lodge, where they arrived before the magician. The daughters were surprized at his return, but Mishosha conducted as if nothing extraordinary had taken place.

On the following day he again addressed the youth. "Come, my son," said he. "I will take you to an island covered with the most beautiful pebbles, looking like silver. I wish you to assist me in gathering some of them. They will make handsome ornaments, and are possessed of great virtues." Entering the canoe, the magician made use of his charm, and they were carried, in a few moments, to a solitary bay in an island, where there was a smooth sandy beach. The young man went ashore as usual. "A little further, a little further," cried the old man. "Up on that rock you will get some finer ones." Then pushing his canoe from land, "Come thou great king of fishes," cried he, "you have long expected an offering from me. Come, and eat the stranger I have put ashore on your island." So saying, he commanded his canoe to return, and was soon out of sight. Immediately a monstrous fish shoved his long snout from the water, moving partially on the beach, and opening wide his jaws to receive his victim.

"When" exclaimed the young man, drawing his knife, and placing himself in a threatening attitude, "when did you ever taste human food. Have a care of yourself. You were given by the Great Spirit to man, and if you, or any of your tribes, taste human flesh, you will fall sick and die. Listen not to the words of that wicked old man, but carry me back to his island, in return for which, I shall present you a piece of red cloth."

The fish complied, raising his back out of water to allow the young man to get on. Then taking his way through the lake, landed his charge safely at the island, before the return of the magician.

The daughters were still more surprized to see him thus escaped a second time, from the arts of their father. But the old man maintained his taciturnity. He could not, however, help saying to himself. "What manner of boy is this, who ever escapes from my power. His spirit shall not however save him. I will entrap him tomorrow. Ha! ha! ha!"

The next day the magician addressed the young man as follows "Come, my son," said he "you must go with me to procure some young eagles. I wish to tame them. I have discovered an island where they exist in great abundance." When they had reached the island, Mishosha led him inland till they came to the foot of a tall pine, upon which the nests were. "Now, my son[,]" said he[, "]climb up this tree, and bring down the birds." The young man obeyed, and when he had with great effort, got up near the nests—"Now," exclaimed the magician, addressing the tree "stretch yourself up, and be very tall." The tree rose up at the command. "Listen ye eagles[,"] continued the old man, "you have long expected a gift from me. I now present you this boy who has had the presumption to molest your young. Stretch forth your claws, and seize him." So saying he left the young man to his fate, and returned.

But the intrepid youth, drawing his knife, and cutting off the head of the first eagle that menaced him, raised his voice and exclaimed—"Thus will I deal with all who come near me. What right have you, ye ravenous birds, to eat living flesh[?] Is it because that old cowardly old magician has bid you do so? He is an old woman. He can neither do you good nor harm. See! I have already slain one of your number[.] Respect my bravery, and carry me back to the lodge of the old man, that I may show you how I shall treat him."

The eagles, pleased with the spirit of the young man, assented, and clustering around him, formed a seat with their backs, and flew towards the enchanted Island. As they crossed the water they passed the magician lying half asleep in his canoe and treated him with great indignity.

The return of the young man was hailed with joy by the daughters, but excited the ire of the magician, who taxed his wits for some new mode of ridding himself of a youth so powerful[ly] aided by his spirit. He therefore invited him to go a hunting. Taking his canoe, they proceeded to an island, and built a lodge to shelter themselves during the night. In the meantime, the magician caused a deep fall of snow and a storm of wind with severe cold.

According to custom the young man pulled off his moccasins and leggons, and hung them before the fire. After he had gone to sleep, the magician, watching his opportunity, got up, and taking one moccasin and one leggon, threw them into the fire. He then went to sleep. In the morning, stretching himself as he arose, and uttering an exclamation of surprize, he exclaimed "My son, what has become of your moccasin and leggon? I believe this is the moon in which fire attracts, and I fear they have been drawn in.["] The young man suspected the true cause of his loss, and rightly attributed it, to a design of the magician to freeze him to death on their march. But he maintained the strictest silence, and drawing his blanket over his head, thus communed with himself. "I have full faith in my spirit, who has preserved me thus far, and I do not fear that he will now forsake me. Great is the power of my Manito; and he shall prevail against this wicked old enemy of mankind."

Then drawing on the remaining moccasin and leggon, he took a coal from the fire and invoking his spirit to give it efficacy, blackened the foot and leg as far as the lost garment usually reached. Then rising announced himself ready for the march. In vain the magician led him snow and over morasses, hoping to see the lad sink at every moment. But in this he was disappointed, and they, for the first time returned home together.

Taking courage from this the young man now determined to try his own power, having previously consulted with the daughters. They all agreed that the life the old man led was detestable, and that whoever would rid the world of him, would entitle himself to the thanks of the human race. On the following day the young man thus addressed the magician. "My grandfather, I have often gone with you on perilous excursions, and never murmured. I must now request that you will accompany me, I wish to visit my little brother, and to bring him home with me.["] They accordingly went on a visit to the main land and found the little lad in the spot where he had been left. After taking him into the canoe, the young man again addressed the magician "My grandfather, will you go and cut me a few of those red willows on the bank. I wish to prepare some smoking mixture." ["]Certainly, my son," replied the old man "What you wish, is not very hard. Ha! ha! ha! do you think me too old to get up there[?]"

No sooner was the magician ashore, than the young man placing himself in the proper position, struck the canoe and repeated the charm N'*chimaun Pall*. And immediately the canoe flew through the water on its passage to the island. It was evening when the two brothers arrived; but the elder daughter informed the young man, that unless he sat up and watched the canoe and kept his hand upon it, such was the power of their father it would slip off and return to him. The young man watched faithfully till near the dawn of day, when he could no longer resist the drowsiness which oppressed him and suffered himself to nod, for a moment. In an instant the canoe slipped off, and sought its master, who soon returned in high glee; "Ha! ha! ha! my son," said he; "you thought to play me a trick; it was very clever; but you see I am too old for you."

A short time after, the youth again addressed the magician[. "]My grandfather, I wish to try my skill in hunting. It is said there is plenty of game on an island not far off and I have to request that you will take me there in your canoe." They accordingly spent the day in hunting, and night coming on, they put up a temporary lodge. When the magician had sunk into a profound sleep, the young man got up, and taking a moccasin and leggon of Mishosha's from the place where they hung before the fire, threw them in; thus retaliating the artifice before played upon himself. He had discovered by some secret means, that the foot and leg were the only assailable parts of the magician's body; which could not be guarded by the spirits who served him and treated him with great indignity.

The return of the young man was hailed with joy by the daughters[.] He then besought his Manito, to cause a storm of snow, with cold wind and icy sleet, and then laid himself down beside the old man. Consternation was depicted in the countenance of the latter, when he awoke in the morning and found his moccasin and leggon missing. "I believe, my grandfather,["] said the young man, "that this is the moon in which fire attracts, and I fear your clothes have been drawn in." Then rising and bidding the old man follow, he began the morning's hunt, frequently he turned his head to see how Mishosha kept up. He saw him faultering at every step and almost benumbed with cold. But encouraged him to follow, saying we shall soon be through and reach the shore. But still leading him round about ways; to let the frost take complete effect. At length the old man reached the brink of the island, where the woods are succeeded by a border of smooth sand. But he could go no further; his legs became stiff and refused all motion, and he found himself fixed to the spot, but he still kept stretching out his arms and swinging his body to and fro. Every moment he found the numbness creeping higher he felt his legs growing downwards like roots, the feathers on his head turned to leaves, and in a few seconds he stood a tall and stiff sycamore, leaning towards the water.

The young man getting into the canoe, and pronouncing the charm, was soon transported to the island, where he related his victory to the daughters. They applauded the deed, agreed to put on mortal shapes, become wives to the young men, and forever quit the enchanted island. They immediately passed over to the main land, where they lived in happiness and Peace.

1827

The Forsaken Brother: A Chippewa Tale[1]

It was a fine summer evening; the sun was scarcely an hour high,—its departing rays beamed through the foliage of the tall, stately elms, that skirted the little green knoll, on which a solitary Indian lodge stood. The deep silence that reigned in this sequestered and romantic spot, seemed to most of the inmates of that lonely hut, like the long sleep of death, that now evidently fast sealing the eyes of the head of this poor family. His low breathing was answered by the sighs of his disconsolate wife and their children. Two of the latter were almost grown up, one was yet a mere child. These were the only human beings near the dying man. The door of the lodge was thrown open to admit the refreshing breeze of the lake, on the banks of which it stood; and as the cool air fanned the head of the poor man, he felt a momentary return of strength, and raising himself a little, he thus addressed his weeping family. "I leave you—thou, who hast been my partner in life, but you will not stay long behind me—You shall soon join me in the happy land of Spirits. Therefore you have not long to suffer in this world. But oh! my children, my poor children! you have just commenced life, and mark me, unkindness, and ingratitude, and every wickedness is in the scene before you. I left my kindred and my tribe, because I found what I have just warned you of. I have contented myself with the company of your mother and yourselves, for many years, and you will find my motives for separating from the haunts of men, were solicitude and anxiety to preserve you from the bad examples you would inevitably have followed. But I shall die content, if you, my children promise me, to cherish each other, and on no account to forsake your youngest brother; of him I give you both particular charge." The man became exhausted, and taking a hand to each of his eldest children, he continued—"My daughter! never forsake your little brother. My son, never forsake your little brother." "Never, never!" they both exclaimed. "Never—never!" repeated the father and expired.

The poor man died happy, because he thought his commands would be obeyed. The sun sank below the trees, and left a golden sky behind, which the family were wont to admire, but no one heeded it now. The lodge that was so still an hour before, was now filled with low and unavailing lamentations. Time wore heavily away—five long moons had passed and the sixth was nearly full, when the mother also died. In her last moments she pressed the fulfilment of their promise to their departed father. They readily renewed their promise, because they were yet free from any selfish motive. The winter passed away, and the beauties of spring cheered the drooping spirits of the bereft little family. The girl, being the eldest, dictated to her brothers, and seemed to feel a tender and sisterly affection for the youngest, who was

[1]Reprinted from *The Sound the Stars Make Rushing through the Sky: The Writings of Jane Johnston Schoolcraft*. The source is a handwritten, unpublished magazine edited by Henry Schoolcraft in 1826 and 1827 and called *The Muzzeniegun or Literary Voyager* (*Muzzeniegun* is Ojibwe for "book" or "magazine"). The manuscript is in Henry Schoolcraft's papers in the Library of Congress.

rather sickly and delicate. The other boy soon showed symptoms of restless-ness, and addressed the sister as follows: "My sister, are we always to live as if there were no other human beings in the world[?] Must I deprive myself the pleasure of associating with my own kind? I shall seek the villages of men; I have determined, and you cannot prevent me." The girl replied. "My brother, I do not say no to what you desire. We were not prohibited the soci-ety of our fellow mortals, but we were told to cherish each other, and that we should do nothing independent of each other—that neither pleasure nor pain ought ever to separate us, particularly from our helpless brother. If we follow our separate gratifications, it will surely make us forget *him* whom we are alike bound to support." The young man made no answer, but taking his bow and arrows left the lodge, and never returned.

Many moons had come and gone, after the young man's departure, and still the girl administered to the wants of her younger brother. At length, how-ever, she began to be weary of her solitude, and of her charge. Years, which added to her strength and capability of directing the affairs of the household, also brought with them the desire of society, and made her solitude irksome. But in meditating a change of life, she thought only for herself, and cruelly sought to abandon her little brother, as her elder brother had done before.

One day after she had collected all the provisions she had set apart for emergencies, and brought a quantity of wood to the door, she said to her brother. "My brother, you must not stray far from the lodge. I am going to seek our brother: I shall soon be back." Then taking her bundle, she set off, in search of habitations. She soon found them, and was so much taken up with the pleasures and amusements of society, that all affection for her brother was obliterated. She accepted a proposal of marriage, and after that, never more thought of the helpless relative she had abandoned.

In the meantime the elder brother had also married, and settled on the shores of the same lake, which contained the bones of his parents, and the abode of his forsaken brother.

As soon as the little boy had eaten all the food left by his sister, he was obliged to pick berries and dig up roots. Winter came on, and the poor child was exposed to all its rigors. He was obliged to quit the lodge in search of food, without a shelter. Sometimes he passed the night in the clefts of old trees, and eat the refuse meats of the wolves. The latter soon became his only resource, and he became so fearless of these animals, that he would sit close to them whilst they devoured their prey, and the animals themselves seemed to pity his condition, and would always leave something. Thus he lived, as it were, on the bounty of fierce wolves until spring. As soon as the lake was free from ice, he followed his new found friends and companions to the shore. It happened his brother was fishing in his canoe in the lake, a considerable distance out, when he thought he heard the cry of a child, and wondered how any could exist on so bleak a part of the shore. He listened again more attentively, and distinctly heard the cry repeated. He made for shore as quick as possible, and as he approached land, discovered and recog-nized his little brother, and heard him singing in a plaintive voice—

> *Neesya, neesya, shyegwuh gushuh!*
> *Ween ne myeengunish!*
> *ne myeengunish!*
> *My brother, my brother,*
> *I am now turning into a Wolf!—*
> *I am turning into a Wolf.*

At the termination of his song, he howled like a Wolf, and the young man was still more astonished, when, on getting nearer shore, he perceived his poor brother half turned into that animal. He however, leapt on shore and strove to catch him in his arms, and soothingly said—"My brother, my brother, come to me." But the boy eluded his grasp, and fled, still singing as he fled—"I am turning into a wolf!—I am turning into a wolf," and howling in the intervals.

The elder brother, conscience struck, and feeling his brotherly affection returning with redoubled force, exclaimed in great anguish, "My brother, my brother, come to me." But the nearer he approached the child, the more rapidly his transformation went on, until he changed into a perfect wolf,— still singing and howling, and naming his brother and sister alternately in his song, as he fled into the woods, until his change was complete. At last he said, "I am a wolf," and bounded out of sight.

The young man felt the bitterness of remorse all his days, and the sister, when she heard of the fate of the little boy whom she had so cruelly left, and whom both she and her brother had solemnly promised to foster and protect, wept bitterly; and never ceased to mourn until she died.

1827

The O-jib-way Maid

Original

Aun dush ween do win ane
Gitchy Mocomaun aince
Caw awzhaw woh da modé
　　We yea, yea haw ha! &c.

Wah yaw bum maud e　　　　　　　　　　5
Ojibway quaince un e
We maw jaw need e
　　We yea, yea haw ha! &c.

Omow e maun e
We nemoshain yun　　　　　　　　　　　10
We maw jaw need e
　　We yea, yea haw ha! &c.

Caw ween gush shá ween
Kin wainzh e we yea
O guh maw e maw seen　　　　　　　　　15
　　We yea, yea haw ha! &c.

Me gosh shá ween e yea
Ke bish quaw bum maud e
Tehe won ain e maud e
  We yea, yea haw ha! &c.

20

Translation

Why! what's the matter with the young American? He crosses the river with tears in his eyes! He sees the young Ojibway Girl preparing to leave the place: he sobs for his sweetheart, because she is going away! but he will not sigh long for her, for as soon as he sees her out of sight, he will forget her.

1826

Two Songs[1]

First Song: Original

I

Kaago! Kaago! moweemizhekain,
Neen deekway meedoag neeboyaun:
Keenahwau aatah keedau moweendim;
Keenahwaa kee gideemaugizim:
Eekwaaweeyaig kee gideemaugizim.

5

II

Nee nundonaawaug, nee nundonaawaug,
Ainuhwaamungig kau nissindjig:
Nindowee tibbisheemaug,—tibbisheemaug!
Ainuhwaamungig kau nissindjig:

III

Naudowaasee! naudowaaseewug!
Guyaa weenahwau tibbishko—
Guyaa weenahwau meesugo,
Kaadowee eezhishee mugwau,—eezhisheemug.
  Kaago, Kaago, &c.

10

First Song: Translation

Do not—do not weep for me
Loved woman, should I die,—

---

[1]Henry Schoolcraft described the first song as "the address of a war party to the women on leaving their village."

For yourselves alone, should you weep.[2]
Poor are ye all, and to be pitied,
Ye women! ye are to be pitied!   5

I seek—I seek our fallen relations;
I go to revenge—revenge the slain;
Our relations, fallen and slain.
And our foes—our foes, they shall lie:
I go—I go, to lay them low—to lay them low!   10
         Do not—do not, &c.

Second Song: Original

I

Neezh ogoone, neezh ogoone;
   Kau weesinissee.
      Neezh, &c.

Aazhee gushkaindumaun;
   Neenemooshain, weeyea!   5
      Aazhee, &c.

II

Kee unee bubbeeshkobee;
Kau unee inausheepun;
   Kee unee, &c.

Neenemooshain, weeyea!   10
Waindjee gushkaindumaun:
   Neenemooshain, &c.

Second Song: Translation

I

'Tis now two days—two long days,
   Since last I tasted food:
'Tis for you—for you, my love!
   That I grieve—that I grieve,
'Tis for you—for you, that I grieve.   5

---

[2]About this line, Henry Schoolcraft wrote, "It is not unusual, for them [Ojibwe speakers] to address a female individual, in the singular number, and almost immediately refer to them, as in this instance, in the plural. It is supposed to result from the strong tendency of the language to personification, and the economy of expression, if I may so say, resulting from it."

II

The waters flow deep and wide
   On which, love! you have sail'd,—
Dividing you far from me:
   'Tis for you—for you, my love!
'Tis for you—for you, that I grieve.   10

1825

■ HENRY WADSWORTH LONGFELLOW ■
1807–1882

Henry Wadsworth Longfellow was born in Portland, Maine, when it was still part of the Commonwealth of Massachusetts. He was educated at Portland Academy and along with his older brother Stephen entered Bowdoin College in Brunswick, Maine, in 1822, at the age of fifteen. He graduated in 1825, in the same class as Nathaniel Hawthorne, and resisting his father's wishes that he follow in his footsteps and take up the law, Longfellow persuaded his father to underwrite informal postgraduate study in Europe. He had been offered a newly created professorship in modern languages at Bowdoin, but the position was contingent upon his undertaking further study of French and Spanish. For the next three years, Longfellow lived and studied in France, Germany, Spain, and Italy, returning to take up his post as professor (and part-time college librarian) in September 1829. During his six years at Bowdoin, Longfellow turned out French, Italian, and Spanish textbooks, published translations, and wrote a travel book, *Outre-Mer: A Pilgrimage Beyond the Sea*, in the fashion of Washington Irving's popular *Sketch Book*.

In 1834, when Harvard College offered him the Smith Professorship of French and Spanish, it was once more conditional upon further study, this time of German. So in April 1835, with his wife, Mary Storer Potter, he sailed once more to Europe. But Mary, after suffering a miscarriage, died in Rotterdam, and Longfellow took himself off to Heidelberg, trying to immerse himself in books to overcome his grief.

The following spring, when Longfellow's passport difficulties forced him to go to the Tyrol, in Switzerland, rather than to Italy, he chanced to meet Fanny Appleton, the daughter of a prominent Beacon Hill family. Seven years later, Fanny, who was initially reluctant and ten years younger than he, finally agreed to marry him, and her family made them a present of Craigie House, a few blocks down Brattle Street from Harvard Yard. Now called the Longfellow Historic Site, the house still stands. Longfellow remained at Harvard until 1854, when he resigned in order to devote himself completely to poetry. He was succeeded in his post by James Russell Lowell.

By all accounts his marriage was a happy one; yet Longfellow's domestic life was to be the source of profound sorrow. They had six children, but two of them did not live much more than a year, and their son Charles was persistently troubled. But most tragically, in July 1861, in the eighteenth year of their marriage, Fanny's dress caught fire in a freak accident and she died of her injuries, Longfellow having been unable to quench the flames in time to save her life. Left to raise the children himself, Longfellow now grew the full beard with which he is always pictured, quite possibly to cover the scars from his badly burned face, and for the next twenty-one years he lived as a widower in Craigie House, becoming increasingly famous with the passing years.

During his first years at Harvard, Longfellow was able to publish several volumes of poetry, including *Voices of the Night* (1839), *Ballads and Other Poems* (1841), and a collection of abolitionist ballads called *Poems on Slavery* (1842), but it was not until 1845 that he began to publish the dramatic compositions for which he earned a great part of his popular reputation. The idyllic *Evangeline*, published in 1847, tells the tragic story of the heroine's search for her lover. Longfellow set his story in America. Indeed, Evangeline wanders through a great deal of America before finding her lover in a Philadelphia almshouse just before his death. The poem is written in unrhymed hexameter lines modeled on the Greek and Latin lines of the epic poems of Homer and Virgil.

Longfellow used the same hexameter line for *The Courtship of Miles Standish* (1856), another dramatic rendering of American legend. As with *The Song of Hiawatha* (1855), for which Longfellow contrived an accentual, unrhymed stanza to imitate the sound of oral folk narrative, *Evangeline* and *The Courtship of Miles Standish* are poems rooted in a scholar's understanding of poetic history and form. In choosing domestic legends and casting them in classical forms, Longfellow was attempting to create an American epic poetry. Unfortunately, poems so easily memorized are sitting targets for parody, and the fact that these three great poems were recited by generations of schoolchildren has inevitably distorted both their importance and Longfellow's achievement.

Always accessible, Longfellow's poems reflect his wide reading and cultural breadth—so much so, in fact, that Poe accused him of poaching. Although the sentiments of old favorites such as "A Psalm of Life" may seem simplistic to our somewhat cynical twenty-first-century ears, Longfellow's uplifting moral verses, like his memorable narrative poems, added inestimably to a growing American literary voice. His seventy-fifth birthday was an occasion for national celebration, and his reputation in England, where he was acknowledged the equal of poets such as Wordsworth and Tennyson, earned him a bust in the poet's corner at Westminster Abbey.

Allison Heisch
San Jose State University

PRIMARY WORKS

Poems, 1886, 1891; *The Poems of Henry Wadsworth Longfellow*, Louis Untermeyer, ed., 1961.

A Psalm of Life

What the Heart of the Young Man Said to the Psalmist

Tell me not, in mournful numbers,[1]
    Life is but an empty dream!—

---

[1] Poetic rhythms.

For the soul is dead that slumbers,
    And things are not what they seem.

Life is real! Life is earnest!   5
    And the grave is not its goal;
Dust thou art, to dust returnest,
    Was not spoken of the soul.

Not enjoyment, and not sorrow,
    Is our destined end or way;   10
But to act, that each to-morrow
    Find us farther than to-day.

Art is long, and Time is fleeting,
    And our hearts, though stout and brave,
Still, like muffled drums, are beating   15
    Funeral marches to the grave.

In the world's broad field of battle,
    In the bivouac[2] of Life,
Be not like dumb, driven cattle!
    Be a hero in the strife!   20

Trust no Future, howe'er pleasant!
    Let the dead Past bury its dead!
Act,—act in the living Present!
    Heart within, and God o'erhead!

Lives of great men all remind us   25
    We can make our lives sublime,
And, departing, leave behind us
    Footprints on the sands of time;

Footprints, that perhaps another,
    Sailing o'er life's solemn main,   30
A forlorn and shipwrecked brother,
    Seeing, shall take heart again.

Let us, then, be up and doing,
    With a heart for any fate;
Still achieving, still pursuing,   35
    Learn to labor and to wait.

                           1838

[2]Temporary battle shelter.

*A Psalm of Life: What the Heart of the Young Woman Said
to the Old Maid [a parody]*

Tell me not, in idle jingle,
　　Marriage is an empty dream,
For the girl is dead that's single,
　　And things are not what they seem.

Married life is real, earnest;　　　　　　　　　　5
　　Single blessedness a fib;
Taken from man, to man returnest,
　　Has been spoken of the rib.

Not enjoyment, and not sorrow,
　　Is our destined end or way;　　　　　　　　　10
But to act, that each to-morrow
　　Nearer brings the wedding-day.

Life is long, and youth is fleeting,
　　And our hearts, if there we search,
Still like steady drums are beating　　　　　　　15
　　Anxious marches to the church.

In the world's broad field of battle,
　　In the bivouac of life,
Be not like dumb, driven cattle!
　　Be a woman, be a wife!　　　　　　　　　　20

Trust no Future, howe'er pleasant!
　　Let the dead Past bury its dead!
Act,—act in the living Present;
　　Heart within, and Man ahead!

Lives of married folks remind us　　　　　　　25
　　We can live our lives as well,
And, departing, leave behind us
　　Such examples as will tell;—

Such examples, that another,
　　Sailing far from Hymen's port,　　　　　　　30
A forlorn, unmarried brother,
　　Seeing, shall take heart, and court.

Let us then be up and doing,
　　With the heart and head begin;
Still achieving, still pursuing,　　　　　　　　35
　　Learn to labor, and to win!

Phoebe Cary (1854), from *The Poems of Alice and Phoebe Cary*, 1903

The Warning[1]

Beware! The Israelite of old, who tore
    The lion in his path,—when, poor and blind,
He saw the blessed light of heaven no more,
    Shorn of his noble strength and forced to grind
In prison, and at last led forth to be   5
A pander to Philistine revelry,—

Upon the pillars of the temple laid
    His desperate hands, and in its overthrow
Destroyed himself, and with him those who made
    A cruel mockery of his sightless woe;   10
The poor, blind Slave, the scoff and jest of all,
Expired, and thousands perished in the fall!

There is a poor, blind Samson in this land,
    Shorn of his strength and bound in bonds of steel,
Who may, in some grim revel, raise his hand,   15
    And shake the pillars of this Commonweal,
Till the vast Temple of our liberties
A shapeless mass of wreck and rubbish lies.

                                  1842

The Arsenal at Springfield[1']

This is the Arsenal. From floor to ceiling,
    Like a huge organ, rise the burnished arms;
But from their silent pipes no anthem pealing
    Startles the villages with strange alarms.

Ah! what a sound will rise, how wild and dreary,   5
    When the death-angel touches those swift keys
What loud lament and dismal Miserere
    Will mingle with their awful symphonies

I hear even now the infinite fierce chorus,
    The cries of agony, the endless groan,   10
Which, through the ages that have gone before us,
    In long reverberations reach our own.

---

[1]Samson, an Israelite who had been captured
and blinded, single-handedly destroyed the
temple of the licentious Philistines and
brought them to ruin.

[1']From *The Belfry of Bruges and Other Poems*
(1846).

On helm and harness rings the Saxon hammer,
    Through Cimbric forest roars the Norseman's song,
And loud, amid the universal clamor,   15
    O'er distant deserts sounds the Tartar gong.

I hear the Florentine, who from his palace
    Wheels out his battle-bell with dreadful din,
And Aztec priests upon their teocallis
    Beat the wild war-drums made of serpent's skin;   20

The tumult of each sacked and burning village;
    The shout that every prayer for mercy drowns;
The soldiers' revels in the midst of pillage;
    The wail of famine in beleaguered towns;

The bursting shell, the gateway wrenched asunder,   25
    The rattling musketry, the clashing blade;
And ever and anon, in tones of thunder,
    The diapason of the cannonade.

Is it, O man, with such discordant noises,
    With such accursed instruments as these,   30
Thou drownest Nature's sweet and kindly voices,
    And jarrest the celestial harmonies?

Were half the power, that fills the world with terror,
    Were half the wealth, bestowed on camps and courts,
Given to redeem the human mind from error,   35
    There were no need of arsenals or forts:

The warrior's name would be a name abhorred!
    And every nation, that should lift again
Its hand against a brother, on its forehead
    Would wear forevermore the curse of Cain!   40

Down the dark future, through long generations,
    The echoing sounds grow fainter and then cease;
And like a bell, with solemn, sweet vibrations,
    I hear once more the voice of Christ say, "Peace!"

Peace! and no longer from its brazen portals   45
    The blast of War's great organ shakes the skies!
But beautiful as songs of the immortals,
    The holy melodies of love arise.

                                            1846

The Jewish Cemetery at Newport

How strange it seems! These Hebrews in their graves,
    Close by the street of this fair seaport town,
Silent beside the never-silent waves,
    At rest in all this moving up and down!

The trees are white with dust, that o'er their sleep   5
    Wave their broad curtains in the south-wind's breath,
While underneath these leafy tents they keep
    The long, mysterious Exodus of Death.

And these sepulchral stones, so old and brown,
That pave with level flags their burial-place,   10
Seem like the tablets of the Law, thrown down
    And broken by Moses at the mountain's base.

The very names recorded here are strange,
    Of foreign accent, and of different climes;
Alvares and Rivera interchange   15
    With Abraham and Jacob of old times.

"Blessed be God! for he created Death!"
    The mourners said, "and Death is rest and peace;"
Then added, in the certainty of faith,
"And giveth Life that nevermore shall cease."   20

Closed are the portals of their Synagogue,
    No Psalms of David now the silence break,
No Rabbi reads the ancient Decalogue
    In the grand dialect the Prophets spake.

Gone are the living, but the dead remain,   25
    And not neglected; for a hand unseen,
Scattering its bounty, like a summer rain,
    Still keeps their graves and their remembrance green.

How came they here? What burst of Christian hate,
    What persecution, merciless and blind,   30
Drove o'er the sea—that desert desolate—
    These Ishmaels and Hagars of mankind?

They lived in narrow streets and lanes obscure,
    Ghetto and Judenstrass, in mirk and mire;
Taught in the school of patience to endure   35
    The life of anguish and the death of fire.

All their lives long, with the unleavened bread
    And bitter herbs of exile and its fears,
The wasting famine of the heart they fed,
And slaked its thirst with marah of their tears.   40

Anathema maranatha![1] was the cry
    That rang from town to town, from street to street;
At every gate the accursed Mordecai
    Was mocked and jeered, and spurned by Christian feet.

Pride and humiliation hand in hand   45
    Walked with them through the world where'er they went;
Trampled and beaten were they as the sand,
    And yet unshaken as the continent.

For in the background figures vague and vast
    Of patriarchs and of prophets rose sublime,   50
And all the great traditions of the Past
    They saw reflected in the coming time.

And thus forever with reverted look
    The mystic volume of the world they read,
Spelling it backward, like a Hebrew book,   55
    Till life became a Legend of the Dead.

But ah! what once has been shall be no more!
    The groaning earth in travail and in pain
Brings forth its races, but does not restore,
And the dead nations never rise again.   60

1852

The Harvest Moon

It is the Harvest Moon! On gilded vanes
    And roofs of villages, on woodland crests
    And their aerial neighborhoods of nests
    Deserted, on the curtained window-panes
Of rooms where children sleep, on country lanes   5
    And harvest-fields, its mystic splendor rests!
    Gone are the birds that were our summer guests;
    With the last sheaves return the laboring wains!

[1]A curse applied by Christians to non-believers,
especially Jews.

All things are symbols: the external shows
    Of Nature have their image in the mind, 10
    As flowers and fruits and falling of the leaves;
The song-birds leave us at the summer's close,
    Only the empty nests are left behind,
    And pipings of the quail among the sheaves.

1876

Nature[1]

As a fond mother, when the day is o'er,
    Leads by the hand her little child to bed,
    Half willing, half reluctant to be led,
And leave his broken playthings on the floor,
Still gazing at them through the open door, 5
    Nor wholly reassured and comforted
    By promises of others in their stead,
    Which, though more splendid, may not please him more;
So Nature deals with us, and takes away
    Our playthings one by one, and by the hand 10
    Leads us to rest so gently, that we go
Scarce knowing if we wish to go or stay,
    Being too full of sleep to understand
    How far the unknown transcends the what we know.

1875

The Tide Rises, the Tide Falls[1']

The tide rises, the tide falls,
The twilight darkens, the curlew calls;
Along the sea-sands damp and brown
The traveller hastens toward the town,
And the tide rises, the tide falls. 5

Darkness settles on roofs and walls,
But the sea, the sea in the darkness calls;
The little waves, with their soft, white hands,
Efface the footprints in the sands,
And the tide rises, the tide falls. 10

The morning breaks; the steeds in their stalls
Stamp and neigh, as the hostler calls;

[1]From *Birds of Passage* (1875).   [1']From *Ultima Thule* (1880).

The day returns, but nevermore
Returns the traveller to the shore,
And the tide rises, the tide falls.   15

                                                                      1880

▪ **FRANCES SARGENT LOCKE OSGOOD** ▪
1811–1850

Frances Sargent Locke Osgood was a popular and versatile poet who wrote both in the high sentimental mode and in a mode of sheer mischief. A focus on children, flowers, and death earns her the designation of sentimental (and that in no reductive sense), but she was also a New York City sophisticate, welcome in the most exalted literary circles, and adept—as Edgar Allan Poe said of her—at literary *espièglerie* (roguishness). In her published poetry, Osgood deals quite seriously with sentimental themes, issues of motherhood and of romantic love, writing about these central human concerns with both personal insight and poetic skill. On the other hand, in a group of "salon poems" composed for social occasions, she wittily destabilizes the underlying premises of the sentimental ethos. In her poetry of relations between the sexes, both published poems and manuscript salon verses, Osgood presents an urbane and sophisticated voice, quite unlike anything our traditional constructs of American literature have led us to expect from either women's or men's writing of the era. A contemporary reviewer claimed Osgood was Elizabeth Barrett Browning's equal as a poet but far superior in "grace and tenderness." Dying of tuberculosis at age thirty-nine, Osgood did not have the opportunity to realize the full promise of that comparison.

Frances Sargent Locke was born in Boston in 1811 to a prosperous mercantile family with a literary bent, including an older sister, Anna Maria Wells, who was also a published poet. The young Fanny Locke's school notebooks show evidence of considerable poetic talent, and she was "discovered" in her youth by writer and editor Lydia Maria Child, who published many of Fanny's verses under the pen name Florence, the first of many Osgood noms de plume, in her "Juvenile Miscellany." Frances met the widely traveled, and self-romanticizing, portrait artist Samuel Stillman Osgood in 1834, and he invited her to sit for her portrait. Married in 1834, the couple spent the next five years in England while Samuel pursued his career among the aristocracy there.

The sophistication of Fanny Osgood's poetic voice was fostered by this cosmopolitan experience. During their years in London, Fanny and Samuel circulated among the social and intellectual elite; in 1838, while living there, she published *A Wreath of Wild Flowers from New England*. As Poe, Osgood's friend during the New York years, tells us, "the fair American authoress grew . . . into high favor with the fashionable literati and the literary fashionables of England." Returning to American shores in 1839, Osgood seems to have imported into New York literary high life the wit and sparkle of the London intelligentsia. At the literary salons of Anne Lynch and Emma Embury, she became acquainted with well-known American writers and editors, among them Poe, Margaret Fuller, N. P. Willis, Grace Greenwood, and Horace Greeley.

By the time the Osgoods settled in New York, they had two daughters, Ellen and May. Osgood's third child, Fanny Fay, was born in 1846, at a time when the marriage seems to have been less than stable. Some writers have speculated that during this period Osgood had a love affair with Poe, but convincing evidence does not, at this time, exist to prove such a claim. Osgood met Poe in 1845, and they quickly became friends. She socialized with Poe at literary salons, visited him and his wife, Virginia, at their home, and published a number of poems in the *Broadway Journal*, of which he was editor. In the pages of the *Journal*, they conducted an open literary flirtation, but, as critic Mary DeJong has said, "For Osgood, writing itself was a kind of performance, and she reveled in drama as much as Poe did." Their flirtatious poems, DeJong speculates, "define their roles as patron and protégé, artist and admirer—not the quality or depth of their emotions."

During the 1840s, Osgood was a much revered popular poet. She thought of herself as a professional writer rather than as a literary artist and took full advantage of the many opportunities presented by a burgeoning print culture. Her work and circumstances embody both the opportunities and the constraints of the contemporary literary marketplace. Osgood published in every venue available to her—books, magazines, pamphlets, anthologies, newspapers. Her poems, including beautiful and poignant expressions of maternal love and impassioned articulations of heterosexual love and enthrallment, were widely sought after by magazines such as *Godey's Lady's Book* and *Sartain's Union Magazine*. Although Osgood does not ever seem to have suffered the kind of dire economic hardship faced by some of her female literary contemporaries, she nonetheless depended on her literary income to support herself and her family.

At their best, Osgood's published poems are either witty or powerfully emotional, skillfully employing, and bringing to vivid life, common literary conventions. With masterful versification, impressive range of subject matter, and compelling imaginative power, Osgood addresses gender politics, not always from a strictly feminist perspective; inscribes the delicate dilemmas of sexual temptation; investigates dynamics of celebrity and reputation; and explores the joys and griefs of motherhood.

Osgood seems to have seen no contradiction between her published verse and a group of more worldly verses she wrote to be shared with an intimate circle of friends—most likely at the salons she attended regularly. This *vers de société*, as Griswold calls it, includes satires, Valentines, billets-doux, and commentary on contemporary current events. In particular, Osgood's "coterie" verses wittily investigate the play of eroticism and social forms, a subject seldom addressed by other writers of the era. Osgood's salon poetry was, according to an obituary writer, produced for the "temporary gratification of her friends, and then thrown aside and forgotten." Treasured in manuscript by friends and kept in draft form by Osgood herself, these poems reveal a far more complex nineteenth-century literary milieu, in terms of class and gender representations, than American literary history has commonly acknowledged.

The complex mechanics of literary reputation have been delineated by many scholars, and Frances Osgood, for any number of reasons, both personal and critical, has been obscured in the scholarly record. Until recently, she has had no advocate. Even the most complete compilation of Osgood's poetry, the 1850 edition, contains less than half her acknowledged pieces. Much work remains to be done in order to recover more fully this poet whose life and poetry significantly enrich our literary record and problematize several major literary historical paradigms, particularly those of gender and class. Osgood testifies to us, for instance, that a mid-nineteenth-century woman was capable of recognizing and dealing with sexual temptation and writing about it as well. She brings a new kind of critical respectability to sentimental poetry, treating its range of domestic, affectional topics with passion and skill. She reveals that the boundaries between British and American writing of the era were not as impermeable as has often been suggested. And, finally, she sketches a portrait of an upper-class, sophisticated, urban society seldom acknowledged in a literary history of the era long dominated by New England literati.

Joanne Dobson
Fordham University

PRIMARY WORKS

A Wreath of Wild Flowers from New England, 1838; *Poems*, 1846; *Poems*, 1850.

The Little Hand

We wandered sadly round the room,—
    We missed the voice's play,
That warbled through our hours of gloom,
    And charmed the cloud away;—

We missed the footstep, loved and light,—   5
    The tiny, twining hand,—
The quick, arch smile, so wildly bright,—
    The brow, with beauty bland!

We wandered sadly round the room,—
    No relic could we find,   10
No toy of hers, to soothe our gloom,—
    She left not one behind!

But look! there is a misty trace,
    Faint, undefined and broken,
Of fingers, on the mirror's face,—   15
    A dear, though simple token!

A cherub hand!—the child we loved
   Had left its impress there,
When first, by young Ambition moved,
   She climbed the easy-chair;—   20

She saw her own sweet self, and tried
   To touch what seemed to be
So near, so beautiful! and cried,—
   "Why! there's another me!"

Dear hand! though from the mirror's face   25
   Thy form did soon depart,
I wore its welcome, tender trace,
   Long after, in my heart!

                                      1838

The Maiden's Mistake[1]

That his eyebrows were false—that his hair
   Was assumed, I was fully aware;
I knew his moustache of a barber was bought.
And that Cartwright provided his teeth;—but I thought
   That his *heart* was, at least, true and fair!   5

I saw that the exquisite glow,
   Spreading over the cheek of my beau,
From a carmine-shell came;—and I often was told,
That his "gras de la jambe," by the tailor was sold;
   I dreamed not his *love* was but show!   10

I was sure, I could easily tell,
   That the form, which deluded each belle,
Was made over his own;—but I could not believe,
That his flattering *tongue*, too, was taught to deceive;
   That his fortune was humbug, as well!   15

I had made up my mind to dispense
   With a figure, hair, teeth, heart and sense—
"La jambe" I'd o'erlook, were it ever so small!
But to think that he is not a *Count*, after all,
   That's a not-to-be pardoned offence!   20

                                      1839

[1]From *The Ladies Companion* [New York], vol.
12 (November 1839–May 1840).

Oh! Hasten to My Side

Oh! hasten to my side, I pray!
    I dare not be alone!
The smile that tempts, when thou'rt away,
    Is fonder than thine own.

The voice that oftenest charms mine ear   5
    Hath such beguiling tone,
'Twill steal my very *soul*, I fear;
    Ah! leave me not alone!

It speaks in accents low and deep,
    It murmurs praise too dear,   10
It makes me passionately weep,
    Then gently soothes my fear;

It calls me sweet, endearing names,
    With Love's own childlike art;
My tears, my doubts, it softly blames—   15
    'Tis *music* to my heart!

And dark, deep, eloquent, soul-fill'd eyes
    Speak tenderly to mine;
Beneath that gaze what feelings rise!
    It is more kind than thine!   20

A hand, even pride can scarce repel,
    Too fondly seeks mine own;
It is not safe!—it is not well!
    Ah! leave me not alone!

I try to calm, in cold repose,   25
    Beneath his earnest eye,
The heart that thrills, the cheek that glows—
    Alas! *in vain* I try!

Oh trust me not—a woman frail—
    To brave the snares of life!   30
Lest—lonely, sad, unloved—I *fail*,
    And shame the name of wife!

Come back! though cold and harsh to me,
    There's *honour* by thy side!
Better unblest, yet safe to be,   35
    Than lost to truth, to pride.

Alas! my peril hourly grows,
    In every thought and dream;
Not—not to *thee* my spirit goes,
    But still—yes! I still to *him!*   40

Return with those cold eyes to me,
    And chill my soul once more
Back to the loveless apathy
    It learn'd so well before!

          1843

A Reply

To One Who Said, Write from Your Heart.

Ah! woman still
    Must veil the shrine,
Where feeling feeds the fire divine,
    Nor sing at will,
    Untaught by art,   5
The music prison'd in her heart!

Still gay the note
    And light the day,
The woodbird warbles on the spray,
    Afar to float;   10
    But homeward flown,
Within his nest, how changed the tone!

Oh! none can know,
    Who have not heard
The music-soul that thrills the bird,   15
    The carol low,
    As coo of dove
He warbles to his woodland love!

The world would say
    'Twas vain and wild,   20
Th'impassion'd lay of Nature's child;
    And Feeling, so
    Should veil the shrine,
Where softly glows her fires divine!

          1846

Lines

Suggested by the announcement that "A Bill for the Protection of the
Property of Married Women has passed both Houses" of our State
Legislature

[For *The New-York Tribune*]

Oh, ye who in those Houses hold
    The sceptre of command!
Thought's sceptre, sunlit, in the soul,
    Not golden, in the hand!

Was there not one among ye all,   5
    No heart, that Love could thrill,
To move some slight amendment there,
    Before you passed the bill?

Ye make our gold and lands secure;
    Maybe you do not know,   10
That we have other property,
    We'd *rather* not forego.

There *are* such things in woman's heart,
    As fancies, tastes, affections;—
Are no encroachments made on these?   15
    Do *they* need no "protections"?

Do we not daily sacrifice,
    To our lords—and Creation's
Some darling wish—some petted whim,
    Ah, me! in vain oblations!   20

These "cold realities" of life,—
    These men, with their intrusions;
Do they not rob us, one by one,
    Of all our "warm illusions"?

These highway robbers, prowling round,   25
    Our "young affections" stealing,
Do they not take our richest store
    Of Truth and Faith and Feeling!

Our "better judgment," "finer sense,"
    We yield with souls that falter,—   30
A costly, dainty holocaust,
    Upon a tyrant's altar;

We waste on them our "golden" hours,
    Our "real estate" of Beauty,
The bloom of Life's young passion-flowers—   35
    And still they talk of "Duty."

Alas for those, whose all of wealth
    Is in their souls and faces,
Whose only "rents" are rents in heart,
    Whose only tenants—graces.   40

How must that poor protection bill
    Provoke their bitter laughter,
Since they themselves are leased for life,
    And no *pay-day* till after!

By all the rest you fondly hope,   45
    When ends this lengthened session,
That household peace, which Woman holds
    Thank Heaven! at *her* discretion.

If a light of generous chivalry,
    This wild appeal arouses,   50
Present a truer, nobler bill!
    And let it pass—*all houses!*

                          1848

To a Slandered Poetess

My brilliant Blue-bell! droop no more;
    But let them mock, and mew and mutter!
I marvel, though a whirlwind roar,
    Your eagle soul should deign to flutter!

So low the pigmies aimed the dart,   5
    (Ah, yes! your looks of scorn reveal it.)
You must have *stooped* your haughty heart,
    Oh, wilful, wayward child!—to feel it.

My dark-eyed darling! don't you know,
    If you were homely, cold, and stupid,   10
Unbent for you were Slander's bow?
    Her shafts but follow those of Cupid.

'Tis but the penalty you pay,
    For wit so rare, and grace so peerless:

So let the snarlers say their say,　　　　　　　　　　　15
　　And smile to hear them, free and fearless.

Nay! hear them *not!* Oh! you should listen
　　To spheral tunes! the angels love you!
The stars with kindred beauty glisten:—
　　No "evil eye" can lower *above* you!　　　　　　　20

Dear child of Genius! strike the lyre,
　　And drown with melody delicious,
Soft answering to your touch of fire,
　　The envious hint—the sneer malicious.

Remember is it Music's law,　　　　　　　　　　　25
　　Each *pure, true* note, though low you sound it,
Is heard through Discord's wildest war
　　Of rage and madness, storming round it.

You smile!—Nay, raise your queenly head;
　　Braid up your hair, lest I upbraid it;　　　　　　30
Be that last coward tear unshed.
　　Or in this dancing dimple shed it!

Serenely go your glorious way,
　　Secure that every footstep onward,
Will lead you from *their* haunts away,　　　　　　35
　　Since you go *up*, and they go—*down*ward.

Yet from your love-lit, heavenly flight,
　　Some pity dole to those who blame you,
You only can forgive them quite.
　　You only, smile, while they defame you.　　　　　40

Oh! think how poor in all the wealth,
　　That makes *your* frame a fairy palace—
The mind's pure light,—the heart's sweet health,—
　　Are they whose dearest joy is malice.

　　　　　　　　　　　　　　　　　　　　　1849

The Indian Maid's Reply to the Missionary[1]

Half earnest, half sportive, yet listening, she stood,
That queenly young creature, the child of the wood;

[1]The friend who related to me this incident
was, I believe, himself an eye-witness to the
scene. [Osgood's note.]

Her curving lips parted—her dark eyes downcast—
Her hands lock'd before her—her heart beating fast;
And around her the forest's majestic arcade,   5
With the pure sunset burning like fire through the shade:
He spake of the goodness, the glory of Him
Whose smile lit the heavens—whose frown made them dim.
And with one flashing glance of the eyes she upraised
Full of rapture impassion'd, her Maker she praised.   10
He spake of the Saviour, his sorrow, his truth,
His pity celestial, the wrong and the ruth;
And quick gushing tears dimm'd the gaze that she turn'd
To his face, while her *soul* on her sunny cheek burn'd.
Then he thought in his fond zeal to wile her within   15
The pale of the church; but as well might he win
Yon cloud that floats changefully on in the light,
A fawn of the forest, a star-ray of light,
As tame to his purpose, or lure from her race
That wild child of freedom, all impulse and grace.   20
She listens in sad, unbelieving surprise;
Then shakes back her dark, glossy locks from her eyes,
And with eloquent gesture points up to the skies.
At last, to awaken her fears he essays;
He threatens God's wrath if thus freely she strays.   25
Wild, sweet, and incredulous rang through the wood
The laugh of the maiden, as proudly she stood.
Soft, thrilling, and glad woke the echo around;
True nature's harmonious reply to that sound.
Then lowly and reverent answer'd the maid:—   30
"God speaketh afar in the forest," she said,
"And he sayeth—'Behold in the woodland so wild,
With its heaven-arch'd aisle, the true church of my child.'"

         1850

The Hand That Swept the Sounding Lyre

The hand that swept the sounding lyre
     With more than mortal skill,
The lightning eye, the heart of fire,
     The fervent lip are still!
No more, in rapture or in wo,   5
     With melody to thrill,
         Ah! nevermore!

Oh! bring the flowers he cherish'd so,
     With eager childlike care;

For o'er his grave they'll love to grow,   10
    And sigh their sorrow there:
Ah me! no more their balmy glow
    May soothe his heart's despair,
        No! nevermore!

But angel hands shall bring him balm   15
    For every grief he knew,
And Heaven's soft harps his soul shall calm
    With music sweet and true,
And teach to him the holy charm
    Of Israfel anew,   20
        For evermore!

Love's silver lyre he play'd so well
    Lies shatter'd on his tomb;
But still in air its music-spell
    Floats on through light and gloom,   25
And in the hearts where soft they fell,
    His words of beauty bloom
        For evermore!

                                       1850

The Wraith of the Rose

An impromptu written on a visiting card

The magic of that name is fled,
The music of that dream is dead,
Long since Love's rose, its perfume, shed,
    And what art *thou* to me?
If you have come to clasp again,   5
The fetter of that fairy chain,
You'd better far at home remain,
    And save your time—and *knee!*
And yet that dream was strangely dear,
And yet that name awakes a tear,
The *wraith* of Love's sweet Rose is here,   10
    It haunts me everywhere!
I wish the chain were still unbroken,
I wish those words again were spoken,
I wish I'd kept that last fond token,   15
    And had not burned your hair!
I wish your voice still sounded sweet,
I wish you dared Love's vow repeat,
I wish you were not all deceit,
    And I so fickle-hearted!   20

I wish we might go back again,
I wish you *could* reclasp the chain!
I wish—*you hadn't drank champagne*,
    So freely since we parted!
Alas! While Flattery baits your line,   25
You fish in shallower hearts than mine!
You'll never find a pearl divine
    Like that *my* spirit wasted!
But should you catch a seeming prise,
A *flying* fish you'll see it rise,   30
Away—beyond your wicked eyes,
    Before the treasure's tasted!
Oh! *if* those eyes were splendid now,
As when they spoke the silent vow!
Oh! *if* the locks that wreath your brow,   35
    Were not—but this is idle!
My wish shall be with kindness rife,
I'll wish you all the joys of life,
A pleasant home—a peerless wife,
    Whose wishes, Sense shall bridle!   40

                                            c. 1849

WALT WHITMAN
1819–1892

The publication of *Leaves of Grass* on or about July 4, 1855, represented a revolutionary departure in American literature. Printed at Whitman's expense, the green, quarto-sized volume bore no author's name. Opposite the title page appeared a daguerreotype engraving of the poet, dressed in workingman's trowsers, a shirt unbuttoned to reveal his undershirt, and a hat cocked casually upon his head. In a rousing Preface, the poet declared America's literary independence, and in verse that rolled freely and dithyrambically across the page, he presented himself as "Walt Whitman, an American, one of the roughs, a kosmos,/Disorderly fleshy and sensual .... eating drinking and breeding." Like his poet as common man, Whitman's act of self-naming represented an assault on literary decorum and the Puritan pieties of the New England literary establishment. "It is as if the beasts spoke," wrote the otherwise sympathetic Thoreau.

In the six editions of *Leaves of Grass* that were published between 1855 and 1881, Whitman opened the field of American and ultimately of modern poetry. His subject was not "the smooth walks, trimm'd hedges, poseys and nightingales of the English poets, but the whole orb, with its geologic history, the Kosmos, carrying fire and snow." He was the poet not only of Darwinian evolution, but of the city and the crowd, science and the machine. Presenting himself as a model democrat who spoke as and for rather than apart from the people, Whitman's poet was a breaker of bounds: he was female and male, farmer and factory worker, prostitute and slave, citizen of America and citizen of the world; shuttling between past, present, and future, he was "an acme of things accomplished" and an "encloser of things to be." His songs were songs not only of occupations but of sex and the body. He sang of masturbation, the sexual organs, and the sexual act; he was one of the first poets to write of the "body electric," of female eroticism, homosexual love, and the anguish of repressed desire.

Puzzled by Whitman's sudden emergence at age thirty-six in 1855 as the American bard, critics have proposed several explanations: a reading of Emerson, a love affair, a mystic experience, an Oedipal crisis. Considered within the context of his time, however, Whitman's emergence seems neither mystifying nor particularly disconnected from his family background and his early life as a radical Democrat, political journalist, and sometime dandy. His mother was an ardent follower of the mystical doctrines of the Quaker preacher Elias Hicks, whom Whitman later described as "the democrat in religion as Jefferson was the democrat in politics." His father was a carpenter who embraced the radical political philosophy of Tom Paine and subscribed to the *Free Enquirer*, edited by Frances Wright and Robert Dale Owen, which sought through the rhetoric of class warfare to unite the grievances of New York City workers in an anticapitalist and anticlerical platform. Raised among eight brothers and sisters whose very names—Andrew Jackson, George Washington, and Thomas Jefferson— bore the inscription of the democratic ideals of his family, Whitman early began to develop a sense of self that was inextricably bound up with the political identity of America.

Although Whitman attended school between 1825 and 1830, he was largely self-educated. During the 1830s, he served as a printer's apprentice, engaged in local politics, and taught for a few years in Long Island schools. He read voraciously but erratically, attended the theater and the opera, and poked about the antiquities at Dr. Abbott's Egyptian Museum. As editor of the *Aurora* in 1842 and later of the Brooklyn *Daily Eagle* (1846–1847), Whitman placed himself at the very center of the political battles over slavery, territorial expansion, the Mexican War, sectionalism, free trade, states' rights, worker strife, and the new market economy. His support for David Wilmot's proposal to forbid the extension of slavery into the new territory led to his being fired as editor of the *Eagle*. Perhaps disillusioned by party politics, he began to experiment with the idea of using poetry as a form of political action. When in his earliest notebook, dated 1847, Whitman breaks for the first time into lines approximating the free verse of *Leaves of Grass*, the lines bear the impress of the slavery issue:

> I am the poet of slaves, and of the masters of slaves
> > I am the poet of the body
> And I am

Similarly, Whitman's first free verse poems, "Blood Money," "House of Friends," and "Resurgemus," which were published in 1850, emerged out of the political passions aroused by slavery, free soil, and the European revolutions of 1848.

Although Whitman continued to support the cause of Free Soil, in the early 1850s he withdrew from party politics. Working part-time as a house builder in Brooklyn, he completed his 1855 edition of *Leaves of Grass*. The poems are propelled by the desire to enlighten and regenerate the people in the ideals of the democratic republic. The drama of identity in the initially untitled "Song of Myself," the first and longest poem in the 1855 *Leaves*, is rooted in the political drama of a nation in crisis. The poet's conflict between separate person and en masse, between pride and sympathy, individualism and equality, nature and the city, the body and the soul, symbolically enacts the larger political conflicts in the nation, which grew out of the controversies over industrialization, wage labor, women's rights, finance, immigration, slavery, territorial expansion, technological progress, and the whole question of the relation of individual and state, state and nation.

Whitman sent a copy of the 1855 *Leaves of Grass* to Ralph Waldo Emerson, whose response was immediate and generous: "I find it the most extraordinary piece of wit and wisdom that America has yet contributed." Spurred by Emerson's words of praise, Whitman published a second edition of *Leaves of Grass* with several new poems in 1856. While he was planning a third edition of *Leaves* as a kind of "New Bible" of democracy, Whitman had an unhappy love affair with a man. This tale of love and loss is the subject of a small sheaf of twelve poems, initially titled "Live Oak with Moss," which was later incorporated into the "Calamus" cluster in the 1860 *Leaves of Grass*. Whitman's homosexual love crisis along with the impending dissolution of the Union caused him to become increasingly doubtful about the future of America and his own future as the bard of democracy.

This doubt is evident in the 1860 edition of *Leaves of Grass*, particularly in the "Chants Democratic" and "Calamus" groupings, and in such individual poems as "Out of the Cradle Endlessly Rocking" and "As I Ebb'd with the Ocean of Life." In the poems of "Calamus," Whitman draws upon the language of democracy and phrenology to name his erotic feeling for men as both comradeship and "adhesiveness" (the phrenological term which Whitman defined as "the personal attachment of man to man"). The love poems of "Calamus" are paired with the procreation poems of "Children of Adam," which focus on "amative" love, the phrenological term for the love between men and women. Although the press and the literary establishment immediately focused on the "sex" poems of "Children of Adam" as Whitman's most provocative grouping, the love poems of "Calamus" were in fact his most radical sequence, sexually and politically. Whitman infused the abstractions of democracy with the intensity of erotic passion, giving literature some of its first and most potent images of democratic comradeship; and by linking homoeroticism with a democratic breaking of bounds, he presents one of the most tender and moving accounts of homosexual love in Western literature.

For Whitman, as for the nation, the Civil War was a period of major crisis. Uncertain of the role of a national poet during a time of fratricidal war, Whitman published little during the war years. In 1862, when he went to the front in search of his brother George, he found the role he would play: he would become a kind of spiritual "wound-dresser" by visiting the sick and dying soldiers in the hospital wards of Washington. Like Lincoln's "Gettysburg Address," the poems of *Drum-Taps and Sequel* (1865–1866) and the prose of *Memoranda during the War* (1875– 1876) were attempts to come to terms with the massive carnage of the war by placing its waste and apparent unreason within some larger providential design. In these volumes, Whitman turns from romance to realism, vision to history, anticipating the naturalistic war writings of Stephen Crane, Ernest Hemingway, and Norman Mailer.

Whitman remained in Washington during and after the war, working first as a clerk in the Indian Bureau and then, after being dismissed in 1865 for moral turpitude by Secretary of the Interior James Harlan, in the Attorney General's office. For all Whitman's effort to (re)present the war as a testing ground for democracy, the Civil War unleashed a hoard of psychic and socioeconomic demons that would continue to haunt his dream of America in the postwar period.

In his incisive political essay *Democratic Vistas* (1871), which was initially composed as a response to Carlyle's attack on the "democratic rabble" in "Shooting Niagara," Whitman seeks to come to terms with the gilded monsters of post–Civil War America. Even before the worst scandals of the Grant administration were exposed, he presents an image of America saturated in corruption and greed from the national to the local level. In "reconstructing, democratizing society," Whitman argues, the true "revolution" would be of the "interior life"; and in bringing about this democratic revolution, the poet would play the leading role by overhauling the "Culture theory" of the past and by providing the language, commonality, and myths by which America named itself.

Whereas Whitman's war poems were merely tagged onto the end of the fourth edition of *Leaves*, which was published in 1867, in the 1871 *Leaves* these poems were incorporated into the main body of his work. By 1872 Whitman came to regard *Leaves of Grass* as essentially complete. In his 1872 Preface to "As a Strong Bird on Pinions Free," he announced his intention of turning away from his former emphasis on "a great composite *democratic individual*, male or female" toward an increased emphasis on "an aggregated, inseparable, unprecedented, vast, composite, electric *democratic nationality*." His plan was cut short by a paralytic stroke, which he suffered at the beginning of 1873. The seizure left him bedridden for several weeks and paralyzed for the rest of his life.

Whitman made a trip to Camden, New Jersey, a few days before his mother's death in May 1873 and never returned to Washington. He spent the remainder of his life in Camden, first at his brother George's house and finally, beginning in 1884, in his own home at 328 Mickle Street. Struggling with occasional spells of dizziness and a prematurely aging body, Whitman mustered enough strength to publish a dual volume of poetry and prose on the occasion of the American centennial in 1876. Invigorated by the visits to the New Jersey farm of Susan and George Stafford that he began making in 1876, by the economic recovery of the nation under the new political regime of Rutherford B. Hayes (1877–1881), and by the attention his work was beginning to receive in England and abroad, Whitman revised, reintegrated, and reordered all of his poems into the final 1881 edition of *Leaves of Grass*. In 1882 he published a prose companion to his poems, titled *Specimen Days*, in which he refigures the events of his life and times as a narrative of personal, national, and cosmic restoration.

The poems that Whitman wrote in the last two decades of his life, such as "Passage to India" and "Prayer of Columbus," are characterized by a leap away from the physical landscape of America toward a more traditionally religious vision of God's providence and spiritual grace. Despite his apparent disillusionment with the material conditions of America, however, Whitman continued to name the possibility of an *other* America. Figuring himself in the image of a New World Columbus, he continued to imagine the possibility of a democratic golden world that, like the dream of a passage to India and a world that was round, might bloom in some future transformation of vision into history.

Betsy Erkkila
Northwestern University

PRIMARY WORKS

Leaves of Grass: The First (1855) Edition, Malcolm Cowley, ed., 1959; *Drum-Taps and Sequel (1865–66): A Facsimile Reproduction*, F. DeWolfe Miller, ed., 1959; *The Correspondence (1842–1892)*, Edwin H. Miller, ed., 1961–1969; *Leaves of Grass: Facsimile of the 1860 Text*, Roy Harvey Pearce, ed., 1961; *Memoranda during the War (1876): Facsimile*, 1962; *The Collected Writings of Walt Whitman*, Gay Wilson Allen and Sculley Bradley, eds., includes: *Prose Works (1892): Specimen Days, Collect, and Other Prose*, Floyd Stovall, ed., 1963; *The Early Poems and the Fiction*, Thomas L. Brasher, ed., 1963; Sculley Bradley and Harold Blodgett, eds., *Leaves of Grass: A Comprehensive Reader's Edition*, 1965; *Daybooks and Notebooks*, William White, ed., 1978; *Leaves of Grass: A Textual Variorum of the Printed Poems*, Sculley Bradley et al., eds., 1980; *Notebooks and Unpublished Prose Manuscripts*, Edward F. Grier, ed., 1984; *Whitman Poetry and Prose*, Justin Kaplan, ed., 1982; *Selected Letters*, Edwin H. Miller, ed., 1990; *The Journalism/Walt Whitman*, Herbert Bergman, Douglas A. Noverr, and Edward J. Recchia, eds., 1998.

Preface to the First Edition of *Leaves of Grass*

America does not repel the past or what it has produced under its forms or amid other politics or the idea of castes or the old religions .... accepts the lesson with calmness ... is not so impatient as has been supposed that the slough still sticks to opinions and manners and literature while the life which served its requirements has passed into the new life of the new forms ... perceives that the corpse is slowly borne from the eating and sleeping rooms of the house ... perceives that it waits a little while in the door ... that it was fittest for its days ... that its action has descended to the stalwart and wellshaped heir who approaches ... and that he shall be fittest for his days.

The Americans of all nations at any time upon the earth have probably the fullest poetical nature. The United States themselves are essentially the greatest poem. In the history of the earth hitherto the largest and most stirring appear tame and orderly to their ampler largeness and stir. Here at last is something in the doings of man that corresponds with the broadcast doings of the day and night. Here is not merely a nation but a teeming nation of nations. Here is action untied from strings necessarily blind to particulars and details magnificently moving in vast masses. Here is the hospitality which forever indicates heroes.... Here are the roughs and beards and space and ruggedness and nonchalance that the soul loves. Here the performance disdaining the trivial unapproached in the tremendous audacity of its crowds and groupings and the push of its perspective spreads with crampless and flowing breadth and showers its prolific and splendid extravagance. One sees it must indeed own the riches of the summer and winter, and need never be bankrupt while corn grows from the ground or the orchards drop apples or the bays contain fish or men beget children upon women.

Other states indicate themselves in their deputies .... but the genius of the United States is not best or most in its executives or legislatures, nor in its ambassadors or authors or colleges or churches or parlors, nor even in its newspapers or inventors ... but always most in the common people. Their manners speech dress friendships—the freshness and candor of their physiognomy—the picturesque looseness of their carriage ... their deathless attachment to freedom—their aversion to anything indecorous or soft or mean—the practical acknowledgment of the citizens of one state by the citizens of all other states—the fierceness of their roused resentment—their curiosity and welcome of novelty—their self-esteem and wonderful sympathy—their susceptibility to a slight—the air they have of persons who never knew how it felt to stand in the presence of superiors—the fluency of their speech—their delight in music, the sure symptom of manly tenderness and native elegance of soul ... their good temper and openhandedness—the terrible significance of their elections—the President's taking off his hat to them not they to him—these too are unrhymed poetry. It awaits the gigantic and generous treatment worthy of it.

The largeness of nature or the nation were monstrous without a corresponding largeness and generosity of the spirit of the citizen. Not nature nor swarming states nor streets and steamships nor prosperous business nor farms nor capital nor learning may suffice for the ideal of man ... nor suffice the poet. No reminiscences may suffice either. A live nation can always cut a deep mark and can have the best authority the cheapest ... namely from its own soul. This is the sum of the profitable uses of individuals or states and of present action and grandeur and of the subjects of poets.—As if it were necessary to trot back generation after generation to the eastern records! As if the beauty and sacredness of the demonstrable must fall behind that of the mythical! As if men do not make their mark out of any times! As if the opening of the western continent by discovery and what has transpired since in North and South America were less than the small theatre of the antique or the aimless sleepwalking of the middle ages! The pride of the United States leaves the wealth and finesse of the cities and all returns of commerce and agriculture and all the magnitude of geography or shows of exterior victory to enjoy the breed of fullsized men or one fullsized man unconquerable and simple.

The American poets are to enclose old and new for America is the race of races. Of them a bard is to be commensurate with a people. To him the other continents arrive as contributions ... he gives them reception for their sake and his own sake. His spirit responds to his country's spirit .... he incarnates its geography and natural life and rivers and lakes. Mississippi with annual freshets and changing chutes, Missouri and Columbia and Ohio and Saint Lawrence with the falls and beautiful masculine Hudson, do not embouchure where they spend themselves more than they embouchure into him. The blue breadth over the inland sea of Virginia and Maryland and the sea off Massachusetts and Maine and over Manhattan bay and over Champlain and Erie and over Ontario and Huron and Michigan and Superior, and over the Texan and Mexican and Floridian and Cuban seas and over the seas off California and Oregon, is not tallied by the blue breadth of the waters below more than the breadth of above and below is tallied by him. When the long Atlantic coast stretches longer and the Pacific coast stretches longer he easily stretches with them north or south. He spans between them also from east to west and reflects what is between them. On him rise solid growths that offset the growths of pine and cedar and hemlock and liveoak and locust and chestnut and cypress and hickory and limetree and cottonwood and tuliptree and cactus and wildvine and tamarind and persimmon .... and tangles as tangled as any canebrake or swamp .... and forests coated with transparent ice and icicles hanging from the boughs and crackling in the wind .... and sides and peaks of mountains .... and pasturage sweet and free as savannah or upland or prairie .... with flights and songs and screams that answer those of the wildpigeon and highhold and orchard-oriole and coot and surf-duck and redshouldered-hawk and fish-hawk and white-ibis and indian-hen and cat-owl and water-pheasant and qua-bird and pied-sheldrake and blackbird and mockingbird and buzzard and condor and night-heron and eagle. To him the hereditary countenance descends both mother's and father's. To him enter the essences of the real things and past and present events—of the enormous diversity of temperature and agriculture and mines—the tribes of red aborigines—the weather-beaten vessels entering new ports or making landings on rocky coasts—the first settlements north or south—the rapid stature and muscle—the haughty defiance of '76, and the war and peace and formation of the constitution .... the union always surrounded by blatherers and always calm and impregnable—the perpetual coming of immigrants—the wharfhem'd cities and superior marine—the unsurveyed interior—the loghouses and clearings and wild animals and hunters and trappers .... the free commerce—the fisheries and whaling and gold-digging—the endless gestation of new states—the convening of Congress every December, the members duly coming up from all climates and the uttermost parts .... the noble character of the young mechanics and of all free American workmen and workwomen .... the general ardor and friendliness and enterprise—the perfect equality of the female with the male .... the large amativeness—the fluid movement of the population—the factories and mercantile life and laborsaving machinery—the Yankee swap—the New-York firemen and the target excursion—the southern plantation life—the character of the northeast and of the northwest and southwest—slavery and the tremulous spreading of hands to protect it, and the stern opposition to it which shall never cease till it ceases or the speaking of tongues and the moving of lips cease. For such the expression of the American poet is to be transcendant and new. It is to be indirect and not direct or descriptive or epic. Its quality goes through these to much more. Let the age and wars of other nations be chanted and their eras and characters be illustrated and that finish the verse. Not so the great psalm of the republic. Here the theme is creative and has vista. Here comes one among the wellbeloved stonecutters and plans with decision and science and sees the solid and beautiful forms of the future where there are now no solid forms.

Of all nations the United States with veins full of poetical stuff most need poets and will doubtless have the greatest and use them the greatest. Their Presidents shall not be their common referee so much as their poets shall. Of all mankind the great poet is the equable man. Not in him but off from him things are grotesque or eccentric or fail of their sanity. Nothing out of its place is good and nothing in its place is bad. He bestows on every object or quality its fit proportions neither more nor less. He is the arbiter of the diverse and he is the key. He is the equalizer of his age and land .... he supplies what wants supplying and checks what wants checking. If peace is the routine out of him speaks the spirit of peace, large, rich, thrifty, building vast and populous cities, encouraging agriculture and the arts and commerce—lighting the study of man, the soul, immortality—federal, state or municipal government, marriage, health, freetrade, intertravel by land and sea .... nothing too close, nothing too far off ... the stars not too far off. In war he is the most deadly force of the war. Who recruits him recruits horse and foot ... he fetches parks of artillery the best that engineer ever knew. If the time becomes slothful and heavy he knows how to arouse it ... he can make every word he speaks draw blood. Whatever stagnates in the flat of custom or obedience or legislation he never stagnates. Obedience does not master him, he masters it. High up out of reach he stands turning a concentrated light ... he turns the pivot with his finger ... he baffles the swiftest runners as he stands and easily overtakes and envelops them. The time straying toward infidelity and confections and persiflage he withholds by his steady faith ... he spreads out his dishes ... he offers the sweet firmfibred meat that grows men and women. His brain is the ultimate brain. He is no arguer ... he is judgment. He judges not as the judge judges but as the sun falling around a helpless thing. As he sees the farthest he has the most faith. His thoughts are the hymns of the praise of things. In the talk on the soul and eternity and God off of his equal plane he is silent. He sees eternity less like a play with a prologue and denouement .... he sees eternity in men and women ... he does not see men and women as dreams or dots. Faith is the antiseptic of the soul ... it pervades the common people and preserves them ... they never give up believing and expecting and trusting. There is that indescribable freshness and unconsciousness about an illiterate person that humbles and mocks the power of the noblest expressive genius. The poet sees for a certainty how one not a great artist may be just as sacred and perfect as the greatest artist..... . The power to destroy or remould is freely used by him but never the power of attack. What is past is past. If he does not expose superior models and prove himself by every step he takes he is not what is wanted. The presence of the greatest poet conquers ... not parleying or struggling or any prepared attempts. Now he has passed that way see after him! there is not left any vestige of despair or misanthropy or cunning or exclusiveness or the ignominy of a nativity or color or delusion of hell or the necessity of hell ..... . and no man thenceforward shall be degraded for ignorance or weakness or sin.

The greatest poet hardly knows pettiness or triviality. If he breathes into any thing that was before thought small it dilates with the grandeur and life of the universe. He is a seer .... he is individual ... he is complete in himself .... the others are as good as he, only he sees it and they do not. He is not one of the chorus .... he does not stop for any regulation ... he is the president of regulation. What the eyesight does to the rest he does to the rest. Who knows the curious mystery of the eyesight? The other senses corroborate themselves, but this is removed from any proof but its own and foreruns the identities of the spiritual world. A single glance of it mocks all the investigations of man and all the instruments and books of the earth and all reasoning. What is marvellous? what is unlikely? what is impossible or baseless or vague? after you have once just opened the space of a peach-pit and given audience to far and near and to the sunset and had all things enter with electric swiftness softly and duly without confusion or jostling or jam.

The land and sea, the animals fishes and birds, the sky of heaven and the orbs, the forests mountains and rivers, are not small themes ... but folks expect of the poet to indicate more than the beauty and dignity which always attach to dumb real objects .... they expect him to indicate the path between reality and their souls. Men and women perceive the beauty well enough . . probably as well as he. The passionate tenacity of hunters, wood-men, early risers, cultivators of gardens and orchards and fields, the love of healthy women for the manly form, seafaring persons, drivers of horses, the passion for light and the open air, all is an old varied sign of the unfailing perception of beauty and of a residence of the poetic in outdoor people. They can never be assisted by poets to perceive ... some may but they never can. The poetic quality is not marshalled in rhyme or uniformity or abstract addresses to things nor in melancholy complaints or good precepts, but is the life of these and much else and is in the soul. The profit of rhyme is that it drops seeds of a sweeter and more luxuriant rhyme, and of uniformity that it conveys itself into its own roots in the ground out of sight. The rhyme and uniformity of perfect poems show the free growth of metrical laws and bud from them as unerringly and loosely as lilacs or roses on a bush, and take shapes as compact as the shapes of chestnuts and oranges and melons and pears, and shed the perfume impalpable to form. The fluency and ornaments of the finest poems or music or orations or recitations are not independent but dependent. All beauty comes from beautiful blood and a beautiful brain. If the greatnesses are in conjunction in a man or woman it is enough .... the fact will prevail through the universe .... but the gaggery and gilt of a million years will not prevail. Who troubles himself about his ornaments or fluency is lost. This is what you shall do: Love the earth and sun and the animals, despise riches, give alms to every one that asks, stand up for the stupid and crazy, devote your income and labor to others, hate tyrants, argue not concerning God, have patience and indulgence toward the people, take off your hat to nothing known or unknown or to any man or number of men, go freely with powerful uneducated persons and with the young and with the mothers of families, read these leaves in the open air every season of every year of your life, re-examine all you have been told at school or church or in any book, dismiss whatever insults you own soul, and your very flesh shall be a great poem and have the richest fluency not only in its words but in the silent lines of its lips and face and between the lashes of your eyes and in every motion and joint of your body .... The poet shall not spend his time in unneeded work. He shall know that the ground is always ready ploughed and manured .... others may not know it but he shall. He shall go directly to the creation. His trust shall master the trust of everything he touches .... and shall master all attachment.

The known universe has one complete lover and that is the greatest poet. He consumes an eternal passion and is indifferent which chance happens and which possible contingency of fortune or misfortune and persuades daily and hourly his delicious pay. What balks or breaks others is fuel for his burning progress to contact and amorous joy. Other proportions of the reception of pleasure dwindle to nothing to his proportions. All expected from heaven or from the highest he is rapport with in the sight of the daybreak or a scene of the winter woods or the presence of children playing or with his arm round the neck of a man or woman. His love above all love has leisure and expanse .... he leaves room ahead of himself. He is no irresolute or suspicious lover ... he is sure ... he scorns intervals. His experience and the showers and thrills are not for nothing. Nothing can jar him .... suffering and darkness cannot—death and fear cannot. To him complaint and jealousy and envy are corpses buried and rotten in the earth .... he saw them buried. The sea is not surer of the shore or the shore of the sea than he is of the fruition of his love and of all perfection and beauty.

The fruition of beauty is no chance of hit or miss ... it is inevitable as life .... it is exact and plumb as gravitation. From the eyesight proceeds another eyesight and from the hearing proceeds another hearing and from the voice proceeds another voice eternally curious of the harmony of things with man. To these respond perfections not only in the committees that were supposed to stand for the rest but in the rest themselves just the same. These understand the law of perfection in masses and floods ... that its finish is to each for itself and onward from itself ... that it is profuse and impartial ... that there is not a minute of the light or dark nor an acre of the earth or sea without it—nor any direction of the sky nor any trade or employment nor any turn of events. This is the reason that about the proper expression of beauty there is precision and balance ... one part does not need to be thrust above another. The best singer is not the one who has the most lithe and powerful organ ... the pleasure of poems is not in them that take the handsomest measure and similes and sound.

Without effort and without exposing in the least how it is done the greatest poet brings the spirit of any or all events and passions and scenes and persons some more and some less to bear on your individual character as you hear or read. To do this well is to compete with the laws that pursue and follow time. What is the purpose must surely be there and the clue of it must be there .... and the faintest indication is the indication of the best and then becomes the clearest indication. Past and present and future are not disjoined but joined. The greatest poet forms the consistence of what is to be from what has been and is. He drags the dead out of their coffins and stands them again on their feet .... he says to the past, Rise and walk before me that I may realize you. He learns the lesson .... he places himself where the future becomes present. The greatest poet does not only dazzle his rays over character and scenes and passions ... he finally ascends and finishes all ... he exhibits the pinnacles that no man can tell what they are for or what is beyond .... he glows a moment on the extremest verge. He is most wonderful in his last half-hidden smile or frown ... by that flash of the moment of parting the one that sees it shall be encouraged or terrified afterward for many years. The greatest poet does not moralize or make applications of morals ... he knows the soul. The soul has that measureless pride which consists in never acknowledging any lessons but its own. But it has sympathy as measurless as its pride and the one balances the other and neither can stretch too far while it stretches in company with the other. The inmost secrets of art sleep with the twain. The greatest poet has lain close betwixt both and they are vital in his style and thoughts.

The art of art, the glory of expression and the sunshine of the light of letters is simplicity. Nothing is better than simplicity .... nothing can make up for excess or for the lack of definiteness. To carry on the heave of impulse and pierce intellectual depths and give all subjects their articulations are powers neither common nor very uncommon. But to speak in literature with the perfect rectitude and insousiance of the movements of animals and the unimpeachableness of the sentiment of trees in the woods and grass by the roadside is the flawless triumph of art. If you have looked on him who has achieved it you have looked on one of the masters of the artists of all nations and times. You shall not contemplate the flight of the graygull over the bay or the mettlesome action of the blood horse or the tall leaning of sunflowers on their stalk or the appearance of the sun journeying through heaven or the appearance of the moon afterward with any more satisfaction than you shall contemplate him. The greatest poet has less a marked style and is more the channel of thoughts and things without increase or diminution, and is the free channel of himself. He swears to his art, I will not be meddlesome, I will not have in my writing any elegance or effect or originality to hang in the way between me and the rest like curtains. I will have nothing hang in the way, not the richest curtains. What I tell I tell for precisely what it is. Let who may exalt or startle or fascinate or soothe I will have purposes as health or heat or snow has and be as regardless of observation. What I experience or portray shall go from my composition without a shred of my composition. You shall stand by my side and look in the mirror with me.

The old red blood and stainless gentility of great poets will be proved by their unconstraint. A heroic person walks at his ease through and out of that custom or precedent or authority that suits him not. Of the traits of the brotherhood of writers savans[1] musicians inventors and artists nothing is finer than silent defiance advancing from new free forms. In the need of poems philosophy politics mechanism science behaviour, the craft of art, an appropriate native grand-opera, ship-craft, or any craft, he is greatest forever and forever who contributes the greatest original practical example. The cleanest expression is that which finds no sphere worthy of itself and makes one.

The messages of great poets to each man and women are, Come to us on equal terms, Only then can you understand us, We are no better than you, What we enclose you enclose, What we enjoy you may enjoy. Did you suppose there could be only one Supreme? We affirm there can be unnumbered Supremes, and that one does not countervail another any more than one eyesight countervails another . . and that men can be good or grand only of the consciousness of their supremacy within them. What do you think is the grandeur of storms and dismemberments and the deadliest battles and wrecks and the wildest fury of the elements and the power of the sea and the motion of nature and of the throes of human desires and dignity and hate and love? It is that something in the soul which says, Rage on, Whirl on, I tread master here and everywhere, Master of the spasms of the sky and of the shatter of the sea, Master of nature and passion and death, And of all terror and all pain.

The American bards shall be marked for generosity and affection and for encouraging competitors . . They shall be kosmos . . without monopoly or secrecy . . glad to pass any thing to any one . . hungry for equals night and day. They shall not be careful of riches and privilege . . . . they shall be riches and privilege . . . . they shall perceive who the most affluent man is. The most affluent man is he that confronts all the shows he sees by equivalents out of the stronger wealth of himself. The American bard shall delineate no class of persons nor one or two out of the strata of interests nor love most nor truth most nor the soul most nor the body most . . . . and not

---

[1]Scientists.

be for the eastern states more than the western or the northern states more than the southern.

Exact science and its practical movements are no checks on the greatest poet but always his encouragement and support. The outset and remembrance are there . . there the arms that lifted him first and brace him best . . . . there he returns after all his goings and comings. The sailor and traveler . . the anatomist chemist astronomer geologist phrenologist spiritualist mathematician historian and lexicographer are not poets, but they are the lawgivers of poets and their construction underlies the structure of every perfect poem. No matter what rises or is uttered they sent the seed of the conception of it . . . of them and by them stand the visible proofs of souls . . . . . always of their fatherstuff must be begotten the sinewy races of bards. If there shall be love and content between the father and the son and if the greatness of the son is the exuding of the greatness of the father there shall be love between the poet and the man of demonstrable science. In the beauty of poems are the tuft and final applause of science.

Great is the faith of the flush of knowledge and of the investigation of the depths of qualities and things. Cleaving and circling here swells the soul of the poet yet is president of itself always. The depths are fathomless and therefore calm. The innocence and nakedness are resumed . . . they are neither modest nor immodest. The whole theory of the special and supernatural and all that was twined with it or educed out of it departs as a dream. What has ever happened . . . . what happens and whatever may or shall happen, the vital laws enclose all . . . . they are sufficient for any case and for all cases . . . none to be hurried or retarded . . . . any miracle of affairs or persons inadmissible in the vast clear scheme where every motion and every spear of grass and the frames and spirits of men and women and all that concerns them are unspeakably perfect miracles all referring to all and each distinct and in its place. It is also not consistent with the reality of the soul to admit that there is anything in the known universe more divine than men and women.

Men and women and the earth and all upon it are simply to be taken as they are, and the investigation of their past and present and future shall be unintermitted and shall be done with perfect candor. Upon this basis philosophy speculates ever looking toward the poet, ever regarding the eternal tendencies of all toward happiness never inconsistent with what is clear to the senses and to the soul. For the eternal tendencies of all toward happiness make the only point of sane philosophy. Whatever comprehends less than that . . . whatever is less than the laws of light and of astronomical motion . . . or less than the laws that follow the thief the liar the glutton and the drunkard through this life and doubtless afterward . . . . . . or less than vast stretches of time or the slow formation of density or the patient upheaving of strata—is of no account. Whatever would put God in a poem or system of philosophy as contending against some being or influence is also of no account. Sanity and ensemble characterise the great master . . . spoilt in one principle all is spoilt. The great master has nothing to do with miracles. He sees health for himself in being one of the mass .... he sees the hiatus in singular eminence. To the perfect shape comes common ground. To be under the general law is great for that is to correspond with it. The master knows that he is unspeakably great and that all are unspeakably great .... that nothing for instance is greater than to conceive children and bring them up well ... that to be is just as great as to perceive or tell.

In the make of the great masters the idea of political liberty is indispensible. Liberty takes the adherence of heroes wherever men and women exist .... but never takes any adherence or welcome from the rest more than from poets. They are the voice and exposition of liberty. They out of ages are worthy the grand idea .... to them it is confided and they must sustain it. Nothing has precedence of it and nothing can warp or degrade it. The attitude of great poets is to cheer up slaves and horrify despots. The turn of their necks, the sound of their feet, the motions of their wrists, are full of hazard to the one and hope to the other. Come nigh them awhile and though they neither speak or advise you shall learn the faithful American lesson. Liberty is poorly served by men whose good intent is quelled from one failure or two failures or any number of failures, or from the casual indifference or ingratitude of the people, or from the sharp show of the tushes of power, or the bringing to bear soldiers and cannon or any penal statutes. Liberty relies upon itself, invites no one, promises nothing, sits in calmness and light, is positive and composed, and knows no discouragement. The battle rages with many a loud alarm and frequent advance and retreat .... the enemy triumphs .... the prison, the handcuffs, the iron necklace and anklet, the scaffold, garrote and leadballs do their work .... the cause is asleep .... the strong throats are choked with their own blood .... the young men drop their eyelashes toward the ground when they pass each other .... and is liberty gone out of that place? No never. When liberty goes it is not the first to go nor the second or third to go . . it waits for all the rest to go . . it is the last... When the memories of the old martyrs are faded utterly away .... when the large names of patriots are laughed at in the public halls from the lips of the orators .... when the boys are no more christened after the same but christened after tyrants and traitors instead .... when the laws of the free are grudgingly permitted and laws for informers and blood-money are sweet to the taste of the people .... when I and you walk abroad upon the earth stung with compassion at the sight of numberless brothers answering our equal friendship and calling no man master—and when we are elated with noble joy at the sight of slaves .... when the soul retires in the cool communion of the night and surveys its experience and has much extasy over the word and deed that put back a helpless innocent person into the gripe of the gripers or into any cruel inferiority .... when those in all parts of these states who could easier realize the true American character but do not yet—when the swarms of cringers, suckers, doughfaces, lice of politics, planners of sly involutions for their own preferment to city offices or state legislatures or the judiciary or congress or the presidency, obtain a response of love and natural deference from the people whether they get

the offices or no .... when it is better to be a bound booby and rogue in
office at a high salary than the poorest free mechanic or farmer with his hat
unmoved from his head and firm eyes and a candid and generous heart ....
and when servility by town or state or the federal government or any
oppression on a large scale or small scale can be tried on without its own
punishment following duly after in exact proportion against the smallest
chance of escape .... or rather when all life and all the souls of men and
women are discharged from that part of the earth.

As the attributes of the poets of the kosmos concentre in the real body
and soul and in the pleasure of things they possess the superiority of genuineness over all fiction and romance. As they emit themselves facts are
showered over with light .... the daylight is lit with more volatile light ....
also the deep between the setting and rising sun goes deeper many fold.
Each precise object or condition or combination or process exhibits a
beauty .... the multiplication table its—old age its—the carpenter's trade
its—the grand-opera its .... the hugehulled clean-shaped New-York clipper
at sea under steam or full sail gleams with unmatched beauty .... the
American circles and large harmonies of government gleam with theirs ....
and the commonest definite intentions and actions with theirs. The poets
of the kosmos advance through all interpositions and coverings and turmoils and stratagems to first principles. They are of use .... they dissolve
poverty from its need and riches from its conceit. You large proprietor they
say shall not realize or perceive more than any one else. The owner of the
library is not he who holds a legal title to it having bought and paid for it.
Any one and every one is owner of the library who can read the same
through all the varieties of tongues and subjects and styles, and in whom
they enter with ease and take residence and force toward paternity and maternity, and make supple and powerful and rich and large......... . These
American states strong and healthy and accomplished shall receive no pleasure from violations of natural models and must not permit them. In paintings or mouldings or carvings in mineral or wood, or in the illustrations of
books or newspapers, or in any comic or tragic prints, or in the patterns of
woven stuffs or any thing to beautify rooms or furniture or costumes, or to
put upon cornices or monuments or on the prows or sterns of ships, or to
put anywhere before the human eye indoors or out, that which distorts honest shapes or which creates unearthly beings or places or contingencies is a
nuisance and revolt. Of the human form especially it is so great it must
never be made ridiculous. Of ornaments to a work nothing outre[2] can be
allowed .. but those ornaments can be allowed that conform to the perfect
facts of the open air and that flow out of the nature of the work and come
irrepressibly from it and are necessary to the completion of the work. Most
works are most beautiful without ornament... Exaggerations will be

[2]Excessive, extravagant. An example of Whitman's many "borrowings" from the French
language.

revenged in human physiology. Clean and vigorous children are jetted and conceived only in those communities where the models of natural forms are public every day..... Great genius and the people of these states must never be demeaned to romances. As soon as histories are properly told there is no more need of romances.

The great poets are also to be known by the absence in them of tricks and by the justification of perfect personal candor. Then folks echo a new cheap joy and a divine voice leaping from their brains: How beautiful is candor! All faults may be forgiven of him who has perfect candor. Henceforth let no man of us lie, for we have seen that openness wins the inner and outer world and that there is no single exception, and that never since our earth gathered itself in a mass have deceit or subterfuge or prevarication attracted its smallest particle or the faintest tinge of a shade—and that through the enveloping wealth and rank of a state or the whole republic of states a sneak or sly person shall be discovered and despised .... and that the soul has never been once fooled and never can be fooled .... and thrift without the loving nod of the soul is only a fœtid puff .... and there never grew up in any of the continents of the globe nor upon any planet or satellite or star, nor upon the asteroids, nor in any part of ethereal space, nor in the midst of density, nor under the fluid wet of the sea, nor in that condition which precedes the birth of babes, nor at any time during the changes of life, nor in that condition that follows what we term death, nor in any stretch of abeyance or action afterward of vitality, nor in any process of formation or reformation anywhere, a being whose instinct hated the truth.

Extreme caution or prudence, the soundest organic health, large hope and comparison and fondness for women and children, large alimentiveness and destructiveness and causality, with a perfect sense of the oneness of nature and the propriety of the same spirit applied to human affairs . . these are called up of the float of the brain of the world to be parts of the greatest poet from his birth out of his mother's womb and from her birth out of her mother's. Caution seldom goes far enough. It has been thought that the prudent citizen was the citizen who applied himself to solid gains and did well for himself and his family and completed a lawful life without debt or crime. The greatest poet sees and admist these economies as he sees the economies of food and sleep, but has higher notions of prudcence than to think he gives much when he gives a few slight attentions at the latch of the gate. The premises of the prudence of life are not the hospitality of it or the ripeness and harvest of it. Beyond the independence of a little sum laid aside for burial-money, and of a few clap-boards around and shingles overhead on a lot of American soil owned, and the easy dollars that supply the year's plain clothing and meals, the melancholy prudence of the abandonment of such a great being as a man is to the toss and pallor of years of moneymaking with all their scorching days and icy nights and all their stifling deceits and underhanded dodgings, or infinitessimals of parlors, or shameless stuffing while others starve . . and all the loss of the bloom and odor of the earth and of the flowers and atmosphere and of the sea and of the true taste of the women and men you pass or have to do with in youth or middle age, and the issuing sickness and desperate revolt at the close of a life without elevation or naivete, and the ghastly chatter of a death without serenity or majesty, is the great fraud upon modern civilization and fore-thought, blotching the surface and system which civilization undeniably drafts, and moistening with tears the immense features it spreads and spreads with such velocity before the reached kisses of the soul... Still the right explanation remains to be made about prudence. The prudence of the mere wealth and respectability of the most esteemed life appears too faint for the eye to observe at all when little and large alike drop quietly aside at the thought of the prudence suitable for immortality. What is wisdom that fills the thinness of a year or seventy or eighty years to wisdom spaced out by ages and coming back at a certain time with strong reinforcements and rich presents and the clear faces of wedding-guests as far as you can look in every direction running gaily toward you? Only the soul is of itself .... all else has reference to what ensues. All that a person does or thinks is of consequence. Not a move can a man or woman make that affects him or her in a day or a month or any part of the direct lifetime or the hour of death but the same affects him or her onward afterward through the indirect lifetime. The indirect is always as great and real as the direct. The spirit receives from the body just as much as it gives to the body. Not one name of word or deed . . not of venereal sores or discolorations . . not the privacy of the onanist . . not of the putrid veins of gluttons or rumdrinkers ... not peculation or cunning or betrayal or murder . . no serpentine poision of those that seduce women . . not the foolish yielding of women . . not prostitution . . not of any depravity of young men . . not of the attainment of gain by discreditable means . . not any nastiness of appetite . . not any harshness of officers to men or judges to prisoners or fathers to sons or sons to fathers or of husbands to wives or bosses to their boys . . not of greedy looks or malignant wishes ... nor any of the wiles practised by people upon themselves ... ever is or ever can be stamped on the programme but it is duly realized and returned, and that returned in further performances ... and they returned again. Nor can the push of charity or personal force ever be any thing else than the profoundest reason, whether it bring arguments to hand or no. No specification is necessary . . to add or subtract or divide is in vain. Little or big, learned or unlearned, white or black, legal or illegal, sick or well, from the first inspiration down the windpipe to the last expiration out of it, all that a male or female does that is vigorous and benevolent and clean is so much sure profit to him or her in the unshakable order of the universe and through the whole scope of it forever. If the savage or felon is wise it is well .... if the greatest poet or savan is wise it is simply the same . . if the President or chief justice is wise it is the same ... if the young mechanic or farmer is wise it is no more or less . . if the prositute is wise it is no more nor less. The interest will come round . . all will come round. All the best actions of war and peace ... all help given to relatives and strangers and the poor and old and sorrowful and young children and widows and the sick, and to all shunned persons . . all furtherance of fugitives and of the escape of slaves . . all the self-denial that stood steady and aloof on wrecks and saw others take the seats of the boats . . . all offering of substance or life for the good old cause, or for a friend's sake or opinion's sake . . . all pains of enthusiasts scoffed at by their neighbors . . all the vast sweet love and precious suffering of mothers . . . all honest men baffled in strifes recorded or unrecorded . . . . all the grandeur and good of the few ancient nations whose fragments of annals we inherit . . and all the good of the hundreds of far mightier and more ancient nations unknown to us by name or date or location . . . . all that was ever manfully begun, whether it succeeded or no . . . . all that has at any time been well suggested out of the divine heart of man or by the divinity of his mouth or by the shaping of his great hands . . and all that is well thought or done this day on any part of the surface of the globe . . or on any of the wandering stars or fixed stars by those there as we are here . . or that is henceforth to be well thought or done by you whoever you are, or by any one—these singly and wholly inured at their time and inure now and will inure always to the identities from which they sprung or shall spring. . . Did you guess any of them lived only its moment? The world does not so exist . . no parts palpable or impalpable so exist . . . no result exists now without being from its long antecedent result, and that from its antecdent, and so backward without the farthest mentionable spot coming a bit nearer the beginning than any other spot. . . . . Whatever satisfies the soul is truth. The prudence of the greatest poet answers at last the craving and glut of the soul, is not contemptuous of less ways of prudence if they conform to its ways, puts off nothing, permits no let-up for its own case or any case, has no particular sabbath or judgment-day, divides not the living from the dead or the righteous from the unrighteous, is satisfied with the present, matches every thought or act by its correlative, knows no possible forgiveness or deputed atonement . . knows that the young man who composedly periled his life and lost it has done exceeding well for himself, while the man who has not periled his life and retains it to old age in riches and ease has perhaps achieved nothing for himself worth mentioning . . and that only that person has no great prudence to learn who has learnt to prefer real longlived things, and favors body and soul the same, and perceives the indirect assuredly following the direct, and what evil or good he does leaping onward and waiting to meet him again—and who in his spirit in any emergency whatever neither hurries or avoids death.

The direct trial of him who would be the greatest poet is today. If he does not flood himself with the immediate age as with vast oceanic tides . . . . . and if he does not attract his own land body and soul to himself and hang on its neck with incomparable love and plunge his semitic[3] muscle into its merits and demerits . . . and if he be not himself the age transfigured . . . . and

---

[3]Whitman's own rather awkward coinage, suggesting the sexual organ through which semen passes.

if to him is not opened the eternity which gives similitude to all periods and locations and processes and animate and inanimate forms, and which is the bond of time, and rises up from its inconceivable vagueness and infiniteness in the swimming shape of today, and is held by the ductile anchors of life, and makes the present spot the passage from what was to what shall be, and commits itself to the representation of this wave of an hour and this one of the sixty beautiful children of the wave—let him merge in the general run and wait his development........ ..... Still the final test of poems or any character or work remains. The prescient poet projects himself centuries ahead and judges performer or performance after the changes of time. Does it live through them? Does it still hold on untired? Will the same style and the direction of genius to similar points be satisfactory now? Has no new discovery in science or arrival at superior planes of thought and judgment and behaviour fixed him or his so that either can be looked down upon? Have the marches of tens and hundreds and thousands of years made willing detours to the right hand and the left hand for his sake? Is he beloved long and long after he is buried? Does the young man think often of him? and the young woman think often of him? and do the middleaged and the old think of him?

A great poem is for ages and ages in common and for all degrees and complexions and all departments and sects and for a woman as much as a man and a man as much as a woman. A great poem is no finish to a man or woman but rather a beginning. Has any one fancied he could sit at last under some due authority and rest satisfied with explanations and realize and be content and full? To no such terminus does the greatest poet bring ... he brings neither cessation or sheltered fatness and ease. The touch of him tells in action. Whom he takes he takes with firm sure grasp into live regions previously unattained .... thenceforward is no rest .... they see the space and ineffable sheen that turn the old spots and lights into dead vacuums. The companion of him beholds the birth and progress of stars and learns one of the meanings. Now there shall be a man cohered out of tumult and chaos .... the elder encourages the younger and shows him how ... they two shall launch off fearlessly together till the new world fits an orbit for itself and looks unabashed on the lesser orbits of the stars and sweeps through the ceaseless rings and shall never be quiet again.

There will soon be no more priests. Their work is done. They may wait awhile . . perhaps a generation or two . . dropping off by degrees. A superior breed shall take their place .... the gangs of kosmos and prophets en masse shall take their place. A new order shall arise and they shall be the priests of man, and every man shall be his own priest. The churches built under their umbrage shall be the churches of men and women. Through the divinity of themselves shall the kosmos and the new breed of poets be interpreters of men and women and of all events and things. They shall find their inspiration in real objects today, symptoms of the past and future .... They shall not deign to defend immortality or God or the perfection of things or liberty or the exquisite beauty and reality of the soul. They shall arise in America and be responded to from the remainder of the earth.

The English language befriends the grand American expression .... it is brawny enough and limber and full enough. On the tough stock of a race who through all change of circumstance was never without the idea of political liberty, which is the animus of all liberty, it has attracted the terms of daintier and gayer and subtler and more elegant tongues. It is the powerful language of resistance ... it is the dialect of common sense. It is the speech of the proud and melancholy races and of all who aspire. It is the chosen tongue to express growth faith self-esteem freedom justice equality friendliness amplitude prudence decision and courage. It is the medium that shall well nigh express the inexpressible.

No great literature nor any like style of behaviour or oratory or social intercourse or household arrangements or public institutions or the treatment by bosses of employed people, nor executive detail or detail of the army or navy, nor spirit of legislation or courts or police or tuition or architecture or songs or amusements or the costumes of young men, can long elude the jealous and passionate instinct of American standards. Whether or no the sign appears from the mouths of the people, it throbs a live interrogation in every freeman's and freewoman's heart after that which passes by or this built to remain. Is it uniform with my country? Are its disposals without ignominious distinctions? Is it for the evergrowing communes of brothers and lovers, large, well-united, proud beyond the old models, generous beyond all models? Is it something grown fresh out of the fields or drawn from the sea for use to me today here? I know that what answers for me an American must answer for any individual or nation that serves for a part of my materials. Does this answer? or is it without reference to universal needs? or sprung of the needs of the less developed society of special ranks? or old needs of pleasure overlaid by modern science and forms? Does this acknowledge liberty with audible and absolute acknowledgement, and set slavery at nought for life and death? Will it help breed one goodshaped and wellhung man, and a woman to be his perfect and independent mate? Does it improve manners? Is it for the nursing of the young of the republic? Does it solve readily with the sweet milk of the nipples of the breasts of the mother of many children? Has it too the old everfresh forbearance and impartiality? Does it look with the same love on the last born and on those hardening toward stature, and on the errant, and on those who disdain all strength of assault outside of their own?

The poems distilled from other poems will probably pass away. The coward will surely pass away. The expectation of the vital and great can only be satisfied by the demeanor of the vital and great. The swarms of the polished deprecating and reflectors and the polite float off and leave no remembrance. America prepares with composure and goodwill for the visitors that have sent word. It is not intellect that is to be their warrant and welcome. The talented, the artist, the ingenious, the editor, the statesman, the erudite ... they are not unappreciated ... they fall in their place and do their work. The soul of the nation also does its work. No disguise can pass on it ... no disguise can conceal from it. It rejects none, it permits all. Only toward as good as itself and toward the like of itself will it advance half-way. An individual is as superb as a nation when he has the qualities which make a superb nation. The soul of the largest and wealthiest and proudest nation may well go half-way to meet that of its poets. The signs are effectual. There is no fear of mistake. If the one is true the other is true. The proof of a poet is that his country absorbs him as affectionately as he has absorbed it.

1855

Song of Myself[1]

[1]   I celebrate myself,
    And what I assume you shall assume,
    For every atom belonging to me as good belongs to you.

    I loafe and invite my soul,
    I lean and loafe at my ease .... observing a spear of summer grass.   5

[2]   Houses and rooms are full of perfumes .... the shelves are crowded
        with perfumes,
    I breathe the fragrance myself, and know it and like it,
    The distillation would intoxicate me also, but I shall not let it.

    The atmosphere is not a perfume .... it has no taste of the
        distillation .... it is odorless,
    It is for my mouth forever .... I am in love with it,   10
    I will go to the bank by the wood and become undisguised and naked,
    I am mad for it to be in contact with me.

    The smoke of my own breath,
    Echos, ripples, and buzzed whispers .... loveroot, silkthread, crotch
        and vine,
    My respiration and inspiration .... the beating of my heart .... the   15
        passing of blood and air through my lungs,
    The sniff of green leaves and dry leaves, and of the shore and
        darkcolored sea-rocks, and of hay in the barn,

---

[1]"Song of Myself" was the first of the twelve untitled poems that followed the Preface in the first edition of *Leaves of Grass* (1855). In the 1856 *Leaves*, it was titled "Poem of Walt Whitman, An American." It was not until the final edition of *Leaves of Grass* in 1881 that the poem was titled "Song of Myself." We have used the 1855 version because in later editions Whitman toned down some of the more radical stylistic, linguistic, and thematic features of the original edition of *Leaves of Grass*. For the convenience of readers familiar with the later version of "Song of Myself," which is divided into fifty-two sections, we have provided the section numbers in marginal brackets at the point at which each section begins in the 1881 edition. The line numbers will not, of course, correspond to those of later versions of the poem, since Whitman added and, less frequently, deleted lines from the text.

The sound of the belched words of my voice .... words loosed to the
  eddies of the wind,
A few light kisses .... a few embraces .... a reaching around of arms,
The play of shine and shade on the trees as the supple boughs wag,
The delight alone or in the rush of the streets, or along the fields   20
  and hillsides,
The feeling of health .... the full-noon trill .... the song of me rising
  from bed and meeting the sun.
Have you reckoned a thousand acres much? Have you reckoned the
  earth much?
Have you practiced so long to learn to read?
Have you felt so proud to get at the meaning of poems?

Stop this day and night with me and you shall possess the origin of   25
  all poems,
You shall possess the good of the earth and sun .... there are millions
  of suns left,
You shall no longer take things at second or third hand .... nor look
  through the eyes of the dead .... nor feed on the spectres in
  books,
You shall not look through my eyes either, nor take things from me,
You shall listen to all sides and filter them from yourself.

[3]   I have heard what the talkers were talking .... the talk of the   30
  beginning and the end,
But I do not talk of the beginning or the end.

There was never any more inception than there is now,
Nor any more youth or age than there is now;
And will never be any more perfection than there is now,
Nor any more heaven or hell than there is now.   35
Urge and urge and urge,
Always the procreant urge of the world.

Out of the dimness opposite equals advance .... Always
  substance and increase,
Always a knit of identity .... always distinction .... always a breed of life.
To elaborate is no avail .... Learned and unlearned feel that it is so.   40

Sure as the most certain sure .... plumb in the uprights, well
  entretied, braced in the beams,
Stout as a horse, affectionate, haughty, electrical,
I and this mystery here we stand.

Clear and sweet is my soul .... and clear and sweet is all that is not
  my soul.

Lack one lacks both .... and the unseen is proved by the seen,   45
Till that becomes unseen and receives proof in its turn.

Showing the best and dividing it from the worst, age vexes age,
Knowing the perfect fitness and equanimity of things, while they
    discuss I am silent, and go bathe and admire myself.

Welcome is every organ and attribute of me, and of any man hearty
    and clean,
Not an inch nor a particle of an inch is vile, and none shall be less   50
    familiar than the rest.
I am satisfied .... I see, dance, laugh, sing;
As God comes a loving bedfellow and sleeps at my side all night and
    close on the peep of the day,
And leaves for me baskets covered with white towels bulging the
    house with their plenty,
Shall I postpone my acceptation and realization and scream at my
    eyes,
That they turn from gazing after and down the road,   55
And forthwith cipher and show me to a cent,
Exactly the contents of one, and exactly the contents of two, and
    which is ahead?

[4]   Trippers and askers surround me,
People I meet ..... the effect upon me of my early life .... of the
    ward and city I live in .... of the nation,
The latest news .... discoveries, inventions, societies .... authors   60
    old and new,
My dinner, dress, associates, looks, business, compliments, dues,
The real or fancied indifference of some man or woman I love,
The sickness of one of my folks—or of myself .... or illdoing.... or
    loss or lack of money .... or depressions or exaltations,
They come to me days and nights and go from me again,
But they are not the Me myself.   65

Apart from the pulling and hauling stands what I am,
Stands amused, complacent, compassionating, idle, unitary,
Looks down, is erect, bends an arm on an impalpable certain rest,
Looks with its sidecurved head curious what will come next,
Both in and out of the game, and watching and wondering at it.   70

Backward I see in my own days where I sweated through fog with
    linguists and contenders,
I have no mockings or arguments .... I witness and wait.

[5]   I believe in you my soul .... the other I am must not abase itself
    to you,
And you must not be abased to the other.

Loafe with me on the grass .... loose the stop from your throat,   75
Not words, not music or rhyme I want .... not custom or lecture, not
    even the best,
Only the lull I like, the hum of your valved voice.

I mind how we lay in June, such a transparent summer morning;
You settled your head athwart my hips and gently turned over
    upon me,
And parted the shirt from my bosom-bone, and plunged your   80
    tongue to my barestript heart,
And reached till you felt my beard, and reached till you held my feet.
Swiftly arose and spread around me the peace and joy and knowledge
    that pass all the art and argument of the earth;
And I know that the hand of God is the elderhand of my own,
And I know that the spirit of God is the eldest brother of my own,
And that all the men ever born are also my brothers .... and the   85
    women my sisters and lovers,
And that a kelson[2] of the creation is love;
And limitless are leaves stiff or drooping in the fields,
And brown ants in the little wells beneath them,
And mossy scabs of the wormfence, and heaped stones, and elder and
    mullen and pokeweed.

[6]   A child said, What is the grass? fetching it to me with full hands;   90

How could I answer the child? .... I do not know what it is any more
    than he.

I guess it must be the flag of my disposition, out of hopeful green
    stuff woven.

Or I guess it is the handkerchief of the Lord,
A scented gift and remembrancer designedly dropped,
Bearing the owner's name someway in the corners, that we may see   95
    and remark, and say Whose?

Or I guess the grass is itself a child .... the produced babe of the
    vegetation.

Or I guess it is a uniform hieroglyphic,
And it means, Sprouting alike in broad zones and narrow zones,
Growing among black folks as among white,

---

[2]A structural unit that connects or reinforces,
like the keelson that braces the keel of a
ship.

Kanuck, Tuckahoe, Congressman, Cuff,[3] I give them the same, I   100
    receive them the same.

And now it seems to me the beautiful uncut hair of graves.

Tenderly will I use you curling grass,
It may be you transpire from the breasts of young men,
It may be if I had known them I would have loved them;
It may be you are from old people and from women, and from   105
    offspring taken soon out of their mothers' laps,
And here you are the mothers' laps.

This grass is very dark to be from the white heads of old mothers,
Darker than the colorless beards of old men,
Dark to come from under the faint red roofs of mouths.
O I perceive after all so many uttering tongues!   110
And I perceive they do not come from the roofs of mouths for
    nothing.

I wish I could translate the hints about the dead young men and
    women,
And the hints about old men and mothers, and the offspring taken
    soon out of their laps.

What do you think has become of the young and old men?
And what do you think has become of the women and children?   115

They are alive and well somewhere;
The smallest sprout shows there is really no death,
And if ever there was it led forward life, and does not wait at the end
    to arrest it,
And ceased the moment life appeared.

All goes onward and outward .... and nothing collapses,   120
And to die is different from what any one supposed, and luckier.

[7]   Has any one supposed it lucky to be born?
I hasten to inform him or her it is just as lucky to die, and I know it.

I pass death with the dying, and birth with the new-washed babe....
    and am not contained between my hat and boots,
And peruse manifold objects, no two alike, and every one good,   125
The earth good, and the stars good, and their adjuncts all good.
I am not an earth nor an adjunct of an earth,

---

[3]Kanuck, a French Canadian; Tuckahoe, a Virginian; Cuff, a black person.

I am the mate and companion of people, all just as immortal and
    fathomless as myself;
They do not know how immortal, but I know.

Every kind for itself and its own .... for me mine male and female,   130
For me all that have been boys and that love women,
For me the man that is proud and feels how it stings to be slighted,
For me the sweetheart and the old maid .... for me mothers and the
    mothers of mothers,
For me lips that have smiled, eyes that have shed tears,
For me children and the begetters of children.   135

Who need be afraid of the merge?
Undrape .... you are not guilty to me, nor stale nor discarded,
I see through the broadcloth and gingham whether or no,
And am around, tenacious, acquisitive, tireless .... and can never be
    shaken away.

[8]   The little one sleeps in its cradle,   140
I lift the gauze and look a long time, and silently brush away flies with
    my hand.
The youngster and the redfaced girl turn aside up the bushy hill,
I peeringly view them from the top.

The suicide sprawls on the bloody floor of the bedroom.
It is so .... I witnessed the corpse .... there the pistol had fallen.   145

The blab of the pave .... the tires of carts and sluff of bootsoles and
    talk of the promenaders,
The heavy omnibus, the driver with his interrogating thumb, the
    clank of the shod horses on the granite floor,
The carnival of sleighs, the clinking and shouted jokes and pelts of
    snowballs;
The hurrahs for popular favorites .... the fury of roused mobs,
The flap of the curtained litter—the sick man inside, borne to the   150
    hospital,
The meeting of enemies, the sudden oath, the blows and fall,
The excited crowd—the policeman with his star quickly working his
    passage to the centre of the crowd;
The impassive stones that receive and return so many echoes,
The souls moving along .... are they invisible while the least atom of
    the stones is visible?
What groans of overfed or half-starved who fall on the flags[4]   155
    sunstruck or in fits,

---

[4]Slabs of flagstone used for paving.

What exclamations of women taken suddenly, who hurry home and
    give birth to babes,
What living and buried speech is always vibrating here .... what howls
    restrained by decorum,
Arrests of criminals, slights, adulterous offers made, acceptances,
    rejections with convex lips,
I mind them or the resonance of them .... I come again and again.

[9]   The big doors of the country-barn stand open and ready,   160
    The dried grass of the harvest-time loads the slow-drawn wagon,
    The clear light plays on the brown gray and green intertinged,
    The armfuls are packed to the sagging mow:
    I am there .... I help .... I came stretched atop of the load,
    I felt its soft jolts .... one leg reclined on the other,   165
    I jump from the crossbeams, and seize the clover and timothy,
    And roll head over heels, and tangle my hair full of wisps.

[10]   Alone far in the wilds and mountains I hunt,
    Wandering amazed at my own lightness and glee,

    In the late afternoon choosing a safe spot to pass the night,   170
    Kindling a fire and broiling the freshkilled game,
    Soundly falling asleep on the gathered leaves, my dog and gun by my
        side.
    The Yankee clipper is under her three skysails .... she cuts the sparkle
        and scud,
    My eyes settle the land .... I bend at her prow or shout joyously from
        the deck.

    The boatmen and clamdiggers arose early and stopped for me,   175
    I tucked my trowser-ends in my boots and went and had a good time,
    You should have been with us that day round the chowder-kettle.

    I saw the marriage of the trapper in the open air in the farwest.... the
        bride was a red girl,
    Her father and his friends sat near by crosslegged and dumbly
        smoking .... they had moccasins to their feet and large thick
        blankets hanging from their shoulders;
    On a bank lounged the trapper .... he was dressed mostly in   180
        skins .... his luxuriant beard and curls protected his neck,
    One hand rested on his rifle .... the other hand held firmly the wrist
        of the red girl,
    She had long eyelashes .... her head was bare .... her coarse straight
        locks descended upon her voluptuous limbs and reached to her
        feet.

The runaway slave[5] came to my house and stopped outside,
I heard his motions crackling the twigs of the woodpile,
Through the swung half-door of the kitchen I saw him limpsey and 185
    weak,
And went where he sat on a log, and led him in and assured him,
And brought water and filled a tub for his sweated body and bruised
    feet,
And gave him a room that entered from my own, and gave him some
    coarse clean clothes,
And remember perfectly well his revolving eyes and his awkwardness,
And remember putting plasters on the galls of his neck and ankles; 190
He staid with me a week before he was recuperated and passed north,
I had him sit next me at table .... my firelock leaned in the corner.

[11]   Twenty-eight young men bathe by the shore,
Twenty-eight young men, and all so friendly,
Twenty-eight years of womanly life, and all so lonesome.   195

She owns the fine house by the rise of the bank,
She hides handsome and richly drest aft the blinds of the window.

Which of the young men does she like the best?
Ah the homeliest of them is beautiful to her.
Where are you off to, lady? for I see you,   200
You splash in the water there, yet stay stock still in your room.

Dancing and laughing along the beach came the twenty-ninth bather,
The rest did not see her, but she saw them and loved them.

The beards of the young men glistened with wet, it ran from their
    long hair,
Little streams passed all over their bodies.   205

An unseen hand also passed over their bodies,
It descended tremblingly from their temples and ribs.

The young men float on their backs, their white bellies swell to the
    sun .... they do not ask who seizes fast to them,
They do not know who puffs and declines with pendant and bending
    arch,
They do not think whom they souse with spray.   210

[12]   The butcher-boy puts off his killing-clothes, or sharpens his knife at
    the stall in the market,

[5]A new and more rigorous Fugitive Slave Act, which required that inhabitants of the free states assist in the capture and return of runaway slaves, was adopted as part of the politically controversial Compromise of 1850.

I loiter enjoying his repartee and his shuffle and breakdown.[6]
Blacksmiths with grimed and hairy chests environ the anvil,
Each has his main-sledge .... they are all out .... there is a great heat
    in the fire.

From the cinder-strewed threshold I follow their movements,   215
The lithe sheer of their waists plays even with their massive arms,
Overhand the hammers roll—overhand so slow—overhand so sure,
They do not hasten, each man hits in his place.

[13]   The negro holds firmly the reins of his four horses .... the block
        swags underneath on its tied-over chain,
The negro that drives the huge dray of the stoneyard .... steady   220
        and tall he stands poised on one leg on the stringpiece,
His blue shirt exposes his ample neck and breast and loosens over his
        hipband,
His glance is calm and commanding .... he tosses the slouch of his
        hat away from his forehead,
The sun falls on his crispy hair and moustache .... falls on the black
        of his polish'd and perfect limbs.

I behold the picturesque giant and love him .... and I do not stop
        there,
I go with the team also.   225

In me the caresser of life wherever moving .... backward as well as
        forward slueing,
To niches aside and junior bending.
Oxen that rattle the yoke or halt in the shade, what is that you
        express in your eyes?
It seems to me more than all the print I have read in my life.

My tread scares the wood-drake and wood-duck on my distant and   230
        daylong ramble,
They rise together, they slowly circle around.... I believe in those
        winged purposes,
And acknowledge the red yellow and white playing within me,
And consider the green and violet and the tufted crown intentional;
And do not call the tortoise unworthy because she is not   235
        something else,
And the mockingbird in the swamp never studied the gamut, yet trills
        pretty well to me,
And the look of the bay mare shames silliness out of me.

[6]Dances popularized by minstrel shows.

[14]   The wild gander leads his flock through the cool night,
Ya-honk! he says, and sounds it down to me like an invitation;
The pert may suppose it meaningless, but I listen closer,   240
I find its purpose and place up there toward the November sky.

The sharphoofed moose of the north, the cat on the housesill, the
      chickadee, the prairie-dog,
The litter of the grunting sow as they tug at her teats,
The brood of the turkeyhen, and she with her halfspread wings,
I see in them and myself the same old law.   245

The press of my foot to the earth springs a hundred affections,
They scorn the best I can do to relate them.
I am enamoured of growing outdoors,
Of men that live among cattle or taste of the ocean or woods,
Of the builders and steerers of ships, of the wielders of axes and   250
      mauls, of the drivers of horses,
I can eat and sleep with them week in and week out.

What is commonest and cheapest and nearest and easiest is Me,
Me going in for my chances, spending for vast returns,
Adorning myself to bestow myself on the first that will take me,
Not asking the sky to come down to my goodwill,   255
Scattering it freely forever.

[15]   The pure contralto sings in the organloft,
The carpenter dresses his plank .... the tongue of his foreplane its
      wild ascending lisp,
The married and unmarried children ride home to their thanksgiving
      dinner,
The pilot seizes the king-pin, he heaves down with a strong arm,   260
The mate stands braced in the whaleboat, lance and harpoon are
      ready,
The duck-shooter walks by silent and cautious stretches,
The deacons are ordained with crossed hands at the altar,
The spinning-girl retreats and advances to the hum of the big wheel,
The farmer stops by the bars of a Sunday and looks at the oats   265
      and rye,
The lunatic is carried at last to the asylum a confirmed case,
He will never sleep any more as he did in the cot in his mother's
      bedroom;
The jour printer with gray head and gaunt jaws works at his case,
He turns his quid of tobacco, his eyes get blurred with the manuscript;
The malformed limbs are tied to the anatomist's table,   270
What is removed drops horribly in a pail;
The quadroon girl is sold at the stand .... the drunkard nods by the
      barroom stove,

The machinist rolls up his sleeves .... the policeman travels his
    beat .... the gate-keeper marks who pass,
The young fellow drives the express-wagon .... I love him though I do
    not know him;
The half-breed straps on his light boots to compete in the race,   275
The western turkey-shooting draws old and young .... some lean on
    their rifles, some sit on logs,
Out from the crowd steps the marksman and takes his position and
    levels his piece;
The groups of newly-come immigrants cover the wharf or levee,
The woollypates hoe in the sugarfield, the overseer views them from
    his saddle;
The bugle calls in the ballroom, the gentlemen run for their   280
    partners, the dancers bow to each other;
The youth lies awake in the cedar-roofed garret and harks to the
    musical rain,
The Wolverine[7] sets traps on the creek that helps fill the Huron,
The reformer ascends the platform, he spouts with his mouth and
    nose,
The company returns from its excursion, the darkey brings up the
    rear and bears the well-riddled target,
The squaw wrapt in her yellow-hemmed cloth is offering moccasins 285
    and beadbags for sale,
The connoisseur peers along the exhibition-gallery with halfshut eyes
    bent sideways,
The deckhands make fast the steamboat, the plank is thrown for the
    shoregoing passengers,
The young sister holds out the skein, the elder sister winds it off in a
    ball and stops now and then for the knots,
The one-year wife is recovering and happy, a week ago she bore her
    first child,
The cleanhaired Yankee girl works with her sewing-machine or   290
    in the factory or mill,
The nine months' gone is in the parturition chamber, her faintness
    and pains are advancing;
The pavingman leans on his twohanded rammer—the reporter's lead
    flies swiftly over the notebook—the signpainter is lettering with
    red and gold,
The canal-boy trots on the towpath—the bookkeeper counts at his
    desk—the shoemaker waxes his thread,
The conductor beats time for the band and all the performers follow
    him,
The child is baptised—the convert is making the first professions,   295
The regatta is spread on the bay .... how the white sails sparkle!

[7] Inhabitant of Michigan.

The drover watches his drove, he sings out to them that would stray,

The pedlar sweats with his pack on his back—the purchaser higgles
about the odd cent,

The camera and plate are prepared, the lady must sit for her
daguerreotype,

The bride unrumples her white dress, the minutehand of the clock 300
moves slowly,

The opium eater reclines with rigid head and just-opened lips,

The prostitute draggles her shawl, her bonnet bobs on her tipsy and
pimpled neck,

The crowd laugh at her blackguard oaths, the men jeer and wink to
each other, (Miserable! I do not laugh at your oaths nor jeer you,)

The President holds a cabinet council, he is surrounded by the   305
great secretaries,

On the piazza walk five friendly matrons with twined arms;

The crew of the fish-smack pack repeated layers of halibut in the hold,

The Missourian crosses the plains toting his wares and his cattle,

The fare-collector goes through the train—he gives notice by the
jingling of loose change,

The floormen are laying the floor—the tinners are tinning the   310
roof—the masons are calling for mortar,

In single file each shouldering his hod pass onward the laborers;

Seasons pursuing each other the indescribable crowd is gathered ....
it is the Fourth of July .... what salutes of cannon and \small
arms!

Seasons pursuing each other the plougher ploughs and the mower
mows and the wintergrain falls in the ground;

Off on the lakes the pikefisher watches and waits by the hole in the
frozen surface,

The stumps stand thick round the clearing, the squatter   315
strikesdeep with his axe,

The flatboatmen make fast toward dusk near the cottonwood or
pekantrees,

The coon-seekers go now through the regions of the Red river, or
through those drained by the Tennessee, or through those of the
Arkansas,

The torches shine in the dark that hangs on the Chattahoochee or
Altamahaw;

Patriarchs sit at supper with sons and grandsons and great grandsons
around them,

In walls of adobe, in canvass tents, rest hunters and trappers after   320
their day's sport.

The city sleeps and the country sleeps,

The living sleep for their time .... the dead sleep for their time,

The old husband sleeps by his wife and the young husband sleeps by
his wife;

And these one and all tend inward to me, and I tend outward to them,
And such as it is to be of these more or less I am.   325

[16]   I am of old and young, of the foolish as much as the wise,
Regardless of others, ever regardful of others,
Maternal as well as paternal, a child as well as a man,
Stuffed with the stuff that is coarse, and stuffed with the stuff that is
    fine,
One of the great nation, the nation of many nations—the smallest 330
    the same and the largest the same,
A southerner soon as a northerner, a planter nonchalant and
    hospitable,
A Yankee bound my own way .... ready for trade .... my joints the
    limberest joints on earth and the sternest joints on earth,
A Kentuckian walking the vale of the Elkhorn in my deerskin leggings,
A boatman over the lakes or bays or along coasts .... a Hoosier, a
    Badger, a Buckeye,[8]
A Louisianian or Georgian, a poke-easy from sandhills and pines, 335
At home on Canadian snowshoes or up in the bush, or with fishermen
    off Newfoundland,
At home in the fleet of iceboats, sailing with the rest and tacking,
At home on the hills of Vermont or in the woods of Maine or the
    Texan ranch,
Comrade of Californians .... comrade of free northwesterners, loving
    their big proportions,
Comrade of raftsmen and coalmen—comrade of all who shake   340
    hands and welcome to drink and meat;
A learner with the simplest, a teacher of the thoughtfulest,
A novice beginning experient of myriads of seasons,
Of every hue and trade and rank, of every caste and religion,
Not merely of the New World but of Africa Europe or Asia .... a
    wandering savage,
A farmer, mechanic, or artist .... a gentleman, sailor, lover or   345
    quaker,
A prisoner, fancy-man, rowdy, lawyer, physician or priest.

I resist anything better than my own diversity,
And breathe the air and leave plenty after me,
And am not stuck up, and am in my place.

The moth and the fisheggs are in their place,   350
The suns I see and the suns I cannot see are in their place,
The palpable is in its place and the impalpable is in its place.

---

[8]Inhabitants of Indiana, Wisconsin, and Ohio,
respectively.

[17]   These are the thoughts of all men in all ages and lands, they are not
original with me,
If they are not yours as much as mine they are nothing or next to
nothing,
If they do not enclose everything they are next to nothing,   355
If they are not the riddle and the untying of the riddle they are
nothing,
If they are not just as close as they are distant they are nothing.
This is the grass that grows wherever the land is and the water is,
This is the common air that bathes the globe.
This is the breath of laws and songs and behaviour,   360
This is the tasteless water of souls .... this is the true sustenance,
It is for the illiterate .... it is for the judges of the supreme court....
it is for the federal capitol and the state capitols,
It is for the admirable communes of literary men and composers and
singers and lecturers and engineers and savans,
It is for the endless races of working people and farmers and seamen.

This is the trill of a thousand clear cornets and scream of the   365
octave flute and strike of triangles.

[18]   I play not a march for victors only .... I play great marches for
conquered and slain persons.

Have you heard that it was good to gain the day?
I also say it is good to fall .... battles are lost in the same spirit in
which they are won.

I sound triumphal drums for the dead .... I fling through my
embouchures[9] the loudest and gayest music to them,
Vivas to those who have failed, and to those whose war-vessels   370
sank in the sea, and those themselves who sank in the sea,
And to all generals that lost engagements, and all overcome heroes,
and the numberless unknown heroes equal to the greatest heroes
known.

[19]   This is the meal pleasantly set .... this is the meat and drink for
natural hunger,
It is for the wicked just the same as the righteous .... I make
appointments with all,
I will not have a single person slighted or left away,
The keptwoman and sponger and thief are hereby invited .... the   375
heavy-lipped slave is invited.... the venerealee is invited,
There shall be no difference between them and the rest.

---

[9]Another borrowing from the French, suggesting an opening, or a mouthpiece of a musical instrument.

This is the press of a bashful hand .... this is the float and odor of
    hair,
This is the touch of my lips to yours .... this is the murmur of
    yearning,
This is the far-off depth and height reflecting my own face,
This is the thoughtful merge of myself and the outlet again.   380
Do you guess I have some intricate purpose?
Well I have .... for the April rain has, and the mica on the side of a
    rock has.

Do you take it I would astonish?
Does the daylight astonish? or the early redstart twittering through
    the woods?
Do I astonish more than they?   385
This hour I tell things in confidence,
I might not tell everybody but I will tell you.

[20]   Who goes there! hankering, gross, mystical, nude?
How is it I extract strength from the beef I eat?

What is a man anyhow? What am I? and what are you?   390
All I mark as my own you shall offset it with your own,
Else it were time lost listening to me.

I do not snivel that snivel the world over,
That months are vacuums and the ground but wallow and filth,
That life is a suck and a sell, and nothing remains at the end but   395
    threadbare crape and tears.

Whimpering and truckling fold with powders for invalids ....
    conformity goes to the fourth-removed,
I cock my hat as I please indoors or out.

Shall I pray? Shall I venerate and be ceremonious?

I have pried through the strata and analyzed to a hair,
And counselled with doctors and calculated close and found no   400
    sweeter fat than sticks to my own bones.

In all people I see myself, none more and not one a barleycorn less,
And the good or bad I say of myself I say of them.

And I know I am solid and sound,
To me the converging objects of the universe perpetually flow,
All are written to me, and I must get what the writing means.   405

And I know I am deathless,
I know this orbit of mine cannot be swept by a carpenter's compass,
I know I shall not pass like a child's carlacue cut with a burnt stick at
      night.

I know I am august,
I do not trouble my spirit to vindicate itself or be understood,   410
I see that the elementary laws never apologize,
I reckon I behave no prouder than the level I plant my house by
      after all.

I exist as I am, that is enough,
If no other in the world be aware I sit content,
And if each and all be aware I sit content.   415

One world is aware, and by far the largest to me, and that is myself,
And whether I come to my own today or in ten thousand or ten
      million years,
I can cheerfully take it now, or with equal cheerfulness I can wait.
My foothold is tenoned and mortised in granite,
I laugh at what you call dissolution,   420
And I know the amplitude of time.

[21]   I am the poet of the body,
And I am the poet of the soul.

The pleasures of heaven are with me, and the pains of hell are
      with me,
The first I graft and increase upon myself .... the latter I translate 425
      into a new tongue.

I am the poet of the woman the same as the man,
And I say it is as great to be a woman as to be a man,
And I say there is nothing greater than the mother of men.
I chant a new chant of dilation or pride,
We have had ducking and deprecating about enough,   430
I show that size is only development.

Have you outstript the rest? Are you the President?
It is a trifle .... they will more than arrive there every one, and still
      pass on.

I am he that walks with the tender and growing night;
I call to the earth and sea half-held by the night.   435

Press close barebosomed night! Press close magnetic nourishing night!
Night of south winds! Night of the large few stars!
Still nodding night! Mad naked summer night!

Smile O voluptuous coolbreathed earth!
Earth of the slumbering and liquid trees!   440
Earth of departed sunset! Earth of the mountains misty-topt!
Earth of the vitreous pour of the full moon just tinged with blue!
Earth of shine and dark mottling the tide of the river!
Earth of the limpid gray of clouds brighter and clearer for my sake!
Far-swooping elbowed earth! Rich apple-blossomed earth!   445
Smile, for your lover comes!

Prodigal! you have given me love! .... therefore I to you give love!
O unspeakable passionate love!

Thruster holding me tight and that I hold tight!
We hurt each other as the bridegroom and the bride hurt   450
     each other.

[22]   You sea! I resign myself to you also .... I guess what you mean,
         I behold from the beach your crooked inviting fingers,
         I believe you refuse to go back without feeling of me;
         We must have a turn together .... I undress .... hurry me out of sight
              of the land,
         Cushion me soft .... rock me in billowy drowse,   455
         Dash me with amorous wet .... I can repay you.

Sea of stretched ground-swells!
Sea breathing broad and convulsive breaths!
Sea of the brine of life! Sea of unshovelled and always-ready graves!
Howler and scooper of storms! Capricious and dainty sea!   460
I am integral with you .... I too am of one phase and of all phases.

Partaker of influx and efflux .... extoler of hate and conciliation,
Extoler of amies[10] and those that sleep in each others' arms.

I am he attesting sympathy;
Shall I make my list of things in the house and skip the house that   465
     supports them?

I am the poet of commonsense and of the demonstrable and of
     immortality;

---

[10]French for girlfriend; Whitman probably
intended to suggest comrades and lovers of
either sex.

And am not the poet of goodness only .... I do not decline to be the
poet of wickedness also.

Washes and razors for foofoos .... for me freckles and a bristling
beard.

What blurt is it about virtue and about vice?
Evil propels me, and reform of evil propels me .... I stand   470
indifferent,
My gait is no faultfinder's or rejecter's gait,
I moisten the roots of all that has grown.

Did you fear some scrofula out of the unflagging pregnancy?
Did you guess the celestial laws are yet to be worked over and
rectified?

I step up to say that what we do is right and what we affirm is   475
right .... and some is only the ore of right,
Witnesses of us .... one side a balance and the antipodal side a
balance,
Soft doctrine as steady help as stable doctrine,
Thoughts and deeds of the present our rouse and early start.

This minute that comes to me over the past decillions,
There is no better than it and now.   480

What behaved well in the past or behaves well today is not such a
wonder,
The wonder is always and always how there can be a mean man or an
infidel.

[23]   Endless unfolding of words of ages!
And mine a word of the modern .... a word en masse.
A word of the faith that never balks,   485
One time as good as another time .... here or henceforward it is all
the same to me.

A word of reality .... materialism first and last imbueing.

Hurrah for positive science! Long live exact demonstration!
Fetch stonecrop and mix it with cedar and branches of lilac;
This is the lexicographer or chemist .... this made a grammar of   490
the old cartouches,[11]
These mariners put the ship through dangerous unknown seas,

[11]Scroll-like tablets used for the inscription of
Egyptian hieroglyphics.

This is the geologist, and this works with the scalpel, and this is a
  mathematician.

Gentlemen I receive you, and attach and clasp hands with you,
The facts are useful and real .... they are not my dwelling .... I enter
  by them to an area of the dwelling.

I am less the reminder of property or qualities, and more the   495
  reminder of life,
And go on the square for my own sake and for others' sakes,
And make short account of neuters and geldings, and favor men and
  women fully equipped,
And beat the gong of revolt, and stop with fugitives and them that
  plot and conspire.

[24]   Walt Whitman, an American, one of the roughs, a kosmos,
Disorderly fleshy and sensual .... eating drinking and breeding,   500
No sentimentalist .... no stander above men and women or apart
  from them .... no more modest than immodest.

Unscrew the locks from the doors!
Unscrew the doors themselves from their jambs!

Whoever degrades another degrades me .... and whatever is done or
  said returns at last to me,
And whatever I do or say I also return.   505

Through me the afflatus[12] surging and surging .... through me the
  current and index.

I speak the password primeval .... I give the sign of democracy;
By God! I will accept nothing which all cannot have their counterpart
  of on the same terms.
Through me many long dumb voices,
Voices of the interminable generations of slaves,   510
Voices of prostitutes and of deformed persons,
Voices of the diseased and despairing, and of thieves and dwarfs,
Voices of cycles of preparation and accretion,
And of the threads that connect the stars—and of wombs, and of the
  fatherstuff,
And of the rights of them the others are down upon,   515
Of the trivial and flat and foolish and despised,
Of fog in the air and beetles rolling balls of dung.

[12]Creative spirit or divine breath.

Through me forbidden voices,
Voices of sexes and lusts .... voices veiled, and I remove the veil,
Voices indecent by me clarified and transfigured.   520
I do not press my finger across my mouth,
I keep as delicate around the bowels as around the head and heart,
Copulation is no more rank to me than death is.

I believe in the flesh and the appetites,
Seeing hearing and feeling are miracles, and each part and tag of   525
    me is a miracle.

Divine am I inside and out, and I make holy whatever I touch or am
    touched from;
The scent of these arm-pits is aroma finer than prayer,
This head is more than churches or bibles or creeds.

If I worship any particular thing it shall be some of the spread of my
    body;
Translucent mould of me it shall be you,   530
Shaded ledges and rests, firm masculine coulter,[13] it shall be you,
Whatever goes to the tilth of me it shall be you,
You my rich blood, your milky stream pale strippings of my life;
Breast that presses against other breasts it shall be you,
My brain it shall be your occult convolutions,   535
Root of washed sweet-flag, timorous pond-snipe, nest of guarded
    duplicate eggs, it shall be you,
Mixed tussled hay of head and beard and brawn it shall be you,
Trickling sap of maple, fibre of manly wheat, it shall be you;
Sun so generous it shall be you,
Vapors lighting and shading my face it shall be you,   540
You sweaty brooks and dews it shall be you,
Winds whose soft-tickling genitals rub against me it shall be you,
Broad muscular fields, branches of liveoak, loving lounger in my
    winding paths, it shall be you,
Hands I have taken, face I have kissed, mortal I have ever touched, it
    shall be you.
I dote on myself .... there is that lot of me, and all so luscious, 545
Each moment and whatever happens thrills me with joy.
I cannot tell how my ankles bend .... nor whence the cause of my
    faintest wish,
Nor the cause of the friendship I emit .... nor the cause of the
    friendship I take again.

To walk up my stoop is unaccountable .... I pause to consider if it
    really be,

---

[13]The iron blade of a plow.

That I eat and drink is spectacle enough for the great authors and   550
    schools,
A morning-glory at my window satisfies me more than the
    metaphysics of books.

To behold the daybreak!
The little light fades the immense and diaphanous shadows,
The air tastes good to my palate.

Hefts of the moving world at innocent gambols, silently rising,   555
    freshly exuding, Scooting obliquely high and low.

Something I cannot see puts upward libidinous[14] prongs,
Seas of bright juice suffuse heaven.

The earth by the sky staid with .... the daily close of their junction,
The heaved challenge from the east that moment over my head,   560
The mocking taunt, See then whether you shall be master!

[25]   Dazzling and tremendous how quick the sunrise would kill me,
If I could not now and always send sunrise out of me.

We also ascend dazzling and tremendous as the sun,
We found our own my soul in the calm and cool of the daybreak.   565

My voice goes after what my eyes cannot reach,
With the twirl of my tongue I encompass worlds and volumes of
    worlds.
Speech is the twin of my vision .... it is unequal to measure itself.

It provokes me forever,
It says sarcastically, Walt, you understand enough .... why don't   570
    you let it out then?

Come now I will not be tantalized .... you conceive too much of
    articulation.

Do you not know how the buds beneath are folded?
Waiting in gloom protected by frost,
The dirt receding before my prophetical screams,
I underlying causes to balance them at last,   575
My knowledge my live parts .... it keeping tally with the meaning of
    things,

---

[14]Full of sexual energy, desire.

Happiness .... which whoever hears me let him or her set out in
    search of this day.

My final merit I refuse you .... I refuse putting from me the
    best I am.

Encompass worlds but never try to encompass me,
I crowd your noisiest talk by looking toward you.   580

Writing and talk do not prove me,
I carry the plenum of proof and every thing else in my face,
With the hush of my lips I confound the topmost skeptic.

[26]   I think I will do nothing for a long time but listen,
And accrue what I hear into myself .... and let sounds contribute   585
    toward me.

I hear the bravuras of birds .... the bustle of growing wheat.... gossip
    of flames .... clack of sticks cooking my meals.

I hear the sound of the human voice .... a sound I love,
I hear all sounds as they are tuned to their uses .... sounds of the city
    and sounds out of the city .... sounds of the day and night;
Talkative young ones to those that like them .... the recitative of fish-
    pedlars and fruit-pedlars .... the loud laugh of workpeople at
    their meals,
The angry base of disjointed friendship .... the faint tones of the   590
    sick,
The judge with hands tight to the desk, his shaky lips pronouncing a
    death-sentence,
The heave'e'yo of stevedores unlading ships by the wharves.... the
    refrain of the anchor-lifters;
The ring of alarm-bells .... the cry of fire .... the whirr of swift-
    streaking engines and hose-carts with premonitory tinkles and
    colored lights,
The steam-whistle .... the solid roll of the train of approaching cars;
The slow-march played at night at the head of the association,   595
They go to guard some corpse .... the flag-tops are draped with black
    muslin.

I hear the violincello or man's heart's complaint,
And hear the keyed cornet or else the echo of sunset.

I hear the chorus .... it is a grand-opera .... this indeed is music!

A tenor large and fresh as the creation fills me,   600
The orbic flex of his mouth is pouring and filling me full.

I hear the trained soprano .... she convulses me like the climax of my
    love-grip;
The orchestra whirls me wider than Uranus flies,
It wrenches unnamable ardors from my breast,
It throbs me to gulps of the farthest down horror,   605
It sails me .... I dab with bare feet .... they are licked by the indolent
    waves,
I am exposed .... cut by bitter and poisoned hail,
Steeped amid honeyed morphine .... my windpipe squeezed in the
    fakes[15] of death,
Let up again to feel the puzzle of puzzles,
And that we call Being.   610

[27]   To be in any form, what is that?
If nothing lay more developed the quahaug and its callous shell were
    enough.

Mine is no callous shell,
I have instant conductors all over me whether I pass or stop,
They seize every object and lead it harmlessly through me.   615

I merely stir, press, feel with my fingers, and am happy,
To touch my person to some one else's is about as much as I can
    stand.

[28]   Is this then a touch? .... quivering me to a new identity,
Flames and ether making a rush for my veins,
Treacherous tip of me reaching and crowding to help them,   620
My flesh and blood playing out lightning, to strike what is hardly
    different from myself,
On all sides prurient provokers stiffening my limbs,
Straining the udder of my heart for its withheld drip,
Behaving licentious toward me, taking no denial,
Depriving me of my best as for a purpose,   625
Unbuttoning my clothes and holding me by the bare waist,
Deluding my confusion with the calm of the sunlight and pasture
    fields,
Immodestly sliding the fellow-senses away,
They bribed to swap off with touch, and go and graze at the edges of
    me,
No consideration, no regard for my draining strength or my anger, 630
Fetching the rest of the herd around to enjoy them awhile,
Then all uniting to stand on a headland and worry me.

The sentries desert every other part of me,
They have left me helpless to a red marauder,

---

[15]Coils of a rope.

They all come to the headland to witness and assist against me.   635
I am given up by traitors;
I talk wildly .... I have lost my wits .... I and nobody else am the
   greatest traitor,
I went myself first to the headland .... my own hands carried me
   there.
You villain touch! what are you doing? .... my breath is tight in its
   throat;
Unclench your floodgates! you are too much for me.   640

[29]   Blind loving wrestling touch! Sheathed hooded sharptoothed touch!
Did it make you ache so leaving me?

Parting tracked by arriving .... perpetual payment of the perpetual
   loan,
Rich showering rain, and recompense richer afterward.

Sprouts take and accumulate .... stand by the curb prolific   645
   and vital,
Landscapes projected masculine full-sized and golden.

[30]   All truths wait in all things,
They neither hasten their own delivery nor resist it,
They do not need the obstetric forceps of the surgeon,
The insignificant is as big to me as any,   650
What is less or more than a touch?

Logic and sermons never convince,
The damp of the night drives deeper into my soul.

Only what proves itself to every man and woman is so,
Only what nobody denies is so.   655

A minute and a drop of me settle my brain;
I believe the soggy clods shall become lovers and lamps,
And a compend of compends is the meat of a man or woman,
And a summit and flower there is the feeling they have for each other,
And they are to branch boundlessly out of that lesson until it   660
   becomes omnific,
And until every one shall delight us, and we them.

[31]   I believe a leaf of grass is no less than the journeywork of the stars,
And the pismire is equally perfect, and a grain of sand, and the egg of
   the wren,
And the tree-toad is a chef-d'ouvre[16] for the highest,
And the running blackberry would adorn the parlors of heaven,   665

---

[16]Masterpiece.

And the narrowest hinge in my hand puts to scorn all machinery,
And the cow crunching with depressed head surpasses any statue,
And a mouse is miracle enough to stagger sextillions of infidels,
    farmer's girl boiling her iron tea-kettle and baking shortcake.

I find I incorporate gneiss and coal and long-threaded moss and   670
    fruits and grains and esculent roots,
And am stucco'd with quadrupeds and birds all over,
And have distanced what is behind me for good reasons,
And call any thing close again when I desire it.

In vain the speeding or shyness,
In vain the plutonic rocks send their old heat against my approach, 675
In vain the mastadon retreats beneath its own powdered bones,
In vain objects stand leagues off and assume manifold shapes,
In vain the ocean settling in hollows and the great monsters lying low,
In vain the buzzard houses herself with the sky,
In vain the snake slides through the creepers and logs,   680
In vain the elk takes to the inner passes of the woods,
In vain the razorbilled auk sails far north to Labrador,
I follow quickly .... I ascend to the nest in the fissure of the cliff.

[32]   I think I could turn and live awhile with the animals .... they are so
    placid and self-contained,
I stand and look at them sometimes half the day long.   685

They do not sweat and whine about their condition,
They do not lie awake in the dark and weep for their sins,
They do not make me sick discussing their duty to God,
Not one is dissatisfied .... not one is demented with the mania of
    owning things,
Not one kneels to another nor to his kind that lived thousands of 690
    years ago,
Not one is respectable or industrious over the whole earth.

So they show their relations to me and I accept them;
They bring me tokens of myself .... they evince them plainly in their
    possession.

I do not know where they got those tokens,
I must have passed that way untold times ago and negligently 695
    dropt them,
Myself moving forward then and now and forever,
Gathering and showing more always and with velocity,
Infinite and omnigenous and the like of these among them;
Not too exclusive toward the reachers of my remembrancers,

Picking out here one that shall be my amie, 700
Choosing to go with him on brotherly terms.

A gigantic beauty of a stallion, fresh and responsive to my caresses,
Head high in the forehead and wide between the ears,
Limbs glossy and supple, tail dusting the ground,
Eyes well apart and full of sparkling wickedness .... ears finely cut 705
    and flexibly moving.

His nostrils dilate .... my heels embrace him .... his well built limbs
    tremble with pleasure .... we speed around and return.
I but use you a moment and then I resign you stallion .... and do not
    need your paces, and outgallop them,
And myself as I stand or sit pass faster than you.

[33] Swift wind! Space! My Soul! Now I know it is true what I guessed at;
What I guessed when I loafed on the grass, 710
What I guessed while I lay alone in my bed .... and again as I walked
    the beach under the paling stars of the morning.

My ties and ballasts[17] leave me .... I travel .... I sail .... my elbows
    rest in the sea-gaps,
I skirt the sierras .... my palms cover continents,
I am afoot with my vision.
By the city's quadrangular houses .... in log-huts, or camping with 715
    lumbermen,
Along the ruts of the turnpike .... along the dry gulch and rivulet bed,
Hoeing my onion-patch, and rows of carrots and parsnips.... crossing
    savannas ... trailing in forests,
Prospecting .... gold-digging .... girdling the trees of a new purchase,
Scorched ankle-deep by the hot sand .... hauling my boat down the
    shallow river;
Where the panther walks to and fro on a limb overhead .... where 720
    the buck turns furiously at the hunter,
Where the rattlesnake suns his flabby length on a rock .... where the
    otter is feeding on fish,
Where the alligator in his tough pimples sleeps by the bayou,
Where the black bear is searching for roots or honey .... where the
    beaver pats the mud with his paddle-tail;
Over the growing sugar .... over the cottonplant .... over the rice in
    its low moist field;
Over the sharp-peaked farmhouse with its scalloped scum and 725
    slender shoots from the gutters;
Over the western persimmon .... over the longleaved corn and the
    delicate blueflowered flax;

---

[17]As of a hot air balloon.

Over the white and brown buckwheat, a hummer and a buzzer there
    with the rest,
Over the dusky green of the rye as it ripples and shades in the breeze;
Scaling mountains .... pulling myself cautiously up .... holding on by
    low scragged limbs,
Walking the path worn in the grass and beat through the leaves of 730
    the brush;
Where the quail is whistling betwixt the woods and the wheatlot,
Where the bat flies in the July eve .... where the great goldbug drops
    through the dark;
Where the flails keep time on the barn floor,
Where the brook puts out of the roots of the old tree and flows to the
    meadow,
Where cattle stand and shake away flies with the tremulous   735
    shuddering of their hides,
Where the cheese-cloth hangs in the kitchen, and andirons straddle
    the hearth-slab, and cobwebs fall in festoons from the rafters;
Where triphammers crash .... where the press is whirling its
    cylinders;
Wherever the human heart beats with terrible throes out of its ribs:
Where the pear-shaped balloon is floating aloft .... floating in it
    myself and looking composedly down:
Where the life-car[18] is drawn on the slipnoose .... where the heat   740
    hatches pale-green eggs in the dented sand,
Where the she-whale swims with her calves and never forsakes them,
Where the steamship trails hindways its long pennant of smoke,
Where the ground-shark's fin cuts like a black chip out of the water,
Where the half-burned brig is riding on unknown currents,
Where shells grow to her slimy deck, and the dead are corrupting   745
    below;
Where the striped and starred flag is borne at the head of the
    regiments;
Approaching Manhattan, up by the long-stretching island,
Under Niagara, the cataract falling like a veil over my countenance;
Upon a door-step .... upon the horse-block of hard wood outside,
Upon the race-course, or enjoying pic-nics or jigs or a good game   750
    of base-ball,
At he-festivals with blackguard jibes and ironical license and bull-
    dances and drinking and laughter,
At the cider-mill, tasting the sweet of the brown sqush[19] .... sucking
    the juice through a straw,
At apple-pealings, wanting kisses for all the red fruit I find,

---

[18]A watertight rescue vessel used to save pas-   [19]Mush.
sengers at sea.

At musters[20] and beach-parties and friendly bees and huskings and
 house-raisings;

Where the mockingbird sounds his delicious gurgles, and cackles   755
 and screams and weeps,

Where the hay-rick stands in the barnyard, and the dry-stalks are
 scattered, and the brood cow waits in the hovel,

Where the bull advances to do his masculine work, and the stud to the
 mare, and the cock is treading the hen,

Where the heifers browse, and the geese nip their food with short
 jerks;

Where the sundown shadows lengthen over the limitless and
 lonesome prairie,

Where the herds of buffalo make a crawling spread of the square   760
 miles far and near;

Where the hummingbird shimmers .... where the neck of the
 longlived swan is curving and winding;

Where the laughing-gull scoots by the slappy shore and laughs her
 near-human laugh;

Where beehives range on a gray bench in the garden half-hid by the
 high weeds;

Where the band-necked partridges roost in a ring on the ground with
 their heads out;

Where burial coaches enter the arched gates of a cemetery;   765

Where winter wolves bark amid wastes of snow and icicled trees;

Where the yellow-crowned heron comes to the edge of the marsh at
 night and feeds upon small crabs;

Where the splash of swimmers and divers cools the warm noon;

Where the katydid works her chromatic reed on the walnut-tree over
 the well;

Through patches of citrons and cucumbers with silver-wired leaves, 770

Through the salt-lick or orange glade .... or under conical firs;

Through the gymnasium .... through the curtained saloon ....
 through the office or public hall;

Pleased with the native and pleased with the foreign .... pleased with
 the new and old,

Pleased with women, the homely as well as the handsome,

Pleased with the quakeress as she puts off her bonnet and talks   775
 melodiously,

Pleased with the primitive tunes of the choir of the whitewashed
 church,

Pleased with the earnest words of the sweating Methodist preacher or
 any preacher .... looking seriously at the camp-meeting;

Looking in at the shop-windows in Broadway the whole forenoon ....
 pressing the flesh of my nose to the thick plate-glass,

[20]Gatherings of people.

Wandering the same afternoon with my face turned up to the clouds;
My right and left arms round the sides of two friends and I in the 780
    middle;
Coming home with the bearded and dark-cheeked bush-boy .... riding
    behind him at the drape of the day;
Far from the settlements studying the print of animals' feet, or the
    moccasin print;
By the cot in the hospital reaching lemonade to a feverish patient,
By the coffined corpse when all is still, examining with a candle;
Voyaging to every port to dicker and adventure; 785
Hurrying with the modern crowd, as eager and fickle as any,
Hot toward one I hate, ready in my madness to knife him;
Solitary at midnight in my back yard, my thoughts gone from me a
    long while,
Walking the old hills of Judea with the beautiful gentle god by my
    side;
Speeding through space .... speeding through heaven and 790
    the stars,
Speeding amid the seven satellites and the broad ring and the
    diameter of eighty thousand miles,
Speeding with tailed meteors .... throwing fire-balls like the rest,
Carrying the crescent child that carries its own full mother in its belly;
Storming enjoying planning loving cautioning,
Backing and filling, appearing and disappearing, 795
I tread day and night such roads.

I visit the orchards of God and look at the spheric product,
And look at quintillions ripened, and look at quintillions green.

I fly the flight of the fluid and swallowing soul,
My course runs below the soundings of plummets. 800
I help myself to material and immaterial,
No guard can shut me off, no law can prevent me.

I anchor my ship for a little while only,
My messengers continually cruise away or bring their returns to me.

I go hunting polar furs and the seal .... leaping chasms with a pike- 805
    pointed staff .... clinging to topples[21] of brittle and blue.

I ascend to the foretruck .... I take my place late at night in the
    crow's nest .... we sail through the arctic sea .... it is plenty light
    enough,
Through the clear atmosphere I stretch around on the wonderful
    beauty,

[21]Pieces of ice.

The enormous masses of ice pass me and I pass them .... the scenery
　　is plain in all directions,
The white-topped mountains point up in the distance .... I fling out
　　my fancies toward them;
We are about approaching some great battlefield in which we are　810
　　soon to be engaged,
We pass the colossal outposts of the encampments .... we pass with
　　still feet and caution;
Or we are entering by the suburbs some vast and ruined city .... the
　　blocks and fallen architecture more than all the living cities of the
　　globe.

I am a free companion .... I bivouac by invading watchfires.

I turn the bridegroom out of bed and stay with the bride myself,
And tighten her all night to my thighs and lips.　　815

My voice is the wife's voice, the screech by the rail of the stairs,
They fetch my man's body up dripping and drowned.

I understand the large hearts of heroes,
The courage of present times and all times;
How the skipper[22] saw the crowded and rudderless wreck of the　820
　　steamship, and death chasing it up and down the storm,
How he knuckled tight and gave not back one inch, and was faithful
　　of days and faithful of nights,
And chalked in large letters on a board, Be of good cheer, We will not
　　desert you;
How he saved the drifting company at last,
How the lank loose-gowned women looked when boated from the side
　　of their prepared graves,
How the silent old-faced infants, and the lifted sick, and the sharp-　825
　　lipped unshaved men;
All this I swallow and it tastes good .... I like it well, and it becomes
　　mine,
I am the man .... I suffered .... I was there.

The disdain and calmness of martyrs,
The mother condemned for a witch and burnt with dry wood, and her
　　children gazing on;
The hounded slave that flags in the race and leans by the fence,　830
　　blowing and covered with sweat,

[22]Whitman describes the shipwreck of the *San Francisco*, which was reported in the *New York Weekly Tribune* on January 21, 1854; he kept a copy of this article among his belongings.

The twinges that sting like needles his legs and neck,
The murderous buckshot and the bullets,
All these I feel or am.

I am the hounded slave .... I wince at the bite of the dogs,
Hell and despair are upon me .... crack and again crack the   835
    marksmen,
I clutch the rails of the fence .... my gore dribs[23] thinned with the
    ooze of my skin,
I fall on the weeds and stones,
The riders spur their unwilling horses and haul close,
They taunt my dizzy ears .... they beat me violently over the head
    with their whip-stocks.

Agonies are one of my changes of garments;   840
I do not ask the wounded person how he feels .... I myself become
    the wounded person,
My hurt turns livid upon me as I lean on a cane and observe.

I am the mashed fireman with breastbone broken .... tumbling walls
    buried me in their debris,
Heat and smoke I inspired .... I heard the yelling shouts of my
    comrades,
I heard the distant click of their picks and shovels;   845
They have cleared the beams away .... they tenderly lift me forth.

I lie in the night air in my red shirt .... the pervading hush is for my
    sake,
Painless after all I lie, exhausted but not so unhappy,
White and beautiful are the faces around me .... the heads are bared
    of their fire-caps,
The kneeling crowd fades with the light of the torches.   850

Distant and dead resuscitate,
They show as the dial or move as the hands of me .... and I am the
    clock myself.
I am an old artillerist, and tell of some fort's bombardment .... and
    am there again.
Again the reveille of drummers .... again the attacking cannon and
    mortars and howitzers,
Again the attacked send their cannon responsive.   855

I take part .... I see and hear the whole,
The cries and curses and roar .... the plaudits for well aimed shots,

---

[23]Short for dribbles.

The ambulanza slowly passing and trailing its red drip,
Workmen searching after damages and to make indispensible repairs,
The fall of grenades through the rent roof .... the fan-shaped   860
    explosion,
The whizz of limbs heads stone wood and iron high in the air.

Again gurgles the mouth of my dying general .... he furiously waves
    with his hand,
He gasps through the clot .... Mind not me .... mind .... the
    entrenchments.

[34]   I tell not the fall of Alamo .... not one escaped to tell the fall of
    Alamo,
The hundred and fifty are dumb yet at Alamo.   865

Hear now the tale of a jetblack sunrise,
Hear of the murder in cold blood of four hundred and twelve young
    men.[24]

Retreating they had formed in a hollow square with their baggage for
    breastworks,
Nine hundred lives out of the surrounding enemy's nine times their
    number was the price they took in advance,
Their colonel was wounded and their ammunition gone,   870
They treated for an honorable capitulation, received writing and seal,
    gave up their arms, and marched back prisoners of war.
They were the glory of the race of rangers,
Matchless with a horse, a rifle, a song, a supper, or a courtship,
Large, turbulent, brave, handsome, generous, proud and affectionate,
Bearded, sunburnt, dressed in the free costume of hunters,   875
Not a single one over thirty years of age.

The second Sunday morning they were brought out in squads and
    massacred .... it was beautiful early summer,
The work commenced about five o'clock and was over by eight.

None obeyed the command to kneel,
Some made a mad and helpless rush .... some stood stark and   880
    straight,
A few fell at once, shot in the temple or heart .... the living and dead
    lay together,
The maimed and mangled dug in the dirt .... the new-comers saw
    them there;
Some half-killed attempted to crawl away,

[24]Whitman tells the story of the death of Captain Fannin and his company of 371 Texans
at the hands of the Mexicans after their surrender at Goliad on March 27, 1836; unlike
Emerson and Thoreau, Whitman supported
the Mexican War (1846–1848).

These were dispatched with bayonets or battered with the blunts of
    muskets;
A youth not seventeen years old seized his assassin till two more   885
    came to release him,
The three were all torn, and covered with the boy's blood.

At eleven o'clock began the burning of the bodies;
And that is the tale of the murder of the four hundred and twelve
    young men,
And that was a jetblack sunrise.

[35]   Did you read in the seabooks of the oldfashioned frigate-fight?[25]   890
Did you learn who won by the light of the moon and stars?

Our foe was no skulk in his ship, I tell you,
His was the English pluck, and there is no tougher or truer, and never
    was, and never will be;
Along the lowered eve he came, horribly raking us.
We closed with him . . . . the yards entangled . . . . the cannon   895
    touched,
My captain lashed fast with his own hands.

We had received some eighteen-pound shots under the water,
On our lower-gun-deck two large pieces had burst at the first fire,
    killing all around and blowing up overhead.

Ten o'clock at night, and the full moon shining and the leaks on the
    gain, and five feet of water reported,
The master-at-arms loosing the prisoners confined in the   900
    after-hold to give them a chance for themselves.

The transit to and from the magazine was now stopped by the
    sentinels,
They saw so many strange faces they did not know whom to trust.

Our frigate was afire . . . . the other asked if we demanded quarters? if
    our colors were struck and the fighting done?

I laughed content when I heard the voice of my little captain,
We have not struck, he composedly cried, We have just begun our   905
    part of the fighting.
Only three guns were in use,
One was directed by the captain himself against the enemy's
    mainmast,

---

[25]Whitman tells the story of the Revolution-   between the *Bonhomme Richard*, commanded
ary sea battle on September 23, 1779,   by John Paul Jones, and the British *Serapis*.

Two well-served with grape and canister silenced his musketry and
    cleared his decks.

The tops alone seconded the fire of this little battery, especially the
    maintop,
They all held out bravely during the whole of the action.   910

Not a moment's cease,
The leaks gained fast on the pumps .... the fire eat toward the
    powder-magazine,
One of the pumps was shot away .... it was generally thought we
    were sinking.
Serene stood the little captain,
He was not hurried .... his voice was neither high nor low,   915
His eyes gave more light to us than our battle-lanterns.

Toward twelve at night, there in the beams of the moon they
    surrendered to us.

[36]   Stretched and still lay the midnight,
Two great hulls motionless on the breast of the darkness,
Our vessel riddled and slowly sinking .... preparations to pass   920
    to the one we had conquered,
The captain on the quarter deck coldly giving his orders through a
    countenance white as a sheet,
Near by the corpse of the child that served in the cabin,
The dead face of an old salt with long white hair and carefully curled
    whiskers,
The flames spite of all that could be done flickering aloft and below,
The husky voices of the two or three officers yet fit for duty,   925
Formless stacks of bodies and bodies by themselves .... dabs of flesh
    upon the masts and spars,
The cut of cordage and dangle of rigging .... the slight shock of the
    soothe of waves,
Black and impassive guns, and litter of powder-parcels, and the strong
    scent,
Delicate sniffs of the seabreeze .... smells of sedgy grass and fields by
    the shore ... death-messages given in charge to survivors,
The hiss of the surgeon's knife and the gnawing teeth of his saw,   930
The wheeze, the cluck, the swash of falling blood .... the short wild
    scream, the long dull tapering groan,
These so .... these irretrievable.

[37]   O Christ! My fit is mastering me!
What the rebel said gaily adjusting his throat to the rope-noose,
What the savage at the stump, his eye-sockets empty, his mouth   935
    spirting whoops and defiance,

What stills the traveler come to the vault at Mount Vernon,
What sobers the Brooklyn boy as he looks down the shores of the
    Wallabout and remembers the prison ships,[26]
What burnt the gums of the redcoat at Saratoga[27] when he
    surrendered his brigades,
These become mine and me every one, and they are but little,
I become as much more as I like.   940

I become any presence or truth of humanity here,
And see myself in prison shaped like another man,
And feel the dull unintermitted pain.

For me the keepers of convicts shoulder their carbines and keep
    watch,
It is I let out in the morning and barred at night.   945

Not a mutineer walks handcuffed to the jail, but I am handcuffed to
    him and walk by his side,
I am less the jolly one there, and more the silent one with sweat on
    my twitching lips.
Not a youngster is taken for larceny, but I go up too and am tried and
    sentenced.

Not a cholera patient lies at the last gasp, but I also lie at the last
    gasp,
My face is ash-colored, my sinews gnarl .... away from me people   950
    retreat.

Askers embody themselves in me, and I am embodied in them,
I project my hat and sit shamefaced and beg.

I rise extatic through all, and sweep with the true gravitation,
The whirling and whirling is elemental within me.

[38]   Somehow I have been stunned. Stand back!   955
Give me a little time beyond my cuffed head and slumbers and dreams
    and gaping,
I discover myself on a verge of the usual mistake.

That I could forget the mockers and insults!
That I could forget the trickling tears and the blows of the bludgeons
    and hammers!

[26]British prison ships along Wallabout Bay,
where American rebels were held captive
during the Revolutionary War.
[27]On October 17, 1777, the British General
Burgoyne surrendered to American forces at
Saratoga; the battle was a turning point
because it enlisted French assistance for the
American cause.

That I could look with a separate look on my own crucifixion and   960
    bloody crowning!
I remember .... I resume the overstaid fraction,[28]
The grave of rock multiplies what has been confided to it .... or to
    any graves,
The corpses rise .... the gashes heal .... the fastenings roll away.

I troop forth replenished with supreme power, one of an average
    unending procession,
We walk the roads of Ohio and Massachusetts and Virginia and   965
    Wisconsin and New York and New Orleans and Texas and
    Montreal and San Francisco and Charleston and Savannah and
    Mexico,
Inland and by the seacoast and boundary lines .... and we pass the
    boundary lines.
Our swift ordinances are on their way over the whole earth,
The blossoms we wear in our hats are the growth of two thousand
    years.

Eleves[29] I salute you,
I see the approach of your numberless gangs .... I see you   970
    understand yourselves and me,
And know that they who have eyes are divine, and the blind and lame
    are equally divine,
And that my steps drag behind yours yet go before them,
And are aware how I am with you no more than I am with everybody.

[39] The friendly and flowing savage .... Who is he?
      Is he waiting for civilization or past it and mastering it?   975

      Is he some southwesterner raised outdoors? Is he Canadian?
      Is he from the Mississippi country? or from Iowa, Oregon or
          California? or from the mountains? or prairie life or bush-life? or
          from the sea?
      Wherever he goes men and women accept and desire him,
      They desire he should like them and touch them and speak to them
          and stay with them.

      Behaviour lawless as snow-flakes .... words simple as grass   980
          uncombed head and laughter and naivete;
      Slowstepping feet and the common features, and the common modes
          and emanations,

[28]Whitman's meaning is unclear. The reference may be temporal, alluding to the poet's
having stayed too long among scenes of suffering and pain. But the words may also

allude to Christ as the "overstaid fraction"
that the poet "resumes" as a living power
within himself.
[29]French for students.

They descend in new forms from the tips of his fingers,
They are wafted with the odor of his body or breath .... they fly out
    of the glance of his eyes.

[40]   Flaunt of the sunshine I need not your bask .... lie over,
You light surfaces only .... I force the surfaces and the depths also. 985
Earth! you seem to look for something at my hands,
Say old topknot! what do you want?

Man or woman! I might tell how I like you, but cannot,
And might tell what it is in me and what it is in you, but cannot,
And might tell the pinings I have .... the pulse of my nights and   990
    days.

Behold I do not give lectures or a little charity,
What I give I give out of myself.

You there, impotent, loose in the knees, open your scarfed chops till I
    blow grit within you,
Spread your palms and lift the flaps of your pockets,
I am not to be denied .... I compel .... I have stores plenty and to 995
    spare,
And any thing I have I bestow.

I do not ask who you are .... that is not important to me,
You can do nothing and be nothing but what I will infold you.

To a drudge of the cottonfields or emptier of privies I lean .... on his
    right cheek I put the family kiss,
And in my soul I swear I never will deny him.   1000
On women fit for conception I start bigger and nimbler babes,
This day I am jetting the stuff of far more arrogant republics.

To any one dying .... thither I speed and twist the knob of the door,
Turn the bedclothes toward the foot of the bed,
Let the physician and the priest go home.   1005

I seize the descending man .... I raise him with resistless will.

O despairer, here is my neck,
By God! you shall not go down! Hang your whole weight upon me.

I dilate you with tremendous breath .... I buoy you up;
Every room of the house do I fill with an armed force .... lovers   1010
    of me, bafflers of graves:

Sleep! I and they keep guard all night;
Not doubt, not decease shall dare to lay finger upon you,
I have embraced you, and henceforth possess you to myself,
And when you rise in the morning you will find what I tell you is so.

[41]   I am he bringing help for the sick as they pant on their backs,   1015
And for strong upright men I bring yet more needed help.

I heard what was said of the universe,
Heard it and heard of several thousand years;
It is middling well as far as it goes .... but is that all?
Magnifying and applying come I,   1020
Outbidding at the start the old cautious hucksters,
The most they offer for mankind and eternity less than a spirt of my
     own seminal wet,
Taking myself the exact dimensions of Jehovah and laying them away,
Lithographing Kronos and Zeus his son, and Hercules his grandson,
Buying drafts of Osiris and Isis and Belus and Brahma and
     Adonai,   1025
In my portfolio placing Manito loose, and Allah on a leaf, and the
     crucifix engraved,
With Odin, and the hideous-faced Mexitli, and all idols and images,[30]
Honestly taking them all for what they are worth, and not a cent
     more,
Admitting they were alive and did the work of their day,
Admitting they bore mites as for unfledged birds who have
     now to rise and fly and sing for themselves,   1030
Accepting the rough deific sketches to fill out better in myself....
     bestowing them freely on each man and woman I see,
Discovering as much or more in a framer framing a house,
Putting higher claims for him there with his rolled-up sleeves, driving
     the mallet and chisel;
Not objecting to special revelations .... considering a curl of smoke or
     a hair on the back of my hand as curious as any revelation;
Those ahold of fire-engines and hook-and-ladder ropes
     more to me than the gods of the antique wars,   1035
Minding their voices peal through the crash of destruction,
Their brawny limbs passing safe over charred laths .... their white
     foreheads whole and unhurt out of the flames;
By the mechanic's wife with her babe at her nipple interceding for
     every person born;

[30]Whitman's list of gods includes sacred fig-
ures from several different religions: Jeho-
vah (the Jewish and Christian God);
Kronos, Zeus, and Hercules (Greek gods);
Osiris and Isis (Egyptian fertility gods);
Belus (a legendary Assyrian king); Brahma

(the supreme Hindu spirit); Adonai (Lord,
in Judaism); Manito (an Algonkian Indian
spirit); Allah (Moslem god); Odin (a Danish
god of war); Mexitli (an Aztec Indian god of
war).

Three scythes at harvest whizzing in a row from three lusty angels
    with shirts bagged out at their waists;
The snag-toothed hostler with red hair redeeming sins past and
    to come,   1040
Selling all he possesses and traveling on foot to fee lawyers for his
    brother and sit by him while he is tried for forgery:
What was strewn in the amplest strewing the square rod about me,
    and not filling the square rod then;
The bull and the bug never worshipped half enough,
Dung and dirt more admirable than was dreamed,
The supernatural of no account .... myself waiting my time to be 1045
    one of the supremes,
The day getting ready for me when I shall do as much good as the
    best, and be as prodigious,
Guessing when I am it will not tickle me much to receive puffs out of
    pulpit or print;
By my life-lumps! becoming already a creator!
Putting myself here and now to the ambushed womb of the shadows!

[42]   .... A call in the midst of the crowd,   1050
My own voice, orotund sweeping and final.

Come my children,
Come my boys and girls, and my women and household and
    intimates,
Now the performer launches his nerve .... he has passed his prelude
    on the reeds within.

Easily written loosefingered chords! I feel the thrum of their 1055
    climax and close.

My head evolves on my neck,
Music rolls, but not from the organ .... folks are around me, but they
    are no household of mine.

Ever the hard and unsunk ground,
Ever the eaters and drinkers .... ever the upward and downward sun
    .... ever the air and the ceaseless tides,
Ever myself and my neighbors, refreshing and wicked and real, 1060
Ever the old inexplicable query .... ever that thorned thumb—that
    breath of itches and thirsts,
Ever the vexer's hoot! hoot! till we find where the sly one hides and
    bring him forth;
Ever love .... ever the sobbing liquid of life,
Ever the bandage under the chin .... ever the tressels of death.

Here and there with dimes on the eyes walking,   1065
To feed the greed of the belly the brains liberally spooning,
Tickets buying or taking or selling, but in to the feast never once
    going;
Many sweating and ploughing and thrashing, and then the chaff for
    payment receiving,
A few idly owning, and they the wheat continually claiming.

This is the city .... and I am one of the citizens;   1070
Whatever interests the rest interests me .... politics, churches,
    newspapers, schools,
Benevolent societies, improvements, banks, tariffs, steamships,
    factories, markets,
Stocks and stores and real estate and personal estate.

They who piddle and patter here in collars and tailed coats .... I am
    aware who they are .... and that they are not worms or fleas,
I acknowledge the duplicates of myself under all the scrape-lipped   1075
    and pipe-legged concealments.
The weakest and shallowest is deathless with me,
What I do and say the same waits for them,
Every thought that flounders in me the same flounders in them.

I know perfectly well my own egotism,
And know my omniverous words, and cannot say any less,   1080
And would fetch you whoever you are flush with myself.

My words are words of a questioning, and to indicate reality;
This printed and bound book .... but the printer and the printing-
    office boy?
The marriage estate and settlement .... but the body and mind of the
    bridegroom? also those of the bride?
The panorama of the sea .... but the sea itself?   1085
The well-taken photographs .... but your wife or friend close and
    solid in your arms?
The fleet of ships of the line and all the modern improvements.... but
    the craft and pluck of the admiral?
The dishes and fare and furniture .... but the host and hostess, and
    the look out of their eyes?
The sky up there .... yet here or next door or across the way?
The saints and sages in history .... but you yourself?   1090
Sermons and creeds and theology .... but the human brain, and what
    is called reason, and what is called love and what is called life?

[43]   I do not despise you priests;
    My faith is the greatest of faiths and the least of faiths,

Enclosing all worship ancient and modern, and all between ancient
    and modern,

Believing I shall come again upon the earth after five thousand   1095
    years,

Waiting responses from oracles .... honoring the gods .... saluting
    the sun,

Making a fetish of the first rock or stump .... powowing with sticks
    in the circle of obis,[31]

Helping the lama[32] or brahmin as he trims the lamps of the idols,

Dancing yet through the streets in a phallic procession .... rapt and
    austere in the woods, a gymnosophist,[33]

Drinking mead from the skull-cup .... to shasta and vedas   1100
    admirant .... minding the koran,[34]

Walking the teokallis,[35] spotted with gore from the stone and knife—
    beating the serpent-skin drum;

Accepting the gospels, accepting him that was crucified, knowing
    assuredly that he is divine,

To the mass kneeling—to the puritan's prayer rising—sitting
    patiently in a pew,

Ranting and frothing in my insane crisis—waiting dead-like till my
    spirit arouses me;

Looking forth on pavement and land, and outside of pavement   1105
    and land,

Belonging to the winders of the circuit of circuits.

One of that centripetal and centrifugal gang,
I turn and talk like a man leaving charges before a journey.
Down-hearted doubters, dull and excluded,
Frivolous sullen moping angry affected disheartened atheistical,   1110
I know every one of you, and know the unspoken interrogatories,
By experience I know them.

How the flukes splash!
How they contort rapid as lightning, with spasms and spouts of blood!

Be at peace bloody flukes of doubters and sullen mopers,   1115
I take my place among you as much as among any;
The past is the push of you and me and all precisely the same,
And the night is for you and me and all,
And what is yet untried and afterward is for you and me and all.

---

[31]Sorcery, of African origin, practiced by blacks in the British West Indies and in the American South.

[32]Tibetan high priest; brahmin, Hindu high priest.

[33]Member of an ancient sect of naked Hindu ascetics.

[34]Shasta and *Vedas*, Hindu sacred texts; the Koran, the sacred text of Islam.

[35]An Aztec temple.

I do not know what is untried and afterward,   1120
But I know it is sure and alive, and sufficient.

Each who passes is considered, and each who stops is considered, and
    not a single one can it fail.

It cannot fail the young man who died and was buried,
Nor the young woman who died and was put by his side,
Nor the little child that peeped in at the door and then drew back 1125
    and was never seen again,
Nor the old man who has lived without purpose, and feels it with
    bitterness worse than gall,
Nor him in the poorhouse tubercled by rum and the bad disorder,
Nor the numberless slaughtered and wrecked . . . . nor the brutish
    koboo,[36] called the ordure of humanity,
Nor the sacs merely floating with open mouths for food to slip in,
Nor any thing in the earth, or down in the oldest graves of the   1130
    earth,
Nor any thing in the myriads of spheres, nor one of the myriads of
    myriads that inhabit them,
Nor the present, nor the least wisp that is known.

[44]   It is time to explain myself . . . . let us stand up.

What is known I strip away . . . . I launch all men and women forward
    with me into the unknown.

The clock indicates the moment . . . . but what does eternity   1135
    indicate?

Eternity lies in bottomless reservoirs . . . . its buckets are rising forever
    and ever,
They pour and they pour and they exhale away.

We have thus far exhausted trillions of winters and summers;
There are trillions ahead, and trillions ahead of them.

Births have brought us richness and variety,   1140
And other births will bring us richness and variety.

I do not call one greater and one smaller,
That which fills its period and place is equal to any.

Were mankind murderous or jealous upon you my brother or my
    sister?

---

[36]Native of Sumatra.

I am sorry for you .... they are not murderous or jealous   1145
    upon me;
All has been gentle with me .... I keep no account with lamentation;
What have I to do with lamentation?

I am an acme of things accomplished, and I am encloser of things
    to be.

My feet strike an apex of the apices of the stairs,
On every step bunches of ages, and larger bunches between the   1150
    steps,
All below duly traveled—and still I mount and mount.

Rise after rise bow the phantoms behind me,
Afar down I see the huge first Nothing, the vapor from the nostrils of
    death,
I know I was even there .... I waited unseen and always,
And slept while God carried me through the lethargic mist,   1155
And took my time .... and took no hurt from the foetid carbon.

Long I was hugged close .... long and long.

Immense have been the preparations for me,
Faithful and friendly the arms that have helped me.

Cycles ferried my cradle, rowing and rowing like cheerful
    boatmen;   1160
For room to me stars kept aside in their own rings,
They sent influences to look after what was to hold me.
Before I was born out of my mother generations guided me,
My embryo has never been torpid .... nothing could overlay it;
For it the nebula cohered to an orb .... the long slow strata piled   1165
    to rest it on .... vast vegetables gave it sustenance,
Monstrous sauroids[37] transported it in their mouths and deposited it
    with care.

All forces have been steadily employed to complete and delight me,
Now I stand on this spot with my soul.

[45]   Span of youth! Ever-pushed elasticity! Manhood balanced and florid
    and full!

My lovers suffocate me!   1170
Crowding my lips, and thick in the pores of my skin,

---

[37]Prehistoric reptiles.

Jostling me through streets and public halls .... coming naked to me
    at night,
Crying by day Ahoy from the rocks of the river .... swinging and
    chirping over my head,
Calling my name from flowerbeds or vines or tangled underbrush,
Or while I swim in the bath .... or drink from the pump at the   1175
    corner .... or the curtain is down at the opera .... or I glimpse
    at a woman's face in the railroad car;
Lighting on every moment of my life,
Bussing[38] my body with soft and balsamic busses,
Noiselessly passing handfuls out of their hearts and giving them to be
    mine.

Old age superbly rising! Ineffable grace of dying days!

Every condition promulges not only itself .... it promulges what   1180
    grows after and out of itself,
And the dark hush promulges as much as any.

I open my scuttle at night and see the far-sprinkled systems,
And all I see, multiplied as high as I can cipher, edge but the rim of
    the farther systems.

Wider and wider they spread, expanding and always expanding,
Outward and outward and forever outward.   1185

My sun has his sun, and round him obediently wheels,
He joins with his partners a group of superior circuit,
And greater sets follow, making specks of the greatest inside them.
There is no stoppage, and never can be stoppage;
If I and you and the worlds and all beneath or upon their surfaces, 1190
    and all the palpable life, were this moment reduced back to a
    pallid float, it would not avail in the long run,
We should surely bring up again where we now stand,
And as surely go as much farther, and then farther and farther.

A few quadrillions of eras, a few octillions of cubic leagues, do not
    hazard the span, or make it impatient,
They are but parts .... any thing is but a part.

See ever so far .... there is limitless space outside of that,   1195
Count ever so much .... there is limitless time around that.
Our rendezvous is fitly appointed .... God will be there and wait till
    we come.

[38]Kissing.

I know I have the best of time and space—and that I was never
measured, and never will be measured.

[46]   I tramp a perpetual journey,
My signs are a rain-proof coat and good shoes and a staff cut from 1200
    the woods;
No friend of mine takes his ease in my chair,
I have no chair, nor church nor philosophy;
I lead no man to a dinner-table or library or exchange,
But each man and each woman of you I lead upon a knoll,
My left hand hooks you round the waist,   1205
My right hand points to landscapes of continents, and a plain public
    road.

Not I, not any one else can travel that road for you,
You must travel it for yourself.

It is not far .... it is within reach,
Perhaps you have been on it since you were born, and did   1210
    not know,
Perhaps it is every where on water and on land.

Shoulder your duds, and I will mine, and let us hasten forth;
Wonderful cities and free nations we shall fetch as we go.

If you tire, give me both burdens, and rest the chuff of your hand on
    my hip,
And in due time you shall repay the same service to me;   1215
For after we start we never lie by again.

This day before dawn I ascended a hill and looked at the crowded
    heaven,
And I said to my spirit, When we become the enfolders of those orbs
    and the pleasure and knowledge of every thing in them, shall we
    be filled and satisfied then?
And my spirit said No, we level that lift to pass and continue beyond.
You are also asking me questions, and I hear you;   1220
I answer that I cannot answer .... you must find out for yourself.

Sit awhile wayfarer,
Here are biscuits to eat and here is milk to drink,
But as soon as you sleep and renew yourself in sweet clothes I will
    certainly kiss you with my goodbye kiss and open the gate for
    your egress hence.

Long enough have you dreamed contemptible dreams,   1225
Now I wash the gum from your eyes,

You must habit yourself to the dazzle of the light and of every
    moment of your life.

Long have you timidly waded, holding a plank by the shore,
Now I will you to be a bold swimmer,
To jump off in the midst of the sea, and rise again and nod to me   1230
    and shout, and laughingly dash with your hair.

[47]   I am the teacher of athletes,
He that by me spreads a wider breast than my own proves the width
    of my own,
He most honors my style who learns under it to destroy the teacher.

The boy I love, the same becomes a man not through derived power
    but in his own right,
Wicked, rather than virtuous out of conformity or fear,   1235
Fond of his sweetheart, relishing well his steak,
Unrequited love or a slight cutting him worse than a wound cuts,
First rate to ride, to fight, to hit the bull's eye, to sail a skiff, to sing a
    song or play on the banjo,
Preferring scars and faces pitted with smallpox over all latherers and
    those that keep out of the sun.

I teach straying from me, yet who can stray from me?   1240
I follow you whoever you are from the present hour;
My words itch at your ears till you understand them.
I do not say these things for a dollar, or to fill up the time while I wait
    for a boat;
It is you talking just as much myself . . . . . I act as the tongue of you,
It was tied in your mouth . . . . in mine it begins to be loosened.   1245

I swear I will never mention love or death inside a house,
And I swear I never will translate myself at all, only to him or her who
    privately stays with me in the open air.
If you would understand me go to the heights or water-shore,
The nearest gnat is an explanation and a drop or the motion of waves
    a key,
The maul the oar and the handsaw second my words.   1250

No shuttered room or school can commune with me,
But roughs and little children better than they.

The young mechanic is closest to me . . . . he knows me pretty well,
The woodman that takes his axe and jug with him shall take me with
    him all day,

The farmboy ploughing in the field feels good at the sound of my 1255
    voice,
In vessels that sail my words must sail . . . . I go with fishermen and
    seamen, and love them,
My face rubs to the hunter's face when he lies down alone in his
    blanket,
The driver thinking of me does not mind the jolt of his wagon,
The young mother and old mother shall comprehend me,
The girl and the wife rest the needle a moment and forget where 1260
    they are,
They and all would resume what I have told them.

[48]   I have said that the soul is not more than the body,
And I have said that the body is not more than the soul,
And nothing, not God, is greater to one than one's-self is,
And whoever walks a furlong without sympathy walks to his own 1265
    funeral, dressed in his shroud,
And I or you pocketless of a dime may purchase the pick of the earth,
And to glance with an eye or show a bean in its pod confounds the
    learning of all times,
And there is no trade or employment but the young man following it
    may become a hero,
And there is no object so soft but it makes a hub for the wheeled
    universe,
And any man or woman shall stand cool and supercilious before a 1270
    million universes.

And I call to mankind, Be not curious about God,
For I who am curious about each am not curious about God,
No array of terms can say how much I am at peace about God and
    about death.

I hear and behold God in every object, yet I understand God not in
    the least,
Nor do I understand who there can be more wonderful 1275
    than myself.

Why should I wish to see God better than this day?
I see something of God each hour of the twenty-four, and each
    moment then,
In the faces of men and women I see God, and in my own face in the
    glass;
I find letters from God dropped in the street, and every one is signed
    by God's name,
And I leave them where they are, for I know that others will 1280
    punctually come forever and ever.

[49]   And as to you death, and you bitter hug of mortality . . . . it is idle to
    try to alarm me.

To his work without flinching the accoucheur[39] comes,
I see the elderhand pressing receiving supporting,
I recline by the sills of the exquisite flexible doors .... and mark the
    outlet, and mark the relief and escape.
And as to you corpse I think you are good manure, but that does   1285
    not offend me,
I smell the white roses sweetscented and growing,
I reach to the leafy lips .... I reach to the polished breasts of melons.

And as to you life, I reckon you are the leavings of many deaths,
No doubt I have died myself ten thousand times before.

I hear you whispering there O stars of heaven,   1290
O suns .... O grass of graves .... O perpetual transfers and
    promotions .... if you do not say anything how can I say
    anything?

Of the turbid pool that lies in the autumn forest,
Of the moon that descends the steeps of the soughing twilight,
Toss, sparkles of day and dusk .... toss on the black stems that decay
    in the muck,
Toss to the moaning gibberish of the dry limbs.   1295

I ascend from the moon .... I ascend from the night,
And perceive of the ghastly glitter the sunbeams reflected,
And debouch[40] to the steady and central from the offspring great or
    small.

[50]   There is that in me .... I do not know what it is .... but I know it is
    in me.

Wrenched and sweaty .... calm and cool then my body becomes;   1300
I sleep .... I sleep long.

I do not know it .... it is without name .... it is a word unsaid,
It is not in any dictionary or utterance or symbol.

Something it swings on more than the earth I swing on,
To it the creation is the friend whose embracing awakes me.   1305
Perhaps I might tell more .... Outlines! I plead for my brothers and
    sisters.

Do you see O my brothers and sisters?
It is not chaos or death .... it is form and union and plan .... it is
    eternal life .... it is happiness.

---

[39]French for midwife.   [40]From the French word *deboucher*, to issue
    forth.

[51]   The past and present wilt .... I have filled them and emptied them,
And proceed to fill my next fold of the future.   1310

Listener up there! Here you .... what have you to confide to me?
Look in my face while I snuff the sidle of evening,
Talk honestly, for no one else hears you, and I stay only a minute
      longer.

Do I contradict myself?
Very well then .... I contradict myself;   1315
I am large .... I contain multitudes.

I concentrate toward them that are nigh .... I wait on the door slab.

Who has done his day's work and will soonest be through with his
      supper?
Who wishes to walk with me?

Will you speak before I am gone? Will you prove already too late?   1320

[52]   The spotted hawk swoops by and accuses me .... he complains of my
      gab and my loitering.

I too am not a bit tamed .... I too am untranslatable,

I sound my barbaric yawp over the roofs of the world.
The last scud of day holds back for me,
It flings my likeness after the rest and true as any on the   1325
      shadowed wilds,
It coaxes me to the vapor and the dusk.

I depart as air .... I shake my white locks at the runaway sun,
I effuse my flesh in eddies and drift it in lacy jags.

I bequeath myself to the dirt to grow from the grass I love,
If you want me again look for me under your bootsoles.   1330

You will hardly know who I am or what I mean,
But I shall be good health to you nevertheless,
And filter and fibre your blood.

Failing to fetch me at first keep encouraged,
Missing me one place search another,   1335
I stop some where waiting for you[41]

      1855

[41]There is no period at the end of the original
version of "Song of Myself."

from **Inscriptions**[1]

One's-Self I Sing

One's-Self I sing, a simple separate person,
Yet utter the word Democratic, the word En-Masse.

Of physiology from top to toe I sing,
Not physiognomy alone nor brain alone is worthy for the Muse, I say
    the Form complete is worthier far,
The Female equally with the Male I sing.   5

Of Life immense in passion, pulse, and power,
Cheerful, for freest action form'd under the laws divine,
The Modern Man I sing.

               1867

I Hear America Singing

I hear America singing, the varied carols I hear,
Those of mechanics, each one singing his as it should be blithe and
    strong,
The carpenter singing his as he measures his plank or beam,
The mason singing his as he makes ready for work, or leaves off work,
The boatman singing what belongs to him in his boat, the deckhand 5
    singing on the steamboat deck,
The shoemaker singing as he sits on his bench, the hatter singing as
    he stands,
The woodcutter's song, the ploughboy's on his way in the morning, or
    at noon intermission or at sundown,
The delicious singing of the mother, or of the young wife at work, or
    of the girl sewing or washing,
Each singing what belongs to him or her and to none else,
The day what belongs to the day—at night the party of young   10
    fellows, robust, friendly,
Singing with open mouths their strong melodious songs.

               1860

[1]*Inscriptions* first appeared as the opening grouping in the 1871 edition of *Leaves of Grass*. Beginning in 1867, "One's-Self I Sing" appeared as the opening poem of all future editions of *Leaves of Grass*.

from **Children of Adam**[1]

To the Garden the World

To the garden the world anew ascending,
Potent mates, daughters, sons, preluding,
The love, the life of their bodies, meaning and being,
Curious here behold my resurrection after slumber,
The revolving cycles in their wide sweep having brought me again,   5
Amorous, mature, all beautiful to me, all wondrous,
My limbs and the quivering fire that ever plays through them, for
    reasons, most wondrous,
Existing I peer and penetrate still,
Content with the present, content with the past,
By my side or back of me Eve following,   10
Or in front, and I following her just the same.

                                            1860

A Woman Waits for Me

A woman waits for me, she contains all, nothing is lacking,
Yet all were lacking if sex were lacking, or if the moisture of the right
    man were lacking.

Sex contains all, bodies, souls,
Meanings, proofs, purities, delicacies, results, promulgations
Songs, commands, health, pride, the maternal mystery, the seminal   5
    milk,
All hopes, benefactions, bestowals, all the passions, loves, beauties,
    delights of the earth,
All the governments, judges, gods, follow'd persons of the earth,
These are contain'd in sex as parts of itself and justifications of itself.

Without shame the man I like knows and avows the deliciousness of
    his sex,
Without shame the woman I like knows and avows hers.   10

Now I will dismiss myself from impassive women,
I will go stay with her who waits for me, and with those women that
    are warm-blooded and sufficient for me,

[1]*Children of Adam* and its companion cluster *Calamus*, which first appeared in the 1860 edition of *Leaves of Grass*, are Whitman's most controversial poetic sequences. In *Children of Adam* he focuses on what he calls "amative love," the phrenological term for the love between men and women. In *Calamus* he focuses on "adhesive love," the phrenological term for the love between men.

I see that they understand me and do not deny me,
I see that they are worthy of me, I will be the robust husband of those
 women.

They are not one jot less than I am,   15
They are tann'd in the face by shining suns and blowing winds,
Their flesh has the old divine suppleness and strength,
They know how to swim, row, ride, wrestle, shoot, run, strike, retreat,
 advance, resist, defend themselves,
They are ultimate in their own right—they are calm, clear, well-
 possess'd of themselves.

I draw you close to me, you women,   20
I cannot let you go, I would do you good,
I am for you, and you are for me, not only for our own sake, but for
 others' sakes,
Envelop'd in you sleep greater heroes and bards,
They refuse to awake at the touch of any man but me.

It is I, you women, I make my way,   25
I am stern, acrid, large, undissuadable, but I love you,
I do not hurt you any more than is necessary for you,
I pour the stuff to start sons and daughters fit for these States, I
 press with slow rude muscle,
I brace myself effectually, I listen to no entreaties,
I dare not withdraw till I deposit what has so long accumulated   30
 within me.

Through you I drain the pent-up rivers of myself,
In you I wrap a thousand onward years,
On you I graft the grafts of the best-beloved of me and America,
The drops I distil upon you shall grow fierce and athletic girls, new
 artists, musicians, and singers,
The babes I beget upon you are to beget babes in their turn,   35
I shall demand perfect men and women out of my love-spendings,
I shall expect them to interpenetrate with others, as I and you
 interpenetrate now,
I shall count on the fruits of the gushing showers of them, as I count
 on the fruits of the gushing showers I give now,
I shall look for loving crops from the birth, life, death, immortality, I
 plant so lovingly now.

                1856

from **Calamus**[1]

In Paths Untrodden

In paths untrodden,
In the growth by margins of pond-waters,
Escaped from the life that exhibits itself,
From all the standards hitherto publish'd, from the pleasures, profits,
    conformities,
Which too long I was offering to feed my soul,   5
Clear to me now standards not yet publish'd, clear to me that my soul,
That the soul of the man I speak for rejoices in comrades,
Here by myself away from the clank of the world,
Tallying and talk'd to here by tongues aromatic,
No longer abash'd, (for in this secluded spot I can respond as I   10
    would not dare elsewhere,)
Strong upon me the life that does not exhibit itself, yet contains all
    the rest,
Resolv'd to sing no songs to-day but those of manly attachment,
Projecting them along that substantial life,
Bequeathing hence types of athletic love,
Afternoon this delicious Ninth-month[2] in my forty-first year,   15
I proceed for all who are or have been young men,
To tell the secret of my nights and days,
To celebrate the need of comrades.

                        1860

Recorders Ages Hence

Recorders ages hence,
Come, I will take you down underneath this impassive exterior, I will
    tell you what to say of me,
Publish my name and hang up my picture as that of the tenderest
    lover,
The friend the lover's portrait, of whom his friend his lover was
    fondest,
Who was not proud of his songs, but of the measureless ocean of   5
    love within him, and freely pour'd it forth,

---

[1]Calamus is another word for sweet flag, a hardy, aromatic grass that grows near ponds and swamps.

[2]Quaker term for September, the ninth month of the year. Whitman associated the pagan names of the days and the months with the feudal past; his substitution of Quaker names was part of his attempt to invent a specifically American idiom expressive of the beliefs and values of the American people.

Who often walk'd lonesome walks thinking of his dear friends, his
    lovers,
Who pensive away from one he lov'd often lay sleepless and
    dissatisfied at night,
Who knew too well the sick, sick dread lest the one he lov'd might
    secretly be indifferent to him,
Whose happiest days were far away through fields, in woods, on hills,
    he and another wandering hand in hand, they twain apart from
    other men,
Who oft as he saunter'd the streets curv'd with his arm the shoulder 10
    of his friend, while the arm of his friend rested upon him also.

                                                                    1860

When I Heard at the Close of the Day

When I heard at the close of the day how my name had been receiv'd
    with plaudits in the capitol, still it was not a happy night for me
    that follow'd,
And else when I carous'd, or when my plans were accomplish'd, still I
    was not happy,
But the day when I rose at dawn from the bed of perfect health,
    refresh'd, singing, inhaling the ripe breath of autumn,
When I saw the full moon in the west grow pale and disappear in the
    morning light,
When I wander'd alone over the beach, and undressing bathed,   5
    laughing with the cool waters, and saw the sun rise,
And when I thought how my dear friend my lover was on his way
    coming, O then I was happy,
O then each breath tasted sweeter, and all that day my food nourish'd
    me more, and the beautiful day pass'd well,
And the next came with equal joy, and with the next at evening came
    my friend,
And that night while all was still I heard the waters roll slowly
    continually up the shores,
I heard the hissing rustle of the liquid and sands as directed to me   10
    whispering to congratulate me,
For the one I love most lay sleeping by me under the same cover in
    the cool night,
In the stillness in the autumn moonbeams his face was inclined
    toward me,
And his arm lay lightly around my breast—and that night I was happy.

                                                                    1860

I Saw in Louisiana a Live-Oak Growing

I saw in Louisiana a live-oak growing,
All alone stood it, and the moss hung down from the branches;
Without any companion it grew there, uttering joyous leaves of dark
    green,
And its look, rude, unbending, lusty, made me think of myself;
But I wonder'd how it could utter joyous leaves, standing alone   5
    there, without its friend, its lover near—for I knew I could not;
And I broke off a twig with a certain number of leaves upon it, and
    twined around it a little moss,
And brought it away—and I have placed it in sight in my room;
It is not needed to remind me as of my own dear friends,
(For I believe lately I think of little else than of them;)
Yet it remains to me a curious token—it makes me think of manly   10
    love;
For all that, and though the live-oak glistens there in Louisiana,
    solitary, in a wide flat space,
Uttering joyous leaves all its life, without a friend, a lover, near,
I know very well I could not.

                                     1860

Here the Frailest Leaves of Me

Here the frailest leaves of me and yet my strongest lasting,
Here I shade and hide my thoughts, I myself do not expose them,
And yet they expose me more than all my other poems.

                                     1860

I Dream'd in a Dream

I dream'd in a dream I saw a city invincible to the attacks of the whole
    of the rest of the earth,
I dream'd that was the new city of Friends,
Nothing was greater there than the quality of robust love, it led the rest,
It was seen every hour in the actions of the men of that city,
And in all their looks and words.   5

                                     1860

Crossing Brooklyn Ferry

1

Flood-tide below me! I see you face to face!
Clouds of the west—sun there half an hour high—I see you also face
    to face.

Crowds of men and women attired in the usual costumes, how curious
    you are to me!
On the ferry-boats the hundreds and hundreds that cross, returning
    home, are more curious to me than you suppose,
And you that shall cross from shore to shore years hence are more   5
    to me, and more in my meditations, than you might suppose.

2

The impalpable sustenance of me from all things at all hours of the
    day,
The simple, compact, well-join'd scheme, myself disintegrated, every
    one disintegrated yet part of the scheme,
The similitudes of the past and those of the future,
The glories strung like beads on my smallest sights and hearings, on
    the walk in the street and the passage over the river,
The current rushing so swiftly and swimming with me far away,   10
The others that are to follow me, the ties between me and them,
The certainty of others, the life, love, sight, hearing of others.

Others will enter the gates of the ferry and cross from shore to shore,
Others will watch the run of the flood-tide,
Others will see the shipping of Manhattan north and west, and the   15
    heights of Brooklyn to the south and east,
Others will see the islands large and small;
Fifty years hence, others will see them as they cross, the sun half an
    hour high,
A hundred years hence, or ever so many hundred years hence, others
    will see them,
Will enjoy the sunset, the pouring-in of the flood-tide, the falling-back
    to the sea of the ebb-tide.

3

It avails not, time nor place—distance avails not,   20
I am with you, you men and women of a generation, or ever so many
    generations hence,
Just as you feel when you look on the river and sky, so I felt,
Just as any of you is one of a living crowd, I was one of a crowd,
Just as you are refresh'd by the gladness of the river and the bright
    flow, I was refresh'd,
Just as you stand and lean on the rail, yet hurry with the swift   25
    current,
I stood yet was hurried,
Just as you look on the numberless masts of ships and the thick-
    stemm'd pipes of steamboats, I look'd.

I too many and many a time cross'd the river of old,
Watched the Twelfth-month sea-gulls, saw them high in the air
    floating with motionless wings, oscillating their bodies,
Saw how the glistening yellow lit up parts of their bodies and left the
    rest in strong shadow,
Saw the slow-wheeling circles and the gradual edging toward the   30
    south,
Saw the reflection of the summer sky in the water,
Had my eyes dazzled by the shimmering track of beams,
Look'd at the fine centrifugal spokes of light round the shape of my
    head in the sunlit water,
Look'd on the haze on the hills southward and south-westward,
Look'd on the vapor as it flew in fleeces tinged with violet,   35
Look'd toward the lower bay to notice the vessels arriving,
Saw their approach, saw aboard those that were near me,
Saw the white sails of schooners and sloops, saw the ships at anchor,
The sailors at work in the rigging or out astride the spars,
The round masts, the swinging motion of the hulls, the slender   40
    serpentine pennants,
The large and small steamers in motion, the pilots in their pilot-
    houses,
The white wake left by the passage, the quick tremulous whirl of the
    wheels,
The flags of all nations, the falling of them at sunset,
The scallop-edged waves in the twilight, the ladled cups, the
    frolicsome crests and glistening,
The stretch afar growing dimmer and dimmer, the gray walls of the 45
    granite storehouses by the docks,
On the river the shadowy group, the big steam-tug closely flank'd on
    each side by the barges, the hay-boat, the belated lighter,
On the neighboring shore the fires from the foundry chimneys
    burning high and glaringly into the night,
Casting their flicker of black contrasted with wild red and yellow light
    over the tops of the houses, and down into the clefts of streets.

4

These and all else were to me the same as they are to you,
I loved well those cities, loved well the stately and rapid river,   50
The men and women I saw were all near to me,
Others the same—others who look back on me because I look'd
    forward to them,
(The time will come, though I stop here to-day and to-night.)

5

What is it then between us?
What is the count of the scores or hundreds of years between us?   55

Whatever it is, it avails not—distance avails not, and place avails not,
I too lived, Brooklyn of ample hills was mine,
I too walk'd the streets of Manhattan island, and bathed in the water
     around it,
I too felt the curious abrupt questionings stir within me.
In the day among crowds of people sometimes they came upon me,   60
In my walks home late at night or as I lay in my bed they came upon
     me,
I too had been struck from the float forever held in solution,
I too had receiv'd identity by my body,
That I was I knew was of my body, and what I should be I knew I
     should be of my body.

6

It is not upon you alone the dark patches fall,   65
The dark threw its patches down upon me also,
The best I had done seem'd to me blank and suspicious,
My great thoughts as I supposed them, were they not in reality
     meagre?
Nor is it you alone who know what it is to be evil,
I am he who knew what it was to be evil,   70
I too knitted the old knot of contrariety,
Blabb'd, blush'd, resented, lied, stole, grudg'd,
Had guile, anger, lust, hot wishes I dared not speak,
Was wayward, vain, greedy, shallow, sly, cowardly, malignant,
The wolf, the snake, the hog, not wanting in me,   75
The cheating look, the frivolous word, the adulterous wish, not
     wanting,
Refusals, hates, postponements, meanness, laziness, none of these
     wanting,
Was one with the rest, the days and haps of the rest,
Was call'd by my nighest name by clear loud voices of young men as
     they saw me approaching or passing,
Felt their arms on my neck as I stood, or the negligent leaning of   80
     their flesh against me as I sat,
Saw many I loved in the street or ferry-boat or public assembly, yet
     never told them a word,
Lived the same life with the rest, the same old laughing, gnawing,
     sleeping,
Play'd the part that still looks back on the actor or actress,

The same old role, the role that is what we make it, as great as we
    like,
Or as small as we like, or both great and small.   85

7

Closer yet I approach you,
What thought you have of me now, I had as much of you—I laid in
    my stores in advance,
I consider'd long and seriously of you before you were born.

Who was to know what should come home to me?
Who knows but I am enjoying this?   90
Who knows, for all the distance, but I am as good as looking at you
    now, for all you cannot see me?

8

Ah, what can ever be more stately and admirable to me than mast-
    hemm'd Manhattan?
River and sunset and scallop-edg'd waves of flood-tide?
The sea-gulls oscillating their bodies, the hay-boat in the twilight, and
    the belated lighter?
What gods can exceed these that clasp me by the hand, and with   95
    voices I love call me promptly and loudly by my nighest name as
    I approach?

What is more subtle than this which ties me to the woman or man
    that looks in my face?
Which fuses me into you now, and pours my meaning into you?

We understand then do we not?
What I promis'd without mentioning it, have you not accepted?
What the study could not teach—what the preaching could not   100
    accomplish is accomplish'd, is it not?

9

Flow on, river! flow with the flood-tide, and ebb with the ebb-tide!
Frolic on, crested and scallop-edg'd waves!
Gorgeous clouds of the sunset! drench with your splendor me, or the
    men and women generations after me!
Cross from shore to shore, countless crowds of passengers!
Stand up, tall masts of Mannahatta! stand up, beautiful hills of   105
    Brooklyn!

Throb, baffled and curious brain! throw out questions and answers!
Suspend here and everywhere, eternal float of solution!
Gaze, loving and thirsting eyes, in the house or street or public
    assembly!
Sound out, voices of young men! loudly and musically call me by my
    nighest name!
Live, old life! play the part that looks back on the actor or actress!   110
Play the old role, the role that is great or small according as one
    makes it!
Consider, you who peruse me, whether I may not in unknown ways be
    looking upon you;
Be firm, rail over the river, to support those who lean idly, yet haste
    with the hasting current;
Fly on, sea-birds! fly sideways, or wheel in large circles high in the air;
Receive the summer sky, you water, and faithfully hold it till all   115
    downcast eyes have time to take it from you!
Diverge, fine spokes of light, from the shape of my head, or any one's
    head, in the sunlit water!
Come on, ships from the lower bay! pass up or down, white-sail'd
    schooners, sloops, lighters!
Flaunt away, flag of all nations! be duly lower'd at sunset!
Burn high your fires, foundry chimneys! cast black shadows at
    nightfall! cast red and yellow light over the tops of the houses!
Appearances, now or henceforth, indicate what you are,   120
You necessary film, continue to envelop the soul,
About my body for me, and your body for you, be hung our divinest
    aromas,
Thrive, cities—bring your freight, bring your shows, ample and
    sufficient rivers,
Expand, being than which none else is perhaps more spiritual,
Keep your places, objects than which none else is more lasting.   125

You have waited, you always wait, you dumb, beautiful ministers,
We receive you with free sense at last, and are insatiate henceforward,
Not you any more shall be able to foil us, or withhold yourselves from
    us,
We use you, and do not cast you aside—we plant you permanently
    within us,
We fathom you not—we love you—there is perfection in you also,   130
You furnish your parts toward eternity,
Great or small, you furnish your parts toward the soul.

                      1856

from **Sea-Drift**

Out of the Cradle Endlessly Rocking

Out of the cradle endlessly rocking,
Out of the mocking-bird's throat, the musical shuttle,
Out of the Ninth-month midnight,
Over the sterile sands and the fields beyond, where the child leaving
    his bed wander'd alone, bareheaded, barefoot,
Down from the shower'd halo,   5
Up from the mystic play of shadows twining and twisting as if they
    were alive,
Out from the patches of briers and blackberries,
From the memories of the bird that chanted to me,
From your memories sad brother, from the fitful risings and fallings I
    heard,
From under that yellow half-moon late-risen and swollen as if with 10
    tears,
From those beginning notes of yearning and love there in the mist,
From the thousand responses of my heart never to cease,
From the myriad thence-arous'd words,
From the word stronger and more delicious than any,
From such as now they start the scene revisiting,   15
As a flock, twittering, rising, or overhead passing,
Borne hither, ere all eludes me, hurriedly,
A man, yet by these tears a little boy again,
Throwing myself on the sand, confronting the waves,
I, chanter of pains and joys, uniter of here and hereafter,   20
Taking all hints to use them, but swiftly leaping beyond them,
A reminiscence sing.
Once Paumanok,[1]
When the lilac-scent was in the air and Fifth-month grass was
    growing,
Up this seashore in some briers,   25
Two feather'd guests from Alabama, two together,
And their nest, and four light-green eggs spotted with brown.
And every day the he-bird to and fro near at hand.
And every day the she-bird crouch'd on her nest, silent, with bright
    eyes,
And every day I, a curious boy, never too close, never disturbing 30
    them,
Cautiously peering, absorbing, translating.

---

[1]Native American Indian name for Long
Island.

Shine! shine! shine!
Pour down your warmth, great sun!
While we bask, we two together.

Two together!   35
Winds blow south, or winds blow north,
Day come white, or night come black,
Home, or rivers and mountains from home,
Singing all time, minding no time,
While we two keep together.   40

Till of a sudden,
May-be kill'd, unknown to her mate,
One forenoon the she-bird crouch'd not on the nest,
Nor return'd that afternoon, nor the next,
Nor ever appear'd again.   45

And thenceforward all summer in the sound of the sea,
And at night under the full of the moon in calmer weather,
Over the hoarse surging of the sea,
Or flitting from brier to brier by day,
I saw, I heard at intervals the remaining one, the he-bird,   50
The solitary guest from Alabama.

Blow! blow! blow!
Blow up sea-winds along Paumanok's shore;
I wait and I wait till you blow my mate to me.

Yes, when the stars glisten'd,   55
All night long on the prong of a moss-scallop'd stake,
Down almost amid the slapping waves,
Sat the lone singer wonderful causing tears.

He call'd on his mate,
He pour'd forth the meanings which I of all men know.   60

Yes my brother I know,
The rest might not, but I have treasur'd every note,
For more than once dimly down to the beach gliding,
Silent, avoiding the moonbeams, blending myself with the shadows,
Recalling now the obscure shapes, the echoes, the sounds and sights 65
    after their sorts,
The white arms out in the breakers tirelessly tossing,
I, with bare feet, a child, the wind wafting my hair,
Listen'd long and long.

Listen'd to keep, to sing, now translating the notes,
Following you my brother. 70

Soothe! soothe! soothe!
Close on its wave soothes the wave behind,
And again another behind embracing and lapping, every one close,
But my love soothes not me, not me.

Low hangs the moon, it rose late, 75
It is lagging—O I think it is heavy with love, with love.

O madly the sea pushes upon the land,
With love, with love.

O night! do I not see my love fluttering out among the breakers?
What is that little black thing I see there in the white? 80

Loud! loud! loud!
Loud I call to you, my love!

High and clear I shoot my voice over the waves,
Surely you must know who is here, is here,
You must know who I am, my love. 85

Low-hanging moon!
What is that dusky spot in your brown yellow?
O it is the shape, the shape of my mate!
O moon do not keep her from me any longer.

Land! land! O land! 90
Whichever way I turn, O I think you could give me my mate back
again if you only would,
For I am almost sure I see her dimly whichever way I look.

O rising stars!
Perhaps the one I want so much will rise, will rise with some of you.

O throat! O trembling throat! 95
Sound clearer through the atmosphere!
Pierce the woods, the earth,
Somewhere listening to catch you must be the one I want.

Shake out carols!
Solitary here, the night's carols! 100
Carols of lonesome love! death's carols!
Carols under that lagging, yellow, waning moon!

O under that moon where she droops almost down into the sea!
O reckless despairing carols.

But soft! sink low!   105
Soft! let me just murmur,
And do you wait a moment you husky-nois'd sea,
For somewhere I believe I heard my mate responding to me,
So faint, I must be still, be still to listen,
But not altogether still, for then she might not come immediately
    to me.   110

Hither my love!
Here I am! here!
With this just-sustain'd note I announce myself to you,
This gentle call is for you my love, for you.

Do not be decoy'd elsewhere,   115
That is the whistle of the wind, it is not my voice,
That is the fluttering, the fluttering of the spray,
Those are the shadows of leaves.

O darkness! O in vain!
O I am very sick and sorrowful.   120

O brown halo in the sky near the moon, drooping upon the sea!
O troubled reflection in the sea!
O throat! O throbbing heart!
And I singing uselessly, uselessly all the night.

O past! O happy life! O songs of joy!   125
In the air, in the woods, over fields,

Loved! loved! loved! loved! loved!
But my mate no more, no more with me!
We two together no more.

The aria sinking,   130
All else continuing, the stars shining,
The winds blowing, the notes of the bird continuous echoing,
With angry moans the fierce old mother incessantly moaning,
On the sands of Paumanok's shore gray and rustling,
The yellow half-moon enlarged, sagging down, drooping, the face   135
    of the sea almost touching,
The boy ecstatic, with his bare feet the waves, with his hair the
    atmosphere dallying,

The love in the heart long pent, now loose, now at last tumultuously
    bursting,
The aria's meaning, the ears, the soul, swiftly depositing,
The strange tears down the cheeks coursing,
The colloquy there, the trio, each uttering,   140
The undertone, the savage old mother incessantly crying,
To the boy's soul's questions sullenly timing, some drown'd secret
    hissing,
To the outsetting bard.

Demon or bird! (said the boy's soul,)
Is it indeed toward your mate you sing? or is it really to me?   145
For I, that was a child, my tongue's use sleeping, now I have heard
    you,
Now in a moment I know what I am for, I awake,
And already a thousand singers, a thousand songs, clearer, louder and
    more sorrowful than yours,
A thousand warbling echoes have started to life within me, never to
    die.
O you singer solitary, singing by yourself, projecting me,   150
O solitary me listening, never more shall I cease perpetuating you,
Never more shall I escape, never more the reverberations,
Never more the cries of unsatisfied love be absent from me,
Never again leave me to be the peaceful child I was before what there
    in the night,
By the sea under the yellow and sagging moon,   155
The messenger there arous'd, the fire, the sweet hell within,
The unknown want, the destiny of me.

O give me the clew! (it lurks in the night here somewhere,)
O if I am to have so much, let me have more!

A word then, (for I will conquer it,)   160
The word final, superior to all,
Subtle, sent up—what is it?—I listen;
Are you whispering it, and have been all the time, you sea-waves?
Is that it from your liquid rims and wet sands?

Whereto answering, the sea,   165
Delaying not, hurrying not,
Whisper'd me through the night, and very plainly before daybreak,
Lisp'd to me the low and delicious word death,
And again death, death, death, death,
Hissing melodious, neither like the bird nor like my arous'd child's   170
    heart,
But edging near as privately for me rustling at my feet,

Creeping thence steadily up to my ears and laving me softly all over,
Death, death, death, death, death.

Which I do not forget,
But fuse the song of my dusky demon and brother,   175
That he sang to me in the moonlight on Paumanok's gray beach,
With the thousand responsive songs at random,
My own songs awaked from that hour,
And with them the key, the word up from the waves,
The word of the sweetest song and all songs,   180
That strong and delicious word which, creeping to my feet,
(Or like some old crone rocking the cradle, swathed in sweet
    garments, bending aside,)
The sea whisper'd me.

                                                                         1859

from **By the Roadside**

Europe[1]

The 72d and 73d Years of These States

Suddenly out of its stale and drowsy lair, the lair of slaves,
Like lightning it le'pt forth half startled at itself,
Its feet upon the ashes and the rags, its hands tight to the throats of
    kings.

O hope and faith!
O aching close of exiled patriots' lives!   5
O many a sicken'd heart!
Turn back unto this day and make yourselves afresh.

And you, paid to defile the People—you liars, mark!
Not for numberless agonies, murders, lusts,
For court thieving in its manifold mean forms, worming from his   10
    simplicity the poor man's wages,
For many a promise sworn by royal lips and broken and laugh'd at in
    the breaking,
Then in their power not for all these did the blows strike revenge, or
    the heads of the nobles fall;
The People scorn'd the ferocity of kings.

---

[1]This poem, which was first published in the *New York Daily Tribune* on June 21, 1850, was included among the initial twelve poems of *Leaves of Grass* in 1855. It was inspired by the 1848 revolutions throughout Europe.

But the sweetness of mercy brew'd bitter destruction, and the
     frighten'd monarchs come back,
Each comes in state with his train, hangman, priest, tax-gatherer,   15
Soldier, lawyer, lord, jailer, and sycophant.

Yet behind all lowering stealing, lo, a shape,
Vague as the night, draped interminably, head, front and form, in
     scarlet folds,
Whose face and eyes none may see,
Out of its robes only this, the red robes lifted by the arm,   20
One finger crook'd pointed high over the top, like the head of a snake
     appears.

Meanwhile corpses lie in new-made graves, bloody corpses of young
     men,
The rope of the gibbet hangs heavily, the bullets of princes are flying,
     the creatures of power laugh aloud,
And all these things bear fruits, and they are good.

Those corpses of young men,   25
Those martyrs that hang from the gibbets, those hearts pierc'd by the
     gray lead,
Cold and motionless as they seem live elsewhere with unslaughter'd
     vitality.

They live in other young men O kings!
They live in brothers again ready to defy you,
They were purified by death, they were taught and exalted.   30

Not a grave of the murder'd for freedom but grows seed for freedom,
     in its turn to bear seed,
Which the winds carry afar and re-sow, and the rains and the snows
     nourish.

Not a disembodied spirit can the weapons of tyrants let loose,
But it stalks invisibly over the earth, whispering, counseling,
     cautioning.

Liberty, let others despair of you—I never despair of you.   35

Is the house shut? is the master away?
Nevertheless, be ready, be not weary of watching,
He will soon return, his messengers come anon.

                                      1850

When I Heard the Learn'd Astronomer

When I heard the learn'd astronomer,
When the proofs, the figures, were ranged in columns before me,
When I was shown the charts and diagrams, to add, divide, and
    measure them,
When I sitting heard the astronomer where he lectured with much
    applause in the lecture-room,
How soon unaccountable I became tired and sick,   5
Till rising and gliding out I wander'd off by myself,
In the mystical moist night-air, and from time to time,
Look'd up in perfect silence at the stars.

                                    1865

To a President[1]

All you are doing and saying is to America dangled mirages,
You have not learn'd of Nature—of the politics of Nature you have
    not learn'd the great amplitude, rectitude, impartiality,
You have not seen that only such as they are for these States,
And that what is less than they must sooner or later lift off from
    these States.

                                    1860

The Dalliance of the Eagles

Skirting the river road, (my forenoon walk, my rest,)
Skyward in air a sudden muffled sound, the dalliance of the eagles,
The rushing amorous contact high in space together,
The clinching interlocking claws, a living, fierce, gyrating wheel,
Four beating wings, two beaks, a swirling mass tight grappling,   5
In tumbling turning clustering loops, straight downward falling,
Till o'er the river pois'd, the twain yet one, a moment's lull,
A motionless still balance in the air, then parting, talons loosing,
Upward again on slow-firm pinions slanting, their separate diverse
    flight,
She hers, he his, pursuing.   10

                                    1880

[1]The poem was initially addressed to James Buchanan, the Democratic president whose support for slavery expansion and other controversial policies seemed, in Whitman's view, to undermine the fundamental values of the American republic.

To the States

To Identify the 16th, 17th, or 18th Presidentiad.[1]

Why reclining, interrogating? why myself and all drowsing?
What deepening twilight—scum floating atop of the waters,
Who are they as bats and night-dogs askant in the capitol?
What a filthy Presidentiad! (O South, your torrid suns! O North, your
    arctic freezings!)
Are those really Congressmen? are those the great Judges?[2] is that   5
    the President?
Then I will sleep awhile yet, for I see that these States sleep, for
    reasons;
(With gathering murk, with muttering thunder and lambent shoots
    we all duly awake,
South, North, East, West, inland and seaboard, we will surely awake.)

              1860

from **Drum-Taps**[1']

Beat! Beat! Drums!

Beat! beat! drums!—blow! bugles! blow!
Through the windows—through doors—burst like a ruthless force,
Into the solemn church, and scatter the congregation,
Into the school where the scholar is studying;
Leave not the bridegroom quiet—no happiness must he have now   5
    with his bride,
Nor the peaceful farmer any peace, ploughing his field or gathering his
    grain,
So fierce you whirr and pound you drums—so shrill you bugles blow.

Beat! beat! drums!—blow! bugles! blow!
Over the traffic of cities—over the rumble of wheels in the streets;
Are beds prepared for sleepers at night in the houses? no sleepers   10
    must sleep in those beds,
No bargainers' bargains by day—no brokers or speculators—would
    they continue?

---

[1]The 16th, 17th, and 18th Presidentiad refers to the presidencies of Millard Fillmore, Franklin Pierce, and James Buchanan, all of whom pursued a policy of compromise on the issue of slavery in order to avoid armed conflict between North and South. The poem, which was included in the 1860 edition of *Leaves of Grass*, appears to predict the imminent outbreak of the Civil War.

[2]Whitman may be referring to Chief Justice Taney's 1857 Dred Scott decision, which denied blacks citizenship under the Constitution of the United States.

[1']*Drum-Taps* was initially published as a separate volume in 1865. It was added to *Leaves of Grass* in 1867.

Would the talkers be talking? would the singer attempt to sing?
Would the lawyer rise in the court to state his case before the judge?
Then rattle quicker, heavier drums—you bugles wilder blow.

Beat! beat! drums!—blow! bugles! blow!   15
Make no parley—stop for no expostulation,
Mind not the timid—mind not the weeper or prayer,
Mind not the old man beseeching the young man,
Let not the child's voice be heard, nor the mother's entreaties,
Make even the trestles to shake the dead where they lie awaiting the 20
    hearses,
So strong you thump O terrible drums—so loud you bugles blow.

                                                                          1861

Cavalry Crossing a Ford

A line in long array where they wind betwixt green islands,
They take a serpentine course, their arms flash in the sun—hark to
    the musical clank,
Behold the silvery river, in it the splashing horses loitering stop to
    drink,
Behold the brown-faced men, each group, each person a picture, the
    negligent rest on the saddles,
Some emerge on the opposite bank, others are just entering the   5
    ford—while,
Scarlet and blue and snowy white,
The guidon flags flutter gayly in the wind.

                                                                          1865

Vigil Strange I Kept on the Field One Night

Vigil strange I kept on the field one night;
When you my son and my comrade dropt at my side that day,
One look I but gave which your dear eyes return'd with a look I shall
    never forget,
One touch of your hand to mine O boy, reach'd up as you lay on the
    ground,
Then onward I sped in the battle, the even-contested battle,   5
Till late in the night reliev'd to the place at last again I made my way,
Found you in death so cold dear comrade, found your body son of
    responding kisses, (never again on earth responding,)
Bared your face in the starlight, curious the scene, cool blew the
    moderate night-wind,
Long there and then in vigil I stood, dimly around me the battle-field
    spreading,

Vigil wondrous and vigil sweet there in the fragrant silent night,   10
But not a tear fell, not even a long-drawn sigh, long, long I gazed,
Then on the earth partially reclining sat by your side leaning my chin
    in my hands,
Passing sweet hours, immortal and mystic hours with you dearest
    comrade—not a tear, not a word,
Vigil of silence, love and death, vigil for you my son and my soldier,
As onward silently stars aloft, eastward new ones upward stole,   15
Vigil final for you brave boy, (I could not save you, swift was your
    death,
I faithfully loved you and cared for you living, I think we shall surely
    meet again,)
Till at latest lingering of the night, indeed just as the dawn appear'd,
My comrade I wrapt in his blanket, envelop'd well his form,
Folded the blanket well, tucking it carefully over head and carefully   20
    under feet,
And there and then and bathed by the rising sun, my son in his grave,
    in his rude-dug grave I deposited,
Ending my vigil strange with that, vigil of night and battle-field dim,
Vigil for boy of responding kisses, (never again on earth responding,)
Vigil for comrade swiftly slain, vigil I never forget, how as day
    brighten'd,
I rose from the chill ground and folded my soldier well in his   25
    blanket,
And buried him where he fell.

1865

Year That Trembled and Reel'd Beneath Me[1]

Year that trembled and reel'd beneath me!
Your summer wind was warm enough, yet the air I breathed froze me,
A thick gloom fell through the sunshine and darken'd me,
Must I change my triumphant songs? said I to myself,
Must I indeed learn to chant the cold dirges of the baffled?   5
And sullen hymns of defeat?

1865

The Wound Dresser

1

An old man bending, I come, among new faces,
Years looking backward, resuming, in answer to children,
Come tell us, old man, as from young men and maidens that love me;

---

[1]The year is probably the crisis year 1863–
1864, when the outcome of the Civil War
was not at all certain.

(Arous'd and angry, I'd thought to beat the alarum, and urge
  relentless war,
But soon my fingers fail'd me, my face droop'd and I resign'd myself, 5
To sit by the wounded and soothe them, or silently watch the dead;)
Years hence of these scenes, of these furious passions, these chances,
Of unsurpass'd heroes, (was one side so brave? the other was equally
  brave;)
Now be witness again—paint the mightiest armies of earth;
Of those armies so rapid, so wondrous, what saw you to tell us?   10
What stays with you latest and deepest? of curious panics,
Of hard-fought engagements, or sieges tremendous, what deepest
  remains?

2

O maidens and young men I love, and that love me,
What you ask of my days, those the strangest and sudden your talking
  recalls;
Soldier alert I arrive, after a long march, cover'd with sweat and   15
  dust;
In the nick of time I come, plunge in the fight, loudly shout in the
  rush of successful charge;
Enter the captur'd works. . . . yet lo! like a swift-running river, they
  fade;
Pass and are gone, they fade—I dwell not on soldiers' perils or
  soldiers' joys;
(Both I remember well—many the hardships, few the joys, yet I was
  content.)

But in silence, in dreams' projections,   20
While the world of gain and appearance and mirth goes on,
So soon what is over forgotten, and waves wash the imprints off the
  sand,
With hinged knees returning, I enter the doors—(while for you up
  there,
Whoever you are, follow me without noise, and be of strong heart.)

3

Bearing the bandages, water and sponge,   25
Straight and swift to my wounded I go,
Where they lie on the ground, after the battle brought in;
Where their priceless blood reddens the grass, the ground;
Or to the rows of the hospital tent, or under the roof'd hospital;
To the long rows of cots, up and down, each side, I return;   30
To each and all, one after another, I draw near—not one do I miss;

An attendant follows, holding a tray—he carries a refuse pail,
Soon to be fill'd with clotted rags and blood, emptied and fill'd again.

I onward go, I stop,
With hinged knees and steady hand, to dress wounds;   35
I am firm with each—the pangs are sharp, yet unavoidable;
One turns to me his appealing eyes—(poor boy! I never knew you,
Yet I think I could not refuse this moment to die for you, if that
     would save you.)

On, on I go!—(open doors of time! open hospital doors!)
The crush'd head I dress, (poor crazed hand, tear not the bandage   40
     away),
The neck of the cavalry-man, with the bullet through and through, I
     examine;
Hard the breathing rattles, quite glazed already the eye, yet life
     struggles hard;
(Come, sweet death! be persuaded, O beautiful death!
In mercy come quickly.)

From the stump of the arm, the amputated hand,   45
I undo the clotted lint, remove the slough, wash off the matter and
     blood;
Back on his pillow the soldier bends, with curv'd neck, and side-falling
     head;
His eyes are closed, his face is pale, he dares not look on the bloody
     stump,
And has not yet look'd on it.

I dress a wound in the side, deep, deep;   50
But a day or two more—for see, the frame all wasted already, and
     sinking,
And the yellow-blue countenance see.

I dress the perforated shoulder, the foot with the bullet wound,
Cleanse the one with a gnawing and putrid gangrene, so sickening, so
     offensive,
While the attendant stands behind aside me, holding the tray and   55
     pail.

I am faithful, I do not give out;
The fractur'd thigh, the knee, the wound in the abdomen,
These and more I dress with impassive hand, (yet deep in my breast a
     fire, a burning flame.)

4

Thus in silence, in dreams' projections,
Returning, resuming, I thread my way through the hospitals;   60
The hurt and wounded I pacify with soothing hand,
I sit by the restless all the dark night—some are so young;
Some suffer so much—I recall the experience sweet and sad;
(Many a soldier's loving arms about this neck have cross'd and rested,
Many a soldier's kiss dwells on these bearded lips).   65

                                                                            1865

Ethiopia Saluting the Colors[1]

Who are you dusky woman, so ancient hardly human,
With your woolly-white and turban'd head, and bare bony feet?
Why rising by the roadside here, do you the colors greet?

('Tis while our army lines Carolina's sands and pines,
Forth from thy hovel door thou Ethiopia com'st to me,   5
As under doughty Sherman[2] I march toward the sea.)

Me master years a hundred since from my parents sunder'd,
A little child, they caught me as the savage beast is caught,
Then hither me across the sea the cruel slaver brought.

No further does she say, but lingering all the day,   10
Her high-borne turban'd head she wags, and rolls her darkling eye,
And courtesies to the regiments, the guidons moving by.

What is it fateful woman, so blear, hardly human?
Why wag your head with turban bound, yellow, red and green?
Are the things so strange and marvelous you see or have seen?   15

                                                                            1870

Reconciliation

Word over all, beautiful as the sky,
Beautiful that war and all its deeds or carnage must in time be utterly
    lost,
That the hands of the sisters Death and Night incessantly softly wash
    again, and ever again, this soil'd world;

[1]Whitman uses Ethiopia as a generic name for Africa or the black race.
[2]Whitman is referring to General William Sherman's famous march from Atlanta to Savannah in 1864; his army was followed by many black refugees seeking freedom.

For my enemy is dead, a man divine as myself is dead,
I look where he lies white-faced and still in the coffin—I draw near,   5
Bend down and touch lightly with my lips the white face in the coffin.

1865–1866

As I Lay with My Head in Your Lap Camerado[1]

As I lay with my head in your lap camerado,
The confession I made I resume, what I said to you and the open air I
    resume,
I know I am restless and make others so,
I know my words are weapons full of danger, full of death,
For I confront peace, security, and all the settled laws, to unsettle   5
    them,
I am more resolute because all have denied me than I could ever have
    been had all accepted me,
I heed not and have never heeded either experience, cautions,
    majorities, nor ridicule,
And the threat of what is call'd hell is little or nothing to me,
And the lure of what is call'd heaven is little or nothing to me;
Dear camerado! I confess I have urged you onward with me, and   10
    still urge you, without the least idea what is our destination,
Or whether we shall be victorious, or utterly quell'd and defeated.

1865–1866

from **Memories of President Lincoln**[1']

When Lilacs Last in the Dooryard Bloom'd[2]

1

When lilacs last in the dooryard bloom'd,
And the great star early droop'd in the western sky in the night,[3]
I mourn'd, and yet shall mourn with ever-returning spring.

Ever-returning spring, trinity sure to me you bring,
Lilac blooming perennial and drooping star in the west,   5
And thought of him I love.

[1]Spanish for comrade.
[1']This is the only place that Lincoln is specifically named as the subject of these poems.
[2]"Lilacs" was written immediately following
Lincoln's death. He was shot on Good Friday,
April 14, 1865, by John Wilkes Booth; Lin-

coln died the next morning. In a long procession through various American cities, his
body was carried by train back to Springfield,
Illinois, where he was buried on May 4,
1865.
[3]The "great star" is the Western star, Venus.

2

O powerful western fallen star!
O shades of night—O moody, tearful night!
O great star disappear'd—O the black murk that hides the star!
O cruel hands that hold me powerless—O helpless soul of me!   10
O harsh surrounding cloud that will not free my soul.

3

In the dooryard fronting an old farm-house near the white-wash'd
      palings,
Stands the lilac-bush tall-growing with heart-shaped leaves of rich
      green,
With many a pointed blossom rising delicate, with the perfume strong
      I love,
With every leaf a miracle—and from this bush in the dooryard,   15
With delicate-color'd blossoms and heart-shaped leaves of rich green,
A sprig with its flower I break.

4

In the swamp in secluded recesses,
A shy and hidden bird is warbling a song.

Solitary the thrush,   20
The hermit withdrawn to himself, avoiding the settlements,
Sings by himself a song.

Song of the bleeding throat,
Death's outlet song of life, (for well dear brother I know,
If thou wast not granted to sing thou would'st surely die.)   25

5

Over the breast of the spring, the land, amid cities,
Amid lanes and through old woods, where lately the violets peep'd
      from the ground, spotting the gray debris,
Amid the grass in the fields each side of the lanes, passing the endless
      grass,
Passing the yellow-spear'd wheat, every grain from its shroud in the
      dark-brown fields uprisen,
Passing the apple-tree blows of white and pink in the orchards,   30
Carrying a corpse to where it shall rest in the grave,
Night and day journeys a coffin.

6

Coffin that passes through lanes and streets,
Through day and night with the great cloud darkening the land,
With the pomp of the inloop'd flags with the cities draped in black,   35
With the show of the States themselves as of crape-veil'd women
      standing,
With processions long and winding and the flambeaus[4] of the night,
With the countless torches lit, with the silent sea of faces and the
      unbared heads,
With the waiting depot, the arriving coffin, and the sombre faces,
With dirges through the night, with the thousand voices rising   40
      strong and solemn,
With all the mournful voices of the dirges pour'd around the coffin,
The dim-lit churches and the shuddering organs—where amid these
      you journey,
With the tolling tolling bells' perpetual clang,
Here, coffin that slowly passes,
I give you my sprig of lilac.   45

7

(Nor for you, for one alone,
Blossoms and branches green to coffins all I bring,
For fresh as the morning, thus would I chant a song for you O sane
      and sacred death.

All over bouquets of roses,
O death, I cover you over with roses and early lilies,   50
But mostly and now the lilac that blooms the first,
Copious I break, I break the sprigs from the bushes,
With loaded arms I come, pouring for you,
For you and the coffins all of you O death.)

8

O western orb sailing the heaven,   55
Now I know what you must have meant as a month since I walk'd,
As I walk'd in silence the transparent shadowy night,
As I saw you had something to tell as you bent to me night after
      night,
As you droop'd from the sky low down as if to my side, (while the
      other stars all look'd on,)

---

[4]Large candlesticks.

As we wander'd together the solemn night, (for something I know   60
  not what kept me from sleep,)
As the night advanced, and I saw on the rim of the west how full you
  were of woe,
As I stood on the rising ground in the breeze in the cool transparent
  night,
As I watch'd where you pass'd and was lost in the netherward black of
  the night,
As my soul in its trouble dissatisfied sank, as where you sad orb,
Concluded, dropt in the night, and was gone.   65

9

Sing on there in the swamp,
O singer bashful and tender, I hear your notes, I hear your call,
I hear, I come presently, I understand you,
But a moment I linger, for the lustrous star has detain'd me,
The star my departing comrade holds and detains me.   70

10

O how shall I warble myself for the dead one there I loved?
And how shall I deck my song for the large sweet soul that has gone?
And what shall my perfume be for the grave of him I love?

Sea-winds blown from east and west,
Blown from the Eastern sea and blown from the Western sea, till   75
  there on the prairies meeting,
These and with these and the breath of my chant,
I'll perfume the grave of him I love.

11

O what shall I hang on the chamber walls?
And what shall the pictures be that I hang on the walls,
To adorn the burial-house of him I love?   80

Pictures of growing spring and farms and homes,
With the Fourth-month eve at sundown, and the gray smoke lucid
  and bright,
With floods of the yellow gold of the gorgeous, indolent, sinking sun,
  burning, expanding the air,
With the fresh sweet herbage under foot, and the pale green leaves of
  the trees prolific,
In the distance the flowing glaze, the breast of the river, with a   85
  wind-dapple here and there,

With ranging hills on the banks, with many a line against the sky, and
    shadows,
And the city at hand with dwellings so dense, and stacks of chimneys,
And all the scenes of life and the workshops, and the workmen
    homeward returning.

12

Lo, body and soul—this land,
My own Manhattan with spires, and the sparkling and hurrying   90
    tides, and the ships,
The varied and ample land, the South and the North in the light,
    Ohio's shores and flashing Missouri,
And ever the far-spreading prairies cover'd with grass and corn.

Lo, the most excellent sun so calm and haughty,
The violet and purple morn with just-felt breezes,
The gentle soft-born measureless light,   95
The miracle spreading bathing all, the fulfill'd noon,
The coming eve delicious, the welcome night and the stars,
Over my cities shining all, enveloping man and land.

13

Sing on, sing on you gray-brown bird,
Sing from the swamps, the recesses, pour your chant from the   100
    bushes,
Limitless out of the dusk, out of the cedars and pines.

Sing on dearest brother, warble your reedy song,
Loud human song, with voice of uttermost woe.

O liquid and free and tender!
O wild and loose to my soul—O wondrous singer!   105
You only I hear—yet the star holds me, (but will soon depart,)
Yet the lilac with mastering odor holds me.

14

Now while I sat in the day and look'd forth,
In the close of the day with its light and the fields of spring, and the
    farmers preparing their crops,
In the large unconscious scenery of my land with its lakes and   110
    forests,
In the heavenly aerial beauty, (after the perturb'd winds and the
    storms,)

Under the arching heavens of the afternoon swift passing, and the
    voices of children and women,
The many-moving sea-tides, and I saw the ships how they sail'd,
And the summer approaching with richness, and the fields all busy
    with labor,
And the infinite separate houses, how they all went on, each with   115
    its meals and minutia of daily usages,
And the streets how their throbbings throbb'd, and the cities pent—
    lo, then and there,
Falling upon them all and among them all, enveloping me with the
    rest,
Appear'd the cloud, appear'd the long black trail,
And I knew death, its thought, and the sacred knowledge of death.
Then with the knowledge of death as walking one side of me,   120
And the thought of death close-walking the other side of me,
And I in the middle as with companions, and as holding the hands of
    companions,
I fled forth to the hiding receiving night that talks not,
Down to the shores of the water, the path by the swamp in the
    dimness,
To the solemn shadowy cedars and ghostly pines so still.   125

And the singer so shy to the rest receiv'd me,
The gray-brown bird I know receiv'd us comrades three,
And he sang the carol of death, and a verse for him I love.
From deep secluded recesses,
From the fragrant cedars and the ghostly pines so still,   130
Came the carol of the bird.

And the charm of the carol rapt me,
As I held as if by their hands my comrades in the night,
And the voice of my spirit tallied the song of the bird.

Come lovely and soothing death,   135
Undulate round the world, serenely arriving, arriving,
In the day, in the night, to all, to each,
Sooner or later delicate death.

Prais'd be the fathomless universe,
For life and joy, and for objects and knowledge curious,   140
And for love, sweet love—but praise! praise! praise!
For the sure-enwinding arms of cool-enfolding death.

Dark mother always gliding near with soft feet,
Have none chanted for thee a chant of fullest welcome?
Then I chant it for thee, I glorify thee above all,   145
I bring thee a song that when thou must indeed come, come unfalteringly.

Approach strong deliveress,
When it is so, when thou hast taken them I joyously sing the dead,
Lost in the loving floating ocean of thee,
Laved in the flood of thy bliss O death.   150

From me to thee glad serenades,
Dances for thee I propose saluting thee, adornments and feastings for thee,
And the sights of the open landscape and the high-spread sky are fitting,
And life and the fields, and the huge and thoughtful night.
The night in silence under many a star,   155
The ocean shore and the husky whispering wave whose voice I know,
And the soul turning to thee O vast and well-veil'd death,
And the body gratefully nestling close to thee.

Over the tree-tops I float thee a song,
Over the rising and sinking waves, over the myriad fields and the   160
prairies wide,
Over the dense-pack'd cities all and the teeming wharves and ways,
I float this carol with joy, with joy to thee O death.

15

To the tally of my soul,
Loud and strong kept up the gray-brown bird,
With pure deliberate notes spreading filling the night.   165

Loud in the pines and cedars dim,
Clear in the freshness moist and the swamp-perfume,
And I with my comrades there in the night.

While my sight that was bound in my eyes unclosed,
As to long panoramas of visions.   170

And I saw askant the armies,
I saw as in noiseless dreams hundreds of battle-flags,
Borne through the smoke of the battles and pierc'd with missiles I saw
    them,
And carried hither and yon through the smoke, and torn and bloody,
And at last but a few shreds left on the staffs, (and all in silence,)   175
And the staffs all splinter'd and broken.

I saw battle-corpses, myriads of them,
And the white skeletons of young men, I saw them,
I saw the debris and debris of all the slain soldiers of the war,
But I saw they were not as was thought,   180
They themselves were fully at rest, they suffer'd not,

The living remain'd and suffer'd, the mother suffer'd,
And the wife and the child and the musing comrade suffer'd,
And the armies that remain'd suffer'd.

16

Passing the visions, passing the night,   185
Passing, unloosing the hold of my comrades' hands,
Passing the song of the hermit bird and the tallying song of my soul,
Victorious song, death's outlet song, yet varying ever-altering song,
As low and wailing, yet clear the notes, rising and falling, flooding the
     night,
Sadly sinking and fainting, as warning and warning, and yet again   190
     bursting with joy,
Covering the earth and filling the spread of the heaven,
As that powerful psalm in the night I heard from recesses,
Passing, I leave thee lilac with heart-shaped leaves,
I leave thee there in the door-yard, blooming, returning with spring.
I cease from my song for thee,   195
From my gaze on thee in the west, fronting the west, communing
     with thee,
O comrade lustrous with silver face in the night.
Yet each to keep and all, retrievements out of the night,
The song, the wondrous chant of the gray-brown bird,
And the tallying chant, the echo arous'd in my soul,   200
With the lustrous and drooping star with the countenance full of woe,
With the holders holding my hand nearing the call of the bird,
Comrades mine and I in the midst, and their memory ever to keep, for
     the dead I loved so well,
For the sweetest, wisest soul of all my days and lands—and this for
     his dear sake,
Lilac and star and bird twined with the chant of my soul,   205
There in the fragrant pines and the cedars dusk and dim.

1865–1866

from Autumn Rivulets

Sparkles from the Wheel

Where the city's ceaseless crowd moves on the livelong day,
Withdrawn I join a group of children watching, I pause aside with
    them.

By the curb toward the edge of the flagging,
A knife-grinder works at his wheel sharpening a great knife,

Bending over he carefully holds it to the stone, by foot and knee,   5
With measur'd tread he turns rapidly, as he presses with light but
    firm hand,
Forth issue then in copious golden jets,
Sparkles from the wheel.

The scene and all its belongings, how they seize and affect me,
The sad sharp-chinn'd old man with worn clothes and broad   10
    shoulder-band of leather,
Myself effusing and fluid, a phantom curiously floating, now here
    absorb'd and arrested,
The group, (an unminded point set in a vast surrounding,)
The attentive, quiet children, the loud, proud, restive base of the
    streets,
The low hoarse purr of the whirling stone, the light-press'd blade,
Diffusing, dropping, sideways-darting, in tiny showers of gold,   15
Sparkles from the wheel.

                1871

from **Whispers of Heavenly Death**

Quicksand Years[1]

Quicksand years that whirl me I know not whither,
Your schemes, politics, fail, lines give way, substances mock and elude
    me,
Only the theme I sing, the great and strong-possess'd soul, eludes not,
One's-self must never give way—that is the final substance—that out
    of all is sure,
Out of politics, triumphs, battles, life, what at last finally remains?   5
When shows break up what but One's-Self is sure?

                1865

A Noiseless Patient Spider

A noiseless patient spider,
I mark'd where on a little promontory it stood isolated,
Mark'd how to explore the vacant, vast surrounding,
It launched forth filament, filament, filament, out of itself.
Ever unreeling them, ever tirelessly speeding them.   5

And you O my soul where you stand,
Surrounded, detatched, in measureless oceans of space,

---

[1]The poem was drafted in 1862–1863.

Ceaselessly musing, venturing, throwing, seeking the spheres to
    connect them.
Till the bridge you will need be form'd, till the ductile anchor hold,
Till the gossamer thread you fling catch somewhere, O my soul.   10

                                    1862–1863

from **From Noon to Starry Night**

To a Locomotive in Winter

Thee for my recitative,
Thee in the driving storm even as now, the snow, the winter-day declining,
Thee in thy panoply, thy measur'd dual throbbing and thy beat
    convulsive,
Thy black cylindric body, golden brass and silvery steel,
Thy ponderous side-bars, parallel and connecting rods, gyrating,   5
    shuttling at thy sides,
Thy metrical, now swelling pant and roar, now tapering in the
    distance,
Thy great protruding head-light fix'd in front,
Thy long, pale, floating vapor-pennants, tinged with delicate purple,
The dense and murky clouds out-belching from thy smoke-stack,
Thy knitted frame, thy springs and valves, the tremulous twinkle of   10
    thy wheels,
Thy train of cars behind, obedient, merrily following,
Through gale or calm, now swift, now slack, yet steadily careering;
Type of the modern—emblem of motion and power—pulse of the
    continent,
For once come serve the Muse and merge in verse, even as here I see
    thee,
With storm and buffeting gusts of wind and falling snow,   15
By day thy warning ringing bell to sound its notes,
By night thy silent signal lamps to swing.

Fierce-throated beauty!
Roll through my chant with all thy lawless music, thy swinging lamps
    at night,
Thy madly-whistled laughter, echoing, rumbling like an earth-quake,   20
    rousing all,
Law of thyself complete, thine own track firmly holding,
(No sweetness debonair of tearful harp or glib piano thine,)
Thy trills of shrieks by rocks and hills return'd,
Launch'd o'er the prairies wide, across the lakes,
To the free skies unpent and glad and strong.   25

                                      1876

from **Songs of Parting**

So Long![1]

To conclude, I announce what comes after me.

I remember I said before my leaves sprang at all,
I would raise my voice jocund and strong with reference to
   consummations.

When America does what was promis'd,
When through these States walk a hundred millions of superb   5
   persons,
When the rest part away for superb persons and contribute to them,
When breeds of the most perfect mothers denote America,
Then to me and mine our due fruition.

I have press'd through in my own right,
I have sung the body and the soul, war and peace have I sung, and   10
   the songs of life and death,
And the songs of birth, and shown that there are many births.

I have offer'd my style to every one, I have journey'd with confident
   step;
While my pleasure is yet at the full I whisper *So long!*
And take the young woman's hand and the young man's hand for the
   last time.

I announce natural persons to arise,   15
I announce justice triumphant,
I announce uncompromising liberty and equality,
I announce the justification of candor and the justification of pride.
I announce that the identity of these States is a single identity only,
I announce the Union more and more compact, indissoluble,   20
I announce splendors and majesties to make all the previous politics
   of the earth insignificant.

I announce adhesiveness,[2] I say it shall be limitless, unloosen'd,
I say you shall yet find the friend you were looking for.

---

[1] In the mid-nineteenth century, "so long" was an idiomatic expression for "good-bye" much used among sailors and street people. This poem concluded *Leaves of Grass* in 1860 and in all subsequent editions.

[2] A term Whitman borrowed from phrenology meaning, he said, the "passion of friendship for man."

I announce a man or woman coming, perhaps you are the one, (*So long!*)

I announce the great individual, fluid as Nature, chaste,   25
    affectionate, compassionate, fully arm'd.

I announce a life that shall be copious, vehement, spiritual, bold,
I announce an end that shall lightly and joyfully meet its translation.

I announce myriads of youths, beautiful, gigantic, sweet-blooded,
I announce a race of splendid and savage old men.

O thicker and faster—(*So long!*)   30
O crowding too close upon me,
I foresee too much, it means more than I thought,
It appears to me I am dying.

Hasten throat and sound your last,
Salute me—salute the days once more. Peal the old cry once more.   35

Screaming electric, the atmosphere using,
At random glancing, each as I notice absorbing,
Swiftly on, but a little while alighting,
Curious envelop'd messages delivering,
Sparkles hot, seed ethereal down in the dirt dropping,   40
Myself unknowing, my commission obeying, to question it never
    daring,
To ages and ages yet the growth of the seed leaving,
To troops out of the war arising, they the tasks I have set promulging,
To women certain whispers of myself bequeathing, their affection me
    more clearly explaining,
To young men my problems offering—no dallier I—I the muscle of   45
    their brains trying,
So I pass, a little time vocal, visible, contrary,
Afterward a melodious echo, passionately bent for, (death making me
    really undying,)
The best of me then when no longer visible, for toward that I have
    been incessantly preparing.

What is there more, that I lag and pause and crouch extended with
    unshut mouth?
Is there a single final farewell?   50

My songs cease, I abandon them,
From behind the screen where I hid I advance personally solely to you.
Camerado, this is no book,
Who touches this touches a man,

(Is it night? are we here together alone?)   55
It is I you hold and who holds you,
I spring from the pages into your arms—decease calls me forth.

O how your fingers drowse me,
Your breath falls around me like dew, your pulse lulls the tympans of
   my ears,
I feel immerged from head to foot,   60
Delicious, enough.

Enough O deed impromptu and secret,
Enough O gliding present—enough O summ'd-up past.

Dear friend whoever you are take this kiss,
I give it especially to you, do not forget me,   65
I feel like one who has done work for the day to retire awhile,
I receive now again of my many translations, from my avataras
   ascending, while others doubtless await me,
An unknown sphere more real than I dream'd, more direct, darts
   awakening rays about me, *So long!*
Remember my words, I may again return,
I love you, I depart from materials,   70
I am as one disembodied, triumphant, dead.

                                                          1860

from Sands at Seventy (First Annex)

Yonnondio

[The sense of the word is lament for the aborigines. *It is an Iroquois term; and
has been used for a personal name.]*

A song, a poem of itself—the word itself a dirge,
Amid the wilds, the rocks, the storm and wintry night,
To me such misty, strange tableaux the syllables calling up;
Yonnondio—I see, far in the west or north, a limitless ravine, with
   plains and mountains dark,
I see swarms of stalwart chieftains, medicine-men, and warriors,   5
As flitting by like clouds of ghosts, they pass and are gone in the
   twilight,
(Race of the woods, the landscapes free, and the falls!
No picture, poem, statement, passing them to the future:)
Yonnondio! Yonnondio!—unlimn'd they disappear;
To-day gives place, and fades—the cities, farms, factories fade;   10

A muffled sonorous sound, a wailing word is borne through the air for
    a moment,
Then blank and gone and still, and utterly lost.

                                      1887

from Good-bye My Fancy (Second Annex)

Good-bye My Fancy!

Good-bye my Fancy!
Farewell dear mate, dear love!
I'm going away, I know not where,
Or to what fortune, or whether I may ever see you again,
So Good-bye my Fancy.   5

Now for my last—let me look back a moment;
The slower fainter ticking of the clock is in me,
Exit, nightfall, and soon the heart-thud stopping.

Long have we lived, joy'd, caress'd together;
Delightful!—now separation—Good-bye my Fancy.   10

Yet let me not be too hasty,
Long indeed have we lived, slept, filter'd, become really blended into
    one;
Then if we die we die together, (yes, we'll remain one,)
If we go anywhere we'll go together to meet what happens,
May-be we'll be better off and blither, and learn something,   15
May-be it is yourself now really ushering me to the true songs, (who
    knows?)
May-be it is you the mortal knob really undoing, turning—so now
    finally,
Good-bye—and hail! my Fancy.

                                        1891

from Democratic Vistas[1]

As the greatest lessons of Nature through the universe are perhaps the lessons of variety and freedom, the same present the greatest lessons also in

---

[1]*Democratic Vistas* was written in response to
Thomas Carlyle's critique of democracy in
"Shooting Niagara" (1867). In this essay,
Carlyle described democratic enfranchisement as an unchaining of the devil—or a suicidal leap over Niagara Falls. Sections of this
essay, originally titled "Democracy" and "Per-
sonalism," appeared in the New York *Galaxy*
in 1867–1868. *Democratic Vistas* was published as a pamphlet in 1871.

New World politics and progress. If a man were ask'd, for instance, the distinctive points contrasting modern European and American political and other life with the old Asiatic cultus, as lingering-bequeath'd yet in China and Turkey, he might find the amount of them in John Stuart Mill's profound essay on Liberty in the future, where he demands two main constituents, or sub-strata, for a truly grand nationality—1st, a large variety of character—and 2d, full play for human nature to expand itself in numberless and even conflicting directions—(seems to be for general humanity much like the influences that make up, in their limitless field, that perennial health-action of the air we call the weather—an infinite number of currents and forces, and contributions, and temperatures, and cross purposes, whose ceaseless play of counterpart upon counterpart brings constant restoration and vitality.) With this thought—and not for itself alone, but all it necessitates, and draws after it—let me begin my speculations.

America, filling the present with greatest deeds and problems, cheerfully accepting the past, including feudalism, (as, indeed, the present is but the legitimate birth of the past, including feudalism,) counts, as I reckon, for her justification and success, (for who, as yet, dare claim success?) almost entirely on the future. Nor is that hope unwarranted. To-day, ahead, though dimly yet, we see, in vistas, a copious, sane, gigantic offspring. For our New World I consider far less important for what it has done, or what it is, than for results to come. Sole among nationalities, these States have assumed the task to put in forms of lasting power and practicality, on areas of amplitude rivaling the operations of the physical kosmos, the moral political speculations of ages, long, long deferr'd, the democratic republican principle, and the theory of development and perfection by voluntary standards, and self-reliance. Who else, indeed, except the United States, in history, so far, have accepted in unwitting faith, and, as we now see, stand, act upon, and go security for, these things?

But preluding no longer, let me strike the key-note of the following strain. First premising that, though the passages of it have been written at widely different times, (it is, in fact, a collection of memoranda, perhaps for future designers, comprehenders,) and though it may be open to the charge of one part contradicting another—for there are opposite sides to the great question of democracy, as to every great question—I feel the parts harmoniously blended in my own realization and convictions, and present them to be read only in such oneness, each page and each claim and assertion modified and temper'd by the others. Bear in mind, too, that they are not the result of studying up in political economy, but of the ordinary sense, observing, wandering among men, these States, these stirring years of war and peace. I will not gloss over the appalling dangers of universal suffrage in the United States. In fact, it is to admit and face these dangers I am writing. To him or her within whose thought rages the battle, advancing, retreating, between democracy's convictions, aspirations, and the people's crudeness, vice, caprices, I mainly write this essay. I shall use the words America and democracy as convertible terms. Not an ordinary one is the issue.

The United States are destined either to surmount the gorgeous history of feudalism, or else prove the most tremendous failure of time. Not the least doubtful am I on any prospects of their material success. The triumphant future of their business, geographic and productive departments, on larger scales and in more varieties than ever, is certain. In those respects the republic must soon (if she does not already) outstrip all examples hitherto afforded, and dominate the world. . . .

I say that democracy can never prove itself beyond cavil, until it founds and luxuriantly grows its own forms of art, poems, schools, theology, displacing all that exists, or that has been produced anywhere in the past, under opposite influences. It is curious to me that while so many voices, pens, minds, in the press, lecture-rooms, in our Congress, &c., are discussing intellectual topics, pecuniary dangers, legislative problems, the suffrage, tariff and labor questions, and the various business and benevolent needs of America, with propositions, remedies, often worth deep attention, there is one need, a hiatus the profoundest, that no eye seems to perceive, no voice to state. Our fundamental want to-day in the United States, with closest, amplest reference to present conditions, and to the future, is of a class, and the clear idea of a class, of native authors, literatures, far different, far higher in grade than any yet known, sacerdotal, modern, fit to cope with our occasions, lands, permeating the whole mass of American mentality, taste, belief, breathing into it a new breath of life, giving it decision, affecting politics far more than the popular superficial suffrage, with results inside and underneath the elections of Presidents or Congresses—radiating, begetting appropriate teachers, schools, manners, and, as its grandest result, accomplishing, (what neither the schools nor the churches and their clergy have hitherto accomplish'd, and without which this nation will no more stand, permanently, soundly, than a house will stand without a substratum,) a religious and moral character beneath the political and productive and intellectual bases of the States. For know you not, dear, earnest reader, that the people of our land may all read and write, and may all possess the right to vote—and yet the main things may be entirely lacking?—(and this to suggest them.)

View'd, to-day, from a point of view sufficiently over-arching, the problem of humanity all over the civilized world is social and religious, and is to be finally met and treated by literature. The priest departs, the divine literatus comes. Never was anything more wanted than, to-day, and here in the States, the poet of the modern is wanted, or the great literatus of the modern. At all times, perhaps, the central point in any nation, and that whence it is itself really sway'd the most, and whence it sways others, is its national literature, especially its archetypal poems. Above all previous lands, a great original literature is surely to become the justification and reliance, (in some respects the sole reliance,) of American democracy.

Few are aware how the great literature penetrates all, gives hue to all, shapes aggregates and individuals, and, after subtle ways, with irresistible power, constructs, sustains, demolishes at will. Why tower, in reminiscence, above all the nations of the earth, two special lands, petty in themselves, yet inexpressibly gigantic, beautiful, columnar? Immortal Judah lives, and Greece immortal lives, in a couple of poems....

In short, as, though it may not be realized, it is strictly true, that a few first-class poets, philosophs, and authors, have substantially settled and given status to the entire religion, education, law, sociology, &c., of the hitherto civilized world, by tinging and often creating the atmospheres out of which they have arisen, such also must stamp, and more than ever stamp, the interior and real democratic construction of this American continent, to-day, and days to come.

For my part, I would alarm and caution even the political and business reader, and to the utmost extent, against the prevailing delusion that the establishment of free political institutions, and plentiful intellectual smartness, with general good order, physical plenty, industry, &c., (desirable and precious advantages as they all are,) do, of themselves, determine and yield to our experiment of democracy the fruitage of success. With such advantages at present fully, or almost fully, possess'd—the Union just issued, victorious, from the struggle with the only foes it need ever fear, (namely, those within itself, the interior ones,) and with unprecedented materialistic advancement—society, in these States, is canker'd, crude, superstitious, and rotten. Political, or law-made society is, and private, or voluntary society, is also. In any vigor, the element of the moral conscience, the most important, the verteber to State or man, seems to me either entirely lacking, or seriously enfeebled or ungrown.

I say we had best look our times and lands searchingly in the face, like a physician diagnosing some deep disease. Never was there, perhaps, more hollowness at heart than at present, and here in the United States. Genuine belief seems to have left us. The underlying principles of the States are not honestly believ'd in, (for all this hectic glow, and these melo-dramatic screamings,) nor is humanity itself believ'd in. What penetrating eye does not everywhere see through the mask? The spectacle is appalling. We live in an atmosphere of hypocrisy throughout. The men believe not in the women, nor the women in the men. A scornful superciliousness rules in literature. The aim of all the *littérateurs* is to find something to make fun of. A lot of churches, sects, &c., the most dismal phantasms I know, usurp the name of religion. Conversation is a mass of badinage. From deceit in the spirit, the mother of all false deeds, the offspring is already incalculable. An acute and candid person, in the revenue department in Washington, who is led by the course of his employment to regularly visit the cities, north, south and west, to investigate frauds, has talk'd much with me about his discoveries. The depravity of the business classes of our country is not less than has been supposed, but infinitely greater. The official services of America, national, state, and municipal, in all their branches and departments, except the judiciary, are saturated in corruption, bribery, falsehood, mal-administration; and the judiciary is tainted. The great cities reek with respectable as much as nonrespectable robbery and scoundrelism. In fashionable life, flippancy, tepid amours, weak infidelism, small aims, or no aims at all, only to kill time. In business, (this all-devouring modern word, business,) the one sole object is, by any means, pecuniary gain. The magician's serpent in the fable ate up all the other serpents; and money-making is our magician's serpent, remaining to-day sole master of the field. The best class we show, is but a mob of fashionably dress'd speculators and vulgarians. True, indeed, behind this fantastic farce, enacted on the visible stage of society, solid things and stupendous labors are to be discover'd, existing crudely and going on in the background, to advance and tell themselves in time. Yet the truths are none the less terrible. I say that our New World democracy, however great a success in uplifting the masses out of their sloughs, in materialistic development, products, and in a certain highly-deceptive superficial popular intellectuality, is, so far, an almost complete failure in its social aspects, and in really grand religious, moral, literary, and esthetic results. In vain do we march with unprecedented strides to empire so colossal, outvying the antique, beyond Alexander's, beyond the proudest sway of Rome. In vain have we annex'd Texas, California, Alaska, and reach north for Canada and south for Cuba. It is as if we were somehow being endow'd with a vast and more and more thoroughly-appointed body, and then left with little or no soul....

Confess that to severe eyes, using the moral microscrope upon humanity, a sort of dry and flat Sahara appears, these cities, crowded with petty grotesques, malformations, phantoms, playing meaningless antics. Confess that everywhere, in shop, street, church, theatre, bar-room, official chair, are pervading flippancy and vulgarity, low cunning, infidelity—everywhere the youth puny, impudent, foppish, prematurely ripe—everywhere an abnormal libidinousness, unhealthy forms, male, female, painted, padded, dyed, chignon'd, muddy complexions, bad blood, the capacity for good motherhood deceasing or deceas'd, shallow notions of beauty, with a range of manners, or rather lack of manners, (considering the advantages enjoy'd,) probably the meanest to be seen in the world.[2]

Of all this, and these lamentable conditions, to breathe into them the breath recuperative of sane and heroic life, I say a new founded literature, not merely to copy and reflect existing surfaces, or pander to what is called taste—not only to amuse, pass away time, celebrate the beautiful, the refined, the past, or exhibit technical, rhythmic, or grammatical dexterity— but a literature underlying life, religious, consistent with science, handling

[2]Of these rapidly-sketch'd hiatuses, the two which seem to me most serious are, for one, the condition, absence, or perhaps the singular abeyance, of moral conscientious fibre all through American society; and, for another, the appalling depletion of women in their powers of sane athletic maternity, their crowning attribute, and ever making the woman, in loftiest spheres, superior to the man.

I have sometimes thought, indeed, that the sole avenue and means of a reconstructed sociology depended, primarily, on a new birth, elevation, expansion, invigoration of woman, affording, for races to come, (as the conditions that antedate birth are indispensable,) a perfect motherhood. Great, great, indeed, far greater than they know, is the sphere of women. But doubtless the question of such new sociology all goes together, includes many varied and complex influences and premises, and the man as well as the woman, and the woman as well as the man. [Whitman's note]

the elements and forces with competent power, teaching and training men—and, as perhaps the most precious of its results, achieving the entire redemption of woman out of these incredible holds and webs of silliness, millinery, and every kind of dyspeptic depletion—and thus insuring to the States a strong and sweet Female Race, a race of perfect Mothers—is what is needed.

And now, in the full conception of these facts and points, and all that they infer, pro and con—with yet unshaken faith in the elements of the American masses, the composites, of both sexes, and even consider'd as individuals—and ever recognizing in them the broadest bases of the best literary and esthetic appreciation—I proceed with my speculations, Vistas. . . .

I say the mission of government, henceforth, in civilized lands, is not repression alone, and not authority alone, not even of law, nor by that favorite standard of the eminent writer, the rule of the best men, the born heroes and captains of the race, (as if such ever, or one time out of a hundred, get into the big places, elective or dynastic)—but higher than the highest arbitrary rule, to train communities through all their grades, beginning with individuals and ending there again, to rule themselves. What Christ appear'd for in the moral-spiritual field for human-kind, namely, that in respect to the absolute soul, there is in the possession of such by each single individual, something so transcendent, so incapable of gradations, (like life,) that, to that extent, it places all beings on a common level, utterly regardless of the distinctions of intellect, virtue, station, or any height or lowliness whatever—is tallied in like manner, in this other field, by democracy's rule that men, the nation, as a common aggregate of living identities, affording in each a separate and complete subject for freedom, worldly thrift and happiness, and for a fair chance for growth, and for protection in citizenship, &c., must, to the political extent of the suffrage or vote, if no further, be placed, in each and in the whole, on one broad, primary, universal, common platform. . . .

Democracy too is law, and of the strictest, amplest kind. Many suppose, (and often in its own ranks the error,) that it means a throwing aside of law, and running riot. But, briefly, it is the superior law, not alone that of physical force, the body, which, adding to, it supersedes with that of the spirit. Law is the unshakable order of the universe forever; and the law over all, and law of laws, is the law of successions; that of the superior law, in time, gradually supplanting and overwhelming the inferior one. (While, for myself, I would cheerfully agree—first covenanting that the formative tendencies shall be administer'd in favor, or at least not against it, and that this reservation be closely construed—that until the individual or community show due signs, or be so minor and fractional as not to endanger the State, the condition of authoritative tutelage may continue, and self-government must abide its time.) Nor is the esthetic point, always an important one, without fascination for highest aiming souls. The common ambition strains for elevations, to become some privileged exclusive. The master sees greatness and health in being part of the mass; nothing will do as well as common ground. Would you have in yourself the divine, vast, general law? Then merge yourself in it.

And, topping democracy, this most alluring record, that it alone can bind, and ever seeks to bind, all nations, all men, of however various and distant lands, into a brotherhood, a family. It is the old, yet ever-modern dream of earth, out of her eldest and her youngest, her fond philosophers and poets. Not that half only, individualism, which isolates. There is another half, which is adhesiveness or love, that fuses, ties and aggregates, making the races comrades, and fraternizing all. Both are to be vitalized by religion, (sole worthiest elevator of man or State,) breathing into the proud, material tissues, the breath of life. For I say at the core of democracy, finally, is the religious element. All the religions, old and new, are there. Nor may the scheme step forth, clothed in resplendent beauty and command, till these, bearing the best, the latest fruit, the spiritual, shall fully appear.

A portion of our pages we might indite with reference toward Europe, especially the British part of it, more than our own land, perhaps not absolutely needed for the home reader. But the whole question hangs together, and fastens and links all peoples. The liberalist of to-day has this advantage over antique or medieval times, that his doctrine seeks not only to individualize but to universalize. The great word Solidarity has arisen. Of all dangers to a nation, as things exist in our day, there can be no greater one than having certain portions of the people set off from the rest by a line drawn— they not privileged as others, but degraded, humiliated, made of no account. Much quackery teems, of course, even on democracy's side, yet does not really affect the orbic quality of the matter. To work in, if we may so term it, and justify God, his divine aggregate, the People, (or, the veritable horn'd and sharp-tail'd Devil, *his* aggregate, if there be who convulsively insist upon it)—this, I say, is what democracy is for; and this is what our America means, and is doing—may I not say, has done? If not, she means nothing more, and does nothing more, than any other land. And as, by virtue of its kosmical, antiseptic power, Nature's stomach is fully strong enough not only to digest the morbific matter always presented, not to be turn'd aside, and perhaps, indeed, intuitively gravitating thither—but even to change such contributions into nutriment for highest use and life—so American democracy's. That is the lesson we, these days, send over to European lands by every western breeze.

And, truly, whatever may be said in the way of abstract argument, for or against the theory of a wider democratizing of institutions in any civilized country, much trouble might well be saved to all European lands by recognizing this palpable fact, (for a palpable fact it is,) that some form of such democratizing is about the only resource now left. *That*, or chronic dissatisfaction continued, mutterings which grow annually louder and louder, till, in due course, and pretty swiftly in most cases, the inevitable crisis, crash, dynastic ruin. Anything worthy to be call'd statesmanship in the Old World, I should say, among the advanced students, adepts, or men of any brains, does not debate to-day whether to hold on, attempting to lean back and monarchize, or to look forward and democratize—but *how*, and in what degree and part, most prudently to democratize....

The true gravitation-hold of liberalism in the United States will be a more universal ownership of property, general homesteads, general comfort—a vast, intertwining reticulation of wealth. As the human frame, or, indeed, any object in this manifold universe, is best kept together by the simple miracle of its own cohesion, and the necessity, exercise and profit thereof, so a great and varied nationality, occupying millions of square miles, were firmest held and knit by the principle of the safety and endurance of the aggregate of its middling property owners. So that, from another point of view, ungracious as it may sound, and a paradox after what we have been saying, democracy looks with suspicious, ill-satisfied eye upon the very poor, the ignorant, and on those out of business. She asks for men and women with occupations, well-off, owners of houses and acres, and with cash in the bank—and with some cravings for literature, too; and must have them, and hastens to make them. Luckily, the seed is already well-sown, and has taken ineradicable root.[3] ...

America has yet morally and artistically originated nothing. She seems singularly unaware that the models of persons, books, manners, &c., appropriate for former conditions and for European lands, are but exiles and exotics here. No current of her life, as shown on the surfaces of what is authoritatively called her society, accepts or runs into social or esthetic democracy; but all the currents set squarely against it. Never, in the Old World, was thoroughly upholster'd exterior appearance and show, mental and other, built entirely on the idea of caste, and on the sufficiency of mere outside acquisition—never were glibness, verbal intellect, more the test, the emulation—more loftily elevated as head and sample—than they are on the surface of our republican States this day. The writers of a time hint the mottoes of its gods. The word of the modern, say these voices, is the word Culture.

We find ourselves abruptly in close quarters with the enemy. This word Culture, or what it has come to represent, involves, by contrast, our whole theme, and has been, indeed, the spur, urging us to engagement. Certain questions arise. As now taught, accepted and carried out, are not the processes of culture rapidly creating a class of supercilious infidels, who believe in nothing? Shall a man lose himself in countless masses of adjustments,

[3]For fear of mistake, I may as well distinctly specify, as cheerfully included in the model and standard of these Vistas, a practical, stirring, worldly, money-making, even materialistic character. It is undeniable that our farms, stores, offices, dry-goods, coal and groceries, enginery, cash-accounts, trades, earnings, markets, &c., should be attended to in earnest, and actively pursued, just as if they had a real and permanent existence. I perceive clearly that the extreme business energy, and this almost maniacal appetite for wealth prevalent in the United States, are parts of amelioration and progress, indispensably needed to prepare the very results I demand. My theory includes riches, and the getting of riches, and the amplest products, power, activity, inventions, movements, &c. Upon them, as upon substrata, I raise the edifice design'd in these Vistas. [Whitman's note]

and be so shaped with reference to this, that, and the other, that the simply good and healthy and brave parts of him are reduced and clipp'd away, like the bordering of box in a garden? You can cultivate corn and roses and orchards—but who shall cultivate the mountain peaks, the ocean, and the tumbling gorgeousness of the clouds? Lastly—is the readily-given reply that culture only seeks to help, systematize, and put in attitude, the elements of fertility and power, a conclusive reply?

I do not so much object to the name, or word, but I should certainly insist, for the purposes of these States, on a radical change of category, in the distribution of precedence. I should demand a programme of culture, drawn out, not for a single class alone, or for the parlors or lecture-rooms, but with an eye to practical life, the west, the working-men, the facts of farms and jack-planes and engineers, and of the broad range of the women also of the middle and working strata, and with reference to the perfect equality of women, and of a grand and powerful motherhood. I should demand of this programme or theory a scope generous enough to include the widest human area. It must have for its spinal meaning the formation of a typical personality of character, eligible to the uses of the high average of men—and *not* restricted by conditions ineligible to the masses. The best culture will always be that of the manly and courageous instincts, and loving perceptions, and of self-respect—aiming to form, over this continent, an idiocrasy of universalism, which, true child of America, will bring joy to its mother, returning to her in her own spirit, recruiting myriads of offspring, able, natural, perceptive, tolerant, devout believers in her, America, and with some definite instinct why and for what she has arisen, most vast, most formidable of historic births, and is, now and here, with wonderful step, journeying through Time....

Of course, in these States, for both man and woman, we must entirely recast the types of highest personality from what the oriental, feudal, ecclesiastical worlds bequeath us, and which yet possess the imaginative and esthetic fields of the United States, pictorial and melodramatic, not without use as studies, but making sad work, and forming a strange anachronism upon the scenes and exigencies around us. Of course, the old undying elements remain. The task is, to successfully adjust them to new combinations, our own days. Nor is this so incredible. I can conceive a community, to-day and here, in which, on a sufficient scale, the perfect personalities, without noise meet; say in some pleasant western settlement or town, where a couple of hundred best men and women, of ordinary worldly status, have by luck been drawn together, with nothing extra of genius or wealth, but virtuous, chaste, industrious, cheerful, resolute, friendly and devout. I can conceive such a community organized in running order, powers judiciously delegated—farming, building, trade, courts, mails, schools, elections, all attended to; and then the rest of life, the main thing, freely branching and blossoming in each individual, and bearing golden fruit. I can see there, in every young and old man, after his kind, and in every woman after hers, a true personality, develop'd, exercised proportionately in body, mind, and spirit. I can imagine this case as one not necessarily rare or difficult, but in buoyant accordance with the municipal and general requirements of our times. And I can realize in it the culmination of something better than any stereotyped *éclat* of history or poems. Perhaps, unsung, undramatized, unput in essays or biographies—perhaps even some such community already exists, in Ohio, Illinois, Missouri, or somewhere, practically fulfilling itself, and thus outvying, in cheapest vulgar life, all that has been hitherto shown in best ideal pictures. . . .

There are still other standards, suggestions, for products of high literatuses. That which really balances and conserves the social and political world is not so much legislation, police, treaties, and dread of punishment, as the latent eternal intuitional sense, in humanity, of fairness, manliness, decorum, &c. Indeed, this perennial regulation, control, and oversight, by self-suppliance, is *sine qua non* to democracy; and a highest widest aim of democratic literature may well be to bring forth, cultivate, brace, and strengthen this sense, in individuals and society. A strong mastership of the general inferior self by the superior self, is to be aided, secured, indirectly, but surely, by the literatus, in his works, shaping, for individual or aggregate democracy, a great passionate body, in and along with which goes a great masterful spirit.

And still, providing for contingencies, I fain confront the fact, the need of powerful native philosophs and orators and bards, these States, as rallying points to come, in times of danger, and to fend off ruin and defection. For history is long, long, long. Shift and turn the combinations of the statement as we may, the problem of the future of America is in certain respects as dark as it is vast. Pride, competition, segregation, vicious wilfulness, and license beyond example, brood already upon us. Unwieldy and immense, who shall hold in behemoth? who bridle leviathan? Flaunt it as we choose, athwart and over the roads of our progress loom huge uncertainty, and dreadful, threatening gloom. It is useless to deny it: Democracy grows rankly up the thickest, noxious, deadliest plants and fruits of all—brings worse and worse invaders—needs newer, larger, stronger, keener compensations and compellers.

Our lands, embracing so much, (embracing indeed the whole, rejecting none,) hold in their breast that flame also, capable of consuming themselves, consuming us all. Short as the span of our national life has been, already have death and downfall crowded close upon us—and will again crowd close, no doubt, even if warded off. Ages to come may never know, but I know, how narrowly during the late secession war—and more than once, and more than twice or thrice—our Nationality, (wherein bound up, as in a ship in a storm, depended, and yet depend, all our best life, all hope, all value,) just grazed, just by a hair escaped destruction. Alas! to think of them! the agony and bloody sweat of certain of those hours! those cruel, sharp, suspended crises!

Even to-day, amid these whirls, incredible flippancy, and blind fury of parties, infidelity, entire lack of first-class captains and leaders, added to the plentiful meanness and vulgarity of the ostensible masses—that problem, the labor question, beginning to open like a yawning gulf, rapidly widening every year—what prospect have we? We sail a dangerous sea of seething currents, cross and under-currents, vortices—all so dark, untried—and whither shall we turn? It seems as if the Almighty had spread before this nation charts of imperial destinies, dazzling as the sun, yet with many a deep intestine difficulty, and human aggregate of cankerous imperfection,— saying, lo! the roads, the only plans of development, long and varied with all terrible balks and ebullitions. You said in your soul, I will be empire of empires, overshadowing all else, past and present, putting the history of old-world dynasties, conquests behind me, as of no account—making a new history, a history of democracy, making old history a dwarf—I alone inaugurating largeness, culminating time. If these, O lands of America, are indeed the prizes, the determinations of your soul, be it so. But behold the cost, and already specimens of the cost. Thought you greatness was to ripen for you like a pear? If you would have greatness, know that you must conquer it through ages, centuries—must pay for it with a proportionate price. For you too, as for all lands, the struggle, the traitor, the wily person in office, scrofulous wealth, the surfeit of prosperity, the demonism of greed, the hell of passion, the decay of faith, the long postponement, the fossil-like lethargy, the ceaseless need of revolutions, prophets, thunderstorms, deaths, births, new projections and invigorations of ideas and men.

Yet I have dream'd, merged in that hidden-tangled problem of our fate, whose long unraveling stretches mysteriously through time—dream'd out, portray'd, hinted already—a little or a larger band—a band of brave and true, unprecedented yet—arm'd and equipt at every point—the members separated, it may be, by different dates and States, or south, or north, or east, or west—Pacific, Atlantic, Southern, Canadian—a year, a century here, and other centuries there—but always one, compact in soul, conscience-conserving, God-inculcating, inspired achievers, not only in literature, the greatest art, but achievers in all art—a new, undying order, dynasty, from age to age transmitted—a band, a class, at least as fit to cope with current years, our dangers, needs, as those who, for their times, so long, so well, in armor or in cowl, upheld and made illustrious, that far-back feudal, priestly world. To offset chivalry, indeed, those vanish'd countless knights, old altars, abbeys, priests, ages and strings of ages, a knightlier and more sacred cause to-day demands, and shall supply, in a New World, to larger, grander work, more than the counterpart and tally of them.

Arrived now, definitely, at an apex for these Vistas, I confess that the promulgation and belief in such a class or institution—a new and greater literatus order—its possibility, (nay certainty,) underlies these entire speculations—and that the rest, the other parts, as superstructures, are all founded upon it. It really seems to me the condition, not only of our future national and democratic development, but of our perpetuation. In the highly artificial and materialistic bases of modern civilization, with the corresponding arrangements and methods of living, the force-infusion of intellect alone, the depraving influences of riches just as much as poverty, the absence of all high ideals in character—with the long series of tendencies, shapings, which few are strong enough to resist, and which now seem, with steam-engine speed, to be everywhere turning out the generations of humanity like uniform iron castings—all of which, as compared with the feudal ages, we can yet do nothing better than accept, make the best of, and even welcome, upon the whole, for their oceanic practical grandeur, and their restless wholesale kneading of the masses—I say of all this tremendous and dominant play of solely materialistic bearings upon current life in the United States, with the results as already seen, accumulating, and reaching far into the future, that they must either be confronted and met by at least an equally subtle and tremendous force-infusion for purposes of spiritualization, for the pure conscience, for genuine esthetics, and for absolute and primal manliness and womanliness—or else our modern civilization, with all its improvements, is in vain, and we are on the road to a destiny, a status, equivalent, in its real world, to that of the fabled damned.

Prospecting thus the coming unsped days, and that new order in them—marking the endless train of exercise, development, unwind, in nation as in man, which life is for—we see, fore-indicated, amid these prospects and hopes, new law-forces of spoken and written language—not merely the pedagogue-forms, correct, regular, familiar with precedents, made for matters of outside propriety, fine words, thoughts definitely told out—but a language fann'd by the breath of Nature, which leaps overhead, cares mostly for impetus and effects, and for what it plants and invigorates to grow—tallies life and character, and seldomer tells a thing than suggests or necessitates it. In fact, a new theory of literary composition for imaginative works of the very first class, and especially for highest poems, is the sole course open to these States. Books are to be call'd for, and supplied, on the assumption that the process of reading is not a halfsleep, but, in highest sense, an exercise, a gymnast's struggle; that the reader is to do something for himself, must be on the alert, must himself or herself construct indeed the poem, argument, history, metaphysical essay—the text furnishing the hints, the clue, the start or frame-work. Not the book needs so much to be the complete thing, but the reader of the book does. That were to make a nation of supple and athletic minds, well-train'd, intuitive, used to depend on themselves, and not on a few coteries of writers.

Investigating here, we see, not that it is a little thing we have, in having the bequeath'd libraries, countless shelves of volumes, records, &c.; yet how serious the danger, depending entirely on them, of the bloodless vein, the nerveless arm, the false application, at second or third hand. We see that the real interest of this people of ours in the theology, history, poetry, politics, and personal models of the past, (the British islands, for instance, and indeed all the past,) is not necessarily to mould ourselves or our literature upon them, but to attain fuller, more definite comparisons, warnings, and the insight to ourselves, our own present, and our own far grander, different, future history, religion, social customs, &c. We see that almost everything that has been written, sung, or stated, of old, with reference to humanity under the feudal and oriental institutes, religions, and for other lands, needs to be re-written, re-sung, re-stated, in terms consistent with the institution of these States, and to come in range and obedient uniformity with them.

We see, as in the universes of the material kosmos, after meteorological, vegetable, and animal cycles, man at last arises, born through them, to prove them, concentrate them, to turn upon them with wonder and love—to command them, adorn them, and carry them upward into superior realms—so, out of the series of the preceding social and political universes, now arise these States. We see that while many were supposing things established and completed, really the grandest things always remain; and discover that the work of the New World is not ended, but only fairly begun.

We see our land, America, her literature, esthetics, &c., as, substantially, the getting in form, or effusement and statement, of deepest basic elements and loftiest final meanings, of history and man—and the portrayal, (under the eternal laws and conditions of beauty,) of our own physiognomy, the subjective tie and expression of the objective, as from our own combination, continuation, and points of view—and the deposit and record of the national mentality, character, appeals, heroism, wars, and even liberties—where these, and all, culminate in native literary and artistic formulation, to be perpetuated; and not having which native, first-class formulation, she will flounder about, and her other, however imposing, eminent greatness, prove merely a passing gleam; but truly having which, she will understand herself, live nobly, nobly contribute, emanate, and, swinging, poised safely on herself, illumin'd and illuming, become a full-form'd world, and divine Mother not only of material but spiritual worlds, in ceaseless succession through time—the main thing being the average, the bodily, the concrete, the democratic, the popular, on which all the superstructures of the future are to permanently rest.

1871

■ PHOEBE CARY ■
1824–1871

Ranked during her lifetime with Mark Twain and Ambrose Bierce as one of the most important humorists before 1900, Phoebe Cary has become part of what critic Nancy Walker has referred to as "a largely invisible tradition" of women humorists. According to Walker, to be a mid-nineteenth-century American female comedic writer was to challenge "the publicly espoused values of the culture, overturning its sacred cows ... to confront and subvert the very power that keeps women powerless, and at the same time to risk alienating those upon whom women are dependent for economic survival."

Nothing could have been truer for Phoebe Cary (1824–1871), who, with her sister Alice Cary (1820–1871), supported universal suffrage, protested slavery, and fought poverty. As part of the growing class of genteel female authors, both sisters objected to the exclusion of women from the literary tradition. They pursued a social and political agenda that demanded rights for the underprivileged and allowed the voices of the traditionally silent—women, slaves, and the poor—to be heard. In contrast to Alice's *Clovernook Stories* (1851), which explored the limitations of small-town life, Phoebe rejected the nostalgic idealization of nature, family, and rural life as an antidote to existential issues. Her witty, irreverent parodies highlighted the shifting class boundaries in the modern city, and her verse speaks to us today because its humor connects with the reader and portrays a realistic view of life in nineteenth-century America.

Originally from Mount Healthy, Ohio, two of nine daughters born on a farm, the sisters had a working-class background and limited formal schooling, which would set them apart from their contemporaries in New York literary society. Describing their home lives in a way that idealized them as models of virtue and piety, their biographer, Mary Clemmer Ames, explains that they had a "tender, loving father, who sang his children to sleep with holy hymns, and habitually went about his work repeating the grand old Hebrew poets, and the sweet and precious promises of the New Testament of our Lord."

According to Alice Cary, their mother was their first teacher and fulfilled a domestic and morally upstanding role as "a woman of superior intellect and of good, well-ordered life. In my memory, she stands apart from all others, wiser, purer, doing more, and living better than any other woman." To relieve the debt on the family farm, the sisters' education relied on the books in their household, which consisted of "a Bible, Hymn Book, the 'History of the Jews,' 'Lewis and Clark's Travels,' 'Pope's Essay,' and 'Charlotte Temple,' a romance founded on fact." As this list suggests, their reading underscores the religious upbringing that would lead to Alice's moral, didactic verse and Phoebe's conventional piety.

Despite their popularity during their lifetimes, Alice and Phoebe Cary struggled to establish literary reputations, and they pursued the social causes that mark them as equalitarian democrats in their writing. Between the 1830s, when they published in newspapers and Universalist church journals, and 1849, when they appeared among the promising "younger" poets of Rufus Griswold's popular anthology, *The Female Poets of America*, they vigorously pursued careers outside their native Ohio.

In 1851, the year that Alice's first series of *Clovernook Stories* appeared, she moved to New York City and invited Phoebe to join her. Partly from the proceeds of their writing for literary magazines such as *Harpers* and *The Atlantic Monthly*, the Cary sisters purchased a home on 20th Street in Greenwich Village, where they held a weekly salon on Sunday evenings that counted among its notables John Greenleaf Whittier, Horace Greeley, James T. Fields, Gail Hamilton, Sara Helen Whitman, William Lloyd Garrison, and Phineas T. Barnum. The salon offered the sisters a private platform for expressing their views on women's rights, slavery, and temperance to a large circle of influential writers, publishers, and critics. This enabled Alice and Phoebe to negotiate the distance between public and private worlds in a way that allowed them to maintain their conservative image while advocating equality for women, slaves, and the poor.

Although the Carys conformed to the self-effacing rhetoric commonly used by female writers of the period, their actions challenged the traditional role of women. Alice, after a visit from Susan B. Anthony, wrote for *The Revolution* and, in 1868, served as the first president of Sorosis, an organization devoted to the social and professional advancement of women. Cultivating a domestic air, Alice recounts her preference for active but unobtrusive engagement in the world's affairs: "I must work in my own way and that is a very quiet one.... I must say my little say, or act and do my little do, at home!"

After the horrified reaction of reviewers to *Poems and Parodies*, published in 1854, Phoebe Cary found it necessary to guard her public self-image. She so challenged the predominant definition of a "woman of sentiment" that one critic called "The City Life," her parody of Bryant's "The Future Life," a "profanation." Indeed, Phoebe used her mordant wit and sarcasm to lambaste the writers who were idolized among her contemporaries but who often romanticized the lives of the working classes and women. While Alice, using a darkly realistic lens, was the more popular poet, Phoebe was touted as a wit and responded to the tribulations of life with irony and humor. According to Ames, "When she was in her best moods, they came like flashes of heat lightning, like a rush of meteors, suddenly and constantly you were dazzled while you were delighted, and afterward found it difficult to single out any distinct flash or separate meteor from the multitude." Indeed, Phoebe praised the value of marriage publicly, yet privately suggested that many women were far from content. In one anecdote, when asked if she and her unmarried sister had ever been disappointed in their affections, she replied, "No, but a great many of my married friends have."

Poems and Parodies gives a fascinating window on the dual image that Phoebe Cary presented to the public throughout her literary career. As its division into conventional poems and literary parodies suggests, the volume reflects a profoundly divided public self-image—on the one hand, domestic, conventional, and pious; on the other, humorous, sardonic, and sarcastic. Religious and domestic poems, including "The Life of Trial," set the tenor of the first half of her volume. In this poem, she sympathizes with the abused woman for whom death brings an "agonizing birth-cry" of deliverance from suffering. Such poems provide evidence of Phoebe's conservative side, as does her hymnody. Her most popular hymn, "Nearer Home" (also known by its first line, "One Sweetly Solemn Thought"), reputedly led to many temperance conversions and furthered her professional dealings with Charles Force Deems, a minister with whom she edited *Hymns for All Christians* (1868).

Many of the themes of Phoebe's poems include popular nineteenth-century forms of social activism, such as temperance, women's rights, suffrage, and abolition. While Alice wrote "local color" stories and poems that center on people in small towns whose lives stand "as 'competent witnesses' to the quality of life in the region," Phoebe used the city as the backdrop for her social critique. In *Poems and Parodies*, she also attacked the class structure that subjected women to poverty and abuse.

As Universalists, the Carys accepted an inherently democratic system of belief that asserts any person may attain salvation. The Universalists advocated equality among the rich and poor, supported education and nonsectarian schools, and advanced a host of issues, including abolition, prison reform, capital punishment, and suffrage. Such progressive attitudes must have influenced Phoebe, who believed in the rights of the poor and observed their tragic lives around her. As she notes, "I have felt so poor myself ... I have cried in the street because I was poor. I am so much *nearer* to poor people than to rich ones."

But Phoebe Cary's parodies amply demonstrate her belief that women were self-deluded regarding their expectations of marriage. In her send-ups of famous poets—such as Longfellow, Whittier, Bryant, Poe, Wordsworth, Goldsmith, Byron, and Shakespeare—she challenges the preeminence of famous authors as she provides an homage to their work. This stance also allows her to provide a witty and irreverent look at the lives of middle-class urban dwellers and their social mores. In her parody of Henry Wadsworth Longfellow's "A Psalm of Life," for example, the ethic of action in the face of life's emptiness is taken to support the beliefs of many women that any "girl is dead that's single" and that "married life is real, earnest; / Single blessedness a fib." As in several other poems, including "Dorothy's Dower," Phoebe exposes the powerlessness of married women who lack economic independence. "Samuel Brown," a parody of the unearthly love that is recounted in Edgar Allan Poe's "Annabel Lee," inverts the expected scenario of an experienced male lover and his childlike bride. Rather, the poem portrays a wealthy woman who crosses class lines when she travels to the speaker's neighborhood and steals away with her working-class lover to her home "In a street quite up in town." "Worser Moments," a send-up of "Better Moments," a poem by Nathaniel Parker Willis (best known as Fanny Fern's brother), underscores the domestic drudgery of a woman's life rather than the romanticized image of his childhood.

The literary careers of Alice and Phoebe Cary are a model of joint female literary production that was common in the nineteenth century, and their devotion to social causes is an important and underappreciated aspect of their writing. The sisters' relationship was indissoluble and profound. After living together as companions for more than thirty years, Phoebe reneged on an offer of marriage in 1867 to care for her ailing sister, who continued to write until, according to Phoebe, "the pen literally fell from her hand at last" in 1871. Five months later, Phoebe died in Newport, Rhode Island. Both sisters were interred in Brooklyn's Greenwood Cemetery. From a contemporary perspective, Phoebe Cary continues to intrigue us both through her aesthetic achievement and political views that resound even today.

Elizabeth Petrino
Fairfield University

PRIMARY WORKS

Poems and Parodies, 1854; *Hymns for All Christians*, Phoebe Cary, ed., 1868; *Poems of Faith, Hope, and Love*, 1868.

SECONDARY WORKS

Mary Clemmer Ames, *A Memorial of Alice and Phoebe Cary*, 1973; Jennie Maria Bingham, *The Cary Sisters*, 1883; Alice Cary, *Clovernook Sketches and Other Stories*, edited and introduced by Judith Fetterley, 1987; Nancy A. Walker, *A Very Serious Thing: Women's Humor and American Culture*, 1988.

The Life of Trial

I am glad her life is over,
    Glad that all her trials are past;
For her pillow was not softened
    Down with roses to the last.

When sharp thorns choked up the pathway   5
    Where she wandered sad and worn,
Never kind hand pressed them backward,
    So her feet were pierced and torn.

And when life's stern course of duty
    Through the fiery furnace ran,   10
Never saw she one beside her,
    Like unto the Son of Man.

Ere the holy dew of baptism
    Cooled her aching forehead's heat,
Heaviest waters of affliction   15
    Many times had touched her feet.

Long for her deliverance waiting,
    Clung she to the cross in vain;
With an agonizing birth-cry
    Was her spirit born again.   20

And her path grew always rougher
    Wearier, wearier, still she trod,
Till, through gates of awful anguish,
    She went in at last to God!

       1854

The City Life[1]

How shall I know thee in that sphere that keeps
    The country youth that to the city goes,

---

[1]A parody of "The Future Life" by William Cullen Bryant.

When all of thee, that change can wither, sleeps
    And perishes among your cast-off clothes?

For I shall feel the sting of ceaseless pain,   5
    If there I meet thy one-horse carriage not;
Nor see the hat I love, nor ride again,
    When thou art driving on a gentle trot.

Wilt thou not for me in the city seek,
    And turn to note each passing shawl and gown?   10
You used to come and see me once a week,—
    Shall I be banished from your thought in town?

In that great street I don't know how to find,
    In the resplendence of that glorious sphere,
And larger movements of the unfettered mind,   15
    Wilt thou forget the love that joined us here?

The love that lived through all the simple past,
    And meekly with my country training bore,
And deeper grew, and tenderer to the last,
    Shall it expire in town, and be no more?   20

A happier lot than mine, and greater praise,
    Await thee there; for thou, with skill and tact,
Hast learnt the wisdom of the world's just ways,
    And dressest well, and knowest how to act.

For me, the country place in which I dwell   25
    Has made me one of a proscribed band;
And work hath left its scar—that fire of hell
    Has left its frightful scar upon my hand.

Yet though thou wear'st the glory of the town,
    Wilt thou not keep the same belovéd name,   30
The same black-satin vest, and morning-gown,
    Lovelier in New York city, yet the same?

Shalt thou not teach me, in that grander home,
    The wisdom that I learned so ill in this,—
The wisdom which is fine,—till I become   35
    Thy fit companion in that place of bliss?

                                        1854

Jacob[1]

He dwelt among "apartments let,"
    About five stories high;
A man I thought that none would get,
    And very few would try.

A boulder, by a larger stone   5
    Half hidden in the mud,
Fair as a man when only one
    Is in the neighborhood.

He lived unknown, and few could tell
    When Jacob was not free;   10
But he has got a wife,—and O!
    The difference to me!

1854

▪ # EMILY DICKINSON ▪
1830–1886

For Emily Dickinson, the immeasurable, unrecorded life was far more real than the verifiable one; the intersections of visible and invisible worlds far more electric than facts recognized by biographers. A sketch of her known dates and places cannot capture or account for Dickinson's extraordinary sensibility or originality, which brought fresh currents into American thought and literature and expanded the possibilities of poetry.

Dickinson lived in Amherst, Massachusetts, where she was born in 1830 and died in 1886. She shared her family's household with her younger sister Lavinia, her mother, Emily Norcross Dickinson, and her father, Edward Dickinson, a lawyer, congressman, and treasurer of Amherst College. Her brother Austin, one year older, a lawyer like his father, lived for most of his life in the house next door, after marrying Dickinson's friend Susan Huntington Gilbert. We know few details about Dickinson's mother: she had a year of higher education, rather unusual for a woman in the early nineteenth century; like Emily, she was a skilled and avid gardener; she shared domestic responsibilities with her daughters, and Lavinia took on much of the household management.

[1]A parody of Wordsworth's Lucy poem "She
Dwelt among the Untrodden Ways."

Squire Edward Dickinson emerges as a dominant and domineering figure in the family, whom Emily Dickinson seems to have both honored and humored. To her brother Austin, away at law school, she wrote:

> We dont have many jokes tho' now, it is pretty much all sobriety, and we do not have much poetry, father having made up his mind that its pretty much all real life. Fathers real life and mine sometimes come into collision, but as yet, escape unhurt!

About ten years later she wrote to a friend: "He buys me many Books—but begs me not to read them—because he fears they joggle the Mind." Dickinson implied that her parents neither comprehended nor aided her development, but we know that their quiet style of living, their secure economic class, and perhaps even their emotional remoteness allowed her the privacy in which to develop her writing. Lavinia protected that privacy; she said after Dickinson's death that Emily was the one of the family who had *thinking* to do.

By the age of twelve, Dickinson was a fluent and prolific writer of letters. Austin described the dramatic effect of her talent at Amherst Academy and Mount Holyoke Female Seminary (now Mount Holyoke College), where she spent one year. "Her compositions were unlike anything ever heard—and always produced a sensation—both with the scholars and Teachers—her imagination sparkled—and she gave it free rein. She was full of courage—but always had a peculiar personal sensitiveness. She saw things directly and just as they were. She abhorred sham...."

Dickinson's early letters reveal a witty, startling, irreverent imagination and a passion for situations that combined friendship, honesty, secrecy, private jokes, and talk about books and ideas. Though her childhood was a time of mass evangelistic conversions, or revivals, in the churches of western Massachusetts, when all souls were urged to commit themselves to Christ, Dickinson refused to think badly of "the world" or believe that greater pleasures could be found in heaven than on earth. Of her family's habits of traditional prayer and church-going she wrote, "[They] are religious—except me—and address an Eclipse, every morning—whom they call 'Father.'" Her letters indicate that she found life exhilarating and sufficient, if only it would last, and that for her, heaven was embodied in familiar surroundings, in nature, in love, and in the power of thought.

After one year of college, Dickinson made only five or six trips away from Amherst, traveling in her twenty-fifth year with her father to Philadelphia and Washington and spending time in Boston in her early thirties when she developed an acute eye problem.

For women of Dickinson's class, the appropriate social institutions were the family and the church; with those came many societal obligations. Women of her day were not expected to be intellectuals, leaders, thinkers, philosophers, or creators. But Dickinson rebelled. She was a woman who created her own avenues of thought, providing a striking example of an alternative sensibility, a dissenting imagination, a re-creating mind.

Attenuated doses of society were enough for Dickinson. She found the electricity between two individuals in a room quite overpowering, when it wasn't stifling, and she needed much time for solitude.

Dickinson rarely, if ever, left her family's house and grounds during the last twenty years of her life, but we should not imagine her disconnected from life. The Dickinson family was prominent in the town and the state, and many visitors came to visit at the two Dickinson houses. Susan, Austin, and their children lived next door. The family holdings included gardens, lawns, a meadow, a stream, an oak grove, a barn, and a conservatory. A number of household workers were employed, including many from among the local community of Irish immigrants. Dickinson's bedroom overlooked the main road from Boston to Amherst, on which there was constant traffic. She could look from the windows of that room, where she wrote most of her poetry, toward the house of her sister-in-law and brother and toward Amherst College and the town's center, with its churches, shops, and citizens coming and going.

We also know that Dickinson was a cosmopolitan and eclectic reader. Her letters indicate that she read newspapers and periodicals, following closely local and national events, and read contemporary poetry and fiction as soon as it came into print. Many of her letters contain requests to borrow books or offers to loan them. She seems to have learned much of the Bible and Shakespeare by heart; her letters are filled with scriptural and literary allusion. She read women writers with particular passion, including Elizabeth Barrett Browning, George Eliot, the Brontës, Harriet Beecher Stowe, and her own friend, Helen Hunt Jackson, who urged her vehemently, and in vain, to publish her poems.

Dickinson was immensely responsive to friendship with those she found interesting and loved both women and men with a passionate intensity expressed in both letters and poems. "My friends are my estate," she once wrote. Throughout her life, she referred to those she loved as "treasures" and "possessions." For her, friendship was like Heaven, and she resented the Calvinistic God, both "burglar" and "banker," who would jealously take those she loved from her. At the same time, she hoped, and believed with "uncertain certainty," that, after death, God would "refund" her "confiscated Gods."

One whom Dickinson loved was her sister-in-law Susan, a woman with whom she was closely connected from her late teens until her death. As far as we know, Susan received more of Dickinson's writing than any other correspondent. The letters and poems sent across the lawn to Susan are evidence of the intimacy and constancy as well as the tensions of this friendship. Those inclined to view Dickinson as emotionally impoverished might think instead of her living for three decades next door to the woman, also a writer, to whom she wrote: "With the exception of Shakespeare, you have told me of more knowledge than any one living—To say that sincerely is strange praise."

Apparently Austin Dickinson, with his mistress, Mabel Loomis Todd, who was editing the poems for publication, mutilated Dickinson's manuscripts, erasing his wife's name and scissoring out references to her. One poem sent to Susan, "One Sister have I in our house," included in our selection, was completely scratched out, line by line. It seems that Susan, too, withheld information. Only after her death in 1913 did she allow her daughter Martha Dickinson Bianchi to publish poems and letters she had received from Dickinson, and it is possible that this writing to be shared with the world was carefully chosen, while other work was destroyed.

It is important to understand the role in Dickinson studies played by homophobia, the fear and hatred of love between people of the same sex. We do not know to what extent Dickinson expressed her sexual desires physically, but we do have clear evidence that her affinities were both lesbian and heterosexual.

One of the most enduring legends in Dickinson studies is the story that the love poems were written to the man Dickinson addressed in several passionate letters as "Master." (It is unclear whether these letters were ever actually sent.) Some argue that "Master" can be identified as the Reverend Charles Wadsworth of Philadelphia and claim that it was Wadsworth who "broke the poet's heart." This story set off the search for "the one true [male] love" of Dickinson's life, which has extended into many contemporary readings of Dickinson.

In the end, though we cannot define the exact nature of Dickinson's bonds with the women and men of her "estate," it is important to realize that she counted each a "treasure."

At the age of thirty-one, Dickinson sent several poems to Thomas Wentworth Higginson, responding to his "Letter to a Young Contributor" in *The Atlantic Monthly*. She asked, "Are you too deeply occupied to say if my Verse is alive?" The Higginson selection in this anthology includes a letter to his wife describing his first visit to Dickinson: "I never was with a person who drained my nerve power so much," he wrote. Even though Higginson stood in awe of the poet, he apparently commented that the poetry was "spasmodic" and "uncontrolled," and despite Dickinson's admiration for her "teacher," she seems never to have taken any of his advice.

Although ten poems by Emily Dickinson were published during her lifetime, we have no evidence that she sought, desired, or welcomed their publication, and considerable evidence that she did not. She enclosed many poems in letters, but no member of the family guessed how seriously she took herself as a poet until after she died, when it was realized that over a period of years she had engaged in what is probably the most remarkable instance of private publication in American letters.

Dickinson copied almost 1,200 poems onto folded sheets of white, unlined stationery, marking with a small "x" certain words and phrases she considered revising, then listed possible alternative word choices at the bottom of the page. She stacked several folded sheets on top of one another, punched two holes, and tied each packet together along one edge with cotton string. Each of the "packets," also called "fascicles" (we have no way of knowing what name Dickinson had for them), contains from sixteen to twenty-four pages and an average of twenty poems. Dickinson's use of and intentions for these packets are unknown. They may have constituted a storage and filing system; some critics believe they have thematic coherence.

Photostatic representations of "fascicle" poems, as well as electronic images, in online editions, of unbound poems, drafts, and fragments, allow us to study Dickinson's manuscripts, observing, for instance, her exact use of punctuation. She used dashes in the place of more traditional marks, such as periods, commas, colons, and semicolons, and some see it as significant that the dashes vary in length and that some slope upward, some downward. One supposition is that Dickinson may have used the dash to direct a reader to stress certain words and phrases. With the dash, Dickinson could avoid what she may have considered the spurious finality of the period. Photostats of the poems also show us Dickinson's line breaks, now a subject of debate among readers, editors, and critics.

When she died, Dickinson left Lavinia and Maggie Maher, a woman who worked in the household, specific instructions to destroy the letters she had received and saved. She made no mention of her poetry. When Lavinia discovered the poems, she was determined to get them into print, and she persuaded Higginson and Mabel Loomis Todd to edit them. Todd and Higginson published volumes of selected poems in 1890 and 1891; in 1896 Todd edited a third volume. The poems were received with great excitement; the 1890 volume went through seven printings in a year, the 1891 volume five printings in two years. Because of complex family feuds that separated the manuscripts, Dickinson's complete poems and all known variant readings were not published until 1955.

In reading Dickinson's poetry, it is best not to look for creeds or statements of belief. Though she reflects her community's Protestant and Calvinistic frames of reference, religious terminology in her poetry does not indicate that she held orthodox religious beliefs. She is by turn satirical, skeptical, awed, reverent, speculative, outraged, tantalized, ironic, or God-like herself.

Dickinson experimented radically with poetic style: she was taut, terse, suggestive, oblique. The words she chose live vividly on the page and invite readers to fill the poems with their own sense of connection. Her tone is often both intimate and stark, especially in the many first lines beginning with "I": "I felt a funeral in my brain ... ," "I dwell in possibility ... ," "I measure every grief I meet...." She rearranged word order, ignored rules of punctuation, evaded rhyme schemes even while suggesting them, and in general tried to ventilate and open up language to the point where it approximated her own sense of the layered complexity of matter, spirit, and consciousness. The English sentence as she inherited it must have seemed to her like a blunt instrument. Her meter suggests not certainty or regularity, but mobility, unfinished business, life in motion. Because she rarely rhymed exactly, one critic has suggested that for her, life did not rhyme. But it seems to have come tantalizingly, agonizingly close before it refused.

Dickinson's explorations of consciousness and the strategies she used to free language from traditional structures and expectations continue to challenge, reward, and astonish readers year after year. Dickinson was a poet who had the courage to resist many authorities, even at the price of being misunderstood. Wresting language back to the service of her own experience, she gives us glimpses of a person too startling to be acceptable to her community, with a mind too exacting to use language as she had learned it, a heart of unacceptable desires and unanswerable demands, and a sensibility embodying in life and language an early and genuine example of the sometimes illusory American trait of self-reliance.

Peggy McIntosh
Wellesley College, Center for Research on Women

Ellen Louise Hart
University of California at Santa Cruz, Cowell College

PRIMARY WORKS

The Poems of Emily Dickinson, Thomas H. Johnson, ed., 3 vols., 1951, 1955; *The Letters of Emily Dickinson*, Thomas H. Johnson and Theodora Ward, eds., 3 vols., 1958; *The Manuscript Books of Emily Dickinson*, R. W. Franklin, ed., 2 vols., 1981; *The Poems of Emily Dickinson (Variorum Edition)*, R. W. Franklin, ed., 3 vols., 1998; *The Poems of Emily Dickinson (Reading Edition)*, R. W. Franklin, ed., 1999; *Open Me Carefully: Emily Dickinson's Intimate Letters to Susan Huntington Dickinson*, Ellen Louise Hart and Martha Nell Smith, eds., 1998; *Radical Scatters: Emily Dickinson's Late Fragments and Related Texts, 1870–1886*, Marta Werner, ed., 1999; Dickinson Electronic Archives, Martha Nell Smith, coordinator, Ellen Louise Hart and Marta Werner, general editors, www.emilydickinson.org.

Poems

One Sister have I in our house,
And one, a hedge away.
There's only one recorded,
But both belong to me.

One came the road that I came—   5
And wore my last year's gown—
The other, as a bird her nest,
Builded our hearts among.

She did not sing as we did—
It was a different tune—   10
Herself to her a music
As Bumble bee of June.

Today is far from Childhood—
But up and down the hills
I held her hand the tighter—   15
Which shortened all the miles—

And still her hum
The years among,
Deceives the Butterfly;
Still in her Eye   20
The Violets lie
Mouldered this many May.

I spilt the dew—
But took the morn—
I chose this single star   25
From out the wide night's numbers—

Sue—forevermore![1]
J. 14   F. 5   1858   1914[2]

_____

I never lost as much but twice,
And that was in the sod.[1']
Twice have I stood a beggar
Before the door of God!

Angels—twice descending   5
Reimbursed my store—
Burglar! Banker—Father!
I am poor once more!
J. 49   F. 39   c. 1858   1890

_____

Success is counted sweetest
By those who ne'er succeed.
To comprehend a nectar[1"]
Requires sorest need.

Not one of all the purple Host   5
Who took the Flag[2'] today
Can tell the definition
So clear of Victory
As he defeated—dying—
On whose forbidden ear   10
The distant strains of triumph
Burst agonized and clear!
J. 67   F. 112   c. 1859   1878

_____

These are the days when Birds come back—
A very few—a Bird or two—
To take a backward look.

These are the days when skies resume
The old—old sophistries[1"'] of June—   5
A blue and gold mistake.

---

[1]This poem was in fascicle 2, which originally contained twenty-four poems. Sometime in 1891, it was canceled out, probably by Austin Dickinson and Mabel Loomis Todd. We have the complete text in a copy sent by Dickinson to Sue Gilbert in 1858.
[2]For each poem, "J" refers to the number of the poem in the Johnson edition and "F" to the number of the poem in the Franklin edition. The year on the left is the date the poem was written, according to Johnson. If "c." precedes the year, the date is approximate. The year on the right is the earliest date of publication.
[1']The sod: i.e., burial.
[1"]Drink of Greek and Roman gods.
[2']Vanquished the enemy.
[1"']Deceptive arguments.

Oh fraud that cannot cheat the Bee—
Almost thy plausibility
Induces my belief.

Till ranks of seeds their witness bear—   10
And softly thro' the altered air
Hurries a timid leaf.

Oh Sacrament of summer days,
Oh Last Communion in the Haze—
Permit a child to join,   15

Thy sacred emblems to partake—
Thy consecrated bread to take
And thine immortal wine![2]
J. 130   F. 122   c. 1859   1890

_____

Come slowly—Eden!
Lips unused to Thee—
Bashful—sip thy Jessamines—[1]
As the fainting Bee—

Reaching late his flower,   5
Round her chamber hums—
Counts his nectars—
Enters—and is lost in Balms.[2']
J. 211   F. 205   c. 1860   1890

_____

I like a look of Agony,
Because I know it's true—
Men do not sham Convulsion,
Nor simulate, a Throe—

The Eyes glaze once—and that is Death—   5
Impossible to feign
The Beads upon the Forehead
By homely Anguish strung.
J. 241   F. 339   c. 1861   1890

_____

[2]Dickinson compares the end of summer to the last supper of Christ, celebrated in some churches as the sacrament of communion.

[1]Jasmines; fragrant flowers.
[2']Healing ointments.

Wild Nights—Wild Nights!
Were I with thee
Wild Nights should be
Our luxury!

Futile—the Winds—   5
To a Heart in port—
Done with the Compass—
Done with the Chart!

Rowing in Eden—
Ah, the Sea!   10
Might I but moor—Tonight—
In Thee![1]
J. 249   F. 269   c. 1861   1891

I can wade Grief—
Whole Pools of it—
I'm used to that—
But the least push of Joy
Breaks up my feet—   5
And I tip—drunken—
Let no Pebble—smile—
'Twas the New Liquor—
That was all!

Power is only Pain—   10
Stranded, thro' Discipline,
Till Weights—will hang—
Give Balm—to Giants—
And they'll wilt, like Men—
Give Himmaleh—[1']   15
They'll Carry—Him!
J. 252   F. 312   c. 1861   1891

There's a certain Slant of light,
Winter Afternoons—
That oppresses, like the Heft[1"]
Of Cathedral Tunes—

---

[1]Dickinson juxtaposes stormy nights with lovers' sheltered ports and moorings.

[1']A personification of the Himalayan mountains.
[1"]Weight or bulk.

Heavenly Hurt, it gives us— 5
We can find no scar,
But internal difference,
Where the Meanings, are—

None may teach it—Any—
'Tis the Seal Despair— 10
An imperial affliction
Sent us of the Air—

When it comes, the Landscape listens—
Shadows—hold their breath—
When it goes, 'tis like the Distance 15
On the look of Death—
J. 258   F. 320   c. 1861   1890

I felt a Funeral, in my Brain,
And Mourners to and fro
Kept treading—treading—till it seemed
That Sense was breaking through—[1]

And when they all were seated, 5
A Service, like a Drum—
Kept beating—beating—till I thought
My Mind was going numb—

And then I heard them lift a Box
And creak across my Soul 10
With those same Boots of Lead, again,
Then Space—began to toll,

As[2] all the Heavens were a Bell,
And Being, but an Ear,
And I, and Silence, some strange Race 15
Wrecked, solitary, here—

And then a Plank in Reason, broke,
And I dropped down, and down—
And hit a World, at every plunge,
And Finished knowing—then— 20
J. 280   F. 340   c. 1861   1896

---

[1] I.e., sense was giving way.   [2] As if. Dickinson often uses "as" in this way.

I'm Nobody! Who are you?
Are you—Nobody—too?
Then there's a pair of us!
Dont tell! they'd banish us—you know!

How dreary—to be—Somebody!   5
How public—like a Frog—
To tell your name—the livelong June—
To an admiring Bog!
J. 288   F. 260   c. 1861   1891

_____

I reason, Earth is short—
And Anguish—absolute—
And many hurt,
But, what of that?

I reason, we could die—   5
The best Vitality
Cannot excel Decay,
But, what of that?

I reason, that in Heaven—
Somehow, it will be even—   10
Some new Equation, given—
But, what of that?
J. 301   F. 403   c. 1862   1890

_____

The Soul selects her own Society—
Then—shuts the Door—
To her divine Majority—
Present no more—

Unmoved—she notes the Chariots—pausing—   5
At her low Gate—
Unmoved—an Emperor be kneeling
Upon her Mat—

I've known her—from an ample nation—
Choose One—   10
Then—close the Valves of her attention—
Like Stone—
J. 303   F. 409   c. 1862   1890

_____

There came a Day at Summer's full,
Entirely for me—
I thought that such were for the Saints,
Where Resurrections—be—

The Sun, as common, went abroad,   5
The flowers, accustomed, blew,
As if no soul the solstice passed
That maketh all things new—

The time was scarce profaned, by speech—
The symbol of a word   10
Was needless, as at Sacrament,
The Wardrobe—of our Lord—

Each was to each The Sealed Church,
Permitted to commune this—time—
Lest we too awkward show   15
At Supper of the Lamb.[1]

The Hours slid fast—as Hours will,
Clutched tight, by greedy hands—
So faces on two Decks, look back,
Bound to opposing lands—   20

And so when all the time had leaked,
Without external sound
Each bound the Other's Crucifix—
We gave no other Bond—

Sufficient troth, that we shall rise—   25
Deposed—at length, the Grave—
To that new Marriage,
Justified—through Calvaries[2] of Love—
J. 322   F. 325   c. 1861   1890

Some keep the Sabbath going to Church—
I keep it, staying at Home—
With a Bobolink for a Chorister—
And an Orchard, for a Dome—

[1]The Last Supper or Lord's Supper.
[2]Calvary was the hill outside Jerusalem on
which Jesus was crucified.

Some keep the Sabbath in Surplice[1]—
I just wear my Wings—
And instead of tolling the Bell, for Church,
Our little Sexton[2]—sings.

God preaches, a noted Clergyman—
And the sermon is never long,
So instead of getting to Heaven, at last—
I'm going, all along.
J. 324   F. 236   c. 1860   1864

———————

A Bird came down the Walk—
He did not know I saw—
He bit an Angleworm in halves
And ate the fellow, raw,

And then he drank a Dew
From a convenient Grass—
And then hopped sidewise to the Wall
To let a Beetle pass—

He glanced with rapid eyes
That hurried all around—
They looked like frightened Beads, I thought—
He stirred his Velvet Head

Like one in danger, Cautious,
I offered him a Crumb
And he unrolled his feathers
And rowed him softer home—

Than Oars divide the Ocean,
Too silver for a seam—
Or Butterflies, off Banks of Noon
Leap, plashless[1'] as they swim.
J. 328   F. 359   c. 1862   1891

———————

I know that He exists.
Somewhere—in Silence—
He has hid his rare life
From our gross eyes.

———

[1]A white gown-like vestment with open sleeves worn by clergymen at services.   [2]Church custodian and keeper of property.
[1']Splashless.

'Tis an instant's play.
'Tis a fond Ambush—
Just to make Bliss
Earn her own surprise!

But—should the play
Prove piercing earnest—
Should the glee—glaze—
In Death's—stiff—stare—

Would not the fun
Look too expensive!
Would not the jest—
Have crawled too far!
J. 338   F. 365   c. 1862   1891

5

10

15

After great pain, a formal feeling comes—
The Nerves sit ceremonious, like Tombs—
The stiff Heart questions was it He, that bore,
And Yesterday, or Centuries before?

The Feet, mechanical, go round—
Of Ground, or Air, or Ought—[1]
A Wooden way
Regardless grown,[2]
A Quartz contentment, like a stone—

This is the Hour of Lead—
Remembered, if outlived,
As Freezing persons, recollect the Snow—
First—Chill—then Stupor—then the letting go—
J. 341   F. 372   c. 1862   1929

5

10

God is a distant—stately Lover—
Woos, as He states us—by His Son—
Verily, a Vicarious Courtship—
"Miles", and "Priscilla", were such an One—

But, lest the Soul—like fair "Priscilla"
Choose the Envoy—and spurn the Groom—
Vouches, with hyperbolic archness—

5

---

[1]Dickinson's spelling of Aught; anything.
[2]Having stopped noticing.

"Miles", and "John Alden" were Synonyme—[1]
J. 357   F. 615   c. 1862   1891

Dare you see a Soul *at the White Heat?*
Then crouch within the door—
Red—is the Fire's common tint—
But when the vivid Ore
Has vanquished Flame's conditions,   5
It quivers from the Forge
Without a color, but the light
Of unannointed Blaze.
Least[1] Village has it's Blacksmith
Whose Anvil's even ring   10
Stands symbol for the finer Forge
That soundless tugs—within—
Refining these impatient Ores
With Hammer, and with Blaze
Until the Designated Light   15
Repudiate[2] the Forge—
J. 365   F. 401   c. 1862   1891

What Soft—Cherubic Creatures—
These Gentlewomen are—
One would as soon assault a Plush—[1"]
Or violate[2'] a Star—

Such Dimity[3] Convictions—   5
A Horror so refined
Of freckled Human Nature—
Of Deity—ashamed—

It's such a common—Glory—
A Fisherman's—Degree—[4]   10
Redemption—Brittle Lady—
Be so—ashamed of Thee—
J. 401   F. 675   c. 1862   1896

---

[1]"Miles": the New England puritan Miles Standish is said to have sent a younger man, John Alden, to propose to Priscilla Mullen for him. Priscilla answered, "Speak for yourself, John," and married the younger man.
[1]The smallest.
[2]Leave behind, disown.

[1"]Piece of upholstery material or upholstered furniture.
[2']Rape; desecrate.
[3]Delicate cotton fabric.
[4]I.e., merely having the status of Christ, who was associated with fishing and later symbolized by a fish.

Much Madness is divinest Sense—
To a discerning Eye—
Much Sense—the starkest Madness—
'Tis the Majority
In this, as All, prevail—   5
Assent—and you are sane—
Demur[1]—you're straightway dangerous—
And handled with a Chain—
J. 435   F. 620   c. 1862   1890

———————

This is my letter to the World
That never wrote to Me—
The simple News that Nature told—
With tender Majesty

Her Message is committed   5
To Hands I cannot see—
For love of Her—Sweet—countrymen—
Judge tenderly—of Me[1]
J. 441   F. 519   c. 1862   1890

———————

I showed her Hights she never saw—
"Would'st Climb," I said?
She said—"Not so"—
"With *me*—" I said—With *me*?
I showed her Secrets—Morning's Nest—   5
The Rope the Nights were put across—
And *now*—"Would'st have me for a Guest?"
She could not find her Yes—
And then, I brake my life—And Lo,
A Light, for her, did solemn glow,   10
The larger, as her face withdrew—
And *could* she, further, "No"?[1]
J. 446   F. 346   c. 1862   1896

———————

[1]Disagree.
[1]This poem was placed by Higginson and Todd just after the table of contents and before the first page of selections in the first edition of Dickinson's poetry, published in 1890. There is no indication that she intended it as an introduction to all of the fascicles; it is lodged in fascicle 24, where it shares a page with part of another poem.

[1]This copy of the poem was sent to Sue in 1862. In the same year, Dickinson copied the poem into a fascicle, with different pronouns:

He showed me Hights I never saw
"Would'st Climb," He said?
I said, "Not so."
"With me—" He said—"With me?" . . .

For further notes, see the Johnson variorum edition.

This was a Poet—It is That
Distills amazing sense
From Ordinary Meanings—
And Attar[1] so immense

From the familiar species   5
That perished by the Door—
We wonder it was not Ourselves
Arrested it—before—

Of Pictures, the Discloser—
The Poet—it is He—   10
Entitles Us—by Contrast—
To ceaseless Poverty—

Of Portion—so unconscious—
The Robbing—could not harm—[2]
Himself—to Him—a Fortune—   15
Exterior—to Time—
J. 448   F. 446   c. 1862   1929

I heard a Fly buzz—when I died—
The Stillness in the Room
Was like the Stillness in the Air—
Between the Heaves of Storm—

The Eyes around—had wrung them dry—   5
And Breaths were gathering firm
For that last Onset—when the King
Be witnessed—in the Room—

I willed my Keepsakes—Signed away
What portion of me be   10
Assignable—and then it was
There interposed a Fly—

With Blue—uncertain—stumbling Buzz—
Between the light—and me—
And then the Windows failed—and then   15
I could not see to see—
J. 465   F. 591   c. 1862   1896

---

[1]Perfume obtained by crushing flower petals.   [2]So unaware of his treasure that stealing could not hurt him.

This World is not Conclusion.
A Species stands beyond—
Invisible, as Music—
But positive, as Sound—
It beckons, and it baffles—   5
Philosophy—dont know—
And through a Riddle, at the last—
Sagacity,[1] must go—
To guess it, puzzles scholars—
To gain it, Men have borne   10
Contempt of Generations
And Crucifixion, shown—
Faith slips—and laughs, and rallies—
Blushes, if any see—
Plucks at a twig of Evidence—   15
And asks a Vane,[2] the way—
Much Gesture, from the Pulpit—
Strong Hallelujahs roll—
Narcotics cannot still the Tooth
That nibbles at the soul—   20

J. 501   F. 373   c. 1862   1896

———————

I'm ceded—I've stopped being Theirs—
The name They dropped upon my face
With water, in the country church
Is finished using, now,
And They can put it with my Dolls,   5
My childhood, and the string of spools,
I've finished threading—too—

Baptized, before, without the choice,
But this time, consciously, of Grace—
Unto supremest name—   10
Called to my Full—The Crescent dropped—
Existence's whole Arc, filled up,
With one small Diadem.

My second Rank—too small the first—
Crowned—Crowing—on my Father's breast—   15
A half unconscious Queen—
But this time—Adequate—Erect
With will to Choose, or to reject,
And I choose, just a Crown—

J. 508   F. 353   c. 1862   1890

———————

[1]Keenness of sense perception.   [2]Weathervane.

I started Early—Took my Dog—
And visited the Sea—
The Mermaids in the Basement
Came out to look at me—

And Frigates—in the Upper Floor   5
Extended Hempen Hands—[1]
Presuming Me to be a Mouse—
Aground—upon the Sands—

But no Man moved Me—till the Tide
Went past my simple Shoe—   10
And past my Apron—and my Belt
And past my Boddice[2]—too—

And made as He would eat me up—
As wholly as a Dew
Upon a Dandelion's Sleeve—   15
And then—I started—too—

And He—He followed—close behind—
I felt His Silver Heel
Upon my Ancle—Then my Shoes
Would overflow with Pearl—   20

Until We met the Solid Town—
No One He seemed to know—
And bowing—with a Mighty look—
At me—The Sea withdrew—
J. 520   F. 656   c. 1862   1891

_____

One Crucifixion is recorded—only—
How many be
Is not affirmed of Mathematics—
Or History—

One Calvary[1']—exhibited to Stranger—   5
As many be
As Persons—or Peninsulas—
Gethsemane—[2']

[1]Ropes.
[2]An article of women's clothing laced and
worn like a vest over a blouse.

[1']Hill of Jesus' crucifixion.
[2']Garden in which Jesus was arrested before
his death.

Is but a Province—in the Being's Centre—
Judea—[3]
For Journey—or Crusade's Achieving—
Too near—

Our Lord—indeed—made Compound Witness—[4]
And yet—
There's newer—nearer Crucifixion
Than That—
J. 553   F. 670   c. 1862   1945

I reckon—when I count at all—
First—Poets—Then the Sun—
Then Summer—Then the Heaven of God—
And then—the List is done—

But, looking back—the First so seems
To Comprehend the Whole—
The Others look a needless Show—
So I write—Poets—All—

Their Summer—lasts a Solid Year—
They can afford a Sun
The East—would deem extravagant—
And if the Further Heaven—

Be Beautiful as they prepare
For Those who worship Them—
It is too difficult a Grace—
To justify the Dream—
J. 569   F. 533   c. 1862   1929

I had been hungry, all the Years—
My Noon had Come—to dine—
I trembling drew the Table near—
And touched the Curious Wine—

'Twas this on Tables I had seen—
When turning, hungry, Home
I looked in Windows, for the Wealth
I could not hope—for Mine—

[3]The Holy Land.   [4]Had many witnesses.

I did not know the ample Bread—
'Twas so unlike the Crumb
The Birds and I, had often shared
In Nature's—Dining Room—   10

The Plenty hurt me—'twas so new—
Myself felt ill—and odd—
As Berry—of a Mountain Bush—   15
Transplanted—to the Road—

Nor was I hungry—so I found
That Hunger—was a way
Of Persons outside Windows—
The Entering—takes away—   20
J. 579   F. 439   c. 1862   1891

They shut me up in Prose—
As when a little Girl
They put me in the Closet—
Because they liked me "still"—

Still! Could themself have peeped—   5
And seen my Brain—go round—
They might as wise have lodged a Bird
For Treason—in the Pound—[1]

Himself has but to will
And easy as a Star   10
Look down upon Captivity—
And laugh—No more have I—[2]
J. 613   F. 445   c. 1862   1935

Ourselves were wed one summer—dear—
Your Vision—was in June—
And when Your little Lifetime failed,
I wearied—too—of mine—

And overtaken in the Dark—   5
Where You had put me down—
By Some one carrying a Light—
I—too—received the Sign.

[1]An enclosure without a roof for livestock or other animals.

[2]I.e., I need do no more than the bird to escape my captivity.

'Tis true—Our Futures different lay—
Your Cottage—faced the sun— 10
While Oceans—and the North must be—
On every side of mine

'Tis true, Your Garden led the Bloom,
For mine—in Frosts—was sown—
And yet, one Summer, we were Queens— 15
But You—were crowned in June—
J. 631   F. 596   c. 1862   1945

The Brain—is wider than the Sky—
For—put them side by side—
The one the other will contain
With ease—and You—beside—

The Brain is deeper than the sea— 5
For—hold them—Blue to Blue—
The one the other will absorb—
As Sponges—Buckets—do—

The Brain is just the weight of God—
For—Heft them—Pound for Pound— 10
And they will differ—if they do—
As Syllable from Sound—
J. 632   F. 598   c. 1862   1896

I cannot live with You—
It would be Life—
And Life is over there—
Behind the Shelf

The Sexton[1] keeps the Key to— 5
Putting up
Our Life—His Porcelain—
Like a Cup—

Discarded of the Housewife—
Quaint—or Broke— 10
A newer Sevres[2] pleases—
Old Ones crack—

---

[1]Custodian of church property; bellringer; gravedigger.   [2]Fine French porcelain china.

I could not die—with You—
For One must wait
To shut the Other's Gaze down—   15
You—could not—

And I—Could I stand by
And see You—freeze—
Without my Right of Frost—
Death's privilege?   20

Nor could I rise—with You—
Because Your Face
Would put out Jesus'—
That New Grace

Glow plain—and foreign   25
On my homesick Eye—
Except that You than He
Shone closer by—

They'd judge Us—How—
For You—served Heaven—You know,   30
Or sought to—
I could not—

Because You saturated Sight—
And I had no more Eyes
For sordid excellence   35
As Paradise

And were You lost, I would be—
Though My Name
Rang loudest
On the Heavenly fame—   40

And were You—saved—
And I—condemned to be
Where You were not—
That self—were Hell to Me—

So We must meet apart—   45
You there—I—here—
With just the Door ajar
That Oceans are—and Prayer—
And that White Sustenance—

Despair— 50
J. 640   F. 706   c. 1862   1890

I dwell in Possibility—
A fairer House than Prose—
More numerous of Windows—
Superior—for Doors—

Of Chambers as the Cedars— 5
Impregnable of Eye—[1]
And for an Everlasting Roof
The Gambrels[2] of the Sky—

Of Visiters—the fairest—
For Occupation—This— 10
The spreading wide my narrow Hands
To gather Paradise—
J. 657   F. 466   c. 1862   1929

Of all the Souls that stand create—
I have elected—One—
When Sense from Spirit—files away—
And Subterfuge—is done—
When that which is—and that which was— 5
Apart—intrinsic—stand—
And this brief Tragedy of Flesh—
Is shifted—like a Sand—
When Figures show their royal Front—
And Mists—are carved away, 10
Behold the Atom—I preferred—
To all the lists[1'] of Clay!
J. 664   F. 279   c. 1862   1891

One need not be a Chamber—to be Haunted—
One need not be a House—
The Brain has Corridors—surpassing
Material Place—
Far safer, of a Midnight Meeting 5

---

[1]Impenetrable, impossible to see through, like some dense cedar trees.
[2]Ridged roofs with two slopes on each side, the lower slope having the steeper pitch.

[1']Probably in the archaic sense of limits, boundaries, borders.

External Ghost
Than it's interior Confronting—
That Cooler Host.

Far safer, through an Abbey gallop,
The Stones a' chase—   10
Than Unarmed, one's a'self encounter—
In lonesome Place—

Ourself behind ourself, concealed—
Should startle most—
Assassin hid in our Apartment   15
Be Horror's least.[1]

The Body—borrows a Revolver—
He bolts the Door—
O'erlooking a superior spectre—[2]
Or More—   20
J. 670   F. 407   c. 1863   1891

Essential Oils—are wrung—
The Attar[1'] from the Rose
Be not expressed[2'] by Suns—alone—
It is the gift of Screws—

The General Rose—decay—   5
But this—in Lady's Drawer
Make Summer—When the Lady lie
In Ceaseless Rosemary—[3]
J. 675   F. 772   c. 1863   1891

Publication—is the Auction
Of the Mind of Man—
Poverty—be justifying
For so foul a thing

Possibly[1"]—but We—would rather   5
From Our Garret go

---

[1] I.e., should be the least horrifying of the things we fear.
[2] Not seeing that there is a greater ghost within.
[1'] Perfume derived from crushing flower petals.

[2'] Pressed out, or brought out.
[3] Herb associated with remembrance, or memory.
[1"] I.e., possibly the alternative of poverty would justify publication.

White—Unto the White Creator—
Than invest—Our Snow—

Thought belong to Him who gave it—
Then—to Him Who Bear   10
It's Corporeal illustration—Sell
The Royal Air—

In the Parcel—Be the Merchant
Of the Heavenly Grace—
But reduce no Human Spirit   15
To Disgrace of Price—
J. 709   F. 788   c. 1863   1929

They say that "Time assuages"—[1]
Time never did assuage—
An actual suffering strengthens
As Sinews do, with age—

Time is a Test of Trouble—   5
But not a Remedy—
If such it prove, it prove too
There was no Malady—
J. 686   F. 861   c. 1863   1896

Because I could not stop for Death—
He kindly stopped for me—
The Carriage held but just Ourselves—
And Immortality.

We slowly drove—He knew no haste   5
And I had put away
My labor and my leisure too,
For His Civility—

We passed the School, where Children strove
At Recess—in the Ring—   10
We passed the Fields of Gazing Grain—
We passed the Setting Sun—

Or rather—He passed Us—
The Dews drew quivering and chill—

-----

[1] Eases or reduces a hurt.

For only Gossamer,[1] my Gown—   15
My Tippet[2]—only Tulle—[3]

We paused before a House that seemed
A Swelling of the Ground—
The Roof was scarcely visible—
The Cornice[4]—in the Ground—   20

Since then—'tis Centuries—and yet
Feels shorter than the Day
I first surmised the Horses Heads
Were toward Eternity—
J. 712   F. 479   c. 1863   1890

She rose to His Requirement—dropt
The Playthings of Her Life
To take the honorable Work
Of Woman, and of Wife—

If ought[1'] She missed in Her new Day,   5
Of Amplitude, or Awe—
Or first Prospective—Or the Gold
In using, wear away,

It lay unmentioned—as the Sea
Develope Pearl, and Weed,   10
But only to Himself—be known
The Fathoms[2'] they abide—
J. 732   F. 857   c. 1863   1890

My Life had stood—a Loaded Gun—
In Corners—till a Day
The Owner passed—identified—
And carried Me away—

And now We roam in Sovreign Woods—   5
And now We hunt the Doe—
And every time I speak for Him—
The Mountains straight reply—

[1]Very fine fabric.
[2]Shoulder cape.
[3]Thin silk netting.
[4]Molding, often decorative, below the roof of
a building.

[1']Aught; anything.
[2']I.e., how deep they lie and in what surroundings. The fathom measures water depth.

And do I smile, such cordial light
Upon the Valley glow—
It is as a Vesuvian[1] face
Had let it's pleasure through—   10

And when at Night—Our good Day done—
I guard My Master's Head—
'Tis better than the Eider-Duck's[2]
Deep Pillow—to have shared—   15

To foe of His—I'm deadly foe—
None stir the second time—
On whom I lay a Yellow Eye—
Or an Emphatic Thumb—   20

Though I than He—may longer live
He longer must—than I—
For I have but the power to kill,
Without—the power to die—
J. 754   F. 764   c. 1863   1929

Presentiment—is that long Shadow—on the Lawn—
Indicative that Suns go down—

The Notice to the startled Grass
That Darkness—is about to pass—
J. 764   F. 487   c. 1863   1890

The Poets light but Lamps—
Themselves—go out—
The Wicks they stimulate—
If vital Light

Inhere as do the Suns—   5
Each Age a Lens
Disseminating their
Circumference—
J. 883   F. 930   c. 1864   1945

---

[1]Volcanic, like Mt. Vesuvius in Italy; capable
of breathing fire, light, and destruction.

[2]I.e., downy (with duck down).

A narrow Fellow in the Grass
Occasionally rides—
You may have met Him—did you not
His notice sudden is—

The Grass divides as with a Comb— 5
A spotted Shaft is seen—
And then it closes at your feet
And opens further on—

He likes a Boggy Acre
A Floor too cool for Corn— 10
Yet when a Boy, and Barefoot—
I more than once at Noon

Have passed, I thought, a Whip lash
Unbraiding in the Sun
When stooping to secure it 15
It wrinkled, and was gone—

Several of Nature's People
I know, and they know me—
I feel for them a transport
Of Cordiality— 20

But never met this Fellow
Attended, or alone
Without a tighter breathing
And Zero at the Bone—
J. 986   F. 1096   c. 1865   1866

_____

Perception of an object costs
Precise the Object's loss—
Perception in itself a Gain
Replying to it's Price—

The Object Absolute—is nought— 5
Perception sets it fair
And then upbraids[1] a Perfectness
That situates so far—
J. 1071   F. 1103   c. 1866   1914

_____

[1]Reproaches.

Title divine—is mine!
The Wife—without the Sign!
Acute Degree—conferred on me—
Empress of Calvary!
Royal—all but the Crown!   5
Betrothed—without the swoon
God sends us Women—
When you—hold—Garnet to Garnet—
Gold—to Gold—
Born—Bridalled—Shrouded—   10
In a Day—
"My Husband"—women say—
Stroking the Melody—
Is *this*—the way?
J. 1072   F. 194   c. 1862   1924

The Bustle in a House
The Morning after Death
Is solemnest of industries
Enacted upon Earth—

The Sweeping up the Heart   5
And putting Love away
We shall not want to use again
Until Eternity.
J. 1078   F. 1108   c. 1866   1890

Tell all the Truth but tell it slant—
Success in Circuit lies
Too bright for our infirm Delight
The Truth's superb surprise
As Lightning to the Children eased   5
With explanation kind
The Truth must dazzle gradually
Or every man be blind—
J. 1129   F. 1263   c. 1868   1945

He preached upon "Breadth" till it argued him narrow—
The Broad are too broad to define
And of "Truth" until it proclaimed him a Liar—
The Truth never flaunted a Sign—

Simplicity fled from his counterfeit presence   5
As Gold the Pyrites[1] would shun—
What confusion would cover the innocent Jesus
To meet so enabled a Man!
J. 1207   F. 1266   c. 1872   1891

———————

[A worksheet draft of this poem printed below reveals some of Dickinson's
characteristic ways of working. For other examples of variant readings, see
the three-volume Johnson edition and the manuscript books edited by
Franklin.]

He preached about Breadth till ~~we~~ knew ~~he was~~ narrow
        upon   *it argued him*
The Broad are too broad to define
And of Truth until it proclaimed him a Liar
The Truth never ~~hoisted~~ a sign—
            flaunted
Simplicity fled from his counterfeit presence
As Gold the Pyrites would shun
       a
What confusion would cover the innocent Jesus
To meet so ~~learned~~ a man—
at meeting   *Religious*
        enabled
         so accomplished
          discerning
          accoutred
          established
          conclusive

———————

Not with a Club, the Heart is broken
Nor with a Stone—
A Whip so small you could not see it
I've known

To lash the Magic Creature   5
Till it fell,
Yet that Whip's Name
Too noble then to tell.

Magnanimous as Bird
By Boy descried—[1']   10

———————

[1] A bright, brassy metal known as fool's gold.
[1'] Sought out, found.

Singing unto the Stone[2]
Of which it died—

Shame need not crouch
In such an Earth as Our's—
Shame—stand erect—   15
The Universe is your's.
    J. 1304   F. 1349   c. 1874   1896

What mystery pervades a well!
The water lives so far—
A neighbor from another world
Residing in a jar

Whose limit none have ever seen,   5
But just his lid of glass—
Like looking every time you please
In an abyss's face!

The grass does not appear afraid,
I often wonder he
Can stand so close and look so bold   10
At what is awe to me.

Related somehow they may be,
The sedge stands next the sea—
Where he is floorless   15
And does no timidity betray

But nature is a stranger yet;
The ones that cite her most[1]
Have never passed her haunted house,
Nor simplified her ghost.[2']   20

To pity those that know her not
Is helped by the regret
That those who know her, know her less
The nearer her they get.[3]
    J. 1400   F. 1433   c. 1877   1896

---

[2]I.e., stone fired from a slingshot.
[1]Refer to her most often as an authority,
example, or proof.
[2']Spirit.
[3]Dickinson sent Sue a variant of the last two
stanzas. It is signed "Emily—"and was written about 1877.
    But Susan is a Stranger yet—

The Ones who cite her most
Have never scaled her Haunted House
Nor compromised her Ghost—
To pity those who know her not
Is helped by the regret
That those who know her know her less
The nearer her they get—

A Route of Evanescence
With a revolving Wheel—
A Resonance of Emerald—
A Rush of Cochineal—[1]
And every Blossom on the Bush   5
Adjusts it's tumbled Head—
The mail from Tunis,[2] probably,
An easy Morning's Ride—[3]
J. 1463   F. 1489   c. 1879   1891

The Bible is an antique Volume—
Written by faded Men
At the suggestion of Holy Spectres—
Subjects—Bethlehem—
Eden—the ancient Homestead—   5
Satan—the Brigadier—
Judas—the Great Defaulter—
David—the Troubadour—
Sin—a distinguished Precipice
Others must resist—   10
Boys that "believe" are very lonesome—
Other Boys are "lost"—
Had but the Tale a warbling Teller—
All the Boys would come—
Orpheus' Sermon captivated—   15
It did not condemn—[1']
J. 1545   F. 1577   c. 1882   1924

Rearrange a "Wife's" affection!
When they dislocate my Brain!
Amputate my freckled Bosom!
Make me bearded like a man!

Blush, my spirit, in thy Fastness—   5
Blush, my unacknowledged clay—
Seven years of troth have taught thee
More than Wifehood ever may!

---

[1]Brilliant red dye.
[2]An African city in Tunisia, near the ancient site of Carthage.
[3]Dickinson sent copies of this poem in several letters to friends and referred to it as "A Humming Bird."

[1']Dickinson sent this poem to her nephew Ned Gilbert when he was twenty-one. She titled an earlier version of the poem "Diagnosis of the Bible, by a Boy—." In Dickinson's view, the Bible's didactic tone alienates many readers.

Love that never leaped its socket—
Trust entrenched in narrow pain—
Constancy thro' fire—awarded—
Anguish—bare of anodyne![1]   10

Burden—borne so far triumphant—
None suspect me of the crown,
For I wear the "Thorns"[2] till *Sunset*—   15
Then—my Diadem[3] put on.

Big my Secret but it's *bandaged*—
It will never get away
Till the Day its Weary Keeper
Leads it through the Grave to thee.[4]   20
J. 1737   F. 267   c. 1861   1945

_____

To make a prairie it takes a clover and one bee,
One clover, and a bee,
And revery.
The revery alone will do,
If bees are few.   5
J. 1755   F. 1779   ?   1896

Letters

To Abiah Root

29 January 1850

Very dear Abiah.[1']

The folks have all gone away—they thought that they left me alone, and
contrived things to amuse me should they stay long, and *I* be lonely. Lonely
indeed—they did'nt look, and they could'nt have seen if they had, who
should bear me company. *Three* here instead of *one*—would'nt it scare
them? A curious trio, part earthly and part spiritual two of us—the other all
heaven, and no earth. *God* is sitting here, looking into my very soul to see if
I think right tho'ts. Yet I am not afraid, for I try to be right and good, and

_____

[1]Painkilling medicine.
[2]A reference to the crown of thorns that Christ
was forced to wear before the crucifixion.
[3]Crown or headband, often of jewels, worn by
royalty.
[4]This poem was originally copied into fascicle
11 by Dickinson around 1861. Seven years
earlier would have been 1854, a year after

Sue became engaged to Austin. Someone
removed the poem from fascicle 11 after
Dickinson's death.
[1']Abiah Root was among Dickinson's early
circle of friends. Letters to Abiah are intimate and affectionate. No correspondence
remains after 1854, the year Abiah Root
married.

he knows every one of my struggles. He looks very gloriously, and everything bright seems dull beside him, and I dont dare to look directly at him for fear I shall die. Then *you* are here—dressed in that quiet black gown and cap—that funny little cap I used to laugh at you about, and you dont appear to be thinking about anything in particular, not in one of your *breaking dish* moods I take it, you seem aware that I'm writing you, and are amused I should think at any such friendly manifestation when you are already present. *Success* however even in making a fool of one's-self is'nt to be despised, so I shall persist in writing, and you may in laughing at me, if you are fully aware of the value of time as regards your immortal spirit. I cant say that I advise you to laugh, but if you are punished, and I warned you, that can be no business of mine. So I fold up my arms, and leave you to fate—may it deal very kindly with you! The trinity winds up with me, as you may have surmised, and I certainly would'nt be at the fag end but for civility to you. This selfsacrificing spirit will be the ruin of me! I am occupied principally with a cold just now, and the dear creature *will* have so much attention that my time slips away amazingly. It has heard *so* much of New Englanders, of their kind attentions to strangers, that it's come all the way from the Alps to determine the truth of the tale—it says the half was'nt told it, and I begin to be afraid it was'nt. Only think, came all the way from that distant Switzerland to find what was the truth! Neither husband—protector—nor friend accompanied it, and so utter a state of loneliness gives friends if nothing else. You are dying of curiosity, let me arrange that pillow to make your exit easier! I stayed at home all Saturday afternoon, and treated some disagreable people who insisted upon calling here as tolerably as I could— when evening shades began to fall, I turned upon my heel, and walked. Attracted by the gaiety visible in the street I still kept walking till a little creature pounced upon a thin shawl I wore, and commenced riding—I stopped, and begged the creature to alight, as I was fatigued already, and quite unable to assist others. It would'nt get down, and commenced talking to itself—"cant be New England—must have made some mistake, disappointed in my reception, dont agree with accounts, Oh what a world of deception, and fraud—Marm, will [you] tell me the name of this country— it's Asia Minor, is'nt it. I intended to stop in New England." By this time I was so completely exhausted that I made no farther effort to rid me of my load, and travelled home at a moderate jog, paying no attention whatever to it, got into the house, threw off both bonnet, and shawl, and out flew my tormentor, and putting both arms around my neck began to kiss me immoderately, and express so much love, it completely bewildered me. Since then it has slept in my bed, eaten from my plate, lived with me everywhere, and will tag me through life for all I know. I think I'll wake first, and get out of bed, and leave it, but early, or late, it is dressed before me, and sits on the side of the bed looking right in my face with such a comical expression it almost makes me laugh in spite of myself. I cant call it interesting, but it certainly *is* curious—has two peculiarities which would quite win your heart, a huge pocket-handkerchief, and a very red nose. The first seems so very *abundant*, it gives you the idea of independence, and prosperity in business. The last brings up the "jovial bowl,[2] my boys," and such an association's worth the having. If it *ever* gets tired of *me*, I will forward it to *you*—you would love it for *my* sake, if not for it's own, it will tell you some queer stories about me—how I sneezed so loud one night that the family thought the last trump[3] was sounding, and climbed into the currant-bushes to get out of the way—how the rest of the people arrayed in long night-gowns folded their arms, and were waiting—but this is a wicked story, it can tell some *better* ones. Now my dear friend, let me tell you that these last thoughts are fictions—vain imaginations to lead astray foolish young women. They are flowers of speech, they both *make*, and *tell* deliberate falsehoods, avoid them as the snake, and turn aside as from the *Bottle* snake, and I dont *think* you will be harmed. Honestly tho', a snake bite is a serious matter, and there cant be too much said, or done about it. The big serpent bites the deepest, and we get so accustomed to it's bites that we dont mind about them. "Verily I say unto you fear *him*." . . .

Your very sincere, and *wicked* friend,
Emily E Dickinson.

Letter 31

To Austin Dickinson

17 October 1851

. . . How glad I am you are well—you must try hard to be careful and not get sick again. I hope you will be better than ever you were in your life when you come home *this time*, for it never seemed so long since we have seen you. I thank you for such a long letter, and yet if I might choose, *the next* should be a longer. I think a letter just about *three days* long would make me happier than any other kind of one—if you please, dated at Boston, but thanks be to our Father, you may conclude it *here*. Everything has changed since my other letter—the doors are shut this morning, and all the kitchen wall is covered with chilly flies who are trying to warm themselves—poor things, they do not understand that there are no summer mornings remaining to them and me and they have a bewildered air which is really very droll, did'nt one feel *sorry* for them. You would say t'was a gloomy morning if you were sitting here—the frost has been severe and the few lingering leaves seem anxious to be going and wrap their faded cloaks more closely about them as if to shield them from the chilly northeast wind. The earth looks like some poor old lady who by dint of pains has bloomed e'en till *now*, yet in a forgetful moment a few silver hairs from out her cap come stealing, and she tucks them back so hastily and thinks nobody *sees*. The cows are going to pasture and little boys with their hands in their pockets are whistling to try to keep warm. Dont think that the sky will frown so the day when you come home! She will smile and look happy, and be full of sunshine *then*—

---

[2]A bowl of alcoholic punch.　　　[3]Trumpet.

and even *should* she frown upon her child returning, there is *another* sky ever serene and fair, and there is *another* sunshine, tho' it be darkness there—never mind faded forests, Austin, never mind silent fields—*here* is a little forest whose leaf is ever green, here is a *brighter* garden, where not a frost has been, in its unfading flowers I hear the bright bee hum, prithee, my Brother, into *my* garden come!¹

Your very aff
Sister.

Letter 58

To Susan Gilbert (Dickinson)

late April 1852

So sweet and still, and Thee, Oh Susie, what need I more, to make my heaven whole?

Sweet Hour, blessed Hour, to carry me to you, and to bring you back to me, long enough to snatch one kiss, and whisper Good bye, again.

I have thought of it all day, Susie, and I fear of but little else, and when I was gone to meeting it filled my mind so full, I could not find a *chink* to put the worthy pastor; when he said "Our Heavenly Father," I said "Oh Darling Sue"; when he read the 100th Psalm, I kept saying your precious letter all over to myself, and Susie, when they sang—it would have made you laugh to hear one little voice, piping to the departed. I made up words and kept singing how I loved you, and you had gone, while all the rest of the choir were singing Hallelujahs. I presume nobody heard me, because I sang *so small*, but it was a kind of a comfort to think I might put them out, singing of you. I a'nt there this afternoon, tho', because I am here, writing a little letter to my dear Sue, and I am very happy. I think of ten weeks—Dear One, and I think of love, and you, and my heart grows full and warm, and my breath stands still. The sun does'nt shine at all, but I can feel a sunshine stealing into my soul and making it all summer, and every thorn, a *rose*. And I pray that such summer's sun shine on my Absent One, and cause her bird to sing!

You have been happy, Susie, and now are sad—and the whole world seems lone; but it wont be so always, "some days *must* be dark and dreary"! You wont cry any more, will you, Susie, for my father will be your father, and my home will be your home, and where you go, I will go, and we will lie side by side in the kirkyard.

I have parents on earth, dear Susie, but your's are in the skies, and I have an earthly fireside, but you have one above, and you have a "Father in Heaven," where I have *none*—and *sister* in heaven, and I know they love you dearly, and think of you every day.

---

¹Note the poem embedded in this letter.

Oh I wish I had half so many dear friends as you in heaven—I could'nt spare them now—but to know they had got there safely, and should suffer nevermore—Dear Susie! ...

Emilie—

Letter 88

To Susan Gilbert (Dickinson)

27 June 1852

... Susie, will you indeed come home next Saturday, and be my own again, and kiss me as you used to? Shall I indeed behold you, not "darkly, but face to face" or am I *fancying* so, and dreaming blessed dreams from which the day will wake me? I hope for you so much, and feel so eager for you, feel that I *cannot* wait, feel that *now* I must have you—that the expectation once more to see your face again, makes me feel hot and feverish, and my heart beats so fast—I go to sleep at night, and the first thing I know, I am sitting there wide awake, and clasping my hands tightly, and thinking of next Saturday, and "never a bit" of you.

Sometimes I must have Saturday before tomorrow comes, and I wonder if it w'd make any difference with God, to give it to me *today*, and I'd let him have Monday, to make him a Saturday; and then I feel so funnily, and wish the precious day would'nt come quite so soon, till I could know how to feel, and get my thoughts ready for it.

Why, Susie, it seems to me as if my absent Lover was coming home so soon—and my heart must be so busy, making ready for him.

While the minister this morning was giving an account of the Roman Catholic system, and announcing several facts which were usually startling, I was trying to make up my mind wh' of the two was prettiest to go and welcome *you* in, my fawn colored dress, or my blue dress. Just as I had decided by all means to wear the blue, down came the minister's fist with a terrible rap on the counter, and Susie, it scared me so, I hav'nt got over it yet, but I'm glad I reached a conclusion! I walked home from meeting with Mattie, and *incidentally* quite, something was said of you, and I think one of us remarked that you would be here next Sunday; well—Susie—what it was *I* dont presume to know, but my gaiters seemed to leave me, and I seemed to move on wings—and I move on wings now, Susie, on wings as white as snow, and as bright as the summer sunshine—because I am with you, and so few short days, you are with me at home. Be patient then, my Sister, for the hours will haste away, and Oh *so* soon! Susie, I write most hastily, and very carelessly too, for it is time for me to get the supper, and my mother is gone and besides, my darling, so near I seem to you, that I *disdain* this pen, and wait for a *warmer* language. With Vinnie's love, and my love, I am once more

Your Emilie—

Letter 96

To Samuel Bowles

about February 1861

Dear friend.[1]

You remember the little "Meeting"—we held for you—last spring? We met again—Saturday—'Twas May—when we "adjourned"—but then Adjourns—are all—The meetings wore alike—Mr Bowles—The Topic—did not tire us—so we chose no new—We voted to remember you—so long as both should live—including Immortality. To count you as ourselves—except sometimes more tenderly—as now—when you are ill—and we—the haler of the two—and so I bring the Bond—we sign so many times—for you to read, when Chaos comes—or Treason—or Decay—still witnessing for Morning.

We hope—it is a tri-Hope—composed of Vinnie's—Sue's—and mine— that you took no more pain—riding in the sleigh.

We hope our joy to see you—gave of it's own degree—to you—We pray for your new health—the prayer that goes not down—when they shut the church—We offer you our cups—stintless—as to the Bee—the Lily, her new Liquors—

Would you like summer? Taste of our's.

Spices? Buy here!

Ill! We have berries, for the parching!

Weary! Furloughs of down!

Perplexed! Estates of violet trouble ne'er looked on!

Captive! We bring reprieve of roses!

Fainting! Flasks of air!

Even for Death, a fairy medicine—

But, which is it, sir?

Emily

Letter 229

To recipient unknown

about 1861

Master.[1']

If you saw a bullet hit a Bird—and he told you he was'nt shot—you might weep at his courtesy, but you would certainly doubt his word.

---

[1]Samuel Bowles was the editor of the *Spring-field Daily Republican*, Amherst's local daily, a politically liberal and nationally influential newspaper. Bowles and his wife were lifelong friends of Dickinson's. Some scholars argue that Dickinson was in love with Bowles, and for some he is a likely candidate for the "Master" whose identity has never been revealed.

[1']Drafts of three letters to "Master" were among Dickinson's papers when she died. It is not known if final copies were ever made and sent. She refers to herself as "Daisy" in two of the letters.

One drop more from the gash that stains your Daisy's bosom—then would you *believe?* Thomas' faith in Anatomy, was stronger than his faith in faith.[2] God made me—[Sir] Master—I did'nt be—myself. I dont know how it was done. He built the heart in me—Bye and bye it outgrew me—and like the little mother—with the big child—I got tired holding him. I heard of a thing called "Redemption"—which rested men and women. You remember I asked you for it—you gave me something else. I forgot the Redemption [in the Redeemed—I did'nt tell you for a long time, but I knew you had altered me—I] and was tired—no more—[so dear did this stranger become that were it, or my breath—the Alternative—I had tossed the fellow away with a smile.] I am older—tonight, Master—but the love is the same—so are the moon and the crescent. If it had been God's will that I might breathe where you breathed—and find the place—myself—at night—if I (can) never forget that I am not with you—and that sorrow and frost are nearer than I—if I wish with a might I cannot repress—that mine were the Queen's place—the love of the Plantagenet[3] is my only apology—To come nearer than presby- teries[4]—and nearer than the new Coat—that the Tailor made—the prank of the Heart at play on the Heart—in holy Holiday—is forbidden me—You make me say it over—I fear you laugh—when I do not see—[but] "Chillon"[5] is not funny. Have you the Heart in your breast—Sir—is it set like mine—a little to the left—has it the misgiving—if it wake in the night—perchance— itself to it—a timbrel is it—itself to it a tune?

These things are [reverent] holy, Sir, I touch them [reverently] hallowed, but persons who pray—dare remark [our] "Father"! You say I do not tell you all—Daisy confessed—and denied not.

Vesuvius dont talk—Etna—dont—[Thy] one of them—said a syllable— a thousand years ago, and Pompeii heard it, and hid forever—[6] She could'nt look the world in the face, afterward—I suppose—Bashfull Pompeii! "Tell you of the want"—you know what a leech is, dont you—and [remember that] Daisy's arm is small—and you have felt the horizon hav'nt you—and did the sea—never come so close as to make you dance?

I dont know what you can do for it—thank you—Master—but if I had the Beard on my cheek—like you—and you—had Daisy's petals—and you cared so for me—what would become of you? Could you forget me in fight, or flight—or the foreign land? Could'nt Carlo,[7] and you and I walk in the meadows an hour—and nobody care but the Bobolink—and *his*—a *silver* scruple? I used to think when I died—I could see you—so I died as fast as I could—but the "Corporation"[8] are going Heaven too so [Eternity] wont be sequestered—now [at all]—Say I may wait for you—say I need go with no stranger to the to me—untried [country] fold—I waited a long time—

---

[2] Doubting Thomas (John 20:25) required physical proof of Christ's resurrection.
[3] The family name of a line of English sover- eigns is used here perhaps as a generic term for royalty.
[4] Priests or ruling elders of a church.

[5] A castle prison in a poem by Lord Byron.
[6] Vesuvius and Etna are volcanoes in Italy and Sicily. Vesuvius, erupting, destroyed the town of Pompeii in the first century A.D.
[7] Dickinson's dog.
[8] Ruling elders, perhaps of a church.

Master—but I can wait more—wait till my hazel hair is dappled—and you carry the cane—then I can look at my watch—and if the Day is too far declined—we can take the chances [of] for Heaven—What would you do with me if I came "in white?"[9] Have you the little chest to put the Alive—in?

I want to see you more—Sir—than all I wish for in this world—and the wish—altered a little—will be my only one—for the skies.

Could you come to New England—[this summer—could] would you come to Amherst—Would you like to come—Master?

[Would it do harm—yet we both fear God—] Would Daisy disappoint you—no—she would'nt—Sir—it were comfort forever—just to look in your face, while you looked in mine—then I could play in the woods till Dark— till you take me where Sundown cannot find us—and the true keep coming—till the town is full. [Will you tell me if you will?]

I did'nt think to tell you, you did'nt come to me "in white," nor ever told me why,

> No Rose, yet felt myself a'bloom,
> No Bird—yet rode in Ether.

Letter 233

To Susan Gilbert Dickinson

date uncertain

Dear Sue—[1]

Your praise is good—to me—because I *know* it *knows*—and *suppose*—it *means*—

Could I make you and Austin—proud—sometime—a great way off— 'twould give me taller feet—

Here is a crumb—for the "Ring dove"—and a spray for *his Nest*,[2] a little while ago—just—"*Sue*."

Emily.

Letter 238

[9]This may mean dressed in white, a color Dickinson associated with immortality. Late in her life she is said to have dressed exclusively in white. Or here she may be associating white with the paper on which she presented herself in letters and poems.
[1]This note is part of an exchange of remarks about "Safe in their Alabaster Chambers," Poem J. 238. Susan seems to have suggested changes in the original version of the poem. After Dickinson sent the next version, Susan praised the first verse but wrote that she was still not suited with the second. So Dickinson sent a third version along with this note. The exchange reveals how exacting a critic Susan could be and how willing Dickinson was to please her.
[2]"Ring dove" was the term Susan had used for her new baby. Dickinson probably sent a "crumb" from her kitchen and a "spray" from her garden with the note.

To T. W. Higginson

15 April 1862

Mr Higginson,[1]

Are you too deeply occupied to say if my Verse is alive?

The Mind is so near itself—it cannot see, distinctly—and I have none to ask—

Should you think it breathed—and had you the leisure to tell me, I should feel quick gratitude—

If I make the mistake—that you dared to tell me—would give me sincerer honor—toward you—

I enclose my name—asking you, if you please—Sir—to tell me what is true?

That you will not betray me—it is needless to ask—since Honor is it's own pawn—

Letter 260

To T. W. Higginson

25 April 1862

Mr Higginson,

Your kindness claimed earlier gratitude—but I was ill—and write today, from my pillow.

Thank you for the surgery[1']—it was not so painful as I supposed. I bring you others[2]—as you ask—though they might not differ—

While my thought is undressed—I can make the distinction, but when I put them in the Gown—they look alike, and numb.[3]

You asked how old I was? I made no verse—but one or two—until this winter—Sir—

I had a terror—since September—I could tell to none—and so I sing, as the Boy does by the Burying Ground—because I am afraid—[4]You inquire my Books—For Poets—I have Keats—and Mr and Mrs Browning. For Prose—Mr Ruskin—Sir Thomas Browne—and the Revelations.[5] I went to

---

[1]Dickinson wrote this unsigned letter to Higginson after reading his "Letter to a Young Contributor" in the *Atlantic Monthly*, April 1862. She enclosed a card with her signature and four poems. The correspondence developed into a friendship that lasted a lifetime.

[1']Perhaps cuts in poems suggested by Higginson.

[2]More poems.

[3]The imagery of "thought," "undressed," and "in the Gown" is unclear, but probably refers to Higginson's previous letter or to his "Letter to a Young Contributor."

[4]There has been much critical speculation on "the terror since September." Biographers have suggested a spiritual crisis, fear of blindness due to an acute eye problem, or an emotional breakdown the result of abandonment by someone Dickinson loved. The exact nature of the "terror" cannot be determined.

[5]Dickinson lists five English writers—three nineteenth-century poets, a nineteenth-century art critic, and a seventeenth-century prose writer—and the last book of the Bible.

school—but in your manner of the phrase—had no education. When a little Girl, I had a friend, who taught me Immortality—but venturing too near, himself—he never returned—Soon after, my Tutor, died—and for several years, my Lexicon—was my only companion—Then I found one more—but he was not contented I be his scholar—so he left the Land.[6]

You ask of my Companions Hills—Sir—and the Sundown—and a Dog—large as myself, that my Father bought me—They are better than Beings—because they know—but do not tell—and the noise in the Pool, at Noon—excels my Piano. I have a Brother and Sister—My Mother does not care for thought—and Father, too busy with his Briefs[7]—to notice what we do—He buys me many Books—but begs me not to read them—because he fears they joggle the Mind. They are religious—except me—and address an Eclipse, every morning—whom they call their "Father." But I fear my story fatigues you—I would like to learn—Could you tell me how to grow—or is it unconveyed—like Melody—or Witchcraft?

You speak of Mr Whitman—I never read his Book—but was told that he was disgraceful—[8]

I read Miss Prescott's "Circumstance," but it followed me, in the Dark—so I avoided her—[9]

Two Editors of Journals came to my Father's House, this winter—and asked me for my Mind—and when I asked them "Why," they said I was penurious—and they, would use it for the World—[10]

I could not weigh myself—Myself—

My size felt small—to me—I read your Chapters in the Atlantic—and experienced honor for you—I was sure you would not reject a confiding question—

Is this—Sir—what you asked me to tell you?

Your friend,
E—Dickinson.

Letter 261

---

[6]None of these—the "friend," the "Tutor," the one who "left the Land"—can be positively identified.
[7]Legal documents.
[8]Walt Whitman's *Leaves of Grass* was first published in 1855. Readers were shocked by the poet's descriptions of his passions and appetites. The innovative appearance of the poetry with its unconventional punctuation may have prompted Higginson to ask if Dickinson had read Whitman. He seems to be looking for stylistic influences.

[9]Harriet Prescott Spofford's "Circumstance," published in the *Atlantic Monthly* in May 1860, is a terrifying story of a woman held hostage "in a tree by a beast which is pacified only when she sings to him."
[10]Dr. Holland and Samuel Bowles, both of the *Springfield Daily Republican*, appear to have urged Dickinson to publish. By this time, Bowles had published one of her poems, probably without her permission.

To T. W. Higginson

7 June 1862

Dear friend.

Your letter gave no Drunkenness, because I tasted Rum before—Domingo comes but once[1]—yet I have had few pleasures so deep as your opinion, and if I tried to thank you, my tears would block my tongue—

My dying Tutor told me that he would like to live till I had been a poet, but Death was much of Mob as I could master—then—And when far afterward—a sudden light on Orchards, or a new fashion in the wind troubled my attention—I felt a palsy, here—the Verses just relieve—

Your second letter surprised me, and for a moment, swung—I had not supposed it. Your first—gave no dishonor, because the True—are not ashamed—I thanked you for your justice—but could not drop the Bells whose jingling cooled my Tramp—Perhaps the Balm, seemed better, because you bled me, first.

I smile when you suggest that I delay "to publish"—that being foreign to my thought, as Firmament to Fin—

If fame belonged to me, I could not escape her—if she did not, the longest day would pass me on the chase—and the approbation of my Dog, would forsake me—then—My Barefoot-Rank is better—

You think my gait "spasmodic"—I am in danger—Sir—

You think me "uncontrolled"[2]—I have no Tribunal.[3]

Would you have time to be the "friend" you should think I need? I have a little shape—it would not crowd your Desk—nor make much Racket as the Mouse, that dents your Galleries—

If I might bring you what I do—not so frequent to trouble you—and ask you if I told it clear—'twould be control, to me—

The Sailor cannot see the North—but knows the Needle[4] can—

The "hand you stretch me in the Dark," I put mine in, and turn away—I have no Saxon,[5] now—

> As if I asked a common Alms,
> And in my wondering hand
> A Stranger pressed a Kingdom,
> And I, bewildered, stand—
> As if I asked the Orient[6]
> Had it for me a Morn—

[1]Santo Domingo is the capital of the rum-producing Dominican Republic. Dickinson is saying that she had tasted praise before, and that the first taste is like no other.

[2]Dickinson is quoting Higginson, who was apparently describing rhythms and phrasing in the poems.

[3]A position from which to judge herself and pronounce her own sentence. It is likely that Dickinson is being ironic. There is no indication that she ever adopted any of Higginson's suggested changes.

[4]Needle of a compass.

[5]The English language. Dickinson is saying that she has no words.

[6]The East.

And it should lift it's purple Dikes,
And shatter me with Dawn!

But, will you be my Preceptor, Mr Higginson?

Your friend
E Dickinson—

Letter 265

To T. W. Higginson

July 1862

Could you believe me—without? I had no portrait, now,[1] but am small, like the Wren, and my Hair is bold, like the Chestnut Bur—and my eyes, like the Sherry in the Glass, that the Guest leaves—Would this do just as well?

It often alarms Father—He says Death might occur, and he has Molds of all the rest—but has no Mold of me, but I noticed the Quick wore off those things, in a few days, and forestall the dishonor—You will think no caprice of me—

You said "Dark." I know the Butterfly—and the Lizard—and the Orchis—

Are not those *your* Countrymen?

I am happy to be your scholar, and will deserve the kindness, I cannot repay.

If you truly consent, I recite, now—

Will you tell me my fault, frankly as to yourself, for I had rather wince, than die. Men do not call the surgeon, to commend—the Bone, but to set it, Sir, and fracture within, is more critical. And for this, Preceptor, I shall bring you—Obedience—the Blossom from my Garden, and every gratitude I know. Perhaps you smile at me. I could not stop for that—My Business is Circumference—An ignorance, not of Customs, but if caught with the Dawn—or the Sunset see me—Myself the only Kangaroo among the Beauty, Sir, if you please, it afflicts me, and I thought that instruction would take it away.

Because you have much business, beside the growth of me—you will appoint, yourself, how often I shall come—without your inconvenience. And if at any time—you regret you received me, or I prove a different fabric to that you supposed—you must banish me—

When I state myself, as the Representative of the Verse—it does not mean—me—but a supposed person. . . .

[1]Here, and in the following paragraph, she explains that she has no photograph of herself to send to Higginson. At age ten a portrait had been painted of the three Dickinson children, and when she was about sixteen, her daguerrotype was made, but, as she tells Higginson, she had never had a photograph taken. This appears to have been the case throughout her life since there are no verified photographs or portraits of Dickinson as an adult.

To thank you, baffles me. Are you perfectly powerful? Had I a pleasure you had not, I could delight to bring it.

Your Scholar

Letter 268

To Mrs. J. G. Holland

early May 1866

Dear Sister,

After you went, a low wind warbled through the house like a spacious bird, making it high but lonely. When you had gone the love came. I supposed it would. The supper of the heart is when the guest has gone.

Shame is so intrinsic in a strong affection we must all experience Adam's reticence. I suppose the street that the lover travels is thenceforth divine, incapable of turnpike aims.

That you be with me annuls fear and I await Commencement[1] with merry resignation. Smaller than David you clothe me with extreme Goliath.

Friday I tasted life. It was a vast morsel. A circus passed the house—still I feel the red in my mind though the drums are out.

The book you mention, I have not met. Thank you for tenderness.

The lawn is full of south and the odors tangle, and I hear today for the first the river in the tree.

You mentioned spring's delaying—I blamed her for the opposite. I would eat evanescence slowly.

Vinnie is deeply afflicted in the death of her dappled cat, though I convince her it is immortal which assists her some. Mother resumes lettuce, involving my transgression—suggestive of yourself, however, which endears disgrace.

"House" is being "cleaned." I prefer pestilence. That is more classic and less fell. . . .

Emily.

Letter 318

To Susan Gilbert Dickinson

about 1870

Oh Matchless Earth—We underrate the chance to dwell in Thee

Letter 347

---

[1]Commencement exercises at Amherst College.

To Susan Gilbert Dickinson

about 1870

We meet no Stranger but Ourself.

Letter 348

To T. W. Higginson

1876

Nature is a Haunted House—but Art—a House that tries to be haunted.

Letter 459A

To Otis P. Lord [rough draft]

about 1878

My lovely Salem smiles at me I seek his Face so often—but I am past disguises (have dropped—) (have done with guises—)[1]
I confess that I love him—I rejoice that I love him—I thank the maker of Heaven and Earth that gave him me to love—the exultation floods me—I can not find my channel—The Creek turned Sea at thoughts of thee—will you punish it—[turn I] involuntary Bankruptcy as the Debtors say. Could that be a Crime—How could that be crime—Incarcerate me in yourself—that will punish me—Threading with you this lovely maze which is not Life or Death tho it has the intangibleness of one and the flush of the other waking for your sake on Day made magical with [before] you before I went to sleep— What pretty phrase—we went to sleep as if it were a country—let us make it one—we could (will) make it one, my native Land—my Darling come oh *be* a patriot now—Love is a patriot now Gave her life for its (its) country Has it meaning now—Oh nation of the soul thou hast thy freedom now

Letter 559

To Susan Gilbert Dickinson

about 1878

I must wait a few Days before seeing you—You are too momentous. But remember it is idolatry, not indifference.

Emily.

Letter 581

---

[1]Dickinson drafted letters as she did poems— writing several words or versions of a line or phrase, and then making a choice. This is a rough copy of a piece of a letter to Judge Otis Lord, a friend of the Dickinson family.

Dickinson corresponded with Lord, who lived in Salem, Massachusetts, from about 1878 to his death in 1884. Her letters indicate that the two were in love with each other.

To Susan Gilbert Dickinson

early October 1883

Dear Sue—

The Vision of Immortal Life has been fulfilled—[1]

How simply at the last the Fathom comes! The Passenger and not the Sea, we find surprises us—

Gilbert rejoiced in Secrets—

His Life was panting with them—With what menace of Light he cried "Dont tell, Aunt Emily"! Now my ascended Playmate must instruct *me*. Show us, prattling Preceptor, but the way to thee!

He knew no niggard movement—His Life was full of Boon—The Playthings of the Dervish were not so wild as his—

No crescent was this Creature—He traveled from the Full—

Such soar, but never set—

I see him in the Star, and meet his sweet velocity in everything that flies—His Life was like the Bugle, which winds itself away, his Elegy an echo—his Requiem ecstasy—

Dawn and Meridian in one.

Wherefore would he wait, wronged only of Night, which he left for us—

Without a speculation, our little Ajax[2] spans the whole—

> Pass to thy Rendezvous of Light,
> Pangless except for us—
> Who slowly ford the Mystery
> Which thou hast leaped across!

Emily.

Letter 868

To Susan Gilbert Dickinson

about 1884

Morning[1']
might come
by Accident—
Sister—
Night comes
by Event—
To believe the
final line of

---

[1]Gilbert, Susan and Austin's youngest child, died of typhoid fever on October 5, 1883.
[2]A hero of Greek mythology known for his size and his courage.

[1']Because Thomas Johnson inaccurately represents margins, line breaks, and spaces between apparent stanzas, we reprint here an exact copy of the original manuscript of what can be seen as a letter-poem.

the Card² would
foreclose Faith—
Faith is *Doubt*—

    Sister—
Show me
Eternity—and
I will show
you Memory—
Both in one
package lain
And lifted
back again—

Be Sue—while
I am Emily—
Be next—what
you have ever
been—Infinity—

Letter 912

²"The final line of the Card" may refer to a standard Victorian greeting card or to a message written on a card. Or the card may be a playing card or a fortune-telling card. By metaphorical extension the "Card" may refer to the Bible.

ACKNOWLEDGMENTS

William Apess. "Eulogy on King Philip," reprinted from *On Our Own Ground: The Complete Writings of William Apess*, edited by Barry O'Connell. Copyright © 1992 by the University of Massachusetts Press and published by the University of Massachusetts Press.

Mary Boykin Chesnut. Excerpts from *Mary Chesnut's Civil War*, edited by C. Vann Woodward. Copyright © 1981 by Yale University Press. Reprinted by permission of the publisher.

Angela Davis. "Reflections on the Black Woman's Role in the Community of Slaves," Black Scholar no. 4 (1971): 4–7. Reprinted by permission of the author.

Emily Dickinson. Reprinted by permission of the publishers and the Trustees of Amherst College from *The Poems of Emily Dickinson*, edited by Thomas H. Johnson, Cambridge, Mass.: The Belknap Press of Harvard University Press. Copyright © 1951, 1955, 1979, 1983 by the President and Fellows of Harvard College.
Reprinted by permission of the publishers from *The Letters of Emily Dickinson*, edited by Thomas H. Johnson, Cambridge, Mass.: The Belknap Press of Harvard University Press. Copyright © 1958, 1986 by The President and Fellows of Harvard College; 1914, 1924, 1932, 1942 by Martha Dickinson Bianchi; 1952 by Alfred Leete Hampson; 1960 by Mary L. Hampson.

José Griego. "La comradre sebastiana," "Los tres hermanos," "El Obispo," and "El indito de las cien vacas," from *Cuentos: Tales from the Hispanic Southwest* selected by José Griego y Maestas, retold in English by Rudolfo A. Anaya. Copyright © 1980 Museum of New Mexico Press. Reprinted with permission.

Julia Ward Howe. "The Hermaphrodite," reprinted from *The Hermaphrodite: Legacies of Nineteenth-Century American Women Writers*

by Julia Howard Howe, edited by Sharon Harris and Karen Danduran. By permission of the University of Nebraska Press. Copyright © 2004 by the University of Nebraska Press.

James Weldon Johnson and J. Rosamond Johnson. "Songs of the Slaves: Lay Dis Body Down," copyright © 1977 James Weldon Johnson and J. Rosamond Johnson, *The Books of American Negro Spirituals*. Reprinted by permission of Da Capo Press, a member of the Perseus Books Group.

Leon Litwack. From "North of Slavery: The Negro in the Free States," Leon F. Litwack, Copyright © University of Chicago Press, 1961.

Herman Melville. "Bartleby, the Scrivener: A Story of Wall-Street," "The Paradise of Bachelors and the Tartarus of Maids," "Benito Cereno," and "Hawthorne and His Mosses: By a Virginian Spending July in Vermont," from *The Piazza Tales: And Other Prose Pieces, 1839–1860* by Herman Melville, edited by Harrison Hayford and Merton M. Sealts, Jr. Copyright © Northwestern University Press, 1987. Pages 43–132 from Billy Budd, Sailor by Herman Melville, edited by Harrison Hayford and Merton M. Sealts, Jr. Copyright © 1962. Reprinted by permission of the University of Chicago Press and the editors.

Victoria Moreno. "La Llorona, Crying Lady of the Creekbeds, 483 Years Old, and Aging," in *The Third Woman: Minority Women Writers of the United States*, edited by Dexter Fisher, 319–320. Boston: Houghton Mifflin, 1977. Reprinted with permission of Carmen Tafolla.

Robert Dale Parker. Excerpts from *The Sound the Stars Make Rushing through the Sky: The Writings of Jane Johnston Schoolcraft*, edited by Robert Dale Parker (University of Pennsylvania Press, 2006), pp. 89–90, 92, 99–100, 108, 116–118, 135–136, 141–143, 166–167, 169–175, 177–180, 190–192, 201,

207–209. Reprinted with permission of the University of Pennsylvania Press.

Pio Pico. *Historical Narrative*, edited by Martin Cole and Henry Welcome, translated by Arthur P. Botello. The Arthur H. Clark Company, California 1973. Reprinted by permission of University of Oklahoma Press.

Lucy Holcombe Pickens. "The Free Flag of Cuba," from *The Lost Novel of Lucy Holcombe Pickens: The Free Flag of Cuba*, edited by Orville Vernon Burton and Georganne B. Burton. Copyright © 2002 by Louisiana State University Press.

John Ross. "Annual Message," from *The Papers of Chief John Ross* by John Ross. Copyright © 1985. Reproduced with permission of University of Oklahoma Press in the format republished in a textbook via Copyright Clearance Center.

José María Tornel. Tejas y los Estados-Unidos de América, en sus relaciones con la República Mexicana (Mexico City: Ignacio Cumplido, 1837), 1; José María Tornel y Mendívil, "Relations Between Texas, the United States of America, and the Mexican Republic," translated by Carlos E. Castañeda, in The Mexican Side of the Texan Revolution (1837) by the Chief Mexican Participants, edited by Carlos E. Castañeda, (Dallas: P.L. Turner, 1928), 287. Used by permission of Consuelo Castañeda de Artaza.

Miguel Teurbe Tolón. "El Segundo Aniversario de La Verdad" is reprinted with permission from the publisher of *El Laud del Esterrado*, edited by Matías Montes-Huidobro (copyright © 1995 Arte Público Press-University of Houston).

Félix Varela. From *Xicoténcatl: An Anonymous Historical Novel about the Events Leading Up to the Conquest of the Aztec Empire*, translated by Guillermo Castillo-Feliú. Copyright © 1999. By permission of the University of Texas Press.

INDEX OF AUTHORS, TITLES, AND FIRST LINES OF POEMS